Leagues Apart

•ANDREW "RUBE" FOSTER•

Leagues Apart

The Men and Times of the Negro Baseball Leagues

Text by
Lawrence S. Ritter

Illustrations by
Richard Merkin

Morrow Junior Books
New York

8/97   Follett $15.00

A special thanks to my friend Luis Muñoz
for sharing his profound knowledge of place and Caribbean baseball with me.
His assistance is always appreciated.
—R.M.

Oil pastels were used for the full-color illustrations.
The text type is 14-point Guardi.

Printed in the United States of America.

1 2 3 4 5 6 7 8 9 10

Library of Congress Cataloging-in-Publication Data
Ritter, Lawrence S.
Leagues apart: the men and times of the Negro baseball leagues/
text by Lawrence S. Ritter; illustrations by Richard Merkin.
p.   cm.
ISBN 0-688-13316-9 (trade)—ISBN 0-688-13317-7 (library)
1. Negro leagues—History—Juvenile literature.   [1. Negro leagues—History.   2. Baseball—History.]
I. Merkin, Richard, ill.   II. Title.   GV875.A1R58 1995   796.357′64′0973—dc20   94-17512   CIP AC

For Luke, Melissa, and Tara
Con Amor
—L.R.

For Robert Peterson, who gave us *Only the Ball Was White*—the
true Old Testament for those who love these great men and
the game that they played. And for my friend Max Manning,
who pitched for the Newark Eagles for seven years and
taught children for twenty-eight.
—R.M.

•GEORGE HERMAN "BABE" RUTH•

Who is the greatest baseball player who ever lived?

That seems like an easy question, doesn't it? But it must be harder than it looks because even the experts can't seem to agree on the answer. For instance, many swear on a stack of Bibles that **George Herman Ruth** is the greatest of all time. Babe Ruth started as a pitcher, became one of the best in the game, and then gave it up and became a phenomenal home run slugger.

The Babe walloped 714 homers during his career. Since it is 360 feet around the bases, he trotted almost 50 miles rounding the bases after hitting the ball into the stands or clear out of the ballpark! (He also received 2,056 bases on balls, which is an additional 35 miles, but that's another story.)

HANK AARON AND WILLIE MAYS

However, not everyone thinks the Babe should be ranked all-time number one. Instead, many would choose **Hank Aaron**, the man who broke Ruth's lifetime home run record. Aaron blasted 755 homers, 41 more than Ruth.

Still others say that the best baseball player ever was neither Babe Ruth nor Hank Aaron. They prefer **Willie Mays**, who was a remarkable fielder and baserunner as well as a marvelous hitter. Mays hit 660 home runs, which is fewer than Ruth or Aaron hit. But he was a better outfielder and stole over 300 bases, which is a lot more than Ruth or Aaron stole.

Something that most people, even most baseball fans, don't know about Henry Louis Aaron and Willie Howard Mays is that they both learned how to play the game from veteran Negro League ballplayers. That's because they both began their careers in the Negro Leagues.

The Negro Leagues . . . if the name isn't familiar or sounds old-fashioned, it's because, like dinosaurs, the Negro Leagues have been extinct for a long time; they faded away in the 1950s.

Before about 1950, if you were black and wanted to earn a living playing baseball, you were not allowed to play on the same team with white ballplayers. Prejudiced team owners, encouraged by bigoted players, established racist rules that prevented black athletes from playing in the major leagues, regardless of their skills.

Take **Smokey Joe Williams**, for example. The tall right-hander pitched from 1905 to 1932, mainly for the Chicago American Giants, the New York Lincoln Giants, and the Homestead Grays. He had a fastball that was said to zip in at well over 90 miles an hour, about as fast as that of the legendary Walter Johnson. Nevertheless, his name is unknown to most baseball fans because he was never permitted to wear a major league uniform.

·SMOKEY JOE WILLIAMS·

CANNONBALL DICK REDDING

Or take **Cannonball Dick Redding**, a hard-throwing righthander who pitched with a scary windup: Kicking high with his left leg, he would pivot on his right foot to face second base, showing the batter his back, then swing around and quickly fire the ball to the catcher. For a number of years he and Smokey Joe made the New York Lincoln Giants the most feared of all black teams.

JAMES "COOL PAPA" BELL

Another example is **James "Cool Papa" Bell**, the swiftest outfielder and fastest runner in the Negro Leagues' history. He played from the early twenties into the forties. Bell specialized in infield singles, stretching doubles into triples, and stealing bases.

Black ballplayers had no choice in those days but to join poorly paid teams made up of black players like themselves. Some of these teams formed leagues—the two most important were the Negro National League and the Negro American League—and, like the major leagues, they played a long schedule of games. They had their own pennant races, all-star games, and often a world series between the two pennant winners.

The guiding light behind the Negro National League was **Andrew "Rube" Foster**, often called the Father of Black Baseball. An excellent pitcher, he also became the manager and owner of the Chicago American Giants. His greatest achievement, however, was organizing the Negro National League, in 1920.

Negro League teams included the Bacharach Giants of Atlantic City, the Birmingham Black Barons (where Willie Mays played), the Chicago American Giants, the Hilldale Club of Philadelphia, the Indianapolis Clowns (Hank Aaron's first team), the Kansas City Monarchs, the Newark Eagles, the New York Black Yankees, the New York Lincoln Giants, the Philadelphia Stars, the Pittsburgh Crawfords, and the Homestead Grays. The Grays had *two* homes: Pittsburgh, Pennsylvania, and Washington, D.C.

•ANDREW "RUBE" FOSTER•

Before passage of the civil rights laws in the 1960s, black Americans often had trouble finding hotels where they could sleep overnight or restaurants where they could sit down and eat. The great Cool Papa Bell once described what life in the Negro Leagues used to be like:

In addition to our regular league games, we'd "barnstorm" a lot. That means we'd play exhibition games, in one city one day and in another city the next. We traveled in our own private bus, not by train or plane, and every night we'd have to find a place to stay if we weren't

in a big city up North. Often no hotel would have us—they were for whites only—and we'd have to stay in rooming houses or with private families, colored families, a few of us in each house.

We went into a lot of small towns where we couldn't find any place to sleep, so we slept on the bus. If we had to, we could convert the seats into beds. We'd pull over to the side of the road, in a cornfield or someplace, and sleep until the break of day, and then we'd go on into the next town, hoping we could find a restaurant that would be willing to serve us. Things like that, today people wouldn't believe it.

•MARTIN DIHIGO•

In the 1920s and 1930s some ballplayers protested against discrimination in the game—Yankee first baseman Lou Gehrig, for one—but it didn't do any good.

Although African American ballplayers were discriminated against in the United States, they were warmly welcomed in many baseball-loving Latin American countries—especially in Mexico, Panama, Venezuela, and the Caribbean islands (Cuba, the Dominican Republic, and Puerto Rico). There they played on integrated teams and did not have to face racial hostility.

Some ballplayers were special favorites in Latin America. One of them was **Martín Dihigo**. Born in Cuba in 1905, Dihigo was a star pitcher who also played infield or outfield and was a terrific hitter. Many old-timers claim he was the greatest all-around player who ever lived. Not surprisingly, he was a national hero in Cuba.

·JOHN HENRY "POP" LLOYD·

Another player, shortstop **John Henry "Pop" Lloyd**, was idolized in Mexico. A six-footer, which is rather tall for a shortstop, he was a sensational fielder and a career .340 hitter from 1905 to 1931. Veteran players say there has never been a better all-around shortstop.

The two best-known Negro Leaguers were pitcher Satchel Paige and catcher Josh Gibson. Everyone agrees that if they had played in the majors, both would have become super-stars.

LeRoy "Satchel" Paige was six feet three and 175 pounds soaking wet. He threw and batted righthanded. Paige is usually ranked as the greatest black pitcher—many say *the* greatest pitcher, black or white—of all time. By the time racial segregation in baseball ended, in 1947, Satchel was already forty-one years old. Even so, the Cleveland Indians signed him on July 7, 1948, his forty-second birthday.

Despite his age, Satchel Paige pitched in the major leagues until 1953. In 1952 he won twelve games, including two shutouts, and saved ten more in relief for a next-to-last-place team. And in 1965, to cap it all off, Paige pitched three scoreless innings for Kansas City against the Boston Red Sox and allowed only one hit. He was fifty-nine years old then and remains the oldest player ever to have participated in a major league game.

•LEROY "SATCHEL" PAIGE•

•JOSH GIBSON•

Catcher **Josh Gibson** did not fare as well. The big right-handed slugger played most of his career with the Homestead Grays. Although the Negro Leagues had a number of great home run hitters, the powerfully built, genial, moon-faced Gibson, whom many called the black Babe Ruth, was the greatest of all. By the time segregation ended, Josh Gibson was dead. He died of a stroke early in 1947, at the age of thirty-five.

Paige and Gibson were the best-known Negro League players, but they were not the only outstanding ones. Three other great pitchers, for example, were Bullet Joe Rogan, Willie Foster, and Jose Mendez.

WILBUR "BULLET JOE" ROGAN

Wilbur "Bullet Joe" Rogan was one of the most versatile players in baseball history. He not only pitched but also batted cleanup for the Kansas City Monarchs during the twenties and early thirties. The Bullet, a righthander, was in the same class as Babe Ruth and Martin Dihigo when it came to the ability to excel in just about every aspect of the game.

·WILLIE FOSTER·

Willie Foster was probably the best lefthanded pitcher in the history of the Negro Leagues. Rube Foster's kid brother pitched brilliantly from the early twenties to the late thirties, mainly for Rube's Chicago American Giants.

Cuban-born **Jose Mendez**, a righthanded fastball pitcher, regularly defeated major league teams visiting Cuba. He also played several infield positions, but he was famous mostly because of his great skill as a pitcher. As a manager, Mendez led the Kansas City Monarchs to three Negro National League pennants.

JOSE MENDEZ

LOUIS SANTOP

Josh Gibson wasn't the only home run slugger in the Negro Leagues. He had plenty of competition.

Catcher **Louis Santop** was the first of the great Negro League power hitters. The burly six-foot-three 230-pounder, a lefthanded batter and righthanded thrower, smashed towering Babe Ruth–type homers that carried great distances. Like the Babe, he was a huge gate attraction.

George "Mule" Suttles played first base from the twenties to the forties for the Birmingham Black Barons and other teams. Righthanded at bat and in the field, Mule hit booming home runs that made him extremely popular with the fans, who delighted in chanting, *"Kick,* Mule, *kick,"* whenever he stepped into the batter's box.

Outfielder Norman "Turkey" Stearnes, a lefthander, was a remarkable long-ball hitter despite his slender build. Loved by the fans for his numerous home runs, he was chosen for four of the first five all-star teams (in 1933, 1934, 1935, and 1937), even though by then he was well past his peak.

GEORGE "MULE" SUTTLES

· CRISTOBAL TORRIENTE ·

Oscar Charleston is the greatest all-around outfielder in the Negro Leagues' history. The barrel-chested lefthander played for the Chicago American Giants and the Pittsburgh Crawfords. He was a league-leading hitter, a whirlwind on the bases, a circus-catch outfielder, and a fine first baseman as well. He was often called the black Ty Cobb, but many thought Ty Cobb should really be called the white Oscar Charleston.

Outfielder **Cristobal Torriente** packed 190 pounds of muscle on a stocky five-foot-ten frame. Born in Cuba in 1895, the lefthander was a line-drive home run slugger who also hit for a high batting average. Torriente starred with the Chicago American Giants and with teams in Latin America, especially in his native Cuba.

WALTER "BUCK" LEONARD

Many skillful infielders snared line drives while in Negro League uniforms. Take first baseman **Walter "Buck" Leonard**, for instance, who was often called the black Lou Gehrig. With Buck playing first base, the Homestead Grays won nine pennants.

Willie "Devil" Wells was Pop Lloyd's chief rival as the Negro Leagues' greatest shortstop. He had a lengthy career, from 1923 to 1949, mainly with the St. Louis Stars, Chicago American Giants, Newark Eagles, and teams in Mexico and the Caribbean. Wells got his nickname because of the many ingenious (and devilish) ways he figured out to beat opponents with his clutch hitting, acrobatic fielding, and quick thinking.

•WILLIE "DEVIL" WELLS•

WILLIAM "JUDY" JOHNSON

William "Judy" Johnson is most often chosen as one of the two best third basemen in the Negro Leagues' history. He played with Philadelphia's Hilldale Club in the twenties and with the Pittsburgh Crawfords in the thirties. The thin third baseman was known for his line drive clutch hitting and dazzling fielding.

Ray "Squatty" (also known as "Hooks") Dandridge is Judy Johnson's chief rival as the greatest third baseman in the Negro Leagues' history. A bowlegged 175-pound spark plug, Ray starred with the Newark Eagles in the thirties and then played mostly in Mexico and Cuba in the forties. He was signed by Minneapolis in the newly integrated American Association in 1949, and in 1950 was voted, at age thirty-seven, that league's most valuable player.

Segregation in baseball started to crumble in 1942, when Branch Rickey became president of the Brooklyn Dodgers. In 1945, when World War II ended, Rickey decided that he would no longer honor the unwritten agreement that banned African Americans from the major leagues.

The man Rickey chose to blaze the trail and desegregate the game was **Jackie Robinson**, then a shortstop for the Kansas City Monarchs. Jack Roosevelt Robinson had been a baseball, football, basketball, *and* track star at UCLA, the University of California at Los Angeles. Signed by Rickey late in 1945, Robinson was sent in 1946 to Montreal, Canada, where Brooklyn had a farm club in the International League, until then an all-white league. That year he led Montreal to a pennant while also leading the league in batting!

On Tuesday, April 15, 1947, at two o'clock in the afternoon, a broad-shouldered Jackie Robinson, wearing a Brooklyn uniform, sprang out of the home team's dugout at Ebbets Field to take his position at first base. He was the first black player in the major leagues.

•JACKIE ROBINSON•

As soon as it was known that Jackie was a Dodger, four of his teammates asked to be traded. During games a barrage of racial insults was directed at him from fans in the stands and from the opposing team's bench. Some players said they would go on strike rather than play with or against a black man.

National League President Ford Frick responded with a blunt ultimatum. "I do not care if half the league strikes," he said. "Those who do will be suspended and I don't care if it wrecks the league for five years. This is the United States of America, and one citizen has as much right to play as another."

This angry statement—which should have been made by someone in authority about fifty years earlier—had such a sobering effect that resistance quickly collapsed.

In his first season with the Dodgers Robinson led the National League in stolen bases and was voted rookie of the year. In 1949 he led the league in hitting and was named its most valuable player. It has been said that Rickey signed Jackie Robinson not for idealistic reasons but because he wanted to win ball games. If so, Rickey knew what he was doing, because Brooklyn won six pennants in the ten years Jackie was there.

• MONTE IRVIN •

    With Robinson's success, other Negro Leaguers were pursued by major league teams. Roy Campanella of the Baltimore Elite Giants joined the Brooklyn (now the Los Angeles) Dodgers in 1948, and **Monte Irvin** of the Newark Eagles reported to the New York (now the San Francisco) Giants in 1949. Ernie Banks of the Kansas City Monarchs signed with the Chicago Cubs in 1953, and the New York Yankees acquired their first black player in 1955—catcher Elston Howard, also of the Monarchs.

As might have been expected, integration meant the end of the trail for the Negro Leagues. Since black and white could now play on the same teams and in the same leagues, the Negro Leagues' fundamental reason for existing disappeared. In addition, African American baseball fans abandoned the Negro League teams and flocked instead to major league

ballparks to see Jackie and Satchel and the others play with and against established major league stars.

The Negro National League got the message right away and shut down at the end of the 1948 season. The Negro American League struggled through the fifties with fewer and fewer teams and then disbanded as well.

And how did former Negro Leaguers do when they got their long-awaited chance in the majors? Not too poorly, thank you: In the dozen years from 1949 through 1960, they won two major league batting crowns, seven runs batted in titles, eight home run crowns, and nine most valuable player awards!

Thus ended an ugly and shameful chapter in American history. When we look back, it is tempting to view the past through rose-colored glasses and glamorize the Negro League experience: busloads of carefree ballplayers barnstorming happily across the land, playing America's national pastime in cities and towns large and small.

But these talented men were not in the Negro Leagues by choice. They were there because of high walls erected in the name of segregation and maintained by racism. Poorly paid and neglected, they were there because they were not allowed to compete against their equals, the Ruths, Gehrigs, and DiMaggios, who were well paid and showered with fame and prestige.

It may be too late to compensate these fine athletes for what they lost through no fault of their own, but the least we can do is remember their names and honor their memories.

Hard-hitting outfielder Gene Benson, who played in the thirties and forties with the Bacharach Giants and Philadelphia Stars, summed up the bittersweet feelings of many Negro Leaguers in a conversation with writer John Holway. "We never thought about the major leagues," Benson said. "We never dreamed that it would come true. But I know we were the pioneers. Without our league, where would Robinson have come from? If we weren't out there suffering and struggling, they wouldn't have any blacks in there now."

African American ballplayers have been outstanding batters, fielders, and pitchers in the major leagues since Jackie Robinson demolished the color barrier in 1947. Their performance since then demonstrates what they could have done in earlier years.

So when we think about the Honor Roll of Great Ballplayers, like Babe Ruth and Mickey Mantle and Hank Aaron, let's not forget the wonderful Negro Leaguers, like Josh and Cool Papa, Cannonball Dick and Bullet Joe, and all the others who never got a chance to show their stuff in the major leagues.

HALL OF FAMERS

The following men, who spent all or most of their careers in the Negro Leagues, have been elected to the Baseball Hall of Fame at Cooperstown. The year each was elected is in parentheses.

LeRoy "Satchel" Paige (1971)

Josh Gibson (1972)

Walter "Buck" Leonard (1972)

Monte Irvin (1973)

James "Cool Papa" Bell (1974)

William "Judy" Johnson (1975)

Oscar Charleston (1976)

Martin Dihigo (1977)

John Henry "Pop" Lloyd (1977)

Andrew "Rube" Foster (1981)

Ray "Squatty" Dandridge (1987)

the Integration of Technology in the Classroom

Online Tutoring from SmarThinking   In partnership with SmarThinking, we offer personalized, online tutoring during typical homework hours. Every new text comes with a one-semester passkey that will allow access to three types of services:

- **Live help** provides access to 20 hours a week of real-time, one-on-one instruction. With Internet access, students may interact live online with an experienced SmarThinking "e-structor" (online tutor) between 9 AM and 1 AM EST, every Sunday through Thursday.
- **Questions anytime** enables students to submit questions 24 hours a day, 7 days a week, for response by an e-structor within 24 hours. Students can even submit spreadsheets for personalized feedback within 24 hours.
- **Independent Study Resources** are available around the clock and provide access to additional educational services, ranging from interactive web sites to Frequently Asked Questions posed to SmarThinking e-structors.

NEW! Introduction to Financial Accounting   An interactive multi-media product that provides practical, intuitive instruction on fundamental accounting concepts. This CD-ROM combines video, audio, and text in an interactive simulation. The user learns accounting by recording a series of business transactions for a real-world company. Each transaction is described and recorded in everyday business language and reconciled to financial statements prepared in accordance with Generally Accepted Accounting Principles ("GAAP"). An accounting coach tutors students as they proceed through the program. They are not able to move ahead without correctly completing each transaction, and they receive a performance evaluation at the end of the program. This program is designed to help students:

- Understand fundamental accounting terminology
- Become intelligent readers of financial statements
- Value, record, and classify business transactions
- Assess how business decisions affect profits and liquidity

The Needles Accounting Resource Center at http://accounting.college.hmco.com

For Students
- **NEW! ACE,** an online self-quizzing program, with over 1,000 new questions, that allows students to check their mastery of the topics covered in each chapter
- **Research Activities** based on the material covered in each chapter
- **Toys "R" Us Annual Report Activities** that make use of the latest Toys "R" Us financial statements
- **Links** to the web sites of over 200 real companies and annual reports referenced in the book
- **A List of Business Readings** from leading periodicals
- **Check Figures** for end-of-chapter problems

For Instructors
- **NEW!** A brand new set of **PowerPoint Slides** that will enhance classroom presentation of text material; the new slides are concise, contain lots of examples of transactions, and explain the accounting process in clear, easy-to-follow steps
- **Text previews,** which highlight new features and provide demonstrations of supplements
- **Sample syllabi** from other first-year accounting faculty
- *Accounting Instructors' Report* newsletter, which explores a wide range of contemporary teaching issues
- **Electronic Solutions,** fully functioning Excel spreadsheets for all text exercises, problems, and cases from the printed Instructor's Solutions Manual

Teaching Accounting Online   This online training course from Faculty Development Programs provides suggestions for integrating new technologies into accounting education. Available within Blackboard.com, the course includes the following modules: Designing Course Basics; Be the Student; Common Online Tools; Designing Teaching Strategies; Designing Learning Activities; Designing Outcomes Assessment; and Delivering a Course. For more information, contact your Houghton Mifflin sales representative or our Faculty Services Center at (800) 733-1717.

To Jennifer, Jeffrey, Annabelle, and Abigail

To Bruce, Brent, and Courtney Crosson and in loving memory of Helen and Bryce Van Valkenburgh

Senior Sponsoring Editor: Bonnie Binkert
Senior Development Editor: Margaret M. Kearney
Project Editor: Claudine Bellanton
Editorial Assistants: Lisa Goodman and Rachel Zanders
Senior Production/Design Coordinator: Sarah L. Ambrose
Senior Manufacturing Coordinator: Priscilla J. Bailey
Marketing Manager: Todd Berman

Cover Illustration © Campbell Laird/SIS

PHOTO CREDITS: page 3, ©Edward Holub/CORBIS; page 5, Courtesy of Intel Corporation; page 45, ©DigitalVision/PictureQuest; page 89, ©Getty Images; page 129, ©Ed Kashi/CORBIS; page 167, ©Getty Images; page 169, Courtesy of Claire's Stores, Inc.; page 213, ©Mark Richards/PhotoEdit; page 323, ©Lester Lefkowitz/Getty Images; page 365, ©Bruce Ayres/Getty Images; page 403, ©Jose Luis Pelaez, Inc./CORBIS; page 441, ©BananaStock/Picturequest; page 443, Courtesy of J.C. Penney Company, Inc.; page 479, ©Ed Young/CORBIS; page 481, Courtesy of Fermi National Accelerator Laboratory; page 525, ©Getty Images; page 557, ©Arthur Tilley/Getty Images; page 593, ©AP/Wide World Photos; page 629, ©Todd Gipstein/CORBIS; page 669, ©Getty Images; page 709, ©DigitalVision/PictureQuest; page 711, Courtesy of Goodyear Tire & Rubber Company; page 751, ©AP/Wide World Photos; page 793, © AFP/Getty Images; page 795, Courtesy of United Parcel Service; page 835, © Scott Olson/Getty Images; page 883, ©Don Smetzer/Getty Images; page 925, Courtesy of England, Inc.; page 965, ©Steve Kagan/Getty Images; page 1003, ©Stephen Marks/Getty Images; page 1005, Courtesy of Enterprise Rent-A-Car; page 1049, ©Sergio Piumatti; page 1091, ©Ken Redding/CORBIS; page 1093, Courtesy of Harley Davidson, Inc. page 1129, © David Young-Wolff/ Getty Images.

The Toys "R" Us Annual Report (excerpts and complete) for the year ended February 1, 2003, which appears at the end of Chapter 6, pages 267–302, is reprinted by permission.

The 2002 Annual Report from Walgreens, which appears at the end of Chapter 6, pages 303–321, is reprinted with permission of Walgreen Co.

This book is written to provide accurate and authoritative information concerning the covered topics. It is not meant to take the place of professional advice.

Printed in the U.S.A.
Library of Congress Control Number: 2003110148
ISBN: 0-618-37989-4

123456789-VH-08 07 06 05 04

BRIEF CONTENTS

CONTENTS

3 Measuring Business Income 88

4 Completing the Accounting Cycle 128

5 Merchandising Operations 166

6 Financial Reporting and Analysis 212

Supplement to Chapter 6 How to Read an Annual Report

7 Accounting Information Systems

8 Internal Control

9 Short-Term Financial Assets

12   Current Liabilities

13   Partnerships

14 Contributed Capital

15 The Corporate Income Statement and the Statement of Stockholders' Equity

16 Long-Term Liabilities

17 The Statement of Cash Flows

18 Financial Performance Evaluation

19 The Changing Business Environment: A Manager's Perspective

20 Cost Concepts and Cost Allocation 834

21 Costing Systems: Job Order and Process Costing

22 Activity-Based Systems: ABM and JIT

23 Cost Behavior Analysis

24 The Budgeting Process

27 Analysis for Decision Making

PREFACE

Recent business and accounting events underscore the fact that accounting matters. Now, more than ever before, accounting students need to learn how to create, analyze, and use financial statements if they are going to be successful managers in the future. They also need to understand how a company's accounting information system works. *Principles of Accounting*, 2005e (9th edition) does just that. It continues a long tradition of teaching students that a company's financial statements and the accounting information system that provides the supporting data are key to guiding a company's prosperity.

We believe that in order to read and interpret financial statements, students have to learn how to think critically. That is why in *Principles of Accounting* we continue to seek ways to help students think critically about what they are reading, how they might make a financial or managerial decision, and what roles they might play as future users of financial accounting information systems. Students also have to learn how to analyze and interpret data—where did the numbers come from? What is the significance of the numbers? What do the numbers reveal about the financial health of the company? Again, we stress the importance of critical analysis in *Principles of Accounting*, 2005e.

Principles of Accounting continues to be the leading text for students—both business and accounting majors—with no previous training in accounting or business. It is part of a well-integrated text and technology program that includes an array of print and electronic support materials for students and professors. The text consists of 27 chapters; the first 18 cover financial accounting, and the remaining 9 chapters focus on managerial accounting.

Principles of Accounting was revised with these major objectives in mind:

- **To support new instructional technologies in today's business environment**

- **To provide a framework for making successful and ethical business decisions**

- **To present real-world events and relevant business practices**

- **To develop skills and abilities critical to life-long learning**

NEW INSTRUCTIONAL TECHNOLOGIES IN TODAY'S BUSINESS ENVIRONMENT

New technologies are a driving force behind business growth and accounting education today. We have therefore developed an integrated text and technology program dedicated to helping instructors take advantage of the opportunities created by new instructional technologies. Our goal with the new 2005 edition is to expand and seamlessly integrate the technology package so users can gain experience with technology tools basic to business. Whether an instructor wants to present a user or procedural orientation, incorporate new instructional strategies, develop students' core skills and competencies, or integrate technology into the classroom, the new 2005e text provides a total solution, making it the leading choice among instructors of first-year financial and managerial accounting courses.

Technology Supplements on the Web

NEW! Eduspace® Eduspace powered by Blackboard™ is Houghton Mifflin's online homework system. The system enables students to complete homework assignments online. After students complete the assignment, they submit it electronically and immediately receive feedback on their answers. Eduspace offers a wealth of other student and instructor resources, including HMTesting (our computerized test bank), brand new PowerPoint slide presentations, and a complete course manual.

SmarThinking   Houghton Mifflin and SmarThinking have partnered to provide state-of-the-art, live, online tutoring. Tutors can assist students with all examples, exercises, problems, and cases found in the text and related student supplements. An interactive interface allows tutors and students to share, annotate, and manipulate resources in real time to help illustrate concepts. A SmarThinking password is available for free and can be packaged with every new copy of the textbook.

The Needles Accounting Resource Center Web Site   The Needles Accounting Resource Center Web Site (http://accounting.college.hmco.com) provides a wealth of free resources for instructors and students. For example, students can access ACE, the very popular online self-testing program that allows them to take sample quizzes and check their mastery of the chapter material. Over 1,200 new questions have been added to the ACE quizzes. An ACE icon at the end of each learning objective section reminds students to check out the ACE online review quizzes. Other resources include

- links to the web sites of over 200 real companies

- a list of relevant readings from leading business and accounting periodicals (such as *BusinessWeek, Forbes, The Wall Street Journal,* and *The Journal of Accountancy*), which examine current business issues, the accounting profession, and career options in a broad context.

- research activities, which present extended investigations of topics covered in the text.

- Toys "R" Us annual report activities, which make use of the latest Toys "R" Us financial statements.

For instructors, the Needles Accounting Resource Center Web Site offers:

- a completely revised set of PowerPoint slides, which contain classroom presentation materials, discussion questions, and figures from the text.

- electronic solutions, available both on the web site and on a CD-ROM, which are fully functioning Excel spreadsheets for exercises, problems, and selected cases in the text.

- sample syllabi, demonstrating how other instructors organize and teach the introductory course.

- the *Accounting Instructors' Report* newsletter, which explores a wide range of contemporary teaching issues.

- Faculty Development Programs' online training, which provides suggestions for integrating new technologies into the classroom or teaching online.

NEW!* Wall Street Journal *Subscription   Students whose instructors have adopted the WSJ version of *Principles of Accounting* will receive, packaged with their book, a registration card for a 10-week print and online subscription to the *Wall Street Journal.* Students fill out and return the registration card to initiate subscription privileges. The text package also includes a copy of the *Wall Street Journal Student Subscriber Handbook,* which explains how to use both print and online versions of the newspaper.

Technology Supplements on CD-ROMs

NEW! HMAccounting Tutor   This new student tutorial CD-ROM, specifically developed for use with *Principles of Accounting,* 2005e, reinforces understanding of accounting concepts covered in the text. Organized by chapter and learning objective, this software program enables students to study more efficiently and learn interactively. The program includes

- demonstration problems with voice-over narration that illustrate important concepts.

- interactive tutorials that allow students to cover text concepts at their own pace.

- Internet case taken directly from the 2005 text, which contain a link to a portal page for information the student needs to complete the cases.

- an interactive quizzing function to reinforce learning.

- a built-in glossary with on-screen pop-up definitions.

NEW! ***Mastering the Accounting Cycle: A Bridge Tutorial***   This new, stand-alone tutorial CD-ROM emphasizes accounting transactions, presents a review of the debit and credit mechanism, and provides a foundation for the preparation and use of financial statements. The CD contains four demonstration problems that show the connection between the balance sheet, income statement, and cash flow statement. It also has an interactive quizzing function and a built-in glossary.

HMClassPrep with HMTesting CD-ROM   This instructor CD contains the computerized version of the test bank as well as other useful instructor aids.

The *computerized test bank* allows instructors to select, edit, and add questions, or generate randomly selected questions to produce a test master for easy duplication. Test questions are organized by learning objective and can be compiled using key words from the text. Online Testing and Gradebook functions allow instructors to administer tests via their school's network or over the Web, set up classes, record grades from tests or assignments, analyze grades, and compile class and individual statistics. This program can be used on both PCs and Macintosh computers. (A printed version of the test bank is also available upon request.)

Other Instructor Aids on HMClassPrep include

- the complete ***Course Manual*** (course planning matrix, time/difficulty chart, chapter-by-chapter instructional materials, and review quizzes).

- the ***Solutions Manual*** (a complete set of solutions to all exercises, problems, and selected cases in the text; also available in print).

- ***PowerPoint Slides*** (brand new PowerPoint slide presentations for every chapter)

- five-minute ***video cases*** tied to the in-text cases, highlighting real companies.

- ***check figures*** for end-of-chapter problems.

- ***web links*** to the Needles Accounting Resource Center Web Site at (http://accounting.college.hmco.com).

NEW! ***Windows General Ledger Software on the Student CD-ROM***   Completely updated for *Principles of Accounting*, 2005e, Houghton Mifflin's Windows General Ledger software offers coverage of accounting concepts and procedures in an extremely simple and user-friendly computerized environment. Most of the text problems in Chapters 1-18 can be solved using this program. The new GLS has an updated interface and expanded features—such as the ability to export files to Peachtree. The GLS software is included on the Student CD, which comes free with new texts purchased from Houghton Mifflin.

Also on the Student CD are check figures for the text problems, the video cases that accompany *Principles of Accounting*, and a full glossary.

Fingraph Financial Analyst CD-ROM   This CD contains the educational version of a patented software program used by financial analysts and certified public accountants to analyze and summarize the financial performance of companies. The financial data reported by over 20 well-known companies have been summarized and loaded into Microsoft Excel spreadsheets that can be accessed through the Needles Accounting Resource Center Web Site at http://accounting.college.hmco.com. Students can also enter data obtained from the annual report of any company. The Fingraph software enables students to prepare financial analyses of real companies in a very short time. The software accommodates a variety of learning styles; analyses are presented in tabular, graphic, and written formats. Most of the financial chapters of *Principles of Accounting,* 2005e contain a case designed to be worked in conjunction with the CD-ROM database, in which students analyze balance sheets, income statements, and statements of cash flows of real companies.

Introduction to Financial Accounting: The Language of Business CD-ROM Bel Needles and Marian Powers developed this competency-based, interactive CD in partnership with Learning Insights. The software is designed to teach accounting to people who have little or no financial background, especially business majors and nonfinancial managers who need to learn the financial impact of operating decisions.

Electronic Working Papers CD-ROM This CD is an electronic version of the printed Working Papers for exercises, problems, and selected cases in the text. By working on these Excel-based templates, students not only learn accounting but also the basic skills required for spreadsheet applications.

A FRAMEWORK FOR SUCCESSFUL AND ETHICAL DECISION MAKING

We know that most instructors want to place more emphasis on critical analysis and on how managers use accounting information to make decisions. We also know that ethical decision making is an important topic in light of the new focus on corporate governance. We are proud to continue our long tradition of emphasizing ethical decision making. At the end of each chapter we present at least one short case, based on real public companies, in which students must address an authentic, work-related, ethical dilemma directly related to the chapter content. The cases reveal how managers must account for their business decisions. Also, we have added within the text several new Focus on Business Ethics boxes that feature examples of how real companies have faced ethical issues.

Comparative Financial Analysis

We have expanded the use of financial information in performance evaluation and measurement by introducing a new comparison case at the end of most of the financial chapters. Students compare Walgreens and Toys "R" Us, using both companies' financial statements, which are bound into the text at the end of Chapter 6. The comparison cases require students to compute ratios, make assumptions, report on the effect of seasonal sales, and describe each company's inventory management system, to name a few tasks. Again, *Principles of Accounting* continues to stress the important role of financial statements in revealing useful information about companies.

Cash Flow

We emphasize the effect of business activities on cash flow throughout the financial chapters. Beginning in Chapter 1, we introduce the statement of cash flows, and we point out the difference between income measurement and cash flow in various chapters, reinforcing it through assignments. An icon in the margin calls attention to cash flow discussions.

Key Ratios

Starting in Chapter 6, we examine financial analysis ratios and integrate them in subsequent financial chapters at appropriate points. We bring all the ratios together in a comprehensive financial analysis of Sun Microsystems, Inc., in Chapter 18. An icon % in the margin calls attention to key ratio presentations.

Management Accounting Coverage

Co-author Susan Crosson has heavily revised most of the managerial chapters (Chapters 19-27). Her efforts were directed at helping students gain confidence in their ability to understand and apply accounting concepts once they leave the classroom and enter the workplace. For example, rather than focusing on the technical details of cost accounting, the managerial chapters emphasize the management cycle critical to operating a successful business. The managerial chapters also emphasize the approaches learned from the most progressive companies, such as how to manage supply chains, analyze value chains, operate in a just-in-time environment, utilize activity-based management, apply the theory of constraints, and focus on quality.

Today, management's use of information goes far beyond computing the cost of products and services. This book explores the full range of innovative managerial systems in a value-centered economy in which managers must make critical decisions concerning product quality, customer service, and long-term relationships. The text discusses the latest in management models and technology, plus it emphasizes that performance measurement, evaluation, and compensation are essential to a manager's success in today's competitive environment. Service businesses, where many students will ultimately work, receive expanded emphasis within the text discussion and the chapter assignments.

REAL-WORLD EVENTS AND BUSINESS PRACTICES

Working toward our goal of reflecting current business practice in a context that is relevant and exciting to students, we have incorporated the following real-world elements of the text.

Actual Financial Statements

To enhance students' appreciation for the usefulness and relevance of accounting information, we include excerpts from annual reports of real companies and articles about them in business journals. In total, we cite more than 200 publicly held companies in the text so that students can apply the concepts to real companies. These companies are identified by a URL in the margin of the text or by a URL within the end-of-chapter case text.

The complete annual report of Toys "R" Us and the financial statements and notes of Walgreen Company appear at the end of Chapter 6. Chapter 6 also presents the financial statements of Dell Computer Corporation in graphical form using the Fingraph Financial Analysis CD-ROM software. Chapter 18 features the financial statements of Sun Microsystems, Inc. to illustrate comprehensive financial analysis. Several of the Financial Reporting and Analysis Cases ask students to select real companies and access their financial statements on the Internet or through the Needles Accounting Resource Center Web Site at http://accounting.college. hmco.com to research the information needed to answer the questions.

Updated Decision Points

Every chapter begins with a Decision Point based on excerpts from a real company's annual report or from articles in the business press. In addition to introducing the concepts to be covered in the chapter, the Decision Point presents a situation that requires a decision by management and then demonstrates how the decision can be made using accounting information. The 2005 edition features several new Decision Points, among them Walgreens, Kelly Services, Cisco, Kraft, Coach, Palm, and Amazon.com. All of the other Decision Points have been revised and updated with the most recent financial information available.

New Focus on Business Boxes

Always a popular feature in the Needles accounting series, the Focus on Business boxes have been redesigned and over a third of them have been replaced with newsworthy feature stories. These boxes contain short summaries of items that show the relevance of accounting in four areas:

- Focus on Business Practice

- Focus on International Business

- Focus on Business Technology

- Focus on Business Ethics

Real-World Graphic Illustrations

We present graphs and tables illustrating how actual business practices relate to chapter topics. Many of these illustrations are based on data from studies of 600 annual reports published in *Accounting Trends and Techniques*. Beginning with Chapter 6, most chapters display a graphic that shows selected ratios for selected industries based on Dun & Bradstreet data. Service industry examples include advertising agencies and interstate trucking companies. Merchandising industry examples include auto and home supply companies and grocery stores. Manufacturing industry examples include machinery and computer companies. All graphs and tables have been updated with the most recent data available.

International Accounting

Recognizing the global economy in which all businesses operate today, we incorporate international accounting examples throughout the text. Each chapter includes a Financial Reporting and Analysis Case or a Managerial Reporting and Analysis Case that features an international company. Some examples include Harrods (British), Heineken (Dutch), Pioneer Corporation (Japan), and Roche (Swiss).

Video Cases

Two new 5-minute video vignettes (Claire's Boutiques and J. C. Penney) have been added to the series of video cases. Each video highlights a real company and is accompanied by an in-text case, which serves as an introduction to the chapter in which it is found. The videos work equally well as individual or group assignments, and all include a critical-thinking component and a writing assignment. The following video cases are included in the 2005 edition.

Intel Corporation (Chapter 1) examines the business goals of liquidity and profitability and the business activities of financing, investing, and operating.

Claire's Stores, Inc. (Chapter 5) describes a merchandising operation that has to regulate its inventories and generate a satisfactory gross margin in order to achieve profitability.

J.C. Penney Company, Inc. (Chapter 10) focuses on the management issues associated with accounting for inventories.

Fermi National Accelerator Laboratory (Chapter 11) demonstrates the importance of long-term assets to a unique scientific laboratory.

Goodyear Tire & Rubber Company (Chapter 17) describes the vision and objectives of the world's largest tire and rubber company and how Goodyear will need strong cash flows to carry out its objectives.

Enterprise Rent-A-Car (Chapter 24) presents the budgeting process in the management cycle and describes the master budget process for a service company.

Harley-Davidson, Inc. (Chapter 26) demonstrates how a company uses the concepts of responsibility accounting and the balanced scorecard in its performance management and evaluation system.

COMPETENCY-BASED SKILL DEVELOPMENT FOR LIFE-LONG LEARNING

Our goal in *Principles of Accounting*, 2005e is to provide the most comprehensive and flexible set of assignments to promote the development of critical knowledge and abilities while still providing the necessary technical skills required of future managers and accountants. Whether you favor more traditional assignments or cases that enhance a broader set of student skills, or a combination of both, we provide ample competency-based assignments—clearly identified—to meet your goals.

We also continue to integrate conceptual learning with procedural learning, especially in our end-of-chapter problems. We have added an analysis component to most of our problem requirements so students learn why a transaction was recorded or how the information in a particular financial statement is used to evaluate liquidity or profitability. In the managerial chapters, students not only make decisions but also must support them with reasoned explanations. We continue to stress the meaning behind the numbers in the financial and managerial reports—the message they contain.

Building Your Knowledge Foundation

This section consists of a variety of questions, exercises, and problems designed to develop basic knowledge, comprehension, and application of the concepts and techniques in the chapter.

- *Questions (Q):* Fifteen to 25 review questions cover the essential topics of the chapter.

- *Short Exercises (SE):* These ten very brief exercises are suitable for classroom use.

- *Exercises (E):* An average of 15 single topic exercises stress application.

- *Problems (P):* These five extensive applications of chapter topics often cover more than one Learning Objective. Most problems in the 2005 edition contain analysis components in which students are asked to explain how the numbers relate to the concepts covered in the chapter. Most problems in the financial chapters can be solved using our General Ledger Software for Windows. These problems are marked with the following icon:

- *Alternate Problems (P):* An alternative set of the most popular problems has been developed based on feedback from our study of users' syllabi.

Skills Development (SD) Cases, Financial Reporting and Analysis (FRA) Cases, and Managerial Reporting and Analysis (MRA) Cases

The Accounting Education Change Commission, the American Accounting Association, The American Institute of CPAs, and the Institute of Management Accountants have all called for the development of a broader set of skills among business and accounting graduates. The ten or more cases in this section answer this need by requiring students to work on their critical-thinking and communication skills, analytical skills, and writing skills. Most of the cases are based on real companies. All require critical-thinking and communication skills in the form of writing. At least one assignment in each chapter requires students to practice good business communication skills by writing a memorandum that reports results and offers recommendations. In addition, all cases are suitable for development of interpersonal skills through group activities. Certain cases are especially appropriate for group activities; they have specific instructions for applying a group methodology. We use icons to identify these cases, as well as to provide guidance in the best use of other assignments. The following is a list of those icons:

 *Cash Flow* icons indicate assignments dealing with cash flow; they also indicate text discussions of cash flow.

Communication icons identify assignments designed to help students develop their ability to understand and communicate accounting information successfully.

Critical Thinking icons indicate assignments intended to strengthen student's critical-thinking skills.

Ethics icons identify assignments that address ethical issues.

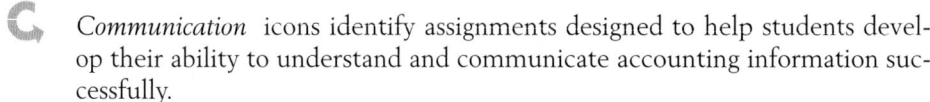 *Group Activity* icons identify assignments especially appropriate for groups or teamwork.

International icons indicate cases involving international companies.

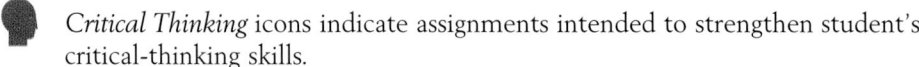 *Key Ratio* icons indicate the presence of financial analysis ratios in both the text and assignments.

 *Memorandum* icons identify cases that require students to write short business memorandums.

Each case has a specific purpose, as described in the following paragraphs:

Conceptual Analysis   Designed so that a written solution is appropriate, these short cases are based on real companies and address conceptual accounting issues.

Ethical Dilemma   The inclusion of ethics training in the business and accounting curriculum has become very important in light of the accounting scandals that have rocked corporate America. Every chapter in *Principles of Accounting, 2005e* contains a short case, often based on a real company, in which students must address an ethical dilemma directly related to the chapter content.

Research Activity   Each chapter has a case that asks students to do research using business periodicals, annual reports, newspaper articles, the library, and the Internet. Some cases are designed to improve students' interviewing and observation skills through field activities at actual businesses.

Decision-Making Practice   Students practice decision making after extracting relevant data from a case and making computations as necessary. Students' role as decision maker may be from the perspective of a manager, investor, analyst, or creditor.

Interpreting Financial (Management) Reports   These short cases are abstracted from business articles and annual reports of well-known companies such as Kmart, Sears, IBM, Toys "R" Us, Chrysler, and many others. All require students to extract relevant data, make computations, and interpret the results.

International Company   Each chapter has an international case that focuses on a foreign company that has had an accounting experience compatible with chapter content.

Toy "R" Us Annual Report   Students read and analyze the actual annual report of Toys "R" Us, which is printed at the end of Chapter 6.

Comparison Case: Toys "R" Us and Walgreen Co.   This is a new case, which appears in most of the financial chapters. Students are asked to compare Toys "R" Us and Walgreens in a number of different ways. Using the Toy "R" Us Annual Report and the financial statements of Walgreens, both of which appear at the end of Chapter 6, students learn how to find information, perform various financial analyses, and then compare the results.

Fingraph Financial Analyst   Most of the financial chapters have a case that requires students to use the Fingraph Financial Analyst CD-ROM. Students can use the Fingraph software to do tabular, graphic, or written analyses. Students can obtain financial data from more than 20 companies by accessing the Needles Accounting Resource Center Web Site at http://accounting.college.hmco.com/students, or they can obtain data from any company of their choice.

Internet Case   Each chapter features an Internet case, which asks students to research a topic on the Internet, answer critical- and analytical-thinking questions, and then prepare a written or oral report on their findings.

Excel Spreadsheet Analysis   These assignments in the managerial accounting chapters provide opportunities for written communication, interpretation, and analysis.

The Annual Report Project   Because the use of real companies' annual reports is the most rapidly growing type of term project in the financial accounting course, we provide an annual report project that we have used in our own classes for several years. Depending on how comprehensive you want the project to be, we have developed four assignment options, including the use of the Fingraph Financial Analyst CD-ROM software.

ORGANIZATION OF *PRINCIPLES OF ACCOUNTING*, 2005E

The chapter organization of *Principles of Accounting*, 2005e reflects an early introduction of financial statements and the relationship of financial accounting to the major activities of a business. *Chapters 1-6* introduce performance measurements, cash flow effects, and ratio analysis, making the integration of these key management techniques throughout the text possible. *Chapters 7-8* cover accounting information systems and internal control, key topics in today's business environment. *Chapters 9-12* are about measuring and reporting assets and current liabilities. *Chapters 13-16* focus on accounting for partnerships and corporations. *Chapters 17-18* conclude the financial chapters by covering the statement of cash flows and emphasizing financial performance evaluation.

Chapters 19-20 introduce the fundamentals of management accounting and cost concepts. *Chapters 21-22* explore cost-based and activity-based systems for management accounting. *Chapters 23-24* focus on information analysis for planning, including cost behavior analysis and the budgeting process. *Chapters 25-26* cover performance measurement using standard costing and performance management and evaluation. *Chapter 27* concludes the managerial chapters with an analysis of decision making.

All 27 chapters of *Principles of Accounting*, 2005e have been thoroughly reviewed and edited. A new and fresh design will engage students as they proceed through the text.

Pedagogical Color

A consistent color scheme throughout the text presents inputs to the accounting system (source documents) in orange, the processing of accounting data (working papers and accounting forms) in green, and outputs of the system (financial statements) in blue.

Stop and Think Questions

We have introduced new "Stop and Think" questions, tied to each learning objective, to motivate students to read actively and think critically. These questions—accompanied by a short answer—are designed to help students think about what they are reading. They can also serve as a valuable review device or as the basis for class discussions.

Pedagogical Annotations

These annotations appear in Chapter 1 only. They introduce each pedagogical element of the text—Learning Objectives, Decision Points, Content Annotations, and Chapter Reviews, to name a few. They describe the purpose of the pedagogy and provide usage suggestions so that students can derive maximum benefit when reading and studying the text.

Content Annotations

These marginal annotations appear throughout the text, offering material that enriches the text discussion as well as strategies and tips for mastering text content. Content annotations fall into the following categories:

- *Key Points* briefly summarize main concepts or ideas.
- *Enrichment Notes* offer interesting insights—such as historical perspectives—to heighten students' appreciation of the material.
- *Terminology Notes* provide succinct definition of key terms and concepts used in the text discussion.
- *Business-World Examples* are short anecdotes drawn from real businesses to help students see the day-to-day relevance of accounting in real companies.
- *Ethical Considerations* highlight practices or behaviors that might engender ethical concern.
- *Study Notes* provide useful strategies and tips to help students avoid common pitfalls.

Related Text Assignments

In the 2005 edition, we have added a list of related text assignments to each learning objective. Students can now see which questions (Q), Short Exercises (SE), exercises (E), Problems (P), Skills Development (SD) Cases, and Financial (Managerial) Reporting and Analysis (FRA/MRA) Cases reinforce a particular learning objective.

ACKNOWLEDGMENTS

The success we have enjoyed over the years with *Principles of Accounting* is due in no small way to the countless comments and suggestions we have received from colleagues, attendees of our annual Conference on Accounting Education, and students who have used our book. While there are too many of you to name individually, we do wish to recognize those who have made special contributions to the 2005 edition of *Principles of Accounting*. We therefore thank Edward H. Julius (California Lutheran University) for his meticulous work on the Study Guide and Test Bank; Gayle Richardson (Bakersfield College) for her contribution to the Test Bank; Gail Mestas for creating the PowerPoint slides; Cathy Larson for her accuracy review of the text and solutions; Jacquie Commanday for her assistance with the Course Manual; and Sarah Evans for her developmental editing of the text and Course Manual and page layout.

We also recognize the constant support we have received over the years and particularly for this edition from senior sponsoring editor, Bonnie Binkert; senior development editor, Margaret Kearney; project editor, Claudine Bellanton; and editorial associate, Jim Dimock.

Others who have been supportive and have had an impact on this book through their reviews, suggestions, and class testing are:

Daneen Adams   *Santa Fe Community College*
Gregory D. Barnes   *Clarion University*
Mohamed E. Bayou   *The University of Michigan—Dearborn*
Charles M. Betts   *Delaware Technical and Community College*
Michael C. Blue   *Bloomsburg University*
Gary R. Bower   *Community College of Rhode Island*
Lee Cannell   *El Paso Community College*
John D. Cunha   *University of California—Berkeley*
Mark W. Dawson   *Duquesne University*
Patricia A. Doherty   *Boston University*
Lizabeth England   *American Language Academy*
David Fetyko   *Kent State University*
Sue Garr   *Wayne State University*
Roxanne Gooch   *Cameron University*
Christine Uber Grosse   *The American Graduate School of International Management*
Dennis A. Gutting   *Orange County Community College*
John Hancock   *University of California—Davis Graduate School of Management*
Yvonne Hatami   *Borough of Manhattan Community College*
Harry Hooper   *Santa Fe Community College*
Marianne James   *California State University, Los Angeles*
Edward H. Julius   *California Lutheran University*
Howard A. Kanter   *DePaul University*
Debbie Luna   *El Paso Community College*
Kevin McClure   *ESL Language Center*
Geroge McGowan
Gail A. Mestas
Jenine Moscove
Beth Brooks Patel   *University of California—Berkeley*
LaVonda Ramey   *Schoolcraft College*
Roberta Rettner   *American Ways*
Gayle Richardson   *Bakersfield College*
James B. Rosa   *Queensborough Community College*
Donald Shannon   *DePaul Univeristy*
S. Murray Simons   *Northeastern University*

Marion Taube   *University of Pittsburgh*
Kathleen Villani   *Queensborough Community College*
Vicki Vorell   *Cuyahoga Community College*
John Weber   *DeVry Institute*
Kay Westerfield   *University of Oregon*
Andy Williams   *Edmunds Community College*

Finally, we want to identify and thank the facilitators for the last five years of COAE (Conference on Accounting Education) and congratulate our recent Technology Award winners:

2003 COAE Facilitators
Charlene Abendroth, California State University
Daneen Adams, Santa Fe Community College
Richard Fern, Eastern Kentucky University
Terry Grant, Mississippi College
Yvonne Hatami, Borough of Manhattan Community College
Rodger Holland, Columbus State University

2002 COAE Facilitators
Sharon Bell, University of North Carolina—Pembroke
Mark Henry, the Victoria College
Harry Hooper, Santa Fe Community College
Richard Irvine, Pensacola Junior College
Nancy Kelly, Middlesex Community College
Paul Mihalek, University of Hartford
Paul Weitzel, Eastern Shore Community College

2001 COAE Facilitators
Salvador Aceves, University of San Francisco
Betty Habershon, Prince George's Community College
Jim Mazza, Heald College
Roselyn Morris, Southwest Texas State University
Ginger Parker, Creighton University
David Rogers, Mesa State College
Jeanne Yamamura, University of Nevada—Reno

2000 COAE Facilitators
Mary Falkey, Prince Georges Community College
Kathy Otero, University of Texas—El Paso
Hubert Gill, University of North Florida
Rick Turpin, University of Tennessee
Lyle Hicks, Danville Area Community College
John Weber, DeVry University

1999 COAE Facilitators
Sidney Askew, Borough of Manhattan Community College
Dahli Gray, Morgan State University
Clarence Coleman, Jr., Francis Marion College
Karen Novey, Robert Morris College
James Dougher, DeVry Institute
Miriam Keller-Perkins, Berkeley College
Suzanne Wright, Penn State University

COAE Technology Award Winners
2003 - Elizabeth Murphy, DePaul University
2002 - Vicki Vorell, Cuyahoga Community College
2001 - Roselyn E. Morris, Southwest Texas State University

—B.N., M.P., and S.C.

TO THE STUDENT

HOW TO STUDY ACCOUNTING SUCCESSFULLY

The introductory accounting course is fundamental to the business curriculum and to success in the business world beyond college. Whether you are majoring in accounting or in another business discipline, it is one of the most important classes you will take. The course has multiple purposes because its students have diverse interests, backgrounds, and reasons for taking it. What are your goals in studying accounting? Being clear about your goals can contribute to your success in this course.

Success in this class also depends on your desire to learn and your willingness to work hard. It depends on your understanding of how the text complements the way your instructor teaches and the way you learn. A familiarity with how this text is structured will help you to study more efficiently, make better use of classroom time, and improve your performance on examinations and other assignments.

To be successful in the business world after you graduate, you will need a broad set of skills, which may be summarized as follows:

Technical/Analytical Skills   A major objective of your accounting course is to give you a firm grasp of the essential business and accounting terminology and techniques that you will need to succeed in a business environment. With this foundation, you then can begin to develop the higher-level perception skills that will help you acquire further knowledge on your own.

An even more crucial objective of this course is to help you develop analytical skills that will allow you to evaluate data. An important aspect of analytical skills is the ability to use technology effectively in making analyses. Well-developed analytical and decision-making skills are among the professional skills most highly valued by employers and will serve you well throughout your academic and professional careers.

Communication Skills   Another skill highly prized by employers is the ability to express oneself in a manner that others correctly understand. This can include writing skills, speaking skills, and presentation skills. Communication skills are developed through particular tasks and assignments and are improved through constructive criticism. Reading skills and listening skills support the direct communication skills.

Interpersonal Skills   Effective interaction between two people requires a solid foundation of interpersonal skills. The success of such interaction depends on empathy, or the ability to identify with and understand the problems, concerns, and motives of others. Leadership, supervision, and interviewing skills also facilitate a professional's interaction with others.

Personal/Self Skills   Personal/self skills form the foundation for growth in the use of all other skills. To succeed, a professional must take initiative, possess self-confidence, show independence, and be ethical in all areas of life. Personal/self skills can be enhanced significantly by the formal learning process and by peers and mentors who provide models upon which one can build. Accounting is just one course in your entire curriculum, but it can play an important role in your skill development. Your instructor is interested in helping you gain both a knowledge of accounting and the more general skills you will need to succeed in the business world. The following sections describe how you can get the most out of this course.

The Teaching/Learning Cycle™

Both teaching and learning have natural, parallel, and mutually compatible cycles. This teaching/learning cycle, as shown in Figure 1, interacts with the basic structure of learning objectives in this text.

The Teaching Cycle   The inner (tan) circle in Figure 1 shows the steps an instructor takes in teaching a chapter. Your teacher *assigns* material, *presents* the subject in lecture, *explains* by going over assignments and answering questions, *reviews* the subject prior to an exam, and *assesses* your knowledge and understanding using examinations and other means of evaluation.

The Learning Cycle   Moving outward, the next circle (green) in Figure 1 shows the steps you should take in studying a chapter. You should *preview* the material, *read* the chapter, *apply* your understanding by working the assignments, *review* the chapter, and *recall* and *demonstrate* your knowledge and understanding of the material in examinations and other assessments.

Integrated Learning Objectives   Your textbook supports the teaching/learning cycle through the use of integrated learning objectives. Learning objectives are simply statements of what you should be able to do after you have completed a chapter. In Figure 1, the outside (blue) circle shows how learning objectives are integrated into your text and other study aids and how they interact with the teaching/learning cycle.

1. Learning objectives listed at the beginning of each chapter aid your teacher in making assignments and help you preview the chapter.
2. Each learning objective is referenced in the margin of the text at the point where that subject is covered. A list of related text assignments below each learning objective identifies the end-of-chapter exercises, problems, and cases that relate to that objective.
3. Every exercise, problem, and case in the end-of-chapter assignments shows the applicable learning objective(s) so you can refer to the text if you need help.
4. A summary of the key points for each learning objective, a list of new concepts and terms referenced by learning objectives, and a review problem covering key learning objectives assist you in reviewing each chapter. The Study Guide, also organized by learning objectives, provides additional review.

Why Students Succeed   Students succeed in their accounting course when they coordinate their personal learning cycle with their instructor's cycle. Students who do a good job of previewing their assignments, reading the chapters before the instructor is ready to present them, preparing homework assignments before they are discussed in class, and reviewing carefully will ultimately achieve their potential on exams. To ensure that your learning cycle is synchronized with your instructor's teaching cycle, check your study habits against the following suggestions.

Previewing the Chapter

1. Read the learning objectives at the beginning of the chapter. These learning objectives specifically describe what you should be able to do after completing the chapter.
2. Study your syllabus. Know where you are in the course and where you are going. Know the rules of the course.
3. Realize that in an accounting course, each assignment builds on previous ones. If you do poorly in Chapter 1, you may have difficulty in Chapter 2 and be lost in Chapter 3.

FIGURE 1
The Teaching/Learning Cycle™ with integrated Learning Objectives

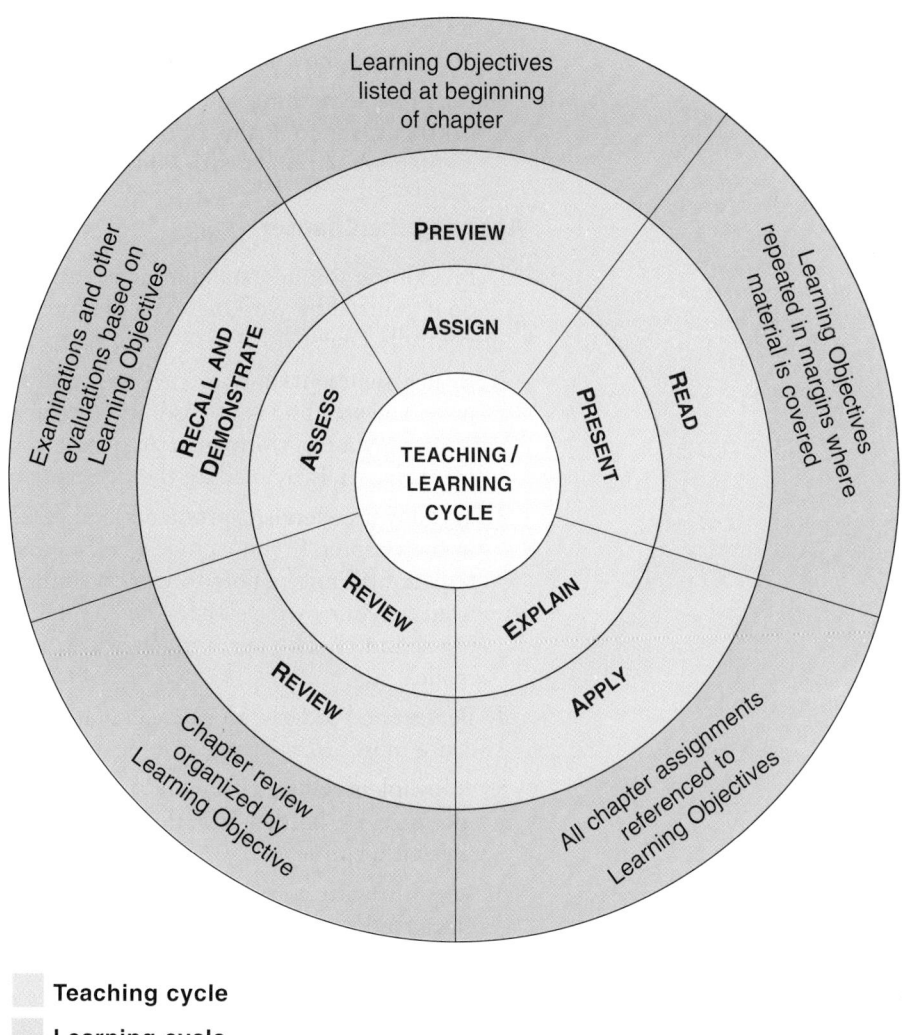

Learning Objectives listed at beginning of chapter

PREVIEW

ASSIGN

Examinations and other evaluations based on Learning Objectives

Learning Objectives repeated in margins where material is covered

RECALL AND DEMONSTRATE

ASSESS

PRESENT

READ

TEACHING/ LEARNING CYCLE

REVIEW

EXPLAIN

REVIEW

APPLY

Chapter review organized by Learning Objective

All chapter assignments referenced to Learning Objectives

Teaching cycle

Learning cycle

Learning Objectives structure

Reading the Chapter

1. As you read each chapter, be aware of the learning objectives in the margins. They will tell you why the material is relevant.

2. Allow yourself plenty of time to read the text. Accounting is a technical subject. Accounting books are so full of information that almost every sentence is important.

3. Strive to understand not only how each procedure is done, but also why it is done. Accounting is logical and requires reasoning. If you understand why something is done in accounting, there is little need to memorize.

4. Relate each new topic to its learning objective and be able to explain it in your own words.

5. Be aware of colors as you read. They are designed to help you understand the text. (For handy reference, the use of color is also explained on the back cover of the book.)
   Orange: All source documents and inputs are in orange.
   Green: All accounting forms, working papers, and accounting processes are shown in green.

Blue: All financial statements, the output or final product of the accounting process, are shown in blue.

6. If there is something you do not understand, prepare specific questions for your instructor. Pinpoint the topic or concept that confuses you. Some students keep a notebook of points with which they have difficulty.

Applying the Chapter

1. In addition to understanding why each procedure is done, you must be able to do it yourself by working exercises, problems, and cases. Accounting is a "do-it-yourself" course.

2. Read assignments and instructions carefully. Each assignment has a specific purpose. The wording is precise, and a clear understanding of it will save time and improve your performance. Acquaint yourself with the end-of-chapter assignment materials by reading the description of them in the Preface.

3. Try to work exercises, problems, and cases without referring to their discussions in the chapter. If you cannot work an assignment without looking in the chapter, you will not be able to work a similar problem on an exam. After you have tried on your own, refer to the chapter (based on the learning objective reference) and check your answer. Try to understand any mistakes you may have made.

4. Be neat and orderly. Sloppy calculations, messy papers, and general carelessness cause most errors on accounting assignments.

5. Allow plenty of time to work the chapter assignments. You will find that assignments seem harder and that you make more errors when you are feeling pressed for time.

6. Keep up with your class. Check your work against the solutions presented in class. Find your mistakes. Be sure you understand the correct solutions.

7. Note the part of each exercise, problem, or case that causes you difficulty so you can ask for help.

8. Attend class. Most instructors design classes to help you and to answer your questions. Absence from even one class can hurt your performance.

Reviewing the Chapter

1. Read the summary of learning objectives in the chapter review. Be sure you know the definitions of all the words in the review of concepts and terminology.

2. Review all assigned exercises, problems, and cases. Know them cold. Be sure you can work the assignments without the aid of the book.

3. Determine the learning objectives for which most of the problems were assigned. They refer to topics that your instructor is most likely to emphasize on an exam. Scan the text for such learning objectives and pay particular attention to the examples and illustrations.

4. Look for and scan other similar assignments that cover the same learning objectives. They may be helpful on an exam.

5. Review quizzes. Similar material will often appear on longer exams.

6. Attend any labs or visit any tutors your school provides, or see your instructor during office hours to get assistance. Be sure to have specific questions ready.

Taking Examinations

1. Arrive at class early so you can get the feel of the room and make a last-minute review of your notes.

2. Have plenty of sharp pencils and your calculator (if allowed) ready.

3. Review the exam quickly when it is handed out to get an overview of your task. Start with a part you know. It will give you confidence and save time.

4. Allocate your time to the various parts of the exam, and stick to your schedule. Every exam has time constraints. You need to move ahead and make sure you attempt all parts of the exam.

5. Read the questions carefully. Some may not be exactly like your homework assignments. They may approach the material from a slightly different angle to test your understanding and ability to reason, rather than your ability to memorize.

6. To avoid unnecessary errors, be neat, use good form, and show calculations.

7. Relax. If you have followed the above guidelines, your effort will be rewarded.

Preparing Other Assignments

1. Understand the assignment. Written assignments, term papers, computer projects, oral presentations, case studies, group activities, individual field trips, video critiques, and other activities are designed to enhance skills beyond your technical knowledge. It is essential to know exactly what your instructor expects. Know the purpose, audience, scope, and expected end product.

2. Allow plenty of time. "Murphy's Law" applies to such assignments: If anything can go wrong, it will.

3. Prepare an outline of each report, paper, or presentation. A project that is done well always has a logical structure.

4. Write a rough draft of each paper and report, and practice each presentation. Professionals always try out their ideas in advance and thoroughly rehearse their presentations. Good results are not accomplished by accident.

5. Make sure that each paper, report, or presentation is of professional quality. Instructors appreciate attention to detail and polish. A good rule of thumb is to ask yourself: Would I give this work to my boss?

ABOUT THE AUTHORS

Central to the success of any accounting text is the expertise of its author team. This team brings a wealth of classroom teaching experience, relevant business insight, and pedagogical expertise, as well as first-hand knowledge of today's students.

Belverd E. Needles, Jr., PhD, CPA, CMA
DePaul University

During his more than 30 years of teaching beginning accounting students, Belverd Needles has been an acknowledged innovator in accounting education. He has won teaching and education awards from DePaul University, the American Accounting Association, the Illinois CPA Society, the American Institute of CPAs, and the national honorary society, Beta Alpha Psi. The Conference on Accounting Education, started by Dr. Needles and sponsored by Houghton Mifflin, is in its 20th year; it has helped more than 2,000 beginning accounting instructors improve their teaching. Dr. Needles is editor of the *Accounting Instructors' Report*, in its 19th year, a newsletter that thousands of accounting teacher's rely on for new ideas in accounting education.

Marian Powers, PhD
Northwestern University

With more than 25 years of teaching experience, Marian Powers has taught beginning accounting at every level, from large lecture halls of 250 students to small classes of graduate students. She is a dynamic teacher who incorporates a variety of instructional strategies designed to broaden students' skills and experiences in critical thinking, group interaction, and communication. Consistently, Dr. Powers receives the highest ratings from students. She also brings practical experience to her students, including examples of how managers in all levels of business use and evaluate financial information. In recent years, Dr. Powers has concentrated on executive education. She has taught thousands of executives from leading companies around the world how to read and analyze the financial statements of their own companies and those of their competitors.

Susan Crosson, MS, CPA
Santa Fe Community College (Florida)

Susan Crosson, with more than 25 years of teaching at the college and university level, is recognized for her pedagogical expertise in teaching managerial accounting. Currently at Santa Fe Community College in Florida, Professor Crosson has a reputation for being able to engage university students in very large course sections and for encouraging community college students to master accounting. She believes in integrating technology into accounting education and actively uses the Internet to teach online, blended, and on-campus courses. Professor Crosson continues to promote the improvement of accounting education by serving the American Accounting Association and the Florida Institute of CPAs on a variety of committees, task forces, and sections. She is a past recipient of an IMA Faculty Development Grant to blend technology into the classroom, the Florida Association of Community Colleges Professor of the Year Award for Instructional Excellence, and the University of Oklahoma's Halliburton Education Award for Excellence.

CHECK FIGURES

Chapter 1 Problems
P 1. Total assets: $21,640
P 2. Total assets: $141,200
P 3. Total assets: $8,060
P 4. Total assets: $143,800
P 5. Total assets: $10,240
P 6. Total assets: $27,450
P 7. Total assets: $115,000
P 8. Total assets: $48,750

Chapter 2 Problems
P 1. No check figure
P 2. Trial balance totals: $21,100
P 3. Trial balance totals: $7,400
P 4. Trial balance totals: $23,100
P 5. Trial balance totals: $47,030
P 6. No check figure
P 7. Trial balance totals: $21,080
P 8. Trial balance totals: $61,420

Chapter 3 Problems
P 1. No check figure
P 2. No check figure
P 3. Adjusted Trial Balance: $212,334
P 4. Adjusted Trial Balance: $26,040
P 5. Adjusted Trial Balance: $29,778
P 6. No check figure
P 7. No check figure
P 8. Adjusted Trial Balance: $121,792

Chapter 4 Problems
P 1. Total assets: $627,800
P 2. Total assets: $56,808
P 3. Oct. Adjusted Trial Balance: $10,288; Total assets: $9,024; Post-Closing Trial Balance: $9,094; Nov. Adjusted Trial Balance: $10,858; Total assets: $9,204; Post-Closing Trial Balance: $9,344
P 4. Total assets: $17,808
P 5. Total assets: $123,574
P 6. Total assets: $193,858
P 7. Total assets: $6,943
P 8. Total assets: $350,868
Comprehensive Problem: Adjusted Trial Balance Totals: $41,260; Total assets: $34,250; Net income: $2,130

Chapter 5 Problems
P 1. Net income: $5,261
P 2. No check figure
P 3. Net income: $71,823
P 4. No check figure
P 5. Net Income: $67,480; Total assets: $244,530
P 6. Net income: $23,812; Total assets: $66,336
P 7. No check figure
P 8. Net income: $30,870
P.9. No check figure
P10. Net income: $3,435
P11. No check figure

Chapter 6 Problems
P 1. No check figure
P 2. Net income (loss): ($1,720)
P 3. Total assets: $595,600
P 4. Current Ratio: 20x4, 2.3; 20x3, 3.5; Return on Assets: 20x4, 12.5%; 20x3 11.0%
P 5. Net income: $72,260; Total assets: $1,083,800
P 6. No check figure
P 7. Net income: $63,626
P 8. Current Ratio: 20x5, 2.0; 20x4, 2.6; Return on Assets: 20x5, 14.8%; 20x4, 13.2%

Chapter 7 Problems
P 1. Maher Company's Total Accounts Receivable: $870; Maher Company's Total Accounts Payable: $2,100
P 2. Cash total in cash receipts journal: $23,340; Cash total in cash payments journal: $17,012
P 3. Accounts Payable total: $22,418
P 4. Trial Balance: $91,616
P 5 Trial Balance: $61,116
P 6. Simons Company's Total Accounts Receivable: $3,020; Simons Company's Total Accounts Payable: $2,600
P 7. Cash total in cash receipts journal: $66,968; Cash total in cash payments journal: $28,644
P 8. Trial Balance: $84,584

Chapter 8 Problems
P 1. Adjusted book balance: $3,930
P 2. Adjusted book balance: $149,473.28
P 3. No check figure
P 4. No check figure
P 5. Total Unpaid Vouchers: $6,216
P 6. No check figure
P 7. Adjusted book balance: $27,242.80
P 8. No check figure

Chapter 9 Problems
P 1. Short-term investments (at market): $354,000
P 2. No check figure
P 3. Amount of adjustment: $73,413
P 4. No check figure
P 5. Short-term investments (at market): $903,875
P 6. No check figure
P 7. Amount of adjustment: $9,533
P 8. No check figure

Chapter 10 Problems
P 1. 1. Cost of goods available for sale: $157,980
P 2. 1. Cost of goods sold for March: $4,578; for April: $15,457
P 3. 1. Cost of goods sold for March: $4,560; for April: $15,424
P 4. Estimated inventory shortage at cost: $6,052; at retail: $8,900
P 5. Estimated loss of inventory in fire: $653,027
P 6. Cost of goods available for sale: $10,560,000

P 7. 1. Cost of goods sold for April: $9,660; for May: $22,119
P 8. 1. Cost of goods sold for April: $9,580; for May: $21,991

Chapter 11 Problems
P 1. Total cost: Land: $361,950; Land Improvements: $71,000; Building: $691,800; Furniture and Equipment: $105,400
P 2. 1. Depreciation, Year 3: a. $165,000; b. $132,000; c. $90,000
P 3. Total Depreciation Expense: 20x5: $13,280; 20x6: $18,760; 20x7: $15,728
P 4. a. Gain on Sale of Road Grader: $1,800; b. Loss on Sale of Road Grader: $2,200; c. Gain on Exchange of Road Grader: $1,800; d. Loss on Exchange of Road Grader: $2,200; e. No gain recognized
P 5. Part A. c. Amortization Expense: $492,000; d. Loss on Exclusive License: $1,476,000; Part B. d. Leasehold Amortization Expense: $1,575; e. Leasehold Improvements Amortization Expense: $2,500
P 6. Totals: Land: $852,424; Land Improvements: $333,120; Buildings: $1,667,880; Machinery: $2,525,280; Expense: $36,240
P 7. 1. Depreciation, Year 3: a. $54,250; b. $81,375; c. $53,407
P 8. Total Depreciation Expense: 20x4: $71,820; 20x5: $103,092; 20x6: $84,072

Chapter 12 Problems
P 1. No check figure
P 2. No check figure
P 3. 1.b. Estimated Product Warranty Liability: $20,160
P 4. 3. Payroll Taxes Expense: $44,221.38
P 5. Net Pay, total: $8,176.32
P 6. No check figure
P 7. 1.b. Estimated Product Warranty Liability: $10,800
P 8. 3. Payroll Taxes Expense: $31,938.70

Chapter 13 Problems
P 1. 2.f. Rivera's income, 20x1: $42,600
P 2. 3. Naomi's share of income: $32,160
P 3. 1.d. Connie, Capital: $48,000
P 4. Cash distribution to Caruso: $336,000
P 5. Cash distribution to Menzer: $254,800
P 6. 1. Jacob's share of income: $225,000
P 7. d. Bob, Capital: $94,000
P 8. 1. Cash distribution to Susi: $104,400

Chapter 14 Problems
P 1. 2. Total stockholders' equity: $175,700
P 2. 1. 20x5 Total dividends: Preferred, $60,000; Common, $34,000
P 3. No check figure
P 4. 2. Total stockholders' equity: $950,080
P 5. 2. Total stockholders' equity: $330,375
P 6. 2. Total stockholders' equity: $1,488,000
P 7. 1. 20x3 Total dividends: Preferred, $420,000; Common, $380,000
P 8. 2. Total stockholders' equity: $475,040

Chapter 15 Problems
P 1. 2. Difference in net income: $48,800
P 2. 1. Income before extraordinary items and cumulative effect of accounting change: $108,000
P 3. 1. Income from continuing operations, December 31, 20x3: $551,250
P 4. 2. Total stockholders' equity, December 31, 20x3: $1,157,000
P 5. 2. Retained earnings: $231,500; Total stockholders' equity: $1,321,500
P 6. 1. Income before extraordinary items and cumulative effect of accounting change: $205,000
P 7. 2. Total stockholders' equity, December 31, 20x5: $2,964,000
P 8. 2. Retained earnings: $207,500; Total stockholders' equity: $1,257,500

Chapter 16 Problems
P 1. 2. Bond Interest Expense: Nov. 30, $1,597,500; Dec. 31, $266,250
P 2. 1. Bond Interest Expense: Sept. 1, $754,400; Nov. 30, $377,071
P 3. Bond Interest Expense: June 30, 20x4, $144,666; Sept. 1, 20x4, $93,290
P 4. 2. Loss on early retirement: $2,261,293
P 5. Bond Interest Expense: Jan. 31, 20x4, $2,400,000; June 30, 20x4, $2,000,000
P 6. 2. Bond Interest Expense: Sept. 1, $192,800; Nov. 30, $96,400
P 7. 1. Bond Interest Expense: Nov. 30, $520,150; Dec. 31, $86,651
P 8. Bond Interest Expense: June 30, 20x3, $46,598; Sept. 30, 20x3, $96,900

Chapter 17 Problems
P 1. No check figure
P 2. 1. Net cash flows from: operating activities, $126,600; investing activities, ($25,800); financing activities, $14,000
P 3. 1. Net cash flows from: operating activities, ($32,600); investing activities, ($7,200); financing activities, $51,000
P 4. 1. Net cash flows from: operating activities, ($106,000); investing activities, $34,000; financing activities, $24,000
P 5. No check figure
P 6. 1. Net Cash flows from: operating activities, $274,000; investing activities, $3,000; financing activities, ($130,000)
P 7. 1. Net cash flows from: operating activities, $46,800; investing activities: ($14,400); financing activities, $87,000

Chapter 18 Problems
P 1. No check figure
P 2. Increase: d, h, i
P 3. 1.c. Receivable turnover, 20x5: 13.9 times; 20x4: 15.6 times; 1.e. Inventory turnover, 20x5: 3.9 times; 20x4: 3.8 times

P 4.   1.b. Quick ratio, Reynard: 0.4 times;
        Bouche: 1.0 times; 2.d. Return on equity,
        Reynard: 11.8%; Bouche: 8.8%
P 5.   Increase: a, b, e, f, l, m
P 6.   1.a. Current ratio, 20x6: 1.9 times; 20x5: 1.0 times;
        2.c. Return on assets, 20x6: 8.4%; 20x5: 6.6%

Chapter 19 Problems
P 1.   No check figure
P 2.   Projected Cost per Unit: $22.25
P 3.   No check figure
P 4.   No check figure
P 5.   Total traffic flow goal, 24,184
P 6.   No check figure
P 7.   2. Decrease in number of rejects: 202
P 8.   Average output, week eight: 92,899

Chapter 20 Problems
P 1.   2. Total unit cost: $13.72
P 2.   Cost of goods manufactured: $10,163,200
P 3.   2a. Gross Margin: $191,800; 2d. Cost of Goods
        Manufactured: $312,100
P 4.   2. Overhead applied to Job 2214: $29,717
P 5.   2. Total costs assigned to the Grater order,
        activity-based costing method: $69,280.40
P 6.   1. Predetermined overhead rate for 20x6:
        $5.014 per machine hour
P 7.   2. Total costs assigned to the Kent order,
        activity-based costing method: $41,805.60
P 8.   1c. Rigger II: $11,665; BioScout: $14,940

Chapter 21 Problems
P 1.   b. $66,500; i. $57,800
P 2.   1. Manufacturing overhead applied,
        January 15: $108,000
P 3.   3. Costs of units sold: $14,834
P 4.   1. Cost per equivalent unit: $6.05; Ending
        inventory: $7,225
P 5.   1. Cost per equivalent unit: $2.00; Ending
        inventory: $5,372
P 6.   2. Cost of units sold: $89,647
P 7.   1. Contract revenue, Job Order No. P-12: $28,990
P 8.   1. Cost per equivalent unit: $7.00; Ending
        inventory: $37,200

Chapter 22 Problems
P 1.   No check figure
P 2.   1. Product unit cost: $270.00; 4. Product unit
        cost: $280.47
P 3.   1a. Total materials handling cost rate:
        30% per dollar of direct materials
P 4.   3. Total direct cost, toy car work cell: $17,000
P 5.   3. Cost of goods sold: $564,400
P 6.   1. Product unit cost: $878.25
P 7.   3. Product unit cost: $10.43
P 8.   3. Cost of goods sold: $391,520

Chapter 23 Problems
P 1.   4. Cost per Job: $81.56
P 2.   1. 7,500 Billable Hours

P 3.   1.a. 3,500 Units
P 4.   2. 190,000 Units
P 5.   3. $806.60 per Job
P 6.   1. 740 Systems
P 7.   1.a. 7,900 Units
P 8.   2. 418 Loans

Chapter 24 Problems
P 1.   1. Total manufacturing costs budgeted,
        November: $1,157,000
P 2.   8. Income from operations: $3,086
P 3.   1. Ending cash balance, August: $1,800
P 4.   1. Projected net income: $101,812
P 5.   Ending cash balance, February, $19,555
P 6.   1. Net income: $1,860,830
P 7.   1. Ending cash balance, February: ($2,900)
P 8.   1. Net income: $52,404

Chapter 25 Problems
P 1.   Total standard unit cost of front entrance: $8,510
P 2.   2. Flexible budget formula: Total Budgeted Costs =
        ($.35 x Units Produced) ı $10,500
P 3.   1. Direct materials price variance—Metal: $832 (F);
        2. Direct labor rate variance—Molding: $510 (F)
P 4.   1.b. Direct materials quantity variance: $3,720 (U);
        1.h. Fixed overhead volume variance: $320 (F)
P 5.   c. Actual variable overhead: $42,500
P 6.   1. Total standard direct materials cost per unit:
        $167.52
P 7.   1. Direct materials price variance—Liquid
        Plastic: $386 (F); 2. Direct labor rate variance—
        Trimming/Packing: $56 (U)
P 8.   1.a. Direct materials price variance—Chemicals:
        $12,200 (F); 1.e. Variable overhead spending
        variance: $100 (U)

Chapter 26 Problems
P 1.   1. Flexible Budget, Total Cost: $7,248,000
P 2.   2. Operating Income: $194,782
P 3.   1. Flexible Budget, Contribution margin: $88,200
P 4.   3. Economic value added for 20x8: $21,850
P 5.   1. Residual income: ($2,500)
P 6.   2. Operating Income: $418,555
P 7.   3a. Actual Return on Investment: 6.3%
P 8.   3. Economic value added: $126,000

Chapter 27 Problems
P 1.   3. Operating income from further processing,
        bagel sandwiches: $.50
P 2.   1. Segment margin for Book X: $223,560
P 3.   2. $68.20
P 4.   1. Net present value: $99,672
P 5.   1. HTZ Machine: 13.4 %; 2. XJS Machine:
        5.5 years
P 6.   1. Total cost to buy: $1,293,750
P 7.   1. Contribution margin per hour for
        phone calls: $130
P 8.   1.a. Net present value: ($26,895)

Principles of Accounting

1

Chapter 1 explores the nature and environment of accounting, with special emphasis on the users and uses of accounting information.

Uses of Accounting Information and the Financial Statements

LEARNING OBJECTIVES

LO1 Define *accounting,* identify business goals and activities, and describe the role of accounting in making informed decisions.

LO2 Identify the many users of accounting information in society.

LO3 Explain the importance of business transactions, money measure, and separate entity to accounting measurement.

LO4 Identify the three basic forms of business organization.

LO5 Define *financial position,* state the accounting equation, and show how they are affected by simple transactions.

LO6 Identify the four financial statements.

LO7 State the relationship of generally accepted accounting principles (GAAP) to financial statements and the independent CPA's report, and identify the organizations that influence GAAP.

LO8 Define *ethics* and describe the ethical responsibilities of accountants.

Look to the learning objectives (LOs) as a guide to help you master the material. You will see many references to LOs throughout each chapter.

Look in the margin for reminders of key concepts or ideas.

KEY POINT: Management must have a good understanding of accounting to set financial goals and to make financial decisions. Management not only must understand how accounting information is compiled and processed but also must realize that accounting information is imperfect and should be interpreted with caution.

DECISION POINT

A USER'S FOCUS

Walgreen Co. <www.walgreens.com>, a nationwide chain of more than 3,800 drugstores and pharmacies, has been a retailing success story, with 28 years of record sales and earnings. During the past five years, Walgreens has opened or remodeled 2,094 stores and by 2010 plans to operate more than 7,000 stores. In fiscal 2002, sales in stores open more than a year rose 10.5 percent.

Why is Walgreens considered successful? Customers appreciate the quality of the products that the company sells and the large selection and good service that its stores offer. Investment companies and others with a financial stake in Walgreens evaluate the success of the company and its management in financial terms, such as those contained in the Financial Highlights from the company's annual report, shown on the opposite page.[1]

Net sales, net earnings, total assets, and stockholders' equity are common financial measures of all companies, large or small. These measures are used to evaluate a company's management and to compare the company to other companies. It is easy to see the large increases at Walgreens over the years in these measures, but what do the terms mean? What financial knowledge do Walgreens' managers need to measure progress toward their financial goals? What financial knowledge does anyone who is evaluating Walgreens in relation to other companies need to understand these measures?

Walgreens' managers must have a thorough knowledge of accounting to understand how the operations for which they are responsible contribute

What kind of information do the people with a financial stake in Walgreens need to have?

to the firm's overall financial health. People with a financial stake in the company, such as owners, investors, creditors, employees, attorneys, and governmental regulators, must also know accounting to evaluate the financial performance of a business. Anyone who aspires to any of these roles in a business requires mastery of accounting terminology and concepts, the process of producing financial information, and how that information is interpreted and analyzed. The purpose of this course and this textbook is to assist you in acquiring that mastery.

A Decision Point at the start of each chapter shows how leading businesses use the accounting information presented in their annual reports to make business decisions.

Walgreens' Financial Highlights
(In millions)

	2002	2001	2000	1999	1998
Net sales	**$28,681**	$24,623	$21,207	$17,839	$15,307
Net earnings	**1,019**	886	777	624	511
Total assets	**9,879**	8,834	7,104	5,907	4,902
Stockholders' equity	**6,230**	5,207	4,234	3,484	2,849

ACCOUNTING AS AN INFORMATION SYSTEM

LO1 Define *accounting*, identify business goals and activities, and describe the role of accounting in making informed decisions.

RELATED TEXT ASSIGNMENTS
Q: 1, 2, 3, 4
E: 1
P: 4, 7
SD: 1, 5
FRA: 2, 4, 6, 7, 8

Today's accountant focuses on the ultimate needs of decision makers who use accounting information, whether those decision makers are inside or outside the business. **Accounting** "is not an end in itself,"[2] but *an information system that measures, processes, and communicates financial information about an identifiable economic entity.* An economic entity is a unit that exists independently—for example, a business, a hospital, or a governmental body. The central focus of this book is on business entities and business activities, although other economic units, such as hospitals and governmental units, are mentioned at appropriate points in the text and assignment material.

Accounting provides a vital service by supplying the information that decision makers need to make "reasoned choices among alternative uses of scarce resources in the conduct of business and economic activities."[3] As shown in Figure 1, accounting is a link between business activities and decision makers. First, accounting measures business activities by recording data about them for future use. Second, the data are stored until needed and then processed to become useful information. Third, the information is communicated, through reports, to decision makers. We might say that data about business activities are the input to the accounting system and that useful information for decision makers is the output.

BUSINESS GOALS, ACTIVITIES, AND PERFORMANCE MEASURES

A **business** is an economic unit that aims to sell goods and services to customers at prices that will provide an adequate return to its owners. The list on the opposite page contains the names of some very well-known businesses and the principal goods or services that they sell.

FIGURE 1
Accounting as an Information System

● STOP AND THINK!
What makes accounting a valuable discipline?
The primary purpose of accounting is to provide decision makers with the financial information they need to make intelligent decisions. It is a valuable discipline because of the usefulness of the information it generates. ■

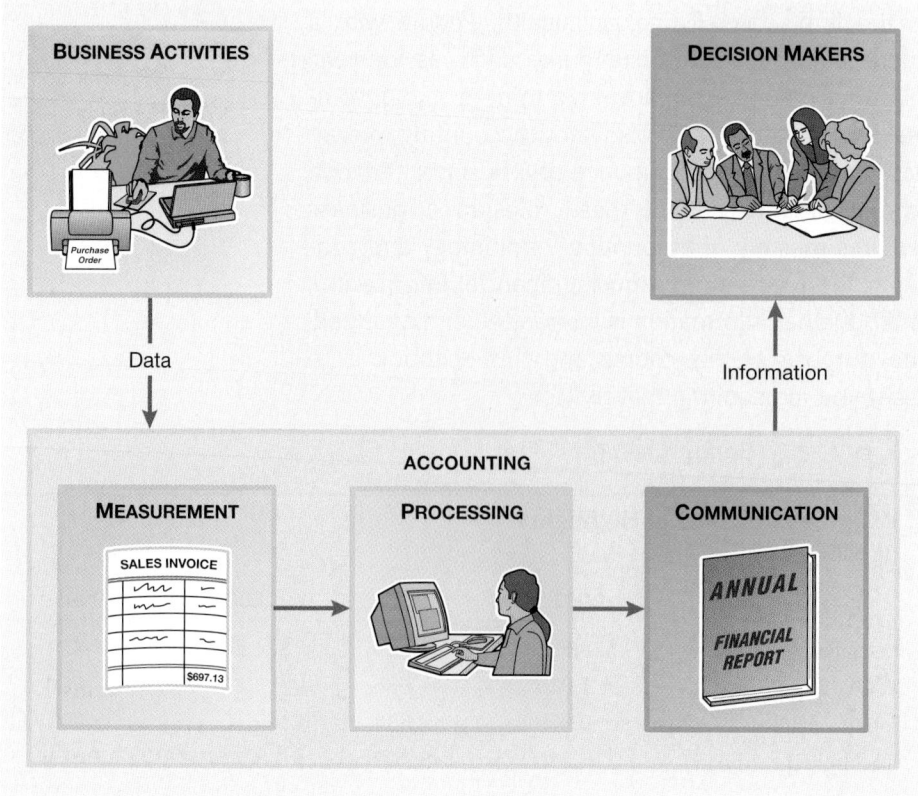

Intel Corporation <www.intel.com>

OBJECTIVES

■ To examine the principal activities of a business enterprise: financing, investing, and operating.

■ To explore the principal performance goals of a business enterprise: liquidity and profitability.

■ To relate these activities and goals to the financial statements.

BACKGROUND FOR THE CASE

Intel Corporation is one of the most successful companies in the world. In 1971, Intel introduced the world's first microprocessor, which made the personal computer (PC) possible. Today, Intel supplies the computing industry with chips, boards, systems, and software. Its principal products include:

■ **Microprocessors.** Also called central processing units (CPUs), these are frequently described as the "brains" of a computer because they act as the central control for the processing of data in PCs. This category includes the famous Pentium® processor.

■ **Networking and Communications Products.** These products enhance the capabilities and ease of use of PC systems by allowing users to talk to each other and to share information.

■ **Semiconductor Products.** Semiconductors facilitate flash memory, making possible easily reprogrammable memory for computers, mobile phones, and many other products. Included in this category are embedded control chips that are programmed to regulate specific functions in such products as automobile engines, laser printers, disk drives, and home appliances.

In addition to PC users, Intel's customers include manufacturers of computers and computer systems, automobiles, and a wide range of industrial and telecommunications equipment.

For more information about Intel Corporation, visit the company's web site directly or access it through the Needles Accounting Resource Center Web Site at **http://accounting.college.hmco.com/students.**

REQUIRED

View the video on Intel Corporation that accompanies this book. As you are watching the video, take notes related to the following:

1. All businesses engage in three basic activities—financing, investing, and operating—but how they engage in them differs from company to company. Describe in your own words the nature of each of these activities and give as many examples as you can of how Intel engages in each activity.

2. To be successful, all businesses must achieve two performance objectives—liquidity and profitability. Describe in your own words the nature of each of these goals and describe how each applies to Intel.

3. Four financial statements apply to business enterprises. Which statements are most closely associated with the goal of liquidity? Which statement is most closely associated with the goal of profitability? Which statement shows the financial position of the company?

> Video cases introduce key concepts and techniques presented in the chapter in the context of a real company.

www.generalmills.com	General Mills, Inc.	Food products
www.reebok.com	Reebok International Ltd.	Athletic footwear and clothing
www.sony.com	Sony Corp.	Consumer electronics
www.wendys.com	Wendy's International Inc.	Food service
www.hilton.com	Hilton Hotels Corp.	Hotels and resorts service
www.southwest.com	Southwest Airlines Co.	Passenger airline service

Icons are visual guides to key features of text and supporting study aids.

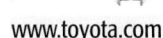

www.toyota.com

Despite their differences, all these businesses have similar goals and engage in similar activities, as shown in Figure 2. Each must take in enough money from customers to pay all the costs of doing business, with enough left over as profit for the owners to want to stay in the business. This need to earn enough income to attract and hold investment capital is the goal of **profitability**. In addition, businesses must meet the goal of liquidity. **Liquidity** means having enough cash available to pay debts when they are due. For example, Toyota may meet the goal of profitability by selling many cars at a price that earns a profit, but if its customers do not pay for their cars quickly enough to enable Toyota to pay its suppliers and employees, the

FIGURE 2
Business Goals and Activities

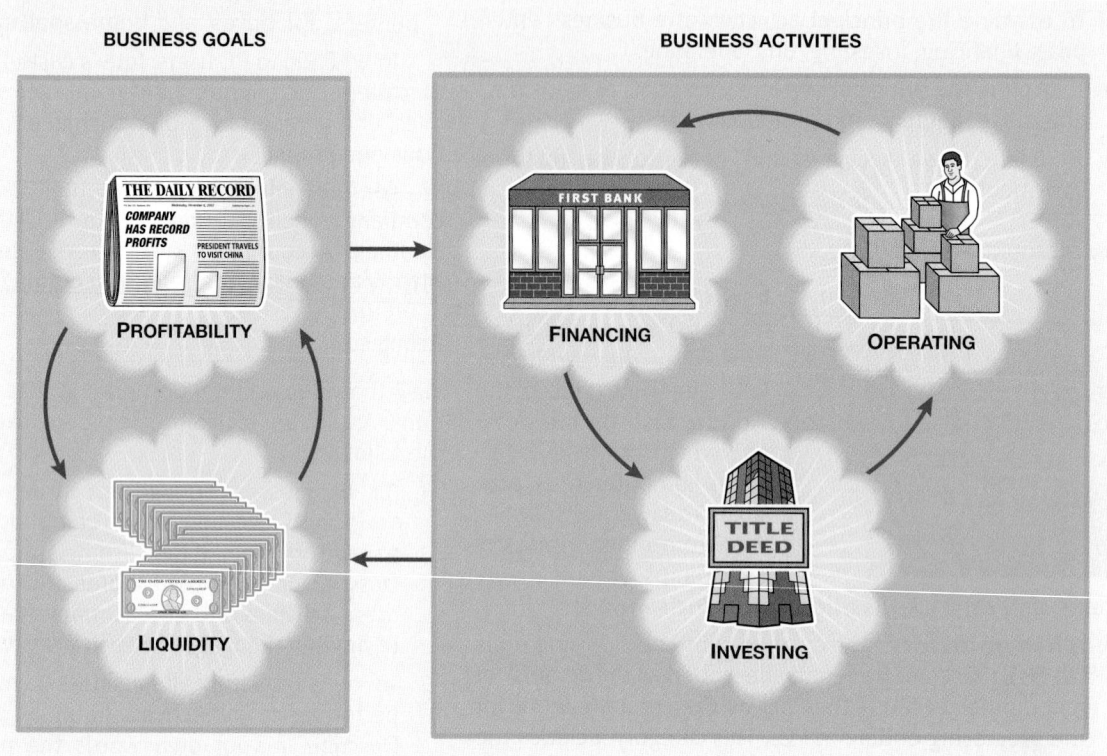

KEY POINT: Multiple financial goals signal that more than one measure of performance is of interest to users of accounting information. For example, lenders are concerned primarily with cash flow, and owners are concerned with earnings and dividends.

The cash flow icon highlights discussion of cash as a measure of liquidity.

The key ratio icon highlights discussion of a measure used to evaluate a company's performance.

company may fail to meet the goal of liquidity. Both goals must be met if a company is to survive and be successful.

All businesses pursue their goals by engaging in similar activities. First, each business must engage in **financing activities** to obtain adequate funds, or capital, to begin and to continue operating. Financing activities include obtaining capital from owners and from creditors, such as banks and suppliers. They also include repaying creditors and paying a return to the owners. Second, each business must engage in **investing activities** to spend the capital it receives in ways that are productive and will help the business achieve its objectives. Investing activities include buying land, buildings, equipment, and other resources that are needed in the operation of the business, and selling these resources when they are no longer needed. Third, each business must engage in **operating activities**. In addition to the selling of goods and services to customers, operating activities include such actions as employing managers and workers, buying and producing goods and services, and paying taxes to the government.

An important function of accounting is to provide **performance measures**, which indicate whether managers are achieving their business goals and whether the business activities are well managed. It is important that these performance measures align with the goals of the business. For example, earned income is a measure of profitability, and cash flow is a measure of liquidity. Ratios of accounting measures are also used as performance measures. For instance, one performance measure for operating activities might be the ratio of expenses to the revenue of the business. A performance measure for financing activities might be the ratio of money owed by the business to total resources controlled by the company. Because managers are usually evaluated on whether targeted levels of specific performance measures are achieved, they must have a knowledge of accounting to understand how they are evaluated and how they can improve their performance. Furthermore,

How Do Performance Measures Relate to Executive Bonuses?

A study of chief executive officers' bonus contracts shows that almost all companies use financial performance measures for determining annual bonuses. The most frequent measures are earnings per share, net income, operating income, return on equity, and cash flow. About one-third of the companies studied also use nonfinancial performance measures to determine bonuses. Examples of nonfinancial measures are customer satisfaction, product or service quality, nonfinancial strategic objectives, efficiency or productivity, and employee safety.[4]

www.gap.com

www.walgreens.com

Notations like these indicate that a direct link to the company's web site is available on the Needles Accounting Resource Center Web Site at http://accounting.college.hmco.com/students.

Focus on Business boxes highlight the relevance of accounting in four different areas: business practice, business technology, business ethics, and international business.

because managers will act to achieve them, the targeted performance measures must be crafted in such a way as to motivate managers to take actions that are in the best interests of the owners of the business.

FINANCIAL AND MANAGEMENT ACCOUNTING

Accounting's role of assisting decision makers by measuring, processing, and communicating information is usually divided into the categories of management accounting and financial accounting. Although there is considerable overlap in the functions of management accounting and financial accounting, the two can be distinguished by who the principal users of their information will be. Management accounting provides internal decision makers who are charged with achieving the goals of profitability and liquidity with information about financing, investing, and operating activities. Managers and employees who conduct the activities of the business need information that tells them how they have done in the past and what they can expect in the future. For example, The Gap, a retail clothing business, needs an operating report on each mall outlet that tells how much was sold at that outlet and what costs were incurred, and it needs a budget for each outlet that projects the sales and costs for the next year. Financial accounting generates reports and communicates them to external decision makers so that they can evaluate how well the business has achieved its goals. These reports to external users are called financial statements. Walgreens, whose stock is traded on the New York Stock Exchange, sends its financial statements to its owners (called *stockholders*), its banks and other creditors, and government regulators. Financial statements report directly on the goals of profitability and liquidity and are used extensively both inside and outside a business to evaluate the business's success. It is important for every person involved with a business to understand financial statements. They are a central feature of accounting and are the primary focus of this book.

PROCESSING ACCOUNTING INFORMATION

To avoid misunderstandings, it is important to distinguish accounting itself from the ways in which accounting information is processed by bookkeeping, computers, and management information systems.

What Does Walgreens Have to Say about Itself?

Walgreens <www.walgreens.com> reports its performance in meeting the major business objectives in its annual report.[5]

Liquidity: "A chunk of our positive cash position is due to a big improvement in inventory levels. . . . Short-term borrowings of $441 million were completely repaid during the year. For my money, the beauty of our 2002 balance sheet rivals Monet, showing a positive cash swing from borrowing to investing of nearly $900 million."

Profitablility: "We completed our 28th consecutive record year—and first billion-dollar earnings year—while opening 471 stores. . . ."

Walgreens' main business activities are shown at the right.

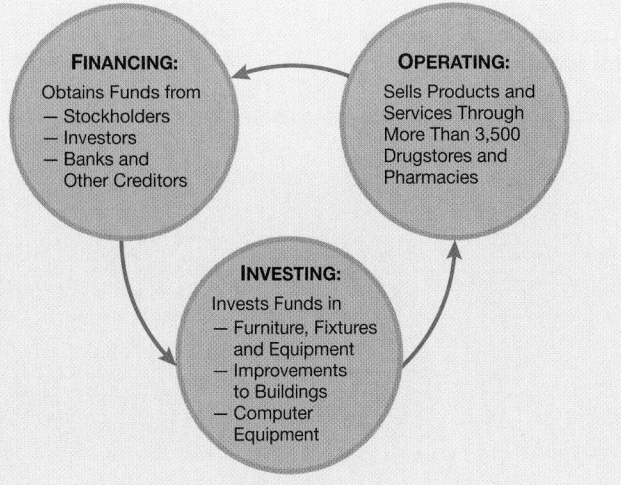

FOCUS ON BUSINESS PRACTICE

How Did Accounting Develop?

Accounting is a very old discipline. Forms of it have been essential to commerce for more than five thousand years. Accounting, in a version close to what we know today, gained widespread use in the 1400s, especially in Italy, where it was instrumental in the development of shipping, trade, construction, and other forms of commerce. This system of double-entry bookkeeping was documented by the famous Italian mathematician, scholar, and philosopher Fra Luca Pacioli. In 1494, Pacioli published his most important work, *Summa de Arithmetica, Geometrica, Proportioni et Proportionalita*, which contained a detailed description of accounting as practiced in that age. This book became the most widely read book on mathematics in Italy and firmly established Pacioli as the "Father of Accounting."

People often fail to understand the difference between accounting and bookkeeping. Bookkeeping is the process of recording financial transactions and keeping financial records. Mechanical and repetitive, bookkeeping is only a small—but important—part of accounting. Accounting, on the other hand, includes the design of an information system that meets the user's needs. The major goals of accounting are the analysis, interpretation, and use of information.

The computer is an electronic tool used to collect, organize, and communicate vast amounts of information with great speed. Accountants were among the earliest and most enthusiastic users of computers, and today they use microcomputers in all aspects of their work. It may appear that the computer is doing the accountant's job; in fact, it is only a tool that is instructed to do routine bookkeeping and to perform complex calculations.

KEY POINT: Computerized accounting information is only as reliable and useful as the data that go into the system. The accountant must have a thorough understanding of the concepts that underlie accounting to ensure the data's reliability and usefulness.

With the widespread use of the computer today, a business's many information needs are organized into what is called a management information system (MIS). A management information system consists of the interconnected subsystems that provide the information needed to run a business. The accounting information system is the most important subsystem because it plays the key role of managing the flow of economic data to all parts of a business and to interested parties outside the business.

 Check out ACE for a Review Quiz at http://accounting.college.hmco.com/students.

DECISION MAKERS: THE USERS OF ACCOUNTING INFORMATION

LO2 Identify the many users of accounting information in society.

RELATED TEXT ASSIGNMENTS
Q: 5, 6, 7, 8, 9
E: 1, 2
SD: 1, 2, 5

As shown in Figure 3, the people who use accounting information to make decisions fall into three categories: (1) those who manage a business; (2) those outside a business enterprise who have a direct financial interest in the business; and (3) those people, organizations, and agencies that have an indirect financial interest in the business. These categories apply to governmental and not-for-profit organizations as well as to profit-oriented ventures.

FIGURE 3
The Users of Accounting Information

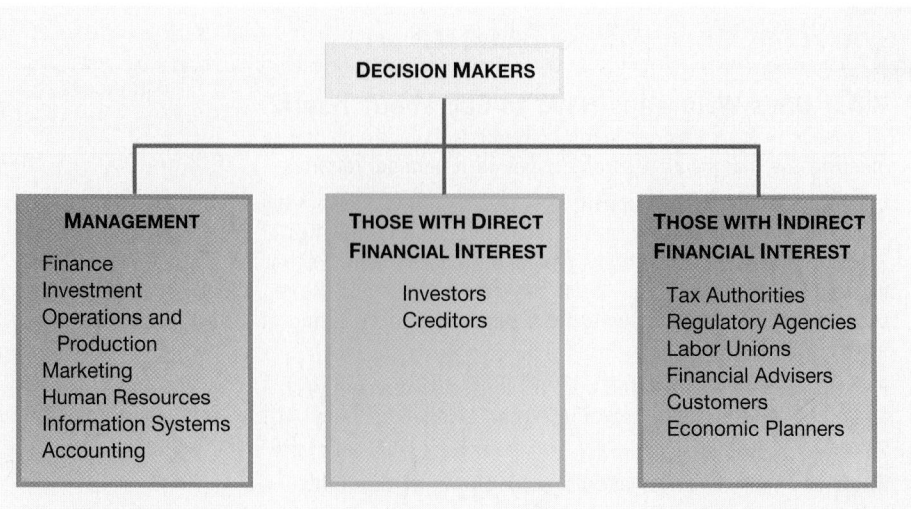

MANAGEMENT

KEY POINT: Managers are internal users of accounting information.

Management refers to the people who have overall responsibility for operating a business and for meeting its profitability and liquidity goals. In a small business, management may consist solely of the owners. In a large business, management more often consists of people who have been hired to do the job. Managers must decide what to do, how to do it, and whether the results match their original plans. Successful managers consistently make the right decisions based on timely and valid information. To make good decisions, managers need answers to such questions as: What was the company's net income during the past quarter? Is the rate of return to the owners adequate? Does the company have enough cash? Which products are most profitable? What is the cost of manufacturing each product? Because so many key decisions are based on accounting data, management is one of the most important users of accounting information.

In carrying out its decision-making process, management performs a set of functions that are essential to the operation of the business. Although large businesses have more elaborate operations than small ones, the same basic functions must be accomplished in all cases, and each requires accounting information for decision making. The basic management functions are:

Financing the business.   Financial management obtains financial resources so that the company can begin and continue operating.

Investing the resources of the business.   Asset management invests the financial resources of the business in productive assets that support the company's goals.

Producing goods and services.   Operations and production management develops and produces goods and services.

Marketing goods and services.   Marketing management sells, advertises, and distributes goods and services.

Managing employees.   Human resource management encompasses the hiring, evaluation, and compensation of employees.

Providing information to decision makers.   Information systems management captures data about all aspects of the company's operations, organizes the data into usable information, and provides reports to internal managers and appropriate outside parties. Accounting plays a key role in this function.

USERS WITH A DIRECT FINANCIAL INTEREST

KEY POINT: The primary external users of accounting information are investors and creditors.

Another group of decision makers who need accounting information are those with a direct financial interest in a business. They depend on accounting to measure and report information about how a business has performed. Most businesses periodically publish a set of general-purpose financial statements that report their success in meeting the goals of profitability and liquidity. These statements show what has happened in the past, and they are important indicators of what will happen in the future. Many people outside the company carefully study these financial reports. The two most important outside groups are investors and creditors.

■ **INVESTORS**   Those who invest or may invest in a business and acquire a part ownership are interested in its past success and its potential earnings. A thorough study of a company's financial statements helps potential investors judge the prospects for a profitable investment. After investing, they must continually review their commitment, again by examining the company's financial statements.

■ **CREDITORS**   Most companies borrow money for both long- and short-term operating needs. Creditors, those who lend money or deliver goods and services before being paid, are interested mainly in whether a company will have the cash to pay interest charges and to repay debt at the appropriate time. They study a

FOCUS ON BUSINESS PRACTICE

What Does the CFO Do?

John Connors, chief financial officer (CFO) of Microsoft <www.microsoft.com>, emphasizes that providing information to decision makers is an important accounting function:

The way I look at it, the [chief financial officer's] principal job is providing information that the business needs to make good decisions. . . . The real purpose is getting the information that managers need to do their jobs better, whether it is in sales and marketing, research and development, in the support groups, or operations.[6]

company's liquidity and cash flow as well as its profitability. Banks, finance companies, mortgage companies, securities firms, insurance firms, suppliers, and other lenders must analyze a company's financial position before they make a loan.

USERS WITH AN INDIRECT FINANCIAL INTEREST

In recent years, society as a whole, through governmental and public groups, has become one of the largest and most important users of accounting information. Users who need accounting information to make decisions on public issues include tax authorities, regulatory agencies, and various other groups.

■ **TAX AUTHORITIES**   Government at every level is financed through the collection of taxes. Under federal, state, and local laws, companies and individuals pay many kinds of taxes, including federal, state, and city income taxes; social security and other payroll taxes; excise taxes; and sales taxes. Each tax requires special tax returns and often a complex set of records as well. Proper reporting is generally a matter of law and can be very complicated. The Internal Revenue Code, for instance, contains thousands of rules governing the preparation of the accounting information used in computing federal income taxes.

■ **REGULATORY AGENCIES**   Most companies must report periodically to one or more regulatory agencies at the federal, state, and local levels. For example, all public

www.sec.gov   corporations must report periodically to the Securities and Exchange Commission (SEC). This body, set up by Congress to protect the public, regulates the issuing, buying, and selling of stocks in the United States. Companies listed on a stock exchange also must meet the special reporting requirements of their exchange.

■ **OTHER GROUPS**   Labor unions study the financial statements of corporations as part of preparing for contract negotiations; a company's income and costs often play an important role in these negotiations. Those who advise investors and creditors— financial analysts, brokers, underwriters, lawyers, economists, and the financial press—also have an indirect interest in the financial performance and prospects of a business. Consumer groups, customers, and the general public have become more concerned about the financing and earnings of corporations as well as the effects that corporations have on inflation, the environment, social problems, and the quality of life. And economic planners, among them the President's Council of Economic Advisers and the Federal Reserve Board, use aggregated accounting information to set and evaluate economic policies and programs.

GOVERNMENTAL AND NOT-FOR-PROFIT ORGANIZATIONS

● **STOP AND THINK!**
Why do managers in governmental and not-for-profit organizations need to understand financial information as much as managers in profit-seeking businesses?

Like managers of profit-seeking businesses, managers of governmental and not-for-profit organizations must report to those who fund them, and they must operate their organizations in a financially prudent way. ■

More than 30 percent of the U.S. economy is generated by governmental and not-for-profit organizations (hospitals, universities, professional organizations, and charities). The managers of these diverse entities need to understand and to use accounting information to perform the same functions as managers in businesses. They need to raise funds from investors, creditors, taxpayers, and donors, and to deploy scarce resources. They need to plan to pay for operations and to repay creditors on a timely basis. Moreover, they have an obligation to report their financial performance to legislators, boards, and donors, as well as to deal with tax authorities, regulators, and labor unions. Although most of the examples throughout this text focus on business enterprises, the same basic principles apply to governmental and not-for-profit organizations.

 Check out ACE for a Review Quiz at http://accounting.college.hmco.com/students.

ACCOUNTING MEASUREMENT

LO3 Explain the importance of business transactions, money measure, and separate entity to accounting measurement.

RELATED TEXT ASSIGNMENTS
Q: 10
SE: 1
E: 3, 4, 5
SD: 3

TERMINOLOGY NOTE:
Measurement means the analysis of transactions in terms of recognition, valuation, and classification. That is, it answers the question: How is this transaction best represented in the accounting records?

↑

Terminology notes define terms used in the text.

◉ STOP AND THINK!
Are all economic events business transactions?
No, because not all economic events involve exchanges of value between a business and someone else. For example, when a customer places an order, it is an economic event, but until the order is fulfilled, no exchange of value has taken place. ■

www.acehardware.com

Accounting is an information system that measures, processes, and communicates financial information. In this section, you begin the study of the measurement aspects of accounting. Here you learn what accounting actually measures and how certain transactions affect a company's financial position.

To make an accounting measurement, the accountant must answer four basic questions:

1. What is measured?
2. When should the measurement be made?
3. What value should be placed on what is measured?
4. How should what is measured be classified?

All these questions deal with basic assumptions and accepted accounting practice, and their answers establish what accounting is and what it is not. Accountants in industry, professional associations, public accounting, government, and academic circles debate the answers to these questions constantly, and the answers change as new knowledge and practice require. But the basis of today's accounting practice rests on a number of widely accepted concepts and conventions, which are described in this book. We begin by focusing on the first question: What is measured?

WHAT IS MEASURED?

The world contains an unlimited number of things to measure and ways to measure them. Consider a machine that makes bottle caps. How many measurements of this machine could you make? You might start with size and then go on to location, weight, cost, and many other units of measurement. Some of these measurements are relevant to accounting; some are not. Every system must define what it measures, and accounting is no exception. Basically, financial accounting uses money measures to gauge the impact of business transactions on separate business entities. The concepts of business transactions, money measure, and separate entity are discussed in the next sections.

BUSINESS TRANSACTIONS AS THE OBJECT OF MEASUREMENT

Business transactions are economic events that affect the financial position of a business entity. Business entities can have hundreds or even thousands of transactions every day. These transactions are the raw material of accounting reports.

A transaction can be an exchange of value (a purchase, sale, payment, collection, or loan) between two or more independent parties. A transaction also can be an economic event that has the same effect as an exchange transaction but does not involve an exchange. Some examples of "nonexchange" transactions are losses from fire, flood, explosion, and theft; physical wear and tear on machinery and equipment; and the day-by-day accumulation of interest.

To be recorded, a transaction must relate directly to a business entity. Suppose a customer buys a shovel from Ace Hardware but has to buy a hoe from a competing store because Ace is out of hoes. The transaction in which the shovel was sold is entered in Ace's records. However, the purchase of the hoe from the competitor is not entered in Ace's records because even though it indirectly affects Ace economically, it does not involve a direct exchange of value between Ace and the customer.

MONEY MEASURE

All business transactions are recorded in terms of money. This concept is termed **money measure**. Of course, information of a nonfinancial nature may be recorded, but it is through the recording of monetary amounts that the diverse transactions

TABLE 1. Examples of Foreign Exchange Rates

Country	Price in $ U.S.	Country	Price in $ U.S.
Australia (dollar)	0.631	Hong Kong (dollar)	0.128
Brazil (real)	0.34	Japan (yen)	0.008
Britain (pound)	1.61	Mexico (peso)	0.10
Canada (dollar)	0.704	Russia (ruble)	0.032
Europe (euro)	1.12	Singapore (dollar)	0.565

Source: The Wall Street Journal, May 5, 2003.

Tables give factual information referred to in the text. ————→

and activities of a business are measured. Money is the only factor common to all business transactions, and thus it is the only practical unit of measure that can produce financial data that are alike and can be compared.

KEY POINT: The common unit of measurement in the United States for financial reporting purposes is the dollar.

The monetary unit a business uses depends on the country in which the business resides. For example, in the United States, the basic unit of money is the dollar. In Japan, it is the yen; in Europe, the euro; and in the United Kingdom, the pound. In international transactions, exchange rates must be used to translate from one currency to another. An **exchange rate** is the value of one currency in terms of another. For example, a British person purchasing goods from a U.S. company and paying in U.S. dollars must exchange British pounds for U.S. dollars before making payment. In effect, the currencies are goods that can be bought and sold. Table 1 illustrates the exchange rates for several currencies in dollars. It shows the exchange rate for British pounds as $1.61 per pound on a particular date. Like the prices of most goods, these prices change daily according to supply and demand for the currencies. For example, a few years earlier the exchange rate for British pounds was $1.43. Although our discussion in this book focuses on dollars, selected examples and certain assignments will be in foreign currencies.

Study notes provide useful tips on ways to avoid common pitfalls.
↓

STUDY NOTE: For accounting purposes, a business is *always* separate and distinct from its owners, creditors, and customers. Note, however, that there is a difference between separate economic entity and separate legal entity.

THE CONCEPT OF SEPARATE ENTITY

For accounting purposes, a business is a **separate entity**, distinct not only from its creditors and customers but also from its owner or owners. It should have a completely separate set of records, and its financial records and reports should refer only to its own financial affairs. For example, the Jones Florist Company should have a bank account separate from the account of Kay Jones, the owner. Kay Jones may own a home, a car, and other property, and she may have personal debts, but these are not the Jones Florist Company's resources or debts. Kay Jones also may own another business, say a stationery shop. If she does, she should have a completely separate set of records for each business.

 Check out ACE for a Review Quiz at http://accounting.college.hmco.com/students.

FORMS OF BUSINESS ORGANIZATION

LO4 Identify the three basic forms of business organization.

RELATED TEXT ASSIGNMENTS
Q: 11
SE: 2
E: 2

There are three basic forms of business organization: sole proprietorships, partnerships, and corporations. Accountants recognize each form as an economic unit separate from its owners, although legally only the corporation is considered separate from its owners. Other legal differences among the three forms are summarized in Table 2 and discussed briefly in the following sections. In this book, we begin with accounting for the sole proprietorship because it is the simplest form of accounting. At critical points, however, we call attention to its essential differences from accounting for partnerships and corporations.

TABLE 2.   Comparative Features of the Forms of Business Organization

	Sole Proprietorship	Partnership	Corporation
1. Legal status	Not a separate legal entity	Not a separate legal entity	Separate legal entity
2. Risk of ownership	Owner's personal resources at stake	Partners' personal resources at stake	Limited to investment in corporation
3. Duration or life	Limited by choice or death of owner	Limited by choice or death of any partner	Indefinite, possibly unlimited
4. Transferability of ownership	Sale by owner establishes new company	Changes in any partner's percentage of interest requires new partnership	Transferable by sale of stock
5. Accounting treatment	Separate economic unit	Separate economic unit	Separate economic unit

SOLE PROPRIETORSHIPS

KEY POINT: In a sole proprietorship or partnership, the owners generally manage the business. In a corporation, however, there is a separation between ownership and management. The owners (stockholders) elect a board of directors to run the corporation for their benefit.

A **sole proprietorship** is a business owned by one person and is not incorporated. This form of organization gives the individual a means of controlling the business apart from his or her personal interests. Legally, however, the proprietorship is the same economic unit as the individual. The individual receives all profits or losses and is liable for all obligations of the business. Proprietorships represent the largest number of businesses in the United States, but they transact far less business in dollar terms than do corporations. In addition, they are typically the smallest in size. The life of a sole proprietorship ends when the owner wants it to or when the owner dies or becomes incapacitated.

PARTNERSHIPS

KEY POINT: A key disadvantage of a partnership is the unlimited liability of its owners. Unlimited liability can be avoided by organizing the business as a corporation.

A **partnership** is like a proprietorship in most ways except that it has more than one owner. A partnership is not a legal entity separate from the owner; it is an unincorporated association that brings together the talents and resources of two or more people. The partners share the profits and losses of the partnership according to an agreed-upon formula. Generally, any partner can obligate the partnership to another party, and the personal resources of each partner can be called on to pay the obligations of the partnership. In some cases, one or more partners limit their liability, but at least one partner must have unlimited liability. A partnership must be dissolved when ownership changes—for example, when a partner leaves or dies. For the business to continue as a partnership, a new partnership must be formed.

FOCUS ON BUSINESS PRACTICE

Are Most Corporations Big or Small Businesses?

Most people think of corporations as large national or global companies whose shares of stock are held by thousands of people and institutions. However, of the approximately 4 million corporations in the United States, only about 15,000 have stock that is publicly bought and sold. The vast majority of corporations are small businesses privately held by a few stockholders. Illinois alone has more than 250,000 corporations. Thus, the study of corporations is just as relevant to small businesses as it is to large ones.

CORPORATIONS

A **corporation** is a business unit chartered by the state and legally separate from its owners (the stockholders). The stockholders, whose ownership is represented by shares of stock, do not directly control the corporation's operations. Instead, they elect a board of directors to run the corporation for their benefit. In exchange for their limited involvement in the corporation's actual operations, stockholders enjoy limited liability; that is, their risk of loss is limited to the amount they paid for their shares. Thus, stockholders are often willing to invest in risky, but potentially

FIGURE 4
Number and Receipts of U.S. Proprietorships, Partnerships, and Corporations, 1999

NUMBER OF BUSINESSES

Proprietorships	17,176
Partnerships	1,758
Corporations	4,710

0 2 4 6 8 10 12 14 16 18 Millions

RECEIPTS OF BUSINESSES

Proprietorships	$ 870
Partnerships	1,141
Corporations	16,610

$0 2,000 4,000 6,000 8,000 10,000 12,000 14,000 16,000 18,000 Billions

Source: U.S. Treasury Department, Internal Revenue Service, *Statistics of Income Bulletin,* Spring 2000.

● **STOP AND THINK!**
Sole proprietorships, partnerships, and corporations differ legally; how and why does accounting treat them alike?
Accounting treats these business forms as entities separate from their owners because the financial performance of each must be measured and reported. ■

www.exxonmobil.com

profitable, activities. Also, because stockholders can sell their shares without dissolving the corporation, the life of a corporation is unlimited and not subject to the whims or health of a proprietor or a partner.

The characteristics of corporations make them very efficient in amassing capital, which enables them to grow extremely large. Even though corporations are fewer in number than sole proprietorships and partnerships, they contribute much more to the economy of the United States in monetary terms (see Figure 4). For example, in 1999, ExxonMobil generated more revenues than all but 30 of the world's countries.

 Check out ACE for a Review Quiz at http://accounting.college.hmco.com/students.

FINANCIAL POSITION AND THE ACCOUNTING EQUATION

LO5 Define *financial position,* state the accounting equation, and show how they are affected by simple transactions.

RELATED TEXT ASSIGNMENTS
Q: 12, 13, 14, 15
SE: 3, 4, 5, 6, 7, 8, 9
E: 6, 7, 8, 9, 10, 11
P: 1, 2, 3, 5, 6, 8
SD: 6
FRA: 6, 8

Financial position refers to the economic resources that belong to a company and the claims against those resources at a point in time. Another term for claims is *equities.* Therefore, a company can be viewed as economic resources and equities:

$$\text{Economic Resources} = \text{Equities}$$

Every company has two types of equities, creditors' equities and owner's equity:

$$\text{Economic Resources} = \text{Creditors' Equities} + \text{Owner's Equity}$$

In accounting terminology, economic resources are called *assets* and creditors' equities are called *liabilities.* So the equation can be written like this:

$$\text{Assets} = \text{Liabilities} + \text{Owner's Equity}$$

This equation is known as the **accounting equation**. The two sides of the accounting equation must always be equal—that is, they must always be in balance. To evaluate the financial effects of business activities, it is important to understand their effects on this equation.

ASSETS

KEY POINT: Assets are the resources of a business, the essence of which is expected future benefits.

Assets are economic resources owned by a business that are expected to benefit future operations. Certain kinds of assets—for example, cash and money owed to the company by customers (called *accounts receivable*)—are monetary items. Other assets—inventories (goods held for sale), land, buildings, and equipment—are nonmonetary, physical items. Still other assets—the rights granted by patents, trademarks, or copyrights—are nonphysical.

LIABILITIES

KEY POINT: A liability is a debt or obligation that is satisfied with the payment of cash or the performance of a service.

Liabilities are present obligations of a business to pay cash, transfer assets, or provide services to other entities in the future. Among these obligations are debts of the business, amounts owed to suppliers for goods or services bought on credit (called *accounts payable*), borrowed money (for example, money owed on loans payable to banks), salaries and wages owed to employees, taxes owed to the government, and services to be performed.

As debts, liabilities are claims recognized by law. That is, the law gives creditors the right to force the sale of a company's assets if the company fails to pay its debts. Creditors have rights over owners and must be paid in full before the owners receive anything, even if payment of a debt uses up all the assets of a business.

OWNER'S EQUITY

Owner's equity represents the claims by the owner of a business to the assets of the business. It equals the residual interest, or *residual equity*, in the assets of an entity that remains after deducting the entity's liabilities. Theoretically, it is what would be left over if all the liabilities were paid, and it is sometimes said to equal net assets. By rearranging the accounting equation, we can define owner's equity this way:

$$\text{Owner's Equity} = \text{Assets} - \text{Liabilities}$$

STUDY NOTE: A mnemonic for remembering which types of accounts affect owner's equity is *WIRE:* Withdrawals, Investments, Revenues, and Expenses.

The four types of transactions that affect owner's equity are shown in Figure 5. Two of these transactions, owner's investments and owner's withdrawals, are assets that the owner either puts into the business or takes out of the business. For instance, if the owner of Shannon Realty, John Shannon, takes cash out of his personal bank account and deposits it in the business bank account, he has made an owner's investment. The assets (cash) of the business increase, and John Shannon's equity in those assets also increases. Conversely, if John Shannon takes cash out of the business bank account and deposits it in his personal bank account, he has made a withdrawal from the business. The assets of the business decrease, and John Shannon's equity in the business also decreases.

FIGURE 5
Four Types of Transactions That Affect Owner's Equity

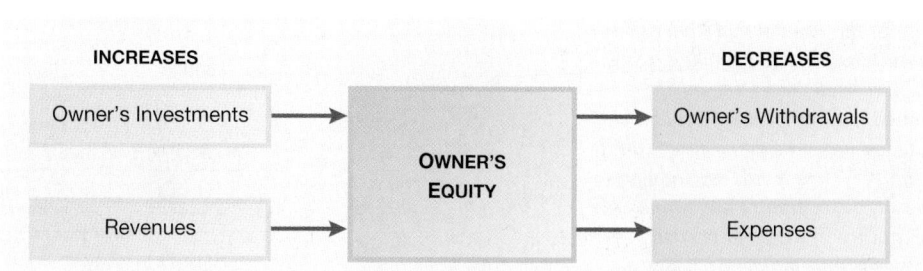

The other two types of transactions that affect owner's equity are revenues and expenses. Simply stated, **revenues** and **expenses** are the increases and decreases in owner's equity that result from operating a business. For example, the amount a customer pays (or agrees to pay in the future) to Shannon Realty in return for a service provided by the company is a revenue. The assets (cash or accounts receivable) of Shannon Realty increase, and the owner's equity in those assets also increases. On the other hand, the amount Shannon Realty pays out (or agrees to pay in the future) in the process of providing a service is an expense. Now the assets (cash) decrease or the liabilities (accounts payable) increase, and the owner's equity in the assets decreases.

Generally speaking, a company is successful if its revenues exceed its expenses. When the revenues exceed the expenses, the difference is called **net income**; when the expenses exceed the revenues, the difference is called **net loss**.

SOME ILLUSTRATIVE TRANSACTIONS

Let us now examine the effects of some of the most common business transactions on the accounting equation. Suppose that John Shannon opens Shannon Realty, a real estate agency, on December 1. During December, his business engages in the transactions described in the following paragraphs.

■ **OWNER'S INVESTMENT**   John starts his business by depositing $50,000 in a bank account in the name of Shannon Realty. The transfer of cash from his personal account to the business account is an owner's investment. The first balance sheet of the new company would show the asset Cash and the owner's equity (John Shannon, Capital):

KEY POINT: The account name is "John Shannon, Capital," not "Owner's Equity" because capital accounts show the equity attributed to the specific owner.

Assets	=	Owner's Equity (OE)	
Cash		John Shannon, Capital	Type of OE Transaction
1. $50,000		$50,000	Owner's Investment

At this point, the company has no liabilities, and assets equal owner's equity. The labels Cash and John Shannon, Capital are called **accounts**. These are used by accountants to accumulate amounts that result from similar transactions. Transactions that affect owner's equity are identified by type so that similar types may later be grouped together on accounting reports.

KEY POINT: The purchase of an asset does not affect owner's equity.

● **STOP AND THINK!**
From the standpoint of operating a business, why is the difference between making a sale for cash and making a sale on credit significant in terms of profitability and liquidity?

Both transactions affect profitability in the same way (owner's equity is increased); when a sale is made on credit, the business must wait to receive payment, which has a negative effect on liquidity. When a sale is made for cash, the company has immediate liquidity in the form of cash to pay its bills and make purchases. ■

■ **PURCHASE OF ASSETS WITH CASH**   John finds a good location and pays cash to purchase a lot for $10,000 and a small building on the lot for $25,000. This transaction does not change Shannon Realty's total assets, liabilities, or owner's equity, but it does change the composition of the assets—it decreases Cash and increases Land and Building:

	Assets			=	Owner's Equity	
	Cash	Land	Building		John Shannon, Capital	Type of OE Transaction
bal.	$50,000				$50,000	
2.	−35,000	+$10,000	+$25,000			
bal.	$15,000	$10,000	$25,000		$50,000	
		$50,000				

KEY POINT: Assets purchased on credit are recorded for the full amount at the time of the purchase.

■ **PURCHASE OF ASSETS BY INCURRING A LIABILITY**   Assets do not always have to be purchased with cash. They may also be purchased on credit, that is, on the basis of an agreement to pay for them later. Suppose the company buys some office supplies for $500 on credit. This transaction increases the assets (Supplies) and increases the liabilities of Shannon Realty. This liability is designated by an account called Accounts Payable:

	Assets				=	Liabilities	+	Owner's Equity	
	Cash	Supplies	Land	Building		Accounts Payable		John Shannon, Capital	Type of OE Transaction
bal.	$15,000		$10,000	$25,000				$50,000	
3.		+$500				+$500			
bal.	$15,000	$500	$10,000	$25,000		$500		$50,000	
		$50,500					$50,500		

Notice that this transaction increases both sides of the accounting equation to $50,500.

KEY POINT: Payment of a liability does not affect owner's equity or the asset purchased on credit.

■ **PAYMENT OF A LIABILITY**   If Shannon Realty later pays $200 of the $500 owed for the supplies, both assets (Cash) and liabilities (Accounts Payable) decrease, but Supplies is unaffected:

	Assets				=	Liabilities	+	Owner's Equity	
	Cash	Supplies	Land	Building		Accounts Payable		John Shannon, Capital	Type of OE Transaction
bal.	$15,000	$500	$10,000	$25,000		$500		$50,000	
4.	−200					−200			
bal.	$14,800	$500	$10,000	$25,000		$300		$50,000	
		$50,300					$50,300		

Notice that both sides of the accounting equation are still equal, although now at a total of $50,300.

KEY POINT: Revenues equal the price charged for the sale of goods or services.

■ **REVENUES**   Shannon Realty earns revenues in the form of commissions by selling houses for clients. Sometimes these commissions are paid to Shannon Realty immediately in the form of cash, and sometimes the client agrees to pay the commission later. In either case, the commission is recorded when it is earned and Shannon Realty has a right to a current or future receipt of cash. First, assume that Shannon Realty sells a house and receives a commission of $1,500 in cash. This transaction increases both assets (Cash) and owner's equity (John Shannon, Capital):

	Assets				=	Liabilities	+	Owner's Equity	
	Cash	Supplies	Land	Building		Accounts Payable		John Shannon, Capital	Type of OE Transaction
bal.	$14,800	$500	$10,000	$25,000		$300		$50,000	
5.	+1,500							+1,500	Commissions Earned
bal.	$16,300	$500	$10,000	$25,000		$300		$51,500	
		$51,800					$51,800		

KEY POINT: Revenues are recorded when they are earned, not necessarily when payments are received.

Now assume that Shannon Realty sells a house, in the process earning a commission of $2,000, and agrees to wait for payment of the commission. Because the commission has been earned now, a bill or invoice is sent to the client, and the transaction is recorded now. This revenue transaction increases both assets and owner's equity as before, but a new asset account, Accounts Receivable, shows that Shannon Realty is awaiting receipt of the commission:

		Assets				= Liabilities +	Owner's Equity	
	Cash	Accounts Receivable	Supplies	Land	Building	Accounts Payable	John Shannon, Capital	Type of OE Transaction
bal.	$16,300		$500	$10,000	$25,000	$300	$51,500	
6.		+$2,000					+2,000	Commissions Earned
bal.	$16,300	$2,000	$500	$10,000	$25,000	$300	$53,500	

$53,800 $53,800

As you progress in your study of accounting, you will be shown the use of separate accounts for revenues, like Commissions Earned.

■ **COLLECTION OF ACCOUNTS RECEIVABLE**   Let us assume that a few days later Shannon Realty receives $1,000 from the client in transaction **6.** At that time, the asset Cash increases and the asset Accounts Receivable decreases:

		Assets				= Liabilities +	Owner's Equity	
	Cash	Accounts Receivable	Supplies	Land	Building	Accounts Payable	John Shannon, Capital	Type of OE Transaction
bal.	$16,300	$2,000	$500	$10,000	$25,000	$300	$53,500	
7.	+1,000	−1,000						
bal.	$17,300	$1,000	$500	$10,000	$25,000	$300	$53,500	

$53,800 $53,800

Notice that this transaction does not affect owner's equity because the commission revenue was already recorded in transaction **6.** Also, notice that the balance of Accounts Receivable is $1,000, indicating that $1,000 is still to be collected.

■ **EXPENSES**   Just as revenues are recorded when they are earned, expenses are recorded when they are incurred. Expenses can be paid in cash when they occur, or they can be paid later. If payment is going to be made later, a liability—for example, Accounts Payable or Wages Payable—increases. In both cases, owner's equity decreases. Assume that Shannon Realty pays $1,000 to rent some equipment for the office and $400 in wages to a part-time helper. These transactions reduce assets (Cash) and owner's equity (John Shannon, Capital):

		Assets				= Liabilities +	Owner's Equity	
	Cash	Accounts Receivable	Supplies	Land	Building	Accounts Payable	John Shannon, Capital	Type of OE Transaction
bal.	$17,300	$1,000	$500	$10,000	$25,000	$300	$53,500	
8.	−1,000						−1,000	Equipment Rental Expense
9.	−400						−400	Wages Expense
bal.	$15,900	$1,000	$500	$10,000	$25,000	$300	$52,100	

$52,400 $52,400

Now assume that Shannon Realty has not paid a $300 bill for utilities expense incurred for December. In this case, the effect on owner's equity is the same as when the expense is paid in cash, but instead of a reduction in assets, there is an increase in liabilities (Accounts Payable):

	Assets					=	Liabilities	+	Owner's Equity	
	Cash	Accounts Receivable	Supplies	Land	Building		Accounts Payable		John Shannon, Capital	Type of OE Transaction
bal.	$15,900	$1,000	$500	$10,000	$25,000		$300		$52,100	
10.							+300		−300	Utilities
bal.	$15,900	$1,000	$500	$10,000	$25,000		$600		$51,800	Expense

$52,400 $52,400

As you progress in your study of accounting, you will be shown the use of separate accounts for expenses, like Equipment Rental Expense, Wages Expense, and Utilities Expense.

STUDY NOTE: Owner's withdrawals do not qualify as expenses because they do not generate revenue.

■ **OWNER'S WITHDRAWALS**   John now withdraws $600 in cash from Shannon Realty and deposits it in his personal account. This transaction reduces assets (Cash) and owner's equity (John Shannon, Capital). Although, as can be seen below, withdrawals have the same effect on the accounting equation as expenses (see transactions 8 and 9), it is important not to confuse them. Withdrawals are not expenses. Withdrawals are personal distributions of assets to the owner; expenses are incurred by the business in its operations.

	Assets					=	Liabilities	+	Owner's Equity	
	Cash	Accounts Receivable	Supplies	Land	Building		Accounts Payable		John Shannon, Capital	Type of OE Transaction
bal.	$15,900	$1,000	$500	$10,000	$25,000		$600		$51,800	
11.	−600								−600	Owner's
bal.	$15,300	$1,000	$500	$10,000	$25,000		$600		$51,200	Withdrawal

$51,800 $51,800

■ **SUMMARY**   Exhibit 1 (page 20) summarizes these 11 illustrative transactions.

 Check out ACE for a Review Quiz at http://accounting.college.hmco.com/students.

COMMUNICATION THROUGH FINANCIAL STATEMENTS

LO6   Identify the four financial statements.

RELATED TEXT ASSIGNMENTS
Q: 16, 17, 18, 19, 20
SE: 10
E: 11, 12, 13, 14, 15
P: 4, 5, 7, 8
SD: 6
FRA: 3, 5, 7, 8

Financial statements are the primary means of communicating important accounting information about a business to those who have an interest in the business. It is helpful to think of these statements as models of the business enterprise because they show the business in financial terms. As is true of all models, however, financial statements are not perfect pictures of the real thing. Rather, they are the accountant's best effort to represent what is real. Four major financial statements are used to communicate accounting information about a business: the income statement, the statement of owner's equity, the balance sheet, and the statement of cash flows.

Exhibit 2 (page 21) illustrates the relationship among the four financial statements by showing how they would appear for Shannon Realty after the eleven sample transactions shown in Exhibit 1. The time period covered is the month of

EXHIBIT 1
Summary of Effects of Illustrative Transactions on Financial Position

Exhibits illustrate financial information.

	Assets					=	Liabilities	+	Owner's Equity	Type of Owner's Equity Transaction
	Cash	Accounts Receivable	Supplies	Land	Building		Accounts Payable		John Shannon, Capital	
1.	$50,000								$50,000	Owner's Investment
2.	−35,000			+$10,000	+$25,000					
bal.	$15,000			$10,000	$25,000				$50,000	
3.			+$500				+$500			
bal.	$15,000		$500	$10,000	$25,000		$500		$50,000	
4.	−200						−200			
bal.	$14,800		$500	$10,000	$25,000		$300		$50,000	
5.	+1,500								+$1,500	Commissions Earned
bal.	$16,300		$500	$10,000	$25,000		$300		$51,500	
6.		+$2,000							+2,000	Commissions Earned
bal.	$16,300	$2,000	$500	$10,000	$25,000		$300		$53,500	
7.	+1,000	−1,000								
bal.	$17,300	$1,000	$500	$10,000	$25,000		$300		$53,500	
8.	−1,000								−1,000	Equipment Rental Expense
9.	−400								−400	Wages Expense
bal.	$15,900	$1,000	$500	$10,000	$25,000		$300		$52,100	
10.							+300		−300	Utilities Expense
bal.	$15,900	$1,000	$500	$10,000	$25,000		$600		$51,800	
11.	−600								−600	Owner's Withdrawal
bal.	$15,300	$1,000	$500	$10,000	$25,000		$600		$51,200	
	$51,800								$51,800	

EXHIBIT 2
Income Statement, Statement of Owner's Equity, Balance Sheet, and Statement of Cash Flows for Shannon Realty

Shannon Realty
Income Statement
For the Month Ended December 31, 20xx

Revenues		
Commissions earned		$3,500
Expenses		
Equipment rental expense	$1,000	
Wages expense	400	
Utilities expense	300	
Total expenses		1,700
Net income		$1,800

Shannon Realty
Statement of Owner's Equity
For the Month Ended December 31, 20xx

John Shannon, Capital, December 1, 20xx		$ 0
Add: Investments by John Shannon	$50,000	
Net income for the month	1,800	51,800
Subtotal		$51,800
Less withdrawals by John Shannon		600
John Shannon, Capital, December 31, 20xx		$51,200

Shannon Realty
Statement of Cash Flows
For the Month Ended December 31, 20xx

Cash flows from operating activities		
Net income		$ 1,800
Adjustments to reconcile net income to net cash flows from operating activities		
Increase in accounts receivable	($ 1,000)*	
Increase in supplies	(500)	
Increase in accounts payable	600	(900)
Net cash flows from operating activities		$ 900
Cash flows from investing activities		
Purchase of land	($10,000)	
Purchase of building	(25,000)	
Net cash flows from investing activities		(35,000)
Cash flows from financing activities		
Investments by John Shannon	$50,000	
Withdrawals by John Shannon	(600)	
Net cash flows from financing activities		49,400
Net increase (decrease) in cash		$15,300
Cash at beginning of month		0
Cash at end of month		$15,300

Shannon Realty
Balance Sheet
December 31, 20xx

Assets		Liabilities	
Cash	$15,300	Accounts payable $	600
Accounts receivable	1,000		
Supplies	500	**Owner's Equity**	
Land	10,000	John Shannon,	
Building	25,000	Capital	51,200
		Total liabilities and owner's	
Total assets	$51,800	equity	$51,800

KEY POINT: Notice the sequence in which these financial statements must be prepared. The statement of owner's equity is a link between the income statement and the balance sheet, and the statement of cash flows is prepared last.

*Parentheses indicate a negative amount.

● STOP AND THINK!
Which financial statement is most closely related to the goal of profitability, and which is most closely related to the goal of liquidity?
The income statement is most closely related to profitability; the statement of cash flows is most closely related to liquidity. ∎

TERMINOLOGY NOTE: The income statement is also called the *statement of earnings,* the *statement of operations,* or the *profit and loss statement.* Its purpose is to measure a company's performance over an accounting period.

TERMINOLOGY NOTE: The statement of owner's equity is also called the *capital statement.* It indicates changes in owner's capital over an accounting period.

TERMINOLOGY NOTE: The balance sheet is also called the *statement of financial position.* It represents two different views of a business: The left side shows the resources of the business; the right side shows who provided those resources (the creditors and the owners).

KEY POINT: The purpose of the statement of cash flows is to explain the change in cash in terms of operating, investing, and financing activities over an accounting period. It provides valuable information that cannot be determined in an examination of the other three financial statements.

December 20xx. Notice that each statement is headed in a similar way. Each heading identifies the company and the kind of statement. The income statement, the statement of owner's equity, and the statement of cash flows give the time period to which they apply; the balance sheet gives the specific date to which it applies. Much of this book deals with developing, using, and interpreting more complete versions of these basic statements.

THE INCOME STATEMENT

The **income statement** summarizes the revenues earned and expenses incurred by a business over a period of time. Many people consider it the most important financial report because it shows whether or not a business achieved its profitability goal of earning an acceptable income. In Exhibit 2, Shannon Realty had revenues in the form of commissions earned of $3,500 ($2,000 of revenue earned on credit and $1,500 of cash). From this amount, total expenses of $1,700 were deducted (equipment rental expense of $1,000, wages expense of $400, and utilities expense of $300), to arrive at a net income of $1,800. To show that it applies to a period of time, the statement is dated "For the Month Ended December 31, 20xx."

THE STATEMENT OF OWNER'S EQUITY

The **statement of owner's equity** shows the change in the owner's capital over a period of time. In Exhibit 2, the beginning capital is zero because the company was started in this accounting period. During the month, John Shannon made an investment in the business of $50,000, and the company earned income (as shown on the income statement) of $1,800, for a total increase of $51,800. Deducted from this amount are the withdrawals for the month of $600, leaving an ending balance of $51,200 in the capital account.

THE BALANCE SHEET

The purpose of a **balance sheet** is to show the financial position of a business on a certain date, usually the end of the month or year. For this reason, it often is called the *statement of financial position* and is dated as of a certain date. The balance sheet presents a view of the business as the holder of resources, or assets, that are equal to the claims against those assets. The claims consist of the company's liabilities and the owner's equity in the company. In Exhibit 2, Shannon Realty has several categories of assets, which total $51,800. These assets equal the total liabilities of $600 (Accounts Payable) plus the ending balance of owner's capital of $51,200. Notice that the owner's capital account amount on the balance sheet comes from the ending balance on the statement of owner's equity.

THE STATEMENT OF CASH FLOWS

Whereas the income statement focuses on a company's profitability goal, the **statement of cash flows** is directed toward the company's liquidity goal. **Cash flows** are the inflows and outflows of cash into and out of a business. Net cash flows are the difference between the inflows and outflows. The statement of cash flows shows the cash produced by operating a business as well as important investing and financing transactions that take place during an accounting period. Notice in Exhibit 2 that the statement of cash flows for Shannon Realty explains how the Cash account changed during the period. Cash increased by $15,300. Operating activities produced net cash flows of $900, and financing activities produced net cash flows of $49,400. Investing activities used cash flows of $35,000.

This statement is related directly to the other three statements. Notice that net income comes from the income statement and that investments and withdrawals by

PARENTHETICAL NOTE:
An entire chapter of this text is devoted to the statement of cash flows.

owners come from the statement of owner's equity. The other items in the statement represent changes in the balance sheet accounts: Accounts Receivable, Supplies, Accounts Payable, Land, and Building.

 Check out ACE for a Review Quiz at http://accounting.college.hmco.com/students.

GENERALLY ACCEPTED ACCOUNTING PRINCIPLES

LO7 State the relationship of generally accepted accounting principles (GAAP) to financial statements and the independent CPA's report, and identify the organizations that influence GAAP.

RELATED TEXT ASSIGNMENTS
Q: 21, 22, 23
E: 1, 16
SD: 2
FRA: 1, 6

🛑 **STOP AND THINK!**
How do generally accepted accounting principles (GAAP) differ from the laws of science?
GAAP differ from the laws of science in that they are not unchanging but rather are constantly evolving. They may change as business conditions change or as improved methods are introduced. ∎

To ensure that financial statements will be understandable to their users, a set of practices, called **generally accepted accounting principles (GAAP)**, has been developed to provide guidelines for financial accounting. Although the term has several meanings in the literature of accounting, perhaps this is the best definition: "Generally accepted accounting principles encompass the conventions, rules, and procedures necessary to define accepted accounting practice at a particular time."[7] In other words, GAAP arise from wide agreement on the theory and practice of accounting at a particular time. These "principles" are not like the unchangeable laws of nature found in chemistry or physics. They are developed by accountants and businesses to serve the needs of decision makers, and they can alter as better methods evolve or as circumstances change.

In this book, we present accounting practice, or GAAP, as it is today. We also try to explain the reasons or theory on which the practice is based. Both theory and practice are important to the study of accounting. However, you should realize that accounting is a discipline that is always growing, changing, and improving. Just as years of research are necessary before a new surgical method or lifesaving drug can be introduced, it may take years for new accounting discoveries to be implemented. As a result, you may encounter practices that seem contradictory. In some cases, we point out new directions in accounting. Your instructor also may mention certain weaknesses in current theory or practice.

FINANCIAL STATEMENTS, GAAP, AND THE INDEPENDENT CPA'S REPORT

Because financial statements are prepared by the management of a company and could be falsified for personal gain, all companies that sell ownership to the public and many companies that apply for sizable loans have their financial statements audited by an independent certified public accountant. **Certified public accountants (CPAs)** are licensed by all states for the same reason that lawyers and doctors are—to protect the public by ensuring the quality of professional service. One important attribute of certified public accountants is independence: They have no financial or other compromising ties with the companies they audit. This gives the public confidence in their work. The firms listed in Table 3 employ about 25 percent of all CPAs.

TABLE 3. Large International Certified Public Accounting Firms

Firm	Home Office	Some Major Clients
Deloitte & Touche	New York	General Motors, Procter & Gamble, Sears
Ernst & Young	New York	Coca-Cola, McDonald's
KPMG	New York	General Electric, Xerox
PricewaterhouseCoopers	New York	Du Pont, ExxonMobil, IBM, Ford

KEY POINT: The purpose of an audit is to lend credibility to a set of financial statements. The auditor does *not* attest to the absolute accuracy of the published information or to the value of the company as an investment. All he or she renders is an opinion, based on appropriate testing, about the fairness of the presentation of the financial information.

An independent CPA performs an **audit**, which is an examination of a company's financial statements and the accounting systems, controls, and records that produced them. The purpose of the audit is to ascertain that the financial statements have been prepared in accordance with generally accepted accounting principles. If the independent accountant is satisfied that this standard has been met, his or her report contains the following language:

> In our opinion, the financial statements . . . present fairly, in all material respects [the company's financial position] and are in conformity with generally accepted accounting principles.

This wording emphasizes the fact that accounting and auditing are not exact sciences. Because the framework of GAAP provides room for interpretation and the application of GAAP necessitates the making of estimates, the auditor can render an opinion or judgment only that the financial statements *present fairly* or conform *in all material respects* to generally accepted accounting principles. The accountant's report does not preclude minor or immaterial errors in the financial statements. However, it does imply that on the whole, investors and creditors can rely on those statements. Historically, auditors have enjoyed a strong reputation for competence and independence. As a result, banks, investors, and creditors are willing to rely on an auditor's opinion when deciding to invest in a company or to make loans to a company. The independent audit is an important factor in the worldwide growth of financial markets.

ORGANIZATIONS THAT INFLUENCE CURRENT PRACTICE

KEY POINT: The FASB is the primary source of GAAP.

KEY POINT: The AICPA is considered the primary organization of certified public accountants.

ENRICHMENT NOTE: The SEC imposes its own strict set of regulations on the companies it regulates, based in part on the standards set by the FASB.

Many organizations directly or indirectly influence GAAP, and they therefore influence much of what is contained in this book. The **Financial Accounting Standards Board (FASB)** is the most important body for developing and issuing rules on accounting practice. This independent body issues *Statements of Financial Accounting Standards*. The **American Institute of Certified Public Accountants (AICPA)** is the professional association of certified public accountants and influences accounting practice through the activities of its senior technical committees. The Securities and Exchange Commission (SEC) is an agency of the federal government that has the legal power to set and enforce accounting practices for companies whose securities are offered for sale to the general public. As such, it has enormous influence on accounting practice. The **Governmental Accounting Standards Board (GASB)**, which was established in 1984 under the same governing body as the Financial Accounting Standards Board, is responsible for issuing accounting standards for state and local governments.

With the growth of financial markets throughout the world, worldwide cooperation in the development of accounting principles has become a priority. The **International Accounting Standards Board (IASB)** has approved more than 30 international standards.

ENRICHMENT NOTE: The primary purpose of the tax law is to generate revenue for the operation of the government, not to measure business income.

U.S. tax laws that govern the assessment and collection of revenue for operating the federal government also influence accounting practice. Because a major source of the government's revenue is the income tax, the tax laws specify the rules for determining taxable income. These rules are interpreted and enforced by the **Internal Revenue Service (IRS)**. In some cases, the rules conflict with good accounting practice, but they still are an important influence on that practice. Businesses use certain accounting practices simply because they are required by the tax laws. Sometimes companies follow an accounting practice specified in the tax laws to take advantage of rules that can help them financially. Cases in which the tax laws affect accounting practice are noted throughout this book.

✓ Check out ACE for a Review Quiz at http://accounting.college.hmco.com/students.

PROFESSIONAL ETHICS AND THE ACCOUNTING PROFESSION

LO8 Define *ethics* and describe the ethical responsibilities of accountants.

RELATED TEXT ASSIGNMENTS
Q: 24
SD: 4

Ethical issues are discussed in each chapter; they relate to real business situations that require ethical judgments.

◆ **STOP AND THINK!**
What are some unethical ways in which a business may do its accounting or prepare its financial statements?

Unethical ways of accounting include recording business transactions that did not occur or being dishonest in recording those that did occur. Financial statements are unethically prepared when they misrepresent a company's financial situation or contain false information. ∎

ENRICHMENT NOTE: The AICPA Code of Professional Ethics is a set of guidelines for appropriate professional behavior. The current guidelines were adopted in 1988 and are based on earlier standards.

Ethics is a code of conduct that applies to everyday life. It addresses the question of whether actions are right or wrong. Ethical actions are the product of individual decisions. You are faced with many situations involving ethical issues every day. Some may be potentially illegal—the temptation to take office supplies from your employer to use when you do homework, for example. Others are not illegal but are equally unethical—for example, deciding not to tell a fellow student who missed class that a test has been announced for the next class meeting. When an organization is said to act ethically or unethically, it means that individuals within the organization have made a decision to act ethically or unethically. When a company uses false advertising, cheats customers, pollutes the environment, treats employees poorly, or misleads investors by presenting false financial statements, members of management and other employees have made a conscious decision to act unethically. In the same way, ethical behavior within a company is a direct result of the actions and decisions of the company's employees.

Professional ethics is a code of conduct that applies to the practice of a profession. Like the ethical conduct of a company, the ethical actions of a profession are a collection of individual actions. As members of a profession, accountants have a responsibility, not only to their employers and clients but to society as a whole, to uphold the highest ethical standards. Historically, accountants have been held in high regard. For example, a survey of over one thousand prominent people in business, education, and government ranked the accounting profession second only to the clergy as having the highest ethical standards.[8] It is the responsibility of every person who becomes an accountant to uphold the high standards of the profession.

To ensure that its members understand the responsibilities of being professional accountants, the AICPA and each state have adopted codes of professional conduct that certified public accountants must follow. Fundamental to these codes is responsibility to the public, including clients, creditors, investors, and anyone else who relies on the work of the certified public accountant. In resolving conflicts among these groups, the accountant must act with integrity. **Integrity** means that the accountant is honest and candid and subordinates personal gain to service and the public trust. The accountant must also be objective. **Objectivity** means that he or she is impartial and intellectually honest. Furthermore, the accountant must be independent. **Independence** means avoiding all relationships that impair or even appear to impair the accountant's objectivity.

One way in which the auditor of a company maintains independence is by having no direct financial interest in the company and by not being an employee of the company. The accountant must exercise **due care** in all activities, carrying out professional responsibilities with competence and diligence. For example, an accountant must not accept a job for which he or she is not qualified, even at the risk of losing a client to another firm, and careless work is not acceptable. These broad principles are supported by more specific rules that public accountants must follow. (For instance, with certain exceptions, client information must be kept strictly confidential.) Accountants who violate the rules can be disciplined or even suspended from practice.

A professional association, the **Institute of Management Accountants (IMA)**, has formally adopted the Code of Professional Conduct for Management

FOCUS ON BUSINESS ETHICS

Good Ethics = Good Business!

Ethics is good business. Many companies, especially those that engage in international trade, adopt codes of ethics. Management sees such self-regulation as a way of avoiding fraud and litigation. A recent survey of 124 companies in 22 countries found that 78 percent of boards of directors had established ethics standards, a fourfold increase over a ten-year period. The study also found that codes of ethics help promote tolerance of diverse practices abroad. In addition, research has shown that over time, companies with codes of ethics tend to do much better in the stock market than those that have not adopted such codes.[9] The recent Enron bankruptcy is an example of the tragic results that can occur when a company's ethical system breaks down.

Accountants. This ethical code emphasizes that management accountants have a responsibility to be competent in their jobs, to keep information confidential except when authorized or legally required to disclose it, to maintain integrity and avoid conflicts of interest, and to communicate information objectively and without bias.[10]

 Check out ACE for Review Quiz at http://accounting.college.hmco.com/students.

Chapter Review ← The Chapter Review restates each learning objective and its main ideas.

REVIEW OF LEARNING OBJECTIVES

LO1 Define *accounting,* identify business goals and activities, and describe the role of accounting in making informed decisions.

Accounting is an information system that measures, processes, and communicates financial information about an identifiable entity for the purpose of making economic decisions. An important type of entity is the business which engages in operating, investing, and financing activities for the purpose of achieving the goals of profitability and liquidity. Management accounting focuses on the preparation of information primarily for internal use by management. Financial accounting is concerned with the development and use of accounting reports that are communicated to those outside the business as well as to management. Accounting is a tool that provides the information necessary to make reasoned choices among alternative uses of scarce resources in the conduct of business and economic activities.

LO2 Identify the many users of accounting information in society.

Accounting plays a significant role in society by providing information to managers of all institutions and to individuals with a direct financial interest in those institutions, including present or potential investors or creditors. Accounting information is also important to those with an indirect financial interest in the business—for example, tax authorities, regulatory agencies, and economic planners.

LO3 Explain the importance of business transactions, money measure, and separate entity to accounting measurement.

To make an accounting measurement, the accountant must determine what is measured, when the measurement should be made, what value should be placed on what is measured, and how what is measured should be classified. The objects of accounting measurement are business transactions that are measured in terms of money and are for separate entities. Relating these concepts, financial accounting uses money measure to gauge the impact of business transactions on a separate business entity.

LO4 Identify the three basic forms of business organization.

The three basic forms of business organization are sole proprietorships, partnerships, and corporations. Legally, sole proprietorships, which are formed by one individual, and partnerships, which are formed by more than one individual, are not separate from their owners. In accounting, however, they are treated as separate. Corporations, whose ownership is represented by shares of stock, are separate entities for both legal and accounting purposes.

LO5 Define *financial position,* state the accounting equation, and show how they are affected by simple transactions.

Financial position refers to the economic resources that belong to a company and the claims against those resources at a point in time. The accounting equation shows financial position as Assets = Liabilities + Owner's Equity. Business transactions affect financial position by decreasing or increasing assets, liabilities, or owner's equity in such a way that the accounting equation is always in balance.

LO6 Identify the four financial statements.

The four financial statements are the income statement, the statement of owner's equity, the balance sheet, and the statement of cash flows. They are the means by which accountants communicate the financial condition and activities of a business to those who have an interest in the business.

LO7 State the relationship of generally accepted accounting principles (GAAP) to financial statements and the independent CPA's report, and identify the organizations that influence GAAP.

Acceptable accounting practice consists of the conventions, rules, and procedures that make up generally accepted accounting principles at a particular time. GAAP are essential to the preparation and interpretation of financial statements and the independent CPA's report. Among the organizations that influence the formulation of GAAP are the Financial Accounting Standards Board, the American Institute of Certified Public Accountants, the Securities and Exchange Commission, and the Internal Revenue Service.

LO8 Define *ethics* and describe the ethical responsibilities of accountants.

All accountants are required to follow a code of professional ethics, the foundation of which is responsibility to the public. Accountants must act with integrity, objectivity, and independence, and they must exercise due care in all their activities.

Want more review? The student *Study Guide* provides a thorough review of each learning objective, a detailed outline, true/false and multiple-choice questions, and exercises. Answers are included. Ask for it at your bookstore.

REVIEW OF CONCEPTS AND TERMINOLOGY

Each chapter has a glossary of the key concepts and terms defined in the chapter. The LO next to each term indicates the section in which it is discussed.

The following concepts and terms were introduced in this chapter:

LO1 **Accounting:** An information system that measures, processes, and communicates financial information about an identifiable economic entity.

LO5 **Accounting equation:** Assets = Liabilities + Owner's Equity.

LO5 **Accounts:** The labels used by accountants to accumulate the amounts produced from similar transactions.

LO7 **American Institute of Certified Public Accountants (AICPA):** The professional association of certified public accountants.

LO5 **Assets:** Economic resources owned by a business that are expected to benefit future operations.

LO7 **Audit:** An examination of a company's financial statements in order to render an independent professional opinion that they have been presented fairly, in all material respects, in conformity with generally accepted accounting principles.

LO6 **Balance sheet:** The financial statement that shows the assets, liabilities, and owner's equity of a business at a point in time. Also called a *statement of financial position*.

LO1 **Bookkeeping:** The process of recording financial transactions and keeping financial records.

LO1 **Business:** An economic unit that aims to sell goods and services to customers at prices that will provide an adequate return to its owners.

LO3 **Business transactions:** Economic events that affect the financial position of a business entity.

LO6 **Cash flows:** The inflows and outflows of cash into and out of a business.

LO7 **Certified public accountants (CPAs):** Public accountants who have met the stringent state licensing requirements.

LO1 **Computer:** An electronic tool for the rapid collection, organization, and communication of large amounts of information.

LO4 **Corporation:** A business unit granted a state charter recognizing it as a separate legal entity having its own rights, privileges, and liabilities distinct from those of its owners.

LO8 **Due care:** Competence and diligence in carrying out professional responsibilities.

LO8 **Ethics:** A code of conduct that addresses whether everyday actions are right or wrong.

LO3 **Exchange rate:** The value of one currency in terms of another.

LO5   **Expenses:** Decreases in owner's equity that result from operating a business.

LO1   **Financial accounting:** The process of generating and communicating accounting information in the form of financial statements to those outside the organization.

LO7   **Financial Accounting Standards Board (FASB):** The most important body for developing and issuing rules on accounting practice, called *Statements of Financial Accounting Standards.*

LO5   **Financial position:** The economic resources that belong to a company and the claims (equities) against those resources at a point in time.

LO1   **Financial statements:** The primary means of communicating important accounting information to users. They include the income statement, statement of owner's equity, balance sheet, and statement of cash flows.

LO1   **Financing activities:** Activities undertaken by management to obtain adequate funds to begin and to continue operating a business.

LO7   **Generally accepted accounting principles (GAAP):** The conventions, rules, and procedures that define accepted accounting practice at a particular time.

LO7   **Governmental Accounting Standards Board (GASB):** The board responsible for issuing accounting standards for state and local governments.

LO6   **Income statement:** The financial statement that summarizes the revenues earned and expenses incurred by a business over a period of time.

LO8   **Independence:** The avoidance of all relationships that impair or appear to impair an accountant's objectivity.

LO8   **Institute of Management Accountants (IMA):** A professional organization made up primarily of management accountants.

LO8   **Integrity:** Honesty, candidness, and the subordination of personal gain to service and the public trust.

LO7   **Internal Revenue Service (IRS):** The federal agency that interprets and enforces the tax laws governing the assessment and collection of revenue for operating the national government.

LO7   **International Accounting Standards Board (IASB):** The organization that encourages worldwide cooperation in the development of accounting principles; it has approved more than 30 international standards of accounting.

LO1   **Investing activities:** Activities undertaken by management to spend capital in ways that are productive and will help a business achieve its objectives.

LO5   **Liabilities:** Present obligations of a business to pay cash, transfer assets, or provide services to other entities in the future.

LO1   **Liquidity:** Having enough cash available to pay debts when they are due.

LO2   **Management:** The people who have overall responsibility for operating a business and meeting its goals.

LO1   **Management accounting:** The process of producing accounting information for the internal use of a company's management.

LO1   **Management information system (MIS):** The interconnected subsystems that provide the information needed to run a business.

LO3   **Money measure:** The recording of all business transactions in terms of money.

LO5   **Net assets:** Assets minus liabilities; owner's equity.

LO5   **Net income:** The difference between revenues and expenses when revenues exceed expenses.

LO5   **Net loss:** The difference between expenses and revenues when expenses exceed revenues.

LO8   **Objectivity:** Impartiality and intellectual honesty.

LO1 **Operating activities:** Activities undertaken by management in the course of running the business.

LO5 **Owner's equity:** The residual interest in the assets of a business entity that remains after deducting the entity's liabilities. Also called *residual equity*.

LO5 **Owner's investments:** The assets that the owner puts into the business.

LO5 **Owner's withdrawals:** The assets that the owner takes out of the business.

LO4 **Partnership:** A business that is owned by two or more people and that is not incorporated.

LO1 **Performance measures:** Indicators of whether managers are achieving business goals and whether the business activities are well managed.

LO8 **Professional ethics:** A code of conduct that applies to the practice of a profession.

LO1 **Profitability:** The ability to earn enough income to attract and hold investment capital.

LO5 **Revenues:** Increases in owner's equity that result from operating a business.

LO2 **Securities and Exchange Commission (SEC):** An agency of the U.S. government set up by Congress to protect the public by regulating the issuing, buying, and selling of stocks. It has the legal power to set and enforce accounting practices for firms whose securities are sold to the general public.

LO3 **Separate entity:** A business that is treated as distinct from its creditors, customers, and owners.

LO4 **Sole proprietorship:** A business that is owned by only one person and that is not incorporated.

LO6 **Statement of cash flows:** The financial statement that shows the inflows and outflows of cash from operating activities, investing activities, and financing activities over a period of time.

LO6 **Statement of owner's equity:** A financial statement that shows the change in owner's captial over a period of time.

Not sure you understood the techniques and calculations, or want to check if you are ready for a chapter test? The Review Problem models main computations or analyses presented in the chapter and other problem assignments. The answer is provided for immediate feedback.

REVIEW PROBLEM

The Effect of Transactions on the Accounting Equation

LO5 Charlene Rudek finished law school in June and immediately set up her own law practice. During the first month that the practice was operating, Rudek completed the following transactions:

a. Began the law practice by placing $2,000 in a bank account established for the business.

b. Purchased a law library for $900 cash.

c. Purchased office supplies for $400 on credit.

d. Accepted $500 in cash for completing a contract.

e. Billed clients $1,950 for services rendered during the month.

f. Paid $200 of the amount owed for office supplies.

g. Received $1,250 in cash from one client who had been billed previously for services rendered.

h. Paid rent expense for the month in the amount of $1,200.

i. Withdrew $400 from the practice for personal use.

REQUIRED ▶

1. Show the effect of each of these transactions on the accounting equation by completing a table similar to Exhibit 1. Identify each owner's equity transaction.

2. Contrast the effects on cash flows of transactions **c** and **f** with transaction **b** and of transactions **e** and **g** with transaction **d**.

ANSWER TO REVIEW PROBLEM

1. Table of effects of transactions on the accounting equation

	Assets				=	Liabilities	+	Owner's Equity	
	Cash	Accounts Receivable	Office Supplies	Law Library		Accounts Payable		C. Rudek, Capital	Type of OE Transaction
a.	$2,000							$2,000	Owner's Investment
b.	−900			+$900					
bal.	$1,100			$900				$2,000	
c.			+$400			+$400			
bal.	$1,100		$400	$900		$400		$2,000	
d.	+500							+ 500	Legal Fees Earned
bal.	$1,600		$400	$900		$400		$2,500	
e.		+$1,950						+1,950	Legal Fees Earned
bal.	$1,600	$1,950	$400	$900		$400		$4,450	
f.	−200					−200			
bal.	$1,400	$1,950	$400	$900		$200		$4,450	
g.	+1,250	−1,250							
bal.	$2,650	$ 700	$400	$900		$200		$4,450	
h.	−1,200							−1,200	Rent Expense
bal.	$1,450	$ 700	$400	$900		$200		$3,250	
i.	−400							−400	Owner's Withdrawal
bal.	$1,050	$ 700	$400	$900		$200		$2,850	
		$3,050						$3,050	

2. Transaction **c**, a purchase on credit, enables the company to use the asset immediately and to defer payment of cash. Cash is expended to partially pay for the asset in transaction **f**. The remainder is to be paid subsequently. This series of transactions contrasts with transaction **b**, in which cash is expended immediately for the asset. In each case, an asset is purchased, but the effects on cash flows differ.

Transaction **e**, a sale on credit, allows the customer to pay later for services provided. This payment is partially received in transaction **g**, and the remainder is to be received later. These transactions contrast with transaction **d**, in which payment is received immediately for the services performed. In each case, the revenue is earned initially, but the effect on cash flows is different.

Chapter Assignments

BUILDING YOUR KNOWLEDGE FOUNDATION

Questions review key concepts, terminology, and topics of the chapter.

QUESTIONS

1. Why is accounting considered an information system?
2. What is the role of accounting in the decision-making process, and what broad business goals and activities does it help management achieve and manage?
3. Distinguish between management accounting and financial accounting.

4. Distinguish among these terms: *accounting, bookkeeping,* and *management information systems.*

5. Which decision makers use accounting information?

6. A business is an economic unit whose goal is to sell goods and services to customers at prices that will provide an adequate return to the business's owners. What functions must management perform to achieve that goal?

7. Why are investors and creditors interested in reviewing the financial statements of a company?

8. Among those who use accounting information are people and organizations that have an indirect interest in the business entity. Briefly describe these people and organizations.

9. Why has society as a whole become one of the largest users of accounting information?

10. Use the terms *business transactions, money measure,* and *separate entity* in a single sentence that demonstrates their relevance to financial accounting.

11. How do sole proprietorships, partnerships, and corporations differ?

12. Define *assets, liabilities,* and *owner's equity.*

13. Arnold Smith's company has assets of $22,000 and liabilities of $10,000. What is the amount of the owner's equity?

14. What four elements affect owner's capital? How?

15. Give examples of the types of transactions that (a) increase assets and (b) increase liabilities.

16. What is the function of the statement of owner's equity?

17. Why is the balance sheet sometimes called the statement of financial position?

18. Contrast the purpose of the balance sheet with that of the income statement.

19. A statement for an accounting period that ends in June can be headed "June 30, 20xx" or "For the Year Ended June 30, 20xx." Which heading is appropriate for (a) a balance sheet and (b) an income statement?

20. How does the income statement differ from the statement of cash flows?

21. What are GAAP? Why are they important to the readers of financial statements?

22. What do auditors mean by the phrase *in all material respects* when they state that financial statements "present fairly, in all material respects . . . in conformity with generally accepted accounting principles"?

23. What organization has the most influence on GAAP?

24. Discuss the importance of professional ethics in the accounting profession.

Short exercises are simple applications of chapter material for a single learning objective. If you need help locating the related text discussions, refer to the LO numbers in the margin.

SHORT EXERCISES

SE 1.

LO3   Accounting Concepts

Tell whether each of the following words or phrases relates most closely to (a) a business transaction, (b) a separate entity, or (c) a money measure:

1. Partnership
2. U.S. dollar
3. Payment of an expense

4. Corporation
5. Sale of an asset

SE 2.

LO4   Forms of Business Enterprises

Match the descriptions on the left with the forms of business enterprise on the right:

_____ 1. Most numerous

_____ 2. Commands most revenues

_____ 3. Two or more co-owners

_____ 4. Has stockholders

_____ 5. Owned by one person

_____ 6. Has a board of directors

a. Sole proprietorship
b. Partnership
c. Corporation

SE 3.

LO5   **The Accounting Equation**

Determine the amount missing from each accounting equation below.

	Assets	=	Liabilities	+	Owner's Equity
1.	?		$25,000		$35,000
2.	$ 78,000		$42,000		?
3.	$146,000		?		$96,000

SE 4.

LO5   **The Accounting Equation**

Use the accounting equation to answer each question below.

1. The assets of Sully Company are $480,000, and the liabilities are $360,000. What is the amount of the owner's equity?
2. The liabilities of Eva Company equal one-fifth of the total assets. The owner's equity is $80,000. What is the amount of the liabilities?

SE 5.

LO5   **The Accounting Equation**

Use the accounting equation to answer each question below.

1. At the beginning of the year, Lanier Company's assets were $180,000, and its owner's equity was $100,000. During the year, the company's assets increased by $60,000, and its liabilities increased by $10,000. What was the owner's equity at the end of the year?
2. At the beginning of the year, Fanto Company had liabilities of $50,000 and owner's equity of $48,000. If assets increased by $20,000 and liabilities decreased by $15,000, what was the owner's equity at the end of the year?

SE 6.

LO5   **The Accounting Equation and Net Income**

Use the following information and the accounting equation to determine the net income for the year for each alternative below.

	Assets	Liabilities
Beginning of the year	$ 70,000	$30,000
End of the year	100,000	50,000

1. No investments were made in the business, and no withdrawals were made during the year.
2. Investments of $10,000 were made in the business, but no withdrawals were made during the year.
3. No investments were made in the business, but withdrawals of $2,000 were made during the year.

SE 7.

LO5   **The Accounting Equation and Net Income**

Meader Company had assets of $140,000 and liabilities of $60,000 at the beginning of the year, and assets of $200,000 and liabilities of $70,000 at the end of the year. During the year, there was an investment of $20,000 in the business, and withdrawals of $24,000 were made. What amount of net income did Meader Company earn during the year?

SE 8.

LO5   **Effect of Transactions on the Accounting Equation**

On a sheet of paper, list the numbers 1 through 6, with columns labeled Assets, Liabilities, and Owner's Equity. In the columns, indicate whether each transaction that follows caused an increase (+), a decrease (−), or no change (NC) in assets, liabilities, and owner's equity.

1. Purchased equipment on credit.
2. Purchased equipment for cash.
3. Billed customers for services performed.
4. Received and immediately paid a utility bill.
5. Received payment from a previously billed customer.
6. The owner made an additional investment.

SE 9.

LO5   **Effect of Transactions on the Accounting Equation**

On a sheet of paper, list the numbers 1 through 6, with columns labeled Assets, Liabilities, and Owner's Equity. In the columns, indicate whether each transaction below caused an increase (+), a decrease (−), or no change (NC) in assets, liabilities, and owner's equity.

1. Purchased supplies on credit.
2. Paid for previously purchased supplies.
3. Paid employee's weekly wages.
4. Cash withdrawal by owner.
5. Purchased a truck with cash.
6. Received a telephone bill to be paid next month.

SE 10.

LO6   Preparation and Completion of a Balance Sheet

Use the following accounts and balances to prepare a balance sheet for Anatole Company at June 30, 20x1, using Exhibit 2 as a model:

Accounts Receivable	$ 800
Wages Payable	250
Owner's Capital	13,750
Building	10,000
Cash	?

Exercises are richer applications of all chapter material referenced by LOs. ➤ **EXERCISES**

E 1.

LO1   The Nature of Accounting
LO2
LO7

Match the terms on the left with the descriptions on the right:

_____ 1. Bookkeeping

_____ 2. Creditors

_____ 3. Measurement

_____ 4. Financial Accounting Standards Board (FASB)

_____ 5. Tax authorities

_____ 6. Computer

_____ 7. Communication

_____ 8. Securities and Exchange Commission (SEC)

_____ 9. Investors

_____ 10. Processing

_____ 11. Management

_____ 12. Management information system

a. Function of accounting
b. Often confused with accounting
c. User(s) of accounting information
d. Organization that influences current practice
e. Tool that facilitates the practice of accounting

E 2.

LO2   Users of Accounting
LO4   Information and Forms of Business Enterprise

Vylex Pharmaceuticals has recently been formed to develop a new type of drug treatment for cancer. Previously a partnership, Vylex has now become a corporation. Identify the various groups that will have an interest in the financial statements of Vylex. What is the difference between a partnership and a corporation, and what advantages does the corporate form have over the partnership?

E 3.

LO3   Business Transactions

Edgar owns and operates a minimart. State which of the actions below are business transactions. Explain why any other actions are not regarded as transactions.

1. Edgar reduces the price of a gallon of milk in order to match the price offered by a competitor.
2. Edgar pays a high school student cash for cleaning up the driveway behind the market.
3. Edgar fills his son's car with gasoline in payment for restocking the vending machines and the snack food shelves.
4. Edgar pays interest to himself on a loan he made to the business three years ago.

E 4.

LO3   Accounting Concepts

Financial accounting uses money measures to gauge the impact of business transactions on a separate business entity. Tell whether each of the following words or phrases relates most closely to (a) a business transaction, (b) a separate entity, or (c) a money measure:

1. Corporation
2. Euro
3. Sales of products
4. Receipt of cash
5. Sole proprietorship
6. U.S. dollar
7. Partnership
8. Owner's investments
9. Japanese yen
10. Purchase of supplies

E 5.

LO3   Money Measure

You have been asked to compare the sales and assets of four companies that make computer chips and to determine which company is the largest in each category. You have gathered the data shown at the top of the next page, but they cannot be used for direct comparison because each company's sales and assets are in its own currency.

Company (Currency)	Sales	Assets
Inchip (U.S. dollar)	20,000,000	13,000,000
Wong (Hong Kong dollar)	80,000,000	24,000,000
Mitzu (Japanese yen)	3,500,000,000	2,500,000,000
Works (Euro)	35,000,000	49,000,000

Assuming that the exchange rates in Table 1 are current and appropriate, convert all the figures to U.S. dollars and determine which company is the largest in sales and which is the largest in assets.

E 6.
LO5   The Accounting Equation

Use the accounting equation to answer each question that follows. Show any calculations you make.

1. The assets of Caton Company are $800,000, and the owner's equity is $310,000. What is the amount of the liabilities?
2. The liabilities and owner's equity of Sung Company are $72,000 and $53,000, respectively. What is the amount of the assets?
3. The liabilities of Plumb Company equal one-third of the total assets, and owner's equity is $240,000. What is the amount of the liabilities?
4. At the beginning of the year, Wilde Company's assets were $220,000 and its owner's equity was $120,000. During the year, assets increased $60,000, and liabilities decreased $18,000. What is the owner's equity at the end of the year?

E 7.
LO5   Owner's Equity Transactions

Identify the following transactions by marking each as an owner's investment (I), owner's withdrawal (W), revenue (R), expense (E), or not an owner's equity transaction (NOE):

a. Received cash for providing a service.
b. Took assets out of the business for personal expenses.
c. Received cash from a customer previously billed for a service.
d. Transferred assets to the business from a personal account.
e. Paid a service station for gasoline for a business vehicle.
f. Performed a service and received a promise of payment.
g. Paid cash to purchase equipment.
h. Paid cash to an employee for services performed.

E 8.
LO5   Effect of Transactions on the Accounting Equation

During the month of April, Cosmos Corporation had the following transactions:

a. Paid salaries for April, $1,800.
b. Purchased equipment on credit, $3,000.
c. Purchased supplies with cash, $100.
d. Additional investment by owner, $4,000.
e. Received payment for services performed, $600.
f. Made partial payment on equipment purchased in transaction **b**, $1,000.
g. Billed customers for services performed, $1,600.
h. Cash withdrawal by owner, $1,500.
i. Received payment from customers billed in transaction **g**, $300.
j. Received utility bill, $70.

On a sheet of paper, list the letters **a** through **j**, with columns labeled Assets, Liabilities, and Owner's Equity. In the columns, indicate whether each transaction caused an increase (+), a decrease (−), or no change (NC) in assets, liabilities, and owner's equity.

E 9.
LO5   Examples of Transactions

For each of the categories below, describe a transaction that would have the required effect on the elements of the accounting equation.

1. Increase one asset and decrease another asset.
2. Decrease an asset and decrease a liability.
3. Increase an asset and increase a liability.
4. Increase an asset and increase owner's equity.
5. Decrease an asset and decrease owner's equity.

E 10.
LO5   Effect of Transactions on the Accounting Equation

The total assets and liabilities at the beginning and end of the year for Flag Company are listed below.

	Assets	Liabilities
Beginning of the year	$140,000	$ 55,000
End of the year	220,000	130,000

Determine Flag Company's net income or loss for the year under each of the following alternatives. The owner made

1. no investments in or withdrawals from the business during the year.
2. no investments in the business but withdrew $22,000 during the year.
3. an investment of $13,000 in the business but no withdrawals during the year.
4. an investment of $10,000 in the business and withdrew $22,000 during the year.

E 11.
LO5 Identification of Accounts
LO6

1. Indicate whether each of the following accounts is an asset (A), a liability (L), or a part of owner's equity (OE):

a. Cash   e. Land
b. Salaries Payable   f. Accounts Payable
c. Accounts Receivable g. Supplies
d. F. Wong, Capital

2. Indicate whether each account below would be shown on the income statement (IS), the statement of owner's equity (OE), or the balance sheet (BS).

a. Repair Revenue   e. Rent Expense
b. Automobile   f. Accounts Payable
c. Fuel Expense   g. F. Wong, Withdrawals
d. Cash

E 12.
LO6 Preparation of a Balance Sheet

Listed in random order below are the balance sheet figures for the Solos Company as of December 31, 20xx.

Accounts Payable	$ 40,000	Accounts Receivable	$50,000
Building	90,000	Cash	20,000
N. Solos, Capital	100,000	Equipment	40,000
Supplies	10,000		

Sort the balances and prepare a balance sheet similar to the one in Exhibit 2.

E 13.
LO6 Completion of Financial Statements

Complete the following independent sets of financial statements by determining the amounts that correspond to the letters. (Assume no new investments by the owner.)

Income Statement	Set A	Set B	Set C
Revenues	$1,100	$ g	$340
Expenses	a	5,200	m
Net income	$ b	$ h	$180
Statement of Owner's Equity			
Beginning balance	$2,900	$15,400	$200
Net income	c	1,600	n
Less withdrawals	200	i	o
Ending balance	$3,000	$ j	$ p
Balance Sheet			
Total assets	$ d	$21,000	$ q
Liabilities	$1,600	$ 5,000	$ r
Owner's equity	e	k	380
Total liabilities and owner's equity	$ f	$ l	$580

E 14.
LO6 Preparation of Financial Statements

Ridge Company engaged in the following activities during the year: Service revenue, $52,800; Rent expense, $4,800; Wages expense, $33,080; Advertising expense, $5,400; Utilities expense, $3,600; and Sy Ridge, Withdrawals, $2,800. In addition, the year-end balances of selected accounts were as follows: Cash, $6,200; Accounts Receivable, $3,000; Supplies, $400; Land, $4,000; Accounts Payable, $1,800; and Sy Ridge, Capital, $8,680.

Using good form, prepare the income statement, statement of owner's equity, and balance sheet for Ridge Company (assume the year ends on June 30, 20x5). (**Hint:** The amount given for Sy Ridge, Capital is the beginning balance.)

E 15.
LO6 Statement of Cash Flows

Waters Company began the year 20x4 with cash of $86,000. In addition to earning a net income of $50,000 and making an owner's withdrawal of $30,000 for his personal use,

Waters borrowed $120,000 from the bank and purchased equipment for $180,000 with cash. Also, Accounts Receivable increased by $12,000, and Accounts Payable increased by $18,000.

Determine the amount of cash on hand at the end of the year (December 31) by preparing a statement of cash flows similar to the one in Exhibit 2.

E 16.

LO7   Accounting Abbreviations

Identify the accounting meaning of each of the following abbreviations: AICPA, SEC, GAAP, FASB, IRS, GASB, IASB, IMA, and CPA.

Problems are comprehensive applications of chapter material, often covering multiple learning objectives.

PROBLEMS

P 1.

LO5   Effect of Transactions on the Accounting Equation

After receiving his degree in computer science, John Unger started his own business, Regency Business Services Company. The company completed the following transactions:

a. John deposited $18,000 in the bank to start the business and purchased a systems library with an additional investment of $1,840.
b. Paid current month's rent on an office, $720.
c. Purchased computers and other systems equipment for cash, $10,000.
d. Purchased computer supplies on credit, $1,200.
e. Received revenue from a client, $1,600.
f. Billed a client on completion of a short project, $1,420.
g. Paid wages, $800.
h. Received a partial payment from the client billed in transaction f, $160.
i. Withdrew cash for personal expenses, $500.
j. Made a partial payment on the computer supplies purchased in transaction d, $400.

REQUIRED ▶

1. Arrange the asset, liability, and owner's equity accounts in an equation similar to that in Exhibit 1, using the following account titles: Cash, Accounts Receivable, Computer Supplies, Equipment, Systems Library, Accounts Payable, and John Unger, Capital.

Curious if you got the right answer? Look at the Check Figures section that precedes Chapter 1.

2. Show by addition and subtraction, as in Exhibit 1, the effects of the transactions on the accounting equation. Show new balances after each transaction, and identify each owner's equity transaction by type.
3. Contrast the effects on cash flows of transactions d and j with transaction c and of transactions f and h with transaction e.

P 2.

LO5   Effect of Transactions on the Accounting Equation

On October 1, Oscar Melendez started a new business, the Melendez Transport Company. During the month of October, the firm completed the following transactions:

a. Deposited $132,000 in a new bank account to establish Melendez Transport Company.
b. Purchased two trucks for cash, $86,000.
c. Purchased equipment on credit, $18,000.
d. Billed a customer for hauling goods, $2,400.
e. Received cash for hauling goods, $4,600.
f. Received cash payment from the customer billed in transaction d, $1,200.
g. Made a payment on the equipment purchased in transaction c, $10,000.
h. Paid wages in cash, $3,400.
i. Withdrew cash from the business for personal use, $2,400.

REQUIRED ▶

1. Arrange the asset, liability, and owner's equity accounts in an equation similar to that in Exhibit 1, using the following account titles: Cash, Accounts Receivable, Trucks, Equipment, Accounts Payable, and Oscar Melendez, Capital.
2. Show by addition and subtraction, as in Exhibit 1, the effects of the transactions on the accounting equation. Show new balances after each transaction, and identify each owner's equity transaction by type.

P 3.

LO5   Effect of Transactions on the Accounting Equation

After completing his M.B.A., Sol Lindberg set up a consulting practice. At the end of his first month of operation, Lindberg had the following account balances: Cash, $2,930; Accounts Receivable, $1,400; Office Supplies, $270; Office Equipment, $4,200; Accounts Payable, $1,900; and Sol Lindberg, Capital, $6,900. Soon thereafter, the following transactions were completed:

a. Paid current month's rent, $800.
b. Made payment toward accounts payable, $450.

c. Billed clients for services performed, $800.
d. Received payment from clients billed last month, $1,000.
e. Purchased office supplies for cash, $80.
f. Paid part-time secretary's salary, $850.
g. Paid utilities expense, $90.
h. Paid telephone expense, $50.
i. Purchased additional office equipment for cash, $400.
j. Received cash from clients for services performed, $1,200.
k. Withdrew cash for personal expenses, $500.

REQUIRED ▶
1. Arrange the following asset, liability, and owner's equity accounts in an equation similar to that in Exhibit 1: Cash, Accounts Receivable, Office Supplies, Office Equipment, Accounts Payable, and Sol Lindberg, Capital.
2. Enter the beginning balances of the assets, liabilities, and owner's equity.
3. Show by addition and subtraction, as in Exhibit 1, the effects of the transactions on the accounting equation. Show new balances after each transaction, and identify each owner's equity transaction by type.

P 4.

LO1 Preparation of Financial
LO6 Statements

General ledger icons indicate that the problem can be solved using Houghton Mifflin General Ledger Software for Windows, with upgraded interface and available on the Student CD.

At the end of August 20xx, the Sheri Alexander, Capital account had a balance of $74,600. After operating during September, her Moon Valley Riding Club had the following account balances:

Cash	$17,400	Building	$60,000
Accounts Receivable	2,400	Horses	20,000
Supplies	2,000	Accounts Payable	35,600
Land	42,000		

In addition, the following transactions affected owner's equity:

Withdrawal by Sheri Alexander	$ 6,400	Salaries expense	$4,600
Investment by Sheri Alexander	32,000	Feed expense	2,000
Riding lesson revenue	12,400	Utilities expense	1,200
Locker rental revenue	3,400		

REQUIRED ▶
1. Using Exhibit 2 as a model, prepare an income statement, a statement of owner's equity, and a balance sheet for Moon Valley Riding Club. (**Hint:** The final balance of Sheri Alexander, Capital is $108,200).
2. Identify the links among the financial statements in part 1.
3. Which of these statements are most closely associated with the goals of profitability and liquidity? Explain your answer. What other financial statement is helpful in evaluating liquidity?

P 5.

LO5 Effect of Transactions
LO6 on the Accounting Equation
and Preparation of Financial
Statements

Arrow Copying Service began operations and engaged in the following transactions during August 20xx:

a. Investment by owner, Myra Lomax, $10,000.
b. Paid current month's rent, $900.
c. Purchased copier for cash, $5,000.
d. Paid cash for paper and other copier supplies, $380.
e. Copying job payments received in cash, $1,780.
f. Copying job billed to major customer, $1,360.
g. Paid wages to part-time employees, $560.
h. Purchased additional copier supplies on credit, $280.
i. Received partial payment from customer in transaction f, $600.
j. Paid current month's utility bill, $180.
k. Made partial payment on supplies purchased in transaction h, $140.
l. Withdrew cash for personal use, $1,400.

REQUIRED ▶
1. Arrange the asset, liability, and owner's equity accounts in an equation similar to that in Exhibit 1, using these account titles: Cash, Accounts Receivable, Supplies, Copier, Accounts Payable, and M. Lomax, Capital.
2. Show by addition and subtraction, as in Exhibit 1, the effects of the transactions on the accounting equation. Show new balances after each transaction, and identify each owner's equity transaction by type.
3. Using Exhibit 2 as a guide, prepare an income statement, a statement of owner's equity, and a balance sheet for Arrow Copying Service. (Optional: Also prepare a statement of cash flows.)

ALTERNATE PROBLEMS ← Looking for more practice? Alternate problems have the same format and learning objectives as the earlier problems.

P 6.

LO5   Effect of Transactions on the Accounting Equation

Rosa Partridge started The Creative Frames Shop in a small shopping center. In the first weeks of operation, the company completed the following transactions:

a. Deposited $21,000 in an account in the name of the company to start the business.
b. Paid the current month's rent, $1,500.
c. Purchased store equipment on credit, $10,800.
d. Purchased framing supplies for cash, $5,100.
e. Received framing revenue, $2,400.
f. Billed customers for services, $2,100.
g. Paid utilities expense, $750.
h. Received payment from customers in transaction f, $600.
i. Made payment on store equipment purchased in transaction c, $5,400.
j. Withdrew cash for personal expenses, $1,200.

REQUIRED ▶

1. Arrange the following asset, liability, and owner's equity accounts in an equation similar to that in Exhibit 1: Cash, Accounts Receivable, Framing Supplies, Store Equipment, Accounts Payable, and Rosa Partridge, Capital.
2. Show by addition and subtraction, as in Exhibit 1, the effects of the transactions on the accounting equation. Show new balances after each transaction, and identify each owner's equity transaction by type.
3. Contrast the effects on cash flows of transactions c and i with transaction d and of transactions f and h with transaction e.

P 7.

LO1   Preparation of Financial
LO6   Statements

At the end of its first month of operation, March 20xx, Ellis Plumbing Company had the following account balances:

Cash	$58,600	Tools	$7,600
Accounts Receivable	10,800	Accounts Payable	8,600
Delivery Truck	38,000		

In addition, during the month of March, the following transactions affected owner's equity:

Original investment by J. Ellis	$40,000	Repair revenue	$ 5,600
Withdrawal by J. Ellis	4,000	Salaries expense	16,600
Further investment by J. Ellis	60,000	Rent expense	1,400
Contract revenue	23,200	Fuel expense	400

REQUIRED ▶

1. Using Exhibit 2 as a model, prepare an income statement, a statement of owner's equity, and a balance sheet for Ellis Plumbing Company. (**Hint:** The final balance of J. Ellis, Capital is $106,400.)
2. Identify the links among the financial statements in part 1.
3. Which financial statement is most closely associated with the goal of liquidity? Which with the goal of profitability? Explain your answers. What other statement is helpful in evaluating liquidity?

P 8.

LO5   Effect of Transactions
LO6   on the Accounting Equation and Preparation of Financial Statements

On April 1, 20xx, AAFast Taxi Service began operation. The company engaged in the following transactions during April:

a. Investment by owner, Madeline Curry, $42,000.
b. Purchased taxi for cash, $19,000.
c. Purchased uniforms on credit, $400.
d. Received taxi fares in cash, $3,200.
e. Paid wages to part-time drivers, $500.
f. Purchased gasoline during month for cash, $800.
g. Purchased car washes during month on credit, $120.
h. Further investment by owner, $5,000.
i. Paid part of the amount owed for the uniforms purchased in transaction c, $200.
j. Billed major client for fares, $900.
k. Paid for automobile repairs, $250.
l. Withdrew cash from business for personal use, $1,000.

REQUIRED ▶

1. Arrange the asset, liability, and owner's equity accounts in an equation similar to that in Exhibit 1, using these account titles: Cash, Accounts Receivable, Uniforms, Taxi, Accounts Payable, and Madeline Curry, Capital.

2. Show by addition and subtraction, as in Exhibit 1, the effects of the transactions on the accounting equation. Show new balances after each transaction, and identify each owner's equity transaction by type.

3. Using Exhibit 2 as a guide, prepare an income statement, a statement of owner's equity, and a balance sheet for AAFast Taxi Service. (Optional: Also prepare a statement of cash flows.)

SKILLS DEVELOPMENT CASES

Conceptual Analysis ← These cases focus on conceptual accounting issues encountered in the real business world.

SD 1.

LO1 Business Activities and
LO2 Management Functions

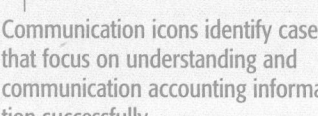

Communication icons identify cases that focus on understanding and communication accounting information successfully.

J.C. Penney Company, Inc., <www.jcpenney.com> is America's largest department store company. According to its letter to stockholders, financial results didn't meet company expectations.

> J.C. Penney is implementing a number of strategic initiatives to ensure our competitiveness, to meet our growth objectives, and to provide a strong return on our stockholders' investment. These initiatives include: accelerated growth in our top 10 markets; expand our women's apparel and accessories business; speed merchandise to market; reduce our cost structure and enhance customer service.[11]

To achieve its strategy, J.C. Penney must organize its management into functions that relate to the principal activities of a business. Discuss the three basic activities J.C. Penney will engage in to achieve its goals, and suggest some examples of each. What is the role of J.C. Penney's management, and what functions must its management perform to accomplish these activities?

SD 2.

LO2 Users of Accounting
LO7 Information

Critical Thinking icons identify cases that reinforce critical thinking skills.

Public companies report quarterly and annually on their success or failure in making a net income. The following item appeared in *The Wall Street Journal*: "Coca-Cola Co.'s <www.coca-cola.com> fourth-quarter net income plunged 27%, a dismal end to a disappointing year, as economic weakness in several overseas markets hurt sales of soft drinks."[12]

Discuss why each of the following individuals or groups might be interested in seeing the accounting reports that support this statement:

1. The management of Coca-Cola
2. The stockholders of Coca-Cola
3. The creditors of Coca-Cola
4. Potential stockholders of Coca-Cola
5. The Internal Revenue Service
6. The Securities and Exchange Commission
7. The Teamsters' union
8. A consumers' group called Public Cause
9. An economic adviser to the president of the United States

The financial statements of Coca-Cola are audited by a CPA firm. Why is the report of these independent auditors important to the users of Coca-Cola's financial statements?

 Group Activity: Assign each of these users to a different group. Ask each group to discuss and present why its user needs accounting information.

SD 3.

LO3 Concept of an Asset

Southwest Airlines Co. <www.southwest.com> is one of the most successful airlines in the United States. Its annual report contains this statement: "We are a company of People, not Planes. That is what distinguishes us from other airlines and other companies. At Southwest Airlines, People are our most important asset."[13] Are employees considered assets in the financial statements? Discuss in what sense Southwest considers its employees to be assets.

Ethical Dilemma ← Ethical dilemmas provide practice in dealing with the tough choices people often face.

SD 4.

LO8 Professional Ethics

Ethics icons identify cases that address ethical issues.

Discuss the ethical choices in the situations below. In each instance, describe the ethical dilemma, determine the alternative courses of action, and tell what you would do.

1. You are the payroll accountant for a small business. A friend asks you how much another employee is paid per hour.

2. As an accountant for the branch office of a wholesale supplier, you discover that several of the receipts the branch manager has submitted for reimbursement as selling expense actually stem from nights out with his spouse.

3. You are an accountant in the purchasing department of a construction company. When you arrive home from work on December 22, you find a large ham in a box marked "Happy Holidays—It's a pleasure to work with you." The gift is from a supplier who has bid on a contract your employer plans to award next week.

4. As an auditor with one year's experience at a local CPA firm, you are expected to complete a certain part of an audit in 20 hours. Because of your lack of experience, you know you cannot finish the job within that time. Rather than admit this, you are thinking about working late to finish the job and not telling anyone.

5. You are a tax accountant at a local CPA firm. You help your neighbor fill out her tax return, and she pays you $200 in cash. Because there is no record of this transaction, you are considering not reporting it on your tax return.

6. The accounting firm for which you work as a CPA has just won a new client, a firm in which you own 200 shares of stock that you received as an inheritance from your grandmother. Because it is only a small number of shares and you think the company will be very successful, you are considering not disclosing the investment.

Group Activity. Assign each case to a different group to resolve and report.

You are asked to gather information from the Internet or business publications and apply it to the accounting concepts in the chapter.

Research Activity

SD 5.

LO1   Need for Knowledge
LO2   of Accounting

What are the relevant numbers, and what do they mean? Practice making business decisions based on accounting information.

Locate an article about a company from one of the following sources: the business section of your local paper or a nearby metropolitan daily, *The Wall Street Journal*, *Business Week*, *Forbes*, or the Needles Accounting Resource Center Web Site at http://accounting. college.hmco.com/students. List all the financial and accounting terms used in the article. Bring the article to class and be prepared to discuss how a knowledge of accounting would help a reader understand the content of the article.

Decision-Making Practice

SD 6.

LO5   Effect of Transactions
LO6   on the Balance Sheet

Memo icons identify cases that require short business memorandums.

Instead of hunting for a summer job after finishing her junior year in college, Lucy Henderson organized a lawn service company in her neighborhood. To start her business on June 1, she deposited $1,350 in a new bank account in the name of her company. The $1,350 consisted of a $500 loan from her father and $850 of her own money. Using the money in this checking account, Henderson rented lawn equipment, purchased supplies, and hired neighborhood high school students to mow and trim the lawns of neighbors who had agreed to pay her for the service. At the end of each month, she mailed bills to her customers.

On August 31, Henderson was ready to dissolve her business and go back to school for the fall quarter. Because she had been so busy, she had not kept any records other than her checkbook and a list of amounts owed to her by customers.

Her checkbook had a balance of $1,760, and the amount owed to her by customers totaled $435. She expected these customers to pay her during October. She planned to return unused supplies to Suburban Landscaping Company for a full credit of $25. When she brought back the rented lawn equipment, Suburban Landscaping also would return a deposit of $100 she had made in June. She owed Suburban Landscaping $260 for equipment rentals and supplies. In addition, she owed the students who had worked for her $50, and she still owed her father $350. Although Henderson feels she did quite well, she is not sure just how successful she was. You have agreed to help her find out.

1. Prepare one balance sheet dated June 1 and another dated August 31 for Henderson Lawn Care Company.

2. Using information that can be inferred from comparing the balance sheets, write a memorandum to Lucy Henderson commenting on her company's performance in achieving profitability and liquidity. (Assume that she used none of the company's assets for personal purposes.) Also, mention the other two financial statements that would be helpful to her in evaluating these business goals.

FINANCIAL REPORTING AND ANALYSIS CASES

Interpreting Financial Reports

FRA 1.

LO7 **Generally Accepted Accounting Principles**

J. P. Morgan Investment Management Inc. <www.jpmorgan.com> is the investment advisory service of the well-known investment bank J.P. Morgan Chase & Company. It makes investments worth billions of dollars in companies listed on the New York Stock Exchange and other stock markets. Generally accepted accounting principles (GAAP) are very important for J.P. Morgan's investment analysts. What are generally accepted accounting principles? Why are financial statements that have been prepared in accordance with GAAP and audited by an independent CPA useful for J.P. Morgan's investment analysts? What organizations influence GAAP? Explain how they do so.

FRA 2.

LO1 **Operating Goals**

Using excerpts from business articles or annual reports of known companies, these cases ask you to extract relevant data, make computations, and interpret your results.

In May 2001, unable to get credit from enough of its lenders, housewares retailer Lechters, Inc., filed for Chapter 11 bankruptcy. It then secured new bank financing in the amount of $86 million. Suppliers, however, remained concerned about Lechters' ability to meet future obligations. Many retracted their term of sale, or the number of days the company had to pay for its merchandise, and asked for cash in advance or on delivery. Smaller home-furnishing retailers like Lechters struggle against big rivals, such as Bed Bath & Beyond, which are more valuable to suppliers and thus can demand better terms and pricing. In spite of these problems and an annual net loss of $101.8 million on sales of $405 million, management believed the company could eventually succeed with its strategy under the bankruptcy.[14] Which is more critical to the short-term survival of a company faced with Lechters' problems: liquidity or profitability? Which is more important in the long term? Explain your answers.

FRA 3.

LO6 **Nature of Cash, Assets, and Net Income**

Charles Schwab Corporation <www.schwab.com> is a well-known financial services firm. Information for 2001 and 2000 from Schwab's annual report appears below.[15]

Charles Schwab Corporation
Condensed Balance Sheets
December 31, 2001 and 2000
(In millions)

	2001	2000
Assets		
Cash	$ 4,407	$ 4,876
Other assets	36,057	33,278
Total assets	$40,464	$38,154
Liabilities		
Total liabilities	$36,301	$33,924
Owner's Equity		
Owner's capital	$ 4,163	$ 4,230
Total liabilities and owner's equity	$40,464	$38,154

Three students who were looking at Charles Schwab's annual report were overheard to make the following comments:

Student A: What a great year Charles Schwab had in 2001! The company earned net income of $2,310,000,000 because its total assets increased from $38,154,000,000 to $40,464,000,000.

Student B: But the change in total assets isn't the same as net income! The company had a net loss of $469,000,000 because cash decreased from $4,876,000,000 to $4,407,000,000.

Student C: I see from the annual report that Charles Schwab had withdrawals (cash distributions to owners) of $209,000,000 in 2001. Don't you have to take that into consideration when analyzing the company's performance?

1. Comment on the interpretations of Students A and B, and then answer Student C's question.
2. Estimate Charles Schwab's net income for 2001. (**Hint:** Reconstruct the statement of owner's equity.)

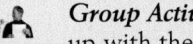 *Group Activity:* After groups discuss **1**, have them compete to see which one can come up with the answer to **2** first.

Explore accounting issues facing international companies.

International Company

FRA 4.

LO1   The Goal of Profitability

International icons identify international cases.

Every chapter has a case on Toys "R" Us; the complete Toys "R" Us annual report for a recent year follows Chapter 6.

In 1998, the celebrated Danish toy company Lego Group <www.lego.com> reported its first loss since the 1930s. In subsequent years, Lego's performance continued to be erratic with profits in 1999, but with a loss in 2000. While its bright plastic bricks were still famous around the globe, Lego was rapidly losing market share to computer and video games. The company's president said, "The Lego Group is not in critical condition, but action is needed. . . . We have to acknowledge that growth and innovation are not enough. We also have to be a profitable business."[16] Discuss the meaning of *profitability*. What other goal must a business achieve? Why is the goal of profitability important to Lego's president? What is the accounting measure of profitability, and on which statement is it determined?

Toys "R" Us Annual Report

FRA 5.

LO6   The Four Basic Financial Statements

Refer to the Toys "R" Us <www.tru.com> annual report in the Supplement to Chapter 6 to answer the questions below. Keep in mind that every company, while following basic principles, adapts financial statements and terminology to its own special needs. Therefore, the complexity of the financial statements and the terminology in the Toys "R" Us statements will sometimes differ from those in the text. (Note that 2002 refers to the year ended February 1, 2003, and 2001 refers to the year ended February 2, 2002.)

1. What names does Toys "R" Us give its four basic financial statements? (Note that the word *consolidated* in the names of the financial statements means that these statements combine those of several companies owned by Toys "R" Us.)
2. Prove that the accounting equation works for Toys "R" Us on February 1, 2003, by finding the amounts for the following equation: Assets = Liabilities + Stockholders' Equity.
3. What were the total revenues of Toys "R" Us for the year ended February 1, 2003?
4. Was Toys "R" Us profitable in the year ended February 1, 2003? How much was net income (loss) in that year, and did it increase or decrease from the year ended February 2, 2002?
5. Did the company's cash and cash equivalents increase from February 2, 2002, to February 1, 2003? By how much? In what two places in the statements can this number be found or computed?
6. Did cash flows from operating activities, cash flows from investing activities, and cash flows from financing activities increase or decrease from 2001 to 2002?

Comparison cases ask you to read the financial statements of Toys "R" Us and Walgreens in the supplement to Chapter 6 and to compare these companies on key financial performance measures and financial disclosures.

Group Activity: Assign the above questions to in-class groups of three or four students. Set a time limit. The first group to answer all questions correctly wins.

Comparison Case: Toys "R" Us and Walgreen Co.

FRA 6.

LO1   Performance Measures
LO5   and Financial Statements
LO7

Refer to the Toys "R" Us <www.tru.com> annual report and the financial statements of Walgreen Co. <www.walgreens.com> in the Supplement to Chapter 6 to answer the following questions:

1. Which company is larger in terms of assets and in terms of revenues? What do you think is the best way to measure the size of a company?
2. Which company is more profitable in terms of net income? What is the trend of profitability over the past three years for both companies?
3. Which company has more cash? Which increased cash most in the last year? Which has more liquidity as measured by cash flows from operating activities?
4. Who is the auditor for each company? Why is the auditor's report that accompanies the financial statements important?

Use the professional software Fingraph® to analyze financial data. ➤ *Fingraph® Financial Analyst™*

FRA 7.

LO1   Financial Statements,
LO6   Business Activities, and Goals

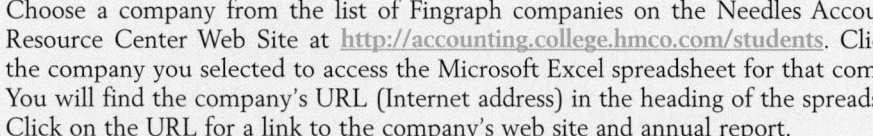

Choose a company from the list of Fingraph companies on the Needles Accounting Resource Center Web Site at <u>http://accounting.college.hmco.com/students</u>. Click on the company you selected to access the Microsoft Excel spreadsheet for that company. You will find the company's URL (Internet address) in the heading of the spreadsheet. Click on the URL for a link to the company's web site and annual report.

1. In the company's annual report, find a description of the business. What business is the company in? How would you describe its operating activities?
2. Find and identify the company's four basic financial statements. Which statement shows the resources of the business and the various claims to those resources? From the balance sheet, prove the accounting equation by showing that the company's assets equal its liabilities plus stockholders' equity. What is the company's largest category of assets? Which statement shows changes in all or part of the company's stockholders' equity during the year? Did the company pay any dividends in the last year?
3. Which statement is most closely associated with the company's profitability goal? How much net income did the company earn in the last year? Which statement is most closely associated with the company's liquidity goal? Did cash (and cash equivalents) increase in the last year? Which provided the most positive cash flows in the last year: operating, investing, or financing activities?
4. Prepare a one-page "executive summary" that highlights what you have learned from steps 1, 2, and 3. An executive summary is a short, easy-to-read report that emphasizes important data and conclusions by putting them in numbered paragraphs or bulleted lists.

Use the Internet to research concepts and applications presented in the chapter. ➤ *Internet Case*

FRA 8.

LO1   Financial Performance
LO5   Comparison of Two
          High-Tech Companies

Microsoft <<u>www.microsoft.com</u>> and Intel <<u>www.intel.com</u>> are two very successful high-tech corporations. Access their web sites using the URLs listed here or go to the Needles Accounting Resource Center Web Site at <u>http://accounting.college.</u> <u>hmco.com/students</u> for a link to their web sites. Access each company's annual report and locate the consolidated balance sheet and consolidated statement of income. Find the amount of total assets, revenues, and net income for the most recent year shown. Then compute net income to revenues (divide net income by revenues) and net income to total assets (divide net income by total assets) for both companies. Which company is larger? Which is more profitable?

2

Chapter 2 continues the exploration of accounting measurement by focusing on the problems of recognition, valuation, and classification and how they are solved in the measuring and recording of business transactions.

Measuring Business Transactions

LEARNING OBJECTIVES

LO1 Explain, in simple terms, the generally accepted ways of solving the measurement issues of recognition, valuation, and classification.

LO2 Describe the chart of accounts and recognize commonly used accounts.

LO3 Define *double-entry system* and state the rules for double entry.

LO4 Apply the steps for transaction analysis and processing to simple transactions.

LO5 Prepare a trial balance and describe its value and limitations.

LO6 Record transactions in the general journal and post transactions from the general journal to the ledger.

DECISION POINT

A USER'S FOCUS

Continental Airlines, Inc. <www.continental.com> & The Boeing Co. <www.boeing.com> In October 2000, Continental Airlines, Inc., announced that it had ordered 15 Boeing 757-300 jetliners.[1] The $1.2 billion order was part of an exclusive agreement Boeing negotiated with Continental. This exclusive 20-year agreement to purchase only Boeing aircraft was Boeing's fourth such agreement with a major airline and positioned the company favorably against Airbus, its European competitor. How should this important order have been recorded, if at all, in the records of Continental and Boeing? When should the purchase and sale that result from this order be recorded in the companies' records?

The order obviously was an important event, one with long-term consequences for both companies. But, as you will see in this chapter, it was not recorded in the accounting records of either company. At the time the order was placed, the aircraft were yet to be manufactured, and the first of them would not be delivered for several years. Even for "firm" orders, Boeing has cautioned that "an economic downturn could result in airline equipment requirements less than currently anticipated resulting in requests to negotiate the rescheduling or possible cancellation of firm orders."[2] The aircraft were not assets of Continental, and the company had not incurred a liability. No aircraft had been delivered or even built, so Continental was not obligated to pay at that point. And Boeing could not record any revenue until it manufactured and delivered the aircraft to Continental, and title to them shifted from Boeing to Continental.

When does Continental record the purchase of a new aircraft it orders from Boeing? When does Boeing record the revenue from the sale?

In fact, Boeing later experienced cancellation or extension of large, previously firm orders because of the economic slowdown in Asia,[3] and also because of the 9-11 attacks and the war in Iraq.

To understand and effectively use financial statements, it is important to know how to analyze events in order to determine the extent of their impact on those statements.

MEASUREMENT ISSUES

LO1 Explain, in simple terms, the generally accepted ways of solving the measurement issues of recognition, valuation, and classification.

RELATED TEXT ASSIGNMENTS
Q: 1, 2, 3, 4, 5
SE: 1, 2
E: 1, 2
P: 3, 4, 7
SD: 1, 2, 3
FRA: 4, 5

Business transactions are economic events that affect the financial position of a business entity. To measure a business transaction, the accountant must decide when the transaction occurred (the recognition issue), what value to place on the transaction (the valuation issue), and how the components of the transaction should be categorized (the classification issue).

These three issues—recognition, valuation, and classification—underlie almost every major decision in financial accounting today. They lie at the heart of accounting for pension plans, for mergers of giant companies, and for international transactions. In discussing the three basic issues, we follow generally accepted accounting principles and use an approach that promotes an understanding of the basic ideas of accounting. Keep in mind, however, that controversy does exist, and that solutions to some problems are not as cut-and-dried as they appear.

THE RECOGNITION ISSUE

TERMINOLOGY NOTE: In accounting, *recognize* means to record a transaction or event.

The **recognition** issue refers to the difficulty of deciding when a business transaction should be recorded. Often the facts of a situation are known, but there is disagreement about *when* the event should be recorded. Suppose, for instance, that a company orders, receives, and pays for an office desk. Which of the following actions constitutes a recordable event?

KEY POINT: A purchase should not be recognized (recorded) before title is transferred because until that point, the vendor has not fulfilled its contractual obligation and the buyer has no liability.

1. An employee sends a purchase requisition to the purchasing department.
2. The purchasing department sends a purchase order to the supplier.
3. The supplier ships the desk.
4. The company receives the desk.
5. The company receives the bill from the supplier.
6. The company pays the bill.

The answer to this question is important because the date on which a purchase is recorded affects amounts in the financial statements. According to accounting tradition, the transaction is recorded when title to the desk passes from the supplier to the purchaser, creating an obligation to pay. Thus, depending on the details of the shipping agreement, the transaction is recognized (recorded) at the time of either action **3** or action **4**. This is the guideline that we generally use in this book. However, in many small businesses that have simple accounting systems, the transaction is not recorded until the bill is received (action **5**) or paid (action **6**) because these are the implied points of title transfer. The predetermined time at which a transaction should be recorded is the **recognition point**.

FOCUS ON BUSINESS PRACTICE

Accounting Policies: Where Do You Find Them?

As noted in the Decision Point at the beginning of this chapter, Continental Airlines' <www.continental.com> order of jetliners from Boeing <www.boeing.com> was not an event that either company should have recorded as a transaction. But when do companies record such events as sales or purchase transactions? The answer to this question and others about a company's accounting policies may be found in the Summary of Significant Accounting Policies in the company's annual report. For example, under the heading "Sales and Other Operating Expenses," Boeing's Summary of Significant Accounting Policies states that "commercial aircraft sales are recorded as deliveries are made."[4]

The recognition issue is not always easy to resolve. Consider an advertising agency that prepares a major advertising campaign for a client. Employees may work on the campaign several hours a day for a number of weeks. They add value to the plan as they develop it. Should this added value be recognized as the campaign is being produced or at the time it is completed? Normally, the increase in value is recorded at the time the plan is finished and the client is billed for it. However, if a plan is going to take a long period to develop, the agency and the client may agree that the client will be billed at key points during its development. A transaction is recorded at each billing.

Here are some more examples of the distinction between business events and transactions:

Business Events That Are *Not* Transactions	Business Events That *Are* Transactions
A customer inquires about the availability of a service.	A customer buys a service.
A company orders a product from a supplier.	A company receives a product previously ordered.
A company hires a new employee.	A company pays an employee for work performed.

THE VALUATION ISSUE

ENRICHMENT NOTE: The value of a transaction usually is based on a business document—a canceled check or an invoice. In general, appraisals or other subjective amounts are not recorded.

◆**STOP AND THINK!**
Which is the most important issue in recording a transaction: recognition, valuation, or classification?
No issue is more important than another. Each must be resolved satisfactorily for a transaction to be recorded correctly.■

Valuation is perhaps the most controversial issue in accounting. The **valuation** issue focuses on assigning a monetary value to a business transaction. Generally accepted accounting principles state that the original cost (often called *historical cost*) is the appropriate value to assign to all business transactions—and therefore to all assets, liabilities, and components of owner's equity, including revenues and expenses, recorded by a business.

Cost is defined here as the exchange price associated with a business transaction at the point of recognition. According to this guideline, the purpose of accounting is not to account for value in terms of worth, which can change after a transaction occurs, but to account for value in terms of cost at the time of the transaction. For example, the cost of an asset is recorded when the asset is acquired, and the value is held at that level until the asset is sold, expires, or is consumed. In this context, *value* means the cost at the time of the transaction. The practice of recording transactions at cost is referred to as the **cost principle**.

Suppose that a person offers a building for sale at $120,000. It may be valued for real estate taxes at $75,000, and it may be insured for $90,000. One prospective buyer may offer $100,000 for the building, and another may offer $105,000. At this point, several different, unverifiable opinions of value have been expressed. Finally, suppose the seller and a buyer settle on a price and complete the sale for $110,000. All these figures are values of one kind or another, but only the last is sufficiently reliable to be used in the records. The market value of the building may vary over the years, but the building will remain on the new buyer's records at $110,000 until it is sold again. At that point, the accountant will record the new transaction at the new exchange price, and a profit or loss will be recognized.

FOCUS ON INTERNATIONAL BUSINESS

No Dollar Amount: How Can That Be?

Determining the valuation of a sale or purchase transaction is often not difficult because it equals the amount of cash, or dollar amount, that changes hands. However, in some areas of the world, valuation is not so easy to determine. In a country where the currency is declining in value and inflation is high, companies often are forced to resort to barter transactions, in which one good or service is traded for another. In Russia, for example, perhaps as many as two-thirds of all transactions are barters. It is not uncommon for Russian companies to end up with piles of goods stacked around their offices and warehouses. In one case, an electric utility company provided a textile-machinery plant with electricity in exchange for wool blankets, which the plant had received in exchange for equipment sold to another company. Determining the value can be difficult in such cases because it becomes a matter of determining the fair value of the goods being traded.[5]

FOCUS ON BUSINESS PRACTICE

Is It Always Cost?

There are sometimes exceptions to the general rules of accounting. For instance, the cost principle is not followed in all parts of the financial statements. Investments, for example, are often accounted for at fair or market value because these investments are available for sale. The fair or market value is the best measure of the potential benefit to the company. Intel Corp. <www.intel.com>, the large microprocessor company, states in its annual report:

Investments designated as available-for-sale on the balance sheet date are reported at fair value.[6]

KEY POINT: Assets, liabilities, and the components of owner's equity are not accounts, but account *classifications*. Cash is a type of asset account, and Notes Payable is a type of liability account.

The cost principle is used because the cost is verifiable. It results from the actions of independent buyers and sellers who come to an agreement on price. An exchange price is an objective price that can be verified by evidence created at the time of the transaction. It is this final price, verified by agreement of the two parties, at which the transaction is recorded.

THE CLASSIFICATION ISSUE

The **classification** issue has to do with assigning all the transactions in which a business engages to appropriate categories, or accounts. Classification of debts can affect a company's ability to borrow money. And classification of purchases can affect its income; for example, purchases of tools may be considered repair expenses (a component of owner's equity) or equipment (assets).

Proper classification depends not only on correctly analyzing the effect of each transaction on the business, but also on maintaining a system of accounts that reflects that effect. The rest of this chapter explains the classification of accounts and the analysis and recording of transactions.

 Check out ACE for a Review Quiz at http://accounting.college.hmco.com/students.

ACCOUNTS AND THE CHART OF ACCOUNTS

LO2 Describe the chart of accounts and recognize commonly used accounts.

RELATED TEXT ASSIGNMENTS
Q: 6, 7, 8, 23
SE: 3
E: 3
FRA: 1, 6

KEY POINT: A chart of accounts is a table of contents for the ledger. Typically, it lists accounts in the order they appear in the ledger, which is usually the order in which they appear on the financial statements, and the numbering scheme allows for some flexibility.

Measuring business transactions often involves gathering large amounts of data. These data require a method of storage that allows businesspeople to retrieve transaction data quickly and in usable form—in other words, a filing system that classifies all transactions according to accounts. Recall that accounts are the basic storage units for accounting data and are used to accumulate amounts from similar transactions. An accounting system has a separate account for each asset, each liability, and each component of owner's equity, including revenues and expenses. Whether a company keeps records by hand or by computer, management must be able to refer to accounts so that it can study the company's financial history and plan for the future. A very small company may need only a few dozen accounts; a multinational corporation may need thousands.

In a manual accounting system, each account is kept on a separate page or card. These pages or cards are placed together in a book or file called the **general ledger**. In the computerized systems that most companies have today, accounts are maintained on magnetic tapes or disks. However, as a matter of convenience, accountants still refer to the group of company accounts as the *general ledger*, or simply the *ledger*.

To help identify accounts in the ledger and to make them easy to find, the accountant often numbers them. A list of these numbers with the corresponding account names is called a **chart of accounts**. A very simple chart of accounts appears in Exhibit 1. Notice that the first digit refers to the major financial statement classification. An account number that begins with the digit 1 represents an asset, an account number that begins with a 2 represents a liability, and so forth. The second and third digits refer to individual accounts. Also notice the gaps in the sequence of numbers. These gaps allow the accountant to expand the number of accounts.

In this chapter and in the next two, we refer to the accounts listed in Exhibit 1 as we discuss the sample case of the Joan Miller Advertising Agency.

EXHIBIT 1
Chart of Accounts for a Small Business

Account Number	Account Name	Description
		Assets
111	Cash	Money and any medium of exchange, including coins, currency, checks, postal and express money orders, and money on deposit in a bank
112	Notes Receivable	Amounts due from others in the form of promissory notes (written promises to pay definite sums of money at fixed future dates)
113	Accounts Receivable	Amounts due from others for revenues or sales on credit (sales on account)
115	Art Supplies	Prepaid expense; art supplies purchased and not used
116	Office Supplies	Prepaid expense; office supplies purchased and not used
117	Prepaid Rent	Prepaid expense; rent paid in advance and not used
118	Prepaid Insurance	Prepaid expense; insurance purchased and not expired; unexpired insurance
141	Land	Property owned for use in the business
142	Buildings	Structures owned for use in the business
143	Accumulated Depreciation, Buildings	Sum of the periodic allocation of the cost of buildings to expense
144	Art Equipment	Art equipment owned for use in the business
145	Accumulated Depreciation, Art Equipment	Sum of the periodic allocation of the cost of art equipment to expense
146	Office Equipment	Office equipment owned for use in the business
147	Accumulated Depreciation, Office Equipment	Sum of the periodic allocation of the cost of office equipment to expense
		Liabilities
211	Notes Payable	Amounts due to others in the form of promissory notes
212	Accounts Payable	Amounts due to others for purchases on credit (purchases on account)
213	Unearned Art Fees	Unearned revenue; advance deposits for artwork to be provided in the future
214	Wages Payable	Amounts due to employees for wages earned and not paid
221	Mortgage Payable	Amounts due on loans that are backed by the company's property and buildings
		Owner's Equity
311	Capital	Owner's investment in the company
312	Withdrawals	Assets withdrawn from the business by the owner for personal use
313	Income Summary	Temporary account used at the end of the accounting period to summarize the revenues and expenses for the period
		Revenues
411	Advertising Fees Earned	Revenues derived from performing advertising services
412	Art Fees Earned	Revenues derived from performing art services

(continued)

EXHIBIT 1
Chart of Accounts for a Small Business *(continued)*

Account Number	Account Name	Description
		Expenses
511	Wages Expense	Amounts earned by employees
512	Utilities Expense	Amounts for utilities, such as water, electricity, and gas, used
513	Telephone Expense	Amounts for telephone services used
514	Rent Expense	Amounts for rent on property and buildings used
515	Insurance Expense	Amounts for insurance expired
516	Art Supplies Expense	Amounts for art supplies used
517	Office Supplies Expense	Amounts for office supplies used
518	Depreciation Expense, Buildings	Amount of buildings' cost allocated to expense
519	Depreciation Expense, Art Equipment	Amount of art equipment cost allocated to expense
520	Depreciation Expense, Office Equipment	Amount of office equipment cost allocated to expense
521	Interest Expense	Amount of interest on debts

● **STOP AND THINK!**

How would the asset accounts in the chart of accounts for Joan Miller Advertising Agency differ if it were a retail company that sold advertising products instead of a service company?

If it were a retail company, it would have an account for inventory.■

OWNER'S EQUITY ACCOUNTS

In the chart of accounts shown in Exhibit 1, the revenue and expense accounts are separated from the other owner's equity accounts. Figure 1 illustrates the relationships of these accounts to each other and to the financial statements. The distinctions among them are important for legal and financial reporting purposes.

First, for income tax reporting, financial reporting, and other purposes, the law requires that Capital and Withdrawals accounts be separated from revenues and expenses. The Capital account represents the owner's interest in the assets of the company. The Withdrawals account is used to record assets taken out of the business by the owner for personal use. These withdrawals are not described as salary or wages, although the owner may think of them as such, because there is no change in the ownership of the money withdrawn. In practice, the Withdrawals account often goes by other names, among them *Personal* and *Drawing*. Corporations do not use a Withdrawals account.

Second, management needs a detailed breakdown of revenues and expenses for budgeting and operating purposes. From these accounts, which are included on the income statement, management can identify the sources of all revenues and the nature of all expenses. In this way, accounting gives management information about whether it has achieved its primary goal of earning a net income.

ACCOUNT TITLES

The names of accounts often confuse beginning accounting students because some words are new or have technical meanings. Also, the same asset, liability, or owner's equity account can have different names in different companies. (Actually, this is not so strange. People, too, often are called different names by their friends, families, and associates.) For example, Fixed Assets, Plant and Equipment, Capital Assets, and Long-Lived Assets are all names for long-term asset accounts. Even the most acceptable names change over time, but out of habit, some companies continue to use names that are out of date.

FIGURE 1
**Relationships of Owner's Equity
Accounts**

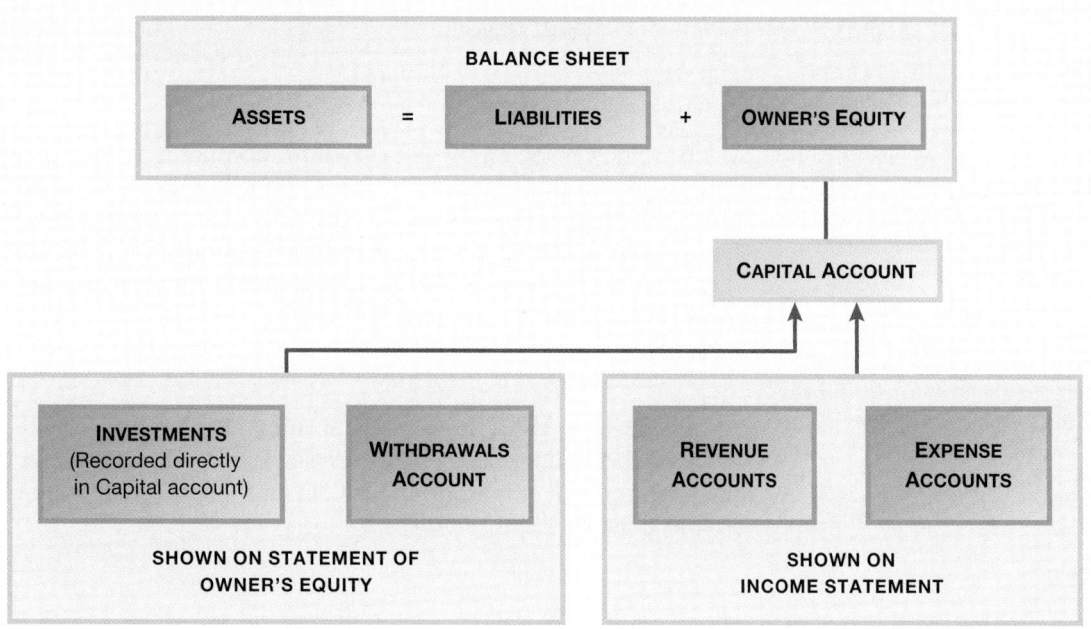

FIGURE 1
**Relationships of Owner's Equity
Accounts**

KEY POINT: Account names must be both concise and descriptive. Although some account names, such as Cash and Land, generally are fixed, others are not.

In general, an account title should describe what is recorded in the account. When you come across an account title that you do not recognize, examine the context of the name—whether it is classified as an asset, liability, or owner's equity component, including revenue or expense, on the financial statements—and look for the kind of transaction that gave rise to the account.

 Check out ACE for a Review Quiz at http://accounting.college.hmco.com/students.

THE DOUBLE-ENTRY SYSTEM: THE BASIC METHOD OF ACCOUNTING

LO3 Define *double-entry system* and state the rules for double entry.

RELATED TEXT ASSIGNMENTS
Q: 9, 10, 11, 12, 13
SE: 2
FRA: 5

KEY POINT: Each transaction must include at least one debit and one credit, and the debit totals must equal the credit totals.

The double-entry system, the backbone of accounting, evolved during the Renaissance. The first systematic description of double-entry bookkeeping appeared in 1494, two years after Columbus discovered America, in a mathematics book by Fra Luca Pacioli. Goethe, the famous German poet and dramatist, referred to double-entry bookkeeping as "one of the finest discoveries of the human intellect." Werner Sombart, an eminent economist-sociologist, believed that "double-entry bookkeeping is born of the same spirit as the system of Galileo and Newton."

What is the significance of the double-entry system? The system is based on the *principle of duality*, which means that every economic event has two aspects—effort and reward, sacrifice and benefit, source and use—that offset or balance each other. In the double-entry system, each transaction must be recorded with at least one debit and one credit, so that the total dollar amount of debits and the total dollar amount of credits equal each other. Because of the way it is designed, the whole system is always in balance. All accounting systems, no matter how sophisticated, are based on the principle of duality.

THE T ACCOUNT

The T account is a good place to begin the study of the double-entry system. In its simplest form, an account has three parts: (1) a title, which describes the asset, the liability, or the owner's equity account; (2) a left side, which is called the **debit** side; and (3) a right side, which is called the **credit** side. This form of an account, called a **T account** because it resembles the letter *T*, is used to analyze transactions. It looks like this:

Title of Account	
Debit (left) side	Credit (right) side

Any entry made on the left side of the account is a debit, or debit entry, and any entry made on the right side of the account is a credit, or credit entry. The terms *debit* (abbreviated Dr., from the Latin *debere*) and *credit* (abbreviated Cr., from the Latin *credere*) are simply the accountant's words for "left" and "right" (not for "increase" or "decrease"). We present a more formal version of the T account, the ledger account form, later in this chapter.

THE T ACCOUNT ILLUSTRATED

As discussed in the last chapter, Shannon Realty had several transactions that involved the receipt or payment of cash. These transactions can be summarized in the Cash account by recording receipts on the left (debit) side of the account and payments on the right (credit) side:

	Cash		
(1)	50,000	(2)	35,000
(5)	1,500	(4)	200
(7)	1,000	(8)	1,000
		(9)	400
		(11)	600
	52,500		37,200
Bal.	15,300		

The cash receipts on the left total $52,500. (The total is written in small figures so that it cannot be confused with an actual debit entry.) The cash payments on the right side total $37,200. These totals are simply working totals, or **footings**. Footings, which are calculated at the end of each month, are an easy way to determine cash on hand. The difference in dollars between the total debit footing and the total credit footing is called the **balance**, or *account balance*. If the balance is a debit, it is written on the left side. If it is a credit, it is written on the right. Shannon Realty's Cash account has a debit balance of $15,300 ($52,500 − $37,200). This is the amount of cash the business has on hand at the end of the month.

ANALYZING AND PROCESSING TRANSACTIONS

The two rules of double-entry bookkeeping are that every transaction affects at least two accounts and that total debits must equal total credits. In other words, for every transaction, one or more accounts must be debited and one or more accounts must be credited, and the total dollar amount of the debits must equal the total dollar amount of the credits.

Look again at the accounting equation:

$$\text{Assets} = \text{Liabilities} + \text{Owner's Equity}$$

You can see that if a debit increases assets, then a credit must be used to decrease assets on the same side of the equal sign or increase liabilities or owner's equity on opposite sides of the equal sign. Likewise, if a credit decreases assets, then a debit must be used to increase assets or decrease liabilities or owner's equity. These rules can be shown as follows:

Assets		=	Liabilities		+	Owner's Equity	
Debit for increases (+)	Credit for decreases (−)		Debit for decreases (−)	Credit for increases (+)		Debit for decreases (−)	Credit for increases (+)

1. Increases in assets are debited to asset accounts. Decreases in assets are credited to asset accounts.

2. Increases in liabilities and owner's equity are credited to liability and owner's equity accounts. Decreases in liabilities and owner's equity are debited to liability and owner's equity accounts.

One of the more difficult points to understand is the application of double-entry rules to the owner's equity components. The key is to remember that withdrawals and expenses are deductions from owner's equity. Thus, transactions that *increase* withdrawals or expenses *decrease* owner's equity. Consider this expanded version of the accounting equation:

Owner's Equity

Assets = Liabilities + Capital − Withdrawals + Revenues − Expenses

This equation may be rearranged by shifting withdrawals and expenses to the left side, as follows:

Assets		+	Withdrawals		+	Expenses		=	Liabilities		+	Capital		+	Revenues	
+ (debits)	− (credits)		+ (debits)	− (credits)		+ (debits)	− (credits)		− (debits)	+ (credits)		− (debits)	+ (credits)		− (debits)	+ (credits)

Note that the rules for double entry for all the accounts on the left of the equal sign are just the opposite of the rules for all the accounts on the right of the equal sign. Assets, withdrawals, and expenses are increased by debits and decreased by credits. Liabilities, capital, and revenues are increased by credits and decreased by debits.

With this basic information about double entry, it is possible to analyze and process transactions by following the five steps illustrated in Figure 2. To show how the steps are applied, assume that on June 1, Koenig Art Supplies borrows $100,000 from its bank on a promissory note. The list that follows describes how this transaction is analyzed and processed.

FIGURE 2
Analyzing and Processing Transactions

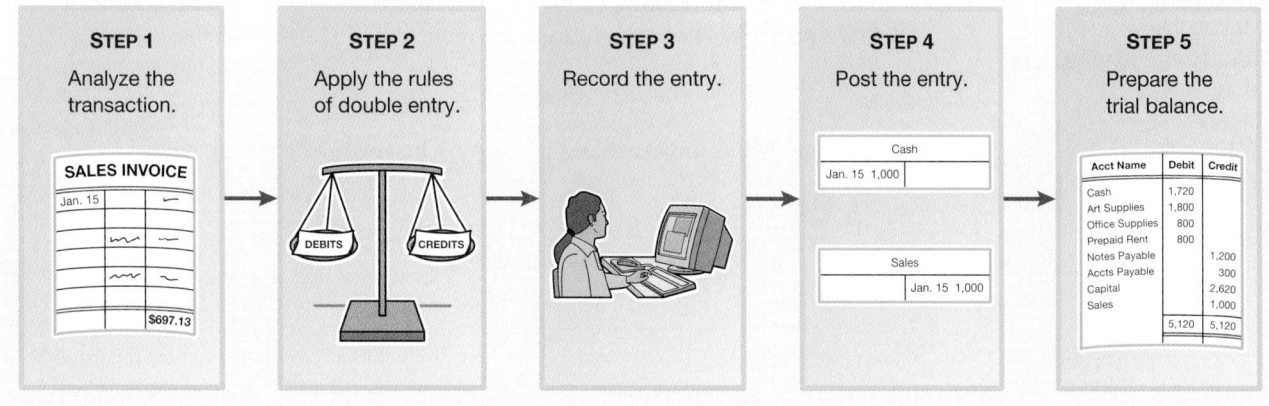

KEY POINT: Identifying the accounts involved in a transaction takes practice. Often, account names are not used in the description of a transaction.

1. *Analyze the transaction to determine its effect on assets, liabilities, and owner's equity.* In this case, both an asset (Cash) and a liability (Notes Payable) increase. A transaction is usually supported by some kind of **source document**—an invoice, receipt, check, or contract; here, it would be a copy of the signed note.

2. *Apply the rules of double entry.* Increases in assets are recorded by debits. Increases in liabilities are recorded by credits.

3. *Record the entry.* Transactions are recorded in chronological order in a journal. In one form of journal, which is explained in more detail later in this chapter, the date, debit account, and debit amount are recorded on one line and the credit account and credit amount, indented, on the next line, as follows:

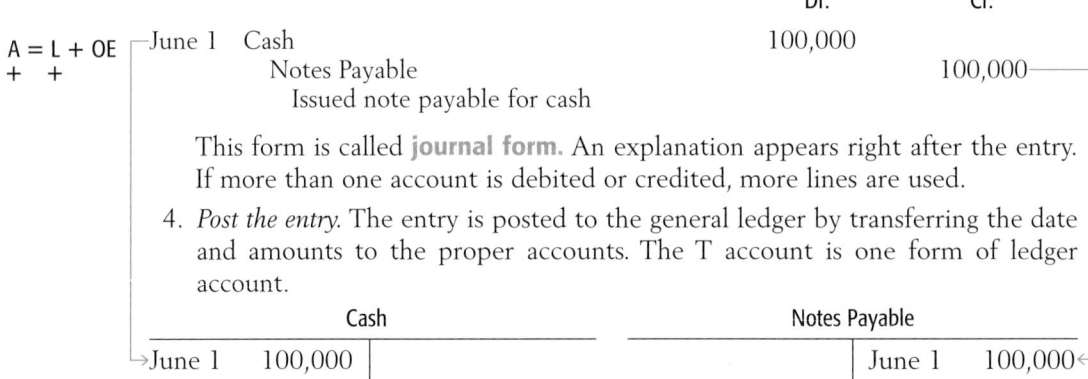

		Dr.	Cr.
June 1	Cash	100,000	
	Notes Payable		100,000
	Issued note payable for cash		

A = L + OE
+   +

This form is called **journal form.** An explanation appears right after the entry. If more than one account is debited or credited, more lines are used.

4. *Post the entry.* The entry is posted to the general ledger by transferring the date and amounts to the proper accounts. The T account is one form of ledger account.

Cash			Notes Payable	
June 1 100,000				June 1 100,000

In formal records, step **3** is never omitted. However, for purposes of analysis, accountants often bypass step **3** and record entries directly in T accounts because doing so clearly and quickly shows the effects of transactions on the accounts. Some of the assignments in this chapter use the same approach to emphasize the analytical aspects of double entry.

5. *Prepare the trial balance to confirm the balance of the accounts.* Periodically, accountants prepare a trial balance to confirm that the accounts are still in balance after the recording and posting of transactions. Preparation of the trial balance is explained later in this chapter.

✓ Check out ACE for a Review Quiz at http://accounting.college.hmco.com/students.

TRANSACTION ANALYSIS ILLUSTRATED

LO4 Apply the steps for transaction analysis and processing to simple transactions.

RELATED TEXT ASSIGNMENTS
Q: 14, 15, 16, 20, 24
SE: 5, 6
E: 4, 5, 7, 12
P: 1, 2, 3, 4, 5, 6, 7, 8
SD: 2, 4, 5
FRA: 1, 2, 3, 5, 6

In the next few pages, we examine the transactions for Joan Miller Advertising Agency during the month of July. In the discussion, we illustrate the principle of duality and show how transactions are recorded in the accounts.

July 1: Joan Miller invests $20,000 to start her own advertising agency.

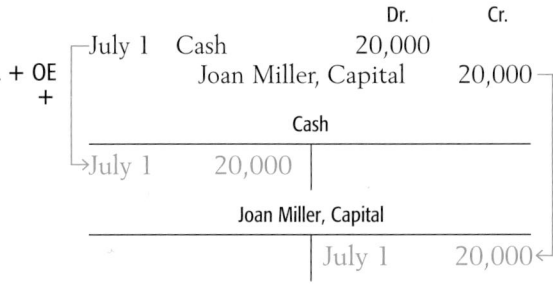

		Dr.	Cr.
July 1	Cash	20,000	
	Joan Miller, Capital		20,000

A = L + OE
+   +

Cash	
July 1 20,000	

Joan Miller, Capital	
	July 1 20,000

Transaction: Owner's investment.
Analysis: Assets increase. Owner's equity increases.
Rules: Increases in assets are recorded by debits. Increases in owner's equity are recorded by credits.
Entry: The increase in assets is recorded by a debit to Cash. The increase in owner's equity is recorded by a credit to Joan Miller, Capital.

Analysis: If Joan Miller had invested assets other than cash in the business, the appropriate asset accounts would be debited.

KEY POINT: Notice the exchange of one asset for another asset.

A = L + OE
\+
\-

July 2: Rents an office, paying two months' rent, $1,600, in advance.

		Dr.	Cr.
July 2	Prepaid Rent	1,600	
	Cash		1,600

Cash

| July 1 | 20,000 | July 2 | 1,600 |

Prepaid Rent

| July 2 | 1,600 | |

Transaction: Rent paid in advance.
Analysis: Assets increase. Assets decrease.
Rules: Increases in assets are recorded by debits. Decreases in assets are recorded by credits.
Entry: The increase in assets is recorded by a debit to Prepaid Rent. The decrease in assets is recorded by a credit to Cash.

July 3: Purchases art equipment, $4,200, with cash.

A = L + OE
\+
\-

		Dr.	Cr.
July 3	Art Equipment	4,200	
	Cash		4,200

Cash

| July 1 | 20,000 | July 2 | 1,600 |
| | | 3 | 4,200 |

Art Equipment

| July 3 | 4,200 | |

KEY POINT: Terms such as *Cash Paid* and *Art Equipment Purchased* are not acceptable account names. *Cash* and *Art Equipment* are the correct account names.

Transaction: Purchase of equipment.
Analysis: Assets increase. Assets decrease.
Rules: Increases in assets are recorded by debits. Decreases in assets are recorded by credits.
Entry: The increase in assets is recorded by a debit to Art Equipment. The decrease in assets is recorded by a credit to Cash.

July 4: Orders art supplies, $1,800, and office supplies, $800.

Analysis: No entry is made because no transaction has occurred. According to the recognition issue, there is no liability until the supplies are shipped or received and there is an obligation to pay for them.

July 5: Purchases office equipment, $3,000, from Morgan Equipment; pays $1,500 in cash and agrees to pay the rest next month.

A = L + OE
\+ \+
\-

		Dr.	Cr.
July 5	Office Equipment	3,000	
	Cash		1,500
	Accounts Payable		1,500

Cash

July 1	20,000	July 2	1,600
		3	4,200
		5	1,500

Office Equipment

| July 5 | 3,000 | |

Accounts Payable

| | July 5 | 1,500 |

KEY POINT: Office equipment is recorded at the full $3,000, even though only half of it has been paid for.

Transaction: Purchase of equipment and partial payment.
Analysis: Assets increase. Assets decrease. Liabilities increase.
Rules: Increases in assets are recorded by debits. Decreases in assets are recorded by credits. Increases in liabilities are recorded by credits.
Entry: The increase in assets is recorded by a debit to Office Equipment. The decrease in assets is recorded by a credit to Cash. The increase in liabilities is recorded by a credit to Accounts Payable.

July 6: Purchases art supplies, $1,800, and office supplies, $800, from Taylor Supply Company, on credit.

		Dr.	Cr.
A = L + OE	July 6 Art Supplies	1,800	
+ +	Office Supplies	800	
+	Accounts Payable		2,600

Art Supplies

July 6 1,800	

Office Supplies

July 6 800	

Accounts Payable

	July 5 1,500
	6 2,600

KEY POINT: Accounts Payable is used when there is a delay between purchase and payment.

Transaction: Purchase of supplies on credit.
Analysis: Assets increase. Liabilities increase.
Rules: Increases in assets are recorded by debits. Increases in liabilities are recorded by credits.
Entry: The increase in assets is recorded by debits to Art Supplies and Office Supplies. The increase in liabilities is recorded by a credit to Accounts Payable.

July 8: Pays for a one-year life insurance policy, $960, with coverage effective July 1.

		Dr.	Cr.
A = L + OE	July 8 Prepaid Insurance	960	
+	Cash		960
−			

Cash

July 1	20,000	July 2	1,600
		3	4,200
		5	1,500
		8	960

Prepaid Insurance

July 8 960	

Transaction: Insurance purchased in advance.
Analysis: Assets increase. Assets decrease.
Rules: Increases in assets are recorded by debits. Decreases in assets are recorded by credits.
Entry: The increase in assets is recorded by a debit to Prepaid Insurance. The decrease in assets is recorded by a credit to Cash.

July 9: Pays Taylor Supply Company $1,000 of the amount owed.

A = L + OE
−   −

KEY POINT: Accounts Payable, not Art Supplies or Office Supplies, is debited. Also, a liability usually is credited before it can be debited.

		Dr.	Cr.
July 9	Accounts Payable	1,000	
	Cash		1,000

Cash

July 1	20,000	July 2	1,600
		3	4,200
		5	1,500
		8	960
		9	1,000

Accounts Payable

July 9	1,000	July 5	1,500
		6	2,600

Transaction: Partial payment on a liability.
Analysis: Assets decrease. Liabilities decrease.
Rules: Decreases in liabilities are recorded by debits. Decreases in assets are recorded by credits.
Entry: The decrease in liabilities is recorded by a debit to Accounts Payable. The decrease in assets is recorded by a credit to Cash.

July 10: Performs a service for an automobile dealer by placing advertisements in a newspaper and collects a fee, $1,400.

A = L + OE
+   +

		Dr.	Cr.
July 10	Cash	1,400	
	Advertising Fees Earned		1,400

Cash

July 1	20,000	July 2	1,600
10	1,400	3	4,200
		5	1,500
		8	960
		9	1,000

Advertising Fees Earned

		July 10	1,400

Transaction: Revenue earned and cash collected.
Analysis: Assets increase. Owner's equity increases.
Rules: Increases in assets are recorded by debits. Increases in owner's equity are recorded by credits.
Entry: The increase in assets is recorded by a debit to Cash. The increase in owner's equity is recorded by a credit to Advertising Fees Earned.

July 12: Pays the secretary two weeks' wages, $1,200.

A = L + OE
−   −

		Dr.	Cr.
July 12	Wages Expense	1,200	
	Cash		1,200

Cash

July 1	20,000	July 2	1,600
10	1,400	3	4,200
		5	1,500
		8	960
		9	1,000
		12	1,200

Wages Expense

July 12	1,200		

Transaction: Payment of wages expense.
Analysis: Assets decrease. Owner's equity decreases.
Rules: Decreases in owner's equity are recorded by debits. Decreases in assets are recorded by credits.
Entry: The decrease in owner's equity is recorded by a debit to Wages Expense. The decrease in assets is recorded by a credit to Cash.

July 15: Accepts an advance fee, $1,000, for artwork to be done for another agency.

			Dr.	Cr.
A = L + OE	July 15	Cash	1,000	
+ +		Unearned Art		
		Fees		1,000

Cash

July	1	20,000	July	2	1,600
	10	1,400		3	4,200
	15	1,000		5	1,500
				8	960
				9	1,000
				12	1,200

Unearned Art Fees

		July	15	1,000

Transaction: Payment received for future services.
Analysis: Assets increase. Liabilities increase.
Rules: Increases in assets are recorded by debits. Increases in liabilities are recorded by credits.
Entry: The increase in assets is recorded by a debit to Cash. The increase in liabilities is recorded by a credit to Unearned Art Fees.

◆ STOP AND THINK!
In what way are unearned revenues the opposite of prepaid expenses?

With unearned revenues (a liability), cash is received in advance for a service to be performed later. With prepaid expenses (an asset), cash is paid in advance of receiving a service. ■

July 19: Performs a service by placing several major advertisements for Ward Department Stores. The fee, $4,800, is billed now but will be collected next month.

			Dr.	Cr.
A = L + OE	July 19	Accounts		
+ +		Receivable	4,800	
		Advertising Fees		
		Earned		4,800

Accounts Receivable

July 19	4,800	

Advertising Fees Earned

	July	10	1,400
		19	4,800

Transaction: Revenue earned, to be received later.
Analysis: Assets increase. Owner's equity increases.
Rules: Increases in assets are recorded by debits. Increases in owner's equity are recorded by credits.
Entry: The increase in assets is recorded by a debit to Accounts Receivable. The increase in owner's equity is recorded by a credit to Advertising Fees Earned.

KEY POINT: Revenue is recognized even though payment has not been received yet. Accounts Receivable is used when there is a delay between the sale of services or merchandise and payment.

July 26: Pays the secretary two more weeks' wages, $1,200.

			Dr.	Cr.
A = L + OE	July 26	Wages Expense	1,200	
− −		Cash		1,200

Cash

July	1	20,000	July	2	1,600
	10	1,400		3	4,200
	15	1,000		5	1,500
				8	960
				9	1,000
				12	1,200
				26	1,200

Wages Expense

July	12	1,200	
	26	1,200	

Transaction: Payment of wages expense.
Analysis: Assets decrease. Owner's equity decreases.
Rules: Decreases in owner's equity are recorded by debits. Decreases in assets are recorded by credits.
Entry: The decrease in owner's equity is recorded by a debit to Wages Expense. The decrease in assets is recorded by a credit to Cash.

July 29: Receives and pays the utility bill, $200.

		Dr.	Cr.
July 29	Utilities Expense	200	
	Cash		200

A = L + OE
−   −

Cash

July	1	20,000	July	2	1,600
	10	1,400		3	4,200
	15	1,000		5	1,500
				8	960
				9	1,000
				12	1,200
				26	1,200
				29	200

Utilities Expense

July 29	200	

Transaction: Payment of utilities expense.
Analysis: Assets decrease. Owner's equity decreases.
Rules: Decreases in owner's equity are recorded by debits. Decreases in assets are recorded by credits.
Entry: The decrease in owner's equity is recorded by a debit to Utilities Expense. The decrease in assets is recorded by a credit to Cash.

July 30: Receives (but does not pay) the telephone bill, $140.

		Dr.	Cr.
July 30	Telephone Expense	140	
	Accounts Payable		140

A = L + OE
    +   −

KEY POINT: The expense and liability are recognized at this point, even though payment has not yet been made, because an expense has been incurred. Telephone services have been used, and the obligation to pay exists.

Accounts Payable

July	9	1,000	July	5	1,500
				6	2,600
				30	140

Telephone Expense

July 30	140	

Transaction: Expense incurred, to be paid later.
Analysis: Liabilities increase. Owner's equity decreases.
Rules: Decreases in owner's equity are recorded by debits. Increases in liabilities are recorded by credits.
Entry: The decrease in owner's equity is recorded by a debit to Telephone Expense. The increase in liabilities is recorded by a credit to Accounts Payable.

July 31: Joan Miller withdraws $1,400 from the business for personal living expenses.

		Dr.	Cr.
July 31	Joan Miller, Withdrawals	1,400	
	Cash		1,400

A = L + OE
−   −

KEY POINT: Withdrawals are not considered an expense. Expenses are costs of operating a business, but withdrawals are assets that the owner takes out of the business.

Cash

July	1	20,000	July	2	1,600
	10	1,400		3	4,200
	15	1,000		5	1,500
				8	960
				9	1,000
				12	1,200
				26	1,200
				29	200
				31	1,400

Joan Miller, Withdrawals

July 31	1,400	

Transaction: Owner's withdrawal for personal use.
Analysis: Assets decrease. Owner's equity decreases.
Rules: Decreases in owner's equity are recorded by debits. Decreases in assets are recorded by credits.
Entry: The decrease in owner's equity is recorded by a debit to Joan Miller, Withdrawals. The decrease in assets is recorded by a credit to Cash.

Exhibit 2
Summary of Transactions for Joan Miller Advertising Agency

| Assets | = | Liabilities | + | Owner's Equity |

Cash

July	1	20,000	July	2	1,600
	10	1,400		3	4,200
	15	1,000		5	1,500
				8	960
				9	1,000
				12	1,200
				26	1,200
				29	200
				31	1,400
		22,400			13,260
Bal.		9,140			

Accounts Receivable

| July | 19 | 4,800 | |

Art Supplies

| July | 6 | 1,800 | |

Office Supplies

| July | 6 | 800 | |

Prepaid Rent

| July | 2 | 1,600 | |

Prepaid Insurance

| July | 8 | 960 | |

Art Equipment

| July | 3 | 4,200 | |

Office Equipment

| July | 5 | 3,000 | |

Accounts Payable

July	9	1,000	July	5	1,500
				6	2,600
				30	140
		1,000			4,240
			Bal.		3,240

Unearned Art Fees

| | | July | 15 | 1,000 |

This account links to the statement of cash flows.

Joan Miller, Capital

| | July | 1 | 20,000 |

Joan Miller, Withdrawals

| July | 31 | 1,400 | |

Advertising Fees Earned

	July	10	1,400
		19	4,800
	Bal.		6,200

Wages Expense

July	12	1,200	
	26	1,200	
Bal.		2,400	

Utilities Expense

| July | 29 | 200 | |

Telephone Expense

| July | 30 | 140 | |

These accounts link to the income statement.

     Exhibit 2 shows the transactions for July in their accounts and in relation to the accounting equation. Note that all transactions have been recorded on the date they are recognized. Most of these transactions involve either the receipt or payment of cash, as reflected in the Cash account. There are important exceptions, however. For instance, on July 19 Advertising Fees were earned, but receipt of cash for these fees will come later. Also, on July 5, 6, and 30 there were transactions recognized that totaled $4,240 in Accounts Payable. This means the company can wait to pay. At the end of the month, only the $1,000 recorded on July 9 had been paid. These lags between recognition of transactions and the subsequent cash inflows or outflows have an impact on achieving the goal of liquidity.

 Check out ACE for a Review Quiz at http://accounting.college.hmco.com/students.

THE TRIAL BALANCE

LO5 Prepare a trial balance and describe its value and limitations.

RELATED TEXT ASSIGNMENTS
Q: 17, 18, 19, 24
SE: 4, 7, 8
E: 3, 6, 8, 9, 10, 11
P: 2, 3, 4, 5, 7, 8
SD: 5

KEY POINT: The trial balance is prepared at the end of the accounting period. It is an initial check that the ledger is in balance.

For every amount debited, an equal amount must be credited. This means that the total of debits and credits in the T accounts must be equal. To test this, the accountant periodically prepares a **trial balance**. Exhibit 3 shows a trial balance for Joan Miller Advertising Agency. It was prepared from the accounts in Exhibit 2.

A trial balance may be prepared at any time but is usually prepared on the last day of the month. Here are the steps in preparing a trial balance:

1. List each T account that has a balance, with debit balances in the left column and credit balances in the right column. Accounts are listed in the order in which they appear in the ledger.

2. Add each column.

3. Compare the totals of the columns.

In accounts in which increases are recorded by debits, the **normal balance** (the usual balance) is a debit balance; in accounts in which increases are recorded by credits, the normal balance is a credit balance. Table 1 summarizes the normal account balances of the major account categories. According to the table, the T account Accounts Payable (a liability) typically has a credit balance and is copied into the trial balance as a credit balance.

EXHIBIT 3
Trial Balance

KEY POINT: The accounts are listed in the same order as in the ledger. At this point, the Capital account does not reflect any revenues, expenses, or withdrawals for the period.

Joan Miller Advertising Agency
Trial Balance
July 31, 20xx

Cash	$ 9,140	
Accounts Receivable	4,800	
Art Supplies	1,800	
Office Supplies	800	
Prepaid Rent	1,600	
Prepaid Insurance	960	
Art Equipment	4,200	
Office Equipment	3,000	
Accounts Payable		$ 3,240
Unearned Art Fees		1,000
Joan Miller, Capital		20,000
Joan Miller, Withdrawals	1,400	
Advertising Fees Earned		6,200
Wages Expense	2,400	
Utilities Expense	200	
Telephone Expense	140	
	$30,440	$30,440

●STOP AND THINK!
Under what conditions would net worth (assets minus liabilities) be negative?

Net worth would be negative if the net amount of all owner's equity accounts is a debit—in other words, if the total of withdrawals and expenses exceeds the total of capital and revenues. In this case, the company's liabilities exceed its assets and it is technically bankrupt. ■

STUDY NOTE: A mnemonic for accounts with normal debit balances is AWE—Assets, Withdrawals, and Expenses.

TABLE 1.   Normal Account Balances of Major Account Categories

Account Category	Increases Recorded by		Normal Balance	
	Debit	Credit	Debit	Credit
Assets	x		x	
Liabilities		x		x
Owner's Equity:				
Capital		x		x
Withdrawals	x		x	
Revenues		x		x
Expenses	x		x	

Once in a while, a transaction leaves an account with a balance that is not "normal." For example, when a company overdraws its account at the bank, its Cash account (an asset) will show a credit balance instead of a debit balance. The "abnormal" balance should be copied into the trial balance columns as it stands, as a debit or a credit.

The trial balance proves whether or not the ledger is in balance. *In balance* means that the total of all debits recorded equals the total of all credits recorded. But the trial balance does not prove that the transactions were analyzed correctly or recorded in the proper accounts. For example, there is no way of determining from the trial balance that a debit should have been made in the Art Equipment account rather than the Office Equipment account. And the trial balance does not detect whether transactions have been omitted, because equal debits and credits will have been omitted. Also, if an error of the same amount is made in both a debit and a credit, it will not be discovered by the trial balance. The trial balance proves only that the debits and credits in the accounts are in balance.

If the debit and credit columns of the trial balance are not equal, look for one or more of the following errors: (1) a debit was entered in an account as a credit, or vice versa; (2) the balance of an account was computed incorrectly; (3) an error was made in carrying the account balance to the trial balance; or (4) the trial balance was summed incorrectly.

Other than simply adding the columns incorrectly, the two most common mistakes in preparing a trial balance are (1) recording an account with a debit balance as a credit, or vice versa, and (2) transposing two digits when transferring an amount to the trial balance (for example, entering $23,459 as $23,549). The first of these mistakes causes the trial balance to be out of balance by an amount evenly divisible by 2. The second causes the trial balance to be out of balance by a number divisible by 9. Thus, if a trial balance is out of balance and the addition has been verified, determine the amount by which the trial balance is out of balance and divide it first by 2 and then by 9. If the amount is divisible by 2, look in the trial balance for an amount that is equal to the quotient. If you find such an amount, it is probably in the wrong column. If the amount is divisible by 9, trace each amount to the ledger account balance, checking carefully for a transposition error. If neither of these techniques identifies the error, first recompute the balance of each account in the ledger.

FOCUS ON BUSINESS TECHNOLOGY

Are All Trial Balances Created Equal?

In computerized accounting systems, posting is done automatically, and the trial balance can be easily prepared as often as needed. Any accounts with abnormal balances are highlighted for investigation. Some general ledger software packages for small businesses list the trial balance amounts in a single column, with credit balances shown as minuses. In such cases, the trial balance is in balance if the total is zero.

Then, if you still have not found the error, retrace each posting from the journal to the ledger.

 Check out ACE for a Review Quiz at http://accounting.college.hmco.com/students.

RECORDING AND POSTING TRANSACTIONS

L06 Record transactions in the general journal and post transactions from the general journal to the ledger.

RELATED TEXT ASSIGNMENTS
Q: 20, 21, 22, 23, 24
SE: 9, 10
E: 12, 13
P: 3, 5, 8

KEY POINT: The journal is a chronological record of events. Only the general journal is discussed in this chapter.

Let us now take a look at the formal process of recording transactions in the general journal and posting them to the ledger.

THE GENERAL JOURNAL

As you have seen, transactions can be entered directly into the accounts. But this method makes identifying individual transactions or finding errors very difficult because the debit is recorded in one account and the credit in another. The solution is to record all transactions chronologically in a journal. The journal is sometimes called the *book of original entry* because it is where transactions first enter the accounting records. Later, the debit and credit portions of each transaction can be transferred to the appropriate accounts in the ledger. A separate journal entry is used to record each transaction, and the process of recording transactions is called journalizing.

Most businesses have more than one kind of journal. The simplest and most flexible type is the general journal, the one we focus on in this chapter. Entries in the general journal include the following information about each transaction:

1. The date
2. The names of the accounts debited and the dollar amounts on the same lines in the debit column
3. The names of the accounts credited and the dollar amounts on the same lines in the credit column
4. An explanation of the transaction
5. The account identification numbers, if appropriate

Exhibit 4 displays two of the transactions for Joan Miller Advertising Agency that we discussed earlier. The procedure for recording transactions in the general journal is as follows:

1. Record the date by writing the year in small figures on the first line at the top of the first column, the month on the next line of the first column, and the day in the second column opposite the month. For subsequent entries on the same page for the same month and year, the month and year can be omitted.

STUDY NOTE: Check your journal for proper form. Frequent errors are forgetting to skip a space between entries, not indenting the credits, using the Post. Ref. column before posting is done, journalizing amounts that do not balance, entering a credit before a debit, and forgetting to enter the explanation.

2. Write the exact names of the accounts debited and credited in the Description column. Starting on the same line as the date, write the name(s) of the account(s) that are debited next to the left margin and indent the name(s) of the account(s) credited. The explanation is placed on the next line and is further indented. The explanation should be brief but sufficient to explain and identify the transaction. A transaction can have more than one debit or credit entry; this is called a compound entry. In a compound entry, all debit accounts are listed before any credit accounts. (The July 6 transaction of Joan Miller Advertising Agency in Exhibit 4 is an example of a compound entry.)

3. Write the debit amounts in the Debit column opposite the accounts to be debited, and write the credit amounts in the Credit column opposite the accounts to be credited.

Exhibit 4
The General Journal

		General Journal			Page 1
Date		Description	Post. Ref.	Debit	Credit
20xx July	6	Art Supplies		1,800	
		Office Supplies		800	
		Accounts Payable			2,600
		Purchase of art and office supplies on credit			
	8	Prepaid Insurance		960	
		Cash			960
		Paid one-year life insurance premium			

A = L + OE
+   +
+

A = L + OE
+
−

4. At the time the transactions are recorded, nothing is placed in the Post. Ref. (posting reference) column. (This column is sometimes called *LP* or *Folio.*) Later, if the company uses account numbers to identify accounts in the ledger, fill in the account numbers to provide a convenient cross-reference from the general journal to the ledger and to indicate that the entry has been posted to the ledger. If the accounts are not numbered, use a checkmark (✔).

5. It is customary to skip a line after each journal entry.

THE GENERAL LEDGER

The general journal is used to record the details of each transaction. The general ledger is used to update each account.

■ **THE LEDGER ACCOUNT FORM**   The T account is a simple, direct means of recording transactions. In practice, a somewhat more complicated form of the account is needed in order to record more information. The **ledger account form**, which contains four columns for dollar amounts, is illustrated in Exhibit 5.

The account title and number appear at the top of the account form. As in the journal, the transaction date appears in the first two columns. The Item column is

Exhibit 5
Accounts Payable in the
General Ledger

		General Ledger					
Accounts Payable						Account No. 212	
			Post. Ref.	Debit	Credit	Balance	
Date		Item				Debit	Credit
20xx July	5		J1		1,500		1,500
	6		J1		2,600		4,100
	9		J1	1,000			3,100
	30		J2		140		3,240

EXHIBIT 6
Posting from the General Journal to the Ledger

A = L + OE
     +   −

STUDY NOTE: When posting, don't forget to use the Post. Ref. columns. They are critical for cross-referencing the components of entries.

General Journal ② Page 2

Date		Description	Post. Ref.	Debit	Credit
20xx ②		①	⑤		③
July	30	Telephone Expense	513	140	
		Accounts Payable	212		140
		Received bill for			
		telephone expense			

General Ledger

Accounts Payable   Account No. 212

Date		Item	Post. Ref.	Debit	Credit	Balance Debit	Balance Credit
20xx							
July	5		J1		1,500		1,500
	6		J1		2,600		4,100
	9		J1	1,000			3,100
	30		J2		140		3,240

General Ledger

Telephone Expense   Account No. 513

Date		Item	Post. Ref.	Debit	Credit	Balance Debit	Balance Credit
20xx						④	
July	30		J2	140		140	

rarely used to identify transactions, because explanations already appear in the journal. The Post. Ref. column is used to note the journal page where the original entry for the transaction can be found. The dollar amount is entered in the appropriate Debit or Credit column, and a new account balance is computed in the final two columns after each entry. The advantage of this account form over the T account is that the current balance of the account is readily available.

STUDY NOTE: Posting is much like sorting mail. It is a tedious, but necessary, procedure, conveniently accomplished by a computer.

■ **POSTING TO THE LEDGER** After transactions have been entered in the journal, they must be transferred to the ledger. The process of transferring journal entry information from the journal to the ledger is called **posting**. Posting is usually done after several entries have been made—for example, at the end of each day or less frequently, depending on the number of transactions. As shown in Exhibit 6, through posting, each amount in the Debit column of the journal is transferred into the Debit column of the appropriate account in the ledger, and each amount in the

Why have both a journal and a ledger? Why not just record all entries in the ledger?

Transactions often need to be verified because mistakes occur. It is much easier to find a transaction and verify that it is correct when it is listed in chronological order in the journal. ■

Credit column of the journal is transferred into the Credit column of the appropriate account in the ledger. The steps in the posting process are as follows:

1. In the ledger, locate the debit account named in the journal entry.
2. Enter the date of the transaction and, in the Post. Ref. column of the ledger, the journal page number from which the entry comes.
3. Enter in the Debit column of the ledger account the amount of the debit as it appears in the journal.
4. Calculate the account balance and enter it in the appropriate Balance column.
5. Enter in the Post. Ref. column of the journal the account number to which the amount has been posted.
6. Repeat the same five steps for the credit side of the journal entry.

Notice that step **5** is the last step in the posting process for each debit and credit. In addition to serving as an easy reference between the journal entry and the ledger account, this entry in the Post. Ref. column of the journal indicates that all steps for the transaction have been completed. This allows accountants who have been called away from their work to easily find where they were before they were interrupted.

SOME NOTES ON PRESENTATION

A ruled line appears in financial reports before each subtotal or total to indicate that the amounts above are added or subtracted. It is common practice to use a double line under a final total to show that it has been checked, or verified.

KEY POINT: Placing a dash in the cents column is preferable to leaving it blank. (It's possible to infer from a blank cents column that the bookkeeper simply forgot to enter the figure for cents.)

Dollar signs ($) are required in all financial statements, including the balance sheet and income statement, and in the trial balance and other schedules. On these statements, a dollar sign should be placed before the first amount in each column and before the first amount in a column following a ruled line. Dollar signs in the same column are aligned. Dollar signs are not used in journals and ledgers.

On unruled paper, commas and decimal points are used in dollar amounts. On paper with ruled columns—like the paper in journals and ledgers—commas and decimal points are not needed. In this book, because most problems and illustrations are in whole dollar amounts, the cents column usually is omitted. When accountants deal with whole dollars, they often use a dash in the cents column to indicate whole dollars rather than taking the time to write zeros.

✓ Check out ACE for a Review Quiz at http://accounting.college.hmco.com/students.

Chapter Review

REVIEW OF LEARNING OBJECTIVES

LO1 Explain, in simple terms, the generally accepted ways of solving the measurement issues of recognition, valuation, and classification.

To measure a business transaction, the accountant determines when the transaction occurred (the recognition issue), what value should be placed on the transaction (the valuation issue), and how the components of the transaction should be categorized (the classification issue). In general, recognition occurs when title passes, and a transaction is valued at the exchange price, the cost at the time the transaction is recognized. Classification refers to the categorizing of transactions according to a system of accounts.

LO2 Describe the chart of accounts and recognize commonly used accounts.

An account is a device for storing data from transactions. There is one account for each asset, liability, and component of owner's equity, including revenues and expenses. The ledger is a book or file containing all of a company's accounts, arranged according to a chart of accounts. Commonly used asset accounts are Cash, Notes Receivable, Accounts

Receivable, Prepaid Expenses, Land, Buildings, and Equipment. Common liability accounts are Notes Payable, Accounts Payable, Wages Payable, and Mortgage Payable. Common owner's equity accounts are Capital, Withdrawals, and revenue and expense accounts.

LO3 Define *double-entry system* and state the rules for double entry.

In the double-entry system, each transaction must be recorded with at least one debit and one credit, so that the total dollar amount of the debits equals the total dollar amount of the credits. The rules for double entry are (1) increases in assets are debited to asset accounts; decreases in assets are credited to asset accounts; and (2) increases in liabilities and owner's equity are credited to those accounts; decreases in liabilities and owner's equity are debited to those accounts.

LO4 Apply the steps for transaction analysis and processing to simple transactions.

The procedure for analyzing transactions is (1) analyze the effect of the transaction on assets, liabilities, and owner's equity; (2) apply the appropriate double-entry rule; (3) record the entry; (4) post the entry; and (5) prepare a trial balance.

LO5 Prepare a trial balance and describe its value and limitations.

A trial balance is used to check that the debit and credit balances are equal. It is prepared by listing each account with its balance in the Debit or Credit column. Then the two columns are added and the totals compared to test the balances. The major limitation of the trial balance is that even if debit and credit balances are equal, this does not guarantee that the transactions were analyzed correctly or recorded in the proper accounts.

LO6 Record transactions in the general journal and post transactions from the general journal to the ledger.

The general journal is a chronological record of all transactions. That record contains the date of each transaction, the names of the accounts and the dollar amounts debited and credited, an explanation of each entry, and the account numbers to which postings have been made. After transactions have been entered in the general journal, they are posted to the ledger. Posting is done by transferring each amount in the Debit column of the general journal to the Debit column of the appropriate account in the ledger, and transferring each amount in the Credit column of the general journal to the Credit column of the appropriate account in the ledger. After each entry is posted, a new balance is entered in the appropriate Balance column.

REVIEW OF CONCEPTS AND TERMINOLOGY

The following concepts and terms were introduced in this chapter:

LO3 **Balance:** The difference in dollars between the total debit footing and the total credit footing of an account. Also called *account balance.*

LO2 **Chart of accounts:** A scheme that assigns a unique number to each account to facilitate finding the account in the ledger; also, the list of account numbers and titles.

LO1 **Classification:** The process of assigning transactions to the appropriate accounts.

LO6 **Compound entry:** An entry that has more than one debit or credit entry.

LO1 **Cost:** The exchange price associated with a business transaction at the point of recognition.

LO1 **Cost principle:** The practice of recording transactions at cost.

LO3 **Credit:** The right side of an account.

LO3 **Debit:** The left side of an account.

LO3 **Double-entry system:** The accounting system in which each transaction is recorded with at least one debit and one credit, so that the total dollar amount of debits and the total dollar amount of credits equal each other.

LO3 **Footings:** Working totals of columns of numbers. *To foot* means to total a column of numbers.

LO6 **General journal:** The simplest and most flexible type of journal.

LO2 **General ledger:** The book or file that contains all of the company's accounts, arranged in the order of the chart of accounts. Also called *ledger*.

LO6 **Journal:** A chronological record of all transactions; the place where transactions first enter the accounting records. Also called *book of original entry*.

LO6 **Journal entry:** Journal notations that record a single transaction.

LO3 **Journal form:** A form of journal in which the date, the debit account, and the debit amount of a transaction are recorded on one line and the credit account and credit amount on the next line.

LO6 **Journalizing:** The process of recording transactions in a journal.

LO6 **Ledger account form:** The form of account that has four dollar amount columns: one column for debit entries, one column for credit entries, and two columns (debit and credit) for showing the balance of the account.

LO5 **Normal balance:** The usual balance of an account; also the side (debit or credit) that increases the account.

LO6 **Posting:** The process of transferring journal entry information from the journal to the ledger.

LO1 **Recognition:** The determination of when a business transaction should be recorded.

LO1 **Recognition point:** The predetermined time at which a transaction should be recorded; usually, the point at which title passes to the buyer.

LO3 **Source document:** An invoice, check, receipt, or other document that supports a transaction.

LO3 **T account:** The simplest form of an account, used to analyze transactions.

LO5 **Trial balance:** A comparison of the total of debit and credit balances in the accounts to check that they are equal.

LO1 **Valuation:** The process of assigning a monetary value to a business transaction.

REVIEW PROBLEM

Transaction Analysis, General Journal, Ledger Accounts, and Trial Balance

LO4
LO5
LO6

After graduation from veterinary school, Laura Stors entered private practice. The transactions of the business through May 27 are as follows:

20xx

May 1   Laura Stors invested $2,000 in her business bank account.
      3   Paid $300 for two months' rent in advance for an office.
      9   Purchased medical supplies for $200 in cash.
     12   Purchased $400 of equipment on credit, making a 25 percent down payment.
     15   Delivered a calf for a fee of $35 (on credit).
     18   Made a partial payment of $50 on the equipment purchased May 12.
     27   Paid a utility bill of $40.

REQUIRED ▶

1. Record these transactions in the general journal.
2. Post the transactions to the following accounts in the ledger: Cash (111); Accounts Receivable (112); Medical Supplies (115); Prepaid Rent (117); Equipment (144); Accounts Payable (212); Laura Stors, Capital (311); Veterinary Fees Earned (411); and Utilities Expense (512).
3. Prepare a trial balance as of May 31.
4. How does the transaction of May 15 relate to recognition and cash flows? Also compare the transactions of May 9 and May 27 with regard to classification.

ANSWER TO REVIEW PROBLEM

1. Journal entries recorded

Date		Description	Post. Ref.	Debit	Credit
20xx					
May	1	Cash	111	2,000	
		Laura Stors, Capital	311		2,000
		Deposited $2,000 in the business bank account			
	3	Prepaid Rent	117	300	
		Cash	111		300
		Paid two months' rent in advance for an office			
	9	Medical Supplies	115	200	
		Cash	111		200
		Purchased medical supplies for cash			
	12	Equipment	144	400	
		Accounts Payable	212		300
		Cash	111		100
		Purchased equipment on credit, paying 25 percent down			
	15	Accounts Receivable	112	35	
		Veterinary Fees Earned	411		35
		Fee on credit for delivery of a calf			
	18	Accounts Payable	212	50	
		Cash	111		50
		Partial payment for equipment purchased May 12			
	27	Utilities Expense	512	40	
		Cash	111		40
		Paid utility bill			

General Journal — Page 1

2. Transactions posted to the ledger accounts

General Ledger

Cash — Account No. 111

Date		Item	Post. Ref.	Debit	Credit	Balance Debit	Balance Credit
20xx							
May	1		J1	2,000		2,000	
	3		J1		300	1,700	
	9		J1		200	1,500	
	12		J1		100	1,400	
	18		J1		50	1,350	
	27		J1		40	1,310	

Accounts Receivable — Account No. 112

Date		Item	Post. Ref.	Debit	Credit	Balance Debit	Balance Credit
20xx							
May	15		J1	35		35	

Medical Supplies — Account No. 115

Date		Item	Post. Ref.	Debit	Credit	Balance Debit	Balance Credit
20xx							
May	9		J1	200		200	

Prepaid Rent — Account No. 117

Date		Item	Post. Ref.	Debit	Credit	Balance Debit	Balance Credit
20xx							
May	3		J1	300		300	

Equipment — Account No. 144

Date		Item	Post. Ref.	Debit	Credit	Balance Debit	Balance Credit
20xx							
May	12		J1	400		400	

Accounts Payable   Account No. 212

Date		Item	Post. Ref.	Debit	Credit	Balance Debit	Balance Credit
20xx May	12		J1		300		300
	18		J1	50			250

Laura Stors, Capital   Account No. 311

Date		Item	Post. Ref.	Debit	Credit	Balance Debit	Balance Credit
20xx May	1		J1		2,000		2,000

Veterinary Fees Earned   Account No. 411

Date		Item	Post. Ref.	Debit	Credit	Balance Debit	Balance Credit
20xx May	15		J1		35		35

Utilities Expense   Account No. 512

Date		Item	Post. Ref.	Debit	Credit	Balance Debit	Balance Credit
20xx May	27		J1	40		40	

3. Trial balance prepared

Laura Stors, Veterinarian Trial Balance May 31, 20xx		
Cash	$1,310	
Accounts Receivable	35	
Medical Supplies	200	
Prepaid Rent	300	
Equipment	400	
Accounts Payable		$ 250
Laura Stors, Capital		2,000
Veterinary Fees Earned		35
Utilities Expense	40	
	$2,285	$2,285

4. The transaction is recorded, or recognized, on May 15, even though no cash is received. The revenue is earned because the service was provided to and accepted by the buyer. The customer now has an obligation to pay the provider of the service. It is recorded as an accounts receivable because the customer has been allowed to pay later. The transaction on May 9 is classified as an asset, Medical Supplies, because these supplies will benefit the company in the future. The transaction on May 27 is classified as an expense, Utilities Expense, because the utilities have already been used and will not benefit the company in the future.

Chapter Assignments

BUILDING YOUR KNOWLEDGE FOUNDATION

QUESTIONS

1. What three issues underlie most accounting measurement decisions?
2. Why is recognition an issue for accountants?
3. A customer asks the owner of a store to save an item for him and says that he will pick it up and pay for it next week. The owner agrees to hold it. Should this transaction be recorded as a sale? Explain your answer.
4. Why is it practical for accountants to rely on original cost for valuation purposes?
5. Under the cost principle, changes in value after a transaction is recorded are not usually recognized in the accounts. Comment on this possible limitation of using original cost in accounting measurements.
6. What is an account, and how is it related to the ledger?
7. Tell whether each of the following accounts is an asset account, a liability account, or an owner's equity account:
    a. Notes Receivable
    b. Land
    c. Withdrawals
    d. Mortgage Payable
    e. Prepaid Rent
    f. Insurance Expense
    g. Service Revenue

8. In the owner's equity accounts, why do accountants maintain separate accounts for revenues and expenses rather than using the Capital account?

9. Why is the system of recording entries called the double-entry system? What is significant about this system?

10. "Double-entry accounting refers to entering a transaction in both the journal and the ledger." Comment on this statement.

11. "Debits are bad; credits are good." Comment on this statement.

12. What are the rules of double entry for (a) assets, (b) liabilities, and (c) owner's equity?

13. Why are the rules of double entry the same for liabilities and owner's equity?

14. What is the meaning of the statement, "The Cash account has a debit balance of $500"?

15. Explain why debits, which decrease owner's equity, also increase expenses, which are a component of owner's equity.

16. What are the five steps in analyzing and processing a transaction?

17. What does a trial balance prove?

18. What is the normal balance of Accounts Payable? Under what conditions could Accounts Payable have a debit balance?

19. Is it possible for errors to be present even though a trial balance balances? Explain your answer.

20. Is it a good idea to forgo the journal and enter a transaction directly into the ledger? Explain your answer.

21. In recording entries in a journal, which is written first, the debit or the credit? How is indentation used in the journal?

22. What is the relationship between the journal and the ledger?

23. Describe each of the following:

    a. Account
    b. Journal
    c. Ledger
    d. Book of original entry
    e. Post. Ref. column
    f. Journalizing
    g. Posting
    h. Footings
    i. Compound entry

24. List the following six items in sequence to illustrate the flow of events through the accounting system:

    a. Analysis of the transaction
    b. Debits and credits posted from the journal to the ledger
    c. Occurrence of the business transaction
    d. Preparation of the financial statements
    e. Entry made in the journal
    f. Preparation of the trial balance

SHORT EXERCISES

LO1 Recognition

SE 1. Which of the following events would be recognized and entered in the accounting records of Heller Company? Why?

Jan. 10   Heller Company places an order for office supplies.
Feb. 15   Heller Company receives the office supplies and a bill for them.
Mar. 1   Heller Company pays for the office supplies.

LO1 Recognition, Valuation,
LO3 and Classification

SE 2. Tell how the concepts of recognition, valuation, and classification apply to this transaction:

Cash			Supplies		
June 1	250		June 1	250	

LO2 Classification of Accounts

SE 3. Tell whether each of the accounts that follows is an asset, a liability, a revenue, an expense, or none of these.

a. Accounts Payable
b. Supplies
c. Withdrawals
d. Fees Earned
e. Supplies Expense
f. Accounts Receivable
g. Unearned Revenue
h. Equipment

SE 4. Tell whether the normal balance of each account in **SE 3** is a debit or a credit.

LO5   Normal Balances

SE 5. For each transaction below, tell which account is debited and which account is credited.

LO4   Transaction Analysis

May   2   Deric Norman started a computer programming business, Norman's Programming Service, by investing $5,000.
       5   Purchased a computer for $2,500 in cash.
       7   Purchased supplies on credit for $300.
      19   Received cash for programming services performed, $500.
      22   Received cash for programming services to be performed, $600.
      25   Paid the rent for May, $650.
      31   Billed a customer for programming services performed, $250.

SE 6. Set up T accounts and record each transaction in **SE 5**. Determine the balance of each account.

**LO4   Recording Transactions in
         T Accounts**

SE 7. From the T accounts created in **SE 6**, prepare a trial balance dated May 31, 20x5.

LO5   Preparing a Trial Balance

SE 8. The trial balance that follows is out of balance. Assuming all balances are normal, place the accounts in proper order and correct the trial balance so that debits equal credits.

**LO5   Correcting Errors in a Trial
         Balance**

Duncan Boating Service
Trial Balance
January 31, 20x5

Cash	$2,000	
Accounts Payable	400	
Fuel Expense	800	
Unearned Service Revenue	250	
Accounts Receivable		$1,300
Prepaid Rent		150
Ann Duncan, Capital		1,500
Service Revenue	1,750	
Wages Expense		300
Ann Duncan, Withdrawals	650	
	$5,850	$3,250

SE 9. Prepare a general journal form like the one in Exhibit 4 and label it Page 4. Record the following transactions in the journal:

**LO6   Recording Transactions in the
         General Journal**

Sept.   6   Billed a customer for services performed, $1,900.
       16   Received partial payment from the customer billed on Sept. 6, $900.

SE 10. Prepare ledger account forms like the ones in Exhibit 5 for the following accounts: Cash (111), Accounts Receivable (113), and Service Revenue (411). Post the transactions that are recorded in **SE 9** to the ledger accounts, at the same time making the proper posting references.

**LO6   Posting to the Ledger
         Accounts**

EXERCISES

LO1   Recognition

E 1. Which of the following events would be recognized and recorded in the accounting records of Raymond Company on the date indicated?

Feb. 17   Raymond Company offers to purchase a tract of land for $280,000. There is a high likelihood that the offer will be accepted.

Mar. 7   Raymond Company receives notice that its rent will be increased from $1,000 per month to $1,200 per month effective April 1.

Apr. 28   Raymond Company receives its utility bill for the month of April. The bill is not due until May 10.

May 19   Raymond Company places a firm order for new office equipment costing $42,000.

June 27   The office equipment ordered on May 19 arrives. Payment is not due until September 1.

LO1   Application of Recognition Point

E 2. Azarian's Body Shop uses a large amount of supplies in its business. The following table summarizes selected transaction data for orders of supplies purchased:

Order	Date Shipped	Date Received	Amount
a	April 28	May 7	$300
b	May 8	13	750
c	10	16	400
d	15	21	600
e	25	June 1	750
f	June 3	9	500

Determine the total purchases of supplies for May alone if:

1. Azarian's Body Shop recognizes purchases when orders are shipped.
2. Azarian's Body Shop recognizes purchases when orders are received.

LO2   Classification of Accounts
LO5

E 3. Listed below are the ledger accounts of Geehan Service Company:

a. Cash
b. Accounts Receivable
c. Deb Geehan, Capital
d. Deb Geehan, Withdrawals
e. Service Revenue
f. Prepaid Rent
g. Accounts Payable
h. Investments in Securities
i. Wages Payable
j. Land
k. Supplies Expense

l. Prepaid Insurance
m. Utilities Expense
n. Fees Earned
o. Unearned Revenue
p. Office Equipment
q. Rent Payable
r. Notes Receivable
s. Interest Expense
t. Notes Payable
u. Supplies
v. Interest Receivable

Complete the following table, indicating with two Xs for each account its classification and its normal balance (whether a debit or credit increases the account):

			Type of Account					
				Owner's Equity				Normal Balance (increases balance)
Item	Asset	Liability	Owner's Capital	Owner's Withdrawals	Revenue	Expense	Debit	Credit
a.	x						x	

LO4   Transaction Analysis

E 4. Analyze transactions **a–g**, following the example on the next page.

a. Liz Cruse established Cruse's Crop Shop by placing $2,400 in a bank account.
b. Paid two months' rent in advance, $840.
c. Purchased supplies on credit, $120.
d. Received cash for scrapbooking services, $100.
e. Paid for supplies purchased in **c**.
f. Paid utility bill, $72.
g. Took cash out of the business for personal expenses, $100.

Example:

a. The asset Cash was increased. Increases in assets are recorded by debits. Debit Cash, $2,400. A component of owner's equity, Liz Cruse, Capital, was increased. Increases in owner's equity are recorded by credits. Credit Liz Cruse, Capital, $2,400.

LO4 Recording Transactions in T Accounts

E 5. Open the following T accounts: Cash; Repair Supplies; Repair Equipment; Accounts Payable; Jessie Sturchio, Capital; Jessie Sturchio, Withdrawals; Repair Fees Earned; Salaries Expense; and Rent Expense. Record the following transactions for the month of June directly in the T accounts; use the letters to identify the transactions in your T accounts. Determine the balance in each account.

a. Jessie Sturchio opened Porcelain Cup Repair Service by investing $4,300 in cash and $1,600 in repair equipment.
b. Paid $400 for the current month's rent.
c. Purchased repair supplies on credit, $500.
d. Purchased additional repair equipment for cash, $300.
e. Paid salary to a helper, $450.
f. Paid $200 of amount purchased on credit in **c.**
g. Accepted cash for repairs completed, $1,860.
h. Withdrew $600 from business for living expenses.

LO5 Trial Balance

E 6. After recording the transactions in **E 5,** prepare a trial balance in proper sequence for Porcelain Cup Repair Service as of June 30, 20xx.

LO4 Analysis of Transactions

E 7. Explain each transaction **(a–h)** entered in the following T accounts:

Cash				Accounts Receivable				Equipment			
a.	60,000	b.	15,000	c.	6,000	g.	1,500	b.	15,000	h.	900
g.	1,500	e.	3,000					d.	9,000		
h.	900	f.	4,500								

Accounts Payable				K. LeMaster, Capital				Service Revenue			
f.	4,500	d.	9,000			a.	60,000			c.	6,000

Wages Expense		
e.	3,000	

LO5 Preparing a Trial Balance

E 8. The accounts of Rounds Service Company as of October 31, 20xx, are listed below in alphabetical order. The amount of Accounts Payable is omitted.

Accounts Payable	$?	Land	$10,400
Accounts Receivable	6,000	Notes Payable	40,000
Building	68,000	Pete Rounds, Capital	62,900
Cash	18,000	Prepaid Insurance	2,200
Equipment	24,000		

Prepare a trial balance with the proper heading (see Exhibit 3) and with the accounts listed in the chart of accounts sequence (see Exhibit 1). Compute the balance of Accounts Payable.

LO5 Effects of Errors on a Trial Balance

E 9. Which of the following errors would cause a trial balance to have unequal totals? Explain your answers.

a. A payment to a creditor was recorded as a debit to Accounts Payable for $172 and as a credit to Cash for $127.
b. A payment of $200 to a creditor for an account payable was debited to Accounts Receivable and credited to Cash.
c. A purchase of office supplies of $560 was recorded as a debit to Office Supplies for $56 and as a credit to Cash for $56.
d. A purchase of equipment for $600 was recorded as a debit to Supplies for $600 and as a credit to Cash for $600.

LO5 Correcting Errors in a Trial Balance

E 10. The trial balance for Fradin Services at the end of September follows. It does not balance because of a number of errors. Fradin's accountant compared the amounts in the

Fradin Services
Trial Balance
September 30, 20xx

Cash	$ 3,840	
Accounts Receivable	5,660	
Supplies	120	
Prepaid Insurance	180	
Equipment	8,400	
Accounts Payable		$ 4,540
F. Fradin, Capital		11,560
F. Fradin, Withdrawals		700
Revenues		5,920
Salaries Expense	2,600	
Rent Expense	600	
Advertising Expense	340	
Utilities Expense	26	
	$21,766	$22,720

trial balance with the ledger, recomputed the account balances, and compared the postings. He found the following errors:

a. The balance of Cash was understated by $400.
b. A cash payment of $420 was credited to Cash for $240.
c. A debit of $120 to Accounts Receivable was not posted.
d. Supplies purchased for $60 were posted as a credit to Supplies.
e. A debit of $180 to Prepaid Insurance was not posted.
f. The Accounts Payable account had debits of $5,320 and credits of $9,180.
g. The Notes Payable account, with a credit balance of $2,400, was not included in the trial balance.
h. The debit balance of F. Fradin, Withdrawals was listed in the trial balance as a credit.
i. A $200 debit to F. Fradin, Withdrawals was posted as a credit.
j. The actual balance of Utilities Expense, $260, was listed as $26 in the trial balance.

Prepare a correct trial balance.

E 11.
LO5 Preparing a Trial Balance

The Breadloaf Construction Company builds foundations for buildings and parking lots. The following alphabetical list shows the company's account balances as of November 30, 20xx.

Accounts Payable	$ 11,700	Notes Payable	$60,000
Accounts Receivable	30,360	Office Trailer	6,600
Cash	?	Prepaid Insurance	13,800
Construction Supplies	5,700	Revenue Earned	52,200
Equipment	73,500	Supplies Expense	21,600
G. Breadloaf, Capital	120,000	Utilities Expense	1,260
G. Breadloaf, Withdrawals	23,400	Wages Expense	26,400

Prepare a trial balance for the company with the proper heading and with the accounts in balance sheet sequence. Determine the correct balance for the Cash account on November 30, 20xx.

E 12.
LO4 Analysis of Unfamiliar
LO6 Transactions

Managers and accountants often encounter transactions with which they are unfamiliar. Use your analytical skills to analyze and record in journal form the transactions below, which have not yet been discussed in the text.

a. Purchased merchandise inventory on account, $1,600.
b. Purchased marketable securities for cash, $4,800.

c. Returned part of merchandise inventory purchased in **a** for full credit, $500.

d. Sold merchandise inventory on account, $1,600 (record sale only).

e. Purchased land and a building for $600,000. Payment is $120,000 cash, and there is a thirty-year mortgage for the remainder. The purchase price is allocated as follows: $200,000 to the land and $400,000 to the building.

f. Received an order for $24,000 in services to be provided. With the order was a deposit of $8,000.

E 13.

LO6   Recording Transactions in the General Journal and Posting to the Ledger Accounts

Open a general journal form like the one in Exhibit 4, and label it Page 10. After opening the form, record the following transactions in the journal:

Dec. 14   Purchased an item of equipment for $6,000, paying $2,000 as a cash down payment.

28   Paid $3,000 of the amount owed on the equipment.

Prepare three ledger account forms like the one shown in Exhibit 5. Use the following account numbers: Cash, 111; Equipment, 144; and Accounts Payable, 212. Then post the two transactions from the general journal to the ledger accounts, being sure to make proper posting references.

Assume that the Cash account has a debit balance of $8,000 on the day prior to the first transaction.

PROBLEMS

P 1.

LO4   Transaction Analysis

The following accounts are applicable to Connie's Scrapbooking Barn:

1. Cash
2. Accounts Receivable
3. Supplies
4. Prepaid Insurance
5. Equipment
6. Notes Payable
7. Accounts Payable
8. Capital
9. Withdrawals
10. Service Revenue
11. Rent Expense
12. Repair Expense

Connie's Scrapbooking Barn completed the following transactions:

	Debit	Credit
a. Paid for supplies purchased on credit last month.	7	1
b. Billed customers for services performed.		
c. Paid the current month's rent.		
d. Purchased supplies on credit.		
e. Received cash from customers for services performed but not yet billed.		
f. Purchased equipment on account.		
g. Received a bill for repairs.		
h. Returned part of the equipment purchased in **f** for a credit.		
i. Received payments from customers previously billed.		
j. Paid the bill received in **g**.		
k. Received an order for services to be performed.		
l. Paid for repairs with cash.		
m. Made a payment to reduce the principal of the note payable.		
n. Withdrew cash for personal expenses.		

REQUIRED ▶   Analyze each transaction and show the accounts affected by entering the corresponding numbers in the appropriate debit or credit column as shown in transaction **a**. Indicate no entry, if appropriate.

LO4 **Transaction Analysis,**
LO5 **T Accounts, and Trial**
      Balance

P 2. Kyle Piu established a small business, Computer Skills Training Center, to teach spreadsheet analysis, word processing, and other techniques on microcomputers.

a. Piu began by transferring the following assets to the business:

Cash	$9,200
Furniture	3,100
Microcomputers	7,300

b. Paid the first month's rent on a small storefront, $580.
c. Purchased computer software on credit, $750.
d. Paid for an advertisement in the school newspaper, $100.
e. Received enrollment applications from five students for a five-day course that is to start next week. Each student will pay $200 if he or she actually begins the course.
f. Paid wages to a part-time helper, $150.
g. Received cash payment from three of the students enrolled in **e**, $600.
h. Billed the two other students in **e**, who attended but did not pay in cash, $400.
i. Paid the utility bill for the current month, $110.
j. Made a payment on the software purchased in **c**, $250.
k. Received payment from one student billed in **h**, $200.
l. Purchased a second microcomputer for cash, $4,700.
m. Transferred cash to personal checking account, $300.

REQUIRED ▶
1. Set up the following T accounts: Cash; Accounts Receivable; Software; Furniture; Microcomputers; Accounts Payable; Kyle Piu, Capital; Kyle Piu, Withdrawals; Tuition Revenue; Wages Expense; Utilities Expense; Rent Expense; and Advertising Expense.
2. Record the transactions by entering debits and credits directly in the T accounts, using the transaction letter to identify each debit and credit.
3. Prepare a trial balance using the current date.
4. Contrast the effects on cash flows of transactions **c** and **j** with **d** and of transactions **h** and **k** with transaction **g**.

LO1 **Transaction Analysis,**
LO4 **General Journal, Ledger**
LO5 **Accounts, and Trial Balance**
LO6

P 3. Dee Strong began an office-cleaning business on October 1 and engaged in the following transactions during the month:

Oct.	1	Began business by transferring $6,000 from her personal bank account to the business bank account.
	2	Ordered cleaning supplies, $500.
	3	Purchased cleaning equipment for cash, $1,400.
	4	Leased a van by making two months' lease payment in advance, $600.
	7	Received the cleaning supplies ordered on October 2 and agreed to pay half the amount in ten days and the rest in thirty days.
	9	Paid for repairs on the van with cash, $40.
	12	Received cash for cleaning offices, $480.
	17	Paid half the amount owed on supplies purchased on October 7, $250.
	21	Billed customers for cleaning offices, $670.
	24	Paid cash for additional repairs on the van, $40.
	27	Received $300 from the customers billed on October 21.
	31	Withdrew $350 from the business for personal use.

REQUIRED ▶
1. Prepare journal entries to record the above transactions in the general journal (Pages 1 and 2). Use the accounts listed below.
2. Set up the following ledger accounts and post the journal entries to the accounts: Cash (111); Accounts Receivable (113); Cleaning Supplies (115); Prepaid Lease (116); Cleaning Equipment (141); Accounts Payable (211); Dee Strong, Capital (311); Dee Strong, Withdrawals (312); Cleaning Revenues (411); and Repair Expense (511).
3. Prepare a trial balance for Strong's Office-Cleaning Service as of October 31, 20xx.
4. Compare and contrast how the issues of recognition, valuation, and classification are settled in the transactions of October 7 and 9.

LO1   Transaction Analysis,
LO4   Journal Form, T Accounts,
LO5   and Trial Balance

P 4.   Ben Aronson is a house painter. During the month of June, he completed the following transactions:

June 3   Began his business with equipment valued at $2,460 and placed $14,200 in a business checking account.
    5   Purchased a used truck costing $3,800. Paid $1,000 in cash and signed a note for the balance.
    7   Purchased supplies on account for $640.
    8   Completed a painting job and billed the customer $960.
   10   Received $300 in cash for painting two rooms.
   11   Hired an assistant to work with him at $12 per hour.
   12   Purchased supplies for $320 in cash.
   13   Received a $960 check from the customer billed on June 8.
   14   Paid $800 for an insurance policy for eighteen months' coverage.
   16   Billed a customer $1,240 for a painting job.
   18   Paid the assistant $300 for twenty-five hours' work.
   19   Paid $80 for a tune-up for the truck.
   20   Paid for the supplies purchased on June 7.
   21   Purchased a new ladder (equipment) for $120 and supplies for $580, on account.
   23   Received a telephone bill for $120, due next month.
   24   Received $660 in cash from the customer billed on June 16.
   25   Transferred $600 to a personal checking account.
   26   Received $720 in cash for painting a five-room apartment.
   28   Paid $400 on the note signed for the truck.
   29   Paid the assistant $360 for thirty hours' work.

REQUIRED ▶   1. Prepare entries to record these transactions in journal form.
2. Set up the following T accounts and post all the journal entries: Cash; Accounts Receivable; Supplies; Prepaid Insurance; Equipment; Truck; Notes Payable; Accounts Payable; Ben Aronson, Capital; Ben Aronson, Withdrawals; Painting Fees Earned; Wages Expense; Telephone Expense; and Repair Expense.
3. Prepare a trial balance for Aronson Painting Service as of June 30, 20xx.
4. Compare how recognition applies to the transactions of June 8 and 10 and their effects on cash flow and how classification applies to the transactions of June 14 and 18.

LO4   Transaction Analysis,
LO5   General Journal, Ledger
LO6   Accounts, and Trial
**   Balance**

P 5.   The Jump-Start Child Development Company provides babysitting and child-care programs. On August 31, 20xx, the company had the following trial balance:

Jump-Start Child Development Company
Trial Balance
August 31, 20xx

Cash (111)	$ 3,740	
Accounts Receivable (113)	3,400	
Equipment (141)	2,080	
Buses (143)	34,800	
Notes Payable (211)		$30,000
Accounts Payable (212)		3,280
Lisa Corvelli, Capital (311)		10,740
	$44,020	$44,020

During the month of September, the company completed the following transactions:

Sept. 3   Paid this month's rent, $540.
     5   Received fees for this month's services, $1,300.
     7   Purchased supplies on account, $170.
     8   Reimbursed the bus driver for gas expenses, $80.
     9   Ordered playground equipment, $2,000.
   10   Paid part-time assistants for two weeks' services, $460.
   12   Made a payment on account, $340.
   13   Received payments from customers on account, $2,400.
   15   Billed customers who had not yet paid for this month's services, $1,400.
   16   Paid for the supplies purchased on September 7.
   18   Purchased playground equipment for cash, $2,000.
   19   Withdrew cash for personal expenses, $220.
   20   Contributed equipment to the business, $580.
   21   Paid this month's utility bill, $290.
   24   Paid part-time assistants for two weeks' services, $460.
   25   Received payment for one month's services from customers previously billed, $1,000.
   26   Purchased gas for the bus on account, $70.
   29   Paid for a one-year insurance policy, $580.

REQUIRED ▶

1. Enter these transactions in the general journal (Pages 17 and 18).
2. Open accounts in the ledger for the accounts in the trial balance and the following accounts: Supplies (115); Prepaid Insurance (116); Lisa Corvelli, Withdrawals (312); Service Revenue (411); Rent Expense (511); Gasoline Expense (512); Wages Expense (513); and Utilities Expense (514).
3. Enter the August 31, 20xx, account balances from the trial balance.
4. Post the entries to the ledger accounts. Be sure to make the appropriate posting references in the journal and ledger as you post.
5. Prepare a trial balance as of September 30, 20xx.
6. What does the trial balance prove? If it is in balance, does this mean there are no errors?

ALTERNATE PROBLEMS

P 6.

LO4   Transaction Analysis

The following accounts are applicable to Smiley's Landscaping Service, a company that maintains condominium grounds:

1. Cash
2. Accounts Receivable
3. Supplies
4. Prepaid Insurance
5. Equipment
6. Accounts Payable
7. Capital
8. Withdrawals
9. Landscaping Services Revenue
10. Wages Expense
11. Rent Expense
12. Utilities Expense

Smiley's Landscaping Service completed the following transactions:

	Debit	Credit
a. Received cash from customers billed last month.	1	2
b. Made a payment on accounts payable.		
c. Purchased a new one-year insurance policy in advance.		
d. Purchased supplies on credit.		

	Debit	Credit
e. Billed a client for landscaping services.	____	____
f. Made a rent payment for the current month.	____	____
g. Received cash from customers for landscaping services.	____	____
h. Paid wages for the staff.	____	____
i. Ordered equipment.	____	____
j. Paid the current month's utility bill.	____	____
k. Received and paid for the equipment ordered in i.	____	____
l. Returned for full credit some of the supplies purchased in d because they were defective.	____	____
m. Paid for supplies purchased in d, less the return in l.	____	____
n. Withdrew cash for personal expenses.	____	____

REQUIRED ▶ Analyze each transaction and show the accounts affected by entering the corresponding numbers in the appropriate debit or credit columns as shown in transaction **a**. Indicate no entry, if appropriate.

P 7.

LO1 Transaction Analysis,
LO4 Journal Form, T Accounts,
LO5 and Trial Balance

Marcus Stahl won a concession to rent bicycles in the local park during the summer. In the month of May, Stahl completed the following transactions for his bicycle rental business:

May	3	Began business by placing $14,400 in a business checking account.
	6	Purchased supplies on account for $300.
	7	Purchased ten bicycles for $5,000, paying $2,400 down and agreeing to pay the rest in thirty days.
	9	Received $940 in cash for rentals during the first week of operation.
	10	Purchased a small shed to hold the bicycles and to use for other operations for $5,800 in cash.
	11	Paid $800 in cash for shipping and installation costs (considered an addition to the cost of the shed) to place the shed at the park entrance.
	14	Received $1,000 in cash for rentals during the second week of operation.
	15	Hired a part-time assistant to help out on weekends at $8 per hour.
	16	Paid a maintenance person $150 to clean the grounds.
	18	Paid the assistant $160 for a weekend's work.
	19	Paid $300 for the supplies purchased on May 6.
	20	Paid a $110 repair bill on bicycles.
	21	Received $1,100 in cash for rentals during the third week of operation.
	23	Paid the assistant $160 for a weekend's work.
	24	Billed a company $220 for bicycle rentals for an employees' outing.
	26	Paid the $200 fee for May to the Park District for the right to the bicycle concession.
	28	Received $820 in cash for rentals during the week.
	30	Paid the assistant $160 for a weekend's work.
	31	Transferred $1,000 to a personal checking account.

REQUIRED ▶
1. Prepare entries in journal form to record these transactions.
2. Set up the following T accounts and post all the journal entries: Cash; Accounts Receivable; Supplies; Shed; Bicycles; Accounts Payable; Marcus Stahl, Capital; Marcus Stahl, Withdrawals; Rental Revenue; Wages Expense; Maintenance Expense; Repair Expense; and Concession Fee Expense.
3. Prepare a trial balance for Stahl Rentals as of May 31, 20xx.
4. Compare how recognition applies to the transactions of May 24 and 28 and their effects on cash flows and how classification applies to the transactions of May 11 and 16.

P 8.

LO4 Transaction Analysis,
LO5 General Journal, Ledger
LO6 Accounts, and Trial Balance

Samantha Young Company is a marketing firm. The company's trial balance as of April 30, 20xx, appears on the opposite page.

During the month of May, the company completed the following transactions:

May	3	Paid rent for May, $1,300.
	5	Received cash from customers on account, $4,600.
	6	Ordered supplies, $760.
	8	Billed customers for services provided, $5,600.

Samantha Young Company
Trial Balance
April 30, 20xx

Cash (111)	$20,400	
Accounts Receivable (113)	11,000	
Supplies (115)	1,220	
Office Equipment (141)	8,400	
Accounts Payable (211)		$ 5,200
Samantha Young, Capital (311)		35,820
	$41,020	$41,020

May 10 Made a payment on accounts payable, $2,200.
13 Received the supplies ordered on May 6 and agreed to pay for them in 30 days, $760.
15 Paid salaries for the first half of May, $3,800.
16 Discovered some of the supplies were not as ordered and returned them for a full credit, $160.
18 Received cash from a customer for services provided, $9,600.
22 Paid the utility bill for May, $320.
23 Paid the telephone bill for May, $240.
27 Received a bill, to be paid in June, for advertisements placed in the local newspaper during the month of May to promote Samantha Young Company, $1,400.
28 Billed a customer for services provided, $5,400.
30 Paid salaries for the last half of May, $3,800.
31 Withdrew cash for personal use, $2,400.

REQUIRED ▶ 1. Enter these transactions in the general journal (Pages 22 and 23).
2. Open accounts in the ledger for the accounts in the trial balance and the following accounts: Samantha Young, Withdrawals (312); Marketing Fees (411); Salaries Expense (511); Rent Expense (512); Utilities Expense (513); Telephone Expense (514); and Advertising Expense (515).
3. Enter the April 30 account balances from the trial balance in the appropriate ledger account.
4. Post the journal entries to the ledger accounts. Be sure to make the appropriate posting references in the journal and ledger as you post.
5. Prepare a trial balance as of May 31, 20xx.
6. What does the trial balance prove? If it is in balance, does this mean there are no errors?

SKILLS DEVELOPMENT CASES

Conceptual Analysis

SD 1. Nike, Inc., <www.nike.com> manufactures athletic shoes and other sports-related products. In one of its annual reports, Nike made the following statement: "Property, plant, and equipment are recorded at cost."[8] Given that the property, plant, and equipment undoubtedly were purchased over several years and that the current value of those assets was likely to be very different from their original cost, explain what authoritative basis there is for Nike's carrying the assets at cost. Does accounting generally recognize

LO1 **Valuation Issue**

changes in value after the purchase of property, plant, and equipment? Assume you are a Nike accountant. Write a memo to management explaining the rationale underlying Nike's approach.

SD 2.

LO1 **Valuation and Classification**
LO4 **Issues for Dot-Coms**

The dot-com business has raised many issues about accounting practices, some of which are of great concern to both the SEC and the FASB. Important ones relate to the valuation and classification of revenue transactions. Many dot-com companies seek to report as much revenue as possible because revenue growth is seen as a key performance measure for these companies. Amazon.com is a good example. Consider the following situations:

a. An Amazon.com <www.amazon.com> customer orders and pays $28 for a Gameboy® electronic game on the Internet. Amazon sends an email to the company that makes the product, which sends the Gameboy to the customer. Amazon collects $28 from the customer and pays $24 to the other company. Amazon never owns the Gameboy.

b. Amazon agrees to place a banner advertisement on its web site for another dot-com company. Instead of paying cash for the advertisement, the other company agrees to let Amazon advertise on its web site.

c. Assume the same facts as in situation **b** except that Amazon agrees to accept the other company's stock in this barter transaction. Over the next six months, the price of the stock received goes down.

Discuss the valuation and classification issues that arise in each of these situations, including how Amazon should account for each transaction.

Group Activity: Divide the class into groups. Assign each group one of the above cases so that one-third of the groups have each case. Debrief and discuss.

Ethical Dilemma

SD 3.

LO1 **Recognition Point and Ethical**
Considerations

Jerry Hasbrow, a sales representative for Penn Office Supplies, is compensated on a commission basis and receives a substantial bonus for meeting his annual sales goal. The company's recognition point for sales is the day of shipment. On December 31, Hasbrow realizes he needs sales of $2,000 to reach his sales goal and receive the bonus. He calls a purchaser for a local insurance company, whom he knows well, and asks him to buy $2,000 worth of copier paper today. The purchaser says, "But Jerry, that's more than a year's supply for us." Hasbrow says, "Buy it today. If you decide it's too much, you can return however much you want for full credit next month." The purchaser says, "Okay, ship it."

The paper is shipped on December 31 and recorded as a sale. On January 15, the purchaser returns $1,750 worth of paper for full credit (approved by Hasbrow) against the bill. Should the shipment on December 31 be recorded as a sale? Discuss the ethics of Jerry Hasbrow's action.

Group Activity: Divide the class into informal groups to discuss and report on the ethical issues of this case.

Research Activity

SD 4.

LO4 **Transactions in a Business**
Article

Locate an article on a company you recognize or on a company in a business that interests you in one of the following sources: a recent issue of a business publication (such as *Barron's, Fortune, The Wall Street Journal, BusinessWeek,* or *Forbes*) or the Needles Accounting Resource Center Web Site at http://accounting.college.hmco.com/students. Read the article carefully, noting any references to transactions in which the company engages. These may be normal transactions (such as sales or purchases) or unusual transactions (such as a merger or the purchase of another company). Bring a copy of the article to class and be prepared to describe how you would analyze and record the transactions you have noted.

Decision-Making Practice

SD 5.

LO4 Transaction Analysis
LO5 and Evaluation of a Trial
Balance

Ben Obi hired an attorney to help him start Obi Repairs Company. On June 1, Obi invested $23,000 in cash in the business. When he paid the attorney's bill of $1,400, the attorney advised him to hire an accountant to keep his records. However, Obi was so busy that it was June 30 before he asked you to straighten out his records. Your first task is to develop a trial balance based on the June transactions, which are described in the next two paragraphs.

After making the investment and paying the attorney, Obi borrowed $10,000 from the bank. He later paid $520, which included interest of $120, on this loan. He also purchased a pickup truck in the company's name, paying $5,000 down and financing $14,800. The first payment on the truck is due July 15. Obi then rented an office and paid three months' rent, $1,800, in advance. Credit purchases of office equipment for $1,400 and repair tools for $1,000 must be paid for by July 13.

In June, Obi Repairs completed repairs of $2,600, of which $800 were cash transactions. Of the credit transactions, $600 were collected during June, and $1,200 remained to be collected at the end of June. Wages of $800 were paid to employees. On June 30, the company received a $150 bill for June utilities and a $100 check from a customer for work to be completed in July.

1. Record the June transactions in journal form.
2. Set up T accounts, post the journal entries to the T accounts, and determine the balance of each account.
3. Prepare a June 30 trial balance for Obi Repairs Company.
4. Ben Obi is unsure how to evaluate the trial balance. His Cash account balance is $24,980, which exceeds his original investment of $23,000 by $1,980. Did he make a profit of $1,980? Explain why the Cash account is not an indicator of business earnings. Cite specific examples to show why it is difficult to determine net income by looking solely at figures in the trial balance.

FINANCIAL REPORTING AND ANALYSIS CASES

Interpreting Financial Reports

 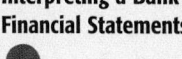

FRA 1.

LO2 Interpreting a Bank's
LO4 Financial Statements

Mellon Bank <www.mellon.com> is a large bank holding company. Selected accounts from a recent annual report are as follows (in millions):[9]

Cash and Due from Banks	$ 3,506
Loans to Customers	26,369
Securities Available for Sale	7,910
Deposits by Customers	36,890

1. Indicate whether each of the accounts just listed is an asset, a liability, or a component of owner's equity on Mellon Bank's balance sheet.
2. Assume that you are in a position to do business with this large company. Prepare the entry on Mellon Bank's books in journal form to record each of the following transactions:
   a. You sell securities in the amount of $2,000 to the bank.
   b. You deposit the $2,000 received in step **a** in the bank.
   c. You borrow $5,000 from the bank.

International Company

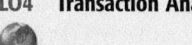

FRA 2.

LO4 Transaction Analysis

Ajinomoto Company <www.ajinomoto.com>, a Japanese company with operations in 22 countries, is primarily engaged in the manufacture and sale of food products. The following selected aggregate cash transactions were reported in the statement of cash flows in Ajinomoto's annual report (amounts in millions of yen):[10]

Purchase of property, plant, and equipment	¥46,381
Proceeds from issuance of long-term debt	10,357
Repayment of long-term debt	11,485

Prepare entries in journal form to record the above transactions.

Toys "R" Us Annual Report

FRA 3.

LO4   Transaction Analysis

Refer to the balance sheet in the Toys "R" Us <www.tru.com> annual report in the Supplement to Chapter 6. Prepare T accounts for the accounts Cash and Cash Equivalents, Accounts and Other Receivables, Prepaid Expenses and Other Current Assets, Accounts Payable, and Income Taxes Payable. Properly place the balance of the account at February 1, 2003, in the T accounts. Below are some typical transactions in which Toys "R" Us would engage. Analyze each transaction, enter it in the T accounts, and determine the balance of each account. Assume all entries are in thousands.

a. Paid cash in advance for certain expenses, $20,000.
b. Received cash from customers billed previously, $35,000.
c. Paid cash for income taxes previously owed, $70,000.
d. Paid cash to suppliers for amounts owed, $120,000.

Comparison Case: Toys "R" Us and Walgreen Co.

FRA 4.

LO1   Recognition, Valuation, and
         Classification

Refer to the Summary of Significant Accounting Policies in the notes to the financial statements in the Toys "R" Us <www.tru.com> annual report and to the financial statements of Walgreens <www.walgreens.com> to answer these questions:

1. How does the concept of recognition apply to advertising costs for both Toys "R" Us and Walgreens?
2. How does the concept of valuation apply to property and equipment for both companies?
3. How does the concept of classification apply to cash and cash equivalents for both companies?

Discuss any differences that you may observe.

Fingraph® Financial Analyst™

FRA 5.

LO1   Transaction Identification
LO3
LO4

Choose a company from the list of Fingraph companies on the Needles Accounting Resource Center Web Site at http://accounting.college.hmco.com/students. Click on the company you selected to access the Microsoft Excel spreadsheet for that company. You will find the company's URL (Internet address) in the heading of the spreadsheet. Click on the URL for a link to the company's web site and annual report.

1. From the company's annual report, determine the industry(ies) in which the company operates.
2. Find the summary of significant accounting policies that follows the financial statements. In these policies, find examples of the application of recognition, valuation, and classification.
3. Identify six types of transactions the company would commonly engage in. Are any of these transactions more common in the industry in which the company operates than in other industries? For each transaction, tell what account would typically be debited and what account would be credited.
4. Prepare a one-page executive summary that highlights what you have learned from steps 1, 2, and 3.

Internet Case

FRA 6.

LO2   Comparison of
LO4   Contrasting Companies

Sun Microsystems <www.sun.com> and Oracle Corporation <www.oracle.com> are leading computer and software companies. Go to their web sites directly using the URLs shown here, or go to the Needles Accounting Resource Center Web Site at http://accounting.college.hmco.com/students for a link to their web sites. Access each company's annual report and find its balance sheet.

1. What differences and similarities do you find in the account titles used by Sun Microsystems and those used by Oracle? What differences and similarities do you find in the account titles used by the two companies and the account titles used in this text?

2. Although the companies are in the same general industry, their businesses differ. How are these differences reflected on the balance sheets? What types of transactions resulted in the differences?

3

Chapter 3 defines the accounting concept of business income, discusses the role of adjusting entries in the measurement of income, and demonstrates the preparation of financial statements.

Measuring Business Income

LEARNING OBJECTIVES

LO1 Define *net income* and its two major components, *revenues* and *expenses*.

LO2 Explain how the income measurement issues of accounting period, continuity, and matching are resolved.

LO3 Define *accrual accounting* and explain three broad ways of accomplishing it.

LO4 State four principal situations that require adjusting entries and prepare typical adjusting entries.

LO5 Prepare financial statements from an adjusted trial balance.

SUPPLEMENTAL OBJECTIVE

SO6 Analyze cash flows from accrual-based information.

D E C I S I O N   P O I N T

A   U S E R ' S   F O C U S

Kelly Services <www.kellyservices.com> Kelly Services is one of the most successful temporary employment agencies. During any given year, Kelly incurs various operating expenses that are recorded as expenses when they are paid. However, at the end of the year, some expenses—including, for example, the wages of employees during the last days before the end of the year—will have been incurred but will not be paid until the next year. If these expenses are not accounted for correctly, they will appear in the wrong year—the year in which they are paid instead of the year in which Kelly benefited from them. The result is a misstatement of the company's income, a key profitability performance measure. How is this problem avoided?

According to the concepts of accrual accounting and the matching rule, which you will learn in this chapter, the amount of expenses that have been incurred but not paid must be determined and then recorded as expenses of the current year with corresponding liabilities to be paid the next year. The accompanying figure shows the liabilities, called *accrued liabilities,* that resulted from this process at Kelly Services.[1] Total accrued liabilities for payroll and related expenses, accrued insurance, and income and other taxes were $227,033,000 in 2001 and $257,215,000 in 2002. If these items had not been recorded in their respective years, income would have been misstated by a significant amount.

How does Kelly Services record wages that have been incurred in December but won't be paid until January?

Financial Highlights: Notes to the Financial Statements

3. ACCRUED LIABILITIES

(In thousands)

	2002	2001
Payroll and related expenses	$181,686	$154,813
Accrued insurance	27,912	24,071
Income and other taxes	47,617	48,149
Total accrued liabilities	$257,215	$227,033

PROFITABILITY MEASUREMENT: THE ROLE OF BUSINESS INCOME

LO1 Define *net income* and its two major components, *revenues* and *expenses*.

RELATED TEXT ASSIGNMENTS
Q: 1
SD: 5
FRA: 5

KEY POINT: Accounting measures and reports a business's profitability. The extent of the reported profit or loss communicates the company's success or failure in meeting this business goal.

◆ **STOP AND THINK!**
When a company has net income, what happens to assets and/or liabilities?
Owner's equity increases, but there is also an increase in assets and/or a decrease in liabilities. ■

Profitability is one of the two major goals of a business (the other being liquidity). For a business to succeed, or even to survive, it must earn a profit. The word **profit**, though, has many meanings. One is the increase in owner's equity that results from business operations. However, even this definition can be interpreted differently by economists, lawyers, businesspeople, and the public. Because the word *profit* has more than one meaning, accountants prefer to use the term *net income*, which can be precisely defined from an accounting point of view. Net income is reported on the income statement and is a performance measure used by management, owners, and others to monitor a business's progress in meeting the goal of profitability. Readers of income statements need to understand how the accountant defines net income and to be aware of its strengths and weaknesses as a measure of company performance.

NET INCOME

Net income is the net increase in owner's equity that results from the operations of a company and is accumulated in the Owner's Capital account. Net income, in its simplest form, is measured by the difference between revenues and expenses when revenues exceed expenses:

$$\text{Net Income} = \text{Revenues} - \text{Expenses}$$

When expenses exceed revenues, a **net loss** occurs.

REVENUES

KEY POINT: The essence of revenue is that something has been *earned* through the sale of goods or services. That is why cash received through a loan does not constitute revenue.

Revenues are increases in owner's equity resulting from selling goods, rendering services, or performing other business activities. Revenues are inflows usually of cash or receivables, received in exchange for products or services. In the simplest case, revenues equal the price of goods sold or services rendered over a specific period of time. When a business delivers a product or provides a service to a customer, it usually receives either cash or a promise to pay cash in the near future. The promise to pay is recorded in either Accounts Receivable or Notes Receivable. The revenue for a given period equals the total of cash and receivables from goods and services provided to customers during that period.

Liabilities generally are not affected by revenues, and some transactions that increase cash and other assets are not revenues. For example, a bank loan increases liabilities and cash but does not produce revenue. The collection of accounts receivable, which increases cash and decreases accounts receivable, does not produce revenue either. Remember that when a sale on credit takes place, the asset account Accounts Receivable increases; at the same time, an owner's equity revenue account increases. So counting the collection of the receivable as revenue later would be counting the same sale twice.

Not all increases in owner's equity arise from revenues. Owner's investments increase owner's equity but are not revenue.

EXPENSES

KEY POINT: The primary purpose of an expense is to generate revenue.

Expenses are decreases in owner's equity resulting from the costs of selling goods, rendering services, or performing other business activities. In other words, expenses are the costs of the goods and services used up in the course of earning revenues. Often called the *cost of doing business*, expenses include the costs of goods sold, of activities needed to carry on a business, and of attracting and serving customers.

BUSINESS-WORLD EXAMPLE: Income measurement is difficult in many industries because of the uncertainties associated with their revenues and expenses. For example, cereal companies must recognize the expense associated with the anticipated redemption of box-tops and coupons during the period of the sale. And construction companies must estimate their revenues based on a project's percentage of completion.

Examples include salaries, rent, advertising, telephone service, expired or used assets, and depreciation (allocation of cost) of a building or office equipment.

Just as not all cash receipts are revenues, not all cash payments are expenses. A cash payment to reduce a liability does not result in an expense. The liability, however, may have come from incurring a previous expense, such as advertising, that is to be paid later. There may also be two steps before an expenditure of cash becomes an expense. For example, prepaid expenses and plant assets (such as machinery and equipment) are recorded as assets when they are acquired. Later, as their usefulness expires in the operation of the business, their cost is allocated to expenses. In fact, expenses sometimes are called *expired costs*.

Not all decreases in owner's equity arise from expenses. Owner withdrawals decrease owner's equity, but they are not expenses.

 Check out ACE for a Review Quiz at http://accounting.college.hmco.com/students.

INCOME MEASUREMENT ISSUES

LO2 Explain how the income measurement issues of accounting period, continuity, and matching are resolved.

RELATED TEXT ASSIGNMENTS
Q: 2, 3, 4
SE: 1
E: 1
SD: 1, 3
FRA: 1, 3, 5, 6

Several issues must be addressed in the measurement of income. These include the accounting period issue, the continuity issue, and the matching issue.

THE ACCOUNTING PERIOD ISSUE

The **accounting period issue** addresses the difficulty of assigning revenues and expenses to a short period of time, such as a month or a year. Not all transactions can be easily assigned to specific time periods. Purchases of buildings and equipment, for example, have effects that extend over many years. Accountants solve this problem by estimating the number of years the buildings or equipment will be in use and the cost that should be assigned to each year. In the process, they make an assumption about **periodicity**: that the net income for any period of time less than the life of the business, although tentative, is still a useful estimate of the entity's profitability for the period.

Generally, to make comparisons easier, the time periods are of equal length. Financial statements may be prepared for any time period. Accounting periods of less than one year—for example, a month or a quarter—are called *interim periods*. The 12-month accounting period used by an organization is called its **fiscal year**. Many organizations use the calendar year, January 1 to December 31, for their fiscal year. Others find it convenient to choose a fiscal year that ends during a slack season rather than a peak season. In this case, the fiscal year corresponds to the yearly cycle of business activity. The time period should always be noted in the financial statements.

FOCUS ON BUSINESS PRACTICE

Fiscal Year-Ends Vary.
The table below shows the diverse fiscal years used by some well-known companies. Many governmental and educational units use fiscal years that end June 30 or September 30.

Company	Last Month of Fiscal Year
Caesars World Inc. <www.caesarsworld.com>	July
The Walt Disney Company <www.disney.go.com>	September
Fleetwood Enterprises, Inc. <www.fleetwood.com>	April
H.J. Heinz, Inc. <www.heinz.com>	March
Kelly Services <www.kellyservices.com>	December
MGM-UA Communications Co. <www.mgm.com>	August
Toys "R" Us <www.tru.com>	January

THE CONTINUITY ISSUE

The process of measuring business income requires that certain expense and revenue transactions be allocated over several accounting periods. The number of accounting periods raises the **continuity issue**. How long will the business entity last? Many businesses survive less than five years, and in any given year, thousands of businesses go bankrupt. To prepare financial

BUSINESS-WORLD EXAMPLE: The continuity assumption is set aside when an organization is formed for a limited venture, such as a World's Fair or the Olympics.

statements for an accounting period, the accountant must make an assumption about the ability of the business to survive. Specifically, unless there is evidence to the contrary, the accountant assumes that the business will continue to operate indefinitely—that it is a **going concern**. Justification for all the techniques of income measurement rests on the assumption of continuity. For example, this assumption allows the cost of certain assets to be held on the balance sheet until a future year, when it will become an expense on the income statement.

Another example has to do with the value of assets on the balance sheet. The accountant records assets at cost and does not record subsequent changes in their value. But the value of assets to a going concern is much higher than the value of assets to a firm facing bankruptcy. In the latter case, the accountant may be asked to set aside the assumption of continuity and to prepare financial statements based on the assumption that the firm will go out of business and sell all of its assets at liquidation value—that is, for what they will bring in cash.

THE MATCHING ISSUE

KEY POINT: Although the cash basis often is used for tax purposes, it seldom produces an accurate measurement of a business's performance for financial reporting purposes.

Revenues and expenses can be accounted for on a cash received and cash paid basis. This practice is known as the **cash basis of accounting**. Individuals and some businesses may use it for income tax purposes. Under this method, revenues are reported in the period in which cash is received, and expenses are reported in the period in which cash is paid. Taxable income, therefore, is calculated as the difference between cash receipts from revenues and cash payments for expenses.

Although the cash basis of accounting works well for some small businesses and many individuals, it does not meet the needs of most businesses. As explained above, revenues can be earned in a period other than the one in which cash is received, and expenses can be incurred in a period other than the one in which cash is paid. To measure net income adequately, revenues and expenses must be assigned to the appropriate accounting period. The accountant solves this problem by applying the **matching rule**:

● **STOP AND THINK!**
Why must a company that gives a guaranty or warranty with its product or service show an expense in the year of sale rather than in a later year when a repair or replacement is made?

To measure a company's performance (net income) accurately, each expense (in this case, guaranty or warranty expense) must be matched with the related revenue in the year in which the product or service was sold. Otherwise, net income will be overstated, and the related liability will be understated. ■

> Revenues must be assigned to the accounting period in which the goods are sold or the services performed, and expenses must be assigned to the accounting period in which they are used to produce revenue.

Direct cause-and-effect relationships seldom can be demonstrated for certain, but many costs appear to be related to particular revenues. The accountant recognizes these expenses and the related revenues in the same accounting period. Examples are the costs of goods sold and sales commissions. When there is no direct means of connecting expenses and revenues, the accountant tries to allocate costs in a systematic way among the accounting periods that benefit from the costs. For example, a building is converted from an asset to an expense by allocating its cost over the years that the company benefits from its use.

 Check out ACE for a Review Quiz at http://accounting.college.hmco.com/students.

ACCRUAL ACCOUNTING

LO3 Define *accrual accounting* and explain three broad ways of accomplishing it.

RELATED TEXT ASSIGNMENTS
Q: 5, 6, 7, 8
SE: 1
E: 1, 2
P: 2, 7
SD: 1, 2, 3
FRA: 3

To apply the matching rule, accountants have developed accrual accounting. **Accrual accounting** "attempts to record the financial effects on an enterprise of transactions and other events and circumstances . . . in the periods in which those transactions, events, and circumstances occur rather than only in the periods in which cash is received or paid by the enterprise."[2] That is, accrual accounting consists of all the techniques developed by accountants to apply the matching rule. It is done in the following general ways: (1) by recording revenues when earned, (2) by recording expenses when incurred, and (3) by adjusting the accounts.

FOCUS ON BUSINESS ETHICS

Aggressive Accounting or Deception? You Judge.

Accounting principles, such as revenue recognition and the matching rule, should not be applied in a way that will distort or obscure financial information. Accounting practices are meant to inform readers of financial statements, not to deceive them. In recent years, the Securities and Exchange Commission <www.sec.gov> has been waging a public campaign against corporate accounting practices that manage or manipulate earnings to meet the expectations of Wall Street analysts.[3] Corporations engage in such practices in the hope of avoiding shortfalls that might cause serious declines in their stock price. The following describes a few of the corporate accounting practices that the SEC has challenged:

- Lucent Technologies <www.lucent.com> sold telecommunications equipment to companies from which there was no reasonable expectation of payment because of the companies' poor financial condition.

- America Online (AOL) <www.aol.com> recorded advertising as an asset rather than as an expense.

- Eclipsys <www.eclipsys.com> recorded software contracts as revenue even though it had not yet rendered the services.

- KnowledgeWare <knowledgeware.itil.com> recorded revenue from sales of software even though it told customers they did not have to pay until they had the software.

KEY POINT: Accrual accounting is a set of *procedures* (such as journal entries) devised to follow the *guideline* known as the matching rule.

RECOGNIZING REVENUES WHEN EARNED

The process of determining when revenue is earned, and consequently when it should be recorded, is called **revenue recognition**. The Securities and Exchange Commission has said that all the following conditions must exist before revenue is recognized:

- Persuasive evidence of an arrangement exists.
- Delivery has occurred or services have been rendered.
- The seller's price to the buyer is fixed or determinable.
- Collectibility is reasonably assured.[4]

For example, when Joan Miller Advertising Agency bills a customer for placing an advertisement, it is recorded as revenue because the transaction meets these four criteria. It is agreed that the customer owes for the service, the service has been rendered, the parties understand the price, and there is a reasonable expectation that the customer will pay the bill. Revenue is recorded by debiting Accounts Receivable and crediting Advertising Fees Earned. Note that it is not necessary for cash to be collected for revenue to be recorded. There only needs to be a reasonable expectation that it will be paid.

RECOGNIZING EXPENSES WHEN INCURRED

Expenses are recorded when there is an agreement to purchase goods or services, the goods have been delivered or the services rendered, a price is established or can be determined, and the goods or services have been used to produce revenue. For example, when Joan Miller Advertising Agency receives its telephone bill, the expense is recognized both as having been incurred and as helping to produce revenue. The transaction is recorded by debiting Telephone Expense and crediting Accounts Payable. Until the bill is paid, Accounts Payable serves as a holding account. Notice that recognition of the expense does not depend on the payment of cash.

ADJUSTING THE ACCOUNTS

A third application of accrual accounting is adjusting the accounts. Adjustments are necessary because the accounting period, by definition, ends on a particular day. The balance sheet must list all assets and liabilities as of the end of that day, and the income statement must contain all revenues and expenses applicable to the period ending on that day. Although operating a business is a continuous process, there

EXHIBIT 1
Trial Balance for Joan Miller Advertising Agency

Joan Miller Advertising Agency Trial Balance July 31, 20xx		
Cash	$ 9,140	
Accounts Receivable	4,800	
Art Supplies	1,800	
Office Supplies	800	
Prepaid Rent	1,600	
Prepaid Insurance	960	
Art Equipment	4,200	
Office Equipment	3,000	
Accounts Payable		$ 3,240
Unearned Art Fees		1,000
Joan Miller, Capital		20,000
Joan Miller, Withdrawals	1,400	
Advertising Fees Earned		6,200
Wages Expense	2,400	
Utilities Expense	200	
Telephone Expense	140	
	$30,440	$30,440

ENRICHMENT NOTE: The accountant waits until the end of an accounting period to update certain revenues and expenses even though the revenues and expenses theoretically have changed during the period. There usually is no need to adjust them until the end of the period, when the financial statements are prepared. In fact, it would be impractical, even impossible, to adjust the accounts each time they are affected.

● **STOP AND THINK!**
Is accrual accounting more closely related to a company's goal of profitability or liquidity?
It is more closely related to profitability because the purpose of accrual accounting is to measure net income. Cash accounting is more closely related to the goal of liquidity. ■

must be a cutoff point for the periodic reports. Some transactions invariably span the cutoff point; thus, some accounts need adjustment.

For example, some of the accounts in the end-of-the-period trial balance for Joan Miller Advertising Agency (Exhibit 1) do not show the correct balances for preparing the financial statements. The July 31 trial balance lists prepaid rent of $1,600. At $800 per month, this represents rent for the months of July and August. So on July 31, one-half of the $1,600, or $800, represents rent expense for July; the remaining $800 represents an asset that will be used in August. An adjustment is needed to reflect the $800 balance in the Prepaid Rent account on the balance sheet and the $800 rent expense on the income statement. As you will see on the following pages, several other accounts in the Joan Miller Advertising Agency trial balance do not reflect their correct balances. Like the Prepaid Rent account, they need to be adjusted.

ACCRUAL ACCOUNTING AND PERFORMANCE MEASURES

Accrual accounting can be difficult to understand. The related adjustments take time to calculate and enter in the records. Also, adjusting entries do not affect cash flows in the current period because they never involve the Cash account. You might ask, "Why go to all the trouble of making them? Why worry about them?" The Securities and Exchange Commission, in fact, has identified issues related to accrual accounting and adjustments as an area of utmost importance because of the potential for abuse and misrepresentation.[5]

All adjustments are important because they are necessary to measure key profitability performance measures. Adjusting entries affect net income on the income statement, and they affect profitability comparisons from one accounting period to the next. They also affect assets and liabilities on the balance sheet and thus provide information about a company's *future* cash inflows and outflows. This information is needed to assess management's short-term goal of achieving sufficient liquidity to meet its need for cash to pay ongoing obligations. The potential for abuse arises because considerable judgment underlies the application of adjusting entries. Misuse of this judgment can result in misleading measures of performance.

 Check out ACE for a Review Quiz at http://accounting.college.hmco.com/students.

THE ADJUSTMENT PROCESS

LO4   State four principal situations that require adjusting entries and prepare typical adjusting entries.

RELATED TEXT ASSIGNMENTS
Q: 9, 10, 11, 12, 13, 14, 15,
    16, 17, 18, 19, 20
SE: 2, 3, 4, 5, 6
E: 1, 3, 4, 5, 6, 7, 8, 9
P: 1, 2, 3, 4, 5, 6, 7, 8
SD: 1, 2, 3, 4, 5
FRA: 1, 2, 4, 5, 6, 7

KEY POINT: Each adjusting entry must include at least one balance sheet account and one income statement account. By definition, it cannot include a debit or a credit to Cash.

KEY POINT: Adjusting entries never involve the Cash account and thus never affect cash flows.

Accountants use adjusting entries to apply accrual accounting to transactions that span more than one accounting period. There are four situations in which adjusting entries are required, as illustrated in Figure 1. As shown, each situation affects one balance sheet account and one income statement account. Adjusting entries never involve the Cash account. The four types of adjusting entries may be stated as follows:

1. Costs have been recorded that must be allocated between two or more accounting periods. Examples are prepaid rent, prepaid insurance, supplies, and costs of a building. The adjusting entry in this case involves an asset account and an expense account.

2. Expenses have been incurred but are not yet recorded. Examples are the wages earned by employees in the current accounting period but after the last pay period. The adjusting entry involves an expense account and a liability account.

3. Revenues have been recorded that must be allocated between two or more accounting periods. An example is payments collected for services yet to be rendered. The adjusting entry involves a liability account and a revenue account.

4. Revenues have been earned but are not yet recorded. An example is fees earned but not yet collected or billed to customers. The adjusting entry involves an asset account and a revenue account.

Accountants often refer to adjusting entries as deferrals or accruals. A deferral is the postponement of the recognition of an expense already paid (Type 1 adjustment) or of a revenue received in advance (Type 3 adjustment). Recording of the receipt or payment of cash precedes the adjusting entry. An accrual is the recognition of a revenue (Type 4 adjustment) or expense (Type 2 adjustment) that has arisen but has not yet been recorded. No cash was received or paid prior to the adjusting entry; this will occur in a future accounting period. Once again, we use Joan Miller Advertising Agency to illustrate the kinds of adjusting entries that most businesses make.

FIGURE 1
The Four Types of Adjustments

	BALANCE SHEET	
	Asset	**Liability**
Expense	1. Recorded costs are allocated between two or more accounting periods.	2. Expenses are incurred but not yet recorded.
Revenue	4. Revenues are earned but not yet recorded.	3. Recorded unearned revenues are allocated between two or more accounting periods.

(Income statement — Expense / Revenue rows)

TYPE 1: ALLOCATING RECORDED COSTS BETWEEN TWO OR MORE ACCOUNTING PERIODS (DEFERRED EXPENSES)

Companies often make expenditures that benefit more than one period. These expenditures are usually debited to an asset account. At the end of the accounting period, the amount that has been used is transferred from the asset account to an expense account. Two of the more important kinds of adjustments are those for prepaid expenses and the depreciation of plant and equipment.

KEY POINT: The expired portion of a prepayment is converted to an expense; the unexpired portion remains an asset.

■ **PREPAID EXPENSES**   Expenses paid in advance are called **prepaid expenses**. They include rent, insurance, and supplies. At the end of an accounting period, some or all of these goods or services will have been used up or expired. An adjusting entry to reduce the asset and increase the expense is always required. As Figure 2 shows, the amount of the adjustment equals the cost of the goods or services used up or expired. If adjusting entries for prepaid expenses are not made at the end of a period, both the balance sheet and income statement will be incorrect; assets will be overstated, and expenses will be understated. Owner's equity on the balance sheet and net income on the income statement will be overstated.

At the beginning of the month, Joan Miller Advertising Agency paid two months' rent in advance, which resulted in an asset: the right to occupy the office for two months. As each day in the month passed, part of the asset's cost expired and became an expense. By July 31, one-half of the asset's cost had expired and should be treated as an expense. Here is the analysis of this economic event:

Prepaid Rent (Adjustment a)

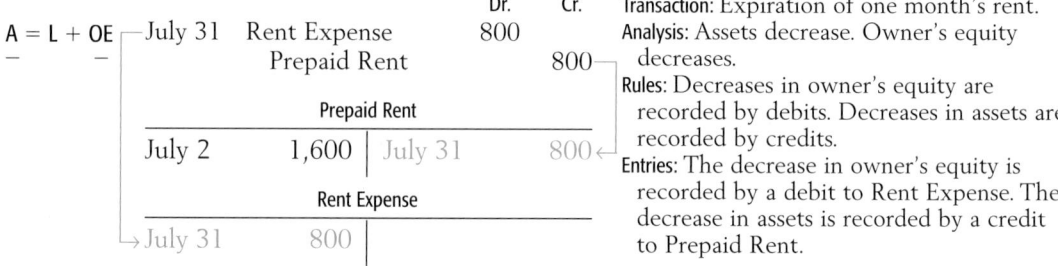

The Prepaid Rent account now has a balance of $800, which represents one month's rent paid in advance. The Rent Expense account reflects the $800 expense for the month of July. Besides rent, Joan Miller Advertising Agency prepaid expenses for insurance, art supplies, and office supplies, all of which call for adjusting entries.

On July 8, the agency purchased a one-year life insurance policy, paying for it in advance. Like prepaid rent, prepaid insurance offers benefits (in this case, protection) that expire day by day. By the end of the month, one-twelfth of the insurance protection had expired. The adjustment is analyzed and recorded like this:

Prepaid Insurance (Adjustment b)

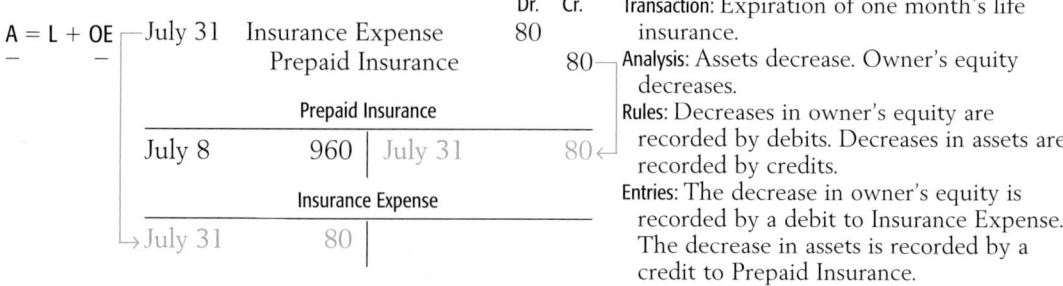

The Prepaid Insurance account now shows the correct balance, $880, and Insurance Expense reflects the expired cost, $80 for the month of July.

Figure 2
Adjustment for Prepaid (Deferred) Expenses

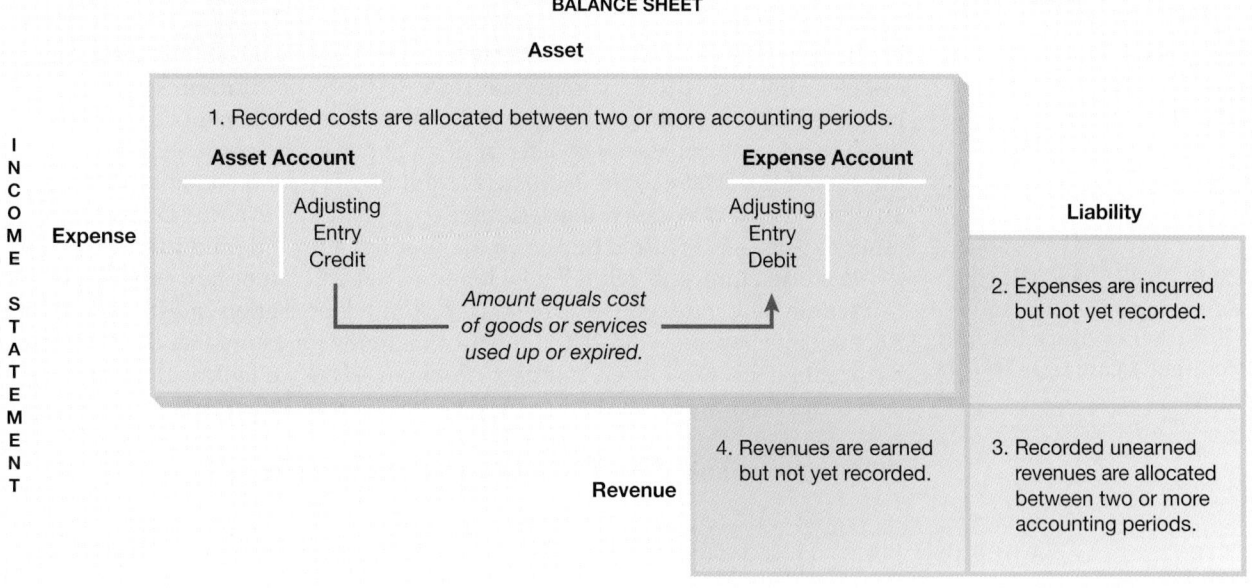

KEY POINT: Notice that the cost of supplies consumed is inferred, not observed.

Early in July, the agency purchased art supplies and office supplies, some of which it consumed during the month. These supplies are not accounted for each day because the financial statements are not prepared until the end of the month and the recordkeeping would involve too much work. Instead, Joan Miller makes a careful inventory of the supplies at the end of the month, recording the number and cost of those not yet consumed and that are thus still assets of the agency.

Suppose the inventory shows that art supplies costing $1,300 and office supplies costing $600 are still on hand. This means that of the $1,800 of art supplies originally purchased, $500 worth were used up (became an expense) in July. Of the original $800 of office supplies, $200 worth were consumed. These transactions are analyzed and recorded as follows:

Art Supplies and Office Supplies (Adjustments c and d)

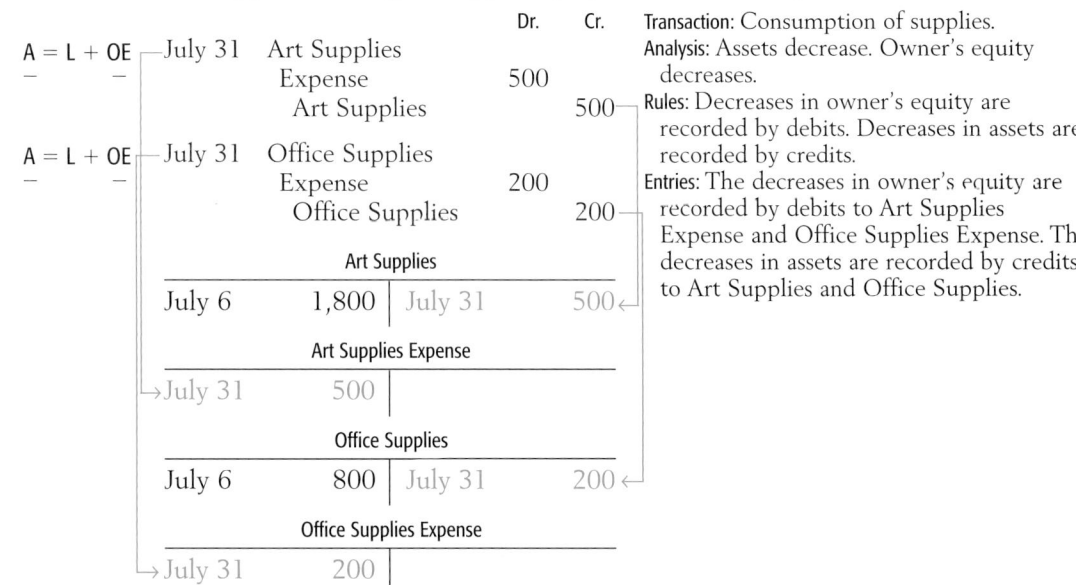

The asset accounts Art Supplies and Office Supplies now reflect the correct balances, $1,300 and $600, respectively, of supplies that are yet to be consumed. In addition, the amount of art supplies used up during the month of July is shown as $500, and the amount of office supplies used up is shown as $200.

KEY POINT: In accounting, depreciation refers only to the *allocation* of an asset's cost, not to the decline in its value.

KEY POINT: The difficulty in estimating an asset's useful life is further evidence that the bottom-line figure is, at best, an estimate.

■ **DEPRECIATION OF PLANT AND EQUIPMENT**   When an organization buys a long-term asset—a building, trucks, computers, store fixtures, or furniture—it is, in effect, prepaying for the usefulness of that asset for as long as it benefits the organization. Because a long-term asset is a deferral of an expense, the accountant must allocate the cost of the asset over its estimated useful life. The amount allocated to any one accounting period is called **depreciation** or *depreciation expense*. Depreciation, like other expenses, is incurred during an accounting period to produce revenue.

It is often impossible to tell how long an asset will last or how much of the asset is used in any one period. For this reason, depreciation must be estimated. Accountants have developed a number of methods for estimating depreciation and for dealing with the related complex problems. Here we look at the simplest case, depreciation on the art and office equipment for Joan Miller Advertising Agency.

Art Equipment and Office Equipment (Adjustments e and f)

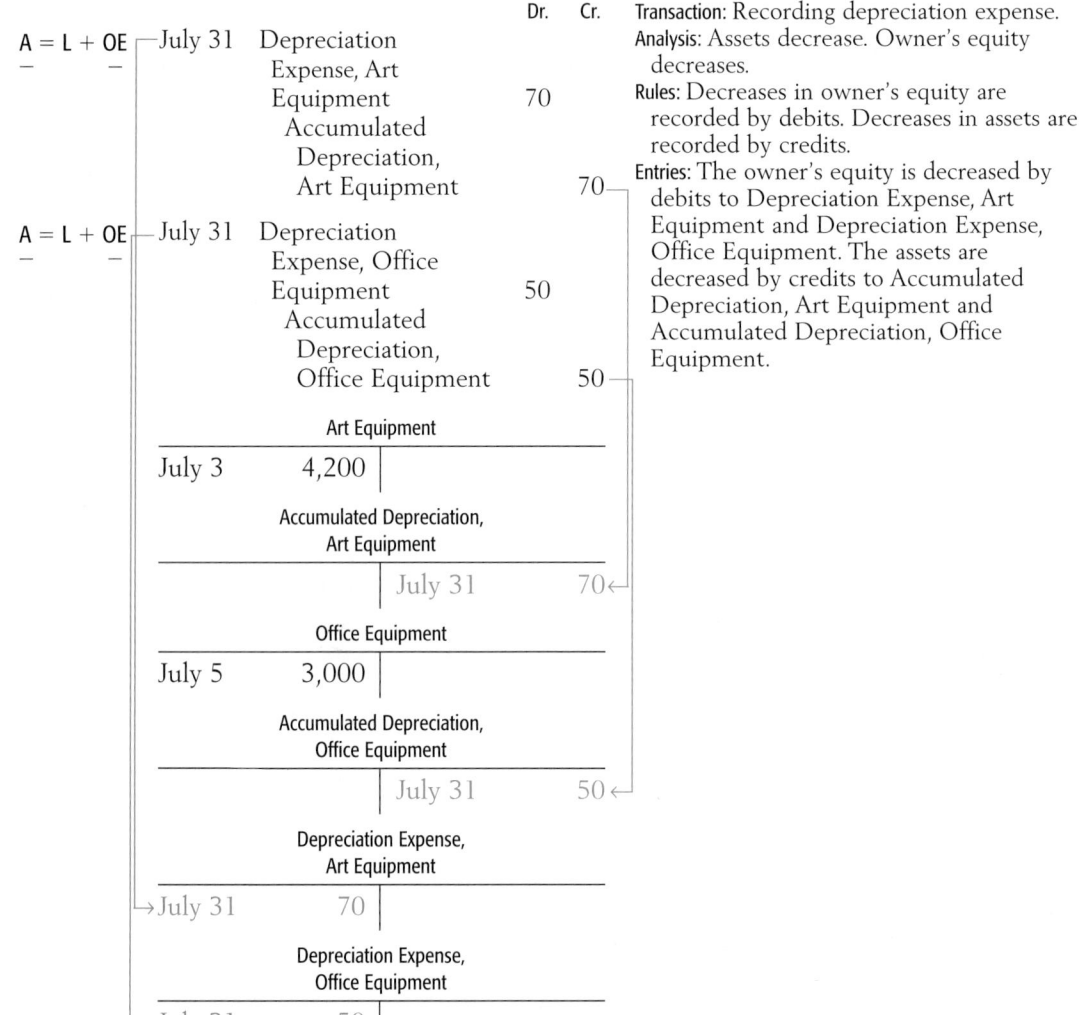

Suppose, for example, that Joan Miller estimates that the art equipment and office equipment for which she paid $4,200 and $3,000, respectively, will last five years (60 months) and will have zero value at the end of that time. The monthly

FIGURE 3
Adjustment for Depreciation

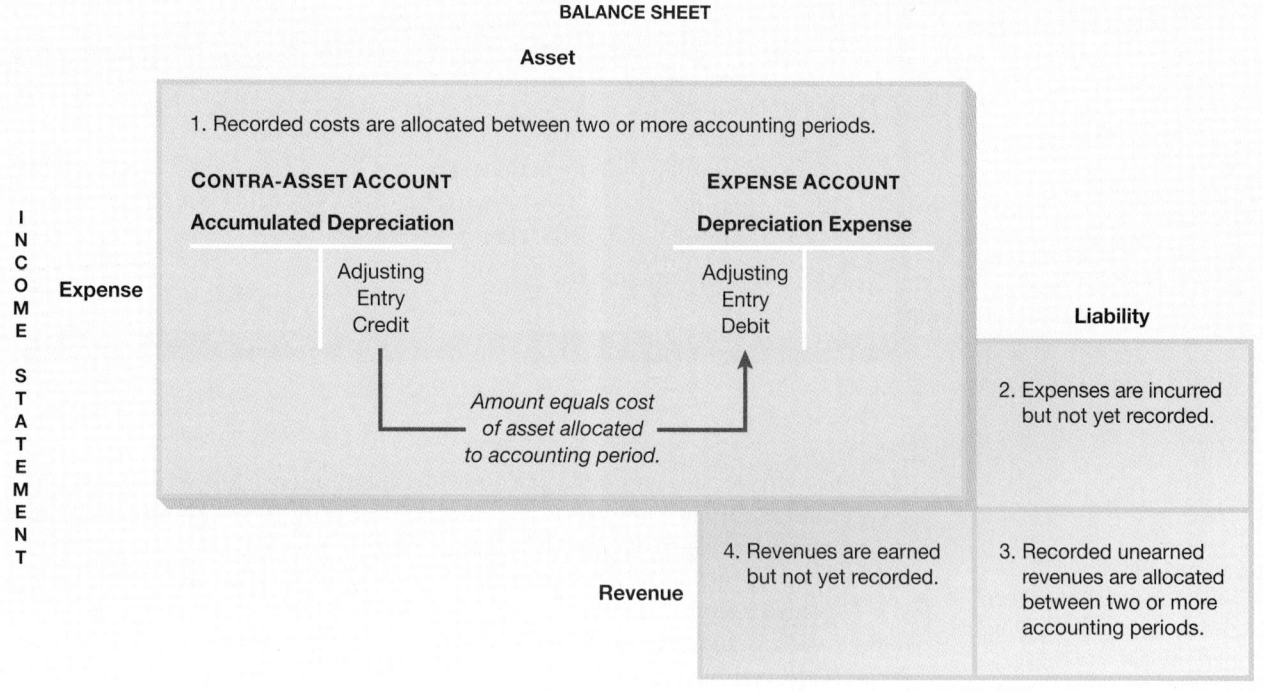

BALANCE SHEET

Asset

1. Recorded costs are allocated between two or more accounting periods.

CONTRA-ASSET ACCOUNT

Accumulated Depreciation

Adjusting
Entry
Credit

EXPENSE ACCOUNT

Depreciation Expense

Adjusting
Entry
Debit

*Amount equals cost
of asset allocated
to accounting period.*

Liability

2. Expenses are incurred
but not yet recorded.

INCOME STATEMENT

Expense

Revenue

4. Revenues are earned
but not yet recorded.

3. Recorded unearned
revenues are allocated
between two or more
accounting periods.

depreciation of art equipment and office equipment is $70 ($4,200 ÷ 60 months) and $50 ($3,000 ÷ 60 months), respectively. These amounts represent the costs allocated to July, and they are the amounts by which the asset accounts must be reduced and the expense accounts increased (reducing owner's equity).

■ **ACCUMULATED DEPRECIATION—A CONTRA ACCOUNT**   Notice that in the previous analysis, the asset accounts are not credited directly. Instead, as shown in Figure 3, new accounts—Accumulated Depreciation, Art Equipment; and Accumulated Depreciation, Office Equipment—are credited. These **accumulated depreciation accounts** are contra-asset accounts used to total the past depreciation expense on specific long-term assets. A **contra account** is a separate account that is paired with a related account—in this case an asset account. The balance of the contra account is shown on the financial statement as a deduction from the related account.

There are several types of contra accounts. In this case, the balance of Accumulated Depreciation, Art Equipment is shown on the balance sheet as a

FOCUS ON INTERNATIONAL BUSINESS

Who Needs Accounting Knowledge?

The privatization of businesses in Eastern Europe and the republics of the former Soviet Union has created a great need for Western accounting knowledge. Many managers from these countries are anxious to study accounting. Under the old governmental systems, the concept of net income as Westerners know it did not exist because the state owned everything and there was no such thing as income.

The new businesses, because they are private, require accounting systems that recognize the importance of net income. In these new systems, it is necessary to make adjusting entries to record such things as depreciation and accrued expenses. Many Eastern European businesses have been suffering losses for years without knowing it and, as a result, are now in poor financial condition.

EXHIBIT 2
Plant and Equipment Section of the Balance Sheet

Joan Miller Advertising Agency Partial Balance Sheet July 31, 20xx		
Plant and equipment		
Art equipment	$4,200	
Less accumulated depreciation	70	$4,130
Office equipment	$3,000	
Less accumulated depreciation	50	2,950
Total plant and equipment		$7,080

⬢ **STOP AND THINK!**
Will the carrying value of a long-term asset normally equal its market value?

The carrying value will equal the market value of the asset only by coincidence because the goal of recording depreciation is to allocate the cost of the asset over its life, not to determine its market value. ■

deduction from the associated account Art Equipment. Likewise, Accumulated Depreciation, Office Equipment is a deduction from Office Equipment. Exhibit 2 shows the plant and equipment section of the balance sheet for Joan Miller Advertising Agency after these adjusting entries have been made.

A contra account is used for two very good reasons. First, it recognizes that depreciation is an estimate. Second, a contra account preserves the original cost of an asset. In combination with the asset account, it shows both how much of the asset has been allocated as an expense and the balance left to be depreciated. As the months pass, the amount of the accumulated depreciation grows, and the net amount shown as an asset declines. In six months, Accumulated Depreciation, Art Equipment will show a balance of $420; when this amount is subtracted from the balance of Art Equipment, a net amount of $3,780 will remain. The net amount is called the **carrying value**, or *book value*, of the asset.

TYPE 2: RECOGNIZING UNRECORDED EXPENSES (ACCRUED EXPENSES)

At the end of an accounting period, there usually are expenses that have been incurred but not recorded in the accounts. These expenses require adjusting entries. One such case is interest on borrowed money. Each day, interest accumulates on the debt. As shown in Figure 4, at the end of the accounting period, an adjusting entry is made to record this accumulated interest, which is an expense of the period, and the corresponding liability to pay the interest. Other common unrecorded expenses are taxes, wages, and utilities. As the expense and the corresponding liability accumulate, they are said to *accrue*—hence the term **accrued expenses**.

■ **ACCRUED WAGES**   Suppose the calendar for the month of July looks like the calendar that follows.

			July			
Su	M	T	W	Th	F	Sa
	1	2	3	4	5	6
7	8	9	10	11	12	13
14	15	16	17	18	19	20
21	22	23	24	25	26	27
28	29	30	31			

FIGURE 4
Adjustment for Unrecorded (Accrued) Expenses

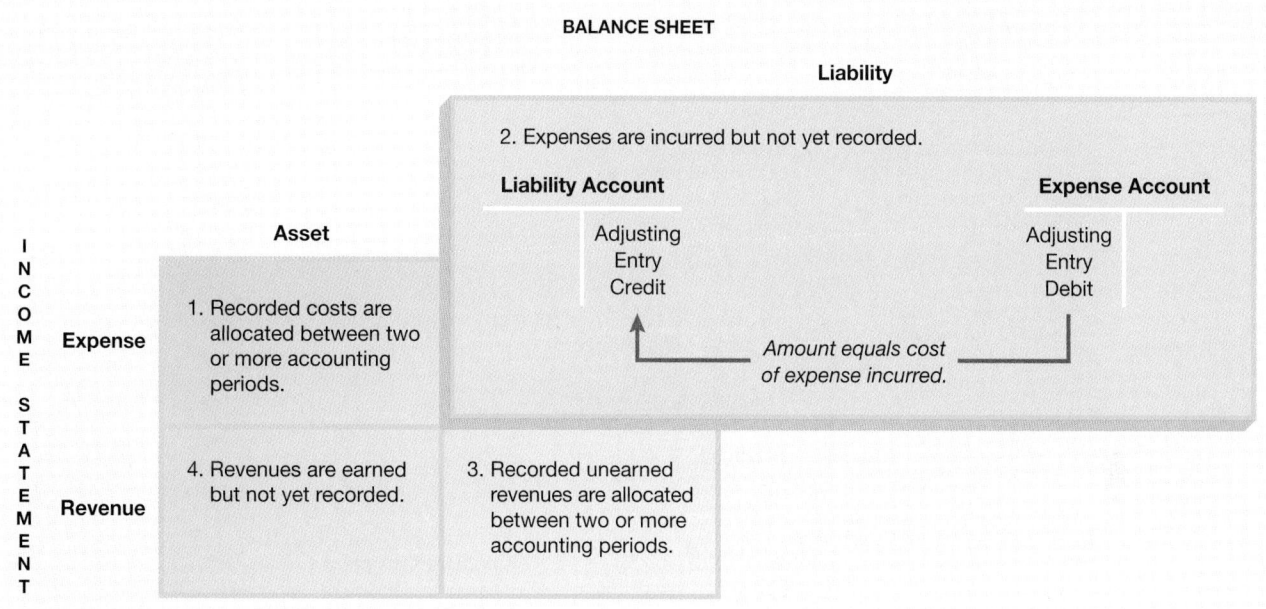

By the end of business on July 31, the secretary at Joan Miller Advertising Agency will have worked three days (Monday, Tuesday, and Wednesday) beyond the last biweekly pay period, which ended on July 26. The employee has earned the wages for these days, but she will not be paid until the regular payday in August. The wages for these three days are rightfully an expense for July, and the liabilities should reflect that the company owes the secretary for those days. Because the secretary's wage rate is $1,200 every two weeks, or $120 per day ($1,200 ÷ 10 working days), the expense is $360 ($120 × 3 days).

Accrued Wages (Adjustment g)

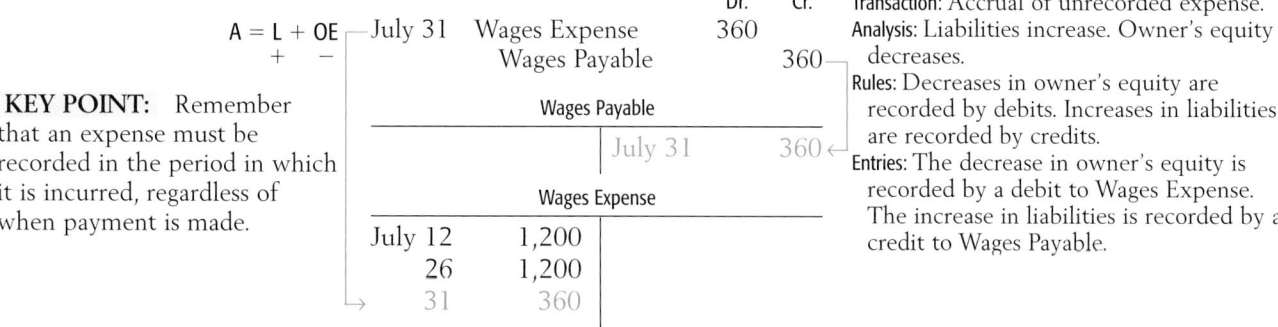

KEY POINT: Remember that an expense must be recorded in the period in which it is incurred, regardless of when payment is made.

The liability of $360 is now reflected correctly in the Wages Payable account. The actual expense incurred for wages during July, $2,760, is also correct.

TYPE 3: ALLOCATING RECORDED UNEARNED REVENUES BETWEEN TWO OR MORE ACCOUNTING PERIODS (DEFERRED REVENUES)

Just as expenses can be paid before they are used, revenues can be received before they are earned. When a company receives revenues in advance, it has an obligation

FIGURE 5
Adjustment for Unearned (Deferred) Revenues

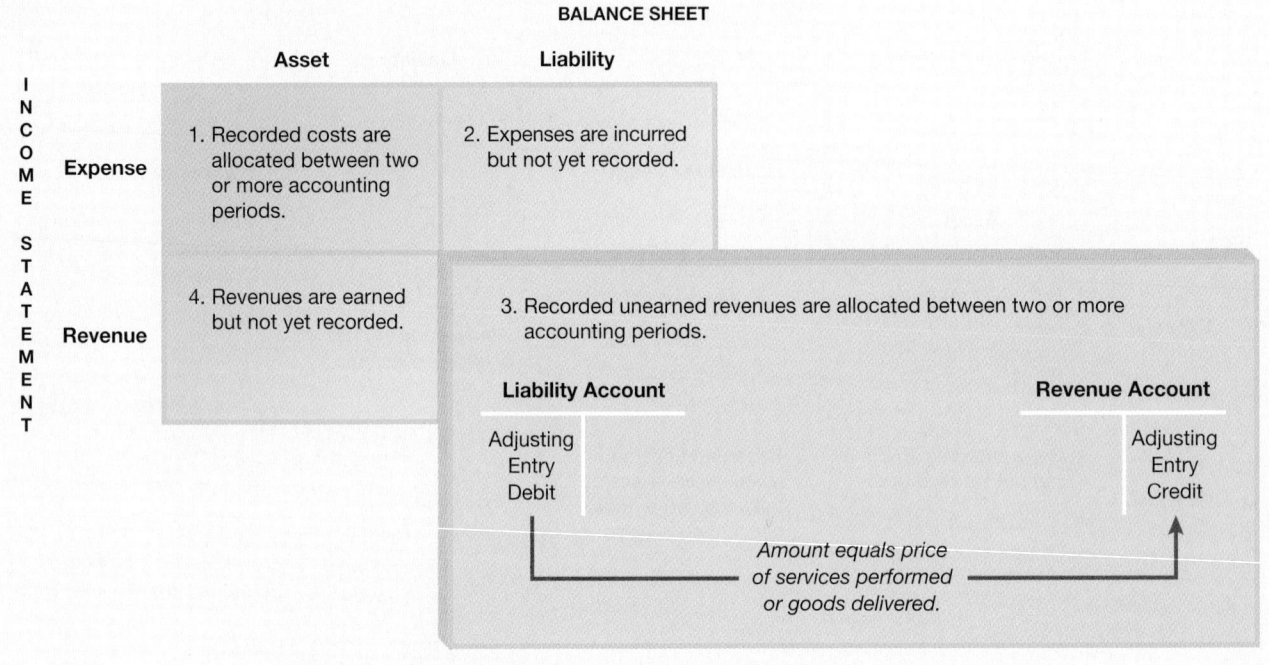

KEY POINT: Unearned Revenue is a liability because there is an obligation to deliver goods or perform a service, or to return the payment. Once the goods have been delivered or the service performed, the liability is converted into revenue.

to deliver goods or perform services. Therefore, unearned revenues are shown in a liability account. For example, publishing companies usually receive payment in advance for magazine subscriptions, and these receipts are recorded in a liability account. If the company fails to deliver the magazines, subscribers are entitled to their money back. As the company delivers each issue of the magazine, it earns a part of the advance payments. This earned portion must be transferred from the Unearned Subscriptions (liability) account to the Subscription Revenue account, as shown in Figure 5.

During the month of July, Joan Miller Advertising Agency received $1,000 as an advance payment for advertising designs to be prepared for another agency. Assume that by the end of the month, $400 of the design was completed and accepted by the other agency. Here is the transaction analysis:

Unearned Art Fees (Adjustment h)

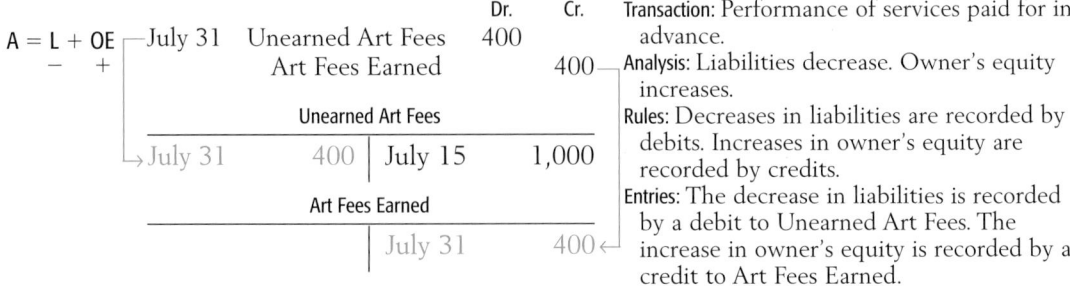

The liability account Unearned Art Fees now reflects the amount of work still to be performed, $600. The revenue account Art Fees Earned reflects the services performed and the revenue earned for them during July, $400.

Type 4: Recognizing Unrecorded Revenues (Accrued Revenues)

STUDY NOTE: When distinguishing between unearned revenues and accrued revenues, be aware that with accrued revenues, cash is not received in advance or by the end of the period.

Accrued revenues are revenues for which a service has been performed or goods delivered but for which no entry has been recorded. Any revenues earned but not recorded during the accounting period call for an adjusting entry that debits an asset account and credits a revenue account, as shown in Figure 6. For example, the interest on a note receivable is earned day by day but may not be received until another accounting period. Interest Receivable should be debited and Interest Income should be credited for the interest accrued at the end of the current period.

Suppose that Joan Miller Advertising Agency has agreed to place a series of advertisements for Marsh Tire Company and that the first ad appears on July 31, the last day of the month. The fee of $200 for this advertisement, which has been earned but not recorded, should be recorded this way:

Accrued Advertising Fees (Adjustment i)

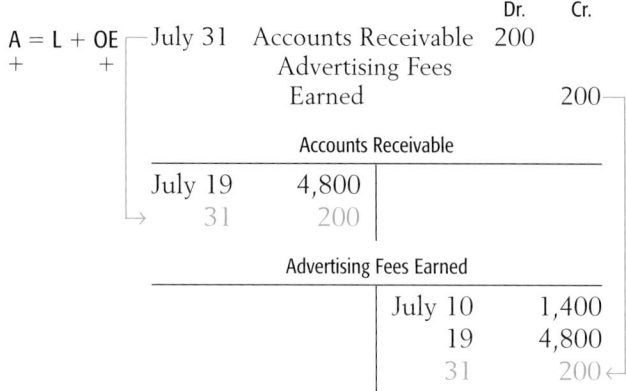

			Dr.	Cr.
July 31	Accounts Receivable		200	
	Advertising Fees Earned			200

A = L + OE
+   +

Accounts Receivable

| July 19 | 4,800 | |
| 31 | 200 | |

Advertising Fees Earned

		July 10	1,400
		19	4,800
		31	200

Transaction: Accrual of unrecorded revenue.
Analysis: Assets increase. Owner's equity increases.
Rules: Increases in assets are recorded by debits. Increases in owner's equity are recorded by credits.
Entries: The increase in assets is recorded by a debit to Accounts Receivable. The increase in owner's equity is recorded by a credit to Advertising Fees Earned.

FIGURE 6
Adjustment for Unrecorded (Accrued) Revenues

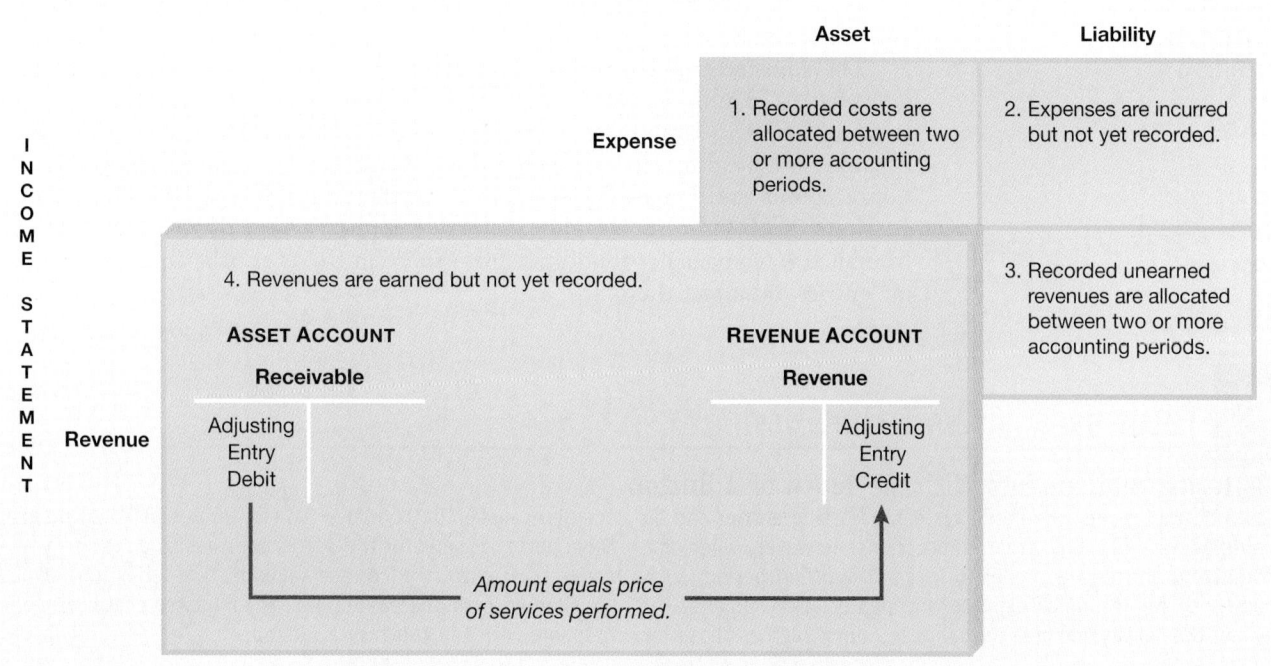

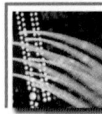

FOCUS ON BUSINESS TECHNOLOGY

Ecommerce: What's Its Impact?

Electronic commerce has received much attention in recent years. Sales and purchases involving Internet-based companies like Amazon.com <www.amazon.com> and Travelocity.com <www.travelocity.com> have grown steadily. The total value of goods and services traded over the Internet was $433 billion in 2002, of which $94 billion were retail sales.[6] It is important to realize that when transactions are made electronically, they are analyzed and recorded just as if they had taken place in a physical store. Internet companies require insurance, employee payrolls, buildings, and other assets and liabilities, and they must make the adjusting entries in the same way as any other business.

Now both the asset and the revenue accounts show the correct balance: The $5,000 in Accounts Receivable is owed to the company, and the $6,400 in Advertising Fees Earned has been earned by the company during July. Marsh Tire Company will be billed for the series of advertisements when they are completed.

A NOTE ABOUT JOURNAL ENTRIES

Thus far, we have presented a full analysis of each journal entry. The analyses showed you the thought process behind each entry. By now, you should be fully aware of the effects of transactions on the accounting equation and the rules of debit and credit. For this reason, in the rest of the book, we present journal entries without full analysis.

 Check out ACE for a Review Quiz at http://accounting.college.hmco.com/students.

USING THE ADJUSTED TRIAL BALANCE TO PREPARE FINANCIAL STATEMENTS

LO5 Prepare financial statements from an adjusted trial balance.

RELATED TEXT ASSIGNMENTS
Q: 21
SE: 7, 8
E: 10
P: 4, 5

After adjusting entries have been recorded and posted, an **adjusted trial balance** is prepared by listing all accounts and their balances. If the adjusting entries have been posted to the accounts correctly, the adjusted trial balance should have equal debit and credit totals.

The adjusted trial balance for Joan Miller Advertising Agency is shown on the left side of Exhibit 3. Notice that some accounts, such as Cash and Accounts Payable, have the same balances as they have in the trial balance (see Exhibit 1) because no adjusting entries affected them. Some new accounts, such as depreciation accounts and Wages Payable, appear in the adjusted trial balance, and other accounts, such as Art Supplies, Office Supplies, Prepaid Rent, and Prepaid Insurance, have balances that differ from those in the trial balance because adjusting entries did affect them.

FOCUS ON BUSINESS TECHNOLOGY

Entering Adjustments With the Touch of a Button

In a computerized accounting system, adjusting entries can be entered just like any other transactions. However, when the adjusting entries are similar for each accounting period, such as those for insurance expense and depreciation expense, or when they always involve the same accounts, such as those for accrued wages, the computer can be programmed to display them automatically. All the accountant has to do is verify the amounts or enter the correct amounts. The adjusting entries are then entered and posted, and the adjusted trial balance is prepared with the touch of a button.

EXHIBIT 3
Relationship of Adjusted Trial Balance to Income Statement

Joan Miller Advertising Agency
Adjusted Trial Balance
July 31, 20xx

Cash	$ 9,140	
Accounts Receivable	5,000	
Art Supplies	1,300	
Office Supplies	600	
Prepaid Rent	800	
Prepaid Insurance	880	
Art Equipment	4,200	
Accumulated Depreciation, Art Equipment		$ 70
Office Equipment	3,000	
Accumulated Depreciation, Office Equipment		50
Accounts Payable		3,240
Unearned Art Fees		600
Wages Payable		360
Joan Miller, Capital		20,000
Joan Miller, Withdrawals	1,400	
Advertising Fees Earned		6,400
Art Fees Earned		400
Wages Expense	2,760	
Utilities Expense	200	
Telephone Expense	140	
Rent Expense	800	
Insurance Expense	80	
Art Supplies Expense	500	
Office Supplies Expense	200	
Depreciation Expense, Art Equipment	70	
Depreciation Expense, Office Equipment	50	
	$31,120	$31,120

Joan Miller Advertising Agency
Income Statement
For the Month Ended July 31, 20xx

Revenues

Advertising fees earned		$6,400
Art fees earned		400
Total revenues		$6,800

Expenses

Wages expense	$2,760	
Utilities expense	200	
Telephone expense	140	
Rent expense	800	
Insurance expense	80	
Art supplies expense	500	
Office supplies expense	200	
Depreciation expense, Art equipment	70	
Depreciation expense, Office equipment	50	
Total expenses		4,800
Net income		**$2,000**

KEY POINT: The adjusted trial balance is a second check that the ledger is still in balance. Because it reflects updated information from the adjusting entries, it may be used to prepare the formal statements.

KEY POINT: The net income figure from the income statement is needed to prepare the statement of owner's equity, and the bottom-line figure of that statement is needed to prepare the balance sheet. Thus, the income statement is prepared before the statement of owner's equity, and that statement is prepared before the balance sheet.

KEY POINT: Notice that the adjusted trial balance figure for Joan Miller, Capital does not reflect net income or withdrawals during the period. The balance is updated when the closing entries are prepared (see Chapter 4).

Using the adjusted trial balance, the financial statements can be easily prepared. The income statement is prepared from the revenue and expense accounts, as shown in Exhibit 3. Then, as shown in Exhibit 4, the statement of owner's equity and the balance sheet are prepared. Notice that the net income from the income statement is combined with withdrawals on the statement of owner's equity to give the net change in the Joan Miller, Capital account. The resulting balance of Joan Miller, Capital on July 31 is used on the balance sheet, as are the asset and liability accounts.

 Check out ACE for a Review Quiz at http://accounting.college.hmco.com/students.

EXHIBIT 4
Relationship of Adjusted Trial Balance to Balance Sheet and Statement of Owner's Equity

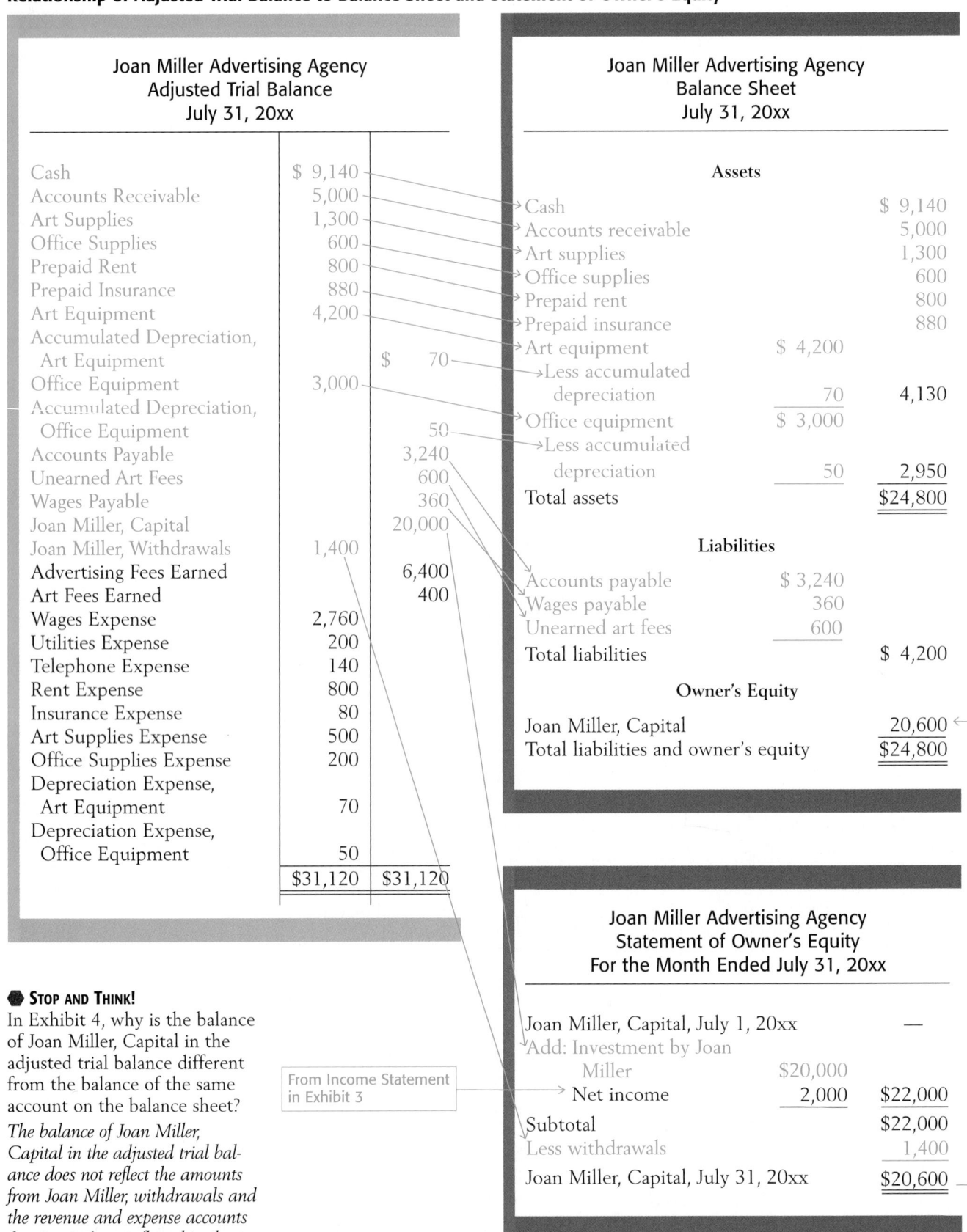

Joan Miller Advertising Agency
Adjusted Trial Balance
July 31, 20xx

Cash	$ 9,140	
Accounts Receivable	5,000	
Art Supplies	1,300	
Office Supplies	600	
Prepaid Rent	800	
Prepaid Insurance	880	
Art Equipment	4,200	
Accumulated Depreciation, Art Equipment		$ 70
Office Equipment	3,000	
Accumulated Depreciation, Office Equipment		50
Accounts Payable		3,240
Unearned Art Fees		600
Wages Payable		360
Joan Miller, Capital		20,000
Joan Miller, Withdrawals	1,400	
Advertising Fees Earned		6,400
Art Fees Earned		400
Wages Expense	2,760	
Utilities Expense	200	
Telephone Expense	140	
Rent Expense	800	
Insurance Expense	80	
Art Supplies Expense	500	
Office Supplies Expense	200	
Depreciation Expense, Art Equipment	70	
Depreciation Expense, Office Equipment	50	
	$31,120	$31,120

Joan Miller Advertising Agency
Balance Sheet
July 31, 20xx

Assets

Cash		$ 9,140
Accounts receivable		5,000
Art supplies		1,300
Office supplies		600
Prepaid rent		800
Prepaid insurance		880
Art equipment	$ 4,200	
Less accumulated depreciation	70	4,130
Office equipment	$ 3,000	
Less accumulated depreciation	50	2,950
Total assets		$24,800

Liabilities

Accounts payable	$ 3,240	
Wages payable	360	
Unearned art fees	600	
Total liabilities		$ 4,200

Owner's Equity

Joan Miller, Capital		20,600
Total liabilities and owner's equity		$24,800

Joan Miller Advertising Agency
Statement of Owner's Equity
For the Month Ended July 31, 20xx

Joan Miller, Capital, July 1, 20xx		—
Add: Investment by Joan Miller	$20,000	
Net income	2,000	$22,000
Subtotal		$22,000
Less withdrawals		1,400
Joan Miller, Capital, July 31, 20xx		$20,600

From Income Statement in Exhibit 3

● **STOP AND THINK!**
In Exhibit 4, why is the balance of Joan Miller, Capital in the adjusted trial balance different from the balance of the same account on the balance sheet?

The balance of Joan Miller, Capital in the adjusted trial balance does not reflect the amounts from Joan Miller, withdrawals and the revenue and expense accounts (net income), as reflected in the statement of owner's equity. ■

CASH FLOWS FROM ACCRUAL-BASED INFORMATION

SO6 Analyze cash flows from accrual-based information.

RELATED TEXT ASSIGNMENTS
Q: 22
SE: 9, 10
E: 11, 12, 13
FRA: 6

Management has the short-range goal of achieving sufficient liquidity to meet its needs for cash to pay its ongoing obligations. It is important for managers to be able to use accrual-based financial information to analyze cash flows in order to plan payments to creditors and assess the need for short-term borrowing.

Every revenue or expense account on the income statement has one or more related accounts on the balance sheet. For instance, Supplies Expense is related to Supplies, Wages Expense is related to Wages Payable, and Art Fees Earned is related to Unearned Art Fees. As we have shown, these accounts are related through adjusting entries whose purpose is to apply the matching rule in the measurement of net income. The cash flows generated or paid by company operations may also be determined by analyzing these relationships. For example, suppose that after receiving the financial statements in Exhibits 3 and 4, management wants to know how much cash was expended for art supplies. On the income statement, Art Supplies Expense is $500, and on the balance sheet, Art Supplies is $1,300. Because July was the company's first month of operation, there was no prior balance of art supplies, so the amount of cash expended for art supplies during the month was $1,800. The cash flow used to purchase art supplies ($1,800) was much greater than the amount expensed in determining income ($500). In planning for August, management can anticipate that the cash needed may be less than the amount expensed because, given the large inventory of art supplies, it will probably not be necessary to buy art supplies for more than a month. Understanding these cash flow effects enables management to better predict the business's need for cash in August.

The general rule for determining the cash flow received from any revenue or paid for any expense (except depreciation, which is a special case not covered here) is to determine the potential cash payments or cash receipts and deduct the amount not paid or received. The application of the general rule varies with the type of asset or liability account, which is shown as follows:

Type of Account	Potential Payment or Receipt	Not Paid or Received	Result
Prepaid Expense	Ending Balance + Expense for the Period	− Beginning Balance =	Cash Payments for Expenses
Unearned Revenue	Ending Balance + Revenue for the Period	− Beginning Balance =	Cash Receipts from Revenues
Accrued Payable	Beginning Balance + Expense for the Period	− Ending Balance =	Cash Payments for Expenses
Accrued Receivable	Beginning Balance + Revenue for the Period	− Ending Balance =	Cash Receipts from Revenues

STUDY NOTE: Balance sheet T accounts also work well for calculating cash receipts and cash payments. You have three pieces of information about the balance sheet account and must solve for one unknown. This approach reinforces the concept of normal balances. After the accrual number is entered, solve for the unknown cash effect.

For instance, assume that on May 31 a company had a balance of $480 in Prepaid Insurance and that on June 30 the balance was $670. If the insurance expense during June was $120, the amount of cash expended on insurance during June can be computed as follows:

Prepaid Insurance at June 30	$670
Insurance Expense during June	120
Potential cash payments for insurance	$790
Less Prepaid Insurance at May 31	480
Cash payments for insurance during June	$310

The beginning balance is deducted because it was paid in a prior accounting period. Note that the cash payments equal the expense plus the increase in the balance of the Prepaid Insurance account [$120 + ($670 − $480) = $310]. In this case, the cash paid was almost three times the amount of insurance expense. In future months, cash payments are likely to be less than the expense.

 Check out ACE for a Review Quiz at http://accounting.college.hmco.com/students.

Chapter Review

REVIEW OF LEARNING OBJECTIVES

LO1 Define *net income* and its two major components, *revenues* and *expenses.*

Net income is the net increase in owner's equity that results from the operations of a company. Net income equals revenues minus expenses, unless expenses exceed revenues, in which case a net loss results. Revenues equal the price of goods sold and services rendered during a specific period. Expenses are the costs of goods and services used up in the process of producing revenues.

LO2 Explain how the income measurement issues of accounting period, continuity, and matching are resolved.

The accounting period issue recognizes that net income measurements for short periods of time are necessarily tentative. The continuity issue recognizes that even though businesses face an uncertain future, without evidence to the contrary, accountants must assume that a business will continue indefinitely. The matching issue has to do with the difficulty of assigning revenues and expenses to a period of time. It is addressed by applying the matching rule: Revenues must be assigned to the accounting period in which the goods are sold or the services performed, and expenses must be assigned to the accounting period in which they are used to produce revenue.

LO3 Define *accrual accounting* and explain three broad ways of accomplishing it.

Accrual accounting consists of all the techniques developed by accountants to apply the matching rule. Three broad ways of accomplishing it are by recognizing revenues when earned, recognizing expenses when incurred, and adjusting the accounts.

LO4 State four principal situations that require adjusting entries and prepare typical adjusting entries.

Adjusting entries are required when (1) recorded costs have to be allocated between two or more accounting periods, (2) unrecorded expenses exist, (3) recorded unearned revenues must be allocated between two or more accounting periods, and (4) unrecorded revenues exist. The preparation of adjusting entries is summarized as follows:

Type of Adjusting Entry	Type of Account		Balance Sheet Account Examples
	Debited	Credited	
1. Allocating recorded costs (previously paid, expired)	Expense	Asset (or contra-asset)	Prepaid Rent Prepaid Insurance Supplies Accumulated Depreciation, Buildings Accumulated Depreciation, Equipment
2. Accrued expenses (incurred, not paid)	Expense	Liability	Wages Payable Interest Payable
3. Allocating recorded unearned revenues (previously received, earned)	Liability	Revenue	Unearned Fees
4. Accrued revenues (earned, not received)	Asset	Revenue	Accounts Receivable Interest Receivable

LO5 Prepare financial statements from an adjusted trial balance.

An adjusted trial balance is prepared after adjusting entries have been posted to the accounts. Its purpose is to test whether the adjusting entries are posted correctly before the financial statements are prepared. The income statement is prepared from the revenue and expense accounts in the adjusted trial balance. The balance sheet is prepared from the asset and liability accounts in the adjusted trial balance and from the statement of owner's equity.

SUPPLEMENTAL OBJECTIVE

SO6 Analyze cash flows from accrual-based information.

Cash flow information relates to management's liquidity goal. The general rule for determining the cash flow effect of any revenue or expense (except depreciation, which is a special case not covered here) is to determine the potential cash payments or cash receipts and deduct the amount not paid or received.

REVIEW OF CONCEPTS AND TERMINOLOGY

The following concepts and terms were introduced in this chapter:

LO2 **Accounting period issue:** The difficulty of assigning revenues and expenses to a short period of time.

LO4 **Accrual:** The recognition of an expense or revenue that has arisen but has not yet been recorded.

LO3 **Accrual accounting:** The attempt to record the financial effects of transactions and other events in the periods in which those transactions or events occur, rather than only in the periods in which cash is received or paid by the business; all the techniques developed by accountants to apply the matching rule.

LO4 **Accrued expenses:** Expenses incurred but not recognized in the accounts; unrecorded expenses.

LO4 **Accrued revenues:** Revenues for which a service has been performed or goods delivered but for which no entry has been made; unrecorded revenues.

LO4 **Accumulated depreciation accounts:** Contra-asset accounts used to accumulate the depreciation expense of specific long-lived assets.

LO5 **Adjusted trial balance:** A trial balance prepared after all adjusting entries have been recorded and posted to the accounts.

LO4 **Adjusting entries:** Entries made to apply accrual accounting to transactions that span more than one accounting period.

LO4 **Carrying value:** The unexpired portion of the cost of an asset. Also called *book value*.

LO2 **Cash basis of accounting:** Accounting for revenues and expenses on a cash received and cash paid basis.

LO2 **Continuity issue:** The difficulty associated with not knowing how long a business entity will survive.

LO4 **Contra account:** An account whose balance is subtracted from an associated account in the financial statements.

LO4 **Deferral:** The postponement of the recognition of an expense that already has been paid or of a revenue that already has been received.

LO4 **Depreciation:** The portion of the cost of a tangible long-term asset allocated to any one accounting period. Also called *depreciation expense*.

LO1 **Expenses:** Decreases in owner's equity resulting from the costs of goods and services used up in the course of earning revenues. Also called *cost of doing business* or *expired costs*.

LO2 **Fiscal year:** Any 12-month accounting period used by an economic entity.

LO2 **Going concern:** The assumption, unless there is evidence to the contrary, that a business entity will continue to operate indefinitely.

LO2 **Matching rule:** Revenues must be assigned to the accounting period in which the goods are sold or the services performed, and expenses must be assigned to the accounting period in which they are used to produce revenue.

LO1 **Net income:** The net increase in owner's equity that results from business operations and is accumulated in the owner's Capital account; revenues less expenses when revenues exceed expenses.

LO1 **Net loss:** The net decrease in owner's equity that results from business operations when expenses exceed revenues. It is accumulated in the owner's Capital account.

LO2 **Periodicity:** The recognition that net income for any period less than the life of the business, although tentative, is still a useful measure.

LO4 **Prepaid expenses:** Expenses paid in advance that have not yet expired; an asset account.

LO1 **Profit:** The increase in owner's equity that results from business operations.

LO3 **Revenue recognition:** In accrual accounting, the process of determining when revenue is earned.

LO1 **Revenues:** Increases in owner's equity resulting from selling goods, rendering services, or performing other business activities.

LO4 **Unearned revenues:** Revenues received in advance for which the goods have not yet been delivered or the services performed; a liability account.

REVIEW PROBLEM

Determining Adjusting Entries, Posting to T Accounts, Preparing Adjusted Trial Balance, and Preparing Financial Statements

LO4
LO5 The following is the unadjusted trial balance for Certified Answering Service on December 31, 20x5:

Certified Answering Service
Trial Balance
December 31, 20x5

Cash	$2,160	
Accounts Receivable	1,250	
Office Supplies	180	
Prepaid Insurance	240	
Office Equipment	3,400	
Accumulated Depreciation, Office Equipment		$ 600
Accounts Payable		700
Unearned Revenue		460
James Neal, Capital		4,870
James Neal, Withdrawals	400	
Answering Service Revenue		2,900
Wages Expense	1,500	
Rent Expense	400	
	$9,530	$9,530

The following information is also available:

a. Insurance that expired during December amounted to $40.
b. Office supplies on hand at the end of December totaled $75.

c. Depreciation for the month of December totaled $100.
d. Accrued wages at the end of December totaled $120.
e. Revenues earned for services performed in December but not yet billed on December 31 totaled $300.
f. Revenues earned in December for services performed that were paid in advance totaled $160.

REQUIRED ▶
1. Prepare T accounts for the accounts in the trial balance and enter the balances.
2. Determine the required adjusting entries and record them directly to the T accounts. Open new T accounts as needed.
3. Prepare an adjusted trial balance.
4. Prepare an income statement, a statement of owner's equity, and a balance sheet for the month ended December 31, 20x5.

ANSWER TO REVIEW PROBLEM

1. T accounts set up and amounts from trial balance entered
2. Adjusting entries recorded

Cash
Bal. 2,160

Accounts Receivable
Bal. 1,250
(e) 300
Bal. 1,550

Office Supplies
Bal. 180 | (b) 105
Bal. 75

Prepaid Insurance
Bal. 240 | (a) 40
Bal. 200

Office Equipment
Bal. 3,400

Accumulated Depreciation, Office Equipment
Bal. 600
(c) 100
Bal. 700

Accounts Payable
Bal. 700

Unearned Revenue
(f) 160 | Bal. 460
Bal. 300

Wages Payable
(d) 120

James Neal, Capital
Bal. 4,870

James Neal, Withdrawals
Bal. 400

Answering Service Revenue
Bal. 2,900
(e) 300
(f) 160
Bal. 3,360

Wages Expense
Bal. 1,500
(d) 120
Bal. 1,620

Rent Expense
Bal. 400

Insurance Expense
(a) 40

Office Supplies Expense
(b) 105

Depreciation Expense, Office Equipment
(c) 100

3. Adjusted trial balance prepared

Certified Answering Service
Adjusted Trial Balance
December 31, 20x5

Cash	$ 2,160	
Accounts Receivable	1,550	
Office Supplies	75	
Prepaid Insurance	200	
Office Equipment	3,400	
Accumulated Depreciation, Office Equipment		$ 700
Accounts Payable		700
Unearned Revenue		300
Wages Payable		120
James Neal, Capital		4,870
James Neal, Withdrawals	400	
Answering Service Revenue		3,360
Wages Expense	1,620	
Rent Expense	400	
Insurance Expense	40	
Office Supplies Expense	105	
Depreciation Expense, Office Equipment	100	
	$10,050	$10,050

4. Financial statements prepared

Certified Answering Service
Income Statement
For the Month Ended December 31, 20x5

Revenues

Answering service revenue		$3,360
Expenses		
Wages expense	$1,620	
Rent expense	400	
Insurance expense	40	
Office supplies expense	105	
Depreciation expense, office equipment	100	
Total expenses		2,265
Net income		$1,095

Financial statements prepared (*continued*)

Certified Answering Service
Statement of Owner's Equity
For the Month Ended December 31, 20x5

James Neal, Capital, November 30, 20x5	$4,870
Net income	1,095
Subtotal	$5,965
Less withdrawals	400
James Neal, Capital, December 31, 20x5	$5,565

Financial statements prepared (*continued*)

Certified Answering Service
Balance Sheet
December 31, 20x5

Assets

Cash		$2,160
Accounts receivable		1,550
Office supplies		75
Prepaid insurance		200
Office equipment	$3,400	
Less accumulated depreciation	700	2,700
Total assets		$6,685

Liabilities

Accounts payable	$ 700
Unearned revenue	300
Wages payable	120
Total liabilities	$1,120

Owner's Equity

James Neal, Capital	5,565
Total liabilities and owner's equity	$6,685

Advance. On December 31, 20x3, the end of the company's fiscal year, the balance of this account was $1,000,000. Expiration of subscriptions revenue is as follows:

During 20x3 $200,000
During 20x4   500,000
During 20x5   300,000

Prepare the adjusting entry in journal form for December 31, 20x3.

E 4.

LO4 Adjusting Entries for Prepaid Insurance

An examination of the Prepaid Insurance account shows a balance of $4,112 at the end of an accounting period, before adjustment. Prepare entries in journal form to record the insurance expense for the period under the following independent assumptions:

1. An examination of the insurance policies shows unexpired insurance that cost $1,974 at the end of the period.
2. An examination of the insurance policies shows that insurance that cost $694 has expired during the period.

E 5.

LO4 Supplies Account: Missing Data

Each of the following columns represents a Supplies account:

	a	b	c	d
Supplies on hand, October 1	$396	$ 651	$294	$?
Supplies purchased during the month	78	?	261	2,892
Supplies consumed during the month	291	1,458	?	2,448
Supplies on hand, October 31	?	654	84	1,782

1. Determine the amounts indicated by the question marks.
2. Make the adjusting entry for column **a**, assuming supplies purchased are debited to an asset account.

E 6.

LO4 Adjusting Entry for Accrued Salaries

Hasterson has a five-day work week and pays salaries of $70,000 each Friday.

1. Make the adjusting entry required on July 31, assuming that August 1 falls on a Wednesday.
2. Make the entry to pay the salaries on August 3.

E 7.

LO4 Revenue and Expense Recognition

Swan Company produces computer software that is sold by Celestial Systems Company. Swan receives a royalty of 15 percent of sales. Royalties are paid by Celestial Systems and received by Swan semiannually on May 1 for sales made July through December of the previous year and on November 1 for sales made January through June of the current year. Royalty expense for Celestial Systems and royalty income for Swan in the amount of $12,000 were accrued on December 31, 20x2. Cash in the amounts of $12,000 and $20,000 was paid and received on May 1 and November 1, 20x3, respectively. Software sales during the July to December 20x3 period totaled $300,000.

1. Calculate the amount of royalty expense for Celestial Systems and royalty income for Swan during 20x3.
2. Record the appropriate adjusting entry made by each company on December 31, 20x3.

E 8.

LO4 Adjusting Entries

Prepare year-end adjusting entries for each of the following:

1. Office Supplies had a balance of $168 on January 1. Purchases debited to Office Supplies during the year amount to $830. A year-end inventory reveals supplies of $570 on hand.
2. Depreciation of office equipment is estimated to be $4,260 for the year.
3. Property taxes for six months, estimated at $1,750, have accrued but have not been recorded.
4. Unrecorded interest receivable on U.S. government bonds is $1,700.
5. Unearned Revenue has a balance of $1,800. Services for $600 received in advance have now been performed.
6. Services totaling $400 have been performed; the customer has not yet been billed.

E 9.

LO4 Accounting for Revenue Received in Advance

Hiski Jurgen, a lawyer, was paid $72,000 on April 1 to represent a client in certain real estate negotiations over the next 12 months.

1. Record the entries required in Jurgen's records on April 1 and at the end of the year, December 31.
2. How would this transaction be reflected on the income statement and balance sheet on December 31?

E 10.

LO5 Preparation of Financial Statements

Prepare the monthly income statement, statement of owner's equity, and balance sheet for Sparkle Bright Services from the data provided in this adjusted trial balance.

Sparkle Bright Services
Adjusted Trial Balance
August 31, 20xx

Cash	$ 4,590	
Accounts Receivable	2,592	
Prepaid Insurance	380	
Prepaid Rent	200	
Cleaning Supplies	152	
Cleaning Equipment	3,200	
Accumulated Depreciation, Cleaning Equipment		$ 320
Truck	7,200	
Accumulated Depreciation, Truck		720
Accounts Payable		420
Wages Payable		80
Unearned Janitorial Revenue		920
Jim Harrington, Capital		15,034
Jim Harrington, Withdrawals	2,000	
Janitorial Revenue		14,620
Wages Expense	5,680	
Rent Expense	1,200	
Gas, Oil, and Other Truck Expenses	580	
Insurance Expense	380	
Supplies Expense	2,920	
Depreciation Expense, Cleaning Equipment	320	
Depreciation Expense, Truck	720	
	$32,114	$32,114

E 11.

SO6 Determination of Cash Flows

After adjusting entries had been made, the 20x4 and 20x5 balance sheets of Akbar Company showed the following asset and liability amounts at the end of each year:

	20x4	20x5
Prepaid insurance	$1,450	$1,200
Wages payable	1,100	600
Unearned fees	950	2,100

From the accounting records, the following amounts of cash disbursements and cash receipts for 20x5 were determined:

Cash disbursed to pay insurance premiums	$1,900
Cash disbursed to pay wages	9,750
Cash received for fees	4,450

Calculate the amount of insurance expense, wages expense, and fees earned that should be reported on the 20x5 income statement.

E 12.

SO6 Determination of Cash Flows

Sun Newspaper Agency delivers morning, evening, and Sunday city newspapers to subscribers who live in the suburbs. Customers can pay a yearly subscription fee in advance (at a savings) or pay monthly after delivery of their newspapers. The following data are available for the Subscriptions Receivable and Unearned Subscriptions accounts at the beginning and end of October 20xx

	October 1	October 31
Subscriptions Receivable	$ 7,600	$ 9,200
Unearned Subscriptions	22,800	19,600

The income statement shows subscriptions revenue for October of $44,800. Determine the amount of cash received from customers for subscriptions during October. Why is this calculation important to management?

E 13.

SO6 Relationship of Expenses to Cash Paid

The income statement for Gemini Company included the following expenses for 20xx:

Rent expense	$ 5,200
Interest expense	7,800
Salaries expense	83,000

Listed below are the related balance sheet account balances at year end for last year and this year:

	Last Year	This Year
Prepaid rent	—	$ 900
Interest payable	$1,200	—
Salaries payable	5,000	9,600

1. Compute the cash paid for rent during the year.
2. Compute the cash paid for interest during the year.
3. Compute the cash paid for salaries during the year.

PROBLEMS

P 1.

LO4 Determining Adjustments

At the end of its fiscal year, the trial balance for Desabrais Cleaners appears as follows:

Desabrais Cleaners
Trial Balance
September 30, 20x4

Cash	$ 11,788	
Accounts Receivable	26,494	
Prepaid Insurance	3,400	
Cleaning Supplies	7,374	
Land	18,000	
Building	185,000	
Accumulated Depreciation, Building		$ 45,600
Accounts Payable		20,400
Unearned Dry Cleaning Revenue		1,600
Mortgage Payable		110,000
Lucille Desabrais, Capital		56,560
Lucille Desabrais, Withdrawals	10,000	
Dry Cleaning Revenue		120,334
Laundry Revenue		37,300
Wages Expense	101,330	
Cleaning Equipment Rental Expense	6,000	
Telephone Expense	4,374	
Interest Expense	11,000	
Other Expenses	7,034	
	$391,794	$391,794

The following information is also available:

a. A study of the company's insurance policies shows that $680 is unexpired at the end of the year.

b. An inventory of cleaning supplies shows $1,244 on hand.

c. Estimated depreciation on the building for the year is $12,800.

d. Accrued interest on the mortgage payable amounts to $1,000.

e. On September 1, the company signed a contract, effective immediately, with Kings County Hospital to dry clean, for a fixed monthly charge of $400, the uniforms used by doctors in surgery. The hospital paid for four months' service in advance.

f. Sales and delivery wages are paid on Saturday. The weekly payroll is $2,520. September 30 falls on a Thursday and the company has a six-day pay week.

REQUIRED ▶ All adjustments affect one balance sheet account and one income statement account. For each of the above situations, show the accounts affected, the amount of the adjustment (using a + or − to indicate an increase or decrease), and the balance of the account after the adjustment in the following format:

Balance Sheet Account	Amount of Adjustment (+ or −)	Balance after Adjustment	Income Statement Account	Amount of Adjustment (+ or −)	Balance after Adjustment

P 2.
LO3
LO4
Preparing Adjusting Entries

On June 30, the end of the current fiscal year, the following information was available to aid the Worcester Company's accountants in making adjusting entries:

a. Among the liabilities of the company is a mortgage payable in the amount of $240,000. On June 30, the accrued interest on this mortgage amounted to $12,000.

b. On Friday, July 2, the company, which is on a five-day workweek and pays employees weekly, will pay its regular salaried employees $19,200.

c. On June 29, the company completed negotiations and signed a contract to provide services to a new client at an annual rate of $3,600.

d. The Supplies account showed a beginning balance of $1,615 and purchases during the year of $3,766. The end-of-year inventory revealed supplies on hand of $1,186.

e. The Prepaid Insurance account showed the following entries on June 30:

Beginning Balance $1,530
January 1 2,900
May 1 3,366

The beginning balance represents the unexpired portion of a one-year policy purchased the previous year. The January 1 entry represents a new one-year policy, and the May 1 entry represents the additional coverage of a three-year policy.

f. The following table contains the cost and annual depreciation for buildings and equipment, all of which were purchased before the current year:

Account	Cost	Annual Depreciation
Buildings	$185,000	$ 7,300
Equipment	218,000	21,800

g. On June 1, the company completed negotiations with another client and accepted a payment of $21,000, representing one year's services paid in advance. The $21,000 was credited to Services Collected in Advance.

h. The company calculated that as of June 30 it had earned $3,500 on a $7,500 contract that will be completed and billed in August.

REQUIRED ▶
1. Prepare adjusting entries for each item listed above.
2. Explain how the conditions for revenue recognition are applied to transactions **c** and **h**.

P 3.
LO4
Determining Adjusting Entries, Posting to T Accounts, and Preparing an Adjusted Trial Balance

The trial balance for the Omega Advisory Company on March 31, 20x4, appears at the top of the next page.

The following information is also available:

a. Ending inventory of office supplies, $172.
b. Prepaid rent expired, $1,400.
c. Depreciation of office equipment for the period, $1,200.
d. Interest accrued on the note payable, $1,200.
e. Salaries accrued at the end of the period, $400.
f. Fees still unearned at the end of the period, $2,820.
g. Fees earned but not billed, $1,200.

REQUIRED ▶
1. Open T accounts for the accounts in the trial balance plus the following: Interest Payable; Salaries Payable; Office Supplies Expense; Depreciation Expense, Office Equipment; and Interest Expense. Enter the balances shown on the trial balance.

Omega Advisory Company
Trial Balance
March 31, 20x4

Cash	$25,572	
Accounts Receivable	49,680	
Office Supplies	1,982	
Prepaid Rent	2,800	
Office Equipment	13,400	
Accumulated Depreciation, Office Equipment		$ 3,200
Accounts Payable		3,640
Notes Payable		20,000
Unearned Service Revenue		5,720
James Georgios, Capital		58,774
James Georgios, Withdrawals	30,000	
Service Revenue		117,000
Salaries Expense	66,000	
Utilities Expense	3,500	
Rent Expense	15,400	
	$208,334	$208,334

2. Determine the adjusting entries and post them directly to the T accounts.
3. Prepare an adjusted trial balance.

P 4.

LO4 **Determining Adjusting Entries**
LO5 **and Tracing Their Effects to**
Financial Statements

Here is the trial balance for Broadway Dance Studio at the end of its current fiscal year.

Broadway Dance Studio
Trial Balance
October 31, 20x4

Cash (111)	$ 1,028	
Accounts Receivable (112)	517	
Supplies (115)	170	
Prepaid Rent (116)	400	
Prepaid Insurance (117)	360	
Equipment (141)	4,100	
Accumulated Depreciation, Equipment (142)		$ 400
Accounts Payable (211)		380
Unearned Dance Fees (213)		900
Margrit Berger, Capital (311)		2,500
Margrit Berger, Withdrawals (312)	12,000	
Dance Fees (411)		20,995
Wages Expense (511)	3,200	
Rent Expense (512)	2,200	
Utilities Expense (515)	1,200	
	$25,175	$25,175

Margrit Berger made no investments in the business during the year. The following information is available to assist in the preparation of adjusting entries:

a. An inventory of supplies reveals $92 still on hand.

b. The prepaid rent reflects the rent for October plus the rent for the last month of the lease.
c. Prepaid insurance consists of a two-year policy purchased on May 1, 20x4.
d. Depreciation on equipment is estimated at $800.
e. Accrued wages are $65 on October 31.
f. Two-thirds of the unearned dance fees have been earned by October 31.

REQUIRED ▶
1. Record the adjusting entries in the general journal (Page 53).
2. Open ledger accounts for the accounts in the trial balance plus the following: Wages Payable (212); Supplies Expense (513); Insurance Expense (514); and Depreciation Expense, Equipment (516). Record the balances shown on the trial balance.
3. Post the adjusting entries from the general journal to the ledger accounts, showing the correct references.
4. Prepare an adjusted trial balance, an income statement, a statement of owner's equity, and a balance sheet.

P 5.
LO4 Determining Adjusting Entries
LO5 and Tracing Their Effects to Financial Statements

Having graduated from college with a degree in accounting, Bonnie Vitali opened a small tax-preparation service. At the end of its second year of operation, Vitali Tax Service had the trial balance shown below.

Vitali Tax Service
Trial Balance
December 31, 20x4

Cash	$ 2,268	
Accounts Receivable	1,031	
Prepaid Insurance	240	
Office Supplies	782	
Office Equipment	4,100	
Accumulated Depreciation, Office Equipment		$ 410
Copier	3,000	
Accumulated Depreciation, Copier		360
Accounts Payable		635
Unearned Service Revenue		219
Bonnie Vitali, Capital		5,439
Bonnie Vitali, Withdrawals	6,000	
Service Revenue		21,926
Office Salaries Expense	8,300	
Advertising Expense	650	
Rent Expense	2,400	
Telephone Expense	218	
	$28,989	$28,989

The following information was also available:

a. Office supplies on hand, December 31, 20x4, were $227.
b. Insurance still unexpired amounted to $120.
c. Estimated depreciation of office equipment was $410.
d. Estimated depreciation of the copier was $360.
e. The telephone expense for December was $19. Bill was received but not recorded.
f. The services for all unearned tax fees had been performed by the end of the year.

REQUIRED ▶
1. Open T accounts for the accounts in the trial balance plus the following: Insurance Expense; Office Supplies Expense; Depreciation Expense, Office Equipment; and Depreciation Expense, Copier. Record the balances shown in the trial balance.
2. Determine the adjusting entries and post them directly to the T accounts.
3. Prepare an adjusted trial balance, an income statement, a statement of owner's equity, and a balance sheet.

ALTERNATE PROBLEMS

P 6.

LO4   Determining Adjustments

At the end of the first three months of operation, the trial balance of Beacon County Answering Service appears as shown below. Ven Lien, the owner of Beacon County, has hired an accountant to prepare financial statements to determine how well the company is doing after three months. Upon examining the accounting records, the accountant finds the following items of interest:

a. An inventory of office supplies reveals supplies on hand of $133.
b. The Prepaid Rent account includes the rent for the first three months plus a deposit for April's rent.
c. Depreciation on the equipment for the first three months is $208.
d. The balance of the Unearned Answering Service Revenue account represents a 12-month service contract paid in advance on February 1.
e. On March 31, accrued wages total $80.

The balance of the Capital acccount represents investments by Ven Lien.

Beacon County Answering Service
Trial Balance
March 31, 20xx

Cash	$ 3,482	
Accounts Receivable	4,236	
Office Supplies	903	
Prepaid Rent	800	
Equipment	4,700	
Accounts Payable		$ 2,673
Unearned Answering Service Revenue		888
Ven Lien, Capital		5,933
Ven Lien, Withdrawals	2,130	
Answering Service Revenue		9,002
Wages Expense	1,900	
Office Cleaning Expense	345	
	$18,496	$18,496

REQUIRED ▶ All adjustments affect one balance sheet account and one income statement account. For each of the above situations, show the accounts affected, the amount of the adjustment (using a + or − to indicate an increase or decrease), and the balance of the account after the adjustment in the following format.

Balance Sheet Account	Amount of Adjustment (+ or −)	Balance after Adjustment	Income Statement Account	Amount of Adjustment (+ or −)	Balance after Adjustment

P 7.

LO3   Preparing Adjusting Entries
LO4

On May 31, the end of the current fiscal year, the following information was available to help Lightfoot Company's accountants make adjusting entries:

a. The Supplies account showed a beginning balance of $4,348. Purchases of supplies during the year totaled $9,052. The end-of-year inventory revealed supplies on hand that cost $2,794.
b. The Prepaid Insurance account showed the following on May 31:

Beginning Balance	$ 7,160
February 1	8,400
April 1	14,544

The beginning balance represents the portion of a one-year policy that remained unexpired at the beginning of the current fiscal year. The February 1 entry represents a new one-year policy, and the April 1 entry represents additional coverage in the form of a three-year policy.

c. The following table contains the cost and annual depreciation for buildings and equipment, all of which were purchased before the current year:

Account	Cost	Annual Depreciation
Buildings	$572,000	$29,000
Equipment	748,000	79,800

d. On March 1, the company completed negotiations with a client and accepted payment of $33,600, which represented one year's services paid in advance. The $33,600 was credited to Unearned Service Revenue.

e. The company calculated that as of May 31, it had earned $8,000 on a $22,000 contract that will be completed and billed in September.

f. Among the liabilities of the company is a note payable in the amount of $600,000. On May 31, the accrued interest on this note amounted to $30,000.

g. On Saturday, June 2, the company, which is on a six-day workweek, will pay its regular salaried employees $24,600.

h. On May 29, the company completed negotiations and signed a contract to provide services to a new client at an annual rate of $35,000.

REQUIRED ▶

1. Prepare adjusting entries for each item listed above.
2. Explain how the conditions for revenue recognition are applied to transactions e and h.

P 8.

LO4   Determining Adjusting Entries, Posting to T Accounts, and Preparing an Adjusted Trial Balance

This is the trial balance for Wu's Transcription Services on December 31, 20x4:

Wu's Transcription Services
Trial Balance
December 31, 20x4

Cash	$ 16,500	
Accounts Receivable	8,250	
Office Supplies	2,662	
Prepaid Rent	1,320	
Office Equipment	9,240	
Accumulated Depreciation, Office Equipment		$ 1,540
Accounts Payable		5,940
Notes Payable		11,000
Unearned Service Revenue		2,970
Stephanie Wu, Capital		24,002
Stephanie Wu, Withdrawals	22,000	
Service Revenue		72,600
Salaries Expense	49,400	
Rent Expense	4,400	
Utilities Expense	4,280	
	$118,052	$118,052

The following information is also available:

a. Ending inventory of office supplies, $264.
b. Prepaid rent expired, $440.
c. Depreciation of office equipment for the period, $660.
d. Accrued interest expense at the end of the period, $550.
e. Accrued salaries at the end of the month, $330.
f. Fees still unearned at the end of the period, $1,166.
g. Fees earned but unrecorded, $2,200.

REQUIRED ▶

1. Open T accounts for the accounts in the trial balance plus the following: Interest Payable; Salaries Payable; Office Supplies Expense; Depreciation Expense, Office Equipment; and Interest Expense. Enter the account balances.
2. Determine the adjusting entries and post them directly to the T accounts.
3. Prepare an adjusted trial balance.

SKILLS DEVELOPMENT CASES

Conceptual Analysis

SD 1.

LO2   **Importance of Adjustments**
LO3
LO4

Never Flake Company, which operated in the northeastern part of the United States, provided a rust-prevention coating for the underside of new automobiles. The company advertised widely and offered its services through new car dealers. When a dealer sold a new car, the dealer's salesperson attempted to sell the rust-prevention coating as an option. The protective coating was supposed to make cars last longer in the severe northeastern winters. An important selling point was Never Flake's warranty, which stated that the company would repair any damage due to rust at no charge for as long as the buyer owned the car.

During the 1990s, Never Flake was very successful in generating enough cash to continue operations. But in 2001 the company suddenly declared bankruptcy. Company officials said that the firm had only $5.5 million in assets against liabilities of $32.9 million. Most of the liabilities represented potential claims under the company's lifetime warranty. It seemed that owners were keeping their cars longer now than previously. Therefore, more damage was being attributed to rust. Discuss what accounting decisions could have helped Never Flake to survive under these circumstances.

Group Activity: Divide the class into groups to discuss this case. Then debrief as a class by asking a person from each group to comment.

SD 2.

LO3   **Application of Accrual**
LO4   **Accounting**

The Lyric Opera of Chicago <www.lyricopera.com> is one of the largest and best-managed opera companies in the United States. Managing opera productions requires advance planning, including the development of scenery, costumes, and stage properties and the sale of tickets. To measure how well the company is operating in any given year, accrual accounting must be applied to these and other transactions. At year end, April 30, 2001, Lyric Opera's balance sheet showed Deferred Production Costs of $1,639,949 and Deferred Ticket Revenue of $19,100,781.[7] Be prepared to discuss what accounting policies and adjusting entries are applicable to these accounts. Why are they important to Lyric Opera's management?

Ethical Dilemma

SD 3.

LO2   **Importance of Adjustments**
LO3
LO4

Central Appliance Service Company has achieved fast growth in the St. Louis area by selling service contracts on large appliances, such as washers, dryers, and refrigerators. For a fee, Central Appliance agrees to provide all parts and labor on an appliance after the regular warranty runs out. For example, by paying a fee of $200, a person who buys a dishwasher can add two years (years 2 and 3) to the regular one-year (year 1) warranty on the appliance. In 2004, the company sold service contracts in the amount of $1.8 million, all of which applied to future years. Management wanted all the sales recorded as revenues in 2004, contending that the amount of the contracts could be determined and the cash had been received.

Discuss whether you agree with the logic of Central Appliance's management. How would you record the cash receipts? What assumptions do you think should be made? Would you consider it unethical to follow management's recommendation? Who might be hurt or helped by this action?

Research Activity

SD 4.

LO4   **Real-World Observation of**
       Business Activities

Choose a company with which you are familiar. Visit the company and observe its operations. For example, it can be where you work, where you eat, or where you buy things. Identify at least two sources of revenue for the company and six types of expenses. For each type of revenue and each type of expense, determine whether it is probable that an adjusting entry is required at the end of the accounting period and specify whether the adjusting entry is a deferred revenue, deferred expense, accrued revenue, or accrued expense.

Decision-Making Practice

SD 5.

LO1 **Adjusting Entries and**
LO4 **Performance Evaluation**

Ginny Baxter, the owner of a newsletter for managers of hotels and restaurants, has prepared the following condensed amounts from her company's financial statements for 20x3:

Revenues	$346,000
Expenses	282,000
Net income	$ 64,000
Total assets	$172,000
Liabilities	$ 48,000
Owner's equity	124,000
Total liabilities and owner's equity	$172,000

Given these figures, Baxter is planning to withdraw $50,000 for personal expenses. However, Baxter's accountant has found that the following items were overlooked:

a. Although the balance of the Printing Supplies account is $32,000, only $14,000 in supplies is on hand at the end of the year.
b. Depreciation of $20,000 on equipment has not been recorded.
c. Wages of $9,400 have been earned by Baxter's employees but not recognized in the accounts.
d. A liability account called Unearned Subscriptions has a balance of $16,200, although it has been determined that one-third of these subscriptions have been mailed to subscribers.

1. Prepare the necessary adjusting entries.
2. Recast the condensed financial statement figures after you have made the necessary adjustments.
3. Discuss the performance of Baxter's business after the adjustments have been made. (**Hint:** Compare net income to revenues (divide net income by revenues) and total assets (divide net income by total assets) before and after the adjustments.) Do you think that making the withdrawal is advisable?

FINANCIAL REPORTING AND ANALYSIS CASES

Interpreting Financial Reports

FRA 1.

LO2 **Analysis of an Asset Account**
LO4

The Walt Disney Company <www.disney.go.com> is engaged in the financing, production, and distribution of motion pictures and television programming. In Disney's annual report, the balance sheet contains an asset called Film and Television Costs. Film and Television Costs, which consist of the cost associated with producing films and television programs less the amount expensed, were $3,606,000,000. The statement of cash flows reveals that the amount of film and television costs expensed (amortized) during the year was $2,469,000,000. The amount spent for new film productions was $2,679,000,000.[8]

1. What are Film and Television Costs, and why would they be classified as an asset?
2. Prepare an entry in T account form to record the amount the company spent on new film and television production during the year (assume all expenditures are paid for in cash).
3. Prepare an adjusting entry in T account form to record the expense for film and television productions.
4. Suggest a method by which The Walt Disney Company might have determined the amount of the expense in **3** in accordance with the matching rule.

FRA 2.

LO4 **Identification of Accruals**

H.J. Heinz Company, <www.heinz.com>, a major food company, had a net income in 2001 of $478,012,000 and the following current liabilities at the end of 2001:[9]

Current Liabilities (in thousands):	2001
Short-term debt	$1,555,869
Portion of long-term debt due within one year	314,965
Accounts payable	962,497
Salaries and wages	54,036
Accrued marketing	146,138
Accrued restructuring costs	134,550
Other accrued liabilities	388,582
Income taxes	98,460
Total current liabilities	$3,655,097

1. Which of the current liabilities definitely arose as the result of an adjusting entry at the end of the year? Which ones may partially have arisen from an adjusting entry? Which ones probably did not arise from an adjusting entry?
2. What effect do adjustments that create new liabilities have on net income or loss? Based on your answer in **1**, what percentage of current liabilities was definitely the result of an adjusting entry? Assuming the adjusting entries for these items had not been performed, what would Heinz's net income or loss have been?

International Company

FRA 3.

LO2   **Account Identification and**
LO3   **Accrual Accounting**

Takashimaya Company, Ltd. <www.takashimaya.co.jp> is Japan's largest department store chain. An account on Takashimaya's balance sheet called Gift Certificates contains ¥41,657 million ($404 million).[10] Is this account an asset or a liability? What transaction gives rise to the account? How is this account an example of the application of accrual accounting? Explain the conceptual issues that must be resolved for an adjusting entry to be valid.

Toys "R" Us Annual Report

FRA 4.

LO4   **Analysis of Balance Sheet and**
        Adjusting Entries

Refer to the balance sheet in the Toys "R" Us <www.tru.com> annual report in the Supplement to Chapter 6. Examine the accounts listed in the current assets, property and equipment, and current liabilities sections. Which accounts are most likely to have had year-end adjusting entries? Describe the nature of the adjusting entries. For more information about the property and equipment section, refer to the notes to the consolidated financial statements.

Comparison Case: Toys "R" Us and Walgreen Co.

FRA 5.

LO1   **Depreciation Expense and**
LO2   **Estimates**
LO4

Depreciation expense is recorded by an adjusting entry and is one of the most important expenses for many companies. In the Supplement to Chapter 6, refer to the Summary of Significant Accounting Policies in the notes to the financial statements in the Toys "R" Us <www.tru.com> annual report and to Walgreens' <www.walgreens.com> financial statements to answer these questions:

1. Where is depreciation (and amortization) expense disclosed on the financial statements for each company? Note that depreciation expense is not listed on Walgreens' income statement. Does this mean it is not a factor in computing net income for the company? (Also, note that amortization expense is similar to depreciation expense and is often included with it.)
2. Determine the importance of depreciation and amortization expense to each company by dividing depreciation and amortization expense by net sales. Why do you think the percentages are small?
3. Each company has a statement on the "Use of Estimates" in its Summary of Significant Accounting Policies. Read these statements and tell how important estimates are to the determination of depreciation expense. What assumptions do accountants make that allow these estimates to be made?

Fingraph® Financial Analyst™

FRA 6.

LO2 **Income Measurement and**
LO4 **Adjustments**
SO6

FRA 6.

Choose a company from the list of Fingraph companies on the Needles Accounting Resource Center Web Site at http://accounting.college.hmco.com/students. Click on the company you selected to access the Microsoft Excel spreadsheet for that company. You will find the company's URL (Internet address) in the heading of the spreadsheet. Click on the URL for a link to the company's web site and annual report.

1. Identify the type of fiscal year that the company uses. Do you think the year end corresponds to the company's natural business year?
2. Find the company's balance sheet. From the asset accounts and liability accounts, find four examples of accounts that might have been related to an adjusting entry at the end of the year. For each example, tell whether it is a deferral or an accrual and suggest an income statement account that might be associated with it.
3. Find the summary of significant accounting policies that appears following the financial statements. In these policies, find examples of the application of going concern and accrual accounting. Explain your choices of examples.
4. Prepare a one-page executive summary that highlights what you have learned from parts 1, 2, and 3.

Internet Case

LO4 **Comparison of Accrued**
Expenses

FRA 7.

How important are accrued expenses? Randomly choose four different companies from the Needles Accounting Resource Center Web Site at http://accounting.college. hmco.com/students. Use the links to get to each company's web site and annual report. For each company, find the section of the balance sheet labeled "Current Liabilities" and identify the current liabilities that are accrued expenses (sometimes called *accrued liabilities*). More than one account may be involved. On a pad, write the information you find in four columns: name of company, total current liabilities, total accrued liabilities, and total accrued liabilities as a percentage of total current liabilities. Write a memorandum to your instructor listing the companies you chose, telling how you obtained their reports, reporting the data you have gathered in the form of a table, and stating a conclusion, with reasons, as to the importance of accrued expenses to the companies you studied. (**Hint:** Compute the average percentage of total accrued expenses for the four companies.)

Chapter 4 focuses on the preparation of closing entries and the completion of the accounting cycle.

Completing the Accounting Cycle

Learning Objectives

LO1 State all the steps in the accounting cycle.
LO2 Explain and prepare closing entries.
LO3 Prepare the post-closing trial balance.
LO4 Prepare reversing entries as appropriate.
LO5 Prepare and use a work sheet.

DECISION POINT

A USER'S FOCUS

Dell Computer Corporation <www.dell.com> Dell Computer Corporation is the world's largest computer company. As a company whose shares are publicly traded, Dell must prepare both annual and quarterly financial statements for its stockholders and file them with the Securities and Exchange Commission. Note the interim income statement from Dell's quarterly report that appears here.[1] It shows that Dell's net revenue (sales) for the three months ended November 1, 2002, was greater than that for the same period of the preceding year by almost $1.7 billion, and net income increased approximately 31 percent from $429,000,000 to $561,000,000 for the same period.

Whether required by law or not, the preparation of *interim financial statements* every quarter, or even every month, is a good idea for all businesses because such reports give management an ongoing view of a company's financial performance. What are the costs and time involved in preparing interim financial statements?

The preparation of interim financial statements throughout the year requires more effort than the preparation of a single set of financial statements for the entire year. Each time the financial statements are prepared, adjusting entries must be determined, prepared, and recorded. Also, the ledger accounts must be prepared to begin the next accounting period. These procedures are time-consuming and costly. However, the advantages of preparing interim financial statements, even when they are not required, usually outweigh the costs, because such statements give management timely information for making decisions that will improve operations. This

Why is it important for a large company like Dell Computer Corporation to prepare interim financial statements?

chapter explains the accounting information systems used to process data and prepare financial statements at the end of an accounting period, whether that period is a month, a quarter, or a year.

Financial Highlights: Interim Income Statement
(Unaudited—in millions)

	Three Months Ended	
	November 1, 2002	November 2, 2001
Net revenue	$9,144	$7,468
Cost of revenue	7,482	6,155
Gross margin	1,662	1,313
Operating expenses:		
Selling, general and administrative	787	662
Research, development and engineering	117	107
Total operating expenses	904	769
Operating income	758	544
Investment and other income (loss), net	44	51
Income before income taxes	802	595
Income tax provision	241	166
Net income	$ 561	$ 429

OVERVIEW OF THE ACCOUNTING CYCLE

LO1 State all the steps in the accounting cycle.

RELATED TEXT ASSIGNMENTS
Q: 1
SE: 1
P: 3
SD: 1, 3, 4, 5
FRA: 2, 3, 5

● **STOP AND THINK!**

Why is the accounting cycle called a "cycle"?

It is so called because its steps are repeated each accounting period. Step 1 of one period follows step 6 of the prior period. ■

KEY POINT: Steps 1 through 3 are carried out throughout the period, whereas steps 4 through 6 are carried out at the end of the period only.

The **accounting cycle** is a series of steps in the accounting system whose purpose is to measure business activities in the form of transactions and to transform these transactions into financial statements that will communicate useful information to decision makers. The steps in the accounting cycle, illustrated in Figure 1, are as follows:

1. *Analyze* business transactions from source documents.

2. *Record* the entries in the journal.

3. *Post* the entries to the ledger and prepare a trial balance.

4. *Adjust* the accounts and prepare an adjusted trial balance.

5. *Close* the accounts and prepare a post-closing trial balance.

6. *Prepare* financial statements.

You are already familiar with steps 1 through 4 and 6. Step 5 is covered in this chapter.

The order of these six steps can vary to some extent depending on the system in place. For instance, the financial statements (step 6) may be completed before the closing entries are prepared (step 5). In fact, in a computerized system, step 6 usually must be performed before step 5. The important point is that all these steps must be accomplished to complete the accounting cycle. At key points in the accounting cycle, trial balances are prepared to ensure that the ledger remains in balance.

 Check out ACE for a Review Quiz at http://accounting.college.hmco.com/students.

CLOSING ENTRIES

LO2 Explain and prepare closing entries.

RELATED TEXT ASSIGNMENTS
Q: 2, 3, 4, 5
SE: 2, 3, 4, 5, 6, 9
E: 1, 8
P: 1, 2, 3, 4, 5, 6, 7, 8
SD: 4, 5
FRA: 1, 2, 4

● **STOP AND THINK!**

Could closing entries be done without using the Income Summary account?

Since the Income Summary account is used to accumulate a balance (steps 1 and 2) that is subsequently transferred to Capital (step 3), it would be possible to eliminate the use of the Income Summary account by closing the accounts in steps 1 and 2 directly to the Capital account and eliminating step 3. ■

Balance sheet accounts are considered **permanent accounts**, or *real accounts*, because they carry their end-of-period balances into the next accounting period. On the other hand, revenue and expense accounts are considered **temporary accounts**, or *nominal accounts*, because they begin each accounting period with a zero balance, accumulate a balance during the period, and are then cleared by means of closing entries.

Closing entries are journal entries made at the end of an accounting period. They have two purposes. First, closing entries set the stage for the next accounting period by clearing revenue, expense, and withdrawal accounts of their balances. Remember that the income statement reports net income (or loss) for a single accounting period and shows revenues and expenses for that period only. For the income statement to present the activity of a single accounting period, the revenue and expense accounts must begin each new period with zero balances. The zero balances are obtained by using closing entries to clear the balances in the revenue and expense accounts at the end of each accounting period. The Withdrawals account is closed in a similar manner.

Second, closing entries summarize a period's revenues and expenses. This is done by transferring the balances of revenue and expense accounts to the **Income Summary** account. This temporary account, which appears in the chart of accounts between the Withdrawals account and the first revenue account, provides a place to summarize all revenues and expenses. It is used only in the closing process and never appears in the financial statements.

FIGURE 1
Overview of the Accounting Cycle

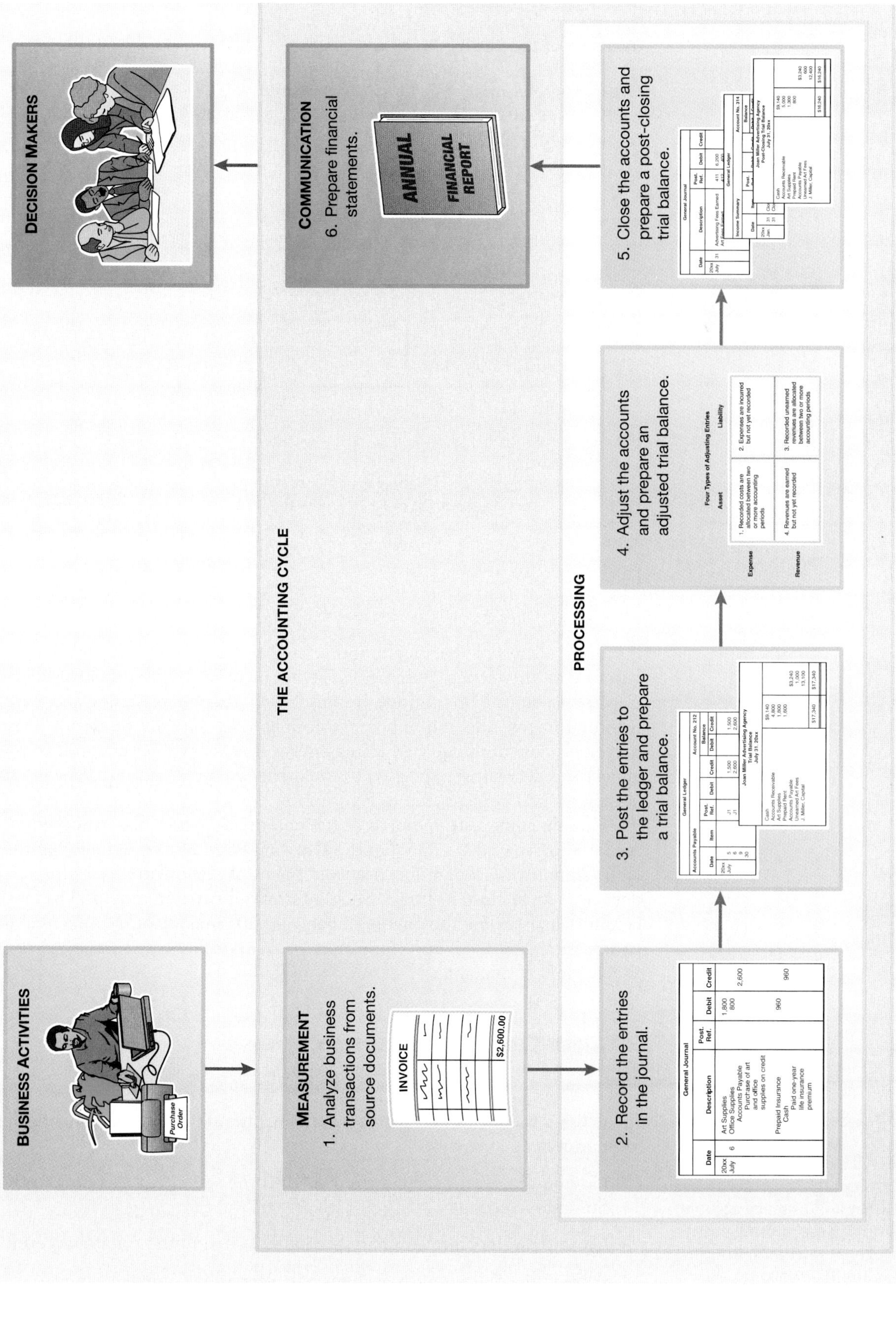

FIGURE 2
Overview of the Closing Process

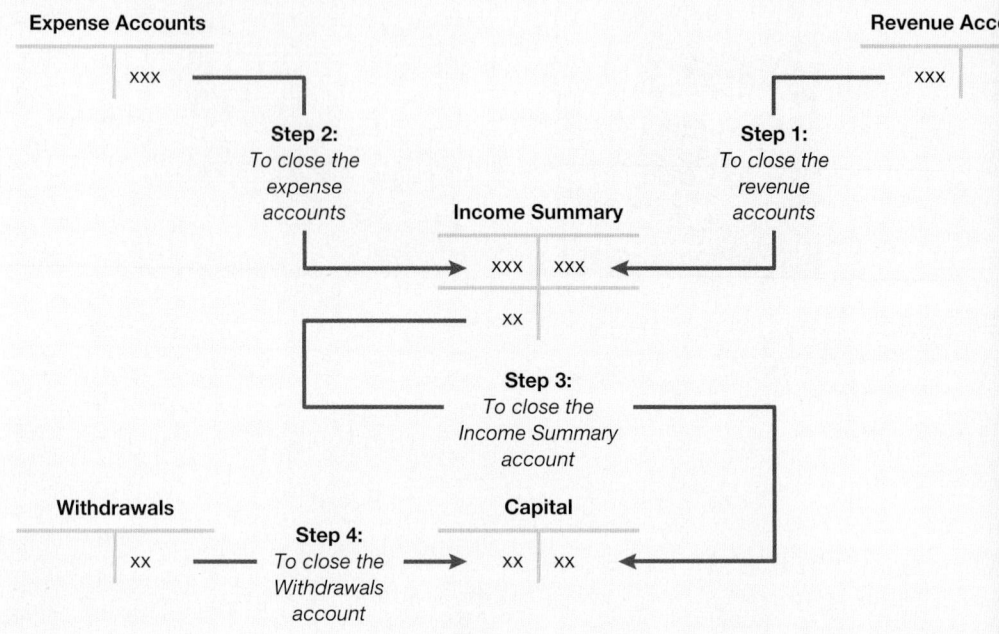

The balance of the Income Summary account equals the net income or loss reported on the income statement. The net income or loss is then transferred to the Capital account. This is done because even though revenues and expenses are recorded in revenue and expense accounts, they actually represent increases and decreases in owner's equity. Closing entries transfer the net effect of increases (revenues) and decreases (expenses) to the owner's capital account. An overview of the closing process is illustrated in Figure 2.

Closing entries are required at the end of any period for which financial statements are prepared. As noted in the Decision Point at the beginning of the chapter, Dell Computer Corporation prepares financial statements each quarter; when it does so, it must close its books. Such interim information is helpful to investors and creditors in assessing the ongoing financial performance of a company. Many companies, including Dell, also close their books monthly to give management a more timely view of ongoing operations.

www.dell.com

REQUIRED CLOSING ENTRIES

There are four important steps in closing the accounts:

1. Closing the credit balances from the income statement accounts to the Income Summary account

2. Closing the debit balances from the income statement accounts to the Income Summary account

3. Closing the Income Summary account balance to the Capital account

4. Closing the Withdrawals account balance to the Capital account

ENRICHMENT NOTE: It is not absolutely necessary to use the Income Summary account when preparing closing entries. However, it does simplify the procedure. The Income Summary account is opened and closed with the preparation of closing entries.

Each step is accomplished by a closing entry. All the data needed to record the closing entries are found in the adjusted trial balance.

EXHIBIT 1
Preparing Closing Entries from the Adjusted Trial Balance

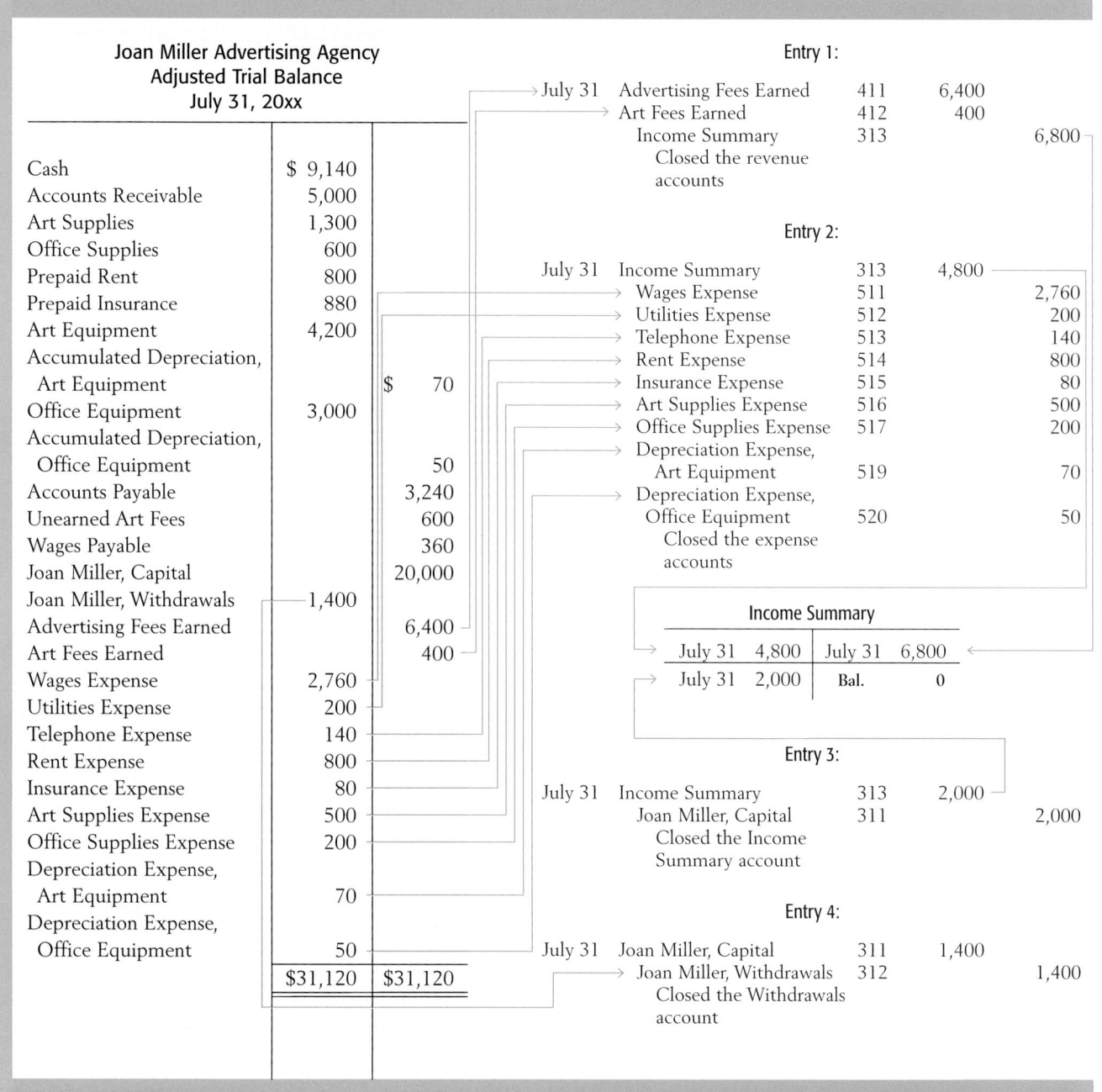

The relationships of the four kinds of entries to the adjusted trial balance are shown in Exhibit 1.

■ **STEP 1: CLOSING THE CREDIT BALANCES FROM INCOME STATEMENT ACCOUNTS TO THE INCOME SUMMARY ACCOUNT** On the credit side of the adjusted trial balance in Exhibit 1, two revenue accounts show balances: Advertising Fees Earned and Art Fees Earned. To close these two accounts, an entry must be made debiting each

Exhibit 2

Posting the Closing Entry of the Credit Balances from the Income Statement Accounts to the Income Summary Account

Advertising Fees Earned   Account No. 411

Date	Item	Post. Ref.	Debit	Credit	Balance Debit	Balance Credit
July 10		J2		1,400		1,400
19		J2		4,800		6,200
31	Adj. (j)	J3		200		6,400
31	Closing	J4	6,400			—

Art Fees Earned   Account No. 412

Date	Item	Post. Ref.	Debit	Credit	Balance Debit	Balance Credit
July 31	Adj. (i)	J3		400		400
31	Closing	J4	400			—

```
          6,400
            400
          6,800
```

Income Summary   Account No. 313

Date	Item	Post. Ref.	Debit	Credit	Balance Debit	Balance Credit
July 31	Closing	J4		6,800		6,800

KEY POINT: The Income Summary account now reflects the account balances that the revenue accounts contained before they were closed.

account in the amount of its balance and crediting the total to the Income Summary account. The effect of posting the entry is illustrated in Exhibit 2. Notice that the entry (1) sets the balances of the revenue accounts to zero and (2) transfers the total revenues to the credit side of the Income Summary account.

■ **Step 2: Closing the Debit Balances from Income Statement Accounts to the Income Summary Account**   Several expense accounts show balances on the debit side of the adjusted trial balance in Exhibit 1. A compound entry is needed to credit each of these expense accounts for its balance and to debit the Income Summary account for the total. The effect of posting the closing entry is shown in Exhibit 3. Notice how the entry (1) reduces the expense account balances to zero and (2) transfers the total of the account balances to the debit side of the Income Summary account.

EXHIBIT 3

Posting the Closing Entry of the Debit Balances from the Income Statement Accounts to the Income Summary Account

Wages Expense — Account No. 511

Date	Item	Post. Ref.	Debit	Credit	Balance Debit	Balance Credit
July 12		J2	1,200		1,200	
26		J2	1,200		2,400	
31	Adj. (g)	J3	360		2,760	
31	Closing	J4		2,760	—	

Utilities Expense — Account No. 512

Date	Item	Post. Ref.	Debit	Credit	Balance Debit	Balance Credit
July 29		J2	200		200	
31	Closing	J4		200	—	

Telephone Expense — Account No. 513

Date	Item	Post. Ref.	Debit	Credit	Balance Debit	Balance Credit
July 30		J2	140		140	
31	Closing	J4		140	—	

Rent Expense — Account No. 514

Date	Item	Post. Ref.	Debit	Credit	Balance Debit	Balance Credit
July 31	Adj. (a)	J3	800		800	
31	Closing	J4		800	—	

Insurance Expense — Account No. 515

Date	Item	Post. Ref.	Debit	Credit	Balance Debit	Balance Credit
July 31	Adj. (b)	J3	80		80	
31	Closing	J4		80	—	

Art Supplies Expense — Account No. 516

Date	Item	Post. Ref.	Debit	Credit	Balance Debit	Balance Credit
July 31	Adj. (c)	J3	500		500	
31	Closing	J4		500	—	

Office Supplies Expense — Account No. 517

Date	Item	Post. Ref.	Debit	Credit	Balance Debit	Balance Credit
July 31	Adj. (d)	J3	200		200	
31	Closing	J4		200	—	

Income Summary — Account No. 313

Date	Item	Post. Ref.	Debit	Credit	Balance Debit	Balance Credit
July 31	Closing	J4		6,800		6,800
31	Closing	J4	4,800			2,000

2,760
200
140
800
80
500
200
50
70
4,800

Depreciation Expense, Art Equipment — Account No. 519

Date	Item	Post. Ref.	Debit	Credit	Balance Debit	Balance Credit
July 31	Adj. (e)	J3	70		70	
31	Closing	J4		70	—	

Depreciation Expense, Office Equipment — Account No. 520

Date	Item	Post. Ref.	Debit	Credit	Balance Debit	Balance Credit
July 31	Adj. (f)	J3	50		50	
31	Closing	J4		50	—	

KEY POINT: The credit balance of the Income Summary account at this point ($2,000) represents the key performance measure of net income.

■ **STEP 3: CLOSING THE INCOME SUMMARY ACCOUNT BALANCE TO THE CAPITAL ACCOUNT**

After the entries closing the revenue and expense accounts have been posted, the balance of the Income Summary account equals the net income or loss for the period. Since revenues are represented by the credit to Income Summary and expenses are represented by the debit to Income Summary, a net income is indicated by a credit balance (where revenues exceed expenses) and a net loss by a

EXHIBIT 4
Posting the Closing Entry of the Income Summary Account Balance to the Capital Account

Income Summary					Account No. 313		Joan Miller, Capital					Account No. 311	
		Post.			Balance				Post.			Balance	
Date	Item	Ref.	Debit	Credit	Debit	Credit	Date	Item	Ref.	Debit	Credit	Debit	Credit
July 31	Closing	J4		6,800		6,800	July 1		J1		20,000		20,000
31	Closing	J4	4,800			2,000	31	Closing	J4		2,000		22,000
31	Closing	J4	2,000			—							

KEY POINT: In a net loss situation, debit the Capital account (to reduce it) and credit Income Summary (to close it).

CLARIFICATION NOTE: If a net loss has been incurred, the Income Summary account would contain a debit balance when the income statement accounts are closed to it.

debit balance (where expenses exceed revenues). At this point, the Income Summary account balance, whatever its nature, must be closed to the Capital account, as shown in Exhibit 1. The effect of posting the closing entry when the company has a net income is shown in Exhibit 4. Notice the dual effect of (1) closing the Income Summary account and (2) transferring the balance, net income in this case, to Joan Miller's Capital account.

■ **STEP 4: CLOSING THE WITHDRAWALS ACCOUNT BALANCE TO THE CAPITAL ACCOUNT**
The Withdrawals account shows the amount by which capital is reduced during the accounting period by withdrawals of cash or other assets from the business for the owner's personal use. The debit balance of the Withdrawals account is closed to the Capital account, as illustrated in Exhibit 1. The effect of this closing entry, as shown in Exhibit 5, is to (1) close the Withdrawals account and (2) transfer the balance to the Capital account.

THE ACCOUNTS AFTER CLOSING

STUDY NOTE: A good way to review is to examine each ledger account and determine where it fits (if at all) into the adjusting and closing procedures. The Cash account, for example, is never part of adjusting or closing entries.

After all the steps in the closing process have been completed and all closing entries have been posted to the accounts, everything is ready for the next accounting period. The ledger accounts of Joan Miller Advertising Agency, as they appear at this point, are shown in Exhibit 6. The revenue, expense, and Withdrawals accounts (temporary accounts) have zero balances. The Capital account has been increased to reflect the agency's net income and decreased for the owner's withdrawals. The balance sheet accounts (permanent accounts) show the correct balances, which are carried forward to the next period.

EXHIBIT 5
Posting the Closing Entry of the Withdrawals Account Balance to the Capital Account

Joan Miller, Withdrawals					Account No. 312		Joan Miller, Capital					Account No. 311	
		Post.			Balance				Post.			Balance	
Date	Item	Ref.	Debit	Credit	Debit	Credit	Date	Item	Ref.	Debit	Credit	Debit	Credit
July 31		J2	1,400		1,400		July 1		J1		20,000		20,000
31	Closing	J4		1,400	—		31	Closing	J4		2,000		22,000
							31	Closing	J4	1,400			20,600

EXHIBIT 6
The Accounts After Closing Entries Are Posted

Cash						Account No. 111
Date	Item	Post. Ref.	Debit	Credit	Balance Debit	Balance Credit
July 1		J1	20,000		20,000	
2		J1		1,600	18,400	
4		J1		4,200	14,200	
5		J1		1,500	12,700	
8		J1		960	11,740	
9		J1		1,000	10,740	
10		J2	1,400		12,140	
12		J2		1,200	10,940	
15		J2	1,000		11,940	
26		J2		1,200	10,740	
29		J2		200	10,540	
31		J2		1,400	9,140	

Accounts Receivable						Account No. 113
Date	Item	Post. Ref.	Debit	Credit	Balance Debit	Balance Credit
July 19		J2	4,800		4,800	
31	Adj. (i)	J3	200		5,000	

Art Supplies						Account No. 115
Date	Item	Post. Ref.	Debit	Credit	Balance Debit	Balance Credit
July 6		J1	1,800		1,800	
31	Adj. (c)	J3		500	1,300	

Office Supplies						Account No. 116
Date	Item	Post. Ref.	Debit	Credit	Balance Debit	Balance Credit
July 6		J1	800		800	
31	Adj. (d)	J3		200	600	

Prepaid Rent						Account No. 117
Date	Item	Post. Ref.	Debit	Credit	Balance Debit	Balance Credit
July 2		J1	1,600		1,600	
31	Adj. (a)	J3		800	800	

Prepaid Insurance						Account No. 118
Date	Item	Post. Ref.	Debit	Credit	Balance Debit	Balance Credit
July 8		J1	960		960	
31	Adj. (b)	J3		80	880	

Art Equipment						Account No. 144
Date	Item	Post. Ref.	Debit	Credit	Balance Debit	Balance Credit
July 4		J1	4,200		4,200	

Accumulated Depreciation, Art Equipment						Account No. 145
Date	Item	Post. Ref.	Debit	Credit	Balance Debit	Balance Credit
July 31	Adj. (e)	J3		70		70

Office Equipment						Account No. 146
Date	Item	Post. Ref.	Debit	Credit	Balance Debit	Balance Credit
July 5		J1	3,000		3,000	

Accumulated Depreciation, Office Equipment						Account No. 147
Date	Item	Post. Ref.	Debit	Credit	Balance Debit	Balance Credit
July 31	Adj. (f)	J3		50		50

Accounts Payable						Account No. 212
Date	Item	Post. Ref.	Debit	Credit	Balance Debit	Balance Credit
July 5		J1		1,500		1,500
6		J1		2,600		4,100
9		J1	1,000			3,100
30		J2		140		3,240

Unearned Art Fees						Account No. 213
Date	Item	Post. Ref.	Debit	Credit	Balance Debit	Balance Credit
July 15		J2		1,000		1,000
31	Adj. (h)	J3	400			600

Wages Payable						Account No. 214
Date	Item	Post. Ref.	Debit	Credit	Balance Debit	Balance Credit
July 31	Adj. (g)	J3		360		360

(continued)

EXHIBIT 6
The Accounts After Closing Entries Are Posted *(continued)*

Joan Miller, Capital — Account No. 311

Date	Item	Post. Ref.	Debit	Credit	Balance Debit	Balance Credit
July 1		J1		20,000		20,000
31	Closing	J4		2,000		22,000
31	Closing	J4	1,400			20,600

Joan Miller, Withdrawals — Account No. 312

Date	Item	Post. Ref.	Debit	Credit	Balance Debit	Balance Credit
July 31		J2	1,400		1,400	
31	Closing	J4		1,400	—	

Income Summary — Account No. 313

Date	Item	Post. Ref.	Debit	Credit	Balance Debit	Balance Credit
July 31	Closing	J4		6,800		6,800
31	Closing	J4	4,800			2,000
31	Closing	J4	2,000			—

Advertising Fees Earned — Account No. 411

Date	Item	Post. Ref.	Debit	Credit	Balance Debit	Balance Credit
July 10		J2		1,400		1,400
19		J2		4,800		6,200
31	Adj. (i)	J3		200		6,400
31	Closing	J4	6,400			—

Art Fees Earned — Account No. 412

Date	Item	Post. Ref.	Debit	Credit	Balance Debit	Balance Credit
July 31	Adj. (h)	J3		400		400
31	Closing	J4	400			—

Wages Expense — Account No. 511

Date	Item	Post. Ref.	Debit	Credit	Balance Debit	Balance Credit
July 12		J2	1,200		1,200	
26		J2	1,200		2,400	
31	Adj. (g)	J3	360		2,760	
31	Closing	J4		2,760	—	

Utilities Expense — Account No. 512

Date	Item	Post. Ref.	Debit	Credit	Balance Debit	Balance Credit
July 29		J2	200		200	
31	Closing	J4		200	—	

Telephone Expense — Account No. 513

Date	Item	Post. Ref.	Debit	Credit	Balance Debit	Balance Credit
July 30		J2	140		140	
31	Closing	J4		140	—	

Rent Expense — Account No. 514

Date	Item	Post. Ref.	Debit	Credit	Balance Debit	Balance Credit
July 31	Adj. (a)	J3	800		800	
31	Closing	J4		800	—	

Insurance Expense — Account No. 515

Date	Item	Post. Ref.	Debit	Credit	Balance Debit	Balance Credit
July 31	Adj. (b)	J3	80		80	
31	Closing	J4		80	—	

Art Supplies Expense — Account No. 516

Date	Item	Post. Ref.	Debit	Credit	Balance Debit	Balance Credit
July 31	Adj. (c)	J3	500		500	
31	Closing	J4		500	—	

Office Supplies Expense — Account No. 517

Date	Item	Post. Ref.	Debit	Credit	Balance Debit	Balance Credit
July 31	Adj. (d)	J3	200		200	
31	Closing	J4		200	—	

Depreciation Expense, Art Equipment — Account No. 519

Date	Item	Post. Ref.	Debit	Credit	Balance Debit	Balance Credit
July 31	Adj. (e)	J3	70		70	
31	Closing	J4		70	—	

Depreciation Expense, Office Equipment — Account No. 520

Date	Item	Post. Ref.	Debit	Credit	Balance Debit	Balance Credit
July 31	Adj. (f)	J3	50		50	
31	Closing	J4		50	—	

FOCUS ON INTERNATIONAL BUSINESS

Closing Doesn't Have to Be Such a Headache.

For companies with extensive international operations, like Caterpillar Inc. <www.caterpillar.com>, Dow Chemical <www.dow.com>, Phillips Petroleum <www.phillips66.com>, Gillette <www.gillette.com>, and Bristol-Myers Squibb <www.bms.com>, closing the records and preparing financial statements on a timely basis used to be a problem. It was common practice for foreign divisions of companies like these to end their fiscal year one month before the end of the fiscal year of their counterparts in the United States. This gave them the extra time they needed to perform closing procedures and mail the results back to U.S. headquarters to be used in preparation of the company's overall financial statements. Such an arrangement is usually unnecessary today because high-speed computers and electronic communications make it possible for companies to close records and prepare financial statements for both foreign and domestic operations in less than a week.

 Check out ACE for a Review Quiz at http://accounting.college.hmco.com/students.

THE POST-CLOSING TRIAL BALANCE

LO3 Prepare the post-closing trial balance.

RELATED TEXT ASSIGNMENTS
Q: 6, 7
P: 3
SD: 4

Because it is possible to make errors in posting the closing entries to the ledger accounts, it is necessary to determine that all temporary accounts have zero balances and to double-check that total debits equal total credits by preparing a new trial balance. This final trial balance, called the **post-closing trial balance**, is shown in Exhibit 7 for Joan Miller Advertising Agency. Notice that only the balance sheet accounts show balances because the income statement accounts and the Withdrawals account have all been closed.

EXHIBIT 7
Post-Closing Trial Balance

● **STOP AND THINK!**
Why does the post-closing trial balance contain only balance sheet accounts?
All the income statement, or temporary, accounts and the Withdrawals account have been closed, thus leaving only the balance sheet, or permanent, accounts to carry over to the next accounting period. ■

KEY POINT: Notice that Joan Miller, Capital now reflects the correct month-end balance, $20,600.

Joan Miller Advertising Agency
Post-Closing Trial Balance
July 31, 20xx

Cash	$ 9,140	
Accounts Receivable	5,000	
Art Supplies	1,300	
Office Supplies	600	
Prepaid Rent	800	
Prepaid Insurance	880	
Art Equipment	4,200	
Accumulated Depreciation, Art Equipment		$ 70
Office Equipment	3,000	
Accumulated Depreciation, Office Equipment		50
Accounts Payable		3,240
Unearned Art Fees		600
Wages Payable		360
Joan Miller, Capital		20,600
	$24,920	$24,920

 Check out ACE for a Review Quiz at http://accounting.college.hmco.com/students.

REVERSING ENTRIES: THE OPTIONAL FIRST STEP IN THE NEXT ACCOUNTING PERIOD

LO4 Prepare reversing entries as appropriate.

RELATED TEXT ASSIGNMENTS
Q: 8, 9
SE: 7, 8
E: 2, 7
P: 4, 5, 8
SD: 2, 4

KEY POINT: Reversing entries are the opposite of adjusting entries and are dated the first day of the new period. They apply only to certain adjusting entries and are never required.

A = L + OE
    +   –

A = L + OE
–   –   –

◆ **STOP AND THINK!**
Why are reversing entries helpful?

Reversing entries enable the bookkeeper to continue preparing routine entries early in the new period. (More complex entries are needed when reversing entries are not used.) ■

At the end of each accounting period, adjusting entries are made to bring revenues and expenses into conformity with the matching rule. A **reversing entry** is a general journal entry made on the first day of a new accounting period; it is the exact reverse of an adjusting entry made at the end of the previous accounting period. Reversing entries are optional. They simplify the bookkeeping process for transactions involving certain types of adjustments. Not all adjusting entries can be reversed. Under the recording system used in this book, only adjustments for accruals (accrued revenues and accrued expenses) are reversed. Deferrals should not be reversed because such reversals would not simplify the bookkeeping process in future accounting periods.

To see how reversing entries can be helpful, consider the adjusting entry made in the records of Joan Miller Advertising Agency to accrue wages expense:

July 31	Wages Expense	360	
	Wages Payable		360
	Accrued unrecorded wages		

When the secretary is paid on the next regular payday, the accountant would make this entry:

Aug. 9	Wages Payable	360	
	Wages Expense	840	
	Cash		1,200
	Paid two weeks'		
	wages to secretary, $360 of		
	which accrued in the		
	previous period		

Notice that when the payment is made, if there is no reversing entry, the accountant must look in the records to find out how much of the $1,200 applies to the current accounting period and how much is applicable to the previous period. This may seem easy in our example, but think how difficult and time-consuming it would be if a company had hundreds of employees working on different schedules. A reversing entry helps solve the problem of applying revenues and expenses to the correct accounting period. It is exactly what its name implies: a reversal made by debiting the credits and crediting the debits of a previously made adjusting entry.

For example, notice the following sequence of entries and their effects on the ledger account Wages Expense:

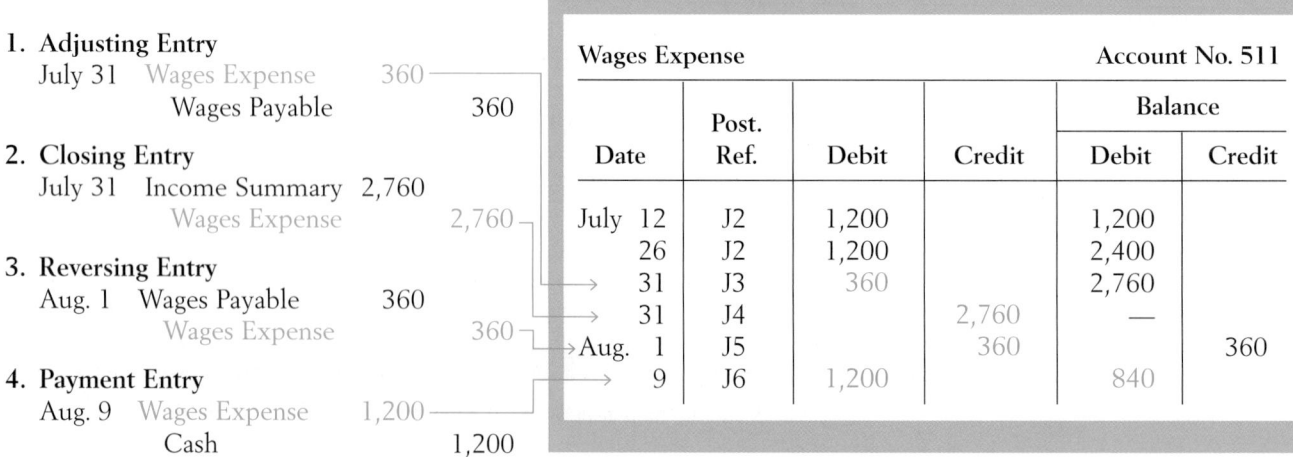

1. Adjusting Entry
July 31   Wages Expense   360
              Wages Payable   360

2. Closing Entry
July 31   Income Summary   2,760
              Wages Expense   2,760

3. Reversing Entry
Aug. 1   Wages Payable   360
              Wages Expense   360

4. Payment Entry
Aug. 9   Wages Expense   1,200
              Cash   1,200

Wages Expense				Account No. 511	
Date	Post. Ref.	Debit	Credit	Balance Debit	Balance Credit
July 12	J2	1,200		1,200	
26	J2	1,200		2,400	
31	J3	360		2,760	
31	J4		2,760	—	
Aug. 1	J5		360		360
9	J6	1,200		840	

Entry **1** adjusted Wages Expense to accrue $360 in the July accounting period.

Entry **2** closed the $2,760 in Wages Expense for July to Income Summary, leaving a zero balance.

KEY POINT: Notice the abnormal credit balance as of August 1. This situation is "corrected" with the August 9 entry, an entry the bookkeeper can easily make.

Entry **3,** the reversing entry, set up a credit balance of $360 on August 1 in Wages Expense, which is the expense recognized through the adjusting entry in July (and also reduced the liability account Wages Payable to a zero balance). The reversing entry always sets up an abnormal balance in the income statement account and produces a zero balance in the balance sheet account.

Entry **4** recorded the $1,200 payment of two weeks' wages as a debit to Wages Expense, automatically leaving a balance of $840, which represents the correct wages expense to date in August. The reversing entry simplified the process of making the payment entry on August 9.

Reversing entries apply to any accrued expenses or revenues. In the case of Joan Miller Advertising Agency, wages expense was the only accrued expense. The adjusting entry for accrued revenue (advertising fees earned) would require the following reversing entry:

A = L + OE
–   –

Aug. 1	Advertising Fees Earned	200	
	Accounts Receivable		200
	Reversed the adjusting entry for accrued fees earned		

When the series of advertisements is finished, the company can credit all the proceeds to Advertising Fees Earned without regard to the amount accrued in the previous period. The credit will automatically be reduced to the amount earned during August by the $200 debit in the account.

As noted earlier, under our system of recording, reversing entries apply only to accruals. They do not apply to deferrals, such as the entries that involve supplies, prepaid rent, prepaid insurance, depreciation, and unearned art fees.

 Check out ACE for a Review Quiz at http://accounting.college.hmco.com/students.

THE WORK SHEET: AN ACCOUNTANT'S TOOL

L05 Prepare and use a work sheet.

RELATED TEXT ASSIGNMENTS
Q: 10, 11, 12, 13, 14, 15, 16, 17, 18, 19
SE: 9
E: 3, 4, 5, 6, 7, 8
P: 4, 5, 8
SD: 4

Accountants must collect relevant data to determine what should be included in financial reports. For example, they must examine insurance policies to see how much prepaid insurance has expired, examine plant and equipment records to determine depreciation, take an inventory of supplies on hand, and calculate the amount of accrued wages. These calculations, along with other computations, analyses, and preliminary drafts of statements, make up the accountants' **working papers**.

Working papers are important for two reasons. First, they help accountants organize their work and thus avoid omitting important data or steps that affect the financial statements. The second reason is that they provide evidence of past work so that accountants or auditors can retrace their steps and support the information in the financial statements.

KEY POINT: The work sheet is extremely useful when an accountant must prepare numerous adjustments. It is not a financial statement, it is not required, and it is not made public.

The **work sheet** is a special kind of working paper. It is often used as a preliminary step in recording adjusting and closing entries and the preparation of financial statements. Using a work sheet lessens the possibility of leaving out an adjustment, helps the accountant check the arithmetical accuracy of the accounts, and facilitates the preparation of financial statements. The work sheet is never published and is rarely seen by management. It is a tool for the accountant. Because preparing a work sheet is a very mechanical process, many accountants use a microcomputer for this purpose. In some cases, accountants use a spreadsheet program to prepare the work sheet. In other cases, they use a general ledger system to prepare financial statements from the adjusted trial balance.

PREPARING THE WORK SHEET

So far, adjusting entries for Joan Miller Advertising Agency have been entered directly in the journal and posted to the ledger, and the financial statements have been prepared from the adjusted trial balance. The process has been relatively simple because of the small size of Joan Miller's company. For larger companies, which may require many adjusting entries, a work sheet is essential. To illustrate the preparation of the work sheet, we continue with our example of the Joan Miller Advertising Agency.

A common form of work sheet has one column for account names and/or numbers and ten more columns with the headings shown in Exhibit 8. Notice that the work sheet is identified by a heading that consists of the name of the company, the title "Work Sheet," and the period of time covered (as on the income statement).

Preparation of a work sheet involves the following five steps:

1. **Enter and total the account balances in the Trial Balance columns.** The titles and balances of the accounts as of July 31 are copied directly from the ledger into the Trial Balance columns, as shown in Exhibit 8. When accountants use a work sheet, they do not have to prepare a separate trial balance.

2. **Enter and total the adjustments in the Adjustments columns.** The required adjustments are entered in the Adjustments columns of the work sheet, as shown in Exhibit 9. As each adjustment is entered, a letter is used to identify its debit and credit parts. The first adjustment, identified by the letter **a,** is to recognize rent expense, which results in a debit to Rent Expense and a credit to Prepaid Rent. In practice, this letter may be used to reference supporting computations or documentation underlying the adjusting entry and may simplify the recording of adjusting entries in the general journal.

   If an adjustment calls for an account that has not been used in the trial balance, the new account is added below the accounts listed in the trial balance. The trial balance includes only those accounts that have balances. For example, Rent Expense has been added in Exhibit 9. The only exception to this rule is the Accumulated Depreciation accounts, which have a zero balance only in the initial period of operation. Accumulated Depreciation accounts are listed immediately after their associated asset accounts.

   When all the adjustments have been made, the two Adjustments columns must be totaled. This procedure proves that the debits and credits of the adjustments are equal, and it generally reduces errors in the preparation of the work sheet.

3. **Enter and total the adjusted account balances in the Adjusted Trial Balance columns.** Exhibit 10 shows the adjusted trial balance. It is prepared by combining the amount of each account in the original Trial Balance columns with the corresponding amount in the Adjustments columns and entering each result in the Adjusted Trial Balance columns.

   Exhibit 10 contains examples of **crossfooting**, or adding and subtracting a group of numbers horizontally. The first line shows Cash with a debit balance of $9,140. Because there are no adjustments to the Cash account, $9,140 is entered in the debit column of the Adjusted Trial Balance columns. On the second line, Accounts Receivable shows a debit of $4,800 in the Trial Balance columns. Since there is a debit of $200 from Adjustment **i** in the Adjustments column, it is added to the $4,800 and carried over to the debit column of the Adjusted Trial Balance columns at $5,000. On the next line, Art Supplies shows a debit of

$1,800 in the Trial Balance columns and a credit of $500 from adjustment **c** in the Adjustments columns. Subtracting $500 from $1,800 results in a $1,300 debit balance in the Adjusted Trial Balance columns. This process is followed for all the accounts, including those added below the trial balance totals. The Adjusted Trial Balance columns are then footed (totaled) to check the accuracy of the crossfooting.

● **STOP AND THINK!**
Under what circumstances would the Income Statement and Balance Sheet columns balance when initially totaled?
When net income equals exactly $0.■

4. **Extend the account balances from the Adjusted Trial Balance columns to the Income Statement columns or the Balance Sheet columns.** Every account in the adjusted trial balance is either a balance sheet account or an income statement account. Each account is extended to its proper place as a debit or credit in either the Income Statement columns or the Balance Sheet columns. The result of extending the accounts is shown in Exhibit 11. Revenue and expense accounts are copied to the Income Statement columns. Assets, liabilities, and the Capital and Withdrawal accounts are extended to the Balance Sheet columns. To avoid overlooking an account, the accounts are extended line by line, beginning with the first line (which is Cash) and not omitting any subsequent lines. For instance, the Cash debit balance of $9,140 is extended to the debit column of the Balance Sheet columns; the Accounts Receivable debit balance of $5,000 is extended to the same debit column, and so forth. Each amount is carried across to only one column.

5. **Total the Income Statement columns and the Balance Sheet columns. Enter the net income or net loss in both pairs of columns as a balancing figure, and recompute the column totals.** This last step, shown in Exhibit 12, is necessary in order to compute net income or net loss and to prove the arithmetical accuracy of the work sheet.

   Net income (or net loss) is equal to the difference between the total debits and credits of the Income Statement columns. It also equals the difference between the total debits and credits of the Balance Sheet columns:

Revenues (Income Statement credit column total)	$6,800
Expenses (Income Statement debit column total)	(4,800)
Net Income	$2,000

In this case, revenues (credit column) exceed expenses (debit column). Thus, the company has a net income of $2,000. The same difference is shown between the total debits and credits of the Balance Sheet columns.

The $2,000 is entered in the debit side of the Income Statement columns to balance the columns, and it is entered in the credit side of the Balance Sheet columns to balance the columns. Remember that the excess of revenues over expenses (net income) increases owner's equity and that increases in owner's equity are recorded by credits.

When a net loss occurs, the opposite rule applies. The excess of expenses over revenues—net loss—is placed in the credit side of the Income Statement columns as a balancing figure. It is then placed in the debit side of the Balance Sheet columns because a net loss decreases owner's equity, and decreases in owner's equity are recorded by debits.

As a final check, the four columns are totaled again. If the Income Statement columns and the Balance Sheet columns do not balance, an account may have been extended or sorted to the wrong column, or an error may have been made in adding the columns. Of course, equal totals in the two pairs of columns are not absolute proof of accuracy. If an asset has been carried to the Income Statement debit column (or an expense has been carried to the Balance Sheet debit column) or a similar error with revenues or liabilities has been made, the work sheet will still balance, but the net income figure will be wrong.

USING THE WORK SHEET

The completed work sheet assists the accountant in (1) recording the adjusting entries, (2) recording the closing entries in the general journal to prepare the records for the next period, and (3) preparing the financial statements.

■ **RECORDING THE ADJUSTING ENTRIES**   For Joan Miller Advertising Agency, the adjustments were determined while completing the work sheet because they are essential to the preparation of the financial statements. The adjusting entries could have been recorded in the general journal at that point.

Recording the adjusting entries with appropriate explanations in the general journal, shown in Exhibit 13, is an easy step. The information can be copied from the work sheet. Adjusting entries are then posted to the general ledger.

EXHIBIT 13
Adjustments from Work Sheet Entered in the General Journal

General Journal					Page 3
Date		Description	Post. Ref.	Debit	Credit
20xx July	31	Rent Expense	514	800	
		Prepaid Rent	117		800
		Recognized expiration of one month's rent			
	31	Insurance Expense	515	80	
		Prepaid Insurance	118		80
		Recognized expiration of one month's insurance			
	31	Art Supplies Expense	516	500	
		Art Supplies	115		500
		Recognized art supplies used during the month			
	31	Office Supplies Expense	517	200	
		Office Supplies	116		200
		Recognized office supplies used during the month			
	31	Depreciation Expense, Art Equipment	519	70	
		Accumulated Depreciation, Art Equipment	145		70
		Recorded depreciation of art equipment for a month			
	31	Depreciation Expense, Office Equipment	520	50	
		Accumulated Depreciation, Office Equipment	147		50
		Recorded depreciation of office equipment for a month			
	31	Wages Expense	511	360	
		Wages Payable	214		360
		Accrued unrecorded wages			
	31	Unearned Art Fees	213	400	
		Art Fees Earned	412		400
		Recognized performance of services paid for in advance			
	31	Accounts Receivable	113	200	
		Advertising Fees Earned	411		200
		Accrued advertising fees earned but unrecorded			

EXHIBIT 14
Income Statement for Joan Miller Advertising Agency

Joan Miller Advertising Agency
Income Statement
For the Month Ended July 31, 20xx

Revenues

Advertising fees earned		$6,400
Art fees earned		400
Total revenues		$6,800

Expenses

Wages expense	$2,760	
Utilities expense	200	
Telephone expense	140	
Rent expense	800	
Insurance expense	80	
Art supplies expense	500	
Office supplies expense	200	
Depreciation expense, art equipment	70	
Depreciation expense, office equipment	50	
Total expenses		4,800
Net income		$2,000

KEY POINT: Notice the ease with which the income statement can be prepared now that the work sheet has been completed.

■ **RECORDING THE CLOSING ENTRIES** The four closing entries for Joan Miller Advertising Agency are entered in the journal and posted to the ledger, as illustrated in Exhibits 1 through 5. All accounts that need to be closed, except for Withdrawals, may be found in the Income Statement columns of the work sheet.

■ **PREPARING THE FINANCIAL STATEMENTS** Once the work sheet has been completed, preparing the financial statements is simple because the account balances have been sorted into Income Statement and Balance Sheet columns. The income statement in Exhibit 14 was prepared from the account balances in the Income Statement columns of Exhibit 12. The account balances for the statement of owner's equity in Exhibit 15 and the balance sheet in Exhibit 16 were drawn from the Balance Sheet columns of

EXHIBIT 15
Statement of Owner's Equity for Joan Miller Advertising Agency

Joan Miller Advertising Agency
Statement of Owner's Equity
For the Month Ended July 31, 20xx

Joan Miller, Capital, July 1, 20xx		—
Add: Investment by Joan Miller	$20,000	
Net income	2,000	$22,000
Subtotal		$22,000
Less withdrawals		1,400
Joan Miller, Capital, July 31, 20xx		$20,600

EXHIBIT 16
Balance Sheet for Joan Miller
Advertising Agency

Joan Miller Advertising Agency
Balance Sheet
July 31, 20xx

Assets

Cash		$ 9,140
Accounts receivable		5,000
Art supplies		1,300
Office supplies		600
Prepaid rent		800
Prepaid insurance		880
Art equipment	$ 4,200	
Less accumulated depreciation	70	4,130
Office equipment	$ 3,000	
Less accumulated depreciation	50	2,950
Total assets		$24,800

Liabilities

Accounts payable	$ 3,240	
Unearned art fees	600	
Wages payable	360	
Total liabilities		$ 4,200

Owner's Equity

Joan Miller, Capital, July 31, 20xx		20,600
Total liabilities and owner's equity		$24,800

the work sheet in Exhibit 12. Notice that the total assets and the total liabilities and owner's equity in the balance sheet are not the same as the totals of the Balance Sheet columns in the work sheet. The reason is that the Accumulated Depreciation and Withdrawals accounts have normal balances that appear in different columns from their associated accounts on the balance sheet. In addition, the owner's Capital account on the balance sheet is the amount determined on the statement of owner's equity. At this point, the financial statements have been prepared from the work sheet, not from the ledger accounts. For the ledger accounts to show the correct balances, the adjusting entries must be journalized and posted to the ledger.

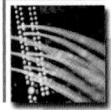

FOCUS ON BUSINESS TECHNOLOGY

Using Electronic Work Sheets

The work sheet is a good application for electronic spreadsheet software programs like Lotus and Microsoft Excel. Constructing a work sheet using spreadsheet software takes time, but once it is done, the work sheet can be used over and over. The principal advantage of electronic preparation over manual preparation is that each time a number is entered or revised, the entire electronic work sheet is updated automatically, without the possibility of addition or extension mistakes. For example, if an error in an adjusting entry is corrected, the proper extensions to the other columns are made, all columns are re-added, and net income is recomputed. Of course, the software is purely mechanical. People are still responsible for inputting the correct numbers and equations initially.

 Check out ACE for a Review Quiz at http://accounting.college.hmco.com/students.

Chapter Review

REVIEW OF LEARNING OBJECTIVES

LO1 State all the steps in the accounting cycle.

The steps in the accounting cycle are (1) analyze business transactions from source documents, (2) record the entries in the journal, (3) post the entries to the ledger and prepare a trial balance, (4) adjust the accounts and prepare an adjusted trial balance, (5) close the accounts and prepare a post-closing trial balance, and (6) prepare the financial statements.

LO2 Explain and prepare closing entries.

Closing entries have two purposes. First, they clear the balances of all temporary accounts (revenue, expense, and owner's Withdrawals accounts) so that they have zero balances at the beginning of the next accounting period. Second, they summarize a period's revenues and expenses in the Income Summary account so that the net income or loss for the period can be transferred as a total to owner's Capital. In preparing closing entries, first the revenue and expense account balances are transferred to the Income Summary account. Then the balance of the Income Summary account is transferred to the owner's Capital account. And, finally, the balance of the owner's Withdrawals account is transferred to the owner's Capital account.

LO3 Prepare the post-closing trial balance.

As a final check on the balance of the ledger and to ensure that all temporary (nominal) accounts have been closed, a post-closing trial balance is prepared after the closing entries are posted to the ledger accounts.

LO4 Prepare reversing entries as appropriate.

Reversing entries are optional entries made on the first day of a new accounting period in order to simplify routine bookkeeping procedures. They reverse certain adjusting entries made in the previous period. As used in this text, they apply only to accruals.

LO5 Prepare and use a work sheet.

There are five steps in the preparation of a work sheet: (1) Enter and total the account balances in the Trial Balance columns; (2) enter and total the adjustments in the Adjustments columns; (3) enter and total the adjusted account balances in the Adjusted Trial Balance columns; (4) extend the account balances from the Adjusted Trial Balance columns to the Income Statement or Balance Sheet columns; and (5) total the Income Statement and Balance Sheet columns, enter the net income or net loss in both pairs of columns as a balancing figure, and recompute the column totals. A work sheet is useful in (1) recording the adjusting entries, (2) recording the closing entries, and (3) preparing the financial statements. The balance sheet and income statement can be prepared directly from the Balance Sheet and Income Statement columns of the completed work sheet. The statement of owner's equity is prepared using owner's Withdrawals, net income, additional investments, and the beginning balance of of the owner's Capital account.

REVIEW OF CONCEPTS AND TERMINOLOGY

The following concepts and terms were introduced in this chapter:

LO1 **Accounting cycle:** The sequence of steps followed in the accounting system to measure business transactions and transform them into financial statements; it includes analyzing and recording transactions, posting entries, adjusting and closing the accounts, and preparing financial statements.

LO2 **Closing entries:** Entries made at the end of an accounting period that set the stage for the next accounting period by clearing the temporary accounts of their balances and transferring them to owner's Capital; they summarize a period's revenues and expenses.

LO5 **Crossfooting:** Adding and subtracting numbers across a row.

LO2 **Income Summary:** A temporary account used during the closing process that holds a summary of all revenues and expenses before the net income or loss is transferred to the owner's Capital account.

LO2   **Permanent accounts:** Balance sheet accounts; accounts whose balances can extend past the end of an accounting period. Also called *real accounts*.

LO3   **Post-closing trial balance:** A trial balance prepared at the end of the accounting period after all adjusting and closing entries have been posted; a final check on the balance of the ledger to ensure that all temporary accounts have zero balances and that total debits equal total credits.

LO4   **Reversing entry:** An entry made on the first day of an accounting period that is the exact reverse of an adjusting entry made on the last day of the previous period.

LO2   **Temporary accounts:** Accounts that show the accumulation of revenues and expenses over one accounting period; at the end of the accounting period, these account balances are transferred to owner's equity. Also called *nominal accounts*.

LO5   **Working papers:** Documents used by accountants to organize their work and to support the information in the financial statements.

LO5   **Work sheet:** A type of working paper used as a preliminary step in recording adjusting and closing entries and in the preparation of financial statements.

REVIEW PROBLEM

Preparation of Closing Entries

LO2   At the end of the current fiscal year, the adjusted trial balance for Westwood Movers Company is as follows:

Westwood Movers Company
Adjusted Trial Balance
June 30, 20xx

Cash	$ 14,200	
Accounts Receivable	18,600	
Packing Supplies	10,400	
Prepaid Insurance	7,900	
Land	4,000	
Building	80,000	
Accumulated Depreciation, Building		$ 7,500
Trucks	106,000	
Accumulated Depreciation, Trucks		27,500
Accounts Payable		7,650
Unearned Storage Fees		5,400
Mortgage Payable		70,000
Art Burton, Capital		104,740
Art Burton, Withdrawals	18,000	
Moving Services Earned		159,000
Storage Fees Earned		26,400
Driver Wages Expense	94,000	
Fuel Expense	19,000	
Office Wages Expense	14,400	
Office Equipment Rental Expense	3,000	
Utilities Expense	4,450	
Insurance Expense	4,200	
Depreciation Expense, Building	4,000	
Depreciation Expense, Trucks	6,040	
	$408,190	$408,190

REQUIRED ▶   Prepare the necessary closing entries.

ANSWER TO REVIEW PROBLEM

Closing entries prepared

June 30	Moving Services Earned	159,000	
	Storage Fees Earned	26,400	
	Income Summary		185,400
	Closed the revenue accounts		
30	Income Summary	149,090	
	Driver Wages Expense		94,000
	Fuel Expense		19,000
	Office Wages Expense		14,400
	Office Equipment Rental Expense		3,000
	Utilities Expense		4,450
	Insurance Expense		4,200
	Depreciation Expense, Building		4,000
	Depreciation Expense, Trucks		6,040
	Closed the expense accounts		
30	Income Summary	36,310	
	Art Burton, Capital		36,310
	Closed the Income Summary account and transferred balance to the Capital account		
30	Art Burton, Capital	18,000	
	Art Burton, Withdrawals		18,000
	Closed the Withdrawals account		

Chapter Assignments

BUILDING YOUR KNOWLEDGE FOUNDATION

QUESTIONS

1. Resequence the following activities **a** through **f** to indicate the correct order of the accounting cycle:
   a. The transactions are entered in the journal.
   b. The financial statements are prepared.
   c. The transactions are analyzed from the source documents.
   d. The adjusting entries are prepared.
   e. The closing entries are prepared.
   f. The transactions are posted to the ledger.

2. What are the two purposes of closing entries?

3. What is the difference between adjusting entries and closing entries?

4. What is the purpose of the Income Summary account?

5. Which of the following accounts do not show a balance after the closing entries are prepared and posted?
   a. Insurance Expense
   b. Accounts Receivable
   c. Commission Revenue
   d. Prepaid Insurance
   e. Owner's Withdrawals
   f. Supplies
   g. Supplies Expense
   h. Owner's Capital

6. What is the significance of the post-closing trial balance?

7. Which of the following accounts would you expect to find in the post-closing trial balance?

   a. Insurance Expense
   b. Accounts Receivable
   c. Commission Revenue
   d. Prepaid Insurance
   e. Owner's Withdrawals
   f. Supplies
   g. Supplies Expense
   h. Owner's Capital

8. How do reversing entries simplify the bookkeeping process?

9. To what types of adjustments do reversing entries apply? To what types do they not apply?

10. Why are working papers important to accountants?

11. Why are work sheets never published and rarely seen by management?

12. Can the work sheet be used as a substitute for the financial statements? Explain your answer.

13. What is the normal balance (debit or credit) of the following accounts?

   a. Cash
   b. Accounts Payable
   c. Prepaid Rent
   d. Sam Jones, Capital
   e. Commission Revenue
   f. Sam Jones, Withdrawals
   g. Rent Expense
   h. Accumulated Depreciation, Office Equipment
   i. Office Equipment

14. Why should the Adjusted Trial Balance columns of the work sheet be totaled before the adjusted amounts are carried to the Income Statement and Balance Sheet columns?

15. What sequence should be followed in extending the amounts in the Adjusted Trial Balance columns to the Income Statement and Balance Sheet columns? Discuss your answer.

16. Do the Income Statement columns and the Balance Sheet columns of the work sheet balance after the amounts from the Adjusted Trial Balance columns are extended?

17. Do the totals of the Balance Sheet columns of the work sheet agree with the totals on the balance sheet? Explain your answer.

18. Should adjusting entries be posted to the ledger accounts before or after the closing entries? Explain your answer.

19. At the end of the accounting period, does the posting of adjusting entries to the ledger precede or follow the preparation of the work sheet?

SHORT EXERCISES

SE 1.

LO1   Accounting Cycle

Resequence the following activities to indicate the usual order of the accounting cycle:

   a. Close the accounts.
   b. Analyze the transactions.
   c. Post the entries to the ledger.
   d. Prepare the financial statements.
   e. Adjust the accounts.
   f. Record the transactions in the journal.
   g. Prepare the post-closing trial balance.
   h. Prepare the initial trial balance.
   i. Prepare the adjusted trial balance.

SE 2.

LO2   Closing Revenue Accounts

Assume that at the end of the accounting period there are credit balances of $3,400 in Patient Services Revenues and $1,800 in Laboratory Fees Revenues. Prepare the required closing entry in journal form. The accounting period ends December 31.

SE 3.
LO2 **Closing Expense Accounts**

Assume that dedit balances at the end of the accounting period are $1,400 in Rent Expense, $1,100 in Wages Expense, and $500 in Other Expenses. Prepare the required closing entry in journal form. The accounting period ends December 31.

SE 4.
LO2 **Closing the Income Summary Account**

Assuming that total revenues were $5,200 and total expenses were $3,000, prepare the entry in journal form to close the Income Summary account to the H. Blake, Capital account. The accounting period ends December 31.

SE 5.
LO2 **Closing the Withdrawals Account**

Assuming that withdrawals during the accounting period were $800, prepare the entry in journal form to close the H. Blake, Withdrawals account to the H. Blake, Capital account. The accounting period ends December 31.

SE 6.
LO2 **Posting Closing Entries**

Show the effects of the transactions in **SE 2, SE 3, SE 4,** and **SE 5** by entering beginning balances in appropriate T accounts and recording the transactions. Assume that the H. Blake, Capital account has a beginning balance of $1,300.

SE 7.
LO4 **Preparation of Reversing Entries**

Below, indicated by letters, are the adjusting entries at the end of March.

Account Name	Debit	Credit
Prepaid Insurance		(a) 180
Accumulated Depreciation, Office Equipment		(b) 1,050
Salaries Expense	(c) 360	
Insurance Expense	(a) 180	
Depreciation Expense, Office Equipment	(b) 1,050	
Salaries Payable		(c) 360
	1,590	1, 590

Prepare the required reversing entry in journal form.

SE 8.
LO4 **Effects of Reversing Entries**

Assume that prior to the adjustments in **SE 7**, Salaries Expense had a debit balance of $1,800 and Salaries Payable had a zero balance. Prepare a T account for each of these accounts. Enter the beginning balance; post the adjustment for accrued salaries, the appropriate closing entry, and the reversing entry; and enter the transaction in the T accounts for a payment of $480 for salaries on April 3.

SE 9.
LO2 **Preparing Closing Entries from**
LO5 **a Work Sheet**

Prepare the required closing entries in journal form for the year ended December 31, using the following items from the Income Statement columns of a work sheet and assuming that withdrawals by the owner, M. Dye, were $6,000:

Account Name	Income Statement	
	Debit	Credit
Repair Revenue		32,860
Wages Expense	12,260	
Rent Expense	1,800	
Supplies Expense	6,390	
Insurance Expense	1,370	
Depreciation Expense, Repair Equipment	2,020	
	23,840	32,860
Net Income	9,020	
	32,860	32,860

EXERCISES

E 1.
LO2 **Preparation of Closing Entries**

The adjusted trial balance for the Featherstone Real Estate Company at the end of its fiscal year is shown below. Prepare the required closing entries in journal form.

Featherstone Real Estate Company
Adjusted Trial Balance
December 31, 20xx

Cash	$ 7,275	
Accounts Receivable	2,325	
Prepaid Insurance	585	
Office Supplies	440	
Office Equipment	6,300	
Accumulated Depreciation, Office Equipment		$ 765
Automobile	6,750	
Accumulated Depreciation, Automobile		750
Accounts Payable		1,700
Unearned Management Fees		1,500
V. Featherstone, Capital		14,535
V. Featherstone, Withdrawals	7,000	
Sales Commissions Earned		31,700
Office Salaries Expense	13,500	
Advertising Expense	2,525	
Rent Expense	2,650	
Telephone Expense	1,600	
	$50,950	$50,950

E 2.
LO4 **Reversing Entries**

Selected September T accounts for Weins Company are presented below.

Supplies			
9/1 Bal.	860	9/30 Adjust.	1,280
Sept. purchases	940		
Bal.	520		

Supplies Expense			
9/30 Adjust.	1,280	9/30 Closing	1,280
Bal.	—		

Wages Payable			
		9/30 Adjust.	640
		Bal.	640

Wages Expense			
Sept. wages	3,940	9/30 Closing	4,580
9/30 Adjust.	640		
Bal.	—		

1. In which of the accounts would a reversing entry be helpful? Why?
2. Prepare the appropriate reversing entry.
3. Prepare the entry to record a payment on October 3 for wages totaling $3,140. How much of this amount represents wages expense for October?

E 3.
LO5 **Preparation of a Trial Balance**

The following alphabetical list presents the accounts and balances for Jessica's Dresses on June 30, 20x4. All the accounts have normal balances.

Accounts Payable	$15,420
Accounts Receivable	7,650
Accumulated Depreciation, Office Equipment	1,350
Advertising Expense	1,800

Cash	7,635
J. Alaria, Capital	30,630
J. Alaria, Withdrawals	27,000
Office Equipment	15,510
Prepaid Insurance	1,680
Rent Expense	7,200
Revenue from Commissions	57,900
Supplies	825
Wages Expense	36,000

Prepare the trial balance by listing the accounts in the correct order, with the balances in the appropriate debit or credit column.

E 4.

LO5   Completion of a Work Sheet

The following is a highly simplified alphabetical list of trial balance accounts and their normal balances for the month ended March 31, 20xx:

Trial Balance Accounts and Balances

Accounts Payable	$4	Prepaid Insurance	$ 2
Accounts Receivable	7	Service Revenue	23
Accumulated Depreciation,		Supplies	4
Office Equipment	1	Terri Julius, Capital	12
Cash	4	Terri Julius, Withdrawals	6
Office Equipment	8	Unearned Revenues	3
		Utilities Expense	2
		Wages Expense	10

1. Prepare a work sheet, entering the trial balance accounts in the order in which they would normally appear and entering the balances in the correct debit or credit column.
2. Complete the work sheet using the following information:

   a. Expired insurance, $1.
   b. Of the unearned revenues balance, $2 has been earned by the end of the month.
   c. Estimated depreciation on office equipment, $1.
   d. Accrued wages, $1.
   e. Unused supplies on hand, $1.

E 5.

LO5   Preparation of a Statement of Owner's Equity

The Capital, Withdrawals, and Income Summary accounts for Sariah's Clip Shop are shown in T account form below. The closing entries have been recorded for the year ended December 31, 20x4.

Sariah Abdul, Capital

12/31/x4	4,500	12/31/x3	13,000
		12/31/x4	9,500
		Bal.	18,000

Income Summary

12/31/x4	21,500	12/31/x4	31,000
12/31/x4	9,500		
Bal.	—		

Sariah Abdul, Withdrawals

4/1/x4	1,500	12/31/x4	4,500
7/1/x4	1,500		
10/1/x4	1,500		
Bal.	—		

Prepare a statement of owner's equity for Sariah's Clip Shop.

E 6.

LO5   Adjusting Entries and Preparation of a Balance Sheet

In the partial work sheet that follows, the Trial Balance and Income Statement columns have been completed. All amounts shown are in dollars.

Account Name	Trial Balance Debit	Trial Balance Credit	Income Statement Debit	Income Statement Credit
Cash	14			
Accounts Receivable	24			
Supplies	22			
Prepaid Insurance	16			
Building	50			
Accumulated Depreciation, Building		16		
Accounts Payable		8		
Unearned Revenues		4		
T. L., Capital		64		
Revenues		88		92
Wages Expense	54		60	
	180	180		
Insurance Expense			8	
Supplies Expense			16	
Depreciation Expense, Building			4	
Wages Payable				
			88	92
Net Income			4	
			92	92

1. Show the adjustments that have been made in journal form without explanation.
2. Prepare a balance sheet.

E 7.
The items that appear below are from the Adjustments columns of a work sheet dated June 30, 20xx.

Account Name	Adjustments Debit	Adjustments Credit
Prepaid Insurance		(a) 240
Office Supplies		(b) 630
Accumulated Depreciation, Office Equipment		(c) 1,400
Accumulated Depreciation, Store Equipment		(d) 2,200
Office Salaries Expense	(e) 240	
Store Salaries Expense	(e) 480	
Insurance Expense	(a) 240	
Office Supplies Expense	(b) 630	
Depreciation Expense, Office Equipment	(c) 1,400	
Depreciation Expense, Store Equipment	(d) 2,200	
Salaries Payable		(e) 720
	5,190	5,190

1. Prepare the adjusting entries in journal form.
2. Where required, prepare appropriate reversing entries in journal form.

E 8.
The items that follow are from the Income Statement columns of the work sheet for O'Malley Repair Shop for the year ended December 31, 20xx.

Account Name	Income Statement	
	Debit	Credit
Repair Revenue		25,620
Wages Expense	8,110	
Rent Expense	1,200	
Supplies Expense	4,260	
Insurance Expense	915	
Depreciation Expense, Repair Equipment	1,345	
	15,830	25,620
Net Income	9,790	
	25,620	25,620

Prepare entries in journal form to close the revenue, expense, Income Summary, and Withdrawals accounts. O'Malley withdrew $5,000 during the year.

PROBLEMS

P 1.

LO2 Closing Entries Using T Accounts and Preparation of Financial Statements

The adjusted trial balance for Applewilde Tennis Club at the end of the company's fiscal year appears below.

Applewilde Tennis Club
Adjusted Trial Balance
June 30, 20x5

	Debit	Credit
Cash	$ 26,200	
Prepaid Advertising	9,600	
Supplies	1,200	
Land	100,000	
Building	645,200	
Accumulated Depreciation, Building		$ 260,000
Equipment	156,000	
Accumulated Depreciation, Equipment		50,400
Accounts Payable		73,000
Wages Payable		29,000
Property Taxes Payable		22,500
Unearned Revenues, Locker Fees		3,000
Susan Wilde, Capital		471,150
Susan Wilde, Withdrawals	54,000	
Revenues from Court Fees		678,100
Revenues from Locker Fees		9,600
Wages Expense	351,000	
Maintenance Expense	51,600	
Advertising Expense	39,750	
Utilities Expense	64,800	
Supplies Expense	26,000	
Depreciation Expense, Building	30,000	
Depreciation Expense, Equipment	12,000	
Property Taxes Expense	22,500	
Miscellaneous Expense	6,900	
	$1,596,750	$1,596,750

REQUIRED ▶

1. Prepare T accounts and enter the balances for Susan Wilde, Capital; Susan Wilde, Withdrawals; Income Summary; and all revenue and expense accounts.
2. Enter the four required closing entries in the T accounts, labeling the components *a*, *b*, *c*, and *d*, as appropriate.
3. Prepare an income statement, a statement of owner's equity, and a balance sheet. Assume no additional investments by the owner.
4. Explain why closing entries are necessary at the end of the accounting period.

P 2.

LO2   Closing Entries Using Journal Form and Preparation of Financial Statements

Lakeside Campgrounds, owned by Anthony Fabrizzi, rents out campsites in a wooded park. The adjusted trial balance for Lakeside Campgrounds on May 31, 20x5, the end of the current fiscal year, is as follows:

Lakeside Campgrounds
Adjusted Trial Balance
March 31, 20x5

Cash	$ 2,040	
Accounts Receivable	3,660	
Supplies	114	
Prepaid Insurance	594	
Land	15,000	
Building	45,900	
Accumulated Depreciation, Building		$ 10,500
Accounts Payable		1,725
Wages Payable		825
Anthony Fabrizzi, Capital		46,535
Anthony Fabrizzi, Withdrawals	18,000	
Campsite Rentals		44,100
Wages Expense	11,925	
Insurance Expense	1,892	
Utilities Expense	900	
Supplies Expense	660	
Depreciation Expense, Building	3,000	
	$103,685	$103,685

REQUIRED ▶

1. Record the closing entries in journal form.
2. From the information given, prepare an income statement, a statement of owner's equity, and a balance sheet. Assume no additional investments by the owner.
3. Assuming that Wages Payable represents wages accrued at the end of the accounting period, record the optional reversing entry on June 1.

P 3.

LO1   The Complete Accounting
LO2   Cycle Without a Work Sheet:
LO3   Two Months (second month optional)

On October 1, 20xx, Jason Dauphinais opened Dauphinais Appliance Service. During the month, he completed the following transactions for the company:

Oct. 1 Began business by depositing $5,000 in a bank account.
       1 Paid the rent for a store for one month, $425.
       1 Paid the premium on a one-year insurance policy, $480.
       2 Purchased repair equipment from Fitzgerald Company, $4,200. Terms were $600 down and $300 per month for one year. First payment is due November 1.
       5 Purchased repair supplies from Deane Company on credit, $468.
       8 Paid cash for an advertisement in a local newspaper, $60.
      15 Received cash repair revenue for the first half of the month, $400.
      21 Paid Deane Company on account, $225.
      31 Received cash repair revenue for the second half of October, $975.
      31 Withdrew cash for personal expenses, $300.

REQUIRED FOR OCTOBER ▶

1. Prepare entries in journal form to record the October transactions.
2. Open the following accounts: Cash (111); Prepaid Insurance (117); Repair Supplies (119); Repair Equipment (144); Accumulated Depreciation, Repair Equipment (145); Accounts Payable (212); J. Dauphinais, Capital (311); J. Dauphinais, Withdrawals (312); Income Summary (313); Repair Revenue (411); Store Rent Expense (511); Advertising Expense (512); Insurance Expense (513); Repair Supplies Expense (514); and Depreciation Expense, Repair Equipment (515). Post the October entries to the ledger accounts.
3. Using the following information, record adjusting entries in journal form and post to the ledger accounts:

   a. One month's insurance has expired.
   b. The remaining inventory of unused repair supplies is $169.
   c. The estimated depreciation on repair equipment is $70.

4. From the accounts in the ledger, prepare an adjusted trial balance. (*Note:* Normally a trial balance is prepared before adjustments but is omitted here to save time.)
5. From the adjusted trial balance, prepare an income statement, a statement of owner's equity, and a balance sheet for October.
6. Prepare and post closing entries.
7. Prepare a post-closing trial balance.

(Optional)   During November, Jason Dauphinais completed these transactions for Dauphinais Appliance Service:

Nov. 1 Paid the monthly rent, $425.
      1 Made the monthly payment to Fitzgerald Company, $300.
      6 Purchased additional repair supplies on credit from Deane Company, $863.
     15 Received cash repair revenue for the first half of the month, $914.
     20 Paid cash for an advertisement in the local newspaper, $60.
     23 Paid Deane Company on account, $600.
     30 Received cash repair revenue for the last half of the month, $817.
     30 Withdrew cash for personal expenses, $300.

REQUIRED FOR NOVEMBER ▶

8. Prepare and post entries in journal form to record the November transactions.
9. Using the following information, record adjusting entries in journal form and post to the ledger accounts:

   a. One month's insurance has expired.
   b. The inventory of unused repair supplies is $413.
   c. The estimated depreciation on repair equipment is $70.

10. From the accounts in the ledger, prepare an adjusted trial balance.
11. From the adjusted trial balance, prepare the November income statement, statement of owner's equity, and balance sheet.
12. Prepare and post closing entries.
13. Prepare a post-closing trial balance.

P 4.
LO2 Preparation of a Work Sheet,
LO4 Financial Statements, and
LO5 Adjusting, Closing, and
Reversing Entries

Jacqueline Woo opened her executive search service on July 1, 20x4. Some customers paid for her services after they were rendered, and others paid in advance for one year of service. After six months of operation, Woo wanted to know how her business stood. The trial balance on December 31 appears at the top of the next page.

REQUIRED ▶

1. Enter the trial balance amounts in the Trial Balance columns of a work sheet. Remember that accumulated depreciation is listed with its asset account. Complete the work sheet using the following information:

   a. One year's rent had been paid in advance when Woo began business.
   b. Inventory of unused office supplies, $75.
   c. One-half year's depreciation on office equipment, $900.
   d. Service rendered that had been paid for in advance, $863.
   e. Executive search services rendered during the month but not yet billed, $270.
   f. Wages earned by employees but not yet paid, $188.

2. Prepare an income statement, a statement of owner's equity, and a balance sheet.

Jacqueline Woo Executive Search Service
Trial Balance
December 31, 20x4

Cash	$ 713	
Accounts Receivable	1,000	
Prepaid Rent	1,800	
Office Supplies	413	
Office Equipment	15,750	
Accounts Payable		$ 3,173
Unearned Revenues		1,823
Jacqueline Woo, Capital		10,000
Jacqueline Woo, Withdrawals	5,200	
Search Revenue		20,140
Utilities Expense	1,260	
Wages Expense	9,000	
	$35,136	$35,136

3. Prepare adjusting, closing, and, if required, reversing entries.
4. What is your evaluation of Jacqueline Woo's first six months in business?

P 5.

LO2 Preparation of a Work Sheet,
LO4 Financial Statements, and
LO5 Adjusting, Closing, and
Reversing Entries

The following trial balance was taken from the ledger of McIntire Express Delivery Company on August 31, 20x4, the end of the company's fiscal year:

McIntire Express Delivery Company
Trial Balance
August 31, 20x4

Cash	$ 5,036	
Accounts Receivable	14,657	
Prepaid Insurance	2,670	
Delivery Supplies	7,350	
Office Supplies	1,230	
Land	7,500	
Building	98,000	
Accumulated Depreciation, Building		$ 26,700
Trucks	51,900	
Accumulated Depreciation, Trucks		15,450
Office Equipment	7,950	
Accumulated Depreciation, Office Equipment		5,400
Accounts Payable		4,698
Unearned Lockbox Fees		4,170
Mortgage Payable		36,000
Matt McIntire, Capital		64,365
Matt McIntire, Withdrawals	15,000	
Delivery Services Revenue		141,735
Lockbox Fees Earned		14,400
Truck Drivers' Wages Expense	63,900	
Office Salaries Expense	22,200	
Gas, Oil, and Truck Repairs Expense	15,525	
	$312,918	$312,918

REQUIRED ▶

1. Enter the trial balance amounts in the Trial Balance columns of a work sheet and complete the work sheet using the following information:

   a. Expired insurance, $1,530.
   b. Inventory of unused delivery supplies, $715.
   c. Inventory of unused office supplies, $93.
   d. Estimated depreciation, building, $7,200.
   e. Estimated depreciation, trucks, $7,725.
   f. Estimated depreciation, office equipment, $1,350.
   g. The company credits the lockbox fees of customers who pay in advance to the Unearned Lockbox Fees account. Of the amount credited to this account during the year, $2,815 had been earned by August 31.
   h. Lockbox fees earned but unrecorded and uncollected at the end of the accounting period, $408.
   i. Accrued but unpaid truck drivers' wages at the end of the year, $960.

2. Prepare an income statement, a statement of owner's equity, and a balance sheet. Assume no additional investments by Matt McIntire.

3. Prepare adjusting, closing, and, if required, reversing entries.

ALTERNATE PROBLEMS

P 6.

LO2 Closing Entries Using T Accounts and Preparation of Financial Statements

The adjusted trial balance for Hartford Go-Cart Lanes at the end of the company's fiscal year is as follows:

Hartford Go-Cart Lanes
Adjusted Trial Balance
December 31, 20x4

Cash	$ 16,214	
Accounts Receivable	7,388	
Supplies	156	
Prepaid Insurance	300	
Land	5,000	
Building	100,000	
Accumulated Depreciation, Building		$ 27,200
Equipment	125,000	
Accumulated Depreciation, Equipment		33,000
Accounts Payable		30,044
Notes Payable		70,000
Unearned Revenues		300
Wages Payable		3,962
Property Taxes Payable		10,000
Tom Wells, Capital		60,813
Tom Wells, Withdrawals	24,000	
Revenues		618,263
Wages Expense	381,076	
Advertising Expense	30,200	
Maintenance Expense	84,100	
Supplies Expense	1,148	
Insurance Expense	1,500	
Depreciation Expense, Building	4,800	
Depreciation Expense, Equipment	11,000	
Utilities Expense	42,200	
Miscellaneous Expense	9,500	
Property Taxes Expense	10,000	
	$853,582	$853,582

REQUIRED ▶ 1. Prepare T accounts and enter the balances for Tom Wells, Capital; Tom Wells, Withdrawals; Income Summary; and all revenue and expense accounts.
2. Enter in the T accounts the four required closing entries, labeling the components *a*, *b*, *c*, and *d* as appropriate.
3. Prepare an income statement, a statement of owner's equity, and a balance sheet.
4. Explain why closing entries are necessary at the end of the accounting period.

P 7.

LO2 **Closing Entries Using Journal Form and Preparation of Financial Statements**

Do-It-Yourself Trailer Rental rents small trailers by the day for local moving jobs. This is its adjusted trial balance at the end of the current fiscal year:

Do-It-Yourself Trailer Rental
Adjusted Trial Balance
June 30, 20x5

Cash	$ 692	
Accounts Receivable	972	
Supplies	119	
Prepaid Insurance	360	
Trailers	12,000	
Accumulated Depreciation, Trailers		$ 7,200
Accounts Payable		271
Wages Payable		200
Selena Perez, Capital		5,694
Selena Perez, Withdrawals	7,200	
Trailer Rentals Revenue		45,546
Wages Expense	23,400	
Insurance Expense	720	
Supplies Expense	266	
Depreciation Expense, Trailers	2,400	
Other Expenses	10,782	
	$58,911	$58,911

REQUIRED ▶ 1. From the information given, record closing entries in journal form.
2. Prepare an income statement, a statement of owner's equity, and a balance sheet. Assume no additional investments by Selena Perez.

P 8.

LO2 **Preparation of a Work Sheet,**
LO4 **Financial Statements, and**
LO5 **Adjusting, Closing, and Reversing Entries**

At the end of the current fiscal year, the trial balance of Flynn Theater appeared as shown at the top of the opposite page.

REQUIRED ▶ 1. Enter the trial balance amounts in the Trial Balance columns of a work sheet and complete the work sheet using the following information.

a. Expired insurance, $8,700.
b. Inventory of unused office supplies, $122.
c. Inventory of unused cleaning supplies, $234.
d. Estimated depreciation, building, $7,000.
e. Estimated depreciation, theater furnishings, $18,000.
f. Estimated depreciation, office equipment, $1,580.
g. The company credits all gift books sold during the year to the Gift Books Liability account. A gift book is a booklet of ticket coupons purchased in advance as a gift. The recipient redeems the coupons at some point in the future. On December 31, it was estimated that $18,900 worth of the gift books had been redeemed.
h. Accrued but unpaid usher wages at the end of the accounting period, $430.

2. Prepare an income statement, a statement of owner's equity, and a balance sheet. Assume no additional investments by Danielle Flynn.
3. Prepare adjusting, closing, and, when possible, reversing entries from the work sheet.

Flynn Theater
Trial Balance
December 31, 20x5

Cash	$ 15,900	
Accounts Receivable	9,272	
Prepaid Insurance	9,800	
Office Supplies	390	
Cleaning Supplies	1,795	
Land	10,000	
Building	200,000	
Accumulated Depreciation, Building		$ 19,700
Theater Furnishings	185,000	
Accumulated Depreciation, Theater Furnishings		32,500
Office Equipment	15,800	
Accumulated Depreciation, Office Equipment		7,780
Accounts Payable		22,753
Gift Books Liability		20,950
Mortgage Payable		150,000
Danielle Flynn, Capital		156,324
Danielle Flynn, Withdrawals	30,000	
Ticket Sales Revenue		205,700
Theater Rental Revenue		22,600
Usher Wages Expense	92,000	
Office Wages Expense	12,000	
Utilities Expense	56,350	
	$638,307	$638,307

SKILLS DEVELOPMENT CASES

Conceptual Analysis

SD 1.

LO1 Interim Financial Statements

Ocean Oil Services Company provides services for drilling operations off the coast of Louisiana. The company has a significant amount of debt to River National Bank in Baton Rouge. The bank requires the company to provide it with quarterly financial statements. Explain what is involved in preparing financial statements every quarter.

SD 2.

LO4 Accounting Efficiency

Way Heaters Company manufactures industrial heaters used in making candy. It sells its heaters to some customers on credit with generous terms specifying payment six months after purchase and an interest rate based on current bank rates. Because the interest on the loans accrues a little every day but is not paid until the note's due date, an adjusting entry must be made at the end of each accounting period to debit Interest Receivable and credit Interest Income for the amount of the interest accrued but not paid to date. The company prepares financial statements every month. Keeping track of what has been accrued in the past is time-consuming because the notes carry different dates and interest rates. Discuss what the accountant can do to simplify the process of making the adjusting entry for accrued interest each month.

Ethical Dilemma

SD 3.

LO1 Ethics and Time Pressure

Jay Wheeler, an accountant for WB Company, has made adjusting entries and is preparing the adjusted trial balance for the first six months of the year. Financial statements must be delivered to the bank by 5 P.M. to support a critical loan agreement. By noon, Wheeler has been unable to balance the adjusted trial balance. The figures are off by $1,320, so he increases the balance of the owner's Capital account by $1,320. He closes the accounts, prepares the statements, and sends them to the bank on time. Wheeler hopes that no one will notice the problem and believes that he can find the error and correct it by the end of next month. Are Wheeler's actions ethical? Why or why not? Did he have other alternatives?

Research Activity

SD 4.

LO1 Interview of a Local
LO2 Businessperson
LO3
LO4
LO5

Arrange to spend about an hour interviewing the owner, manager, or accountant of a local service or retail business. Your goal is to learn as much as you can about the accounting cycle of the person's business. Ask the interviewee to show you his or her accounting records and to tell you how such transactions as sales, purchases, payments, and payroll are handled. Examine the documents used to support the transactions. Look at any journals, ledgers, or work sheets. Does the business use a computer? Does it use its own accounting system, or does it use an outside or centralized service? Does it use the cash or the accrual basis of accounting? When does it prepare adjusting entries? When does it prepare closing entries? How often does it prepare financial statements? Does it prepare reversing entries? How do its procedures differ from those described in the text? When the interview is finished, organize and write up your findings and be prepared to present them in class.

 Group Activity: Divide the class into groups and have each group investigate a different type of business, such as a shoe store, grocery store, hardware store, and fast-food restaurant. Have the groups give presentations in class.

Decision-Making Practice

SD 5.

LO1 Conversion from Accrual to
LO2 Cash Statement

Adele, owner of Adele's Secretarial Service, is puzzled by the income statement that appears below. She knows she withdrew $15,600 in cash from the company for personal expenses; yet the cash balance in the company's bank account increased from $460 to $3,100 from last June 30 to this June 30. She wants to know how her net income could be less than the cash she took out of the business if there is an increase in the cash balance. Her accountant has completed the closing entries and shows her the balance sheets for June 30, 20x4, and June 30, 20x3. He explains that besides the change in the cash balance, Accounts Receivable decreased by $1,480 and Accounts Payable increased by $380 (supplies are the only items Adele buys on credit). The only other asset or liability account that changed during the year was Accumulated Depreciation, Office Equipment, which increased by $2,200.

Adele's Secretarial Service
Income Statement
For the Year Ended June 30, 20x4

Revenues		
Word processing services		$20,980
Expenses		
Rent expense	$2,400	
Depreciation expense, office equipment	2,200	
Supplies expense	960	
Other expenses	1,240	
Total expenses		6,800
Net income		$14,180

1. Verify the cash balance increase by preparing a statement that lists the receipts of cash and the expenditures of cash during the year.
2. Write a memorandum to Adele explaining why the accountant is answering her question by pointing out year-to-year changes in the balance sheet. Include an explanation of your treatment of depreciation expense.

FINANCIAL REPORTING AND ANALYSIS CASES

Interpreting Financial Reports

FRA 1.

LO2   **Closing Entries**

H&R Block, Inc., <www.hrblock.com> is the world's largest tax preparation service firm. Adapted information from the statement of earnings (in thousands, without earnings per share information) in its annual report for the year ended April 30, 2002, follows.[2] The firm reported distributing cash in the amount of $115,725 to the owners in 2002.

Revenues	
Service revenues	$2,333,064
Other revenues	986,084
Total revenues	$3,319,148
Expenses	
Employee compensation and benefits	$1,308,705
Occupancy and equipment expense	305,387
Depreciation expense	155,386
Marketing and advertising expense	155,729
Supplies, freight, and postage expense	75,710
Bad debt	76,804
Interest expense	116,141
Other operating expenses	408,446
Total expenses	$2,602,308
Earnings before income taxes	$ 716,840
Income taxes	282,435
Net earnings	$ 434,405

1. Prepare in journal form the closing entries H&R Block would have made on April 30, 2002. Treat income taxes as an expense and cash distributions as withdrawals.
2. Based on the way you handled expenses and cash distributions in step 1 and their ultimate effect on the owner's capital, what theoretical reason can you give for not including expenses and cash distributions in the same closing entry?

International Company

FRA 2.

LO1   **Accounting Cycle and Closing**
LO2   **Entries**

Nestlé S.A. <www.nestle.com>, maker of such well-known products as Nescafé, Lean Cuisine, and Perrier, is one of the largest and most internationally diverse companies in the world. Only 2 percent of its $81.4 billion in revenues comes from its home country of Switzerland; the rest comes from sales in almost every other country. Nestlé has over 224,000 employees in 70 countries, and many of its divisions operate as separate companies.[3] How would the accounting cycle, including the closing process, be the same for Nestlé as for Joan Miller Advertising Agency? How would it differ?

Toys "R" Us Annual Report

FRA 3.

LO1   **Fiscal Year, Closing Process, and Interim Reports**

Refer to the notes to the financial statements in the Toys "R" Us <www.tru.com> annual report. When does Toys "R" Us end its fiscal year? For what reasons might it have chosen this date? From the standpoint of completing the accounting cycle, what advantages does this date have? Does Toys "R" Us prepare interim financial statements? What are the implications of interim financial statements for the accounting cycle?

Comparison Case: Toys "R" Us and Walgreen Co.

FRA 4.

LO2   Interim Financial Reporting and Seasonality

Both Walgreens <www.walgreens.com> and Toys "R" Us <www.tru.com> provide quarterly financial information in their financial statements. Quarterly financial reports provide important information about the "seasonality" of a company's operations. *Seasonality* refers to how dependent a company is on sales during one season of the year, such as the Christmas season, and it affects a company's need to plan for cash flows and inventory. From the quarterly financial information for Walgreens and for Toys "R" Us in the Supplement to Chapter 6, determine which company has more seasonal sales and income by calculating for the most recent year the percentage of quarterly net sales and net earnings to annual net sales and net earnings. Discuss the results.

Fingraph® Financial Analyst™

This activity is not applicable to this chapter.

Internet Case

FRA 5.

LO1   Interim Financial Statements

Go to Dell Computer Corporation's web site <www.dell.com> and find the latest quarterly financial report. Compare the results of the latest quarter available to you with the results in the Decision Point at the beginning of this chapter. Are Dell's net revenue (sales) and net income greater or less in the more recent quarter? What other information do you find in the quarterly report?

COMPREHENSIVE PROBLEM: JOAN MILLER ADVERTISING AGENCY

This comprehensive problem involving the Joan Miller Advertising Agency covers all the learning objectives in this chapter and in the chapters on measuring business transactions and measuring business income. To complete the problem, you may sometimes have to refer to this material.

The July 31, 20xx, post-closing trial balance for the Joan Miller Advertising Agency appears on the facing page. During August, the agency engaged in these transactions:

Aug. 1   Received an additional investment of cash from Joan Miller, $6,300.
      2   Purchased additional office equipment with cash, $1,200.
      5   Received art equipment transferred to the business from Joan Miller, $1,400.
      6   Purchased additional office supplies with cash, $90.
      7   Purchased additional art supplies on credit from Taylor Supply Company, $450.
      8   Completed the series of advertisements for Marsh Tire Company that began on July 31 (see page 103) and billed Marsh Tire Company for the total services performed, including the accrued revenues (fees receivable) that had been recognized in an adjusting entry in July, $800.
      9   Paid the secretary for two weeks' wages, $1,200.
    12   Paid the amount due to Morgan Equipment for the office equipment purchased last month, $1,500.
    13   Accepted an advance in cash for artwork to be done for another agency, $1,600.
    14   Purchased a copier (office equipment) from Morgan Equipment for $2,100, paying $350 in cash and agreeing to pay the rest in equal payments over the next five months.
    15   Performed advertising services and received a cash fee, $1,450.
    16   Received payment on account from Ward Department Stores for services performed last month, $2,800.

Joan Miller Advertising Agency
Post-Closing Trial Balance
July 31, 20xx

Cash	$ 9,140	
Accounts Receivable	5,000	
Art Supplies	1,300	
Office Supplies	600	
Prepaid Rent	800	
Prepaid Insurance	880	
Art Equipment	4,200	
Accumulated Depreciation, Art Equipment		$ 70
Office Equipment	3,000	
Accumulated Depreciation, Office Equipment		50
Accounts Payable		3,240
Unearned Art Fees		600
Wages Payable		360
Joan Miller, Capital		20,600
	$24,920	$24,920

Aug. 19 Paid amount due for the telephone bill that was received and recorded at the end of July, $140.

20 Performed advertising services for Ward Department Stores and agreed to accept payment next month, $3,200.

21 Performed art services for cash, $580.

22 Received and paid the utility bill for August, $220.

23 Paid the secretary for two weeks' wages, $1,200.

26 Paid the rent for September in advance, $800.

27 Received the telephone bill for August, which is to be paid next month, $160.

30 Paid cash to Joan Miller as a withdrawal for personal expenses, $1,400.

REQUIRED ▶

1. Record entries in journal form and post to the ledger accounts the optional reversing entries on August 1 for Wages Payable and Accounts Receivable (see Adjustment **g** on page 101 and Adjustment **i** on page 103). (Begin the general journal on Page 5.)

2. Record the transactions for August in journal form.

3. Post the August transactions to the ledger accounts.

4. Prepare a trial balance in the Trial Balance columns of a work sheet.

5. Prepare adjusting entries and complete the work sheet using the information below.

   a. One month's prepaid rent has expired, $800.
   b. One month's prepaid insurance has expired, $80.
   c. An inventory of art supplies reveals $600 still on hand on August 31.
   d. An inventory of office supplies reveals $410 still on hand on August 31.
   e. Depreciation on art equipment for August is calculated to be $100.
   f. Depreciation on office equipment for August is calculated to be $100.
   g. Art services performed for which payment had been received in advance totaled $1,300.
   h. Advertising services performed that will not be billed until September total $290.
   i. Three days' wages had accrued by the end of August (assume a five-day week).

6. From the work sheet prepare an income statement, a statement of owner's equity, and a balance sheet.

7. Record the adjusting entries in journal form, and post them to the ledger accounts.

8. Record the closing entries in journal form, and post them to the ledger accounts.

9. Prepare a post-closing trial balance.

5

Chapter 5 introduces merchandising accounting, including the operating cycle and the perpetual and periodic inventory systems for merchandising businesses.

Merchandising Operations

LEARNING OBJECTIVES

LO1 Identify the management issues related to merchandising businesses.

LO2 Compare the income statements for service and merchandising concerns, and define the components of the merchandising income statement.

LO3 Define and distinguish the terms of sale for merchandising transactions.

LO4 Prepare an income statement and record merchandising transactions under the perpetual inventory system.

LO5 Prepare an income statement and record merchandising transactions under the periodic inventory system.

SUPPLEMENTAL OBJECTIVES

SO6 Prepare a work sheet and closing entries for a merchandising concern using the perpetual inventory system.

SO7 Prepare a work sheet and closing entries for a merchandising concern using the periodic inventory system.

SO8 Apply sales and purchases discounts to merchandising transactions.

Target Stores <<u>www.target.com</u>> Merchandising businesses have two key decisions to make: the price at which they sell merchandise and the level of service they provide. A department store may set the price of its merchandise at a relatively high level and provide a great deal of service. A discount store, on the other hand, may price its merchandise at a relatively low level and provide limited service. Target Stores, a division of Target Corp., is a successful discount retailer, as the figures in the Financial Highlights show.[1] What decisions did Target Stores' management make about pricing and service to achieve this success?

Target distinguishes itself from other discounters by providing its customers with high-quality, name-brand merchandise, superior service, a convenient shopping experience, and competitive prices. Target's merchandise might be sold at full price in specialty stores; Target sells it at prices that are competitive with those of other discount stores that sell less well-known merchandise. Target's chief executive officer says, "We continue to open stores across the country.... Even in our most populated states, our market presence has expanded by 40 percent [since 1997] indicating ample opportunity for profitable growth well into the future."[2]

What decisions did Target's management make about pricing and service that resulted in Target's becoming a leading discount retailer?

Financial Highlights

(In millions, except stores and square feet)

	2002	2001
Revenues	**$43,917**	$39,826
Net earnings	**1,654**	1,386
Stores	**1,475**	1,381
Retail square feet*	**176,525**	161,624

*In thousands, reflects total square feet, less office, warehouse, and vacant space.

MANAGEMENT ISSUES IN MERCHANDISING BUSINESSES

LO1   Identify the management issues related to merchandising businesses.

RELATED TEXT ASSIGNMENTS
Q: 1, 2, 3, 4, 5, 6, 7
SE: 1
E: 1, 2
P: 1, 3, 8, 10
SD: 1, 2, 4
FRA: 3, 4, 5, 6

KEY POINT: The operating cycle is average day's inventory on hand plus the average number of days to collect credit sales.

Up to this point you have studied business and accounting issues related to the simplest type of business—the service business. **Service businesses**, such as advertising agencies and law firms, perform services for fees or commissions. **Merchandising businesses**, on the other hand, earn income by buying and selling goods. These companies, whether wholesale or retail, use the same basic accounting methods as service companies, but the buying and selling of goods adds to the complexity of the process. As a foundation for discussing the accounting issues of merchandising businesses, we must first identify the management issues involved in running such a business.

CASH FLOW MANAGEMENT

Cash flow management involves planning a company's receipts and payments of cash. If a company is not able to pay its bills when they are due, it may be forced out of business. This is particularly true for merchandising businesses, which differ from service businesses in that they must have goods on hand so that they are available for sale to customers. These goods are called **merchandise inventory**.

Merchandising businesses engage in a series of transactions called the **operating cycle**, which is illustrated in Figure 1. The transactions in the operating cycle consist of (1) purchases of merchandise inventory for cash or on credit, (2) payment for purchases made on credit, (3) sales of merchandise inventory for cash or on credit, and (4) collection of cash from credit sales. Purchases of merchandise are usually made on credit, so the merchandiser has a period of time before payment is due, but this period is generally less than the time it takes to sell the merchandise. To finance the inventory until it is sold and the resulting cash is collected, management must plan for cash flows from within the company or from borrowing.

The need for cash flow management is demonstrated in Figure 2, which shows the financing period. Sometimes referred to as the *cash gap*, the **financing period** is the amount of time from the purchase of inventory until it is sold and payment is collected, less the amount of time creditors give the company to pay for the inventory. Thus, if it takes 60 days to sell inventory, 60 days to collect for the sale, and creditors' payment terms are 30 days, the financing period is 90 days. During the

FIGURE 1
The Operating Cycle of Merchandising Businesses

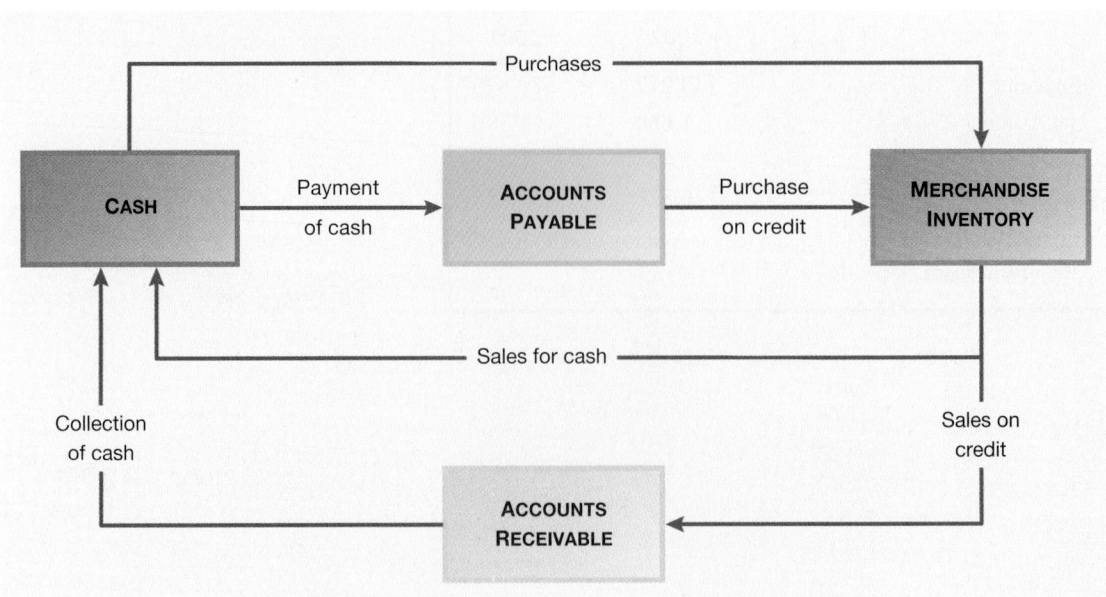

Claire's Stores, Inc. <<u>www.clairestores.com</u>>

OBJECTIVES

■ To become familiar with the nature of merchandising operations.

■ To identify the management issues associated with a merchandising business.

■ To show how gross margin and operating expenses affect the business goal of profitability.

BACKGROUND FOR THE CASE

Claire's Stores, Inc. is a leading international retailer offering value-priced costume jewelry, accessories, and cosmetics to fashion-aware teens and young adults. Claire's Accessories is the company's core business. In the 1980s, the company sold its capital-intensive manufacturing businesses to concentrate on the specialty retailing of women's fashion accessories. The company has grown steadily and now has about 2,200 stores throughout North America, Europe, and Japan. Claire's Accessories stores are approximately 1,000 square feet in size in North America and 600 square feet in Europe and Japan. Claire's expansion into Europe has been particularly successful, with high store traffic and sales per square foot at 250 percent of that in North America. Keys to the company's success are the merchan-

dising and marketing practices that reinforce its position as the place for customers to find new accessories. Constant product testing, test placement of successful items in all departments, and an efficient distribution system all enable Claire's to make quick responses to "what's new." The company's North American distribution center receives and ships merchandise on the same day, and the retail outlets receive shipments three to five times per week.

For more information about Claire's Stores, Inc., visit the company's web site through the Needles Accounting Resource Center Web Site at **http://accounting.college. hmco.com/students.**

REQUIRED

View the video on Claire's Stores, Inc., that accompanies this book. As you are watching the video, take notes related to the following questions:

1. All merchandising companies have inventories. What is inventory, and why is it important to implement controls over it? Identify the types of products that Claire's Accessories stores typically have in inventory and some ways in which the company might control its inventory.

2. All merchandising companies have an operating cycle. Describe the operating cycle and explain how Claire's successfully manages its operating cycle.

3. All merchandising companies try to achieve the goal of profitability by producing a satisfactory gross margin and maintaining acceptable levels of operating expenses. Describe how Claire's operations affect gross margin and operating expenses in a way that enables the company to achieve superior profitability.

financing period, the company will be without cash from this series of transactions and will need either to have funds available internally or to borrow from a bank.

The financing period for a merchandising company can be less than 120 days. For example, Dillard Dept. Stores, Inc., a successful chain of U.S. department stores, has a financing period of 101 days. It consists of inventory on hand for an average

www.dillards.com

FIGURE 2
The Financing Period

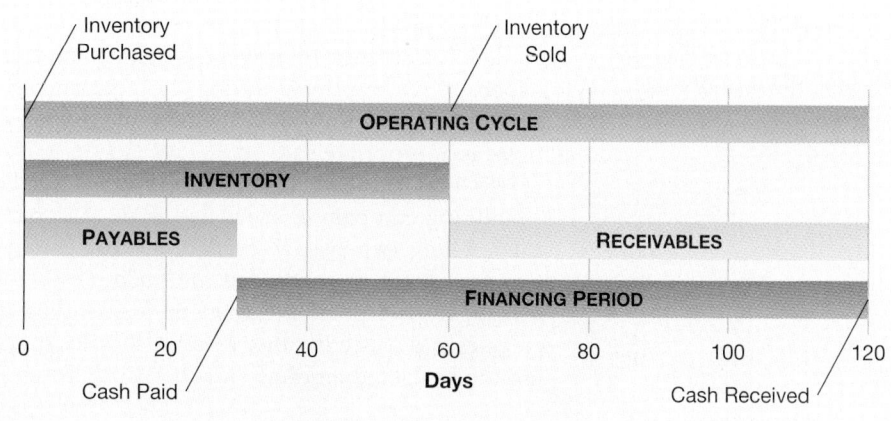

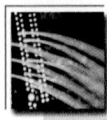

FOCUS ON BUSINESS TECHNOLOGY

Credit Cards or Debit Cards?

An increasing percentage of merchandising transactions are conducted electronically. Credit cards have long been in use, but debit, purchase, and Smart cards are becoming integral parts of the so-called cashless society. The debit card allows consumers to access their bank accounts for ATM transactions or with any seller that accepts major credit cards. The price of the sale is withdrawn immediately from the customer's account when purchases are made at grocery stores, drugstores, gas stations, dry cleaners, or hardware stores. The purchase card, the business equivalent of a debit card, allows employees to purchase merchandise for their business. Smart cards have an embedded integrated circuit that stores information, such as prepaid amounts from which purchases are deducted at the point of purchase.

www.target.com

● **STOP AND THINK!**

Can a company have a "negative" financing period?

Yes, if its merchandise is held for a very short time, if its sales are made mostly for cash, or if it has long terms to pay its suppliers. For example, Dell makes its computers to order (resulting in small inventories), sells on credit cards (which reduces accounts receivable), and takes 30 days or more to pay its suppliers. ■

of 102 days, plus an average of 42 days to collect its receivables, minus an average of 43 days to pay for its merchandise. Target, on the other hand, has a much shorter financing period, only 29 days. Its period consists of inventory on hand for an average of 61 days, plus an average of 20 days to collect its receivables, minus an average of 52 days to pay for its merchandise. Target derives its advantage from selling most of its merchandise for cash, which results in very low receivables.

As Target demonstrates, a company can help its cash flow by reducing its financing period. Many retailers, including Target, do this by selling as much as possible for cash. Cash sales include sales on bank credit cards, such as Visa or MasterCard, and on debit cards, which draw directly on the purchaser's bank account. They are considered cash sales because funds from them are available to the merchandiser immediately. In the case of credit sales, the company must wait a period of time before receiving the cash. Small retail stores may have mostly cash sales and very few credit sales, whereas large wholesale concerns may have almost all credit sales. Most merchandising businesses, however, have a combination of cash and credit sales.

PROFITABILITY MANAGEMENT

In addition to managing cash flow, management must achieve a satisfactory level of profitability. It must sell merchandise at a price that exceeds its cost by a sufficient margin to pay operating expenses and have enough left to provide sufficient income, or profitability. **Profitability management** is a complex activity that includes, first, achieving a satisfactory gross margin and, second, maintaining acceptable levels of operating expenses. Achieving a satisfactory gross margin depends on setting appropriate prices for merchandise and purchasing merchandise at favorable prices and terms. Maintaining acceptable levels of operating expenses depends on controlling expenses and operating efficiently.

One of the more effective ways of controlling expenses is to use operating budgets. An **operating budget** reflects management's operating plans and consists of detailed listings of projected selling expenses and general and administrative expenses. At key times during the year and at the end of the year, management should compare the budget with actual expenses and make adjustments to operations as appropriate.

Exhibit 1 shows an operating budget for Fenwick Fashions Company, a merchandising company that we use as an example throughout this chapter. Fenwick's total selling expenses exceeded the budget by only $80, but four of its selling expense categories exceeded the budget by a total of $2,080. Management should investigate the possibility that underspending in advertising of $2,000 hid inefficiencies and waste in other areas. Also, sales may have been penalized by not spending the budgeted amount on advertising. Total general and administrative expenses

KEY POINT: An operating budget is a financial plan for achieving the goal of profitability.

EXHIBIT 1
An Example of an Operating Budget

Fenwick Fashions Company
Operating Budget
For the Year Ended December 31, 20x3

Operating Expenses	Budget	Actual	Difference Under (Over) Budget
Selling expenses			
Sales salaries expense	$22,000	$22,500	($ 500)
Freight out expense	5,500	5,740	(240)
Advertising expense	12,000	10,000	2,000
Insurance expense, selling	800	1,600	(800)
Store supplies expense	1,000	1,540	(540)
Total selling expenses	$41,300	$41,380	($ 80)
General and administrative expenses			
Office salaries expense	$23,000	$26,900	($3,900)
Insurance expense, general	2,100	4,200	(2,100)
Office supplies expense	500	1,204	(704)
Depreciation expense, building	2,600	2,600	—
Depreciation expense, office equipment	2,000	2,200	(200)
Total general and administrative expenses	$30,200	$37,104	($6,904)
Total operating expenses	$71,500	$78,484	($6,984)

exceeded the budget by $6,904. Management should determine why large differences occurred for office salaries expense, insurance expense, and office supplies expense. The amount of insurance expense is usually set by the insurance company; thus, an error in the initial budgeting of insurance expense may have caused the unfavorable result. The operating budget helps management focus on specific areas that need attention.

CHOICE OF INVENTORY SYSTEM

Another issue the management of a merchandising business must address is the choice of inventory system. Management must choose the system or combination of systems that is best for achieving the company's goals. There are two basic systems of accounting for the many items in the merchandise inventory: the perpetual inventory system and the periodic inventory system.

Under the **perpetual inventory system**, continuous records are kept of the quantity and, usually, the cost of individual items as they are bought and sold. The detailed data available from the perpetual inventory system enable management to respond to customers' inquiries about product availability, to order inventory more effectively and thus avoid running out of stock, and to control the financial costs associated with investments in inventory. Under this system, the cost of each item

KEY POINT: Under the perpetual inventory system, the Merchandise Inventory account and the Cost of Goods Sold account are updated with every sale.

FOCUS ON BUSINESS TECHNOLOGY

Bar Codes—How Have They Influenced Choice of Inventory Systems?

Many grocery stores, which traditionally used the periodic inventory system, now employ bar coding to update the physical inventory as items are sold. At the checkout counter, the cashier scans the electronic marking on each product, called a *bar code* or *universal product code* (UPC), into the cash register, which is linked to a computer that records the sale. Bar coding has become common in all types of retail companies, and in manufacturing firms and hospitals as well. It has also become a major factor in the increased use of the perpetual inventory system. Interestingly, some retail businesses now use the perpetual inventory system for keeping track of the physical flow of inventory and the periodic inventory system for preparing their financial statements.

KEY POINT: The valuation of ending inventory on the balance sheet is determined by multiplying the quantity of each inventory item by its unit cost.

is recorded in the Merchandise Inventory account when it is purchased. As merchandise is sold, its cost is transferred from the Merchandise Inventory account to the Cost of Goods Sold account. Thus, at all times the balance of the Merchandise Inventory account equals the cost of goods on hand, and the balance in Cost of Goods Sold equals the cost of merchandise sold to customers.

Under the **periodic inventory system**, the inventory not yet sold, or on hand, is counted periodically, usually at the end of the accounting period. No detailed records of the inventory on hand are maintained during the accounting period. The figure for inventory on hand is accurate only on the balance sheet date. As soon as any purchases or sales are made, the inventory figure becomes a historical amount, and it remains so until the new ending inventory amount is entered at the end of the next accounting period.

Some retail and wholesale businesses use the periodic inventory system because it reduces the amount of clerical work. If a business is fairly small, management can maintain control over its inventory simply through observation or by using an offline system of cards or computer records. But for larger businesses, the lack of detailed records may lead to lost sales or high operating costs.

KEY POINT: Although computerization has made the perpetual inventory system more popular in recent years, a physical count still should be made periodically to ensure that the actual number of goods on hand matches the quantity indicated by the computer records.

Because of the difficulty and expense of accounting for the purchase and sale of each item, companies that sell items of low value in high volume have traditionally used the periodic inventory system. Examples of such companies are drugstores, automobile parts stores, department stores, and discount stores. In contrast, companies that sell items of high unit value, such as appliances or automobiles, have tended to use the perpetual inventory system. The distinction between high and low unit value for inventory systems has blurred considerably in recent years because of the widespread use of computers. Although the periodic inventory system is still widely used, use of the perpetual inventory system has increased greatly.

CONTROL OF MERCHANDISING OPERATIONS

Buying and selling, the principal transactions of merchandising businesses, involve assets—cash, accounts receivable, and merchandise inventory—that are vulnerable to theft and embezzlement. One reason for this vulnerability is that cash and inventory may be fairly easy to steal. Another is the difficulty of monitoring the large number of transactions (including cash receipts, receipts on account, payments for purchases, and receipts and shipments of inventory) in which these assets are usually involved. If a merchandising company does not take steps to protect its assets, it may suffer high losses of cash and inventory. Management's responsibility is to establish an environment, accounting systems, and control procedures that will protect the company's assets. These systems and procedures are called **internal controls**.

Maintaining control over merchandise inventory is facilitated by taking a **physical inventory**. This process involves an actual count of all merchandise on hand. It can be a difficult task because it is easy to accidentally omit items or to count them twice. A physical inventory must be taken under both the periodic and the perpetual inventory systems. Under the perpetual inventory system, the records need to be compared with the physical inventory to determine whether any inventory shortages exist.

Merchandise inventory includes all goods intended for sale that are owned by a business, regardless of where they are located—on shelves, in storerooms, in warehouses, or in trucks between warehouses and stores. It also includes goods in transit from suppliers if title to the goods has passed to the merchant. Ending inventory does not include merchandise that has been sold but not yet delivered to customers or goods that cannot be sold because they are damaged or obsolete. If the damaged or obsolete goods can be sold at a reduced price, however, they should be included in ending inventory at their reduced value.

The actual count is usually taken after the close of business on the last day of the fiscal year. To facilitate taking the physical inventory, many companies end their fiscal year in a slow season, when inventories are at relatively low levels. Retail department stores often end their fiscal year in January or February, for example. After hours, at night, or on the weekend, employees count all items and record the results on numbered inventory tickets or sheets, following procedures to ensure no items will be missed. Sometimes a store closes for all or part of a day for inventory taking. The use of bar coding to take inventory electronically has greatly facilitated the process in many companies.

ENRICHMENT NOTE:
Inventory shortages can result from honest mistakes, such as accidentally tagging inventory with the wrong number.

Most companies experience losses of merchandise inventory from spoilage, shoplifting, and theft by employees. When such losses occur, the periodic inventory system provides no means of identifying them because the costs are automatically included in the cost of goods sold. For example, assume that a company has lost $1,250 in stolen merchandise during an accounting period. When the physical inventory is taken, the missing items are not in stock, so they cannot be counted. Because the ending inventory does not contain these items, the amount subtracted from goods available for sale is less than it would be if the goods were in stock. The cost of goods sold, then, is overstated by $1,250. In a sense, the cost of goods sold is inflated by the amount of merchandise that has been lost.

KEY POINT: An adjustment to the Merchandise Inventory account will be needed if the physical inventory reveals a difference between the actual inventory and the amount in the records.

The perpetual inventory system makes it easier to identify such losses. Because the Merchandise Inventory account is continuously updated for sales, purchases, and returns, the loss will show up as the difference between the inventory records and the physical inventory taken at the end of the accounting period. Once the amount of the loss has been identified, the ending inventory is updated by crediting the Merchandise Inventory account. The offsetting debit is usually an increase in Cost of Goods Sold because the loss is considered a cost that reduces the company's gross margin.

Check out ACE for a Review Quiz at http://accounting.college.hmco.com/students.

INCOME STATEMENT FOR A MERCHANDISING CONCERN

LO2 Compare the income statements for service and merchandising concerns, and define the components of the merchandising income statement.

RELATED TEXT ASSIGNMENTS
Q: 8, 9, 10
SE: 2
E: 3
SD: 4, 5
FRA: 1, 5

Many service companies require only a simple income statement. For those companies, as shown in Figure 3, net income represents the difference between revenues and expenses. But merchandising companies, because they buy and sell merchandise inventory, require a more complex income statement. As shown in Figure 3, the income statement for a merchandiser consists of three major parts: (1) net sales, (2) cost of goods sold, and (3) operating expenses. There is also a subtotal for gross margin.

The main difference between a merchandiser's income statement and the income statement of a service business is that the merchandiser must compute gross

FIGURE 3
The Components of Income Statements for Service and Merchandising Companies

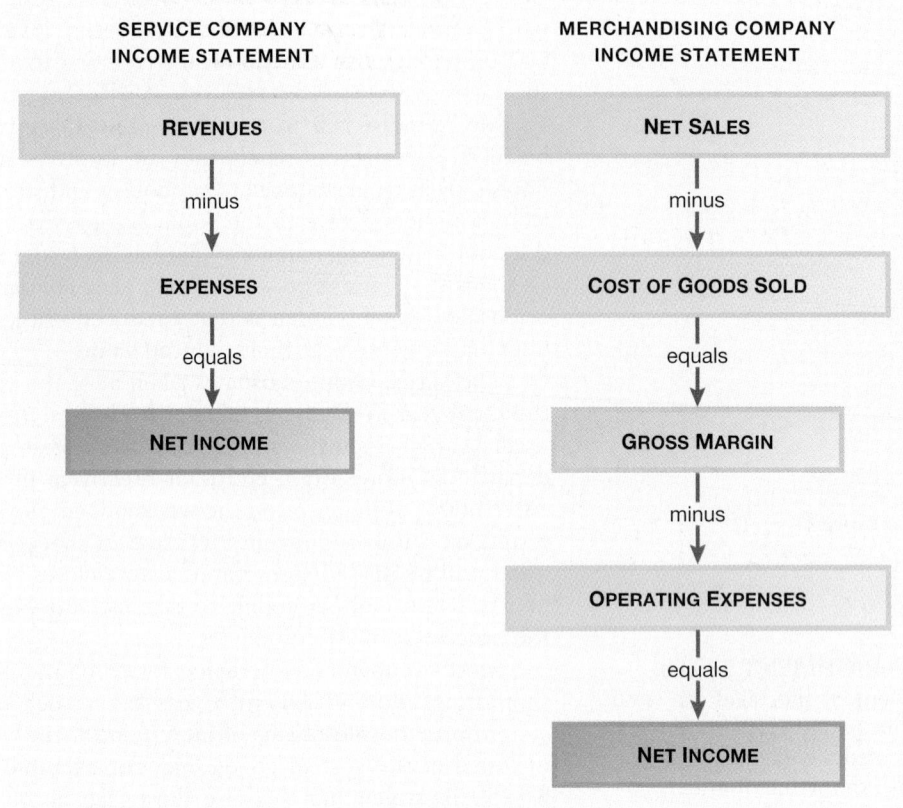

⬡ STOP AND THINK!

Why do merchandising companies have a more complex income statement than service companies?

Because merchandising companies buy and sell merchandising inventory, they require a Cost of Goods Sold account, which makes the income statement more complex. ■

margin before operating expenses are deducted. In the following discussion, the income statement for Fenwick Fashions Company, presented in Exhibit 2, will serve as an example of a merchandising income statement.

NET SALES

KEY POINT: A sale takes place when title to the goods transfers to the buyer.

The first major part of the merchandising income statement is **net sales**, often simply called *sales*. Net sales consist of the gross proceeds from sales of merchandise, or gross sales, less sales returns and allowances. **Gross sales** consist of total cash sales and total credit sales during an accounting period. Even though the cash may not be collected until the following accounting period under the revenue recognition rule, revenue is recorded as earned when title for merchandise passes from seller to buyer at the time of sale. **Sales Returns and Allowances** is a contra-revenue account used to accumulate cash refunds, credits on account, and allowances off selling prices made to customers who have received defective or otherwise unsatisfactory products. If other discounts or allowances are given to customers (see supplemental objective 8, for instance), they also should be deducted from gross sales.

Management, investors, and others often use the amount of sales and trends suggested by sales as indicators of a firm's progress. Increasing sales suggest growth; decreasing sales indicate the possibility of decreased future earnings and other financial problems. To detect trends, comparisons are frequently made between the net sales of different accounting periods.

COST OF GOODS SOLD

The second part of the income statement for a merchandiser or manufacturer is **cost of goods sold**, or simply *cost of sales*. Cost of goods sold is the amount a

EXHIBIT 2
Income Statement Under the Perpetual Inventory System

Fenwick Fashions Company
Income Statement
For the Year Ended December 31, 20x3

Net sales			
Gross sales			$246,350
Less sales returns and allowances			7,025
Net sales			$239,325
Cost of goods sold*			131,360
Gross margin			$107,965
Operating expenses			
Selling expenses			
Sales salaries expense	$22,500		
Freight out expense	5,740		
Advertising expense	10,000		
Insurance expense, selling	1,600		
Store supplies expense	1,540		
Total selling expenses		$41,380	
General and administrative expenses			
Office salaries expense	$26,900		
Insurance expense, general	4,200		
Office supplies expense	1,204		
Depreciation expense, building	2,600		
Depreciation expense, office equipment	2,200		
Total general and administrative expenses		37,104	
Total operating expenses			78,484
Net income			$ 29,481

*Freight in has been included in cost of goods sold.

KEY POINT: The matching rule precludes the cost of inventory from being expensed until the inventory has been sold.

KEY POINT: Gross margin is an important measure of profitability.

ENRICHMENT NOTE: When gross margin is insufficient to cover operating expenses, the company has suffered a net loss.

merchandiser paid for the merchandise sold during an accounting period or the cost to a manufacturer of making the products sold during an accounting period.

GROSS MARGIN

The difference between net sales and cost of goods sold on the merchandising income statement is **gross margin**, or *gross profit*. To be successful, merchants must sell goods for an amount greater than cost—that is, gross margin must be great enough to pay operating expenses and provide an adequate income. Management is interested in both the amount and the percentage of gross margin. The percentage of gross margin is computed by dividing the amount of gross margin by net sales. In the case of Fenwick Fashions, the amount of gross margin is $107,965 and the percentage of gross margin is 45.1 percent ($107,965 ÷ $239,325). This information is helpful in planning business operations. For instance, management may try to increase total sales dollars by reducing the selling price. This strategy reduces the percentage of gross margin, but it will work if the total items sold increase enough to raise the absolute amount of gross margin. This is the strategy of discount

www.samsclub.com
www.costco.com

www.neimanmarcus.com
www.tiffany.com

warehouse stores like Sam's Clubs and Costco Wholesale Corporation. On the other hand, management may keep a high gross margin and attempt to increase sales and the amount of gross margin by increasing operating expenses, such as advertising. This is the strategy followed by upscale specialty stores like Neiman Marcus and Tiffany & Co. Other strategies to increase gross margin include reducing cost of goods sold by better purchasing methods.

OPERATING EXPENSES

KEY POINT: The most common types of operating expenses are selling expenses and general and administrative expenses. They are deducted from gross margin on the income statement.

BUSINESS-WORLD EXAMPLE: Companies that are restructuring their operations often focus on reducing operating expenses.

The third major area of the merchandising income statement consists of **operating expenses**, which are the expenses other than cost of goods sold that are incurred in running a business. It is customary to group operating expenses into categories, such as selling expenses and general and administrative expenses. Selling expenses include the costs of storing goods and preparing them for sale, displaying, advertising, and otherwise promoting sales; making sales; and delivering goods to the buyer, if the seller bears the cost of delivery. The latter cost is often accumulated in an account called **Freight Out Expense** or *Delivery Expense*. Among the general and administrative expenses are general office expenses, which include expenses for accounting, personnel, credit and collections, and any other expenses that apply to overall operation. General occupancy expenses, such as rent expense, insurance expense, and utilities expense, are often classified as general and administrative expenses. However, they may also be allocated between the selling and the general and administrative categories. Careful planning and control of operating expenses can improve a company's profitability.

NET INCOME

Net income, the final figure or "bottom line" of the income statement, is what remains after operating expenses are deducted from gross margin. It is an important performance measure because it represents the amount of business earnings that accrue to the owners. It is the amount that is transferred to owner's equity from all the income-generating activities during the period. Both management and owners often use net income to measure whether a business has operated successfully during the past accounting period.

 Check out ACE for a Review Quiz at http://accounting.college.hmco.com/students.

TERMS OF SALE

LO3 Define and distinguish the terms of sale for merchandising transactions.

RELATED TEXT ASSIGNMENTS
Q: 11, 12
SE: 3, 4
E: 4
FRA: 2, 6

KEY POINT: A trade discount applies to the list or catalogue price. A sales discount applies to the sales price.

When goods are sold on credit, both parties should understand the amount and timing of payment as well as other terms of the purchase, such as who pays delivery charges and what warranties or rights of return apply. Sellers quote prices in different ways. Many merchants quote the price at which they expect to sell their goods. Others, particularly manufacturers and wholesalers, quote prices as a percentage (usually 30 percent or more) off their list or catalogue prices. Such a reduction is called a **trade discount**. For example, if an article is listed at $1,000 with a trade discount of 40 percent, or $400, the seller records the sale at $600 and the buyer records the purchase at $600. The seller may raise or lower the trade discount depending on the quantity purchased. The list or catalogue price and related trade discount are used only to arrive at the agreed-upon price; they do not appear in the accounting records.

The terms of sale are usually printed on the sales invoice and thus constitute part of the sales agreement. Customary terms differ from industry to industry. In

FOCUS ON BUSINESS TECHNOLOGY

How Are Web Sales Doing?

In spite of the well-publicized dot-com meltdown and the demise of "pure-play" Internet retailers like eToys.com and Pets.com, merchandise sales over the Internet are thriving. Internet sales amounted to $44.5 billion in 2001 and were expected to double in the next few years. As it has turned out, the most successful Internet retailing companies are established retailers that use the Internet to enhance their current operations. For example, mail-order catalogue companies like Lands' End <www.landsend.com> and L.L. Bean <www.llbean.com> have profitable Internet operations. Circuit City <www.circuitcity.com> allows customers to purchase online and pick up the products at stores near their homes. Office Depot <www.officedepot.com>, which focuses primarily on business-to-business Internet sales, has set up customized web pages for 37,000 corporate clients. These web sites allow customers to make online purchases or to check store inventories.[3] Although Internet transactions are recorded in the same way as on-site transactions, the technology adds a level of complexity to the transaction.

ENRICHMENT NOTE:
Early collection also has the advantage of reducing the probability of a customer's defaulting.

● STOP AND THINK!
Assume a large shipment of uninsured merchandise to your company was destroyed when the delivery truck had an accident and burned. Would you want the terms to be FOB shipping point or FOB destination?

You would want the terms to be FOB destination because the loss of merchandise would be the responsibility of the shipper. If the terms were FOB shipping point, the merchandise would belong to you when it left the shipper and would be your loss. ∎

some industries, payment is expected in a short period of time, such as 10 or 30 days. In these cases, the invoice is marked "n/10" ("net 10") or "n/30" ("net 30"), meaning that the amount of the invoice is due either 10 days or 30 days after the invoice date. If the invoice is due 10 days after the end of the month, it is marked "n/10 eom."

In some industries, it is customary to give a discount for early payment. This discount, called a **sales discount**, is intended to increase the seller's liquidity by reducing the amount of money tied up in accounts receivable. An invoice that offers a sales discount might be labeled "2/10, n/30," which means that the buyer either can pay the invoice within 10 days of the invoice date and take a 2 percent discount or can wait 30 days and pay the full amount of the invoice. It is almost always advantageous for a buyer to take the discount because the saving of 2 percent over a period of 20 days (from the eleventh day to the thirtieth day) represents an effective annual rate of 36.5 percent (365 days ÷ 20 days × 2% = 36.5%). Most companies would be better off borrowing money to take the discount. The practice of giving sales discounts has been declining because it is costly to the seller and because, from the buyer's viewpoint, the amount of the discount is usually very small in relation to the price of the purchase. Accounting for sales discounts is covered in Supplemental Objective 8.

In some industries, the seller usually pays transportation costs and charges a price that includes those costs. In other industries, it is customary for the purchaser to pay transportation charges. Special terms designate whether the seller or the purchaser pays the freight charges. **FOB shipping point** means that the seller places the merchandise "free on board" at the point of origin and the buyer bears the shipping costs. The title to the merchandise passes to the buyer at that point. For example, when the sales agreement for the purchase of a car says "FOB factory," the buyer must pay the freight from where the car was made to wherever he or she is located, and the buyer owns the car from the time it leaves the factory.

On the other hand, **FOB destination** means that the seller bears the transportation costs to the place where the merchandise is delivered. The seller retains title until the merchandise reaches its destination and usually prepays the shipping costs, in which case the buyer makes no accounting entry for freight. The effects of these special shipping terms are summarized as follows:

Shipping Term	Where Title Passes	Who Pays the Cost of Transportation
FOB shipping point	At origin	Buyer
FOB destination	At destination	Seller

Many retailers allow customers to charge their purchases to a third-party company that the customer will pay later. These transactions are normally handled with credit cards. Five of the most widely used credit cards are American Express, Discover Card, Diners Club, MasterCard, and Visa. The customer establishes credit with the lender (the credit card issuer) and receives a plastic card to use in making charge purchases. If the seller accepts the card, an invoice is prepared and signed by the customer at the time of the sale. The seller then deposits the invoice in the bank and receives cash. Thus, the seller does not have to establish the customer's credit, collect from the customer, or tie up money in accounts receivable. As payment, the lender, rather than paying the total amount of the credit card sales, takes a discount of 2 to 6 percent. The discount is a selling expense for the merchandiser. For example, assume that a restaurant made sales of $1,000 on Visa credit cards and that Visa takes a 4 percent discount on the sales. Assume also that the sales invoices are deposited in a special Visa bank account in the name of the company, in much the same way that checks from cash sales are deposited. The sales are recorded as follows:

$A = L + OE$	Cash	960
$+$ $-$	Credit Card Discount Expense	40
$+$	Sales	1,000
	Made sales on Visa cards	

Check out ACE for a Review Quiz at http://accounting.college.hmco.com/students.

APPLYING THE PERPETUAL INVENTORY SYSTEM

LO4   Prepare an income statement and record merchandising transactions under the perpetual inventory system.

RELATED TEXT ASSIGNMENTS
Q: 13, 14, 16, 17
SE: 5, 6
E: 5, 6, 7
P: 1, 2, 8, 9
SD: 2
FRA: 2, 6

Exhibit 2 previously showed the income statement for Fenwick Fashions Company as it would appear if the company used the perpetual inventory system. The focal point of this income statement is cost of goods sold, which is deducted from net sales to arrive at gross margin. Under the perpetual inventory system, this account is continually updated during the accounting period as purchases, sales, and other inventory transactions take place. The Merchandise Inventory account on the balance sheet is updated at the same time.

TRANSACTIONS RELATED TO PURCHASES OF MERCHANDISE

The following sections illustrate the recording of typical transactions related to purchases of merchandise under the perpetual inventory system. Transactions related to sales made by Fenwick Fashions Company follow.

KEY POINT: The Merchandise Inventory account is increased when a purchase is made.

Purchases of Merchandise on Credit

Oct. 3   Received merchandise purchased on credit from Neebok Company, invoice dated October 1, terms n/10, FOB shipping point, $4,890.

$A = L + OE$
$+$ $+$

Oct. 3	Merchandise Inventory	4,890	
	Accounts Payable		4,890
	Purchased merchandise from Neebok Company, terms n/10, FOB shipping point, invoice dated Oct. 1		

● **STOP AND THINK!**
Under the perpetual inventory system, the Merchandise Inventory account is constantly updated. What would cause it to have the wrong balance?
The balance would be wrong if an error were made in updating the account or if merchandise had been lost or stolen. ■

Under the perpetual inventory system, the cost of merchandise purchased is placed in the Merchandise Inventory account at the time of purchase.

Transportation Costs on Purchases

Oct. 4   Received bill from Transfer Freight Company for transportation costs on October 3 shipment, invoice dated October 1, terms n/10, $160.

A = L + OE   Oct. 4   Freight In   160
    +   −   Accounts Payable   160
                                Received transportation charges on
                                Oct. 3 purchase, Transfer Freight
                                Company, terms n/10,
                                invoice dated Oct. 1

KEY POINT: Freight in appears within the cost of goods sold section of the income statement, and Freight Out Expense appears as an operating expense.

Freight in, also called *transportation in*, is the transportation cost of receiving merchandise. Transportation costs are accumulated in a Freight In account because most shipments contain multiple items. It is usually not practical to identify the specific cost of shipping each item of inventory. In Exhibit 2, freight in is included in cost of goods sold. Theoretically, freight in should be allocated between ending inventory and cost of goods sold, but most companies choose to include the cost of freight in with the cost of goods sold on the income statement because it is a relatively small amount.

In some cases, the seller pays the freight charges and bills them to the buyer as a separate item on the invoice. When this occurs, the entries are the same as in the October 3 example, except that an additional debit is made to Freight In for the amount of the freight charges and Accounts Payable is increased by a like amount.

Purchases Returns and Allowances

Oct. 6   Returned merchandise received from Neebok Company on October 3 for credit, $480.

A = L + OE   Oct. 6   Accounts Payable   480
    −   −   Merchandise Inventory   480
                                Returned merchandise from purchase
                                of Oct. 3 to Neebok Company for
                                full credit

If a seller sends the wrong product or one that is otherwise unsatisfactory, the buyer may be allowed to return the item for a cash refund or credit on account, or the buyer may be given an allowance off the sales price. Under the perpetual inventory system, the returned merchandise is removed from the Merchandise Inventory account.

Payments on Account

Oct. 10   Paid in full the amount due to Neebok Company for the purchase of October 3, part of which was returned on October 6.

A = L + OE   Oct. 10   Accounts Payable   4,410
    −   −   Cash   4,410
                                Made payment on account to
                                Neebok Company
                                $4,890 − $480 = $4,410

TRANSACTIONS RELATED TO SALES OF MERCHANDISE

KEY POINT: The Cost of Goods Sold account is increased and the Merchandise Inventory account is decreased when a sale is made.

Under the perpetual inventory system, at the time of a sale, the cost of the merchandise is transferred from the Merchandise Inventory account to the Cost of Goods Sold account. In the case of a return of sold merchandise, the cost of the merchandise is transferred from Cost of Goods Sold back to Merchandise Inventory. Transactions related to sales made by Fenwick Fashions Company follow.

Sales of Merchandise on Credit

Oct. 7   Sold merchandise on credit to Gonzales Distributors, terms n/30, FOB destination, $1,200; the cost of the merchandise was $720.

A = L + OE   Oct. 7   Accounts Receivable   1,200
    +   +   Sales   1,200
                                    Sold merchandise to Gonzales
                                    Distributors, terms n/30,
                                    FOB destination

A = L + OE   Cost of Goods Sold   720
    −   −   Merchandise Inventory   720
                                    Transferred cost of merchandise inventory
                                    sold to Cost of Goods Sold account

KEY POINT: More entries are associated with a perpetual inventory system than with a periodic inventory system.

Under the perpetual inventory system, two entries are necessary. First, the sale is recorded. Second, Cost of Goods Sold is updated by a transfer from Merchandise Inventory. In the case of cash sales, Cash rather than Accounts Receivable is debited for the amount of the sale.

Payment of Delivery Costs

Oct. 8   Paid transportation costs for the sale on October 7, $78.

A = L + OE   Oct. 8   Freight Out Expense   78
    −   −   Cash   78
                                    Paid delivery costs on Oct. 7 sale

A seller will often absorb delivery or freight out costs in the belief that doing so will facilitate the sale of its products. These costs are accumulated in an account called Freight Out Expense, or *Delivery Expense*, which is shown as a selling expense on the income statement.

Returns of Merchandise Sold

Oct. 9   Return of merchandise sold on October 7 accepted from Gonzales Distributors for full credit and returned to merchandise inventory, $300; the cost of the merchandise was $180.

A = L + OE   Oct. 9   Sales Returns and Allowances   300
    −   −   Accounts Receivable   300
                                    Accepted return of merchandise from
                                    Gonzales Distributors

A = L + OE   Oct. 9   Merchandise Inventory   180
    +   +   Cost of Goods Sold   180
                                    Transferred cost of merchandise
                                    returned to the Merchandise Inventory
                                    account

Returns and allowances to customers for wrong or unsatisfactory merchandise are often an indicator of customer dissatisfaction. Such amounts are accumulated in a Sales Returns and Allowances account, which gives management a readily available

FOCUS ON BUSINESS PRACTICE

Are Sales Returns Worth Accounting For?

Some industries routinely have a high percentage of sales returns. More than 6 percent of all nonfood items sold in stores are eventually returned to vendors. This amounts to more than $100 billion a year, or more than the gross national product of two-thirds of the world's nations.[4] Book publishers like Simon & Schuster <www.simonsays.com> often have returns as high as 30 to 50 percent of books shipped because to gain the attention of potential buyers, large numbers of copies must be distributed to various outlets. Magazine publishers like AOL Time Warner <www.aoltw.com> expect to sell no more than 35 to 38 percent of the magazines they send to newsstands and other outlets.[5] In all these businesses, it pays for management to scrutinize the Sales Returns and Allowances account for ways to reduce returns and increase profitability.

KEY POINT: Because the Sales account is established with a credit, its contra account, Sales Returns and Allowances, is established with a debit.

measure of unsatisfactory products and dissatisfied customers. This contra-revenue account has a normal debit balance and is deducted from sales on the income statement. Under the perpetual inventory system, the cost of the merchandise must also be transferred from the Cost of Goods Sold account back into the Merchandise Inventory account. If an allowance is made instead of accepting a return, or if the merchandise cannot be returned to inventory and resold, this transfer is not made.

Receipts on Account

Nov. 5   Received payment in full from Gonzales Distributors for sale of merchandise on October 7, less the return on October 9.

A = L + OE
\+
−

Nov. 5	Cash	900	
	Accounts Receivable		900
	Received on account from		
	Gonzales Distributors		
	$1,200 − $300 = $900		

 Check out ACE for a Review Quiz at http://accounting.college.hmco.com/students.

APPLYING THE PERIODIC INVENTORY SYSTEM

LO5   Prepare an income statement and record merchandising transactions under the periodic inventory system.

RELATED TEXT ASSIGNMENTS
Q: 13, 14, 15, 16, 17, 18
SE: 7, 8, 9
E: 8, 9, 10, 11
P: 3, 4, 7, 10, 11
SD: 2, 5
FRA: 2

Exhibit 3 shows the income statement for Fenwick Fashions Company as it would appear if the company used the periodic inventory system. A major feature of this income statement is the computation of cost of goods sold. Cost of goods sold must be computed because it is not updated for purchases, sales, and other transactions during the accounting period, as it is under the perpetual inventory system. Figure 4 illustrates the components of cost of goods sold.

COST OF GOODS SOLD

The method of computing cost of goods sold when using the periodic inventory method is sometimes confusing because it must take into account both merchandise inventory on hand at the beginning of the accounting period, called the **beginning inventory**, and merchandise inventory on hand at the end of the accounting period, called the **ending inventory**. The ending inventory appears on the balance sheet at the end of the accounting period and becomes the beginning inventory for the next accounting period.

To calculate cost of goods sold, the **goods available for sale** must first be determined. The goods available for sale during the year is the sum of two factors, beginning inventory and the net cost of purchases during the year. In this case, the goods available for sale is $179,660 ($52,800 + $126,860).

If a company sold all the goods available for sale during an accounting period, the cost of goods sold would equal the goods available for sale. In most businesses, however, some merchandise remains unsold and on hand at the end of the period. This merchandise, or ending inventory, must be deducted from the goods available for sale to determine the cost of goods sold. In the case of Fenwick Fashions Company, the ending inventory on December 31, 20x3, is $48,300. Thus, the cost of goods sold is $131,360 ($179,660 − $48,300).

An important component of the cost of goods sold section is **net cost of purchases**, which consists of net purchases plus any freight charges on the purchases. **Net purchases** equal total purchases less any deductions, such as purchases returns and allowances and any discounts allowed by suppliers for early payment (see supplemental objective 8). Because transportation charges, or freight in, are a necessary cost of receiving merchandise for sale, they are added to net purchases to arrive at the net cost of purchases, as shown in Exhibit 3.

Exhibit 3
Income Statement Under the Periodic Inventory System

ENRICHMENT NOTE:
Most published financial statements are condensed, eliminating much of the detail shown here.

Fenwick Fashions Company
Income Statement
For the Year Ended December 31, 20x3

Net sales			
Gross sales			$246,350
Less sales returns and allowances			7,025
Net sales			$239,325
Cost of goods sold			
Merchandise inventory, December 31, 20x2		$ 52,800	
Purchases	$126,400		
Less purchases returns and allowances	7,776		
Net purchases	$118,624		
Freight in	8,236		
Net cost of purchases		126,860	
Goods available for sale		$179,660	
Less merchandise inventory, December 31, 20x3		48,300	
Cost of goods sold			131,360
Gross margin			$107,965
Operating expenses			
Selling expenses			
Sales salaries expense	$ 22,500		
Freight out expense	5,740		
Advertising expense	10,000		
Insurance expense, selling	1,600		
Store supplies expense	1,540		
Total selling expenses		$ 41,380	
General and administrative expenses			
Office salaries expense	$ 26,900		
Insurance expense, general	4,200		
Office supplies expense	1,204		
Depreciation expense, building	2,600		
Depreciation expense, office equipment	2,200		
Total general and administrative expenses		37,104	
Total operating expenses			78,484
Net income			$ 29,481

TRANSACTIONS RELATED TO PURCHASES OF MERCHANDISE

The primary difference between the perpetual and periodic inventory systems is that in the perpetual inventory system, the Merchandise Inventory account is adjusted each time a purchase, sale, or other inventory transaction occurs, whereas in the periodic inventory system, the Merchandise Inventory account stays at its

FIGURE 4
The Components of Cost of Goods Sold

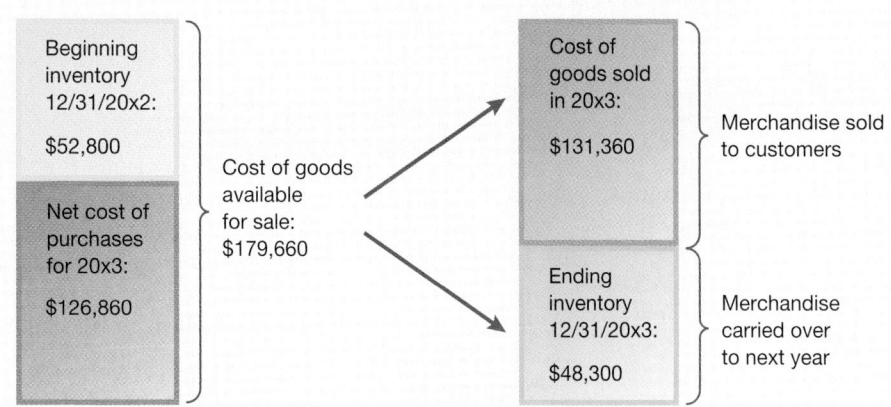

beginning balance until the physical inventory is recorded at the end of the period. In the periodic system, a Purchases account is used to accumulate the purchases of merchandise during the accounting period, and a Purchases Returns and Allowances account is used to accumulate returns of and allowances on purchases.

The following sections illustrate how purchase transactions made by Fenwick Fashions Company would be recorded under the periodic inventory system.

KEY POINT: The Purchases account is increased when a purchase is made under the periodic inventory system.

Purchases of Merchandise on Credit

Oct. 3   Received merchandise purchased on cedit from Neebok Company, invoice dated October 1, terms n/10, FOB shipping point, $4,890.

A = L + OE
   +   −

Oct. 3	Purchases	4,890	
	Accounts Payable		4,890
	Purchased merchandise from Neebok Company, terms n/10, FOB shipping point, invoice dated Oct. 1		

Purchases is a temporary account used under the periodic inventory system. Its sole purpose is to accumulate the total cost of merchandise purchased for resale during an accounting period. (Purchases of other assets, such as equipment, are recorded in the appropriate asset account, not in the Purchases account.) The Purchases account does not indicate whether merchandise has been sold or is still on hand.

Transportation Costs on Purchases

Oct. 4   Received bill from Transfer Freight Company for transportation costs on October 3 shipment, invoice dated October 1, terms n/10, $160.

A = L + OE
   +   −

Oct. 4	Freight In	160	
	Accounts Payable		160
	Received transportation charges on Oct. 3 purchase, Transfer Freight Company, terms n/10, invoice dated Oct. 1		

Transportation costs on purchases are usually accumulated in a Freight In account. In some cases, the seller pays the freight charges and bills them to the buyer as a separate item on the invoice. When this occurs, the entries are the same as in the October 3 example, except that a debit is made to Freight In for the amount of the freight charges and Accounts Payable is increased by a like amount.

ENRICHMENT NOTE: Accounts like Purchases and Purchases Returns and Allowances are used only in conjunction with a periodic inventory system.

Purchases Returns and Allowances

Oct. 6   Returned merchandise received from Neebok Company on October 3 for credit, $480.

A = L + OE   Oct. 6   Accounts Payable   480
  −   +   Purchases Returns and Allowances   480
                              Returned merchandise from purchase
                              of Oct. 3 to Neebok Company for
                              full credit

KEY POINT: Because the Purchases account is established with a debit, its contra accounts, Purchases Returns and Allowances and Purchases Discounts, are established with a credit.

If a seller sends the wrong product or one that is otherwise unsatisfactory, the buyer may be allowed to return the item for a cash refund or credit on account, or the buyer may be given an allowance off the sales price. Under the periodic inventory system, the amount of the return or allowance is recorded in the **Purchases Returns and Allowances** account. This account is a contra-purchases account with a normal credit balance, and it is deducted from purchases on the income statement.

Payments on Account

Oct. 10   Paid in full the amount due to Neebok Company for the purchase of October 3, part of which was returned on October 6.

A = L + OE   Oct. 10   Accounts Payable   4,410
  − −   Cash   4,410
                              Made payment on account to
                              Neebok Company
                              $4,890 − $480 = $4,410

TRANSACTIONS RELATED TO SALES OF MERCHANDISE

The Cost of Goods Sold account, which is updated for sales and returns under the perpetual inventory system, is not used under the periodic inventory system because the Merchandise Inventory account is not updated until the end of the accounting period. Transactions related to Fenwick Fashions' sales follow.

Sales of Merchandise on Credit

Oct. 7   Sold merchandise on credit to Gonzales Distributors, terms n/30, FOB destination, $1,200; the cost of the merchandise was $720.

A = L + OE   Oct. 7   Accounts Receivable   1,200
+   +   Sales   1,200
                              Sold merchandise to
                              Gonzales Distributors, terms n/30,
                              FOB destination

In the case of cash sales, Cash rather than Accounts Receivable is debited for the amount of the sale.

Payment of Delivery Costs

Oct. 8   Paid transportation costs for the sale on October 7, $78.

A = L + OE   Oct. 8   Freight Out Expense   78
  −   −   Cash   78
                              Paid delivery costs on Oct. 7 sale

Delivery costs are accumulated in the Freight Out Expense account. This account is shown as a selling expense on the income statement.

Returns of Merchandise Sold

Oct. 9   Return of merchandise sold on October 7 accepted from Gonzales Distributors for full credit and returned to merchandise inventory, $300.

A = L + OE   Oct. 9   Sales Returns and Allowances   300
  −   −   Accounts Receivable   300
                              Accepted return of merchandise from
                              Gonzales Distributors

Returns and allowances to customers for wrong or unsatisfactory merchandise are accumulated in the Sales Returns and Allowances account. This account is a contra-revenue account with a normal debit balance and is deducted from sales on the income statement.

Receipts on Account

Nov. 5   Received payment in full from Gonzales Distributors for sale of merchandise on October 7, less the return on October 9.

A = L + OE
+
−

Nov. 5	Cash	900	
	Accounts Receivable		900
	Received on account from		
	Gonzales Distributors		
	$1,200 − $300 = $900		

Check out ACE for a Review Quiz at http://accounting.college.hmco.com/students.

THE MERCHANDISING WORK SHEET AND CLOSING ENTRIES: THE PERPETUAL INVENTORY SYSTEM

SO6   Prepare a work sheet and closing entries for a merchandising concern using the perpetual inventory system.

RELATED TEXT ASSIGNMENTS

Q: 19, 20
SE: 10
E: 12
P: 5

The work sheet for a merchandising company is basically the same as for a service business, except that it includes the additional accounts needed to handle merchandising transactions. The treatment of these additional accounts differs depending on whether a company uses the perpetual or the periodic inventory system.

The accounts for a merchandising company using the perpetual inventory system generally include Sales, Sales Returns and Allowances, Cost of Goods Sold, and Freight In. The Merchandise Inventory account is up to date at the end of the accounting period and therefore is not involved in the closing process. The reason for this is that, under the perpetual inventory system, purchases of merchandise are recorded directly in the Merchandise Inventory account and costs are transferred from the Merchandise Inventory account to the Cost of Goods Sold account as merchandise is sold. The work sheet for Fenwick Fashions Company, assuming the company uses the perpetual inventory system, is shown in Exhibit 4. You are already familiar with the first step in preparing a work sheet, which is to enter the balances from the ledger accounts into the Trial Balance columns. Each of the other pairs of columns in the work sheet and the closing entries are discussed in the following paragraphs. Note that the ending merchandise inventory is $48,300 in both the Trial Balance and the Balance Sheet columns.

ADJUSTMENTS COLUMNS

The adjusting entries are entered in the Adjustments columns just as they are for service companies. Fenwick's adjusting entries involve insurance expired during the period (adjustment **a**), store and office supplies used during the period (adjustments **b** and **c**), and the depreciation of building and office equipment (adjustments **d** and **e**). No adjusting entry is made for merchandise inventory. After the adjusting entries are entered on the work sheet, the columns are totaled to prove that total debits equal total credits.

OMISSION OF ADJUSTED TRIAL BALANCE COLUMNS

KEY POINT: No inventory-related entries are entered in the Adjustments columns of the work sheet.

These two columns, which appear in the work sheet for a service company, can be omitted. They are optional and are used when there are many adjusting entries to record. When only a few adjusting entries are required, as is the case for Fenwick Fashions Company, these columns are not necessary and may be omitted to save time.

EXHIBIT 4
Work Sheet for Fenwick Fashions Company: Perpetual Inventory System

Fenwick Fashions Company
Work Sheet
For the Year Ended December 31, 20x3

Account Name	Trial Balance Debit	Trial Balance Credit	Adjustments Debit	Adjustments Credit	Income Statement Debit	Income Statement Credit	Balance Sheet Debit	Balance Sheet Credit
Cash	29,410						29,410	
Accounts Receivable	42,400						42,400	
Merchandise Inventory	48,300						48,300	
Prepaid Insurance	17,400			(a) 5,800			11,600	
Store Supplies	2,600			(b) 1,540			1,060	
Office Supplies	1,840			(c) 1,204			636	
Land	4,500						4,500	
Building	20,260						20,260	
Accumulated Depreciation, Building		5,650		(d) 2,600				8,250
Office Equipment	8,600						8,600	
Accumulated Depreciation, Office Equipment		2,800		(e) 2,200				5,000
Accounts Payable		25,683						25,683
Gloria Fenwick, Capital		118,352						118,352
Gloria Fenwick, Withdrawals	20,000						20,000	
Sales		246,350				246,350		
Sales Returns and Allowances	7,025				7,025			
Cost of Goods Sold	123,124				123,124			
Freight In	8,236				8,236			
Sales Salaries Expense	22,500				22,500			
Freight Out Expense	5,740				5,740			
Advertising Expense	10,000				10,000			
Office Salaries Expense	26,900				26,900			
	398,835	398,835						
Insurance Expense, Selling			(a) 1,600		1,600			
Insurance Expense, General			(a) 4,200		4,200			
Store Supplies Expense			(b) 1,540		1,540			
Office Supplies Expense			(c) 1,204		1,204			
Depreciation Expense, Building			(d) 2,600		2,600			
Depreciation Expense, Office Equipment			(e) 2,200		2,200			
			13,344	13,344	216,869	246,350	186,766	157,285
Net Income					29,481			29,481
					246,350	246,350	186,766	186,766

INCOME STATEMENT AND BALANCE SHEET COLUMNS

KEY POINT: The Income Summary account does not appear on this work sheet.

After the Trial Balance columns have been totaled, the adjustments entered, and the equality of the columns proved, the balances are extended to the Income Statement and Balance Sheet columns. Again, begin with the Cash account at the top of the

Exhibit 5
Closing Entries for Fenwick Fashions Company: Perpetual Inventory System

Date		Description	Post. Ref.	Debit	Credit
		General Journal			Page 10
20x3 Dec.	31	*Closing entries:*			
		Income Summary		216,869	
		Sales Returns and Allowances			7,025
		Cost of Goods Sold			123,124
		Freight In			8,236
		Sales Salaries Expense			22,500
		Freight Out Expense			5,740
		Advertising Expense			10,000
		Office Salaries Expense			26,900
		Insurance Expense, Selling			1,600
		Insurance Expense, General			4,200
		Store Supplies Expense			1,540
		Office Supplies Expense			1,204
		Depreciation Expense, Building			2,600
		Depreciation Expense, Office Equipment			2,200
		Closed the temporary expense and revenue accounts having debit balances			
	31	Sales		246,350	
		Income Summary			246,350
		Closed the temporary revenue account having a credit balance			
	31	Income Summary		29,481	
		Gloria Fenwick, Capital			29,481
		Closed the Income Summary account			
	31	Gloria Fenwick, Capital		20,000	
		Gloria Fenwick, Withdrawals			20,000
		Closed the Withdrawals account			

sheet and move sequentially down the sheet, one account at a time, entering each account balance in the correct Income Statement or Balance Sheet column.

ADJUSTING ENTRIES

The adjusting entries from the work sheet are now entered into the general journal and posted to the ledger, as they would be in a service company. There is no difference in this procedure between a service company and a merchandising company.

CLOSING ENTRIES

Exhibit 5 shows the closing entries for Fenwick Fashions Company. The Cost of Goods Sold account is closed to Income Summary along with the expense accounts because the Cost of Goods Sold account has a debit balance. No closing entries affect the Merchandise Inventory account.

 Check out ACE for a Review Quiz at http://accounting.college.hmco.com/students.

THE MERCHANDISING WORK SHEET AND CLOSING ENTRIES: THE PERIODIC INVENTORY SYSTEM

SO7 Prepare a work sheet and closing entries for a merchandising concern using the periodic inventory system.

RELATED TEXT ASSIGNMENTS

Q: 18, 19, 20
SE: 10
E: 13
P: 6

STUDY NOTE: The mnemonic BEE reflects the treatment of inventory in the Income Statement and Balance Sheet columns: Beginning, Ending, and Ending amounts, starting with the debit side of the Income Statement columns.

The accounts for a merchandising company using the periodic system generally include Sales, Sales Returns and Allowances, Purchases, Purchases Returns and Allowances, Freight In, and Merchandise Inventory. Like a service company's revenue and expense accounts, these accounts (except for Merchandise Inventory) are extended to the work sheet's Income Statement columns. During closing, they are transferred to the Income Summary account.

The Merchandise Inventory account requires special treatment under the periodic inventory system because purchases of merchandise are accumulated in the Purchases account. No entries are made to Merchandise Inventory during the accounting period. Thus, its balance is the same at the end of the period as at the beginning. To calculate net income, the closing entries must (1) remove the beginning inventory from the Merchandise Inventory account, (2) enter the ending inventory in the Merchandise Inventory account, and (3) transfer both inventory amounts to the Income Summary account. The following T accounts illustrate the flow of the inventory amounts for Fenwick Fashions.

Merchandise Inventory

Dec. 31, 20x2	Beg. Bal.	52,800	Dec. 31, 20x3	52,800
Dec. 31, 20x3	End. Bal.	48,300		

Income Summary

Dec. 31, 20x3	52,800	Dec. 31, 20x3 48,300

STUDY NOTE: Asset accounts are increased with debits and decreased with credits. Ending inventory must be established with a debit, and beginning inventory eliminated with a credit.

Beginning inventory ($52,800) is removed from the Merchandise Inventory account by a credit, leaving a zero balance, and transferred to the Income Summary account by a debit. Ending inventory ($48,300) is entered in the Merchandise Inventory account by a debit and recorded in the Income Summary account by a credit. The results of the two closing entries mirror the calculation of cost of goods sold, in which beginning inventory is added to net cost of purchases and ending inventory is then subtracted. When beginning inventory is debited to the Income Summary account, it is, in effect, added to net purchases because the balance in the Purchases account is also debited to Income Summary by a closing entry. And when ending inventory is credited to Income Summary, it is, in effect, deducted from the sum of beginning inventory and net cost of purchases. Keep these effects in mind while studying Fenwick Fashions' work sheet in Exhibit 6.

INCOME STATEMENT AND BALANCE SHEET COLUMNS

KEY POINT: The Income Summary account does not appear on this work sheet.

As explained earlier, the Merchandise Inventory row requires special treatment. The beginning inventory balance of $52,800 (which is already in the trial balance) is extended to the debit column of the Income Statement columns, as in Exhibit 6. This procedure has the effect of adding beginning inventory to net purchases because the Purchases account is also in the debit column of the Income Statement columns. The ending inventory balance of $48,300 (which is determined by the physical inventory and is not in the trial balance) is then inserted in the credit column of the Income Statement columns. This has the effect of subtracting the ending inventory from goods available for sale in order to calculate the cost of goods sold. Finally, the ending merchandise inventory ($48,300) is inserted in the debit side of the Balance Sheet columns because it will appear on the balance sheet.

After all the items have been extended into the correct columns, the four columns are totaled. The net income or net loss is the difference between the debit

EXHIBIT 6
Work Sheet for Fenwick Fashions Company: Periodic Inventory System

Fenwick Fashions Company
Work Sheet
For the Year Ended December 31, 20x3

Account Name	Trial Balance Debit	Trial Balance Credit	Adjustments Debit	Adjustments Credit	Income Statement Debit	Income Statement Credit	Balance Sheet Debit	Balance Sheet Credit
Cash	29,410						29,410	
Accounts Receivable	42,400						42,400	
Merchandise Inventory	52,800				52,800	48,300	48,300	
Prepaid Insurance	17,400			(a) 5,800			11,600	
Store Supplies	2,600			(b) 1,540			1,060	
Office Supplies	1,840			(c) 1,204			636	
Land	4,500						4,500	
Building	20,260						20,260	
Accumulated Depreciation, Building		5,650		(d) 2,600				8,250
Office Equipment	8,600						8,600	
Accumulated Depreciation, Office Equipment		2,800		(e) 2,200				5,000
Accounts Payable		25,683						25,683
Gloria Fenwick, Capital		118,352						118,352
Gloria Fenwick, Withdrawals	20,000						20,000	
Sales		246,350				246,350		
Sales Returns and Allowances	7,025				7,025			
Purchases	126,400				126,400			
Purchases Returns and Allowances		7,776				7,776		
Freight In	8,236				8,236			
Sales Salaries Expense	22,500				22,500			
Freight Out Expense	5,740				5,740			
Advertising Expense	10,000				10,000			
Office Salaries Expense	26,900				26,900			
	406,611	406,611						
Insurance Expense, Selling			(a) 1,600		1,600			
Insurance Expense, General			(a) 4,200		4,200			
Store Supplies Expense			(b) 1,540		1,540			
Office Supplies Expense			(c) 1,204		1,204			
Depreciation Expense, Building			(d) 2,600		2,600			
Depreciation Expense, Office Equipment			(e) 2,200		2,200			
			13,344	13,344	272,945	302,426	186,766	157,285
Net Income					29,481			29,481
					302,426	302,426	186,766	186,766

and credit Income Statement columns. In this case, Fenwick Fashions Company has earned a net income of $29,481, which is extended to the credit side of the Balance Sheet columns. The four columns are then added to prove that total debits equal total credits.

CLOSING ENTRIES

Exhibit 7 shows the closing entries for Fenwick Fashions. Notice that Merchandise Inventory is credited for the amount of the beginning inventory ($52,800) in the first entry and debited for the amount of the ending inventory ($48,300) in the second entry. Otherwise, these closing entries are very similar to those for a service company except that the merchandising accounts also must be closed to Income Summary. All income statement accounts with debit balances, including the merchandising accounts of Sales Returns and Allowances, Purchases, and Freight In, are

EXHIBIT 7
Closing Entries for Fenwick Fashions Company: Periodic Inventory System

General Journal					Page 10
Date		Description	Post. Ref.	Debit	Credit
20x3 Dec.	31	Closing entries: Income Summary		272,945	
		Merchandise Inventory			52,800
		Sales Returns and Allowances			7,025
		Purchases			126,400
		Freight In			8,236
		Sales Salaries Expense			22,500
		Freight Out Expense			5,740
		Advertising Expense			10,000
		Office Salaries Expense			26,900
		Insurance Expense, Selling			1,600
		Insurance Expense, General			4,200
		Store Supplies Expense			1,540
		Office Supplies Expense			1,204
		Depreciation Expense, Building			2,600
		Depreciation Expense, Office Equipment			2,200
		Closed the temporary expense and revenue accounts having debit balances and removed the beginning inventory			
	31	Merchandise Inventory		48,300	
		Sales		246,350	
		Purchases Returns and Allowances		7,776	
		Income Summary			302,426
		Closed the temporary expense and revenue accounts having credit balances and established the ending inventory			
	31	Income Summary		29,481	
		Gloria Fenwick, Capital			29,481
		Closed the Income Summary account			
	31	Gloria Fenwick, Capital		20,000	
		Gloria Fenwick, Withdrawals			20,000
		Closed the Withdrawals account			

credited in the first entry. The total of these accounts ($272,945) equals the total of the debit column in the Income Statement columns of the work sheet. All income statement accounts with credit balances—Sales and Purchases Returns and Allowances—are debited in the second entry. The total of these accounts ($302,426) equals the total of the Income Statement credit column in the work sheet. The third and fourth entries are used to close the Income Summary account and transfer net income to the Capital account, and to close the Withdrawals account to the Capital account.

Check out ACE for a Review Quiz at http://accounting.college.hmco.com/students.

ACCOUNTING FOR DISCOUNTS

SO8 Apply sales and purchases discounts to merchandising transactions.

RELATED TEXT ASSIGNMENTS
Q: 21
SE: 11
E: 13, 14, 15, 16
P: 7
SD: 3

A = L + OE
+   +

KEY POINT: Accounts Receivable must be credited for the full $300 even though only $294 has been received.

A = L + OE
+   −
−

A = L + OE
+
−

SALES DISCOUNTS

As mentioned earlier, sales discounts for early payment are customary in some industries. Because it usually is not possible to know at the time of the sale whether the customer will pay in time to take advantage of sales discounts, the discounts are recorded only at the time the customer pays. For example, assume that Fenwick Fashions Company sells merchandise to a customer on September 20 for $300, on terms of 2/10, n/60. This is the entry at the time of the sale:

Sept. 20	Accounts Receivable	300	
	Sales		300
	Sold merchandise on credit, terms 2/10, n/60		

The customer can take advantage of the sales discount any time on or before September 30, ten days after the date of the invoice. If the customer pays on September 29, the entry in Fenwick's records would look like this:

Sept. 29	Cash	294	
	Sales Discounts	6	
	Accounts Receivable		300
	Received payment for Sept. 20 sale; discount taken		

If the customer does not take advantage of the sales discount but waits until November 19 to pay for the merchandise, the entry would be as follows:

Nov. 19	Cash	300	
	Accounts Receivable		300
	Received payment for Sept. 20 sale; no discount taken		

At the end of the accounting period, the Sales Discounts account has accumulated all the sales discounts taken during the period. Because sales discounts reduce revenues from sales, Sales Discounts is a contra-revenue account with a normal debit balance that is deducted from sales on the income statement. Sales Discounts is treated the same as Sales Returns and Allowances on the work sheet and in the closing entries.

PURCHASES DISCOUNTS

Merchandise purchases are usually made on credit and sometimes involve **purchases discounts** for early payment. Purchases discounts are discounts taken for early payment for merchandise purchased for resale. They are to the buyer what sales discounts are to the seller. The amount of discounts taken is recorded in a separate account. Assume that Fenwick Fashions Company made a credit purchase of merchandise on November 12 for $1,500 with terms of 2/10, n/30 and returned

$200 in merchandise on November 14. When payment is made within the discount period, Fenwick's entry looks like this:

A = L + OE
−   −   +

Nov. 22	Accounts Payable		1,300	
	Purchases Discounts			26
	Cash			1,274
	Paid the invoice of Nov. 12			
	Purchase Nov. 12	$1,500		
	Less return Nov. 14	200		
	Net purchase	$1,300		
	Discount: 2%	26		
	Cash paid	$1,274		

KEY POINT: Accounts Payable must be debited for the full $1,300 even though only $1,274 has been paid.

If Fenwick does not pay for the purchase within the discount period, the entry would be as follows:

A = L + OE
−   −

Dec. 12	Accounts Payable	1,300	
	Cash		1,300
	Paid the invoice of Nov. 12,		
	less the return, on due date;		
	no discount taken		

Like Purchases Returns and Allowances, Purchases Discounts is a contra-purchases account with a normal credit balance that is deducted from purchases on the income statement. If a company makes only a partial payment on an invoice, most creditors allow the company to take the discount applicable to the partial payment. The discount usually does not apply to freight, postage, taxes, or other charges that might appear on the invoice.

Check out ACE for a Review Quiz at http://accounting.college.hmco.com/students.

Chapter Review

REVIEW OF LEARNING OBJECTIVES

LO1   Identify the management issues related to merchandising businesses.

Merchandising companies differ from service companies in that they earn income by buying and selling goods. The buying and selling of goods adds to the complexity of the business and raises four issues that management must address. First, the series of transactions in which merchandising companies engage (the operating cycle) requires careful cash flow management. Second, to achieve the goal of profitability, management must price goods and control operating costs by using budgets to ensure an adequate income after operating expenses have been paid. Third, management must choose whether to use the perpetual or the periodic inventory system. Fourth, management must establish an internal control structure that protects the company's assets—its cash, merchandise inventory, and accounts receivable.

LO2   Compare the income statements for service and merchandising concerns, and define the components of the merchandising income statement.

In the simplest case, the income statement for a service company consists only of revenues and expenses. The income statement for a merchandising company has three major parts: (1) net sales, (2) cost of goods sold, and (3) operating expenses. Gross margin is the difference between revenues from net sales and the cost of goods sold. Net income is the "bottom line" after operating expenses are deducted from the gross margin.

LO3   Define and distinguish the terms of sale for merchandising transactions.

A trade discount is a reduction from the list or catalogue price of a product. A sales discount is a discount given for early payment of a sale on credit. FOB shipping point means that the buyer bears the cost of transportation and that title to the goods passes to the buyer at the shipping origin. FOB destination means that the seller bears the cost of transportation and that title does not pass to the buyer until the goods reach their destination.

LO4 Prepare an income statement and record merchandising transactions under the perpetual inventory system.

The Merchandise Inventory account is continuously adjusted by entering purchases, sales, and other inventory transactions as the transactions occur. Purchases increase the Merchandise Inventory account, and purchases returns decrease it. As goods are sold, their cost is transferred from the Merchandise Inventory account to the Cost of Goods Sold account.

LO5 Prepare an income statement and record merchandising transactions under the periodic inventory system.

When the periodic inventory system is used, the cost of goods sold section of the income statement must include the following elements:

$$\begin{array}{c} \text{Gross} \\ \text{Purchases} \end{array} - \begin{array}{c} \text{Purchases Returns} \\ \text{and Allowances} \end{array} + \begin{array}{c} \text{Freight} \\ \text{In} \end{array} = \begin{array}{c} \text{Net Cost of} \\ \text{Purchases} \end{array}$$

$$\begin{array}{c} \text{Beginning} \\ \text{Merchandise Inventory} \end{array} + \begin{array}{c} \text{Net Cost of} \\ \text{Purchases} \end{array} = \begin{array}{c} \text{Goods} \\ \text{Available for Sale} \end{array}$$

$$\begin{array}{c} \text{Goods} \\ \text{Available for Sale} \end{array} - \begin{array}{c} \text{Ending} \\ \text{Merchandise Inventory} \end{array} = \begin{array}{c} \text{Cost of} \\ \text{Goods Sold} \end{array}$$

Under the periodic inventory system, the Merchandise Inventory account stays at the beginning level until the physical inventory is recorded at the end of the accounting period. A Purchases account is used to accumulate purchases of merchandise during the accounting period, and a Purchases Returns and Allowances account is used to accumulate returns of and allowances on purchases.

SUPPLEMENTAL OBJECTIVES

SO6 Prepare a work sheet and closing entries for a merchandising concern using the perpetual inventory system.

Preparing a work sheet for a merchandising concern is much like preparing one for a service concern, except that there are additional accounts relating to merchandising transactions, such as Sales, Sales Returns and Allowances, Cost of Goods Sold, and Freight In. These accounts must be extended to the appropriate Income Statement columns. Also, since the Merchandise Inventory account is kept up to date, its ending balance is extended directly to the debit column of the Balance Sheet columns. There is no need to place it in the Income Statement columns. The closing entries for a merchandising concern under the perpetual inventory system are the same as those for a service business. There is no need to include the Merchandise Inventory account.

SO7 Prepare a work sheet and closing entries for a merchandising concern using the periodic inventory system.

The work sheet under the periodic inventory system is the same as under the perpetual inventory system with the exception that the beginning merchandise inventory from the trial balance is extended to the debit column of the Income Statement columns, and the ending balance of Merchandise Inventory is inserted in both the credit column of the Income Statement columns and the debit column of the Balance Sheet columns. The closing entries for a merchandising concern under the periodic inventory system are similar to those for a service business, with one exception. The exception is that the closing entries include a credit to Merchandise Inventory for the amount of the beginning inventory and a debit to Merchandise Inventory for the amount of the ending inventory.

SO8 Apply sales and purchases discounts to merchandising transactions.

Sales discounts are discounts for early payment. Terms of 2/10, n/30 mean that the buyer can take a 2 percent discount if the invoice is paid within ten days of the invoice date. Otherwise, the buyer is obligated to pay the full amount in 30 days. Discounts on sales are recorded in the Sales Discounts account, and discounts on purchases are recorded in the Purchases Discounts account.

REVIEW OF CONCEPTS AND TERMINOLOGY

The following concepts and terms were introduced in this chapter:

LO5 **Beginning inventory:** Merchandise on hand at the start of an accounting period.

LO1 **Cash flow management:** The planning of a company's receipts and payments of cash.

LO2 **Cost of goods sold:** The amount a merchant paid for the merchandise sold during an accounting period. Also called *cost of sales*.

LO5   Ending inventory: Merchandise on hand at the end of an accounting period.

LO1   Financing period: The amount of time from the purchase of inventory until it is sold and payment is collected, less the amount of time creditors allow for payment of the inventory. Also called the *cash gap*.

LO3   FOB destination: A shipping term that means that the seller bears transportation costs to the place of delivery.

LO3   FOB shipping point: A shipping term that means that the buyer bears transportation costs from the point of origin.

LO4   Freight in: The transportation cost of receiving merchandise. Also called *transportation in*.

LO2   Freight Out Expense: The account that accumulates transportation charges on merchandise sold, which are shown as a selling expense. Also called *Delivery Expense*.

LO5   Goods available for sale: The sum of beginning inventory and the net cost of purchases during the period; the total goods available for sale to customers during an accounting period.

LO2   Gross margin: The difference between net sales and cost of goods sold. Also called *gross profit*.

LO2   Gross sales: Total sales for cash and on credit occurring during an accounting period.

LO1   Internal controls: The environment, accounting systems, and control procedures established by management and designed to safeguard the assets of a business and provide reliable accounting records.

LO1   Merchandise inventory: The goods on hand at any one time that are available for sale to customers.

LO1   Merchandising businesses: Businesses that earn income by buying and selling goods.

LO5   Net cost of purchases: Net purchases plus any freight charges on the purchases.

LO2   Net income: For merchandising companies, what is left after deducting operating expenses from gross margin.

LO5   Net purchases: Total purchases less any deductions, such as purchases returns and allowances and purchases discounts.

LO2   Net sales: The gross proceeds from sales of merchandise less sales returns and allowances and any discounts. Also called *sales* on income statements.

LO1   Operating budget: Management's operating plans as reflected by detailed listings of projected selling expenses and general and administrative expenses.

LO1   Operating cycle: A series of transactions that includes purchases of merchandise inventory for cash or on credit, payment for purchases made on credit, sales of merchandise inventory for cash or on credit, and collection of cash from the sales.

LO2   Operating expenses: The expenses other than cost of goods sold that are incurred in running a business.

LO1   Periodic inventory system: A system for determining inventory on hand by taking a physical count at the end of an accounting period.

LO1   Perpetual inventory system: A system for determining inventory on hand by keeping continuous records of the quantity and, usually, the cost of individual items as they are bought and sold.

LO1   Physical inventory: An actual count of all merchandise on hand.

LO1   Profitability management: The process of achieving a satisfactory gross margin and maintaining acceptable levels of operating expenses.

LO5   Purchases: A temporary account that is used under the periodic inventory system to accumulate the total cost of merchandise purchased for resale during an accounting period.

SO8 **Purchases discounts:** Discounts taken for prompt payment for merchandise purchased for resale; the Purchases Discounts account is a contra-purchases account.

LO5 **Purchases Returns and Allowances:** A contra-purchases account used under the periodic inventory system to accumulate cash refunds, credits on account, and other allowances made by suppliers.

LO3 **Sales discount:** A discount given to a buyer for early payment of a sale made on credit; the Sales Discounts account is a contra-revenue account.

LO2 **Sales Returns and Allowances:** A contra-revenue account used to accumulate cash refunds, credits on account, and other allowances made to customers who have received defective or otherwise unsatisfactory products.

LO1 **Service business:** Businesses that earn income by performing a service for fees or commissions.

LO3 **Trade discount:** A deduction (usually 30 percent or more) off a list or catalogue price that is not recorded in the accounting records.

REVIEW PROBLEM

Merchandising Transactions: Perpetual and Periodic Inventory Systems

LO4
LO5
Dawkins Company engaged in the following transactions during October.

Oct. 1 Sold merchandise to Ernie Devlin on credit, terms n/30, FOB shipping point, $1,050 (cost, $630).
2 Purchased merchandise on credit from Ruland Company, terms n/30, FOB shipping point, $1,900.
2 Paid Custom Freight $145 for freight charges on merchandise received.
6 Purchased store supplies on credit from Arizin Supply House, terms n/30, $318.
9 Purchased merchandise on credit from LNP Company, terms n/30, FOB shipping point, $1,800, including $100 freight costs paid by LNP Company.
11 Accepted from Ernie Devlin a return of merchandise, which was returned to inventory, $150 (cost, $90).
14 Returned for credit $300 of merchandise received on October 2.
15 Returned for credit $100 of store supplies purchased on October 6.
16 Sold merchandise for cash, $500 (cost, $300).
22 Paid Ruland Company for purchase of October 2 less return of October 14.
23 Received full payment from Ernie Devlin for his October 1 purchase, less return on October 11.

REQUIRED ▶ 1. Prepare entries in journal form to record the transactions, assuming the perpetual inventory system is used.
2. Prepare entries in journal form to record the transactions, assuming the periodic inventory system is used.

ANSWER TO REVIEW PROBLEM

Accounts that differ under the two systems are highlighted.

1. Perpetual Inventory System

Oct. 1	Accounts Receivable	1,050	
	Sales		1,050

Sold merchandise on account to Ernie Devlin, terms n/30, FOB shipping point

	Cost of Goods Sold	630	
	Merchandise Inventory		630

Transferred cost of merchandise sold to Cost of Goods Sold account

2. Periodic Inventory System

Accounts Receivable	1,050		
Sales		1,050	

Sold merchandise on account to Ernie Devlin, terms n/30, FOB shipping point

1. Perpetual Inventory System			2. Periodic Inventory System		
Oct. 2 Merchandise Inventory	1,900		Purchases	1,900	
Accounts Payable		1,900	Accounts Payable		1,900
Purchased merchandise on account from Ruland Company, terms n/30, FOB shipping point			Purchased merchandise on account from Ruland Company, terms n/30, FOB shipping point		
Freight In	145		Freight In	145	
Cash		145	Cash		145
Paid freight on previous purchase			Paid freight on previous purchase		
6 Store Supplies	318		Store Supplies	318	
Accounts Payable		318	Accounts Payable		318
Purchased store supplies on account from Arizin Supply House, terms n/30			Purchased store supplies on account from Arizin Supply House, terms n/30		
9 Merchandise Inventory	1,700		Purchases	1,700	
Freight In	100		Freight In	100	
Accounts Payable		1,800	Accounts Payable		1,800
Purchased merchandise on account from LNP Company, terms n/30, FOB shipping point, freight paid by supplier			Purchased merchandise on account from LNP Company, terms n/30, FOB shipping point, freight paid by supplier		
11 Sales Returns and Allowances	150		Sales Returns and Allowances	150	
Accounts Receivable		150	Accounts Receivable		150
Accepted return of merchandise from Ernie Devlin			Accepted return of merchandise from Ernie Devlin		
Merchandise Inventory	90				
Cost of Goods Sold		90			
Transferred cost of merchandise returned to Merchandise Inventory account					
14 Accounts Payable	300		Accounts Payable	300	
Merchandise Inventory		300	Purchases Returns and Allowances		300
Returned portion of merchandise purchased from Ruland Company			Returned portion of merchandise purchased from Ruland Company		
15 Accounts Payable	100		Accounts Payable	100	
Store Supplies		100	Store Supplies		100
Returned store supplies (not merchandise) purchased on October 6 for credit			Returned store supplies (not merchandise) purchased on October 6 for credit		
16 Cash	500		Cash	500	
Sales		500	Sales		500
Sold merchandise for cash			Sold merchandise for cash		
Cost of Goods Sold	300				
Merchandise Inventory		300			
Transferred cost of merchandise sold to Cost of Goods Sold account					
22 Accounts Payable	1,600		Accounts Payable	1,600	
Cash		1,600	Cash		1,600
Made payment on account to Ruland Company $1,900 − $300 = $1,600			Made payment on account to Ruland Company $1,900 − $300 = $1,600		
23 Cash	900		Cash	900	
Accounts Receivable		900	Accounts Receivable		900
Received payment on account of Ernie Devlin $1,050 − $150 = $900			Received payment on account of Ernie Devlin $1,050 − $150 = $900		

Chapter Assignments

BUILDING YOUR KNOWLEDGE FOUNDATION

QUESTIONS

1. What four issues must managers of merchandising businesses address?

2. What is the operating cycle of a merchandising business, and why is it important?

3. What is the primary difference between the operations of a merchandising business and those of a service business?

4. What is the difference between the perpetual inventory system and the periodic inventory system?

5. Under the periodic inventory system, how must the amount of inventory at the end of the year be determined?

6. What are the principal differences in the handling of merchandise inventory in the accounting records under the perpetual inventory system and the periodic inventory system?

7. Discuss this statement: "The perpetual inventory system is the best system because management always needs to know how much inventory it has."

8. What is the primary difference in the income statement of a merchandising company from that of a service company? Define *gross margin*. Why is it important?

9. During its first year in operation, Molinari Nursery had a cost of goods sold of $64,000 and a gross margin equal to 40 percent of sales. What was the dollar amount of the company's sales?

10. Could Molinari Nursery (in Question 9) have a net loss for the year? Explain your answer.

11. What is the difference between a trade discount and a sales discount?

12. Two companies quoted the following prices and terms on 50 units of product. Which supplier is quoting the better deal? Explain your answer.

	Price	Terms
Supplier A	$20 per unit	FOB shipping point
Supplier B	$21 per unit	FOB destination

13. What is the principal difference in accounting for the purchase and sale of merchandise under the perpetual inventory system and the periodic inventory system?

14. Is *freight in* an operating expense? Explain your answer.

15. Lorres Hardware purchased the following items: (a) a delivery truck, (b) two dozen hammers, (c) supplies for its office workers, and (d) a broom for the janitor. Which items should be debited to the Purchases account under the periodic inventory system?

16. Under which inventory system is a Cost of Goods Sold account maintained? Why?

17. Why is it advisable to maintain a Sales Returns and Allowances account when the same result could be obtained by debiting each return or allowance to the Sales account?

18. Why is special treatment of the Merchandise Inventory account at the end of the accounting period of particular importance in the determination of net income under the periodic inventory system? What must be achieved in the account?

19. What are the principal differences between the work sheet for a merchandising company and that for a service company? Discuss in terms of the periodic and the perpetual inventory systems.

20. What are the principal differences between the closing entries for a merchandising company using the perpetual inventory system and those for a company using the periodic inventory system?

21. What is the normal balance of the Sales Discounts account? Is it an asset, a liability, an expense, or a contra-revenue account?

SHORT EXERCISES

SE 1.
LO1   Identification of Management Issues

Identify each of the following decisions as most directly related to (a) cash flow management, (b) profitability management, (c) choice of inventory system, or (d) control of merchandising operations:

1. Determination of how to protect cash from theft or embezzlement
2. Determination of the selling price of goods for sale
3. Determination of policies governing sales of merchandise on credit
4. Determination of whether to use the periodic or the perpetual inventory system

SE 2.
LO2   Merchandising Income Statement

Using the following data, prepare an income statement for Martin's Hardware for the month ended February 28:

Cost of goods sold	$30,000
General and administrative expenses	8,000
Net sales	50,000
Selling expenses	7,000

SE 3.
LO3   Terms of Sale

A dealer buys tooling machines from a manufacturer and resells them to its customers.

a. The manufacturer sets a list or catalogue price of $6,000 for a machine. The manufacturer offers its dealers a 40 percent trade discount.
b. Freight charges are FOB shipping point. The cost of shipping a machine is $350.
c. The manufacturer offers a sales discount of 2/10, n/30. The sales discount does not apply to shipping costs.

What is the net cost of the tooling machine to the dealer, assuming it is paid for within ten days of purchase?

SE 4.
LO3   Credit Card Sales Transaction

Record in journal form the following transaction for Jenny's Crafts Store:

Apr. 19   A tabulation at the end of the day showed $400 in Visa® invoices, which are deposited in a special bank account at full value less 5 percent discount.

SE 5.
LO4   Purchases of Merchandise: Perpetual Inventory System

Record in journal form each of the following transactions, assuming the perpetual inventory system is used:

Aug. 2   Purchased merchandise on credit from Bean Company, invoice dated August 1, terms n/10, FOB shipping point, $2,300.
       3   Received bill from Ace Shipping Company for transportation costs on August 2 shipment, invoice dated August 1, terms n/30, $210.
       7   Returned damaged merchandise received from Bean Company on August 2 for credit, $360.
      10   Paid in full the amount due to Bean Company for the purchase of August 2, part of which was returned on August 7.

SE 6.
LO4   Sales of Merchandise: Perpetual Inventory System

Record in journal form the following transactions, assuming the perpetual inventory system is used:

Aug. 4   Sold merchandise on credit to Konner Company, terms n/30, FOB destination, $1,200. (Cost = $720.)
       5   Paid transportation costs for sale of August 4, $110.
       9   Part of the merchandise sold on August 4 was accepted back from Konner Company for full credit and returned to the merchandise inventory, $350. (Cost = $210.)
Sept. 3   Received payment in full from Konner Company for merchandise sold on August 4, less the return on August 9.

SE 7.
LO5   Purchases of Merchandise: Periodic Inventory System

Record in journal form the transactions in **SE 5**, assuming the periodic inventory system is used.

SE 8.
LO5   Cost of Goods Sold: Periodic Inventory System

Using the following data and assuming cost of goods sold is $230,000, prepare the cost of goods sold section of a merchandising income statement (periodic inventory system), including computation of the amount of purchases for the month of October:

Freight in	$12,000
Merchandise inventory, Sept. 30, 20xx	33,000
Merchandise inventory, Oct. 31, 20xx	44,000
Purchases	?
Purchases returns and allowances	9,000

SE 9.

LO5 Sales of Merchandise: Periodic Inventory System

Record in journal form the transactions in **SE 6** using the periodic inventory system.

SE 10.

SO6 Merchandise Inventory
SO7 on the Work Sheet and in Closing Entries

Forrester Company had beginning merchandise inventory of $14,800 and ending merchandise inventory of $19,200. Where would these numbers appear on the work sheet and in the closing entries under (1) the perpetual inventory system and (2) the periodic inventory system?

SE 11.

SO8 Sales and Purchases Discounts

On April 15, Farid Company sold merchandise to Smarte Company for $1,500 on terms of 2/10, n/30. Record the entries in both Farid's and Smarte's records for (1) the sale, (2) a return of merchandise on April 20 of $300, and (3) payment in full on April 25. Assume both companies use the periodic inventory system.

EXERCISES

E 1.

LO1 Management Issues and Decisions

The decisions that follow were made by the management of Shanahan Shoe Company. Indicate whether each decision pertains primarily to (a) cash flow management, (b) profitability management, (c) choice of inventory system, or (d) control of merchandise operations.

1. Decided to mark each item of inventory with a magnetic tag that sets off an alarm if the tag is removed from the store before being deactivated
2. Decided to reduce the credit terms offered to customers from 30 days to 20 days to speed up collection of accounts
3. Decided that the benefits of keeping track of each item of inventory as it is bought and sold would exceed the costs of such a system
4. Decided to raise the price of each item of inventory to achieve a higher gross margin to offset an increase in rent expense
5. Decided to purchase a new type of cash register that can be operated only by a person who knows a predetermined code
6. Decided to switch to a new cleaning service that will provide the same service at a lower cost

E 2.

LO1 Operating Budget

The operating budget and actual performance for the six months ended June 30, 20x3, for Pacific Hardware Company appear below.

	Budget	Actual
Selling expenses		
Sales salaries expense	$ 90,000	$102,030
Sales supplies expense	2,000	1,642
Rent expense, selling space	18,000	18,000
Utilities expense, selling space	12,000	11,256
Advertising expense	15,000	21,986
Depreciation expense, selling fixtures	6,500	6,778
Total selling expenses	$143,500	$161,692
General and administrative expenses		
Office salaries expense	$ 50,000	$ 47,912
Office supplies expense	1,000	782
Rent expense, office space	4,000	4,000
Depreciation expense, office equipment	3,000	3,251
Utilities expense, office space	3,000	3,114
Postage expense	500	626
Insurance expense	2,000	2,700
Miscellaneous expense	500	481
Total general and administrative expenses	$ 64,000	$ 62,866
Total operating expenses	$207,500	$224,558

1. Prepare an operating report that shows budget, actual, and difference.
2. Discuss the results, identifying which differences most likely should be investigated by management.

E 3. Compute the dollar amount of each item indicated by a letter in the following table. Treat each horizontal row of numbers as a separate problem.

LO2 Parts of the Income Statement: Missing Data

Sales	Cost of Goods Sold	Gross Margin	Operating Expenses	Net Income (Loss)
$250,000	$ a	$ 80,000	$ b	$24,000
c	216,000	120,000	80,000	40,000
460,000	d	100,000	e	(2,000)
780,000	f	g	240,000	80,000

E 4. A household appliance dealer buys refrigerators from a manufacturer and resells them to its customers.

LO3 Terms of Sale

a. The manufacturer sets a list or catalogue price of $1,000 for a refrigerator. The manufacturer offers its dealers a 30 percent trade discount.
b. The manufacturer sells the machine under terms of FOB destination. The cost of shipping is $100.
c. The manufacturer offers a sales discount of 2/10, n/30. Sales discounts do not apply to shipping costs.

What is the net cost of the refrigerator to the dealer, assuming it is paid for within ten days of purchase?

E 5. Using the selected account balances at December 31, 20xx, for City Rental that follow, prepare an income statement for the year ended December 31, 20xx. Show the detail of net sales. The company uses the perpetual inventory system, and Freight In has not been included in Cost of Goods Sold.

LO4 Preparation of the Income Statement: Perpetual Inventory System

Account Name	Debit	Credit
Sales		$237,500
Sales Returns and Allowances	$ 11,750	
Cost of Goods Sold	140,000	
Freight In	6,750	
Selling Expenses	21,500	
General and Administrative Expenses	43,500	

E 6. Give the entries to record each of the following transactions under the perpetual inventory system:

LO4 Recording Purchases: Perpetual Inventory System

a. Purchased merchandise on credit, terms n/30, FOB shipping point, $2,500.
b. Paid freight on the shipment in transaction **a,** $135.
c. Purchased merchandise on credit, terms n/30, FOB destination, $1,400.
d. Purchased merchandise on credit, terms n/30, FOB shipping point, $2,600, which includes freight paid by the supplier of $200.
e. Returned part of the merchandise purchased in transaction **c,** $500.
f. Paid the amount owed on the purchase in transaction **a.**
g. Paid the amount owed on the purchase in transaction **d.**
h. Paid the amount owed on the purchase in transaction **c** less the return in **e.**

E 7. On June 15, Tunnale Company sold merchandise for $1,300 on terms of n/30 to Whist Company. On June 20, Whist Company returned some of the merchandise for a credit of $300, and on June 25, Whist paid the balance owed. Give Tunnale's entries to record the sale, return, and receipt of payment under the perpetual inventory system. The cost of the merchandise sold on June 15 was $750, and the cost of the merchandise returned to inventory on June 20 was $175.

LO4 Recording Sales: Perpetual Inventory System

E 8.

Using the selected year-end account balances at December 31, 20x4, for the Atlanta General Store shown below, prepare a 20x4 income statement. Show the detail of net sales. The company uses the periodic inventory system. Beginning merchandise inventory was $52,000; ending merchandise inventory is $44,000.

Account Name	Debit	Credit
Sales		$594,000
Sales Returns and Allowances	$ 30,400	
Purchases	229,600	
Purchases Returns and Allowances		8,000
Freight In	11,200	
Selling Expenses	97,000	
General and Administrative Expenses	74,400	

E 9.

Determine the missing data for each letter in the following three income statements for Leominster Wholesale Paper Company (in thousands):

	20x4	20x3	20x2
Gross sales	$ o	$ h	$286
Sales returns and allowances	24	19	a
Net sales	p	317	b
Merchandise inventory, beginning	q	i	38
Purchases	192	169	c
Purchases returns and allowances	31	j	17
Freight in	r	29	22
Net cost of purchases	189	k	d
Goods available for sale	222	212	182
Merchandise inventory, ending	39	l	42
Cost of goods sold	s	179	e
Gross margin	142	m	126
Selling expenses	t	78	f
General and administrative expenses	39	n	33
Total operating expenses	130	128	g
Net income	u	10	27

E 10.

Using the data in **E 6,** give the entries to record each of the transactions under the periodic inventory system.

E 11.

Using the relevant data in **E 7,** give the entries to record each of the transactions under the periodic inventory system.

E 12.

Below are selected account balances of Linley Company for the year ended December 31, 20xx.

Account Name	Debit	Credit
Sales		$297,000
Sales Returns and Allowances	$ 15,200	
Cost of Goods Sold	113,000	
Freight In	5,600	
Selling Expenses	48,500	
General and Administrative Expenses	37,200	

Prepare closing entries, assuming that the owner of Linley Company, Sandra Linley, withdrew $40,000 for personal expenses during the year.

SO7 Preparation of Closing Entries:
SO8 Periodic Inventory System

E 13. Selected account balances of the Lakeside Grocery Store for the year ended December 31, 20xx, follow.

Account Name	Debit	Credit
Sales		$297,000
Sales Returns and Allowances	$ 11,000	
Sales Discounts	4,200	
Purchases	114,800	
Purchases Returns and Allowances		1,800
Purchases Discounts		2,200
Freight In	5,600	
Selling Expenses	48,500	
General and Administrative Expenses	37,200	

Beginning merchandise inventory was $26,000, and ending merchandise inventory is $22,000. Prepare closing entries, assuming that the owner of Lakeside Grocery, John Grover, withdrew $34,000 for personal expenses during the year.

SO8 Sales Involving Discounts

E 14. Give the entries to record the following transactions engaged in by Ramos Company, which uses the periodic inventory system:

Mar. 1   Sold merchandise on credit to Smythe Company, terms 2/10, n/30, FOB shipping point, $500.
     3   Accepted a return from Smythe Company for full credit, $200.
    10   Received payment from Smythe Company for the sale, less the return and discount.
    11   Sold merchandise on credit to Smythe Company, terms 2/10, n/30, FOB shipping point, $800.
    31   Received payment for amount due from Smythe Company for the sale of March 11.

SO8 Purchases Involving Discounts

E 15. Give the entries to record the following transactions engaged in by Amal Company, which uses the periodic inventory system:

July 2   Purchased merchandise on credit from Olney Company, terms 2/10, n/30, FOB destination, invoice dated July 1, $800.
     6   Returned some merchandise to Olney Company for full credit, $100.
    11   Paid Olney Company for purchase of July 2 less return and discount.
    14   Purchased merchandise on credit from Olney Company, terms 2/10, n/30, FOB destination, invoice dated July 12, $900.
    31   Paid amount owed Olney Company for purchase of July 14.

SO8 Purchases and Sales Involving Discounts

E 16. The Melody Company purchased $9,200 of merchandise, terms 2/10, n/30, from Mirro Company and paid for the merchandise within the discount period. Give the entries (1) by the Melody Company to record the purchase and payment and (2) by Mirro Company to record the sale and receipt of payment. Both companies use the periodic inventory system.

PROBLEMS

LO1 Merchandising Income
LO4 Statement: Perpetual
      Inventory System

P 1. Selected accounts from the adjusted trial balance for Bear Camera Store at the end of the fiscal year, June 30, 20x4, follow.

Bear Camera Store
Partial Adjusted Trial Balance
June 30, 20x4

Sales		$433,912
Sales Returns and Allowances	$ 11,250	
Cost of Goods Sold	221,185	
Freight In	10,078	
Store Salaries Expense	107,550	
Office Salaries Expense	26,500	
Advertising Expense	18,200	
Rent Expense	14,400	
Insurance Expense	2,800	
Utilities Expense	8,760	
Store Supplies Expense	2,464	
Office Supplies Expense	1,814	
Depreciation Expense, Store Equipment	1,800	
Depreciation Expense, Office Equipment	1,850	

REQUIRED ▶ 1. Prepare an income statement for Bear Camera Store. Freight In should be combined with Cost of Goods Sold. Store Salaries Expense; Advertising Expense; Store Supplies Expense; and Depreciation Expense, Store Equipment are selling expenses. The other expenses are general and administrative expenses. The company uses the perpetual inventory system. Show details of net sales and operating expenses.

2. Based on your knowledge at this point in the course, how would you use the income statement for Bear Camera Store to evaluate the company's profitability? What other financial statement should be considered and why?

P 2. Sweet Company engaged in the following transactions in July 20xx:

LO4 Merchandising Transactions:
Perpetual Inventory System

July	1	Sold merchandise to Rick Lee on credit, terms n/30, FOB shipping point, $4,200 (cost, $2,520).
	3	Purchased merchandise on credit from Cobalt Company, terms n/30, FOB shipping point, $7,600.
	5	Paid Rapid Freight for freight charges on merchandise received, $580.
	6	Purchased store supplies on credit from DGE Supply Company, terms n/20, $1,272.
	8	Purchased merchandise on credit from Holt Company, terms n/30, FOB shipping point, $7,200, which includes $400 freight costs paid by Holt Company.
	12	Returned some of the merchandise purchased on July 3 for credit, $1,200.
	15	Sold merchandise on credit to Bob Wagner, terms n/30, FOB shipping point, $2,400 (cost, $1,440).
	16	Returned some of the store supplies purchased on July 6 for credit, $400.
	17	Sold merchandise for cash, $2,000 (cost, $1,200).
	18	Accepted for full credit a return from Rick Lee and returned merchandise to inventory, $400 (cost, $240).
	24	Paid Cobalt Company for purchase of July 3 less return of July 12.
	25	Received full payment from Rick Lee for his July 1 purchase less the return on July 18.

REQUIRED ▶ 1. Prepare entries in journal form to record the transactions, assuming use of the perpetual inventory system.

2. Why is it important to keep purchases of merchandise in a separate account from purchases of store supplies?

P 3. The data at the top of the next page are from Pat's Sports Equipment's adjusted trial balance on September 30, 20x5, the fiscal year end. The company's beginning merchandise inventory was $243,666; ending merchandise inventory is $229,992 for the period.

LO1 Merchandising Income
LO5 Statement: Periodic Inventory
System

Pat's Sports Equipment
Partial Adjusted Trial Balance
September 30, 20x5

Sales		$1,301,736
Sales Returns and Allowances	$ 33,750	
Purchases	663,555	
Purchases Returns and Allowances		90,714
Freight In	30,234	
Store Salaries Expense	322,650	
Office Salaries Expense	79,500	
Advertising Expense	54,600	
Rent Expense	43,200	
Insurance Expense	8,400	
Utilities Expense	56,280	
Store Supplies Expense	1,392	
Office Supplies Expense	2,442	
Depreciation Expense, Store Equipment	5,400	
Depreciation Expense, Office Equipment	5,550	

REQUIRED ▶ 1. Prepare an income statement for Pat's Sports Equipment. Store Salaries Expense; Advertising Expense; Store Supplies Expense; and Depreciation Expense, Store Equipment are selling expenses. The other expenses are general and administrative expenses. The company uses the periodic inventory system. Show details of net sales and operating expenses.

2. How would you use the income statement you prepared in **1** to evaluate the company's profitability? What other financial statements should be considered and why?

P 4. Use the relevant data in **P 2** for this problem.

LO5 Merchandising Transactions: Periodic Inventory System

REQUIRED ▶ Prepare entries in journal form to record the transactions, assuming use of the periodic inventory system.

P 5. The year-end trial balance at the top of the opposite page was taken from the ledger of the Clay Party Costumes Company at the end of its annual accounting period on June 30, 20x4. The company uses the perpetual inventory system.

SO6 Merchandiser's Work Sheet, Financial Statements, and Closing Entries: Perpetual Inventory System

REQUIRED ▶ 1. Enter the trial balance on a work sheet, and complete the work sheet using the following information: ending store supplies inventory, $550; expired insurance, $2,400; estimated depreciation on store equipment, $5,000; sales salaries payable, $650; and accrued utilities expense, $100.

2. Prepare an income statement, a statement of owner's equity, and a balance sheet. Sales Salaries Expense; Other Selling Expenses; Store Supplies Expense; and Depreciation Expense, Store Equipment are all selling expenses.

3. From the work sheet, prepare the closing entries.

P 6. The trial balance at the bottom of the opposite page was taken from the ledger of East End Bookstore at the end of its annual accounting period. The company uses the periodic inventory system.

SO7 Merchandiser's Work Sheet, Financial Statements, and Closing Entries: Periodic Inventory System

REQUIRED ▶ 1. Enter the trial balance on a work sheet, and complete the work sheet using this information: ending merchandise inventory, $33,227; ending store supplies inventory, $304; unexpired prepaid insurance, $200; estimated depreciation on store equipment, $4,300; sales salaries payable, $80; and accrued utilities expense, $150.

Clay Party Costumes Company
Trial Balance
June 30, 20x4

Cash	$ 7,050	
Accounts Receivable	24,830	
Merchandise Inventory	88,900	
Store Supplies	3,800	
Prepaid Insurance	4,800	
Store Equipment	151,300	
Accumulated Depreciation, Store Equipment		$ 25,500
Accounts Payable		38,950
Jarrott Clay, Capital		161,350
Jarrott Clay, Withdrawals	24,000	
Sales		475,250
Sales Returns and Allowances	4,690	
Cost of Goods Sold	231,840	
Freight In	10,400	
Sales Salaries Expense	64,600	
Rent Expense	48,000	
Other Selling Expenses	32,910	
Utilities Expense	3,930	
	$701,050	$701,050

East End Bookstore
Trial Balance
June 30, 20x3

Cash	$ 6,025	
Accounts Receivable	9,280	
Merchandise Inventory	29,450	
Store Supplies	1,911	
Prepaid Insurance	1,600	
Store Equipment	37,200	
Accumulated Depreciation, Store Equipment		$ 15,600
Accounts Payable		12,300
Ellen Donnelly, Capital		41,994
Ellen Donnelly, Withdrawals	12,000	
Sales		102,250
Sales Returns and Allowances	987	
Purchases	63,200	
Purchases Returns and Allowances		21,011
Freight In	2,261	
Sales Salaries Expense	21,350	
Rent Expense	3,600	
Other Selling Expenses	2,614	
Utilities Expense	1,677	
	$193,155	$193,155

2. Prepare an income statement, a statement of owner's equity, and a balance sheet. Sales Salaries Expense; Other Selling Expenses; Store Supplies Expense; and Depreciation Expense, Store Equipment are all selling expenses.

3. From the work sheet, prepare the closing entries.

P 7.

LO5   Merchandising Transactions,
SO8   Including Discounts: Periodic
Inventory System

Kimbassa Authentics Company engaged in these transactions in January 20xx:

Jan. 2   Purchased merchandise on credit from Chang Company, terms 2/10, n/30, FOB destination, $7,400.

3   Sold merchandise on credit to B. St. Pierre, terms 1/10, n/30, FOB shipping point, $1,000.

5   Sold merchandise for cash, $700.

6   Purchased and received merchandise on credit from Oakland Company, terms 2/10, n/30, FOB shipping point, $4,200.

7   Received freight bill from North Port Express for shipment received on January 6, $570.

9   Sold merchandise on credit to R. Hayden, terms 1/10, n/30, FOB destination, $3,800.

10   Purchased merchandise from Chang Company, terms 2/10, n/30, FOB shipping point, $2,650, including freight costs of $150.

11   Received freight bill from North Port Express for sale to R. Hayden on January 9, $291.

12   Paid Chang Company for purchase of January 2.

13   Received payment in full for B. St. Pierre's purchase of January 3.

14   Paid Oakland Company half the amount owed on the January 6 purchase. A discount is allowed on partial payment.

15   Returned faulty merchandise worth $300 to Chang Company for credit against purchase of January 10.

16   Purchased office supplies from GHI Co., terms n/10, $478.

17   Received payment from R. Hayden for half of the purchase of January 9. A discount is allowed on partial payment.

18   Paid Chang Company in full for amount owed on purchase of January 10, less return on January 15.

19   Sold merchandise on credit to M. Perez, terms 2/10, n/30, FOB shipping point, $780.

20   Returned for credit several items of office supplies purchased on January 16, $128.

22   Issued a credit to M. Perez for returned merchandise, $180.

25   Paid for January 16 purchase, less return on January 20.

26   Paid North Port Express for freight charges of January 7 and 11.

27   Received payment of amount owed by M. Perez for purchase of January 19, less credit of January 22.

28   Paid Oakland Company for balance of January 6 purchase.

31   Sold merchandise for cash, $973.

REQUIRED ▶   Prepare entries in journal form to record the transactions, assuming that the periodic inventory system is used.

ALTERNATE PROBLEMS

P 8.

LO1   Merchandising Income
LO4   Statement: Perpetual
Inventory System

At the end of the fiscal year, August 31, 20x4, selected accounts from the adjusted trial balance for Holiday Merchandise were as shown at the top of the next page. The company uses the perpetual inventory system.

REQUIRED ▶   1. Using the information given, prepare an income statement for Holiday Merchandise. Combine Freight In with Cost of Goods Sold. Store Salaries Expense; Advertising Expense; Store Supplies Expense; and Depreciation Expense, Store Equipment are selling expenses. The other expenses are general and administrative expenses. Show details of net sales and operating expenses.

Holiday Merchandise
Partial Adjusted Trial Balance
August 31, 20x4

Sales		$324,000
Sales Returns and Allowances	$ 4,000	
Cost of Goods Sold	122,800	
Freight In	4,600	
Store Salaries Expense	65,250	
Office Salaries Expense	25,750	
Advertising Expense	48,600	
Rent Expense	4,800	
Insurance Expense	2,400	
Utilities Expense	3,120	
Store Supplies Expense	5,760	
Office Supplies Expense	2,350	
Depreciation Expense, Store Equipment	2,100	
Depreciation Expense, Office Equipment	1,600	

2. Based on your knowledge at this point in the course, how would you use the income statement for Holiday Merchandise to evaluate the company's profitability? What other financial statement should be considered and why?

P 9.

LO4 Merchandising Transactions: Perpetual Inventory System

Garden Company engaged in the following transactions in October 20x4:

Oct. 7 Sold merchandise on credit to Sonia Mendes, terms n/30, FOB shipping point, $6,000 (cost, $3,600).

8 Purchased merchandise on credit from DaCosta Company, terms n/30, FOB shipping point, $12,000.

9 Paid Jay Company for shipping charges on merchandise purchased on October 8, $508.

10 Purchased merchandise on credit from Paige Company, terms n/30, FOB shipping point, $19,200, including $1,200 freight costs paid by Paige.

13 Purchased office supplies on credit from Hayami Company, terms n/30, $4,800.

14 Sold merchandise on credit to Eliza Samms, terms n/30, FOB shipping point, $4,800 (cost, $2,880).

14 Returned damaged merchandise received from DaCosta Company on October 8 for credit, $1,200.

17 Received check from Sonia Mendes for her purchase of October 7.

18 Returned a portion of the office supplies purchased on October 13 for credit because the wrong items were sent, $800.

19 Sold merchandise for cash, $3,600 (cost, $2,160).

20 Paid Paige Company for purchase of October 10.

21 Paid DaCosta Company the balance from the transactions of October 8 and October 14.

24 Accepted from Eliza Samms a return of merchandise, which was put back in inventory, $400 (cost, $240).

REQUIRED ▶

1. Prepare entries in journal form to record the transactions, assuming the perpetual inventory system is used.
2. Why is it important to keep purchases of merchandise in a separate account from purchases of office supplies?

P 10.

LO1 Merchandising Income
LO5 Statement: Periodic Inventory System

Selected accounts from the adjusted trial balance for Gourmet Gadgets Shop at the end of the fiscal year, March 31, 20x4, appear at the top of the next page. Gourmet Gadgets' merchandise inventory was $38,200 at the beginning of the year and $29,400 at the end of the year. The company uses the periodic inventory system.

Gourmet Gadgets Shop Partial Adjusted Trial Balance March 31, 20x4		
Sales		$165,000
Sales Returns and Allowances	$ 2,000	
Purchases	70,200	
Purchases Returns and Allowances		2,600
Freight In	2,300	
Store Salaries Expense	32,625	
Office Salaries Expense	12,875	
Advertising Expense	24,300	
Rent Expense	2,400	
Insurance Expense	1,200	
Utilities Expense	1,560	
Store Supplies Expense	2,880	
Office Supplies Expense	1,175	
Depreciation Expense, Store Equipment	1,050	
Depreciation Expense, Office Equipment	800	

REQUIRED ▶

1. Using the information given, prepare an income statement for Gourmet Gadgets Shop. Store Salaries Expense; Advertising Expense; Store Supplies Expense; and Depreciation Expense, Store Equipment are selling expenses. The other expenses are general and administrative expenses. Show details of net sales and operating expenses.

2. Based on your knowledge at this point in the course, how would you use the income statement for Gourmet Gadgets Shop to evaluate the company's profitability? What other financial statements should be considered and why?

P 11. Use the relevant data in **P 9** for this problem.

LO5 **Merchandising Transactions:**
Periodic Inventory System

REQUIRED ▶ Prepare entries in journal form to record the transactions, assuming the periodic inventory system is used.

SKILLS DEVELOPMENT CASES

Conceptual Analysis

SD 1.

LO1 **Cash Flow Management**

Matson Audio and Video Source has operated in a middle-size Midwest city for 30 years. The company has always prided itself on individual attention to its customers. It carries a large inventory so it can offer a good selection and deliver purchases quickly. It accepts credit cards and checks in payment but also provides 90 days credit to reliable customers who have purchased from the company in the past. The company maintains good relations with suppliers by paying invoices soon after they are received. In the past year, the company has been strapped for cash and has had to borrow from the bank to pay its bills. An analysis of its financial statements reveals that, on average, inventory is on hand for 70 days before being sold and receivables are held for 90 days before being paid. Accounts payable are paid, on average, in 20 days. What are the operating cycle and the financing period, and how long are Matson's? In what three ways can Matson improve its cash flow management? Make a suggestion for implementing each.

SD 2.

LO1 **Periodic Versus Perpetual**
LO4 **Inventory Systems**
LO5

Books Unlimited is a well-established chain of 20 bookstores in eastern Michigan. In recent years the company has grown rapidly, adding five new stores in regional malls. Management has relied on the manager of each store to place orders keyed to the market in his or her region; the managers select from a master list of available titles provided

by the central office. Every six months, a physical inventory is taken, and financial statements are prepared using the periodic inventory system. At that time, books that have not sold well are placed on sale or, whenever possible, returned to the publisher. As a result of the company's fast growth, there are many new store managers, and management has found that they are not as able to judge the market as are managers of the older, established stores. Thus, management is considering implementing a perpetual inventory system and carefully monitoring sales from the central office. Do you think Books Unlimited should switch to the perpetual inventory system or stay with the periodic inventory system? Discuss the advantages and disadvantages of each system.

Group Activity: Divide the class into groups. Ask half the groups to develop reasons to keep a periodic inventory system and half to list reasons to change to a perpetual inventory system. Debrief by writing parallel lists on the board.

Ethical Dilemma

SD 3.

**SO8   Ethics and Purchases
Discounts**

The purchasing power of some customers is such that they can exert pressure on suppliers to go beyond the suppliers' customary allowances. For example, Wal-Mart <www.walmart.com> represents more than 10 percent of annual sales for many suppliers, including Fruit of the Loom <www.fruit.com>, Sunbeam <www.sunbeam.com>, Rubbermaid <www.rubbermaid.com>, and Coleman <www.coleman.com>. *Forbes* magazine reports that while many of these suppliers allow a 2 percent discount if bills are paid within 15 days, "Wal-Mart routinely pays its bills closer to 30 days and takes the 2 percent discount anyway on the gross amount of the invoice, not the net amount, which deducts for [trade] discounts and things like freight costs."[6]

Identify two ways in which Wal-Mart's practice benefits Wal-Mart. Do you think this practice is unethical, or is it just good cash management on the part of Wal-Mart? Are the suppliers harmed by it?

Research Activity

SD 4.

**LO1   Merchandising Companies
LO2**

Conduct an individual field trip by visiting any retail or wholesale business. It may be a business where you buy a product, a company where you work, or a family business. It is not necessary for you to talk to anyone at the business, but it may be helpful to do so. Determine why the business is a merchandising business. List the products or groups of products that the company sells. Does the company offer any services? How do services differ from merchandise? Make a list of the types of transactions the business engages in. Also identify and list all the operating expenses you can think of that would be relevant to this business. Organize your findings in the form of a memo to your instructor.

Decision-Making Practice

SD 5.

**LO2   Analysis of Merchandising
LO5   Income Statement**

In 20x5, Les Solty opened a small retail store in a suburban mall. Called Solty Denim Company, the shop sold designer jeans. Solty worked 14 hours a day and controlled all aspects of the operation. All sales were for cash or bank credit card. The business was such a success that in 20x6, Solty decided to open a second store in another mall. Because the new shop needed his attention, he hired a manager to work in the original store with two sales clerks. During 20x6, the new store was successful, but the operations of the original store did not match the first year's performance.

Concerned about this turn of events, Solty compared the two years' results for the original store. The figures were as follows:

	20x6	20x5
Net sales	$325,000	$350,000
Cost of goods sold	225,000	225,000
Gross margin	$100,000	$125,000
Operating expenses	75,000	50,000
Net income	$ 25,000	$ 75,000

In addition, Solty's analysis revealed that the cost and selling price of jeans were about the same in both years and that the level of operating expenses was roughly the same in both years, except for the new manager's $25,000 salary. Sales returns and allowances were insignificant amounts in both years.

Studying the situation further, Solty discovered the following facts about the cost of goods sold:

	20x6	20x5
Purchases	$200,000	$271,000
Total purchases allowances	15,000	20,000
Freight in	19,000	27,000
Physical inventory, end of year	32,000	53,000

Still not satisfied, Solty went through all the individual sales and purchase records for the year. Both sales and purchases were verified. However, the 20x6 ending inventory should have been $57,000, given the unit purchases and sales during the year. After puzzling over all this information, Solty comes to you for accounting help.

1. Using Solty's new information, recompute the cost of goods sold for 20x5 and 20x6, and account for the difference in net income between 20x5 and 20x6.
2. Suggest at least two reasons for the discrepancy in the 20x6 ending inventory.

FINANCIAL REPORTING AND ANALYSIS CASES

Interpreting Financial Reports

FRA 1.

LO2 **Comparison of Operating Performance**

Wal-Mart <www.walmart.com> and Kmart <www.kmartcorp.com>, two of the largest retailers in the United States, have different approaches to retailing. Their success has been different also. At one time, Kmart was larger than Wal-Mart. Today, Wal-Mart is almost three times as large and Kmart has declared bankruptcy. You can see the difference by analyzing their respective income statements and merchandise inventories. Selected information from their annual reports for the year ended January 31, 2001, is presented below.[7] (All amounts are in millions.)

Wal-Mart: Net sales, $191,329; Cost of goods sold, $150,255; Operating expenses, $31,550; Ending inventory, $21,442

Kmart: Net sales, $37,028; Cost of goods sold, $29,658; Operating expenses, $7,415; Ending inventory, $6,412

1. Prepare a schedule computing the gross margin and income from operations for both companies as dollar amounts and as percentages of net sales. Also compute inventory as a percentage of the cost of goods sold.
2. From what you know about the different retailing approaches of these two companies, do the gross margins and incomes from operations you computed in **1** seem compatible with these approaches? What is it about the nature of Wal-Mart's operations that produces higher gross margin and lower operating expenses in percentages in comparison to Kmart? Which company's approach was more successful in the fiscal year ending January 31, 2001? Explain your answer.
3. Both companies have chosen a fiscal year that ends on January 31. Why do you suppose they made this choice? How realistic do you think the inventory figures are as indicators of inventory levels during the rest of the year? Which company appears to make the most efficient use of its inventory?

International Company

FRA 2.

LO3 **British Terminology for**
LO4 **Merchandising Transactions**
LO5

Harrods <www.harrods.com> is a large British retailer with department stores throughout the United Kingdom and Europe. British and American merchandising terms differ. For instance, in the United Kingdom, the income statement is called the *profit and loss account*, sales is called *turnover*, merchandise inventory is called *stocks*, accounts receivable is called *debtors*, and accounts payable is called *creditors*. Of course, the amounts are stated in terms of the pound (£). In today's business world, it is important to understand terminology employed by professionals from other countries. Explain in your own words why the British may use the terms *profit and loss account*, *turnover*, *stocks*, *debtors*, and *creditors* rather than the American equivalents.

Toys "R" Us Annual Report

FRA 3.

LO1 **Operating Cycle and Financing Period**

Refer to the Toys "R" Us <www.tru.com> annual report in the Supplement to Chapter 6 and to Figures 1 and 2 in this chapter. Write a memorandum to your instructor briefly describing the Toys "R" Us operating cycle and financing period. This memorandum should identify the most common transactions in the operating cycle as it applies to Toys "R" Us. It should refer to the importance of accounts receivable, accounts payable, and merchandise inventory in the Toys "R" Us financial statements. Complete the memorandum by explaining why the operating cycle and financing period are favorable to the company.

Comparison Case: Toys "R" Us and Walgreen Co.

FRA 4.

LO1 **Income Statement Analysis**

Refer to the Toys "R" Us <www.tru.com> annual report and the financial statements of Walgreens <www.walgreens.com> in the Supplement to Chapter 6. Determine which company—Toys "R" Us or Walgreens—has more profitable merchandising operations by preparing a schedule that compares the companies based on net sales, cost of sales, gross margin, total operating expenses, and income from operations as a percentage of sales. (*Hint:* You should put the income statements in comparable formats.) In addition, for each company, compute inventory as a percentage of the cost of sales. Which company has the highest prices in relation to costs of sales? Which company is more efficient in its operating expenses? Which company manages its inventory better? Overall, on the basis of the income statement, which company is more profitable? Explain your answers.

Fingraph® Financial Analyst™

FRA 5.

LO1 **Income Statement Analysis**
LO2

Choose any retail company from the list of Fingraph companies on the Needles Accounting Resource Center Web Site at http://accounting.college.hmco.com/students. Access the Microsoft Excel spreadsheets for the company you selected. Using the Fingraph CD-ROM software, display the Income Statements Analysis: Income from Operations in tabular and graphic form for the company.

Write an executive summary that analyzes the change in the company's income from operations from the first to the second year. In preparing the summary, focus on the reasons the change occurred by answering the following questions: Did the company's income from operations improve or decline from the first to the second year? What was the relationship of the change to the change in net sales? Was the change in income from operations primarily due to a change in gross margin or to a change in operating expenses? Suggest some possible reasons for the change in gross margin or operating expenses. Use percentages to support your answer.

Internet Case

FRA 6.

LO1 **Comparison of Traditional**
LO3 **Merchandising with**
LO4 **Ecommerce**

Ecommerce is a word coined to describe business conducted over the Internet. Ecommerce is similar in some ways to traditional retailing, but it presents new challenges. Choose a company with traditional retail outlets that is also selling over the Internet and go to its web site. Some examples are Wal-Mart <www.walmart.com>, Kmart <www.kmartcorp.com>, Toys "R" Us <www.tru.com>, Barnes & Noble <www.bn.com>, and Lands' End <www.landsend.com>. Investigate and list the steps a customer makes to purchase an item on the site. How do these steps differ from those in a traditional retail store? What are some of the accounting challenges in recording Internet transactions? Be prepared to discuss your results in class.

6

Chapter 6 introduces the objectives and qualitative aspects of financial information and demonstrates how much more useful classified financial statements are than simple financial statements in presenting information to statement users.

Financial Reporting and Analysis

DECISION POINT
A USER'S FOCUS

General Mills, Inc. <www.generalmills.com> The management of a corporation is judged by the company's financial performance. Financial performance is reported to stockholders and others outside the business in the company's annual report, which includes the financial statements and other relevant information. Performance measures are usually based on the relationships of key data in the financial statements. For large companies, this often means condensing a tremendous amount of information to a few numbers that management considers important. For example, what key measures does the management of General Mills, Inc., a successful food products company that recently acquired its long-time rival Pillsbury and offers such well-known brands as Cheerios, Wheaties, Hamburger Helper, and Progresso Soups, choose to focus on as its goals?

In its letter to shareholders, General Mills states its financial goals as follows:

> Our target is 7 percent compound annual sales growth between now and 2010. With this faster topline growth, . . . our Earnings Per Share (EPS) growth should accelerate, too. Our target is to deliver 11 to 15 percent annual earnings per share growth over the balance of this decade. We believe achieving these goals will represent superior performance when benchmarked against major consumer products companies.[1]

General Mills' management has thus set forth measurable performance goals by which it can be evaluated. The graph on the opposite page shows that the company reached its growth in sales target in only

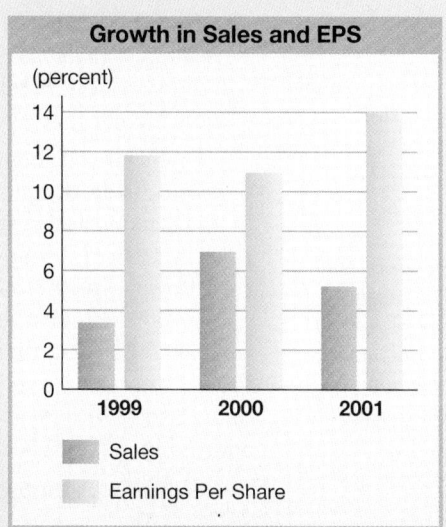

What key performance measures does the management of General Mills choose to focus on as its goals?

one of the past three years. However, it reached its growth in EPS in all three years.

Of course, investors and creditors will want to do their own analysis of General Mills. This will require reading and interpreting the financial statements and calculating other ratios. However, the analysis will be meaningless unless the reader understands financial statements and generally accepted accounting principles, on which the statements are based. Also important to learning how to read and interpret financial statements is a comprehension of the categories and classifications used in balance sheets and income statements. Key financial ratios used in financial statement analysis are based on those categories. This chapter begins by describing the objectives, characteristics, and conventions that underlie the preparation of financial statements.

213

OBJECTIVES OF FINANCIAL INFORMATION

LO1   State the objectives of financial reporting.
RELATED TEXT ASSIGNMENTS
Q: 1
SE: 1
E: 1

The United States has a highly developed exchange economy. In this kind of economy, most goods and services are exchanged for money or claims to money instead of being used or bartered by their producers. Most business is carried on through corporations, including many extremely large firms that buy, sell, and obtain financing in U.S. and world markets.

By issuing stocks and bonds that are traded in financial markets, businesses can raise capital for production and marketing activities. Investors are interested mainly in returns from dividends and increases in the market price of their investments. Creditors want to know if the business can repay a loan plus interest in accordance with required terms. Thus, both investors and creditors need to know if a company can generate adequate cash flows. Financial statements are important to both groups in making that judgment. They offer valuable information that helps investors and creditors judge a company's ability to pay dividends and repay debts with interest. In this way, the market puts scarce resources to work in the companies that can use them most efficiently.

The information needs of users and the general business environment are the basis for the three objectives of financial reporting established by the Financial Accounting Standards Board (FASB):[2]

KEY POINT: Although reading financial reports requires some understanding of business, it does not require the skills of a CPA.

1. *To furnish information that is useful in making investment and credit decisions.* Financial reporting should offer information that can help current and potential investors and creditors make rational investment and credit decisions. The reports should be in a form that makes sense to those who have some understanding of business and are willing to study the information carefully.

2. *To provide information useful in assessing cash flow prospects.* Financial reporting should supply information to help current and potential investors and creditors predict the amounts, timing, and risk of cash receipts from dividends or interest and proceeds from the sale, redemption, or maturity of stocks or loans.

3. *To provide information about business resources, claims to those resources, and changes in them.* Financial reporting should give information about the company's assets, liabilities, and stockholders' equity, and the effects of transactions on the company's assets, liabilities, and stockholders' equity.

● **STOP AND THINK!**
How do the four basic financial statements meet the third objective of financial reporting?
The balance sheet provides information about a company's resources (assets) and claims to those resources (liabilities and owners' equity). The income statement, statement of cash flows, and statement of owner's equity provide information about changes in resources and claims to them. ■

Financial statements are the most important way of periodically presenting to parties outside the business the information that has been gathered and processed in the accounting system. For this reason, the financial statements—the balance sheet, the income statement, the statement of owner's equity, and the statement of cash flows—are the most important output of the accounting system. These financial statements are "general purpose" because of their wide audience. They are "external" because their users are outside the business. Because of a potential conflict of interest between managers, who must prepare the statements, and investors or creditors, who invest in or lend money to the business, these statements often are audited by outside accountants to increase confidence in their reliability.

 Check out ACE for a Review Quiz at http://accounting.college.hmco.com/students.

QUALITATIVE CHARACTERISTICS OF ACCOUNTING INFORMATION

LO2   State the qualitative characteristics of accounting information and describe their interrelationships.
RELATED TEXT ASSIGNMENTS
Q: 2
SE: 1
E: 1

It is easy for students in their first accounting course to get the idea that accounting is 100 percent accurate. This idea is reinforced by the fact that all the problems in this and other introductory books can be solved. The numbers all add up; what is supposed to equal something else does. Accounting seems very much like mathematics in its precision. In this book, the basics of accounting are presented in a simple form to help you understand them. In practice, however, accounting information

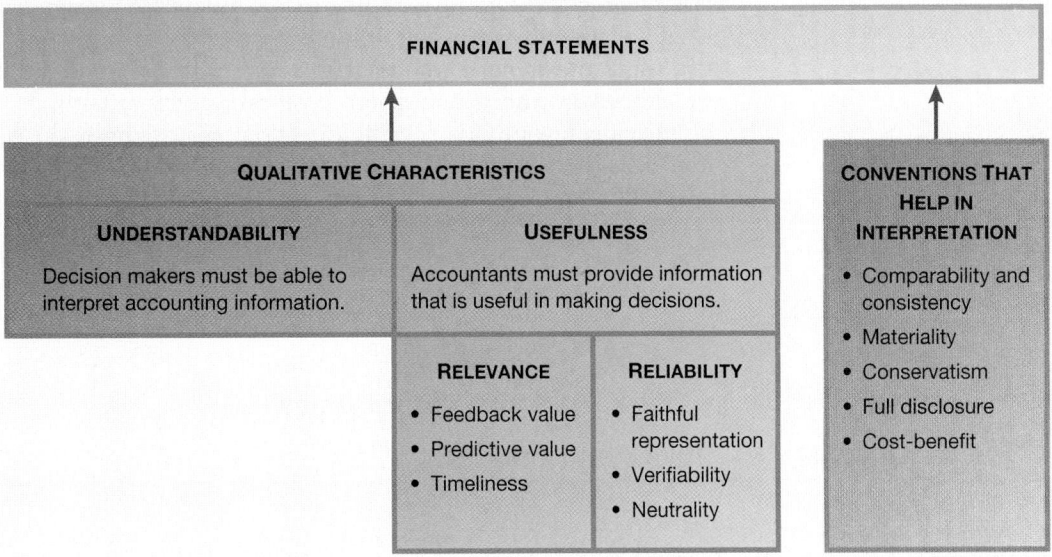

FIGURE 1
Qualitative Characteristics and the Conventions of Accounting Information

is neither simple nor precise, and it rarely satisfies all criteria. The FASB emphasizes this fact in the following statement:

> The information provided by financial reporting often results from approximate, rather than exact, measures. The measures commonly involve numerous estimates, classifications, summarizations, judgments and allocations. The outcome of economic activity in a dynamic economy is uncertain and results from combinations of many factors. Thus, despite the aura of precision that may seem to surround financial reporting in general and financial statements in particular, with few exceptions the measures are approximations, which may be based on rules and conventions, rather than exact amounts.[3]

The goal of accounting information—to provide the basic data that different users need to make informed decisions—is an ideal. The gap between the ideal and the actual provides much of the interest and controversy in accounting. To facilitate interpretation, the FASB has described the **qualitative characteristics** of accounting information, which are standards for judging that information. In addition, there are generally accepted conventions for recording and reporting that simplify interpretation. The relationships among these concepts are shown in Figure 1.

The most important qualitative characteristics are understandability and usefulness. **Understandability** depends on both the accountant and the decision maker. The accountant prepares the financial statements in accordance with accepted practices, generating important information that is believed to be understandable. But the decision maker must interpret the information and use it in making decisions. The decision maker must judge what information to use, how to use it, and what it means.

For accounting information to meet the standard of **usefulness**, it must have two major qualitative characteristics: relevance and reliability. **Relevance** means that the information can affect the outcome of a decision. In other words, a different decision would be made if the relevant information were not available. To be relevant, information must provide feedback, help predict future conditions, and be timely. For example, the income statement provides information about how a company performed over the past year (feedback), and it helps in planning for the next

● STOP AND THINK!
What are some areas that require estimates to record transactions under the matching rule?
To record depreciation expense, it is necessary to estimate the useful life of the asset. To record the amount of unearned revenue that is now earned or the amount of accrued revenue on a project in process, it is necessary to estimate the amount of revenue earned. ■

KEY POINT: Financial statements should be free of material misstatements.

year (prediction). To be useful, however, it also must be communicated soon enough after the end of the accounting period to enable the reader to make decisions (timeliness).

In addition to being relevant, accounting information must have **reliability**. In other words, the user must be able to depend on the information. It must represent what it is meant to represent. It must be credible and verifiable by independent parties using the same methods of measuring. It also must be neutral. Accounting should convey information about business activity as faithfully as possible without influencing anyone in a specific direction. For example, the balance sheet should represent the economic resources, obligations, and owner's equity of a business as faithfully as possible in accordance with generally accepted accounting principles, and it should be verifiable by an auditor.

✅ Check out ACE for a Review Quiz at http://accounting.college.hmco.com/students.

CONVENTIONS THAT HELP IN THE INTERPRETATION OF FINANCIAL INFORMATION

LO3 Define and describe the conventions of *comparability* and *consistency, materiality, conservatism, full disclosure,* and *cost-benefit.*

RELATED TEXT ASSIGNMENTS
Q: 3
SE: 2
E: 1, 2
P: 1, 6
SD: 1, 2

To a large extent, financial statements are based on estimates and the application of accounting rules for recognition and allocation. In this book, we point out a number of difficulties with financial statements. One is failing to recognize the changing value of the dollar caused by inflation. Another is treating intangibles, such as research and development costs, as assets if they are purchased outside the company and as expenses if they are developed within the company. Such problems do not mean that financial statements are useless; they are essential. However, users must know how to interpret them. To help in this interpretation, accountants depend on five **conventions**, or rules of thumb, in recording transactions and preparing financial statements: (1) comparability and consistency, (2) materiality, (3) conservatism, (4) full disclosure, and (5) cost-benefit.

COMPARABILITY AND CONSISTENCY

A characteristic that increases the usefulness of accounting information is comparability. Information about a company is more useful if it can be compared with similar facts about the same company over several time periods or about another company for the same time period. **Comparability** means that the information is presented in such a way that a decision maker can recognize similarities, differences, and trends over different time periods or between different companies.

Consistent use of accounting measures and procedures is important in achieving comparability. The **consistency** convention requires that once an accounting procedure is adopted by a company, it remain in use from one period to the next unless users of the financial statements are informed of the change. Thus, without a note to the contrary, the users can assume that there has been no change in the treatment of a particular transaction, account, or item that would affect the interpretation of the statements.

If management decides that a certain procedure is no longer appropriate and should be changed, or if reporting requirements change, generally accepted accounting principles require that the change and its dollar effect be described in the notes to the financial statements:

> The nature of and justification for a change in accounting principle and its effect on income should be disclosed in the financial statements of the period in which the change is made. The justification for the change should explain clearly why the newly adopted accounting principle is preferable.[4]

🔴 **STOP AND THINK!**

How can financial information be consistent but not comparable?

Consistency in accounting applies only to the use of the accounting principles for presenting the financial information. It does not apply to the conditions that are represented in the financial statements. For example, changes in business operations or the economy may make financial information incomparable from year to year, even though the same accounting policies have been followed. ∎

FOCUS ON BUSINESS PRACTICE

How Much Is Material? It's Not Only a Matter of Numbers.

The materiality issue has been a pet peeve of the SEC <www.sec.gov>, which contends that companies have increasingly abused the convention to protect their stocks from taking a pounding when earnings do not reach their targets. Over the years, companies have excluded from earnings any losses that they deem so small as to have virtually no effect on net income. Accountants and companies have typically used a rule of thumb of 5 percent of net income. The SEC has issued a new rule that puts stricter requirements on the use of materiality in that it calls for qualitative considerations in addition to quantitative guides. The percentage assessment is acceptable as an initial screening, but now companies cannot decline to book items in order to meet earnings estimates, preserve a growing earnings trend, convert a loss to a profit, increase management compensation, or hide an illegal transaction, such as a bribe.[5]

www.rmc.com

For example, Reynolds Metals Company changed its method of accounting for business start-up costs because the American Institute of Certified Public Accountants (AICPA) changed the requirements for accounting for this type of cost.[6]

MATERIALITY

BUSINESS-WORLD EXAMPLE: By definition, a $10 stapler is a long-term asset that, theoretically, should be capitalized and depreciated over its useful life. However, the convention of materiality allows the stapler to be expensed entirely in the year of purchase because its cost is small and writing it off in one year has no effect on anyone's decision making.

KEY POINT: Illegal acts involving even small dollar amounts should be investigated.

Materiality refers to the relative importance of an item or event. If an item or event is material, it is probably relevant to users of the financial statements. In other words, an item is material if users would have done something differently if they had not known about the item. The accountant is often faced with decisions about small items or events that make little difference to users no matter how they are handled. For example, a large company may decide that expenditures for durable items of less than $500 should be charged as expenses rather than recorded as long-term assets and depreciated.

In general, an item is material if there is a reasonable expectation that knowing about it would influence the decisions of users of financial statements. The materiality of an item normally is determined by relating its dollar value to an element of the financial statements, such as net income or total assets. Some accountants feel that when an item is 5 percent or more of net income, it is material. However, materiality also depends on the nature of the item, not just its value. For example, in a multimillion-dollar company, a mistake of $5,000 in recording an item may not be important, but the discovery of a $5,000 bribe or theft can be very important. Also, many small errors can combine into a material amount. Accountants judge the materiality of many things, and the users of financial statements depend on their judgments being fair and accurate. The SEC has recently questioned whether a desire to avoid showing certain items in the financial statements has influenced some companies' judgment about materiality.

CONSERVATISM

KEY POINT: The purpose of conservatism is not to produce the lowest net income and lowest asset value. It is a guideline for choosing among GAAP alternatives, and it should be used with care.

Accountants try to base their decisions on logic and evidence that lead to the fairest report of what happened. In judging and estimating, however, accountants often are faced with uncertainties. In these cases, they look to the convention of conservatism. This convention means that when accountants face major uncertainties about which accounting procedure to use, they generally choose the one that is least likely to overstate assets and income.

One of the most common applications of the conservatism convention is the use of the lower-of-cost-or-market method in accounting for inventories. Under this method, if an item's market value is greater than its cost, the more conservative cost figure is used. If the market value falls below the cost, the more conservative market value is used. The latter situation often occurs in the computer industry.

Conservatism can be a useful tool in doubtful cases, but its abuse leads to incorrect and misleading financial statements. Suppose that someone incorrectly applies

FOCUS ON BUSINESS PRACTICE

When Is "Full Disclosure" Too Much? It's a Matter of Cost and Benefits.

The large accounting firm of Ernst & Young <www.ey.com> reports that over a 20-year period, the total number of pages in the annual reports of 25 large, well-known companies has increased an average of 84 percent and the number of pages of notes has increased 325 percent—from 4 to 17 pages. Management's discussion and analysis increased 300 percent, from 3 pages to 12.[7] Because some people feel that "these documents are so daunting that people don't read them at all," the SEC allows companies to issue to the public "summary reports" in which the bulk of the notes can be reduced.

Although more accessible and less costly, summary reports are controversial because many analysts feel that it is in the notes that one gets the detailed information necessary to understand complex business operations. One analyst remarked, "To banish the notes for fear they will turn off readers would be like eliminating fractions from math books on the theory that the average student prefers to work with whole numbers."[8] Where this controversy will end, nobody knows. Detailed reports still must be filed with the SEC, but more and more companies are providing summary reports to the public.

---

the conservatism convention by expensing a long-term asset of material cost in the period of purchase. In this case, there is no uncertainty. Income and assets for the current period would be understated, and income in future periods would be overstated. For this reason, accountants depend on the conservatism convention only when there is uncertainty about which accounting procedure to use.

FULL DISCLOSURE

The convention of **full disclosure** requires that financial statements and their notes present all information that is relevant to the users' understanding of the statements. That is, the statements should offer any explanation needed to keep them from being misleading. Explanatory notes are considered an integral part of the financial statements. For instance, a change from one accounting procedure to another should be reported. In general, the form of the financial statements can affect their usefulness in making certain decisions—for example, the categories used to group accounts in the statements convey information about the accounts. Also, certain items, such as the amount of depreciation expense on the income statement and the accumulated depreciation on the balance sheet, are essential to the readers of financial statements.

Other examples of disclosures required by the FASB and other official bodies are the accounting procedures used in preparing the statements, important terms of the company's debt, commitments and contingencies, and important events taking place after the date of the statements. However, the statements can become so cluttered with notes that they impede rather than help understanding. Beyond required disclosures, the application of the full-disclosure convention is based on the judgment of management and of the accountants who prepare the financial statements.

In recent years, the principle of full disclosure also has been influenced by investors and creditors. To protect them, independent auditors, the stock exchanges, and the SEC have made more demands for disclosure by publicly owned companies. The SEC has been pushing especially hard for the enforcement of full disclosure. As a result, more and better information about corporations is available to the public today than ever before.

COST-BENEFIT

The **cost-benefit** convention underlies all the qualitative characteristics and conventions. It holds that the benefits to be gained from providing accounting information should be greater than the costs of providing it. Of course, minimum levels of relevance and reliability must be reached if accounting information is to be useful. Beyond the minimum levels, however, it is up to the FASB and the SEC, which

BUSINESS-WORLD EXAMPLE: Firms use the convention of cost-benefit for both accounting and nonaccounting decisions. Department stores could almost completely stop shoplifting if they were to hire five times as many clerks to watch customers. The benefit would be reduced shoplifting. The cost would be reduced sales (customers do not like being watched closely) and increased wages expense. Although shoplifting is a serious problem for department stores, the benefit of reducing shoplifting in this way does not outweigh the cost.

require the information, and the accountant, who provides the information, to judge the costs and benefits in each case. Most of the costs of providing information fall at first on the preparers; the benefits are reaped by both preparers and users. Finally, both the costs and the benefits are passed on to society in the form of prices and social benefits from more efficient allocation of resources.

The costs and benefits of a particular requirement for accounting disclosure are both direct and indirect, immediate and deferred. For example, it is hard to judge the final costs and benefits of a far-reaching and costly regulation. The FASB, for instance, allows certain large companies to make a supplemental disclosure in their financial statements of the effects of changes in current costs. Most companies choose not to present this information because they believe the costs of producing and providing it exceed its benefits to the readers of their financial statements. Cost-benefit is a question faced by all regulators, including the FASB and the SEC. Even though there are no definitive ways of measuring costs and benefits, much of an accountant's work deals with these concepts.

 Check out ACE for a Review Quiz at http://accounting.college.hmco.com/students.

MANAGEMENT'S RESPONSIBILITY FOR ETHICAL REPORTING

LO4 Explain management's responsibility for ethical financial reporting and define *fraudulent financial reporting*.

RELATED TEXT ASSIGNMENTS
Q: 4
SD: 3, 4, 5

www.generalmills.com

The users of financial statements depend on the good faith of those who prepare these statements. This dependence places a duty on a company's management and its accountants to act ethically in the reporting process. That duty is often expressed in the report of management that accompanies financial statements. For example, the report of the management of General Mills, Inc., a company known for strong financial reporting and controls, states:

> The management . . . is responsible for the fairness and accuracy of the consolidated financial statements. The consolidated financial statements have been prepared in accordance with accounting principles that are generally accepted in the United States, using management's best estimates and judgments where appropriate.[9]

General Mills' management also tells how it meets this responsibility:

> Management has established a system of internal controls that provides reasonable assurance that assets are adequately safeguarded and transactions are recorded accurately in all material respects, in accordance with management's authorization. We maintain a strong audit program that independently evaluates the adequacy and effectiveness of internal controls.[10]

● **STOP AND THINK!**

What is the difference between aggressive accounting and fraudulent financial reporting?

There is often a fine line between aggressive accounting, which is the use of legitimate accounting methods to achieve business purposes, and fraudulent financial reporting, which is the intentional misrepresentation of financial information. The former is acceptable, whereas the latter is unethical and sometimes illegal. ■

www.worldcom.com
www.enron.com

The intentional preparation of misleading financial statements is called **fraudulent financial reporting**.[11] It can result from the distortion of records (e.g., the manipulation of inventory records), falsified transactions (e.g., fictitious sales), or the misapplication of accounting principles (e.g., treating as an asset an item that should be expensed). There are a number of possible motives for fraudulent reporting—for instance, to obtain a higher price when a company is sold, meet the expectations of stockholders, or obtain a loan. Sometimes, the incentive is personal gain, such as additional compensation, promotion, or avoidance of penalties for poor performance. The personal costs of such actions can be high. Individuals who authorize or prepare fraudulent financial statements may face prison sentences and fines. A company's investors and lenders, employees, and customers suffer from fraudulent financial reporting as well.

Due to recent abuses in financial reporting that have come to light in companies like WorldCom and Enron, Congress passed the Sarbanes-Oxley Act in 2002. This legislation orders the SEC to draw up rules requiring chief executives and chief

FOCUS ON BUSINESS ETHICS

Questionable Accounting Practices Are Under Scrutiny.

There is a difference between management's choosing to follow accounting principles that are favorable to its actions and fraudulent financial reporting. Because of recent, highly visible accounting misstatements by such companies as WorldCom <www.worldcom.com>, Enron <www.enron.com>, Sunbeam Corporation <www.sunbeam.com>, and many others attempting to meet the earnings expectations of stock analysts, the SEC is cracking down on what it sees as the main abuses, which the chairman of the SEC has called "accounting hocus-pocus." These are cases in which real transactions are accounted for in such a way as to distort reality. Examples include one-time "big bath" restructuring charges that overstate current expenses to benefit future periods, creative acquisition accounting in mergers, writing off purchased research and development inappropriately, miscellaneous "cookie jar reserves" involving unrealistic assumptions about such items as sales returns and warranty costs, and the abuse of the materiality convention.[12] The SEC brings about 100 accounting actions each year. In recent times, executives at WorldCom and Sunbeam have been indicted. Executives at Enron are under investigation.[13]

financial officers of all 15,000 publicly traded companies to file statements each quarter swearing that, based on their knowledge, their company's quarterly and annual statements are accurate and complete. Violation can result in criminal penalties. To comply with this law and meet ethical reporting requirements, a company's accountants and auditors must apply financial accounting concepts in such a way as to present a fair view of the company's operations and financial position and to avoid misleading readers of the financial statements.

 Check out ACE for a Review Quiz at http://accounting.college.hmco.com/students.

CLASSIFIED BALANCE SHEET

LO5 Identify and describe the basic components of a classified balance sheet.

RELATED TEXT ASSIGNMENTS
Q: 5, 6, 7, 8, 9, 10, 11, 12, 13
SE: 3, 4
E: 3, 4
P: 3, 5
FRA: 4, 5

The balance sheets you have seen in the chapters thus far categorize accounts as assets, liabilities, and owner's equity. Because even a fairly small company can have hundreds of accounts, simply listing accounts in these broad categories is not particularly helpful to a statement user. Setting up subcategories within the major categories often makes financial statements much more useful. Investors and creditors study and evaluate the relationships among the subcategories. General-purpose external financial statements that are divided into subcategories are called **classified financial statements**.

The balance sheet presents the financial position of a company at a particular time. The subdivisions of the classified balance sheet shown in Exhibit 1 are typical of those used by most companies in the United States. The subdivisions under owner's equity depend, of course, on the form of business.

ASSETS

REAL-WORLD EXAMPLE: Examples of accounts that would be classified as "other assets" are long-term receivables and bond issue costs.

A company's assets are often divided into four categories: (1) current assets; (2) investments; (3) property, plant, and equipment; and (4) intangible assets. These categories are listed in the order of their presumed ease of conversion into cash. For example, current assets are usually more easily converted to cash than are property, plant, and equipment. For simplicity, some companies group investments, intangible assets, and other miscellaneous assets into a category called "**other assets**."

■ **CURRENT ASSETS** Current assets are cash and other assets that are reasonably expected to be converted to cash, sold, or consumed within one year or within the normal operating cycle of the business, whichever is longer. The normal operating cycle of a company is the average time needed to go from cash to cash. For example,

EXHIBIT 1
Classified Balance Sheet for
Shafer Auto Parts Company

Shafer Auto Parts Company
Balance Sheet
December 31, 20xx

Assets

Current assets			
Cash		$10,360	
Short-term investments		2,000	
Notes receivable		8,000	
Accounts receivable		35,300	
Merchandise inventory		60,400	
Prepaid insurance		6,600	
Store supplies		1,060	
Office supplies		636	
Total current assets			$124,356
Investments			
Land held for future use			5,000
Property, plant, and equipment			
Land		$ 4,500	
Building	$20,650		
Less accumulated depreciation	8,640	12,010	
Delivery equipment	$18,400		
Less accumulated depreciation	9,450	8,950	
Office equipment	$ 8,600		
Less accumulated depreciation	5,000	3,600	
Total property, plant, and equipment			29,060
Intangible assets			
Trademark			500
Total assets			$158,916

Liabilities

Current liabilities			
Notes payable		$15,000	
Accounts payable		23,883	
Salaries payable		2,000	
Current portion of mortgage payable		1,800	
Total current liabilities			$ 42,683
Long-term liabilities			
Mortgage payable			17,800
Total liabilities			$ 60,483

Owner's Equity

Fred Shafer, Capital			98,433
Total liabilities and owner's equity			$158,916

www.boeing.com

KEY POINT: Use one year as the current period unless the normal operating cycle happens to be longer.

KEY POINT: A firm does not consume prepaid expenses, but it does enjoy the benefit of the space rented, the insurance protection provided, and so forth.

KEY POINT: For an investment to be classified as current, management must intend to sell it within the next year or the current operating cycle, and it must be readily marketable.

⬤ **STOP AND THINK!**
Why is it that land held for future use and equipment not currently used in the business are classified as investments rather than as property, plant, and equipment?

They are classified as investments because doing so helps users of financial statements assess the performance of the company using such measures as return on assets. Also, the investment category gives users some idea of resources the company may be able to draw on without disturbing the current business operations. ■

cash is used to buy merchandise inventory, which is sold for cash or for a promise of cash if the sale is made on account. If a sale is made on account, the resulting receivable must be collected before the cycle is completed.

The normal operating cycle for most companies is less than one year, but there are exceptions. Boeing Company, for example, can take more than one year to make commerical aircraft. The cost of those aircraft are considered current asssets while they are being made because they will be sold in the current operating cycle. The payments for a television set or a refrigerator can be extended over 24 or 36 months, but these receivables are still considered current assets.

Cash is obviously a current asset. Short-term investments, notes and accounts receivable, and inventory are also current assets because they are expected to be converted to cash within the next year or during the normal operating cycle. On the balance sheet, they are listed in the order of their ease of conversion into cash.

Prepaid expenses, such as rent and insurance paid in advance, and inventories of supplies bought for use rather than for sale also should be classified as current assets. Such assets are current in the sense that if they had not been bought earlier, a current outlay of cash would be needed to obtain them.[14]

In deciding whether an asset is current or noncurrent, the idea of "reasonable expectation" is important. For example, Short-Term Investments, also called "Marketable Securities," is an account used for temporary investments of "idle" cash—that is, cash not immediately required for operating purposes. Management can reasonably expect to sell these securities as cash needs arise over the next year or operating cycle. Investments in securities that management does not expect to sell within the next year and that do not involve the temporary use of idle cash should be shown in the investments category of a classified balance sheet.

■ **INVESTMENTS**   The investments category includes assets, usually long term, that are not used in the normal operation of the business and that management does not plan to convert to cash within the next year. Items in this category are securities held for long-term investment, long-term notes receivable, land held for future use, plant or equipment not used in the business, and special funds established to pay off a debt or buy a building. Also included are large permanent investments in another company for the purpose of controlling that company.

■ **PROPERTY, PLANT, AND EQUIPMENT**   Property, plant, and equipment are tangible long-term assets used in the continuing operation of the business. They represent a place to operate (land and buildings) and the equipment to produce, sell, deliver, and service the company's goods. They are therefore also called *operating assets* or, sometimes, *fixed assets, tangible assets, long-lived assets,* or *plant assets.* Through depreciation, the costs of these assets (except land) are spread over the periods they benefit. Past depreciation is recorded in the Accumulated Depreciation accounts. The order in which property, plant, and equipment are listed on the balance sheet is not the same everywhere. In practice, accounts are often combined to make the financial statements less cluttered. For example:

Property, Plant, and Equipment

Land		$ 4,500
Buildings and equipment	$47,650	
Less accumulated depreciation	23,090	24,560
Total property, plant, and equipment		$29,060

Many companies simply show a single line with a total for property, plant, and equipment and provide the details in a note to the financial statements.

The property, plant, and equipment category also includes natural resources owned by the company, such as forest lands, oil and gas properties, and coal mines, if they are used in the regular course of business. If they are not, they are listed in the investments category, as noted above.

■ **INTANGIBLE ASSETS**   Intangible assets are long-term assets with no physical substance whose value stems from the rights or privileges they extend to their owners. Examples are patents, copyrights, goodwill, franchises, and trademarks. These assets are recorded at cost, which is spread over the expected life of the right or privilege.

LIABILITIES

Liabilities are divided into two categories, based on when the liabilities fall due: current liabilities and long-term liabilities.

BUSINESS-WORLD EXAMPLE: The portion of a mortgage paid monthly for 120 months that is due during the next year or the current operating cycle would be classified as a current liability. The portion due after the next year or the current operating cycle would be classified as a long-term liability.

■ **CURRENT LIABILITIES**   The category of current liabilities consists of obligations due to be paid or performed within one year or within the normal operating cycle of the business, whichever is longer. Current liabilities are typically paid from current assets or by incurring new short-term liabilities. They include notes payable, accounts payable, the current portion of long-term debt, salaries and wages payable, taxes payable, and customer advances (unearned revenues).

■ **LONG-TERM LIABILITIES**   The debts of a business that fall due more than one year in the future or beyond the normal operating cycle, which will be paid out of noncurrent assets, are long-term liabilities. Mortgages payable, long-term notes, bonds payable, employee pension obligations, and long-term lease liabilities generally fall into the category of long-term liabilities.

OWNER'S EQUITY

The terms *owner's equity*, *proprietorship*, *capital*, and *net worth* are used interchangeably. They all stand for the owner's interest in the company. The first three terms are preferred to *net worth* because most assets are recorded at original cost rather than at current value. For this reason, the ownership section will not represent "worth." It is really a claim against the assets of the company.

Although the form of business organization does not usually affect the accounting treatment of assets and liabilities, the equity section of the balance sheet differs depending on whether the business is a sole proprietorship, a partnership, or a corporation.

■ **SOLE PROPRIETORSHIP**   You are already familiar with the owner's equity section of a sole proprietorship, like the one shown in the balance sheet for Shafer Auto Parts Company in Exhibit 1:

Owner's Equity

Fred Shafer, Capital	$98,433

KEY POINT: The only difference in equity between a sole proprietorship and a partnership is in the number of capital accounts.

■ **PARTNERSHIP**   The equity section of the balance sheet for a partnership is called *partners' equity* and is much like that for the sole proprietorship. It might appear as follows:

Partners' Equity

A. J. Martin, Capital	$21,666	
R. C. Moore, Capital	35,724	
Total partners' equity		$57,390

■ **CORPORATION**   Corporations are by law separate, legal entities that are owned by their stockholders. The equity section of a balance sheet for a corporation is called stockholders' equity and has two parts: contributed, or paid-in, capital and retained earnings. It might appear like this:

Stockholders' Equity

Contributed capital		
Common stock, $10 par value, 5,000 shares authorized, issued, and outstanding	$50,000	
Paid-in capital in excess of par value	10,000	
Total contributed capital		$60,000
Retained earnings		37,500
Total stockholders' equity		$97,500

Remember that owner's equity accounts show the sources of and claims on assets. Of course, the claims are not on any particular asset but on the assets as a whole. It follows, then, that a corporation's contributed and earned capital accounts measure its stockholders' claims on assets and also indicate the sources of the assets. The **contributed capital**, also called *paid-in capital*, accounts reflect the amounts of assets invested by stockholders. Generally, contributed capital is shown on corporate balance sheets by two amounts: (1) the face, or par, value of issued stock and (2) the amounts paid in, or contributed, in excess of the par value per share. In the illustration above, stockholders invested amounts equal to the par value of the outstanding stock (5,000 × $10) plus $10,000 more.

The **Retained Earnings** account is sometimes called *Earned Capital* because it represents the stockholders' claim to the assets that are earned from operations and reinvested in corporate operations. Distributions of assets to shareholders, which are called *dividends*, reduce the Retained Earnings account balance just as withdrawals of assets by the owner of a business lower the Capital account balance. Thus the Retained Earnings account balance, in its simplest form, represents the earnings of the corporation less dividends paid to stockholders over the life of the business.

READING AND GRAPHING REAL COMPANY BALANCE SHEETS

www.dell.com

Although financial statements usually follow the same general form as illustrated for Shafer Auto Parts Company, no two companies have statements that are exactly alike. The balance sheet of Dell Computer Corporation, the world's leading direct seller of computer systems, is a good example of some of the variations. As shown in Exhibit 2, it provides data for two years so that the change from one year to the next can be evaluated. Note that its major classifications are similar but not identical to Shafer's. For instance, Shafer's assets include investments and intangible assets categories, whereas Dell has an asset category called "other non-current assets," which is a small amount of its total assets. Also note that Dell has a category called "other liabilities." Because this category appears after long-term debt, it represents longer-term liabilities, due more than one year from the balance sheet dates.

Dell's stockholders' equity section also differs from the owner's equity section of Shafer Auto Parts Company because it is a corporation. However, it is possible to look at the total stockholders' equity and know that this amount relates to the stockholders' claims on the company and is similar to the capital account for Shafer.

When we look at columns of numbers, it is sometimes difficult to see the patterns. Graphic presentation of the numbers can be helpful in visualizing the changes taking place in a company's financial position. Figure 2, which was prepared with the Fingraph® Financial Analyst™ CD-ROM software that accompanies this text, is a graphic presentation of a portion of the balance sheet shown in Exhibit 2. Total

Exhibit 2
Balance Sheet for Dell Computer Corporation

Dell Computer Corporation
Consolidated Statement of Financial Position
(in millions)

	January 31, 2003	February 1, 2002
ASSETS		
Current assets:		
Cash and cash equivalents	$ 4,232	$ 3,641
Short-term investments	406	273
Accounts receivable, net	2,586	2,269
Inventories	306	278
Other	1,394	1,416
Total current assets	8,924	7,877
Property, plant and equipment, net	913	826
Investments	5,267	4,373
Other non-current assets	366	459
Total assets	$15,470	$13,535
LIABILITIES AND STOCKHOLDERS' EQUITY		
Current liabilities:		
Accounts payable	$ 5,989	$ 5,075
Accrued and other	2,944	2,444
Total current liabilities	8,933	7,519
Long-term debt	506	520
Other liabilities	1,158	802
Total liabilities	10,597	8,841
Stockholders' equity:		
Common stock and capital in excess of $.01 par value; shares authorized: 7,000; shares issued: 2,681 and 2,654, respectively	6,018	5,605
Treasury stock, at cost; 102 and 52 shares, respectively	(4,539)	(2,249)
Retained earnings	3,486	1,364
Other comprehensive income (loss)	(33)	38
Other	(59)	(64)
Total stockholders' equity	4,873	4,694
Total liabilities and stockholders' equity	$15,470	$13,535

Source: Dell Computer Corporation, *Annual Report,* 2002.

assets and its components are graphed on the left side, and total liabilities and its components, together with total stockholders' equity, are on the right. The composition of the assets and liabilities, their relation to stockholders' equity, and the changes in them from 2001 to 2002 are easily seen. These graphs show that overall Dell was relatively stable in both totals and components from 2001 to 2002, but overall the assets increased. Also note that the graphic presentation of the balance sheet reduces the detailed clutter of the statement. For instance, all current assets are combined and represented by a single component line.

FIGURE 2
Graphic Presentation of Dell Computer Corporation's Balance Sheet

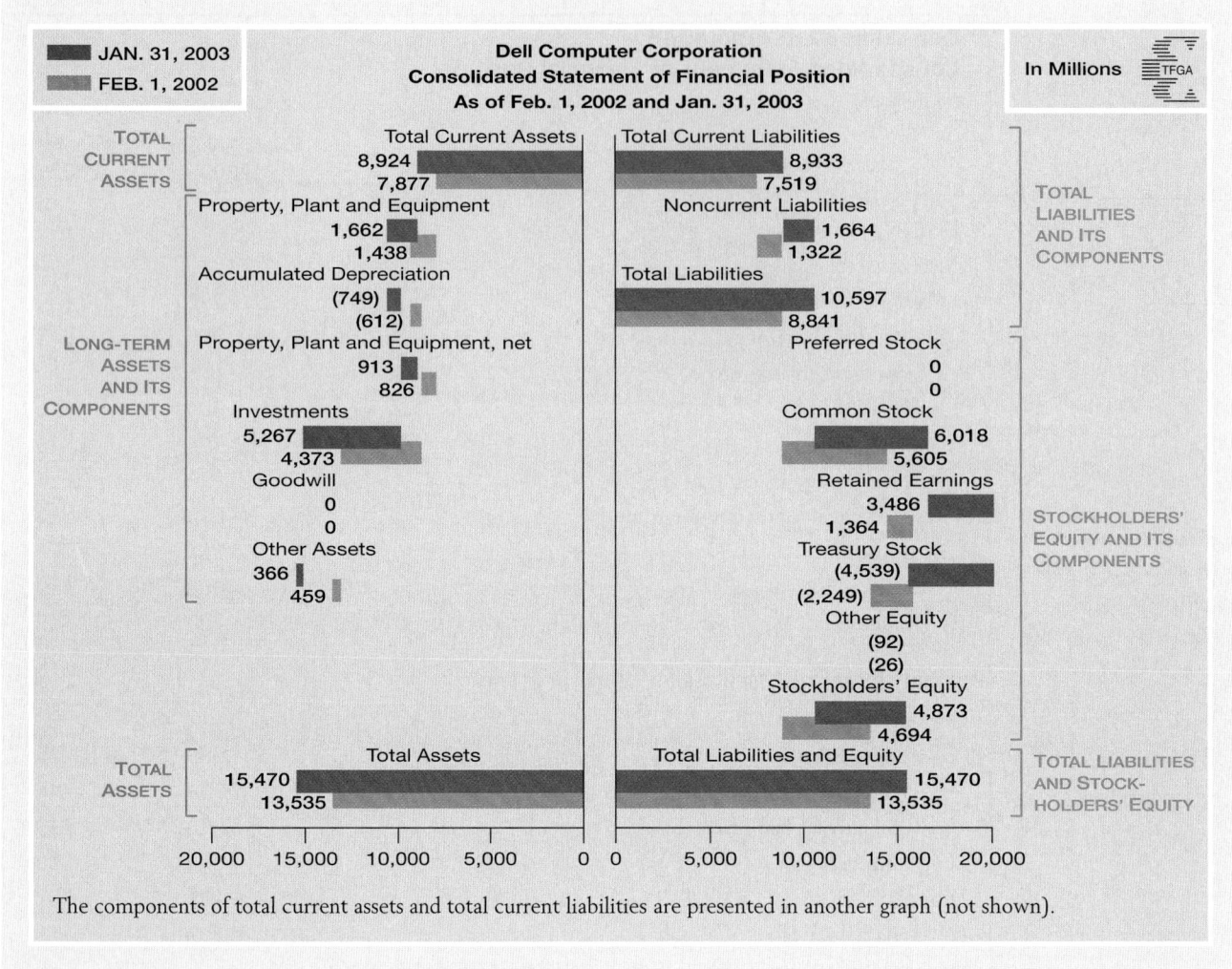

The components of total current assets and total current liabilities are presented in another graph (not shown).

✔ Check out ACE for a Review Quiz at http://accounting.college.hmco.com/students.

FORMS OF THE INCOME STATEMENT

LO6 Prepare multistep and single-step classified income statements.

RELATED TEXT ASSIGNMENTS
Q: 14, 15
SE: 5, 6, 7
E: 5, 6, 7
P: 2, 5, 7
FRA: 5

For internal management, a detailed income statement is helpful in analyzing the company's performance. But for external reporting purposes, the income statement is usually presented in condensed form. **Condensed financial statements** present only the major categories of the detailed financial statements. The two common forms of the condensed income statement are the multistep and single-step forms. The **multistep form**, illustrated in Exhibit 3, derives net income in the same step-by-step fashion as a detailed income statement, but it gives only the totals of significant categories. Usually, it shows some breakdown for operating expenses, such as the totals for selling expenses and general and administrative expenses. In the Shafer Auto Parts Company statement, gross margin less operating expenses is called **income from operations** and a new section, **other revenues and expenses**, has been added to include nonoperating revenues and expenses. The latter section includes revenues from investments (such as dividends and interest from stocks, bonds, and savings accounts) and interest earned on credit or notes extended to customers. It

BUSINESS-WORLD EXAMPLE: The multistep income statement is a valuable analytical tool that is often overlooked. Analysts frequently convert a single-step statement into a multistep one because the latter separates operating sources of income from nonoperating ones. Investors want income to result primarily from operations, not from one-time gains or losses.

KEY POINT: Financial analysts often focus on income from operations as a key profitability measure.

Shafer Auto Parts Company
Income Statement
For the Year Ended December 31, 20xx

Net sales		$289,656
Cost of goods sold		181,260
Gross margin		$108,396
Operating expenses		
Selling expenses	$54,780	
General and administrative expenses	34,504	
Total operating expenses		89,284
Income from operations		$ 19,112
Other revenues and expenses		
Interest income	$ 1,400	
Less interest expense	2,631	
Excess of other expenses over other revenues		1,231
Net income		$ 17,881

also includes interest expense and other expenses that result from borrowing money or from credit extended to the company. If the company has other revenues and expenses not related to normal business operations, they too are included in this part of the income statement. Thus, an analyst who wants to compare two companies independent of their financing methods—that is, before considering other revenues and expenses—would focus on income from operations.

The **single-step form** of income statement, illustrated in Exhibit 4, derives net income in a single step by putting the major categories of revenues in the first part

STOP AND THINK!
Which is the better measure of a company's performance: income from operations or net income?

Neither measure is better than the other. Both measure different aspects of profitability. Income from operations measures the income from a company's ongoing operations before considering issues of financing (interest expense), nonoperating revenues, and income taxes. Net income measures whether a business has been operating successfully. ◼

Shafer Auto Parts Company
Income Statement
For the Year Ended December 31, 20xx

Revenues		
Net sales		$289,656
Interest income		1,400
Total revenues		$291,056
Costs and expenses		
Cost of goods sold	$181,260	
Selling expenses	54,780	
General and administrative expenses	34,504	
Interest expense	2,631	
Total costs and expenses		273,175
Net income		$ 17,881

of the statement and the major categories of costs and expenses in the second part. The multistep form and the single-step form both have advantages. The multistep form shows the components that are used in deriving net income; the single-step form has the advantage of simplicity. Approximately an equal number of large U.S. companies use each form in their public reports.

Net income from the income statement becomes an element of the statement of owner's equity.

READING AND GRAPHING REAL COMPANY INCOME STATEMENTS

Income statements, like balance sheets, vary among companies. You will rarely, if ever, find an income statement exactly like the one for Shafer Auto Parts Company. You will encounter terms and structure that differ, such as those on the multistep income statement for Dell Computer Corporation in Exhibit 5, in which management provides three years of data for comparison purposes. You may also encounter components that are not covered in this chapter. If this occurs, refer to the index at the end of the book to find the topic and read about it.

www.dell.com

Figure 3, which was prepared with the Fingraph® Financial Analyst™ CD-ROM software that is available with this text, is a graphic presentation of a portion of

EXHIBIT 5
Income Statement for Dell Computer Corporation

Dell Computer Corporation
Consolidated Statement of Income
(in millions, except per share amounts)

	Fiscal Year Ended		
	January 31, 2003	February 1, 2002	February 2, 2001
Net revenue	$35,404	$31,168	$31,888
Cost of revenue	29,055	25,661	25,445
Gross margin	6,349	5,507	6,443
Operating expenses:			
Selling, general and administrative	3,050	2,784	3,193
Research, development and engineering	455	452	482
Special charges	—	482	105
Total operating expenses	3,505	3,718	3,780
Operating income	2,844	1,789	2,663
Investment and other income (loss), net	183	(58)	531
Income before income taxes and cumulative effect of change in accounting principle	3,027	1,731	3,194
Provision for income taxes	905	485	958
Income before cumulative effect of change in accounting principle	2,122	1,246	2,236
Cumulative effect of change in accounting principle, net	—	—	(59)
Net income	$ 2,122	$ 1,246	$ 2,177

Source: Dell Computer Corporation, *Annual Report,* 2002.

FIGURE 3
Graphic Presentation of a Portion of Dell Computer Corporation's Income Statement

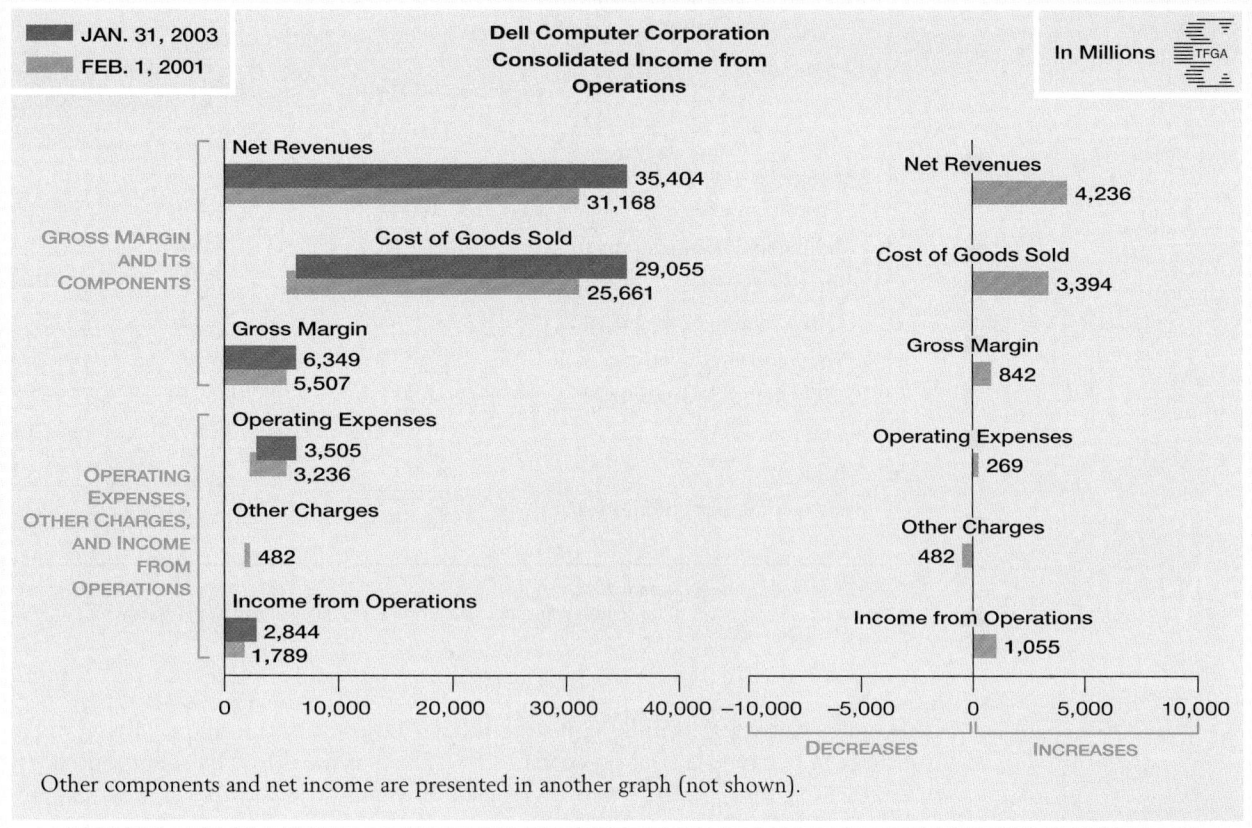

Other components and net income are presented in another graph (not shown).

Dell's income statement. It helps show the company's progress in meeting its profitability objectives. On the left side of the graph are the components of income from operations, beginning with net revenues at the top and ending with income from operations at the bottom. The right side graphs the percentage changes in the components. Increases are shown on the right of the vertical column, and decreases are shown on the left. Except for special charges, there was little change in the components from 2001 to 2002 but overall the company grew during the year.

www.nike.com   Exhibit 6 shows the single-step income statement used by Nike, Inc., the footwear company. When a company uses the single-step form, most analysts will still calculate gross margin, income from operations, and each component's percentage of revenues. Such calculations for Nike would be as follows (in millions):

	2002	Percent	2001	Percent
Revenues	$9,893.0	100.0	$9,488.8	100.0
Cost of sales	6,004.7	60.7	5,784.9	61.0
Gross margin	$3,888.3	39.3	$3,703.9	39.0
Selling and administrative expenses	2,820.4	28.5	2,689.7	28.3
Income from operations	$1,067.9	10.8	$1,014.2	10.7

This analysis shows that Nike's income from operations increased slightly, from 10.7 to 10.8 percent. The difference of 0.1 percent may not seem like a lot; however on

EXHIBIT 6
Single-Step Income Statement for Nike, Inc.

Nike, Inc.
Consolidated Statements of Income
(In millions, except per share data)

	Year Ended May 31,		
	2002	2001	2000
Revenues	$9,893.0	$9,488.8	$8,995.1
Costs and expenses:			
Costs of sales	6,004.7	5,784.9	5,403.8
Selling and administrative	2,820.4	2,689.7	2,606.4
Interest expense	47.6	58.7	45.0
Other income/expense, net	3.0	34.1	20.7
Total costs and expenses	8,875.7	8,567.4	8,075.9
Income before income taxes	1,017.3	921.4	919.2
Income taxes	349.0	331.7	340.1
Net income	$ 668.3	$ 589.7	$ 579.1
Basic income per common share	$ 2.50	$ 2.18	$ 2.10

Source: Nike, Inc., *Annual Report,* 2002.
The accompanying notes to consolidated financial statements are an integral part of this statement.

revenues of $9,893.0 million, it amounts to almost $10.0 million. The company's efficiency declined by 0.2 percent (28.5 − 28.3) as measured by selling and administrative expenses, but this was more than offset by the increase in gross margin of 0.3 percent (39.3 minus 39.0).

 Check out ACE for a Review Quiz at http://accounting.college.hmco.com/students.

USING CLASSIFIED FINANCIAL STATEMENTS

LO7 Evaluate liquidity and profitability using classified financial statements.

RELATED TEXT ASSIGNMENTS
Q: 16, 17, 18, 19, 20
SE: 8, 9
E: 8, 9, 10
P: 4, 5, 8
SD: 6
FRA: 1, 2, 3, 4, 5, 6, 7, 8

Earlier in this chapter, you learned that the objectives of financial reporting established by the Financial Accounting Standards Board are to provide information that is useful in making investment and credit decisions, in judging cash flow prospects, and in understanding business resources, claims to those resources, and changes in them. These objectives are related to two important goals of management: maintaining adequate liquidity and achieving satisfactory profitability. Investors and creditors base their decisions largely on their assessment of a company's potential liquidity and profitability. The following analysis shows how ratios make use of the components in classified financial statements to reflect a company's performance with respect to these important goals.

EVALUATION OF LIQUIDITY

KEY POINT: It is imperative that accounts be classified correctly before the ratios are computed. If accounts are not classified correctly, the ratios will not be correct.

Liquidity means having enough money on hand to pay bills when they are due and to take care of unexpected needs for cash. Two measures of liquidity are working capital and the current ratio.

■ **WORKING CAPITAL**   The first measure, **working capital**, is the amount by which total current assets exceed total current liabilities. This is an important measure of liquidity because current liabilities are debts that must be paid or obligations that

FIGURE 4
Average Current Ratio for Selected Industries

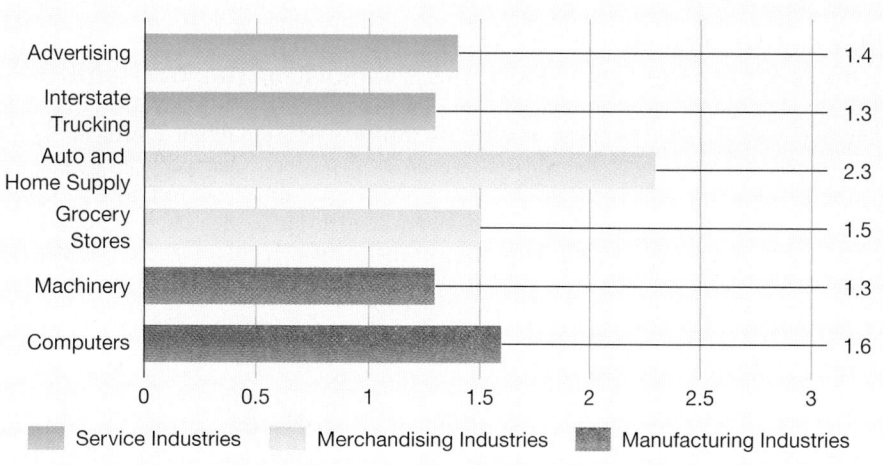

Source: Data from Dun & Bradstreet, *Industry Norms and Key Business Ratios,* 2001–2002.

must be performed within one year, and current assets are assets that will be realized in cash or used up within one year or one operating cycle, whichever is longer. By definition, current liabilities are paid out of current assets. So the excess of current assets over current liabilities is the net current assets, or working capital, on hand to continue business operations. Working capital can be used to buy inventory, obtain credit, and finance expanded sales. Lack of working capital can lead to a company's failure.

For Shafer Auto Parts Company, working capital is computed as follows:

Current assets	$124,356
Less current liabilities	42,683
Working capital	$ 81,673

■ **CURRENT RATIO** The second measure of liquidity, the current ratio, is closely related to working capital and is believed by many bankers and other creditors to be a good indicator of a company's ability to pay its bills and to repay outstanding loans. The **current ratio** is the ratio of current assets to current liabilities. For Shafer Auto Parts Company, it would be computed like this:

$$\text{Current Ratio} = \frac{\text{Current Assets}}{\text{Current Liabilities}} = \frac{\$124,356}{\$42,683} = 2.9$$

Thus, Shafer has $2.90 of current assets for each $1.00 of current liabilities. Is that good or bad? The answer requires the comparison of this year's ratio with ratios for earlier years and with similar measures for successful companies in the same industry. The average current ratio varies widely from industry to industry, as shown in Figure 4. For the advertising industry, which has no merchandise inventory, the current ratio is 1.4. In contrast, auto and home supply, which carries large merchandise inventories, has an average current ratio of 2.3. The current ratio for Shafer Auto Parts Company, 2.9, exceeds the average for its industry. A very low current ratio, of course, can be unfavorable, but so can a very high one. The latter may indicate that the company is not using its assets effectively.

EVALUATION OF PROFITABILITY

Just as important as paying bills on time is **profitability**—the ability to earn a satisfactory income. As a goal, profitability competes with liquidity for managerial attention because liquid assets, although important, are not the best profit-producing resources. Cash, for example, means purchasing power, but a satisfactory profit can

FOCUS ON BUSINESS PRACTICE

Who Is Right: The Credit-Worthiness Analyst or the Profitability Analyst?

The answer depends on your point of view. For example, the future of Amazon.com, the online retailer, has sparked controversy in the big investment company of Lehman Brothers Inc. <www.lehman.com>. One Lehman analyst, who focuses on debt and credit worthiness, has provided a very bearish prediction of the future of Amazon.com because of the company's high level of debt and lack of cash flows to make debt pay-

ments. Another Lehman analyst, who focuses on growth and future profitability, is bullish on Amazon.com because the company is growing fast and reducing costs, which should lead to future profitability. Credit analysts tend to look at the downside of future prospects, whereas profitability analysts look at the upside. Which view of Amazon.com's future will prevail? Only time will tell.[15]

be made only if purchasing power is used to buy profit-producing (and less liquid) assets, such as inventory and long-term assets.

Among the common measures of a company's ability to earn income are (1) profit margin, (2) asset turnover, (3) return on assets, (4) debt to equity ratio, and (5) return on equity. To evaluate a company meaningfully, one must relate its current profit performance to its past performance and prospects for the future, as well as to the averages for other companies in the same industry.

■ **PROFIT MARGIN**   The **profit margin** shows the percentage of each sales dollar that results in net income. It is figured by dividing net income by net sales. It should not be confused with gross margin, which is not a ratio but rather the amount by which revenues exceed the cost of goods sold.

Shafer Auto Parts Company has a profit margin of 6.2 percent:

$$\text{Profit Margin} = \frac{\text{Net Income}}{\text{Net Sales}} = \frac{\$17,881}{\$289,656} = .062 \ (6.2\%)$$

On each dollar of net sales, Shafer made 6.2 cents. A difference of 1 or 2 percent in a company's profit margin can mean the difference between a fair year and a very profitable one.

KEY POINT: Average total assets equals assets at the beginning of the year plus assets at the end of the year, divided by 2.

■ **ASSET TURNOVER**   **Asset turnover** measures how efficiently assets are used to produce sales. Computed by dividing net sales by average total assets, it shows how many dollars of sales were generated by each dollar of assets. A company with a higher asset turnover uses its assets more productively than one with a lower asset turnover. Average total assets is computed by adding total assets at the beginning of the year to total assets at the end of the year and dividing by 2.

Assuming that total assets for Shafer Auto Parts Company were $148,620 at the beginning of the year, its asset turnover is computed as follows:

$$\text{Asset Turnover} = \frac{\text{Net Sales}}{\text{Average Total Assets}}$$

$$= \frac{\$289,656}{(\$158,916 + \$148,620) \div 2} = \frac{\$289,656}{\$153,768} = 1.9 \text{ times}$$

Shafer produces $1.90 in sales for each $1.00 invested in average total assets. This ratio shows a meaningful relationship between an income statement figure and a balance sheet figure.

■ **RETURN ON ASSETS**   Both the profit margin and the asset turnover ratios have some limitations. The profit margin ratio does not take into consideration the assets necessary to produce income, and the asset turnover ratio does not take into account the amount of income produced. The **return on assets** ratio overcomes these deficiencies by relating net income to average total assets. For Shafer Auto Parts, it is computed like this:

FIGURE 5
Average Profit Margin for Selected Industries

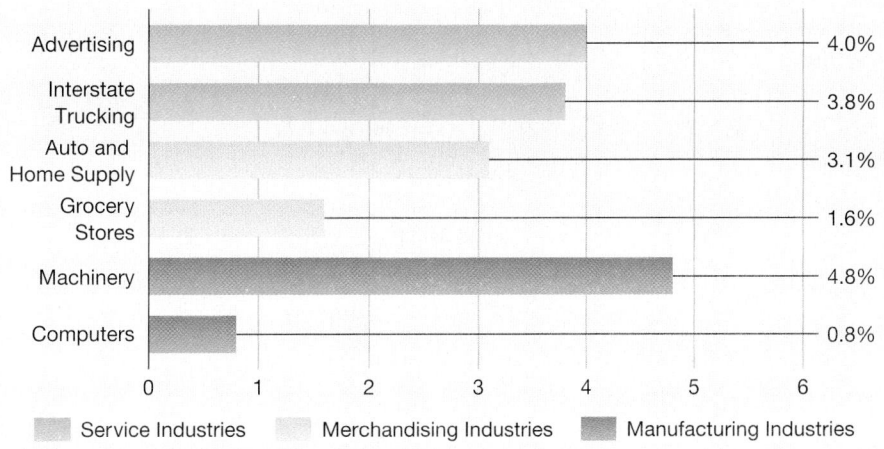

Source: Data from Dun & Bradstreet, *Industry Norms and Key Business Ratios,* 2001–2002.

$$\text{Return on Assets} = \frac{\text{Net Income}}{\text{Average Total Assets}}$$

$$= \frac{\$17,881}{(\$158,916 + \$148,620) \div 2} = \frac{\$17,881}{\$153,768} = .116 \ (11.6\%)$$

KEY POINT: Return on assets is one of the most widely used measures of profitability because it reflects both the profit margin and asset turnover.

For each dollar invested, Shafer's assets generated 11.6 cents of net income. This ratio indicates the income-generating strength (profit margin) of the company's resources and how efficiently the company is using all its assets (asset turnover).

Return on assets, then, combines profit margin and asset turnover as follows:

$$\frac{\text{Net Income}}{\text{Net Sales}} \times \frac{\text{Net Sales}}{\text{Average Total Assets}} = \frac{\text{Net Income}}{\text{Average Total Assets}}$$

$$\text{Profit Margin} \times \quad \text{Asset Turnover} \quad = \quad \text{Return on Assets}$$

$$6.2\% \quad \times \quad 1.9 \text{ times} \quad = \quad 11.8\%^*$$

*The slight difference between 11.6 and 11.8 is due to rounding.

Thus, a company's management can improve overall profitability by increasing the profit margin, the asset turnover, or both. Similarly, in evaluating a company's overall profitability, the financial statement user must consider the interaction of both ratios to produce return on assets.

Careful study of Figures 5, 6, and 7 shows the different ways in which the selected industries combine profit margin and asset turnover to produce return on

FIGURE 6
Asset Turnover for Selected Industries

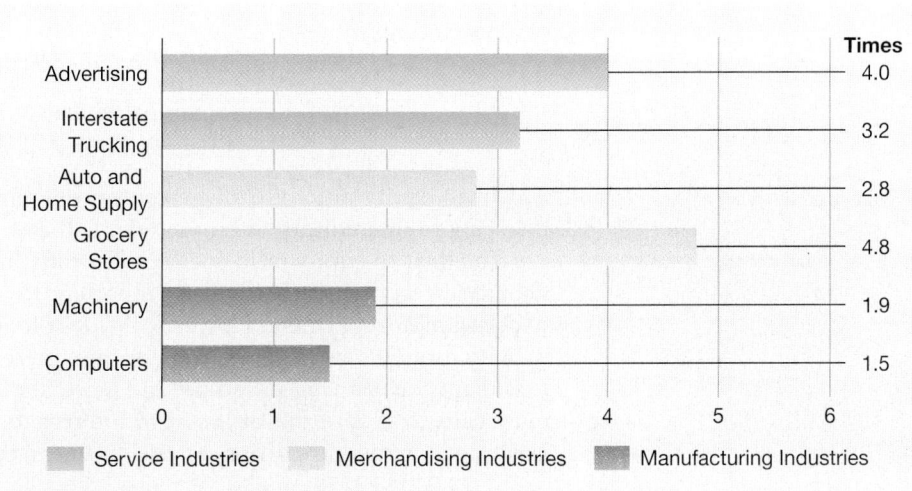

Source: Data from Dun & Bradstreet, *Industry Norms and Key Business Ratios,* 2001–2002.

FIGURE 7
Return on Assets for Selected Industries

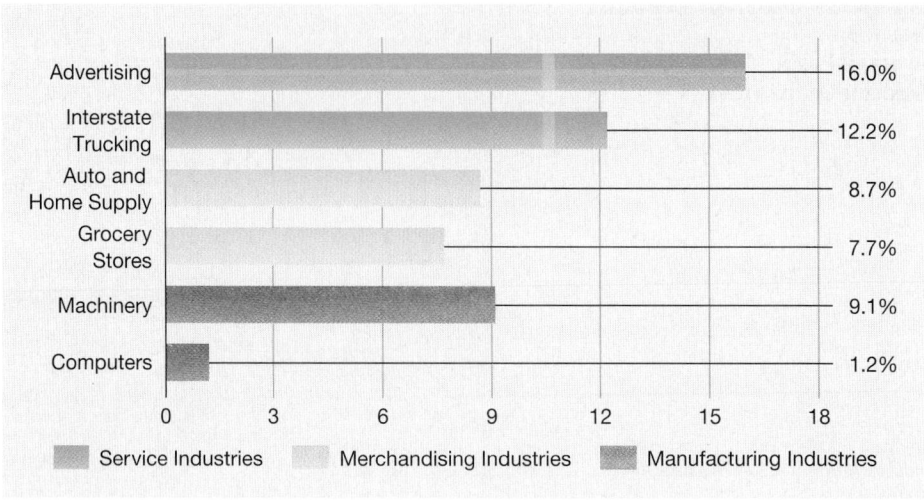

Source: Data from Dun & Bradstreet, *Industry Norms and Key Business Ratios,* 2001–2002.

⬢ **STOP AND THINK!**

Why is it important to compare a company's financial performance with industry averages?

When calculating ratios to measure performance, analysts need benchmarks to measure whether the performance was good or bad. Past performance of the company is one measure, but a better measure is the financial performance of similar companies. This is done by examining industry averages. ∎

KEY POINT: A company with a low debt to equity ratio has a better chance of surviving in rough times. Debt requires additional expenses (interest) that must be paid.

---

assets. For instance, by comparing the return on assets for grocery stores and machinery manufacturers, you can see how they achieve it in very different ways. The grocery store industry has a profit margin of 1.6 percent, which when multiplied by an asset turnover of 4.8 times, gives a return on assets of 7.7 percent. The machinery industry, on the other hand, has a higher profit margin, 4.8 percent, and a lower asset turnover, 1.9 times, and produces a return on assets of 9.1 percent.

Shafer's profit margin of 6.2 percent is well above the auto and home supply industry average of 3.1 percent, but its asset turnover of 1.9 times lags behind the industry average of 2.8 times. Shafer is sacrificing asset turnover to achieve a higher profit margin. It is clear that this strategy is working, because Shafer's return on assets of 11.6 percent exceeds the industry average of 8.7 percent.

■ **DEBT TO EQUITY RATIO**   Another useful measure of profitability is the **debt to equity ratio**, which shows the proportion of the company financed by creditors in comparison with that financed by owners. This ratio is computed by dividing total liabilities by owner's equity. Since the balance sheets of many companies do not show total liabilities, a short way of determining total liabilities is to deduct owner's equity from total assets. A debt to equity ratio of 1.0 means that total liabilities equal owner's equity—that half of the company's assets are financed by creditors. A ratio of 0.5 means that one-third of the assets are financed by creditors. A company with a high debt to equity ratio is at risk in poor economic times because it must continue to repay creditors. Owner's investments, on the other hand, do not have to be repaid, and withdrawals can be deferred when the company suffers because of a poor economy.

Shafer Auto Parts Company's debt to equity ratio is computed as follows:

$$\text{Debt to Equity} = \frac{\text{Total Liabilities}}{\text{Owner's Equity}} = \frac{\$60{,}483}{\$98{,}433} = .614 \ (61.4\%)$$

A debt to equity ratio of 61.4 percent means that Shafer receives less than half its financing from creditors and more than half from its owner, Fred Shafer.

The debt to equity ratio does not fit neatly into either the liquidity or the profitability category. It is clearly very important to liquidity analysis because it relates to debt and its repayment. However, the debt to equity ratio is also relevant to profitability for two reasons. First, creditors are interested in the proportion of the business that is debt financed because the more debt a company has, the more profit it must earn to ensure the payment of interest to its creditors. Second, an owner is interested in the proportion of the business that is debt financed because the

FIGURE 8
Average Debt to Equity Ratio for Selected Industries

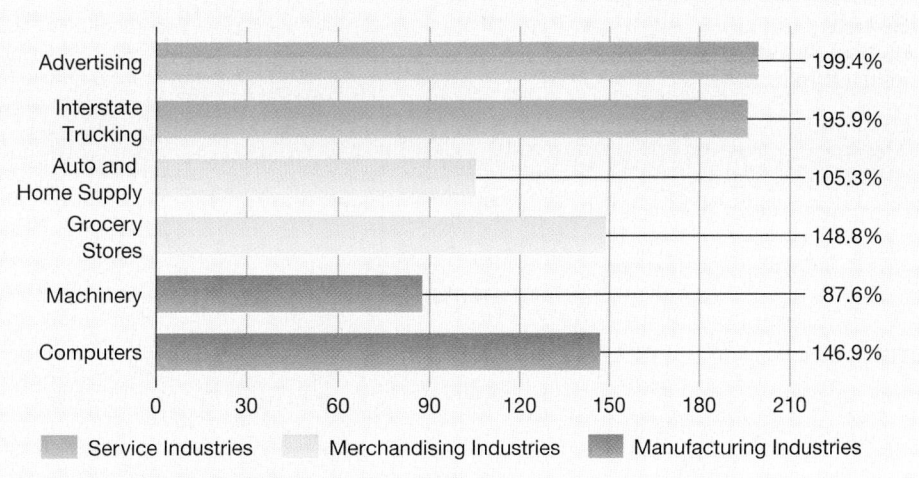

Advertising	199.4%
Interstate Trucking	195.9%
Auto and Home Supply	105.3%
Grocery Stores	148.8%
Machinery	87.6%
Computers	146.9%

Service Industries   Merchandising Industries   Manufacturing Industries

Source: Data from Dun & Bradstreet, *Industry Norms and Key Business Ratios,* 2001–2002.

amount of interest that must be paid on the debt affects the amount of profit that is left to provide a return on the owner's investments. The debt to equity ratio also shows how much expansion is possible by borrowing additional long-term funds. Figure 8 shows that the debt to equity ratio in our selected industries varies from a low of 87.6 percent in the machinery industry to a high of 199.4 percent in the advertising industry.

■ **RETURN ON EQUITY**   Of course, Fred Shafer is interested in how much he has earned on his investment in the business. His **return on equity** is measured by the ratio of net income to average owner's equity. Taking the ending owner's equity from the balance sheet and assuming that beginning owner's equity is $100,553, Shafer's return on equity is computed as follows:

$$\text{Return on Equity} = \frac{\text{Net Income}}{\text{Average Owner's Equity}}$$

$$= \frac{\$17,881}{(\$98,433 + \$100,553) \div 2} = \frac{\$17,881}{\$99,493} = .180 \ (18.0\%)$$

In 20xx, Shafer Auto Parts Company earned 18.0 cents for every dollar invested by the owner, Fred Shafer.

Whether this is an acceptable return depends on several factors, such as how much the company earned in previous years and how much other companies in the

FOCUS ON BUSINESS PRACTICE

To What Level of Profitability Should a Company Aspire?

At one time, a company earning a 20 percent return on equity ranked among the elite. Only Disney <www.disney.go.com>, Wal-Mart <www.walmart.com>, Coca-Cola <www.coca-cola.com>, and a few other companies were able to achieve this level of profitability. However, in the first quarter of 1995, for the first time, the average company of the Standard & Poor's 500 companies made a return on equity of 20.12 percent. *The Wall Street Journal* described this performance as "akin to the average ball player hitting .350."[16] This meant that stockholders' equity would double every four years.

Why did this happen? First, a good business environment and cost cutting led to more profitable operations. Second, special charges and other accounting transactions reduced stockholders' equity for many companies. In this way, the denominator of the ratio is reduced, thus increasing the ratio.

Until 2000, the number of companies with a return on equity of more than 20 percent continued to increase, but during the recession of 2001 and 2002, this number declined. When earnings are declining, companies tend to emphasize measures of performance other than profitability.

FIGURE 9
Average Return on Equity for Selected Industries

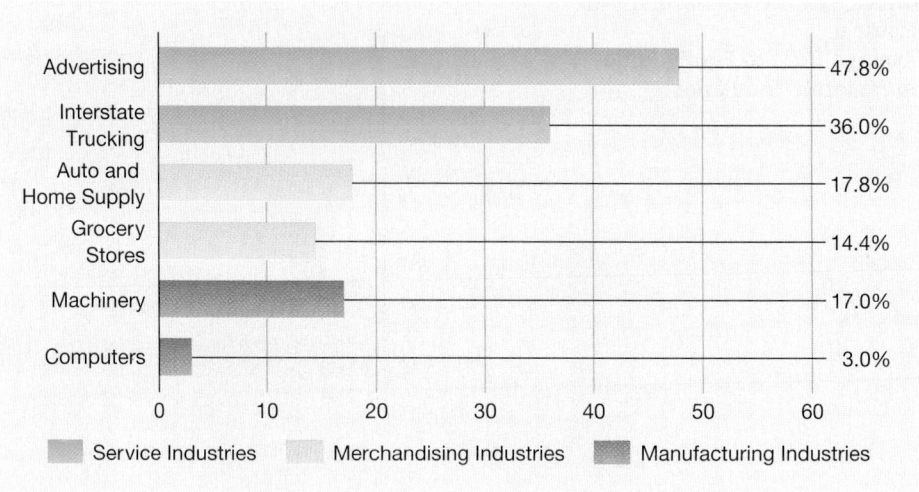

Source: Data from Dun & Bradstreet, *Industry Norms and Key Business Ratios,* 2001–2002 .

same industry earned. As measured by return on equity (Figure 9), the advertising industry is the most profitable of our sample industries, with a return on equity of 47.8 percent. Shafer Auto Parts Company's average return on equity of 18.0 percent is slightly more than the average of 17.8 percent for the auto and home supply industry.

FIGURE 10
Graphic Presentation of Dell Computer Corporation's Profitability Ratios

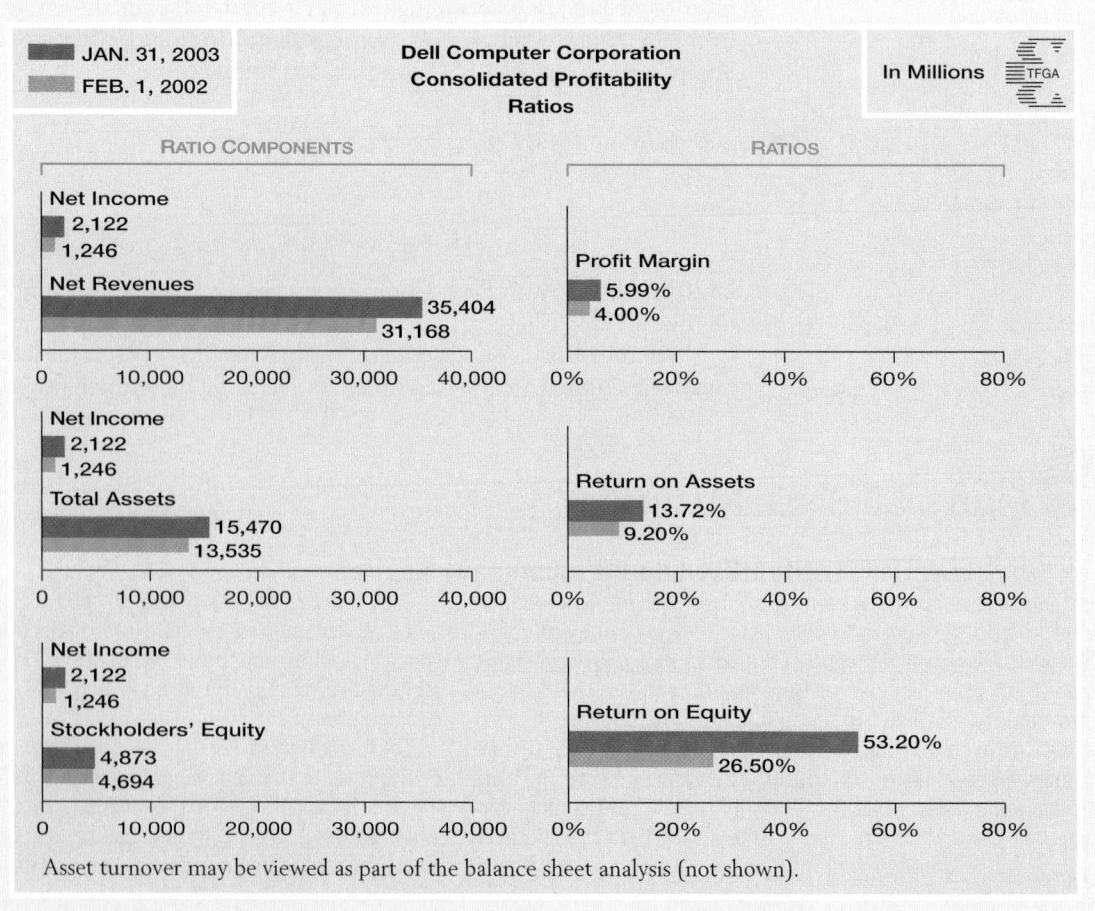

www.dell.com

■ **GRAPHING RATIO ANALYSIS**   Figure 10, prepared with the Fingraph® Financial Analyst™ software that is available with this text, graphically presents Dell Computer Corporation's profitability ratios involving net income. It helps us visualize the progress of the company in meeting its profitability objectives. On the left of the figure are the components of the ratios. On the right are the ratios for the past two years. Notice that the changes in return on equity and return on assets are linked to changes in profit margin or asset turnover. The Fingraph Financial Analyst CD-ROM software graphs all the ratios used in this book and provides narrative analysis. The asset turnover ratio is shown graphically with the Fingraph balance sheet analysis.

✔ Check out ACE for a Review Quiz at http://accounting.college.hmco.com/students.

Chapter Review

REVIEW OF LEARNING OBJECTIVES

LO1   State the objectives of financial reporting.

The objectives of financial reporting are (1) to furnish information that is useful in making investment and credit decisions, (2) to provide information that can be used to assess cash flow prospects, and (3) to provide information about business resources, claims to those resources, and changes in them.

LO2   State the qualitative characteristics of accounting information and describe their interrelationships.

Understandability depends on the knowledge of the user and the ability of the accountant to provide useful information. Usefulness is a function of two primary characteristics: relevance and reliability. Information is relevant when it affects the outcome of a decision. Information that is relevant has feedback value and predictive value, and is timely. To be reliable, information must represent what it is supposed to represent and be verifiable and neutral.

LO3   Define and describe the conventions of *comparability* and *consistency, materiality, conservatism, full disclosure,* and *cost-benefit.*

Because accountants' measurements are not exact, certain conventions are applied in current practice to help users interpret financial statements. The first of these conventions is comparability and consistency. Consistency requires the use of the same accounting procedures from period to period and enhances the comparability of financial statements. The second is materiality, which has to do with the relative importance of an item. The third is conservatism, which entails using the procedure that is least likely to overstate assets and income. The fourth is full disclosure, which means including all relevant information in the financial statements. The fifth is cost-benefit, which suggests that above a minimum level of information, additional information should be provided only if the benefits derived from the information exceed the costs of providing it.

LO4   Explain management's responsibility for ethical financial reporting and define *fraudulent financial reporting.*

Management is responsible for the preparation of financial statements in accordance with generally accepted accounting principles and for the internal controls that provide assurance that this objective is achieved. Fraudulent financial reporting is the intentional preparation of misleading financial statements.

LO5   Identify and describe the basic components of a classified balance sheet.

The classified balance sheet is subdivided as follows:

Assets	Liabilities
Current assets	Current liabilities
Investments	Long-term liabilities
Property, plant, and equipment	**Owner's Equity**
Intangible assets	(Content depends on the
(Other assets)	form of business)

A current asset is an asset that can reasonably be expected to be realized in cash or consumed during the next year or the normal operating cycle, whichever is longer. Investments are assets, usually long term, that are not used in the normal operation of a business. Property, plant, and equipment are tangible long-term assets used in day-to-day operations. Intangible assets are long-term assets with no physical substance whose value stems from the rights or privileges they extend to the owners. A current liability is an obligation that can reasonably be expected to be paid or performed during the next year or the normal operating cycle, whichever is longer. Long-term liabilities are debts that fall due more than one year in the future or beyond the normal operating cycle. The equity section of the balance sheet for a corporation differs from that for a proprietorship or partnership in that it has subdivisions of contributed capital (the value of assets invested by stockholders) and retained earnings (stockholders' claim to assets earned from operations and reinvested in operations).

LO6 Prepare multistep and single-step classified income statements.

Classified income statements for external reporting can be in multistep or single-step form. The multistep form arrives at net income through a series of steps; the single-step form arrives at net income in a single step. There is usually a separate section in the multistep form for other revenues and expenses.

LO7 Evaluate liquidity and profitability using classified financial statements.

One use of classified financial statements is to evaluate a company's liquidity and profitability. Two measures of liquidity are working capital and the current ratio. Five measures of profitability are profit margin, asset turnover, return on assets, debt to equity ratio, and return on equity. Referring to industry averages aids interpretation of these ratios.

REVIEW OF CONCEPTS AND TERMINOLOGY

The following concepts and terms were introduced in this chapter:

LO7 **Asset turnover:** A measure of profitability that shows how efficiently assets are used to produce sales; net sales divided by average total assets.

LO5 **Classified financial statements:** General-purpose external financial statements that are divided into subcategories.

LO3 **Comparability:** The convention of presenting information in a way that enables decision makers to recognize similarities, differences, and trends over different time periods or between different companies.

LO6 **Condensed financial statements:** Financial statements for external reporting that present only the major categories of information.

LO3 **Conservatism:** The convention that when faced with two equally acceptable alternatives, the accountant must choose the one least likely to overstate assets and income.

LO3 **Consistency:** The convention requiring that once an accounting procedure is adopted, it not be changed from one period to the next unless users of the financial statements are informed of the change.

LO5 **Contributed capital:** The accounts that reflect the owner's investment in a corporation. Also called *paid-in capital*.

LO3 **Conventions:** Rules of thumb, or general principles, for recording transactions and preparing financial statements.

LO3 **Cost-benefit:** The convention that the benefits gained from providing accounting information should be greater than the costs of providing that information.

LO5 **Current assets:** Cash and other assets that are reasonably expected to be converted to cash, sold, or consumed within one year or within a normal operating cycle, whichever is longer.

LO5 **Current liabilities:** Obligations due to be paid or performed within one year or within the normal operating cycle, whichever is longer.

LO7 **Current ratio:** A measure of liquidity; current assets divided by current liabilities.

LO7 **Debt to equity ratio:** A measure of profitability that shows the relationship of assets financed by creditors to those financed by owners; total liabilities divided by owner's equity.

LO4 **Fraudulent financial reporting:** The intentional preparation of misleading financial statements.

LO3   **Full disclosure:** The convention requiring that financial statements and their notes present all information relevant to the users' understanding of the statements.

LO6   **Income from operations:** Gross margin less operating expenses. Also called *operating income*.

LO5   **Intangible assets:** Long-term assets with no physical substance whose value stems from the rights or privileges they extend to their owners.

LO5   **Investments:** Assets, usually long term, that are not used in the normal operation of a business and that management does not intend to convert to cash within the next year.

LO7   **Liquidity:** Having enough money on hand to pay bills when they are due and to take care of unexpected needs for cash.

LO5   **Long-term liabilities:** Debts that fall due more than one year in the future or beyond the normal operating cycle.

LO3   **Materiality:** The convention that refers to the relative importance of an item or event in a financial statement and its influence on the decisions of the users of financial statements.

LO6   **Multistep form:** A form of condensed income statement that arrives at net income in the same steps as a detailed income statement but presents only the totals of significant categories.

LO5   **Other assets:** A balance sheet category that some companies use to group all assets other than current assets and property, plant, and equipment.

LO6   **Other revenues and expenses:** The section of a multistep income statement that includes revenues and expenses not related to business operations. Also called *nonoperating revenues and expenses*.

LO7   **Profitability:** The ability of a business to earn a satisfactory income.

LO7   **Profit margin:** A measure of profitability that shows the percentage of each sales dollar that results in net income; net income divided by net sales.

LO5   **Property, plant, and equipment:** Tangible long-term assets used in the continuing operation of a business. Also called *operating assets, fixed assets, tangible assets, long-lived assets*, or *plant assets*.

LO2   **Qualitative characteristics:** Standards for judging the information that accountants give to decision makers.

LO2   **Relevance:** The qualitative characteristic of information that bears directly on the outcome of a decision.

LO2   **Reliability:** The qualitative characteristic of information that represents what it is supposed to represent and is verifiable and neutral.

LO5   **Retained Earnings:** The account that reflects the stockholders' claim to the assets earned from operations and reinvested in corporate operations. Also called *Earned Capital*.

LO7   **Return on assets:** A measure of profitability that shows how efficiently a company uses its assets to produce income; net income divided by average total assets.

LO7   **Return on equity:** A measure of profitability that relates the amount earned by a business to the owner's investment in the business; net income divided by average owner's equity.

LO6   **Single-step form:** A form of condensed income statement that arrives at net income in a single step.

LO2   **Understandability:** The qualitative characteristic of information that communicates an intended meaning.

LO2   **Usefulness:** The qualitative characteristic of information that is relevant and reliable.

LO7   **Working capital:** A measure of liquidity that shows the net current assets on hand to continue business operations; total current assets minus total current liabilities.

REVIEW PROBLEM

Analyzing Liquidity and Profitability Using Ratios

LO7 Flavin Shirt Company has faced increased competition from overseas shirtmakers in recent years. Presented below is summary information for the last two years:

	20x5	20x4
Current assets	$ 200,000	$ 170,000
Total assets	880,000	710,000
Current liabilities	90,000	50,000
Long-term liabilities	150,000	50,000
Owner's equity	640,000	610,000
Sales	1,200,000	1,050,000
Net income	60,000	80,000

Total assets and owner's equity at the beginning of 20x4 were $690,000 and $590,000, respectively.

REQUIRED ▶ Use (1) liquidity analysis and (2) profitability analysis to document the declining financial position of Flavin Shirt Company.

ANSWER TO REVIEW PROBLEM

1. Liquidity analysis

	Current Assets	Current Liabilities	Working Capital	Current Ratio
20x4	$170,000	$50,000	$120,000	3.40
20x5	200,000	90,000	110,000	2.22
Decrease in working capital			$ 10,000	
Decrease in current ratio				1.18

Both working capital and the current ratio declined from 20x4 to 20x5 because the $40,000 increase in current liabilities ($90,000 − $50,000) was greater than the $30,000 increase in current assets.

2. Profitability analysis

	Net Income	Sales	Profit Margin	Average Total Assets	Asset Turnover	Return on Assets	Average Owner's Equity	Return on Equity
20x4	$80,000	$1,050,000	7.6%	$700,000[1]	1.50	11.4%	$600,000[3]	13.3%
20x5	60,000	1,200,000	5.0	795,000[2]	1.51	7.5	625,000[4]	9.6
Increase (decrease)	($20,000)	$ 150,000	(2.6)%	$ 95,000	0.01	(3.9)%	$ 25,000	(3.7)%

[1]($710,000 + $690,000) ÷ 2   [3]($610,000 + $590,000) ÷ 2
[2]($880,000 + $710,000) ÷ 2   [4]($640,000 + $610,000) ÷ 2

Net income decreased by $20,000 despite an increase in sales of $150,000 and an increase in average total assets of $95,000. The results were decreases in profit margin from 7.6 percent to 5.0 percent and in return on assets from 11.4 percent to 7.5 percent. Asset turnover showed almost no change and so did not contribute to the decline in profitability. The decrease in return on equity, from 13.3 percent to 9.6 percent, was not as great as the decrease in return on assets because the growth in total assets was financed by debt instead of by owner's equity, as shown by the capital structure analysis below.

	Total Liabilities	Owner's Equity	Debt to Equity Ratio
20x4	$100,000	$610,000	16.4%
20x5	240,000	640,000	37.5
Increase	$140,000	$ 30,000	21.1%

Total liabilities increased by $140,000, while owner's equity increased by $30,000. As a result, the amount of the business financed by debt in relation to the amount of the business financed by owner's equity increased from 20x4 to 20x5.

Chapter Assignments

BUILDING YOUR KNOWLEDGE FOUNDATION

QUESTIONS

1. What are the three objectives of financial reporting?
2. What are the qualitative characteristics of accounting information, and what is their significance?
3. What are the accounting conventions? How does each help in the interpretation of financial information?
4. Who is responsible for the preparation of reliable financial statements, and what is a principal way of achieving this objective?
5. What is the purpose of classified financial statements?
6. What are four common categories of assets?
7. What criteria must an asset meet to be classified as current? Under what condition is an asset considered current even though it will not be realized as cash within a year? What are two examples of assets that fall into this category?
8. In what order should current assets be listed?
9. What is the difference between a short-term investment in the current assets section of the balance sheet and a security in the investments section?
10. What is an intangible asset? Give at least three examples.
11. Name the two major categories of liabilities.
12. What are the primary differences between the equity section of the balance sheet for a sole proprietorship or partnership and the corresponding section for a corporation?
13. Explain the difference between contributed capital and retained easrnings.
14. Explain how the multistep form of income statement differs from the single-step form. What are the relative merits of each?

15. Why are other revenues and expenses separated from operating revenues and expenses on the multistep income statement?

16. Define *liquidity*, and name two measures of liquidity.

17. How is the current ratio computed, and why is it important?

18. Which is the more important goal: liquidity or profitability? Explain your answer.

19. Name five measures of profitability.

20. "Return on assets is a better measure of profitability than profit margin." Evaluate this statement.

SHORT EXERCISES

SE 1.

LO1 Objectives and Qualitative
LO2 Characteristics

Identify each of the following statements as either an objective (O) of financial information or a qualitative (Q) characteristic of accounting information:

1. Information about business resources, claims to those resources, and changes in them should be provided.
2. Decision makers must be able to interpret accounting information.
3. Information that is useful in making investment and credit decisions should be furnished.
4. Accounting information must be relevant and reliable.
5. Information useful in assessing cash flow prospects should be provided.

SE 2.

LO3 Accounting Conventions

State which of the accounting conventions—comparability and consistency, materiality, conservatism, full disclosure, or cost-benefit—is being followed in each of the cases listed below.

1. Management provides detailed information about the company's long-term debt in the notes to the financial statements.
2. A company does not account separately for discounts received for prompt payment of accounts payable because few of these transactions occur and the total amount of the discounts is small.
3. Management eliminates a weekly report on property, plant, and equipment acquisitions and disposals because no one finds it useful.
4. A company follows the policy of recognizing a loss on inventory when the market value of an item falls below its cost but does nothing if the market value rises.
5. When several accounting methods are acceptable, management chooses a single method and follows that method from year to year.

SE 3.

LO5 Classification of Accounts:
Balance Sheet

Tell whether each of the following accounts is a current asset; an investment; property, plant, and equipment; an intangible asset; a current liability; a long-term liability; owner's equity; or not on the balance sheet:

1. Delivery Trucks
2. Accounts Payable
3. Note Payable (due in 90 days)
4. Delivery Expense
5. T. Woo, Capital

6. Prepaid Insurance
7. Trademark
8. Investment to Be Held Six Months
9. Interest Payable
10. Factory Not Used in Business

SE 4.

LO5 Classified Balance Sheet

Using the following accounts, prepare a classified balance sheet at year end, May 31, 20xx: Accounts Payable, $400; Accounts Receivable, $550; Accumulated Depreciation, Equipment, $350; Cash, $100; Equipment, $2,000; Franchise, $100; Investments (long-term), $250; Merchandise Inventory, $300; Notes Payable (long-term), $200; R. Strong, Capital, ?; Wages Payable, $50.

SE 5.

LO6 Classification of Accounts:
Income Statement

Tell whether each of the following accounts is part of net sales, cost of goods sold, operating expenses, other revenues and expenses, or is not on the income statement:

1. Delivery Expense
2. Interest Expense
3. Unearned Revenue
4. Sales Returns and Allowances

5. Cost of Goods Sold
6. Depreciation Expense
7. Investment Income
8. Withdrawals

SE 6.

LO6 Single-Step Income Statement

Using the following accounts, prepare a single-step income statement at year end, May 31, 20xx: Cost of Goods Sold, $280; General Expenses, $150; Interest Expense, $70; Interest Income, $30; Net Sales, $800; Selling Expenses, $185.

SE 7.

LO6 Multistep Income Statement

Using the accounts presented in **SE 6,** prepare a multistep income statement.

SE 8.

LO7 Liquidity Ratios

Using the following accounts and balances taken from a year-end balance sheet, compute working capital and the current ratio:

Accounts Payable	$ 7,000
Accounts Receivable	10,000
Cash	4,000
J. Matson, Captial	20,000
Marketable Securities	2,000
Merchandise Inventory	12,000
Notes Payable in Three Years	13,000
Property, Plant, and Equipment	40,000

SE 9.

LO7 Profitability Ratios

Using the following information from a balance sheet and an income statement, compute the (1) profit margin, (2) asset turnover, (3) return on assets, (4) debt to equity ratio, and (5) return on equity. (The previous year's total assets were $100,000 and owner's equity was $70,000.)

Total assets	$120,000
Total liabilities	30,000
Total owner's equity	90,000
Net sales	130,000
Cost of goods sold	70,000
Operating expenses	45,000

EXERCISES

E 1.

LO1 Financial Accounting Concepts
LO2
LO3

The lettered items below represent a classification scheme for the concepts of financial accounting. Match each numbered term with the letter of the category in which it belongs.

a. Decision makers (users of accounting information)
b. Business activities or entities relevant to accounting measurement
c. Objectives of accounting information
d. Accounting measurement considerations
e. Accounting processing considerations
f. Qualitative characteristics
g. Accounting conventions
h. Financial statements

1. Conservatism	13. Specific business entities
2. Verifiability	14. Classification
3. Statement of cash flows	15. Management
4. Materiality	16. Neutrality
5. Reliability	17. Internal accounting control
6. Recognition	18. Valuation
7. Cost-benefit	19. Investors
8. Understandability	20. Timeliness
9. Business transactions	21. Relevance
10. Consistency	22. Furnishing information that is useful in assessing cash flow prospects
11. Full disclosure	
12. Furnishing information that is useful to investors and creditors	

E 2.

LO3 Accounting Concepts and Conventions

Each of the statements below violates a convention in accounting. State which of the following accounting conventions is violated: comparability and consistency, materiality, conservatism, full disclosure, or cost-benefit.

1. A series of reports that are time-consuming and expensive to prepare is presented to the board of directors each month even though the reports are never used.
2. A company changes its method of accounting for depreciation.
3. The company in **2** does not indicate in the financial statements that the method of depreciation was changed, nor does it specify the effect of the change on net income.

4. A new office building next to the factory is debited to the Factory account because it represents a fairly small dollar amount in relation to the factory.

5. The asset account for a pickup truck still used in the business is written down to what the truck could be sold for even though the carrying value under conventional depreciation methods is higher.

E 3.

LO5   Classification of Accounts: Balance Sheet

The lettered items below represent a classification scheme for a balance sheet, and the numbered items are account titles. Match each account with the letter of the category in which it belongs.

a. Current assets
b. Investments
c. Property, plant, and equipment
d. Intangible assets

e. Current liabilities
f. Long-term liabilities
g. Owner's equity
h. Not on balance sheet

1. Patent
2. Building Held for Sale
3. Prepaid Rent
4. Wages Payable
5. Note Payable in Five Years
6. Building Used in Operations
7. Fund Held to Pay Off Long-Term Debt
8. Inventory

9. Prepaid Insurance
10. Depreciation Expense
11. Accounts Receivable
12. Interest Expense
13. Unearned Revenue
14. Short-Term Investments
15. Accumulated Depreciation
16. M. Capelli, Capital

E 4.

LO5   Classified Balance Sheet Preparation

The following data pertain to a corporation: Cash, $31,200; Investment in Six-Month Government Securities, $16,400; Accounts Receivable, $38,000; Inventory, $40,000; Prepaid Rent, $1,200; Investment in Corporate Securities (long-term), $20,000; Land, $8,000; Building, $70,000; Accumulated Depreciation, Building, $14,000; Equipment, $152,000; Accumulated Depreciation, Equipment, $17,000; Copyright, $6,200; Accounts Payable, $51,000; Revenue Received in Advance, $2,800; Bonds Payable, $60,000; Common Stock, $10 par, 10,000 shares authorized, issued, and outstanding, $100,000; Paid-in Capital in Excess of Par Value, $50,000; and Retained Earnings, $88,200.

Prepare a classified balance sheet; omit the heading.

E 5.

LO6   Classification of Accounts: Income Statement

Using the classification scheme below for a multistep income statement, match each account with the letter of the category in which it belongs.

a. Net sales
b. Cost of goods sold
c. Selling expenses
d. General and administrative expenses
e. Other revenues and expenses
f. Not on income statement

1. Purchases
2. Sales Discounts
3. Merchandise Inventory (beginning)
4. Interest Income
5. Advertising Expense
6. Office Salaries Expense
7. Freight Out Expense
8. Prepaid Insurance
9. Utilities Expense

10. Sales Salaries Expense
11. Rent Expense
12. Purchases Returns and Allowances
13. Freight In
14. Depreciation Expense, Delivery Equipment
15. Wages Payable
16. Interest Expense

E 6.

LO6   Preparation of Income Statements

The following data pertain to a sole proprietorship: Sales, $405,000; Cost of Goods Sold, $220,000; Selling Expenses, $90,000; General and Administrative Expenses, $60,000; Interest Expense, $4,000; and Interest Income, $3,000.

1. Prepare a condensed single-step income statement.
2. Prepare a condensed multistep income statement.

E 7.

LO6   Multistep Income Statement

A condensed single-step income statement for Harrington Housewares Company appears at the top of the next page. Present the information in a condensed multistep

Harrington Housewares Company
Income Statement
For the Year Ended June 30, 20xx

Revenues
Net sales		$1,197,132
Interest income		5,720
Total revenues		$1,202,852

Costs and expenses
Cost of goods sold	$777,080	
Selling expenses	203,740	
General and administrative expenses	100,688	
Interest expense	13,560	
Total costs and expenses		1,095,068
Net income		$ 107,784

income statement, and tell what insights can be obtained from the multistep form as opposed to the single-step form.

LO7   Liquidity Ratios

E 8. The following accounts and balances are from the general ledger of Swan Company.

Accounts Payable	$ 49,800
Accounts Receivable	30,600
Cash	4,500
Current Portion of Long-Term Debt	30,000
Long-Term Investments	31,200
Marketable Securities	37,800
Merchandise Inventory	76,200
Notes Payable, 90 days	45,000
Notes Payable, 2 years	60,000
Notes Receivable, 90 days	78,000
Notes Receivable, 2 years	30,000
Prepaid Insurance	1,200
Property, Plant, and Equipment	180,000
C. Swan, Capital	84,900
Salaries Payable	2,550
Supplies	1,050
Property Taxes Payable	3,750
Unearned Revenue	2,250

Compute the (1) working capital and (2) current ratio.

LO7   Profitability Ratios

E 9. The following end-of-year amounts are from the financial statements of Laliberte Company: Total assets, $852,000; Total liabilities, $344,000; Owner's equity, $508,000; Net sales, $1,564,000; Cost of goods sold, $972,000; Operating expenses, $404,000; and Withdrawals, $80,000. During the past year, total assets increased by $150,000. Total owner's equity was affected only by net income and withdrawals.

Compute (1) profit margin, (2) asset turnover, (3) return on assets, (4) debt to equity ratio, and (5) return on equity.

LO7   Computation of Ratios

E 10. A simplified balance sheet and income statement for a sole proprietorship appear at the top of the next page. Total assets and owner's equity at the beginning of 20xx were $360,000 and $280,000, respectively.

1. Compute the following liquidity measures: (a) working capital and (b) current ratio.
2. Compute the following profitability measures: (a) profit margin, (b) asset turnover, (c) return on assets, (d) debt to equity ratio, and (e) return on equity.

Balance Sheet
December 31, 20xx

Assets		Liabilities	
Current assets	$100,000	Current liabilities	$ 40,000
Investments	20,000	Long-term liabilities	60,000
Property, plant, and		Total liabilities	$100,000
equipment	293,000	**Owner's Equity**	
Intangible assets	27,000		
		P. Cavafy, Capital	340,000
		Total liabilities and	
Total assets	$440,000	owner's equity	$440,000

Income Statement
For the Year Ended December 31, 20xx

Net sales	$820,000
Cost of goods sold	500,000
Gross margin	$320,000
Operating expenses	270,000
Net income	$ 50,000

PROBLEMS

P 1.

LO3 Accounting Conventions

In each case below, accounting conventions *may* have been violated.

1. After careful study, Hawthorne Company, which has offices in 40 states, decided to change its method of depreciating office furniture. The new method is adopted for the current year, and the change is noted in the financial statements.

2. In the past, Ruggio Corporation has recorded operating expenses in general accounts for each classification (e.g., Salaries Expense, Depreciation Expense, and Utilities Expense). Management has determined that despite the additional recordkeeping costs, the company's income statement should break down each operating expense into its components of selling expense and administrative expense.

3. Connie Watts, Pine Corporation's auditor, discovered that a company officer had authorized the payment of a $3,000 bribe to a local government official. Pine's management argued that because the item was so small in relation to the size of the company ($3 million in sales), the illegal payment should not be disclosed.

4. Dearleap Bookstore built a small addition to its main building to house a new computer games section. Because no one could be sure that the section would succeed, the accountant took a conservative approach and recorded the addition as an expense.

5. Since its origin ten years ago, Hsu Company has used the same generally accepted inventory method. Because there has been no change in the inventory method, the company does not declare in its financial statements what inventory method it uses.

REQUIRED ▶   In each case, identify the convention that applies, state whether the treatment is in accord with the convention and generally accepted accounting principles, and briefly explain your answer.

P 2.

LO6 Forms of the Income Statement

The July 31, 20x5, year-end income statement accounts that follow are for Inge Robotics Company. Beginning merchandise inventory was $172,800 and ending merchandise inventory is $145,000. Inge Robotics Company is a sole proprietorship.

Account Name	Debit	Credit
Sales		$922,200
Sales Returns and Allowances	$ 53,800	
Purchases	449,000	
Purchases Returns and Allowances		23,840
Freight In	34,800	
Sales Salaries Expense	124,320	
Sales Supplies Expense	3,280	
Rent Expense, Selling Space	14,400	
Utilities Expense, Selling Space	5,920	
Advertising Expense	33,600	
Depreciation Expense, Delivery Equipment	8,800	
Office Salaries Expense	58,480	
Office Supplies Expense	19,520	
Rent Expense, Office Space	4,800	
Utilities Expense, Office Space	2,000	
Postage Expense	4,640	
Insurance Expense	5,360	
Miscellaneous Expense	2,880	
General Management Salaries Expense	84,000	
Interest Expense	11,200	
Interest Income		840

REQUIRED ▶ 1. Prepare (a) a detailed income statement, (b) a condensed income statement in multi-step form, and (c) a condensed income statement in single-step form.

2. Which form is most useful to management? Which is most useful to an investor?

P 3.

LO5   Classified Balance Sheet

The following information is taken from the July 31, 20x4, post-closing trial balance of Theopoulos Machine Company.

Account Name	Debit	Credit
Cash	$ 31,000	
Short-Term Investments	33,000	
Notes Receivable	10,000	
Accounts Receivable	276,000	
Merchandise Inventory	145,000	
Prepaid Rent	1,600	
Prepaid Insurance	4,800	
Sales Supplies	1,280	
Office Supplies	440	
Deposit for Future Advertising	3,680	
Building, Not in Use	49,600	
Land	22,400	
Delivery Equipment	41,200	
Accumulated Depreciation, Delivery Equipment		$ 28,400
Franchise Fee	4,000	
Accounts Payable		114,600
Salaries Payable		5,200
Interest Payable		840
Long-Term Notes Payable		80,000
Pete Theopoulos, Capital		394,960

REQUIRED ▶ From the information provided, prepare a classified balance sheet for Theopoulos Machine Company.

P 4.

LO7 Ratio Analysis: Liquidity and Profitability

O'Malley Products Company has been disappointed with its operating results for the past two years. As the accountant for the company, you have the following information available to you.

	20x4	20x3
Current assets	$ 45,000	$ 35,000
Total assets	145,000	110,000
Current liabilities	20,000	10,000
Long-term liabilities	20,000	—
Owner's equity	105,000	100,000
Net sales	262,000	200,000
Net income	16,000	11,000

Total assets and owner's equity at the beginning of 20x3 were $90,000 and $80,000, respectively.

REQUIRED ▶ 1. Compute the following liquidity measures for 20x3 and 20x4: (a) working capital and (b) current ratio. Comment on the differences between the years.
2. Compute the following measures of profitability for 20x3 and 20x4: (a) profit margin, (b) asset turnover, (c) return on assets, (d) debt to equity ratio, and (e) return on equity. Comment on the change in performance from 20x3 to 20x4.

P 5.

LO5 Classified Financial
LO6 Statement Preparation
LO7 and Evaluation

Folino Company is in the auto supply business. At the December 31, 20x6, year end, the following financial information was available from the income statement: administrative expenses, $175,600; cost of goods sold, $700,840; interest expense, $45,280; interest income, $5,600; net sales, $1,428,780; and selling expenses, $440,400.

The following information was available from the balance sheet (after closing entries were made): accounts payable, $65,200; accounts receivable, $209,600; accumulated depreciation, delivery equipment, $34,200; accumulated depreciation, store fixtures, $84,440; cash, $56,800; Cindy Folino, Capital, $718,600; delivery equipment, $177,000; inventory, $273,080; investment in Tsung Corporation (long-term), $112,000; investment in U.S. government securities (short-term), $79,200; long-term notes payable, $200,000; short-term notes payable, $100,000; prepaid expenses, $11,520; and store fixtures, $283,240.

Total assets on December 31, 20x5, were $1,048,800 and withdrawals for the year were $120,000.

REQUIRED ▶ 1. From the information above, prepare (a) an income statement in single-step form, (b) a statement of owner's equity, and (c) a classified balance sheet.
2. From the statements you have prepared, compute the following measures: (a) working capital and current ratio (for liquidity); and (b) profit margin, asset turnover, return on assets, debt to equity ratio, and return on equity (for profitability).
3. Using the industry averages for the auto and home supply business in Figures 4–9 in this chapter, determine whether Folino Company needs to improve its liquidity or its profitability. Explain your answer, making recommendations as to specific areas on which Folino Company should concentrate.

P 6.

LO3 Accounting Conventions

In each case below, accounting conventions *may* have been violated.

1. Mt. Shasta Manufacturing Company uses the cost method for computing the balance sheet amount of inventory unless the market value of the inventory is less than the cost, in which case the market value is used. At the end of the current year, the market value is $221,000, and the cost is $240,000. Mt. Shasta uses the $221,000 figure to compute current assets because management feels it is the more cautious approach.
2. Herlihan Company has annual sales of $15,000,000. It follows the practice of charging any items costing less than $300 to expenses in the year purchased. During the current year, it purchased several chairs for the executive conference rooms at $291 each, including freight. Although the chairs were expected to last for at least ten years, they were charged as an expense in accordance with company policy.
3. Svrcek Company closed its books on December 31, 20x4, before preparing its annual report. A day later, a fire destroyed one of its two factories. Although Svrcek

Company had fire insurance and would not suffer a loss on the building, it expected a significant decrease in sales in 20x5 because of the fire. The company did not report the fire damage in its 20x4 financial statements because the fire did not affect that year's operations.

4. Geehan Chemical Company spends a substantial portion of its profits on research and development. The company has been reporting its $7,500,000 expenditure for research and development as a lump sum, but management recently decided to begin classifying the expenditures by project even though the recordkeeping costs will increase.

5. During the current year, Kern Company changed from one generally accepted method of accounting for inventories to another method.

REQUIRED ▶ In each case, identify the convention that applies, state whether the treatment is in accord with the convention and generally accepted accounting principles, and briefly explain why.

ALTERNATE PROBLEMS

P 7.

LO6 Forms of the Income Statement

The income statement accounts from the June 30, 20x5, year-end adjusted trial balance of Kansas City Appliance Company follow. Beginning merchandise inventory was $175,200 and ending merchandise inventory is $157,650. The company is a sole proprietorship.

Account Name	Debit	Credit
Sales		$541,230
Sales Returns and Allowances	$ 15,298	
Purchases	212,336	
Purchases Returns and Allowances		6,159
Freight In	11,221	
Sales Salaries Expense	102,030	
Sales Supplies Expense	1,642	
Rent Expense, Selling Space	18,000	
Utilities Expense, Selling Space	11,256	
Advertising Expense	21,986	
Depreciation Expense, Selling Fixtures	6,778	
Office Salaries Expense	47,912	
Office Supplies Expense	782	
Rent Expense, Office Space	4,000	
Depreciation Expense, Office Equipment	3,251	
Utilities Expense, Office Space	3,114	
Postage Expense	626	
Insurance Expense	2,700	
Miscellaneous Expense	481	
Interest Expense	3,600	
Interest Income		800

REQUIRED ▶

1. From the information provided, prepare the following:
   a. a detailed income statement,
   b. a condensed income statement in multistep form, and
   c. a condensed income statement in single-step form.
2. Which of these forms do you think is most useful to management and which is most useful to investment analysts?

P 8.

LO7   Ratio Analysis: Liquidity and Profitability

Below is a summary of data from the income statements and balance sheets for Leominster Plastics Company for 20x4 and 20x5.

	20x5	20x4
Current assets	$ 366,000	$ 310,000
Total assets	2,320,000	1,740,000
Current liabilities	180,000	120,000
Long-term liabilities	800,000	580,000
Owner's equity	1,340,000	1,040,000
Net sales	4,600,000	3,480,000
Net income	300,000	204,000

Total assets and owner's equity at the beginning of 20x4 were $1,360,000 and $840,000, respectively.

REQUIRED ▶

1. Compute the following liquidity measures for 20x4 and 20x5: (a) working capital and (b) current ratio. Comment on the differences between the years.
2. Compute the following measures of profitability for 20x4 and 20x5: (a) profit margin, (b) asset turnover, (c) return on assets, (d) debt to equity ratio, and (e) return on equity. Comment on the change in performance from 20x4 to 20x5.

SKILLS DEVELOPMENT CASES

Conceptual Analysis

SD 1.

LO3   Accounting Conventions

Central Parking, which operates a seven-story parking building in downtown Chicago, has a calendar year end. It serves daily and hourly parkers, as well as monthly parkers, who pay a fixed monthly rate in advance. The company traditionally has recorded all cash receipts as revenues when received. Most monthly parkers pay in full during the month prior to that in which they have the right to park. The company's auditors have said that beginning in 20x5, the company should consider recording the cash receipts from monthly parking on an accrual basis, crediting Unearned Revenues. Total cash receipts for 20x5 were $2,500,000, and the cash receipts received in 20x5 and applicable to January 20x6 were $125,000. Discuss the relevance of the accounting conventions of consistency, materiality, and full disclosure to the decision to record the monthly parking revenues on an accrual basis.

SD 2.

LO3   Materiality

Sophia Electronics, Inc., operates a chain of consumer electronics stores in the Atlanta area. This year the company achieved annual sales of $50 million, on which it earned a net income of $2 million. At the beginning of the year, management implemented a new inventory system that enabled it to track all purchases and sales. At the end of the year, a physical inventory revealed that the actual inventory was $80,000 below what the new system indicated it should be. The inventory loss, which probably resulted from shoplifting, is reflected in a higher cost of goods sold. The problem concerns management but seems to be less important to the company's auditors. What is materiality? Why might the inventory loss concern management more than it does the auditors? Do you think the amount is material?

Ethical Dilemma

SD 3.

LO4   Ethics and Financial Reporting

Sensor Software, located outside Boston, develops computer software and licenses it to financial institutions. The firm uses an aggressive accounting method that records revenues from the software it has developed on a percentage of completion basis. Consequently, revenue for partially completed projects is recognized based on the proportion of the project that is completed. If a project is 50 percent completed, then 50 percent of the contracted revenue is recognized. In 20x4, preliminary estimates for a $5 million project are that the project is 75 percent complete. Because the estimate of completion is a matter of judgment, management asks for a new report showing the project to be 90 percent complete. The change will enable senior managers to meet their financial goals for the year and thus receive substantial year-end bonuses. Do you think management's action is ethical? If you were the company controller and were asked to prepare the new report, would you do it? What action would you take?

 Group Activity: Use in-class groups to debate the ethics of the action.

SD 4.

LO4 **Ethics and Financial Reporting**

The SEC is conducting an investigation into possible fraudulent accounting practices at Lucent Technologies, Inc. <www.lucent.com>. The probe focuses on whether Lucent improperly booked $679 million in revenue. The SEC is looking at how Lucent recognized revenue on sales to its distribution partners, who may not have sold the products or even may not have been able to sell the products. This practice is known as "stuffing the channels." In an adjustment, the company took back $452 million in revenue it had sent to its distribution partners but never actually sold to end customers. Normal accounting practice does not allow recording as revenue shipments to distributors on consignment—that is, with the right of return if not sold. It is not clear what rights of return exist in this case, but analysts have been critical of Lucent's aggressive practice. Lucent maintains the practice is legal.[17] What is the difference between aggressive accounting and fraudulent financial reporting? Can Lucent's revenue recognition practice be legal but also fraudulent?

Research Activity

SD 5.

LO4 **Accounting and Fraud**

Most university and public libraries have access to indexes of leading newspapers, such as *The Wall Street Journal* and *The New York Times*, on CD-ROM. Go to a library and do a search for a recent year using the key words "accounting and fraud," "accounting and restatement," or "accounting and irregularities." Choose one of the articles you find and read it. What company is involved, and how is accounting connected with the fraud, restatement, or irregularity? Describe the situation. Does it involve an apparently legal or illegal activity? Does it involve fraudulent financial reporting? Explain your answer, and be prepared to discuss it in class.

Decision-Making Practice

SD 6.

LO7 **Financial Analysis for Loan Decision**

Steve Sulong was recently promoted to loan officer at First National Bank. He has authority to issue loans up to $50,000 without approval from a higher bank official. This week two small companies, Handy Harvey Company, and Sheila's Fashions Company, have each submitted a proposal for a six-month, $50,000 loan. To prepare financial analyses of the two companies, Sulong has obtained the information summarized below.

Handy Harvey Company, is a local lumber and home improvement company. Because sales have increased so much during the past two years, owner Harvey Cushing has had to raise additional working capital, especially as represented by receivables and inventory. The $50,000 loan is needed to ensure that the company has enough working capital for the next year. Handy Harvey began the year with total assets of $740,000 and owner's equity of $260,000. During the past year, the company had a net income of $40,000 on net sales of $760,000. Handy Harvey's unclassified balance sheet as of the current date appears as follows:

Assets		Liabilities and Owner's Equity	
Cash	$ 30,000	Accounts payable	$200,000
Accounts receivable (net)	150,000	Notes payable	
Inventory	250,000	(short term)	100,000
Land	50,000	Notes payable	
Buildings (net)	250,000	(long term)	200,000
Equipment (net)	70,000	H. Cushing, Capital	300,000
		Total liabilities and	
Total assets	$800,000	owner's equity	$800,000

Sheila's Fashions has for three years been a successful clothing store for young professional women. The leased store is located in the downtown financial district. Owner Sheila Willard's loan proposal asks for $50,000 to pay for stocking a new line of women's suits during the coming season. At the beginning of the year, the company had total assets of $200,000 and total owner's equity of $114,000. Over the past year, the company earned a net income of $36,000 on net sales of $480,000. The firm's unclassified balance sheet at the current date is as follows:

Assets		Liabilities and Owner's Equity	
Cash	$ 10,000	Accounts payable	$ 80,000
Accounts receivable (net)	50,000	Accrued liabilities	10,000
Inventory	135,000	S. Willard, Capital	150,000
Prepaid expenses	5,000		
Equipment (net)	40,000	Total liabilities and	
Total assets	$240,000	owner's equity	$240,000

1. Prepare a financial analysis of each company's liquidity before and after receiving the proposed loan. Also compute profitability ratios before and after, as appropriate. Write a brief summary of the effect of the proposed loan on each company's financial position.
2. Assume you are Sulong and can make a loan to only one of these companies. Write a memorandum to the bank's vice president outlining your decision and naming the company to which you would lend $50,000. Be sure to state what positive and negative factors could affect each company's ability to pay back the loan in the next year. Also indicate what other information of a financial or nonfinancial nature would be helpful in making a final decision.

FINANCIAL REPORTING AND ANALYSIS CASES

Interpreting Financial Reports

FRA 1.
LO7   Comparison of Profitability

Two of the largest chains of grocery stores in the United States are Albertson's Inc. <www.albertsons.com> and the Great Atlantic & Pacific Tea Company (A&P) <www.aptea.com>. In a recent fiscal year, Albertson's had a net income of $765 million, and A&P had a net income of $14 million. It is difficult to judge which company is more profitable from those figures alone because they do not take into account the relative sales, sizes, and investments of the companies. Data (in millions) to complete a financial analysis of the two companies follow:[18]

	Albertson's	A&P
Net sales	$36,762	$10,151
Beginning total assets	15,719	3,335
Ending total assets	16,078	3,309
Beginning total liabilities	10,017	2,489
Ending total liabilities	10,394	2,512
Beginning stockholders' equity	5,702	846
Ending stockholders' equity	5,684	797

1. Determine which company was more profitable by computing profit margin, asset turnover, return on assets, debt to equity ratio, and return on equity for the two companies. Comment on the relative profitability of the two companies.

2. What do the ratios tell you about the factors that go into achieving an adequate return on assets in the grocery industry? For industry data, refer to Figures 5 through 9 in this chapter.

3. How would you characterize the use of debt financing in the grocery industry and the use of debt by the two companies?

Group Activity: Assign each ratio or company to a group, and hold a class discussion.

FRA 2.

LO7 Evaluation of Profitability

Carla Cruz is the owner and president of Cruz Tapestries, which wholesales fine tapestries to retail stores. Because Cruz was not satisfied with the company earnings in 20x3, she raised prices in 20x4, increasing gross margin from sales from 30 percent in 20x3 to 35 percent in 20x4. Cruz is pleased that net income went up from 20x3 to 20x4, as shown in the following comparative income statements:

	20x4	20x3
Revenues		
Net sales	$611,300	$693,200
Costs and expenses		
Cost of goods sold	$397,345	$485,240
Selling and administrative expenses	169,199	166,504
Total costs and expenses	$566,544	$651,744
Net income	$ 44,756	$ 41,456

Total assets for Cruz Tapestries at year end for 20x2, 20x3, and 20x4 were $623,390, $693,405, and $768,455, respectively.

Has Cruz Tapestries' profitability really improved? (**Hint:** Compute profit margin and return on assets, and comment.) What factors has Cruz overlooked in evaluating the profitability of the company? (**Hint:** Compute asset turnover and comment on the role it plays in profitability.)

FRA 3.

LO7 Financial Analysis with Industry Comparison

Exhibits 2 and 5 in this chapter contain the comparative balance sheet and income statement for Dell Computer Corporation <www.dell.com>. Assume you are the chief financial officer.

1. Compute liquidity ratios (working capital and current ratio) and profitability ratios (profit margin, asset turnover, return on assets, debt to equity ratio, and return on equity) for 2001 and 2002 and show the industry ratios (except working capital) from Figures 4 to 9 in this chapter. Use income from continuing operations and end-of-year assets and stockholders' equity to compute the ratios.

2. Write a memorandum to the board of directors in executive summary form describing changes in Dell's liquidity and profitability performance from 2001 to 2002 compared with the industry averages.

International Company

FRA 4.

LO5 Interpretation and Analysis
LO7 of British Financial Statements

Presented on the next page are the classified balance sheets for the British company GlaxoSmithKline PLC <www.gsk.com>, a pharmaceutical firm with marketing and manufacturing operations in 57 countries.[19]

In the United Kingdom, the format of classified financial statements usually differs from that used in the United States. To compare the financial statements of companies in different countries, it is important to know how to interpret a variety of formats.

GlaxoSmithKline PLC and Subsidiaries
Consolidated Balance Sheets

	2000 £m	1999 £m
Goodwill	170	160
Intangible assets	966	926
Tangible assets	6,642	6,402
Investments	2,544	1,804
Fixed assets	10,322	9,292
Equity investments	171	52
Stocks	2,277	2,243
Debtors	5,399	4,828
Liquid investments	2,138	1,780
Cash at bank	1,283	579
Current assets	11,268	9,482
Loans and overdrafts	(2,281)	(2,819)
Other creditors	(6,803)	(5,629)
Creditors: amounts due within one year	(9,084)	(8,448)
Net current assets	2,184	1,034
Total assets less current liabilities	12,506	10,326
Loans	(1,751)	(1,897)
Other creditors	(143)	(147)
Creditors: amounts due after one year	(1,894)	(2,044)
Provisions for liabilities and charges	(1,657)	(1,675)
Net assets	8,955	6,607
Called up share capital	1,556	1,549
Share premium account	30	—
Other reserves	6,125	3,915
Equity shareholders' funds	7,711	5,464
Non-equity minority interest	1,039	961
Equity minority interests	205	182
Capital employed	8,955	6,607

1. For each line on GlaxoSmithKline's balance sheet, indicate the corresponding term that would be found on a U.S. balance sheet. (For this exercise, consider Provisions for liabilities and Charges to be long-term liabilities.) What is the focus or rationale behind the format of the U.K. balance sheet?

2. Assuming that GlaxoSmithKline earned a net income of £4,147 million and £2,543 million in 2000 and 1999, respectively, compute the current ratio, debt to equity

ratio, return on assets, and return on equity for 2000 and 1999. (Use year-end amounts to compute ratios.)

Toys "R" Us Annual Report

FRA 5.

LO5 Reading and Analyzing an
LO6 Annual Report
LO7

Refer to the Toys "R" Us <www.tru.com> annual report to answer the following questions. (Note that 2001 refers to the year ended February 2, 2002, and 2002 refers to the year ended February 1, 2003.)

1. Consolidated balance sheets: (a) Did the amount of working capital increase or decrease from 2001 to 2002? By how much? (b) Did the current ratio improve from 2001 to 2002? (c) Does the company have long-term investments or intangible assets? (d) Did the debt to equity ratio of Toys "R" Us change from 2001 to 2002? (e) What is the contributed capital for 2002? How does contributed capital compare with retained earnings?

2. Consolidated statements of earnings: (a) Does Toys "R" Us use a multistep or single-step income statement? (b) Is it a comparative statement? (c) What is the trend of net earnings? (d) How significant are income taxes for Toys "R" Us? (e) Did the profit margin increase from 2001 to 2002? (f) Did asset turnover improve from 2001 to 2002? (g) Did the return on assets increase from 2001 to 2002? (h) Did the return on equity increase from 2001 to 2002? Total assets and total stockholders' equity for 2000 may be obtained from the financial highlights.

3. Multistep income statement: In the 1987 Toys "R" Us annual report, management stated that the company's "[operating] expense levels were among the best controlled in retailing [at] 18.8 percent. . . .We were able to operate with lower merchandise margins and still increase our earnings and return on sales."[20] Prepare a multistep income statement for Toys "R" Us down to income from operations for 2001 and 2002, and compute the ratios of gross margin, operating expenses, and income from operations to net sales. Comment on whether the company continued, as of 2002, to maintain the level of performance indicated by management in 1987. In 1987, gross margin was 31.2 percent and income from operations was 12.4 percent of net sales.

Comparison Case: Toys "R" Us and Walgreen Co.

FRA 6.

LO7 Financial Analysis
Comparison: Toys "R" Us vs.
Walgreens

Compare the financial performance of Toys "R" Us <www.tru.com> and Walgreens <www.walgreens.com> on the basis of liquidity and profitability for 2002 and 2001. Use the following ratios: working capital, current ratio, debt to equity ratio, profit margin, asset turnover, return on assets, and return on equity. In 2000, Walgreens' total assets were $7,103,700,000, and total stockholders' equity was $4,234,000,000. Comment on the relative performance of the two companies. (If you have done **FRA 5**, use the computations you made in that solution for Toys "R" Us.) In general, how does Walgreens' performance compare with the performance of Toys "R" Us with respect to liquidity and profitability? What distinguishes Walgreens' profitability performance from that of Toys "R" Us?

Fingraph® Financial Analyst™

FRA 7.

LO7 Analysis of Dell Computer
Corporation or Toys "R" Us

Choose one or both of the following analyses:

1. *Alternative to FRA 3:* Analyze the balance sheet and income statement of Dell Computer Corporation <www.dell.com> using Fingraph Financial Analyst CD-ROM software. To do this assignment, you will need to enter the data from Dell's financial statements shown in this chapter. Complete part 1 of **FRA 3.** Prepare the memorandum required in part 2 of **FRA 3** separately.

2. *Alternative to FRA 5:* Refer to the Toys "R" Us <www.tru.com> annual report in the Supplement to this chapter. Analyze the Toys "R" Us balance sheet and income statement using Fingraph Financial Analyst CD-ROM software. Your instructor will specify which year to analyze. Complete requirements 1, 2, and 3 of **FRA 5.**

Internet Case

LO7   **Annual Reports and Financial
Analysis**

FRA 8.

Select a large, well-known company and access its annual report online. Or, choose a company on the Needles Accounting Resource Center Web Site at http://accounting.college.hmco.com/students and use the links provided there to access the company's web site and its annual report. In the annual report of the company you have chosen, identify the four basic financial statements and the notes to the financial statements. Perform a liquidity analysis, including the calculation of working capital and the current ratio. Perform a profitability analysis, calculating profit margin, asset turnover, return on assets, debt to equity ratio, and return on equity. Be prepared to present your findings in class.

Supplement to Chapter 6
How to Read an Annual Report

More than 4 million corporations are chartered in the United States. Most of these are small, family-owned businesses. They are called *private* or *closely held corporations* because their common stock is held by only a few people and is not available for sale to the public. Larger companies usually find it desirable to raise investment funds from many investors by issuing common stock to the public. These companies are called *public companies*. Although they are fewer in number than private companies, their total economic impact is much greater.

Public companies must register their common stock with the Securities and Exchange Commission (SEC), which regulates the issuance and subsequent trading of the stock of public companies. One important responsibility of the management of public companies under SEC rules is to report each year to the company's stockholders on the financial performance of the company. This report, called an *annual report*, contains the annual financial statements and other information about the company. Annual reports, which are a primary source of financial information about public companies, are distributed to all the company's stockholders and filed with the SEC. When filed with the SEC, the annual report is called the 10-K because a Form 10-K is used to file the report. The general public may obtain an annual report by calling or writing the company or accessing it online at the company's web site. If a company has filed its 10-K electronically with the SEC, it may be accessed at **http://www.sec.gov/edgar.shtml**. Many libraries also maintain files of annual reports or have them available on electronic media, such as *Compact Disclosure*.

This supplement describes the major sections of the typical annual report and contains the annual report of one of the most successful retailers of this generation, Toys "R" Us, Inc. In addition to operating stores that sell toys and other items for children, the company has a chain of stores that sell children's clothes, called Kids "R" Us and a chain of stores devoted exclusively to babies, called Babies "R" Us. The Toys "R" Us annual report should be referred to in completing the case assignments related to the company in each chapter. For purposes of comparison, the supplement also includes the financial statements and notes to the financial statements of Walgreens, one of the largest drugstore chains in the United States.

THE COMPONENTS OF AN ANNUAL REPORT

In addition to listing the corporation's directors and officers, an annual report contains a letter to the stockholders, a multiyear summary of financial highlights, a description of the company, management's discussion of operating results and financial conditions, the financial statements, notes to the financial statements, a report of management's responsibilities, the auditors' report, and supplementary information notes.

LETTER TO THE STOCKHOLDERS

Traditionally, an annual report begins with a letter in which the top officers of the corporation tell stockholders about the performance and prospects of the company. In its 2002 annual report, the president and chief executive officer of Toys "R" Us wrote to the stockholders about the highlights of the past year, the key priorities for the new year, store format and redeployment plans, corporate citizenship, and other aspects of the business. He reported on results as follows:

2002 was a year of encouraging progress, but a time of disappointments as well. Three divisions in our portfolio of businesses—Babies "R" Us, Toys "R" Us International, and Toysrus.com—enjoyed the best performances in their history. Those results, coupled with improved expense discipline, resulted in a 19% gain in net earnings, before restructuring and other charges in 2001, for Toys "R" Us, Inc. However, weaker results in Toys "R" Us U.S. and Kids "R" Us were very disappointing, despite progress in strategic execution in both divisions. . . .

Nonetheless, we were encouraged by the progress we made in the execution of our strategy, which we believe further strengthened our ability to improve our performance in 2003 and beyond.

FINANCIAL HIGHLIGHTS

The financial highlights section of an annual report presents key statistics for a ten-year period and is often accompanied by graphs. The Toys "R" Us annual report, for example, gives key figures for operations, financial position, and number of stores at year end. Note that the financial highlights section often includes nonfinancial data, such as the number of stores.

DESCRIPTION OF THE COMPANY

An annual report contains a detailed description of the products and divisions of the company. Some analysts tend to scoff at this section of the annual report because it often contains glossy photographs and other image-building material, but it should not be overlooked because it may provide useful information about past results and future plans.

MANAGEMENT'S DISCUSSION AND ANALYSIS

Management also presents a discussion and analysis of financial condition and results of operations. In this section, management explains the difference from one year to the next. For example, the management of Toys "R" Us describes the company's net sales in the following way:

Comparison of Fiscal Year 2002 to 2001
We reported consolidated net sales of $11.3 billion for the 52-week fiscal year ended February 1, 2003 versus $11.0 billion for the 52-week fiscal year ended February 2, 2002, or a 3% increase in consolidated net sales. Our consolidated net sales were $11.2 billion for 2002, after excluding the impact of foreign currency translation, representing a 1% increase over 2001 net sales.

 Its management of cash flows is described as follows:

The seasonal nature of our business typically causes cash balances to decline from the beginning of the year through October as inventory increases for the holiday selling season and funds are used for construction of new stores, remodeling and other initiatives that normally occur in this period. The fourth quarter, including the holiday season, accounts for more than 40% of our net sales and substantially all of our operating earnings.

FINANCIAL STATEMENTS

All companies present four basic financial statements in their annual reports. As you can see in the annual report included with this supplement, Toys "R" Us presents statements of earnings (income statements), balance sheets, statements of cash flows, and statements of stockholders' equity (retained earnings).

The headings of all Toys "R" Us financial statements are preceded by the word *consolidated*. A corporation issues *consolidated* financial statements when it consists of more than one company and has combined their data for reporting purposes. For example, Toys "R" Us has combined the financial data of Kids "R" Us and Babies "R" Us with those of the Toys "R" Us stores.

Toys "R" Us provides several years of data for each financial statement: two years for the balance sheet and three years for the others. Financial statements presented in this fashion are called *comparative financial statements*. Such statements are in accordance with generally accepted accounting principles and help readers assess the company's performance over several years.

You may notice that the fiscal year for Toys "R" Us ends on the Saturday nearest the end of January, rather than on the same date each year. The reason is that Toys "R" Us is a retail company. It is common for retailers to end their fiscal years at a slow period after the busiest time of year.

In a note at the bottom of each page of the financial statements, Toys "R" Us reminds the reader that the accompanying notes are an integral part of the statements and must be consulted in interpreting the data.

■ **STATEMENTS OF EARNINGS**   Toys "R" Us uses a multistep form of the income statement that shows gross margin as the difference between net sales and cost of sales (goods sold). Total operating expenses are deducted from gross margin to arrive at operating earnings (income). Interest expense is shown separately, and income taxes are deducted in another step. *Net earnings* is an alternative name for *net income*. The company also discloses the earnings per share, which is the net earnings divided by the weighted average number of shares of common stock held by stockholders during the year.

■ **BALANCE SHEETS**   Toys "R" Us has a typical balance sheet for a merchandising company. In the assets and liabilities sections, the company separates out the current assets and the current liabilities. Current assets will become available as cash or be used up in the next year; current liabilities will have to be paid or satisfied in the next year. These groupings help in understanding the company's liquidity.

Several items in the stockholders' equity section need additional explanation. Common stock represents the number of shares outstanding at par value. Additional paid-in capital represents amounts invested by stockholders in excess of the par value of the common stock. Treasury shares is a deduction from stockholders' equity that represents the cost of previously issued shares that have been bought back and held by the company.

 ■ **STATEMENTS OF CASH FLOWS**   Whereas the income statement reflects a company's profitability, the statement of cash flows reflects its liquidity. This statement provides information about a company's cash receipts, cash payments, and investing and financing activities during an accounting period.

Refer to the consolidated statements of cash flows in the Toys "R" Us annual report. The first major section shows cash flows from operating activities. It begins with the net earnings (income) from the consolidated statements of earnings and adjusts that figure to a figure that represents the net cash from operating activities. Among the adjustments are increases for depreciation and amortization, which are expenses that do not require the use of cash, and increases and decreases for the changes in the working capital accounts. In the year ended February 1, 2003, Toys "R" Us had net earnings of $229,000,000, and its net cash from operating activities was $574,000,000. Added to net income are such expenses as depreciation and amortization. Two small negative items were more than offset by a positive amount associated with deferred income taxes. Accounts and other receivables showed little change. Increases in merchandise inventories, prepaid expenses, and other operating assets contributed to declines in cash, as did a decrease in income taxes payable. An increase of $112,000,000 in accounts payable, accrued expenses, and other liabilities was a significant source of cash.

The second major section of the consolidated statements of cash flows is cash flows from investing activities. The main item in this category is capital expenditures, net, of $388,000,000. This figure demonstrates that Toys "R" Us is a growing company.

The third major section of the consolidated statements of cash flows is cash flows from financing activities. You can see here that the sources of cash from financing are long-term borrowings of $548,000,000 and issuance of stock of $266,000,000, which were helpful in making debt repayments of $141,000,000. In total, the company generated $613,000,000 in cash from financing activities during the year.

At the bottom of the consolidated statements of cash flows, the net effect of the operating, investing, and financing activities on the cash balance may be seen. Toys "R" Us had an increase in cash and cash equivalents during the year of $740,000,000 and ended the year with $1,023,000,000 of cash and cash equivalents on hand.

The supplemental disclosures of cash flow information show income tax and interest payments for the last three years.

■ **STATEMENTS OF STOCKHOLDERS' EQUITY**   Instead of a simple statement of retained earnings, Toys "R" Us presents a *statement of stockholders' equity*. This statement explains the changes in five components of stockholders' equity.

NOTES TO THE FINANCIAL STATEMENTS

To meet the requirements of full disclosure, a company must add *notes to the financial statements* to help users interpret some of the more complex items. The notes are considered an integral part of the financial statements. In recent years, the need for explanation and further details has become so great that the notes often take more space than the statements themselves. The notes to the financial statements include a summary of significant accounting policies and explanatory notes.

■ **SUMMARY OF SIGNIFICANT ACCOUNTING POLICIES**   Generally accepted accounting principles require that the financial statements include a *Summary of Significant Accounting Policies*. In most cases, this summary is presented in the first note to the financial statements or as a separate section just before the notes. In this summary, the company tells which generally accepted accounting principles it has followed in preparing the statements. For example, in the Toys "R" Us report, the company states the principles followed for property and equipment:

> Property and equipment are recorded at cost. Leasehold improvements represent capital improvements made to leased locations. Depreciation and amortization are provided using the straight-line method over the estimated useful lives of the assets or, where applicable, the terms of the respective leases, whichever is shorter.

Other important accounting policies listed by Toys "R" Us deal with fiscal year; reclassification; principles of consolidation; use of estimates; revenue recognition; advertising costs; cash and cash equivalents; merchandise inventories; credits and allowances received from vendors; cost of sales and selling, general, and administrative expenses; costs of computer software; financial instruments; and stock options.

■ **EXPLANATORY NOTES**   Other notes explain some of the items in the financial statements. For example, Toys "R" Us showed the details of its Property and Equipment account, which is reproduced below.

	Useful Life (in years)	February 1, 2003	February 2, 2002
Property and Equipment			
Land		$ 825	$ 811
Buildings	45–50	2,009	1,980
Furniture and equipment	5–20	1,786	1,800
Leasehold improvements	12½–35	1,726	1,542
Costs of computer software	5	192	127
Construction in progress		33	41
Leased property and equipment under capital lease		53	53
		6,624	6,354
Less accumulated depreciation and amortization		1,861	1,810
		$4,763	$4,544

Other notes had to do with restricted cash, merchandise inventories, goodwill, investment in Toys–Japan, seasonal financing and long-term debt, derivative instruments and hedging activities, issuance of common stock and equity security units, stockholders' equity, earnings per share, stock purchase warrants, leases, taxes on income, stock options, replacement of certain stock option grants with restricted stock, profit-sharing plan, Toysrus.com, segments, restructuring and other charges, gain from initial public offering of Toys–Japan, subsequent events, and other matters.

REPORT OF MANAGEMENT'S RESPONSIBILITIES

A statement of management's responsibility for the financial statements and the internal control structure may accompany the financial statements. The management report of Toys "R" Us acknowledges management's responsibility for the integrity and objectivity of the financial information and for the system of internal controls. It mentions the company's internal audit program and its distribution of company policies to employees. It also mentions the Audit Committee of the Board of Directors and states that the company's financial statements have been audited.

REPORT OF CERTIFIED PUBLIC ACCOUNTANTS

The *independent auditors' report* deals with the credibility of the financial statements. This report by independent certified public accountants gives the accountants' opinion about how fairly these statements have been presented. Using financial statements prepared by managers without an independent audit would be like having a judge hear a case in which he or she was personally involved. Management, through its internal accounting system, is logically responsible for recordkeeping because it needs similar information for its own use in operating the business. The

FIGURE 11
Auditors' Report for Toys "R" Us, Inc.

REPORT OF INDEPENDENT AUDITORS

To the Board of Directors and Stockholders
Toys"R"Us, Inc.

(1) We have audited the accompanying consolidated balance sheets of Toys"R"Us, Inc. and subsidiaries as of February 1, 2003 and February 2, 2002, and the related consolidated statements of earnings, stockholders' equity and cash flows for each of the three years in the period ended February 1, 2003. These financial statements are the responsibility of the company's management. Our responsibility is to express an opinion on these financial statements based on our audits.

(2) We conducted our audits in accordance with auditing standards generally accepted in the United States. Those standards require that we plan and perform the audit to obtain reasonable assurance about whether the financial statements are free of material misstatement. An audit includes examining, on a test basis, evidence supporting the amounts and disclosures in the financial statements. An audit also includes assessing the accounting principles used and significant estimates made by management, as well as evaluating the overall financial statement presentation. We believe that our audits provide a reasonable basis for our opinion.

(3) In our opinion, the financial statements referred to above present fairly, in all material respects, the consolidated financial position of Toys"R"Us, Inc. and subsidiaries at February 1, 2003 and February 2, 2002, and the consolidated results of their operations and their cash flows for each of the three years in the period ended February 1, 2003, in conformity with accounting principles generally accepted in the United States.

(4) As discussed in the note entitled "Goodwill," the company adopted SFAS No. 142, Goodwill and Other Intangible Assets, effective February 3, 2002.

Ernst & Young LLP

Ernst & Young LLP
New York, New York
March 5, 2003

Source: Reprinted by permission of Toys "R" Us. The notes to the financial statement, which are an integral part of the report, are not included.

certified public accountants, acting independently, add the necessary credibility to management's figures for interested third parties. They report to the board of directors and the stockholders rather than to management.

In form and language, most auditors' reports are like the one shown in Figure 11. Usually such a report is short, but its language is very important. The report is usually divided into three parts, but it can have a fourth part if there is a need for further explanation.

1. The first paragraph identifies the financial statements subject to the auditors' report. This paragraph also identifies responsibilities. Company management is responsible for the financial statements, and the auditor is responsible for expressing an opinion on the financial statements based on the audit.

2. The second paragraph, or *scope section*, states that the examination was made in accordance with generally accepted auditing standards. These standards call for an acceptable level of quality in ten areas established by the American Institute of Certified Public Accountants. This paragraph also contains a brief description of the objectives and nature of the audit.

3. The third paragraph, or *opinion section*, states the results of the auditors' examination. The use of the word *opinion* is very important because the auditor does not certify or guarantee that the statements are absolutely correct. To do so would go beyond the truth, since many items, such as depreciation, are based on estimates. Instead, the auditors simply give an opinion about whether, overall, the financial statements "present fairly," in all material respects, the financial position, results of operations, and cash flows. This means that the statements are

prepared in accordance with generally accepted accounting principles. If, in the auditors' opinion, the statements do not meet accepted standards, the auditors must explain why and to what extent.

4. The optional fourth paragraph mentions the adoption of a new accounting standard.

SUPPLEMENTARY INFORMATION NOTES

In recent years, the FASB and the SEC have ruled that certain supplemental information must be presented with financial statements. Examples are the quarterly reports that most companies present to their stockholders and to the SEC. These quarterly reports, called *interim financial statements,* are in most cases reviewed but not audited by the company's independent CPA firm. In its annual report, Toys "R" Us presents unaudited quarterly financial data from its 2002 quarterly statements, which are shown in the following table (for the year ended February 1, 2003; dollars in millions, except per share amounts):

	First Quarter	Second Quarter	Third Quarter	Fourth Quarter
Year Ended February 1, 2003				
Net Sales	$2,095	$2,070	$2,271	$4,869
Gross Margin	682	670	722	1,432
Net (Loss)/Earnings	(4)	(17)	(28)	278
Basic (Loss)/ Earnings per Share	$ (0.02)	$ (0.08)	$ (0.13)	$ 1.31
Diluted (Loss)/ Earnings per Share	$ (0.02)	$ (0.08)	$ (0.13)	$ 1.30

Interim data are presented for the prior year as well. Toys "R" Us also provides supplemental information on the market price of its common stock during the years and data on its store locations.

The Annual Report Project

Many instructors assign a term project that requires reading and analyzing a real annual report. The Annual Report Project described here has proved successful in the authors' classes. It may be used with the annual report of any company, including the Toys "R" Us annual report and the financial statements from the Walgreen Co. annual report that are provided with this supplement.

The extent to which financial analysis is required depends on the point in the course at which the Annual Report Project is assigned. Several options are provided in Instruction 3E, below.

INSTRUCTIONS:

1. Select any company from the list of Fingraph companies on the Needles Accounting Resource Center Web Site at **http://accounting.college. hmco.com/students**. Click on the company to access the Microsoft Excel spreadsheet for that company. Then click on the URL in the heading of the spreadsheet for a link to the company's web site and annual report. You may also obtain the annual report of a company of your own choice and access the company's annual report online or obtain it through your library or another source.

2. Library and Internet Research

   Go to the library or the Needles Accounting Resource Center Web Site (**http://accounting.college.hmco.com/students**) to learn about the company you have chosen and the industry in which it operates. Find at least two articles or other references to the industry and the company and summarize your findings.

   Also, access the company's Internet home page directly or through the Needles Accounting Resource Center. Review the company's products and services and find its financial information. Summarize what you have learned.

3. Your term project should consist of five or six double-spaced pages organized according to the following outline:

   A. **Introduction**
      Identify your company by writing a summary that includes the following elements:
      - Name of the chief executive officer
      - Location of the home office
      - Ending date of latest fiscal year
      - Description of the principal products or services that the company provides
      - Main geographic area of activity
      - Name of the company's independent accountants (auditors). In your own words, explain what the accountants said about the company's financial statements.
      - The most recent price of the company's stock and its dividend per share. Be sure to provide the date for this information.

   B. **Industry Situation and Company Plans**
      Describe the industry and its outlook; then summarize the company's future plans based on your library research and on reading the annual report. Be sure to read the letter to the stockholders. Include relevant information about the company's plans from that discussion.

C. **Financial Statements**

Income Statement: Is the format more like a single-step or multistep format? Determine gross profit, income from operations, and net income for the last two years; comment on the increases or decreases in these amounts.

Balance Sheet: Show that Assets = Liabilities + Stockholders' Equity for the past two years.

Statement of Cash Flows: Are cash flows from operations more or less than net income for the past two years? Is the company expanding through investing activities? What is the company's most important source of financing? Overall, has cash increased or decreased over the past two years?

D. **Accounting Policies**

What are the significant accounting policies, if any, relating to revenue recognition, cash, short-term investments, merchandise inventories, and property and equipment?

What are the topics of the notes to the financial statements?

E. **Financial Analysis**

For the past two years, calculate and discuss the significance of the following ratios:

Option (a): Basic (After Completing Chapters 1–6)

Liquidity Ratios
  Working capital
  Current ratio

Profitability Ratios
  Profit margin
  Asset turnover
  Return on assets
  Debt to equity ratio
  Return on equity

Option (b): Basic with Enhanced Liquidity Analysis (After Completing Chapters 1–10)

Liquidity Ratios
  Working capital
  Current ratio
  Receivable turnover
  Average days' sales uncollected
  Inventory turnover
  Average days' inventory on hand
  Operating cycle

Profitability Ratios
  Profit margin
  Asset turnover
  Return on assets
  Debt to equity ratio
  Return on equity

Option (c): Comprehensive (After Completing Chapters 1–18)

Liquidity Ratios
  Working capital
  Current ratio
  Receivable turnover
  Average days' sales uncollected
  Inventory turnover

Average days' inventory on hand
Payables turnover
Average days' payable
Operating cycle
Financing period

Profitability Ratios
Profit margin
Asset turnover
Return on assets
Return on equity

Long-Term Solvency Ratios
Debt to equity ratio
Interest coverage

Cash Flow Adequacy
Cash flow yield
Cash flows to sales
Cash flows to assets
Free cash flow

Market Strength Ratios
Price/earnings per share
Dividends yield

***Option (d): Comprehensive Using Fingraph® Financial Analyst™
Software on the CD-ROM That Accompanies This Text***

TOYS*R*US®

Annual Report
2002

Shaping
our future and
our brands

This annual report is for the year ended February 1, 2003. Pages 1–5 and 20–48 reprinted by permission of Toys "R" Us, Inc.

Company Profile

We are one of the world's leading retailers of toys, children's apparel and baby products based on our consolidated net sales in 2002. As of February 1, 2003, we operated 1,595 "R"Us retail stores worldwide. These consist of 1,051 United States locations comprised of 681 toy stores under the name "Toys"R"Us," 183 infant-toddler stores under the name "Babies"R"Us," 146 children's clothing stores under the name "Kids"R"Us," 37 educational specialty stores under the name "Imaginarium" and 4 "Geoffrey" stores that include products from Toys"R"Us, Kids"R"Us and Babies"R"Us as well as many interactive events. Internationally, as of February 1, 2003, we operated 544 stores, including licensed and franchised stores, under the "R"Us name. We also sell merchandise through Internet sites at www.toysrus.com, www.babiesrus.com, www.imaginarium.com and www.giftsrus.com. Toys"R"Us, Inc. is incorporated in the state of Delaware.

Our History

Toys"R"Us got its start in 1948 when founder Charles Lazarus opened a baby furniture store, Children's Bargain Town, in Washington D.C. Lazarus quickly realized the potential of fulfilling customer's requests for baby toys and toys for older children.

In 1957, Lazarus introduced a "supermarket environment." That same year, the Toys"R"Us name made its debut, complete with a backwards "R". By 1966, Lazarus had four stores with approximately $12 million in annual sales. Around this time, Lazarus sold his stores to retail conglomerate Interstate Stores. He maintained responsibility for running Toys"R"Us, which continued to grow profitably. Interstate, however, faced major difficulties and was forced to declare bankruptcy. During this critical period, Lazarus led and restructured the company. In 1978, when Interstate emerged from bankruptcy it was renamed Toys"R"Us, Inc.

The 1980s were a time of major expansion for Toys"R"Us, Inc. In 1983, the company had 169 toy stores in 26 states and had added four stores under its new Kids"R"Us brand. The company opened its first international stores in Singapore and Canada in 1984. Just 10 years later, the company completed its 1993 fiscal year with 581 U.S. toy stores, 217 Kids"R"Us stores and 234 stores in international locations. In 2001, Toys"R"Us opened its flagship store in Times Square.

In 1996, the company opened its first Babies"R"Us store. The acquisition of Baby Superstore in 1997 added 76 locations and helped Babies"R"Us become the undisputed leader in the juvenile market. Imaginarium was acquired in 1998 to bring the learning and educational toy categories to the "R"Us family of retail stores. Between 2000 and 2002, Imaginarium boutiques were added to U.S. toy stores as part of the division's Mission Possible renovation. In addition, Imaginarium also operates 37 freestanding locations.

Geoffrey the Giraffe was first introduced in 1960. However, he didn't receive his name until 1970 when a contest was held among company associates to name him. In 2000, Geoffrey was reintroduced, in his current animatronic form, as the company's lovable wisecracking "spokesanimal." Today he's one of the world's most recognized icons by kids and grown-ups alike, representative of a worldwide chain of stores that has forever changed the way the world shops for toys.

financial highlights

Toys"R"Us, Inc. and Subsidiaries

(Dollars in millions, except per share data)   Fiscal Year Ended

	Feb. 1, 2003	Feb. 2, 2002	Feb. 3, 2001	Jan. 29, 2000	Jan. 30, 1999	Jan. 31, 1998	Feb. 1, 1997	Feb. 3, 1996	Jan. 28, 1995	Jan. 29, 1994
Operations										
Total Enterprise Sales*	**$13,067**	$12,630	$12,774	$12,118	$11,459	$11,315	$10,113	$9,498	$8,819	$8,018
Net Sales	**11,305**	11,019	11,332	11,862	11,170	11,038	9,932	9,427	8,746	7,946
Net Earnings/(Loss)	**229**	67	404	279	(132)	490	427	148	532	483
Basic Earnings/(Loss) Per Share	**1.10**	0.34	1.92	1.14	(0.50)	1.72	1.56	0.54	1.88	1.66
Diluted Earnings/(Loss) Per Share	**1.09**	0.33	1.88	1.14	(0.50)	1.70	1.54	0.53	1.85	1.63
Financial Position at Year End										
Working Capital	**$ 1,182**	$ 657	$ 575	$ 35	$ 106	$ 579	$ 619	$ 326	$ 484	$ 633
Real Estate - Net	**2,398**	2,313	2,348	2,342	2,354	2,435	2,411	2,336	2,271	2,036
Total Assets	**9,397**	8,076	8,003	8,353	7,899	7,963	8,023	6,738	6,571	6,150
Long-Term Debt	**2,139**	1,816	1,567	1,230	1,222	851	909	827	785	724
Stockholders' Equity	**4,030**	3,414	3,418	3,680	3,624	4,428	4,191	3,432	3,429	3,148
Common Shares Outstanding	**212.5**	196.7	197.5	239.3	250.6	282.4	287.8	273.1	279.8	289.5
Number of Stores at Year End										
Toys"R"Us – U.S.	**681**	701	710	710	704	700	682	653	618	581
Toys"R"Us – International**	**544**	507	491	462	452	441	396	337	293	234
Babies"R"Us – U.S.	**183**	165	145	131	113	98	82	–	–	–
Kids"R"Us – U.S.	**146**	184	198	205	212	215	212	213	204	217
Imaginarium – U.S.	**37**	42	37	40	–	–	–	–	–	–
Geoffrey – U.S.	**4**	–	–	–	–	–	–	–	–	–
Total Stores	**1,595**	1,599	1,581	1,548	1,481	1,454	1,372	1,203	1,115	1,032

*Total enterprise sales consist of all Toys"R"Us branded net sales, which include net sales from all the company's stores and from the company's internet businesses, in addition to net sales from licensed and franchised stores.

**Includes licensed and franchised stores.

contents

Building
our portfolio of
brands

Performance *and Progress*

A year in review

2002 was a year of encouraging progress, but a time of disappointments as well. Three divisions in our portfolio of businesses – Babies"R"Us, Toys"R"Us International and Toysrus.com – enjoyed the best performances in their history. Those results, coupled with improved expense discipline resulted in a 19% gain in net earnings, before restructuring and other charges in 2001, for Toys"R"Us, Inc. However, weaker results in Toys"R"Us U.S. and Kids"R"Us were very disappointing, despite progress in strategic execution in both divisions.

The performance of our U.S. toy stores did not meet our expectations. Our comparable store sales declined 1% for the year and, in a difficult retail environment, our operating earnings declined as well.

Nonetheless, we were encouraged by the progress we made in the execution of our strategy; which we believe further strengthened our ability to improve our performance in 2003 and beyond. For example, by working closely with our vendors last year, we gained market share in core toy, defined as the Boys and Girls, Learning (i.e. Imaginarium) and Preschool categories. Our core toy sales outpaced toy industry performance, as reported by the Toy Industry Association, by 4% for the year.

John Eyler
Chairman and Chief
Executive Officer

We continued to improve our in-stock position, content, presentation and service levels. In addition, we experienced significant improvements in customer satisfaction scores related to pricing and value perception. Both messages were effectively reinforced through our award-winning television commercials featuring our charismatic "spokesanimal," Geoffrey the Giraffe.

We enjoyed historically high levels of success in several of our divisions in 2002. Babies"R"Us and Toys"R"Us International both turned in record-setting operating earnings for the fourth quarter and full year of 2002. In addition, Toysrus.com achieved operating profitability in the fourth quarter – a full year ahead of schedule. Our Kids"R"Us division has been struggling in its stand-alone stores for some time now, but we have seen positive results from sourcing apparel through Kids"R"Us for our Babies"R"Us stores as well as our Toys"R"Us/Kids"R"Us combo stores. Currently, our total apparel business represents approximately $900 million in sales per year, at above company average profit margins, and we expect continued growth. Approximately 65% of these sales come from exclusive products that generate higher margins than nationally branded items. We'll talk about these divisions in greater detail in this report.

Geoffrey the Giraffe
helped boost consumer
awareness for
Toys"R"Us in 2002.

Imaginarium®   TOYSЯUS.COM®   Geoffrey™

We worked diligently in 2002 to improve our productivity, reduce expenses and enhance our financial strength.

We took steps to strengthen our balance sheet and improve our liquidity. As a result, we had substantial excess liquidity in early November during our seasonal borrowing peak, and ended the fiscal year with more than $1 billion in cash.

We reduced capital spending significantly in 2002. Net capital expenditures were $398 million in 2002 as compared to $705 million in 2001.

We made solid progress on our commitment to reduce selling, general and administrative (SG&A) expenses by 200 basis points by 2005. We were able to achieve a reduction of 70 basis points in 2002, so we're approximately a third of the way to achieving our four-year objectives in the first year.

We will also continue to find ways to strengthen and expand our portfolio, and, in fact, made progress in the development of new businesses for the future in 2002. Our test of Toys"R"Us ToyBox, our store concept within grocery stores which first opened in the summer of 2001, is generating positive results. By the end of the year, we expanded our initial test to more than 30 stores, and we are currently evaluating further expansion opportunities for 2003.

The customer response to our recently launched Geoffrey stores has been positive.

We also launched Geoffrey, which is a combination Toys"R"Us, Kids"R"Us and Babies"R"Us store, in four smaller markets in 2002. The customer response has been positive, and we've already derived some key learnings from Geoffrey that may be applicable to our other divisions. We plan to move forward carefully with this concept, but we are encouraged by the results we've seen.

Challenges for 2003

We are committed to doing all it takes to turn the U.S. toy stores around and to expand further on the successes that we've seen. This progress clearly indicates that we are on the right track with our strategies. Our challenge and our commitment is to build on what we've accomplished. We will accelerate execution of our merchandising, presentation, customer service, pricing and advertising efforts designed to drive traffic and increase profitable sales. Knowing that we also need the support of our vendor community to succeed, we continue to work in partnership with them to build excitement for their brands and to re-energize underperforming product categories.

We will accelerate execution of our strategies in 2003.

We will also continue to improve our cost effectiveness to reduce our SG&A even further in 2003. In March, we reduced our national headquarters staff by approximately 200 positions, or 10%. We also announced that we would combine our Kids"R"Us and Babies"R"Us management teams into one group. This will help Kids"R"Us reduce its operating costs. In addition, we will ensure that our balance sheet remains strong and that we have ample liquidity now and into the future.

I think it truly says something about the strength of our portfolio that even in a year where we did not see the kind of success we expected in the largest division of our company, we were still able to announce a meaningful earnings increase. As we look to the future, I'm very proud of the steps that we've taken to manage the business in an undeniably difficult operating environment.

Babies"R"Us registers more expectant parents than any other retailer in the U.S.

Conclusion

As I write this letter, our associates from all divisions and all disciplines are working with tremendous commitment to make ours a more profitable organization. They share my absolute conviction that in 2003 we will seize upon every opportunity to drive sales and profits across every division. Given the solid improvement in our earnings in 2002, despite very difficult and uncertain economic and world environments, we believe we have ample evidence that we're on the right track. We will build on that progress, and we will not stop until we can deliver a better value for your investment and repay your faith in our company.

John H. Eyler, Jr.

John H. Eyler, Jr.
Chairman, President and Chief Executive Officer
March 29, 2003

Responding
to our
World

corporate responsibility

The Demand for Corporate **Responsibility**

Corporate Governance

Corporate governance is a joint responsibility requiring the involvement of and interaction between the Board of Directors and the senior management of the company.

Toys"R"Us, Inc. is fortunate to have a talented Board of Directors committed to the success of the company. For example, during fiscal year 2002, 11 Board meetings and 34 additional Board committee meetings were held. At several of the Board meetings, the Board met in executive session, outside the presence of senior management, to further discuss and examine issues of importance to the company.

After many months of careful research, investigation and thought, the Board adopted Corporate Governance Guidelines of the company in March 2002 to reflect the Board's commitment to monitor the effectiveness of policy and decision-making, both at the Board and management level, and to enhance stockholder value over the long term. Those Guidelines covered such issues as conflicts of interest, the compensation of the company's Chief Executive Officer and other Board members, the process and criteria for selecting Board members and the requirements that the Audit, Compensation and former Corporate Governance Committees be comprised solely of independent Board members and that independent Board members constitute a substantial majority of the Board.

In the past year, the Board has adopted Amended and Restated Corporate Governance Guidelines of the company that further address those issues and cover such issues as director orientation and continuing education and the Board's retention of independent advisors, as well as the requirement that the new Corporate Governance and Nominating Committee be comprised solely of independent Board members. The current Guidelines and committee charters are published in the company's proxy materials filed with the SEC in 2003.

The Toys"R"Us Board of Directors is fully engaged in and focused on the strategic issues facing our business. Each year, the Board devotes one meeting to develop, discuss and refine the company's long-range operating plan and overall corporate strategy. Following the Board's annual strategic meeting, the Board reviews the progress of one or more strategic initiatives at each scheduled meeting. Through the established procedures, the Board, consistent with good corporate governance, encourages the long-term success of the company by exercising sound and independent business judgment on the strategic issues that are important to the company's business.

Code of Conduct for Suppliers

There is growing concern in the global community about working conditions in many nations, including the United States, which may fall below the basic standards of fair and humane treatment. In an effort to source products in a manner that is both socially responsible and profitable, Toys"R"Us, Inc. developed its Code of Conduct for Suppliers program in 1997.

Implementation of the Code and the use of SA8000®, an independent monitoring and factory certification program, enable the company and its business partners to continually improve their performance in relation to workers' rights, labor standards and other human rights issues integral to the manufacturing process.

Developed by Social Accountability International (SAI) in 1998 and currently in use by businesses and governments around the world, SA8000® assessments are widely recognized by trade unions and non-governmental organizations as a powerful tool for creating environments where both workers and management benefit. Facilities in more than 20 nations and 15 industries have been SA8000® certified.

Participation in the Toys"R"Us Code of Conduct program and compliance with all of its provisions is mandatory for all suppliers who sell products, for the purpose of resale, to any Toys"R"Us, Inc. division. The company will terminate its business relationship with any supplier that elects not to participate in the Code of Conduct program or fails to abide by any of its stated provisions.

The Toys"R"Us Code of Conduct includes provisions covering the following issues: Child Labor, Forced Labor, Worker Environment, Working Conditions, Discrimination, Wages & Hours, and Freedom of Association.

Suppliers must post copies of the Toys"R"Us Code of Conduct for all workers to view. The company also encourages suppliers to implement their own Code of Conduct that meets or exceeds the provisions of the Toys"R"Us, Inc. program.

Inquiries about the Toys"R"Us Code of Conduct can be directed to: Vice President of Product Development, Safety Assurance & Imports, Toys"R"Us, Inc., 461 From Road, Paramus, NJ 07652.

management's discussion and analysis

Management's Discussion and Analysis
of Results of Operations and Financial Condition

RESULTS OF OPERATIONS

Comparison of Fiscal Year 2002 to 2001

We reported consolidated net sales of $11.3 billion for the 52-week fiscal year ended February 1, 2003 versus $11.0 billion for the 52-week fiscal year ended February 2, 2002, or a 3% increase in consolidated net sales. Our consolidated net sales were $11.2 billion for 2002, after excluding the impact of foreign currency translation, representing a 1% increase over 2001 net sales.

Total enterprise sales consist of all Toys"R"Us branded net sales from all of our stores and from our internet businesses, and the net sales from international licensed and franchised stores. We believe that enterprise sales are useful in analyzing the worldwide strength of our family of brands:

(In billions)	2002	2001	2000
Consolidated net sales	$ 11.3	$ 11.0	$ 11.3
Licensed and franchised net sales	1.8	1.6	1.5
Total enterprise sales	$ 13.1	$ 12.6	$ 12.8

Our consolidated comparable store sales, in local currencies, were flat for the fourth quarter and the fiscal year. Comparable store sales for our U.S. toy store division declined 1% for both the fourth quarter and the full year. Video game sales, which include sales of video hardware, software and accessories, were the primary factor contributing to these decreases. The video game category posted an 18% decline for the fourth quarter and a 13% decline for the year. The introduction of three video platforms (X-Box, Gamecube and Gameboy Advance) drove strong video sales in 2001. The performance of the video game category was also negatively impacted by significant reductions in the retail prices of video game platforms this year, such as the reduction in retail price from $299 to $199 for X-Box and PlayStation 2, and a reduction in retail price from $199 to $149 for Gamecube. Video game sales accounted for approximately 19% of our total U.S. toy store sales, excluding apparel sales, in the fourth quarter of 2002, down from 22% in 2001. Juvenile product sales in our U.S. toy stores declined 8% for the full year, mainly due to a shift of some sales to Babies"R"Us stores in the same markets. However, our core toy sales, which include boys and girls, learning and preschool toy categories, increased 3% in 2002.

Our International division reported comparable toy store sales increases, in local currencies, of 5% for the fourth quarter and 6% for the full year. These increases were primarily driven by the strong performance of our toy stores in the United Kingdom and Spain. We continued to expand the presence of in-store shops, such as Universe of Imagination (learning and educational products), Animal Alley (plush), Teentronics (electronic entertainment products) and Babies"R"Us (newborn and infant products). In addition, the penetration of exclusive products in the International division continues to grow, and, as a result, contributed to the improvement of our gross margin in this division.

Our Babies"R"Us division reported 12% net sales growth for the full year, primarily driven by the opening of 19 new Babies"R"Us stores in the United States this year. This division reported a 2% increase in comparable store sales for the fourth quarter and a 3% increase for the full year. A variety of initiatives helped to drive sales and guest traffic, including the rollout of extended apparel sizing to all stores and the addition of in-store photo studios in 21 Babies"R"Us stores.

Toysrus.com reported a net sales increase of 11% for the fourth quarter and 23% for the full year. Growth in the on-line toy business and the Babiesrus.com (baby products), Imaginarium.com (learning products) and the new Giftsrus.com (personalized gifts) on-line stores were factors in the sales performance of Toysrus.com.

We record the costs associated with operating our distribution network as a part of selling, general and administrative expenses (SG&A), including those costs that primarily relate to moving merchandise from distribution centers to stores. Therefore, our consolidated gross margin may not be comparable to some other retailers which include similar costs in their cost of sales. Our consolidated gross margin, as a percentage of sales, increased by 0.4% for the fourth quarter and was flat at 31.0% for the full year. Our consolidated gross margin for the fourth quarter of 2001 included $27 million of store closing markdowns, which were recorded as part of the restructuring and other charges announced in January 2002. Credits and allowances from vendors, which are netted against our cost of sales, have a positive impact on our consolidated gross margin. These credits and allowances increased our consolidated gross margin by 0.4% for the year, primarily in support of our increased promotional activities. Our U.S. toy store division reported a 0.7% decline in gross margin for the fourth quarter and a 0.8% decline for the full year. These declines were primarily attributed to the impact of increased promotional activity, such as our "Low Price Super Stars" pricing campaign, as well as the impact of higher markdowns recorded to keep our inventories fresh. Our International toy store division reported a 0.3% increase in gross margin to 32.2% for the year, primarily due to our continued emphasis on exclusive products which carry higher margins. Our Babies"R"Us division reported a 1.0% improvement in gross margin to 36.0%, primarily due to a shift in sales mix to higher margin import product. Gross margin for Toysrus.com improved 2.7% to 24.8%, reflecting an ongoing mix shift toward higher margin juvenile and learning products, as well as lower markdowns due to decreased inventory levels this year.

Our consolidated SG&A, as a percentage of net sales, increased 0.3% to 18.3% for the fourth quarter of 2002. This increase was primarily due to an increase in net advertising expense as a result of our decision to defer certain of our advertising activities to this year's fourth quarter. Our consolidated SG&A, as a percentage of sales, decreased 0.7% to 24.0% for the full year, primarily as a result of our continued focus on expense control. During 2002, we implemented shared services in a variety of functional groups, which, along with other efforts, helped us to achieve the overall reduction in SG&A as a percentage of sales. Advertising allowances, which are netted against

SG&A and have a positive impact on our SG&A, did not significantly vary year over year. SG&A for our U.S. toy store division decreased in absolute dollars, however it remained flat as a percentage of sales at 22.6% for the year. SG&A for the Babies"R"Us division decreased 0.2% to 23.6% for the year, primarily as a function of expense control coupled with higher sales productivity. SG&A for our International toy store business was reduced by 0.2% to 22.6% for the year. SG&A for Toysrus.com decreased for the year, due to lower fulfillment costs associated with product bundling, and a reduction in net advertising costs. The SG&A decrease, as well as an increase in Toysrus.com's net sales for the year, contributed to the overall reduction in consolidated SG&A, as a percentage of sales.

Depreciation and amortization increased by $9 million to $317 million for the year. Depreciation and amortization for 2001 included $13 million related to the amortization of goodwill. We ceased amortizing this goodwill on February 3, 2002 when we adopted the provisions of Statement of Financial Accounting Standard No. 142, "Goodwill and Other Intangible Assets,"(SFAS No. 142) (see the section "Recent Accounting Pronouncements"). Therefore, excluding the 2001 goodwill amortization, depreciation and amortization increased by $22 million for the year. This increase was primarily due to our Mission Possible store remodeling program, new store openings, and strategic investments to improve our management information systems. These increases were partially offset by the impact of closed stores. As part of the restructuring initiatives announced in January 2002, we closed 37 Kids"R"Us stores and 27 Toys"R"Us stores in the United States.

Interest expense, net of interest income, increased by $4 million to $23 million for the fourth quarter of 2002 and increased by $1 million to $110 million for the full year. These increases in net interest expense are mainly attributable to increased long-term borrowings, partly offset by increased cash investments, lower short-term borrowings and a decrease in interest rates.

Our effective tax rate was 36.5% versus 26.9% in the prior year. Our 2001 effective tax rate was impacted by the reversal of prior years' charges included in restructuring and other charges recorded in 2001.

Foreign currency translation had a 3% favorable impact on our consolidated net earnings for the fourth quarter of 2002 and a 4% favorable impact on our consolidated net earnings for the full year of 2002. Inflation did not have a significant impact on our full year consolidated net earnings for 2002.

Fourth Quarter Results

Our business is highly seasonal, with net sales and net earnings typically highest in the fourth quarter due to the inclusion of the holiday selling season. Fourth quarter 2002 net earnings were $278 million compared with $158 million in 2001. Diluted earnings per share were $1.30 for the fourth quarter of 2002 compared with $0.78 in 2001. Total consolidated comparable store sales, in local currencies, were flat in the fourth quarter of 2002 compared with an increase of 2% in 2001. Our results for 2001 included restructuring and other charges of $213 million ($126 million, net of taxes). Excluding the impact of these charges, net earnings were $284 million and diluted earnings per share were $1.39 for the fourth quarter of 2001.

Fourth Quarter Net Sales by Segment

(In millions)	2002	2001	2000
Toys"R"Us – U.S.	$3,114	$3,202	$3,270
Toys"R"Us – International	1,069	915	907
Babies"R"Us	381	342	335
Toysrus.com[1]	193	174	140
Other[2]	112	126	147
Total	$4,869	$4,759	$4,799

Fourth Quarter Operating Earnings by Segment

(In millions)	2002	2001	2000
Toys"R"Us – U.S.[3]	$ 271	$ 331	$ 335
Toys"R"Us – International	157	131	128
Babies"R"Us	40	29	29
Toysrus.com, net of minority interest[4]	3	(17)	(54)
Other[3],[5]	(9)	(35)	(13)
Restructuring and other charges	–	(186)	–
Total	$ 462	$ 253	$ 425

(1) Includes the sales of Toysrus.com – Japan.

(2) Includes the sales of the Kids"R"Us and Geoffrey divisions.

(3) Includes markdowns related to the store closings announced as part of the restructuring in 2001.

(4) Includes the operations of Toysrus.com – Japan, net of minority interest.

(5) Includes corporate expenses, the operating results of the Kids"R"Us and Geoffrey divisions and the equity in net earnings of Toys"R"Us – Japan, Ltd. (Toys – Japan).

management's discussion and analysis

Comparison of Fiscal Year 2001 to 2000

We reported consolidated net sales of $11.0 billion for the 52-week fiscal year ended February 2, 2002 versus $11.3 billion for the 53-week fiscal year ended February 3, 2001. Net sales of Toys – Japan, which has been accounted for on the "equity method" since its initial public offering, are included in our consolidated net sales in the first quarter of 2000 and excluded from our net sales thereafter. Our consolidated net sales were $11.0 billion for both years, after excluding sales of Toys – Japan. Currency translation did not have a significant impact on our consolidated net sales in 2001.

Total enterprise sales, which consist of all Toys"R"Us branded net sales from all of our stores and from our internet businesses, and the net sales from international licensed and franchised stores, were $12.6 billion in 2001 versus $12.8 billion in 2000.

Our consolidated comparable store sales, in local currencies, declined 1%. Comparable store sales for our U.S. toy store division increased 2% for the fourth quarter and declined 1% for the fiscal year. Video game sales were the primary drivers of the fourth quarter increase due to the introduction of X-Box, Gamecube and Gameboy Advance in the latter half of the year. Video game sales accounted for approximately 22% of our total U.S. toy store sales, excluding apparel sales, in the fourth quarter of 2001 as compared to 18% in the fourth quarter of the prior year. We had 433 stores in the Mission Possible format by the start of the 2001 holiday season, which also contributed to the comparable store sales increase in the fourth quarter. This gain partially offset the negative impact of 268 stores under construction during the first nine months of 2001 that were retrofitted to the Mission Possible format, as well as the negative impact resulting from the events of the September 11th terrorist attacks. Our International division reported comparable toy store sales increases of 5%, in local currencies, primarily driven by the performance of our toy stores in the United Kingdom, which reported double-digit comparable store sales growth. Our Babies"R"Us division reported 8% net sales growth, primarily driven by the opening of 20 new Babies"R"Us stores in the United States this year, as well as a 2% comparable store sales increase. Toysrus.com reported a net sales increase of 24% for the fourth quarter and 54% for the full year, which continued to reflect increases in its market share and the impact of the Toysrus.com alliance with Amazon.com that began in 2000.

Our consolidated gross margin, as a percentage of net sales, remained flat at 31.0%. Our consolidated margin for 2001 included $27 million of store closing markdowns, which were recorded as part of the restructuring and other charges announced in January 2002, and our consolidated margin for 2000 included $10 million of markdowns resulting from the alliance between Toysrus.com and Amazon.com. Excluding the impact of these items, our consolidated gross margin would have increased from 31.0% to 31.2%. Credits and allowances from our vendors, which are netted against our gross margin and have a positive impact on our cost of sales, did not vary significantly. Gross margin for the U.S. toy store division decreased 0.2% to 30.1% due to the impact of $15 million in store closing markdowns, that we recorded with the 2001 restructuring and other charges. The Babies"R"Us division reported a 1.2% improvement in gross margin to

35.0%, primarily due to a favorable sales shift to higher margin juvenile import and proprietary product. Our International toy store business reported a 0.2% increase in gross margin to 31.9%, primarily due to our continued emphasis on exclusive products.

Our consolidated SG&A, as a percentage of net sales, remained flat at 24.7% for the full year. Our consolidated SG&A for 2000 included $85 million of non-recurring charges related to the alliance between Toysrus.com and Amazon.com. Excluding these charges, our 2000 consolidated SG&A would have been 24.0% of sales. A reduction in advertising allowances, which are netted against SG&A and have a positive impact on SG&A, accounted for 0.3% of the increase in consolidated SG&A. SG&A for our U.S. toy store division increased 1.1% to 22.6%, reflecting the strategic investments we made in our business, including the renovation of our U.S. toy stores to the Mission Possible format and certain guest focused initiatives, both of which accounted for approximately 1.0% of this increase. Additional SG&A expenses resulting from the September 11th events accounted for approximately 0.1% of this increase. SG&A for our International toy store business increased 0.1% to 22.8%. SG&A for the Babies"R"Us division increased 0.4% to 23.8%, primarily attributable to increased payroll costs to support our emphasis on guest focused initiatives.

Depreciation and amortization increased by $18 million, primarily due to the Mission Possible store remodeling program, continued new store expansion and strategic investments to improve our management information systems.

Interest expense decreased by $10 million, primarily due to lower interest rates, partially offset by the impact of higher average total debt outstanding during the year. Interest and other income decreased by $15 million, primarily due to lower average investments outstanding, as well as lower interest rates.

Our effective tax rate declined to 26.9% from 36.5%. The reduction in our effective tax rate was due to the impact of the restructuring and other charges recorded in 2001.

Neither foreign currency exchange nor inflation had a significant impact on our consolidated net earnings in 2001.

Restructuring and Other Charges

In January 2002, we announced plans to reposition our business and, as part of this plan, we closed 27 non-Mission Possible format Toys"R"Us stores and 37 Kids"R"Us stores. In conjunction with the Kids"R"Us store closings in most all of these locations, we converted the nearest Toys"R"Us store into a Toys"R"Us/Kids"R"Us combo store.

As part of this plan, we eliminated approximately 1,700 staff positions in our stores and our headquarters. In addition, these plans included the costs of consolidating five of our store support center facilities into our new headquarters in Wayne, New Jersey, in 2003.

The costs associated with the facilities' consolidation, elimination of positions, and other actions designed to improve efficiency in support functions were $79 million, of which $15 million related to severance. The costs associated with store closings were $73 million for Kids"R"Us and $85 million for Toys"R"Us, of which $27 million was recorded in cost of sales. The fair value of the facilities to be consolidated and stores identified for closure were obtained from third party appraisals. We also reversed $24 million of previously accrued charges ($11 million from the 1998 charge and $13 million from the 1995 charge) that we determined to be no longer needed. Accordingly, based on these actions, we recorded $213 million of pre-tax ($126 million after-tax) restructuring and other charges in the fourth quarter of the fiscal year ending February 2, 2002. Details on the components of the charges are as follows:

Description (in millions)	Initial charge	Utilized in 2001	Reserve balance at 2/02/02	Utilized in 2002	Adjustments to charge in 2002	Reserve balance at 2/01/03
Store closing:						
Lease commitments	$ 52	$ –	$ 52	$ (11)	$ –	$ 41
Severance	4	–	4	(4)	–	–
Write-down of property and equipment	75	(75)	–	–	–	–
Markdowns	27	–	27	(27)	–	–
Store support center consolidation:						
Lease commitments	28	–	28	–	11*	39
Write-down of property and equipment	29	(29)	–	–	–	–
Severance	15	–	15	(9)	(1)	5
Other	7	(7)	–	–	–	–
Total restructuring and other charges	**$237**	**$(111)**	**$126**	**$ (51)**	**$ 10**	**$ 85**

In the fourth quarter of 2002, we determined that the reserve for lease costs for the disposition of one of our store support center facilities needed to be increased and, accordingly, recorded an additional charge of $11 million.

In 2000, Toysrus.com, our internet subsidiary, recorded $118 million in non-recurring charges as a result of the transition to its co-branded on-line store with Amazon.com, of which $10 million was included in cost of sales and $108 million was included in SG&A. These costs and charges related primarily to the closure of three distribution centers, as well as web-site asset write-offs and other costs. We had remaining lease commitment reserves of $3 million at February 1, 2003, that will be utilized in 2003 and thereafter.

We previously announced strategic initiatives to reposition our world-wide business and recorded related restructuring and other charges of $698 million in 1998 and $396 million in 1995 to complete these initiatives. As of February 1, 2003, we substantially completed all announced initiatives. We reversed reserves of $10 million in the fourth quarter of 2002 that were determined to no longer be needed. We also reversed reserves of $29 million in 2001, $24 million of which were reversed in the fourth quarter of 2001 and is discussed above, and $11 million in 2000 that were determined to no longer be needed. We had $42 million of reserves remaining at February 1, 2003, primarily for long-term lease commitments that will be utilized in 2003 and thereafter.

We believe that the remaining reserves at February 1, 2003 are reasonable estimates of what is required to complete all remaining initiatives.

Liquidity and Capital Resources

Our contractual obligations mainly consist of operating leases related to real estate used in the operation of our business and long-term debt. The table below shows the amounts we are obligated to pay for operating leases and principal amounts due under long-term debt issuances by fiscal period:

Contractual Obligations at February 1, 2003 (in millions)

	Amounts due in Fiscal 2003	Amounts due in Fiscal 2004 and Fiscal 2005	Amounts due in Fiscal 2006 and Fiscal 2007	Amounts due subsequent to 2007	Total
Operating leases*	$ 317	$ 615	$ 552	$ 1,786	$ 3,270
Sub-leases to third parties	17	26	20	40	103
Net operating lease obligations	300	589	532	1,746	3,167
Capital lease obligations	6	9	2	1	18
Long-term debt	367	541	697**	723	2,328
Minimum royalty obligations	14	7	–	–	21
Other obligations	2	4	–	–	6
Total contractual obligations	**$ 689**	**$ 1,150**	**$ 1,231**	**$ 2,470**	**$ 5,540**

Includes synthetic lease obligation for our new headquarters facility in Wayne, New Jersey as described in the section "Critical Accounting Policies" and the note to our consolidated financial statements entitled "LEASES."

**Includes $390 million of equity security units, due 2007, which we are obligated to remarket in 2005. See the section "Financing Activities" and the note to our consolidated financial statements entitled "ISSUANCE OF COMMON STOCK AND EQUITY UNITS."*

We are in compliance with all covenants associated with the above contractual obligations. The covenants include, among other things, requirements to provide financial information and public filings, and to comply with specified financial ratios. Non-compliance with associated covenants could give rise to accelerated payments, requirements to provide collateral, or changes in terms contained in the respective agreements.

At February 1, 2003, we had available over $1 billion of cash and cash equivalents. Our current portion of long-term debt of $379 million at February 1, 2003 includes a 475 million Swiss Franc note, due on January 28, 2004. In addition, our long-term debt at February 1, 2003 includes a 500 million Euro bond, due on February 13, 2004. See the section "Other Matters" and the note to our consolidated financial statements entitled "SUBSEQUENT EVENTS" for a discussion regarding the registration of $800 million of debt securities in March 2003 and the sale and issuance of $400 million of notes in April 2003.

We have $985 million in unsecured committed revolving credit facilities from a syndicate of financial institutions. These credit facilities are available for seasonal borrowings. There were no outstanding balances under these credit facilities at the end of fiscal 2002, 2001 or 2000. Additionally, we have lines of credit with various banks to meet certain of the short-term financing needs of our foreign subsidiaries. The following table shows our commercial commitments with their related expirations and availability:

management's discussion and analysis

Commercial Commitments at February 1, 2003 (in millions)

	Total amounts committed	Fiscal 2003	Fiscal 2004 and Fiscal 2005	Fiscal 2006 and Fiscal 2007	Fiscal 2008 and subsequent	Amounts available at February 1, 2003
			Amount of commitment expiration per fiscal period			
Unsecured revolving credit facilities:						
Facility expiring in September 2006	$ 685	$ –	$ –	$ 685	$ –	$ 685
364-day facility expiring August 25, 2003	300	300	–	–	–	300
Total unsecured revolving credit facilities	$ 985	$ 300	$ –	$ 685	$ –	$ 985

Cash requirements for operating and investing activities will be met primarily through use of our exisiting cash and cash equivalents, cash flows from operating activities, and utilization of our unsecured committed revolving credit facilities. At February 1, 2003, we had in place stand-by letters of credit of $360 million, primarily as a guarantee for a debt obligation and $75 million of outstanding letters of credit related to import merchandise.

Credit Ratings

	Moody's	Standard & Poor's
Long-term debt	Baa3	BBB-
Commercial paper	P-3	A-3
Outlook	Negative	Stable
Date of last rating update	March 19, 2003	March 5, 2003

Our debt instruments do not contain provisions requiring acceleration of payment upon a debt rating downgrade. We continue to be confident in our ability to refinance maturing debt. Other credit ratings for our debt are available; however we disclosed above only ratings of the two largest nationally recognized statistical rating organizations because we believe these are the most relevant to our business.

The seasonal nature of our business typically causes cash balances to decline from the beginning of the year through October as inventory increases for the holiday selling season and funds are used for construction of new stores, remodeling and other initiatives that normally occur in this period. The fourth quarter, including the holiday season, accounts for more than 40% of our net sales and substantially all of our operating earnings.

Operating Activities

Our net cash inflows from operating activities increased to $574 million in 2002 from net cash inflows of $504 million in 2001 and net cash outflows of $151 in 2000. Net earnings, as adjusted for non-cash items, of $600 million in 2002 and $425 million in 2001 were the primary drivers of the net cash inflows from operations in those years. The net cash outflows from operations in 2000 were primarily driven by an increase in merchandise inventories of $486 million, and a net decrease in accounts payable, accrued expenses and other liabilities of $178 million, and was partially offset by net earnings, as adjusted for non-cash items, of $444 million for that year.

Investing Activities

Capital expenditures, net of dispositions, were $398 million in 2002, $705 million in 2001 and $402 million in 2000. Capital expenditures during these periods include investments to: open 55 new Babies"R"Us stores in the United States; open 18 new Toys"R"Us stores internationally; reformat our existing Toys"R"Us store base in the United States to our Mission Possible format and remodel 41 existing Kids"R"Us stores to our R-Generation store format; convert 286 existing Toys"R"Us stores into Toys"R"Us/Kids"R"Us combo stores; improve and enhance our management information systems.

During 2003, we plan to reduce our capital expenditures for our business to less than $350 million. We plan to open approximately 20 new Babies"R"Us stores in the United States and approximately five new international Toys"R"Us stores, and we also plan to continue to improve and enhance our management information systems in 2003.

Financing Activities

Net cash inflows from financing activities were $613 million in 2002, primarily driven by net long-term borrowings of $407 million, as well as proceeds received from the issuance of our common stock and contracts to purchase common stock totaling $266 million. In May 2002, we issued 14,950,000 shares of our common stock at a price of $17.65 per share and received net proceeds of $253 million. On the same date, we issued 8,050,000 equity security units with a stated amount of $50 per unit and received net proceeds of $390 million. Each security unit consists of a contract to purchase, for $50, a specified number of shares of Toys"R"Us common stock in August 2005, and a senior note due in 2007 with a principal amount of $50. The fair value of the contract to purchase shares of Toys"R"Us common stock was estimated at $1.77 per equity security unit. The fair value of the senior note was estimated at $48.23 per equity security unit. Interest on the senior notes is payable quarterly at an initial rate of 6.25%. We are obligated to remarket the notes in May 2005 at the then prevailing interest rate for similar notes. If the remarketing were not to be successful, we would be entitled to take possession of the senior notes, and the holder's obligation under the contracts to purchase shares of our common stock would be deemed to have been satisfied. The net proceeds from these public offerings were used to refinance short-term borrowings and for other general corporate purposes.

Net cash inflows from financing activities were $191 million in 2001, primarily as a result of net borrowings of $216 million during the year. In July 2001, we issued and sold $750 million of notes, comprised of $500 million of notes bearing interest at 7.625% per annum, maturing in 2011, and $250 million of notes bearing interest at 6.875% per annum, maturing in 2006. The proceeds from these notes were used to reduce outstanding commercial paper obligations. Simultaneously with the sale of the notes, we entered into interest rate swap agreements. As a result of the interest rate swap agreements, interest on the $500 million notes accrues at an effective rate of LIBOR plus 1.5120% and interest on the $250 million notes accrues at an effective rate of LIBOR plus 1.1515%. In October 2002, we terminated a portion of the interest rate swap agreeements and received a payment of $27 million, which is being amortized over the remaining lives of the related notes. Concurrently, we entered into new interest rate swap agreements. Of the $500 million notes, $200 million accrues interest at an effective rate of LIBOR plus 3.06%, and $125 million of the $250 million notes accrues interest at an effective rate of LIBOR plus 3.54%. Interest is payable on both notes semi-annually on February 1 and August 1 of each year. In February 2001, we borrowed 500 million EURO through the public issuance of a EURO bond bearing interest at 6.375% per annum. The obligation was swapped into a $466 million fixed rate obligation with an effective rate of 7.43% per annum with interest payments due annually and principal due February 13, 2004.

Net cash outflows from financing activities were $2 million for 2000. Net borrowings for 2000 were $521 million and were used primarily to repurchase 42 million shares of our common stock, to fund increased inventory levels, and to fund our Toysrus.com internet subsidiary. In 2000, we received a total of $97 million from SOFTBANK Venture Capital and affiliates representing their 20% minority interest investment in Toysrus.com.

Other Matters
On March 24, 2003, we filed a "shelf" registration statement with the Securities and Exchange Commission giving us the capability to sell up to $800 million of debt securities that would be used to repay outstanding debt and for general corporate purposes. In April 2003, we sold and issued $400 million in notes bearing interest at a coupon rate of 7.875%, maturing on April 15, 2013. The notes were sold at a price of 98.305%, resulting in an effective yield of 8.125%. Simultaneously with the sale of the notes, we entered into interest rate swap agreements. As a result of these swap agreements, interest will accrue at the effective rate of LIBOR plus 3.622%. Interest is payable semi-annually commencing on October 15, 2003. We plan to use the proceeds from these notes for the repayment of indebtedness maturing in the 2004 calendar year, and pending such repayment, for working capital needs and other general corporate purposes.

In August 2000, eleven purported class action lawsuits were filed (six in the United States District Court for the District of New Jersey, three in the United States District Court for the Northern District of California, one in the United States District Court for the Western District of Texas and one in the Superior Court of the State of California, County of San Bernardino), against us and our affiliates

Toysrus.com, Inc. and Toysrus.com, LLC. In September 2000, three additional purported class action lawsuits were filed (two in the United States District Court for the District of New Jersey and one in the United States District Court for the Western District of Texas). These actions generally purport to bring claims under federal privacy and computer fraud statutes, as well as under state statutory and common law, on behalf of all persons who have visited one or more of our web-sites and either made an online purchase or allegedly had information about them unlawfully "intercepted," "monitored," "transmitted," or "used." All the suits (except one filed in the United States District Court for the District of New Jersey) also named Coremetrics, Inc. (Coremetrics) as a defendant. Coremetrics is an internet marketing company with whom we have an agreement. These suits seek damages in unspecified amounts and other relief under state and federal law.

With Coremetrics, we filed a joint application with the Multidistrict litigation panel which resulted in all of the federal actions being consolidated and transferred to the United States District Court for the Northern District of California. Plaintiffs voluntarily dismissed the action in the Superior Court of the State of California, County of San Bernardino without prejudice. On October 16, 2001, plaintiffs filed an amended complaint in the United States District Court for the Northern District of California. We believe that we have substantial defenses to all of these claims. On November 13, 2002, we entered into a settlement agreement with plaintiffs in connection with all causes of action. This settlement agreement is subject to the court's review and approval and will not have a material impact on our consolidated financial statements.

We are party to certain other litigation, which, in our judgment, based in part on the opinion of legal counsel, will not have a material adverse effect on our consolidated financial statements.

In August 2000, Toysrus.com entered into a 10-year strategic alliance with Amazon.com to operate a co-branded toy and video game on-line store, which was launched in the third quarter of 2000. In addition, a co-branded baby products on-line store was launched in May 2001 and a co-branded creative and learning products on-line store was launched in July 2001. Under this alliance, Toysrus.com and Amazon.com are responsible for specific aspects of the on-line stores. Toysrus.com is responsible for merchandising, marketing and content for the co-branded store. Toysrus.com also identifies, buys, owns and manages the inventory. Amazon.com handles web-site development, order fulfillment, guest service, and the housing of Toysrus.com's inventory in Amazon.com's U.S. distribution centers. Also in August 2000, Amazon.com was granted a warrant entitling it to acquire up to 5% (subject to dilution under certain circumstances) of the capital of Toysrus.com at the then market value. This warrant has not been exercised.

We recorded a non-operating gain of $315 million ($200 million net of taxes) resulting from the initial public offering of shares of Toys – Japan, which was completed in April 2000. Of this gain, $91 million resulted from an adjustment to the basis of our investment in Toys – Japan, and $224 million was related to the sale of a portion of company-owned common stock of Toys – Japan, for which we received net cash proceeds of $267 million. In connection with this transaction, we

management's discussion and analysis

recorded a provision for current income taxes of $82 million and a provision for deferred income taxes of $33 million. As a result of this transaction, our ownership percentage in the common stock of Toys – Japan was reduced from 80% to 48%. Toys – Japan is a licensee of our company.

Quantitative and Qualitative Disclosures About Market Risks

We are exposed to market risk from potential changes in interest rates and foreign exchange rates. The countries in which we own assets and operate stores are politically stable, and we regularly evaluate these risks and have taken the following measures to mitigate these risks: our foreign exchange risk management objectives are to stabilize cash flow from the effects of foreign currency fluctuations; we do not participate in speculative hedges; and we will, whenever practical, offset local investments in foreign currencies with liabilities denominated in the same currencies. We also enter into derivative financial instruments to hedge a variety of risk exposures, including interest rate and currency risks.

Our foreign currency exposure is primarily concentrated in the United Kingdom, Europe, Canada, Australia and Japan. We face currency exposures that arise from translating the results of our worldwide operations into U.S. dollars from exchange rates that have fluctuated from the beginning of the period. We also face transactional currency exposures relating to merchandise that we purchase in foreign currencies. We enter into forward exchange contracts to minimize and manage the currency risks associated with these transactions. The counter-parties to these contracts are highly rated financial institutions and we do not have significant exposure to any one counter-party. Gains or losses on these derivative instruments are largely offset by the gains or losses on the underlying hedged transactions. For foreign currency derivative instruments, market risk is determined by calculating the impact on fair value of an assumed one-time change in foreign rates relative to the U.S. dollar. Fair values were estimated based on market prices, where available, or dealer quotes. With respect to derivative instruments outstanding at February 1, 2003, a 10% appreciation of the U.S. dollar would have increased pre-tax earnings in 2002 by $39 million, while a 10% depreciation of the U.S. dollar would have decreased pre-tax earnings in 2002 by $42 million. Comparatively, considering our derivative instruments outstanding at February 2, 2002, a 10% appreciation of the U.S. dollar would have increased pre-tax earnings in 2001 by $13 million, while a 10% depreciation of the U.S. dollar would have decreased pre-tax earnings in 2001 by $13 million.

We are faced with interest rate risks resulting from interest rate fluctuations. We have a variety of fixed and variable rate debt instruments. In an effort to manage interest rate exposures, we strive to achieve an acceptable balance between fixed and variable rate debt and have entered into interest rate swaps to maintain that balance. For interest rate derivative instruments, market risk is determined by calculating the impact to fair value of an assumed

one-time change in interest rates across all maturities. Fair values were estimated based on market prices, where available, or dealer quotes. A change in interest rates on variable rate debt is assumed to impact earnings and cash flow, but not the fair value of debt. A change in interest rates on fixed rate debt is assumed to impact the fair value of debt, but not earnings and cash flow. Based on our overall interest rate exposure at February 1, 2003 and February 2, 2002, a 1% increase in interest rates would have decreased pre-tax earnings by $15 million in 2002 and $11 million in 2001, respectively. A 1% decrease in interest rates would have increased pre-tax earnings by $15 million in 2002 and $11 million in 2001. A 1% increase in interest rates would decrease the fair value of our long-term debt at February 1, 2003 and February 2, 2002 by approximately $90 million and $79 million, respectively. A 1% decrease in interest rates would increase the fair value of our long-term debt at February 1, 2003 and February 2, 2002 by approximately $98 million and $87 million, respectively.

See notes to our consolidated financial statements for additional discussion of our outstanding derivative financial instruments at February 1, 2003.

Critical Accounting Policies

Our consolidated financial statements have been prepared in accordance with accounting principles generally accepted in the United States. The preparation of these financial statements requires us to make certain estimates and assumptions that affect the reported amounts of assets, liabilities, revenues and expenses, and the related disclosure of contingent assets and liabilities as of the date of the financial statements and during the applicable periods. We base these estimates on historical experience and on other various assumptions that we believe to be reasonable under the circumstances. Actual results may differ materially from these estimates under different assumptions or conditions and could have a material impact on our consolidated financial statements.

We believe the following are some of the critical accounting policies that include significant judgments and estimates used in the preparation of our consolidated financial statements.

Inventories and Vendor Allowances:

Merchandise inventories for the U.S. toy store division, which represent approximately 60% of total merchandise inventories, are stated at the lower of LIFO (last-in, first-out) cost or market value, as determined by the retail inventory method. All other merchandise inventories are stated at the lower of FIFO (first-in, first-out) cost or market value, as determined by the retail inventory method.

We receive various types of merchandise and other types of allowances from our vendors, which are based on negotiated terms. We use estimates at interim periods to record our provisions for inventory shortage and to record vendor funded merchandise allowances. These estimates are based on available data and other factors and are adjusted to actual amounts at the completion of our physical inventories and finalization of all vendor allowances.

Deferred Tax Assets:

As part of the process of preparing our consolidated financial statements, we are required to estimate our income taxes in each of the jurisdictions in which we operate. This process involves estimating our actual current tax exposure, together with assessing temporary differences resulting from differing treatment of items for tax and accounting purposes. These differences result in deferred tax assets and liabilities, which are included within our consolidated balance sheet. The measurement of deferred tax assets is adjusted by a valuation allowance to recognize the extent to which, more likely than not, the future tax benefits will be recognized.

At February 1, 2003, we recorded deferred tax assets, net of valuation allowances, of $317 million. We believe it is more likely than not that we will be able to realize these assets through the reduction of future taxable income. We base this belief upon the levels of taxable income historically generated by our businesses, as well as projections of future taxable income. If future levels of taxable income are not consistent with our expectations, we may be required to record an additional valuation allowance, which could reduce our net earnings by a material amount.

Derivatives and Hedging Activities:

We enter into derivative financial arrangements to hedge a variety of risk exposures, including interest rate and currency risks associated with our long-term debt, as well as foreign currency risk relating to import merchandise purchases. We account for these hedges in accordance with SFAS No. 133, "Accounting for Derivative Instruments and Hedging Activities," and we record the fair value of these instruments within our consolidated balance sheet. Gains and losses from derivative financial instruments are largely offset by gains and losses on the underlying transactions. At February 1, 2003, we increased the carrying amount of our long-term debt by $172 million, representing the fair value of debt in excess of the carrying amount on that date. Also at February 1, 2003, we recorded derivative assets of $158 million and derivative liabilities of $10 million. While we intend to continue to meet the conditions for hedge accounting, if hedges were not to be highly effective in offsetting cash flows attributable to the hedged risk, the changes in the fair value of the derivatives used as hedges could have a material effect on our consolidated financial statements.

Insurance Risks:

We insure a substantial portion of our general liability and workers' compensation risks through a wholly-owned insurance subsidiary, in addition to third party insurance coverage. Provisions for losses related to self-insured risks are based upon independent actuarially determined estimates. While we believe these provisions for losses to be adequate, the ultimate liabilities may be in excess of, or less than, the amounts recorded.

Stock Options:

We account for stock options under Accounting Principles Board Opinion No. 25, "Accounting for Stock Issued to Employees", which does not require compensation costs related to stock options to be recorded in net income, as all options granted under the various stock option plans had an exercise price equal to the market value of the underlying common stock at grant date. SFAS No. 148 "Accounting for Stock-Based Compensation – Transition and Disclosure – an amendment of SFAS No. 123," provides guidance on acceptable approaches to the implementation of SFAS No. 123, and requires more prominent disclosures of pro forma net earnings and earnings per share determined as if the fair value method of accounting for stock options had been applied in measuring compensation cost. Stock options are further detailed in the note to our consolidated financial statements entitled "STOCK OPTIONS."

Synthetic Lease:

Our new corporate headquarters facility, located in Wayne, New Jersey, is financed under a lease arrangement commonly referred to as a "synthetic lease." Under this lease, unrelated third parties, arranged by Wachovia Development Corporation, a multi-purpose real estate investment company, will fund up to $125 million for the acquisition and construction of the facility. Upon completion of the construction, which is expected to be in 2003, we will begin to pay rent on the facility until the lease expires in 2011. The rent will be based on a mix of fixed and variable interest rates, which will be applied against the final amount funded. Upon expiration of the lease, we would expect to either: renew the lease arrangement; purchase the facility from the lessor; or remarket the property on behalf of the owner. The lease agreement provides the lessor with a residual value guarantee equal to the funding for the acquisition and construction of the facility. Under accounting principles generally accepted in the United States, this arrangement is required to be treated as an operating lease for accounting purposes and as a financing for tax purposes.

Recent Accounting Pronouncements

In 2002, the FASB Emerging Issues Task Force issued EITF issue No. 02-16, "Accounting by a Reseller for Cash Consideration Received from a Vendor" (EITF 02-16). EITF 02-16 considers vendor allowances as a reduction in the price of a vendor's product that should be recognized as a reduction of cost of sales. Advertising allowances that are received for specific, identifiable and incremental costs are considered a reduction of advertising expenses and should be recognized as a reduction of SG&A. The provisions of EITF 02-16 are effective for all new arrangements, or modifications to existing arrangements, beginning after December 31, 2002. We are currently evaluating the potential impact of the provisions of EITF 02-16 on our consolidated financial statements for 2003.

In January 2003, the Financial Accounting Standards Board (FASB) issued Interpretation No. 46, "Consolidation of Variable Interest Entities" (FIN 46), which will require the consolidation of entities that are controlled by a company through interests other than voting interests. Under the requirements of this interpretation, an entity that maintains a majority of the risks or rewards associated with Variable Interest Entities (VIEs), commonly known as special purpose entities, is effectively in the same position as the parent in a parent-subsidiary relationship. Disclosure requirements of VIEs are effective in all financial statements issued after January 31, 2003. The consolidation requirements apply to all VIEs created after January 31, 2003. FIN 46 requires public companies to apply the consolidation requirements to VIEs that existed prior to February 1, 2003 and remained in existence as of the beginning of annual or interim periods

management's discussion and analysis

beginning after June 15, 2003. Our new corporate headquarters facility, located in Wayne, New Jersey, is leased from unrelated third parties, arranged by a multi-purpose real estate investment company that we do not control. In addition, we do not have the majority of the associated risks or rewards. Accordingly, we believe that FIN 46 will have no impact on the accounting for this synthetic lease. The synthetic lease is discussed above and in the note to our consolidated financial statements entitled "LEASES." We believe that FIN 46 will not have a material impact on our consolidated financial statements.

In November 2002, the FASB issued Interpretation No. 45, "Guarantor's Accounting and Disclosure Requirements for Guarantees, Including Indirect Guarantees of Indebtedness of Others" (FIN 45), which imposes new disclosure and liability-recognition requirements for financial guarantees, performance guarantees, indemnifications and indirect guarantees of the indebtedness of others. FIN 45 requires certain guarantees to be recorded at fair value. This is different from previous practice, where a liability would typically be recorded only when a loss is probable and reasonably estimable. The initial recognition and initial measurement provisions are applicable on a prospective basis to guarantees issued or modified after December 31, 2002. FIN 45 also requires new disclosures, even when the likelihood of making any payments under the guarantee is remote. The disclosure requirements are effective for interim and annual periods ending after December 15, 2002. We have procedures to identify guarantees contained in the various legal documents and agreements that have been executed, and those to be executed in the future, that fall within the scope of FIN 45. We expect that FIN 45 will not have a material impact on our consolidated financial statements.

In July 2002, the FASB issued SFAS No. 146, "Accounting for Costs Associated with Exit or Disposal Activities" (SFAS No. 146), which addresses the recognition, measurement, and reporting of costs associated with exit or disposal activities and supercedes Emerging Issues Task Force issue No. 94-3, "Liability Recognition for Certain Employee Termination Benefits and Other Costs to Exit an Activity (including Certain Costs Incurred in a Restructuring)," (EITF No. 94-3). The fundamental difference between SFAS No. 146 and EITF No. 94-3 is the requirement that a liability for a cost associated with an exit or disposal activity be recognized when the liability is incurred rather than at the date an entity commits to an exit plan. A fundamental conclusion of SFAS No. 146 is that an entity's commitment to a plan, by itself, does not create an obligation that meets the definition of a liability. SFAS No. 146 also establishes that the initial measurement of a liability recognized be recorded at fair value. The provisions of this statement are effective for exit or disposal activities that are initiated after December 31, 2002, with early application encouraged. We believe that the adoption of this pronouncement will not have a significant effect on our consolidated financial statements.

In August 2001, the FASB issued SFAS No. 144, "Accounting for the Impairment or Disposal of Long-Lived Assets" (SFAS No. 144), which addresses financial accounting and reporting for the impairment or disposal of long-lived assets and supersedes SFAS No. 121, "Accounting for the Impairment of Long-Lived Assets and for Long-Lived Assets to be Disposed Of." We adopted SFAS No. 144 as of February 3, 2002 and the adoption did not have a significant effect on our consolidated financial statements.

In July 2001, the FASB issued SFAS No. 142, "Goodwill and Other Intangible Assets" (SFAS No. 142), which is effective for fiscal years beginning after December 15, 2001. SFAS No. 142 changes the accounting for goodwill from an amortization method to an impairment only approach. We adopted this pronouncement on February 3, 2002. As a result of this adoption, amortization of $348 million of goodwill, which was to be amortized ratably through 2037, ceased. Based on the historical and projected operating results of the reporting units to which the goodwill relates, we determined that no impairment of this goodwill exists. Application of the non-amortization provisions of SFAS No. 142 resulted in an increase in net earnings of $2 million for the fourth quarter of 2002 and $8 million for the 2002 fiscal year.

Forward Looking Statements

This annual report contains "forward looking" statements within the meaning of Section 27A of the Securities Act of 1933, as amended, and Section 21E of the Securities Exchange Act of 1934, which are intended to be covered by the safe harbors created thereby. All statements that are not historical facts, including statements about our beliefs or expectations, are forward-looking statements. We generally identify these statements by words or phrases such as "anticipate," "estimate," "plan," "expect," "believe," "intend," "foresee," "will," "may," and similar words or phrases. These statements discuss, among other things, our strategy, store openings and renovations, future performance and anticipated cost savings, results of our restructuring, anticipated international development and other goals and targets. Such statements involve risks and uncertainties that exist in our operations and business environment that could render actual outcomes and results materially different than predicted. Our forward-looking statements are based on assumptions about many factors, including, but not limited to, ongoing competitive pressures in the retail industry, changes in consumer spending and consumer preferences, general economic conditions in the United States and other jurisdictions in which we conduct our business (such as interest rates, currency exchange rates and consumer confidence) and normal business uncertainty. While we believe that our assumptions are reasonable at the time forward-looking statements were made, we caution that it is impossible to predict the actual outcome of numerous factors and, therefore, readers should not place undue reliance on such statements. Forward-looking statements speak only as of the date they are made, and we undertake no obligation to update such statements in light of new information or future events that involve inherent risks and uncertainties. Actual results may differ materially from those contained in any forward-looking statement.

Consolidated Statements of Earnings

Toys"R"Us, Inc. and Subsidiaries

					Year Ended	
(in millions, except per share data)		**February 1,** **2003**		February 2, 2002		February 3, 2001
Net sales	$	**11,305**	$	11,019	$	11,332
Cost of sales		**7,799**		7,604		7,815
Gross margin		**3,506**		3,415		3,517
Selling, general and administrative expenses		**2,718**		2,721		2,801
Depreciation and amortization		**317**		308		290
Restructuring and other charges		**–**		186		–
Total operating expenses		**3,035**		3,215		3,091
Operating earnings		**471**		200		426
Other (expense) income:						
Interest expense		**(119)**		(117)		(127)
Interest and other income		**9**		8		23
Gain from IPO of Toys – Japan		**–**		–		315
Earnings before income taxes		**361**		91		637
Income taxes		**132**		24		233
Net earnings	$	**229**	$	67	$	404
Basic earnings per share	$	**1.10**	$	0.34	$	1.92
Diluted earnings per share	$	**1.09**	$	0.33	$	1.88

See notes to consolidated financial statements.

consolidated financial statements

Consolidated Balance Sheets
Toys"R"Us, Inc. and Subsidiaries

(In millions)	February 1, 2003	February 2, 2002
Assets		
Current Assets:		
Cash and cash equivalents	$ 1,023	$ 283
Restricted cash	60	–
Accounts and other receivables	202	210
Merchandise inventories	2,190	2,041
Prepaid expenses and other current assets	85	97
Total current assets	3,560	2,631
Property and Equipment:		
Real estate, net	2,398	2,313
Other, net	2,365	2,231
Total property and equipment	4,763	4,544
Goodwill, net	348	348
Derivative assets	158	42
Other assets	568	511
	$ 9,397	$ 8,076
Liabilities and Stockholders' Equity		
Current Liabilities:		
Short-term borrowings	$ –	$ –
Accounts payable	896	878
Accrued expenses and other current liabilities	824	738
Income taxes payable	279	319
Current portion of long-term debt	379	39
Total current liabilities	2,378	1,974
Long-term debt	2,139	1,816
Deferred income taxes	545	447
Derivative liabilities	10	122
Other liabilities	282	276
Minority interest in Toysrus.com	13	27
Stockholders' Equity:		
Common stock	30	30
Additional paid-in capital	414	444
Retained earnings	5,457	5,228
Accumulated other comprehensive loss	(149)	(267)
Treasury shares, at cost	(1,722)	(2,021)
Total stockholders' equity	4,030	3,414
	$ 9,397	$ 8,076

See notes to consolidated financial statements.

Consolidated Statements of Cash Flows
Toys"R"Us, Inc. and Subsidiaries

		Year Ended	
(In millions)	February 1, 2003	February 2, 2002	February 3, 2001
Cash Flows from Operating Activities			
Net earnings	$ 229	$ 67	$ 404
Adjustments to reconcile net earnings to net cash from operating activities:			
Depreciation and amortization	317	308	290
Deferred income taxes	99	(6)	67
Minority interest in Toysrus.com	(14)	(24)	(52)
Other non-cash items	(31)	(29)	50
Restructuring and other charges	–	109	–
Gain from initial public offering of Toys – Japan	–	–	(315)
Changes in operating assets and liabilities:			
Accounts and other receivables	8	15	(69)
Merchandise inventories	(100)	217	(486)
Prepaid expenses and other operating assets	(18)	36	(54)
Accounts payable, accrued expenses and other liabilities	112	(241)	(178)
Income taxes payable	(28)	52	192
Net cash from operating activities	574	504	(151)
Cash Flows from Investing Activities			
Capital expenditures, net	(398)	(705)	(402)
Net proceeds from sale of Toys – Japan common stock	–	–	267
Reduction in cash due to deconsolidation of Toys – Japan	–	–	(15)
Net cash from investing activities	(398)	(705)	(150)
Cash Flows from Financing Activities			
Short-term borrowings, net	–	(588)	419
Long-term borrowings	548	1,214	147
Long-term debt repayment	(141)	(410)	(45)
Proceeds from issuance of stock and contracts to purchase stock	266	–	–
Increase in restricted cash	(60)	–	–
Exercise of stock options	–	19	2
Proceeds received from investors in Toysrus.com	–	–	97
Share repurchase program	–	(44)	(632)
Issuance of stock warrants	–	–	10
Net cash from financing activities	613	191	(2)
Effect of exchange rate changes on cash and cash equivalents	(49)	18	(6)
Cash and Cash Equivalents			
Increase/(decrease) during year	740	8	(309)
Beginning of year	283	275	584
End of year	$ 1,023	$ 283	$ 275
Supplemental Disclosures of Cash Flow Information			
Income tax payments (refunds), net	$ 32	$ (22)	$ (2)
Interest payments	$ 93	$ 85	$ 128

See notes to consolidated financial statements.

Consolidated Statements of Stockholders' Equity

Toys"R"Us, Inc. and Subsidiaries

(In millions)	Common Stock Issued Shares	Issued Amount	In Treasury Shares	In Treasury Amount	Additional paid-in capital	Accumulated other comprehensive loss	Retained earnings	Total stockholders' equity
Balance, January 29, 2000	300.4	$ 30	(61.1)	$ (1,423)	$ 453	$ (137)	$ 4,757	$ 3,680
Net earnings for the year	–	–	–	–	–	–	404	404
Foreign currency translation adjustments	–	–	–	–	–	(74)	–	(74)
Comprehensive income								330
Share repurchase program	–	–	(42.1)	(632)	–	–	–	(632)
Issuance of restricted stock, net	–	–	–	50	(21)	–	–	29
Exercise of stock options, net	–	–	0.3	4	(3)	–	–	1
Issuance of stock warrants	–	–	–	–	10	–	–	10
Balance, February 3, 2001	300.4	$ 30	(102.9)	$ (2,001)	$ 439	$ (211)	$ 5,161	$ 3,418
Net earnings for the year	–	–	–	–	–	–	67	67
Foreign currency translation adjustments	–	–	–	–	–	(55)	–	(55)
Unrealized loss on hedged transactions	–	–	–	–	–	(1)	–	(1)
Comprehensive income								11
Share repurchase program	–	–	(2.1)	(44)	–	–	–	(44)
Issuance of restricted stock, net	–	–	0.5	5	4	–	–	9
Exercise of stock options, net	–	–	0.8	19	1	–	–	20
Balance, February 2, 2002	300.4	$ 30	(103.7)	$ (2,021)	$ 444	$ (267)	$ 5,228	$ 3,414
Net earnings for the year	–	–	–	–	–	–	229	229
Foreign currency translation adjustments	–	–	–	–	–	127	–	127
Unrealized loss on hedged transactions	–	–	–	–	–	(9)	–	(9)
Comprehensive income								347
Common stock equity offering	–	–	14.9	301	(35)	–	–	266
Issuance of restricted stock, net	–	–	0.9	(2)	5	–	–	3
Balance, February 1, 2003	300.4	$ 30	(87.9)	$(1,722)	$ 414	$ (149)	$ 5,457	$ 4,030

See notes to consolidated financial statements.

Notes to Consolidated Financial Statements

Toys"R"Us, Inc. and Subsidiaries

(Amounts in millions, except per share data)

SUMMARY OF SIGNIFICANT ACCOUNTING POLICIES

Fiscal Year

The company's fiscal year ends on the Saturday nearest to January 31. References to 2002, 2001, and 2000 are for the 52 weeks ended February 1, 2003 and February 2, 2002 and the 53 weeks ended February 3, 2001.

Reclassification

Certain reclassifications have been made to prior periods to conform to current presentations.

Principles of Consolidation

The consolidated financial statements include the accounts for the company and its subsidiaries. All material intercompany balances and transactions have been eliminated. Assets and liabilities of foreign operations are translated at current rates of exchange at the balance sheet date while results of operations are translated at average rates in effect for the period. Unrealized translation gains or losses are shown as a component of accumulated other comprehensive loss within stockholders' equity.

Use of Estimates

The preparation of financial statements in conformity with accounting principles generally accepted in the United States requires management to make estimates and assumptions that affect the amounts reported in the consolidated financial statements and accompanying notes. Actual results could differ from those estimates.

Revenue Recognition

The company recognizes sales revenue at the time the guest takes possession of merchandise or at the point of sale in our stores, or at the time of delivery for products purchased from our web-sites. Layaway transactions are recognized as revenue when the guest satisfies all payment obligations and takes possession of the merchandise. Revenues from the sale of gift cards and issuance of store credits are recognized as they are redeemed.

Advertising Costs

Net advertising costs are included in selling, general and administrative expenses and are expensed at the point of first broadcast or distribution. Net advertising costs were $147, $160, and $135 for 2002, 2001 and 2000, respectively.

Cash and Cash Equivalents

The company considers its highly liquid investments with original maturities of less than three months to be cash equivalents.

Merchandise Inventories

Merchandise inventories for the U.S. toy store division, which represent approximately 60% of total inventories, are stated at the lower of LIFO (last-in, first-out) cost or market, as determined by the retail inventory method. All other merchandise inventories are stated at the lower of FIFO (first-in, first-out) cost or market, as determined by the retail inventory method.

Credits and Allowances Received from Vendors

Credits and allowances are received from vendors and are related to formal agreements negotiated with such vendors. These credits and allowances are predominantly for cooperative advertising, promotions, and volume related purchases. These credits and allowances, excluding advertising allowances, are netted against cost of sales. The company's policy is to recognize credits, that are related directly to inventory purchases, as the related inventory is sold. Cooperative advertising allowances offset the cost of cooperative advertising that is agreed to by the company and its vendors, and are netted against advertising expenses included in selling, general and administrative expenses. The company's policy is to recognize cooperative advertising allowances in the period that the related advertising media is run.

Cost of Sales and Selling, General and Administrative Expenses

The significant components of the line item "Cost of sales" include the cost to acquire merchandise from vendors; freight in; markdowns; provision for inventory shortages; and discounts and allowances related to merchandise inventories.

The significant components of the line item "Selling, general and administrative expenses" include store payroll and related payroll benefits; rent and other store operating expenses; net advertising expenses; costs associated with operating the company's distribution network that primarily relate to moving merchandise from distribution centers to stores; and other corporate-related expenses.

Property and Equipment

Property and equipment are recorded at cost. Leasehold improvements represent capital improvements made to leased locations. Depreciation and amortization are provided using the straight-line method over the estimated useful lives of the assets or, where applicable, the terms of the respective leases, whichever is shorter. Accelerated depreciation methods are used for income tax reporting purposes with recognition of deferred income taxes for the resulting temporary differences. The company periodically evaluates the need to recognize impairment losses relating to long-lived assets. If indications of impairment exist and if the value of the assets are impaired, an impairment loss would be recognized.

Costs of Computer Software

The company capitalizes certain costs associated with computer software developed or obtained for internal use in accordance with the provisions of Statement Of Position No. 98-1, "Accounting for the Costs of Computer Software Developed or Obtained for Internal Use," issued by the American Institute of Certified Public Accountants. The company's policy provides for the capitalization of costs from the acquisition of external materials and services associated with developing or obtaining internal use computer software. Certain payroll costs for employees that are directly associated with internal use computer software projects are capitalized once specific criteria are met. The amount of payroll costs capitalized is limited to the time directly

notes to consolidated financial statements

spent on computer software projects. Costs associated with preliminary stage activities, training, maintenance and all other post-implementation stage activities are expensed as incurred. All costs capitalized in connection with internal use computer software projects are amortized on a straight-line basis over a useful life of five years.

Financial Instruments

The company adopted the provisions of Statement of Financial Accounting Standards No. 133, "Accounting for Derivative Instruments and Hedging Activities" (SFAS No. 133), as amended, effective February 4, 2001, as discussed in the footnote entitled "DERIVATIVE INSTRUMENTS AND HEDGING ACTIVITIES." This statement requires that all derivatives be recorded on the balance sheet at fair value and that changes in fair value be recognized currently in earnings unless specific hedge accounting criteria is met.

The company enters into forward foreign exchange contracts to minimize the risk associated with currency movement relating to its short-term intercompany loan program with foreign subsidiaries. Gains and losses, which offset the movement in the underlying transactions, are recognized as part of such transactions. Gross deferred unrealized losses on the forward contracts were not material at either February 1, 2003 or at February 2, 2002. The related receivable, payable and deferred gain or loss are included on a net basis in the balance sheet. The company had $205 and $108 of short-term outstanding forward contracts at February 1, 2003 and February 2, 2002, maturing in 2003 and 2002, respectively. These contracts are entered into with counter-parties that have high credit ratings and with which the company has the contractual right to net forward currency settlements.

Stock Options

The company accounts for stock options in accordance with the provisions of Accounting Principles Board Opinion No. 25, "Accounting for Stock Options Issued to Employees" (APB 25). The company has adopted the disclosure only provisions of SFAS No. 123 "Accounting for Stock Based Compensation" (FAS 123), issued in 1995.

In accordance with the provisions of SFAS No. 123, the company applies APB Opinion No. 25 and related interpretations in accounting for its stock option plans and, accordingly, does not recognize compensation cost. If the company had elected to recognize compensation cost based on the fair value of the options granted at grant date as prescribed by SFAS No. 123, net earnings and earnings per share would have been reduced to the pro forma amounts indicated in the following table:

	2002	2001	2000
Net earnings – as reported	$ 229	$ 67	$ 404
Net earnings – pro forma	190	28	385
Basic earnings per share – as reported	1.10	0.34	1.92
Basic earnings per share – pro forma	0.92	0.14	1.83
Diluted earnings per share – as reported	1.09	0.33	1.88
Diluted earnings per share – pro forma	0.91	0.14	1.79

The weighted-average fair value at the date of grant for options granted in 2002, 2001, 2000 was $6.42, $9.16 and $5.88, respectively. The fair value of each option grant is estimated on the date of grant using the Black-Scholes option pricing model. As there were a number of options granted during the years of 2000 through 2002, a range of assumptions are provided below:

	2002	2001	2000
Expected stock price volatility	.407 –.507	.407 –.567	.434 –.585
Risk-free interest rate	2.6% – 5.0%	3.6% – 5.1%	5.0% – 6.8%
Weighted average expected life of options	5 years	5 years	5 years

The effects of applying SFAS No. 123 and the results obtained through the use of the Black-Scholes option pricing model are not necessarily indicative of future values.

RESTRICTED CASH

The company had restricted cash of $60 at February 1, 2003. Included in this amount is $45 being used as support for a letter of credit in exchange for reduced letter of credit fees. This letter of credit partially supports the company's 475 Swiss Franc note, due January 28, 2004. The remaining $15 relates to a pending real estate transaction that is expected to close in 2003.

MERCHANDISE INVENTORIES

Merchandise inventories for the U.S. toy store division are stated at the lower of LIFO (last-in, first-out) cost or market. If inventories had been valued at the lower of FIFO (first-in, first-out) cost or market, inventories would show no change at February 1, 2003 or February 2, 2002.

	February 1, 2003	February 2, 2002
Toys"R"Us – U.S.	$ 1,387	$ 1,328
Toys"R"Us – International	362	278
Babies"R"Us	287	282
Toysrus.com	34	52
Other	120	101
	$ 2,190	$ 2,041

PROPERTY AND EQUIPMENT

	Useful life (in years)	**February 1, 2003**	February 2, 2002
Land		$ **825**	$ 811
Buildings	45-50	**2,009**	1,980
Furniture and equipment	5-20	**1,786**	1,800
Leasehold improvements	12½-35	**1,726**	1,542
Costs of computer software	5	**192**	127
Construction in progress		**33**	41
Leased property and equipment under capital lease		**53**	53
		6,624	6,354
Less accumulated depreciation and amortization		**1,861**	1,810
		$ **4,763**	$ 4,544

GOODWILL

In July 2001, the Financial Accounting Standards Board ("FASB") issued SFAS No. 142, "Goodwill and Other Intangible Assets" (SFAS No. 142), which is effective for fiscal years beginning after December 15, 2001. SFAS No. 142 changes the accounting for goodwill from an amortization method to an impairment only approach. The company adopted this pronouncement on February 3, 2002. As a result of this adoption, amortization of $348 of goodwill, which was to be amortized ratably through 2037, ceased. The carrying amount of goodwill at February 1, 2003 relates to the acquisition of Baby Super Stores, Inc. in 1997 ($319), which is now part of the Babies"R"Us division, and the acquisition of Imaginarium Toy Centers, Inc. in 1999 ($29), which is part of the Toys"R"Us – U.S. division. Based on the estimated fair market values (calculated using historical operating results of the reporting units to which the goodwill relates and relative industry multiples) of these divisions compared with the related book values, the company has determined that no impairment of this goodwill exists. Application of the non-amortization provisions of SFAS No. 142 resulted in an increase in net earnings of $8 for 2002. Had the non-amortization provisions of SFAS No. 142 been applied for 2001 and 2000, the company would have reported net earnings of $75 and $412, respectively, and diluted earnings per share of $0.36 and $1.92, respectively.

INVESTMENT IN TOYS – JAPAN

The company is accounting for its 48% ownership investment in the common stock of Toys – Japan on the "equity method" of accounting since the initial public offering in April 2000. Toys – Japan operates as a licensee of the company. As part of the initial public offering, Toys – Japan issued 1.3 shares of common stock to the public at a price of 12,000 yen or $113.95 per share. In November 2001, the common stock of Toys - Japan split 3 for 1. The company's accounting policy for the sales of subsidiaries' stock is to recognize gains or losses for value received in excess of or less than its basis in such subsidiary. No similar issuances of subsidiaries' stock are contemplated at this time. The carrying value of the investment is reflected on the consolidated balance sheets as part of "Other Assets" and was $140 and $123 at February 1, 2003 and February 2, 2002, respectively. At February 1, 2003, the quoted market value of the company's

investment was $188, which exceeds the carrying value of the investment. The valuation represents a mathematical calculation based on the closing quotation published by the Tokyo over-the-counter market and is not necessarily indicative of the amount that could be realized upon sale. The company is a guarantor of 80% of a 10 billion yen ($84) loan from third parties in Japan with an annual rate of 6.47%, due in 2012, for which Toys – Japan is the borrower.

SEASONAL FINANCING AND LONG-TERM DEBT

	February 1, 2003	February 2, 2002
7.625% notes, due fiscal 2011	$ **554**	$ 505
6.875% notes, due fiscal 2006	**267**	254
500 Euro bond, due February 13, 2004	**538**	431
475 Swiss Franc note, due January 28, 2004[a]	**348**	277
Equity Security Units	**408**	–
8¾% debentures, due fiscal 2021, net of expenses[b]	**198**	198
Note at an effective cost of 2.32% due in semi-annual installments through fiscal 2005[c]	**158**	126
Industrial revenue bonds, net of expenses	**21**	34
Obligation under capital leases	**18**	21
Mortgage notes at annual interest rates from 10.16% to 11.00%	**8**	9
	2,518	1,855
Less current portion	**379**	39
	$ **2,139**	$ 1,816

Long-term debt balances as of February 1, 2003 and February 2, 2002 have been impacted by certain interest rate and currency swaps that have been designated as fair value and cash flow hedges, as discussed in the note entitled, "DERIVATIVE INSTRUMENTS AND HEDGING ACTIVITIES."

(a) Supported by a 475 Swiss Franc bank letter of credit. This note has been converted by an interest rate and currency swap to a floating rate, U.S. dollar obligation at 3 month LIBOR.

(b) Fair value was $192 and $204 at February 1, 2003 and February 2, 2002, respectively. The fair value was estimated using quoted market rates for publicly traded debt and estimated interest rates for non-public debt.

(c) Amortizing note secured by the expected future yen cash flows from license fees due from Toys – Japan.

On May 28, 2002, the company completed public offerings of Toys"R"Us common stock and equity security units, as described in the note entitled "ISSUANCE OF COMMON STOCK AND EQUITY SECURITY UNITS."

In February 2001, the company issued and sold 500 EURO through the public issuance of a EURO bond bearing interest at 6.375% per annum. Through the use of derivative instruments, this obligation was swapped into a $466 fixed rate obligation at an effective rate of 7.43% per annum with interest payments due annually and principal due on February 13, 2004.

In July 2001, the company issued and sold $750 of notes comprised of $500 of notes bearing interest at 7.625% per annum, maturing in August 2011, and $250 of notes bearing interest at 6.875% per annum, maturing in August 2006. Simultaneously with the issuance of these notes, the company entered into interest rate swap

notes to consolidated financial statements

agreements. As a result of the interest rate swap agreements, interest on the $500 notes will accrue at the rate of LIBOR plus 1.5120% per annum and interest on the $250 notes accrues at the rate of LIBOR plus 1.1515% per annum. Interest is payable on both notes semi-annually on February 1 and August 1, commencing on February 1, 2002. In October 2002, the company terminated a portion of the interest rate swap agreements and received a payment of $27, which is being amortized over the lives of the related notes. Concurrently, the company entered into new interest rate swap agreements. Of the $500 notes, $200 accrues interest at the rate of LIBOR plus 3.06%, and $125 of the $250 notes accrues interest at the rate of LIBOR plus 3.54%.

As of February 1, 2003, the company had $985 in unsecured committed revolving credit facilities from a syndicate of financial institutions. These credit facilities consist of a $685 facility expiring September 2006 and a $300 facility expiring on August 25, 2003. The facilities are used for seasonal borrowings and to support the company's domestic commercial paper borrowings. As of February 1, 2003, all of the $685 facility expiring September 2006 and all of the $300 facility expiring on August 25, 2003 were available.

The annual maturities of long-term debt at February 1, 2003 are as follows:

	Annual maturities	Fair value hedging adjustment	Annual maturities, including fair value hedging adjustment
2003	$ 373	$ 6	$ 379
2004	499	75	574
2005	51	–	51
2006	279	17	296
2007	420*	19	439
2008 and subsequent	724	55	779
	$ 2,346	$ 172	$ 2,518

Long-term debt balances as of February 1, 2003 have been impacted by certain interest rate and currency swaps that have been designated as fair value and cash flow hedges, as discussed in the note entitled, "DERIVATIVE INSTRUMENTS AND HEDGING ACTIVITIES."

*Includes $390 of equity security units, due 2007, which the company is obligated to remarket in 2005. See the note entitled "ISSUANCE OF COMMON STOCK AND EQUITY SECURITY UNITS."

DERIVATIVE INSTRUMENTS AND HEDGING ACTIVITIES

The company is exposed to market risk from potential changes in interest rates and foreign exchange rates. The company continues to regularly evaluate these risks and continues to take measures to mitigate these risks, including, among other measures, entering into derivative financial instruments to hedge a variety of risk exposures including interest rate and currency risks. The company enters into forward exchange contracts to minimize and manage the currency risks related to its import merchandise purchase program. The company enters into interest rate swaps to manage interest rate risk and strives to achieve what it believes is an acceptable balance between fixed and variable rate debt.

The company purchases forward exchange contracts to minimize and manage the foreign currency risks related to its import merchandise purchase program. The counter-parties to these contracts are highly rated financial institutions and the company does not have significant exposure to any one counter-party. These forward exchange contracts are designated as cash flow hedges, as defined by SFAS No. 133, and are effective as hedges. Accordingly, changes in the effective portion of the fair value of these forward exchange contracts are included in other comprehensive income. Once the hedged transactions are completed, or when merchandise is sold, the unrealized gains and losses on the forward contracts are reclassified from accumulated other comprehensive income and recognized in earnings. The unrealized losses related to the import merchandise purchase program contracts, that were recorded in other comprehensive income, were not material at February 1, 2003 or February 2, 2002.

The company is faced with interest rate risks resulting from interest rate fluctuations. The company has a variety of fixed and variable rate debt instruments. In an effort to manage interest rate exposures, the company strives to achieve an acceptable balance between fixed and variable rate debt and has entered into interest rate swaps to maintain that balance.

On May 28, 2002, the company entered into an interest rate swap agreement on its Equity-Linked Securities. Under the agreement, the company will pay interest at a variable rate in exchange for fixed rate payments, effectively transforming these debentures to floating rate obligations. This swap is designated as a highly effective fair value hedge, as defined by SFAS No. 133. Changes in the fair value of the interest rate swap offset changes in the fair value of the fixed rate debt due to changes in market interest rates with some ineffectiveness present. The amount of ineffectiveness did not have a material effect on earnings.

On March 19, 2002, the company refinanced a note payable originally due in 2005 and increased the amount outstanding to $160 from $100. This borrowing is repayable in semi-annual installments of principal and interest, with the final installment due on February 20, 2008. The effective cost of this borrowing is 2.23% and is secured by expected future cash flows from license fees due from Toys – Japan. The company also entered into a contract to swap yen to U.S. dollars, within exact terms of the loan. This cross currency swap has been designated as a foreign currency cash flow hedge, as defined by SFAS No. 133, and is effective as a hedge.

In July 2001, the company entered into interest rate swap agreements on its 7.625% $500 notes, due August 1, 2011, and its 6.875% $250 notes, due August 1, 2006. Under these agreements, the company will pay interest at a variable rate in exchange for fixed rate payments, effectively transforming the debentures to floating rate obligations. These swaps are designated as highly effective fair value hedges, as defined by SFAS No. 133. Changes in the fair value of the interest rate swaps perfectly offset changes in the fair value of the fixed rate debt due to changes in market interest rates. As such, there were no ineffective hedge portions recognized in earnings during 2001.

notes to consolidated financial statements

In February 2001, the company issued and sold 500 EURO through the public issuance of a EURO bond bearing interest at 6.375% per annum. The obligation was swapped into a $466 fixed rate obligation with an effective rate of 7.43% per annum with interest payments due annually and principal due February 13, 2004. This cross currency swap is designated as a cash flow hedge, as defined by SFAS No. 133, and is effective as a hedge. The portion of the fair value of the swap attributable to changes in the spot rate is matched in earnings against changes in the fair value of debt.

The company entered into a Swiss Franc floating rate loan with a financial institution in January 1999, due January, 28 2004. The company also entered into a contract to swap U.S. dollars to Swiss Francs, within exact terms of the loan. This cross currency swap has been designated as a foreign currency fair value hedge, as defined by SFAS No. 133, and is effective as a hedge.

The company increased the carrying amount of its long-term debt by $172 at February 1, 2003, representing the fair value of debt in excess of the carrying amount on that date. Also at February 1, 2003, the company recorded derivative assets of $158 and derivative liabilities of $10, representing the fair value of these derivatives at that date.

ISSUANCE OF COMMON STOCK AND EQUITY SECURITY UNITS

On May 28, 2002, the company completed public offerings of Toys"R"Us common stock and equity security units. On that date, the company issued 15.0 shares of its common stock at a price of $17.65 per share and received net proceeds of $253. Also on that date, the company issued 8.0 equity security units with a stated amount of $50 per unit and received net proceeds of $390. Each security unit consists of a contract to purchase, for $50, a specified number of shares of Toys"R"Us common stock in August 2005, and a senior note due in 2007 with a principal amount of $50. The fair value of the contract to purchase shares of Toys"R"Us common stock was estimated at $1.77 per equity security unit. The fair value of the senior note was estimated at $48.23 per equity security unit. Interest on the senior notes is payable quarterly at an initial rate of 6.25%, which commenced in August 2002. The company is obligated to remarket the notes in May 2005 at the then prevailing market interest rate for similar notes. If the remarketing were not to be successful, the company would be entitled to take possession of the senior notes, and the holder's obligation under the contracts to purchase shares of Toys"R"Us common stock would be deemed to have been satisfied. The proceeds allocated to the purchase contracts were recorded in stockholders' equity on the consolidated balance sheet. The fair value of the senior notes is reflected as long-term debt on the consolidated balance sheet. The net proceeds from the public offerings were used to refinance short-term borrowings and for other general corporate purposes. As a result of the interest rate swap agreements, interest on the senior notes will accrue at the rate of LIBOR plus 3.43% per annum. Interest is payable quarterly each year, beginning in August 2002.

STOCKHOLDERS' EQUITY

The common shares of the company, par value $0.10 per share, were as follows:

	February 1, 2003	February 2, 2002
Authorized shares	650.0	650.0
Issued shares	300.4	300.4
Treasury shares	87.9	103.7
Issued and outstanding shares	212.5	196.7

EARNINGS PER SHARE

The following table sets forth the computation of basic and diluted earnings per share:

	2002	2001	2000
Numerator:			
Net earnings available to common stockholders	$ 229	$ 67	$ 404
Denominator for basic earnings per share – weighted average shares	207.6	197.6	210.9
Impact of dilutive securities	2.0	8.4	4.1
Denominator for diluted earnings per share – weighted average shares	209.6	206.0	215.0
Basic earnings per share	$ 1.10	$ 0.34	$ 1.92
Diluted earnings per share	$ 1.09	$ 0.33	$ 1.88

Options to purchase approximately 32.5, 10.3 and 3.0 shares of common stock were outstanding during 2002, 2001 and 2000, respectively, but were not included in the computation of diluted earnings per share because the option exercise prices were greater than the average market price of the common shares.

STOCK PURCHASE WARRANTS

The company issued 1.2 stock purchase warrants to SOFTBANK Venture Capital and affiliates ("SOFTBANK") for $8.33 per warrant. Each warrant gives the holder thereof the right to purchase one share of Toys"R"Us common stock at an exercise price of $13 per share, until the expiration date of February 24, 2010. In addition, the company granted a warrant on August 9, 2000 entitling Amazon.com to acquire up to 5% (subject to dilution under certain circumstances) of the capital of Toysrus.com at the then market value. As of February 1, 2003, none of these warrants have been exercised.

notes to consolidated financial statements

LEASES

The company leases a portion of the real estate used in its operations. Most leases require the company to pay real estate taxes and other expenses; some require additional amounts based on percentages of sales.

Minimum rental commitments under noncancelable operating leases having a term of more than one year as of February 1, 2003 are as follows:

	Gross minimum rentals	Sublease income	Net minimum rentals
2003	$ 317	$ 17	$ 300
2004	314	14	300
2005	301	12	289
2006	285	11	274
2007	267	9	258
2008 and subsequent	1,786	40	1,746
	$ 3,270	$ 103	$ 3,167

Total rent expense, net of sublease income, was $267, $261 and $291 in 2002, 2001 and 2000, respectively. The company remains contingently liable for lease payments related to the sub-lease of locations to third parties. To the extent that sub-lessees fail to perform, the company's total net rent expense would be increased.

The company's new corporate headquarters facility, located in Wayne, New Jersey, is financed under a lease arrangement commonly referred to as a "synthetic lease." Under this lease, unrelated third parties, arranged by Wachovia Development Corporation, a multi-purpose real estate investment company, will fund up to $125 for the acquisition and construction of the facility. Upon completion of the construction, which is expected to be in 2003, the company will begin to pay rent on the facility until the lease expires in 2011. The rent will be based on a mix of fixed and variable interest rates that will be applied against the final amount funded. Upon expiration of the lease, the company would expect to either: renew the lease arrangement; purchase the facility from the lessor; or remarket the property on behalf of the owner. The lease agreement provides the lessor with a residual value guarantee equal to the funding for the acquisition and construction of the facility. Under accounting principles generally accepted in the United States, this arrangement is required to be treated as an operating lease for accounting purposes and as a financing for tax purposes.

TAXES ON INCOME

The provisions for income taxes consist of the following:

	2002	2001	2000
Current:			
Federal	$ 4	$ 63	$ 120
Foreign	31	10	36
State	(2)	9	10
	$ 33	$ 82	$ 166
Deferred:			
Federal	62	(61)	50
Foreign	23	16	13
State	14	(13)	4
	99	(58)	67
Total tax provision	$ 132	$ 24	$ 233

At February 1, 2003 and February 2, 2002, the company had gross deferred tax assets, before valuation allowances, of $612 and $576, respectively, and gross deferred tax liabilities of $600 and $484, respectively. Deferred tax assets of $32 and $45 were included in "Prepaid Expenses and Other Current Assets" at February 1, 2003 and February 2, 2002, respectively. Deferred tax assets, net of valuation allowances, of $285 and $245 were included in "Other Assets" at February 1, 2003 and February 2, 2002, respectively. Deferred tax liabilities of $55 and $36 were included in "Accrued Expenses and Other Current Liabilities" at February 1, 2003 and February 2, 2002, respectively. The tax effects of temporary differences and carryforwards that give rise to significant portions of deferred tax assets and liabilities consist of the following:

	February 1, 2003	February 2, 2002
Deferred tax assets:		
Foreign loss carryforwards	$ 305	$ 296
Restructuring	116	131
Other	143	115
Depreciation and amortization	30	22
Derivative instruments and hedging activities	11	–
LIFO reserves	7	12
Valuation allowances, related to foreign loss carryforwards	(295)	(287)
	$ 317	$ 289
Deferred tax liabilities:		
Depreciation and amortization	$ (404)	$ (344)
Other	(169)	(131)
LIFO reserves	(27)	(9)
	$ (600)	$ (484)
Net deferred liabilities	$ (283)	$ (195)

On February 1, 2003, the company had foreign loss carryforwards available to reduce future taxable income of certain foreign subsidiaries. The foreign loss carryforwards, as well as the related tax benefits associated with the foreign loss carryforwards, will expire as follows:

Expiration	Net operating loss carryforwards	Tax benefit
1 – 5 years	$ 208	$ 71
6 – 7 years	9	4
Indefinitely	572	230
	$ 789	$ 305

At February 1, 2003, the company had valuation allowances of $295 against the tax benefit of foreign loss carryforwards of $305.

A reconciliation of the federal statutory tax rate with the effective tax rate follows:

	2002	2001	2000
Statutory tax rate	35.0%	35.0%	35.0%
State income taxes, net of federal income tax benefit	1.4	1.8	1.4
Foreign taxes, net of valuation allowance	(2.4)	(9.4)	1.1
Reversal of deferred tax asset	–	(6.5)	–
Subpart F income	1.5	5.4	0.6
Amortization of goodwill	–	3.5	0.5
Other, net	1.0	(2.9)	(2.1)
Effective tax rate	36.5%	26.9%	36.5%

Deferred income taxes are not provided on un-remitted earnings of foreign subsidiaries that are intended to be indefinitely invested. Exclusive of amounts that, if remitted, would result in little or no tax under current U.S. tax laws, unremitted earnings were approximately $607 at February 1, 2003. Net income taxes of approximately $120 would be due if these earnings were remitted.

STOCK OPTIONS

The company has stock option plans (the "Plans") that provide for the granting of options to purchase the company's common stock. The Plans cover employees and directors of the company and provide for the issuance of non-qualified options, incentive stock options, performance share options, performance units, stock appreciation rights, restricted shares, restricted units and unrestricted shares. The Plans provide for a variety of vesting dates with the majority of the options vesting approximately three years from the date of grant, 50% over the first two years and the remaining 50% over three years. Options granted to directors are exercisable one-third on a cumulative basis commencing on the third, fourth and fifth anniversaries from the date of the grant.

The exercise price per share of all options granted has been the average of the high and low market price of the company's common stock on the date of grant. All options must be exercised within ten years from the date of grant.

At February 1, 2003, an aggregate of 47.7 shares of authorized common stock were reserved for all of the Plans noted above, including 1.6 shares reserved for the future issuance of restricted shares, restricted units, performance units, unrestricted shares and 2 shares reserved for the restricted shares of units granted but not yet vested. Of these amounts, 11.5 were available for future grants. All outstanding options expire at dates ranging from February 17, 2003 to December 30, 2012.

Stock option transactions are summarized as follows:

	Shares	Exercise price per share	Weighted-average exercise price
Outstanding at January 29, 2000	39.8	$11.69 – $40.94	$24.59
Granted	7.5	10.25 – 26.25	15.29
Exercised	(0.4)	14.78 – 22.06	18.96
Canceled	(22.2)	14.63 – 40.94	28.60
Outstanding at February 3, 2001	24.7	$10.25 – $40.94	$18.36
Granted	8.6	15.53 – 38.36	28.03
Exercised	(1.1)	14.63 – 25.44	16.21
Canceled	(1.6)	11.50 – 39.88	24.26
Outstanding at February 2, 2002	30.6	$10.25 – $40.94	$20.39
Granted	6.0	9.83 – 20.41	20.08
Exercised	0.0	0.00 – 0.00	0.00
Canceled	(4.0)	10.25 – 38.19	19.62
Outstanding at February 1, 2003	**32.6**	**$ 9.83 – $40.94**	**$20.43**

The following table summarizes information about stock options outstanding at February 1, 2003:

		Outstanding		Exercisable (Vested)	
Range of exercise prices	Number of options	Weighted average remaining years of contractual life	Weighted average exercise price	Number of options	Weighted average exercise price
$ 9.83 – $14.99	2.0	6	$12.83	1.9	$12.84
$15.00 – $19.99	15.2	6	$17.60	12.6	$17.81
$20.00 – $24.99	7.3	8	$21.00	3.4	$21.47
$25.00 – $29.99	7.1	7	$25.85	3.7	$26.08
$30.00 – $40.94	1.0	4	$35.57	1.0	$35.57
Outstanding at February 1, 2003	32.6	7	$20.43	22.6	$20.07

Options exercisable and the weighted-average exercise prices were 11.3 and $19.60 at February 3, 2001; 16.1 and $20.74 at February 2, 2002; and 22.6 and $20.07 at February 1, 2003, respectively.

At February 1, 2003 and February 2, 2002, Toysrus.com, the company's internet subsidiary, had approximately 11.3 stock options outstanding to both employees and non-employees of the company. This represents approximately 11% of the authorized common stock of Toysrus.com at February 1, 2003 and February 2, 2002. These outstanding options, with exercise prices ranging between $0.30 and $2.25 per share, entitle each option holder the right to purchase one share of the common stock of Toysrus.com.

The company utilizes a restoration feature to encourage the early exercise of certain options and retention of shares, thereby promoting increased employee ownership. This feature provides for the grant of new options when previously owned shares of company stock are used to exercise existing options. Restoration option grants are non-dilutive, as they do not increase the combined number of shares of company stock and options held by an employee prior to exercise. The new options are granted at a price equal to the fair market value on the date of the new grant and generally expire on the same date as the original options that were exercised.

REPLACEMENT OF CERTAIN STOCK OPTION GRANTS WITH RESTRICTED STOCK

In 2000, the company authorized the exchange of certain stock options having an exercise price above $22 per share for an economically equivalent grant of restricted stock. The exchange, which was voluntary, replaced approximately 14.4 options with approximately 1.7 restricted shares. Shares of restricted stock resulting from the exchange vest over a period of three years. One-half of the grant vested on April 1, 2002 and the remainder vests on April 1, 2003. Accordingly, the company recognizes compensation expense throughout the vesting period of the restricted stock. The company recorded $3 in compensation expense related to this restricted stock in 2002 and $8 in both 2001 and 2000.

notes to consolidated financial statements

PROFIT SHARING PLAN

The company has a profit sharing plan with a 401(k) salary deferral feature for eligible domestic employees. The terms of the plan call for annual contributions by the company as determined by the Board of Directors, subject to certain limitations. The profit sharing plan may be terminated at the company's discretion. Provisions of $34, $46 and $50 have been charged to earnings in 2002, 2001 and 2000, respectively.

TOYSRUS.COM

Toysrus.com operates a co-branded toy and video game on-line store (Toysrus.com), a co-branded baby products on-line store (Babiesrus.com), and a co-branded learning products and information on-line store (Imaginarium.com) under a strategic alliance with Amazon.com.

The Toysrus.com strategic alliance with Amazon.com was launched in the third quarter of 2000 and expires in 2010. Under this alliance, each company is responsible for specific aspects of the on-line stores. Toysrus.com is responsible for merchandising, marketing and content for the co-branded stores. Toysrus.com also identifies, buys, owns and manages the inventory. Amazon.com handles web-site development, order fulfillment, customer service, and the housing of Toysrus.com's inventory in Amazon.com's U.S. distribution centers. The company recognizes revenue for Toysrus.com at the point in time when merchandise is shipped to customers, in accordance with the shipping terms (FOB shipping point) that exist under the agreement with Amazon.com.

Toysrus.com also opened a personalized gifts for all ages on-line store (Giftsrus.com) in November 2002. Visitors can choose from hundreds of products, ranging from exclusive stuffed animals, toys, clothing, home décor, and keepsakes, have them personalized with messages, monogrammed, hand-painted or engraved, gift wrapped, and then delivered. Giftsrus.com does not operate as part of the strategic alliance with Amazon.com.

In February 2000, the company entered into an agreement with SOFTBANK that included an investment of $60 by SOFTBANK in Toysrus.com. Accordingly, the company records a 20% minority interest in the net losses of Toysrus.com in selling, general and administrative expenses. Toysrus.com received additional capital contributions of $37 from SOFTBANK, representing its proportionate share of funding required for the operations of Toysrus.com.

SEGMENTS

The company's reportable segments are Toys"R"Us – U.S., which operates toy stores in 49 states and Puerto Rico; Toys"R"Us – International, which operates, licenses or franchises toy stores in 29 countries outside the United States; Babies"R"Us, which operates stores in 35 states; and Toysrus.com, the company's internet subsidiary.

Information on segments and reconciliation to earnings before income taxes, are as follows:

	February 1, 2003	February 2, 2002	February 3, 2001
Net sales			
Toys"R"Us – U.S.	$ 6,743	$ 6,877	$ 7,073
Toys"R"Us – International	2,161	1,889	1,872
Babies"R"Us	1,595	1,421	1,310
Toysrus.com[(1)]	340	277	180
Other[(2)]	466	555	897
Total	$11,305	$11,019	$11,332
Operating earnings			
Toys"R"Us – U.S.[(3)]	$ 280	$ 308	$ 431
Toys"R"Us – International	160	131	124
Babies"R"Us	174	138	120
Toysrus.com, net of minority interest[(4)]	(37)	(76)	(212)
Other[(3), (5)]	(106)	(115)	(37)
Restructuring and other charges	–	(186)	–
Operating earnings	$ 471	$ 200	$ 426
Interest expense, net	(110)	(109)	(104)
Gain from IPO of Toys – Japan	–	–	315
Earning before income taxes	$ 361	$ 91	$ 637
Identifiable assets			
Toys"R"Us – U.S.	$ 5,513	$ 5,412	$ 5,384
Toys"R"Us – International	1,430	1,146	1,235
Babies"R"Us	758	574	486
Toysrus.com	58	84	141
Other[(6)]	1,638	860	757
Total	$ 9,397	$ 8,076	$ 8,003
Depreciation and amortization			
Toys"R"Us – U.S.	$ 176	$ 166	$ 143
Toys"R"Us – International	49	41	42
Babies"R"Us	24	29	26
Toysrus.com	4	6	6
Other[(6)]	64	66	73
Total	$ 317	$ 308	$ 290

(1) Includes the net sales of Toysrus.com – Japan.

(2) Includes the net sales of the Kids"R"Us and Geoffrey divisions, and the net sales of the Toys – Japan division prior to its initial public offering on April 24, 2000.

(3) Includes markdowns related to the store closings announced as part of the restructuring in 2001.

(4) Includes the operations of Toysrus.com – Japan, net of minority interest.

(5) Includes corporate expenses, the operating results of the Kids"R"Us and Geoffrey divisions, and the equity in net earnings of Toys – Japan.

(6) Includes the Kids"R"Us and Geoffrey divisions, as well as corporate assets and related depreciation.

RESTRUCTURING AND OTHER CHARGES

In January 2002, the company announced plans to reposition its business, and as part of this plan, the company closed 27 non-Mission Possible format Toys"R"Us stores and closed 37 Kids"R"Us stores. In conjuction with the Kids"R"Us store closings in most of these locations, the company converted the nearest Toys"R"Us store into a Toys"R"Us/Kids"R"Us combo store.

notes to consolidated financial statements

As part of this plan, the company eliminated approximately 1,700 staff positions in its stores and its headquarters. In addition, these plans include the cost of consolidating five of the company's store support center facilities into its new headquarters in Wayne, New Jersey in 2003.

The costs associated with the facilities consolidation, elimination of positions, and other actions designed to improve efficiency in support functions were $79, of which $15 related to severance. The costs associated with store closings were $73 for Kids"R"Us and $85 for Toys"R"Us, of which $27 was recorded in cost of sales. The fair value of the facilities to be consolidated and store closings were obtained from third party appraisals. The company also reversed $24 of previously accrued charges ($11 from the 1998 charge and $13 from the 1995 charge) that the company determined to be no longer needed. Accordingly, based on these actions, the company recorded $213 million of pre-tax ($126 after-tax) restructuring and other charges in the fourth quarter of its fiscal year ending February 2, 2002. Details on the components of the charges are as follows:

Description	Initial charge	Utilized in 2001	Reserve balance at 2/02/02	Utilized in 2002	Adjustments to charge in 2002	Reserve balance at 2/01/03
Store closing:						
Lease commitments	$ 52	$ –	$ 52	$ (11)	$ –	$ 41
Severance	4	–	4	(4)	–	–
Write-down of property and equipment	75	(75)	–	–	–	–
Markdowns	27	–	27	(27)	–	–
Store support center consolidation:						
Lease commitments	28	–	28	–	11*	39
Write-down of property and equipment	29	(29)	–	–	–	–
Severance	15	–	15	(9)	(1)	5
Other	7	(7)	–	–	–	–
Total restructuring and other charges	**$237**	**$(111)**	**$126**	**$ (51)**	**$ 10**	**$ 85**

In the fourth quarter of 2002, we determined that a reserve for lease costs for the disposition of one of our store support center facilities was no longer adequate and, accordingly, recorded an additional charge of $11 million.

In 2000, Toysrus.com the company's internet subsidiary, recorded $118 in non-recurring charges as a result of the transition to its co-branded on-line store with Amazon.com, of which, $10 were included in cost of sales and $108 were included in selling, general and administrative expenses. These costs and charges related primarily to the closure of three distribution centers, as well as web-site asset write-offs and other costs. The company had remaining lease commitment reserves of $3 at February 1, 2003, that will be utilized in 2003 and thereafter.

The company previously announced strategic initiatives to reposition its worldwide business and recorded related restructuring and other charges of $698 in 1998 and $396 in 1995 to complete these initiatives. As of February 1, 2003, the company had substantially completed all announced initiatives. The company reversed unused reserves of $10 in the fourth quarter of 2002, and also reversed unused reserves of $29 in 2001, $24 of which were reversed in the fourth quarter of 2001 and are discussed above, and $11 in 2000, as these reserves were concluded to be no longer necessary. The company had $42 of reserves remaining at February 1, 2003, primarily for long-term lease commitments that will be utilized in 2003 and thereafter. The company believes that remaining reserves at February 1, 2003 are reasonable estimates of what is required to complete all remaining initiatives.

GAIN FROM INITIAL PUBLIC OFFERING OF TOYS – JAPAN

The company recorded a pre-tax non-operating gain of $315 ($200 net of taxes) in the first quarter of fiscal 2000 resulting from the initial public offering of shares of Toys – Japan. Of this gain, $91 resulted from an adjustment to the basis of the company's investment in Toys – Japan and $224 was related to the sale of a portion of the company-owned common stock of Toys – Japan, for which the company received net cash proceeds of $267. In connection with this transaction, the company recorded a provision for current income taxes of $82 and a provision for deferred income taxes of $33, respectively. As a result of this transaction, the company's ownership percentage in the common stock of Toys – Japan was reduced from 80% to 48%. Toys – Japan is a licensee of the company.

SUBSEQUENT EVENTS

On March 24, 2003, the company filed a "shelf" registration statement with the Securities and Exchange Commission, giving the company the capability to sell up to $800 of debt securities that would be used to repay outstanding debt and for general corporate purposes. In April 2003, the company sold and issued $400 million in notes bearing interest at a coupon rate of 7.875%, maturing on April 15, 2013. The notes were sold at a price of 98.305%, resulting in an effective yield of 8.125%. Simultaneously with the sale of the notes, we entered into interest rate swap agreements. As a result of these swap agreements, interest will accrue at the rate of LIBOR plus 3.622%. Interest is payable semi-annually commencing on October 15, 2003. The company plans to use the proceeds from these notes for the repayment of indebtedness maturing in the 2004 calendar year, and pending such repayment, for working capital needs and other general corporate purposes.

On March 5, 2003 the company announced that it would be eliminating approximately 200 positions in its store support facilities in 2003, representing approximately 10% of total headquarters staff.

OTHER MATTERS

In August 2000, eleven purported class action lawsuits were filed (six in the United States District Court for the District of New Jersey, three in the United States District Court for the Northern District of California, one in the United States District Court for the Western District of Texas and one in the Superior Court of the State of California, County of San Bernardino), against the company and our affiliates Toysrus.com, Inc. and Toysrus.com, LLC. In September 2000, three additional purported class action lawsuits were filed (two in the United

notes to consolidated financial statements

States District Court for the District of New Jersey and one in the United States District Court for the Western District of Texas). These actions generally purport to bring claims under federal privacy and computer fraud statutes, as well as under state statutory and common law, on behalf of all persons who have visited one or more of the company's web sites and either made an online purchase or allegedly had information about them unlawfully "intercepted," "monitored," "transmitted," or "used." All the suits (except one filed in the United States District Court for the District of New Jersey) also named Coremetrics, Inc. ("Coremetrics"), as a defendant. Coremetrics is an internet marketing company with whom the company has an agreement. These suits seek damages in unspecified amounts and other relief under state and federal law.

With Coremetrics the company filed a joint application with the Multidistrict litigation panel which resulted in all of the federal actions being consolidated and transferred to the United States District Court for the Northern District of California. Plaintiffs voluntarily dismissed the action in the Superior Court of the State of California, County of San Bernardino without prejudice. On October 16, 2001, plaintiffs filed an amended complaint in the United States District Court for the Northern District of California. The company believes that it has substantial defenses to all of these claims. On November 13, 2002, the company entered into a settlement agreement with plaintiffs in connection with all causes of action. This settlement agreement is subject to the court's review and approval and will not have a material impact on the company's consolidated financial statements.

RECENT ACCOUNTING PRONOUNCEMENTS

In 2002, the FASB Emerging Issues Task Force issued EITF issue No. 02-16, "Accounting by a Reseller for Cash Consideration Received from a Vendor" (EITF 02-16). EITF 02-16 considers vendor allowances as a reduction in the price of a vendor's product that should be recognized as a reduction of cost of sales. Advertising allowances that are received for specific, identifiable and incremental costs are considered a reduction of advertising expenses and should be recognized as a reduction of SG&A. The provisions of EITF 02-16 are effective for all new arrangements, or modifications to existing arrangements, beginning after December 31, 2002. The company is currently evaluating the potential impact of the provisions of EITF 02-16 on its consolidated financial statements for 2003.

In January 2003, the FASB issued Interpretation No. 46, "Consolidation of Variable Interest Entities" (FIN 46), which will require the consolidation of entities that are controlled by a company through interests other than voting interests. Under the requirements of this interpretation, an entity that maintains a majority of the risks or rewards associated with Variable Interest Entities ("VIEs"), commonly known as special purpose entities, is effectively in the same position as the parent in a parent-subsidiary relationship. Disclosure requirements of VIEs are effective in all financial statements issued after January 31, 2003. The consolidation requirements apply to all VIEs created after January 31, 2003. FIN 46 requires public companies to apply the consolidation requirements to VIEs that existed prior to February 1, 2003 and remained in existence as of the beginning of annual or interim periods beginning after June 15, 2003. The company's new corporate headquarters facility, located in

Wayne, New Jersey, is leased from unrelated third parties, arranged by a multi-purpose real estate investment company that the company does not control. In addition the company does not have the majority of the associated risks or rewards. Accordingly, the company believes that FIN 46 will have no impact on the accounting for the synthetic lease for such facility. The synthetic lease is discussed in the note entitled "LEASES." The company believes that FIN 46 will not have a material impact on its consolidated financial statements.

In November 2002, the FASB issued Interpretation No. 45, "Guarantor's Accounting and Disclosure Requirements for Guarantees, Including Indirect Guarantees of Indebtedness of Others" (FIN 45), which imposes new disclosure and liability-recognition requirements for financial guarantees, performance guarantees, indemnifications and indirect guarantees of the indebtedness of others. FIN 45 requires certain guarantees to be recorded at fair value. This is different from previous practice, where a liability would typically be recorded only when a loss was probable and reasonably estimable. The initial recognition and initial measurements provisions are applicable on a prospective basis to guarantees issued or modified after December 31, 2002. FIN 45 also requires additional disclosures, even when the likelihood of making any payments under the guarantee is remote. The disclosure requirements are effective for interim and annual periods ending after December 15, 2002. The company instituted procedures to identify guarantees contained in the various legal documents and agreements, already executed and those to be executed in the future that fall within the scope of FIN 45. The company expects that FIN 45 will not have a material impact on its consolidated financial statements.

In July 2002, the FASB issued SFAS No. 146 "Accounting for Costs Associated with Exit or Disposal Activities" (SFAS No. 146), which addresses the recognition, measurement, and reporting of costs associated with exit or disposal activities and supercedes Emerging Issues Task Force Issue No. 94-3, "Liability Recognition for Certain Employee Termination Benefits and Other Costs to Exit an Activity (including Certain Costs Incurred in a Restructuring)" (EITF No. 94.3). The fundamental difference between SFAS No. 146 and EITF No. 94-3 is the requirement that a liability for a cost associated with an exit or disposal activity be recognized when the liability is incurred rather than at the date an entity commits to an exit plan. A fundamental conclusion of SFAS No. 146 is that an entity's commitment to a plan, by itself, does not create an obligation that meets the definition of a liability. SFAS No. 146 also establishes that the initial measurement of a liability recognized be recorded at fair value. The provisions of this statement are effective for exit or disposal activities that are initiated after December 31, 2002, with early application encouraged. The company believes that adoption of this pronouncement will not have a significant effect on the company's consolidated financial statements.

In August 2001, the FASB issued SFAS No. 144, "Accounting for the Impairment or Disposal of Long-Lived Assets" (SFAS No. 144), which addresses financial accounting and reporting for the impairment or disposal of long-lived assets and supersedes SFAS No. 121, "Accounting for the Impairment of Long-Lived Assets and for Long-Lived Assets to be Disposed Of." The company adopted SFAS No. 144 as of February 3, 2002. The adoption did not have a significant effect on the company's consolidated financial statements.

reports

Report of Management

Responsibility for the integrity and objectivity of the financial information presented in this Annual Report resides with the management of Toys"R"Us. The accompanying financial statements have been prepared from accounting records which management believes fairly and accurately reflect the operations and financial position of the company.

Management has established a system of internal controls to provide reasonable assurance that assets are maintained and accounted for in accordance with its policies and that transactions are recorded accurately on the company's books and records. The company's disclosure controls provide reasonable assurance that appropriate information is accumulated and communicated to senior management to allow decisions regarding accurate, complete and timely financial disclosures.

The company's comprehensive internal audit program provides for constant evaluation of the adequacy of the adherence to management's established policies and procedures. The company has distributed to key employees its policies for conducting business affairs in a lawful and ethical manner.

The Audit Committee of the Board of Directors, which is comprised solely of outside directors, provides oversight of the financial reporting process through periodic meetings with our independent auditors, internal auditors, and management.

The financial statements of the company have been audited by Ernst & Young LLP, the company's independent auditors, in accordance with auditing standards generally accepted in the United States, including a review of financial reporting matters and internal controls to the extent necessary to express an opinion on the consolidated financial statements.

John H. Eyler, Jr.
Chairman, President and
Chief Executive Officer
March 5, 2003

Louis Lipschitz
Executive Vice President
and Chief Financial Officer

Report of Independent Auditors

The Board of Directors and Stockholders
Toys"R"Us, Inc.

We have audited the accompanying consolidated balance sheets of Toys"R"Us, Inc. and subsidiaries as of February 1, 2003 and February 2, 2002, and the related consolidated statements of earnings, stockholders' equity and cash flows for each of the three years in the period ended February 1, 2003. These financial statements are the responsibility of the company's management. Our responsibility is to express an opinion on these financial statements based on our audits.

We conducted our audits in accordance with auditing standards generally accepted in the United States. Those standards require that we plan and perform the audit to obtain reasonable assurance about whether the financial statements are free of material misstatement. An audit includes examining, on a test basis, evidence supporting the amounts and disclosures in the financial statements. An audit also includes assessing the accounting principles used and significant estimates made by management, as well as evaluating the overall financial statement presentation. We believe that our audits provide a reasonable basis for our opinion.

In our opinion, the financial statements referred to above present fairly, in all material respects, the consolidated financial position of Toys"R"Us, Inc. and subsidiaries at February 1, 2003 and February 2, 2002, and the consolidated results of their operations and their cash flows for each of the three years in the period ended February 1, 2003, in conformity with accounting principles generally accepted in the United States.

As discussed in the note entitled "Goodwill", the company adopted SFAS No. 142, Goodwill and Other Intangible Assets, effective February 3, 2002.

Ernst & Young LLP
New York, New York
March 5, 2003

board of directors

The Board of Directors

Charles Lazarus
Chairman Emeritus and founder
Toys"R"Us, Inc.
Board member since 1969

Charles Lazarus, founder of Toys"R"Us, Inc., is a pioneer of off-price specialty retailing. He opened his first retail establishment totally dedicated to children's needs in 1948 in Washington D.C. Mr. Lazarus continued to lead Toys"R"Us, Inc. as Chairman of the Board and Chief Executive Officer until 1994. Under his leadership, the company expanded internationally and launched its Kids"R"Us and Babies"R"Us brands. Mr. Lazarus remained Chairman of the Board from 1994 until 1998 when he became Chairman Emeritus.

Mr. Lazarus is a Director of Loral Space Systems and has served on the boards of Wal-Mart and Automatic Data Processing. He also served on the Advisory Board for Trade Policy under both President George Bush and President Bill Clinton. He is a member of the Toy Industry Hall of Fame.

John H. Eyler, Jr. [1]
Chairman, President and
Chief Executive Officer
Toys"R"Us, Inc.
Board member since 2000

John H. Eyler Jr. joined Toys"R"Us, Inc. as President and Chief Executive Officer in January 2000. He was named Chairman of the Board in 2001. Prior to joining the company, Mr. Eyler was Chairman and Chief Executive Officer of FAO Schwarz in New York, where he had been employed since 1992.

Mr. Eyler's previous positions include Chief Executive Officer of Chicago's Hartmarx retail subsidiary, and Chairman and Chief Executive Officer of MainStreet, a division of Federated Department Stores, Inc.

He serves on the Board of Directors for the National Retail Federation and The Andre Agassi Charitable Foundation. Mr. Eyler is also on the Board of NYC 2012, an effort to bring the 2012 Olympic Games to New York City. He holds a degree in Finance from the University of Washington and an M.B.A. from Harvard Business School.

RoAnn Costin [2]
President
Reservoir Capital Management, Inc.
Board member since 1996

RoAnn Costin is the President of Reservoir Capital Management, Inc., an investment advisory firm. She has worked in investment management since 1981, holding the position of Senior Vice President, Investment Manager for The Putnam Companies and Portfolio Manager for State Street Research and Management, Inc.

Ms. Costin holds an M.B.A. from the Stanford University Graduate School of Business and a B.A. in Government from Harvard University. In addition to Toys"R"Us, Inc., she serves on the Board of Directors for the Paul Taylor Dance Company in New York and on the Board of Trustees for The Boston Conservatory.

Roger N. Farah [1,4]
President and Chief Operating Officer
Polo Ralph Lauren
Board member since 2001

Roger N. Farah, has been President and Chief Operating Officer of Polo Ralph Lauren and a member of its Board of Directors since 2000.

From 1994 to 2000, Mr. Farah was Chairman of the Board and Chief Executive Officer of Venator Group, Inc. Prior to that, he held positions as President and Chief Operating Officer of Macy's Inc., Chairman and Chief Executive Officer of Federated Merchandising Services, and Chairman and Chief Executive Officer of Rich's Department Stores. From 1998 until 2000, he served on the Board of Directors at Liz Claiborne, Inc.

Mr. Farah received his B.S. in Economics from the University of Pennsylvania, Wharton School. He currently serves on the Wharton School's Board of Directors.

Peter A. Georgescu [2,4]
Chairman Emeritus
Young & Rubicam, Inc.
Board member since 2001

Peter A. Georgescu is Chairman Emeritus of Young & Rubicam, Inc. where he served as the company's Chairman and CEO from 1994 until 2000. He also served as President of Young and Rubicam Advertising and President of the company's former International division. Under Mr. Georgescu's tenure, Young & Rubicam transformed from a private to a publicly-held company and built an extensive database for global branding.

Mr. Georgescu also serves on the Board of Directors for EMI Group PLC, International Flavors & Fragrances Inc. and Levi Strauss & Co. He is Vice Chairman/Director of New York Presbyterian Hospital and a Director of A Better Chance. He received his B.A. from Princeton and an M.B.A. from the Stanford Business School. He was elected to the Advertising Hall of Fame in 2001.

Michael Goldstein [1]
Chairman, The Toys"R"Us
Children's Fund, Inc.
Board member since 1989

Michael Goldstein is Chairman of The Toys"R"Us Children's Fund, Inc. and Toys"R"Us.com, Inc. He has spent 19 years with Toys"R"Us, Inc. serving as both Chairman of the Board and Chief Executive Officer. Prior to 1983, Mr. Goldstein held positions as Sr. Executive Vice President-Operations & Finance with Lerner Stores Corporation and as a Partner with Ernst & Young.

Mr. Goldstein is a Director of Finlay Enterprises, Inc., United Retail Group, 4 Kids Entertainment, Inc. and Columbia House. He is President-elect of the 92nd Street Y, a Director of The Special Contributions Fund of the NAACP, and serves on the Advisory Boards of the For All Kids Foundation, USA Tennis Foundation and the New York Restoration Project. Mr. Goldstein is President and Director of the Northside Center for Child Development. He serves on the Board and Executive Committee of Reading is Fundamental and on the Board and Executive Committee of the Queens College Foundation. He is an inductee into the Toy Industry Hall of Fame and was appointed by President George W. Bush to serve on the Advisory Committee for Trade Policy and Negotiation. He is a graduate of Queens College with a B.S. in Economics.

Calvin Hill [3]
Consultant
Board member since 1997

Calvin Hill is a consultant to The Dallas Cowboys Football Club, Mental Health Management, Inc., Fleet Financial Services and Alexander & Associates, Inc. Mr. Hill was Vice President with the Baltimore Orioles from 1987 to 1994, also serving on its Board of Directors. From 1993 to 2000, he served on President Bill Clinton's Council on Physical Fitness.

Mr. Hill currently serves on the Boards of the Rand Corporation Drug Policy and Research Center, the NCAA Foundation, Duke Divinity School, and International Special Olympics. He launched his professional athletic career with the Dallas Cowboys in 1969 and has played professional football in both the World Football League and the NFL. He is a graduate of Yale University.

Nancy Karch [2,4]
Senior Partner (retired)
McKinsey & Company
Board member since 2000

Nancy Karch is a retired Director of the international consulting firm McKinsey & Company and a member of the McKinsey Advisory Council, comprised of former partners who provide advice to the firm. During 26 years with McKinsey, she held several leadership positions, including Managing Partner of the Retail and Consumer Industries Sector, and Managing Partner of McKinsey Southeast United States.

Ms. Karch is a recognized expert in the field of general merchandise retailing and an active speaker in the retailing and consumer goods fields. She also serves on the Board of Directors of Liz Claiborne, Inc., Gillette, and the Corporate Executive Board, a business research firm. Ms. Karch holds a B.A. in mathematics from Cornell University, an M.S. in mathematics from Northeastern University, and an M.B.A. from Harvard Business School.

company officers

Corporate and Administrative Officers

Norman S. Matthews [1, 3, 4]
Consultant
Board member since 1996

Norman S. Matthews has worked in consulting and venture capital since 1989. Prior to that he held various executive positions with Federated Department stores, including President, Vice Chairman and Executive Vice President. He was also Chairman of Federated's Gold Circle Stores Division.

In addition to Toys"R"Us, Inc., Mr. Matthews serves on the Board of Directors for The Progressive Corporation, Sunoco, Eye Care Centers of America, Finlay Enterprises, Inc., Galyan's Trading Company, and Henry Schein, Inc. He holds a B.A. degree from Princeton University and an M.B.A. from Harvard Business School.

Arthur B. Newman [1, 2, 3]
Senior Managing Director,
The Blackstone Group, L.P.
Board member since 1997

Arthur B. Newman has been a Senior Managing Director and head of The Restructuring Group of The Blackstone Group, L.P., a private investment bank, since 1991. Previously, Mr. Newman was a Managing Director and head of the Restructuring and Reorganization Group of Chemical Bank and a senior partner at Ernst & Young. Mr. Newman has been an advisor in many of this country's largest reorganizations, including AMF Bowling, Arch Wireless, The Charter Company, Chiquita Banana, Dow Corning Corporation, Eastern Airlines, Exide Technologies, Global Crossing, Iridium, LTV Corporation, Levitz Furniture, Macy's, Manville Corporation, Mobile Media Corporation, Montgomery Ward, Texaco, Inc., White Motor Corporation and the Wickes Corporation.

Mr. Newman is a member of the America College of Bankruptcy and was the recipient of the 1990 award by the Bankruptcy & Reorganization Group, Lawyers Division of UJA-Federation. Mr. Newman holds a B.S. degree in economics and an M.B.A. from Rutgers University. He is a certified public accountant in New York.

1 Executive Committee
2 Audit Committee
3 Compensation & Organizational
  Development Committee
4 Corporate Governance and
  Nominating Committee

John H. Eyler, Jr.
Chairman, President and
Chief Executive Officer

Francesca L. Brockett
Executive Vice President –
Strategic Planning &
Business Development

Michael D'Ambrose
Executive Vice President –
Human Resources

Karen Duvall
Executive Vice President –
Supply Chain

John Holohan
Executive Vice President –
Chief Information Officer

Christopher K. Kay
Executive Vice President –
Operations & General Counsel,
Corporate Secretary

Warren F. Kornblum
Executive Vice President –
Chief Marketing Officer

Louis Lipschitz
Executive Vice President –
Chief Financial Officer

Jon W. Kimmins
Sr. Vice President – Treasurer

Dorvin D. Lively
Sr. Vice President –
Corporate Controller

Peter W. Weiss
Sr. Vice President – Taxes

Rebecca A. Caruso
Vice President –
Corporate Communications

Ursula H. Moran
Vice President –
Investor Relations

Divisional Officers

Richard L. Markee
Executive Vice President and
President – Specialty Businesses
and International Operations

Raymond L. Arthur
President – Toysrus.com

John Barbour
Executive Vice President and
President – Toys"R"Us International

James E. Feldt
Executive Vice President and
President – Merchandising
and Marketing, Toys"R"Us U.S.

Elliott Wahle
President – Babies"R"Us & Kids"R"Us

Joan W. Donovan
Sr. Vice President –
General Merchandise Manager,
Toys"R"Us International

Jonathan M. Friedman
Sr. Vice President –
Chief Financial Officer,
Toys"R"Us U.S.

Andrew R. Gatto
Sr. Vice President –
Product Development,
Toys"R"Us U.S.

Steven J. Krajewski
Sr. Vice President –
Operations, Toys"R"Us U.S.

James G. Parros
Sr. Vice President –
Stores & Distributions Center
Operations, Kids"R"Us

David Schoenbeck
Sr. Vice President –
Operations, Babies"R"Us

Pamela B. Wallack
Sr. Vice President –
General Merchandise Manager,
Babies"R"Us & Kids"R"Us

International Country Presidents
and Managing Directors

David Rurka
Managing Director –
Toys"R"Us U.K.

Jacques LeFoll
President – Toys"R"Us France

Monika Merz
President – Toys"R"Us Canada

John Schryver
Managing Director –
Toys"R"Us Australia

Michael C. Taylor
Managing Director –
Toys"R"Us Central Europe

Antonio Urcelay
Managing Director –
Toys"R"Us Iberia

A Heartfelt Tribute

After decades of much appreciated leadership and service, Charles Lazarus and Michael Goldstein will be leaving the Board at the end of this year's (2002-2003) term. Charles and Mike have both served many years as Chief Executive Officer and as Chairman of the Board of Directors of Toys"R"Us, Inc., where they both played significant roles in the growth of the company. Thereafter, they served the company with distinction as members of the Board of Directors. We are extremely grateful for their leadership, their inspiration, their compassion and their commitment to the Toys"R"Us family of stockholders, colleagues and guests.

Quarterly Financial Data and Market Information

Toys"R"Us, Inc. and Subsidiaries

Quarterly Financial Data

(In millions except per share data)

The following table sets forth certain unaudited quarterly financial information:

	First Quarter	Second Quarter	Third Quarter	Fourth Quarter
Year Ended February 1, 2003				
Net Sales	$ 2,095	$ 2,070	$ 2,271	$ 4,869
Gross Margin	682	670	722	1,432
Net (Loss)/Earnings	(4)	(17)	(28)	278
Basic (Loss)/ Earnings per Share	$ (0.02)	$ (0.08)	$ (0.13)	$ 1.31
Diluted (Loss)/ Earnings per Share	$ (0.02)	$ (0.08)	$ (0.13)	$ 1.30

	First Quarter	Second Quarter	Third Quarter	Fourth Quarter[a]
Year Ended February 2, 2002				
Net Sales	$ 2,061	$ 2,021	$ 2,178	$ 4,759
Gross Margin	665	661	710	1,379
Net (Loss)/Earnings	(18)	(29)	(44)	158
Basic (Loss)/ Earnings per Share	$ (0.09)	$ (0.15)	$ (0.22)	$ 0.80
Diluted (Loss)/ Earnings per Share	$ (0.09)	$ (0.15)	$ (0.22)	$ 0.78

(a) Includes restructuring and other charges
    of $213 ($126 net of tax, or $0.61 per share).

Market Information

The company's common stock is listed on the New York Stock Exchange. The following table reflects the high and low prices (rounded to the nearest hundredth) based on New York Stock Exchange trading since February 3, 2001.

The company has not paid any cash dividends, however, the Board of Directors of the company periodically reviews this policy.

The company had approximately 30,736 Stockholders of Record on March 12, 2003.

			High	Low
2001	1st	Quarter	$ 26.52	$ 23.00
	2nd	Quarter	31.00	22.30
	3rd	Quarter	25.10	16.81
	4th	Quarter	24.00	18.25
2002	1st	Quarter	$ 20.31	$ 16.18
	2nd	Quarter	18.28	12.58
	3rd	Quarter	14.09	8.70
	4th	Quarter	13.81	9.04

Why Walgreens?

2002 ANNUAL REPORT

This annual report is for the year ended August 31, 2002. Pages 1–5 and 18–31 reprinted by permission of Walgreen Co.

Financial Highlights
For the Years Ended August 31, 2002 and 2001

(In Millions, except per share data)	2002	2001	Increase
Net Sales	$28,681.1	$24,623.0	16.5%
Net Earnings	$ 1,019.2	$ 885.6	15.1%
Net Earnings per Common Share (diluted)	$ .99	$ .86	15.1%
Shareholders' Equity	$ 6,230.2	$ 5,207.2	19.6%
Return on Average Shareholders' Equity	17.8%	18.8%	
Closing Stock Price per Common Share	$ 34.75	$ 34.35	
Total Market Value of Common Stock	$ 35,616	$ 35,017	1.7%
Dividends Declared per Common Share	$ .145	$ .140	3.6%
Average Shares Outstanding (diluted)	1,032.3	1,028.9	0.3%

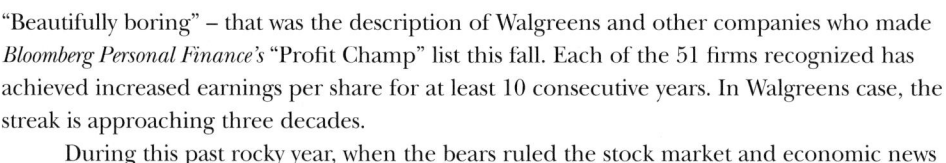

Questions and Answers for Our Shareholders
November 18, 2002

Chairman L. Daniel Jorndt
(left) with president and
chief executive officer
David W. Bernauer.

"Beautifully boring" – that was the description of Walgreens and other companies who made *Bloomberg Personal Finance's* "Profit Champ" list this fall. Each of the 51 firms recognized has achieved increased earnings per share for at least 10 consecutive years. In Walgreens case, the streak is approaching three decades.

During this past rocky year, when the bears ruled the stock market and economic news turned morning coffee bitter, we completed our 28th consecutive record year – and first billion-dollar earnings year – while opening 471 stores and investing nearly $1 billion in new stores, distribution centers and technology improvements. And in a world where cash is now king, we ended 2002 with over $400 million in the bank, nearly $3 billion in owned real estate, virtually no debt and the wherewithal to self-finance accelerating growth and customer service innovations. As one analyst commented recently: "Profits are opinion, but cash is a fact."

It was a record year, but fourth quarter earnings came in a penny light of expectations. Why?
Dave Bernauer: Pure and simple, this was a sales problem. Prescriptions were excellent – up 20 percent for the quarter and more than 21 percent for the year. But fourth quarter front-end – non-pharmacy – sales were anemic, particularly for promotional and summer seasonal merchandise. Those weak sales held our profit below Wall Street's expectations. A company with our stock market valuation isn't allowed a toe-stub, and our stock took a hit.

Why the weak sales?
Dan Jorndt: The easiest culprit is the economy, but we're not taking that bait. One of the beauties of our admittedly "boring" business is its staying power – we sell everyday, consumable items that people *need* more than *want*. Some times are tougher than others, but since the mid-1970s – through recessions and boom times – we've never had a down year. So when sales are tight, we look in the mirror…and adjust. We've made lots of corrections, especially in our advertising, to ensure that fall and holiday sales are more "Walgreen-like," that is, good, strong front-end sales.

Quite frankly, we got out of balance this summer. We were less promotion-oriented, which helped increase our gross profits, but hurt the top sales line. Advertising is always a delicate balance and we're moving the pendulum a little more in favor of traffic building. But we're seeking middle ground. Walgreens is not a retailer that sacrifices all to drive sales. We will get the top line moving…sensibly.

Walgreens keeps adding stores despite the economic slowdown. Is this smart?

Bernauer: There's never been a better time for us to expand. We have the sites, the cash, the people…and America has the need. The only retail segment where sales are outpacing store growth is drugstores. In 2001, the number of retail prescriptions climbed 5 percent, while drugstore outlets grew only 1 percent. Although we're the largest prescription provider in the nation, we still fill only 12 percent of the total, which gives us outstanding growth opportunity.

What about Wal*Mart?

Bernauer: What about *any* competitor? Any store that sells what we sell is on our radar screen. Our strategy has always been to define our segment – convenient healthcare and basic need retailing – and do it better than anyone else. We've seriously – and successfully – competed head-on with Wal*Mart for a quarter century now. They're not new competition. They *are* excellent, respected competition…and they're also one of the few retailers expanding at the same pace we are. Top competitors like Wal*Mart make us better. We watch them… they watch us.

Inventory was high going into fiscal 2002. How did you end up?

Bernauer: A chunk of our positive cash position is due to a big improvement in inventory levels. We had a bad case of indigestion last year, but ended 2002 with inventories up just 5 percent, despite a 16.5 percent sales increase and opening a record 363 net new stores plus new distribution centers in Jupiter, Florida, and Waxahachie, Texas. More importantly, we didn't just blow out product with severe price cuts. We used our systems to attack overages on an orderly basis without hurting gross profit margins and in-stock conditions.

Short-term borrowings of $441 million were completely repaid during the year. For my money, the beauty of our 2002 balance sheet rivals Monet, showing a positive cash swing from borrowing to investing of nearly $900 million.

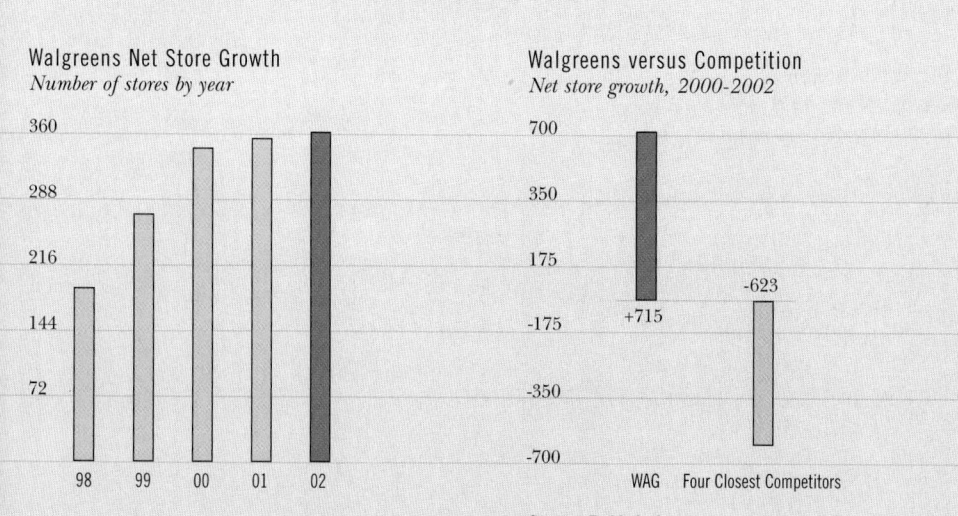

Walgreens Net Store Growth
Number of stores by year

Walgreens versus Competition
Net store growth, 2000-2002

WAG +715   Four Closest Competitors -623

Source: Published company reports

3,883 AND GROWING

Walgreens is the most "national" – and fastest growing – drugstore chain in America. In 2002, we filled 361 million prescriptions – 12 percent of the U.S. retail market and more per store than all major competitors. Our stores average $7.1 million or $654 per square foot in annual sales. Looking ahead, in 2003 we plan to open 450 new stores (approximately 360 net), add 12,000 new jobs and open our third new distribution center in just two years.

Dan Jorndt retires in January after 40 years with Walgreens. Since 1990 he's served as president, CEO and then chairman, leading this company through its period of greatest expansion and innovation. Dan Jorndt's two favorite words are "thank you." On behalf of all shareholders, we thank him for his leadership, honesty, retail savvy, tough decisions, long days and nights, sense of humor and the example he's set. Quite simply, he's made all of those whose lives he's touched a little richer. We wish him and his wife, Pat, the best — and most active — of retirements.

What was the impact of generic drug introductions last year?

Jorndt: Very positive. Generics save money for patients and their providers, both private insurance companies and state Medicaid plans. For Walgreens, while the higher mix of generics to brands slowed our top-line sales growth trend slightly last year, it had a healthy impact on the bottom line. The most important metric in pharmacy is the number of prescriptions. We filled 361 million in 2002, up almost 12 percent from the previous year, and more than double the national increase.

Is there still a pharmacist shortage?

Bernauer: There is a shortage…a big one. But aside from a few markets, we're in good shape. At the end of fiscal 2002, we had 1,600 more pharmacists working for us than a year ago. We're meeting ongoing needs and staffing over 360 net new drugstores a year. We also have the pharmacists to cover 900 24-hour stores. That's more than half of *all* 24-hour pharmacies in America.

If you could stress just one thing to shareholders this year, what would it be?

Jorndt: The quality of our earnings. Warren Buffet has a good quote: "It's only when the tide goes out that you learn who's been swimming naked." A lot of skinny-dippers have surfaced in the past year, bringing down high-flying companies and millions of shareholders. Believe me, we at Walgreens have our swimsuits on, and they're those scratchy knee-to-neck getups beach lovers wore in the 1920s. More boring than bikinis and thongs? You'd better believe it. But accounting works best when it's boring.

Our earnings are all about quality. Our financial statements are straightforward…what you see is what you get. We pay as we go and, other than store leases, everything is on our balance sheet. With no one-time charges and virtually no debt, WAG made the "Top 10" on a recent Merrill Lynch list of firms with quality earnings.

What worries you?

Bernauer: Mostly, stuff that's difficult to control. That includes the current economy as well as government actions. As our population ages, healthcare costs are going up, up, up. This will require government at all levels to make some very tough decisions about resource allocation. We believe it's our job to invest, create jobs, serve customer needs and get a return for these efforts, a return on which we pay significant taxes. It's the government's job to provide social

WHAT ARE WE WORTH?

As of August 31, 2002, Walgreens market capitalization was $35.6 billion. That ranks us third among U.S. retailers and third in the world. In terms of sales volume, we rank No. 78 in the *Fortune 100.* Walgreens has paid dividends in every quarter since 1933 and has raised them for 27 consecutive years. Since 1980, we've had seven two-for-one stock splits.

Sales
Billions of dollars

Earnings
Millions of dollars

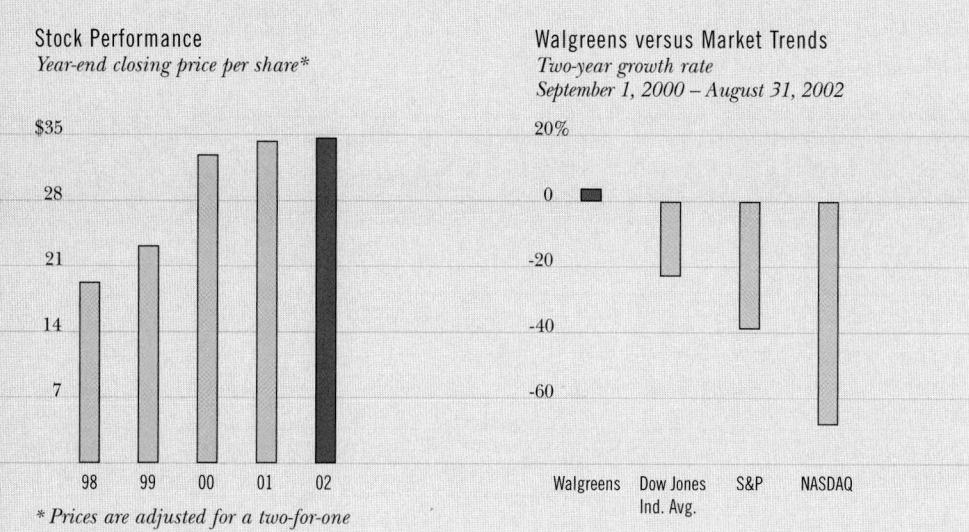

Stock Performance
*Year-end closing price per share**

$35
28
21
14
7

98 99 00 01 02

* Prices are adjusted for a two-for-one
stock split in 1999.

Walgreens versus Market Trends
Two-year growth rate
September 1, 2000 – August 31, 2002

20%
0
-20
-40
-60

Walgreens | Dow Jones | S&P | NASDAQ
| Ind. Avg. | |

WALGREENS STOCK PERFORMANCE

10 YEARS
On August 31, 1992, 100 shares of Walgreen stock sold for $3,838. Ten years later, on August 31, 2002, those 100 shares, having split three times, were 800 shares worth $27,800, for a gain of 624 percent.

20 YEARS
On August 31, 1982, 100 shares of Walgreen stock sold for $3,600. Twenty years later, those 100 shares, having split six times, were 6,400 shares worth $222,400, for a gain of 6,078 percent.

services. Although pharmacy consumes only 10 percent of the nation's healthcare bill and is the most cost-effective form of treatment, there have been moves recently to slash state Medicaid reimbursement to levels below the filling cost. We and other community pharmacies cannot accept plans – public or private – on which we lose money.

January marks a new era, as Dan Jorndt retires and Dave Bernauer adds "chairman" to his CEO position. What will change?

Jorndt: I've had a great 40-year run with this company, but it's time for new blood. Same core strategy, same execution…someone else calling the shots. These moves are part of our long-term succession plan. We're blessed in not having to go outside for CEOs. Dave Bernauer and our new president, Jeff Rein, are both pharmacists who started in the stores and have spent long careers here. They, and what I call the "new generation" of Walgreen leaders behind them, are among the top retailers in the country. These men and women know drugstores inside out and bring amazing energy and relentless character to their work. It will be a pleasure to watch their progress.

IN A TOUGH BUSINESS ENVIRONMENT, where confidence in corporate America has plummeted, we feel compelled to say, "No, Chicken Little, the sky isn't falling." We read volumes about the failures…while the thousands of successful companies receive little press. We can't solve the world's ills, but we can promise you, our shareholders and employees, that we'll do our level best to restore faith in what's good about American business. At Walgreens, we know who we are and what we're about. We have a competitive format and clearly defined strategy…a growing demand for our products and services…healthy cash and inventory positions…superior real estate and technology…and motivated, seasoned people at every level. Thanks for your faith in our long-term future…it's a solid one.

Jeffrey A. Rein will become president and chief operating officer in January 2003.

L. Daniel Jorndt
Chairman

David W. Bernauer
President and Chief Executive Officer

Eleven-Year Summary of Selected Consolidated Financial Data

Walgreen Co. and Subsidiaries (Dollars in Millions, except per share data)

Fiscal Year		2002	2001	2000
Net Sales		$28,681.1	$24,623.0	$21,206.9
Costs and Deductions	Cost of sales	21,076.1	18,048.9	15,465.9
	Selling, occupancy and administration	5,980.8	5,175.8	4,516.9
	Other (income) expense (1)	(13.1)	(24.4)	(39.2)
	Total Costs and Deductions	27,043.8	23,200.3	19,943.6
Earnings	Earnings before income tax provision and cumulative effect of accounting changes	1,637.3	1,422.7	1,263.3
	Income tax provision	618.1	537.1	486.4
	Earnings before cumulative effect of accounting changes	1,019.2	885.6	776.9
	Cumulative effect of accounting changes (2)	—	—	—
	Net Earnings	$ 1,019.2	$ 885.6	$ 776.9
Per Common Share (3)	Net earnings (2)			
	Basic	$ 1.00	$ .87	$ .77
	Diluted	.99	.86	.76
	Dividends declared	.15	.14	.14
	Book value	6.08	5.11	4.19
Non-Current Liabilities	Long-term debt	$ 11.2	$ 20.8	$ 18.2
	Deferred income taxes	176.5	137.0	101.6
	Other non-current liabilities	505.7	457.2	446.2
Assets and Equity	Total assets	$ 9,878.8	$ 8,833.8	$ 7,103.7
	Shareholders' equity	6,230.2	5,207.2	4,234.0
	Return on average shareholders' equity	17.8%	18.8%	20.1%
Drugstore Units	Year-end: Units (4)	3,883	3,520	3,165

(1) Fiscal 2002, 2001 and 2000 include pre-tax income of $6.2 million ($.004 per share), $22.1 million ($.01 per share) and $33.5 million ($.02 per share), respectively, from the partial payments of the brand name prescription drugs litigation settlement. Fiscal 1998 includes a pre-tax gain of $37.4 million ($.02 per share) from the sale of the company's long-term care pharmacy business.

(2) Fiscal 1998 includes the after-tax $26.4 million ($.03 per share) charge from the cumulative effect of accounting change for system development costs. Fiscal 1993 includes the after-tax $23.6 million ($.02 per share) costs from the cumulative effect of accounting changes for postretirement benefits and income taxes.

(3) Per share data have been adjusted for two-for-one stock splits in 1999, 1997 and 1995.

(4) Units include mail service facilities.

1999	1998	1997	1996	1995	1994	1993	1992
$17,838.8	$15,306.6	$13,363.0	$11,778.4	$10,395.1	$9,235.0	$8,294.8	$7,475.0
12,978.6	11,139.4	9,681.8	8,514.9	7,482.3	6,614.4	5,959.0	5,377.7
3,844.8	3,332.0	2,972.5	2,659.5	2,392.7	2,164.9	1,929.6	1,738.8
(11.9)	(41.9)	(3.9)	(2.9)	(3.6)	(2.7)	6.5	5.5
16,811.5	14,429.5	12,650.4	11,171.5	9,871.4	8,776.6	7,895.1	7,122.0
1,027.3	877.1	712.6	606.9	523.7	458.4	399.7	353.0
403.2	339.9	276.1	235.2	202.9	176.5	154.4	132.4
624.1	537.2	436.5	371.7	320.8	281.9	245.3	220.6
—	(26.4)	—	—	—	—	(23.6)	—
$ 624.1	$ 510.8	$ 436.5	$ 371.7	$ 320.8	$ 281.9	$ 221.7	$ 220.6
$ .62	$ .51	$ .44	$ .38	$ .33	$ .29	$ .23	$ .22
.62	.51	.44	.37	.32	.29	.23	.22
.13	.13	.12	.11	.11	.09	.08	.07
3.47	2.86	2.40	2.08	1.82	1.60	1.40	1.25
$ 18.0	$ 13.6	$ 3.3	$ 3.4	$ 2.4	$ 1.8	$ 6.2	$ 18.7
74.8	89.1	112.8	145.2	142.3	137.7	144.2	171.8
405.8	369.9	279.2	259.9	237.6	213.8	176.2	103.8
$ 5,906.7	$ 4,901.6	$ 4,207.1	$ 3,633.6	$ 3,252.6	$2,872.8	$2,506.0	$2,346.9
3,484.3	2,848.9	2,373.3	2,043.1	1,792.6	1,573.6	1,378.8	1,233.3
19.7%	19.6%	19.8%	19.4%	19.1%	19.1%	18.8%	19.1%
2,821	2,549	2,358	2,193	2,085	1,968	1,836	1,736

Management's Discussion and Analysis of Results of Operations and Financial Condition

Results of Operations

Fiscal 2002 was the 28th consecutive year of record sales and earnings. Net earnings were $1.019 billion or $.99 per share (diluted), an increase of 15.1% from last year's earnings of $885.6 million or $.86 per share. Included in this year's results was a $6.2 million pre-tax gain ($.004 per share) for a partial payment of the company's share of the brand name prescription drugs antitrust litigation settlement. Last year's results included a $22.1 million ($.01 per share) comparable payment. Excluding these gains, fiscal year earnings rose 16.5%.

Total net sales increased by 16.5% to $28.7 billion in fiscal 2002 compared to increases of 16.1% in 2001 and 18.9% in 2000. Drugstore sales increases resulted from sales gains in existing stores and added sales from new stores, each of which include an indeterminate amount of market-driven price changes. Comparable drugstore (those open at least one year) sales were up 10.5% in 2002, 10.5% in 2001 and 11.7% in 2000. New store openings accounted for 9.6% of the sales gains in 2002, 11.3% in 2001 and 10.6% in 2000. The company operated 3,883 drugstores as of August 31, 2002, compared to 3,520 a year earlier.

Prescription sales increased 21.2% in 2002, 20.9% in 2001 and 25.3% in 2000. Comparable drugstore prescription sales were up 16.3% in 2002, 17.6% in 2001 and 19.0% in 2000. Prescription sales were 59.8% of total sales for fiscal 2002 compared to 57.5% in 2001 and 55.2% in 2000. Third party sales, where reimbursement is received from managed care organizations and government and private insurance, were 89.8% of pharmacy sales in 2002, 88.4% in 2001 and 86.1% in 2000. Pharmacy sales trends are expected to continue primarily because of increased penetration in existing markets, availability of new drugs and demographic changes such as the aging population.

Gross margins as a percent of total sales were 26.5% in 2002, 26.7% in 2001 and 27.1% in 2000. The decrease in gross margin was caused by a number of factors. Non-pharmacy margins declined as a result of more aggressive advertising and in-store promotions. Although prescription margins increased, due in part to the shift to more generic medications, the trend in sales mix continued toward pharmacy, which carries lower margins than the rest of the store. Within the pharmacy, third party sales, which typically have lower profit margins than cash prescriptions, continue to become a larger portion of prescription sales.

The company uses the last-in, first-out (LIFO) method of inventory valuation. The effective LIFO inflation rates were 1.42% in 2002, 1.93% in 2001 and 1.36% in 2000, which resulted in charges to cost of sales of $55.9 million in 2002, $62.8 million in 2001 and $38.8 million in 2000. Inflation on prescription inventory was 4.3% in 2002, 4.9% in 2001 and 3.5% in 2000.

Selling, occupancy and administration expenses were 20.9% of sales in fiscal 2002, 21.0% of sales in fiscal 2001 and 21.3% of sales in fiscal 2000. The decrease in fiscal 2002, as a percent to sales, was

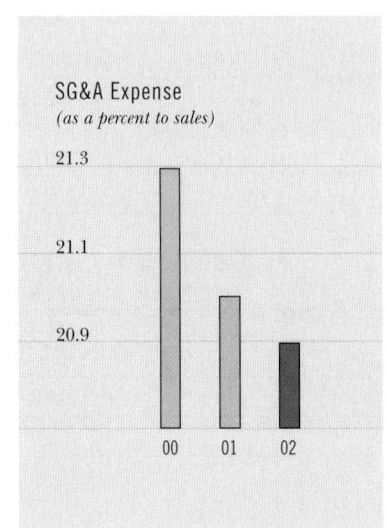

SG&A Expense
(as a percent to sales)

caused by lower store direct expenses, which were partially offset by higher occupancy costs. The decline in fiscal 2001 resulted from lower advertising and headquarters expense. Fixed costs continue to be spread over a larger base of stores.

Interest income net of interest expense increased in 2002 principally due to higher investment levels. Average net investment levels were approximately $162 million in 2002, $31 million in 2001 and $64 million in 2000.

The fiscal 2002 and 2001 effective income tax rates were 37.75% compared to 38.50% in 2000. The decrease in rates compared to 2000 was principally the result of lower state income taxes and the settlement of various IRS matters.

Critical Accounting Policies

The consolidated financial statements are prepared in accordance with accounting principles generally accepted in the United States of America and include amounts based on management's prudent judgments and estimates. Actual results may differ from these estimates. Management believes that any reasonable deviation from those judgments and estimates would not have a material impact on the company's consolidated financial position or results of operations. However, to the extent that the estimates used differ from actual results, adjustments to the statement of earnings and corresponding balance sheet accounts would be necessary. Some of the more significant estimates include liability for closed locations, liability for insurance reserves, vendor allowances, allowance for doubtful accounts, and cost of sales. The company uses the following techniques to determine estimates:

Liability for closed locations – The present value of future rent obligations and other related costs to the first lease option date or estimated sublease date.

Liability for insurance reserves – Incurred losses by policy year extended by historical growth factors to derive ultimate losses.

Vendor allowances – Vendor allowances are principally received as a result of meeting defined purchase levels or promoting vendors' products. Those received as a result of purchase levels are accrued as a reduction of merchandise purchase prices over the incentive period based on estimates. Those received for promoting vendors' products are offset against advertising expense and result in a reduction of selling, occupancy and administration expense.

Allowance for doubtful accounts – Based on both specific receivables and historic write-off percents.

Cost of sales – Based primarily on point-of-sale scanning information with an estimate for shrinkage and adjusted based on periodic inventories.

Financial Condition

Cash and cash equivalents were $449.9 million at August 31, 2002, compared to $16.9 million at August 31, 2001. Short-term investment objectives are to minimize risk, maintain liquidity and maximize after-tax yields. To attain these objectives, investment limits are placed on the amount, type and issuer of securities. Investments are principally in top-tier money market funds, tax exempt bonds and commercial paper.

Net cash provided by operating activities for fiscal 2002 was $1.5 billion compared to $719.2 million a year ago. The change between periods was principally due to tighter control over inventory levels. The company's profitability is the principal source for providing funds for expansion and remodeling programs, dividends to shareholders and funding for various technological improvements.

Net cash used for investing activities was $551.9 million in fiscal 2002 and $1.1 billion in 2001. Additions to property and equipment were $934.4 million compared to $1.2 billion last year. During the year, 471 new or relocated drugstores were opened. This compares to 474 new or relocated drugstores opened in the same period last year. New stores are owned or leased. There were 150 owned locations opened during the year or under construction at August 31, 2002, versus 245 for the same period last year. During the year, two new distribution centers opened, one in West Palm Beach (Jupiter), Florida, and the other in the Dallas metropolitan area.

During fiscal 2002, the company entered into two sale-leaseback transactions. These transactions involved 86 drugstore locations and resulted in proceeds of $302 million.

Capital expenditures for fiscal 2003 are expected to exceed $1 billion. The company expects to open more than 450 new stores in fiscal 2003 and have a total of 7,000 drugstores by the year 2010. The company is continuing to relocate stores to more convenient and profitable freestanding locations. In addition to new stores, a significant portion of the expenditures will be made for technology and distribution centers. A new distribution center is under construction in Ohio. Another is planned in Southern California.

Net cash used for financing activities was $488.9 million compared to $419.4 million provided a year ago. The change was principally due to payments of short-term borrowings this year versus proceeds from borrowings last year. There were no short-term borrowings at August 31, 2002, compared to $440.7 million at August 31, 2001. Borrowings were needed during each year to support working capital needs and store and distribution center growth, which included purchases of new store property, equipment and inventory. At August 31, 2002, the

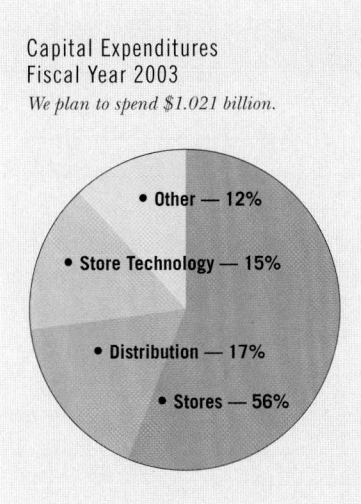

**Capital Expenditures
Fiscal Year 2003**
We plan to spend $1.021 billion.

- Other — 12%
- Store Technology — 15%
- Distribution — 17%
- Stores — 56%

company had a syndicated bank line of credit facility of $600 million to support the company's short-term commercial paper program. On July 2, 2002, the company deregistered the remaining $100 million of unissued authorized debt securities, previously filed with the Securities and Exchange Commission.

Recent Accounting Pronouncements

During the first quarter of 2002, the company adopted Statement of Financial Accounting Standards (SFAS) No. 142, "Goodwill and Other Intangible Assets." Under this pronouncement, goodwill is no longer amortized but periodically tested for impairment. No significant impact to the consolidated financial position or results of operations occurred as a result of adopting this standard.

The adoption of SFAS No. 144, "Accounting for the Impairment or Disposal of Long-Lived Assets," resulted in additional disclosures which can be found under "Impaired Assets and Liabilities for Store Closings" in the Summary of Major Accounting Policies.

During the fourth quarter of 2002, the company early adopted SFAS No. 146, "Accounting for Costs Associated with Exit or Disposal Activity." As a result, beginning in June 2002, the remaining lease obligations for closed locations were no longer recognized at the time management made the decision to close the location but were recognized at the time of closing. The adoption of this pronouncement did not have a material impact in the fourth quarter and is not expected to have a material impact on the company's consolidated financial position or results of operations in the future.

Cautionary Note Regarding Forward-Looking Statements

Certain statements and projections of future results made in this report constitute forward-looking information that is based on current market, competitive and regulatory expectations that involve risks and uncertainties. Those risks and uncertainties include changes in economic conditions generally or in the markets served by the company; consumer preferences and spending patterns; changes in state or federal legislation or regulations; the availability and cost of real estate and construction; competition; and risks of new business areas. Please see Walgreen Co.'s Form 10-K for the period ended August 31, 2002, for a discussion of certain other important factors as they relate to forward-looking statements. Actual results could differ materially.

Consolidated Statements of Earnings and Shareholders' Equity

Walgreen Co. and Subsidiaries for the Years Ended August 31, 2002, 2001 and 2000 (Dollars in Millions, except per share data)

Earnings		2002	2001	2000
Net Sales		$28,681.1	$24,623.0	$21,206.9
Costs and Deductions	Cost of sales	21,076.1	18,048.9	15,465.9
	Selling, occupancy and administration	5,980.8	5,175.8	4,516.9
		27,056.9	23,224.7	19,982.8
Other (Income) Expense	Interest income	(6.9)	(5.4)	(6.1)
	Interest expense	—	3.1	.4
	Other income	(6.2)	(22.1)	(33.5)
		(13.1)	(24.4)	(39.2)
Earnings	Earnings before income tax provision	1,637.3	1,422.7	1,263.3
	Income tax provision	618.1	537.1	486.4
	Net Earnings	$ 1,019.2	$ 885.6	$ 776.9
Net Earnings per Common Share	Basic	$ 1.00	$ .87	$ .77
	Diluted	.99	.86	.76
	Average shares outstanding	1,022,554,460	1,016,197,785	1,007,393,572
	Dilutive effect of stock options	9,716,486	12,748,828	12,495,236
	Average shares outstanding assuming dilution	1,032,270,946	1,028,946,613	1,019,888,808

Shareholders' Equity	Common Stock		Paid-in Capital	Retained Earnings
	Shares	Amount		
Balance, August 31, 1999	1,004,022,258	$78.4	$258.9	$3,147.0
Net earnings	—	—	—	776.9
Cash dividends declared ($.135 per share)	—	—	—	(136.1)
Employee stock purchase and option plans	6,796,632	.6	108.3	—
Balance, August 31, 2000	1,010,818,890	79.0	367.2	3,787.8
Net earnings	—	—	—	885.6
Cash dividends declared ($.14 per share)	—	—	—	(142.5)
Employee stock purchase and option plans	8,606,162	.6	229.5	—
Balance, August 31, 2001	1,019,425,052	79.6	596.7	4,530.9
Net earnings	—	—	—	1,019.2
Cash dividends declared ($.145 per share)	—	—	—	(148.4)
Employee stock purchase and option plans	5,483,224	.5	151.7	—
Balance, August 31, 2002	1,024,908,276	$80.1	$748.4	$5,401.7

The accompanying Summary of Major Accounting Policies and the Notes to Consolidated Financial Statements are integral parts of these statements.

Consolidated Balance Sheets

Walgreen Co. and Subsidiaries at August 31, 2002 and 2001 (Dollars in Millions)

	Assets	2002	2001
Current Assets	Cash and cash equivalents	$ 449.9	$ 16.9
	Accounts receivable, net	954.8	798.3
	Inventories	3,645.2	3,482.4
	Other current assets	116.6	96.3
	Total Current Assets	5,166.5	4,393.9
Non-Current Assets	Property and equipment, at cost, less accumulated depreciation and amortization	4,591.4	4,345.3
	Other non-current assets	120.9	94.6
	Total Assets	$9,878.8	$8,833.8
	Liabilities and Shareholders' Equity		
Current Liabilities	Short-term borrowings	$ —	$ 440.7
	Trade accounts payable	1,836.4	1,546.8
	Accrued expenses and other liabilities	1,017.9	937.5
	Income taxes	100.9	86.6
	Total Current Liabilities	2,955.2	3,011.6
Non-Current Liabilities	Deferred income taxes	176.5	137.0
	Other non-current liabilities	516.9	478.0
	Total Non-Current Liabilities	693.4	615.0
Shareholders' Equity	Preferred stock, $.0625 par value; authorized 32 million shares; none issued	—	—
	Common stock, $.078125 par value; authorized 3.2 billion shares; issued and outstanding 1,024,908,276 in 2002 and 1,019,425,052 in 2001	80.1	79.6
	Paid-in capital	748.4	596.7
	Retained earnings	5,401.7	4,530.9
	Total Shareholders' Equity	6,230.2	5,207.2
	Total Liabilities and Shareholders' Equity	$9,878.8	$8,833.8

The accompanying Summary of Major Accounting Policies and the Notes to Consolidated Financial Statements are integral parts of these statements.

Consolidated Statements of Cash Flows

Walgreen Co. and Subsidiaries for the Years Ended August 31, 2002, 2001 and 2000 (In Millions)

Fiscal Year		**2002**	2001	2000
Cash Flows from Operating Activities	Net earnings	**$1,019.2**	$ 885.6	$ 776.9
	Adjustments to reconcile net earnings to net cash provided by operating activities –			
	Depreciation and amortization	**307.3**	269.2	230.1
	Deferred income taxes	**22.9**	46.9	21.0
	Income tax savings from employee stock plans	**56.8**	67.3	38.5
	Other	**(8.6)**	2.1	13.6
	Changes in operating assets and liabilities –			
	Inventories	**(162.8)**	(651.6)	(368.2)
	Trade accounts payable	**289.6**	182.8	233.7
	Accounts receivable, net	**(170.6)**	(177.3)	(135.4)
	Accrued expenses and other liabilities	**75.0**	82.2	101.2
	Income taxes	**14.3**	(5.4)	28.6
	Other	**30.7**	17.4	31.7
	Net cash provided by operating activities	**1,473.8**	719.2	971.7
Cash Flows from Investing Activities	Additions to property and equipment	**(934.4)**	(1,237.0)	(1,119.1)
	Disposition of property and equipment	**368.1**	43.5	22.9
	Net proceeds from corporate-owned life insurance	**14.4**	59.0	58.8
	Net cash used for investing activities	**(551.9)**	(1,134.5)	(1,037.4)
Cash Flows from Financing Activities	(Payments of) proceeds from short-term borrowings	**(440.7)**	440.7	—
	Cash dividends paid	**(147.0)**	(140.9)	(134.6)
	Proceeds from employee stock plans	**111.1**	126.1	79.2
	Other	**(12.3)**	(6.5)	(7.9)
	Net cash (used for) provided by financing activities	**(488.9)**	419.4	(63.3)
Changes in Cash and Cash Equivalents	Net increase (decrease) in cash and cash equivalents	**433.0**	4.1	(129.0)
	Cash and cash equivalents at beginning of year	**16.9**	12.8	141.8
	Cash and cash equivalents at end of year	**$ 449.9**	$ 16.9	$ 12.8

The accompanying Summary of Major Accounting Policies and the Notes to Consolidated Financial Statements are integral parts of these statements.

Summary of Major Accounting Policies

Description of Business

The company is principally in the retail drugstore business and its operations are within one reportable segment. Stores are located in 43 states and Puerto Rico. At August 31, 2002, there were 3,880 retail drugstores and 3 mail service facilities. Prescription sales were 59.8% of total sales for fiscal 2002 compared to 57.5% in 2001 and 55.2% in 2000.

Basis of Presentation

The consolidated statements include the accounts of the company and its subsidiaries. All significant intercompany transactions have been eliminated. The consolidated financial statements are prepared in accordance with accounting principles generally accepted in the United States of America and include amounts based on management's prudent judgments and estimates. While actual results may differ from these estimates, management does not expect the differences, if any, to have a material effect on the consolidated financial statements.

Cash and Cash Equivalents

Cash and cash equivalents include cash on hand and all highly liquid investments with an original maturity of three months or less. The company's cash management policy provides for the bank disbursement accounts to be reimbursed on a daily basis. Checks issued but not presented to the banks for payment of $317 million and $233 million at August 31, 2002 and 2001, respectively, are included in cash and cash equivalents as reductions of other cash balances.

Financial Instruments

The company had approximately $37 million and $53 million of outstanding letters of credit at August 31, 2002 and 2001, respectively, which guaranteed foreign trade purchases. Additional outstanding letters of credit of $84 million and $71 million at August 31, 2002 and 2001, respectively, guaranteed payments of casualty claims. The casualty claim letters of credit are annually renewable and will remain in place until the casualty claims are paid in full. The company pays a nominal facility fee to the financing bank to keep this line of credit facility active. The company also had purchase commitments of approximately $70 million and $162 million at August 31, 2002 and 2001, respectively, related to the purchase of store locations. There were no investments in derivative financial instruments during fiscal 2002 and 2001.

Inventories

Inventories are valued on a lower of last-in, first-out (LIFO) cost or market basis. At August 31, 2002 and 2001, inventories would have been greater by $693.5 million and $637.6 million, respectively, if they had been valued on a lower of first-in, first-out (FIFO) cost or market basis. Included in inventory are product cost and in-bound freight. Cost of sales is primarily derived based upon point-of-sale scanning information with an estimate for shrinkage and adjusted based on periodic inventories. At August 31, 2001 and 2000, the company experienced lower inventory levels in certain LIFO pools compared with the previous year-end inventory levels which caused a liquidation of LIFO inventories which were carried at lower costs prevailing in prior years. The effect of this liquidation was a reduction in cost of sales of $4.2 million in fiscal 2001 and $3.1 million in fiscal 2000.

Vendor Allowances

The company receives vendor allowances principally as a result of meeting defined purchase levels or promoting vendors' products. Those received as a result of purchase levels are accrued as a reduction of merchandise purchase price over the incentive period and result in a reduction of cost of sales. Those received for promoting vendors' products are offset against advertising expense and result in a reduction of selling, occupancy and administration expense.

Property and Equipment

Depreciation is provided on a straight-line basis over the estimated useful lives of owned assets. Leasehold improvements and leased properties under capital leases are amortized over the estimated physical life of the property or over the term of the lease, whichever is shorter. Estimated useful lives range from 12½ to 39 years for land improvements, buildings and building improvements and 5 to 12½ years for equipment. Major repairs, which extend the useful life of an asset, are capitalized in the property and equipment accounts. Routine maintenance and repairs are charged against earnings. The composite method of depreciation is used for equipment; therefore, gains and losses on retirement or other disposition of such assets are included in earnings only when an operating location is closed, completely remodeled or impaired. Fully depreciated property and equipment are removed from the cost and related accumulated depreciation and amortization accounts.

Property and equipment consists of *(In Millions)*:

	2002	2001
Land and land improvements		
Owned stores	$1,080.4	$1,109.2
Distribution centers	57.8	38.7
Other locations	9.3	18.6
Buildings and building improvements		
Owned stores	1,185.9	1,156.6
Leased stores (leasehold improvements only)	425.6	411.1
Distribution centers	364.9	309.1
Other locations	58.2	70.6
Equipment		
Stores	1,609.6	1,440.3
Distribution centers	499.4	350.2
Other locations	464.9	462.7
Capitalized system development costs	144.1	117.4
Capital lease properties	17.8	18.8
	5,917.9	5,503.3
Less: accumulated depreciation and amortization	1,326.5	1,158.0
	$4,591.4	$4,345.3

The company capitalizes application stage development costs for significant internally developed software projects, including "SIMS Plus," an inventory management system, and "Basic Department Management," a marketing system. These costs are amortized over a five-year period. Amortization of these costs was $19.5 million in 2002, $17.3 million in 2001 and $13.1 million in 2000. Unamortized costs as of August 31, 2002 and 2001, were $73.2 million and $66.1 million, respectively.

Revenue Recognition

For all sales other than third party pharmacy sales, the company recognizes revenue at the time of the sale. For third party sales, revenue is recognized at the time the prescription is filled, adjusted by an estimate for those that will be unclaimed by customers. Customer returns are immaterial.

Impaired Assets and Liabilities for Store Closings

The company tests long-lived assets for impairment whenever events or circumstances indicate. Store locations that have been open at least five years are periodically reviewed for impairment indicators. Once identified, the amount of the impairment is computed by comparing the carrying value of the assets to the fair value, which is based on the discounted estimated future cash flows. Included in selling, occupancy and administration expense were impairment charges of $8.4 million in 2002, $9.7 million in 2001, and $15.1 million in 2000.

Summary of Major Accounting Policies
(continued)

During the fourth quarter of fiscal 2002, the company implemented SFAS No. 146, "Accounting for Costs Associated with Exit or Disposal Activities." Since implementation, the present value of expected future lease costs are charged against earnings when the location is closed. Prior to this, the liability was recognized at the time management made the decision to relocate or close the store.

Insurance
The company obtains insurance coverage for catastrophic exposures as well as those risks required to be insured by law. It is the company's policy to retain a significant portion of certain losses related to worker's compensation, property losses, business interruptions relating from such losses and comprehensive general, pharmacist and vehicle liability. Provisions for these losses are recorded based upon the company's estimates for claims incurred. The provisions are estimated in part by considering historical claims experience, demographic factors and other actuarial assumptions.

Pre-Opening Expenses
Non-capital expenditures incurred prior to the opening of a new or remodeled store are charged against earnings as incurred.

Advertising Costs
Advertising costs, which are reduced by the portion funded by vendors, are expensed as incurred. Net advertising expenses which are included in selling, occupancy and administration expense were $64.5 million in 2002, $54.1 million in 2001 and $76.7 million in 2000.

Stock-Based Compensation Plans
As permitted by SFAS No. 123, the company applies Accounting Principles Board (APB) Opinion No. 25 and related interpretations in accounting for its plans. Under APB 25, compensation expense is recognized for stock option grants if the exercise price is below the fair value of the underlying stock at the date of grant. The company complies with the disclosure provisions of SFAS No. 123, which requires presentation of pro forma information applying the fair-value based method of accounting.

Income Taxes
The company provides for federal and state income taxes on items included in the Consolidated Statements of Earnings regardless of the period when such taxes are payable. Deferred taxes are recognized for temporary differences between financial and income tax reporting based on enacted tax laws and rates.

Earnings Per Share
In fiscal year 2002 and 2001, the diluted earnings per share calculation excluded certain stock options, because the options' exercise price was greater than the average market price of the common shares for the year. If they were included, anti-dilution would have resulted. At August 31, 2002 and August 31, 2001, options to purchase 3,186,227 and 3,316,906 common shares granted at a price ranging from $35.90 to $45.625 and $36.875 to $45.625 per share were excluded from the fiscal year 2002 and 2001 calculations, respectively.

Notes to Consolidated Financial Statements

Interest Expense
The company capitalized $8.5 million, $15.6 million and $4.0 million of interest expense as part of significant construction projects during fiscal 2002, 2001 and 2000, respectively. Interest paid, net of amounts capitalized, was $.3 million in 2002, $3.4 million in 2001 and $.2 million in 2000.

Other Income
In fiscal 2002, 2001 and 2000, the company received partial payments of the brand name prescription drug antitrust litigation settlement for pre-tax income of $6.2 million ($.004 per share), $22.1 million ($.01 per share) and $33.5 million ($.02 per share), respectively. These payments, which are now concluded, were a result of a pharmacy class action against drug manufacturers, which resulted in a $700 million settlement for all recipients.

Leases
Although some locations are owned, the company generally operates in leased premises. Original non-cancelable lease terms typically are 20-25 years and may contain escalation clauses, along with options that permit renewals for additional periods. The total amount of the minimum rent is expensed on a straight-line basis over the term of the lease. In addition to minimum fixed rentals, most leases provide for contingent rentals based upon sales.

Minimum rental commitments at August 31, 2002, under all leases having an initial or remaining non-cancelable term of more than one year are shown below (In Millions):

2003	$ 897.9
2004	943.3
2005	933.4
2006	914.0
2007	895.0
Later	10,659.2
Total minimum lease payments	$15,242.8

The above minimum lease payments include minimum rental commitments related to capital leases amounting to $10.7 million at August 31, 2002. Total minimum lease payments have not been reduced by minimum sublease rentals of approximately $49.1 million on leases due in the future under non-cancelable subleases.

During fiscal 2002, the company entered into two sale-leaseback transactions. The properties were sold at net book value and resulted in proceeds of $302 million. The related leases are accounted for as operating leases.

Rental expense was as follows (In Millions):

	2002	2001	2000
Minimum rentals	$873.0	$730.1	$605.7
Contingent rentals	23.6	26.2	31.4
Less: Sublease rental income	(11.1)	(10.4)	(7.6)
	$885.5	$745.9	$629.5

Notes to Consolidated Financial Statements

(continued)

Income Taxes

The provision for income taxes consists of the following *(In Millions)*:

	2002	2001	2000
Current provision –			
Federal	$510.2	$417.1	$400.9
State	85.0	73.1	64.5
	595.2	490.2	465.4
Deferred provision –			
Federal	24.0	47.1	17.7
State	(1.1)	(.2)	3.3
	22.9	46.9	21.0
	$618.1	$537.1	$486.4

The deferred tax assets and liabilities included in the Consolidated Balance Sheets consist of the following *(In Millions)*:

	2002	2001
Deferred tax assets –		
Employee benefit plans	$106.2	$146.3
Accrued rent	56.5	52.7
Insurance	82.7	68.3
Inventory	35.6	28.1
Other	95.3	39.0
	376.3	334.4
Deferred tax liabilities –		
Accelerated depreciation	401.9	341.7
Inventory	98.9	92.9
Other	14.7	16.1
	515.5	450.7
Net deferred tax liabilities	$139.2	$116.3

Income taxes paid were $528.0 million, $432.1 million and $398.4 million during the fiscal years ended August 31, 2002, 2001 and 2000, respectively. The difference between the statutory income tax rate and the effective tax rate is principally due to state income tax provisions.

Short-Term Borrowings

The company obtained funds through the placement of commercial paper, as follows *(Dollars in Millions)*:

	2002	2001	2000
Average outstanding during the year	$250.2	$304.9	$14.0
Largest month-end balance	689.0	461.2	98.0
	(Nov)	(Nov)	(Nov)
Weighted-average interest rate	2.3%	5.2%	5.9%

At August 31, 2002, the company had a syndicated bank line of credit facility of $600 million to support the company's short-term commercial paper program. On July 2, 2002, the company deregistered the remaining $100 million of unissued authorized debt securities, previously filed with the Securities and Exchange Commission.

Contingencies

The company is involved in various legal proceedings incidental to the normal course of business. Company management is of the opinion, based upon the advice of General Counsel, that although the outcome of such litigation cannot be forecast with certainty, the final disposition should not have a material adverse effect on the company's consolidated financial position or results of operations.

Capital Stock

The company's common stock is subject to a Rights Agreement under which each share has attached to it a Right to purchase one one-hundredth of a share of a new series of Preferred Stock, at a price of $37.50 per Right. In the event an entity acquires or attempts to acquire 15% of the then outstanding shares, each Right, except those of an acquiring entity, would entitle the holder to purchase a number of shares of common stock pursuant to a formula contained in the Agreement. These non-voting Rights will expire on August 21, 2006, but may be redeemed at a price of $.0025 per Right at any time prior to a public announcement that the above event has occurred.

As of August 31, 2002, 102,738,392 shares of common stock were reserved for future stock issuances under the company's various employee benefit plans. Preferred stock of 10,249,083 shares has been reserved for issuance upon the exercise of Preferred Share Purchase Rights.

Stock Compensation Plans

The Walgreen Co. Executive Stock Option Plan provides to key employees the granting of options to purchase company common stock over a 10-year period, at a price not less than the fair market value on the date of the grant. Under this Plan, options may be granted until October 9, 2006, for an aggregate of 38,400,000 shares of common stock of the company. Compensation expense related to the plan was less than $1 million in fiscal 2002, $1.4 million in fiscal 2001 and less than $1 million in fiscal 2000. The options granted during fiscal 2002, 2001 and 2000 have a minimum three-year holding period.

The Walgreen Co. Stock Purchase/Option Plan (Share Walgreens) provides for the granting of options to purchase company common stock over a period of 10 years to eligible employees upon the purchase of company shares subject to certain restrictions. Under the terms of the Plan, the option price cannot be less than 85% of the fair market value at the date of grant. Compensation expense related to the Plan was $10.9 million in fiscal 2002, $9.6 million in fiscal 2001 and less than $1 million in fiscal 2000. Options may be granted under this Plan until September 30, 2012, for an aggregate of 42,000,000 shares of common stock of the company. The options granted during fiscal 2002, 2001 and 2000 have a two-year holding period.

The Walgreen Co. Restricted Performance Share Plan provides for the granting of up to 32,000,000 shares of common stock to certain key employees, subject to restrictions as to continuous employment except in the case of death, normal retirement or total and permanent disability. Restrictions generally lapse over a four-year period from the date of grant. Compensation expense is recognized in the year of grant. Compensation expense related to the Plan was $5.4 million in fiscal 2002, $3.6 million in fiscal 2001 and $5.1 million in fiscal 2000. The number of shares granted was 81,416 in 2002, 61,136 in 2001 and 84,746 in 2000.

Under the Walgreen Co. 1982 Employees Stock Purchase Plan, eligible employees may purchase company stock at 90% of the fair market value at the date of purchase. Employees may purchase shares through cash purchases, loans or payroll deductions up to certain limits. The aggregate number of shares for which all participants have the right to purchase under this Plan is 64,000,000.

On May 11, 2000, substantially all employees, in conjunction with opening the company's 3,000th store, were granted a stock option award to purchase from 75 to 500 shares, based on years of service. The stock option award, issued at fair market value on the date of the grant, represents a total of 14,859,275 shares of Walgreen Co. common stock. The options vest after three years and are exercisable up to 10 years after the grant date.

The Walgreen Co. Broad Based Employee Stock Option Plan provides for the granting of options to eligible employees to purchase common stock over a 10-year period, at a price not less than the fair market value on the date of the grant, in connection with the achievement of store opening milestones. Options may be granted for an aggregate of 15,000,000 shares of company common stock until all options have either been exercised or have expired. There is a holding period of three years for options granted under this plan.

Notes to Consolidated Financial Statements
(continued)

A summary of information relative to the company's stock option plans follows:

| | Options Outstanding | | Options Exercisable | |
	Shares	Weighted-Average Exercise Price	Shares	Weighted-Average Exercise Price
August 31, 1999	28,479,238	$ 7.89		
Granted	17,040,383	28.43		
Exercised	(5,055,842)	5.59		
Canceled/Forfeited	(1,086,118)	27.39		
August 31, 2000	39,377,661	$16.55	19,267,211	$6.45
Granted	5,354,388	36.68		
Exercised	(5,532,895)	5.75		
Canceled/Forfeited	(2,943,030)	28.02		
August 31, 2001	36,256,124	$20.24	14,824,227	$7.40
Granted	2,886,365	34.05		
Exercised	(3,525,955)	7.28		
Canceled/Forfeited	(1,315,499)	30.32		
August 31, 2002	34,301,035	$22.35	13,786,657	$9.71

Net options granted as a percentage of outstanding shares at fiscal year-end were 0.2% in fiscal 2002, 0.2% in fiscal 2001 and 1.6% in fiscal 2000.

The following table summarizes information concerning currently outstanding and exercisable options:

| | Options Outstanding | | | Options Exercisable | |
Range of Exercise Prices	Number Outstanding at 8/31/02	Weighted-Average Remaining Contractual Life	Weighted-Average Exercise Price	Number Exercisable at 8/31/02	Weighted-Average Exercise Price
$ 4 to 14	11,511,707	3.13 yrs.	$ 7.64	11,511,707	$ 7.64
15 to 30	14,869,487	7.31	26.65	2,212,570	19.81
31 to 46	7,919,841	8.48	35.67	62,380	34.17
$ 4 to 46	34,301,035	6.18 yrs.	$22.35	13,786,657	$ 9.71

The company applies Accounting Principles Board (APB) Opinion No. 25 and related interpretations in accounting for its plans. Accordingly, no compensation expense has been recognized based on the fair value of its grants under these plans. Had compensation costs been determined consistent with the method of SFAS No. 123 for options granted in fiscal 2002, 2001 and 2000, pro forma net earnings and net earnings per common share would have been as follows (In Millions, except per share data):

	2002	2001	2000
Net earnings			
As reported	$1,019.2	$885.6	$776.9
Pro forma	958.7	833.3	754.3
Net earnings per common share – Basic			
As reported	1.00	.87	.77
Pro forma	.94	.82	.75
Net earnings per common share – Diluted			
As reported	.99	.86	.76
Pro forma	.93	.81	.74

The weighted-average fair value and exercise price of options granted for fiscal 2002, 2001 and 2000 were as follows:

	2002	2001	2000
Granted at market price –			
Weighted-average fair value	$13.60	$14.28	$12.17
Weighted-average exercise price	34.40	32.88	28.44
Granted below market price –			
Weighted-average fair value	11.86	20.78	10.56
Weighted-average exercise price	33.21	38.78	24.12

The fair value of each option grant used in the pro forma net earnings and net earnings per share was determined using the Black-Scholes option pricing model with weighted-average assumptions used for grants in fiscal 2002, 2001 and 2000:

	2002	2001	2000
Risk-free interest rate	4.56%	6.16%	6.64%
Average life of option (years)	7	7	7
Volatility	27.58%	25.95%	25.86%
Dividend yield	.22%	.16%	.27%

Retirement Benefits

The principal retirement plan for employees is the Walgreen Profit-Sharing Retirement Trust to which both the company and the employees contribute. The company's contribution, which is determined annually at the discretion of the Board of Directors, has historically related to pre-tax income. The profit-sharing provision was $145.7 million in 2002, $126.6 million in 2001 and $112.4 million in 2000.

The company provides certain health and life insurance benefits for retired employees who meet eligibility requirements, including age and years of service. The costs of these benefits are accrued over the period earned. The company's postretirement health and life benefit plans currently are not funded.

Components of net periodic benefit costs (In Millions):

	2002	2001	2000
Service cost	$ 6.0	$ 4.8	$ 4.7
Interest cost	10.5	8.7	7.7
Amortization of actuarial loss	1.4	.3	—
Amortization of prior service cost	(0.4)	—	—
Total postretirement benefit cost	$17.5	$13.8	$12.4

Change in benefit obligation (In Millions):

	2002	2001
Benefit obligation at September 1	$142.7	$118.6
Service cost	6.0	4.8
Interest cost	10.5	8.7
Amendments	—	(7.1)
Actuarial loss	72.6	23.1
Benefit payments	(6.6)	(6.3)
Participants contributions	1.2	.9
Benefit obligation at August 31	$226.4	$142.7

Notes to Consolidated Financial Statements

(continued)

Change in plan assets *(In Millions)*:

	2002	2001
Plan assets at fair value at September 1	$ —	$ —
Plan participants contributions	1.2	.9
Employer contributions	5.4	5.4
Benefits paid	(6.6)	(6.3)
Plan assets at fair value at August 31	$ —	$ —

Funded status *(In Millions)*:

	2002	2001
Funded status	$(226.4)	$(142.7)
Unrecognized actuarial loss	99.1	27.9
Unrecognized prior service cost	(6.7)	(7.1)
Accrued benefit cost at August 31	$(134.0)	$(121.9)

The discount rate assumptions used to compute the postretirement benefit obligation at year-end were 7.0% for 2002 and 7.5% for 2001.

Future benefit costs were estimated assuming medical costs would increase at a 9% annual rate decreasing to 5.25% over the next seven years and then remaining at a 5.25% annual growth rate thereafter. A one percentage point change in the assumed medical cost trend rate would have the following effects *(In Millions)*:

	1% Increase	1% Decrease
Effect on service and interest cost	$ 4.0	$ (3.0)
Effect on postretirement obligation	49.0	(37.8)

Supplementary Financial Information

Included in the Consolidated Balance Sheets captions are the following assets and liabilities *(In Millions)*:

	2002	2001
Accounts receivable –		
Accounts receivable	$ 974.9	$819.2
Allowances for doubtful accounts	(20.1)	(20.9)
	$ 954.8	$798.3
Accrued expenses and other liabilities –		
Accrued salaries	$ 323.8	$272.7
Taxes other than income taxes	179.9	155.5
Profit sharing	143.3	122.1
Other	370.9	387.2
	$1,017.9	$937.5

Summary of Quarterly Results *(Unaudited)*
(Dollars in Millions, except per share data)

		Quarter Ended				
		November	February	May	August	Fiscal Year
Fiscal 2002	Net sales	$6,559.4	$7,488.5	$7,397.9	$7,235.3	$28,681.1
	Gross profit	1,697.9	2,033.9	1,937.2	1,936.0	7,605.0
	Net earnings	185.9	326.6	259.0	247.7	1,019.2
	Per Common Share – Basic	$ .18	$ .32	$ .25	$ .25	$ 1.00
	Diluted	.18	.32	.25	.24	.99
Fiscal 2001	Net sales	$5,614.2	$6,429.0	$6,296.2	$6,283.6	$24,623.0
	Gross profit	1,488.1	1,770.8	1,651.6	1,663.6	6,574.1
	Net earnings	158.4	296.9	213.4	216.9	885.6
	Per Common Share – Basic	$ .16	$ .29	$ .21	$ .21	$ .87
	Diluted	.15	.29	.21	.21	.86

Comments on Quarterly Results: In further explanation of and supplemental to the quarterly results, the 2002 fourth quarter LIFO adjustment was a credit of $9.9 million compared to a 2001 charge of $2.8 million. If the 2002 interim results were adjusted to reflect the actual inventory inflation rates and inventory levels as computed at August 31, 2002, earnings per share would have increased in the first quarter by $.01 and decreased in the fourth quarter by $.01. Similar adjustments in 2001 would have increased earnings per share in the second quarter by $.01 and decreased earnings per share in the fourth quarter by $.01.

The quarter ended November 30, 2001, includes the pre-tax income of $5.5 million (less than $.01 per share) from the partial payment of the brand name prescription drugs antitrust litigation settlement. The quarter ended August 31, 2002, includes the pre-tax income of $.7 million (less than $.01 per share). The quarter ended February 28, 2001, includes the pre-tax income of $22.1 million ($.01 per share) from the second partial payment.

Common Stock Prices
Below is the New York Stock Exchange high and low sales price for each quarter of fiscal 2002 and 2001.

		Quarter Ended				
		November	February	May	August	Fiscal Year
Fiscal 2002	High	$36.00	$40.70	$40.29	$39.49	$40.70
	Low	28.70	30.72	36.10	30.20	28.70
Fiscal 2001	High	$45.75	$45.00	$45.29	$42.40	$45.75
	Low	32.75	35.38	37.13	31.00	31.00

Reports of Independent Public Accountants

To the Board of Directors and Shareholders of Walgreen Co.:
We have audited the accompanying consolidated balance sheet of Walgreen Co. and subsidiaries (the "Company") as of August 31, 2002, and the related consolidated statements of earnings, shareholders' equity, and cash flows for the year then ended. These consolidated financial statements are the responsibility of the Company's management. Our responsibility is to express an opinion on these consolidated financial statements based on our audit. The consolidated financial statements of the Company for the years ended August 31, 2001 and 2000 were audited by other auditors who have ceased operations. Those auditors expressed in their report dated September 28, 2001 an unqualified opinion on those statements.

We conducted our audit in accordance with auditing standards generally accepted in the United States of America. Those standards require that we plan and perform the audit to obtain reasonable assurance about whether the consolidated financial statements are free of material misstatement. An audit includes examining, on a test basis, evidence supporting the amounts and disclosures in the financial statements. An audit also includes assessing the accounting principles used and significant estimates made by management, as well as evaluating the overall financial statement presentation. We believe that our audit provides a reasonable basis for our opinion.

In our opinion, such consolidated financial statements present fairly, in all material respects, the financial position of Walgreen Co. and subsidiaries as of August 31, 2002, and the results of their operations and their cash flows for the year then ended, in conformity with accounting principles generally accepted in the United States of America.

Deloitte & Touche LLP

Deloitte & Touche LLP
Chicago, Illinois
September 27, 2002

To the Board of Directors and Shareholders of Walgreen Co.:
We have audited the accompanying consolidated balance sheets of Walgreen Co. (an Illinois corporation) and Subsidiaries as of August 31, 2001 and 2000, and the related consolidated statements of earnings, shareholders' equity and cash flows for each of the three years in the period ended August 31, 2001. These financial statements are the responsibility of the company's management. Our responsibility is to express an opinion on these financial statements based on our audits.

We conducted our audits in accordance with auditing standards generally accepted in the United States. Those standards require that we plan and perform the audit to obtain reasonable assurance about whether the financial statements are free of material misstatement. An audit includes examining, on a test basis, evidence supporting the amounts and disclosures in the financial statements. An audit also includes assessing the accounting principles used and significant estimates made by management, as well as evaluating the overall financial statement presentation. We believe that our audits provide a reasonable basis for our opinion.

In our opinion, the financial statements referred to above present fairly, in all material respects, the financial position of Walgreen Co. and Subsidiaries as of August 31, 2001 and 2000 and the results of their operations and their cash flows for each of the three years in the period ended August 31, 2001 in conformity with accounting principles generally accepted in the United States.

Arthur Andersen LLP

Arthur Andersen LLP (1)
Chicago, Illinois
September 28, 2001

(1) This report is a copy of the previously issued report covering fiscal years 2001 and 2000. The predecessor auditor has not reissued their report.

Management's Report

The primary responsibility for the integrity and objectivity of the consolidated financial statements and related financial data rests with the management of Walgreen Co. The financial statements were prepared in conformity with accounting principles generally accepted in the United States of America appropriate in the circumstances and included amounts that were based on management's most prudent judgments and estimates relating to matters not concluded by fiscal year-end. Management believes that all material uncertainties have been either appropriately accounted for or disclosed. All other financial information included in this annual report is consistent with the financial statements.

The firm of Deloitte & Touche LLP, independent public accountants, was engaged to render a professional opinion on Walgreen Co.'s consolidated financial statements as of August 31, 2002. Their report contains an opinion based on their audit, which was made in accordance with auditing standards generally accepted in the United States of America and procedures, which they believed were sufficient to provide reasonable assurance that the consolidated financial statements, considered in their entirety, are not misleading and do not contain material errors. The financial statements for the years ended August 31, 2001 and 2000 were audited by other auditors whose report expressed an unqualified opinion on those statements.

Four outside members of the Board of Directors constitute the company's Audit Committee, which meets at least quarterly and is responsible for reviewing and monitoring the company's financial and accounting practices. Deloitte & Touche LLP and the company's General Auditor meet alone with the Audit Committee, which also meets with the company's management to discuss financial matters, auditing and internal accounting controls.

The company's systems are designed to provide an effective system of internal accounting controls to obtain reasonable assurance at reasonable cost that assets are safeguarded from material loss or unauthorized use and transactions are executed in accordance with management's authorization and properly recorded. To this end, management maintains an internal control environment which is shaped by established operating policies and procedures, an appropriate division of responsibility at all organizational levels, and a corporate ethics policy which is monitored annually. The company also has an Internal Control Evaluation Committee, composed primarily of senior management from the Accounting and Auditing Departments, which oversees the evaluation of internal controls on a company-wide basis. Management believes it has appropriately responded to the internal auditors' and independent public accountants' recommendations concerning the company's internal control system.

David W. Bernauer
President
and Chief Executive Officer

William M. Rudolphsen
Controller
and Chief Accounting Officer

Roger L. Polark
Senior Vice President
and Chief Financial Officer

Board of Directors
As of November 18, 2002

Directors

L. Daniel Jorndt*
Chairman
Elected 1990

David W. Bernauer*
President and
Chief Executive Officer
Elected 1999

William C. Foote
Chairman of the Board,
Chief Executive Officer
and President
USG Corporation
Elected 1997

James J. Howard
Chairman Emeritus
Xcel Energy, Inc.
Elected 1986

Alan G. McNally
Chairman
Harris Bankcorp Inc.
Elected 1999

Cordell Reed
Former Senior Vice President
Commonwealth Edison Co.
Elected 1994

David Y. Schwartz
Former Partner
Arthur Andersen LLP
Elected 2000

John B. Schwemm
Former Chairman and
Chief Executive Officer
R.R. Donnelley & Sons Co.
Elected 1985

Marilou M. von Ferstel
Former Executive Vice President
and General Manager
Ogilvy Adams & Rinehart
Elected 1987

Charles R. Walgreen III
Chairman Emeritus
Elected 1963

* L. Daniel Jorndt will retire in January
2003. David W. Bernauer will become
chairman and chief executive officer.
Jeffrey A. Rein will become president and
chief operating officer. George J. Riedl will
become senior vice president–Marketing.

Committees

Audit Committee
John B. Schwemm,
Chairman
William C. Foote
David Y. Schwartz
Marilou M. von Ferstel

Compensation Committee
Cordell Reed,
Chairman
James J. Howard
John B. Schwemm

Finance Committee
David Y. Schwartz,
Chairman
David W. Bernauer
L. Daniel Jorndt
Alan G. McNally
Cordell Reed
Charles R. Walgreen III

**Nominating and
Governance Committee**
William C. Foote,
Chairman
James J. Howard
Alan G. McNally
John B. Schwemm
Marilou M. von Ferstel

Officers
As of November 18, 2002

Corporate

Chairman
L. Daniel Jorndt*

President
David W. Bernauer*
Chief Executive Officer

Executive Vice Presidents
Jerome B. Karlin
Store Operations
Jeffrey A. Rein*
Marketing

Senior Vice Presidents
R. Bruce Bryant
Western Store Operations
George C. Eilers
Eastern Store Operations
J. Randolph Lewis
Distribution & Logistics
Julian A. Oettinger
General Counsel and
Corporate Secretary
Roger L. Polark
Chief Financial Officer
William A. Shiel
Facilities Development
Trent E. Taylor
Chief Information Officer
Mark A. Wagner
Central Store Operations

Vice Presidents
John W. Gleeson
Corporate Strategy and Treasurer
Dana I. Green
Human Resources
Dennis R. O'Dell
Health Services
Gregory D. Wasson
President
Walgreens Health Initiatives

Operational and Divisional

Store Operations Vice Presidents
James F. Cnota
Kermit R. Crawford
George C. Eilers Jr.
Debra M. Ferguson
John J. Foley
David L. Gloudemans
John W. Grant
Frank C. Grilli
William M. Handal
Patrick E. Hanifen
Barry L. Markl
Richard Robinson
Michael D. Tovian
Kevin P. Walgreen
Christine D. Whelan
Bruce C. Zarkowsky
Barry W. Zins

Divisional Vice Presidents
Thomas L. Bergseth
Facilities Planning and Design
Donald A. Churchill
Construction and Facilities
Thomas J. Connolly
Real Estate
Robert M. Kral
Operations/Merchandising
Development
Laurie L. Meyer
Corporate Communications
Allan M. Resnick
Law
George J. Riedl*
Purchasing
Robert E. Rogan
Distribution Centers
Jerry A. Rubin
Real Estate
William M. Rudolphsen
Controller
James M. Schultz
Performance Development
Craig M. Sinclair
Advertising
Patrick W. Tupa
Real Estate
Terry R. Watkins
Distribution Centers
Kenneth R. Weigand
Employee Relations
Denise K. Wong
Supply Chain Systems
Chester G. Young
General Auditor
Robert G. Zimmerman
Vice President – Administration
Walgreens Health Initiatives

7

Chapter 7 focuses on the principles of designing accounting information systems and on the preparation and the role and types of special-purpose journals.

Accounting Information Systems

LEARNING OBJECTIVES

LO1 Identify the principles of designing accounting information systems.

LO2 Describe the use and structure of spreadsheet software and general ledger systems in computerized accounting systems.

LO3 Explain how accountants and businesses use the Internet.

LO4 Describe the role of special-purpose journals and their relationship to controlling accounts and subsidiary ledgers.

LO5 Construct and use a sales journal, purchases journal, cash receipts journal, and cash payments journal.

DECISION POINT

A USER'S FOCUS

RR Donnelley <www.rrdonnelley.com> With sales of more then $6 billion per year, RR Donnelley is one of the largest printing firms in the world. Most of the catalogues and magazines you receive in the mail are printed in Donnelley's plants.

Donnelley recently decided it needed a new accounting information system. Like all companies, it wanted a system that would provide more than just financial statements—one that would enable it to be more competitive and more responsive to customers' needs. The system also had to be flexible enough to deal with Donnelley's expanding business, and its benefits had to outweigh its costs. In addition, it had to be compatible with Donnelley's operations so that it could be put in place without causing schedules to break down. Such problems are not uncommon; for example, when Hershey Foods <www.hersheys.com>, a major supplier of chocolate candy, implemented its new software system during the peak Halloween season, key retailers failed to receive shipments. If Donnelley did not print and ship magazines and catalogues on time, it would have highly dissatisfied customers. How did Donnelley implement an accounting information system that met all these needs?

Donnelley's managers went to a Dutch software firm that had experience in developing programs for the printing industry. They tested the Dutch firm's software and formed a dedicated team of 55 Donnelley personnel to work with the software company. The result was a Web-based system that manages printing presses and binding lines and that allows customers

Why did RR Donnelley choose a software vendor with expertise in the printing industry to design its Web-based accounting information system?

to enter their own orders, check the status of jobs remotely, and do away with paper-order processing. By selecting a software vendor with large-scale printing expertise, Donnelley's managers obtained a system that fulfilled the company's needs. Because the system did not need extensive customization, it not only saved Donnelley money, but also facilitated implementation.[1]

ACCOUNTING INFORMATION SYSTEMS: PRINCIPLES OF DESIGN

LO1   Identify the principles of designing accounting information systems.

RELATED TEXT ASSIGNMENTS
Q: 1, 2
SE: 1
SD: 1
FRA: 1, 2, 3

www.sap.com
www.peoplesoft.com
www.oracle.com

⬢ **STOP AND THINK!**

Certainly, it is important to make right decisions and avoid wrong decisions, but what is the cost of making no decisions?

The cost can be high. For example, assume a product suddenly becomes so popular that it will soon be sold out. If the retailer's accounting information system is not set up to provide this information to the sales manager quickly, the sales manager's failure to make the decision to reorder could cause the company to lose valuable sales. ∎

KEY POINT: The cost of making a wrong decision is an intangible cost that can easily be overlooked in designing an accounting system. It is the systems analyst's job to strike the optimal balance between expected benefits and costs.

KEY POINT: An accounting information system should help protect the company's assets and provide reliable data.

Accounting information systems summarize financial data about a business and organize the data into useful forms. Accountants communicate the results to management. The means by which an accounting system accomplishes these objectives is called **data processing**. Management uses the resulting information to make a variety of business decisions.

As businesses have grown larger and more complex, the role of accounting information systems has grown. Today, many organizations use comprehensive, computerized information systems that integrate financial and nonfinancial information about customers, operations, and suppliers in a single database. Though integrated with a wide variety of other information, accounting information serves as the base for these integrated information systems, which are known as **enterprise resource planning (ERP) systems**. Three companies that specialize in ERP software are the German-based company SAP and the U.S.-based companies PeopleSoft and Oracle.

ERP systems are most often set up, monitored, and operated by accountants. The primary purpose of these systems is to integrate all functions of a company to provide timely information to decision makers throughout the organization. For this reason, accountants must understand all phases of their company's operations as well as the latest developments in systems design and technology. Additionally, while a computerized accounting system may automate many or all bookkeeping functions, it does not eliminate the need to understand the accounting process. In fact, it is impossible to use any accounting information system, manual or computerized, without a basic knowledge of accounting.

The design of an accounting information system involves four general principles: (1) the cost-benefit principle, (2) the control principle, (3) the compatibility principle, and (4) the flexibility principle.

COST-BENEFIT PRINCIPLE

The most important systems principle, the **cost-benefit principle**, holds that the benefits derived from an accounting information system must be equal to or greater than the system's cost. In addition to performing certain routine tasks—preparing payroll and tax reports and financial statements, and maintaining internal control—the accounting system may be called upon to provide other information that management wants or needs. The benefits from that information must be weighed against both the tangible and the intangible costs of gathering it. In the Decision Point at the beginning of this chapter, we saw how Donnelley's new system significantly improved customer service while reducing costs.

Among the tangible costs are those for personnel, forms, and equipment. One of the intangible costs is the cost of wrong decisions stemming from the lack of good information. For instance, wrong decisions can lead to loss of sales, production stoppages, or inventory losses. Some companies have spent thousands of dollars on computerized systems that do not offer enough benefits. On the other hand, some have failed to realize the important benefits that could be gained from investing in more advanced systems. It is the job of the accountant and the systems designer or analyst to weigh the costs and benefits.

CONTROL PRINCIPLE

The **control principle** requires that an accounting information system provide all the features of internal control needed to protect a firm's assets and to ensure that data are reliable. For example, before expenditures are made, a responsible member of management should approve them.

FOCUS ON BUSINESS PRACTICE

How Much Is a Used Computerized Accounting System Worth?

Apparently, a second-hand computerized accounting system has value in the marketplace, if it's a good one. When it declared bankruptcy, the old-line retailer Montgomery Ward had many problems, but accounting, inventory, and sales software wasn't one of them. When the company auctioned off its custom-designed software system, bids started at $100 million.[2]

COMPATIBILITY PRINCIPLE

The **compatibility principle** holds that the design of an accounting information system must be in harmony with the organizational and human factors of the business. Donnelley, as explained in the Decision Point, chose a software supplier with experience in the printing industry to ensure the compatibility of its new system.

The organizational factors of business have to do with the nature of a company's business and the formal roles its units play in meeting business objectives. For example, a company can organize its marketing efforts by region or by product. If a company is organized by region, its accounting information system should report revenues and expenses by region. If a company is organized by product, its system should report revenues and expenses first by product and then by region.

The human factors of business have to do with the people within the organization and their abilities, behaviors, and personalities. The interest, support, and competence of a company's employees are very important to the success or failure of systems design. In changing systems or installing new ones, the accountant must deal with the people who are carrying out or supervising existing procedures. Such people must understand, accept, and, in many cases, be trained in the new procedures. The new system cannot succeed unless the system and the people in the organization are compatible.

KEY POINT: A systems analyst must carefully consider a business's activities, objectives, and performance measures, as well as the behavioral characteristics of its employees.

KEY POINT: To work effectively with a computerized accounting system, you must understand how a manual accounting system works. A computerized system functions exactly like a manual system, except that it processes information at lightning speed.

FLEXIBILITY PRINCIPLE

The **flexibility principle** holds that an accounting information system must be flexible enough to allow for growth in the volume of transactions and for organizational changes. Businesses do not stay the same. They grow, they offer new products, they add new branch offices, they sell existing divisions, or they make other changes that require adjustments in the accounting system. A carefully designed accounting system allows a business to grow and change without having to make major alterations in the system. For example, the chart of accounts should be designed to accommodate the addition of new asset, liability, owner's equity, revenue, and expense accounts.

 Check out ACE for a Review Quiz at http://accounting.college.hmco.com/students.

COMPUTERIZED ACCOUNTING SYSTEMS

LO2 Describe the use and structure of spreadsheet software and general ledger systems in computerized accounting systems.

RELATED TEXT ASSIGNMENTS
Q: 3, 4, 5, 6
SE: 2
SD: 1, 2, 3

Businesses use computerized systems for accounting and many other purposes. Large, multinational companies have vast computer resources and use very powerful computers that are linked together to provide communication and data transfer around the world. However, even in these large companies and in most small companies, the microcomputer, or PC, is a critical element in the processing of information. It has become even more critical as companies have expanded their use of the Internet to communicate and transact business directly with vendors, suppliers, and clients. Two kinds of microcomputer programs on which accountants rely heavily are spreadsheet software and general ledger systems.

SPREADSHEET SOFTWARE

Spreadsheet software is used to analyze data. A **spreadsheet** is a computerized grid of columns and rows into which the user places data or formulas related to

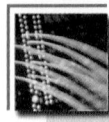

FOCUS ON BUSINESS TECHNOLOGY

Networking: How to Get It Done

Many businesses achieve the computing power of mainframes (large computers) by linking many microcomputers in a network. In a daisy chain network, the microcomputers are linked in a type of circle, or daisy chain. With this network, a person may have to go through several other microcomputers to reach a file or communicate with a person at another computer. In a home base, or star, network, all microcomputers are linked to a central switching point, or home base. A separate microcomputer called a *server* contains all the common data files, such as the accounting records. The server is also connected to the home base. All users can access accounting records and other data files by going through the home base. This type of network is faster and more efficient than the daisy chain network.

KEY POINT: Five kinds of transactions—credit sales, credit purchases, cash receipts, cash payments, and miscellaneous—are common in the typical business. In a manual system, a separate journal should be used for each type of transaction, and a general journal should be used for all other transactions. In a computerized system, a separate function is chosen for each type.

🔴 **STOP AND THINK!**

Why is knowledge of accounting necessary when a computerized general ledger system will do the steps in the accounting cycle automatically?

Knowledge of accounting is necessary for two reasons. First, transactions must be entered in the proper way and in the proper accounts. Second, an understanding of the financial statements that the system produces is a necessary component in making business decisions. ■

financial planning, cost estimating, and other accounting tasks. Windows® Excel and Lotus are popular commercial spreadsheet programs used for financial analysis and other purposes.

GENERAL LEDGER SYSTEMS

General ledger systems is the terminology commonly used to identify the group of integrated software programs that accountants use to perform major functions, such as accounting for sales and accounts receivable, purchases and accounts payable, cash receipts and disbursements, and payroll.

Today, most general ledger systems are written using the Windows® operating system, which has a **graphical user interface (GUI)**. A graphical user interface employs symbols, called **icons**, to represent operations. Examples of icons include a file folder, eraser, hourglass, and magnifying glass. The keyboard can be used in the traditional way, or a *mouse* or *trackball* may be used. When a program uses Windows as its graphical user interface, the program is termed *Windows-compatible*. The visual format and the ability to use a mouse or trackball make Windows-compatible software easy to use. Figure 1 shows how Peachtree Complete Accounting™ for Windows (PCW) uses a combination of text and icons. It is an example of what a graphical user interface looks like on your computer.

One of the benefits of Windows-compatible programs is that they use standardized terms and operations. Once you have mastered one Windows-compatible program, such as Peachtree Complete Accounting, you will be able to use other Windows-compatible applications.

Three software programs available for this book are (1) General Ledger Software, (2) Peachtree Complete Accounting for Windows, and (3) Quickbooks®. General Ledger Software is used to work end-of-chapter problems. It is designed for educational use and cannot be purchased commercially. Peachtree Complete and Quickbooks can be purchased through retail stores. They, too, can be used with selected end-of-chapter problems.

STRUCTURE OF GENERAL LEDGER SYSTEMS

Most general ledger systems are organized so that each module performs a major task of the accounting information system. Figure 2 shows a typical configuration of general ledger systems. Note that there is a software module for each major accounting function: sales/accounts receivable, purchases/accounts payable, cash receipts, cash disbursements, payroll, and general journal. When these features interact with one another, the software is called an *integrated program*.

Source documents, or written evidence, should support each transaction entered into the accounting system. Source documents verify that a transaction occurred and provide the details of the transaction. For example, a customer's invoice should support each sale on account, and a vendor's invoice should support each purchase. Even though the transactions are recorded in a computer file

FIGURE 1
Graphical User Interface

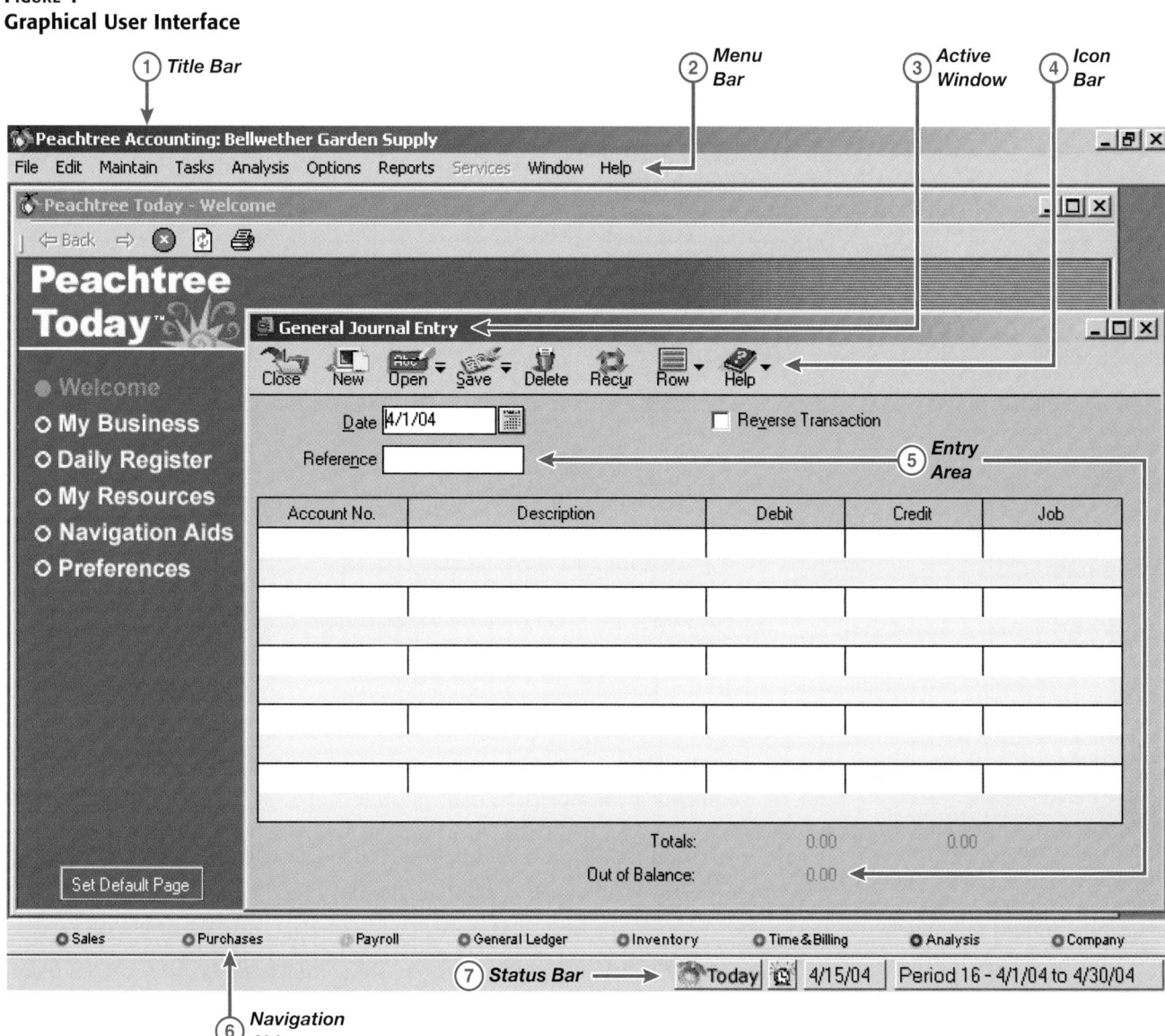

1. **Title Bar:** The title bar at the top of the screen identifies the program and the company under consideration.

2. **Menu Bar:** When you click on one of the menu bar headings, a submenu of options opens. You select an option with a mouse or by holding down the <Alt> key and pressing the letter underlined in the desired option.

3. **Active Window:** This bar shows what window is open, or "active." Here, the "General Journal Entry" window is active.

4. **Icon Bar:** The icon bar shows visual images that pertain to the window. Some icons are common to all windows, whereas others are specific to a particular window. You click on an icon to perform the associated function.

5. **Entry Area:** This part of the screen is where you enter information for the journal entry.

6. **Navigation Aid:** The navigation aid offers a graphical supplement to the menu bar. The major functions of the program are represented as icons or pictures that show you how tasks flow through the system.

7. **Status Bar:** The gray bar (screen colors may vary) at the bottom of the window shows the current date and the current accounting period.

FIGURE 2
Computerized Accounting System Using a General Ledger System

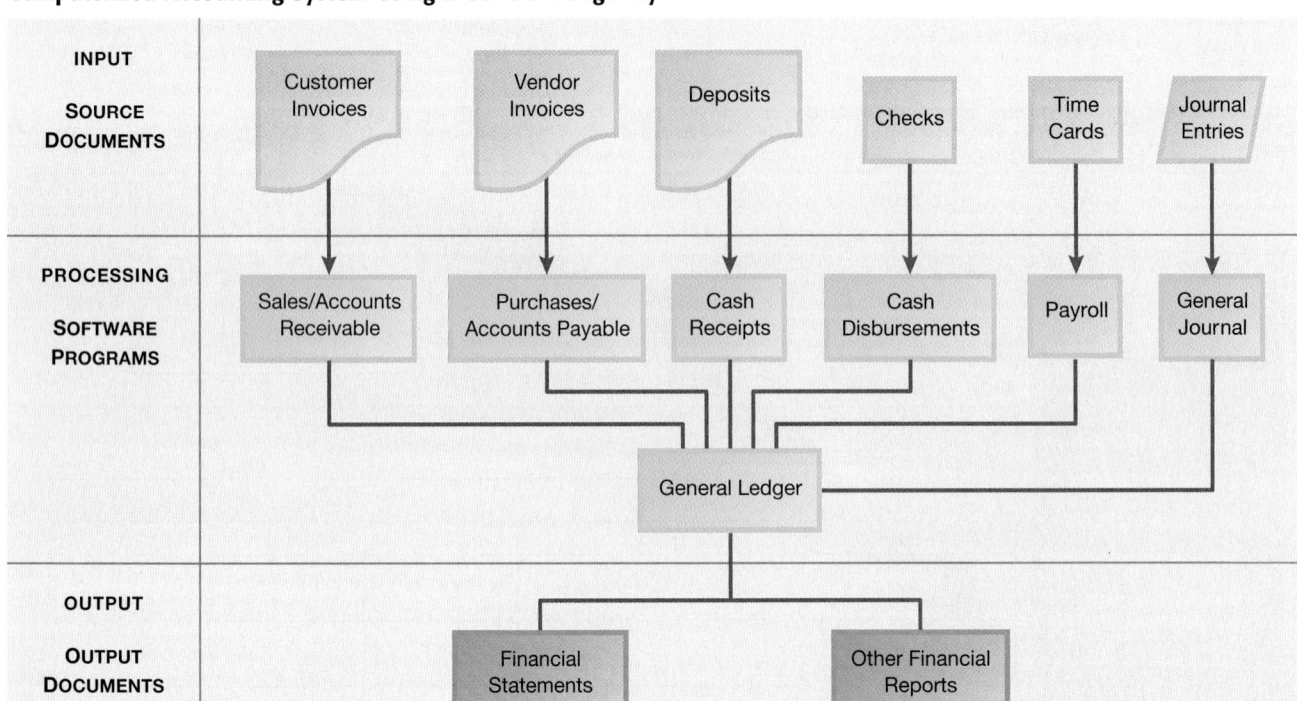

KEY POINT: At least one source document should support each business transaction entered in the records. The accounting system should provide easy reference to the source documents to facilitate subsequent examination (e.g., by an auditor). For instance, canceled checks should be filed by check number.

(on floppy disks or hard disks), the original documents should be stored so that they can be examined at a later date if a question arises about the accuracy of the accounting records.

After transactions are processed in a general ledger system, there is a procedure for posting them, updating the ledgers, and preparing the trial balance. Finally, the financial statements and other accounting reports are printed.

Peachtree Complete Accounting for Windows allows either *batch* posting or *real-time* posting. In a batch posting system, source documents are recorded in the appropriate journal and saved; posting is done at the end of the day, week, or month. In a real-time posting system, documents are posted as they are recorded in the journal. The basic goal of a general ledger system is to make accounting tasks less time-consuming and more accurate and dependable. However, it is important to understand just what the computer is accomplishing. Knowledge of the underlying accounting process helps ensure that the accounting records are accurate and that the assets of the business are protected.

 Check out ACE for a Review Quiz at http://accounting.college.hmco.com/students.

ACCOUNTANTS, BUSINESSES, AND THE INTERNET

LO3 Explain how accountants and businesses use the Internet.

RELATED TEXT ASSIGNMENTS
Q: 7
SE: 3
SD: 5
FRA: 1

The Internet is the world's largest computer network. The Internet allows any computer on the network to communicate with any other computer on the network. Computer access to the Internet is generally gained via a modem connected to a phone line or cable.

Most people are well aware of the Internet's ability to provide access to the World Wide Web (WWW), electronic mail (email), and electronic bulletin boards. Recent research shows that even businesses with fewer than ten employees are users of the Internet. More than 50 percent of these small businesses have Internet

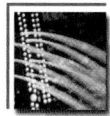

FOCUS ON BUSINESS TECHNOLOGY

The Top Ten Technological Challenges Businesses Face

Every year, the American Institute of Certified Public Accountants publishes a list of the ten most important technological challenges facing businesses. In recent years, the list has emphasized the growing role of the Internet in business activities. In 2003, the list identified the following items as the top ten technological priorities:[3]

1. Information Security
2. Business Information Management
3. Application Integration
4. Web Services
5. Disaster Recovery Planning
6. Wireless Technologies
7. Intrusion Detection
8. Remote Connectivity
9. Customer Relationship Management
10. Privacy

access, and more than 20 percent have their own web sites.[4] Among the ways in which accountants and businesses of all sizes use the Internet are the following:

www.sec.gov/edgar.shtml

● **STOP AND THINK!**
Why do you think small businesses may be reluctant to establish their own web sites?
There are several possible reasons. A web site is costly to set up and maintain; management may lack knowledge or expertise about web sites and may fail to see their benefits; or the business may be of a type that would not benefit from the principal features of a web site. ■

- **Financial reporting.** Companies today commonly make their financial statements available on the Internet. Large companies are required to file their financial information electronically with the SEC, and it is available on Edgar, the SEC's online warehouse of financial information. Additionally, most companies publish electronic versions of their annual reports on their web sites.

- **XBRL. Extensible Business Reporting Language (XBRL)** is a new computer language developed by accountants and others for the express purpose of identifying and communicating financial information. It allows businesses to post information on the Web in a uniform way so that users can access the information, summarize it, perform computations, and format the output in any manner they wish.

- **Ecommerce. Electronic commerce (ecommerce)** is the conduct of business transactions on computer networks, including the Internet. Most people are familiar with the buying and selling of products from business to consumers (B to C) on the Internet, but the Internet is used far more widely in business-to-business (B to B) and business to government (B to G) transactions. These transactions include buying and selling products and services, collecting receivables, and paying bills.

- **EDI.** Ecommerce is often facilitated through private links, referred to as **Electronic Data Interchange (EDI).** For example, companies in many industries, such as retail chemicals, oil, and automobile parts, have formed private networks to use EDI for buying and selling goods and services.

- **Supply-chain management. Supply-chain management** is a system that uses the Internet to track the supplies and materials a manufacturer will need on a day-to-day—sometimes hour-to-hour—basis. Such a system may also link the manufacturer to its customers.

FOCUS ON BUSINESS PRACTICE

B to B and EDI: How Much Can They Save?

An officer of Target Corporation <www.target.com>, the large discount retailer, is quoted as saying, B to B is "real, and it's big, and it's growing. In five years all of our purchasing activity will be done over the Internet." Most executives agree with this statement. Sales and purchases that in the past would have been made by telephone or fax are now transacted by electronic data interchange (EDI). For example, Target participates in a worldwide Retail Exchange, an electronic marketplace formed by over 50 large retailers, including J.C. Penney <www.jcpenney.com> and Safeway Inc. <www.safeway.com>. The purpose of the Retail Exchange is to provide a market for online sales and purchases. When Target wants to purchase something—for instance, fax paper, cleaning products, or jeans—it posts its needs, and other companies bid on the business. Retailers participating in the exchange have seen a 12 to 15 percent reduction in purchasing costs. Even greater reductions are likely because at present only about 50 percent of purchases are made this way.[5]

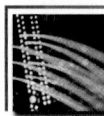

FOCUS ON BUSINESS TECHNOLOGY

E2K: How Much Time Can It Save?

E2K, or event-to-knowledge, is the concept of the time it takes to turn the results of a transaction, such as a sale or a purchase, into useful information for managers. It involves the application of the just-in-time management philosophy to accounting. The goal of just-in-time accounting (JITA) is to reduce the time it takes to produce and distribute financial reports from days or weeks to a single business day so that

managers receive them when they need them, or "just in time." Cisco Systems <www.cisco.com>, the large software company, believes it has achieved a breakthrough with a "virtual close" program that gives managers the financial results of one day by 2 P.M. the next day. A reduction in E2K time means that managers have more time to consider the information and can thus make better decisions.[6]

- **E2K. Event-to-knowledge (E2K) management** means that the Internet is used to get information to users within and outside a company in the quickest possible way after an event like a sale or a purchase has occurred.

- **Document-less transactions.** One of the limitations on the growth of electronic commerce is that although the transactions are conducted electronically, source documents, such as those used in general ledger systems, are still often needed to back up the transactions. For example, a purchase is made on the Internet, but a confirmation is emailed, faxed, or mailed to provide documentation of the transaction. Gradually, methods that eliminate the need for source documents are being developed.

 Check out ACE for a Review Quiz at http://accounting.college.hmco.com/students.

ROLE OF SPECIAL-PURPOSE JOURNALS IN AN ACCOUNTING INFORMATION SYSTEM

LO4 Describe the role of special-purpose journals and their relationship to controlling accounts and subsidiary ledgers.

RELATED TEXT ASSIGNMENTS
Q: 8, 9, 12
SE: 4, 6, 8, 9, 10
E: 1, 2, 5, 6, 7, 8
P: 1, 3, 4, 5, 6, 8
SD: 1, 4, 6

The method of accounting described in prior chapters, and presented in Figure 3, is a form of **manual data processing**. It has been a useful way to present basic accounting theory and practice in small businesses. Data are fed into the system manually by entering each transaction from a source document into the general journal. Then each debit and credit is posted to the correct ledger account. A work sheet is used as a tool to prepare the financial statements that are distributed to users. This system, although useful for explaining the basic concepts of accounting, is actually used in only the smallest of companies.

Companies involved in more transactions, perhaps hundreds or thousands every week or every day, must have a more efficient and economical way of recording transactions in the journal and posting entries to the ledger. The easiest approach is to group typical transactions into common categories and use an input device called a **special-purpose journal** for each category. Special-purpose journals promote efficiency, economy, and control. Although manual special-purpose journals are used by

FOCUS ON BUSINESS TECHNOLOGY

Why Are Customer Numbers Necessary?

In manual accounting systems, subsidiary ledgers are often maintained in alphabetical order because that is a convenient way for people to organize information. With computers, however, numbers are much faster and easier to process than letters. For this reason, numbers are essential for all types of computer data processing. There are customer numbers, order

numbers, social security numbers, product numbers, credit card numbers, and many more. When numbers are used, every account can be given a unique identification number. Then the potential confusion of having more than one Janet Smith or Juan Sanchez as customers can be avoided because each customer is assigned a different number.

FIGURE 3
Steps and Devices in a Manual Accounting System

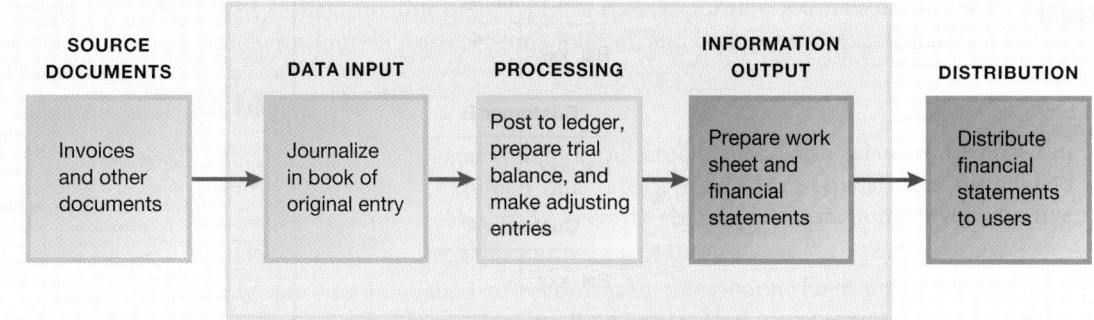

companies that have not yet computerized their systems, the concepts that underlie these journals also underlie the programs that drive computerized general ledger
accounting systems.

Most business transactions—90 to 95 percent—fall into one of four categories.
Each kind of transaction can be recorded in a special-purpose journal.

KEY POINT: Although a
transaction could fall outside
the four categories listed to the
right, a transaction cannot fall
into more than one category.

Transaction	Special-Purpose Journal	Posting Abbreviation
Sale of merchandise on credit	Sales journal	S
Purchase on credit	Purchases journal	P
Receipt of cash	Cash receipts journal	CR
Disbursement of cash	Cash payments journal	CP

Notice that these special-purpose journals correspond to the accounting functions
shown in the computerized system in Figure 2, except for payroll.

The general journal is used to record transactions that do not fall into any of
these special categories. For example, purchase returns, sales returns, and adjusting
and closing entries are recorded in the general journal. (When transactions are
posted from the general journal to the ledger accounts, the posting abbreviation
used is **J**.)

Using special-purpose journals greatly reduces the work involved in entering and
posting transactions in the general ledger. For example, in most cases, instead of posting every debit and credit for each transaction, only the total amounts of the transactions are posted. In addition, labor can be divided by assigning each journal to a
different employee. This division of labor is important in establishing good internal
control.

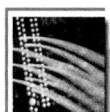

FOCUS ON BUSINESS TECHNOLOGY

How Can Accounting Information Systems Help Satisfy Customers?

Accounting information systems are obviously important for
financial reporting, but they are increasingly becoming a
means of providing good customer service as well. For
instance, Walgreens, the world's largest prescription pharmacy
company, has established direct communications with the
insurance companies, employers, and government agencies
that pay the bills of Walgreens' customers. From an accounting perspective, such links enhance Walgreens' profitability by
eliminating rejected prescriptions, facilitating billing, and
speeding collections. From the customers' point of view,
instant communication with payers means faster service and
immediate confirmation of payments—no forms, no paperwork, and no-hassle service.[7]

EXHIBIT 2
Relationship of Sales Journal, General Ledger, and Accounts Receivable Subsidiary Ledger and the Posting Procedure

KEY POINT: Accounts in the subsidiary ledger are maintained in alphabetical order. If account numbers are used to identify customers, the accounts would be listed in account number order.

KEY POINT: Subsidiary accounts are posted daily to prevent customers from exceeding their credit limits and to have up-to-date balances for customers wishing to pay their accounts.

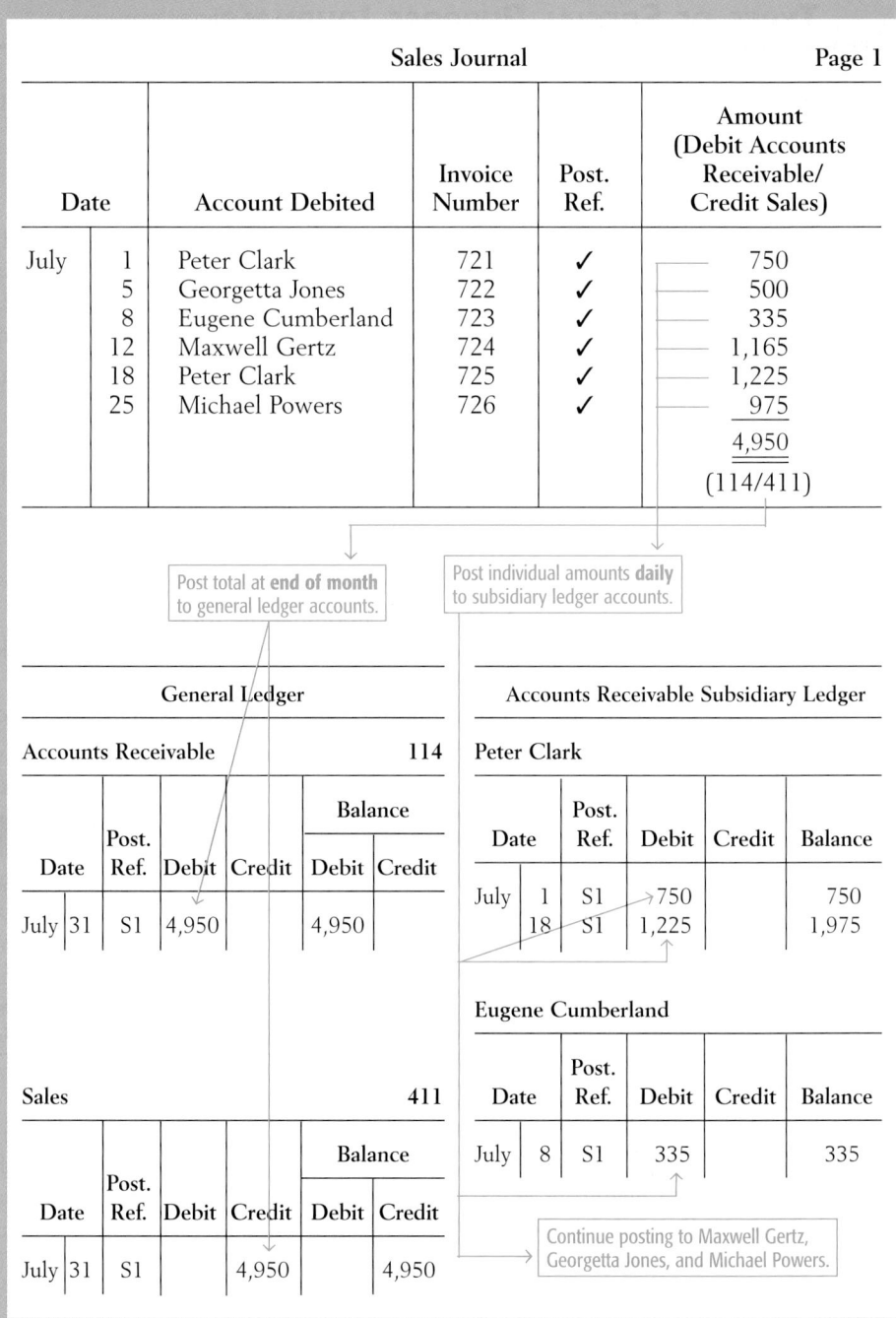

Exhibit 2 illustrates the procedure for using a sales journal:

1. Enter each sales invoice in the sales journal on a single line. Record the date, the customer's name, the invoice number, and the amount. No column is needed for the terms if the terms on all sales are the same.

2. At the end of each day, post each individual sale to the customer's account in the accounts receivable subsidiary ledger. As each sale is posted, place a checkmark (or customer account number, if used) in the Post. Ref. (posting reference) column of the sales journal to indicate that it has been posted. In the Post. Ref. column of each customer's account, place an *S* and the sales journal page number (*S1* means Sales Journal—Page 1) to indicate the source of the entry.

EXHIBIT 3
Schedule of Accounts Receivable

Mitchell's Used Car Sales
Schedule of Accounts Receivable
July 31, 20xx

Peter Clark	$1,975
Eugene Cumberland	335
Maxwell Gertz	1,165
Georgetta Jones	500
Michael Powers	975
Total Accounts Receivable	$4,950

KEY POINT: In theory, the sum of the account balances from the subsidiary accounts must equal the balance in the related general ledger controlling account. In practice, however, the equality is verified only at the end of the month, when the general ledger is posted.

KEY POINT: Columns can be added to a special-purpose journal for accounts that are commonly used.

3. At the end of the month, sum the Amount column in the sales journal to determine the total credit sales, and post the total to the general ledger accounts (debit Accounts Receivable and credit Sales). Place the numbers of the accounts debited and credited beneath the total in the sales journal to indicate that this step has been completed. In the general ledger, indicate the source of the entry in the Post. Ref. column of each account.

4. Verify the accuracy of the posting by adding the account balances of the accounts receivable subsidiary ledger and comparing the total with the balance of the Accounts Receivable controlling account in the general ledger. You can do this by listing the accounts in a schedule of accounts receivable, like the one in Exhibit 3, in the order in which the accounts are maintained. This step is performed after posting collections on account in the cash receipts journal.

Many cities and states require retailers to collect a sales tax from their customers and periodically remit the total collected to the city or state. In this case, an additional column is needed in the sales journal to record the credit to Sales Taxes Payable on credit sales. The form of the entry is shown in Exhibit 4. The procedure for posting to the ledger is exactly the same as described above, except that the total of the Sales Taxes Payable column must be posted as a credit to the Sales Taxes Payable account at the end of the month.

PURCHASES JOURNAL

The **purchases journal** is used to record purchases on credit. It can take the form of either a single-column journal or a multicolumn journal. In the single-column

EXHIBIT 4
Section of a Sales Journal with a Column for Sales Taxes

				Sales Journal		Page 2
				Debit	Credits	
Date	Account Debited	Invoice Number	Post. Ref.	Accounts Receivable	Sales Taxes Payable	Sales
Aug. 1	Ralph P. Hake	727	✓	206	6	200

EXHIBIT 5
Relationship of Single-Column Purchases Journal to the General Ledger and the Accounts Payable Subsidiary Ledger

ENRICHMENT NOTE: The single-column purchases journal works exactly the same way as a sales journal, except that different ledger accounts are used.

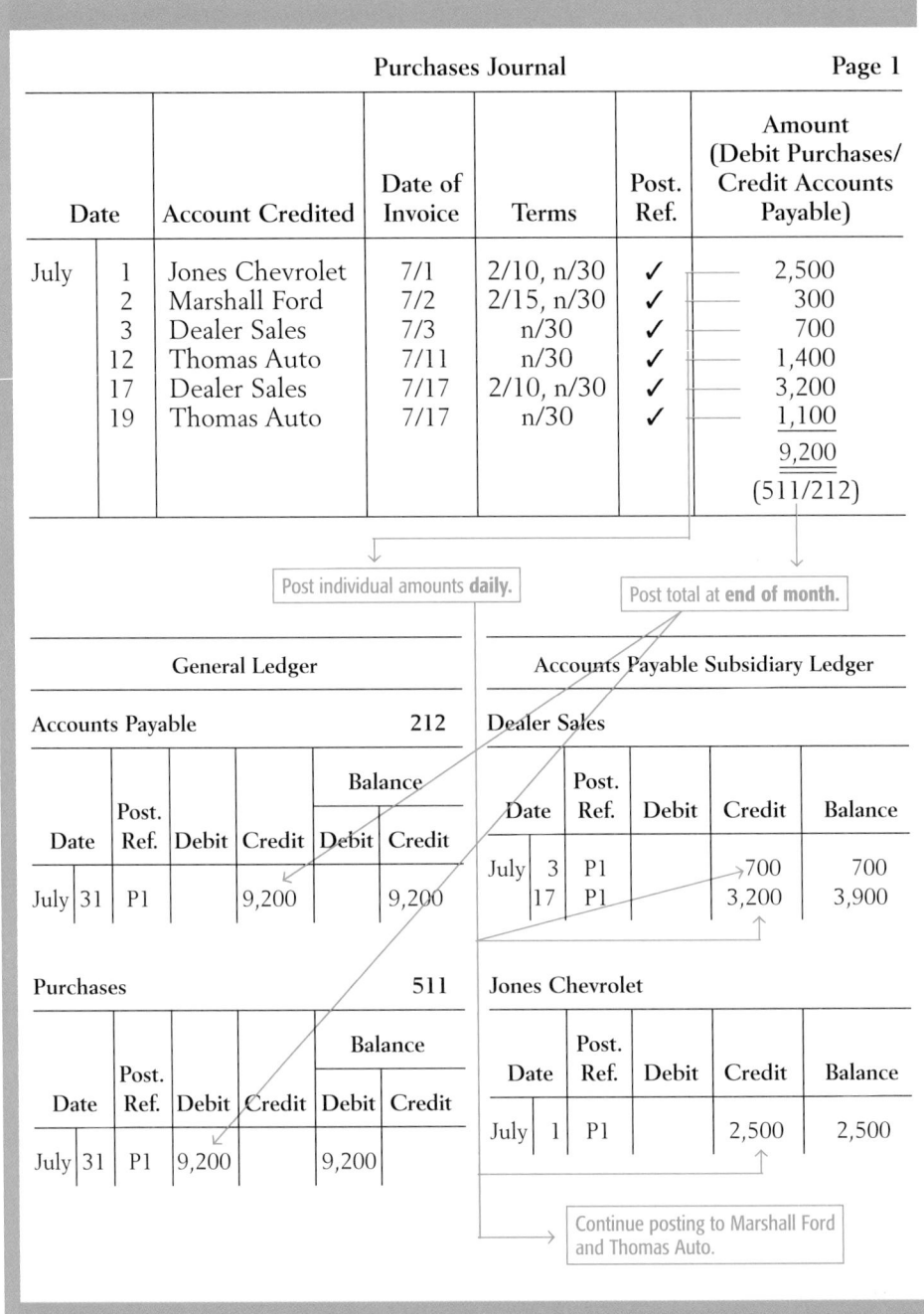

ENRICHMENT NOTE: It is easy to forget that a cash purchase is entered into the cash payments journal, not into the purchases journal.

journal shown in Exhibit 5, only credit purchases of merchandise for resale to customers are recorded. This kind of transaction is recorded with a debit to Purchases and a credit to Accounts Payable. When the single-column purchases journal is used, credit purchases of items other than merchandise are recorded in the general journal. Cash purchases are never recorded in the purchases journal; they are recorded in the cash payments journal, which we explain later.

Like the Accounts Receivable account, the Accounts Payable account in the general ledger is generally used as a controlling account. So that the company knows how much it owes each supplier, it keeps a separate account for each supplier in an accounts payable subsidiary ledger.

The procedure for using the purchases journal is much like that for using the sales journal:

1. Enter each purchase invoice in the purchases journal on a single line. Record the date, the supplier's name, the invoice date, the terms (if given), and the amount. It is not necessary to record the shipping terms in the terms column because they do not affect the payment date.

2. At the end of each day, post each individual purchase to the supplier's account in the accounts payable subsidiary ledger. As each purchase is posted, place a checkmark in the Post. Ref. column of the purchases journal to show that it has been posted. Also place a *P* and the page number of the purchases journal (*P1* stands for Purchases Journal—Page 1) in the Post. Ref. column of each supplier's account to show the source of the entry.

3. At the end of the month, sum the Amount column in the purchases journal, and post the total to the general ledger accounts (a debit to Purchases and a credit to Accounts Payable). Place the numbers of the accounts debited and credited beneath the totals in the purchases journal to show that this step has been carried out. In the general ledger, indicate the source of the entry in the Post. Ref. column of each account.

4. Check the accuracy of the posting by adding the account balances of the accounts payable subsidiary ledger and comparing the total with the balance of the Accounts Payable controlling account in the general ledger. This step can be done by preparing a schedule of accounts payable from the subsidiary ledger.

KEY POINT: The multicolumn purchases journal can accommodate the purchase of *anything* on credit. Each column total (except the total of Other Accounts) must be posted at the end of the month.

The single-column purchases journal can be expanded to record credit purchases of items other than merchandise by adding separate debit columns for other accounts that are used often. For example, the multicolumn purchases journal in Exhibit 6 has columns for Freight In, Store Supplies, Office Supplies, and Other Accounts. Here, the total credits to Accounts Payable ($9,637) equal the total debits to Purchases, Freight In, Store Supplies, Office Supplies, and Parts ($9,200 + $50 + $145 + $42 + $200). Again, the individual transactions in the Accounts

EXHIBIT 6
A Multicolumn Purchases Journal

						Credit		Debits			Other Accounts		
Date	Account Credited	Date of Invoice	Terms	Post. Ref.	Accounts Payable	Purchases	Freight In	Store Supplies	Office Supplies	Account	Post. Ref.	Amount
July 1	Jones Chevrolet	7/1	2/10, n/30	✓	2,500	2,500						
2	Marshall Ford	7/2	2/15, n/30	✓	300	300						
2	Shelby Car Delivery	7/2	n/30	✓	50		50					
3	Dealer Sales	7/3	n/30	✓	700	700						
12	Thomas Auto	7/11	n/30	✓	1,400	1,400						
17	Dealer Sales	7/17	2/10, n/30	✓	3,200	3,200						
19	Thomas Auto	7/17	n/30	✓	1,100	1,100						
25	Osborne Supply	7/21	n/10	✓	187			145	42			
28	Auto Supply	7/28	n/10	✓	200					Parts	120	200
					9,637	9,200	50	145	42			200
					(212)	(511)	(514)	(132)	(133)			(✓)

Purchases Journal — Page 1

Payable column are posted daily to the accounts payable subsidiary ledger, and the totals of each column in the purchases journal are posted monthly to the corresponding general ledger accounts. Entries in the Other Accounts column are posted individually to the named accounts, and the column total is not posted.

CASH RECEIPTS JOURNAL

KEY POINT: The cash receipts journal can accommodate *all* receipts of cash. Daily postings are made, not only to the subsidiary accounts, but also to the "other accounts." The Other Accounts column totals, therefore, are not posted at the end of the month. Only at the end of the month are the control account balances meaningful or correct.

All transactions involving receipts of cash are recorded in the **cash receipts journal**. Examples of these transactions are cash from cash sales and cash from credit customers in payment of their accounts. Although all cash receipts are alike in that they require a debit to Cash, they differ in that they require a variety of credit entries. Thus, the cash receipts journal must have several columns. The Other Accounts column is used to record credits to accounts not specifically represented by a column. The account numbers are entered in the Post. Ref. column, and the amounts are posted daily to the appropriate account in the general ledger.

The cash receipts journal shown in Exhibit 7 has three debit columns and three credit columns. The three debit columns are as follows:

1. *Cash*   Each entry must have an amount in this column because each transaction involves a receipt of cash.

2. *Sales Discounts*   This company allows a 2 percent discount for prompt payment. Therefore, it is useful to have a column for sales discounts. Notice that in the transactions of July 8 and 28, the debits to Cash and Sales Discounts equal the credits to Accounts Receivable.

3. *Other Accounts*   The Other Accounts column (sometimes called *Sundry Accounts*) is used for transactions that involve both a debit to Cash and a debit to some account other than Sales Discounts.

These are the credit columns:

1. *Accounts Receivable*   This column is used to record collections on account from customers. The name of the customer is written in the Account Debited/Credited column so that the payment can be entered in the corresponding account in the accounts receivable subsidiary ledger. Posting to the individual accounts receivable accounts is usually done daily so that each customer's balance is up to date.

2. *Sales*   This column is used to record all cash sales during the month. Retail firms that use cash registers would make an entry at the end of each day for the total sales from each cash register for that day. The debit, of course, is in the Cash debit column.

3. *Other Accounts*   This column is used for the credit portion of any entry that is neither a cash collection from accounts receivable nor a cash sale. The name of the account to be credited is indicated in the Account Debited/Credited column. For example, the transactions of July 1, 20, and 24 involve credits to accounts other than Accounts Receivable or Sales. These individual postings should be done daily (or weekly if there are just a few of them). If a company finds that it consistently is crediting a certain account in the Other Accounts column, it can add another credit column to the cash receipts journal for that particular account.

The procedure for posting the cash receipts journal, as shown in Exhibit 7, is as follows:

1. Post the transactions in the Accounts Receivable column daily to the individual accounts in the accounts receivable subsidiary ledger. The amount credited to the customer's account is the same as that credited to Accounts Receivable. A checkmark in the Post. Ref. column of the cash receipts journal indicates that the amount has been posted, and a *CR1* (Cash Receipts Journal—Page 1) in the

EXHIBIT 7

Relationship of the Cash Receipts Journal to the General Ledger and the Accounts Receivable Subsidiary Ledger

Cash Receipts Journal   Page 1

Date		Account Debited/Credited	Post. Ref.	Debits			Credits		
				Cash	Sales Discounts	Other Accounts	Accounts Receivable	Sales	Other Accounts
July	1	Henry Mitchell, Capital	311	20,000					20,000
	5	Sales		1,200				1,200	
	8	Georgetta Jones	✓	490	10		500		
	13	Sales		1,400				1,400	
	16	Peter Clark	✓	750			750		
	19	Sales		1,000				1,000	
	20	Store Supplies	132	500					500
	24	Notes Payable	213	5,000					5,000
	26	Sales		1,600				1,600	
	28	Peter Clark	✓	588	12		600		
				32,528	22		1,850	5,200	25,500
				(111)	(412)		(114)	(411)	(✓)

Post individual amounts in Accounts Receivable Susidiary Ledger column **daily.**

Post totals at **end of month.**

Total not posted.

Post individual amounts in Other Accounts column **daily.**

General Ledger

Cash   111

Date	Post. Ref.	Debit	Credit	Balance Debit	Balance Credit
July 31	CR1	32,528		32,528	

Accounts Receivable   114

Date	Post. Ref.	Debit	Credit	Balance Debit	Balance Credit
July 31	S1	4,950		4,950	
31	CR1		1,850	3,100	

Store Supplies   132

Date	Post. Ref.	Debit	Credit	Balance Debit	Balance Credit
Bal.				500	
July 20	CR1		500	—	

Accounts Receivable Subsidiary Ledger

Peter Clark

Date	Post. Ref.	Debit	Credit	Balance
July 1	S1	750		750
16	CR1		750	—
18	S1	1,225		1,225
28	CR1		600	625

Georgetta Jones

Date	Post. Ref.	Debit	Credit	Balance
July 5	S1	500		500
8	CR1		500	—

Continue posting to Notes Payable and Henry Mitchell, Capital.

Continue posting to Sales and Sales Discounts.

Post. Ref. column of each subsidiary ledger account indicates the source of the entry.

2. Post the debits/credits in the Other Accounts columns daily, or at convenient short intervals during the month, to the general ledger accounts. Write the account number in the Post. Ref. column of the cash receipts journal as the individual items are posted to indicate that the posting has been done, and write *CR1* in the Post. Ref. column of the general ledger account to indicate the source of the entry.

3. At the end of the month, total the columns in the cash receipts journal, as shown below. The sum of the Debits column totals must equal the sum of the Credits column totals:

Debits Column Totals		Credits Column Totals	
Cash	$32,528	Accounts Receivable	$ 1,850
Sales Discounts	22	Sales	5,200
Other Accounts	0	Other Accounts	25,500
Total Debits	$32,550	Total Credits	$32,550

This step is called *crossfooting.*

4. Post the Debits column totals as follows:
   a. *Cash*   Posted as a debit to the Cash account.
   b. *Sales Discounts*   Posted as a debit to the Sales Discounts account.

5. Post the Credits column totals as follows:
   a. *Accounts Receivable*   Posted as a credit to the Accounts Receivable controlling account.
   b. *Sales*   Posted as a credit to the Sales account.

6. Write the account numbers below each column in the cash receipts journal as they are posted to indicate that these steps have been completed. *CR1* is written in the Post. Ref. column of each account in the general ledger to indicate the source of the entry.

7. Notice that the total of the Other Accounts column is not posted because each entry was posted separately when the transaction occurred. The individual accounts were posted in step **2.** Place a checkmark at the bottom of the column to show that postings in that column have been made and that the total is not posted.

CASH PAYMENTS JOURNAL

KEY POINT: The cash payments journal can accommodate *all* cash payments. It functions like the cash receipts journal, although it uses some different general ledger accounts.

All transactions involving payments of cash are recorded in the **cash payments journal** (also called the *cash disbursements journal*). Examples of these transactions are cash purchases and payments of obligations resulting from earlier purchases on credit. The form of the cash payments journal is much like that of the cash receipts journal.

The cash payments journal shown in Exhibit 8 has three credit columns and two debit columns.

The credit columns for the cash payments journal are as follows:

1. *Cash*   Each entry must have an amount in this column because each transaction involves a payment of cash.

2. *Purchases Discounts*   When purchases discounts are taken, they are recorded in this column.

3. *Other Accounts*   This column is used to record credits to accounts other than Cash or Purchases Discounts. Notice that the July 31 transaction shows a purchase of Land for $15,000, with a check for $5,000 and a note payable for $10,000.

EXHIBIT 8
Relationship of the Cash Payments Journal to the General Ledger and the Accounts Payable Subsidiary Ledger

Cash Payments Journal   Page 1

| | Ck. No. | Payee | Account Credited/Debited | Post. Ref. | Credits | | | Debits | |
Date					Cash	Purchases Discounts	Other Accounts	Accounts Payable	Other Accounts
July 2	101	Sondra Tidmore	Purchases	511	400				400
6	102	Daily Journal	Advertising Expense	612	200				200
8	103	Siviglia Agency	Rent Expense	631	250				250
11	104	Jones Chevrolet		✓	2,450	50		2,500	
16	105	Charles Kuntz	Salaries Expense	611	600				600
17	106	Marshall Ford		✓	294	6		300	
24	107	Grabow & Co.	Prepaid Insurance	119	480				480
27	108	Dealer Sales		✓	3,136	64		3,200	
30	109	A&B Equipment	Office Equipment	144	900				400
		Company	Service Equipment	146					500
31	110	Burns Real Estate	Notes Payable	213	5,000		10,000		
			Land	141					15,000
					13,710	120	10,000	6,000	17,830
					(111)	(512)	(✓)	(212)	(✓)

Post individual amounts in Other Accounts column **daily.**

Post individual amounts in Accounts Payable Subsidiary Ledger column **daily.**

Post totals at **end of month.**

Totals not posted.

General Ledger

Cash   111

Date	Post. Ref.	Debit	Credit	Balance Debit	Balance Credit
July 31	CR1	32,528		32,528	
31	CP1		13,710	18,818	

Prepaid Insurance   119

Date	Post. Ref.	Debit	Credit	Balance Debit	Balance Credit
July 24	CP1	480		480	

Continue posting to Land, Office Equipment, Service Equipment, Notes Payable, Purchases, Salaries Expense, Advertising Expense, and Rent Expense.

Continue posting to Purchases Discounts and Accounts Payable.

Accounts Payable Subsidiary Ledger

Dealer Sales

Date	Post. Ref.	Debit	Credit	Balance
July 3	P1		700	700
17	P1		3,200	3,900
27	CP1	3,200		700

Jones Chevrolet

Date	Post. Ref.	Debit	Credit	Balance
July 1	P1		2,500	2,500
11	CP1	2,500		—

Marshall Ford

Date	Post. Ref.	Debit	Credit	Balance
July 2	P1		300	300
17	CP1	300		—

The debit columns are as follows:

1. *Accounts Payable* This column is used to record payments to suppliers that have extended credit to the company. Each supplier's name is written in the Payee column so that the payment can be entered in the supplier's account in the accounts payable subsidiary ledger.

2. *Other Accounts* Cash can be expended for many reasons. Therefore, an Other Accounts or Sundry Accounts column is needed in the cash payments journal. The title of the account to be debited is written in the Account Credited/Debited column, and the amount is entered in the Other Accounts debit column. If a company finds that a particular account appears often in the Other Accounts column, it can add another debit column to the cash payments journal.

The procedure for posting the cash payments journal, shown in Exhibit 8, is as follows:

1. Post the transactions in the Accounts Payable column daily to the individual accounts in the accounts payable subsidiary ledger. Place a checkmark in the Post. Ref. column of the cash payments journal to indicate that the posting has been made.

2. Post the debits/credits in the Other Accounts debit/credit columns to the general ledger daily or at convenient short intervals during the month. Write the account number in the Post. Ref. column of the cash payments journal as the individual items are posted to indicate that the posting has been completed and CP1 (Cash Payments Journal—Page 1) in the Post. Ref. column of each general ledger account.

3. At the end of the month, the columns are footed and crossfooted. That is, the sum of the Credits column totals must equal the sum of the Debits column totals, as follows:

Credits Column Totals		Debits Column Totals	
Cash	$13,710	Accounts Payable	$ 6,000
Purchases Discounts	120	Other Accounts	17,830
Other Accounts	10,000		
Total Credits	$23,830	Total Debits	$23,830

4. At the end of the month, post the column totals for Cash, Purchases Discounts, and Accounts Payable to their respective accounts in the general ledger. Write the account number below each column in the cash payments journal as it is

FOCUS ON BUSINESS ETHICS

Why Is Confidentiality Important to Accountants?

Confidentiality is an important issue in the design and use of accounting information systems. For example, computer operators and other employees who have access to accounting records may know customers' credit histories as well as what they have purchased, how much they owe the company, and how punctually they pay their bills. In many cases, customers may include friends, neighbors, and acquaintances. The payroll records also contain such sensitive information as salary lev-els. To avoid problems, it is good practice for businesses to restrict access to sensitive records to only those employees whose work depends on them and to make it clear that strict confidentiality must be maintained. The Institute of Management Accountants states that information should not be communicated to anyone inside or outside the company who is not authorized to receive it, except when disclosure is required by law.

EXHIBIT 9
Transactions Recorded in the General Journal

KEY POINT: The general journal is used only to record transactions that cannot be accommodated by the special-purpose journals. Whenever a controlling account is recorded, it must be "double posted" to the general ledger and the subsidiary accounts. All general journal entries are posted daily; column totals are neither obtained nor posted.

Date		Description	Post. Ref.	Debit	Credit
July	25	Accounts Payable, Thomas Auto	212/✓	700	
		Purchases Returns and			
		Allowances	513		700
		Returned used car for			
		credit; invoice date: 7/11			
	26	Sales Returns and Allowances	413	35	
		Accounts Receivable, Maxwell			
		Gertz	114/✓		35
		Allowance for faulty tire			

General Journal   Page 1

posted to indicate that this step has been completed and *CP1* in the Post. Ref. column of each general ledger account. Place a checkmark under the total of each Other Accounts column in the cash payments journal to indicate that the postings in the column have been made and that the total is not posted.

TRANSACTIONS THAT ARE NOT RECORDED IN A SPECIAL-PURPOSE JOURNAL

Adjusting and closing entries are recorded in the general journal. Transactions that do not involve sales, purchases, cash receipts, or cash payments should also be recorded in the general journal. Usually, there are only a few of these transactions. Two examples of entries that do not fit in a special-purpose journal are a return of merchandise bought on account and an allowance from a supplier for credit.

These entries are shown in Exhibit 9. Notice that the entries include a debit or a credit to a controlling account (Accounts Payable or Accounts Receivable). The name of the customer or supplier also is given here. When this kind of debit or credit is made to a controlling account in the general ledger, the entry must be posted twice: once to the controlling account and once to the individual account in the subsidiary ledger. This procedure keeps the subsidiary ledger equal to the controlling account. Notice that the July 26 transaction is posted by a debit to Sales Returns and Allowances in the general ledger (shown by the account number 413), a credit to the Accounts Receivable controlling account in the general ledger (account number 114), and a credit to the Maxwell Gertz account in the accounts receivable subsidiary ledger (checkmark).

THE FLEXIBILITY OF SPECIAL-PURPOSE JOURNALS

Special-purpose journals reduce and simplify the work of accounting and allow for the division of labor. Such journals should be designed to fit the business in which they are used. As noted earlier, if certain accounts show up often in the Other Accounts column of a journal, it is a good idea to add a column for them when a new page of a special-purpose journal is prepared. Also, if certain transactions appear repeatedly in the general journal, it is a good idea to set up a new special-purpose journal.

 Check out ACE for a Review Quiz at http://accounting.college.hmco.com/students.

Chapter Review

REVIEW OF LEARNING OBJECTIVES

LO1 Identify the principles of designing accounting information systems.

The developers of an accounting information system must keep in mind the four principles of systems design: the cost-benefit principle, the control principle, the compatibility principle, and the flexibility principle.

LO2 Describe the use and structure of spreadsheet software and general ledger systems in computerized accounting systems.

Most companies today have computerized accounting systems that use spreadsheet software and general ledger systems. Spreadsheet software, such as Windows® Excel and Lotus, is used widely by accountants for analysis of data. General ledger systems are a group of integrated software programs that perform major accounting functions, such as accounting for purchases and accounts payable, sales and accounts receivable, and payroll. Some software uses icons in a graphical user interface to guide the accountant through the tasks.

LO3 Explain how accountants and businesses use the Internet.

In addition to using the Internet for access to the Web, email, and electronic bulletin boards, accountants and businesses use it for financial reporting, Extensible Business Reporting Language (XBRL), electronic commerce (ecommerce), electronic data interchange (EDI), supply-chain management, event-to-knowledge management (E2K), and document-less transactions.

LO4 Describe the role of special-purpose journals and their relationship to controlling accounts and subsidiary ledgers.

The typical manual data processing system uses several special-purpose journals, each designed to record one kind of transaction. Recording only one kind of transaction in each journal reduces and simplifies the accounting task and allows for the division of labor. The division of labor is important for internal control. Subsidiary ledgers contain individual accounts of a specific kind, such as customers' accounts (accounts receivable) or suppliers' accounts (accounts payable). The individual account records are kept separately in a subsidiary ledger to avoid making the general ledger too bulky. The total of the balances of the subsidiary ledger accounts should equal the balance of the controlling account in the general ledger because the individual items are posted daily to the subsidiary ledger accounts and the column totals are posted to the general ledger account monthly from the special-purpose journal.

LO5 Construct and use a sales journal, purchases journal, cash receipts journal, and cash payments journal.

A special-purpose journal is constructed by devoting a single column to a particular account (for example, debits to Cash in the cash receipts journal and credits to Cash in the cash payments journal). Other columns in the journal depend on the kinds of transactions in which the company normally engages. Special-purpose journals also have columns for transaction dates, explanations or subsidiary account names, and posting references.

REVIEW OF CONCEPTS AND TERMINOLOGY

The following concepts and terms were introduced in this chapter:

LO1 **Accounting information systems:** The processes that gather data, put them into useful form, and communicate the results to management.

LO5 **Cash payments journal:** A multicolumn special-purpose journal used to record payments of cash. Also called *cash disbursements journal.*

LO5 **Cash receipts journal:** A multicolumn special-purpose journal used to record transactions involving the receipt of cash.

LO1 **Compatibility principle:** The principle that holds that the design of an accounting information system must be in harmony with the organizational and human factors of the business.

LO4 **Controlling account:** An account in the general ledger that summarizes the total balance of a group of related accounts in a subsidiary ledger. Also called *control account*.

LO1 **Control principle:** The principle that holds that an accounting information system must provide all the features of internal control needed to protect the firm's assets and ensure that data are reliable.

LO1 **Cost-benefit principle:** The principle that holds that the benefits derived from an accounting information system must be equal to or greater than its cost.

LO1 **Data processing:** The means by which an accounting system gathers data, organizes them into useful forms for business decision making, and issues the resulting information to users.

LO3 **Electronic commerce (ecommerce):** The conduct of business transactions on computer networks, including the Internet.

LO3 **Electronic Data Interchange (EDI):** Private links that facilitate the conduct of electronic commerce.

LO1 **Enterprise resource planning (ERP) systems:** Comprehensive, computerized information systems that integrate financial and nonfinancial information about customers, operations, and suppliers in a single database.

LO3 **Event-to-knowledge (E2K) management:** A system that uses the Internet to get information to users within and outside a company in the quickest possible way after an event like a sale or a purchase has occurred.

LO3 **Extensible Business Reporting Language (XBRL):** A new computer language developed by accountants and others for the express purpose of identifying and communicating financial information.

LO1 **Flexibility principle:** The principle that holds that an accounting information system must be flexible enough to allow for growth in the volume of transactions and for organizational changes.

LO2 **General ledger systems:** A group of integrated software programs that accountants use to perform the major accounting functions.

LO2 **Graphical user interface (GUI):** The employment of symbols, called *icons*, to represent operations, which makes software easier to use.

LO2 **Icons:** Symbols representing operations that appear on a computer screen as part of a graphical user interface.

LO3 **Internet:** The world's largest computer network.

LO4 **Manual data processing:** A system of accounting in which each transaction is entered manually from a source document into the general journal (input device) and each debit and credit is posted manually to the correct ledger account (processor and memory device) for the eventual preparation of financial statements (output devices).

LO5 **Purchases journal:** A single-column or multicolumn special-purpose journal used to record all purchases on credit.

LO5 **Sales journal:** A type of special-purpose journal used to record credit sales.

LO2 **Source documents:** The written evidence that supports each accounting transaction for each major accounting function.

LO4 **Special-purpose journal:** An input device in an accounting system that is used to record a single type of transaction.

LO2 **Spreadsheet:** A computerized grid of columns and rows into which the user places data or formulas related to financial planning, cost estimating, and other accounting tasks.

LO4 **Subsidiary ledger:** A ledger separate from the general ledger that contains a group of related accounts; the total of the balances in the subsidiary ledger accounts must equal the balance of the related controlling account in the general ledger.

LO3 **Supply-chain management:** A system that uses the Internet to track the supplies and materials a manufacturer will need on a day-to-day basis.

REVIEW PROBLEM

Purchases Journal

LO1
LO4
LO5
Caraban Company is a retail seller of hiking and camping gear. The company is installing a manual accounting system, and the accountant is trying to decide whether to use a single-column or a multicolumn purchases journal. Here is a list of several transactions related to purchases in the month of January.

Jan. 5   Received a shipment of merchandise from Simons Corporation, terms 2/10, n/30, FOB shipping point, invoice dated January 4, $2,875.
     10   Received a bill from Allied Freight for the freight charges on the January 5 shipment, terms n/30, invoice dated January 4, $416.
     15   Returned some of the merchandise received from Simons Corporation because it was not what was ordered, $315.
     20   Purchased store supplies of $56 and office supplies of $117 from Mason Company, terms n/30, invoice dated January 20.
     25   Received a shipment from Thomas Manufacturing, $1,882, which included supplier-paid freight charges of $175, terms n/30, FOB shipping point, invoice dated January 23.

REQUIRED ▶
1. Record the transactions using a single-column purchases journal and a general journal, and show the posting reference for each journal entry. Use the following accounts: Store Supplies (116), Office Supplies (117), Accounts Payable (211), Purchases (611), Purchases Returns and Allowances (612), and Freight In (613).
2. Record the transactions using a multicolumn purchases journal and a general journal, total the purchases journal, and show the posting reference for each entry.
3. Using the principles of systems design, compare the single-column and multicolumn journals in terms of the number of entries and postings.

ANSWER TO REVIEW PROBLEM

1. Record the transactions in a single-column purchases journal and the general journal. Show the posting references.

Purchases Journal						Page 1
Date		Account Credited	Date of Invoice	Terms	Post. Ref.	Amount
Jan.	5	Simons Corporation	1/4	2/10, n/30	✓	2,875

		General Journal			Page 1
Date		Description	Post. Ref.	Debit	Credit
Jan.	10	Freight In	613	416	
		Accounts Payable, Allied Freight	211/✓		416
		Freight charges on Simons Corporation shipment, terms n/30, invoice dated January 4			
	15	Accounts Payable, Simons Corporation	211/✓	315	
		Purchases Returns and			
		Allowances	612		315
		Returned merchandise not ordered			
	20	Store Supplies	116	56	
		Office Supplies	117	117	
		Accounts Payable, Mason Company	211/✓		173
		Purchased supplies, terms n/30, invoice dated January 20			
	25	Purchases	611	1,707	
		Freight In	613	175	
		Accounts Payable, Thomas Manufacturing	211/✓		1,882
		Purchased merchandise, terms n/30; supplier paid shipping, invoice dated January 23			

2. Record the transactions in a multicolumn purchases journal and the general journal. Total the purchases journal and show posting references.

						Credit		Debits		
Date		Account Credited	Date of Invoice	Terms	Post. Ref.	Accounts Payable	Purchases	Freight In	Store Supplies	Office Supplies
Jan.	5	Simons Corporation	1/4	2/10, n/30	✓	2,875	2,875			
	10	Allied Freight	1/4	n/30	✓	416		416		
	20	Mason Company	1/20	n/30	✓	173			56	117
	25	Thomas Manufacturing	1/23	n/30	✓	1,882	1,707	175		
						5,346	4,582	591	56	117
						(211)	(611)	(613)	(116)	(117)

Purchases Journal — Page 1

Each of these amounts is posted **daily** to the appropriate account in the subsidiary ledger.

Each of these totals is posted **monthly** to the applicable general ledger account.

	General Journal			Page 1
Date	**Description**	**Post. Ref.**	**Debit**	**Credit**
Jan. 15	Accounts Payable, Simons Corporation	211/✓	→ 315	
	Purchases Returns and			
	Allowances	612		315 ↩
	Returned merchandise			
	not ordered			

> This amount is posted both to the controlling account and to the subsidiary account.

> This amount is posted to the general ledger account.

3. The single-column purchases journal requires four general journal entries plus one purchases journal entry, or 20 separate lines, including explanations. In addition, 15 postings to the general ledger and the accounts payable subsidiary ledger are necessary. (Also, the total of the purchases journal must be posted twice at the end of the month: once as a debit to Purchases and once as a credit to Accounts Payable.) The multicolumn purchases journal calls for just one general journal entry and four purchases journal entries. Only eight lines need to be written, and only seven postings must be made. (In addition, the column totals in the purchases journal must be posted at the end of the month.)

In applying the cost-benefit principle, the benefits of the multicolumn purchases journal in terms of journalizing and posting time saved are clear from this analysis. In addition, there are fewer chances for error when using the multicolumn purchases journal. So the control principle is better achieved under the second system. It is not possible to decide which system better meets the compatibility principle because we do not know the relative proportion of transaction types. For instance, if the number of transactions like the one for January 5 exceeds all the others by ten to one, the first system may be more compatible with the needs of the company. On the other hand, if there are many transactions like those for January 10, 20, and 25, the second system may be more compatible. Finally, in terms of the flexibility principle, the multicolumn purchases journal is obviously more flexible because it can handle more kinds of transactions and can be expanded to include columns for other accounts if necessary.

Chapter Assignments

BUILDING YOUR KNOWLEDGE FOUNDATION

QUESTIONS

1. What is the relationship of accounting information systems to data processing?
2. Describe the four principles of accounting information systems design.
3. Why is a graphical user interface important to the successful use of general ledger systems?
4. Define and contrast *enterprise resource planning* (ERP) *systems, electronic commerce,* and *electronic data interchange* (EDI).
5. Data are the raw material of a computer system. Trace the flow of data through the different parts of a computerized accounting system.

6. How does a computerized accounting system using a general ledger system relate to the major accounting functions?

7. In what ways can the Internet assist businesses in their operations?

8. How do special-purpose journals save time in entering and posting transactions?

9. What is the purpose of the Accounts Receivable controlling account? What is its relationship to the accounts receivable subsidiary ledger?

10. Lake Transit had 1,700 sales on credit during the current month.

    a. If the firm uses a two-column general journal to record sales, how many times will the word *Sales* be written?
    b. How many postings to the Sales account will have to be made?
    c. If the firm uses a sales journal, how many times will the word *Sales* be written?
    d. How many postings to the Sales account will have to be made?

11. Why are the cash receipts journal and cash payments journal crossfooted? When is this step performed?

12. A company has the following accounts with balances: 18 asset accounts, including the Accounts Receivable account but not the individual customers' accounts; 200 customer accounts; 8 liability accounts, including the Accounts Payable account but not the individual creditors' accounts; 100 creditor accounts; and 35 owner's equity accounts, including income statement accounts—a total of 361 accounts. How many accounts in total would appear in the general ledger?

SHORT EXERCISES

SE 1.

LO1 Principles of Accounting Information System Design

Indicate whether each of the following statements concerning a newly installed accounting information system is most closely related to the (a) cost-benefit principle, (b) control principle, (c) compatibility principle, or (d) flexibility principle:

1. Procedures are in place to ensure that the data entered into the system are reliable.
2. The system allows for growth in the number and types of transactions entered into by the company.
3. The system was installed after its costs were carefully weighed against the improved decision making that will result.
4. The system takes into account the various operations of the business and the capabilities of the people who will interact with the system.

SE 2.

LO2 Computerized Accounting System

Assuming that a company uses a general ledger package for its computerized accounting system, indicate whether each of the following source documents would provide input to (a) sales/accounts receivable, (b) purchases/accounts payable, (c) cash receipts, (d) cash disbursements, (e) payroll, or (f) the general journal:

1. Deposit slips
2. Time cards
3. Vendor invoices
4. Checks issued
5. Customer invoices
6. Documents for other journal entries

SE 3.

LO3 Use of the Internet

Define and contrast the following uses of the Internet:

1. Electronic commerce (ecommerce)
2. Electronic Data Interchange (EDI)
3. Supply-chain management

SE 4.

LO4 Transactions and Special-Purpose Journals

Indicate whether each transaction listed below should be recorded in the (a) sales journal, (b) multicolumn purchases journal, (c) cash receipts journal, (d) cash payments journal, or (e) general journal:

1. Receipt on account
2. Purchase return on account
3. Sale on account
4. Purchase on account
5. Sale for cash
6. Payment on account

SE 5.

LO5 Sales Journal Transactions

Using Exhibit 2 as a model, show how each of the following transactions should be entered in a sales journal. All terms are 2/10, n/30. If a transaction should not appear in the sales journal, tell where it should be recorded. Total and rule the journal.

Oct. 1 Sold merchandise to S. Rush on credit, invoice no. 301, $350.
       8 Sold merchandise to J. Sussman for cash, $150.
      15 Sold merchandise to F. Thomaso on credit, invoice no. 302, $200.

LO4   Sales Journal Postings
LO5   and Subsidiary Ledger

SE 6.   Assuming the transactions in **SE 5** are the only sales transactions for the month of October, describe all the postings that would be made from the sales journal to the general ledger and the accounts receivable subsidiary ledger.

LO5   Multicolumn Purchases
Journal

SE 7.   Using Exhibit 6 as a model, show how each of the following transactions should be entered in a multicolumn purchases journal. If a transaction should not appear in this journal, tell where it should be recorded. Total and rule the journal.

Oct. 2   Purchased merchandise on credit from Farmington Electronics, invoice dated October 1, terms 2/10, n/30, $500.

4   Purchased merchandise on credit from Ciarri Electrics, invoice dated October 2, terms 2/10, n/30, $650, including freight charges of $50.

6   Purchased supplies on credit from Avon Supplies, invoice dated October 5, terms n/30, $180, to be allocated one-third to store and two-thirds to office.

8   Purchased postage stamps at the post office for cash (check no. 101), $58.

9   Purchased equipment on credit from Simsbury Furniture Co., invoice dated October 9, terms n/EOM, $1,000.

LO4   Purchases Journal Postings
LO5   and Subsidiary Ledger

SE 8.   Assuming the transactions in **SE 7** are the only purchases transactions for the month of October, describe all the postings that would be made from the purchases journal to the general ledger and the accounts payable subsidiary ledger.

LO4   Cash Receipts Journal
LO5

SE 9.   Using Exhibit 7 as a model, show how each of the following transactions should be entered in the cash receipts journal. If a transaction should not appear in this journal, tell where it should be recorded.

Oct. 8   Sold merchandise for cash to J. Sussman, $150.

9   Received payment on account from S. Rush, $350 less 2 percent discount.

17   F. Thomaso returned purchase of October 15 for full credit, $200.

Describe the postings that are required for each transaction.

LO4   Cash Payments Journal
LO5

SE 10.   Using Exhibit 8 as a model, show how each of the following transactions should be entered in the cash payments journal. If a transaction should not appear in this journal, tell where it should be recorded.

Oct. 8   Issued check no. 101 to the U.S. Postal Service for postage, $58.

12   Issued check no. 102 to Farmington Electronics, $500 less 2 percent discount.

Describe the postings that are required for each transaction.

EXERCISES

LO4   Matching Transactions to
Special-Purpose Journals

E 1.   A company uses a single-column sales journal, a single-column purchases journal, a cash receipts journal, a cash payments journal, and a general journal. In which journal would each of the following transactions be recorded?

1. Sold merchandise on credit
2. Sold merchandise for cash
3. Gave a customer credit for merchandise purchased on credit and returned
4. Paid a creditor
5. Paid office salaries
6. Received a customer's payment for merchandise previously purchased on credit
7. Recorded adjusting and closing entries
8. Purchased merchandise on credit
9. Purchased sales department supplies on credit
10. Purchased office equipment for cash
11. Returned merchandise purchased on credit
12. Paid sales commissions

LO4   Characteristics of Special-
LO5   Purpose Journals

E 2.   Fallow Corporation uses a single-column sales journal, a single-column purchases journal, a cash receipts journal, a cash payments journal, and a general journal.

1. In which of the journals listed above would you expect to find the fewest transactions recorded?

2. At the end of the accounting period, to which account or accounts should the total of the sales journal be posted as a debit and/or credit?
3. At the end of the accounting period, to which account or accounts should the total of the purchases journal be posted as a debit and/or credit?
4. What two subsidiary ledgers would probably be associated with the journals listed above? From which journals would postings normally be made to each of the two subsidiary ledgers?
5. In which of the journals are adjusting and closing entries made?

E 3. Shown below is a page from a special-purpose journal.

LO5 Identifying the Content of a Special-Purpose Journal

| | | Account Debited/Credited | Post. Ref. | Debits | | Credits | | |
				Cash	Sales Discount	Accounts Receivable	Sales	Other Accounts
		Balance Forward		79,598	1,574	20,408	8,564	52,200
May	25	Sally Juno	✓	980	20	1,000		
	26	Notes Receivable	115	2,240				2,000
		Interest Income	715					240
	27	Cash Sale		1,920			1,920	
	31	Kevin LaPorte	✓	400		400		
				85,138	1,594	21,808	10,484	54,440
				(111)	(412)	(114)	(411)	(√)

1. What kind of journal is this?
2. Explain each transaction.
3. Explain the following: (a) the numbers under the double rule, (b) the checkmarks entered in the Post. Ref. column, (c) the numbers 115 and 715 in the Post. Ref. column, and (d) the checkmark below the Other Accounts credit column.

E 4. Herlihy Company uses a multicolumn purchases journal similar to the one shown in Exhibit 6. During the month of July, Herlihy made the following purchases:

LO5 Multicolumn Purchases Journal

July 1 Purchased merchandise from Burlington Company on account for $5,400, invoice dated July 1, terms 2/10, n/30.
    3 Received freight bill dated July 1 from SuLong Freight for merchandise purchased July 1, $350, terms n/30.
    18 Purchased supplies from Leddin Company for $240; allocated half to the store and half to the office; invoice dated July 16, terms n/30.
    23 Purchased merchandise from Valera Company on account for $1,974; total included freight in of $174; invoice dated July 20, terms n/30, FOB shipping point.
    27 Purchased office supplies from Leddin Company for $96, invoice dated July 27, terms n/30.
    31 Purchased a one-year insurance policy from Southbury Associates, $480, invoice dated July 31, terms n/30.

1. Set up a multicolumn purchases journal similar to the one in Exhibit 6 and label it page 1.
2. Enter the transactions listed above in the purchases journal. Then foot and crossfoot the columns.

LO4   Finding Errors in Special-
LO5   Purpose Journals

E 5. A company records purchases in a single-column purchases journal and records purchases returns in its general journal. During the past month, an accounting clerk made each of the errors described below.

1. Correctly recorded a $191 purchase in the purchases journal but posted it to the creditor's account as a $119 purchase.
2. Made an error in totaling the Amount column of the purchases journal.
3. Posted a purchases return from the general journal to the Purchases Returns and Allowances account and the Accounts Payable account but did not post it to the creditor's account.
4. Made an error in determining the balance of a creditor's account.
5. Posted a purchases return to the Accounts Payable account but did not post it to the Purchases Returns and Allowances account.

Explain how each error might be discovered.

LO4   Posting from a Sales
LO5   Journal

E 6. Figaro Company began business on June 1. The company maintains a sales journal. The sales journal at the end of the month is shown below.

	Sales Journal				Page 1
Date		Account Debited	Invoice Number	Post. Ref.	Amount
June	3	Sue Longo	1001		516
	8	Ed Kohen	1002		951
	12	Ye Tang	1003		642
	18	Sue Longo	1004		291
	27	Gina Touloumos	1005		1,299
					3,699

1. Open general ledger accounts for Accounts Receivable (112) and Sales (411) and an accounts receivable subsidiary ledger with an account for each customer. Make the appropriate postings from the sales journal, inserting the posting references in the sales journal and in the ledger accounts as you work.
2. Prove the accounts receivable subsidiary ledger by preparing a schedule of accounts receivable.

LO4   Identification of
LO5   Transactions

E 7. Conomacos Company uses a manual accounting system with a sales journal, purchases journal, cash receipts journal, cash payments journal, and general journal similar to those illustrated in the text. On October 31, the Sales account in the general ledger looked like this:

Sales							Page 411
						Balance	
Date		Item	Post. Ref.	Debit	Credit	Debit	Credit
Oct.	31		S11		74,842		74,842
	31		CR7		42,414		117,256
	31		J17	117,256			—

On October 31, the M. Kern account in the accounts receivable subsidiary ledger looked like this:

M. Kern   Account No. 10012

Date		Item	Post. Ref.	Debit	Credit	Balance
Oct.	8		S10	4,216		4,216
	12		J14		564	3,652
	18		CR6		1,000	2,652

1. Write an explanation of each entry in the Sales account; include the journal from which the entry was posted.
2. Write an explanation of each entry in the M. Kern account in the accounts receivable subsidiary ledger; include the journal from which the entry was posted.

LO4 Identification of
LO5 Transactions

E 8. Randall Company uses a sales journal, single-column purchases journal, cash receipts journal, cash payments journal, and general journal similar to those shown in the text. On April 30, the D. Amir account in the accounts receivable subsidiary ledger appeared as shown below.

D. Amir

Date		Item	Post. Ref.	Debit	Credit	Balance
Mar.	31		S4	2,448		2,448
Apr.	7		J7		192	2,256
	12		CR5		600	1,656
	17		S6	684		2,340

On April 30, the Wong Company account in the accounts payable subsidiary ledger appeared as follows:

Wong Company

Date		Item	Post. Ref.	Debit	Credit	Balance
Apr.	18		P7		6,078	6,078
	20		J9	636		5,442
	25		CP8	5,442		—

1. Write an explanation of each entry that affected the D. Amir account receivable, including the journal from which the entry was posted.
2. Write an explanation of each entry that affected the Wong Company account payable, including the journal from which the entry was posted.

PROBLEMS

P 1.

LO4   Special-Purpose Journals and
LO5   Subsidiary Ledgers

Maher Company is a small retail business that uses a manual accounting system similar to the one described in this chapter. At the end of April 20xx, the firm's accounts receivable and accounts payable subsidiary ledgers showed the following balances:

Accounts Receivable		Accounts Payable	
A. Barrel	$430	Bayle Company	$1,300
L. Lozocek	330	Centro Company	890
Total Accounts Receivable	$760	Total Accounts Payable	$2,190

During May, the company engaged in the following transactions:

May 2   Sold merchandise on credit to R. Woodman, a new customer, $570, terms 2/10, n/30, invoice no. 1001.

4   Received payment in full from L. Lozocek, no discount allowed.

5   Paid Bayle Company the full amount owed less a 2 percent discount, check no. 201.

8   Accepted a return of merchandise for credit from R. Woodman, $170.

9   Paid Centro Company the full amount owed, no discount allowed, check no. 202.

12   Received payment from R. Woodman for amount due less discount.

15   Received partial payment from A. Barrel, no discount allowed, $230.

22   Purchased merchandise from Bayle Company, $1,200, terms 2/10, n/30, FOB destination, invoice dated May 22.

23   Sold merchandise on credit to L. Lozocek, $670, terms 2/10, n/30, invoice no. 1002.

26   Purchased merchandise from Centro Company, $1,500, terms 2/10, n/30, FOB destination, invoice dated May 23.

31   Returned merchandise to Centro Company for full credit, $600.

REQUIRED ▶

1. Prepare a single-column sales journal, a single-column purchases journal, a cash receipts journal, a cash payments journal, and a general journal similar to the ones illustrated in the chapter. Use Page 1 for all references.

2. Open the following general ledger accounts: Accounts Receivable (112) and Accounts Payable (211).

3. Open the following accounts receivable subsidiary ledger accounts: A. Barrel, L. Lozocek, and R. Woodman.

4. Open the following accounts payable subsidiary ledger accounts: Bayle Company and Centro Company.

5. Enter the transactions in the journals and post to the appropriate subsidiary ledger and general ledger accounts.

6. Foot and crossfoot the journals, and make the end-of-month postings applicable to Accounts Receivable and Accounts Payable.

7. Prove the control balances of Accounts Receivable and Accounts Payable by preparing schedules of accounts receivable and accounts payable.

8. When in the accounting cycle will (a) the total of all the customer accounts in the accounts receivable subsidiary ledger equal the balance of the accounts receivable controlling account and (b) the total of all the supplier accounts in the accounts payable subsidiary ledger equal the balance of the accounts payable controlling account?

P 2.

LO5   Cash Receipts and Cash
**   Payments Journals**

Kimball Company is a small retail business that uses a manual data processing system similar to the one described in the chapter. Among its special-purpose journals are multicolumn cash receipts and cash payments journals. These were the cash transactions for Kimball Company during the month of November:

Nov. 1   Paid November rent to R. Carello, $1,000, with check no. 782.

3   Paid Stavos Wholesale on account, $2,300 less a 2 percent discount, check no. 783.

4   Received payment on account of $1,000, within the 2 percent discount period, from J. Walker.

5   Cash sales, $2,632.

8   Paid Moving Freight on account, $598, with check no. 784.

Nov. 9   The owner, Fred Kimball, invested an additional $10,000 in cash and a truck valued at $14,000 in the business.

11   Paid Escobedo Supply on account, $284, with check no. 785.

14   Cash sales, $2,834.

15   Paid Moving Freight $310 for the freight on a shipment of merchandise received today, with check no. 786.

16   Paid Ludman Company on account, $1,568 net a 2 percent discount, with check no. 787.

17   Received payment on account from P. Sivula, $120.

18   Cash sales, $1,974.

19   Received payment on a note receivable, $1,800 plus $36 interest.

20   Purchased office supplies from Escobedo Supply, $108, with check no. 788.

21   Paid a note payable in full to Kenington Bank, $4,100 including $100 interest, with check no. 789.

24   Cash sales, $2,964.

25   Paid $500 less a 2 percent discount to Stavos Wholesale, with check no. 790.

26   Paid sales clerk Tracy Dye $1,100 for her monthly salary, with check no. 791.

27   Purchased equipment from Standard Corporation for $16,000, paying $4,000 with check no. 792 and signing a note payable for the difference.

30   Fred Kimball withdrew $1,200 from the business, using check no. 793.

REQUIRED ▶

1. Enter these transactions in the cash receipts and cash payments journals.
2. Foot and crossfoot the journals.
3. If a manager wanted to know the total sales for the accounting period, where else would the manager need to refer to obtain the data needed?.

P 3.

LO4   Purchases and General
LO5   Journals

Meloon Lawn Supply Company uses a multicolumn purchases journal and a general journal similar to those illustrated in the text. The company also maintains an accounts payable subsidiary ledger. The items below represent the company's credit transactions for the month of July.

July 2   Purchased merchandise from Diego Fertilizer Company, $2,640.

3   Purchased office supplies of $166 and store supplies of $208 from Laronne Supply, Inc.

5   Purchased cleaning equipment from Whitman Company, $1,856.

7   Purchased display equipment from Laronne Supply, Inc., $4,700.

10   Purchased lawn mowers from Brandon Lawn Equipment Company, for resale, $8,400 (which included transportation charges of $350).

14   Purchased merchandise from Diego Fertilizer Company, $3,444.

18   Purchased a lawn mower from Brandon Lawn Equipment Company to be used in the business, $950 (which included transportation charges of $70).

23   Purchased store supplies from Laronne Supply, Inc., $54.

27   Returned a defective lawn mower purchased on July 10 for full credit, $750.

REQUIRED ▶

1. Enter the preceding transactions in the purchases journal and the general journal. Assume that all terms are n/30 and that invoice dates are the same as the transaction dates. Use Page 1 for all references.
2. Foot and crossfoot the purchases journal.
3. Open the following general ledger accounts: Store Supplies (116), Office Supplies (117), Lawn Equipment (142), Display Equipment (144), Cleaning Equipment (146), Accounts Payable (211), Purchases (611), Purchases Returns and Allowances (612), and Freight In (613). Open accounts payable subsidiary ledger accounts as needed. Post from the journals to the ledger accounts.

P 4.

LO4   Comprehensive Use of
LO5   Special-Purpose Journals

Ye Olde Book Store opened its doors for business on May 1. During May, the following transactions took place:

May 1   Linda Berrill began the business by depositing $42,000 in the new company's bank account.

3   Issued check no. C001 to Remax Rentals for one month's rent, $1,000.

4   Received a shipment of books from Chassman Books, Inc., invoice dated May 3, terms 5/10, n/60, FOB shipping point, $15,680.

5   Received a bill for freight from Menden Shippers for the previous day's shipment, terms n/30, $790.

May 6   Received a shipment from Lakeside Books, invoice dated May 6, terms 2/10, n/30, FOB shipping point, $11,300.

7   Issued check no. C002 to Pappanopoulos Freight for transportation charges on the previous day's shipment, $574.

8   Issued check no. C003 to Yun Chao Equipment Company for store equipment, $10,400.

9   Sold books to Midtown Center, terms 5/10, n/30, invoice no. 1001, $1,564.

10   Returned books to Chassman Books, Inc., for credit, $760.

11   Issued check no. C004 to WCAM for radio commercials, $470.

12   Issued check no. C005 to Chassman Books, Inc., for balance of amount owed less discount.

13   Cash sales for the first two weeks, $4,018. (For this problem, cash sales are recorded every two weeks, not daily as they are in actual practice.)

14   Issued check no. C006 to Lakeside Books, $6,000 less discount.

15   Signed a 90-day, 10 percent note for a bank loan and received $20,000 in cash.

15   Sold books to Steve Oahani, terms n/30, invoice no. 1002, $260.

16   Issued a credit memorandum to Midtown Center for returned books, $124.

17   Received full payment from Midtown Center of balance owed less discount.

18   Sold books to Missy Porter, terms n/30, invoice no. 1003, $194.

19   Received a shipment from Perspectives Publishing Company, invoice dated May 18, terms 5/10, n/60, $4,604.

20   Returned additional books purchased on May 4 to Chassman Books, Inc., for credit at gross price, $1,436.

21   Sold books to Midtown Center, terms 5/10, n/30, invoice no. 1004, $1,634.

23   Received a shipment from Chassman Books, Inc., invoice dated May 19, terms 5/10, n/60, FOB shipping point, $2,374.

24   Issued check no. C007 to Menden Shippers for balance owed on account plus shipping charges of $194 on previous day's shipment.

27   Cash sales for the second two weeks, $7,488.

29   Issued check no. C008 to Payroll for sales salaries for first four weeks of the month, $1,400.

31   Cash sales for the last four days of the month, $554.

REQUIRED ▶

1. Prepare a sales journal, a multicolumn purchases journal, a cash receipts journal, a cash payments journal, and a general journal. Use Page 1 for all journal references.

2. Open the following general ledger accounts: Cash (111); Accounts Receivable (112); Store Equipment (141); Accounts Payable (211); Notes Payable (212); Linda Berrill, Capital (311); Sales (411); Sales Discounts (412); Sales Returns and Allowances (413); Purchases (511); Purchases Discounts (512); Purchases Returns and Allowances (513); Freight In (514); Sales Salaries Expense (611); Advertising Expense (612); and Rent Expense (613).

3. Open accounts receivable subsidiary ledger accounts for Midtown Center, Steve Oahani, and Missy Porter.

4. Open accounts payable subsidiary ledger accounts for Chassman Books, Inc.; Lakeside Books; Menden Shippers; and Perspectives Publishing Company.

5. Enter the transactions in the journals and post as appropriate.

6. Foot and crossfoot the journals, and make the end-of-month postings.

7. Prepare a trial balance of the general ledger and prove the control balances of Accounts Receivable and Accounts Payable by preparing schedules of accounts receivable and accounts payable.

LO4 Comprehensive Use of
LO5 Special-Purpose Journals

P 5.   During October, Fahner Refrigeration Company completed the following transactions:

Oct. 1   Received merchandise from Tate Company, $5,000, invoice dated September 29, terms 2/10, n/30, FOB shipping point.

3   Issued check no. 230 to Wallace Realtors for October rent, $4,000.

4   Received merchandise from LaRocke Manufacturing, $10,800, invoice dated October 1, terms 2/10, n/30, FOB shipping point.

6   Issued check no. 231 to Babbitt Company for repairs, $1,120.

7   Received $800 credit memorandum pertaining to October 4 shipment from LaRocke Manufacturing for return of unsatisfactory merchandise.

8   Issued check no. 232 to Esmerelda Company for freight charges on October 1 and October 4 shipments, $368.

Oct.	9	Sold merchandise to J. Koppel, $2,000, terms 1/10, n/30, invoice no. 725.
	10	Issued check no. 233 to Tate Company for full payment less discount.
	11	Sold merchandise to K. Hanama for $2,500, terms 1/10, n/30, invoice no. 726.
	12	Issued check no. 234 to LaRocke Manufacturing for balance of account less discount.
	13	Purchased advertising on credit from WRRT, invoice dated October 13, $900, terms n/20.
	15	Issued credit memorandum to K. Hanama for $100 for merchandise returned.
	16	Cash sales for the first half of the month, $19,340. (For this problem, cash sales are recorded twice a month, not daily, as they are in actual practice.)
	17	Sold merchandise to H. Blake, $1,400, terms 1/10, n/30, invoice no. 727.
	18	Received check from J. Koppel for October 9 sale less discount.
	19	Received check from K. Hanama for balance of account less discount.
	20	Received merchandise from Tate Company, $5,600, invoice dated October 19, terms 2/10, n/30, FOB shipping point.
	21	Received freight bill from Winters Company for merchandise received on October 20, invoice dated October 19, $1,140, terms n/5.
	22	Issued check no. 235 for advertising purchase of October 13.
	24	Received merchandise from LaRocke Manufacturing, $7,200, invoice dated October 23, terms 2/10, n/30, FOB shipping point.
	25	Issued check no. 236 for freight charge of October 21.
	26	Sold merchandise to J. Koppel, $1,600, terms 1/10, n/30, invoice no. 728.
	28	Received credit memorandum from LaRocke Manufacturing for defective merchandise received October 24, $600.
	29	Issued check no. 237 to Woo Company for purchase of office equipment, $700.
	30	Issued check no. 238 to Tate Company for half of October 20 purchase less discount.
	30	Received check in full from H. Blake, no discount allowed.
	31	Cash sales for the last half of the month, $23,120.
	31	Issued check no. 239 to Payroll for monthly sales salaries, $8,600.

REQUIRED ▶

1. Prepare a sales journal, a multicolumn purchases journal, a cash receipts journal, a cash payments journal, and a general journal for Fahner Refrigeration Company. Use Page 1 for all journal references.
2. Open the following general ledger accounts: Cash (111); Accounts Receivable (112); Office Equipment (141); Accounts Payable (211); Sales (411); Sales Discounts (412); Sales Returns and Allowances (413); Purchases (511); Purchases Discounts (512); Purchases Returns and Allowances (513); Freight In (514); Sales Salaries Expense (521); Advertising Expense (522); Rent Expense (531); and Repairs Expense (532).
3. Open accounts receivable subsidiary ledger accounts for H. Blake, K. Hanama, and J. Koppel.
4. Open accounts payable subsidiary ledger accounts for LaRocke Manufacturing, Tate Company, Winters Company, and WRRT.
5. Enter the transactions in the journals and post as appropriate.
6. Foot and crossfoot the journals, and make the end-of-month postings.
7. Prepare a trial balance of the general ledger and prove the control balances of Accounts Receivable and Accounts Payable by preparing schedules of accounts receivable and accounts payable.

ALTERNATE PROBLEMS

P 6.
LO4 Special-Purpose Journals and
LO5 Subsidiary Ledgers

Simons Company, a small retail business, uses a manual accounting system similar to the one illustrated in this chapter. At the end of May 20xx, the accounts in the accounts receivable and accounts payable subsidiary ledgers showed the following balances:

Accounts Receivable		Accounts Payable	
T. Bacon	$ 870	Shalkor Inc.	$2,900
R. Banks	650	Ventman Company	460
Total Accounts Receivable	$1,520	Total Accounts Payable	$3,360

During June, the company engaged in the following transactions:

June 2 Sold merchandise on credit to R. Banks, $920, terms 2/10, n/30, invoice no. 4001.

4 Received payment in full from R. Banks for the amount due at the beginning of June less a 2 percent discount.

5 Paid Shalkor Inc. the full amount owed less a 2 percent discount, check no. 501.

8 Accepted a return of merchandise from R. Banks, $220.

9 Paid Ventman Company the full amount owed, no discount allowed, check no. 502.

12 Received payment from R. Banks for the amount due less the discount.

15 Received partial payment from T. Bacon, no discount allowed, $300.

22 Purchased merchandise from Ventman Company, $1,700, terms 2/10, n/30, FOB destination, invoice dated June 21.

23 Sold merchandise on credit to M. Abdul, $2,450, terms 2/10, n/30, invoice no. 4002.

26 Purchased merchandise from Shalkor Inc., $1,500, terms 2/10, n/30, FOB destination, invoice dated June 24.

30 Returned merchandise to Ventman Company for full credit, $600.

REQUIRED ▶ 1. Prepare a sales journal, a single-column purchases journal, a cash receipts journal, a cash payments journal, and a general journal similar to the ones illustrated in the chapter. Use Page 1 for all references.

2. Open the following general ledger accounts: Accounts Receivable (112) and Accounts Payable (211).

3. Open accounts receivable subsidiary ledger accounts for M. Abdul, T. Bacon, and R. Banks.

4. Open accounts payable subsidiary ledger accounts for Shalkor Inc. and Ventman Company.

5. Enter the transactions in the journals and post to the appropriate subsidiary ledger and general ledger accounts.

6. Foot and crossfoot the journals, and make the end-of-month postings applicable to Accounts Receivable and Accounts Payable.

7. Prove the control balances of Accounts Receivable and Accounts Payable by preparing schedules of accounts receivable and accounts payable.

8. When in the accounting cycle will (a) the total of all the customer accounts in the accounts receivable subsidiary ledger equal the balance of the accounts receivable controlling account and (b) the total of all the supplier accounts in the accounts payable subsidiary ledger equal the balance of the accounts payable controlling account?

P 7.

LO5 **Cash Receipts and Cash Payments Journals**

The items below detail all cash transactions by O'Malley Company for the month of October. The company uses multicolumn cash receipts and cash payments journals similar to those illustrated in the chapter.

Oct. 1 The owner, Michael O'Malley, invested $50,000 cash and $24,000 in equipment in the business.

2 Paid rent to Bellamy Agency, $600, with check no. 75.

3 Cash sales, $2,200.

6 Purchased store equipment for $5,000 from Quantum Company, with check no. 76.

7 Purchased merchandise for cash, $6,500, from Hoffman Company, with check no. 77.

8 Paid Boronski Company invoice, $1,800, less 2 percent discount, with check no. 78 (assume that a payable has already been recorded).

9 Paid advertising bill, $350, to WKBD, with check no. 79.

10 Cash sales, $3,910.

12 Received $800 on account from L. Saluna.

13 Purchased used truck for cash, $3,520, from Denecker Company, with check no. 80.

19 Received $4,180 from Precision Company, in settlement of a $4,000 note plus interest.

Oct. 20 Received $1,078 ($1,100 less $22 cash discount) from I. Fraden.

21 Paid O'Malley $2,000 from business for personal use by issuing check no. 81.

23 Paid Rinardi Company invoice, $2,500, less 2 percent discount, with check no. 82.

26 Paid Curran Company for freight on merchandise received, $60, with check no. 83.

27 Cash sales, $4,800.

28 Paid C. Shegley for monthly salary, $1,400, with check no. 84.

31 Purchased land from O. Dante for $20,000, paying $5,000 with check no. 85 and signing a note payable for $15,000.

REQUIRED ▶

1. Enter the preceding transactions in the cash receipts and cash payments journals.
2. Foot and crossfoot the journals.
3. If a manager wanted to know the total sales for the accounting period, where else would the manager need to refer to obtain the data needed?

P 8.

LO4 Comprehensive Use of
LO5 Special-Purpose Journals

The following transactions were completed by Stackpole's Men's Wear during the month of May, its first month of operation:

May 1 Garrett Stackpole deposited $40,000 in the new company's bank account.

2 Issued check no. 101 to Bannister Realty for one month's rent, $2,400.

3 Received merchandise from Seagal Company, $14,000, invoice dated May 2, terms 2/10, n/60, FOB shipping point.

4 Received from Gallagher Company freight bill on merchandise purchased, $1,928, terms n/20.

5 Issued check no. 102 to Kenawahi Company for store equipment, $14,800.

6 Borrowed $16,000 from the bank on a 90-day, 9 percent note.

7 Cash sales for the first week, $3,964. (To shorten this problem, cash sales are recorded weekly instead of daily, as they would be in actual practice.)

8 Sold merchandise to Avon Old Farms School, $1,800, terms 2/10, n/30, invoice no. 1001.

9 Sold merchandise to Missy Cavanaugh, $600, terms n/20, invoice no. 1002.

10 Purchased advertising in the *Sentinel-Gazette*, $300, terms n/15.

11 Issued check no. 103 for purchase of May 3 less discount.

12 Issued a credit memorandum for merchandise returned by Missy Cavanaugh, $60.

15 Cash sales for the second week, $6,984.

16 Received merchandise from Seagal Company, $3,800, invoice dated May 15, terms 2/10, n/60, FOB shipping point.

17 Received from Gallagher Company freight bill on merchandise purchased, $524, terms n/20.

18 Received merchandise from Cronos Company, $2,800, invoice dated May 16, terms 1/10, n/60, FOB destination.

18 Received payment in full less discount from Avon Old Farms School.

20 Received a credit memorandum from Seagal Company for merchandise returned, $200.

21 Cash sales for the third week, $5,824.

23 Issued check no. 104 for the total amount owed Gallagher Company.

24 Sold merchandise to Avon Old Farms School, $1,368, terms 2/10, n/30, invoice no. 1003.

25 Issued check no. 105 in payment of the amount owed Seagal Company less discount.

26 Sold merchandise to Alicia Menotte, $744, terms n/20, invoice no. 1004.

27 Issued check no. 106 for the amount owed the *Sentinel-Gazette*.

28 Cash sales for the fourth week, $3,948.

31 Issued check no. 107 to Payroll for sales salaries for the month of May, $7,200.

REQUIRED ▶

1. Prepare a sales journal, a multicolumn purchases journal, a cash receipts journal, a cash payments journal, and a general journal. Use Page 1 for all journal references.
2. Open the following general ledger accounts: Cash (111); Accounts Receivable (112); Store Equipment (141); Accounts Payable (211); Notes Payable (212); Garrett Stackpole, Capital (311); Sales (411); Sales Discounts (412); Sales Returns and

Allowances (413); Purchases (511); Purchases Discounts (512); Purchases Returns and Allowances (513); Freight In (514); Sales Salaries Expense (611); Advertising Expense (612); and Rent Expense (613).

3. Open accounts receivable subsidiary ledger accounts for Avon Old Farms School, Missy Cavanaugh, and Alicia Menotte.

4. Open accounts payable subsidiary ledger accounts for Cronos Company, Gallagher Company, the *Sentinel-Gazette*, and Seagal Company.

5. Enter the transactions in the journals and post as appropriate.

6. Foot and crossfoot the journals, and make the end-of-month postings.

7. Prepare a trial balance of the general ledger and prove the control balances of Accounts Receivable and Accounts Payable by preparing schedules of accounts receivable and accounts payable.

SKILLS DEVELOPMENT CASES

Conceptual Analysis

LO1 Accounting System
LO2 Evaluation
LO4

SD 1. Asian Accent Interiors is an interior design company that was started three years ago by Agnes Hiramata. For the first two years of the company's life, Hiramata helped clients plan the decorating of their luxury apartments in Manhattan. Hiramata did not sell any furnishings herself but was paid an hourly fee plus a percentage of the total purchases made by her clients. Although the business was successful, it was very simple. And it required just a simple manual accounting system consisting of a general journal and a general ledger. During the past year, Hiramata expanded. She opened a second-floor studio and began displaying and selling selected furnishings. She hired her first employees and began buying and selling on credit. As the number of daily transactions multiplied, Hiramata began to find the manual accounting system very burdensome. It was taking far too much time to record and post all the transactions. The company does not have a computer at present, but Hiramata is thinking about buying one. She has come to you for help. Evaluate Hiramata's current accounting system in terms of the principles of systems design (excluding the control principle) and make a recommendation about the types of accounting systems Hiramata should consider installing. Write a memorandum to Hiramata providing your analysis and recommendation.

LO2 General Ledger Systems

SD 2. Fine Arts Gallery and Framing, located in the South Fork Mall, was established two years ago to provide framing services. At the time, Gary Hoben, the owner, set up an accounting system. His business is a sole proprietorship service business that uses a general journal and general ledger. Because all sales were for cash or by credit card and because Hoben made a practice of paying all bills by the end of the month, the gallery had few receivables or payables. Over the past year, however, Hoben has added an inventory of color prints and posters, which carry a high profit margin. In addition, the new suppliers offer generous terms for payment. As a result, Hoben has allowed customers who buy framed prints or posters to pay over a period of three months. With the increased number of transactions involving inventory, accounts receivable, and accounts payable, Hoben's general journal/general ledger accounting system is now outdated. What kind of accounting system could Hoben use to handle the increased number and complexity of the store's transactions?

LO2 Switching to a General Ledger Accounting System

SD 3. Krock's & Marici's operates a growing full-service bookstore in the Louisville area. The firm is known for excellent service and large inventories of books in a wide number of fields, such as art, history, business, technology, travel, fiction, and juvenile. To increase traffic and project a casual image, the company has a coffee shop in the bookstore. The owner's accountant has recommended that it install a general ledger software system. Describe a general ledger software system and identify the source documents, software function, and output documents that would constitute the system. What do you think the advantages of this system will be?

Ethical Dilemma

SD 4.

LO4 **Confidentiality of Accounting Records**

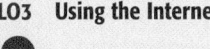

Frank Santino is the accounting manager at the Ford and Toyota dealership in Petersburg, Texas, a town with a population of 50,000. At a barbecue, José Martinez, a close friend, mentions that he is planning to sell some land to Louis Johnson for $20,000 and will allow Johnson to pay him over a five-year period. Santino, who happened to have been reviewing the delinquent accounts at the dealership earlier in the day, knows that Johnson has a poor payment history and that his car may have to be repossessed. Martinez asks Santino what he thinks about the sale. What ethical issue is involved here? If you were Santino, would you warn Martinez about Johnson's credit record?

Research Activity

SD 5.

LO3 **Using the Internet**

Assume you have been asked by your boss, the owner of a small dress shop, to investigate general ledger software for her business. Both Peachtree Software and Intuit Software, the publisher of Quickbooks®, have web pages. Access these web sites through the Needles Accounting Resource Center Web Site at http://accounting.college.hmco.com/students. Study the information you find, and write a summary of the information and its usefulness. Can you assess the differences in the software approaches of the two companies and their applicability to a small dress shop?

Decision-Making Practice

SD 6.

LO4 **Design of Special-Purpose**
LO5 **Journals**

RW Finer Foods Company, owned by Robert Washington, is a neighborhood grocery store that accepts cash or checks in payment for food. Known for its informality, the store has been very successful and has grown with the community. Along with that growth, however, has come an increase in the number of bad checks customers have written for purchases. Washington is concerned about the difficulty of accounting for these returned checks, so he has asked you to look into the problem.

In addition to a purchases journal and a cash payments journal, the company has a combination single-column sales and cash receipts journal. The combination journal has worked in the past because all sales are for cash (including checks), and almost all cash receipts represent sales transactions. Thus, the single column represents a debit to Cash and a credit to Sales.

The bad checks are recorded individually in the general journal by debiting Accounts Receivable and crediting Cash for the amount of the check. When a customer pays off a bad check, another entry is made in the general journal debiting Cash and crediting Accounts Receivable. Returned Check Revenue for the amount of $10, which represents reimbursement of the service charge by the bank, will be recorded in the Sales/Cash Receipts journal when the bad check is collected. Washington keeps the returned checks in an envelope. When a customer comes in to pay one off, Washington gives the check back. No other records of the returned checks are maintained.

In studying the problem, you discover that the company is averaging ten returned checks per day, totaling $1,000. As part of the solution, you recommend that Washington issue check-cashing cards to customers whose credit is approved in advance. The card must be presented when a customer offers a check in payment for groceries. You recommend further that a special-purpose journal be established for the returned checks and returned check revenue, that a subsidiary ledger be maintained, and that the combination sales/cash receipts journal be expanded.

1. Draw and label the columns for the new returned checks journal and the expanded sales/cash receipts journal.
2. Assume that there are 300 returned checks and 280 collections per month and that the records are closed each month. How many written lines can be saved each month by recording returned checks and subsequent collections in the special journals? How many postings can be saved each month? (Ignore the effect of the subsidiary ledger.)
3. Describe the nature and use of the subsidiary ledger. What advantages do you see in having a subsidiary ledger?
4. Assuming that it takes approximately two and a half minutes to make each entry and related postings under the old system of recording bad checks and one minute to

make each entry and related postings under the new system, what are the monthly savings if the cost is $20 an hour? What further, and possibly more significant, savings may be realized by using the new system?

 Group Activity: After presenting parts **1** and **3** in class, divide the class into teams to work on parts **2** and **4**. Compare and discuss results.

FINANCIAL REPORTING AND ANALYSIS CASES

Interpreting Financial Reports

FRA 1.

LO1 Electronic Commerce on the
LO3 Internet

Amazon.com, <<u>www.amazon.com</u>> which describes itself as the "Earth's Biggest Bookstore," is the leading Internet book seller. It might be described as a "virtual" bookstore because it carries only a relatively few books in its Seattle warehouse, far fewer than the average superstore, like Borders or Barnes & Noble. Buyers choose from a selection of 2.5 million books on the Internet and give credit card information to place an order. Amazon.com verifies the information and electronically sends the order to a wholesaler that packages and sends the order, usually within one day. Ninety-five percent of the books Amazon.com sells are delivered by these wholesalers, which charge a wholesale markup for handling and shipping. The cost of having to rely on wholesalers for distribution is one reason that Amazon.com has not yet reached profitability in spite of its success. As a result, the company is planning to expand its own distribution capability, which it believes it can do at a lower cost.[8]

1. Define electronic commerce and describe generally how conducting business on the Internet differs from conducting business in a retail store.
2. Describe how you believe the four principles of systems design apply to Amazon.com's sale and distribution of books as compared to a more traditional bookstore.
3. What changes in the application of these principles will occur if Amazon.com begins to do more of its own distribution?

International Company

This category is not applicable to this chapter.

Toys "R" Us Annual Report

FRA 2.

LO1 Principles of Accounting
Systems Design

In its Annual Report, the management of Toys "R" Us <<u>www.tru.com</u>> described the success of Toysrus.com, whose sales have increased by 23 percent in the past year, as follows:

> Toysrus.com recorded its first operating profit of $3 million during the fourth quarter of 2002 versus an operating loss of $(17) million for the prior year's fourth quarter. . . . A number of factors contributed to this significant improvement in operating performance including higher merchandise margins, . . . diligent expense control, reduced inventory levels, and increased integration between Babiesrus.com and Babies "R" Us stores

Explain how these efforts to improve operating results are facilitated by computer systems that comply with the principles of cost-benefit, control, compatibility, and flexibility. Give an example from this quote to support each principle.

Comparison Case

This category is not applicable to this chapter.

Fingraph® Financial Analyst™

This category is not applicable to this chapter.

Internet Case

**LO1 Accounting and Systems
Careers**

FRA 3. Many accountants are involved in systems careers. Go to the Needles Accounting Resource Center Web Site at http://accounting.college.hmco.com/students. Under Companies Web Links, go to the annual reports on the web sites for PeopleSoft <www.peoplesoft.com>, Accenture (formerly Andersen Consulting) <www.accenture.com>, and PricewaterhouseCoopers <www.pwc.com>. Find information describing these firms' businesses and look for the sections on career opportunities that relate to accounting and systems. For each firm, summarize its business and the career opportunities and be prepared to discuss what you find in class.

8

Chapter 8 focuses on the basic components and control activities of an effective internal control system, with emphasis on internal control over merchandising transactions.

Internal Control

LEARNING OBJECTIVES

LO1 Define *internal control*, explain its basic components and limitations, and give examples of control activities.

LO2 Apply internal control activities to common merchandising transactions.

LO3 Demonstrate the control of cash by preparing a bank reconciliation.

SUPPLEMENTAL OBJECTIVES

SO4 Demonstrate the use of a simple imprest system.

SO5 Define *voucher system* and describe the components and operation of a voucher system.

DECISION POINT

A USER'S FOCUS

Oxford Health Plans, Inc. <www.oxhp.com>   After a decade of rapid growth, Oxford Health Plans, Inc., surprised Wall Street analysts with losses of more than $200 million. How did disaster strike so quickly? Ironically, Oxford's dazzling growth was its undoing. Its systems were unable to handle the expanding business as it grew from 217,000 plan members to over 1.9 million. As Oxford was signing up hordes of new members, the company was unable to send out monthly bills to thousands of member accounts, and it couldn't track payments to hundreds of doctors and hospitals. As a result, uncollected receivables from customers tripled to more than $400 million. Also, amounts owed to caregivers soared to more than $650 million. As one analyst said, "If you drive a train at 150 miles an hour without good tracks, you derail".[1] What could Oxford's management have done to avoid these problems?

Problems with controls and systems are serious for all companies. At Oxford, they led to an inability to collect from members and to overpayments to caregivers, which contributed to the company's losses. Oxford's management was forced to institute new systems and internal controls over billing, accounts receivable, and cash receipts. Further, the company had to establish internal controls over accounts payable and cash disbursements so that it did not under- or overpay. Such controls are critical to managing cash, protecting revenues, and restraining costs. As you will see in the following section, these goals can be achieved through an internal control structure that

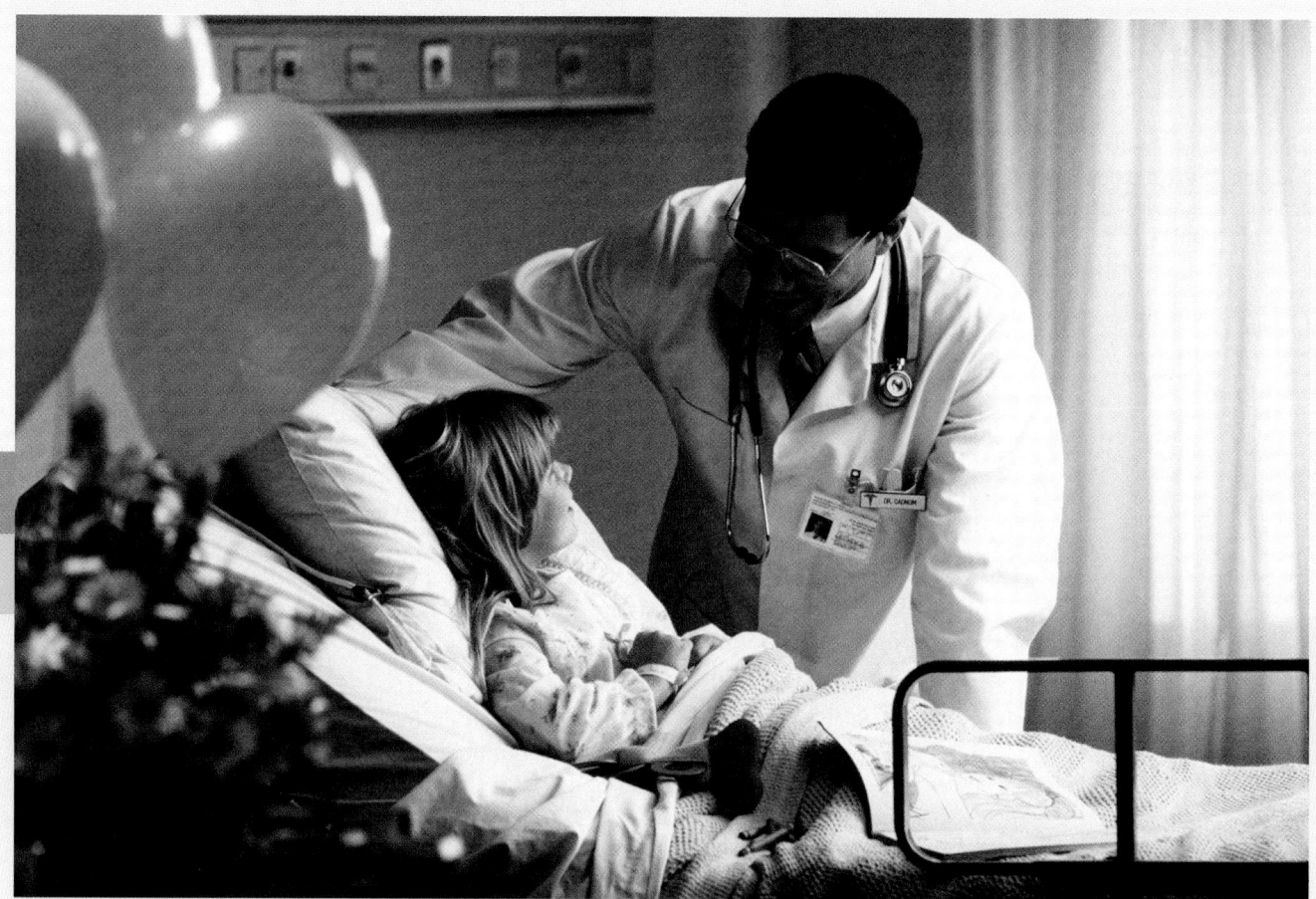

Why are good internal controls critical for a company like Oxford Health Plans, Inc.?

includes an accounting information system with procedures specifically designed to prevent losses. Fortunately, Oxford was able to resolve its systems and control weaknesses and is now a Fortune 500 company with annual revenues of almost $5 million.

INTERNAL CONTROL: BASIC COMPONENTS AND CONTROL ACTIVITIES

LO1 Define *internal control,* explain its basic components and limitations, and give examples of control activities.

RELATED TEXT ASSIGNMENTS
Q: 1, 2, 3, 4
SE: 1, 2, 3, 4
E: 1, 2, 3, 4, 5
P: 2, 4, 6, 7
SD: 1, 2, 4, 5
FRA: 1, 2, 3, 4

www.circuitcity.com

KEY POINT: A good system of internal control safeguards a company's assets, produces reliable accounting records, promotes operational efficiency, and encourages adherence to management's policies.

◆ STOP AND THINK!
Which of the following accounts would be assigned a higher level of risk: Buildings or Merchandise Inventory?
Merchandise Inventory would because there is a greater risk of human error in recording the large number of transactions involved and because there is a greater risk of theft. ■

A merchandising company can have inaccurate accounting records as well as high losses of cash and inventory if it does not take steps to protect its assets. The best way to do this is to set up and maintain a good system of internal control.

MANAGEMENT'S RESPONSIBILITY FOR INTERNAL CONTROL

Management is responsible for establishing a satisfactory system of internal control. **Internal control** is defined as all the policies and procedures management uses to ensure the reliability of financial reporting, compliance with laws and regulations, and the effectiveness and efficiency of operations. In other words, management must safeguard the firm's assets and have reliable accounting records. It must ensure that employees comply with legal requirements and operate the company in the best way possible.

Management comments on its responsibility and effectiveness in achieving the goals of internal control in the "Report of Management" in the company's annual report to stockholders. A portion of this statement from the annual report of Circuit City Stores, Inc., follows:

> Management is responsible for maintaining an internal control structure designed to provide reasonable assurance that the books and records reflect the transactions of the Company and that the Company's established policies and procedures are carefully followed. Because of inherent limitations in any system, there can be no absolute assurance that errors or irregularities will not occur. Nevertheless, management believes that the internal control structure provides reasonable assurance that assets are safeguarded and that financial information is objective and reliable.[2]

COMPONENTS OF INTERNAL CONTROL

To accomplish the objectives of internal control, management must establish five interrelated components of internal control:[3]

1. *Control environment* The **control environment** is created by the overall attitude, awareness, and actions of management. It includes management's integrity and ethics, philosophy and operating style, organizational structure, method of assigning authority and responsibility, and personnel policies and practices. Personnel should be qualified to handle responsibilities, which means that employees must be trained and informed. For example, the manager of a retail store should train employees to follow prescribed procedures for handling cash sales, credit card sales, and returns and refunds.

2. *Risk assessment* **Risk assessment** is the identification of areas in which risks of loss of assets or inaccuracies in the accounting records are high so that adequate controls can be implemented. Among the greater risks in a retail store are that employees will take cash or that customers will shoplift merchandise.

3. *Information and communication* **Information and communication** relates to the accounting system established by management to identify, assemble, analyze, classify, record, and report a company's transactions, and to the need for clear communication of individual responsibilities in performing the accounting functions.

4. *Control activities* **Control activities** are the policies and procedures management puts in place to see that its directives are carried out. Control activities are discussed in more detail in the next section.

5. *Monitoring*   Monitoring involves management's regular assessment of the quality of internal control, including periodic review of compliance with all policies and procedures. For example, large companies often have a staff of internal auditors who review the company's system of internal control to determine if it is working properly and if procedures are being followed. In smaller businesses, owners and managers conduct these reviews.

CONTROL ACTIVITIES

Control activities are a principal way in which companies implement internal control in an accounting information system. These activities safeguard a company's assets and ensure the reliability of accounting records. Control activities include the following:

1. *Authorization*   All transactions and activities should be properly authorized by management. In a retail store, for example, some transactions, such as normal cash sales, are authorized routinely; others, such as issuing a refund, may require a manager's approval.

2. *Recording transactions*   To facilitate preparation of financial statements and to establish accountability for assets, all transactions should be recorded. For example, in a retail store, the cash register records sales, refunds, and other transactions internally on a paper tape or computer disk so that the cashier can be held responsible for the cash received and the merchandise removed during his or her shift.

3. *Documents and records*   Using well-designed documents helps ensure the proper recording of transactions. For example, to ensure that all transactions are recorded, invoices and other documents should be prenumbered, and all numbers should be accounted for.

4. *Physical controls*   Physical controls permit access to assets only with management's authorization. For example, retail stores should use cash registers, and only the cashier responsible for the cash in a register should have access to it. Other employees should not be able to open the cash drawer if the cashier is not present. Likewise, warehouses and storerooms should be accessible only to authorized personnel. Access to accounting records, including those stored in company computers, should also be controlled.

5. *Periodic independent verification*   The records should be periodically checked against the assets by someone other than the persons responsible for those records and assets. For example, at the end of each shift or day, the owner or store manager should count the cash in the cash drawer and compare the amount with the amount recorded on the tape or computer disk in the cash

FOCUS ON BUSINESS ETHICS

Which Frauds Are Most Common?

A survey of 5,000 large U.S. businesses disclosed that 21 percent suffered frauds in excess of $1 million. The most common were credit card frauds, check frauds, inventory theft, false invoices and phantom vendors, and expense account abuse. Major factors in allowing these frauds to take place were poor internal controls, management override of internal controls, and collusion. The most common methods of detection were notification by an employee, internal controls, internal auditor review, notification by a customer, and accidental discovery. Companies successful in preventing fraud have a good system of internal control and a formal code of ethics with a program to monitor compliance that includes a system for reporting incidents of fraud. These companies routinely communicate the existence of the program to their employees.[4]

register. Other examples of independent verification are the monthly bank reconciliation and periodic counts of physical inventory.

6. *Separation of duties* The organizational plan should separate functional responsibilities. Within a department, no one person should be in charge of authorizing transactions, operating the department, handling assets, and keeping records of assets. For example, in a stereo store, each employee should oversee only a single part of a transaction. A sales employee takes the order and creates an invoice. Another employee receives the customer's cash or credit card payment and issues a receipt. Once the customer has a paid receipt, and only then, a third employee obtains the item from the warehouse and gives it to the customer. A person in the accounting department subsequently records the sales from the tape or disk in the cash register, comparing them with the sales invoices and updating the inventory in the records. The separation of duties means that a mistake, careless or not, cannot be made without being seen by at least one other person.

KEY POINT: No control procedure can guarantee the prevention of theft. However, the more procedures there are in place, the less likely it is that a theft will occur.

7. *Sound personnel procedures* Sound practices should be followed in managing the people who carry out the functions of each department. Among those practices are supervision, rotation of key people among different jobs, insistence that employees take vacations, and bonding of personnel who handle cash or inventories. **Bonding** is the process of carefully checking an employee's background and insuring the company against theft by that person. Bonding does not guarantee against theft, but it does prevent or reduce economic loss if theft occurs. Prudent personnel procedures help ensure that employees know their jobs, are honest, and will find it difficult to carry out and conceal embezzlement over time.

LIMITATIONS OF INTERNAL CONTROL

No system of internal control is without weaknesses. As long as control procedures are performed by people, the internal control system will be vulnerable to human error. Errors may arise from misunderstandings, mistakes in judgment, carelessness, distraction, or fatigue. Separation of duties can be defeated through collusion by employees who secretly agree to deceive the company. In addition, established procedures may be ineffective against employees' errors or dishonesty, and controls that were initially effective may become ineffective when conditions change.[5] In some cases, the costs of establishing and maintaining elaborate systems may exceed the benefits. In a small business, for example, active involvement by the owner can be a practical substitute for the separation of some duties.

 Check out ACE for a Review Quiz at http://accounting.college.hmco.com/students.

INTERNAL CONTROL OVER MERCHANDISING TRANSACTIONS

LO2 Apply internal control activities to common merchandising transactions.

RELATED TEXT ASSIGNMENTS
Q: 5, 6, 7, 8, 16
SE: 4, 5
E: 5
P: 4, 6
SD: 1, 2, 4, 5
FRA: 1, 3

Sound internal control activities are needed in all aspects of a business, but particularly when assets are involved. Assets are especially vulnerable when they enter or leave a business. When sales are made, for example, cash or other assets enter the business, and goods or services leave the business. Activities must be set up to prevent theft during those transactions.

Likewise, purchases of assets and payments of liabilities must be controlled. The majority of those transactions can be safeguarded by adequate purchasing and payment systems. In addition, assets on hand, such as cash, investments, inventory, plant, and equipment, must be protected. Lack of adequate internal controls can lit-

www.oxhp.com erally bring a company to its knees as we saw with Oxford Health Plans, Inc., in the Decision Point at the beginning of the chapter.

In this section, you will see how internal control activities are applied to such merchandising transactions as cash sales receipts, purchases, and cash payments. Similar activities are applicable to service and manufacturing businesses.

INTERNAL CONTROL AND MANAGEMENT GOALS

KEY POINT: Maintaining internal control is especially complex and difficult for a merchandiser. Management must not only establish controls for cash sales receipts, purchases, and cash payments, but also go to great lengths to manage and protect its inventory.

When a system of internal control is applied effectively to merchandising transactions, it can achieve important management goals. For example, two key goals for the success of a merchandising business are:

1. To prevent losses of cash or inventory owing to theft or fraud
2. To provide accurate records of merchandising transactions and account balances

Three broader goals for management are:

1. To keep enough inventory on hand to sell to customers without overstocking
2. To keep enough cash on hand to pay for purchases in time to receive discounts
3. To keep credit losses as low as possible by making credit sales only to customers who are likely to pay on time

One control used in meeting broad management goals is the cash budget, which projects future cash receipts and disbursements. By maintaining adequate cash balances, a company is able to take advantage of discounts on purchases, prepare to borrow money when necessary, and avoid the damaging effects of being unable to pay bills when they are due. By investing excess cash, the company can earn interest until the cash is needed.

KEY POINT: The separation of duties *can* be defeated through the collusion of two or more people.

A more specific accounting control is the separation of duties that involve the handling of cash. Such separation makes theft without detection extremely unlikely, unless two or more employees conspire. The separation of duties is easier in large businesses than in small ones, where one person may have to carry out several duties. The effectiveness of internal control over cash varies, based on the size and nature of the company. Most firms, however, should use the following procedures:

1. Separate the functions of authorization, recordkeeping, and custodianship of cash.
2. Limit the number of people who have access to cash.
3. Designate specific people who are responsible for handling cash.
4. Use banking facilities as much as possible, and keep the amount of cash on hand to a minimum.
5. Bond all employees who have access to cash.
6. Physically protect cash on hand by using cash registers, cashiers' cages, and safes.
7. Have a person who does not handle or record cash make periodic independent verifications of the cash on hand.
8. Record all cash receipts promptly.
9. Deposit all cash receipts promptly.
10. Make payments by check rather than by currency.
11. Have a person who does not authorize, handle, or record cash transactions reconcile the Cash account.

Notice that each of the foregoing procedures helps safeguard cash by making it more difficult for any one individual who has access to cash to steal or misuse it without being detected.

CONTROL OF CASH SALES RECEIPTS

Cash receipts for sales of goods and services can be received by mail or over the counter in the form of checks, credit or debit cards, or currency. Whatever the source of the payments, cash should be recorded immediately upon receipt. This is usually done by making an entry in a cash receipts journal. Such a journal establishes a written record of cash receipts that should prevent errors and make theft more difficult.

■ **CONTROL OF CASH RECEIVED THROUGH THE MAIL**   Payment by mail is increasing because of the expansion of mail-order sales. Cash receipts that arrive by mail are vulnerable to theft by the employees who handle them. To control mailed receipts, companies should urge customers to pay by check or by credit card instead of with currency.

Cash received through the mail should be handled by two or more employees. The employee who opens the mail should make a list in triplicate of the money received. The list should contain each payer's name, the purpose for which the money was sent, and the amount. One copy goes with the cash to the cashier, who deposits the money. The second copy goes to the accounting department for recording. The third copy is kept by the person who opens the mail. Errors can be easily caught because the amount deposited by the cashier must agree with the amount received and the amount recorded in the cash receipts journal.

■ **CONTROL OF CASH RECEIVED OVER THE COUNTER**   Two common tools for controlling cash sales receipts are cash registers and prenumbered sales tickets. The amount of a cash sale should be rung up on a cash register at the time of the sale. The cash register should be placed so that the customer can see the amount recorded. Each cash register should have a locked-in tape on which it prints the day's transactions. At the end of the day, the cashier counts the cash in the cash register and turns it in to the cashier's office. Another employee takes the tape out of the cash register and records the cash receipts for the day in the cash receipts journal. The amount of cash turned in and the amount recorded on the tape should agree; if not, any differences must be explained. Large retail chains commonly monitor cash receipts by having each cash register tied directly into a computer that records each transaction as it occurs. Whether the elements are performed manually or by computer, separating responsibility for cash receipts, cash deposits, and record-keeping is necessary to ensure good internal control.

In some stores, internal control is further strengthened by the use of prenumbered sales tickets and a central cash register or cashier's office, where all sales are rung up and collected by a person who does not participate in the sale. The sales-

● **STOP AND THINK!**

Why is it important to write down the amount of cash received through the mail or over the counter?

It is important because until there is a written record of the cash, there is no accountability. This is why some stores offer a reward to customers who report making a purchase without receiving a receipt. ■

KEY POINT: The cashier should not be allowed to remove the cash register tape or to record the day's cash receipts.

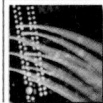

FOCUS ON BUSINESS TECHNOLOGY

How Do Computers Influence Internal Controls?

One of the more difficult challenges facing computer programmers is to build good internal controls into computerized accounting programs. Such computer programs must include controls that prevent unintentional errors as well as unauthorized access and tampering. The programs prevent errors through reasonableness checks (such as not allowing any transactions over a specified amount), mathematical checks that verify the arithmetic of transactions, and sequence checks that require documents and transactions to be in proper order. They typically use passwords and questions about randomly selected personal data to prevent unauthorized access to computer records. They may also use firewalls, which are strong electronic barriers to unauthorized access, as well as data encryption. Data encryption is a way of coding data so that if they are stolen, they are useless to the thief.

FIGURE 1
Internal Control for Purchasing and Paying for Goods and Services

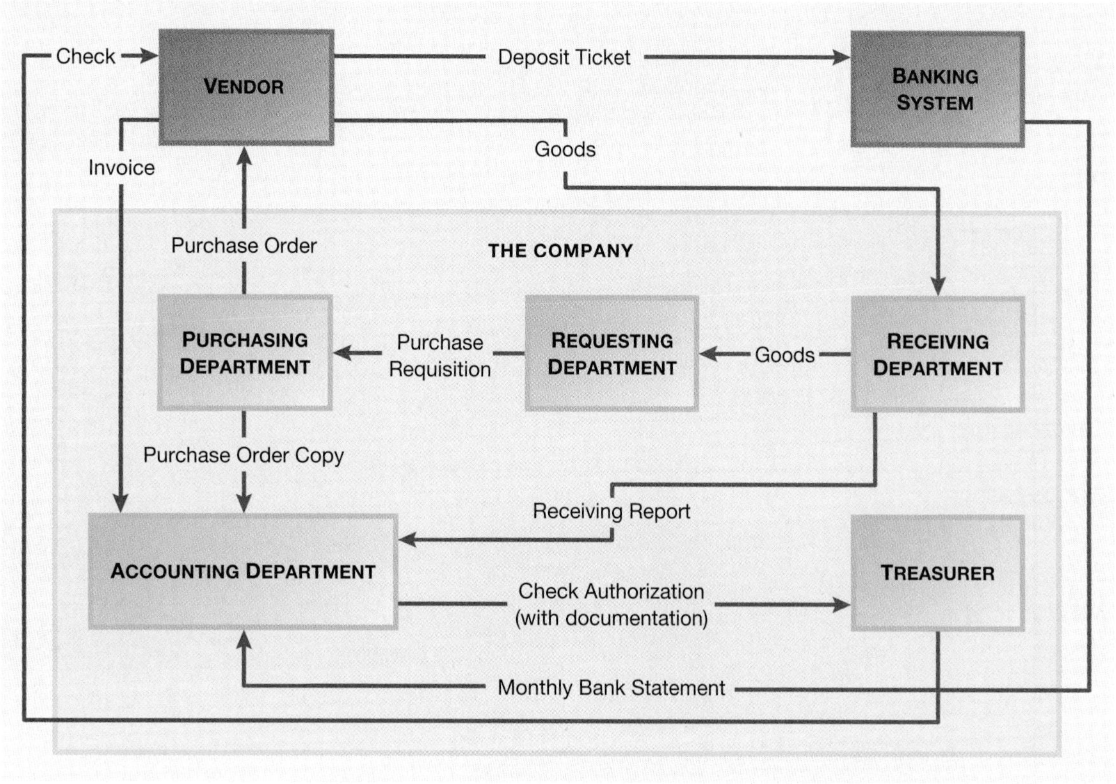

person completes a prenumbered sales ticket at the time of the sale, giving one copy to the customer and keeping a copy. At the end of the day, all sales tickets must be accounted for, and the sales total computed from the sales tickets should equal the total sales recorded on the cash register.

CONTROL OF PURCHASES AND CASH DISBURSEMENTS

Purchases and cash disbursements are particularly vulnerable to fraud and embezzlement. Lack of internal controls in these areas can cause other problems as well. For example, at Oxford Health Plans, Inc., discussed in this chapter's Decision Point, inadequate controls over cash disbursements resulted in overpayments that contributed to the company's huge losses, and failure to pay bills in a timely manner had a negative effect on the company's relations with caregivers.

www.oxhp.com

To avoid such situations, cash should be paid only after the receipt of specific authorization supported by documents that establish the validity and amount of the claim. In addition, maximum possible use should be made of the principle of separation of duties in the purchase of goods and services and the payment for them. The degree of separation of duties varies, depending on the size of the business. Figure 1 shows how separation of duties can be maximized in large companies. Five internal units (the requesting department, the purchasing department, the accounting department, the receiving department, and the treasurer) and two external contacts (the vendor and the banking system) all play a role in the internal control plan. Notice that business documents are also crucial components of the plan.

As shown in Figure 2, every action is documented and verified by at least one other person. Thus, the requesting department cannot work out a kickback scheme

FIGURE 2
Internal Control Plan for Purchases and Cash Disbursements

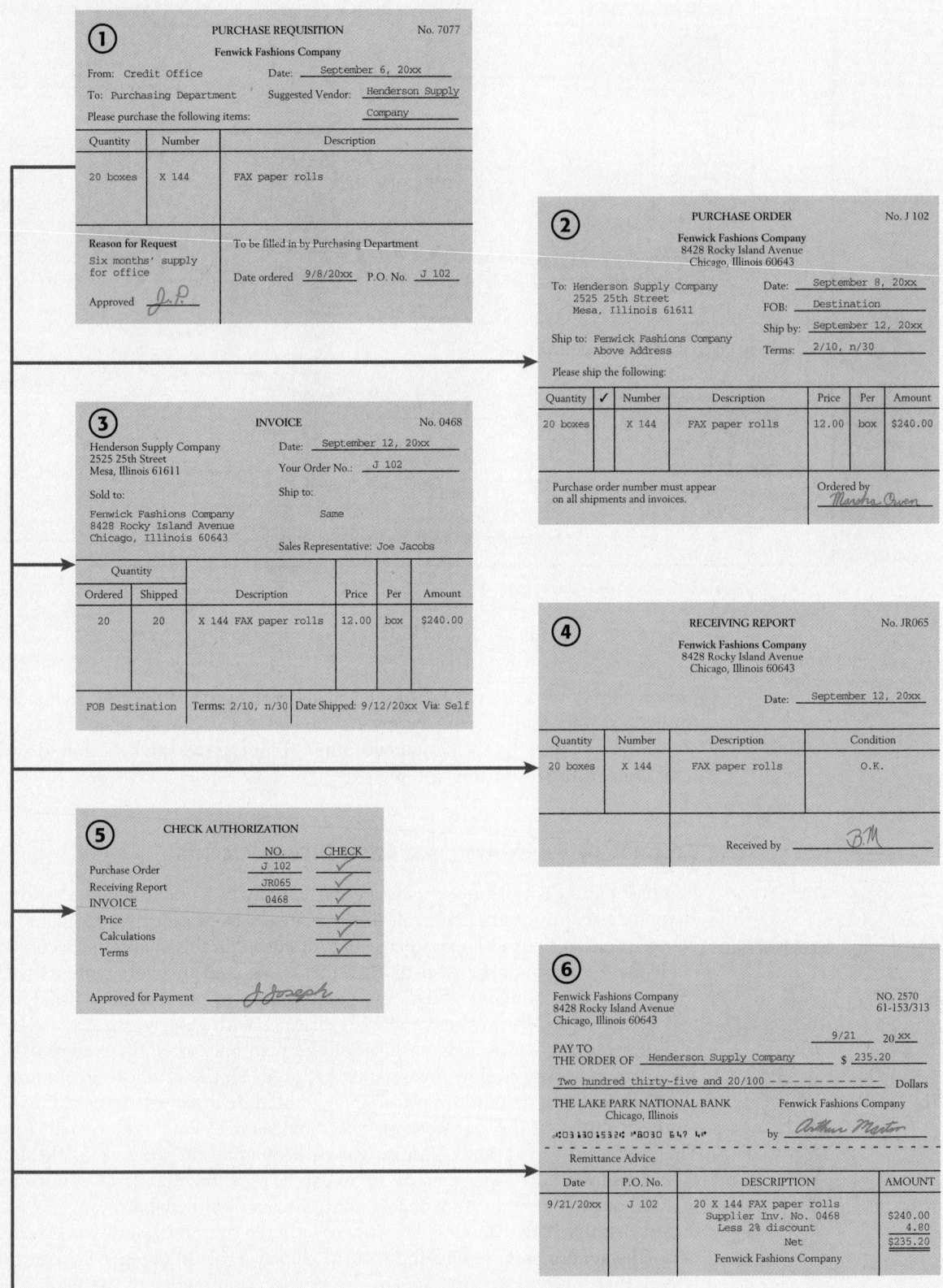

Business Document	Prepared by	Sent to	Verification and Related Procedures
① Purchase requisition	Requesting department	Purchasing department	Purchasing verifies authorization.
② Purchase order	Purchasing department	Vendor	Vendor sends goods or services in accordance with purchase order.
③ Invoice	Vendor	Accounting department	Accounting receives invoice from vendor.
④ Receiving report	Receiving department	Accounting department	Accounting compares invoice, purchase order, and receiving report. Accounting verifies prices.
⑤ Check authorization	Accounting department	Treasurer	Accounting attaches check authorization to invoice, purchase order, and receiving report.
⑥ Check	Treasurer	Vendor	Treasurer verifies all documents before preparing check.
⑦ Bank statement	Buyer's bank	Accounting department	Accounting compares amount and payee's name on returned check with check authorization.

⑦

Statement of Account with
THE LAKE PARK NATIONAL BANK
Chicago, Illinois

Fenwick Fashions Company
8428 Rocky Island Avenue
Chicago, Illinois 60643

Checking Acct No
8030-647-4
Period covered
Sept.30-Oct.31,20xx

Previous Balance	Checks/Debits—No.	Deposits/Credits—No.	S.C.	Current Balance
$2,645.78	$4,319.33 --16	$5,157.12 --7	$12.50	$3,471.07

CHECKS/DEBITS			DEPOSITS/CREDITS		DAILY BALANCES	
Posting Date	Check No.	Amount	Posting Date	Amount	Date	Amount
					09/30	2,645.78
10/01	2564	100.00	10/01	586.00	10/01	2,881.78
10/01	2565	250.00	10/05	1,500.00	10/04	2,825.60
10/04	2567	56.18	10/06	300.00	10/05	3,900.46
10/05	2566	425.14	10/16	1,845.50	10/06	4,183.34
10/06	2568	17.12	10/21	600.00	10/12	2,242.34
10/12	2569	1,705.80	10/24	300.00CM	10/16	3,687.84
10/12	2570	235.20	10/31	25.62IN	10/17	3,589.09
10/16	2571	400.00			10/21	4,189.09
10/17	2572	29.75			10/24	3,745.59
10/17	2573	69.00			10/25	3,586.09
10/24	2574	738.50			10/28	3,457.95
10/24		5.00DM			10/31	3,471.07
10/25	2575	7.50				
10/25	2577	152.00				
10/28		118.14NSF				
10/28		10.00DM				
10/31		12.50SC				

Explanation of Symbols:

CM – Credit Memo
DM – Debit Memo
NSF – Non-Sufficient Funds

SC – Service Charge
EC – Error Correction
OD – Overdraft
IN – Interest on Average Balance

The last amount
in this column
is your balance.

Please examine; if no errors are reported within ten (10) days, the account will be considered to be correct.

FOCUS ON BUSINESS ETHICS

Throw It or Shred It?

What happens to all the paper—records and documents of all sorts—generated by a company's accounting system? Some of it, of course, must be saved for tax and legal purposes, but much of it is discarded after a time. Because accounting records and documents contain much information that companies want to keep confidential, management is reluctant to simply throw the paper in the trash. As a result, a nationwide industry of information-destruction firms has grown up and prospers. Companies such as DocuShred, Inc., <www.docushred.com> of Pennsylvania specialize in picking up paper and shredding it in a confidential way. Some shredding machines can make confetti of up to ten tons of paper per hour at seven to fifteen cents per pound. This method is cheaper, faster, and more secure than any method the companies themselves could employ. Data-destruction companies recycle about 95 percent of the shredded paper.[6] Of course, documents that may be the subject of an investigation should not be destroyed, as happened in the infamous case of Enron <www.enron.com> and its auditor, Arthur Andersen.

KEY POINT: A purchase requisition is not the same as a purchase order. A purchase requisition is sent to the purchasing department; a purchase order is sent to the vendor.

TERMINOLOGY NOTE:

Invoice is the business term for "bill." Every business document must have a number for purposes of reference.

to make illegal payments to the supplier because the receiving department independently records receipts and the accounting department verifies prices. The receiving department cannot steal goods because the receiving report must equal the invoice. For the same reason, the supplier cannot bill for more goods than it ships. The accounting department's work is verified by the treasurer, and the treasurer ultimately is checked by the accounting department.

Figure 2 illustrates the typical sequence of documents used in an internal control plan for purchases and cash disbursements. To begin, the credit office (requesting department) of Fenwick Fashions Company fills out a formal request for a purchase, or **purchase requisition**, for 20 boxes of fax paper rolls (item 1). The department head approves it and forwards it to the purchasing department. The people in the purchasing department prepare a **purchase order**, as shown in item 2. The purchase order is addressed to the vendor (seller) and contains a description of the items ordered; the expected price, terms, and shipping date; and other shipping instructions. Fenwick Fashions Company does not pay any bill that is not accompanied by a purchase order number.

After receiving the purchase order, the vendor, Henderson Supply Company, ships the goods and sends an **invoice** or bill (item 3) to Fenwick Fashions Company. The invoice gives the quantity and description of the goods delivered, the price, and the terms of payment. If goods cannot all be shipped immediately, the estimated date for shipment of the remainder is indicated.

When the goods reach the receiving department of Fenwick Fashions Company, an employee writes the description, quantity, and condition of the goods on a form called a **receiving report** (item 4). The receiving department does not receive a copy of the purchase order or the invoice, so its employees do not know what should be received or its value. Thus, they are not tempted to steal any excess that may be delivered.

The receiving report is sent to the accounting department, where it is compared with the purchase order and the invoice. If everything is correct, the accounting department completes a **check authorization** and attaches it to the three supporting documents. The check authorization form shown in item 5 has a space for each item to be checked off as it is examined. Notice that the accounting department has all the documentary evidence for the transaction but does not have access to the assets purchased. Nor does it write the check for payment. This means that the people performing the accounting function cannot gain by falsifying documents in an effort to conceal fraud.

Finally, the treasurer examines all the documents and issues an order to the bank for payment, called a **check** (item 6), for the amount of the invoice less any appropriate discount. In some systems, the accounting department fills out the check so that all the treasurer has to do is inspect and sign it. The check is then sent to the supplier, with a remittance advice that shows what the check is for. A supplier who is not paid the proper amount will complain, of course, thus providing a form of outside control over the payment. Using a deposit ticket, the supplier deposits the check in the bank, which returns the canceled check with Fenwick Fashions Company's next bank statement (item 7). If the treasurer has made the check out for the wrong amount (or altered a pre-filled-in check), the problem will show up in the bank reconciliation.

There are many variations of the system just described. This example is offered as a simple system that provides adequate internal control.

 Check out ACE for a Review Quiz at http://accounting.college.hmco.com/students.

PREPARING A BANK RECONCILIATION

LO3 Demonstrate the control of cash by preparing a bank reconciliation.

RELATED TEXT ASSIGNMENTS
Q: 9, 10
SE: 6, 7
E: 6, 7, 8
P: 1, 2, 7
SD: 3

ENRICHMENT NOTE:
Periodically, banks detect individuals who are *kiting*. Kiting is the illegal issuing of checks when there isn't enough money to cover them. Before one kited check clears the bank, a kited check from another account is deposited to cover it, making an endless circle.

● **STOP AND THINK!**
How could a small business use information from bank statements and technology to reduce its cash management costs?

Using computer software to reconcile the cash balance with the bank statement will save time monthly. A detailed listing by category of all bank charges for previous periods may highlight areas where costs are controllable and could be reduced. Even small companies can save money by evaluating how they conduct business. ∎

It is rare that the balance of a company's Cash account will exactly equal the cash balance shown on the bank statement. Certain transactions shown in the company's records may not have been recorded by the bank, and certain bank transactions may not appear in the company's records. Therefore, a necessary step in internal control is to prove both the balance shown on the bank statement and the balance of Cash in the accounting records.

A **bank reconciliation** is the process of accounting for the difference between the balance appearing on the bank statement and the balance of the Cash account in the company's records. This process involves making additions to and subtractions from both balances to arrive at the adjusted cash balance.

The most common transactions shown in the company's records but not entered in the bank's records are the following:

1. *Outstanding checks* These are checks that the company has issued and recorded but that do not yet appear on the bank statement.

2. *Deposits in transit* These are deposits mailed or taken to the bank but not received in time to be recorded on the bank statement.

Transactions that may appear on the bank statement but not in the company's records include the following:

1. *Service charges (SC)* Banks often charge a fee, or service charge, for the use of a checking account. Many banks base the service charge on a number of factors, such as the average balance of the account during the month or the number of checks drawn.

2. *NSF (nonsufficient funds) checks* An NSF check is a check that the company has deposited in its bank account but that is not paid when the bank presents it to the issuer's bank. The bank charges the company's account and returns the check so that the company can try to collect the amount due. If the bank has deducted the NSF check from the bank statement but the company has not deducted it from its book balance, an adjustment must be made in the bank reconciliation. The company usually reclassifies the NSF check from Cash to Accounts Receivable because it must now collect from the person or company that wrote the check.

3. *Miscellaneous debits and credits* Banks charge for other services as well, including stopping payment on checks and printing checks. The bank notifies the

depositor of each deduction by including a debit memorandum with the monthly statement. A bank will also sometimes serve as an agent in collecting on promissory notes for the depositor. In such a case, a credit memorandum will be included in the statement, along with a debit memorandum of the service charge.

4. *Interest income*   Banks commonly pay interest on a company's average balance. Accounts that pay interest are sometimes called NOW or money market accounts. Such interest is reported on the bank statement.

An error by either the bank or the depositor will, of course, require immediate correction.

ILLUSTRATION OF A BANK RECONCILIATION

KEY POINT: The ending bank statement balance does not represent the amount that should appear on the balance sheet for cash. There are events and items, such as deposits in transit and outstanding checks, that the bank is unaware of at the cutoff date. This is why a bank reconciliation must be prepared.

Assume that the October bank statement for Fenwick Fashions Company indicates a balance on October 31 of $3,471.07, and that in its records, Fenwick Fashions Company has a cash balance on October 31 of $2,415.91. The purpose of a bank reconciliation is to identify the items that make up the difference between these amounts and to determine the correct cash balance. The bank reconciliation for Fenwick Fashions Company is shown in Exhibit 1. The numbered items in the exhibit refer to the following:

1. A deposit in the amount of $276.00 was mailed to the bank on October 31 and has not been recorded by the bank.

2. Five checks issued in October or prior months have not yet been paid by the bank, as follows:

Check No.	Date	Amount
551	Sept. 14	$150.00
576	Oct. 30	40.68
578	Oct. 31	500.00
579	Oct. 31	370.00
580	Oct. 31	130.50

3. The deposit for cash sales of October 6 was incorrectly recorded in Fenwick Fashions Company's records as $330.00. The bank correctly recorded the deposit as $300.00.

STUDY NOTE: A credit memorandum means that an amount was *added* to the bank balance; a debit memorandum means that an amount was *deducted*.

4. Among the returned checks was a credit memorandum showing that the bank had collected a promissory note from A. Jacobs in the amount of $280.00, plus $20.00 in interest on the note. A debit memorandum was also enclosed for the $5.00 collection fee. No entry had been made on Fenwick Fashions Company's records.

5. Also returned with the bank statement was an NSF check for $128.14. This check had been received from a customer named Arthur Clubb. The NSF check from Clubb was not reflected in the company's accounting records.

6. A debit memorandum was enclosed for the regular monthly service charge of $12.50. This service charge had not yet been recorded by Fenwick Fashions Company.

7. Interest earned by Fenwick Fashions Company on the average balance was reported as $15.62.

Note in Exhibit 1 that starting from their separate balances, both the bank and book amounts are adjusted to the amount of $2,555.89. This adjusted balance is the

EXHIBIT 1
Bank Reconciliation

KEY POINT: Even though the September 14 check was deducted on the September 30 reconciliation, it must be deducted again in each subsequent month in which it remains outstanding.

STUDY NOTE: It is possible to place an item in the wrong section of a bank reconciliation and still have it balance. The *correct* adjusted balance must be obtained.

Fenwick Fashions Company
Bank Reconciliation
October 31, 20xx

Balance per bank, October 31		$3,471.07
① Add deposit of October 31 in transit		276.00
		$3,747.07
② Less outstanding checks:		
No. 551	$150.00	
No. 576	40.68	
No. 578	500.00	
No. 579	370.00	
No. 580	130.50	1,191.18
Adjusted bank balance, October 31		**$2,555.89**
Balance per books, October 31		$2,415.91
Add:		
④ Note receivable collected by bank	$280.00	
④ Interest income on note	20.00	
⑦ Interest income	15.62	315.62
		$2,731.53
Less:		
③ Overstatement of deposit of October 6	$ 30.00	
④ Collection fee	5.00	
⑤ NSF check of Arthur Clubb	128.14	
⑥ Service charge	12.50	175.64
Adjusted book balance, October 31		**$2,555.89**

Note: The circled numbers refer to the items listed in the text.

amount of cash owned by the company on October 31 and thus is the amount that should appear on its October 31 balance sheet.

RECORDING TRANSACTIONS AFTER RECONCILIATION

The adjusted balance of cash differs from both the bank statement and Fenwick Fashions Company's records. The bank balance will automatically become correct when outstanding checks are presented for payment and the deposit in transit is received and recorded by the bank. Entries must be made, however, for the transactions necessary to update the book balance. All the items reported by the bank but not yet recorded by the company must be recorded in the general journal by means of the following entries:

KEY POINT: Notice that only those transactions the company has not recorded before receiving the bank statement are recorded.

$$A = L + OE$$
$$+ \quad\quad +$$
$$-$$

KEY POINT: Every entry involves either a debit or a credit to Cash.

Oct. 31	Cash	300.00	
	Notes Receivable		280.00
	Interest Income		20.00
	Note receivable of $280.00		
	and interest of $20.00 collected		
	by bank from A. Jacobs		

A = L + OE
+   +
	Oct. 31	Cash
		    Interest Income
		    Interest on average bank
		    account balance
			15.62	15.62

A = L + OE
–   –
	31	Sales
		    Cash
		    Correction of error in recording
		    a $300.00 deposit as $330.00
			30.00	30.00

A = L + OE
+
–
	31	Accounts Receivable
		    Cash
		    NSF check of Arthur Clubb
		    returned by bank
			128.14	128.14

A = L + OE
–   –
	31	Bank Service Charges Expense
		    Cash
		    Bank service charge ($12.50)
		    and collection fee ($5.00) for October
			17.50	17.50

It is acceptable to record these entries in one or two compound entries to save time and space.

 Check out ACE for a Review Quiz at http://accounting.college.hmco.com/students.

PETTY CASH PROCEDURES

SO4 Demonstrate the use of a simple imprest system.

RELATED TEXT ASSIGNMENTS
Q: 11, 12, 13, 14, 15, 16
SE: 8
E: 9, 10
P: 3, 8

It is not always practical to make every disbursement by check. For example, it is sometimes necessary to make small payments of cash for such things as postage stamps, incoming postage, shipping charges due, or minor purchases of pens, paper, and the like.

For situations in which it is inconvenient to pay by check, most companies set up a **petty cash fund**. One of the best ways to control a petty cash fund is through the use of an **imprest system**. Under this system, a petty cash fund is established for a fixed amount. Each cash payment from the fund is documented by a voucher. The fund is periodically reimbursed, based on the vouchers, by the exact amount necessary to restore its original cash balance.

ESTABLISHING THE PETTY CASH FUND

Some companies have a regular cashier or other employee who administers the petty cash fund. To establish the fund, the company issues a check for an amount intended to cover two to four weeks of small expenditures. The check is cashed and the money placed in the petty cash box, drawer, or envelope.

The only entry required when the fund is established is to record the check.

A = L + OE
+
–
	Oct. 14	Petty Cash
		    Cash
		    To establish the petty cash fund
			100.00	100.00

MAKING DISBURSEMENTS FROM THE PETTY CASH FUND

The custodian of the petty cash fund should prepare a **petty cash voucher**, or written authorization, for each expenditure, as shown in Figure 3. On each petty cash

FIGURE 3
Petty Cash Voucher

PETTY CASH VOUCHER

No. X 744

Date   Oct. 23, 20xx

For   Postage due

Charge to   Postage Expense

Amount $2.86

_____W.S._____   _____Tom L._____
Approved by   Received by

KEY POINT: Even though withdrawals from petty cash are generally small, the cumulative total over time can represent a substantial amount. Accordingly, an effective system of internal control must be established for the management of the fund.

voucher, the custodian enters the date, amount, and purpose of the expenditure. The voucher is signed by the person who receives the payment.

The custodian should be informed that unannounced audits of the fund will be made occasionally. The cash in the fund plus the sum of the petty cash vouchers should at all times equal the amount shown in the Petty Cash account.

REIMBURSING THE PETTY CASH FUND

KEY POINT: When the petty cash fund is replenished, the Petty Cash account is neither debited nor credited. But if the size of the fund is changed, there should be an entry to Petty Cash.

At specified intervals, when the fund becomes low, and at the end of an accounting period, the petty cash fund is replenished by a check issued to the custodian for the exact amount of the expenditures. From time to time, there may be minor discrepancies in the amount of cash left in the fund at the time of reimbursement. In those cases, the amount of the discrepancy is recorded in a Cash Short or Over account—as a debit if short or as a credit if over.

Assume that after two weeks the petty cash fund established earlier has a cash balance of $14.27 and petty cash vouchers as follows: postage, $25.00; supplies, $30.55; and freight in, $30.00. The entry to replenish, or replace, the fund would be:

$A = L + OE$
$+$ $-$
$-$ $-$

Oct. 28	Postage Expense	25.00	
	Supplies	30.55	
	Freight In	30.00	
	Cash Short or Over	.18	
	Cash		85.73
	To replenish the petty cash fund		

Notice that the Petty Cash account was not affected by the entry to replenish the fund. The Petty Cash account is debited when the fund is established or the fund level is changed. Expense or asset accounts are debited each time the fund is replenished, including in this case $.18 to Cash Short or Over for a small cash shortage. In most cases, no further entries to the Petty Cash account are needed unless the firm wants to change the fixed amount of the fund.

The petty cash fund should be replenished at the end of an accounting period to bring it up to its fixed amount and ensure that changes in the other accounts involved are reflected in the current period's financial statements. If, through an oversight, the petty cash fund is not replenished at the end of the period, expenditures for the period still must appear on the income statement. They are shown through an adjusting entry debiting the expense accounts and crediting Petty Cash. The result is a reduction in the petty cash fund and the Petty Cash account by the amount of the adjusting entry. On the financial statements, the balance of the Petty Cash account is usually combined with other cash accounts.

✓ Check out ACE for a Review Quiz at http://accounting.college.hmco.com/students.

VOUCHER SYSTEMS

S05 Define *voucher system* and describe the components and operation of a voucher system.

RELATED TEXT ASSIGNMENTS
Q: 17, 18, 19, 20, 21
SE: 9, 10
P: 5

KEY POINT: The purpose of a voucher system is to control expenditures through mandatory documentation and written authorization.

A voucher system is any system that gives documentary proof of and written authorization for business transactions. In this section, we present a voucher system designed to keep the tightest possible control over a company's expenditures. It consists of records and procedures for systematically gathering, recording, and paying expenditures. The system provides strong internal control by separating duties and responsibilities in the following functions:

1. Authorization of expenditures

2. Receipt of goods and services

3. Validation of liability by examination of invoices from suppliers for correctness of prices, extensions (quantity times price), shipping costs, and credit terms

4. Payment of expenditure by check, taking discounts when possible

Under a voucher system, every liability must be recorded as soon as it is incurred. A written authorization, called a **voucher**, is prepared for each expenditure when it becomes an obligation to pay, and checks are written only for approved vouchers. No one person has the authority both to incur expenses and to issue checks. In large companies, the duties of authorizing expenditures, verifying receipt of goods and services, checking invoices, recording liabilities, and issuing checks are divided among different people. So, for both accounting and management control, every expenditure must be carefully and routinely reviewed and verified before payment. For each transaction, the written approval leaves a trail of documentary evidence, or what is called an **audit trail**.

COMPONENTS OF A VOUCHER SYSTEM

Although there is more than one way to set up a voucher system, most systems use (1) vouchers, (2) voucher checks, (3) a voucher register, and (4) a check register.

KEY POINT: A voucher serves the same purpose as a check authorization form.

■ **VOUCHERS**   Any business can use vouchers to control expenditures. A voucher serves as the basis of an accounting entry. To facilitate tracking, all vouchers are sequentially numbered, and a separate voucher is attached to each bill as it comes in. In the cash disbursement system introduced earlier in this chapter, a voucher would replace the check authorization form. Figure 4 shows the front and back of a typical voucher. On the front is important information about the expenditure and the authorizing signatures required for payment. On the back of the voucher is

FOCUS ON BUSINESS PRACTICE

Which Is More Important: B to C or B to B?

E-tailing, the selling of business (goods) to consumers (B to C), gets the most publicity, but the most rapidly growing segment of business use of the Internet is business to business (B to B) transactions. It is projected that B to B transactions will exceed $14 trillion, compared with $7 trillion for B to C transactions. Industries leading in B to B transactions are automotive, chemicals, paper and office products, computers and electronics, and utilities. Manual voucher systems are obviously not sufficient for this heavy volume of activity. B to B voucher systems will require strong internal controls that ensure proper delivery, precise product specifications, high levels of customer service, and timely, accurate bill payment.[7]

FIGURE 4
Front and Back of a Typical Voucher Form

Thomas Appliance Company

Payee	Belmont Products	Voucher No.	704
Address	Gary, Indiana	Date Due	7/13
		Date Paid	7/13
Terms	2/10, n/30	Check No.	205

Date	Invoice No.	Description	Amount
7/3	XL1066	10 cases Model 70X14	1,200--

Approved _____M. N._____   Approved _____a. Thomas_____
          Controller   Treasurer

STUDY NOTE: A voucher not only provides for the necessary signatures but also includes information and document numbers that are important in creating an audit trail.

BACK OF VOUCHER

Account Debited	Acct. No.	Amount
Purchases	511	1,200.00
Freight In	512	
Rent Expense	631	
Salary Expense	611	
Utilities Expense	635	
Total		$1,200.00

Voucher No.	704
Payee	Belmont Products
Address	Gary, Indiana
Invoice Amount	1,200.00
Less Discount	24.00
Net	1,176.00
Date Due	7/13
Date Paid	7/13
Check No.	205

information about the accounts and amounts to be debited and credited. The voucher identifies the transaction by both voucher number and check number and is recorded in both the voucher register and the check register, as described in the following sections.

KEY POINT: Payment is made with a voucher check.

■ **VOUCHER CHECKS** Although regular checks can be used effectively with a voucher system, many businesses use a form of **voucher check**, which tells the payee the reason the check was issued. The information is written either on the check itself or on a detachable stub.

KEY POINT: All approved vouchers are recorded in the voucher register.

■ **VOUCHER REGISTER** The **voucher register** is the book of original entry in which vouchers are recorded after they have been approved. The voucher register takes the place of the purchases journal in companies that use special-purpose journals. There is one important difference between the two journals: All expenditures—expenses, payroll, plant, and equipment, as well as purchases of merchandise—are

EXHIBIT 2
Voucher Register

KEY POINT: The voucher register contains a Vouchers Payable column that functions exactly like the Accounts Payable column in a purchases journal.

Voucher Register

Date		Voucher No.	Payee	Payment		Credit	Debits		
				Date	Check No.	Vouchers Payable	Purchases	Freight In	Store Supplies
20xx									
July	1	701	Common Utility	7/6	203	75			
	2	702	Ade Realty	7/2	201	400			
	2	703	Buy Rite Supplies	7/6	202	25			
	3	704	Belmont Products	7/13	205	1,200	1,200		
	6	705	M&M Freight			60		60	
	7	706	J. Jay, Petty Cash	7/7	204	50			
	8	707	Belmont Products	7/18	208	600	600		
	11	708	M&M Freight			30		30	
	11	709	Mack Truck			5,600			
	12	710	Livingstone Wholesale	7/22	209	785	750	35	
	14	711	Payroll	7/14	206	2,200			
	17	712	First National Bank	7/17	207	4,250			
	20	713	Livingstone Wholesale			525	500	25	
	21	714	Belmont Products			400	400		
	24	715	M&M Freight			18		18	
	30	716	Payroll	7/30	210	2,200			
	31	717	J. Jay, Petty Cash	7/31	211	47		17	
	31	718	Maintenance Company			175			
	31	719	Store Supply Company			350			350
						18,990	3,450	185	350
						(211)	(511)	(512)	(116)

recorded in a voucher register; only purchases of merchandise on credit are recorded in a single-column purchases journal.

A voucher register appears in Exhibit 2. Notice that a column called Vouchers Payable replaces the Accounts Payable column. As you can see, the first entry in the voucher register records the receipt of a utility bill. It is recorded as a debit to Utilities Expense and a credit to Vouchers Payable (not Accounts Payable). On July 6, this utility bill was paid with check number 203.

KEY POINT: A check register serves the same purpose as a cash payments journal.

■ **CHECK REGISTER** In a voucher system, the **check register**, as shown in Exhibit 3, is the journal in which checks are listed as they are written. Consequently, it

ENRICHMENT NOTE: The Other Accounts column enables the voucher register to accommodate any type of expenditure. The total of the Other Accounts column is not posted because it represents several different accounts, each of which is posted the day the transaction is entered into the voucher register.

Page 1

				Debits					
			Main-tenance	Main-tenance		Other Accounts			
Office Supplies	Sales Salaries Expense	Office Salaries Expense	Expense, Selling	Expense, Office	Utilities Expense	Name	No.	Amount	
25					75	Rent Expense	631	400	
						Petty Cash	121	50	
						Trucks	148	5,600	
	1,400	800				Notes Payable	212	4,000	
						Interest Expense	645	250	
20	1,400	800				Misc. Expense	649	10	
			100	75					
45	2,800	1,600	100	75	75			10,310	
(117)	(611)	(612)	(621)	(622)	(635)			(✓)	

replaces the cash payments journal. Carefully study the connection between the voucher register and the check register. The incurrence of a liability is recorded in the voucher register; its payment is recorded in the check register.

OPERATION OF A VOUCHER SYSTEM

There are five steps in the operation of a voucher system:

1. *Preparing the voucher*   A voucher is prepared for each expenditure. All documents—purchase orders, invoices, and receiving reports—should be attached to the voucher when it is submitted for approval.

EXHIBIT 3
Check Register

Check Register

Date		Check No.	Payee	Voucher No.	Debit	Credits	
					Vouchers Payable	Purchases Discounts	Cash
20xx							
July	2	201	Ade Realty	702	400		400
	6	202	Buy Rite Supplies	703	25		25
	6	203	Common Utility	701	75		75
	7	204	J. Jay, Petty Cash	706	50		50
	13	205	Belmont Products	704	1,200	24	1,176
	14	206	Payroll	711	2,200		2,200
	17	207	First National Bank	712	4,250		4,250
	18	208	Belmont Products	707	600	12	588
	22	209	Livingstone Wholesale	710	785	15	770
	30	210	Payroll	716	2,200		2,200
	31	211	J. Jay, Petty Cash	717	47		47
					11,832	51	11,781
					(211)	(513)	(111)

STUDY NOTE: The check register in Exhibit 3 assumes the use of the gross method to handle discounts.

Many companies pay their employees out of a separate payroll account. In such cases, a voucher is prepared to cover the total payroll. The check for the voucher is then deposited in the payroll account, and individual payroll checks are drawn on that account.

2. *Recording the voucher* All approved vouchers should be recorded in the voucher register, as shown in Exhibit 2. For example, the entry for Voucher 704 corresponds to the information that is presented in Figure 4. Vouchers that do not have appropriate approvals or supporting documents should be investigated immediately.

3. *Paying the voucher* After a voucher has been recorded, it is placed in an unpaid voucher file. Many companies file their vouchers by due date and by vendor within due date, so that checks can be written at the appropriate times. Such a practice ensures that all discounts for prompt payment can be taken. After payment, vouchers are filed by voucher number.

   A few days before a voucher is due, a check for the correct amount, accompanied by the voucher and supporting documents, is presented to the individual who is authorized to sign checks. The payment is entered in the check register, as shown in Exhibit 3. For example, Belmont Products is paid with check no. 205. Both the date of payment and the check number are then entered in the voucher register on the same line as the corresponding voucher. This information is helpful in the preparation of a schedule of unpaid vouchers, which is described in step **5**.

   Extra steps are required when there has been a purchase return or allowance that applies to a voucher. For example, suppose that part of a ship-

EXHIBIT 4
Schedule of Unpaid Vouchers

Thomas Appliance Company
Schedule of Unpaid Vouchers
July 31, 20xx

Payee	Voucher Number	Amount
M&M Freight	705	$ 60
M&M Freight	708	30
Mack Truck	709	5,600
Livingstone Wholesale	713	525
Belmont Products	714	400
M&M Freight	715	18
Maintenance Company	718	175
Store Supply Company	719	350
Total Unpaid Vouchers		$7,158

KEY POINT: The schedule total of $7,158 would appear as a liability on the July 31 balance sheet, usually labeled Accounts Payable.

ment of merchandise is defective and is returned to the supplier for credit. At the time the merchandise is returned or the allowance is given, an entry should be made in the general journal debiting Vouchers Payable and crediting Purchases Returns and Allowances, and a notation should be made on the voucher in the voucher file. At the time of payment, only the *net amount* of the voucher—the original amount less the return or allowance and any applicable discount—should be paid and recorded in the check register. Rather than noting the change on the voucher, some companies cancel the original voucher and prepare a new one for the amount to be paid.

4. *Posting the voucher and check registers*   Posting the voucher and check registers is very similar to posting the purchases journal and cash payments journal. The only difference is that the Vouchers Payable account is substituted for the Accounts Payable account.

5. *Summarizing unpaid vouchers*   Because the sum of the vouchers in the unpaid vouchers file should always equal the credit balance of the Vouchers Payable account, a subsidiary ledger is unnecessary. At the end of each accounting period, the unpaid voucher file should be totaled to prove the balance of the Vouchers Payable account. Exhibit 4 shows a schedule of unpaid vouchers, which is a list of all the unpaid vouchers according to the voucher register in Exhibit 2. The voucher register and the check register (Exhibit 3) are reconciled by simple subtraction:

Vouchers Payable credit from the voucher register	$18,990
Less Vouchers Payable debit from the check register	11,832
Vouchers Payable credit balance from the schedule of unpaid vouchers	$ 7,158

Sometimes the account title *Vouchers Payable* appears on a company's balance sheet. The preferred practice, however, is to use the more widely known and accepted term *Accounts Payable*, even when a voucher system is in place.

 Check out ACE for a Review Quiz at http://accounting.college.hmco.com/students.

Chapter Review

REVIEW OF LEARNING OBJECTIVES

LO1 Define *internal control*, explain its basic components and limitations, and give examples of control activities.

Internal control consists of all the policies and procedures a company uses to ensure the reliability of financial reporting, compliance with laws and regulations, and the effectiveness and efficiency of operations. Internal control has five components: the control environment, risk assessment, information and communication, control activities, and monitoring. Examples of control activities are proper authorization of transactions; recording all transactions to facilitate preparation of financial statements and to establish accountability for assets; use of well-designed documents to ensure proper recording of transactions; physical controls; periodic checks of records and assets; separation of duties into the functions of authorization, operations, custody of assets, and recordkeeping; and use of sound personnel policies. A system of internal control relies on the people who implement it. Thus, the effectiveness of internal control is limited by the people involved. Human error, collusion, and failure to recognize changed conditions all can contribute to a system's failure.

LO2 Apply internal control activities to common merchandising transactions.

Certain procedures strengthen internal control over cash sales receipts, purchases, and cash disbursements. First, the functions of authorization, recordkeeping, and custody should be kept separate. Second, the accounting system should provide for physical protection of assets (especially cash and merchandise inventory), use of banking services, prompt recording and deposit of cash receipts, and payment by check. Third, the people who have access to cash and merchandise inventory should be specifically designated and their number limited. Fourth, employees who have access to cash or merchandise inventory should be bonded. Fifth, the Cash account should be reconciled each month, and unannounced audits of cash on hand should be made by an individual who does not authorize, handle, or record cash transactions.

LO3 Demonstrate the control of cash by preparing a bank reconciliation.

A bank reconciliation accounts for the difference between the balance that appears on the bank statement and the balance in the company's Cash account. It involves adjusting both balances to arrive at the adjusted cash balance. The bank balance is adjusted for outstanding checks and deposits in transit. The depositor's book balance is adjusted for service charges, NSF checks, interest earned, and miscellaneous debits and credits.

SUPPLEMENTAL OBJECTIVES

SO4 Demonstrate the use of a simple imprest system.

An imprest system is a method of controlling small cash expenditures by setting up a fund at a fixed amount and periodically reimbursing the fund by the amount necessary to restore the original balance. A petty cash fund, one example of an imprest system, is established by a debit to Petty Cash and a credit to Cash. It is replenished by debits to various expense or asset accounts and a credit to Cash. Each expenditure should be supported by a petty cash voucher.

SO5 Define *voucher system* and describe the components and operation of a voucher system.

A voucher system is any system that gives documentary proof of and written authorization for business transactions. It consists of authorizations (vouchers), voucher checks, a special journal to record the vouchers (voucher register), and a special journal to record the voucher checks (check register). The five steps in operating a voucher system are (1) preparing the voucher, (2) recording the voucher, (3) paying the voucher, (4) posting the voucher and check registers, and (5) summarizing unpaid vouchers.

REVIEW OF CONCEPTS AND TERMINOLOGY

The following concepts and terms were introduced in this chapter:

SO5   **Audit trail:** The documentary evidence of written approval created by key people as they routinely review and verify an expenditure before payment is made.

LO3 **Bank reconciliation:** The process of accounting for the difference between the balance appearing on the bank statement and the balance of the Cash account in the company's records.

LO1 **Bonding:** The process of carefully checking an employee's background and insuring the company against theft by that person.

LO2 **Check:** A written order to a bank to pay the amount specified from funds on deposit.

LO2 **Check authorization:** A form prepared by the accounting department after it has compared the receiving report with the purchase order and the invoice. It permits the issuance of a check to pay the invoice.

SO5 **Check register:** In a voucher system, the journal in which voucher checks are listed as they are written.

LO1 **Control activities:** Policies and procedures established by management to ensure that the objectives of internal control are met.

LO1 **Control environment:** The overall attitude, awareness, and actions of management, as reflected in the company's philosophy and operating style, organizational structure, method of assigning authority and responsibility, and personnel policies and practices.

SO4 **Imprest system:** A system for controlling small cash disbursements by establishing a fund at a fixed amount and periodically reimbursing the fund by the amount necessary to restore the original cash balance.

LO1 **Information and communication:** The accounting system established by management and the communication of responsibilities with regard to the accounting system.

LO1 **Internal control:** All the policies and procedures a company uses to ensure the reliability of financial reporting, compliance with laws and regulations, and the effectiveness and efficiency of operations.

LO2 **Invoice:** A form sent to the purchaser by the vendor describing the goods delivered, the quantity, price, and terms of payment.

LO1 **Monitoring:** Management's regular assessment of the quality of internal control.

SO4 **Petty cash fund:** A fund for making small payments of cash when it is inconvenient to pay by check.

SO4 **Petty cash voucher:** A form signed by a person who receives a cash payment from a petty cash fund; lists the date, amount, and purpose of the expenditure.

LO2 **Purchase order:** A form prepared by a company's purchasing department and sent to a vendor describing the items ordered; the expected price, terms, and shipping date; and other shipping instructions.

LO2 **Purchase requisition:** A formal written request for a purchase, prepared by the requesting department in an organization and sent to the purchasing department.

LO2 **Receiving report:** A form prepared by the receiving department of a company describing the quantity and condition of goods received.

LO1 **Risk assessment:** The identification of areas in which risks of loss of assets or inaccuracies in the accounting records are high.

SO5 **Voucher:** A written authorization prepared for each business expenditure when it becomes a liability or obligation to pay.

SO5 **Voucher check:** A form of check, used in a voucher system, that describes the reason for issuing the check.

SO5 **Voucher register:** The book of original entry in which vouchers are recorded after they have been approved.

SO5 **Voucher system:** Any system that gives documentary proof of and written authorization for business transactions.

REVIEW PROBLEM

Bank Reconciliation

LO3 The information that follows comes from the records of the Maynard Company. The credit memorandum on April 15 is for the collection of a note and includes $100 in interest. Checks numbered 1714 for $210 and 1715 for $70 were outstanding on March 31.

From the Cash Receipts Journal		Page 14
Date		Debit Cash
Apr. 1		560
10		1,440
17		780
30		2,900
		5,680

From the Cash Payments Journal		Page 18
Date	Check Number	Credit Cash
Apr. 4	1716	580
6	1717	800
17	1718	1,050
25	1719	110
		2,540

From the General Ledger

Cash   Account No. 111

Date		Item	Post. Ref.	Debit	Credit	Balance Debit	Balance Credit
Mar.	31	Balance				4,200	
Apr.	30		CR14	5,680		9,880	
	30		CP18		2,540	7,340	

From the Company's Bank Statement

Checks and Other Debits

Date	Check Number	Amount	Deposits		Balance	
					4/1	4,480
4/5	1714	210	4/2	560	4/2	5,040
4/5	1716	580	4/11	1,440	4/5	4,250
4/12	1717	800	4/15	1,500CM	4/11	5,690
4/28		20SC	4/17	780	4/12	4,890
			4/28	10IN	4/15	6,390
					4/17	7,170
					4/28	7,160

CM—Credit Memo   SC—Service Charge   IN—Interest

REQUIRED ▶ 1. Prepare a bank reconciliation as of April 30, 20xx.
2. Prepare the necessary entries in journal form.

ANSWER TO REVIEW PROBLEM

1. Prepare a bank reconciliation.

Maynard Company
Bank Reconciliation
April 30, 20xx

Balance per bank, April 30, 20xx		$ 7,160
Add deposit of April 30, in transit		2,900
		$10,060
Less outstanding checks:		
No. 1715	$ 70	
No. 1718	1,050	
No. 1719	110	1,230
Adjusted bank balance, April 30, 20xx		$ 8,830
Balance per books, April 30, 20xx		$ 7,340
Add: Note collected by bank	$1,400	
Interest income on note	100	
Interest income	10	1,510
		$ 8,850
Less service charge		20
Adjusted book balance, April 30, 20xx		$ 8,830

2. Prepare the entries in journal form.

Apr. 30	Cash		1,500	
		Notes Receivable		1,400
		Interest Income		100
		Collection of note by bank		
30	Cash		10	
		Interest Income		10
		Interest on bank account		
30	Bank Service Charges Expense		20	
		Cash		20
		Bank service charge for April		

Chapter Assignments

BUILDING YOUR KNOWLEDGE FOUNDATION

QUESTIONS

1. Most people think of internal control as a means of making fraud harder to commit and easier to detect. What are some other important purposes of internal control?

2. What are the five components of internal control?

3. What are some examples of control activities?

4. Why is the separation of duties necessary to ensure sound internal control? What does this principle assume about the relationships of employees in a company and the possibility of two or more of them stealing from the company?

5. In a small business, it is sometimes impossible to separate duties completely. What are three other practices that a small business can follow to achieve the objectives of internal control over cash?

6. At Thrifty Variety Store, each sales clerk counts the cash in his or her cash drawer at the end of the day, then removes the cash register tape and prepares a daily cash form, noting any discrepancies. This information is checked by an employee in the cashier's office, who counts the cash, compares the total with the form, and then gives the cash to the cashier. What is the weakness in this system of internal control?

7. How does a movie theater control cash receipts?

8. For each of the following business documents, tell what department or person prepares it and what department or person receives it: purchase requisition, purchase order, invoice, receiving report, check authorization, check, deposit ticket, and bank statement.

9. Why is a bank reconciliation prepared?

10. Assume that each of the following items appeared on a bank reconciliation. Which item would be (1) an addition to the balance on the bank statement, (2) a deduction from the balance on the bank statement, (3) an addition to the balance on the books, or (4) a deduction from the balance on the books? Write the correct number next to each item.

    a. Outstanding checks   d. NSF check returned with statement
    b. Deposits in transit   e. Note collected by bank
    c. Bank service charge

    Which of the above items requires an entry?

11. What is the purpose of a petty cash fund? From the standpoint of internal control, what is the significance of the level at which the fund is established?

12. What account or accounts are debited when a petty cash fund is established? What account or accounts are debited when a petty cash fund is replenished?

13. What does a credit balance in the Cash Short or Over account indicate?

14. At the end of the day, the combined count of cash for all cash registers in a store reveals a cash shortage of $17.20. In what account would this cash shortage be recorded? Would the account be debited or credited?

15. Should a petty cash fund be replenished as of the last day of the accounting period? Explain your answer.

16. Explain how each of the following can contribute to internal control over cash: (a) a bank reconciliation; (b) a petty cash fund; (c) a cash register with printed receipts; (d) printed, prenumbered cash sales receipts; (e) regular vacations for the cashier; (f) two signatures on checks; and (g) prenumbered checks.

17. What is the greatest advantage of a voucher system?

18. Before a voucher for the purchase of merchandise is approved for payment, three documents should be compared to verify the amount of the liability. What are the three documents?

19. A company that presently uses a general journal, a sales journal, a purchases journal, a cash receipts journal, and a cash payments journal decides to adopt the voucher system. Which of the five journals would be changed or replaced? What would replace them?

20. What is the correct order for filing (a) unpaid vouchers and (b) paid vouchers?

21. When the voucher system is used, is there an Accounts Payable controlling account and an accounts payable subsidiary ledger? Be prepared to explain your answer.

SHORT EXERCISES

SE 1.
LO1 Purposes of Internal Control

Ann Mogen owns a gourmet coffee shop. Identify four ways in which good internal controls can help her operate her business.

SE 2.
LO1 Components of Internal Control

Schell Company is a men's clothing store. Indicate whether each of the following components of internal control is part of the (a) control environment, (b) risk assessment, (c) information and communication, (d) control activities, or (e) monitoring:

1. An organization plan calls for separation of duties in the handling of cash sales.
2. Charles Schell emphasizes to employees the importance of following specific procedures in the handling of cash.
3. All cash transactions are recorded automatically in the company's computer when the sales are rung up on the cash register.
4. Management identifies the ways clothes could be stolen.
5. Management observes that employees are following proper procedures.

SE 3.
LO1 Limitations of Internal Control

Internal control is subject to several inherent limitations. Indicate whether each of the following situations is an example of (a) human error, (b) collusion, (c) changed conditions, or (d) cost-benefit considerations:

1. Effective separation of duties in a restaurant is impractical because the business is too small.
2. The cashier and the manager of a retail shoe store work together to circumvent the internal controls for the purpose of embezzling funds.
3. The cashier in a pizza shop does not understand the procedures for operating the cash register and thus fails to ring up all sales and to count the cash at the end of the day.
4. At a law firm, computer supplies were mistakenly delivered to the reception area instead of the receiving area because the supplier began using a different means of shipment. As a result, the receipt of supplies was not recorded.

SE 4.
LO1 Internal Control Activities
LO2

Match the check-writing policy for a small business described below to these control activities:

a. Authorization
b. Recording transactions
c. Documents and records
d. Physical controls
e. Periodic independent verification
f. Separation of duties
g. Sound personnel policies

1. The person who writes the checks to pay bills is different from the persons who authorize the payments and who keep the records of the payments.
2. The checks are kept in a locked drawer. The only person who has the key is the person who writes the checks.
3. The person who writes the checks is bonded.
4. Once each month the owner compares and reconciles the amount of money shown in the accounting records with the amount in the bank account.
5. Each check is approved by the owner of the business before it is mailed.
6. A check stub recording pertinent information is completed for each check.
7. Every day, all checks are recorded in the accounting records, using the information on the check stubs.

SE 5.
LO2 Internal Control Documents for Purchases and Payments

Indicate the letter of where each of the following documents would be prepared and the letter of where each document would be sent:

1. Purchase requisition
2. Receiving report
3. Invoice
4. Check authorization
5. Check

a. Requesting department
b. Purchasing department
c. Receiving department
d. Accounting department
e. Treasurer
f. Supplier

SE 6.
LO3 Elements of a Bank Reconciliation

When a bank reconciliation is performed, is each of the following items (a) an addition to the balance per bank, (b) a deduction from the balance per bank, (c) an addition to the balance per books, or (d) a deduction from the balance per books?

1. Service charges (by the bank)
2. Deposits in transit

3. Interest income (shown on bank statement)
4. Outstanding checks

LO3   Bank Reconciliation

SE 7. Prepare a bank reconciliation from the following information:

a. Balance per bank statement as of June 30, $2,586.58
b. Balance per books as of June 30, $1,308.87
c. Deposits in transit, $348.00
d. Outstanding checks, $1,611.11
e. Interest on average balance, $14.60

SO4   Petty Cash Fund

SE 8. A petty cash fund was established at $100. At the end of May, the fund has a cash balance of $36 and petty cash vouchers for postage, $29, and office supplies, $34. Prepare the entry on May 31 to replenish the fund.

SO5   Components of a Voucher System

SE 9. Identify which of the following statements describes the purpose of a (a) voucher, (b) voucher check, (c) voucher register, and (d) check register:

1. Provides a record of the payment of vouchers
2. Serves as a means of payment and notes the reason for the issuance of the payment
3. Provides a written authorization for each expenditure
4. Provides a record of all authorized expenditures

SO5   Operation of a Voucher System

SE 10. Arrange the following actions in the order in which they would take place in the operation of a voucher system:

1. A voucher check is written for each recorded voucher on the due date and is recorded in the check register.
2. A voucher is prepared authorizing each expenditure.
3. A list of unpaid vouchers is prepared to prove the balance of the Vouchers Payable account.
4. Each authorized voucher is recorded in the voucher register.
5. Column totals in the voucher register and the check register and individual items in the Other Accounts column of the voucher register are posted to the appropriate accounts.

EXERCISES

LO1   Use of Accounting Records in Internal Control

E 1. Careful scrutiny of accounting records and financial statements can lead to the discovery of fraud or embezzlement. Each of the following situations may indicate a possible breakdown in internal control. Indicate the nature of the possible fraud or embezzlement in each situation:

1. Wages expense for a branch office was 30 percent higher in 20x2 than in 20x1, even though the office was authorized to employ only the same four employees and raises were only 5 percent in 20x2.
2. Sales returns and allowances increased from 5 percent to 20 percent of sales in the first two months of 20x2, after record sales in 20x1 resulted in large bonuses for the sales staff.
3. Gross margin decreased from 40 percent of net sales in 20x1 to 30 percent in 20x2, even though there was no change in pricing. Ending inventory was 50 percent less at the end of 20x2 than it was at the beginning of the year. There is no immediate explanation for the decrease in inventory.
4. A review of daily records of cash register receipts shows that one cashier consistently accepts more discount coupons for purchases than do the other cashiers.

LO1   Internal Control Activities

E 2. Jessie's Video Store maintains the following policies with regard to purchases of new videotapes at each of its branch stores:

1. Employees are required to take vacations, and the duties of employees are rotated periodically.
2. Once each month a person from the home office visits each branch store to examine the receiving records and to compare the inventory of videos with the accounting records.
3. Purchases of new videos must be authorized by purchase order in the home office and paid for by the treasurer in the home office. Receiving reports are prepared in each branch and sent to the home office.

4. All new personnel receive one hour of training in how to receive and catalogue new videos.

5. The company maintains a perpetual inventory system that keeps track of all videos purchased, sold, and on hand.

Match the following control activities to each of the above policies. (Some may have several answers.)

a. Authorization
b. Recording transactions
c. Documents and records
d. Physical controls

e. Periodic independent verification
f. Separation of duties
g. Sound personnel policies

LO1 Internal Control Evaluation

E 3. Developing a convenient means of providing sales representatives with cash for their incidental expenses, such as entertaining a client at lunch, is a problem many companies face. Under one company's plan, the sales representatives receive advances in cash from the petty cash fund. Each advance is supported by an authorization from the sales manager. The representative returns the receipt for the expenditure and any unused cash, which is replaced in the petty cash fund. The cashier of the petty cash fund is responsible for seeing that the receipt and the cash returned equal the advance. When the petty cash fund is reimbursed, the amount of the representative's expenditure is debited to Direct Sales Expense.

What is the weak point in this system? What fundamental principle of internal control is being ignored? What improvement in the procedure can you suggest?

LO1 Internal Control Evaluation

E 4. An accountant is responsible for the following procedures: (1) receiving all cash; (2) maintaining the general ledger; (3) maintaining the accounts receivable subsidiary ledger that includes the individual records of each customer; (4) maintaining the journals for recording sales, purchases, and cash receipts; and (5) preparing monthly statements to be sent to customers. As a service to customers and employees, the company allows the accountant to cash checks of up to $50 with money from the cash receipts. When deposits are made, the checks are included in place of the cash receipts.

What weakness in internal control exists in this system?

LO1 Internal Control Activities
LO2

E 5. Ted Songe, who operates a small grocery store, has established the following policies with regard to the checkout cashiers:

1. Each cashier has his or her own cash drawer, to which no one else has access.
2. Each cashier may accept checks for purchases under $50 with proper identification. Checks over $50 must be approved by Songe before they are accepted.
3. Every sale must be rung up on the cash register and a receipt given to the customer. Each sale is recorded on a tape inside the cash register.
4. At the end of each day, Songe counts the cash in the drawer and compares it with the amount on the tape inside the cash register.

Match the following conditions for internal control to each of the policies listed above:

a. Transactions are executed in accordance with management's general or specific authorization.
b. Transactions are recorded as necessary to permit preparation of financial statements and maintain accountability for assets.
c. Access to assets is permitted only as allowed by management.
d. At reasonable intervals, the records of assets are compared with the existing assets.

LO3 Bank Reconciliation

E 6. Prepare a bank reconciliation from the following information:

a. Balance per bank statement as of August 31, $8,454.54
b. Balance per books as of August 31, $6,138.04
c. Deposits in transit, $1,134.42
d. Outstanding checks, $3,455.92
e. Bank service charge, $5.00

LO3 Bank Reconciliation: Missing Data

E 7. Compute the correct amounts to replace each letter in the following table:

Balance per bank statement	$ a	$26,700	$945	$5,970
Deposits in transit	1,800	b	150	375
Outstanding checks	4,500	3,000	c	225
Balance per books	10,350	28,200	675	d

**LO3   Collection of a Note
        by a Bank**

E 8. Haskell Corporation received a notice with its bank statement that the bank had collected a note for $4,000 plus $20 interest from L. Peters and credited Haskell Corporation's account for the total less a collection charge of $30.

Explain the effect that these items have on the bank reconciliation. Prepare an entry in journal form to record the information on the books of Haskell Corporation.

SO4   Petty Cash Entries

E 9. The petty cash fund of Sachs Company appeared as follows on July 31, 20xx (the end of the accounting period):

Cash on hand		$122.46
Petty cash vouchers		
Freight in	$45.72	
Postage	42.38	
Flowers for a sick employee	37.00	
Office supplies	52.44	177.54
Total		$300.00

Because there is cash on hand, is there a need to replenish the petty cash fund on July 31? Explain your answer. Prepare, in journal form, an entry to replenish the fund.

SO4   Petty Cash Transactions

E 10. A small company maintains a petty cash fund for minor expenditures. In June and July, the following transactions took place:

a. The fund was established in the amount of $100.00 on June 1 from the proceeds of check no. 2707.

b. On June 30, the petty cash fund had cash of $15.46 and the following receipts on hand: postage, $40.00; supplies, $24.94; delivery service, $12.40; and rubber stamp, $7.20. Check no. 2778 was drawn to replenish the fund.

c. On July 31, the petty cash fund had cash of $22.06 and these receipts on hand: postage, $34.20; supplies, $32.84; and delivery service, $6.40. The petty cash custodian could not account for the shortage. Check no. 2847 was drawn to replenish the fund.

Prepare entries in journal form necessary to record each transaction.

PROBLEMS

LO3   Bank Reconciliation

P 1. The information presented below and on the opposite page comes from the records of Costa Company:

From the Cash Receipts Journal		Page 9
Date		Debit Cash
Apr. 1		914
8		1,012
15		3,240
22		2,646
30		1,942
		9,754

From the Cash Payments Journal		Page 12
Date	Check Number	Credit Cash
Apr. 1	531	14
3	532	283
4	533	416
5	534	27
	535 (voided)	
6	536	5
11	537	5,746
12	538	709
21	539	1,246
22	540	76
		8,522

From the General Ledger

Cash — Account No. 111

Date		Item	Post. Ref.	Debit	Credit	Balance Debit	Balance Credit
Mar.	31	Balance				2,465	
Apr.	30		CR9	9,754		12,219	
	30		CP12		8,522	3,697	

TURNBULL NATIONAL BANK — Statement of Costa Company
Jarvis and Oak Streets

Checks/Debits			Deposits/Credits		Daily Balances	
Posting Date	Check No.	Amount	Posting Date	Amount	Date	Amount
					4/01	3,785.00
4/03	500	100.00	4/03	914.00	4/03	4,099.00
4/03	505	500.00	4/09	1,012.00	4/05	3,625.00
4/05	530	460.00	4/16	3,240.00	4/07	3,209.00
4/05	531	14.00	4/23	2,646.00	4/09	4,194.00
4/07	533	416.00	4/27	408.00CM	4/13	4,174.00
4/09	534	27.00	4/30	42.00IN	4/15	3,267.00
4/13	536	5.00			4/16	6,507.00
4/13		15.00NSF			4/23	9,153.00
4/15	538	907.00			4/25	3,407.00
4/25	537	5,746.00			4/27	3,739.00
4/27	540	76.00			4/30	3,777.00
4/30		4.00SC				

Code: CM–Credit Memo   IN–Interest   NSF–Nonsufficient Funds
DM–Debit Memo   SC–Service Charge

The NSF check was received from customer S. Tilvie for merchandise. The credit memorandum represents a $400 note, plus interest, collected by the bank. Check number 535 was prepared improperly and has been voided. Check number 538 for a purchase of merchandise was recorded incorrectly in the cash payments journal as $709 instead of $907. On April 1, the following checks were outstanding: no. 500 for $100, no. 505 for $500, no. 529 for $260, and no. 530 for $460.

REQUIRED ▶

1. Prepare a bank reconciliation as of April 30, 20xx.
2. Prepare the journal entries necessary to adjust the accounts.
3. What amount should appear on the balance sheet for Cash as of April 30?

P 2.

LO1 Bank Reconciliation
LO3

The following information is available for Sultani Company as of November 30, 20xx:

a. Cash on the books as of November 30 amounted to $113,675.28. Cash on the bank statement for the same date was $141,717.08.
b. A deposit of $14,249.84, representing cash receipts of November 30, did not appear on the bank statement.
c. Outstanding checks totaled $7,293.64.

d. A check for $2,420.00 returned with the statement was recorded in the cash payments journal as $2,024.00. The check was for advertising.
e. The bank service charge for November amounted to $26.00.
f. The bank collected $36,400.00 for Sultani Company on a note. The face value of the note was $36,000.00.
g. An NSF check for $1,140.00 from a customer, Estelle Maxx, was returned with the statement.
h. The bank mistakenly deducted a check for $800.00 drawn by Mooney Corporation.
i. The bank reported a credit of $960.00 for interest on the average balance.

REQUIRED ▶

1. Prepare a bank reconciliation for Sultani Company as of November 30, 20xx.
2. Prepare the journal entries necessary from the reconciliation.
3. State the amount of cash that should appear on the balance sheet as of November 30.
4. What control activity in the internal control structure does the bank reconciliation accomplish? How does it accomplish this activity and how should the person to prepare the bank reconciliation be chosen?

P 3.

SO4　Petty Cash Transactions

A small company maintains a petty cash fund for minor expenditures. The following transactions occurred in June and July.

a. The fund was established in the amount of $300.00 on June 1 from the proceeds of check no. 1515.
b. On June 30, the petty cash fund had cash of $46.38 and the following receipts on hand: postage, $120.00; supplies, $74.82; delivery service, $37.20; and rubber stamp, $21.60. Check no. 1527 was drawn to replenish the fund.
c. On July 31, the petty cash fund had cash of $66.18 and the following receipts on hand: postage, $102.60; supplies, $98.52; and delivery service, $19.20. The petty cash custodian could not account for the shortage. Check no. 1621 was written to replenish the fund.

REQUIRED ▶　Prepare the journal entries necessary to record each transaction.

P 4.

LO1
LO2　Internal Control Procedures

Eyles Sports Shop is a small neighborhood sporting goods store. The shop's owner, Samantha Eyles, has set up a system of internal control over sales to prevent theft and to ensure the accuracy of the accounting records.

When a customer buys a product, the cashier writes up a sales invoice that describes the purchase, including the total price. All sales invoices are prenumbered sequentially.

If the sale is by credit card, the cashier runs the credit card through a scanner that verifies the customer's credit. The scanner prints out a receipt and a slip for the customer to sign. The signed slip is put in the cash register, and the customer is given the receipt and a copy of the sales invoice.

If the sale is by cash or check, the cashier rings it up on the cash register and gives change, if appropriate. Checks must be written for the exact amount of the purchase and must be accompanied by identification. The sale is recorded on a tape inside the cash register that cannot be accessed by the cashier. The cash register may be locked with a key. The cashier is the only person other than Eyles who has a key. The cash register must be locked when the cashier is not present. Refunds are made only with Eyles's approval, are recorded on prenumbered credit memorandum forms, and are rung up on the cash register.

At the end of each day, Eyles counts the cash and checks in the cash register and compares the total with the amount recorded on the tape inside the register. Eyles totals all the signed credit card slips and ensures that the total equals the amount recorded by the scanner. Eyles also makes sure that all sales invoices and credit memoranda are accounted for. Eyles prepares a bank deposit ticket for the cash, checks, and signed credit card slips, less $40 in change to be put in the cash register the next day, and removes the record of the day's credit card sales from the scanner. All the records are placed in an envelope that is sealed and sent to the company's accountant for verification and recording in the company records. On the way home, Eyles places the bank deposit in the night deposit box.

The company hires experienced cashiers who are bonded. The owner spends the first half-day with new cashiers, showing them the procedures and overlooking their work.

REQUIRED ▶　Give an example of how each of the following control procedures is applied to internal control over sales and cash at Eyles Sports Shop: authorization, recording transactions, documents and records, physical controls, periodic independent verification, separation of duties, and sound personnel procedures. Do not address controls over inventory.

P 5.

SO5   Voucher System Transactions

During the month of July, Second Star Toy Shop had the following transactions.

July 1 Prepared voucher no. 205, payable to the petty cash cashier, to establish a petty cash fund, $500.

2 Issued check no. 330 for voucher no. 205.

3 Prepared voucher no. 206, payable to Fortunato Distributing, for a shipment of merchandise, $1,600, invoice dated July 3, terms 2/10, n/60, FOB shipping point. Fortunato prepaid freight of $120 and added it to the invoice, for a total of $1,720.

5 Prepared voucher no. 207, payable to Moynihan Realty, for July rent, $2,400.

5 Issued check no. 331 for voucher no. 207.

6 Prepared voucher no. 208, payable to Sheehan Distributors, for merchandise, $2,000, invoice dated July 6, terms 2/10, n/60, FOB shipping point.

7 Prepared voucher no. 209, payable to Gaines Express, for freight in on July 6 shipment, $128, terms n/10.

8 Prepared voucher no. 210, payable to Best Buy Hardware, for office equipment, $800, terms n/30.

10 Received credit memorandum from Sheehan Distributors for damaged merchandise returned, $200.

11 Prepared voucher no. 211, payable to Sheehan Distributors, for merchandise, $2,600, invoice dated July 10, terms 2/10, n/60, FOB shipping point.

12 Prepared voucher no. 212, payable to Gaines Express, for freight in on July 11, $188, terms n/10.

13 Issued check no. 332 for voucher no. 206.

14 Prepared voucher no. 213, payable to the company's owner, Patti Paul, for her personal expenses, $2,000.

16 Issued check no. 333 for voucher no. 213.

16 Issued check no. 334 for voucher no. 208. There was a return on July 10.

17 Issued check no. 335 for voucher no. 209.

18 Prepared vouchers no. 214, 215, 216, and 217, for $1,200 each, payable to Kusak Furniture, for office furniture having an invoice price of $4,800, terms one-fourth down and one-fourth each month for three months.

19 Issued check no. 336 for voucher no. 214.

19 Issued check no. 337 for voucher no. 211.

20 Issued check no. 338 for voucher no. 212.

21 Prepared voucher no. 218, payable to Mohansa Supply, $540 ($380 to be charged to Store Supplies and $160 to Office Supplies), terms n/10.

22 Prepared voucher no. 219, payable to Schmitt Videocassettes, for merchandise, $660, invoice dated July 20, terms 2/10, n/30, FOB shipping point. Freight paid by shipper and included in invoice total, $60.

23 Prepared voucher no. 220, payable to Southern National Bank, in payment of an $8,000 note plus $200 interest.

23 Issued check no. 339 for voucher no. 220.

25 Prepared voucher no. 221, payable to Hassad Insurance Company, for a one-year policy, $960.

26 Issued check no. 340 for voucher no. 221.

27 Prepared voucher no. 222, payable to Sheehan Distributors, for merchandise, $1,200, invoice dated July 26, terms 2/10, n/60, FOB shipping point.

28 Prepared voucher no. 223, payable to Gaines Express, for freight in on shipment of July 27, $76.

29 Prepared voucher no. 224, payable to the Payroll Account, for monthly salaries, $15,800 (to be divided as follows: Sales Salaries Expense, $8,800, and Office Salaries Expense, $7,000).

29 Issued check no. 341 for voucher no. 224.

30 Issued check no. 342 for voucher no. 219.

31 Prepared voucher no. 225 to reimburse the petty cash fund. A count of the fund revealed cash on hand of $100 and the following receipts: postage, $88; office supplies, $68; collect telegram, $12; flowers for sick employee, $60; and

delivery service, $108. The total of cash on hand and receipts was $64 less than the book balance of petty cash.

July 31   Issued check no. 343 for voucher no. 225.

REQUIRED ▶

1. Record the transactions in a voucher register (Page 18), a check register (Page 12), and a general journal (Page 10). Record purchases at gross amounts. Total the voucher and check registers.
2. Prepare a Vouchers Payable account (211) and post those portions of the journal and register entries that affect this account. Assume the Vouchers Payable account had a zero balance on June 30.
3. Prove the balance of Vouchers Payable by preparing a schedule of unpaid vouchers.

ALTERNATE PROBLEMS

P 6.

LO1 **Internal Control Procedures**
LO2

VueWay Printers makes printers for personal computers and maintains a factory outlet showroom through which it sells its products to the public. The company's management has set up a system of internal controls over the inventory of printers to prevent theft and to ensure the accuracy of the accounting records.

All printers in inventory at the factory outlet are kept in a secured warehouse behind the showroom, except for the sample printers on display. Only authorized personnel may enter the warehouse. When a customer buys a printer, a sales invoice is written in triplicate by the cashier and is marked "paid." The sales invoices are sequentially numbered, and all must be accounted for. The cashier sends the pink copy of the completed invoice to the warehouse, gives the blue copy to the customer, and keeps the green copy. The customer drives around to the warehouse entrance. The warehouse attendant takes the blue copy of the invoice from the customer and gives the customer the printer and the pink copy of the invoice.

The company maintains a perpetual inventory system for the printers at the outlet. The warehouse attendant at the outlet signs an inventory transfer sheet for each printer received. An accountant at the factory is assigned responsibility for maintaining the inventory records based on copies of the inventory transfer sheets and the sales invoices. The records are updated daily and may be accessed by computer but not modified by the sales personnel and the warehouse attendant. The accountant also sees that all prenumbered inventory transfer sheets are accounted for and compares copies of them with the ones signed by the warehouse attendant. Once every three months the company's internal auditor takes a physical count of the printer inventory and compares the results with the perpetual inventory records.

All new employees are required to read a sales and inventory manual and receive a two-hour training session about the internal controls. They must demonstrate that they can perform the functions required of them.

REQUIRED ▶

Give an example of how each of the following internal control procedures is applied to the printer inventory at VueWay Printers' outlet showroom: authorization, recording transactions, documents and records, physical controls, periodic independent verification, separation of duties, and sound personnel procedures. Do not address controls over cash.

P 7.

LO1 **Bank Reconciliation**
LO3

The following information is available for Manuel Suarez Company as of October 31, 20xx:

a. Cash on the books as of October 31 amounted to $21,327.08. Cash on the bank statement for the same date was $26,175.73.
b. A deposit of $2,610.47, representing cash receipts of October 31, did not appear on the bank statement.
c. Outstanding checks totaled $1,968.40.
d. A check for $960.00 returned with the statement was recorded incorrectly in the check register as $690.00. The check was made for a cash purchase of merchandise.
e. Bank service charges for October amounted to $12.50.
f. The bank collected for Manuel Suarez Company $6,120.00 on a note. The face value of the note was $6,000.00.
g. An NSF check for $91.78 from a client, Liz Fahll, came back with the statement.
h. The bank mistakenly charged to the company account a check for $425.00 drawn by another company.

i. The bank reported that it had credited the account for $170.00 in interest on the average balance for October.

REQUIRED ▶

1. Prepare a bank reconciliation for Manuel Suarez Company as of October 31, 20xx.
2. Prepare the journal entries necessary to adjust the accounts.
3. State the amount of cash that should appear on the balance sheet as of October 31.
4. What control activity in the internal control structure does the bank reconciliation accomplish? How does it accomplish this activity and how should the person to prepare the bank reconciliation be chosen?

SO4   Petty Cash Transactions

P 8. The Appalachian Theater Company established a petty cash fund in its snack bar so that payment can be made for small deliveries on receipt. The following transactions occurred in July and August:

July 1   The fund was established in the amount of $400.00 from the proceeds of a check drawn for that purpose.

   31   The petty cash fund has cash of $31.42 and the following receipts on hand: for merchandise received, $204.30; freight in, $65.74; laundry service, $84.00; and miscellaneous expense, $14.54. A check was drawn to replenish the fund.

Aug.31   The petty cash fund has cash of $55.00 and the following receipts on hand: merchandise, $196.84; freight in, $76.30; laundry service, $84.00; and miscellaneous expense, $7.86. The petty cash custodian cannot account for the excess cash in the fund. A check is drawn to replenish the fund.

REQUIRED ▶

In journal form, prepare the entries necessary to record each of these transactions.

SKILLS DEVELOPMENT CASES

Conceptual Analysis

SD 1.

LO1   Internal Control Lapse
LO2

Starbucks Corporation <www.starbucks.com> has accused an employee and her husband of embezzling $3.7 million by billing the company for services from a fictitious consulting firm. The employee and her husband created a phony company called RAD Services Inc. and charged Starbucks for work they never provided. The employee worked in the information technology department. RAD Services Inc. charged Starbucks for as much as $492,800 in consulting services in a single week.[8] For such a fraud to have taken place, certain control activities were likely not implemented. Identify and describe these activities.

SD 2.

LO1   System for Control of Supplies
LO2

Industrial Services Company provides maintenance services to factories in the West Bend, Wisconsin, area. The company, which buys large amounts of cleaning supplies, has consistently been over budget in its expenditures for those items. In the past, supplies were left open in the warehouse so that the on-site supervisors could take them as needed. Periodically, a clerk in the accounting department ordered additional supplies from a long-time supplier. The only records maintained were records of purchases. Once a year, an inventory of supplies was made for the preparation of the financial statements.

To solve the budgetary problem, management recently implemented a new system for controlling and purchasing supplies. Under the new system, the cleaning supplies were placed in a secured storeroom overseen by a supplies clerk. Supplies are requisitioned by the supervisors of specific jobs. Each job receives a predetermined amount of supplies based on a study of the needs of that job. In the storeroom, the supplies clerk notes the levels of supplies and completes a purchase requisition when supplies are needed. The purchase requisition goes to the purchasing clerk, a new position, who is solely responsible for authorizing purchases and who prepares the purchase orders for suppliers. The prices of several suppliers are constantly monitored to ensure that the lowest price is obtained. When supplies are received from a vendor, the supplies clerk checks them in and prepares a receiving report, which is sent to accounting, where each payment to a supplier is documented by the purchase requisition, the purchase order, and the receiving report. The accounting department also maintains a record of supplies inventory, supplies requisitioned by supervisors, and supplies received. Once each month, a physical inventory of cleaning supplies in the storeroom is made by the warehouse manager and compared against the supplies inventory records maintained by the accounting department.

Demonstrate how the new system applies or does not apply to each of the seven control activities described in this chapter. Is each new control activity an improvement over the old system?

Ethical Dilemma

SD 3.

LO3   Inflating the Cash Account and the Bank Reconciliation

Jean McGuire is the accountant for Slate Company. Among her responsibilities are the payment of bills and the preparation of the monthly bank reconciliation. On December 31, year end, McGuire's boss, Lydia Grunwald, instructed her to write checks for all the outstanding bills so that their amounts could be deducted for income tax purposes. Since payment of all the outstanding bills would have overdrawn the company's checking account by $78,000, McGuire had to hold the checks until sufficient funds were received. On January 2, a check for $100,000 was received from a customer in payment of an account receivable. Grunwald did not want to report the negative balance of cash on the previous year's balance sheet. She thus instructed McGuire to record the receipt as of December 31 and to show the check as a deposit in transit on the bank reconciliation. The checks written by McGuire on December 31 were mailed on January 3 and listed as outstanding checks on the bank reconciliation. Which, if any, of McGuire's and Grunwald's actions are unethical? Who may be harmed by their actions? What alternative actions could McGuire have taken?

Research Activity

SD 4.

**LO1   Internal Controls
LO2**

Go to a retail business, such as a bookstore, a clothing shop, a gift shop, a grocery, a hardware store, or a car dealership, in your local shopping area or a local shopping mall. Speak to someone who is knowledgeable about the store's internal controls. Find out the answers to the following questions, and be prepared to discuss your findings in class:

1. How does the company protect against inventory theft and loss?
2. What control activities, including authorization, recording transactions, documents and records, physical controls, periodic independent verification, separation of duties, and sound personnel policies, does the company use?
3. Can you see these control procedures in use?

 Group Activity: Assign teams to carry out the above assignment.

Decision-Making Practice

SD 5.

**LO1   Identifying Internal
LO2   Control Weaknesses**

Fleet's is a retail store with several departments. Its internal control procedures for cash sales and purchases are described in the following paragraphs:

Cash sales. Every cash sale is rung up on the department cash register by the sales clerk assigned to that department. The cash register produces a sales slip that is given to the customer with the merchandise. A carbon copy of the sales ticket is made on a continuous tape locked inside the machine. At the end of each day, a "total" key is pressed, and the machine prints the total sales for the day on the continuous tape. Then, the sales clerk unlocks the machine, reads the total sales figure, and makes the entry in the accounting records for the day's cash sales. Next, she counts the cash in the drawer, places the basic $100 change fund back in the drawer, and gives the cash received to the cashier. Finally, she files the cash register tape and is ready for the next day's business.

Purchases. All goods are ordered by the purchasing agent upon the requests of the various department heads. When the goods are received, the receiving clerk prepares a receiving report in triplicate. One copy is sent to the purchasing agent, one copy is forwarded to the department head, and one copy is kept by the receiving clerk. Invoices are forwarded immediately to the accounting department to ensure payment before the discount period elapses. After payment, the invoice is forwarded to the purchasing agent for comparison with the purchase order and the receiving report and is then returned to the accounting office for filing.

Fleet's president has asked you to evaluate these control procedures for cash sales and purchases. Write a memorandum to the president identifying the significant internal control weakness for each of the above situations and in each case recommend changes that would improve the current system.

FINANCIAL REPORTING AND ANALYSIS CASES

Interpreting Financial Reports

FRA 1.

LO1 **Effect of Ecommerce on**
LO2 **Internal Control**

Many retailers, such as Crate & Barrel <www.crateandbarrel.com>, Eddie Bauer Inc. <www.eddiebauer.com>, and Sears, Roebuck and Co.<www.sears.com>, are selling to customers on the Internet. In what ways do Internet transactions differ from retail store transactions? How will each difference affect internal controls?

Group Activity: Divide the class into teams and ask each team to identify as many differences as they can. Debrief by asking each team to give one difference and describe its effect on internal controls. Write the results on the board. Continue until no team can add another difference.

International Company

FRA 2.

LO1 **Internal Control and**
Accounting Education in a
Developing Country

Zambia, a country in southern Africa, has 8.5 million inhabitants. It has an elected government and is moving toward capital markets through privatization of government-owned business. For example, the government-owned beer company was recently sold to private interests for $13 million. One national priority calls for the training of competent professional accountants, and the Zambian Centre for Accountancy Studies has been established with the assistance of the World Bank. There are only about 250 native-born certified accountants in all of Zambia. A state with a comparable population in the United States would have more than 20,000 certified public accountants. One reason for placing a priority on the training of accountants is the importance of good internal controls to the development of a country like Zambia. What are the purposes of internal control, and what are some ways in which such controls would aid the development of a country like Zambia? What are some other reasons for making accounting education a high national priority?

Toys "R" Us Annual Report

FRA 3.

LO1 **Internal Control**
LO2 **Considerations**

Refer to the annual report for Toys "R" Us <www.tru.com> in the Supplement to Chapter 6. How many stores did Toys "R" Us operate in the United States and abroad in the most recent year? The typical store contains a showroom where customers wheel carts down aisles to select items for purchase, a warehouse where larger items may be picked up after purchase, a bank of cash registers, and a service desk where returns and other unusual transactions can be authorized. Identify the main activities or transactions for which Toys "R" Us management would need to establish internal controls in each new store. Discuss the objectives of internal controls in each case.

Fingraph® Financial Analyst™

This activity is not appropriate for this chapter.

Comparison Case

The comparison case is not applicable to this chapter.

Internet Case

FRA 4.

LO1 **Comparison of Reports of**
Management on Internal
Control

Through the Needles Accounting Resource Center Web site at http://accounting. hmco.com/students, go to the annual reports in the web sites for Tandy Corporation <www.tandy.com> and Circuit City Stores, Inc. <www.circuitcity.com>. Find the "Report of Management on Internal Accounting Controls" in the case of Tandy and "Management's Report" in the case of Circuit City in the companies' respective annual reports. A portion of the Circuit City's report is quoted in the text. Compare management statements. What similarities do you find in the content? What is a difference in the reports? Which company in your opinion, does a better job of explaining what management has done to fulfill its responsibility of internal control?

9

Chapter 9 focuses on management of, and accounting for, several types of short-term assets: cash and cash equivalents, short-term investments, accounts receivable, and notes receivable.

Short-Term Financial Assets

LEARNING OBJECTIVES

LO1 Identify and explain the management issues related to short-term financial assets.

LO2 Explain *cash, cash equivalents,* and the importance of electronic funds transfer.

LO3 Identify types of short-term investments and explain the financial reporting implications.

LO4 Define *accounts receivable* and apply the allowance method of accounting for uncollectible accounts.

LO5 Define *promissory note,* and compute and record promissory notes receivable.

D E C I S I O N   P O I N T

A   U S E R ' S   F O C U S

Pioneer Corporation <www.pioneer.co.jp> A company must use its assets to maximize income earned while maintaining liquidity. Pioneer Corporation, a leading Japanese manufacturer of electronics for home, commerce, and industry, manages about $2.4 billion in short-term financial assets. Short-term financial assets are assets that arise from cash transactions, the investment of cash, and the extension of credit. What is the composition of these assets? Why are they important to Pioneer's management?

Pioneer's short-term financial assets, as reported on the balance sheet in the company's annual report, are shown in the table on the opposite page.[1] These assets make up almost 41 percent of Pioneer's total assets, and they are very important to the company's strategy for meeting its goals. Effective asset management techniques ensure that these assets remain liquid and usable for the company's operations.

A commonly used ratio for measuring the adequacy of short-term financial assets is the quick ratio. The quick ratio is the ratio of short-term financial assets to current liabilities. Because Pioneer's current liabilities are (in millions) ¥177,825 ($1,434.1), its quick ratio is 1.39, which is computed as follows:

$$\text{Quick Ratio} = \frac{\text{Short-Term Financial Assets}}{\text{Current Liabilities}}$$

$$= \frac{\$1,995,200,000}{\$1,434,100,000} = 1.39$$

A quick ratio of about 1.0 has historically been the minimum common benchmark. However, it is more

How does Pioneer Electric, a leading manufacturer of electronics for the home, manage its short-term financial assets?

important to look at industry characteristics and at the trends for a particular company to see if the ratio is improving or not. A lower ratio may mean that a company is a very good manager of its short-term financial assets. Pioneer has maintained a quick ratio of over 1.0 for several years. Through good cash management, the company has not tied up excess funds in quick assets relative to current liabilities. This chapter emphasizes management of, and accounting for, short-term financial assets to achieve liquidity.

Financial Highlights
(In millions)

	Yen	Dollars
Cash and cash equivalents	¥121,127	$ 976.8
Short-term investments	1,598	12.9
Accounts receivable, net of allowances of ¥5,895 ($47.5)	116,594	940.3
Notes receivable	8,079	65.2
Total short-term financial assets	¥247,398	$1,995.2

MANAGEMENT ISSUES RELATED TO SHORT-TERM FINANCIAL ASSETS

LO1   Identify and explain the management issues related to short-term financial assets.

RELATED TEXT ASSIGNMENTS
Q: 1, 2
SE: 1, 2
E: 1, 2
P: 2, 6
SD: 1, 2, 3, 4, 5
FRA: 1, 3, 4, 5, 6

www.homedepot.com

The management of short-term financial assets is critical to the goal of maintaining adequate liquidity. In dealing with short-term financial assets, management must address three key issues: managing cash needs during seasonal cycles, setting credit policies, and financing receivables.

MANAGING CASH NEEDS DURING SEASONAL CYCLES

Most companies experience seasonal cycles of business activity during the year. During some periods, sales are weak; during others, they are strong. There are also periods when expenditures are high and periods when expenditures are low. For toy companies, college textbook publishers, amusement parks, construction companies, and sports equipment companies, the cycles are dramatic, but all companies experience them to some degree.

Seasonal cycles require careful planning of cash inflows, cash outflows, borrowing, and investing. Figure 1 shows the seasonal cycles typical of a home improvement company, such as The Home Depot, Inc. As you can see, cash receipts from sales are highest in the late spring, summer, and fall because that is when most people make home improvements. Sales are relatively low in the winter months. On the other hand, cash expenditures are highest in late winter and spring as the company builds up inventory for spring and summer selling. During the late summer, fall, and winter, the company has excess cash on hand that it needs to invest in a way that will earn a return but still permit access to cash as needed. During the late spring

FIGURE 1
Seasonal Cycles and Cash Requirements for a Home Improvement Company

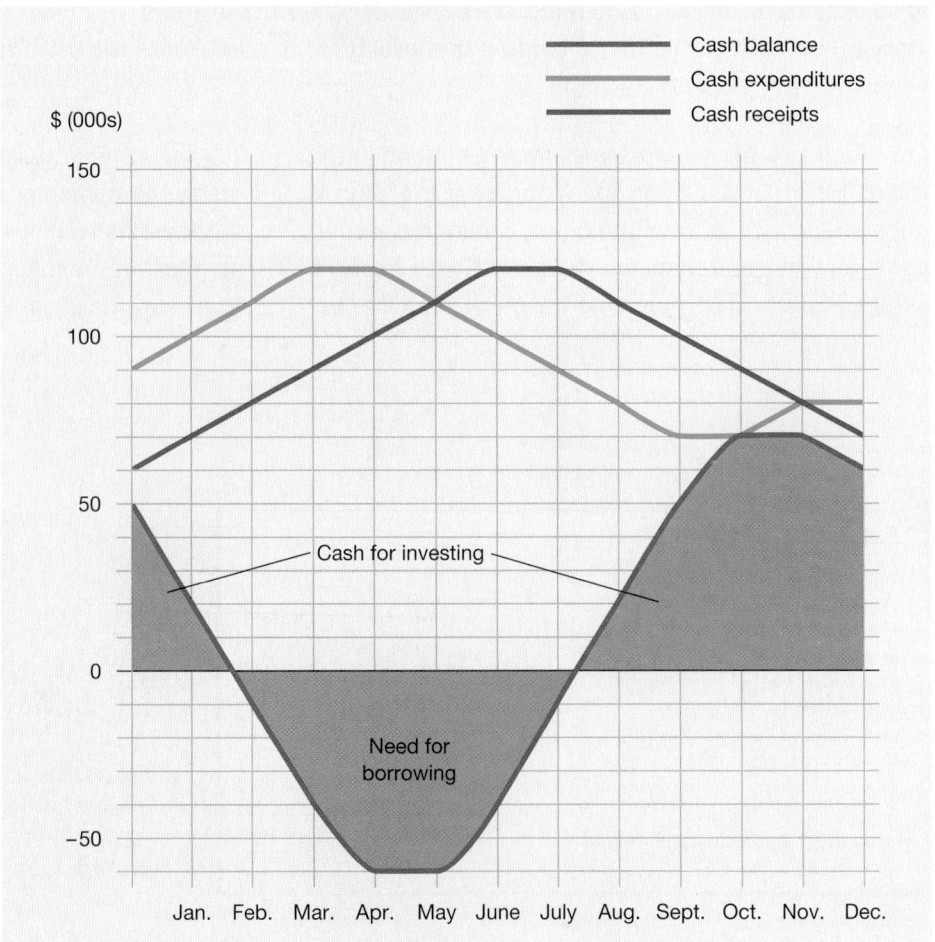

FOCUS ON BUSINESS PRACTICE

What a Difference a Year Makes!

It's hard to know how much cash reserve a company should have. Analysts are often critical of companies that build cash reserves because the cash is not earning as much as other assets might. But having a cash reserve may be a good thing, especially in a cyclical industry like the auto industry. For example, just about two years ago, the Big Three automakers— General Motors <www.gm.com>, Ford <www.ford.com>, and DaimlerChrysler <www.daimlerchrysler.com>—were awash in cash. However, in little over two years, the three companies went through $28 billion in cash through various purchases, losses, dividends, and share buybacks. Then, with increasing losses from rising costs, big rebates, and 0 percent financing, the companies were suddenly faced with a shortage of cash. As a result, Standard & Poor's lowered their credit ratings, which raises the interest cost of borrowing money. Perhaps the Big Three should have held on to some of that cash.[2]

ENRICHMENT NOTE:
Here is a chance to apply the economic concept of profit maximization. Profit is maximized when marginal revenue equals marginal cost. Thus, credit policy should equate the additional gross profit from credit sales with the cost of credit sales (i.e., bad debts).

● **STOP AND THINK!**
To increase sales, a company decides to increase its credit terms from 15 days to 30 days. What effect will this change in policy have on receivable turnover, average days' sales uncollected, and cash flows?

Receivable turnover will become smaller because average net accounts receivable will increase relative to sales. Consequently, the average days' sales uncollected will increase. This will have an adverse effect on cash flows because, on average, the company will have to wait longer to receive cash from sales. ■

and early summer, the company needs to plan for short-term borrowing to tide it over until cash receipts pick up later in the year. The discussion in this chapter of accounting for cash and cash equivalents and for short-term investments is directly related to managing the seasonal cycles of a business.

SETTING CREDIT POLICIES

Companies that sell on credit do so to be competitive and to increase sales. In setting credit terms, management must keep in mind both the terms the company's competitors are offering and the needs of customers. Obviously, companies that sell on credit want to have customers who will pay the debts they incur. To increase the likelihood of selling only to customers who will pay on time, most companies develop control procedures and maintain a credit department. The credit department's responsibilities include the examination of each person or company that applies for credit and the approval or rejection of a credit sale to that customer. Typically, the credit department asks for information about the customer's financial resources and debts. It may also check personal references and credit bureaus for further information. Then, based on the information it has gathered, the credit department decides whether to extend credit to the customer.

Two common measures of the effect of a company's credit policies are **receivable turnover** and **average days' sales uncollected**. The receivable turnover reflects the relative size of a company's accounts receivable and the success of its credit and collection policies. It may also be affected by external factors, such as seasonal conditions and interest rates. It shows how many times, on average, the receivables were turned into cash during the accounting period. The average days' sales uncollected is a related measure that shows, on average, how long it takes to collect accounts receivable.

FOCUS ON BUSINESS PRACTICE

Why Powerful Buyers Can Cause Headaches for Small Businesses

Big buyers often have significant power over small suppliers, and their cash management decisions can cause severe cash flow problems for the little companies that depend on them. For instance, in an effort to control costs and optimize cash flow, Ameritech Corp. <www.ameritech.com> told 70,000 suppliers that it would begin paying its bills in 45 days instead of 30. Other large companies routinely take 90 days or more to pay. Some small suppliers are so anxious to get the big companies' business that they fail to realize the implications of the deals they make until it is too late. When Earthly Elements, Inc., accepted a $10,000 order for dried floral gifts from a national home shopping network, its management was ecstatic because the deal increased sales by 25 percent. But in four months, the resulting cash crunch forced the company to close down. When the shopping network finally paid for the big order six months later, it was too late to revive Earthly Elements.[3]

Turnover ratios usually consist of one balance sheet account and one income statement account. The receivable turnover is computed by dividing net sales by average net accounts receivable. Theoretically, the numerator should be net credit sales, but the amount of net credit sales is rarely made available in public reports, so total net sales is used. Pioneer Corporation, discussed in the Decision Point at the start of the chapter, had net sales in 2001 of $5,052,700,000. Its net trade accounts receivable in 2001 and 2000 were $940,300,000 and $805,564,000, respectively. Its receivable turnover is computed as follows:[4]

www.pioneer.co.jp

$$\text{Receivable Turnover} = \frac{\text{Net Sales}}{\text{Average Net Accounts Receivable}}$$

$$= \frac{\$5,052,700,000}{(\$940,300,000 + \$805,564,000) \div 2}$$

$$= \frac{\$5,052,700,000}{\$872,932,000} = 5.8 \text{ times}$$

To find the average days' sales uncollected, the number of days in a year is divided by the receivable turnover, as follows:

$$\text{Average Days' Sales Uncollected} = \frac{365 \text{ days}}{\text{Receivable Turnover}} = \frac{365 \text{ days}}{5.8} = 62.9 \text{ days}$$

BUSINESS-WORLD EXAMPLE: For many businesses with seasonal sales activity, such as Nordstrom, Dillard, Marshall Field's, and Macy's, the fourth quarter produces more than 25 percent of annual sales. For such businesses, receivables are highest at the balance sheet date, resulting in an artificially low receivable turnover and high average days' sales uncollected.

Pioneer turns its receivables 5.8 times a year, for an average of every 62.9 days. While this turnover period is longer than that of many companies, it is not unusual for electronics companies because their credit terms allow retail outlets to receive and sell products before paying for them. This example demonstrates the need to interpret ratios in light of the specific industry's practice.

As Figure 2 shows, the receivable turnover ratio varies substantially from industry to industry. Grocery stores, for example, have a high turnover because that type of business has few receivables; the turnover in interstate trucking is 11.4 times because the typical credit terms in that industry are 30 days. The turnover in the machinery and computer industries is lower because those industries tend to have longer credit terms.

Figure 3 shows the average days' sales uncollected for the industries listed in Figure 2. Grocery stores, which have the lowest ratio (3.8 days) require the least amount of receivables financing; the computer industry, with average days' sales uncollected of 52.9 days, requires the most.

FIGURE 2
Receivable Turnover for Selected Industries

Industry	Times
Advertising	8.4
Interstate Trucking	11.4
Auto and Home Supply	15.2
Grocery Stores	96.6
Machinery	7.8
Computers	6.9

Service Industries   Merchandising Industries   Manufacturing Industries

Source: Data from Dun and Bradstreet, *Industry Norms and Key Business Ratios,* 2001–2002.

FIGURE 3
Average Days' Sales Uncollected for Selected Industries

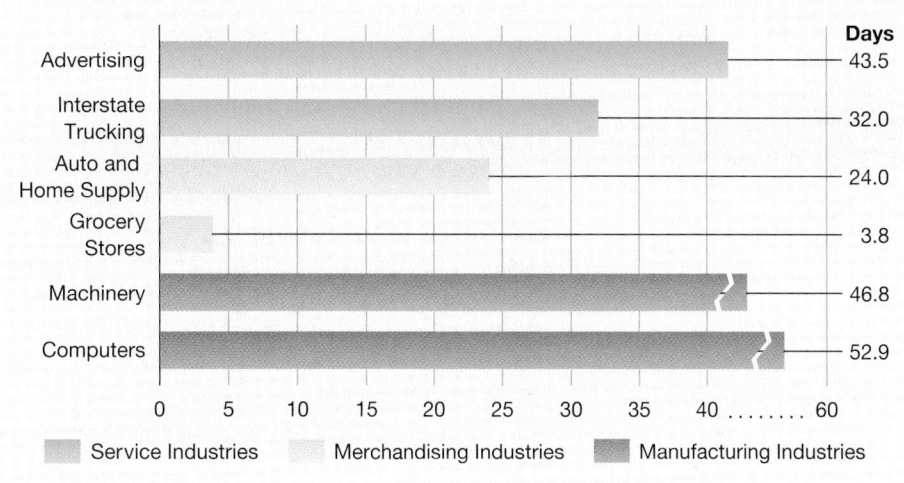

Source: Data from Dun and Bradstreet, *Industry Norms and Key Business Ratios,* 2001–2002.

FINANCING RECEIVABLES

Financial flexibility is important to most companies. Companies that have significant amounts of assets tied up in accounts receivable may be unwilling or unable to wait until cash from the receivables is collected. Many companies have set up finance companies to help their customers pay for the purchase of their products; for example, Ford has set up Ford Motor Credit Co. (FMCC), General Motors has set up General Motors Acceptance Corp. (GMAC), and Sears has set up Sears Roebuck Acceptance Corp. (SRAC). Some companies borrow funds by pledging their accounts receivable as collateral. If a company does not pay back its loan, the creditor can take the collateral (in this case, the accounts receivable) and convert it to cash to satisfy the loan.

www.ford.com
www.gm.com
www.sears.com

Companies can also raise funds by selling or transferring accounts receivable to another entity, called a **factor**. The sale or transfer of accounts receivable, called **factoring**, can be done with or without recourse. *With recourse* means that the seller of the receivables is liable to the purchaser if a receivable is not collected. *Without recourse* means that the factor that buys the accounts receivable bears any losses from uncollectible accounts. A company's acceptance of credit cards like Visa, MasterCard, or American Express is an example of factoring without recourse because the credit card issuers accept the risk of nonpayment.

The factor, of course, charges a fee for its service. The fee for sales with recourse is usually about 1 percent of the accounts receivable. The fee is higher for sales without recourse because the factor's risk is greater. In accounting terminology, the seller of the receivables with recourse is said to be contingently liable. A **contingent liability** is a potential liability that can develop into a real liability if a particular subsequent event occurs. In this case, the subsequent event would be nonpayment of the receivable by the customer. A contingent liability generally requires disclosure in the notes to the financial statements.

KEY POINT: The receivable turnover and average days' sales uncollected will appear better for a company that factors receivables than for a company that does not factor.

www.circuitcity.com

Circuit City Stores, Inc., is one of the nation's largest electronics and appliance retailers. To sell its products, the company offers generous terms through its installment programs, under which customers pay over a number of months. The company is growing rapidly and needs the cash from these installment receivables sooner than the customers have agreed to pay. To generate cash immediately from these receivables, the company sells them through a process called securitization. Under **securitization**, the company groups its receivables in batches and sells them at a discount to companies and investors. When the receivables are paid, the buyers of the receivables receive the full amount; their revenue is the amount of the discount. Circuit City sells all its receivables without recourse, which means that after

STUDY NOTE: An example will help here. If Company A holds a note from company B of $10,000 that will pay $600 in interest, a bank may be willing to buy it for $9,600. The bank will receive $10,600 at maturity while earning $1,000 in interest.

selling the receivables, it has no further liability, even if the customers do not pay. If the receivables were with recourse, it would mean that if a customer did not pay, Circuit City would have to make good on the debt.[5]

Another method of financing receivables is through the **discounting**, or selling, of promissory notes held as notes receivable. Selling notes receivable is called discounting because the bank deducts the interest from the maturity value of the note to determine the proceeds. The holder of the note (usually the payee) endorses the note and delivers it to the bank. The bank expects to collect the maturity value of the note (principal plus interest) on the maturity date but also has recourse against the endorser or seller of the note. If the maker fails to pay, the endorser is liable to the bank for payment. The endorser has a contingent liability in the amount of the discounted notes plus interest that must be disclosed in the notes to the financial statements.

✔ Check out ACE for a Review Quiz at http://accounting.college.hmco.com/students.

CASH AND CASH EQUIVALENTS

LO2 Explain *cash, cash equivalents,* and the importance of electronic funds transfer.

RELATED TEXT ASSIGNMENTS
Q: 3, 4
SE: 3
E: 3
SD: 1
FRA: 4

ENRICHMENT NOTE:
Most reporting practices are set by the FASB. This is an example of an SEC requirement for disclosure of information.

www.pioneer.co.jp

🔴 **STOP AND THINK!**
A cash register can be considered a type of imprest system. If a cashier in a supermarket started the day with $100 in change, what should the amount of cash in the drawer equal at the end of the day?

The amount of cash in the drawer should equal the total cash sales less any refunds plus $100. ▪

The annual report of Pioneer Corporation refers to *cash and cash equivalents.* Of the two terms, *cash* is the easier to understand. It is the most liquid of all assets and the most readily available to pay debts. On the balance sheet, **cash** normally consists of currency and coins on hand, checks and money orders from customers, and deposits in bank checking and savings accounts. Cash may also include a **compensating balance**, an amount that is not entirely free to be spent. A compensating balance is a minimum amount that a bank requires a company to keep in its bank account as part of a credit-granting arrangement. Such an arrangement restricts cash; in effect, increases the interest of the loan; and reduces a company's liquidity. Therefore, the SEC requires companies to disclose the amount of any compensating balances in a note to the financial statements.

The term *cash equivalents* is a little harder to understand. At times a company may find that it has more cash on hand than it needs to pay current obligations. Excess cash should not remain idle, especially during periods of high interest rates. Thus, management may periodically invest idle funds in time deposits or certificates of deposit at banks and other financial institutions, in government securities (such as U.S. Treasury notes), or in other securities. Such actions are rightfully called investments. However, if the investments have a term of 90 days or less when they are purchased, they are called **cash equivalents** because the funds revert to cash so quickly that they are regarded as cash on the balance sheet. Pioneer Corporation follows this practice. Its policy is stated as follows: "The Company considers all highly liquid investments with a maturity of 90 days or less when purchased to be cash equivalents. Cash equivalents are stated at cost, which approximates market value."[6] A survey of 600 large U.S. corporations found that 53 of them, or 9 percent, used the term *cash* as the balance sheet caption and 510, or 85 percent, used the phrase *cash and cash equivalents* or *cash and equivalents.* Twenty-seven companies, or 5 percent, combined cash with marketable securities.[7] The average amount of cash held can also vary by industry.

Most companies need to keep some currency and coins on hand. Currency and coins are needed for cash registers, for paying expenses that are impractical to pay by check, and for situations that require cash advances—for example, when sales representatives need cash for travel expenses. One way to control a cash fund or cash advances is through the use of an imprest system. A common form of imprest system is a petty cash fund, which is established at a fixed amount. Each cash payment from the fund is documented by a receipt. The fund is periodically reimbursed, based on the documented expenditures, by the exact amount necessary to restore its original cash balance. The person responsible for the petty cash fund must

Focus on Business Ethics

What About the Unlawful Use of EFT?

Electronic Funds Transfer (EFT) has made it easy to transfer funds around the world. It has facilitated the huge growth in international business, but what about the unlawful use of EFT? To combat the laundering of money by drug dealers, U.S. law requires banks to report cash transactions in excess of $10,000. However, terrorist groups have circumvented this law by electronically transferring amounts of less than $10,000. In response, the Treasury Department has set up rules that require banks to keep records about the sources and recipients of electronic transfers. But it is questionable how much effect this action will have. Since most of the millions of EFT transactions that occur every day look pretty much alike, looking for transactions that support illegal activities is like looking for a needle in a haystack.

always be able to account for its contents by having cash and receipts whose total equals the originally fixed amount.

All businesses rely on banks to control cash receipts and cash disbursements. Banks serve as safe depositories for cash, negotiable instruments, and other valuable business documents, such as stocks and bonds. The checking accounts that banks provide improve control by minimizing the amount of currency a company needs to keep on hand and by supplying permanent records of all cash payments. Banks also serve as agents in a variety of transactions, such as the collection and payment of certain kinds of debts and the exchange of foreign currencies.

Many companies commonly conduct transactions through a type of electronic communication called **electronic funds transfer (EFT)**. Instead of writing checks to pay for purchases or to repay loans, the company arranges to have cash transferred electronically from its bank to another company's bank. Wal-Mart Stores, Inc., for example, makes 75 percent of its payments to suppliers through EFT. The actual cash, of course, is not transferred. For the banks, an electronic transfer is simply a bookkeeping entry.

www.walmart.com

In serving customers, banks also offer automated teller machines (ATMs) for making deposits, withdrawing cash, transferring funds among accounts, and paying bills. Large consumer banks like Citibank, BankOne, and Bank of America process hundreds of thousands of ATM transactions each week. Many banks also give customers the option of paying bills over the telephone and with *debit cards*. When a customer makes a retail purchase using a debit card, the amount of the purchase is deducted directly from the buyer's bank account. The bank usually documents debit card transactions for the retailer, but the retailer must develop new internal controls to ensure that the transactions are recorded properly and that unauthorized transfers are not permitted. It is expected that within a few years, 25 percent of all retail activity will be handled electronically.

www.citigroup.com
www.bankone.com
www.bankofamerica.com

✓ Check out ACE for a Review Quiz at http://accounting.college.hmco.com/students.

Short-Term Investments

LO3 Identify types of short-term investments and explain the financial reporting implications.

RELATED TEXT ASSIGNMENTS
Q: 5, 6
SE: 4, 5
E: 4, 5
P: 1, 5
SD: 1, 5, 6

When investments have a maturity of more than 90 days but are intended to be held only until cash is needed for current operations, they are called **short-term investments** or **marketable securities**. Investments intended to be held for more than one year are called *long-term investments*. Long-term investments are reported in an investments section of the balance sheet, not in the current assets section. Although long-term investments may be just as marketable as short-term assets, management intends to hold them for an indefinite period of time.

Securities that may be held as short-term or long-term investments fall into three categories, as specified by the Financial Accounting Standards Board: held-to-maturity securities, trading securities, and available-for-sale securities.[8] Trading securities are classified as short-term investments. Held-to-maturity securities and available-for-sale securities may be classified as either short-term or long-term investments, depending on their length to maturity or management's intent to hold them. The three categories of securities when held as short-term investments are discussed here.

HELD-TO-MATURITY SECURITIES

KEY POINT: Any broker costs or taxes paid to acquire securities are part of the cost of the securities.

Held-to-maturity securities are debt securities that management intends to hold to their maturity date and whose cash value is not needed until that date. Such securities are recorded at cost and valued on the balance sheet at cost adjusted for the effects of interest. For example, suppose that on December 1, 20x4, Webber Company pays $97,000 for U.S. Treasury bills, which are short-term debt of the federal government. The bills will mature in 120 days at $100,000. Webber would make the following entry:

20x4

A = L + OE
+
−

Dec. 1   Short-Term Investments   97,000
        Cash   97,000
           Purchase of U.S. Treasury bills
           that mature in 120 days

At Webber's year end on December 31, the entry to accrue the interest income earned to date would be as follows:

20x4

A = L + OE
+   +

Dec. 31   Short-Term Investments   750
        Interest Income   750
          Accrual of interest on U.S. Treasury bills
          $3,000 × 30/120 = $750

On December 31, the U.S. Treasury bills would be shown on the balance sheet as a short-term investment at their amortized cost of $97,750 ($97,000 + $750). When Webber receives the maturity value on March 31, 20x5, the entry is as follows:

20x5

A = L + OE
+   +
−

Mar. 31 Cash   100,000
        Short-Term Investments   97,750
        Interest Income   2,250
          Receipt of cash at maturity of
          U.S. Treasury bills and recognition
          of related income

TRADING SECURITIES

Trading securities are debt and equity securities bought and held principally for the purpose of being sold in the near term. Debt securities are to be redeemed at a specified time and pay a return in the form of interest. Equity securities are an ownership interest in an entity and are subject to market fluctuations. Return takes the form of dividends and increases in the price of the securities.

Trading securities are frequently bought and sold to generate profits on short-term changes in their prices. Trading securities are classified as current assets on the balance sheet and are valued at fair value, which is usually the same as market value—for example, when securities are traded on a stock exchange or in the over-the-counter market.

An increase or decrease in the fair value of the total trading portfolio (the group of securities held for trading purposes) is included in net income in the accounting period in which the increase or decrease occurs. For example, assume that Franklin Company purchases 10,000 shares of Exxon Mobil Corporation for $900,000 ($90 per share) and 5,000 shares of Texaco Inc. for $300,000 ($60 per share) on October 25, 20x4. The purchase is made for trading purposes; that is, management intends

www.exxonmobil.com
www.texaco.com

to realize a gain by holding the shares for only a short period. The entry to record the investment at cost follows:

A = L + OE
+
−

20x4			
Oct. 25	Short-Term Investments	1,200,000	
	Cash		1,200,000
	Investment in stocks for trading		
	($900,000 + $300,000 = $1,200,000)		

Assume that at year end Exxon Mobil's stock price has decreased to $80 per share and Texaco's has risen to $64 per share. The trading portfolio is now valued at $1,120,000:

Security	Market Value	Cost	Gain (Loss)
Exxon Mobil (10,000 shares)	$ 800,000	$ 900,000	
Texaco (5,000 shares)	320,000	300,000	
Totals	$1,120,000	$1,200,000	($80,000)

Because the current fair value of the portfolio is $80,000 less than the original cost of $1,200,000, an adjusting entry is needed, as follows:

A = L + OE
−   −

20x4			
Dec. 31	Unrealized Loss on Investments	80,000	
	Allowance to Adjust Short-Term		
	Investments to Market		80,000
	Recognition of unrealized loss		
	on trading portfolio		

KEY POINT: The Allowance to Adjust Short-Term Investments to Market account is never changed when securities are sold. It changes only with an adjusting entry at year end.

The unrealized loss will appear on the income statement as a reduction in income. The loss is unrealized because the securities have not been sold; unrealized gains are treated the same way if they occur. The Allowance to Adjust Short-Term Investments to Market account appears on the balance sheet as a contra-asset, as follows:

Short-term investments (at cost)	$1,200,000
Less allowance to adjust short-term investments to market	80,000
Short-term investments (at market)	$1,120,000

or, more simply,

Short-term investments (at market value, cost is $1,200,000)	$1,120,000

If Franklin sells its 5,000 shares of Texaco for $70 per share on March 2, 20x5, a realized gain on trading securities is recorded as follows:

A = L + OE
+   +
−

20x5			
Mar. 2	Cash	350,000	
	Short-Term Investments		300,000
	Realized Gain on Investments		50,000
	Sale of 5,000 shares of Texaco		
	for $70 per share; cost was $60 per share		

The realized gain will appear on the income statement. Note that the realized gain is unaffected by the adjustment for the unrealized loss at the end of 20x4. The two transactions are treated independently. If the stock had been sold for less than cost, a realized loss on investments would have been recorded. Realized losses also appear on the income statement.

www.bp.com

Let's assume that during 20x5 Franklin buys 2,000 shares of BP Corporation at $64 per share and has no transactions involving Exxon Mobil. Also assume that by December 31, 20x5, the price of Exxon Mobil's stock has risen to $95 per share, or $5 per share more than the original cost, and that BP's stock price has fallen to $58, or $6 less than the original cost. The trading portfolio now can be analyzed as follows:

Security	Market Value	Cost	Gain (Loss)
Exxon Mobil (10,000 shares)	$ 950,000	$ 900,000	
BP (2,000 shares)	116,000	128,000	
Totals	$1,066,000	$1,028,000	$38,000

KEY POINT: The entry to the Allowance to Adjust Short-Term Investments to Market account is equal to the change in the market value. Compute the new allowance, and then compute the amount needed to change the account. The unrealized loss or gain is the other half of the entry.

$$A = L + OE$$
$$+ \qquad +$$

● **STOP AND THINK!**
What would cause an Allowance to Adjust Short-Term Investments to Market account that has a negative (credit) balance at the beginning of the year to have a positive (debit) balance at the end of the year?
The total market value of the portfolio of trading securities would have increased enough during the year to exceed the negative (credit) balance at the beginning of the year. ■

The market value of the portfolio now exceeds the cost by $38,000 ($1,066,000 − $1,028,000). This amount represents the targeted ending balance for the Allowance to Adjust Short-Term Investments to Market account. Recall that at the end of 20x4, that account had a credit balance of $80,000, meaning that the market value of the trading portfolio was less than the cost. The account has no entries during 20x5 and thus retains its balance until adjusting entries are made at the end of the year. The adjustment for 20x5 must be $118,000—enough to result in a debit balance of $38,000 in the allowance account.

20x5
Dec. 31   Allowance to Adjust Short-Term
               Investments to Market   118,000
                  Unrealized Gain on Investments   118,000
                  Recognition of unrealized gain
                  on trading portfolio
                  ($80,000 + $38,000 = $118,000)

The 20x5 ending balance of the allowance account may be determined as follows:

Allowance to Adjust Short-Term Investments to Market

Dec. 31, 20x5 adj.	118,000	Dec. 31, 20x4 bal.	80,000
Dec. 31, 20x5 bal.	38,000		

The balance sheet presentation of short-term investments is as follows:

Short-term investments (at cost)	$1,028,000
Plus allowance to adjust short-term investments to market	38,000
Short-term investments (at market)	$1,066,000

or, more simply,

Short-term investments (at market value, cost is $1,028,000)	$1,066,000

If the company also holds held-to-maturity securities, they are included in short-term investments at cost adjusted for the effects of interest if they will mature within one year.

AVAILABLE-FOR-SALE SECURITIES

Available-for-sale securities are debt and equity securities that do not meet the criteria for either held-to-maturity or trading securities. They are accounted for in exactly the same way as trading securities, except that the unrealized gain or loss is not reported on the income statement, but as a special item in the stockholders' equity section of the balance sheet. For example, Pioneer Corporation states in its annual report that "all debt securities and marketable equity securities held by the Company are classified as available-for-sale securities, and are carried at their fair values with unrealized gains and losses reported as a component of shareholders' equity."[9] This component is called accumulated other comprehensive income.

www.pioneer.co.jp

DIVIDEND AND INTEREST INCOME

Dividend and interest income for all three categories of investments appears in the other income and expenses section of the income statement.

 Check out ACE for a Review Quiz at http://accounting.college.hmco.com/students.

ACCOUNTS RECEIVABLE

www.jcpenney.com
www.sears.com

The other major types of short-term financial assets are accounts receivable and notes receivable. Both result from credit sales to customers. Retailers like Sears, Roebuck and Co. have made credit available to nearly every responsible person in the United States. Every field of retail trade has expanded by allowing customers to make payments a month or more after the date of sale. What is not so apparent is that credit has expanded even more in the wholesale and manufacturing industries than at the retail level. The levels of accounts receivable in selected industries are shown in Figure 4.

Accounts receivable are short-term financial assets that arise from sales on credit to customers by wholesalers or retailers. This type of credit is often called **trade credit**. Terms on trade credit usually range from 5 to 60 days, depending on industry practice. For some companies that sell to consumers, **installment accounts receivable** constitute a significant portion of accounts receivable. Installment accounts receivable arise from the sale of goods on terms that allow the buyer to make a series of time payments. Department stores, appliance stores, furniture stores, used car companies, and other retail businesses often offer installment credit. Retailers like J.C. Penney Company, Inc., and Sears, Roebuck and Co. have millions of dollars in installment accounts receivable. Although the payment period may be 24 months or more, installment accounts receivable are classified as current assets if such credit policies are customary in the industry.

On the balance sheet, the title "accounts receivable" is used for amounts arising from credit sales made to customers in the ordinary course of business. If loans or credit sales are made to employees, officers of the corporation, or owners, they should be shown separately, with an asset title like "receivables from employees," because of the increased risk of uncollectibility and conflict of interest.

Normally, individual customer accounts receivable have debit balances, but sometimes customers overpay their accounts either by mistake or in anticipation of future purchases. When these accounts show credit balances, the total of the credits should be shown on the balance sheet as a current liability because the amounts must be refunded if future sales are not made to those customers.

UNCOLLECTIBLE ACCOUNTS AND THE DIRECT CHARGE-OFF METHOD

A company will always have some customers who cannot or will not pay their debts. The accounts owed by such customers are called **uncollectible accounts**, or *bad debts,* and are a loss or an expense of selling on credit. Why does a company sell

FIGURE 4
Accounts Receivable as a Percentage of Total Assets for Selected Industries

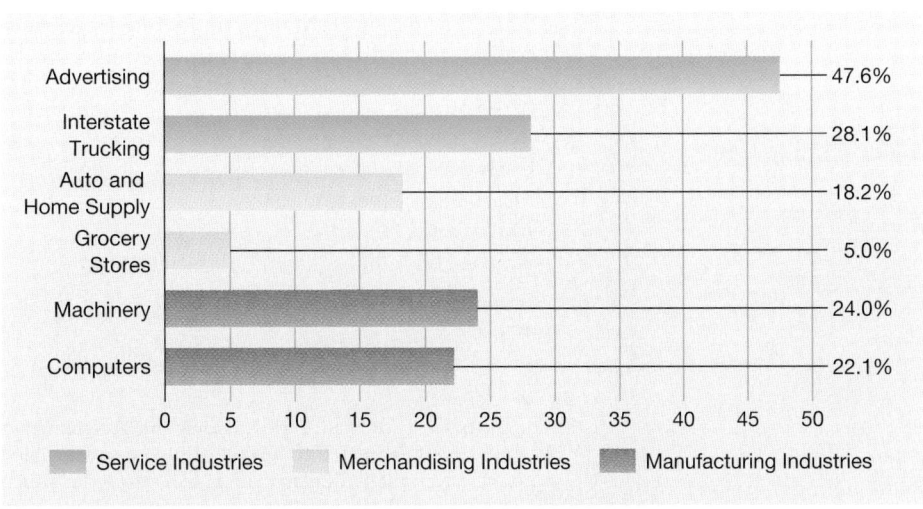

Source: Data from Dun and Bradstreet, *Industry Norms and Key Business Ratios,* 2001–2002.

on credit if it expects that some of its accounts will not be paid? The answer is that the company expects to sell much more than it would if it did not sell on credit, thereby increasing its earnings.

Some companies recognize the loss from an uncollectible account receivable at the time it is determined to be uncollectible by reducing Accounts Receivable directly and increasing Uncollectible Accounts Expense. Many small companies use this method, called the **direct charge-off method**, because it is required in computing taxable income under federal tax regulations. However, companies that follow generally accepted accounting principles do not use it in their financial statements because it does not conform to the matching rule. The direct charge-off is often recorded in a different accounting period from the one in which the sale takes place. Companies that follow GAAP prefer the allowance method, which is explained in the next section.

KEY POINT: The direct charge-off method does not conform to the matching rule.

UNCOLLECTIBLE ACCOUNTS AND THE ALLOWANCE METHOD

KEY POINT: The allowance method relies on an estimate of uncollectible accounts but is in accord with the matching rule.

Under the **allowance method** of accounting for uncollectible accounts, bad debt losses are matched against the sales they help to produce. As mentioned earlier, when management extends credit to increase sales, it knows that it will incur some losses from uncollectible accounts. Those losses are expenses that occur at the time sales on credit are made and should be matched to the revenues they help to generate. Of course, at the time the sales are made, management cannot identify which customers will not pay their debts, nor can it predict the exact amount of money that will be lost. Therefore, to observe the matching rule under generally accepted accounting principles, losses from uncollectible accounts must be estimated, and the estimate becomes an expense in the fiscal year in which the sales are made.

For example, let us assume that Cottage Sales Company made most of its sales on credit during its first year of operation, 20x4. At the end of the year, accounts receivable amounted to $100,000. On December 31, 20x4, management reviewed the collectible status of the accounts receivable. Approximately $6,000 of the $100,000 of accounts receivable were estimated to be uncollectible. Therefore, the uncollectible accounts expense for the first year of operation was estimated to be $6,000. The following adjusting entry would be made on December 31 of that year:

20x4

$A = L + OE$
$-\quad\ -$

Dec. 31	Uncollectible Accounts Expense	6,000	
	Allowance for Uncollectible Accounts		6,000
	To record the estimated uncollectible		
	accounts expense for the year		

Uncollectible Accounts Expense appears on the income statement as an operating expense. **Allowance for Uncollectible Accounts** appears on the balance sheet as a contra account that is deducted from accounts receivable.* It reduces the accounts receivable to the amount expected to be realized, or collected, in cash, as follows:

Current assets		
Cash		$ 10,000
Short-term investments		15,000
Accounts receivable	$100,000	
Less allowance for uncollectible accounts	6,000	94,000
Inventory		56,000
Total current assets		$175,000

*The purpose of Allowance for Uncollectible Accounts is to reduce the gross accounts receivable to the amount estimated to be collectible (net realizable value). The purpose of another contra account, Accumulated Depreciation, is *not* to reduce the gross plant and equipment accounts to realizable value. Rather, its purpose is to show how much of the cost of the plant and equipment has been allocated as an expense to previous accounting periods.

FOCUS ON BUSINESS PRACTICE

Selling Goods and Services Is Only Half the Problem.

To be profitable, a company must not only sell goods and services; it must also generate cash flows by collecting on those sales. The latter has been a problem for the five leading North American manufacturers of telecommunications equipment. In the late 1990s, to make sales to start-up telecom companies, these manufacturers made loans of $17 billion to their customers. Nortel Networks <www.nortelnetworks.com> had $4.1 billion in customer financing; Cisco Systems <www.cisco.com>, $2.4 bil-

lion; Lucent Technologies <www.lucent.com>, $5.4 billion; Motorola <www.motorola.com>, $3.8 billion; and Qualcomm <www.qualcomm.com>, $1.18 billion. While not all of these loans were bad debts, many became so when the telecom industry experienced a major recession in 2001. All five companies had to increase their allowances for uncollectible accounts, actions that eliminated previously reported earnings and caused the companies' stock prices to fall.[10]

Accounts receivable may also be shown on the balance sheet as follows:

Accounts receivable (net of allowance for uncollectible accounts of $6,000)	$94,000

Or they may be shown at "net," with the amount of the allowance for uncollectible accounts identified in a note to the financial statements. The estimated uncollectible amount cannot be identified with any particular customer; therefore, it is credited to a separate contra-asset account—Allowance for Uncollectible Accounts.

The allowance account often has other titles, such as *Allowance for Doubtful Accounts* and *Allowance for Bad Debts*. Once in a while, the older phrase *Reserve for Bad Debts* will be seen, but in modern practice it should not be used. *Bad Debts Expense* is a title often used for Uncollectible Accounts Expense.

ESTIMATING UNCOLLECTIBLE ACCOUNTS EXPENSE

As noted, it is necessary to estimate the expense to cover the expected losses for the year. Of course, estimates can vary widely. If management takes an optimistic view and projects a small loss from uncollectible accounts, the resulting net accounts receivable will be larger than if management takes a pessimistic view. The net income will also be larger under the optimistic view because the estimated expense will be smaller. The company's accountant makes an estimate based on past experience and current economic conditions. For example, losses from uncollectible accounts are normally expected to be greater in a recession than during a period of economic growth. The final decision, made by management, on the amount of the expense will depend on objective information, such as the accountant's analyses, and on certain qualitative factors, such as how investors, bankers, creditors, and others may view the performance of the debtor company. Regardless of the qualitative considerations, the estimated losses from uncollectible accounts should be realistic.

Two common methods of estimating uncollectible accounts expense are the percentage of net sales method and the accounts receivable aging method.

■ **PERCENTAGE OF NET SALES METHOD**   The **percentage of net sales method** asks the question, How much of this year's net sales will not be collected? The answer determines the amount of uncollectible accounts expense for the year. For example, the following balances represent the ending figures for Hassel Company for 20x9:

KEY POINT: The accountant looks at the local economic conditions as well as national conditions in setting the estimated uncollectible accounts expense.

◆ **STOP AND THINK!**
How might the receivable turnover and the average days' sales uncollectible ratios reveal that management is consistently underestimating the amount of losses from uncollectible accounts?

A decrease in receivables turnover and an increase in average days' sales uncollectible from period to period, especially in the absence of changes in credit policies, might mean that management is underestimating the amount of losses from uncollectible accounts. ■

KEY POINT: The percentage of net sales method can be described as the income statement method to emphasize that the percentage of the net sales calculated is the amount expensed. That is, any previous balance in the allowance account is irrelevant in preparing the adjustment.

Sales		Sales Returns and Allowances	
	Dec. 31 645,000	Dec. 31 40,000	

Sales Discounts		Allowance for Uncollectible Accounts	
Dec. 31 5,000			Dec. 31 3,600

PARENTHETICAL NOTE:
The percentage of net sales method, unlike the direct charge-off method, matches revenues with expenses.

Below are Hassel's actual losses from uncollectible accounts for the past three years:

Year	Net Sales	Losses from Uncollectible Accounts	Percentage
20x6	$ 520,000	$10,200	1.96
20x7	595,000	13,900	2.34
20x8	585,000	9,900	1.69
Total	$1,700,000	$34,000	2.00

In many businesses, net sales is understood to approximate net credit sales. If there are substantial cash sales, then net credit sales should be used because they generate accounts receivable. Hassel's management believes that uncollectible accounts will continue to average about 2 percent of net sales. The uncollectible accounts expense for the year 20x9 is therefore estimated to be

$$.02 \times (\$645,000 - \$40,000 - \$5,000) = .02 \times \$600,000 = \$12,000$$

The entry to record this estimate is as follows:

$A = L + OE$
$-\quad\quad -$

20x9			
Dec. 31	Uncollectible Accounts Expense	12,000	
	Allowance for Uncollectible Accounts		12,000
	To record uncollectible accounts expense at 2 percent of $600,000 net sales		

After the above entry is posted, Allowance for Uncollectible Accounts will have a balance of $15,600:

Allowance for Uncollectible Accounts

	Dec. 31	3,600
	Dec. 31 adj.	12,000
	Dec. 31 bal.	15,600

The balance consists of the $12,000 estimated uncollectible accounts receivable from 20x9 sales and the $3,600 estimated uncollectible accounts receivable from previous years.

■ **ACCOUNTS RECEIVABLE AGING METHOD**   The accounts receivable aging method asks the question, How much of the year-end balance of accounts receivable will not be collected? Under this method, the year-end balance of Allowance for Uncollectible Accounts is determined directly by an analysis of accounts receivable. The difference between the amount determined to be uncollectible and the actual balance of Allowance for Uncollectible Accounts is the expense for the year. In theory, this method should produce the same result as the percentage of net sales method, but in practice it rarely does.

The aging of accounts receivable is the process of listing each customer's receivable account according to the due date of the account. If the customer's account is past due, there is a possibility that the account will not be paid. And that possibility increases as the account extends further beyond the due date. The aging of accounts receivable helps management evaluate its credit and collection policies and alerts it to possible problems.

FOCUS ON INTERNATIONAL BUSINESS

Why Companies in Emerging Economies Must Adapt Accounting Practices

Companies in emerging economies do not always follow the accounting practices accepted in the United States. The Shanghai Stock Exchange is one of the fastest-growing stock markets in the world. Few Chinese companies acknowledge that uncollected receivables are not worth full value even when the receivables have been outstanding for a year or more. It is common practice in the United States to write off receivables more than six months old. Now that Chinese companies like Shanghai Steel Tube and Shanghai Industrial Sewing Machine are making their shares of stock available to outsiders, they must estimate uncollectible accounts in accordance with international accounting standards. Recognition of this expense could easily wipe out annual earnings.[11]

EXHIBIT 1
Analysis of Accounts Receivable by Age

			Myer Company			
			Analysis of Accounts Receivable by Age			
			December 31, 20x5			
Customer	Total	Not Yet Due	1–30 Days Past Due	31–60 Days Past Due	61–90 Days Past Due	Over 90 Days Past Due
A. Arnold	$ 150		$ 150			
M. Benoit	400			$ 400		
J. Connolly	1,000	$ 900	100			
R. Deering	250				$ 250	
Others	42,600	21,000	14,000	3,800	2,200	$1,600
Totals	$44,400	$21,900	$14,250	$4,200	$2,450	$1,600
Estimated percentage uncollectible		1.0	2.0	10.0	30.0	50.0
Allowance for Uncollectible Accounts	$ 2,459	$ 219	$ 285	$ 420	$ 735	$ 800

ENRICHMENT NOTE: The aging method is often superior to the percentage of net sales method during changing economic times. For example, during a recession, more bad debts occur. The aging method automatically reflects the economic change as accounts receivable age because customers are unable to pay. A company using the percentage of net sales method must anticipate the change and modify the percentage it uses.

KEY POINT: When the write-offs in an accounting period exceed the amount of the allowance, a debit balance in the Allowance for Uncollectible Accounts account results.

The aging of accounts receivable for Myer Company is illustrated in Exhibit 1. Each account receivable is classified as being not yet due or as being 1–30 days, 31–60 days, 61–90 days, or over 90 days past due. The estimated percentage uncollectible in each of these catagories is multiplied by the amount in each category in order to determine the estimated, or target, balance of Allowance for Uncollectible Accounts. In total, it is estimated that $2,459 of the $44,400 accounts receivable will not be collected.

Once the target balance for Allowance for Uncollectible Accounts has been found, it is necessary to determine how much the adjustment is. The amount of the adjustment depends on the current balance of the allowance account. Let us assume two cases for the December 31 balance of Myer Company's Allowance for Uncollectible Accounts: (1) a credit balance of $800 and (2) a debit balance of $800.

In the first case, an adjustment of $1,659 is needed to bring the balance of the allowance account to a $2,459 credit balance, calculated as follows:

Targeted balance for allowance for uncollectible accounts	$2,459
Less current credit balance of allowance for uncollectible accounts	800
Uncollectible accounts expense	$1,659

The uncollectible accounts expense is recorded as follows:

A = L + OE
–   –

20x5			
Dec. 31	Uncollectible Accounts Expense	1,659	
	Allowance for Uncollectible Accounts		1,659
	To bring the allowance for		
	uncollectible accounts to the		
	level of estimated losses		

The resulting balance of Allowance for Uncollectible Accounts is $2,459, as follows:

Allowance for Uncollectible Accounts

		Dec. 31	800
		Dec. 31 adj.	1,659
		Dec. 31 bal.	2,459

In the second case, because Allowance for Uncollectible Accounts has a debit balance of $800, the estimated uncollectible accounts expense for the year will have to be $3,259 to reach the targeted balance of $2,459. This calculation is as follows:

Targeted balance for allowance for uncollectible accounts	$2,459
Plus current debit balance of allowance for uncollectible accounts	800
Uncollectible accounts expense	$3,259

The uncollectible accounts expense is recorded as follows:

$A = L + OE$
$-\quad\ -$

20x5				
Dec. 31	Uncollectible Accounts Expense		3,259	
	Allowance for Uncollectible Accounts			3,259
	To bring the allowance for uncollectible accounts to the level of estimated losses			

After this entry, Allowance for Uncollectible Accounts has a credit balance of $2,459:

Allowance for Uncollectible Accounts

Dec. 31	800	Dec. 31 adj.	3,259
		Dec. 31 bal.	2,459

■ **COMPARISON OF THE TWO METHODS**   Both the percentage of net sales method and the accounts receivable aging method estimate the uncollectible accounts expense in accordance with the matching rule, but as shown in Figure 5, they do so in different ways. The percentage of net sales method is an income statement

FIGURE 5
Two Methods of Estimating Uncollectible Accounts

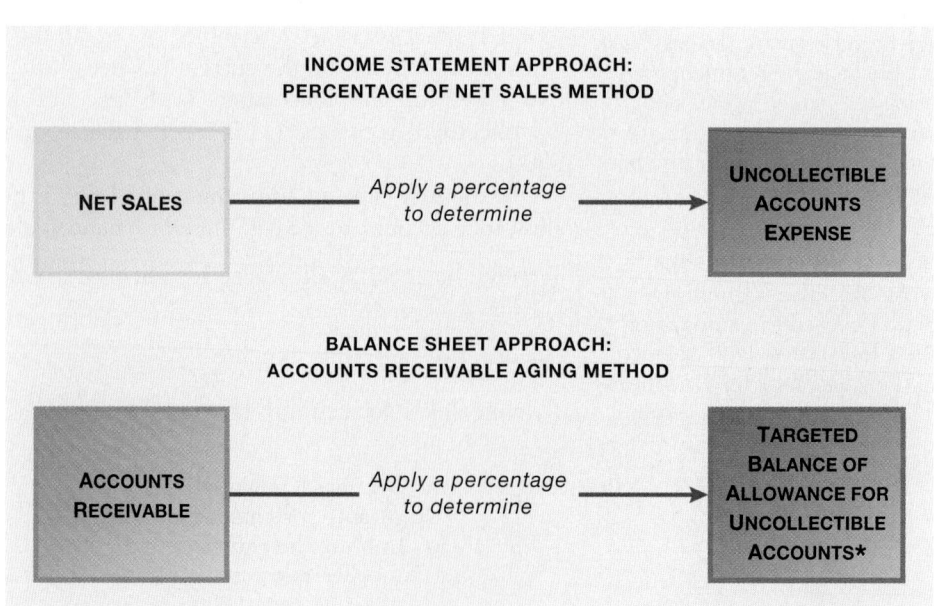

*Add current debit balance or subtract current credit balance to determine uncollectible accounts expense.

approach. It assumes that a certain proportion of sales will not be collected, and this proportion is the *amount of Uncollectible Accounts Expense* for the accounting period. The accounts receivable aging method is a balance sheet approach. It assumes that a certain proportion of accounts receivable outstanding will not be collected. This proportion is the *targeted balance of the Allowance for Uncollectible Accounts account*. The expense for the accounting period is the difference between the targeted balance and the current balance of the allowance account.

■ **WHY ACCOUNTS WRITTEN OFF WILL DIFFER FROM ESTIMATES** Regardless of the method used to estimate uncollectible accounts, the total of accounts receivable written off in any given year will rarely equal the estimated uncollectible amount. The allowance account will show a credit balance when the total of accounts written off is less than the estimated uncollectible amount. The allowance account will show a debit balance when the total of accounts written off is greater than the estimated uncollectible amount.

WRITING OFF AN UNCOLLECTIBLE ACCOUNT

When it becomes clear that a specific account receivable will not be collected, the amount should be written off to Allowance for Uncollectible Accounts. Remember that the uncollectible amount was already accounted for as an expense when the allowance was established. For example, assume that on January 15, 20x6, R. Deering, who owes Myer Company $250, is declared bankrupt by a federal court. The entry to *write off* this account is as follows:

```
20x6
A = L + OE    Jan. 15   Allowance for Uncollectible Accounts      250
  +                        Accounts Receivable                          250
  −                          To write off receivable
                             from R. Deering as uncollectible;
                             Deering declared bankrupt on
                             January 15
```

Although the write-off removes the uncollectible amount from Accounts Receivable, it does not affect the estimated net realizable value of accounts receivable. The write-off simply reduces R. Deering's account to zero and reduces Allowance for Uncollectible Accounts by a similar amount, as shown below:

	Balances Before Write-off	Balances After Write-off
Accounts receivable	$44,400	$44,150
Less allowance for uncollectible accounts	2,459	2,209
Estimated net realizable value of accounts receivable	$41,941	$41,941

RECOVERY OF ACCOUNTS RECEIVABLE WRITTEN OFF

Occasionally, a customer whose account has been written off as uncollectible will later be able to pay some or all of the amount owed. When this happens, two entries must be made: one to reverse the earlier write-off (which is now incorrect) and another to show the collection of the account. For example, assume that on September 1, 20x6, R. Deering, after his bankruptcy on January 15, notified Myer Company that he could pay $100 of his account and sent a check for $50. The entries to record this transaction are as follows:

20x6

A = L + OE + −	Sept. 1	Accounts Receivable	100	
		Allowance for Uncollectible Accounts		100
		To reinstate the portion of		
		the account of R. Deering		
		now considered collectible;		
		originally written off January 15		

A = L + OE + −	Sept. 1	Cash	50	
		Accounts Receivable		50
		Collection from R. Deering		

The collectible portion of R. Deering's account must be restored to his account and credited to Allowance for Uncollectible Accounts for two reasons. First, it turned out to be wrong to write off the full $250 on January 15 because only $150 was actually uncollectible. Second, the accounts receivable subsidiary account for R. Deering should reflect his ability to pay a portion of the money he owed despite his declaration of bankruptcy. Documentation of this action will give a clear picture of R. Deering's credit record for future credit action.

 Check out ACE for a Review Quiz at http://accounting.college.hmco.com/students.

NOTES RECEIVABLE

L05 Define *promissory note,* and compute and record promissory notes receivable.

RELATED TEXT ASSIGNMENTS
Q: 18, 19
SE: 9
E: 12, 13, 14, 15
P: 4, 8

A **promissory note** is an unconditional promise to pay a definite sum of money on demand or at a future date. The entity who signs the note and thereby promises to pay is called the *maker* of the note. The entity to whom payment is to be made is called the *payee.*

The promissory note illustrated in Figure 6 is dated May 20, 20x5, and is an unconditional promise by the maker, Samuel Mason, to pay a definite sum, or principal ($1,000), to the payee, Cook County Bank & Trust Company, on the future date of August 18, 20x5. The promissory note bears an interest rate of 8 percent. The payee regards all promissory notes it holds that are due in less than one year as **notes receivable** in the current assets section of the balance sheet. The maker regards them as **notes payable** in the current liabilities section of the balance sheet.

This portion of the chapter is concerned primarily with notes received from customers. The nature of a company's business generally determines how frequently it receives promissory notes from customers. Firms selling durable goods of high value, such as farm machinery and automobiles, will often accept promissory notes. Among the advantages of promissory notes are that they produce interest income and represent a stronger legal claim against a debtor than do accounts receivable. In addition, selling, or discounting, promissory notes to banks is a common financing method. Almost all companies occasionally receive a note, and many companies obtain notes receivable in settlement of past-due accounts.

COMPUTATIONS FOR PROMISSORY NOTES

In accounting for promissory notes, the following terms are important to remember: (1) *maturity date,* (2) *duration of note,* (3) *interest and interest rate,* and (4) *maturity value.*

■ **MATURITY DATE** The **maturity date** is the date on which a promissory note must be paid. This date must either be stated on the note or be determinable from the facts stated on the note. Among the most common statements of maturity date are the following:

1. A specific date, such as "November 14, 20xx"

2. A specific number of months after the date of the note, for example, "three months after date"

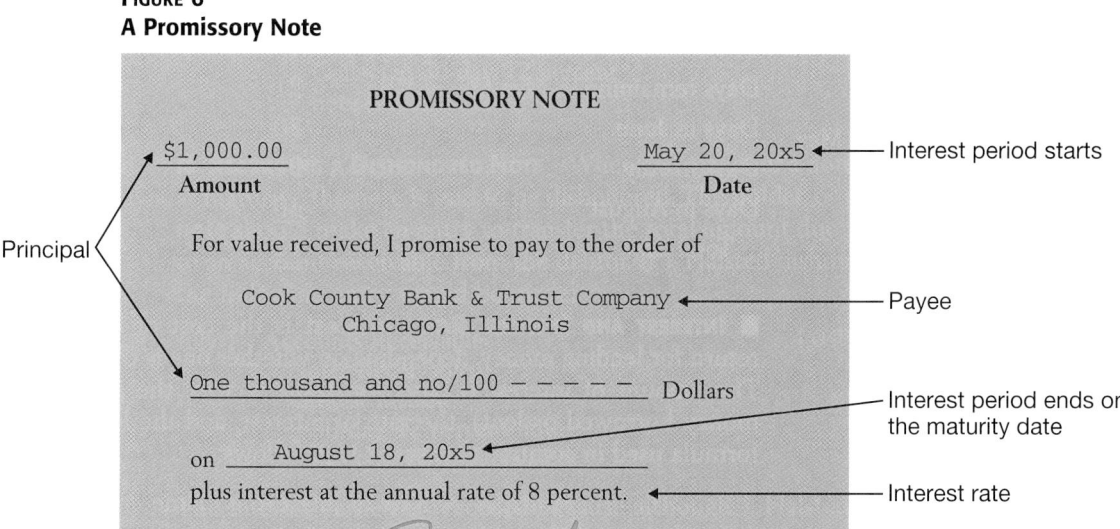

FIGURE 6
A Promissory Note

PROMISSORY NOTE

$1,000.00   May 20, 20x5 ◄——— Interest period starts
Amount   Date

Principal ◄ — For value received, I promise to pay to the order of

Cook County Bank & Trust Company ◄———————— Payee
Chicago, Illinois

One thousand and no/100 — — — — — Dollars
———————————————————————————— ◄——— Interest period ends on
                                                                          the maturity date

on _____August 18, 20x5_____ ◄

plus interest at the annual rate of 8 percent. ◄————————— Interest rate

Samuel Mason ◄————————— Maker

3. A specific number of days after the date of the note, for example, "60 days after date"

The maturity date is obvious when a specific date is stated. And when the maturity date is a number of months from the date of the note, one simply uses the same day in the appropriate future month. For example, a note that is dated January 20 and that is due in two months would be due on March 20.

When the maturity date is a specific number of days from the date of the note, however, the exact maturity date must be determined. In computing the maturity date, it is important to exclude the date of the note. For example, a note dated May 20 and due in 90 days would be due on August 18, computed as follows:

Days remaining in May (31 − 20)	11
Days in June	30
Days in July	31
Days in August	18
Total days	90

■ **DURATION OF NOTE**   The **duration of note** is the length of time in days between a promissory note's issue date and its maturity date. Knowing the duration of the note is important because interest is calculated for the exact number of days. Identifying the duration is easy when the maturity date is stated as a specific number of days from the date of the note because the two numbers are the same.

FOCUS ON BUSINESS PRACTICE

How Long Is a Year? It Depends.

Most banks use a 365-day year to compute interest for all loans, but some use a 360-day year for commercial loans. For example, the brokerage firm of May SWS Securities <www.maysws.com> of Dallas, Texas, states in its customer loan agreement, "Interest is calculated on a 360-day basis."

In Europe, use of a 360-day year is common. Financial institutions that use the 360-day basis earn slightly more interest than those that use the 365-day basis. In this book, we use a 360-day year to keep the computations simple.

Chapter Review

REVIEW OF LEARNING OBJECTIVES

LO1 Identify and explain the management issues related to short-term financial assets.

In managing short-term financial assets, management must (1) consider the need for short-term investing and borrowing as the business's balance of cash fluctuates during seasonal cycles, (2) establish credit policies that balance the need for sales with the ability to collect, and (3) assess the need to increase cash flows through the financing of receivables.

LO2 Explain *cash, cash equivalents,* and the importance of electronic funds transfer.

Cash consists of coins and currency on hand, checks and money orders received from customers, and deposits in bank accounts. Cash equivalents are investments that have a term of 90 days or less. Conducting transactions through electronic funds transfer (EFT) is important because of its efficiency. It eliminates much of the paperwork associated with traditional recordkeeping.

LO3 Identify types of short-term investments and explain the financial reporting implications.

Short-term investments are classified as held-to-maturity securities, trading securities, or available-for-sale securities. Held-to-maturity securities are debt securities that management intends to hold to the maturity date; they are valued on the balance sheet at cost adjusted for the effects of interest. Trading securities are debt and equity securities bought and held principally for the purpose of being sold in the near term; they are valued at fair value or at market value. Unrealized gains or losses on trading securities appear on the income statement. Available-for-sale securities are debt and equity securities that do not meet the criteria for either held-to-maturity or trading securities. They are accounted for in the same way as trading securities, except that an unrealized gain or loss is reported as a special item in the stockholders' equity section of the balance sheet.

LO4 Define *accounts receivable* and apply the allowance method of accounting for uncollectible accounts.

Accounts receivable are amounts still to be collected from credit sales to customers. Because credit is offered to increase sales, uncollectible accounts associated with credit sales should be charged as expenses in the period in which the sales are made. However, because of the time lag between the sales and the time the accounts are judged uncollectible, the accountant must use the allowance method to match the amount of uncollectible accounts against revenues in any given period.

Uncollectible accounts expense is estimated by either the percentage of net sales method or the accounts receivable aging method. When the first method is used, bad debts are judged to be a certain percentage of net sales during the period. When the second method is used, certain percentages are applied to groups of accounts receivable that have been arranged by due dates.

Allowance for Uncollectible Accounts is a contra-asset account to Accounts Receivable. The estimate of uncollectible accounts is debited to Uncollectible Accounts Expense and credited to the allowance account. When an individual account is determined to be uncollectible, it is removed from Accounts Receivable by debiting the allowance account and crediting Accounts Receivable. If the written-off account should later be collected, the earlier entry should be reversed and the collection should be recorded in the normal way.

LO5 Define *promissory note,* and compute and record promissory notes receivable.

A promissory note is an unconditional promise to pay a definite sum of money on demand or at a future date. Companies selling durable goods of high value, such as farm machinery and automobiles, often accept promissory notes. Selling these notes to banks is a common financing method.

In accounting for promissory notes, it is important to know how to calculate the maturity date, duration of note, interest and interest rate, and maturity value. The accounting entries for promissory notes receivable fall into four groups: recording receipt of a note, recording collection on a note, recording a dishonored note, and recording adjusting entries.

REVIEW OF CONCEPTS AND TERMINOLOGY

The following concepts and terms were introduced in this chapter:

LO4 **Accounts receivable:** Short-term financial assets that arise from sales on credit at the wholesale or retail level.

LO4 **Accounts receivable aging method:** A method of estimating uncollectible accounts based on the assumption that a predictable proportion of each dollar of accounts receivable outstanding will not be collected.

LO4 **Aging of accounts receivable:** The process of listing each customer's receivable account according to the due date of the account.

LO4 **Allowance for Uncollectible Accounts:** A contra-asset account that reduces accounts receivable to the amount expected to be collected in cash. Also called *Allowance for Doubtful Accounts* and *Allowance for Bad Debts.*

LO4 **Allowance method:** A method of accounting for uncollectible accounts by expensing estimated uncollectible accounts in the period in which the related sales take place.

LO3 **Available-for-sale securities:** Debt and equity securities that do not meet the criteria for either held-to-maturity or trading securities.

LO1 **Average days' sales uncollected:** A ratio that shows on average how long it takes to collect accounts receivable; 365 days divided by receivable turnover.

LO2 **Cash:** Coins and currency on hand, checks and money orders from customers, and deposits in bank checking and savings accounts.

LO2 **Cash equivalents:** Short-term investments that will revert to cash in 90 days or less from the time they are purchased.

LO2 **Compensating balance:** A minimum amount that a bank requires a company to keep in its bank account as part of a credit-granting arrangement.

LO1 **Contingent liability:** A potential liability that can develop into a real liability if a particular subsequent event occurs.

LO4 **Direct charge-off method:** A method of accounting for uncollectible accounts by directly debiting an expense account when bad debts are discovered instead of using the allowance method; this method violates the matching rule but is required for federal income tax computations.

LO1 **Discounting:** A method of selling notes receivable in which the bank deducts the interest from the maturity value of the note to determine the proceeds.

LO5 **Dishonored note:** A promissory note that the maker cannot or will not pay at the maturity date.

LO5 **Duration of note:** The length of time in days between a promissory note's issue date and its maturity date.

LO2 **Electronic funds transfer (EFT):** The transfer of funds from one bank to another through electronic communication.

LO1 **Factor:** An entity that buys accounts receivable.

LO1 **Factoring:** The selling or transferring of accounts receivable.

LO3 **Held-to-maturity securities:** Debt securities that management intends to hold to their maturity or payment date and whose cash value is not needed until that date.

LO4 **Installment accounts receivable:** Accounts receivable that are payable in a series of time payments.

LO5 **Interest:** The cost of borrowing money or the return for lending money, depending on whether one is the borrower or the lender.

LO3 **Marketable securities:** Short-term investments intended to be held only until needed to pay current obligations. Also called *short-term investments.*

LO5 **Maturity date:** The date on which a promissory note must be paid.

LO5 **Maturity value:** The total proceeds of a promissory note—principal plus interest—at the maturity date.

LO5 **Notes payable:** Collective term for promissory notes owed by the entity (maker) who promises payment to other entities.

LO5 **Notes receivable:** Collective term for promissory notes held by the entity to whom payment is promised (payee).

LO4 **Percentage of net sales method:** A method of estimating uncollectible accounts based on the assumption that a predictable proportion of each dollar of sales will not be collected.

LO5 **Promissory note:** An unconditional promise to pay a definite sum of money on demand or at a future date.

LO1 **Quick ratio:** A ratio for measuring the adequacy of short-term financial assets; short-term financial assets divided by current liabilities.

LO1 **Receivable turnover:** A ratio for measuring the average number of times receivables were turned into cash during an accounting period; net sales divided by average net accounts receivable.

LO1 **Securitization:** The grouping of receivables into batches for sale at a discount to companies and investors.

LO1 **Short-term financial assets:** Assets that arise from cash transactions, the investment of cash, and the extension of credit.

LO3 **Short-term investments:** Temporary investments of excess cash that are intended to be held only until they are needed to pay current obligations. Also called *marketable securities*.

LO4 **Trade credit:** Credit granted to customers by wholesalers or retailers.

LO3 **Trading securities:** Debt and equity securities bought and held principally for the purpose of being sold in the near term.

LO4 **Uncollectible accounts:** Accounts receivable owed by customers who cannot or will not pay. Also called *bad debts*.

REVIEW PROBLEM

Estimating Uncollectible Accounts, Receivables Analysis, and Notes Receivable Transactions

LO1
LO4
LO5
The Farm Implement Company sells merchandise on credit and also accepts notes for payment. During the year ended June 30, the company had net sales of $1,200,000. At the end of the year, it had Accounts Receivable of $400,000 and a debit balance in Allowance for Uncollectible Accounts of $2,100. In the past, approximately 1.5 percent of net sales has proved uncollectible. Also, an aging analysis of accounts receivable reveals that $17,000 in accounts receivable appears to be uncollectible.

The Farm Implement Company sold a tractor to R. C. Sims. Payment was received in the form of a 90-day, 9 percent, $15,000 note dated March 16. On June 14, Sims dishonored the note. On June 29, the company received payment in full from Sims plus additional interest from the date of the dishonored note.

REQUIRED ▶
1. Compute Uncollectible Accounts Expense and determine the ending balance of Allowance for Uncollectible Accounts and Accounts Receivable, Net under (a) the percentage of net sales method and (b) the accounts receivable aging method.
2. Compute the receivable turnover and average days' sales uncollected using the data from the accounts receivable aging method in 1 and assuming that the prior year's net accounts receivable were $353,000.
3. Prepare entries in journal form relating to the note received from R. C. Sims.

ANSWER TO REVIEW PROBLEM

1. Uncollectible Accounts Expense computed and balances determined

   a. Percentage of net sales method:

Uncollectible Accounts Expense $= 1.5$ percent $\times \$1,200,000 = \$18,000$

Allowance for Uncollectible Accounts $= \$18,000 - \$2,100 = \$15,900$

Accounts Receivable, Net $= \$400,000 - \$15,900 = \$384,100$

   b. Accounts receivable aging method:

Uncollectible Accounts Expense $= \$2,100 + \$17,000 = \$19,100$

Allowance for Uncollectible Accounts $= \$17,000$

Accounts Receivable, Net $= \$400,000 - \$17,000 = \$383,000$

2. Receivable turnover and average days' sales uncollected computed

$$\text{Receivable Turnover} = \frac{\$1,200,000}{(\$383,000 + \$353,000) \div 2} = 3.3 \text{ times}$$

$$\text{Average Days' Sales Uncollected} = \frac{365 \text{ days}}{3.3} = 110.6 \text{ days}$$

3. Entries related to the note prepared

A = L + OE	Mar. 16	Notes Receivable	15,000.00	
+ +		Sales		15,000.00
		Tractor sold to R. C. Sims;		
		terms of note: 90 days, 9 percent		

A = L + OE	June 14	Accounts Receivable	15,337.50	
+ +		Notes Receivable		15,000.00
−		Interest Income		337.50
		The note was dishonored by R. C. Sims		
		Maturity value:		
		$15,000 + (\$15,000 \times 9/100$		
		$\times 90/360) = \$15,337.50$		

A = L + OE	June 29	Cash	15,395.02	
+ +		Accounts Receivable		15,337.50
−		Interest Income		57.52
		Received payment in full from R. C. Sims		
		$15,337.50 + (\$15,337.50 \times 9/100 \times$		
		$15/360)$		
		$\$15,337.50 + \$57.52 = \$15,395.02$		

Chapter Assignments

BUILDING YOUR KNOWLEDGE FOUNDATION

QUESTIONS

1. Why does a business need short-term financial assets? What three issues does management face in dealing with short-term financial assets?
2. What is a factor, and what do the terms *factoring with recourse* and *factoring without recourse* mean?
3. What items are included in the Cash account? What is a compensating balance?

4. How do cash equivalents differ from cash? From short-term investments?

5. What are the three kinds of securities held as short-term investments, and how are they valued at the balance sheet date?

6. What are unrealized gains and losses on trading securities? On what statement are they reported?

7. Which of the following items should be in accounts receivable? If an item does not belong in accounts receivable, tell where on the balance sheet it does belong: (a) installment accounts receivable from regular customers, due monthly for three years; (b) debit balances in customers' accounts; and (c) receivables from employees; (d) credit balances in customers' accounts; and (e) receivables from officers of the company.

8. Why does a company sell on credit if it expects that some of the accounts will not be paid? What role does a credit department play in selling on credit?

9. What accounting rule is violated by the direct charge-off method of recognizing uncollectible accounts? Why?

10. According to generally accepted accounting principles, at what point in the cycle of selling and collecting does a loss on an uncollectible account occur?

11. Do the following terms differ in any way: *allowance for bad debts, allowance for doubtful accounts, allowance for uncollectible accounts*?

12. What is the effect on net income of management's taking an optimistic versus a pessimistic view of estimated uncollectible accounts?

13. In what ways is Allowance for Uncollectible Accounts similar to Accumulated Depreciation? In what ways is it different?

14. What is the reasoning behind the percentage of net sales method and the accounts receivable aging method of estimating uncollectible accounts?

15. What is the procedure for estimating uncollectible accounts that also gives management a view of the status of collections and the overall quality of accounts receivable?

16. After adjusting and closing the accounts at the end of the year, suppose that Accounts Receivable is $176,000 and Allowance for Uncollectible Accounts is $14,500. (a) What is the collectible value of Accounts Receivable? (b) If the $450 account of a bankrupt customer is written off in the first month of the new year, what will be the resulting collectible value of Accounts Receivable?

17. Why should an account that has been written off as uncollectible be reinstated if the amount owed is subsequently collected?

18. What is a promissory note? Who is the maker? Who is the payee?

19. What are the maturity dates of the following notes: (a) a three-month note that is dated August 16, (b) a 90-day note that is dated August 16, and (c) a 60-day note that is dated March 25?

SHORT EXERCISES

SE 1.

LO1   Management Issues

Indicate whether each of the following actions is related to (a) managing cash needs during seasonal cycles, (b) setting credit policies, or (c) financing receivables:

1. Selling accounts receivable to a factor
2. Borrowing funds for short-term needs during slow periods
3. Conducting thorough checks of new customers' ability to pay
4. Investing cash that is not currently needed for operations

SE 2.

LO1   Short-Term Liquidity Ratios

Ravena Company has cash of $20,000, short-term investments of $25,000, net accounts receivable of $45,000, inventory of $44,000, accounts payable of $60,000, and net sales of $360,000. Last year's net accounts receivable were $35,000. Ravena has no current liabilities other than accounts payable.

Compute the following ratios: quick ratio, receivable turnover, and average days' sales uncollected.

SE 3.
LO2 Cash and Cash Equivalents

Compute the amount of cash and cash equivalents on Dalester Company's balance sheet if on the balance sheet date, it has currency and coins on hand of $500, deposits in checking accounts of $3,000, U.S. Treasury bills due in 80 days of $30,000, and U.S. Treasury bonds due in 200 days of $50,000.

SE 4.
LO3 Held-to-Maturity Securities

On May 31, Levinson Company invested $49,000 in U.S. Treasury bills. The bills mature in 120 days at $50,000. Prepare entries to record the purchase on May 31; the adjustment to accrue interest on June 30, which is the end of the fiscal year; and the receipt of cash at the maturity date of September 28.

SE 5.
LO3 Trading Securities

Hi Light Corporation began investing in trading securities in 20x1. At the end of 20x1, it had the following trading portfolio:

Security	Cost	Market Value
C-Thru Rulers (10,000 shares)	$220,000	$330,000
Magenta (5,000 shares)	100,000	75,000
Totals	$320,000	$405,000

Prepare the necessary year-end adjusting entry on December 31 and the entry for the sale of all the Magenta shares on the following March 23 for $95,000.

SE 6.
LO4 Percentage of Net Sales Method

At the end of October, Yao Company's management estimates the uncollectible accounts expense to be 1 percent of net sales of $2,770,000. Give the entry to record the uncollectible accounts expense, assuming that the Allowance for Uncollectible Accounts has a debit balance of $14,000.

SE 7.
LO4 Accounts Receivable Aging Method

An aging analysis on June 30 of the accounts receivable of Multiview Corporation indicates that uncollectible accounts amount to $43,000. Give the entry to record uncollectible accounts expense under each of the following independent assumptions: (a) Allowance for Uncollectible Accounts has a credit balance of $9,000 before adjustment, and (b) Allowance for Uncollectible Accounts has a debit balance of $7,000 before adjustment.

SE 8.
LO4 Write-off of Accounts Receivable

Platt Company, which uses the allowance method, has an account receivable from Patty Greer of $4,400 that it deems to be uncollectible. Prepare the entries on May 31 to write off the account and on August 13 to record an unexpected receipt of $1,000 from Greer. The company does not expect to collect more from Greer.

SE 9.
LO5 Notes Receivable Entries

On August 25, Morgan Company received a 90-day, 9 percent note in settlement of an account receivable in the amount of $10,000. Record the receipt of the note, the accrual of interest at the end of the fiscal year on September 30, and the collection of the note on the due date.

EXERCISES

E 1.
LO1 Management Issues

Indicate whether each of the following actions is primarily related to (a) managing cash needs during seasonal cycles, (b) setting credit policies, or (c) financing receivables:

1. Buying a U.S. Treasury bill with cash that is not needed for a few months
2. Comparing receivable turnovers for two years
3. Setting a policy that allows customers to buy on credit
4. Selling notes receivable to a financing company
5. Borrowing funds for short-term needs during the period of the year when sales are low
6. Changing the terms for credit sales in an effort to reduce the average days' sales uncollected
7. Using a factor to provide operating funds
8. Establishing a department whose responsibility is to approve customers' credit

E 2.
LO1 Short-Term Liquidity Ratios

Using the following data from the financial statements of Renard Company, compute the quick ratio, the receivable turnover, and the average days' sales uncollected:

Current assets	
Cash	$ 70,000
Short-term investments	170,000
Notes receivable	240,000
Accounts receivable, net	200,000
Inventory	500,000
Prepaid assets	50,000
Total current assets	$1,230,000
Current liabilities	
Notes payable	$ 300,000
Accounts payable	150,000
Accrued liabilities	20,000
Total current liabilities	$ 470,000
Net sales	$1,600,000
Last period's accounts receivable, net	$ 180,000

E 3.

LO2   Cash and Cash Equivalents

At year end, Tarski Company had currency and coins in cash registers of $2,800, money orders from customers of $5,000, deposits in checking accounts of $32,000, U.S. Treasury bills due in 80 days of $90,000, certificates of deposits at the bank that mature in six months of $100,000, and U.S. Treasury bonds due in one year of $50,000. Calculate the amount of cash and cash equivalents that will be shown on the company's year-end balance sheet.

E 4.

LO3   Held-to-Maturity Securities

Valera Company experiences heavy sales in the summer and early fall, after which time it has excess cash to invest until the next spring. On November 1, 20x1, the company invested $194,000 in U.S. Treasury bills. The bills mature in 180 days at $200,000. Prepare entries to record the purchase on November 1; the adjustment to accrue interest on December 31, which is the end of the fiscal year; and the receipt of cash at the maturity date of April 30.

E 5.

LO3   Trading Securities

Bolton Corporation, which has begun investing in trading securities, engaged in the following transactions:

Jan.   6   Purchased 7,000 shares of General Mills stock, $30 per share.
Feb. 15   Purchased 9,000 shares of Delta, $22 per share.

At year end on June 30, General Mills was trading at $40 per share, and Delta was trading at $18 per share.
     Record the entries for the purchases. Then record the necessary year-end adjusting entry. (Include a schedule of the trading portfolio cost and market in the explanation.) Also record the entry for the sale of all the Delta shares on August 20 for $16 per share. Is the last entry affected by the June 30 adjustment?

E 6.

LO4   Percentage of Net Sales Method

At the end of the year, Simonic Enterprises estimates the uncollectible accounts expense to be .7 percent of net sales of $30,300,000. The current credit balance of Allowance for Uncollectible Accounts is $51,600. Prepare the entry in journal form to record the uncollectible accounts expense. What is the balance of Allowance for Uncollectible Accounts after this adjustment?

E 7.

LO4   Accounts Receivable Aging Method

Accounts Receivable of Soo Company shows a debit balance of $52,000 at the end of the year. An aging analysis of the individual accounts indicates estimated uncollectible accounts to be $3,350.
     Prepare the entry in journal form to record the uncollectible accounts expense under each of the following independent assumptions: (a) Allowance for Uncollectible Accounts has a credit balance of $400 before adjustment, and (b) Allowance for Uncollectible Accounts has a debit balance of $400 before adjustment. What is the balance of Allowance for Uncollectible Accounts after each of these adjustments?

E 8.

LO4   Aging Method and Net Sales Method Contrasted

At the beginning of 20xx, the balances for Accounts Receivable and Allowance for Uncollectible Accounts were $430,000 and $31,400, respectively. During the year, credit sales were $3,200,000, and collections on account were $2,950,000. In addition, $35,000 in uncollectible accounts were written off.
     Using T accounts, determine the year-end balances of Accounts Receivable and Allowance for Uncollectible Accounts. Then make the year-end adjusting entry to record

the uncollectible accounts expense and show the year-end balance sheet presentation of Accounts Receivable and Allowance for Uncollectible Accounts under each of the following conditions:

a. Management estimates the percentage of uncollectible credit sales to be 1.2 percent of total credit sales.
b. Based on an aging of accounts receivable, management estimates the end-of-year uncollectible accounts receivable to be $38,700.

Post the results of each of the entries to the T account for Allowance for Uncollectible Accounts.

E 9.
LO4   Aging Method and Net Sales Method Contrasted

During 20x1, Alpine Supply Company had net sales of $2,850,000. Most of the sales were on credit. At the end of 20x1, the balance of Accounts Receivable was $350,000, and Allowance for Uncollectible Accounts had a debit balance of $12,000. Alpine Supply Company's management uses two methods of estimating uncollectible accounts expense: (a) The percentage of uncollectible sales is 1.5 percent of net sales, and (b) based on an aging of accounts receivable, the end-of-year uncollectible accounts total $35,000. Make the end-of-year adjusting entry to record the uncollectible accounts expense under each method, and tell what the balance of Allowance for Uncollectible Accounts will be after each adjustment. Why are the results different? Which method is likely to be more reliable?

E 10.
LO4   Aging Method and Net Sales Method Contrasted

The Georgia Parts Company sells merchandise on credit. During the fiscal year ended July 31, the company had net sales of $4,600,000. At the end of the year, it had Accounts Receivable of $1,200,000 and a debit balance in Allowance for Uncollectible Accounts of $6,800. In the past, approximately 1.4 percent of net sales has proved uncollectible. Also, an aging analysis of accounts receivable reveals that $60,000 of the receivables appear to be uncollectible. Prepare entries in journal form to record uncollectible accounts expense using (a) the percentage of net sales method and (b) the accounts receivable aging method.

What is the resulting balance of Allowance for Uncollectible Accounts under each method? How would your answers under each method change if Allowance for Uncollectible Accounts had a credit balance of $6,800 instead of a debit balance? Why do the methods result in different balances?

E 11.
LO4   Accounts Receivable Transactions

Assuming that the allowance method is used, prepare entries in journal form to record the following transactions:

July 12, 20x4   Sold merchandise to Erin Lane for $1,800, terms n/10.
Oct. 18, 20x4   Received $600 from Erin Lane on account.
May   8, 20x5   Wrote off as uncollectible the balance of the Erin Lane account when she declared bankruptcy.
June 22, 20x5   Unexpectedly received a check for $200 from Erin Lane.

E 12.
LO5   Interest Computations

Determine the interest on the following notes:

a. $22,800 at 10 percent for 90 days
b. $16,000 at 12 percent for 60 days
c. $18,000 at 9 percent for 30 days
d. $30,000 at 15 percent for 120 days
e. $10,800 at 6 percent for 60 days

E 13.
LO5   Notes Receivable Transactions

Prepare entries in journal form to record the following transactions:

Jan. 16   Sold merchandise to Rounds Corporation on account for $36,000, terms n/30.
Feb. 15   Accepted a 90-day, 10 percent, $36,000 note from Rounds Corporation in lieu of payment of account.
May 16   Rounds Corporation dishonored the note.
June 15   Received payment in full from Rounds Corporation, including interest at 10 percent from the date the note was dishonored.

E 14.
LO5   Adjusting Entries: Interest Income

Prepare entries in journal form (assuming reversing entries were not made) to record the following:

Dec. 1   Received a 90-day, 12 percent note for $10,000 from a customer for a sale of merchandise.
     31   Made end-of-year adjustment for interest income.
Mar. 1   Received payment in full for note and interest.

E 15.

Prepare entries in journal form to record these transactions:

Jan. 5   Accepted a 60-day, 10 percent, $4,800 note dated this day in granting a time extension on the past-due account of K. Napoli.

Mar. 6   K. Napoli paid the maturity value of her $4,800 note.

      9   Accepted a 60-day, 12 percent, $3,000 note dated this day in granting a time extension on the past-due account of S. Plechette.

May 8   When asked for payment, S. Plechette dishonored his note.

June 7   S. Plechette paid in full the maturity value of the note plus interest at 12 percent for the period since May 8.

PROBLEMS

P 1.

Lahore Distributions follows a policy of investing excess cash until it is needed. During 20x1 and 20x2, the company engaged in the following transactions:

20x1

Feb. 1   Invested $97,000 in 120-day U.S. Treasury bills that had a maturity value of $100,000.

Mar. 30   Purchased 20,000 shares of Baser Company common stock at $16 per share and 12,000 shares of Jim's Fruit, Inc., common stock at $10 per share as trading securities.

June 1   Received maturity value of U.S. Treasury bills in cash.

     10   Received dividends of $.50 per share from Baser Company and $.25 per share from Jim's Fruit, Inc.

     30   Made year-end adjusting entry for trading securities. Market price of Baser Company shares is $13 per share and of Jim's Fruit, Inc., shares is $12 per share.

Dec. 3   Sold all the shares of Baser Company for $12 per share.

20x2

Mar. 17   Purchased 15,000 shares of CPS, Inc., for $9 per share.

May 31   Invested $116,000 in 120-day U.S. Treasury bills that had a maturity value of $120,000.

June 10   Received dividend of $.30 per share from Jim's Fruit, Inc.

     30   Made year-end adjusting entry for held-to-maturity securities.

     30   Made year-end adjusting entry for trading securities. Market price of Jim's Fruit, Inc., shares is $6 per share, and market price of CPS, Inc., shares is $11 per share.

REQUIRED ▶

1. Prepare entries in journal form to record these transactions, assuming that Lahore Distributions' fiscal year ends on June 30.

2. Show the balance sheet presentation of Lahore Distributions' short-term investments on June 30, 20x2.

P 2.

Cavanaugh Company had an Accounts Receivable balance of $320,000 and a credit balance in Allowance for Uncollectible Accounts of $16,700 at January 1, 20xx. During the year, the company recorded the following transactions:

a. Sales on account, $1,052,000

b. Sales returns and allowances by credit customers, $53,400

c. Collections from customers, $993,000

d. Worthless accounts written off, $19,800

The company's past history indicates that 2.5 percent of its net credit sales will not be collected.

REQUIRED ▶

1. Prepare T accounts for Accounts Receivable and Allowance for Uncollectible Accounts. Enter the beginning balances, and show the effects on these accounts of the items listed above, summarizing the year's activity. Determine the ending balance of each account.

2. Compute Uncollectible Accounts Expense and determine the ending balance of Allowance for Uncollectible Accounts under (a) the percentage of net sales method and (b) the accounts receivable aging method, assuming an aging of the accounts receivable shows that $24,000 may be uncollectible.

3. Compute the receivable turnover and average days' sales uncollected, using the data from the accounts receivable aging method in **2.**
4. How do you explain that the two methods used in **2** result in different amounts for Uncollectible Accounts Expense? What rationale underlies each method?

P 3.

LO4 Accounts Receivable Aging Method

Avioni Fashions Store uses the accounts receivable aging method to estimate uncollectible accounts. On February 1, 20x1, the balance of the Accounts Receivable account was a debit of $446,341, and the balance of Allowance for Uncollectible Accounts was a credit of $43,000. During the year, the store had sales on account of $3,724,000, sales returns and allowances of $63,000, worthless accounts written off of $44,300, and collections from customers of $3,214,000. As part of the end-of-year (January 31, 20x2) procedures, an aging analysis of accounts receivable is prepared. The totals of the analysis, which is partially complete, follow:

Customer Account	Total	Not Yet Due	1–30 Days Past Due	31–60 Days Past Due	61–90 Days Past Due	Over 90 Days Past Due
Balance Forward	$793,791	$438,933	$149,614	$106,400	$57,442	$41,402

To finish the analysis, the following accounts need to be classified:

Account	Amount	Due Date
B. Sunni	$10,977	Jan. 15
S. Hoffman	9,314	Feb. 15 (next fiscal year)
D. Ywahoo	8,664	Dec. 20
P. Blaine	780	Oct. 1
K. Matson	14,810	Jan. 4
J. Laberge	6,316	Nov. 15
A. Ming	4,389	Mar. 1 (next fiscal year)
	$55,250	

From past experience, the company has found that the following rates are realistic for estimating uncollectible accounts:

Time	Percentage Considered Uncollectible
Not yet due	2
1–30 days past due	5
31–60 days past due	15
61–90 days past due	25
Over 90 days past due	50

REQUIRED ▶

1. Complete the aging analysis of accounts receivable.
2. Compute the end-of-year balances (before adjustments) of Accounts Receivable and Allowance for Uncollectible Accounts.
3. Prepare an analysis computing the estimated uncollectible accounts.
4. Prepare the entry in journal form to record Avioni Fashion Store's estimated uncollectible accounts expense for the year (round the adjustment to the nearest whole dollar).

P 4.

LO5 Notes Receivable Transactions

Northern Importing Company engaged in the following transactions involving promissory notes:

Jan. 14 Sold merchandise to Maguire Company for $37,000, terms n/30.
Feb. 13 Received $8,400 in cash from Maguire Company and received a 90-day, 8 percent promissory note for the balance of the account.
May 14 Received payment in full from Maguire Company.
15 Received a 60-day, 12 percent note from Rocky Mount Company in payment of a past-due account, $12,000.
July 14 When asked to pay, Rocky Mount Company dishonored the note.
20 Received a check from Rocky Mount Company for payment of the maturity value of the note and interest at 12 percent for the six days beyond maturity.
25 Sold merchandise to Trisha Geehan Company for $36,000, with payment of $6,000 cash down and the remainder on account.

July 31   Received a 45-day, 10 percent, $30,000 promissory note from Trisha Geehan Company for the outstanding account receivable.

Sept. 14   When asked to pay, Trisha Geehan Company dishonored the note.

25   Wrote off the Trisha Geehan Company account as uncollectible following news that the company had declared bankruptcy.

REQUIRED ▶   Prepare entries in journal form to record the above transactions.

ALTERNATE PROBLEMS

P 5.
LO3 Held-to-Maturity and Trading Securities

During certain periods, Wong Suu Company invests its excess cash until it is needed. During 20x1 and 20x2, the company engaged in the following transactions:

20x1

Jan. 16   Invested $146,000 in 120-day U.S. Treasury bills that had a maturity value of $150,000.

Apr. 15   Purchased 10,000 shares of Morris Tools common stock at $40 per share and 5,000 shares of D'Alleinne Gas common stock at $30 per share as trading securities.

May 16   Received maturity value of U.S. Treasury bills in cash.

June 2   Received dividends of $2.00 per share from Morris Tools and $1.50 per share from D'Alleinne Gas.

30   Made year-end adjusting entry for trading securities. Market price of Morris Tools shares is $32 per share and of D'Alleinne Gas shares is $35 per share.

Nov. 14   Sold all the shares of Morris Tools for $42 per share.

20x2

Feb. 15   Purchased 9,000 shares of BSC Communications for $50 per share.

Apr. 1   Invested $195,500 in 120-day U.S. Treasury bills that had a maturity value of $200,000.

June 1   Received dividend of $2.20 per share from D'Alleinne Gas.

30   Made year-end adjusting entry for held-to-maturity securities.

30   Made year-end adjusting entry for trading securities. Market price of D'Alleinne Gas shares is $33 per share and of BSC Communications shares is $60 per share.

REQUIRED ▶   1. Prepare entries in journal form to record the preceding transactions, assuming that Wong Suu Company's fiscal year ends on June 30.

2. Show the balance sheet presentation of short-term investments on June 30, 20x2.

P 6.
LO1 Methods of Estimating
LO4 Uncollectible Accounts and Receivables Analysis

On December 31 of last year, the balance sheet of Vince Company had Accounts Receivable of $298,000 and a credit balance in Allowance for Uncollectible Accounts of $20,300. During the current year, Vince Company's records included the following selected activities: (a) sales on account, $1,195,000; (b) sales returns and allowances, $73,000; (c) collections from customers, $1,150,000; and (d) accounts written off as worthless, $16,000. In the past, 1.6 percent of Vince Company's net sales has been uncollectible.

REQUIRED ▶   1. Prepare T accounts for Accounts Receivable and Allowance for Uncollectible Accounts. Enter the beginning balances, and show the effects on these accounts of the items listed above, summarizing the year's activity. Determine the ending balance of each account.

2. Compute Uncollectible Accounts Expense and determine the ending balance of Allowance for Uncollectible Accounts under (a) the percentage of net sales method and (b) the accounts receivable aging method, assuming an aging of the accounts receivable shows that $20,000 may be uncollectible.

3. Compute the receivable turnover and average days' sales uncollected, using the data from the accounts receivable aging method in **2**.

4. How do you explain that the two methods used in **2** result in different amounts for Uncollectible Accounts Expense? What rationale underlies each method?

P 7.
LO4 Accounts Receivable Aging Method

Pinero Company uses the accounts receivable aging method to estimate uncollectible accounts. The Accounts Receivable account had a debit balance of $88,430 and

Allowance for Uncollectible Accounts had a credit balance of $7,200 at the beginning of the year. During the year, the company had sales on account of $473,000, sales returns and allowances of $4,200, worthless accounts written off of $7,900, and collections from customers of $450,730. At the end of the year (December 31), a junior accountant for the company was preparing an aging analysis of accounts receivable. At the top of page 6 of the report, the following totals appeared:

Customer Account	Total	Not Yet Due	1–30 Days Past Due	31–60 Days Past Due	61–90 Days Past Due	Over 90 Days Past Due
Balance Forward	$89,640	$49,030	$24,110	$9,210	$3,990	$3,300

The following accounts remained to be classified to finish the analysis:

Account	Amount	Due Date
A. Miele	$ 930	Jan. 14 (next year)
L. Dzud	620	Dec. 24
P. Chao	1,955	Sept. 28
W. North	2,100	Aug. 16
B. Ojito	375	Dec. 14
J. Taub	2,685	Jan. 23 (next year)
D. Frost	295	Nov. 5
	$8,960	

From past experience, the company has found that the following rates are realistic to estimate uncollectible accounts:

Time	Percentage Considered Uncollectible
Not yet due	2
1–30 days past due	4
31–60 days past due	20
61–90 days past due	30
Over 90 days past due	50

REQUIRED ▶ 1. Complete the aging analysis of accounts receivable.
2. Determine the end-of-year balances (before adjustments) of Accounts Receivable and Allowance for Uncollectible Accounts.
3. Prepare an analysis computing the estimated uncollectible accounts.
4. Prepare the entry in journal form to record the estimated uncollectible accounts expense for the year (round the adjustment to the nearest whole dollar).

P 8.
LO5 Notes Receivable Transactions

Carlotta Manufacturing Company sells engines. The company engaged in the following transactions involving promissory notes:

Jan. 10 Sold engines to Tilton Company for $60,000, terms n/10.
     20 Accepted a 90-day, 12 percent promissory note in settlement of the account from Tilton.
Apr. 20 Received payment from Tilton Company for the note and interest.
May 5 Sold engines to Marsden Company for $40,000, terms n/10.
     15 Received $8,000 cash and a 60-day, 13 percent note for $32,000 in settlement of the Marsden account.
July 14 When asked to pay, Marsden dishonored the note.
Aug. 2 Wrote off the Marsden account as uncollectible after receiving news that the company declared bankruptcy.
      5 Received a 90-day, 11 percent note for $30,000 from Carlson Company in settlement of an account receivable.
Nov. 3 When asked to pay, Carlson dishonored the note.
      9 Received payment in full from Carlson, including 15 percent interest for the six days since the note was dishonored.

REQUIRED ▶ Prepare entries in journal form to record the preceding transactions.

SKILLS DEVELOPMENT CASES

Conceptual Analysis

LO1 **Management of Cash**
LO2
LO3

SD 1. Collegiate Publishing Company publishes college textbooks in the sciences and humanities. More than 50 percent of Collegiate Publishing's sales occur in July, August, and December. Its cash balances are largest in August, September, and January. During the rest of the year, its cash receipts are low. The company's treasurer keeps the cash in a bank checking account earning little or no interest and pays bills from this account as they come due. To survive periods when cash receipts are low, Collegiate Publishing Company sometimes borrows money, and it repays the loans in the months when cash receipts are largest.

A management consultant has suggested that Collegiate Publishing Company institute a new cash management plan under which cash would be invested in marketable securities as it is received and securities would be sold when the funds are needed. In this way, the company would earn income on the cash and might realize a gain through an increase in the value of the securities, thus reducing the need for borrowing. The president of the company has asked you to assess the plan. Write a memorandum to the president that lays out the accounting implications of the plan for cash and cash equivalents and for the three types of marketable securities. Include in your assessment any disadvantages the plan might have.

LO1 **Role of Credit Sales**
LO4

SD 2. Mitsubishi Corp. <www.mitsubishi.com>, a broadly diversified Japanese corporation, instituted a credit plan called Three Diamonds for customers who buy its major electronic products, such as large-screen televisions and videotape recorders, from specified retail dealers.[12] Under the plan, approved customers who make purchases in July of one year do not have to make any payments until September of the next year and pay no interest during the intervening months. Mitsubishi pays the dealer the full amount less a small fee, sends the customer a Mitsubishi credit card, and collects from the customer at the specified time.

What was Mitsubishi's motivation for establishing such generous credit terms? What costs are involved? What are the accounting implications?

LO1 **Receivables Financing**

SD 3. Goldstein Appliances, Inc., is a small manufacturer of washing machines and dryers located in central Michigan. Goldstein sells most of its appliances to large, established discount retail companies that market the appliances under their own names. Goldstein sells the appliances on trade credit terms of n/60. If a customer wants a longer term, however, Goldstein will accept a note with a term of up to nine months. At present, the company is having cash flow troubles and needs $5 million immediately. Its cash balance is $200,000, its accounts receivable balance is $2.3 million, and its notes receivable balance is $3.7 million.

How might Goldstein Appliance's management use its accounts receivable and notes receivable to raise the cash it needs? What are the company's prospects for raising the needed cash?

  Group Activity: Assign to in-class groups and debrief.

Ethical Dilemma

LO1 **Ethics, Uncollectible Accounts,**
LO4 **and Short-Term Objectives**

SD 4. Waddell Interiors, a successful retail furniture company, is located in an affluent suburb where a major insurance company has just announced a restructuring that will lay off 4,000 employees. Waddell Interiors sells quality furniture, usually on credit. Accounts Receivable are one of its major assets. Although the company's annual uncollectible accounts losses are not out of line, they represent a sizable amount. The company depends on bank loans for its financing. Sales and net income have declined in the past year, and some customers are falling behind in paying their accounts.

Henry Waddell, the owner of the business, knows that the bank's loan officer likes to see a steady performance. He has therefore instructed the company's controller to underestimate the uncollectible accounts this year to show a small growth in earnings. Waddell believes this action is justified because earnings in future years will average out the losses, and since the company has a history of success, he believes the adjustments are meaningless accounting measures anyway. Are Waddell's actions ethical? Would any parties be harmed by his actions? How important is it to try to be accurate in estimating losses from uncollectible accounts?

 Group Activity: Assign in-class groups to debate the ethical issues of this case.

Research Activity

SD 5.

LO1   **Stock and Treasury Investments**
LO3

Locate the listing of New York Stock Exchange (NYSE) stocks in a recent issue of *The Wall Street Journal*. Find five companies whose names you recognize (such as IBM, McDonald's, or Ford). Write down the range of each company's stock price for the last year and the current closing price. Also note the dividend, if any, per share. How much did the market values of the common stocks you picked vary in the last year? Do these data demonstrate the need to value short-term investments of this type at market value? How does accounting for short-term investments in these common stocks differ from accounting for short-term investments in U.S. Treasury bills? How are dividends received on investments in these common stocks accounted for?

Be prepared to hand in your notes and to discuss the results of your investigation during class.

Decision-Making Practice

SD 6.

LO3   **Accounting for Short-Term Investments**

Jackson Christmas Tree Company's business—the growing and selling of Christmas trees—is seasonal. By January 1, after its heavy selling season, the company has cash on hand that will not be needed for several months. It has minimal expenses from January to October and heavy expenses during the harvest and shipping months of November and December. The company's management follows the practice of investing the idle cash in marketable securities, which can be sold as funds are needed for operations. The company's fiscal year ends on June 30.

On January 10 of the current year, Jackson has cash of $597,300 on hand. It keeps $20,000 on hand for operating expenses and invests the rest as follows:

$100,000 three-month Treasury bills	$ 97,800
1,000 shares of Ford Motor Co. ($50 per share)	50,000
2,500 shares of McDonald's ($50 per share)	125,000
2,100 shares of IBM ($145 per share)	304,500
Total short-term investments	$577,300

On February 10 and on May 10, Jackson receives quarterly cash dividends from each company in which it has invested: $.50 per share from Ford Motor Co., $.05 per share from McDonald's, and $.25 per share from IBM. The Treasury bills are redeemed at face value on April 10. On June 1, management sells 500 shares of McDonald's at $55 per share.

On June 30, the market values of the investments are as follows:

Ford Motor Co.	$ 61 per share
McDonald's	$ 46 per share
IBM	$140 per share

Jackson receives another quarterly dividend from each company on August 10. It sells all its remaining shares on November 1 at the following prices:

Ford Motor Co.	$ 55 per share
McDonald's	$ 44 per share
IBM	$160 per share

1. Record the investment transactions that occurred on January 10, February 10, April 10, May 10, and June 1. The Treasury bills are accounted for as held-to-maturity securities, and the stocks are trading securities. Prepare the required adjusting entry on June 30, and record the investment transactions on August 10 and November 1.
2. Explain how the short-term investments would be shown on the balance sheet on June 30.
3. After November 1, what is the balance of Allowance to Adjust Short-Term Investments to Market, and what will happen to this account next June?
4. What is your assessment of Jackson Christmas Tree Company's strategy with regard to idle cash?

FINANCIAL REPORTING AND ANALYSIS CASES

Interpreting Financial Reports

FRA 1.

LO1 Role of Estimates in
LO4 Accounting for Receivables

CompuCredit <www.compucredit.com> is a credit card issuer in Atlanta. It prides itself on making credit cards available to almost anybody in a matter of seconds over the Internet. The cost to the consumer is an interest rate of 28 percent, about double that of companies that provide cards only to customers with good credit. CompuCredit has been successful. It has 1.9 million accounts and achieved an income of over $100 million in a recent year. To arrive at net income, the company estimates that 10 percent of its $1.3 billion in accounts receivable will not be paid; the industry average is 7 percent. Some analysts have been critical of CompuCredit for being too optimistic in its projections of losses.[13] Why are estimates necessary in accounting for receivables? If CompuCredit were to use the same estimate of losses as other companies in its industry, what would its net income have been for the year? How would one determine if CompuCredit's estimate of losses is reasonable?

FRA 2.

LO4 Accounting for Accounts
Receivable

Dodge Products Co. is a major consumer goods company that sells over 3,000 products in 135 countries. The company's annual report to the Securities and Exchange Commission presented the following data (in thousands) pertaining to net sales and accounts related to accounts receivable for 1999, 2000, and 2001.

	2001	2000	1999
Net sales	$4,910,000	$4,865,000	$4,888,000
Accounts receivable	523,000	524,000	504,000
Allowance for uncollectible accounts	18,600	21,200	24,500
Uncollectible accounts expense	15,000	16,700	15,800
Uncollectible accounts written off	19,300	20,100	17,700
Recoveries of accounts previously written off	1,700	100	1,000

1. Compute the ratio of Uncollectible Accounts Expense to Net Sales and to Accounts Receivable and the ratio of Allowance for Uncollectible Accounts to Accounts Receivable for 1999, 2000, and 2001.
2. Compute the receivable turnover and average days' sales uncollected for each year, assuming 1998 net accounts receivable were $465,000,000.
3. What is your interpretation of the ratios? Describe management's attitude toward the collectibility of accounts receivable over the three-year period.

International Company

FRA 3.

LO1 Comparison and
**   Interpretation of Ratios**

Philips Electronics N.V. <www.philips.com> and Heineken N.V. <www.heinekencorp.nl> are two well-known Dutch companies. Philips is a large, diversified electronics, music, and media company, and Heineken makes a popular beer. Philips is about three and a half times bigger than Heineken. Its 2001 revenues were 32.3 billion euros, versus 9.1 billion euros for Heineken. Ratios can help in comparing and understanding companies. For example, the receivable turnovers for Philips and Heineken in 2000 and 2001 were as follows:[14]

	2001	2000
Philips	5.2 times	5.6 times
Heineken	7.7 times	7.9 times

What do the ratios tell you about the credit policies of the two companies? How long does it take each, on average, to collect a receivable? What do the ratios tell about the companies' relative needs for capital to finance receivables? Can you tell which company has a better credit policy? Explain your answers.

Toys "R" Us Annual Report

FRA 4.

LO1 Analysis of Short-Term
LO2 Financial Assets
LO4

Refer to the Toys "R" Us <www.tru.com> annual report in the Supplement to Chapter 6 to answer the following questions:

1. How much cash and cash equivalents did Toys "R" Us have on February 1, 2003? Do you suppose most of that amount is cash in the bank or cash equivalents?

2. Toys "R" Us does not disclose an allowance for uncollectible accounts. How do you explain the lack of disclosure?
3. Compute the quick ratios for 2002 and 2001 and comment on them.
4. Compute receivable turnover and average days' sales uncollected for 2002 and 2001 and comment on Toys "R" Us credit policies. Accounts Receivable in 2000 were $225,000,000.

Comparison Case: Toys "R" Us and Walgreen Co.

FRA 5.
LO1 Quick Ratio and Seasonality of Cash Flows

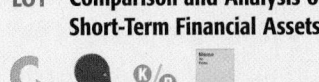

Refer to the Toys "R" Us <www.tru.com> annual report and the financial statements of Walgreens <www.walgreens.com> in the Supplement to Chapter 6 to answer the following questions:

1. What is the quick ratio for both companies for the last two years? Comment on the results of your calculation. (If you were assigned **FRA 4**, use the calculation from that case for Toys "R" Us.)
2. Do you think the seasonal need for cash is different or the same for Toys "R" Us and Walgreens? Explain. Identify the place in the financial statements where the seasonality of sales is discussed.

Fingraph® Financial Analyst™

FRA 6.
LO1 Comparison and Analysis of Short-Term Financial Assets

Choose any two companies in the same industry from the list of Fingraph companies on the Needles Accounting Resource Center Web Site at http://accounting.college. hmco.com/students. The industry should be one in which accounts receivable is likely to be an important current asset—for example, manufacturing, consumer products, consumer food and beverage, or computers. Retail companies should be avoided because they usually have low accounts receivables. Access the Microsoft Excel spreadsheets for the companies you selected. Click on the URL at the top of each company's spreadsheet for a link to the company's web site and annual report.

1. In the summary of significant accounting policies or notes to the financial statements in the annual reports of the companies you have selected, find any reference to cash and cash equivalents, short-term (marketable) securities, and accounts receivable.
2. Using the Fingraph Financial Analyst CD-ROM software, display and print for the companies you have selected (a) the Current Assets and Current Liabilities Analysis page and (b) the Liquidity and Asset Utilization Analysis page in tabular and graphic form. Prepare a table that compares the quick ratio, receivable turnover, and average days' sales uncollected for both companies for two years.
3. Find and read the liquidity analysis section of management's discussion and analysis in each annual report.
4. Write a one-page executive summary that highlights the accounting policies for short-term financial assets and compares the short-term liquidity position of the two companies. Include your assessment of the companies' relative liquidity, and make reference to management's assessment. Include the Fingraph pages and your table with your report.

Internet Case

FRA 7.
LO4 Comparison of J.C. Penney and Sears

Access the annual reports of J.C. Penney, Inc. <www.jcpenney.com> and Sears, Roebuck and Co. <www.sears.com> directly, or go to the Needles Accounting Resource Center Web Site at http://accounting.college.hmco.com/students for a link to their web sites. Find the accounts receivable and marketable securities (if any) on each company's balance sheet and the notes related to these accounts in the notes to the financial statements. If either company has marketable securities, what is their cost and market value? Does the company currently have a gain or loss on the securities? Which company has the most accounts receivable as a percentage of total assets? What is the percentage of the allowance account to gross accounts receivable for each company? Which company experienced the highest loss rate on its receivables? Why do you think there is a difference? Do the companies finance their receivables? Be prepared to discuss your findings in class.

10

Chapter 10 presents the management issues associated with inventories, including the costing of inventories for financial reporting.

Inventories

LEARNING OBJECTIVES

LO1 Identify and explain the management issues associated with accounting for inventories.

LO2 Define *inventory cost* and relate it to goods flow and cost flow.

LO3 Calculate the pricing of inventory, using the cost basis under the periodic inventory system.

LO4 Apply the perpetual inventory system to the pricing of inventories at cost.

LO5 State the effects of inventory methods and misstatements of inventory on income determination, income taxes, and cash flows.

LO6 Apply the lower-of-cost-or-market (LCM) rule to inventory valuation.

SUPPLEMENTAL OBJECTIVE

SO7 Estimate the cost of ending inventory using the retail method and gross profit method.

DECISION POINT
A USER'S FOCUS

J.C. Penney Company, Inc. <www.jcpenney.com> Managing inventory for profit is one of management's most complex and challenging tasks. In terms of dollars, the inventory of goods held for sale is one of the largest assets of a merchandising business. As may be seen in the financial highlights on the opposite page, J.C. Penney Company, Inc., a major retailer with department stores in all 50 states and Puerto Rico, devotes more than 27 percent, or $4.9 billion, of its $17.9 billion in assets to inventories. What challenges does J.C. Penney's management face in managing its inventory?

Not only must J.C. Penney's management purchase merchandise that customers will want to buy; it must also have the merchandise available in the right locations at the times when customers want to buy it. Management also must try to minimize the cost of inventory while maintaining quality. To these ends, J.C. Penney maintains purchasing offices in cities throughout the world, including Hong Kong, Taipei, Osaka, Seoul, Bangkok, Singapore, Bombay, and Florence. Further, because of the high cost of borrowing funds and storing inventory, management must control the amount of money tied up in inventory. Important accounting decisions include what assumptions to make about the flow of inventory costs, what prices to put on inventory, what inventory systems to use, and how to protect inventory against loss.

Proper management of inventory has helped J.C. Penney reduce its inventory (and total assets) and increase its level of retail sales. The company has

440

What challenges does J.C. Penney's management face in managing its inventory?

improved its income from operations from a negative $886 million in 2000 to a positive $584 million in 2002. The company plans to improve the profitability of its core department stores by further improving inventory management, controlling costs, and closing underperforming stores.[1]

Financial Highlights
(In millions)

	2002	2001	2000
Retail sales, net	$32,347	$32,004	$31,846
Cost of goods sold	22,573	22,789	23,031
(Loss)/income from operations	584	203	(886)
Merchandise inventories	4,945	4,930	5,269
Total assets	$17,867	$18,048	$19,742

MANAGEMENT ISSUES ASSOCIATED WITH ACCOUNTING FOR INVENTORIES

LO1 Identify and explain the management issues associated with accounting for inventories.

RELATED TEXT ASSIGNMENTS

Q: 1, 2, 3
SE: 1, 2
E: 1, 2
P: 1, 2, 6, 7
SD: 1, 4
FRA: 1, 4, 5, 6, 7

www.jcpenney.com
www.tru.com
www.itwinc.com

Inventory is considered a current asset because it is normally sold within a year or within a company's operating cycle. For a merchandising business like J.C. Penney or Toys "R" Us, **merchandise inventory** consists of all goods owned and held for sale in the regular course of business.

Inventories are important for manufacturing companies as well. Because manufacturers are engaged in the actual making of products, they have three kinds of inventory: raw materials to be used in the production of goods, partially completed products (often called *work in process*), and finished goods ready for sale. For example, in its annual report for the year 2002, Illinois Tool Works, Inc., disclosed the following inventories:[2]

Financial Highlights
(In thousands)

	2002	2001
Inventories		
Raw materials	$275,902	$287,067
Work in process	98,678	101,418
Finished goods	588,166	605,671
Total inventories	$962,746	$994,156

In manufacturing operations, the costs of the work in process and the finished goods inventories include not only the cost of the raw materials that go into the product, but also the cost of the labor used to convert the raw materials to finished goods and the overhead costs that support the production process. Included in this last category are such costs as indirect materials (e.g., paint, glue, and nails), indirect labor (such as the salaries of supervisors), factory rent, depreciation of plant assets, utilities costs, and insurance costs. The methods for maintaining and pricing inventory explained in this chapter are applicable to manufactured goods, but because the details of accounting for manufacturing companies are usually covered as a management accounting topic, this chapter focuses on accounting for merchandising firms.

APPLYING THE MATCHING RULE TO INVENTORIES

The American Institute of Certified Public Accountants states, "A major objective of accounting for inventories is the proper determination of income through the process of matching appropriate costs against revenues."[3] Note that the objective is the proper determination of income through the matching of costs and revenues, not the determination of the most realistic inventory value. These two objectives are sometimes incompatible, in which case the objective of income determination takes precedence.

KEY POINT: Merchandise inventory affects both the income statement and the balance sheet.

The reason inventory accounting is so important to income measurement is linked to the way income is measured on the merchandising income statement. Recall that gross margin is computed as the difference between net sales and cost of goods sold and that cost of goods sold is dependent on the cost assigned to inventory or goods not sold. Because of those relationships, the higher the cost of ending inventory, the lower the cost of goods sold and the higher the resulting gross margin. Conversely, the lower the value assigned to ending inventory, the higher the cost of goods sold and the lower the gross margin. Because the amount of gross mar-

VIDEO CASE

J.C. Penney Company, Inc.

<www.jcpenney.com>

OBJECTIVES

■ To explain why merchandise inventories represent one of the most important assets of a retail company

■ To understand the difference between goods flow and cost flow

■ To identify and explain four methods of determining inventory cost

■ To define and explain the lower-of-cost-or-market (LCM) rule

BACKGROUND FOR THE CASE

 J.C. Penney Company, Inc., as profiled in the Decision Point in this chapter, is a major department store retailer. Merchandise inventories represent a substantial portion of the company's assets. J.C. Penney stores sell fashion at value prices. The company's target customers fall in the middle of the American population. They have a household income ranging from $30,000 to $80,000. The company's goal is "to be the customer's first choice for its products and services." The company faces intense competition not only from other department stores like Sears <www.sears.com> or Macy's <www.macys.com>, but also from discount stores like Target <www.target.com> and specialty stores like The Limited <www.limitedbrands.com>. To a great extent,

J.C. Penney's future success depends on its ability to manage its inventory. Proper management of inventory has helped the company reduce its inventory (and total assets) and increase its level of retail sales, but the company still faces challenges. The company has announced plans to improve the profitability of its core department stores by further improving inventory management, controlling costs, and closing underperforming stores.

For more information about J.C. Penney Company, Inc., visit the company's web site through the Needles Accounting Resource Center Web Site at **http://accounting. college.hmco.com/students.**

REQUIRED

View the video on J.C. Penney Company, Inc., that accompanies this book. As you are watching the video, take notes related to the following questions:

1. Merchandise inventories make up more than 25 percent of J.C. Penney's assets. Explain how inventories affect the profitability of a retailer like J.C. Penney, and give both positive and negative reasons why the level of inventory is important to the company's operations.

2. Explain the difference between goods flow and cost flow as they relate to inventories, and tell which is more important in determining the cost of inventory.

3. Identify and explain the four methods of determining the cost of inventory available to J.C. Penney. Which method does J.C. Penney use?

4. What is the lower-of-cost-or-market (LCM) rule and why is it appropriate for J.C. Penney to use it? Why is LCM considered a conservative approach to inventory valuation?

gin has a direct effect on the amount of net income, the amount assigned to ending inventory directly affects the amount of net income. In effect, the value assigned to the ending inventory determines what portion of the cost of goods available for sale is assigned to cost of goods sold and what portion is assigned to the balance sheet as inventory to be carried over into the next accounting period.

ASSESSING THE IMPACT OF INVENTORY DECISIONS

Figure 1 summarizes the choices management has with regard to inventory systems and methods. The decisions usually result in different amounts of reported net income. Thus, the choices affect both the external evaluation of the company by investors and creditors and such internal evaluations as performance reviews, which determine bonuses and executive compensation. Because income is affected, the valuation of inventory may also have a considerable effect on the amount of income taxes paid. Federal income tax authorities have specific regulations about the acceptability of different methods. As a result, management is sometimes faced with balancing the goal of proper income determination with that of minimizing income taxes. Another consideration is that since the choice of inventory valuation method affects the amount of income taxes paid, it also affects a company's cash flows.

FIGURE 1
**Management Choices in
Accounting for Inventories**

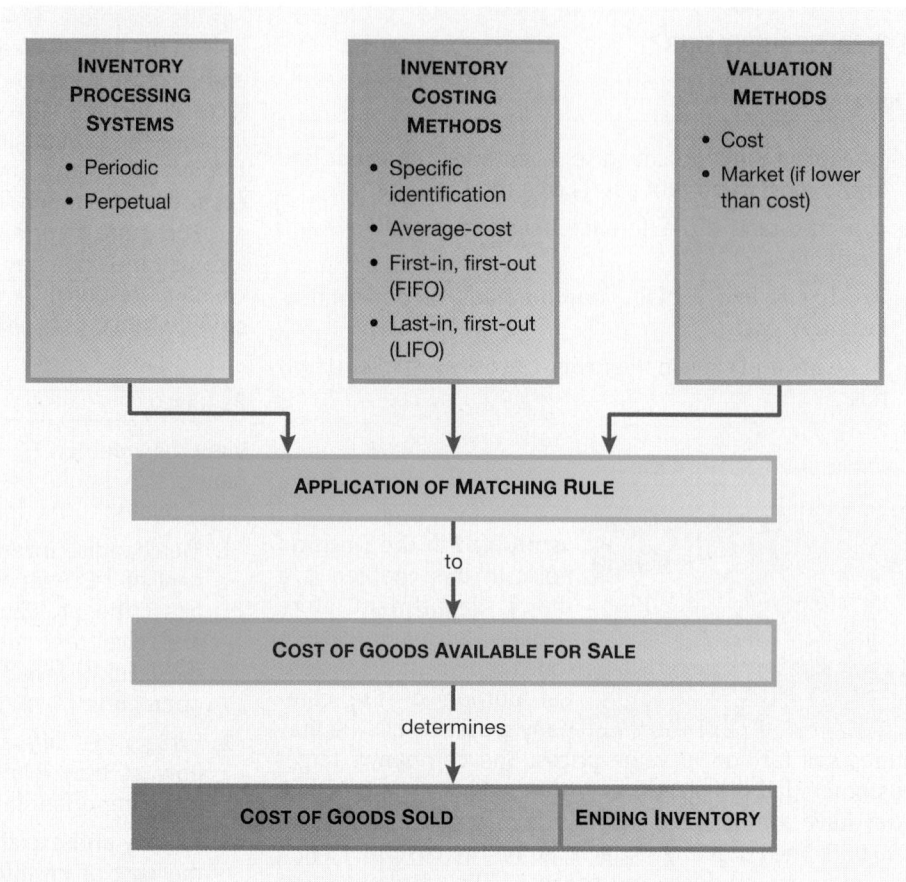

ENRICHMENT NOTE:
Management considers the
behavior of inventory prices
over time when selecting
inventory costing methods.

EVALUATING THE LEVEL OF INVENTORY

The level of inventory has important economic consequences for a company. Ideally, a company should have a great variety and quantity on hand so that customers have a large choice and do not have to wait for an item to be restocked. Such an inventory policy is not costless, however. Handling and storage costs and the interest on the funds needed to maintain high inventory levels can be substantial. But low inventory levels may result in disgruntled customers and lost sales. Common measures for evaluating inventory levels are inventory turnover and its related measure, average days' inventory on hand. **Inventory turnover** is similar to receivable turnover. It indicates the number of times a company's average inventory is sold during an accounting period. It is computed by dividing cost of goods sold by average inventory. For example, J.C. Penny's cost of goods sold was

ENRICHMENT NOTE:
Some of the costs associated
with carrying inventory are
insurance, property taxes, and
storage costs. There is also the
possibility of additional
spoilage and employee theft.

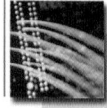

FOCUS ON BUSINESS TECHNOLOGY

Dell's Inventory Turnover Can Make Your Head Spin.

Dell Computer <www.dell.com> turns its inventory every six days. How can it do this when other companies have inventory on hand for 60, 100, or even more days? Technology and good inventory management are a big part of the answer.

Dell's speed from order to delivery sets the industry standard. Consider that a computer ordered by 9 A.M. can be delivered the next day by 9 P.M. How can Dell do this when it does not start ordering components and assembling computers until an order is placed? First, Dell's suppliers keep components warehoused just minutes from Dell's factories, making efficient,

just-in-time operations possible. Another time and money saver is the handling of computer monitors. Monitors are no longer shipped first to Dell and then on to buyers. Dell sends an email message to a shipper, such as United Parcel Service <www.ups.com>, and the shipper picks up a monitor from a supplier and schedules it to arrive with the PC. In addition to contributing to a high inventory turnover, this practice saves Dell about $30 per monitor in freight costs. Dell is showing the world how to run a business in the cyber age by selling more than $1 million worth of computers a day on its web site.[4]

FIGURE 2
Inventory Turnover for Selected Industries

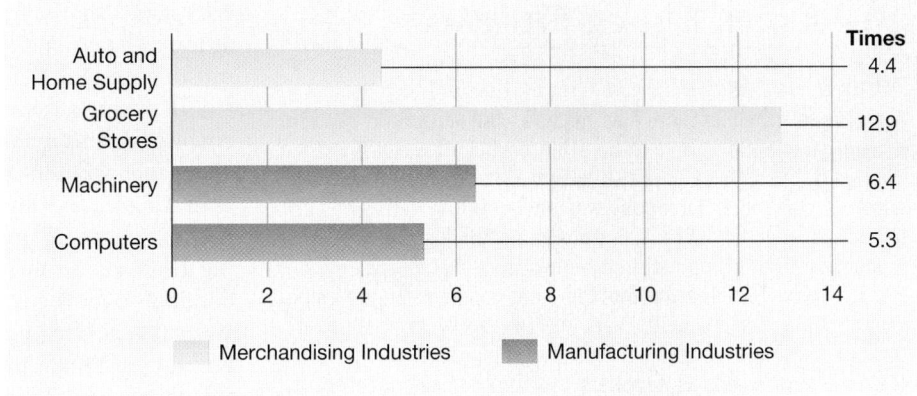

Source: Data from Dun & Bradstreet, *Industry Norms and Key Business Ratios,* 2001–2002.

ENRICHMENT NOTE:
Inventory turnover will be systematically higher if year-end inventory levels are low. For example, Toys "R" Us inventory levels on January 30 are at their lowest point of the year.

$22,573 million in 2002; its ending inventory was $4,945 million in 2002 and $4,930 million in 2001. Its inventory turnover is computed as follows:

$$\text{Inventory Turnover} = \frac{\text{Cost of Goods Sold}}{\text{Average Inventory}}$$

$$= \frac{\$22,573,000,000}{(\$4,945,000,000 + \$4,930,000,000) \div 2}$$

$$= \frac{\$22,573,000,000}{\$4,937,500,000} = 4.6 \text{ times}$$

The **average days' inventory on hand** indicates the average number of days required to sell the inventory on hand. It is found by dividing the number of days in a year by the inventory turnover, as follows:

$$\text{Average Days' Inventory on Hand} = \frac{\text{Number of Days in a Year}}{\text{Inventory Turnover}}$$

$$= \frac{365 \text{ days}}{4.6 \text{ times}} = 79.3 \text{ days}$$

STOP AND THINK!
Is it good or bad for a retail store to have a large inventory?
It depends. Obviously, a large inventory means customers have choices, and they are less likely to be disappointed because the items they want are out of stock. On the other hand, maintaining a large inventory is expensive, and if the items do not sell, they may have to be sold at a discount. The challenge to management is finding the right balance in the size of inventory. ■

J.C. Penney turned its inventory over 4.6 times in 2002, or, on average, every 79.3 days. These figures represent an improvement over the previous two years, and they are also reasonable because J.C. Penney is in a business in which fashions change every season, or about every 90 days. Management wants to sell all of each season's inventory within 80 to 90 days, even while purchasing inventory for the next season.

There are natural levels of inventory in every industry, as shown for selected merchandising and manufacturing industries in Figures 2 and 3. Nonetheless,

FIGURE 3
Average Days' Inventory on Hand for Selected Industries

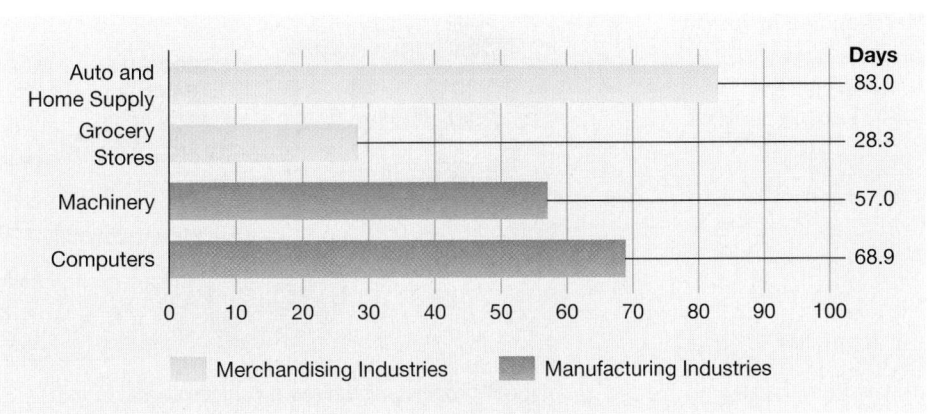

Source: Data from Dun & Bradstreet, *Industry Norms and Key Business Ratios,* 2001–2002.

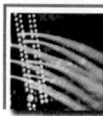

FOCUS ON BUSINESS TECHNOLOGY

What a Headache!

A single seat belt can have as many as 50 parts, and getting them from suppliers used to be a big problem for Autoliv, Inc. <www.autoliv.com>, a Swedish maker of auto safety devices. Autoliv's plant in Indianapolis was encountering constant bottlenecks in dealing with 125 different suppliers. To keep the production lines going required high-priced, rush shipments on a daily basis. To solve the problem, the company began using supply-chain management, keeping in touch with suppliers through the Internet rather than through faxes and phone calls. The new system allows suppliers to monitor the inventory at Autoliv and thus to anticipate problems. It also provides information on quantity and time of recent shipments, as well as continuously updated forecasts of parts that will be needed in the next 12 weeks. With the new system, Autoliv has reduced inventory by 75 percent and rush freight costs by 95 percent.[5]

companies that are able to maintain their inventories at lower levels and still satisfy customer needs are the most successful.

To reduce their levels of inventory, many merchandising and manufacturing companies use supply-chain management in conjunction with a just-in-time operating environment. With **supply-chain management**, a company manages its inventory and purchasing through business-to-business transactions that it conducts over the Internet. In a **just-in-time operating environment**, the company works closely with suppliers to coordinate and schedule shipments so that the shipments arrive just at the time they are needed. The benefits of using supply-chain management in a just-in-time operating environment are that the company has less money tied up in inventory, and the cost associated with carrying the inventory is reduced.

 Check out ACE for a Review Quiz at http://accounting.college.hmco.com/students.

INVENTORY COST AND GOODS FLOW

LO2 Define *inventory cost* and relate it to goods flow and cost flow.

RELATED TEXT ASSIGNMENTS
Q: 4, 5, 6
SD: 5
FRA: 1

BUSINESS-WORLD EXAMPLE: When customers order merchandise from a catalogue company, they pay not only the price listed in the catalogue, but also such charges as shipping and insurance. Consequently, the cost is greater than the catalogue price.

According to the AICPA, "The primary basis of accounting for inventories is cost, which has been defined generally as the price paid or consideration given to acquire an asset."[6] This definition of **inventory cost** has generally been interpreted as including the following costs: invoice price less purchases discounts; freight in, including insurance in transit; and applicable taxes and tariffs. Other costs—for ordering, receiving, and storing—should in principle also be included in inventory cost, but in practice it is so difficult to allocate such costs to specific inventory items that they are instead usually considered expenses of the accounting period.

MERCHANDISE IN TRANSIT

Because merchandise inventory includes all items owned by a company and held for sale, the status of any merchandise in transit, whether the company is selling it or buying it, must be examined to determine if the merchandise should be included in the inventory count. As Figure 4 illustrates, neither the seller nor the buyer has *phys-*

FIGURE 4
Merchandise in Transit

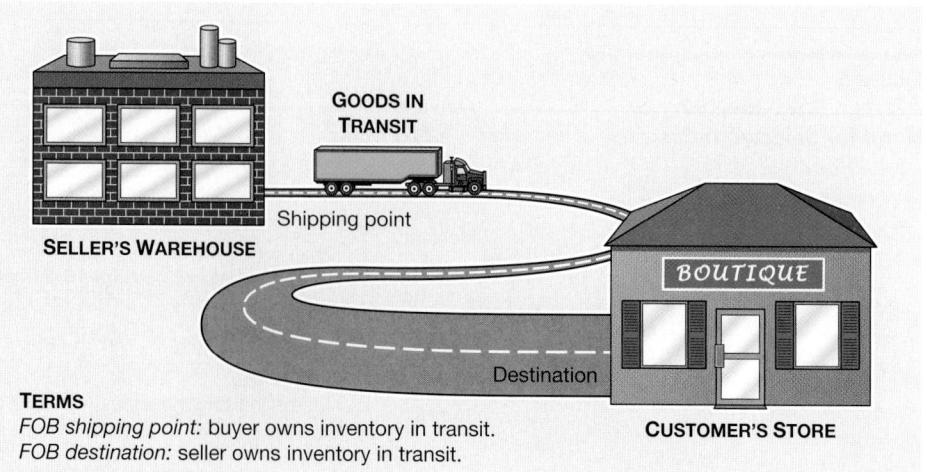

TERMS
FOB shipping point: buyer owns inventory in transit.
FOB destination: seller owns inventory in transit.

ical possession of merchandise in transit. Ownership of goods in transit is determined by the terms of the shipping agreement, which indicate when title passes. Outgoing goods shipped FOB (free on board) destination would be included in the seller's merchandise inventory, whereas those shipped FOB shipping point would not. Conversely, incoming goods shipped FOB shipping point would be included in the buyer's merchandise inventory, but those shipped FOB destination would not.

MERCHANDISE ON HAND NOT INCLUDED IN INVENTORY

KEY POINT: The consignor will count as inventory all merchandise placed (consigned) at other locations.

At the time a company takes a physical inventory, it may have merchandise on hand to which it does not hold title. One category of such goods is merchandise that has been sold and is awaiting delivery to the buyer. Since the sale has been completed, title to the goods has passed to the buyer, and the merchandise should be included in the inventory of the buyer, not of the seller. A second category is goods held on consignment. A **consignment** is merchandise that its owner (known as the *consignor*) places on the premises of another company (the *consignee*) with the understanding that payment is expected only when the merchandise is sold and that unsold items may be returned to the consignor. Title to consigned goods remains with the consignor until the consignee sells the goods. Consigned goods should not be included in the physical inventory of the consignee because they still belong to the consignor.

GOODS FLOW VERSUS COST FLOW

KEY POINT: The assumed flow of costs for inventory pricing does not have to correspond to the natural flow of goods.

The prices of most kinds of merchandise vary during the year. Identical lots of merchandise may have been purchased at different prices. Also, when identical items are bought and sold, it is often impossible to tell which have been sold and which are still in inventory. It is therefore necessary to make an assumption about the order in which items have been sold. Because the assumed order of sale may or may not be the same as the actual order of sale, the assumption is really about the *flow of costs* rather than the *flow of physical inventory*.

● **STOP AND THINK!**

Which is more important from the standpoint of inventory costing: the flow of goods or the flow of costs?

Flow of costs is more important because inventory costing ignores the actual flow of goods and assumes a flow of costs. ■

The term **goods flow** refers to the actual physical movement of goods in the operations of a company, and the term **cost flow** refers to the association of costs with their *assumed* flow in the operations of a company. The assumed cost flow may or may not be the same as the actual goods flow. The possibility of a difference between cost flow and goods flow may seem strange at first, but it arises because several choices of assumed cost flow are available under generally accepted accounting principles. In fact, it is sometimes preferable to use an assumed cost flow that bears no relationship to goods flow because it gives a better estimate of income, which is the main goal of inventory valuation.

✓ Check out ACE for a Review Quiz at http://accounting.college.hmco.com/students.

METHODS OF PRICING INVENTORY AT COST UNDER THE PERIODIC INVENTORY SYSTEM

LO3 Calculate the pricing of inventory, using the cost basis under the periodic inventory system.

RELATED TEXT ASSIGNMENTS
Q: 7, 8, 9
SE: 3, 4, 5, 6
E: 3, 4, 5, 7, 9
P: 1, 2, 6, 7
SD: 7

The value assigned to ending inventory is the result of two measurements: quantity and price. Quantity is determined by taking a physical inventory. The pricing of inventory is usually based on the assumed cost flow of the goods as they are bought and sold. Accountants usually price inventory by using one of the following generally accepted methods, each based on a different assumption of cost flow: (1) specific identification method; (2) average-cost method; (3) first-in, first-out (FIFO) method; and (4) last-in, first-out (LIFO) method. The choice of method depends on the nature of the business, the financial effects of the method, and the cost of implementing the method. To illustrate the four methods under the periodic inventory system, we use the following data for the month of June:

Inventory Data—June 30

June 1	Inventory	50 units @ $1.00	$ 50
6	Purchase	50 units @ $1.10	55
13	Purchase	150 units @ $1.20	180
20	Purchase	100 units @ $1.30	130
25	Purchase	150 units @ $1.40	210
Goods available for sale		500 units	$625
Sales		280 units	
On hand June 30		220 units	

Notice that a total of 500 units is available for sale at a total cost of $625. Stated simply, the problem of inventory pricing is to divide the $625 between the 280 units sold and the 220 units on hand. Recall that under the periodic inventory system, the inventory is not updated after each purchase and sale. Thus, it is not necessary to know when the individual sales take place.

SPECIFIC IDENTIFICATION METHOD

If the units in the ending inventory can be identified as coming from specific purchases, the **specific identification method** may be used. This method prices the inventory by identifying the cost of each item in ending inventory. For instance, if the June 30 inventory consisted of 50 units from the June 1 inventory, 100 units from the June 13 purchase, and 70 units from the June 25 purchase, the specific identification method would assign a cost of $268 to the inventory, as follows:

Periodic Inventory System—Specific Identification Method

50 units @ $1.00	$ 50	Cost of goods available	
100 units @ $1.20	120	for sale	$625
70 units @ $1.40	98	Less June 30 inventory	268
220 units at a cost of	$268	Cost of goods sold	$357

BUSINESS-WORLD EXAMPLE: Even if it were possible to track each individual inventory item, a company would not do so because it would be excessively expensive to track which items were left in inventory. The cost would clearly exceed the benefit.

The specific identification method may appear logical, and it might be used in the purchase and sale of high-priced articles, such as automobiles and works of art, but it is not used by many companies because of two definite disadvantages. First, it is often difficult and impractical to keep track of the purchase and sale of individual items. Second, when a company deals in items that are identical but that it bought at different costs, deciding which items were sold becomes arbitrary; thus, the company can raise or lower income by choosing the lower- or higher-cost items.

AVERAGE-COST METHOD

BUSINESS-WORLD EXAMPLE: The physical flow of goods may sometimes seem to dictate a particular method, such as in a milk producer's operations in which the perishable nature of the product apparently requires a *physical flow* of FIFO. However, the milk producer's management can choose an inventory method based on an assumed *cost flow* that differs from FIFO, such as average-cost or LIFO.

Under the **average-cost method**, inventory is priced at the average cost of the goods available for sale during the period. Average cost is computed by dividing the total cost of goods available for sale by the total units available for sale. This gives an average unit cost that is applied to the units in ending inventory. In our illustration, the ending inventory would be $275, or $1.25 per unit, determined as follows:

Periodic Inventory System—Average-Cost Method

Cost of Goods Available for Sale ÷ Units Available for Sale = Average Unit Cost

$625 ÷ 500 units = $1.25

Ending inventory: 220 units @ $1.25 =	$275
Cost of goods available for sale	$625
Less June 30 inventory	275
Cost of goods sold	$350

The average-cost method tends to level out the effects of cost increases and decreases because the cost for the ending inventory calculated under this method is influenced by all the prices paid during the year and by the beginning inventory price. Some, however, criticize the average-cost method because they believe recent costs are more relevant for income measurement and decision making.

FIRST-IN, FIRST-OUT (FIFO) METHOD

The **first-in, first-out (FIFO) method** is based on the assumption that the costs of the first items acquired should be assigned to the first items sold. The costs of the goods on hand at the end of a period are assumed to be from the most recent purchases, and the costs assigned to goods that have been sold are assumed to be from beginning inventory and the earliest purchases. The FIFO method of determining inventory cost may be adopted by any business, regardless of the actual physical flow of goods, because the assumption is made regarding the flow of costs and not the flow of goods. In our illustration, the June 30 inventory would be $301 when the FIFO method is used. It is computed as follows:

Periodic Inventory System—First-In, First-Out Method

150 units @ $1.40 from purchase of June 25	$210
70 units @ $1.30 from purchase of June 20	91
220 units at a cost of	$301
Cost of goods available for sale	$625
Less June 30 inventory	301
Cost of goods sold	$324

ENRICHMENT NOTE: When you make a FIFO cost flow assumption, you use it even if you can prove that one of the first-purchased items is still in inventory. Let's say that for the first week of January, perfume was packaged in blue boxes, and then the company changed to red packaging. When you price inventory using the FIFO method, you assume the blue boxes (the older merchandise) were sold, even if you have some of them left in inventory.

The effect of the FIFO method is to value the ending inventory at the most recent costs and include earlier costs in cost of goods sold. During periods of consistently rising prices, the FIFO method yields the highest possible amount of net income because cost of goods sold will show the earliest costs incurred, which are lower during periods of inflation. Another reason for this result is that businesses tend to increase selling prices as costs rise, even when inventories were purchased before the price rise. The reverse effect occurs in periods of price decreases. Consequently, a major criticism of FIFO is that it magnifies the effects of the business cycle on income.

LAST-IN, FIRST-OUT (LIFO) METHOD

The **last-in, first-out (LIFO) method** of costing inventories is based on the assumption that the costs of the last items purchased should be assigned to the first items sold and that the cost of ending inventory reflects the cost of the goods purchased earliest. Under LIFO, the June 30 inventory would be $249, computed as follows:

Periodic Inventory System—Last-In, First-Out Method

50 units @ $1.00 from June 1 inventory	$ 50
50 units @ $1.10 from purchase of June 6	55
120 units @ $1.20 from purchase of June 13	144
220 units at a cost of	$249
Cost of goods available for sale	$625
Less June 30 inventory	249
Cost of goods sold	$376

BUSINESS-WORLD EXAMPLE: Physical flow under LIFO can be likened to the changes in a gravel pile. As gravel on top is sold, more is purchased and added on top. The gravel on the bottom may never be sold. Despite the physical flow of LIFO, any acceptable cost flow assumption may be made.

The effect of LIFO is to value inventory at the earliest prices and to include in cost of goods sold the cost of the most recently purchased goods. This assumption, of course, does not agree with the actual physical movement of goods in most businesses.

FIGURE 5

Impact of Cost Flow Assumptions on the Income Statement and Balance Sheet Using the Periodic Inventory System

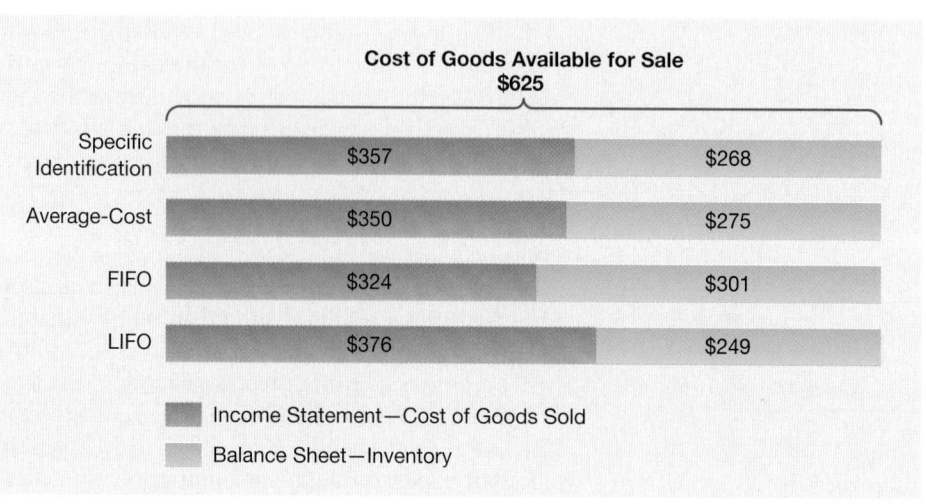

There is, however, a strong logical argument to support LIFO, based on the fact that a certain size of inventory is necessary in a going concern. When inventory is sold, it must be replaced with more goods. The supporters of LIFO reason that the fairest determination of income occurs if the current costs of merchandise are matched against current sales prices, regardless of which physical units of merchandise are sold. When prices are moving either upward or downward, the cost of goods sold will, under LIFO, show costs closer to the price level at the time the goods were sold. As a result, the LIFO method tends to show a smaller net income during inflationary times and a larger net income during deflationary times than other methods of inventory valuation. The peaks and valleys of the business cycle tend to be smoothed out. In inventory valuation, the flow of costs—and hence income determination—is more important than the physical movement of goods and balance sheet valuation.

An argument may also be made against LIFO. Because the inventory valuation on the balance sheet reflects earlier prices, it often gives an unrealistic picture of the current value of the inventory. Such balance sheet measures as working capital and current ratio may be distorted and must be interpreted carefully.

Figure 5 summarizes the impact of the four inventory cost allocation methods on the cost of goods sold as reported on the income statement and on inventory as reported on the balance sheet when a company uses the periodic inventory system. In periods of rising prices, the FIFO method yields the highest inventory valuation, the lowest cost of goods sold, and hence a higher net income; the LIFO method yields the lowest inventory valuation, the highest cost of goods sold, and thus a lower net income.

 Check out ACE for a Review Quiz at http://accounting.college.hmco.com/students.

● **STOP AND THINK!**

Under what condition would all four methods of inventory pricing produce exactly the same results?

They would produce the same results if there were no price changes after the purchase of beginning inventory. ■

FOCUS ON BUSINESS PRACTICE

What's a "Category Killer?"

A new type of retail company called the "category killer" seems to ignore the tenets of good inventory management. The category killers include Home Depot <www.homedepot.com>, Barnes & Noble <www.bn.com>, Wal-Mart <www.walmart.com>, Toys "R" Us <www.tru.com>, and Blockbuster Entertainment Corporation <www.blockbuster.com>. These retailers maintain huge inventories of the goods in which they specialize and sell them at such low prices that smaller competitors find it hard to compete. Although the category killers have large amounts of money tied up in inventories, they maintain very sophisticated just-in-time operating environments that require suppliers to meet demanding standards for delivery of products and reduction of inventory costs. Some suppliers are required to stock the shelves and keep track of inventory levels. By minimizing handling and overhead costs and buying at favorably low prices, the category killers achieve great success.

PRICING INVENTORY UNDER THE PERPETUAL INVENTORY SYSTEM

LO4 Apply the perpetual inventory system to the pricing of inventories at cost.

RELATED TEXT ASSIGNMENTS
Q: 10
SE: 7, 8, 9
E: 6, 7
P: 3, 8
SD: 5

The pricing of inventories under the perpetual inventory system differs from pricing under the periodic inventory system. The difference occurs because under the perpetual inventory system, a continuous record of quantities and costs of merchandise is maintained as purchases and sales are made. Under the periodic inventory system, only the ending inventory is counted and priced, and cost of goods sold is determined by deducting the cost of the ending inventory from the cost of goods available for sale. Under the perpetual inventory system, cost of goods sold is accumulated as sales are made and costs are transferred from the Inventory account to the Cost of Goods Sold account. The cost of the ending inventory is the balance of the Inventory account. To illustrate pricing methods under the perpetual inventory system, we use the same data as in the last section, but we add specific sales dates and amounts, as follows:

Inventory Data—June 30

June	1	Inventory	50 units @ $1.00
	6	Purchase	50 units @ $1.10
	10	Sale	70 units
	13	Purchase	150 units @ $1.20
	20	Purchase	100 units @ $1.30
	25	Purchase	150 units @ $1.40
	30	Sale	210 units
	30	Inventory	220 units

Pricing the inventory and cost of goods sold using the specific identification method is the same under the perpetual system as under the periodic system because cost of goods sold and ending inventory are based on the cost of the identified items sold and on hand. The perpetual system facilitates the use of the specific identification method because detailed records of purchases and sales are maintained.

Pricing the inventory and cost of goods sold using the average-cost method differs when the perpetual system is used. Under the periodic system, the average cost is computed for all goods available for sale during the month. Under the perpetual system, an average is computed after each purchase or series of purchases, as follows:

ENRICHMENT NOTE: An automated perpetual system has considerable costs. They include the costs of automating the system, maintaining the system, and taking a physical inventory to check against the perpetual records.

Perpetual Inventory System—Average-Cost Method

June	1	Inventory	50 units @ $1.00	$ 50.00
	6	Purchase	50 units @ $1.10	55.00
	6	Balance	100 units @ $1.05	$105.00
	10	Sale	70 units @ $1.05	(73.50)
	10	Balance	30 units @ $1.05	$ 31.50
	13	Purchase	150 units @ $1.20	180.00
	20	Purchase	100 units @ $1.30	130.00
	25	Purchase	150 units @ $1.40	210.00
	25	Balance	430 units @ $1.28*	$551.50
	30	Sale	210 units @ $1.28	(268.80)
	30	Inventory	220 units @ $1.29*	$282.70
Cost of goods sold			($73.50 + $268.80)	$342.30

*Rounded.

● **STOP AND THINK!**
Under the perpetual inventory system, why is the cost of goods sold not determined by deducting the ending inventory from goods available for sale, as it is under the periodic method?

Under the perpetual inventory system, the cost of goods sold and the inventory balance are determined after every transaction. ■

The sum of the costs applied to sales becomes the cost of goods sold, $342.30. The ending inventory is the balance, or $282.70.

When pricing the inventory using the FIFO and LIFO methods, it is necessary to keep track of the components of inventory at each step of the way because as sales are made, the costs must be assigned in the proper order. To apply the FIFO method, the approach is as follows:

Perpetual Inventory System—FIFO Method

June	1	Inventory	50 units @ $1.00		$ 50.00
	6	Purchase	50 units @ $1.10		55.00
	10	Sale	50 units @ $1.00	($ 50.00)	
			20 units @ $1.10	(22.00)	(72.00)
	10	Balance	30 units @ $1.10		$ 33.00
	13	Purchase	150 units @ $1.20		180.00
	20	Purchase	100 units @ $1.30		130.00
	25	Purchase	150 units @ $1.40		210.00
	30	Sale	30 units @ $1.10	($ 33.00)	
			150 units @ $1.20	(180.00)	
			30 units @ $1.30	(39.00)	(252.00)
	30	Inventory	70 units @ $1.30	$ 91.00	
			150 units @ $1.40	210.00	$301.00
Cost of goods sold			($72.00 + $252.00)		$324.00

Note that the ending inventory of $301 and the cost of goods sold of $324 are the same as the figures computed earlier under the periodic inventory system. This will always occur because the ending inventory under both systems consists of the last items purchased—in this case, the entire purchase of June 25 and 70 units from the purchase of June 20.

To apply the LIFO method, the approach is as follows:

Perpetual Inventory System—LIFO Method

June	1	Inventory	50 units @ $1.00		$ 50.00
	6	Purchase	50 units @ $1.10		55.00
	10	Sale	50 units @ $1.10	($ 55.00)	
			20 units @ $1.00	(20.00)	(75.00)
	10	Balance	30 units @ $1.00		$ 30.00
	13	Purchase	150 units @ $1.20		180.00
	20	Purchase	100 units @ $1.30		130.00
	25	Purchase	150 units @ $1.40		210.00
	30	Sale	150 units @ $1.40	($210.00)	
			60 units @ $1.30	(78.00)	(288.00)
	30	Inventory	30 units @ $1.00	$ 30.00	
			150 units @ $1.20	180.00	
			40 units @ $1.30	52.00	$262.00
Cost of goods sold			($75.00 + $288.00)		$363.00

Note that the ending inventory of $262 includes 30 units from the beginning inventory, all units from the June 13 purchase, and 40 units from the June 20 purchase.

A comparison of the average-cost, FIFO, and LIFO methods using the perpetual inventory system is shown in Figure 6. The results are the same as under the periodic inventory system, but some amounts have changed. For example, LIFO has

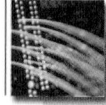

FOCUS ON BUSINESS TECHNOLOGY

More Companies Enjoy LIFO!

Using the LIFO method under the perpetual inventory system is a tedious process, especially if done manually. The development of faster and less expensive computer systems has made it easier for many companies to switch to LIFO and still use the perpetual inventory system. The availability of better technology may partially account for the increasing use of LIFO in the United States and may enable more companies to enjoy LIFO's economic benefits.

FIGURE 6
Impact of Cost Flow Assumptions on the Income Statement and Balance Sheet Using the Perpetual Inventory System

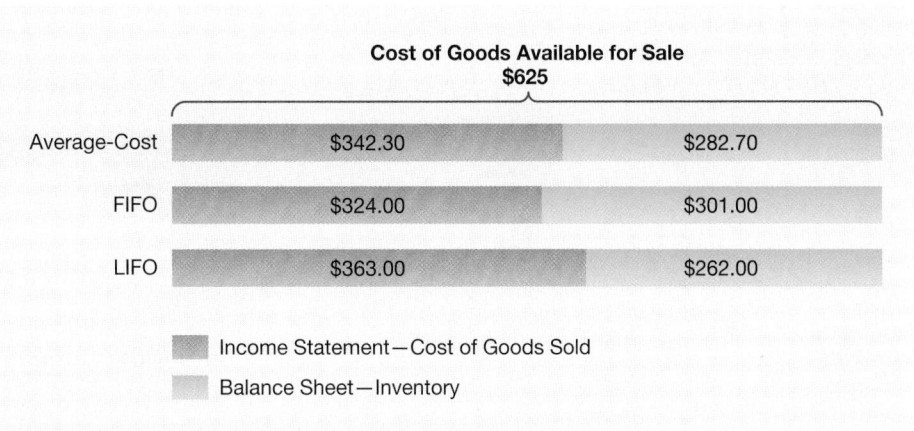

the lowest inventory valuation regardless of the inventory system used, but the amount is $262 using the perpetual system versus $249 using the periodic system.

✓ Check out ACE for a Review Quiz at http://accounting.college.hmco.com/students.

COMPARISON AND IMPACT OF INVENTORY DECISIONS AND MISSTATEMENTS

LO5 State the effects of inventory methods and misstatements of inventory on income determination, income taxes, and cash flows.

RELATED TEXT ASSIGNMENTS
Q: 11, 12, 13, 14
SE: 10
E: 8, 9, 10
SD: 2, 4, 6, 7
FRA: 1, 2, 3, 4, 5, 8

Exhibit 1 shows how the specific identification, average-cost, FIFO, and LIFO methods of pricing inventory under both the periodic and the perpetual inventory systems affect gross margin. The exhibit uses the same data as before and assumes June sales of $500. Because the specific identification method is based on actual cost, it is the same under both systems.

Keeping in mind that June was a period of rising prices, we can see that LIFO, which charges the most recent, and, in this case, the highest, prices to cost of goods sold, resulted in the lowest gross margin under both systems. Conversely, FIFO, which charges the earliest, and, in this case, the lowest, prices to cost of goods sold,

EXHIBIT 1
Effects of Inventory Systems and Costing Methods on Gross Margin

		Periodic Inventory System			Perpetual Inventory System*		
	Specific Identification Method	Average-Cost Method	First-In, First-Out Method	Last-In, First-Out Method	Average-Cost Method	First-In, First-Out Method	Last-In, First-Out Method
Sales	$500	$500	$500	$500	$500	$500	$500
Cost of goods sold							
Beginning inventory	$ 50	$ 50	$ 50	$ 50			
Purchases	575	575	575	575			
Cost of goods available for sale	$625	$625	$625	$625			
Less ending inventory	268	275	301	249	$283†	$301	$262
Cost of goods sold	$357	$350	$324	$376	$342†	$324	$363
Gross margin	$143	$150	$176	$124	$158	$176	$137

*Ending inventory under the perpetual inventory system is provided for comparison only. It is not used in the computation of cost of goods sold.
†Rounded.

Figure 7
Inventory Costing Methods Used by 600 Large Companies

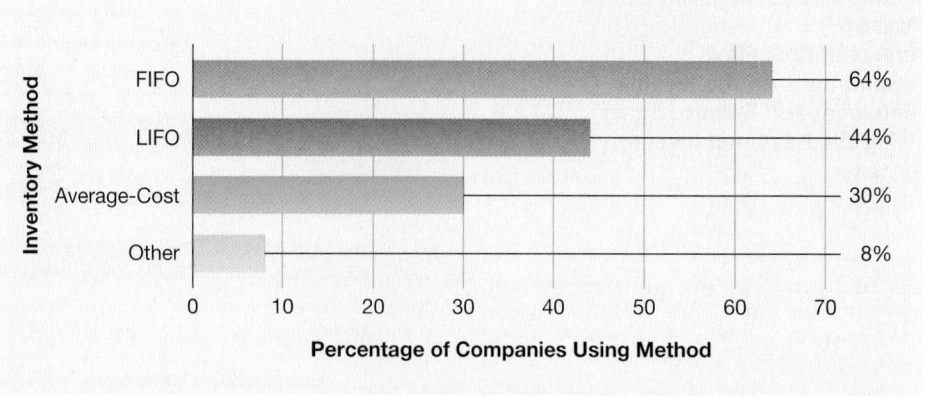

Total percentage exceeds 100 because some companies used different methods for different types of inventory.

Source: "Inventory Costing Methods Used by 600 Large Companies." Reprinted with permission from *Accounting Trends and Techniques.* Copyright © 2002 by the American Institute of Certified Public Accountants, Inc.

produced the highest gross margin. The gross margin under the average-cost method is in between the gross margins under LIFO and FIFO; thus, this method clearly has a less pronounced effect. Note that ending inventory and gross margin under FIFO are the same under both the periodic and the perpetual inventory systems.

During a period of declining prices, the reverse would occur. The LIFO method would produce a higher gross margin than the FIFO method. It is apparent that the method of inventory valuation has the greatest importance during prolonged periods of price changes in one direction, either up or down.

Because the specific identification method depends on the particular items sold, no generalization can be made about the effect of changing prices.

EFFECTS ON THE FINANCIAL STATEMENTS

KEY POINT: The assumption of inventory cost flows is necessary because of changes in merchandise prices.

Each of the four methods of inventory pricing is acceptable for use in published financial statements. The FIFO, LIFO, and average-cost methods are widely used, as can be seen in Figure 7, which shows the inventory costing methods used by 600 large companies. Each method has its advantages and disadvantages, and none can be considered best or perfect. The factors that should be considered in choosing an inventory method are the trend of prices and the effects of each method on financial statements, income taxes, and cash flows.

A basic problem in determining the best inventory measure for a particular company is that inventory affects both the balance sheet and the income statement. As we have seen, the LIFO method is best suited for the income statement because it matches revenues and cost of goods sold. But it is not the best measure of the current balance sheet value of inventory, particularly during a prolonged period of price increases or decreases. FIFO, on the other hand, is best suited to the balance sheet because the ending inventory is closest to current values and thus gives a more realistic view of the current financial assets of a business. Readers of financial statements must be alert to inventory methods and be able to assess their effects.

EFFECTS ON INCOME TAXES

The Internal Revenue Service has developed several rules for valuing inventories for federal income tax purposes. A company has a wide choice of methods, including specific identification, average-cost, FIFO, and LIFO, as well as lower-of-cost-or-market, discussed later in the chapter. But once a method has been chosen, it must be used consistently from one year to the next. The IRS must approve any change in the inventory valuation method for income tax purposes.* This requirement

*A single exception to this rule is that although taxpayers must notify the IRS of a change to LIFO from another method, they do not need to have advance IRS approval.

FOCUS ON BUSINESS PRACTICE

Does a Company's Accounting Method Affect Management's Operating Decisions?

It certainly does when taxes are involved! Research has shown that among firms that use the LIFO inventory method, those with high tax rates are more likely to buy extra inventory at year end than are those with low tax rates.[7] This behavior is predictable because LIFO deducts the most recent purchases, which are likely to have higher costs than earlier purchases, in determining taxable income. This action will result in lower income taxes.

KEY POINT: In periods of rising prices, LIFO results in lower net income and thus lower taxes.

agrees with the consistency convention, since changes in inventory method may cause income to fluctuate too much and would make income statements hard to interpret from year to year. A company may change its inventory method if there is a good reason for doing so. The nature and effect of the change must be shown on the company's financial statements.

Many accountants believe that using the FIFO and average-cost methods in periods of rising prices causes businesses to report more than their true profit, resulting in the payment of excess income taxes. The profit is overstated because cost of goods sold is understated relative to current prices. The company must buy replacement inventory at higher prices, but additional funds are also needed to pay income taxes. During the rapid inflation of 1979 to 1982, billions of dollars reported as profits and paid in income taxes were believed to be the result of poor matching of current costs and revenues under the FIFO and average-cost methods. Consequently, many companies, believing that prices would continue to rise, switched to the LIFO inventory method.

If a company uses the LIFO method in reporting income for tax purposes, the IRS requires that the same method be used in the accounting records. Also, the IRS will not allow the use of the lower-of-cost-or-market rule if LIFO is used to determine inventory cost. In such a case, only the LIFO cost can be used. This rule, however, does not preclude a company from using lower-of-LIFO-cost-or-market for financial reporting purposes (discussed later in this chapter).

Over a period of rising prices, a business that uses the LIFO method may find that for balance sheet purposes, its inventory is valued at a cost figure far below what it currently pays for the same items. Management must monitor this situation carefully, because if it should let the inventory quantity at year end fall below the beginning-of-the-year level, the company will find itself paying higher income taxes. Higher income before taxes results because the company expenses historical costs of inventory, which are below current costs. When this occurs, it is called a **LIFO liquidation** because sales have reduced inventories below the levels set in prior years; that is, units sold exceed units purchased for the period.

A LIFO liquidation may be prevented by making enough purchases prior to year end to restore the desired inventory level. Sometimes a LIFO liquidation cannot be avoided because products are discontinued or supplies are interrupted, as in the case of a strike. In a recent year, 27 out of 600 large companies reported a LIFO liquidation in which net income was increased because of the matching of older historical cost with present sales dollars.[8]

EFFECTS OF MISSTATEMENTS IN INVENTORY MEASUREMENT

The basic problem of separating goods available for sale into two components—goods sold and goods not sold—is that of assigning a cost to the goods not sold, the ending inventory. The portion of the goods available for sale not assigned to the ending inventory is used to determine the cost of goods sold.

Because the figures for ending inventory and cost of goods sold are related, a misstatement in the inventory figure at the end of the period will cause an equal misstatement in gross margin and income before income taxes on the income statement. The amount of assets and owner's equity on the balance sheet will also be misstated by the same amount. The consequences of overstatement and understatement of inventory are illustrated in the three simplified examples that follow. In each case, beginning inventory, net cost of purchases, and cost of goods available for sale have been stated correctly. In the first example, ending inventory has been stated correctly. In the second example, ending inventory is overstated by $6,000; in the third example, ending inventory is understated by $6,000.

Example 1. Ending Inventory Correctly Stated at $10,000

Cost of Goods Sold for the Year		Income Statement for the Year	
Beginning inventory	$12,000	Net sales	$100,000
Net cost of purchases	58,000	Cost of goods sold	60,000
Cost of goods available for sale	$70,000	Gross margin	$ 40,000
Ending inventory	10,000	Operating expenses	32,000
		Income before income	
Cost of goods sold	$60,000	taxes	$ 8,000

Example 2. Ending Inventory Overstated by $6,000

Cost of Goods Sold for the Year		Income Statement for the Year	
Beginning inventory	$12,000	Net sales	$100,000
Net cost of purchases	58,000	Cost of goods sold	54,000
Cost of goods available for sale	$70,000	Gross margin	$ 46,000
Ending inventory	16,000	Operating expenses	32,000
		Income before income	
Cost of goods sold	$54,000	taxes	$ 14,000

Example 3. Ending Inventory Understated by $6,000

Cost of Goods Sold for the Year		Income Statement for the Year	
Beginning inventory	$12,000	Net sales	$100,000
Net cost of purchases	58,000	Cost of goods sold	66,000
Cost of goods available for sale	$70,000	Gross margin	$ 34,000
Ending inventory	4,000	Operating expenses	32,000
		Income before income	
Cost of goods sold	$66,000	taxes	$ 2,000

KEY POINT: A misstatement in inventory affects not only the current year, but also has the opposite effect on the next year.

KEY POINT: Inventory errors will correct (counterbalance) themselves over a two-year period.

In all three examples, the total cost of goods available for sale was $70,000. The difference in income before income taxes resulted from how this $70,000 was divided between ending inventory and cost of goods sold.

Because the ending inventory in one period becomes the beginning inventory in the following period, it is important to recognize that a misstatement in inventory valuation affects not only the current period but also the following period. Over a two-year period, the errors in income before income taxes will offset, or counterbalance, each other. If we assume that Example 2 represents year 1, for instance, the overstatement of ending inventory in year 1 will cause a $6,000 overstatement of beginning inventory in year 2, resulting in an understatement of income by $6,000 in the second year.

FOCUS ON BUSINESS ETHICS

The Temptation to Overstate Inventories

Net income can be easily manipulated when accounting for inventory. For example, it is easy to overstate or understate inventory by including end-of-the-year purchase and sales transactions in the wrong fiscal year or by simply misstating inventory. In one spectacular case, Rite Aid Corp. <www.riteaid.com>, the large drugstore chain, falsified income by manipulating its computerized inventory system to cover losses from shrinkage, which includes shoplifting, employee theft, and spoilage. In another case, bookkeepers at RentWay, Inc. <www.rentway.com>, a company that rents furniture to apartment dwellers, boosted income artificially over several years by overstating inventory in small increments that were not noticed by top management.[9]

● STOP AND THINK!

Why is misstatement of inventory one of the most common means of financial statement fraud?

For one thing, the value put on inventory has a direct dollar-for-dollar effect on net income. For another, it is relatively easy to falsify the value placed on the ending inventory and to cover up the falsification. ■

Because the total income before income taxes for the two years is the same, it may appear that one need not worry about inventory misstatements. However, the misstatements violate the matching rule. In addition, management, creditors, and investors make many decisions on an annual basis and depend on the accountant's determination of net income. The accountant has an obligation to make the net income figure for each year as useful as possible.

The effects of misstatements in inventory on income before income taxes are as follows:

Year 1	Year 2
Ending inventory overstated	**Beginning inventory overstated**
Cost of goods sold understated	Cost of goods sold overstated
Income before income taxes overstated	Income before income taxes understated
Ending inventory understated	**Beginning inventory understated**
Cost of goods sold overstated	Cost of goods sold understated
Income before income taxes understated	Income before income taxes overstated

A misstatement in inventory results in a misstatement in income before income taxes of the same amount. Thus, the measurement of inventory is important.

INVENTORY MEASUREMENT AND CASH FLOWS

www.internationalpaper.com

A company's inventory methods affect not only its reported profitability but also its reported liquidity and cash flows. In the case of a large company like International Paper Co., these effects can be complex and material. In a note on inventories, International Paper provides more detail about these effects:

> The last-in, first-out inventory method is used to value most of International Paper's U.S. inventories. Approximately 68% of total raw materials and finished products inventories were valued using this method. If the first-in, first-out method had been used, it would have increased total inventory balances by approximately $264 million and $250 million at December 31, 2000 and 1999, respectively.[10]

By using LIFO, the company usually reports a lower income before taxes. This will have a favorable effect on cash flows because of the lower amount of income taxes to be paid. The reader of the financial statements may determine what International Paper's inventory value would have been if it were valued at current prices under FIFO rather than older prices under LIFO. Thus, a more realistic comparison of the company's liquidity ratios can be made. For example, the more realistic FIFO figure would show a better short-term liquidity position as measured by the current ratio than the LIFO figures reported on the balance sheet would seem to indicate. However, the company's inventory turnover and average days' inventory on hand will be adversely affected if the more realistic FIFO figures are used.

 Check out ACE for a Review Quiz at http://accounting.college.hmco.com/students.

VALUING INVENTORY AT THE LOWER OF COST OR MARKET (LCM)

LO6 Apply the lower-of-cost-or-market (LCM) rule to inventory valuation.

RELATED TEXT ASSIGNMENTS
Q: 15, 16
SE: 11
E: 11
SD: 3
FRA: 5

Although cost is usually the most appropriate basis for valuation of inventory, there are times when inventory may properly be shown in the financial statements at less than its cost. If the market value of inventory falls below its cost because of physical deterioration, obsolescence, or decline in price level, a loss has occurred. This loss may be recognized by writing the inventory down to **market**, or current replacement cost, of inventory. For a merchandising company, market is the amount that the company would pay at the present time for the same goods, purchased from the usual suppliers and in the usual quantities. The **lower-of-cost-or-market (LCM) rule**

FOCUS ON BUSINESS PRACTICE

How Bad Can It Get?

Pretty bad! When the lower-of-cost-or-market rule comes into play, it can be an indicator of how bad. For example, when the market for Internet and telecommunications equipment soured in 2001, Cisco Systems, Inc. <www.cisco.com>, found itself faced with probably the largest inventory loss in history. It had to write down to zero almost two-thirds of its $2.5 billion inventory, 80 percent of which consisted of raw materials that would never be made into final product. In another case, through poor management, a downturn in the economy, and underperforming stores, Kmart <www.kmartcorp.com> found itself with a huge amount of excess merchandise, including more than 5,000 truckloads of goods stored in parking lots, which it could not sell except at drastically reduced prices. The company had to mark down its inventory by $1 billion in order to sell it, resulting in a loss for the year.[12]

◆ **STOP AND THINK!**

Given that the LCM rule is an application of the conservatism convention in the current accounting period, is the effect of this application also conservative in the next period?

It probably is not because a reduction in inventory in the current period resulting in lower net income will cause the beginning inventory in the next period to be smaller and will thus increase net income in that period. ■

STUDY NOTE: Cost must first be determined by the specific identification, FIFO, LIFO, or average-cost method before it can be compared with replacement cost.

requires that when the replacement cost of inventory falls below historical cost, based on one of the conventional inventory costing methods, the inventory is written down to the lower value and a loss is recorded. This rule is an example of the application of the convention of conservatism because the loss is recognized before an actual transaction takes place. Under historical cost accounting, the inventory remains at cost until it is sold. It may help in applying the LCM rule to think of it as the "lower-of-cost-or-replacement-cost" rule.* Approximately 90 percent of 600 large companies report applying the LCM rule to their inventories.[11]

There are two basic methods of valuing inventories at the lower of cost or market accepted both by GAAP and the IRS for federal income tax purposes: (1) the item-by-item method and (2) the major category method. For example, a stereo shop could determine lower of cost or market for each kind of speaker, receiver, and turntable (item by item) or for all speakers, all receivers, and all turntables (major categories).

ITEM-BY-ITEM METHOD

When the **item-by-item method** is used, cost and market values are compared for each item in inventory. Each individual item is then valued at its lower price, as shown in Table 1:

TABLE 1. Lower of Cost or Market with Item-by-Item Method

		Per Unit		Lower of
	Quantity	Cost	Market	Cost or Market
Category I				
Item a	200	$1.50	$1.70	$ 300
Item b	100	2.00	1.80	180
Item c	100	2.50	2.60	250
Category II				
Item d	300	5.00	4.50	1,350
Item e	200	4.00	4.10	800
Inventory at the lower of cost or market				$2,880

MAJOR CATEGORY METHOD

Under the **major category method**, the total cost and total market values for each category of items are compared. Each category is then valued at its lower amount, as shown in Table 2:

---

*In some cases, the *realizable value* of the inventory determines the *market value*—the amount for which the goods can be sold—rather than by the amount for which the goods can be replaced. The circumstances in which realizable value determines market value are encountered in practice only occasionally, and the valuation procedures are technical enough to be addressed in a more advanced accounting course.

TABLE 2. Lower of Cost or Market with Major Category Method

| | Quantity | Per Unit | | Total | | Lower of Cost or Market |
		Cost	Market	Cost	Market	
Category I						
Item a	200	$1.50	$1.70	$ 300	$ 340	
Item b	100	2.00	1.80	200	180	
Item c	100	2.50	2.60	250	260	
Totals				$ 750	$ 780	$ 750
Category II						
Item d	300	5.00	4.50	$1,500	$1,350	
Item e	200	4.00	4.10	800	820	
Totals				$2,300	$2,170	2,170
Inventory at the lower of cost or market						$2,920

 Check out ACE for a Review Quiz at http://accounting.college.hmco.com/students.

VALUING INVENTORY BY ESTIMATION

SO7 Estimate the cost of ending inventory using the retail method and gross profit method.

RELATED TEXT ASSIGNMENTS
Q: 17, 18, 19
E: 12, 13
P: 4, 5
FRA: 5

It is sometimes necessary or desirable to estimate the value of ending inventory. The retail method and gross profit method are most commonly used for this purpose.

RETAIL METHOD OF INVENTORY ESTIMATION

The **retail method**, as its name implies, is used in retail merchandising businesses to estimate the cost of ending inventory by using the ratio of cost to retail price. There are two principal reasons for its use. First, since preparing financial statements each month requires a knowledge of the cost of inventory, the retail method can be used to estimate the cost without the time or expense of determining the cost of items in the inventory. Second, because items in a retail store normally have a price tag or a universal product code, it is common practice to take the physical inventory at retail from these price tags or codes and to reduce the total value to cost through use of the retail method. The term *at retail* means the amount of the inventory at the marked selling prices of the inventory items.

KEY POINT: When estimating inventory by the retail method, the inventory need not be counted.

When the retail method is used to estimate ending inventory, the records must show the beginning inventory at cost and at retail. The records must also show the amount of goods purchased during the period both at cost and at retail. The net sales at retail is, of course, the balance of the Sales account less returns and allowances. A simple example of the retail method is shown in Table 3.

Goods available for sale is determined both at cost and at retail by listing beginning inventory and net purchases for the period at cost and at their expected selling price, adding freight to the cost column, and totaling. The ratio of these two amounts (cost to retail price) provides an estimate of the cost of each dollar of retail sales value. The estimated ending inventory at retail is then determined by deducting sales for the period from the retail price of the goods that were available for sale during the period. The inventory at retail is then converted to cost on the basis of the ratio of cost to retail.

The cost of ending inventory may also be estimated by applying the ratio of cost to retail price to the total retail value of the physical count of the ending inventory.

STUDY NOTE: Freight in is not placed under the Retail column when using the retail method of inventory estimation because businesses automatically price their goods high enough to cover freight charges.

TABLE 3.   Retail Method of Inventory Estimation

	Cost	Retail
Beginning inventory	$ 40,000	$ 55,000
Net purchases for the period (excluding freight in)	107,000	145,000
Freight in	3,000	
Merchandise available for sale	$150,000	$200,000
Ratio of cost to retail price: $\frac{\$150,000}{\$200,000} = 75\%$		
Net sales during the period		160,000
Estimated ending inventory at retail		$ 40,000
Ratio of cost to retail	75%	
Estimated cost of ending inventory	$ 30,000	

Applying the retail method in practice is often more difficult than this simple example because of such complications as changes in retail price during the year, different markups on different types of merchandise, and varying volumes of sales for different types of merchandise.

GROSS PROFIT METHOD OF INVENTORY ESTIMATION

BUSINESS-WORLD EXAMPLE: It is highly desirable to maintain financial records off site. If records were destroyed, it would be difficult, if not impossible, to reconstruct the data necessary for an insurance claim.

The **gross profit method** (also known as the *gross margin method*) assumes that the ratio of gross margin for a business remains relatively stable from year to year. The gross profit method is used in place of the retail method when records of the retail prices of beginning inventory and purchases are not kept. It is considered acceptable for estimating the cost of inventory for interim reports, but it is not acceptable for valuing inventory in the annual financial statements. It is also useful in estimating the amount of inventory lost or destroyed by theft, fire, or other hazards. Insurance companies often use this method to verify loss claims.

As Table 4 shows, the gross profit method is simple to use. First, figure the cost of goods available for sale in the usual way (add purchases to beginning inventory). Second, estimate the cost of goods sold by deducting the estimated gross margin of 30 percent from sales. Finally, deduct the estimated cost of goods sold from the goods available for sale to arrive at the estimated cost of ending inventory.

TABLE 4.   Gross Profit Method of Inventory Estimation

1. Beginning inventory at cost		$ 50,000
Purchases at cost (including freight in)		290,000
Cost of goods available for sale		$340,000
2. Less estimated cost of goods sold		
Sales at selling price	$400,000	
Less estimated gross margin (30% × 400,000)	120,000	
Estimated cost of goods sold		280,000
3. Estimated cost of ending inventory		$ 60,000

✓ Check out ACE for a Review Quiz at http://accounting.college.hmco.com/students.

Chapter Review

REVIEW OF LEARNING OBJECTIVES

LO1 Identify and explain the management issues associated with accounting for inventories.

Included in inventory are goods owned, whether produced or purchased, that are held for sale in the normal course of business. Manufacturing companies also include raw materials and work in process. Among the issues management must face in accounting for inventories are allocating the cost of inventories in accordance with the matching rule, assessing the impact of inventory decisions, and evaluating the level of inventory. The objective of accounting for inventories is the proper determination of income through the matching of costs and revenues, not the determination of the most realistic inventory value. Because the valuation of inventory has a direct effect on a company's net income, the choice of inventory systems and methods affects not only the amount of income taxes and cash flows, but also the external and internal evaluation of the company. The level of inventory as measured by the inventory turnover and its related measure, average days' inventory on hand, is important to managing the amount of investment a company needs.

LO2 Define *inventory cost* and relate it to goods flow and cost flow.

The cost of inventory includes (1) invoice price less purchases discounts; (2) freight in, including insurance in transit; and (3) applicable taxes and tariffs. Goods flow refers to the actual physical flow of merchandise, whereas cost flow refers to the assumed flow of costs in the operations of the business.

LO3 Calculate the pricing of inventory, using the cost basis under the periodic inventory system.

The value assigned to ending inventory is the result of two measurements: quantity and price. Quantity is determined by taking a physical inventory. The pricing of inventory is usually based on the assumed cost flow of the goods as they are bought and sold. One of four assumptions is usually made regarding cost flow. These assumptions are represented by four inventory methods. Inventory pricing can be determined by the specific identification method, which associates the actual cost with each item of inventory, but this method is rarely used. The average-cost method assumes that the cost of inventory is the average cost of goods available for sale during the period. The first-in, first-out (FIFO) method assumes that the costs of the first items acquired should be assigned to the first items sold. The last-in, first-out (LIFO) method assumes that the costs of the last items acquired should be assigned to the first items sold. The inventory method chosen may or may not be equivalent to the actual physical flow of goods.

LO4 Apply the perpetual inventory system to the pricing of inventories at cost.

The pricing of inventories under the perpetual and periodic inventory systems differs because under the perpetual system a continuous record of quantities and costs of merchandise is maintained as purchases and sales are made. Cost of goods sold is accumulated as sales are made and costs are transferred from the Inventory account to the Cost of Goods Sold account. The cost of the ending inventory is the balance of the Inventory account. The specific identification method and the FIFO method produce the same results under the perpetual and periodic inventory systems. The results differ for the average-cost method because an average is calculated after each purchase rather than at the end of the accounting period, and for the LIFO method because the cost components of inventory change constantly as goods are bought and sold.

LO5 State the effects of inventory methods and misstatements of inventory on income determination, income taxes, and cash flows.

During periods of rising prices, the LIFO method will show the lowest net income; FIFO, the highest; and average-cost, in between. The opposite effects occur in periods of falling prices. No generalization can be made regarding the specific identification method. The Internal Revenue Service requires that if LIFO is used for tax purposes, it must also be used for financial statements; it also does not allow the lower-of-cost-or-market rule to be applied to the LIFO method. If the value of ending inventory is understated or overstated, a corresponding error—dollar for dollar—will be made in income before income taxes. Furthermore, because the ending inventory of one period is the beginning inventory of the next, the misstatement affects two accounting periods, although the effects are opposite.

LO6 Apply the lower-of-cost-or-market (LCM) rule to inventory valuation.

The lower-of-cost-or-market rule can be applied to the above methods of determining inventory at cost. This rule states that if the replacement cost (market) of the inventory is lower than the inventory cost, the lower figure should be used. Valuation can be determined on an item-by-item or major category basis.

SUPPLEMENTAL OBJECTIVE

SO7 Estimate the cost of ending inventory using the retail method and gross profit method.

Two methods of estimating the value of inventory are the retail method and the gross profit method. Under the retail method, inventory is determined at retail prices and is then reduced to estimated cost by applying a ratio of cost to retail price. Under the gross profit method, cost of goods sold is estimated by reducing sales by estimated gross margin. The estimated cost of goods sold is then deducted from the cost of goods available for sale to estimate the inventory.

REVIEW OF CONCEPTS AND TERMINOLOGY

The following concepts and terms were introduced in this chapter:

LO3 **Average-cost method:** An inventory costing method in which inventory is priced at the average cost of the goods available for sale during the period.

LO1 **Average days' inventory on hand:** The average number of days required to sell the inventory on hand; number of days in a year divided by inventory turnover.

LO2 **Consignment:** Merchandise that its owner (the *consignor*) places on the premises of another company (the *consignee*) with the understanding that payment is expected only when the merchandise is sold and that unsold items may be returned to the consignor.

LO2 **Cost flow:** The association of costs with their assumed flow in the operations of a company.

LO3 **First-in, first-out (FIFO) method:** An inventory costing method based on the assumption that the costs of the first items acquired should be assigned to the first items sold.

LO2 **Goods flow:** The actual physical movement of goods in the operations of a company.

SO7 **Gross profit method:** A method of inventory estimation based on the assumption that the ratio of gross margin for a business remains relatively stable from year to year. Also called *gross margin method*.

LO2 **Inventory cost:** The price paid or consideration given to acquire an asset; includes invoice price less purchases discounts, plus freight in, plus applicable taxes and tariffs.

LO1 **Inventory turnover:** A ratio indicating the number of times a company's average inventory is sold during an accounting period; cost of goods sold divided by average inventory.

LO6 **Item-by-item method:** A lower-of-cost-or-market method of valuing inventory in which cost and market values are compared for each item in inventory and each item is then valued at its lower price.

LO1 **Just-in-time operating environment:** A system of reducing levels of inventory by working closely with suppliers to coordinate and schedule deliveries so that goods arrive just at the time they are needed.

LO3 **Last-in, first-out (LIFO) method:** An inventory costing method based on the assumption that the costs of the last items purchased should be assigned to the first items sold.

LO5 **LIFO liquidation:** The reduction of inventory below previous levels so that income is increased by the amount by which current prices exceed the historical cost of the inventory under LIFO.

LO6 **Lower-of-cost-or-market (LCM) rule:** A method of valuing inventory at an amount less than cost when the replacement cost falls below historical cost.

LO6   **Major category method:** A lower-of-cost-or-market method of valuing inventory in which the total cost and total market values for each category of items are compared and each category is then valued at its lower amount.

LO6   **Market:** Current replacement cost of inventory.

LO1   **Merchandise inventory:** All goods owned and held for sale in the regular course of business.

SO7   **Retail method:** A method of inventory estimation, used in retail merchandising businesses, in which inventory at retail value is reduced by the ratio of cost to retail price.

LO3   **Specific identification method:** An inventory costing method in which the price of inventory is computed by identifying the cost of each item in ending inventory as coming from a specific purchase.

LO1   **Supply-chain management:** A system of managing inventory and purchasing through business-to-business transactions conducted over the Internet.

REVIEW PROBLEM

Periodic and Perpetual Inventory Systems

LO1
LO3   The table below summarizes the beginning inventory, purchases, and sales of Psi Company's single product during January.
LO4

	Beginning Inventory and Purchases			
Date	Units	Cost	Total	Sales Units
Jan. 1 Inventory	1,400	$19	$26,600	
4 Sale				300
8 Purchase	600	20	12,000	
10 Sale				1,300
12 Purchase	900	21	18,900	
15 Sale				150
18 Purchase	500	22	11,000	
24 Purchase	800	23	18,400	
31 Sale				1,350
Totals	4,200		$86,900	3,100

REQUIRED ▶   1. Assuming that the company uses the periodic inventory system, compute the cost that should be assigned to ending inventory and to cost of goods sold using (a) the average-cost method, (b) the FIFO method, and (c) the LIFO method.

2. Assuming that the company uses the perpetual inventory system, compute the cost that should be assigned to ending inventory and to cost of goods sold using (a) the average-cost method, (b) the FIFO method, and (c) the LIFO method.

K/R   3. Compute inventory turnover and average days' inventory on hand under each of the inventory cost flow assumptions in 1. What conclusion can be made from this comparison?

ANSWER TO REVIEW PROBLEM

	Units	Amount
Beginning inventory	1,400	$26,600
Purchases	2,800	60,300
Available for sale	4,200	$86,900
Sales	3,100	
Ending inventory	1,100	

1. Periodic inventory system:

    a. Average-cost method

Cost of goods available for sale	$86,900
Less ending inventory consisting of 1,100 units at $20.69*	22,759
Cost of goods sold	$64,141

    *$86,900 ÷ 4,200 = $20.69 (rounded).

    b. FIFO method

Cost of goods available for sale		$86,900
Less ending inventory consisting of		
Jan. 24 purchase (800 × $23)	$18,400	
Jan. 18 purchase (300 × $22)	6,600	25,000
Cost of goods sold		$61,900

    c. LIFO method

Cost of goods available for sale	$86,900
Less ending inventory consisting of beginning inventory (1,100 × $19)	20,900
Cost of goods sold	$66,000

2. Perpetual inventory system:

    a. Average-cost method

Date		Units	Cost*	Amount*
Jan. 1	Inventory	1,400	$19.00	$26,600
4	Sale	(300)	19.00	(5,700)
4	Balance	1,100	19.00	$20,900
8	Purchase	600	20.00	12,000
8	Balance	1,700	19.35	$32,900
10	Sale	(1,300)	19.35	(25,155)
10	Balance	400	19.36	$ 7,745
12	Purchase	900	21.00	18,900
12	Balance	1,300	20.50	$26,645
15	Sale	(150)	20.50	(3,075)
15	Balance	1,150	20.50	$23,570
18	Purchase	500	22.00	11,000
24	Purchase	800	23.00	18,400
24	Balance	2,450	21.62	$52,970
31	Sale	(1,350)	21.62	(29,187)
31	Inventory	1,100	21.62	$23,783

    Cost of goods sold ($5,700 + $25,155 + $3,075 + $29,187) $63,117

    *Rounded.

    b. FIFO method

Date		Units	Cost	Amount
Jan. 1	Inventory	1,400	$19	$26,600
4	Sale	(300)	19	(5,700)
4	Balance	1,100	19	$20,900
8	Purchase	600	20	12,000

Date		Units	Cost	Amount
Jan. 8	Balance	1,100	19	
		600	20	$32,900
10	Sale	(1,100)	19	
		(200)	20	(24,900)
10	Balance	400	20	$ 8,000
12	Purchase	900	21	18,900
12	Balance	400	20	
		900	21	$26,900
15	Sale	(150)	20	(3,000)
15	Balance	250	20	
		900	21	$23,900
18	Purchase	500	22	11,000
24	Purchase	800	23	18,400
24	Balance	250	20	
		900	21	
		500	22	
		800	23	$53,300
31	Sale	(250)	20	
		(900)	21	
		(200)	22	(28,300)
31	Inventory	300	22	
		800	23	$25,000
Cost of goods sold ($5,700 + $24,900 + $3,000 + $28,300)				$61,900

c. LIFO method

Date		Units	Cost	Amount
Jan. 1	Inventory	1,400	$19	$26,600
4	Sale	(300)	19	(5,700)
4	Balance	1,100	19	$20,900
8	Purchase	600	20	12,000
8	Balance	1,100	19	
		600	20	$32,900
10	Sale	(600)	20	
		(700)	19	(25,300)
10	Balance	400	19	$ 7,600
12	Purchase	900	21	18,900
12	Balance	400	19	
		900	21	$26,500
15	Sale	(150)	21	(3,150)
15	Balance	400	19	
		750	21	$23,350
18	Purchase	500	22	11,000
24	Purchase	800	23	18,400
24	Balance	400	19	
		750	21	
		500	22	
		800	23	$52,750
31	Sale	(800)	23	
		(500)	22	
		(50)	21	(30,450)
31	Inventory	400	19	
		700	21	$22,300
Cost of goods sold ($5,700 + $25,300 + $3,150 + $30,450)				$64,600

3. Ratios computed:

	Average-Cost	FIFO	LIFO
Cost of goods sold	$64,141	$61,900	$66,000
Average inventory	$24,680* ($22,759 + $26,600) ÷ 2	$25,800 ($25,000 + $26,600) ÷ 2	$23,750 ($20,900 + $26,600) ÷ 2
Inventory turnover	2.6 times ($64,141 ÷ $24,680)	2.4 times ($61,900 ÷ $25,800)	2.8 times ($66,000 ÷ $23,750)
Average days' inventory on hand	140.4 days (365 days ÷ 2.6 times)	152.1 days (365 days ÷ 2.4 times)	130.4 days (365 days ÷ 2.8 times)

*Rounded.

In periods of rising prices, the LIFO method will always result in a higher inventory turnover and lower average days' inventory on hand. When comparing inventory ratios for two or more companies, the inventory methods used by the companies should be considered.

Chapter Assignments

BUILDING YOUR KNOWLEDGE FOUNDATION

QUESTIONS

1. What is merchandise inventory, and what is the primary objective of inventory measurement?
2. How does inventory for a manufacturing company differ from that for a merchandising company?
3. Why is the level of inventory important, and what are two common measures of inventory level?
4. What items should be included in the cost of inventory?
5. Fargo Sales Company is very busy at the end of its fiscal year on June 30. It has an order for 130 units of product in its warehouse. Although the shipping department tries, it cannot ship the product by June 30, and title has not yet passed. Should the 130 units be included in the year-end count of inventory? Why or why not?
6. What is the difference between goods flow and cost flow?
7. Do the FIFO and LIFO inventory methods result in different quantities of ending inventory?
8. Under which method of cost flow are (a) the earliest costs assigned to inventory, (b) the latest costs assigned to inventory, and (c) the average costs assigned to inventory?
9. What are the relative advantages and disadvantages of FIFO and LIFO from management's point of view?
10. Why do you think it is more expensive to maintain a perpetual inventory system?
11. In periods of steadily rising prices, which inventory method—average-cost, FIFO, or LIFO—will give the (a) highest ending inventory cost, (b) lowest ending inventory cost, (c) highest net income, and (d) lowest net income?
12. May a company change its inventory cost method from year to year? Explain.
13. What is the relationship between income tax rules and the inventory valuation methods?
14. If the merchandise inventory is mistakenly overstated at the end of 20x0, what is the effect on the (a) 20x0 net income, (b) 20x0 year-end balance sheet value, (c) 20x1 net income, and (d) 20x1 year-end balance sheet value?
15. In the phrase *lower of cost or market*, what is meant by the word *market*?

16. What methods can be used to determine the lower of cost or market?

17. Does using the retail method mean that inventories are measured at retail value on the balance sheet? Explain.

18. For what reasons might management use the gross profit method of estimating inventory?

19. Which of the following inventory systems or methods do not require the taking of a physical inventory: (a) perpetual, (b) periodic, (c) retail, and (d) gross profit?

SHORT EXERCISES

SE 1.

LO1 Management Issues

Indicate whether each of the following items is associated with (a) allocating the cost of inventories in accordance with the matching rule, (b) assessing the impact of inventory decisions, or (c) evaluating the level of inventory:

1. Calculating the average days' inventory on hand
2. Ordering a supply of inventory to satisfy customer needs
3. Calculating the income tax effect of an inventory method
4. Deciding the cost to place on ending inventory

SE 2.

LO1 Inventory Turnover and Average Days' Inventory on Hand

During 20x1, Louisville Clothiers had beginning inventory of $240,000, ending inventory of $280,000, and cost of goods sold of $1,100,000. Compute the inventory turnover and average days' inventory on hand.

SE 3.

LO3 Specific Identification Method

Assume the following data with regard to inventory for Ambrose Company:

Aug. 1	Inventory	80 units @ $10 per unit	$ 800
8	Purchase	100 units @ $11 per unit	1,100
22	Purchase	70 units @ $12 per unit	840
Goods available for sale		250 units	$2,740
Aug. 15	Sale	90 units	
28	Sale	50 units	
Inventory, Aug. 31		110 units	

Assuming that the inventory consists of 60 units from the August 8 purchase and 50 units from the purchase of August 22, calculate the cost of ending inventory and cost of goods sold.

SE 4.

LO3 Average-Cost Method– Periodic Inventory System

Using the data in **SE 3**, calculate the cost of ending inventory and cost of goods sold according to the average-cost method under the periodic inventory system.

SE 5.

LO3 FIFO Method–Periodic Inventory System

Using the data in **SE 3**, calculate the cost of ending inventory and cost of goods sold according to the FIFO method under the periodic inventory system.

SE 6.

LO3 LIFO Method–Periodic Inventory System

Using the data in **SE 3**, calculate the cost of ending inventory and cost of goods sold according to the LIFO method under the periodic inventory system.

SE 7.

LO4 Average-Cost Method– Perpetual Inventory System

Using the data in **SE 3**, calculate the cost of ending inventory and cost of goods sold according to the average-cost method under the perpetual inventory system.

SE 8.

LO4 FIFO Method–Perpetual Inventory System

Using the data in **SE 3**, calculate the cost of ending inventory and cost of goods sold according to the FIFO method under the perpetual inventory system.

SE 9.

LO4 LIFO Method–Perpetual Inventory System

Using the data in **SE 3**, calculate the cost of ending inventory and cost of goods sold according to the LIFO method under the perpetual inventory system.

SE 10.

LO5 Effects of Methods and Changing Prices

Using Exhibit 1 as an example, prepare a table with seven columns that shows the ending inventory and cost of goods sold for each of the results from your calculations in SE 3 through SE 9. Comment on the results, including the effects of the different prices at which the merchandise was purchased. Which method(s) would result in the lowest income taxes?

SE 11.
LO6   Lower of Cost or Market

The following schedule is based on a physical inventory and replacement costs for one product line of men's shirts:

Item	Quantity	Cost per Unit	Market per Unit
Short sleeve	280	$24	$20
Long sleeve	190	28	29
Extra-long sleeve	80	34	35

Determine the value of this category of inventory at the lower of cost or market using (1) the item-by-item method and (2) the major category method.

EXERCISES

E 1.
LO1   Management Issues

Indicate whether each of the following items is associated with (a) allocating the cost of inventories in accordance with the matching rule, (b) assessing the impact of inventory decisions, or (c) evaluating the level of inventory:

1. Computing inventory turnover
2. Application of the just-in-time operating environment
3. Determining the effects of inventory decisions on cash flows
4. Apportioning the cost of goods available for sale to ending inventory and cost of goods sold
5. Determining the effects of inventory methods on income taxes
6. Determining the assumption about the flow of costs into and out of the company

E 2.
LO1   Inventory Ratios

SaveMore Discount Stores is assessing its levels of inventory for 20x2 and 20x3 and has gathered the following data:

	20x3	20x2	20x1
Ending inventory	$128,000	$108,000	$92,000
Cost of goods sold	640,000	600,000	

Compute the inventory turnover and average days' inventory on hand for 20x3 and 20x2 and comment on the results.

E 3.
LO3   Periodic Inventory System and Inventory Costing Methods

Paul's Farm Store recorded the following purchases and sales of fertilizer during the past year:

Jan. 1	Beginning inventory	250 cases @ $23	$ 5,750
Feb. 25	Purchased	100 cases @ $26	2,600
June 15	Purchased	400 cases @ $28	11,200
Aug. 15	Purchased	100 cases @ $26	2,600
Oct. 15	Purchased	300 cases @ $28	8,400
Dec. 15	Purchased	200 cases @ $30	6,000
	Goods available for sale	1,350	$36,550
	Total sales	1,000 cases	
Dec. 31	Ending inventory	350 cases	

Assume that Paul's Farm Store sold all of the June 15 purchase and 200 cases each from the January 1 beginning inventory, the October 15 purchase, and the December 15 purchase.

Determine the costs that should be assigned to ending inventory and cost of goods sold under each of the following assumptions: (1) costs are assigned by the specific identification method; (2) costs are assigned by the average-cost method; (3) costs are assigned by the FIFO method; (4) costs are assigned by the LIFO method. What conclusions can be drawn about the effect of each method on the income statement and the balance sheet of Paul's Farm Store? Round your answers to the nearest whole number and assume the periodic inventory system.

E 4.
LO3   Periodic Inventory System and Inventory Costing Methods

During its first year of operation, Bingham Company purchased 5,600 units of a product at $21 per unit. During the second year, it purchased 6,000 units of the same product at $24 per unit. During the third year, it purchased 5,000 units at $30 per unit.

Bingham Company managed to have an ending inventory each year of 1,000 units. The company uses the periodic inventory system.

Prepare cost of goods sold statements that compare the value of ending inventory and the cost of goods sold for each of the three years using (1) the FIFO inventory costing method and (2) the LIFO method. From the resulting data, what conclusions can you draw about the relationships between changes in unit price and changes in the value of ending inventory?

E 5.

LO3 Periodic Inventory System and Inventory Costing Methods

In chronological order, the inventory, purchases, and sales of a single product for a recent month are as follows:

		Units	Amount per Unit
June 1	Beginning inventory	300	$30
4	Purchase	800	33
8	Sale	400	60
12	Purchase	1,000	36
16	Sale	700	60
20	Sale	500	66
24	Purchase	1,200	39
28	Sale	600	66
29	Sale	400	66

Using the periodic inventory system, compute the cost of ending inventory, cost of goods sold, and gross margin. Use the average-cost, FIFO, and LIFO inventory costing methods. Explain the differences in gross margin produced by the three methods. Round unit costs to cents and totals to dollars.

E 6.

LO4 Perpetual Inventory System and Inventory Costing Methods

Using the data provided in **E 5** and assuming the perpetual inventory system, compute the cost of ending inventory, cost of goods sold, and gross margin. Use the average-cost, FIFO, and LIFO inventory costing methods. Explain the reasons for the differences in gross margin produced by the three methods. Round unit costs to cents and totals to dollars.

E 7.

LO3 Periodic and Perpetual
LO4 Systems and Inventory Costing Methods

During July 20x1, Downes, Inc., sold 250 units of its product Velt for $4,000. The following units were available:

	Units	Cost
Beginning inventory	100	$ 2
Purchase 1	40	4
Purchase 2	60	6
Purchase 3	70	8
Purchase 4	80	10
Purchase 5	90	12

A sale of 100 units was made after purchase 1, and a sale of 150 units was made after purchase 4. Of the units sold, 100 came from beginning inventory and 150 from purchases 3 and 4.

Determine goods available for sale and ending inventory in units. Then determine the costs that should be assigned to cost of goods sold and ending inventory under each of the following assumptions: (1) Costs are assigned under the periodic inventory system using (a) the specific identification method, (b) the average-cost method, (c) the FIFO method, and (d) the LIFO method. (2) Costs are assigned under the perpetual inventory system using (a) the average-cost method, (b) the FIFO method, and (c) the LIFO method. For each alternative, show the gross margin. Round unit costs to cents and totals to dollars.

E 8.

LO5 Effects of Inventory Methods on Cash Flows

Lao Products, Inc., sold 120,000 cases of glue at $40 per case during 20x1. Its beginning inventory consisted of 20,000 cases at a cost of $24 per case. During 20x1, it purchased 60,000 cases at $28 per case and later 50,000 cases at $30 per case. Operating expenses were $1,100,000, and the applicable income tax rate was 30 percent.

Using the periodic inventory system, compute net income using the FIFO method and the LIFO method for costing inventory. Which alternative produces the larger cash flow? The company is considering a purchase of 10,000 cases at $30 per case just before the year end. What effect on net income and on cash flow will this proposed purchase have under each method? (**Hint:** What are the income tax consequences?)

E 9.
LO3 Characteristics of Inventory
LO5 Costing Methods

Match each of the descriptions listed below to these inventory costing methods:

a. Specific identification   c. First-in, first-out (FIFO)
b. Average-cost   d. Last-in, first-out (LIFO)

1. Matches recent costs with recent revenues
2. Assumes that each item of inventory is identifiable
3. Results in the most realistic balance sheet valuation
4. Results in the lowest net income in periods of deflation
5. Results in the lowest net income in periods of inflation
6. Matches the oldest costs with recent revenues
7. Results in the highest net income in periods of inflation
8. Results in the highest net income in periods of deflation
9. Tends to level out the effects of inflation
10. Is unpredictable as to the effects of inflation

E 10.
LO5 Effects of Inventory Errors

Condensed income statements for Earle Company for two years are shown below.

	20x5	20x4
Sales	$126,000	$105,000
Cost of goods sold	75,000	54,000
Gross margin	$ 51,000	$ 51,000
Operating expenses	30,000	30,000
Income before income taxes	$ 21,000	$ 21,000

After the end of 20x5, the company discovered that an error had resulted in a $9,000 understatement of the 20x4 ending inventory.

Compute the corrected income before income taxes for 20x4 and 20x5. What effect will the error have on income before income taxes and owner's equity for 20x6?

E 11.
LO6 Lower-of-Cost-or-Market Rule

Rasmin Company values its inventory, shown below, at the lower of cost or market. Compute Rasmin's inventory value using (1) the item-by-item method and (2) the major category method.

	Quantity	Per Unit Cost	Per Unit Market
Category I			
Item aa	200	$ 2.00	$ 1.80
Item bb	240	4.00	4.40
Item cc	400	8.00	7.50
Category II			
Item dd	300	12.00	13.00
Item ee	400	18.00	18.20

E 12.
S07 Retail Method

Isabel's Dress Shop had net retail sales of $500,000 during the current year. The following additional information was obtained from the accounting records:

	At Cost	At Retail
Beginning inventory	$ 80,000	$120,000
Net purchases (excluding freight in)	280,000	440,000
Freight in	20,800	

1. Using the retail method, estimate the company's ending inventory at cost.
2. Assume that a physical inventory taken at year end revealed an inventory on hand of $36,000 at retail value. What is the estimated amount of inventory shrinkage (loss due to theft, damage, etc.) at cost using the retail method?

E 13.
S07 Gross Profit Method

Lance Borkowski was at home watching television when he received a call from the fire department telling him his store had burned. His business was a total loss. The insurance company asked him to prove his inventory loss. For the year, until the date of the fire, Borkowski's company had sales of $450,000 and purchases of $280,000. Freight in amounted to $13,700, and the beginning inventory was $45,000. It was Borkowski's custom to price goods to achieve a gross margin of 40 percent. Compute Borkowski's estimated inventory loss.

PROBLEMS

P 1.

LO1   Periodic Inventory System and
LO3   Inventory Costing Methods

K/R

The Champlain Cabinet Company sold 2,200 cabinets during 20x2 at $160 per cabinet. Its beginning inventory on January 1 was 130 cabinets at $56. Purchases made during the year were as follows:

February	225 cabinets @ $62
April	350 cabinets @ $65
June	700 cabinets @ $70
August	300 cabinets @ $66
October	400 cabinets @ $68
November	250 cabinets @ $72

The company's selling and administrative expenses for the year were $101,000, and the company uses the periodic inventory system.

REQUIRED ▶   1. Prepare a schedule to compute the cost of goods available for sale.
2. Compute income before income taxes under each of the following inventory cost flow assumptions: (a) the average-cost method; (b) the FIFO method; and (c) the LIFO method.
3. Compute inventory turnover and average days' inventory on hand under each of the inventory cost flow assumptions in **2.** What conclusion can be made from this comparison?

P 2.

LO1   Periodic Inventory System and
LO3   Inventory Costing Methods

The inventory, purchases, and sales of Product ABO for March and April follow. The company closes its books at the end of each month and uses the periodic inventory system.

Mar.	1	Beginning inventory	60 units @ $49
	7	Sale	20 units
	10	Purchase	100 units @ $52
	19	Sale	70 units
	31	Ending inventory	70 units
Apr.	4	Purchase	120 units @ $53
	11	Sale	110 units
	15	Purchase	50 units @ $54
	23	Sale	80 units
	25	Purchase	100 units @ $55
	27	Sale	100 units
	30	Ending inventory	50 units

REQUIRED ▶   1. Compute the cost of the ending inventory on March 31 and April 30 using the average-cost method. In addition, determine cost of goods sold for March and April. Round unit costs to cents and totals to dollars.
2. Compute the cost of the ending inventory on March 31 and April 30 using the FIFO method. In addition, determine cost of goods sold for March and April.
3. Compute the cost of the ending inventory on March 31 and April 30 using the LIFO method. In addition, determine cost of goods sold for March and April.
4. Do the cash flows from operations for March and April differ depending on the inventory costing method—average-cost, FIFO, or LIFO—used? Explain.

P 3.

LO4   Perpetual Inventory System
and Inventory Costing
Methods

Use the data provided in **P 2,** but assume that the company uses the perpetual inventory system. (**Hint:** In preparing the solutions required below, it is helpful to determine the balance of inventory after each transaction, as shown in the Review Problem in this chapter.)

REQUIRED ▶   1. Determine the cost of ending inventory and cost of goods sold for March and April using the average-cost method. Round unit costs to cents and totals to dollars.
2. Determine the cost of ending inventory and cost of goods sold for March and April using the FIFO method.
3. Determine the cost of ending inventory and cost of goods sold for March and April using the LIFO method.

P 4.

SO7   Retail Method

Lopez Company operates a large discount store and uses the retail method to estimate the cost of ending inventory. Management suspects that in recent weeks there have been unusually heavy losses from shoplifting or employee pilferage. To estimate the amount of the loss, the company has taken a physical inventory and will compare the results with the estimated cost of inventory. Data from the accounting records of Lopez Company are as follows:

	At Cost	At Retail
October 1 beginning inventory	$51,488	$ 74,300
Purchases	71,733	108,500
Purchases returns and allowances	(2,043)	(3,200)
Freight in	950	
Sales		109,183
Sales returns and allowances		(933)
October 31 physical inventory at retail		62,450

REQUIRED ▶

1. Using the retail method, prepare a schedule to estimate the dollar amount of the store's month-end inventory at cost.
2. Use the store's cost to retail ratio to reduce the retail value of the physical inventory to cost.
3. Calculate the estimated amount of inventory shortage at cost and at retail.

P 5.
SO7 **Gross Profit Method**

Sabatino Sisters is a large retail furniture company that operates in two adjacent warehouses. One warehouse is a showroom, and the other is used to store merchandise. On the night of April 22, 20x2, a fire broke out in the storage warehouse and destroyed the merchandise stored there. Fortunately, the fire did not reach the showroom, so all the merchandise on display was saved.

Although the company maintained a perpetual inventory system, its records were rather haphazard, and the last reliable physical inventory had been taken on December 31. In addition, there was no control of the flow of the goods between the showroom and the warehouse. Thus, it was impossible to tell what goods should have been in either place. As a result, the insurance company required an independent estimate of the amount of loss. The insurance company examiners were satisfied when they were provided with the following information.

Merchandise inventory on December 31, 20x1	$ 727,400
Purchases, January 1 to April 22, 20x2	1,206,100
Purchases returns, January 1 to April 22, 20x2	(5,353)
Freight in, January 1 to April 22, 20x2	26,550
Sales, January 1 to April 22, 20x2	1,979,525
Sales returns, January 1 to April 22, 20x2	(14,900)
Merchandise inventory in showroom on April 22, 20x2	201,480
Average gross margin	44%

REQUIRED ▶ Prepare a schedule that estimates the amount of the inventory lost in the fire.

ALTERNATE PROBLEMS

P 6.
LO1 **Periodic Inventory System and**
LO3 **Inventory Costing Methods**
Ⓚ/ⓡ

McDougal Company merchandises a single product called Gailen. The following data represent beginning inventory and purchases of Gailen during the past year: January 1 inventory, 68,000 units at $11.00; February purchases, 80,000 units at $12.00; March purchases, 160,000 units at $12.40; May purchases, 120,000 units at $12.60; July purchases, 200,000 units at $12.80; September purchases, 160,000 units at $12.60; and November purchases, 60,000 units at $13.00. Sales of Gailen totaled 786,000 units at $20.00 per unit. Selling and administrative expenses totaled $5,102,000 for the year, and McDougal Company uses the periodic inventory system.

REQUIRED ▶

1. Prepare a schedule to compute the cost of goods available for sale.
2. Compute income before income taxes under each of the following inventory cost flow assumptions: (a) the average-cost method; (b) the FIFO method; and (c) the LIFO method.
3. Compute inventory turnover and average days' inventory on hand under each of the inventory cost flow assumptions listed in **2.** What conclusion can be drawn from this comparison?

P 7.
LO1 **Periodic Inventory System and**
LO3 **Inventory Costing Methods**

The inventory of Product H and data on purchases and sales for a two-month period follow. The company closes its books at the end of each month. It uses a periodic inventory system.

Apr.	1	Beginning inventory	50 units @ $102
	5	Sale	30 units
	10	Purchase	100 units @ $110

Apr.	17	Sale	60 units
	30	Ending inventory	60 units
May	2	Purchase	100 units @ $108
	8	Sale	110 units
	14	Purchase	50 units @ $112
	18	Sale	40 units
	22	Purchase	60 units @ $117
	26	Sale	30 units
	30	Sale	20 units
	31	Ending inventory	70 units

REQUIRED ▶

1. Compute the cost of ending inventory of Product H on April 30 and May 31 using the average-cost method. In addition, determine cost of goods sold for April and May. Round unit costs to cents and totals to dollars.

2. Compute the cost of the ending inventory on April 30 and May 31 using the FIFO method. In addition, determine cost of goods sold for April and May.

3. Compute the cost of the ending inventory on April 30 and May 31 using the LIFO method. In addition, determine cost of goods sold for April and May.

4. Do the cash flows from operations for April and May differ depending on the inventory costing method—average-cost, FIFO, or LIFO—used? Explain.

P 8.

LO4 Perpetual Inventory System and Inventory Costing Methods

Use the data provided in **P 7**, but assume that the company uses the perpetual inventory system. (**Hint:** In preparing the solutions required below, it is helpful to determine the balance of inventory after each transaction, as shown in the Review Problem in this chapter.)

REQUIRED ▶

1. Determine the cost of ending inventory and cost of goods sold for April and May using the average-cost method. Round unit costs to cents and totals to dollars.

2. Determine the cost of ending inventory and cost of goods sold for April and May using the FIFO method.

3. Determine the cost of ending inventory and cost of goods sold for April and May using the LIFO method.

SKILLS DEVELOPMENT CASES

Conceptual Analysis

SD 1.

LO1 Evaluation of Inventory Levels

J.C. Penney <www.jcpenney.com> has an inventory turnover of 4.6 times. Dell Computer Corporation <www.dell.com> has an inventory turnover of 75.7. Dell achieves its high turnover through supply-chain management in a just-in-time operating environment. Why is inventory turnover important to companies like J.C. Penney and Dell? Why are comparisons among companies important? Are J.C. Penney and Dell a good match for comparison? What are supply-chain management and a just-in-time operating environment? Why are they important to achieving a favorable inventory turnover?

SD 2.

LO5 LIFO Inventory Method

Eighty-six percent of chemical companies use the LIFO inventory method for the costing of inventories, whereas only 9 percent of computer equipment companies use LIFO.[13] Describe the LIFO inventory method. What effects does it have on reported income, cash flows, and income taxes during periods of price changes? Why do you think so many chemical companies use LIFO while most companies in the computer industry do not?

SD 3.

LO6 LCM and Conservatism

Exxon Mobil Corporation <www.exxonmobil.com> uses the LIFO inventory method for most of its inventories. The cost of inventories is heavily dependent on the cost of oil. In a recent year when the price of oil was down, Exxon Mobil, following the lower-of-cost-or-market (LCM) rule, wrote down its inventory by $325 million. In the next year, when the price of oil recovered, the company reported that market price exceeded the LIFO carrying values by $6.7 billion.[14] Explain why the LCM rule resulted in a writedown in the first year. What is the inconsistency between the first and second year treatment of the change in the price of oil? How does the accounting convention of conservatism explain the inconsistency? If the price of oil declines substantially in the third year, what will be the likely consequence?

Ethical Dilemma

LO1 Inventories, Income
LO5 Determination, and Ethics

SD 4. Flare, Inc., which has a December 31 year end, designs and sells fashions for young professional women. Sandra Mason, president of the company, feared that the forecasted 20x5 profitability goals would not be reached. She was pleased when Flare received a large order on December 30 from The Executive Woman, a retail chain of upscale stores for businesswomen. Mason immediately directed the controller to record the sale, which represented 13 percent of Flare's annual sales, but directed the inventory control department not to separate the goods for shipment until after January 1. Separated goods are not included in inventory because they have been sold. On December 31, the company's auditors arrived to observe the year-end taking of the physical inventory under the periodic inventory system. What will be the effect of Sandra Mason's action on Flare's 20x5 profitability? What will be the effect on Flare's 20x6 profitability? Was Mason's action ethical?

Research Activity

LO2 Retail Business Inventories
LO4

SD 5. Make an appointment to visit a local retail business—a grocery, clothing, book, music, or appliance store—and interview the manager for 30 minutes about the company's inventory accounting system. The store may be a branch of a larger company. Ask the following questions, summarize your findings in a paper, and be prepared to discuss your results in class:

1. What is the physical flow of merchandise into the store, and what documents are used in connection with this flow?
2. What documents are prepared when merchandise is sold?
3. Does the store keep perpetual inventory records? If so, does it keep the records in units only, or does it keep track of cost as well? If not, what system does the store use?
4. How often does the company take a physical inventory?
5. How are financial statements generated for the store?
6. What method does the company use to cost its inventory for financial statements?

 Group Activity: Assign teams to various types of businesses in your community.

Decision-Making Practice

LO5 Inventory Costing Methods,
Income Taxes, and Cash Flows

SD 6. The Osaka Trading Company began business in 20x4 for the purpose of importing and marketing an electronic component widely used in digital appliances. It is now December 20, 20x4, and Osaka Trading Company's management is considering its options. Among its considerations is whether to choose the FIFO or LIFO inventory method. Under the periodic inventory system, the effects on net income of using the two methods are as follows:

	FIFO Method	LIFO Method
Sales (500,000 units × $12)	$6,000,000	$6,000,000
Cost of goods sold		
Purchases		
200,000 × $4	$ 800,000	$ 800,000
400,000 × $6	2,400,000	2,400,000
Total purchases	$3,200,000	$3,200,000
Less ending inventory		
FIFO (100,000 × $6)	(600,000)	
LIFO (100,000 × $4)		(400,000)
Cost of goods sold	$2,600,000	$2,800,000
Gross margin	$3,400,000	$3,200,000
Operating expenses	2,400,000	2,400,000
Income before income taxes	$1,000,000	$ 800,000
Income taxes	300,000	240,000
Net income	$ 700,000	$ 560,000

Also, management has an option to purchase an additional 100,000 units of inventory before year end at a price of $8 per unit, the price that is expected to prevail during 20x5. The income tax rate applicable to the company in 20x4 is 30 percent.

Business conditions are expected to be favorable in 20x5, as they were in 20x4. Management has asked you for advice. Analyze the effects of making the additional purchase. Then prepare a memorandum to Osaka's management in which you compare cash outcomes under the four alternatives (Option 1: FIFO and LIFO and Option 2: FIFO and LIFO) and advise management which inventory method to choose and whether to order the additional inventory. Be prepared to discuss your recommendations in class.

SD 7.

LO3 **FIFO versus LIFO Analysis**
LO5

Refrigerated Truck Sales Company (RTS Company) buys large refrigerated trucks from the manufacturer and sells them to companies and independent truckers who haul perishable goods over long distances. RTS has been successful in this specialized niche of the industry. Because of the high cost of the trucks and of financing inventory, RTS tries to maintain as small an inventory as possible. In fact, at the beginning of July the company had no inventory or liabilities, as shown on the balance sheet below.

On July 9, RTS took delivery of a truck at a price of $300,000. On July 19, an identical truck was delivered to the company at a price of $320,000. On July 28, the company sold one of the trucks for $390,000. During July, expenses totaled $30,000. All transactions were paid in cash.

RTS Company
Balance Sheet
July 1, 20x4

Assets		Stockholders' Equity	
Cash	$800,000	Common stock	$800,000
Total assets	$800,000	Total stockholders' equity	$800,000

1. Prepare income statements and balance sheets for RTS on July 31 using (a) the FIFO method of inventory valuation and (b) the LIFO method of inventory valuation. Assume an income tax rate of 40 percent. Explain the effects of each method on the financial statements.
2. Assume that the management of RTS Company follows the policy of declaring a cash dividend each period that is exactly equal to net income. What effects does this action have on each balance sheet prepared in **1,** and how do the resulting balance sheets compare with the balance sheet at the beginning of the month? Which inventory method, if either, do you feel is more realistic in representing RTS's income?
3. Assume that RTS receives notice of another price increase of $20,000 on refrigerated trucks, to take effect on August 1. How does this information relate to management's dividend policy, and how will it affect next month's operations?

FINANCIAL REPORTING AND ANALYSIS CASES

Interpreting Financial Reports

FRA 1.

LO1 **FIFO and LIFO**
LO2
LO5

Hershey Foods Corp. <www.hersheys.com> is famous for its chocolate and confectionary products. In 2000, the company had net sales of $4,220 million, cost of goods sold of $2,471 million, and net income of $334 million. The company uses LIFO to determine cost of inventories. The following disclosure was made to show the relationship of LIFO cost to FIFO cost (dollars are in millions):[15]

	2000	1999
Raw materials	$264	$271
Goods in process	48	49
Finished goods	338	365
Inventories at FIFO	650	685
Adjustment to LIFO	(45)	(83)
Total inventories	$605	$602

1. Prepare a schedule comparing net income for 2000 using the LIFO and FIFO methods. Use a corporate income tax rate of 40 percent. Did prices of cocoa and sugar, the main ingredients of Hershey's products, go up or down in 2000? Explain.
2. Why do you suppose Hershey's management chooses to use the LIFO inventory method? On what economic conditions, if any, do those reasons depend? Given your calculations in **1,** do you believe the economic conditions relevant to Hershey were advantageous for using LIFO in 2000? Explain your answer.
3. Compute inventory turnover and average days' inventory on hand under the LIFO and FIFO methods. What conclusion can be drawn from this comparison?

FRA 2.

LO5　**Misstatement of Inventory**

Crazy Eddie, Inc. <www.crazyeddie.com>, a discount consumer electronics chain, seemed to be missing $52 million in merchandise inventory. "It was a shock," the new management was quoted as saying. It was also one of the nation's largest swindles. Investors lost $145.6 million when the company declared bankruptcy. A count turned up only $75 million in inventory, compared with $126.7 million reported by former management. Net sales could account for only $6.7 million of the difference. At the time, it was not clear whether bookkeeping errors in prior years or an actual physical loss created the shortfall, although at least one store manager felt it was a bookkeeping error because security was strong. "It would be hard for someone to steal anything," he said. Former management was eventually fined $72.7 million.[16]

1. What is the effect of the misstatement of inventory on Crazy Eddie's reported earnings in prior accounting periods?
2. Is this a situation you would expect in a company that is experiencing financial difficulty? Explain.

FRA 3.

LO5　**LIFO Liquidation**

Crane Company <www.crane.com> reported approximately $259 million and $236 million of inventories valued under the LIFO method in 2000 and 1999, respectively. As explained in the company's annual report:

> The reduction of inventory quantities has resulted in a liquidation of LIFO inventories acquired at lower costs prevailing in prior years. Liquidations have reduced cost of sales by $1.3 million in 2000, $2.7 million in 1999, and $.6 million in 1998. Replacement cost would have been higher by $21.4 million and $23.1 million at December 31, 2000 and 1999, respectively.[17]

Assume Crane's average income tax rates for 1999 and 2000 were 40 percent.

1. Explain why a reduction in the quantity of inventory resulted in an increase in net income. Would the same result have occurred if Crane had used the FIFO method to value inventory? Explain your answer.
2. What is the income tax effect of the LIFO liquidation? Is this a favorable outcome?

International Company

FRA 4.

LO1　**Comparison of Inventory**
LO5　**Levels and Methods**

Yamaha Motor Co., Ltd. <www.yamaha-motor.co.jp> and Pioneer Corporation <www.pioneer.co.jp> are two large, diversified Japanese electronics companies. Both use the average-cost method and the lower-of-cost-or-market rule to account for inventories. The following data are for their 2001 fiscal years (in millions of yen):[18]

	Yamaha	Pioneer
Beginning inventory	¥139,625	¥ 91,517
Ending inventory	166,074	84,429
Cost of goods sold	668,992	447,389

Compare the inventory efficiency of Yamaha and Pioneer by computing the inventory turnover and average days' inventory on hand for both companies in 2001. Comment on the results. Most companies in the United States use the LIFO inventory method.

How would inventory method affect your evaluation if you were to compare Pioneer and Yamaha to a U.S. company? What could you do to make the results comparable?

Toys "R" Us Annual Report

FRA 5.

LO1 **Retail Method and Inventory**
LO5 **Ratios**
LO6
SO7

Refer to the note related to inventories in the Toys "R" Us <www.tru.com> annual report in the Supplement to Chapter 6 to answer the following questions: What inventory method(s) does Toys "R" Us use? If LIFO inventories had been valued at FIFO, why would there be no difference? Do you think many of the company's inventories are valued at market? Few companies use the retail method; why do you think Toys "R" Us uses it? Compute and compare the inventory turnover and average days' inventory on hand for Toys "R" Us for 2001 and 2002. Beginning 2001 inventory was $1,902 million.

Comparison Case: Toys "R" Us and Walgreen Co.

FRA 6.

LO1 **Inventory Efficiency**

Refer to the financial statements for Toys "R" Us <www.tru.com> and Walgreens <www.walgreens.com> in the Supplement to Chapter 6. Beginning inventory for 2001 for Toys "R" Us was $2,307 million and for Walgreens, $2,830.8 million. Calculate inventory turnover and average days' inventory on hand for the past two years. If you did **FRA 5**, refer to your answer there for Toys "R" Us. Has either company improved its performance over the past two years? If so, what advantage does it have? Which company seems to make the most efficient use of inventory? Explain.

Fingraph® Financial Analyst™

FRA 7.

LO1 **Comparative Analysis of**
Inventories and Operating
Cycle

Select any two companies from the same industry from the list of Fingraph companies on the Needles Accounting Resource Center Web Site at http://accounting.college. hmco.com/students. Choose an industry, such as manufacturing, consumer products, consumer food and beverage, or computers, in which inventory is likely to be an important current asset. Access the Microsoft Excel spreadsheets for the companies you selected. Click on the URL at the top of each company's spreadsheet for a link to the company's web site and annual report.

1. In the annual reports of the companies you have selected, read any reference to inventories in the summary of significant accounting policies or notes to the financial statements. What inventory method does the company use? What are the changes in and the relative importance of raw materials, work in process, and finished goods inventories?
2. Using the Fingraph Financial Analyst CD-ROM software, display and print in tabular and graphic form the Liquidity and Asset Utilization Analysis page. Prepare a table that compares the inventory turnover and average days' inventory on hand for both companies for two years. Also include in your table the operating cycle by combining average days' inventory on hand with average days' sales uncollected.
3. Find and read references to inventories in the liquidity analysis section of management's discussion and analysis in each annual report.
4. Write a one-page executive summary that highlights the accounting policies for inventories, the relative importance and changes in raw materials, work in process, and finished goods, and compares the inventory utilization of the two companies, including reference to management's assessment. Comment specifically on the financing implications of the companies' relative operating cycles. Include the Fingraph page and your table with your report.

Internet Case

FRA 8.

LO5 **Effect of LIFO on Income and**
Cash Flows

Maytag Corporation <www.maytag.com>, an appliance manufacturer, uses the LIFO inventory method. Go to its web site and select "About Maytag." Then select "Financial Center." After finding the income statement and inventory note, calculate what net income would have been had the company used FIFO. Calculate how much cash the company saved for the year and cumulatively by using LIFO. What is the difference between the LIFO and FIFO gross margin and profit margin results? Which reporting alternative is better for the company?

Chapter 11 explores the management issues associated with the acquisition, operation, and disposal of property, plant, and equipment, natural resources, and intangible assets, as well as the concepts and techniques of depreciation, depletion, and amortization.

Long-Term Assets

LEARNING OBJECTIVES

LO1 Identify the types of long-term assets and explain the management issues related to accounting for them.

LO2 Distinguish between capital and revenue expenditures, and account for the cost of property, plant, and equipment.

LO3 Define *depreciation* and compute depreciation under the straight-line, production, and declining-balance methods.

LO4 Account for the disposal of depreciable assets.

LO5 Identify the issues related to accounting for natural resources and compute depletion.

LO6 Identify the issues related to accounting for intangible assets, including research and development costs and goodwill.

SUPPLEMENTAL OBJECTIVE

SO7 Apply depreciation methods to problems of partial years, revised rates, groups of similar items, special types of capital expenditures, and cost recovery.

DECISION POINT

A USER'S FOCUS

H. J. Heinz Company <www.heinz.com> The effects of management's decisions regarding long-term assets are most apparent in the areas of reported total assets, net income, and cash flows related to investing activities. How does one learn about the significance of those items to a company? An idea of the extent of a company's long-term assets and their importance can be gained from the financial statements. For example, the list of assets in the Financial Highlights is from the annual report of H. J. Heinz Company, one of the world's largest food companies. Of the company's $10 billion in total assets, property, plant, and equipment represent about 23 percent, and other non-current assets represent about 47 percent.

With 69 percent of Heinz's total assets classified as long-term, management's decisions regarding choice of expected useful life and residual value of the assets can have a material impact on the amount expensed on the income statement. The income statement shows that depreciation and amortization expenses associated with those assets are more than $207 million, or about 25 percent of net income. While depreciation and amortization expenses have no cash effect, the statement of cash flows indicates the amount paid for newly purchased property, plant, and equipment and to what extent a company is reinvesting in its operations. Heinz spent more than $213 million on new long-term assets. In addition to annual expense recognition, long-term assets are reviewed annually to determine if the assets have lost some of their service potential, resulting in asset impairment. Finally, disposals of long-term assets may result in

What do Heinz's financial statements reveal about the company's long-term assets?

gains or losses on the income statement. Each of these financial-statement issues falls within the scope of accounting for the acquisition, use, and disposal of long-term assets and the related management judgments.[1]

Financial Highlights (In thousands)	**2002**	2001
Total Current Assets	$ 3,373,566	$3,116,814
Property, Plant, and Equipment:		
Land	$ 63,075	$ 54,774
Buildings and leasehold improvements	880,490	878,028
Equipment, furniture, and other	2,929,082	2,947,978
	3,872,647	3,880,780
Less accumulated depreciation	1,622,573	1,712,400
Total property, plant, and equipment, net	$ 2,250,074	$2,168,380
Other Noncurrent Assets:		
Goodwill (net of amortization: 2002— $393,972 and 2001—$334,907)	$ 2,528,942	$2,077,451
Trademarks (net of amortization: 2002— $144,884 and 2001—$118,254)	808,884	567,692
Other intangibles (net of amortization: 2002—$160,230 and 2001—$157,678)	152,249	120,749
Other noncurrent assets	1,164,639	984,064
Total other noncurrent assets	$ 4,654,714	$3,749,956
Total Assets	$10,278,354	$9,035,150

MANAGEMENT ISSUES RELATED TO ACCOUNTING FOR LONG-TERM ASSETS

LO1   Identify the types of long-term assets and explain the management issues related to accounting for them.

RELATED TEXT ASSIGNMENTS

Q: 1, 2, 3, 4, 5, 6, 7
SE: 1
E: 1, 2
SD: 1, 6, 7
FRA: 3, 4, 5

STUDY NOTE: For an asset to be classified as property, plant, and equipment, it must be "put in use." This means that it is available for its intended purpose. An emergency generator is "put in use" when it is available for emergencies, even if it is never used.

KEY POINT: A computer used in the office would be considered plant and equipment, whereas an identical computer held for sale to customers would be considered inventory.

● **STOP AND THINK!**
Is carrying value ever the same as market value?

On the date of acquisition, the carrying value equals the current market value. After that, it would be a coincidence if it equaled the market value. ■

Long-term assets are assets that (1) have a useful life of more than one year, (2) are acquired for use in the operation of a business, and (3) are not intended for resale to customers. For many years, it was common to refer to long-term assets as *fixed assets*, but use of this term is declining because the word *fixed* implies that they last forever. The relative importance of long-term assets to various industries is shown in Figure 1. Long-term assets range from 17.7 percent of total assets in the advertising industry to 51.2 percent in interstate trucking.

Although there is no strict rule for defining the useful life of a long-term asset, the most common criterion is that the asset be capable of repeated use for at least a year. Included in this category is equipment used only in peak or emergency periods, such as generators.

Assets not used in the normal course of business should not be included in this category. Thus, land held for speculative reasons or buildings no longer used in ordinary business operations should not be included in the property, plant, and equipment category. Instead, they should be classified as long-term investments.

Finally, if an item is held for resale to customers, it should be classified as inventory—not plant and equipment—no matter how durable it is. For example, a printing press held for sale by a printing press manufacturer would be considered inventory, whereas the same printing press would be considered plant and equipment if a printing company buys it for use in operations.

Long-term assets differ from current assets in that they support the operating cycle instead of being a part of it. They are also expected to benefit the business for a longer period than do current assets. Current assets are expected to be used up or converted to cash within one year or during the operating cycle, whichever is longer. Long-term assets are expected to last beyond that period. Long-term assets and their related expenses are summarized in Figure 2 on page 482.

Generally, long-lived assets are reported at carrying value, as presented in Figure 3 on page 482. **Carrying value** is the unexpired part of the cost of an asset, not its market value; it is also called *book value*. If a long-lived asset loses some or all of its revenue-generating potential before the end of its useful life, the asset may be deemed impaired, and its carrying value reduced. **Asset impairment** occurs when the sum of the expected cash flows from the asset is less than the carrying value of the asset.[2] Reducing carrying value to fair value, as measured by the present value

FIGURE 1
Long-Term Assets as a Percentage of Total Assets for Selected Industries

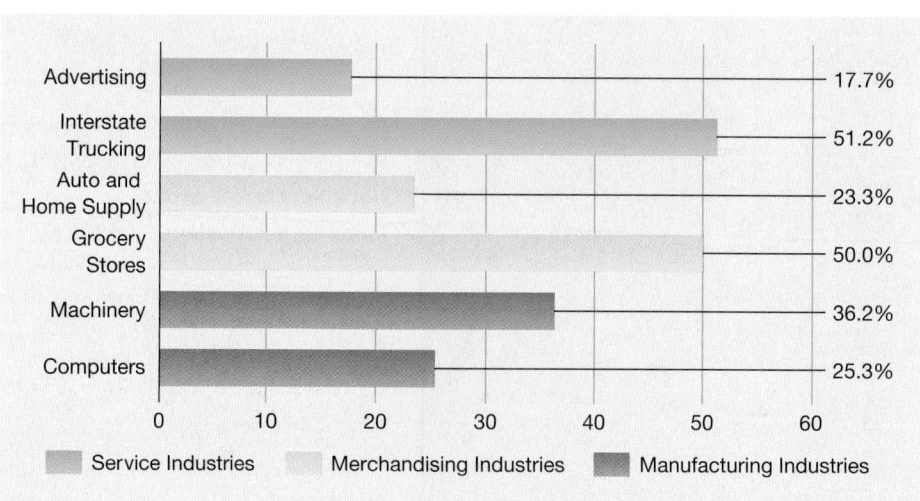

Source: Data from Dun & Bradstreet, *Industry Norms and Key Business Ratios,* 2001–02.

Fermi National Accelerator Laboratory <www.fnal.gov>

OBJECTIVES

- To describe the characteristics of long-term assets
- To identify the four issues that must be addressed in applying the matching rule to long-term assets
- To define depreciation and state the principal causes of depreciation
- To identify the issues related to intangible assets, including research and development

BACKGROUND FOR THE CASE

 Fermi National Accelerator Laboratory (Fermilab), located 30 miles west of Chicago, is run by the U.S. Department of Energy. Its primary mission is to advance the understanding of the fundamental nature of matter and energy.

Fermilab operates the world's highest-energy particle accelerator, the Trevatron, or "atom-smasher." Circling through rings of magnets four miles in circumference, particle beams generate experimental conditions equivalent to those that existed in the first quadrillionth of a second after the birth of the universe. This capability to re-create such high energy levels places Fermilab at the frontier of global physics research. The facility provides leadership and resources for qualified experimenters to conduct basic research at the leading edge of high-energy physics and related disciplines. In the year 2000, with Collider Run II, scientists at Fermilab began probing the smallest dimen-

sions that humans have ever examined. These scientists have the opportunity to make discoveries that could answer some important questions in particle physics.

Although a unit of the U.S. government, Fermilab is a financially independent nonprofit corporation with a governing body consisting of the presidents of 87 affiliated research universities. With annual revenues of about $300 million, consisting mostly of government contracts, and annual expenses of about $260 million, Fermilab faces the same management challenges as a for-profit corporation. It must make huge investments in long-term assets. Other than salaries, depreciation is the lab's largest expense. In addition, Fermilab creates intellectual capital through basic research that it shares with U.S. industry to encourage economic development.

For more information about Fermi National Accelerator Laboratory, visit its web site through the Needles Accounting Resource Center Web Site at **http://accounting.college.hmco.com/students** or directly through Fermilab's web site.

REQUIRED

View the video on Fermi National Accelerator Laboratory that accompanies this book. As you are watching the video, take notes related to the following questions:

1. What characteristics distinguish long-term assets? What are some examples of long-term assets at Fermilab?

2. What four issues must be addressed in applying the matching rule to long-term assets?

3. What is depreciation, and what are its two major causes?

4. What are research and development costs, and how does Fermilab account for them? How might this method understate the assets of Fermilab?

of future cash flows, is an application of conservatism. All long-term assets are subject to an asset impairment evaluation. A reduction in carrying value as a result of impairment is recorded as a loss.

www.amazon.com
www.cisco.com
www.lucent.com

Because of a slowdown in the growth of Internet, telecommunications, and technology companies, companies like Amazon.com, Cisco Systems, and Lucent Technologies took write-downs totaling billions of dollars. The carrying value of certain long-term tangible and intangible assets no longer exceeded the cash flows that they would help generate, due to declining revenues or slowing revenue growth. The write-downs caused the companies to report operating losses.[3]

DECIDING TO ACQUIRE LONG-TERM ASSETS

The decision to acquire a long-term asset involves a complex process. Methods of evaluating data to make rational decisions in this area are grouped under a topic called capital budgeting, which is usually covered as a managerial accounting topic. However, an awareness of the general nature of the problem can be helpful in

FIGURE 2
Classification of Long-Term Assets and Corresponding Expenses

BALANCE SHEET
Long-Term Assets

INCOME STATEMENT
Expenses

Tangible Assets: long-term assets that have physical substance

Land

Plant, Buildings, Equipment (plant assets)

Land is not expensed because it has an unlimited life.

Depreciation: periodic allocation of the cost of a tangible long-lived asset (other than land and natural resources) over its estimated useful life

Natural Resources: long-term assets purchased for the economic value that can be taken from the land and used up, as with ore, lumber, oil, and gas or other resources contained in the land

Mines

Timberland

Oil and Gas Fields

Depletion: exhaustion of a natural resource through mining, cutting, pumping, or other extraction, and the way in which the cost is allocated

Intangible Assets: long-term assets that have no physical substance but have a value based on rights or advantages accruing to the owner

Patents, Copyrights, Trademarks, Franchises, Leaseholds, Leasehold Improvements, Goodwill

Amortization: periodic allocation of the cost of an intangible asset to the periods it benefits

Goodwill is not expensed, but its value is reviewed annually.

KEY POINT: For an asset to be classified as intangible, it must lack physical substance, be long term, and (normally) represent a legal right or advantage.

understanding the accounting issues related to long-term assets. To illustrate the acquisition decision, let us assume that Irena Markova, M.D., is considering the purchase of a $5,000 computer system for her office. She estimates that if she purchases the computer, she can reduce the hours of a part-time employee sufficiently to save net cash flows of $2,000 per year for four years and that the computer will be worth $1,000 at the end of that period. These data are summarized as follows:

FIGURE 3
Carrying Value of Long-Term Assets on the Balance Sheet

Plant Assets	Natural Resources	Intangible Assets
Less Accumulated Depreciation	Less Accumulated Depletion	Less Accumulated Amortization
Carrying Value	Carrying Value	Carrying Value

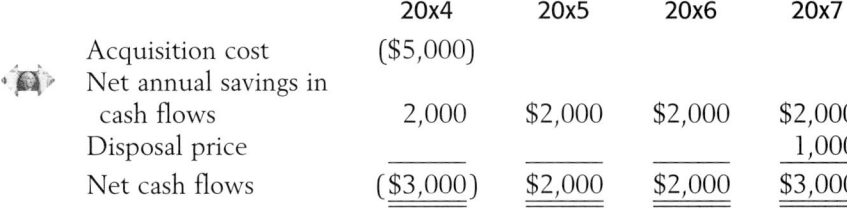

	20x4	20x5	20x6	20x7
Acquisition cost	($5,000)			
Net annual savings in cash flows	2,000	$2,000	$2,000	$2,000
Disposal price				1,000
Net cash flows	($3,000)	$2,000	$2,000	$3,000

To place the cash flows on a comparable basis, it is helpful to use present value tables, such as Tables 3 and 4 in the appendix on future value and present value tables. Assuming that the appropriate interest rate is 10 percent compounded annually, the purchase may be evaluated as follows:

		Present Value
Acquisition cost	Present value factor = 1.000 1.000 × $5,000	($5,000)
Net annual savings in cash flows	Present value factor = 3.170 (Table 4: 4 periods, 10%) 3.170 × $2,000	6,340
Disposal price	Present value factor = .683 (Table 3: 4 periods, 10%) .683 × $1,000	683
Net present value		$2,023

As long as the net present value is positive, Dr. Markova will earn at least 10 percent on the investment. In this case, the return is greater than 10 percent because the net present value is a positive $2,023. Based on this analysis, Dr. Markova makes the decision to purchase. However, there are other important considerations that have to be taken into account, such as the costs of training and maintenance, and the possibility that because of unforeseen circumstances, the savings may not be as great as expected. In Dr. Markova's case, the decision to purchase is likely to be a good one because the net present value is both positive and large relative to the investment.

Information about a company's acquisitions of long-term assets may be found under investing activities in the statement of cash flows. For example, in referring to this section of its 2002 annual report, the management of H. J. Heinz Company makes the following statement:

www.heinz.com

> Capital expenditures totaled $213.4 million compared to $411.3 million last year. . . . In fiscal 2003, the company expects capital expenditures to be consistent with fiscal 2002.[4]

FINANCING LONG-TERM ASSETS

In addition to deciding whether to acquire a long-term asset, management must decide how to finance the asset if it is acquired. Some companies are profitable enough to pay for long-term assets out of cash flows from operations, but when financing is needed, some form of long-term arrangement related to the life of the asset is usually most appropriate. For example, an automobile loan generally spans 4 or 5 years, whereas a mortgage on a house may span as many as 30 years.

For a major long-term acquisition, a company may issue capital stock, long-term notes, or bonds. A good place to study a company's long-term financing is in the financing activities section of the statement of cash flows. For instance, in discussing this section, Ford Motor Company's management states, "At December 31, 2002, the Automotive sector had total debt of $14.2 billion, up $400 million from a year ago. The weighted average maturity of our long-term debt . . . is approximately 27 years."[5]

www.ford.com

FIGURE 4
Issues of Accounting for Long-Term Assets

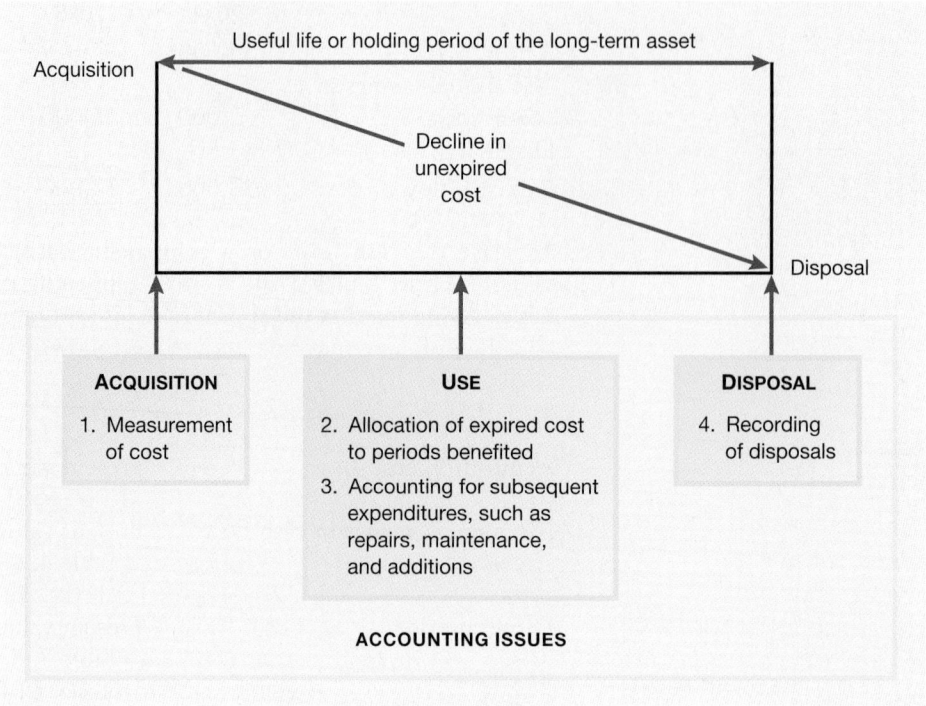

APPLYING THE MATCHING RULE TO LONG-TERM ASSETS

Accounting for long-term assets requires the proper application of the matching rule through the resolution of two important issues. The first is how much of the total cost to allocate to expense in the current accounting period. The second is how much to retain on the balance sheet as an asset to benefit future periods. To resolve these issues, four important questions about the acquisition, use, and disposal of each long-term asset must be answered (see Figure 4):

1. How is the cost of the long-term asset determined?

2. How should the expired portion of the cost of the long-term asset be allocated against revenues over time?

3. How should subsequent expenditures, such as repairs and additions, be treated?

4. How should disposal of the long-term asset be recorded?

STUDY NOTE: Useful life is measured by the service units a business expects to receive from an asset. It should not be confused with physical life, which is often much longer. If the management of a new business is having difficulty determining an asset's estimated useful life, it may obtain help from trade magazines. Nearly every industry has at least one.

Because of the long life of long-term assets and the complexity of the transactions relating to them, management has many choices and estimates to make. For example, acquisition cost may be complicated by group purchases, trade-ins, or construction costs. In addition, to allocate the cost of the asset to future periods effectively, management must estimate how long the asset will last and what it will be worth at the end of its use. In making such estimates, it is helpful to think of a long-term asset as a bundle of services to be used in the operation of the business over a period of years. A delivery truck may provide 100,000 miles of service over its life. A piece of equipment may have the potential to produce 500,000 parts. A building may provide shelter for 50 years. As each of those assets is purchased, the company is paying in advance for 100,000 miles, the capacity to produce 500,000 parts, or 50 years of service. In essence, each asset is a type of long-term prepaid expense. The accounting problem is to spread the cost of the services over the useful life of the asset. As the services benefit the company over the years, the cost becomes an expense rather than an asset.

 Check out ACE for a Review Quiz at http://accounting.college.hmco.com/students.

ACQUISITION COST OF PROPERTY, PLANT, AND EQUIPMENT

LO2 Distinguish between capital and revenue expenditures, and account for the cost of property, plant, and equipment.

RELATED TEXT ASSIGNMENTS
Q: 8, 9, 10
SE: 2, 3
E: 3, 4, 5, 14
P: 1, 6
SD: 4, 5, 6
FRA: 3

STUDY NOTE: Although dyeing a carpet may make it look almost new, it is not considered a capital expenditure because even though the carpet looks better, its fibers are not stronger, and it probably will not last significantly longer than it would have before the color was changed.

STUDY NOTE: The cost of mailing lists may be recorded as an asset because the mailing lists will be used over and over and will benefit future accounting periods.

KEY POINT: Expenditures necessary to prepare an asset for its intended use are a cost of the asset.

Expenditure refers to a payment or an obligation to make future payment for an asset, such as a truck, or a service, such as a repair. Expenditures may be classified as capital expenditures or revenue expenditures. A **capital expenditure** is an expenditure for the purchase or expansion of a long-term asset. Capital expenditures are recorded in the asset accounts because they benefit several future accounting periods. A **revenue expenditure** is an expenditure related to the repair, maintenance, and operation of a long-term asset. These expenditures do not extend the asset's original useful life but are necessary to enable the asset to fulfill its original useful life. Revenue expenditures are recorded in the expense accounts because their benefits are realized in the current period.

THE IMPORTANCE OF CLASSIFYING EXPENDITURES CORRECTLY

Careful distinction between capital and revenue expenditures is important to the proper application of the matching rule. For example, if the purchase of an automobile is mistakenly recorded as a revenue expenditure, the total cost of the automobile is recorded as an expense on the income statement. As a result, current net income is reported at a lower amount (understated) and assets are understated. In future periods net income will be overstated because depreciation expense is understated. Assets are also understated because the asset was completely expensed in the period that it was purchased. If, on the other hand, a revenue expenditure, such as the painting of a building, were charged to an asset account, the expense of the current period would be understated. Current net income and assets would be overstated by the same amount, and the net income of future periods would be understated because of the erroneous future depreciation expense that was recorded.

Determining when a payment is an expense and when it is an asset is a matter of judgment, in the exercise of which management takes a leading role. For example, inconsistencies have existed in accounting for the costs of computer programs that run the systems for businesses. Some companies immediately write off the expenditure as an expense, whereas others treat it as a long-term intangible asset and amortize it year after year. Companies spend billions of dollars a year on this type of software, and it is an important variable in the profitability of many companies. Although the AICPA has issued new rules to try to bring more standardization to these accounting issues, considerable latitude does still exist, such as in determining how long the economic life of the software will be.[6]

GENERAL APPROACH TO ACQUISITION COSTS

The acquisition cost of property, plant, and equipment includes all expenditures reasonable and necessary to get the asset in place and ready for use. For example, the cost of installing and testing a machine is a legitimate cost of the machine. However, if the machine is damaged during installation, the cost of repairs is an operating expense and not an acquisition cost.

Cost is easiest to determine when a purchase is made for cash. In that case, the cost of the asset is equal to the cash paid for the asset plus expenditures for freight, insurance while in transit, installation, and other necessary related costs. If a debt is incurred in the purchase of the asset, the interest charges are not a cost of the asset, but a cost of borrowing the money to buy the asset. They are therefore an operating expense. An exception to this principle is that interest costs incurred during the construction of an asset are properly included as a cost of the asset.[7]

Expenditures like freight, insurance while in transit, and installation are included in the cost of the asset because they are necessary if the asset is to function. Following the matching rule, they are allocated to the useful life of the asset rather than charged as expenses in the current period.

For practical purposes, many companies establish policies defining when an expenditure should be recorded as an expense or an asset. For example, small expenditures for items that would normally be treated as assets may be treated as expenses because the amounts involved are not material in relation to net income. Thus, a wastebasket, which might last for years, would be recorded as a supplies expense rather than as a depreciable asset.

Some of the problems of determining the cost of long-lived plant assets are discussed in the next sections.

KEY POINT: Many costs may be incurred to prepare land for its intended use and condition. All such costs are a cost of land.

■ **LAND**   There are often expenditures in addition to the purchase price of land that should be debited to the Land account. Some examples are commissions to real estate agents; lawyers' fees; accrued taxes paid by the purchaser; costs of preparing the land to build on, such as the costs of tearing down old buildings and draining, clearing, and grading the land; and assessments for local improvements, such as putting in streets and sewage systems. The cost of landscaping is usually debited to the Land account because such improvements are relatively permanent. Land is not subject to depreciation because it does not have a limited useful life.

ENRICHMENT NOTE: The costs of tearing down existing buildings can be major. For example, companies may spend millions of dollars imploding buildings so they can remove them and build new ones.

Let us assume that a company buys land for a new retail operation. It pays a net purchase price of $170,000, pays brokerage fees of $6,000 and legal fees of $2,000, pays $10,000 to have an old building on the site torn down, receives $4,000 salvage from the old building, and pays $1,000 to have the site graded. The cost of the land is $185,000:

Net purchase price		$170,000
Brokerage fees		6,000
Legal fees		2,000
Tearing down old building	$10,000	
Less salvage	4,000	6,000
Grading		1,000
Total cost		$185,000

■ **LAND IMPROVEMENTS**   Some improvements to real estate, such as driveways, parking lots, and fences, have a limited life and are thus subject to depreciation. They should be recorded in an account called Land Improvements rather than in the Land account.

■ **BUILDINGS**   When an existing building is purchased, its cost includes the purchase price plus all repairs and other expenditures required to put it in usable condition. Buildings are subject to depreciation because they have a limited useful life. When a business constructs its own building, the cost includes all reasonable and necessary expenditures, such as those for materials, labor, part of the overhead and other indirect costs, architects' fees, insurance during construction, interest on construction loans during the period of construction, lawyers' fees, and building permits. If outside contractors are used in the construction, the net contract price plus other expenditures necessary to put the building in usable condition are included in the cost.

ENRICHMENT NOTE: The electrical wiring and plumbing of a dental chair are included in the cost of the asset because they are a necessary cost of preparing the asset for use.

■ **EQUIPMENT**   The cost of equipment includes all expenditures connected with purchasing the equipment and preparing it for use. Those expenditures include the invoice price less cash discounts; freight, including insurance; excise taxes and tariffs; buying expenses; installation costs; and test runs to ready the equipment for operation. Equipment is subject to depreciation.

FOCUS ON BUSINESS ETHICS

Is It an Asset or Expense? The Answer Matters.

Determining whether an expenditure is a long-term asset or an expense is not always as clear-cut as some might imagine. Management has considerable leeway in how to record transactions, but the financial statements must be prepared in accordance with generally accepted accounting principles and the result cannot be deceptive. If management's choices are questioned, the results can sometimes have drastic consequences.

For example, *The Wall Street Journal* reported that the chief financial officer of WorldCom <www.worldcom.com> used an unorthodox and unusually aggressive technique to account for one of the long-distance company's biggest expenses. The company recorded charges paid to local telephone networks to complete calls as long-term assets instead of operating expenses. This increased income in the year in question by deferring the costs to a future year, effectively turning a net loss for the year into a net income. In total, the company says that at least $3.8 billion was accounted for in this way. As a result of the report, the company's stock price dropped from a high of $64.50 to less than one dollar. The SEC filed civil fraud charges against WorldCom, saying the company "falsely portrayed itself as a profitable business."[8] Criminal charges may follow and the company will likely face bankruptcy.

This and other notable cases show that accounting is not a passive part of business that can be manipulated at will, but must be taken seriously. The financial statements must reveal the substance of the business's activities.

● STOP AND THINK!

What incentive does a company have to allocate more of a group purchase price to the land rather than to the building?

A higher land valuation has the effect of increasing income because a smaller building valuation results in a lower amount to depreciate over its useful life. ■

■ **GROUP PURCHASES** Land and other assets are sometimes purchased for a lump sum. Because land is a nondepreciable asset that has an unlimited life, it must have a separate ledger account, and the lump-sum purchase price must be apportioned between the land and the other assets. For example, assume that a building and the land on which it is situated are purchased for a lump-sum payment of $85,000. The apportionment can be made by determining the price of each if purchased separately and applying the appropriate percentages to the lump-sum price. Assume that appraisals yield estimates of $10,000 for the land and $90,000 for the building if purchased separately. In that case, 10 percent of the lump-sum price, or $8,500, would be allocated to the land, and 90 percent, or $76,500, would be allocated to the building, as follows:

	Appraisal	Percentage	Apportionment
Land	$ 10,000	10% ($10,000 ÷ $100,000)	$ 8,500 ($85,000 × 10%)
Building	90,000	90% ($90,000 ÷ $100,000)	76,500 ($85,000 × 90%)
Totals	$100,000	100%	$85,000

✔ Check out ACE for a Review Quiz at http://accounting.college.hmco.com/students.

ACCOUNTING FOR DEPRECIATION

LO3 Define *depreciation* and compute depreciation under the straight-line, production, and declining-balance methods.

RELATED TEXT ASSIGNMENTS
Q: 11, 12, 13, 14, 15, 16
SE: 4, 5, 6
E: 5, 6, 7, 10
P: 2, 3, 7, 8
SD: 1, 2, 6
FRA: 1, 3, 5, 6

The AICPA describes depreciation accounting as follows:

> The cost of a productive facility is one of the costs of the services it renders during its useful economic life. Generally accepted accounting principles require that this cost be spread over the expected useful life of the facility in such a way as to allocate it as equitably as possible to the periods during which services are obtained from the use of the facility. This procedure is known as depreciation accounting, a system of accounting which aims to distribute the cost or other basic value of tangible capital assets, less salvage (if any), over the estimated useful life of the unit . . . in a systematic and rational manner. It is a process of allocation, not of valuation.[9]

This description contains several important points. First, all tangible assets except land have a limited useful life. Because of this, their costs must be distributed as expenses over the years they benefit. Physical deterioration and obsolescence are the major causes of the limited useful life of a depreciable asset. The physical deterioration of tangible assets results from use and from exposure to the elements, such as wind and sun. Periodic repairs and a sound maintenance policy may keep buildings and equipment in good operating order and extract the maximum useful life from them, but every machine or building at some point must be discarded. Repairs do not eliminate the need for depreciation. Obsolescence is the process of becoming out of date. Because of fast-changing technology and fast-changing demands, machinery and even buildings often become obsolete before they wear out. Accountants do not distinguish between physical deterioration and obsolescence because they are interested in the length of an asset's useful life, not in what limits that useful life.

Second, the term *depreciation*, as used in accounting, does not refer to an asset's physical deterioration or decrease in market value over time. Depreciation means the allocation of the cost of a plant asset to the periods that benefit from the services of that asset. The term is used to describe the gradual conversion of the cost of the asset into an expense.

Third, depreciation is not a process of valuation. Accounting records are kept in accordance with the cost principle; they are not indicators of changing price levels. It is possible that because of an advantageous purchase and specific market conditions, the market value of a building may rise. Nevertheless, depreciation must continue to be recorded because it is the result of an allocation, not a valuation, process. Eventually, the building will wear out or become obsolete regardless of interim fluctuations in market value.

Factors That Affect the Computation of Depreciation

Four factors affect the computation of depreciation: (1) cost, (2) residual value, (3) depreciable cost, and (4) estimated useful life.

■ **Cost**   As explained earlier in the chapter, cost is the net purchase price plus all reasonable and necessary expenditures to get the asset in place and ready for use.

■ **Residual Value**   The residual value of an asset is its estimated net scrap, salvage, or trade-in value as of the estimated date of disposal. Other terms often used to describe residual value are *salvage value* and *disposal value*.

■ **Depreciable Cost**   The depreciable cost of an asset is its cost less its residual value. For example, a truck that costs $12,000 and has a residual value of $3,000 would have a depreciable cost of $9,000. Depreciable cost must be allocated over the useful life of the asset.

■ **Estimated Useful Life**   Estimated useful life is the total number of service units expected from a long-term asset. Service units may be measured in terms of years

Focus on Business Practice

The Useful Life of an Aircraft Is How Long?

Most airlines depreciate airplanes over an estimated useful life of 10 to 20 years. But how long will a properly maintained airplane really last? Western Airlines <www.westernairlines.com> paid $3.3 million for a new Boeing 737 in July 1968. More than 78,000 flights and 30 years later, this aircraft was still flying for Vanguard Airlines <www.flyvanguard.com>, a no-frills airline. Among the other airlines that have owned this aircraft during the course of its life are Piedmont, Delta <www.delta.com>, and US Airways <www.usairways.com>.

Virtually every part of the plane has been replaced over the years. Boeing believes the plane could theoretically make double the number of flights before it is retired.

The useful lives of many types of assets can be extended indefinitely if the assets are correctly maintained, but proper accounting in accordance with the matching rule requires depreciation over a "reasonable" useful life. Each airline that owned the plane would have accounted for the plane in this way.

the asset is expected to be used, units expected to be produced, miles expected to be driven, or similar measures. In computing the estimated useful life of an asset, an accountant should consider all relevant information, including (1) past experience with similar assets, (2) the asset's present condition, (3) the company's repair and maintenance policy, (4) current technological and industry trends, and (5) local conditions, such as weather.

Depreciation is recorded at the end of the accounting period by an adjusting entry that takes the following form:

$A = L + OE$
$-$ $-$

Depreciation Expense, Asset Name	xxx	
Accumulated Depreciation, Asset Name		xxx
To record depreciation for the period		

METHODS OF COMPUTING DEPRECIATION

Many methods are used to allocate the cost of plant assets to accounting periods through depreciation. Each is proper for certain circumstances. The most common methods are (1) the straight-line method, (2) the production method, and (3) an accelerated method known as the declining-balance method.

■ **STRAIGHT-LINE METHOD**   When the straight-line method is used to calculate depreciation, the depreciable cost of the asset is spread evenly over the estimated useful life of the asset. The straight-line method is based on the assumption that depreciation depends only on the passage of time. The depreciation expense for each period is computed by dividing the depreciable cost (cost of the depreciating asset less its estimated residual value) by the number of accounting periods in the asset's estimated useful life. The rate of depreciation is the same in each year. Suppose, for example, that a delivery truck costs $10,000 and has an estimated residual value of $1,000 at the end of its estimated useful life of five years. The annual depreciation would be $1,800 under the straight-line method, calculated as follows:

$$\frac{\text{Cost} - \text{Residual Value}}{\text{Estimated Useful Life}} = \frac{\$10,000 - \$1,000}{5 \text{ years}} = \$1,800 \text{ per year}$$

The depreciation for the five years would be as follows:

Depreciation Schedule, Straight-Line Method

	Cost	Yearly Depreciation	Accumulated Depreciation	Carrying Value
Date of purchase	$10,000	—	—	$10,000
End of first year	10,000	$1,800	$1,800	8,200
End of second year	10,000	1,800	3,600	6,400
End of third year	10,000	1,800	5,400	4,600
End of fourth year	10,000	1,800	7,200	2,800
End of fifth year	10,000	1,800	9,000	1,000

There are three important points to note from the depreciation schedule for the straight-line depreciation method. First, the depreciation is the same each year. Second, the accumulated depreciation increases uniformly. Third, the carrying value decreases uniformly until it reaches the estimated residual value.

■ **PRODUCTION METHOD**   The production method of depreciation is based on the assumption that depreciation is solely the result of use and that the passage of time plays no role in the depreciation process. If we assume that the delivery truck in the previous example has an estimated useful life of 90,000 miles, the depreciation cost per mile would be determined as follows:

$$\frac{\text{Cost} - \text{Residual Value}}{\text{Estimated Units of Useful Life}} = \frac{\$10,000 - \$1,000}{90,000 \text{ miles}} = \$.10 \text{ per mile}$$

If we assume that the use of the truck was 20,000 miles for the first year,
30,000 miles for the second, 10,000 miles for the third, 20,000 miles for the fourth,
and 10,000 miles for the fifth, the depreciation schedule for the delivery truck
would be as follows:

Depreciation Schedule, Production Method

	Cost	Miles	Yearly Depreciation	Accumulated Depreciation	Carrying Value
Date of purchase	$10,000	—	—	—	$10,000
End of first year	10,000	20,000	$2,000	$2,000	8,000
End of second year	10,000	30,000	3,000	5,000	5,000
End of third year	10,000	10,000	1,000	6,000	4,000
End of fourth year	10,000	20,000	2,000	8,000	2,000
End of fifth year	10,000	10,000	1,000	9,000	1,000

There is a direct relation between the amount of depreciation each year and the
units of output or use. Also, the accumulated depreciation increases each year in
direct relation to units of output or use. Finally, the carrying value decreases each
year in direct relation to units of output or use until it reaches the estimated residual value.

Under the production method, the unit of output or use employed to measure
the estimated useful life of each asset should be appropriate for that asset. For
example, the number of items produced may be an appropriate measure for one
machine, but the number of hours of use may be a better measure for another. The
production method should be used only when the output of an asset over its useful
life can be estimated with reasonable accuracy.

■ **DECLINING-BALANCE METHOD**   An **accelerated method** of depreciation results in
relatively large amounts of depreciation in the early years of an asset's life and
smaller amounts in later years. Such a method, which is based on the passage of
time, assumes that many kinds of plant assets are most efficient when new, and so
provide more and better service in the early years of their useful life. It is consistent
with the matching rule to allocate more depreciation to earlier years than to later
years if the benefits or services received in the earlier years are greater than those
received later.

An accelerated method also recognizes that fast-changing technologies cause
some equipment to become obsolescent and lose service value rapidly. Thus, it is
realistic to allocate more to depreciation in earlier years than in later ones. Another
argument in favor of an accelerated method is that repair expense is likely to be
greater in later years than in earlier years. Thus, the total of repair and depreciation
expense remains fairly constant over a period of years. This result naturally assumes
that the services received from the asset are roughly equal from year to year.

The **declining-balance method** is the most common accelerated method of
depreciation. Under this method, depreciation is computed by applying a fixed rate
to the carrying value (the declining balance) of a tangible long-lived asset, resulting
in higher depreciation charges during the early years of the asset's life. Though any
fixed rate can be used, the most common rate is a percentage equal to twice the
straight-line depreciation percentage. When twice the straight-line rate is used, the
method is usually called the **double-declining-balance method**.

In our earlier example, the delivery truck had an estimated useful life of five
years. Consequently, under the straight-line method, the depreciation rate for each
year was 20 percent (100 percent ÷ 5 years).

Under the double-declining-balance method, the fixed rate is 40 percent (2 ×
20 percent). This fixed rate is applied to the *remaining carrying value* at the end of
each year. Estimated residual value is not taken into account in figuring depreciation except in a year when calculated depreciation exceeds the amount necessary to

KEY POINT: Under the double-declining-balance method, depreciation in the last year rarely equals the exact amount needed to reduce carrying value to residual value. Depreciation in the last year is limited to the amount necessary to reduce carrying value to residual value.

PARENTHETICAL NOTE: An asset remains on the books as long as it is in use. Even if the asset is fully depreciated, the company should not remove it from the books until it is taken out of service.

● **STOP AND THINK!** Which depreciation method would best reflect the risk of obsolescence from rapid technological changes? *An accelerated depreciation method is best. Companies facing rapid technological change use it to minimize the risk of obsolescence.* ■

bring the carrying value down to the estimated residual value. The depreciation schedule for this method is as follows:

Depreciation Schedule, Double-Declining-Balance Method

	Cost	Yearly Depreciation		Accumulated Depreciation	Carrying Value
Date of purchase	$10,000	—		—	$10,000
End of first year	10,000	(40% × $10,000)	$4,000	$4,000	6,000
End of second year	10,000	(40% × $6,000)	2,400	6,400	3,600
End of third year	10,000	(40% × $3,600)	1,440	7,840	2,160
End of fourth year	10,000	(40% × $2,160)	864	8,704	1,296
End of fifth year	10,000		296*	9,000	1,000

*Depreciation limited to amount necessary to reduce carrying value to residual value: $296 = $1,296 (previous carrying value) − $1,000 (residual value).

Note that the fixed rate is always applied to the carrying value at the end of the previous year. The depreciation is greatest in the first year and declines each year after that. Finally, the depreciation in the fifth year is limited to the amount necessary to reduce carrying value to residual value.

■ **COMPARISON OF THE THREE METHODS**   A visual comparison may provide a better understanding of the three depreciation methods described above. Figure 5 compares yearly depreciation and carrying value under the three methods. In the left-hand graph, which shows yearly depreciation, straight-line depreciation is uniform at $1,800 per year over the five-year period. However, the double-declining-balance method begins at an amount greater than straight-line ($4,000) and decreases each year to amounts that are less than straight-line (ultimately, $296). The production method does not generate a regular pattern because of the random fluctuation of the depreciation from year to year. The three yearly depreciation patterns are reflected in the graph of carrying value. In that graph, each method starts in the same place (cost of $10,000) and ends at the same place (residual value of $1,000). It is the patterns during the useful life of the asset that differ for each method. For instance, the carrying value under the straight-line method is always greater than that under the double-declining-balance method, except at the beginning and end of useful life.

FIGURE 5
Graphic Comparison of Three Methods of Determining Depreciation

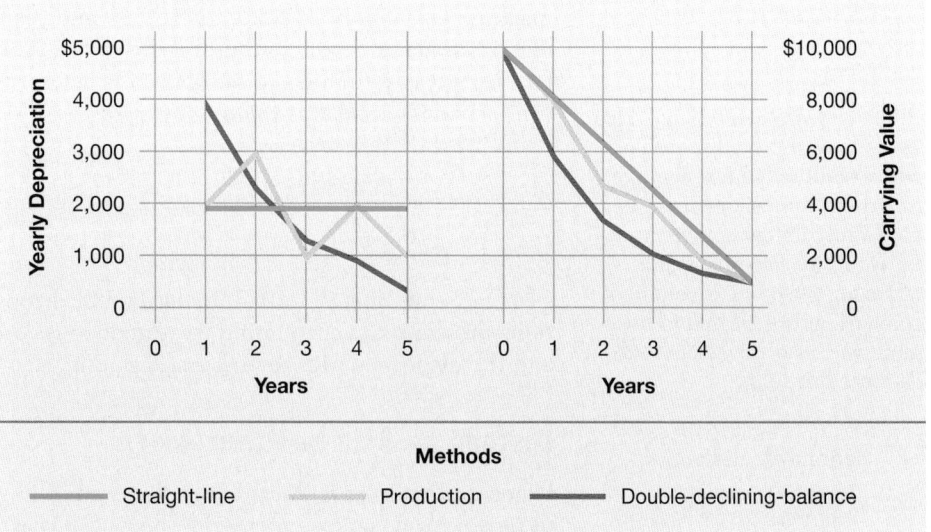

FOCUS ON BUSINESS PRACTICE

Accelerated Methods Save Money!

An AICPA study of 600 large companies found that the overwhelming majority used the straight-line method of depreciation for financial reporting purposes, as shown in Figure 6. Only about 13 percent used some type of accelerated method, and 5 percent used the production method. These figures tend to be misleading about the importance of accelerated depreciation methods, however, especially when it comes to income taxes. Federal income tax laws allow either the straight-line method or an accelerated method, and for tax purposes, about 75 percent of the 600 companies studied preferred using an accelerated method. Companies use different methods of depreciation for good reason. The straight-line method can be advantageous for financial reporting because it can produce the highest net income, and an accelerated method can be beneficial for tax purposes because it can result in lower income taxes.

FIGURE 6
Depreciation Methods Used by 600 Large Companies for Financial Reporting

CLARIFICATION NOTE: For financial reporting purposes, the objective is to measure performance accurately. For tax purposes, the objective is to minimize tax liability.

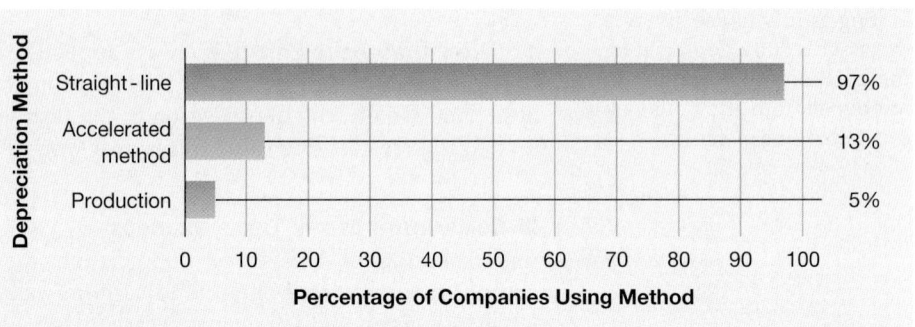

Total percentage exceeds 100 because some companies used different methods for different types of depreciable assets.

Reprinted with permission from *Accounting Trends & Techniques*. Copyright © 2002 by the American Institute of Certified Public Accountants, Inc.

 Check out ACE for a Review Quiz at http://accounting.college.hmco.com/students.

DISPOSAL OF DEPRECIABLE ASSETS

LO4   Account for the disposal of depreciable assets.

RELATED TEXT ASSIGNMENTS
Q: 17, 18
SE: 7, 8
E: 8, 9
P: 4
FRA: 6

ENRICHMENT NOTE: Plant assets may also be disposed of by involuntary conversion (e.g., fire, theft, mud slide, flood) or condemnation by a governmental authority. For financial reporting purposes, involuntary conversions are treated in the same way as if the assets were discarded or sold.

When plant assets are no longer useful because they are worn out or obsolete, they may be discarded, sold, or traded in on the purchase of new plant and equipment. For accounting purposes, a plant asset may be disposed of in one of three ways: It may be (1) discarded, (2) sold for cash, or (3) exchanged for another asset. To illustrate how each of these cases is recorded, assume that MGC Company purchased a machine on January 2, 20x0, for $6,500 and planned to depreciate it on a straight-line basis over an estimated useful life of ten years. The residual value at the end of ten years was estimated to be $500. On January 2, 20x7, the balances of the relevant accounts appear as follows:

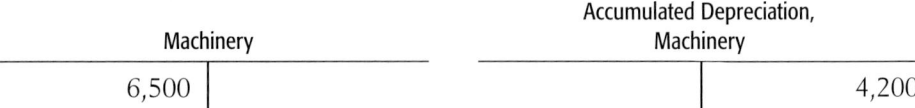

On September 30, 20x7, management disposes of the asset. The next few sections illustrate the accounting treatment to record depreciation for the partial year and the disposal under several assumptions.

DISCARD OR SALE OF PLANT ASSETS

When a plant asset is discarded or disposed of in some other way, it is first necessary to record depreciation expense for the partial year up to the date of disposal. This step is required because the asset was used until that date and, under the matching rule, the accounting period should receive the proper allocation of depreciation expense.

In this illustration, MGC Company disposes of the machinery on September 30. The entry to record the depreciation for the first nine months of 20x7 (nine-twelfths of a year) is as follows:

A = L + OE
−   −

Sept. 30   Depreciation Expense, Machinery   450
                Accumulated Depreciation, Machinery   450
                To record depreciation up to date of
                disposal

$$\frac{\$6,500 - \$500}{10} \times \frac{9}{12} = \$450$$

KEY POINT: When it disposes of an asset, a company must do two things. First, it must bring the depreciation up to date. Second, it must remove all evidence of ownership of the asset, including the contra account Accumulated Depreciation.

The relevant accounts appear as follows after the entry is posted:

Machinery		Accumulated Depreciation, Machinery	
6,500			4,650

After updating the depreciation, it is then necessary to remove the carrying value of the asset as shown in the following sections.

■ **DISCARDED PLANT ASSETS**   A plant asset rarely lasts exactly as long as its estimated life. If it lasts longer than its estimated life, it is not depreciated past the point at which its carrying value equals its residual value. The purpose of depreciation is to spread the depreciable cost of an asset over the estimated life of the asset. Thus, the total accumulated depreciation should never exceed the total depreciable cost. If an asset remains in use beyond the end of its estimated life, its cost and accumulated depreciation remain in the ledger accounts. Proper records will thus be available for maintaining control over plant assets. If the residual value is zero, the carrying value of a fully depreciated asset is zero until the asset is disposed of. If such an asset is discarded, no gain or loss results.

KEY POINT: A fully depreciated asset is kept on the books as long as it is still being used in the business. When a physical count of plant assets is made and reconciled with the general ledger control account and the subsidiary ledger, all assets must be accounted for.

In the illustration, however, the discarded equipment has a carrying value of $1,850 at the time of its disposal. The carrying value is computed from the T accounts above as machinery of $6,500 less accumulated depreciation of $4,650. A loss equal to the carrying value should be recorded when the machine is discarded, as follows:

A = L + OE
+   −
−

Sept. 30   Accumulated Depreciation, Machinery   4,650
              Loss on Disposal of Machinery   1,850
                Machinery   6,500
                Discarded machine no longer used
                in the business

Gains and losses on disposals of plant assets are classified as other revenues and expenses on the income statement.

● **STOP AND THINK!**
When would the disposal of long-term assets result in no gain or loss?
If cash received for the assets equals their residual value, then no gain or loss occurs. ■

■ **PLANT ASSETS SOLD FOR CASH**   The entry to record a plant asset sold for cash is similar to the one just illustrated, except that the receipt of cash should also be recorded. The following entries show how to record the sale of a machine under three assumptions about the selling price. In the first case, the $1,850 cash received is exactly equal to the $1,850 carrying value of the machine; therefore, no gain or loss occurs.

A = L + OE
+
+
−

Sept. 30   Cash   1,850
              Accumulated Depreciation, Machinery   4,650
                Machinery   6,500
                Sale of machine for carrying value;
                no gain or loss

In the second case, the $1,000 cash received is less than the carrying value of $1,850, so a loss of $850 is recorded.

A = L + OE
\+   −
\+
−

Sept. 30	Cash	1,000	
	Accumulated Depreciation, Machinery	4,650	
	Loss on Sale of Machinery	850	
	Machinery		6,500
	Sale of machine at less than carrying		
	value; loss of $850 ($1,850 − $1,000)		
	recorded		

KEY POINT: For an asset discarded or sold for cash, the gain (loss) on disposal of the asset equals cash received minus carrying value.

In the third case, the $2,000 cash received exceeds the carrying value of $1,850, so a gain of $150 is recorded.

A = L + OE
\+   \+
\+
−

Sept. 30	Cash	2,000	
	Accumulated Depreciation, Machinery	4,650	
	Gain on Sale of Machinery		150
	Machinery		6,500
	Sale of machine at more than the		
	carrying value; gain of $150		
	($2,000 − $1,850) recorded		

EXCHANGES OF PLANT ASSETS

Businesses also dispose of plant assets by trading them in on the purchase of other plant assets. Exchanges may involve similar assets, such as an old machine traded in on a newer model, or dissimilar assets, such as a cement mixer traded in on a truck. In either case, the purchase price is reduced by the amount of the trade-in allowance.

Basically, accounting for exchanges of plant assets is similar to accounting for sales of plant assets for cash. If the trade-in allowance received is greater than the carrying value of the asset surrendered, there has been a gain. If the allowance is less, there has been a loss. There are special rules for recognizing these gains and losses, depending on the nature of the assets exchanged:

Exchange	Losses Recognized	Gains Recognized
For financial accounting purposes		
Of dissimilar assets	Yes	Yes
Of similar assets	Yes	No
For income tax purposes		
Of dissimilar assets	Yes	Yes
Of similar assets	No	No

CLARIFICATION NOTE: For assets to be similar, they must be used for similar purposes. A desktop computer, for example, is similar to a laptop computer. Dissimilar assets, such as a truck and a cement mixer, are not used for similar purposes.

PARENTHETICAL NOTE: Recognizing losses but not gains on similar assets follows the convention of conservatism.

KEY POINT: For exchanges of dissimilar assets, the gain or loss on exchange equals the trade-in allowance minus carrying value of the old asset.

For both financial accounting and income tax purposes, both gains and losses are recognized when a company exchanges dissimilar assets. Assets are dissimilar when they perform different functions or do not meet specific monetary and business criteria for being considered similar assets. For financial accounting purposes, most exchanges are considered exchanges of dissimilar assets. In rare cases, when exchanges meet the specific criteria for exchanges of similar assets, the gains are not recognized. In these cases, you could think of the trade-in as an extension of the life and usefulness of the original machine. Instead of recognizing a gain at the time of the exchange, the company records the new machine at the sum of the carrying value of the older machine plus any cash paid.[10]

For income tax purposes, similar assets are defined as those performing the same function. Neither gains nor losses on exchanges of these assets are recognized in computing a company's income tax liability. Thus, in practice, accountants face cases in which both gains and losses are recognized (exchanges of dissimilar assets), cases in which losses are recognized and gains are not (exchanges of similar assets for financial reporting purposes), and cases in which neither gains nor losses are recognized (exchanges of similar assets for income tax purposes). Since all these options are used in practice, they are all illustrated in the following sections.

CLARIFICATION NOTE:
There is no relationship between carrying value and trade-in value. Carrying value is original cost minus accumulated depreciation to date, whereas trade-in value is fair market value on the date of the exchange.

■ **LOSS ON THE EXCHANGE RECOGNIZED**   A loss is recognized for financial accounting purposes on all exchanges in which a material loss occurs. A loss occurs when the trade-in allowance is less than the carrying value of the old asset. To illustrate the recognition of a loss, let us assume that the firm in our earlier example exchanges the machine for a newer, more modern machine on the following terms:

List price of new machine	$12,000
Trade-in allowance for old machine	(1,000)
Cash payment required	$11,000

In this case, the trade-in allowance ($1,000) is less than the carrying value ($1,850) of the old machine. The loss on the exchange is $850 ($1,850 − $1,000). This entry records the transaction under the assumption that the loss is to be recognized:

```
A = L + OE     Sept. 30  Machinery (new)                                12,000
   +      −                  Accumulated Depreciation, Machinery          4,650
   +                          Loss on Exchange of Machinery                 850
   −                              Machinery (old)                                      6,500
   −                              Cash                                                11,000
                                      Exchange of machines
```

KEY POINT: For income tax purposes, gains and losses on the exchange of similar assets are not recognized.

■ **LOSS ON THE EXCHANGE NOT RECOGNIZED**   In the previous example, in which a loss was recognized, the new asset was recorded at the purchase price of $12,000 and a loss of $850 was recorded. If the transaction involves similar assets and is to be recorded for income tax purposes, the loss should not be recognized. In this case, the cost basis of the new asset will reflect the effect of the unrecorded loss. The cost basis is computed by adding the cash payment to the carrying value of the old asset:

Carrying value of old machine	$ 1,850
Cash paid	11,000
Cost basis of new machine	$12,850

Note that no loss is recognized in the entry to record this transaction:

```
A = L + OE     Sept. 30  Machinery (new)                                12,850
   +                          Accumulated Depreciation, Machinery          4,650
   +                              Machinery (old)                                      6,500
   −                              Cash                                                11,000
   −                                  Exchange of machines
```

Note that the new machinery is reported at the purchase price of $12,000 plus the unrecognized loss of $850. The nonrecognition of the loss on the exchange is, in effect, a postponement of the loss. Since depreciation of the new machine will be computed based on a cost of $12,850 instead of $12,000, the "unrecognized" loss results in more depreciation each year on the new machine than if the loss had been recognized.

KEY POINT: For exchanges of assets, the cash payment on the exchange equals list price of the new asset minus trade-in allowance of the old asset.

■ **GAIN ON THE EXCHANGE RECOGNIZED**   Gains on exchanges are recognized for accounting purposes when dissimilar assets are involved. To illustrate the recognition of a gain, we continue with our example, assuming the following terms and assuming the machines being exchanged serve different functions:

List price of new machine	$12,000
Trade-in allowance for old machine	(3,000)
Cash payment required	$ 9,000

Here, the trade-in allowance ($3,000) exceeds the carrying value ($1,850) of the old machine by $1,150. Thus, there is a gain on the exchange, assuming the price of the new machine has not been inflated to allow for an excessive trade-in value. In other words, a gain exists if the trade-in allowance represents the fair market value of the old machine. In that case, the transaction is recorded as follows:

A = L + OE
+   +
+
−
−

Sept. 30	Machinery (new)	12,000	
	Accumulated Depreciation, Machinery	4,650	
	Gain on Exchange of Machinery		1,150
	Machinery (old)		6,500
	Cash		9,000
	Exchange of machines		

■ **GAIN ON THE EXCHANGE NOT RECOGNIZED**   When similar assets are exchanged, gains are not recognized for either accounting or income tax purposes. The cost basis of the new machine must reflect the effect of the unrecorded gain. This cost basis is computed by adding the cash payment to the carrying value of the old asset:

Carrying value of old machine	$ 1,850
Cash paid	9,000
Cost basis of new machine	$10,850

The entry to record the transaction is as follows:

A = L + OE
+
|
−
−

Sept. 30	Machinery (new)	10,850	
	Accumulated Depreciation, Machinery	4,650	
	Machinery (old)		6,500
	Cash		9,000
	Exchange of machines		

As with the nonrecognition of losses, the nonrecognition of the gain on an exchange is, in effect, a postponement of the gain. In this illustration, when the new machine is eventually discarded or sold, its cost basis will be $10,850 instead of its original price of $12,000. Since depreciation will be computed on the cost basis of $10,850, the "unrecognized" gain is reflected in lower depreciation each year on the new machine than if the gain had been recognized.

 Check out ACE for a Review Quiz at http://accounting.college.hmco.com/students.

ACCOUNTING FOR NATURAL RESOURCES

LO5 Identify the issues related to accounting for natural resources and compute depletion.

RELATED TEXT ASSIGNMENTS
Q: 19, 20
SE: 9
E: 10
FRA: 5

CLARIFICATION NOTE:
Natural resources are not intangible assets. Natural resources are correctly classified as components of property, plant, and equipment.

Natural resources are shown on the balance sheet as long-term assets with such descriptive titles as Timberlands, Oil and Gas Reserves, and Mineral Deposits. The distinguishing characteristic of these assets is that they are converted to inventory by cutting, pumping, mining, or other extraction methods. Natural resources are recorded at acquisition cost, which may include some costs of development. As the resource is extracted and converted to inventory, the asset account must be proportionally reduced. The carrying value of oil reserves on the balance sheet, for example, is reduced by a small amount for each barrel of oil pumped. As a result, the original cost of the oil reserves is gradually reduced, and depletion is recognized in the amount of the decrease.

DEPLETION

The term *depletion* is used to describe not only the exhaustion of a natural resource but also the proportional allocation of the cost of a natural resource to the units extracted. The costs are allocated in a way that closely resembles the production method used to calculate depreciation. When a natural resource is purchased or developed, there must be an estimate of the total units that will be available, such as barrels of oil, tons of coal, or board-feet of lumber. The depletion cost per unit is determined by dividing the cost of the natural resource (less residual value, if any) by the estimated number of units available. The amount of the depletion cost for each accounting period is then computed by multiplying the depletion cost per unit by the number of units extracted and sold. For example, for a mine having an estimated 1,500,000 tons of coal, a cost of $1,800,000, and an estimated residual value of $300,000, the depletion charge per ton of coal is $1:

$$\frac{\$1,800,000 - \$300,000}{1,500,000 \text{ tons}} = \$1 \text{ per ton}$$

Thus, if 115,000 tons of coal are mined and sold during the first year, the depletion charge for the year is $115,000. This charge is recorded as follows:

Dec. 31	Depletion Expense, Coal Deposits	115,000	
	Accumulated Depletion, Coal Deposits		115,000
	To record depletion of coal mine: $1 per ton for 115,000 tons mined and sold		

On the balance sheet, data for the mine would be presented as follows:

| Coal deposits | $1,800,000 | |
| Less accumulated depletion | 115,000 | $1,685,000 |

Sometimes a natural resource is not sold in the year it is extracted. It is important to note that it would then be recorded as a depletion *expense* in the year it is *sold*. The part not sold is considered inventory.

DEPRECIATION OF CLOSELY RELATED PLANT ASSETS

The extraction of natural resources generally requires special on-site buildings and equipment (e.g., conveyors, drills, and pumps). If the useful life of those assets is longer than the estimated time it will take to deplete the resource, a special problem arises. Because such long-term assets are often abandoned and have no useful purpose once all the resources have been extracted, they should be depreciated on the same basis as the depletion. For example, if machinery with a useful life of ten years is installed on an oil field that is expected to be depleted in eight years, the machinery should be depreciated over the eight-year period, using the production method. That way, each year's depreciation will be proportional to the year's depletion. If one-sixth of the oil field's total reserves is pumped in one year, then the depreciation should be one-sixth of the machinery's cost minus the residual value. If the useful life of a long-term plant asset is less than the expected life of the resource, the shorter life should be used to compute depreciation. In such cases, or when an asset will not be abandoned once all reserves have been depleted, other depreciation methods, such as straight-line or declining-balance, are appropriate.

DEVELOPMENT AND EXPLORATION COSTS IN THE OIL AND GAS INDUSTRY

The costs of exploring and developing oil and gas resources can be accounted for under one of two methods. Under the **successful efforts method**, the cost of successful exploration—for example, producing an oil well—is a cost of the resource. It should be recorded as an asset and depleted over the estimated life of the resource. The cost of an unsuccessful exploration—such as the cost of a dry well—is written off immediately as a loss. Because of these immediate write-offs, successful efforts accounting is considered the more conservative method and is used by most large oil companies. Exploration-minded independent oil companies, on the other hand, argue that the cost of dry wells is part of the overall cost of the systematic development of an oil field and is thus a part of the cost of producing wells. Under this **full-costing method**, all costs, including the cost of dry wells, are recorded as assets and depleted over the estimated life of the producing resources. This method tends to improve a company's earnings performance in its early years. Either method is permitted by the Financial Accounting Standards Board.[11]

 Check out ACE for a Review Quiz at http://accounting.college.hmco.com/students.

ACCOUNTING FOR INTANGIBLE ASSETS

LO6   Identify the issues related to accounting for intangible assets, including research and development costs and goodwill.

RELATED TEXT ASSIGNMENTS
Q: 21, 22, 23, 24, 25, 26
SE: 10
E: 11
P: 5
SD: 3, 5, 6
FRA: 2, 3, 5, 6

www.heinz.com

KEY POINT: Generally, intangible assets, including goodwill, are recorded only when purchased. An exception is the cost of internally developed computer software after a working prototype has been developed.

The purchase of an intangible asset is a special kind of capital expenditure. An intangible asset is both long term and nonphysical. Its value comes from the long-term rights or advantages it offers its owner. The most common examples—goodwill, trademarks, brand names, copyrights, patents, licenses or franchises, leaseholds, leasehold improvements, technology, noncompete covenants, and customer lists— are described in Table 1. Some current assets, such as accounts receivable and certain prepaid expenses, also have no physical substance, but they are not classified as intangible assets because they are short term.

Figure 7 shows the percentage of companies that report the various types of intangible assets. For some companies, intangible assets make up a substantial portion of total assets. As noted in the Decision Point at the beginning of the chapter, goodwill, trademarks, and other intangible assets of H. J. Heinz Company amount to almost $3.5 billion, or 35 percent of total assets. How these assets are accounted for will have a substantial effect on Heinz's performance.

Intangible assets are accounted for at acquisition cost—that is, the amount that was paid for them. Some intangible assets, such as goodwill and trademarks, may be acquired at little or no cost. Even though they may have great value and be needed for profitable operations, they should not appear on the balance sheet unless they have been purchased from another party at a price established in the marketplace.

The accounting issues connected with intangible assets, other than goodwill, are the same as those connected with other long-lived assets. The Accounting Principles Board, in its *Opinion No. 17*, lists them as (1) determining an initial carrying amount, (2) accounting for that amount after acquisition under normal business conditions—that is through periodic write-off or amortization—in a manner similar to depreciation, and (3) accounting for that amount if the value declines substantially and permanently.[12] In addition to these three problems, an intangible

FIGURE 7
Intangible Assets Separately Reported by 600 Large Companies

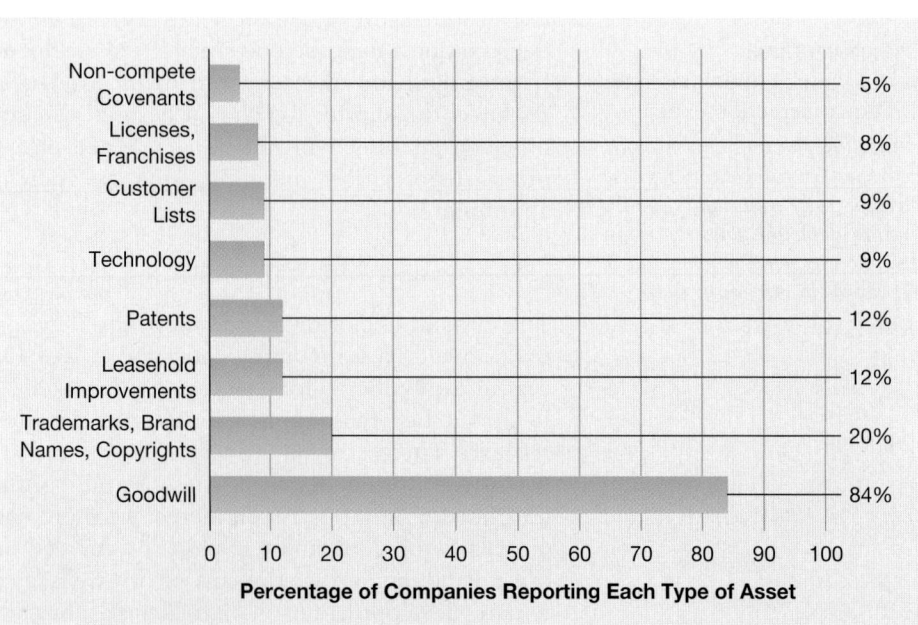

Source: Data from *Accounting Trends and Techniques,* 2002

TABLE 1. Accounting for Intangible Assets

Type	Description	Accounting Treatment
Goodwill	The excess of the amount paid for the purchase of a business over the fair market value of the net assets.	Debit Goodwill for the acquisition cost, and perform impairment review annually.
Trademark, brand name	A registered symbol or name that can be used only by its owner to identify a product or service.	Debit Trademark or Brand Name for the acquisition cost, and amortize it over a reasonable life.
Copyright	An exclusive right granted by the federal government to reproduce and sell literary, musical, and other artistic materials and computer programs for a period of the author's life plus 70 years.	Record at acquisition cost, and amortize over the useful life, which is often much shorter than the legal life. For example, the cost of paperback rights to a popular novel would typically be amortized over a useful life of two to four years.
Patent	An exclusive right granted by the federal government for a period of 20 years to make a particular product or use a specific process. A design may be granted a patent for 14 years.	The cost of successfully defending a patent in a patent infringement suit is added to the acquisition cost of the patent. Amortize over the useful life, which may be less than the legal life.
License, franchise	A right to an exclusive territory or market, or the right to use a formula, technique, process, or design.	Debit License or Franchise for the acquisition cost, and amortize it over a reasonable life.
Leasehold	A right to occupy land or buildings under a long-term rental contract. For example, Company A, which owns the right to use but does not want to use a retail location, sells or subleases to Company B the right to use it for ten years in return for one or more rental payments. Company B has purchased a leasehold.	Debit Leasehold for the amount of the rental payment, and amortize it over the remaining life of the lease. Payments to the lessor during the life of the lease should be debited to Lease Expense.
Leasehold improvements	Improvements to leased property that become the property of the lessor (the owner of the property) at the end of the lease.	Debit Leasehold Improvements for the cost of improvements, and amortize the cost of the improvements over the remaining life of the lease.
Technology	Capitalized costs associated with software developed for sale, lease, or internal use.	Record the amount of capitalizable software production costs, and amortize over the estimated economic life of the product.
Noncompete covenant	A contract limiting the rights of others to compete in a specific industry or line of business for a specified period.	Record at the acquisition cost, and amortize over the contract period.
Customer list	A list of customers or subscribers.	Debit Customer Lists for amount paid, and amortize over the expected life.

FOCUS ON BUSINESS PRACTICE

Take a Closer Look at Subscriber Lists!

One of the most valuable intangible assets some companies have is a list of subscribers. For example, the Newark Morning Ledger Co., a newspaper chain, purchased a chain of Michigan newspapers whose list of 460,000 subscribers was valued at $68 million. The U.S. Supreme Court upheld the company's right to amortize the value of the subscriber list because the company showed that the list had a limited useful life. The Internal Revenue Service had argued that the list had an indefinite life and therefore could not provide tax deductions through amortization. This ruling will benefit other types of businesses that purchase everything from bank deposits to pharmacy prescription files.[13]

CLARIFICATION NOTE:
Useful life refers to how long an intangible asset will be contributing income to a firm.

asset, because it has no physical substance, may sometimes be impossible to identify. For these reasons, its value and its useful life may be quite hard to estimate.

The Accounting Principles Board has decided that a company should record the costs of intangible assets acquired from others as assets. However, the company should record as expenses the costs of developing intangible assets. Also, intangible assets that have a determinable useful life, such as patents, copyrights, and leaseholds, should be written off through periodic amortization over that useful life in much the same way that plant assets are depreciated. Even though some intangible assets, such as brand names and trademarks, have no measurable limit on their lives, they should still be amortized over a reasonable length of time.

To illustrate these procedures, assume that Soda Bottling Company purchases a patent on a unique bottle cap for $18,000. The entry to record the patent would include $18,000 in the asset account Patents. Note that if Soda Bottling Company had developed the bottle cap internally instead of purchasing it from others, the costs of developing the cap, such as salaries of researchers, supplies used in testing, and costs of equipment, would have been expensed as incurred.

Assume now that Soda's management determines that although the patent for the bottle cap will last for 20 years, the product using the cap will be sold only for the next six years. The entry to record the annual amortization expense would be for $3,000 ($18,000 ÷ 6 years). Note that the Patents account is reduced directly by the amount of the amortization expense. This is in contrast to the treatment of other long-term asset accounts, for which depreciation or depletion is accumulated in separate contra accounts.

If the patent becomes worthless before it is fully amortized, the remaining carrying value is written off as a loss by removing it from the Patents account.

RESEARCH AND DEVELOPMENT COSTS

Most successful companies carry out research and development (R&D) activities, often in a separate department. R&D activities include development of new products, testing of existing and proposed products, and pure research. The costs of these activities are substantial for many companies. In a recent year, General Motors spent $6.6 billion on R&D, or about 4 percent of its revenues.[14] R&D costs can be even greater in high-tech fields like pharmaceuticals. For example, Abbott Laboratories recently spent $1.4 billion, or almost 10 percent of revenues, on R&D, and Roche Group spent almost $4 billion, or 14 percent of revenues.[15]

In the past, some companies recorded as assets R&D costs that could be directly traced to the development of specific patents, formulas, or other rights. Other costs,

www.gm.com

www.abbott.com
www.roche.com

FOCUS ON INTERNATIONAL BUSINESS

Lack of Comparability Is a Real Problem!

Worldwide variability in accounting practice causes problems for those who want to compare the financial statements of companies from different countries. For example, the method of accounting for R&D costs differs, depending on the country in which a company files its financial report. In Germany, Mexico, and the United States, a company must expense its R&D costs, whereas in France, Australia, and Japan, a company

may expense R&D or capitalize it (record it as an asset) if it meets certain criteria. Companies complying with the European Directives (European laws affecting financial reporting) have a choice of expensing or capitalizing R&D costs, but companies complying with International Accounting Standards (IAS) must expense research costs and capitalize development costs that meet certain conditions.[16]

such as those for testing and pure research, were treated as expenses of the accounting period and deducted from income. Since then, the Financial Accounting Standards Board has stated that all R&D costs should be treated as revenue expenditures and charged to expense in the period in which they are incurred.[17] The board argues that it is too hard to trace specific costs to specific profitable developments. Also, the costs of research and development are continuous and necessary for the success of a business and so should be treated as current expenses. To support this conclusion, the board cites studies showing that 30 to 90 percent of all new products fail and that 75 percent of new-product expenses go to unsuccessful products. Thus, their costs do not represent future benefits.

COMPUTER SOFTWARE COSTS

The costs that companies incur in developing computer software for sale or lease or for their own internal use are considered research and development costs until the product has proved technologically feasible. Thus, costs incurred before that point should be charged to expense when incurred. A product is deemed technologically feasible when a detailed working program has been designed. Once that occurs, all software production costs are recorded as assets, such as Technology, and are amortized over the estimated economic life of the product using the straight-line method. If at any time the company cannot expect to realize from a software product the amount of its unamortized costs on the balance sheet, the asset should be written down to the amount expected to be realized.[18]

LEASEHOLD IMPROVEMENTS

As noted in Table 1, improvements to leased property that become the property of the lessor (the owner of the property) at the end of the lease are called leasehold improvements. Such improvements are common for both small and large businesses. A study of large companies showed that 19 percent list leasehold improvements separately; the percentage is likely to be much higher for small businesses, since they generally operate in leased premises.[19] The improvement costs are amortized over the remaining term of the lease or the useful life of the improvement, whichever is shorter. Leasehold improvements are often classified as tangible assets in the property, plant, and equipment section of the balance sheet but are included in the intangible asset section because the improvements revert to the lessor at the end of the lease and are therefore more of a right than a tangible asset.

GOODWILL

⬢ STOP AND THINK!
Why would a company spend millions of dollars on goodwill?
The company must be paying for anticipated superior earnings and believes it will more than recoup the goodwill it purchased. ∎

The term *goodwill* means different things to different people. In most cases, the term is taken to mean the good reputation of a company. From an accounting standpoint, goodwill exists when a purchaser pays more for a business than the fair market value of the net assets if purchased individually. Because the purchaser has paid more than the fair market value of the physical assets, there must be intangible assets. If the company being purchased does not have patents, copyrights, trademarks, or other identifiable intangible assets of value, the excess payment is assumed to be for goodwill. Goodwill exists because most businesses are worth more as going concerns than as collections of assets. Goodwill reflects all the factors that allow a company to earn a higher-than-market rate of return on its assets, including customer satisfaction, good management, manufacturing efficiency, the advantages of holding a monopoly, good locations, and good employee relations. The payment above and beyond the fair market value of the tangible assets and other specific intangible assets is properly recorded in the Goodwill account.

The FASB has stated that purchased goodwill is an asset to be reported as a separate line item on the balance sheet and is subject to an annual impairment review. The impairment review requires a company to determine the reporting-unit level

FOCUS ON BUSINESS PRACTICE

Wake up, Goodwill Is Growing!

As Figure 7 shows, 84 percent of 600 large companies separately report goodwill as an asset. Because much of the growth of these companies has come through purchasing other companies, goodwill as a percentage of total assets has also grown. For some, the amount of goodwill is material:[20]

	Goodwill (in billions)	Percentage of Total Assets
General Mills <www.generalmills.com>	$8,473	51.2
Sara Lee Corporation <www.saralee.com>	$3,314	24.1
Tribune Company <www.tribune.com>	$5,419	38.5

KEY POINT: Goodwill equals purchase price minus adjusted net asset value.

on which goodwill is to be tested and the specific methodology to calculate the fair value of the reporting unit. If the fair value of goodwill is less than its carrying value on the balance sheet, then goodwill is considered impaired. Impairment results in reducing goodwill to its fair value and reporting the impairment charge on the income statement. A company can perform the fair value measurement for each reporting unit at any time as long as the measurement date is consistent from year to year.[21]

Goodwill should not be recorded unless it is paid for in connection with the purchase of a whole business. The amount to be recorded as goodwill can be determined by writing the identifiable net assets up to their fair market values at the time of purchase and subtracting the total from the purchase price. For example, assume that the owners of Company A agree to sell the company for $11,400,000. If the net assets (total assets − total liabilities) are fairly valued at $10,000,000, then the amount of the goodwill is $1,400,000 ($11,400,000 − $10,000,000). If the fair market value of the net assets is later determined to be more or less than $10,000,000, an entry is made in the accounting records to adjust the assets to the fair market value. The goodwill would then represent the difference between the adjusted net assets and the purchase price of $11,400,000.

 Check out ACE for a Review Quiz at http://accounting.college.hmco.com/students.

SPECIAL PROBLEMS OF DEPRECIATING PLANT ASSETS

S07 Apply depreciation methods to problems of partial years, revised rates, groups of similar items, special types of capital expenditures, and cost recovery.

RELATED TEXT ASSIGNMENTS
Q: 27, 28, 29, 30, 31, 32
E: 12, 13, 14, 15
P: 3, 8
FRA: 1

The illustrations used so far in this chapter have been simplified to explain the concepts and methods of depreciation. In actual business practice, there is often a need to (1) calculate depreciation for partial years, (2) revise depreciation rates based on new estimates of useful life or residual value, (3) group like items when calculating depreciation, (4) account for special types of capital expenditures, and (5) use the accelerated cost recovery method for tax purposes. The next sections discuss these five cases.

DEPRECIATION FOR PARTIAL YEARS

So far, most illustrations of depreciation methods have assumed that plant assets were purchased at the beginning or end of an accounting period. Usually, however, businesses buy assets when they are needed and sell or discard them when they are no longer useful or needed. The time of year is normally not a factor in the decision. Consequently, it is often necessary to calculate depreciation for partial years.

For example, assume that a piece of equipment is purchased for $3,600 and that it has an estimated useful life of six years and an estimated residual value of $600. Assume also that it is purchased on September 5 and that the yearly accounting period ends on December 31. Depreciation must be recorded for four months, September through December, or four-twelfths of the year. This factor is applied to the calculated depreciation for the entire year. The four months' depreciation under the straight-line method is calculated as follows:

$$\frac{\$3,600 - \$600}{6 \text{ years}} \times 4/12 = \$167$$

For the other depreciation methods, most companies compute the first year's depreciation and then multiply by the partial year factor. For example, if the company used the double-declining-balance method on the preceding equipment, the depreciation on the asset would be computed as follows:

$$\$3,600 \times 1/3 \times 4/12 = \$400$$

Typically, the depreciation calculation is rounded off to the nearest whole month because a partial month's depreciation is rarely material and the calculation is easier. In this case, depreciation was recorded from the beginning of September even though the purchase was made on September 5.

For all methods, the remainder (eight-twelfths) of the first year's depreciation is recorded in the next annual accounting period together with four-twelfths of the second year's depreciation.

REVISION OF DEPRECIATION RATES

ENRICHMENT NOTE:
A poor estimate can occur when a defective piece of equipment is purchased.

CLARIFICATION NOTE:
A change in an accounting estimate is not considered the correction of an error, but rather a revision based on new information.

Because a depreciation rate is based on an estimate of an asset's useful life, the periodic depreciation charge is seldom precise. It is sometimes very inadequate or excessive. This situation may result from an underestimate or overestimate of the asset's useful life or from a wrong estimate of the residual value. What action should be taken when it is found that after several years of use, a piece of equipment will last less time—or longer—than originally thought? Sometimes, it is necessary to revise the estimate of useful life so that the periodic depreciation expense increases or decreases. Then, to reflect the revised situation, the remaining depreciable cost of the asset is spread over the remaining years of useful life.

With this technique, the annual depreciation expense is increased or decreased to reduce the asset's carrying value to its residual value at the end of its remaining useful life. For example, assume that a delivery truck was purchased for $7,000 and has a residual value of $1,000. At the time of the purchase, the truck was expected to last six years, and it was depreciated on the straight-line basis. However, after two years of intensive use, it is determined that the truck will last only two more years, but that its estimated residual value at the end of the two years will still be $1,000. In other words, at the end of the second year, the truck's estimated useful life is reduced from six years to four years. At that time, the asset account and its related accumulated depreciation account would appear as follows:

KEY POINT: Allocate the remaining depreciable cost over the estimated remaining life.

Delivery Truck		Accumulated Depreciation, Delivery Truck	
Cost 7,000		Depreciation, year 1	1,000
		Depreciation, year 2	1,000

The remaining depreciable cost is computed as follows:

Cost	minus	Depreciation Already Taken	minus	Residual Value	
$7,000	−	$2,000	−	$1,000	= $4,000

The new annual periodic depreciation charge is computed by dividing the remaining depreciable cost of $4,000 by the remaining useful life of two years. Therefore, the new periodic depreciation charge is $2,000. The annual adjusting entry for depreciation for the next two years would be as follows:

A = L + OE   Dec. 31   Depreciation Expense, Delivery Truck   2,000
                                Accumulated Depreciation, Delivery Truck   2,000
                                   To record depreciation expense for the
                                   year

This method of revising depreciation is used widely in industry. It is also supported by *Opinion No. 9* and *Opinion No. 20* of the Accounting Principles Board of the AICPA.

GROUP DEPRECIATION

To say that the estimated useful life of an asset, such as a piece of equipment, is six years means that the average piece of equipment of that type is expected to last six years. In reality, some pieces may last only two or three years, and others may last eight or nine years, or longer. For this reason, and for reasons of convenience, large companies group similar items, such as trucks or pieces of office equipment, to calculate depreciation. This method is called **group depreciation**. Group depreciation is widely used in all fields of industry and business. A survey of large businesses indicated that 65 percent used group depreciation for all or part of their plant assets.[22]

SPECIAL TYPES OF CAPITAL EXPENDITURES

Companies make capital expenditures not only for plant assets, natural resources, and intangible assets but also for additions and betterments. An **addition** is an enlargement to the physical layout of a plant asset. As an example, if a new wing is added to a building, the benefits from the expenditure will be received over several years, and the amount paid for it should be debited to the asset account. A **betterment** is an improvement that does not add to the physical layout of a plant asset. For example, installing an air-conditioning system is a betterment that will offer benefits over a period of years; thus, its cost should be charged to an asset account.

Revenue expenditures for plant equipment include the repairs necessary to keep an asset in good working condition. Repairs fall into two categories: ordinary repairs and extraordinary repairs. **Ordinary repairs** are necessary to maintain an asset in good operating condition to achieve its originally intended useful life. Trucks must have periodic tune-ups, their tires and batteries must be regularly replaced, and other routine repairs must be made. Offices must be painted regularly, and broken tiles or woodwork must be replaced. Such repairs are a current expense.

Extraordinary repairs are repairs of a more significant nature—they affect the estimated residual value or estimated useful life of an asset. For example, a boiler for heating a building may be given a complete overhaul, at a cost of several thousand dollars, that will extend its useful life by five years. Typically, extraordinary repairs are recorded by debiting the Accumulated Depreciation account, under the assumption that some of the depreciation previously recorded has now been eliminated. The effect of this reduction in the Accumulated Depreciation account is to increase the carrying value of the asset by the cost of the extraordinary repair. Consequently, the new carrying value of the asset should be depreciated over the new estimated useful life.

Let us assume that a machine that cost $10,000 has no residual value and an estimated useful life of ten years. After eight years, the accumulated depreciation under the straight-line method is $8,000, and the carrying value is $2,000 ($10,000 − $8,000). At that point, the machine is given a major overhaul costing $1,500. This expenditure extends the machine's useful life three years beyond the original ten years. The entry for the extraordinary repair would be as follows:

A = L + OE   Jan. 4   Accumulated Depreciation, Machinery   1,500
\+   Cash   1,500
\−   Extraordinary repair
                                        to machinery

The annual periodic depreciation for each of the five years remaining in the machine's useful life would be calculated as follows:

Carrying value before extraordinary repairs	$2,000
Extraordinary repairs	1,500
Total	$3,500

$$\text{Annual periodic depreciation} = \frac{\$3,500}{5 \text{ years}} = \$700$$

ENRICHMENT NOTE:
Other examples of betterments include replacing stairs with an escalator in a department store and paving a gravel parking lot.

ENRICHMENT NOTE:
Putting a new motor in a cement mixer or replacing the roof on a building, thereby extending the useful life of the asset, are other examples of extraordinary repairs.

If the machine remains in use for the five years expected after the major overhaul, the total of the five annual depreciation charges of $700 will exactly equal the new carrying value, including the cost of the extraordinary repair.

COST RECOVERY FOR FEDERAL INCOME TAX PURPOSES

The Tax Reform Act of 1986 is arguably the most sweeping revision of federal tax laws since the original enactment of the Internal Revenue Code in 1913. First, it allows a company to expense the first $17,500 (which increases to $25,000 by tax year 2003) of equipment expenditures rather than recording them as an asset. Second, it allows a new method of writing off expenditures recorded as assets, the Modified Accelerated Cost Recovery System (MACRS). MACRS discards the concepts of estimated useful life and residual value. Instead, it requires that a cost recovery allowance be computed (1) on the unadjusted cost of property being recovered, and (2) over a period of years prescribed by the law for all property of similar types. The accelerated method prescribed under MACRS for most property other than real estate is 200 percent declining balance with a half-year convention (only one half-year's depreciation is allowed in the year of purchase, and one half-year's depreciation is taken in the last year). In addition, the period over which the cost may be recovered is specified. Recovery of the cost of property placed in service after December 31, 1986, is calculated as prescribed in the 1986 law.

Congress hoped that MACRS would encourage businesses to invest in new plant and equipment by allowing them to write off such assets rapidly. MACRS accelerates the write-off of these investments in two ways. First, the prescribed recovery periods are often shorter than the estimated useful lives used for calculating depreciation for the financial statements. Second, the accelerated method allowed under the new law enables businesses to recover most of the cost of their investments early in the depreciation process.

CLARIFICATION NOTE: MACRS depreciation is used for tax purposes only. It cannot be used for financial reporting.

Tax methods of depreciation are not usually acceptable for financial reporting under generally accepted accounting principles because the recovery periods are shorter than the depreciable assets' estimated useful lives.

Chapter Review

REVIEW OF LEARNING OBJECTIVES

LO1 Identify the types of long-term assets and explain the management issues related to accounting for them.

Long-term assets are assets that are used in the operation of a business, are not intended for resale, and have a useful life of more than one year. Long-term assets are either tangible or intangible. In the former category are land, plant assets, and natural resources. In the latter are trademarks, patents, franchises, goodwill, and other rights. The accounting issues associated with long-term assets relate to the decision to acquire the assets, the means of financing the assets, and the methods of accounting for the assets.

LO2 Distinguish between capital and revenue expenditures, and account for the cost of property, plant, and equipment.

It is important to distinguish between capital expenditures, which are recorded as assets, and revenue expenditures, which are recorded as expenses of the current period. The error of classifying one as the other will have an important effect on net income. The acquisition cost of property, plant, and equipment includes all expenditures that are reasonable and necessary to get such an asset in place and ready for use. Among these expenditures are purchase price, installation cost, freight charges, and insurance during transit.

LO3 Define *depreciation* and compute depreciation under the straight-line, production, and declining-balance methods.

Depreciation is the periodic allocation of the cost of a plant asset over its estimated useful life. It is recorded by debiting Depreciation Expense and crediting a related contra-asset account called Accumulated Depreciation. Factors that affect the computation of depreciation are cost, residual value, depreciable cost, and estimated useful life. Depreciation is commonly computed by the straight-line method, the production method, or an accelerated method. The straight-line method is related directly to the passage of time, whereas the production method is related directly to use. An accelerated method, which results in relatively large amounts of depreciation in earlier years and reduced amounts in later years, is based on the assumption that plant assets provide greater economic benefit in their earlier years than in later years. The most common accelerated method is the declining-balance method.

LO4 Account for the disposal of depreciable assets.

Long-term depreciable assets may be disposed of by being discarded, sold, or exchanged. When long-term assets are disposed of, it is necessary to record the depreciation up to the date of disposal and to remove the carrying value from the accounts by removing the cost from the asset account and the depreciation to date from the accumulated depreciation account. If a long-term asset is sold at a price that differs from its carrying value, the gain or loss should be recorded and reported on the income statement. In recording exchanges of similar plant assets, a gain or loss may arise. Losses, but not gains, should be recognized at the time of the exchange. When a gain is not recognized, the new asset is recorded at the carrying value of the old asset plus any cash paid. For income tax purposes, neither gains nor losses are recognized in the exchange of similar assets. When dissimilar assets are exchanged, gains and losses are recognized under both accounting and income tax rules.

LO5 Identify the issues related to accounting for natural resources and compute depletion.

Natural resources are depletable assets that are converted to inventory by cutting, pumping, mining, or other forms of extraction. Natural resources are recorded at cost as long-term assets. They are allocated as expenses through depletion charges as the resources are sold. The depletion charge is based on the ratio of the resource extracted to the total estimated resource. A major issue related to this subject is accounting for oil and gas reserves.

LO6 Identify the issues related to accounting for intangible assets, including research and development costs and goodwill.

The purchase of an intangible asset should be treated as a capital expenditure and recorded at acquisition cost, which in turn should be amortized over the useful life of the asset. The FASB requires that research and development costs be treated as revenue expenditures and charged as expenses in the periods of expenditure. Software costs are treated as research and development costs and expensed until a feasible working program is developed, after which time the costs may be capitalized and amortized over a reasonable estimated life. Goodwill is the excess of the amount paid for the purchase of a business over the fair market value of the net assets and is usually related to the superior earning potential of the business. It should be recorded only if paid for in connection with the purchase of a business, and it should be reviewed annually for possible impairment.

SUPPLEMENTAL OBJECTIVE

SO7 Apply depreciation methods to problems of partial years, revised rates, groups of similar items, special types of capital expenditures, and cost recovery.

In actual business practice, many factors affect depreciation calculations. It may be necessary to calculate depreciation for partial years because assets are bought and sold throughout the year, or to revise depreciation rates because of changed conditions. Because it is often difficult to estimate the useful life of a single item, and because it is more convenient, many large businesses group similar items for purposes of depreciation. Companies must also consider certain special capital expenditures when calculating depreciation. For example, expenditures for additions and betterments are capital expenditures. Extraordinary repairs, which increase the residual value or extend the life of an asset, are also treated as capital expenditures, but ordinary repairs are revenue expenditures. For income tax purposes, rapid write-offs of depreciable assets are allowed under the Modified Accelerated Cost Recovery System. Such rapid write-offs are not usually acceptable for financial accounting because the shortened recovery periods violate the matching rule.

REVIEW OF CONCEPTS AND TERMINOLOGY

The following concepts and terms were introduced in this chapter:

LO3 **Accelerated method:** A method of depreciation that allocates relatively large amounts of the depreciable cost of an asset to earlier years and reduced amounts to later years.

SO7 **Addition:** An enlargement to the physical layout of a plant asset.

LO1   **Amortization:** The periodic allocation of the cost of an intangible asset to the periods it benefits.

LO1   **Asset impairment:** Loss of revenue-generating potential of a long-lived asset before the end of its useful life; the difference between an asset's carrying value and its fair value, as measured by the present value of the expected cash flows.

SO7   **Betterment:** An improvement that does not add to the physical layout of a plant asset.

LO6   **Brand name:** A registered name that can be used only by its owner to identify a product or service.

LO2   **Capital expenditure:** An expenditure for the purchase or expansion of a long-term asset, recorded in an asset account.

LO1   **Carrying value:** The unexpired part of the cost of an asset, not its market value. Also called *book value*.

LO6   **Copyright:** An exclusive right granted by the federal government to reproduce and sell literary, musical, and other artistic materials and computer programs for a period of the author's life plus 70 years.

LO6   **Customer list:** A list of customers or subscribers.

LO3   **Declining-balance method:** An accelerated method of depreciation in which depreciation is computed by applying a fixed rate to the carrying value (the declining balance) of a tangible long-lived asset.

LO1   **Depletion:** The exhaustion of a natural resource through mining, cutting, pumping, or other extraction, and the way in which the cost is allocated.

LO3   **Depreciable cost:** The cost of an asset less its residual value.

LO1   **Depreciation:** The periodic allocation of the cost of a tangible long-lived asset (other than land and natural resources) over its estimated useful life.

LO3   **Double-declining-balance method:** An accelerated method of depreciation in which a fixed rate equal to twice the straight-line percentage is applied to the carrying value (the declining balance) of a tangible long-lived asset.

LO3   **Estimated useful life:** The total number of service units expected from a long-term asset.

LO2   **Expenditure:** A payment or an obligation to make future payment for an asset or a service.

SO7   **Extraordinary repairs:** Repairs that affect the estimated residual value or estimated useful life of an asset thereby increasing its carrying value.

LO6   **Franchise:** The right or license to an exclusive territory or market.

LO5   **Full-costing method:** A method of accounting for the costs of exploring and developing oil and gas resources in which all costs are recorded as assets and depleted over the estimated life of the producing resources.

LO6   **Goodwill:** The excess of the cost of a group of assets (usually a business) over the fair market value of the net assets if purchased individually.

SO7   **Group depreciation:** The grouping of similar items to calculate depreciation.

LO1   **Intangible assets:** Long-term assets with no physical substance whose value is based on rights or advantages accruing to the owner.

LO6   **Leasehold:** A right to occupy land or buildings under a long-term rental contract.

LO6   **Leasehold improvements:** Improvements to leased property that become the property of the lessor at the end of the lease.

LO6   **License:** The right to use a formula, technique, process, or design.

LO1   **Long-term assets:** Assets that have a useful life of more than one year, are acquired for use in the operation of a business, and are not intended for resale. Less commonly called *fixed assets*.

SO7   **Modified Accelerated Cost Recovery System (MACRS):** A mandatory system of depreciation for income tax purposes, enacted by Congress in 1986, that requires a cost recovery allowance to be computed (1) on the unadjusted cost of property being recovered, and (2) over a period of years prescribed by the law for all property of similar types.

LO1   **Natural resources:** Long-term assets purchased for the economic value that can be taken from the land and used up.

LO6   **Noncompete covenant:** A contract limiting the rights of others to compete in a specific industry or line of business for a specified period.

LO3   **Obsolescence:** The process of becoming out of date, which is a factor in the limited useful life of tangible assets.

SO7   **Ordinary repairs:** Repairs necessary to maintain an asset in good operating condition, which are recorded as current period expenses.

LO6   **Patent:** An exclusive right granted by the federal government for a period of 20 years to make a particular product or use a specific process or design.

LO3   **Physical deterioration:** Limitations on the useful life of a depreciable asset resulting from use and from exposure to the elements.

LO3   **Production method:** A method of depreciation that assumes depreciation is solely the result of use and that allocates depreciation based on the units of output or use during each period of an asset's useful life.

LO3   **Residual value:** The estimated net scrap, salvage, or trade-in value of a tangible asset at the estimated date of disposal. Also called *salvage value* or *disposal value.*

LO2   **Revenue expenditure:** An expenditure related to repair, maintenance, and operation of a long-term asset, recorded by a debit to an expense account.

LO3   **Straight-line method:** A method of depreciation that assumes depreciation depends only on the passage of time and that allocates an equal amount of depreciation to each accounting period in an asset's useful life.

LO5   **Successful efforts method:** A method of accounting for the costs of exploring and developing oil and gas resources in which successful exploration is recorded as an asset and depleted over the estimated life of the resource and all unsuccessful efforts are immediately written off as losses.

LO1   **Tangible assets:** Long-term assets that have physical substance.

LO6   **Technology:** Capitalized costs associated with software developed for sale, lease, or internal use and amortized over the estimated economic life of the software.

LO6   **Trademark:** A registered symbol or brand name that can be used only by its owner to identify a product or service.

REVIEW PROBLEM

Comparison of Depreciation Methods

LO3   Norton Construction Company purchased a cement mixer on January 2, 20x4, for $14,500. The mixer was expected to have a useful life of five years and a residual value of $1,000. The company engineers estimated that the mixer would have a useful life of 7,500 hours. It was used 1,500 hours in 20x4, 2,625 hours in 20x5, 2,250 hours in 20x6, 750 hours in 20x7, and 375 hours in 20x8. Norton Construction Company's year end is December 31.

REQUIRED ▶   1. Compute the depreciation expense and carrying value for 20x4 to 20x8, using the following methods: (a) straight-line, (b) production, and (c) double-declining-balance.

2. Prepare the adjusting entry to record the depreciation for 20x4 that you calculated in 1(a).

3. Show the balance sheet presentation for the cement mixer after the entry in **2** on December 31, 20x4.
4. What conclusions can you draw from the patterns of yearly depreciation?

ANSWER TO REVIEW PROBLEM

1. Depreciation computed:

Depreciation Method	Year	Computation	Depreciation	Carrying Value
a. Straight-line	20x4	$13,500 × 1/5	$2,700	$11,800
	20x5	13,500 × 1/5	2,700	9,100
	20x6	13,500 × 1/5	2,700	6,400
	20x7	13,500 × 1/5	2,700	3,700
	20x8	13,500 × 1/5	2,700	1,000
b. Production	20x4	$13,500 × $\frac{1,500}{7,500}$	$2,700	$11,800
	20x5	13,500 × $\frac{2,625}{7,500}$	4,725	7,075
	20x6	13,500 × $\frac{2,250}{7,500}$	4,050	3,025
	20x7	13,500 × $\frac{750}{7,500}$	1,350	1,675
	20x8	13,500 × $\frac{375}{7,500}$	675	1,000
c. Double-declining-balance	20x4	$14,500 × .4	$5,800	$ 8,700
	20x5	8,700 × .4	3,480	5,220
	20x6	5,220 × .4	2,088	3,132
	20x7	3,132 × .4	1,253*	1,879
	20x8		879*†	1,000

* Rounded.
† Remaining depreciation to reduce carrying value to residual value ($1,879 − $1,000 = $879).

2. Adjusting entry prepared—straight-line method:

20x4
Dec. 31   Depreciation Expense, Cement Mixer   2,700
                Accumulated Depreciation, Cement Mixer   2,700
                To record depreciation expense,
                straight-line method

3. Balance sheet presentation for 20x4 shown:

Property, plant, and equipment
   Cement mixer $14,500
   Less accumulated depreciation   2,700
                                                      $11,800

4. Conclusions drawn from depreciation patterns: The pattern of depreciation for the straight-line method differs significantly from that for the double-declining-balance method. In the earlier years, the amount of depreciation under the double-declining-balance method is significantly greater than the amount under the straight-line method. In the later years, the opposite is true. The carrying value under the straight-line method is greater than that under the double-declining-balance method at the end of all years except the fifth year. Depreciation under the production method differs from that under the other methods in that it follows no regular pattern. It varies with the amount of use. Consequently, depreciation is greatest in 20x5 and 20x6, which are the years of greatest use. Use declined significantly in the last two years.

Chapter Assignments

BUILDING YOUR KNOWLEDGE FOUNDATION

QUESTIONS

1. What are the characteristics of long-term assets?

2. Which of the following items would be classified as plant assets on the balance sheet? (a) A truck held for sale by a truck dealer, (b) an office building that was once the company headquarters but is now to be sold, (c) a typewriter used by a secretary of the company, (d) a machine that is used in manufacturing operations but is now fully depreciated, (e) pollution-control equipment that does not reduce the cost or improve the efficiency of a factory, (f) a parking lot for company employees.

3. Why is land different from other long-term assets?

4. What do accountants mean by the term *depreciation*, and what is its relationship to depletion and amortization?

5. What is asset impairment, and how does it affect the valuation of long-term assets?

6. How do cash flows relate to the decision to acquire a long-term asset, and how does the useful life of an asset relate to the means of financing it?

7. Why is it useful to think of a plant asset as a bundle of services?

8. What is the distinction between revenue expenditures and capital expenditures, why is it important, and what in general is included in the cost of a long-term asset?

9. Which of the following expenditures stemming from the purchase of a computer system would be charged to the asset account? (a) The purchase price of the equipment, (b) interest on the debt incurred to purchase the equipment, (c) freight charges, (d) installation charges, (e) the cost of special communications outlets at the computer site, (f) the cost of repairing a door that was damaged during installation, (g) the cost of adjustments to the system during the first month of operation.

10. Bert's Grocery obtained bids on the construction of a receiving dock at the back of its store. The lowest bid was $22,000. The company decided to build the dock itself, however, and was able to do so for $20,000, which it borrowed. The activity was recorded as a debit to Buildings for $22,000 and credits to Notes Payable for $20,000 and Gain on Construction for $2,000. Do you agree with the entry?

11. A firm buys technical equipment that is expected to last twelve years. Why might the equipment have to be depreciated over a shorter period of time?

12. A company purchased a building five years ago. The market value of the building is now greater than it was when the building was purchased. Explain why the company should continue depreciating the building.

13. Evaluate the following statement: "A parking lot should not be depreciated because adequate repairs will make it last forever."

14. Is the purpose of depreciation to determine the value of equipment? Explain your answer.

15. Contrast the assumption underlying the straight-line depreciation method with the assumption underlying the production depreciation method.

16. What is the principal argument supporting an accelerated depreciation method?

17. If a plant asset is sold during the year, why should depreciation be computed for the partial year prior to the date of the sale?

18. If a plant asset is discarded before the end of its useful life, how is the amount of loss measured?

19. Blackfeet Mining Company computes the depletion rate of ore to be $2 per ton. During 20xx the company mined 400,000 tons of ore and sold 370,000 tons. What is the total depletion expense for the year?

20. Under what circumstances can a mining company depreciate its plant assets over a period of time that is less than their useful lives?

21. Because accounts receivable have no physical substance, can they be classified as intangible assets?

22. Under what circumstances can a company have intangible assets that do not appear on the balance sheet?

23. How does the Financial Accounting Standards Board recommend that research and development costs be treated?

24. After spending three years developing a new software program for designing office buildings, Drew Mason Architects recently completed the detailed working program. How does accounting for the costs of software development differ before and after the completion of a successful working program?

25. How is accounting for software development costs similar to and different from accounting for research and development costs?

26. Under what conditions should goodwill be recorded? Should it remain in the records permanently once it is recorded?

27. What basic procedure should be followed in revising a depreciation rate?

28. On what basis can depreciation be taken on a group of assets rather than on individual items?

29. What will be the effect on future years' income of charging an addition to a building to repair expense?

30. In what ways do an addition, a betterment, and an extraordinary repair differ?

31. How does an extraordinary repair differ from an ordinary repair? What is the accounting treatment for each?

32. What is the difference between depreciation for accounting purposes and the Modified Accelerated Cost Recovery System for income tax purposes?

SHORT EXERCISES

LO1 Management Issues

SE 1. Indicate whether each of the following actions is primarily related to (a) acquisition of long-term assets, (b) financing of long-term assets, or (c) choosing methods and estimates related to long-term assets:

1. Deciding between common stock and long-term notes for the raising of funds
2. Relating the acquisition cost of a long-term asset to the cash flows generated by the asset
3. Determining how long an asset will benefit the company
4. Deciding to use cash flows from operations to purchase long-term assets
5. Determining how much an asset will sell for when it is no longer useful to the company

LO2 Determining Cost of Long-Term Assets

SE 2. Standard Auto purchased a neighboring lot for a new building and parking lot. Indicate whether each of the following expenditures is properly charged to (a) Land, (b) Land Improvements, or (c) Buildings.

1. Paving costs
2. Architects' fee for building design
3. Cost of clearing the property
4. Cost of the property
5. Building construction costs
6. Lights around the property
7. Building permit
8. Interest on the construction loan

LO2 Group Purchase

SE 3. Arney Company purchased property with a warehouse and parking lot for $750,000. An appraiser valued the components of the property if purchased separately as follows:

Land	$200,000
Land improvements	100,000
Building	500,000
Total	$800,000

Determine the cost to be assigned to each component.

LO3 Straight-Line Method

SE 4. Waybury Fitness Center purchased a new step machine for $5,500. The apparatus is expected to last four years and have a residual value of $500. What will be the depreciation expense for each year under the straight-line method?

SE 5.
LO3 Production Method

Assuming that the step machine in **SE 4** has an estimated useful life of 8,000 hours and was used for 2,400 hours in year 1, for 2,000 hours in year 2, for 2,200 hours in year 3, and for 1,400 hours in year 4, how much would depreciation expense be in each year?

SE 6.
LO3 Double-Declining-Balance Method

Assuming that the step machine in **SE 4** is depreciated using the double-declining-balance method, how much would depreciation expense be in each year?

SE 7.
LO4 Disposal of Plant Assets: No Trade-In

West Coast Printing had a piece of equipment that cost $8,100 and on which $4,500 of accumulated depreciation had been recorded. The equipment was disposed of on January 4, the first day of business of the current year.

1. Calculate the carrying value of the equipment.
2. Calculate the gain or loss on the disposal under each of the following assumptions:

   a. It was discarded as having no value.
   b. It was sold for $1,500 cash.
   c. It was sold for $4,000 cash.

SE 8.
LO4 Disposal of Plant Assets: Trade-In

For each of the following assumptions and referring to the equipment mentioned in **SE 7**, compute the gain (loss) on the exchange, the cash payment required, and the amount at which the new equipment would be recorded:

1. The equipment was traded in on dissimilar equipment that had a list price of $12,000. A $3,800 trade-in was allowed, and the balance was paid in cash. Gains and losses are to be recognized.
2. The equipment was traded in on dissimilar equipment that had a list price of $12,000. A $1,750 trade-in was allowed, and the balance was paid in cash. Gains and losses are to be recognized.
3. Same as **2**, except the items are similar and gains and losses are not to be recognized.

SE 9.
LO5 Natural Resources

Ledgemore Company purchased land containing an estimated 4,000,000 tons of ore for $8,000,000. The land will be worth $1,200,000 without the ore after eight years of active mining. Although the equipment needed for the mining will have a useful life of 20 years, it is not expected to be usable and will have no value after the mining on this site is complete. Compute the depletion charge per ton and the amount of depletion expense for the first year of operation, assuming that 600,000 tons of ore were mined and sold. Also, compute the first-year depreciation on the mining equipment using the production method, assuming a cost of $9,600,000 with no residual value.

SE 10.
LO6 Intangible Assets: Computer Software

Osaka created a new software application for PCs. Its costs during research and development were $500,000, and its costs after the working program was developed were $350,000. Although its copyright may be amortized over 40 years, management believes that the product will be viable for only five years. How should the costs be accounted for? At what value will the software appear on the balance sheet after one year?

EXERCISES

E 1.
LO1 Management Issues

Indicate whether each of the following actions is primarily related to (a) acquisition of long-term assets, (b) financing of long-term assets, or (c) choosing methods and estimates related to long-term assets:

1. Deciding to use the production method of depreciation
2. Allocating costs on a group purchase
3. Determining the total units a machine will produce
4. Deciding to borrow funds to purchase equipment
5. Estimating the savings a new machine will yield and comparing the amount to cost
6. Deciding whether to rent or buy a piece of equipment

E 2.
LO1 Purchase Decision–Present Value Analysis

Management is considering the purchase of a new machine for a cost of $12,000. It is estimated that the machine will generate positive net cash flows of $3,000 per year for five years and will have a disposal price at the end of that time of $1,000. Assuming an interest rate of 9 percent, determine if management should purchase the machine. Use Tables 3 and 4 in the appendix on future value and present value tables to determine the net present value of the new machine.

E 3.
LO2 Determining Cost of Long-Term Assets

Denver Manufacturing purchased land next to its factory to be used as a parking lot. Expenditures were as follows: purchase price, $150,000; broker's fees, $12,000; title search and other fees, $1,100; demolition of a shack on the property, $4,000; general grading of property, $2,100; paving parking lots, $20,000; lighting for parking lots,

$16,000; and signs for parking lots, $3,200. Determine the amounts that should be debited to the Land account and the Land Improvements account.

LO2 Group Purchase

E 4. Jodie Williams purchased a car wash for $480,000. If purchased separately, the land would have cost $120,000, the building $270,000, and the equipment $210,000. Determine the amount that should be recorded in the new business's records for land, building, and equipment.

LO2 Cost of Long-Term Asset
LO3 and Depreciation

E 5. Dewees Brown purchased a used tractor for $35,000. Before the tractor could be used, it required new tires, which cost $2,200, and an overhaul, which cost $2,800. Its first tank of fuel cost $150. The tractor is expected to last six years and have a residual value of $4,000. Determine the cost and depreciable cost of the tractor and calculate the first year's depreciation under the straight-line method.

LO3 Depreciation Methods

E 6. North End Oil Company purchased a drilling truck for $90,000. North End expected the truck to last five years or 200,000 miles, with an estimated residual value of $15,000 at the end of that time. During 20x5, the truck was driven 48,000 miles. North End's year end is December 31. Compute the depreciation for 20x5 under each of the following methods, assuming that the truck was purchased on January 13, 20x4: (1) straight-line, (2) production, and (3) double-declining-balance. Using the amount computed in **3,** prepare the entry in journal form to record depreciation expense for the second year and show how the Drilling Truck account would appear on the 20x5 balance sheet.

LO3 Double-Declining-Balance
Method

E 7. Aburri Burglar Alarm Systems Company purchased a word processor for $2,240. It has an estimated useful life of four years and an estimated residual value of $240. Compute the depreciation charge for each of the four years using the double-declining-balance method.

LO4 Disposal of Plant Assets

E 8. A piece of equipment that cost $32,400 and on which $18,000 of accumulated depreciation had been recorded was disposed of on January 2, the first day of business of the current year. For each of the following assumptions, compute the gain (loss) on the disposal or exchange. In addition, for assumptions **4, 5** and **6,** compute the cash payment required and the amount at which the new equipment would be recorded.

1. It was discarded as having no value.
2. It was sold for $6,000 cash.
3. It was sold for $18,000 cash.
4. It was traded in on dissimilar equipment having a list price of $48,000. A $16,200 trade-in was allowed, and the balance was paid in cash. Gains and losses are to be recognized.
5. It was traded in on dissimilar equipment having a list price of $48,000. A $7,500 trade-in was allowed, and the balance was paid in cash. Gains and losses are to be recognized.
6. Same as **5,** except the items are similar and gains and losses are not to be recognized.

LO4 Disposal of Plant Assets

E 9. Sunshire Company purchased a computer on January 2, 20x4, at a cost of $5,000. It is expected to have a useful life of five years and a residual value of $500. Assuming that the computer is disposed of on July 1, 20x7, record the partial year's depreciation for 20x7 using the straight-line method, and record the disposal under each of the following assumptions:

1. The computer is discarded.
2. The computer is sold for $800.
3. The computer is sold for $2,200.
4. The computer is exchanged for a new computer with a list price of $9,000. A $1,200 trade-in is allowed on the cash purchase. The accounting approach to gains and losses is followed.
5. Same as **4,** except a $2,400 trade-in is allowed.
6. Same as **4,** except the income tax approach is followed.
7. Same as **5,** except the income tax approach is followed.
8. Same as **4,** except the computer is exchanged for dissimilar office equipment.
9. Same as **5,** except the computer is exchanged for dissimilar office equipment.

LO3 Natural Resource Depletion
LO5 and Depreciation of Related
Plant Assets

E 10. Seropoulos Mining Company purchased land containing an estimated 10 million tons of ore for a cost of $8,800,000. The land without the ore is estimated to be worth $1,600,000. The company expects that all the usable ore can be mined in 10 years. Buildings costing $1,000,000 with an estimated useful life of 30 years were erected on the site. Equipment costing $960,000 with an estimated useful life of 10 years was installed. Because of the remote location, neither the buildings nor the equipment has an estimated residual value. During its first year of operation, the company mined and sold 800,000 tons of ore.

1. Compute the depletion charge per ton.
2. Compute the depletion expense that Seropoulos Mining should record for the year.
3. Determine the depreciation expense for the year for the buildings, making it proportional to the depletion.
4. Determine the depreciation expense for the year for the equipment under two alternatives: (a) making the expense proportional to the depletion and (b) using the straight-line method.

LO6   Amortization of Copyrights and Trademarks

E 11. 1. Maddox Publishing Company purchased the copyright to a basic computer textbook for $20,000. The usual life of a textbook is about four years. However, the copyright will remain in effect for another 50 years. Calculate the annual amortization of the copyright.

2. Weyland Company purchased a trademark from a well-known supermarket for $160,000. The management of the company argued that because the trademark's value would last forever and might even increase, no amortization should be charged. Calculate the minimum amount of annual amortization that should be charged, according to guidelines of the appropriate Accounting Principles Board opinion.

SO7   Depreciation Methods and Partial Years

E 12. Using the data given for North End Oil Company in **E 6,** compute the depreciation for calendar year 20x4 under each of the following methods, assuming that the truck was purchased on July 1, 20x4, and was driven 20,000 miles during 20x4: (1) straight-line, (2) production, and (3) double-declining-balance.

SO7   Revision of Depreciation Rates

E 13. Mt. Sinai Hospital purchased a special x ray machine. The machine, which cost $311,560, was expected to last ten years, with an estimated residual value of $31,560. After two years of operation (and depreciation charges using the straight-line method), it became evident that the x-ray machine would last a total of only seven years. The estimated residual value, however, would remain the same. Given this information, determine the new depreciation charge for the third year on the basis of the revised estimated useful life.

LO2   Special Types of Capital
SO7   Expenditures

E 14. Tell whether each of the following transactions related to an office building is a revenue expenditure (RE) or a capital expenditure (CE). In addition, indicate whether each transaction is an ordinary repair (OR), an extraordinary repair (ER), an addition (A), a betterment (B), or none of these (N).

1. The hallways and ceilings in the building are repainted at a cost of $8,300.
2. The hallways, which have tile floors, are carpeted at a cost of $28,000.
3. A new wing is added to the building at a cost of $175,000.
4. Furniture is purchased for the entrance to the building at a cost of $16,500.
5. The air-conditioning system is overhauled at a cost of $28,500. The overhaul extends the useful life of the air-conditioning system by ten years.
6. A cleaning firm is paid $200 per week to clean the newly installed carpets.

SO7   Extraordinary Repairs

E 15. Marino Manufacturing has an incinerator that originally cost $187,200 and now has accumulated depreciation of $132,800. The incinerator has completed its 15th year of service in an estimated useful life of 20 years. At the beginning of the 16th year, the company spent $42,800 repairing and modernizing the incinerator to comply with pollution-control standards. Therefore, the incinerator is now expected to last 10 more years instead of 5. It will not, however, have more capacity than it did in the past or a residual value at the end of its useful life.

1. Prepare the entry in journal form to record the cost of the repair.
2. Compute the carrying value of the incinerator after the entry.
3. Prepare the entry to record straight-line depreciation for the current year.

PROBLEMS

LO2   Determining Cost of Assets

P 1. Constanza Computers constructed a new training center in 20x4. You have been hired to manage the training center. A review of the accounting records shows the following expenditures debited to an asset account called Training Center:

Attorney's fee, land acquisition	$ 17,450
Cost of land	299,000
Architect's fee, building design	51,000
Building	510,000
Parking lot and sidewalk	67,800
Electrical wiring, building	82,000
Landscaping	27,500
Cost of surveying land	4,600
Training equipment, tables, and chairs	68,200
Installation of training equipment	34,000
Cost of grading the land	7,000
Cost of changes in building to soundproof rooms	29,600
Total account balance	$1,198,150

During the center's construction, an employee of Constanza Computers worked full time overseeing the project. He spent two months on the purchase and preparation of the site, six months on the construction, one month on land improvements, and one month on equipment installation and training room furniture purchase and setup. His salary of $32,000 during this ten-month period was charged to Administrative Expense. The training center was placed in operation on November 1.

REQUIRED ▶ Prepare a schedule with the following four column (Account) headings: Land, Land Improvements, Building, and Equipment. Place each of the above expenditures in the appropriate column. Total the columns.

P 2.
LO3 Comparison of Depreciation Methods

Harrington Manufacturing Company purchased a robot for $720,000 at the beginning of year 1. The robot has an estimated useful life of four years and an estimated residual value of $60,000. The robot, which should last 20,000 hours, was operated 6,000 hours in year 1; 8,000 hours in year 2; 4,000 hours in year 3; and 2,000 hours in year 4.

REQUIRED ▶ 1. Compute the annual depreciation and carrying value for the robot for each year assuming the following depreciation methods: (a) straight-line, (b) production, and (c) double-declining-balance.

2. Prepare the adjusting entry in journal form that would be made each year to record the depreciation calculated under the straight-line method.

3. Show the balance sheet presentation for the robot after the adjusting entry in year 2 using the straight-line method.

4. What conclusions can you draw from the patterns of yearly depreciation and carrying value in 1?

P 3.
LO3 Depreciation Methods and SO7 Partial Years

Ellen Leblanc purchased a laundry company. In addition to the washing machines, Leblanc installed a tanning machine and a refreshment center. Because each type of asset performs a different function, Leblanc has decided to use different depreciation methods. Data on each type of asset are summarized in the table below. The tanning machine was operated for 2,100 hours in 20x5, 3,000 hours in 20x6, and 2,400 hours in 20x7.

Asset	Date Purchased	Cost	Installation Cost	Residual Value	Estimated Life	Depreciation Method
Washing machines	3/5/x5	$15,000	$2,000	$2,600	4 years	Straight-line
Tanning machine	4/1/x5	34,000	3,000	1,000	7,500 hours	Production
Refreshment center	10/1/x5	3,400	600	600	10 years	Double-declining-balance

REQUIRED ▶ Assume the fiscal year ends December 31. Compute the depreciation expense for each item and the total depreciation expense for 20x5, 20x6, and 20x7. Round your answers to the nearest dollar and present them in a table with the headings shown below.

			Depreciation		
Asset	Year	Computations	20x5	20x6	20x7

P 4.
LO4 Recording Disposals

Masterson Construction Company purchased a road grader for $29,000. The machine is expected to have a useful life of five years and a residual value of $2,000.

REQUIRED ▶ Prepare entries in journal form to record the disposal of the road grader at the end of the second year, after the depreciation is recorded, assuming that the straight-line method is used and making the following separate assumptions:

a. The road grader is sold for $20,000 cash.

b. The road grader is sold for $16,000 cash.

c. The road grader is traded in on a dissimilar piece of machinery costing $33,000, a trade-in allowance of $20,000 is given, the balance is paid in cash, and gains or losses are recognized.

d. The road grader is traded in on a dissimilar piece of machinery costing $33,000, a trade-in allowance of $16,000 is given, the balance is paid in cash, and gains or losses are recognized.

e. Same as **c,** except it is traded for a similar road grader and Masterson Construction Company follows accounting rules for the recognition of gains or losses.

f. Same as **d,** except it is traded for a similar road grader and Masterson Construction Company follows accounting rules for the recognition of gains or losses.

g. Same as **c,** except it is traded for a similar road grader and gains or losses are not recognized for income tax purposes.

h. Same as **d,** except it is traded for a similar road grader and gains or losses are not recognized for income tax purposes.

P 5.

LO6   Amortization of License, Leasehold, and Leasehold Improvements

Part A: On January 2, Baby Doll, Inc., purchased the exclusive license to make dolls based on the characters in a popular new television series called "Sky Pirates." The license cost $2,100,000, and there was no termination date on the rights. Immediately after signing the contract, the company sued a rival firm that claimed it had already received the exclusive license to the series characters. Baby Doll successfully defended its rights at a cost of $360,000.

During the first year and the next, Baby Doll marketed toys based on the series. Because a successful television series lasts about five years, the company felt it could market the toys for three more years. However, before the third year of the series could get under way, a controversy arose between its two stars and its producer. As a result, the stars refused to work the third year, and the show was canceled, rendering the exclusive rights worthless.

REQUIRED ▶ Prepare entries in journal form to record the following: (a) purchase of the exclusive license; (b) successful defense of the license; (c) amortization expense, if any, for the first year; and (d) write-off of the license as worthless.

Part B: Valerie Spare purchased a six-year sublease on a building from the estate of the former tenant. It was a good location for her business, and the annual rent of $3,600, which had been established ten years before, was low. The cost of the sublease was $9,450.

To use the building, Spare had to make certain alterations. She moved some panels at a cost of $1,700 and installed others for $6,100. She also added carpet, lighting fixtures, and a sign at costs of $2,900, $3,100, and $1,200, respectively. All items except the carpet would last for at least twelve years. The expected life of the carpet was six years. None of the improvements would have a residual value.

REQUIRED ▶ Prepare entries in journal form to record the following: (a) the payment for the sublease; (b) the payments for the alterations, panels, carpet, lighting fixtures, and sign; (c) the lease payment for the first year; (d) the amortization expense, if any, associated with the sublease; and (e) the amortization expense, if any, associated with the alterations, panels, carpet, lighting fixtures, and sign.

ALTERNATE PROBLEMS

P 6.

LO2   Determining Cost of Assets

Patroni Company began operation on January 2 of 20x5. At the end of the year, the company's auditor discovered that all expenditures involving long-term assets had been debited to an account called Fixed Assets. An analysis of the Fixed Assets account, which had a year-end balance of $5,289,944, disclosed that it contained the following items:

Cost of land	$ 633,200
Surveying costs	8,200
Transfer of title and other fees required by the county	1,840
Broker's fees for land	42,288
Attorney's fees associated with land acquisition	14,096
Cost of removing timber from land	100,800
Cost of grading land	8,400
Cost of digging building foundation	69,200
Architect's fee for building and land improvements (80 percent building)	129,600
Cost of building construction	1,420,000
Cost of sidewalks	22,800
Cost of parking lots	108,800
Cost of lighting for grounds	160,600
Cost of landscaping	23,600
Cost of machinery	1,978,000
Shipping cost on machinery	110,600
Cost of installing machinery	352,400
Cost of testing machinery	44,200
Cost of changes in building to comply with safety regulations pertaining to machinery	25,080
Cost of repairing building that was damaged in the installation of machinery	17,800
Cost of medical bill for injury received by employee while installing machinery	4,800
Cost of water damage to building during heavy rains prior to opening the plant for operation	13,640
Account balance	$5,289,944

Patroni Company sold the timber it cleared from the land to a firewood dealer for $10,000. This amount was credited to Miscellaneous Income.

During the construction period, two of Patroni's supervisors devoted full time to the construction project. They earn annual salaries of $96,000 and $84,000, respectively. They spent two months on the purchase and preparation of the land, six months on the construction of the building (approximately one-sixth of which was devoted to improvements on the grounds), and one month on machinery installation. The plant began operation on October 1, and the supervisors returned to their regular duties. Their salaries were debited to Factory Salaries Expense.

REQUIRED ▶ Prepare a schedule with the following column headings: Land, Land Improvements, Buildings, Machinery, and Expense. Place each of the above expenditures in the appropriate column. Negative amounts should be shown in parentheses. Total the columns.

P 7.
LO3 Comparison of Depreciation Methods

Mount Royal Construction Company purchased a new crane for $360,500 at the beginning of year 1. The crane has an estimated residual value of $35,000 and an estimated useful life of six years. The crane is expected to last 10,000 hours. It was used 1,800 hours in year 1; 2,000 in year 2; 2,500 in year 3; 1,500 in year 4; 1,200 in year 5; and 1,000 in year 6.

REQUIRED ▶
1. Compute the annual depreciation and carrying value for the new crane for each of the six years (round to nearest dollar where necessary) under each of the following methods: (a) straight-line, (b) production, and (c) double-declining-balance.
2. Prepare the adjusting entry that would be made each year to record the depreciation calculated under the straight-line method.
3. Show the balance sheet presentation for the crane after the adjusting entry in year 2 using the straight-line method.
4. What conclusions can you draw from the patterns of yearly depreciation and carrying value in 1?

P 8.
LO3 Depreciation Methods and
SO7 Partial Years

Sao Company operates three types of equipment. Because of the equipment's varied functions, company accounting policy requires the application of three different depreciation methods. Data on this equipment are summarized in the table that follows.

Equipment	Date Purchased	Cost	Installation Cost	Estimated Residual Value	Estimated Life	Depreciation Method
1	1/12/x4	$171,000	$ 9,000	$18,000	10 years	Double-declining-balance
2	7/9/x4	191,100	15,900	21,000	10 years	Straight-line
3	10/2/x4	290,700	8,100	33,600	20,000 hours	Production

Equipment 3 was used for 2,000 hours in 20x4; for 4,200 hours in 20x5; and for 3,200 hours in 20x6.

REQUIRED ▶ Assuming that the fiscal year ends December 31, compute the depreciation expense on each type of equipment and the total depreciation expense for 20x4, 20x5, and 20x6 by filling in a table with the headings shown below.

		Depreciation		
Equipment No.	Computations	20x4	20x5	20x6

SKILLS DEVELOPMENT CASES

Conceptual Analysis

SD 1.

LO1   Nature of Depreciation and
LO3   Amortization and Estimated
Useful Lives

A change in the estimated useful lives of long-term assets can have a significant effect. For instance, General Motors Corp. <www.gm.com> states,

> . . . the Corporation revised the estimated service lives of its plants and equipment and special tools retroactive to January 1, 1987. These revisions, which were based on 1987 studies of actual useful lives and periods of use, recognized current estimates of service lives of the assets and had the effect of reducing 1987 depreciation and amortization charges by $1,236.6 million or $2.53 per share of $1⅔ par value common stock.[23]

General Motors' income before income taxes for the year was $2,005.4 million. Discuss the purpose of depreciation and amortization. What is estimated service life, and on what basis did General Motors change the estimates of the service lives of plants and equipment and special tools? What was the effect of this change on the corporation's income before income taxes? Is it likely that the company is in better condition economically as a result of the change? Does the company have more cash at the end of the year as a result? (Ignore income tax effects.)

SD 2.

LO3   Change of Depreciation
Method

Several years ago, Polaroid Corporation <www.polaroid.com>, a manufacturer of instant cameras and film, changed from an accelerated depreciation method for financial reporting purposes to the straight-line method for newly acquired assets. As noted in its annual report:

> The company changed its method of depreciation for financial reporting for the cost of buildings, machinery, and equipment . . . from a primarily accelerated method to the straight-line method.[24]

What reasons can you give for Polaroid's choosing to switch to a straight-line method of depreciation? Discuss which of the two depreciation methods is more conservative. Polaroid's deteriorating financial position led it to declare bankruptcy in 2001. Could this accounting change have been a signal that the company was in trouble?

SD 3.

LO6   Brands

Hilton Hotels Corporation <www.hilton.com> and Marriott International <www.marriott.com> provide hospitality services. Hilton Hotels' well-known brands include Hilton, Doubletree, Hampton Inn, Embassy Suites, Red Lion Hotels and Inns, and Homewood Suites. Marriott also owns or manages properties with recognizable brand names, such as Marriott Hotels, Resorts and Suites; Ritz-Carlton; Renaissance Hotels; Residence Inn; Courtyard; and Fairfield Inn.

On its balance sheet, Hilton Hotels Corporation includes brands (net of amortization) of $1,048 million, or 11.3 percent of total assets. Marriott International, however, does not list brands among its intangible assets.[25] What principles of accounting for intangibles would cause Hilton to record brands as an asset while Marriott does not? How will these differences in accounting for brands generally affect the net income and return on assets of these two competitors?

Ethical Dilemma

SD 4.

LO2 Ethics and Allocation of Acquisition Costs

Signal Company has purchased land and a warehouse for $18,000,000. The warehouse is expected to last 20 years and to have a salvage value equal to 10 percent of its cost. The chief financial officer (CFO) and the controller are discussing the allocation of the purchase price. The CFO believes that the largest amount possible should be assigned to the land because this action will improve reported net income in the future. Depreciation expense will be lower because land is not depreciated. He suggests allocating one-third, or $6,000,000, of the cost to the land. This results in depreciation expense each year of $540,000 [($12,000,000 − $1,200,000) ÷ 20 years]. The controller disagrees, arguing that the smallest amount possible, say one-fifth of the purchase price, should be allocated to the land, thereby saving income taxes, since the depreciation, which is tax deductible, will be greater. Under this plan, annual depreciation would be $648,000 [($14,400,000 − $1,440,000) ÷ 20 years]. The annual tax savings at a 30 percent tax rate is $32,400 [($648,000 − $540,000) × .30]. How will this decision affect the company's cash flows? Ethically, how should the purchase cost be allocated? Who will be affected by the decision?

 Group Activity: Divide the class into groups and have each develop the position of the CFO or controller for presentation and debate.

SD 5.

LO2 Ethics of Aggressive
LO6 Accounting Policies

Is it ethical to choose aggressive accounting practices to advance a company's business? During the 1990s, America Online (AOL) <www.aol.com>, the largest Internet service provider in the United States, was one of the hottest stocks on Wall Street. After its initial stock offering in 1992, its stock price shot up several thousand percent. Accounting is very important to a company like AOL because earnings enable it to sell shares of stock and raise more cash to fund its growth. In its early years, AOL was one of the most aggressive companies in its choice of accounting principles. AOL's strategy called for building the largest customer base in the industry. Consequently, it spent many millions of dollars each year marketing its services to new customers. Such costs are usually recognized as operating expenses in the year in which they are incurred. However, AOL treated these costs as long-term assets, called "deferred subscriber acquisition costs," and expensed them over several years, because it said the average customer was going to stay with the company for three years or more. The company also recorded research and development costs as "product development costs" and amortized them over five years. Both of these practices are justifiable theoretically, but they are not common practice. If the standard, more conservative practice had been followed, the company would have had a net loss in every year it has been in business.[26] This result would have greatly limited AOL's ability to raise money and grow.

Explain in your own words AOL management's rationale for adopting the accounting policies that it did. What could go wrong with such a plan? How would you evaluate the ethics of AOL's actions? Who benefits from the actions? Who is harmed by these actions?

Research Activity

SD 6.

LO1 Individual Field Trip
LO2
LO3
LO6

Visit a fast-food restaurant. Make a list of all the intangible and property, plant, and equipment assets you can identify. For each one, identify one management issue that relates to that asset. In addition, give examples of at least one capital expenditure and one revenue expenditure that is applicable to property, plant, and equipment assets. Bring your list to class for discussion.

Decision-Making Practice

Morningside Machine Works has obtained a subcontract to manufacture parts for a new military aircraft. The parts are to be delivered over the next five years, and the company will be paid as the parts are delivered.

To make the parts, Morningside Machine Works will have to purchase new equipment. Two types are available. Type A is conventional equipment that can be put into service immediately; Type B requires one year to be put into service but is more efficient than Type A. Type A requires an immediate cash investment of $1,000,000 and will produce enough parts to provide net cash receipts of $340,000 each year for the five years. Type B may be purchased by signing a two-year non-interest-bearing note for $1,346,000. It is projected that Type B will produce net cash receipts of zero in year 1, $500,000 in year 2, $600,000 in year 3, $600,000 in year 4, and $200,000 in year 5. Neither type of equipment can be used on other contracts or will have any useful life remaining at the end of the contract. Morningside currently pays an interest rate of 16 percent to borrow money.

1. What is the present value of the investment required for each type of equipment? (Use Table 3 in the appendix on future value and present value tables.)
2. Compute the net present value of each type of equipment based on your answer in **1** and the present value of the net cash receipts projected to be received. (Use Tables 3 and 4 in the appendix on future value and present value tables.)
3. Write a memorandum to the board of directors that recommends the option that appears to be best for Morningside. Explain your reasoning and include **1** and **2** as attachments.

FINANCIAL REPORTING AND ANALYSIS CASES

Interpreting Financial Reports

Depreciation expense is a significant cost for companies in which plant assets are a high proportion of assets. The amount of depreciation expense in a given year is affected by estimates of useful life and choice of depreciation method. In 2004, Century Steelworks Company, a major integrated steel producer, changed the estimated useful lives for its major production assets. It also changed the method of depreciation for other steel-making assets from straight-line to the production method.

The company's 2004 annual report states, "A recent study conducted by management shows that actual years-in-service figures for our major production equipment and machinery are, in most cases, higher than the estimated useful lives assigned to these assets. We have recast the depreciable lives of such assets so that equipment previously assigned a useful life of 8 to 26 years now has an extended depreciable life of 10 to 32 years."

The report goes on to explain that the new production method of depreciation "recognizes that depreciation of production equipment and machinery correlates directly to both physical wear and tear and the passage of time. The production method of depreciation, which we have now initiated, more closely allocates the cost of these assets to the periods in which products are manufactured."

The report summarizes the effects of both actions on the year 2004 as shown in the following table:

Incremental Increase in Net Income	In Millions	Per Share
Lengthened lives	$11.0	$ .80
Production method		
Current year	7.3	.53
Prior years	2.8	.20
Total increase	$21.1	$1.53

During 2004, Century Steelworks reported a net loss of $83,156,500 ($6.03 per share). Depreciation expense for 2004 was $87,707,200.

In explaining the changes the company has made, the controller of Century Steelworks was quoted in an article in *Business Journal* as follows: "There is no reason for Century Steelworks to continue to depreciate our assets more conservatively than our competitors do." But the article also quotes an industry analyst who argues that by slowing its method of depreciation, Century Steelworks could be viewed as reporting lower-quality earnings.

1. Explain the accounting treatment when there is a change in the estimated lives of depreciable assets. What circumstances must exist for the production method to produce the effect it did in relation to the straight-line method? What would Century Steelworks' net income or loss have been if the changes had not been made? What might have motivated management to make the changes?
2. What does the controller of Century Steelworks mean when he says that Century had been depreciating "more conservatively than our competitors do"? Why might the changes at Century Steelworks indicate, as the analyst asserts, "lower-quality earnings"? What risks might Century face as a result of its decision to use the production method of depreciation?

International Company

FRA 2.
LO6   **Accounting for Goodwill: U.S. and IAS rules**

For most pharmaceutical companies, intangible assets, such as goodwill, patents, licenses, and trademarks, make up a significant percentage of total assets. For example, for Roche Group <www.roche.com>, intangible assets constitute 22.8 percent of total assets, and for Baxter International <www.baxter.com>, 14.2 percent.[27] For both companies, goodwill represents the largest portion of intangible assets.

Before 2000, Roche Group, a Swiss company, charged any goodwill resulting from acquisitions against equity immediately. However, in 2000, in accordance with a change in International Accounting Standards (IAS), Roche began recording goodwill as an asset and amortizing it over a period of up to 20 years. This IAS change brought U.S. and IAS companies into closer agreement on accounting for goodwill. At that time, companies like Baxter International, which comply with U.S. GAAP, recorded goodwill resulting from acquisitions as an asset and amortized it over periods not to exceed 40 years. However, as of 2002, U.S. companies, while continuing to record purchased goodwill as an asset, were no longer required to amortize any existing or new goodwill. Both IAS and U.S. GAAP require companies to apply the impairment test annually to ensure that goodwill is not overvalued.

What impact did accounting for goodwill under IAS and U.S. GAAP have on cash flows and net income in the year 2002? In your opinion, which accounting treatment for goodwill (U.S. or IAS) is better? State your reasons.

Toys "R" Us Annual Report

FRA 3.
LO1   **Long-Term Assets**
LO2
LO3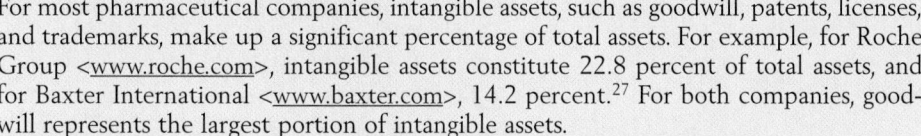
LO6

1. Refer to the balance sheets and to the note on property and equipment in the notes to the financial statements in the Toys "R" Us <www.tru.com> annual report to answer the following questions: What percentage of total assets in the most recent year was property and equipment? What is the most significant type of property and equipment? Does Toys "R" Us have a significant investment in land? What other kinds of things are included in the property and equipment category? (Ignore leased property under capital leases for now.)
2. Refer to the summary of significant accounting policies and to the note on property and equipment in the Toys "R" Us annual report. What method of depreciation does Toys "R" Us use? How long does management estimate its buildings to last as compared with furniture and equipment? What does this say about the company's need to remodel its stores?
3. Refer again to the note on property and equipment. What are leasehold improvements? How significant are leasehold improvements, and what are their effects on the earnings of the company?

Comparison Case: Toys "R" Us and Walgreen Co.

FRA 4.

LO1   **Long-Term Assets and Cash Flows**

Refer to the annual report of Toys "R" Us <www.tru.com> and to the financial statements of Walgreens <www.walgreens.com> in the Supplement to Chapter 6 to answer the following:

1. Prepare a table that shows the net amount each company spent on property and equipment (from the statement of cash flows), the total property and equipment (from the balance sheet), and the percentage of the first figure to the second for each of the past two years. Which company grew its property and equipment at a faster rate?

2. Which other note to the financial statements is helpful in evaluating the cash flows related to property and equipment? (**Hint:** In what way do Toys "R" Us and Walgreens gain use of property and equipment other than by purchase?) How important is this method of obtaining use of assets to these companies? Which company makes greater use of the method?

Fingraph® Financial Analyst™

FRA 5.

LO1   **Comparison of Long-Term**
LO3   **Assets**
LO5
LO6

Choose any two companies from the list of Fingraph companies on the Needles Accounting Resource Center Web Site at http://accounting.college.hmco.com/students. The industry should be one in which long-term assets are likely to be important, such as the airline, manufacturing, consumer products, consumer food and beverage, or computer industry. Access the Microsoft Excel spreadsheets for the companies you selected. For parts **1**, **3**, and **4**, click on the URL at the top of each company's spreadsheet for a link to the company's web site and annual report.

1. In the annual reports of the companies you have selected, read the long-term asset section of the balance sheet and any reference to long-term assets in the summary of significant accounting policies or notes to the financial statements. What are the most important long-term assets for each company? What depreciation methods do the companies use? Do any long-term assets appear to be characteristic of the industry? What intangible assets do the companies have, and how important are they?

2. Using the Fingraph CD-ROM software, display and print in tabular and graphic form the Balance Sheet Analysis page. Prepare a table that compares the gross and net amounts for property, plant, and equipment.

3. Locate the statements of cash flows in the two companies' annual reports. Prepare another table that compares depreciation (and amortization) expense from the operating activities section with the net purchases of property, plant, and equipment (net capital expenditures) from the investing activities section for two years. Does depreciation (and amortization) expense exceed replacement of long-term assets? Are the companies expanding or reducing their property, plant, and equipment?

4. Find and read references to long-term assets and capital expenditures in management's discussion and analysis in each annual report.

5. Write a one-page executive summary that highlights the most important long-term assets and the accounting policies for long-term assets, and that compares the investing activities of the two companies, including reference to management's assessment. Include the Fingraph page and your tables with your report.

Internet Case

FRA 6.

LO3   **SEC and Forms 10-K**
LO4
LO6

Public corporations are required not only to communicate with their stockholders by means of an annual report but also to submit an annual report to the Securities and Exchange Commission (SEC). The annual report to the SEC is called a Form 10-K and is a source of the latest information about a company. Through the Needles Accounting Resource Center Web Site at http://accounting.college.hmco.com/students, access the SEC's EDGAR files to locate either H. J. Heinz Company's <www.heinz.com> or Ford Motor Company's <www.ford.com> Form 10-K. Find the financial statements and the notes to the financial statements. Scan through the notes to the financial statements and prepare a list of information related to long-term assets, including intangibles. For instance, what depreciation methods does the company use? What are the useful lives of its property, plant, and equipment? What intangible assets does the company have? Does the company have goodwill? How much does the company spend on research and development? In the statement of cash flows, how much did the company spend on new property, plant, and equipment (capital expenditures)? Summarize your results and be prepared to discuss them as well as your experience in using the SEC's EDGAR database.

 Group Activity: Divide students into groups according to the company researched and have each group compile a comprehensive list of information about its company.

Chapter 12 presents the management issues associated with current liabilities and payroll accounting.

Current Liabilities

DECISION POINT

A USER'S FOCUS

US Airways, Inc. <www.usairways.com> Liabilities are one of the three major parts of the balance sheet. They are legal obligations for the future payment of assets or the future performance of services that result from past transactions. The current and long-term liabilities of US Airways, Inc., which has total assets of almost $8 billion, are shown in the Financial Highlights.[1] Current maturities of long-term debt; accounts payable; accrued aircraft rent; accrued salaries, wages, and vacation; and other accrued expenses will for the most part require an outlay of cash in the next year. Traffic balances payable will require payments to other airlines, but those may be partially offset by amounts owed by other airlines. Unused tickets are tickets already paid for by passengers and represent services that must be performed. Long-term debt will require cash outlays in future years. Altogether these liabilities represent over 75 percent of total assets. How does the decision of US Airways' management to incur so much debt relate to the goals of the business?

Liabilities are important because they are closely related to the goals of profitability and liquidity. Liabilities are sources of cash for operating and financing activities when they are incurred, but they are also obligations that use cash when they are paid. Achieving the appropriate level of liabilities is critical to business success. A company that has too few liabilities may not be earning up to its potential. A company that has too many liabilities, however, may be incurring excessive risks. In the case of US Airways, the company became vulnerable when there was a down-

What factors other than a downturn in air travel caused US Airways to file for bankruptcy?

turn in air travel as occurred in 2001–2002. Because of problems with liquidity, US Airways had to file for bankruptcy in 2002 in order to continue operating. This chapter focuses on the management and accounting issues involving current liabilities, including payroll liabilities and contingent liabilities.

Financial Highlights
(In millions)

Current Liabilities	2001	2000
Current maturities of long-term debt	$ 159	$ 284
Accounts payable	598	506
Traffic balances payable and unused tickets	817	890
Accrued aircraft rent	249	349
Accrued salaries, wages, and vacation	367	319
Other accrued expenses	742	475
Total current liabilities	$2,932	$2,823
Long-term debt, net of current maturities	$3,515	$2,688

MANAGEMENT ISSUES RELATED TO ACCOUNTING FOR CURRENT LIABILITIES

LO1 Identify the management issues related to recognition, valuation, classification, and disclosure of current liabilities.

RELATED TEXT ASSIGNMENTS
Q: 1, 2, 3, 4, 5
SE: 1, 2
E: 1, 2
P: 1
SD: 5
FRA: 1, 3, 4, 5, 6

The primary reason for incurring current liabilities is to meet needs for cash during the operating cycle. The proper identification and management of current liabilities requires an understanding of how these liabilities are recognized, valued, classified, and disclosed.

MANAGING LIQUIDITY AND CASH FLOWS

The operating cycle is the process of converting cash to purchases, to sales, to accounts receivable, and back to cash. Most current liabilities arise in support of this cycle, as when accounts payable arise from purchases of inventory, accrued expenses arise from operating costs, and unearned revenues arise from customers' advance payments. Short-term debt is used to raise cash during periods of inventory buildup or while waiting for collection of receivables. Cash is used to pay current maturities of long-term debt and to pay off liabilities arising from operations.

Failure to manage the cash flows related to current liabilities can have serious consequences for a business. For instance, if suppliers are not paid on time, they may withhold shipments that are vital to a company's operations. Continued failure to pay current liabilities can lead to bankruptcy. To evaluate a company's ability to pay its current liabilities, three measures of liquidity—working capital, the current ratio, and the quick ratio—are often used. Current liabilities are a key component of each of these measures. They typically equal from 25 to 50 percent of total assets.

www.usairways.com

As shown below (in millions of dollars), US Airways' short-term liquidity as measured by working capital was negative in 2000 and 2001:

	Current Assets	−	Current Liabilities	=	Working Capital
2001	$1,793	−	$2,932	=	($1,139)
2000	$2,571	−	$2,823	=	($ 252)

ENRICHMENT NOTE:
Unused tickets are often a significant liability for airlines and other service providers. The receipt of cash is usually incidental to revenue recognition.

This measure highlights the reason why US Airways faced a problem with short-term liquidity. It is common for airlines to have low or negative working capital because unearned ticket revenue is a current liability, but the cash from these ticket sales is quickly consumed in operations. On the assumption that only a small portion of unearned ticket revenues will be repaid to customers, unearned ticket revenue might be excluded from current liabilities for purposes of analysis. The healthiest airlines have positive working capital when unearned ticket revenue is excluded. However, for US Airways, the negative working capital of $1,139 million exceeded the traffic balances and unused tickets of $817 million in 2001.

Another consideration in managing liquidity and cash flows is the amount of time creditors are willing to give a company to pay its accounts payable. Common measures of this time are the **payables turnover** and the **average days' payable**. The payables turnover is the number of times, on average, that accounts payable are paid in an accounting period and shows the relative size of a company's accounts payable. The average days' payable shows how long, on average, a company takes to pay its accounts payables.

www.radioshack.com

For example, RadioShack Corporation, which operates more than 8,000 electronics stores, must carefully plan its purchases and payables. It had accounts payable of $312.6 million in 2002 and $206.7 million in 2001. Its purchases are determined by cost of goods sold adjusted for the change in inventory. An increase in inventory means purchases were more than cost of goods sold; a decrease in inventory means that purchases were less than cost of goods sold. RadioShack's cost of goods sold in 2002 was $2,338.9 million, and its inventory increased by $21.4 million.[2] Its payables turnover is computed as follows:

FIGURE 1
Payables Turnover for Selected Industries

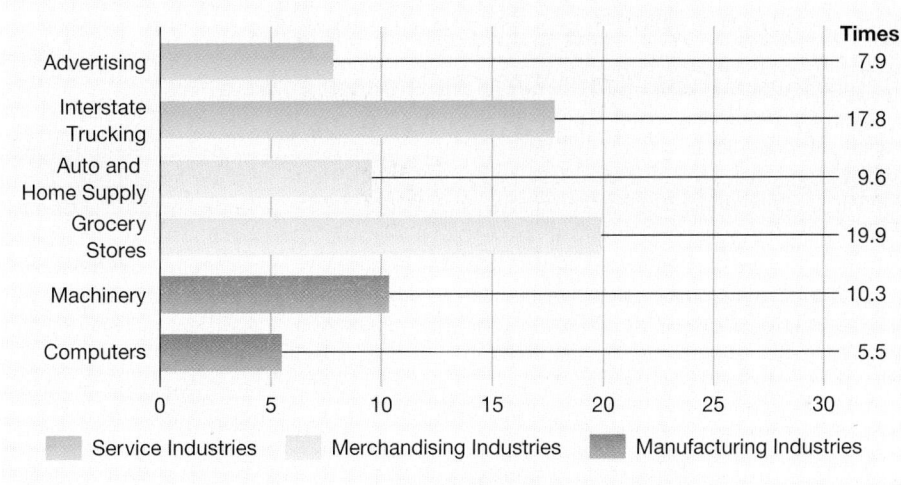

Source: Data from Dun & Bradstreet, *Industry Norms and Key Business Ratios,* 2001–2002.

● **STOP AND THINK!**
Is a decreasing payables turnover good or bad for a company?

Other things being equal, a decreasing payables turnover is good because it means the average days' payable is greater, thus allowing the company more time to pay its bills. The company will not have to borrow as much to finance its operating cycle of inventory turnover and receivables turnover. ■

$$\text{Payables Turnover} = \frac{\text{Cost of Goods Sold} \pm \text{Change in Merchandise Inventory}}{\text{Average Accounts Payable}}$$

$$= \frac{\$2,338.9 + \$21.4}{(\$312.6 + \$206.7) \div 2}$$

$$= \frac{\$2,360.3}{\$259.7} = 9.1 \text{ times}$$

To find the average days' payable, the number of days in a year is divided by the payables turnover:

$$\text{Average Days' Payable} = \frac{365 \text{ days}}{\text{Payables Turnover}} = \frac{365 \text{ days}}{9.1} = 40.1 \text{ days}$$

The payables turnover of 9.1 times and the resulting average days' payable of 40.1 days are consistent with customary 30-day credit terms.

Figures 1 and 2 show the payables turnover and average days' payable for various industries. To get a full picture of a company's operating cycle and liquidity position, these ratios should be considered in relation to the inventory turnover and the receivables turnover and their related days' ratios.

FIGURE 2
Average Days' Payable for Selected Industries

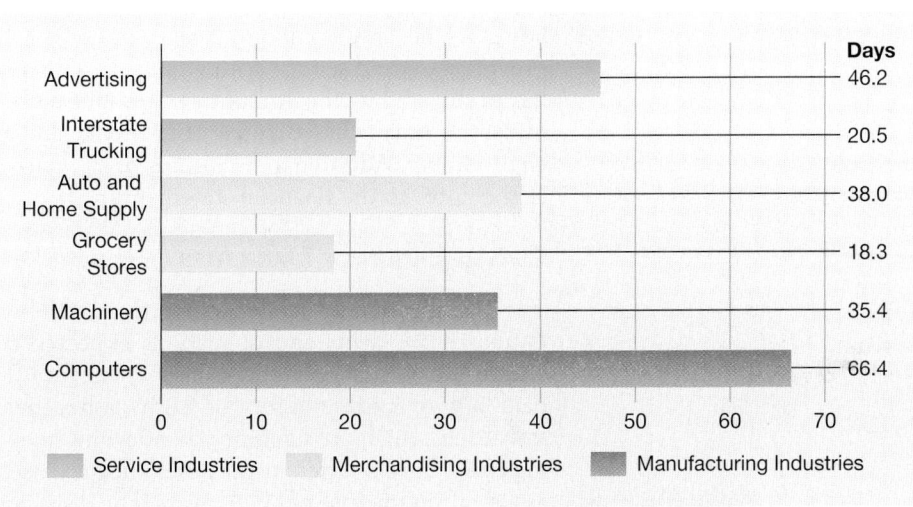

Source: Data from Dun & Bradstreet, *Industry Norms and Key Business Ratios,* 2001–2002.

FOCUS ON BUSINESS PRACTICE

Debt Problems Can Plague Even Well-Known Companies.

In a recent Wall Street horror story that illustrates the importance of managing current liabilities, Xerox Corporation <www.xerox.com>, one of the most storied names in American business, found itself combating rumors that it was facing bankruptcy. Following a statement by Xerox's CEO that the company's financial model was "unsustainable," management was forced to defend the company's liquidity by saying it had adequate funds to continue operations. But in a report filed with the SEC, management acknowledged that it had tapped into its $7 billion line of bank credit for more than $3 billion to pay off short-term debt that was coming due. Unable to secure more money from any other source to pay such debts, Xerox had no choice but to turn to the line of credit from its bank. Had it run out, the company might well have gone bankrupt.[3] Fortunately, Xerox was able to restructure its line of credit to stay in business, but it is still in a perilous position and may have to sell itself to another company to survive.

RECOGNITION OF LIABILITIES

Timing is important in the recognition of liabilities. Failure to record a liability in an accounting period very often goes along with failure to record an expense. The two errors lead to an understatement of expense and an overstatement of income.

A liability is recorded when an obligation occurs. This rule is harder to apply than it might appear. When a transaction obligates a company to make future payments, a liability arises and is recognized, as when goods are bought on credit. However, current liabilities often are not represented by direct transactions. One of the key reasons for making adjusting entries at the end of an accounting period is to recognize unrecorded liabilities. Among these accrued liabilities are salaries payable and interest payable. Other liabilities that can only be estimated, such as taxes payable, must also be recognized through adjusting entries.

On the other hand, companies often enter into agreements for future transactions. For instance, a company may agree to pay an executive $150,000 a year for a period of three years, or a public utility may agree to buy an unspecified quantity of coal at a certain price over the next five years. Such contracts, though they are definite commitments, are not considered liabilities because they are for future—not past—transactions. As there is no current obligation, no liability is recognized.

VALUATION OF LIABILITIES

On the balance sheet, a liability is generally valued at the amount of money needed to pay the debt or at the fair market value of goods or services to be delivered. For most liabilities, the amount is definitely known, but for some, it must be estimated. For example, an automobile dealer who sells a car with a one-year warranty must provide parts and service during the year. The obligation is definite because the sale has occurred, but the amount of the obligation can only be estimated. Such estimates are usually based on past experience and anticipated changes in the business environment. Additional disclosures of the fair value of liabilities may be required in the notes to the financial statements.

CLASSIFICATION OF LIABILITIES

The classification of liabilities directly matches the classification of assets. **Current liabilities** are debts and obligations expected to be satisfied within one year or within the normal operating cycle, whichever is longer. Such liabilities are normally paid out of current assets or with cash generated from operations. **Long-term liabilities**, which are liabilities due beyond one year or beyond the normal operating cycle, have a different purpose. They are used to finance long-term assets, such as aircraft in the case of US Airways. The distinction between current and long-term liabilities is important because it affects the evaluation of a company's liquidity.

www.usairways.com

DISCLOSURE OF LIABILITIES

To explain some accounts, supplemental disclosure in the notes to the financial statements may be required. For example, if a company has a large amount of notes payable, an explanatory note may disclose the balances, maturities, interest rates, and other features of the debts. Any special credit arrangements, such as issues of commercial paper and lines of credit, should also be disclosed. For example, Goodyear Tire & Rubber Company, which manufactures and sells tires, vehicle components, industrial rubber products, and rubber-related chemicals, disclosed its short-term debt arrangements in the notes to its financial statements, as follows:

www.goodyear.com

Short Term Debt and Financing Arrangements
At December 31, 2002, Goodyear had short term committed and uncommitted credit arrangements totaling $.97 billion, of which $.68 billion were unused. These arrangements are available to the Company or certain of its international subsidiaries through various domestic and international banks at quoted market interest rates. There are no commitment fees or compensating balances associated with these arrangements. Goodyear had outstanding debt obligations, which by their terms are due within one year, amounting to $653.2 million at December 31, 2002, compared to $364.7 million at December 31, 2001.[4]

This type of disclosure is helpful in assessing whether a company has additional borrowing power, because unused lines of credit allow a company to borrow on short notice, up to the agreed credit limit, with little or no negotiations.

 Check out ACE for a Review Quiz at http://accounting.college.hmco.com/students.

COMMON CATEGORIES OF CURRENT LIABILITIES

LO2 Identify, compute, and record definitely determinable and estimated current liabilities.

RELATED TEXT ASSIGNMENTS
Q: 6, 7, 8, 9, 10, 11, 12, 13, 14, 15, 16
SE: 3, 4, 5, 6, 7, 8
E: 3, 4, 5, 6, 7, 8
P: 1, 2, 3, 4, 6, 7, 8
SD: 1, 2, 3, 4, 5
FRA: 3, 6

Current liabilities fall into two major groups: (1) definitely determinable liabilities and (2) estimated liabilities.

DEFINITELY DETERMINABLE LIABILITIES

Current liabilities that are set by contract or by statute and can be measured exactly are called **definitely determinable liabilities**. The related accounting problems are to determine the existence and amount of each such liability and to see that it is recorded properly. Definitely determinable liabilities include accounts payable, bank loans and commercial paper, notes payable, accrued liabilities, dividends payable, sales and excise taxes payable, current portions of long-term debt, payroll liabilities, and unearned revenues.

■ **ACCOUNTS PAYABLE** Accounts payable, sometimes called *trade accounts payable*, are short-term obligations to suppliers for goods and services. The amount in the Accounts Payable account is generally supported by an accounts payable subsidiary ledger, which contains an individual account for each person or company to which money is owed.

www.usairways.com

■ **BANK LOANS AND COMMERCIAL PAPER** Management often establishes a **line of credit** with a bank; this arrangement allows the company to borrow funds when they are needed to finance current operations. For example, US Airways states in a note to its financial statements that "the Company has in place a $190 million 364-day secured revolving credit facility and a $250 million three-year secured revolving credit facility to provide liquidity for its operations."[5] Although a promissory note for the full amount of the line of credit is signed when the credit is granted, the company has great flexibility in using the available funds. The company can increase its borrowing up to the limit when it needs cash and reduce the amount borrowed when it generates enough cash of its own. Both the amount borrowed and the interest rate charged by the bank may change daily. The bank may require the company to meet certain financial goals (such as maintaining specific profit margins, current ratios, or debt to equity ratios) to retain the line of credit.

CLARIFICATION NOTE:
Only the used portion of the line of credit is recognized as a liability in the financial statements.

Companies with excellent credit ratings may borrow short-term funds by issuing **commercial paper**, unsecured loans that are sold to the public, usually through professionally managed investment firms. The portion of a line of credit currently borrowed and the amount of commercial paper issued are usually combined with notes payable in the current liabilities section of the balance sheet. Details are disclosed in a note to the financial statements.

■ **Notes Payable**   Short-term notes payable are obligations represented by promissory notes. These notes may be used to secure bank loans, to pay suppliers for goods and services, and to secure credit from other sources.

The interest may be stated separately on the face of the note (Case 1 in Figure 3), or it may be deducted in advance by discounting it from the face value of the note (Case 2 in Figure 3). The entries to record the note in each case are as follows:

	Case 1—Interest Stated Separately			Case 2—Interest in Face Amount		
Case 1						
A = L + OE	Aug. 31 Cash	5,000		Aug. 31 Cash	4,900	
+ +	Notes Payable		5,000	Discount on Notes Payable	100	
Case 2	Issued 60-day,			Notes Payable		5,000
A = L + OE	12% promissory			Issued 60-day		
+ −	note with interest			promissory note with		
+	stated separately			$100 interest included		
				in face amount		

CLARIFICATION NOTE:
The effective interest rate on the loan in Case 2 is 12.24% ($100/$4,900 × 360/60). For ease of computation, 360 days are used to compute interest on notes.

Note that in Case 1 the money received equaled the face value of the note, whereas in Case 2 the money received ($4,900) was less than the face value ($5,000) of the note. The amount of the discount equals the amount of the interest for 60 days. Although the dollar amount of interest on each of these notes is the same, the effective interest rate is slightly higher in Case 2 because the amount

FIGURE 3
Two Promissory Notes: One with Interest Stated Separately; One with Interest in Face Amount

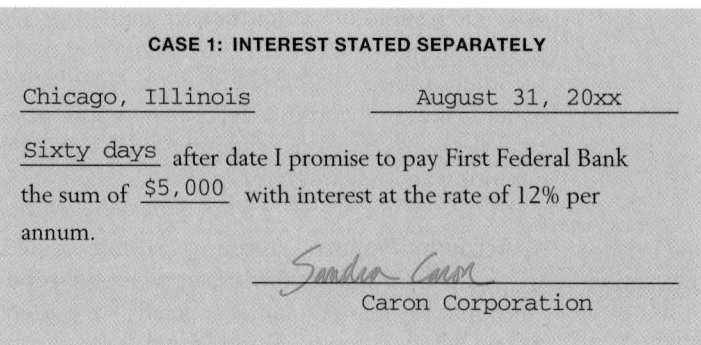

CASE 1: INTEREST STATED SEPARATELY

Chicago, Illinois   August 31, 20xx

Sixty days after date I promise to pay First Federal Bank the sum of $5,000 with interest at the rate of 12% per annum.

             Sandra Caron
             Caron Corporation

CASE 2: INTEREST IN FACE AMOUNT

Chicago, Illinois   August 31, 20xx

Sixty days after date I promise to pay First Federal Bank the sum of $5,000.

             Sandra Caron
             Caron Corporation

received is slightly less ($4,900 in Case 2 versus $5,000 in Case 1). Discount on Notes Payable is a contra account to Notes Payable and is deducted from Notes Payable on the balance sheet.

On October 30, when the note is paid, each alternative is recorded as follows:

Case 1—Interest Stated Separately

Case 1
A = L + OE
−   −   −

Case 2
A = L + OE
−   −

A = L + OE
+   −

Oct. 30	Notes Payable	5,000	
	Interest Expense	100	
	Cash		5,100
	Payment of note with interest stated separately		

$$\$5,000 \times .12 \times \frac{60}{360} = \$100$$

Case 2—Interest in Face Amount

Oct. 30	Notes Payable	5,000	
	Cash		5,000
	Payment of note with interest included in face amount		
30	Interest Expense	100	
	Discount on Notes Payable		100
	Interest expense on note payable		

■ **ACCRUED LIABILITIES** A key reason for making adjusting entries at the end of an accounting period is to recognize and record any liabilities that are not already in the accounting records. This practice applies to any type of liability. As you will see, accrued liabilities can include estimated liabilities.

Here the focus is on interest payable, a definitely determinable liability. Interest accrues daily on interest-bearing notes. At the end of the accounting period, an adjusting entry should be made in accordance with the matching rule to record the interest obligation up to that point. Let us again use the example of the two notes presented in Figure 3. If we assume that the accounting period ends on September 30, or 30 days after the issuance of the 60-day notes, the adjusting entries for each case would be as follows:

Case 1—Interest Stated Separately

Case 1
A = L + OE
+   −

Case 2
A = L + OE
+   −

Sept. 30	Interest Expense	50	
	Interest Payable		50
	To record interest expense for 30 days on note with interest stated separately		

$$\$5,000 \times .12 \times \frac{30}{360} = \$50$$

Case 2—Interest in Face Amount

Sept. 30	Interest Expense	50	
	Discount on Notes Payable		50
	To record interest expense for 30 days on note with interest included in face amount		

$$\$100 \times \frac{30}{60} = \$50$$

KEY POINT: Both of these entries have exactly the same impact on the financial statements.

In Case 2, Discount on Notes Payable will now have a debit balance of $50, which will become interest expense during the next 30 days.

■ **DIVIDENDS PAYABLE** Cash dividends are a distribution of earnings by a corporation. The payment of dividends is solely the decision of the corporation's board of directors. A liability does not exist until the board declares the dividends. There is usually a short time between the date of declaration and the date of payment of dividends. During that short time, the dividends declared are considered current liabilities of the corporation.

■ **SALES AND EXCISE TAXES PAYABLE** Most states and many cities levy a sales tax on retail transactions. There is a federal excise tax on some products, such as automobile tires. A merchant who sells goods subject to these taxes must collect the taxes and forward them periodically to the appropriate government agency. The amount of tax collected represents a current liability until it is remitted to the government. For example, assume that a merchant makes a $100 sale that is subject to a 5 percent sales tax and a 10 percent excise tax. Assuming that the sale takes place on June 1, the entry to record the sale is as follows:

A = L + OE
+   +   +
        +

	June 1	Cash	115	
		Sales		100
		Sales Tax Payable		5
		Excise Tax Payable		10
		Sales of merchandise and collection		
		of sales and excise tax		

The sale is properly recorded at $100, and the taxes collected are recorded as liabilities to be remitted at the proper times to the appropriate government agencies.

■ **CURRENT PORTIONS OF LONG-TERM DEBT**   If a portion of long-term debt is due within the next year and is to be paid from current assets, then that current portion is properly classified as a current liability. For example, suppose that a $500,000 debt is to be paid in installments of $100,000 per year for the next five years. The $100,000 installment due in the current year should be classified as a current liability. The remaining $400,000 should be classified as a long-term liability. Note that no journal entry is necessary. The total debt of $500,000 is simply reclassified when the financial statements are prepared, as follows:

Current liabilities

    Current portion of long-term debt $100,000

Long-term liabilities

    Long-term debt   400,000

■ **PAYROLL LIABILITIES**   For most organizations, the cost of labor and related payroll taxes is a major expense. In some industries, such as banking and airlines, payroll costs represent more than half of all operating costs. Payroll accounting is important because complex laws and significant liabilities are involved. The employer is liable to employees for wages and salaries and to various agencies for amounts withheld from wages and salaries and for related taxes. The term **wages** refers to payment for the services of employees at an hourly rate. The term **salaries** refers to the compensation of employees who are paid at a monthly or yearly rate.

Because payroll accounting applies only to the employees of an organization, it is important to distinguish between employees and independent contractors. Employees are paid a wage or salary by the organization and are under its direct supervision and control. Independent contractors are not employees of the organization, so they are not accounted for under the payroll system. They offer services to the organization for a fee, but they are not under its direct control or supervision. Certified public accountants, advertising agencies, and lawyers, for example, may act as independent contractors.

Figure 4 provides an illustration of payroll liabilities and their relationship to employee earnings and employer taxes and other costs. Two important observations may be made. First, the amount payable to employees is less than the amount of earnings. This occurs because employers are required by law or are requested by employees to withhold certain amounts from wages and send them directly to government agencies or other organizations. Second, the total employer liabilities exceed employee earnings because the employer must pay additional taxes and make other contributions, such as for pensions and medical care, that increase the cost and liabilities. The most common withholdings, taxes, and other payroll costs are described next.

FOCUS ON BUSINESS PRACTICE

Small Businesses Offer Benefits, Too.

A survey of small businesses in the Midwest shows the percentages of respondents that offer the following benefits:[6]

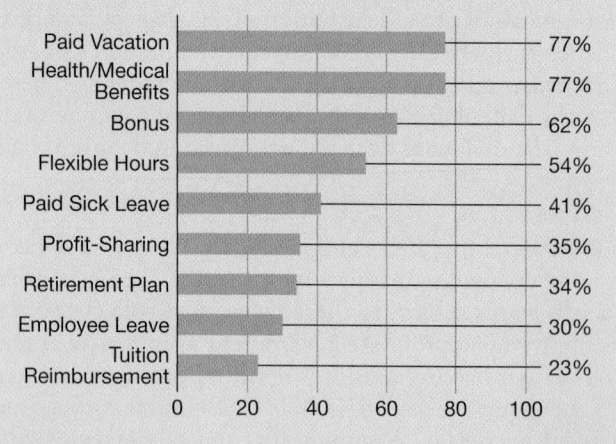

FIGURE 4
Illustration of Payroll Liabilities

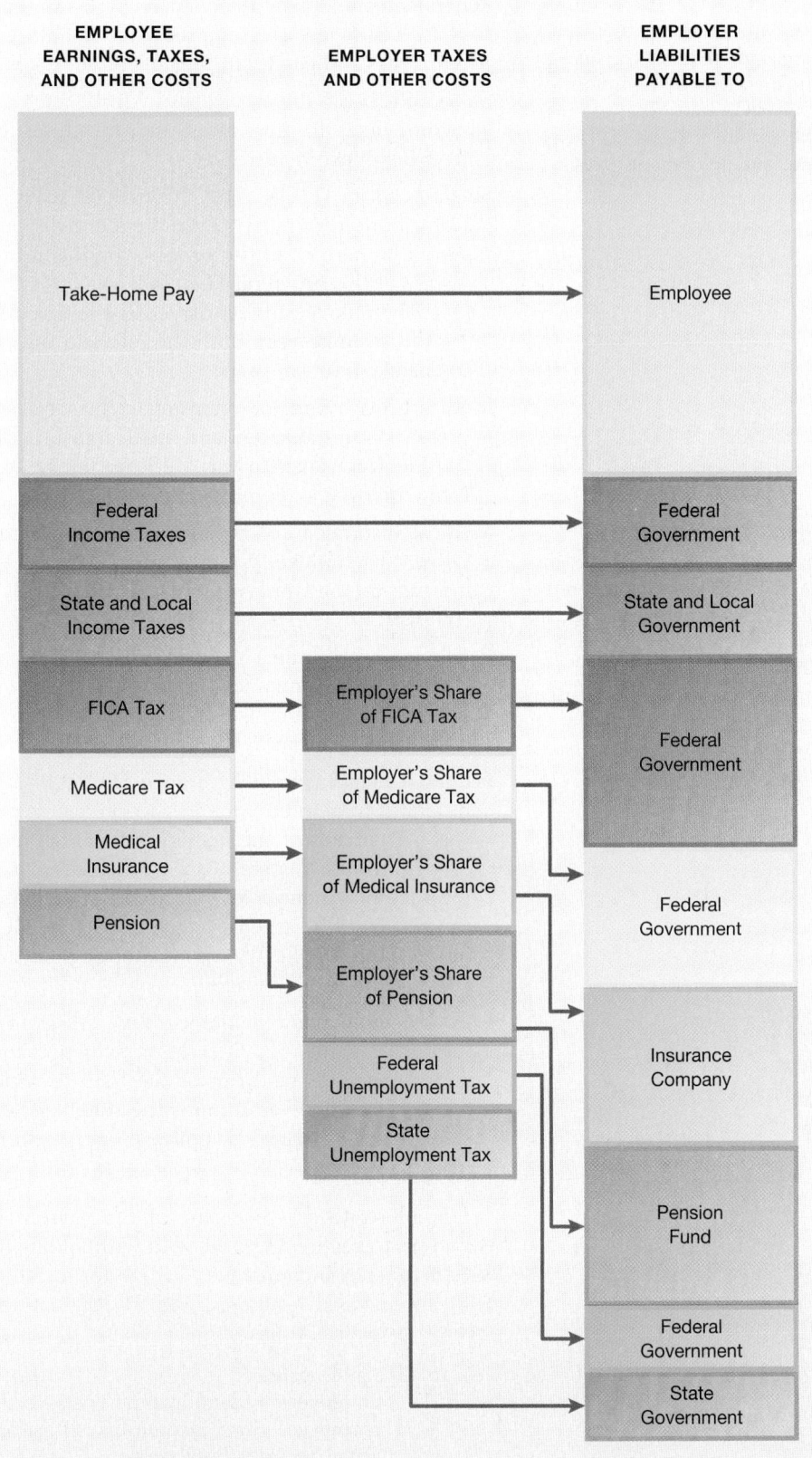

Federal Income Taxes   Federal income taxes are collected on a "pay as you go" basis. Employers are required to withhold appropriate taxes from employees' paychecks and pay them to the United States Treasury.

State and Local Income Taxes   Most states and some local governments have income taxes. In most cases, the procedures for withholding are similar to those for federal income taxes.

Social Security (FICA) Tax   The social security program (the Federal Insurance Contribution Act) offers retirement and disability benefits and survivor's benefits. About 90 percent of the people working in the United States fall under the provisions of this program. The 2003 social security tax rate of 6.2 percent was paid by *both* employee and employer on the first $87,000 earned by an employee during the calendar year. Both the rate and the base to which it applies are subject to change in future years.

Medicare Tax   A major extension of the social security program is Medicare, which provides hospitalization and medical insurance for persons over age 65. In 2003, the Medicare tax rate was 1.45 percent of gross income, with no limit, paid by *both* employee and employer.

Medical Insurance   Many organizations provide medical benefits to employees. Often, the employee contributes a portion of the cost through withholdings from income and the employer pays the rest, usually a greater amount, to the insurance company.

Pension Contributions   Many organizations also provide pension benefits to employees. In a manner similar to that for medical insurance, a portion of the pension contribution is withheld from the employee's income and the rest is paid by the organization to the pension fund.

Federal Unemployment Insurance (FUTA) Tax   This tax is intended to pay for programs to help unemployed workers. It is paid *only* by employers and recently was 6.2 percent of the first $7,000 earned by each employee (this amount may vary from state to state). Against this federal tax, the employer is allowed a credit for unemployment taxes paid to the state. The maximum credit is 5.4 percent of the first $7,000 earned by each employee. Most states set their rate at this maximum. Thus, the FUTA tax most often paid is .8 percent (6.2 percent − 5.4 percent) of the taxable wages.

State Unemployment Insurance Tax   All state unemployment programs provide for unemployment compensation to be paid to eligible unemployed workers. This compensation is paid out of the fund provided by the 5.4 percent of the first $7,000 (or whatever amount the state sets) earned by each employee. In some states, employers with favorable employment records may be entitled to pay less than 5.4 percent.

To illustrate the recording of the payroll, assume that on February 15 total employee wages are $32,500, with withholdings of $5,400 for federal income taxes, $1,200 for state income taxes, $2,015 for social security tax, $471 for Medicare tax, $900 for medical insurance, and $1,300 for pension contributions. The entry to record this payroll follows:

A = L + OE				
+	Feb. 15	Wages Expense	32,500	
+		Employees' Federal Income Taxes Payable		5,400
+		Employees' State Income Taxes Payable		1,200
+		Social Security Tax Payable		2,015
+		Medicare Tax Payable		471
+		Medical Insurance Premiums Payable		900
+		Pension Contributions Payable		1,300
		Wages Payable		21,214
		To record payroll		

Note that the employees' take-home pay is $21,214, although $32,500 was earned.

Using the same data, the additional employer taxes and other benefits costs would be recorded as follows, assuming that the payroll taxes correspond to the discussion above and that the employer pays 80 percent of the medical insurance premiums and half of the pension contributions:

A = L + OE
   +   –
   +
   +
   +
   +
   +

Feb. 15	Payroll Taxes and Benefits Expense	9,401	
	Social Security Tax Payable		2,015
	Medicare Tax Payable		471
	Medical Insurance Premiums Payable		3,600
	Pension Contributions Payable		1,300
	Federal Unemployment Tax Payable		260
	State Unemployment Tax Payable		1,755
	To record payroll taxes and other costs		

Note that the payroll taxes and benefits increase the total cost of the payroll to $41,901 ($9,401 + $32,500), which exceeds by almost 29 percent the amount earned by employees. This is a typical situation.

■ **UNEARNED REVENUES**   Unearned revenues represent obligations for goods or services that the company must provide in a future accounting period in return for an advance payment from a customer. For example, a publisher of a monthly magazine who receives annual subscriptions totaling $240 would make the following entry:

A = L + OE
+ +

Cash	240	
Unearned Subscriptions		240
Receipt of annual subscriptions in advance		

The publisher now has a liability of $240 that will be reduced gradually as monthly issues of the magazine are mailed:

A = L + OE
– +

Unearned Subscriptions	20	
Subscription Revenues		20
Delivery of monthly magazine issues		

Many businesses, such as repair companies, construction companies, and special-order firms, ask for a deposit or advance from a customer before they will begin work. Such advances are also current liabilities until the goods or services are actually delivered.

ESTIMATED LIABILITIES

KEY POINT: Estimated liabilities are recorded and presented on the financial statements in the same way as definitely determinable liabilities. The only difference is that estimated liabilities involve some uncertainty in their computation.

Estimated liabilities are definite debts or obligations whose exact dollar amount cannot be known until a later date. Since there is no doubt about the existence of the legal obligation, the primary accounting problem is to estimate and record the amount of the liability. Examples of estimated liabilities are income taxes, property taxes, product warranties, and vacation pay.

■ **INCOME TAXES**   The income of a corporation is taxed by the federal government, most state governments, and some cities and towns. The amount of income taxes liability depends on the results of operations. Often the results are not known until after the end of the year. However, because income taxes are an expense in the year in which income is earned, an adjusting entry is necessary to record the estimated tax liability. The entry is as follows:

A = L + OE
   +   –

Dec. 31	Income Taxes Expense	53,000	
	Estimated Income Taxes Payable		53,000
	To record estimated federal income taxes		

Sole proprietorships and partnerships do *not* pay income taxes. Their owners must report their share of the firm's income on their individual tax returns.

ENRICHMENT NOTE: The process of accruing property tax each month could be applied to income taxes if a company desires monthly financial statements.

■ **PROPERTY TAX PAYABLE**   Property taxes are levied on real property, such as land and buildings, and on personal property, such as inventory and equipment. Property taxes are a main source of revenue for local governments. They are usually assessed annually against the real and personal property involved. Because the fiscal years of local governments and their assessment dates rarely correspond to a company's fiscal year, it is necessary to estimate the amount of property tax that applies to each month of the year.

KEY POINT: Recording product warranty expense in the year of the sale follows the matching rule.

■ **PRODUCT WARRANTY LIABILITY**   When a firm places a warranty on its product (or its service) at the time of sale, a liability exists for the length of the warranty. The cost of the warranty is properly debited to an expense account in the period of sale because it is a feature of the product sold and thus is included in the price the customer pays for the product. On the basis of experience, it should be possible to estimate the amount the warranty will cost in the future. Some products will require little warranty service; others may require much. Thus, there will be an average cost per product.

For example, assume a muffler company guarantees that it will replace free of charge any muffler it sells that fails during the time the buyer owns the car. The company charges a small service fee for replacing the muffler. This warranty is an important selling feature for the firm's mufflers. In the past, 6 percent of the mufflers sold have been returned for replacement under the warranty. The average cost of a muffler is $50. Assume that during July, the company sold 350 mufflers. The accrued liability would be recorded as an adjustment at the end of July as shown below:

A = L + OE
    +   −

July 31	Product Warranty Expense	1,050	
	Estimated Product Warranty Liability		1,050
	To record estimated product warranty expense:		
	Number of units sold	350	
	Rate of replacement under warranty	× .06	
	Estimated units to be replaced	21	
	Estimated cost per unit	× $ 50	
	Estimated liability for product warranty	$1,050	

When a muffler is returned for replacement under the warranty, the cost of the muffler is charged against the Estimated Product Warranty Liability account. For example, assume that on December 5, a customer returns with a defective muffler

FOCUS ON BUSINESS PRACTICE

Those Little Coupons Can Add Up.

Many companies promote their products by issuing coupons that offer "cents off" or other enticements. Since four out of five shoppers use coupons, companies are forced by competition to distribute them. The total value of unredeemed coupons, each of which represents a potential liability for the issuing company, is truly staggering. NCH Promotional Services <www.wattsgroup.com>, a company owned by Dun & Bradstreet, estimates that almost 300 billion coupons are issued annually. Of course, the liability depends on how many of the coupons will actually be redeemed. NCH estimates that number at approximately 6 billion, or about 2 percent. Thus, a big advertiser that puts a cents-off coupon in Sunday papers to reach 60 million people can be faced with liability for 1,200,000 coupons. The total value of coupons redeemed each year is estimated at more than $4 billion.[7]

FOCUS ON BUSINESS PRACTICE

Are Frequent-Flier Miles a Liability or a Revenue?

In the early 1980s, American Airlines, Inc. <www.aa.com> developed a frequent-flier program that gives free trips and other awards to customers based on the number of miles they fly on the airline. Since then, many other airlines have instituted similar programs, and it is estimated that 38 million people now participate in them. Today, U.S. airlines have more than 3 trillion "miles" outstanding. Seven to eight percent of all passengers are traveling on free tickets. Estimated liabilities for these tickets have become an important consideration

in evaluating an airline's financial position. Complicating the estimate is that almost half the miles have been earned on purchases from hotels, car rental and telephone companies, and Internet service providers like AOL, and through the use of credit cards. In these cases, the companies giving the miles must pay the airlines at the rate of $.02 per mile. Thus, a free ticket obtained with 25,000 miles provides revenue to the airline of $500. In a recent year, airlines took in more than $2 billion from this source.[8]

and pays a $20 service fee to have the muffler replaced. Assume that this particular muffler cost $40. The entry is as follows:

A = L + OE
\+ – +
  –

	Dec. 5	Cash	20	
		Estimated Product Warranty Liability	40	
		Service Revenue		20
		Merchandise Inventory		40
		Replacement of muffler under warranty		

● **STOP AND THINK!**

Do adjusting entries involving estimated liabilities and accruals ever affect cash flows?

They never affect cash flows at the time of the entry, but they may require the payment of a liability in the future. ■

www.usairways.com

■ **VACATION PAY LIABILITY**   In most companies, employees accrue paid vacation as they work during the year. For example, an employee may earn two weeks of paid vacation for each 50 weeks of work. Therefore, the person is paid 52 weeks' salary for 50 weeks' work. Theoretically, the cost of the two weeks' vacation should be allocated as an expense over the whole year so that month-to-month costs will not be distorted. The vacation pay represents 4 percent (two weeks' vacation divided by 50 weeks) of a worker's pay. Every week worked earns the employee a small fraction (4 percent) of vacation pay.

Vacation pay liability can represent a substantial amount of money. As noted in this chapter's Decision Point, US Airways reported at its 2001 year end accrued salaries, wages, and vacation liabilities of $367 million.

Suppose that a company with a vacation policy of two weeks of paid vacation for each 50 weeks of work has a payroll of $21,000, of which $1,000 was paid to employees on vacation for the week ended April 20. Because of turnover and rules regarding term of employment, it is assumed that only 75 percent of employees will ultimately collect vacation pay. The computation of vacation pay expense based on the payroll of employees not on vacation ($21,000 − $1,000) is as follows: $20,000 × 4 percent × 75 percent = $600. The entry to record vacation pay expense for the week ended April 20 is as follows:

A = L + OE
\+ –

	Apr. 20	Vacation Pay Expense	600	
		Estimated Liability for Vacation Pay		600
		Estimated vacation pay expense		

At the time employees receive their vacation pay, an entry is made debiting Estimated Liability for Vacation Pay and crediting Cash or Wages Payable. This entry records the $1,000 paid to employees on vacation during August:

A* = L + OE
  – –
*Assumes cash paid.

	Aug. 31	Estimated Liability for Vacation Pay	1,000	
		Cash (or Wages Payable)		1,000
		Wages of employees on vacation		

The treatment of vacation pay presented in this example may also be applied to other payroll costs, such as bonus plans and contributions to pension plans.

 Check out ACE for a Review Quiz at http://accounting.college.hmco.com/students.

CONTINGENT LIABILITIES AND COMMITMENTS

LO3   Distinguish *contingent liabilities* from *commitments.*

RELATED TEXT ASSIGNMENTS
Q: 17, 18
SE: 3
SD: 2, 4
FRA: 2, 3, 5, 6, 7

KEY POINT: Contingencies are recorded when they are probable and can be reasonably estimated.

www.gm.com

The FASB requires companies to disclose in a note to their financial statements any contingent liabilities and commitments they may have. A **contingent liability** is not an existing obligation. Rather, it is a potential liability because it depends on a future event arising out of a past transaction. For instance, a construction company that built a bridge may have been sued by the state for using poor materials. The past transaction is the building of the bridge under contract. The future event is the outcome of the lawsuit, which is not yet known.

The FASB has established two conditions for determining when a contingency should be entered in the accounting records: (1) the liability must be probable, and (2) it can be reasonably estimated.[9] Estimated liabilities like the income taxes liability, warranty liability, and vacation pay liability that we described earlier meet those conditions. Therefore, they are accrued in the accounting records.

In a survey of 600 large companies, the most common types of contingencies reported were litigation, which can involve many different issues, and environmental concerns.[10] The notes in an annual report of General Motors Corporation, the world's largest automobile maker, describe contingent liabilities as follows:

> Litigation is subject to uncertainties and the outcome of individual litigated matters is not predictable with assurance. Various legal actions, governmental investigations, claims, and proceedings are pending against the Corporation, including those arising out of alleged product defects; employment-related matters; governmental regulations relating to safety, emissions, and fuel economy; product warranties; financial services; dealer, supplier, and other contractual relationships and environmental matters. . . . After discussion with counsel, it is the opinion of management that such liability is not expected to have a material adverse effect on the Corporation's consolidated financial condition or results of operations.[11]

⬟ Stop and Think!
When would a commitment be recognized in the records?
When a transaction has occurred, such as when a purchase agreement is followed up and completed or when a lease payment is made. ■

www.usairways.com

A **commitment** is a legal obligation that does not meet the technical requirements for recognition as a liability. The most common examples are purchase agreements and leases.[12] For example, in a note to its financial statements, US Airways states: "The Company had 65 A320 aircraft on firm order, 182 aircraft subject to reconfirmation prior to scheduled delivery, and options for 63 additional aircraft." The note goes on to say, "The company leases certain aircraft and ground equipment, in addition to the majority of the ground facilities."[13] It then summarizes the amounts of the lease obligations.

 Check out ACE for a Review Quiz at http://accounting.college.hmco.com/students.

PAYROLL ACCOUNTING ILLUSTRATED

SO4   Compute and record the liabilities associated with payroll accounting.

RELATED TEXT ASSIGNMENTS
Q: 19, 20, 21
SE: 9, 10
E: 9, 10, 11
P: 5
SD: 5

Earlier in this chapter, the liabilities associated with payroll accounting were identified and discussed. This section will focus on the calculations, records, and control requirements of payroll accounting. To demonstrate the concepts, the illustrations are shown in manual format, but, in actual practice, most businesses (including small businesses) use a computer to process payroll.

COMPUTATION OF AN EMPLOYEE'S TAKE-HOME PAY

Besides setting minimum wage levels, the federal Fair Labor Standards Act (also called the Wages and Hours Law) regulates overtime pay. Employers who take part in interstate commerce must pay overtime to employees who work beyond 40 hours a week or more than eight hours a day. This pay must be at least one and one-half times the regular rate. Work on Saturdays, Sundays, or holidays may also call for overtime pay or some sort of premium pay under separate wage agreements. Overtime pay under union or other employment contracts may exceed these minimums.

For example, suppose that the employment contract of Robert Jones calls for a regular wage of $8 an hour, one and one-half times the regular rate for work over eight hours in any weekday, and twice the regular rate for work on Saturdays, Sundays, or holidays. He works the following days and hours during the week of January 18, 20xx:

Day	Total Hours Worked	Regular Time	Overtime
Monday	10	8	2
Tuesday	8	8	0
Wednesday	8	8	0
Thursday	9	8	1
Friday	10	8	2
Saturday	2	0	2
	47	40	7

Jones's wages would be calculated as follows:

Regular time	40 hours $\times$ $8	$320
Overtime, weekdays	5 hours $\times$ $8 $\times$ 1.5	60
Overtime, weekend	2 hours $\times$ $8 $\times$ 2	32
Total wages		$412

Once Jones's wages are known, his take-home pay can be calculated. Since his total earnings for the week of January 18 are $412.00, his social security tax is 6.2 percent, or $25.54 (he has not earned over $87,000), and his Medicare tax is 1.45 percent, or $5.97. The amount to be withheld for federal income taxes depends in part on Jones's earnings and in part on the number of his exemptions. All employees are required by law to indicate exemptions by filing a Form W-4 (Employee's Withholding Exemption Certificate). Every employee is entitled to one exemption for himself or herself and one for each dependent.

Based on the information in Form W-4, the amount of withholding is determined by referring to a withholding table provided by the Internal Revenue Service. For example, the withholding table in Figure 5 shows that for Jones, a married employee who has a total of four exemptions and is paid weekly, the withholding on total wages of $412 is $31. Actual withholding tables change periodically to reflect changes in tax rates and tax laws. Assume also that Jones's union dues are $2.00, his medical insurance premiums are $7.60, his life insurance premium is $6.00, he places $15.00 per week in savings bonds, and he contributes $1.00 per week to United Charities. Jones's net (take-home) pay can now be computed:

KEY POINT: The expense to the company is the gross earnings, not the net take-home pay.

Total earnings		$412.00
Deductions		
Federal income taxes withheld	$31.00	
Social security tax	25.54	
Medicare tax	5.97	
Union dues	2.00	
Medical insurance	7.60	
Life insurance	6.00	
Savings bonds	15.00	
United Charities contribution	1.00	
Total deductions		94.11
Net (take-home) pay		$317.89

FIGURE 5
Sample Withholding Table

WEEKLY PAYROLL PERIOD — EMPLOYEE MARRIED												
		And the number of withholding allowances claimed is —										
And the wages are —		0	1	2	3	4	5	6	7	8	9	10 or more
At least	But less than	The amount of income tax to be withheld will be —										
$300	$310	$37	$31	$26	$20	$14	$ 9	$ 3	$ 0	$ 0	$0	$0
310	320	38	33	27	22	16	10	5	0	0	0	0
320	330	40	34	29	23	17	12	6	1	0	0	0
330	340	41	36	30	25	19	13	8	2	0	0	0
340	350	43	37	32	26	20	15	9	4	0	0	0
350	360	44	39	33	28	22	16	11	5	0	0	0
360	370	46	40	35	29	23	18	12	7	1	0	0
370	380	47	42	36	31	25	19	14	8	2	0	0
380	390	49	43	38	32	26	21	15	10	4	0	0
390	400	50	45	39	34	28	22	17	11	5	0	0
400	410	52	46	41	35	29	24	18	13	7	1	0
410	420	53	48	42	37	31	25	20	14	8	3	0
420	430	55	49	44	38	32	27	21	16	10	4	0

PAYROLL REGISTER

The **payroll register**, which is prepared each pay period, is a detailed listing of the firm's total payroll. A payroll register is presented in Exhibit 1. Note that the name, hours, earnings, deductions, and net pay of each employee are listed. Compare the entry for Robert Jones in the payroll register with the January 18 entry in Robert Jones's employee earnings record, presented in Exhibit 2. Except for the first column, which lists the employee names, and the last two columns, which show

EXHIBIT 1
Payroll Register

		Earnings			Deductions								Payment		Distribution	
Employee	Total Hours	Regular	Overtime	Gross	Federal Income Taxes	Social Security Tax	Medicare Tax	Union Dues	Medical Insurance	Life Insurance	Savings Bonds	Other: A—United Charities	Net Earnings	Check No.	Sales Wages Expense	Office Wages Expense
Linda Duval	40	160.00		160.00	11.00	9.92	2.32		5.80				130.96	923		160.00
John Franks	44	160.00	24.00	184.00	14.00	11.41	2.67	2.00	7.60			A 10.00	136.32	924	184.00	
Samuel Goetz	40	400.00		400.00	53.00	24.80	5.80		10.40	14.00		A 3.00	289.00	925	400.00	
Robert Jones	47	320.00	92.00	412.00	31.00	25.54	5.97	2.00	7.60	6.00	15.00	A 1.00	317.89	926	412.00	
Billie Matthews	40	160.00		160.00	14.00	9.92	2.32		5.80				127.96	927		160.00
Rosaire O'Brien	42	200.00	20.00	220.00	22.00	13.64	3.19	2.00	5.80				173.37	928	220.00	
James Van Dyke	40	200.00		200.00	20.00	12.40	2.90		5.80				158.90	929		200.00
		1,600.00	136.00	1,736.00	165.00	107.63	25.17	6.00	48.80	20.00	15.00	14.00	1,334.40		1,216.00	520.00

Payroll Register   Pay Period: Week ended January 18

EXHIBIT 2
Employee Earnings Record

Employee Earnings Record

Employee's Name   Robert Jones   Social Security Number   444-66-9999

Address   777 20th Street   Sex   Male   Employee No.   705

　　　　 Marshall, Michigan 52603   Single _____   Married   X   Weekly Pay Rate _____

Date of Birth   September 20, 1962   Exemptions (W-4)   4   Hourly Rate $8

Position   Sales Assistant   Date of Employment   July 15, 1988   Date Employment Ended _____

20xx		Earnings			Deductions								Payment		
Period Ended	Total Hours	Regular	Overtime	Gross	Federal Income Taxes	Social Security Tax	Medicare Tax	Union Dues	Medical Insurance	Life Insurance	Savings Bonds	Other: A—United Charities	Net Earnings	Check No.	Cumulative Gross Earnings
Jan 4	40	320.00	0	320.00	17.00	19.84	4.64	2.00	7.60	6.00	15.00	A 1.00	246.92	717	320.00
11	44	320.00	48.00	368.00	23.00	22.82	5.34	2.00	7.60	6.00	15.00	A 1.00	285.24	822	688.00
18	47	320.00	92.00	412.00	31.00	25.54	5.97	2.00	7.60	6.00	15.00	A 1.00	317.89	926	1,100.00

the wage or salary as either sales or office expense, the columns are the same. The columns help employers record the payroll in the accounting records and meet legal reporting requirements. The last two columns in Exhibit 1 are needed to divide the expenses in the accounting records into selling and administrative categories.

RECORDING THE PAYROLL

The journal entry for recording the payroll is based on the column totals from the payroll register. The journal entry to record the January 18 payroll follows. Note that each account debited or credited is a total from the payroll register. If the payroll register is considered a special-purpose journal, the column totals can be posted directly to the ledger accounts, with the correct account numbers shown at the bottom of each column.

ENRICHMENT NOTE:
The credits in the January 18 entry would be presented as current liabilities on the financial statements. Because most of them are small, they probably would be aggregated into "Other Payables" or a similar category.

$$A = L + OE$$
$$+ \quad -$$
$$+$$
$$+$$
$$+$$
$$+$$

Jan. 18	Sales Wages Expense	1,216.00	
	Office Wages Expense	520.00	
	Employees' Federal Income Taxes Payable		165.00
	Social Security Tax Payable		107.63
	Medicare Tax Payable		25.17
	Union Dues Payable		6.00
	Medical Insurance Premiums Payable		48.80
	Life Insurance Premiums Payable		20.00
	Savings Bonds Payable		15.00
	United Charities Payable		14.00
	Wages Payable		1,334.40
	To record payroll		

EMPLOYEE EARNINGS RECORD

KEY POINT: Payroll is one of the easiest elements of a business to computerize.

Each employer must keep a record of earnings and withholdings for each employee. Most companies today use computers to maintain such records, but some small companies may still use manual records. The manual form of *employee earnings*

Why Is Payroll Fraud Common?

Payroll fraud is a common form of financial wrongdoing because there are strong motivations for both the employee and the employer to cheat. Some employees want to be paid cash "under the table" to avoid income, social security, and Medicare taxes. Some employers may wish to avoid paying their share of social security and Medicare taxes as well as other payroll taxes and employee benefits. Therefore, the Internal Revenue Service cracks down on cheaters. It investigates, for example, the relationships between restaurants' revenues and the tip income that employees report on their tax returns. Severe penalties, including prison terms, can result from false reporting. Good accounting records and controls over payroll help ensure compliance with the law.

record for Robert Jones is shown in Exhibit 2. This form is designed to help the employer meet legal reporting requirements. Each deduction must be shown to have been paid to the proper agency, and the employee must receive a report of the deductions made each year.

Most of the columns in Exhibit 2 are self-explanatory. Note, however, the column on the far right for cumulative gross earnings (total earnings to date). This record helps the employer comply with the rule of applying social security and unemployment taxes only up to the maximum wage levels. At the end of the year, the employer reports to the employee on Form W-2, the Wage and Tax Statement, the total earnings and tax deductions for the year, which the employee uses to complete his or her individual tax return. The employer sends a copy of the W-2 to the Internal Revenue Service. Thus, the IRS can check whether the employee has reported all income earned from that employer.

RECORDING PAYROLL TAXES

According to Exhibit 1, the gross payroll for the week ended January 18 was $1,736.00. Because it was the first month of the year, all employees had accumulated less than the $87,000 and $7,000 maximum taxable salaries. Therefore, the total social security tax was $107.63 and the total Medicare tax was $25.17 (equal to the tax on employees), the total FUTA tax was $13.89 (.008 × $1,736.00), and the total state unemployment tax was $93.74 (.054 × $1,736.00). The entry to record this expense and related liability is as follows:

A = L + OE				
+ −	Jan. 18	Payroll Taxes Expense	240.43	
+		Social Security Tax Payable		107.63
+		Medicare Tax Payable		25.17
+		Federal Unemployment Tax Payable		13.89
		State Unemployment Tax Payable		93.74
		To record payroll taxes		

PAYMENT OF PAYROLL AND PAYROLL TAXES

After the weekly payroll is recorded, as illustrated earlier, a liability of $1,334.40 exists for wages payable. How this liability will be paid depends on the system used by the company. Many companies use a special payroll account against which payroll checks are drawn. Under this system, a check for total net earnings for this payroll ($1,334.40) must be drawn on the regular checking account and deposited in the special payroll account before the payroll checks are issued to the employees. If a voucher system is combined with a special payroll account, a voucher for the total wages payable is prepared and recorded in the voucher register as a debit to Payroll Bank Account and a credit to Vouchers Payable.

The combined social security and Medicare taxes (both employees' and employer's shares) and the federal income taxes must be paid at least quarterly. More frequent payments are required when the total liability exceeds $500. The federal unemployment insurance tax is paid yearly if the amount is less than $100. If the liability for the federal unemployment insurance tax exceeds $100 at the end of any quarter, a payment is necessary. Payment dates vary among the states. Other payroll deductions must be paid in accordance with the particular contracts or agreements involved.

✔ Check out ACE for a Review Quiz at http://accounting.college.hmco.com/students.

Chapter Review

REVIEW OF LEARNING OBJECTIVES

LO1 Identify the management issues related to recognition, valuation, classification, and disclosure of current liabilities.

Liabilities are legal obligations for future payment of assets or future performance of services. They result from past transactions and should be recognized at the time a transaction obligates a company to make future payments. They are valued at the amount of money necessary to satisfy the obligation or at the fair value of goods or services that must be delivered. Liabilities are classified as current or long term. Supplemental disclosure is required when the nature or details of the obligations would help in understanding the liability. Liabilities are an important consideration in assessing a company's liquidity. Key measures are working capital, payables turnover, and average days' payable.

LO2 Identify, compute, and record definitely determinable and estimated current liabilities.

Two principal categories of current liabilities are definitely determinable liabilities and estimated liabilities. Although definitely determinable liabilities, such as accounts payable, notes payable, accrued liabilities, dividends payable, and the current portion of long-term debt, can be measured exactly, the accountant must still be careful not to overlook existing liabilities in these categories. Estimated liabilities, such as liabilities for income taxes, property taxes, and product warranties, definitely exist, but the amounts must be estimated and recorded properly.

LO3 Distinguish *contingent liabilities* from *commitments*.

A contingent liability is a potential liability that arises from a past transaction and is dependent on a future event. Examples of contingent liabilities are lawsuits, income tax disputes, discounted notes receivable, guarantees of debt, and failure to follow government regulations. A commitment is a legal obligation, such as a purchase agreement, that is not recorded as a liability.

SUPPLEMENTAL OBJECTIVE

SO4 Compute and record the liabilities associated with payroll accounting.

Computations for payroll liabilities must be made for the compensation to each employee, for withholdings from each employee's total pay, and for the employer's portion of payroll taxes. The salary and deductions for each employee are recorded each pay period in the payroll register. From the payroll register, the details of each employee's earnings are transferred to the employee's earnings record. The column totals of the payroll register are used to prepare an entry that records the payroll and accompanying liabilities. The employer's share of social security and Medicare taxes and the federal and state unemployment taxes as well as any liabilities for other fringe benefits must then be recorded.

REVIEW OF CONCEPTS AND TERMINOLOGY

The following concepts and terms were introduced in this chapter:

LO1 **Average days' payable:** How long, on average, a company takes to pay its accounts payable; 365 days divided by payables turnover.

LO2 **Commercial paper:** Unsecured loans sold to the public, usually through professionally managed investment firms, as a means of borrowing short-term funds.

LO3   **Commitment:** A legal obligation that does not meet the technical requirements for recognition as a liability.

LO3   **Contingent liability:** A potential liability that arises from a past transaction and is dependent on a future event.

LO1   **Current liabilities:** Debts and obligations expected to be satisfied within one year or within the normal operating cycle, whichever is longer.

LO2   **Definitely determinable liabilities:** Current liabilities that are set by contract or statute and that can be measured exactly.

SO4   **Employee earnings record:** A record of earnings and withholdings for an individual employee.

LO2   **Estimated liabilities:** Definite debts or obligations whose exact amounts cannot be known until a later date.

LO2   **Line of credit:** An arrangement with a bank that allows a company to borrow funds as needed.

LO1   **Long-term liabilities:** Debts or obligations due beyond one year or beyond the normal operating cycle.

LO1   **Payables turnover:** The number of times, on average, that accounts payable are paid in an accounting period; cost of goods sold plus (or minus) change in merchandise inventory divided by average accounts payable.

SO4   **Payroll register:** A detailed listing of a firm's total payroll that is prepared each pay period.

LO2   **Salaries:** Compensation of employees who are paid at a monthly or yearly rate.

LO2   **Unearned revenues:** Revenues received in advance for goods or services that will not be delivered during the current accounting period.

LO2   **Wages:** Payment for services of employees at an hourly rate.

REVIEW PROBLEM

Notes Payable Transactions and End-of-Period Entries

LO2   McLaughlin, Inc., whose fiscal year ends June 30, 20xx, completed the following transactions involving notes payable:

May 11   Purchased a small crane by issuing a 60-day, 12 percent note for $54,000. The face of the note does not include interest.
    16   Obtained a $40,000 bank loan to finance a temporary increase in receivables by signing a 90-day, 10 percent note. The face value includes interest.
June 30   Made the end-of-year adjusting entry to accrue interest expense.
    30   Made the end-of-year adjusting entry to recognize interest expired on the note.
    30   Made the end-of-year closing entry pertaining to interest expense.
July 10   Paid the note plus interest on the crane purchase.
Aug. 14   Paid off the note to the bank.

REQUIRED ▶   Prepare entries in journal form for the above transactions.

ANSWER TO REVIEW PROBLEM

20xx
May 11   Equipment   54,000
                Notes Payable   54,000
                    Purchased crane with 60-day,
                    12% note

May 16	Cash	39,000	
	Discount on Notes Payable	1,000	
	Notes Payable		40,000
	Obtained loan from bank by signing		
	90-day, 10% note; discount equals		
	$40,000 \times .10 \times 90/360 = \$1,000$		
June 30	Interest Expense	900	
	Interest Payable		900
	Accrued interest expense		
	$54,000 \times .12 \times 50/360 = \$900$		
30	Interest Expense	500	
	Discount on Notes Payable		500
	Recognized interest on note		
	$\$1,000 \times 45/90 = \$500$		
30	Income Summary	1,400	
	Interest Expense		1,400
	Closed interest expense		
July 10	Notes Payable	54,000	
	Interest Payable	900	
	Interest Expense	180	
	Cash		55,080
	Paid note on equipment		
	$54,000 \times .12 \times 10/360 = \$180$		
Aug. 14	Notes Payable	40,000	
	Cash		40,000
	Paid bank loan		
14	Interest Expense	500	
	Discount on Notes Payable		500
	Interest expense on matured note		
	$\$1,000 - \$500 = \$500$		

Chapter Assignments

BUILDING YOUR KNOWLEDGE FOUNDATION

QUESTIONS

1. What are liabilities?

2. Why is the timing of liability recognition important in accounting?

3. At the end of the accounting period, Janson Company had a legal obligation to accept delivery of and pay for a truckload of hospital supplies the following week. Is this legal obligation a liability?

4. Ned Johnson, a star college basketball player, received a contract from the Midwest Blazers to play professional basketball. The contract calls for a salary of $300,000 a year for four years, dependent on his making the team in each of those years. Should this contract be considered a liability and recorded on the books of the basketball team?

5. What is the rule for classifying a liability as current?

6. What are a line of credit and commercial paper? Where do they appear on the balance sheet?

7. A bank is offering Diane Wedge two alternatives for borrowing $2,000. The first alternative is a $2,000, 12 percent, 30-day note. The second alternative is a $2,000, 30-day note discounted at 12 percent. (a) What entries are required by

Diane Wedge to record the two loans? (b) What entries are needed by Wedge to record the payment of the two loans? (c) Which alternative favors Wedge, and why?

8. Where should the Discount on Notes Payable account appear on the balance sheet?

9. When can a portion of long-term debt be classified as a current liability?

10. What are three types of employer-related payroll liabilities?

11. How does an employee differ from an independent contractor?

12. Who pays social security and Medicare taxes?

13. Why are unearned revenues classified as liabilities?

14. What is definite about an estimated liability?

15. Why are income taxes payable considered to be estimated liabilities?

16. When does a company incur a liability for a product warranty?

17. What is a contingent liability, and how does it differ from a commitment?

18. What are some examples of contingent liabilities? For what reason is each a contingent liability?

19. What role does the W-4 form play in determining the withholding for estimated federal income taxes?

20. How can the payroll register be used as a special-purpose journal?

21. Why is an employee earnings record necessary, and how does it relate to the W-2 form?

SHORT EXERCISES

LO1 Issues in Accounting for Liabilities

SE 1. Indicate whether each of the following actions relates to (a) managing liquidity and cash flow, (b) recognition of liabilities, (c) valuation of liabilities, (d) classification of liabilities, or (e) disclosure of liabilities:

1. Determining that a liability will be paid in less than one year
2. Estimating the amount of a liability
3. Providing information about when liabilities are due and their interest rates
4. Determining when a liability arises
5. Assessing working capital and payables turnover

LO1 Measuring Short-Term Liquidity

SE 2. Stratton Company has current assets of $130,000 and current liabilities of $80,000, of which accounts payable are $70,000. Stratton's cost of goods sold is $460,000, its merchandise inventory increased by $20,000, and accounts payable were $50,000 the prior year. Calculate Stratton's working capital, payables turnover, and average days' payable.

LO2 Types of Liabilities
LO3

SE 3. Indicate whether each of the following is (a) a definitely determinable liability, (b) an estimated liability, (c) a commitment, or (d) a contingent liability:

1. Dividends Payable
2. Pending litigation
3. Income Taxes Payable
4. Current portion of long-term debt
5. Vacation Pay Liability
6. Guaranteed loans of another company
7. Purchase agreement

LO2 Interest Expense: Interest Not Included in Face Value of Note

SE 4. On the last day of August, Swift Company borrowed $60,000 on a bank note for 60 days at 10 percent interest. Assume that interest is stated separately. Prepare the following entries in journal form: (1) August 31, recording of note; and (2) October 30, payment of note plus interest.

LO2 Interest Expense: Interest Included in Face Value of Note

SE 5. Assume the same facts as in **SE 4,** except that interest of $1,000 is included in the face amount of the note and the note is discounted at the bank on August 31. Prepare the following entries in journal form: (1) August 31, recording of note; and (2) October 30, payment of note and recording of interest expense.

LO2 **Payroll Entries**

SE 6. The following payroll totals for the month of April are from the payroll register of Corelli Corporation: salaries, $223,000.00; federal income taxes withheld, $31,440.00; social security tax withheld, $13,826.00; Medicare tax withheld, $3,233.50; medical insurance deductions, $6,580.00; and salaries subject to unemployment taxes, $156,600.00. Prepare entries in journal form to record (1) the monthly payroll and (2) employer's payroll expense, assuming social security and Medicare taxes equal to the amounts for employees, a federal unemployment insurance tax of .8 percent, a state unemployment tax of 5.4 percent, and medical insurance premiums for which the employer pays 80 percent of the cost.

LO2 **Product Warranty Liability**

SE 7. Diamante Corp. manufactures and sells travel clocks. Each clock costs $25 to produce and sells for $50. In addition, each clock carries a warranty that provides for free replacement if it fails during the two years following the sale. In the past, 5 percent of the clocks sold have had to be replaced under the warranty. During October, Diamante sold 52,000 clocks, and 2,800 clocks were replaced under the warranty. Prepare entries in journal form to record the estimated liability for product warranties during the month and the clocks replaced under warranty during the month.

LO2 **Vacation Pay Liability**

SE 8. The employees of Larue Services receive two weeks of paid vacation each year. Seventy percent of the employees qualify for vacation. Assuming the September payroll is $150,000, including $12,000 paid to employees on vacation, how much is the vacation pay expense for September? What is the ending balance of the Estimated Liability for Vacation Pay account, assuming a beginning balance of $16,000?

SO4 **Payroll Taxes**

SE 9. Karma Company and its employees are subject to a 6.2 percent social security tax on wages up to $87,000 and a 1.45 percent Medicare tax with no limit. The company is subject to a 5.4 percent state unemployment tax and a .8 percent federal unemployment tax up to $7,000 per employee. The company has two employees: A. Ballo, who has cumulative earnings of $88,000 and earned $7,000 in the month of December, and C. Dureo, who has cumulative earnings of $5,000 and earned $1,000 during December. Compute the total payroll taxes for the employees and the employer for December.

SO4 **Payroll Earnings, Withholdings, and Taxes**

SE 10. Last week, Manuel Karmelo worked 44 hours. He is paid $10 per hour and receives one and one-half times his regular rate for hours worked over 40. Karmelo has withholdings of $45 for federal income taxes, $10 for state income taxes, $23 for health insurance, 6.2 percent for social security tax, and 1.45 percent for Medicare tax. Compute Karmelo's take-home pay. Also compute the total cost of Karmelo to his employer, assuming that Karmelo's cumulative wages are over the limit for unemployment taxes and that the company makes a health-care contribution of $75.

EXERCISES

LO1 **Issues in Accounting for Liabilities**

E 1. Indicate whether each of the following actions relates to (a) managing liquidity and cash flows, (b) recognition of liabilities, (c) valuation of liabilities, (d) classification of liabilities, or (e) disclosure of liabilities:

1. Setting a liability at the fair market value of goods to be delivered
2. Relating the payment date of a liability to the length of the operating cycle
3. Recording a liability in accordance with the matching rule
4. Providing information about financial instruments on the balance sheet
5. Estimating the amount of "cents-off" coupons that will be redeemed
6. Categorizing a liability as long-term debt
7. Measuring working capital
8. Comparing average days' payable with last year

LO1 **Measuring Short-Term Liquidity**

E 2. In 20x1, Telos Company had current assets of $310,000 and current liabilities of $200,000, of which accounts payable were $130,000. Cost of goods sold was $850,000, merchandise inventory increased by $40,000, and accounts payable were $110,000 in the prior year. In 20x2, Telos had current assets of $420,000 and current liabilities of $320,000, of which accounts payable were $150,000. Cost of goods sold was $950,000, and merchandise inventory decreased by $30,000. Calculate Telos's working capital, payables turnover, and average days' payable for 20x1 and 20x2. Assess Telos's liquidity and cash flows in relation to the change in payables turnover from 20x1 to 20x2.

E 3.
LO2 Interest Expense: Interest Not Included in Face Value of Note

On the last day of October, Shealy Company borrows $30,000 on a bank note for 60 days at 12 percent interest. Interest is not included in the face amount. Prepare the following entries in journal form: (1) October 31, recording of note; (2) November 30, accrual of interest expense; and (3) December 30, payment of note plus interest.

E 4.
LO2 Interest Expense: Interest Included in Face Value of Note

Assume the same facts as in **E 3,** except that interest is included in the face amount of the note and the note is discounted at the bank on October 31. Prepare the following entries in journal form: (1) October 31, recording of note; (2) November 30, recognition of interest accrued on note; and (3) December 30, payment of note and recording of interest expense.

E 5.
LO2 Sales and Excise Taxes

Web Design Service billed its customers a total of $980,400 for the month of August, including 9 percent federal excise tax and 5 percent sales tax.

1. Determine the proper amount of service revenue to report for the month.
2. Prepare an entry in journal form to record the revenue and related liabilities for the month.

E 6.
LO2 Payroll Entries

At the end of October, the payroll register for Lakeside Tool and Die Corporation contained the following totals: wages, $185,500; federal income taxes withheld, $47,442; state income taxes withheld, $7,818; social security tax withheld, $11,501; Medicare tax withheld, $2,689.75; medical insurance deductions, $6,435; and wages subject to unemployment taxes, $28,620.

Prepare entries in journal form to record the (1) monthly payroll and (2) employer payroll expenses, assuming social security and Medicare taxes equal to the amount for employees, a federal unemployment insurance tax of .8 percent, a state unemployment tax of 5.4 percent, and medical insurance premiums for which the employer pays 80 percent of the cost.

E 7.
LO2 Product Warranty Liability

Hoopes Company manufactures and sells electronic games. Each game costs $25 to produce and sells for $45. In addition, each game carries a warranty that provides for free replacement if it fails during the two years following the sale. In the past, 7 percent of the games sold had to be replaced under the warranty. During July, Hoopes sold 26,000 games, and 2,800 games were replaced under the warranty.

1. Prepare an entry in journal form to record the estimated liability for product warranties during the month.
2. Prepare an entry in journal form to record the games replaced under warranty during the month.

E 8.
LO2 Vacation Pay Liability

Syracuse Corporation gives three weeks' paid vacation to each employee who has worked at the company for one year. Based on studies of employee turnover and previous experience, management estimates that 65 percent of the employees will qualify for vacation pay this year.

1. Assume that Syracuse's July payroll is $600,000, of which $40,000 is paid to employees on vacation. Figure the estimated employee vacation benefit for the month.
2. Prepare an entry in journal form to record the employee benefit for July.
3. Prepare an entry in journal form to record the pay to employees on vacation.

E 9.
SO4 Social Security, Medicare, and Unemployment Taxes

Munro Company is subject to a 5.4 percent state unemployment insurance tax and a .8 percent federal unemployment insurance tax after credits. Assume both federal and state unemployment taxes apply to the first $7,000 earned by each employee. Social security and Medicare taxes in effect at this time are 6.2 and 1.45 percent, respectively. The social security tax is levied for both employee and employer on the first $87,000 earned by each employee during the year.

During the current year, the cumulative earnings for each employee of the company are as follows:

Employee	Cumulative Earnings	Employee	Cumulative Earnings
Basmani, J.	$28,620	Van Trapp, M.	$16,760
Cohen, A.	5,260	Harwit, P.	6,420
Derbye, G.	32,820	Lemaire, C.	51,650
Carbone, R.	30,130	Papyani, D.	32,100
Sourdiffe, B.	89,000	Menzek, V.	36,645
Conniger, N.	5,120	Woo, S.	5,176

1. Prepare and complete a schedule with the following columns: Employee Name, Cumulative Earnings, Earnings Subject to Social Security Tax, Earnings Subject to Medicare Tax, and Earnings Subject to Unemployment Taxes. Total the columns.

2. Compute the social security and Medicare taxes and the federal and state unemployment taxes for Munro Company for the year.

SO4 Net Pay Calculation and Payroll Entries

E 10. Lynne Featherstone is an employee whose overtime pay is regulated by the Fair Labor Standards Act. Her hourly rate is $8, and during the week ended July 11, she worked 42 hours. She claims two exemptions on her W-4 form. So far this year she has earned $8,650. Each week $12 is deducted from her paycheck for medical insurance.

1. Compute the following items related to the pay for Lynne Featherstone for the week of July 11: (a) total pay, (b) federal income taxes withholding (use Figure 4), (c) social security and Medicare taxes (assume rates of 6.2 percent and 1.45 percent, respectively), and (d) net pay.

2. Prepare an entry in journal form to record the wages expense and related liabilities for Lynne Featherstone for the week ended July 11.

SO4 Payroll Transactions

E 11. Jian-Jin Loo earns a salary of $90,000 per year. Social security and Medicare taxes are, respectively, 6.2 percent on salary up to $87,000 and 1.45 percent on total salary. Federal unemployment insurance taxes are 6.2 percent of the first $7,000; however, a credit is allowed equal to the state unemployment insurance taxes of 5.4 percent on the $7,000. During the year, $15,000 was withheld for federal income taxes, $3,000 for state income taxes, and $1,500 for medical insurance.

1. Prepare an entry in journal form summarizing the payment of $90,000 to Loo during the year.

2. Prepare an entry in journal form summarizing the employer payroll taxes and other costs on Loo's salary for the year. Assume the company pays 80 percent of the total premiums for medical insurance.

3. Determine the total amount paid by Jian-Jin Loo's employer to employ Loo for the year.

PROBLEMS

LO1 Identification of Current
LO2 Liabilities

P 1. Neil Fusco opened a small television repair shop, Fusco Television Repair, on January 2, 20x0. The shop also sells a limited number of television sets. In January 20x1, Fusco realized he had never filed any tax reports for his business and therefore probably owes a considerable amount of taxes. Since he has limited experience in running a business, he has brought you all his business records, including a checkbook, canceled checks, deposit slips, suppliers' invoices, a notice of annual property taxes of $4,620 due to the city, and a promissory note to his father-in-law for $5,000. He wants you to determine what his business owes the government and other parties.

You analyze all his records and determine the following as of December 31, 20x0:

Unpaid invoices for televisions	$ 18,000
Television sales (excluding sales tax)	88,540
Cost of Televisions Sold	62,250
Workers' salaries	20,400
Repair revenues	120,600
Current assets	32,600
Television inventory	23,500

You learn that the company has deducted $952 from the two employees' salaries for federal income taxes owed to the government. The current social security tax is 6.2 percent on maximum earnings of $87,000 for each employee, and the current Medicare tax is 1.45 percent (no maximum earnings). The FUTA tax is 5.4 percent to the state and .8 percent to the federal government on the first $7,000 earned by each employee, and each employee earned more than $7,000. Fusco has not filed a sales tax report to the state (5 percent of sales).

REQUIRED ▶

1. Given these limited facts, determine Fusco Television Repair's current liabilities as of December 31, 20x0.

2. What additional information would you want from Fusco to satisfy yourself that all current liabilities have been identified?

3. Evaluate Fusco's liquidity by calculating working capital, payables turnover, and average days' payable. Comment on the results. (Assume average accounts payable were the same as year-end accounts payable.)

P 2.

LO2   Notes Payable Transactions and End-of-Period Entries

Iron's Paper Company, whose fiscal year ends December 31, completed the following transactions involving notes payable:

20x3

Nov. 25   Purchased a new loading cart by issuing a 60-day, 10 percent note for $43,200.

Dec. 16   Borrowed $50,000 from the bank to finance inventory by signing a 90-day note. The face value of the note includes interest of $1,500. Proceeds received were $48,500.

31   Made the end-of-year adjusting entry to accrue interest expense.

31   Made the end-of-year adjusting entry to recognize the discount expired on the note.

20x4

Jan. 24   Paid off the loading cart note.

Mar. 16   Paid off the inventory note to the bank.

REQUIRED ▶

1. Prepare entries in journal form for the notes payable transactions.

2. In the transaction of December 16, would the bank be better off making the loan with the interest stated separately instead of included in the $50,000? Why or why not?

P 3.

LO2   Product Warranty Liability

The Galway Company manufactures and sells food processors, which it guarantees for five years. If a processor fails, it is replaced free, but the customer is charged a service fee for handling. In the past, management has found that only 3 percent of the processors sold required replacement under the warranty. The average food processor costs the company $240. At the beginning of September, the account for estimated liability for product warranties had a credit balance of $208,000. During September, 250 processors were returned under the warranty. Service fees of $9,860 were collected for handling. During the month, the company sold 2,800 food processors.

REQUIRED ▶

1. Prepare entries in journal form to record (a) the cost of food processors replaced under warranty and (b) the estimated liability for product warranties for processors sold during the month.

2. Compute the balance of the Estimated Product Warranty Liability account at the end of the month.

3. If the company's product warranty liability is underestimated, what are the effects on current and future years' income?

P 4.

LO2   Payroll Entries

At the end of October, the payroll register for Golinski Corporation contained the following totals: sales salaries, $176,220; office salaries, $80,880; administrative salaries, $113,900; federal income taxes withheld, $94,884; state income taxes withheld, $15,636; social security tax withheld, $23,002; Medicare tax withheld, $5,379.50; medical insurance premiums, $12,870; life insurance premiums, $11,712; union dues deductions, $1,368; and salaries subject to unemployment taxes, $57,240. Fifty percent of medical and life insurance premiums are paid by the employer.

REQUIRED ▶

Prepare entries in journal form to record the (1) accrual of the monthly payroll, (2) payment of the net payroll, (3) accrual of employer's payroll taxes and expenses (assuming social security and Medicare taxes equal to the amount for employees, a federal unemployment insurance tax of .8 percent, and a state unemployment tax of 5.4 percent), and (4) payment of all liabilities related to the payroll (assuming that all are paid at the same time).

P 5.

SO4   Payroll Register and Related Entries

Hendrik Dairy Company has seven employees. Employees paid hourly receive a set rate for regular hours plus one and one-half times their hourly rate for overtime hours. They are paid every two weeks. The salaried employees are paid monthly on the last biweekly payday of each month. The employees and company are subject to social security tax of 6.2 percent up to a maximum of $87,000 for each employee and to Medicare tax of 1.45 percent. The unemployment insurance tax rates are 5.4 percent for the state and .8 percent for the federal government. The unemployment insurance tax applies to the first $7,000 earned by each employee and is levied only on the employer.

The company maintains a supplemental benefits plan that includes medical insurance, life insurance, and additional retirement funds for employees. Under the plan, each employee contributes 4 percent of her or his gross income as a payroll withholding, and the company matches the amount. Data for the November 30 payroll, the last payday of November, follow.

	Hours			Cumulative Gross Pay Excluding Current Pay Period	Federal Income Taxes to Be Withheld
Employee	Regular	Overtime	Pay Rate		
Eggers, D.	80	5	$ 8.00	$ 4,867.00	$ 71.00
Gosligan, W.	80	4	6.50	3,954.00	76.00
Valmont, P.*	Salary	—	5,000.00	55,000.00	985.00
Norelli, V.	80	—	5.00	8,250.00	32.00
Appia, L.*	Salary	—	2,000.00	20,000.00	294.00
Tou, M.	80	20	10.00	12,000.00	103.00
Voss, B.*	Salary	—	1,500.00	15,000.00	210.00

*Denotes administrative personnel; the rest are sales. P. Valmont's cumulative gross pay includes a $5,000 bonus paid early in the year.

REQUIRED ▶

1. Prepare a payroll register for the pay period ended November 30. The payroll register should have the following columns:

Employee	Deductions	Net Pay
Total Hours	Federal Income Taxes	Distribution
Earnings	Social Security Tax	Sales Wages Expense
Regular	Medicare Tax	Administrative Salaries Expense
Overtime	Supplemental Benefits Plan	
Gross		
Cumulative		

2. Prepare an entry in journal form to record the payroll and related liabilities for deductions for the period ended November 30.
3. Prepare entries in journal form to record the employer's payroll taxes and contribution to the supplemental benefits plan.
4. Prepare the November 30 entries (a) to transfer sufficient cash from the company's regular checking account to a special payroll disbursement account and (b) to pay the employees.

ALTERNATE PROBLEMS

P 6.

LO2   Notes Payable Transactions and End-of-Period Entries

Aragian Corporation, whose fiscal year ends June 30, completed the following transactions involving notes payable:

20xx

May 11   Signed a 90-day, $132,000 note payable to Eastern Shore Bank for a working capital loan. The face value included interest of $3,960. Proceeds received were $128,040.

21   Obtained a 60-day extension on a $36,000 trade account payable owed to a supplier by signing a 60-day, $36,000 note. Interest is in addition to the face value, at the rate of 14 percent.

June 30   Made the end-of-year adjusting entry to accrue interest expense.

30   Made the end-of-year adjusting entry to recognize discount expired on the note.

July 20   Paid off the note plus interest due the supplier.

Aug. 9   Paid the amount due to the bank on the 90-day note.

REQUIRED ▶

1. Prepare entries in journal form for the notes payable transactions.
2. In the transaction of May 11, would the bank be better off making the loan with the interest stated separately or with it included in the loan amount? Why or why not?

LO2   Product Warranty Liability

P 7. Sparkle Bright Company is engaged in the retail sale of washing machines. Each machine has a 24-month warranty on parts. If a repair under warranty is required, a charge for the labor is made. Management has found that 20 percent of the machines sold require some work before the warranty expires. Furthermore, the average cost of replacement parts has been $120 per repair. At the beginning of June, the account for the estimated liability for product warranties had a credit balance of $28,600. During June, 112 machines were returned under the warranty. The cost of the parts used in repairing the machines was $17,530, and $18,884 was collected as service revenue for the labor involved. During the month, Sparkle Bright Company sold 450 new machines.

REQUIRED ▶ 1. Prepare entries in journal form to record each of the following: (a) the warranty work completed during the month, including related revenue; (b) the estimated liability for product warranties for machines sold during the month.

2. Compute the balance of the Estimated Product Warranty Liability account at the end of the month.

3. If the company's product warranty liability is overestimated, what are the effects on current and future years' income?

LO2   Payroll Entries

P 8. The following payroll amounts for the month of April were taken from the payroll register of Weiskauf Corporation: sales salaries, $116,400; office salaries, $57,000; general salaries, $49,600; social security tax withheld, $13,826; Medicare tax withheld, $3,233.50; income taxes withheld, $31,440; medical insurance premiums, $3,290; life insurance premiums, $1,880; salaries subject to unemployment taxes, $156,600. Fifty percent of medical and life insurance premiums are paid by the employee. The rest are paid by the employer.

REQUIRED ▶ Prepare entries in journal form to record the following: (1) accrual of the monthly payroll, (2) payment of the net payroll, (3) accrual of employer's payroll taxes and expenses (assuming social security and Medicare taxes equal to the amounts for employees, a federal unemployment insurance tax of .8 percent, and a state unemployment tax of 5.4 percent), and (4) payment of all liabilities related to the payroll (assuming that all are paid at the same time).

SKILLS DEVELOPMENT CASES

Conceptual Analysis

LO2   Frequent-Flier Plan

SD 1. America South Airways instituted a frequent-flier program under which passengers accumulate points toward a free flight based on the number of miles they fly on the airline. One point was awarded for each mile flown, with a minimum of 750 miles being given for any flight. Because of competition in 2001, the company began a bonus plan under which passengers receive triple the normal mileage points. In the past, about 1.5 percent of passenger miles were flown by passengers who had converted points to free flights. With the triple mileage program, it is expected that a 2.5 percent rate will be more appropriate for future years. During 2001, the company had passenger revenues of $966.3 million and passenger transportation operating expenses of $802.8 million before depreciation and amortization. Operating income was $86.1 million. What is the appropriate rate to use to estimate free miles? What would be the effect of the estimated liability for free travel by frequent fliers on 2001 net income? Describe several ways to estimate the amount of this liability. Be prepared to discuss the arguments for and against recognizing this liability.

LO2   Nature and Recognition of an
LO3   Estimated Liability

SD 2. The decision to recognize and record a liability is sometimes a matter of judgment. People who use General Motors <www.gm.com> credit cards earn rebates toward the purchase or lease of GM vehicles in relation to the amount of purchases they make with their cards. General Motors chooses to treat these outstanding rebates as a commitment in the notes to its financial statements:

> GM sponsors a credit card program . . . that offers rebates that can be applied primarily against the purchase or lease of GM vehicles. The amount of rebates available to qualified cardholders (net of deferred program income) was $4.0 billion, $3.9 billion, and $3.8 billion at December 31, 2002, 2001, and 2000, respectively.[14]

Using the two criteria established by the FASB for recording a contingency, explain GM's reasoning in treating this liability as a commitment in the notes, where it will likely receive less attention by analysts, rather than including it on the income statement as an expense and on the balance sheet as an estimated liability. Do you agree with this position? (**Hint:** Apply the matching rule.)

Ethical Dilemma

LO2 Known Legal Violations

SD 3. Chop Shop Restaurant is a large steak restaurant in the suburbs of Chicago. Joe Murray, an accounting student at a nearby college, recently secured a full-time accounting job at the restaurant. He felt fortunate to have a good job that accommodated his class schedule because the local economy was very bad. After a few weeks on the job, Murray realized that his boss, the owner of the business, was paying the kitchen workers in cash and was not withholding federal and state income taxes or social security and Medicare taxes. Murray understands that federal and state laws require these taxes to be withheld and paid to the appropriate agency in a timely manner. He also realizes that if he raises this issue, he could lose his job. What alternatives are available to Murray? What action would you take if you were in his position? Why did you make this choice?

 Group Activity: Use in class groups. Debrief by asking each group for an alternative. Then debate the ethics of each alternative.

Research Activity

LO2 Basic Research Skills
LO3

SD 4. Indexes for business periodicals, in which you can look up topics of interest, are available in your school library. Three of the most important of these indexes are the *Business Periodicals Index*, *The Wall Street Journal Index*, and the *Accountants' Index*. Using one or more of these indexes, locate and photocopy two articles related to bank financing, commercial paper, product warranties, airline frequent-flier plans, or contingent liabilities. Keep in mind that you may have to look under related topics to find an article. For example, to find articles about contingent liabilities, you might look under litigation, debt guarantees, or environmental losses. For each of the two articles, write a short summary of the situation and tell how it relates to accounting for the topic as described in the text. Be prepared to discuss your results in class.

Decision-Making Practice

LO1 Identification of Current
LO2 Liabilities
SO4

SD 5. Sandra Miller opened a bicycle repair shop, Miller Bicycles, in 20x3. She also sold bicycles. The new business was such a success that she hired two assistants on June 1, 20x3. In December, Miller realized that she had failed to file any tax reports for her business since its inception and therefore probably owed a considerable amount of taxes. Since Miller has limited experience in running a business, she has brought all her business records to you and is asking for help. The records include a checkbook, canceled checks, deposit slips, invoices from her suppliers, a notice of annual property taxes of $9,240 due to the city on January 1, 20x4, and a one-year promissory note to the bank for $10,000. She wants you to determine what her business owes the government and other parties. You analyze all her records and determine the following:

Unpaid supplies invoices	$ 6,320
Sales (excluding sales tax)	177,080
Workers' salaries	40,800
Repair revenues	241,200

You learn that the company has deducted $1,904 from the two employees' salaries for federal income taxes owed to the government. The current social security tax is 6.2 percent on maximum earnings of $87,000 for each employee, and the current Medicare tax is 1.45 percent (no maximum earnings). The FUTA tax is 5.4 percent to the state and .8 percent to the federal government on the first $7,000 earned by each employee, and each employee earned more than $7,000. Miller has not filed a sales tax report to the state (5 percent of sales).

1. Given these limited facts, determine Miller Bicycle's current liabilities as of December 31, 20x4.
2. What additional information would you want from Miller to satisfy yourself that all current liabilities have been identified?

FINANCIAL REPORTING AND ANALYSIS CASES

Interpreting Financial Reports

FRA 1.

LO1 **Comparison of Two Companies' Ratios with Industry Ratios**

Both Sun Microsystems Inc. <www.sun.com> and Cisco Systems <www.cisco.com> are in the computer industry. These data (in thousands) are for their fiscal year ends:[15]

	Sun	Cisco
Accounts payable	$ 1,050,000	$ 644,000
Cost of goods sold	10,049,000	11,221,000
Increase (decrease) in inventory	492,000	452,000

Compare the payables turnover ratio and average days' payable for both companies. Comment on the results. How are cash flows affected by average days' payable? How do Sun Microsystems' and Cisco Systems' ratios compare with the computer industry ratios shown in Figures 1 and 2 in this chapter? (Use year-end amounts for ratios.)

FRA 2.

LO3 **Classic Case: Contingent Liabilities**

In its 1986 annual report, Texaco, Inc. <www.texaco.com>, one of the world's largest oil companies, reported its loss in the biggest damage judgment rendered to that date:

> **Note 17.** Contingent Liabilities
> Pennzoil Litigation
>
> *State Court Action.* On December 10, 1985, the 151st District Court of Harris County, Texas, entered judgment for Pennzoil Company of $7.5 billion actual damages, $3 billion punitive damages, and approximately $600 million prejudgment interest in *Pennzoil Company v. Texaco, Inc.*, an action in which Pennzoil claims that Texaco, Inc., tortiously interfered with Pennzoil's alleged contract to acquire a ³/₇ths interest in Getty. Interest began accruing on the judgment at the simple rate of 10% per annum from the date of judgment. Texaco, Inc., believes that there is no legal basis for the judgment, which it believes is contrary to the evidence and applicable law. Texaco, Inc., is pursuing all available remedies to set aside or to reverse the judgment. . . .
>
> The outcome of the appeal on the preliminary injunction and the ultimate outcome of the Pennzoil litigation are not presently determinable, but could have a material adverse effect on the consolidated financial position and the results of the consolidated operations of Texaco, Inc.[16]

At December 31, 1986, Texaco's retained earnings were $12.882 billion, and its cash and marketable securities totaled $3.0 billion. Its net income for 1986 was $.725 billion.

After a series of court reversals and filing for bankruptcy in 1987, Texaco announced in December 1987 an out-of-court settlement with Pennzoil for $3.0 billion. Although less than the original amount, it is still the largest damage payment in history.

1. What two conditions established by the FASB must a contingent liability meet before it is recorded in the accounting records? Does the situation described in "Note 17. Contingent Liabilities" meet those conditions? Explain your answer.
2. Do the events of 1987 change your answer to 1? Explain your response.
3. How would the settlement have affected Texaco's retained earnings, cash and marketable securities, and net income?

International Company

FRA 3.

LO1 **Classification and Disclosure**
LO2 **of Current Liabilities and**
LO3 **Contingent Liabilities**

Man Nutzfahrzeuge Aktiengesellschaft <www.mannutzfahrzeuge.de>, a German firm, is one of the world's largest truck companies. Accounting in Germany differs in some respects from that in the United States. A good example is the placement and classification of liabilities. On the balance sheet, Man places liabilities below a detailed stockholders' equity section. Man does not distinguish between current and long-term liabilities; however, a note to the financial statements does disclose the amount of the liabilities due within one year. Those liabilities are primarily what we call *definitely determinable liabilities*, such as loans, accounts payable, and notes payable. Estimated liabilities do not seem to appear in this category. There is an asset category called *current assets*, similar to that used in the United States. In another note to the financial statements, Man lists what it calls *contingent liabilities*, which have not been recorded and do not appear on the balance sheet. These include liabilities for hire and leasing contracts, guarantees of loans of other companies, and warranties on trucks.[17] What do you think of combining all liabilities, short- and long-term, in a single item on the balance sheet? Should any contingent liabilities be recorded and shown on the balance sheet?

Toys "R" Us Annual Report

FRA 4.

LO1 **Short-Term Liabilities and Seasonality**

Refer to the balance sheet and the liquidity and capital resources section of management's discussion in the Toys "R" Us annual report <www.tru.com>. Compute the payables turnover for 2002 for Toys "R" Us. How does it compare with the payables turnover ratios for the industries shown in Figure 1? Toys "R" Us is a seasonal business. Would you expect short-term borrowings and accounts payable to be unusually high or unusually low at the balance sheet date of February 1, 2003? How does management use short-term financing to meet its needs for cash during the year?

Comparison Case: Toys "R" Us and Walgreen Co.

FRA 5.

LO1 **Payables Analysis and**
LO3 **Commitments and Contingencies**

Refer to the financial statements and notes for Toys "R" Us <www.tru.com> and Walgreens <www.walgreens.com> in the Supplement to Chapter 6.

1. Compute the payables turnover and average days' payable for Toys "R" Us and Walgreens for the past two years. Accounts payable in 2000 were $1,152 million for Toys "R" Us and $1,364.0 million for Walgreens. The merchandise inventory for Toys "R" Us in 2000 was $2,307 million, and for Walgreens, $2,830.8 million. Which company makes most use of creditors to finance the operating cycle's needs?
2. Read each company's note on commitments and contingencies. What commitments and contingencies do the companies have in common? For which company does this information seem to be most important? Why is it important to consider this information in connection with payables analysis?

Fingraph® Financial Analyst™

FRA 6.

LO1 **Comparison of Current**
LO2 **Liabilities and Working**
LO3 **Capital**

Choose any two companies from the list of Fingraph companies on the Needles Accounting Resource Center Web Site at http://accounting.college.hmco.com/students. The industry should be one in which current liabilities are likely to be important, such as the airline, manufacturing, consumer products, or computer industry. Access the Microsoft Excel spreadsheets for the companies you selected. Click the URL at the top of each company's spreadsheet to link to the company's web site and annual report.

1. In the annual reports of the companies you have selected, read the current liability section of the balance sheet and any reference to current liabilities in the summary of significant accounting policies or notes to the financial statements. What are the most important current liabilities for each company? Do any current liabilities appear to be characteristic of the industry? Which current liabilities are definitely determinable, and which appear to be accrued liabilities?
2. Using the Fingraph CD-ROM software, display and print in tabular and graphic form the Current Assets and Current Liabilities Analysis page. Prepare a table that compares the current ratio and working capital for both companies for two years.
3. Find and read references to current liabilities in the liquidity analysis section of management's discussion and analysis in each annual report.
4. Write a one-page executive summary that highlights the most important types of current liabilities for this industry and that compares the current ratio and working capital trends of the two companies, including reference to management's assessment. Include the Fingraph page and your table with your report.

Internet Case

FRA 7.

LO3 **Investigation of Status of Famous Contingencies**

In addition to the Texaco <www.texaco.com> case in **FRA 2,** other famous contingency liability cases include suits against RJR Nabisco <www.nabisco.com>, Philip Morris <www.philipmorris.com>, and Waste Management, Inc. <www.wm.com>. Investigate the current status of any one of these cases by going to the company's web site and finding its latest annual report. Look in the notes to the financial statements under "Contingencies." Report what you find about the case, including whether it has been settled or is no longer being reported.

13

Chapter 13 discusses the characteristics of the partnership form of business and examines accounting issues relating to formation, division of income, dissolution, and liquidation of partnerships.

Partnerships

LEARNING OBJECTIVES

LO1 Identify the principal characteristics, advantages, and disadvantages of the partnership form of business.

LO2 Record partners' investments of cash and other assets when a partnership is formed.

LO3 Compute and record the income or losses that partners share, based on stated ratios, capital balance ratios, and partners' salaries and interest.

LO4 Record a person's admission to or withdrawal from a partnership.

LO5 Compute the distribution of assets to partners when they liquidate their partnership.

DECISION POINT

A USER'S FOCUS

KPMG LLP <www.kpmg.com> Many people think of partnerships as relatively small business organizations, and usually they are right. However, some partnerships, among them law firms, investment companies, real estate companies, and accounting firms, are very large. An example is KPMG LLP, which is a member firm in KPMG International, a professional services organization with offices in 150 countries. KPMG LLP provides accounting and auditing services, tax services, and management consulting services. With over 1,500 partners and 98,000 employees, it is one of the largest partnerships in the world. In 2002, the firm was growing rapidly, with revenues of over $10 billion, about half of which came from outside the United States. How does a partnership this large organize to accomplish its objectives?[1]

KPMG LLP is organized as a limited liability partnership. In a normal partnership, the personal financial resources of all partners are subject to risk of loss if the partnership suffers a loss it cannot bear. Accounting firms are at risk of suffering large losses as a result of lawsuits from investors who lose money investing in a company audited by the accounting firm. Because KPMG is organized as a limited liability partnership, the partners are liable to the extent of their partnership interest in the firm, but their personal assets are not subject to risk.

Why did KPMG organize itself as a limited liability partnership?

Financial Highlights
(in millions of dollars)

	2002	2001
Annual revenue	$10,720	$10,320

PARTNERSHIP CHARACTERISTICS

LO1   Identify the principal characteristics, advantages, and disadvantages
of the partnership form of business.

RELATED TEXT ASSIGNMENTS
Q: 1, 2, 3, 4, 5, 6, 7
SE: 1
SD: 1, 3, 4
FRA: 1, 2, 3

KEY POINT: Partnerships and
sole proprietorships are not
legal entities; corporations are.
All three, however, are considered accounting entities.

The Uniform Partnership Act, which has been adopted by most states, defines a
partnership as "an association of two or more persons to carry on as co-owners of a
business for profit." Partnerships are treated as separate entities in accounting, but
legally there is no economic separation between them and their owners. They differ
in many ways from the other forms of business. Here we describe some of their
important characteristics.

VOLUNTARY ASSOCIATION

A partnership is a voluntary association of individuals rather than a legal entity in
itself. Therefore, a partner is responsible under the law for his or her partners'
actions within the scope of the business. A partner also has unlimited liability for
the debts of the partnership. Because of these potential liabilities, a partner must be
allowed to choose the people who join the partnership. A person should select as
partners individuals who share his or her business objectives.

■ **PARTNERSHIP AGREEMENT**   A partnership is easy to form. Two or more competent
people simply agree to be partners in a common business purpose. Their agreement
is known as a **partnership agreement**. The partnership agreement does not have to
be in writing. However, good business practice calls for a written document that
clearly states the details of the arrangement, including the name, location, and
purpose of the business; the names of the partners and their respective duties; the
investments of each partner; the method of distributing income and losses; and the
procedures for the admission and withdrawal of partners, the withdrawal of assets
allowed each partner, and the liquidation (termination) of the business.

■ **LIMITED LIFE**   Because a partnership is formed by an agreement between
partners, it has a **limited life**. It may be dissolved when a new partner is admitted;
a partner withdraws, goes bankrupt, is incapacitated (to the point that he or she
cannot perform as obligated), retires, or dies; or the terms of the partnership
agreement are met (e.g., when the project for which the partnership was formed is
completed). However, if the partners want the partnership to continue legally, the
partnership agreement can be written to cover each of these situations. For example,
the partnership agreement can state that if a partner dies, the remaining partner or
partners must purchase the deceased partner's capital at book value from the heirs.

■ **MUTUAL AGENCY**   Each partner is an agent of the partnership within the scope of
the business. Because of this **mutual agency**, any partner can bind the partnership
to a business agreement as long as he or she acts within the scope of the company's
normal operations. For example, a partner in a used-car business can bind the
partnership through the purchase or sale of used cars. But this partner cannot bind
the partnership to a contract to buy men's clothing or any other goods that are not
related to the used-car business. Because of mutual agency, it is very important for
an individual to choose business partners who have integrity and who share his or
her business objectives.

KEY POINT: Unlimited liability means that potential
responsibility for debts is not
limited by one's investment, as
it is in a corporation. Each person is personally liable for all
debts of the partnership,
including those arising from
contingent liabilities such as
lawsuits. Liability can be
avoided only by filing for personal bankruptcy.

■ **UNLIMITED LIABILITY**   All partners have **unlimited liability** for their company's
debt, which means that each partner is personally liable for all the debts of the
partnership. If a partnership cannot pay its debts, creditors must first satisfy their
claims from the assets of the business. If these assets are not enough to pay all debts,
the creditors can seek payment from the personal assets of each partner. If one
partner's personal assets are used up before the debts are paid, the creditors can

FOCUS ON INTERNATIONAL BUSINESS

How Do Partnerships Facilitate International Investment?

American businesses are expanding into emerging markets throughout the world. Many of these markets, such as those of Hungary, Poland, the Czech Republic, India, and China, are in the process of privatizing public entities. This means that operations such as steel mills, cement factories, and utilities that were previously run by the government are being converted into private enterprises. Many countries require that local investors own a substantial proportion of the newly formed businesses. One way of accomplishing this is to form joint ventures, which match a country's need for outside capital and operational know-how with investors' interest in business expansion and profitability. Joint ventures often take the form of partnerships among two or more corporations and other investors. Any income or losses from operations will be divided among the participants according to a predetermined agreement.

---

claim additional assets from the remaining partners who are able to pay. Each partner, then, can be required by law to pay all the debts of the partnership.

■ **CO-OWNERSHIP OF PARTNERSHIP PROPERTY** When individuals invest property in a partnership, they give up the right to their separate use of the property. The property becomes an asset of the partnership and is owned jointly by the partners.

■ **PARTICIPATION IN PARTNERSHIP INCOME** Each partner has the right to share in the company's income and the responsibility to share in its losses. The partnership agreement should state the method of distributing income and losses to each partner. If the agreement describes how income should be shared but does not mention losses, losses are distributed in the same way as income. If the agreement does not describe the method of income and loss distribution, the partners must by law share income and losses equally.

■ **ADVANTAGES AND DISADVANTAGES OF PARTNERSHIPS** Partnerships have both advantages and disadvantages. One advantage is that a partnership is easy to form, change, and dissolve. Also, a partnership facilitates the pooling of capital resources and individual talents; it has no corporate tax burden (because a partnership is not a legal entity for tax purposes, it does not have to pay a federal income tax, as do corporations, but must file an informational return); and it gives the partners a certain amount of freedom and flexibility.

On the other hand, partnerships have the following disadvantages: the life of a partnership is limited; one partner can bind the partnership to a contract (mutual agency); the partners have unlimited personal liability; and it is more difficult for a

---

FOCUS ON BUSINESS PRACTICE

Corporations That Look Like Partnerships

Several types of corporations have been created to mimic the characteristics of partnerships in certain ways. *S corporations* are corporations that U.S. tax laws treat in a manner similar to partnerships. S corporations do not pay income taxes like normal corporations. The income or loss of the S corporation is distributed to the stockholders (which are limited to a small number), who report and pay taxes on the income or loss on their personal tax returns. This avoids the problem of double taxation. *Limited liability corporations* are corporations that professional firms such as accounting and consultancy firms mostly use to limit the liability of the partners, who in this form of business are stockholders. *Special-purpose entities (SPEs)*, which have gained notoriety because of the Enron case, are actually quite common. They are separately distinct from the company that forms them and are used by companies to raise money by selling certain assets such as receivables. By meeting certain conditions, the company that sets them up can legitimately avoid including the debt of the SPEs on its balance sheet. Enron used SPEs extensively and fraudulently to hide debt and other commitments of the company.

FOCUS ON BUSINESS PRACTICE

How Do Limited Partnerships Help Finance Big Projects?

Limited partnerships are sometimes used in place of the corporate form to raise funds from the public. Because possible investor losses are normally restricted to the amount of the investment, the limited partnership has some characteristics of the corporate form. Limited partnerships are used to obtain financing for many projects, such as locating and drilling oil and gas wells, manufacturing airplanes, and developing real estate (including shopping centers, office buildings, and apartment complexes). For example, Alliance Capital Management Limited Partnership is one of the largest investment advisors, managing more than $90 billion in assets for corporate and individual investors. The company's partnership units, or shares of ownership, sell on the New York Stock Exchange and can be purchased by the individual investor. In 2003, the units were selling at about $28 each and paid an annual dividend of $2.50 per share.[2]

partnership to raise large amounts of capital and to transfer ownership interests than it is for a corporation.

OTHER FORMS OF ASSOCIATION

Two other common forms of association that are a type of partnership or similar to a partnership are limited partnerships and joint ventures.

ENRICHMENT NOTE:
Many types of organizations have been created by law. They include S corporations and limited partnerships. Each provides legal (especially tax) advantages and disadvantages.

■ **LIMITED PARTNERSHIPS**   A limited partnership is a special type of partnership that, like corporations, confines the limited partner's potential loss to the amount of his or her investment. Under this type of partnership the unlimited liability disadvantage of a partnership can be overcome. Usually, the limited partnership has a general partner who has unlimited liability but allows other partners to limit their potential loss. The potential loss of all partners in an ordinary partnership is limited only by personal bankruptcy laws.

■ **JOINT VENTURES**   In today's global environment, more companies are looking to form alliances similar to partnerships, called *joint ventures*, with other companies rather than to venture out on their own. A joint venture is an association of two or more entities for the purpose of achieving a specific goal, such as the manufacture of a product in a new market. Many joint ventures have an agreed-upon limited life. The entities forming joint ventures usually involve companies but can sometimes involve governments, especially in emerging economies. A joint venture brings together the resources, technical skills, political ties, and other assets of each of the parties for a common goal. Profits and losses are shared on an agreed-upon basis.

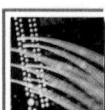

FOCUS ON BUSINESS TECHNOLOGY

Joint Ventures and the Internet

The Internet is fostering the formation of many joint ventures by companies that are normally competitors. Among recent developments of this type are the following:
- Eight metals companies, including Allegheny Technologies Inc. and Alcoa Inc. <www.alcoa.com>, have formed a joint venture to establish online service to provide products to businesses in the metals industries.
- Accor <www.accorhotels.com>, Europe's largest hotel chain; Hilton International <www.hilton.com>; and Forte Hotels <www.forte-hotels.com> have launched an Internet joint venture enabling customers to make online bookings at their hotels. This counters a similar effort involving seven other hotel chains including Marriott <www.marriott.com>, Hyatt <www.hyatt.com>, and Holiday Inn <www.holidayinn.com>.
- General Motors Corporation <www.gm.com> and other companies have formed an Internet joint venture to consolidate and coordinate the purchase of parts and supplies in the manufacture of automobiles.

 Check out ACE for a Review Quiz at http://accounting.college.hmco.com/students.

ACCOUNTING FOR PARTNERS' EQUITY

LO2 Record partners' investments of cash and other assets when a partnership is formed.

RELATED TEXT ASSIGNMENTS
Q: 8
SE: 2
E: 1
P: 1, 5
SD: 3

Although accounting for a partnership is very similar to accounting for a sole proprietorship, there are differences. One is that the owner's equity in a partnership is called **partners' equity**. In accounting for partners' equity, it is necessary to maintain separate Capital and Withdrawals accounts for each partner and to divide the income and losses of the company among the partners.

The differences in the Capital accounts of a sole proprietorship and a partnership are as follows:

SOLE PROPRIETORSHIP

Blake, Capital	
	50,000

PARTNERSHIP

Desmond, Capital		Frank, Capital	
	30,000		40,000

Blake, Withdrawals		Desmond, Withdrawals		Frank, Withdrawals	
12,000		5,000		6,000	

In the partners' equity section of the balance sheet, the balance of each partner's Capital account is listed separately:

Liabilities and Partners' Equity

Total liabilities		$28,000
Partners' equity		
Desmond, capital	$25,000	
Frank, capital	34,000	
Total partners' equity		59,000
Total liabilities and partners' equity		$87,000

STOP AND THINK!

When accounts receivable are transferred into a partnership, at what amount should they be recorded?

Accounts receivable should be transferred in at their net realizable value. Thus, the gross amount of accounts receivable should be recorded, and a related contra account Allowance for Uncollected Accounts should also be recorded so that the net amount is the amount that the partnership will realize. ■

Each partner invests cash, other assets, or both in the partnership according to the partnership agreement. Noncash assets should be valued at their fair market value on the date they are transferred to the partnership. The assets invested by a partner are debited to the proper account, and the total amount is credited to the partner's Capital account.

To show how partners' investments are recorded, let's assume that Jerry Adcock and Rose Villa have agreed to combine their capital and equipment in a partnership to operate a jewelry store. According to their partnership agreement, Adcock will invest $28,000 in cash and $37,000 worth of furniture and displays, and Villa will invest $40,000 in cash and $30,000 worth of equipment. Related to the equipment is a note payable for $10,000, which the partnership assumes. The entries to record the partners' initial investments are as follows:

	20x3		
A = L + OE	July 1 Cash	28,000	
+ +	Furniture and Displays	37,000	
+	Jerry Adcock, Capital		65,000
	Initial investment of Jerry		
	Adcock in Adcock and Villa		
A = L + OE	1 Cash	40,000	
+ + +	Equipment	30,000	
+	Notes Payable		10,000
	Rose Villa, Capital		60,000
	Initial investment of Rose		
	Villa in Adcock and Villa		

KEY POINT: Old book values from previous entities are irrelevant to the new entity.

KEY POINT: Villa's noncash contribution is equal to the fair market value of the equipment less the amount owed on the equipment.

The values assigned to the assets would be included in the partnership agreement. These values can differ from those carried on the partners' personal books. For example, the equipment that Rose Villa contributed had a value of only $22,000 on her books, but its market value had increased considerably after she purchased it. The book value of Villa's equipment is not important. The fair market value of the equipment at the time of transfer *is* important, however, because that value represents the amount of money Villa has invested in the partnership. Later investments are recorded in the same way.

 Check out ACE for a Review Quiz at http://accounting.college.hmco.com/students.

DISTRIBUTION OF PARTNERSHIP INCOME AND LOSSES

LO3 Compute and record the income or losses that partners share, based on stated ratios, capital balance ratios, and partners' salaries and interest.

RELATED TEXT ASSIGNMENTS
Q: 9, 10, 11
SE: 3, 4, 5
E: 2, 3, 4
P: 1, 2, 5, 6
SD: 2
FRA: 1

KEY POINT: The division of income is one area in which a partnership differs from a corporation. In corporations, each common share receives an equal dividend. Partners can use any method they agree on to divide partnership income.

A partnership's income and losses can be distributed according to whatever method the partners specify in the partnership agreement. Income in this form of business normally has three components: return to the partners for the use of their capital (called *interest on partners' capital*), compensation for services the partners have rendered (partners' salaries), and other income for any special contributions individual partners may make to the partnership or risks they may take. The breakdown of total income into its three components helps clarify how much each partner has contributed to the firm.

If all partners contribute equal capital, have similar talents, and spend the same amount of time in the business, then an equal distribution of income and losses would be fair. However, if one partner works full time in the firm and another devotes only a fourth of his or her time, then the distribution of income or losses should reflect the difference. (This concept would apply to any situation in which the partners contribute unequally to the business.)

Distributing income and losses among partners can be accomplished by using stated ratios or capital balance ratios or by paying the partners' salaries and interest on their capital and sharing the remaining income according to stated ratios. *Salaries* and *interest* here are not *salaries expense* or *interest expense* in the ordinary sense of the terms. They do not affect the amount of reported net income. Instead, they refer to ways of determining each partner's share of net income or loss on the basis of time spent and money invested in the partnership.

STATED RATIOS

One method of distributing income and losses is to give each partner a stated ratio of the total income or loss. If each partner is making an equal contribution to the firm, each can assume the same share of income and losses. It is important to understand that an equal contribution to the firm does not necessarily mean an equal capital investment in the firm. One partner may be devoting more time and talent to the firm, whereas another may have made a larger capital investment. And if the partners contribute unequally to the firm, unequal stated ratios can be appropriate.

KEY POINT: The computations of each partner's share of net income are relevant to the closing entries in which the Income Summary account is closed to the partners' Capital accounts.

Let's assume that Adcock and Villa had a net income last year of $30,000. Their partnership agreement states that the percentages of income and losses distributed to Jerry Adcock and Rose Villa should be 60 percent and 40 percent, respectively. The computation of each partner's share of the income and the entry to show the distribution are as follows:

Adcock ($30,000 × .60)	$18,000
Villa ($30,000 × .40)	12,000
Net income	$30,000

20x4

$A = L + OE$
$-$
$+$
$+$

June 30	Income Summary	30,000	
	Jerry Adcock, Capital		18,000
	Rose Villa, Capital		12,000
	Distribution of income for the year to the partners' Capital accounts		

CAPITAL BALANCE RATIOS

If invested capital produces the most income for the partnership, then income and losses may be distributed according to capital balances. The ratio used to distribute income and losses here may be based on each partner's capital balance at the beginning of the year or on the average capital balance of each partner during the year. The partnership agreement must describe the method to be used.

■ **RATIOS BASED ON BEGINNING CAPITAL BALANCES**   To show how the first method works, let's look at the beginning capital balances of the partners in Adcock and Villa. At the start of the fiscal year, July 1, 20x3, Jerry Adcock, Capital showed a $65,000 balance and Rose Villa, Capital showed a $60,000 balance. (Actually, these balances reflect the partners' initial investment; the partnership was formed on July 1, 20x3.) The total partners' equity in the firm, then, was $125,000. Each partner's capital balance at the beginning of the year divided by the total partners' equity at the beginning of the year is that partner's beginning capital balance ratio:

	Beginning Capital Balance	Beginning Capital Balance Ratio
Jerry Adcock	$ 65,000	65,000 ÷ 125,000 = .52 = 52%
Rose Villa	60,000	60,000 ÷ 125,000 = .48 = 48%
	$125,000	

The income that each partner should receive when distribution is based on beginning capital balance ratios is determined by multiplying the total income by each partner's capital ratio. If we assume that income for the year was $140,000, Jerry Adcock's share of that income was $72,800, and Rose Villa's share was $67,200.

Jerry Adcock	$140,000 × .52 = $ 72,800
Rose Villa	140,000 × .48 = 67,200
	$140,000

■ **RATIOS BASED ON AVERAGE CAPITAL BALANCES**   If Adcock and Villa use beginning capital balance ratios to determine the distribution of income, they do not consider any investments or withdrawals made during the year. But investments and withdrawals usually change the partners' capital ratios. If the partners believe their capital balances will change dramatically during the year, they can choose average capital balance ratios as a fairer means of distributing income and losses.

The following T accounts show the activity over the year in Adcock and Villa's partners' Capital and Withdrawals accounts:

Jerry Adcock, Capital			Jerry Adcock, Withdrawals		
	7/1/x3	65,000	1/1/x4	10,000	

Rose Villa, Capital			Rose Villa, Withdrawals		
	7/1/x3	60,000	11/1/x3	10,000	
	2/1/x4	8,000			

Jerry Adcock withdrew $10,000 on January 1, 20x4, and Rose Villa withdrew $10,000 on November 1, 20x3, and invested an additional $8,000 of equipment on February 1, 20x4. Again, the income for the year's operation (July 1, 20x3, to June 30, 20x4) was $140,000. The calculations for the average capital balances and the distribution of income are as follows:

Average Capital Balances

Partner	Date	Capital Balance $\times$	Months Unchanged	=	Total	Average Capital Balance
Adcock	July–Dec.	$65,000 $\times$	6	=	$390,000	
	Jan.–June	55,000 $\times$	6	=	330,000	
			12		$720,000 $\div$ 12 =	$ 60,000
Villa	July–Oct.	$60,000 $\times$	4	=	$240,000	
	Nov.–Jan.	50,000 $\times$	3	=	150,000	
	Feb.–June	58,000 $\times$	5	=	290,000	
			12		$680,000 $\div$ 12 =	56,667
					Total average capital	$116,667

Average Capital Balance Ratios

$$\text{Adcock} = \frac{\text{Adcock's Average Capital Balance}}{\text{Total Average Capital}} = \frac{\$60,000}{\$116,667} = .514 = 51.4\%$$

$$\text{Villa} = \frac{\text{Villa's Average Capital Balance}}{\text{Total Average Capital}} = \frac{\$56,667}{\$116,667} = .486 = 48.6\%$$

Distribution of Income

Partner	Income	$\times$	Ratio	=	Share of Income
Adcock	$140,000	$\times$	.514	=	$ 71,960
Villa	140,000	$\times$	.486	=	68,040
				Total income	$140,000

Notice that to determine the distribution of income (or loss), you must determine the average capital balances, the average capital balance ratios, and each partner's share of income or loss. To compute each partner's average capital balance, you must examine the changes that have occured during the year in each partner's capital balance, changes that are the product of further investments and withdrawals. The partner's beginning capital is multiplied by the number of months the balance remains unchanged. After the balance changes, the new balance is multiplied by the number of months it remains unchanged. The process continues until the end of the year. The totals of these computations are added, and then they are divided by 12 to determine the average capital balances. Once the average capital balances are determined, the method of figuring capital balance ratios for sharing income and losses is the same as the method used for beginning capital balances.

SALARIES, INTEREST, AND STATED RATIOS

KEY POINT: Partnership income or loss cannot be divided solely on the basis of salaries or interest. An additional component, such as stated ratios, is needed.

Partners' contributions to a firm are usually not equal. To make up for the inequality, a partnership agreement can allow for partners' salaries, interest on partners' capital balances, or both in the distribution of income. Again, salaries and interest of this kind are not deducted as expenses before the partnership income is determined. They represent a method of arriving at an equitable distribution of income or loss.

To illustrate an allowance for partners' salaries, we assume that Adcock and Villa agree to annual salaries of $8,000 and $7,000, respectively, and to divide any

● **Stop and Think!**

What is a disadvantage of receiving a large salary as part of a partner's distribution of income?

If the partnership is not very profitable, partners with the large salaries will see reductions in their respective capital accounts to the extent that the salary distribution exceeds their distributions for income or loss for the year. ■

remaining income equally between them. Each salary is charged to the appropriate partner's Withdrawals account when paid. Assuming the same $140,000 income for the first year, the calculations for Adcock and Villa are as follows:

	Income of Partner		Income Distributed
	Adcock	Villa	
Total Income for Distribution			$140,000
Distribution of Salaries			
Adcock	$ 8,000		
Villa		$ 7,000	(15,000)
Remaining Income After Salaries			$125,000
Equal Distribution of Remaining Income			
Adcock ($125,000 × .50)	62,500		
Villa ($125,000 × .50)		62,500	(125,000)
Remaining Income			—
Income of Partners	$70,500	$69,500	$140,000

Salaries allow for differences in the services that partners provide the business. However, they do not take into account differences in invested capital. To allow for capital differences, each partner can receive, in addition to salary, a stated interest on his or her invested capital. Suppose that Jerry Adcock and Rose Villa agree to annual salaries of $8,000 and $7,000, respectively, as well as 10 percent interest on their beginning capital balances, and to share any remaining income equally. The calculations for Adcock and Villa, assuming income of $140,000, are as follows:

CLARIFICATION NOTE: If there is a negative balance after salaries or salaries and interest have been distributed, the terms *Remaining Income After Salaries* and *Remaining Income After Salaries and Interest* become *Negative Balance After Salaries* and *Negative Balance After Salaries and Interest.* The computation proceeds in exactly the same way, regardless of whether the balance is positive or negative.

	Income of Partner		Income Distributed
	Adcock	Villa	
Total Income for Distribution			$140,000
Distribution of Salaries			
Adcock	$ 8,000		
Villa		$ 7,000	(15,000)
Remaining Income After Salaries			$125,000
Distribution of Interest			
Adcock ($65,000 × .10)	6,500		
Villa ($60,000 × .10)		6,000	(12,500)
Remaining Income After Salaries and Interest			$112,500
Equal Distribution of Remaining Income			
Adcock ($112,500 × .50)	56,250		
Villa ($112,500 × .50)		56,250	(112,500)
Remaining Income			—
Income of Partners	$70,750	$69,250	$140,000

FOCUS ON BUSINESS PRACTICE

What Are the Risks of Being a Partner in an Accounting Firm?

Partners in large accounting firms can make over $250,000 per year, with top partners drawing over $800,000. However, consideration of those incomes should take into account the risks that partners take and the fact that the incomes of partners in small accounting firms are often much lower.

Partners are not compensated in the same way as managers in corporations. Partners' income is not guaranteed, but rather is based on the performance of the partnership. Also,

each partner is required to make a substantial investment of capital in the partnership. This capital remains at risk for as long as the partner chooses to stay in the partnership. For instance, in one notable instance, when a large firm was convicted of destroying evidence in the Enron case, the partners lost their total investments as well as their income when their firm was subjected to lawsuits and other losses. The firm was eventually liquidated.

ENRICHMENT NOTE:
When negotiating a partnership agreement, be sure to look at (and negotiate) the impact of both profits (net income) and losses.

If the partnership agreement allows for the distribution of salaries or interest or both, the amounts must be allocated to the partners even if profits are not enough to cover the salaries and interest. In fact, even if the company has a loss, these allocations must still be made. The negative balance, or loss, after the allocation of salaries and interest must be distributed according to the stated ratio in the partnership agreement, or equally if the agreement does not mention a ratio.

For example, let's assume that Adcock and Villa agreed to the following conditions, with much higher annual salaries, for the distribution of income and losses:

	Salaries	Interest	Beginning Capital Balance
Adcock	$70,000	10 percent of beginning	$65,000
Villa	60,000	capital balances	60,000

The computations for the distribution of the income and loss, again assuming income of $140,000, are as follows:

KEY POINT: Using salaries and interest to divide income or loss among partners has no effect on the income statement. They are not expenses. Partners' salaries and interest are used only to allow the equitable division of the partnership's net income.

	Income of Partner		Income Distributed
	Adcock	Villa	
Total Income for Distribution			$140,000
Distribution of Salaries			
Adcock	$70,000		
Villa		$60,000	(130,000)
Remaining Income After Salaries			$ 10,000
Distribution of Interest			
Adcock ($65,000 × .10)	6,500		
Villa ($60,000 × .10)		6,000	(12,500)
Negative Balance After Salaries and Interest			($ 2,500)
Equal Distribution of Negative Balance*			
Adcock ($2,500 × .50)	(1,250)		
Villa ($2,500 × .50)		(1,250)	2,500
Remaining Income			—
Income of Partners	$75,250	$64,750	$140,000

*Notice that the negative balance is distributed equally because the agreement does not indicate how income and losses should be distributed after salaries and interest are paid.

EXHIBIT 1
Partial Income Statement for Adcock and Villa

Adcock and Villa
Partial Income Statement
For the Year Ended June 30, 20x4

Net income		$140,000
Distribution to the partners		
Adcock		
Salary distribution	$70,000	
Interest on beginning capital balance	6,500	
Total	$76,500	
One-half of remaining negative amount	(1,250)	
Share of net income		$ 75,250
Villa		
Salary distribution	$60,000	
Interest on beginning capital balance	6,000	
Total	$66,000	
One-half of remaining negative amount	(1,250)	
Share of net income		64,750
Net income distributed		$140,000

On the income statement for the partnership, the distribution of income or losses is shown below the net income figure. Exhibit 1 shows how this is done.

 Check out ACE for a Review Quiz at http://accounting.college.hmco.com/students.

DISSOLUTION OF A PARTNERSHIP

LO4 Record a person's admission to or withdrawal from a partnership.

RELATED TEXT ASSIGNMENTS
Q: 12, 13
SE: 6, 7, 8, 9
E: 5, 6
P: 3, 5, 7
SD: 3, 5

Dissolution of a partnership occurs whenever there is a change in the original association of partners. When a partnership is dissolved, the partners lose their authority to continue the business as a going concern. The fact that the partners lose this authority does not necessarily mean that the business operation is ended or interrupted. However, it does mean—from a legal and accounting standpoint—that the separate entity ceases to exist. The remaining partners can act for the partnership in finishing the affairs of the business or in forming a new partnership that will be a new accounting entity. The dissolution of a partnership takes place through, among other events, the admission of a new partner, the withdrawal of a partner, or the death of a partner.

ADMISSION OF A NEW PARTNER

BUSINESS-WORLD EXAMPLE: Dissolution of a partnership is a legal issue. Consider Ernst & Young, which admits over one hundred partners each year. The entity continues to operate despite the legal changes it must make.

The admission of a new partner dissolves the old partnership because a new association has been formed. Dissolving the old partnership and creating a new one requires the consent of all the original partners and the ratification of a new partnership agreement. When a new partner is admitted, a new partnership agreement should be in place.

An individual can be admitted to a partnership in one of two ways: by purchasing an interest in the partnership from one or more of the original partners or by investing assets in the partnership.

KEY POINT: Admission of a new partner never has an impact on net income. Regardless of the price a new partner pays, there are never any income statement accounts in the entry to admit a new partner.

A = L + OE
−
+

KEY POINT: When a partner sells his or her interest directly to a new partner, the partner, not the partnership, realizes the gain or loss. In this case, Adcock has a gain of $30,000, but the assets, liabilities, and total equity of the partnership do not change.

A = L + OE
−
−
+

CLARIFICATION NOTE: If the account did not reflect the current value of the assets, the asset accounts (and Capital accounts) would need to be adjusted before admitting the new partner.

A = L + OE
+   +

■ **PURCHASING AN INTEREST FROM A PARTNER**   When a person purchases an interest in a partnership from an original partner, the transaction is a personal one between these two people. However, the interest purchased must be transferred from the Capital account of the selling partner to the Capital account of the new partner.

Suppose that Jerry Adcock decides to sell his interest of $70,000 in Adcock and Villa to Richard Davis for $100,000 on August 31, 20x5, and that Rose Villa agrees to the sale. The entry to record the sale on the partnership books looks like this:

20x5
Aug. 31   Jerry Adcock, Capital   70,000
           Richard Davis, Capital   70,000
             Transfer of Jerry Adcock's equity
             to Richard Davis

Notice that the entry records the book value of the equity, not the amount Davis pays. The amount Davis pays is a personal matter between Adcock and him. Because the amount paid does not affect the assets or liabilities of the firm, it is not entered in the records.

Here's another example of a purchase: Assume that Richard Davis purchases half of Jerry Adcock's $70,000 interest in the partnership and half of Rose Villa's interest, assumed to be $80,000, by paying a total of $100,000 to the two partners on August 31, 20x5. The entry to record this transaction on the partnership books would be as follows:

20x5
Aug. 31   Jerry Adcock, Capital   35,000
      Rose Villa, Capital   40,000
           Richard Davis, Capital   75,000
             Transfer of half of Jerry Adcock's
             and Rose Villa's equity to
             Richard Davis

■ **INVESTING ASSETS IN A PARTNERSHIP**   When a new partner is admitted through an investment in the partnership, both the assets and the partners' equity in the firm increase. The increase occurs because the assets the new partner invests become partnership assets, and as partnership assets increase, partners' equity increases. For example, assume that Jerry Adcock and Rose Villa have agreed to allow Richard Davis to invest $75,000 in return for a one-third interest in their partnership. The Capital accounts of Jerry Adcock and Rose Villa are $70,000 and $80,000, respectively. Davis's $75,000 investment equals a one-third interest in the firm after the investment is added to the previously existing capital of the partnership:

Jerry Adcock, Capital	$ 70,000
Rose Villa, Capital	80,000
Davis's investment	75,000
Total capital after Davis's investment	$225,000
One-third interest = $225,000 ÷ 3 =	$ 75,000

The entry to record Davis's investment is as follows:

20x5
Aug. 31   Cash   75,000
           Richard Davis, Capital   75,000
             Admission of Richard Davis for a
             one-third interest in the company

■ **BONUS TO THE OLD PARTNERS**   A partnership is sometimes so profitable or otherwise advantageous that a new investor is willing to pay more than the actual dollar interest he or she receives in the partnership. For instance, suppose an individual pays $100,000 for an $80,000 interest in a partnership. The $20,000 excess of the payment over the interest purchased is a **bonus** to the original partners. The bonus must be distributed to the original partners according to the partnership agreement. When the agreement does not cover the distribution of bonuses, a bonus should be distributed to the original partners in accordance with the method for distributing income and losses.

Assume that the Adcock and Villa Company has operated for several years and that the partners' capital balances and the stated ratios for distribution of income and loss are as follows:

Partners	Capital Balances	Stated Ratios
Adcock	$160,000	55%
Villa	140,000	45
	$300,000	100%

Richard Davis wants to join the firm. He offers to invest $100,000 on December 1 for a one-fifth interest in the business and income. The original partners agree to the offer. This is the computation of the bonus to the original partners:

Partners' equity in the original partnership		$300,000
Cash investment by Richard Davis		100,000
Partners' equity in the new partnership		$400,000
Partners' equity assigned to Richard Davis ($400,000 × ⅕)		$ 80,000
Bonus to the original partners		
Investment by Richard Davis	$100,000	
Less equity assigned to Richard Davis	80,000	$ 20,000
Distribution of bonus to original partners		
Jerry Adcock ($20,000 × .55)	$ 11,000	
Rose Villa ($20,000 × .45)	9,000	$ 20,000

This is the entry that records Davis's admission to the partnership:

20x5			
Dec. 1	Cash	100,000	
	Jerry Adcock, Capital		11,000
	Rose Villa, Capital		9,000
	Richard Davis, Capital		80,000
	Investment by Richard Davis for a one-fifth interest in the firm, and the bonus distributed to the original partners		

A = L + OE
+   +
     +
     +

■ **BONUS TO THE NEW PARTNER**   There are several reasons that a partnership might want a new partner. A partnership in financial trouble might need additional cash. Or the partners might want to expand the firm's markets and need more capital for this purpose than they themselves can provide. Also, the partners might know a person who would bring a unique talent to the firm. Under these conditions, a new partner may be admitted to the partnership with the understanding that part of the original partners' capital will be transferred (credited) to the new partner's Capital account as a bonus.

For example, suppose that Jerry Adcock and Rose Villa have invited Richard Davis to join the firm. Davis is going to invest $60,000 on December 1 for a one-fourth interest in the company. The stated ratios for distribution of income or loss

● **Stop and Think!**
If the value of a partnership is worth far more than the book value of the assets on the balance sheet, would a new partner entering the partnership be more likely to pay a bonus to the old partners or receive a bonus from the old partners?

The new partner would more likely pay a bonus to the old partners because the value of the incoming partner's share of the partnership would be more than the amounts on the balance sheet. The old partners will want compensation for the value of the proportionate share the new partner is getting. ■

for Adcock and Villa are 55 percent and 45 percent, respectively. If Davis is to receive a one-fourth interest in the firm, the interest of the original partners represents a three-fourths interest in the business. The computation of Davis's bonus is as follows:

Total equity in partnership		
Jerry Adcock, Capital		$160,000
Rose Villa, Capital		140,000
Investment by Richard Davis		60,000
Partners' equity in the new partnership		$360,000
Partners' equity assigned to Richard Davis ($360,000 × ¼)		$ 90,000
Bonus to new partner		
Equity assigned to Richard Davis	$90,000	
Less cash investment by Richard Davis	60,000	$ 30,000
Distribution of bonus from original partners		
Jerry Adcock ($30,000 × .55)	$16,500	
Rose Villa ($30,000 × .45)	13,500	$ 30,000

The entry to record the admission of Richard Davis to the partnership is shown below:

A = L + OE
+
−
−
+

20x5			
Dec. 1	Cash	60,000	
	Jerry Adcock, Capital	16,500	
	Rose Villa, Capital	13,500	
	Richard Davis, Capital		90,000
	To record the investment by Richard Davis of cash and a bonus from Adcock and Villa		

WITHDRAWAL OF A PARTNER

KEY POINT: There is no impact on the income statement of a partnership when a partner withdraws. The only change is on the balance sheet.

Since a partnership is a voluntary association, a partner usually has the right to withdraw at any time. However, to avoid disputes when a partner does decide to withdraw or retire, a partnership agreement should describe the procedures to be followed. The agreement should specify (1) whether an audit will be performed, (2) how the assets will be reappraised, (3) how a bonus will be determined, and (4) by what method the withdrawing partner will be paid.

A partner who wants to withdraw from a partnership can do so in one of several ways. The partner can sell his or her interest to another partner or to an out-

FOCUS ON BUSINESS PRACTICE

Can Withdrawal of Partners Harm a Partnership?

The withdrawal of partners can cause a financial strain on a partnership, as when Goldman, Sachs & Co., the last major Wall Street investment company still organized as a partnership, was scrambling to raise more than $250 million to compensate for the withdrawal of twenty-three partners. The retirements caused a decrease in equity capital of about $400 million, which represented almost 10 percent of the firm's capital.

Goldman was looking for private investors to make up for the losses.[3] The majority of Wall Street investment companies, such as Merrill Lynch & Co., Inc., and Salomon Brothers Inc., are organized as corporations. An advantage of this form of organization is that managers who want to leave their jobs can sell their stock to other investors without affecting the firm's capital.

FIGURE 1
Alternative Ways for a Partner to Withdraw

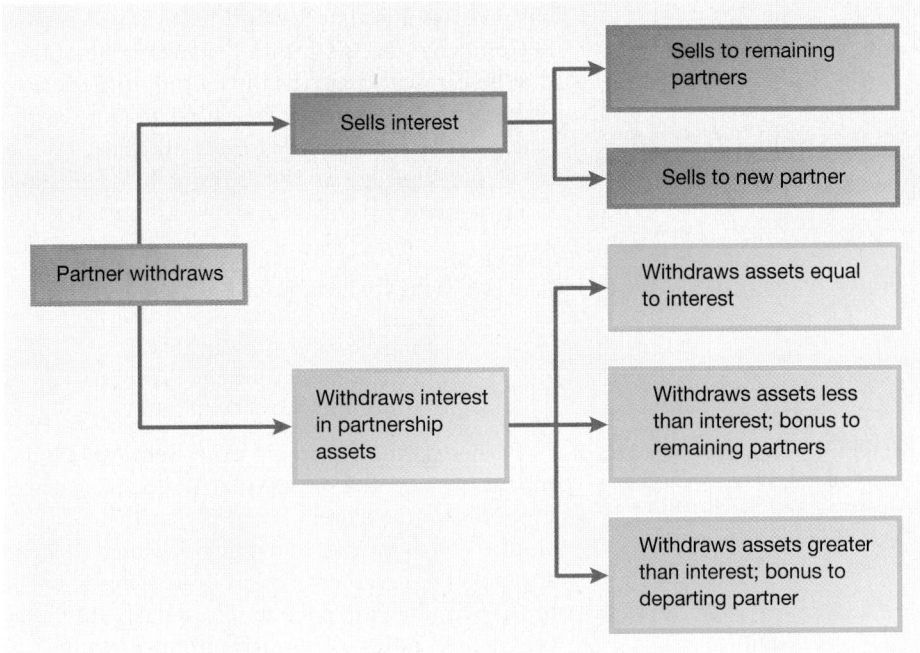

sider with the consent of the remaining partners, or the partner can withdraw assets equal to his or her capital balance, less than his or her capital balance (in this case, the remaining partners receive a bonus), or greater than his or her capital balance (in this case, the withdrawing partner receives a bonus). These alternatives are illustrated in Figure 1.

KEY POINT: Selling a partnership interest does not affect the assets and liabilities of the partnership. Therefore, total equity remains unchanged. The only effect of a partner's selling his or her interest to the existing partners or to a new partner is the change of names in the partners' equity section of the balance sheet.

■ **WITHDRAWAL BY SELLING INTEREST**   When a partner sells his or her interest to another partner or to an outsider with the consent of the other partners, the transaction is personal; it does not change the partnership assets or the partners' equity. For example, let's assume that the capital balances of Adcock, Villa, and Davis are $140,000, $100,000, and $60,000, respectively, for a total of $300,000.

Villa wants to withdraw from the partnership and is reviewing two offers for her interest. The offers are (1) to sell her interest to Davis for $110,000 or (2) to sell her interest to Judy Jones for $120,000. The remaining partners have agreed to either potential transaction. Because Davis and Jones would pay for Villa's interest from their personal assets, the partnership accounting records would show only the transfer of Villa's interest to Davis or Jones. The entries to record these possible transfers are as follows:

1. If Villa's interest is purchased by Davis:

$A = L + OE$
$-$
$+$

Rose Villa, Capital	100,000	
Richard Davis, Capital		100,000
Sale of Villa's partnership interest to Davis		

2. If Villa's interest is purchased by Jones:

$A = L + OE$
$-$
$+$

Rose Villa, Capital	100,000	
Judy Jones, Capital		100,000
Sale of Villa's partnership interest to Jones		

■ **WITHDRAWAL BY REMOVING ASSETS**   A partnership agreement can allow a withdrawing partner to remove assets from the firm equal to his or her capital balance. Assume that Richard Davis decides to withdraw from Adcock, Villa, Davis & Company. Davis's capital balance is $60,000. The partnership agreement states that he can withdraw cash from the firm equal to his capital balance. If there is not enough cash, he must accept a promissory note from the new partnership for the balance. The remaining partners ask that Davis take only $50,000 in cash because of a cash shortage at the time of his withdrawal; he agrees to this request. The following entry records Davis's withdrawal:

A = L + OE
− + −

20x5			
Jan. 21	Richard Davis, Capital	60,000	
	Cash		50,000
	Notes Payable, Richard Davis		10,000
	Withdrawal of Richard Davis from the partnership		

KEY POINT: Even if a bonus was involved, Davis's Capital account would be debited for $60,000 to eliminate it.

When a withdrawing partner removes assets that represent less than his or her capital balance, the equity that the partner leaves in the business is divided among the remaining partners according to their stated ratios. This distribution is considered a bonus to the remaining partners. When a withdrawing partner takes out assets that are greater than his or her capital balance, the excess is treated as a bonus to the withdrawing partner. The remaining partners absorb the bonus according to their stated ratios. Alternative arrangements can be spelled out in the partnership agreement.

DEATH OF A PARTNER

When a partner dies, the partnership is dissolved because the original association has changed. The partnership agreement should state the actions to be taken. Normally, the books are closed, and financial statements are prepared. Those actions are necessary to determine the capital balance of each partner on the date of the death. The agreement may also indicate whether an audit should be conducted, assets appraised, and a bonus recorded, as well as the procedures for settling with the deceased partner's heirs. The remaining partners may purchase the deceased's equity, sell it to outsiders, or deliver specified business assets to the estate. If the firm intends to continue, a new partnership must be formed.

 Check out ACE for a Review Quiz at http://accounting.college.hmco.com/students.

LIQUIDATION OF A PARTNERSHIP

LO5 Compute the distribution of assets to partners when they liquidate their partnership.

RELATED TEXT ASSIGNMENTS
Q: 14, 15
SE: 10
E: 7, 8
P: 4, 5, 8

The **liquidation** of a partnership is the process of ending the business, of selling enough assets to pay the partnership's liabilities, and distributing any remaining assets among the partners. Liquidation is a special form of dissolution. When a partnership is liquidated, the business will not continue.

The partnership agreement should indicate the procedures to be followed in the case of liquidation. Usually, the books are adjusted and closed, with the income or loss distributed to the partners. As the assets of the business are sold, any gain or loss should be distributed to the partners according to the stated ratios. As cash becomes available, it must be applied first to outside creditors, then to loans from partners, and finally to the partners' capital balances.

The process of liquidation can have a variety of financial outcomes. We look at two: (1) assets sold for a gain and (2) assets sold for a loss. For both alternatives, we make the assumptions that the books have been closed for Adcock, Villa, Davis & Company and that the following balance sheet exists before liquidation:

STUDY NOTE: Be sure to consider the liquidation procedure step by step. To liquidate a partnership, the partners first must sell the assets and pay the liabilities (or distribute them to the partners). Second, any gains or losses from the sales of assets must be allocated to the partners. Third, when only cash remains, it is paid to the partners. Fourth, when a partner has a negative capital balance, he or she is obligated to pay the deficiency. Otherwise, the remaining partners must absorb the deficiency.

Adcock, Villa, Davis & Company
Balance Sheet
February 2, 20x6

Assets		Liabilities	
Cash	$ 60,000	Accounts payable	$120,000
Accounts receivable	40,000	**Partners' Equity**	
Merchandise inventory	100,000		
Plant assets (net)	200,000	Adcock, Capital	85,000
Total assets	$400,000	Villa, Capital	95,000
		Davis, Capital	100,000
		Total liabilities and partners' equity	$400,000

● **STOP AND THINK!**
When a partnership is dissolved, what is an alternate approach to selling all the assets and distributing the proceeds, and what decisions will have to be made if this approach is taken?

The partners may decide to divide up the assets among themselves. In this case, they will have to decide on the value of the assets and who gets which assets. They will also have to decide how to pay the liabilities. And they will have to settle the capital accounts, just as they would if cash were involved. ■

TERMINOLOGY NOTE:
Notice the proper use of the term *realization* in the February 13 and 14 entries. *Realization* means "conversion into cash."

The stated ratios of Adcock, Villa, and Davis are 3:3:4, or 30, 30, and 40 percent, respectively.

GAIN ON SALE OF ASSETS

Suppose that the following transactions took place in the liquidation of Adcock, Villa, Davis & Company:

1. The accounts receivable were collected for $35,000.
2. The inventory was sold for $110,000.
3. The plant assets were sold for $200,000.
4. The accounts payable of $120,000 were paid.
5. The gain of $5,000 from the realization of the assets was distributed according to the partners' stated ratios.
6. The partners received cash equivalent to the balances of their Capital accounts.

These transactions are summarized in the statement of liquidation in Exhibit 2. The journal entries with their assumed transaction dates are as follows:

				Explanation on Statement of Liquidation	
	20x6				

A = L + OE
+
−
	Feb. 13	Cash
		Gain or Loss from Realization
		    Accounts Receivable
		        Collection of accounts
		        receivable
			35,000
			5,000
				
				40,000
					1

A = L + OE
+
−
	14	Cash
		    Merchandise Inventory
		    Gain or Loss from Realization
		        Sale of inventory
			110,000	
				100,000
				10,000
					2

EXHIBIT 2
Statement of Liquidation Showing Gain on Sale of Assets

Adcock, Villa, Davis & Company
Statement of Liquidation
February 2–20, 20x6

Explanation	Cash	Other Assets	Accounts Payable	Adcock, Capital (30%)	Villa, Capital (30%)	Davis, Capital (40%)	Gain (or Loss) from Realization
Balance 2/2/x6	$ 60,000	$340,000	$120,000	$85,000	$95,000	$100,000	
1. Collection of Accounts Receivable	35,000	(40,000)					($ 5,000)
	$ 95,000	$300,000	$120,000	$85,000	$95,000	$100,000	($ 5,000)
2. Sale of Inventory	110,000	(100,000)					10,000
	$205,000	$200,000	$120,000	$85,000	$95,000	$100,000	$ 5,000
3. Sale of Plant Assets	200,000	(200,000)					
	$405,000	—	$120,000	$85,000	$95,000	$100,000	$ 5,000
4. Payment of Liabilities	(120,000)		(120,000)				
	$285,000		—	$85,000	$95,000	$100,000	$ 5,000
5. Distribution of Gain (or Loss) from Realization				1,500	1,500	2,000	(5,000)
	$285,000			$86,500	$96,500	$102,000	—
6. Distribution of Cash to Partners	(285,000)			(86,500)	(96,500)	(102,000)	
	—			—	—	—	

A = L + OE	Feb. 16	Cash		200,000		3
+		Plant Assets			200,000	
−		Sale of plant assets				
A = L + OE	16	Accounts Payable		120,000		4
− −		Cash			120,000	
		Payment of accounts payable				
A = L + OE	20	Gain or Loss from Realization		5,000		5
−		Jerry Adcock, Capital			1,500	
+		Rose Villa, Capital			1,500	
+		Richard Davis, Capital			2,000	
+		Distribution of the gain on assets ($10,000 gain minus $5,000 loss) to the partners				

A = L + OE	Feb. 20	Jerry Adcock, Capital	86,500		6
-	-	Rose Villa, Capital	96,500		
-		Richard Davis, Capital	102,000		
-		Cash		285,000	
		Distribution of cash to the partners			

Notice that the cash distributed to the partners is the balance in their respective Capital accounts. Cash is not distributed according to the partners' stated ratios.

LOSS ON SALE OF ASSETS

KEY POINT: The case here is almost the same as the previous one because losses are allocated on the same basis as gains. The only difference is that entry 3 in this case (a loss) and entry 5 in the first case (a gain) switch the debits and credits.

We discuss two cases involving losses on the sale of a company's assets. In the first, the losses are small enough to be absorbed by the partners' capital balances. In the second, one partner's share of the losses is too large for his capital balance to absorb.

When a firm's assets are sold at a loss, the partners share the loss on liquidation according to their stated ratios. For example, assume that during the liquidation of Adcock, Villa, Davis & Company, the total cash received from the collection of accounts receivable and the sale of inventory and plant assets was $140,000. The statement of liquidation appears in Exhibit 3.

EXHIBIT 3
Statement of Liquidation Showing Loss on Sale of Assets

Adcock, Villa, Davis & Company
Statement of Liquidation
February 2–20, 20x6

Explanation	Cash	Other Assets	Accounts Payable	Adcock, Capital (30%)	Villa, Capital (30%)	Davis, Capital (40%)	Gain (or Loss) from Realization
Balance 2/2/x6	$ 60,000	$340,000	$120,000	$85,000	$95,000	$100,000	
1. Collection of Accounts Receivable and Sale of Inventory and Plant Assets	140,000	(340,000)					($200,000)
	$200,000	—	$120,000	$85,000	$95,000	$100,000	($200,000)
2. Payment of Liabilities	(120,000)		(120,000)				
	$ 80,000		—	$85,000	$95,000	$100,000	($200,000)
3. Distribution of Gain (or Loss) from Realization				(60,000)	(60,000)	(80,000)	200,000
	$ 80,000			$25,000	$35,000	$ 20,000	—
4. Distribution of Cash to Partners	(80,000)			(25,000)	(35,000)	(20,000)	
	—			—	—	—	

The journal entries for the transactions summarized in the statement of liquidation in Exhibit 3 are as follows:

Explanation on Statement of Liquidation

	20x6				
A = L + OE	Feb. 15	Cash	140,000		1
+		Gain or Loss from Realization	200,000		
−		Accounts Receivable		40,000	
−		Merchandise Inventory		100,000	
−		Plant Assets		200,000	
		Collection of accounts			
		receivable and the sale of			
		inventory and plant assets			
A = L + OE	16	Accounts Payable	120,000		2
− −		Cash		120,000	
		Payment of accounts payable			
A = L + OE	20	Jerry Adcock, Capital	60,000		3
−		Rose Villa, Capital	60,000		
−		Richard Davis, Capital	80,000		
−		Gain or Loss from Realization		200,000	
+		Distribution of the loss on			
		assets to the partners			
A = L + OE	20	Jerry Adcock, Capital	25,000		4
− −		Rose Villa, Capital	35,000		
−		Richard Davis, Capital	20,000		
−		Cash		80,000	
		Distribution of cash to			
		the partners			

KEY POINT: This example (a loss) uses a compound entry for what was included in entries 1, 2, and 3 in the first example (a gain). If you have difficulty with the concept, here is an opportunity to break the entry down into its three component parts.

In some liquidations, a partner's share of the loss is greater than his or her capital balance. In such a situation, because partners are subject to unlimited liability, the partner must make up the deficit in his or her Capital account from personal assets. For example, suppose that after the sale of assets and the payment of liabilities, the remaining assets and partners' equity of Adcock, Villa, Davis & Company look like this:

Assets
  Cash $ 30,000

Partners' Equity
  Adcock, Capital $25,000
  Villa, Capital   20,000
  Davis, Capital   (15,000) $ 30,000

Richard Davis must pay $15,000 into the partnership from personal funds to cover his deficit. If he pays cash to the partnership, the following entry would record the cash contribution:

	20x6			
A = L + OE	Feb. 20	Cash	15,000	
+ +		Richard Davis, Capital		15,000
		Additional investment of		
		Richard Davis to cover the		
		negative balance in his		
		Capital account		

After Davis pays $15,000, there is enough cash to pay Adcock and Villa their capital balances and, thus, to complete the liquidation. The transaction is recorded in the following way:

			20x6			
A = L + OE			Feb. 20	Jerry Adcock, Capital	25,000	
−	−			Rose Villa, Capital	20,000	
		−		Cash		45,000
				Distribution of cash to		
				the partners		

If a partner does not have the cash to cover his or her obligations to the partnership, the remaining partners share the loss according to their established stated ratios. Remember that all partners have unlimited liability. As a result, if Richard Davis cannot pay the $15,000 deficit in his Capital account, Adcock and Villa must share the deficit according to their stated ratios. Each has a 30 percent stated ratio, so each must pay 50 percent of the losses that Davis cannot pay. The new stated ratios are computed as follows:

	Old Ratios	New Ratios		
Adcock	30%	30 ÷ 60 = .50 =	50%
Villa	30	30 ÷ 60 = .50 =	50
	60%		100%

And the entries to record the transactions are as follows:

			20x6			
A = L + OE			Feb. 20	Jerry Adcock, Capital	7,500	
−				Rose Villa, Capital	7,500	
−				Richard Davis, Capital		15,000
		+		Transfer of Davis's deficit		
				to Adcock and Villa		
A = L + OE			20	Jerry Adcock, Capital	17,500	
−	−			Rose Villa, Capital	12,500	
		−		Cash		30,000
				Distribution of cash to the partners		

Davis's inability to meet his obligations at the time of liquidation does not relieve him of his liabilities to Adcock and Villa. If he is able to pay his liabilities at some time in the future, Adcock and Villa can collect the amount of Davis's deficit that they absorbed.

✔ Check out ACE for a Review Quiz at http://accounting.college.hmco.com/students.

Chapter Review

REVIEW OF LEARNING OBJECTIVES

LO1 Identify the principal characteristics, advantages, and disadvantages of the partnership form of business.

A partnership has several major characteristics that distinguish it from the other forms of business. It is a voluntary association of two or more people who combine their talents and resources to carry on a business. Their joint effort should be supported by a partnership agreement that spells out the venture's operating procedures. A partnership is dissolved by a partner's admission, withdrawal, or death, and therefore has a limited life. Each partner acts as an agent of the partnership within the scope of normal operations and is personally liable for the partnership's debts. Property invested in the partnership becomes an asset of the partnership, owned jointly by all the partners. And, finally, each partner has the right to share in the company's income and the responsibility to share in its losses.

The advantages of a partnership are the ease of its formation and dissolution, the opportunity to pool several individuals' talents and resources, the lack of corporate tax burden, and the freedom of action each partner enjoys. The disadvantages are the limited life of a partnership, mutual agency, the unlimited personal liability of the partners, and the difficulty of raising large amounts of capital and transferring partners' interest. Two other common forms of association that are a type of partnership or similar to a partnership are limited partnerships and joint ventures.

LO2   Record partners' investments of cash and other assets when a partnership is formed.

A partnership is formed when the partners contribute cash, other assets, or a combination of both to the business. The details are stated in the partnership agreement. Initial investments are recorded with a debit to Cash or another asset account and a credit to the investing partner's Capital account. The recorded amount of the other assets should be their fair market value on the date of transfer to the partnership. In addition, a partnership can assume an investing partner's liabilities. When this occurs, the partner's Capital account is credited with the difference between the assets invested and the liabilities assumed.

LO3   Compute and record the income or losses that partners share, based on stated ratios, capital balance ratios, and partners' salaries and interest.

The partners must share income and losses in accordance with the partnership agreement. If the agreement says nothing about the distribution of income and losses, the partners share them equally. Common methods used for distributing income and losses include stated ratios, capital balance ratios, and salaries and interest on capital investments. Each method tries to measure the individual partner's contribution to the operations of the business.

Stated ratios usually are based on the partners' relative contributions to the partnership. When capital balance ratios are used, income or losses are divided strictly on the basis of each partner's capital balance. The use of salaries and interest on capital investment takes into account both efforts (salary) and capital investment (interest) in dividing income or losses among the partners.

LO4   Record a person's admission to or withdrawal from a partnership.

An individual is admitted to a partnership by purchasing a partner's interest or by contributing additional assets. When an interest is purchased, the withdrawing partner's capital is transferred to the new partner. When the new partner contributes assets to the partnership, it may be necessary to recognize a bonus shared or borne by the original partners or by the new partner.

A person can withdraw from a partnership by selling his or her interest in the business to the remaining partners or a new partner or by withdrawing company assets. When assets are withdrawn, the amount can be equal to, less than, or greater than the partner's capital interest. When assets that have a value less than or greater than the partner's interest are withdrawn, a bonus is recognized and distributed among the remaining partners or to the departing partner.

LO5   Compute the distribution of assets to partners when they liquidate their partnership.

The liquidation of a partnership entails selling the assets necessary to pay the company's liabilities and then distributing any remaining assets to the partners. Any gain or loss on the sale of the assets is shared by the partners according to their stated ratios. When a partner has a deficit balance in a Capital account, that partner must contribute personal assets equal to the deficit. When a partner does not have personal assets to cover a capital deficit, the deficit must be absorbed by the solvent partners according to their stated ratios.

REVIEW OF CONCEPTS AND TERMINOLOGY

The following concepts and terms were introduced in this chapter:

LO4 **Bonus:** An amount that accrues to the original partners when a new partner pays more to the partnership than the interest received or that accrues to the new partner when the amount paid to the partnership is less than the interest received.

LO4 **Dissolution:** The loss of authority to continue a partnership as a separate entity due to a change in the original association of partners.

LO1 **Joint venture:** An association of two or more entities for the purpose of achieving a specific goal, such as the manufacture of a product in a new market.

LO1 **Limited life:** A characteristic of a partnership; the fact that any event that breaches the partnership agreement—including the admission, withdrawal, or death of a partner—terminates the partnership.

LO1 **Limited partnership:** A form of partnership in which limited partners' liabilities are limited to their investment.

LO5 **Liquidation:** A special form of dissolution in which a business ends by selling assets, paying liabilities, and distributing any remaining assets to the partners.

LO1 **Mutual agency:** A characteristic of a partnership; the authority of each partner to act as an agent of the partnership within the scope of the business's normal operations.

LO2 **Partners' equity:** The owner's equity in a partnership.

LO1 **Partnership:** An association of two or more people to carry on as co-owners of a business for profit.

LO1 **Partnership agreement:** The contractual relationship between partners that identifies the details of their partnership.

LO1 **Unlimited liability:** A characteristic of a partnership; the fact that each partner has personal liability for all the debts of the partnership.

REVIEW PROBLEM

Distribution of Income and Admission of a Partner

LO3
LO4 Jack Holder and Dan Williams reached an agreement in 20x7 to pool their resources and form a partnership to manufacture and sell university T-shirts. In forming the partnership, Holder and Williams contributed $100,000 and $150,000, respectively. They drafted a partnership agreement stating that Holder was to receive an annual salary of $6,000 and Williams was to receive 3 percent interest annually on his original investment of $150,000 in the business. Income and losses after salary and interest were to be shared by Holder and Williams in a 2:3 ratio.

REQUIRED ▶ 1. Compute the income or loss that Holder and Williams share, and prepare the required entries in journal form, assuming the partnership made $27,000 income in 20x7 and suffered a $2,000 loss in 20x8 (before salary and interest).

2. Assume that Jean Ratcliffe offers Holder and Williams $60,000 for a 15 percent interest in the partnership on January 1, 20x9. Holder and Williams agree to Ratcliffe's offer because they need her resources to expand the business. On January 1, 20x9, the balance in Holder's Capital account is $113,600, and the balance in Williams's Capital account is $161,400. Record the admission of Ratcliffe to the partnership, assuming that her investment represents a 15 percent interest in the total partners' capital and that a bonus will be distributed to Holder and Williams in the ratio of 2:3.

ANSWER TO REVIEW PROBLEM

1. Compute the income or loss distribution to the partners.

| | Income of Partner | | Income |
	Holder	Williams	Distributed
20x7			
Total Income for Distribution			$27,000
Distribution of Salary			
Holder	$ 6,000		(6,000)
Remaining Income After Salary			$21,000
Distribution of Interest			
Williams ($150,000 × .03)		$ 4,500	(4,500)
Remaining Income After Salary and Interest			$16,500
Distribution of Remaining Income			
Holder ($16,500 × ⅖)	6,600		
Williams ($16,500 × ⅗)		9,900	(16,500)
Remaining Income			—
Income of Partners	$12,600	$14,400	$27,000
20x8			
Total Loss for Distribution			($ 2,000)
Distribution of Salary			
Holder	$ 6,000		(6,000)
Negative Balance After Salary			($ 8,000)
Distribution of Interest			
Williams ($150,000 × .03)		$ 4,500	(4,500)
Negative Balance After Salary and Interest			($12,500)
Distribution of Negative Balance			
Holder ($12,500 × ⅖)	(5,000)		
Williams ($12,500 × ⅗)		(7,500)	12,500
Remaining Loss			—
Income and Loss of Partners	$ 1,000	($ 3,000)	($ 2,000)

Entry in Journal Form—20x7

Income Summary	27,000	
Jack Holder, Capital		12,600
Dan Williams, Capital		14,400
Distribution of income for the year to the partners' Capital accounts		

Entry in Journal Form—20x8

Dan Williams, Capital	3,000	
Income Summary		2,000
Jack Holder, Capital		1,000
Distribution of the loss for the year to the partners' Capital accounts		

2. Record the admission of a new partner.

Capital Balance and Bonus Computation

$$\text{Ratcliffe, Capital} = (\text{Original Partners' Capital} + \text{New Partner's Investment}) \times 15\%$$
$$= (\$113,600 + \$161,400 + \$60,000) \times .15 = \$50,250$$
$$\text{Bonus} = \text{New Partner's Investment} - \text{Ratcliffe, Capital}$$
$$= \$60,000 - \$50,250$$
$$= \$9,750$$

Distribution of Bonus

Holder = $\$9,750 \times \frac{2}{5}$ = $\$3,900$

Williams = $\$9,750 \times \frac{3}{5}$ = $\underline{5,850}$

Total bonus $\underline{\underline{\$9,750}}$

Entry in Journal Form

20x9			
Jan. 1	Cash	60,000	
	Jack Holder, Capital		3,900
	Dan Williams, Capital		5,850
	Jean Ratcliffe, Capital		50,250
	Sale of a 15 percent interest in the partnership to Jean Ratcliffe and the bonus paid to the original partners		

Chapter Assignments

BUILDING YOUR KNOWLEDGE FOUNDATION

QUESTIONS

1. Briefly define *partnership*, and list several important characteristics of the partnership form of business.

2. Leon and Jon are partners in a drilling operation. Leon purchased a drilling rig to be used in the partnership's operations. Is Leon's purchase binding on Jon even though Jon was not involved in it? Explain your answer.

3. What is the meaning of unlimited liability when applied to a partnership? Describe a form of partnership that limits investors' liability.

4. The partnership agreement for Anne and Jin-Li does not disclose how they will share income and losses. How would the income and losses be shared in this partnership?

5. What are several key advantages of a partnership? What are some disadvantages?

6. How does a limited partnership overcome a key disadvantage of ordinary partnerships?

7. What form of association is becoming more prevalent in conducting global business? Define it.

8. Charles contributes $10,000 in cash and a building with a book value of $40,000 and fair market value of $50,000 to the Charles and Dean partnership. What is the balance of Charles's Capital account in the partnership?

9. Oscar Perez and Leah Torn are forming a partnership. What are some factors they should consider in deciding how income is to be divided?

10. Sue and Ari share income and losses in their partnership in a 3:2 ratio. The firm's net income for the current year is $80,000. How would the distribution of income be recorded in the journal?

11. Kathy and Roger share income in their partnership in a 2:4 ratio. Kathy and Roger receive salaries of $6,000 and $10,000, respectively. How would they share a net income of $22,000 before salaries?

12. Carol purchases Mary's interest in the Mary and Leo partnership for $62,000. Mary has a $57,000 capital interest in the partnership. How would this transaction be recorded in the partnership books?

13. Dan and Augie each own a $50,000 interest in a partnership. They agree to admit Bea as a partner by selling her a one-third interest for $80,000. How large a bonus will be distributed to Dan and Augie?

14. Describe the ways in which the dissolution of a partnership differs from the liquidation of a partnership.

15. In the liquidation of a partnership, José's Capital account showed a $5,000 debit balance after all the creditors had been paid. What obligation does José have to the partnership?

SHORT EXERCISES

SE 1.
LO1 Partnership Characteristics

Indicate whether each statement below is a reflection of (a) voluntary association, (b) a partnership agreement, (c) limited life, (d) mutual agency, or (e) unlimited liability.

1. A partner may be required to pay the debts of the partnership out of personal assets.
2. A partnership must be dissolved when a partner is admitted, withdraws, retires, or dies.
3. Any partner can bind the partnership to a business agreement.
4. A partner does not have to remain a partner if he or she does not want to.
5. Details of the arrangements among partners are specified in a written contract.

SE 2.
LO2 Partnership Formation

Bob contributes cash of $12,000, and Kim contributes office equipment that cost $10,000 but is valued at $8,000 to the formation of a new partnership. Prepare the entry in journal form to form the partnership.

SE 3.
LO3 Distribution of Partnership Income

During the first year, the Bob and Kim partnership (see **SE 2**) earned an income of $5,000. Assume the partners agreed to share income and losses in the ratio of the beginning balances of their capital accounts. How much income should be transferred to each Capital account?

SE 4.
LO3 Distribution of Partnership Income

During the first year, the Bob and Kim partnership (see **SE 2**) earned an income of $5,000. Assume the partners agreed to share income and losses by figuring interest on the beginning capital balances at 10 percent and dividing the remainder equally. How much income should be transferred to each Capital account?

SE 5.
LO3 Distribution of Partnership Income

During the first year, the Bob and Kim partnership (see **SE 2**) earned an income of $5,000. Assume the partners agreed to share income and losses by figuring interest on the beginning capital balances at 10 percent, allowing a salary of $6,000 to Bob, and dividing the remainder equally. How much income (or loss) should be transferred to each Capital account?

SE 6.
LO4 Withdrawal of a Partner and Admission of a Partner

After the partnership has been operating for a year, the Capital accounts of Bob and Kim are $15,000 and $10,000, respectively. Kim withdraws from the partnership by selling her interest in the business to Sonia for $8,000. What will be the Capital account balances of the partners in the new Bob and Sonia partnership? Prepare the journal entry to record the transfer of ownership on the partnership books.

SE 7.
LO4 Admission of a New Partner

After the partnership has been operating for a year, the Capital accounts of Bob and Kim are $15,000 and $10,000, respectively. Sonia buys a one-sixth interest in the partnership by investing cash of $11,000. What will be the Capital account balances of the partners in the new Bob, Kim, and Sonia partnership, assuming a bonus to the old partners, who share income and losses equally? Prepare the entry in journal form to record the transfer of ownership on the partnership books.

SE 8.
LO4 Admission of a New Partner

After the partnership has been operating for a year, the Capital accounts of Bob and Kim are $15,000 and $10,000, respectively. Sonia buys a one-fourth interest in the partnership by investing cash of $5,000. What will be the Capital account balances of the partners in the new Bob, Kim, and Sonia partnership, assuming that the new partner receives a bonus and that Bob and Kim share income and losses equally? Prepare the entry in journal form to record the transfer of ownership on the partnership books.

SE 9.
LO4 Withdrawal of a Partner

After the partnership has been operating for several years, the Capital accounts of Bob, Kim, and Sonia are $25,000, $16,000, and $9,000, respectively. Sonia decides to leave the partnership and is allowed to withdraw $9,000 in cash. Prepare the entry in journal form to record the withdrawal on the partnership books.

SE 10.
LO5 Liquidation of a Partnership

After the partnership has been operating for a year, the Capital accounts of Bob and Kim are $15,000 and $10,000, respectively. The firm has cash of $12,000 and office equipment of $13,000. The partners decide to liquidate the partnership. The office equipment is sold for only $4,000. Assuming the partners share income and losses in the ratio of one-third to Bob and two-thirds to Kim, how much cash will be distributed to each partner in liquidation?

EXERCISES

E 1.
LO2 Partnership Formation

Henri Mikels and Alex Jamison are watch repairmen who want to form a partnership and open a jewelry store. They have an attorney prepare their partnership agreement, which indicates that assets invested in the partnership will be recorded at their fair market value and that liabilities will be assumed at book value.

The assets contributed by each partner and the liabilities assumed by the partnership are as follows:

Assets	Henri Mikels	Alex Jamison	Total
Cash	$40,000	$30,000	$70,000
Accounts receivable	52,000	20,000	72,000
Allowance for uncollectible accounts	4,000	3,000	7,000
Supplies	1,000	500	1,500
Equipment	20,000	10,000	30,000
Liabilities			
Accounts payable	32,000	9,000	41,000

Prepare the entry in journal form necessary to record the original investments of Mikels and Jamison in the partnership.

E 2.
LO3 Distribution of Income

Elijah Samuels and Tony Winslow agreed to form a partnership. Samuels contributed $200,000 in cash, and Winslow contributed assets with a fair market value of $400,000. The partnership, in its initial year, reported net income of $120,000. Calculate the distribution of the first year's income to the partners under each of the following conditions:

1. Samuels and Winslow failed to include stated ratios in the partnership agreement.
2. Samuels and Winslow agreed to share income and losses in a 3:2 ratio.
3. Samuels and Winslow agreed to share income and losses in the ratio of their original investments.
4. Samuels and Winslow agreed to share income and losses by allowing 10 percent interest on original investments and sharing any remainder equally.

E 3.
LO3 Distribution of Income or Losses: Salary and Interest

Assume that the partnership agreement of Samuels and Winslow in E 2 states that Samuels and Winslow are to receive salaries of $20,000 and $24,000, respectively; that Samuels is to receive 6 percent interest on his capital balance at the beginning of the year; and that the remainder of income and losses are to be shared equally. Calculate the distribution of the income or losses under the following conditions:

1. Income totaled $120,000 before deductions for salaries and interest.
2. Income totaled $48,000 before deductions for salaries and interest.
3. There was a loss of $2,000.
4. There was a loss of $40,000.

LO3 Distribution of Income: Average Capital Balance

E 4. Barbara and Karen operate a furniture rental business. Their capital balances on January 1, 20x7, were $160,000 and $240,000, respectively. Barbara withdrew cash of $32,000 from the business on April 1, 20x7. Karen withdrew $60,000 cash on October 1, 20x7. Barbara and Karen distribute partnership income based on their average capital balances each year. Income for 20x7 was $160,000. Compute the income to be distributed to Barbara and Karen using their average capital balances in 20x7.

LO4 Admission of a New Partner: Recording a Bonus

E 5. Ernie, Ron, and Denis have equity in a partnership of $40,000, $40,000, and $60,000, respectively, and they share income and losses in a ratio of 1:1:3. The partners have agreed to admit Henry to the partnership. Prepare entries in journal form to record the admission of Henry to the partnership under the following conditions:

1. Henry invests $60,000 for a 20 percent interest in the partnership, and a bonus is recorded for the original partners.
2. Henry invests $60,000 for a 40 percent interest in the partnership, and a bonus is recorded for Henry.

LO4 Withdrawal of a Partner

E 6. Danny, Steve, and Luis are partners. They share income and losses in the ratio of 3:2:1. Luis's Capital account has a $120,000 balance. Danny and Steve have agreed to let Luis take $160,000 of the company's cash when he retires from the business. What entry in journal form must be made on the partnership's books when Luis retires, assuming that a bonus to Luis is recognized and absorbed by the remaining partners?

LO5 Partnership Liquidation

E 7. Assume the following assets, liabilities, and partners' equity in the Ming and Demmick partnership on December 31, 20xx:

$$\text{Assets} = \text{Liabilities} + \text{Ming, Capital} + \text{Demmick, Capital}$$
$$\$160,000 = \$10,000 + \$90,000 + \$60,000$$

The partnership has no cash. When the partners agree to liquidate the business, the assets are sold for $120,000, and the liabilities are paid. Ming and Demmick share income and losses in a ratio of 3:1.

1. Prepare a statement of liquidation.
2. Prepare entries in journal form for the sale of assets, payment of liabilities, distribution of loss from realization, and final distribution of cash to Ming and Demmick.

LO5 Partnership Liquidation

E 8. Ariel, Mandy, and Tisha are partners in a tanning salon. The assets, liabilities, and capital balances as of July 1, 20x7, are as follows:

Assets	$480,000
Liabilities	160,000
Ariel, Capital	140,000
Mandy, Capital	40,000
Tisha, Capital	140,000

Because competition is strong, business is declining, and the partnership has no cash, the partners have decided to sell the business. Ariel, Mandy, and Tisha share income and losses in a ratio of 3:1:1, respectively. The assets were sold for $260,000, and the liabilities were paid. Mandy has no other assets and will not be able to cover any deficits in her Capital account. How will the ending cash balance be distributed to the partners?

PROBLEMS

LO2 Partnership Formation
LO3 and Distribution of Income

P 1. In January 20x3, Edie Rivera and Babs Bacon agreed to produce and sell chocolate candies. Rivera contributed $240,000 in cash to the business. Bacon contributed the building and equipment, valued at $220,000 and $140,000, respectively. The partnership had an income of $84,000 during 20x3 but was less successful during 20x4, when income was only $40,000.

REQUIRED ▶

1. Prepare the entry to record the investment of both partners in the partnership.
2. Determine the share of income for each partner in 20x3 and 20x4 under each of the following conditions: (a) The partners agreed to share income equally. (b) The partners failed to agree on an income-sharing arrangement. (c) The partners agreed to share income according to the ratio of their original investments. (d) The partners agreed to share income by allowing interest of 10 percent on their original investments and dividing the remainder equally. (e) The partners agreed to share income by allowing salaries of $40,000 for Rivera and $28,000 for Bacon, and dividing the remainder equally. (f) The partners agreed to share income by paying salaries of

$40,000 to Rivera and $28,000 to Bacon, allowing interest of 9 percent on their original investments, and dividing the remainder equally.

3. What are some of the factors that need to be considered in choosing the plan of partners' income sharing among the options shown in Part 2?

P 2.
LO3 Distribution of Income: Salary and Interest

Naomi and Petri are partners in a tennis shop. They have agreed that Naomi will operate the store and receive a salary of $104,000 per year. Petri will receive 10 percent interest on his average capital balance during the year of $500,000. The remaining income or losses are to be shared by Naomi and Petri in a 2:3 ratio.

REQUIRED ▶

Determine each partner's share of income and losses under each of the following conditions. In each case, the income or loss is stated before the distribution of salary and interest.

1. Income was $168,000.
2. Income was $88,000.
3. The loss was $25,600.

P 3.
LO4 Admission and Withdrawal of a Partner

Marnie, Stacie, and Samantha are partners in Woodware Company. Their capital balances as of July 31, 20x4, are as follows:

Marnie, Capital	Stacie, Capital	Samantha, Capital
45,000	15,000	30,000

Each partner has agreed to admit Connie to the partnership.

REQUIRED ▶

1. Prepare the journal entries to record Connie's admission to or Marnie's withdrawal from the partnership under each of the following conditions: (a) Connie pays Marnie $12,500 for 20 percent of Marnie's interest in the partnership. (b) Connie invests $20,000 cash in the partnership and receives an interest equal to her investment. (c) Connie invests $30,000 cash in the partnership for a 20 percent interest in the business. A bonus is to be recorded for the original partners on the basis of their capital balances. (d) Connie invests $30,000 cash in the partnership for a 40 percent interest in the business. The original partners give Connie a bonus according to the ratio of their capital balances on July 31, 20x4. (e) Marnie withdraws from the partnership, taking $52,500. The excess of withdrawn assets over Marnie's partnership interest is distributed according to the balances of the Capital accounts. (f) Marnie withdraws by selling her interest directly to Connie for $60,000.
2. When a new partner enters a partnership, why would the new partner pay a bonus to the old partners, or why would the old partners pay a bonus to the new partner?

P 4.
LO5 Partnership Liquidation

Caruso, Evans, and Weisman are partners in a retail lighting store. They share income and losses in the ratio of 2:2:1, respectively. The partners have agreed to liquidate the partnership. Here is the partnership balance sheet before the liquidation:

Caruso, Evans, and Weisman Partnership
Balance Sheet
August 31, 20x7

Assets		Liabilities	
Cash	$ 280,000	Accounts payable	$ 360,000
Other assets	880,000	**Partners' Equity**	
Total assets	$1,160,000		
		Caruso, Capital	400,000
		Evans, Capital	240,000
		Weisman, Capital	160,000
		Total liabilities and partners' equity	$1,160,000

The other assets were sold on September 1, 20x7, for $720,000. Accounts payable were paid on September 4, 20x7. The remaining cash was distributed to the partners on September 11, 20x7.

REQUIRED ▶

1. Prepare a statement of liquidation.
2. Prepare the following entries in journal form: (a) the sale of the other assets, (b) payment of the accounts payable, (c) the distribution of the loss from realization, and (d) the distribution to the partners of the remaining cash.

P 5.

LO2 **Comprehensive Partnership**
LO3 **Transactions**
LO4
LO5

The following events pertain to a partnership formed by Mark Raymond and Stan Bryden to operate a floor-cleaning company:

20x4
Feb. 14   The partnership was formed. Raymond transferred to the partnership $80,000 cash, land worth $80,000, a building worth $480,000, and a mortgage on the building of $240,000. Bryden transferred to the partnership $40,000 cash and equipment worth $160,000.

Dec. 31   During 20x4, the partnership earned income of just $84,000. The partnership agreement specifies that income and losses are to be divided by paying salaries of $40,000 to Raymond and $60,000 to Bryden, allowing 8 percent interest on beginning capital investments, and dividing any remainder equally.

20x5
Jan. 1   To improve the prospects for the company, the partners decided to take in a new partner, Chuck Menzer, who had experience in the floor-cleaning business. Menzer invested $156,000 for a 25 percent interest in the business. A bonus was transferred in equal amounts from the original partners' Capital accounts to Menzer's Capital account.

Dec. 31   During 20x5, the company earned income of $87,200. The new partnership agreement specified that income and losses would be divided by paying salaries of $60,000 to Bryden and $80,000 to Menzer (no salary to Raymond), allowing 8 percent interest on beginning capital balances after Menzer's admission, and dividing the remainder equally.

20x6
Jan. 1   Because it appeared that the business could not support the three partners, the partners decided to liquidate the partnership. The asset and liability accounts of the partnership were as follows: Cash, $407,200; Accounts Receivable (net), $68,000; Land, $80,000; Building (net), $448,000; Equipment (net), $236,000; Accounts Payable, $88,000; and Mortgage Payable, $224,000. The equipment was sold for $200,000. The accounts payable were paid. The loss was distributed equally to the partners' Capital accounts. A statement of liquidation was prepared, and the remaining assets and liabilities were distributed. Raymond agreed to accept cash plus the land and building at book value and the mortgage payable as payment for his share. Bryden accepted cash and the accounts receivable for his share. Menzer was paid in cash.

REQUIRED ▶

Prepare entries in journal form to record all of the facts above. Support your computations with schedules, and prepare a statement of liquidation in connection with the January 1, 20x6, entries.

ALTERNATE PROBLEMS

P 6.

LO3 **Distribution of Income:**
Salaries and Interest

Jacob, Deric, and Jason are partners in the South Central Company. The partnership agreement states that Jacob is to receive 8 percent interest on his capital balance at the beginning of the year, Deric is to receive a salary of $100,000 a year, and Jason will be paid interest of 6 percent on his average capital balance during the year. Jacob, Deric, and Jason will share any income or loss after salary and interest in a 5:3:2 ratio. Jacob's capital balance at the beginning of the year was $600,000, and Jason's average capital balance for the year was $720,000.

REQUIRED ▶

Determine each partner's share of income and losses under the following conditions. In each case, the income or loss is stated before the distribution of salary and interest.

1. Income was $545,200.
2. Income was $155,600.
3. The loss was $56,800.

P 7.

LO4 Admission and Withdrawal of a Partner

Peter, Mara, and Vanessa are partners in the Image Gallery. As of November 30, 20xx, the balance in Peter's Capital account was $50,000, the balance in Mara's was $60,000, and the balance in Vanessa's was $90,000. Peter, Mara, and Vanessa share income and losses in a ratio of 2:3:5.

REQUIRED ▶

1. Prepare entries in journal form for each of the following independent conditions: (a) Bob pays Vanessa $100,000 for four-fifths of Vanessa's interest. (b) Bob is to be admitted to the partnership with a one-third interest for a $100,000 cash investment. (c) Bob is to be admitted to the partnership with a one-third interest for a $160,000 cash investment. A bonus, based on the partners' ratio for income and losses, is to be distributed to the original partners when Bob is admitted. (d) Bob is to be admitted to the partnership with a one-third interest for an $82,000 cash investment. A bonus is to be given to Bob on admission. (e) Peter withdraws from the partnership, taking $66,000 in cash. (f) Peter withdraws from the partnership by selling his interest directly to Bob for $70,000.
2. In general, when a new partner enters a partnership, why would the new partner pay a bonus to the old partners, or why would the old partners pay a bonus to the new partner?

P 8.

LO5 Partnership Liquidation

The balance sheet of the Rose Partnership as of July 31, 20xx, follows.

Rose Partnership
Balance Sheet
July 31, 20xx

Assets		Liabilities	
Cash	$ 6,000	Accounts payable	$480,000
Accounts receivable	120,000	**Partners' Equity**	
Inventory	264,000		
Equipment (net)	462,000		
Total assets	$852,000	Gerri, Capital	72,000
		Susi, Capital	180,000
		Mari, Capital	120,000
		Total liabilities and partners' equity	$852,000

The partners—Gerri, Susi, and Mari—share income and losses in the ratio of 5:3:2. Because of a mutual disagreement, Gerri, Susi, and Mari have decided to liquidate the business.

Assume that Gerri cannot contribute any additional personal assets to the company during liquidation and that the following transactions occurred during liquidation: (a) Accounts receivable were sold for 60 percent of their book value. (b) Inventory was sold for $276,000. (c) Equipment was sold for $300,000. (d) Accounts payable were paid in full. (e) Gain or loss from realization was distributed to the partners' Capital accounts. (f) Gerri's deficit was transferred to the remaining partners in their new income and loss ratio. (g) The remaining cash was distributed to Susi and Mari.

REQUIRED ▶

1. Prepare a statement of liquidation.
2. Prepare entries in journal form to liquidate the partnership and distribute any remaining cash.

SKILLS DEVELOPMENT CASES

Conceptual Analysis

LO1   Partnership Agreement

SD 1. Form a partnership with one or two of your classmates. Assume that the two or three of you are forming a small service business. For example, you might form a company that hires college students to paint houses during the summer or to provide landscaping services.

Working together, draft a partnership agreement for your business. The agreement can be a simple one, with just a sentence or two for each provision. However, it should include the name, location, and purpose of the business; the names of the partners and their respective duties; the investments of each partner; methods for distributing profits and losses; and procedures for dealing with the admission or withdrawal of partners, the withdrawal of assets, the death of a partner, and liquidation of the business. Include a title, date, and signature lines.

Group Activity: Assign groups to prepare partnership agreements.

LO3   Distribution of Partnership Income and Losses

SD 2. Landow, Donovan, and Hansa, who are forming a partnership to operate an antiques gallery, are discussing how income and losses should be distributed. Among the facts they are considering are the following:

a. Landow will contribute cash for operations of $100,000, Donovan will contribute a collection of antiques that is valued at $300,000, and Hansa will not contribute any assets.

b. Landow and Hansa will handle day-to-day business operations. Hansa will work full time, and Landow will devote about half-time to the partnership. Donovan will not devote time to day-to-day operations. A full-time clerk in a retail store would make about $20,000 in a year, and a full-time manager would receive about $30,000.

c. The current interest rate on long-term bonds is 8 percent.

Landow, Donovan, and Hansa have just hired you as the partnership's accountant. Write a memorandum describing an equitable plan for distributing income and losses. Outline the reasons why you believe this plan is equitable. According to your plan, which partner will gain the most if the partnership is very profitable, and which will lose the most if the partnership has large losses?

Ethical Dilemma

LO1   Death of a Partner
LO2
LO4

SD 3. South Shore Realty was started 20 years ago when T. S. Tyler, R. C. Strong, and A. J. Hibbert established a partnership to sell real estate near Galveston, Texas. The partnership has been extremely successful. In 20xx, Tyler, the senior partner, who in recent years had not been very active in the partnership, died. Unfortunately, the partnership agreement is vague about how the partnership interest of a partner who dies should be valued. It simply states that "the estate of a deceased partner shall receive compensation for his or her interest in the partnership in a reasonable time after death." The attorney for Tyler's family believes that the estate should receive one-third of the assets of the partnership based on the fair market value of the net assets (total assets less total liabilities). The total assets of the partnership are $10 million in the accounting records, but the assets are worth at least $20 million. Because the firm's total liabilities are $4 million, the attorney is asking for $5.3 million (one-third of $16 million). Strong and Hibbert do not agree, but all parties want to avoid a protracted, expensive lawsuit. They have decided to put the question to an arbitrator, who will make a determination of the settlement.

Here are some other facts that may or may not be relevant. The current balances in the partners' Capital accounts are $1.5 million for Tyler, $2.5 million for Strong, and $2.0 million for Hibbert. Net income in 20xx is to be distributed to the Capital accounts in the ratio of 1:4:3. Before Tyler's semiretirement, the distribution ratio was 3:3:2. Assume you or your group is the arbitrator, and develop what you would consider a fair distribution of assets to Tyler's estate. Defend your solution.

Research Activity

SD 4.   The limited partnership is a form of business that was particularly important to the U.S. economy in the 1980s. To find the latest developments or to study the practical applications of a particular subject, such as limited partnerships, it is helpful to use periodical indexes in the library to find articles relating to that subject. Three periodical indexes relevant to accounting and business are *The Accountant's Index*, the *Business Periodicals Index*, and *The Wall Street Journal Index*. Use one or more of those periodical indexes in your college or university library to find three articles about limited partnerships. Sometimes the articles are not listed under the heading "Limited Partnerships"; instead, they appear under the uses of limited partnerships. Some examples are real estate, investments, research and development, and cattle or livestock. Write a short summary of each article, relating the content of the article to the content of this chapter or explaining why the limited partnership form of business was important in the situation described in the article.

Decision-Making Practice

SD 5.   The A-One Fitness Center, owned by Abe Hines and Mario Saconi, has been very successful since its inception five years ago. Hines and Saconi work 10 to 11 hours a day at the business. They have decided to expand by opening up another fitness center in the north part of town. Hines has approached you about becoming a partner in the business. He and Saconi are interested in you because of your experience in operating a small gym. Also, they need additional funds to expand their business. Projected income after the expansion but before partners' salaries for the next five years is as follows:

20x3	20x4	20x5	20x6	20x7
$100,000	$120,000	$130,000	$140,000	$150,000

Currently, Hines and Saconi each draw a $25,000 salary and share remaining profits equally. They are willing to give you an equal share of the business for $142,000. You will receive a $25,000 salary and one-third of the remaining profits. You would work the same hours as Hines and Saconi. Your salary for the next five years where you currently work is expected to be as follows:

20x3	20x4	20x5	20x6	20x7
$34,000	$38,000	$42,000	$45,000	$50,000

Here is financial information for the A-One Fitness Center:

Current Assets	$ 45,000	Long-Term Liabilities	$100,000
Plant and Equipment, net	365,000	Abe Hines, Capital	140,000
Current Liabilities	50,000	Mario Saconi, Capital	120,000

1. Compute your capital balance if you decide to join Hines and Saconi in the fitness center partnership.
2. Analyze your expected income for the next five years.
3. Should you invest in the A-One Fitness Center?
4. Assume that you do not consider Hines and Saconi's offer of partnership to be a good one. Develop a counteroffer that you would be willing to accept (be realistic).

FINANCIAL REPORTING AND ANALYSIS CASES

Interpreting Financial Reports

FRA 1.   The Springfield Clinic is owned and operated by ten local doctors as a partnership. Recently, a paralyzed patient sued the clinic for malpractice, for a total of $20 million. The clinic carries malpractice liability insurance in the amount of $10 million. There is no provision for the possible loss from this type of lawsuit in the partnership's financial statements. The condensed balance sheet for 20xx is as follows:

```
                        Springfield Clinic
                     Condensed Balance Sheet
                       December 31, 20xx
    _____

                            Assets

    Current assets                       $246,000
    Property, plant, and equipment (net)  750,000
    Total assets                                        $996,000


                 Liabilities and Partners' Equity

    Current liabilities                  $180,000
    Long-term debt                        675,000
    Total liabilities                                   $855,000
    Partners' equity                                     141,000
    Total liabilities and partners' equity              $996,000
```

1. How should information about the lawsuit be disclosed in the December 31, 20xx, financial statements of the partnership?
2. Assume that the clinic and its insurance company settle out of court by agreeing to pay a total of $10.1 million, of which $100,000 must be paid by the partnership. What effect will the payment have on the clinic's December 31, 20xx, financial statements? Discuss the effect of the settlement on the Springfield Clinic doctors' personal financial situations.

International Company

FRA 2.
LO1   International Joint Ventures

Nokia <www.nokia.com>, the Finnish telecommunications company, has formed an equally owned joint venture with Capital Corporation, a state-owned Chinese company, to develop a center for the manufacture and development of telecommunications equipment in China, the world's fastest-growing market for this kind of equipment. The main aim of the development is to persuade Nokia's suppliers to move close to the company's main plant. The Chinese government looks favorably on companies that involve local suppliers.[4] What advantages does a joint venture have over a single company in entering a new market in another country? What are the potential disadvantages?

Toys "R" Us Annual Report

This activity is not appropriate for this chapter.

Fingraph® Financial Analysis™

This activity is not appropriate for this chapter.

Comparison Case

This activity is not appropriate for this chapter.

Internet Case

LO1 **Comparison of Career Opportunities in Partnerships and Corporations**

FRA 3. Accounting firms are among the world's largest partnerships and provide a wide range of attractive careers for business and accounting majors. Through the Needles Accounting Resource Center Web Site at http://accounting.college.hmco.com/students, you can explore careers in public accounting by linking to the web site of one of the Big Four accounting firms. The firms are Deloitte & Touche, Ernst & Young, KPMG International, and PricewaterhouseCoopers. Each firm's home page has a career opportunity section. For the firm you choose, compile a list of facts about the firm—size, locations, services, and career opportunities. Do you have the interest and background for a career in public accounting? Why or why not? How do you think working for a large partnership would differ from or be the same as working for a large corporation? Be prepared to discuss your findings in class.

14

Chapter 14 focuses on long-term equity financing, including the types of equity securities and transactions that affect the stockholders' equity section of the balance sheet, such as stock issues, dividends, and treasury stock purchases.

Contributed Capital

LEARNING OBJECTIVES

LO1 Identify and explain the management issues related to contributed capital.

LO2 Identify the components of stockholders' equity.

LO3 Account for cash dividends.

LO4 Identify the characteristics of preferred stock, including the effect on distribution of dividends.

LO5 Account for the issuance of stock for cash and other assets.

LO6 Account for treasury stock.

DECISION POINT

A USER'S FOCUS

Cisco Systems, Inc. <www.cisco.com> One way corporations raise new capital is by issuing stock. Cisco Systems, Inc., a major manufacturer of telecommunications equipment, issued almost $3.5 billion of common stock in a recent three-year period, as shown in the Financial Highlights on the opposite page.[1] Why does Cisco Systems' management choose to issue common stock to satisfy some of its needs for new capital? What are some of the advantages and disadvantages of this approach?

Financing with common stock has several advantages. First, it is less risky than financing with bonds because dividends on common stock are not paid unless the board of directors decides to pay them. Cisco Systems does not currently pay any dividends. In contrast, if the interest on bonds is not paid, a company can be forced into bankruptcy. Second, when a company does not pay a cash dividend, the cash generated by profitable operations can be invested in the company's operations. Third, a company may need the proceeds of a common stock issue to maintain or improve the balance between liabilities and stockholders' equity. By issuing common stock in 2001, Cisco Systems offset the impact on stockholders' equity of a $1 billion net loss in 2001. The balance between total liabilities and total equity remains a relatively low 30 percent.

On the other hand, issuing common stock comes with certain disadvantages. Unlike the interest on bonds, dividends paid on stock are not tax-deductible. Furthermore, when it issues more stock, the corpora-

Why does Cisco Systems, Inc. choose to issue common stock to satisfy some of its needs for new capital?

tion dilutes its ownership. This means that the current stockholders must yield some control to the new stockholders. It is important for accountants to understand the nature and characteristics of corporations as well as the process of accounting for a stock issue and other types of stock transactions.

LO3   **Date of declaration:** The date on which the board of directors declares a dividend.

LO3   **Date of payment:** The date on which payment of a dividend is made.

LO3   **Date of record:** The date on which ownership of stock for the purpose of receiving a dividend is determined.

LO1   **Dividends:** The distribution of a corporation's assets (usually cash generated by past earnings) to its stockholders.

LO4   **Dividends in arrears:** Past dividends on cumulative preferred stock that remain unpaid.

LO1   **Dividends yield:** Current return to stockholders in the form of dividends; dividends per share divided by market price per share.

LO1   **Double taxation:** Taxation of corporate earnings twice—once as income of the corporation and once again as income to stockholders based on the dividends they receive.

LO3   **Ex-dividend:** A description of capital stock between the date of record and the date of payment, when the right to a dividend already declared on the stock remains with the person who sells the stock and does not transfer to the person who buys it.

LO1   **Initial public offering (IPO):** A company's first issue of capital stock to the public.

LO2   **Issued stock:** The shares of stock sold or otherwise transferred to stockholders.

LO1   **Legal capital:** The number of shares of stock issued times the par value; the minimum amount that can be reported as contributed capital.

LO3   **Liquidating dividend:** A dividend that exceeds retained earnings; usually paid when a corporation goes out of business or reduces its operations.

LO4   **Noncumulative preferred stock:** Preferred stock that does not oblige the issuer to make up a missed dividend in a subsequent year.

LO5   **No-par stock:** Capital stock that does not have a par value.

LO2   **Outstanding stock:** Stock that has been issued and is still in circulation.

LO1   **Par value:** An arbitrary amount assigned to each share of stock; constitutes the legal capital of a corporation.

LO2   **Preferred stock:** Stock that has preference over common stock, usually in terms of dividends and the distribution of assets.

LO1   **Price/earnings (P/E) ratio:** A measure of confidence in a company's future; market price per share divided by earnings per share.

LO2   **Residual equity:** The common stock of a corporation.

LO1   **Return on equity:** A measure of management performance; net income divided by average stockholders' equity.

LO1   **Share of stock:** A unit of ownership in a corporation.

LO1   **Start-up and organization costs:** The costs of forming a corporation.

LO5   **Stated value:** A value assigned by the board of directors of a corporation to no-par stock.

LO1   **Stock certificate:** A document issued to a stockholder indicating the number of shares of stock the stockholder owns.

LO1   **Stock option plan:** An agreement to issue stock to employees according to specified terms.

LO6   **Treasury stock:** Capital stock, either common or preferred, that the issuing company has reacquired but has not subsequently resold or retired.

LO1   **Underwriter:** An intermediary between the corporation and the investing public who facilitates an issue of stock or other securities for a fee.

REVIEW PROBLEM

Stock Entries and Stockholders' Equity

LO1
LO2
LO3
LO4
LO5
LO6

The Beta Corporation was organized in 20x4 in the state of Arizona. Its charter authorized the corporation to issue 1,000,000 shares of $1 par value common stock and an additional 25,000 shares of 4 percent, $20 par value cumulative convertible preferred stock. Here are the transactions related to the company's stock during 20x4:

Feb. 1 Issued 100,000 shares of common stock for $125,000.
15 Issued 3,000 shares of common stock for accounting and legal services. The services were billed to the company at $3,600.
Mar. 15 Issued 120,000 shares of common stock to Edward Jackson in exchange for a building and land appraised at $100,000 and $25,000, respectively.
Apr. 2 Purchased 20,000 shares of common stock for the treasury at $1.25 per share from a person who changed his mind about investing in the company.
July 1 Issued 25,000 shares of preferred stock for $500,000.
Sept. 30 Sold 10,000 of the shares in the treasury for $1.50 per share.
Dec. 31 The board declared dividends of $24,910 payable on January 15 to stockholders of record on January 8. Dividends included preferred stock cash dividends for one-half year.

For the period ended December 31, 20x4, the company reported net income of $40,000 and earnings per common share of $.14. At December 31, the market price per common share was $1.60.

REQUIRED ▶

1. Record these transactions in journal form. In the explanation for the December 31 entry to record dividends, show dividends payable to each class of stock.
2. Prepare the stockholders' equity section of the Beta Corporation balance sheet as of December 31, 20x4. (**Hint:** Use net income and dividends to calculate retained earnings.)
3. Calculate dividends yield on common stock, price/earnings ratio of common stock, and return on equity.

ANSWER TO REVIEW PROBLEM

1. Entries prepared in journal form:

Feb.	1	Cash	125,000	
		Common Stock		100,000
		Paid-in Capital in Excess of Par Value, Common		25,000
		Issued 100,000 shares of $1 par value common stock for $1.25 per share		
	15	Start-up and Organization Expense	3,600	
		Common Stock		3,000
		Paid-in Capital in Excess of Par Value, Common		600
		Issued 3,000 shares of $1 par value common stock for billed accounting and legal services of $3,600		
Mar.	15	Building	100,000	
		Land	25,000	
		Common Stock		120,000
		Paid-in Capital in Excess of Par Value, Common		5,000
		Issued 120,000 shares of $1 par value common stock for a building and land appraised at $100,000 and $25,000, respectively		

Apr.	2	Treasury Stock, Common	25,000	
		Cash		25,000
		Purchased 20,000 shares of common stock for the treasury at $1.25 per share		
July	1	Cash	500,000	
		Preferred Stock		500,000
		Issued 25,000 shares of $20 par value preferred stock for $20 per share		
Sept.	30	Cash	15,000	
		Treasury Stock, Common		12,500
		Paid-in Capital, Treasury Stock		2,500
		Sold 10,000 shares of treasury stock at $1.50 per share; original cost was $1.25 per share		
Dec.	31	Cash Dividends Declared	24,910	
		Cash Dividends Payable		24,910
		Declared a $24,910 cash dividend to preferred and common stockholders		

Total dividend	$24,910	
Less preferred stock cash dividend		
$500,000 × .04 × 6/12	10,000	
Common stock cash dividend	$14,910	

2. Stockholders' equity section of the balance sheet prepared:

Beta Corporation
Balance Sheet
December 31, 20x4

Stockholders' Equity

Contributed capital		
Preferred stock, 4 percent cumulative convertible, $20 par value, 25,000 shares authorized, issued, and outstanding		$500,000
Common stock, $1 par value, 1,000,000 shares authorized, 223,000 shares issued, and 213,000 shares outstanding	$223,000	
Paid-in capital in excess of par value, common	30,600	
Paid-in capital, treasury stock	2,500	256,100
Total contributed capital		$756,100
Retained earnings		15,090*
Total contributed capital and retained earnings		$771,190
Less treasury stock, common (10,000 shares, at cost)		12,500
Total stockholders' equity		$758,690

*Retained Earnings = $40,000 − $24,910 = $15,090.

3. Dividends yield on common stock, price/earnings ratio of common stock, and return on equity calculated:

$$\text{Dividends per Share} = \$14{,}910 \text{ Common Stock Dividend} \div 213{,}000 \text{ Common Shares Outstanding} = \$.07$$

$$\text{Dividends Yield} = \frac{\text{Dividends per Share}}{\text{Market Price per Share}} = \frac{\$.07}{\$1.60} = 4.4\%$$

$$\text{Price/Earnings (P/E) Ratio} = \frac{\text{Market Price per Share}}{\text{Earnings per Share}} = \frac{\$1.60}{\$.14} = 11.4 \text{ times}$$

The opening balance of stockholders' equity on February 1, 20x1, was $125,000.

$$\text{Return on Equity} = \frac{\text{Net Income}}{\text{Average Stockholders' Equity}}$$

$$= \frac{\$40{,}000}{(\$758{,}690 + \$125{,}000) \div 2}$$

$$= 9.1\%$$

Chapter Assignments

BUILDING YOUR KNOWLEDGE FOUNDATION

QUESTIONS

1. What management issues are related to contributed capital?
2. Identify and explain several advantages of the corporate form of business.
3. Identify and explain several disadvantages of the corporate form of business.
4. What is dividends yield, and what do investors learn from it?
5. What is the price/earnings (P/E) ratio, and what does it measure?
6. What are the start-up and organization costs of a corporation?
7. What is the proper accounting treatment of start-up and organization costs?
8. What is a stock option plan, and why would a company have one?
9. What is the legal capital of a corporation, and what is its significance?
10. Describe the significance of the following dates as they relate to dividends: (a) date of declaration, (b) date of record, and (c) date of payment.
11. Explain the accounting treatment of cash dividends.
12. What are dividends in arrears, and how should they be disclosed in the financial statements?
13. Define *cumulative*, *convertible*, and *callable* as they apply to preferred stock.
14. How is the value of stock determined when stock is issued for noncash assets?
15. Define *treasury stock* and explain why a company would purchase its own stock.
16. What is the proper classification of the accounts listed below on the balance sheet? Indicate whether stockholders' equity accounts are contributed capital, retained earnings, or contra stockholders' equity.
    a. Common Stock
    b. Treasury Stock
    c. Paid-in Capital, Treasury Stock
    d. Paid-in Capital in Excess of Par Value, Common
    e. Paid-in Capital in Excess of Stated Value, Common
    f. Retained Earnings

SHORT EXERCISES

LO1   Management Issues

SE 1. Indicate whether each of the following actions is related to (a) managing under the corporate form of business, (b) using equity financing, (c) determining dividend policies, or (d) evaluating performance using return on equity:

1. Considering whether to make a distribution to stockholders
2. Controlling day-to-day operations
3. Determining whether to issue preferred or common stock
4. Compensating management based on the company's meeting or exceeding the targeted return on equity
5. Issuing shares
6. Transferring shares without the approval of other owners

LO1   Advantages and Disadvantages of a Corporation

SE 2. Identify whether each of the following characteristics is an advantage or a disadvantage of the corporate form of business:

1. Ease of transfer of ownership
2. Taxation
3. Separate legal entity
4. Lack of mutual agency
5. Government regulation
6. Continuous existence

LO1   Effect of Start-up and Organization Costs

SE 3. At the beginning of 20x3, Shiran Company incurred the following start-up and organization costs: (1) attorneys' fees with a market value of $5,000, paid with 3,000 shares of $1 par value common stock, and (2) incorporation fees paid of $3,000. Calculate total start-up and organization costs. What will be the effect of these costs on the balance sheet and income statement?

LO1   Exercise of Stock Options

SE 4. On June 6, Heda Corday exercised her option to purchase 10,000 shares of Antonia Corporation $1 par value common stock at an option price of $4. The market price per share was $4 on the grant date and $18 on the exercise date. Record the transaction on Antonia's books.

LO2   Stockholders' Equity

SE 5. Prepare the stockholders' equity section of Keech Corporation's balance sheet from the following accounts and balances on December 31, 20xx:

Account	Balance	
	Debit	Credit
Common Stock, $10 par value, 60,000 shares authorized, 40,000 shares issued, and 39,000 shares outstanding		$400,000
Paid-in Capital in Excess of Par Value, Common		200,000
Retained Earnings		30,000
Treasury Stock, Common (1,000 shares, at cost)	$15,000	

LO3   Cash Dividends

SE 6. Powers Corporation has authorized 100,000 shares of $1 par value common stock, of which 80,000 are issued and 70,000 are outstanding. On May 15, the board of directors declared a cash dividend of $.10 per share payable on June 15 to stockholders of record on June 1. Prepare the entries, as necessary, for each of the three dates.

LO4   Preferred Stock Dividends with Dividends in Arrears

SE 7. Maddox Corporation has 1,000 shares of $100, 8 percent cumulative preferred stock outstanding and 20,000 shares of $1 par value common stock outstanding. In the company's first three years of operation, its board of directors paid cash dividends as follows: 20x3, none; 20x4, $20,000; and 20x5, $40,000. Determine the total cash dividends and dividends per share paid to the preferred and common stockholders during each of the three years.

LO5   Issuance of Stock

SE 8. Brianna Corporation is authorized to issue 100,000 shares of common stock. The company sold 5,000 shares at $12 per share. Prepare entries in journal form to record the sale of stock for cash under each of the following independent alternatives: (1) The stock has a par value of $5, and (2) the stock has no par value but a stated value of $1 per share.

SE 9.

LO5 Issuance of Stock for Noncash Assets

Rheimes Corporation issued 8,000 shares of its $1 par value common stock in exchange for land that had a fair market value of $50,000. Prepare in journal form the entries necessary to record the issuance of the stock for the land under each of the following conditions: (1) The stock was selling for $7 per share on the day of the transaction, and (2) management attempted to place a value on the common stock but could not do so.

SE 10.

LO6 Treasury Stock Transactions

Prepare in journal form the entries necessary to record the following stock transactions of Oahanii Company during 20xx:

Oct. 1 Purchased 1,000 shares of its own $2 par value common stock for $20 per share, the current market price.
    17 Sold 250 shares of treasury stock purchased on October 1 for $25 per share.
    21 Sold 400 shares of treasury stock purchased on October 1 for $18 per share.

SE 11.

LO6 Retirement of Treasury Stock

On October 28, 20xx, Oahanii Company (**SE 10**) retired the remaining 350 shares of treasury stock. The shares were originally issued at $5 per share. Prepare the necessary entry in journal form.

EXERCISES

E 1.

LO1 Dividends Yield and Price/Earnings Ratio

In 20x5, Palladin Corporation earned $2.20 per share and paid a dividend of $1.00 per share. At year end, the price of its stock was $33 per share. Calculate the dividends yield and the price/earnings ratio.

E 2.

LO2 Stockholders' Equity
LO6

The following accounts and balances are from the records of Halloran Corporation on December 31, 20xx:

	Balance	
Account	Debit	Credit
Preferred Stock, $100 par value, 9 percent cumulative, 20,000 shares authorized, 12,000 shares issued and outstanding		$1,200,000
Common Stock, $12 par value, 90,000 shares authorized, 60,000 shares issued, and 57,000 shares outstanding		720,000
Paid-in Capital in Excess of Par Value, Common		388,000
Retained Earnings		46,000
Treasury Stock, Common (3,000 shares, at cost)	$60,000	

Prepare the stockholders' equity section for Halloran Corporation's balance sheet.

E 3.

LO2 Characteristics of Common
LO4 and Preferred Stock

Indicate whether each of the following characteristics is more closely associated with common stock (C) or preferred stock (P):

1. Often receives dividends at a set rate
2. Is considered the residual equity of a company
3. Can be callable
4. Can be convertible
5. More likely to have dividends that vary in amount from year to year
6. Can be entitled to receive dividends not paid in past years
7. Likely to have full voting rights
8. Receives assets first in liquidation
9. Generally receives dividends before other classes of stock

E 4.

LO2 Stock Entries Using
LO5 T Accounts; Stockholders'
Equity

The Wallace Hospital Supply Corporation was organized in 20xx. It was authorized to issue 100,000 shares of no-par common stock with a stated value of $5 per share, and 20,000 shares of $100 par value, 6 percent noncumulative preferred stock. On March 1, the company issued 60,000 shares of its common stock for $15 per share and 8,000 shares of its preferred stock for $100 per share.

1. Record the issuance of the stock in T accounts.
2. Prepare the stockholders' equity section of Wallace Hospital Supply Corporation's balance sheet as it would appear immediately after the company issued the common and preferred stock.

LO3   Cash Dividends

E 5.   Estey Corporation secured authorization from the state for 200,000 shares of $10 par value common stock. It has 160,000 shares issued and 140,000 shares outstanding. On June 5, the board of directors declared a $.50 per share cash dividend to be paid on June 25 to stockholders of record on June 15. Prepare entries in journal form to record these events.

LO3
LO6   Cash Dividends

E 6.   Santori Corporation has 500,000 authorized shares of $1 par value common stock, of which 400,000 are issued, including 40,000 shares of treasury stock. On October 15, the board of directors declared a cash dividend of $.25 per share payable on November 15 to stockholders of record on November 1. Prepare entries in journal form for each of the three dates.

LO4   Cash Dividends with
Dividends in Arrears

E 7.   Amsco Corporation has 10,000 shares of its $100 par value, 7 percent cumulative preferred stock outstanding, and 50,000 shares of its $1 par value common stock outstanding. In Amsco's first four years of operation, its board of directors paid cash dividends as follows: 20x3, none; 20x4, $120,000; 20x5, $140,000; 20x6, $140,000. Determine the dividends per share and total cash dividends paid to the preferred and common stockholders during each of the four years.

LO4   Cash Dividends on Preferred
and Common Stock

E 8.   Caron Corporation pays dividends at the end of each year. The dividends that it paid for 20x3, 20x4, and 20x5 were $80,000, $60,000, and $180,000, respectively. Calculate the total amount of dividends the Caron Corporation paid in each of these years to its common and preferred stockholders under both of the following capital structures: (1) 20,000 shares of $100 par, 6 percent noncumulative preferred stock and 60,000 shares of $10 par common stock; (2) 10,000 shares of $100 par, 7 percent cumulative preferred stock and 60,000 shares of $10 par common stock. No dividends were in arrears at the beginning of 20x3.

LO5   Issuance of Stock

E 9.   Montana Company is authorized to issue 200,000 shares of common stock. On August 1, the company issued 10,000 shares at $25 per share. Prepare entries in journal form to record the issuance of stock for cash under each of the following alternatives:

1. The stock has a par value of $25.
2. The stock has a par value of $10.
3. The stock has no par value.
4. The stock has a stated value of $1 per share.

LO5   Issuance of Stock for Noncash
Assets

E 10.   On July 1, 20xx, Florine, a new corporation, issued 20,000 shares of its common stock to finance a corporate headquarters building. The building has a fair market value of $600,000 and a book value of $400,000. Because Florine is a new corporation, it is not possible to establish a market value for its common stock. Record the issuance of stock for the building, assuming the following conditions: (1) the par value of the stock is $10 per share; (2) the stock is no-par stock; and (3) the stock has a stated value of $4 per share.

LO6   Treasury Stock Transactions

E 11.   Record in T accounts the following stock transactions of Mahtani Company, which represent all the company's treasury stock transactions during 20xx:

May   5   Purchased 400 shares of its own $2 par value common stock for $20 per share, the current market price.
          17   Sold 150 shares of treasury stock purchased on May 5 for $22 per share.
          21   Sold 100 shares of treasury stock purchased on May 5 for $20 per share.
          28   Sold the remaining 150 shares of treasury stock purchased on May 5 for $19 per share.

LO6   Treasury Stock Transactions
Including Retirement

E 12.   Record in T accounts the following stock transactions of Theoharis Corporation, which represent all its treasury stock transactions for the year:

June   1   Purchased 2,000 shares of its own $30 par value common stock for $70 per share, the current market price.
          10   Sold 500 shares of treasury stock purchased on June 1 for $80 per share.
          20   Sold 700 shares of treasury stock purchased on June 1 for $58 per share.
          30   Retired the remaining shares purchased on June 1. The original issue price was $42 per share.

PROBLEMS

P 1.

LO1 **Start-up and Organization**
LO2 **Costs, Stock and Dividend**
LO3 **Entries Using T Accounts, and**
LO5 **Stockholders' Equity**

On March 1, 20xx, Jung Corporation began operations with a charter from the state that authorized 100,000 shares of $2 par value common stock. Over the next quarter, the firm engaged in the following transactions:

Mar. 1   Issued 30,000 shares of common stock, $100,000.
     2   Paid fees associated with obtaining the charter and starting up and organizing the corporation, $12,000.
Apr. 10   Issued 13,000 shares of common stock, $65,000.
May 31   The board of directors declared a $.10 per share cash dividend to be paid on June 15 to shareholders of record on June 10.

REQUIRED ▶

1. Record the above transactions in T accounts.
2. Prepare the stockholders' equity section of Jung Corporation's balance sheet on May 31, 20xx. Net income earned during the first quarter was $15,000.

P 2.

LO1 **Preferred and Common Stock**
LO4 **Dividends and Dividends Yield**

Ⓚ/Ⓡ

Taswell Corporation had the following stock outstanding from 20x3 through 20x6:

Preferred stock: $50 par value, 8 percent cumulative, 10,000 shares authorized, issued, and outstanding

Common stock: $5 par value, 200,000 shares authorized, issued, and outstanding

The company paid $30,000, $30,000, $94,000, and $130,000 in dividends during 20x3, 20x4, 20x5, and 20x6, respectively. The market price per common share was $7.25 and $8.00 per share at year end 20x5 and 20x6, respectively.

REQUIRED ▶

1. Determine the dividends per share and the total dividends paid to common stockholders and preferred stockholders in 20x3, 20x4, 20x5, and 20x6.
2. Perform the same computations, with the assumption that the preferred stock was noncumulative.
3. Calculate the 20x5 and 20x6 dividends yield for common stock, using the dividends per share computed in **2.**
4. How are cumulative preferred stock and noncumulative preferred stock similar to long-term bonds? How do they differ from long-term bonds?

P 3.

LO1 **Treasury Stock Transactions**
LO6

Bendix Company was involved in the following treasury stock transactions during 20xx:

Jan. 10   Purchased 52,000 shares of its $2 par value common stock on the market for $40 per share.
     20   Sold 16,000 shares of the treasury stock for $42 per share.
Feb. 8   Sold 12,000 shares of the treasury stock for $38 per share.
     16   Sold 20,000 shares of the treasury stock for $34 per share.
Mar. 14   Purchased an additional 8,000 shares for $36 per share.
     25   Retired all the remaining shares of treasury stock. All shares originally were issued at $16 per share.

REQUIRED ▶

1. Record these transactions in journal form.
2. What effect does the purchase of treasury stock have on return on equity? Why might management prefer to buy treasury stock rather than pay dividends?

P 4.

LO1 **Comprehensive Stockholders'**
LO2 **Equity Transactions and**
LO3 **Financial Ratios**
LO4
LO5
LO6

Ⓚ/Ⓡ

Arkazian, Inc., was organized and authorized to issue 10,000 shares of $100 par value, 9 percent preferred stock and 100,000 shares of no-par, $10 stated value common stock on July 1, 20xx. Stock-related transactions for Arkazian were as follows:

July 1   Issued 20,000 shares of common stock at $22 per share.
     1   Issued 1,000 shares of common stock at $22 per share for services rendered in connection with the organization of the company.
     2   Issued 4,000 shares of preferred stock at par value for cash.
     10   Issued 5,000 shares of common stock for land on which the asking price was $120,000. Market value of the stock was $24. Management wishes to record the land at full market value of the stock.
Aug. 2   Purchased 3,000 shares of its common stock at $26 per share.
     10   Declared a cash dividend for one month on the outstanding preferred stock and $.04 per share on common stock outstanding, payable on August 22 to stockholders of record on August 12.
     12   Date of record for cash dividends.
     22   Paid cash dividends.

REQUIRED ▶

1. Record the transactions in T accounts.
2. Prepare the stockholders' equity section of the balance sheet as it would appear on August 31, 20xx. Net income for July and August was $50,000.
3. Calculate dividends yield, price/earnings ratio, and return on equity. Assume earnings per common share are $1.97 and market price per common share is $25. For beginning stockholders' equity, use the balance at the close of business on July 1, 20xx.

P 5.

LO1   **Comprehensive Stockholders'**
LO2   **Equity Transactions and**
LO3   **T Accounts**
LO4
LO5
LO6

In January 20xx, Hammond Corporation was organized and authorized to issue 2,000,000 shares of no-par common stock and 50,000 shares of 5 percent, $50 par value, noncumulative preferred stock. The stock-related transactions for the first year's operations were as follows:

Jan. 19   Sold 15,000 shares of the common stock for $31,500. State law requires a minimum of $1 stated value per share.

     21   Issued 5,000 shares of common stock to attorneys and accountants for services valued at $11,000 and provided during the organization of the corporation.

Feb. 7   Issued 30,000 shares of common stock for a building that had an appraised value of $78,000.

Mar. 22   Purchased 10,000 shares of its common stock at $3 per share.

July 15   Issued 5,000 shares of common stock to employees under a stock option plan that allows any employee to buy shares at the current market price, which is now $3 per share.

Aug. 1   Sold 2,500 shares of treasury stock for $4 per share.

Sept. 1   Declared a cash dividend of $.15 per common share to be paid on September 25 to stockholders of record on September 15.

     15   Cash dividends date of record.

     25   Paid cash dividends to stockholders of record on September 15.

Oct. 30   Issued 4,000 shares of common stock for a piece of land. The stock was selling for $3 per share, and the land had a fair market value of $12,000.

Dec. 15   Issued 2,200 shares of preferred stock for $50 per share.

REQUIRED ▶

1. Record the above transactions in T accounts. Prepare T accounts for Cash; Land; Building; Cash Dividends Payable; Preferred Stock; Common Stock; Paid-in Capital in Excess of Stated Value, Common; Paid-in Capital, Treasury Stock; Retained Earnings; Treasury Stock, Common; Cash Dividends Declared; and Start-up and Organization Expense.
2. Prepare the stockholders' equity section of Hammond Corporation's balance sheet as of December 31, 20xx. Net income earned during the year was $100,000.

ALTERNATE PROBLEMS

P 6.

LO1   **Start-up and Organization**
LO2   **Costs, Stock and Dividend**
LO3   **Entries, and Stockholders'**
LO5   **Equity**

Quesnel Corporation began operations on September 1, 20xx. The corporation's charter authorized 300,000 shares of $8 par value common stock. Quesnel Corporation engaged in the following transactions during its first quarter:

Sept. 1   Issued 50,000 shares of common stock, $500,000.

     1   Paid an attorney $32,000 to help start up and organize the corporation and obtain a corporate charter from the state.

Oct. 2   Issued 80,000 shares of common stock, $960,000.

Nov. 30   Declared a cash dividend of $.40 per share to be paid on December 15 to stockholders of record on December 10.

REQUIRED ▶

1. Prepare entries in journal form to record the above transactions.
2. Prepare the stockholders' equity section of Quesnel Corporation's balance sheet on November 30, 20xx. Net income for the quarter was $80,000.

P 7.

LO1   **Preferred and Common Stock**
LO4   **Dividends and Dividends Yield**

DeMarcello Corporation had both common stock and preferred stock outstanding from 20x2 through 20x4. Information about each stock for the three years is as follows:

Type	Par Value	Shares Outstanding	Other
Preferred	$100	40,000	7% cumulative
Common	20	600,000	

The company paid $140,000, $800,000, and $1,100,000 in dividends for 20x2 through 20x4, respectively. The market price per common share was $15 and $17 per share at the end of years 20x3 and 20x4, respectively.

REQUIRED ▶

1. Determine the dividends per share and total dividends paid to the common and preferred stockholders each year.
2. Assuming that the preferred stock was noncumulative, repeat the computations performed in **1**.
3. Calculate the 20x3 and 20x4 dividends yield for common stock using dividends per share computed in **2**.
4. How are cumulative preferred stock and noncumulative preferred stock similar to long-term bonds? How do they differ from long-term bonds?

P 8.

LO1 **Comprehensive Stockholders'**
LO2 **Equity Transactions**
LO3
LO4
LO5
LO6

Czerepak, Inc., was organized and authorized to issue 10,000 shares of $100 par value, 9 percent preferred stock and 100,000 shares of no-par, $5 stated value common stock on July 1, 20xx. Stock-related transactions for Czerepak are as follows:

July 1 Issued 20,000 shares of common stock at $11 per share.
      1 Issued 1,000 shares of common stock at $11 per share for services rendered in connection with the organization of the company.
      2 Issued 2,000 shares of preferred stock at par value for cash.
     10 Issued 5,000 shares of common stock for land on which the asking price was $70,000. Market value of the stock was $12. Management wishes to record the land at full market value of the stock.
Aug. 2 Purchased 3,000 shares of its common stock at $13 per share.
     10 Declared a cash dividend for one month on the outstanding preferred stock and $.02 per share on common stock outstanding, payable on August 22 to stockholders of record on August 12.
     12 Date of record for cash dividends.
     22 Paid cash dividends.

REQUIRED ▶

1. Record the transactions in journal form.
2. Prepare the stockholders' equity section of the balance sheet as it would appear on August 31, 20xx. Net income for July and August was $25,000.

SKILLS DEVELOPMENT CASES

Conceptual Analysis

SD 1.

LO1 **Reasons for Issuing Common**
LO2 **Stock**

In a recent year, Avaya, Inc. <www.avaya.com>, an East Coast telecommunications company, issued 34,300,000 shares of common stock for a total of $212,000,000.[15] As a growing company, Avaya could have raised this significant amount of money by issuing long-term bonds, but the company's bond rating had recently been lowered. What are some advantages of issuing common stock as opposed to bonds? What are some disadvantages?

SD 2.

LO4 **Reasons for Issuing Preferred**
         Stock

Preferred stock is a hybrid security; it has some of the characteristics of stock and some of the characteristics of bonds. Historically, preferred stock has not been a popular means of financing. In the past few years, however, it has become more attractive to companies and individual investors alike, and investors are buying large amounts because of high yields. Large preferred stock issues have been made by such banking firms as Chase <www.chase.com>, Citibank <www.citigroup.com>, HSBC Bank USA <www.us.hsbc.com>, and Wells Fargo <www.wellsfargo.com>, as well as by other companies. The dividends yields on these stocks are over 9 percent, higher than the interest rates on bonds of comparable risk.[16] Especially popular are preferred equity redemption convertible stocks, or PERCs, which are automatically convertible into common stock after three years if the company does not call them first and retire them. What reasons can you give for the popularity of preferred stock, and of PERCs in particular, when the tax-deductible interest on bonds is lower? Discuss from both the company's and the investor's standpoint.

SD 3.

LO6 **Purposes of Treasury Stock**

Many companies in recent years have bought back their common stock. For example, IBM <www.ibm.com>, with large cash holdings, spent almost $27 billion over five years repurchasing its stock. What are the reasons companies buy back their own shares? What is the effect of common stock buybacks on earnings per share, return on equity, return on assets, debt to equity, and the current ratio?

Ethical Dilemma

LO1   **Ethics, Management**
LO6   **Compensation, and Treasury**
      Stock

SD 4. Compensation of senior management is often tied to earnings per share or return on equity. Treasury stock purchases have a favorable impact on both these measures. In the recent buyback boom, many companies borrowed money to purchase treasury shares, resulting in a higher debt to equity ratio. In some cases, the motivation for the borrowing and repurchase of shares was the desire of executives to secure their year-end cash bonuses. Did these executives act ethically? Were their actions in the best interests of stockholders? Why or why not? How might such behavior be avoided in the future?

Research Activity

LO1   **Comparison of Stockholders'**
LO2   **Equity Characteristics**
LO3
LO4
LO5

SD 5. Select the annual reports of three corporations from sources in your library or from the Fingraph® Financial Analyst™ CD-ROM software that accompanies this text. You can choose them from the same industry or at random, at the direction of your instructor. (**Note:** You may be asked to use these companies again in the Research Activity cases in later chapters.) Prepare a table with a column for each corporation. Then answer the following questions for each corporation: Does it have preferred stock? If so, what are the preferred stock's par value and dividend, and is the stock cumulative or convertible? Is the common stock par value or no-par? What is its par value or stated value? What cash dividends, if any, did the corporation pay in the past year? What is the dividends yield? From the notes to the financial statements, determine whether the corporation has an employee stock option plan. If so, what are some of its provisions? What is the return on equity? Be prepared to discuss the characteristics of the stocks and dividends of the three corporations in class.

Decision-Making Practice

LO1   **Analysis of Alternative**
LO2   **Financing Methods**

SD 6. Northeast Servotech Corporation, which offers services to the computer industry, has expanded rapidly in recent years. Because of its profitability, the company has been able to grow without obtaining external financing. This fact is reflected in its current balance sheet, which contains no long-term debt. The liabilities and stockholders' equity sections of the balance sheet on March 31, 20xx, appear below.

Northeast Servotech Corporation
Balance Sheet
March 31, 20xx

Liabilities

Current liabilities	$ 500,000

Stockholders' Equity

Common stock, $10 par value, 500,000 shares authorized, 100,000 shares issued and outstanding	$1,000,000	
Paid-in capital in excess of par value, common	1,800,000	
Retained earnings	1,700,000	
Total stockholders' equity		4,500,000
Total liabilities and stockholders' equity		$5,000,000

The company now has the opportunity to double its size by purchasing the operations of a rival company for $4,000,000. If the purchase goes through, Northeast Servotech will become one of the top companies in its specialized industry. The problem for management is how to finance the purchase. After much study and discussion with bankers and underwriters, management has prepared the following three financing alternatives to present to the board of directors, which must authorize the purchase and the financing:

Alternative A   The company could issue $4,000,000 of long-term debt. Given the company's financial rating and the current market rates, management believes the company will have to pay an interest rate of 12 percent on the debt.

Alternative B   The company could issue 40,000 shares of 8 percent, $100 par value preferred stock.

Alternative C   The company could issue 100,000 additional shares of $10 par value common stock at $40 per share.

Management explains to the board that the interest on the long-term debt is tax-deductible and that the applicable income tax rate is 40 percent. The board members know that a dividend of $.80 per share of common stock was paid last year, up from $.60 and $.40 per share in the two years before that. The board has had a policy of regular increases in dividends of $.20 per share. It believes each of the three financing alternatives is feasible and now wants to study the financial effects of each one.

1. Prepare a schedule to show how the liabilities and stockholders' equity sections of Northeast Servotech's balance sheet would look under each alternative, and compute the debt to equity ratio (total liabilities ÷ total stockholders' equity) for each.
2. Compute and compare the cash needed to pay the interest or dividends for each kind of new financing, net of income taxes, in the first year.
3. How might the cash needed to pay for the financing change in future years under each alternative?
4. Prepare a memorandum to the board of directors that evaluates the alternatives in order of preference based on cash flow effects, giving arguments for and against each.

 Group Activity: Assign the alternatives to different groups to analyze and present to members of the class who act as the board of directors.

FINANCIAL REPORTING AND ANALYSIS CASES

Interpreting Financial Reports

LO1   **Effect of Stock Issue**
LO2
LO5

FRA 1.   Netscape Communications Corporation <www.netscape.com>, now part of AOL–Time Warner, is a leading provider of software that links people and information over the Internet and intranets. It is one of the great success stories of the Internet age. When Netscape went public with an IPO, it issued stock at $14 per share. In its second year as a public company, it advertised a common stock issue in *The Wall Street Journal:*

6,440,000 Shares
NETSCAPE
Common Stock
Price $53¾ a share

If Netscape sold all these shares at the offering price of $53.75, the net proceeds before issue costs would have been $346.15 million. Below is a portion of the stockholders' equity section of the balance sheet adapted from Netscape's annual report, which was issued prior to this stock offering.

Stockholders' Equity
(In thousands)

Common stock, $.0001 par value, 200,000,000	
shares authorized, 81,063,158 shares issued	
and outstanding	$ 8
Additional paid-in capital	196,749
Accumulated deficit	(16,314)

1. Assume the net proceeds from the sale of 6,440,000 shares at $53.75 were $342.6 million after issue costs. Record the stock issuance on Netscape's accounting records in journal form.
2. Prepare the portion of the stockholders' equity section of the balance sheet shown at the bottom of the previous page after the issue of the common stock, based on the information given. Round all answers to the nearest thousand.
3. Based on your answer in **2**, did Netscape have to increase its authorized shares to undertake this stock issue?
4. What amount per share did Netscape receive and how much did Netscape's underwriters receive to help in issuing the stock if investors paid $53.75 per share? What do underwriters do to earn their fee?

FRA 2.

LO4 **Effect of Deferring Preferred Dividends**

US Airways <www.usairways.com> had indefinitely deferred the quarterly dividend on its $358 million of cumulative convertible 9¼ percent preferred stock.[17] According to a US Airways spokesperson, the company did not want to "continue to pay a dividend while the company is losing money." Others interpreted the action as "an indication of a cash crisis situation."

At the time, Berkshire Hathaway <www.berkshirehathaway.com>, the large company run by Warren Buffett and the owner of the preferred stock, was not happy, but US Airways was able to turn around, become profitable, and return to paying its cumulative dividends on preferred stock. Berkshire Hathaway was able to convert the preferred stock into 9.24 million common shares of US Airways' common stock at $38.74 per share at a time when the market value had risen to $62.[18]

What is cumulative convertible preferred stock? Why is deferring dividends on those shares a drastic action? What is the impact on profitability and liquidity? Why did using preferred stock instead of long-term bonds as a financing method probably save the company from bankruptcy? What was Berkshire Hathaway's gain on its investment at the time of the conversion?

International Company

FRA 3.

LO2 **Stockholders' Equity and**
LO3 **Dividends**

Roche Group <www.roche.com> is a giant Swiss pharmaceutical company. Its stockholders' equity shows how little importance common stock, which the Swiss call *share capital*, typically has in the financing of Swiss companies:[19]

	2001	2000
Shareholders' equity (in millions of Swiss francs)		
Share capital	160	160
Retained earnings	32,273	31,614
Total shareholders' equity	32,433	31,774

When Swiss companies need financing, they often rely on debt financing from large Swiss banks and other debt markets. With only 160 million Swiss francs (835 million shares) in share capital, Roche has had few stock issues in its history. In contrast, the company has over 42 billion Swiss francs in liabilities. Roche has been profitable, having built up retained earnings of more than 32 billion Swiss francs over the years. The company also pays a substantial dividend that totaled 981 million Swiss francs in 2001. Calculate the dividends per share and dividends yield assuming a share price of 118.5 Swiss francs. Assuming that dividends and net income were the only factors that affected retained earnings during 2001, how much did Roche earn in 2001 in U.S. dollars (use an exchange rate of 1.7 Swiss francs to the dollar)? What was Roche's return on equity? Comment on Roche's dividend policy and its level of earnings.

Toys "R" Us Annual Report

FRA 4.

LO1   **Stockholders' Equity**
LO2
LO6

Refer to the Toys "R" Us <www.tru.com> annual report to answer the following questions:

1. What type of capital stock does Toys "R" Us have? What is the par value? How many shares were authorized, issued, and outstanding at the end of fiscal 2002?
2. What is the dividends yield for Toys "R" Us and its relationship to the investors' total return? Does the company rely mostly on stock or on earnings for its stockholders' equity?
3. Does the company have a stock option plan? To whom do the stock options apply? Do employees have significant stock options? Given the market price of the stock shown in the report, do these options represent significant value to the employees?
4. Calculate and discuss the price/earnings ratio and return on equity for 2001 and 2002. The average share price for the fourth quarter was $21.13 and $11.43 for 2001 and 2002, respectively.

Comparison Case: Toys "R" Us and Walgreen Co.

FRA 5.

LO1   **Return on Equity, Treasury Stock, and Dividends Policy**

Refer to the annual report of Toys "R" Us <www.tru.com> and the financial statements and notes of Walgreens <www.walgreens.com> in the Supplement to Chapter 6.

1. Compute the return on equity for both companies for the most recent two years.
2. Did either company purchase treasury stock during these years? How will the purchase of treasury stock affect return on equity and earnings per share?
3. Did either company issue stock during these years? What are the details?
4. Compare the dividend policy of the two companies.

Fingraph® Financial Analyst™

FRA 6.

LO1   **Comparative Analysis of**
LO2   **Stockholders' Equity**
LO6

Select any two companies from the list of Fingraph companies on the Needles Accounting Resource Center Web Site at http://accounting.college.hmco.com/students. Access the Microsoft Excel spreadsheets for the companies you selected.

1. In the Fingraph spreadsheet for each company, identify the equity section of the balance sheet information. Do the companies have more than one kind of capital stock? Do the companies have treasury stock?
2. Using the Fingraph CD-ROM software, prepare a page of text that summarizes the price/earnings ratio and dividends yield for each company.
3. Using the Fingraph CD-ROM software, prepare a page of text that summarizes the financing section of each company's statement of cash flows.
4. Write a one-page summary highlighting the types of capital stock and the significance of treasury stock for these companies. Mention the extent to which they raised cash from recent stock issues or used cash to repurchase capital stock. Describe the impact on total equity. Also compare the price/earnings ratio and dividends yield trends of the two companies. Include your Fingraph pages with your report.

Internet Case

FRA 7.

LO1   **Comparison of Financing of**
LO3   **Internet Companies**
LO4
LO5
LO6

Many Internet start-up companies have gone public in recent years. These companies are generally unprofitable and require a great deal of cash to finance expansion. They also reward their employees with stock options. Choose any two of the following Internet companies: Amazon.com <www.amazon.com>, Yahoo! <www.yahoo.com>, eBay Inc. <www.ebay.com>, or AOL-Time Warner <www.aoltw.com>. Go to the web sites of the two companies you have selected. In their latest annual reports, look at the financing section of the statement of cash flows for the last three years. How have these two companies financed their businesses? Have they issued stock or long-term debt? Have they purchased treasury stock, paid dividends, or issued stock under stock option plans? Are the companies profitable (see net income or earnings at the top of the statement)? Are your findings in line with your expectations about these Internet companies? Find each company's stock price, either on its web site or in a newspaper, and compare it with the average issue price of that company's past stock issues. Summarize your findings.

Chapter 15 focuses on the components of the corporate income statement and the statement of stockholders' equity within the context of evaluating quality of earnings. The chapter also covers earnings per share, stock dividends, stock splits, and book value per share.

The Corporate Income Statement and the Statement of Stockholders' Equity

LEARNING OBJECTIVES

LO1 Prepare a corporate income statement and identify the issues related to evaluating the quality of earnings.

LO2 Show the relationships among income taxes expense, deferred income taxes, and net of taxes.

LO3 Describe the disclosure on the income statement of discontinued operations, extraordinary items, and accounting changes.

LO4 Compute earnings per share.

LO5 Prepare a statement of stockholders' equity.

LO6 Account for stock dividends and stock splits.

LO7 Calculate book value per share.

DECISION POINT

A USER'S FOCUS

AMR Corporation <www.amrcorp.com> AMR Corporation, American Airlines' parent company, is one of the two largest airline companies in the United States. Its operating results are of interest to many people, but interpreting these results is not always easy. Net earnings per share is the "bottom line" by which many investors judge a company's success or failure. For instance, we know that during 2001 and 2002, the airline industry was adversely affected by the 9/11 attacks and the impending war in Iraq. This is reflected in AMR's basic earnings per share over the past three years, as shown in the Financial Highlights. Net earnings (loss) per share have declined from a positive in 2000 to substantial losses in 2001 and 2002. Note, however, that other factors affect earnings per share. The results in 2002 were also adversely affected by the cumulative effect of an accounting change of $6.35 per share, which made the results appear worse than the company's loss from continuing operations of $16.22. Also, in 2000, the company had discontinued operations and an extraordinary loss.[1] To truly understand a company's "bottom line," it is important to know the various components. In fact, many analysts consider income (loss) from continuing operations to be a better indicator than the "bottom-line" numbers of a company's future operations. In this chapter, we examine the components of the corporate income statement and the statement of stockholders' equity with a view to understanding their impact on a company's future operations.

Is American Airlines' income from operations a better measure than its "bottom-line" numbers?

Financial Highlights

Earnings (Loss) per Share: Basic	2002	2001	2000
Income (loss) from continuing operations	$(16.22)	$(11.43)	$ 5.20
Discontinued operations	—	—	0.30
Extraordinary loss	—	—	(0.07)
Cumulative effect of accounting change	(6.35)	—	—
Net earnings (loss)	$(22.57)	$(11.43)	$ 5.43

PERFORMANCE MEASUREMENT: QUALITY OF EARNINGS ISSUES

LO1 Prepare a corporate income statement and identify the issues related to evaluating the quality of earnings.

RELATED TEXT ASSIGNMENTS
Q: 1, 2, 3, 4, 5
SE: 1, 2
E: 1, 2, 3
P: 1, 2, 3, 6
SD: 1, 2, 4
FRA: 1, 4, 6, 7

The Financial Accounting Standards Board (FASB) has taken the position that income for a period should be all-inclusive, comprehensive income, which is different from net income.[2] **Comprehensive income** is the change in a company's equity from sources other than owners during a period; it includes net income, changes in unrealized investment gains and losses, and other items affecting equity. Companies are reporting comprehensive income and its components as a separate financial statement or as a part of another financial statement.

In a recent survey of 600 large companies, 519 reported comprehensive income. Of these, 81 percent reported comprehensive income on the statement of stockholders' equity, 13 percent reported it on a separate statement, and only 6 percent reported it on the income statement.[3] In the illustration of comprehensive income later in this chapter, we follow the most common practice and show it as a part of the statement of stockholders' equity.

THE CORPORATE INCOME STATEMENT

www.aimr.org

Net income is the most commonly used measure of earnings because current and expected earnings are important factors in evaluating a company's performance and analyzing its prospects. In fact, a survey of 2,000 members of the Association for Investment Management and Research indicated that the two most important economic measures in evaluating common stocks were expected changes in earnings per share and expected return on equity;[4] net income is a key component of both measures. The corporate income statement is the statement that shows how a company's net income is derived.

KEY POINT: It is important to know which items included in earnings are recurring and which are one-time items. Income from continuing operations before nonoperating items gives a clear signal about future results. In assessing the company's future earnings potential, nonoperating items are excluded because they are not expected to continue.

Net income or loss for a period includes all revenues, expenses, gains, and losses over the period, with the exception of prior period adjustments. Thus, the corporate income statement may consist of several components, as illustrated in Exhibit 1. When a company has both continuing and discontinued operations, the operating income section is called **income from continuing operations**. Income from continuing operations before income taxes is affected by choices of accounting methods and estimates and may contain such items as gains and losses, write-downs, and restructurings. The income taxes expense section of the statement is also subject to special accounting rules. The lower part of the statement may contain such nonoperating items as discontinued operations, extraordinary gains and losses, and effects of accounting changes. Another item that may appear in this section is the write-off of goodwill when its value has been impaired. Finally, earnings per share information appears at the bottom of the statement. We discuss these components of the corporate income statement in more detail later in the chapter.

FOCUS ON BUSINESS PRACTICE

Why Do Investors Study Quality of Earnings?

Analysts for Twentieth Century Mutual Funds, a major investment company, now merged with American Century Services Corp. <www.americancentury.com>, make adjustments to a company's reported financial performance to create a more accurate picture of the company's ongoing operations. Assume a paper company reports earnings of $1.30 per share, which makes year-to-year comparisons unusually strong. Upon further investigation, however, it is found that the per share number includes a one-time gain on the sale of assets of $.25 per share. Twentieth Century would list the company in its data base as earning only $1.05 per share. "These kinds of adjustments help assure long-term decisions aren't based on one-time events."[5]

Because of the importance of net income, or the "bottom line," in measuring a company's prospects, there is significant interest in evaluating the quality of the net income figure, or the **quality of earnings**. The quality of a company's earnings refers to the substance of earnings and their sustainability into future accounting periods. For example, if earnings increase because of a gain on the sale of an asset, analysts may not view this portion of earnings as sustainable. The quality of earnings may be affected by the accounting methods and estimates the company's management chooses and by the gains and losses, the write-downs and restructurings, and the nature of the nonoperating items reported on the income statement. Since management has choices in the content and positioning of these income-

EXHIBIT 1
Corporate Income Statement

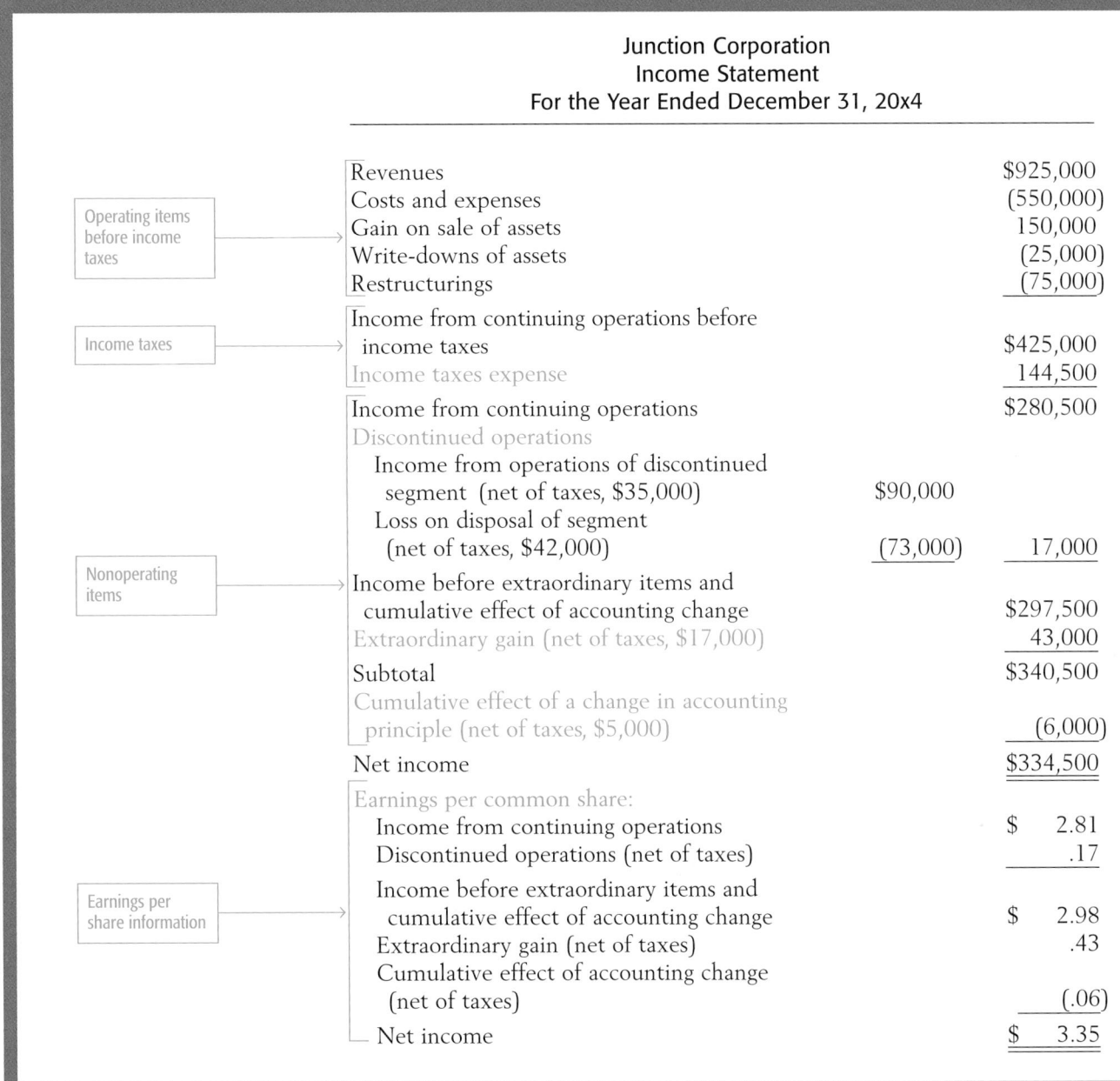

Junction Corporation
Income Statement
For the Year Ended December 31, 20x4

Revenues		$925,000
Costs and expenses		(550,000)
Gain on sale of assets		150,000
Write-downs of assets		(25,000)
Restructurings		(75,000)
Income from continuing operations before income taxes		$425,000
Income taxes expense		144,500
Income from continuing operations		$280,500
Discontinued operations		
Income from operations of discontinued segment (net of taxes, $35,000)	$90,000	
Loss on disposal of segment (net of taxes, $42,000)	(73,000)	17,000
Income before extraordinary items and cumulative effect of accounting change		$297,500
Extraordinary gain (net of taxes, $17,000)		43,000
Subtotal		$340,500
Cumulative effect of a change in accounting principle (net of taxes, $5,000)		(6,000)
Net income		$334,500
Earnings per common share:		
Income from continuing operations		$ 2.81
Discontinued operations (net of taxes)		.17
Income before extraordinary items and cumulative effect of accounting change		$ 2.98
Extraordinary gain (net of taxes)		.43
Cumulative effect of accounting change (net of taxes)		(.06)
Net income		$ 3.35

Labels: Operating items before income taxes; Income taxes; Nonoperating items; Earnings per share information

ENRICHMENT NOTE: Management is responsible for the content of financial statements. Financial statements report on the performance of management. When a group is responsible for reporting on its own activity, usually the best or most favorable position will be reported.

statement categories, there is the potential for managing earnings to achieve specific income targets. Thus, users of income statements must understand these factors and take them into consideration when evaluating a company's performance.

CHOICE OF ACCOUNTING METHODS AND ESTIMATES

Choices of accounting methods and estimates affect a firm's operating income. To assure proper matching of revenues and expenses, accounting requires cost allocations and estimates of data that will not be known with certainty until some future date. For example, accountants estimate the useful life of assets when they are acquired. However, technological obsolescence could shorten the expected useful life, and excellent maintenance and repairs could lengthen it. The actual useful life will not be known with certainty until some future date. The estimate affects both current and future operating income.

Because there is considerable latitude in assumptions underlying estimates, management and other financial statement users must be aware of the impact of accounting estimates on reported operating income. Estimates include percentage of uncollectible accounts receivable, sales returns, useful life, residual or salvage value, total units of production, total recoverable units of natural resources, amortization period, expected warranty claims, and expected environmental cleanup costs.

These estimates are not equally important to all firms. Their relative importance depends on the industry in which a firm operates. For example, the estimate of uncollectible receivables for a credit card firm, such as American Express, or a financial services firm, such as Bank of America, can have a material impact on earnings, but the estimate of useful life may be less important because depreciable assets represent only a small percentage of total assets. Toys "R" Us has very few receivables, but it has substantial investment in depreciable assets; thus, estimates of useful life and residual value are much more important than the estimate of uncollectible accounts receivable.

The choice of methods also affects a firm's operating income. Generally accepted accounting methods include uncollectible receivable methods (percentage of net sales and aging of accounts receivable), inventory methods (last-in, first-out [LIFO]; first-in, first-out [FIFO]; and average-cost), depreciation methods (accelerated, production, and straight-line), and revenue recognition methods. These methods are designed to match revenues and expenses. Costs are allocated based on a determination of the benefits to the current period (expenses) versus the benefits to future periods (assets). The expenses are estimates, and the period or periods benefited cannot be demonstrated conclusively. The estimates are also subjective, because in practice it is hard to justify one method of estimation over another.

For these reasons, management, the accountant, and the financial statement user need to understand the possible effects of different accounting procedures on net income and financial position. Some methods and estimates are more conservative than others because they tend to produce a lower net income in the current period. For example, suppose that two companies have similar operations, but one uses FIFO for inventory costing and straight-line (SL) for computing depreciation, whereas the other uses LIFO for inventory costing and double-declining-balance (DDB) for computing depreciation. The income statements of the two companies might appear as follows:

www.americanexpress.com
www.bankofamerica.com

www.tru.com

KEY POINT: Two companies in the same industry may have comparable earnings quantity but not comparable earnings quality. To assess the quality of reported earnings, one must know the methods and estimates used to compute income. GAAP allow several methods and estimates, all yielding different results.

	FIFO and SL	LIFO and DDB
Net sales	$875,000	$875,000
Goods available for sale	$400,000	$400,000
Less ending inventory	60,000	50,000
Cost of goods sold	$340,000	$350,000
Gross margin	$535,000	$525,000
Less depreciation expense	$ 40,000	$ 80,000
Less other expenses	170,000	170,000
Total operating expenses	$210,000	$250,000
Income from continuing operations before income taxes	$325,000	$275,000

The income from continuing operations before income taxes (operating income) for the firm using LIFO and DDB is lower because in periods of rising prices, the LIFO inventory costing method produces a higher cost of goods sold, and, in the early years of an asset's useful life, accelerated depreciation yields a higher depreciation expense. The result is lower operating income. However, future operating income is expected to be higher. It is also important that the choice of accounting method does not affect cash flows except for possible differences in income taxes caused by the use of one method instead of another.

The $50,000 difference in operating income stems only from the differences in accounting methods. Differences in the estimated lives and residual values of the plant assets could lead to an even greater variation. In practice, of course, differences in net income occur for many reasons, but the user must be aware of the discrepancies that can occur as a result of the accounting methods chosen by management. In general, an accounting method or estimate that results in lower current earnings is considered to produce a better quality of operating income.

The existence of such alternatives could cause problems in the interpretation of financial statements were it not for the conventions of full disclosure and consistency. As noted in an earlier chapter, full disclosure requires that management explain the significant accounting policies used in preparing the financial statements in a note to the statements. Consistency requires that the same accounting procedures be followed from year to year. If a change in procedure is made, the nature of the change and its monetary effect must be explained in a note.

GAINS AND LOSSES

When a company sells or otherwise disposes of operating assets or marketable securities, a gain or loss generally results. These gains or losses appear in the operating portion of the income statement, but they usually represent one-time events. They are not sustainable, ongoing operations, and management often has some choice as to their timing. Thus, from an analyst's point of view, they should be ignored when considering operating income.

WRITE-DOWNS AND RESTRUCTURINGS

Management has considerable latitude in deciding when an asset is no longer of value to the company. If the value of an asset is impaired, management may decide to record a write-down. A **write-down**, also referred to as a *write-off*, is the recording of a decrease in the value of an asset below the carrying value on the balance sheet and the reduction of income in the current period by the amount of the decrease. If operations have changed, management may decide to record a restructuring. A **restructuring** is the estimated cost associated with a change in a company's operations, usually involving the closing of facilities and the laying off of personnel. Both write-downs and restructurings reduce current operating income and boost future income by shifting future costs to the current accounting period.

Write-downs and restructurings are important to consider because they often are an indication of bad management decisions in the past, such as paying too much for the assets of another company or making operational changes that do not work out. Companies sometimes take all possible losses in the current year so that future years will be "clean" of these costs. Such "big baths," as they are called, commonly occur when a company is having a bad year. They also often occur in years when there is a change in management. The new management takes a "big bath" in the current year so it can show improved results in future years.

Write-downs and restructurings are common. In a recent year, 27 percent of 600 large companies had write-downs, and 26 percent had restructurings. Another 24 percent had write-downs or charges involving intangible assets.[6] As discussed in the chapter on long-term assets, goodwill is subject to an annual impairment test to determine if its current fair value is below cost.

NATURE OF NONOPERATING ITEMS

The nonoperating items that appear on the income statement, such as discontinued operations, extraordinary gains and losses, and effects of accounting changes, can also significantly affect the bottom line, or net income. In fact, in Exhibit 1, earnings

⬢ **STOP AND THINK!**
Is it unethical for new management to take a "big bath" in order to enhance future performance?
It is not unethical as long as new management stays within the accounting rules and properly discloses its actions. An investor or analyst must be aware of these actions and take them into consideration when evaluating the company's performance. ∎

FOCUS ON BUSINESS ETHICS

Whistle-Blowing

External users of financial statements depend on management's honesty and openness in disclosing factual information about a company. In the vast majority of cases, management's reports are reliable, but there are exceptions. Whistle-blowers— employees who step forward to disclose such exceptions and other types of wrongdoing they observe in their companies— run various risks, including losing their jobs, with no assurance that their actions will have any effect. In the recent Enron case, the largest bankruptcy in U.S. history, the whistle-blower was a company accountant who, well before the firm's collapse, informed her CEO and the firm's external auditors of Enron's questionable accounting practices. Although her warnings were ignored then, they made headlines during the SEC and congressional investigations, as well as the criminal prosecutions that followed the collapse.[7]

ENRICHMENT NOTE:

Discontinued operations, extraordinary items, and cumulative effects of a change in accounting principle are more likely to occur in large, public corporations. A knowledge of these items is important when analyzing **www.sears.com** the financial results of such companies. These items do not occur as frequently in small, private corporations.

per common share for income from continuing operations are $2.81, but net income per share is $3.35 when all the nonoperating items are taken into consideration.

For practical reasons, the calculations of trends and ratios are based on the assumption that net income and other components are comparable from year to year and from company to company. However, in making interpretations, the astute analyst will always look beyond the ratios to the quality of the components. For example, write-downs, restructurings, and nonoperating items, if the charges are large enough, can have a significant effect on a company's return on equity.

A company may boost income by including one-time gains. For example, Sears, Roebuck and Co. used a gain from the change of an accounting principle to bolster its net income by $136 million or by $.35 per share. Without the gain, earnings per share (EPS) would have decreased from $3.12 to $2.92, not increased as Sears reported.[8] The quality of Sears's earnings is, in fact, lower than it might appear on the surface. Unless analysts are prepared to go beyond the "bottom line" in analyzing and interpreting financial reports, they can come to the wrong conclusions.

EFFECT OF QUALITY OF EARNINGS ON CASH FLOWS AND PERFORMANCE MEASURES

The reason for considering quality of earnings issues is to assess their effects on cash flows and performance measures. Generally speaking, except for possible income tax effects, none of the gains and losses, asset write-downs, restructurings, and non-operating items has any effect on cash flows. The cash expenditures for these items were made previously. For this reason, the focus of analysis is on sustainable earnings, which generally have a relationship to future cash flows.

Since management's performance and compensation are often linked to return on assets or return on equity, it is important to understand the nature of both the numerator and denominator of these performance measures. Most commonly, the numerator in these ratios is net income. However, when a company has a complex income statement with items that affect quality of earnings, such as those discussed above, it is important not to take net income at face value. Consider the example of Junction Corporation in Exhibit 1. The reported net income is $334,500, whereas income from continuing operations is $280,500. Even the latter amount is a questionable measure of sustainable earnings because of the gain, write-down, and restructuring, which collectively added $50,000 to income from continuing operations before income taxes. With a tax rate of 34 percent, the sustainable earnings after income taxes are probably close to $247,500 [$280,500 − ($50,000 × .66)].

It also pays to examine how quality of earnings issues affect the denominator of the return on assets and return on equity ratios. If a company has a write-down or restructuring of assets, in addition to a reduction in net income, there is also a reduction in assets and in stockholders' equity, which tends to improve these ratios in both current and future years. This contributes to the motivation to take "big-bath" write-offs in years that are poor anyway so that it will be easier to show improvement in future ratios.

 Check out ACE for a Review Quiz at http://accounting.college.hmco.com/students.

INCOME TAXES EXPENSE

LO2 Show the relationships among income taxes expense, deferred income taxes, and net of taxes.

RELATED TEXT ASSIGNMENTS
Q: 6, 7
SE: 3
E: 3, 4, 5
P: 2, 3, 6
SD: 4
FRA: 2

Corporations determine their taxable income (the amount on which taxes are paid) by subtracting allowable business deductions from includable gross income. The federal tax laws determine which business expenses may be deducted and which cannot be deducted from taxable gross income. (Rules for calculating and reporting taxable income in specialized industries, such as banking, insurance, mutual funds, and cooperatives, are highly technical and may vary significantly from the ones we discuss in this chapter.)

Table 1 shows the tax rates that apply to a corporation's taxable income. A corporation with taxable income of $70,000 would have a federal income tax liability of $12,500: $7,500 (the tax on the first $50,000 of taxable income) plus $5,000 (25 percent of the $20,000 earned in excess of $50,000).

Income taxes expense is the expense recognized in the accounting records on an accrual basis that applies to income from continuing operations. This expense may or may not equal the amount of taxes actually paid by the corporation and recorded as income taxes payable in the current period. The amount payable is determined from taxable income, which is measured according to the rules and regulations of the income tax code.

ENRICHMENT NOTE:
Most people think it is illegal to keep accounting records on a different basis from income tax records. However, the Internal Revenue Code and GAAP often do not agree. To work with two conflicting sets of guidelines, the accountant must keep two sets of records.

For the sake of convenience, most small businesses keep their accounting records on the same basis as their tax records, so that the income taxes expense on the income statement equals the income taxes liability to be paid to the U.S. Treasury. This practice is acceptable when there is no material difference between the income on an accounting basis and the income on an income tax basis. However, the purpose of accounting is to determine net income in accordance with generally accepted accounting principles, not to determine taxable income and tax liability.

Management has an incentive to use methods that minimize the firm's tax liability, but accountants, who are bound by accrual accounting and the materiality concept, cannot let tax procedures dictate their method of preparing financial statements if the result would be misleading. As a consequence, there can be a material

TABLE 1. Tax Rate Schedule for Corporations, 2002

Taxable Income		Tax Liability	
Over	But Not Over		Of the Amount Over
—	$ 50,000	0 + 15%	—
$ 50,000	75,000	$ 7,500 + 25%	$ 50,000
75,000	100,000	13,750 + 34%	75,000
100,000	335,000	22,250 + 39%	100,000
335,000	10,000,000	113,900 + 34%	335,000
10,000,000	15,000,000	3,400,000 + 35%	10,000,000
15,000,000	18,333,333	5,150,000 + 38%	15,000,000
18,333,333	—	6,416,667 + 35%	18,333,333

ENRICHMENT NOTE: The federal income tax is progressive. That is, the rate increases as taxable income increases.

Note: Tax rates are subject to change by Congress.

difference between accounting income and taxable income, especially in larger businesses. This discrepancy can result from differences in the timing of the recognition of revenues and expenses under the two accounting methods. Some possible variations are shown below.

	Accounting Method	Tax Method
Expense recognition	Accrual or deferral	At time of expenditure
Accounts receivable	Allowance	Direct charge-off
Inventories	Average-cost	FIFO
Depreciation	Straight-line	Modified Accelerated Cost Recovery System

DEFERRED INCOME TAXES

KEY POINT: The discrepancy between GAAP-based tax expense and Internal Revenue Code-based tax liability produces the need for the Deferred Income Taxes account.

The accounting method used to accrue income taxes expense on the basis of accounting income whenever there are differences between accounting and taxable income is called **income tax allocation**. The account used to record the difference between the income taxes expense and income taxes payable is called **Deferred Income Taxes**. For example, Junction Corporation shows income taxes expense of $144,500 on its income statement in Exhibit 1, but it has actual income taxes payable to the U.S. Treasury of $92,000. The following entry records the estimated income taxes expense applicable to income from continuing operations using the income tax allocation procedure:

A = L + OE
    +   −
        +

Dec. 31	Income Taxes Expense	144,500	
	Income Taxes Payable		92,000
	Deferred Income Taxes		52,500
	To record estimated current and deferred income taxes		

● **STOP AND THINK!**
What is an argument against the recording of deferred income taxes?
Because the recording of deferred income taxes depends on future actions of management, which may or may not happen, critics of deferred taxes argue that the income taxes for a particular year should simply be the amount of income taxes paid. Thus, each year is allowed to stand on its own. ■

In other years, it is possible for Income Taxes Payable to exceed Income Taxes Expense, in which case the same entry is made except that Deferred Income Taxes is debited.

The Financial Accounting Standards Board has issued specific rules for recording, measuring, and classifying deferred income taxes.[9] Deferred income taxes are recognized for the estimated future tax effects resulting from temporary differences in the valuation of assets, liabilities, equity, revenues, expenses, gains, and losses for tax and financial reporting purposes. Temporary differences include revenues and expenses or gains and losses that are included in taxable income before or after they are included in financial income. In other words, the recognition point for revenues, expenses, gains, and losses is not the same for tax and financial reporting. For example, advance payments for goods and services, such as magazine subscriptions, are not recognized in financial income until the product is shipped, but for tax purposes they are usually recognized as revenue when cash is received. The result is that taxes paid exceed taxes expense, which creates a deferred income taxes asset (or prepaid taxes).

STUDY NOTE: Deferred Income Taxes is classified as a liability when it has a credit balance and as an asset when it has a debit balance. It is further classified as either current or long-term depending on when it is expected to reverse.

Classification of deferred income taxes as current or noncurrent depends on the classification of the related asset or liability that created the temporary difference. For example, the deferred income taxes asset mentioned above would be classified as current if unearned subscription revenue is classified as a current liability. On the other hand, the temporary difference arising from depreciation is related to a long-term depreciable asset. Therefore, the resulting deferred income taxes would be classified as long-term. However, if a temporary difference is not related to an asset or liability, then it is classified as current or noncurrent based on its expected date of reversal. Temporary differences and the classification of deferred income taxes that results are covered in depth in more advanced courses.

Each year, the balance of the Deferred Income Taxes account is evaluated to determine whether it still accurately represents the expected asset or liability in light of legislated changes in income tax laws and regulations. If changes have occurred, an adjusting entry to bring the account balance into line with current laws is required. For example, a decrease in corporate income tax rates, like the one that occurred in 1987, means that a company with a deferred income taxes liability will pay less in taxes in future years than the amount indicated by the credit balance of its Deferred Income Taxes account. As a result, the company would debit Deferred Income Taxes to reduce the liability and credit Gain from Reduction in Income Tax Rates. This credit increases the reported income on the income statement. If the tax rate increases in future years, a loss would be recorded and the deferred income taxes liability would be increased.

In any given year, the amount a company pays in income taxes is determined by subtracting (or adding, as the case may be) the deferred income taxes for that year, as reported in the notes to the financial statements, from (or to) income taxes expense, which is reported in the financial statements. In subsequent years, the amount of deferred income taxes can vary based on changes in tax laws and rates.

Some understanding of the importance of deferred income taxes to financial reporting can be gained from studying a survey of the financial statements of 600 large companies. About 65 percent reported deferred income taxes with a credit balance in the long-term liability section of the balance sheet.[10]

NET OF TAXES

The phrase **net of taxes**, as used in Exhibit 1, means that the effect of applicable taxes (usually income taxes) has been considered in determining the overall effect of an item on the financial statements. The phrase is used on the corporate income statement when a company has items that must be disclosed in a separate section. Each such item should be reported net of the applicable income taxes to avoid distorting the income taxes expense associated with ongoing operations and the resulting net operating income. For example, assume that a corporation with operating income before income taxes of $120,000 has a total tax expense of $66,000 and that the total income includes a gain of $100,000 on which a tax of $30,000 is due. Also assume that the gain is not part of normal operations and must be disclosed separately on the income statement as an extraordinary item (explained later). This is how the income taxes expense would be reported on the income statement:

Operating income before income taxes	$120,000
Income taxes expense	36,000
Income before extraordinary item	$ 84,000
Extraordinary gain (net of taxes, $30,000)	70,000
Net income	$154,000

If all the income taxes expense were deducted from operating income before income taxes, both the income before extraordinary item and the extraordinary gain would be distorted.

A company follows the same procedure in the case of an extraordinary loss. For example, assume the same facts as before except that the total income taxes expense is only $6,000 because of a $100,000 extraordinary loss. The result is a $30,000 tax savings, shown as follows:

Operating income before income taxes	$120,000
Income taxes expense	36,000
Income before extraordinary item	$ 84,000
Extraordinary loss (net of taxes, $30,000)	(70,000)
Net income	$ 14,000

In Exhibit 1, the total of the income tax items for Junction Corporation is $149,500. That amount is allocated among five statement components, as follows:

Income taxes expense on income from continuing operations	$144,500
Income taxes on income from a discontinued segment	35,000
Income tax savings on the loss on the disposal of the segment	(42,000)
Income taxes on the extraordinary gain	17,000
Income tax savings on the cumulative effect of a change in accounting principle	(5,000)
Total income taxes expense	$149,500

✔ Check out ACE for a Review Quiz at http://accounting.college.hmco.com/students.

NONOPERATING ITEMS

LO3   Describe the disclosure on the income statement of discontinued operations, extraordinary items, and accounting changes.

RELATED TEXT ASSIGNMENTS
Q: 8, 9, 10
E: 3
P: 2, 3, 6
SD: 2, 4
FRA: 4, 6

www.amrcorp.com

● **STOP AND THINK!**
Why is it useful to disclose discontinued operations separately on the income statement?

Users of financial statements want to assess the effects of past performance on the future performance of a company. Separating discontinued operations on the income statement helps accomplish that objective. ∎

Nonoperating items are items not related to the company's normal operations. They appear in a separate section of the income statement because they are considered one-time items that will not affect future results. There are three principal kinds of nonoperating items: discontinued operations, extraordinary items, and accounting changes.

DISCONTINUED OPERATIONS

Large companies in the United States usually have many **segments**. A segment may be a separate major line of business or serve a separate class of customer. For example, a company that makes heavy drilling equipment may also have another line of business, such as the manufacture of mobile homes. A large company may discontinue or otherwise dispose of certain segments of its business that do not fit its future plans or are not profitable. **Discontinued operations** are segments of a business that are no longer part of its ongoing operations. Generally accepted accounting principles require that gains and losses from discontinued operations be reported separately on the income statement. Such separation makes it easier to evaluate the ongoing activities of the business. For example, the Financial Highlights in the Decision Point in this chapter show that AMR's discontinued operations are a significant factor in its "bottom-line" earnings per share. The discontinued operations are AMR's Sabre reservation services, one of the steadiest and most profitable parts of the company's business, which it is divesting to the shareholders of the company. For the analyst, this important piece of information means that in the future, the company is going to be more dependent on the volatile airline business.

In Exhibit 1, the disclosure of discontinued operations has two parts. One part shows that after the decision to discontinue, the income from operations of the disposed segment was $90,000 (net of $35,000 taxes). The other part shows that the loss from the disposal of the segment was $73,000 (net of $42,000 tax savings). Computation of the gains or losses is covered in more advanced accounting courses. We have described the disclosure to give a complete view of the corporate income statement.

EXTRAORDINARY ITEMS

In its *Opinion No. 30*, the Accounting Principles Board defines **extraordinary items** as "events or transactions that are distinguished by their unusual nature *and* by the infrequency of their occurrence."[11] Unusual and infrequent occurrences are explained in the opinion as follows:

Unusual Nature—the underlying event or transaction should possess a high degree of abnormality and be of a type clearly unrelated to, or only incidentally related to, the ordinary and typical activities of the entity, taking into account the environment in which the entity operates.

KEY POINT: To qualify as extraordinary, an event must be unusual (not in the ordinary course of business) and must not be expected to occur again in the foreseeable future. Occasionally, it is not clear whether an event meets these two criteria, and the decision then becomes a matter of judgment.

Infrequency of Occurrence—the underlying event or transaction should be of a type that would not reasonably be expected to recur in the foreseeable future, taking into account the environment in which the entity operates.[12]

If an item is both unusual and infrequent (and material in amount), it should be reported separately from continuing operations on the income statement. The disclosure allows readers to identify gains or losses in income that would not be expected to happen again soon. Items usually treated as extraordinary include (1) an uninsured loss from flood, earthquake, fire, or theft; (2) a gain or loss resulting from the passage of a new law; and (3) the expropriation (taking) of property by a foreign government.

Gains or losses from extraordinary items should be reported on the income statement after discontinued operations. And they should be shown net of applicable taxes. In a recent year, 78 (13 percent) of 600 large companies reported extraordinary items on their income statements.[13] In Exhibit 1, the extraordinary gain was $43,000 after applicable taxes of $17,000.

ACCOUNTING CHANGES

ENRICHMENT NOTE: A change in accounting method (principle) violates the convention of consistency. Such a change is allowed, however, when it can be demonstrated that the new method will produce more useful financial statements. The effect of the change is disclosed just above net income on the income statement.

ETHICAL CONSIDERATION: Some accounting changes can produce a significant increase in net income without an accompanying improvement in performance. The user of financial statements should be aware that some businesses implement an accounting change solely for the increase in net income that results.

In a departure from the consistency convention, a company is allowed to make accounting changes if current procedures are incorrect or inappropriate. For example, a change from the FIFO to the LIFO inventory method can be made if there is adequate justification for the change. Adequate justification usually means that if the change occurs, the financial statements will better show the financial activities of the company. A company's desire to lower the amount of income taxes it pays is not considered adequate justification for an accounting change. If justification does exist and an accounting change is made, generally accepted accounting principles require the disclosure of the change in the financial statements.

The **cumulative effect of an accounting change** is the effect that the new accounting principle would have had on net income in prior periods if it had been applied instead of the old principle. This effect is shown on the income statement immediately after extraordinary items.[14] For example, assume that in the five years prior to 20x4, Junction Corporation had used the straight-line method to depreciate its machinery. This year, the company retroactively changed to the double-declining-balance method of depreciation. The controller computed the cumulative effect of the change in depreciation charges (net of taxes) as $6,000, as follows:

Cumulative, five-year double-declining-balance depreciation	$29,000
Less cumulative, five-year straight-line depreciation	18,000
Before tax effect	$11,000
Income tax savings	5,000
Cumulative effect of accounting change	$ 6,000

FOCUS ON INTERNATIONAL BUSINESS

Were Preussag's Year-End Results Really "Remarkable"?

The big German travel company Preussag <www.preussag.com> reported that the year 2000 was "a remarkable year" in which the company achieved "all-time high" results and "profit rose by 16.5 percent." The financial reports reveal that profits would not have been so remarkable if the effects of four voluntary accounting changes had not been taken into account. Profits would have increased by only 6.7 percent if Preussag had not made these changes. The company began recognizing revenue from holiday packages at the beginning of the holiday instead of at the stage of completion, but it began deferring the cost of brochures over future tourist seasons. In addition, the cost of "empty-leg flights" at the beginning and the end of each tourist season are now amortized over the season. Finally the inventory method was changed from LIFO to the average-cost method. None of these cosmetic changes affect future cash flows or change the company's operations for the better.[15]

Relevant information about the accounting change is shown in the notes to the financial statements. The change results in $11,000 of depreciation expense for prior years being deducted in the current year, in addition to the current year's depreciation costs included in the $550,000 costs and expenses section of the income statement. This expense must be shown in the current year's income statement as a reduction in income (see Exhibit 1). In a recent year, over 90 percent of 600 large companies reported changes in accounting procedures, mostly in order to conform to new FASB pronouncements.[16] Further study of accounting changes is left to more advanced accounting courses.

> Check out ACE for a Review Quiz at http://accounting.college.hmco.com/students.

EARNINGS PER SHARE

LO4   Compute earnings per share.

RELATED TEXT ASSIGNMENTS
Q: 11, 12, 13
SE: 4
E: 3, 6
P: 2, 3, 6
FRA: 6, 7

Readers of financial statements use earnings per share information to judge a company's performance and to compare it with the performance of other companies. Because such information is so important, the Accounting Principles Board concluded that earnings per share of common stock should be presented on the face of the income statement.[17] As shown in Exhibit 1, the information is usually disclosed just below the net income.

An earnings per share amount is always shown for (1) income from continuing operations, (2) income before extraordinary items and cumulative effect of accounting change, (3) cumulative effect of accounting change, and (4) net income. If the statement shows a gain or loss from discontinued operations or a gain or loss on extraordinary items, earnings per share amounts can also be presented for them.

The following per share data from the income statement of Minnesota Mining and Manufacturing Company (3M) show why it is a good idea to study the components of earnings per share:[18]

www.3m.com

ENRICHMENT NOTE:
Earnings per share is a measure of a corporation's profitability. It is one of the most closely watched financial statement ratios in the business world. Its disclosure on the income statement is required.

Financial Highlights

	2000	1999	1998
Earnings per share—basic			
Income before extraordinary loss and cumulative effect of accounting change	$ 4.69	$ 4.39	$ 3.01
Extraordinary loss	—	—	(.10)
Cumulative effect of accounting change	(.19)	—	—
Net income	$ 4.50	$ 4.39	$ 2.91

Note that net income was influenced by special items in 1998 and 2000: An extraordinary loss decreased income from continuing operations by $.10 per share in 1998, and the cumulative effect of an accounting change decreased earnings by $.19 in 2000. In 1999, the company had no special items; thus, 100 percent of 3M's basic earnings per share were attributable to continuing operations.

Basic earnings per share is net income applicable to common stock divided by the weighted-average number of common shares outstanding. To compute this figure, one must determine if the number of common shares outstanding changed during the year, and if the company paid preferred stock dividends.

When a company has only common stock and has the same number of shares outstanding throughout the year, the earnings per share computation is simple. From Exhibit 1, we know that Junction Corporation reported net income of $334,500.

● **STOP AND THINK!**
What is one action a company can take to improve its earnings per share without improving its earnings or net income? **K/R**

Many companies attempt to improve their earnings per share by reducing the number of shares outstanding through buybacks of their own stock. ■

Assume that the company had 100,000 shares of common stock outstanding for the entire year. The earnings per share of common stock is computed as follows:

$$\text{Earnings per Share} = \frac{\$334,500}{100,000} = \$3.35 \text{ per share}$$

If the number of shares outstanding changes during the year, it is necessary to figure the weighted-average number of shares outstanding for the year. Suppose that during various periods of the year, Junction Corporation had the following amounts of common shares outstanding: January–March, 100,000 shares; April–September, 120,000 shares; and October–December, 130,000 shares. The weighted-average number of common shares outstanding and basic earnings per share would be calculated this way:

100,000 shares × 3/12 year	25,000
120,000 shares × 6/12 year	60,000
130,000 shares × 3/12 year	32,500
Weighted-average common shares outstanding	117,500

K/R

$$\text{Basic Earnings per Share} = \frac{\text{Net Income}}{\text{Weighted-Average Common Shares Outstanding}}$$

$$= \frac{\$334,500}{117,500 \text{ shares}} = \$2.85 \text{ per share}$$

If a company has nonconvertible preferred stock outstanding, the dividend for that stock must be subtracted from net income before earnings per share for common stock are computed. Suppose that Junction Corporation has preferred stock on which the annual dividend is $23,500. Earnings per share on common stock would be $2.65 [($334,500 − $23,500) ÷ 117,500 shares].

Companies with a capital structure in which there are no bonds, stocks, or stock options that can be converted into common stock are said to have a **simple capital structure**. The earnings per share for these companies is computed as shown above. Some companies, however, have a **complex capital structure**, which includes exercisable stock options or convertible preferred stocks and bonds. Those convertible securities have the potential of diluting the earnings per share of common stock. *Potential dilution* means that a stockholder's proportionate share of ownership in a company could be reduced through the conversion of stocks or bonds or the exercise of stock options, which would increase the total number of shares the company has outstanding.

For example, suppose that a person owns 10,000 shares of a company, which equals 2 percent of the outstanding shares of 500,000. Now suppose that holders of convertible bonds convert the bonds into 100,000 shares of stock. The person's 10,000 shares would then equal only 1.67 percent (10,000 ÷ 600,000) of the outstanding shares. In addition, the added shares outstanding would lower earnings per share and would most likely lower market price per share.

KEY POINT: A company with potentially dilutive securities (such as convertible preferred stock or bonds) has a complex capital structure and must present two earnings per share figures—basic and diluted. The latter figure is the more conservative of the two.

Because stock options and convertible preferred stocks or bonds have the potential to dilute earnings per share, they are referred to as **potentially dilutive securities**. When a company has a complex capital structure, it must report two earnings per share figures: basic earnings per share and diluted earnings per share.[19] **Diluted earnings per share** are calculated by adding all potentially dilutive securities to the denominator of the basic earnings per share calculation. This figure shows stockholders the maximum potential effect of dilution on their ownership position in the company.

The difference between basic and diluted earnings per share can be significant. For example, consider the results reported by Tribune Company:

www.amrcorp.com

Financial Highlights

	2002	2001	2000
Basic earnings per share	$1.38	$.28	$.74
Diluted earnings per share	1.30	.28	.70

Note that in 2000 and 2002, diluted earnings per share are about 5-6 percent less than basic earnings per share.[20] The basic earnings per share is used in various ratios, including the price/earnings ratio.

The computation of diluted earnings per share is a complex process and is reserved for more advanced courses.

 Check out ACE for a Review Quiz at http://accounting.college.hmco.com/students.

THE STATEMENT OF STOCKHOLDERS' EQUITY

LO5   Prepare a statement of stock-holders' equity.

RELATED TEXT ASSIGNMENTS
Q: 14, 15, 16
SE: 5, 6, 7
E: 7, 8
P: 4, 5, 7, 8
SD: 4, 5
FRA: 1, 3, 4, 6, 7

● **STOP AND THINK!**
In Exhibit 2, what is the total amount of comprehensive income?

The total amount of compre-hensive income includes all changes in stockholders' equity not involving the owners. In Exhibit 2, it is the net income of $270,000 and accumulated other comprehensive income (foreign currency translation adjustment) of ($10,000), or $260,000. ■

KEY POINT: In accounting, a deficit is a negative (debit) balance in Retained Earnings. It is not the same thing as a net loss, which reflects the per-formance in just one account-ing period.

The **statement of stockholders' equity**, also called the *statement of changes in stock-holders' equity*, summarizes the changes in the components of the stockholders' equity section of the balance sheet. More and more companies are using this state-ment in place of the statement of retained earnings because it reveals much more about the year's stockholders' equity transactions. In the statement of stockholders' equity in Exhibit 2, for example, the first line shows the beginning balance of each account in the stockholders' equity section. Each subsequent line discloses the effects of transactions on those accounts. Tri-State earned net income of $270,000 and had a foreign currency translation loss of $10,000, reported as accumulated other comprehensive income. These two items together resulted in comprehensive income of $260,000. The statement also shows that during 20x4 Tri-State Corporation issued 5,000 shares of common stock for $250,000, had a conversion of $100,000 of preferred stock into common stock, declared and issued a 10 per-cent stock dividend on common stock, had a net purchase of treasury shares of $24,000, and paid cash dividends on both preferred and common stock. The end-ing balances of the accounts are presented at the bottom of the statement. Those accounts and balances make up the stockholders' equity section of Tri-State's bal-ance sheet on December 31, 20x4, as shown in Exhibit 3.

RETAINED EARNINGS

Notice that in Exhibit 2 the Retained Earnings column has the same components as the statement of retained earnings. The **retained earnings** of a company are the part of stockholders' equity that represents stockholders' claims to assets arising from the earnings of the business. Retained earnings equal a company's profits since the date of its inception, less any losses, dividends to stockholders, or transfers to contributed capital.

It is important to remember that retained earnings are not the assets them-selves. The existence of retained earnings means that assets generated by profitable operations have been kept in the company to help it grow or meet other business needs. A credit balance in Retained Earnings is *not* directly associated with a specific amount of cash or designated assets. Rather, such a balance means that assets as a whole have been increased.

Retained Earnings can carry a debit balance. Generally, this happens when a company's dividends and subsequent losses are greater than its accumulated profits from operations. In such a case, the firm is said to have a **deficit** (debit balance) in Retained Earnings. A deficit is shown in the stockholders' equity section of the bal-ance sheet as a deduction from contributed capital.

EXHIBIT 2
Statement of Stockholders' Equity

Tri-State Corporation
Statement of Stockholders' Equity
For the Year Ended December 31, 20x4

	Preferred Stock $100 Par Value 8% Convertible	Common Stock $10 Par Value	Paid-in Capital in Excess of Par Value, Common	Retained Earnings	Treasury Stock	Accumulated Other Comprehensive Income	Total
Balance, December 31, 20x3	$400,000	$300,000	$300,000	$600,000	—		$1,600,000
Net income				270,000			270,000
Foreign currency translation adjustment						($10,000)	(10,000)
Issuance of 5,000 shares of common stock		50,000	200,000				250,000
Conversion of 1,000 shares of preferred stock to 3,000 shares of common stock	(100,000)	30,000	70,000				—
10 percent stock dividend on common stock, 3,800 shares		38,000	152,000	(190,000)			—
Purchase of 500 shares of treasury stock					($24,000)		(24,000)
Cash dividends							
Preferred stock				(24,000)			(24,000)
Common stock				(47,600)			(47,600)
Balance, December 31, 20x4	$300,000	$418,000	$722,000	$608,400	($24,000)	($10,000)	$2,014,400

EXHIBIT 3
Stockholders' Equity Section of a Balance Sheet

KEY POINT: The ending balances on the statement of stockholders' equity are transferred to the stockholders' equity section of the balance sheet.

Tri-State Corporation
Stockholders' Equity
December 31, 20x4

Contributed capital		
Preferred stock, $100 par value, 8 percent convertible, 10,000 shares authorized, 3,000 shares issued and outstanding		$ 300,000
Common stock, $10 par value, 100,000 shares authorized, 41,800 shares issued, 41,300 shares outstanding	$418,000	
Paid-in capital in excess of par value, common	722,000	1,140,000
Total contributed capital		$1,440,000
Retained earnings		608,400
Total contributed capital and retained earnings		$2,048,400
Less: Treasury stock, common (500 shares, at cost)	$ 24,000	
Foreign currency translation adjustment	10,000	34,000
Total stockholders' equity		$2,014,400

Focus on International Business

Why Are Reserves Common in Other Countries?

Restrictions on retained earnings, called *reserves,* are much more common in some foreign countries than in the United States. In Sweden, for instance, reserves are used to respond to fluctuations in the economy. The Swedish tax code allows companies to set up contingency reserves for the purpose of maintaining financial stability. Appropriations to those reserves reduce taxable income and income taxes. The reserves become taxable when they are reversed, but they are available to absorb losses should they occur. For example, Skandia Group <www.skandia.com>, a large Swedish insurance company, reported a net income of only SK2,826 million in 2000, considerably less than the SK3,456 million in 1999. An examination of its statement of stockholders' equity shows restricted reserves in 2000 of SK10.2 billion. Skandia also increased its dividends in 2000 to SK512 million and still had SK9.5 billion in unrestricted reserves.[21]

Restriction on Retained Earnings

A corporation may be required or may want to restrict all or a portion of its retained earnings. A **restriction on retained earnings** means that dividends can be declared only to the extent of the *unrestricted* retained earnings. The following are reasons a company might restrict retained earnings:

1. *A contractual agreement.* For example, bond indentures may place a limitation on the dividends the company can pay.

2. *State law.* Many states do not allow a corporation to distribute dividends or purchase treasury stock if doing so reduces equity to a level that would impair the legal capital of the company.

3. *Voluntary action by the board of directors.* Often, a board decides to retain assets in the business for future needs. For example, the company may want to limit dividends to save enough money for a new building or to offset a possible future loss of assets resulting from a lawsuit.

A restriction on retained earnings does not change the total retained earnings or stockholders' equity of the company. It simply divides retained earnings into two parts: restricted and unrestricted. The unrestricted amount represents earnings kept in the business that the company can use for dividends and other purposes. Also, the restriction of retained earnings does not restrict cash or other assets in any way. It simply explains to the readers of the financial statements that a certain amount of assets generated by earnings will remain in the business for the purpose stated. It is still management's job to make sure enough cash or assets are on hand to fulfill the purpose. The removal of a restriction does not necessarily mean that the board of directors can then declare a dividend.

The most common way to disclose restricted retained earnings is by reference to a note to the financial statements. For example:

Retained earnings (Note 15) $900,000

Note 15:
Because of plans to expand the capacity of the company's clothing division, the board of directors has restricted retained earnings available for dividends by $300,000.

 Check out ACE for a Review Quiz at http://accounting.college.hmco.com/students.

Accounting for Stock Dividends and Stock Splits

LO6 Account for stock dividends and stock splits.

RELATED TEXT ASSIGNMENTS
Q: 17, 18
SE: 6, 8, 9
E: 9, 10, 11
P: 4, 5, 7, 8
SD: 3, 4, 5
FRA: 6

Two common transactions that can modify the content of stockholders' equity are stock dividends and stock splits.

Stock Dividends

A **stock dividend** is a proportional distribution of shares among a corporation's stockholders. Unlike a cash dividend, it involves no distribution of assets, so it has no effect on a firm's assets and liabilities. A board of directors may declare a stock dividend for several reasons:

1. It may want to give stockholders some evidence of the company's success without paying a cash dividend, which would affect working capital.

2. It may want to reduce the stock's market price by increasing the number of shares outstanding. (This goal is, however, more often met by a stock split.)

3. It may want to make a nontaxable distribution to stockholders. Stock dividends that meet certain conditions are not considered income, so they are not taxed.

4. It may wish to increase the company's permanent capital by transferring an amount from retained earnings to contributed capital.

The total stockholders' equity is not affected by a stock dividend. The effect of a stock dividend is to transfer a dollar amount from retained earnings to contributed capital on the date of declaration. The amount transferred is the fair market value (usually, the market price) of the additional shares to be issued. The laws of most states specify the minimum value of each share transferred under a stock dividend, which is normally the minimum legal capital (par or stated value). However, generally accepted accounting principles state that market value reflects the economic effect of small stock distributions (less than 20 to 25 percent of a company's outstanding common stock) better than par or stated value does. For this reason, market price should be used to account for small stock dividends.[22]

To illustrate how to account for a stock dividend, let us assume that Caprock Corporation has the following stockholders' equity structure:

Contributed capital	
Common stock, $5 par value, 100,000 shares authorized, 30,000 shares issued and outstanding	$ 150,000
Paid-in capital in excess of par value, common	30,000
Total contributed capital	$ 180,000
Retained earnings	900,000
Total stockholders' equity	$1,080,000

Suppose that the board of directors declares a 10 percent stock dividend on February 24, distributable on March 31 to stockholders of record on March 15, and that the market price of the stock on February 24 is $20 per share. The entries to record the declaration and distribution of the stock dividend are as follows:

Date of Declaration

A = L + OE	Feb. 24	Stock Dividends Declared	60,000	
−		Common Stock Distributable		15,000
+		Paid-in Capital in Excess of Par		
+		Value, Common		45,000

Declared a 10 percent stock dividend on common stock, distributable on March 31 to stockholders of record on March 15:
30,000 shares × .10 = 3,000 shares
3,000 shares × $20/share = $60,000
3,000 shares × $5/share = $15,000

KEY POINT: For a small stock dividend, the portion of retained earnings transferred is determined by multiplying the number of shares to be distributed by the stock's market price on the date of declaration.

Date of Record

Mar. 15 No entry required.

Date of Distribution

A = L + OE	Mar. 31	Common Stock Distributable	15,000	
−		Common Stock		15,000
+		Distributed a stock dividend of 3,000 shares		

The effect of this stock dividend is to permanently transfer the market value of the stock, $60,000, from retained earnings to contributed capital and to increase the

KEY POINT: The declaration of a stock dividend results in a reshuffling of stockholders' equity. That is, a portion of retained earnings is converted into contributed capital (by closing the Stock Dividends Declared account). Total stockholders' equity is not affected. Retained earnings are transferred at the time of the recording (date of declaration) and not at the closing of the Stock Dividends Declared account.

KEY POINT: Common Stock Distributable is a contributed capital (stockholders' equity) account, not a liability. When the shares are issued, this account is converted to the Common Stock account.

number of shares outstanding by 3,000. The Stock Dividends Declared account is used to record the total amount of the stock dividend. Retained Earnings is reduced by the amount of the stock dividend when the Stock Dividends Declared account is closed to Retained Earnings at the end of the accounting period. Common Stock Distributable is credited for the par value of the stock to be distributed ($3,000 \times \$5 = \$15,000$).

In addition, when the market value is greater than the par value of the stock, Paid-in Capital in Excess of Par Value, Common must be credited for the amount by which the market value exceeds the par value. In this case, the total market value of the stock dividend ($60,000) exceeds the total par value ($15,000) by $45,000. No entry is required on the date of record. On the distribution date, the common stock is issued by debiting Common Stock Distributable and crediting Common Stock for the par value of the stock ($15,000).

Common Stock Distributable is not a liability account because there is no obligation to distribute cash or other assets. The obligation is to distribute additional shares of capital stock. If financial statements are prepared between the date of declaration and the date of distribution, Common Stock Distributable should be reported as part of contributed capital:

Contributed capital	
Common stock, $5 par value, 100,000 shares authorized, 30,000 shares issued and outstanding	$ 150,000
Common stock distributable, 3,000 shares	15,000
Paid-in capital in excess of par value, common	75,000
Total contributed capital	$ 240,000
Retained earnings	840,000
Total stockholders' equity	$1,080,000

● **STOP AND THINK!**
The receipt of additional shares of stock resulting from a stock dividend has no effect on a stockholder's income. Why not?
Although the stockholder receives additional shares of stock, that stockholder's share of ownership remains unchanged because all other stockholders receive the same proportionate increase in the number of shares owned. The company's net worth remains unchanged since net assets have not increased or decreased. Therefore, the stockholder still owns the same percentage of the company's unchanged net worth. ■

Three points can be made from this example. First, the total stockholders' equity is the same before and after the stock dividend. Second, the assets of the corporation are not reduced as they are with a cash dividend. Third, the proportionate ownership in the corporation of any individual stockholder is the same before and after the stock dividend. To illustrate these points, assume that a stockholder owns 1,000 shares before the stock dividend. After the 10 percent stock dividend is distributed, this stockholder would own 1,100 shares, as illustrated below.

Stockholders' Equity	Before Dividend	After Dividend
Common stock	$ 150,000	$ 165,000
Paid-in capital in excess of par value, common	30,000	75,000
Total contributed capital	$ 180,000	$ 240,000
Retained earnings	900,000	840,000
Total stockholders' equity	$1,080,000	$1,080,000
Shares outstanding	30,000	33,000
Stockholders' equity per share	$ 36.00	$ 32.73

Stockholders' Investment

Shares owned	1,000	1,100
Shares outstanding	30,000	33,000
Percentage of ownership	3⅓%	3⅓%
Proportionate investment ($1,080,000 × .03⅓)	$36,000	$36,000

Both before and after the stock dividend, the stockholders' equity totals $1,080,000 and the stockholder owns 3⅓ percent of the company. The proportionate investment (stockholders' equity times percentage ownership) remains at $36,000.

KEY POINT: When a large (greater than 20 to 25 percent) stock dividend is declared, the transfer from retained earnings is based on the stock's par or stated value, not on its market value.

All stock dividends have an effect on the market price of a company's stock. But some stock dividends are so large that they have a material effect. For example, a 50 percent stock dividend would cause the market price of the stock to drop about 33 percent because the increase is now one-third of shares outstanding. The AICPA has decided that large stock dividends, those greater than 20 to 25 percent, should be accounted for by transferring the par or stated value of the stock on the date of declaration from retained earnings to contributed capital.[23]

STOCK SPLITS

KEY POINT: Stock splits and stock dividends reduce earnings per share because they increase the number of shares issued and outstanding. Cash dividends have no effect on earnings per share.

www.gillette.com

A **stock split** occurs when a corporation increases the number of issued shares of stock and reduces the par or stated value proportionally. A company may plan a stock split when it wants to lower the stock's market value per share and increase the demand for the stock at this lower price. This action may be necessary if the market value per share has become so high that it hinders the trading of the stock or if the company wants to signal to the market its success in achieving its operating goals. The Gillette Company achieved these strategic objectives in a recent year by declaring a 2-for-1 stock split and raising its cash dividend. The market viewed these actions positively, pushing Gillette's share price from $77 to $106. After the stock split, the number of shares outstanding doubled, thereby cutting the share price in half and also the dividend per share. Most important, each stockholder's total wealth was unchanged as a result of the stock split.

ENRICHMENT NOTE: Stock splits greater than 2 for 1 are unusual. Splits such as 3 for 2 or 4 for 3 are far more common. On occasion, companies whose stock sells for a very low price will perform a reverse stock split, which reduces the number of shares and increases the market price.

To illustrate a stock split, suppose that Caprock Corporation has 30,000 shares of $5.00 par value stock outstanding. The market value is $70.00 per share. The corporation plans a 2-for-1 split. This split will lower the par value to $2.50 and increase the number of shares outstanding to 60,000. A stockholder who previously owned 400 shares of the $5.00 par value stock would own 800 shares of the $2.50 par value stock after the split. When a stock split occurs, the market value tends to fall in proportion to the increase in outstanding shares of stock. For example, a 2-for-1 stock split would cause the price of the stock to drop by approximately 50 percent, to about $35.00. It would also halve earnings per share and cash dividends per share (if the board does not increase the dividend). The lower price and the increase in shares tend to promote the buying and selling of shares.

A stock split does not increase the number of shares authorized. Nor does it change the balances in the stockholders' equity section of the balance sheet. It simply changes the par value and number of shares issued, both shares outstanding and treasury stock. Thus, an entry is unnecessary. However, it is appropriate to document the change with a memorandum entry in the general journal. For example:

July 15   The 30,000 shares of $5 par value common stock issued and outstanding were split 2 for 1, resulting in 60,000 shares of $2.50 par value common stock issued and outstanding.

FOCUS ON BUSINESS PRACTICE

Do Stock Splits Help Increase a Company's Market Price?

Stock splits tend to follow the market. When the market went up dramatically in 1998, 1999, and 2000, there were record numbers of stock splits—more than 1,000 per year. At the height of the market in early 2000, stock splitters included such diverse companies as Alcoa <www.alcoa.com>, Apple Computer <www.apple.com>, Chase Manhattan <www.chase.com>, Intel <www.intel.com>, Nvidia <www.nvidia.com>, Juniper Networks <www.juniper.net>, and Tiffany & Co. <www.tiffany.com>. Some analysts liken stock splits to the air a pastry chef whips into a mousse: it doesn't make it any sweeter, just frothier. There is no fundamental reason a stock should go up because of a stock split. When Rambus Inc. <www.rambus.com>, a developer of high-speed memory technology, announced a four-for-one split on March 10, 2000, its stock rose more than 50 percent, to $471 per share.[24] But when the market deflated in 2001, its stock dropped to less than $10 per share. Research shows that stock splits have no long-term effect on stock prices.

The change for the Caprock Corporation is as follows:

Before Stock Split

Contributed capital
    Common stock, $5 par value, 100,000 shares
        authorized, 30,000 shares issued and outstanding $ 150,000
        Paid-in capital in excess of par value, common   30,000
                Total contributed capital $ 180,000
Retained earnings   900,000
Total stockholders' equity $1,080,000

After Stock Split

Contributed capital
    Common stock, $2.50 par value, 100,000 shares
        authorized, 60,000 shares issued and outstanding $ 150,000
        Paid-in capital in excess of par value, common   30,000
                Total contributed capital $ 180,000
Retained earnings   900,000
Total stockholders' equity $1,080,000

KEY POINT: A stock split affects only the common stock calculation. In this case, there are twice as many shares after the split, but par value is now half of what it was.

KEY POINT: As long as the newly outstanding shares do not exceed the previously authorized shares, permission from the state is not needed for a stock split.

Although the amount of stockholders' equity per share is half as much, each stockholder's proportionate interest in the company remains the same.

If the number of split shares will exceed the number of authorized shares, the board of directors must secure state and stockholders' approval before it can issue additional shares.

✓ Check out ACE for a Review Quiz at http://accounting.college.hmco.com/students.

BOOK VALUE

LO7 Calculate book value per share.

RELATED TEXT ASSIGNMENTS
Q: 19
SE: 10
E: 12
P: 4, 5, 7, 8
SD: 4, 5
FRA: 5, 6

KEY POINT: Book value per share represents the equity of one share of stock in the net assets (assets minus liabilities) of a corporation. It can apply to both common and preferred stock.

The word *value* is associated with shares of stock in several ways. Par value or stated value is set when the stock is authorized and establishes the legal capital of a company. Neither par value nor stated value has any relationship to a stock's book value or market value. The **book value** of a company's stock represents the total assets of the company less its liabilities. It is simply the stockholders' equity of the company or, to look at it another way, the company's net assets. The **book value per share** therefore represents the equity of the owner of one share of stock in the net assets of the corporation. That value, of course, does not necessarily equal the amount the shareholder would receive if the company were sold or liquidated. It differs in most cases because assets are usually recorded at historical cost, not at the current value at which they could be sold.

When a company has only common stock outstanding, book value per share is calculated by dividing the total stockholders' equity by the total common shares outstanding. In computing the shares outstanding, common stock distributable is included. Treasury stock (shares previously issued and now held by the company), however, is not included. For example, suppose that Caprock Corporation has total stockholders' equity of $1,030,000 and 29,000 shares outstanding after recording the purchase of treasury shares. The book value per share of Caprock's common stock is $35.52 ($1,030,000 ÷ 29,000 shares).

If a company has both preferred and common stock, the determination of book value per share is not so simple. The general rule is that the call value (or par value, if a call value is not specified) of the preferred stock plus any dividends in arrears is subtracted from total stockholders' equity to determine the equity pertaining to common stock. As an illustration, refer to the stockholders' equity section of Tri-

What is the effect of a stock dividend or a stock split on book value per share?

Both a stock dividend and a stock split reduce the book value per share because they increase the number of shares outstanding without changing the total of stockholders' equity. ■

State Corporation's balance sheet in Exhibit 3. Assuming that no dividends are in arrears and that the preferred stock is callable at $105, the equity pertaining to common stock is calculated as follows:

Total stockholders' equity	$2,014,400
Less equity allocated to preferred shareholders (3,000 shares × $105)	315,000
Equity pertaining to common shareholders	$1,699,400

There are 41,300 shares of common stock outstanding (41,800 shares issued less 500 shares of treasury stock). The book values per share are computed as follows:

Preferred Stock: $315,000 ÷ 3,000 shares = $105 per share
Common Stock: $1,699,400 ÷ 41,300 shares = $41.15 per share

If we assume the same facts except that the preferred stock is 8 percent cumulative and that one year of dividends is in arrears, the stockholders' equity would be allocated as follows:

Total stockholders' equity		$2,014,400
Less: Call value of outstanding preferred shares	$315,000	
Dividends in arrears ($300,000 × .08)	24,000	
Equity allocated to preferred shareholders		339,000
Equity pertaining to common shareholders		$1,675,400

The book values per share are then as follows:

Preferred Stock: $339,000 ÷ 3,000 shares = $113 per share
Common Stock: $1,675,400 ÷ 41,300 shares = $40.57 per share

Undeclared preferred dividends fall into arrears on the last day of the fiscal year (the date shown on the financial statements). Also, dividends in arrears do not apply to unissued preferred stock.

✓ Check out ACE for a Review Quiz at http://accounting.college.hmco.com/students.

Chapter Review

REVIEW OF LEARNING OBJECTIVES

LO1 Prepare a corporate income statement and identify the issues related to evaluating the quality of earnings.

The operating income section on the income statement of a corporation with both continuing and discontinued operations is called income from continuing operations. Income from continuing operations before income taxes is affected by choices of accounting methods and estimates and may contain such items as gains and losses, write-downs, and restructurings. The income taxes expense section of the statement is also subject to special accounting rules. The lower part of the statement may contain such nonoperating items as discontinued operations, extraordinary gains and losses, and effects of accounting changes. Earnings per share information appears at the bottom of the statement. The quality of a company's earnings refers to the substance of earnings and their sustainability into future accounting periods. The quality of earnings may be affected by the accounting methods and estimates the company's management chooses and by the gains and losses, the write-downs and restructurings, and the nature of the nonoperating items reported on the income statement. The reason for considering quality of earnings issues is to assess their effects on cash flows and performance measures. Generally speaking, except for possible income tax effects, none of the gains and losses, asset write-downs, restructurings, and nonoperating items has any effect on cash flows. Quality of earnings issues can affect key performance ratios like return on assets and return on equity.

LO2 Show the relationships among income taxes expense, deferred income taxes, and net of taxes.

Income taxes expense is the taxes applicable to income from operations on an accrual basis. Income tax allocation is necessary when differences between accrual-based accounting income and taxable income cause a material difference between income taxes expense as shown on the income statement and actual income tax liability. The difference between income taxes expense and income taxes payable is debited or credited to an account called Deferred Income Taxes. *Net of taxes* is a phrase used to indicate that the effect of income taxes has been considered when showing an item on the income statement.

LO3 Describe the disclosure on the income statement of discontinued operations, extraordinary items, and accounting changes.

Because of their unusual nature, a gain or loss on discontinued operations and on extraordinary items and the cumulative effect of accounting changes must be disclosed on the income statement separately from continuing operations and net of income taxes. Relevant information about any accounting change is shown in the notes to the financial statements.

LO4 Compute earnings per share.

Stockholders and other readers of financial statements use earnings per share data to evaluate a company's performance and to compare it with the performance of other companies. Therefore, earnings per share data are presented on the face of the income statement. The amounts are computed by dividing the income applicable to common stock by the number of common shares outstanding for the year. If the number of shares outstanding has varied during the year, then the weighted-average number of common shares outstanding should be used in the computation. When the company has a complex capital structure, both basic and diluted earnings per share must be disclosed on the face of the income statement.

LO5 Prepare a statement of stockholders' equity.

A statement of stockholders' equity shows changes over the period in each component of the stockholders' equity section of the balance sheet. This statement reveals much more about the transactions that affect stockholders' equity than does the statement of retained earnings.

LO6 Account for stock dividends and stock splits.

A stock dividend is a proportional distribution of shares among a corporation's stockholders. Here is a summary of the key dates and accounting treatment of stock dividends:

Key Date	Stock Dividend
Date of declaration	Debit Stock Dividends Declared for the market value of the stock to be distributed (if it is a small stock dividend), and credit Common Stock Distributable for the stock's par value and Paid-in Capital in Excess of Par Value, Common for the excess of the market value over the stock's par value.
Date of record	No entry.
Date of distribution	Debit Common Stock Distributable and credit Common Stock for the par value of the stock that has been distributed.

A stock split is usually undertaken to reduce the market value of a company's stock and improve the demand for the stock. Because there is normally a decrease in the par value of the stock in proportion to the number of additional shares issued, a stock split has no effect on the dollar amounts in the stockholders' equity accounts. The split should be recorded in the general journal by a memorandum entry only.

LO7 Calculate book value per share.

Book value per share is the stockholders' equity per share. It is calculated by dividing stockholders' equity by the number of common shares outstanding plus shares distributable. When a company has both preferred and common stock, the call or par value of the preferred stock plus any dividends in arrears is deducted from total stockholders' equity before dividing by the common shares outstanding.

REVIEW OF CONCEPTS AND TERMINOLOGY

The following concepts and terms were introduced in this chapter:

LO4 Basic earnings per share: The net income applicable to common stock divided by the weighted-average number of common shares outstanding.

LO7 Book value: The total assets of a company less its liabilities; stockholders' equity or net assets.

LO7 Book value per share: The equity of the owner of one share of stock in the net assets of the corporation.

LO4 Complex capital structure: A capital structure that includes exercisable stock options or convertible preferred stocks and bonds.

LO1 Comprehensive income: The change in a company's equity from sources other than owners during a period; it includes net income, changes in unrealized investment gains and losses, and other items affecting equity.

LO3 Cumulative effect of an accounting change: The effect that a different accounting principle would have had on the net income of prior periods if it had been used instead of the old principle.

LO2 Deferred Income Taxes: The account used to record the difference between the Income Taxes Expense and Income Taxes Payable accounts.

LO5 Deficit: A debit balance in the Retained Earnings account.

LO4 Diluted earnings per share: The net income applicable to common stock divided by the sum of the weighted-average number of common shares outstanding plus potentially dilutive securities.

LO3 Discontinued operations: Segments of a business that are no longer part of its ongoing operations.

LO3 Extraordinary items: Events or transactions that are both unusual in nature and infrequent in occurrence.

LO1 Income from continuing operations: The operating income section of the income statement when a company has both continuing and discontinued operations.

LO2 Income tax allocation: An accounting method used to accrue income taxes expense on the basis of accounting income whenever there are differences between accounting and taxable income.

LO2 Net of taxes: A phrase indicating that the effect of applicable taxes (most often, income taxes) has been considered in determining the overall effect of an item on the financial statements.

LO4 Potentially dilutive securities: Stock options and convertible preferred stocks or bonds, which have the potential to dilute earnings per share.

LO1 Quality of earnings: The substance of earnings and their sustainability into future accounting periods.

LO5 Restriction on retained earnings: The required or voluntary identification of a portion of retained earnings that cannot be used to declare dividends.

LO1 Restructuring: The estimated cost associated with a change in a company's operations, usually involving the closing of facilities and the laying off of personnel.

LO5 Retained earnings: Stockholders' claims to assets arising from the earnings of the business; the accumulated earnings of a corporation from its inception, minus any losses, dividends, or transfers to contributed capital.

LO3 Segments: Distinct parts of business operations, such as a line of business or a class of customer.

LO4 Simple capital structure: A capital structure in which there are no stocks, bonds, or stock options that can be converted into common stock.

LO5 **Statement of stockholders' equity:** A financial statement that summarizes changes in the components of the stockholders' equity section of the balance sheet. Also called *statement of changes in stockholders' equity.*

LO6 **Stock dividend:** A proportional distribution of shares among a corporation's stockholders.

LO6 **Stock split:** An increase in the number of outstanding shares of stock accompanied by a proportionate reduction in the par or stated value.

LO1 **Write-down:** The recording of a decrease in the value of an asset below the carrying value on the balance sheet and the reduction of income in the current period by the amount of the decrease. Also called *write-off.*

REVIEW PROBLEM

Comprehensive Stockholders' Equity Transactions

LO5
LO6
LO7
The stockholders' equity of Szatkowski Company on June 30, 20x4, was as follows:

Contributed capital	
Common stock, no par value, $6 stated value, 1,000,000 shares authorized, 250,000 shares issued and outstanding	$1,500,000
Paid-in capital in excess of stated value, common	820,000
Total contributed capital	$2,320,000
Retained earnings	970,000
Total stockholders' equity	$3,290,000

Stockholders' equity transactions for the next fiscal year were as follows:

a. The board of directors declared a 2-for-1 stock split.
b. The board of directors obtained authorization to issue 50,000 shares of $100 par value, 6 percent noncumulative preferred stock, callable at $104.
c. Issued 12,000 shares of common stock for a building appraised at $96,000.
d. Purchased 8,000 shares of the company's common stock for $64,000.
e. Issued 20,000 shares of preferred stock for $100 per share.
f. Sold 5,000 shares of treasury stock for $35,000.
g. Declared cash dividends of $6 per share on preferred stock and $.20 per share on common stock.
h. Declared a 10 percent stock dividend on common stock. The market value was $10 per share. The stock dividend is distributable after the end of the fiscal year.
i. Closed Net Income for the year, $340,000.
j. Closed the Cash Dividends Declared and Stock Dividends Declared accounts to Retained Earnings.

Because of a loan agreement, the company is not allowed to reduce retained earnings below $100,000. The board of directors determined that this restriction should be disclosed in the notes to the financial statements.

REQUIRED ▶
1. Record the stockholders' equity components of the preceding transactions in T accounts. Indicate when there is no entry.
2. Prepare the stockholders' equity section of the company's balance sheet on June 30, 20x5, including appropriate disclosure of the restriction on retained earnings.
3. Compute the book values per share of common stock on June 30, 20x4 and 20x5, and of preferred stock on June 30, 20x5, using end-of-year shares outstanding.

ANSWER TO REVIEW PROBLEM

1. Entries in T accounts:
   a. No entry: memorandum in journal
   b. No entry: memorandum in journal

Preferred Stock				Common Stock			
		e.	2,000,000			Beg. bal.	1,500,000
						c.	36,000
						End. Bal	1,536,000

Common Stock Distributable				Paid-in Capital in Excess of Stated Value, Common			
		h.	152,700			Beg. bal.	820,000
						c.	60,000
						h.	356,300
						End. Bal.	1,236,300

Retained Earnings				Treasury Stock, Common			
f.	5,000	Beg. bal.	970,000	d.	64,000	f.	40,000
j.	730,800	i.	340,000	End. Bal.	24,000		
		End. bal.	574,200				

Cash Dividends Declared				Stock Dividend Declared			
g.	221,800*	j.	221,800	h.	509,000**	j.	509,000

* $20,000 \times \$6 = \$120,000$
$509,000 \times \$.20 = \$101,800$
Total $= \$221,800$

**$509,000$ shares $\times .10 \times \$10 = \$509,000$

2. Stockholders' equity section of the balance sheet:

Szatkowski Company
Stockholders' Equity
June 30, 20x5

Contributed capital			
Preferred stock, $100 par value, 6 percent noncumulative, 50,000 shares authorized, 20,000 shares issued and outstanding		$2,000,000	
Common stock, no par value, $3 stated value, 1,000,000 shares authorized, 512,000 shares issued, 509,000 shares outstanding	$1,536,000		
Common stock distributable, 50,900 shares	152,700		
Paid-in capital in excess of stated value, common	1,236,300	2,925,000	
Total contributed capital		$4,925,000	
Retained earnings (Note x)		574,200	
Total contributed capital and retained earnings		$5,499,200	
Less treasury stock, common (3,000 shares, at cost)		24,000	
Total stockholders' equity		$5,475,200	

Note x: The board of directors has restricted retained earnings available for dividends by the amount of $100,000 as required under a loan agreement.

3. Book values:

June 30, 20x4
Common Stock: $3,290,000 ÷ 250,000 shares = $13.16 per share

June 30, 20x5
    Preferred Stock: Call price of $104 per share equals book value per share
    Common Stock:
        ($5,475,200 − $2,080,000) ÷ (509,000 shares + 50,900 shares) =
        $3,395,200 ÷ 559,900 shares = $6.06 per share

Chapter Assignments

BUILDING YOUR KNOWLEDGE FOUNDATION

QUESTIONS

1. What is comprehensive income? How does it differ from net income?

2. What is quality of earnings, and what are four ways in which quality of earnings may be affected?

3. Why would the reader of financial statements be interested in management's choice of accounting methods and estimates? Give an example.

4. What is the difference between a write-down and a restructuring, and where do they appear on the corporate income statement?

5. In the first quarter of 1994, AT&T, the giant telecommunications company, reported a net loss because it reduced its income by $1.3 billion, or $.96 per share, as a result of changing its method of accounting for disability and severance payments. Without this charge, the company would have earned $1.15 billion, or $.85 per share. Where on the corporate income statement do you find the effects of changes in accounting principles? As an analyst, how would you treat this accounting change?

6. "Accounting income should be geared to the concept of taxable income because the public understands that concept." Comment on this statement, and tell why income tax allocation is necessary.

7. Nabisco had about $1.3 billion of deferred income taxes in 1996, equal to about 11 percent of total liabilities. This percentage had risen or remained steady for many years. Given management's desire to put off the payment of taxes for as long as possible, the long-term growth of the economy and inflation, and the definition of a liability (probable future sacrifice of economic benefits arising from present obligations), make an argument for not accounting for deferred income taxes.

8. Why should a gain or loss on discontinued operations be disclosed separately on the income statement?

9. Explain the two major criteria for extraordinary items. How should extraordinary items be disclosed in the financial statements?

10. When an accounting change occurs, what disclosures must be made in the financial statements?

11. How are earnings per share disclosed in the financial statements?

12. When does a company have a simple capital structure? A complex capital structure?

13. What is the difference between basic and diluted earnings per share?

14. What is the difference between the statement of stockholders' equity and the stockholders' equity section of the balance sheet?

15. When does a company have a deficit in retained earnings?

16. What is the purpose of a restriction on retained earnings? Why might a company have restrictions on its retained earnings?

17. Explain how the accounting treatment of stock dividends differs from that of cash dividends.

18. What is the difference between a stock dividend and a stock split? What is the effect of each on the capital structure of the corporation?

19. Would you expect a corporation's book value per share to equal its market value per share? Why or why not?

SHORT EXERCISES

LO1 Quality of Earnings

SE 1. Each of the items listed below is a quality of earnings issue. Indicate whether the item is (a) an accounting method, (b) an accounting estimate, or (c) a nonoperating item. For any item for which the answer is (a) or (b), indicate which alternative is usually the more conservative choice.

1. LIFO versus FIFO
2. Extraordinary loss
3. 10-year useful life versus 15-year useful life
4. Effect of change in accounting principle
5. Straight-line versus accelerated method
6. Discontinued operations
7. Immediate write-off versus amortization
8. Increase versus decrease in percentage of uncollectible accounts

LO1 Corporate Income Statement

SE 2. Assume that Bedard Company's chief financial officer gave you the following information: Net Sales, $720,000; Cost of Goods Sold, $350,000; Loss from Discontinued Operations (net of income tax benefit of $70,000), $200,000; Loss on Disposal of Discontinued Operations (net of income tax benefit of $16,000), $50,000; Operating Expenses, $130,000; Income Taxes Expense on Continuing Operations, $80,000. From this information, prepare the company's income statement for the year ended June 30, 20xx. (Ignore earnings per share information.)

LO2 Corporate Income Tax Rate Schedule

SE 3. Using the corporate tax rate schedule in Table 1, compute the income tax liability for taxable income of (1) $400,000 and (2) $20,000,000.

LO4 Earnings per Share

SE 4. During 20x4, Halmut Corporation reported a net income of $669,200. On January 1, Halmut had 360,000 shares of common stock outstanding. The company issued an additional 240,000 shares of common stock on August 1. In 20x4, the company had a simple capital structure. During 20x5, there were no transactions involving common stock, and the company reported net income of $870,000. Determine the weighted-average number of common shares outstanding for 20x4 and 20x5. Also, compute earnings per share for 20x4 and 20x5.

LO5 Statement of Stockholders' Equity

SE 5. Refer to the statement of stockholders' equity for Tri-State Corporation in Exhibit 2 to answer the following questions: (1) At what price per share were the 5,000 shares of common stock sold? (2) What was the conversion price per share of the common stock? (3) At what price was the common stock selling on the date of the stock dividend? (4) At what price per share was the treasury stock purchased?

**LO5 Effects of Stockholders' Equity Actions
LO6**

SE 6. Tell whether each of the following actions will increase, decrease, or have no effect on total assets, total liabilities, and total stockholders' equity:

1. Declaration of a stock dividend
2. Declaration of a cash dividend
3. Stock split
4. Restriction of retained earnings
5. Purchase of treasury stock

LO5 Restriction of Retained Earnings

SE 7. Jasmine Company has a lawsuit filed against it. The board took action to restrict retained earnings in the amount of $2,500,000 on May 31, 20x4, pending the outcome of the suit. On May 31, the company had retained earnings of $3,725,000. Show how the restriction on retained earnings would be disclosed as a note to the financial statements.

LO6 Stock Dividends

SE 8. On February 15, Purple Mountain Corporation's board of directors declared a 2 percent stock dividend applicable to the outstanding shares of its $10 par value common stock, of which 200,000 shares are authorized, 130,000 are issued, and 20,000 are held in the treasury. The stock dividend was distributable on March 15 to stockholders of record on March 1. On February 15, the market value of the common stock was $15 per share. On March 30, the board of directors declared a $.50 per share cash dividend. No other stock transactions have occurred. Record, as necessary, the transactions of February 15, March 1, March 15, and March 30.

LO6   Stock Split

SE 9.   On August 10, the board of directors of Torrinni International declared a 3-for-1 stock split of its $9 par value common stock, of which 800,000 shares were authorized and 250,000 were issued and outstanding. The market value on that date was $60 per share. On the same date, the balance of paid-in capital in excess of par value, common was $6,000,000, and the balance of retained earnings was $6,500,000. Prepare the stock-holders' equity section of the company's balance sheet after the stock split. What entry, if any, is needed to record the stock split?

LO7   Book Value for Preferred and Common Stock

SE 10.   Using data from the stockholders' equity section of Gerhardt Corporation's balance sheet shown below, compute the book value per share for both the preferred and the common stock.

Contributed capital		
Preferred stock, $100 par value, 8 percent cumulative, 10,000 shares authorized, 500 shares issued and outstanding*		$ 50,000
Common stock, $10 par value, 100,000 shares authorized, 40,000 shares issued and outstanding	$400,000	
Paid-in capital in excess of par value, common	516,000	916,000
Total contributed capital		$ 966,000
Retained earnings		275,000
Total stockholders' equity		$1,241,000

*The preferred stock is callable at $104 per share, and one year's dividends are in arrears.

EXERCISES

LO1   Effect of Alternative Accounting Methods

E 1.   At the end of its first year of operations, a company calculated its ending merchandise inventory according to three different accounting methods, as follows: FIFO, $95,000; average-cost, $90,000; LIFO, $86,000. If the company used the average-cost method, its net income for the year would be $34,000.

1. Determine net income if the company used the FIFO method.
2. Determine net income if the company used the LIFO method.
3. Which method is more conservative?
4. Will the consistency convention be violated if the company chooses to use the LIFO method?
5. Does the full-disclosure convention require disclosure of the inventory method used in the financial statements?

LO1   Corporate Income Statement

E 2.   Assume that the Sedgeway Furniture Company's chief financial officer gave you the following information: net sales, $1,900,000; cost of goods sold, $1,050,000; extraordinary gain (net of income taxes of $3,500), $12,500; loss from discontinued operations (net of income tax benefit of $30,000), $50,000; loss on disposal of discontinued operations (net of income tax benefit of $13,000), $35,000; selling expenses, $50,000; administrative expenses, $40,000; income taxes expense on continuing operations, $300,000. From this information, prepare the company's income statement for the year ended June 30, 20xx. (Ignore earnings per share information.)

LO1   Corporate Income Statement
LO2
LO3
LO4

E 3.   The following items are components of Asheville Corporation's income statement for the year ended December 31, 20x4:

Sales	$555,000
Cost of goods sold	(275,000)
Operating expenses	(112,500)
Restructuring	(55,000)
Total income taxes expense for period	(82,350)
Income from operations of a discontinued segment	80,000
Gain on disposal of segment	70,000
Extraordinary gain	36,000
Cumulative effect of a change in accounting principle	(24,000)
Net income	$192,150
Earnings per share	$.96

Recast the income statement in proper multistep form, including allocating income taxes to appropriate items (assume a 30 percent income tax rate) and showing earnings per share figures (200,000 shares outstanding).

LO2   Corporate Income Tax Rate Schedule

E 4. Using the corporate tax rate schedule in Table 1, compute the income tax liability for the following situations:

Situation	Taxable Income
A	$ 70,000
B	85,000
C	320,000

LO2   Income Tax Allocation

E 5. Ft. Worth Corporation reported the following accounting income before income taxes, income taxes expense, and net income for 20x2 and 20x3:

	20x2	20x3
Income before income taxes	$280,000	$280,000
Income taxes expense	88,300	88,300
Net income	$191,700	$191,700

On the balance sheet, deferred income taxes liability increased by $38,400 in 20x2 and decreased by $18,800 in 20x3.

1. How much did Ft. Worth Corporation actually pay in income taxes for 20x2 and 20x3?
2. Prepare entries in journal form to record income taxes expense for 20x2 and 20x3.

LO4   Earnings per Share

E 6. During 20x3, Portland Corporation reported a net income of $1,529,500. On January 1, Portland had 700,000 shares of common stock outstanding. The company issued an additional 420,000 shares of common stock on October 1. In 20x3, the company had a simple capital structure. During 20x4, there were no transactions involving common stock, and the company reported net income of $2,016,000.

1. Determine the weighted-average number of common shares outstanding each year.
2. Compute earnings per share for each year.

LO5   Restriction of Retained Earnings

E 7. The board of directors of the Sunset Company has approved plans to acquire another company during the coming year. The acquisition should cost approximately $550,000. The board took action to restrict retained earnings of the company in the amount of $550,000 on July 17, 20x4. On July 31, the company had retained earnings of $975,000. Show how the restriction on retained earnings would be disclosed in a note to the financial statements.

LO5   Statement of Stockholders' Equity

E 8. The stockholders' equity section of Mallory Corporation's balance sheet on December 31, 20x4, appears as follows:

Contributed capital	
Common stock, $2 par value, 500,000 shares authorized, 400,000 shares issued and outstanding	$ 800,000
Paid-in capital in excess of par value, common	1,200,000
Total contributed capital	$2,000,000
Retained earnings	4,200,000
Total stockholders' equity	$6,200,000

Prepare a statement of stockholders' equity for the year ended December 31, 20x5, assuming the following transactions occurred in sequence during 20x5:

a. Issued 10,000 shares of $100 par value, 9 percent cumulative preferred stock at par after obtaining authorization from the state.
b. Issued 40,000 shares of common stock in connection with the conversion of bonds having a carrying value of $600,000.
c. Declared and issued a 2 percent common stock dividend. The market value on the date of declaration was $14 per share.
d. Purchased 10,000 shares of common stock for the treasury at a cost of $16 per share.
e. Earned net income of $460,000.
f. Declared and paid the full year's dividend on preferred stock and a dividend of $.40 per share on common stock outstanding at the end of the year.
g. Had foreign currency translation adjustment of minus $100,000.

LO6   Journal Entries: Stock Dividends

E 9. Perfect Rest Company has 30,000 shares of its $1 par value common stock outstanding. Record in journal form the following transactions as they relate to the company's common stock:

July 17   Declared a 10 percent stock dividend on common stock to be distributed on August 10 to stockholders of record on July 31. Market value of the stock was $5 per share on this date.

31   Record date.

Aug. 10   Distributed the stock dividend declared on July 17.

Sept. 1   Declared a $.50 per share cash dividend on common stock to be paid on September 16 to stockholders of record on September 10.

LO6   Stock Split

E 10. Teuong Company currently has 500,000 shares of $1 par value common stock authorized with 200,000 shares outstanding. The board of directors declared a 2-for-1 split on May 15, when the market value of the common stock was $2.50 per share. The retained earnings balance on May 15 was $700,000. Paid-in capital in excess of par value, common on this date was $20,000. Prepare the stockholders' equity section of the company's balance sheet before and after the stock split. What entry, if any, would be necessary to record the stock split?

LO6   Stock Split

E 11. On January 15, the board of directors of Exavier International declared a 3-for-1 stock split of its $12 par value common stock, of which 800,000 shares were authorized and 200,000 were issued and outstanding. The market value on that date was $45 per share. On the same date, the balance of paid-in capital in excess of par value, common was $4,000,000, and the balance of retained earnings was $8,000,000. Prepare the stockholders' equity section of the company's balance sheet before and after the stock split. What entry, if any, is needed to record the stock split?

LO7   Book Value for Preferred and Common Stock

E 12. Below is the stockholders' equity section of Village Corporation's balance sheet. Determine the book value per share for both the preferred and the common stock.

Contributed capital		
Preferred stock, $100 per share, 6 percent cumulative, 10,000 shares authorized, 200 shares issued and outstanding*		$ 20,000
Common stock, $5 par value, 100,000 shares authorized, 10,000 shares issued, 9,000 shares outstanding	$50,000	
Paid-in capital in excess of par value, common	28,000	78,000
Total contributed capital		$ 98,000
Retained earnings		95,000
Total contributed capital and retained earnings		$193,000
Less treasury stock, common (1,000 shares at cost)		15,000
Total stockholders' equity		$178,000

*The preferred stock is callable at $105 per share, and one year's dividends are in arrears.

PROBLEMS

LO1   Effect of Alternative Accounting Methods

P 1. Carsey Company began operations in 20xx. At the beginning of the year, the company purchased plant assets of $450,000, with an estimated useful life of ten years and no salvage value. During the year, the company had net sales of $650,000, salaries expense of $100,000, and other expenses of $40,000, excluding depreciation. In addition, Carsey Company purchased inventory as follows:

Jan. 15	400 units at $200	$ 80,000
Mar. 20	200 units at $204	40,800
June 15	800 units at $208	166,400
Sept. 18	600 units at $206	123,600
Dec. 9	300 units at $210	63,000
Total	2,300 units	$473,800

At the end of the year, a physical inventory disclosed 500 units still on hand. The managers of Carsey Company know they have a choice of accounting methods, but they are unsure how those methods will affect net income. They have heard of the FIFO and LIFO inventory methods and the straight-line and double-declining-balance depreciation methods.

REQUIRED ▶
1. Prepare two income statements for Carsey Company, one using the FIFO and straight-line methods and the other using the LIFO and double-declining-balance methods. Ignore income taxes.
2. Prepare a schedule accounting for the difference in the two net income figures obtained in **1.**
3. What effect does the choice of accounting method have on Carsey's inventory turnover? What conclusions can you draw?
4. How does the choice of accounting methods affect Carsey's return on assets? Assume the company's only assets are cash of $40,000, inventory, and plant assets. Use year-end balances to compute the ratios. Is your evaluation of Carsey's profitability affected by the choice of accounting methods?

P 2.

LO1 Corporate Income Statement
LO2
LO3
LO4

Ⓚ/Ⓡ

Income statement information for Dimsum Corporation during 20x3 is as follows:

a. Administrative expenses, $110,000.
b. Cost of goods sold, $440,000.
c. Restructuring charge, $125,000.
d. Cumulative effect of a change in inventory methods that decreased income (net of taxes, $28,000), $60,000.
e. Extraordinary loss from a storm (net of taxes, $10,000), $20,000.
f. Income taxes expense, continuing operations, $42,000.
g. Net sales, $1,015,000.
h. Selling expenses, $190,000.

REQUIRED ▶
1. Prepare Dimsum Corporation's income statement for 20x3, including earnings per share, assuming a weighted average of 200,000 shares of common stock outstanding for 20x3.
2. What is a restructuring charge, and why is it deducted before income from operations before income taxes?

P 3.

LO1 Corporate Income Statement
LO2 and Evaluation of Business
LO3 Operations
LO4

Ⓚ/Ⓡ

During 20x3, Burston Corporation engaged in a number of complex transactions to improve the business—selling off a division, retiring bonds, and changing accounting methods. The company has always issued a simple single-step income statement, and the accountant has accordingly prepared the December 31 year-end income statements for 20x2 and 20x3, as shown below.

Burston Corporation
Income Statements
For the Years Ended December 31, 20x3 and 20x2

	20x3	20x2
Net sales	$3,500,000	$4,200,000
Cost of goods sold	(1,925,000)	(2,100,000)
Operating expenses	(787,500)	(525,000)
Income taxes expense	(576,450)	(472,500)
Income from operations of a discontinued segment	560,000	
Gain on disposal of discontinued segment	490,000	
Extraordinary gain	252,000	
Cumulative effect of a change in accounting principle	(168,000)	
Net income	$1,345,050	$1,102,500
Earnings per share	$ 6.73	$ 5.51

Theodore Burston, the president of Burston Corporation, is pleased to see that both net income and earnings per share increased by 22 percent from 20x2 to 20x3 and intends to announce to the company's stockholders that the plan to improve the business has been successful.

REQUIRED ▶

1. Recast the 20x3 and 20x2 income statements in proper multistep form, including allocating income taxes to appropriate items (assume a 30 percent income tax rate) and showing earnings per share figures (200,000 shares outstanding).
2. What is your assessment of Burston Corporation's plan and business operations in 20x3?

P 4.

LO5 Dividends, Stock Splits, and
LO6 Stockholders' Equity
LO7

Ⓚ/Ⓡ

The stockholders' equity section of Montpelior Linen Mills, Inc., as of December 31, 20x2, was as follows:

Contributed capital	
Common stock, $6 par value, 500,000 shares authorized, 80,000 shares issued and outstanding	$ 480,000
Paid-in capital in excess of par value, common	150,000
Total contributed capital	$ 630,000
Retained earnings	480,000
Total stockholders' equity	$1,110,000

A review of the stockholders' equity records of Montpelior Linen Mills, Inc., disclosed the following transactions during 20x3:

Mar. 25 The board of directors declared a 5 percent stock dividend to stockholders of record on April 20 to be distributed on May 1. The market value of the common stock was $11 per share.
Apr. 20 Date of record for the stock dividend.
May 1 Distributed the stock dividend.
Sept. 10 Declared a 3-for-1 stock split.
Dec. 15 Declared a 10 percent stock dividend to stockholders of record on January 15 to be distributed on February 15. The market price on this date is $3.50 per share.

REQUIRED ▶

1. Record the stockholders' equity components of the transactions for Montpelior Linen Mills, Inc., in T accounts.
2. Prepare the stockholders' equity section of the company's balance sheet as of December 31, 20x3. Assume net income for 20x3 is $47,000.
3. Calculate book value per share before and after the above transactions.

P 5.

LO5 Dividends, Stock Splits, and
LO6 Stockholders' Equity
LO7

Ⓚ/Ⓡ

The balance sheet of O'Malley Woolen Company disclosed the following stockholders' equity as of September 30, 20x3:

Contributed capital	
Common stock, $2 par value, 1,000,000 shares authorized, 300,000 shares issued and outstanding	$ 600,000
Paid-in capital in excess of par value, common	370,000
Total contributed capital	$ 970,000
Retained earnings	350,000
Total stockholders' equity	$1,320,000

The following stockholders' equity transactions were completed during the next fiscal year in the order presented:

20x3
Dec. 17 Declared a 10 percent stock dividend to be distributed January 20 to stockholders of record on January 1. The market value per share on the date of declaration was $4.

20x4
Jan. 1 Date of record.
    20 Distributed the stock dividend.
Apr. 14 Declared a $.25 per share cash dividend. The cash dividend is payable May 15 to stockholders of record on May 1.

May   1   Date of record.
      15   Paid the cash dividend.
June 17   Split its stock 2 for 1.
Sept. 15 Declared a cash dividend of $.10 per share payable October 10 to stock-
          holders of record on October 1.

On September 14, the board of directors restricted retained earnings for plant expansion in the amount of $175,000. The restriction should be shown in the notes to the
financial statements.

REQUIRED ▶
1. Record the above transactions in journal form.
2. Prepare the stockholders' equity section of the company's balance sheet as of
   September 30, 20x4, with an appropriate disclosure of the restriction of retained
   earnings. Assume net income for the year is $150,000.
3. Calculate book value per share before and after the transactions.

ALTERNATE PROBLEMS

P 6.
LO1   **Corporate Income Statement**
LO2
LO3
LO4

Information concerning operations of MacFarland Weather Gear Corporation during
20xx is as follows:

a. Administrative expenses, $90,000.
b. Cost of goods sold, $420,000.
c. Write-down of assets, $75,000.
d. Cumulative effect of an accounting change in depreciation methods that increased
   income (net of taxes, $20,000), $42,000.
e. Extraordinary loss from an earthquake (net of taxes, $36,000), $60,000.
f. Sales (net), $975,000.
g. Selling expenses, $80,000.
h. Income taxes expense applicable to continuing operations, $105,000.

REQUIRED ▶
1. Prepare the corporation's income statement for the year ended December 31, 20xx,
   including earnings per share information. Assume a weighted average of 100,000
   common shares outstanding during the year.
2. What is a write-down, and why is it deducted before income from operations?

P 7.
LO5   **Dividends, Stock Splits, and**
LO6   **Stockholders' Equity**
LO7

The stockholders' equity section of the balance sheet of Boysan Corporation as of
December 31, 20x4, was as follows:

Contributed capital	
Common stock, $4 par value, 500,000 shares authorized,	
200,000 shares issued and outstanding	$ 800,000
Paid-in capital in excess of par value, common	1,000,000
Total contributed capital	$1,800,000
Retained earnings	1,200,000
Total stockholders' equity	$3,000,000

The following transactions occurred in 20x5 for Boysan Corporation:

Feb. 28   The board of directors declared a 10 percent stock dividend to stockholders
          of record on March 25 to be distributed on April 5. The market value on this
          date is $16.
Mar. 25   Date of record for stock dividend.
Apr. 5   Distributed the stock dividend.
Aug. 3   Declared a 2-for-1 stock split.
Nov. 20   Purchased 18,000 shares of the company's common stock at $8 per share for
          the treasury.
Dec. 31   Declared a 5 percent stock dividend to stockholders of record on January 25
          to be distributed on February 5. The market value per share was $9.

REQUIRED ▶
1. Record the stockholders' equity components of the transactions for Boysan
   Corporation in T accounts.
2. Prepare the stockholders' equity section of the company's balance sheet as of
   December 31, 20x5. Assume net income for 20x5 is $108,000.
3. Calculate book value per share before and after the above transactions.

LO5   **Dividends, Stock Splits, and**
LO6   **Stockholders' Equity**
LO7

P 8. The stockholders' equity section of Blue Ridge Furniture Restoration Company's balance sheet as of December 31, 20x2, was as follows:

Contributed capital

Common stock, $1 par value, 3,000,000 shares authorized, 500,000 shares issued and outstanding	$ 500,000
Paid-in capital in excess of par value, common	200,000
Total contributed capital	$ 700,000
Retained earnings	540,000
Total stockholders' equity	$1,240,000

The company engaged in the following stockholders' equity transactions during 20x3:

Mar.   5   Declared a $.20 per share cash dividend to be paid on April 6 to stockholders of record on March 20.

      20   Date of record.

Apr.   6   Paid the cash dividend.

June 17   Declared a 10 percent stock dividend to be distributed August 17 to stockholders of record on August 5. The market value of the stock was $7 per share.

Aug.   5   Date of record.

      17   Distributed the stock dividend.

Oct.   2   Split its stock 3 for 1.

Dec. 27   Declared a cash dividend of $.05 payable January 27, 20x4, to stockholders of record on January 14, 20x4.

On December 9, the board of directors restricted retained earnings for a pending lawsuit in the amount of $100,000. The restriction should be shown in the notes to the firm's financial statements.

REQUIRED ▶

1. Record the 20x3 transactions in journal form.
2. Prepare the stockholders' equity section of the company's balance sheet as of December 31, 20x3, with an appropriate disclosure of the restriction on retained earnings. Assume net income for the year is $200,000.
3. Calculate book value per share before and after the above transactions.

SKILLS DEVELOPMENT CASES

Conceptual Analysis

SD 1.

LO1   **Interpretation of Earnings**
       Reports

In a recent year, analysts expected International Business Machines (IBM) <www.ibm.com> to earn $1.32 per share. The company actually earned $1.33. Microsoft Corporation <www.microsoft.com> was expected to earn $.43 per share, but it earned only $.41. The corporate income statements of these companies show that Microsoft had a special charge (with corresponding liability) of $660 million, or $.06 per share, based on settlement of a class-action law suit filed on behalf of consumers, whereas IBM had no such a charge.[25] Who did better, Microsoft or IBM? Use quality of earnings to support your answer. Also, what is the effect of Microsoft's special charge on current and future cash flows?

SD 2.

LO1   **Classic Quality of Earnings**
LO3

On Tuesday, January 19, 1988, IBM <www.ibm.com> reported greatly increased earnings for the fourth quarter of 1987. Despite this reported gain in earnings, the price of IBM's stock on the New York Stock Exchange declined by $6 per share to $111.75. In sympathy with this move, most other technology stocks also declined.[26]

     IBM's fourth-quarter net earnings rose from $1.39 billion, or $2.28 a share, to $2.08 billion, or $3.47 a share, an increase of 49.6 percent and 52.2 percent over the same period a year earlier. Management declared that these results demonstrated the effectiveness of IBM's efforts to become more competitive and that, despite the economic uncertainties of 1988, the company was planning for growth.

     The apparent cause of the stock price decline was that the huge increase in income could be traced to nonrecurring gains. Investment analysts pointed out that IBM's high earnings stemmed primarily from such factors as a lower tax rate. Despite most analysts' expectations of a tax rate between 40 and 42 percent, IBM's was a low 36.4 percent, down from the previous year's 45.3 percent. Analysts were also disappointed in IBM's revenue growth. Revenues within the United States were down, and much of the company's growth in revenues came through favorable currency translations, increases that might not be repeated. In fact, some estimates of IBM's fourth-quarter earnings attributed $.50 per share to currency translations and another $.25 to tax-rate changes.

Other factors contributing to IBM's rise in earnings were one-time transactions, such as the sale of Intel Corporation stock and bond redemptions, along with a corporate stock buyback program that reduced the amount of stock outstanding in the fourth quarter by 7.4 million shares.

The analysts were concerned about the quality of IBM's earnings. Identify four quality of earnings issues reported in the case and the analysts' concern about each. In percentage terms, what is the impact of the currency changes on fourth-quarter earnings? Comment on management's assessment of IBM's performance. Do you agree with management? (Optional question: What has IBM's subsequent performance been?) Be prepared to discuss your answers in class.

Ethical Dilemma

SD 3.

LO6 Ethics and Stock Dividends

For 20 years Bass Products Corporation, a public corporation, has followed the practice of paying a cash dividend every quarter and has promoted itself to investors as a stable, reliable company. Recent competition from Asian companies has negatively affected its earnings and cash flows. As a result, Sandra Bass, president of the company, is proposing that the board of directors declare a stock dividend of 5 percent this year instead of a cash dividend. She says, "This will maintain our consecutive dividend record and will not require any cash outflow." What is the difference between a cash dividend and a stock dividend? Why does a corporation usually distribute either kind of dividend, and how does each affect the financial statements? Is the action that Sandra Bass has proposed ethical?

Research Activity

SD 4.

LO1 Corporate Income Statement,
LO2 Statement of Stockholders'
LO3 Equity, and Book Value per
LO5 Share
LO6
LO7

Select the annual reports of three corporations, using one or more of the following sources: your library, the Internet, or the Needles Accounting Resource Center Web Site at http://accounting.college.hmco.com/students. You may choose companies from the same industry or at random, at the direction of your instructor. (If you completed the related research activity in the chapter on contributed capital, use the same three companies.) Prepare a table with a column for each corporation. Then, for any year covered by the balance sheet, the statement of stockholders' equity, and the income statement, answer the following questions: Does the company own treasury stock? Did it buy or retire any treasury stock? Did it declare a stock dividend or a stock split? What other transactions appear in the statement of stockholders' equity? Has the company deferred any income taxes? Were there any discontinued operations, extraordinary items, or accounting changes? Compute the book value per common share for the company. In *The Wall Street Journal* or the financial section of another daily newspaper, find the current market price of each company's common stock and compare it with the book value you computed. Should there be any relationship between the two values? Be prepared to discuss your answers in class.

Decision-Making Practice

SD 5.

LO5 Analyzing Effects of
LO6 Stockholders' Equity
LO7 Transactions

Metzger Steel Corporation (MSC) is a small specialty steel manufacturer located in northern Alabama. It has been owned by the Metzger family for several generations. Arnold Metzger is a major shareholder in MSC by virtue of his having inherited 200,000 shares of common stock in the company. Metzger has not shown much interest in the business because of his enthusiasm for archaeology, which takes him to far parts of the world. However, when he received the minutes of the last board of directors meeting, he questioned a number of transactions involving stockholders' equity. He asks you, as a person with a knowledge of accounting, to help him interpret the effect of these transactions on his interest in MSC.

You begin by examining the stockholders' equity section of MSC's December 31, 20x4, balance sheet:

Metzger Steel Corporation Stockholders' Equity December 31, 20x4		
Contributed capital		
Common stock, $10 par value, 5,000,000 shares		
authorized, 1,000,000 shares issued and outstanding		$10,000,000
Paid-in capital in excess of par value, common		25,000,000
Total contributed capital		$35,000,000
Retained earnings		20,000,000
Total stockholders' equity		$55,000,000

Then you read the relevant parts of the minutes of the board of directors meeting on December 15, 20x5:

Item A The president reported the following transactions involving the company's stock during the last quarter:

October 15. Sold 500,000 shares of authorized common stock through the investment banking firm of T.R. Kendall at a net price of $50 per share.

November 1. Purchased 100,000 shares for the corporate treasury from Lucy Metzger at a price of $55 per share.

Item B The board declared a 2-for-1 stock split (accomplished by halving the par value and doubling each stockholder's shares), followed by a 10 percent stock dividend. The board then declared a cash dividend of $2 per share on the resulting shares. Cash dividends are declared on outstanding shares and shares distributable. All these transactions are applicable to stockholders of record on December 20 and are payable on January 10. The market value of MSC stock on the board meeting date after the stock split was estimated to be $30.

Item C The chief financial officer stated that he expected the company to report net income for the year of $4,000,000.

1. Prepare a stockholders' equity section of MSC's balance sheet as of December 31, 20x5, that reflects the above transactions. (**Hint:** Use T accounts to analyze the transactions. Also use a T account to keep track of the shares of common stock outstanding.)
2. Write a memorandum to Arnold Metzger that shows the book value per share and Metzger's percentage of ownership at the beginning and end of the year. Explain the difference and state whether Metzger's position has improved during the year. Tell why or why not and state how Metzger may be able to maintain his percentage of ownership.

FINANCIAL REPORTING AND ANALYSIS CASES

Interpreting Financial Reports

FRA 1.
LO1 Interpretation of Statement
LO5 of Stockholders' Equity

The consolidated statement of stockholders' equity for Jackson Electronics, Inc., a manufacturer of a broad line of electrical components, is presented at the top of the next page.

This statement has nine summary transactions. (1) Show that you understand it by preparing an entry in journal form with an explanation for each entry. In each case,

Jackson Electronics, Inc.
Consolidated Statement of Stockholders' Equity
(In thousands)

	Preferred Stock $100 Par Value	Common Stock $1 Par Value	Paid-in Capital in Excess of Par Value, Common	Retained Earnings	Treasury Stock, Common	Accumulated Other Comprehensive Income	Total
Balance at September 30, 20x4	$2,756	$3,902	$14,149	$119,312	($ 942)		$139,177
Net income	—	—	—	18,753	—		18,753
Unrealized gain on available for sale securities						$12,000	12,000
Redemption and retirement of preferred stock (27,560 shares)	(2,756)	—	—	—	—		(2,756)
Stock options exercised (89,000 shares)	—	89	847	—	—		936
Purchases of common stock for treasury (501,412 shares)	—	—	—	—	(12,552)		(12,552)
Issuance of common stock (148,000 shares) in exchange for convertible subordinated debentures	—	148	3,635	—	—		3,783
Issuance of common stock (715,000 shares) for cash	—	715	24,535	—	—		25,250
Issuance of 500,000 shares of common stock in exchange for investment in Electrix Company shares	—	500	17,263	—	—		17,763
Cash dividends—common stock ($.80 per share)	—	—	—	(3,086)	—		(3,086)
Balance at September 30, 20x5	$ —	$5,354	$60,429	$134,979	($13,494)	$12,000	$199,268

if applicable, determine the average price per common share. At times, you will have to make assumptions about an offsetting part of the entry. For example, assume debentures (long-term bonds) are recorded at face value and that employees pay cash for stock purchased under company incentive plans. (2) Define comprehensive income and determine the amount for Jackson Electronics.

Group Activity: Assign each transaction to a different group to develop the entry and present the explanation to the class.

FRA 2.
LO2 Analysis of Income Taxes from Annual Report

In its 2000 annual report, The Washington Post Company <www.washingtonpost.com>, a newspaper publishing and television broadcasting company based in Washington, D.C., provided the following data about its current and deferred income tax provisions (in millions):[27]

	2000	
	Current	Deferred
U.S. federal	$ 77.5	$ 4.9
Foreign	1.0	—
State	22.6	(12.7)
	$101.1	($7.8)

1. What was the 2000 income taxes expense? Record in journal form the overall income tax liability for 2000, using income tax allocation procedures.
2. In the long-term liability section of its balance sheet, The Washington Post Company shows deferred income taxes of $117.7 million in 2000 versus $114.0 million in 1999. This shows an increase in the amount of deferred income taxes. How do such deferred income taxes arise? What would cause deferred income taxes to increase? Give an example of this process. Given the definition of a liability, do you see a potential problem with the company's classifying deferred income taxes as a liability?

International Company

FRA 3.

LO5 **Restriction of Retained Earnings**

In some countries, including Japan, the availability of retained earnings for the payment of dividends is restricted. The following disclosure appeared in the annual report of Yamaha Motor Company, Ltd. <www.yamaha.com>, the Japanese motorcycle manufacturer:[28]

> The Commercial Code of Japan provides that an amount not less than 10 percent of the total of cash dividends and bonuses [paid] to directors and corporate auditors be appropriated as a legal reserve until such reserve equals 25 percent of stated capital. The legal reserve may be used to reduce a deficit or may be transferred to stated capital, but is not available as dividends.

"Stated capital" is equivalent to common stock. For Yamaha, this legal reserve amounted to ¥34.4 billion, or $290 million. How does this practice differ from that in the United States? Why do you think it is government policy in Japan? Do you think it is a good idea?

Toys "R" Us Annual Report

FRA 4.

LO1 **Corporate Income Statement,**
LO3 **Statement of Stockholders'**
LO5 **Equity, and Book Value per Share**

Refer to the Toys "R" Us <www.tru.com> annual report to answer the following questions:

1. Does Toys "R" Us have discontinued operations, extraordinary items, or cumulative effects from accounting changes? Would you say the income statement for Toys "R" Us is relatively simple or relatively complex?
2. What transactions most commonly affect the stockholders' equity section of the balance sheet of Toys "R" Us? Examine the statements of stockholders' equity.

Comparison Case: Toys "R" Us and Walgreen Co.

FRA 5.

LO7 **Book Value and Market Value**

Refer to the annual report for Toys "R" Us <www.tru.com> and the financial statements for Walgreens <www.walgreens.com> in the Supplement to Chapter 6. Compute the 2002 and 2001 book value per share for both companies and compare the results to the average stock price of each in the fourth quarter of 2002 as shown in the notes to the financial statements. How do you explain the differences in book value per share, and how do you interpret their relationship to market prices?

Fingraph® Financial Analyst™

FRA 6.

LO1 **Stockholders' Equity Analysis**
LO3
LO4
LO5
LO6
LO7

Choose any two companies in the same industry from the list of Fingraph companies on the Needles Accounting Resource Center Student Web Site at http://accounting.college.hmco.com/students. Access the Microsoft Excel spreadsheets for the companies you selected. Click on the URL at the top of each company's spreadsheet for a link to the company's web site and annual report.

1. In the annual reports of the companies you have selected, find the corporate income statement and summary of significant accounting policies (usually the first note to the financial statements). Did the companies report any discontinued operations, extraordinary items, or accounting changes? What percentage impact did these items have on earnings per share? Summarize the methods and estimates each company

uses in a table. If the company changed its accounting methods, was the change the result of a new accounting standard or a voluntary choice by management? Evaluate the quality of earnings for each company.

2. Did the companies provide a statement of stockholders' equity or summarize changes in stockholders' equity in the notes only? Did the companies declare any stock dividends or stock splits? Calculate book value per common share.

3. Find in the financial section of your local paper the current market prices of the companies' common stock. Discuss the difference between market price per share and book value per share.

4. Find and read references to earnings per share in management's discussion and analysis in each annual report.

5. Write a one-page executive summary that highlights the quality of earnings for these companies, the relationship of book value and market value, and the existence or absence of stock splits or dividends, including reference to management's assessment. Include your table with your report.

Internet Case

FRA 7.

LO1 **Comparison of Comprehensive**
LO4 **Income Disclosures**
LO5

When the FASB ruled that public companies should report comprehensive income, it did not issue specific guidelines for how this amount and its components should be disclosed. Choose two companies in the same industry from the Needles Accounting Resource Center Web Site at http://accounting.college.hmco.com/students. Using web links, go to the annual reports on the web sites of the two companies you have selected. In the latest annual report, look at the financial statements. How have your two companies reported comprehensive income—as a part of the income statement, a part of stockholders' equity, or a separate statement? What items create a difference between net income and comprehensive income? Is comprehensive income greater or less than net income? Is comprehensive income more volatile than net income? Which measure of income is used to compute basic earnings per share?

16

Chapter 16 covers the management issues related to sources of long-term financing, with an emphasis on bond liabilities.

Long-Term Liabilities

DECISION POINT

A USER'S FOCUS

AT&T Corporation <www.att.com> During 2002, AT&T Corporation reduced its debt financing. How much to borrow and how much debt should be financed long term are two questions management must consider. What is the impact of AT&T's lower debt level on its capital structure and its interest-paying ability?

Decisions related to the issuance of long-term debt are among the most important that management has to make because, next to the success or failure of a company's operations, how the company finances its operations is the most important factor in the company's long-term viability. Long-term liabilities, or long-term debt, are obligations of a business that are due to be paid after one year or beyond the operating cycle, whichever is longer. Even after reducing its debt, AT&T's capital structure includes a large amount of long-term debt, as shown by the figures for 2002 in the Financial Highlights.[1] Total liabilities are greater than stockholders' equity, and the debt to equity ratio is 3.5 ($42,960 ÷ $12,312). What factors might have influenced AT&T's management to incur a large amount of debt?

In the past, AT&T was the nation's largest long-distance telephone company. The investments in power lines, transformers, computers, and other types of property, plant, and equipment required for this business are enormous. These are mostly long-term assets, and the most sensible way to finance them is through long-term financing. When the business was protected from competition, management could reasonably predict sufficient earnings and cash flow to

Now that AT&T is facing competition for its markets, why must management reassess the company's long-term liabilities?

meet the debt and interest obligations. Now that AT&T is facing open competition for its markets, the company must reassess not only the kind of business it is but also the amount and kinds of debt it carries. The amount and type of debt a company incurs depends on many factors, including the nature of the business, its competitive environment, the state of the financial markets, and the predictability of its earnings.

Financial Highlights: Capital Structure
(In millions)

Liabilities	
Total current liabilities	$12,024
Long-term debt	$18,812
Long-term benefit-related liabilities	4,001
Deferred income taxes	4,739
Other long-term liabilities and deferred credits	3,384
Total long-term liabilities	$30,936
Total liabilities	$42,960
Stockholders' equity	12,312
Total liabilities and stockholders' equity	$55,272

MANAGEMENT ISSUES RELATED TO ISSUING LONG-TERM DEBT

LO1 Identify the management issues related to issuing long-term debt.

RELATED TEXT ASSIGNMENTS
Q: 1
SE: 1
E: 1
SD: 6
FRA: 1, 3, 4, 5, 6

Profitable operations and short-term credit seldom provide sufficient cash for a growing business. Growth often requires investment in long-term assets and in research and development and other activities that will produce income in future years. To finance such assets and activities, the company requires funds that will be available for longer periods. Two key sources of long-term funds are the issuance of capital stock and the issuance of long-term debt in the form of bonds, notes, mortgages, and leases. The management issues related to issuing long-term debt are (1) whether to take on long-term debt, (2) how much long-term debt to carry, (3) what types of long-term debt to incur, and (4) how to handle debt repayment.

THE DECISION TO ISSUE LONG-TERM DEBT

KEY POINT: Although carrying a lot of debt is risky, there are some advantages to issuing bonds instead of stock. First, bond interest expense is tax-deductible for the issuing corporation, whereas dividends paid on stock are not. Second, issuing bonds is a way to raise capital without diluting ownership of the corporation. The challenge is to determine the optimal balance between stocks and bonds so that the advantages of each can be enjoyed.

A key decision for management is whether to rely solely on stockholders' equity—capital stock issued and retained earnings—for long-term funds for the business or to rely partially on long-term debt for those funds. Since long-term debts represent financial commitments that must be paid at maturity and interest or other payments that must be paid periodically, common stock would seem to have two advantages over long-term debt: it does not have to be paid back, and dividends on common stock are usually paid only if the company earns sufficient income. Long-term debt does, however, have the following advantages over common stock:

1. **Stockholder control.** Since bondholders and other creditors do not have voting rights, common stockholders do not relinquish any control of the company.

2. **Tax effects.** The interest on debt is tax-deductible, whereas dividends on common stock are not. For example, if a corporation pays $100,000 in interest and the income tax rate is 30 percent, the net cost to the corporation is $70,000 because it will save $30,000 on its income taxes. To pay $100,000 in dividends, the company would have to earn $142,857 before taxes ($100,000 ÷ .70).

3. **Financial leverage.** If a corporation is able to earn more on its assets than it pays in interest on debt, the excess will increase its earnings for stockholders. This concept is called **financial leverage** or *trading on the equity*. For example, if a company is able to earn 12 percent, or $120,000, on a $1,000,000 investment financed by long-term 10 percent notes, it will earn $20,000 before taxes ($120,000 − $100,000). Financial leverage makes heavily debt-financed investments in office buildings and shopping centers attractive to investors, who hope to earn a return that exceeds the cost of the interest on the underlying debt. The debt to equity ratio is considered an overall measure of the financial leverage of a company.

Despite these advantages, using debt financing is not always in a company's best interest. First, since cash is required to make periodic interest payments and to pay back the principal amount of the debt at the maturity date, a company whose plans for earnings do not pan out, whose operations are subject to ups and downs, or whose cash flow is weak can be in danger. If the company fails to meet its obligations, it can be forced into bankruptcy by creditors. In other words, a company may become overcommitted. Consider, for example, the heavily debt-financed airline industry. Both TWA and Continental Airlines filed for bankruptcy protection because they could not make payments on their long-term debt and other liabilities. (While in bankruptcy both firms restructured their debt and interest payments, but only Continental survived.) And Swiss Air and Midway Airlines shut down all operations because of insufficient cash to pay creditors and employees. Second, financial leverage can work against a company if the earnings from its investments do not exceed its interest payments. This happened during the savings and loan crisis when long-term debt was used to finance the construction of office buildings that subsequently could not be leased for enough money to cover interest payments.

www.continental.com

FOCUS ON INTERNATIONAL BUSINESS

Pushed to the Brink of Failure

Due to recent declines in passenger revenue, a record number of airlines are shutting down operations, operating under bankruptcy protection, seeking purchase by another airline, or relying on government loan guarantees for their short-term survival. Air Afrique, Canada 3000, Swiss Air, and Midway Airlines have been among those hardest hit.[2] Subsequently, TWA and US Airways joined the group as the largest airline bankruptcies. In a weak economy, the large amount of debt financing that airlines use to fund operations and purchases of aircraft adds to their troubles. With lower cash flows, the airlines find it harder to make payments of interest and principal on debt, thereby increasing the risk of default.

HOW MUCH DEBT TO CARRY

The amount of total debt that companies carry varies widely. Many companies carry less than 100 percent of their stockholders' equity. However, as can be seen from Figure 1, the average debt to equity for these selected industries exceeds 100 percent of stockholders' equity. The range is from about 105 percent to 200 percent of equity. Clearly the use of debt financing varies widely across industries. Firms that own a high percentage of long-term assets would be looking to long-term financing as an option. We saw previously that AT&T has a debt to equity ratio of 3.5 times. Financial leverage makes it advantageous to have long-term debt so long as the company earns a satisfactory income and is able to make interest payments and repay the debt at maturity. Since failure to make timely interest payments could force a company into bankruptcy, it is important for companies to assess the risk of default or nonpayment of interest or principal.

A common measure of how much risk a company is undertaking with its debt is the **interest coverage ratio**. It measures the degree of protection a company has from default on interest payments. For AT&T, which in 2002 had income before taxes and special items of $2,836 million and interest expense of $1,448 million, this ratio is computed as follows:

$$\text{Interest Coverage Ratio} = \frac{\text{Income Before Taxes} + \text{Interest Expense}}{\text{Interest Expense}}$$

$$= \frac{\$2,836,000,000 + \$1,448,000,000}{\$1,448,000,000}$$

$$= 3.0 \text{ times}$$

This ratio shows that the interest expense for AT&T was covered 3.0 times in 2002. AT&T's interest coverage ratio was much higher in 2001 (6.1 times). Its income

www.att.com

FIGURE 1
Average Debt to Equity for Selected Industries

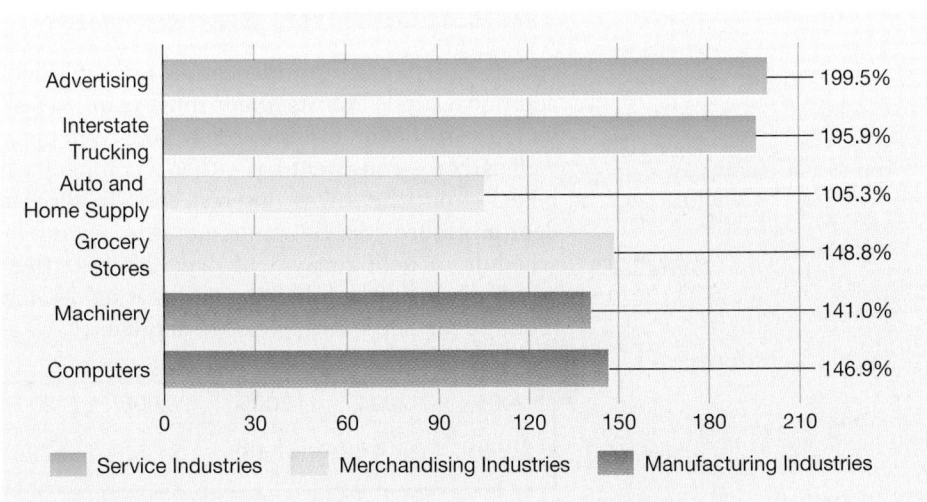

Source: Data from Dun & Bradstreet, *Industry Norms and Key Business Ratios,* 2000–2001.

● **STOP AND THINK!**
How does a lender assess the
risk that a borrower may
default—that is, not pay interest and principal when due?

*The lender reviews the enterprise's
current earnings and cash flows as
well as its debt to equity and
interest coverage ratios. The analysis may also include a historical
comparison that reflects both good
and poor economic times. The
lender can then judge how well the
company has met its past debt
obligations.* ■

before taxes in 2002 was 63 percent lower, and its interest expense was about the
same, resulting in the dramatic decline in interest coverage. The risk for lenders
increased substantially, and a lower debt rating is likely if earnings before taxes do
not return to levels of previous years.

TYPES OF LONG-TERM DEBT

Long-term bonds (most of which are also called debentures) are the most common
type of long-term debt. They can have many different characteristics, including the
time until repayment, amount of interest, whether the company can elect to repay
early, and whether they can be converted into common stock or other securities.
But there are many other types of long-term debt, such as long-term notes, mortgages, and long-term leases. AT&T, for example, has a mixture of long-term obligations, as shown by the following excerpt from its 2002 annual report:[3]

www.att.com

Financial Highlights: Long-Term Obligations
(This table shows the outstanding long-term debt obligations,
in millions, at December 31.)

Interest Rates (b)	Maturities	2002
Debentures and Notes		
4.59%–6.00%	2004–2009	$ 1,455
6.06%–6.50%	2004–2029	6,678
6.75%–7.50%	2004–2006	2,449
7.75%–8.85%	2003–2031	6,796
9.90%–19.95%	2004–2004	13
Variable rate	2003–2054	3,012
Total debentures and notes		20,403
Other		105
Less: Unamortized discount—net		(115)
Total long-term obligations		20,393
Less: Currently maturing long-term debt		1,581
Net long-term obligations		$18,812

To structure long-term financing to the best advantage of their companies, managers
must know the characteristics of the various types of long-term debt.

TIMING OF LONG-TERM DEBT REPAYMENT

Ability to repay debt influences a company's debt rating and the cost of borrowing
additional funds. Management must plan its cash flows carefully to ensure that it
will have sufficient funds to repay long-term debt when it comes due. If this is done
well and on a consistent basis, then a company can achieve the best debt rating and
benefit from the lowest interest cost. To show the potential effects of long-term
debt on future cash flows, the notes to a company's financial statements provide a

www.att.com

schedule of debt repayment over the next five years. For example, in its notes,
AT&T disclosed the following information detailing cash payments totaling $20,393
required for 2003 through 2007 and later:[4]

2003	2004	2005	2006	2007	Later years
$1,581	$2,437	$1,185	$4,328	$296	$10,566

 Check out ACE for a Review Quiz at http://accounting.college.hmco.com/students.

THE NATURE OF BONDS

LO2 Identify and contrast the major characteristics of bonds.

RELATED TEXT ASSIGNMENTS
Q: 2, 3
SD: 4, 6
FRA: 6, 7

● **STOP AND THINK!**
If a company with a high debt to equity ratio wants to increase its debt when the economy is weak, what kind of bond might it issue?
It would most likely issue a secured bond because, rather than being issued on the company's general credit, certain assets are pledged as a guarantee of repayment. ■

TERMINOLOGY NOTE:
Do not confuse the terms *indenture* and *debenture*. They sound alike, but an indenture is a bond contract, whereas a debenture is an unsecured bond.

STUDY NOTE: A debenture of a solid company actually might be a less risky investment than a secured bond of an unstable company.

STUDY NOTE: An advantage of issuing serial bonds is that the organization retires the bonds over a period of years, rather than all at once.

A bond is a security, usually long term, representing money that a corporation or other entity borrows from the investing public. (Bonds are also issued by the U.S. government, state and local governments, and foreign countries to raise money.) A bond must be repaid at a specified time and requires periodic payments of interest.* Interest is usually paid semiannually (twice a year). Bonds must not be confused with stocks. Because stocks are shares of ownership, stockholders are owners. Bondholders are creditors. Bonds are promises to repay the amount borrowed, called the *principal*, and interest at a specified rate on specified future dates.

Often, a bondholder receives a bond certificate as evidence of the organization's debt. In most cases, the face value (denomination) of the bond is $1,000 or some multiple of $1,000. A bond issue is the total value of bonds issued at one time. For example, a $1,000,000 bond issue could consist of a thousand $1,000 bonds. Because a bond issue can be bought and held by many investors, the organization usually enters into a supplementary agreement called a bond indenture. The bond indenture defines the rights, privileges, and limitations of the bondholders. It generally describes such things as the maturity date of the bonds, interest payment dates, and interest rate. It may also cover repayment plans and restrictions.

The prices of bonds are stated in terms of a percentage of face value. A bond issue quoted at 103½ means that a $1,000 bond costs $1,035 ($1,000 × 1.035). When a bond sells at exactly 100, it is said to sell at face or par value. When it sells above 100, it is said to sell at a premium; below 100, at a discount. A $1,000 bond quoted at 87.62 would be selling at a discount and would cost the buyer $876.20.

A bond indenture can be written to fit the financing needs of an individual organization. As a result, the bonds being issued in today's financial markets have many different features. Several of the more important ones are described in the following paragraphs.

SECURED OR UNSECURED BONDS

Bonds can be either secured or unsecured. If issued on the general credit of the organization, they are unsecured bonds (also called *debenture bonds*). Secured bonds give the bondholders a pledge of certain assets as a guarantee of repayment. The security identified by a secured bond can be any specific asset of the organization or a general category of asset, such as property, plant, or equipment.

TERM OR SERIAL BONDS

When all the bonds of an issue mature at the same time, they are called term bonds. For instance, an organization may decide to issue $1,000,000 worth of bonds, all due 20 years from the date of issue. When the bonds in an issue mature on different dates, the bonds are called serial bonds. An example of serial bonds would be a $1,000,000 issue that calls for retiring $200,000 of the principal every five years. This arrangement means that after the first $200,000 payment is made, $800,000 of the bonds would remain outstanding for the next five years. In other words, $1,000,000 is outstanding for the first five years, $800,000 for the second five years, and so on. An organization may issue serial bonds to ease the task of retiring its debt.

REGISTERED OR COUPON BONDS

Most bonds issued today are registered bonds. The names and addresses of the owners of such bonds must be recorded with the issuing organization. The organization keeps a register of the owners and pays interest by check to the bondholders

*At the time this chapter was written, the market interest rates on corporate bonds were volatile. We therefore use a variety of interest rates to demonstrate the concepts.

FOCUS ON INTERNATIONAL BUSINESS

Choice of Bank Debt Cripples Japanese Firms.

When U.S. companies need cash, one ready source is a bond issue, but this source of funds is not available in many other countries. For instance, surprising as it may seem, Japan, with one of the world's largest economies and financial systems, has only a fledgling corporate bond market. Whereas corporate bonds account for 31 percent of U.S. corporate debt, only 57 of the 2,500 publicly listed companies in Japan have any domestic bonds outstanding. Japanese companies have traditionally relied on loans from big Japanese banks when they need cash. Reliance on bank debt has caused problems for Japanese companies because, as a result of the collapse of the real estate industry in Japan, Japanese banks do not have the funds to lend them.[5] Similar problems have occurred recently in other Asian countries.

---

of record on the interest payment date. **Coupon bonds** generally are not registered with the organization; instead, they bear interest coupons stating the amount of interest due and the payment date. The bondholder removes the coupons from the bonds on the interest payment dates and presents them at a bank for collection.

 Check out ACE for a Review Quiz at http://accounting.college.hmco.com/students.

ACCOUNTING FOR BONDS PAYABLE

LO3 Record the issuance of bonds at face value and at a discount or premium.

RELATED TEXT ASSIGNMENTS
Q: 4, 5
SE: 2, 3, 5, 7
E: 2, 3, 4, 5, 10, 12
P: 1, 2, 3, 4, 5, 6, 7, 8
SD: 1, 5

When the board of directors of a public corporation decides to issue bonds, the company must submit the appropriate legal documents to the Securities and Exchange Commission for permission to borrow the funds. The SEC reviews the corporation's financial health and the specific terms of the bond agreement. Once approved, the company has a limited time in which to issue the authorized bonds. It is not necessary to make an entry for the bond authorization, but most companies prepare a memorandum in the Bonds Payable account describing the issue. This note lists the number and value of bonds authorized, the interest rate, the interest payment dates, and the life of the bonds.

Once the bonds are issued, the corporation must pay interest to the bondholders over the life of the bonds (in most cases, semiannually) and the principal of the bonds at maturity.

BALANCE SHEET DISCLOSURE OF BONDS

KEY POINT: Bonds payable are presented on the balance sheet as either a current or a long-term liability, depending on the maturity date and method of retiring the bonds.

Bonds payable and unamortized discounts or premiums (which we explain later) are typically shown on a company's balance sheet as long-term liabilities. However, if the maturity date of the bond issue is one year or less and the bonds will be retired using current assets, bonds payable should be listed as a current liability. If the issue is to be paid with segregated assets or replaced by another bond issue, the bonds should still be shown as a long-term liability.

Important provisions of the bond indenture are reported in the notes to the financial statements, as illustrated by the Financial Highlights excerpted from the AT&T annual report. Often reported with them is a list of all bond issues, the kinds of bonds, any securities connected with the bonds, interest payment dates, maturity dates, and interest rates.

www.att.com

BONDS ISSUED AT FACE VALUE

Suppose that the Vason Corporation has authorized the issuance of $100,000 of 9 percent, five-year bonds on January 1, 20x4. According to the bond indenture, interest is to be paid on January 1 and July 1 of each year. Assume that the bonds are sold on January 1, 20x4, for their face value. The entry to record the issuance is as follows:

20x4

A = L + OE + +	Jan. 1	Cash	100,000	
		Bonds Payable		100,000
		Sold $100,000 of 9%, 5-year bonds at face value		

STUDY NOTE: When calculating semiannual interest, do not use the annual rate (9 percent in this case) by mistake. Rather, use half the annual rate.

As stated above, interest is paid on January 1 and July 1 of each year. Therefore, the corporation would owe the bondholders $4,500 interest on July 1, 20x4:

$$\text{Interest} = \text{Principal} \times \text{Rate} \times \text{Time}$$

$$= \$100,000 \times .09 \times \frac{6}{12} \text{ year}$$

$$= \$4,500$$

The interest paid to the bondholders on each semiannual interest payment date (January 1 or July 1) would be recorded as follows:

$A^* = L + OE$
$-$ $-$
*assumes cash paid

Bond Interest Expense	4,500	
Cash (or Interest Payable)		4,500
Paid (or accrued) semiannual interest to bondholders of 9%, 5-year bonds		

FACE INTEREST RATE AND MARKET INTEREST RATE

KEY POINT: A bond sells at face value when the face interest rate of the bond is identical to the market interest rate for similar bonds on the date of issue.

KEY POINT: When bonds with an interest rate different from the market rate are issued, they sell at a discount or premium. The discount or premium acts as an equalizing factor.

When issuing bonds, most organizations try to set the face interest rate as close as possible to the market interest rate. The **face interest rate** is the rate of interest paid to bondholders based on the face value, or principal, of the bonds. The rate and amount are fixed over the life of the bond. An organization must decide in advance what the face interest rate will be to allow time to file with regulatory bodies, publicize the issue, and print the certificates.

The **market interest rate** is the rate of interest paid in the market on bonds of similar risk. It is also referred to as the *effective interest rate*. The market interest rate fluctuates daily. Because an organization has no control over the market interest rate, it often differs from the face interest rate on the issue date. As a result, the issue price of the bonds does not always equal their face value. If the market interest rate is higher than the face interest rate, the issue price will be less than the face value and the bonds are said to be issued at a **discount**. The discount equals the excess of the face value over the issue price. On the other hand, if the market interest rate is

FOCUS ON BUSINESS PRACTICE

Check Out Those Bond Prices!

The price of many bonds can be found daily in business publications like *The Wall Street Journal*. For instance, shown to the right are the quotations for a number of AT&T <www.att.com> bonds. The first is a bond with a face interest rate of 6¾ percent that is due in 2004. The current yield is 6.5 percent based on the closing price of 103. The volume of $1,000 bonds traded was 70, and the last sale was up by .22 point from the previous day's last sales.

Corporation bond price/change (5/30/03), from *Wall Street Journal*. Copyright 2003 by Dow Jones & Co. Inc. Reproduced with permission of Dow Jones & Co. Inc. in the format textbook via Copyright Clearance Center.

Bonds	Cur Yld	Vol	Close	Net Chg
ATT 6¾04	6.5	70	103	0.22
ATT 5⅝04	5.5	15	102.06	...
ATT 7½04	7.2	37	103.59	0.06
ATT 7½06	6.8	362	111.13	1.13
ATT 7¾07	6.9	25	111.75	...
ATT 6s09	5.8	1136	103.63	0.13
ATT 6½13	6.2	86	105.25	0.38
ATT 8⅛22	7.9	200	102.75	0.25
ATT 8⅛24	7.9	190	103.25	...
ATT 8.35s25	7.9	101	105.13	0.63
ATT 6½29	6.7	263	97.50	0.75
ATT 8⅝31	8.3	41	104.25	0.63

lower than the face interest rate, the issue price will be more than the face value and the bonds are said to be issued at a **premium**. The premium equals the excess of the issue price over the face value.

BONDS ISSUED AT A DISCOUNT

Suppose that the Vason Corporation issues $100,000 of 9 percent, five-year bonds at 96.149 on January 1, 20x4, when the market interest rate is 10 percent. In this case, the bonds are being issued at a discount because the market interest rate exceeds the face interest rate. The following entry records the issuance of the bonds at a discount:

A = L + OE
+   +
    −

20x4

Jan. 1	Cash	96,149	
	Unamortized Bond Discount	3,851	
	Bonds Payable		100,000
	Sold $100,000 of 9%, 5-year		
	bonds at 96.149		

Face amount of bonds	$100,000	
Less purchase price of bonds		
($100,000 × .96149)	96,149	
Unamortized bond discount	$ 3,851	

KEY POINT: The carrying amount is always the face value of the bonds plus the unamortized premium or less the unamortized discount. The carrying amount always approaches the face value over the life of the bond.

In the entry, Cash is debited for the amount received ($96,149), Bonds Payable is credited for the face amount ($100,000) of the bond liability, and the difference ($3,851) is debited to Unamortized Bond Discount. If a balance sheet is prepared right after the bonds are issued at a discount, the liability for bonds payable is reported as follows:

KEY POINT: The unamortized bond discount is subtracted from bonds payable on the balance sheet. The carrying value will be below the face value until the maturity date.

Long-term liabilities		
9% bonds payable, due 1/1/x9	$100,000	
Less unamortized bond discount	3,851	$96,149

Unamortized bond discount is a contra-liability account: its balance is deducted from the face amount of the bonds to arrive at the carrying value, or present value, of the bonds. The bond discount is described as unamortized because it will be amortized (written off) over the life of the bonds.

⬢ **STOP AND THINK!**
What determines whether bonds are issued at a discount, premium, or face value?
The relationship between the prevailing market interest rate and the face interest rate on the issue date is the determinant. ∎

BONDS ISSUED AT A PREMIUM

When bonds have a face interest rate above the market interest rate for similar investments, they are issued at a price above the face value, or at a premium. For example, assume that the Vason Corporation issues $100,000 of 9 percent, five-year bonds for $104,100 on January 1, 20x4, when the market interest rate is 8 percent. This means that investors will purchase the bonds at 104.1 percent of their face value. The issuance would be recorded as follows:

A = L + OE
+   +
    +

20x4

Jan. 1	Cash	104,100	
	Unamortized Bond Premium		4,100
	Bonds Payable		100,000
	Sold $100,000 of 9%, 5-year bonds		
	at 104.1 ($100,000 × 1.041)		

KEY POINT: The unamortized bond premium is *added* to bonds payable on the balance sheet. The carrying value will be above the face value until the maturity date.

Right after this entry is made, bonds payable would be presented on the balance sheet as follows:

Long-term liabilities		
9% bonds payable, due 1/1/x9	$100,000	
Unamortized bond premium	4,100	$104,100

FOCUS ON BUSINESS PRACTICE

100-Year Bonds Are Not for Everyone.

In 1993, interest rates on long-term debt were at historically low levels, which induced some companies to attempt to lock in those low costs for long periods. One of the most aggressive companies in that regard was The Walt Disney Company <www.disney.go.com>, which issued $150 million of 100-year bonds at a yield of only 7.5 percent. It was the first time since 1954 that 100-year bonds had been issued. Among the others that followed Walt Disney's lead by issuing 100-year bonds were the Coca-Cola Company <www.coca-cola.com>, Columbia HCA Healthcare <www.hcahealthcare.com>, Bell South <www.bellsouth.com>, IBM <www.ibm. com>, and even the People's Republic of China. Some analysts wondered if even Mickey Mouse could survive 100 years. Investors who purchase such bonds take a financial risk because if interest rates rise, which would seem likely, then the market value of the bonds will decrease.[6]

The carrying value of the bonds payable is $104,100, which equals the face value of the bonds plus the unamortized bond premium. The cash received from the bond issue is also $104,100. This means that the purchasers were willing to pay a premium of $4,100 to buy these bonds because their face interest rate was higher than the market interest rate.

BOND ISSUE COSTS

KEY POINT: A separate Bond Issue Costs account is usually established and amortized over the life of the issue.

Most bonds are sold through underwriters, who receive a fee for taking care of the details of marketing the issue or for taking a chance on receiving the selling price. Such costs are connected with the issuance of bonds. Because bond issue costs benefit the whole life of a bond issue, it makes sense to spread the costs over that period. It is generally accepted practice to establish a separate account for bond issue costs and to amortize them over the life of the bonds. However, issue costs decrease the amount of money a company receives from a bond issue. They have the effect, then, of raising the discount or lowering the premium on the issue. As a result, bond issue costs can be spread over the life of the bonds through the amortization of a discount or premium. Because this method simplifies recordkeeping, we assume in the text and problems of this book that all bond issue costs increase the discounts or decrease the premiums of bond issues.

 Check out ACE for a Review Quiz at http://accounting.college.hmco.com/students.

USING PRESENT VALUE TO VALUE A BOND

LO4 Use present values to determine the value of bonds.

RELATED TEXT ASSIGNMENTS
SE: 4
E: 6, 7, 8, 13

Present value is relevant to the study of bonds because the value of a bond is based on the present value of two components of cash flow: (1) a series of fixed interest payments and (2) a single payment at maturity. The amount of interest a bond pays is fixed over its life. However, the market interest rate varies from day to day. Thus, the amount investors are willing to pay for a bond changes as well.

Assume, for example, that a bond has a face value of $10,000 and pays fixed interest of $450 every six months (a 9 percent annual rate). The bond is due in five years. If the market interest rate today is 14 percent, what is the present value of the bond?

To determine the present value of the bond, we use Table 4 in the appendix on future value and present value tables to calculate the present value of the periodic interest payments of $450, and we use Table 3 in the same appendix to calculate the present value of the single payment of $10,000 at maturity. Since interest payments are made every six months, the compounding period is half a year. Because of this, it is necessary to convert the annual rate to a semiannual rate of 7 percent (14 percent divided by two six-month periods per year) and to use ten periods (five

STUDY NOTE: The amount buyers are willing to pay for an investment is normally based on what they expect to receive in return, taken at present value. In the case of a bond, the theoretical value equals the present value of the periodic interest payments plus the present value of the maturity value. The discount rate is set at the market rate (what investors are looking for), not at the face rate. ■

years multiplied by two six-month periods per year). Using this information, we compute the present value of the bond as follows:

Present value of 10 periodic payments at 7% (from Table 4 in the appendix on future value and present value tables): $450 × 7.024	$3,160.80
Present value of a single payment at the end of 10 periods at 7% (from Table 3 in the appendix on future value and present value tables): $10,000 × .508	5,080.00
Present value of $10,000 bond	$8,240.80

The market interest rate has increased so much since the bond was issued (from 9 percent to 14 percent) that the value of the bond is only $8,240.80 today. That amount is all investors would be willing to pay at this time for a bond that provides income of $450 every six months and a return of the $10,000 principal in five years.

If the market interest rate falls below the face interest rate, say to 8 percent (4 percent semiannually), the present value of the bond will be greater than the face value of $10,000:

Present value of 10 periodic payments at 4% (from Table 4 in the appendix on future value and present value tables): $450 × 8.111	$ 3,649.95
Present value of a single payment at the end of 10 periods at 4% (from Table 3 in the appendix on future value and present value tables): $10,000 × .676	6,760.00
Present value of $10,000 bond	$10,409.95

 Check out ACE for a Review Quiz at http://accounting.college.hmco.com/students.

● **STOP AND THINK!**

Why do bond prices vary over time?

Bond price is the present value of the principal and interest cash flows at the market interest rate; therefore, as the market interest rate changes over time, bond prices will change. ■

AMORTIZATION OF BOND DISCOUNTS AND PREMIUMS

LO5 Amortize bond discounts and bond premiums using the straight-line and effective interest methods.

RELATED TEXT ASSIGNMENTS
Q: 6, 7
SE: 2, 3, 7
E: 2, 3, 4, 5, 9, 12
P: 1, 2, 3, 4, 5, 6, 7, 8
SD: 2

A bond discount or premium represents the amount by which the total interest cost is higher or lower than the total interest payments. To record interest expense properly and ensure that at maturity the carrying value of bonds payable equals its face value, systematic reduction of the bond discount or premium over the bond term is required. That is, the discount or premium has to be amortized over the life of the bonds. This is accomplished by using either the straight-line method or the effective interest method.

AMORTIZING A BOND DISCOUNT

In one of the examples on page 676, Vason Corporation issued $100,000 of five-year bonds at a discount because the market interest rate of 10 percent exceeded the face interest rate of 9 percent. The bonds were sold for $96,149, resulting in an unamortized bond discount of $3,851. Because this discount affects interest expense in each year of the bond issue, the bond discount should be amortized (reduced gradually) over the life of the issue. This means that the unamortized bond discount will decrease gradually over time, and that the carrying value of the bond issue (face value less unamortized discount) will increase gradually. By the maturity date of the bond, the carrying value of the issue will equal its face value, and the unamortized bond discount will be zero. In the following sections, the total interest cost is calculated, and the bond discount is amortized using the straight-line and the effective interest methods.

KEY POINT: A bond discount is considered a component of total interest cost because a bond discount represents the amount in excess of the issue price that the corporation must pay on the maturity date.

■ **CALCULATION OF TOTAL INTEREST COST** When bonds are issued at a discount, the effective (or market) interest rate paid by the company is greater than the face interest rate on the bonds. The reason is that the interest cost to the company is the stated interest payments *plus* the amount of the bond discount. That is, although the company does not receive the full face value of the bonds on issue, it still must pay back the full face value at maturity. The difference between the issue price and the face value must be added to the total interest payments to arrive at the actual interest expense. The full cost to the corporation of issuing the bonds at a discount is as follows:

Cash to be paid to bondholders
Face value at maturity	$100,000
Interest payments ($100,000 × .09 × 5 years)	45,000
Total cash paid to bondholders	$145,000
Less cash received from bondholders	96,149
Total interest cost	$ 48,851 ←

Or, alternatively:

Interest payments ($100,000 × .09 × 5 years)	$ 45,000
Bond discount	3,851
Total interest cost	$ 48,851 ←

The total interest cost of $48,851 is made up of $45,000 in interest payments and the $3,851 bond discount, so the bond discount increases the interest paid on the bonds from the face interest rate to the market interest rate. The *market (effective) interest rate* is the real interest cost of the bond over its life.

For each year's interest expense to reflect the market interest rate, the discount must be allocated over the remaining life of the bonds as an increase in the interest expense each period. The process of allocation is called *amortization of the bond discount*. Thus, interest expense for each period will exceed the actual payment of interest by the amount of the bond discount amortized over the period.

Some companies and governmental units issue bonds that do not require periodic interest payments. These bonds, called **zero coupon bonds**, are simply a promise to pay a fixed amount at the maturity date. They are issued at a large discount because the only interest earned by the buyer or paid by the issuer is the discount. For example, a five-year, $100,000 zero coupon bond issued at a time when the market rate is 14 percent, compounded semiannually, would sell for only $50,800. That amount is the present value of a single payment of $100,000 at the end of five years. The discount of $49,200 ($100,000 − $50,800) is the total interest cost; it is amortized over the life of the bond.

KEY POINT: The discount on a zero coupon bond represents the interest that will be paid (in its entirety) on the maturity date.

■ **STRAIGHT-LINE METHOD** The **straight-line method** assumes equal amortization of the bond discount for each interest period. Suppose that the interest payment dates for the Vason Corporation bond issue are January 1 and July 1. The amount of the bond discount amortized and the interest expense for each semiannual period are calculated in four steps:

1. Total Interest Payments = Interest Payments per Year × Life of Bonds
$$= 2 \times 5 = 10$$

2. Amortization of Bond Discount per Interest Period = $\dfrac{\text{Bond Discount}}{\text{Total Interest Payments}}$

$$= \frac{\$3,851}{10} = \$385^*$$

*Rounded.

3. Cash Interest Payment = Face Value × Face Interest Rate × Time

    = $100,000 × .09 × 6/12 = $4,500

4. Interest Expense per Interest Period = Interest Payment + Amortization of
    Bond Discount

    = $4,500 + $385 = $4,885

On July 1, 20x4, the first semiannual interest date, the entry would be as follows:

20x4

July 1	Bond Interest Expense	4,885	
	Unamortized Bond Discount		385
	Cash (or Interest Payable)		4,500
	Paid (or accrued) semiannual interest		
	to bondholders and amortized the		
	discount on 9%, 5-year bonds		

A* = L + OE
−   +   −
*assumes cash paid

Notice that the bond interest expense is $4,885, but the amount paid to the bondholders is the $4,500 face interest payment. The difference of $385 is the credit to Unamortized Bond Discount. This lowers the debit balance of Unamortized Bond Discount and raises the carrying value of the bonds payable by $385 each interest period. Assuming that no changes occur in the bond issue, this entry will be made every six months for the life of the bonds. When the bond issue matures, there will be no balance in the Unamortized Bond Discount account, and the carrying value of the bonds will be $100,000—exactly equal to the amount due the bondholders.

The straight-line method has long been used, but it has a certain weakness. Because the carrying value goes up each period and the bond interest expense stays the same, the rate of interest falls over time. Conversely, when the straight-line method is used to amortize a premium, the rate of interest rises over time. Therefore, the Accounting Principles Board has ruled that the straight-line method can be used only when it does not lead to a material difference from the effective interest method.[7] An amount is material if it affects a decision on the evaluation of the company.

STOP AND THINK!

When is it acceptable to use the straight-line method to amortize a bond discount or premium?

It is acceptable only when it does not produce a result materially different from that produced by the effective interest method. ■

■ EFFECTIVE INTEREST METHOD   To compute the interest and amortization of a bond discount for each interest period under the **effective interest method**, a constant interest rate is applied to the carrying value of the bonds at the beginning of the interest period. This constant rate equals the market rate, or effective rate, at the time the bonds were issued. The amount to be amortized each period is the difference between the interest computed by using the market rate and the actual interest paid to bondholders. As an example, we use the same facts presented earlier—a $100,000 bond issue at 9 percent, with a five-year maturity and interest to be paid twice a year. The market, or effective, interest rate at the time the bonds were issued was 10 percent. The bonds were sold for $96,149, a discount of $3,851. The interest and amortization of the bond discount are shown in Table 1.

The amounts in the table (using period 1) were computed as follows:

Column A: The carrying value of the bonds is their face value less the unamortized bond discount ($100,000 − $3,851 = $96,149).

Column B: The interest expense to be recorded is the effective interest. It is found by multiplying the carrying value of the bonds by the effective (market) interest rate for one-half year ($96,149 × .10 × %12 = $4,807).

Column C: The interest paid in the period is a constant amount computed by multiplying the face value of the bonds by their face interest rate by the interest time period ($100,000 × .09 × %12 = $4,500).

Column D: The discount amortized is the difference between the effective interest expense to be recorded and the interest to be paid on the interest payment date ($4,807 − $4,500 = $307).

TABLE 1.   Interest and Amortization of a Bond Discount: Effective Interest Method

	A	B	C	D	E	F
Semiannual Interest Period	Carrying Value at Beginning of Period	Semiannual Interest Expense at 10% to Be Recorded* (5% × A)	Semiannual Interest Payment to Bondholders (4½% × $100,000)	Amortization of Bond Discount (B − C)	Unamortized Bond Discount at End of Period (E − D)	Carrying Value at End of Period (A + D)
0					$3,851	$ 96,149
1	$96,149	$4,807	$4,500	$307	3,544	96,456
2	96,456	4,823	4,500	323	3,221	96,779
3	96,779	4,839	4,500	339	2,882	97,118
4	97,118	4,856	4,500	356	2,526	97,474
5	97,474	4,874	4,500	374	2,152	97,848
6	97,848	4,892	4,500	392	1,760	98,240
7	98,240	4,912	4,500	412	1,348	98,652
8	98,652	4,933	4,500	433	915	99,085
9	99,085	4,954	4,500	454	461	99,539
10	99,539	4,961†	4,500	461	—	100,000

*Rounded to the nearest dollar.

†Last period's interest expense equals $4,961 ($4,500 + $461); it does not equal $4,977 ($99,539 × .05) because of the cumulative effect of rounding.

Column E: The unamortized bond discount is the balance of the bond discount at the beginning of the period less the current period amortization of the discount ($3,851 − $307 = $3,544). The unamortized discount decreases each interest payment period because it is amortized as a portion of interest expense.

Column F: The carrying value of the bonds at the end of the period is the carrying value at the beginning of the period plus the amortization during the period ($96,149 + $307 = $96,456). Notice that the sum of the carrying value and the unamortized discount (Column F + Column E) always equals the face value of the bonds ($96,456 + $3,544 = $100,000).

The entry to record the interest expense is like the one used with the straight-line method, but the amounts debited and credited to the various accounts differ. With the effective interest method, the entry for July 1, 20x4, would be as follows:

A* = L + OE
−   +   −
*assumes cash paid

KEY POINT: The bond interest expense recorded exceeds the amount of interest paid because of the amortization of the bond discount. The matching rule dictates that the discount be amortized over the life of the bond.

20x4
July 1   Bond Interest Expense   4,807
        Unamortized Bond Discount   307
        Cash (or Interest Payable)   4,500
         Paid (or accrued) semiannual
         interest to bondholders and
         amortized the discount on 9%,
         5-year bonds

Notice that it is not necessary to prepare an interest and amortization table to determine the amortization of a discount for any one interest payment period. It is necessary only to multiply the carrying value by the effective interest rate and subtract the interest payment from the result. For example, the amount of discount to be amortized in the seventh interest payment period is $412, calculated as follows: ($98,240 × .05) − $4,500.

■ **VISUAL SUMMARY OF THE EFFECTIVE INTEREST METHOD**   The effect on carrying value and interest expense of the amortization of a bond discount using the effective

TABLE 2. Interest and Amortization of a Bond Premium: Effective Interest Method

	A	B	C	D	E	F
Semiannual Interest Period	Carrying Value at Beginning of Period	Semiannual Interest Expense at 8% to Be Recorded* (4% × A)	Semiannual Interest Payment to Bondholders (4½% × $100,000)	Amortization of Bond Premium (C − B)	Unamortized Bond Premium at End of Period (E − D)	Carrying Value at End of Period (A − D)
0					$4,100	$104,100
1	$104,100	$4,164	$4,500	$336	3,764	103,764
2	103,764	4,151	4,500	349	3,415	103,415
3	103,415	4,137	4,500	363	3,052	103,052
4	103,052	4,122	4,500	378	2,674	102,674
5	102,674	4,107	4,500	393	2,281	102,281
6	102,281	4,091	4,500	409	1,872	101,872
7	101,872	4,075	4,500	425	1,447	101,447
8	101,447	4,058	4,500	442	1,005	101,005
9	101,005	4,040	4,500	460	545	100,545
10	100,545	3,955†	4,500	545	—	100,000

*Rounded to the nearest dollar.

†Last period's interest expense equals $3,955 ($4,500 − $545); it does not equal $4,022 ($100,545 × .04) because of the cumulative effect of rounding.

the effective interest rate is determined by comparing the fixed interest expense with a carrying value that changes as a result of amortizing the discount or premium. To apply a fixed interest rate over the life of the bonds based on the actual market rate at the time of the bond issue requires the use of the effective interest method. Under this method, the interest expense decreases slightly each period (see Table 2, Column B) because the amount of the bond premium amortized increases slightly (Column D). This occurs because a fixed rate is applied each period to the gradually decreasing carrying value (Column A).

The first interest payment is recorded as follows:

$A^* = L + OE$

*assumes cash paid

	20x4			
	July 1	Bond Interest Expense	4,164	
		Unamortized Bond Premium	336	
		Cash (or Interest Payable)		4,500
		Paid (or accrued) semiannual interest to bondholders and amortized the premium on 9%, 5-year bonds		

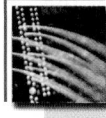

FOCUS ON BUSINESS TECHNOLOGY

Speed Up the Calculations!

Interest and amortization tables like those in Tables 1 and 2 are ideal applications for computer spreadsheet software, such as Lotus and Microsoft Excel. Once the tables have been set up with the proper formula in each cell, only five variables must be entered to produce the entire table. These variables are the face value of the bonds, selling price, life of the bonds, face interest rate, and market interest rate.

Notice that the unamortized bond premium (Column E) decreases gradually to zero as the carrying value decreases to the face value (Column F). To find the amount of premium amortized in any one interest payment period, subtract the effective interest expense (the carrying value times the effective interest rate, Column B) from the interest payment (Column C). In semiannual interest period 5, for example, the amortization of premium is $393, which is calculated in the following manner: $4,500 − ($102,674 × .04).

KEY
inter
perio
value
pal o
culat

FIGURE 3
Carrying Value and Interest Expense—Bonds Issued at a Premium

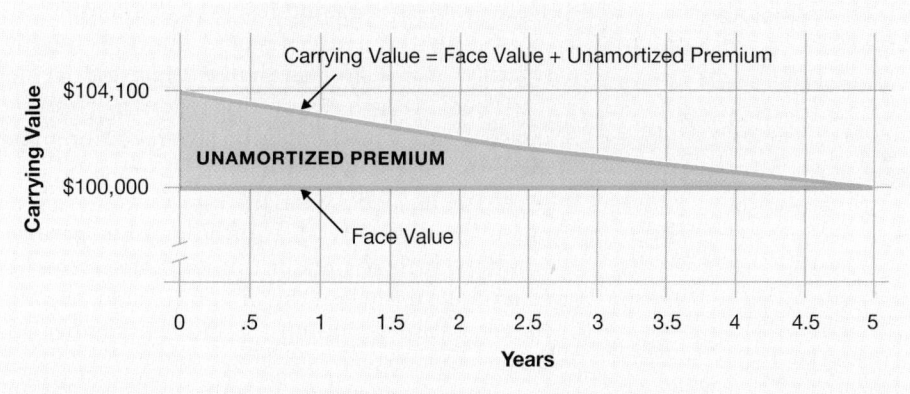

KEY POINT: Over the life of a bond, the premium or discount amortized increases each period.

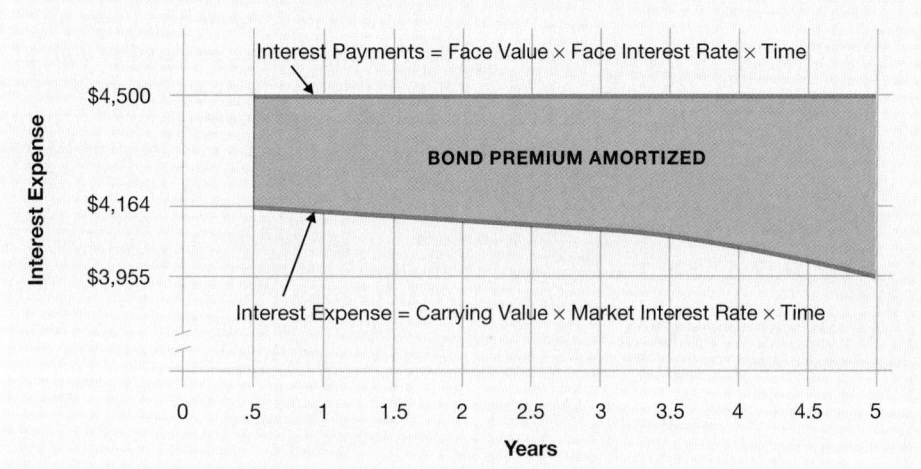

■ **VISUAL SUMMARY OF THE EFFECTIVE INTEREST METHOD**   The effect on carrying value and interest expense of the amortization of a bond premium using the effective interest method can be seen in Figure 3 (which is based on data from Table 2). Notice that initially the carrying value (issue price) is greater than the face value, but that it gradually decreases toward the face value over the life of the bond issue. Notice also that interest payments exceed interest expense by the amount of the premium amortized and that interest expense decreases gradually over the life of the bond because it is based on the gradually decreasing carrying value (multiplied by the market interest rate).

 Check out ACE for a Review Quiz at http://accounting.college.hmco.com/students.

OTHER BONDS PAYABLE ISSUES

LO6   Record bonds issued between interest dates and year-end adjustments.

RELATED TEXT ASSIGNMENTS
Q: 8
SE: 3, 5, 6, 7
E: 4, 5, 9, 10, 11, 12
P: 1, 2, 3, 5, 6, 7, 8

Several other issues arise in accounting for bonds payable. Among them are the sale of bonds between interest payment dates and the year-end accrual of bond interest expense.

SALE OF BONDS BETWEEN INTEREST DATES

Bonds may be issued on an interest payment date, as in the previous examples, but they are often issued between interest payment dates. The generally accepted method of handling bonds issued in this manner is to collect from investors the interest that would have accrued for the partial period preceding the issue date.

Then, when the first interest period is completed, the corporation pays investors the interest for the entire period. Thus, the interest collected when bonds are sold is returned to investors on the next interest payment date.

There are two reasons for following this procedure. The first is a practical one. If a company issued bonds on several different days and did not collect the accrued interest, records would have to be maintained for each bondholder and date of purchase. In such a case, the interest due each bondholder would have to be computed on the basis of a different time period. Clearly, large bookkeeping costs would be incurred under this kind of system. On the other hand, if accrued interest is collected when the bonds are sold, the corporation can pay the interest due for the entire period on the interest payment date, eliminating the extra computations and costs.

The second reason for collecting accrued interest in advance is that when that amount is netted against the full interest paid on the interest payment date, the resulting interest expense represents the amount for the time the money was borrowed. For example, assume that Vason Corporation sold $100,000 of 9 percent, five-year bonds for face value on May 1, 20x4, rather than on January 1, 20x4, the issue date. The entry to record the sale of the bonds is as follows:

A = L + OE
+   +   +

20x4

May 1	Cash	103,000	
	Bond Interest Expense		3,000
	Bonds Payable		100,000
	Sold 9%, 5-year bonds at face value		
	plus 4 months' accrued interest		
	$100,000 \times .09 \times \frac{4}{12} = \$3,000$		

ENRICHMENT NOTE:
This is one of the few times an expense account is credited (other than when it is closed). The ledger account demonstrates that the net effect is the recording of two months' interest (May and June).

As shown, Cash is debited for the amount received, $103,000 (the face value of $100,000 plus four months' accrued interest of $3,000). Bond Interest Expense is credited for the $3,000 of accrued interest, and Bonds Payable is credited for the face value of $100,000.

When the first semiannual interest payment date arrives, this entry is made:

A* = L + OE
  −   −

*assumes cash paid

20x4

July 1	Bond Interest Expense	4,500	
	Cash (or Interest Payable)		4,500
	Paid (or accrued) semiannual interest		
	$100,000 \times .09 \times \frac{6}{12} = \$4,500$		

Notice that the entire half-year interest is both debited to Bond Interest Expense and credited to Cash because the corporation pays bond interest only once every six months, in full six-month amounts. This process is illustrated in Figure 4. The actual interest expense for the two months that the bonds were outstanding is $1,500. This amount is the net balance of the $4,500 debit to Bond Interest Expense on July 1 less the $3,000 credit to Bond Interest Expense on May 1. You can see these steps clearly in the following T account:

Bond Interest Expense

Bal.	0	May 1	3,000
July 1	4,500		
Bal.	1,500		

YEAR-END ACCRUAL OF BOND INTEREST EXPENSE

Bond interest payment dates rarely correspond with a company's fiscal year. Therefore, an adjustment must be made at the end of the accounting period to

FIGURE 4
Effect on Bond Interest Expense When Bonds Are Issued Between Interest Dates

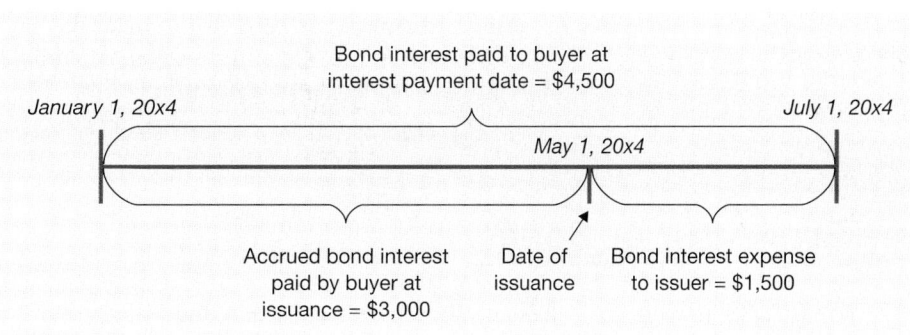

Bond interest paid to buyer at
interest payment date = $4,500

January 1, 20x4   July 1, 20x4

May 1, 20x4

Accrued bond interest   Date of   Bond interest expense
paid by buyer at   issuance   to issuer = $1,500
issuance = $3,000

accrue the interest expense on the bonds from the last payment date to the end of the fiscal year. Further, if there is any discount or premium on the bonds, it must also be amortized for the fractional period.

KEY POINT: Remember that adjusting entries never affect cash.

Remember that in the example of bonds issued at a premium, Vason Corporation issued $100,000 in bonds on January 1, 20x4, at 104.1 percent of face value. Suppose the company's fiscal year ends on September 30, 20x4. In the period since the interest payment and amortization of the premium on July 1, three months' worth of interest has accrued, and the following adjusting entry under the effective interest method must be made:

$$A = L + OE$$
$$- \quad -$$
$$+$$

20x0			
Sept. 30	Bond Interest Expense	2,075.50	
	Unamortized Bond Premium	174.50	
	Interest Payable		2,250.00
	To record accrual of interest on 9% bonds payable for 3 months and amortization of one-half of the premium for the second interest payment period		

CLARIFICATION NOTE: The matching rule dictates that both the accrued interest and the amortization of a premium or discount be recorded at year end.

This entry covers one-half of the second interest period. Unamortized Bond Premium is debited for $174.50, which is one-half of $349, the amortization of the premium for the second period from Table 2. Interest Payable is credited for $2,250, three months' interest on the face value of the bonds ($100,000 × .09 × ³⁄₁₂). The net debit figure of $2,075.50 ($2,250.00 − $174.50) is the bond interest expense for the three-month period.

When the January 1, 20x5, payment date arrives, the entry to pay the bondholders and amortize the premium is as follows:

$$A = L + OE$$
$$- \quad - \quad -$$
$$-$$

20x1			
Jan. 1	Bond Interest Expense	2,075.50	
	Interest Payable	2,250.00	
	Unamortized Bond Premium	174.50	
	Cash		4,500.00
	Paid semiannual interest, including interest previously accrued, and amortized the premium for the period since the end of the fiscal year		

● **STOP AND THINK!**
Why must the accrual of bond interest expense be recorded?
Bond interest expense must be accrued at the close of each accounting period to ensure proper matching of all the borrowing costs associated with bonds payable. Interest payment dates rarely coincide with the end of the accounting period. ■

As shown here, one-half ($2,250) of the amount paid ($4,500) was accrued on September 30. Unamortized Bond Premium is debited for $174.50, the remaining amount to be amortized for the period ($349.00 − $174.50). The resulting bond interest expense is the amount that applies to the three-month period from October 1 to December 31.

Bond discounts are recorded at year end in the same way as bond premiums. The difference is that the amortization of a bond discount increases interest expense instead of decreasing it as a premium does.

 Check out ACE for a Review Quiz at http://accounting.college.hmco.com/students.

RETIREMENT OF BONDS

SO7　Account for the retirement of bonds and the conversion of bonds into stock.

RELATED TEXT ASSIGNMENTS
Q: 9, 10
SE: 8, 9
E: 13, 14, 15
P: 4, 5
FRA: 2

ENRICHMENT NOTE:
When interest rates drop, corporations frequently refinance their bonds at the lower rate, much like homeowners who refinance their mortgage loans when interest rates go down. Even though a call premium is usually paid to extinguish the bonds, the interest saved makes the refinancing cost-effective in the long run.

Usually, bonds are paid when due—on the stated maturity date. However, it can be advantageous not to wait until maturity, as is sometimes the case with callable bonds and convertible bonds.

CALLABLE BONDS

Callable bonds give the issuer the right to buy back and retire the bonds at a specified **call price**, usually above face value, before maturity. Such bonds give the company flexibility in financing its operations. For example, if bond interest rates drop, the company can call its bonds and reissue debt at a lower interest rate. A company might also call its bonds if it has earned enough to pay off the debt, if the reason for having the debt no longer exists, or if it wants to restructure its debt to equity ratio. The bond indenture states the time period and the prices at which the bonds can be redeemed. The retirement of a bond issue before its maturity date is called **early extinguishment of debt**.

Let's assume that Vason Corporation can call or retire at 105 the $100,000 of bonds it issued at a premium (104.1) and that it decides to do so on July 1, 20x7. (To simplify the example, the retirement is made on an interest payment date.) Because the bonds were issued on January 1, 20x4, the retirement takes place on the seventh interest payment date. Assume that the entry for the required interest payment and the amortization of the premium has been made. The entry to retire the bonds is as follows:

A = L + OE	20x7		
− − −	July 1　Bonds Payable	100,000	
−	Unamortized Bond Premium	1,447	
	Loss on Retirement of Bonds	3,553	
	Cash		105,000
	Retired 9% bonds at 105		

In this entry, the cash paid is the face value times the call price ($100,000 × 1.05 = $105,000). The unamortized bond premium can be found in Column E of Table 2. The loss on retirement of bonds occurs because the call price of the bonds is greater than the carrying value ($105,000 − $101,447 = $3,553).

Sometimes, a rise in the market interest rate can cause the market value of bonds to fall considerably below their face value. If it has the cash to do so, the company may find it advantageous to purchase the bonds on the open market and retire them, rather than wait and pay them off at face value. A gain is recognized for the difference between the purchase price of the bonds and the carrying value of the retired bonds. For example, assume that because of a rise in interest rates, Vason Corporation is able to purchase the $100,000 bond issue on the open market at 85. The entry would be as follows:

STUDY NOTE:　The goal is to eliminate from the books any reference to the bonds being retired.

A = L + OE	20x7		
− − +	July 1　Bonds Payable	100,000	
−	Unamortized Bond Premium	1,447	
	Cash		85,000
	Gain on Retirement of Bonds		16,447
	Purchased and retired		
	9% bonds at 85		

CONVERTIBLE BONDS

Bonds that can be exchanged for common stock or other securities of the corporation are called convertible bonds. Convertibility enables an investor to make more money if the market price of the common stock rises, because the value of the bonds then rises. However, if the common stock price does not rise, the investor still holds the bonds and receives both the periodic interest payments and the principal at the maturity date.

Several factors related to the issuance of convertible bonds are favorable to the company. First, the interest rate is usually less than the company would have to offer if the bonds were not convertible. An investor is willing to give up some current interest for the prospect that the value of the stock will increase and therefore the value of the bonds will also increase. Another advantage is that management will not have to give up any current control of the company. Unlike stockholders, bondholders do not have voting rights. A third benefit is tax savings. Interest paid on bonds is fully deductible for income tax purposes, whereas cash dividends on common stock are not. Fourth, the company's income will be affected favorably if the company earns a return that exceeds the interest cost of the bonds. Finally, the convertible feature offers financial flexibility. If the market value of the stock rises to a level at which the bond is worth more than face value, management can avoid repaying the bonds by calling them for redemption, thereby forcing the bondholders to convert their bonds into common stock. The bondholders will agree to convert because no gain or loss results from the transaction.

One major disadvantage of bonds is that interest must be paid semiannually. Inability to make an interest payment could force the company into bankruptcy. Common stock dividends are declared and paid only when the board of directors decides to do so. Another disadvantage of bonds is that when the bonds are converted, they become new outstanding common stock. These new shares give the bondholders stockholders' rights and reduce the proportional ownership of the existing stockholders.

When a bondholder wishes to convert bonds into common stock, the common stock is recorded at the carrying value of the bonds. The bond liability and the associated unamortized discount or premium are written off the books. For this reason, no gain or loss on the transaction is recorded. For example, suppose that Vason Corporation's bonds are not called on July 1, 20x7. Instead, the corporation's bondholders decide to convert all the bonds to $8 par value common stock under a convertible provision of 40 shares of common stock for each $1,000 bond. The entry would be as follows:

A = L + OE
−   +
−   +

20x7				
July 1	Bonds Payable		100,000	
	Unamortized Bond Premium		1,447	
	Common Stock			32,000
	Paid-in Capital in Excess of Par			
	Value, Common			69,447
	Converted 9% bonds payable into			
	$8 par value common stock at a rate			
	of 40 shares for each $1,000 bond			

STUDY POINT: The credits to the contributed capital accounts are based on the carrying value of the bonds converted. As a result, no gain or loss is recognized. If only a portion of the bonds had been converted, proportionate shares of the balances in Bonds Payable and Unamortized Bond Premium would be eliminated.

The unamortized bond premium is found in Column E of Table 2. At a rate of 40 shares for each $1,000 bond, 4,000 shares will be issued, with a total par value of $32,000 (4,000 × $8). The Common Stock account is credited for the amount of the par value of the stock issued. In addition, Paid-in Capital in Excess of Par Value, Common is credited for the difference between the carrying value of the bonds and the par value of the stock issued ($101,447 − $32,000 = $69,447). No gain or loss is recorded.

Check out ACE for a Review Quiz at http://accounting.college.hmco.com/students.

OTHER LONG-TERM LIABILITIES

S08 Explain the basic features of mortgages payable, long-term leases, and pensions and other post-retirement benefits as long-term liabilities.

RELATED TEXT ASSIGNMENTS
Q: 11, 12, 13, 14, 15
SE: 10
E: 16, 17
SD: 3, 6
FRA: 4, 6

A company may have other long-term liabilities besides bonds. The most common are mortgages payable, long-term leases, and pensions and other postretirement benefits.

MORTGAGES PAYABLE

A **mortgage** is a long-term debt secured by real property. It is usually paid in equal monthly installments. Each monthly payment includes interest on the debt and a reduction in the debt. Table 3 shows the first three monthly payments on a $50,000, 12 percent mortgage. The mortgage was obtained on June 1, and the monthly payments are $800. According to the table, the entry to record the July 1 payment would be as follows:

$A = L + OE$
$-\ \ -\ \ -$

July 1	Mortgage Payable	300	
	Mortgage Interest Expense	500	
	Cash		800
	Made monthly mortgage payment		

Notice from the entry and from Table 3 that the July 1 payment represents interest expense of $500 ($50,000 × .12 × $\frac{1}{12}$) and a reduction in the debt of $300 ($800 − $500). Therefore, the unpaid balance is reduced to $49,700 by the July payment. August's interest expense is slightly less than July's because of the decrease in the debt.

LONG-TERM LEASES

A company can obtain new operating assets in several ways. One way is to borrow money and buy the asset. Another is to rent the equipment on a short-term lease. A third way is to obtain the equipment on a long-term lease. The first two methods do not create accounting problems. In the first case, the asset and liability are recorded at the amount paid, and the asset is subject to periodic depreciation. In the second case, the lease is short term in relation to the useful life of the asset, and the risks of ownership remain with the lessor. This type of agreement is called an **operating lease**. It is proper accounting procedure to treat operating lease payments as an expense and to debit the amount of each monthly payment to Rent Expense.

The third alternative, a long-term lease, is one of the fastest-growing ways of financing operating equipment in the United States today. It has several advantages.

TABLE 3. Monthly Payment Schedule on a $50,000, 12 Percent Mortgage

	A	B	C	D	E
Payment Date	Unpaid Balance at Beginning of Period	Monthly Payment	Interest for 1 Month at 1% on Unpaid Balance* (1% × A)	Reduction in Debt (B − C)	Unpaid Balance at End of Period (A − D)
June 1					$50,000
July 1	$50,000	$800	$500	$300	49,700
Aug. 1	49,700	800	497	303	49,397
Sept. 1	49,397	800	494	306	49,091

*Rounded to the nearest dollar.

TABLE 4.   Payment Schedule on a 16 Percent Capital Lease

Year	A Lease Payment	B Interest (16%) on Unpaid Obligation* (D × 16%)	C Reduction of Lease Obligation (A − B)	D Balance of Lease Obligation (D − C)
Beginning				$14,740
1	$ 4,000	$2,358	$ 1,642	13,098
2	4,000	2,096	1,904	11,194
3	4,000	1,791	2,209	8,985
4	4,000	1,438	2,562	6,423
5	4,000	1,028	2,972	3,451
6	4,000	549[†]	3,451	—
	$24,000	$9,260	$14,740	

*Computations are rounded to the nearest dollar.

[†]The last year's interest equals $549 ($4,000 − $3,451); it does not exactly equal $552 ($3,451 × .16) because of the cumulative effect of rounding.

TERMINOLOGY NOTE:
From the lessee's point of view, a lease is treated as either an operating lease or a capital lease. An operating lease is a true lease and is treated as such. A capital lease, however, is in substance an installment purchase, and the leased asset and related liability must be recognized at their present value.

KEY POINT: Under a capital lease, the lessee must record depreciation, using any allowable method. Depreciation is *not* recorded under an operating lease, however, because the leased asset is not recognized on the lessee's books.

For instance, a long-term lease requires no immediate cash payment, the rental payment is deducted in full for tax purposes, and it costs less than a short-term lease. Acquiring the use of plant assets under long-term leases does create several accounting challenges, however. Often, such leases cannot be canceled. Also, their duration may be about the same as the useful life of the asset. Finally, they stipulate that the lessee has the option to buy the asset at a nominal price at the end of the lease. The lease is much like an installment purchase because the risks of ownership are transferred to the lessee. Both the lessee's available assets and its legal obligations (liabilities) increase because the lessee must make a number of payments over the life of the asset.

The Financial Accounting Standards Board has described this kind of long-term lease as a **capital lease**. The term reflects the provisions of such a lease, which make the transaction more like a purchase or sale on installment. The FASB has ruled that in the case of a capital lease, the lessee must record an asset and a long-term liability equal to the present value of the total lease payments during the lease term. In doing so, the lessee must use the present value at the beginning of the lease.[8] Much like a mortgage payment, each lease payment consists partly of interest expense and partly of repayment of debt. Further, depreciation expense is figured on the asset and entered on the records of the lessee.

Suppose, for example, that Isaacs Company enters into a long-term lease for a machine used in its manufacturing operations. The lease terms call for an annual payment of $4,000 for six years, which approximates the useful life of the machine (see Table 4). At the end of the lease period, the title to the machine passes to Isaacs. This lease is clearly a capital lease and should be recorded as an asset and a liability according to FASB *Statement No. 13*.

A lease is a contract that provides for a periodic payment for the right to use an asset or assets. Present value techniques can be used to place a value on the asset and on the corresponding liability associated with a capital lease. If Isaacs's interest cost is 16 percent, the present value of the lease payments can be computed as follows:

Periodic Payment × Factor (Table 4 in the appendix on future value and present value tables: 16%, 6 periods) = Present Value

$4,000 × 3.685   = $14,740

The entry to record the lease contract is as follows:

A = L + OE
+   +

Capital Lease Equipment	14,740	
Capital Lease Obligations		14,740
To record capital lease on machinery		

Capital Lease Equipment is classified as a long-term asset; Capital Lease Obligations is classified as a long-term liability. Each year, Isaacs must record depreciation on the leased asset. Using straight-line depreciation, a six-year life, and no salvage value, the following entry would record the depreciation:

A = L + OE
–   –

Depreciation Expense, Capital Lease Equipment	2,457	
Accumulated Depreciation, Capital Lease		
Equipment		2,457
To record depreciation expense on capital lease		

The interest expense for each year is computed by multiplying the interest rate (16 percent) by the amount of the remaining lease obligation. Table 4 shows these calculations. Using the data in the table, the first lease payment would be recorded as follows:

A = L + OE
–   –   –

Interest Expense (Column B)	2,358	
Capital Lease Obligations (Column C)	1,642	
Cash		4,000
Made payment on capital lease		

PENSIONS

Most employees who work for medium-sized and large companies are covered by some sort of pension plan. A **pension plan** is a contract between a company and its employees in which the company agrees to pay benefits to the employees after they retire. Many companies pay the full cost of the pension, but frequently the employees also contribute part of their salary or wages. The contributions from both parties are typically paid into a **pension fund**, from which benefits are paid to retirees. In most cases, pension benefits consist of monthly payments to retired employees and other payments upon disability or death.

There are two kinds of pension plans. Under a *defined contribution plan*, the employer is required to contribute an annual amount specified by an agreement between the company and its employees or by a resolution of the board of directors. Retirement payments depend on the amount of pension payments the accumulated contributions can support. Under a *defined benefit plan*, the employer's annual contribution is the amount required to fund pension liabilities arising from employment in the current year, but the exact amount will not be determined until the retirement and death of the current employees. Under a defined benefit plan, the amount of future benefits is fixed, but the annual contributions vary depending on assumptions about how much the pension fund will earn. Under a defined contribution plan, each year's contribution is fixed, but the benefits vary depending on how much the pension fund earns.

Accounting for annual pension expense under a defined contribution plan is simple. After the required contribution is determined, Pension Expense is debited and a liability (or Cash) is credited. Accounting for annual expense under a defined benefit plan is, however, one of the most complex topics in accounting; thus, the intricacies are reserved for advanced courses. In concept, though, the procedure is simple. First, the amount of pension expense is determined. Then, if the amount of cash contributed to the fund is less than the pension expense, a liability results, which is reported on the balance sheet. If the amount of cash paid to the pension plan exceeds the pension expense, a prepaid expense arises and appears on the asset side of the balance sheet. For example, the annual report for Philip Morris Companies, Inc., includes among assets on the balance sheet a prepaid pension of $628 million.[9]

ENRICHMENT NOTE:
Companies prefer defined contribution plans because the employees assume the risk that their pension assets will earn a sufficient return to meet their retirement needs.

www.philipmorris.com

ENRICHMENT NOTE:
Accounting for a defined benefit plan is far more complex than accounting for a defined contribution plan. Fortunately, accountants can rely on the calculations of professional actuaries, whose expertise includes the mathematics of pension plans.

In accordance with the FASB's *Statement No. 87*, all companies should use the same actuarial method to compute pension expense.[10] However, because actuarial methods require the estimation of many factors, such as the average remaining service life of active employees, the long-run return on pension plan assets, and future salary increases, the computation of pension expense is not simple. In addition, terminology further complicates pension accounting. In nontechnical terms, the pension expense for the year includes not only the cost of the benefits earned by people working during the year but also interest costs on the total pension obligation (which are calculated on the present value of future benefits to be paid) and other adjustments. Those costs are reduced by the expected return on the pension fund assets.

Since 1989, all employers whose pension plans do not have sufficient assets to cover the present value of their pension benefit obligations (on a termination basis) must record the amount of the shortfall as a liability on their balance sheets. Thus, investors don't have to read the notes to the financial statements to learn whether the pension plan is fully funded. If a pension plan does have sufficient assets to cover its obligations, no balance sheet reporting is required or permitted.

OTHER POSTRETIREMENT BENEFITS

KEY POINT: Other postretirement benefits should be expensed when earned by the employee, not when received after retirement. This practice conforms to the matching rule.

Many companies provide retired employees not only with pensions but also with health care and other benefits. In the past, these other postretirement benefits were accounted for on a cash basis; that is, they were expensed when the benefits were paid, after an employee had retired. The FASB has concluded, however, that those benefits are earned by the employee and that, in accordance with the matching rule, they should be estimated and accrued during the period of time the employee is working.[11]

The estimates must take into account assumptions about retirement age, mortality, and, most significantly, future trends in health care benefits. Like pension benefits, such future benefits should be discounted to the current period. A field test conducted by the Financial Executives Research Foundation determined that the change to accrual accounting increased postretirement benefits by two to seven times the amount recognized on a cash basis.

✓ Check out ACE for a Review Quiz at http://accounting.college.hmco.com/students.

Chapter Review

REVIEW OF LEARNING OBJECTIVES

LO1   Identify the management issues related to issuing long-term debt.

Long-term debt is used to finance long-term assets and business activities that have long-term earnings potential, such as property, plant, and equipment and research and development. In issuing long-term debt, management must decide (1) whether to take on long-term debt, (2) how much long-term debt to carry, (3) what types of long-term debt to incur, and (4) how to handle debt repayment. Among the advantages of long-term debt financing are that (1) common stockholders do not relinquish any control, (2) interest on debt is tax deductible, and (3) financial leverage may increase earnings. Disadvantages of long-term financing are that (1) interest and principal must be repaid on schedule, and (2) financial leverage can work against a company if an investment is not successful.

LO2   Identify and contrast the major characteristics of bonds.

A bond is a security that represents money borrowed from the investing public. When a corporation issues bonds, it enters into a contract, called a bond indenture, with the bondholders. The bond indenture identifies the major conditions of the bonds. A corporation can issue several types of bonds, each having different characteristics. For example, a bond issue may or may not require security (secured versus unsecured bonds). It may be payable at a single time (term bonds) or at several times (serial bonds). And the holder may receive interest automatically (registered bonds) or may have to return coupons to receive interest payable (coupon bonds).

LO3   Record the issuance of bonds at face value and at a discount or premium.

When bonds are issued, the bondholders pay an amount equal to, less than, or greater than the bonds' face value. Bondholders pay face value for bonds when the interest rate on the bonds approximates the market rate for similar investments. The issuing corporation records the bond issue at face value as a long-term liability in the Bonds Payable account.

Bonds are issued at an amount less than face value when their face interest rate is lower than the market rate for similar investments. The difference between the face value and the issue price is called a discount and is debited to Unamortized Bond Discount.

When the face interest rate on bonds is greater than the market interest rate on similar investments, investors are willing to pay more than face value for the bonds. The difference between the issue price and the face value is called a premium and is credited to Unamortized Bond Premium.

LO4   Use present values to determine the value of bonds.

The value of a bond is determined by summing the present values of (1) the series of fixed interest payments of the bond issue and (2) the single payment of the face value at maturity. Tables 3 and 4 in the appendix on future value and present value tables should be used in making these computations.

LO5   Amortize bond discounts and bond premiums using the straight-line and effective interest methods.

When bonds are sold at a discount or a premium, the interest rate is adjusted from the face rate to an effective rate that is close to the market rate when the bonds were issued. Therefore, bond discounts or premiums have the effect of increasing or decreasing the interest expense on the bonds over their life. Under these conditions, it is necessary to amortize the discount or premium over the life of the bonds by using either the straight-line method or the effective interest method.

The straight-line method allocates a fixed portion of the bond discount or premium each interest period to adjust the interest payment to interest expense. The effective interest method, which is used when the effects of amortization are material, results in a constant rate of interest on the carrying value of the bonds. To find interest and the amortization of discounts or premiums, the effective interest rate is applied to the carrying value of the bonds (face value minus the discount or plus the premium) at the beginning of the interest period. The amount of the discount or premium to be amortized is the difference between the interest figured by using the effective rate and that obtained by using the face rate. The results of using the effective interest method on bonds issued at a discount or a premium are summarized below and compared with issuance at face value.

	Bonds Issued At		
	Face Value	**Discount**	**Premium**
Trend in carrying value over bond term	Constant	Increasing	Decreasing
Trend in interest expense over bond term	Constant	Increasing	Decreasing
Interest expense versus interest payments	Interest expense = interest payments	Interest expense > interest payments	Interest expense < interest payments
Classification of bond discount or premium	Not applicable	Contra-liability (deducted from Bonds Payable)	Liability (added to Bonds Payable)

LO6 Record bonds issued between interest dates and year-end adjustments.

When bonds are sold on dates between the interest payment dates, the issuing corporation collects from investors the interest that has accrued since the last interest payment date. When the next interest payment date arrives, the corporation pays the bondholders interest for the entire interest period.

When the end of a corporation's fiscal year does not fall on an interest payment date, the corporation must accrue bond interest expense from the last interest payment date to the end of the company's fiscal year. This accrual results in the inclusion of the interest expense in the year incurred.

SUPPLEMENTAL OBJECTIVES

SO7 Account for the retirement of bonds and the conversion of bonds into stock.

Callable bonds can be retired before maturity at the option of the issuing corporation. The call price is usually an amount greater than the face value of the bonds, in which case the corporation recognizes a loss on the retirement of the bonds. A gain can be recognized on the early extinguishment of debt when a company purchases its bonds on the open market at a price below carrying value. This happens when a rise in the market interest rate causes the market value of the bonds to fall below face value.

Convertible bonds allow the bondholder to convert bonds to common stock in the issuing corporation. In this case, the common stock issued is recorded at the carrying value of the bonds being converted. No gain or loss is recognized.

SO8 Explain the basic features of mortgages payable, long-term leases, and pensions and other postretirement benefits as long-term liabilities.

A mortgage is a long-term debt secured by real property. It usually is paid in equal monthly installments. Each payment is partly interest expense and partly debt repayment. If a long-term lease is a capital lease, the risks of ownership lie with the lessee. Like a mortgage payment, each lease payment is partly interest and partly a reduction of debt. For a capital lease, both an asset and a long-term liability should be recorded. The liability should be equal to the present value at the beginning of the lease of the total lease payments over the lease term. The recorded asset is subject to depreciation. Pension expense must be recorded in the current period. Other postretirement benefits should be estimated and accrued while the employee is still working.

REVIEW OF CONCEPTS AND TERMINOLOGY

The following concepts and terms were introduced in this chapter:

LO2 **Bond:** A security, usually long term, representing money that a corporation or other entity borrows from the investing public.

LO2 **Bond certificate:** Evidence of an organization's debt to a bondholder.

LO2 **Bond indenture:** A supplementary agreement to a bond issue that defines the rights, privileges, and limitations of bondholders.

LO2 **Bond issue:** The total value of bonds issued at one time.

SO7 **Callable bonds:** Bonds that an organization can buy back and retire at a call price before maturity.

SO7 **Call price:** A specified price, usually above face value, at which a corporation may buy back and retire bonds before maturity.

SO8 **Capital lease:** A long-term lease in which the risk of ownership lies with the lessee and whose terms resemble those of a purchase or sale on installment.

SO7 **Convertible bonds:** Bonds that can be exchanged for common stock or other securities of the corporation.

LO2 **Coupon bonds:** Bonds that are usually not registered with the issuing organization but instead bear interest coupons stating the amount of interest due and the payment date.

LO3 **Discount:** The amount by which the face value of a bond exceeds the issue price, which occurs when the market interest rate is higher than the face interest rate.

SO7 **Early extinguishment of debt:** The retirement of a bond issue before its maturity date.

LO5   **Effective interest method:** A method of amortizing bond discounts or premiums that applies a constant interest rate (the market rate at the time the bonds were issued) to the carrying value of the bonds at the beginning of each interest period.

LO3   **Face interest rate:** The rate of interest paid to bondholders based on the face value of the bonds.

LO1   **Financial leverage:** The ability to increase earnings for stockholders by earning more on assets than is paid in interest on debt incurred to finance the assets. Also called *trading on the equity*.

LO1   **Interest coverage ratio:** A measure of the degree of protection a company has from default on interest payments; income before taxes plus interest expense divided by interest expense.

LO3   **Market interest rate:** The rate of interest paid in the market on bonds of similar risk. Also called *effective interest rate*.

SO8   **Mortgage:** A long-term debt secured by real property.

SO8   **Operating lease:** A short-term lease in which the risks of ownership remain with the lessor and whose payments are recorded as rent expense.

SO8   **Other postretirement benefits:** Health care and other nonpension benefits paid to a worker after retirement but earned while the employee is still working.

SO8   **Pension fund:** A fund established through contributions by an employer, and often by employees, from which payments are made to employees after retirement or on disability or death.

SO8   **Pension plan:** A contract between a company and its employees under which the company agrees to pay benefits to the employees after they retire.

LO3   **Premium:** The amount by which the issue price of a bond exceeds its face value, which occurs when the market interest rate is lower than the face interest rate.

LO2   **Registered bonds:** Bonds for which the names and addresses of bondholders are recorded with the issuing organization.

LO2   **Secured bonds:** Bonds that give the bondholders a pledge of certain assets as a guarantee of repayment.

LO2   **Serial bonds:** Bonds in an issue that mature on different dates.

LO5   **Straight-line method:** A method of amortizing bond discounts or premiums that allocates the discount or premium equally over each interest period of the life of a bond.

LO2   **Term bonds:** Bonds in an issue that mature at the same time.

LO2   **Unsecured bonds:** Bonds issued on the general credit of an organization. Also called *debenture bonds*.

LO5   **Zero coupon bonds:** Bonds that do not pay periodic interest but that promise to pay a fixed amount on the maturity date.

REVIEW PROBLEM

Interest and Amortization of a Bond Discount, Bond Retirement, and Bond Conversion

LO3   When Merrill Manufacturing Company was expanding its metal window division, it did
LO5   not have enough capital to finance the expansion. So, management sought and received
SO7   approval from the board of directors to issue bonds. The company planned to issue $5,000,000 of 8 percent, five-year bonds in 20x4. Interest would be paid on June 30 and December 31 of each year. The bonds would be callable at 104, and each $1,000 bond would be convertible into 30 shares of $10 par value common stock.

On January 1, 20x4, the bonds were sold at 96 because the market rate of interest for similar investments was 9 percent. The company decided to amortize the bond discount by using the effective interest method. On July 1, 20x6, management called and retired half the bonds, and investors converted the other half into common stock.

REQUIRED ▶ 1. Prepare an interest and amortization schedule for the first five interest periods.
2. Prepare entries in journal form to record the sale of the bonds, the first two interest payments, the bond retirement, and the bond conversion.

ANSWER TO REVIEW PROBLEM

1. Schedule prepared for the first five interest periods:

Interest and Amortization of Bond Discount

Semiannual Interest Payment Date	Carrying Value at Beginning of Period	Semiannual Interest Expense* (9% × ½)	Semiannual Interest Payment (8% × ½)	Amorti- zation of Discount	Unamortized Bond Discount at End of Period	Carrying Value at End of Period
Jan. 1, 20x4					$200,000	$4,800,000
June 30, 20x4	$4,800,000	$216,000	$200,000	$16,000	184,000	4,816,000
Dec. 31, 20x4	4,816,000	216,720	200,000	16,720	167,280	4,832,720
June 30, 20x5	4,832,720	217,472	200,000	17,472	149,808	4,850,192
Dec. 31, 20x5	4,850,192	218,259	200,000	18,259	131,549	4,868,451
June 30, 20x6	4,868,451	219,080	200,000	19,080	112,469	4,887,531

*Rounded to the nearest dollar.

2. Entries made in journal form:

20x4
Jan. 1 Cash 4,800,000
        Unamortized Bond Discount 200,000
          Bonds Payable 5,000,000
          Sold $5,000,000 of 8%,
          5-year bonds at 96

June 30 Bond Interest Expense 216,000
          Unamortized Bond Discount 16,000
          Cash 200,000
          Paid semiannual interest and
          amortized the discount on 8%,
          5-year bonds

Dec. 31 Bond Interest Expense 216,720
          Unamortized Bond Discount 16,720
          Cash 200,000
          Paid semiannual interest and
          amortized the discount on 8%,
          5-year bonds

20x6
July 1 Bonds Payable 2,500,000
        Loss on Retirement of Bonds 156,235
          Unamortized Bond Discount 56,235
          Cash 2,600,000
          Called $2,500,000 of 8% bonds and
          retired them at 104
          $112,469 × ½ = $56,235*

    1 Bonds Payable 2,500,000
          Unamortized Bond Discount 56,234
          Common Stock 750,000
          Paid-in Capital in Excess of Par
          Value, Common 1,693,766
          Converted $2,500,000 of 8% bonds into
          common stock:
          2,500 × 30 shares = 75,000 shares
          75,000 shares × $10 = $750,000
          $112,469 − $56,235 = $56,234
          $2,500,000 − ($56,234 + $750,000) =
          $1,693,766

*Rounded.

Chapter Assignments

BUILDING YOUR KNOWLEDGE FOUNDATION

QUESTIONS

1. What are the advantages and disadvantages of issuing long-term debt?

2. What are a bond certificate, a bond issue, and a bond indenture? What information is in a bond indenture?

3. What are the essential differences between (a) secured and debenture bonds, (b) term and serial bonds, and (c) registered and coupon bonds?

4. Napier Corporation sold $500,000 of 5 percent $1,000 bonds on the interest payment date. What would the proceeds from the sale be if the bonds were issued at 95, at 100, and at 102?

5. If you were about to buy bonds on which the face interest rate was less than the market interest rate, would you expect to pay more or less than par value for the bonds?

6. Why does the amortization of a bond discount increase interest expense to an amount greater than interest paid? Why does the amortization of a premium have the opposite effect?

7. When the effective interest method of amortizing a bond discount or premium is used, why does the amount of interest expense change from period to period?

8. When bonds are issued between interest dates, why is it necessary for the issuer to collect an amount equal to accrued interest from the buyer?

9. Why would a company want to exercise the call provision of a bond when it can wait to pay off the debt?

10. What are the advantages of convertible bonds to the company issuing them and to the investor?

11. What are the two components of a uniform monthly mortgage payment?

12. What is a capital lease? Why should an accountant record both an asset and a liability in connection with this type of lease? What items should appear on the income statement as the result of a capital lease?

13. What is a pension plan? What is a pension fund?

14. What is the difference between a defined contribution plan and a defined benefit plan? In general, how is expense determined under each plan? What assumptions must be made to account for the expenses of a defined benefit plan?

15. What are other postretirement benefits, and how is the matching rule applied?

SHORT EXERCISES

SE 1.
LO1 **Bond Versus Common Stock Financing**

Indicate whether each of the following is an advantage or a disadvantage of using long-term bond financing rather than issuing common stock:

1. Interest paid on bonds is tax deductible.
2. Investments are sometimes not as successful as planned.
3. Financial leverage can have a negative effect when investments do not earn as much as the interest payments on the related debt.
4. Bondholders do not have voting rights in a corporation.
5. Positive financial leverage may be achieved.

SE 2.
LO3 **Entries for Interest Using**
LO5 **the Straight-Line Method**

On April 1, 20x4, Agaki Corporation issued $4,000,000 in 8.5 percent, five-year bonds at 98. The semiannual interest payment dates are April 1 and October 1. Prepare entries in journal form for the issue of the bonds by Agaki on April 1, 20x4, and the first two interest payments on October 1, 20x4, and April 1, 20x5. Use the straight-line method and ignore year-end accruals.

SE 3.

LO3 **Entries for Interest Using the**
LO5 **Effective Interest Method**
LO6

On March 1, 20xx, Westward Freight Company sold $100,000 of its 9.5 percent, 20-year bonds at 106. The semiannual interest payment dates are March 1 and September 1. The market interest rate is about 8.9 percent. The company's fiscal year ends August 31. Prepare entries in journal form to record the sale of the bonds on March 1, the accrual of interest and amortization of premium on August 31, and the first interest payment on September 1. Use the effective interest method to amortize the premium.

SE 4.

LO4 **Valuing Bonds Using Present Value**

Cap Art, Inc., is considering the sale of two bond issues. Choice A is a $400,000 bond issue that pays semiannual interest of $32,000 and is due in 20 years. Choice B is a $400,000 bond issue that pays semiannual interest of $30,000 and is due in 15 years. Assume that the market interest rate for each bond is 12 percent. Calculate the amount that Cap Art will receive if both bond issues occur. (Calculate the present value of each bond issue and sum.)

SE 5.

LO3 **Entries for Bond Issues**
LO6

League Company is authorized to issue $900,000 in bonds on June 1. The bonds carry a face interest rate of 8 percent, with interest to be paid on June 1 and December 1. Prepare entries in journal form for the issue of the bonds under the independent assumptions that (a) the bonds are issued on September 1 at 100 and (b) the bonds are issued on June 1 at 103.

SE 6.

LO6 **Sale of Bonds Between Interest Dates**

Eisley Corporation sold $200,000 of 9 percent, ten-year bonds for face value on September 1, 20xx. The issue date of the bonds was May 1, 20xx. The company's fiscal year ends on December 31, and this is its only bond issue. Record the sale of the bonds on September 1 and the first semiannual interest payment on November 1, 20xx. What is the bond interest expense for the year ended December 31, 20xx?

SE 7.

LO3 **Year-End Accrual of Bond**
LO5 **Interest**
LO6

On October 1, 20x4, Knight Corporation issued $500,000 of 9 percent bonds at 96. The bonds are dated October 1 and pay interest semiannually. The market rate of interest is 10 percent, and the company's year end is December 31. Prepare the entries to record the issuance of the bonds, the accrual of the interest on December 31, 20x4, and the payment of the first semiannual interest on April 1, 20x5. Assume that the company does not use reversing entries and uses the effective interest method to amortize the bond discount.

SE 8.

SO7 **Entry for Bond Retirement**

Ross Corporation has outstanding $800,000 of 8 percent bonds callable at 104. On December 1, immediately after the payment of the semiannual interest and the amortization of the bond discount were recorded, the unamortized bond discount equaled $21,000. On that date, $480,000 of the bonds were called and retired. Prepare the entry to record the retirement of the bonds on December 1.

SE 9.

SO7 **Entry for Bond Conversion**

Hui Corporation has $1,000,000 of 6 percent bonds outstanding. There is $20,000 of unamortized discount remaining on the bonds after the March 1, 20x5, semiannual interest payment. The bonds are convertible at the rate of 20 shares of $10 par value common stock for each $1,000 bond. On March 1, 20x5, bondholders presented $600,000 of the bonds for conversion. Prepare the entry to record the conversion of the bonds.

SE 10.

SO8 **Mortgage Payable**

Sedaka Corporation purchased a building by signing a $300,000 long-term mortgage with monthly payments of $2,400. The mortgage carries an interest rate of 8 percent. Prepare a monthly payment schedule showing the monthly payment, the interest for the month, the reduction in debt, and the unpaid balance for the first three months. (Round to the nearest dollar.)

EXERCISES

E 1.

LO1 **Interest Coverage Ratio**

Compute the interest coverage ratios for 20x4 and 20x5 from the partial income statements of Ivy Wall Company that appear below. State whether the ratio improved or worsened over time.

	20x5	20x4
Income from operations	$23,890	$18,460
Interest expense	5,800	3,300
Income before income taxes	$18,090	$15,160
Income taxes	5,400	4,500
Net income	$12,690	$10,660

E 2.
LO3   **Entries for Interest Using the**
LO5   **Straight-Line Method**

Agga Corporation issued $4,000,000 in 10.5 percent, ten-year bonds on February 1, 20x4, at 104. The semiannual interest payment dates are February 1 and August 1. Prepare entries in journal form for the issue of bonds by Agga on February 1, 20x4, and the first two interest payments on August 1, 20x4, and February 1, 20x5. Use the straight-line method and ignore year-end accruals.

E 3.
LO3   **Entries for Interest Using**
LO5   **the Straight-Line Method**

Famina Corporation issued $8,000,000 in 8.5 percent, five-year bonds on March 1, 20x5, at 96. The semiannual interest payment dates are March 1 and September 1. Prepare entries in journal form for the issue of the bonds by Famina on March 1, 20x5, and the first two interest payments on September 1, 20x5, and March 1, 20x6. Use the straight-line method and ignore year-end accruals.

E 4.
LO3   **Entries for Interest Using the**
LO5   **Effective Interest Method**
LO6

Whistle Toy Company sold $500,000 of 9.5 percent, 20-year bonds on April 1, 20xx, at 106. The semiannual interest payment dates are April 1 and October 1. The market interest rate is 8.9 percent. The company's fiscal year ends September 30. Prepare entries in journal form to record the sale of the bonds on April 1, the accrual of interest and amortization of premium on September 30, and the first interest payment on October 1. Use the effective interest method to amortize the premium.

E 5.
LO3   **Entries for Interest Using**
LO5   **the Effective Interest Method**
LO6

On March 1, 20x4, Eddy Corporation issued $1,200,000 of 10 percent, five-year bonds. The semiannual interest payment dates are March 1 and September 1. Because the market rate for similar investments was 11 percent, the bonds had to be issued at a discount. The discount on the issuance of the bonds was $48,670. The company's fiscal year ends February 28. Prepare entries in journal form to record the bond issue on March 1, 20x4; the payment of interest and the amortization of the discount on September 1, 20x4; the accrual of interest and the amortization of the discount on February 28, 20x5; and the payment of interest on March 1, 20x5. Use the effective interest method. (Round answers to the nearest dollar.)

E 6.
LO4   **Valuing Bonds Using Present**
Value

Octogon, Inc., is considering the sale of two bond issues. Choice A is an $800,000 bond issue that pays semiannual interest of $64,000 and is due in 20 years. Choice B is an $800,000 bond issue that pays semiannual interest of $60,000 and is due in 15 years. Assume that the market interest rate for each bond is 12 percent. Calculate the amount that Octogon, Inc., will receive if both bond issues are made. (**Hint:** Calculate the present value of each bond issue and sum.)

E 7.
LO4   **Valuing Bonds Using Present**
Value

Use the present value tables in the appendix on future value and present value tables to calculate the issue price of a $1,200,000 bond issue in each of the following independent cases, assuming that interest is paid semiannually:

a. A ten-year, 8 percent bond issue; the market interest rate is 10 percent.
b. A ten-year, 8 percent bond issue; the market interest rate is 6 percent.
c. A ten-year, 10 percent bond issue; the market interest rate is 8 percent.
d. A 20-year, 10 percent bond issue; the market interest rate is 12 percent.
e. A 20-year, 10 percent bond issue; the market interest rate is 6 percent.

E 8.
LO4   **Zero Coupon Bonds**

The state of Idaho needs to raise $100,000,000 for highway repairs. Officials are considering issuing zero coupon bonds, which do not require periodic interest payments. The current market interest rate for the bonds is 10 percent. What face value of bonds must be issued to raise the needed funds, assuming the bonds will be due in 30 years and compounded annually? How would your answer change if the bonds were due in 50 years? How would both answers change if the market interest rate were 8 percent instead of 10 percent?

E 9.
LO5   **Entries for Interest Payments**
LO6   **Using the Effective Interest**
Method

The long-term debt section of the Sanchos Corporation's balance sheet at the end of its fiscal year, December 31, 2005, was as follows:

Long-term liabilities
  Bonds payable—8%, interest payable
    1/1 and 7/1, due 12/31/13 $1,000,000
    Less unamortized bond discount   80,000 $920,000

Prepare entries in journal form relevant to the interest payments on July 1, 2006, December 31, 2006, and January 1, 2007. Use the effective interest rate method and assume a market interest rate of 10 percent.

E 10.
LO3   **Entries for Bond Issue**
LO6

Water Symphonics, Inc., is authorized to issue $1,800,000 in bonds on June 1. The bonds carry a face interest rate of 9 percent, which is to be paid on June 1 and December 1. Prepare entries in journal form for the issue of the bonds by Water Symphonics, Inc., under the assumptions that (a) the bonds are issued on September 1 at 100 and (b) the bonds are issued on June 1 at 105.

E 11.

LO6 Sale of Bonds Between Interest Dates

Margi Corporation sold $400,000 of 12 percent, ten-year bonds at face value on September 1, 20xx. The issue date of the bonds was May 1, 20xx.

1. Record the sale of the bonds on September 1 and the first semiannual interest payment on November 1, 20xx.
2. The company's fiscal year ends on December 31, and this is its only bond issue. What is the bond interest expense for the year ended December 31, 20xx?

E 12.

LO3 Year-End Accrual of Bond
LO5 Interest
LO6

Lon Corporation issued $1,000,000 of 9 percent bonds on October 1, 20x3, at 96. The bonds are dated October 1 and pay interest semiannually. The market interest rate is 10 percent, and Lon's fiscal year ends on December 31. Prepare the entries to record the issuance of the bonds, the accrual of the interest on December 31, 20x3, and the first semiannual interest payment on April 1, 20x4. Assume the company does not use reversing entries and uses the effective interest method to amortize the bond discount.

E 13.

LO4 Time Value of Money and
SO7 Early Extinguishment of Debt

Brown, Inc., has a $1,400,000, 8 percent bond issue that was issued a number of years ago at face value. There are now ten years left on the bond issue, and the market interest rate is 16 percent. Interest is paid semiannually.

1. Using present value tables, figure the current market value of the bond issue.
2. Record the retirement of the bonds, assuming the company purchases the bonds on the open market at the calculated value.

E 14.

SO7 Entry for Bond Retirement

The Pucinski Corporation has outstanding $1,600,000 of 8 percent bonds callable at 104. On September 1, immediately after recording the payment of the semiannual interest and the amortization of the discount, the unamortized bond discount equaled $42,000. On that date, $960,000 of the bonds were called and retired. Prepare the entry to record the retirement of the bonds on September 1.

E 15.

SO7 Entry for Bond Conversion

The Daglar Corporation has $400,000 of 6 percent bonds outstanding. There is $20,000 of unamortized discount remaining on these bonds after the July 1, 20x8, semiannual interest payment. The bonds are convertible at the rate of 40 shares of $5 par value common stock for each $1,000 bond. On July 1, 20x8, bondholders presented $300,000 of the bonds for conversion. Prepare the entry to record the conversion of the bonds.

E 16.

SO8 Mortgage Payable

Fiery Corporation purchased a building by signing a $150,000 long-term mortgage with monthly payments of $2,000. The mortgage carries an interest rate of 12 percent.

1. Prepare a monthly payment schedule showing the monthly payment, the interest for the month, the reduction in debt, and the unpaid balance for the first three months. (Round to the nearest dollar.)
2. Prepare entries in journal form to record the purchase and the first two monthly payments.

E 17.

SO8 Recording Lease Obligations

Foxx Corporation has leased a piece of equipment that has a useful life of 12 years. The terms of the lease are $43,000 per year for 12 years. Foxx currently is able to borrow money at a long-term interest rate of 15 percent. Round answers to the nearest dollar.)

1. Calculate the present value of the lease.
2. Prepare the entry to record the lease agreement.
3. Prepare the entry to record depreciation of the equipment for the first year using the straight-line method.
4. Prepare the entries to record the lease payments for the first two years.

PROBLEMS

P 1.

LO3 Bond Transactions—Straight-
LO5 Line Method
LO6

REQUIRED ▶

Gala Corporation has $30,000,000 of 10.5 percent, 20-year bonds dated June 1, with interest payment dates of May 31 and November 30. The company's fiscal year ends on December 31. It uses the straight-line method to amortize bond premiums or discounts.

1. Assume the bonds are issued at 103 on June 1. Prepare entries in journal form for June 1, November 30, and December 31.
2. Assume the bonds are issued at 97 on June 1. Prepare entries in journal form for June 1, November 30, and December 31.
3. Assume the bonds are issued at face value plus accrued interest on August 1. Prepare entries in journal form for August 1, November 30, and December 31.

P 2.

LO3 **Bond Transactions–Effective**
LO5 **Interest Method**
LO6

Paco Corporation has $16,000,000 of 9.5 percent, 25-year bonds dated March 1, with interest payable on March 1 and September 1. The company's fiscal year ends on November 30. It uses the effective interest method to amortize bond premiums or discounts. (Round amounts to the nearest dollar.)

REQUIRED ▶

1. Assume the bonds are issued at 102.5 on March 1 to yield an effective interest rate of 9.2 percent. Prepare entries in journal form for March 1, September 1, and November 30.
2. Assume the bonds are issued at 97.5 on March 1 to yield an effective interest rate of 9.8 percent. Prepare entries in journal form for March 1, September 1, and November 30.
3. Assume the bonds are issued on June 1 at face value plus accrued interest. Prepare entries in journal form for June 1, September 1, and November 30.

P 3.

LO3 **Bonds Issued at a Discount**
LO5 **and a Premium**
LO6

Reiser Corporation issued bonds twice during 20x4. A summary of the transactions involving the bonds follows.

20x4
Jan.   1   Issued $3,000,000 of 9.9 percent, 10-year bonds dated January 1, 20x4, with interest payable on June 30 and December 31. The bonds were sold at 102.6, resulting in an effective interest rate of 9.4 percent.
Mar.   1   Issued $2,000,000 of 9.2 percent, 10-year bonds dated March 1, 20x4, with interest payable March 1 and September 1. The bonds were sold at 98.2, resulting in an effective interest rate of 9.5 percent.
June 30   Paid semiannual interest on the January 1 issue and amortized the premium, using the effective interest method.
Sept.   1   Paid semiannual interest on the March 1 issue and amortized the discount, using the effective interest method.
Dec.   31   Paid semiannual interest on the January 1 issue and amortized the premium, using the effective interest method.
        31   Made an end-of-year adjusting entry to accrue interest on the March 1 issue and to amortize two-thirds of the discount applicable to the second interest period.

20x5
Mar.   1   Paid semiannual interest on the March 1 issue and amortized the remainder of the discount applicable to the second interest period.

REQUIRED ▶

Prepare entries in journal form to record the bond transactions. (Round amounts to the nearest dollar.)

P 4.

LO3 **Bond Interest and**
LO5 **Amortization Table, and**
SO7 **Bond Retirements**

In 20x3, the Boston Corporation was authorized to issue $60,000,000 of six-year unsecured bonds. The bonds carried a face interest rate of 9 percent, payable semiannually on June 30 and December 31. The bonds were callable at 105 any time after June 30, 20x6. All of the bonds were issued on July 1, 20x3 at 95.568, a price yielding an effective interest rate of 10 percent. On July 1, 20x6, the company called and retired half the outstanding bonds.

REQUIRED ▶

1. Prepare a table similar to Table 1 to show the interest and amortization of the bond discount for 12 interest payment periods, using the effective interest method. (Round results to the nearest dollar.)
2. Calculate the amount of loss on early retirement of one-half of the bonds on July 1, 20x6.

P 5.

LO3 **Comprehensive Bond**
LO5 **Transactions**
LO6
SO7

The Ingolls Corporation, a company whose fiscal year ends on June 30, engaged in the following long-term bond transactions over a three-year period:

20x3
Nov.   1   Issued $40,000,000 of 12 percent debenture bonds at face value plus accrued interest. Interest is payable on January 31 and July 31, and the bonds are callable at 104.

20x4
Jan.   31   Made the semiannual interest payment on the 12 percent bonds.
June 30   Made the year-end accrual of interest payment on the 12 percent bonds.
July   1   Issued $20,000,000 of 10 percent, 15-year convertible bonds at 105. Interest is payable on June 30 and December 31, and each $1,000 bond is convertible into 30 shares of $10 par value common stock. The market rate of interest is 9 percent.

July 31 Made the semiannual interest payment on the 12 percent bonds.

Dec. 31 Made the semiannual interest payment on the 10 percent bonds and amortized the bond premium.

20x5

Jan. 31 Made the semiannual interest payment on the 12 percent bonds.

Feb. 28 Called and retired all of the 12 percent bonds, including accrued interest.

June 30 Made the semiannual interest payment on the 10 percent bonds and amortized the bond premium.

July 1 Accepted for conversion into common stock all of the 10 percent bonds.

REQUIRED ▶ Prepare entries in journal form to record the bond transactions, making all necessary accruals and using the effective interest method. (Round all calculations to the nearest dollar.)

ALTERNATE PROBLEMS

P 6.

LO3 **Bond Transactions–Straight-**
LO5 **Line Method**
LO6

Raol Corporation has $4,000,000 of 9.5 percent, 25-year bonds dated March 1, with interest payable on March 1 and September 1. The company's fiscal year ends on November 30, and it uses the straight-line method to amortize bond premiums or discounts.

REQUIRED ▶

1. Assume the bonds are issued at 103.5 on March 1. Prepare entries in journal form for March 1, September 1, and November 30.
2. Assume the bonds are issued at 96.5 on March 1. Prepare entries in journal form for March 1, September 1, and November 30.
3. Assume the bonds are issued on June 1 at face value plus accrued interest. Prepare entries in journal form for June 1, September 1, and November 30.

P 7.

LO3 **Bond Transactions–Effective**
LO5 **Interest Method**
LO6

Dubchec Corporation has $10,000,000 of 10.5 percent, 20-year bonds dated June 1, with interest payment dates of May 31 and November 30. The company's fiscal year ends December 31. It uses the effective interest method to amortize bond premiums or discounts.

REQUIRED ▶

1. Assume the bonds are issued at 103 on June 1 to yield an effective interest rate of 10.1 percent. Prepare entries in journal form for June 1, November 30, and December 31. (Round amounts to the nearest dollar.)
2. Assume the bonds are issued at 97 on June 1 to yield an effective interest rate of 10.9 percent. Prepare entries in journal form for June 1, November 30, and December 31. (Round amounts to the nearest dollar.)
3. Assume the bonds are issued at face value plus accrued interest on August 1. Prepare entries in journal form for August 1, November 30, and December 31. (Round amounts to the nearest dollar.)

P 8.

LO3 **Bonds Issued at a Discount**
LO5 **and a Premium**
LO6

Fils Corporation issued bonds twice during 20x3. The transactions were as follows:

20x3

Jan. 1 Issued $1,000,000 of 9.2 percent, 10-year bonds dated January 1, 20x3, with interest payable on June 30 and December 31. The bonds were sold at 98.1, resulting in an effective interest rate of 9.5 percent.

Apr. 1 Issued $2,000,000 of 9.8 percent, 10-year bonds dated April 1, 20x3, with interest payable on March 31 and September 30. The bonds were sold at 102, resulting in an effective interest rate of 9.5 percent.

June 30 Paid semiannual interest on the January 1 issue and amortized the discount, using the effective interest method.

Sept. 30 Paid semiannual interest on the April 1 issue and amortized the premium, using the effective interest method.

Dec. 31 Paid semiannual interest on the January 1 issue and amortized the discount, using the effective interest method.

31 Made an end-of-year adjusting entry to accrue interest on the April 1 issue and to amortize half the premium applicable to the second interest period.

20x4

Mar. 31 Paid semiannual interest on the April 1 issue and amortized the premium applicable to the second half of the second interest period.

REQUIRED ▶ Prepare entries in journal form to record the bond transactions. (Round amounts to the nearest dollar.)

issuing common stock directly? Are there any disadvantages to this approach? If the price of the company's common stock returns to $200 per share, what would be the total theoretical value of the notes? If the holders of the notes were to elect to convert the notes into common stock, what would be the effect on the company's debt to equity ratio, and what would be the effect on the percentage ownership of the company by other stockholders?

International Company

FRA 3.

**LO1 Comparison of Interest
       Coverage**

Japanese companies have historically relied more on debt financing and are more highly leveraged than U.S. companies. For instance, NEC Corporation <www.nec.com> and Sanyo Electric Co. <www.sanyo.com>, two large Japanese electronics companies, had debt to equity ratios of about 4.3 and 3.5, respectively, in 2001. From the selected data from the companies' annual reports shown below (in millions of yen), compute the interest coverage ratios for the two companies for the two years. Comment on the riskiness of the companies and on the trends they show.[16]

	NEC		Sanyo	
	2001	2000	2001	2000
Interest expense	63,873	70,211	26,427	27,914
Income before income taxes	92,323	30,183	73,484	36,953

Group Activity: Assign the two companies to different groups to calculate the ratios and discuss the results. Debrief by discussing the advantages and disadvantages of a debt-laden capital structure.

Toys "R" Us Annual Report

FRA 4.

**LO1 Business Practice, Long-Term
 SO8 Debt, and Leases**

Refer to the financial statements and the notes to the financial statements in the Toys "R" Us <www.tru.com> annual report to answer the following questions:

1. Is it the practice of Toys "R" Us to own or lease most of its property and equipment?
2. Does Toys "R" Us lease property predominantly under capital leases or under operating leases? How much was rental expense for operating leases in 2002?

Comparison Case: Toys "R" Us and Walgreen Co.

FRA 5.

LO1 Use of Debt Financing

Refer to the annual report of Toys "R" Us <www.tru.com> and the financial statements of Walgreens <www.walgreens.com> in the Supplement to Chapter 6. Calculate the debt to equity ratio and the interest coverage ratio for both companies' most recent two years. Evaluate and comment on the relative performance of the two companies with regard to debt financing. Which company has more risk of not being able to meet its interest obligations? Explain.

FRA 6.

**LO1 Long-Term Liabilities
 LO2
 SO8**

Fingraph® Financial Analyst™

Select any two companies from the same industry from the list of Fingraph companies on the Needles Accounting Resource Center Web Site at http://accounting. college.hmco.com/students. Access the Microsoft Excel spreadsheets for the companies you selected. For parts 1, 3, and 4, click on the URL at the top of each company's spreadsheet for a link to the company's web site and annual report.

1. In the annual reports of the companies you have selected, identify the long-term liabilities on the balance sheet and read any reference to long-term liabilities in the summary of significant accounting policies or notes to the financial statements. There is likely to be a separate note for each type of long-term liability. What are the most important long-term liabilities for each company?
2. Using the Fingraph CD-ROM software, display and print in tabular and graphic form the Balance Sheet Analysis page. Prepare a table that compares the debt to equity and interest coverage ratios for both companies for two years.
3. Read the statements of cash flows in both annual reports. Have the companies been increasing or decreasing their long-term debt? If increasing, what were each com-

pany's most important sources of long-term financing over the past two years? If decreasing, which liabilities are being decreased?

4. Find and read references to long-term liabilities in management's discussion and analysis in each annual report.

5. Write a one-page executive summary that highlights the most important types of long-term liabilities for these companies, identifies their accounting policies for specific long-term liabilities, and compares their debt to equity and interest coverage trends. The summary should refer to management's assessment. Include the Fingraph page and your table with your report.

Internet Case

LO2   Bond Rating Changes

FRA 7.   Go to the Needles Accounting Resource Center Web Site at http://accounting. college.hmco.com/students. Under Web Links, select Standard & Poor's or access their web site directly at <www.standardandpoors.com>. In times of economic or industry recessions, it is common to see downward revisions of bond ratings. From the Standard & Poor's list of companies with lowered bond ratings, identify three whose names you recognize. For each company, give reasons that you believe contributed to the ratings downgrade.

17

Chapter 17 presents the statement of cash flows and explains the changes in cash flows from operating, investing, and financing activities. The chapter also focuses on how to analyze the statement of cash flows to determine a company's cash-generating ability and its free cash flow.

The Statement of Cash Flows

LEARNING OBJECTIVES

LO1 State the principal purposes and uses of the statement of cash flows, and identify its components.

LO2 Analyze the statement of cash flows.

LO3 Use the indirect method to determine cash flows from operating activities.

LO4 Determine cash flows from investing activities.

LO5 Determine cash flows from financing activities.

DECISION POINT

A USER'S FOCUS

Marriott International, Inc. <www.marriott.com> Marriott International, Inc., is a world leader in lodging and contract hotel services. The balance sheet, income statement, and statement of stockholders' equity presented in Marriott's annual report give an excellent picture of the company's philosophy and performance.

Although these three financial statements are essential to the evaluation of any company, they do not tell the entire story. A fourth statement, the statement of cash flows, contains some additional information, as shown in the Financial Highlights on page 710.[1] This statement shows how much cash the company's operations generated during the past three years and how much cash investing and financing activities used or provided.

Marriott feels that maintaining adequate cash flows is important to the future of the company. In fact, Marriott's emphasis on cash flows is reflected in its compensation plan for top executives. A review of the plan indicates that cash flows, at the firm or business group level, are the financial measure given the greatest weight in determining compensation. Why would Marriott emphasize cash flows to such an extent?

Strong cash flows are essential to management's key goal of liquidity. If cash flows exceed the amount needed for operations and expansion, the company will not have to borrow additional funds. The excess cash flows will be available to reduce the company's debt and improve its financial position by lowering its debt to equity ratio. Another reason for the emphasis

What does Marriott's statement of cash flows reveal about the company's success in providing top-notch lodging and hotel services?

on cash flows may be the belief that strong cash flows from operations generate shareholder value and increase the market value of the company's stock.

The statement of cash flows demonstrates management's commitments in ways that are not readily apparent in the other financial statements. For exam-

ple, it can show whether management's focus is on the short term or the long term. This statement, which is required by the FASB,[2] satisfies the board's long-held position that a primary objective of financial statements is to provide investors and creditors with information about a company's cash flows.

Financial Highlights: Consolidated Statement of Cash Flows

Marriott International, Inc., and Subsidiaries

(In millions)

	2002	2001	2000
OPERATING ACTIVITIES			
Net income	$ 448	$ 236	$ 479
Adjustments to reconcile to cash provided by operations:			
Depreciation and amortization	187	222	195
Income taxes	(105)	9	133
Timeshare activity, net	(63)	(358)	(195)
Loss on discontinued operations	(171)	—	—
Other	223	278	54
Working capital changes:			
Accounts receivable	(31)	57	(53)
Other current assets	60	(20)	24
Accounts payable and accruals	(32)	(21)	219
Cash provided by operations	516	403	856
INVESTING ACTIVITIES			
Capital expenditures	(292)	(560)	(1,095)
Dispositions	729	554	742
Loan advances	(237)	(367)	(389)
Loan collections and sales	124	71	93
Other	(7)	(179)	(377)
Cash used in investing activities	317	(481)	(1,026)
FINANCING ACTIVITIES			
Commercial paper, net	102	(827)	46
Issuance of long-term debt	26	1,329	338
Repayment of long-term debt	(946)	(123)	(26)
Redemption of convertible subordinated debt	(347)	405	—
Issuance of Class A common stock	35	76	58
Dividends paid	(65)	(61)	(55)
Purchase of treasury stock	(252)	(235)	(340)
Cash provided by financing activities	(1,447)	564	21
(DECREASE) INCREASE IN CASH AND EQUIVALENTS	(614)	486	(149)
CASH AND EQUIVALENTS, beginning of year	812	326	475
CASH AND EQUIVALENTS, end of year	$ 198	$ 812	$ 326

Goodyear Tire & Rubber Company

<www.goodyear.com>

OBJECTIVES

- To state the purposes of the statement of cash flows
- To identify the three components of the statement of cash flows
- To identify the reasons why cash flows from operating activities usually differ from net income
- To understand the importance of cash flows from investing and financing activities

BACKGROUND FOR THE CASE

Goodyear was founded in 1898 by Frank Seiberling, who borrowed $3,500 to start a bicycle tire factory and

subsequently began making tires for horseless carriages. Today, Goodyear is the world's largest tire and rubber company, with factories in 28 countries and more than 100,000 employees. In a recent year, sales exceeded $14 billion. In addition to producing Goodyear tires, the company makes Dunlop, Kelly, Fulda, Lee, Sava, and Debica tires and rubber products for the automotive and industrial markets.

Goodyear's goal is to be ranked by all measures as the best tire and rubber company in the world. It intends to accomplish this by doing the following:

- having fast and profitable growth in all core businesses.
- achieving a number one or two market position.
- making strategic acquisitions and expansions.
- being the lowest cost producer.

To achieve these objectives, especially "fast and profitable growth" and "strategic acquisitions and expansions," Goodyear will need adequate funding. Management expects the funding to come from strong cash flows; divestiture of underperforming, nonstrategic assets; and debt issues. Within this framework, management must maintain the company's financial health and a strong balance sheet, with a debt to debt plus equity ratio of 25 to 30 percent.

Understanding Goodyear's performance in meeting the challenge of achieving adequate funding requires an ability to read and understand the statement of cash flows.

For more information about Goodyear Tire & Rubber Company, visit the company's web site through the Needles Accounting Resource Center Web Site at **http://accounting.college.hmco.com/students**.

REQUIRED

1. What are the purposes and three main components of the statement of cash flows?

2. What is the most important amount in the statement of cash flows? Why is it the most important?

3. What is the relationship of cash flows from operating activities to net income for Goodyear, and how do you account for the difference?

4. What are Goodyear's principal investing and financing activities?

OVERVIEW OF THE STATEMENT OF CASH FLOWS

LO1 State the principal purposes and uses of the statement of cash flows, and identify its components.

RELATED TEXT ASSIGNMENTS
Q: 1, 2, 3, 4, 5, 6
SE: 1, 8
E: 1
P: 1, 5
SD: 1, 2, 3
FRA: 3

The **statement of cash flows** shows how a company's operating, investing, and financing activities have affected cash during an accounting period. It explains the net increase (or decrease) in cash during the period. For purposes of preparing this statement, **cash** is defined as including both cash and cash equivalents. The FASB defines **cash equivalents** as short-term, highly liquid investments, including money market accounts, commercial paper, and U.S. Treasury bills. A company maintains cash equivalents to earn interest on cash that would otherwise remain unused temporarily. Suppose, for example, that a company has $1,000,000 that it will not need for 30 days. To earn a return on this amount, the company may place the cash in an account that earns interest (such as a money market account), it may lend the cash to another corporation by purchasing that corporation's short-term notes (commercial paper), or it may purchase a short-term obligation of the U.S. government (Treasury bills). In this context, short-term refers to original maturities of 90 days or less. Since cash and cash equivalents are considered the same, transfers between the Cash account and cash equivalents are not treated as cash receipts or cash payments. In effect, cash equivalents are combined with the Cash account on the statement of cash flows.

KEY POINT: Money market accounts, commercial paper (short-term notes), and U.S. Treasury bills are considered cash equivalents because they are highly liquid, temporary (90 days or less) holding places for cash not currently needed to operate the business. They can be quickly converted into cash if the need arises.

● **STOP AND THINK!**
Which statement is more useful—the income statement or the statement of cash flows?
The statements are equally useful. The income statement relates most directly to the goal of profitability, whereas the statement of cash flows is more closely tied to the goal of liquidity. ■

KEY POINT: Management uses the statement of cash flows to make various investing and financing decisions. Investors and creditors, on the other hand, use the statement primarily to assess cash flow prospects.

KEY POINT: Operating activities arise from the day-to-day sale of goods and services, investing activities involve long-term assets and investments, and financing activities deal with stockholders' equity accounts and debt (borrowing).

Cash equivalents should not be confused with short-term investments or marketable securities, which are not combined with the Cash account on the statement of cash flows. Purchases of marketable securities are treated as cash outflows and sales of marketable securities as cash inflows on the statement of cash flows. In this chapter, we assume that cash includes cash and cash equivalents.

PURPOSES OF THE STATEMENT OF CASH FLOWS

The primary purpose of the statement of cash flows is to provide information about a company's cash receipts and cash payments during an accounting period. A secondary purpose of the statement is to provide information about a company's operating, investing, and financing activities during the accounting period. Some information about those activities may be inferred from other financial statements, but it is on the statement of cash flows that all the transactions affecting cash are summarized.

INTERNAL AND EXTERNAL USES OF THE STATEMENT OF CASH FLOWS

The statement of cash flows is useful internally to management and externally to investors and creditors. Management uses the statement to assess liquidity, to determine dividend policy, and to evaluate the effects of major policy decisions involving investments and financing. In other words, management may use the statement to determine if short-term financing is needed to pay current liabilities, to decide whether to raise or lower dividends, and to plan for investing and financing needs.

Investors and creditors find the statement useful in assessing the company's ability to manage cash flows, to generate positive future cash flows, to pay its liabilities, to pay dividends and interest, and to anticipate its need for additional financing. Also, they may use the statement to explain the differences between net income on the income statement and the net cash flows generated from operations. In addition, the statement shows both the cash and the noncash effects of investing and financing activities during the accounting period.

CLASSIFICATION OF CASH FLOWS

The statement of cash flows classifies cash receipts and cash payments into the categories of operating, investing, and financing activities. The components of these activities are illustrated in Figure 1 and summarized below.

1. **Operating activities** include the cash effects of transactions and other events that enter into the determination of net income. Included in this category as cash inflows are cash receipts from customers for goods and services, interest and dividends received on loans and investments, and sales of trading securities. Included as cash outflows are cash payments for wages, inventory, expenses, interest, taxes, and purchases of trading securities. In effect, the income statement is changed from an accrual to a cash basis.

2. **Investing activities** include the acquisition and sale of long-term assets and marketable securities, other than trading securities or cash equivalents, and the making and collecting of loans. Cash inflows include the cash received from selling long-term assets and marketable securities and from collecting loans. Cash outflows include the cash expended for purchases of long-term assets and marketable securities and the cash lent to borrowers.

3. **Financing activities** include obtaining resources from stockholders and providing them with a return on their investments, and obtaining resources from creditors and repaying the amounts borrowed or otherwise settling the obligations. Cash inflows include the proceeds from issues of stocks and from short-term and long-term borrowing. Cash outflows include the repayments of loans (excluding interest) and payments to owners, including cash dividends. Treasury stock transactions are also considered financing activities. Repayments of

Figure 1
Classification of Cash Inflows and Cash Outflows

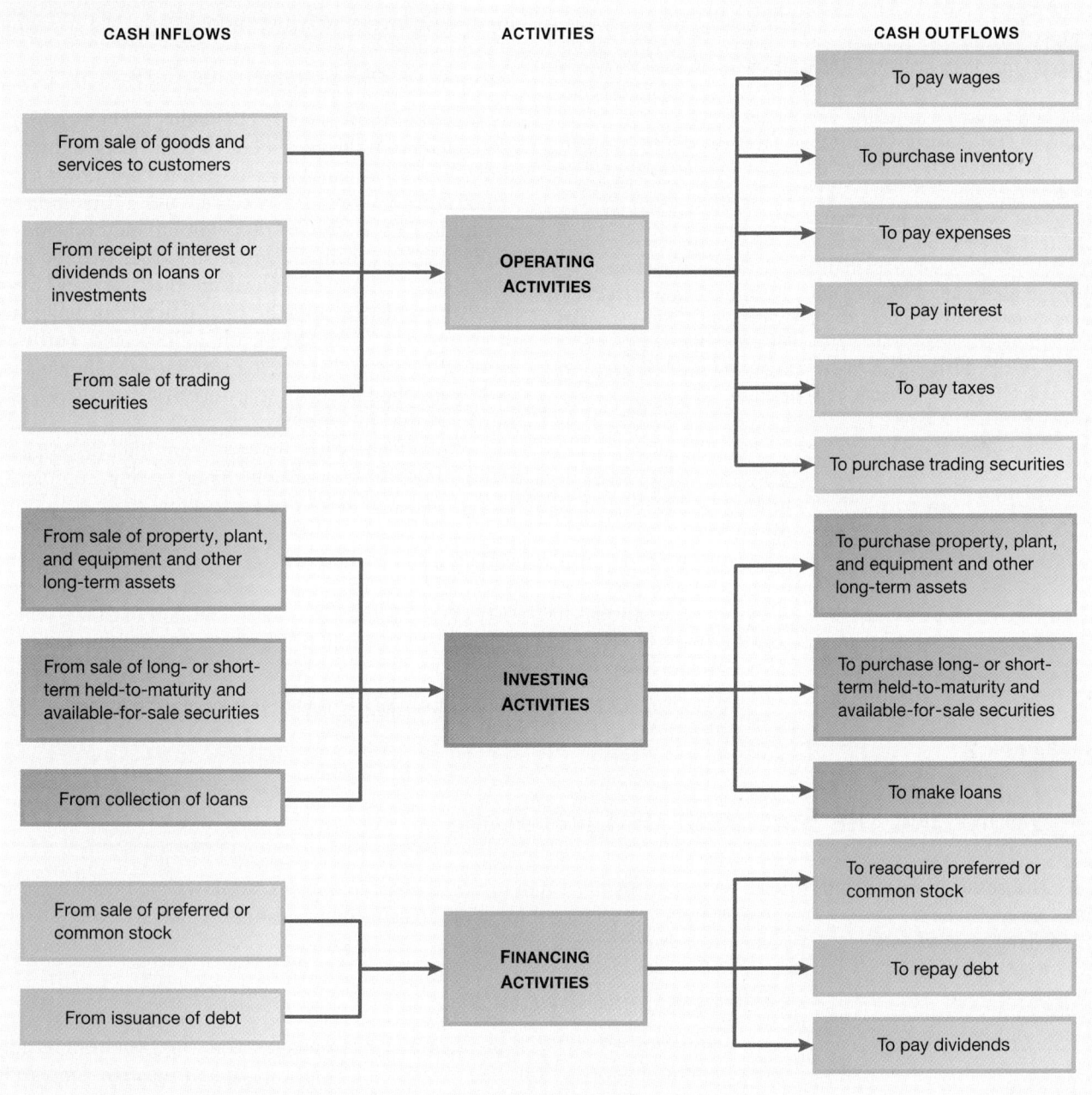

accounts payable or accrued liabilities are not considered repayments of loans under financing activities; they are classified as cash outflows under operating activities.

Companies occasionally engage in significant **noncash investing and financing transactions** involving only long-term assets, long-term liabilities, or stockholders' equity. For instance, a company might exchange a long-term asset for a long-term liability, settle a debt by issuing capital stock, or take out a long-term mortgage for the purchase of land and a building. Such transactions represent significant investing and financing activities, but they would not be reflected on the statement of cash flows because they do not involve either cash inflows or outflows. However, because such transactions will affect future cash flows, the FASB has determined

FOCUS ON INTERNATIONAL BUSINESS

How Universal Is the Statement of Cash Flows?

Despite the importance of the statement of cash flows in assessing the liquidity of companies in the United States, considerable variation in its use and format has existed in other countries. For example, the principal directives related to financial reporting for the European Union do not address the statement of cash flows. In many countries, the statement shows the change in working capital instead of the change in cash and cash equivalents. However, international accounting standards require the statement of cash flows, and international financial markets expect it to be presented. As a result, most multinational companies include the statement in their financial reports. Most European countries will adopt the statement of cash flows by 2006, when the European Union will require the use of international accounting standards.

that they should be disclosed in a separate schedule as part of the statement of cash flows. In this way, the reader of the statement can see the company's investing and financing activities more clearly.

FORMAT OF THE STATEMENT OF CASH FLOWS

As shown in the Financial Highlights at the beginning of this chapter, the statement of cash flows is divided into three sections. The first section, cash flows from operating activities, is presented using the indirect method. This is the most common method and is explained later in the chapter. The other two sections of the statement of cash flows are the cash flows from investing activities and the cash flows from financing activities. The individual cash inflows and outflows from investing and financing activities are shown separately in their respective categories. Normally, cash outflows for the purchase of plant assets are shown separately from cash inflows from the disposal of plant assets. However, because the inflows are not usually material, some companies follow the practice of combining these two lines in order to show the net amount of outflow.

www.marriott.com

A reconciliation of the beginning and ending balances of cash appears near the bottom of the statement. Again referring to the Financial Highlights, note that Marriott International had a net decrease in cash of $614 million in 2002, which together with the beginning balance of $812 million results in $198 million of cash and cash equivalents on hand at the end of the year.

✓ Check out ACE for a Review Quiz at http://accounting.college.hmco.com/students.

ANALYZING THE STATEMENT OF CASH FLOWS

LO2 Analyze the statement of cash flows.

RELATED TEXT ASSIGNMENTS
Q: 7, 8
SE: 2, 3
E: 2
P: 2, 3, 4, 6, 7
SD: 3, 4
FRA: 1, 2, 3, 4, 5, 6

www.marriott.com

Like the other financial statements, the statement of cash flows can be analyzed to reveal significant relationships. Two areas analysts examine when studying a company are cash-generating efficiency and free cash flow.

CASH-GENERATING EFFICIENCY

Cash-generating efficiency is the ability of a company to generate cash from its current or continuing operations. Three ratios are helpful in measuring cash-generating efficiency: cash flow yield, cash flows to sales, and cash flows to assets. We compute these ratios for Marriott International in 2002 using data from the Financial Highlights at the beginning of this chapter and those presented below.[3] All dollar amounts are stated in millions.

Financial Highlights for Marriott International
(In millions of dollars)

	2002	2001	2000
Net Sales	$8,441	$7,786	$7,911
Total Assets	8,296	9,107	8,237

ENRICHMENT NOTE: The
cash flow yield enables users to
assess whether sufficient cash
flows underlie earnings. Serious
questions would be raised if
cash flow yield was less than
1.0. For example, receivables
and inventories might be growing too fast, perhaps signaling a
slowdown in sales growth or a
problem in managing receivables collection or inventory
levels.

Cash flow yield is the ratio of net cash flows from operating activities to net
income, computed as follows:

$$\text{Cash Flow Yield} = \frac{\text{Net Cash Flows from Operating Activities}}{\text{Net Income}}$$

$$= \frac{\$516}{\$448}$$

$$= 1.2 \text{ times}$$

Marriott International has a good cash flow yield of 1.2 times; that is, the corporation's operating activities are generating about 20 percent more cash flow than net
income. If special items, such as discontinued operations, appear on the income
statement and are material, income from continuing operations should be used as
the denominator.

Cash flows to sales is the ratio of net cash flows from operating activities to
sales, computed as follows:

$$\text{Cash Flows to Sales} = \frac{\text{Net Cash Flows from Operating Activities}}{\text{Net Sales}}$$

$$= \frac{\$516}{\$8,441}$$

$$= 6.1\%$$

Marriott generates cash flows to sales of 6.1 percent. The company generated a positive but relatively small percentage of net cash from sales.

Cash flows to assets is the ratio of net cash flows from operating activities to
average total assets, computed as follows:

$$\text{Cash Flows to Assets} = \frac{\text{Net Cash Flows from Operating Activities}}{\text{Average Total Assets}}$$

$$= \frac{\$516}{(\$8,296 + \$9,107) \div 2}$$

$$= 5.9\%$$

● **STOP AND THINK!**
If cash flow yield is less than
1.0, would cash flows to sales
and cash flows to assets be
greater or less than profit margin and return on assets, respectively?
*Cash flows to sales and cash
flows to assets would be less than
profit margin and return on
assets, respectively, because a
cash flow yield of less than 1.0
means that cash flows from operations are less than net income.
Both are numerators in ratios
that have the same denomina-
tors.* ■

The cash flows to assets ratio is slightly less than the cash flows to sales ratio because
Marriott International has a good asset turnover ratio (sales ÷ average total assets)
of approximately .97 times (5.9% ÷ 6.1%). Cash flows to sales and cash flows to
assets are closely related to the profitability measures of profit margin and return on
assets. They exceed those measures by the amount of the cash flow yield ratio
because cash flow yield is the ratio of net cash flows from operating activities to
net income.

Although Marriott's cash flow yield and cash flows to assets are relatively good,
its efficiency at generating cash flows from operating activities, as measured by cash
flows to sales, could be improved.

FREE CASH FLOW

www.marriott.com

In 2002, Marriott had a net cash outflow of $317 million for investing activities,
which could indicate that the company was expanding. However, that figure
mixes capital expenditures for plant assets, which reflect management's expansion of operations, with loan advances and collections. Cash flows from financing
activities used $1,447 million, but that figure combines financing activities asso-
ciated with long-term debt and stocks with dividends paid to stockholders. While
something can be learned by looking at those broad categories, many analysts

FOCUS ON BUSINESS PRACTICE

What Do You Mean, "Free Cash Flow"?

Because the statement of cash flows has been around for less than 20 years, no generally accepted analyses have yet been developed. For example, the term *free cash flow* is commonly used in the business press, but there is no agreement on its definition. An article in *Forbes* defines *free cash flow* as "cash available after paying out capital expenditures and dividends, *but before taxes and interest*"[4] [emphasis added]. An article in

The Wall Street Journal defines it as "operating income less maintenance-level capital expenditures."[5] The definition with which we are most in agreement is the one used in *Business Week:* free cash flow is net cash flows from operating activities less net capital expenditures and dividends. This "measures truly discretionary funds—company money that an owner could pocket without harming the business."[6]

KEY POINT: Free cash flow should be interpreted in light of the company's overall need for cash. For instance, the purchase of treasury stock will reduce the amount of cash that is free for operating uses.

find it more informative to go beyond them to focus on a computation called free cash flow.

Free cash flow is the amount of cash that remains after deducting the funds a company must commit to continue operating at its planned level. The commitments must cover current or continuing operations, interest, income taxes, dividends, and net capital expenditures. Cash requirements for current or continuing operations, interest, and income taxes must be paid or the company's creditors and the government can take legal action. Although the payment of dividends is not strictly required, dividends normally represent a commitment to stockholders. If these payments are reduced or eliminated, stockholders will be unhappy and the price of the company's stock will fall. Net capital expenditures represent management's plans for the future.

If free cash flow is positive, it means that the company has met all its planned cash commitments and has cash available to reduce debt or to expand. A negative free cash flow means that the company will have to sell investments, borrow money, or issue stock in the short term to continue at its planned level. If free cash flow remains negative for several years, a company may not be able to raise cash by issuing stock or bonds.

Since cash commitments for current or continuing operations, interest, and income taxes are incorporated in cash flows from current operations, free cash flow for Marriott is computed as follows (in millions):

$$\text{K/R} \quad \text{Free Cash Flow} = \begin{array}{l} \text{Net Cash Flows from Operating Activities} - \text{Dividends} \\ - \text{Purchases of Plant Assets} + \text{Sales of Plant Assets} \end{array}$$

$$= \$516 - \$65 - \$292 + \$729$$

$$= \$888$$

FOCUS ON BUSINESS PRACTICE

Cash Flows Tell All.

In early 2001, the telecommunications industry began one of the biggest market crashes in history. Could it have been predicted? The telecommunications industry depends on heavy capital expenditures in equipment, such as cable lines and computers. When the cash flows from sales of 41 telecommunications companies are compared with their capital expenditures (a negative component of free cash flow) over the six years preceding the crash, an interesting pattern emerges. In the first three years, both cash flows from sales and capital expenditures were about 20 percent of sales. In other words,

free cash flows were neutral, with operations generating enough cash flows to cover capital expenditures. In the next three years, these measures diverged. Cash flows to sales stayed at about 20 percent of sales, but the companies increased capital expenditures dramatically, to 35 percent of sales. Thus, free cash flows turned very negative, and almost half of capital expenditures had to be financed by debt instead of operations, making these companies more vulnerable to the downturn in the economy that occurred in 2001.[7]

Purchases and sales of plant assets appear in the investing activities section of the statement of cash flows; Marriott reported both capital expenditures and dispositions of property and equipment. Dividends are in the financing activities section. Marriott had positive free cash flow of $888 million due mainly to its strong operating cash flow of $516 million and $729 million cash received on disposal of property and equipment. The cash used by financing activities was the largest in three years, $1,447 million, because Marriott repaid long-term debt of $946 million and convertible subordinated debt of $347 million. Marriott also issued common stock in the amount of $35 million and purchased treasury stock for $252 million.

Cash flows can vary from year to year, so it is best to look at trends in cash flow measures over several years when analyzing a company's cash flows. Marriott's cash flow yield was less in 2002 than in 2001 and thus should be watched in 2003. Management summed this up in the company's annual report:

Liquidity and Capital Resources
We consider [our credit] resources, together with cash we expect to generate from operations, adequate to meet our short-term and long-term liquidity requirements.[8]

 Check out ACE for a Review Quiz at http://accounting.college.hmco.com/students.

PREPARING THE STATEMENT OF CASH FLOWS: OPERATING ACTIVITIES

LO3 Use the indirect method to determine cash flows from operating activities.

RELATED TEXT ASSIGNMENTS
Q: 9, 10, 11, 12
SE: 4, 5, 8
E: 3, 4, 5, 9
P: 2, 3, 4, 6, 7
SD: 1, 4
FRA: 3, 5

KEY POINT: The direct and indirect methods relate only to the operating activities section of the statement of cash flows. They are both acceptable for financial reporting purposes.

To demonstrate the preparation of the statement of cash flows, we will work through an example step by step. The data for this example are presented in Exhibits 1 and 2, which show Ryan Corporation's balance sheets for December 31, 20x5 and 20x4, and its 20x5 income statement. Exhibit 1 shows the balance sheet accounts that we use for analysis and whether the change in each account is an increase or a decrease. Exhibit 2 contains data about transactions that affected non-current accounts. The company's accountants would identify those transactions from the records.

The first step in preparing the statement of cash flows is to determine cash flows from operating activities. The income statement indicates a business's success or failure in earning an income from its operating activities. However, because the income statement is prepared on an accrual basis, it does not reflect the inflow and outflow of cash from those activities. Revenues are recorded even though the cash for them may not have been received, and expenses are recorded even though the cash for them may not have been expended. Thus, to arrive at cash flows from operations, the figures on the income statement must be converted from an accrual basis to a cash basis. There are two methods of accomplishing this: the direct method and the indirect method. Under the **direct method**, each item on the income statement is adjusted from the accrual basis to the cash basis. The result is a statement that begins with cash receipts from sales and interest and deducts cash payments for purchases, operating expenses, interest payments, and income taxes to arrive at net cash flows from operating activities. The **indirect method** does not require the individual adjustment of each item on the income statement; it lists only the adjustments necessary to convert net income to cash flows from operations.

The direct and indirect methods always produce the same net figure. The direct method is more easily understood by the average reader because it results in a more straightforward presentation of operating cash flows than does the indirect method. However, the indirect method is the overwhelming choice of most companies and accountants. A survey of large companies shows that 99 percent use this method.[9] The indirect method is superior to the direct method from the analysts' perspective because its format begins with net income and derives cash flows from operations.

EXHIBIT 1
Comparative Balance Sheets with Changes in Accounts Indicated

Ryan Corporation
Comparative Balance Sheets
December 31, 20x5 and 20x4

	20x5	20x4	Change	Increase or Decrease
Assets				
Current assets				
Cash	$ 46,000	$ 15,000	$ 31,000	Increase
Accounts receivable (net)	47,000	55,000	(8,000)	Decrease
Inventory	144,000	110,000	34,000	Increase
Prepaid expenses	1,000	5,000	(4,000)	Decrease
Total current assets	$238,000	$185,000	$ 53,000	
Investments available for sale	$115,000	$127,000	($ 12,000)	Decrease
Plant assets				
Plant assets	$715,000	$505,000	$210,000	Increase
Accumulated depreciation	(103,000)	(68,000)	(35,000)	Increase
Total plant assets	$612,000	$437,000	$175,000	
Total assets	$965,000	$749,000	$216,000	
Liabilities				
Current liabilities				
Accounts payable	$ 50,000	$ 43,000	$ 7,000	Increase
Accrued liabilities	12,000	9,000	3,000	Increase
Income taxes payable	3,000	5,000	(2,000)	Decrease
Total current liabilities	$ 65,000	$ 57,000	$ 8,000	
Long-term liabilities				
Bonds payable	295,000	245,000	50,000	Increase
Total liabilities	$360,000	$302,000	$ 58,000	
Stockholders' Equity				
Common stock, $5 par value	$276,000	$200,000	$ 76,000	Increase
Paid-in capital in excess of par value, common	214,000	115,000	99,000	Increase
Retained earnings	140,000	132,000	8,000	Increase
Treasury stock	(25,000)	0	(25,000)	Increase
Total stockholders' equity	$605,000	$447,000	$158,000	
Total liabilities and stockholders' equity	$965,000	$749,000	$216,000	

KEY POINT: The indirect method begins with net income and adjusts up or down to produce net cash flows from operating activities.

The analyst can readily identify the factors that cause cash flows from operations. Further, from the company's standpoint, the indirect method is easier and less expensive to prepare. For these reasons, we use the indirect method in this book.

As illustrated in Figure 2, the indirect method focuses on items from the income statement that must be adjusted to reconcile net income to net cash flows

EXHIBIT 2
Income Statement and Other Information on Noncurrent Accounts

Ryan Corporation
Income Statement
For the Year Ended December 31, 20x5

Net sales		$698,000
Cost of goods sold		520,000
Gross margin		$178,000
Operating expenses (including depreciation expense of $37,000)		147,000
Operating income		$ 31,000
Other income (expenses)		
Interest expense	($23,000)	
Interest income	6,000	
Gain on sale of investments	12,000	
Loss on sale of plant assets	(3,000)	(8,000)
Income before income taxes		$ 23,000
Income taxes		7,000
Net income		$ 16,000

Other transactions affecting noncurrent accounts during 20x5:

1. Purchased investments in the amount of $78,000.
2. Sold investments that cost $90,000 for $102,000.
3. Purchased plant assets in the amount of $120,000.
4. Sold plant assets that cost $10,000 with accumulated depreciation of $2,000 for $5,000.
5. Issued $100,000 of bonds at face value in a noncash exchange for plant assets.
6. Repaid $50,000 of bonds at face value at maturity.
7. Issued 15,200 shares of $5 par value common stock for $175,000.
8. Purchased treasury stock in the amount of $25,000.
9. Paid cash dividends in the amount of $8,000.

from operating activities. The items that require adjustment are those that affect net income but not net cash flows from operating activities. They include depreciation and amortization, gains and losses, and changes in the balances of current asset and current liability accounts. The reconciliation of Ryan Corporation's net income to net cash flows from operating activities is shown in Exhibit 3. Each adjustment is discussed in the sections that follow.

FIGURE 2
Indirect Method of Determining Net Cash Flows from Operating Activities

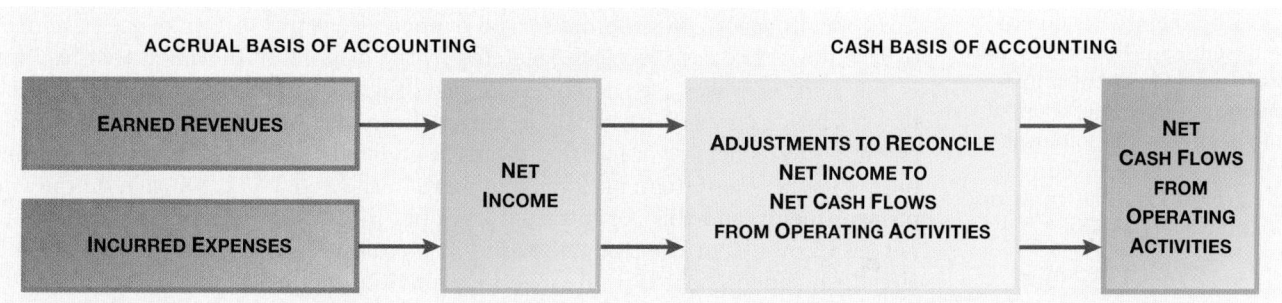

EXHIBIT 3
Schedule of Cash Flows from Operating Activities: Indirect Method

Ryan Corporation
Schedule of Cash Flows from Operating Activities
For the Year Ended December 31, 20x5

Cash flows from operating activities		
Net income		$16,000
Adjustments to reconcile net income to net		
cash flows from operating activities		
Depreciation expense	$37,000	
Gain on sale of investments	(12,000)	
Loss on sale of plant assets	3,000	
Changes in current assets and current liabilities		
Decrease in accounts receivable	8,000	
Increase in inventory	(34,000)	
Decrease in prepaid expenses	4,000	
Increase in accounts payable	7,000	
Increase in accrued liabilities	3,000	
Decrease in income taxes payable	(2,000)	14,000
Net cash flows from operating activities		$30,000

● **STOP AND THINK!**
If a company has positive earnings, can cash flows from operating activities ever be negative?

If a company has large gains, large increases in current assets, or decreases in current liabilities, the results could overwhelm the earnings and create negative cash flows from operating activities. ■

DEPRECIATION

Cash payments for plant assets, intangibles, and natural resources occur when the assets are purchased and are reflected as investing activities on the statement of cash flows at that time. When depreciation expense, amortization expense, and depletion expense appear on the income statement, they simply indicate allocations of the costs of the original purchases to the current accounting period; they do not affect net cash flows in the current period. The amount of such expenses can usually be found by referring to the income statement or a note to the financial statements. For Ryan Corporation, the income statement reveals depreciation expense of $37,000, which would have been recorded as follows:

KEY POINT: Operating expenses on the income statement include depreciation expense, which does not require a cash outlay.

A = L + OE
–   –

Depreciation Expense	37,000	
Accumulated Depreciation		37,000
To record annual depreciation on plant assets		

The recording of depreciation involved no outlay of cash even though depreciation expense appears on the income statement. Thus, to derive cash flows from operations, an adjustment for depreciation is needed to increase net income by the amount of depreciation recorded.

GAINS AND LOSSES

STUDY NOTE: Gains and losses by themselves do not represent cash flows; they are merely bookkeeping adjustments. For example, when a long-term asset is sold, it is the *proceeds* (cash received), not the gain or loss, that constitute cash flow.

Gains and losses that appear on the income statement also do not affect cash flows from operating activities and need to be removed from this section of the statement of cash flows. The cash receipts generated by the disposal of the assets that resulted in the gains or losses are shown in the investing section of the statement of cash flows. Thus, gains and losses are removed from net income (preventing double counting) to reconcile net income to cash flows from operating activities. For example, on its income statement, Ryan Corporation showed a $12,000 gain on the sale of investments, and this is subtracted from net income to reconcile net income to net cash flows from operating activities. The reason for this is that the $12,000 is already included (added) in the investing activities section as part of the $102,000 cash from the sale of the investment. Because the gain is included in the calculation of net income, the $12,000 gain needs to be subtracted to prevent double counting. Also, Ryan Corporation showed a $3,000 loss on the sale of plant assets. Following the same logic, the $3,000 loss is already reflected in the $5,000 sale of plant assets in the investing activities section. Thus, the $3,000 is added to net income to reconcile net income to net cash flows from operating activities.

CHANGES IN CURRENT ASSETS

Decreases in current assets other than cash have positive effects on cash flows, and increases in current assets have negative effects on cash flows. A decrease in a current asset frees up invested cash, thereby increasing cash flow. An increase in a current asset consumes cash, thereby decreasing cash flow. For example, refer to the balance sheets and income statement for Ryan Corporation in Exhibits 1 and 2. Note that net sales in 20x5 were $698,000 and that Accounts Receivable decreased by $8,000. Thus, cash received from sales was $706,000, calculated as follows:

$$\$706,000 = \$698,000 + \$8,000$$

Collections were $8,000 more than sales recorded for the year. This relationship may be illustrated as follows:

Accounts Receivable

Sales to Customers	Beg. Bal.	55,000	706,000 → Cash Receipts from Customers
	→	698,000	
	End. Bal.	47,000	

Thus, to reconcile net income to net cash flows from operating activities, the $8,000 decrease in Accounts Receivable is added to net income.

Inventory may be analyzed in the same way. For example, Exhibit 1 shows that Inventory increased by $34,000 from 20x4 to 20x5. This means that Ryan Corporation expended $34,000 more in cash for purchases than was included in cost of goods sold on the income statement. As a result of this expenditure, net income is higher than the net cash flows from operating activities, so $34,000 must be deducted from net income. Using the same logic, the decrease of $4,000 in Prepaid Expenses is added to net income to reconcile net income to net cash flows from operating activities.

CHANGES IN CURRENT LIABILITIES

Changes in current liabilities have the opposite effects on cash flows from those of changes in current assets. Increases in current liabilities are added to net income, and decreases in current liabilities are deducted from net income to reconcile net income to net cash flows from operating activities. An increase in a current liability represents a postponement of a cash payment, which frees up cash and increases cash flow in the current period. A decrease in current liabilities consumes cash, thereby decreasing cash flow. For example, Exhibit 1 shows that Ryan Corporation had a $7,000 increase in accounts payable from 20x4 to 20x5. This means that Ryan Corporation paid $7,000 less to creditors than the amount of purchases indicates in cost of goods sold on the income statement. This relationship may be visualized as follows:

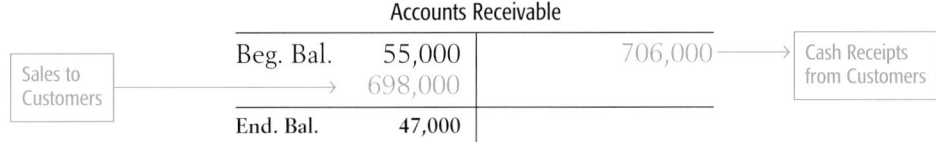

Accounts Payable

Cash Payments to Suppliers	← 547,000	Beg. Bal.	43,000
			554,000* ← Purchases
		End. Bal.	50,000

*Purchases = Cost of Goods Sold ($520,000) + Increase in Inventory ($34,000).

FOCUS ON BUSINESS PRACTICE

What's Your "Burn Rate"?

Why would a company have a total market value less than the amount of cash it has on hand? The answer is "burn rate." Burn rate is the pace at which companies use cash in their operations. A major contributor to the market crash of the stocks of dot-com companies was the difficulty these firms had in generating enough revenue to produce positive cash flows from operations. For example, when investors thought Webvan Group, Inc., the Internet grocer, would be the delivery service model of the future, the company was valued as high as $11.4 billion. However, as Webvan's burn rate reached $55 million a month, its market value dropped to a mere $132 million, even though the company had $212 million in cash.[10] The company was never able to generate sufficient revenues and soon declared bankruptcy.

As a result, $7,000 is added to net income to reconcile net income to net cash flows from operating activities. By the same logic, the increase of $3,000 in accrued liabilities is added to net income, and the decrease of $2,000 in income taxes payable is deducted from net income.

SCHEDULE OF CASH FLOWS FROM OPERATING ACTIVITIES

In summary, Exhibit 3 shows that by using the indirect method, net income of $16,000 has been adjusted by reconciling items totaling $14,000 to arrive at net cash flows from operating activities of $30,000. This means that although net income was $16,000, Ryan actually had net cash flows of $30,000 available from operating activities to use for purchasing assets, reducing debts, or paying dividends.

The effects of items on the income statement that do not affect cash flows may be summarized as follows:

	Add to or Deduct from Net Income
Depreciation expense	Add
Amortization expense	Add
Depletion expense	Add
Losses	Add
Gains	Deduct

The adjustments for increases and decreases in current assets and current liabilities may be summarized as follows:

	Add to Net Income	Deduct from Net Income
Current assets		
Accounts receivable (net)	Decrease	Increase
Inventory	Decrease	Increase
Prepaid expenses	Decrease	Increase
Current liabilities		
Accounts payable	Increase	Decrease
Accrued liabilities	Increase	Decrease
Income taxes payable	Increase	Decrease

✓ Check out ACE for a Review Quiz at http://accounting.college.hmco.com/students.

PREPARING THE STATEMENT OF CASH FLOWS: INVESTING ACTIVITIES

LO4 Determine cash flows from investing activities.

RELATED TEXT ASSIGNMENTS
Q: 13
SE: 6, 8
E: 6, 7, 8, 9
P: 2, 3, 4, 6, 7
SD: 4
FRA: 3, 5

To determine cash flows from investing activities, accounts involving cash receipts and cash payments from investing activities are examined individually. The objective is to explain the change in each account balance from one year to the next.

Investing activities center on the long-term assets shown on the balance sheet, but they also include transactions affecting short-term investments from the current assets section of the balance sheet and investment gains and losses from the income statement. The balance sheets in Exhibit 1 show that Ryan Corporation had long-term assets of investments and plant assets, but no short-term investments. The income statement in Exhibit 2 shows that Ryan had investment-related items in the form of a gain on the sale of investments and a loss on the sale of plant assets.

The schedule at the bottom of Exhibit 2 lists the following five items pertaining to investing activities in 20x5:

1. Purchased investments in the amount of $78,000.
2. Sold investments that cost $90,000 for $102,000.
3. Purchased plant assets in the amount of $120,000.
4. Sold plant assets that cost $10,000 with accumulated depreciation of $2,000 for $5,000.
5. Issued $100,000 of bonds at face value in a noncash exchange for plant assets.

The following sections analyze the accounts related to investing activities to determine their effects on Ryan Corporation's cash flows.

INVESTMENTS

The objective here is to explain Ryan Corporation's $12,000 decrease in investments, all of which are classified as available-for-sale securities. This is accomplished by analyzing the increases and decreases in the Investments account to determine the effects on the Cash account. Purchases increase investments, and sales decrease investments.

Item 1 in Ryan's list of investing activities shows purchases of $78,000 during 20x5. This transaction is recorded as follows:

A = L + OE
\+
−

Investments	78,000	
Cash		78,000
Purchase of investments		

The entry shows that the effect of this transaction is a $78,000 decrease in cash flows.

Item 2 in the list shows that Ryan sold investments that cost $90,000 for $102,000, resulting in a gain of $12,000. This transaction is recorded as follows:

A = L + OE
\+   +
−

Cash	102,000	
Investments		90,000
Gain on Sale of Investments		12,000
Sale of investments for a gain		

The effect of this transaction is a $102,000 increase in cash flows. Note that the gain on sale of investments is included in the $102,000. This is why we excluded it in computing cash flows from operations. If it had been included in that section, it would have been counted twice.

The $12,000 decrease in the Investments account (unrelated to the $12,000 gain above) during 20x5 has now been explained, as seen in the following T account:

Investments

Beg. Bal.	127,000	Sales	90,000
Purchases	78,000		
End. Bal.	115,000		

The cash flow effects from these transactions are shown in the investing activities section on the statement of cash flows as follows:

Purchase of investments	($ 78,000)
Sale of investments	102,000

Notice that purchases and sales are listed separately as cash outflows and inflows to give readers of the statement a complete view of investing activity. Some companies prefer to combine them into a single net amount.

If Ryan Corporation had short-term investments or marketable securities, the analysis of cash flows would be the same.

PLANT ASSETS

In the case of plant assets, it is necessary to explain the changes in both the Plant Assets account and the related Accumulated Depreciation account. According to Exhibit 1, Ryan Corporation's plant assets increased by $210,000, and accumulated depreciation increased by $35,000. Purchases increase plant assets, and sales decrease plant assets. Accumulated depreciation is increased by the amount of depreciation expense and decreased by the removal of the accumulated depreciation associated with plant assets that are sold. Three items listed in Exhibit 2 affect plant assets. Item **3** in the list indicates that Ryan Corporation purchased plant assets totaling $120,000 during 20x5, as shown by the following entry:

A = L + OE
+
−

Plant Assets	120,000	
Cash		120,000
Purchase of plant assets		

This transaction results in a cash outflow of $120,000.

Item **4** states that Ryan Corporation sold for $5,000 plant assets that cost $10,000 and had accumulated depreciation of $2,000, which resulted in a loss of $3,000. The entry to record this transaction is as follows:

A = L + OE
+   −
+
−

Cash	5,000	
Accumulated Depreciation	2,000	
Loss on Sale of Plant Assets	3,000	
Plant Assets		10,000
Sale of plant assets at a loss		

KEY POINT: Even though Ryan had a loss on the sale, it realized a positive cash flow of $5,000, which will be reported in the investing activities section of the statement of cash flows. When the indirect approach is used, the loss is eliminated with an "add-back" to net income.

Note that in this transaction the positive cash flow is equal to the amount of cash received, or $5,000. The loss on the sale of plant assets is included here, and excluded from the operating activities section (see page 721), by adjusting net income for the amount of the loss. The amount of a loss or gain on the sale of an asset is determined by the amount of cash received and does not represent a cash outflow or inflow.

The disclosure of these two transactions in the investing activities section of the statement of cash flows is as follows:

| Purchase of plant assets | ($120,000) |
| Sale of plant assets | 5,000 |

Cash outflows and cash inflows are listed separately here, though companies sometimes combine them into a single net amount, as they do the purchase and sale of investments.

Item **5** in Exhibit 2 is a noncash exchange that affects two long-term accounts, Plant Assets and Bonds Payable. It is recorded as follows:

A = L + OE
+   +

Plant Assets	100,000	
Bonds Payable		100,000
Issued bonds at face value for plant assets		

Although this transaction does not involve an inflow or outflow of cash, it is a significant transaction involving both an investing activity (the purchase of plant assets) and a financing activity (the issue of bonds payable). Because one purpose of the statement of cash flows is to show important investing and financing activities, the transaction is listed in a separate schedule, either at the bottom of the statement of cash flows or accompanying the statement, as follows:

Schedule of Noncash Investing and Financing Transactions

| Issue of bonds payable for plant assets | $100,000 |

Through our analysis of the preceding transactions and the depreciation expense for plant assets, we have now accounted for all the changes in the Plant Assets accounts, as shown in the following T accounts:

Plant Assets

Beg. Bal.	505,000	Sale	10,000
Cash Purchase	120,000		
Noncash Purchase	100,000		
End. Bal.	715,000		

Accumulated Depreciation

Sale	2,000	Beg. Bal.	68,000
		Dep. Expense	37,000
		End. Bal.	103,000

Had the balance sheet included specific plant asset accounts (e.g., Buildings and Equipment and related accumulated depreciation accounts) or other long-term asset accounts (e.g., Intangibles), the analysis would have been the same.

 Check out ACE for a Review Quiz at http://accounting.college.hmco.com/students.

PREPARING THE STATEMENT OF CASH FLOWS: FINANCING ACTIVITIES

LO5 Determine cash flows from financing activities.

RELATED TEXT ASSIGNMENTS
Q: 14
SE: 7, 8
E: 8, 9
P: 2, 3, 4, 6, 7
SD: 4
FRA: 3, 5

KEY POINT: Financing activities involve stockholders' equity accounts and short- and long-term borrowings. Because dividends paid involve retained earnings, they are appropriately included in this category.

The procedure for determining cash flows from financing activities is like the analysis of investing activities, including treatment of related gains or losses, but the accounts analyzed are short-term borrowings, long-term liabilities, and stockholders' equity accounts. Cash dividends from the statement of stockholders' equity must also be considered. Since Ryan Corporation does not have short-term borrowings, we deal only with long-term liabilities and stockholders' equity accounts.

These items from Exhibit 2 pertain to Ryan's financing activities in 20x5:

5. Issued $100,000 of bonds at face value in a noncash exchange for plant assets.
6. Repaid $50,000 of bonds at face value at maturity.
7. Issued 15,200 shares of $5 par value common stock for $175,000.
8. Purchased treasury stock for $25,000.
9. Paid cash dividends in the amount of $8,000.

BONDS PAYABLE

Exhibit 1 shows that Bonds Payable increased by $50,000 in 20x5. This account is affected by items **5** and **6**. Item **5** was analyzed in connection with plant assets. As noted above, it is reported on the schedule of noncash investing and financing transactions, but it must be remembered here in preparing the T account for Bonds Payable. Item **6** results in a cash outflow, which is recorded as follows:

A = L + OE
−   −

Bonds Payable	50,000	
Cash		50,000

    Repayment of bonds at face value
    at maturity

This appears in the financing activities section of the statement of cash flows as:

Repayment of bonds   ($50,000)

The following T account explains the change in Bonds Payable:

Bonds Payable

Repayment	50,000	Beg. Bal.	245,000
		Noncash Issue	100,000
		End. Bal.	295,000

If Ryan Corporation had any notes payable, the analysis would be the same.

COMMON STOCK

Like the Plant Asset account and its related accounts, related stockholders' equity accounts should be analyzed together. For example, Paid-in Capital in Excess of Par Value, Common should be examined with Common Stock. In 20x5, Ryan Corporation's Common Stock account increased by $76,000, and Paid-in Capital in Excess of Par Value, Common increased by $99,000. Those increases are explained by item 7 in the list in Exhibit 2, which states that Ryan issued 15,200 shares of $5 par value common stock for $175,000. The entry to record the cash inflow is as follows:

$A = L + OE$
$+ \quad +$
$+$

Cash	175,000	
Common Stock		76,000
Paid-in Capital in Excess of Par Value, Common		99,000
Issued 15,200 shares of $5 par value common stock		

STUDY NOTE: The purchase of treasury stock would also qualify as a financing activity, but would appear as a cash outflow.

This appears in the financing activities section of the statement of cash flows as:

Issue of common stock $175,000

The following analysis of this transaction is all that is needed to explain the changes in the two accounts during 20x5:

Common Stock			Paid-in Capital in Excess of Par Value, Common		
	Beg. Bal.	200,000		Beg. Bal.	115,000
	Issue	76,000		Issue	99,000
	End. Bal.	276,000		End. Bal.	214,000

RETAINED EARNINGS

At this point, we have dealt with several items that affect retained earnings. For instance, we used Ryan's net income in the analysis of cash flows from operating activities. The only other item affecting Ryan's retained earnings is the payment of $8,000 in cash dividends (item 9 in Exhibit 2), which is recorded as follows:

$A = L + OE$
$- \quad -$

Retained Earnings	8,000	
Cash		8,000
Cash dividends for 20x5		

Ryan Corporation would have declared the dividend before paying it and therefore would have debited the Cash Dividends Declared account instead of Retained Earnings, but after paying the dividend and closing the Cash Dividends Declared account to Retained Earnings, the effect is as shown. Cash dividends are displayed in the financing activities section of the statement of cash flows as follows:

KEY POINT: It is dividends paid, not dividends declared, that appear on the statement of cash flows.

Payment of dividends   ($8,000)

The following T account shows the change in the Retained Earnings account:

Retained Earnings			
Dividends	8,000	Beg. Bal.	132,000
		Net Income	16,000
		End. Bal.	140,000

TREASURY STOCK

As noted in the chapter on contributed capital, many companies buy back their own stock on the open market. These buybacks use cash, as this entry shows:

$A = L + OE$
$- \quad -$

Treasury Stock	25,000	
Cash		25,000

This use of cash is classified in the statement of cash flows as a financing activity:

● **Stop and Think!**
In computing free cash flow, what is an argument for treating purchases of treasury stock like dividend payments?

Both purchases of treasury stock and dividend payments represent payments to stockholders. Each diverts cash from productive use in the business (as assets), and thus each reduces free cash flow. ■

Exhibit 4
Statement of Cash Flows: Indirect Method

Purchase of treasury stock   ($25,000)

The T account for this transaction is as follows:

Treasury Stock	
Purchase 25,000	

We have now analyzed all Ryan's income statement items, explained all balance sheet changes, and taken all additional data into account. The resulting information can now be assembled into the statement of cash flows shown in Exhibit 4.

Ryan Corporation
Statement of Cash Flows
For the Year Ended December 31, 20x5

Cash flows from operating activities		
Net income		$ 16,000
Adjustments to reconcile net income to net cash flows from operating activities		
Depreciation expense	$ 37,000	
Gain on sale of investments	(12,000)	
Loss on sale of plant assets	3,000	
Changes in current assets and current liabilities		
Decrease in accounts receivable	8,000	
Increase in inventory	(34,000)	
Decrease in prepaid expenses	4,000	
Increase in accounts payable	7,000	
Increase in accrued liabilities	3,000	
Decrease in income taxes payable	(2,000)	14,000
Net cash flows from operating activities		$ 30,000
Cash flows from investing activities		
Purchase of investments	($ 78,000)	
Sale of investments	102,000	
Purchase of plant assets	(120,000)	
Sale of plant assets	5,000	
Net cash flows from investing activities		(91,000)
Cash flows from financing activities		
Repayment of bonds	($ 50,000)	
Issue of common stock	175,000	
Payment of dividends	(8,000)	
Purchase of treasury stock	(25,000)	
Net cash flows from financing activities		92,000
Net increase (decrease) in cash		$ 31,000
Cash at beginning of year		15,000
Cash at end of year		$ 46,000
Schedule of Noncash Investing and Financing Transactions		
Issue of bonds payable for plant assets		$100,000

✔ Check out ACE for a Review Quiz at http://accounting.college.hmco.com/students.

Chapter Review

REVIEW OF LEARNING OBJECTIVES

LO1 State the principal purposes and uses of the statement of cash flows, and identify its components.

The statement of cash flows explains the changes in cash and cash equivalents from one accounting period to the next by showing cash inflows and outflows from the operating, investing, and financing activities of a company for an accounting period. For the statement of cash flows, *cash* is defined as including both cash and cash equivalents. The primary purpose of the statement is to provide information about a firm's cash receipts and cash payments during an accounting period. A secondary purpose is to provide information about a firm's operating, investing, and financing activities.

Cash flows may be classified as stemming from (1) operating activities, which include the cash effects of transactions and other events that enter into the determination of net income; (2) investing activities, which include the acquisition and sale of marketable securities and property, plant, and equipment, and the making and collecting of loans, excluding interest; or (3) financing activities, which include obtaining resources from stockholders and creditors and providing the former with a return on their investments and the latter with repayment. Noncash investing and financing transactions are also important because they affect future cash flows; these exchanges of long-term assets or liabilities are of interest to potential investors and creditors.

LO2 Analyze the statement of cash flows.

In analyzing a firm's statement of cash flows, analysts tend to focus on cash-generating efficiency and free cash flow. Cash-generating efficiency is a firm's ability to generate cash from its current or continuing operations. Three ratios used in measuring cash-generating efficiency are cash flow yield, cash flows to sales, and cash flows to assets. Free cash flow is the cash that remains after deducting the funds a firm must commit to continue operating at its planned level. Such commitments must cover current or continuing operations, interest, income taxes, dividends, and net capital expenditures.

LO3 Use the indirect method to determine cash flows from operating activities.

The indirect method adjusts net income for all noncash effects and for items that need to be converted from an accrual to a cash basis to arrive at a cash flow basis, as follows:

Cash flows from operating activities
Net income		xxx
Adjustments to reconcile net income to net cash flows from operating activities (list of individual items)	xxx	xxx
Net cash flows from operating activities		xxx

LO4 Determine cash flows from investing activities.

Cash flows from investing activities are determined by identifying the cash flow effects of the transactions that affect each account relevant to investing activities. Such accounts include all long-term assets and short-term marketable securities.

LO5 Determine cash flows from financing activities.

The procedure for determining cash flows from financing activities is almost identical to that for investing activities. The difference is that the accounts involved are short-term borrowings, long-term liabilities, and stockholders' equity. The effects of gains and losses reported on the income statement must also be considered. After the changes in the balance sheet accounts from one accounting period to the next have been explained, all the cash flow effects should have been identified.

REVIEW OF CONCEPTS AND TERMINOLOGY

The following concepts and terms were introduced in this chapter:

LO1 **Cash:** For purposes of the statement of cash flows, both cash and cash equivalents.

LO1 **Cash equivalents:** Short-term (90 days or less), highly liquid investments, including money market accounts, commercial paper, and U.S. Treasury bills.

LO2 **Cash flows to assets:** The ratio of net cash flows from operating activities to average total assets.

LO2 Cash flows to sales: The ratio of net cash flows from operating activities to sales.

LO2 Cash flow yield: The ratio of net cash flows from operating activities to net income.

LO2 Cash-generating efficiency: The ability of a company to generate cash from its current or continuing operations.

LO3 Direct method: The procedure for converting the income statement from an accrual basis to a cash basis by separately adjusting each item on the income statement.

LO1 Financing activities: Business activities that involve obtaining resources from stockholders and creditors and providing the former with a return on their investments and the latter with repayment.

LO2 Free cash flow: The amount of cash that remains after deducting the funds a company must commit to continue operating at its planned level; net cash flows from operating activities minus dividends paid minus net capital expenditures.

LO3 Indirect method: The procedure for converting the income statement from an accrual basis to a cash basis by adjusting net income for items that do not affect cash flows, including depreciation, amortization, depletion, gains, losses, and changes in current assets and current liabilities.

LO1 Investing activities: Business activities that involve the acquisition and sale of long-term assets and marketable securities, other than trading securities or cash equivalents, and the making and collecting of loans.

LO1 Noncash investing and financing transactions: Significant investing and financing transactions involving only long-term assets, long-term liabilities, or stockholders' equity that do not affect current cash inflows or outflows.

LO1 Operating activities: Business activities that involve the cash effects of transactions and other events that enter into the determination of net income.

LO1 Statement of cash flows: A financial statement that shows how a company's operating, investing, and financing activities have affected cash during an accounting period.

REVIEW PROBLEM

The Statement of Cash Flows

LO2
LO3 Northwest Corporation's 20x5 income statement appears below. Its comparative bal-
LO4 ance sheets for 20x5 and 20x4 are presented on the next page.
LO5

Northwest Corporation
Income Statement
For the Year Ended December 31, 20x5

Net sales		$1,650,000
Cost of goods sold		920,000
Gross margin		$ 730,000
Operating expenses (including depreciation expense of $12,000 on buildings and $23,100 on equipment, and amortization expense of $4,800)		470,000
Operating income		$ 260,000
Other income (expenses)		
Interest expense	($ 55,000)	
Dividend income	3,400	
Gain on sale of investments	12,500	
Loss on disposal of equipment	(2,300)	(41,400)
Income before income taxes		$ 218,600
Income taxes		52,200
Net income		$ 166,400

Northwest Corporation
Comparative Balance Sheets
December 31, 20x5 and 20x4

	20x5	20x4	Change	Increase or Decrease
Assets				
Cash	$ 105,850	$ 121,850	($16,000)	Decrease
Accounts receivable (net)	296,000	314,500	(18,500)	Decrease
Inventory	322,000	301,000	21,000	Increase
Prepaid expenses	7,800	5,800	2,000	Increase
Long-term investments	36,000	86,000	(50,000)	Decrease
Land	150,000	125,000	25,000	Increase
Buildings	462,000	462,000	—	—
Accumulated depreciation, buildings	(91,000)	(79,000)	(12,000)	Increase
Equipment	159,730	167,230	(7,500)	Decrease
Accumulated depreciation, equipment	(43,400)	(45,600)	2,200	Decrease
Intangible assets	19,200	24,000	(4,800)	Decrease
Total assets	$1,424,180	$1,482,780	($58,600)	
Liabilities and Stockholders' Equity				
Accounts payable	$ 133,750	$ 233,750	($100,000)	Decrease
Notes payable (current)	75,700	145,700	(70,000)	Decrease
Accrued liabilities	5,000	—	5,000	Increase
Income taxes payable	20,000	—	20,000	Increase
Bonds payable	210,000	310,000	(100,000)	Decrease
Mortgage payable	330,000	350,000	(20,000)	Decrease
Common stock, $10 par value	400,000	340,000	60,000	Increase
Paid-in capital in excess of par value, common	90,000	50,000	40,000	Increase
Retained earnings	209,730	93,330	116,400	Increase
Treasury stock	(50,000)	(40,000)	(10,000)	Increase
Total liabilities and stockholders' equity	$1,424,180	$1,482,780	($ 58,600)	

The company's records for 20x5 provide the following additional information:

a. Long-term investments (available-for-sale securities) that cost $70,000 were sold at a gain of $12,500; additional long-term investments were made in the amount of $20,000.

b. Five acres of land to build a parking lot were purchased for $25,000.

c. Equipment that cost $37,500 with accumulated depreciation of $25,300 was sold at a loss of $2,300; new equipment costing $30,000 was purchased.

d. Notes payable in the amount of $100,000 were repaid; an additional $30,000 was borrowed by signing notes payable.

e. Bonds payable in the amount of $100,000 were converted into 6,000 shares of common stock.

f. The Mortgage Payable account was reduced by $20,000.

g. Cash dividends declared and paid were $50,000.

h. Treasury stock was purchased for $10,000.

REQUIRED ▶ 1. Prepare a statement of cash flows using the indirect method.

2. Compute cash flow yield, cash flows to sales, cash flows to assets, and free cash flow for 20x5.

ANSWER TO REVIEW PROBLEM

1. Statement of cash flows using the indirect method:

Northwest Corporation
Statement of Cash Flows
For the Year Ended December 31, 20x5

Cash flows from operating activities		
Net income		$166,400
Adjustments to reconcile net income		
to net cash flows from operating activities		
Depreciation expense, buildings	$ 12,000	
Depreciation expense, equipment	23,100	
Amortization expense, intangible assets	4,800	
Gain on sale of investments	(12,500)	
Loss on disposal of equipment	2,300	
Changes in current assets and current		
liabilities		
Decrease in accounts receivable	18,500	
Increase in inventory	(21,000)	
Increase in prepaid expenses	(2,000)	
Decrease in accounts payable	(100,000)	
Increase in accrued liabilities	5,000	
Increase in income taxes payable	20,000	(49,800)
Net cash flows from operating activities		$116,600
Cash flows from investing activities		
Sale of long-term investments	$ 82,500[a]	
Purchase of long-term investments	(20,000)	
Purchase of land	(25,000)	
Sale of equipment	9,900[b]	
Purchase of equipment	(30,000)	
Net cash flows from investing activities		17,400
Cash flows from financing activities		
Repayment of notes payable	($100,000)	
Issuance of notes payable	30,000	
Reduction in mortgage	(20,000)	
Payment of dividends	(50,000)	
Purchase of treasury stock	(10,000)	
Net cash flows from financing activities		(150,000)
Net increase (decrease) in cash		($ 16,000)
Cash at beginning of year		121,850
Cash at end of year		$105,850

Schedule of Noncash Investing and Financing Transactions

Conversion of bonds payable into common stock	$100,000

[a]$70,000 + $12,500 (gain) = $82,500
[b]$37,500 − $25,300 = $12,200 (book value) − $2,300 (loss) = $9,900

2. Cash flow yield, cash flows to sales, cash flows to assets, and free cash flow for 20x5:

$$\text{Cash Flow Yield} = \frac{\$116,600}{\$166,400} = .7 \text{ times}$$

$$\text{Cash Flows to Sales} = \frac{\$116,600}{\$1,650,000} = 7.1\%$$

$$\text{Cash Flows to Assets} = \frac{\$116,600}{(\$1,424,180 + \$1,482,780) \div 2} = 8.0\%$$

$$\text{Free Cash Flow} = \$116,600 - \$50,000 - \$25,000 - \$30,000 + \$9,900$$
$$= \$21,500$$

Chapter Assignments

BUILDING YOUR KNOWLEDGE FOUNDATION

QUESTIONS

1. In the statement of cash flows, what does cash include?

2. To earn a return on cash on hand during 20x3, Sallas Corporation transferred $45,000 from its checking account to a money market account, purchased a $25,000 Treasury bill, and invested $35,000 in common stocks. How will each of these transactions affect the statement of cash flows?

3. What are the purposes of the statement of cash flows?

4. Why is the statement of cash flows needed when most of the information in it is available from a company's comparative balance sheets and income statement?

5. What are the three classifications of cash flows? Give some examples of each.

6. Why is it important to disclose certain noncash transactions? How should they be disclosed?

7. Define *cash-generating efficiency* and identify three ratios that measure it.

8. Define *free cash flow* and identify its components. What do *positive* and *negative* free cash flows mean?

9. What is the basic difference between the direct method and the indirect method of determining cash flows from operations?

10. In determining net cash flows from operating activities (assuming the indirect method is used), what are the effects on cash generated by the following items: (a) an increase in accounts receivable, (b) a decrease in inventory, (c) an increase in accounts payable, (d) a decrease in wages payable, (e) depreciation expense, and (f) amortization of patents?

11. In 20x1, Cell-Borne Corporation had a net loss of $12,000 but positive cash flows from operations of $9,000. What conditions might have caused this situation?

12. Glen Corporation has the following other income and expense items: interest expense, $12,000; interest income, $3,000; dividend income, $5,000; and loss on the retirement of bonds, $6,000. Where does each of these items appear on the statement of cash flows, or how does the item affect the statement?

13. What is the proper treatment on the statement of cash flows of a transaction in which a building that cost $50,000 with accumulated depreciation of $32,000 was sold at a loss of $5,000?

14. What is the proper treatment on the statement of cash flows of (a) a transaction in which buildings and land were purchased by the issuance of a mortgage for

$234,000 and (b) a conversion of $50,000 in bonds payable into 2,500 shares of $6 par value common stock?

SHORT EXERCISES

<table>
<tr><td>

LO1 **Classification of Cash Flow Transactions**

</td><td>

SE 1. Stahl Corporation engaged in the transactions listed below. Identify each as (a) an operating activity, (b) an investing activity, (c) a financing activity, (d) a noncash transaction, or (e) none of the above.

1. Sold land.
2. Declared and paid a cash dividend.
3. Paid interest.
4. Issued common stock for plant assets.
5. Issued preferred stock.
6. Borrowed cash on a bank loan.

</td></tr>
<tr><td>

LO2 **Cash-Generating Efficiency Ratios and Free Cash Flow**

</td><td>

SE 2. In 20x5, Portillo Corporation had year-end assets of $550,000, net sales of $790,000, net income of $90,000, net cash flows from operating activities of $180,000, purchases of plant assets of $120,000, and sales of plant assets of $20,000, and it paid dividends of $40,000. In 20x4, year-end assets were $500,000. Calculate the cash-generating efficiency ratios of cash flow yield, cash flows to sales, and cash flows to assets. Also calculate free cash flow.

</td></tr>
<tr><td>

LO2 **Cash-Generating Efficiency Ratios and Free Cash Flow**

</td><td>

SE 3. Examine the cash flow measures in part **2** of the review problem in this chapter. Discuss the meaning of these ratios.

</td></tr>
<tr><td>

LO3 **Computing Cash Flows from Operating Activities: Indirect Method**

</td><td>

SE 4. Global Market Corporation had a net income of $33,000 during 20x4. During the year, the company had depreciation expense of $14,000. Accounts Receivable increased by $11,000, and Accounts Payable increased by $5,000. Those were the company's only current assets and current liabilities. Use the indirect method to determine net cash flows from operating activities.

</td></tr>
<tr><td>

LO3 **Computing Cash Flows from Operating Activities: Indirect Method**

</td><td>

SE 5. During 20x4, Cheng Corporation had a net income of $72,000. Included on its income statement were depreciation expense of $8,000 and amortization expense of $900. During the year, Accounts Receivable decreased by $4,100, Inventories increased by $2,700, Prepaid Expenses decreased by $500, Accounts Payable decreased by $7,000, and Accrued Liabilities decreased by $850. Use the indirect method to determine net cash flows from operating activities.

</td></tr>
<tr><td>

LO4 **Cash Flows from Investing Activities and Noncash Transactions**

</td><td>

SE 6. During 20x5, Okee Company purchased land for $750,000. It paid $250,000 in cash and signed a $500,000 mortgage for the rest. The company also sold a building that originally cost $180,000, on which it had $140,000 of accumulated depreciation, for $190,000 cash, making a gain of $150,000. Prepare the cash flows from investing activities and schedule of noncash investing and financing transactions sections of the statement of cash flows.

</td></tr>
<tr><td>

LO5 **Cash Flows from Financing Activities**

</td><td>

SE 7. During 20x4, Dakota Company issued $1,000,000 in long-term bonds at 96, repaid $150,000 of bonds at face value, paid interest of $80,000, and paid dividends of $50,000. Prepare the cash flows from the financing activities section of the statement of cash flows.

</td></tr>
<tr><td>

LO1 **Identifying Components of the**
LO3 **Statement of Cash Flows**
LO4
LO5

</td><td>

SE 8. Assuming the indirect method is used to prepare the statement of cash flows, tell whether each of the following items would appear (a) in cash flows from operating activities, (b) in cash flows from investing activities, (c) in cash flows from financing activities, (d) in the schedule of noncash investing and financing transactions, or (e) not on the statement of cash flows at all:

1. Dividends paid
2. Cash receipts from sales
3. Decrease in accounts receivable
4. Sale of plant assets
5. Gain on sale of investment
6. Issue of stock for plant assets
7. Issue of common stock
8. Net income

</td></tr>
</table>

EXERCISES

E 1.
LO1 Classification of Cash Flow Transactions

Trout Corporation engaged in the transactions listed below. Identify each transaction as (a) an operating activity, (b) an investing activity, (c) a financing activity, (d) a noncash transaction, or (e) not on the statement of cash flows. (Assume the indirect method is used.)

1. Declared and paid a cash dividend.
2. Purchased a long-term investment.
3. Increased accounts receivable.
4. Paid interest.
5. Sold equipment at a loss.
6. Issued long-term bonds for plant assets.
7. Increased dividends receivable on securities held.
8. Issued common stock.
9. Declared and issued a stock dividend.
10. Repaid notes payable.
11. Decreased wages payable.
12. Purchased a 60-day Treasury bill.
13. Purchased land.

E 2.
LO2 Cash-Generating Efficiency Ratios and Free Cash Flow

In 20x5, Ignatz Corporation had year-end assets of $4,800,000, net sales of $6,600,000, net income of $560,000, net cash flows from operating activities of $780,000, dividends of $240,000, and net capital expenditures of $820,000. In 20x4, year-end assets were $4,200,000.

Calculate the cash-generating efficiency ratios of cash flow yield, cash flows to sales, and cash flows to assets. Also calculate free cash flow.

E 3.
LO3 Cash Flows from Operating Activities: Indirect Method

The condensed single-step income statement for the year ended December 31, 20x4, of Gro-More Chem Company, a distributor of farm fertilizers and herbicides, appears as follows:

Sales		$6,500,000
Less: Cost of goods sold	$3,800,000	
Operating expenses (including depreciation of $410,000)	1,900,000	
Income taxes	200,000	5,900,000
Net income		$ 600,000

Selected accounts from Gro-More Chem Company's balance sheets for 20x4 and 20x3 are as follows:

	20x4	20x3
Accounts receivable, net	$1,200,000	$850,000
Inventory	420,000	510,000
Prepaid expenses	130,000	90,000
Accounts payable	480,000	360,000
Accrued liabilities	30,000	50,000
Income taxes payable	70,000	60,000

Present in good form a schedule of cash flows from operating activities using the indirect method.

E 4.
LO3 Computing Cash Flows from Operating Activities: Indirect Method

During 20x5, Germaine Corporation had net income of $41,000. Included on its income statement were depreciation expense of $2,300 and amortization expense of $300. During the year, Accounts Receivable increased by $3,400, Inventories decreased by $1,900, Prepaid Expenses decreased by $200, Accounts Payable increased by $5,000, and Accrued Liabilities decreased by $450. Determine net cash flows from operating activities using the indirect method.

E 5.
LO3 Preparing a Schedule of Cash Flows from Operating Activities: Indirect Method

For the year ended June 30, 20xx, net income for Pine Corporation was $7,400. Depreciation expense was $2,000. During the year, Accounts Receivable increased by $4,400, Inventories increased by $7,000, Prepaid Rent decreased by $1,400, Accounts Payable increased by $14,000, Salaries Payable increased by $1,000, and Income Taxes Payable decreased by $600. Use the indirect method to prepare a schedule of cash flows from operating activities.

E 6.
LO4 **Computing Cash Flows from Investing Activities: Investments**

FBR Company's T account for long-term available-for-sale investments at the end of 20x3 is as follows:

Investments			
Beg. Bal.	38,000	Sales	39,000
Purchases	58,000		
End Bal.	57,000		

In addition, FBR's income statement shows a loss on the sale of investments of $6,500. Compute the amounts to be shown as cash flows from investing activities and show how they are to appear in the statement of cash flows.

E 7.
LO4 **Computing Cash Flows from Investing Activities: Plant Assets**

The T accounts for plant assets and accumulated depreciation for FBR Company at the end of 20x3 are as follows:

Plant Assets					Accumulated Depreciation			
Beg. Bal.	65,000	Disposals	23,000		Disposals	14,700	Beg. Bal.	34,500
Purchases	33,600						Depreciation	10,200
End. Bal.	75,600						End. Bal.	30,000

In addition, FBR Company's income statement shows a gain on sale of plant assets of $4,400. Compute the amounts to be shown as cash flows from investing activities and show how they are to appear on the statement of cash flows.

E 8.
LO4 **Determining Cash Flows from**
LO5 **Investing and Financing Activities**

All transactions involving Notes Payable and related accounts of Wix Company during 20x4 are as follows:

Cash	18,000	
Notes Payable		18,000
Bank loan		
Patent	30,000	
Notes Payable		30,000
Purchase of patent by issuing note payable		
Notes Payable	5,000	
Interest Expense	500	
Cash		5,500
Repayment of note payable at maturity		

Determine the amounts of the transactions affecting financing activities and show how they are to appear on the statement of cash flows for 20x4.

E 9.
LO3 **Preparing the Statement of**
LO4 **Cash Flows: Indirect Method**
LO5

Margol Corporation's 20x5 income statement appears below. Its comparative balance sheets for June 30, 20x5 and 20x4 are on the next page.

Margol Corporation
Income Statement
For the Year Ended June 30, 20x5

Sales	$468,000
Cost of goods sold	312,000
Gross margin	$156,000
Operating expenses	90,000
Operating income	$ 66,000
Interest expense	5,600
Income before income taxes	$ 60,400
Income taxes	24,600
Net income	$ 35,800

Margol Corporation
Comparative Balance Sheets
June 30, 20x5 and 20x4

	20x5	20x4
Assets		
Cash	$139,800	$ 25,000
Accounts receivable (net)	42,000	52,000
Inventory	86,800	96,800
Prepaid expenses	6,400	5,200
Furniture	110,000	120,000
Accumulated depreciation, furniture	(18,000)	(10,000)
Total assets	$367,000	$289,000
Liabilities and Stockholders' Equity		
Accounts payable	$ 26,000	$ 28,000
Income taxes payable	2,400	3,600
Notes payable (long-term)	74,000	70,000
Common stock, $10 par value	230,000	180,000
Retained earnings	34,600	7,400
Total liabilities and stockholders' equity	$367,000	$289,000

The following information is also available: The company issued a $44,000 note payable for purchase of furniture; sold furniture that cost $54,000 with accumulated depreciation of $30,600 at carrying value; recorded depreciation on the furniture during the year, $38,600; repaid a note in the amount of $40,000; issued $50,000 of common stock at par value; and declared and paid dividends of $8,600.

Prepare Margol Corporation's statement of cash flows for the year 20x5 using the indirect method.

PROBLEMS

LO1 Classification of Cash Flow Transactions

P 1. Analyze each transaction listed in the table that follows and place X's in the appropriate columns to indicate the transaction's classification and its effect on cash flows using the indirect method.

Transaction	Cash Flow Classification				Effect on Cash Flows		
	Operating Activity	Investing Activity	Financing Activity	Noncash Transaction	Increase	Decrease	No Effect
1. Incurred a net loss.							
2. Declared and issued a stock dividend.							
3. Paid a cash dividend.							
4. Decreased accounts receivable.							
5. Increased inventory.							
6. Retired long-term debt with cash.							
7. Sold available-for-sale securities at a loss.							
8. Issued stock for equipment.							
9. Decreased prepaid insurance.							
10. Purchased treasury stock with cash.							
11. Retired a fully depreciated truck (no gain or loss).							
12. Increased interest payable.							
13. Decreased dividends receivable on investment.							
14. Sold treasury stock.							
15. Increased income taxes payable.							
16. Transferred cash to money market account.							
17. Purchased land and building with a mortgage.							

LO2 Statement of Cash Flows:
LO3 Indirect Method
LO4
LO5

P 2. Maron Corporation's comparative balance sheets as of December 31, 20x5 and 20x4 and its income statement for the year ended December 31, 20x5 are presented on the next page.

During 20x5, Maron Corporation sold furniture and fixtures that cost $35,600, on which it had accumulated depreciation of $28,800, at a gain of $7,000. The corporation also purchased furniture and fixtures in the amount of $39,600; paid a $20,000 note payable and borrowed $40,000 on a new note; converted bonds payable in the amount of $100,000 into 2,000 shares of common stock; and declared and paid $6,000 in cash dividends.

REQUIRED ▶ 1. Using the indirect method, prepare a statement of cash flows for Maron Corporation. Include a supporting schedule of noncash investing and financing transactions.

Maron Corporation
Comparative Balance Sheets
December 31, 20x5 and 20x4

	20x5	20x4
Assets		
Cash	$164,800	$ 50,000
Accounts receivable (net)	165,200	200,000
Merchandise inventory	350,000	450,000
Prepaid rent	2,000	3,000
Furniture and fixtures	148,000	144,000
Accumulated depreciation, furniture and fixtures	(42,000)	(24,000)
Total assets	$788,000	$823,000
Liabilities and Stockholders' Equity		
Accounts payable	$143,400	$200,400
Income taxes payable	1,400	4,400
Notes payable (long-term)	40,000	20,000
Bonds payable	100,000	200,000
Common stock, $20 par value	240,000	200,000
Paid-in capital in excess of par value, common	181,440	121,440
Retained earnings	81,760	76,760
Total liabilities and stockholders' equity	$788,000	$823,000

Maron Corporation
Income Statement
For the Year Ended December 31, 20x5

Net sales		$1,609,000
Cost of goods sold		1,127,800
Gross margin		$ 481,200
Operating expenses (including depreciation expense of $46,800)		449,400
Income from operations		$ 31,800
Other income (expenses)		
Gain on sale of furniture and fixtures	$ 7,000	
Interest expense	(23,200)	(16,200)
Income before income taxes		$ 15,600
Income taxes		4,600
Net income		$ 11,000

2. What are the primary reasons for Maron Corporation's large increase in cash from 20x4 to 20x5, despite its low net income?
3. Compute and assess cash flow yield and free cash flow for 20x5.

P 3. The comparative balance sheets for Pierre Fabrics, Inc., for December 31, 20x5, and 20x4 appear below.

LO2 **Statement of Cash Flows:**
LO3 **Indirect Method**
LO4
LO5

Pierre Fabrics, Inc.
Comparative Balance Sheets
December 31, 20x5 and 20x4

	20x5	20x4
Assets		
Cash	$ 38,560	$ 27,360
Accounts receivable (net)	102,430	75,430
Inventory	112,890	137,890
Prepaid expenses	—	20,000
Land	25,000	—
Building	137,000	—
Accumulated depreciation, building	(15,000)	—
Equipment	33,000	34,000
Accumulated depreciation, equipment	(14,500)	(24,000)
Patents	4,000	6,000
Total assets	$423,380	$276,680
Liabilities and Stockholders' Equity		
Accounts payable	$ 10,750	$ 36,750
Notes payable (current)	10,000	—
Accrued liabilities	—	12,300
Mortgage payable	162,000	—
Common stock, $10 par value	180,000	150,000
Paid-in capital in excess of par value, common	57,200	37,200
Retained earnings	3,430	40,430
Total liabilities and stockholders' equity	$423,380	$276,680

Additional information about Pierre Fabrics' operations during 20x5 is as follows: net loss, $28,000; building and equipment depreciation expense amounts, $15,000 and $3,000, respectively; equipment that cost $13,500 with accumulated depreciation of $12,500 sold for a gain of $5,300; equipment purchases, $12,500; patent amortization, $3,000; purchase of patent, $1,000; funds borrowed by issuing notes payable, $25,000; notes payable repaid, $15,000; land and building purchased for $162,000 by signing a mortgage for the total cost; 3,000 shares of $10 par value common stock issued for a total of $50,000; and cash dividend paid, $9,000.

REQUIRED ▶ 1. Using the indirect method, prepare a statement of cash flows for Pierre Fabrics, Inc.
2. Why did Pierre Fabrics have an increase in cash in a year in which it recorded a net loss of $28,000? Discuss and interpret.
3. Compute and assess cash flow yield and free cash flow for 20x5.

P 4. The comparative balance sheets for Maggio Masonry, Inc., for December 31, 20x5 and 20x4 are presented on the next page. During 20x5, the company had net income of $96,000 and building and equipment depreciation expenses of $80,000 and $60,000, respectively. It amortized intangible assets in the amount of $20,000; purchased

LO2 **Statement of Cash Flows:**
LO3 **Indirect Method**
LO4
LO5

Maggio Masonry, Inc.
Comparative Balance Sheets
December 31, 20x5 and 20x4

	20x5	20x4
Assets		
Cash	$ 257,600	$ 305,600
Accounts receivable (net)	738,800	758,800
Inventory	960,000	800,000
Prepaid expenses	14,800	26,800
Long-term investments	440,000	440,000
Land	361,200	321,200
Building	1,200,000	920,000
Accumulated depreciation, building	(240,000)	(160,000)
Equipment	480,000	480,000
Accumulated depreciation, equipment	(116,000)	(56,000)
Intangible assets	20,000	40,000
Total assets	$4,116,400	$3,876,400
Liabilities and Stockholders' Equity		
Accounts payable	$ 470,800	$ 660,800
Notes payable (current)	40,000	160,000
Accrued liabilities	10,800	20,800
Mortgage payable	1,080,000	800,000
Bonds payable	1,000,000	760,000
Common stock	1,300,000	1,300,000
Paid-in capital in excess of par value, common	80,000	80,000
Retained earnings	254,800	194,800
Treasury stock	(120,000)	(100,000)
Total liabilities and stockholders' equity	$4,116,400	$3,876,400

investments for $116,000; sold investments for $150,000, on which it recorded a gain of $34,000; issued $240,000 of long-term bonds at face value; purchased a warehouse and land through a $320,000 mortgage; paid $40,000 to reduce the mortgage; borrowed $60,000 by issuing notes payable; repaid notes payable in the amount of $180,000; declared and paid cash dividends in the amount of $36,000; and purchased treasury stock in the amount of $20,000.

REQUIRED ▶

1. Using the indirect method, prepare a statement of cash flows for Maggio Masonry, Inc.
2. Why did Maggio Masonry experience a decrease in cash in a year in which it had a net income of $96,000? Discuss and interpret.
3. Compute and assess cash flow yield and free cash flow for 20x5.

ALTERNATE PROBLEMS

P 5.

LO1 Classification of Cash Flow Transactions

Analyze each transaction listed in the table that follows and place X's in the appropriate columns to indicate the transaction's classification and its effect on cash flows using the indirect method.

Transaction	Cash Flow Classification				Effect on Cash Flows		
	Operating Activity	Investing Activity	Financing Activity	Noncash Trans-action	Increase	Decrease	No Effect
1. Earned a net income.							
2. Declared and paid a cash dividend.							
3. Issued stock for cash.							
4. Retired long-term debt by issuing stock.							
5. Increased accounts payable.							
6. Decreased inventory.							
7. Increased prepaid insurance.							
8. Purchased a long-term investment with cash.							
9. Sold trading securities at a gain.							
10. Sold a machine at a loss.							
11. Retired fully depreciated equipment.							
12. Decreased interest payable.							
13. Purchased available-for-sale securities (long-term).							
14. Decreased dividends receivable.							
15. Decreased accounts receivable.							
16. Converted bonds to common stock.							
17. Purchased 90-day Treasury bill.							

P 6.   Sulyat Corporation's income statement for 20x7 appears below.

LO2   **Statement of Cash Flows:**
LO3   **Indirect Method**
LO4
LO5

Sulyat Corporation
Income Statement
For the Year Ended June 30, 20x7

Net sales		$1,040,900
Cost of goods sold		656,300
Gross margin		$ 384,600
Operating expenses (including depreciation expense of $60,000)		189,200
Income from operations		$ 195,400
Other income (expenses)		
Loss on sale of equipment	($ 4,000)	
Interest expense	(37,600)	(41,600)
Income before income taxes		$ 153,800
Income taxes		34,200
Net income		$ 119,600

Sulyat Corporation's comparative balance sheets as of June 30, 20x7 and 20x6 are as follows:

Sulyat Corporation
Comparative Balance Sheets
June 30, 20x7 and 20x6

	20x7	20x6
Assets		
Cash	$167,000	$ 20,000
Accounts receivable (net)	100,000	120,000
Inventory	180,000	220,000
Prepaid expenses	600	1,000
Property, plant, and equipment	628,000	552,000
Accumulated depreciation, property, plant, and equipment	(183,000)	(140,000)
Total assets	$892,600	$773,000
Liabilities and Stockholders' Equity		
Accounts payable	$ 64,000	$ 42,000
Notes payable (due in 90 days)	30,000	80,000
Income taxes payable	26,000	18,000
Mortgage payable	360,000	280,000
Common stock, $5 par value	200,000	200,000
Retained earnings	212,600	153,000
Total liabilities and stockholders' equity	$892,600	$773,000

During 20x7, Sulyat Corporation sold equipment that cost $24,000, on which it had accumulated depreciation of $17,000, at a loss of $4,000. The corporation also purchased land and a building for $100,000 through an increase of $100,000 in Mortgage Payable; made a $20,000 payment on the mortgage; repaid notes of $80,000 but borrowed an additional $30,000 through the issuance of a new note payable; and declared and paid a $60,000 cash dividend.

REQUIRED ▶

1. Using the indirect method, prepare a statement of cash flows. Include a supporting schedule of noncash investing and financing transactions.
2. What are the primary reasons for Sulyat Corporation's large increase in cash from 20x6 to 20x7?
3. Compute and assess cash flow yield and free cash flow for 20x7.

P 7.

LO2   Statement of Cash Flows:
LO3   Indirect Method
LO4
LO5

The comparative balance sheets for Fernandez Fashions, Inc., for December 31, 20x6 and 20x5 appear on the next page. Additional information about Fernandez Fashions' operations during 20x6 is as follows: net income, $56,000; building and equipment depreciation expense amounts, $30,000 and $6,000, respectively; equipment that cost $27,000 with accumulated depreciation of $25,000 sold at a gain of $10,600; equipment purchases, $25,000; patent amortization, $6,000; purchase of patent, $2,000; funds borrowed by issuing notes payable, $50,000; notes payable repaid, $30,000; land and building purchased for $324,000 by signing a mortgage for the total cost; 3,000 shares of $20 par value common stock issued for a total of $100,000; cash dividend paid $18,000; and treasury stock purchased, $15,000.

Fernandez Fashions, Inc.
Comparative Balance Sheets
December 31, 20x6 and 20x5

	20x6	20x5
Assets		
Cash	$174,120	$ 54,720
Accounts receivable (net)	204,860	150,860
Inventory	225,780	275,780
Prepaid expenses	—	40,000
Land	50,000	—
Building	274,000	—
Accumulated depreciation, building	(30,000)	—
Equipment	66,000	68,000
Accumulated depreciation, equipment	(29,000)	(48,000)
Patents	8,000	12,000
Total assets	$943,760	$553,360
Liabilities and Stockholders' Equity		
Accounts payable	$ 21,500	$ 73,500
Notes payable	20,000	—
Accrued liabilities (current)	—	24,600
Mortgage payable	324,000	—
Common stock, $20 par value	370,000	310,000
Paid-in capital in excess of par value, common	114,400	74,400
Retained earnings	118,860	80,860
Treasury stock	(25,000)	(10,000)
Total liabilities and stockholders' equity	$943,760	$553,360

REQUIRED ▶

1. Using the indirect method, prepare a statement of cash flows for Fernandez Fashions, Inc.
2. Why did Fernandez Fashions have an increase in cash of $119,400 when it recorded net income of $56,000? Discuss and interpret.
3. Compute and assess cash flow yield and free cash flow for 20x6.

SKILLS DEVELOPMENT CASES

Conceptual Analysis

SD 1.
LO1   EBITDA and the Statement of
LO3   Cash Flows

When Fleetwood Enterprises, Inc. <www.fleetwood.com>, a large producer of recreational vehicles and manufactured housing, warned that it might not be able to generate enough cash to satisfy debt requirements and avoid default of a loan agreement, its cash flow, defined in the financial press as "EBITDA" (earnings before interest, taxes, depreciation, and amortization), was a negative $2.7 million. The company would have had to generate $17.7 million in the next accounting period to comply with the loan terms.[11] To what section of the statement of cash flows does EBITDA most closely relate? Is EBITDA a good approximation for this section of the statement of cash flows?

Explain your answer, which should include an identification of the major differences between EBITDA and the section of the statement of cash flows you chose.

Ethical Dilemma

LO1 **Ethics and Cash Flow Classifications**

SD 2. Chemical Waste Treatment, Inc., a fast-growing company that disposes of chemical wastes, has an $800,000 line of credit at its bank. One section in the credit agreement says that the ratio of cash flows from operations to interest expense must exceed 3.0. If this ratio falls below 3.0, the company must reduce the balance outstanding on its line of credit to one-half the total line if the funds borrowed against the line of credit exceed one-half of the total line.

After the end of the fiscal year, the company's controller informs the president: "We will not meet the ratio requirements on our line of credit in 20x5 because interest expense was $1.2 million and cash flows from operations were $3.2 million. Also, we have borrowed 100 percent of our line of credit. We do not have the cash to reduce the credit line by $400,000." The president says, "This is a serious situation. To pay our ongoing bills, we need our bank to increase our line of credit, not decrease it. What can we do?" "Do you recall the $500,000 two-year note payable for equipment?" replied the controller. "It is now classified as 'Proceeds from Notes Payable' in cash flows provided from financing activities in the statement of cash flows. If we move it to cash flows from operations and call it 'Increase in Payables,' it would increase cash flows from operations to $3.7 million and put us over the limit." "Well, do it," ordered the president. "It surely doesn't make any difference where it is on the statement. It is an increase in both places. It would be much worse for our company in the long term if we failed to meet this ratio requirement."

What is your opinion of the president's reasoning? Is the president's order ethical? Who benefits and who is harmed if the controller follows the president's order? What are management's alternatives? What would you do?

 Group Activity. Assign in-class groups to develop a position in support of or against the president's reasoning and have them defend that position in a debate.

Research Activity

LO1 **Basic Research Skills**
LO2

SD 3. Find the statement of cash flows in the annual reports of three corporations, using sources in your library or the Fingraph® Financial Analyst™ CD-ROM software that accompanies this text. You may choose corporations from the same industry or at random, at the direction of your instructor. (If you did a Research Activity in a previous chapter, use the same three companies.)

For any year covered by these companies' statements of cash flows, answer the following questions: Does the company use the direct or the indirect method? Is its net income more or less than its net cash flows from operating activities? What are the major causes of differences between net income and net cash flows from operating activities? Compute cash flow efficiency ratios and free cash flow for each company. Does the dividend appear secure? Did the company make significant capital expenditures during the year? How did the company finance the expenditures? Do you notice anything unusual about the investing and financing activities of these three companies? Do the investing and financing activities provide any insights into management's plan for each company? If so, what are they?

Be prepared to discuss your findings in class.

Decision-Making Practice

LO2 **Analysis of Cash Flow**
LO3 **Difficulty**
LO4
LO5

SD 4. Lou Klein, certified public accountant, has just given his employer May Hashimi, the president of Hashimi Print Gallery, Inc., the income statement that appears at the top of the next page.

Hashimi Print Gallery, Inc.
Income Statement
For the Year Ended December 31, 20x4

Net sales	$884,000
Cost of goods sold	508,000
Gross margin	$376,000
Operating expenses (including depreciation expense of $20,000)	204,000
Operating income	$172,000
Interest expense	24,000
Income before income taxes	$148,000
Income taxes	28,000
Net income	$120,000

After examining the statement, Hashimi said to Klein, "Lou, the statement seems to be well done, but what I need to know is why I don't have enough cash to pay my bills this month. You show that I earned $120,000 in 20x4, but I have only $24,000 in the bank. I know I bought a building on a mortgage and paid a cash dividend of $48,000, but what else is going on?" Klein replied, "To answer your question, we have to look at comparative balance sheets and prepare another type of statement. Take a look at these balance sheets." The statement handed to Hashimi follows.

Hashimi Print Gallery, Inc.
Comparative Balance Sheets
December 31, 20x4 and 20x3

	20x4	20x3
Assets		
Cash	$ 24,000	$ 40,000
Accounts receivable (net)	178,000	146,000
Inventory	240,000	180,000
Prepaid expenses	10,000	14,000
Building	400,000	—
Accumulated depreciation	(20,000)	—
Total assets	$832,000	$380,000
Liabilities and Stockholders' Equity		
Accounts payable	$ 74,000	$ 96,000
Income taxes payable	6,000	4,000
Mortgage payable	400,000	—
Common stock	200,000	200,000
Retained earnings	152,000	80,000
Total liabilities and stockholders' equity	$832,000	$380,000

1. To what statement is Klein referring? From the information given, prepare the additional statement using the indirect method.
2. Hashimi Print Gallery, Inc., has a cash problem despite profitable operations. Why is this the case?

FINANCIAL REPORTING AND ANALYSIS CASES

Interpreting Financial Reports

FRA 1.

LO2   Anatomy of a Disaster

On October 16, 2001, Kenneth Lay, chairman and CEO of Enron Corporation <www.enron.com>, announced the company's earnings for the first nine months of 2001 as follows:

> Our 26 percent increase in recurring earnings per diluted share shows the very strong results of our core wholesale and retail energy businesses and our natural gas pipelines. The continued excellent prospects in these businesses and Enron's leading market position make us very confident in our strong earnings outlook.[12]

Less than six months later, the company filed for the biggest bankruptcy in U.S. history. Its stock dropped to less than $1 per share, and a major financial scandal was underway. Presented on the opposite page is Enron's statement of cash flows for the first nine months of 2001 and 2000 (restated to correct the previous accounting errors). Assume you report to an investment analyst who has asked you to analyze this statement for clues as to why the company went under.

1. For the two time periods shown, compute the cash-generating efficiency ratios of cash flow yield, cash flows to sales (Enron's revenues were $133,762 million in 2001 and $55,494 million in 2000), and cash flows to assets (use total assets of $61,783 million for 2001 and $64,926 million for 2000). Also compute free cash flows for the two years.
2. Prepare a memorandum to the investment analyst that assesses Enron's cash-generating efficiency in light of the chairman's remarks and that evaluates its available free cash flow, taking into account its financing activities. Identify significant changes in operating items and any special operating items that should be considered. Include your computations as an attachment.

International Company

FRA 2.

LO2   Cash-Generating Efficiency Ratios and Free Cash Flow

The following data pertain to two of Japan's best-known and most successful companies, Sony Corporation <www.sony.com> and Canon, Inc. <www.canon.com>.[13] (Numbers are in billions of yen.)

	Sony Corporation		Canon, Inc.	
	2000	1999	2000	1999
Net sales	¥6,238	¥6,415	¥2,781	¥2,622
Net income	122	179	134	70
Average total assets	6,579	6,351	2,711	2,658
Net cash flows from operating activities	597	663	347	309
Dividends	21	25	15	15
Net capital expenditures	374	340	165	194

Calculate the ratios of cash flow yield, cash flows to sales, and cash flows to assets, as well as free cash flow, for the two years for both Sony Corporation and Canon, Inc.

Enron Corporation
Statement of Cash Flows
For the Nine Months Ending September 30, 2001 and 2002

	2001	2000
	(In millions)	
Cash Flows from Operating Activities		
Reconciliation of net income to net cash provided by operating activities		
Net income	$ 225	$ 797
Cumulative effect of accounting changes, net of tax	(19)	0
Depreciation, depletion and amortization	746	617
Deferred income taxes	(134)	8
Gains on sales of non-trading assets	(49)	(135)
Investment losses	768	0
Changes in components of working capital		
Receivables	987	(3,363)
Inventories	1	339
Payables	(1,764)	2,899
Other	464	(455)
Trading investments		
Net margin deposit activity	(2,349)	541
Other trading activities	173	(555)
Other, net	198	(566)
Net Cash Provided by (Used in) Operating Activities	$ (753)	$ 127
Cash Flows from Investing Activities		
Capital expenditures	(1,584)	(1,539)
Equity investments	(1,172)	(858)
Proceeds from sales of non-trading investments	1,711	222
Acquisition of subsidiary stock	0	(485)
Business acquisitions, net of cash acquired	(82)	(773)
Other investing activities	(239)	(147)
Net Cash Used in Investing Activities	$(1,366)	$(3,580)
Cash Flows from Financing Activities		
Issuance of long-term debt	4,060	2,725
Repayment of long-term debt	(3,903)	(579)
Net increase in short-term borrowings	2,365	1,694
Issuance of common stock	199	182
Net redemption of company-obligated preferred securities of subsidiaries	0	(95)
Dividends paid	(394)	(396)
Net (acquisition) disposition of treasury stock	(398)	354
Other financing activities	(49)	(12)
Net Cash Provided by Financing Activities	$ 1,880	$ 3,873
Increase (Decrease) in Cash and Cash Equivalents	$ (239)	$ 420
Cash and Cash Equivalents, Beginning of Period	1,240	333
Cash and Cash Equivalents, End of Period	$ 1,001	$ 753

Source: Adapted from Enron Corporation, SEC filings, 2001.

Which company is most efficient in generating cash flow? Which company has the best year-to-year trend? Which company do you think will most probably need external financing?

Toys "R" Us Annual Report

FRA 3.

LO1 **Analysis of the Statement of**
LO2 **Cash Flows**
LO3
LO4
LO5

Refer to the statement of cash flows in the Toys "R" Us <www.tru.com> annual report to answer the following questions:

1. Does Toys "R" Us use the indirect method of reporting cash flows from operating activities? Other than net earnings, what are the most important factors affecting the company's cash flows from operating activities? Explain the trend of each of these factors.
2. Based on the cash flows from investing activities, would you say that Toys "R" Us is a contracting or an expanding company? Explain.
3. Has Toys "R" Us used external financing? If so, where did it come from?

Comparison Case: Toys "R" Us and Walgreen Co.

FRA 4.

LO2 **Cash Flows Analysis**

Refer to the annual report of Toys "R" Us <www.tru.com> and the financial statements of Walgreens <www.walgreens.com> in the Supplement to Chapter 6. Calculate for two years each company's cash flow yield, cash flows to sales ratio, cash flows to assets ratio, and free cash flows. In 2000, Walgreens' total assets were $7,103,700,000. Discuss and compare the trends of the cash-generating ability of both Toys "R" Us and Walgreens. Comment on each company's change in cash and cash equivalents over the two-year period.

Fingraph® Financial Analyst™

FRA 5.

LO2 **Cash Flow Analysis**
LO3
LO4
LO5

Choose any two companies in the same industry from the list of Fingraph companies on the Needles Accounting Resource Center Web Site at http://accounting.college.hmco.com/students. Access the Microsoft Excel spreadsheets for the companies you selected. Click on the URL at the top of each company's spreadsheet for a link to the company's web site and annual report.

1. In the annual reports of the companies you have selected, find the statement of cash flows. Do the companies use the direct or indirect method of preparing the statement?
2. Using the Fingraph CD-ROM software, display and print in tabular and graphic form the Statement of Cash Flows: Operating Activities Analysis page. Prepare a table that compares the cash flow yield, cash flows to sales, and cash flows to assets ratios for both companies for two years. Are the ratios moving in the same direction or opposite ones? Study the operating activities sections of the statements to determine the main causes of differences between the net income and cash flows from operations. How do the companies compare?
3. Using the Fingraph CD-ROM software, display and print in tabular and graphic form the Statement of Cash Flows: Investing and Financing Activities Analysis page. Prepare a table that compares the free cash flow for both companies for two years. How do the companies compare? Are the companies growing or contracting? Study the investing and financing activities sections of the statements to determine the main causes of differences between the companies.
4. Find and read references to cash flows in the liquidity analysis section of management's discussion and analysis in each annual report.
5. Write a one-page executive summary that reports your findings from parts 1–4, including your assessment of the companies' comparative liquidity. Include the Fingraph pages and your tables with your report.

Internet Case

FRA 6.

LO2 **Follow-up Analysis of Cash Flows**

Go to Marriott International's web site <www.marriott.com> and find the statement of cash flows in the company's latest annual report. Compare it with the 2002 statement at the beginning of this chapter by (1) identifying major changes in operating, investing, and financing activities; (2) reading management's financial review of cash flows; and (3) calculating the cash flow ratios (cash flow yield, cash flows to sales, cash flows to assets) and free cash flow for the most recent year. How does Marriott's cash flow performance differ between these two years? Be prepared to discuss your conclusions in class.

Chapter 18 focuses on financial performance evaluation by internal and external users. The chapter describes the tools and techniques of financial analysis and ratio analysis.

Financial Performance Evaluation

LEARNING OBJECTIVES

LO1 Describe and discuss financial performance evaluation by internal and external users.

LO2 Describe and discuss the standards for financial performance evaluation.

LO3 Identify the sources of information for financial performance evaluation.

LO4 Apply horizontal analysis, trend analysis, vertical analysis, and ratio analysis to financial statements.

LO5 Apply ratio analysis to financial statements in a comprehensive evaluation of a company's financial performance.

DECISION POINT

A USER'S FOCUS

Sun Microsystems <www.sun.com> Sun Microsystems is a global leader in providing products and services for computer networking. A committee of its board of directors has developed a compensation package for top management that is linked to, among other things, financial performance measures, some of which are presented in the Financial Highlights. These measures are, in turn, linked to creating shareholder value. How does Sun Microsystems make these links?

The company's executive compensation package consists primarily of the following three components:

- Base salary
- Long-term incentives
- Annual incentive bonus

Executives' base salaries are competitive within the industry, and long-term incentives are tied to stock options that will become more valuable if the stock price goes up, thereby creating shareholder value. Of the three components, the annual incentive bonus is most closely linked to financial performance in any given year. Although the company was profitable and its revenues increased in 2001, no annual incentive bonuses were awarded because growth in revenues and in earnings per share was below the company's plan. These results contrast sharply with those in 2000, when financial performance was outstanding and several executives received bonuses in excess of $1 million.[1]

Thus, at Sun Microsystems, as at many other companies that demand outstanding results, financial

How is financial performance tied to the annual incentive bonuses that executives at Sun hope to receive?

performance is an important factor in management compensation. Managers who work in such an environment must understand the comprehensive framework that internal and external users of financial statements commonly employ to evaluate a company's results. This chapter presents that framework.

Financial Highlights
(In millions except earnings per share)

	2001	2000	1999
Net revenues	$18,250	$15,721	$11,806
Net income	927	1,854	1,030
Earnings per share—basic	0.28	0.59	0.33

FINANCIAL PERFORMANCE EVALUATION BY INTERNAL AND EXTERNAL USERS

LO1   Describe and discuss financial performance evaluation by internal and external users.

RELATED TEXT ASSIGNMENTS
Q: 1, 2
SE: 1
E: 1

Financial performance evaluation, also called *financial statement analysis*, comprises all the techniques users of financial statements employ to show important relationships in a firm's financial statements and to relate them to important financial objectives. Users of financial statements who evaluate financial performance fall into two categories: internal users and external users. Both groups have a strong interest in financial performance. Internal users include top managers, who set and strive to achieve financial performance objectives; middle-level managers of business processes; and employee stockholders. External users are creditors and investors who want to assess management's accomplishment of financial objectives, as well as customers who have cooperative agreements with the company.

INTERNAL USERS

⬥ **STOP AND THINK!**
Why is it essential that management compensation, including bonuses, be linked to financial goals and strategies that achieve shareholder value?

If the overall financial plan is expected to increase the owners' wealth, then aligning managers' compensation and bonuses with achieving or exceeding these financial targets encourages managers to act in their own and the owners' best interests. ■

Setting financial performance objectives is a major function of management's plan to achieve the company's strategic goals. All strategic and operating plans established by management must eventually be stated in terms of financial objectives. A primary objective of management is to increase the wealth of the owners or stockholders of the business, but this objective must be divided into categories. A complete financial plan should have balanced financial performance objectives in all the following categories:

Business Objectives	Links to Financial Performance
Liquidity	Ability to pay bills when due and to meet unexpected needs for cash
Profitability	Ability to earn a satisfactory net income
Long-term solvency	Ability to survive for many years
Cash flow adequacy	Ability to generate sufficient cash through operating, investing, and financing activities
Market strength	Ability to increase the wealth of owners

Management's main responsibility is to put into action and to carry out its plan to achieve the financial performance objectives. Management must constantly monitor key financial performance measures, determine the cause of any deviations in the measures, and propose corrective actions. Annual measures provide data for long-term trend analysis. Management develops monthly, quarterly, and annual reports that compare actual performance with objectives for key financial measures in each of the above categories. These reports should be formatted to highlight key performance measures.

EXTERNAL USERS

Creditors make loans in the form of trade accounts, notes, or bonds. They expect them to be repaid according to specified terms and to receive interest on the notes and bonds payable. Investors buy capital stock, from which they hope to receive dividends and an increase in value. Both groups face risks. The creditor faces the risk that the debtor will fail to pay back the loan. The investor faces the risks that dividends will be reduced or not paid and that the market price of the stock will drop. For both groups, the goal is to achieve a return that makes up for the risk. In general, the greater the risk taken, the greater the return required as compensation.

Any one loan or any one investment can turn out badly. As a result, most creditors and investors put their funds into a **portfolio**, which is a group of loans or investments. The portfolio is designed to average the returns and the risks. Nevertheless, individual decisions about the loans or stock in the portfolio must still be made. It is in making those individual decisions that financial performance evaluation is most useful. Creditors and investors use financial performance evaluation in two general ways: to judge past performance and current position, and to judge future potential and the risk connected with that potential.

■ **ASSESSMENT OF PAST PERFORMANCE AND CURRENT POSITION**   Past performance is often a good indicator of future performance. Therefore, an investor or creditor looks at the trends of past sales, expenses, net income, cash flow, and return on investment not only as means of judging management's past performance but also as possible indicators of future performance. In addition, an evaluation of current position will tell, for example, what assets the business owns and what liabilities it must pay. It will also tell what the company's cash position is, how much debt it has in relation to equity, and what levels of inventories and receivables exist. Knowing a company's past performance and current position is often important in judging future potential and the related risk.

■ **ASSESSMENT OF FUTURE POTENTIAL AND RELATED RISK**   Information about the past and present is useful only insofar as it bears on decisions about the future. An investor evaluates a company's potential earning ability because that ability will affect the market price of the company's stock and the amount of dividends the company will pay. A creditor evaluates the company's potential debt-paying ability.

The riskiness of an investment or loan depends on how easy it is to predict future profitability or liquidity. If an investor can predict with confidence that a company's earnings per share will be between $2.50 and $2.60 in the next year, the investment is less risky than if the earnings per share are expected to fall between $2.00 and $3.00. For example, the potential associated with an investment in an established and stable electric utility, or a loan to it, is relatively easy to predict on the basis of the company's past performance and current position. The potential associated with investment in a small Internet firm, on the other hand, may be much harder to predict. For this reason, the investment in or loan to the electric utility carries less risk than the investment in or loan to the small Internet company.

Often, in return for taking a greater risk, an investor in the small Internet company will demand a higher expected return (increase in market price plus dividends) than will an investor in the established utility company. Also, a creditor of the Internet company will demand a higher interest rate and possibly more assurance of repayment (a secured loan, for instance) than a creditor of the utility company. The higher interest rate reimburses the creditor for assuming a higher risk.

FINANCIAL REPORTING UNDER THE SARBANES-OXLEY ACT

www.enron.com
www.worldcom.com

In response to the financial reporting issues raised by the cases of Enron, WorldCom, and others, the U.S. Congress passed broad legislation, referred to as the **Sarbanes-Oxley Act**, in an attempt to rectify the problems. This act includes numerous provisions designed to improve investor confidence in the financial reporting system as it applies to publicly traded companies, including the following:

- Establishes a Public Oversight Board for the accounting profession, which will establish auditing standards and oversee other regulations involving auditors.
- Requires the chief executor officer and chief financial officer to take responsibility for the accuracy of annual and quarterly financial statements under criminal penalties.
- Requires the audit committee of public corporations to be made up of independent (nonofficer) board members, some of whom must have financial expertise.
- Requires that the audit committee appoint the company's auditor and that the auditor not be allowed to do any consulting for the company.

The Sarbanes-Oxley Act does not apply to private (nonpublic) companies.

 Check out ACE for a Review Quiz at http://accounting.college.hmco.com/students.

STANDARDS FOR FINANCIAL STATEMENT ANALYSIS

LO2   Describe and discuss the standards for financial performance evaluation.

RELATED TEXT ASSIGNMENTS
Q: 3, 4
SE: 1
E: 1
SD: 1
FRA: 6

www.dunandbradstreet.com

ENRICHMENT NOTE:
Rules of thumb evolve and change as the environment changes. Not long ago, an acceptable current ratio was higher than today's 2:1.

STOP AND THINK!
How are past performance and industry norms useful in evaluating a company's performance?
A company's past performance indicates whether performance is improving. Industry norms tell how well a company is performing in relation to its peer group. ■

When analyzing financial statements, decision makers must judge whether the relationships they find are favorable or unfavorable. Three commonly used standards of comparison are rule-of-thumb measures, past performance of the company, and industry norms.

RULE-OF-THUMB MEASURES

Many financial analysts, investors, and lenders employ general standards, or rule-of-thumb measures, for key financial ratios. For example, most analysts today agree that a current ratio (current assets divided by current liabilities) of 2:1 is acceptable. The credit-rating firm of Dun & Bradstreet, in its *Industry Norms and Key Business Ratios*, offers such rules of thumb as the following:

Current debt to tangible net worth   Ordinarily, a business begins to pile up trouble when this relationship exceeds 80 percent.

Inventory to net working capital   Ordinarily, this relationship should not exceed 80 percent.

Although such measures may suggest areas that need further investigation, there is no proof that the specified levels are applicable to all companies. A company with a current ratio higher than 2:1 may have a poor credit policy (resulting in accounts receivable being too large), too much inventory, or poor cash management. Another company may have a ratio lower than 2:1 but still have excellent management in all three of those areas. Thus, rule-of-thumb measures must be used with great care.

PAST PERFORMANCE OF THE COMPANY

An improvement over rule-of-thumb measures is the comparison of financial measures or ratios of the same company over time. Such a comparison gives the analyst some basis for judging whether the measure or ratio is getting better or worse. It may also be helpful in showing possible future trends. However, trends reverse at times, so such projections must be made with care. Another problem with trend analysis is that past performance may not be enough to meet present needs. For example, even if a company has improved its return on total investment from 3 percent one year to 4 percent the next, the 4 percent return may, in fact, not be adequate for the company's needs.

INDUSTRY NORMS

One way of making up for the limitations of using past performance as a standard is to use industry norms. Such norms show how a company compares with others in the same industry. For example, if companies in the same industry have an average rate of return on total investment of 8 percent, returns on investment of 3 and 4 percent are probably not adequate. Industry norms can also be used to judge trends. Suppose a company's profit margin dropped from 12 to 10 percent because of a downward turn in the economy. If the average drop in profit margin of other companies in the same industry was from 12 to 4 percent, this norm would indicate that the company had done relatively well. Sometimes, instead of industry averages, data for the industry leader or a specific competitor are analyzed.

Using industry norms as standards has three limitations. First, companies in the same industry may not be strictly comparable. Consider two companies in the oil industry. One purchases oil products and markets them through service stations. The other, an international company, discovers, produces, refines, and markets its

EXHIBIT 1
Selected Segment Information for Goodyear Tire & Rubber Co.

(In millions)	2002	2001	2000
Sales			
North American Tire	$ 6,703.3	$ 7,152.3	$ 7,111.3
European Union Tire	3,314.9	3,128.0	3,198.1
Eastern Europe, Africa, and Middle East Tire	807.1	703.1	793.0
Latin American Tire	947.6	1,012.6	1,047.9
Asia Tire	531.7	493.9	524.6
Total Tires	**12,304.6**	**12,489.9**	**12,674.9**
Engineered Products	1,126.5	1,122.3	1,174.2
Chemical Products	937.9	1,037.3	1,129.7
Total Segment Sales	**14,369.0**	**14,649.5**	**14,978.8**
Income			
North American Tire	$ (35.5)	$ 107.8	$ 260.7
European Union Tire	102.6	57.2	88.7
Eastern Europe, Africa, and Middle East Tire	91.9	20.2	54.6
Latin American Tire	102.4	89.8	69.8
Asia Tire	43.9	19.9	17.9
Total Tires	**305.3**	**294.9**	**491.7**
Engineered Products	45.6	11.6	43.1
Chemical Products	69.4	60.2	64.2
Total Segment Income	**420.3**	**366.7**	**599.0**
Assets			
North American Tire	$ 4,594.8	$ 4,856.7	$ 5,268.5
European Union Tire	3,124.4	2,836.9	3,088.1
Eastern Europe, Africa, and Middle East Tire	899.4	747.7	903.6
Latin American Tire	642.8	753.9	796.5
Asia Tire	604.0	600.9	668.5
Total Tires	**9,865.4**	**9,796.1**	**10,725.2**
Engineered Products	678.2	681.3	736.8
Chemical Products	636.9	601.6	742.9
Total Segment Assets	**11,180.5**	**11,079.0**	**12,204.9**

Source: Goodyear Tire & Rubber Co., *Annual Report,* 2002.

KEY POINT: Each segment represents an investment that the home office or parent company evaluates and reviews frequently. The segment can remain an active investment or be replaced by a more attractive one.

own oil products. Because of their different operations, these two companies cannot be compared.

Second, many large companies today operate in more than one industry or segment. Some of these **diversified companies**, or *conglomerates*, operate in many unrelated industries. The individual segments of a diversified company generally have different rates of profitability and different degrees of risk. In analyzing the consolidated financial statements of such companies, it is often impossible to use industry norms as standards. There are simply no comparable companies. A requirement of the Financial Accounting Standards Board, presented in *Statement No. 131*, provides

FOCUS ON BUSINESS ETHICS

Take the Numbers with a Grain of Salt.

Traditionally, pro-forma statements presented financial statements as they would appear after certain agreed-upon transactions, such as mergers or acquisitions, took place. In recent years, pro-forma statements have become more widely used as a way for companies to present a better picture of their operations than would be the case under GAAP. According to a survey by the National Investor Relations Institute, 57 percent of companies across a range of industries use pro-forma reporting.[2] In one quarter, Amazon.com <www.amazon.com> reported a "pro-forma operating" loss of $49 million and a "pro-forma

net" loss of $76 million; had the company used GAAP, it would have reported a net loss of $234 million. Among many other examples, JDS Uniphase <www.jdsu.com> reported a "pro-forma" gain of $.14 per share, when, in fact, its net loss using GAAP was $1.13 per share. Pro-forma statements, which are unaudited, have come to mean whatever a company's management wants them to mean. Thus, the analyst should rely exclusively on financial statements that are prepared using GAAP and that are audited by an independent CPA.[3]

www.goodyear.com

a partial solution to this problem. It states that diversified companies must report profit or loss, certain revenue and expense items, and assets for each of their segments. Depending on how the company is organized for assessing performance, segment information may be reported for operations in different industries or different geographical areas, or for major customers.[4]

Exhibit 1 on page 755 shows an example of segment reporting. Goodyear Tire & Rubber Co., well known as a tire manufacturer, also has significant engineered and chemical products divisions. The data on sales, income, and assets for these segments, shown in Exhibit 1, allow the analyst to compute important profitability performance measures, such as profit margin, asset turnover, and return on assets, for each segment and to compare them with the appropriate industry norms.

The third limitation of industry norms is that companies in the same industry with similar operations may use different acceptable accounting procedures. That is, they may use different methods to value inventories and different methods to depreciate assets. Even so, if little information about a company's past performance is available, industry norms probably offer the best available standards for judging current performance—as long as they are used with care.

 Check out ACE for a Review Quiz at http://accounting.college.hmco.com/students.

SOURCES OF INFORMATION

LO3   Identify the sources of information for financial performance evaluation.

RELATED TEXT ASSIGNMENTS
Q: 5
SE: 2
E: 1
SD: 2, 3, 4, 5
FRA: 6

The external analyst is often limited to using publicly available information about a company. The major sources of information about publicly held corporations are reports published by the company, SEC reports, business periodicals, and credit and investment advisory services.

REPORTS PUBLISHED BY THE COMPANY

A publicly held corporation's annual report is an important source of financial information. From a financial analyst's perspective, its main parts are management's analysis of the past year's operations; the financial statements; the notes to the financial statements, which include a summary of significant accounting policies; the auditors' report; and financial highlights for a five- or ten-year period.

Most publicly held companies also publish **interim financial statements** each quarter. Those reports present limited information in the form of condensed financial statements, which need not be subjected to a full audit by the independent auditor. The financial community watches the interim statements closely for early signs of important changes in a company's earnings trend.

FOCUS ON BUSINESS TECHNOLOGY

Find It on the Internet.

Performance reports and other financial information, including stock quotes, reference data, and news about companies and markets, are available instantaneously through such Internet services as CompuServe <www.compuserve.com>, America Online, <www.aol.com>, Yahoo <www.yahoo.com>, and Wall Street Journal Interactive Edition <http://online.wsj.com>.

With access to these online services and those of brokers like Charles Schwab & Co., Inc. <www.schwab.com>, which allow customers to use their own computers to buy and sell stock and other securities, individuals today can avail themselves of resources equivalent to those used by many professional analysts.

● STOP AND THINK!

Why would ratios that include one balance sheet account and one income statement or statement of cash flows account, such as receivable turnover or return on assets, be questionable if they came from quarterly or other interim financial reports?

On quarterly financial statements, all numbers on the income statement and statement of cash flows are for less than one year, whereas the balance sheet figures are full values similar to those at year end. Thus, any ratios that use data from the income statement or statement of cash flows as their basis will be less than they might be on a full-year basis. ■

www.moodys.com
www.standardpoor.com
www.dunandbradstreet.com

www.rmahq.com

www.pepsi.com

SEC REPORTS

Publicly held corporations in the United States must file annual reports, quarterly reports, and current reports with the Securities and Exchange Commission (SEC). If they have more than $10 million in assets and more than 500 shareholders, they must file these reports electronically at www.sec.gov/edgar.shtml, where anyone can access them free of charge.

The Securities and Exchange Commission requires companies to use a standard form, called Form 10-K, for the annual report. Form 10-K contains more information than the annual reports published by companies. For that reason, it is a valuable source of information.

Companies file their quarterly reports with the SEC on Form 10-Q. This report presents important facts about interim financial performance. The current report, filed on Form 8-K must be submitted to the SEC within a few days of the date of certain significant events, such as the sale or purchase of a division of the company or a change in the company's auditors. The current report is often the first indicator of important changes that may affect a company's financial performance in the future.

BUSINESS PERIODICALS AND CREDIT AND INVESTMENT ADVISORY SERVICES

Financial analysts must keep up with current events in the financial world. Probably the best source of financial news is *The Wall Street Journal*, which is published every business day and is the most complete financial newspaper in the United States. Some helpful magazines, published every week or every two weeks, are *Forbes*, *Barron's*, *Fortune*, and the *Financial Times*.

For further details about the financial history of companies, the publications of such services as Moody's Investors Service, Inc., and Standard & Poor's are useful. Data on industry norms, average ratios and relationships, and credit ratings are available from such agencies as The Dun & Bradstreet Corp. In its publication entitled *Industry Norms and Key Business Ratios*, Dun & Bradstreet offers an annual analysis of 14 ratios for each of 125 industry groups, classified as retailing, wholesaling, manufacturing, and construction. *Annual Statement Studies*, published by the Risk Management Association (formerly Robert Morris Associates), presents many facts and ratios for 223 different industries. A number of private services are also available for a yearly fee.

An example of specialized financial reporting readily available to the public is Mergent's *Handbook of Dividend Achievers*, which profiles companies that have increased their dividends consistently over the past ten years. A listing from that publication—for PepsiCo Inc.—is shown in Exhibit 2. A wealth of information about the company is summarized on one page, including the market action of its stock; its business operations, recent developments, and prospects; earnings and dividend data; and annual financial data for the past ten years. The kind of data in these profiles is used in many of the analyses and ratios explained in this chapter.

EXHIBIT 2
Listing from Mergent's
Handbook of Dividend
Achievers

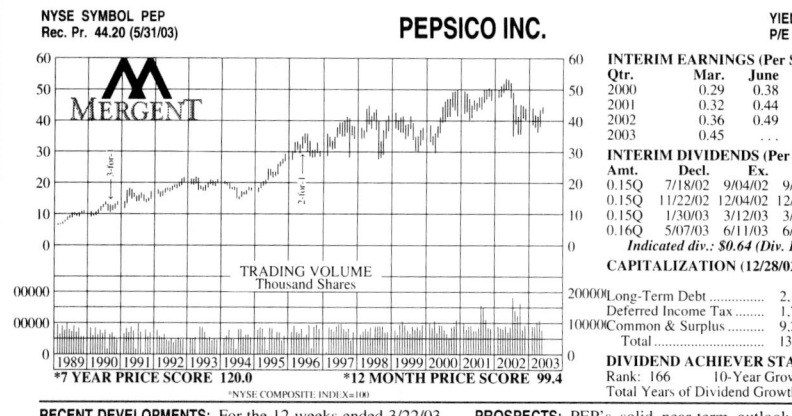

NYSE SYMBOL PEP
Rec. Pr. 44.20 (5/31/03)

PEPSICO INC.

YIELD 1.4%
P/E RATIO 22.8

INTERIM EARNINGS (Per Share):

Qtr.	Mar.	June	Sept.	Dec.
2000	0.29	0.38	0.40	0.41
2001	0.32	0.44	0.34	0.37
2002	0.36	0.49	0.54	0.46
2003	0.45	...	...	...

INTERIM DIVIDENDS (Per Share):

Amt.	Decl.	Ex.	Rec.	Pay.
0.15Q	7/18/02	9/04/02	9/06/02	9/27/02
0.15Q	11/22/02	12/04/02	12/06/02	1/02/03
0.15Q	1/30/03	3/12/03	3/14/03	3/31/03
0.16Q	5/07/03	6/11/03	6/13/03	6/30/03

Indicated div.: $0.64 (Div. Reinv. Plan)

CAPITALIZATION (12/28/02):

	($000)	(%)
Long-Term Debt	2,187,000	16.6
Deferred Income Tax	1,718,000	13.0
Common & Surplus	9,298,000	70.4
Total	13,203,000	100.0

DIVIDEND ACHIEVER STATUS:
Rank: 166   10-Year Growth Rate: 8.97%
Total Years of Dividend Growth: 31

TRADING VOLUME
Thousand Shares

1989|1990|1991|1992|1993|1994|1995|1996|1997|1998|1999|2000|2001|2002|2003
*7 YEAR PRICE SCORE 120.0   *12 MONTH PRICE SCORE 99.4
*NYSE COMPOSITE INDEX=100

RECENT DEVELOPMENTS: For the 12 weeks ended 3/22/03, net income was $777.0 million versus $689.0 million in the same period a year earlier. Results for 2003 and 2002 included pre-tax merger-related costs of $11.0 million and $36.0 million, respectively. Results for 2003 also included an after-tax gain of $16.0 million on Quaker's Mission pasta business. Net sales grew 4.1% to $5.53 billion, and operating profit rose 13.5% to $1.14 billion.

PROSPECTS: PEP's solid near-term outlook is supported by the roll-out of new products and market programs designed to fuel growth over the balance of 2003. They include the introduction of MOUNTAIN DEW LIVEWIRE, an orange-flavored version of MOUNTAIN DEW that is expected to be available from Memorial Day through Labor Day; new packaging and re-designed graphics for PEPSI; and a number of new Quaker products.

BUSINESS

PEPSICO INC. is a worldwide consumer products company. Worldwide snacks (57.1% of 2002 division net sales and 56.4% of operating profit) manufactures, markets, sells and distributes primarily salty, sweet and grain-based snacks including such brands as LAY'S, DORITOS, CHEETOS, ROLD GOLD, SABRITAS and WALKERS. Worldwide beverages (36.9%, 34.6%) includes such brands as PEPSI, DIET PEPSI, MOUNTAIN DEW, MUG, AQUAFINA, SOBE, TROPICANA PURE PREMIUM, GATORADE and MIRINDA and 7-UP internationally. Quaker Foods North America (6.0%, 9.0%) manufactures, markets and sells a variety of food products. PEP also has various ownership interests in a number of bottling concerns. In August 2001, PEP acquired The Quaker Oats Company.

ANNUAL FINANCIAL DATA

	12/28/02	12/29/01	12/30/00	12/25/99	12/26/98	12/27/97	12/28/96
Earnings Per Share	⑦1.85	⑤1.47	1.48	④1.37	③1.31	①0.95	⑧0.72
Cash Flow Per Share	2.47	2.07	2.13	2.06	2.12	1.65	1.79
Tang. Book Val. Per Share	2.37	2.17	1.91	1.47	...	0.72	...
Dividends Per Share	0.59	0.57	0.55	0.53	0.51	0.48	0.43
Dividend Payout %	31.9	38.8	37.2	38.7	38.9	50.5	59.7

INCOME STATEMENT (IN MILLIONS):

Total Revenues	25,112.0	26,935.0	20,438.0	20,367.0	22,348.0	20,917.0	31,645.0
Costs & Expenses	19,270.0	21,832.0	16,253.0	16,517.0	18,530.0	17,149.0	27,380.0
Depreciation & Amort.	1,112.0	1,082.0	960.0	1,032.0	1,234.0	1,106.0	1,719.0
Operating Income	4,730.0	4,021.0	3,225.0	2,818.0	2,584.0	2,662.0	2,546.0
Net Interest Inc./(Exp.)	d142.0	d152.0	d145.0	d245.0	d321.0	d353.0	d499.0
Income Before Income Taxes	4,868.0	4,029.0	3,210.0	3,656.0	2,263.0	2,309.0	2,047.0
Income Taxes	1,555.0	1,367.0	1,027.0	1,606.0	270.0	818.0	898.0
Net Income	⑦3,313.0	⑤2,662.0	2,183.0	④2,050.0	③1,993.0	①1,491.0	⑧1,149.0
Cash Flow	4,421.0	3,740.0	3,143.0	3,082.0	3,227.0	2,597.0	2,868.0
Average Shs. Outstg. (000)	1,789,000	1,807,000	1,475,000	1,496,000	1,519,000	1,570,000	1,606,000

BALANCE SHEET (IN MILLIONS):

Cash & Cash Equivalents	1,845.0	1,649.0	1,330.0	1,056.0	394.0	2,883.0	786.0
Total Current Assets	6,413.0	5,853.0	4,604.0	4,173.0	4,362.0	6,251.0	5,139.0
Net Property	7,390.0	6,876.0	5,438.0	5,266.0	7,318.0	6,261.0	10,191.0
Total Assets	23,474.0	21,695.0	18,339.0	17,551.0	22,660.0	20,101.0	24,512.0
Total Current Liabilities	6,052.0	4,998.0	3,935.0	3,788.0	7,914.0	4,257.0	5,139.0
Long-Term Obligations	2,187.0	2,651.0	2,346.0	2,812.0	4,028.0	4,946.0	8,439.0
Net Stockholders' Equity	9,298.0	8,648.0	7,249.0	6,881.0	6,401.0	6,936.0	6,623.0
Net Working Capital	361.0	855.0	669.0	385.0	d3,552.0	1,994.0	...
Year-end Shs. Outstg. (000)	1,722,000	1,756,000	1,446,000	1,455,000	1,471,000	1,502,000	1,545,000

STATISTICAL RECORD:

Operating Profit Margin %	18.8	14.9	15.8	13.8	11.6	12.7	8.0
Net Profit Margin %	13.2	9.9	10.7	10.1	8.9	7.1	3.6
Return on Equity %	35.6	30.8	30.1	29.8	31.1	21.5	17.3
Return on Assets %	14.1	12.3	11.9	11.7	8.8	7.4	4.7
Debt/Total Assets %	9.3	12.2	12.8	16.0	17.8	24.6	34.4
Price Range	53.50-35.01	50.46-40.25	49.94-29.69	42.56-30.13	44.81-27.56	41.31-28.25	35.88-27.25
P/E Ratio	28.9-18.9	34.3-27.4	33.7-20.1	31.1-22.0	34.2-21.0	43.5-29.7	49.8-37.8
Average Yield %	1.3	1.3	1.4	1.5	1.4	1.4	1.4

Statistics are as originally reported. ① Incl. non-recurr. chrgs. of $290.0 mill.; bef. disc. oper. gain of $651.0 mill. ② Incl. non-recurr. chrgs. of $716.0 mill. ③ Incl. non-recurr. chrg. of $288.0 mill. ④ Incl. non-recurr. chrg. of $65.0 mill. ⑤ Incl. after-tax merger-rel. chrgs. of $322.0 mill. and oth. asset impairmnt. & restruct. chrgs. of $19.0 mill. ⑥ Refl. 10/6/97 spin-off of TRICON Global Restaurants. ⑦ Incl. merger-rel. chrgs. of $224.0 mill.

OFFICERS:	**TELEPHONE NUMBER:** (914) 253-2000	**INSTITUTIONAL HOLDINGS:**
S. S. Reinemund, Chmn., C.E.O.	**FAX:** (914) 253-2070	No. of Institutions: 1,072
I. K. Nooyi, Pres., C.F.O.	**WEB:** www.pepsico.com	Shares Held: 1,123,709,222
D. R. Andrews, Sr. V.P., Sec., Gen. Couns.	**NO. OF EMPLOYEES:** 142,000 (approx.)	% Held: 65.4
INVESTOR CONTACT: Kathleen Luke, V.P., Inv. Rel., (914) 253-3691	**SHAREHOLDERS:** 220,000 (approx.)	**INDUSTRY:** Bottled and canned soft drinks (SIC: 2086)
	ANNUAL MEETING: In May	
PRINCIPAL OFFICE: 700 Anderson Hill Road, Purchase, NY 10577-1444	**INCORPORATED:** DE, Sept., 1919; reincorp., NC, Dec., 1986	**TRANSFER AGENT(S):** The Bank of New York, Newark, NJ

Source: Sample listing from *Handbook of Dividend Achievers, 2002.* Reprinted by permission of Mergent, Inc.

 Check out ACE for a Review Quiz at http://accounting.college.hmco.com/students.

TOOLS AND TECHNIQUES OF FINANCIAL ANALYSIS

LO4 Apply horizontal analysis, trend analysis, vertical analysis, and ratio analysis to financial statements.

RELATED TEXT ASSIGNMENTS

Q: 6, 7, 8, 9
SE: 3, 4, 5   www.sun.com
E: 2, 3, 4
P: 1
SD: 6
FRA: 1

Few numbers are very significant when looked at individually. It is their relationship to other numbers or their change from one period to another that is important. The tools of financial analysis are intended to show relationships and changes. Among the more widely used tools are horizontal analysis, trend analysis, vertical analysis, and ratio analysis. To illustrate how these tools are used, we devote the rest of this chapter to a comprehensive financial analysis of Sun Microsystems, Inc. Sun Microsystems was formed in 1982 and, as noted in this chapter's Decision Point, it has emerged as a global leader in network computing. It developed many of the networking technologies that are the basis of the Internet and corporate intranets, including the widely adopted Java technology.

HORIZONTAL ANALYSIS

Generally accepted accounting principles require the presentation of comparative financial statements that give financial information for the current year and the previous year. A common starting point for studying such statements is **horizontal analysis**, which computes changes from the previous year to the current year in both dollar amounts and percentages. The percentage change relates the size of the change to the size of the dollar amounts involved.

Exhibits 3 and 4 present the comparative balance sheets and income statements of Sun Microsystems and show both the dollar and percentage changes. The percentage change is computed as follows:

$$\%\ \ \ \text{Percentage Change} = 100 \times \left(\frac{\text{Amount of Change}}{\text{Base Year Amount}} \right)$$

The **base year** in any set of data is always the first year to be considered. For example, when studying data from 2000 and 2001, 2000 is the base year. As the balance sheets in Exhibit 3 show, between 2000 and 2001, Sun Microsystems' total current assets increased by $1,057 million, from $6,877 million to $7,934 million, or by 15.4 percent. This is computed as follows:

$$\%\ \ \ \text{Percentage Change} = 100 \times \left(\frac{\$1,057\ \text{million}}{\$6,877\ \text{million}} \right) = 15.4\%$$

ENRICHMENT NOTE:
Traditional horizontal analysis presents trends in terms of nominal dollars. Advanced analysis might adjust data over several time periods to remove any inflation effect or price-level changes.

The company's total current liabilities also increased—by $600 million, or 13.2 percent—in this two-year period. When examining such changes, it is important to consider both the dollar amount of the change as well as the percentage change in each component. For example, the difference between the percentage increase in warranty reserve (48.8 percent) and deferred revenues and customer deposits (41.7 percent) is not great. However, the dollar increase in deferred revenues and customer deposits is more than five times the dollar increase in warranty reserve ($538 million versus $103 million).

Sun Microsystems' balance sheets for this period also show an increase in total assets of $4,029 million, or 28.5 percent, which included an increase of $602 million, or 28.7 percent, in property, plant, and equipment, net. In addition, they show that stockholders' equity increased by $3,277 million, or 44.8 percent. All of this indicates that Sun Microsystems is a rapidly growing company.

The most important findings from the income statements in Exhibit 4 are that net revenues increased by $2,529 million, or 16.1 percent; operating income decreased by $1,082 million, or 45.2 percent; and net income decreased by $927 million, or 50.0 percent. These extremely negative results occurred in part because net revenues grew at a slower rate (16.1 percent) than cost of sales (33.0 percent) and operating expenses (19.4 percent).

EXHIBIT 3
Comparative Balance Sheets with Horizontal Analysis

Sun Microsystems, Inc.
Consolidated Balance Sheets
June 30, 2001 and 2000

			Increase (Decrease)	
(Dollar amounts in millions)	2001	2000	Amount	Percentage
Assets				
Current assets:				
Cash and cash equivalents	$ 1,472	$ 1,849	($377)	(20.4)
Short-term investments	387	626	(239)	(38.2)
Accounts receivable, net of allowances				
of $410 in 2001 and $534 in 2000	2,955	2,690	265	9.9
Inventories	1,049	557	492	88.3
Deferred tax assets	1,102	673	429	63.7
Prepaids and other current assets	969	482	487	101.0
Total current assets	$ 7,934	$ 6,877	$1,057	15.4
Property, plant and equipment, net	2,697	2,095	602	28.7
Long-term investments	4,677	4,496	181	4.0
Goodwill, net of accumulated amortization				
of $349 in 2001 and $88 in 2000	2,041	163	1,878	1,152.1
Other assets, net	832	521	311	59.7
Total assets	$18,181	$14,152	$4,029	28.5
Liabilities and Stockholders' Equity				
Current liabilities:				
Short-term borrowings	$ 3	$ 7	$ (4)	(57.1)
Accounts payable	1,050	924	126	13.6
Accrued payroll-related liabilities	488	751	(263)	(35.0)
Accrued liabilities and other	1,374	1,155	219	19.0
Deferred revenues and customer deposits	1,827	1,289	538	41.7
Warranty reserve	314	211	103	48.8
Income taxes payable	90	209	(119)	(56.9)
Total current liabilities	$ 5,146	$ 4,546	$ 600	13.2
Deferred income taxes	744	577	167	28.9
Long-term debt and other obligations	1,705	1,720	(15)	(0.9)
Stockholders' equity	10,586	7,309	3,277	44.8
Total liabilities and stockholders' equity	$18,181	$14,152	$4,029	28.5

Source: Sun Microsystems, Inc., *Annual Report,* 2001.

TREND ANALYSIS

A variation of horizontal analysis is **trend analysis**, in which percentage changes are calculated for several successive years instead of for two years. Trend analysis, with its long-run view, is important because it may point to basic changes in the nature of a business. In addition to presenting comparative financial statements, most companies present a summary of key data for five or more years. Exhibit 5 (page 762)

Exhibit 4
Comparative Income Statements with Horizontal Analysis

Sun Microsystems, Inc.
Consolidated Income Statements
For the Years Ended June 30, 2001 and 2000

(Dollar amounts in millions, except per share amounts)	2001	2000	Increase (Decrease) Amount	Increase (Decrease) Percentage
Net revenues	$18,250	$15,721	$ 2,529	16.1
Cost of sales	10,041	7,549	2,492	33.0
Gross margin	$ 8,209	$ 8,172	37	0.5
Operating expenses				
Research and development	$ 2,016	$ 1,630	$ 386	23.7
Selling, general and administrative	4,544	4,072	472	11.6
Goodwill amortization	261	65	196	301.5
Purchased in-process R&D	77	12	65	541.7
Total operating expenses	$ 6,898	$ 5,779	$ 1,119	19.4
Operating income	$ 1,311	$ 2,393	($ 1,082)	(45.2)
Gain (loss) on investments	(90)	208	(298)	(143.3)
Interest income	463	254	209	82.3
Interest expense	(100)	(84)	(16)	19.0
Income before income taxes	$ 1,584	$ 2,771	($ 1,187)	(42.8)
Provision for income taxes	603	917	(314)	(34.2)
Income before cumulative effect of change in accounting principle	$ 981	$ 1,854	$ (873)	(47.1)
Cumulative effect of change in accounting principle	(54)	—	(54)	NA
Net income	$ 927	$ 1,854	($ 927)	(50.0)
Net income per common share—basic	$0.28	$0.59	($0.31)	(52.2)
Net income per common share—diluted	$0.27	$0.55	($0.28)	(50.9)
Shares used in calculation of net income per common share—basic	3,234	3,151	83	2.6
Shares used in calculation of net income per common share—diluted	3,417	3,379	38	1.1

Source: Sun Microsystems, Inc., *Annual Report,* 2001

shows a trend analysis of Sun Microsystems' five-year summary of net revenues and operating income.

Trend analysis uses an **index number** to show changes in related items over time. For index numbers, the base year is equal to 100 percent. Other years are measured in relation to that amount. For example, the 2001 index for Sun Microsystems' net revenues is figured as follows (dollar amounts in millions):

$$\text{Index} = 100 \times \left(\frac{\text{Index Year Amount}}{\text{Base Year Amount}} \right)$$

$$= 100 \times \left(\frac{\$18,250}{\$8,661} \right) = 210.7\%$$

ENRICHMENT NOTE:
Trend analysis is usually done for a five-year period to reflect the general five-year economic cycle that affects the U.S. economy. Cycles of other lengths exist and are tracked by the National Bureau of Economic Research. Trend analysis needs to use the appropriate cycle time to cover the complete cycle's impact on the business being studied.

Sun Microsystems, Inc.
Net Revenues and Operating Income
Trend Analysis

	2001	2000	1999	1998	1997
Dollar values (in millions)					
Net revenues	$18,250	$15,721	$11,806	$9,862	$8,661
Operating income	1,311	2,393	1,520	1,114	1,033
Trend analysis (in percentages)					
Net revenues	210.7	181.5	136.3	113.9	100.0
Operating income	126.9	231.7	147.1	107.8	100.0

Source: Sun Microsystems, Inc., *Annual Report,* 2001.

The trend analysis in Exhibit 5 shows that net revenues at Sun Microsystems increased over the five-year period, as did operating income in every year except 2001, when it declined dramatically. Figure 1 illustrates these trends.

VERTICAL ANALYSIS

⊛/®   In **vertical analysis**, percentages are used to show the relationship of the different parts to a total in a single statement. The analyst sets a total figure in the statement equal to 100 percent and computes each component's percentage of that total. (The figure would be total assets or total liabilities and stockholders' equity on the balance sheet, and net revenues or net sales on the income statement.) The resulting statement of percentages is called a **common-size statement**. Common-size balance sheets and common-size income statements for Sun Microsystems are shown in pie-chart form in Figures 2 and 3, and in financial statement form in Exhibits 6 and 7.

Vertical analysis is useful for comparing the importance of specific components in the operation of a business. Also, comparative common-size statements can be used to identify important changes in the components from one year to the next. As shown in Figure 2 and Exhibit 6, from 2000 to 2001 the composition of Sun

FIGURE 1
Graph of Trend Analysis Shown in Exhibit 5

⬣ **STOP AND THINK!**
In a five-year trend analysis, why do the dollar values remain the same for their respective years while the percentages usually change when a new five-year period is chosen?

In a five-year trend analysis for a new five-year period, the base year changes. Unless two successive base years have exactly the same dollar values, the trend analysis percentages will be different each year. ■

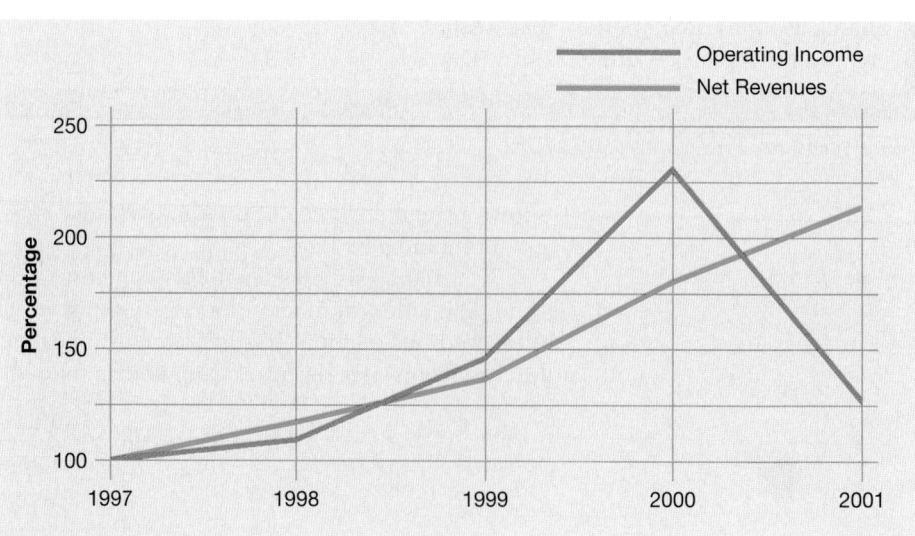

FIGURE 2
Common-Size Balance Sheets Presented Graphically

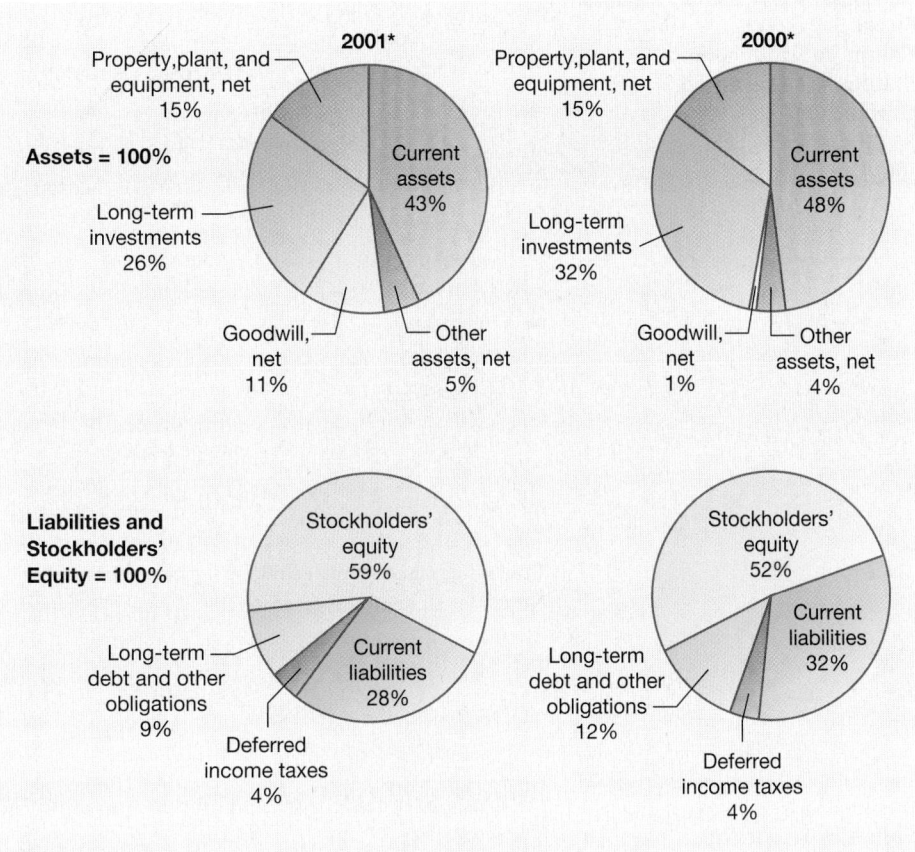

* Rounding causes some additions not to total precisely.

EXHIBIT 6
Common-Size Balance Sheets

Sun Microsystems, Inc.
Common-Size Balance Sheets
June 30, 2001 and 2000

	2001*	2000*
Assets		
Current assets	43.6%	48.6%
Property, plant and equipment, net	14.8	14.8
Long-term investments	25.7	31.8
Goodwill, net	11.2	1.2
Other assets, net	4.6	3.7
Total assets	100.0%	100.0%
Liabilities and Stockholders' Equity		
Current liabilities	28.3%	32.1%
Deferred income taxes	4.1	4.1
Long-term debt and other obligations	9.4	12.2
Stockholders' equity	58.2	51.6
Total liabilities and stockholders' equity	100.0%	100.0%

*Amounts do not precisely total 100 percent in all cases due to rounding.
Source: Sun Microsystems, Inc., *Annual Report,* 2001.

FIGURE 3
Common-Size Income Statements Presented Graphically

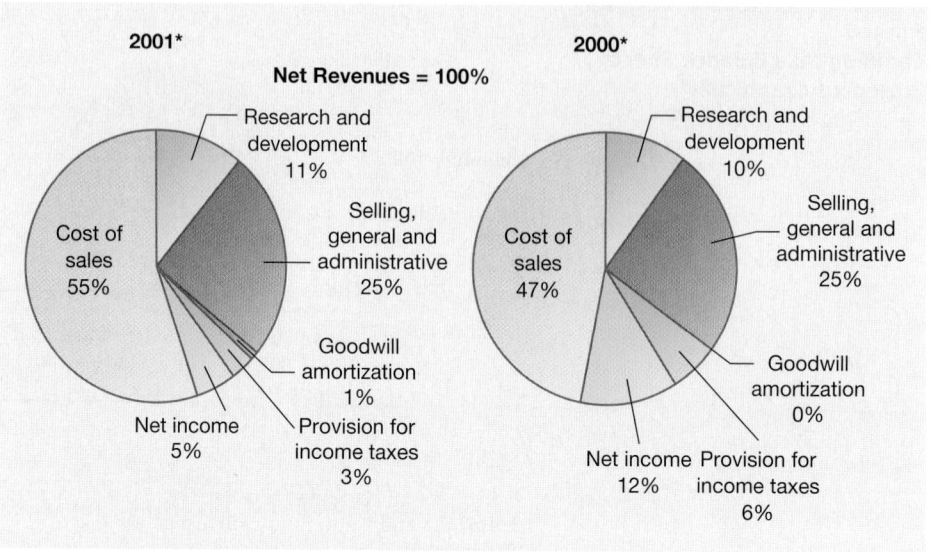

* Rounding causes some additions not to total precisely.
Note: Not all items are presented.

EXHIBIT 7
Common-Size Income Statements

Sun Microsystems, Inc. Common-Size Income Statements For the Years Ended June 30, 2001 and 2000		
	2001*	2000*
Net revenues	100.0%	100.0%
Cost of sales	55.0	48.0
Gross margin	45.0%	52.0%
Operating expenses:		
Research and development	11.0%	10.4%
Selling, general, and administrative	24.9	25.9
Goodwill amortization	1.4	0.4
Purchased in-process R&D	0.4	0.1
Total operating expenses	37.8%	36.8%
Operating income	7.2%	15.2%
Other income (expense)	1.5	2.4
Income before income taxes	8.7%	17.6%
Provision for income taxes	3.3	5.8
Income before cumulative effect of change in accounting principle	5.4%	11.8%
Cumulative effect of change in accounting principle	(0.3)	—
Net income	5.1%	11.8%

*Rounding causes some additions and subtractions not to total precisely.
Source: Sun Microsystems, Inc., *Annual Report,* 2001.

KEY POINT: It is important to discern what base amount is used when a percentage describes an item. For example, inventory may be 50 percent of *total current assets* but only 10 percent of *total assets*.

Microsystems' assets shifted from current assets and long-term investments toward goodwill, while current liabilities decreased and stockholders' equity increased. The main conclusions to be drawn from this analysis are that current assets and current liabilities make up a large portion of Sun Microsystems' financial structure and that the company has few long-term liabilities. The graphs in Figure 2 and the common-size balance sheets in Exhibit 6 show that the composition of assets at Sun Microsystems shifted from long-term investments and current assets toward goodwill. In the relationship of liabilities and stockholders' equity, there was a shift from total liabilities to stockholders' equity.

The common-size income statements in Exhibit 7, illustrated in Figure 3, show that Sun Microsystems reduced its selling, general, and administrative expenses from 2000 to 2001 by 1.0 percent of revenues (25.9% − 24.9%). This reduction was offset by an increase in goodwill amortization of 1.0 percent (1.4% − 0.4%).

PARENTHETICAL NOTE: Common-size statements can be used to compare characteristics of firms reporting in different currencies.

Common-size statements are often used to make comparisons between companies. They allow an analyst to compare the operating and financing characteristics of two companies of different size in the same industry. For example, the analyst might want to compare Sun Microsystems with other companies in terms of percentage of total assets financed by debt or in terms of selling, general, and administrative expenses as a percentage of net revenues. Common-size statements would show those and other relationships.

Ratio Analysis

 Ratio analysis is a technique of financial performance evaluation that identifies meaningful relationships between the components of the financial statements. To be most meaningful, the interpretation of ratios must include a study of the underlying data. Ratios are useful guides or shortcuts in evaluating a company's financial position and operations and in comparing financial data for several years or for several companies. The primary purpose of ratios is to point out areas needing further investigation. To interpret ratios correctly, an analyst must have a general understanding of the company and its environment. Ratios may be expressed in several ways. For example, a ratio of net income of $100,000 to sales of $1,000,000 may be stated as:

1. Net income is 1/10 or 10 percent of sales.
2. The ratio of sales to net income is 10 to 1 (10:1), or sales are 10 times net income.
3. For every dollar of sales, the company has an average net income of 10 cents.

 Check out ACE for a Review Quiz at http://accounting.college.hmco.com/students.

COMPREHENSIVE ILLUSTRATION OF RATIO ANALYSIS

LO5 Apply ratio analysis to financial statements in a comprehensive evaluation of a company's financial performance.

RELATED TEXT ASSIGNMENTS
Q: 10, 11, 12, 13, 14, 15
SE: 6, 7, 8, 9, 10
E: 5, 6, 7, 8, 9
P: 2, 3, 4, 5, 6
SD: 1, 6
FRA: 2, 3, 4, 5   www.sun.com

To illustrate how analysts apply ratio analysis to a company's financial statements in order to evaluate the company's financial situation, we will perform a comprehensive ratio analysis of Sun Microsystems' financial performance for 2000 and 2001. In the discussion and analysis section in Sun Microsystems' annual report, management states: "While we reported significant growth in our products net revenues on a year-over-year basis, all of this growth occurred in the first half of fiscal 2001. . . . If the current macro economic conditions persist, we expect demand, and therefore products net revenue in the first half of fiscal 2002, will be less than the comparable period in fiscal 2001."[5] These statements provide the context for evaluating Sun Microsystems' liquidity, profitability, long-term solvency, cash flow adequacy, and market strength. Most data for the analyses come from the financial statements presented in Exhibits 3 and 4. Other data are presented as needed.

● **STOP AND THINK!**

Why does a decrease in receivable turnover or inventory turnover create the need for cash from operating activities?

When receivable turnover or inventory turnover decreases, it means that the company has more average days' sales uncollected or more average days' inventory on hand to finance. Consequently, the company needs more cash to pay for the increase in receivables or inventory. ∎

EVALUATING LIQUIDITY

Liquidity is a company's ability to pay bills when they are due and to meet unexpected needs for cash. All the ratios that relate to liquidity involve working capital or some part of it, because it is out of working capital that debts are paid. The objective of liquidity is also closely related to the cash flow ratios.

The liquidity ratios from 2000 to 2001 for Sun Microsystems are presented in Exhibit 8. The **current ratio** and the **quick ratio** are measures of short-term debt-paying ability. The principal difference between the two is that the numerator of the current ratio includes inventories and prepaid expenses. Inventories take longer to convert to cash than do the current assets included in the numerator of the quick ratio. The quick ratio was 1.1 times in 2000 and 0.9 times in 2001. The current ratio was 1.5 times in both years primarily because current assets and current liabilities grew at similar rates. However, the composition of current assets shows a decline in quick ratio assets offset by increases in the remaining current assets.

Two major components of current assets, receivables and inventories, show improving trends. The relative size of the accounts receivable and the effectiveness of credit policies are measured by the **receivable turnover**, which rose from 6.3 times in 2000 to 6.5 times in 2001. The related ratio of **average days' sales uncollected** decreased by about one day, from 57.9 days in 2000 to 56.2 days in 2001. The major change in this category of ratios is in the inventory turnover. The **inventory turnover**, which measures the relative size of inventories, worsened. Inventory turnover decreased from 17.4 times in 2000 to 12.5 times in 2001. This results in an unfavorable increase in **average days' inventory on hand**, from 21.0 days in 2000 to 29.2 days in 2001. When taken together this means that Sun Microsystems' **operating cycle**, or the time it takes to sell products and collect for them, increased from 78.9 days in 2000 (57.9 days + 21.0 days or the average days' sales uncollected plus the average days' inventory on hand) to 85.4 days in 2001 (56.2 days + 29.2 days). Related to the operating cycle is the number of days the company takes to pay its accounts payable. The **payables turnover** increased from 9.3 times in 2000 to 10.7 times in 2001. This results in average days' payable of 39.2 days in 2000 and 34.1 days in 2001. Thus, if the **average days' payable** is subtracted from the operating cycle, the financing period, or days of financing required, are 39.7 days in 2000 and 51.3 days in 2001, a significant decline (see Figure 4). Overall, Sun Microsystems' liquidity declined.

EVALUATING PROFITABILITY

Profitability relates to a company's ability to earn a satisfactory income so that investors and stockholders will continue to provide capital to the company. Profitability is also closely linked to liquidity because earnings ultimately produce

FIGURE 4
Financing Period for Sun Microsystems, 2001

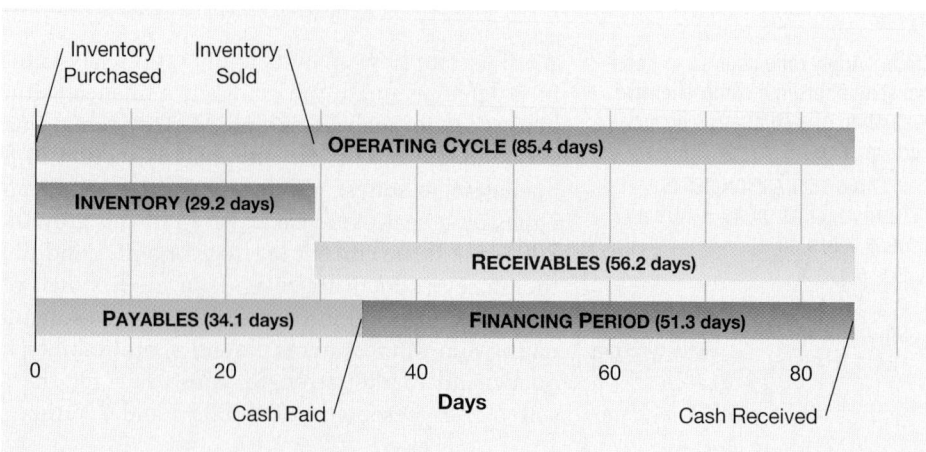

EXHIBIT 8
Liquidity Ratios of Sun Microsystems, Inc.

(Dollar amounts in millions)	2001	2000

Current ratio: Measure of short-term debt-paying ability

$$\frac{\text{Current Assets}}{\text{Current Liabilities}} \qquad \frac{\$7,934}{\$5,146} = 1.5 \text{ times} \qquad \frac{\$6,877}{\$4,546} = 1.5 \text{ times}$$

Quick ratio: Measure of short-term debt-paying ability

$$\frac{\text{Cash} + \text{Marketable Securities} + \text{Receivables}}{\text{Current Liabilities}}$$

$$\frac{\$1,472 + \$387 + \$2,955}{\$5,146} \qquad \frac{\$1,849 + \$626 + \$2,690}{\$4,546}$$

$$= \frac{\$4,814}{\$5,146} = .9 \text{ times} \qquad = \frac{\$5,165}{\$4,546} = 1.1 \text{ times}$$

Receivable turnover: Measure of relative size of accounts receivable and effectiveness of credit policies

$$\frac{\text{Net Sales}}{\text{Average Accounts Receivable}} \qquad \frac{\$18,250}{(\$2,955 + \$2,690) \div 2} \qquad \frac{\$15,721}{\$2,690 + \$2,287^* \div 2}$$

$$= \frac{\$18,250}{\$2,823} = 6.5 \text{ times} \qquad = \frac{\$15,721}{\$2,489} = 6.3 \text{ times}$$

Average days' sales uncollected: Measure of average days taken to collect receivables

$$\frac{\text{Days in Year}}{\text{Receivable Turnover}} \qquad \frac{365 \text{ days}}{6.5 \text{ times}} = 56.2 \text{ days} \qquad = \frac{365 \text{ days}}{6.3 \text{ times}} = 57.9 \text{ days}$$

Inventory turnover: Measure of relative size of inventory

$$\frac{\text{Costs of Goods Sold}}{\text{Average Inventory}} \qquad \frac{\$10,041}{(\$1,049 + \$557) \div 2} \qquad \frac{\$7,549}{\$557 + \$308^* \div 2}$$

$$= \frac{\$10,041}{\$803} = 12.5 \text{ times} \qquad = \frac{\$7,549}{\$433} = 17.4 \text{ times}$$

Average days' inventory on hand: Measure of average days taken to sell inventory

$$\frac{\text{Days in Year}}{\text{Inventory Turnover}} \qquad \frac{365 \text{ days}}{12.5 \text{ times}} = 29.2 \text{ days} \qquad = \frac{365 \text{ days}}{17.4 \text{ times}} = 21.0 \text{ days}$$

Payables turnover: Measure of relative size of accounts payable

$$\frac{\text{Costs of Goods Sold} +/- \text{Change in Inventory}}{\text{Average Accounts Payable}}$$

$$\frac{\$10,041 + \$492}{(\$1,050 + \$924) \div 2} \qquad \frac{\$7,549 + \$249^*}{(\$924 + \$754^*) \div 2}$$

$$= \frac{\$10,533}{\$987} = 10.7 \text{ times} \qquad = \frac{\$7,798}{\$839} = 9.3 \text{ times}$$

Average days' payable: Measure of average days taken to pay accounts payable

$$\frac{\text{Days in Year}}{\text{Payables Turnover}} \qquad = \frac{365 \text{ days}}{10.7 \text{ times}} = 34.1 \text{ days} \qquad = \frac{365 \text{ days}}{9.3 \text{ times}} = 39.2 \text{ days}$$

*1999 figures are derived from the statement of cash flows in Sun Microsystems' annual report.
Source: Sun Microsystems, Inc., *Annual Report,* 2001.

FOCUS ON BUSINESS PRACTICE

There's More Than One Way to Measure Profitability.

Efforts to link management compensation to the company's performance measures and to the creation of shareholder wealth are increasing. One such measure compares the company's return on assets with the cost of debt and equity capital. If the return on assets exceeds the cost of financing the assets with debt and equity, then management is indeed creating value for the shareholders. This measure is referred to in various ways. The originators refer to it as *Economic Value Added,* or *EVA®*. Coca-Cola <www.coca-cola.com>, which uses this measure to evaluate management performance, calls it by its more generic name, *economic profit.* In its annual report, Coca-Cola reports economic profit along with other key financial measures, such as free cash flow and return on equity.

ENRICHMENT NOTE: In both asset turnover and return on assets, the analysis is improved if only productive assets are used in the calculations. For example, unfinished new plant construction or investments in obsolete or nonoperating plants could be removed from the asset base to give a better picture of the productivity of assets.

cash flow. For this reason, evaluating profitability is important to both investors and creditors. The profitability ratios of Sun Microsystems, Inc., are shown in Exhibit 9.

Profit margin, which measures the net income produced by each dollar of sales, decreased from 11.8 to 5.1 percent. **Asset turnover**, which measures how efficiently assets are used to produce sales, decreased from 1.4 to 1.1 times. The result is a decrease in the company's earning power, or **return on assets**, from 16.4 percent in 2000 to 5.7 percent in 2001. These computations show the relationships:

Profit Margin		Asset Turnover		Return on Assets
$\dfrac{\text{Net Income}}{\text{Net Sales}}$	$\times$	$\dfrac{\text{Net Sales}}{\text{Average Total Assets}}$	$=$	$\dfrac{\text{Net Income}}{\text{Average Total Assets}}$
2000 11.8%	$\times$	1.4	$=$	16.5%
2001 5.1%	$\times$	1.1	$=$	5.6%

KEY POINT: Profit often is expressed in different ways in accounting literature. Examples are income before income taxes, income after income taxes, and net operating income. Being aware of the content of net income data in profitability ratios enables analysts to draw appropriate conclusions about the results of ratio computations.

(The small difference in the two sets of return on assets figures results from the rounding of the ratios.) The profitability of stockholders' investments, or **return on equity**, also declined, from 30.5 percent in 2000 to 10.4 percent in 2001.

Although we have used net income in computing profitability ratios for Sun Microsystems, net income is not always a good indicator of a company's sustainable earnings. For instance, if a company has discontinued operations, then income from continuing operations may be a better measure of sustainable earnings. For a company that has one-time items on the income statement, such as restructurings, gains, or losses, income from operations before these items may be a better measure. Some analysts like to use earnings before interest and taxes, or EBIT, for the earnings measure because it excludes the effects of the company's borrowings and the tax rates from the analysis. Whatever figure one uses for earnings, it is important to try to determine the effects of various components on future operations.

EVALUATING LONG-TERM SOLVENCY

KEY POINT: Liquidity is a firm's ability to meet its current obligations, whereas solvency is a firm's ability to meet its maturing obligations as they come due, without losing the ability to continue operations.

Long-term solvency has to do with a company's ability to survive for many years. The aim of long-term solvency analysis is to detect early signs that a company is headed for financial difficulty. Studies have indicated that accounting ratios can show as much as five years in advance that a company may fail.[6] Declining profitability and liquidity ratios are key indicators of possible business failure. Two other ratios that analysts often consider when assessing long-term solvency are debt to equity and interest coverage, which are shown in Exhibit 10.

Increasing amounts of debt in a company's capital structure mean the company is becoming more heavily leveraged. Because of increasing legal obligations to pay interest periodically and the principal at maturity, this condition negatively affects long-term solvency. Failure to make those payments can result in bankruptcy. The **debt to equity ratio** measures capital structure and leverage by showing the amount of assets provided by creditors in relation to the amount provided by stockholders. Sun Microsystems' debt to equity ratio was only .9 times in 2000 and .7 times in 2001. Recall from Exhibit 3 that the company has primarily short-term debt and

EXHIBIT 9
Profitability Ratios of Sun Microsystems, Inc.

(Dollar amounts in millions)	2001	2000

Profit margin: Measure of net income produced by each dollar of sales

$$\frac{\text{Net Income}}{\text{Net Sales}} \qquad \frac{\$927}{\$18,250} = 5.1\% \qquad \frac{\$1,854}{\$15,721} = 11.8\%$$

Asset turnover: Measure of how efficiently assets are used to produce sales

$$\frac{\text{Net Sales}}{\text{Average Total Assets}} \qquad \frac{\$18,250}{(\$18,181+ \$14,152) \div 2} \qquad \frac{\$15,721}{(\$14,152+ \$8,499^*) \div 2}$$

$$= \frac{\$18,250}{\$16,167} = 1.1 \text{ times} \qquad = \frac{\$15,721}{\$11,326} = 1.4 \text{ times}$$

Return on assets: Measure of overall earning power or profitability

$$\frac{\text{Net Income}}{\text{Average Total Assets}} \qquad \frac{\$927}{\$16,167} = 5.7\% \qquad \frac{\$1,854}{\$11,326} = 16.4\%$$

Return on equity: Measure of the profitability of stockholders' investments

$$\frac{\text{Net Income}}{\text{Average Stockholders' Equity}} \qquad \frac{\$927}{(\$10,586 + \$7,309) \div 2} \qquad \frac{\$1,854}{(\$7,309 + \$4,867^*) \div 2}$$

$$= \frac{\$927}{\$8,948} = 10.4\% \qquad = \frac{\$1,854}{\$6,088} = 30.5\%$$

*1999 figures are from the 11-year financial history and the statement of stockholders' equity in Sun Microsystems' annual report.
Source: Sun Microsystems, Inc., *Annual Report,* 2001.

EXHIBIT 10
Long-Term Solvency Ratios of Sun Microsystems, Inc.

(Dollar amounts in millions)	2001	2000

Debt to equity ratio: Measure of capital structure and leverage

$$\frac{\text{Total Liabilities}}{\text{Stockholders' Equity}} \qquad \frac{\$7,595}{\$10,586} = .7 \text{ times} \qquad \frac{\$6,843}{\$7,309} = .9 \text{ times}$$

Interest coverage ratio: Measure of creditors' protection from default on interest payments

$$\frac{\text{Income Before Income Taxes + Interest Expense}}{\text{Interest Expense}} \qquad \frac{\$1,584 + \$100}{\$100} \qquad \frac{\$2,771 + \$84}{\$84}$$

$$= 16.8 \text{ times} \qquad = 34.0 \text{ times}$$

Source: Sun Microsystems, Inc., *Annual Report,* 2001.

The **price/earnings (P/E) ratio**, which measures investor confidence in a company, is the ratio of the market price per share to earnings per share. The P/E ratio is useful in comparing the relative values placed on the earnings of different companies and in comparing the value placed on a company's shares in relation to the overall market. With a lower P/E ratio, the investor obtains more underlying earnings per dollar invested.

Sun Microsystems' P/E ratio decreased from 73.7 times in 2000 to 65.0 times in 2001, which signals that investors have less confidence in the company. The **dividends yield** measures a stock's current return to an investor in the form of dividends. Because Sun Microsystems pays no dividend, it may be concluded that investors expect their return to come from increases in the stock's market value.

SUMMARY OF THE FINANCIAL ANALYSIS OF SUN MICROSYSTEMS, INC.

Our analysis clearly shows that Sun Microsystems' financial condition declined from 2000 to 2001, as measured by its liquidity, profitability, long-term solvency, and cash flow adequacy ratios. This performance resulted in a lower market price per share.

 Check out ACE for a Review Quiz at http://accounting.college.hmco.com/students.

Chapter Review

REVIEW OF LEARNING OBJECTIVES

LO1 Describe and discuss financial performance evaluation by internal and external users.	Creditors and investors use financial performance evaluation to judge the past performance and current position of a company, and its future potential with the associated risk. Creditors use the information gained from their analysis to make reliable loans that will be repaid with interest. Investors use the information to make investments that will provide a return worth the risk. The Sarbanes-Oxley Act is intended to improve investor confidence in the financial reporting system.
LO2 Describe and discuss the standards for financial performance evaluation.	Three commonly used standards for financial performance evaluation are rule-of-thumb measures, the company's past performance, and industry norms. Rule-of-thumb measures are weak because of the lack of evidence that they can be widely applied. The past performance of a company can offer a guideline for measuring improvement but is not helpful in judging performance relative to other companies. Although the use of industry norms overcomes this last problem, its disadvantage is that firms are not always comparable, even in the same industry.
LO3 Identify the sources of information for financial performance evaluation.	The main sources of information about publicly held corporations are company-published reports, such as annual reports and interim financial statements; SEC reports; business periodicals; and credit and investment advisory services.
LO4 Apply horizontal analysis, trend analysis, vertical analysis, and ratio analysis to financial statements.	Horizontal analysis involves the computation of changes in both dollar amounts and percentages from year to year. Trend analysis is an extension of horizontal analysis in that it calculates percentage changes for several years. The changes are computed by setting a base year equal to 100 and calculating the results for subsequent years as percentages of that base year. Vertical analysis uses percentages to show the relationship of the component parts to a total in a single statement. The resulting financial statements, which are expressed entirely in percentages, are called common-size statements. Ratio analysis is a technique of financial performance evaluation that identifies meaningful relationships between the components of the financial statements.
LO5 Apply ratio analysis to financial statements in a comprehensive evaluation of a company's financial performance.	A comprehensive ratio analysis includes the evaluation of a company's liquidity, profitability, long-term solvency, cash flow adequacy, and market strength. The ratios for measuring these characteristics are shown in Exhibits 8 to 12.

REVIEW OF CONCEPTS AND TERMINOLOGY

The following concepts and terms were introduced in this chapter:

LO5 **Asset turnover:** Net sales divided by average total assets; a measure of how efficiently assets are used to produce sales.

LO5 **Average days' inventory on hand:** Days in the year divided by inventory turnover; a measure that shows the average number of days taken to sell inventory.

LO5 **Average days' payable:** Days in the year divided by payables turnover; a measure that shows the average number of days taken to pay accounts payable.

LO5 **Average days' sales uncollected:** Days in the year divided by receivable turnover; a measure that shows the number of days, on average, that a company must wait to receive payment for credit sales.

LO4 **Base year:** In financial analysis, the first year to be considered in any set of data.

LO5 **Cash flows to assets:** Net cash flows from operating activities divided by average total assets; a measure of the ability of assets to generate operating cash flows.

LO5 **Cash flows to sales:** Net cash flows from operating activities divided by net sales; a measure of the ability of sales to generate operating cash flows.

LO5 **Cash flow yield:** Net cash flows from operating activities divided by net income; a measure of a company's ability to generate operating cash flows in relation to net income.

LO4 **Common-size statement:** A financial statement in which the components of a total figure are stated in terms of percentages of that total.

LO5 **Current ratio:** Current assets divided by current liabilities; a measure of short-term debt-paying ability.

LO5 **Debt to equity ratio:** Total liabilities divided by stockholders' equity; a measure that shows the relationship of debt financing to equity financing, or the extent to which a company is leveraged.

LO2 **Diversified companies:** Companies that operate in more than one industry. Also called *conglomerates*.

LO5 **Dividends yield:** Dividends per share divided by market price per share; a measure of a stock's current return to an investor.

LO1 **Financial performance evaluation:** All the techniques used to show important relationships in financial statements and to relate them to important financial objectives. Also called *financial statement analysis*.

LO5 **Free cash flow:** Net cash flows from operating activities minus dividends minus net capital expenditures; a measure of cash generated or cash deficiency after providing for commitments.

LO4 **Horizontal analysis:** A technique for analyzing financial statements that involves the computation of changes from the previous to the current year in both dollar amounts and percentages.

LO4 **Index number:** In trend analysis, a number that shows changes in related items over time, which is calculated by setting the base year equal to 100 percent.

LO5 **Interest coverage ratio:** Income before income taxes plus interest expense divided by interest expense; a measure of the degree of protection creditors have from default on interest payments.

LO3 **Interim financial statements:** Financial statements issued for a period of less than one year, usually a quarter or a month.

LO5 **Inventory turnover:** The cost of goods sold divided by average inventory; a measure of the relative size of inventory.

LO5 **Operating cycle:** Average days' inventory on hand plus average days' sales uncollected; the time it takes to sell products and collect for them.

LO5 **Payables turnover:** Cost of goods sold plus or minus change in inventory divided by average accounts payable; a measure of the relative size of accounts payable.

LO1 **Portfolio:** A group of loans or investments designed to average the returns and risks of a creditor or investor.

LO5 **Price/earnings (P/E) ratio:** Market price per share divided by earnings per share; a measure of investor confidence in a company and a means of comparing stock values.

LO5 **Profit margin:** Net income divided by net sales; a measure that shows the percentage of each revenue dollar that contributes to net income.

LO5 **Quick ratio:** The more liquid current assets—cash, marketable securities or short-term investments, and receivables—divided by current liabilities; a measure of short-term debt-paying ability.

LO4 **Ratio analysis:** A technique of financial performance evaluation that identifies meaningful relationships between the components of the financial statements.

LO5 **Receivable turnover:** Net sales divided by average accounts receivable; a measure of the relative size of accounts receivable and the effectiveness of credit policies.

LO5 **Return on assets:** Net income divided by average total assets; a measure of overall earning power, or profitability, that shows the amount earned on each dollar of assets invested.

LO5 **Return on equity:** Net income divided by average stockholders' equity; a measure of how much income was earned on each dollar invested by stockholders.

LO1 **Sarbanes-Oxley Act:** Legislation passed by the U.S. Congress to improve the financial reporting system.

LO4 **Trend analysis:** A type of horizontal analysis in which percentage changes are calculated for several successive years instead of for two years.

LO4 **Vertical analysis:** A technique for analyzing financial statements that uses percentages to show the relationships of the different parts to a total in a single statement.

REVIEW PROBLEM

Comparative Analysis of Two Companies

LO5
Ⓚ/Ⓡ
Maggie Washington is considering an investment in one of two fast-food restaurant chains because she believes the trend toward eating out more often will continue. She has narrowed her choices to Quik Burger and Big Steak, whose balance sheets and income statements are presented on the opposite page.

The statements of cash flows show that net cash flows from operating activities were $2,200,000 for Quik Burger and $3,000,000 for Big Steak. Net capital expenditures were $2,100,000 for Quik Burger and $1,800,000 for Big Steak. Dividends of $500,000 were paid by Quik Burger and $600,000 by Big Steak. The market prices of the stocks of Quik Burger and Big Steak were $30 and $20, respectively. Financial information pertaining to prior years is not readily available to Maggie Washington. Assume that all notes payable of these two companies are current liabilities and that all their bonds payable are long-term liabilities.

REQUIRED ▶ Conduct a comprehensive ratio analysis of Quik Burger and Big Steak and compare the results. Perform the analysis by following the steps outlined below. Use end-of-year balances for averages, assume no change in inventory, and round all ratios and percentages to one decimal place.

1. Prepare an analysis of liquidity.
2. Prepare an analysis of profitability.
3. Prepare an analysis of long-term solvency.
4. Prepare an analysis of cash flow adequacy.
5. Prepare an analysis of market strength.
6. Indicate in each analysis the company that apparently had the more favorable ratio. (Consider differences of .1 or less to be neutral.)
7. In what ways would having access to prior years' information aid this analysis?

Balance Sheets
December 31, 20xx
(in thousands)

	Quik Burger	Big Steak
Assets		
Cash	$ 2,000	$ 4,500
Accounts receivable (net)	2,000	6,500
Inventory	2,000	5,000
Property, plant, and equipment (net)	20,000	35,000
Other assets	4,000	5,000
Total assets	$30,000	$56,000
Liabilities and Stockholders' Equity		
Accounts payable	$ 2,500	$ 3,000
Notes payable	1,500	4,000
Bonds payable	10,000	30,000
Common stock, $1 par value	1,000	3,000
Paid-in capital in excess of par value, common	9,000	9,000
Retained earnings	6,000	7,000
Total liabilities and stockholders' equity	$30,000	$56,000

Income Statements
For the Year Ended December 31, 20xx
(in thousands, except per share amounts)

	Quik Burger	Big Steak
Net sales	$53,000	$86,000
Costs and expenses		
Cost of goods sold	$37,000	$61,000
Selling expenses	7,000	10,000
Administrative expenses	4,000	5,000
Total costs and expenses	$48,000	$76,000
Income from operations	$ 5,000	$10,000
Interest expense	1,400	3,200
Income before income taxes	$ 3,600	$ 6,800
Income taxes	1,800	3,400
Net income	$ 1,800	$ 3,400
Earnings per share	$ 1.80	$ 1.13

ANSWER TO REVIEW PROBLEM

Ratio Name	Quik Burger	Big Steak	6. Company with More Favorable Ratio*
1. Liquidity analysis			
a. Current ratio	$\dfrac{\$2,000 + \$2,000 + \$2,000}{\$2,500 + \$1,500}$	$\dfrac{\$4,500 + \$6,500 + \$5,000}{\$3,000 + \$4,000}$	
	$= \dfrac{\$6,000}{\$4,000} = 1.5$ times	$= \dfrac{\$16,000}{\$7,000} = 2.3$ times	Big Steak
b. Quick ratio	$\dfrac{\$2,000 + \$2,000}{\$2,500 + \$1,500}$	$\dfrac{\$4,500 + \$6,500}{\$3,000 + \$4,000}$	
	$= \dfrac{\$4,000}{\$4,000} = 1.0$ times	$= \dfrac{\$11,000}{\$7,000} = 1.6$ times	Big Steak
c. Receivable turnover	$\dfrac{\$53,000}{\$2,000} = 26.5$ times	$\dfrac{\$86,000}{\$6,500} = 13.2$ times	Quik Burger
d. Average days' sales uncollected	$\dfrac{365}{26.5} = 13.8$ days	$\dfrac{365}{13.2} = 27.7$ days	Quik Burger
e. Inventory turnover	$\dfrac{\$37,000}{\$2,000} = 18.5$ times	$\dfrac{\$61,000}{\$5,000} = 12.2$ times	Quik Burger
f. Average days' inventory on hand	$\dfrac{365}{18.5} = 19.7$ days	$\dfrac{365}{12.2} = 29.9$ days	Quik Burger
g. Payables turnover	$\dfrac{\$37,000 + \$0}{\$2,500} = 14.8$ times	$\dfrac{\$61,000 + \$0}{\$3,000} = 20.3$ times	Quik Burger
h. Average days' payable	$\dfrac{365}{14.8} = 24.7$ days	$\dfrac{365}{20.3} = 18.0$ days	Quik Burger
2. Profitability analysis			
a. Profit margin	$\dfrac{\$1,800}{\$53,000} = 3.4\%$	$\dfrac{\$3,400}{\$86,000} = 4.0\%$	Big Steak
b. Asset turnover	$\dfrac{\$53,000}{\$30,000} = 1.8$ times	$\dfrac{\$86,000}{\$56,000} = 1.5$ times	Quik Burger
c. Return on assets	$\dfrac{\$1,800}{\$30,000} = 6.0\%$	$\dfrac{\$3,400}{\$56,000} = 6.1\%$	Neutral
d. Return on equity	$\dfrac{\$1,800}{\$1,000 + \$9,000 + \$6,000}$	$\dfrac{\$3,400}{\$3,000 + \$9,000 + \$7,000}$	
	$= \dfrac{\$1,800}{\$16,000} = 11.3\%$	$= \dfrac{\$3,400}{\$19,000} = 17.9\%$	Big Steak
3. Long-term solvency analysis			
a. Debt to equity ratio	$\dfrac{\$2,500 + \$1,500 + \$10,000}{\$1,000 + \$9,000 + \$6,000}$	$\dfrac{\$3,000 + \$4,000 + \$30,000}{\$3,000 + \$9,000 + \$7,000}$	
	$= \dfrac{\$14,000}{\$16,000} = .9$ times	$= \dfrac{\$37,000}{\$19,000} = 1.9$ times	Quik Burger

*This analysis indicates the company with the apparently more favorable ratio. Class discussion may focus on conditions under which different conclusions may be drawn.

Ratio Name	Quik Burger	Big Steak	6. Company with More Favorable Ratio
b. Interest coverage ratio	$\dfrac{\$3,600 + \$1,400}{\$1,400}$ $= \dfrac{\$5,000}{\$1,400} = 3.6$ times	$\dfrac{\$6,800 + \$3,200}{\$3,200}$ $= \dfrac{\$10,000}{\$3,200} = 3.1$ times	Quik Burger

4. Cash flow adequacy analysis

a. Cash flow yield	$\dfrac{\$2,200}{\$1,800} = 1.2$ times	$\dfrac{\$3,000}{\$3,400} = .9$ times	Quik Burger
b. Cash flows to sales	$\dfrac{\$2,200}{\$53,000} = 4.2\%$	$\dfrac{\$3,000}{\$86,000} = 3.5\%$	Quik Burger
c. Cash flows to assets	$\dfrac{\$2,200}{\$30,000} = 7.3\%$	$\dfrac{\$3,000}{\$56,000} = 5.4\%$	Quik Burger
d. Free cash flow	$\$2,200 - \$500 - \$2,100$ $= (\$400)$	$\$3,000 - \$600 - \$1,800$ $= \$600$	Big Steak

5. Market strength analysis

a. Price/earnings ratio	$\dfrac{\$30}{\$1.80} = 16.7$ times	$\dfrac{\$20}{\$1.13} = 17.7$ times	Big Steak
b. Dividends yield	$\dfrac{\$500,000/1,000,000}{\$30} = 1.7\%$	$\dfrac{\$600,000/3,000,000}{\$20} = 1.0\%$	Quik Burger

7. Usefulness of prior years' information
Prior years' information would be helpful in two ways. First, turnover, return, and cash flows to assets ratios could be based on average amounts. Second, a trend analysis could be performed for each company.

Chapter Assignments

BUILDING YOUR KNOWLEDGE FOUNDATION

QUESTIONS

1. How are the objectives of investors and creditors in using financial performance evaluation similar? How do they differ?
2. What role does risk play in making loans and investments?
3. What standards of comparison are commonly used to evaluate financial statements, and what are their relative merits?
4. Why would a financial analyst compare the ratios of Steelco, a steel company, with the ratios of other companies in the steel industry? What factors might invalidate such a comparison?
5. Where can investors find information about a publicly held company in which they are thinking of investing?
6. Why would an investor want to see both horizontal and trend analyses of a company's financial statements?
7. What does the following sentence mean: "Based on 1996 equaling 100, net income increased from 240 in 2002 to 260 in 2003"?

8. What is the difference between horizontal and vertical analysis?

9. What is the purpose of ratio analysis?

10. In a period of high interest rates, why are receivable turnover and inventory turnover especially important?

11. The following statements were made on page 35 of the November 6, 1978, issue of *Fortune* magazine: "Supermarket executives are beginning to look back with some nostalgia on the days when the standard profit margin was 1 percent of sales. Last year the industry overall margin came to a thin 0.72 percent." How could a supermarket earn a satisfactory return on assets with such a small profit margin?

12. Company A and Company B both have net incomes of $1,000,000. Is it possible to say that these companies are equally successful? Why or why not?

13. Circo Company has a return on assets of 12 percent and a debt to equity ratio of .5. Would you expect return on equity to be more or less than 12 percent?

14. What amount is common to all cash flow adequacy ratios? To what other groups of ratios are the cash flow adequacy ratios most closely related?

15. The market price of Company J's stock is the same as that of Company Q's. How might you determine whether investors are equally confident about the future of these companies?

SHORT EXERCISES

LO1 **Objectives and Standards**
LO2 **of Financial Performance**
        Evaluation

SE 1. Indicate whether each of the following items is (a) an objective or (b) a standard of comparison of financial statement analysis:

1. Industry norms
2. Assessment of a company's past performance
3. The company's past performance
4. Assessment of future potential and related risk
5. Rule-of-thumb measures

LO3 **Sources of Information**

SE 2. For each piece of information listed below, indicate whether the *best* source would be (a) reports published by the company, (b) SEC reports, (c) business periodicals, or (d) credit and investment advisory services.

1. Current market value of a company's stock
2. Management's analysis of the past year's operations
3. Objective assessment of a company's financial performance
4. Most complete body of financial disclosures
5. Current events affecting the company

LO4 **Trend Analysis**

SE 3. Using 20x4 as the base year, prepare a trend analysis for the following data, and tell whether the results suggest a favorable or unfavorable trend. (Round your answers to one decimal place.)

	20x6	20x5	20x4
Net sales	$158,000	$136,000	$112,000
Accounts receivable (net)	43,000	32,000	21,000

LO4 **Horizontal Analysis**

SE 4. The comparative income statements and balance sheets of SiteWorks, Inc., appear on the opposite page. Compute the amount and percentage changes for the income statements, and comment on the changes from 20x4 to 20x5. (Round the percentage changes to one decimal place.)

LO4 **Vertical Analysis**

SE 5. Express the comparative balance sheets of SiteWorks, Inc., as common-size statements, and comment on the changes from 20x4 to 20x5. (Round computations to one decimal place.)

LO5 **Liquidity Analysis**

SE 6. Using the information for SiteWorks, Inc., in **SE 4** and **SE 5,** compute the current ratio, quick ratio, receivable turnover, average days' sales uncollected, inventory turnover, average days' inventory on hand, payables turnover, and average days' payable for 20x4 and 20x5. Inventories were $4,000 in 20x3, $5,000 in 20x4, and $7,000 in 20x5. Accounts Receivable were $6,000 in 20x3, $8,000 in 20x4, and $10,000 in 20x5. Accounts Payable were $9,000 in 20x3, $10,000 in 20x4, and $12,000 in 20x5. The company had no marketable securities or prepaid assets. Comment on the results. (Round computations to one decimal place.)

**SiteWorks, Inc.
Comparative Income Statements
For the Years Ended December 31, 20x5 and 20x4**

	20x5	20x4
Net sales	$180,000	$145,000
Cost of goods sold	112,000	88,000
Gross margin	$ 68,000	$ 57,000
Operating expenses	40,000	30,000
Operating income	$ 28,000	$ 27,000
Interest expense	7,000	5,000
Income before income taxes	$ 21,000	$ 22,000
Income taxes	7,000	8,000
Net income	$ 14,000	$ 14,000
Earnings per share	$ 1.40	$ 1.40

**SiteWorks, Inc.
Comparative Balance Sheets
December 31, 20x5 and 20x4**

	20x5	20x4
Assets		
Current assets	$ 24,000	$ 20,000
Property, plant, and equipment (net)	130,000	100,000
Total assets	$154,000	$120,000
Liabilities and Stockholders' Equity		
Current liabilities	$ 18,000	$ 22,000
Long-term liabilities	90,000	60,000
Stockholders' equity	46,000	38,000
Total liabilities and stockholders' equity	$154,000	$120,000

SE 7.
LO5 Profitability Analysis

Using the information for SiteWorks, Inc., in **SE 4** and **SE 5,** compute the profit margin, asset turnover, return on assets, and return on equity for 20x4 and 20x5. In 20x3, total assets were $100,000 and total stockholders' equity was $30,000. Comment on the results. (Round computations to one decimal place.)

SE 8.
LO5 Long-Term Solvency Analysis

Using the information for SiteWorks, Inc., in **SE 4** and **SE 5,** compute the debt to equity ratio and the interest coverage ratio for 20x4 and 20x5. Comment on the results. (Round computations to one decimal place.)

SE 9.
LO5 Cash Flow Adequacy Analysis

Using the information for SiteWorks, Inc., in **SE 4, SE 5,** and **SE 7,** compute the cash flow yield, cash flows to sales, cash flows to assets, and free cash flow for 20x4 and 20x5. Net cash flows from operating activities were $21,000 in 20x4 and $16,000 in 20x5. Net capital expenditures were $30,000 in 20x4 and $40,000 in 20x5. Cash dividends were $6,000 in both years. Comment on the results. (Round computations to one decimal place.)

SE 10.
LO5 Market Strength Analysis

Using the information for SiteWorks, Inc., in **SE 4, SE 5,** and **SE 9,** compute the price/earnings ratio and dividends yield for 20x4 and 20x5. The company had 10,000 shares of common stock outstanding in both years. The price of SiteWorks' common stock was $30 in 20x4 and $20 in 20x5. Comment on the results. (Round computations to one decimal place.)

EXERCISES

E 1.
LO1 Objectives, Standards, and
LO2 Sources of Information for
LO3 Financial Performance
**   Evaluation**

Identify each of the following as (a) an objective of financial statement analysis, (b) a standard for financial statement analysis, or (c) a source of information for financial statement analysis:

1. Average ratios of other companies in the same industry
2. Assessment of the future potential of an investment
3. Interim financial statements
4. Past ratios of the company
5. SEC Form 10-K
6. Assessment of risk
7. A company's annual report

E 2.
LO4 Horizontal Analysis

Compute the amount and percentage changes for the following balance sheets, and comment on the changes from 20x3 to 20x4. (Round the percentage changes to one decimal place.)

Trumpet Company
Comparative Balance Sheets
December 31, 20x4 and 20x3

	20x4	20x3
Assets		
Current assets	$ 37,200	$ 25,600
Property, plant, and equipment (net)	218,928	194,400
Total assets	$256,128	$220,000
Liabilities and Stockholders' Equity		
Current liabilities	$ 22,400	$ 6,400
Long-term liabilities	70,000	80,000
Stockholders' equity	163,728	133,600
Total liabilities and stockholders' equity	$256,128	$220,000

E 3.
LO4 Trend Analysis

Using 20x3 as the base year, prepare a trend analysis of the following data, and tell whether the situation shown by the trends is favorable or unfavorable. (Round your answers to one decimal place.)

	20x7	20x6	20x5	20x4	20x3
Net sales	$25,520	$23,980	$24,200	$22,880	$22,000
Cost of goods sold	17,220	15,400	15,540	14,700	14,000
General and administrative expenses	5,280	5,184	5,088	4,896	4,800
Operating income	3,020	3,396	3,572	3,284	3,200

E 4.
LO4 Vertical Analysis

Express the comparative income statements that follow as common-size statements, and comment on the changes from 20x5 to 20x6. (Round computations to one decimal place.)

```
                        Trumpet Company
                  Comparative Income Statements
              For the Years Ended December 31, 20x6 and 20x5
```

	20x6	20x5
Net sales	$424,000	$368,000
Cost of goods sold	254,400	239,200
Gross margin	$169,600	$128,800
Selling expenses	$106,000	$ 73,600
General expenses	50,880	36,800
Total operating expenses	$156,880	$110,400
Operating income	$ 12,720	$ 18,400

LO5 Liquidity Analysis

E 5. Partial comparative balance sheet and income statement information for Helig Company is as follows:

	20x4	20x3
Cash	$ 6,800	$ 5,200
Marketable securities	3,600	8,600
Accounts receivable (net)	22,400	17,800
Inventory	27,200	24,800
Total current assets	$ 60,000	$ 56,400
Accounts payable	$ 20,000	$ 14,100
Net sales	$161,280	$110,360
Cost of goods sold	108,800	101,680
Gross margin	$ 52,480	$ 8,680

In 20x2, the year-end balances for Accounts Receivable and Inventory were $16,200 and $25,600, respectively. Accounts Payable was $15,300 in 20x2 and is the only current liability. Compute the current ratio, quick ratio, receivable turnover, average days' sales uncollected, inventory turnover, average days' inventory on hand, payables turnover, and average days' payable for each year. (Round computations to one decimal place.) Comment on the change in the company's liquidity position, including its operating cycle and required days of financing from 20x3 to 20x4.

LO5 Turnover Analysis

E 6. Main Tuxedo Shop has been in business for four years. Because the company has recently had a cash flow problem, management wonders whether there is a problem with receivables or inventories. Here are selected figures from the company's financial statements (in thousands):

	20x4	20x3	20x2	20x1
Net sales	$288	$224	$192	$160
Cost of goods sold	180	144	120	96
Accounts receivable (net)	48	40	32	24
Merchandise inventory	56	44	32	20
Accounts payable	25	20	15	10

Compute the receivable turnover, inventory turnover, and payables turnover for each of the four years, and comment on the results relative to the cash flow problem that Main Tuxedo Shop has been experiencing. Merchandise inventory was $22,000, accounts receivable was $22,000, and accounts payable was $8,000 in 20x0. (Round computations to one decimal place.)

LO5 Profitability Analysis

E 7. D.J. Company had total assets of $640,000 in 20x3, $680,000 in 20x4, and $760,000 in 20x5. Its debt to equity ratio was .67 times in all three years. In 20x4, the company had net income of $77,112 on revenues of $1,224,000. In 20x5, the company had net income of $98,952 on revenues of $1,596,000. Compute the profit margin, asset turnover, return on assets, and return on equity for 20x4 and 20x5. Comment on the apparent cause of the increase or decrease in profitability. (Round the percentages and other ratios to one decimal place.)

LO5   Long-Term Solvency and Market Strength Ratios

E 8.   An investor is considering investing in the long-term bonds and common stock of Companies M and N. Both companies operate in the same industry. In addition, both companies pay a dividend per share of $4 and have a yield of 10 percent on their long-term bonds. Other data for the two companies are as follows:

	Company M	Company N
Total assets	$2,400,000	$1,080,000
Total liabilities	1,080,000	594,000
Income before income taxes	288,000	129,600
Interest expense	97,200	53,460
Earnings per share	3.20	5.00
Market price of common stock	40	47.50

Compute the debt to equity, interest coverage, price/earnings (P/E), and dividends yield ratios, and comment on the results. (Round computations to one decimal place.)

LO5   Cash Flow Adequacy Analysis

E 9.   Using the data below from the financial statements of Cheng, Inc., compute the company's cash flow yield, cash flows to sales, cash flows to assets, and free cash flow. (Round computations to one decimal place.)

Net sales	$6,400,000
Net income	704,000
Net cash flows from operating activities	912,000
Total assets, beginning of year	5,780,000
Total assets, end of year	6,240,000
Cash dividends	240,000
Net capital expenditures	596,000

PROBLEMS

LO4   Horizontal and Vertical Analyses

P 1.   The condensed comparative income statements and balance sheets for Rochelle Corporation follow.

Rochelle Corporation
Comparative Income Statements
For the Years Ended December 31, 20x5 and 20x4

	20x5	20x4
Net sales	$1,600,800	$1,485,200
Costs and expenses		
Cost of goods sold	$ 908,200	$ 792,400
Selling expenses	260,200	209,200
Administrative expenses	280,600	231,000
Total costs and expenses	$1,449,000	$1,232,600
Income from operations	$ 151,800	$ 252,600
Interest expense	50,000	40,000
Income before income taxes	$ 101,800	$ 212,600
Income taxes	28,000	70,000
Net income	$ 73,800	$ 142,600
Earnings per share	$ 1.23	$ 2.38

Rochelle Corporation
Comparative Balance Sheets
December 31, 20x5 and 20x4

	20x5	20x4
Assets		
Cash	$ 62,200	$ 54,400
Accounts receivable (net)	145,000	85,400
Inventory	245,200	215,600
Property, plant, and equipment (net)	1,155,400	1,015,000
Total assets	$1,607,800	$1,370,400
Liabilities and Stockholders' Equity		
Accounts payable	$ 209,400	$ 144,600
Notes payable	100,000	100,000
Bonds payable	400,000	220,000
Common stock, $10 par value	600,000	600,000
Retained earnings	298,400	305,800
Total liabilities and stockholders' equity	$1,607,800	$1,370,400

REQUIRED ▶ Perform the following analyses. (Round all ratios and percentages to one decimal place.)

1. Prepare schedules showing the amount and percentage changes from 20x4 to 20x5 for the comparative income statements and the balance sheets.
2. Prepare common-size income statements and balance sheets for 20x4 and 20x5.
3. Comment on the results in **1** and **2** by identifying favorable and unfavorable changes in the components and composition of the statements.

P 2.
LO5 Effects of Transactions on Ratios

Jamal Corporation, a clothing retailer, engaged in the transactions listed in the first column of the table below. Opposite each transaction is a ratio and space to mark the effect of each transaction on the ratio.

		Effect		
Transaction	Ratio	Increase	Decrease	None
a. Issued common stock for cash.	Asset turnover			
b. Declared cash dividend.	Current ratio			
c. Sold treasury stock.	Return on equity			
d. Borrowed cash by issuing note payable.	Debt to equity ratio			
e. Paid salaries expense.	Inventory turnover			
f. Purchased merchandise for cash.	Current ratio			
g. Sold equipment for cash.	Receivable turnover			
h. Sold merchandise on account.	Quick ratio			
i. Paid current portion of long-term debt.	Return on assets			
j. Gave sales discount.	Profit margin			
k. Purchased marketable securities for cash.	Quick ratio			
l. Declared 5% stock dividend.	Current ratio			
m. Purchased a building.	Free cash flow			

REQUIRED ▶ Place an X in the appropriate column to show whether the transaction increased, decreased, or had no effect on the indicated ratio.

LO5   Ratio Analysis

P 3.   Data for Rochelle Corporation in 20x5 and 20x4 follow. These data should be used in conjunction with the data in **P 1.**

	20x5	20x4
Net cash flows from operating activities	$128,000	$198,000
Net capital expenditures	$238,000	$76,000
Dividends paid	$62,800	$70,000
Number of common shares	60,000	60,000
Market price per share	$40	$60

Selected balances at the end of 20x3 were accounts receivable (net), $105,400; inventory, $198,800; total assets, $1,295,600; accounts payable, $134,400; and stockholders' equity, $753,200. All Rochelle's notes payable were current liabilities; all its bonds payable were long-term liabilities.

REQUIRED ▶   Perform a ratio analysis following the steps outlined below. Round all answers to one decimal place, and consider changes of .1 or less to be neutral. After making the calculations, indicate whether each ratio improved or deteriorated from 20x4 to 20x5 (use *F* for favorable and *U* for unfavorable).

1. Prepare a liquidity analysis by calculating for each year the (a) current ratio, (b) quick ratio, (c) receivable turnover, (d) average days' sales uncollected, (e) inventory turnover, (f) average days' inventory on hand, (g) payables turnover, and (h) average days' payable.
2. Prepare a profitability analysis by calculating for each year the (a) profit margin, (b) asset turnover, (c) return on assets, and (d) return on equity.
3. Prepare a long-term solvency analysis by calculating for each year the (a) debt to equity ratio and (b) interest coverage ratio.
4. Prepare a cash flow adequacy analysis by calculating for each year the (a) cash flow yield, (b) cash flows to sales, (c) cash flows to assets, and (d) free cash flow.
5. Prepare a market strength analysis by calculating for each year the (a) price/earnings ratio and (b) dividends yield.
6. Based on your analysis, assess Rochelle's performance in each of the following areas: liquidity, profitability, long-term solvency, and cash flow adequacy. Explain your evaluations.

LO5   Comprehensive Ratio Analysis of Two Companies

P 4.   Juanita Maxwell has decided to invest some of her savings in common stock. She feels that the chemical industry has good growth prospects, and she has narrowed her choice to two companies in that industry. As a final step in making the choice, she has decided to perform a comprehensive ratio analysis of the two companies, Reynard and Bouche. Income statement and balance sheet data for these two companies follow.

	Reynard	Bouche
Net sales	$9,486,200	$27,287,300
Costs and expenses		
Cost of goods sold	$5,812,200	$18,372,400
Selling expenses	1,194,000	1,955,700
Administrative expenses	1,217,400	4,126,000
Total costs and expenses	$8,223,600	$24,454,100
Income from operations	$1,262,600	$ 2,833,200
Interest expense	270,000	1,360,000
Income before income taxes	$ 992,600	$ 1,473,200
Income taxes	450,000	600,000
Net income	$ 542,600	$ 873,200
Earnings per share	$ 1.55	$ .87

	Reynard	Bouche
Assets		
Cash	$ 126,100	$ 514,300
Marketable securities (at cost)	117,500	1,200,000
Accounts receivable (net)	456,700	2,600,000
Inventories	1,880,000	4,956,000
Prepaid expenses	72,600	156,600
Property, plant, and equipment (net)	5,342,200	19,356,000
Intangibles and other assets	217,000	580,000
Total assets	$8,212,100	$29,362,900
Liabilities and Stockholders' Equity		
Accounts payable	$ 517,400	$ 2,342,000
Notes payable	1,000,000	2,000,000
Income taxes payable	85,200	117,900
Bonds payable	2,000,000	15,000,000
Common stock, $1 par value	350,000	1,000,000
Paid-in capital in excess of par value, common	1,747,300	5,433,300
Retained earnings	2,512,200	3,469,700
Total liabilities and stockholders' equity	$8,212,100	$29,362,900

During the year, Reynard paid a total of $140,000 in dividends, and its current price per share is $20. Bouche paid a total of $600,000 in dividends during the year, and its current market price per share is $9. Reynard had net cash flows from operating activities of $771,500 and net capital expenditures of $450,000. Bouche had net cash flows from operating activities of $843,000 and net capital expenditures of $1,550,000.

Information pertaining to these companies' prior years is not readily available. Assume that all their notes payable are current liabilities and that all their bonds payable are long-term liabilities.

REQUIRED ▶ Conduct a comprehensive ratio analysis of Reynard and of Bouche following the steps outlined below. (Round all ratios and percentages except earnings per share to one decimal place.)

1. Prepare a liquidity analysis by calculating for each company the (a) current ratio, (b) quick ratio, (c) receivable turnover, (d) average days' sales uncollected, (e) inventory turnover, (f) average days' inventory on hand, (g) payables turnover, and (h) averages days' payables.
2. Prepare a profitability analysis by calculating for each company the (a) profit margin, (b) asset turnover, (c) return on assets, and (d) return on equity.
3. Prepare a long-term solvency analysis by calculating for each company the (a) debt to equity ratio and (b) interest coverage ratio.
4. Prepare a cash flow adequacy analysis by calculating for each company the (a) cash flow yield, (b) cash flows to sales, (c) cash flows to assets, and (d) free cash flow.
5. Prepare an analysis of market strength by calculating for each company the (a) price/earnings ratio and (b) dividends yield.
6. Compare the two companies by inserting the ratio calculations from 1 through 5 in a table with the following column headings: Ratio Name, Reynard, Bouche, and Company with More Favorable Ratio. Indicate in the last column which company had the more favorable ratio in each case.
7. How could the analysis be improved if information about these companies' prior years were available?

ALTERNATE PROBLEMS

P 5.

LO5   **Effects of Transactions on Ratios**

Ⓚ/ᵣ

Mankato Corporation engaged in the transactions listed in the first column of the following table. Opposite each transaction is a ratio and space to indicate the effect of each transaction on the ratio.

Transaction	Ratio	Effect		
		Increase	Decrease	None
a. Sold merchandise on account.	Current ratio			
b. Sold merchandise on account.	Inventory turnover			
c. Collected on accounts receivable.	Quick ratio			
d. Wrote off an uncollectible account.	Receivable turnover			
e. Paid on accounts payable.	Current ratio			
f. Declared cash dividend.	Return on equity			
g. Incurred advertising expense.	Profit margin			
h. Issued stock dividend.	Debt to equity ratio			
i. Issued bonds payable.	Asset turnover			
j. Accrued interest expense.	Current ratio			
k. Paid previously declared cash dividend.	Dividends yield			
l. Purchased treasury stock.	Return on assets			
m. Recorded depreciation expense.	Cash flow yield			

REQUIRED ▶ Place an X in the appropriate column to show whether the transaction increased, decreased, or had no effect on the indicated ratio.

P 6.

LO5   **Ratio Analysis**

Ⓚ/ᵣ

The condensed comparative income statements and balance sheets of Lisle Corporation follow. All figures are in thousands of dollars, except earnings per share.

Lisle Corporation
Comparative Income Statements
For the Years Ended December 31, 20x6 and 20x5

	20x6	20x5
Net sales	$1,638,400	$1,573,200
Costs and expenses		
Cost of goods sold	$1,044,400	$1,004,200
Selling expenses	238,400	259,000
Administrative expenses	223,600	211,600
Total costs and expenses	$1,506,400	$1,474,800
Income from operations	$ 132,000	$ 98,400
Interest expense	32,800	19,600
Income before income taxes	$ 99,200	$ 78,800
Income taxes	31,200	28,400
Net income	$ 68,000	$ 50,400
Earnings per share	$ 1.70	$ 1.26

Lisle Corporation
Comparative Balance Sheets
December 31, 20x6 and 20x5

	20x6	20x5
Assets		
Cash	$ 40,600	$ 20,400
Accounts receivable (net)	117,800	114,600
Inventory	287,400	297,400
Property, plant, and equipment (net)	375,000	360,000
Total assets	$820,800	$792,400
Liabilities and Stockholders' Equity		
Accounts payable	$133,800	$238,600
Notes payable	100,000	200,000
Bonds payable	200,000	—
Common stock, $5 par value	200,000	200,000
Retained earnings	187,000	153,800
Total liabilities and stockholders' equity	$820,800	$792,400

Additional data for Lisle Corporation in 20x6 and 20x5 are as follows:

	20x6	20x5
Net cash flows from operating activities	$106,500,000	$86,250,000
Net capital expenditures	$22,500,000	$16,000,000
Dividends paid	$22,000,000	$17,200,000
Number of common shares	40,000,000	40,000,000
Market price per share	$9	$15

Selected balances (in thousands) at the end of 20x4 were accounts receivable (net), $103,400; inventory, $273,600; total assets, $732,800; accounts payable $193,300; and stockholders' equity, $320,600. All Lisle Corporation's notes payable were current liabilities. All its bonds payable were long-term liabilities.

REQUIRED ▶ Perform a ratio analysis following the steps outlined below. Round percentages and ratios to one decimal place, and consider changes of .1 or less to be neutral. After making the calculations, indicate whether each ratio had a favorable (F) or unfavorable (U) change from 20x5 to 20x6.

1. Conduct a liquidity analysis by calculating for each year the (a) current ratio, (b) quick ratio, (c) receivable turnover, (d) average days' sales uncollected, (e) inventory turnover, (f) average days' inventory on hand, (g) payables turnover, and (h) average days' payable.
2. Conduct a profitability analysis by calculating for each year the (a) profit margin, (b) asset turnover, (c) return on assets, and (d) return on equity.
3. Conduct a long-term solvency analysis by calculating for each year the (a) debt to equity ratio and (b) interest coverage ratio.
4. Conduct a cash flow adequacy analysis by calculating for each year the (a) cash flow yield, (b) cash flows to sales, (c) cash flows to assets, and (d) free cash flow.
5. Conduct a market strength analysis by calculating for each year the (a) price/earnings ratio and (b) dividends yield.
6. Based on your analysis, assess Lisle's performance in each of the following areas: liquidity, profitability, long-term solvency, and cash flow adequacy. Explain your evaluations.

Chapter 19 describes the approaches that businesses have developed to meet the challenges of today's changing business environment and the role that management accounting plays in meeting those challenges.

The Changing Business Environment: A Manager's Perspective

LEARNING OBJECTIVES

LO1 Distinguish management accounting from financial accounting and explain the role of management accounting in the management cycle.

LO2 Describe the value chain and its usefulness in analyzing a business.

LO3 Identify the management tools used for continuous improvement and describe how they work to meet the demands of global competition and how management accounting supports them.

LO4 Explain the balanced scorecard and its relationship to performance measures.

LO5 Prepare an analysis of nonfinancial data.

LO6 Identify the standards of ethical conduct for management accountants.

DECISION POINT

A MANAGER'S FOCUS

Honda Motor Company <www.honda.com> If organizations are to prosper, they must identify the factors that are critical to their success. Key success factors include satisfying customer needs, developing efficient manufacturing processes and advanced technologies, and being a leader in marketing innovative products. Honda Motor Company had all these factors in mind when it introduced a "green car" called the Insight to the U.S. market. Like other green cars, the Insight is a hybrid vehicle, running on both a gasoline engine and an electric motor. Priced at less than $20,000, it gets more than 60 miles to the gallon. The Insight thus meets regulators' demands for vehicles that emit fewer air-polluting fumes and consumers' demands for inexpensive, practical transportation.[1]

Using new technology and innovative design to address both customers' needs and environmental concerns is just part of Honda's strategy to stay agile, flexible, and ahead of its competitors. Equally important to Honda's success is the development of efficient manufacturing operations.[2] The company is standardizing manufacturing tools and eliminating the need to modify its assembly lines. Its model-specific sub-assembly lines will feed their products to a new and shorter assembly line.

All these innovations demonstrate Honda's resolve to remain an industry leader. What role does management accounting play in this endeavor?

Management accounting provides the information necessary for effective decision making. Honda's managers use management accounting information in

What managment accounting tools does Honda utilize to stay ahead of its competitors?

making decisions about everything from buying materials to developing and implementing new production processes to pricing, marketing, and distributing vehicles. Management accounting also provides Honda's managers with objective data by which they can measure the company's performance in terms of its key success factors. Among the tools of management accounting are budgets, which set daily operating goals for workers and provide targets for evaluating the workers' performance. Performance measures for the production process may include the time to complete one cycle of the process, the number of setups, and the time to rework errors in production. Performance measures of customer satisfaction may include number of customer complaints, number of service change notices, and number of customer referrals. As Honda strives to improve its products and maintain its record of success with vehicles like the Insight, it will continue to rely on the information that management accounting provides.

THE ROLE OF MANAGEMENT ACCOUNTING

LO1   Distinguish management accounting from financial accounting and explain the role of management accounting in the management cycle.

RELATED TEXT ASSIGNMENTS
Q: 1, 2, 3, 4, 5, 6, 7, 8
SE: 1, 2, 3, 4
E: 1, 2, 3, 4, 5
P: 1, 6
SD: 5
MRA: 1, 2

● **STOP AND THINK!**
A financial report often contains estimates and projections. How does the writer of such a report make sure the reader understands the uncertainties involved?

The writer should include a clear statement of the assumptions underlying the report and the conditions under which the estimates and projections were made. This will enable the reader to assess how valid the estimates and projections are. ∎

To plan and control an organization's operations, to measure its performance, and to make decisions about pricing products or services and many other matters, managers need accurate and timely accounting information. To do their jobs efficiently, employees who handle daily operations, such as managing the flow of materials into a production system, also rely on accurate and timely accounting information. The role of management accounting is to provide an information system that enables persons throughout an organization to make informed decisions, to be more effective at their jobs, and to improve the organization's performance.

The need for management accounting information exists regardless of the type of organization—manufacturing, retail, service, or governmental—or its size. Although multidivisional corporations need more information and more complex accounting systems than small ones, even small businesses need certain types of management accounting information to ensure efficient operating conditions. The precise type of information needed depends on an organization's goals and the nature of its operations.

In 1982, the Institute of Management Accountants (IMA) defined **management accounting** as

> the process of identification, measurement, accumulation, analysis, preparation, interpretation, and communication of financial information used by management to plan, evaluate, and control within the organization and to assure appropriate use of and accountability for its resources.[3]

Since this definition was written, the importance of nonfinancial information has increased significantly. Today, management accounting information includes such nonfinancial data as the time needed to complete one cycle of the production process or to rework production errors, as well as nonfinancial data pertaining to customer satisfaction.

MANAGEMENT ACCOUNTING AND FINANCIAL ACCOUNTING: A COMPARISON

Both management accounting and financial accounting assist decision makers by identifying, measuring, and processing relevant information and communicating

FOCUS ON BUSINESS PRACTICE

Why Is Management Accounting Vitally Important to Excellent Companies?

Futura Industries <www.futuraind.com> is not a famous company, but it is one of the best. Based in Utah, it is rated as that state's top privately owned employer. An international company with more than 50 years' experience in aluminum extruding, finishing, fabrication, machining, and design, Futura serves a high-end niche in such diverse markets as floor covering, electronics, transportation, and shower doors.

In achieving its success, Futura has used a management accounting technique called the balanced scorecard. The balanced scorecard focuses on four key dimensions of a company's operations: learning and growth among employees, internal business processes, satisfaction of customers, and financial goals. Using the balanced scorecard, Futura has developed measures of performance in each of these dimensions. For example, employee turnover is a measure of employee learning

and growth. Percentage of sales from new products and total production cost per standard hour are measures of how well the company's internal processes are performing, and number of customers' complaints and percentage of materials returned are measures of customer satisfaction. Finally, income and gross margin are among the measures of financial performance. To be truly successful, Futura must excel in all four dimensions.[4]

Management accounting plays an important role in helping companies attain their goals, providing information for making operating decisions, developing budgets, determining costs of products, measuring performance, and evaluating results. Without the interplay of information, decisions, and performance measurement that management accounting facilitates, companies like Futura could not be so successful.

TABLE 1.   Comparison of Management and Financial Accounting

Areas of Comparison	Management Accounting	Financial Accounting
Primary users	Managers, employees	Owners or stockholders, lenders, customers, governmental agencies
Report format	Flexible, driven by user's needs	Based on generally accepted accounting principles
Purpose of reports	Provide information for planning, control, performance measurement, and decision making	Report on past performance
Nature of information	Objective and verifiable for decision making; more subjective for planning (relies on estimates)	Objective and verifiable
Units of measure	Dollars at historical, market, or projected values; physical measures of time or number of objects	Dollars at historical and market values
Frequency of reports	Prepared as needed; may or may not be on a periodic basis	Prepared on a periodic basis

KEY POINT: Management accounting is *not* a subordinate activity to financial accounting. Rather, management accounting is a process that includes financial accounting, tax accounting, information analysis, and other accounting activities.

KEY POINT: Financial accounting requires consistency and comparability to ensure the usefulness of information to those outside the firm. Management accounting can use innovative analyses and presentation techniques to enhance information's usefulness to management within the firm.

this information through reports. Both provide managers with key measures of a company's performance and with cost information for valuing inventories on the balance sheet. Despite the overlap in their functions, management accounting and financial accounting differ in a number of ways. Table 1 summarizes these differences.

As we have indicated, management accounting provides managers and employees with the information they need to make informed decisions, to perform their jobs effectively, and to achieve their organization's goals. Thus, the primary users of management accounting information are people inside the organization. Financial accounting takes the actual results of management decisions about operating, investing, and financing activities and prepares financial statements for parties outside the organization—owners or stockholders, lenders, customers, and governmental agencies. Although these reports are prepared primarily for external use, managers also rely on them in evaluating an organization's performance.

Because management accounting reports are for internal use, their format can be flexible, driven by the user's needs. They may report either historical or future-oriented information without any formal guidelines or restrictions. In contrast, financial accounting reports, which focus on past performance, must follow standards and procedures specified by generally accepted accounting principles.

The information in management accounting reports may be objective and verifiable, expressed in terms of dollar amounts or physical measures of time or objects; if needed for planning purposes, the information may be based on estimates, and it will thus be more subjective. In contrast, the statements that financial accounting provides must be based on objective and verifiable information, which is generally

statement, a forecasted statement of cash flows, and a forecasted balance sheet for both years.

Because Wang does not have a financial background, she will consult a local accounting firm to help her develop the business plan. To provide relevant input for the plan, she will have to determine the types of candy she wants to sell; the volume of sales she anticipates; the selling price for each product; the monthly costs of leasing or purchasing facilities, employing personnel, and maintaining the facilities; and the number of display counters, storage units, and cash registers that she will need.

■ **EXECUTING**   Planning alone does not guarantee satisfactory operating results. Management must implement the business plan in ways that make optimal use of available resources. Smooth operations require one or more of the following: hiring and training personnel, matching human and technical resources to the work that must be done, purchasing or leasing facilities, maintaining an inventory of products for sale, and identifying operating activities, or tasks, that minimize waste and improve the quality of the products or services.

Managers execute the business plan by overseeing the daily operations of the organization. In small organizations, managers generally have frequent direct contact with their employees. They supervise them and interact with them to help them learn a task or to improve their performance. In larger, more complex organizations, there is usually less direct contact between managers and employees. Instead of directly observing employees, managers in large companies monitor employees' performance by measuring the time taken to complete an activity (such as the number of inspection hours) or the frequency of an activity (such as the number of inspections).

To illustrate how management accounting provides information to support the executing stage of the management cycle, let's assume that Abbie Wang has obtained the bank loan, and Sweet Treasures Candy Store is now open for business. The budget prepared for the store's first two years of business provides the link between the business plan and executing the plan. Items that relate to the business plan appear in the budget and become authorizations for expenditures. They include such matters as spending on store fixtures, hiring employees, developing advertising campaigns, and pricing items for special sales.

Critical to managing any retail business is the supply chain. As Figure 3 shows, the **supply chain** (also called the *supply network*) is the path that leads from the suppliers of the materials from which a product is made to the final consumer. In the supply chain for candy, sugar and other ingredients flow from suppliers to manufacturers to distributors to retailers to consumers. Wang's business is toward the end of the supply chain. She buys from distributors and sells to consumers. She must coordinate deliveries from distributors so that she meets the demands of her customers without having too much inventory on hand, which would tie up cash, or being out of stock when a customer asks for a certain type of candy. Management

KEY POINT: The supply chain is primarily concerned with logistics and with shortening the cycle time of suppliers to customers.

FIGURE 3
The Supply Chain

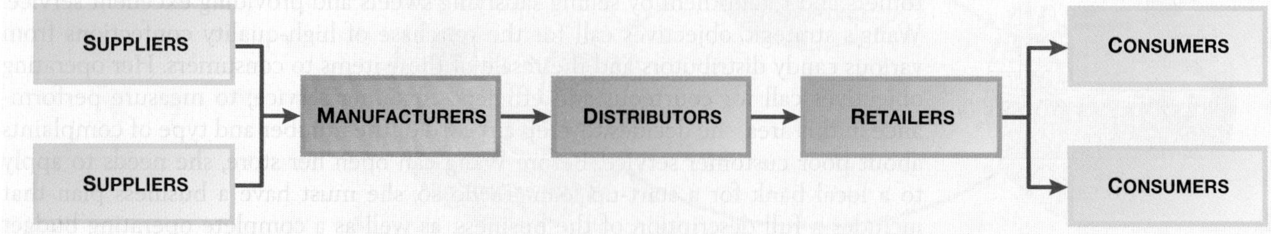

FIGURE 4
The Value Chain

Research and Development   Design

www.enron.com
www.worldcom.com

KEY POINT: Revenues and expenses accumulated in accounting systems for financial reporting purposes are also used in management accounting to support budgeting of next year's business activities.

● STOP AND THINK!

Is it better for a company to have a primary process or a support service as a core competency?

A company needs to be good at both. However, it is more important to have a primary process as a core competency because primary processes add value to the final product, and it is on the basis of primary processes that a company distinguishes itself from its competitors. ■

PRIMAR'

Let's assi
Wang no
of candy.

Research
plans t
confec

Design: c
For ex
of Wa

Supply: p
high-c
qualit

Productic
Wang

Marketir
them.

Distribu
cient :
want

Custome
For e
the cu

accounting information about deliveries and sales will help her manage the supply chain.

■ **REVIEWING** In the reviewing stage of the management cycle, managers compare actual performance with the performance levels they established in the planning stage. They earmark any significant variations for further analysis so that they can correct the problems. If the problems result from a change in the organization's operating environment, they may revise the original objectives. Ideally, the adjustments made in the reviewing stage will improve the company's performance.

To evaluate how well Sweet Treasures Candy Store is doing, Abbie Wang will compare the amounts estimated in the budget with information about actual results. If any differences occur, she will analyze why they have occurred. Reasons for these differences may lead Wang to change parts of her original business plan. In addition to reviewing employees' performance in regard to financial goals, such as avoiding waste, Wang will want to review how well her employees served customers. As noted earlier, she decided to monitor service quality by keeping a record of the number and type of complaints about poor customer service. Her review of this record may help her develop new and better business strategies.

■ **REPORTING** Whether accounting reports are prepared for internal or external use, it is essential that they provide accurate information and that they clearly communicate this information to the reader. Internal reports that provide inaccurate information or that present information in such a way that it is unclear to the employee or manager can have a negative effect on a company's operations and ultimately on its profitability. Full disclosure and transparency in financial statements issued to external parties is a fundamental of generally accepted accounting principles, and violation of this precept can now result in stiff penalties. After reporting violations by Enron, WorldCom, and other companies, Congress passed legislation that requires top management of companies that file financial statements with the Securities and Exchange Commission to certify that these statements are accurate; the penalty for issuing false public reports can be loss of compensation, fines, and jail time.

The key to producing a management accounting report that communicates accurate and useful information in such a way that the meaning is transparent to the reader is to apply the four *w*'s: why, who, what, and when.

- *Why?* Know the purpose of the report. Focus on it as you write.

- *Who?* Identify the audience for your report. Communicate at a level that matches your readers' understanding of the issue and their familiarity with accounting information. A detailed, informal report may be appropriate for your manager, but a more concise summary may be necessary for other audiences, such as the president or board of directors of your organization.

- *What?* What information is needed, and what method of presentation is best? Select relevant information from reliable sources. You may draw information from pertinent documents or from interviews with knowledgeable managers and employees. The information should be not only relevant, but also easy to read and understand. You may need to include visual aids, such as bar charts or graphs, to present the information clearly.

- *When?* Know the due date for the report. Strive to prepare an accurate report on a timely basis. If the report is urgently needed, you may have to sacrifice some accuracy in the interest of timeliness.

The four *w*'s are also applicable to financial accounting reports. Assume that Abbie Wang has hired Salvador Chavez to be her company's accountant. In the financial statements that he prepares, the purpose—or *why*—is to report on the financial health of Sweet Treasures Candy Store. In this case, Wang, her bank and

EXHIBIT 1
A Management Accounting Report

When:	Today's Date
Who:	To: Abbie Wang, Swee[...]
	From: Salvador Chavez, A[...]
Why:	Re: Ordering and Ship[...]
What:	As you requested, I have a[...]
	distributors. I found that d[...]
	of sales, or $36,000.
	On average, we are placing[...]
	order requires about two a[...]
	a service fee for each order,[...]
	My recommendations are ([...]
	affected if we order at least[...]
	web sites (our distributors[...]
	mendations, I project that t[...]
	$16,000, annually—a savin[...]

● STOP AND THINK!

A financial report often contains estimates and projections. How does the writer of such a report make sure the reader understands the uncertainties involved?

The writer should include a clear statement of the assumptions underlying the report and the conditions under which the estimates and projections were made. This will enable the reader to assess how valid the estimates and projections are. ■

other c[...]
about a[...]
the acc[...]
    Wa[...]
For exa[...]
distribu[...]
appear[...]
results[...]
Exhibi[...]
    In[...]
inform[...]
ment c[...]
and rev[...]
plan, c[...]
of emp[...]
a critic[...]

VALUE CHAIN ANALYSIS

LO2 Describe the value chain and its usefulness in analyzing a business.

RELATED TEXT ASSIGNMENTS
Q: 9, 10
SE: 4, 5
E: 6
P: 2
SD: 1

Each
though[...]
cept of[...]
As sho[...]
from [...]
proces[...]
manag[...]
add va[...]
ing the[...]

EXHIBIT 4
Standards of Ethical Conduct for Practitioners of Management Accounting and Financial Management

Practitioners of management accounting and financial management have an obligation to the public, their profession, the organization they serve, and themselves, to maintain the highest standards of ethical conduct. In recognition of this obligation, the Institute of Management Accountants has promulgated the following standards of ethical conduct for practitioners of management accounting and financial management. Adherence to these standards, both domestically and internationally, is integral to achieving the Objectives of Management Accounting. Practitioners of management accounting and financial management shall not commit acts contrary to these standards nor shall they condone the commission of such acts by others within their organizations.

Competence.   Practitioners of management accounting and financial management have a responsibility to:

- Maintain an appropriate level of professional competence by ongoing development of their knowledge and skills.
- Perform their professional duties in accordance with relevant laws, regulations, and technical standards.
- Prepare complete and clear reports and recommendations after appropriate analysis of relevant and reliable information.

Confidentiality.   Practitioners of management accounting and financial management have a responsibility to:

- Refrain from disclosing confidential information acquired in the course of their work except when authorized, unless legally obligated to do so.
- Inform subordinates as appropriate regarding the confidentiality of information acquired in the course of their work and monitor their activities to assure the maintenance of that confidentiality.
- Refrain from using or appearing to use confidential information acquired in the course of their work for unethical or illegal advantage either personally or through third parties.

Integrity.   Practitioners of management accounting and financial management have a responsibility to:

- Avoid actual or apparent conflicts of interest and advise all appropriate parties of any potential conflict.
- Refrain from engaging in any activity that would prejudice their ability to carry out their duties ethically.
- Refuse any gift, favor, or hospitality that would influence or would appear to influence their actions.
- Refrain from either actively or passively subverting the attainment of the organization's legitimate and ethical objectives.
- Recognize and communicate professional limitations or other constraints that would preclude responsible judgment or successful performance of an activity.

FOCUS ON BUSINESS ETHICS

What Is Management's Responsibility for the Financial Statements?

Top-level managers have not only an ethical responsibility to ensure that the financial statements issued by their companies adhere to the principles of full disclosure and transparency; today, they have a legal responsibility as well. Strong concerns about the integrity of financial reporting created by the collapse of the Enron Corporation <www.enron.com> in 2001 fueled widespread support for accounting reform. An important outcome of the reform efforts was the passage of the Sarbanes-Oxley Act in 2002. Among the provisions of this law is one that directed the Securities and Exchange Commission (SEC) to adopt a rule requiring the chief executive officers and chief financial officers of companies filing reports with the SEC to certify that those reports contain no untrue statements and include all facts needed to ensure that the reports are not misleading. In addition to issuing this rule, the SEC adopted one requiring managers to ensure that the information in reports filed with the SEC "is recorded, processed, summarized and reported on a timely basis."[8]

- Communicate unfavorable as well as favorable information and professional judgments or opinions.
- Refrain from engaging in or supporting any activity that would discredit the profession.

Objectivity.   Practitioners of management accounting and financial management have a responsibility to:

- Communicate information fairly and objectively.
- Disclose fully all relevant information that could reasonably be expected to influence an intended user's understanding of the reports, comments, and recommendations presented.

Resolution of Ethical Conflict.   In applying the standards of ethical conduct, practitioners of management accounting and financial management may encounter problems in identifying unethical behavior or in resolving an ethical conflict. When faced with significant ethical issues, practitioners of management accounting and financial management should follow the established policies of the organization bearing on the resolution of such conflict. If these policies do not resolve the ethical conflict, such practitioner should consider the following courses of action:

- Discuss such problems with the immediate superior except when it appears that the superior is involved, in which case the problem should be presented initially to the next higher managerial level. If a satisfactory resolution cannot be achieved when the problem is initially presented, submit the issues to the next higher managerial level.
- If the immediate superior is the chief executive officer, or equivalent, the acceptable reviewing authority may be a group such as the audit committee, executive committee, board of directors, board of trustees, or owners. Contact with levels above the immediate superior should be initiated only with the superior's knowledge, assuming the superior is not involved. Except where legally prescribed, communication of such problems to authorities or individuals not employed or engaged by the organization is not considered appropriate.
- Clarify relevant ethical issues by confidential discussion with an objective advisor (e.g., IMA Ethics Counseling Service) to obtain a better understanding of possible courses of action.
- Consult your own attorney as to legal obligations and rights concerning the ethical conflict.
- If the ethical conflict still exists after exhausting all levels of internal review, there may be no other recourse on significant matters than to resign from the organization and to submit an informative memorandum to an appropriate representative of the organization. After resignation, depending on the nature of the ethical conflict, it may also be appropriate to notify other parties.

Source: From *Standards of Ethical Conduct for Practitioners of Management Accounting and Financial Management.*. Institute of Management Accountants, July 1997. Reprinted by permission.

🛑 **STOP AND THINK!**

If you encounter financial irregularities in your company, what should your first step be? What is your last recourse?

Your first step should be to discuss the situation with your immediate superior unless he or she is involved, in which case you should discuss the situation with someone at at higher level. You may have to take the matter to the board of directors or to the authorities. If you cannot resolve it, your last resort is to resign. ■

management could achieve higher profits for the owners by purchasing a less expensive, less effective antipollution device that would not protect the community as well. Such conflicts between external parties can create ethical dilemmas for management and for accountants.

To be viewed credibly by the various parties that rely on the information they provide, management accountants must adhere to the highest standards of performance. To provide guidance, the Institute of Management Accountants has issued standards of ethical conduct for practitioners of management accounting and financial management. Those standards, presented in Exhibit 4, emphasize that management accountants have responsibilities in the areas of competence, confidentiality, integrity, and objectivity.

✔ Check out ACE for a Review Quiz at http://accounting.college.hmco.com/students.

Chapter Review

REVIEW OF LEARNING OBJECTIVES

LO1 Distinguish management accounting from financial accounting and explain the role of management accounting in the management cycle.

Management accounting is the process of identifying, measuring, accumulating, analyzing, preparing, interpreting, and communicating information that management uses to plan, evaluate, and control an organization and to ensure that its resources are used and accounted for appropriately. Management accounting reports provide information for planning, control, performance measurement, and decision making to managers and employees when they need such information. These reports follow a flexible format and may present either historical or future-oriented information expressed in dollar amounts or physical measures. In contrast, financial accounting reports provide information about an organization's past performance to owners, lenders, customers, and government agencies on a periodic basis. Financial accounting reports follow strict guidelines defined by generally accepted accounting principles.

Management accounting supports each stage of the management cycle. In the planning stage, managers use the information that management accounting provides to establish strategic and operating objectives that reflect their company's mission and to formulate a comprehensive business plan for achieving those objectives. The plan is usually expressed in financial terms in the form of budgets. In the executing stage, managers use the information in the budgets to implement the plan. In the reviewing stage, they compare actual performance with planned performance and take steps to correct any problems. Reports reflect the results of planning, executing, and reviewing operations and may be prepared for external or internal use.

LO2 Describe the value chain and its usefulness in analyzing a business.

The value chain conceives of each step in the manufacture of a product or the delivery of a service as a link in a chain that adds value to the product or service. These value-adding steps—research and development, design, supply, production, marketing, distribution, and customer service—are known as primary processes. The value chain also includes support services—human resources, legal services, information services, and management accounting. Support services facilitate the primary processes but do not add value to the final product. Value chain analysis enables a company to focus on its core competencies. Parts of the value chain that are not core competencies are frequently outsourced.

LO3 Identify the management tools used for continuous improvement and describe how they work to meet the demands of global competition and how management accounting supports them.

Management tools for continuous improvement include the just-in-time (JIT) operating philosophy, total quality management (TQM), activity-based management (ABM), and the theory of constraints (TOC). These tools are designed to help businesses meet the demands of global competition by reducing resource waste and costs and improving product or service quality, thereby increasing customer satisfaction. Management accounting responds to a JIT operating environment by providing an information system that is sensitive to changes in production processes. In a TQM environment, management accounting provides information about the costs of quality. ABM's assignment of overhead costs to products or services relies on the accounting practice known as activity-based costing (ABC). In businesses that use TOC, management accounting identifies process or product constraints.

LO4 Explain the balanced scorecard and its relationship to performance measures.

The balanced scorecard links the perspectives of an organization's stakeholder groups—financial (investors and owners), learning and growth (employees), internal business processes, and customers—with the organization's mission, objectives, resources, and performance measures. Performance measures are used to assess whether the objectives of each of the four perspectives are being met. Benchmarking is a technique for determining a company's competitive advantage by comparing its performance with that of its industry peers.

LO5 Prepare an analysis of non-financial data.

Using management tools like TQM and ABM and comprehensive frameworks like the balanced scorecard requires analysis of both financial and nonfinancial data. In analyzing nonfinancial data, it is important to compare performance measures with the objectives that are to be achieved.

LO6 Identify the standards of ethical conduct for management accountants.

Standards of ethical conduct for management accountants emphasize practitioners' responsibilities in the areas of competence, confidentiality, integrity, and objectivity. These standards of conduct help management accountants recognize and avoid situations that could compromise their ability to supply management with accurate and relevant information.

REVIEW OF CONCEPTS AND TERMINOLOGY

The following concepts and terms were introduced in this chapter:

LO3 **Activity-based costing (ABC):** A management accounting practice that identifies all of an organization's major operating activities (both production and nonproduction), traces costs to those activities, and then assigns costs to the products or services that use the resources and services supplied by those activities.

LO3 **Activity-based management (ABM):** An approach to managing an organization that identifies all major operating activities, determines the resources consumed by each of those activities and the cause of the resource usage, categorizes the activities as either adding value to a product or service or not adding value, and seeks to eliminate or reduce nonvalue-adding activities.

LO4 **Balanced scorecard:** A framework that links the perspectives of an organization's stakeholder groups with the organization's mission, objectives, resources, and performance measures.

LO4 **Benchmarking:** A technique for determining a company's competitive advantage by comparing its performance with that of its best competitors.

LO4 **Benchmarks:** Measures of the best practices in an industry.

LO1 **Business plan:** A comprehensive statement of how a company will achieve its objectives.

LO3 **Continuous improvement:** The management concept that one should never be satisfied with what is but should instead constantly seek improved efficiency and lower cost through better methods, products, services, processes, or resources.

LO2 **Core competency:** What a company does best and what gives it an advantage over its competitors.

LO3 **Costs of quality:** Both the costs of achieving quality and the costs of poor quality in the manufacture of a product or the delivery of a service.

LO3 **Just-in-time (JIT) operating philosophy:** A management tool aimed at improving productivity and eliminating waste by requiring that all resources—materials, personnel, and facilities—be acquired and used only as needed.

LO1 **Management accounting:** The process of identifying, measuring, accumulating, analyzing, preparing, interpreting, and communicating information that management uses to plan, evaluate, and control an organization and to ensure that its resources are used and accounted for appropriately.

LO1 **Mission:** A statement of the fundamental way in which a business will achieve its goal of increasing the value of the owners' interest in the business.

LO3 **Nonvalue-adding activities:** Activities that add cost to a product or service but do not increase its market value.

LO1 **Operating objectives:** Short-term goals that outline expectations for the performance of day-to-day operations.

LO2 **Outsourcing:** The engagement of other companies to perform a process or service of the value chain that is not among an organization's core competencies.

LO4 **Performance measures:** Quantitative tools that gauge an organization's performance in relation to a specific goal or expected outcome.

LO2 **Primary processes:** Components of the value chain that add value to a product or service.

LO1 **Strategic objectives:** Broad, long-term goals that determine the fundamental nature and direction of a business and that serve as a guide for decision making.

LO1 **Supply chain:** The path that leads from the suppliers of the materials from which a product is made to the final consumer. Also called the *supply network*.

LO2 **Support services:** Components of the value chain that facilitate the primary processes but do not add value to a product or service.

LO3 **Theory of constraints (TOC):** A management theory that contends that limiting factors, or bottlenecks, occur during the production of any product or service, but that once managers identify such a constraint, they can focus attention and resources on it and thus achieve significant improvements.

LO3 **Total quality management (TQM):** A management tool that requires that all parts of a business work together to build quality into the business's product or service.

LO3 **Value-adding activities:** Activities that add value to a product or service as perceived by the customer.

LO2 **Value chain:** A way of defining a business as a set of primary processes and support services that link together to add value to a business's products or services, thus fulfilling the business's mission and objectives.

REVIEW PROBLEM

Analysis of Nonfinancial Data

LO5 Youngdale Painting, Inc., employs painters who specialize in interior walls and exterior trim. George Youngdale, the owner, recently assigned two interior painters and three exterior trim painters to jobs at Yakima High School and Jerome Elementary School. He prepared the following table estimating the number of hours that the painters would work during June:

Estimated Hours to Be Worked

	Week 1	Week 2	Week 3	Week 4	Totals
Interior	80	80	80	80	320
Exterior	120	120	120	120	480

On July 2, Youngdale assembled the following data on the actual number of hours worked:

Actual Hours Worked

	Week 1	Week 2	Week 3	Week 4	Totals
Interior	96	108	116	116	436
Exterior	104	108	116	108	436

Youngdale is concerned about the excess hours worked during June.

REQUIRED ▶

1. For each group of painters (interior and exterior), prepare an analysis that shows the estimated hours, the actual hours worked, and the number of hours under or over the estimates for each week and in total.
2. Using the same information, prepare a line graph for the interior painters and another line graph for the exterior painters. Place the weeks on the X axis and the number of hours on the Y axis.

3. Using the information from 1 and 2, identify which group of painters worked more hours than George Youngdale planned and offer several reasons for the additional hours.

ANSWER TO REVIEW PROBLEM

1.

Interior Painters

Week	Estimated Hours	Actual Hours	Hours Under or (Over) Estimate
1	80	96	(16)
2	80	108	(28)
3	80	116	(36)
4	80	116	(36)
Total	320	436	(116)

Exterior Painters

Week	Projected Hours	Actual Hours	Hours Under or (Over) Estimate
1	120	104	16
2	120	108	12
3	120	116	4
4	120	108	12
Total	480	436	44

2.

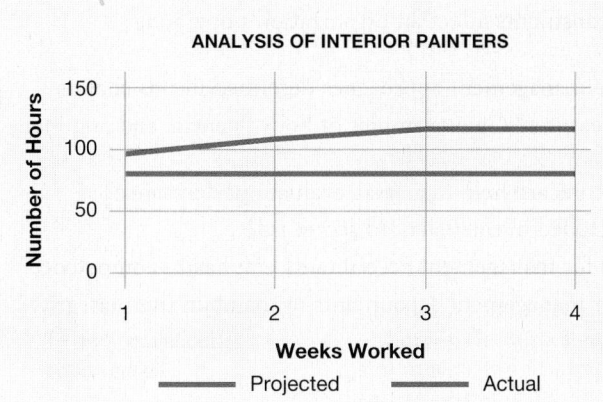

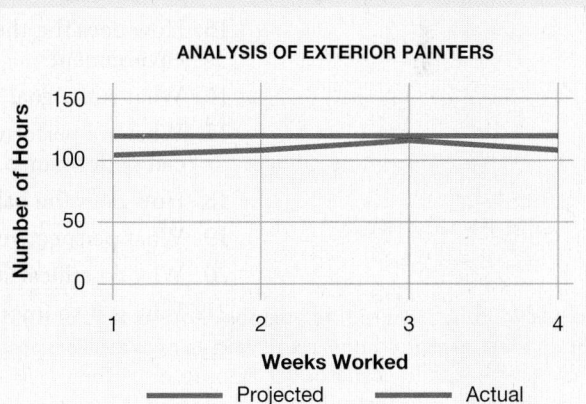

3. The interior painters worked more hours than Youngdale had planned. The following are possible reasons for the additional hours:

a. The quality of the paint or painting materials may have been poor, which would have required the painters to apply extra coats.

b. One of the painters may have been recently hired and inexperienced. He would therefore have worked more slowly than anticipated, and the other painter may have taken extra time to train him.

c. The customer may have requested a change in color or finish after the painting had started, in which case the painters would have had to repaint some areas.

d. Youngdale may have underestimated the time required for the interior painting.

3. Low-priced products
4. Improved return on investment
5. Job security
6. Cost-effective production processes

SE 9.
LO5   Analysis of Nonfinancial Data

Precision Technologies has been having a problem with the computerized welding operation in its extractor assembly line. The extractors are used to separate metal shavings into piles of individual metals for recycling and scrap sales. The time for each welding operation has been increasing at an erratic rate. Management has asked that the time intervals be analyzed to see if the cause of the problem can be determined. The number of parts welded per shift during the previous week is as follows:

	Machine Number	Monday	Tuesday	Wednesday	Thursday	Friday
First shift:						
Kovacs	1	642	636	625	617	602
Abington	2	732	736	735	729	738
Geisler	3	745	726	717	694	686
Second shift:						
Deragon	1	426	416	410	404	398
Berwager	2	654	656	661	664	670
Grass	3	526	524	510	504	502

What can you deduce from this information that may help management solve the welding operation problem?

SE 10.
LO6   Ethical Conduct

Tyler Jones, a management accountant for Pegstone Cosmetics Company, has lunch every day with his friend Joe Blaik, a management accountant for Shepherd Cosmetics, Inc., a competitor of Pegstone. Last week, Jones couldn't decide how to treat some information in a report he was preparing, so he discussed it with Blaik. Is Jones adhering to the ethical standards of management accountants? Defend your answer.

EXERCISES

E 1.
LO1   Management Accounting Versus Financial Accounting

Explain this statement: "It is impossible to distinguish the point at which financial accounting ends and management accounting begins."

E 2.
LO1   The Management Cycle

Indicate whether each of the following management activities in a community hospital is part of the planning stage (P), the executing stage (E), the reviewing stage (REV), or the reporting stage (REP) of the management cycle:

1. Leasing five ambulances for the current year
2. Comparing the actual number with the planned number of patient days in the hospital for the year
3. Developing a strategic plan for a new pediatric wing
4. Preparing a report showing the past performance of the emergency room
5. Developing standards, or expectations, for performance in the hospital admittance area for next year
6. Preparing and distributing the hospital's balance sheet and income statement to the board of directors
7. Maintaining an inventory of bed linens and bath towels
8. Formulating a corporate policy for the treatment and final disposition of hazardous waste materials
9. Preparing a report of the types and amounts of hazardous waste materials removed from the hospital in the last three months
10. Recording the time taken to deliver food trays to patients

E 3.
LO1   Report Preparation

Jeff Johnson is the sales manager for Sunny Days Greeting Cards, Inc. At the beginning of the year, the organization introduced a new line of humorous birthday cards to the U.S. market. Management will hold a strategic planning meeting on August 31 to discuss next year's operating activities. One item on the agenda is to review the success of the new line of cards and decide if there is a need to change the selling price or to stimulate sales volume in the five sales territories. Johnson has been asked to prepare a report addressing those issues and to present it at the meeting. His report is to include profits generated in each sales territory by the new card line only.

On August 31, Johnson arrived at the meeting late and immediately distributed his report to the strategic planning team. The report consisted of comments made by seven of Johnson's leading sales representatives. The comments were broad in scope and touched only lightly on the success of the new card line. Johnson was pleased that he had met the deadline for distributing the report, but the other team members were disappointed in the information he had provided.

Using the four *w*'s for report presentation, comment on Johnson's effectiveness in preparing his report.

LO1 The Planning Framework

E 4. Edward Ortez has just opened a company that imports fine ceramic gifts from Mexico and sells them over the Internet. In planning his business, Ortez did the following:

1. Listed his expected expenses and revenues for the first six months of operations
2. Decided that he wanted the company to provide him with income for a good lifestyle and funds for retirement
3. Determined that he would keep his expenses low and generate enough revenues during the first two months of operations so that he would have a positive cash flow by the third month
4. Decided to focus his business on providing customers with the finest Mexican ceramics at a favorable price
5. Developed a complete list of goals, objectives, procedures, and policies relating to how he would find, buy, store, sell, and ship goods and collect payment
6. Decided not to have a retail operation but to rely solely on the Internet to market the products

Match each of Ortez's actions to the components of the planning framework: goal, mission, strategic objectives, operating objectives, business plan, and budget.

LO1 The Supply Chain

E 5. In recent years, United Parcel Service (UPS) has been positioning itself as a solver of supply chain issues. Visit its web site at www.ups-scs.com and read one of the case studies related to its supply chain solutions. Explain how UPS helped improve the supply chain of the business featured in the case.

LO2 The Value Chain

E 6. As mentioned in **E4**, Edward Ortez recently opened his own company. He has been thinking of ways to improve the business. Here is a list of the actions that he will be undertaking:

1. Engaging an accountant to help analyze progress in meeting the objectives of the company
2. Hiring a company to handle payroll records and employee benefits
3. Developing a logo for labeling and packaging the ceramics
4. Making gift packages by placing gourmet food products in ceramic pots and wrapping them in plastic
5. Engaging an attorney to write contracts
6. Traveling to Mexico himself to arrange for purchase and shipment of products back to the company
7. Arranging new ways of taking orders over the Internet and shipping the products
8. Keeping track of the characteristics of customers and the number and types of products they buy
9. Following up with customers to see if they received the products and if they are happy with them
10. Arranging for an outside firm to keep the accounting records
11. Distributing brochures that display the ceramics and refer to the web site

Classify each of Ortez's actions as one of the value chain's primary processes—research and development, design, supply, production, marketing, distribution, or customer service—or as a support service—human resources, legal services, information systems, or management accounting. Of the eleven actions, which are the most likely candidates for outsourcing? Why?

LO3 Management Tools

E 7. Recently, you were dining with four chief financial officers who were attending a seminar on management tools and approaches to improving operations. During dinner, they shared information about their organizations' current operating environments. Excerpts from the dinner conversation appear on the following page. Indicate whether each excerpt describes activity-based management (ABM), the just-in-time (JIT) operating philosophy, total quality management (TQM), or the theory of constraints (TOC).

CFO 1: We think quality can be achieved through carefully designed production processes. We focus on minimizing the time needed to move, store, queue, and inspect our materials and products. We've reduced inventories by purchasing and using materials only when they're needed.

CFO 2: Your approach is good. But we're more concerned with our total operating environment, so we have a strategy that asks all employees to contribute to the quality of both our products and our work environment. We focus on eliminating poor product quality by reducing waste and inefficiencies in our current operating methods.

CFO 3: Our organization has adopted a strategy for producing high-quality products that incorporates many of your approaches. We also want to manage our resources effectively, but we do it by monitoring operating activities. We analyze all activities to eliminate or reduce the ones that don't add value to products.

CFO 4: All of your approaches are good, but how do you set priorities for your management efforts? We find that we achieve the greatest improvements by focusing our time and resources on the bottlenecks in our production processes.

LO3   TQM and Value

E 8. De Silva Dry Cleaners recently adopted total quality management. Jorge De Silva, the owner, has hired you as a consultant. Classify each of the following activities as either value-adding (V) or nonvalue-adding (NV):

1. Providing same-day service
2. Closing store on weekends
3. Providing free delivery service
4. Having seamstress on site
5. Making customers pay for parking

LO4   The Balanced Scorecard

E 9. Connie's Takeout caters to young professionals who want a good meal at home but do not have time to prepare it. Connie's has developed the following business objectives:

1. To provide fast, courteous service
2. To manage its inventory of food carefully
3. To have repeat customers
4. To be profitable and grow

Connie's has also developed the following performance measures:

5. Growth in revenues per quarter and net margin
6. Average unsold food at the end of the business day as a percentage of the total food purchased that day
7. Average customer time at counter before being waited on
8. Percentage of customers who have shopped in the store before

Match each of these objectives and performance measures with the four perspectives of the balanced scorecard: financial perspective, learning and growth perspective, internal business processes perspective, and customer perspective.

LO5   Nonfinancial Data Analysis

E 10. Bluegrass Landscaping specializes in lawn installations requiring California bluegrass sod. The sod comes in 1-yard squares. To evaluate performance in laying sod layers, Bluegrass Landscaping uses the guideline of 500 square yards per person per hour. The company collected the following data about its operations during the first week of March:

Employee	Hours Worked	Square Yards of Sod Planted
S. Elway	38	18,240
R. Mahoney	45	22,500
N. Fencereaux	40	19,800
O. Pfister	42	17,640
B. Onski	44	22,880
J. Mantero	45	21,500

Evaluate the performance of the six employees.

E 11.

LO5 Nonfinancial Data Analysis

Mother's Cookie Company recently adopted total quality management. According to a quality performance measure set by Elián Gomez, the vice president in charge of production, no more than ten cookies should be rejected per day. Data gathered for a recent week showed that the actual number of rejected cookies per day was as follows.

Day	Actual Number of Rejected Cookies
Monday	5
Tuesday	6
Wednesday	7
Thursday	4
Friday	8
Total	30

Analyze the activity for the week by preparing a table showing each day's maximum number of rejected cookies allowed, actual number of rejected cookies, and variance from the maximum number allowed. Compute the daily average for each column. Based on the information in your table, how successful was Gomez in increasing the quality of the company's cookies?

E 12.

LO5 Nonfinancial Data Analysis

Sara Fowler, who is in charge of information technology at Cergo Corporation, must decide whether to purchase additional memory for her department's three computers or to buy additional new computers to increase her department's productivity. Six weeks ago, Fowler installed additional memory on Computer CM. She is impressed with the processing improvement, but she has yet to decide between the two courses of action. Information on the number of bytes processed per nanosecond by each computer for the past ten weeks is as follows:

	Weeks									
Computer	One	Two	Three	Four	Five	Six	Seven	Eight	Nine	Ten
CM	51	52	53	50	80	82	84	87	88	89
CN	52	51	52	52	54	54	53	54	54	54
CP	50	49	50	48	50	52	51	50	52	50

Fowler has asked you to analyze the two courses of action based on the assumption that two memory upgrades can be purchased for the price of one new computer. Your analysis is to include the computation of the average weekly output per nanosecond for Computers CN and CP, a comparison of that average with the output of Computer CM, and the computation of the weekly difference between the average output and the output of Computer CM. What course of action do you recommend?

E 13.

LO6 Ethical Conduct

Katrina Kim went to work for Billings Industries five years ago. She was recently promoted to cost accounting manager and now has a new boss, Vic Howard, the corporate controller. Last week, Kim and Howard went to a two-day professional development program on accounting changes in the manufacturing environment. During the first hour of the first day's program, Howard disappeared, and Kim didn't see him again until the cocktail hour. The same thing happened on the second day. During the trip home, Kim asked Howard if he had enjoyed the conference. He replied:

> Katrina, the golf course was excellent. You play golf. Why don't you join me during the next conference? I haven't sat in on one of those sessions in ten years. This is my R&R time. Those sessions are for the new people. My experience is enough to keep me current. Plus, I have excellent people to help me as we adjust our accounting system to the changes being implemented on the production floor.

Does Katrina Kim have an ethical dilemma? If so, what is it? What are her options? How would you solve her problem? Be prepared to defend your answer.

E 14.

LO6 Ethical Responsibility

Rank in order of importance the management accountant's four areas of responsibility: competence, confidentiality, integrity, and objectivity. Explain the reasons for your ranking.

E 15.

LO6 Corporate Ethics

To answer the following questions, conduct a search of several companies' web sites: (1) Does the company have an ethics statement? (2) Does it express a commitment to environmental or social issues? (3) In your opinion, is the company ethically responsible? Select one of the companies you researched and write a brief description of your findings.

PROBLEMS

LO1   Report Preparation

P 1. Classic Industries, Inc., is deciding whether to expand its line of women's clothing called Pants by Olene. Sales in units of this product were 22,500, 28,900, and 36,200 in 20x4, 20x5, and 20x6, respectively. The product has been very profitable, averaging 35 percent profit (above cost) over the three-year period. Classic has ten sales representatives covering seven states in the Northeast. Present production capacity is about 40,000 pants per year. There is adequate plant space for additional equipment, and the labor needed can be easily hired and trained.

The organization's management is made up of four vice presidents: the vice president of marketing, the vice president of production, the vice president of finance, and the vice president of management information systems. Each vice president is directly responsible to the president, Teresa Jefferson.

REQUIRED ▶
1. What types of information will Jefferson need before she can decide whether to expand the Pants by Olene line?
2. Assume that one report needed to support Jefferson's decision is an analysis of sales, broken down by sales representatives, over the past three years. How would each of the four *w*'s pertain to this report?
3. Design a format for the report described in **2**.

LO2   The Value Chain

P 2. Zeigler Electronics is a manufacturer of cell phones, a highly competitive business. Zeigler's phones carry a price of $99, but competition forces the company to offer significant discounts and rebates. As a result, the average price of Zeigler's cell phones has dropped to around $50, and the company is losing money. Management is applying value chain analysis to the company's operations in an effort to reduce costs and improve product quality. A study by the company's management accountant has determined the following per unit costs for primary processes:

Primary Process	Cost per Unit
Research and development	$ 2.50
Design	3.50
Supply	4.50
Production	6.70
Marketing	8.00
Distribution	1.90
Customer service	.50
Total cost	$27.60

To generate a gross margin large enough for the company to cover overhead costs and earn a profit, Zeigler must lower its total cost per unit for primary processes to at least $20. After analyzing operations, management reached the following conclusions with regard to primary processes:

- Research and development and design are critical functions because the market and competition require constant development of new features with "cool" designs at lower cost. Nevertheless, management feels that the cost per unit of these processes must be reduced by 10 percent.
- Six different suppliers currently provide the components for the cell phones. Ordering these components from just two suppliers and negotiating lower prices could result in a savings of 15 percent.
- The cell phones are currently manufactured in Mexico. By shifting production to China, the unit cost of production can be lowered by 20 percent.
- Most cell phones are sold through wireless communication companies that are trying to attract new customers with low-priced cell phones. Management believes these companies should bear more of the marketing costs and that it is feasible to renegotiate its marketing arrangements with them so that they will bear 35 percent of the current marketing costs.

- Distribution costs are already very low, but management will set a target of reducing the cost per unit by 10 percent.
- Customer service is a weakness of the company and has resulted in lost sales. Management therefore proposes increasing the cost per unit of customer service by 50 percent.

REQUIRED ▶

1. Prepare a table showing the current cost per unit of primary processes and the projected cost per unit based on management's proposals for cost reduction.
2. Will management's proposals for cost reduction achieve the targeted total cost per unit? What further steps should management take to reduce costs? Which steps that management is proposing do you believe will be the most difficult to accomplish?
3. What are the company's support services? What role should these services play in the value chain analysis?

P 3.

LO4   The Balanced Scorecard and Benchmarking

Bychowski Associates is an independent insurance agency that sells business, automobile, home, and life insurance. Myra Bychowski, senior partner of the agency, recently attended a workshop at the local university in which the balanced scorecard was presented as a way of focusing all of a company's functions on its mission. After the workshop, she met with her managers in a weekend brainstorming session. The group determined that the agency's mission was to provide high-quality, innovative risk-protection services to individuals and businesses. To ensure that the agency would fulfill this mission, the group established the following objectives:

- To provide a sufficient return on investment by increasing sales and maintaining the liquidity needed to support operations
- To add value to the agency's services by training employees to be knowledgeable and competent
- To retain customers and attract new customers
- To operate an efficient and cost-effective office support system for customer agents

To determine the agency's progress in meeting these objectives, the group established the following performance measures:

- Number of new ideas for customer insurance
- Percentage of customers who rate services as excellent
- Average time for processing insurance applications
- Number of dollars spent on training
- Growth in revenues for each type of insurance
- Average time for processing claims
- Percentage of employees who complete 40 hours of training during the year
- Percentage of new customer leads that result in sales
- Cash flow
- Number of customer complaints
- Return on assets
- Percentage of customers who renew policies
- Percentage of revenue devoted to office support system (information systems, accounting, orders, and claims processing)

REQUIRED ▶

1. Prepare a balanced scorecard for Bychowski Associates by stating the agency's mission and matching its four objectives to the four stakeholder perspectives: the financial, learning and growth, internal business processes, and customer perspectives. Indicate which of the agency's performance measures would be appropriate for each objective.
2. Bychowski Associates is a member of an association of independent insurance agents that provides industry statistics about many aspects of operating an insurance agency. What is benchmarking, and in what ways would the industry statistics assist Bychowski Associates in further developing its balanced scorecard?

P 4.

LO5   Nonfinancial Data Analysis

Action Skateboards, Inc., manufactures state-of-the-art skateboards and related equipment. Lindy Raymond is the manager of the California branch. The production process involves the following departments and tasks: the Molding Department, where the board's base is molded; the Sanding Department, where the base is sanded after being taken out of the mold; the Fiber-Ap Department, where a fiberglass coating is applied; and the Assembling Department, where the wheels are attached and the board is inspected. After the board is molded, all processes are performed by hand.

Raymond is concerned about the number of hours her employees are working. The plant has a two-shift labor force. The actual hours worked for the past four weeks are as follows:

Actual Hours Worked—First Shift

Department	Week 1	Week 2	Week 3	Week 4	Totals
Molding	420	432	476	494	1,822
Sanding	60	81	70	91	302
Fiber-Ap	504	540	588	572	2,204
Assembling	768	891	952	832	3,443

Actual Hours Worked—Second Shift

Department	Week 1	Week 2	Week 3	Week 4	Totals
Molding	360	357	437	462	1,616
Sanding	60	84	69	99	312
Fiber-Ap	440	462	529	506	1,937
Assembling	670	714	782	726	2,892

Expected labor hours per product for each operation are Molding, 3.4 hours; Sanding, .5 hour; Fiber-Ap, 4.0 hours; and Assembling, 6.5 hours. Actual units completed are as follows:

Week	First Shift	Second Shift
1	120	100
2	135	105
3	140	115
4	130	110

REQUIRED ▶

1. Prepare an analysis of each week to determine the average actual labor hours worked per board for each phase of the production process and for each shift. Carry your solution to two decimal places.
2. Using the information from 1 and the expected labor hours per board for each department, prepare an analysis showing the differences in each phase of each shift. Identify possible reasons for the differences.

P 5.
LO5   Nonfinancial Data Analysis

The flow of passenger traffic is an important factor in airport management, and over the past year, heightened security measures at Winnebago County Airport in Rockford, Illinois, have slowed passenger flow significantly. The airport uses eight metal detectors to screen passengers for weapons. The facility is open from 6:00 A.M. to 10:00 P.M. daily, and present machinery allows a maximum of 45,000 passengers to be checked each day.

Management has selected four of the metal detectors for special analysis to determine if additional equipment is needed or if a passenger traffic director could solve the problem. The passenger traffic director would be responsible for guiding people to different machines and instructing them on the detection process. Because this solution would be less expensive than acquiring new machines, management decides to assign a suitable person to this function on a trial basis. Management hopes this procedure will speed up the flow of passenger traffic by at least 10 percent. Manufacturers of the machinery have stated that each machine can handle an average of 400 passengers per hour. Data on passenger traffic through the four machines for the past 10 days are shown at the top of the next page.

In the past, passenger flow has favored Machine 1 because of its location. Overflow traffic goes to Machine 2, Machine 3, and Machine 4, in that order.

The passenger traffic director, Lynn Hedlund, began her duties on March 13. If her work results in at least a 10 percent increase in the number of passengers handled, management plans to hire a second traffic director for the other four machines rather than purchasing additional metal detectors.

REQUIRED ▶

1. Calculate the average daily traffic flow for the period March 6–12 and then calculate management's traffic flow goal.
2. Calculate the average traffic flow for the period March 13–15. Did the passenger traffic director's work result in the minimum increase in flow set by management, or should airport officials purchase additional metal directors?

Passengers Checked by Metal Detectors

Date	Machine 1	Machine 2	Machine 3	Machine 4	Totals
March 6	5,620	5,490	5,436	5,268	21,814
March 7	5,524	5,534	5,442	5,290	21,790
March 8	5,490	5,548	5,489	5,348	21,875
March 9	5,436	5,592	5,536	5,410	21,974
March 10	5,404	5,631	5,568	5,456	22,059
March 11	5,386	5,667	5,594	5,496	22,143
March 12	5,364	5,690	5,638	5,542	22,234
March 13	5,678	6,248	6,180	6,090	24,196
March 14	5,720	6,272	6,232	6,212	24,436
March 15	5,736	6,324	6,372	6,278	24,710

3. Is there anything unusual in the analysis of passenger traffic flow that management should look into? Explain your answer.

ALTERNATE PROBLEMS

P 6.
LO1 Report Preparation

Sam Ratha recently purchased Yard & More, Inc., a wholesale distributor of equipment and supplies for lawn and garden care. The organization, headquartered in Baltimore, has four distribution centers that service 14 eastern states. The centers are located in Boston; Rye, New York; Reston, Virginia; and Lawrenceville, New Jersey. Company profits for 20x2, 20x3, and 20x4 were $225,400, $337,980, and $467,200, respectively.

Shortly after purchasing the organization, Ratha appointed people to the following positions: vice president, marketing; vice president, distribution; corporate controller; and vice president, research and development. Ratha has called a meeting of his management group. He wants to create a deluxe retail lawn and garden center that would include a large, fully landscaped plant and tree nursery. The purposes of the retail center would be (1) to test equipment and supplies before selecting them for sales and distribution and (2) to showcase the effects of using the company's products. The retail center must also make a profit on sales.

REQUIRED ▶

1. What types of information will Ratha need before deciding whether to create the retail lawn and garden center?
2. To support his decision, Ratha will need a report from the vice president of research and development analyzing all possible plants and trees that could be planted and their ability to grow in the places where the new retail center might be located. How would each of the four w's pertain to this report?
3. Design a format for the report in **2**.

P 7.
LO5 Nonfinancial Data Analysis

Holiday Candy Company, which has recently developed a strategic plan based on total quality management, wants its candy canes to have the highest quality of color, texture, shape, and taste possible. To ensure that quality standards are met, management has chosen many quality performance measures, including the number of rejected candy canes. Working with Luisa Ortes, the production supervisor, management has decided that no more than 50 candy canes should be rejected each day.

Using data on rejections in Week 1 of 20x4, Luisa Ortes prepared the following summary and the graph that appears on the next page.

Week 1, 20x4	Maximum Number of Rejected Candy Canes Allowed	Actual Number of Rejected Candy Canes	Variance Under (Over) Allowed Maximum
Monday	50	60	(10)
Tuesday	50	63	(13)
Wednesday	50	58	(8)
Thursday	50	59	(9)
Friday	50	62	(12)
Total for the week	250	302	(52)
Daily average	50	60.4	

ANALYSIS OF REJECTED CANDY CANES
WEEK 1, 20X4

Maximum Number of Rejected Candy Canes Allowed
Actual Number of Rejected Candy Canes

Because the variance was 20.8 percent (52 ÷ 250), Ortes decided to analyze the data further. She found that the rejected candy canes contained too little sugar (ingredients), were not circular in shape (shaping), or were undercooked (cooking time). The number of rejects in each category appears below.

Week 1, 20x4	Reasons for Rejects
Ingredients	40
Shaping	195
Cooking time	67
Total	302

The following week, Ortes reviewed the recipe with the cooks. She trained them to measure ingredients more precisely, to shape the candy more carefully, and to time the cooking process more accurately. Then, in Week 3 of 20x4, she gathered the following information on the actual number of rejected candy canes and reasons for the rejects:

Week 3, 20x4	Actual Number of Rejects	Week 3, 20x4	Reasons for Rejects
Monday	20	Ingredients	7
Tuesday	21	Shaping	63
Wednesday	22	Cooking time	30
Thursday	19	Total	100
Friday	18		
Total	100		

REQUIRED ▶

1. Analyze the activity in Week 3 of 20x4 by preparing a table showing each day's maximum number of rejected candy canes allowed, actual number of rejected candy canes, and variance under (over) the maximum number allowed. In addition, prepare a graph comparing the maximum and actual numbers for each day of Week 3.

2. Analyze how the reasons for rejecting candy canes changed from Week 1 to Week 3 by preparing a table showing the number of times each reason occurred each week. In addition, prepare a graph comparing the reasons for rejects each week.

3. How successful was Ortes in increasing the quality of Holiday's candy canes? What recommendations, if any, would you make about monitoring candy production in the future?

P 8.

LO5 Nonfinancial Data Analysis

Texas State Bank was founded in 1869. It has had a record of slow, steady growth since its inception. Management has always kept the processing of information as current as technology allows. Leslie Oistins, manager of the Brazas branch, is upgrading the check-sorting equipment in her office. There are ten check-sorting machines in operation. Information on the number of checks sorted by machine during the past eight weeks is as follows:

Machine	Weeks							
	One	Two	Three	Four	Five	Six	Seven	Eight
AA	89,260	89,439	89,394	90,288	90,739	90,658	90,676	90,630
AB	91,420	91,237	91,602	91,969	91,950	92,502	92,446	92,816
AC	94,830	95,020	94,972	95,922	96,401	96,315	96,334	96,286
AD	91,970	91,786	92,153	92,522	92,503	93,058	93,002	93,375
AE	87,270	87,445	87,401	88,275	88,716	88,636	88,654	88,610
BA	92,450	92,265	92,634	93,005	92,986	93,544	93,488	93,862
BB	91,910	92,094	92,048	92,968	93,433	93,349	93,368	93,321
BC	90,040	89,860	90,219	90,580	90,562	91,105	91,051	91,415
BD	87,110	87,190	87,210	130,815	132,320	133,560	134,290	135,770
BE	94,330	94,519	94,471	95,416	95,893	95,807	95,826	95,778

The Brazas branch has increased its checking business significantly over the past two years. Oistins must decide whether to purchase additional check-sorting machines or attachments for the existing machines to increase productivity. Five weeks ago the Colonnade Company convinced her to experiment with one such attachment, and it was placed on Machine BD. Oistins is impressed with the attachment but has yet to decide between the two courses of action. Labor costs are not a factor in her decision.

REQUIRED ▶

1. Compute the average weekly output of all machines except BD.
2. Compare the weekly output of Machine BD with the average weekly output of the nine machines without the attachment. Compute the weekly difference in the number of checks and the percentage change (difference divided by the average weekly output of the nine machines).
3. Assume that Colonnade's attachment costs about the same as a new check-sorting machine. Which alternative would you recommend that Oistins choose?
4. Would you change your recommendation if two attachments could be purchased for the price of one check-sorting machine? Does this decision require more data?
5. Assume three attachments could be purchased for the price of one check-sorting machine. What action would you recommend?

SKILLS DEVELOPMENT CASES

Conceptual Analysis

SD 1.

LO2 The Value Chain and Core Competency

Medical Products Company (MPC) is known for developing innovative and high-quality products for use in hospitals and medical and dental offices. Its latest product is a nonporous, tough, and very thin disposable glove that will not leak or split and molds tightly to the hand, making it ideal for use in medical and dental procedures. MPC buys the material it uses in making the gloves from another company, which manufactures it according to MPC'S exact specifications and quality standards. MPC makes two models of the glove—one white, and one transparent—in its own plant and sells them through independent agents who represent various manufacturers. When an agent informs MPC of a sale, MPC ships the order directly to the buyer. MPC advertises the gloves in professional journals and gives free samples to physicians and dentists. It provides a product warranty and periodically surveys users about the product's quality.

Briefly explain how MPC accomplishes each of the primary processes of the value chain. What is a core competency? Which one of the primary processes would you say is MPC's core competency? Explain your choice.

SD 2.

LO3 Continuous Improvement

Achieving high quality requires high standards of performance. To maintain high standards of quality, individuals and organizations must continuously improve their performance. To illustrate this concept, select your favorite sport or hobby.

1. Answer the following questions:

    a. What standards do you have for assessing your performance?
    b. What processes have you designed for achieving high quality in your performance?
    c. How do you know when you have achieved high quality in your performance?
    d. Once you know you perform well, how easy will it be for you to maintain that level of expertise?
    e. What can you do to ensure that you are continuously improving your performance?

2. If you owned a business, which of the above questions would be important to answer?

3. Answer the questions in 1, assuming you own a business.

SD 3.

LO4 Performance Measures and the Balanced Scorecard

General Motors Corporation <www.gm.com> had a plan to revamp the way it makes small cars. Called Project Yellowstone, the plan called for GM to build two U.S. plants that would use modular assembly systems. GM's suppliers would develop and send large chunks of cars, like dashboards, to the two new plants for final assembly. The amount of GM's investment and the number of employees needed to assemble the cars would be greatly reduced. The United Auto Workers union blasted the new approach as an attempt to eliminate union jobs, and GM retreated from the plan.[9]

1. What financial performance measures mentioned in the chapter would have prompted GM to try this new approach?

2. The balanced scorecard uses performance measures that are linked to the perspectives of all stakeholder groups. Who are GM's stakeholders, and what performance measures do they value?

3. Refer to the discussion of Honda Motor Company <www.honda.com> in the Decision Point at the beginning of this chapter. How does Honda's modular assembly plan differ from the one GM proposed?

4. In your opinion, what options does GM have if it wishes to pursue the use of modular assembly systems?

Ethical Dilemma

SD 4.

LO6 Professional Ethics

Mark Taylor is the controller for Krohm Corporation. Taylor has been with the company for 17 years and is being considered for the job of chief financial officer (CFO). His boss, the current CFO and former company controller, will be Krohm Corporation's new president. Taylor has just discussed the year-end closing with his boss, who made the following statement during the conversation:

> Mark, why are you being so inflexible? I'm only asking you to postpone the $2,500,000 write-off of obsolete inventory for ten days so that it won't appear on this year's financial statements. Ten days! Do it. Your promotion is coming up, you know. Make sure you keep all the possible outcomes in mind as you complete your year-end work. Oh, and keep this conversation confidential—just between you and me. Okay?

Identify the ethical issue or issues involved and state the appropriate solution to the problem. Be prepared to defend your answer.

Research Activity

SD 5.

LO1 Report Preparation

The registrar's office of Polk Community College is responsible for maintaining a record of each student's grades and credits for use by students, instructors, and administrators.

1. Assume you are a manager in the registrar's office and that you recently joined a team of managers to review the grade-reporting process. Explain how you would prepare a report of grades for students' use and the same report for instructors' use by answering the following questions:

    a. Who will read the grade report?
    b. Why is the grade report necessary?
    c. What information should the grade report contain?
    d. When is the grade report due?

2. Why does the information in a grade report for students' use and in a grade report for instructors' use differ?
3. Visit the registrar's office of your school in person or through your school's web site. Obtain a copy of your grade report and a copy of the form the registrar's office uses to report grades to instructors. Compare the information that these reports supply with the information you listed in 1. Explain any differences.
4. What can the registrar's office do to make sure that its grade reports are effective in communicating all necessary information to readers?

Decision-Making Practice

SD 6.

LO5   Nonfinancial Data Analysis

Aviation Products Company is a subcontractor that specializes in producing housings for landing gears on jet airplanes. Its production process begins with Machine 1, which bends pieces of metal into cylinder-shaped housings and trims off the rough edges. Machine 2 welds the seam of the cylinder and pushes the entire piece into a large die to mold the housing into its final shape.

Joe Mee, the production supervisor, believes the current process creates too much scrap (i.e., wasted metal). To verify this, James Kincaid, the company's accountant, began comparing the amounts of scrap generated in the last four weeks with the amounts of scrap the company anticipated for that period. Because of a death in his family, Kincaid could not complete his analysis. His incomplete report appears below. Mee asks you to complete the report and submit a recommendation to him.

Aviation Products Company
Comparison of Actual Scrap and Expected Scrap
Four-Week Period

	Scrap in Pounds		Difference	
	Actual	Expected	Pounds	Percentage
Machine 1				
Week 1	36,720	36,720		
Week 2	54,288	36,288		
Week 3	71,856	35,856		
Week 4	82,440	35,640		
Machine 2				
Week 1	43,200	18,180		
Week 2	39,600	18,054		
Week 3	7,200	18,162		
Week 4	18,000	18,108		

1. Present the information in two ways:
   a. Prepare a table that shows the difference between the actual and the expected scrap in pounds per machine per week. Calculate the difference in pounds and as a percentage (divide the difference in pounds by the expected pounds of scrap for each week). If the actual poundage of scrap is less than the expected poundage, record the difference as a negative. (This means there is less scrap than expected.)
   b. Prepare a line graph for each machine showing the weeks on the X axis and the pounds of scrap on the Y axis.
2. Examine the differences for the four weeks for each machine and determine which machine operation is creating excessive scrap.
3. What could be causing this problem?
4. What could Mee do to encourage early identification of the specific cause of such problems?

MANAGERIAL REPORTING AND ANALYSIS CASES

Interpreting Management Reports

MRA 1.

LO1 **Management Information**

Obtain a copy of a recent annual report of a publicly held organization in which you have a particular interest. (Copies of annual reports are available at your campus library, at a local public library, on the Internet, or by direct request to an organization.) Assume that you have just been appointed to a middle-management position in a division of the organization you have chosen. You are interested in obtaining information that will help you better manage the activities of your division and have decided to study the contents of the annual report in an attempt to learn as much as possible. You particularly want to know about the following:

1. Size of inventory maintained
2. Ability to earn income
3. Reliance on debt financing
4. Types, volume, and prices of products or services sold
5. Type of production process used
6. Management's long-range strategies
7. Success (profitability) of the division's various product lines
8. Efficiency of operations
9. Operating details of your division

1. Write a brief description of the organization and its products or services and activities.
2. Based on a review of the financial statements and the accompanying disclosure notes, prepare a written summary of information pertaining to items 1 through 9 above.
3. Is any of the information in which you are interested in other sections of the annual report? If so, which information, and in which sections of the report is it?
4. The annual report also includes other types of information you may find helpful in your new position. In outline form, summarize this additional information.

Formulating Management Reports

MRA 2.

LO1 **Management Information Needs**

In **MRA 1**, you examined your new employer's annual report and found some useful information. However, you are interested in knowing whether your division's products or services are competitive, and you were unable to find the necessary information in the annual report.

1. What kinds of information about your competition do you want to find?
2. Why is this information relevant? (Link your response to a particular decision about your organization's products or services. For example, you might seek information to help you determine a new selling price.)
3. From what sources could you obtain the information you need?
4. When would you want to obtain this information?
5. Create a report that will communicate your findings to your superior.

International Company

MRA 3.

LO5 **Management Information Needs**

McDonald's <www.mcdonalds.com> is a leading competitor in the fast-food restaurant business. One component of McDonald's marketing strategy is to increase sales by expanding its foreign markets. At present, more than 40 percent of McDonald's restaurants are located outside the United States. In making decisions about opening restaurants in foreign markets, the company uses quantitative and qualitative financial and nonfinancial information. For example, the following types of information would be important to such a decision: the cost of a new building (quantitative financial information), the estimated number of hamburgers to be sold in the first year (quantitative nonfinancial information), and site desirability (qualitative information).

You are a member of a management team that must decide whether or not to open a new restaurant in England. Identify at least two examples each of the (a) quantitative financial, (b) quantitative nonfinancial, and (c) qualitative information you will need before you can make a decision.

 Group Activity: Divide the class into groups and ask them to discuss this case. Then debrief the entire class by asking one person from each group to summarize his or her group's discussion.

Excel Spreadsheet Analysis

MRA 4.
LO5   Nonfinancial Data Analysis

Refer to assignment **P 2** in this chapter. Lindy Raymond needs to analyze the work performed by each shift in each department during Weeks 1 through 4.

1. For each department, calculate the average labor hours worked per board for each shift during Weeks 1 through 4. Carry your solution to two decimal places. (Note: Hours worked per board = hours worked each week ÷ boards produced each week.)
2. Using the ChartWizard and the information from **1**, prepare a line graph for each department that compares the hours per board worked by the first and second shifts and the estimate for that department during Weeks 1 through 4. The following is the suggested format to use for the information table necessary to complete the line graph for the Molding Department:

Molding Department

	Week 1	Week 2	Week 3	Week 4
First shift	3.50	3.20	3.40	3.80
Second shift	3.60	3.40	3.80	4.20
Estimated	3.40	3.40	3.40	3.40

3. Examine the four graphs that you prepared in **2**. Which shift is more efficient in all four departments? List some reasons for the differences between the shifts.

Internet Case

MRA 5.
LO4   Comparison of Performance Measures

As noted in this chapter's Decision Point, Honda Motor Company <www.honda.com> makes a green car called the Insight. Toyota Motor Company <www.toyota.com> also makes a green car, which it calls the Prius. Search the web sites of both these companies for data concerning the success of their green cars. (**Hint:** Review annual reports and press releases, or use the company's search engine.)

1. List the financial and nonfinancial performance measures that Toyota uses. List the measures used by Honda.
2. Use the data you found to prepare a brief comparison of the two cars. Do the two companies use comparable performance measures? If so, use these measures to evaluate the performance of the Prius and the Insight. If the measures are not comparable, how do they differ?

Chapter 20 describes how managers use information about costs, classify costs, compile product unit costs, and allocate costs using the traditional method and the newer activity-based approach.

Cost Concepts and Cost Allocation

LEARNING OBJECTIVES

LO1 Describe how managers use information about costs in the management cycle.

LO2 Explain how managers classify costs and how they use these cost classifications.

LO3 Define and give examples of the three elements of product cost and compute the unit cost of a product.

LO4 Describe the flow of costs through a manufacturer's inventory accounts.

LO5 Compare how service, retail, and manufacturing organizations report costs on their financial statements and how they account for inventories.

LO6 Define *cost allocation* and explain how cost objects, cost pools, and cost drivers are used to assign manufacturing overhead costs.

LO7 Using the traditional method of allocating manufacturing overhead costs, calculate product unit cost.

LO8 Using activity-based costing to assign manufacturing overhead costs, calculate product unit cost.

LO9 Apply costing concepts to a service organization.

DECISION POINT

A MANAGER'S FOCUS

Southwest Airlines <www.southwest.com> With approximately 2,800 flights a day, an average trip length of 715 miles, and an average one-way fare of $82.84, Southwest Airlines is the nation's leading high-frequency, short-haul, low-fare carrier. It is also the only large domestic airline to have remained profitable for more than 30 years. In both 2001 and 2002, the Official Airline Guide <www.oag.com>, an independent provider of travel information, products, and services, named Southwest "Best Low-Cost Airline."

To have achieved such a status and to maintain it, Southwest managers must know the costs the airline is incurring, including the cost of selling tickets and of flight operations. For example, knowing that selling a ticket through a travel agent costs Southwest as much as $6 to $8 whereas selling a ticket through its web site costs the airline just $1 enables managers to offer lower fares to customers who buy tickets online. Online ticket sales at southwest.com generated approximately 46 percent, or $500 million, of the company's passenger revenues for the first quarter of 2002.[1]

Determining the cost of selling tickets online or the cost of operating a flight requires complex analyses of many costs. What are some of these costs, and how do they bear on Southwest's management decisions?

When determining the cost of online ticket sales, Southwest's managers analyze the costs of direct labor and materials (if a paper ticket is issued), as well

How does Southwest Airlines determine the cost of selling tickets or operating a flight?

as the costs of activities needed to support these sales, such as supervision, equipment maintenance, depreciation, and utilities. When determining the cost of operating a flight, they analyze the costs of the materials (e.g., peanuts, drinks, jet fuel) and labor used (e.g., flight attendants, pilot), as well as overhead costs, such as aircraft maintenance and depreciation. Southwest's managers also consider any other relevant selling, administrative, or general operating costs that the flight incurs.

To help managers make decisions that will sustain Southwest's profitability, all costs must be analyzed in terms of their traceability and behavior, whether they add value, and how they affect the financial statements. Because many costs cannot be directly traced to specific flights, activities, or departments, management must use a method of allocation to assign them. Possibilities include traditional allocation methods and a newer method called activity-based costing, which we introduce in this chapter.

COST INFORMATION AND THE MANAGEMENT CYCLE

LO1 Describe how managers use information about costs in the management cycle.

RELATED TEXT ASSIGNMENTS
Q: 1
E: 1
SD: 1

One of a company's primary goals is to be profitable. Because owners expect to earn profits, managers have a responsibility to use resources wisely and to generate revenues that will exceed the costs of the company's operating, investing, and financing activities. In this chapter, we focus on costs related to the operating activities of manufacturing, retail, and service organizations. We begin by looking at how managers in these different organizations use information about costs during the management cycle.

USE OF COST INFORMATION IN THE MANAGEMENT CYCLE

During the management cycle, managers use information about operating costs to plan, execute, review, and report the results of operating activities. Figure 1 provides an overview of operating costs and the management cycle.

www.johndeere.com
www.motorola.com
www.gm.com
www.sears.com
www.pepboys.com
www.chicos.com
www.citibank.com
www.humana.com
www.usaa.com

■ **PLANNING**   In the planning stage, managers of manufacturing companies, such as John Deere, Motorola, and General Motors, use estimates of product costs to develop budgets for production, materials, labor, and overhead, as well as to determine the selling price or sales level required to cover all costs. In retail companies, such as Sears, Pep Boys, and Chico's, managers work with estimates of the cost of merchandise purchases to develop budgets for purchases and net income, as well as to determine the selling prices or sales units required to cover all costs. In service organizations, like Citibank, Humana, and USAA, managers use the estimated costs

FIGURE 1
Operating Costs and the Management Cycle

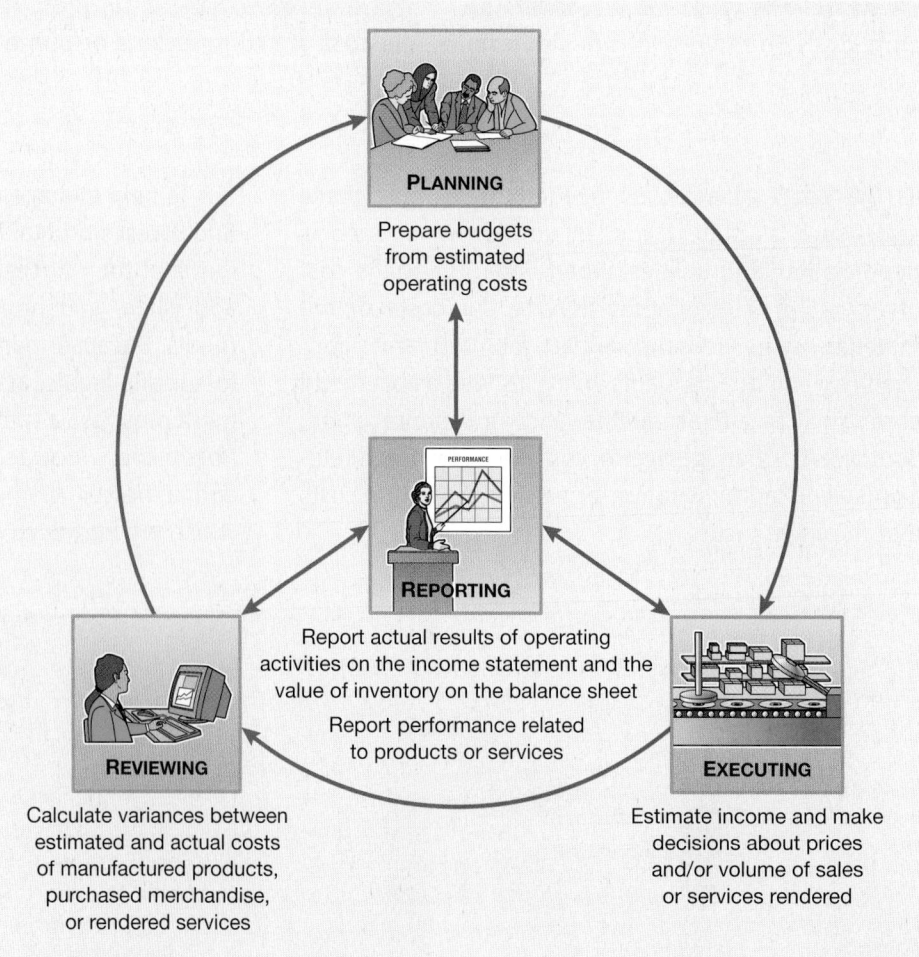

of rendering services to develop budgets, estimate revenues, and manage the organization's work force.

■ **EXECUTING** In the executing stage, managers of manufacturing companies use estimated product costs to predict the gross margin and operating income on sales and to make decisions about such matters as dropping a product line, outsourcing the manufacture of a part to another company, bidding on a special order, or negotiating a selling price. In retail organizations, managers work with the estimated cost of merchandise purchases to predict gross margin, operating income, and value of merchandise sold and to make decisions about such matters as reducing selling prices for clearance sales, lowering selling prices for bulk sales, or dropping a product line. In service organizations, managers find the estimated cost of services helpful in estimating profitability and making decisions about such matters as bidding on future business, lowering or negotiating their fees, or dropping one of their services.

■ **REVIEWING** In the reviewing stage, managers want to know about significant differences between the estimated costs and actual costs of their products, merchandise purchases, or services. The identification of variances between estimated and actual costs helps them determine the causes of cost overruns, which may enable them to make decisions that will avoid such problems in the future.

■ **REPORTING** In the reporting stage, managers expect to see income statements that show the actual costs of operating activities and balance sheets that show the value of inventory. They also expect performance reports that summarize the variance analyses done in the reviewing stage.

COST INFORMATION AND ORGANIZATIONS

Although all organizations use cost information to determine profits and selling prices and to value inventories, different types of organizations have different types of costs. Manufacturing organizations need information about the costs of manufacturing products. Product costs include the costs of direct materials, direct labor, and manufacturing overhead. Retail organizations need information about the costs of purchasing products for resale. These costs include adjustments for freight-in costs, purchase returns and allowances, and purchase discounts. Service organizations need information about the costs of providing services, which include the costs of labor and related overhead. Among the other costs that these organizations incur are the costs of marketing, distributing, installing, and repairing a product or the costs of marketing and supporting the delivery of services. Ultimately, a company is profitable only when its revenues from sales or services rendered exceed all costs.

✓ Check out ACE for a Review Quiz at http://accounting.college.hmco.com/students.

● **STOP AND THINK!**
Do managers in all organizations need the same type of cost information?

The type of cost information managers need varies according to the type of organization. Managers in manufacturing organizations need information about the cost of manufacturing a product, those in retail organizations need information about the cost of purchasing a product, and those in service organizations need information about the cost of providing a service. ■

COST CLASSIFICATIONS AND THEIR USES

LO2 Explain how managers classify costs and how they use these cost classifications.

RELATED TEXT ASSIGNMENTS
Q: 2, 3, 4, 5
SE: 1
E: 2
SD: 1, 4
MRA: 2, 5

A single cost can be classified and used in several ways, depending on the purpose of the analysis. Figure 2 provides an overview of commonly used cost classifications. These classifications enable managers to (1) control costs by determining which are traceable to a particular cost object, such as a service or product; (2) calculate the number of units that must be sold to obtain a certain level of profit (cost behavior); (3) identify the costs of activities that do and do not add value to a product or service; and (4) classify costs for the preparation of financial statements. Cost classifications are important in all types of organizations. They help managers select and use relevant information to improve the efficiency of operations, provide quality products or services, and satisfy customer needs.

FIGURE 2
Overview of Cost Classifications

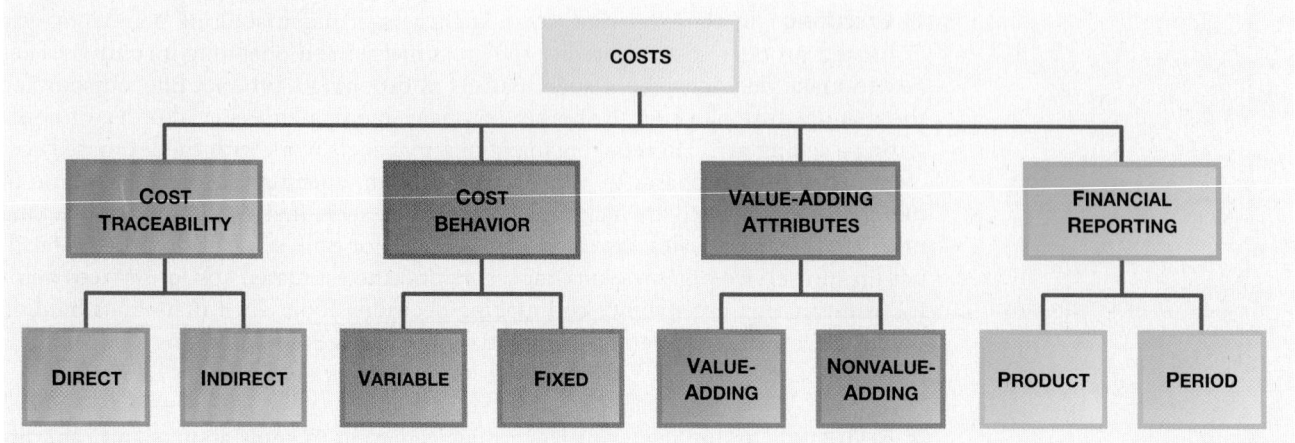

COST TRACEABILITY

Managers trace costs to cost objects, such as products or services, sales territories, departments, or operating activities, to develop a fairly accurate measurement of costs. They use both direct and indirect measures of costs to support pricing decisions or decisions to reallocate resources to other cost objects.

www.southwest.com

Direct costs are costs that can be conveniently and economically traced to a cost object. For example, the wages of a Southwest Airlines flight crew can be conveniently traced to a flight because the time worked and the hourly wages are shown on time cards and payroll records. Similarly, jet fuel costs for a flight can be easily traced.

In some cases, even though a material becomes part of a finished product, the expense of tracing its cost is too great. Some examples include the nails used in furniture, the salt used in cookies, and the rivets used in airplanes. Such costs are considered indirect costs of the product. **Indirect costs** are costs that cannot be conveniently and economically traced to a cost object. For the sake of accuracy, however, indirect costs must be included in the cost of a product or service. Because they are difficult to trace, management uses a formula to assign them. For example, Southwest Airlines' insurance costs cannot be conveniently traced to individual flights; management solves the problem by assigning a portion of the insurance costs to each flight flown.

⬤ **STOP AND THINK!**
Are the costs of a product always traceable as direct or indirect costs?

Because products are cost objects, their costs can always be classified as direct or indirect. ∎

The following examples illustrate cost objects and their direct and indirect costs in service, retail, and manufacturing organizations:

- In a service organization, such as an accounting firm, costs can be traced to a specific service, such as preparation of tax returns. Direct costs for such a service include the costs of government reporting forms, computer usage, and the accountant's labor. Indirect costs include the costs of supplies, office rental, utilities, secretarial labor, telephone usage, and depreciation of office furniture.

- In a retail organization, such as a department store, costs can be traced to a department. For example, the direct costs of the shoe department include the costs of shoes and the wages of employees working in that department. Indirect costs include the costs of utilities, insurance, property taxes, storage, and handling.

- In a manufacturing organization, costs can be traced to the product. Direct costs include the costs of the materials and labor needed to make the product. Indirect costs include the costs of utilities, depreciation of plant and equipment, insurance, property taxes, inspection, supervision, maintenance of machinery, storage, and handling.

COST BEHAVIOR

Managers are also interested in the way costs respond to changes in volume or activity. By analyzing those patterns of behavior, they gain information about how changes in selling prices or operating costs affect the company's net income, and they can then make adjustments so that the company obtains a certain level of profit.

Costs can be separated into variable costs and fixed costs. A **variable cost** is a cost that changes in direct proportion to a change in productive output (or any other measure of volume). A **fixed cost** is a cost that remains constant within a defined range of activity or time period.

All types of organizations have variable and fixed costs. The following are a few examples:

- The variable costs of a landscaping service include the costs of landscaping materials and labor to plant the materials. Fixed costs include the costs of depreciation on trucks and equipment, rent, insurance, and property taxes.
- The variable costs of a used-car dealer include the cost of cars sold and sales commissions. Fixed costs include the costs of building and lot rental, depreciation on office equipment, and receptionist's and accountant's salaries.
- The variable costs of a lawn-mower manufacturer include the costs of direct materials, direct labor, indirect materials (e.g., bolts, nails, lubricants), and indirect labor (e.g., inspection and maintenance labor). Fixed costs include the costs of supervisors' salaries and depreciation on buildings.

As a landscaping service plants more trees, as a used-car dealer sells more cars, or as a lawn-mower manufacturer increases its output of products, its variable costs will increase proportionately. But its fixed costs will remain the same for a specified period; rent, for example, will not change over the term of the lease, and property taxes will remain the same until the next assessment.

VALUE-ADDING VERSUS NONVALUE-ADDING COSTS

A **value-adding cost** is the cost of an activity that increases the market value of a product or service. A **nonvalue-adding cost** is the cost of an activity that adds cost to a product or service but does not increase its market value. For example, the depreciation of a machine that shapes a part used in the final product is a value-adding cost; the depreciation of a car used by the Sales Department is a nonvalue-adding cost. Managers examine the value-adding attributes of their company's operating activities and, wherever possible, reduce or eliminate those that do not directly add value to the company's products or services. Managers also identify which characteristics of their company's products or services customers value and are willing to pay for. This information influences the design of future products or services.

Costs incurred to improve the quality of a product are value-adding costs if the customer is willing to pay more for the higher-quality product; otherwise, they are nonvalue-adding costs because they do not increase the product's market value. The costs of administrative activities, such as accounting and human resource management, are nonvalue-adding costs; they are necessary for the operation of the business, but they do not add value to the product.

COST CLASSIFICATIONS FOR FINANCIAL REPORTING

For purposes of preparing financial statements, managers classify costs as product costs or period costs. **Product costs**, or *inventoriable* costs, are costs assigned to inventory; they include direct materials, direct labor, and manufacturing overhead.

KEY POINT: Product costs remain assets until they are expensed and transferred from the Finished Goods Inventory account to Cost of Goods Sold.

BUSINESS WORLD EXAMPLE: The length of time costs remain in inventory is not a consideration in determining product cost. For example, fast-food operations maintain a direct materials inventory, have a rapid turnover in work in process inventory, and have virtually no finished goods inventory at any given time.

TABLE 1. Examples of Cost Classifications for a Candy Manufacturer

Cost Examples	Traceability to Product	Cost Behavior	Value Attribute	Financial Reporting
Sugar for candy	Direct	Variable	Value-adding	Product (direct materials)
Labor for mixing	Direct	Variable	Value-adding	Product (direct labor)
Labor for supervision	Indirect	Fixed	Nonvalue-adding	Product (manufacturing overhead)
Depreciation on mixing machine	Indirect	Fixed	Value-adding	Product (manufacturing overhead)
Sales commission	—*	Variable	Value-adding†	Period
Accountant's salary	—*	Fixed	Nonvalue-adding	Period

*Sales commissions and accountants' salaries cannot be directly or indirectly traced to a cost object; they are not product costs.
†Sales commissions can be value-adding because customers' perceptions of the salesperson and the selling experience can strongly affect their perceptions of the product's market value.

STUDY NOTE: Product costs and period costs can be explained using the matching rule. Product costs must be charged to the period in which the product generates revenue, and period costs are charged against the revenue of the current period.

Product costs appear on the income statement as cost of goods sold and on the balance sheet as finished goods inventory. **Period costs**, or *noninventoriable* costs, are costs of resources used during the accounting period and not assigned to products. They appear as operating expenses on the income statement. For example, selling and administrative expenses are period costs.

Table 1 shows how some costs of a candy manufacturer can be classified in terms of traceability, behavior, value attribute, and financial reporting.

✓ Check out ACE for a Review Quiz at http://accounting.college.hmco.com/students.

ELEMENTS OF PRODUCT COSTS

LO3 Define and give examples of the three elements of product cost and compute the unit cost of a product.

RELATED TEXT ASSIGNMENTS
Q: 6, 7, 8, 9
SE: 2, 3
E: 3
P: 1
MRA: 5

KEY POINT: Direct materials and direct labor are costs that can be conveniently and economically traced to the product. This is an application of cost-benefit analysis.

As noted above, product costs include all costs related to the manufacturing process. The three elements of product cost are direct materials costs, direct labor costs, and manufacturing overhead costs, which are indirect costs.

Direct materials costs are the costs of materials used in making a product that can be conveniently and economically traced to specific units of the product. Some examples of direct materials are the iron ore used in making steel, the sheet metal used in making automobiles, and the sugar used in making candy. Direct materials may also include parts purchased from another manufacturer.

Direct labor costs are the costs of the labor needed to make a product that can be conveniently and economically traced to specific units of the product. For example, the wages of production-line workers are direct labor costs.

Manufacturing overhead costs (also called *factory overhead, factory burden,* or *indirect manufacturing costs*) are production-related costs that cannot be practically or conveniently traced directly to an end product. They include **indirect materials costs**, such as the costs of nails, rivets, lubricants, and small tools, and **indirect labor costs**, such as the costs of labor for machinery and tool maintenance, inspection, engineering design, supervision, and materials handling. Other indirect manufacturing costs include the costs of building maintenance, property taxes, property insurance, depreciation on plant and equipment, rent, and utilities. As indirect costs, manufacturing overhead costs are allocated to a product's cost using traditional or activity-based costing methods, which we discuss later in the chapter.

To illustrate product costs and the manufacturing process, we'll refer throughout the chapter to Candy Company, Inc., a manufacturer of chocolate candy bars. Olga Santee, the company's founder and president, has identified the following elements of the product cost of one candy bar:

• *Direct materials costs:* costs of sugar, chocolate, and wrapper

FOCUS ON BUSINESS TECHNOLOGY

Has Technology Shifted the Elements of Product Costs?

New technology and manufacturing processes have produced new patterns of product costs. The three elements of product costs are still direct materials, direct labor, and manufacturing overhead, but the percentage that each contributes to the total cost of a product has changed. From the 1950s through the 1970s, direct labor was the dominant element, making up over 40 percent of total product cost, while direct materials contributed 35 percent and manufacturing overhead, around 25 percent. Thus, 75 percent of total product cost was a direct cost, traceable to the product. Improved production technology caused a dramatic shift in the three product cost elements. Machines replaced people, significantly reducing direct labor costs. Today, only 50 percent of the cost of a product is

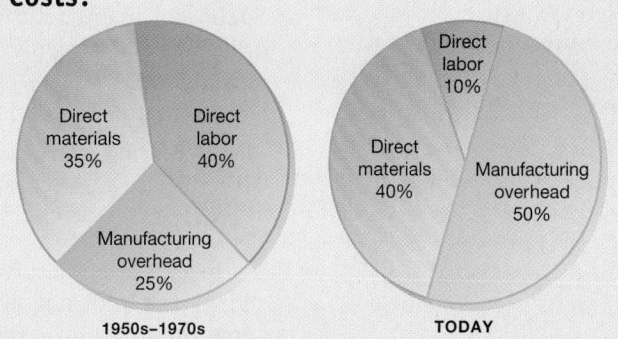

directly traceable to the product; the other 50 percent is manufacturing overhead, an indirect cost.

- *Direct labor costs:* costs of labor used in making the candy bar
- *Manufacturing overhead costs:* indirect materials costs, including the costs of salt and flavorings; indirect labor costs, including the costs of labor to move materials to the production area and to inspect the candy bars during production; other indirect overhead costs, including depreciation on the building and equipment, utilities, property taxes, and insurance

COMPUTING PRODUCT UNIT COST

● **STOP AND THINK!**

How do the costing methods used to compute a product's cost per unit affect the three elements of product cost?

The three elements of product cost, direct materials, direct labor, and manufacturing overhead, may differ in amount depending on whether the actual, normal, or standard costing method is used. ■

Product unit cost is the cost of manufacturing a single unit of a product. It is made up of the costs of direct materials, direct labor, and manufacturing overhead. These three cost elements are accumulated as a batch of products is being produced. When the batch has been completed, the product unit cost is computed either by dividing the total cost of direct materials, direct labor, and manufacturing overhead by the total number of units produced, or by determining the cost per unit for each element of the product cost and summing those per-unit costs.

Unit cost information helps managers price products and calculate gross margin and net income. Managers and accountants can calculate product unit cost by using actual costing, normal costing, or standard costing methods. Table 2 summarizes how these three cost-measurement methods use actual and estimated costs.

■ **ACTUAL COSTING METHOD**   The **actual costing** method uses the costs of direct materials, direct labor, and manufacturing overhead at the end of an accounting period or when actual costs become known to calculate the product unit cost. The actual product unit cost is assigned to the finished goods inventory on the balance sheet and to the cost of goods sold on the income statement. For example, assume

TERMINOLOGY NOTE:
Estimated costs are also called *projected, standard, predetermined,* or *budgeted costs.*

TABLE 2.   Use of Actual and Estimated Costs in Three Cost-Measurement Methods

Product Cost Elements	Actual Costing	Normal Costing	Standard Costing
Direct materials	Actual costs	Actual costs	Estimated costs
Direct labor	Actual costs	Actual costs	Estimated costs
Manufacturing overhead	Actual costs	Estimated costs	Estimated costs

KEY POINT: Many management decisions require estimates of future costs. Managers often use actual cost as a basis for estimating future cost.

that Candy Company, Inc., produced 3,000 candy bars on December 28, 20x6, for a corporate customer in Seattle. Maya Kee, the company's accountant, calculated that the actual costs for the Seattle order were direct materials, $540; direct labor, $420; and manufacturing overhead, $240. The actual product unit cost for the order was $.40, calculated as follows:

Direct materials ($540 ÷ 3,000 candy bars)	$.18
Direct labor ($420 ÷ 3,000 candy bars)	.14
Manufacturing overhead ($240 ÷ 3,000 candy bars)	.08
Product cost per candy bar	
($1,200 ÷ 3,000 candy bars)	$.40

In this case, the product unit cost was computed after the job was completed and all cost information was known. Sometimes, however, a manufacturer needs to know product unit cost during production, when the actual direct materials costs and direct labor costs are known but the actual manufacturing overhead costs are uncertain. In that case, the computation of product unit cost will include an estimate of the manufacturing overhead, and the normal costing method will be helpful.

■ **NORMAL COSTING METHOD**   The **normal costing** method combines actual direct costs of materials and labor with estimated manufacturing overhead costs to determine a product unit cost. The normal costing method is simple and allows a smoother, more even assignment of manufacturing overhead costs to production during an accounting period than is possible with the actual costing method. It also contributes to better pricing decisions and profitability estimates. However, at the end of the accounting period, any difference between the estimated and actual costs must be identified and removed so that the financial statements show only the actual product costs.

Assume that Maya Kee used normal costing to price the Seattle order for 3,000 candy bars and that manufacturing overhead was applied to the product's cost using an estimated rate of 60 percent of direct labor costs. In this case, the costs for the order would include the actual direct materials cost of $540, the actual direct labor cost of $420, and an estimated manufacturing overhead cost of $252 ($420.00 × 60%). The product unit cost would be $.404:

Direct materials ($540.00 ÷ 3,000 candy bars)	$.180
Direct labor ($420.00 ÷ 3,000 candy bars)	.140
Manufacturing overhead ($252.00 ÷ 3,000 candy bars)	.084
Product cost per candy bar	
($1,212 ÷ 3,000 candy bars)	$.404

■ **STANDARD COSTING METHOD**   Managers sometimes need product cost information before the accounting period begins so that they can control the cost of operating activities or price a proposed product for a customer. In such situations, product unit costs must be estimated, and the **standard costing** method can be helpful. This method uses estimated, or standard, costs of direct materials, direct labor, and manufacturing overhead to calculate the product unit cost.

Assume that Candy Company is placing a bid to manufacture 2,000 candy bars for a new customer. From standard cost information developed at the beginning of the period, Kee estimates the following costs: $.20 per unit for direct materials, $.15 per unit for direct labor, and $.09 per unit for manufacturing overhead (assuming a standard overhead rate of 60 percent of direct labor cost). The standard cost per unit would be $.44:

Direct materials	$.20
Direct labor	.15
Manufacturing overhead ($.15 × 60%)	.09
Product cost per candy bar	$.44

FIGURE 3
Relationships Among Product Cost Classifications

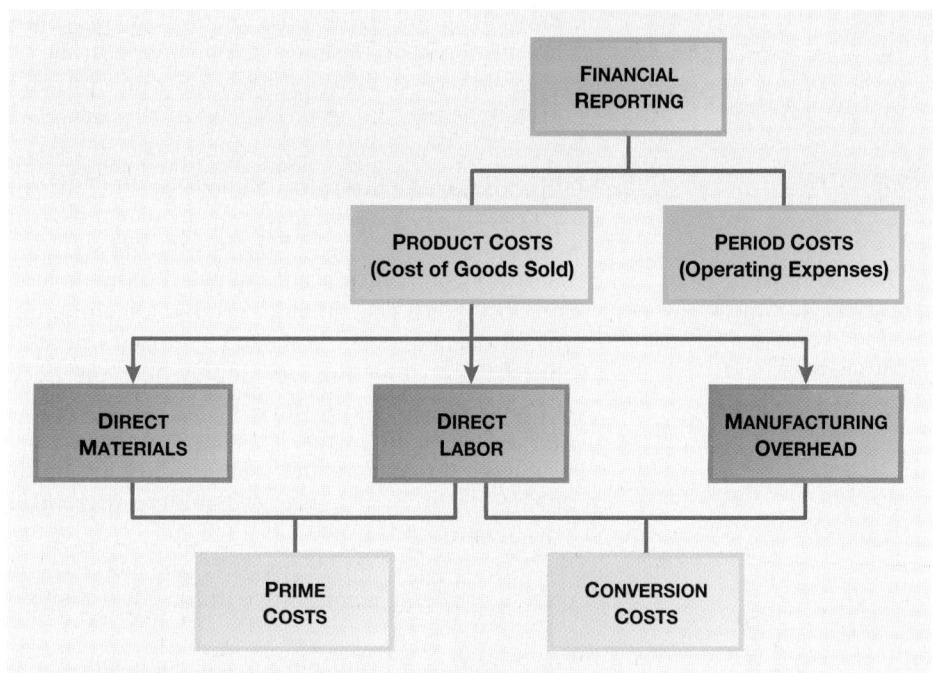

The $.44 product unit cost is useful in determining the cost of the bid, $880 ($.44 × 2,000 candy bars), estimating the gross margin for the job, and deciding the price to bid for the business. We cover standard costing in more detail in another chapter.

PRIME COSTS AND CONVERSION COSTS

The three elements of manufacturing costs can be grouped into prime costs and conversion costs. **Prime costs** are the primary costs of production; they are the sum of the direct materials costs and direct labor costs. **Conversion costs** are the costs of converting direct materials into a finished product; they are the sum of direct labor costs and manufacturing overhead costs. Using the figures for Candy Company's actual unit cost, the per-unit prime costs and conversion costs are as follows:

	Prime Costs	Conversion Costs
Direct materials	$.18	—
Direct labor	.14	$.14
Manufacturing overhead	—	.08
Totals	$.32	$.22

These classifications are important for understanding the costing methods discussed in later chapters. Figure 3 summarizes the relationships among the product cost classifications presented so far.

 Check out ACE for a Review Quiz at http://accounting.college.hmco.com/students.

INVENTORY ACCOUNTS IN MANUFACTURING ORGANIZATIONS

LO4 Describe the flow of costs through a manufacturer's inventory accounts.

RELATED TEXT ASSIGNMENTS
Q: 10, 11, 12
SE: 4, 5
E: 4, 5

Transforming materials into finished products ready for sale requires a number of production and production-related activities, including purchasing, receiving, inspecting, storing, and moving materials; converting them into finished products using labor, equipment, and other resources; and moving, storing, and shipping the finished products. A manufacturing organization's accounting system tracks these activities as product costs flowing through the Materials Inventory, Work in Process Inventory, and Finished Goods Inventory accounts. The **Materials Inventory** account shows the balance of the cost of unused materials, the **Work in Process Inventory account** shows the manufacturing costs that have been incurred and assigned to partially completed units of product, and the **Finished Goods Inventory account** shows the costs assigned to all completed products that have not been sold.

DOCUMENT FLOWS AND COST FLOWS THROUGH THE INVENTORY ACCOUNTS

● STOP AND THINK!
Are paper documents always used in accounting for manufacturing costs?
Although paper documents have traditionally been used, many companies today use electronic documents. ■

In many companies, accountants accumulate and report manufacturing costs based on documents pertaining to production and production-related activities. Although paper documents are still used for this purpose, electronic documents have become increasingly common. Looking at how the documents for the three elements of product cost relate to the flow of costs through the three inventory accounts provides insight into when an activity must be recorded in the accounting records. Figure 4 summarizes the relationships among the production activities, the documents for each of the three cost elements, and the inventory accounts affected by the activities.

To illustrate the document flow and changes in inventory balances for production activities, we continue with our example of Candy Company, Inc.

ENRICHMENT NOTE:
Some companies use sophisticated computer programs to match receiving reports to purchase orders.

■ **PURCHASE OF MATERIALS**   The same process is used for purchasing both direct and indirect materials. The purchasing process starts with a *purchase request* for specific quantities of materials needed in the manufacturing process but not currently available in the materials storeroom. A qualified manager approves the request. Based on the information in the purchase request, the Purchasing Department sends a *purchase order* to a supplier. When the materials arrive, an employee on the receiving dock counts and examines them and prepares a *receiving report*. Later, an accounting clerk matches the information on the receiving report with the descriptions and quantities listed on the purchase order. A materials handler moves the newly arrived materials from the receiving area to the materials storeroom. Soon, Candy Company receives a *vendor's invoice* from the supplier requesting payment for the purchased materials. The cost of those materials increases the balance of the Materials Inventory account.

■ **PRODUCTION OF GOODS**   When candy bars are scheduled for production, the storeroom clerk receives a *materials request form*. The materials request form is essential for controlling materials. In addition to showing the supervisor's signature of approval, it describes the types and quantities of materials the storeroom clerk is to send to the production area, and it authorizes the release of those materials from the materials inventory into production. If the appropriate manager has approved the materials request form, the storeroom clerk has the materials handler move the materials to the production floor. The cost of the direct materials transferred will increase the balance of the Work in Process Inventory account and decrease the balance of the Materials Inventory account. The cost of the indirect materials transferred will increase the balance of the Manufacturing Overhead account and decrease the balance of the Materials Inventory account. (We discuss overhead in more detail later in this chapter.)

Each of the production employees who make the candy bars prepares a *time card* to record the number of hours he or she has worked on this and other orders each day. The costs of the direct labor and manufacturing overhead used to manufacture the candy bars increase the balance of the Work in Process Inventory account. A *job order cost card* is used to record all costs incurred as the products move through production.

■ **PRODUCT COMPLETION AND SALE**   Employees place completed candy bars in cartons and then move the cartons to the finished goods storeroom, where they are kept until shipped to customers. The cost of the completed candy bars increases the

FIGURE 4
Activities, Documents, and Cost Flows Through the Inventory Accounts of a Manufacturing Organization

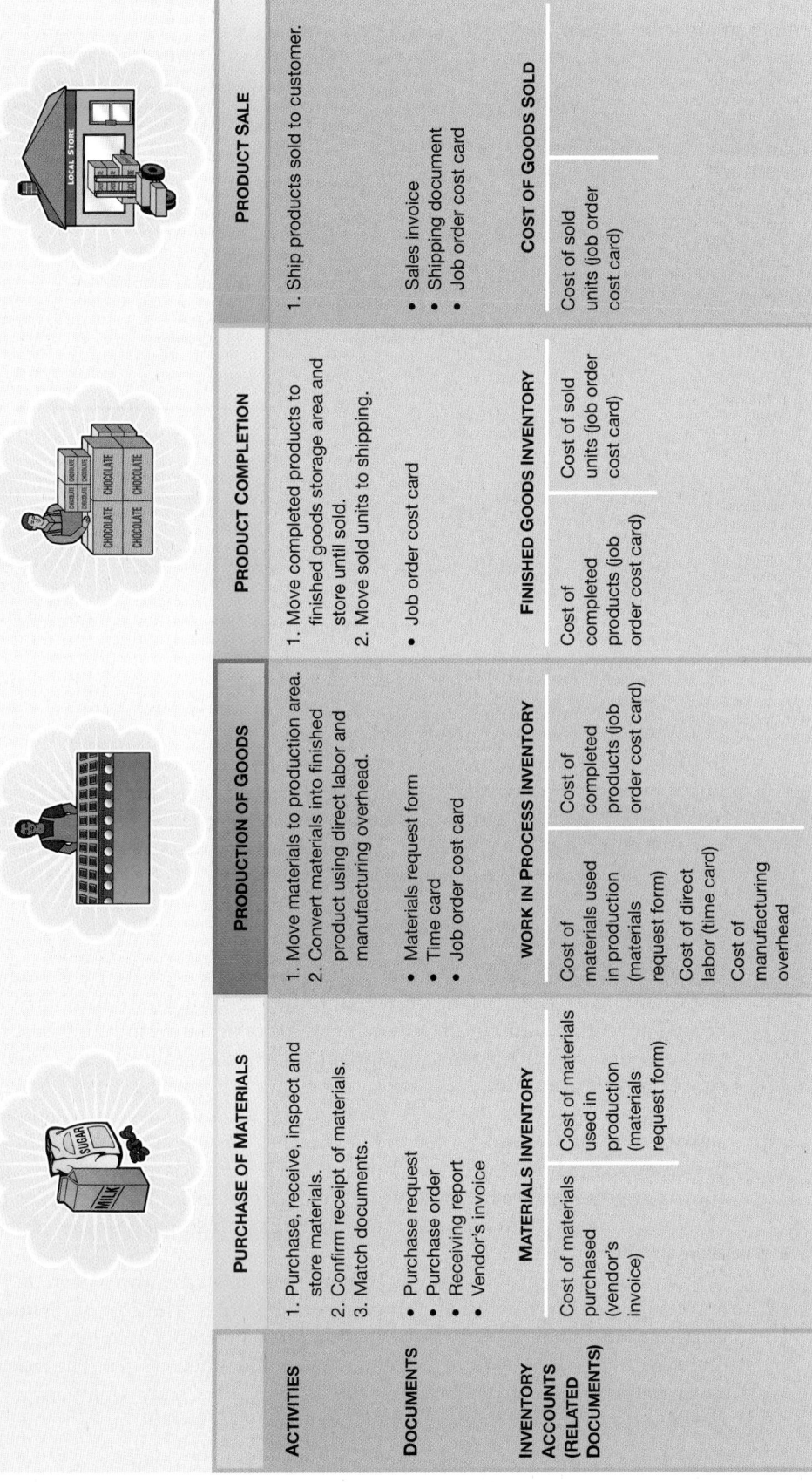

PURCHASE OF MATERIALS

ACTIVITIES
1. Purchase, receive, inspect and store materials.
2. Confirm receipt of materials.
3. Match documents.

DOCUMENTS
- Purchase request
- Purchase order
- Receiving report
- Vendor's invoice

INVENTORY ACCOUNTS (RELATED DOCUMENTS)

MATERIALS INVENTORY

Cost of materials purchased (vendor's invoice)	Cost of materials used in production (materials request form)

PRODUCTION OF GOODS

ACTIVITIES
1. Move materials to production area.
2. Convert materials into finished product using direct labor and manufacturing overhead.

DOCUMENTS
- Materials request form
- Time card
- Job order cost card

WORK IN PROCESS INVENTORY

Cost of materials used in production (materials request form)	Cost of completed products (job order cost card)
Cost of direct labor (time card)	
Cost of manufacturing overhead	

PRODUCT COMPLETION

ACTIVITIES
1. Move completed products to finished goods storage area and store until sold.
2. Move sold units to shipping.

DOCUMENTS
- Job order cost card

FINISHED GOODS INVENTORY

Cost of completed products (job order cost card)	Cost of sold units (job order cost card)

PRODUCT SALE

ACTIVITIES
1. Ship products sold to customer.

DOCUMENTS
- Sales invoice
- Shipping document
- Job order cost card

COST OF GOODS SOLD

Cost of sold units (job order cost card)	

FIGURE 5
Manufacturing Cost Flow: An Example Using Actual Costing for Candy Company, Inc.

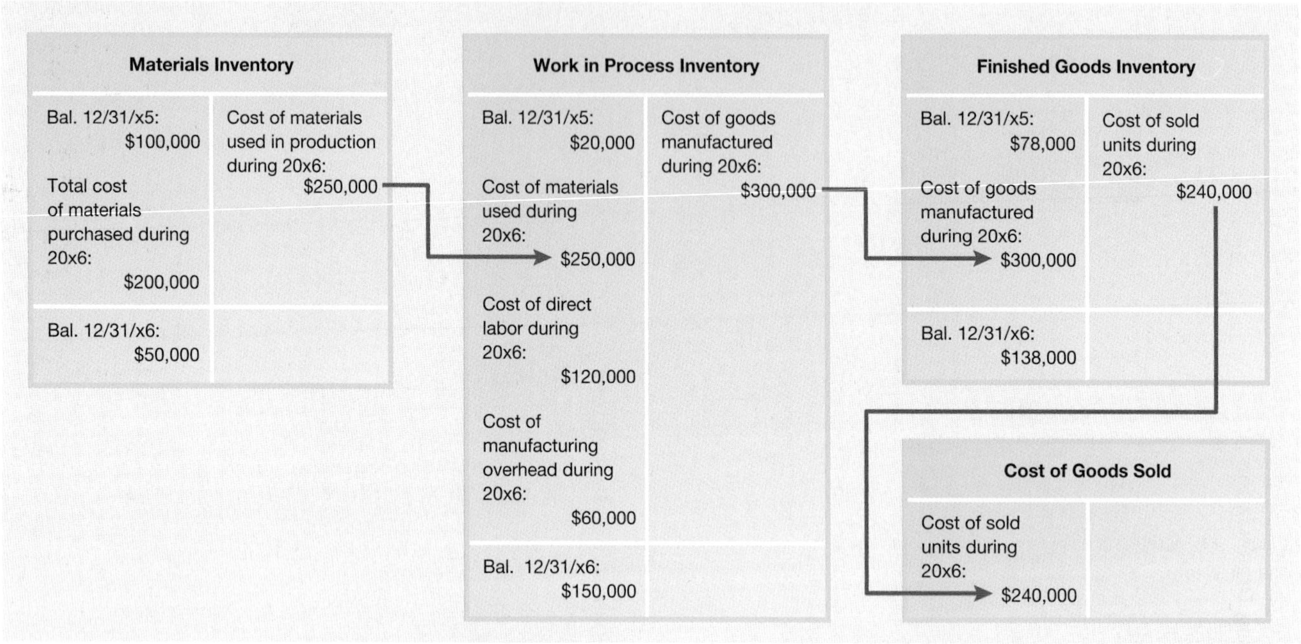

Materials Inventory		Work in Process Inventory		Finished Goods Inventory	
Bal. 12/31/x5: $100,000	Cost of materials used in production during 20x6: $250,000	Bal. 12/31/x5: $20,000	Cost of goods manufactured during 20x6: $300,000	Bal. 12/31/x5: $78,000	Cost of sold units during 20x6: $240,000
Total cost of materials purchased during 20x6: $200,000		Cost of materials used during 20x6: $250,000		Cost of goods manufactured during 20x6: $300,000	
Bal. 12/31/x6: $50,000		Cost of direct labor during 20x6: $120,000		Bal. 12/31/x6: $138,000	
		Cost of manufacturing overhead during 20x6: $60,000			

Cost of Goods Sold	
Cost of sold units during 20x6: $240,000	

Work in Process Inventory — Bal. 12/31/x6: $150,000

balance of the Finished Goods Inventory account and decreases the balance of the Work in Process Inventory account.

When candy bars are sold, a clerk prepares a *sales invoice*, and another employee fills the order by removing the candy bars from the storeroom, packaging them, and shipping them to the customer. A *shipping document* shows the quantity of the products that are shipped and gives a description of them. The cost of the candy bars sold, which is shown on the job order cost card, increases the Cost of Goods Sold account and decreases the balance of the Finished Goods Inventory account.

THE MANUFACTURING COST FLOW

Manufacturing cost flow is the flow of manufacturing costs (direct materials, direct labor, and manufacturing overhead) through the Materials Inventory, Work in Process Inventory, and Finished Goods Inventory accounts into the Cost of Goods Sold account. A defined, structured manufacturing cost flow is the foundation for product costing, inventory valuation, and financial reporting. Figure 5 summarizes the manufacturing cost flow as it relates to the inventory accounts and production activity of Candy Company for the year ended December 31, 20x6. To show the basic flows in this example, we assume that all materials can be traced directly to the candy bars. This means there are no indirect materials in the Materials Inventory account. We also work with the actual amount of manufacturing overhead, rather than an estimated amount.

Because there are no indirect materials in this case, the Materials Inventory account shows the balance of unused direct materials. The cost of direct materials purchased increases the balance of the Materials Inventory account, and the cost of direct materials used by the Production Department decreases it. The following formula may be used to summarize the activity of Candy Company's Materials Inventory account during the year:

Materials Inventory, Ending Balance	=	Materials Inventory, Beginning Balance	+	Cost of Materials Purchased	−	Cost of Materials Used
$50,000	=	$100,000	+	$200,000	−	$250,000

The Work in Process Inventory account records the balance of partially completed units of the product. As direct materials and direct labor are used, their costs are added to the Work in Process Inventory account. The cost of manufacturing overhead for the current period is also added. The total costs of direct materials, direct labor, and manufacturing overhead incurred and transferred to work in process inventory during an accounting period are called **total manufacturing costs** (also called *current manufacturing costs*). These costs increase the balance of the Work in Process Inventory account.

The cost of all units completed and moved to finished goods storage during an accounting period is the **cost of goods manufactured**. The cost of goods manufactured for the period decreases the balance of the Work in Process Inventory account. The following formulas show the activity in Candy Company's Work in Process Inventory account during the year:

KEY POINT: When costs are transferred from one inventory account to another in a manufacturing company, they remain assets. They are inventoriable product costs and are not expensed until the finished goods are sold.

Total Manufacturing Costs		Cost of Direct Materials Used		Direct Labor Costs		Manufacturing Overhead Costs
	=		+		+	
$430,000	=	$250,000	+	$120,000	+	$60,000

KEY POINT: Materials Inventory and Work in Process Inventory support the production process, while Finished Goods Inventory supports the sales and distribution functions.

Work in Process Inventory, Ending Balance		Work in Process Inventory, Beginning Balance		Total Manufacturing Costs		Cost of Goods Manufactured
	=		+		−	
$150,000	=	$20,000	+	$430,000	−	$300,000

The Finished Goods Inventory account holds the balance of costs assigned to all completed products that a manufacturing company has not yet sold. The cost of goods manufactured increases the balance, and the cost of goods sold decreases the balance. The following formula shows the activity in Candy Company's Finished Goods Inventory account during the year:

KEY POINT: When a credit sale occurs, Accounts Receivable and Sales are increased by the *revenue* amount. Cost of Goods Sold is increased and Finished Goods Inventory is decreased by the *cost* amount, or inventory carrying value.

Finished Goods Inventory, Ending Balance		Finished Goods Inventory, Beginning Balance		Cost of Goods Manufactured		Cost of Goods Sold
	=		+		−	
$138,000	=	$78,000	+	$300,000	−	$240,000

 Check out ACE for a Review Quiz at http://accounting.college.hmco.com/students.

FINANCIAL STATEMENTS AND THE REPORTING OF COSTS

LO5 Compare how service, retail, and manufacturing organizations report costs on their financial statements and how they account for inventories.

RELATED TEXT ASSIGNMENTS
Q: 13, 14
SE: 6, 7
E: 6, 7, 8, 9, 10
P: 2, 3
MRA: 1, 3

The key to preparing an income statement for a manufacturing organization is to determine the cost of goods manufactured. This dollar amount is calculated on the statement of cost of goods manufactured, a special report based on an analysis of the Work in Process Inventory account.

STATEMENT OF COST OF GOODS MANUFACTURED

At the end of an accounting period, the flow of all manufacturing costs incurred during the period is summarized in the **statement of cost of goods manufactured**. Exhibit 1 shows Candy Company's statement of cost of goods manufactured for the year ended December 31, 20x6. (The company's flow of manufacturing costs for the same period appears in Figure 5.) It is helpful to think of the statement of cost of goods manufactured as being developed in three steps, as described below.

■ **STEP 1** *Compute the cost of direct materials used during the accounting period.* To do so, add the beginning balance in the Materials Inventory account to the direct materials purchased ($100,000 + $200,000). The subtotal ($300,000) represents

Exhibit 1
Statement of Cost of Goods Manufactured and Partial Income Statement for a Manufacturing Organization

Candy Company, Inc.
Statement of Cost of Goods Manufactured
For the Year Ended December 31, 20x6

Direct materials used		
Materials inventory, December 31, 20x5	$100,000	
Direct materials purchased	200,000	
Cost of direct materials available for use	$300,000	
Less materials inventory, December 31, 20x6	50,000	
Cost of direct materials used		$250,000
Direct labor		120,000
Manufacturing overhead		60,000
Total manufacturing costs		$430,000
Add work in process inventory,		
December 31, 20x5		20,000
Total cost of work in process during the year		$450,000
Less work in process inventory,		
December 31, 20x6		150,000
Cost of goods manufactured		$300,000

Candy Company, Inc.
Income Statement
For the Year Ended December 31, 20x6

Sales		$500,000
Cost of goods sold		
Finished goods inventory, December 31, 20x5	$ 78,000	
Cost of goods manufactured	300,000	
Total cost of finished goods available for sale	$378,000	
Less finished goods inventory,		
December 31, 20x6	138,000	
Cost of goods sold		240,000
Gross margin		$260,000
Selling and administrative expenses		160,000
Operating income		$100,000

● **STOP AND THINK!**
What inventory accounts accumulate the cost information used in the statement of cost of goods manufactured?

The Materials Inventory and Work in Process Inventory accounts accumulate this information. ■

the cost of direct materials available for use during the accounting period. Next, subtract the ending balance of the Materials Inventory account from the cost of direct materials available for use. The difference is the cost of direct materials used during the period ($300,000 − $50,000 = $250,000).

■ **STEP 2** *Calculate total manufacturing costs for the period.* As shown in Exhibit 1, the costs of direct materials used ($250,000) and direct labor ($120,000) are added to total manufacturing overhead costs incurred during the period ($60,000) to arrive at total manufacturing costs ($430,000).

ENRICHMENT NOTE: An
alternative to the cost of goods
manufactured calculation uses
the cost flow concept. Current
manufacturing costs (direct
materials, direct labor, and
manufacturing overhead)
become the cost of goods manufactured if the Work in
Process Inventory balance
remains unchanged in the
accounting period. Similarly,
the cost of goods manufactured
becomes the cost of goods sold
if the Finished Goods Inventory
remains unchanged in the
period.

■ **STEP 3** *Determine total cost of goods manufactured for the period.* To do so, add the beginning balance in the Work in Process Inventory account to total manufacturing costs to arrive at the total cost of work in process during the period. From this amount, subtract the ending balance in the Work in Process Inventory account to arrive at the cost of goods manufactured ($450,000 − $150,000 = $300,000).

Total manufacturing costs should not be confused with the cost of goods manufactured. To understand the difference between these two amounts, look again at the computations in Exhibit 1. Total manufacturing costs of $430,000 incurred during the period are added to the $20,000 beginning balance in the Work in Process Inventory account to arrive at the total cost of work in process during the period ($430,000 + $20,000 = $450,000). The costs of products still in process ($150,000) are then subtracted from the total cost of work in process during the year. The remainder, $300,000, is the cost of goods manufactured (completed) during the current year. Note that the costs attached to the ending balance of Work in Process Inventory come from the current period's total manufacturing costs; they will not become part of the cost of goods manufactured until the next period, when the products are completed.

COST OF GOODS SOLD AND A MANUFACTURING ORGANIZATION'S INCOME STATEMENT

STUDY NOTE: It is impor-
tant not to confuse the cost of
goods manufactured with the
cost of goods sold.

Exhibit 1 demonstrates the relationship between Candy Company's income statement and its statement of cost of goods manufactured. The total amount of the cost of goods manufactured during the period is carried over to the income statement, where it is used to compute the cost of goods sold. The beginning balance of the Finished Goods Inventory account is added to the cost of goods manufactured to arrive at the total cost of finished goods available for sale during the period ($78,000 + $300,000 = $378,000). The cost of goods sold is then computed by subtracting the ending balance in Finished Goods Inventory (the cost of goods completed but not sold) from the total cost of finished goods available for sale ($378,000 − $138,000 = $240,000). The cost of goods sold is considered an expense in the period in which the goods are sold.

COST REPORTING AND ACCOUNTING FOR INVENTORIES IN SERVICE, RETAIL, AND MANUFACTURING ORGANIZATIONS

Because the operations of service and retail concerns differ from those of manufacturing organizations, the accounts presented in their financial statements differ as well. For example, because service organizations, such as Southwest Airlines, United Parcel Service (UPS), and Enterprise Rent-a-Car, sell services, not products, they maintain no inventories for sale or resale and thus, unlike manufacturing and retail organizations, have no inventory accounts on the balance sheet. When preparing income statements, they calculate the cost of sales rather than the cost of goods sold, using the following equation:

www.southwest.com
www.ups.com
www.enterprise.com

Cost of Sales = Net Cost of Services Sold

Suppose, for instance, that Sweet Treasures Candy Store, the retail shop that we used as an example in the last chapter, employs UPS to deliver 50 boxes of candy. The cost of sales for UPS would include the wages and salaries of personnel plus the expense of trucks, planes, supplies, and anything else UPS used to deliver the packages for Sweet Treasures Candy Store.

Retail organizations, such as Wal-Mart, Toys "R" Us, and Sweet Treasures Candy Store, which purchase

FOCUS ON BUSINESS PRACTICE

What Candy Company Has the Sweetest Share of the U.S. Market?

Among the top U.S. candy vendors are Hershey <www.hershey.com>, Mars <www.mars.com>, Wrigley's <www.wrigley.com>, Nestlé <www.nestle.com>, Philip Morris <www.altria.com>, and Russell Stover Candies <www.russellstover.com>. Hershey has the sweetest share of the market, leading with 30 percent. Mars is second with a 17.1 percent market share, and Wrigley's, Nestlé, and Phillip Morris vie for third place, with 6.7 percent, 6.5 percent, and 6.3 percent, respectively.[3]

FIGURE 6
Financial Statements of Service, Retail, and Manufacturing Organizations

	Service Company	Retail Company	Manufacturing Company
Income Statement	Sales − Cost of sales Gross margin − Operating expenses Net income	Sales − Cost of goods sold* Gross margin − Operating expenses Net income *Cost of goods sold: Beginning merchandise inventory + Net cost of purchases Cost of goods available for sale − Ending merchandise inventory Cost of goods sold	Sales − Cost of goods sold† Gross margin − Operating expenses Net income †Cost of goods sold: Beginning finished goods inventory + Cost of goods manufactured Cost of goods available for sale − Ending finished goods inventory Cost of goods sold

Balance Sheet (current assets section)	No inventory accounts	One inventory account:
		   Merchandise Inventory
		   (finished product ready for sale)
			Three inventory accounts:
			   Materials Inventory
			   (unused materials)
			   Work in Process Inventory
			   (unfinished product)
			   Finished Goods Inventory
			   (finished product ready for sale)

Example with numbers		Income Statement: Beg. merchandise inventory $ 3,000 Net cost of purchases 23,000 Cost of goods available for sale $26,000 End. merchandise inventory 4,500 Cost of goods sold $21,500 Balance Sheet: Merchandise inventory, ending $ 4,500	Income Statement: Beg. finished goods inventory $ 52,000 Cost of goods manufactured 144,000 Cost of goods available for sale $196,000 End. finished goods inventory 78,000 Cost of goods sold $118,000 Balance Sheet: Finished goods inventory, ending $ 78,000

www.walmart.com
www.tru.com

products ready for resale, maintain just one inventory account on the balance sheet. Called the Merchandise Inventory account, it reflects the costs of goods held for resale. Retail organizations include the cost of purchases in the calculation of cost of goods sold, as follows:

$$\text{Cost of Goods Sold} = \text{Beginning Merchandise Inventory} + \textbf{Net Cost of Purchases} - \text{Ending Merchandise Inventory}$$

Suppose that Sweet Treasures Candy Store had a balance of $3,000 in its Merchandise Inventory account on December 31, 20x4. During the next year, its purchases of candy products totaled $23,000 (adjusted for purchase discounts, returns and allowances, and freight-in). On December 31, 20x5, its Merchandise Inventory balance was $4,500. The cost of goods sold for 20x5 is thus $21,500:

$$\text{Cost of Goods Sold} = \$3,000 + \$23,000 - \$4,500 = \$21,500$$

www.motorola.com
www.sony.com

As we have seen, manufacturing organizations, such as Motorola, Sony, and Candy Company, which make products for sale, maintain three inventory accounts on the balance sheet: the Materials Inventory, Work in Process Inventory, and

Finished Goods Inventory accounts. The Materials Inventory account shows the balance of the cost of materials purchased but unused in the production process. During the production process, the costs of manufacturing the product are accumulated in the Work in Process Inventory account; the balance of this account represents the costs of the unfinished product. Once the product is complete and ready for sale, the cost of the goods manufactured is transferred to the Finished Goods Inventory account; the balance in this account is the cost of the unsold completed product. When the product is sold, the manufacturing organization uses the following equation to calculate the cost of goods sold:

$$\text{Cost of Goods Sold} = \begin{array}{c}\text{Beginning}\\\text{Finished Goods}\\\text{Inventory}\end{array} + \begin{array}{c}\textbf{Cost of}\\\textbf{Goods}\\\textbf{Manufactured}\end{array} - \begin{array}{c}\text{Ending}\\\text{Finished Goods}\\\text{Inventory}\end{array}$$

For example, suppose that Candy Company had a balance of $52,000 in its Finished Goods Inventory account on December 31, 20x4. During the next year, the cost of the products that Candy Company manufactured totaled $144,000. On December 31, 20x5, its Finished Goods Inventory balance was $78,000. The cost of goods sold for 20x5 is thus $118,000:

$$\text{Cost of Goods Sold} = \$52,000 + \$144,000 - \$78,000 = \$118,000$$

Remember that all organizations—service, retail, and manufacturing—use the following income statement format:

$$\text{Sales} - \begin{array}{c}\text{Cost of Sales}\\\text{or}\\\text{Cost of Goods Sold}\end{array} = \begin{array}{c}\text{Gross}\\\text{Margin}\end{array} - \begin{array}{c}\text{Operating}\\\text{Expenses}\end{array} = \text{Net Income}$$

Figure 6 compares the financial statements of service, retail, and manufacturing organizations. Note in particular the differences in inventory accounts and cost of goods sold. As pointed out earlier, product costs, or inventoriable costs, appear as finished goods inventory on the balance sheet and as cost of goods sold on the income statement; period costs, or noninventoriable costs, are reflected in the operating expenses on the income statement.

 Check out ACE for a Review Quiz at http://accounting.college.hmco.com/students.

COST ALLOCATION

LO6 Define *cost allocation* and explain how cost objects, cost pools, and cost drivers are used to assign manufacturing overhead costs.

RELATED TEXT ASSIGNMENTS
Q: 15, 16, 17
SE: 8, 9, 10
E: 11, 12, 13
P: 4, 6, 8
SD: 2
MRA: 4

ENRICHMENT NOTE:
Because allocation by its very nature is a relatively arbitrary process, a rational allocation scheme is best. Rational allocation approaches help avoid behavior problems for management.

As noted earlier, the costs of direct materials and direct labor can be easily traced to a product, but manufacturing overhead costs are indirect costs that must be collected and allocated in some manner. **Cost allocation** is the process of assigning a collection of indirect costs to a specific **cost object**, such as a product or service, a department, or an operating activity, using an allocation base known as a **cost driver**. A cost driver might be direct labor hours, direct labor costs, units produced, or another activity base that is important to a business. As the cost driver increases in volume, it causes the **cost pool**—the collection of indirect costs assigned to a cost object—to increase in amount. For example, suppose Candy Company has a machine-maintenance cost pool. The cost pool consists of overhead costs for the supplies and labor needed to maintain the machines, the cost object is the product, and the cost driver is machine hours. As more machine hours are used, the amount of the cost pool increases, thus increasing the costs assigned to the product.

For purposes of product costing, cost allocation is defined as the assignment of manufacturing overhead costs to the product (cost object) during an accounting period. It requires (1) the pooling of manufacturing overhead costs that are affected by a common activity (e.g., machine maintenance) and (2) the selection of a cost driver whose activity level causes a change in the cost pool (e.g., machine hours).

ALLOCATING THE COSTS OF MANUFACTURING OVERHEAD

Allocating manufacturing overhead costs is a four-step process that corresponds to the four stages of the management cycle. In the first step (the planning stage), managers estimate manufacturing overhead costs and calculate a rate at which they will assign those costs to products. In the second step (the executing stage), this rate is applied to products as manufacturing overhead costs are incurred and recorded during production. In the third step (the reviewing stage), actual manufacturing overhead costs are recorded as they are incurred, and managers calculate the difference between the estimated and actual costs. In the fourth step (the reporting stage), managers report on this difference. Figure 7 summarizes these four steps in terms of their timing, the procedures involved, and the journal entries they require. It also shows how the cost flows in the various steps affect the accounting records.

■ **PLANNING THE OVERHEAD RATE**   Before an accounting period begins, managers determine cost pools and cost drivers and calculate a **predetermined overhead rate** by dividing the cost pool of total estimated overhead costs by the total estimated cost driver level. Grouping all estimated overhead costs into one cost pool and using direct labor hours or machine hours as the cost driver results in a single, plantwide overhead rate. By applying this predetermined rate in the same way to all units of production during the period, managers can better estimate product costs. This step requires no journal entry because no business activity has occurred.

■ **APPLYING THE OVERHEAD RATE**   As units of the product are manufactured during the accounting period, the estimated manufacturing overhead costs are assigned to the product's costs at the predetermined overhead rate. The overhead rate for each cost pool is multiplied by that pool's actual cost driver level (e.g., the actual number of direct labor hours used to complete the product). The purpose of this calculation is to assign a consistent manufacturing overhead cost to each unit produced during the accounting period. A journal entry records the allocation of overhead to the product as an increase in the Work in Process Inventory account and a decrease in the Manufacturing Overhead account.

■ **RECORDING ACTUAL OVERHEAD COSTS**   The actual manufacturing overhead costs are recorded as they are incurred during the accounting period. These costs, which include the costs of indirect materials, indirect labor, depreciation, property taxes, and other production costs, will be part of the actual product cost. The journal entry made for the actual manufacturing overhead costs records an increase in the Manufacturing Overhead account and a decrease in asset accounts or an increase in contra-asset or liability accounts.

■ **RECONCILING THE APPLIED AND ACTUAL OVERHEAD AMOUNTS**   At the end of the accounting period, the difference between the applied and actual manufacturing overhead costs is calculated and reconciled. If the manufacturing overhead costs applied to production during the period are greater than the actual manufacturing overhead costs, the difference in the amounts represents **overapplied overhead costs**. If this difference is immaterial, the Manufacturing Overhead account is increased and the Cost of Goods Sold account is decreased by the difference. If the difference is material, adjustments are made to the accounts affected—that is, the Work in Process Inventory, Finished Goods Inventory, and Cost of Goods Sold accounts. If the manufacturing overhead costs applied to production during the period are less than the actual manufacturing overhead costs, the difference represents **underapplied overhead costs**. The Cost of Goods Sold account is increased and the Manufacturing Overhead account is decreased by this difference, assuming the difference is not material. The adjustment for overapplied or underapplied overhead costs, whether they are immaterial or material, is necessary to reflect the actual manufacturing overhead costs on the income statement.

FIGURE 7
Allocating Manufacturing Overhead Costs: A Four-Step Process

Year 20x5 ——————————|—————————— Year 20x6 ——————————▶
January 1   December 31

	Step 1: Planning the Overhead Rate	Step 2: Applying the Overhead Rate	Step 3: Recording Actual Overhead Costs	Step 4: Reconciling Applied and Actual Overhead Costs
Timing and Procedure	Before the accounting period begins, determine cost pools and cost drivers. Calculate the overhead rate by dividing the cost pool of total estimated overhead costs by the total estimated cost driver level.	During the accounting period, as units are produced, apply overhead costs to products by multiplying the predetermined overhead rate for each cost pool by the actual cost driver level for that pool. Record costs.	Record actual manufacturing overhead costs as they are incurred during the accounting period.	At the end of the accounting period, calculate and reconcile the difference between applied and actual manufacturing overhead costs.
Journal Entry	None	Increase Work in Process Inventory account and decrease Manufacturing Overhead account: Dr. Work in Process XX Cr. Manufacturing Overhead XX	Increase Manufacturing Overhead account and decrease asset accounts or increase contra-asset or liability accounts: Dr. Manufacturing Overhead XX Cr. Various Accounts XX	Entry will vary depending on how costs have been applied. If overapplied, increase Manufacturing Overhead and decrease Cost of Goods Sold. If underapplied, increase Cost of Goods Sold and decrease Manufacturing Overhead.
Cost Flow Through the Accounts		Manufacturing Overhead — Overhead applied using predetermined rate Work in Process Inventory — Overhead applied using predetermined rate	Manufacturing Overhead — Actual overhead costs recorded Various Asset and Liability Accounts — Actual costs recorded	**Overapplied:** Manufacturing Overhead: Actual overhead costs recorded / Overhead applied using predetermined rate; Overapplied; Bal. $0. Cost of Goods Sold: Bal. / Overapplied; Actual bal. **Underapplied:** Manufacturing Overhead: Actual overhead costs recorded / Overhead applied using predetermined rate; Underapplied; Bal. $0. Cost of Goods Sold: Bal. / Underapplied; Actual bal.

THE IMPORTANCE OF GOOD ESTIMATES

A predetermined, or estimated, manufacturing overhead rate has two main uses. First, it enables managers to make decisions about pricing products and controlling costs before some of the actual costs are known. The product cost calculated at the end of a period, when all product costs are known, is, of course, more accurate. But when the overhead portion of product cost is estimated in advance, managers can compare actual and estimated costs throughout the year and more quickly correct any problems that may cause the under- or overallocation of overhead costs.

Second, an advance estimate allows managers to apply manufacturing overhead costs to each unit produced in an equitable and timely manner. Actual manufacturing overhead costs fluctuate from month to month as a result of the timing of the costs and the variability of the amounts. For example, some manufacturing overhead costs (such as supervisors' salaries and depreciation on equipment) may be expensed monthly. Others (like payroll taxes) may be paid quarterly, and still others (like property taxes and insurance) may be paid annually. In addition, indirect hourly labor costs (such as the costs of machine maintenance and materials handling) fluctuate with changes in production levels.

The successful allocation of manufacturing overhead costs depends on two factors. One is a careful estimate of the total manufacturing overhead costs. The other is a good forecast of the cost driver level.

An accurate estimate of total manufacturing overhead costs is crucial. If the estimate is wrong, the manufacturing overhead rate will be wrong. This will cause an overstatement or understatement of the product unit cost. If an organization relies on information that overstates product unit cost, it may fail to bid on profitable projects because the costs appear too high. If it relies on information that understates product unit cost, it may accept business that is not as profitable as expected. So, to provide managers with reliable product unit costs, the management accountant must be careful to include all manufacturing overhead items and to forecast the costs of those items accurately.

The budgeting process usually includes estimating manufacturing overhead costs. Managers who use production-related resources will provide cost estimates for direct and indirect production activities. For example, the managers for materials handling and inspection at Candy Company, Inc., estimate the costs related to their departments' activities, and Maya Kee, the accountant, includes their cost estimates in developing total manufacturing overhead costs.

Managers also need to provide accurate estimates of cost driver levels. An understated cost driver level will cause an overstatement of the predetermined manufacturing overhead rate (the cost is spread over a lesser level), and an overstated cost driver level will cause an understatement of the predetermined manufacturing overhead rate (the cost is spread over a greater level).

In the following sections, we present two approaches to allocating manufacturing overhead. We use the first two steps of the four-step overhead allocation process to demonstrate these approaches.

 Check out ACE for a Review Quiz at http://accounting.college.hmco.com/students.

ALLOCATING MANUFACTURING OVERHEAD: THE TRADITIONAL APPROACH

L07   Using the traditional method of allocating manufacturing overhead costs, calculate product unit cost.

RELATED TEXT ASSIGNMENTS

Q: 18   P: 4, 6, 8
SE: 9, 10   SD: 2
E: 11, 12, 13, 14   MRA: 4

The traditional approach to applying manufacturing overhead costs to a product cost is to use a single predetermined overhead rate. This approach is especially useful when companies manufacture only one product or a few very similar products that require the same production processes and production-related activities, such as setup, inspection, and materials handling. The total manufacturing overhead costs constitute one cost pool, and a traditional activity base—such as direct labor hours, direct labor costs, machine hours, or units of production—is the cost driver.

FIGURE 8
Using the Traditional Approach to Assign Manufacturing Overhead Costs to Production

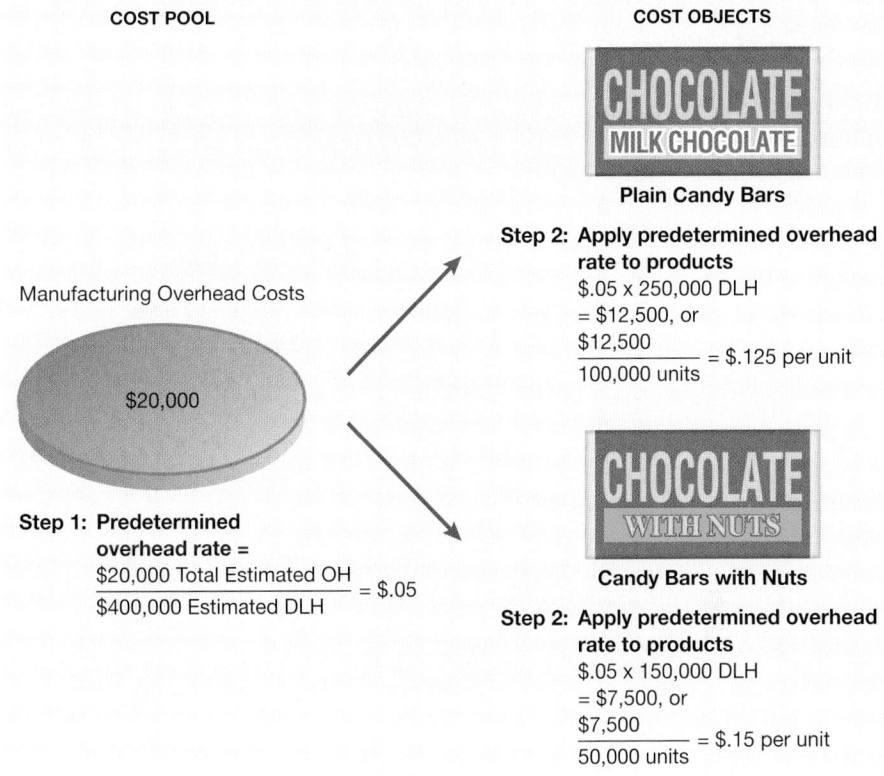

COST POOL

COST OBJECTS

Plain Candy Bars

Step 2: Apply predetermined overhead rate to products
$.05 x 250,000 DLH
= $12,500, or
$$\frac{\$12,500}{100,000 \text{ units}} = \$.125 \text{ per unit}$$

Manufacturing Overhead Costs

$20,000

Step 1: Predetermined overhead rate =
$$\frac{\$20,000 \text{ Total Estimated OH}}{\$400,000 \text{ Estimated DLH}} = \$.05$$

Candy Bars with Nuts

Step 2: Apply predetermined overhead rate to products
$.05 x 150,000 DLH
= $7,500, or
$$\frac{\$7,500}{50,000 \text{ units}} = \$.15 \text{ per unit}$$

Figure 8 illustrates the application of one cost pool of manufacturing overhead costs to two product lines. As we continue with our example of Candy Company, Inc., let's assume that the company will be selling two product lines in 20x7—plain candy bars and candy bars with nuts—and that Maya Kee chooses direct labor hours as the cost driver. Kee estimates that total manufacturing overhead costs for the next year will be $20,000 and that total direct labor hours (DLH) worked will be 400,000 hours.

Table 3 summarizes the first two steps in the traditional approach to allocating manufacturing overhead costs. In the first step, Kee uses the following formula to compute the rate at which manufacturing overhead costs will be applied:

$$\text{Predetermined Overhead Rate} = \frac{\$20,000}{400,000 \text{ DLH}} = \$.05 \text{ per DLH}$$

In the second step, Kee applies the predetermined overhead rate to the products. During the year, Candy Company used 250,000 direct labor hours to produce 100,000 plain candy bars and 150,000 direct labor hours to produce 50,000 candy bars with nuts. When Kee applies the predetermined overhead rate, the portion of the manufacturing overhead cost applied to the plain candy bars totals $12,500 ($.05 × 250,000 DLH), or $.125 per unit ($12,500 ÷ 100,000 units), and the portion applied to the candy bars with nuts totals $7,500 ($.05 × 150,000 DLH), or $.15 per unit ($7,500 ÷ 50,000 units).

Kee also wanted to calculate the product unit cost for the accounting period using normal costing. She gathered the following data for the two product lines:

	Plain Candy Bars	Candy Bars with Nuts
Actual direct materials cost per unit	$.18	$.21
Actual direct labor cost per unit	.14	.16
Prime cost per unit	$.32	$.37

● STOP AND THINK!
How many overhead cost pools are used in the traditional approach to cost allocation?
In the traditional approach to cost allocation, total manufacturing overhead costs constitute one cost pool. ■

STUDY NOTE: Don't make the mistake of thinking that because a cost is not traced directly to a product it is not a product cost. All manufacturing costs, both direct and indirect, are product costs.

TABLE 3. Allocating Manufacturing Overhead Costs and Calculating Product Unit Cost: Traditional Approach

Step 1. Calculate overhead rate for cost pool:

$$\frac{\text{Estimated Total Overhead Costs}}{\text{Estimated Total Cost Driver Level}} = \frac{\$20,000}{400,000 \text{ (DLH)}} = \$.05 \text{ per DLH}$$

Step 2. Apply predetermined overhead rate to products:

	Plain Candy Bars	Candy Bars with Nuts
	Predetermined Overhead Rate × Actual Cost Driver Level = Cost Applied to Production	Predetermined Overhead Rate × Actual Cost Driver Level = Cost Applied to Production
Manufacturing overhead applied: $.05 per DLH	$.05 × 250,000 DLH = $12,500	$.05 × 150,000 DLH = $7,500
Manufacturing overhead cost per unit: Cost Applied ÷ Number of Units	$12,500 ÷ 100,000 = $.125	$7,500 ÷ 50,000 = $.15

Product unit cost using normal costing:

	Plain Candy Bars	Nut Candy Bars
Product costs per unit:		
Direct materials	$.180	$.21
Direct labor	.140	.16
Applied manufacturing overhead	.125	.15
Product unit cost	$.445	$.52

At the bottom of Table 3 is Kee's calculation of the normal product unit cost for each product line. The nut candy bar's product unit cost ($.52) is higher than the plain candy bar's ($.445) because producing the candy bar with nuts required more expensive materials and more labor time.

 Check out ACE for a Review Quiz at http://accounting.college.hmco.com/students.

ALLOCATING MANUFACTURING OVERHEAD: THE ABC APPROACH

LO8 Using activity-based costing to assign manufacturing overhead costs, calculate product unit cost.

RELATED TEXT ASSIGNMENTS
Q: 19
SE: 11
E: 14
P: 5, 7, 8
SD: 2
MRA: 4

Activity-based costing (ABC) is a more accurate method of assigning overhead costs to products than the traditional approach. It categorizes all indirect costs by activity, traces the indirect costs to those activities, and assigns activity costs to products using a cost driver related to the cause of the cost. A company that uses ABC identifies production-related activities and the events and circumstances that cause, or drive, those activities, such as number of inspections or maintenance hours. As a result, many smaller activity pools are created from the single manufacturing overhead cost pool used in the traditional method. This means that managers will calculate an overhead rate, or activity cost rate, for each activity pool and then use that rate and a cost driver amount to determine the portion of manufacturing overhead costs to assign to a product. Managers must select an appropriate number of activity pools for manufacturing overhead, and a system must be designed to capture the actual cost driver amounts. Because each activity pool requires a cost driver, the

FOCUS ON BUSINESS ETHICS

What Can a Company Do to Be Resource-Responsible?

United Parcel Service <www.ups.com> has taken a proactive role in its commitment to efficient and responsible management of resources. UPS recycles computer paper, letter envelopes, and delivery notices, and it records delivery information electronically, which saves an estimated 30,000 trees annually. UPS also helps customers protect the environment by using packaging methods that prevent product damage and minimize waste and by operating a national recycling program for its customer's packaging materials. For example, Ethan Allen, Inc. <www.ethanallen.com>, a furniture maker and retailer, uses UPS's services to retrieve foam-sheet shipping material, which makes money for Ethan Allen in addition to reducing its disposal costs.[4]

benefit of grouping manufacturing overhead costs into several smaller pools to obtain more accurate estimates of product costs is offset by the additional costs of measuring many different cost drivers.

ABC will improve the accuracy of product cost estimates for organizations that sell many different types of products (product diversity) or that use varying, significant amounts of different production-related activities to complete the products (process complexity). To remain competitive in today's global marketplace, many organizations are selling a wider range of products or services than in the past. For example, 20 years ago, Taco Bell had only 6 food items on its menu; today, it has more than 25. This diversity of product lines requires more careful cost allocation, especially when it comes to making decisions about pricing products, outsourcing processes to other organizations, or choosing to keep a food item or drop it from the menu.

For other organizations, some products are more complicated to manufacture, store, move, package, or ship than others (process complexity). For example, an auto parts distributor receives, stores, selects, moves, consolidates, packs, and ships auto parts to auto dealers. The distributor's greatest costs are overhead costs, which under the traditional method are assigned based on what it costs to purchase a part for resale. With the traditional method, more expensive parts, such as car radios, receive a greater allocation of overhead costs than do less expensive parts, such as windshields. However, because a glass windshield is more delicate than a car radio, it costs the distributor more to move, store, pack, and ship. If ABC were used, the cost of the windshield would increase to reflect a fairer allocation of the distributor's overhead costs. Thus, by assigning overhead costs based on the relative use of overhead resources, ABC would provide managers with better information for making decisions, such as pricing car radios, windshields, and other auto parts; choosing to discontinue selling windshields; or reducing the amount of storage space.

PLANNING OVERHEAD RATES

As discussed earlier, Maya Kee, the accountant for Candy Company, Inc., calculated product unit cost by computing one manufacturing overhead rate for one cost pool and applying that rate to the direct labor hours used to manufacture plain candy bars and candy bars with nuts. As we continue with our example, we find that Olga Santee, president of Candy Company, is concerned about the product cost for each type of candy bar. Santee believes that the difference in cost between the plain and nut candy bars should be more than $.075 ($.52 − $.445). She has asked Kee to review her estimate. Kee found no error when she rechecked the calculation of direct materials costs and direct labor costs. However, she believes the traditional approach to assigning manufacturing overhead cost could be misleading, so she wants to use activity-based costing to obtain a more accurate estimate of product cost. Figure 9 illustrates the use of ABC to assign manufacturing overhead costs to two product lines.

Kee analyzed the production-related activities and decided that the estimated $20,000 in manufacturing overhead cost could be grouped into four activity pools. The first activity, setup, includes estimated total costs of $7,000 for indirect labor and indirect materials used in preparing machines for each batch of production. The second activity, inspection, includes $6,000 for salaries and indirect materials costs, indirect labor, and depreciation on testing equipment. The third activity, packaging,

FIGURE 9
Using ABC to Assign Manufacturing Overhead Costs to Production

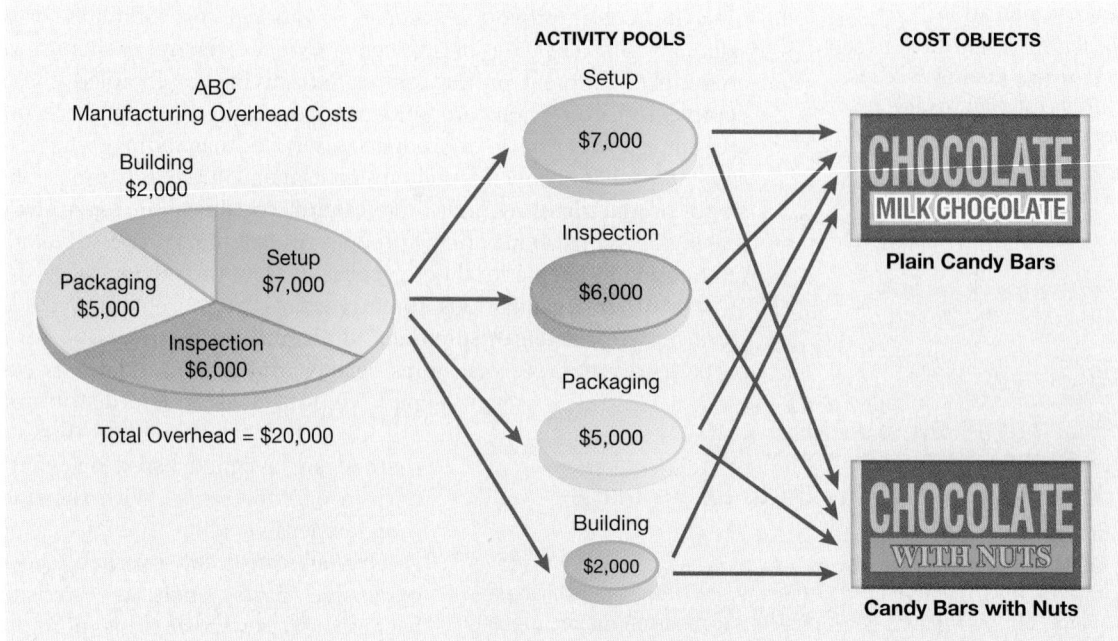

includes estimated total costs of $5,000 for indirect materials, indirect labor, and equipment depreciation. The last activity, building operations, includes estimated total overhead costs of $2,000 for building depreciation, maintenance, janitorial wages, property taxes, insurance, security, and all other costs not related to the first three activities.

After identifying the four activity pools, Kee selected a cost driver and estimated the cost driver level for each activity pool. The following schedule shows those amounts by product line and in total:

KEY POINT: Under ABC, activity pools are allocated to cost objects using multiple cost drivers.

Estimated Cost Driver Level

Cost Driver	Plain	Nut	Total
Number of setups	300	400	700
Number of inspections	150	350	500
Packaging hours	600	1,400	2,000
Machine hours	4,000	6,000	10,000

After identifying activity pools, estimated activity pool amounts, cost drivers, and estimated cost driver levels, Kee performed Step 1 of the overhead allocation process by calculating the activity cost rate for each activity pool. The activity cost rate is the estimated activity pool amount divided by the estimated cost driver level. Step 1 of Table 4 shows the activity cost rates to be $10 per setup, $12 per inspection, $2.50 per packaging hour, and $.20 per machine hour.

APPLYING THE OVERHEAD RATES

In Step 2, Kee applied manufacturing overhead to the two product lines using the cost driver level for each cost driver multiplied by the activity cost rate shown in the preceding schedule. Step 2 of Table 4 shows those calculations. For example, Kee applied $3,000 in setup costs ($10 × 300 setups) to the plain candy bar line and $4,000 ($10 × 400 setups) to the nut candy bar line. After applying the over-

TABLE 4. Allocating Manufacturing Overhead Costs and Calculating Product Unit Cost: ABC Approach

Step 1. Calculate activity cost rate for cost pool:

$$\frac{\text{Estimated Total Activity Costs}}{\text{Estimated Total Cost Driver Level}} = \text{Activity Cost Rate for Cost Pool}$$

Activity	Estimated Total Activity Costs	Estimated Total Cost Driver Level	Activity Cost Rate for Cost Pool
Setup	$ 7,000	700 setups	$7,000 ÷ 700 = $10 per setup
Inspection	6,000	500 inspections	$6,000 ÷ 500 = $12 per inspection
Packaging	5,000	2,000 packaging hours	$5,000 ÷ 2,000 = $2.50 per packaging hour
Building	2,000	10,000 machine hours	$2,000 ÷ 10,000 = $.20 per machine hour
	$20,000		

Step 2. Apply predetermined activity cost rates to products:

	Plain Candy Bars		Nut Candy Bars	
Activity Pool	Predetermined Overhead Rate × Actual Cost Driver Level = Cost Applied to Production		Predetermined Overhead Rate × Actual Cost Driver Level = Cost Applied to Production	
Setup	$10 × 300 =	$3,000	$10 × 400 =	$4,000
Inspection	$12 × 150 =	1,800	$12 × 350 =	4,200
Packaging	$2.50 × 600 =	1,500	$2.50 × 1,400 =	3,500
Building	$.20 × 4,000 =	800	$.20 × 6,000 =	1,200
Total overhead applied		$7,100		$12,900
Applied overhead cost per unit: Cost Applied ÷ Number of Units	$7,100 ÷ 100,000 =	$.071	$12,900 ÷ 50,000 =	$.258

Product unit cost using normal costing:

	Plain Candy Bars	Nut Candy Bars
Product costs per unit:		
Direct materials	$.180	$.210
Direct labor	.140	.160
Applied manufacturing overhead	.071	.258
Product unit cost	$.391	$.628

head costs from the four activity pools to the product lines, Kee estimated that total manufacturing overhead costs of $7,100, or $.071 per bar ($7,100 ÷ 100,000 units), should be applied to the plain candy bar line and that $12,900, or $.258 per bar ($12,900 ÷ 50,000 units), should be applied to the nut candy bar line.

Kee also wanted to calculate the unit cost for each product line using normal costing. Her calculations appear at the bottom of Table 4. The product unit cost is $.391 for the plain line and $.628 for the nut line.

Kee presented the following information to Olga Santee:

	Plain	Nut
Product unit cost: Traditional approach with one manufacturing overhead cost pool	$.445	$.520
Product unit cost: ABC with four activity pools	.391	.628
Difference: decrease (increase)	$.054	($.108)

FOCUS ON BUSINESS PRACTICE

How Costly Is Television Talent?

If salary is measured per unit, your perspective on the cost of television talent may change. Compare the salaries and cost per viewer (salary divided by number of viewers per season) for the following television personalities in 2002. In your opinion, who is the highest paid talent?[5]

	2002 Salary	Season Viewers	Cost per Viewer
Larry King	$7 million	1.3 million	$5.39
Conan O'Brien	$8 million	2.55 million	$3.14
Katie Couric	$13 million	6.1 million	$2.13
David Letterman	$16 million	4.35 million	$3.68

Because ABC assigned more costs to the product line that used more resources, it provided a more accurate estimate of product unit cost. The increased information about the production requirements for the nut candy bar line that went into the ABC calculation of product unit cost also provided valuable insights. Santee found that the nut candy bars cost more to manufacture because the changes in the ingredients require more setups and machine hours and because more inspections are needed to test the candy quality. Because the nut candy bar line requires more production and production-related activities, its product unit cost is higher. Based on this analysis, Santee may want to reconsider some of her decisions about the manufacture and sale of these two product lines.

 Check out ACE for a Review Quiz at http://accounting.college.hmco.com/students.

COST ALLOCATION IN SERVICE ORGANIZATIONS

LO9 Apply costing concepts to a service organization.

RELATED TEXT ASSIGNMENTS
Q: 20
SE: 12
E: 15
SD: 3, 5
MRA: 2

● **STOP AND THINK!**
How should a manager in a service organization handle materials costs?

Any materials costs in a service organization would be for supplies used in providing services. Because these are indirect materials costs, the manager should include them in service overhead. ■

Processing loans, representing people in courts of law, selling insurance policies, and computing people's income taxes are typical of the services performed by professionals in many service organizations. Like other services, these are labor-intensive processes supported by indirect labor and overhead costs.

Because no products are manufactured in the course of providing services, service organizations have no direct materials costs. As noted, however, they do have both labor and overhead costs, which must be included when computing the cost of providing a service. The most important cost in a service organization is the direct cost of professional labor, and the usual standard is applicable; that is, the direct labor cost must be traceable to the service rendered. The indirect costs incurred in performing a service are similar to those incurred in manufacturing a product. They are classified as service overhead and, along with professional labor costs, are considered service costs rather than period costs. Just as product costs appear on manufacturers' income statements as cost of goods sold, service costs appear on service organizations' income statements as cost of sales.

To illustrate how overhead costs are applied in service organizations, assume that the Loan Department of the Campus Bank wants to determine the total costs incurred in processing a typical loan application. Its policy for the past five years has been to charge a $150 fee for processing a home-loan application. Jerome Hill, the chief loan officer, thinks the fee is far too low. Because of the way operating costs have soared in the past five years, he proposes that the fee be doubled. The bank has asked you to compute the cost of processing a typical home-loan application and has given you the following information about its processing of loan applications:

Direct professional labor

Loan processors' monthly salaries:
  4 people at $3,000 each $12,000

Indirect monthly overhead costs

Chief loan officer's salary	$ 4,500
Telephone	750
Depreciation	5,750
Legal advice	2,460
Customer relations	640
Credit check function	1,980
Internal audit function	2,400
Utilities	1,690
Clerical personnel	3,880
Miscellaneous	1,050
Total overhead costs	$25,100

The Loan Department usually processes 100 home-loan applications each month.

The Loan Department performs several other functions in addition to processing home-loan applications. Roughly one-half of the department is involved in loan collection. After determining how many of the processed loans were not home loans, you conclude that only 25 percent of the overhead costs of the Loan Department were applicable to the processing of home-loan applications. The cost of processing one home-loan application can be computed as follows:

Direct professional labor cost:		
$12,000 ÷ 100		$120.00
Service overhead cost:		
$25,100 × 25% ÷ 100		62.75
Total processing cost per loan		$182.75

Finally, you conclude that the chief loan officer was correct; the present fee does not cover the current costs of processing a typical home-loan application. However, doubling the loan fee seems too extreme. To allow for a profit margin, the loan fee could be raised to $225 or $250.

 Check out ACE for a Review Quiz at http://accounting.college.hmco.com/students.

Chapter Review

REVIEW OF LEARNING OBJECTIVES

LO1 Describe how managers use information about costs in the management cycle.

During the management cycle, managers in manufacturing, retail, and service organizations use information about operating costs and product or service costs to prepare budgets, make pricing and other decisions, calculate variances between estimated and actual costs, and report results.

LO2 Explain how managers classify costs and how they use these cost classifications.

A single cost can be classified as a direct or indirect cost, a variable or fixed cost, a value-adding or nonvalue-adding cost, and a product or period cost. These cost classifications enable managers to control costs by tracing them to cost objects, to calculate the number of units that must be sold to obtain a certain level of profit, to identify the costs of activities that do and do not add value to a product or service, and to prepare financial statements for parties outside the organization.

LO3 Define and give examples of the three elements of product cost and compute the unit cost of a product.

Direct materials costs are the costs of materials used in making a product that can be conveniently and economically traced to specific product units. Direct labor costs include all labor costs needed to make a product that can be conveniently and economically traced to specific product units. All other production-related costs are classified and accounted for as manufacturing overhead costs. Such costs cannot be conveniently or economically traced to end products, so a cost allocation method is used to assign them to products.

When a batch of products has been completed, the product unit cost is computed by dividing the total cost of direct materials, direct labor, and manufacturing overhead by the total number of units produced. The product unit cost can be calculated using actual, normal, or standard costing methods. Under normal costing, the actual costs of direct materials and direct labor are combined with the estimated cost of manufacturing overhead to determine the product unit cost. Under standard costing, the estimated costs of direct materials, direct labor, and manufacturing overhead are used to calculate the product unit cost. The components of product cost may be classified as prime costs or conversion costs. Prime costs are the primary costs of production; they are the sum of direct materials costs and direct labor costs. Conversion costs are the costs of converting direct materials into finished product; they are the sum of direct labor costs and manufacturing overhead costs.

LO4 Describe the flow of costs through a manufacturer's inventory accounts.

The flow of costs through the inventory accounts begins when costs are incurred for direct materials, direct labor, and manufacturing overhead. Materials costs flow first into the Materials Inventory account, which is used to record the costs of materials when they are received and again when they are issued for use in a production process. All manufacturing-related costs—direct materials, direct labor, and manufacturing overhead—are recorded in the Work in Process Inventory account as the production process begins. When products are completed, their costs are transferred from the Work in Process Inventory account to the Finished Goods Inventory account. Costs remain in the Finished Goods Inventory account until the products are sold, at which time they are transferred to the Cost of Goods Sold account.

LO5 Compare how service, retail, and manufacturing organizations report costs on their financial statements and how they account for inventories.

Because the operations of service, retail, and manufacturing organizations differ, their financial statements differ as well. A service organization maintains no inventory accounts on its balance sheet. The cost of sales on its income statement reflects the net cost of the services sold. A retail organization, which purchases products ready for resale, maintains only a Merchandise Inventory account, which is used to record and account for items in inventory. The cost of goods sold is simply the difference between the cost of goods available for sale and the ending merchandise inventory. A manufacturing organization, because it creates a product, maintains three inventory accounts: Materials Inventory, Work in Process Inventory, and Finished Goods Inventory. Manufacturing costs flow through all three inventory accounts. During the accounting period, the cost of completed products is transferred to the Finished Goods Inventory account; the cost of units that have been manufactured and sold is transferred to the Cost of Goods Sold account.

LO6 Define *cost allocation* and explain how cost objects, cost pools, and cost drivers are used to assign manufacturing overhead costs.

Cost allocation is the process of assigning collected indirect costs to a specific cost object using an allocation base known as a cost driver. The allocation of manufacturing overhead costs requires the pooling of overhead costs that are affected by a common activity and the selection of a cost driver whose activity level causes a change in the cost pool. A cost pool is the collection of overhead costs assigned to a cost object. A cost driver is an activity base that causes the cost pool to increase in amount as the cost driver increases.

Allocating manufacturing overhead is a four-step process that involves planning a rate at which overhead costs will be assigned to products, assigning overheard costs at this predetermined rate to product costs during production, recording actual manufacturing overhead costs as they are incurred, and reconciling the difference between the actual and applied overhead costs. The Cost of Goods Sold account is corrected for an immaterial amount of over- or underapplied manufacturing overhead costs assigned to the products. If the difference is material, adjustments are made to the Work in Process Inventory, Finished Goods Inventory, and Cost of Goods Sold accounts.

LO7 Using the traditional method of allocating manufacturing overhead costs, calculate product unit cost.

The traditional method applies manufacturing overhead costs to a product's cost by estimating a predetermined overhead rate and multiplying that rate by the actual cost driver level. The product unit cost is computed either by dividing the total product cost (the sum of the total applied manufacturing overhead cost and the actual costs of direct materials and direct labor) by the total number of units produced or by determining the cost per unit for each element of the product cost and summing those per-unit costs.

LO8 Using activity-based costing to assign manufacturing overhead costs, calculate product unit cost.

When ABC is used, manufacturing overhead costs are grouped into a number of cost pools related to specific activities. Cost drivers are identified, and cost driver levels are estimated for each activity pool. Each activity cost rate is calculated by dividing the estimated activity pool amount by the estimated cost driver level. Manufacturing overhead, which is divided into the activity pools, is applied to the product's cost by multiplying the various activity cost rates by their actual cost driver levels. The product unit cost is computed by dividing the total product cost (the sum of the total applied cost pools and the actual costs of direct materials and direct labor) by the total number of units produced.

LO9 Apply costing concepts to a service organization.

Because no products are manufactured in the course of providing services, service organizations have no materials costs. They do, however, have both direct labor costs and overhead costs, which are similar to those in manufacturing organizations. To determine the cost of performing a service, professional labor and service-related overhead costs are included in the analysis.

REVIEW OF CONCEPTS AND TERMINOLOGY

The following concepts and terms were introduced in this chapter:

LO8 **Activity-based costing (ABC):** A method of assigning overhead costs that categorizes all indirect costs by activity, traces the indirect costs to those activities, and assigns activity costs to products using a cost driver related to the cause of the cost.

LO3 **Actual costing:** A method of cost measurement that uses the actual costs of direct materials, direct labor, and manufacturing overhead to calculate a product unit cost.

LO3 **Conversion costs:** The costs of converting direct materials into a finished product; the sum of direct labor costs and manufacturing overhead costs.

LO6 **Cost allocation:** The process of assigning a collection of indirect costs to a specific cost object using an allocation base known as a cost driver.

LO6 **Cost driver:** An activity base that causes a cost pool to increase in amount as the cost driver increases in volume.

LO6 **Cost object:** The destination of an assigned, or allocated, cost.

LO4 **Cost of goods manufactured:** The cost of all units completed and moved to finished goods storage during an accounting period.

LO6 **Cost pool:** The collection of overhead costs assigned to a cost object.

LO2 **Direct costs:** Costs that can be conveniently and economically traced to a cost object.

LO3 **Direct labor costs:** The costs of the labor needed to make a product that can be conveniently and economically traced to specific units of the product.

LO3 **Direct materials costs:** The costs of the materials used in making a product that can be conveniently and economically traced to specific units of the product.

LO4 **Finished Goods Inventory account:** An inventory account that shows the costs assigned to all completed products that have not been sold.

LO2 **Fixed cost:** A cost that remains constant within a defined range of activity or time period.

LO2 **Indirect costs:** Costs that cannot be conveniently or economically traced to a cost object.

LO3 **Indirect labor costs:** The costs of labor for production-related activities that cannot be conveniently or economically traced to a unit of the product.

LO3 **Indirect materials costs:** The costs of materials that cannot be conveniently and economically traced to a unit of the product.

LO4 **Manufacturing cost flow:** The flow of manufacturing costs (direct materials, direct labor, and overhead) through the Materials Inventory, Work in Process

Inventory, and Finished Goods Inventory accounts into the Cost of Goods Sold account.

LO3   Manufacturing overhead costs: Production-related costs that cannot be practically or conveniently traced to an end product. Also called *factory overhead, factory burden,* or *indirect manufacturing costs.*

LO4   Materials Inventory account: An inventory account that shows the balance of the cost of unused materials.

LO2   Nonvalue-adding cost: The cost of an activity that adds cost to a product or service but does not increase its market value.

LO3   Normal costing: A method of cost measurement that combines the actual direct costs of materials and labor with estimated manufacturing overhead costs to determine a product unit cost.

LO6   Overapplied overhead costs: The amount that overhead costs applied using the predetermined overhead rate exceed the actual overhead costs for the accounting period.

LO2   Period costs: The costs of resources used during an accounting period and not assigned to products. Also called *noninventoriable costs.*

LO6   Predetermined overhead rate: The rate calculated before an accounting period begins by dividing the cost pool of total estimated overhead costs by the total estimated cost driver for that pool.

LO3   Prime costs: The primary costs of production; the sum of direct materials costs and direct labor costs.

LO2   Product costs: The costs assigned to inventory, which include the costs of direct materials, direct labor, and manufacturing overhead. Also called *inventoriable costs.*

LO3   Product unit cost: The cost of manufacturing a single unit of a product, computed either by dividing the total cost of direct materials, direct labor, and manufacturing overhead by the total number of units produced, or by determining the cost per unit for each element of the product cost and summing those per-unit costs.

LO3   Standard costing: A method of cost measurement that uses the estimated costs of direct materials, direct labor, and manufacturing overhead to calculate a product unit cost.

LO5   Statement of cost of goods manufactured: A formal statement summarizing the flow of all manufacturing costs incurred during an accounting period.

LO4   Total manufacturing costs: The total costs of direct materials, direct labor, and manufacturing overhead incurred and transferred to Work in Process Inventory during an accounting period. Also called *current manufacturing costs.*

LO6   Underapplied overhead costs: The amount that actual overhead costs exceed the overhead costs applied using the predetermined overhead rate for the accounting period.

LO2   Value-adding cost: The cost of an activity that increases the market value of a product or service.

LO2   Variable cost: A cost that changes in direct proportion to a change in productive output (or any other measure of volume).

LO4   Work in Process Inventory account: An inventory account used to record the manufacturing costs incurred and assigned to partially completed units of product.

REVIEW PROBLEM

Calculating Cost of Goods Manufactured: Three Fundamental Steps

LO3
LO4
LO5
Nikita Company requires its controller to prepare not only a year-end balance sheet and income statement, but also a statement of cost of goods manufactured. During 20x6, Nikita purchased $361,920 of direct materials. The company's direct labor costs for the year were $99,085 (10,430 hours at $9.50 per hour); its indirect labor costs totaled $126,750 (20,280 hours at $6.25 per hour). Account balances for 20x6 were as follows:

Account	Balance
Plant Supervision	$ 42,500
Factory Insurance	8,100
Utilities, Factory	29,220
Depreciation, Factory Building	46,200
Depreciation, Factory Equipment	62,800
Factory Security	9,460
Factory Repair and Maintenance	14,980
Selling and Administrative Expenses	76,480
Materials Inventory, December 31, 20x5	26,490
Work in Process Inventory, December 31, 20x5	101,640
Finished Goods Inventory, December 31, 20x5	148,290
Materials Inventory, December 31, 20x6	24,910
Work in Process Inventory, December 31, 20x6	100,400
Finished Goods Inventory, December 31, 20x6	141,100

REQUIRED ▶

1. Compute the cost of materials used during the year.
2. Given the cost of materials used, compute the total manufacturing costs for the year.
3. Given the total manufacturing costs for the year, compute the cost of goods manufactured during the year.
4. If 13,397 units were manufactured during the year, what was the actual product unit cost? (Round your answer to two decimal places.)

ANSWER TO REVIEW PROBLEM

1. Cost of materials used:

Materials inventory, December 31, 20x5	$ 26,490
Add direct materials purchased (net)	361,920
Cost of materials available for use	$388,410
Less materials inventory, December 31, 20x6	24,910
Cost of materials used	$363,500

2. Total manufacturing costs:

Cost of materials used		$363,500
Add direct labor costs		99,085
Add total manufacturing overhead costs		
Plant supervision	$ 42,500	
Indirect labor	126,750	
Factory insurance	8,100	
Utilities, factory	29,220	
Depreciation, factory building	46,200	
Depreciation, factory equipment	62,800	
Factory security	9,460	
Factory repair and maintenance	14,980	
Total manufacturing overhead costs		340,010
Total manufacturing costs		$802,595

3. Cost of goods manufactured:

Total manufacturing costs	$802,595
Add work in process inventory, December 31, 20x5	101,640
Total cost of work in process during the year	$904,235
Less work in process inventory, December 31, 20x6	100,400
Cost of goods manufactured	$803,835

4. Actual product unit cost:

$$\frac{\text{Cost of Goods Manufactured}}{\text{Number of Units Manufactured}} = \frac{\$803,835}{13,397} = \$60.00$$

Chapter Assignments

BUILDING YOUR KNOWLEDGE FOUNDATION

QUESTIONS

1. How do managers use information about costs?
2. Why do managers use different classifications of costs?
3. What is the difference between a direct cost and an indirect cost?
4. What is the difference between a value-adding cost and a nonvalue-adding cost?
5. What are product costs and period costs?
6. What three kinds of costs are included in a product's cost?
7. What characteristics identify a cost as part of manufacturing overhead?
8. What is the difference between actual costing and normal costing?
9. What is the difference between prime costs and conversion costs?
10. Identify and describe the inventory accounts used by a manufacturing company.
11. What does the term *manufacturing cost flow* mean?
12. How do total manufacturing costs differ from the cost of goods manufactured?
13. How do service, retail, and manufacturing organizations differ, and how do these differences affect accounting for inventories?
14. How is the cost of goods manufactured used in computing the cost of goods sold?
15. What is cost allocation?
16. Explain the relationship among cost objects, cost pools, and cost drivers. Give an example of each.
17. List the four steps involved in allocating manufacturing overhead costs. Briefly explain each step.
18. How does traditional overhead allocation differ from ABC overhead allocation?
19. What allocation measure does ABC use to relate an activity pool to a cost object? Explain.
20. "The concept of product costs is not applicable to service organizations." Is this statement correct? Defend your answer.

SHORT EXERCISES

LO2   Cost Classifications

SE 1. Indicate whether each of the following is a direct (D) or indirect (ID) cost and a variable (V) or fixed (F) cost. Also indicate whether each adds value (VA) or does not add value (NVA) to the product and whether each is a product cost (PD), period cost (PER), or neither (N).

1. Production supervisor's salary
2. Sales commission
3. Wages of a production-line worker

LO3   Elements of Manufacturing Costs

SE 2. Daisy Luna, the bookkeeper at Candlelight, Inc., must group the costs of manufacturing candles. Indicate whether each of the following items should be classified as direct materials (DM), direct labor (DL), manufacturing overhead (MO), or none of these (N). Also indicate whether each is a prime cost (PC), conversion cost (CC), or neither (N).

1. Depreciation of the cost of vats to hold melted wax
2. Cost of wax
3. Rent on the factory where candles are made
4. Cost of George's time to dip the wicks into the wax
5. Cost of coloring for candles
6. Cost of Ray's time to design candles for Halloween
7. Sam's commission to sell candles to Candles Plus

SE 3.
LO3 Computation of Product Unit Cost

What is the product unit cost for Job 14, which consists of 300 units and has total manufacturing costs of direct materials, $4,500; direct labor, $7,500; and manufacturing overhead, $3,600? What are the prime costs and conversion costs per unit?

SE 4.
LO4 Cost Flow in a Manufacturing Organization

Given the following information, compute the ending balances of the Materials Inventory, Work in Process Inventory, and Finished Goods Inventory accounts:

Materials Inventory, beginning balance	$ 23,000
Work in Process Inventory, beginning balance	25,750
Finished Goods Inventory, beginning balance	38,000
Direct materials purchased	85,000
Direct materials placed into production	74,000
Direct labor costs	97,000
Manufacturing overhead costs	35,000
Cost of goods completed	123,000
Cost of goods sold	93,375

SE 5.
LO4 Document Flows in a Manufacturing Organization

Identify the document needed to support each of the following activities in a manufacturing organization:

1. Placing an order for direct materials with a supplier
2. Recording direct labor time at the beginning and end of each work shift
3. Receiving direct materials at the shipping dock
4. Recording the costs of a specific job requiring direct materials, direct labor, and overhead
5. Issuing direct materials into production
6. Billing the customer for a completed order
7. Fulfilling a request from the Production Scheduling Department for the purchase of direct materials

SE 6.
LO5 Income Statement for a Manufacturing Organization

Using the following information from Hakim Company, prepare an income statement through operating income for 20x6:

Sales	$900,000
Finished goods inventory, December 31, 20x5	45,000
Cost of goods manufactured	585,000
Finished goods inventory, December 31, 20x6	60,000
Operating expenses	275,000

SE 7.
LO5 Comparison of Income Statement Formats

Indicate whether each of these equations applies to a service organization (SER), retail organization (RET), or manufacturing organization (MANF):

1. Cost of Goods Sold = Beginning Merchandising Inventory + Net Cost of Purchases − Ending Merchandise Inventory
2. Cost of Sales = Net Cost of Services Sold
3. Cost of Goods Sold = Beginning Finished Goods Inventory + Cost of Goods Manufactured − Ending Finished Goods Inventory

SE 8.
LO6 Calculation of Underapplied or Overapplied Overhead

At year end, records show that actual manufacturing overhead costs incurred were $25,870 and the amount of manufacturing overhead costs applied to production was $27,000. Identify the amount of under- or overapplied manufacturing overhead, and indicate whether the Cost of Goods Sold account should be increased or decreased to reflect actual manufacturing overhead costs.

SE 9.
LO6 Computation of Overhead
LO7 Rate

Compute the overhead rate per service request for the Maintenance Department if estimated overhead costs are $18,290 and the number of estimated service requests is 3,100.

SE 10.
LO6 Allocation of Manufacturing
LO7 Overhead to Production

Calculate the amount of manufacturing overhead costs applied to production if the predetermined overhead rate is $4 per direct labor hour and 1,200 direct labor hours were worked.

SE 11.
LO8 Activity-Based Costing and Cost Drivers

Mazzola Clothiers Company relies on the information from its activity-based costing system when setting prices for its products. Compute ABC rates from the following estimated data for each of the activity centers:

Estimated Activity	Pool Amount	Cost Driver Level
Cutting/Stitching	$5,220,000	145,000 machine hours
Trimming/Packing	998,400	41,600 operator hours
Designing	1,187,500	62,500 designer hours

LO9   Unit Costs in a Service Business

SE 12. Fickle Picking Services provides inexpensive, high-quality labor for farmers growing vegetable and fruit crops. In September, Fickle Picking Services paid laborers $4,000 to harvest 500 acres of apples. The company incurred overhead costs of $2,400 for apple-picking services in September. This amount included the costs of transporting the laborers to the orchards; of providing facilities, food, and beverages for the laborers; and of scheduling, billing, and collecting from the farmers. Of this amount, 50 percent was related to picking apples. Compute the cost per acre to pick apples.

EXERCISES

LO1   The Management Cycle and Operating Costs

E 1. Indicate whether each of the following activities takes place during the planning (P), executing (E), reviewing (RV), or reporting (RP) stage of the management cycle:

1. Changing regular price to clearance price
2. Communicating results to appropriate personnel
3. Preparing budgets of operating costs
4. Comparing estimated and actual costs to determine variances

LO2   Cost Classifications

E 2. Indicate whether each of the following costs for a bicycle manufacturer is a direct or indirect cost of the bicycle, a variable or fixed cost, a value-adding or nonvalue-adding cost, and a product or period cost:

	Cost Classification			
	Direct or Indirect	Variable or Fixed	Value-adding or Nonvalue-adding	Product or Period
Example: Bicycle tire	Direct	Variable	Value-adding	Product

1. Depreciation on office computer
2. Labor to assemble bicycle
3. Labor to inspect bicycle
4. Internal auditor's salary
5. Lubricant for wheels

LO3   Unit Cost Determination

E 3. The Pattia Winery is one of the finest wineries in the country. One of its famous products is a red wine called Old Vines. Recently, management has become concerned about the increasing cost of making Old Vines and needs to determine if the current selling price of $10 per bottle is adequate. The winery wants to achieve a 25 percent gross profit on the sale of each bottle. The following information is given to you for analysis:

Batch size		10,550 bottles
Costs		
Direct materials		
Olen Millot grapes	$22,155	
Chancellor grapes	9,495	
Bottles	5,275	
Total direct materials costs	$36,925	
Direct labor		
Pickers/loaders	2,110	
Crusher	422	
Processors	8,440	
Bottler	$13,293	
Total direct labor costs	$24,265	
Manufacturing overhead		
Depreciation, equipment	2,743	
Depreciation, building	5,275	
Utilities	1,055	
Indirect labor	6,330	
Supervision	7,385	
Supplies	9,917	
Repairs	1,477	
Miscellaneous	633	
Total manufacturing overhead costs	$34,815	
Total production costs	$96,005	

1. Compute the unit cost per bottle for materials, labor, and overhead.
2. How would you advise management regarding the price per bottle of wine?
3. Compute the prime costs per unit and the conversion costs per unit.

LO4 Documentation

E 4. Lisette Company manufactures music boxes. Seventy percent of its products are standard items produced in long production runs. The other 30 percent are special orders with specific requests for tunes. The latter cost from three to six times as much as the standard product because they require additional materials and labor.

Reza Seca, the controller, recently received a complaint memorandum from Iggy Paulo, the production supervisor, about the new network of source documents that was added to the existing cost accounting system. The new documents include a purchase request, a purchase order, a receiving report, and a materials request. Paulo claims that the forms create extra work and interrupt the normal flow of production.

Prepare a written memorandum from Reza Seca to Iggy Paulo that fully explains the purpose of each type of document.

LO4 Cost Flows and Inventory Accounts

E 5. For each of the following activities, identify the inventory account (Materials Inventory, Work in Process Inventory, Finished Goods Inventory), if any, that is affected. If an inventory account is affected, indicate whether the account balance will increase or decrease. (*Example:* Moved completed units to finished goods inventory. *Answer:* Increase Finished Goods Inventory; decrease Work in Process Inventory.) If no inventory account is affected, use "None of these" as your answer.

1. Moved materials requested by production
2. Sold units of product
3. Purchased and received direct materials for production
4. Used direct labor and manufacturing overhead in the production process
5. Received payment from customer
6. Purchased office supplies and paid cash
7. Paid monthly office rent

LO5 Statement of Cost of Goods Manufactured

E 6. During August 31, 20x5, Rao Company's purchases of direct materials totaled $139,000; direct labor for the month was 3,400 hours at $8.75 per hour. Rao also incurred the following manufacturing overhead costs: utilities, $5,870; supervision, $16,600; indirect materials, $6,750; depreciation, $6,200; insurance, $1,830; and miscellaneous, $1,100.

Inventory accounts on July 31 were as follows: Materials Inventory, $48,600; Work in Process Inventory, $54,250; and Finished Goods Inventory, $38,500. Inventory accounts on August 31 were as follows: Materials Inventory, $50,100; Work in Process Inventory, $48,400; and Finished Goods Inventory, $37,450.

From the information given, prepare a statement of cost of goods manufactured.

LO5 Statement of Cost of Goods Manufactured and Cost of Goods Sold

E 7. Treetec Corp. makes irrigation sprinkler systems for tree nurseries. Rama Shih, Treetec's new controller, can find only the following partial information for the past year:

	Oak Division	Loblolly Division	Maple Division	Spruce Division
Direct materials used	$3	$ 7	$ g	$ 8
Total manufacturing costs	6	d	h	14
Manufacturing overhead	1	3	2	j
Direct labor	a	6	4	4
Ending work in process inventory	b	3	2	5
Cost of goods manufactured	7	20	12	k
Beginning work in process inventory	2	e	3	l
Ending finished goods inventory	2	6	i	9
Beginning finished goods inventory	3	f	5	7
Cost of goods sold	c	18	13	9

Using the information given, compute the unknown values. List the accounts in the proper order and show subtotals and totals as appropriate.

LO5 Characteristics of Organizations

E 8. Indicate whether each of the following is typical of a service organization (SER), retail organization (RET), or manufacturing organization (MANF):

1. Maintains only one balance sheet inventory account
2. Maintains no balance sheet inventory accounts
3. Maintains three balance sheet inventory accounts
4. Purchases products ready for resale
5. Designs and makes products for sale

6. Sells services
7. Determines the cost of sales
8. Includes the cost of goods manufactured in calculating cost of goods sold
9. Includes the cost of purchases in calculating cost of goods sold

E 9. Presented below are incomplete inventory and income statement data for Trevor Corporation. Determine the missing amounts.

LO5 Missing Amounts– Manufacturing

	Cost of Goods Sold	Cost of Goods Manufactured	Beginning Finished Goods Inventory	Ending Finished Goods Inventory
1.	$ 10,000	$12,000	$ 1,000	?
2.	$140,000	?	$45,000	$60,000
3.	?	$89,000	$23,000	$20,000

E 10. The data presented below are for a retail organization and a manufacturing organization.

LO5 Inventories, Cost of Goods Sold, and Net Income

1. Fill in the missing data for the retail organization:

	First Quarter	Second Quarter	Third Quarter	Fourth Quarter
Sales	$9	$ e	$15	$ k
Gross margin	a	4	5	l
Ending merchandise inventory	5	f	5	m
Beginning merchandise inventory	4	g	h	5
Net cost of purchases	b	7	9	n
Operating income	3	2	i	2
Operating expenses	c	2	2	4
Cost of goods sold	5	6	j	11
Cost of goods available for sale	d	12	15	15

2. Fill in the missing data for the manufacturing organization:

	First Quarter	Second Quarter	Third Quarter	Fourth Quarter
Ending finished goods inventory	$a	$3	$h	$6
Cost of goods sold	6	3	5	l
Operating income	1	3	1	m
Cost of goods available for sale	8	d	10	13
Cost of goods manufactured	5	e	i	8
Gross margin	4	f	j	7
Operating expenses	3	g	5	6
Beginning finished goods inventory	b	2	3	n
Sales	c	10	k	14

E 11. The overhead costs that Lucca Industries, Inc., used to compute its overhead rate for 20x6 are as follows:

LO6 Computation of Overhead
LO7 Rate

Indirect materials and supplies	$ 79,200
Repairs and maintenance	14,900
Outside service contracts	17,300
Indirect labor	79,100
Factory supervision	42,900
Depreciation, machinery	85,000
Factory insurance	8,200
Property taxes	6,500
Heat, light, and power	7,700
Miscellaneous manufacturing overhead	5,760
	$346,560

The allocation base for 20x6 was 45,600 total machine hours. In 20x7, all overhead costs except depreciation, property taxes, and miscellaneous manufacturing overhead are expected to increase by 10 percent. Depreciation should increase by 12 percent, and property taxes and miscellaneous manufacturing overhead are expected to increase by 20 percent. Plant capacity in terms of machine hours used will increase by 4,400 hours.

1. Compute the 20x6 overhead rate. (Carry your answer to three decimal places.)
2. Compute the overhead rate for 20x7. (Carry your answer to three decimal places.)

E 12.

LO6   Computation and Application
LO7   of Overhead Rate

Compumatics specializes in the analysis and reporting of complex inventory costing projects. Materials costs are minimal, consisting entirely of operating supplies (DVDs, inventory sheets, and other recording tools). Labor is the highest single expense, totaling $693,000 for 75,000 hours of work in 20x8. Manufacturing overhead costs for 20x8 were $916,000 and were applied to specific jobs on the basis of labor hours worked. In 20x9, the company anticipates a 25 percent increase in manufacturing overhead costs. Labor costs will increase by $130,000, and the number of hours worked is expected to increase by 20 percent.

1. Determine the total amount of manufacturing overhead anticipated in 20x9.
2. Compute the manufacturing overhead rate for 20x9. (Round your answer to the nearest cent.)
3. During April 20x9, 11,980 labor hours were worked. Calculate the manufacturing overhead amount assigned to April production.

E 13.

LO6   Disposition of Overapplied
LO7   Overhead

At the end of 20x9, Compumatics had compiled a total of 89,920 labor hours worked. The actual manufacturing overhead incurred was $1,143,400.

1. Using the overhead rate computed in **E 12**, determine the total amount of manufacturing overhead applied to operations during 20x9.
2. Compute the amount of overapplied overhead for the year.
3. Will the Cost of Goods Sold account be increased or decreased to correct the over-application of manufacturing overhead?

E 14.

LO7   Activities and Activity-Based
LO8   Costing

Zone Enterprises produces wireless components used in telecommunications equipment. One of the most important features of the company's new just-in-time production process is quality control. Initially, a traditional allocation method was used to assign the costs of quality control to products; all these costs were included in the plant's overhead cost pool and allocated to products based on direct labor dollars. Recently, the firm implemented an activity-based costing system. The activities, cost drivers, and rates for the quality control function are summarized below, along with cost allocation information from the traditional method. Also shown is information related to one order, Order HL14. Compute the quality control cost that would be assigned to the order under both the traditional method and the activity-based costing method.

Traditional costing method:
Quality control costs were assigned at a rate of 12 percent of direct labor dollars. Order HL14 was charged with $9,350 of direct labor costs.

Activity-based costing method:

Activity	Activity Cost Driver	Activity Cost Rate	Activity Usage for Order HL14
Incoming materials inspection	Types of materials used	$17.50 per type of material used	17 types of materials
In-process inspection	Number of products	$.06 per product	2,400 products
Tool and gauge control	Number of processes per cell	$26.50 per process per cell	11 processes
Product certification	Per order	$94.00 per order	1 order

E 15.

LO9   Unit Costs in a Service
Business

Walden Green provides custom farming services to owners of five-acre wheat fields. In July, he earned $2,400 by cutting, turning, and baling 3,000 bales. In the same month, he incurred the following costs: gas, $150; tractor maintenance, $115; and labor, $600. His annual tractor depreciation was $1,500. What was Green's cost per bale? What was his revenue per bale? Should he increase the amount he charges for his services?

PROBLEMS

P 1.

LO3   Computation of Unit Cost

Carola Industries, Inc., manufactures discs for several of the leading recording studios in the United States and Europe. Department 60 is responsible for the electronic circuitry within each disc. Department 61 applies the plastic-like surface to the discs and packages them for shipment. Carola recently produced 4,000 discs for the Milo Company. In fulfilling this order, the departments incurred the following costs:

	Department	
	60	61
Direct materials used	$29,440	$3,920
Direct labor	6,800	2,560
Manufacturing overhead	7,360	4,800

REQUIRED ▶

1. Compute the unit cost for each department.
2. Compute the total unit cost for the Milo Company order.
3. The selling price for this order was $14 per unit. Was the selling price adequate? List the assumptions and/or computations upon which you based your answer. What suggestions would you make to Carola Industries' management about the pricing of future orders?
4. Compute the prime costs and conversion costs per unit for each department.

P 2.

LO5   Statement of Cost of Goods Manufactured

Dillo Vineyards, a large winery in Texas, produces a full line of varietal wines. The company, whose fiscal year begins on November 1, has just completed a record-breaking year. Its inventory account balances on October 31, 20x7, were Materials Inventory, $1,803,800; Work in Process Inventory, $2,764,500; and Finished Goods Inventory, $1,883,200. On October 31, 20x6, the inventory account balances were Materials Inventory, $2,156,200; Work in Process Inventory, $3,371,000; and Finished Goods Inventory, $1,596,400.

During the 20x6–20x7 fiscal year, the company's purchases of direct materials totaled $6,750,000. Direct labor hours totaled 142,500, and the average labor rate was $8.20 per hour. The following manufacturing overhead costs were incurred during the year: depreciation, plant and equipment, $685,600; indirect labor, $207,300; property tax, plant and equipment, $94,200; plant maintenance, $83,700; small tools, $42,400; utilities, $96,500; and employee benefits, $76,100.

REQUIRED ▶

Prepare a statement of cost of goods manufactured for the fiscal year ended October 31, 20x7.

P 3.

LO5   A Manufacturing Organization's Balance Sheet

The following information is from the balance sheet of Mills Manufacturing Company:

	Debit	Credit
Cash	$ 34,000	
Accounts receivable	27,000	
Materials inventory, 12/31/x6	31,000	
Work in process inventory, 12/31/x6	47,900	
Finished goods inventory, 12/31/x6	54,800	
Production supplies	5,700	
Small tools	9,330	
Land	160,000	
Factory building	575,000	
Accumulated depreciation, factory building		$ 199,000
Factory equipment	310,000	
Accumulated depreciation, factory equipment		137,000
Patents	33,500	
Accounts payable		26,900
Insurance premiums payable		6,700
Income taxes payable		41,500
Mortgage payable		343,000
Common stock		200,000
Retained earnings, 12/31/x6		334,130
	$1,288,230	$1,288,230

REQUIRED ▶

1. Manufacturing organizations use asset accounts that are not needed by merchandising organizations.
   a. List the titles of the asset accounts that are specifically related to manufacturing organizations.
   b. List the titles of the asset, liability, and equity accounts that you would see on the balance sheets of both manufacturing and merchandising organizations.

2. Assuming that the following information reflects the results of operations for 20x6, calculate the (a) gross margin, (b) cost of goods sold, (c) cost of goods available for sale, and (d) cost of goods manufactured:

Operating income	$138,130
Operating expenses	53,670
Sales	500,000
Finished goods inventory, 12/31/x5	50,900

3. Does Mills Manufacturing use the periodic or perpetual inventory system?

P 4.
LO6 Allocation of Manufacturing
LO7 Overhead

Natural Cosmetics Company applies manufacturing overhead costs on the basis of machine hours. The overhead rate is computed by analyzing data from the previous two years and projecting figures for the current year, adjusted for expected changes. The controller prepared the overhead rate analysis for 20x7 using the following information:

	20x5	20x6
Machine hours	47,800	57,360
Manufacturing overhead costs		
Indirect labor	$ 18,100	$ 23,530
Employee benefits	22,000	28,600
Manufacturing supervision	16,800	18,480
Utilities	10,350	14,490
Factory insurance	6,500	7,800
Janitorial services	11,000	12,100
Depreciation, factory and machinery	17,750	21,300
Miscellaneous manufacturing overhead	5,750	7,475
Total manufacturing overhead	$108,250	$133,775

In 20x7, the cost of utilities is expected to increase by 40 percent over 20x6; the cost of indirect labor, employee benefits, and miscellaneous manufacturing overhead is expected to increase by 30 percent; the cost of insurance and depreciation is expected to increase by 20 percent; and the cost of supervision and janitorial services is expected to increase by 10 percent. Machine hours are expected to total 68,832.

REQUIRED ▶

1. Compute the projected costs and the overhead rate for 20x7 using the information about expected cost increases. (Carry your answer to three decimal places.)
2. Jobs completed during 20x7 and the machine hours used were as follows:

Job No.	Machine Hours
2214	12,300
2215	14,200
2216	9,800
2217	13,600
2218	11,300
2219	8,100

Determine the amount of manufacturing overhead to be applied to each job and to total production during 20x7. (Round answers to whole dollars.)

3. Actual manufacturing overhead costs for 20x7 were $165,845. Was overhead underapplied or overapplied? By how much? Should the Cost of Goods Sold account be increased or decreased to reflect actual overhead costs?

P 5.
LO8 Activities and Activity-Based
Costing

Byte Computer Company, a manufacturing organization, has been in operation for ten years. It has just completed an order that Grater, Ltd., placed for 80 computers. Byte recently shifted from a traditional system of allocating costs to an activity-based costing system. Simone Faure, Byte's controller, wants to know the impact that the ABC system had on the Grater order. Raw materials, purchased parts, and direct labor costs for the Grater order are as follows:

Cost of direct materials	$36,750.00	Direct labor hours	220
Cost of purchased parts	$21,300.00	Average direct labor pay rate	$15.25

Other operating costs are as follows:

Traditional costing data:
Manufacturing overhead costs were applied at a single, plant-wide overhead rate of 270 percent of direct labor dollars.

Activity-based costing data:

Activity	Cost Driver	Activity Cost Rate	Activity Usage for Grater Order
Electrical engineering design	Engineering hours	$19.50 per engineering hour	32 engineering hours
Setup	Number of setups	$29.40 per setup	11 setups
Parts production	Machine hours	$26.30 per machine hour	134 machine hours
Product testing	Product testing hours	$32.80 per product testing hour	52 product testing hours
Packaging	Packaging hours	$17.50 per packaging hour	22 packaging hours
Building occupancy	Machine hours	$9.80 per machine hour	134 machine hours

REQUIRED ▶

1. Using the traditional costing method, compute the total cost of the Grater order.
2. Using the activity-based costing method, compute the total cost of the Grater order.
3. What difference in the amount of cost assigned to the Grater order resulted from the shift to activity-based costing? Was Byte Computer Company's shift to activity-based costing a good management decision?

ALTERNATE PROBLEMS

P 6.

LO6   Allocation of Manufacturing
LO7   Overhead

Lund Products, Inc., uses a predetermined manufacturing overhead rate in its production, assembly, and testing departments. One rate is used for the entire company; it is based on machine hours. The rate is determined by analyzing data from the previous two years and projecting figures for the current year, adjusted for expected changes. Lise Jensen is about to compute the rate for 20x6 using the following data:

	20x4	20x5
Machine hours	38,000	41,800
Manufacturing overhead costs		
Indirect materials	$ 44,500	$ 57,850
Indirect labor	21,200	25,440
Supervision	37,800	41,580
Utilities	9,400	11,280
Labor-related costs	8,200	9,020
Depreciation, factory	9,800	10,780
Depreciation, machinery	22,700	27,240
Property taxes	2,400	2,880
Insurance	1,600	1,920
Miscellaneous manufacturing overhead	4,400	4,840
Total manufacturing overhead	$162,000	$192,830

In 20x6, the cost of indirect materials is expected to increase by 30 percent over the previous year. The cost of indirect labor, utilities, machinery depreciation, property taxes, and insurance is expected to increase by 20 percent. All other expenses are expected to increase by 10 percent. Machine hours for 20x6 are estimated at 45,980.

REQUIRED ▶

1. Compute the projected costs and the manufacturing overhead rate for 20x6 using the information about expected cost increases. (Round your answer to three decimal places.)
2. During 20x6, Lund Products completed the following jobs using the machine hours shown:

Job No.	Machine Hours	Job No.	Machine Hours
H–142	7,840	H–201	10,680
H–164	5,260	H–218	12,310
H–175	8,100	H–304	2,460

Determine the amount of manufacturing overhead applied to each job. What was the total manufacturing overhead applied during 20x6? (Round answers to the nearest dollar.)
3. Actual manufacturing overhead costs for 20x6 were $234,485. Was overhead underapplied or overapplied in 20x6? By how much? Should the Cost of Goods Sold account be increased or decreased to reflect actual overhead costs?

4. At what point during 20x6 was the manufacturing overhead rate computed? When was it applied? Finally, when was underapplied or overapplied overhead determined and the Cost of Goods Sold account adjusted to reflect actual costs?

P 7.
LO8   Activities and Activity-Based Costing

Fraser Products, Inc., which produces fax machines for wholesale distributors in the Pacific Northwest, has just completed packaging an order from Kent Company for 150 Model 14 fax machines. Fraser recently switched from a traditional system of allocating costs to an activity-based costing system. Before the Kent order is shipped, the controller wants a unit cost analysis comparing the amounts computed under the traditional costing system with those computed under the ABC system. Raw materials, purchased parts, and direct labor costs for the Kent order are as follows:

Cost of direct materials	$17,450.00	Direct labor hours	140
Cost of purchased parts	$14,800.00	Average direct labor pay rate	$16.50

Other operating costs are as follows:

Traditional costing data:
Manufacturing overhead costs were applied at a single, plant-wide overhead rate of 240 percent of direct labor dollars.

Activity-based costing data:

Activity	Cost Driver	Activity Cost Rate	Activity Usage for Kent Order
Engineering systems design	Engineering hours	$28.00 per engineering hour	18 engineering hours
Setup	Number of setups	$42.00 per setup	8 setups
Parts production	Machine hours	$37.50 per machine hour	84 machine hours
Assembly	Assembly hours	$44.00 per assembly hour	36 assembly hours
Packaging	Packaging hours	$28.50 per packaging hour	28 packaging hours
Building occupancy	Machine hours	$10.40 per machine hour	84 machine hours

REQUIRED ▶
1. Using the traditional costing approach, compute the total cost of the Kent order.
2. Using the activity-based costing approach, compute the total cost of the Kent order.
3. What difference in the amount of cost assigned to the Kent order resulted from the shift to activity-based costing? Does the use of activity-based costing guarantee cost reduction for every product?

P 8.
LO6   Allocation of Manufacturing
LO7   Overhead: Traditional and
LO8   Activity-Based Costing
**   Methods**

Sea Scout, Inc., manufactures two types of underwater vehicles. Oil companies use the vehicle called Rigger II to examine offshore oil rigs, and marine biology research foundations use the BioScout to study coastlines. The company's San Diego factory is not fully automated and requires some direct labor. Using estimated manufacturing overhead costs of $220,000 and an estimated 16,000 hours of direct labor, Oz Parson, the company's controller, calculated a traditional overhead rate of $13.75 per direct labor hour. He used normal costing to calculate the product unit cost for both product lines, as shown in the following summary:

	Rigger II	BioScout
Product costs per unit		
Direct materials	$ 10,000.00	$12,000.00
Direct labor	1,450.00	1,600.00
Applied manufacturing overhead	412.50*	550.00†
Product unit cost	$11,862.50	$14,150.00
Units of production	400	100
Direct labor hours	12,000	4,000

*$13.75 per Direct Labor Hour × 30 Direct Labor Hours per Unit = $412.50
†$13.75 per Direct Labor Hour × 40 Direct Labor Hours per Unit = $550

Parson believes the product unit cost for the BioScout is too low. After carefully observing the production process, he has concluded that the BioScout requires much more attention than the Rigger II. Because of BioScout's more intricate design, it requires more production activities, and fewer subassemblies by suppliers are possible. He has therefore created four overhead activity pools, estimated the manufacturing overhead costs of the activity pools, selected a cost driver for each pool, and estimated the cost driver levels for each product line, as shown in the following summary:

Activity Pool	Estimated Manufacturing Overhead Cost
Setup	$ 70,000
Inspection	20,000
Engineering	50,000
Assembly	80,000
Total	$220,000

Cost Driver	Rigger II Cost Driver Level	BioScout Cost Driver Level	Total Cost Driver Level
Number of setups	250	450	700
Number of inspections	150	350	500
Engineering hours	600	1,400	2,000
Machine hours	5,000	5,000	10,000

REQUIRED ▶

1. Use activity-based costing to do the following:

   a. Calculate the activity cost rate for each activity pool.
   b. Compute the overhead costs applied to each product line by activity pool and in total.
   c. Calculate the product unit cost for each product line.

2. What differences in the costs assigned to the two product lines resulted from the shift to activity-based costing?

SKILLS DEVELOPMENT CASES

Conceptual Analysis

SD 1.

LO1 **Comparison of Costs in**
LO2 **Different Types of Businesses**

H & R Block <www.hrblock.com> is a service company that prepares tax returns; Borders <www.bordersstores.com> is a retail company that sells books and CDs; Indian Motorcycle Corporation <www.indianmotorcycle.com> is a manufacturing company that makes motorcycles. Show that you understand how these companies differ by giving for each one an example of a direct and indirect cost, a variable and fixed cost, a value-adding and nonvalue-adding cost, and a product and period cost. Discuss the use of cost classifications in these three types of organizations.

SD 2.

LO6 **Comparison of Approaches to**
LO7 **Developing Overhead Rates**
LO8

Both Matos Company and Stubee Corporation use predetermined overhead rates for product costing, inventory valuation, and sales quotations. The two businesses are about the same size, and they compete in the corrugated box industry. Because the overhead rate is an estimated measure, Matos Company's management believes that the controller's department should spend little effort in developing it. The company computes the rate annually based on an analysis of the previous year's costs. No one monitors its accuracy during the year. Stubee Corporation takes a different approach. One person in the controller's office is responsible for developing overhead rates on a monthly basis. All cost estimates are checked carefully to make sure they are realistic. Accuracy checks are done routinely at the end of each month, and forecasts of changes in business activity are taken into account.

Assume that Cooke Corporation, an East Coast manufacturer of corrugated boxes, has hired you as a consultant. Asimina Hiona, Cooke's controller, wants you to recommend the best method of developing overhead rates. Based on your knowledge of Matos's and Stubee's practices, write a memo to Hiona that answers the following questions:

1. What are the advantages and disadvantages of Matos's and Stubee's approaches to developing overhead rates?
2. Which company has taken the more cost-effective approach to developing overhead rates? Defend your answer.
3. Is an accurate overhead rate most important for product costing, inventory valuation, or sales quotations? Why?
4. What is activity-based costing (ABC)? Would it be better than the two approaches discussed above? Explain.

Ethical Dilemma

SD 3.

LO9   Preventing Pollution and the Costs of Waste Disposal

Lake Weir Power Plant provides power to a metropolitan area of 4 million people. Sundeep Guliani, the plant's controller, has just returned from a conference on the Environmental Protection Agency's regulations concerning pollution prevention. She is meeting with Alton Guy, the president of the company, to discuss the impact of the EPA's regulations on the plant.

"Alton, I'm really concerned. We haven't been monitoring the disposal of the radioactive material we send to the Willis Disposal Plant. If Willis is disposing of our waste material improperly, we could be sued," said Guliani. "We also haven't been recording the costs of the waste as part of our product cost. Ignoring those costs will have a negative impact on our decision about the next rate hike."

"Sundeep, don't worry. I don't think we need to concern ourselves with the waste we send to Willis. We pay them to dispose of it. They take it off of our hands, and it's their responsibility to manage its disposal. As for the cost of waste disposal, I think we would have a hard time justifying a rate increase based on a requirement to record the full cost of waste as a cost of producing power. Let's just forget about waste and its disposal as a component of our power cost. We can get our rate increase without mentioning waste disposal," replied Guy.

What responsibility does Lake Weir Power Plant have to monitor the condition of the waste at the Willis Disposal Plant? Should Guliani take Guy's advice to ignore waste disposal costs in calculating the cost of power? Be prepared to discuss your response.

Research Activity

SD 4.

LO2   Cost Classifications

Visit a local fast-food restaurant. Observe all aspects of the operation and take notes on the entire process. Describe the procedures used to take, process, and fill an order and deliver the food to the customer. Based on your observations, make a list of the costs incurred by the owner. Then create a table similar to Table 1 in the text, in which you classify the costs you have identified by their traceability (direct or indirect), cost behavior (variable or fixed), value attribute (value-adding or nonvalue-adding), and implications for financial reporting (product or period costs). Bring your notes and your table to class and be prepared to discuss your findings.

 Group Activity: Divide the class into groups and ask them to discuss their findings. Then ask a person from each group to summarize his or her group's discussion.

Decision-Making Practice

SD 5.

LO9   Unit Costs in a Service Business

Municipal Hospital relies heavily on cost data to keep its pricing structures in line with those of competitors. The hospital provides a wide range of services, including intensive care, intermediate care, and a neonatal nursery. Joo Young, the hospital's controller, is concerned about the profits generated by the 30-bed intensive care unit (ICU), so she is reviewing current billing procedures for that unit. The focus of her analysis is the hospital's billing per ICU patient day. This billing equals the per diem cost of intensive care plus a 40 percent markup to cover other operating costs and generate a profit. ICU patient costs include the following:

Doctors' care	2 hours per day @ $360 per hour (actual)
Special nursing care	4 hours per day @ $85 per hour (actual)
Regular nursing care	24 hours per day @ $28 per hour (average)
Medications	$237 per day (average)
Medical supplies	$134 per day (average)
Room rental	$350 per day (average)
Food and services	$140 per day (average)

One other significant ICU cost is equipment, which is about $185,000 per room. Young has determined that the cost per patient day for the equipment is $179.

Wiley Dix, the hospital director, has asked Young to compare the current billing procedure with another that uses industry averages to determine the billing per patient day.

1. Compute the cost per patient per day.
2. Compute the billing per patient day using the hospital's existing markup rate. (Round answers to whole dollars.)

3. Industry averages for markup rates are as follows:

Equipment	30%	Medications	50%
Doctors' care	50	Medical supplies	50
Special nursing care	40	Room rental	30
Regular nursing care	50	Food and services	25

Using these rates, compute the billing per patient day. (Round answers to the nearest whole dollars.)

4. Based on your findings in **2** and **3**, which billing procedure would you recommend to the hospital's director? Why? Be prepared to discuss your response.

MANAGERIAL REPORTING AND ANALYSIS CASES

Interpreting Management Reports

MRA 1.

LO5   Financial Performance Measures

Tarbox Manufacturing Company makes sheet metal products for heating and air conditioning installations. For the past several years, the company's income has been declining. Its statements of cost of goods manufactured and income statements for 20x7 and 20x6 follow.

Tarbox Manufacturing Company
Statements of Cost of Goods Manufactured
For the Years Ended December 31, 20x7 and 20x6

	20x7		20x6	
Direct materials used				
Materials inventory, beginning	$ 91,240		$ 93,560	
Direct materials purchased (net)	987,640		959,940	
Cost of direct materials available for use	$1,078,880		$1,053,500	
Less materials inventory, ending	95,020		91,240	
Cost of direct materials used		$ 983,860		$ 962,260
Direct labor		571,410		579,720
Manufacturing overhead				
Indirect labor	$ 182,660		$ 171,980	
Power	34,990		32,550	
Insurance	22,430		18,530	
Supervision	125,330		120,050	
Depreciation	75,730		72,720	
Other manufacturing costs	41,740		36,280	
Total manufacturing overhead		482,880		452,110
Total manufacturing costs		$2,038,150		$1,994,090
Add work in process inventory, beginning		148,875		152,275
Total cost of work in process during the period		$2,187,025		$2,146,365
Less work in process inventory, ending		146,750		148,875
Cost of goods manufactured		$2,040,275		$1,997,490

Tarbox Manufacturing Company
Income Statements
For the Years Ended December 31, 20x7 and 20x6

	20x7		20x6	
Sales		$2,942,960		$3,096,220
Cost of goods sold				
Finished goods inventory,				
beginning	$ 142,640		$ 184,820	
Cost of goods manufactured	2,040,275		1,997,490	
Total cost of finished goods				
available for sale	$2,182,915		$2,182,310	
Less finished goods				
inventory, ending	186,630		142,640	
Cost of goods sold		1,996,285		2,039,670
Gross margin		$ 946,675		$1,056,550
Selling and administrative expenses				
Sales salaries and				
commission expense	$ 394,840		$ 329,480	
Advertising expense	116,110		194,290	
Other selling expenses	82,680		72,930	
Administrative expenses	242,600		195,530	
Total selling and administrative expenses		836,230		792,230
Income from operations		$ 110,445		$ 264,320
Other revenues and expenses				
Interest expense		54,160		56,815
Income before income taxes		$ 56,285		$ 207,505
Income taxes expense		19,137		87,586
Net income		$ 37,148		$ 119,919

You have been asked to comment on why Tarbox's profitability has deteriorated.

1. In preparing your comments, compute the following ratios for each year:

   a. Ratios of cost of direct materials used to total manufacturing costs, direct labor to total manufacturing costs, and total manufacturing overhead to total manufacturing costs. (Round to one decimal place.)

   b. Ratios of sales salaries and commission expense, advertising expense, other selling expenses, administrative expenses, and total selling and administrative expenses to sales. (Round to one decimal place.)

   c. Ratios of gross margin to sales and net income to sales. (Round to one decimal place.)

2. From your evaluation of the ratios computed in 1, state the probable causes of the decline in net income.

3. What other factors or ratios do you believe should be considered in determining the cause of the company's decreased income?

Formulating Management Reports

MRA 2.

LO2   Management Decision About a
LO9   Supporting Service Function

As the manager of grounds maintenance for Latchey, a large insurance company in Missouri, you are responsible for maintaining the grounds surrounding the company's three buildings, the six entrances to the property, and the recreational facilities, which

Chapter 21 describes the two basic types of product costing systems—job order costing and process costing.

Costing Systems: Job Order and Process Costing

DECISION POINT

A MANAGER'S FOCUS

John H. Daniel Company <<u>www.johnhdaniel.com</u>>
Whatever a man's size, John H. Daniel Company has a suit to fit him. In addition to having a division that produces large quantities of ready-to-wear men's suits for retailers, the company has a division that manufactures made-to-order suits for individual customers. The made-to-order process begins when one of over 300 custom tailors from around the United States visits a customer at his home or office to show him the latest fabrics and suit styles. When the customer has made his selections, the tailor takes the measurements to guarantee a proper fit. The tailor then transmits the customer's measurements and choices of fabric, suit model, leg finish, and pocket type to John H. Daniel Company's manufacturing plant in Knoxville, Tennessee. At the factory, workers use state-of-the-art technology to cut the fabric to the order's specifications. A skilled, specialized team sews the pieces together and presses the finished suit. The suit is then shipped to the custom tailor, who delivers it for final fitting and approval at a time convenient for the customer. The whole process generally takes less than five weeks.

Is the product costing system that is used when making a large quantity of ready-to-wear suits appropriate when making suits to an individual customer's specifications? Why might John H. Daniel Company implement a different product costing system for each of its divisions? What performance measures would be most useful in evaluating the results of each division?

What product costing system is appropriate for John H. Daniel Company?

The appropriateness of a product costing system depends on the nature of the production process. Because the manufacture of custom orders and the manufacture of large quantities of similar products involve different processes, they generally require different costing systems. When a product is custom-made, it is possible to collect the costs of each order. When a product is mass-produced, the costs of a specific unit cannot be collected because there is a continuous flow of similar products; in this case, costs are collected by process, department, or work cell. Thus, each of John H. Daniel Company's two divisions will probably need its own costing system to determine the cost of a suit.

Performance measures will also differ for John H. Daniel Company's two divisions. For the custom suit division, management can measure the profitability of each order by comparing the order's cost and price. For the retail suit division, management will measure performance by comparing the budgeted and actual costs for a process, department, or work cell.

PRODUCT COST INFORMATION AND THE MANAGEMENT CYCLE

LO1 Discuss the role information about costs plays in the management cycle and explain why unit cost is important.

RELATED TEXT ASSIGNMENTS
Q: 1, 2, 3
SE: 1
SD: 1
MRA: 1, 4

www.toyota.com
www.harley-davidson.com
www.levistrauss.com
www.century21.com
www.hrblock.com
www.orkin.com

Managers depend on relevant and reliable information about costs to manage their organizations. The role of the management accountant is to develop a management information system that provides managers with the cost information they need. Although companies vary in their approaches to gathering, analyzing, and reporting information about costs, managers share the same basic concerns as they move through the management cycle. Figure 1 summarizes the management cycle and the concerns that managers address with relevant and timely information about costs.

PLANNING

During the planning stage, managers use information about costs to set performance expectations and estimate unit costs. In manufacturing companies, such as Toyota, Harley-Davidson, and Levi Strauss & Co., managers use cost information to develop budgets, establish product prices, and plan production volumes. In service organizations, such as Century 21, H&R Block, and Orkin Exterminating Company, managers use cost information to develop budgets, establish prices, set sales goals, and determine human resource needs. During the planning stage, knowledge of unit costs helps managers of both manufacturing and service companies set reasonable selling prices and estimate the cost of their products or services.

FIGURE 1
Uses of Information about Costs in the Management Cycle

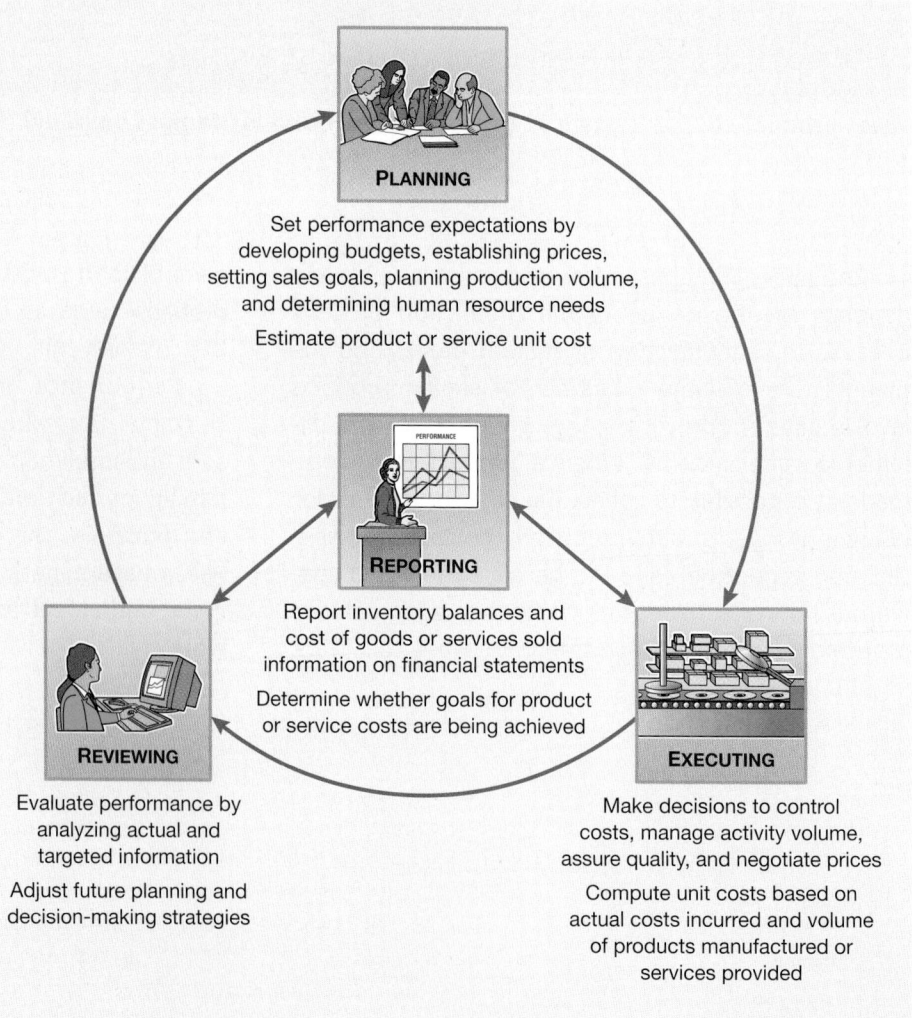

EXECUTING

During the executing stage, managers make decisions about controlling costs, managing the company's activity volume, ensuring quality, and negotiating prices. They use timely cost and volume information and actual unit costs to support their decision making. In manufacturing companies, managers use information about costs to decide whether to drop a product line, add a production shift, outsource the manufacture of a subassembly to another company, bid on a special order, or negotiate a selling price. In service organizations, managers use cost information to make decisions about bidding on jobs, dropping a current service, outsourcing a task to an independent contractor, adding staff, or negotiating a price. All of these decisions can have far-reaching effects, including possible changes in unit cost or quality.

REVIEWING

During the reviewing stage, managers watch for changes in cost and quality. They compare actual and targeted total and unit costs and monitor relevant price and volume information. They analyze the information to evaluate their performance, and on the basis of this evaluation, they adjust their planning and decision-making strategies. For example, if a product's quality is suffering, managers may study the design, materials purchasing, and manufacturing processes to determine the source of the problem so that they can make changes that will ensure the product's quality. If operating costs in a service business have risen too high, managers may break a unit cost of service down into its many components to analyze where costs can be cut or how the service can be performed more efficiently.

REPORTING

Finally, during the reporting stage, managers prepare financial statements. In manufacturing companies, managers use product unit costs to determine inventory balances for the organization's balance sheet and the cost of goods sold for its income statement. In service organizations, managers use unit costs of services to determine cost of sales for the income statement. During this stage, managers also prepare performance evaluation reports for internal use. These reports compare actual unit costs and targeted costs, as well as actual and targeted nonfinancial measures of performance. Managers in both manufacturing and service organizations analyze the data in the performance evaluation reports to determine whether cost goals for products or services are being achieved.

 Check out ACE for a Review Quiz at http://accounting.college.hmco.com/students.

JOB ORDER VERSUS PROCESS COSTING

LO2 Distinguish between the two basic types of product costing systems and identify the information each provides.

RELATED TEXT ASSIGNMENTS
Q: 4, 5, 6, 7
SE: 2, 3
E: 1, 2

For an organization to succeed, its managers must sell its products or services at prices that exceed the costs of creating and delivering them, thus ensuring a profit. To do so, managers need extensive information about such product-related costs as setup, production, and distribution. To meet managers' needs for cost information, it is necessary to have a highly reliable product costing system specifically designed to record and report the organization's operations. A **product costing system** is a set of procedures used to account for an organization's product costs and to provide timely and accurate unit cost information for pricing, cost planning and control, inventory valuation, and financial statement preparation.

The product costing system enables managers to track costs throughout the management cycle. It provides a structure for recording the revenue earned from sales and the costs incurred for direct materials, direct labor, and manufacturing overhead.

TABLE 1.   Characteristics of Job Order Costing and Process Costing Systems

Job Order Costing System	Process Costing System
Traces manufacturing costs to a specific job order	Traces manufacturing costs to processes, departments, or work cells and then assigns the costs to products manufactured
Measures the cost of each completed unit	Measures costs in terms of units completed during a specific period
Uses a single Work in Process Inventory account to summarize the cost of all job orders	Uses several Work in Process Inventory accounts: one for each process, department, or work cell
Typically used by companies that make large, unique, or special-order products, such as customized publications, built-in cabinets, or made-to-order draperies	Typically used by companies that make large amounts of similar products or liquid products or that have long, continuous production runs of identical products, such as makers of paint, soft drinks, candy, bricks, and paper

KEY POINT: In job order costing, costs are assigned to jobs; in process costing, costs are assigned to production processes.

KEY POINT: The product cost arrived at by both job order and process costing systems is an average cost. Process costing usually averages cost over a greater volume of product.

www.toyota.com
www.gm.com

Two basic types of product costing systems have been developed: job order costing and process costing systems. A **job order costing system** is used by companies that make large, unique, or special-order products, such as customized publications, specially built cabinets, made-to-order draperies, or custom-tailored suits. Such a system uses a single Work in Process Inventory account to record the costs of all job orders. It traces the costs of direct materials, direct labor, and manufacturing overhead to a specific batch of products or a specific **job order** (i.e., a customer order for a specific number of specially designed, made-to-order products) by using a subsidiary ledger of job order cost cards. **A job order cost card** is the document on which all costs incurred in the production of a particular job order are recorded. The costs that a job order costing system gathers are used to measure the cost of each completed unit.

Companies that produce large amounts of similar products or liquid products or that have long, continuous production runs of identical products use a **process costing system.** Makers of paint, soft drinks, candy, bricks, and paper would use such a system, as would John H. Daniel Company's retail suit division. A process costing system first traces the costs of direct materials, direct labor, and manufacturing overhead to processes, departments, or work cells and then assigns the costs to the products manufactured by those processes, departments, or work cells during a specific period. A process costing system uses several Work in Process Inventory accounts—-one for each process, department, or work cell. Table 1 summarizes the characteristics of job order costing and process costing systems.

In reality, few production processes are a perfect match for either a job order costing system or a process costing system. The typical product costing system therefore combines parts of job order costing and process costing to create a hybrid system designed specifically for an organization's production process. For example, an automobile maker like Toyota or General Motors may use process costing to track the costs of manufacturing a standard car and job order costing to track the costs of customized features, such as a convertible top or a stick shift. Managers who know the terms and procedures related to both job order and process costing can

FOCUS ON INTERNATIONAL BUSINESS

Why Does Toyota Use a Hybrid Product Costing System?

Thanks to its virtual production line, Toyota <www.toyota.com> can now manufacture custom vehicles in five days. Computer software allows Toyota to calculate the exact number of parts needed at each precise point on its production line for a certain mix of cars. The mix can be modified up to five days in advance of actual production, allowing Toyota to modify a production run to include custom orders. When Toyota announced its hybrid approach, General Motors <www.gm.com> was taking 17 to 18 days to assemble a custom vehicle, and DaimlerChrysler <www.daimlerchrysler.com> needed an average of 10 to 12 days. Because most vehicles are mass-produced either in batches or on continuous flow assembly lines, manufacturers' process costing systems have not handled custom orders well. With its virtual production line and a hybrid product costing system, Toyota has gained a competitive advantage.[1]

● **STOP AND THINK!**

What kind of product costing system do most companies use?

Most companies use hybrid systems that combine features of both job order costing and process costing to meet the specific needs of the business. ■

help design product costing systems that fit their information needs in any operating environment.

In recent years, global competition, technology, and the shifting mix of materials, labor, and overhead in the manufacturing process have changed the way companies approach product costing. The use of multidisciplinary teams of managers has fostered the development of new management accounting practices to improve product costing. These new practices emphasize the elimination of waste, the importance of quality, value-added processing, and increased customer satisfaction. We discuss some of the new practices, including the value chain, process value analysis, activity-based management, and the just-in-time operating environment elsewhere in the text.

 Check out ACE for a Review Quiz at http://accounting.college.hmco.com/students.

THE JOB ORDER COSTING SYSTEM

LO3 Explain cost flow in a job order costing system, prepare a job order cost card, and compute product unit cost.

RELATED TEXT ASSIGNMENTS
Q: 8, 9, 10, 11, 12
SE: 4, 5, 6, 7
E: 3, 4, 5, 6, 7, 8
P: 1, 2, 3, 6, 7
SD: 3, 4
MRA: 5

A job order costing system traces the costs of a specific order or batch of products to provide timely, accurate cost information and to facilitate the smooth and continuous flow of that information. Because such a system emphasizes cost flow, it is important to understand how costs are incurred, recorded, and transferred within the system. A basic part of a job order costing system is the set of procedures, documents, and accounts that a company uses when it incurs costs for materials, labor, and manufacturing overhead. Job order cost cards and subsidiary ledgers for materials and finished goods inventories form the core of a job order costing system.

COST FLOW IN A JOB ORDER COSTING SYSTEM FOR A MANUFACTURING COMPANY

KEY POINT: In a job order costing system, the specific job or batch of product, not a department or work center, is the focus of cost accumulation.

To study the cost flows in a job order costing system, let's look at how Jon Lyman, the owner of Augusta, Inc., operates his business. For the past few years, Lyman has been building both customized and general-purpose golf carts. The direct materials costs for a golf cart include the costs of a cart frame, wheels, upholstered seats, a windshield, a motor, and a rechargeable battery. Direct labor costs include the wages of the two production workers who assemble the golf carts. Manufacturing overhead includes indirect materials costs for upholstery zippers, cloth straps to hold equipment in place, wheel lubricants, screws and fasteners, and silicon to attach the windshield. It also includes indirect labor costs for moving materials to the production area and inspecting a golf cart during its construction; depreciation on the manufacturing plant and equipment used to make the golf carts; and utilities, insurance, and property taxes related to the manufacturing plant. Exhibit 1 shows the flow of each of these costs. Notice that all three inventory accounts have subsidiary ledgers backing up their totals. The beginning balance in the Materials Inventory account

During the month, Augusta made two purchases. In transaction **1**, the company purchased cart frames costing $572 and wheels costing $340 from one of its vendors. As shown in Exhibit 1, these purchases increase the balances in the Materials Inventory account and the corresponding accounts in the materials ledger. In transaction **2**, the company purchased indirect materials costing $82 from another vendor. This purchase also increases the balance in the Materials Inventory account, as well as the balance in the Indirect Materials account in the materials ledger.

When golf carts are scheduled for production, direct materials are sent to the production area. Transaction **3** shows the request for materials for the production of two jobs. Of the $1,880 of direct materials requested, the materials ledger shows that $1,240 was for cart frames and $640 was for wheels. Job CC, a batch run of two general-purpose golf carts already in production, required $1,038 of the additional direct materials. Job JB, a customized golf cart made to the specifications of an individual customer, required $842 of the direct materials. Notice that the $1,880 of direct materials requested appears as a debit in the Work in Process Inventory account because that account records the costs of partially completed units of product. The cost of direct materials requested is also recorded on the corresponding job order cost cards. In addition, transaction **3** accounts for the $96 of indirect materials requested for production. As you will see in our discussion of overhead, because the $96 was for indirect materials rather than direct materials, it flows to the Manufacturing Overhead account instead of to a specific job.

STUDY NOTE: Parts of transaction 4 are not posted in Exhibit 1. Although transaction 4 is necessary for an accurate payroll, it does not deal directly with product costs. Exhibit 1 focuses only on the flow of product costs through the accounts.

■ **LABOR** As noted earlier, Augusta's two production employees assemble the golf carts. Several other employees support production by moving materials and inspecting the products. Transaction **4** shows the total wages earned by these employees during the period as a $2,400 debit to the Factory Payroll account. (The corresponding credit, not shown here, is to Augusta's Wages Payable account.) Factory Payroll is a clearing account—it holds costs for only a short time, until they are distributed to the various production accounts. This distribution is shown in transaction **5**. Job CC required direct labor of $1,320, and Job JB required $320. The total direct labor cost of $1,640 ($1,320 + $320) is shown as a debit to the Work in Process Inventory account. The indirect labor cost of $760, shown in transaction **5**, flows to the Manufacturing Overhead account instead of to a particular job.

■ **MANUFACTURING OVERHEAD** Thus far, indirect materials and indirect labor have been the only costs debited to the Manufacturing Overhead account. Other indirect production costs, such as utilities, property taxes, insurance, and depreciation, are also charged to the Manufacturing Overhead account as they are incurred during the period. Transaction **6** shows that other indirect costs amounting to $295 were paid. Transaction **7** records the $240 adjustment for factory-related depreciation.

During the period, to recognize all product-related costs for a job, an overhead cost estimate is applied using a predetermined rate. Based on its budget and past experience, Augusta currently uses a predetermined overhead rate of 85 percent of direct labor costs. In transaction **8**, total manufacturing overhead of $1,394 is applied, with $1,122 going to Job CC (85 percent of $1,320) and $272 to Job JB (85 percent of $320). Notice that the Work in Process Inventory account is debited for $1,394.

FOCUS ON BUSINESS PRACTICE

How Long Does Production Take?
As the following list shows, throughput time—the time it takes to manufacture products—varies according to the product:[2]

Yogurt	Up to eight hours
Beer	Two weeks or longer
Processed foods	Less than two hours
Paint	Less than an hour
Refined oil	Less than two hours
Cement	Less than three hours

■ **COMPLETED UNITS** When a custom job or a batch of general-purpose golf carts is completed, the products are moved from the manufacturing area to the finished goods storeroom. As shown in transaction **9**, when Job CC is completed and moved to the finished goods storeroom, its cost of $3,880 is transferred from the Work in Process Inventory account to the Finished

Figure 2
Job Order Cost Card—
Manufacturing Company

JOB ORDER COST CARD
Augusta, Inc.
Spring Hill, Florida

Job Order: _CC_

Customer: _Stock_   Batch: _X_   Custom: _____
Specifications: _Two general-purpose golf carts_
Date of Order: _2/26/x7_
Date of Completion: _3/6/x7_

Costs Charged to Job	Previous Months	Current Month	Cost Summary
Direct materials	$165	$1,038	$1,203
Direct labor	127	1,320	1,447
Manufacturing overhead (85% of direct labor cost)	108	1,122	1,230
Totals	$400	$3,480	$3,880
Units completed			2
Product unit cost			$1,940

Goods Inventory account. Its job order cost card is also completed and transferred to the finished goods file. Figure 2 shows the job order cost card for Job CC. Notice that the product unit cost for each of the two golf carts in the job is computed.

ENRICHMENT NOTE: This example shows the company using a perpetual inventory system. In a periodic inventory system, the cost of goods sold is calculated at the end of the period.

■ **SOLD UNITS**   When a company uses a perpetual inventory system, as Augusta does, two accounting entries are made when products are sold. One is prompted by the sales invoice and records the quantity and selling price of the products sold. This entry, which is not shown in Exhibit 1, is a debit to the Accounts Receivable or Cash account and a credit to the Sales account. The other entry, prompted by the delivery of products to a customer, records the quantity and cost of the products shipped. In transaction 10, the $1,940 cost of the one general-purpose golf cart that was sold during the period is transferred from the Finished Goods Inventory account to the Cost of Goods Sold account. The $1,940 cost of the unsold cart remains in the Finished Goods Inventory account.

● **STOP AND THINK!**
Why do financial statements require the reconciliation of manufacturing overhead costs?
Financial statements report actual cost information; therefore, estimated manufacturing overhead costs applied during the accounting period must be adjusted to reflect actual manufacturing overhead costs. ■

■ **RECONCILIATION OF MANUFACTURING OVERHEAD COSTS**   To prepare financial statements at the end of the accounting period, the actual manufacturing overhead cost for the period ($1,391) and the estimated manufacturing overhead that was applied during the period ($1,394) must be reconciled. In transaction 11, the Manufacturing Overhead account is closed by transferring its balance of $3 to the Cost of Goods Sold account. Because the applied overhead exceeded the actual overhead by $3, Cost of Goods Sold must be reduced by the amount of the overcharge. It will then reflect the actual overhead costs incurred. Given that the amount is minor, the company prefers to subtract it from the cost of the cart that was sold rather than tracing it back to the individual units worked on during the period. Thus, $3 is deducted from the Cost of Goods Sold account, making the ending balance of that account $1,937.

FOCUS ON BUSINESS ETHICS

Does a Product's Unit Cost Tell the Whole Story?

In response to a tip from the fraud hotline maintained by the Department of Defense <www.defenselink.mil>, the Office of the Inspector General <www.oig.hhs.gov>, the watchdog agency for the Pentagon, conducted an audit of The Boeing Company <www.boeing.com>. The audit found several instances in which Boeing had evidently overcharged the government for parts. For example, it had charged $1.24 for each of 31,108 springs previously priced at $.05 and $403 each for 246 actuator sleeves priced earlier at $24.72.

Boeing spokesperson Dick Dalton said, "This is a story that looks a whole lot worse than it is." According to Boeing, the audit cited prices from 15 to 20 years ago, when the Pentagon bought and stored large quantities of products. Today, the Pentagon receives small deliveries of parts on short notice, as needed. The new system saves the Pentagon huge inventory storage costs, but the price per part is higher because of the higher cost of frequent deliveries and on-demand ordering. The inspector general, Eleanor Hill, told the Senate Armed Services Subcommittee, "We found considerable evidence that the Department of Defense had not yet learned how to be an astute buyer in the commercial marketplace."[3]

THE JOB ORDER COST CARD AND COMPUTATION OF PRODUCT UNIT COST

As is evident from the preceding discussion, job order cost cards play a key role in a job order costing system. Because all manufacturing costs are accumulated in one Work in Process Inventory account, a separate accounting procedure is needed to trace those costs to specific jobs. The solution is the subsidiary ledger made up of job order cost cards. Each job being worked on has a job order cost card. As costs are incurred, they are classified by job and recorded on the appropriate card.

As you can see in Figure 2, a manufacturer's job order cost card has space for direct materials, direct labor, and manufacturing overhead costs. It also includes the job order number, product specifications, the name of the customer, the date of the order, the projected completion date, and a cost summary. As a job incurs direct materials and direct labor costs, its job order cost card is updated. Manufacturing overhead is also posted to the job order cost card at the predetermined rate. Job order cost cards for incomplete jobs make up the subsidiary ledger for the Work in Process Inventory account. To ensure correctness, the ending balance in the Work in Process Inventory account is compared with the total of the costs shown on the job order cost cards.

KEY POINT: Product unit cost in a job order costing system is the total cost of the job or batch divided by the number of items in the job or batch. This is an average cost for the good units manufactured for that job or batch.

A job order costing system simplifies the calculation of product unit costs. When a job is finished, the costs of direct materials, direct labor, and manufacturing overhead that have been recorded on its job order cost card are totaled. The product unit cost is computed by dividing the total costs for the job by the number of good (i.e., salable) units produced. The product unit cost is entered on the job order cost card and will be used to value items in inventory. The job order cost card in Figure 2 shows the costs for completed Job CC. Two golf carts were produced at a total cost of $3,880, so the product unit cost was $1,940.

JOB ORDER COSTING IN A SERVICE ORGANIZATION

Many service organizations use a job order costing system to compute the cost of rendering services. As pointed out elsewhere in the text, the costs of service organizations are different from those of a manufacturing organization in that they are not associated with a physical product that can be assembled, stored, and valued as inventory. Because these organizations sell services rather than making products for sale, the costs that they incur for materials are usually negligible. Their most important cost is labor, which is carefully accounted for through the use of time cards.

KEY POINT: Job order cost cards for service businesses may record costs by activities done for the job. Notice the activity cost includes supplies, labor, and overhead.

The cost flow of services is similar to the cost flow of manufactured products. Job order cost cards are used to keep track of the costs incurred for each job. Job costs include labor, materials and supplies, and service overhead. To cover these costs and earn a profit, many service organizations base jobs on **cost-plus contracts**.

FIGURE 3
Job Order Cost Card—Service Organization

JOB ORDER COST CARD
Gartner Landscaping Services

Customer: Rico Corporation
Job Order Number: _____
Contract Type: Cost-Plus
Type of Service: Landscape Corporate Headquarters
Date Completed: May 31, 20xx

Costs Charged to Job	Previous Months	Current Month	Total Cost
Landscape design			
Supplies	$ 100	$ –	$ 100
Design labor	850	–	850
Service overhead (40% of design labor)	340	–	340
Totals	$1,290	$ –	$1,290
Landscape installation			
Planting materials	$ 970	$1,200	$2,170
Installation labor	400	620	1,020
Service overhead (50% of installation labor)	200	310	510
Totals	$1,570	$2,130	$3,700
Job-site cleanup			
Janitorial service cost	$ 90	$ 320	$ 410
Totals	$2,950	$2,450	$5,400

Cost Summary to Date	Total Cost
Landscape design	$ 1,290
Landscape installation	3,700
Job-site cleanup	410
Totals	$ 5,400
Profit margin (15%)	810
Contract revenue	$6,210

Such contracts require the customer to pay all costs incurred in performing the job plus a predetermined amount of profit, which is based on the amount of costs incurred. When the job is complete, the costs on the completed job order cost card become the cost of services. The cost of services is adjusted at the end of the accounting period for the difference between the applied service overhead costs and the actual service overhead costs.

To illustrate how a service organization uses a job order costing system, let's assume that a company called Gartner Landscaping Services employs 15 people and serves the San Francisco Bay area. The company earns its revenue by designing and installing landscapes for homes and offices. Figure 3 shows Gartner's job order cost card for the landscaping of Rico Corporation's corporate headquarters. Costs have been categorized into three separate activities: landscape design, landscape installation, and job-site cleanup. Costs have been tracked to the Rico Corporation job throughout its duration, and now that the job is finished, it is time to complete the job order cost card. The service overhead cost for landscape design is 40 percent of design labor cost, and the service overhead cost for landscape installation is 50 percent of installation labor cost. Total costs incurred for this job were $5,400. Gartner's cost-plus contract with Rico has a 15 percent profit guarantee; therefore, $810 of profit margin is added to the total cost to arrive at the total contract revenue of $6,210, which is the amount billed to Rico.

✅ Check out ACE for a Review Quiz at http://accounting.college.hmco.com/students.

THE PROCESS COSTING SYSTEM

LO4 Explain product flow and cost flow in a process costing system.

RELATED TEXT ASSIGNMENTS
Q: 13
SD: 2, 5
MRA: 3, 4, 6

As discussed earlier, a process costing system is used by businesses that produce large amounts of similar products or liquid products or that have long, continuous production runs of identical products. Companies that produce paint, beverages, bricks, canned foods, milk, and paper are typical users of a process costing system. Tracking costs to individual products in a continuous flow environment would be too difficult and too expensive and would not reveal significantly different product costs. One gallon of green paint is identical to the next gallon of green paint; one brick looks just like the next brick. Because the products are alike, they should cost the same amount to produce. A process costing system accumulates the costs of direct materials, direct labor, and manufacturing overhead for each process, department, or work cell and assigns those costs to the products as they are produced during a particular period.

PATTERNS OF PRODUCT FLOWS AND COST FLOWS

In companies that use process costing, the steps in the production process can be combined in hundreds of ways. Two basic production flows are illustrated in Figure 4. Example 1 shows a series of three processing steps, or departments. The completed product from one department becomes the direct materials for the next department. Such a production flow can include from two to a dozen or more departments or processes. The product unit cost is the sum of the cost elements in all departments.

Example 2 in Figure 4 shows a different kind of production flow. Again there are three departments, but the product does not flow through all the departments in a simple 1-2-3 order. Instead, two separate products are developed: one in Department X and the other in Department Y. Both products then go to Department Z, where they are joined with a third direct material, Material AH. The unit cost transferred to the Finished Goods Inventory account when the products are completed includes cost elements from Departments X, Y, and Z.

To further illustrate this linear pattern of production flow, let's consider an example from the computer chip–making industry. The steps below, which describe the production flow during the manufacture of computer chips, are shown in Figure 5.

• Producing the silicon wafer. Silicon, which is extracted from sand and then purified, is the direct material from which computer chips are made. Through a process of crystallization, the refined, molten silicon is converted to a cylindrical ingot. The ingot is then sliced into wafers, and the wafers are polished to meet flatness and thickness specifications. The workers involved in these steps provide direct labor. Overhead includes the costs of the equipment the workers use and the resources necessary to operate and maintain the equipment.

• Fabricating the chips. Fabrication includes photolithography, etching, ion implantation, and all the other steps needed to create the electronic circuits that make

FIGURE 4
Production Flows for Process Costing

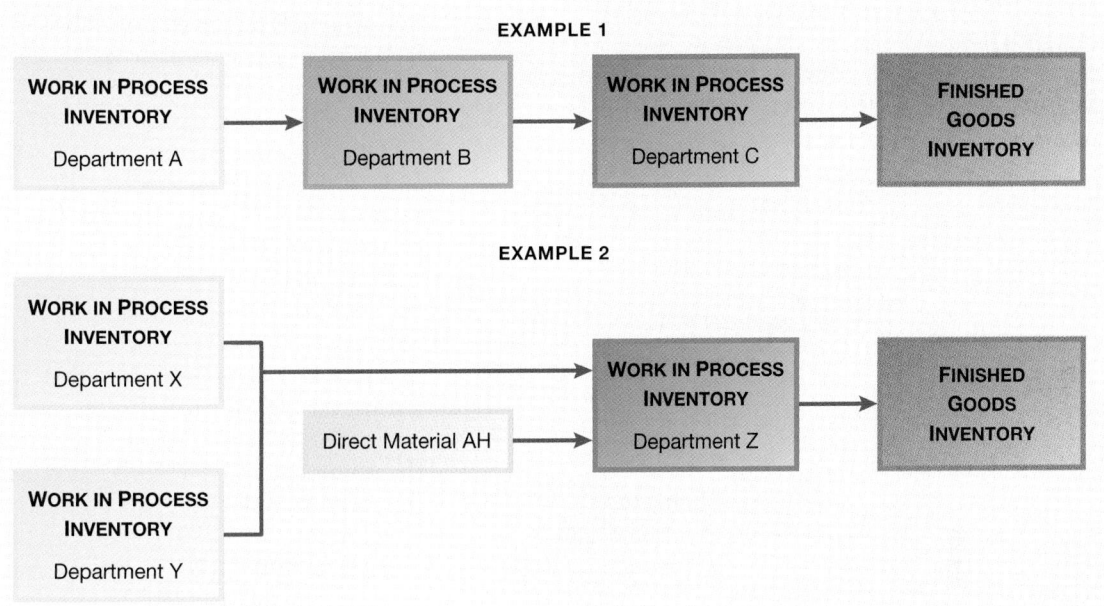

up each chip on a wafer. Additional direct labor and overhead costs are incurred during fabrication.

- Final testing, assembly, and packaging of the chips: Although the wafers are tested at each step in the fabrication process, each chip on a wafer is tested again when fabrication is complete. Those that pass this test are cut from the wafer, placed in metal or plastic packages, tested once again, and transferred to finished goods inventory in the warehouse. These steps incur additional direct labor, direct materials, and overhead costs.

FIGURE 5
Product Flows in a Process Costing System for Computer Chip Making

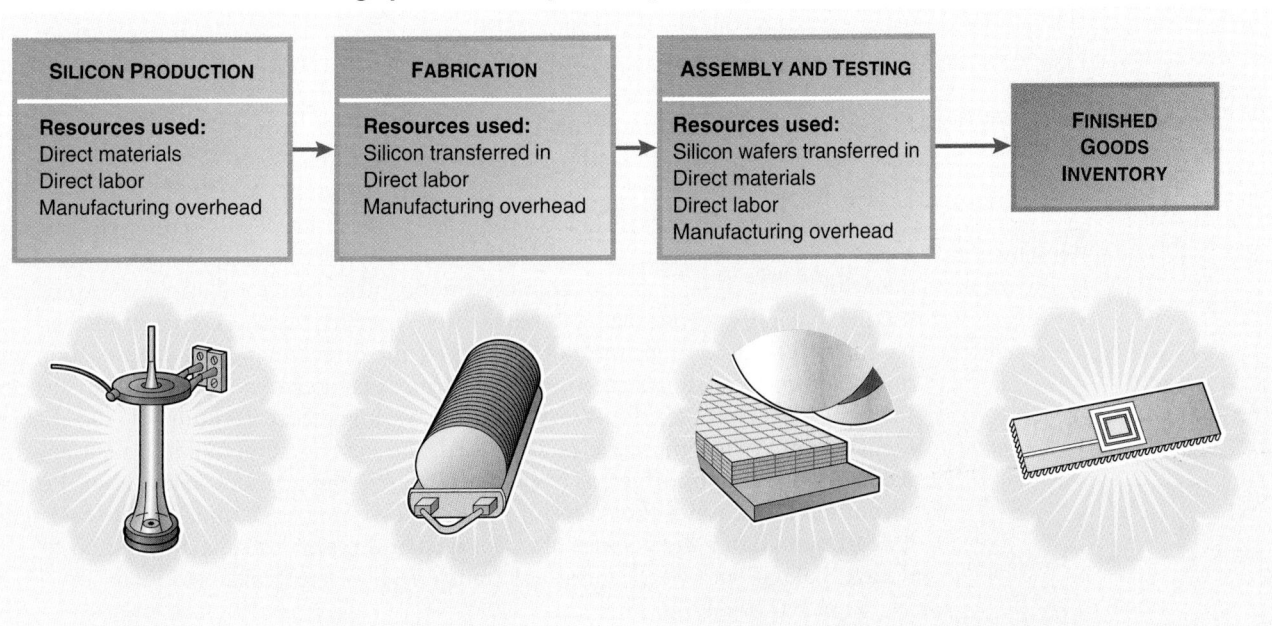

What Kinds of Companies Use Process Costing?

Process costing is appropriate for companies in many types of industries. The following list provides some examples:

Industry	Company
Aluminum	Alcoa, Inc. <www.alcoa.com>
Beverages	Coors <www.coors.com>
Building materials	Owens Corning <www.owenscorning.com>
Chemicals	Engelhard Corporation <www.englehard.com>
Computers	Apple Computer <www.apple.com>
Containers	Crown Cork & Seal <www.crowncork.com>
Electrical equipment	Emerson Electric <www.emersonelectric.com>
Foods	Kellogg Company <www.kelloggs.com>
Machinery	Caterpillar Inc. <www.caterpillar.com>
Manufacturing	Minnesota Mining & Manufacturing <www.3m.com>
Oil and gas	Exxon <www.exxon.com>
Paper products	Boise Cascade <www.boisecascade.com>
Photography	Eastman Kodak <www.eastmankodak.com>
Plastic products	Tupperware <www.tupperware.com>
Soft drinks	Coca-Cola <www.cocacola.com>

Process costing environments can be considerably less complex than the one we have just described, but even in simple process costing environments, production generally involves a number of separate manufacturing processes, departments, or works cells. For example, the separate processes involved in manufacturing sofas include making the frames and cushions, upholstering the frames, and assembling the frames and cushions into finished products.

As products pass through each manufacturing process, department, or work cell, the process costing system accumulates their costs and passes them on to the next process, department, or work cell. At the end of every accounting period, the system generates a report that assigns the costs that have accumulated during the period to the units that have transferred out of the process, department, or work cell and to the units that are still work in process. Managers use this report, called a **process cost report**, to assign costs using the FIFO costing method. In the **FIFO costing method**, the cost flow follows the logical physical flow of production—the costs assigned to the first materials processed are the first costs transferred out when those materials flow to the next process, department, or work cell. Thus, in Figure 5, the costs assigned to the production of the silicon wafers would be the first costs transferred to the fabrication of the chips. How process cost reports are prepared using the FIFO costing method is covered later in this chapter.

COSTS FLOWS THROUGH THE WORK IN PROCESS INVENTORY ACCOUNTS

How many Work in Process Inventory accounts does a process costing system require?

A process costing system requires a Work in Process Inventory account for each process, department, or work cell in the production process. ■

www.nabisco.com

As we pointed out earlier in the chapter, a job order costing system uses a single Work in Process Inventory account, whereas a process costing system has a separate Work in Process Inventory account for each process, department, or work cell. These accounts are the focal point of process costing. As products move from one process, department, or work cell to the next, the costs of the direct materials, direct labor, and manufacturing overhead associated with them flow to the Work in Process Inventory account of that process, department, or work cell. Once the products are completed, packaged, and ready for sale, their costs are transferred to the Finished Goods Inventory account.

To illustrate how costs flow through the Work in Process Inventory accounts in a process costing system, let's consider a company like Nabisco, which makes large quantities of identical cookies in a continuous flow. Such a company would have mixing, baking, and packaging departments. After its Mixing Department has prepared the cookie dough, the costs incurred for direct materials, direct labor, and manufacturing overhead are transferred from that department's Work in Process Inventory account to the Work in Process Inventory account of the Baking Department. When the cookies are baked, the costs of the cookie dough and the baking costs are transferred from the Baking Department's Work in Process Inventory account to the Work in Process Inventory account of the Packaging Department. After the cookies are packaged and ready for sale, all their costs—for dough, baking, and packaging—are transferred to the Finished Goods Inventory account. When the packages of cookies are sold, their costs transfer from the Finished Goods Inventory account to the Cost of Goods Sold account.

Because the production of homogeneous products like packaged cookies, paint, or computer chips is continuous, it would be impractical to try to assign their costs to a specific batch of products, as is done with a job order costing system. Instead, as we have noted, in a process costing system, the process cost report prepared at the end of every accounting period assigns the costs that have accumulated in each Work in Process Inventory account to the units transferred out and to the units still in process. Managers use the process cost report to compute the unit cost of all products worked on during the period. Thus, the product unit cost includes all costs from all processes, departments, or work cells.

KEY POINT: Total product cost is a flow-through concept in which each department's work adds cost to the product.

To compute the unit cost, the total cost of direct materials, direct labor, and manufacturing overhead is divided by the total number of units worked on during the period. Thus, a critical question is exactly how many units were worked on during the period? Do we count only units started and completed during the period? Or should we include partially completed units in the beginning work in process inventory? And what about incomplete products in the ending work in process inventory? The answers to these questions relate to the concept of equivalent production, which is discussed next.

 Check out ACE for a Review Quiz at http://accounting.college.hmco.com/students.

COMPUTING EQUIVALENT PRODUCTION

LO5 Define *equivalent production* and compute equivalent units.

RELATED TEXT ASSIGNMENTS
Q: 14, 15, 16
SE: 8
E: 9, 10, 11
P: 4, 5, 8
SD: 5
MRA: 2, 3

STUDY NOTE: The number of units started and completed is not the same as the total number of units completed during the period. Total units completed includes two categories: units in beginning work in process inventory and units started and completed.

A process costing system, because it makes no attempt to associate costs with particular job orders, assigns the costs incurred in a process, department, or work cell to the units worked on during an accounting period by computing an average cost per unit. **Equivalent production** (also called *equivalent units*) is a measure that applies a percentage-of-completion factor to partially completed units to calculate the equivalent number of whole units produced in an accounting period for each type of input (i.e., direct materials, direct labor, and manufacturing overhead). The number of equivalent units produced is the sum of (1) total units started and completed during the period and (2) an amount representing the work done on partially completed products in both the beginning and the ending work in process inventories. Equivalent production must be computed separately for each type of input because of differences in the ways the costs are incurred. Direct materials are usually added to production at the beginning of the process. The costs of direct labor and manufacturing overhead are often incurred uniformly throughout the production process. Thus, it is convenient to combine direct labor and manufacturing overhead when calculating equivalent units. These combined costs are called **conversion costs**.

ENRICHMENT NOTE: Don't make the mistake of thinking that direct materials are always placed into production at the beginning of the process. In reality, direct materials are often added at different stages of production (e.g., for paint, cans for packaging are added at the end).

We will explain the computation of equivalent production by using a simplified example. Soda Products Company makes bottled soft drinks. As illustrated in Figure 6, the company started Week 2 with one half-completed drink in process. During Week 2, it started and completed three drinks, and at the end of Week 2, it had one drink that was three-quarters completed.

EQUIVALENT PRODUCTION FOR DIRECT MATERIALS

At Soda Products, all direct materials, including the liquids and the bottles, are added at the beginning of production. Thus, the drink that was half-completed at the beginning of Week 2 had had all its direct materials added during the previous week. For this reason, no direct materials costs for this drink are included in the computation of Week 2's equivalent units.

FIGURE 6
Computation of Equivalent Production

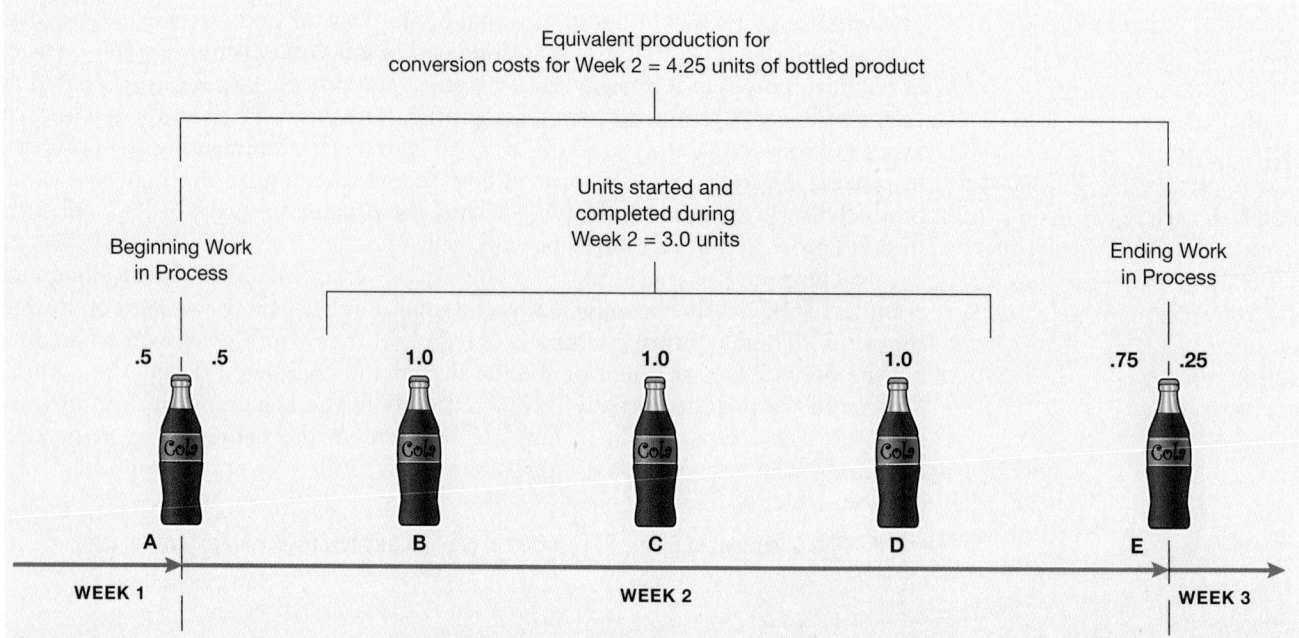

Note: Conversion costs (the cost of direct labor and manufacturing overhead) are incurred uniformly as each physical unit of drink moves through production. Equivalent production for Week 2 is 4.25 units for conversion costs. But direct materials costs are all added to production at the beginning of the process. Because four physical units of drinks entered production in Week 2, equivalent production for the week is 4.0 units of effort for direct materials costs.

During Week 2, Soda Products began work on four new drinks—the three drinks that were completed and the drink that was three-quarters completed at the end of the week. Because all direct materials are added at the beginning of the production process, all four drinks were 100 percent complete in regard to direct materials at the end of Week 2. Thus, for Week 2, the equivalent production for direct materials was 4.0 units. This figure includes direct materials for both the 3.0 units that were started and completed and the 1.0 unit that was three-quarters completed.

EQUIVALENT PRODUCTION FOR CONVERSION COSTS

Because conversion costs at Soda Products are incurred uniformly throughout the production process, the equivalent production for conversion costs during Week 2 consists of three components: the cost to finish the half-completed unit in beginning work in process inventory (0.5), the cost to begin and finish three completed units (3.0), and the cost to begin work on the three-quarters completed unit in ending work in process inventory (0.75). For Week 2, the total equivalent production for conversion costs was 4.25 (0.5 + 3.0 + 0.75) units.

In reality, Soda Products would make many more drinks during an accounting period and would have many more partially completed drinks in its beginning and ending work in process inventories. The number of partially completed drinks would be so great that it would be impractical to take a physical count of them. So, instead of taking a physical count, Soda Products would estimate an average percentage of completion for all drinks in process.

✓ Check out ACE for a Review Quiz at http://accounting.college.hmco.com/students.

PREPARING A PROCESS COST REPORT USING THE FIFO COSTING METHOD

L06 Prepare a process cost report using the FIFO costing method.

RELATED TEXT ASSIGNMENTS
Q: 17, 18, 19
SE: 8, 9
E: 9, 10, 11, 12, 13, 14
P: 4, 5, 8
SD: 5
MRA: 2, 3

STUDY NOTE: The FIFO method focuses on the work done in the current period only.

As mentioned earlier, a process cost report is a report that managers use to track and analyze costs for a process, department, or work cell in a process costing system. In a process cost report that uses the FIFO costing method, the cost flow follows the logical physical flow of production—that is, the costs assigned to the first materials processes are the first costs transferred out when those materials flow to the next process, department, or work cell.

As illustrated in Exhibit 2, the preparation of a process cost report has five steps. The first two steps account for the units of product being processed. The next two steps account for the costs of the direct material, direct labor, and manufacturing overhead that are being incurred. The final step assigns costs to products transferring out of the area and to those remaining behind in ending work in process inventory.

ACCOUNTING FOR UNITS

Managers must account for the physical flow of products through their areas (Step 1) before they can compute equivalent production for the accounting period (Step 2). To continue with the Soda Products example, assume the following facts for the accounting period of February 20x6:

KEY POINT: The process cost report is developed for the purpose of assigning a value to one transaction: the transfer of goods from one department to another or to finished goods inventory. The ending balance in the Work in Process Inventory account represents the costs that remain after this transfer.

- The beginning work in process inventory consists of 6,200 partially completed units (60 percent processed in the previous period).

- During the period, the 6,200 units in beginning inventory were completed, and 57,500 units were started into production.

- Of the 57,500 units started during the period, 52,500 units were completed. The other 5,000 units remain in ending work in process inventory and are 45 percent complete.

In Step 1 of Exhibit 2, Soda Products' department manager computes the total units to be accounted for by adding the 6,200 units in beginning inventory to the 57,500 units started into production in this period. These 63,700 units are the actual physical units that the manager is responsible for during the period. Step 2 continues accounting for physical units. As shown in the "Physical Units" column of Exhibit 2, the 6,200 units in beginning inventory that were completed during the period, the 52,500 units that were started and finished in the period, and the 5,000 units remaining in the department at the end of the period are summed, and the total is listed as "units accounted for." (Notice that the "units accounted for" in Step 2 must equal the "units to be accounted for" in Step 1.) These amounts are used to compute equivalent production for the department's direct materials and conversion costs for the month, as described below.

ENRICHMENT NOTE:
The percentage of completion for beginning work in process inventory is the amount of work completed the prior period. Under FIFO, the amount of effort required to complete beginning work in process inventory is the relevant percentage.

■ **BEGINNING INVENTORY**   Because all direct materials are added at the beginning of the production process, the 6,200 partially completed units that began February as work in process were already 100 percent complete in regard to direct materials. They were 60 percent complete in regard to conversion costs on February 1. The remaining 40 percent of their conversion costs were incurred as they were completed during the month. Thus, as shown in the far right column of Exhibit 2, the equivalent production for their conversion costs is 2,480 units (40% × 6,200).

■ **UNITS STARTED AND COMPLETED DURING THE PERIOD**   All the costs of the 52,500 units started and completed during February were incurred during this accounting

EXHIBIT 2
Process Cost Report: FIFO Costing Method

Step 1:
Account for physical units.

Beginning inventory (units started last period)		6,200
Units started this period		57,500
Units to be accounted for		63,700

Step 2:
Account for equivalent units.

		Direct Materials Costs	% Incurred During Period	Conversion Costs	% Incurred During Period
Beginning inventory (units completed this period)	6,200	0	0%	2,480	40%
Units started and completed this period	52,500	52,500	100%	52,500	100%
Ending inventory (units started but not completed this period)	5,000	5,000	100%	2,250	45%
Units accounted for	63,700	57,500		57,230	

Step 3:
Account for costs.

	Total Costs				
Beginning inventory	$ 41,540	=	$ 20,150	+	$ 21,390
Current costs	510,238	=	189,750	+	320,488
Total costs	$551,778				

Step 4:
Compute cost per equivalent unit.

Current Costs			$189,750		$320,488
Equivalent units			57,500		57,230
Cost per equivalent unit	$8.90	=	$3.30	+	$5.60

Step 5:
Assign costs to cost of goods manufactured and ending inventory.

Cost of goods manufactured and transferred out:					
From beginning inventory	$ 41,540				
Current costs to complete	13,888	=	0	+	(2,480 × $5.60)
Units started and completed this period	467,250	=	(52,500 × $3.30) +		(52,500 × $5.60)
Cost of goods manufactured	$522,678		(No rounding necessary)		
Ending inventory	29,100	=	(5,000 × $3.30) +		(2,250 × $5.60)
Total costs	$551,778				

Work in Process Inventory Account: Cost Recap		
Beg. Bal.	$ 41,540	$522,678 (Cost of goods manufactured and transferred out)
Direct Materials	$189,750	
Conversion Costs	$320,488	
End. Bal.	$29,100	

Work in Process Inventory Account: Unit Recap		
Beg. Bal.	6,200	58,700 (FIFO units transferred out from the 6,200 in beginning inventory plus the 52,500 started and completed)
Direct Materials and Conversion Costs	57,500	
End. Bal.	5,000	

period. Thus, the full amount of 52,500 is entered as the equivalent units for both direct materials costs and conversion costs.

■ **ENDING INVENTORY**   Because the materials for the 5,000 drinks still in process at the end of February were added when the drinks went into production during the month, the full amount of 5,000 is entered as the equivalent units for their direct materials cost. However, these drinks are only 45 percent complete in terms of conversion costs. Thus, as shown in the far right column of Exhibit 2, the equivalent production for their conversion costs is 2,250 units (45% × 5,000).

KEY POINT: Units in beginning work in process inventory represent work accomplished in the previous accounting period that has already been assigned a certain portion of its total cost. Those units must be completed in the current period, incurring additional costs.

■ **TOTALS**   Step 2 is completed by summing all the physical units to be accounted for, all equivalent units for direct materials costs, and all equivalent units for conversion costs. Exhibit 2 shows that for February, Soda Products accounted for 63,700 units. Equivalent units for direct materials costs totaled 57,500, and equivalent units for conversion costs totaled 57,230. Once Soda Products knows February's equivalent unit amounts, it can complete the remaining three steps in the preparation of a process cost report.

ACCOUNTING FOR COSTS

Thus far, we have focused on accounting for units of productive output—in our example, bottled soft drinks. We now turn our focus to cost information. Step 3 in preparing a process cost report accumulates and analyzes all costs charged to the Work in Process Inventory account of each production process, department, or work cell. Step 4 computes the cost per equivalent unit for direct materials costs and conversion costs.

The following information about Soda Products' manufacture of soft drinks during February 20x6 enables us to complete Steps 3 and 4:

Work in Process Inventory

Costs from beginning inventory	
Direct materials costs	$ 20,150
Conversion costs	21,390
Current period costs	
Direct materials costs	189,750
Conversion costs	320,488

As shown in Step 3 of Exhibit 2, all costs for the period are accumulated in the "Total Costs" column. Beginning inventory's direct material costs of $20,150 are added to the conversion costs of $21,390 to determine the total cost of beginning inventory ($41,540). Current period costs for direct materials ($189,750) are added to conversion costs ($320,488) to determine the total current manufacturing costs ($510,238). The grand total of $551,778 is the sum of beginning inventory costs ($41,540) and current period costs ($510,238). Notice that only the "Total Costs" column is totaled. Since only the current period costs for materials and conversion are used in Step 4, there is no need to find the total costs of the direct materials and conversion columns in Step 3.

KEY POINT: The cost per equivalent unit using the FIFO method measures the current cost divided by current effort. Notice the cost of beginning work in process inventory is omitted.

In Step 4, the direct materials costs and conversion costs for the current period are divided by their respective units of equivalent production to arrive at the cost per equivalent unit. Prior period costs attached to units in beginning inventory are not included in these computations because the FIFO costing method uses separate costing analyses for each accounting period. (The FIFO method treats the costs of beginning inventory separately, in Step 5.) Exhibit 2 shows that the total current cost of $8.90 per equivalent unit consists of $3.30 per equivalent unit for direct materials costs ($189,750 ÷ 57,500 equivalent units) plus $5.60 per equivalent unit for conversion costs ($320,488 ÷ 57,230 equivalent units). (Note that the equivalent units are taken from Step 2 of Exhibit 2.)

ASSIGNING COSTS

Step 5 in the preparation of a process costing report uses information from Steps 2 and 4 to assign costs, as shown in Exhibit 2. This final step determines the costs that are transferred out either to the next production process, department, or work cell or to the Finished Goods Inventory account (i.e., the cost of goods manufactured), as well as the costs that remain in the ending balance in the Work in Process Inventory account. The total costs assigned to units completed and transferred out and to ending inventory must equal the total costs in Step 3.

■ **COST OF GOODS MANUFACTURED AND TRANSFERRED OUT**   Step 5 of Exhibit 2 shows that the costs transferred to the Finished Goods Inventory account include the $41,540 in direct materials and conversion costs for completing the 6,200 units in beginning inventory. Step 2 in the exhibit shows that 2,480 equivalent units of conversion costs were required to complete these 6,200 units. Because the equivalent unit conversion cost for February is $5.60, the cost to complete the units carried over from January is $13,888 (2,480 units × $5.60).

Each of the 52,500 units started and completed in February cost $8.90 to produce. Their combined cost of $467,250 is added to the $41,540 and $13,888 of costs required to produce the 6,200 units from beginning inventory to arrive at the total of $522,678 that is transferred to the Finished Goods Inventory account.

■ **ENDING INVENTORY**   All costs remaining in Soda Products' Work in Process Inventory account after the cost of goods manufactured have been transferred out represent the costs of the drinks still in production at the end of February. As shown in Step 5 of Exhibit 2, the balance of $29,100 in the ending Work in Process Inventory is made up of $16,500 of direct materials costs (5,000 units × $3.30 per unit) and $12,600 of conversion costs (5,000 × 45% × $5.60 per unit).

■ **ROUNDING DIFFERENCES**   As you perform Step 5 in any process cost report, remember that the total costs in Steps 3 and 5 must always be the same number. In Exhibit 2, for example, they are both $551,778. If the numbers are not the same, first check for omission of any costs and for calculation errors. If that does not solve the problem, check if any rounding was necessary in computing the costs per equivalent unit in Step 4. If rounding was done in Step 4, rounding differences will occur when assigning costs in Step 5. Adjust the total costs transferred out for any rounding difference so that the total costs in Step 5 equal the total costs in Step 3.

■ **RECAP OF WORK IN PROCESS INVENTORY ACCOUNT**   When the process cost report is complete, an account recap may be prepared to show the effects of the report on the Work in Process Inventory account for the period. Two recaps of Soda Products' Work in Process Inventory account for February—one for costs and one for units—appear at the end of Exhibit 2.

PROCESS COSTING FOR TWO OR MORE PRODUCTION DEPARTMENTS

Because Soda Products Company has only one production department, it needs only one Work in Process Inventory account. However, a company that has more than one production department must have a Work in Process Inventory account for each department. For instance, a soft drink maker that has a production department for formulation, another for bottling, and another for packaging needs three Work in Process Inventory accounts. When products flow from the Formulation Department to the Bottling Department, their costs flow from the Formulation Department's Work in Process Inventory account to the Bottling Department's Work in Process Inventory account. The costs transferred into the Bottling Department's Work in Process Inventory account are treated in the same way as the cost of direct materials added at the beginning of the production process. When pro-

KEY POINT: All costs must be accounted for, including costs from both beginning inventory and costs incurred during the current period. All costs must be assigned to either ending inventory or the goods transferred out.

STUDY NOTE: Rounding product unit costs to even dollars may lead to a significant difference in total costs, giving the impression that costs have been miscalculated. Carry product unit costs to two decimal places where appropriate.

⬢ **STOP AND THINK!**
How many process cost reports are prepared each period?
One process cost report is prepared for every Work in Process Inventory account. ■

duction flows to the Packaging Department, the accumulated costs (incurred in the two previous departments) are transferred to that department's Work in Process Inventory account. At the end of the accounting period, a separate process cost report is prepared for each department.

 Check out ACE for a Review Quiz at http://accounting.college.hmco.com/students.

USING INFORMATION ABOUT PRODUCT COST TO EVALUATE PERFORMANCE

LO7 Evaluate operating performance using information about product cost.

RELATED TEXT ASSIGNMENTS
Q: 20
SE: 10
E: 15
SD: 5
MRA: 1, 2, 3

● STOP AND THINK!
How can information about product cost help managers evaluate operating performance?

By analyzing the information from a job order or process costing system, managers can compare budgeted and actual costs for a process, department, or work cell. They can also track units produced per time period and monitor labor costs to evaluate operating performance. ■

A product costing system—whether it's a job order or a process costing system—provides managers with valuable information. As we have noted, managers use the information that such a system provides in determining a product's price and in computing the balances in the Materials Inventory, Work in Process Inventory, and Finished Goods Inventory accounts on the balance sheet and the Cost of Goods Sold account on the income statement. Managers also use product costing information to evaluate operating performance. Such an analysis may include consideration of the following:

- Cost trends of a product or product line
- Units produced per time period
- Materials usage per unit produced
- Labor cost per unit produced
- Special needs of customers
- Cost-effectiveness of changing to a more advanced production process

Cost trends can be developed from product cost data over several time periods. Such trends help managers identify areas of rising costs or areas in which cost-effectiveness has improved. Tracking units produced per time period, a figure easily pulled from a product cost analysis, can help managers evaluate operating efficiency.

Direct materials and labor costs are significant parts of a product's cost and should be monitored constantly. Trends in direct materials usage and labor costs per unit produced can help managers determine optimal resource usage.

Anticipating customers' needs is very important to managers. By tracking the size, cost, and type of products ordered by customers, managers can see which customers are increasing or reducing their orders and take action to improve customer relations.

STUDY NOTE: Performance measures are quantitative tools that help managers assess the performance of a specific process or expected outcome.

Finally, decisions to purchase new machinery and equipment are often based on the savings that the change is expected to produce. Information from a product costing system helps managers make such decisions in that it enables them to estimate unit costs for the new equipment and to compare them with cost trends for the existing equipment.

 Check out ACE for a Review Quiz at http://accounting.college.hmco.com/students.

Chapter Review

REVIEW OF LEARNING OBJECTIVES

LO1 Discuss the role information about costs plays in the management cycle and explain why unit cost is important.

During the planning stage of the management cycle, information about costs helps managers develop budgets, establish prices, set sales goals, plan production volumes, estimate product or service unit costs, and determine human resource needs. During the executing stage, managers use cost information to make decisions about controlling costs, managing the company's volume of activity, ensuring quality, and negotiating prices. During the reviewing stage, they analyze actual and targeted information to evaluate performance and make any necessary adjustments to their planning and decision-making strategies. During the reporting stage, they use unit costs to determine inventory balances and the cost of goods or services sold for the financial statements. They also analyze internal reports that compare the organization's measures of actual and targeted performance to determine whether cost goals for products or services are being achieved.

LO2   Distinguish between the two basic types of product costing systems and identify the information each provides.

A job order costing system is a product costing system used by companies that make large, unique, or special-order products. Such a system traces the costs of direct materials, direct labor, and manufacturing overhead to a specific batch of products or a specific job order. A job order costing system measures the cost of each complete unit and summarizes the cost of all jobs in a single Work in Process Inventory account that is supported by job order cost cards.

A process costing system is a product costing system used by companies that produce large amounts of similar products or liquid products or long, continuous production runs of identical products. Such a system first traces the costs of direct materials, direct labor, and manufacturing overhead to processes, departments, or work cells and then assigns the costs to the products manufactured by those processes, departments, or work cells. A process costing system uses several Work in Process Inventory accounts: one for each department, process, or work cell.

LO3   Explain cost flow in a job order costing system, prepare a job order cost card, and compute product unit cost.

In a manufacturer's job order costing system, the costs of materials are first charged to the Materials Inventory account and to the respective materials accounts in the subsidiary ledger. Labor costs are first accumulated in the Factory Payroll account. The various manufacturing overhead costs are charged to the Manufacturing Overhead account. As products are manufactured, the costs of direct materials and direct labor are transferred to the Work in Process Inventory account and are recorded on the job's job order cost card. Manufacturing overhead costs are applied and charged to the Work in Process Inventory account using a predetermined overhead rate. Those charges are used to reduce the balance in the Manufacturing Overhead account. They too are recorded on the job order cost card. When products and jobs are completed, the costs assigned to them are transferred to the Finished Goods Inventory account. Then, when the products are sold and shipped, their costs are transferred to the Cost of Goods Sold account.

All costs of direct materials, direct labor, and manufacturing overhead for a particular job are accumulated on a job order cost card. When the job has been completed, those costs are totaled. The total is then divided by the number of good units produced to find the product unit cost for that order. The product unit cost is entered on the job order cost card and will be used to value items in inventory.

Job order costing in a service organization differs in that the costs are not associated with a physical product but rather with services, for which the most important cost is labor. Job order cost cards are kept and include the costs for labor, materials and supplies, and service overhead.

LO4   Explain product flow and cost flow in a process costing system.

Process costing is used by companies that produce large amounts of similar products or liquids or that have a continuous production flow. A process costing system accumulates the costs of direct materials, direct labor, and manufacturing overhead for each process, department, or work cell and assigns those costs to the products as they are produced during a particular period. The cost flow follows the logical physical flow of production using the FIFO costing method—that is, the costs assigned to the first materials processed are the first costs transferred out when those materials flow to the next process, department, or work cell.

LO5   Define *equivalent production* and compute equivalent units.

Equivalent production is a measure that applies a percentage-of-completion factor to partially completed units to compute the equivalent number of whole units produced in an accounting period for each type of input. Equivalent units are computed from (1) units in the beginning work in process inventory and their percentage of completion, (2) units started and completed during the period, and (3) units in the ending work in process inventory and their percentage of completion.

LO6   Prepare a process cost report using the FIFO costing method.

In a process cost report that uses the FIFO costing method, the cost flow follows the logical physical flow of production—that is, the costs assigned to the first materials processed are the first costs transferred when those materials flow to the next process, department, or work cell. Preparation of a process cost report involves five steps. Steps 1 and 2 account for the physical flow of products and compute the equivalent units of production. Once equivalent production has been determined, the focus of the report shifts to accounting for costs. In Step 3, all direct materials and conversion costs for the current period are added to arrive at total costs. In Step 4, the cost per equivalent unit for both direct materials and conversion costs is found by dividing those costs by their respective equivalent units. In Step 5, costs are assigned to the units completed and transferred out during the period, as well as to the ending work in process inventory. The costs assigned to units completed and transferred out include the costs incurred in the preceding period and the conversion costs needed to complete those units during the current period. That amount is added to the total cost of producing all units started and completed during the period. The result is the total cost transferred out for the units completed during the period. Step 5 also assigns costs to units still in process at the end of the period by multiplying their direct materials and conversion costs by their respective equivalent units. The total equals the balance in the Work in Process Inventory account at the end of the period.

LO7 Evaluate operating performance using information about product cost.

Both the job order and the process costing systems supply information that managers can use to evaluate operating performance. Such an analysis may include consideration of the following: cost trends of a product or product line, units produced per time period, materials usage per unit produced, labor cost per unit produced, special needs of customers, and the cost-effectiveness of changing to a more advanced production process.

REVIEW OF CONCEPTS AND TERMINOLOGY

The following concepts and terms were introduced in this chapter:

LO5 **Conversion costs:** The combined total costs of direct labor and manufacturing overhead.

LO3 **Cost-plus contracts:** Job contracts that require the customer to pay all costs incurred in performing the job plus a predetermined amount of profit.

LO5 **Equivalent production:** A measure that applies a percentage-of-completion factor to partially completed units to compute the equivalent number of whole units produced in an accounting period for each type of input. Also called *equivalent units*.

LO4 **FIFO costing method:** A process costing method in which the cost flow follows the actual flow of production, so that the costs assigned to the first materials processed are the first costs transferred out when those materials flow to the next process, department, or work cell.

LO2 **Job order:** A customer order for a specific number of specially designed, made-to-order products.

LO2 **Job order cost card:** A document on which all costs incurred in the production of a particular job order are recorded; part of the subsidiary ledger for the Work in Process Inventory account.

LO2 **Job order costing system:** A product costing system that traces the costs of direct materials, direct labor, and manufacturing overhead to a specific batch of products or a specific job order; used by companies that make large, unique, or special-order products.

LO2 **Process costing system:** A product costing system that traces the costs of direct materials, direct labor, and manufacturing overhead to processes, departments, or work cells and then assigns the costs to the products manufactured by those processes, departments, or work cells; used by companies that produce large amounts of similar products or liquid products or that have long, continuous production runs of identical products.

LO4 **Process cost report:** A report that managers use to track and analyze costs in a process costing system.

LO2   **Product costing system:** A set of procedures used to account for an organization's product costs and to provide timely and accurate unit cost information for pricing, cost planning and control, inventory valuation, and financial statement preparation.

REVIEW PROBLEM

Process Costing Using the FIFO Costing Method

LO5
LO6
LO7

Pop Chewing Gum Company produces several flavors of bubble gum. Two basic direct materials, gum base and flavored sweetener, are blended at the beginning of the manufacturing process. No materials are lost in the process, so 1 kilogram of materials input produces 1 kilogram of bubble gum. Direct labor and manufacturing overhead costs are incurred uniformly throughout the blending process. On June 30, 20x4, 16,000 units were in process. All direct materials had been added, but the units were only 70 percent complete in regard to conversion costs. Direct materials costs of $8,100 and conversion costs of $11,800 were attached to the beginning inventory. During July, 135,000 kilograms of gum base and 270,000 kilograms of flavored sweetener were used at costs of $122,500 and $80,000, respectively. Direct labor charges were $299,200, and manufacturing overhead costs applied during July were $284,000. The ending work in process inventory was 21,600 kilograms. All direct materials have been added to those units, and 25 percent of the conversion costs have been assigned. Output from the Blending Department is transferred to the Packaging Department.

REQUIRED ▶

1. Prepare a process cost report using the FIFO costing method for the Blending Department for July.
2. Identify the amount that should be transferred out of the Work in Process Inventory account, and state where those dollars should be transferred.

ANSWER TO REVIEW PROBLEM

1. Process cost report using the FIFO costing method:

Pop Chewing Gum Company
Blending Department
Process Cost Report: FIFO Method
For the Month Ended July 31, 20x4

Step 1:
Account for physical units.

Beginning inventory (units started last period)	16,000
Units started this period	405,000
Units to be accounted for	421,000

Step 2:
Account for equivalent units.

		Direct Materials Costs	% Incurred During Period	Conversion Costs	% Incurred During Period
Beginning inventory (units completed this period)	16,000	0	0%	4,800	30%
Units started and completed this period	383,400	383,400	100%	383,400	100%
Ending inventory (units started but not completed this period)	21,600	21,600	100%	5,400	25%
Units accounted for	421,000	405,000		393,600	

(continued)

Step 3:
Account for costs.

	Total Costs		Direct Materials Costs		Conversion Costs
Beginning inventory	$ 19,900	=	$ 8,100	+	$ 11,800
Current costs	785,700	=	$202,500	+	$583,200
Total costs	$805,600				

Step 4:
Compute cost per equivalent unit.

			Direct Materials Costs		Conversion Costs
Current Costs			$202,500		$583,200
Equivalent Units			405,000		393,600
Cost per equivalent unit	$1.98	=	$ .50	+	$ 1.48*

*Rounded to nearest cent

Step 5:
Assign costs to cost of goods manufactured and ending inventory.

Cost of goods manufactured and transferred out:

	Total Costs		Direct Materials Costs		Conversion Costs
From beginning inventory	$19,900				
Current costs to complete	7,104	=	0	+	$(4,800 \times \$1.48)$
Units started and completed this period	759,132	=	$(383,400 \times \$.50)$	+	$(383,400 \times \$1.48)$
Cost of goods manufactured	$786,808		(Add rounding, $672)		
Ending inventory	18,792	=	$(21,600 \times \$.50)$	+	$(5,400 \times \$1.48)$
Total costs	$805,600				

Work in Process Inventory Account: Cost Recap

Beg. Bal.	$ 19,900	$786,808 (cost of goods manufactured and transferred out)	
Direct Materials	$202,500		
Conversion Costs	$583,200		
End. Bal.	$18,792		

Work in Process Inventory Account: Unit Recap

Beg. Bal.	16,000	399,400 (FIFO units transferred out from the 16,000 in beginning inventory plus the 383,400 started and completed)
Direct Materials and Conversion Costs	405,000	
End. Bal.	21,600	

2. The amount of $786,808 should be transferred to the Work in Process Inventory account of the Packaging Department.

Chapter Assignments

BUILDING YOUR KNOWLEDGE FOUNDATION

QUESTIONS

1. How do managers in manufacturing and service organizations use cost information during the planning stage of the management cycle?
2. Managers use cost information to support their decision making during the executing stage of the management cycle. What kinds of decisions do they make at this stage?
3. How do managers use cost information during the reviewing stage of the management cycle?
4. What is a product costing system?
5. What is a job order costing system? Identify the kinds of companies that use such a system.

6. What is a job order?

7. What are the main similarities and differences between a job order costing system and a process costing system? (Focus on the characteristics of each type of system.)

8. What is the purpose of the Work in Process Inventory account?

9. Why is the Manufacturing Overhead account reconciled at the end of an accounting period?

10. What is the purpose of a job order cost card? Identify the kinds of information recorded on that document.

11. How is product unit cost in a job order costing system computed? How are the necessary data accumulated?

12. How do the costs of a service organization and a manufacturing organization differ? How do these differences affect the job order costing system of a service organization?

13. "In job order costing, only one Work in Process Inventory account is used for all jobs processed. In process costing, several Work in Process Inventory accounts are used." Explain these statements. Why does process costing require multiple Work in Process Inventory accounts?

14. What is *equivalent production* (also called *equivalent units*)?

15. Why must actual unit data be changed to equivalent unit data to cost products in a process costing system?

16. What are *conversion costs*? Why does a process costing system compute conversion costs?

17. What five steps does a process cost report entail?

18. What are the purposes of accounting for costs in a process cost report?

19. What two important dollar amounts come from the assignment of costs in Step 5 of a process cost report? How do they relate to the year-end financial statements?

20. What type of operating performance can be evaluated with the information that a product costing system provides about (a) units produced per time period, (b) labor cost per unit produced, and (c) special needs of customers?

SHORT EXERCISES

LO1 Uses of Product Costing Information

SE 1. Shelley's Kennel provides boarding for dogs and cats. Shelley, the owner of the kennel, must make several business decisions in the near future. Write *yes* or *no* to indicate whether knowing the cost to board one animal per day (i.e., the product unit cost) can help Shelley answer the following questions:

1. Is the boarding fee high enough to cover the kennel's costs?
2. How much profit will the kennel make if it boards an average of 10 dogs per day for 50 weeks?
3. What costs can be reduced to make the kennel's boarding fee competitive with that of its competitor?

LO2 Companies That Use Job Order Costing

SE 2. Write *yes* or *no* to indicate whether each of the following companies would typically use a job order costing system:

1. Soft drink producer
2. Jeans manufacturer
3. Submarine contractor
4. Office building contractor
5. Stuffed toy maker

LO2 Job Order Versus Process Costing Systems

SE 3. State whether a job order costing system or a process costing system would typically be used to account for the costs of the following:

1. Manufacturing cat collars
2. Manufacturing custom-designed fencing for outdoor breeding kennels
3. Providing pet grooming
4. Manufacturing one-gallon aquariums
5. Manufacturing dog food
6. Providing veterinary services

SE 4.

LO3   Transactions in a Manufacturer's Job Order Costing System

For each of the following transactions, state which account(s) would be affected in a job order costing system:

1. Purchased materials, $12,890
2. Charged direct labor to production, $3,790
3. Requested direct materials for production, $6,800
4. Applied manufacturing overhead to jobs in process, $3,570

SE 5.

LO3   Transactions in a Manufacturer's Job Order Costing System

Enter the following transactions into T accounts:

1. Incurred $34,000 of direct labor and $18,000 of indirect labor
2. Applied manufacturing overhead based on 12,680 labor hours @ $6.50 per labor hour

SE 6.

LO3   Accounts for Job Order Costing

Identify the accounts in which each of the following transactions for Dom's Furniture, a custom manufacturer of oak tables and chairs, would be recorded:

1. Issued oak materials into production for Job ABC
2. Recorded direct labor time for the first week in February for Job ABC
3. Received indirect materials from a vendor
4. Received a production-related electricity bill
5. Applied manufacturing overhead to Job ABC
6. Completed but did not yet sell Job ABC

SE 7.

LO3   Computation of Product Unit Cost

Complete the following job order cost card for six custom-built computer systems:

Job Order ___168___

JOB ORDER COST CARD
Keeper 3000
Apache City, North Dakota

Customer: _Brian Patcher_   Batch: _____   Custom: _X_

Specifications: _6 Custom Computer Systems_

Date of Order: _4/4/x7_   Date of Completion: _6/8/x7_

Costs Charged to Job	Previous Months	Current Month	Cost Summary
Direct materials	$3,540	$2,820	$___
Direct labor	2,340	1,620	___
Manufacturing overhead applied	2,880	2,550	___
Totals	$___	$___	$___
Units completed			___
Product unit cost			$___

SE 8.

LO5   Equivalent Production: FIFO
LO6   Costing Method

Blue Blaze adds direct materials at the beginning of its production process and adds conversion costs uniformly throughout the process. Given the following information from Blue Blaze's records for July 20x7 and using Steps 1 and 2 of the FIFO costing method, compute the equivalent units of production:

Units in beginning inventory	3,000
Units started during the period	17,000
Units partially completed	2,500
Percentage of completion of ending work in process inventory	70%
Percentage of completion of beginning inventory	100% for direct materials; 40% for conversion costs

SE 9.

LO6   Determining Unit Cost: FIFO Costing Method

Using the information from **SE 8** and the following data, compute the total cost per equivalent unit:

	Costs for the Period	Beginning Work in Process
Direct materials costs	$20,400	$7,600
Conversion costs	32,490	2,545

SE 10.

LO7   Measuring Performance with Product Costing Data

The following table presents the weekly average of direct materials costs per unit for two products. How could the manager of the department that makes these products use this information?

Week	Product A	Product B
1	$45.20	$23.90
2	46.10	23.80
3	48.30	23.80
4	49.60	23.60

EXERCISES

E 1.

LO2   Product Costing

Anniversary Printing Company specializes in wedding invitations. Anniversary needs information to budget next year's activities. Write *yes* or *no* to indicate whether each of the following costs is likely to be available in the company's product costing system:

1. Cost of paper and envelopes
2. Printing machine setup costs
3. Depreciation of printing machinery
4. Advertising costs
5. Repair costs for printing machinery
6. Costs to deliver stationery to customers
7. Office supplies costs
8. Costs to design a wedding invitation
9. Cost of ink
10. Sales commissions

E 2.

LO2   Costing Systems: Industry Linkage

Which of the following products would typically be accounted for using a job order costing system? Which would be accounted for using a process costing system? (a) Paint, (b) jelly beans, (c) jet aircraft, (d) bricks, (e) large milling machines, (f) liquid detergent, (g) aluminum compressed-gas cylinders of standard size and capacity, and (h) aluminum compressed-gas cylinders with a special fiberglass wrap for a Mount Everest expedition.

E 3.

LO3   Work in Process Inventory: T Account Analysis

On June 30, Specialty Company's Work in Process Inventory account showed a beginning balance of $29,400. Production activity for July was as follows: Direct materials costing $238,820 were requested for production; total manufacturing payroll was $140,690, of which $52,490 was used to pay for indirect labor; indirect materials costing $28,400 were purchased and used; and manufacturing overhead was applied at a rate of 150 percent of direct labor costs.

1. Record Specialty's materials, labor, and manufacturing overhead costs for July in T accounts.
2. Compute the ending balance in the Work in Process Inventory account. Assume a transfer of $461,400 to the Finished Goods Inventory account during the period.

E 4.

LO3   T Account Analysis with Unknowns

Partial operating data for Starke Company are presented below. Management has set the predetermined overhead rate for the current year at 80 percent of direct labor costs.

Account/Transaction	December
Beginning Materials Inventory	$ 42,000
Beginning Work in Process Inventory	66,000
Beginning Finished Goods Inventory	29,000
Direct materials used	168,000
Direct materials purchased	a
Direct labor costs	382,000
Manufacturing overhead applied	b
Cost of units completed	c
Cost of goods sold	808,000

Ending Materials Inventory	38,000	
Ending Work in Process Inventory	138,600	
Ending Finished Goods Inventory	d	

Using T accounts and the data provided, compute the unknown values. Show all your computations.

LO3 Job Order Cost Card and Computation of Product Unit Cost

E 5. During January, the Cabinet Company worked on six different job orders for specialty kitchen cabinets. It began Job A-62 for Thomas Cabinets, Inc., on January 10 and completed the job on January 24. Partial data for Job A-62 are as follows:

	Costs	Machine Hours Used
Direct materials		
Cedar	$7,900	
Pine	6,320	
Hardware	2,930	
Assembly supplies	988	
Direct labor		
Sawing	$2,840	120
Shaping	2,200	220
Finishing	2,250	180
Assembly	2,890	50

The Cabinet Company produced a total of 34 cabinets for Job A-62. Its current predetermined manufacturing overhead rate is $21.60 per machine hour. From the information given, prepare a job order cost card and compute the job order's product unit cost. (Round to whole dollars.)

LO3 Computation of Product Unit Cost

E 6. Wild Things, Inc., manufactures custom-made stuffed animals. Last month, the company produced 4,540 stuffed bears with stethoscopes for the local children's hospital to sell at a fundraising event.

Using job order costing, determine the product unit cost of a stuffed bear based on the following costs incurred during the month: manufacturing utilities, $500; depreciation on manufacturing equipment, $450; indirect materials, $300; direct materials, $1,300; indirect labor, $800; direct labor, $2,400; sales commissions, $3,000; president's salary, $4,000; insurance on manufacturing plant, $600; advertising expense, $500; rent on manufacturing plant, $5,000; rent on sales office, $4,000; and legal expense, $250. Carry your answer to two decimal places.

LO3 Computation of Product Unit Cost

E 7. Style Corporation manufactures specialty lines of women's apparel. During February, the company worked on three special orders: A-25, A-27, and B-14. Cost and production data for each order are as follows:

	Job A-25	Job A-27	Job B-14
Direct materials			
Fabric Q	$10,840	$12,980	$17,660
Fabric Z	11,400	12,200	13,440
Fabric YB	5,260	6,920	10,900
Direct labor			
Garment maker	8,900	10,400	16,200
Layout	6,450	7,425	9,210
Packaging	3,950	4,875	6,090
Manufacturing overhead (120% of direct labor costs)	?	?	?
Number of units produced	700	775	1,482

1. Compute the total cost associated with each job. Show the subtotals for each cost category.
2. Compute the product unit cost for each job. (Round your computations to the nearest cent.)

LO3 Job Order Costing in a Service Organization

E 8. A job order cost card for Personal Trainers, Inc., appears at the top of the next page. Compute the missing information.

Job Order   H.W.

JOB ORDER COST CARD
Personal Trainers, Inc.

Customer: Hillary White   Batch: _____   Custom: X

Specifications: Marathon Training

Date of Order: 4/2/xx   Date of Completion: 7/24/xx

Costs Charged to Job	Previous Months	Current Month	Total
In-person consultation			
Training logbook	$ 20.00	$ 0	$20.00
Labor ($10 per hour)	20.00	?	50.00
Overhead (10% of in-person labor costs)	?	3.00	5.00
Total	$?	$?	$?
Training			
Bike rental	$ 30.00	$?	$60.00
Labor ($5 per hour)	150.00	300.00	?
Overhead (25% of labor costs)	37.50	?	?
Total	$?	$?	$?
Telephone consultations			
Cell phone calls ($1 per call)	$ 30.00	$ 10.00	?
Labor ($10 per hour)	10.00	10.00	?
Overhead (50% of telephone labor costs)	?	?	?
Total	$?	$?	$?
Total cost			$?

Job Revenue and Profit

Logbook and bike rental	$?
Service fee: 97 hours* $\times$ $30	?
Job revenue	$2,990.00
Less total cost	?
Profit	$2,222.50

*5 + 90 + 2 = 97 hours

E 9.

LO5   Equivalent Production:
LO6   FIFO Costing Method

McCabe Stone Company produces bricks. Though the company has been in operation for only twelve months, it already enjoys a good reputation. During its first year, it put 600,000 bricks into production and completed and transferred 586,000 bricks to finished goods inventory. The remaining bricks were still in process at the end of the year and were 60 percent complete. The company's process costing system adds all direct materials costs at the beginning of the process; conversion costs are incurred uniformly throughout the production process. From this information, compute the equivalent units of production for direct materials and conversion costs for the company's first year, which ended December 31, 20x7. Use the FIFO costing approach.

E 10.

LO5   Equivalent Production:
LO6   FIFO Costing Method

Olivares Enterprises makes Rainberry Shampoo for professional hair stylists. On July 31, 20x5, it had 5,200 liters of shampoo in process, which were 80 percent complete in regard to conversion costs and 100 percent complete in regard to direct materials costs. During August, it put 212,500 liters of direct materials into production. Data for work in process inventory on August 31, 20x5, were as follows: shampoo, 4,500 liters; stage of completion, 60 percent for conversion costs and 100 percent for direct materials.

From this information, compute the equivalent units of production for direct materials and conversion costs for the month. Use the FIFO costing approach.

LO5 Equivalent Production:
LO6 FIFO Costing Method

E 11. Cunningham Paper Corporation produces wood pulp that is used in making paper. The following data pertain to the company's production of pulp during September:

		Percentage Complete	
	Tons	Direct Materials	Conversion Costs
Work in process, Aug. 31	40,000	100%	60%
Placed into production	250,000	—	—
Work in process, Sept. 30	80,000	100%	40%

Compute the equivalent units of production for direct materials and conversion costs for September using the FIFO costing method.

LO6 Work in Process Inventory
Accounts: Total Unit Cost

E 12. Scientists at Anschultz Laboratories, Inc., have just perfected Dentalite, a liquid substance that dissolves tooth decay. The substance, which is generated by a complex process involving five departments, is very expensive. Cost and equivalent unit data for the latest week are as follows (units are in ounces):

	Direct Materials Costs		Conversion Costs	
Dept.	Dollars	Equivalent Units	Dollars	Equivalent Units
A	$12,000	1,000	$33,825	2,050
B	21,835	1,985	13,065	1,005
C	23,896	1,030	20,972	2,140
D	—	—	22,086	2,045
E	—	—	15,171	1,945

From these data, compute the unit cost for each department and the total unit cost of producing one ounce of Dentalite.

LO6 Determining Unit Cost:
FIFO Costing Method

E 13. Turner's Pots, Inc., manufactures sets of heavy-duty cookware. It has just completed production for August 20x2. At the beginning of August, its Work in Process Inventory account showed direct materials costs of $31,700 and conversion costs of $29,400. The cost of direct materials used in August was $275,373; conversion costs were $175,068. During the month, the company started and completed 15,190 sets. For August, a total of 16,450 equivalent sets for direct materials and 16,210 equivalent sets for conversion costs have been computed.

From this information, determine the cost per equivalent unit for August. Use the FIFO costing method.

LO6 Assigning Costs: FIFO
Costing Method

E 14. The Beach Bakery produces Healthnut coffee bread. It uses a process costing system. In March 20x9, its beginning inventory was 450 units, which were 100 percent complete for direct materials costs and 10 percent complete for conversion costs. The cost of beginning inventory was $655. Units started and completed during the month totaled 14,200. Ending inventory was 410 units, which were 100 percent complete for direct materials costs and 70 percent complete for conversion costs. Costs per equivalent unit for March were $1.40 for direct materials costs and $.80 for conversion costs.

From this information, compute the cost of goods transferred to the Finished Goods Inventory account, the cost remaining in the Work in Process Inventory account, and the total costs to be accounted for. Use the FIFO costing method.

LO7 Measuring Performance with
Nonfinancial Product Data

E 15. During December, Carola Products Company conducted a study of the productivity of its metal-trimming operation, which requires the use of three machines. The data were condensed into product units per hour so that managers could analyze the productivity of the three workers who operate the machines. The target output established for the year was 125 units per hour.

From the following data, analyze the productivity of Carola Products' three machine operators:

Week	Operator 1	Operator 2	Operator 3
1	119 per hour	129 per hour	124 per hour
2	120 per hour	127 per hour	124 per hour
3	122 per hour	125 per hour	123 per hour
4	124 per hour	122 per hour	124 per hour

PROBLEMS

P 1.

LO3   T Account Analysis with Unknowns

Flagstaff Enterprises makes peripheral equipment for computers. Dana Dona, Flagstaff's new controller, can find only the following partial information for the past two months:

Account/Transaction	May	June
Materials Inventory, Beginning	$ 36,240	$ e
Work in Process Inventory, Beginning	56,480	f
Finished Goods Inventory, Beginning	44,260	g
Materials purchased	a	96,120
Direct materials requested	82,320	h
Direct labor costs	b	72,250
Manufacturing overhead applied	53,200	i
Cost of units completed	c	221,400
Cost of units sold	209,050	j
Materials Inventory, Ending	38,910	41,950
Work in Process Inventory, Ending	d	k
Finished Goods Inventory, Ending	47,940	51,180

The current year's predetermined overhead rate is 80 percent of direct labor cost.

REQUIRED ▶   Using the data provided and T accounts, compute the unknown values.

P 2.

LO3   Job Order Costing: T Account Analysis

Par Carts Manufacturing, Inc., produces electric golf carts. The carts are special-order items, so the company uses a job order costing system. Manufacturing overhead is applied at the rate of 90 percent of direct labor cost. The following is a list of transactions for January:

Jan.   1   Purchased direct materials on account, $215,400.
    2   Purchased indirect materials on account, $49,500.
    4   Requested direct materials costing $193,200 (all used on Job X) and indirect materials costing $38,100 for production.
    10   Paid the following manufacturing overhead costs: utilities, $4,400; manufacturing rent, $3,800; and maintenance charges, $3,900.
    15   Recorded the following gross wages and salaries for employees: direct labor, $120,000 (all for Job X) and indirect labor, $60,620.
    15   Applied manufacturing overhead to production.
    19   Purchased indirect materials costing $27,550 and direct materials costing $190,450 on account.
    21   Requested direct materials costing $214,750 (Job X, $178,170; Job Y, $18,170; Job Z, $18,410) and indirect materials costing $31,400 for production.
    31   Recorded the following gross wages and salaries for employees: direct labor, $132,000 (Job X, $118,500; Job Y, $7,000; Job Z, $6,500) and indirect labor, $62,240.
    31   Applied manufacturing overhead to production.
    31   Completed and transferred Job X (375 carts) and Job Y (10 carts) to finished goods inventory; total cost was $855,990.
    31   Shipped Job X to the customer; total production cost was $824,520 and sales invoice totaled $996,800.
    31   Recorded these manufacturing overhead costs (adjusting entries): prepaid insurance expired, $3,700; property taxes (payable at year end), $3,400; and depreciation, machinery, $15,500.

REQUIRED ▶   1. Record the entries for all transactions in January using T accounts for the following: Materials Inventory, Work in Process Inventory, Finished Goods Inventory, Manufacturing Overhead, Cash, Accounts Receivable, Prepaid Insurance, Accumulated Depreciation—Machinery, Accounts Payable, Factory Payroll, Property Taxes Payable, Sales, and Cost of Goods Sold. Use job order cost cards for Job X, Job Y, and Job Z. Determine the partial account balances. Assume no beginning inventory balances.

2. Compute the amount of underapplied or overapplied overhead as of January 31, and transfer it to the Cost of Goods Sold account.

3. Why should the Manufacturing Overhead account's underapplied or overapplied overhead be transferred to the Cost of Goods Sold account?

LO3   Job Order Cost Flow

P 3. On May 31, the inventory balances of Abbey Designs, a manufacturer of high-quality children's clothing, were as follows: Materials Inventory, $21,360; Work in Process Inventory, $15,112; and Finished Goods Inventory, $17,120. Job order cost cards for jobs in process as of June 30 had these totals:

Job No.	Direct Materials	Direct Labor	Manufacturing Overhead
24-A	$1,596	$1,290	$1,677
24-B	1,492	1,380	1,794
24-C	1,984	1,760	2,288
24-D	1,608	1,540	2,002

The predetermined overhead rate is 130 percent of direct labor cost. Materials purchased and received in June were as follows:

June 4 $33,120
June 16   28,600
June 22   31,920

Direct labor costs for June were as follows:

June 15 payroll $23,680
June 29 payroll   25,960

Direct materials requested by production during June were as follows:

June 6 $37,240
June 23   38,960

During June, Abbey Designs sold finished goods with a 75 percent markup over cost for $320,000.

REQUIRED ▶

1. Using T accounts for Materials Inventory, Work in Process Inventory, Finished Goods Inventory, Manufacturing Overhead, Accounts Receivable, Factory Payroll, Sales, and Cost of Goods Sold, reconstruct the transactions in June.
2. Compute the cost of units completed during the month.
3. What was the total cost of units sold during June?
4. Determine the ending inventory balances.
5. Jobs 24-A and 24-C were completed during the first week of July. No additional materials costs were incurred, but Job 24-A required $960 more of direct labor, and Job 24-C needed an additional $1,610 of direct labor. Job 24-A was composed of 1,200 pairs of trousers; Job 24-C, of 950 shirts. Compute the product unit cost for each job. (Round your answers to two decimal places.)

LO5   Process Costing: FIFO
LO6   Costing Method

P 4. Lightning Industries specializes in making Flash, a low-alkaline wax used to protect and preserve skis. The company began producing a new, improved brand of Flash on January 1, 20x5. Materials A-14 and C-9 and a wax base are introduced at the beginning of the production process. During January, 640 pounds of A-14, 1,860 pounds of C-9, and 12,800 pounds of wax base were used at costs of $15,300, $29,070, and $2,295, respectively. Direct labor of $17,136 and manufacturing overhead costs of $25,704 were incurred uniformly throughout the month. By January 31, 13,600 pounds of Flash had been completed and transferred to the finished goods inventory (one pound of input equals one pound of output). Since no spoilage occurred, the leftover materials remained in production and were 40 percent complete on average.

REQUIRED ▶

1. Using the FIFO costing method, prepare a process cost report for January.
2. From the information in the process cost report, identify the amount that should be transferred out of the Work in Process Inventory account, and state where those dollars should be transferred.

LO5   Process Costing: FIFO
LO6   Costing Method

P 5. Liquid Extracts Company produces a line of fruit extracts for home use in making wine, jams and jellies, pies, and meat sauces. Fruits enter the production process in pounds; the product emerges in quarts (one pound of input equals one quart of output). On May 31, 20x6, 4,250 units were in process. All direct materials had been added, and the units were 70 percent complete for conversion costs. Direct materials costs of $4,607 and conversion costs of $3,535 were attached to the units in beginning work in process inventory. During June, 61,300 pounds of fruit were added: 23,500 pounds of apples costing $20,915, 22,600 pounds of grapes costing $28,153, and 15,200 pounds of bananas costing $22,040. Direct labor for the month totaled $19,760, and overhead costs applied were $31,375. On June 30, 20x6, 3,400 units remained in process. All direct materials for these units had been added, and 50 percent of conversion costs had been incurred.

REQUIRED ▶
1. Using the FIFO costing method, prepare a process cost report for June.
2. From the information in the process cost report, identify the amount that should be transferred out of the Work in Process Inventory account, and state where those dollars should be transferred.

ALTERNATE PROBLEMS

P 6.

LO3   Job Order Cost Flow

Dori Hatami is the chief financial officer of Gotham Industries, a company that makes special-order printers for personal computers. Her records for February revealed the following information:

Beginning inventory balances	
Materials Inventory	$27,450
Work in Process Inventory	22,900
Finished Goods Inventory	19,200
Direct materials purchased and received	
February 6	$ 7,200
February 12	8,110
February 24	5,890
Direct labor costs	
February 14	$13,750
February 28	13,230
Direct materials requested for production	
February 4	$ 9,080
February 13	5,940
February 25	7,600

Job order cost cards for jobs in process on February 28 had the following totals:

Job No.	Direct Materials	Direct Labor	Manufacturing Overhead
AJ-10	$3,220	$1,810	$2,534
AJ-14	3,880	2,110	2,954
AJ-30	2,980	1,640	2,296
AJ-16	4,690	2,370	3,318

The predetermined manufacturing overhead rate for the month was 140 percent of direct labor costs. Sales for February totaled $152,400, which represented a 70 percent markup over the cost of production.

REQUIRED ▶
1. Using T accounts for Materials Inventory, Work in Process Inventory, Finished Goods Inventory, Manufacturing Overhead, Accounts Receivable, Factory Payroll, Sales, and Cost of Goods Sold, reconstruct the February transactions.
2. Compute the cost of units completed during the month.
3. What was the total cost of units sold during February?
4. Determine the ending balances in the inventory accounts.
5. During the first week of March, Jobs AJ-10 and AJ-14 were completed. No additional direct materials costs were incurred, but Job AJ-10 needed $720 more of direct labor, and Job AJ-14 needed an additional $1,140 of direct labor. Job AJ-10 was 40 units; Job AJ-14, 55 units. Compute the product unit cost for each completed job (round to two decimal places).

P 7.

LO3   Job Order Costing in a Service Organization

Peruga Engineering Company specializes in designing automated characters and displays for theme parks. It uses cost-plus profit contracts, and its profit factor is 30 percent of total cost. A job order costing system is used to track the costs of developing each job. Costs are accumulated for three primary activities: bid and proposal, design, and prototype development. Current service overhead rates based on engineering hours are as follows: bid and proposal, $18 per hour; design, $22 per hour; and prototype development, $20 per hour. Supplies are treated as direct materials, traceable to each job. Peruga worked on jobs P-12, P-15, and P-19 during January. The following table shows the costs for those jobs:

	P-12	P-15	P-19
Beginning Balances			
Bid and proposal	$2,460	$2,290	$ 940
Design	1,910	460	0
Prototype development	2,410	1,680	0
Costs During January			
Bid and proposal			
Supplies	0	$ 280	$2,300
Labor: hours	12	20	68
dollars	$ 192	$ 320	$1,088
Design			
Supplies	$ 400	$ 460	$ 290
Labor: hours	64	42	26
dollars	$1,280	$ 840	$ 520
Prototype development			
Special materials	$6,744	$7,216	$2,400
Labor: hours	120	130	25
dollars	$2,880	$3,120	$ 600

REQUIRED ▶

1. Using the format shown in Figure 3, create the job order cost card for each of the three jobs.
2. Peruga completed Jobs P-12 and P-15, and the customers approved of the prototype products. Customer A plans to produce 12 special characters using the design and specifications created by Job P-12. Customer B plans to make 18 displays from the design developed by Job P-15. What dollar amount will each customer use as the cost of design for each of those products (i.e., what is the product unit cost for Jobs P-12 and P-15)? Round to the nearest dollar.
3. What is the January ending balance of Peruga's Contract in Process account for the three jobs?
4. Rank the jobs in order of most costly to least costly based on each job's total cost. From the rankings of cost, what observations can you make?
5. Speculate on the price Peruga should charge for such jobs.

P 8.

LO5 Process Costing: FIFO
LO6 Costing Method

Canned fruits and vegetables are the main products made by Good Foods, Inc. All direct materials are added at the beginning of the Mixing Department's process. When the ingredients have been mixed, they go to the Cooking Department. There the mixture is heated to 100° Celsius and simmered for 20 minutes. When cooled, the mixture goes to the Canning Department for final processing. Throughout the operations, direct labor and manufacturing overhead costs are incurred uniformly. No direct materials are added in the Cooking Department.

Cost data and other information for the Mixing Department for January 20x8 are as follows:

Production Cost Data	Direct Materials Costs	Conversion Costs
Mixing Department		
Beginning inventory	$ 28,560	$ 5,230
Current period costs	$450,000	$181,200
Work in process inventory		
Beginning inventory		
Mixing Department (40% complete)	5,000 liters	
Ending inventory		
Mixing Department (60% complete)	6,000 liters	
Unit production data		
Units started during January	90,000 liters	
Units transferred out during January	89,000 liters	

Assume that Good Foods, Inc., experienced no spoilage or evaporation loss during the month of January.

REQUIRED ▶   1. Using the FIFO costing method, prepare a process cost report for the Mixing Department for January.
2. Explain how the analysis for the Cooking Department will differ from the analysis for the Mixing Department.

SKILLS DEVELOPMENT CASES

Conceptual Analysis

SD 1.

LO1   Business Plans

In the past 20 years, Fortune 500 companies have eliminated over 5 million jobs, and yet the U.S. economy has grown by almost 30 million jobs. New businesses have created most of the new employment. A key step in starting a new business is a realistic analysis of the people, opportunities, context, risks, and rewards of the venture and the formulation of a business plan. Notice the similarities between the questions accountants answer in the management cycle and the nine questions every great business plan should answer:[4]

- Who is the new company's customer?
- How does the customer make decisions about buying this product or service?
- To what degree is the product or service a compelling purchase for the customer?
- How will the product or service be priced?
- How will the company reach all the identified customer segments?
- How much does it cost (in time and resources) to acquire a customer?
- How much does it cost to produce and deliver the product or service?
- How much does it cost to support a customer?
- How easy is it to retain a customer?

Assume a new business has hired you as a consultant because of your knowledge of the management cycle. Write a memo that discusses how the nine questions fit into the management cycle.

SD 2.

LO4   Concept of Process Costing Systems

For more than 60 years, Dow Chemical Company <www.dow.com> has made and sold a tasteless, odorless, and calorie-free substance called Methocel. When heated, this liquid plastic (methyl cellulose) has the unusual characteristic (for plastics) of becoming a gel that resembles cooked egg whites. It is used in over 400 food products, including gravies, soups, and puddings. It was also used as wampa drool in *The Empire Strikes Back* and dinosaur sneeze in *Jurassic Park*. What kind of costing system is most appropriate for the manufacture of Methocel? Why is that system most appropriate? Describe the system; include in the description a general explanation of how costs are determined.

Ethical Dilemma

SD 3.

LO3   Costing Procedures and Ethics

Jennifer Martin, the production manager of Fabricated Products Company, entered the office of controller Joe Barnes and asked, "Joe, what gives here? I was charged for 330 direct labor hours on Job AD22, and my records show that we spent only 290 hours on that job. That 40-hour difference caused the total cost of direct labor and manufacturing overhead for the job to increase by over $5,500. Are my records wrong, or was there an error in the direct labor assigned to the job?"

Barnes replied, "Don't worry about it, Jennifer. This job won't be used in your quarterly performance evaluation. Job AD22 was a federal government job, a cost-plus contract, so the more costs we assign to it, the more profit we make. We decided to add a few hours to the job in case there is some follow-up work to do. You know how fussy the feds are."

What should Martin do? Discuss Barnes's costing procedure.

Research Activity

LO3 Job Order Costing

SD 4. Many businesses accumulate costs for each job performed. Examples of businesses that use a job order costing system include print shops, car repair shops, health clinics, and kennels.

Visit a local business that uses job order costing, and interview the owner, manager, or accountant about the process and the documents the business uses to accumulate product costs. Write a paper that summarizes the information you obtained. Include the following in your summary:

1. The name of the business and the type of operations performed
2. The name and position of the individual you interviewed
3. A description of the process of starting and completing a job
4. A description of the accounting process and the documents used to track a job
5. Your responses to these questions:

    a. Did the person you interviewed know the actual amount of materials, labor, and overhead charged to a particular job? If the job includes some estimated costs, how are the estimates calculated? Do the costs affect the determination of the selling price of the product or service?

    b. Compare the documents discussed in this chapter with the documents used by the company you visited. How are they similar, and how are they different?

    c. In your opinion, does the business record and accumulate its product costs effectively? Explain your answer.

 Group Activity: Group students according to the type of business they selected and ask them to discuss their responses to the questions in **5**.

Decision-Making Practice

LO4 Setting a Selling Price
LO5
LO6
LO7

SD 5. For the past four years, three companies have dominated the soft drink industry, holding a combined 85 percent of market share. Wonder Cola, Inc., ranks second nationally in soft drink sales; it had gross revenues of $27,450,000 last year. Its management is thinking about introducing a new low-calorie drink called Zero Cola.

Wonder soft drinks are processed in a single department. All ingredients are added at the beginning of the process. At the end of the process, the beverage is poured into bottles that cost $.24 per case produced. Direct labor and manufacturing overhead costs are applied uniformly throughout the process.

Corporate controller Adam Daneen believes that costs for the new cola will be very much like those for the company's Cola Plus drink. Last year (20x8), he collected the following data about Cola Plus:

	Units*	Costs
Work in process inventory		
December 31, 20x7†	2,200	
Direct materials costs		$ 2,080
Conversion costs		620
December 31, 20x8‡	2,000	
Direct materials costs		1,880
Conversion costs		600
Units started during 20x8	458,500	
Costs for 20x8		
Liquid materials added		430,990
Direct labor and manufacturing overhead		229,400
Bottles		110,068

*Each unit is a 24-bottle case.

†50% complete.

‡60% complete.

The company's variable general administrative and selling costs are $1.10 per unit. Fixed administrative and selling costs are assigned to products at the rate of $.50 per unit. Each of Wonder Cola's two main competitors is already marketing a diet cola. Company A's product sells for $4.10 per unit; Company B's, for $4.05. All costs are expected to increase by 10 percent in the next three years. Wonder Cola tries to earn a profit of at least 15 percent on the total unit cost.

1. What factors should Wonder Cola, Inc., consider in setting a unit selling price for a case of Zero Cola?
2. Using the FIFO costing approach, compute (a) equivalent units for direct materials, cases of bottles, and conversion costs; (b) the total production cost per unit; and (c) the total cost per unit of Cola Plus for 20x8.
3. What is the expected unit cost of Zero Cola for 20x9?
4. Recommend a unit selling price range for a case of Zero Cola for 20x9, and give the reason(s) for your choice.

MANAGERIAL REPORTING AND ANALYSIS CASES

Interpreting Management Reports

MRA 1.

LO1   **Interpreting Nonfinancial**
LO7   **Data**

Eagle Manufacturing supplies engine parts to Cherokee Cycle Company, a major U.S. manufacturer of motorcycles. Like all of Cherokee's other suppliers, Eagle has always added a healthy profit margin to its cost when quoting selling prices to Cherokee. Recently, however, several companies have offered to supply engine parts to Cherokee for lower prices than Eagle has been charging.

Because Eagle Manufacturing wants to keep Cherokee Cycle Company's business, a team of Eagle's managers analyzed their company's product costs and decided to make minor changes in the company's manufacturing process. No new equipment was purchased, and no additional labor was required. Instead, the machines were rearranged, and some of the work was reassigned.

To monitor the effectiveness of the changes, Eagle Manufacturing introduced three new performance measures to its information system: inventory levels, lead time (total time required for a part to move through the production process), and productivity (number of parts manufactured per employee per day). The company's goal was to reduce the quantities of the first two performance measures and to increase the quantity of the third.

A section of a recent management report, shown below, summarizes the quantities for each performance measure before and after the changes in the manufacturing process were made.

Measure	Before	After	Improvement
Inventory in dollars	$21,444	$10,772	50%
Lead time in minutes	17	11	35
Productivity			
(parts per person per day)	515	1,152	124

1. Do you believe Eagle improved the quality of its manufacturing process and the quality of its engine parts? Explain your answer.
2. Can Eagle lower its selling price to Cherokee? Explain your answer.
3. Did the introduction of the new measures affect the design of the product costing system? Explain your answer.
4. Do you believe that the new measures caused a change in Eagle's cost per engine part? If so, how did they cause the change?

MRA 2.

LO5   **Analysis of Product Cost**
LO6
LO7

Ready Tire Corporation makes several lines of automobile and truck tires. The company operates in a competitive marketplace, so it relies heavily on cost data from its FIFO-based process costing system. It uses that information to set prices for its most competitive tires. The company's radial line has lost some of its market share during each of the past four years. Management believes that price breaks allowed by the company's three biggest competitors are the main reason for the decline in sales.

The company controller, Sara Birdsong, has been asked to review the product costing information that supports price decisions on the radial line. In preparing her report, she collected the following data for 20x8, the most recent full year of operations:

		Units	Dollars
Equivalent units:	Direct materials costs	84,200	
	Conversion costs	82,800	
Manufacturing costs:	Direct materials		$1,978,700
	Direct labor		800,400
	Manufacturing overhead		1,600,800
Unit cost data:	Direct materials costs		23.50
	Conversion costs		29.00
Work in process inventory:	Beginning (70% complete)	4,200	
	Ending (30% complete)	3,800	

Units started and completed during 20x8 totaled 80,400. Attached to the beginning Work in Process Inventory account were direct materials costs of $123,660 and conversion costs of $57,010. Birdsong found that little spoilage had occurred. The proper cost allowance for spoilage was included in the predetermined overhead rate of $2 per direct labor dollar. The review of direct labor cost revealed, however, that $90,500 had been charged twice to the production account, the second time in error. This resulted in overly high overhead costs being charged to the production account.

So far in 20x9, the radial has sold for $92 per tire. This price was based on the 20x8 unit data plus a 75 percent markup to cover operating costs and profit. During 20x9, Ready Tire's three main competitors have charged about $87 for a tire of comparable quality. The company's process costing system adds all direct materials at the beginning of the process, and conversion costs are incurred uniformly throughout the process.

1. Identify what inaccuracies in costs, inventories, and selling prices result from the company's cost-charging error.
2. Prepare a revised process cost report for 20x8.
3. What should have been the minimum selling price per tire in 20x9?
4. Suggest ways of preventing such errors in the future.

Formulating Management Reports

MRA 3.

LO4   **Using the Process Costing**
LO5   **System**
LO6
LO7

You are the production manager for Great Grain Corporation, a manufacturer of four cereal products. The company's best-selling product is Smackaroos, a sugar-coated puffed rice cereal. Yesterday, Clark Winslow, the controller, reported that the production cost for each box of Smackaroos has increased approximately 22 percent in the past four months. Because the company is unable to increase the selling price for a box of Smackaroos, the increased production costs will reduce profits significantly.

Today, you received a memo from Gilbert Rom, the company president, asking you to review your production process to identify inefficiencies or waste that can be eliminated. Once you have completed your analysis, you are to write a memo presenting your findings and suggesting ways to reduce or eliminate the problems. The president will use your information during a meeting with the top management team in ten days.

You are aware of previous problems in the Baking Department and the Packaging Department. At your request, Winslow has provided you with process cost reports for the two departments. He has also given you the following detailed summary of the cost per equivalent unit for a box of Smackaroos cereal:

	April	May	June	July
Baking Department				
Direct materials	$1.25	$1.26	$1.24	$1.25
Direct labor	.50	.61	.85	.90
Manufacturing overhead	.25	.31	.34	.40
Department totals	$2.00	$2.18	$2.43	$2.55
Packaging Department				
Direct materials	$ .35	$ .34	$ .33	$ .33
Direct labor	.05	.05	.04	.06
Manufacturing overhead	.10	.16	.15	.12
Department totals	$ .50	$ .55	$ .52	$ .51
Total cost per equivalent unit	$2.50	$2.73	$2.95	$3.06

REQUIRED ▶

1. In preparation for writing your memo, answer the following questions:

    a. For whom are you preparing the memo? Does this affect the length of the memo? Explain.

    b. Why are you preparing the memo?

    c. What actions should you take to gather information for the memo? What information is needed? Is the information that Winslow provided sufficient for analysis and reporting?

    d. When is the memo due? What can be done to provide accurate, reliable, and timely information?

2. Based on your analysis of the information that Winslow provided, where is the main problem in the production process?

3. Prepare an outline of the sections you would want in your memo.

International Company

MRA 4.

LO1 **Process Costing and Work in**
LO4 **Process Inventory Accounts**

SvenskStål, AB, is a steel-producing company located in Solentuna, Sweden. The company originally produced only specialty steel products that were made to order for customers. A job order product costing system is used for the made-to-order products. This year, after purchasing three continuous processing work cells, the company created a new division that produces three types of sheet steel in continuous rolls. Ingrid Bjorn, the company controller, has redesigned the management accounting system to accommodate these changes and has installed a process costing system for the new division.

At a recent meeting of the company's executive committee, Bjorn explained that the new product costing system uses three new Work in Process Inventory accounts, one for each of the three work cells. Lars Karlsson, the production superintendent, questioned the need to change product costing approaches and did not understand why so many new Work in Process Inventory accounts were necessary.

Why did Bjorn install a process costing system in the new division? Was a new division necessary, or could the three new work cells have been merged with the specialty production facilities? Why were three new Work in Process Inventory accounts required? Could the single Work in Process Inventory account used for the specialty orders have tracked and accumulated the costs incurred in the three new work cells?

Excel Spreadsheet Analysis

MRA 5.

LO3 **Job Order Costing in a**
     Service Organization

Refer to assignment **P 7** in this chapter. Peruga Engineering Company needs to analyze its jobs in process during the month of January.

1. Using the Chart Wizard and the job order cost cards that you created for Jobs P-12, P-15, and P-19, prepare a bar chart that compares the bid and proposal costs, design costs, and prototype development costs of the jobs. Below is the suggested format to use for the information table necessary to complete the bar chart.

	A	B	C	D
1		P-12	P-15	P-19
2	Bid and proposal			
3	Design			
4	Prototype development			
5	Total job cost			

2. Examine the chart you prepared in **1**. List some reasons for the differences between the costs of the various jobs.

Internet Case

MRA 6.

LO4 **Comparison of Companies**
     That Use Process Costing
     Systems

A Focus on Business Practice box in this chapter lists many companies for which process costing systems are appropriate. Access the web sites of at least two of these companies. Find as much information as you can about the products the companies make and how they make them, including the manufacturing processes involved. For which products would process costing be most appropriate? For which products would it be inappropriate? Identify differences in the nature of the business conducted by the companies you chose. Do you think those differences have any bearing on the type of product costing system the company uses? Explain your reasoning. Do the companies make any products that might require a costing system other than process costing? Be prepared to present the results of your research in class.

22

Chapter 22 describes activity-based management and the just-in-time operating philosophy, demonstrating how these two activity-based systems help managers improve operating processes and make better pricing decisions.

Activity-Based Systems: ABM and JIT

LEARNING OBJECTIVES

LO1 Explain the role of activity-based systems in the management cycle.

LO2 Define *activity-based management (ABM)* and discuss its relationship to the supply chain and the value chain.

LO3 Distinguish between value-adding and nonvalue-adding activities, and describe process value analysis.

LO4 Define *activity-based costing* and explain how a cost hierarchy and a bill of activities are used.

LO5 Define the *just-in-time (JIT) operating philosophy* and identify the elements of a JIT operating environment.

LO6 Identify the changes in product costing that result when a firm adopts a JIT operating environment.

LO7 Define and apply *backflush costing*, and compare the cost flows in traditional and backflush costing.

LO8 Compare ABM and JIT as activity-based systems.

DECISION POINT

A MANAGER'S FOCUS

England, Inc. England, Inc., is a division of La-Z-Boy, Inc. <www.lazboy.com>. A critical factor in the success of this company is the speed of its value chain. England makes about 11,000 built-to-order sofas and chairs each week in its Tennessee plant, and it generally delivers them less than three weeks after customers have placed their orders with a retailer. This is quite a feat, especially since the company offers 85 styles of sofas and a choice of 550 fabrics. It also gives England, Inc., a competitive advantage. How does the company maintain this advantage?

England's managers use activity-based management (ABM) and a just-in-time (JIT) operating environment to identify and reduce or eliminate activities that do not add value to the company's products. These systems focus on minimizing waste, reducing costs, improving the allocation of resources, and ensuring that suppliers deliver materials just at the time a company needs them. They help managers make better decisions about costing and pricing products, adding or dropping product styles, changing production and delivery systems, and contracting with suppliers. The continuous flow of information that ABM and JIT provide has enabled England's managers to improve production processes; for example, they are able to adjust labor needs each week to meet order requirements. It has also enabled them to schedule timely deliveries from suppliers and thus maintain appropriate inventory levels, as well as to keep track of England's own fleet of delivery trucks.

England's disciplined monitoring of order, production, and delivery activities is the factor that gives it a

How have ABM and JIT helped England, Inc.'s managers to improve production processes and reduce delivery time?

competitive edge. By using ABM and JIT, England has achieved higher productivity than other furniture manufacturers, is able to offer more than 40,000 product variations, and over five years has cut its delivery time by one-half to one-third.[1]

ACTIVITY-BASED SYSTEMS AND MANAGEMENT

www.dell.com

Many companies operate in volatile business environments that are strongly influenced by customer demands. Managers know that customers buy value, usually in the form of quality products or services that are delivered on a timely basis for a reasonable price. Companies generate revenue when customers see value and buy their products or services. Thus, companies measure value as revenue (customer value = revenue generated).

Value exists when some characteristic of a product or service satisfies customers' wants or needs. For example, customers who appreciate convenience are an important market segment for Dell Computer Corporation. In response to their needs, Dell creates value and increases revenue by selling customized computer systems that include the latest microprocessor, monitor, graphics card, CD-ROM or DVD drive, sound card, modem, speakers, and preinstalled software products.

Creating value by satisfying customers' needs for quality, reasonable price, and timely delivery requires that managers do the following:

- Work with suppliers and customers.
- View the organization as a collection of value-adding activities.
- Use resources for value-adding activities.
- Reduce or eliminate nonvalue-adding activities.
- Know the total cost of creating value for a customer.

If an organization's business plan focuses on providing products or services that customers esteem, then managers will work with suppliers and customers to find ways of improving quality, reducing costs, and shortening delivery time. Managers will also focus their attention internally to find the best ways of using resources to create and maintain the value of their products or services. This requires matching resources to the operating activities that add value to a product or service. Managers will examine all business activities, including research and development, purchasing, production, storing, selling, shipping, and customer service, so that they can allocate resources effectively. In addition, managers need to know the **full product cost**, which includes not only the costs of direct materials and direct labor, but also the costs of all production and nonproduction activities required to satisfy the customer. For example, the full product cost of a Dell computer system includes the cost of the computer components and software, as well as the costs of taking the sales order, processing the order, packaging and shipping the system, and providing subsequent customer service for warranty work and software upgrades. If the activities are executed well and in agreement with the business plan, and if costs are assigned fairly, the company can improve product pricing and quality, increase productivity, and generate revenues (value) and profits.

ACTIVITY-BASED SYSTEMS

Organizations that focus on customers design their accounting information systems to provide customer-related, activity-based information. **Activity-based systems** are information systems that provide quantitative information about an organization's activities. They create opportunities to improve the cost information supplied to managers. They also help managers view their organization as a collection of activities. Activity-based cost information helps managers improve operating processes and make better pricing decisions.

Activity-based systems developed because traditional accounting systems failed to produce the types of information today's managers need for decision making. Traditional systems focused primarily on measurements needed for financial reporting and auditing, such as the measurement of cost of goods sold and the valuation

● **STOP AND THINK!**
What is the main focus of an activity-based system?
An activity-based system's main focus is on managing activities rather than costs. ■

of inventory. Because they were not designed to capture data on activities or to trace the full cost of a product, these systems could not isolate the cost of unnecessary activities, penalize for overproduction, or quantify measures that improved quality or reduced throughput time.

In this chapter, we explore two types of activity-based systems—activity-based management (ABM) and the just-in-time (JIT) operating environment—and consider how they affect product costing. Both systems help organizations manage activities, not costs, but by managing activities, organizations can reduce or eliminate many nonvalue-adding activities, which leads to reduced costs and hence to increased income.

KEY POINT: ABM and JIT focus on value-adding activities—not costs—to increase income.

USING ACTIVITY-BASED COST INFORMATION IN THE MANAGEMENT CYCLE

In this section, we look at the ways in which managers use activity-based cost information to answer basic questions during the management cycle. Figure 1 summarizes those uses.

■ **PLANNING** In the planning stage, managers want answers to questions like "Which activities add value to a product or service?" "What resources are needed to perform those activities?" and "How much should the product or service cost?" By examining their company's value-adding activities and the related costs, managers

FIGURE 1
Activity-Based Systems and the Management Cycle

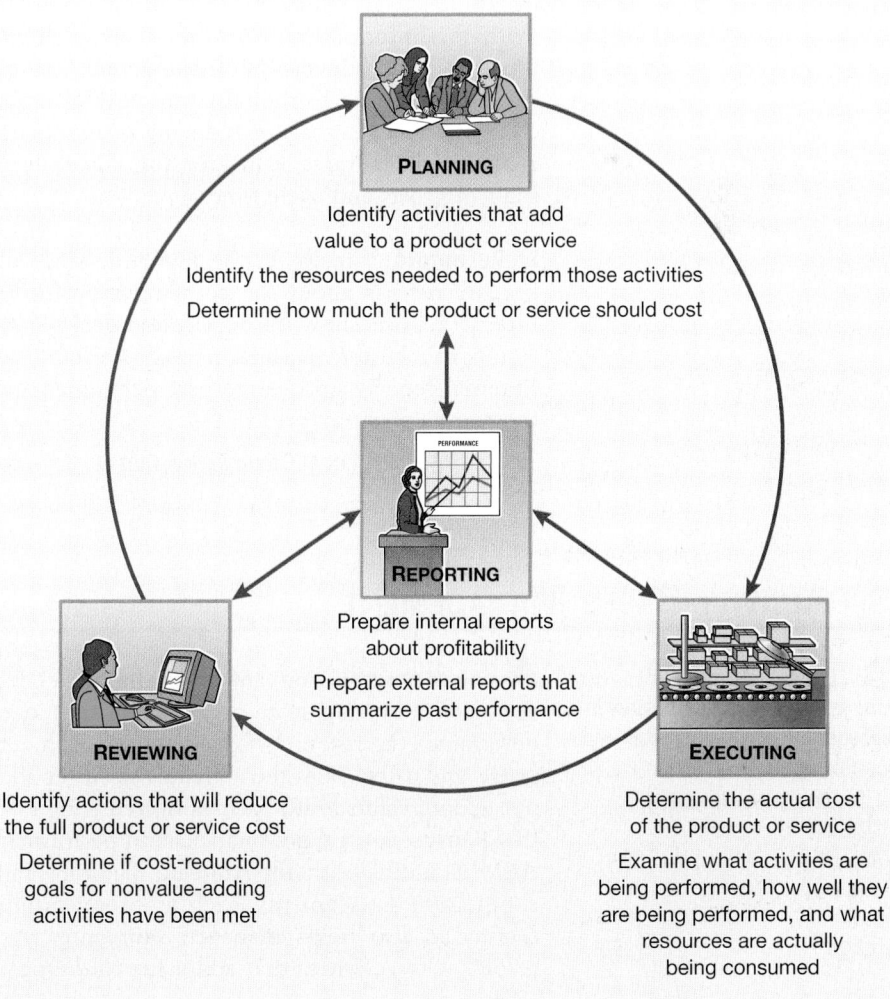

PLANNING

Identify activities that add
value to a product or service

Identify the resources needed to perform those activities

Determine how much the product or service should cost

REPORTING

Prepare internal reports
about profitability

Prepare external reports that
summarize past performance

REVIEWING

Identify actions that will reduce
the full product or service cost

Determine if cost-reduction
goals for nonvalue-adding
activities have been met

EXECUTING

Determine the actual cost
of the product or service

Examine what activities are
being performed, how well they
are being performed, and what
resources are actually
being consumed

can ensure that the company is offering quality products or services at the lowest cost. With budgeted costs prepared for each activity, they can not only better allocate resources to cost objects (such as product or service lines, customer groups, or sales territories) and estimate product or service unit cost more accurately, but also measure operating performance. If managers assume that resource-consuming activities cause costs and that products and services incur costs by the activities they require, the estimated unit cost will be more accurate.

■ **EXECUTING**   In the executing stage, managers want an answer to the question "What is the actual cost of making our product or providing our service?" They want to know what activities are being performed, how well they are being performed, and what resources they are consuming. Although managers focus on the activities that create the most value for customers, they also monitor some nonvalue-adding activities that have been reduced but not completely eliminated. An activity-based accounting information system measures actual quantities of activity (a quantitative nonfinancial measure) and accumulates related activity costs (a quantitative financial measure). Gathering quantitative information at the activity level allows managers the flexibility to create cost pools for different types of cost objects. For example, the costs of the selling activity can be assigned to a customer, a sales territory, or a product or service line.

■ **REVIEWING**   In the reviewing stage, managers want answers to the questions "What actions will reduce the full product and service cost?" and "Did we meet our cost-reduction goals for nonvalue-adding activities?" Managers measure an activity's performance by reviewing the difference between its actual and budgeted costs. With this information, they can analyze the variances in activity levels, identify waste and inefficiencies, and take action to improve processes and activities. They can also continue to monitor the costs of nonvalue-adding activities to see if the company met its goals of reducing or eliminating those costs. Careful review and analysis will increase value for the customer by improving product quality and reducing costs and cycle time.

■ **REPORTING**   Finally, in the reporting stage of the management cycle, managers prepare reports about the company's performance for internal and external use. Internal reports show the application of the costs of activities to cost objects, which results in a better measurement of profitability, as we discuss later in the chapter. External reports summarize past performance and answer such questions as "Did the company earn a profit?"

✓ Check out ACE for a Review Quiz at http://accounting.college.hmco.com/students.

ACTIVITY-BASED MANAGEMENT

LO2 Define *activity-based management (ABM)* and discuss its relationship to the supply chain and the value chain.

RELATED TEXT ASSIGNMENTS

Q: 6, 7
SE: 2, 3
E: 2, 3
P: 1
SD: 2

As you may recall from an earlier chapter, **activity-based management (ABM)** is an approach to managing an organization that identifies all major operating activities, determines the resources consumed by each activity and the cause of the resource usage, and categorizes the activities as either adding value to a product or service or not adding value. ABM focuses on reducing or eliminating nonvalue-adding activities. Because it provides financial and performance information at the activity level, ABM is useful both for strategic planning and for making operational decisions about business segments, such as product lines, market segments, and customer groups. It also helps managers eliminate waste and inefficiencies and redirect resources to activities that add value to the product or service. Activity-based cost-

FOCUS ON BUSINESS PRACTICE

How Do Traditional and ABC Reports Differ?

Many companies are finding that ABC enhances managerial reporting and decision making because it reflects the cause-and-effect relationships between indirect costs and individual processes, products, services, or customers. ABC is not a replacement for traditional general ledger accounting, which collects costs by departments. Rather, it is a practical spreadsheet translation of general ledger data into a format aimed at estimating true cost. The table on the right compares the reports of a department in a health-related company. Identify the report that would be used for financial purposes and the one that would be used for decision making.[2]

Chart of Accounts View		Activity-Based Costing View	
Salaries	$621,400	Enter claims into system	$ 32,000
Equipment	161,200	Analyze claims	121,000
Travel Expenses	58,000	Suspend claims	32,500
Supplies	43,900	Receive provider inquiries	101,500
Use and Occupancy	30,000	Resolve member problems	83,400
Total	$914,500	Process batches	45,000
		Determine eligibility	119,000
		Make copies	145,000
		Write correspondence	77,100
		Attend training	158,000
		Total	$914,500

ENRICHMENT NOTE:
Some activities or functions occur before production; their costs are sometimes called *upstream costs*. Other activities or functions occur after production; their costs are called *downstream costs*. In the new operating environment, both upstream and downstream costs are part of a product's total cost.

ing (ABC) is the tool used in an ABM environment to assign activity costs to cost objects. ABC helps managers make better pricing decisions, inventory valuations, and profitability decisions.

VALUE CHAINS AND SUPPLY CHAINS

As we noted earlier in the text, a **value chain** is a sequence of activities, or primary processes, that add value to a company's product or service; the value chain also includes support services, such as management accounting, that facilitate the primary processes. ABM enables managers to see their organization's value chain as part of a larger system that includes the value chains of suppliers and customers. This larger system is the **supply chain**—the path that leads from the suppliers of the materials from which a product is made to the final customer. The supply chain (also called the *supply network*) includes both suppliers and suppliers' suppliers, and customers and customers' customers.

As Figure 2 shows, in the supply chain for automobiles, a metal manufacturer supplies metal to an engine manufacturer, which supplies engines to the car manufacturer. The car manufacturer supplies cars to car dealerships, which supply cars to the final customers. Except for the metal manufacturer, each organization in this supply chain is a customer of an earlier supplier, and each, including the metal manufacturer, has its own value chain. The sequence of primary processes in the value chain varies from company to company depending on a number of factors, including the size of the company and the types of products or services it sells. Figure 2 shows the primary processes that add value for a car manufacturer—marketing, research and development, purchasing, production, sales, shipping, and customer service.

Value chains and supply chains give managers a better grasp of their company's internal and external operations. Managers who understand the supply

FOCUS ON BUSINESS PRACTICE

How Can a Changing Business Economy Cause Strategy Shifts in a Company's Value Chain?

Because of an economic downturn and overcapacity in the technology sector, high-tech companies like Oracle <www.oracle.com>, SAP <www.sap.com>, and PeopleSoft <www.peoplesoft.com> have shifted the emphasis of their value chain from marketing to customer service. Measures once used to gauge the performance of an aggressive sales force, such as sales volume, are no longer relevant and have been replaced by measures of customer satisfaction and retention.[3]

FIGURE 2
Supply Chain and Value Chain for a Manufacturing Company

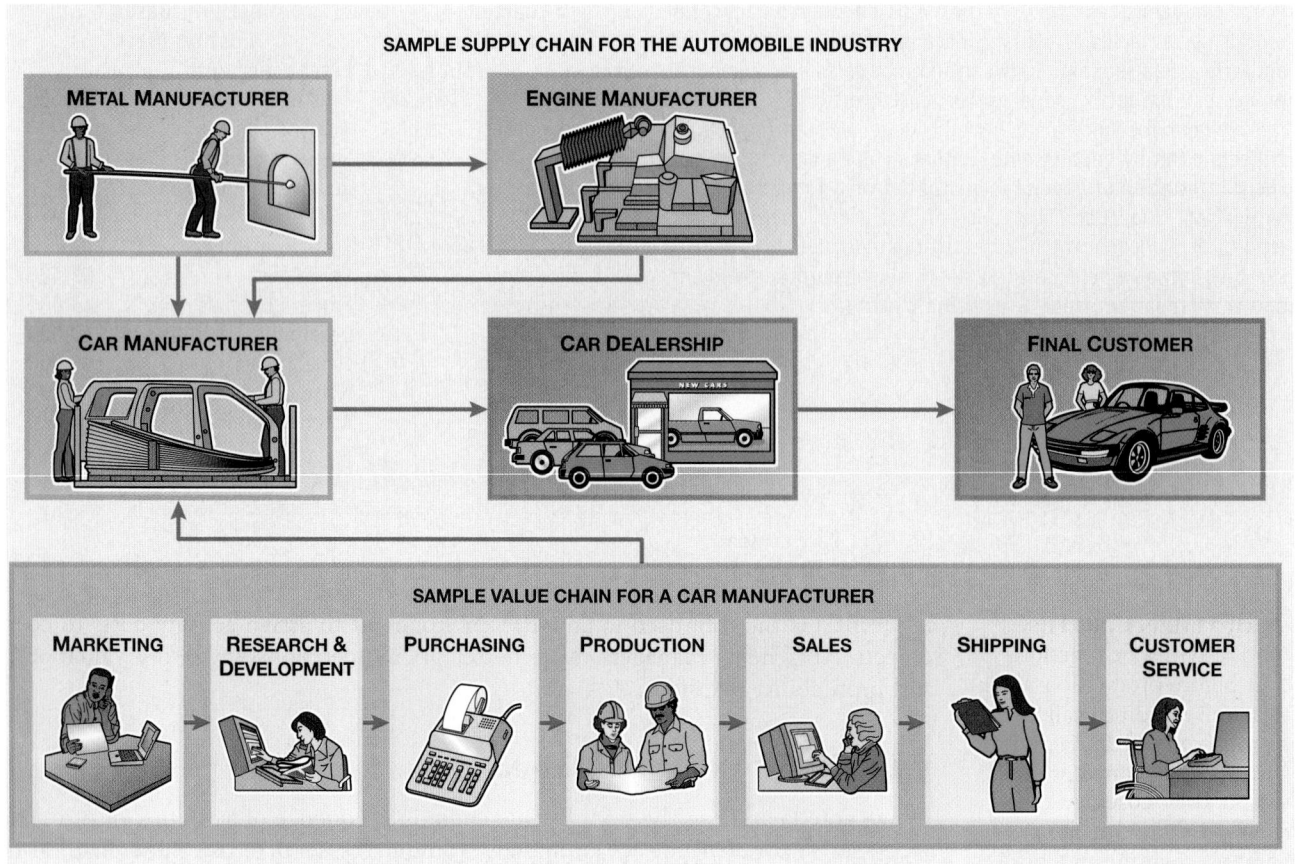

SAMPLE SUPPLY CHAIN FOR THE AUTOMOBILE INDUSTRY

METAL MANUFACTURER → ENGINE MANUFACTURER

CAR MANUFACTURER → CAR DEALERSHIP → FINAL CUSTOMER

SAMPLE VALUE CHAIN FOR A CAR MANUFACTURER

MARKETING → RESEARCH & DEVELOPMENT → PURCHASING → PRODUCTION → SALES → SHIPPING → CUSTOMER SERVICE

● **STOP AND THINK!**

How does the focus of a supply chain differ from that of a value chain?

A supply chain focuses on external relationships, whereas a value chain focuses on internal relationships. ■   **www.ford.com**

chain and how their company's value-adding activities fit into their suppliers' and customers' value chains can see their company's role in the overall process of creating and delivering products or services. Such an understanding can also make a company more profitable. By working with suppliers and customers across the entire supply chain, managers may be able to reduce the total cost of making a product, even though costs for one activity may increase. For example, assume that Ford Motor Company decided to place computers for online order entry in its car dealerships. The new computers would streamline the processing of orders and make the orders more accurate. In this case, even though Ford would incur the cost of the computers, the total cost of making and delivering a car would decrease because the cost of order processing would decrease. When organizations work cooperatively with others in their supply chain, they can develop new processes that reduce the total costs of their products or services.

ABM IN A SERVICE ORGANIZATION

To illustrate how a service organization can use ABM, let's assume that a firm called Western Data Services, Inc. (WDSI), offers database marketing strategies to help companies increase their sales. WDSI's basic package of services includes the design of a mailing piece (either a Classic Letter with or without inserts or a Self-Mailer),

FIGURE 3
Supply Chain and Value Chain
for a Service Organization

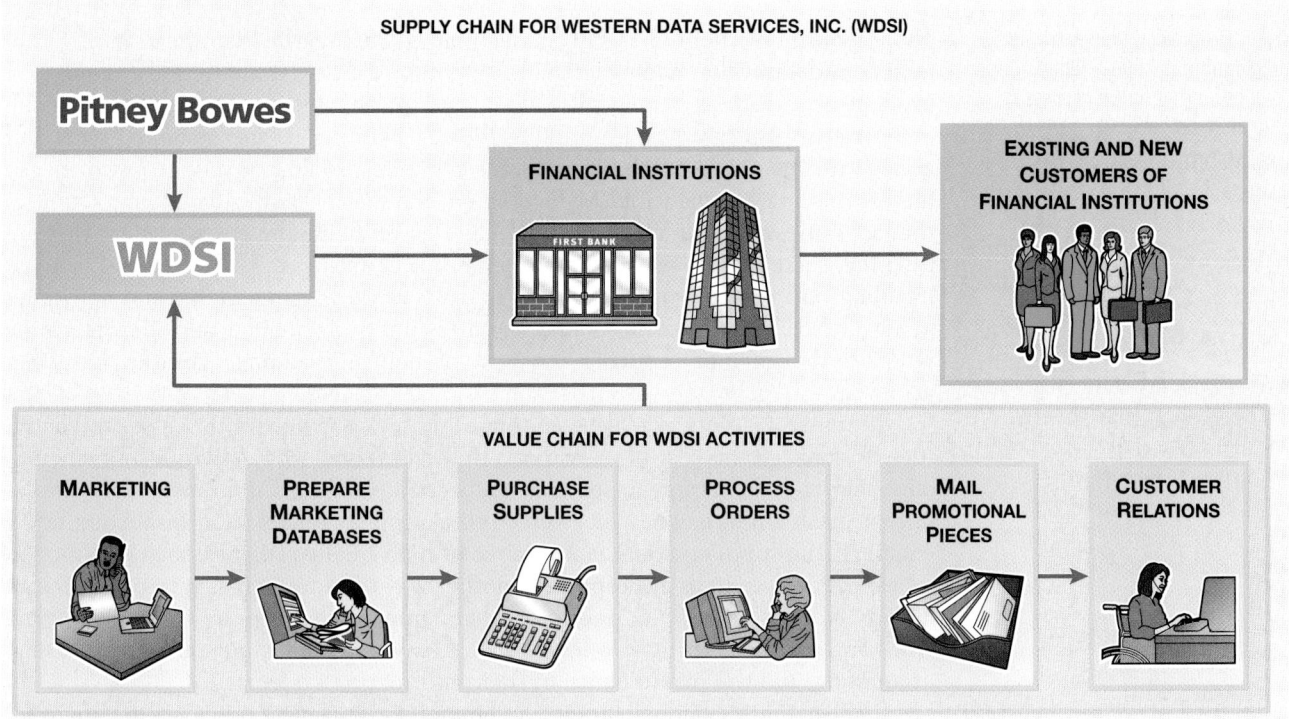

SUPPLY CHAIN FOR WESTERN DATA SERVICES, INC. (WDSI)

creation and maintenance of marketing databases containing information about the client's target group, and a production process that prints a promotional piece and prepares it for mailing. WDSI's primary customers are financial institutions throughout the western states, but the company also serves small businesses and nonprofit organizations.

In preparing WSDI's business plan, Carl Marcus, the owner and manager of WDSI, reviewed the company's supply chain. As Figure 3 shows, this supply chain includes one supplier (Pitney Bowes), WDSI as a service provider, one customer group (financial institutions), and the customer group's customers. WDSI had a number of suppliers, including office supply companies, printers, and computer stores, but Marcus chose to include only Pitney Bowes because of the significant cost savings from using this supplier's equipment to fold, insert, address, seal, and meter mailing pieces. Marcus chose financial institutions as the supply chain's primary customer group because they represent 75 percent of revenues. The customers of the financial institutions are included in the supply chain because those individuals and businesses receive the mailing pieces that WDSI prepares. Based on his review of the supply chain, Marcus concluded that WDSI's strategy to work with Pitney Bowes and the financial institutions to improve WDSI's services was sound.

www.pb.com

Marcus also decided to use ABM to manage processes and activities. He developed a value chain of activities for the company so that he could identify all major operating activities, the resources each activity consumes, and the cause of the resource usage. As shown in Figure 3, the activities that add value to WDSI's services are marketing, preparing marketing databases, purchasing supplies, processing orders, mailing promotional pieces, and customer relations.

 Check out ACE for a Review Quiz at http://accounting.college.hmco.com/students.

VALUE-ADDING AND NONVALUE-ADDING ACTIVITIES AND PROCESS VALUE ANALYSIS

LO3 Distinguish between value-adding and nonvalue-adding activities, and describe process value analysis.

RELATED TEXT ASSIGNMENTS
Q: 8, 9
SE: 4
E: 4, 5
P: 1
SD: 2, 5
MRA: 1, 4, 5

KEY POINT: The customer's perspective is what governs whether an activity adds value to a product or service.

An important element of activity-based management is the identification of value-adding and nonvalue-adding activities. A **value-adding activity** adds value to a product or service as perceived by the customer. Examples include designing the components of a new car, assembling the car, painting it, and installing seats and airbags. A **nonvalue-adding activity** adds cost to a product or service but does not increase its market value. ABM focuses on eliminating nonvalue-adding activities that are not essential to an organization and on reducing the costs of those that are essential, such as legal services, management accounting, machine repair, materials handling, and building maintenance. The costs of both value-adding and nonvalue-adding activities are accumulated to measure performance and to determine whether the goal of reducing the cost of nonvalue-adding activities has been achieved.

To minimize costs, managers continuously seek to improve processes and activities. To manage the cost of an activity, they can reduce the activity's frequency or eliminate it. For example, inspection costs can be reduced if an inspector samples one of every three engines received from a supplier rather than inspecting every engine. If the supplier is a reliable source of high-quality engines, such a reduction in inspection activity is appropriate. Another way to reduce costs is to outsource an activity—that is, to have it done by another company that is more competent at the work and can perform it at a lower cost. Many companies outsource purchasing, accounting, and the maintenance of their information systems.

Some activities can be eliminated completely if business processes are changed. For example, when a company adopts a just-in-time operating philosophy, it can eliminate some recordkeeping activities. Because it purchases materials just in time for production and manufactures products just in time for customer delivery, it no longer needs to accumulate costs as the product is made.

VALUE-ADDING AND NONVALUE-ADDING ACTIVITIES IN A SERVICE ORGANIZATION

To illustrate how service organizations deal with value-adding and nonvalue-adding activities, let's suppose Carl Marcus, the owner and manager of WDSI, has examined the activities related to the design, processing, and mailing of his company's Classic Letters and drawn up the list of value-adding activities shown in Table 1. When Marcus's customers ask for database marketing services, these are the activities they pay for. Marcus also identified the following nonvalue-adding activities:

- Preparing a job order form and scheduling the job
- Ordering, receiving, inspecting, and storing paper, envelopes, and other supplies
- Setting up machines to process a specific letter size
- Logging the total number of items processed in a batch
- Billing the client and recording and depositing payments from the client

After reviewing the list of nonvalue-adding activities, Marcus arranged with his suppliers to have paper, envelopes, and other supplies delivered the day a job is performed. This helped reduce WDSI's storage costs. Marcus was also able to reduce the costs of some value-adding activities. For example, he reduced the cost of the labor involved in verifying the conformity of mailings with United States Postal Service (USPS) requirements by purchasing computer software that verifies addresses, determines postage, and automatically sorts the letters.

● **STOP AND THINK!**
Are customers willing to pay for nonvalue-adding activities?
Customers are not willing to pay for such activities, which is why businesses try to minimize or eliminate them. ■

FOCUS ON BUSINESS PRACTICE

What Is VBM?

Value-based management (VBM) is a long-term strategy that many businesses use to reward managers who create and sustain shareholder wealth and value. In other words, VBM encourages managers to think like business owners. Three elements are essential for a successful VBM program. First, VBM must have the full support of top management. Second, performance and compensation must be linked because "what gets measured and rewarded gets done." Finally, everyone involved must understand the what, why, and how of the program. Since a variety of VBM approaches exist, each company can tailor its VBM performance metrics and implementation strategy to meet its particular needs.[4]

www.westinghouseelectric.com
www.pepsico.com
www.landolakes.com

PROCESS VALUE ANALYSIS

Process value analysis (PVA) is a technique that managers use to identify and link all the activities involved in the value chain. It analyzes business processes by relating activities to the events that prompt the activities and to the resources that the activities consume. PVA forces managers to look critically at all phases of their operations. Managers who use ABM find it an effective way of reducing nonvalue-adding activities and their costs. PVA improves cost traceability and results in significantly more accurate product costs, which in turn improves management decisions and increases profitability.

By using PVA to identify nonvalue-adding activities, companies can reduce costs and redirect resources to value-adding activities. For example, PVA has enabled companies like Westinghouse Electric, Pepsi-Cola North America, and Land O'Lakes to reduce the processing costs of purchasing and accounts payable. After identifying the nonvalue-adding activities involved in small-dollar purchases (e.g., recording and paying small bills, setting up accounts, and establishing credit with seldom-used suppliers) and their costs, managers of these companies decided to stop performing such activities internally. Instead, they chose the less expensive alternative of using a special credit card known as a procurement (or purchasing)

TABLE 1. Value-Adding Activities for a Service Organization

Western Data Services, Inc.
Value-Adding Activities for the Classic Letter

Value-Adding Activities	How the Activity Adds Value
Designing the letter	Enhances the effectiveness of the communication
Creating a database of customers' names and addresses sorted in ZIP code order	Increases the probability that the client will efficiently and effectively reach the targeted customer group
Verifying the conformity of mailings with USPS requirements	Ensures that the client's mailing will receive the best postal rate
Processing the job: A computer prints a personalized letter A machine folds the letter, inserts it and other information into an envelope, prints the address on the envelope, and seals and meters the envelope.	Creates the client mailing
Delivering the letters to the post office	Begins the delivery process

card from Visa, MasterCard, or American Express to handle large volumes of small-dollar purchases.

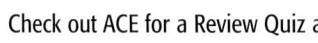 Check out ACE for a Review Quiz at http://accounting.college.hmco.com/students.

ACTIVITY-BASED COSTING

LO4 Define *activity-based costing* and explain how a cost hierarchy and a bill of activities are used.

RELATED TEXT ASSIGNMENTS
Q: 10, 11, 12, 13
SE: 5, 6
E: 6, 7, 8
P: 2, 3, 6, 7
MRA: 1, 3, 4

KEY POINT: Indirect costs are assigned to cost objects using an appropriate allocation scheme.

As access to value chain data has improved, management accountants have refined the issue of how to assign costs fairly to products or services to determine unit costs. You may recall from an earlier chapter that traditional methods of allocating manufacturing overhead costs to products use such cost drivers as direct labor hours, direct labor costs, or machine hours. In the mid-1980s, organizations began realizing that these methods did not accurately assign manufacturing overhead costs to their product lines and that the resulting inaccuracy in product unit costs was causing poor pricing decisions. In their search for more accurate product costing, many organizations embraced activity-based costing.

Activity-based costing (ABC) is a method of assigning costs that calculates a more accurate product cost than traditional methods. It does so by categorizing all indirect costs by activity, tracing the indirect costs to those activities, and assigning those costs to products using a cost driver related to the cause of the cost. Since ABC was introduced, organizations in all parts of the world have chosen it as their cost allocation method.

Activity-based costing is an important tool of activity-based management because it improves the allocation of activity-driven costs to cost objects. To implement activity-based costing, managers

1. Identify and classify each activity.
2. Estimate the cost of resources for each activity.
3. Identify a cost driver for each activity and estimate the quantity of each cost driver.
4. Calculate an activity cost rate for each activity.
5. Assign costs to cost objects based on the level of activity required to make the product or provide the service.

THE COST HIERARCHY AND THE BILL OF ACTIVITIES

Two tools help in the implementation of ABC—a cost hierarchy and a bill of activities.

■ **THE COST HIERARCHY** A cost hierarchy is a framework for classifying activities according to the level at which their costs are incurred. Many companies use this framework to allocate activity-based costs to products or services. In a manufacturing company, the cost hierarchy typically has four levels: the unit level, the batch level, the product level, and the facility level.

• **Unit-level activities** are performed each time a unit is produced. For example, when a car manufacturer installs an engine, unit-level activities include assembling engine subassemblies, testing engines, and connecting engines to car frames. These activities have a direct correlation to the number of cars produced since each car contains only one engine.

• **Batch-level activities** are performed each time a batch of goods is produced. Examples of batch-level activities in an engine-installation process include setup,

TABLE 2. Sample Activities in Cost Hierarchies

Activity Level	Car Manufacturer: Engine Installation	Direct Mail Service: Preparing a Mailing to Bank Customers
Unit level	Install engine Test engine	Print and fold letter Insert letter and other information into envelope
Batch level	Set up installation process Move engines Inspect engines	Retool machines Verify correct postage Bill client
Product or service level	Redesign installation process	Train employees Develop and maintain computer systems and databases
Facility or operations level	Provide facility management, maintenance, lighting, and security	Provide facility management, maintenance, lighting, and security

inspection, scheduling, and materials handling. These activities vary with the number of batches prepared.

- **Product-level activities** are performed to support the diversity of products in a manufacturing plant. Examples of product-level activities include implementing engineering changes and redesigning the installation process.

- **Facility-level activities** are performed to support a facility's general manufacturing process. Examples for a car manufacturer include managing, maintaining, lighting, securing, and insuring the manufacturing plant.

Note that the frequency of activities varies across levels and that the cost hierarchy includes both value-adding and nonvalue-adding activities. Service organizations can also use a cost hierarchy to group activities; the four levels typically are the unit level, the batch level, the service level, and the operations level. Table 2 lists examples of activities in the cost hierarchies of a manufacturing company and a service organization.

KEY POINT: A bill of activities summarizes costs relating to a product or service and supports the calculation of the product or service unit cost.

■ **THE BILL OF ACTIVITIES** Once managers have created the cost hierarchy, they group the activities into the specified levels and prepare a summary of the activity costs assigned to the selected cost objects. A **bill of activities** is a list of activities and related costs that is used to compute the costs assigned to activities and the product unit cost. More complex bills of activities group activities into activity pools and include activity cost rates and the cost driver levels used to assign costs to cost objects. A bill of activities may be used as the primary document or as a supporting schedule to calculate the product unit cost in both job order and process costing systems and in both manufacturing and service organizations.

Exhibit 1 illustrates a bill of activities for WDSI. In this example, Carl Marcus uses the bill of activities to see how activity costs contribute to unit costs. WDSI provides two types of mailing pieces:

- Preparing the Classic Letter involves printing, folding, collating, and inserting letters and other materials into a printed, addressed envelope and then metering and

Exhibit 1
Bill of Activities for a Service Organization

Western Data Services, Inc.
Bill of Activities for Classic Letter and Self-Mailer
For the Month Ended May 31, 20x6

Activity	Activity Cost Rate	Classic Letter (110,000 letters) Cost Driver Level	Activity Cost	Self-Mailer (48,000 self-mailers) Cost Driver Level	Activity Cost
Unit level					
Process letters	$20 per machine hour	300 machine hours	$ 6,000	120 machine hours	$ 2,400
Batch level					
Prepare databases	$85 per 1,000 names	50,000 names	4,250	20,000 names	1,700
Set up machines	$10 per direct labor hour	220 direct labor hours	2,200	100 direct labor hours	1,000
Inspect for USPS compliance	$12 per inspection hour	100 inspection hours	1,200	80 inspection hours	960
Service level					
Develop databases	$25 per design hour	118 design hours	2,950	81 design hours	2,025
Solicit new customers	$3 per solicitation	300 solicitations	900	95 solicitations	285
Operations level					
Provide utilities and space	$15 per machine hour	300 machine hours	4,500	50 machine hours	750
Total activity costs assigned to services			$ 22,000		$ 9,120
Total volume			÷110,000		÷48,000
Activity costs per unit (total activity costs ÷ total volume)			$ 0.20		$ 0.19
Cost summary					
Direct materials cost			$ 7,700		$ 5,280
Postage costs			17,600		7,680
Activity costs (includes labor and overhead)			22,000		9,120
Total costs for month			$ 47,300		$22,080
Product unit cost (total costs for month ÷ total volume)			$ 0.43		$ 0.46

sealing the envelope. The cost of the Classic Letter includes the costs of direct materials (envelopes, letters, other materials), postage, and service overhead.

- The Self-Mailer is a one-page solicitation that can be refolded and returned to the client's address. Its cost includes the costs of direct materials (a single piece of paper for each mailer), postage, and service overhead.

The volume of mailings for a customer can vary from 150 to 20,000 addresses in a single mailing. The sizes of the databases that are prepared and the number of machine setups and inspection hours also vary from job to job. The service overhead costs for the activities identified in the cost hierarchy are assigned using ABC. The activity costs are calculated for the service overhead related to each type of mailing piece. These are then added to the costs of direct materials and postage to calculate a unit cost.

Marcus chose to group activities by unit, batch, service, and operations levels:

- At the unit level, Marcus included the costs of all activities needed to process each Classic Letter and Self-Mailer. He used machine hours as the cost driver.

- At the batch level, for each job, he included the costs of all activities required to prepare the database of names and addresses for mailing, to set up the machines, and to inspect the letters for compliance with postal regulations. He used the number of names in the database, direct labor hours, and inspection hours as the cost drivers.

- At the service level, he included the costs of all activities required to develop databases for new clients and to solicit new business for WDSI. He used design hours and number of solicitations as the cost drivers.

- At the operations level, he included the costs of all activities related to providing utilities and space. He used machine hours as the cost driver.

Marcus prepared a bill of activities for one month ending May 31, 20x6. He supported each activity's cost with information about the activity cost rate and the cost driver level. He also calculated the total activity costs and activity cost per unit for each type of mailing piece. At the bottom of the bill of activities for the month, he prepared a summary of the total costs of the mailings and calculated the unit cost for each type (the total costs divided by the number of units mailed).

The cost information gathered in the bill of activities helped Marcus estimate the company's profits by allowing him to compare costs with revenues. To be competitive, he is currently offering the Classic Letter for $.50 per letter and the Self-Mailer for $.45 per mailer. The Classic Letter is generating a positive gross margin of $.07 ($.50 − $.43) per letter, but the Self-Mailer shows a negative gross margin of $.01 ($.45 − $.46) per mailer. Marcus must find ways to increase fee revenue, reduce costs, or increase volume for the Self-Mailer. ABC can help him reduce costs because the activity costs, including labor and overhead, are categorized by activities and grouped into activity levels. Marcus can examine those activities to identify and reduce or eliminate some of the company's nonvalue-adding activities.

ACTIVITY-BASED COSTING FOR SELLING AND ADMINISTRATIVE ACTIVITIES

Activity-based costing can also be used to assign the costs of selling and administrative activities. The costs of these activities include salaries, benefits, depreciation on buildings and equipment, sales commissions, and utilities. ABC groups such costs into activity pools and assigns them to cost objects using cost drivers like the number of sales calls, sales orders, invoices, or billings. The cost objects might be products, services, customers, or sales territories. Because it is difficult to assign costs to individual customers, many companies treat similar customers, such as distributors or retailers, as a single group.

Because customer groups and sales territories differ in their complexity and diversity, each should support its related costs. For example, some customers place

STOP AND THINK!
How does a bill of activities differ from a job order cost card?
A bill of activities includes not only the product or service costs found on a job order cost card, but also the costs of all relevant operating activities. ∎

KEY POINT: Activity-based costing reflects the cause-and-effect relationships between costs and individual processes, products, services, or customers.

EXHIBIT 2
Income Statement for a Cost Object

Western Data Services, Inc.
Customer-Related Income Statement
Gila State Bank
For the Month Ended May 31, 20x6

Fee revenue ($.50 × 12,000 Classic Letters)				$6,000
Cost of processing order ($.43 × 12,000 Classic Letters)				5,160
Gross margin				$ 840
Less: Selling and administrative activity costs				

Activity	Activity Cost Rate	Cost Driver Level	Activity Cost	
Make sales calls	$12 per sales call	10 sales calls	$120	
Prepare sales orders	$6 per sales order	25 sales orders	150	
Handle inquiries	$.50 per minute	120 minutes	60	
Process credits	$20 per notice	1 notice	20	
Process invoices	$10 per invoice	12 invoices	120	
Follow-ups	$8 per follow-up	20 follow-ups	160	
Process billings and collections	$4 per billing	24 billings	96	

Total selling and administrative activity costs			726
Operating income contributed by Gila State Bank			$ 114

larger or more frequent orders than others, and a larger portion of the costs of selling and administrative activities can therefore be traced to them. Sales territories differ in the size and number of customers served; thus, some sales territories may require more support services than others.

Exhibit 2 presents a customer-related income statement for WDSI. A similar format can be used to create an income statement for any cost object. Service organizations typically group clients according to significant characteristics, such as the length of time required to perform the service or the frequency of the service. In our example, Carl Marcus can use the ABC information to review the profitability of each customer or customer group. He can also use it to compare selling and administrative costs across customer groups and as a basis for making changes in selling and administrative activities that will increase his company's profitability.

 Check out ACE for a Review Quiz at http://accounting.college.hmco.com/students.

THE NEW MANUFACTURING ENVIRONMENT AND JIT OPERATIONS

LO5 Define the *just-in-time (JIT) operating philosophy* and identify the elements of a JIT operating environment.

RELATED TEXT ASSIGNMENTS
Q: 14, 15, 16, 17
SE: 7
E: 9, 10
SD: 1, 3, 4, 5
MRA: 2

To remain competitive in today's changing business environment, companies have had to rethink their organizational processes and basic operating methods. One of the operating philosophies that managers have devised for the new manufacturing environment is JIT. The just-in-time (JIT) operating philosophy requires that all resources—materials, personnel, and facilities—be acquired and used only as needed. Its objectives are to enhance productivity, eliminate waste, reduce costs, and improve product quality.

Traditionally, a company operated with large amounts of inventory, including finished goods stored in anticipation of customers' orders; purchased materials infrequently but in large amounts; had long production runs with infrequent setups; manufactured large batches of products; and trained each member of its work force to perform a limited number of tasks. Managers determined a change was necessary because

- Large amounts of an organization's space and money were tied up in inventory.
- The source of poor-quality materials, products, or services was hard to pinpoint.
- The number of nonvalue-adding manufacturing activities was growing.
- Accounting for the manufacturing process was becoming ever more complex.

To achieve JIT's objectives, a company must redesign its operating systems, plant layout, and basic management methods to conform to several basic concepts:

- Simple is better.
- The quality of the product or service is critical.
- The work environment must emphasize continuous improvement.
- Maintaining large inventories wastes resources and may hide poor work.
- Activities or functions that do not add value to a product or service should be eliminated or reduced.
- Goods should be produced only when needed.
- Workers must be multiskilled and must participate in improving efficiency and product quality.

Application of these concepts creates a JIT operating environment. The elements used in a JIT operating environment to enhance productivity, eliminate waste, reduce costs, and improve product quality are described below.

MINIMUM INVENTORY LEVELS

Maintaining minimum inventory levels is fundamental to the JIT operating philosophy. In the traditional manufacturing environment, parts, materials, and supplies are purchased far in advance and stored until the production department needs them. In contrast, in a JIT environment, materials and parts are purchased and received only when needed. The JIT system lowers costs by reducing the space needed for inventory storage, the amount of materials handling, and the amount of inventory obsolescence. It also reduces the need for inventory control facilities, personnel, and recordkeeping. In addition, it significantly decreases the amount of work in process inventory and the amount of working capital tied up in all inventories.

Maintaining minimum inventory levels does increase the risk of stock depletions and downtime, which can be costly and result in late revenues. Before adopting the JIT operating philosophy, managers need to plan for such risks.

PULL-THROUGH PRODUCTION

A JIT operating environment requires **pull-through production**, a system in which a customer's order triggers the purchase of materials and the scheduling of production for the products that have been ordered. In contrast, the **push-through method** used in traditional manufacturing operations manufactures products in long production runs and stores them in anticipation of customers' orders. With pull-through production, the size of a customer's order determines the size of a production run, and the company purchases materials and parts as needed. Inventory levels are kept low, but machines must be set up more frequently, resulting in more work stoppages.

QUICK SETUP AND FLEXIBLE WORK CELLS

In the past, managers felt that it was more cost effective to produce large batches of goods because producing small batches increases the number of machine setups.

KEY POINT: In the JIT environment, normal operating activities—setup, production, and maintenance—still take place. But the timing of those activities is altered to promote smoother operations and to minimize downtime.

The success of JIT has disproved this. By placing machines in more efficient locations, setup time can be minimized. In addition, when workers perform frequent setups, they become more efficient at it.

In a traditional factory layout, similar machines are grouped together, forming functional departments. Products are routed through each department in sequence, so that all necessary operations are completed in order. This process can take several days or weeks, depending on the size and complexity of the job. By changing the factory layout so that all the machines needed for sequential processing are placed together, the JIT operating environment may cut the manufacturing time of a product from days to hours, or from weeks to days. The new cluster of machinery forms a flexible **work cell**, an autonomous production line that can perform all required operations efficiently and continuously. The flexible work cell handles a "family of products"—that is, products of similar shape or size. Product families require minimal setup changes as workers move from one job to the next. The more flexible the work cell is, the greater the potential to minimize total production time.

A MULTISKILLED WORK FORCE

In the flexible work cells of a JIT environment, one worker may be required to operate several types of machines simultaneously. That worker may have to set up and retool the machines and even perform routine maintenance on them. A JIT operating environment thus requires a multiskilled work force, and multiskilled workers have been very effective in contributing to high levels of productivity.

HIGH LEVELS OF PRODUCT QUALITY

KEY POINT: The fact that inspections are necessary is an admission that problems with quality do occur. Continuous inspection throughout production as opposed to inspection only at the end of the process creates awareness of a problem at the point where it occurs.

JIT operations result in quality products because high-quality direct materials are used and because inspections are made throughout the production process. According to the JIT philosophy, inspection as a separate step does not add value to a product, so inspection is incorporated into ongoing operations. A JIT machine operator inspects the products as they pass through the manufacturing process. If the operator detects a flaw, he or she shuts down the work cell to prevent the production of similarly flawed products while the cause of the problem is being determined. The operator either fixes the problem or helps the engineer or quality control person find a way to correct it. This integrated inspection procedure, combined with quality raw materials, produces high-quality finished goods.

EFFECTIVE PREVENTIVE MAINTENANCE

When a company rearranges its machinery into flexible work cells, each machine becomes an integral part of its cell. If one machine breaks down, the entire cell stops functioning. Because the product cannot be easily routed to another machine while the malfunctioning machine is being repaired, continuous JIT operations require an effective system of preventive maintenance. Preventing machine breakdowns is considered more important and more cost-effective than keeping machines running continuously. Machine operators are trained to perform minor repairs as they detect problems. Machines are serviced regularly—much as an automobile is—to help guarantee continued operation. The machine operator conducts routine maintenance during periods of downtime between orders. (Remember that in a JIT setting, the work cell does not operate unless there is a customer order for the product. Machine operators take advantage of such downtime to perform routine maintenance.)

CONTINUOUS IMPROVEMENT OF THE WORK ENVIRONMENT

KEY POINT: The JIT operating philosophy must be adopted by everyone in a company before its total benefits can be realized.

A JIT environment fosters loyalty among workers, who are likely to see themselves as part of a team because they are so deeply involved in the production process. Machine operators must have the skills to run several types of machines, detect defective products, suggest measures to correct problems, and maintain the machinery within their work cells. In addition, each worker is encouraged to suggest improvements to the production process. Companies with a JIT operating environment receive thousands of employee suggestions and implement a high percentage of them, and they reward workers for suggestions that improve the process. Such an environment fosters workers' initiative and benefits the company.

 Check out ACE for a Review Quiz at http://accounting.college.hmco.com/students.

ACCOUNTING FOR PRODUCT COSTS IN THE NEW MANUFACTURING ENVIRONMENT

LO6 Identify the changes in product costing that result when a firm adopts a JIT operating environment.

RELATED TEXT ASSIGNMENTS

Q: 18
SE: 8
E: 11
P: 4
SD: 5

When a firm shifts to the new manufacturing environment, the management accounting system must take a new approach to evaluating costs and controlling operations. The changes in the manufacturing operations will affect how costs are determined and what measures are used to monitor performance.

When a company adopts a JIT operating environment, the work cells and goal of reducing or eliminating nonvalue-adding activities change the way costs are classified and assigned. In this section, we examine those changes.

CLASSIFYING COSTS

The traditional production process can be divided into five time frames:

⬢ STOP AND THINK!
Which time frame in the production process is value adding?
Processing time is value adding. ■

Processing time	The actual amount of time spent working on a product
Inspection time	The time spent looking for product flaws or reworking defective units
Moving time	The time spent moving a product from one operation or department to another
Queue time	The time a product spends waiting to be worked on once it arrives at the next operation or department
Storage time	The time a product spends in materials storage, work in process inventory, or finished goods inventory

STUDY NOTE: Although separate inspection costs are reduced in a JIT operating environment, some additional time is added to production because the machine operator is now performing the inspection function. The objectives are to reduce *total* costs and to increase quality.

In product costing under JIT, costs associated with processing time are classified as either direct materials costs or conversion costs. **Conversion costs** are the sum of the direct labor costs and manufacturing overhead costs incurred by a production department, work cell, or other work center. According to the JIT philosophy, costs associated with inspection, moving, queue, and storage time should be reduced or eliminated because they do not add value to the product.

ASSIGNING COSTS

In a JIT operating environment, managers focus on **throughput time**, the time it takes to move a product through the entire production process. Measures of product movement, such as machine time, are used to apply conversion costs to products.

Sophisticated computer monitoring of the work cells allows many costs to be traced directly to the cells where products are manufactured. As Table 3 shows, several costs that in a traditional environment are treated as indirect costs and applied to products using a manufacturing overhead rate are treated as the direct costs of a

TABLE 3.   Direct and Indirect Costs in Traditional and JIT Environments

Costs in a Traditional Environment		Costs in a JIT Environment
Direct	Direct materials	Direct
Direct	Direct labor	Direct
Indirect	Repairs and maintenance	Direct to work cell
Indirect	Materials handling	Direct to work cell
Indirect	Operating supplies	Direct to work cell
Indirect	Utilities costs	Direct to work cell
Indirect	Supervision	Direct to work cell
Indirect	Depreciation	Direct to work cell
Indirect	Supporting service functions	Mostly direct to work cell
Indirect	Building occupancy	Indirect
Indirect	Insurance and taxes	Indirect

JIT work cell. Because the products that a work cell manufactures are similar in nature, direct materials and conversion costs should be nearly uniform for each product in a cell. The costs of repairs and maintenance, materials handling, operating supplies, utilities, and supervision can be traced directly to work cells as they are incurred. Depreciation charges are based on units of output, not on time, so depreciation can be charged directly to work cells based on the number of units produced. Building occupancy costs, insurance premiums, and property taxes remain indirect costs and must be assigned to the work cells for inclusion in the conversion cost.

 Check out ACE for a Review Quiz at http://accounting.college.hmco.com/students.

BACKFLUSH COSTING

LO7 Define and apply *backflush costing*, and compare the cost flows in traditional and backflush costing.

RELATED TEXT ASSIGNMENTS
Q: 19
SE: 9
E: 12, 13
P: 5, 8

KEY POINT: Backflush costing eliminates the need to make journal entries during the period to track cost flows as the product is made.

Managers in a just-in-time operating environment continuously seek ways of reducing wasted resources and time. So far, we have focused on how they can trim waste from manufacturing operations, but they can reduce waste in other areas as well, including the accounting process. Because a JIT environment reduces labor costs, the accounting system can combine the costs of direct labor and manufacturing overhead into the single category of conversion costs, and because materials arrive just in time to be used in the production process, there is little reason to maintain a separate Materials Inventory account. Thus, by simplifying cost flows through the accounting records, a JIT environment makes it possible to reduce the time it takes to record and account for the costs of the manufacturing process.

A JIT organization can also streamline its accounting process by using backflush costing. In **backflush costing**, all product costs are first accumulated in the Cost of Goods Sold account, and at the end of the accounting period, they are "flushed back," or worked backward, into the appropriate inventory accounts. By having all product costs flow straight to a final destination and working back to determine the proper balances for the inventory accounts at the end of the period, this method saves recording time. As illustrated in Figure 4, it eliminates the need to record several transactions that must be recorded in traditional manufacturing environments.

When direct materials arrive at a factory in which traditional costing methods are used, their costs flow into the Materials Inventory account. Then, when the direct materials are requisitioned into production, their costs flow into the Work in Process Inventory account. When direct labor is used, its costs are added to the

FIGURE 4
Comparison of Cost Flows in Traditional and Backflush Costing

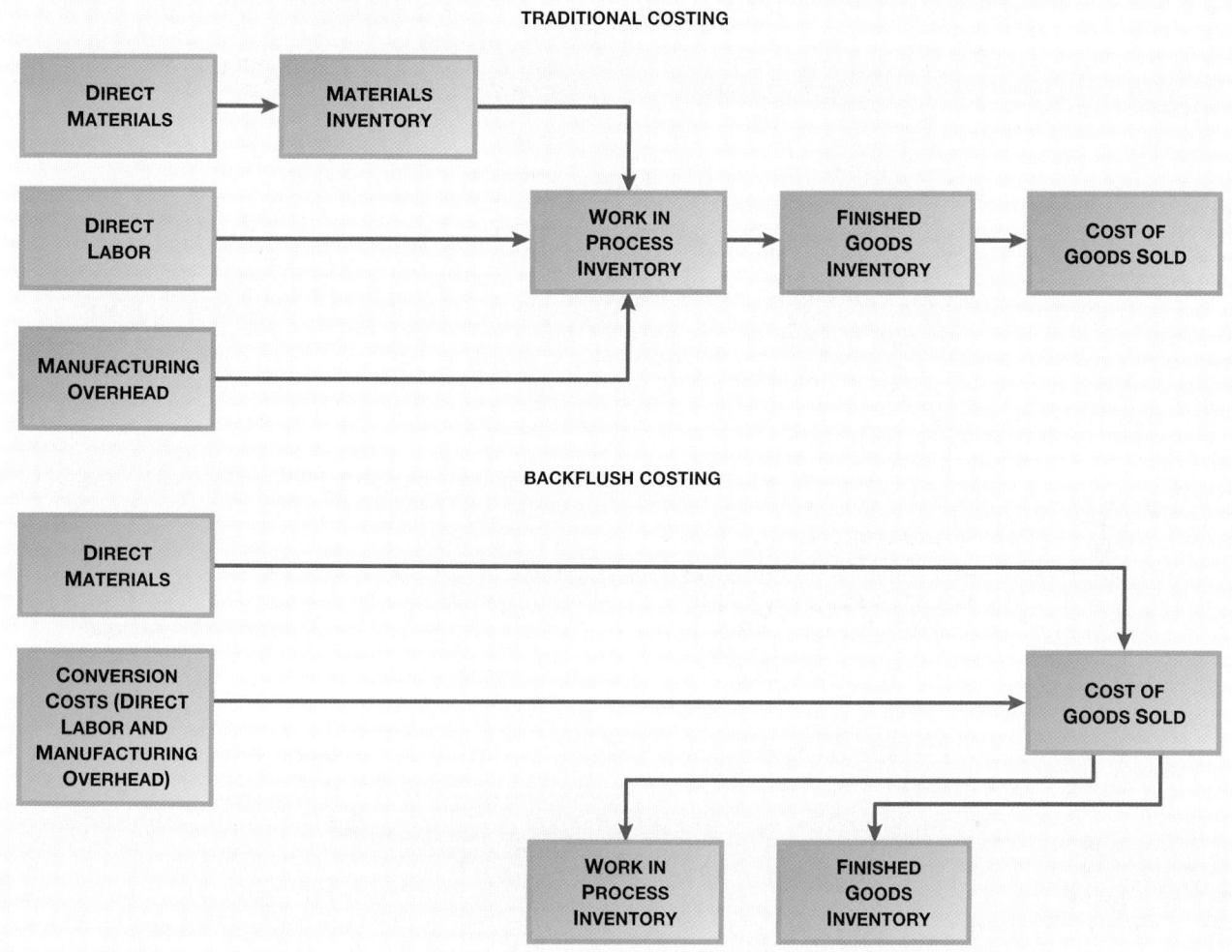

Work in Process Inventory account. Manufacturing overhead is applied to production using a base like direct labor hours, machine hours, or number of units produced. The amount of applied overhead is added to the other costs in the Work in Process Inventory account. At the end of the manufacturing process, the costs of the finished units are transferred to the Finished Goods Inventory account, and when the units are sold, their costs are transferred to the Cost of Goods Sold account.

In a JIT setting, direct materials arrive just in time to be placed into production. As you can see in Figure 4, when backflush costing is used, the direct materials costs and the conversion costs (direct labor and manufacturing overhead) are immediately charged to the Cost of Goods Sold account. At the end of the period, the costs of goods in work in process inventory and in finished goods inventory are determined, and those costs are flushed back to the Work in Process Inventory account and the Finished Goods Inventory account. Once those costs have been flushed back, the Cost of Goods Sold account contains only the costs of units completed and sold during the period.

To illustrate, assume that the following transactions occurred at Allegro Company last month:

1. Purchased $20,000 of direct materials on account.

2. Used all of the direct materials in production during the month.

KEY POINT: All costs flow directly to the Cost of Goods Sold account during the month.

KEY POINT: In backflush costing, entries to the Work in Process Inventory and Finished Goods Inventory accounts are made at the end of the period.

Figure 5

Cost Flows Through T Accounts in Traditional and Backflush Costing

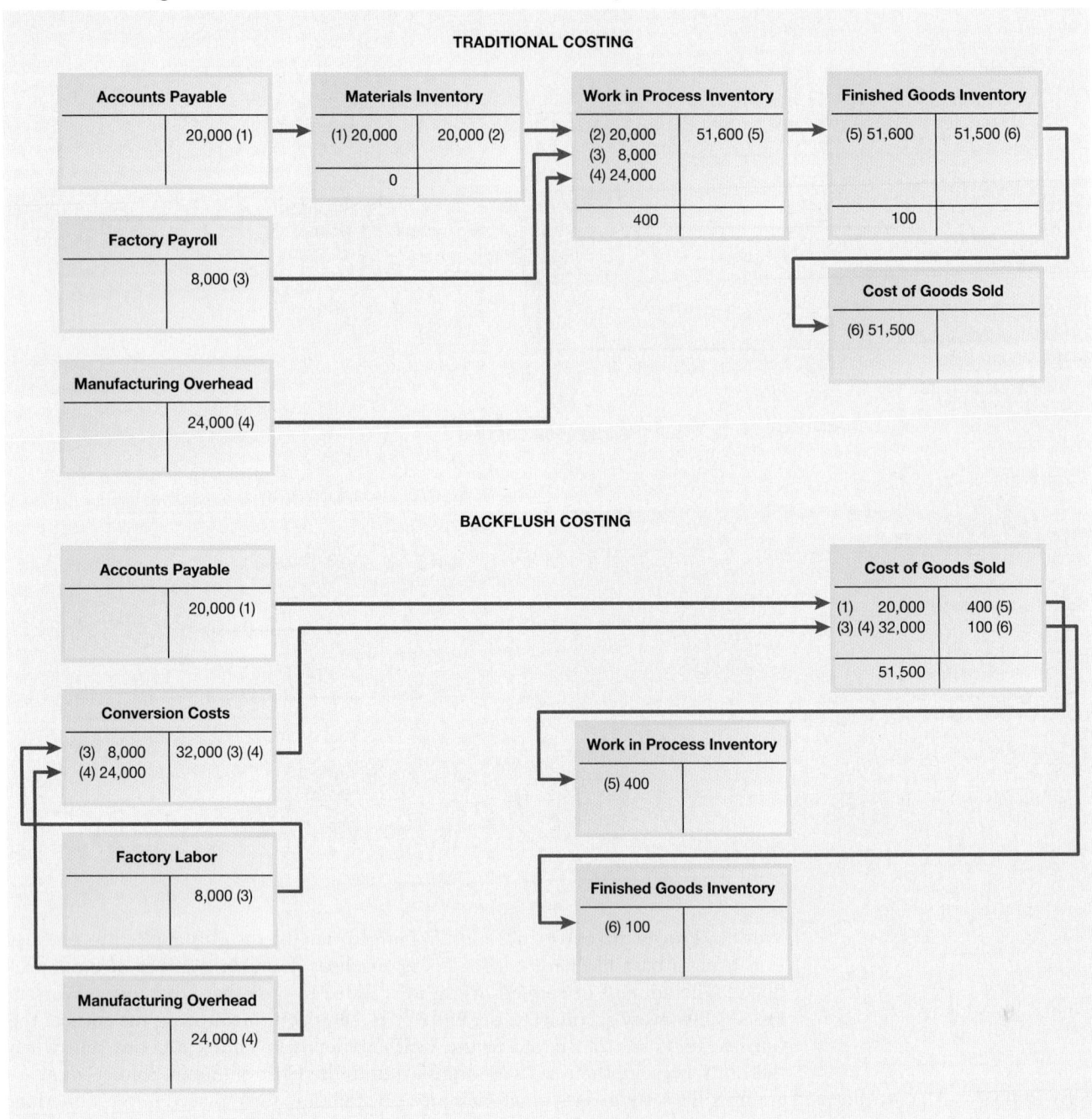

3. Incurred direct labor costs of $8,000.

4. Applied $24,000 of manufacturing overhead to production.

5. Completed units costing $51,600 during the month.

6. Sold units costing $51,500 during the month.

The top diagram in Figure 5 shows how those transactions would be entered in T accounts when traditional product costing is used. You can trace the flow of each cost by following its transaction number.

The bottom diagram in Figure 5 shows how backflush costing in a JIT environment would treat the same transactions. The cost of direct materials (Transaction 1) is charged directly to the Cost of Goods Sold account. Transaction 2 in the traditional method is not included because there is no Materials Inventory account when backflush costing is used. The costs of direct labor (Transaction 3) and manufacturing overhead (Transaction 4) are combined in the Conversion Costs account and transferred to the Cost of Goods Sold account. The total in the Cost of Goods Sold account is then $52,000 ($20,000 for direct materials and $32,000 for conversion costs).

Once all product costs for the period have been entered in the Cost of Goods Sold account, the amounts to be transferred back to the inventory accounts are calculated. The amount transferred to the Finished Goods Inventory account is the difference between the cost of units sold (Transaction 6) and the cost of completed units (Transaction 5) ($51,600 − $51,500 = $100). The remaining difference in the Cost of Goods Sold account represents the cost of the work still in production at the end of the period. It is the amount charged to the Cost of Goods Sold account during the period less the actual cost of goods finished during the period (Transaction 5) [($20,000 + $8,000 + $24,000) − $51,600 = $400]; this amount is transferred to the Work in Process Inventory account. Notice that the ending balance in the Cost of Goods Sold account, $51,500, is the same as the ending balance when traditional costing is used. The difference is that backflush costing enabled us to use fewer accounts and to avoid recording several transactions.

✔ Check out ACE for a Review Quiz at http://accounting.college.hmco.com/students.

● **STOP AND THINK!**
How is the ending balance in the Finished Goods Inventory account determined when backflush costing is used?
The ending balance in this account is the difference between the cost of goods sold and the cost of goods completed. ∎

COMPARISON OF ABM AND JIT

LO8 Compare ABM and JIT as activity-based systems.

RELATED TEXT ASSIGNMENTS
Q: 20
SE: 10
E: 14, 15

KEY POINT: ABM's primary goal is to calculate product cost accurately. JIT's primary goal is to simplify and standardize business processes.

● **STOP AND THINK!**
Can a business use both ABM and JIT?
A business can use both of these activity-based systems. ∎

ABM and JIT have several things in common. As activity-based systems, both analyze processes and identify value-adding and nonvalue-adding activities. Both seek to eliminate waste and reduce nonvalue-adding activities to improve product or service quality, reduce costs, and improve an organization's efficiency and productivity. Both improve the quality of the information managers use to make decisions about bidding, pricing, product lines, and outsourcing. However, the two systems differ in their methods of costing and cost assignment.

ABM's tool, ABC, calculates product cost by using cost drivers to assign the indirect costs of production to cost objects. ABC affects only the assignment of manufacturing overhead costs to the products; the costs of direct materials and direct labor are traced directly to products and are unaffected by ABC. ABC is often a fairly complex accounting method used with job order and process costing systems. Note that the ABC method can also be used to examine nonproduction-related activities, such as marketing and shipping.

JIT reorganizes many activities so that they are performed within work cells. The costs of those activities become direct costs of the work cell and of the products made in that cell. The total production costs within the cell can then be assigned by using simple cost drivers, such as process hours or direct materials cost. Companies that have implemented JIT manufacturing may use backflush costing rather than job order costing or process costing. This approach focuses on the output at the end of the production process and simplifies the accounting system. Table 4 summarizes the characteristics of ABM and JIT.

A company can use both ABM and JIT. ABM and ABC will improve the accuracy of its product or service costing and help the company reduce or eliminate business activities that do not add value for its customers. It can apply the JIT operating philosophy to simplify processes, use resources effectively, and eliminate

TABLE 4. Comparison of ABM and JIT Activity-Based Systems

	ABM	JIT
Primary purpose	To eliminate or reduce nonvalue-adding activities	To eliminate or reduce waste
Cost assignment	Uses ABC to assign manufacturing overhead costs to the product cost by using appropriate cost drivers	Reorganizes activities so that they are performed within work cells; manufacturing overhead costs incurred in the work cell become direct costs of the products made in that cell
Costing method	Integrates ABC with job order or process costing to calculate product costs	May use backflush costing to calculate product costs when the products are completed

waste. To remain competitive in today's fast-changing business environment, many organizations rely on both of these activity-based systems.

 Check out ACE for a Review Quiz at http://accounting.college.hmco.com/students.

Chapter Review

REVIEW OF LEARNING OBJECTIVES

LO1 Explain the role of activity-based systems in the management cycle.

Activity-based systems are information systems that provide quantitative information about an organization's activities. They help managers view the organization as a collection of related activities. Activity-based cost information enables managers to improve operating processes and make better pricing decisions. During the planning stage of the management cycle, activity-based systems help managers identify value-adding activities, determine the resources needed for those activities, and estimate product costs. In the executing and reviewing stages, these systems help managers determine the full product or service cost, identify actions that will reduce that cost, and establish whether cost-reduction goals for nonvalue-adding activities were reached. Activity-based systems also help managers report the cost of inventory and determine the degree to which product goals were achieved.

LO2 Define *activity-based management (ABM)* and discuss its relationship to the supply chain and the value chain.

Activity-based management (ABM) is an approach to managing an organization that identifies all major operating activities, determines the resources consumed by each activity and the cause of the resource usage, and categorizes the activities as either adding value to a product or service or not adding value. ABM enables managers to see their organization as a collection of value-creating activities (a value chain) operating as part of a larger system that includes suppliers' and customers' value chains (a supply chain). This perspective helps managers work cooperatively both inside and outside their organizations to reduce costs by eliminating waste and inefficiencies and by redirecting resources toward value-adding activities.

LO3 Distinguish between value-adding and nonvalue-adding activities, and describe process value analysis.

A value-adding activity adds value to a product or service as perceived by the customer. Examples include designing the components of a new car, assembling the car, painting it, and installing seats and airbags. A nonvalue-adding activity adds cost to a product or service but does not increase its market value. Examples include legal services, management accounting, machine repair, materials handling, and building maintenance. PVA is a technique that managers use to identify and link all the activities involved in the value chain. It analyzes business processes by relating activities to the events that prompt the activities and to the resources that the activities consume.

LO4 Define *activity-based costing* and explain how a cost hierarchy and a bill of activities are used.

Activity-based costing (ABC) is a method of assigning costs that calculates a more accurate product cost than traditional methods. It does so by categorizing all indirect costs by activity, tracing the indirect costs to those activities, and assigning those costs to products using a cost driver related to the cause of the cost. To implement ABC, managers (1) identify and classify each activity, (2) estimate the cost of resources for each activity, (3) identify a cost driver for each activity and estimate the quantity of each cost driver, (4) calculate an activity cost rate for each activity, and (5) assign costs to cost objects based on the level of activity required to make the product or provide the service.

Two tools—a cost hierarchy and a bill of activities—help in the implementation of ABC. To create a cost hierarchy, managers classify activities into four levels. Unit-level activities are performed each time a unit is produced. Batch-level activities are performed each time a batch of goods is produced. Product-level activities are performed to support the diversity of products in a manufacturing plant. Facility-level activities are performed to support a facility's general manufacturing process. A bill of activities is then used to compute the costs assigned to activities and the product or service unit cost.

LO5 Define the *just-in-time (JIT) operating philosophy* and identify the elements of a JIT operating environment.

The just-in-time (JIT) operating philosophy is a management philosophy that requires that all resources—materials, personnel, and facilities—be acquired and used only as needed. Its objectives are to enhance productivity, eliminate waste, reduce costs, and improve product quality. The elements in a JIT operating environment that are designed to achieve those objectives are minimum inventory levels, pull-through production, quick setup and flexible work cells, a multiskilled work force, high levels of product quality, effective preventive maintenance, and continuous improvement of the work environment.

LO6 Identify the changes in product costing that result when a firm adopts a JIT operating environment.

In product costing under JIT, processing costs are classified as either direct materials costs or conversion costs. The costs associated with inspection time, moving time, queue time, and storage time are reduced or eliminated. With computerized monitoring of the work cells, many costs that are treated as indirect or overhead costs in traditional manufacturing settings, such as the costs of utilities and operating supplies, can be traced directly to work cells. The only costs that remain indirect costs and that must be assigned to the work cells for inclusion in the conversion cost are those associated with building occupancy, insurance, and property taxes.

LO7 Define and apply *backflush costing*, and compare the cost flows in traditional and backflush costing.

In backflush costing, all product costs are first accumulated in the Cost of Goods Sold account, and at the end of the accounting period, they are "flushed back," or worked backward, into the appropriate inventory accounts. Backflush costing is commonly used to account for product costs in a JIT operating environment. It differs from the traditional costing approach, which records the costs of materials purchased in the Materials Inventory account and uses the Work in Process Inventory account to record the costs of direct materials, direct labor, and manufacturing overhead during the production process. The objective of backflush costing is to save recording time, which cuts costs.

LO8 Compare ABM and JIT as activity-based systems.

As activity-based systems, both ABM and JIT seek to eliminate waste and reduce nonvalue-adding activities. However, they differ in their approaches to cost assignment and calculation of product cost. ABM uses ABC to assign indirect costs to products using cost drivers; JIT reorganizes activities so that they are performed within work cells, and the manufacturing overhead costs incurred in a work cell become direct costs of the products made in that cell. ABM uses job order or process costing to calculate product costs, whereas JIT may use backflush costing.

REVIEW OF CONCEPTS AND TERMINOLOGY

The following concepts and terms were introduced in this chapter:

LO4 **Activity-based costing:** A method of assigning costs that calculates a more accurate product cost than traditional methods by categorizing all indirect costs by activity, tracing the indirect costs to those activities, and assigning those costs to products using a cost driver related to the cause of the cost.

LO2   Activity-based management (ABM): An approach to managing an organization that identifies all major operating activities, determines the resources consumed by each activity and the cause of the resource usage, and categorizes the activities as either adding value to a product or service or not adding value; focuses on reducing or eliminating nonvalue-adding activities.

LO1   Activity-based systems: Information systems that provide quantitative information about an organization's activities.

LO7   Backflush costing: A product costing approach in which all product costs are first accumulated in the Cost of Goods Sold account and at the end of the period are "flushed back," or worked backward, into the appropriate inventory accounts.

LO4   Batch-level activities: Activities performed each time a batch of goods is produced.

LO4   Bill of activities: A list of activities and related costs that is used to compute the costs assigned to activities and the product unit cost.

LO6   Conversion costs: The sum of the direct labor costs and manufacturing overhead costs incurred by a production department, work cell, or other work center.

LO4   Cost hierarchy: A framework for classifying activities according to the level at which their costs are incurred.

LO4   Facility-level activities: Activities performed to support a facility's general manufacturing process.

LO1   Full product cost: A cost that includes not only the costs of direct materials and direct labor, but also the costs of all production and nonproduction activities required to satisfy the customer.

LO6   Inspection time: The time spent looking for product flaws or reworking defective units.

LO5   Just-in-time (JIT) operating philosophy: An operating philosophy that requires that all resources—materials, personnel, and facilities—be acquired and used only as needed; focuses on eliminating or reducing waste.

LO6   Moving time: The time spent moving a product from one operation or department to another.

LO3   Nonvalue-adding activity: An activity that adds cost to a product or service but does not increase its market value.

LO6   Processing time: The actual amount of time spent working on a product.

LO3   Process value analysis (PVA): A technique that analyzes business processes by relating activities to the events that prompt the activities and to the resources that the activities consume.

LO4   Product-level activities: Activities performed to support the diversity of products in a manufacturing plant.

LO5   Pull-through production: A production system in which a customer's order triggers the purchase of materials and the scheduling of production for the required products.

LO5   Push-through method: A production system in which products are manufactured in long production runs and stored in anticipation of customers' orders.

LO6   Queue time: The time a product spends waiting to be worked on once it enters a new operation or department.

LO6   Storage time: The time a product spends in materials storage, work in process inventory, or finished goods inventory.

LO2   Supply chain: The path that leads from the suppliers of the materials from which a product is made to the final customer.

LO6   Throughput time: The time it takes to move a product through the entire production process.

LO4   Unit-level activities: Activities performed each time a unit is produced.

L03 Value-adding activity: An activity that adds value to a product or service as perceived by the customer.

L02 Value chain: A sequence of activities, or primary processes, that add value to a product or service; also includes support services that facilitate these activities.

L05 Work cell: An autonomous production line that can perform all required operations efficiently and continuously.

REVIEW PROBLEM

Activity-Based Costing

L04 Alvelo Corporation produces more than a dozen types of boat motors. The 240-horsepower motor is the most difficult to produce and the most expensive. The 60-horsepower model, which is the company's leading seller, is the easiest to produce. The other models range from 70 to 220 horsepower, and the difficulty of producing them increases as the horsepower increases. Rodak Company recently ordered 175 of the 80-horsepower model. Because Alvelo Corporation is considering a shift to activity-based costing, its controller, Song Shin, is interested in using this order to compare ABC with traditional costing. Costs directly traceable to the Rodak order are as follows:

Direct materials	$57,290
Purchased parts	$76,410
Direct labor hours	1,320
Average direct labor pay rate per hour	$14.00

With the traditional costing approach, Song Shin applies manufacturing overhead costs at a rate of 320 percent of direct labor costs.

For activity-based costing of the Rodak order, Song Shin uses the following data:

Activity	Cost Driver	Activity Cost Rate	Activity Usage
Product design	Engineering hours	$62 per engineering hour	76 engineering hours
Work cell setup	Number of setups	$90 per setup	16 setups
Parts production	Machine hours	$38 per machine hour	380 machine hours
Assembly	Assembly labor hours	$40 per assembly labor hour	500 assembly labor hours
Product simulation	Testing hours	$90 per testing hour	28 testing hours
Packaging and shipping	Product units	$26 per unit	175 units
Building occupancy	Direct labor cost	125% of direct labor cost	$18,480 direct labor cost

REQUIRED ▶

1. Use the traditional costing approach to compute the total cost and product unit cost of the Rodak order.
2. Using the cost hierarchy for manufacturing companies, classify each activity of the Rodak order according to the level at which it occurs.
3. Prepare a bill of activities for the operating costs.
4. Use ABC to compute the total cost and product unit cost.
5. What is the difference between the product unit cost you computed using the traditional approach and the one you computed using ABC? Does the use of ABC guarantee cost reduction for every order?

ANSWER TO REVIEW PROBLEM

1. Traditional costing approach:

Direct materials	$ 57,290
Purchased parts	76,410
Direct labor	18,480
Manufacturing overhead (320% of direct labor cost)	59,136
Total cost of order	$ 211,316
Product unit cost (total cost ÷ 175 units)	$1,207.52

2. Activities classified by level of the manufacturing cost hierarchy:

Unit level:	Parts production
	Assembly
	Packaging and shipping
Batch level:	Work cell setup
Product level:	Product design
	Product simulation
Facility level:	Building occupancy

3, 4. Bill of activities and total cost and product unit cost computed with ABC:

Alvelo Corporation
Bill of Activities
Rodak Order

Activity	Activity Cost Rate	Cost Driver Level	Activity Cost
Unit level			
Parts production	$38 per machine hour	380 machine hours	$ 14,440
Assembly	$40 per assembly labor hour	500 assembly labor hours	20,000
Packaging and shipping	$26 per unit	175 units	4,550
Batch level			
Work cell setup	$90 per setup	16 setups	1,440
Product level			
Product design	$62 per engineering hour	76 engineering hours	4,712
Product simulation	$90 per testing hour	28 testing hours	2,520
Facility level			
Building occupancy	125% of direct labor cost	$18,480 direct labor cost	23,100
Total activity costs assigned to job			$ 70,762
Total job units			÷ 175
Activity costs per unit (total activity costs ÷ total units)			$ 404.35
Cost summary			
Direct materials			$ 57,290
Purchased parts			76,410
Activity costs (includes labor and overhead)			70,762
Total cost of order			$ 204,462
Product unit cost (total cost ÷ 175 units)			$1,168.35

5. Product unit cost computed using traditional costing approach: $1,207.52
   Product unit cost computed using activity-based costing approach: 1,168.35

   Difference: $ 39.17

Although the ABC product unit cost here is lower than the one computed using the traditional costing approach, ABC does not guarantee cost reduction for every product. It does improve cost traceability, which often identifies products undercosted or overcosted by a traditional product costing system.

Chapter Assignments

BUILDING YOUR KNOWLEDGE FOUNDATION

QUESTIONS

1. How do companies measure customer value? What do managers do to create value and satisfy customers' needs?

2. Define an activity-based system and identify two such systems. What are some of the benefits of using activity-based systems?

3. How do managers use activity-based cost information in each stage of the management cycle?

4. What assumption should managers make about resource-consuming activities when they estimate a product or service unit cost?

5. What is the value of gathering quantitative information at the activity level?

6. What is activity-based management (ABM)? How is ABM useful for strategic planning and operational decision making?

7. How does a supply chain differ from a value chain?

8. What is the difference between a value-adding activity and a nonvalue-adding activity? Give an example of each.

9. Define process value analysis.

10. What is activity-based costing?

11. List the five steps involved in implementing activity-based costing.

12. List and define the four levels in the cost hierarchy for a manufacturing company.

13. What is a bill of activities?

14. What is pull-through production, and how is it different from push-through production?

15. What are the responsibilities of a machine operator in a JIT operating environment? How are they different from those of a machine operator in a traditional environment?

16. How does the inspection function change in a JIT operating environment?

17. Why is preventive maintenance of machinery critical to the operation of a JIT work cell?

18. How do JIT operations affect the classification of costs?

19. Does JIT or ABM use backflush costing? How does it reduce the time spent on recordkeeping?

20. How do ABM and JIT differ in their approaches to product costing?

SHORT EXERCISES

LO1 Activity-Based Systems

SE 1. Amber Lutz started a retail clothing business two years ago. Lutz's first year was very successful, but sales dropped 50 percent in the second year. A friend who is a business consultant analyzed Lutz's business and came up with two basic reasons for the decline in sales: (1) Lutz has been placing orders late in each season, and (2) shipments of clothing have been arriving late and in poor condition. What measures can Lutz take to improve her business and persuade customers to return?

LO2 The Value Chain

SE 2. Which of the following activities would be part of the value chain of a manufacturing company? Which activities do not add value?

1. Product inspection
2. Machine drilling
3. Materials storage
4. Product engineering
5. Product packing
6. Cost accounting
7. Moving work in process
8. Inventory control

LO2   The Supply Chain

SE 3.   Thom DuBois is developing plans to open a restaurant called Ribs 'n Slaw. He has located a building and will lease all the furniture and equipment he needs for the restaurant. Food Servers, Inc., will supply all the restaurant's personnel. Identify the components of Ribs 'n Slaw's supply chain.

LO3   Value-Adding and Nonvalue-Adding Activities

SE 4.   Indicate whether the following activities of a submarine sandwich shop are value-adding (V) or nonvalue-adding (NV):

1. Purchasing sandwich ingredients
2. Storing condiments
3. Making sandwiches
4. Cleaning up the shop
5. Making home deliveries
6. Accounting for sales and costs

LO4   The Cost Hierarchy

SE 5.   Engineering design is an activity vital to the success of any motor vehicle manufacturer. Identify the level at which engineering design would be classified in the cost hierarchy used with ABC for each of the following:

1. A maker of unique editions of luxury automobiles
2. A maker of built-to-order city and county emergency vehicles (orders are usually placed for 10 to 12 identical vehicles)
3. A maker of a line of automobiles sold throughout the world

LO4   The Cost Hierarchy

SE 6.   Match the four levels of the cost hierarchy to the following activities of a dress manufacturer that uses activity-based management:

1. Routine maintenance of sewing machines
2. Designing a pattern for a new dress style
3. Sewing seams on a garment
4. Producing 100 blue dresses of a certain style

LO5   Elements of a JIT Operating Environment

SE 7.   Maintaining minimum inventory levels and using pull-through production are important elements of a just-in-time operating environment. How does pull-through production help minimize inventories?

LO6   Product Costing Changes in a JIT Environment

SE 8.   Tool Products Company is in the process of adopting the just-in-time operating philosophy for its tool-making operations. Indicate which of the following manufacturing overhead costs are nonvalue-adding costs (NVA) and which can be traced directly to the new tool-making work cell (D):

1. Storage barrels for work in process inventory
2. Inspection labor
3. Machine electricity
4. Machine repairs
5. Depreciation of the storage barrel movers
6. Machine setup labor

LO7   Backflush Costing

SE 9.   For work done during August, Printing Press Company incurred direct materials costs of $123,450 and conversion costs of $265,200. The company employs a just-in-time operating philosophy and backflush costing. At the end of August, it was determined that the Work in Process Inventory account had been assigned $980 of costs, and the ending balance of the Finished Goods Inventory account was $1,290. There were no beginning inventory balances.

How much was charged to the Cost of Goods Sold account during August? What was the ending balance of the Cost of Goods Sold account?

LO8   Comparison of ABM and JIT

SE 10.   Hwang Corp. recently installed three just-in-time work cells in its screen-making division. The work cells will make large quantities of products for major window and door manufacturers. Should Hwang use JIT and backflush costing or ABM and ABC to account for product costs? Defend your choice of activity-based system.

EXERCISES

LO1   Management Reports

E 1.   The reports that follow are from a department in an insurance company. Which report would be used for financial purposes, and which would be used for activity-based decision making? Why?

Salaries	$ 1,400	Enter claims into system	$ 2,000
Equipment	1,200	Analyze claims	1,000
Travel expenses	8,000	Suspend claims	1,500
Supplies	300	Receive inquiries	1,500
Use and occupancy	3,000	Resolve problems	400
		Process batches	3,000
		Determine eligibility	4,000
		Make copies	200
		Write correspondence	100
		Attend training	200
Total	$13,900	Total	$13,900

LO2 The Supply Chain and Value Chain

E 2. Indicate which of the following persons and activities associated with a lawn and garden nursery are part of the supply chain (S) and which are part of the value chain (V):

1. Plant and tree vendor
2. Purchasing potted trees
3. Computer and software salesperson
4. Creating marketing plans
5. Advertising company manager
6. Scheduling delivery trucks
7. Customer service

LO2 The Supply Chain and Value Chain

E 3. The items listed below are associated with a hotel. Indicate which are part of the supply chain (S) and which are part of the value chain (V).

1. Travel agency
2. Housekeeping supplies
3. Special events and promotions
4. Customer service
5. Travel web site
6. Tour agencies

LO3 Value Analysis

E 4. Libbel Enterprises has been in business for 30 years. Last year, the company purchased Chemcraft Laboratory and entered the chemical processing business. Libbel's controller prepared a process value analysis of the new operation and identified the following activities:

New product research	Product sales	Product bottling process
Solicitation of vendor bids	Packaging process	Product warranty work
Materials storage	Materials inspection	Product engineering
Product curing process	New product marketing	Purchasing of direct materials
Product scheduling	Product inspection	Finished goods storage
Product spoilage	Product delivery	Cleanup of processing areas
Customer follow-up	Materials delivery	Product mixing process

Identify the value-adding activities in this list, and classify them into the activity areas of the value chain illustrated in Figure 2 in this chapter. Prepare a separate list of the nonvalue-adding activities.

LO3 Value-Adding Activities

E 5. When Courtney Tybee prepared a process value analysis for her company, she identified the following primary activities. Identify the value-adding activities.

1. Production scheduling
2. Customer follow-up
3. Materials moving
4. Product inspection
5. Engineering design
6. Product marketing
7. Product sales

LO4 The Cost Hierarchy

E 6. Copia Electronics makes speaker systems. Its customers range from new hotels and restaurants that need specially designed sound systems to nationwide retail outlets that order large quantities of similar products. The following activities are part of the company's operating process:

New product design	Purchasing of materials	Assembly labor
Product line marketing	Building repair	Assembly line setup
Unique system design	Sales commissions	Building security
Unique system packaging	Bulk packing of orders	Production line supervision

Classify each activity as unit level (UL), batch level (BL), product level (PL), or facility level (FL).

LO4 The Bill of Activities

E 7. Lake Corporation has received an order for handheld computers from Union, LLC. A partially complete bill of activities for that order appears at the top of the next page. Fill in the missing data.

Lake Corporation
Bill of Activities for
Order from Union, LLC

Activity	Activity Cost Rate	Cost Driver Level	Activity Cost
Unit level			
Parts production	$50 per machine hour	200 machine hours	$?
Assembly	$20 per direct labor hour	100 direct labor hours	?
Packaging and shipping	$12.50 per unit	400 units	?
Batch level			
Work cell setup	$100 per setup	16 setups	?
Product level			
Product design	$60 per engineering hour	80 engineering hours	?
Product simulation	$80 per testing hour	30 testing hours	?
Facility level			
Building occupancy	200% of assembly labor cost	?	?
Total activity costs assigned to job			$?
Total job units			400
Activity costs per unit (total activity costs ÷ total units)			$?
Cost summary			
Direct materials			$60,000
Purchased parts			80,000
Activity costs			?
Total cost of order			$?
Product unit cost (total cost ÷ 400 units)			$?

LO4   Activity Cost Rates

E 8. Compute the activity cost rates for materials handling, assembly, and design based on these data:

Materials
Cloth	$26,000
Fasteners	4,000
Purchased parts	40,000

Materials handling
Labor	8,000
Equipment depreciation	5,000
Electrical power	2,000
Maintenance	6,000

Assembly
Machinists	5,000

Design
Labor	5,000
Electrical power	1,000
Overhead	8,000

Output totaled 40,000 units. Each unit requires three machine hours of effort. Materials handling costs are allocated to the products based on direct materials cost. Design costs are allocated based on units produced. Assembly costs are allocated based on 500 machinist hours.

E 9.

The numbered items below are concepts that underlie activity-based systems, such as ABM and JIT. Match each concept to the related lettered element(s) of a JIT operating environment.

1. Business processes are simplified.
2. The quality of the product or service is critical.
3. Employees are cross-trained.
4. Large inventories waste resources and may hide bad work.
5. Goods should be produced only when needed.
6. Equipment downtime is minimized.

a. Minimum inventory levels
b. Pull-through production
c. Quick machine setups and flexible work cells
d. A multiskilled work force
e. High levels of product quality
f. Effective preventive maintenance

E 10.

Identify which of the following exist in a traditional manufacturing environment and which exist in a JIT environment:

1. Large amounts of inventory
2. Complex manufacturing processes
3. A multiskilled labor force
4. Flexible work cells
5. Push-through production methods
6. Materials purchased infrequently but in large lot sizes
7. Infrequent setups

E 11.

The cost categories in this list are typical of many manufacturing operations:

Direct materials	Direct labor	Depreciation, machinery
Sheet steel	Engineering labor	Supervisory salaries
Iron castings	Indirect labor	Electrical power
Assembly parts	Operating supplies	Insurance and taxes, plant
Part 24RE6	Small tools	President's salary
Part 15RF8	Depreciation, plant	Employee benefits

Identify each cost as direct or indirect assuming it was incurred in (1) a traditional manufacturing setting and (2) a JIT environment. State the reasons for changes in classification.

E 12.

Conda Products Company implemented a JIT work environment in its trowel division eight months ago, and the division has been operating at near capacity since then. Its accounting system was changed to combine direct labor and manufacturing overhead into a Conversion Costs account. The following transactions took place last week:

May 28   Ordered, received, and used handles and sheet metal costing $11,340.
29   Direct labor costs incurred, $5,400.
29   Manufacturing overhead costs incurred, $8,100.
30   Completed trowels costing $24,800.
31   Sold trowels costing $24,000.

Using backflush costing, calculate the ending balance in the Work in Process Inventory and Finished Goods Inventory accounts.

E 13.

Good Morning Enterprises produces digital alarm clocks. It has a just-in-time assembly process and uses backflush costing to record production costs. Manufacturing overhead is assigned at a rate of $17 per assembly labor hour. There were no beginning inventories in March. During March, the following operating data were generated:

Cost of direct materials purchased and used	$53,200
Direct labor costs incurred	$27,300
Manufacturing overhead costs assigned	?
Assembly hours worked	3,840 hours
Ending work in process inventory	$1,050
Ending finished goods inventory	$960

Using T accounts, show the flow of costs through the backflush costing system. What was the total cost of goods sold in March?

E 14.

Identify each of the following as a characteristic of ABM or JIT:

1. Backflush costing
2. ABC used to assign manufacturing overhead costs to the product cost
3. ABC integrated with job order or process costing systems

4. Complexity reduced by using work cells, minimizing inventories, and reducing or eliminating nonvalue-adding activities
5. Activities reorganized so that they are performed within work cells

LO8   Comparison of ABM and JIT

E 15. The following are excerpts from a conversation between two managers about their companies' activity-based systems. Identify the manager who works for a company that emphasizes ABM and the one who works for a company that emphasizes a JIT system.

Manager 1: We try to manage our resources effectively by monitoring operating activities. We analyze all major operating activities, and we focus on reducing or eliminating the ones that don't add value to our products.

Manager 2: We're very concerned with eliminating waste. We've designed our operations to reduce the time it takes to move, store, queue, and inspect materials. We've also reduced our inventories by buying and using materials only when we need them.

PROBLEMS

P 1.

LO2   The Value Chain and Process
LO3   Value Analysis

Lindstrom Industries, Inc., produces chain saws, weed whackers, and lawn mowers for major retail chains. Lindstrom makes these products to order in large quantities for each customer. It has adopted activity-based management, and its controller is in the process of developing an activity-based costing system. The controller has identified the following primary activities of the company:

Production scheduling	Materials moving
Product delivery	Production—assembly
Customer follow-up	Engineering design
Materials and parts purchasing	Product inspection
Materials storage	Processing areas cleanup
Materials inspection	Product marketing
Production—drilling	Building maintenance
Product packaging	Product sales
New product testing	Product rework
Finished goods storage	Production—grinding
Production—machine setup	Personnel services

REQUIRED ▶

1. Identify the activities that do not add value to Lindstrom's products.
2. Assist the controller's process value analysis by grouping the value-adding activities into the activity areas of the value chain illustrated in Figure 2 of this chapter.
3. State whether each nonvalue-adding activity is necessary or unnecessary. Suggest how the controller could reduce or eliminate each unnecessary activity.

P 2.

LO4   Activity-Based Costing

Boulware Products, Inc., produces a line of printers for wholesale distributors. It has just completed packaging an order from Shawl Company for 150 of its Model G printers. Before the order is shipped, the controller wants to compare the unit costs computed under the company's new activity-based costing system with the unit costs computed under its traditional costing system. Data for the Shawl order are as follows:

Direct materials	$17,552
Purchased parts	$14,856
Direct labor hours	140
Average direct labor pay rate per hour	$17

Boulware's traditional costing system assigned manufacturing overhead costs at a rate of 240 percent of direct labor cost.

Data for activity-based costing of the Shawl order are as follows:

Activity	Cost Driver	Activity Cost Rate	Activity Usage
Engineering systems design	Engineering hours	$28 per engineering hour	18 engineering hours
Setup	Number of setups	$36 per setup	12 setups
Parts production	Machine hours	$37 per machine hour	82 machine hours
Product assembly	Labor hours	$42 per labor hour	96 labor hours
Packaging	Number of packages	$28 per package	30 packages
Building occupancy	Machine hours	$10 per machine hour	82 machine hours

REQUIRED ▶

1. Use the traditional costing approach to compute the total cost and the product unit cost of the Shawl order.

2. Using the cost hierarchy, identify each activity as unit level, batch level, product level, or facility level.
3. Prepare a bill of activities for the operating costs.
4. Use ABC to compute the total cost and product unit cost of the Shawl order.
5. What is the difference between the product unit cost you computed using the traditional approach and the one you computed using ABC? Does the use of activity-based costing guarantee cost reduction for every order?

P 3.

LO4   Activity Cost Rates

Noir Company produces four versions of its model J17-21 bicycle seat in its Santa Clara plant. The four versions have different shapes, but their processing operations and production costs are identical. During July, the following costs were incurred:

Direct materials

Leather	$25,430
Metal frame	39,180
Bolts	3,010

Materials handling

Labor	8,232
Equipment depreciation	4,410
Electrical power	2,460
Maintenance	5,184

Assembly

Machinists	13,230

Engineering design

Labor	4,116
Electrical power	1,176
Engineering overhead	7,644

Overhead

Equipment depreciation	7,056
Indirect labor	30,870
Supervision	17,640
Operating supplies	4,410
Electrical power	10,584
Repairs and maintenance	21,168
Building occupancy overhead	52,920

July's output totaled 29,400 units. Each unit requires three machine hours of effort. Materials handling costs are allocated to the products based on direct materials cost, engineering design costs are allocated based on units produced, and overhead is allocated based on machine hours. Assembly costs are allocated based on machinist hours, which are estimated at 882 for July.

During July, Noir completed 500 bicycle seats for Job 142. The activity usage for Job 142 was as follows: direct materials, $1,150; machinist hours, 15.

REQUIRED

1. Compute the following activity cost rates: (a) The materials handling cost rate; (b) assembly cost rate, (c) engineering design cost rate, and (d) overhead rate.
2. Prepare a bill of activities for Job 142.
3. Use activity-based costing to compute the job's total cost and product unit cost.

P 4.

LO6   Direct and Indirect Costs in JIT and Traditional Manufacturing Environments

Funz Company, which produces wooden toys, is about to adopt a JIT operating environment. In anticipation of the change, Letty Hernando, Funz's controller, prepared the following list of costs for December:

Wood	$3,200	Insurance, plant	$ 324
Bolts	32	President's salary	4,000
Small tools	54	Engineering labor	2,700
Depreciation, plant	450	Utilities	1,250
Depreciation, machinery	275	Building occupancy	1,740
Direct labor	2,675	Supervision	2,686
Indirect labor	890	Operating supplies	254
Purchased parts	58	Repairs and maintenance	198
Materials handling	74	Employee benefits	2,654

REQUIRED

1. Identify each cost as direct or indirect assuming it was incurred in a traditional manufacturing setting.

2. Identify each cost as direct or indirect assuming it was incurred in a just-in-time (JIT) environment.

3. Assume that the costs incurred in the JIT environment are for a work cell that completed 1,250 toy cars in December. Compute the total direct cost and the direct cost per unit for the cars produced.

LO7   Backflush Costing

P 5. Automotive Parts Company produces 12 parts for car bodies and sells them to three automobile assembly companies in the United States. The company implemented just-in-time operating and costing procedures three years ago. Manufacturing overhead is applied at a rate of $26 per work cell hour used. All direct materials and purchased parts are used as they are received.

One of the company's work cells produces automotive fenders that are completely detailed and ready to install when received by the customer. The cell is operated by four employees and involves a flexible manufacturing system with 14 workstations. Operating details for February for this cell are as follows:

Beginning work in process inventory	—
Beginning finished goods inventory	$420
Cost of direct materials purchased on account and used	$213,400
Cost of parts purchased on account and used	$111,250
Direct labor costs incurred	$26,450
Costs of goods completed during February	$564,650
Manufacturing overhead costs assigned	?
Work cell hours used	8,260 work cell hours
Ending work in process inventory	$1,210
Ending finished goods inventory	$670

REQUIRED ▶

1. Using T accounts, show the flow of costs through a backflush costing system.
2. Using T accounts, show the flow of costs through a traditional costing system.
3. What was the total cost of goods sold for the month?

ALTERNATE PROBLEMS

LO4   Activity-Based Costing

P 6. Kaui Company produces cellular phones. It has just comleted an order for 80 phones placed by Many Hands, Ltd. Kaui recently shifted to an activity-based costing system, and its controller is interested in the impact the ABC system had on the Many Hands order. Data for that order are as follows: direct materials $36,950; purchased parts, $21,100; direct labor hours, 220; average direct labor pay rate per hour, $15.

Under Kaui's traditional costing system, manufacturing overhead costs were assigned at a rate of 270 percent of direct labor cost.

Data for activity-based costing of the Many Hands order are as follows:

Activity	Cost Driver	Activity Cost Rate	Activity Usage
Electrical engineering design	Engineering hours	$19 per engineering hour	32 engineering hours
Setup	Number of setups	$29 per setup	11 setups
Parts production	Machine hours	$26 per machine hour	134 machine hours
Product testing	Number of tests	$32 per test	52 tests
Packaging	Number of packages	$17 per package	22 packages
Building occupancy	Machine hours	$9.80 per machine hour	134 machine hours
Assembly	Direct labor hours	$15 per direct labor hour	220 direct labor hours

REQUIRED ▶

1. Use the traditional costing approach to compute the total cost and the product unit cost of the Many Hands order.
2. Using the cost hierarchy, identify each activity as unit level, batch level, product level, or facility level.
3. Prepare a bill of activities for the operating costs.
4. Use ABC to compute the total cost and product unit cost of the order.
5. What is the difference between the product unit cost you computed using the traditional approach and the one you computed using ABC? Does the use of activity-based costing guarantee cost reduction for every order?

LO4   Activity Cost Rates

P 7.   Alligood Company produces three models of aluminum skateboards in its Kansas City plant. The models have minor differences, but their processing operations and production costs are identical. During June, the following costs were incurred:

Direct materials

Aluminum frame	$162,524
Bolts	3,876

Purchased parts

Wheels	74,934
Decals	5,066

Materials handling (assigned based on direct materials cost)

Labor	17,068
Utilities	4,438
Maintenance	914
Depreciation	876

Assembly line (assigned based on labor hours)

Labor	46,080

Setup (assigned based on number of setups)

Labor	6,385
Supplies	762
Overhead	3,953

Product testing (assigned based on number of tests)

Labor	2,765
Supplies	435

Building occupancy (assigned based on machine hours)

Insurance	5,767
Depreciation	2,452
Repairs and maintenance	3,781

June's output totaled 32,000 skateboards. Each board required 1.5 machine hours of effort. During June, Alligood's assembly line worked 2,304 hours, performed 370 setups and 64,000 product tests, and completed an order for 1,000 skateboards placed by Executive Toys Company. The job incurred costs of $5,200 for direct materials and $2,500 for purchased parts. It required 3 setups, 2,000 tests, and 72 assembly line hours.

REQUIRED ▶   1. Compute the following activity cost rates:

   a. Materials handling cost rate
   b. Assembly line cost rate
   c. Setup cost rate
   d. Product testing cost rate
   e. Building occupancy cost rate

2. Prepare a bill of activities for the Executive Toys job.
3. Use activity-based costing to compute the job's total cost and product unit cost. (Round your answer to two decimal places.)

LO7   Backflush Costing

P 8.   Reilly Corporation produces metal fasteners using six work cells, one for each of its product lines. It implemented just-in-time operations and costing methods two years ago. Manufacturing overhead is assigned using a rate of $14 per machine hour for the Machine Snap Work Cell. There were no beginning inventories on April 1. All direct materials and purchased parts are used as they are received. Operating details for April for the Machine Snap Work Cell are as follows.

Cost of direct materials purchased on account and used	$104,500
Cost of parts purchased on account and used	$78,900
Direct labor costs incurred	$39,000
Costs of goods completed during April	$392,540
Manufacturing overhead costs assigned	?
Machine hours used	12,220 machine hours
Ending work in process inventory	$940
Ending finished goods inventory	$1,020

REQUIRED ▶   1. Using T accounts, show the flow of costs through a backflush costing system.
2. Using T accounts, show the flow of costs through a traditional costing system.
3. What was the total cost of goods sold for the month?

SKILLS DEVELOPMENT CASES

Conceptual Analysis

LO5   JIT in a Service Business

SD 1. The initiation banquet for new members of your business club is being held at an excellent restaurant. You are sitting next to two college students who are majoring in marketing. In discussing the accounting course they are taking, they mention that they are having difficulty understanding the just-in-time philosophy. They have read that the elements of a company's JIT operating system support the concepts of simplicity, continuous improvement, waste reduction, timeliness, and efficiency. They realize that to understand JIT in a complex manufacturing environment, they must first understand JIT in a simpler context. They ask you to explain the philosophy and provide an example.

Briefly explain the JIT philosophy. Apply the elements of a JIT operating system to the restaurant where the banquet is being held. Do you believe the JIT philosophy applies in all restaurant operations? Explain.

LO2   Adding Value
LO3

SD 2. In a new business model called "zero time," time is the primary focus that drives everything else in an organization. According to this model, instantaneous, or "zero-time," Internet access to relevant information allows a company to add value for customers at every point along its value chain—from marketing, research and development, purchasing, production, sales, and shipping to customer service.[6]

1. Identify and comment on the primary focus of traditional business models, such as job order or process costing.
2. Speculate about how focusing on time would add value for customers throughout an organization's value chain.

Ethical Dilemma

LO5   Ethics and JIT Implementation

SD 3. For almost a year, Traki Company has been changing its manufacturing process from a traditional to a JIT approach. Management has asked for employees' assistance in the transition and has offered bonuses for suggestions that cut time from the production operation. Deb Hinds and Jack Snow each identified a timesaving opportunity and turned in their suggestions to their manager, Randall Soder.

Soder sent the suggestions to the committee charged with reviewing employees' suggestions, which inadvertently identified them as being Soder's own. The committee decided that the two suggestions were worthy of reward and voted a large bonus for Soder. When notified of this, Soder could not bring himself to identify the true authors of the suggestions.

When Hinds and Snow heard about Soder's bonus, they confronted him with his fraudulent act and expressed their grievances. He told them that he needed the recognition to be eligible for an upcoming promotion and promised that if they kept quiet about the matter, he would make sure that they both received significant raises. Prepare written responses to the following questions so that you can discuss them in class:

1. Should Hinds and Snow keep quiet? What other options are open to them?
2. How should Soder have dealt with Hinds's and Snow's complaints?

Research Activity

LO5   JIT Production

SD 4. To compete for new domestic and foreign business, many large, multinational companies, as well as many smaller firms, have installed automated just-in-time production processes. Locate an article about a company that has recently installed a JIT system or an annual report from such a company. Conduct your search using an Internet search engine like Google, a business periodical like *The Wall Street Journal*, or the Needles Accounting Resource Center Web Site at http://accounting.college.hmco.com/students.

Choose a source that describes the changes the company made to its plant to increase product quality and to compete as a world-class manufacturer. Prepare a one-page description of those changes. Include in your report the name of the company, its location, the name of the chief executive officer and/or president, and, if available, the dollar amount of the company's total sales for the most recent year. Be prepared to present your findings in class.

Decision-Making Practice

SD 5.

LO3 Activities, Cost Drivers, and
LO5 JIT
LO6

Fifteen years ago, Bruce Sable, together with 10 financial supporters, founded Sable Corporation. Located in Atlanta, the company originally manufactured roller skates, but 12 years ago, on the advice of its marketing department, it switched to making skateboards. More than 4 million skateboards later, Sable Corporation finds itself an industry leader in both volume and quality. To retain market share, it has decided to automate its manufacturing process. It has ordered flexible manufacturing systems for wheel assembly and board shaping. Manual operations will be retained for board decorating because some hand painting is involved. All operations will be converted to a just-in-time environment.

Bruce Sable wants to know how the JIT approach will affect the company's product costing practices and has called you in as a consultant.

1. Summarize the elements of a JIT environment.
2. How will the automated systems change product costing?
3. What are some cost drivers that the company should employ? In what situations?

MANAGERIAL REPORTING AND ANALYSIS CASES

Interpreting Management Reports

MRA 1.

LO3 ABC and Selling and
LO4 Administrative Expenses

Sandy Star, the owner of Star Bakery, wants to know the profitability of each of her bakery's customer groups. She is especially interested in the State Institutions customer group, which is one of the company's largest customer groups. Currently, the bakery is selling doughnuts and snack foods to ten state institutions in three states. The controller has prepared the following income statement for the State Institutions customer group:

Star Bakery
Income Statement for State Institutions Customer Group
For the Year Ended December 31, 20x7

Sales ($5 per case × 50,000 cases)				$250,000
Cost of goods sold ($3.50 per case × 50,000 cases)				175,000
Gross margin				$ 75,000

Less: Selling and administrative activity costs

Activity	Activity Cost Rate	Cost Driver Level	Activity Cost	
Make sales calls	$60 per sales call	60 sales calls	$ 3,600	
Prepare sales orders	$10 per sales order	900 sales orders	9,000	
Handle inquiries	$5 per minute	1,000 minutes	5,000	
Ship products	$1 per case sold	50,000 cases	50,000	
Process invoices	$20 per invoice	950 invoices	19,000	
Process credits	$20 per notice	40 notices	800	
Process billings and collections	$7 per billing	1,050 billings	7,350	
Total selling and administrative activity costs				94,750
Income (loss) contributed by State Institutions customer group				($ 19,750)

The controller has also provided information about selling and administrative activities for customer groups that have similar characteristics. For 20x7, the planned activity cost rates and the annual cost driver levels for each selling and administrative activity are as follows:

Activity	Activity Cost Rate	Planned Annual Cost Driver Level
Make sales calls	$60 per sales call	59 sales calls
Prepare sales orders	$10 per sales order	850 sales orders
Handle inquiries	$5.10 per minute	1,000 minutes
Ship products	$.60 per case sold	50,000 cases
Process invoices	$1 per invoice	500 invoices
Process credits	$10 per notice	5 notices
Process billings and collections	$4 per billing	600 billings

You have been called in as a consultant on the State Institutions customer group.

1. Calculate the planned activity cost for each activity.
2. Calculate the differences between the planned activity cost and the State Institutions customer group's activity costs for 20x7.
3. From your evaluation of the differences calculated in 2 and your review of the income statement, identify the nonvalue-adding activities and state which selling and administrative activities should be examined.
4. What actions might the company take to reduce the costs of nonvalue-adding selling and administrative activities?

 Group Activity: Provide groups with data for 1 and 2 and ask them to discuss and answer 3 and 4.

Formulating Management Reports

MRA 2.

LO5   Manufacturing Processes

Classic Clubs, Inc., manufactures professional golf clubs. Demand has been so great that the company has built a special plant that makes only custom-crafted clubs. The clubs are shaped by machines but vary according to the customer's sex, height, weight, and arm length. Ten basic sets of clubs are produced, five for females and five for males. Slight variations in machine setup produce the differences in the club weights and lengths. In the past six months, several problems have developed. Even though one computer-controlled machine is used in the manufacturing process, the company's backlog is growing rapidly, and customers are complaining that delivery is too slow. Quality is declining because clubs are being pushed through production without proper inspection. Working capital is tied up in excessive amounts of inventory and storage space. Workers are complaining about the pressure to produce the backlogged orders. Machine breakdowns are increasing. Production control reports are not useful because they are not timely and contain irrelevant information. The company's profitability and cash flow are suffering.

Classic Clubs has hired you as a consultant to analyze its problems and suggest a solution. Denise Rodeburg, the president, asks that you complete your work within a month so that she can prepare a plan to present to the board of directors at the mid-year board meeting.

1. In memo form, prepare a report for Rodeburg recommending specific changes in the manufacturing processes.
2. In preparing the report, answer the following questions:
   a. Why are you preparing the report? What is its purpose?
   b. Who is the audience for this report?
   c. What kinds of information do you need to prepare the report, and where will you find it (i.e., what sources will you use)?
   d. When do you need to obtain the information?

International Company

MRA 3.
LO4   ABM and ABC in a Service Business

Kendle and Watson, a CPA firm, has provided audit, tax, and management advisory services to businesses in the London area for over 50 years. Recently, the firm decided to use ABM and activity-based costing to assign its overhead costs to those service functions. Bellamy Kendle is interested in seeing how the traditional and the activity-based costing

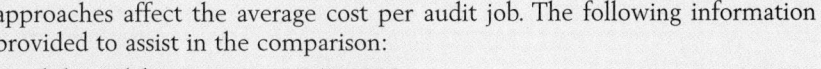

approaches affect the average cost per audit job. The following information has been provided to assist in the comparison:

Total direct labor costs	£400,000
Other direct costs	120,000
Total direct costs	£520,000

The traditional costing approach assigned overhead costs at a rate of 120 percent of direct labor costs.

Data for activity-based costing of the audit function are as follows:

Activity	Cost Driver	Activity Cost Rate	Activity Usage
Professional development	Number of employees	£2,000 per employee	50 employees
Administration	Number of jobs	£1,000 per job	50 jobs
Client development	Number of new clients	£5,000 per new client	29 new clients

1. Using direct labor cost as the cost driver, calculate the total costs for the audit function. What is the average cost per job?
2. Using activity-based costing to assign overhead, calculate the total costs for the audit function. What is the average cost per job?
3. Calculate the difference in total costs between the two approaches. Why would activity-based costing be the better approach to assigning overhead to the audit function?

Excel Spreadsheet Analysis

MRA 4.
LO3 ABC in Planning and Control
LO4

Refer to the income statement in **MRA 1** for the State Institutions customer group for the year ended December 31, 20x7. Sandy Star, the owner of Star Bakery, is in the process of budgeting income for 20x8. She has asked the controller to prepare a budgeted income statement for the State Institutions customer group. She estimates that the selling price per case, the number of cases sold, the cost of goods sold per case, and the activity costs for making sales calls, preparing sales orders, and handling inquiries will remain the same for 20x8. She has contracted with a new freight company to ship the 50,000 cases at $.60 per case sold. She has also analyzed the procedures for invoicing, processing credits, billing, and collecting and has decided it would be less expensive for a customer service agency to do the work. The agency will charge the bakery 1.5 percent of the total sales revenue.

1. Prepare a budgeted income statement for the State Institutions customer group for the year ended December 31, 20x8.
2. Refer to the information in **MRA 1**. Assuming the planned activity cost rate and planned annual cost driver level for each selling and administrative activity remain the same in 20x8, calculate the planned activity cost for each activity.
3. Calculate the differences between the planned activity costs (determined in requirement **2**) and the State Institutions customer group's activity costs for 20x8 (determined in **1**).
4. Evaluate the results of changing freight companies and outsourcing the customer service activities.

Internet Case

MRA 5.
LO3 Value-Adding and Nonvalue-Adding Activities

Levi Strauss & Co. <www.levistrauss.com> has been making jeans since 1853. Today, it manufactures different jeans for different market segments. For example, Wal-Mart <www.walmart.com> sells Levi Strauss's Signature brand of jeans for about $15 less than department stores sell the company's Type One brand.[7] Visit the Levi Strauss web site to learn more about the company's brands. What value-adding production and non-production activities do you think might account for the higher price of the Type One brand? Which of these activities do you think Levi Strauss would eliminate for the less costly Signature brand? (By visiting the web site, you can also discover what Levi Strauss called jeans when it first sold them 150 years ago, as well as the year in which the company officially changed the name to "jeans.")

23

Chapter 23 focuses on the analysis of cost behavior and its role in achieving profitability.

Cost Behavior Analysis

LEARNING OBJECTIVES

LO1 Define *cost behavior* and explain how managers use this concept in the management cycle.

LO2 Identify variable, fixed, and mixed costs, and separate mixed costs into their variable and fixed components.

LO3 Define *cost-volume-profit (C-V-P) analysis* and discuss how managers use it as a tool for planning and control.

LO4 Define *breakeven point* and use contribution margin to determine a company's breakeven point for multiple products.

LO5 Use C-V-P analysis to project the profitability of products and services.

DECISION POINT

A MANAGER'S FOCUS

Kraft Foods <www.kraft.com> Kraft, Philadelphia, Maxwell House, Nabisco, Oscar Mayer, and Post are among the brands that Kraft Foods brings to households around the world. The company has five core sectors—snacks, beverages, cheese, grocery, and convenience meals—and it holds the largest market share in 21 of its 25 top categories, both in the United States and abroad. Located in more than 150 countries around the globe, Kraft's 109,000 employees work to make food a simpler, easier, and more enjoyable part of life by adding innovative products and optimizing line and geographic extensions of current products.[1] The types and numbers of products that Kraft makes and sells vary from year to year depending on market demand. How does the mix of production and sales affect Kraft management's planning for profitability? How does it affect the computation of product costs?

Kraft's management must consider the behavior of the many costs of making products and determine a selling price that will take into account the variability of demand. For example, the costs of the direct materials and direct labor the company uses to make each one-pound package of cheese are roughly the same, but the total cost of direct materials will vary according to the number of packages produced in any one year. Similarly, the costs of operating the factories and of the manufacturing equipment used in making the cheese will not change significantly from year to year in relation to the number of pounds produced, but the portion of those costs applied to each pound of product will vary depending on the number of

Why does Kraft's management analyze cost behavior to project the profitability of it's core sectors?

pounds actually produced. To project the profitability of a particular year, Kraft's management must take into account both the selling price and the estimated production and sales mix of products and the effects those estimates have on a product's unit cost.

COST BEHAVIOR AND THE MANAGEMENT CYCLE

LO1 Define *cost behavior* and explain how managers use this concept in the management cycle.

RELATED TEXT ASSIGNMENTS
Q: 1, 2
SE: 1
SD: 1

Cost behavior—the way costs respond to changes in volume or activity—is a factor in almost every decision managers make. Managers commonly use it to analyze alternative courses of action so that they can select the course that will best generate income for an organization's owners and maintain liquidity for its creditors. Figure 1 shows how managers use cost behavior throughout the management cycle.

PLANNING

In the planning stage, managers use cost behavior to determine how many units of products or services must be sold to generate a targeted amount of profit and how changes in planned operating, investing, and financing activities will affect operating income. For example, when Kraft's managers launched a product called Boca, they used cost behavior to analyze how offering two flavors of this meatless soy-based burger would contribute to the organization's operating income.

www.kraft.com

www.daimlerchysler.com

Manufacturers of cars and trucks, such as DaimlerChrysler, use cost behavior to decide how to adjust output to meet changing sales demand. If increased demand for trucks suggests the need to increase truck production and decrease car production, management can use cost behavior analysis to estimate the changes in operating income for those product lines. Cost behavior analysis is also useful to service businesses. For example, Blockbuster's managers use cost behavior in the planning stage to determine the optimal mix of DVD or VCR movies to rent and whether to price rentals to subscribers on a per movie or flat monthly fee basis.

www.blockbuster.com

EXECUTING

As we have noted, managers use information about cost behavior in almost every decision they make. Throughout the executing stage of the management cycle, managers at Kraft and at service businesses like Sprint and Verizon must understand and anticipate cost behavior to determine the impact of their decisions on operating income. For example, Kraft's managers must understand the changes in income that can result from a decision to buy new, more productive manufacturing equipment or to launch a Saturday morning advertising campaign to promote a new Post cereal.

www.sprint.com
www.verizon.com

REVIEWING AND REPORTING

When reviewing operations and preparing reports for various product or service lines or geographic regions, managers in all types of organizations, including serv-

FOCUS ON BUSINESS ETHICS

Core Values Guide Kraft Foods.

Six core values—focus, innovation, passion, speed, trust, and teamwork—guide Kraft Foods <www.kraft.com> in its mission to be recognized as the undisputed leader of the global food industry. Kraft's *focus* is on what matters most to consumers and on what's most important for its employees, brands, and business. The company encourages *innovation* to create ideas that will satisfy consumers, contribute to better service, and improve management. It values individuals who set high goals and have an uncompromising drive, or *passion*, to achieve them. *Speed* is important to Kraft in that it expects its decision makers to move quickly, with appropriate discipline, to stay ahead of the competition. The company regards *trust* as the foundation of all relationships and emphasizes the importance of integrity, respect, and responsibility. Finally, Kraft values *teamwork* because it recognizes that the power of working together across functions and business units around the world is what will make all the difference in the world.[2]

FIGURE 1
The Use of Cost Behavior in the Management Cycle

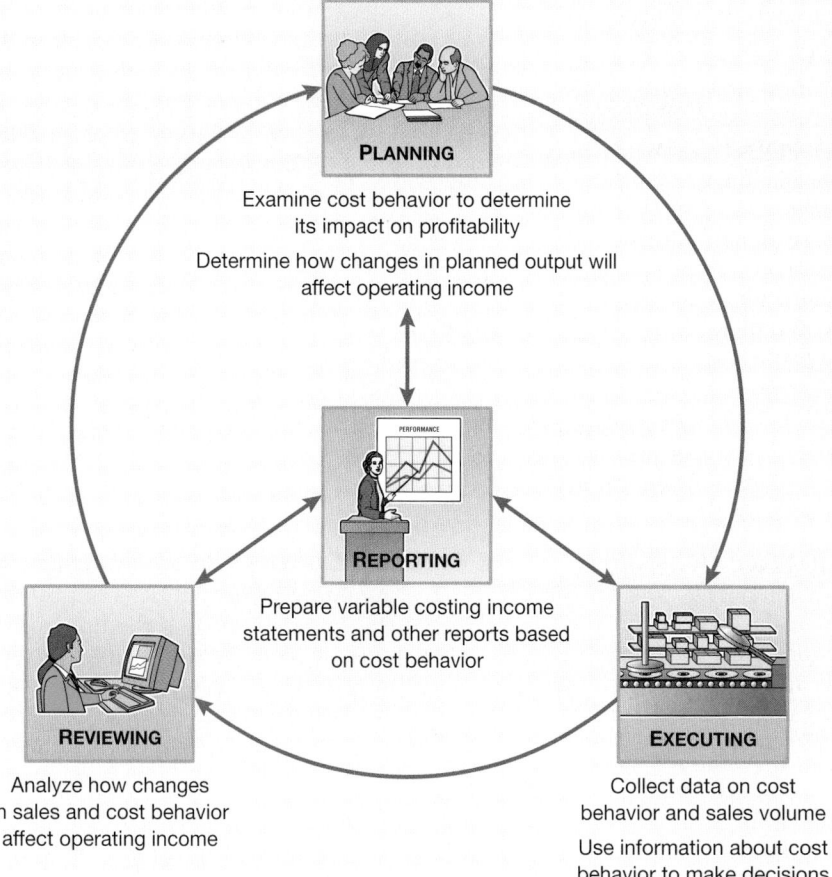

PLANNING
Examine cost behavior to determine its impact on profitability
Determine how changes in planned output will affect operating income

REPORTING
Prepare variable costing income statements and other reports based on cost behavior

REVIEWING
Analyze how changes in sales and cost behavior affect operating income

EXECUTING
Collect data on cost behavior and sales volume
Use information about cost behavior to make decisions

 STOP AND THINK!

Why do managers need to understand cost behavior?

Almost every decision managers make involves cost ramifications; to make good decisions, managers must understand the ways costs respond to changes in volume or activity. ∎

www.fedex.com
www.ups.com

ice businesses like Federal Express and UPS, need to understand cost behavior. Variable costing income statements are commonly used to analyze how changes in cost and sales affect the profitability of product lines, sales territories, customers, departments, and other segments. Other reports based on cost behavior are used when deciding whether to eliminate a product line, accept a special order, or outsource services.

✅ Check out ACE for a Review Quiz at http://accounting.college.hmco.com/students.

THE BEHAVIOR OF COSTS

LO2 Identify variable, fixed, and mixed costs, and separate mixed costs into their variable and fixed components.

RELATED TEXT ASSIGNMENTS
Q: 3, 4, 5, 6, 7, 8, 9, 10, 11
SE: 2, 3
E: 1, 2, 3, 4
P: 1, 5
SD: 1, 4, 5

Although our focus in this chapter is on cost behavior as it relates to products and services, cost behavior can also be observed in selling, administrative, and general activities. For example, increases in the number of shipments affect shipping costs; the number of units sold or total sales revenue affects the cost of sales commissions; and the number of customers billed or the number of hours needed to bill affects total billing costs. If managers can predict how costs behave, then costs become manageable.

Some costs vary with volume or operating activity (variable costs). Others remain fixed as volume changes (fixed costs). Between those two extremes are costs that exhibit characteristics of each type (mixed costs).

KEY POINT: Variable costs are incurred in all functional areas, not just in manufacturing.

www.landrover.com

KEY POINT: Variable costs change in *direct proportion* to changes in activity; that is, they increase *in total* with an increase in volume and decrease *in total* with a decrease in volume, but they remain the same on a *per unit* basis.

www.goodyear.com
www.wellsfargo.com
www.walmart.com

TERMINOLOGY NOTE: By definition, no variable costs exist at the level of zero production, which is why variable costs are sometimes described as the direct costs of production, sales, and administration.

ENRICHMENT NOTE: In a just-in-time operating environment, theoretical (ideal) capacity is used as a benchmark, a relatively constant reference point against which to measure improvement.

TERMINOLOGY NOTE: Practical capacity is sometimes called *engineering capacity*.

◆ **STOP AND THINK!**
What is the most realistic measure of operating capacity?
Normal capacity is the most realistic measure of operating capacity because it measures what a company is likely to produce, not what it can produce. ■

VARIABLE COSTS

Total costs that change in direct proportion to changes in productive output (or any other measure of volume) are called **variable costs**. To explore how variable costs work, consider the tire costs of Land Rover, a maker of off-road vehicles. Each new vehicle has four tires, and each tire costs $48. The total cost of tires, then, is $192 for one vehicle, $384 for two, $960 for five, $1,920 for ten, $19,200 for one hundred, and so on. In the production of off-road vehicles, the total cost of tires is a variable cost. On a per unit basis, however, a variable cost remains constant. In this case, the cost of tires per vehicle is $192 whether the automaker produces one vehicle or one hundred vehicles. True, the cost of tires will vary depending on the number purchased if discounts are available for purchases of large quantities. But once the purchase has been made, the cost per tire is established.

Figure 2 illustrates other examples of variable costs. All those costs—whether incurred by a manufacturer like Goodyear Tires, a service business like Wells Fargo Bank, or a merchandiser like Wal-Mart—are variable based on either productive output or total sales.

■ **OPERATING CAPACITY**   Because variable costs increase or decrease in direct proportion to volume or output, it is important to know an organization's operating capacity. **Operating capacity** is the upper limit of an organization's productive output capability, given its existing resources. It describes just what an organization can accomplish in a given period. Operating capacity can be expressed in several ways, including total labor hours, total machine hours, and total units of output. Any increase in volume or activity over operating capacity requires additional expenditures for buildings, machinery, personnel, and operations. When additional operating capacity is added, cost behavior patterns can change. In our discussion of those patterns, we assume that operating capacity is constant and that all activity occurs within the limits of current operating capacity.

There are three common measures, or types, of operating capacity: theoretical, or ideal, capacity; practical capacity; and normal capacity. **Theoretical (ideal) capacity** is the maximum productive output for a given period in which all machinery and equipment are operating at optimum speed, without interruption. In a just-in-time operating environment, the long-term goal is to approach theoretical capacity through continuous improvement; however, no company ever actually operates at such an ideal level. **Practical capacity** is theoretical capacity reduced by normal and expected work stoppages, such as machine breakdowns; downtime for retooling, repairs, and maintenance; and employees' breaks. Although theoretical capacity and practical capacity are useful when estimating maximum production levels, neither measure is realistic when planning operations.

When planning operations, managers use **normal capacity**, which is the average annual level of operating capacity needed to meet expected sales demand. The sales demand figure is adjusted for seasonal changes and industry and economic cycles. Normal capacity is therefore a realistic measure of what an organization is *likely* to produce, not what it *can* produce. Each variable cost should be related to an appropriate measure of normal capacity, but in many cases, more than one measure of normal capacity applies. Operating costs can be related to machine hours used or total units produced. Sales commissions, on the other hand, usually vary in direct proportion to total sales dollars.

The basis for measuring the activity of variable costs should be carefully selected for two reasons. First, an appropriate activity base simplifies cost planning and control. Second, the management accountant must combine (aggregate) many variable costs with the same activity base so that the costs can be analyzed in a reasonable way. Such aggregation also provides information that allows management to predict future costs.

FIGURE 2
Examples of Variable, Fixed, and Mixed Costs

Costs	Manufacturing Company— Tire Manufacturer	Merchandising Company— Department Store	Service Company—Bank
VARIABLE	Direct materials Direct labor (hourly) Indirect labor (hourly) Operating supplies Small tools	Merchandise to sell Sales commissions Shelf stockers (hourly)	Computer equipment leasing (based on usage) Computer operators (hourly) Operating supplies Data storage disks

FIXED	Depreciation, machinery
	  and building
	Insurance premiums
	Labor (salaried)
	Supervisory salaries
	Property taxes
		Depreciation, building
		Insurance premiums
		Buyers (salaried)
		Supervisory salaries
		Property taxes (on equipment
		  and building)
			Depreciation, furniture and fixtures
			Insurance premiums
			Salaries:
			  Programmers
			  Systems designers
			  Bank administrators
			Rent, buildings

MIXED	Electrical power Telephone Heat	Electrical power Telephone Heat	Electrical power Telephone Heat

TERMINOLOGY NOTE:
An activity base is often called *denominator activity*; it is the activity for which relationships are established. The basic relationships should not change greatly if activity fluctuates around the level of denominator activity.

The general guide for selecting an activity base is to relate costs to their most logical or causal factor. For example, machinery setup costs should be considered variable in relation to the number of setups needed for a particular job. This will allow machinery setup costs to be budgeted and controlled more effectively.

■ **LINEAR RELATIONSHIPS AND THE RELEVANT RANGE** The traditional definition of a variable cost assumes that costs go up or down as volume increases or decreases, as demonstrated by the linear relationship in the tire example we cited earlier. Figure 3 shows a similar straight-line relationship. There, each unit of output requires $2.50 of labor cost. Total labor costs grow in direct proportion to the increase in units of output. For two units, total labor costs are $5.00; for six units, the organization incurs $15.00 in labor costs.

CLARIFICATION NOTE:
Nonlinear costs can be roughly estimated by treating them as if they were linear (variable) costs within set limits of volume.

Many costs, however, vary with operating activity in a nonlinear fashion. Graph A in Figure 4 shows the behavior of power costs as usage increases and the unit cost of power consumption falls. Graph B shows the behavior of rental costs when each additional hour of computer usage costs more than the previous hour. Graph C shows how labor costs vary as efficiency increases and decreases. These three nonlinear cost patterns are variable in nature, but they differ from the linear variable cost pattern shown in Figure 3.

FIGURE 3
A Common Variable Cost Behavior Pattern: A Linear Relationship

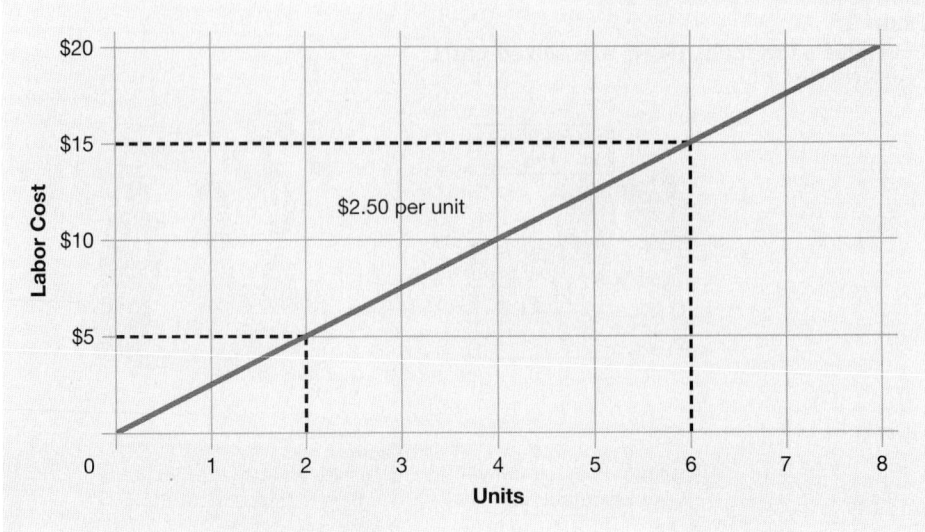

TERMINOLOGY NOTE:
Relevant range is the range of activity in which costs are expected to behave as predicted.

Variable costs with linear relationships to a volume measure are easy to analyze and project for cost planning and control. Nonlinear variable costs are not easy to use. But all costs must be included in an analysis if the results are to be useful to management. To simplify cost analysis procedures and make variable costs easier to use, accountants have developed a method of converting nonlinear variable costs into linear variable costs. Called *linear approximation*, this method relies on the concept of relevant range. **Relevant range** is the span of activity in which a company expects to operate. Within the relevant range, it is assumed that both total fixed costs and per unit variable costs are constant. Under that assumption, many nonlinear costs can be estimated using the linear approximation approach illustrated in Figure 5. Those estimated costs can then be treated as part of the other variable costs.

A linear approximation of a nonlinear variable cost is not a precise measure, but it allows the inclusion of nonlinear variable costs in cost behavior analysis, and the loss of accuracy is usually not significant. The goal is to help management estimate costs and prepare budgets, and linear approximation helps accomplish that goal.

FIGURE 4
Other Variable Cost Behavior Patterns: Nonlinear Relationships

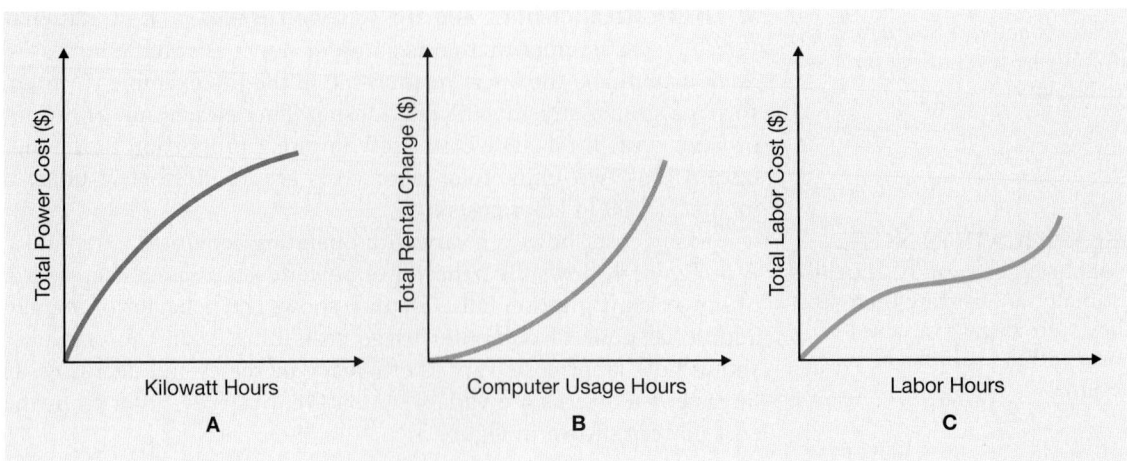

FIGURE 5
The Relevant Range and Linear Approximation

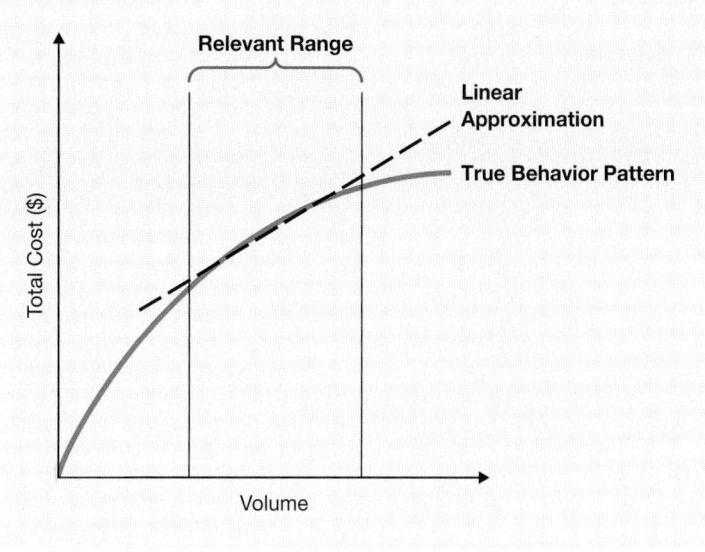

FIXED COSTS

Fixed costs behave very differently from variable costs. **Fixed costs** are total costs that remain constant within a relevant range of volume or activity—that is, the range in which actual operations are likely to occur. Look back at Figure 2 for examples of fixed costs. The manufacturer, the department store, and the bank all incur depreciation costs and fixed annual insurance premiums. In addition, all salaried personnel have fixed earnings for a particular period. The manufacturer and the department store own their buildings and pay annual property taxes, and the bank pays an annual fixed rental charge for the use of its building.

According to economic theory, all costs tend to be variable in the long run; thus, as the examples in Figure 2 suggest, a cost is fixed only within a limited period. A change in plant capacity, machinery, labor needs, or other production factors causes fixed costs to increase or decrease. For planning, management usually considers a one-year period, and fixed costs are expected to be constant within that period.

Of course, fixed costs change when activity exceeds the relevant range. For example, assume that a manufacturer of aluminum cans needs one supervisor for an eight-hour work shift. Production can range from zero to 500,000 units (cans) per month per shift. The relevant range, then, is from zero to 500,000 units. The supervisor's salary is $4,000 per month. The cost behavior analysis is as follows:

Units of Output per Month	Total Supervisory Salaries per Month
0–500,000	$4,000
Over 500,000–1,000,000	**$8,000**

If a maximum of 500,000 units can be produced per month per shift, output over 500,000 units would require another shift and another supervisor. Like all fixed costs, the new fixed cost remains constant in total within the new relevant range.

What about unit costs? Fixed unit costs vary inversely with activity or volume. On a per unit basis, fixed costs go down as volume goes up, as long as a firm is operating within the relevant range of activity. Look at how supervisory costs per unit fall as the volume of activity increases within the relevant range:

Volume of Activity	Cost per Unit
100,000 units	$4,000 ÷ 100,000 = $.0400
300,000 units	$4,000 ÷ 300,000 = $.0133
500,000 units	$4,000 ÷ 500,000 = $.0080
600,000 units	**$8,000 ÷ 600,000 = $.0133**

FIGURE 6
A Common Fixed Cost Behavior Pattern

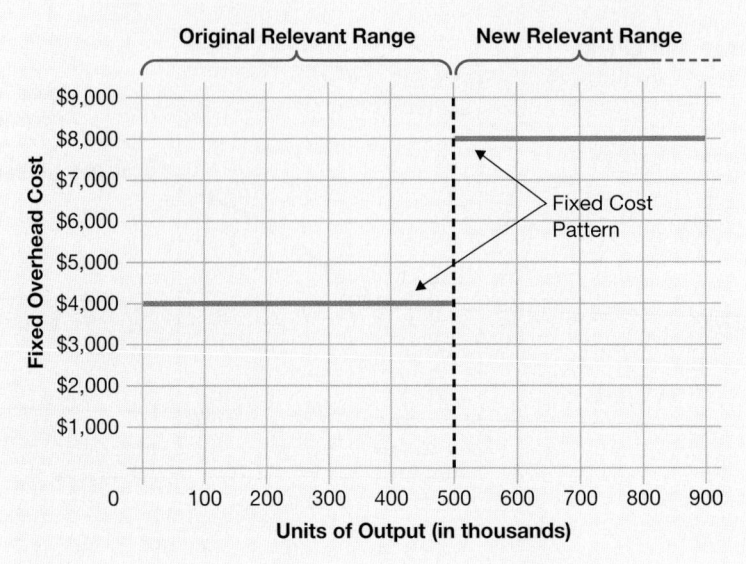

At 600,000 units, the activity level is above the relevant range, which means another shift must be added and another supervisor must be hired; thus, the per unit cost increases to $.0133.

Figure 6 shows this behavior pattern. The fixed supervisory costs for the first 500,000 units of production are $4,000. Those costs hold steady at $4,000 for any level of output within the relevant range. But if output goes above 500,000 units, another supervisor must be hired, pushing fixed supervisory costs to $8,000.

MIXED COSTS

KEY POINT: A business's cost accounts often fall into the mixed-cost category.

Mixed costs have both variable and fixed cost components. Part of a mixed cost changes with volume or usage, and part is fixed over a particular period. Monthly electricity costs are an example. Such costs include charges per kilowatt-hour used plus a basic monthly service charge. The kilowatt-hour charges are variable because they depend on the amount of use; the monthly service charge is a fixed cost. Graph A in Figure 7 depicts an organization's total electricity cost. The monthly bill begins with a fixed charge for the service and increases as kilowatt-hours are consumed. Graph B illustrates a special contractual arrangement. Here, the annual cost of equipment maintenance provided by an outside company increases for each maintenance hour worked, up to a maximum amount per period. After the maximum is reached, additional maintenance is done at no cost.

FIGURE 7
Behavior Patterns of Mixed Costs

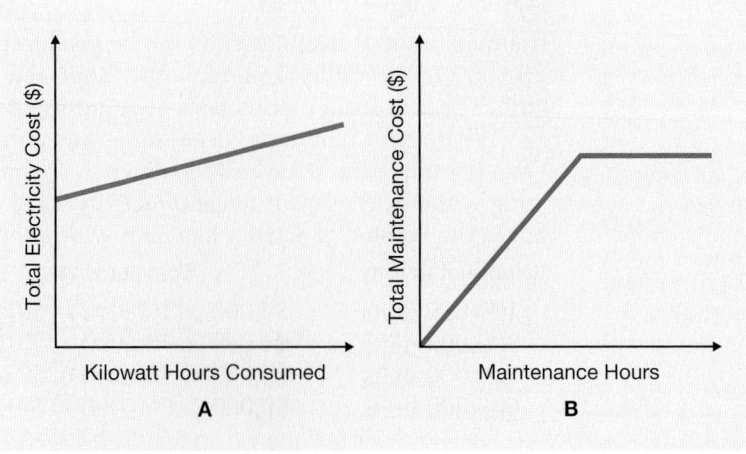

FOCUS ON BUSINESS TECHNOLOGY

High-Priced vs. Low-Priced Seats

Airline companies, such as Southwest <www.southwest.com>, Continental <www.continental.com>, and Delta <www.delta.com>, have a unique cost structure, which they use to make pricing decisions that will increase profitability. These companies have a high proportion of fixed costs relative to the variable costs associated with an additional passenger. In other words, it does not cost much more to include an additional passenger on a flight as long as a seat is available. In principle, the objective is simple: keep the prices high on seats that will sell anyway and reduce prices on seats that are less likely to sell, with the goal of filling as many seats as possible on every flight. In practice, this is a very complex process; it is made possible by sophisticated software that often results in minute-to-minute price changes. After years of developing the system, the airlines have refined it so that they can increase their profitability by increasing the revenue from each flight.

For cost planning and control purposes, mixed costs must be divided into their variable and fixed components. The separate components can then be grouped with other variable and fixed costs for analysis. Four methods are commonly used to separate costs into their variable and fixed components: the engineering, scatter diagram, high-low, and statistical methods. Because the results yielded by each of these methods are likely to differ, managers often use multiple approaches before determining the best possible estimate for a mixed cost.

■ **THE ENGINEERING METHOD** The engineering method of separating costs measures the work required by performing a step-by-step analysis of the tasks, costs, and processes involved. It is generally used to estimate the cost of activities and new products. For example, the U.S. Postal Service conducts periodic audits of how many letters a postal worker should be able to delivery on a particular mail route within a certain period. This type of analysis is sometimes called a *time and motion study*. The engineering method is expensive to use because it is so detailed. In addition, this method requires the expertise of engineers to determine the cost of a new product or activity for which no prior data exist.

KEY POINT: A scatter diagram is a useful tool for cost analysis. The original data in the diagram can be updated as new information becomes available. As time passes, the diagram presents a visual display of cost behavior and any changes that have occurred. In addition, such a diagram is easy to create and maintain.

■ **THE SCATTER DIAGRAM METHOD** When there is doubt about the behavior pattern of a particular cost, especially a mixed cost, it helps to plot past costs and related measures of volume in a scatter diagram. A scatter diagram is a chart of plotted points that helps determine whether a linear relationship exists between a cost item and its related activity measure. It is a form of linear approximation. If the diagram suggests a linear relationship, a cost line can be imposed on the data by either visual means or statistical analysis.

Suppose, for example, that the Piedmont Corporation's Park Division incurred the following machine hours and electricity costs last year:

Month	Machine Hours	Electricity Costs
January	6,250	$ 24,000
February	6,300	24,200
March	6,350	24,350
April	6,400	24,600
May	6,300	24,400
June	6,200	24,300
July	6,100	23,900
August	6,050	23,600
September	6,150	23,950
October	6,250	24,100
November	6,350	24,400
December	6,450	24,700
Totals	75,150	$290,500

FIGURE 8
Scatter Diagram of Machine Hours and Electricity Costs

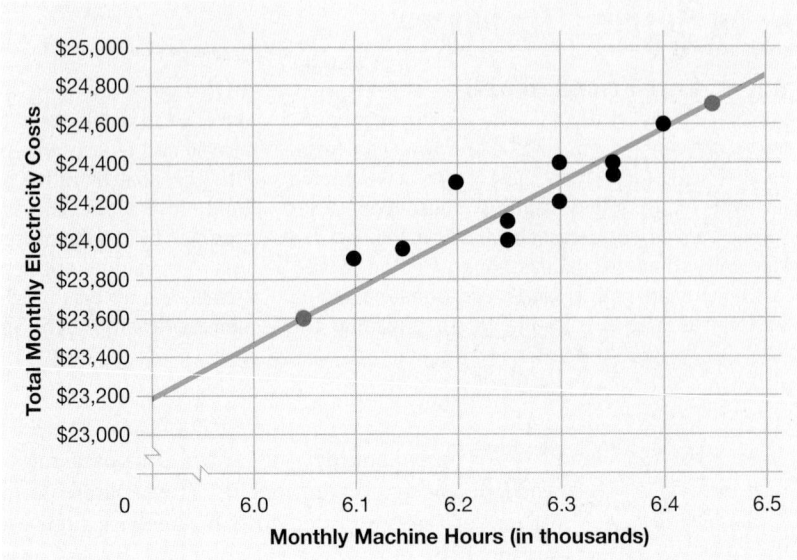

KEY POINT: A scatter diagram shows how closely volume and costs are correlated. A tight, closely associated group of data is better for linear approximation than a random or circular pattern of data points.

Figure 8 shows a scatter diagram of these data. The diagram suggests a linear relationship between machine hours and the cost of electricity. If we were to add a line to the diagram to represent the linear relationship, the estimated fixed electricity cost would occur at the point at which the line intersects the vertical axis. The variable cost per unit can be estimated by determining the slope of the line, much as is done in Step 1 of the high-low method.

KEY POINT: The high-low method is based on the premise that only two data points are necessary to define a linear cost-volume relationship. The disadvantage of this method is that if one or both data points are not representative of the remaining data set, the estimate of variable and fixed costs may not be accurate. Its advantage is that it can be used when only limited data are available.

CLARIFICATION NOTE: If the highest or lowest level of activity occurs more than once in the data set and each occurrence has a different cost value, the *average* of all the values for that level of activity should be used.

■ **THE HIGH-LOW METHOD** The high-low method is a common, three-step approach to determining the variable and fixed components of a mixed cost. It is a relatively crude method since it uses only the high and low data observations to predict cost behavior. The three steps of this method are as follows:

Step 1. *Calculate the variable cost per activity base.* Select the periods of highest and lowest activity within the accounting period. In our example, the Park Division experienced its highest machine-hour activity in December and its lowest machine-hour activity in August. Find the difference between the highest and lowest amounts for both the machine hours and their related electricity costs:

Volume	Month	Activity Level	Cost
Highest	December	6,450 machine hours	$24,700
Lowest	August	6,050 machine hours	23,600
Difference		400 machine hours	$ 1,100

To determine the variable cost per machine hour, divide the difference in cost by the difference in machine hours:

$$\text{Variable Cost per Machine Hour} = \$1,100 \div 400 \text{ Machine Hours}$$
$$= \$2.75 \text{ per Machine Hour}$$

Step 2. *Calculate the total fixed costs.* Compute total fixed costs for a month by selecting the information from the month with either the highest or the lowest volume. Here, we use the month with the highest volume:

$$\text{Total Fixed Costs} = \text{Total Costs} - \text{Total Variable Costs}$$
$$\text{Total Fixed Costs for December} = \$24,700.00 - (6,450 \times \$2.75) = \$6,962.50$$

You can check your answer by recalculating total fixed costs using the month with the lowest activity. Total fixed costs will be the same:

$$\text{Total Fixed Costs for August} = \$23,600.00 - (6,050 \times \$2.75) = \$6,962.50$$

Step 3. *Calculate the formula to estimate the total costs within the relevant range:*

Total Cost per Month = $6,962.50 + $2.75 per Machine Hour

Remember that the cost formula will work only within the relevant range. In this example, the formula would work for amounts between 6,050 machine hours and 6,450 machine hours. To estimate the electricity costs for machine hours outside the relevant range (in this case, below 6,050 machine hours or above 6,450 machine hours), a new cost formula must be calculated.

■ **STATISTICAL METHODS**   Statistical methods, such as regression analysis, mathematically describe the relationship between costs and activities. Because all data observations are used, the resulting linear equation is more representative of cost behavior than either the high-low or scatter diagram methods. Regression analysis can be performed using one or more activities to predict costs. For example, overhead costs can be predicted using only machine hours (a simple regression analysis), or they can be predicted using both machine hours and labor hours (a multiple regression analysis) because both activities affect overhead. We leave further description of regression analysis to statistics courses, which provide detailed coverage of this method.

 Check out ACE for a Review Quiz at http://accounting.college.hmco.com/students.

COST-VOLUME-PROFIT ANALYSIS

LO3 Define *cost-volume-profit (C-V-P) analysis* and discuss how managers use it as a tool for planning and control.

RELATED TEXT ASSIGNMENTS
Q: 12, 13, 14
SE: 4
MRA: 1, 3

www.kraft.com
www.sony.com

● **STOP AND THINK!**
How does C-V-P analysis help managers identify relevant costs for decision making?

C-V-P analysis helps managers identify relevant costs because it groups costs by behavior. Variable costs are often relevant to a decision, but many fixed costs are not. ■

KEY POINT: One of the important benefits of C-V-P analysis is that it allows managers to adjust different variables and to evaluate how these changes affect profit.

Like Kraft Foods, many companies produce and distribute a variety of products. For example, a division of Sony Corporation, Sony Records, makes compact disks (CDs). Producing these CDs is a complex process that requires hiring and organizing hundreds of people, including musicians, and maintaining studios and offices. The company hopes, of course, that all its CDs will be hits, but the reality is that only some will be. At the least, the company wants to break even—that is, not lose any money—on each CD. Cost-volume-profit analysis is an important tool that enables Sony's managers to determine how many CDs they must sell to avoid losing money and what their profit will be if they have a hit. It is also an important tool in setting sales targets.

Cost-volume-profit (C-V-P) analysis is an examination of the cost behavior patterns that underlie the relationships among cost, volume of output, and profit. C-V-P analysis usually applies to a single product, product line, or division of a company. For that reason, *profit*, which is only part of an entire company's operating income, is the term used in the C-V-P equation. The equation is expressed as

Sales Revenue − Variable Costs − Fixed Costs = Profit

or as

S − VC − FC = P

In cases involving the income statement of an entire company, the term *operating income* is more appropriate than *profit*. In the context of C-V-P analysis, however, *profit* and *operating income* mean the same thing.

C-V-P analysis is a tool for both planning and control. The techniques and the problem-solving procedures involved in the process express relationships among revenue, sales mix, cost, volume, and profit. Those relationships provide a general model of financial activity that managers can use for short-range planning and for evaluating performance and analyzing alternative courses of action.

For planning, managers can use C-V-P analysis to calculate net income when sales volume is known, or they can decide the level of sales needed to reach a targeted amount of net income. C-V-P analysis is used extensively in budgeting as well.

C-V-P Analysis in Grams and Liters

How does C-V-P analysis in Japan, Germany, Sweden, and Canada differ from C-V-P analysis in the United States? The only difference is in the measures used. The procedures and formulas remain the same. Instead of expressing volume in pounds or gallons, those countries use metric measures, such as grams and liters. Whereas our cost and profit amounts are expressed in dollars, Japan's amounts would be in yen, Germany's in euros, Sweden's in kronor, and Canada's in Canadian dollars. Most management accounting procedures and analyses are appropriate for use by companies in any free economy. All that changes are the units of measurement.

C-V-P analysis is also a way of measuring how well an organization's departments are performing. At the end of a period, sales volume and related actual costs are analyzed to find actual net income. A department's performance is measured by comparing actual costs with expected costs—costs that have been computed by applying C-V-P analysis to actual sales volume. The result is a performance report on which managers can base the control of operations.

In addition, managers use C-V-P analysis to measure the effects of alternative courses of action, such as changing variable or fixed costs, expanding or contracting sales volume, and increasing or decreasing selling prices. C-V-P analysis is useful in making decisions about product pricing, product mix (when an organization makes more than one product or offers more than one service), adding or dropping a product line, and accepting special orders.

C-V-P analysis has many applications, all of which managers use to plan and control operations effectively. However, it is useful only under certain conditions and only when certain assumptions hold true. Those conditions and assumptions are as follows:

1. The behavior of variable and fixed costs can be measured accurately.

2. Costs and revenues have a close linear approximation. For example, if costs rise, revenues rise proportionately.

3. Efficiency and productivity hold steady within the relevant range of activity.

4. Cost and price variables also hold steady during the period being planned.

5. The sales mix does not change during the period being planned.

6. Production and sales volume are roughly equal.

If one or more of these conditions and assumptions are absent, the C-V-P analysis may be misleading.

 Check out ACE for a Review Quiz at http://accounting.college.hmco.com/students.

BREAKEVEN ANALYSIS

LO4 Define *breakeven point* and use contribution margin to determine a company's breakeven point for multiple products.

RELATED TEXT ASSIGNMENTS
Q: 15, 16
SE: 5, 6, 7, 8, 9
E: 5, 6, 7, 8, 9, 10, 11, 12
P: 2, 3, 4, 6, 7
SD: 3, 4
MRA: 1, 5

Breakeven analysis uses the basic elements of cost-volume-profit relationships. The **breakeven point** is the point at which total revenues equal total costs. It is thus the point at which an organization can begin to earn a profit. When a new venture or product line is being planned, the likelihood of the project's success can be quickly measured by finding its breakeven point. If, for instance, the breakeven point is 50,000 units and the total market is only 25,000 units, the margin of safety would be very low, and the idea should be abandoned promptly. The **margin of safety** is the number of sales units or amount of sales dollars by which actual sales can fall below planned sales without resulting in a loss.

Sales (S), variable costs (VC), and fixed costs (FC) are used to compute the breakeven point, which can be stated in terms of sales units or sales dollars. The general equation for finding the breakeven point is as follows:

$$S - VC - FC = 0$$

Suppose, for example, that a company called Valley Metal Products, Inc., makes ornamental iron plant stands. Variable costs are $50 per unit, and fixed costs average $20,000 per year. Each plant stand sells for $90. Given this information, we can compute the breakeven point for this product in sales units (x equals sales units):

$$S - VC - FC = 0$$
$$\$90x - \$50x - \$20,000 = 0$$
$$\$40x = \$20,000$$
$$x = 500 \text{ Units}$$

We can also compute it in sales dollars:

$$\$90 \times 500 \text{ Units} = \$45,000$$

In addition, we can make a rough estimate of the breakeven point using a scatter graph. This method is less exact, but it does yield meaningful data. Figure 9 shows a breakeven graph for Valley Metal Products. As you can see there, the graph has five parts:

1. A horizontal axis for units of output

2. A vertical axis for dollars of revenue

3. A line running horizontally from the vertical axis at the level of fixed costs

4. A total cost line that begins at the point where the fixed cost line crosses the vertical axis and slopes upward to the right (The slope of the line depends on the variable cost per unit.)

5. A total revenue line that begins at the origin of the vertical and horizontal axes and slopes upward to the right (The slope depends on the selling price per unit.)

At the point at which the total revenue line crosses the total cost line, revenues equal total costs. The breakeven point, stated in either sales units or dollars of sales, is found by extending broken lines from this point to the axes. As Figure 9 shows, Valley Metal Products will break even when it has sold 500 plant stands for $45,000.

KEY POINT: Graphs can be powerful management tools because they visually depict relationships between revenues and expenses that otherwise might not be evident.

⬤ **STOP AND THINK!**
Why does the total revenue line in a breakeven graph start at the origin (zero units, zero dollars) while the total cost line usually starts higher on the vertical axis?

At zero sales, there is zero revenue; at zero sales and production, there is no variable cost, yet fixed costs still exist. ∎

FIGURE 9
Graphic Breakeven Analysis for Valley Metal Products, Inc.

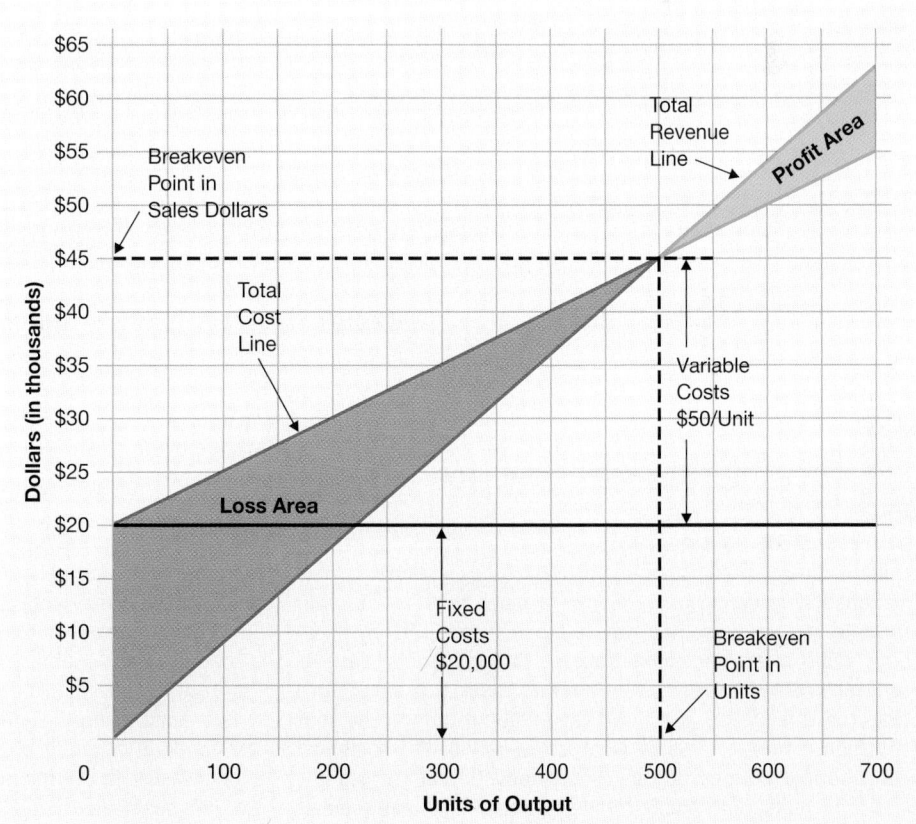

BUSINESS WORLD EXAMPLE: The C-V-P model shown in Figure 9 is a static model. The modern business environment is dynamic—selling prices, advertising costs, and wages fluctuate. Those variables can be expressed in computer simulation languages to produce a dynamic model.

USING CONTRIBUTION MARGIN TO DETERMINE THE BREAKEVEN POINT

KEY POINT: Contribution margin equals sales minus variable costs, whereas gross margin equals sales minus the cost of goods sold.

KEY POINT: The maximum contribution a unit of product can make is its selling price. After paying for itself (variable costs), a product provides a contribution margin to help pay total fixed costs and then earn a profit.

A simpler method of determining the breakeven point uses contribution margin. **Contribution margin** (CM) is the amount that remains after all variable costs are subtracted from sales:

$$S - VC = CM$$

A product line's contribution margin represents its net contribution to paying off fixed costs and earning a profit. Profit (P) is what remains after fixed costs are paid and subtracted from the contribution margin:

$$CM - FC = P$$

The example that follows uses contribution margin to determine the profitability of Valley Metal Products.

		Units Produced and Sold		
Symbols		250	500	750
S	Sales revenue ($90 per unit)	$22,500	$45,000	$67,500
VC	Less variable costs ($50 per unit)	12,500	25,000	37,500
CM	Contribution margin ($40 per unit)	$10,000	$20,000	$30,000
FC	Less fixed costs	20,000	20,000	20,000
P	Profit (loss)	($10,000)	$ 0	$10,000

The breakeven point (BE) can be expressed as the point at which contribution margin minus total fixed costs equals zero (or the point at which contribution margin equals total fixed costs). In terms of units of product, the equation for the breakeven point looks like this:

$$(CM \text{ per Unit} \times BE \text{ Units}) - FC = 0$$

It can also be expressed like this:

$$BE \text{ Units} = \frac{FC}{CM \text{ per unit}}$$

To show how the formula works, we use the data for Valley Metal Products:

$$BE \text{ Units} = \frac{FC}{CM \text{ per unit}} = \frac{\$20,000}{\$90 - \$50} = \frac{\$20,000}{\$40} = 500 \text{ Units}$$

The breakeven point in total sales dollars may be determined by multiplying the breakeven point in units by the selling price (SP) per unit:

$$BE \text{ Dollars} = SP \times BE \text{ Units} = \$90 \times 500 \text{ Units} = \$45,000$$

FOCUS ON BUSINESS PRACTICE

Supersizing Value Meals

Understanding their costs helps fast-food restaurants like McDonald's <www.mcdonalds.com> increase their profitability in at least two ways. One way is to encourage customers to buy "value meals"—combinations of three products, such as sandwich, drink, and fries—by offering them at a lower price than the three items purchased separately. Although the contribution margin of a value meal is lower than the combined contribution margins of the three products sold separately, fast-food restaurants know from experience that value meals lead to higher total sales. Another way fast-food restaurants increase profitability is by offering "supersized" orders for only a few cents more than the price of a regular order. Supersizing increases the total contribution margin because the additional variable cost of the larger size is very small. Profitability is enhanced even though revenue increases by only a small amount. Selling larger sizes is so important to a fast-food restaurant's profitability that a common performance measure in the industry is the percentage of value meals that are supersized.

FIGURE 10
Sales Mix for Valley Metal Products, Inc.

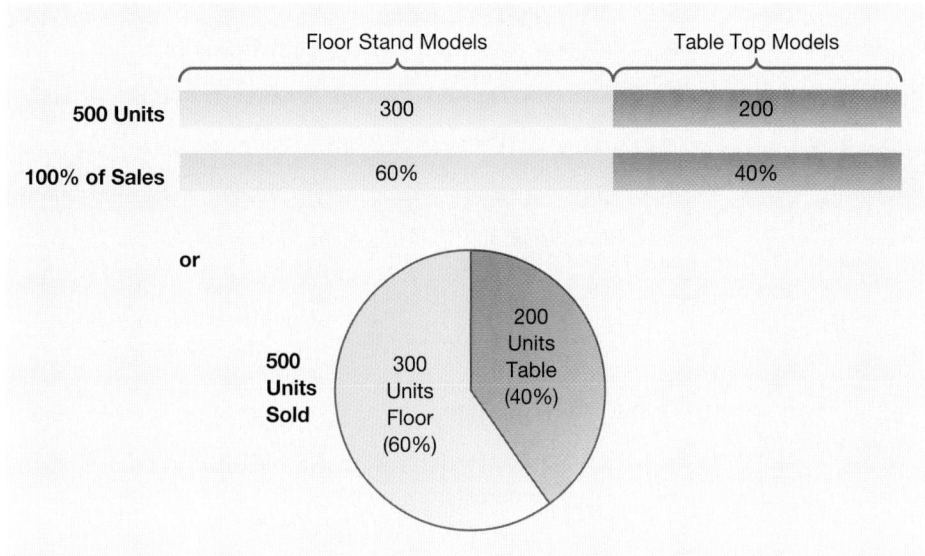

An alternative way of determining the breakeven point in total sales dollars is to divide the fixed costs by the contribution margin ratio. The contribution margin ratio is the contribution margin divided by the selling price:

$$CM\ Ratio = \frac{CM}{SP} = \frac{\$40}{\$90} = .444, \text{ or } 4/9$$

$$BE\ Dollars = \frac{FC}{CM\ Ratio} = \frac{\$20,000}{.444} = \$45,045^*$$

*Difference due to rounding up.

THE BREAKEVEN POINT FOR MULTIPLE PRODUCTS

To satisfy the needs of different customers, many manufacturers sell a variety of products, which often have different variable and fixed costs and different selling prices. To calculate the breakeven point for each product, its unit contribution margin must be weighted by the sales mix. The **sales mix** is the proportion of each product's unit sales relative to the organization's total unit sales. Let's assume that Valley Metal Products sells two types of plant stands: a floor stand model and a smaller tabletop model. If the company sells 500 units, of which 300 units are floor stands and 200 are tabletops, the sales mix would be 3:2. For every three floor stands sold, two tabletops are sold. The sales mix can also be stated in percentages. Of the 500 units sold, 60 percent (300 ÷ 500) are floor stand sales, and 40 percent (200 ÷ 500) are tabletop sales (see Figure 10).

The breakeven point for multiple products can be computed in three steps. To illustrate, we will use Valley Metal Products' sales mix of 60 percent floor stands to 40 percent tabletops and total fixed costs of $32,000; the selling price, variable cost, and contribution margin per unit for each product line are shown in Step 1 below.

Step 1. *Compute the weighted-average contribution margin.* To do so, multiply the contribution margin for each product by its percentage of the sales mix, as follows:

	Selling Price		Variable Costs		Contribution Margin (CM)		Percentage of Sales Mix		Weighted-Average CM
Floor stand	$90	−	$50	=	$40	×	.60	=	$24
Tabletop	$40	−	$20	=	$20	×	.40	=	8
Weighted-average contribution margin									$32

KEY POINT: A company's sales mix can be very dynamic. If the mix is constantly changing, an assumption of stability may undermine the C-V-P analysis.

Step 2. *Calculate the weighted-average breakeven point.* Divide total fixed costs by the weighted-average contribution margin:

$$\text{Weighted-Average Breakeven Point} = \text{Total Fixed Costs} \div \text{Weighted-Average Contribution Margin}$$
$$= \$32,000 \div \$32$$
$$= 1,000 \text{ Units}$$

Step 3. *Calculate the breakeven point for each product.* Multiply the weighted-average breakeven point by each product's percentage of the sales mix:

	Weighted-Average Breakeven Point		Sales Mix		Breakeven Point
Floor stand	1,000 units	×	.60	=	600 units
Tabletop	1,000 units	×	.40	=	400 units

To verify, determine the contribution margin of each product and subtract the total fixed costs:

Contribution margin		
Floor stand	600 × $40 =	$24,000
Tabletop	400 × $20 =	8,000
Total contribution margin		$32,000
Less fixed costs		32,000
Profit		$ 0

✅ Check out ACE for a Review Quiz at http://accounting.college.hmco.com/students.

USING C-V-P ANALYSIS TO PLAN FUTURE SALES, COSTS, AND PROFITS

LO5 Use C-V-P analysis to project the profitability of products and services.

RELATED TEXT ASSIGNMENTS
Q: 17, 18, 19
SE: 9, 10
E: 6, 9, 12, 13, 14, 15
P: 1, 2, 3, 4, 5, 6, 7, 8
SD: 2
MRA: 2, 4, 5

The primary goal of a business venture is not to break even; it is to generate profits. C-V-P analysis adjusted for targeted profit can be used to estimate the profitability of a venture. This approach is excellent for "what-if" analysis, in which managers select several scenarios and compute the profit that may be anticipated from each. For instance, what if sales increase by 17,000 units? What effect will the increase have on profit? What if sales increase by only 6,000 units? What if fixed costs are reduced by $14,500? What if the variable unit cost increases by $1.40? Each scenario generates a different amount of profit or loss.

APPLYING C-V-P TO A MANUFACTURING BUSINESS

To illustrate how a manufacturing business can apply C-V-P analysis, assume that Van Bryce, the president of Valley Metal Products, Inc., has set $4,000 in profit as this year's goal for the plant stands. If all the data in our earlier example remain the same, how many plant stands must Valley Metal Products sell to reach the targeted profit? Again, x equals the number of units.

$$S = VC + FC + P$$
$$\$90x = \$50x + \$20,000 + \$4,000$$
$$\$40x = \$24,000$$
$$x = 600 \text{ Units}$$

To check the answer, insert all known data into the equation:

$$S - VC - FC = P$$
$$(600 \times \$90) - (600 \times \$50) - \$20,000 = \$4,000$$
$$\$54,000 - \$30,000 - \$20,000 = \$4,000$$

The contribution margin approach can also be used for profit planning. To do so, simply add the targeted profit to the numerator of the contribution margin breakeven equation:

$$\text{Targeted Sales Units} = \frac{FC + P}{CM \text{ per Unit}}$$

The number of sales units Valley Metal Products needs to generate $4,000 in profit is computed this way:

$$\text{Targeted Sales Units} = \frac{FC + P}{CM \text{ per Unit}} = \frac{\$20,000 + \$4,000}{\$40} = \frac{\$24,000}{\$40} = 600 \text{ Units}$$

Contribution income statements, which are prepared for internal use, are also useful to managers in planning and making decisions about their company's operations. As you can see in the contribution income statement for Valley Metal Products that appears below, the focus of such a statement is on cost behavior, not cost function. All variable costs related to production, selling, and administration are subtracted from sales to determine the total contribution margin. All fixed costs related to production, selling, and administration are subtracted from the total contribution margin to determine operating income. (As we noted earlier, in income statements involving an entire company, the term *operating income* is more appropriate than *profit*.)

Valley Metal Products, Inc.
Contribution Income Statement
For the Year Ended December 31, 20x8

	Per Unit	Total for 600 Units
Sales revenue	$90	$54,000
Less variable costs	50	30,000
Contribution margin	$40	$24,000
Less fixed costs		20,000
Operating income		$ 4,000

Van Bryce wants Valley Metal Products' planning team to consider three alternatives to the original plan shown in the contribution income statement. In the following sections, we examine each of these alternatives and its impact on operating income. In the summary, we review our work and analyze the different breakeven points.

■ **ALTERNATIVE 1: DECREASE VARIABLE COSTS, INCREASE SALES VOLUME**   The planning team worked with production, purchasing, and sales employees to determine what operating income would be if the company purchased and used aluminum rather than iron to make the plant stands. If aluminum were used, the direct materials cost per unit would decrease by $3 to $47. If the company painted the aluminum to meet the needs of a new customer group, it would increase sales volume by 10 percent to 660 units. What is the estimated operating income for this alternative? How does this alternative affect operating income?

	Per Unit	Total for 660 units
Sales revenue	$90	$59,400
Less variable costs	47	31,020
Contribution margin	$43	$28,380
Less fixed costs		20,000
Operating income		$ 8,380
Increase in operating income ($8,380 − $4,000)		$ 4,380

A different way to determine the impact of changes in selling price, cost, or sales volume on operating income is to analyze only the data that change between the original plan and the proposed alternative. If Alternative 1 is used, variable costs will decrease by $3 (from $50 to $47), which will increase the contribution margin per unit by $3 (from $40 to $43). This will increase the total contribution margin and operating income by $1,800 ($3 × 600). In addition, a sales increase of 60 units (.10 × 600) will increase the total contribution margin and operating income by $2,580 ($43 × 60). The total increase in operating income due to the decrease in variable costs and the increase in sales volume will be $4,380.

Analysis of Changes Only

Increase in contribution margin from	
Planned sales [($43 − $40) × 600 units]	$1,800
Additional sales ($43 × 60 units)	2,580
Increase in operating income	$4,380

■ **ALTERNATIVE 2: INCREASE FIXED COSTS, INCREASE SALES VOLUME**   Instead of changing the direct materials, the Marketing Department suggested that a $500 increase in advertising costs would increase sales volume by 5 percent. What is the estimated operating income for this alternative? How does this alternative affect operating income?

	Per Unit	Total for 630 units
Sales revenue	$90	$56,700
Less variable costs	50	31,500
Contribution margin	$40	$25,200
Less fixed costs		20,500
Operating income		$ 4,700
Increase in operating income ($4,700 − $4,000)		$ 700

Additional advertising costs will affect both sales volume and fixed costs. The sales volume will increase by 30 plant stands, from 600 units to 630 units (600 × 1.05), which increases the total contribution margin and operating income by $1,200 (from $24,000 to $25,200). Fixed costs will increase from $20,000 to $20,500, which decreases operating income by $500. The increase in operating income will be $700 ($1,200 − $500).

Analysis of Changes Only

Increase in contribution margin from	
additional units sold [($40 × (600 × .05)]	$1,200
Less increase in fixed costs	500
Increase in operating income	$ 700

■ **ALTERNATIVE 3: INCREASE SELLING PRICE, DECREASE SALES VOLUME**   Van Bryce asked the planning team to evaluate the impact of a $10 increase in selling price on the company's operating income. If the selling price is increased, the team estimates that the sales volume will decrease by 15 percent to 510 units. What is the estimated operating income for this alternative? How does this alternative affect operating income?

	Per Unit	Total for 510 Units
Sales revenue	$100	$51,000
Less variable costs	50	25,500
Contribution margin	50	$25,500
Less fixed costs		
		20,000
Operating income		$ 5,500
Increase in operating income ($5,500 − $4,000)		$ 1,500

Analysis of Changes Only

Increase in contribution margin from increase in selling price ($10 increase in selling price × 510 units sold)	$5,100
Decrease in contribution margin from decrease in sales volume ($40 contribution margin per unit × 90 sales units lost)	(3,600)
Increase in operating income	$1,500

■ **COMPARATIVE SUMMARY**   In preparation for a meeting with Van Bryce, the planning team at Valley Metal Products compiled the summary presented in Exhibit 1. It compares the three alternatives with the original plan and shows how changes in variable and fixed costs, selling price, and sales volume affect the breakeven point.

EXHIBIT 1
Comparative Summary of Alternatives at Valley Metal Products, Inc.

	Original Plan — Totals for 600 Units	Alternative 1 — Decrease Direct Materials Costs for 660 Units	Alternative 2 — Increase Advertising Costs for 630 Units	Alternative 3 — Increase Selling Price for 510 Units
Sales revenue	$54,000	$59,400	$56,700	$51,000
Less variable costs	30,000	31,020	31,500	25,500
Contribution margin	$24,000	$28,380	$25,200	$25,500
Less fixed costs	20,000	20,000	20,500	20,000
Operating income	$ 4,000	$ 8,380	$ 4,700	$ 5,500

Breakeven point in whole units				
$20,000 FC ÷ $40 CM	500			
$20,000 FC ÷ $43 CM		466*		
$20,500 FC ÷ $40 CM			513	
$20,000 FC ÷ $50 CM				400

*Rounded up to next whole unit.

Note that the decrease in variable costs (direct materials) proposed in Alternative 1 increases the contribution margin per unit (from $40 to $43), which reduces the breakeven point. Because fewer sales dollars are required to cover variable costs, the breakeven point is reached sooner than in the original plan—at a sales volume of 466 units rather than at 500 units. In Alternative 2, the increase in fixed costs has no effect on the contribution margin per unit, but it does require the total contribution margin to cover more fixed costs before reaching the breakeven point. Thus, the breakeven point is higher than in the original plan—513 units as opposed to 500. The increase in selling price in Alternative 3 increases the contribution margin per unit, which reduces the breakeven point. Because more sales dollars are available to cover fixed costs, the breakeven point of 400 units is lower than the breakeven point in the original plan.

Which plan should Bryce choose? If he wants the highest operating income, he will choose Alternative 1. If, however, he wants the company to begin generating operating income more quickly, he will choose the plan with the lowest breakeven point, Alternative 3. Remember that the breakeven point provides a rough estimate of the number of units that must be sold to cover the total costs. Additional qualitative information may help Bryce make a better decision. Will customers perceive that the quality of the plant stands is lower if the company uses aluminum rather than iron, as proposed in Alternative 1? Will increased expenditures on advertising yield a 5 percent increase in sales volume, as Alternative 2 postulates? Will the increase in selling price suggested in Alternative 3 create more than a 15 percent decline in unit sales? Quantitative information is essential for planning, but managers must also be sensitive to qualitative factors, such as product quality, reliability and quality of suppliers, and availability of human and technical resources.

APPLYING C-V-P ANALYSIS TO A SERVICE BUSINESS

In this section, we look at how a service business can use C-V-P analysis in planning its operations. Assume that Glenda Haley, the manager of the Appraisal Department at Edmunds Mortgage Company, wants to plan the home appraisal activities that each mortgage loan application requires. She estimates that over the next year, her department will perform an average of 100 appraisals per month and service fee revenue will be $400 per appraisal. Other estimated data for the year are as follows:

Variable costs: direct professional labor, $160 per appraisal; county survey map fee, $99 per appraisal

Mixed costs (monthly service overhead):

Volume	Month	Activity Level	Cost
Highest	March	180 appraisals	$23,380
Lowest	February	98 appraisals	20,018

■ **ESTIMATING SERVICE OVERHEAD COSTS**   Haley wants to estimate the total service overhead cost of appraisals for next year. She uses the high-low method to do so:

Step 1.   *Calculate the variable service overhead cost per appraisal.*

Variable Service Overhead Cost per Appraisal = (Highest Cost − Lowest Cost) ÷ (Highest Volume − Lowest Volume)
= ($23,380 − $20,018) ÷ (180 − 98)
= $3,362 ÷ 82 Appraisals = $41

Step 2.   *Calculate the total fixed service overhead costs.*

Total Fixed Service Overhead Costs = Total Service Overhead Costs − Total Variable Service Overhead Costs

Total Fixed Service Overhead Costs for March = $23,380 − ($41 × 180)
= $16,000

Step 3. *Calculate the total service overhead costs for one month.*

Total Service Overhead Costs = Total Fixed Service Overhead Costs +
(Variable Rate × Estimated Number of Appraisals)
= $16,000 + ($41 per Appraisal × Number of Appraisals)

Step 4. *Calculate the total service overhead costs for one month assuming that 100 appraisals will be made.*

Total Overhead Service Costs = $16,000 + ($41 × 100) = $20,100

■ **DETERMINING THE BREAKEVEN POINT**   Glenda Haley also wants to know how many appraisals her department must perform each month to cover the fixed and variable appraisal costs. She calculates the breakeven point as follows:

Let x = Number of Appraisals per Month at Breakeven Point
S = VC + FC
$400x = $300x + $16,000
$100x = $16,000
x = 160 Appraisals per Month

The variable rate of $300 per appraisal includes the variable service overhead rate, the direct professional labor, and the county survey map fee ($41 + $160 + $99).

■ **DETERMINING THE EFFECT OF A CHANGE IN OPERATING COSTS**   Haley is worried because her department can perform an average of only 100 appraisals each month, but the estimated breakeven point is 160 appraisals per month. Because of strong competition, increasing the appraisal fee is not an option; to make the appraisals profitable, the mortgage company has asked Haley to find ways of reducing costs. In reviewing the situation, Haley has determined that improved scheduling of appraisals will reduce appraisers' travel time. Travel time is included in the current professional labor cost of $160 per appraisal (four hours of an appraiser's time at $40 per hour). By scheduling the jobs according to location, Haley can reduce the appraisers' travel time enough to reduce the total time required by 50 percent, thus cutting the professional labor cost to $80 per appraisal [(.50 × 4 hours) × $40 per hour]. The new scheduling process will increase fixed costs by $200 per month. Given these circumstances, what will the breakeven point be?

Let x = Number of Appraisals per Month at Breakeven Point
S = VC + FC
$400x = $220x + $16,200
$180x = $16,200
x = 90 Appraisals per Month

Variable costs become $220 ($300 − $80) per appraisal due to the reduced labor costs. This change increases the contribution margin by $80 per appraisal. Fixed costs increase from $16,000 to $16,200. The increase in the contribution margin is greater than the increase in the fixed costs, so the breakeven point decreases from 160 appraisals per month to 90 appraisals per month.

■ **ACHIEVING A TARGETED PROFIT**   How many appraisals would Glenda Haley's department have to perform each month to achieve a targeted profit of $18,000 per month?

Let x = Targeted Sales in Units
S = VC + FC + P
$400x = $220x + $16,200 + $18,000
$180x = $34,200
x = 190 Units

 Check out ACE for a Review Quiz at http://accounting.college.hmco.com/students.

Chapter Review

REVIEW OF LEARNING OBJECTIVES

LO1   Define *cost behavior* and explain how managers use this concept in the management cycle.

Cost behavior is the way costs respond to changes in volume or activity. In the planning stage of the management cycle, managers use cost behavior to determine how many units of products or services must be sold to generate a targeted amount of profit and how changes in planned activities will affect operating income. In the executing stage, managers must understand and anticipate cost behavior to determine the impact of their decisions on operating income. In the reviewing and reporting stages, managers analyze how changes in cost and sales affect the profitability of product lines, sales territories, customers, departments, and other business segments by preparing reports using variable costing.

LO2   Identify variable, fixed, and mixed costs, and separate mixed costs into their variable and fixed components.

Some costs vary in relation to volume or operating activity; other costs remain fixed as volume changes. Cost behavior depends on whether the focus is total costs or cost per unit. Total costs that change in direct proportion to changes in productive output (or any other volume measure) are called *variable costs*. They include hourly wages, the cost of operating supplies, direct materials costs, and the cost of merchandise. Total *fixed costs* remain constant within a relevant range of volume or activity. They change only when volume or activity exceeds the relevant range—for example, when new equipment or new buildings must be purchased, higher insurance premiums and property taxes must be paid, or additional supervisory personnel must be hired to accommodate increased activity. A *mixed cost*, such as the cost of electricity, has both variable and fixed cost components. For cost planning and control, mixed costs must be separated into their variable and fixed components. To separate them, managers use a variety of methods, including the engineering, scatter diagram, high-low, and statistical methods.

LO3   Define *cost-volume-profit (C-V-P) analysis* and discuss how managers use it as a tool for planning and control.

Cost-volume-profit analysis is an examination of the cost behavior patterns that underlie the relationships among cost, volume of output, and profit. It is a tool for both planning and control. The techniques and problem-solving procedures involved in C-V-P analysis express relationships among revenue, sales mix, cost, volume, and profit. Those relationships provide a general model of financial activity that management can use for short-range planning and for evaluating performance and analyzing alternatives.

LO4   Define *breakeven point* and use contribution margin to determine a company's breakeven point for multiple products.

The *breakeven point* is the point at which total revenues equal total costs—in other words, the point at which net sales equal variable costs plus fixed costs. Once the number of units needed to break even is known, the number can be multiplied by the product's selling price to determine the breakeven point in sales dollars. *Contribution margin* is the amount that remains after all variable costs have been subtracted from sales. A product's contribution margin represents its net contribution to paying off fixed costs and earning a profit. The breakeven point in units can be computed by using the following formula:

$$\text{BE Units} = \frac{\text{FC}}{\text{CM per Unit}}$$

A sales mix is used to calculate the breakeven point for each product when a company sells more than one product.

LO5   Use C-V-P analysis to project the profitability of products and services.

The addition of targeted profit to the breakeven equation makes it possible to plan levels of operation that yield the targeted profit. The formula in terms of contribution margin is

$$\text{Targeted Sales Units} = \frac{\text{FC} + \text{P}}{\text{CM per Unit}}$$

C-V-P analysis, whether used by a manufacturing company or a service organization, enables managers to select several "what if" scenarios and evaluate the outcome of each to determine which will generate the desired amount of profit.

REVIEW OF CONCEPTS AND TERMINOLOGY

The following concepts and terms were introduced in this chapter:

LO4 **Breakeven point:** The point at which total revenues equal total costs.

LO4 **Contribution margin:** The amount that remains after all variable costs are subtracted from sales.

LO1 **Cost behavior:** The way costs respond to changes in volume or activity.

LO3 **Cost-volume-profit (C-V-P) analysis:** An examination of the cost behavior patterns that underlie the relationships among cost, volume of output, and profit.

LO2 **Engineering method:** A method that separates costs into their fixed and variable components by performing a step-by-step analysis of the tasks, costs, and processes involved in completing an activity or product.

LO2 **Fixed costs:** Total costs that remain constant within a relevant range of volume or activity.

LO2 **High-low method:** A three-step approach to separating a mixed cost into its variable and fixed components.

LO4 **Margin of safety:** The number of sales units or amount of sales dollars by which actual sales can fall below planned sales without resulting in a loss.

LO2 **Mixed costs:** Costs that have both variable and fixed components.

LO2 **Normal capacity:** The average annual level of operating capacity needed to meet expected sales demand.

LO2 **Operating capacity:** The upper limit of an organization's productive output capability, given its existing resources.

LO2 **Practical capacity:** Theoretical capacity reduced by normal and expected work stoppages.

LO2 **Regression analysis:** A mathematical approach to separating a mixed cost into its variable and fixed components.

LO2 **Relevant range:** The span of activity in which a company expects to operate.

LO4 **Sales mix:** The proportion of each product's unit sales relative to the organization's total unit sales.

LO2 **Scatter diagram:** A chart of plotted points that helps determine whether a linear relationship exists between a cost item and its related activity measure.

LO2 **Theoretical (ideal) capacity:** The maximum productive output for a given period in which all machinery and equipment are operating at optimum speed, without interruption.

LO2 **Variable costs:** Total costs that change in direct proportion to changes in productive output or any other measure of volume.

REVIEW PROBLEM

Breakeven Analysis and Profitability Planning

LO4
LO5 Olympia, Inc., is a major producer of golf clubs. Its oversized putter has a large potential market. The following is a summary of data from the company's operations in 20x5:

Total fixed costs
Manufacturing overhead	195,000
Advertising	55,000
Administrative expense	68,000

Variable costs per unit
Direct materials	$ 23
Direct labor	8
Manufacturing overhead	6
Selling expense	5
Selling price per unit	95

REQUIRED ▶ 1. Compute the breakeven point in units for 20x5.
2. Olympia sold 6,500 putters in 20x5. How much profit did the company realize?
3. To improve profitability in 20x6, management is considering the four alternative courses of action indicated below. (In performing the required steps, use the figures from item **2** and treat each alternative independently.)
   a. Calculate the number of units Olympia must sell to generate a targeted profit of $95,400. Assume that costs and selling price remain constant.
   b. Calculate the operating income if the company increases the number of units sold by 20 percent and cuts the selling price by $5 per unit.
   c. Determine the number of units that must be sold to break even if advertising costs are increased by $47,700.
   d. Find the number of units that must be sold to generate a targeted profit of $120,000 if variable costs are cut by 10 percent.

ANSWER TO REVIEW PROBLEM

1. Breakeven point in units for 20x5:

$$\text{Breakeven Units} = \frac{FC}{CM \text{ per Unit}} = \frac{\$318,000}{\$95 - \$42} = \frac{\$318,000}{\$53} = 6,000 \text{ Units}$$

2. Profit from sale of 6,500 units:

Units sold	6,500
Units required to break even	6,000
Units over breakeven	500

20x5 profit = $53 per unit × 500 = $26,500

Contribution margin equals sales minus all variable costs. Contribution margin per unit equals the amount left to cover fixed costs and earn a profit after variable costs have been subtracted from sales dollars. If all fixed costs have been absorbed by the time breakeven is reached, the entire contribution margin of each unit sold in excess of breakeven represents profit.

3. a. Number of units that must be sold to generate a targeted profit of $95,400:

$$\text{Targeted Sales Units} = \frac{FC + P}{CM \text{ per Unit}}$$

$$\frac{\$318,000 + \$95,400}{\$53} = \frac{\$413,400}{\$53} = 7,800 \text{ Units}$$

b. Operating income if unit sales increase 20 percent and unit selling price decreases by $5:

Sales revenue [7,800 (6,500 × 1.20) units at $90 per unit]	$702,000
Less variable costs (7,800 units × $42)	327,600
Contribution margin	$374,400
Less fixed costs	318,000
Operating income	$ 56,400

c. Number of units needed to break even if advertising costs (fixed costs) increase by $47,700:

$$\text{BE Units} = \frac{FC}{CM \text{ per Unit}}$$

$$\frac{\$318,000 + \$47,700}{\$53} = \frac{\$365,700}{\$53} = 6,900 \text{ Units}$$

d. Number of units that must be sold to generate a targeted profit of $120,000 if variable costs decrease by 10 percent:

$$CM \text{ per Unit} = \$95.00 - (\$42.00 \times .9) = \$95.00 - \$37.80 = \$57.20$$

$$\text{Targeted Sales Units} = \frac{FC + P}{CM \text{ per Unit}}$$

$$\frac{\$318,000 + \$120,000}{\$57.20} = \frac{\$438,000}{\$57.20} = 7,658 \text{ Units*}$$

*Note that the answer is rounded up to the next whole unit.

Chapter Assignments

BUILDING YOUR KNOWLEDGE FOUNDATION

QUESTIONS

1. Define *cost behavior*.
2. Why is an understanding of cost behavior useful to managers?
3. What is the difference between theoretical capacity and practical capacity?
4. Why does a company never operate at theoretical capacity?
5. What is normal capacity? Why is normal capacity considered more relevant and useful than either theoretical or practical capacity?
6. What does *relevant range of activity* mean?
7. What makes variable costs different from fixed costs?
8. "Fixed costs remain constant in total but decrease per unit as productive output increases." Explain this statement.
9. What is a mixed cost? Give an example.
10. What is a scatter diagram?
11. Describe the high-low method of separating mixed costs.
12. Define *cost-volume-profit analysis*.
13. Identify two uses of C-V-P analysis and explain their significance to management.
14. What conditions must be met for C-V-P computations to be accurate?
15. Define *breakeven point*. Why is information about the breakeven point important to managers?
16. Define *contribution margin* and describe its use in breakeven analysis.
17. State the equation that uses fixed costs, targeted profit, and contribution margin per unit to determine targeted sales units.
18. Give examples of the ways in which a service business can use C-V-P analysis.
19. Identify the differences and similarities in breakeven analysis for manufacturing organizations and service organizations.

SHORT EXERCISES

SE 1.
LO1 Concept of Cost Behavior

Dapper Hat Makers is in the business of designing and producing specialty hats. The material used for derbies costs $4.50 per unit, and Dapper pays each of its two full-time employees $250 per week. If Employee A makes 15 derbies in one week, what is the variable cost per derby, and what is this worker's fixed cost per derby? If Employee B makes only 12 derbies in one week, what are this worker's variable and fixed costs per derby? (Round to two decimal places where necessary.)

SE 2.
LO2 Identification of Variable, Fixed, and Mixed Costs

Identify the following as fixed costs, variable costs, or mixed costs:

1. Direct materials   4. Personnel manager's salary
2. Telephone expense   5. Factory building rent payment
3. Operating supplies

SE 3.
LO2 Mixed Costs: High-Low Method

Using the high-low method and the information below, compute the monthly variable cost per telephone hour and total fixed costs for Sadiko Corporation.

Month	Telephone Hours Used	Telephone Expenses
April	96	$4,350
May	93	4,230
June	105	4,710

SE 4.
LO3 C-V-P Analysis

DeLuca, Inc., wants to make a profit of $20,000. It has variable costs of $80 per unit and fixed costs of $12,000. How much must it charge per unit if 4,000 units are sold?

	SE 5.	How many units must Braxton Company sell to break even if the selling price per unit is $8.50, variable costs are $4.30 per unit, and fixed costs are $3,780? What is the breakeven point in total dollars of sales?

LO4 Breakeven Analysis

	SE 6.	Using the contribution margin approach, find the breakeven point in units for Norcia Consumer Products if the selling price per unit is $11, the variable cost per unit is $6, and the fixed costs are $5,500.

LO4 Contribution Margin

	SE 7.	Using the information in **SE 6**, compute the breakeven point in total sales dollars using the contribution margin ratio.

LO4 Contribution Margin Ratio

	SE 8.	Using the contribution margin approach, find the breakeven point in units for Sardinia Company's two products. Product A's selling price per unit is $10, and its variable cost per unit is $4. Product B's selling price per unit is $8, and its variable cost per unit is $5. Fixed costs are $15,000, and the sales mix of Product A to Product B is 2:1.

LO4 Breakeven Analysis for Multiple Products

	SE 9.	If Oui Watches sells 300 watches at $48 per watch and has variable costs of $18 per watch and fixed costs of $4,000, what is the projected profit?

LO4 Contribution Margin and
LO5 Projected Profit

LO5 Cost Behavior in a Service Business

SE 10. Guy Spy, a private investigation firm, has the following costs for December:

Direct labor: $190 per case
Service overhead

Salary for director of investigations	$ 4,800
Telephone	930
Depreciation	8,300
Legal advice	2,300
Supplies	590
Advertising	360
Utilities	1,560
Wages for clerical personnel	2,000
Total service overhead	$20,840

Service overhead for October was $21,150; for November, it was $21,350.

The number of cases investigated during October, November, and December was 93, 97, and 91, respectively. Compute the variable and fixed cost components of service overhead. Then determine the variable and fixed costs per case for December. (Round to nearest dollar where necessary.)

EXERCISES

LO2 Identification of Variable and Fixed Costs

E 1. Indicate whether each of the following costs of productive output is usually variable or fixed: (1) packing materials for stereo components, (2) real estate taxes, (3) gasoline for a delivery truck, (4) property insurance, (5) depreciation expense of buildings (calculated with the straight-line method), (6) supplies, (7) indirect materials, (8) bottles used to package liquids, (9) license fees for company cars, (10) wiring used in radios, (11) machine helper's wages, (12) wood used in bookcases, (13) city operating license, (14) machine depreciation based on machine hours used, (15) machine operator's hourly wages, and (16) cost of required outside inspection of each unit produced.

LO2 Variable Cost Analysis

E 2. Zero Time Oil Change has been in business for six months. The company pays $.50 per quart for the oil it uses in servicing cars, and each job requires an average of four quarts of oil. The company estimates that in the next three months, it will service 240, 288, and 360 cars.

1. Compute the cost of oil for each of the three months and the total cost for all three months.

Month	Cars to Be Serviced	Required Quarts/Car	Cost/Quart	Total Cost/Month
1	240	4	$.50	____
2	288	4	.50	____
3	360	4	.50	____
Three-month total	888			____

2. Complete the following sentences by choosing the words that best describe the cost behavior at Zero Time Oil Change:

Cost per unit (increased, decreased, remained constant).
Total variable cost per month (increased, decreased) as the quantity of oil used (increased, decreased).

E 3.

LO2 Mixed Costs: High-Low Method

Whitehouse Company manufactures major appliances. Because of increased interest in its refrigerators, it has just had its most successful year. In preparing the budget for next year, Jackson Harper, the company's controller, compiled these data:

Month	Volume in Machine Hours	Electricity Costs
July	6,000	$60,000
August	5,000	53,000
September	4,500	49,500
October	4,000	46,000
November	3,500	42,500
December	3,000	39,000

Using the high-low method, determine (1) the variable electricity cost per machine hour, (2) the monthly fixed electricity cost, and (3) the total variable electricity costs and fixed electricity costs for the six-month period.

E 4.

LO2 Mixed Costs: High-Low Method

When Jerome Company's monthly costs were $75,000, sales were $80,000; when its monthly costs were $60,000, sales were $50,000. Use the high-low method to develop a monthly cost formula for Jerome Company's coming year.

E 5.

LO4 Contribution Margin

Senora Company manufactures a single product that sells for $110 per unit. The company projects sales of 500 units per month. Projected costs are as follows:

Type of Cost	Manufacturing	Nonmanufacturing
Variable	$10,000	$5,000
Nonvariable	$12,500	$7,500

1. What is the company's contribution margin per unit?
2. What is the contribution margin ratio?
3. What volume, in terms of units, must the company sell to break even?

E 6.

LO4 Breakeven Point and C-V-P
LO5 Analysis

Using the data in the contribution income statement for Sedona, Inc., that appears below, calculate (1) selling price, (2) variable costs, and (3) breakeven point in sales.

Sedona, Inc.
Contribution Income Statement
For the Year Ended December 31, 20x7

Sales (10,000 units)		$16,000,000
Less variable costs		
Cost of goods sold	$8,000,000	
Selling, administrative, and general	4,000,000	
Total variable costs		12,000,000
Contribution margin		$ 4,000,000
Less fixed costs		
Overhead	$1,200,000	
Selling, administrative, and general	800,000	
Total fixed costs		2,000,000
Operating Income		$ 2,000,000

LO4 **Graphic Breakeven Analysis**

E 7.   Identify the letter of the point, line segment, or area of the breakeven graph shown below that correctly completes each of the following statements:

1. The maximum possible operating loss is

   a. *A.*   c. *B.*
   b. *D.*   d. *F.*

2. The breakeven point in sales dollars is

   a. *C.*   c. *A.*
   b. *D.*   d. *G.*

3. At volume F, total contribution margin is

   a. *C.*   c. *E.*
   b. *D.*   d. *G.*

4. Net income is represented by area

   a. *KDL.*   c. *BDC.*
   b. *KCJ.*   d. *GCJ.*

5. At volume J, total fixed costs are represented by

   a. *H.*   c. *I.*
   b. *G.*   d. *J.*

6. If volume increases from F to J, the change in total costs is

   a. *HI* minus *DE.*   c. *BC* minus *DF.*
   b. *DF* minus *HJ.*   d. *AB* minus *DE.*

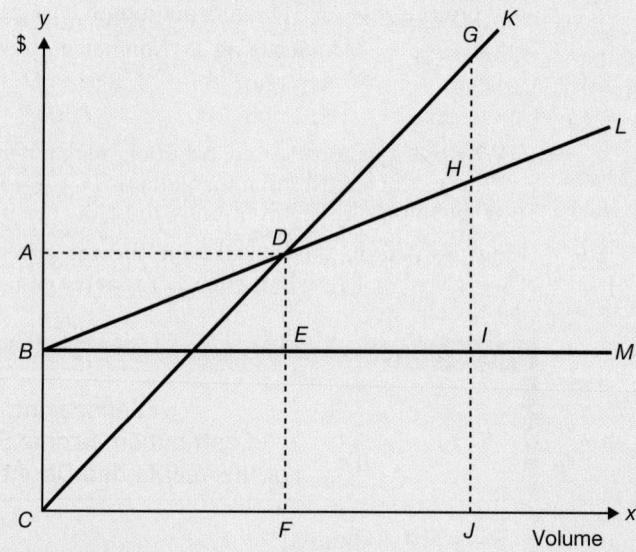

LO4 **Breakeven Analysis**

E 8.   Techno Designs Company produces head covers for golf clubs. The company expects to generate a profit next year. It anticipates fixed manufacturing costs of $126,500 and fixed general and administrative expenses of $82,030 for the year. Variable manufacturing and selling costs per set of head covers will be $4.65 and $2.75, respectively. Each set will sell for $13.40.

1. Compute the breakeven point in sales units.
2. Compute the breakeven point in sales dollars.
3. If the selling price is increased to $14 per unit and fixed general and administrative expenses are cut by $33,465, what will the new breakeven point be in units?
4. Prepare a graph to illustrate the breakeven point computed in **2**.

LO4 **Breakeven Analysis and**
LO5 **Pricing**

E 9.   McLennon Company has a plant capacity of 100,000 units per year, but its budget for 20x6 indicates that only 60,000 units will be produced and sold. The entire budget for 20x6 is as follows:

Sales (60,000 units at $4)		$240,000
Less cost of goods produced (based on production of 60,000 units)		
Direct materials (variable)	$60,000	
Direct labor (variable)	30,000	
Variable manufacturing costs	45,000	
Fixed manufacturing costs	75,000	
Total cost of goods produced		210,000
Gross margin		$ 30,000
Less selling and administrative expenses		
Selling (fixed)	$24,000	
Administrative (fixed)	36,000	
Total selling and administrative expenses		60,000
Operating income (loss)		($ 30,000)

1. Given the budgeted selling price and cost data, how many units would McLennon have to sell to break even? (**Hint:** Be sure to consider selling and administrative expenses.)
2. Market research indicates that if McLennon were to drop its selling price to $3.80 per unit, it could sell 100,000 units in 20x6. Would you recommend the drop in price? What would the new operating income or loss be?

E 10.
LO4 Breakeven Point for Multiple Products

Saline Aquarium, Inc., manufactures and sells aquariums, water pumps, and air filters. The sales mix is 1:2:2 (i.e., for every one aquarium sold, two water pumps and air filters are sold). Using the contribution margin approach, find the breakeven point in units for each product. The company's fixed costs are $26,000. Other information is as follows:

	Selling Price per Unit	Variable Cost per Unit
Aquariums	$60	$25
Water pumps	20	12
Air filters	10	3

E 11.
LO4 Sales Mix Analysis

Ella Mae Simpson is the owner of a hairdressing salon in Palm Coast, Florida. Her salon provides three basic services: shampoo and set, permanents, and cut and blow dry. The following are its operating results from the past quarter:

Type of Service	Number of Customers	Total Sales	Contribution Margin Dollars
Shampoo and set	1,200	$24,000	$14,700
Permanents	420	21,000	15,120
Cut and blow dry	1,000	15,000	10,000
	2,620	$60,000	$39,820
Total fixed costs			30,000
Profit			$ 9,820

Compute the breakeven point in units based on the weighted average contribution margin for the sales mix.

E 12.
LO4 Contribution Margin and
LO5 Profit Planning

Target Systems, Inc., makes heat-seeking missiles. It has just been offered a government contract from which it may realize a profit. The contract purchase price is $130,000 per missile, but the number of units to be purchased has not yet been decided. The company's fixed costs are budgeted at $3,973,500, and variable costs are $68,500 per unit.

1. Compute the number of units the company should agree to make at the stated contract price to earn a profit of $1,500,000.
2. Using a lighter material, the variable unit cost can be reduced by $1,730, but total fixed overhead will increase by $27,500. How many units must be produced to make $1,500,000 in profit?
3. Given the figures in **2**, how many additional units must be produced to increase profit by $1,264,600?

LO5   Planning Future Sales

E 13.   Short-term automobile rentals are the specialty of ASAP Auto Rentals, Inc. Average variable operating costs have been $12.50 per day per automobile. The company owns 60 cars. Fixed operating costs for the next year are expected to be $145,500. Average daily rental revenue per automobile is expected to be $34.50. Management would like to earn a profit of $47,000 during the year.

1. Calculate the total number of daily rentals the company must have during the year to earn the targeted profit.
2. On the basis of your answer to 1, determine the average number of days each automobile must be rented.
3. Determine the total revenue needed to achieve the targeted profit of $47,000.
4. What would the total rental revenue be if fixed operating costs could be lowered by $5,180 and the targeted profit increased to $70,000?

LO5   Cost Behavior in a Service Business

E 14.   Luke Ricci, CPA, is the owner of a firm that provides tax services. The firm charges $50 per return for the direct professional labor involved in preparing standard short-form tax returns. In January, the firm prepared 850 such returns; in February, 1,000; and in March, 700. Service overhead (telephone and utilities, depreciation on equipment and building, tax forms, office supplies, and wages of clerical personnel) for January was $18,500; for February, $20,000; and for March, $17,000.

1. Determine the variable and fixed cost components of the firm's Service Overhead account.
2. What would the estimated total cost per tax return be if the firm prepares 825 standard short-form tax returns in April?

LO5   C-V-P Analysis in a Service Business

E 15.   Flossmoor Inspection Service specializes in inspecting cars that have been returned to automobile leasing companies at the end of their leases. Flossmoor's charge for each inspection is $50; its average cost per inspection is $15. Tony Lomangeno, Flossmoor's owner, wants to expand his business by hiring another employee and purchasing an automobile. The fixed costs of the new employee and automobile would be $3,000 per month. How many inspections per month would the new employee have to perform to earn Lomangeno a profit of $1,200?

PROBLEMS

LO2   Cost Behavior and Projection
LO5

P 1.   Luster Auto, Inc., specializes in "detailing" automobile exteriors—that is, revitalizing them so the cars look as if they had just rolled off the showroom floor. The company charges $100 for a full exterior detailing. It has just completed its first year of business and has asked its accountants to analyze the operating results. Management wants costs divided into variable, fixed, and mixed components and would like them projected for the coming year. Anticipated volume for next year is 1,100 jobs.

The process used to detail a car's exterior is as follows:

1. One $20-per-hour employee spends 20 minutes cleaning the car's exterior.
2. One can per car of Bugg-Off, a cleaning compound, is used on trouble spots.
3. A chemical compound called Buff Glow is used to remove oxidants from the paint surface and restore the natural oils to the paint.
4. Poly Wax is applied by hand, allowed to sit for 10 minutes, and then buffed off.
5. The final step is an inspection to see that all wax and debris have been removed.

On average, two hours are spent on each car, including cleaning time and drying time for the wax. Operating information for Luster Auto's first year is as follows:

Number of automobiles detailed	840
Labor per auto	2 hours at $20.00 per hour
Containers of Bugg-Off consumed	840 at $3.50 per can
Pounds of Buff Glow consumed	105 pounds at $32.00 per pound
Pounds of Poly Wax consumed	210 pounds at $8.00 per pound
Rent	$1,400.00 per month

During the year, utilities costs ranged from $800 for 40 jobs in March to $1,801 for 110 jobs in August.

REQUIRED ▶   1. Classify the costs as variable, fixed, or mixed.
2. Using the high-low method, separate the mixed costs into their variable and fixed components. Use number of jobs as the basis.

3. Project the same costs for next year, assuming that the anticipated increase in activity will occur and that fixed costs will remain constant.
4. Compute the unit cost per job for next year.
5. Given your answer to **4**, should the price remain at $100 per job?

P 2.

LO4   Breakeven Analysis
LO5

Luce & Morgan, a law firm in downtown Jefferson City, is considering opening a legal clinic for middle- and low-income clients. The clinic would bill at a rate of $18 per hour. It would employ law students as paraprofessional help and pay them $9 per hour. Other variable costs are anticipated to be $5.40 per hour, and annual fixed costs are expected to total $27,000.

REQUIRED ▶

1. Compute the breakeven point in billable hours.
2. Compute the breakeven point in total billings.
3. Find the new breakeven point in total billings if fixed costs should go up by $2,340.
4. Using the original figures, compute the breakeven point in total billings if the billing rate decreases by $1 per hour, variable costs decrease by $.40 per hour, and fixed costs go down by $3,600.

P 3.

LO4   Planning Future Sales:
LO5   Contribution Margin Approach

Icon Industries is considering a new product for its Trophy Division. The product, which would feature an alligator, is expected to have global market appeal and to become the mascot for many high school and university athletic teams. Expected variable unit costs are as follows: direct materials, $18.50; direct labor, $4.25; production supplies, $1.10; selling costs, $2.80; and other, $1.95. Annual fixed costs are depreciation, building and equipment, $36,000; advertising, $45,000; and other, $11,400. Icon Industries plans to sell the product for $55.00.

REQUIRED ▶

1. Using the contribution margin approach, compute the number of units the company must sell to (a) break even and (b) earn a profit of $70,224.
2. Using the same data, compute the number of units that must be sold to earn a profit of $139,520 if advertising costs rise by $40,000.
3. Using the original information and sales of 10,000 units, compute the selling price the company must use to make a profit of $131,600. (**Hint:** Calculate contribution margin per unit first.)
4. According to the vice president of marketing, Albert Flora, the most optimistic annual sales estimate for the product would be 15,000 units, and the highest competitive selling price the company can charge is $52 per unit. How much more can be spent on fixed advertising costs if the selling price is $52, if the variable costs cannot be reduced, and if the targeted profit for 15,000 unit sales is $251,000?

P 4.

LO4   Breakeven Analysis and
LO5   Planning Future Sales

Write Company has a maximum capacity of 200,000 units per year. Variable manufacturing costs are $12 per unit. Fixed manufacturing overhead is $600,000 per year. Variable selling and administrative costs are $5 per unit, and fixed selling and administrative costs are $300,000 per year. The current sales price is $23 per unit.

REQUIRED ▶

1. What is the breakeven point in (a) sales units and (b) sales dollars?
2. How many units must Write Company sell to earn a profit of $240,000 per year?
3. A strike at one of the company's major suppliers has caused a shortage of materials, so the current year's production and sales are limited to 160,000 units. To partially offset the effect of the reduced sales on profit, management is planning to reduce fixed costs to $841,000. Variable cost per unit is the same as last year. The company has already sold 30,000 units at the regular selling price of $23 per unit.

   a. What amount of fixed costs was covered by the total contribution margin of the first 30,000 units sold?
   b. What contribution margin per unit will be needed on the remaining 130,000 units to cover the remaining fixed costs and to earn a profit of $210,000 this year?

P 5.

LO2   Cost Behavior and Projection
LO5   for a Service Business

Power Brite Painting Company specializes in refurbishing exterior painted surfaces that have been hard hit by humidity and insect debris. It uses a special technique, called pressure cleaning, before priming and painting the surface. The refurbishing process involves the following steps:

1. Unskilled laborers trim all trees and bushes within two feet of the structure.
2. Skilled laborers clean the building with a high-pressure cleaning machine, using about six gallons of chlorine per job.

3. Unskilled laborers apply a coat of primer.
4. Skilled laborers apply oil-based exterior paint to the entire surface.

On average, skilled laborers work 12 hours per job, and unskilled laborers work 8 hours. The refurbishing process generated the following operating results during 20x5:

Skilled labor	$20.00 per hour
Unskilled labor	$8.00 per hour
Gallons of chlorine used	3,768 gallons at $5.50 per gallon
Paint primer	7,536 gallons at $15.50 per gallon
Paint	6,280 gallons at $16.00 per gallon
Paint spraying equipment	$600.00 per month depreciation
Two leased vans	$800.00 per month total
Rent for storage building	$450.00 per month

Data on utilities for the year are as follows:

Month	Number of Jobs	Cost	Hours Worked
January	42	$ 3,950	840
February	37	3,550	740
March	44	4,090	880
April	49	4,410	980
May	54	4,720	1,080
June	62	5,240	1,240
July	71	5,820	1,420
August	73	5,890	1,460
September	63	5,370	1,260
October	48	4,340	960
November	45	4,210	900
December	40	3,830	800
Totals	628	$55,420	12,560

REQUIRED ▶
1. Classify the costs as variable, fixed, or mixed.
2. Using the high-low method, separate mixed costs into their variable and fixed components. Use total hours worked as the basis.
3. Compute the average cost per job for 20x5. (**Hint**: Divide the total of all costs for 20x5 by the number of jobs completed.)
4. Project the average cost per job in 20x6 if variable costs per job increase 20 percent.

ALTERNATE PROBLEMS

P 6.
LO4 Breakeven Analysis
LO5

At the beginning of each year, the Accounting Department at Moon Glow Lighting, Ltd., must find the point at which projected sales revenue will equal total budgeted variable and fixed costs. The company produces custom-made, low-voltage outdoor lighting systems. Each system sells for an average of $435. Variable costs per unit are $210. Total fixed costs for the year are estimated to be $166,500.

REQUIRED ▶
1. Compute the breakeven point in sales units.
2. Compute the breakeven point in sales dollars.
3. Find the new breakeven point in sales units if the fixed costs go up by $10,125.
4. Using the original figures, compute the breakeven point in sales units if the selling price decreases to $425 per unit, fixed costs go up by $15,200, and variable costs decrease by $15 per unit.

P 7.
LO4 Planning Future Sales:
LO5 Contribution Margin Approach

Garden Marbles manufactures birdbaths, statues, and other decorative items, which it sells to florists and retail home and garden centers. The company's Design Department has proposed a new product, a statue of a frog, that it believes will be popular with home gardeners. Expected variable unit costs are as follows: direct materials, $9.25; direct labor, $4.00; production supplies, $.55; selling costs, $2.40; and other, $3.05. The following are fixed costs: depreciation, building and equipment, $33,000; advertising, $40,000; and other, $6,000. Management plans to sell the product for $29.25.

REQUIRED ▶
1. Using the contribution margin approach, compute the number of statues the company must sell to (a) break even and (b) earn a profit of $50,000.
2. Using the same data, compute the number of statues that must be sold to earn a profit of $70,000 if advertising costs rise by $20,000.

3. Using the original data and sales of 15,000 units, compute the selling price the company must charge to make a profit of $100,000.

4. According to the vice president of marketing, Yvonne Palmer, if the price of the statues is reduced and advertising is increased, the most optimistic annual sales estimate is 25,000 units. How much more can be spent on fixed advertising costs if the selling price is reduced to $28.00 per statue, if the variable costs cannot be reduced, and if the targeted profit for sales of 25,000 statues is $120,000?

P 8.

LO5 Planning Future Sales for a Service Business

Lending Hand Financial Corporation is a subsidiary of Gracey Enterprises. Its main business is processing loan applications. Last year, Bettina Brent, the manager of the corporation's Loan Department, established a policy of charging a $250 fee for every loan application processed. Next year's variable costs have been projected as follows: loan consultant's wages, $15.50 per hour (a loan application takes five hours to process); supplies, $2.40 per application; and other variable costs, $5.60 per application. Annual fixed costs include depreciation of equipment, $8,500; building rental, $14,000; promotional costs, $12,500; and other fixed costs, $8,099.

REQUIRED ▶

1. Using the contribution margin approach, compute the number of loan applications the company must process to (a) break even and (b) earn a profit of $14,476.

2. Using the same approach and assuming promotional costs increase by $5,662, compute the number of applications the company must process to earn a profit of $20,000.

3. Assuming the original information and the processing of 500 applications, compute the loan application fee the company must charge if the targeted profit is $41,651.

4. Brent's staff can handle a maximum of 750 loan applications. How much more can be spent on promotional costs if the highest fee tolerable to the customer is $280, if variable costs cannot be reduced, and if the targeted profit for the loan applications is $50,000?

SKILLS DEVELOPMENT CASES

Conceptual Analysis

SD 1.

LO1 Concept of Cost Behavior
LO2

Gulf Coast Shrimp Company is a small company. It owns an icehouse and processing building, a refrigerated van, and three shrimp boats. Bob Jones inherited the company from his father three months ago. The company employs three boat crews of four people each and five processing workers. Trey Goodfellow of Bayou Accountants, a local accounting firm, has kept the company's financial records for many years. In his last analysis of operations, Goodfellow stated that the company's fixed cost base of $100,000 is satisfactory for its type and size of business. However, variable costs have averaged 70 percent of sales over the last two years, which is too high for the volume of business. Last year, only 30 percent of the sales revenue of $300,000 contributed to covering fixed costs. As a result, the company reported a $10,000 operating loss.

Jones wants to improve the company's net income, but he is confused by Goodfellow's explanation of the fixed and variable costs. Prepare a response to Jones from Goodfellow in which you explain the concept of cost behavior as it relates to Gulf Coast's operations. Include ideas for improving the company's net income based on changes in fixed and variable costs.

SD 2.

LO5 Comparison of Cost Behavior

Allstate Insurance Co. <www.allstate.com> and USAA <www.usaa.com> are two well-known insurers of motorists. Allstate has agents and offices all over the country. USAA sells only through the mail and over the telephone or Internet. In addition to offering collision and liability coverage for automobiles, each company offers life insurance and homeowners' insurance. When a motorist buys auto insurance from Allstate, the agent generally offers life insurance and homeowners' insurance as well—a strategy that helps increase Allstate's profitability. Although USAA usually sells its policies at lower prices than Allstate does, it is a very profitable company.

Identify and discuss the role that fixed costs, sales mix, and contribution margin can play in increasing profitability. Suggest a performance measure that could be used to evaluate agents who sell auto insurance. What is the role of variable costs? What is it about the relationship of USAA's fixed and variable costs that allows the company to sell policies at lower prices than Allstate and yet remain profitable?

Group Activity: Divide the class into groups and have them discuss this case. Ask one student from each group to summarize his or her group's discussion, and use the presentations to review the material in LO5.

Ethical Dilemma

LO4   Breaking Even and Ethics

SD 3. Lesley Chomski is the supervisor of the New Product Division of MCO Corporation. Her annual bonus is based on the success of new products and is computed on the number of sales that exceed each new product's projected breakeven point. In reviewing the computations supporting her most recent bonus, Chomski found that although an order for 7,500 units of a new product called R56 had been refused by a customer and returned to the company, the order had been included in the calculations. She later discovered that the company's accountant had labeled the return an overhead expense and had charged the entire cost of the returned order to the plantwide Manufacturing Overhead account. The result was that R56 appeared to exceed breakeven by more than 5,000 units and Chomski's bonus from this product amounted to over $800. What actions should Chomski take? Be prepared to discuss your response in class.

Research Activity

LO2   Cost Behavior and
LO4   Contribution Margin

SD 4. Make a trip to a local fast-food restaurant. Observe all aspects of the operation and take notes on the entire process. Describe the procedures used to take, process, and fill an order and deliver the order to the customer. Based on your observations, make a list of the costs incurred by the operation. Identify at least three variable costs and three fixed costs. Can you identify any potential mixed costs? Why is the restaurant willing to sell a large drink for only a few cents more than a medium drink? How is the restaurant able to offer a "value meal" (e.g., sandwich, drink, and fries) for considerably less than those items would cost if they were bought separately? Bring your notes to class and be prepared to discuss your findings.

Decision-Making Practice

LO2   Mixed Costs

SD 5. Officials of the Hidden Hills Golf and Tennis Club are in the process of preparing a budget for the year ending December 31, 20x6. Because Ramon Saud, the club treasurer, has had difficulty with two expense items, the process has been delayed by more than four weeks. The two items are mixed costs—expenses for electricity and for repairs and maintenance—and Saud has been having trouble breaking them down into their variable and fixed components. An accountant friend and golfing partner has suggested that he use the high-low method to divide the costs into their variable and fixed parts. The spending patterns and activity measures related to each cost during the past year are as follows:

Month	Electricity Expense Amount	Kilowatt-Hours	Repairs and Maintenance Amount	Labor Hours
January	$ 7,500	210,000	$ 7,578	220
February	8,255	240,200	7,852	230
March	8,165	236,600	7,304	210
April	8,960	268,400	7,030	200
May	7,520	210,800	7,852	230
June	7,025	191,000	8,126	240
July	6,970	188,800	8,400	250
August	6,990	189,600	8,674	260
September	7,055	192,200	8,948	270
October	7,135	195,400	8,674	260
November	8,560	252,400	8,126	240
December	8,415	246,600	7,852	230
Totals	$92,550	2,622,000	$96,416	2,840

1. Using the high-low method, compute the variable cost rates used last year for each expense. What was the monthly fixed cost for electricity and for repairs and maintenance?
2. Compute the total variable cost and total fixed cost for each expense category for last year.
3. Saud believes that in the coming year, the electricity rate will increase by $.005 and the repairs rate, by $1.20. Usage of all items and their fixed cost amounts will remain constant. Compute the projected total cost for each category. How will those increases in costs affect the club's profits and cash flow?

MANAGERIAL REPORTING AND ANALYSIS CASES

Interpreting Management Reports

LO3 **C-V-P Analysis**
LO4

MRA 1.   Established in 1963 in Datura, Italy, Datura, Ltd., is an international importer-exporter of pottery with distribution centers in the United States, Europe, and Australia. The company was very successful in its early years, but since then, its profitability has steadily declined. As a member of a management team selected to gather information for Datura's next strategic planning meeting, you have been asked to review its most recent contribution income statement, which appears below.

Datura, Ltd.
Contribution Income Statement
For the Year Ended December 31, 20x4

Sales revenue		€13,500,000
Less variable costs		
Purchases	€ 6,000,000	
Distribution	2,115,000	
Sales commissions	1,410,000	
Total variable costs		9,525,000
Contribution margin		€ 3,975,000
Less fixed costs		
Distribution	€ 985,000	
Selling	1,184,000	
General and administrative	871,875	
Total fixed costs		3,040,875
Operating income		€ 934,000

In 20x4, Datura sold 15,000 sets of pottery.

1. For each set of pottery sold in 20x4, calculate the (a) selling price, (b) variable purchases cost, (c) variable distribution cost, (d) variable sales commission, and (e) contribution margin.
2. Calculate the breakeven point in units and in sales euros.
3. Historically, Datura's variable costs have been about 60 percent of sales. What was the ratio of variable costs to sales in 20x4? List three actions Datura could take to correct the difference.
4. How would fixed costs have been affected if Datura had sold only 14,000 sets of pottery in 20x4?

Formulating Management Reports

MRA 2.

LO5   **C-V-P Analysis Applied**

Refer to the information in **MRA 1**. In January 20x5, Sophia Callas, the president and chief executive officer of Datura, Ltd., conducted a strategic planning meeting. During the meeting, Phillipe Mazzeo, vice president of distribution, noted that because of a new contract with an international shipping line, the company's fixed distribution costs for 20x5 would be reduced by 10 percent and its variable distribution costs by 4 percent. Gino Roma, vice president of sales, offered the following information:

> We plan to sell 15,000 sets of pottery again in 20x5, but based on review of the competition, we are going to lower the selling price to €890 per set. To encourage increased sales, we will raise sales commissions to 12 percent of the selling price.

Sophia Callas is concerned that the changes described by Roma and Mazzeo may not improve operating income sufficiently in 20x5. If operating income does not increase by at least 10 percent, she will want to find other ways to reduce the company's costs. She asks you to evaluate the situation in a written report. Because it is already January of 20x5 and changes need to be made quickly, she requests your report within five days.

1. Prepare a budgeted contribution income statement for 20x5. Your report should show the budgeted (estimated) operating income based on the information provided above and in **MRA 1**. Will the changes improve operating income sufficiently? Explain.
2. In preparation for writing your report, answer the following questions:
   a. Why are you preparing the report?
   b. Who needs the report?
   c. What sources of information will you use?
   d. When is the report due?

International Company

MRA 3.

LO3   **C-V-P Analysis and Decision Making**

The Goslar Corporation cuts granite, marble, and sandstone for use in the construction and restoration of cathedrals throughout Europe. The German-based company has operations in Italy and Switzerland. Gunder Shillar, the controller, recently determined that the breakeven point was €325,000 in sales. In preparation for a quarterly planning meeting, Shillar must provide information for the following six proposals, which will be discussed individually by the planning team:

1. Increase the selling price of marble slabs by 10 percent.
2. Change the sales mix to respond to an increased demand for marble slabs—that is, increase production and sales of marble slabs and decrease the production and sales of sandstone slabs, the least profitable product.
3. Increase fixed production costs by €40,000 annually to cover depreciation on new stone-cutting equipment.
4. Increase variable costs by 1 percent to cover higher export duties on foreign sales.
5. Decrease the sales volume of sandstone slabs because of a reduction in demand in Eastern Europe.
6. Decrease the number of days a customer can defer payment without being charged interest.

1. For each proposal, determine whether cost-volume-profit (C-V-P) analysis would provide useful financial information.
2. Indicate how each proposal that lends itself to C-V-P analysis would affect profit.

Excel Spreadsheet Analysis

MRA 4.

LO5   **Planning Future Sales**

As noted in **MRA 2**, Datura, Ltd., had targeted sales of 15,000 sets of pottery for 20x5 and was reducing the selling price to €890 per set. It was increasing sales commissions to 12 percent of the selling price and decreasing its fixed distribution costs by 10 percent and its variable distribution costs by 4 percent. Based on analysis of these changes, Sophia Callas has concluded that they would not increase Datura's 20x5 operating income by 10 percent over the previous year's income. Now, however, Gino Roma has reported that a new salesperson has just obtained a sales contract with an Australian distributor for 4,500 sets of pottery. The selling price, variable purchases cost per unit, sales commission, and total fixed costs will remain the same, but the variable distribution costs will be €160 per unit.

Using an Excel spreadsheet, complete the following:

1. Calculate the targeted operating income for 20x5.
2. Prepare a budgeted contribution income statement for 20x5 based on the information in **MRA 1** and the adjustments presented in **MRA 2**. Do you agree with Sophia Callas that Datura's projected operating income for 20x5 will be less than the operating income for 20x4? Explain.
3. Calculate the total contribution margin from the Australian sales.
4. Prepare a revised budgeted contribution income statement for 20x5 by combining the information from **2** and **3** above.
5. Does Datura need the Australian sales to achieve its targeted operating income for 20x5?

Internet Case

MRA 5.
LO4 Planning Future Sales and
LO5 Costs

Find a recent annual report on the Internet and read management's letter to the stockholders. This section of an annual report typically discusses initiatives or actions that the company implemented during the year as part of its strategic plan. (1) Identify at least three such initiatives or actions that you believe affected the company's annual sales or costs. (2) Also identify one initiative or action the company is planning for the coming year that you believe will affect revenue or expenses.

Chapter 24 describes the budgeting process, identifies the elements of a master budget, and demonstrates the preparation of operating budgets and financial budgets.

The Budgeting Process

LEARNING OBJECTIVES

LO1 Define *budgeting* and explain its role in the management cycle.

LO2 Identify the elements of a master budget in different types of organizations and the guidelines for preparing budgets.

LO3 Prepare the operating budgets that support the financial budgets.

LO4 Prepare a budgeted income statement, a cash budget, and a budgeted balance sheet.

LO5 Describe management's role in budget implementation.

DECISION POINT

A MANAGER'S FOCUS

Johnson & Johnson <www.jnj.com> With products that range from baby powder, Band-Aids, Tylenol, and contact lenses to diagnostic and surgical devices, Johnson & Johnson is the largest and most diversified manufacturer of health care products in the world. It has had affiliated companies operating in Latin America, Europe, Africa, and Australia for more than fifty years. Today, it is a global family of over 200 decentralized companies. Unifying the strategic planning of these companies' management teams are the set of common values and ethical principles expressed in Johnson & Johnson's credo, or mission statement. The strategic direction and major developments of the various companies are discussed at board meetings throughout the year and at meetings between management and board members. This ongoing dialogue provides managers with insight into the activities and direction of the company's businesses and is the basis for Johnson & Johnson's budgeting decisions.[1]

How does Johnson & Johnson's budgeting process work? First, sales and marketing teams from the decentralized companies develop sales budgets by product, geographic territory, and distribution channel. Senior management and staff then review the sales budgets to see that they meet the goals of Johnson & Johnson's strategic plan. Second, scheduling teams prepare production and shipping schedules to coordinate activities at the different manufacturing plants. Third, the managers responsible for functional areas (such as research and development, production, marketing, distribution, and customer service)

How is Johnson & Johnson's budgeting process linked to the company's long-term goals and objectives?

prepare cost and expense budgets. Fourth, the company accounting group reviews all budgets from the decentralized companies and analyzes their contents to determine whether they are in accord with the overall strategic plan. Fifth, Johnson & Johnson's controller prepares a complete set of companywide budgeted financial statements.

The budgeting process can be a highly effective way of linking strategic planning to operations, especially when it is coupled with ongoing discussions about a company's activities and direction, as is the case at Johnson & Johnson. Because a budget sets forth a company's objectives in concrete terms, it enables managers and employees to act in ways that will attain those objectives; it also gives them a means of monitoring the results of their actions. At Johnson & Johnson, the budgeting process and ongoing dialogue about strategy foster rapid improvements in productivity and customer service, as well as innovation in product and market development.

THE BUDGETING PROCESS

LO1   Define *budgeting* and explain its role in the management cycle.

RELATED TEXT ASSIGNMENTS
Q: 1, 2, 3, 4, 5, 6, 7, 8
SE: 1, 2, 3, 4
E: 1, 2, 3, 4
SD: 1, 3, 5
MRA: 1, 2, 5

www.jnj.com
www.merck.com
www.national.unitedway.org
www.unitednations.org

TERMINOLOGY NOTE:
For-profit organizations often use the term *profit planning* rather than *budgeting*.

ENRICHMENT NOTE: Any budget, even a poorly prepared one, is probably better than no budget at all. As the budgeting process is refined, the benefits to the organization will increase.

Budgeting is the process of identifying, gathering, summarizing, and communicating financial and nonfinancial information about an organization's future activities. It is an essential part of the continuous planning an organization must do to accomplish its long-term goals. The budgeting process provides managers of all types of organizations—including for-profit organizations, such as Johnson & Johnson and Merck, and not-for-profit organizations, such as the United Way and the United Nations—the opportunity to match organizational goals with the resources necessary to accomplish those goals. As part of the ongoing budgeting process, managers evaluate operational, tactical, value chain, and capacity issues; assess how resources for operating, investing, and financial activities are currently being used and how they can be efficiently used in the future; and develop contingency budgets as business conditions change.

Budgets—plans of action based on forecasted transactions, activities, and events—are synonymous with managing an organization. They are essential to accomplishing the goals articulated in an organization's strategic plan. They are used to communicate information, coordinate activities and resource usage, motivate employees, and evaluate performance. For example, a board of directors may use budgets to determine managers' areas of responsibility and to measure managers' performance in those areas. Budgets are, of course, also used to manage and account for cash. Such budgets establish minimum or targeted levels of cash receipts and limits on the spending of cash for particular purposes.

Budgets come in many forms. For example, a cash budget focuses on financial information; it shows, among other things, how cash resources will be allotted to operating, investing, and financing activities over a future period. A production budget, on the other hand, focuses on nonfinancial information; it shows planned production in units and identifies the activities needed to meet certain requirements or standards established in the planning stage of the management cycle.

To compete successfully in today's fast-paced global market, an organization must ensure that its managers have continuously updated operating data against which to measure performance. Thus, an ongoing budgeting process is especially important in the current business environment.

BUDGETING AND GOALS

■ **LONG-TERM GOALS**   Strategic planning is the process by which management establishes an organization's long-term goals. These goals define the strategic direction an organization will take over a five- to ten-year period and are the basis for making annual operating plans and preparing budgets. Long-term goals should take into consideration economic and industry forecasts, employee management relations, the structure and role of management, value chain considerations, organizational capacity, and any other operational and tactical issues facing the organization, such as the expected quality of products or services, growth rates, and desired market share.

Long-term goals cannot be vague; they must set specific targets and timetables and assign responsibility for achieving the goals to specific personnel. For example, a long-term goal for a company that currently holds only 4 percent of its product's market share might specify that the vice president of market-

FOCUS ON BUSINESS PRACTICE

What Can Cause the Planning Process to Fail?
When chief financial officers were asked what caused their planning process to fail, the six factors they most commonly cited were as follows:[2]

- An inadequately defined strategy
- No clear link between strategy and the operational budget
- Lack of individual accountability for results
- Lack of meaningful performance measures
- Inadequate pay for performance
- Lack of appropriate data

Enterprise Rent-A-Car

<www.enterprise.com>

OBJECTIVES

- To become familiar with the budgeting process and budgets
- To understand the relationship between strategic plans and operating budgets
- To describe the role of budgeting in the management cycle

BACKGROUND FOR THE CASE

Because its core business is not the airport market, Enterprise Rent-A-Car does not have the high profile most of its competitors enjoy. However, with over $6.5 billion in annual revenues, more than 4,800 locations worldwide, and offices within 15 miles of 90 percent of the U.S. population, it is the largest car rental company in North America. Founded in 1947 in St. Louis, Missouri, where it operated out of the basement of a car dealership, Enterprise now employs more than 50,000 people. It focuses on two market segments: people who need a replacement vehicle when their own car is unavailable—for instance, when it is undergoing repairs—and people who want a car for a business or leisure trip or for a special occasion.

Enterprise prides itself on providing excellent customer service, including free customer pickup. To accomplish its goals, the company has an incentive plan for employees and a decentralized organization that allows great latitude in decision making. Enterprise's managers prepare budgets to integrate, coordinate, and communicate the operating plans necessary to achieve the company's strategic objectives. The budgeting system includes measurement of performance at each location and for each employee. Good systems and budgeting also facilitate the company's objective of expanding its business in Canada, the United Kingdom, Ireland, and Germany.[3]

REQUIRED

View the video on Enterprise Rent-A-Car that accompanies this book. As you are watching the video, take notes pertaining to the following:

1. In your own words, explain what a budget is and list all the reasons you believe a company like Enterprise would prepare a set of budgets.
2. What is the relationship between Enterprise's strategic plans and its operating budgets?
3. What is the role of budgeting in the management cycle?

ENRICHMENT NOTE: Long-term goals are often expressed in subjective terms, such as increasing market share, becoming the industry leader, or having the best product on the market.

ing is to develop strategies to ensure that the company controls 10 percent of the market in five years and 15 percent by the end of ten years. An organization's strategic plan should include a range of long-term goals and give direction to its efforts to achieve those goals. It should include profit projections and describe new products or services in general terms.

KEY POINT: As plans are formulated for time periods closer to the current date, they become more specific and quantified. The annual budget is a very specific plan of action.

■ **SHORT-TERM GOALS** Annual operating plans involve every part of an enterprise and are much more detailed than long-term strategic plans. To formulate an annual operating plan, an organization must restate its long-term goals in terms of what it needs to accomplish during the next year. The process entails making decisions about sales and profit targets, human resource needs, and the introduction of new products or services. The short-term goals identified in an annual operating plan are the basis of an organization's operating budgets for the year.

Once management has established short-term goals, the organization's controller takes charge of coordinating the budgeting process. This person designs a complete set of budget-development directions, including a timetable complete with deadlines for all parts of the year's operating plan, and assigns clearly defined responsibilities for carrying out each part of the budget's development to specific individuals or management teams.

Depending on organizational practice, a budget may be reviewed and revised during the year. As pointed out in the focus box that follows, there is a growing trend to more frequent budget revisions.

FOCUS ON INTERNATIONAL BUSINESS

Budget Revision Practices in the United Kingdom

A recent survey of 1,000 leading U.K. companies has suggested that to keep pace in today's fast-changing business environment, managers would like more frequent budget revisions. The survey asked participants how often they revise their budgets and how often they believe budget revisions should be done. The survey results, summarized in the table to the right, show the trend to more frequent revisions.[4]

Frequency	Current Practice	Desired Practice
Daily	—	1%
Weekly	—	4%
Monthly	24%	44%
Quarterly	36%	33%
Twice a year	15%	17%
Once a year	15%	—
No revision	10%	1%

THE IMPORTANCE OF PARTICIPATION

Because an organization's main activities—such as production, sales, and employee training—take place at its lower levels, information necessary for establishing a budget flows from the supervisors of those activities through middle managers to senior executives. Each person in this chain of communication thus plays a role in developing a budget, as well as in implementing it. If these individuals feel they have a voice in setting the budget targets, they will feel personally motivated to ensure that their departments attain those targets and stay within the budget. If they do not feel they have a role in the budgeting process, motivation will suffer. The key to a successful budget is therefore **participative budgeting**, a process in which personnel at all levels of an organization actively engage in making decisions about the budget.

Because the controller is at the center of the budgeting process—collecting and distributing information and coordinating all budgeting activities—that person has considerable influence over the nature of the budgeting process. Participative budgeting depends on joint decision making, and to foster a climate in which that can take place, a controller must be able to communicate and negotiate effectively with people at all levels of an organization—from the senior executives who formulate the organization's long- and short-term goals to the middle managers and supervisors responsible for daily operations.

Senior executives also play a central role in determining the nature of the budgeting process. If they dictate targets instead of allowing middle managers and supervisors a voice in setting them, the budgeting process will be authoritative rather than participative. Without input from personnel at operational levels, the targets may be unrealistic and impossible to attain, which will further undermine the motivation of the managers and supervisors whose cooperation is essential for successful budget implementation. Problems may also arise if senior executives allow the controller to develop the budget without consulting other managers. In that case, managers may feel that budgeting is not a top priority and that budgets need not be taken seriously. Such difficulties can be avoided if senior executives recognize the importance of allowing personnel at all levels to play meaningful roles in the budgeting process.

BUDGETING AND THE MANAGEMENT CYCLE

● STOP AND THINK!

Why are budgets important at every stage of the management cycle?

An organization's budgets constitute its master plan for profitable operations. ■

As Figure 1 shows, budgeting is helpful to managers at each stage of the management cycle. To illustrate the relationship between budgeting and the management cycle, we will refer to the budgeting activities of Framecraft Company, a manufacturer that specializes in high-quality plastic picture frames. Framecraft's owner, Chase Vittel, believes the future growth of his company depends on a good budgeting process.

FIGURE 1
Budgeting and the Management Cycle

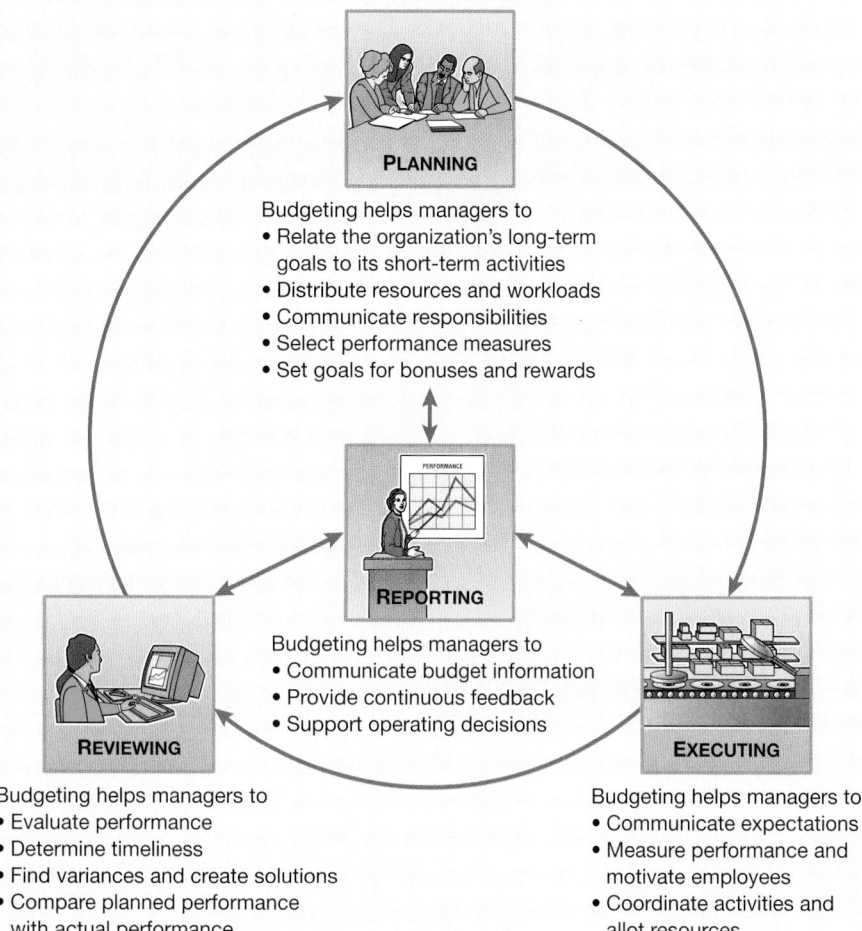

PLANNING

Budgeting helps managers to
• Relate the organization's long-term goals to its short-term activities
• Distribute resources and workloads
• Communicate responsibilities
• Select performance measures
• Set goals for bonuses and rewards

REPORTING

Budgeting helps managers to
• Communicate budget information
• Provide continuous feedback
• Support operating decisions

REVIEWING

Budgeting helps managers to
• Evaluate performance
• Determine timeliness
• Find variances and create solutions
• Compare planned performance with actual performance

EXECUTING

Budgeting helps managers to
• Communicate expectations
• Measure performance and motivate employees
• Coordinate activities and allot resources

KEY POINT: Although we present the four stages of the management cycle linearly, organizations are dynamic and managers may move through one stage, such as the executing stage, more often than another, such as the planning stage. For example, as part of the reviewing stage, a manager may evaluate performance reports on a weekly basis. On the other hand, as part of the planning stage, a manager may prepare a capital expenditures budget for new equipment only once a year.

PLANNING   Budgets originate in the planning stage of the management cycle. They reflect an organization's long- and short-term plans for achieving key success factors, such as high-quality products, reasonable costs, and timely delivery. Chase Vittel believes that by carefully distributing workloads and allotting resources to specific products, departments, and sales territories, budgets help his managers orchestrate short-term activities to accomplish long-term goals. Because he recognizes the benefits of participative budgeting, Vittel includes personnel from all levels of the company in the budgeting process. To motivate employees to achieve the targets set forth in the budget, Framecraft Company awards bonuses for good performance. As measures of performance, managers have selected profits, number of units sold, number of defective units, and cycle time (the time to obtain, manufacture, and ship an order).

KEY POINT: Budgeting is not only an essential part of planning; it also helps in controlling operations.

EXECUTING   During the executing stage, managers use budget information for communication, performance measurement, and resource allocation. The managers of Framecraft Company use budget information daily, weekly, and monthly to communicate expectations about performance, to measure performance and motivate employees, and to coordinate activities and allot resources among various departments. For example, Geoff Vukovic, the production manager, uses the units of production specified in the budget as an operating target for his workers and the number of defective units as a performance measure to motivate them to manufacture quality products. Chase Vittel uses standard product costs, generated in the planning process, to submit bids and estimate profits.

■ **REVIEWING**   In the reviewing stage, managers evaluate performance, including its timeliness. They look for variances between planned and actual performance and create solutions for the variances they detect. As we have already indicated, Framecraft Company's managers use the targets established in the planning stage as targets for actual performance in the executing stage. During the reviewing stage, they compare planned performance with actual performance. If they identify variances, they focus on finding solutions to the problems, which promotes continuous improvement of the company's products and processes. Framecraft Company's managers review their budgets on a regular basis because doing so helps them evaluate past performance and chart the course of future operations.

■ **REPORTING**   Because budgets are plans of action based on forecasts of transactions, activities, and events, they serve as a reference point for many kinds of reports. For example, performance reports that support bonuses and promotions are based on budget information. Other budget-based reports support operating decisions. To provide continuous feedback about an organization's operating, investing, and financing activities, managers prepare and distribute reports based on budget information throughout the year.

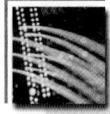 Check out ACE for a Review Quiz at http://accounting.college.hmco.com/students.

THE MASTER BUDGET

LO2   Identify the elements of a master budget in different types of organizations and the guidelines for preparing budgets.

RELATED TEXT ASSIGNMENTS
Q: 9, 10, 11, 12
SE: 5
E: 5
SD: 1
MRA: 1, 2

TERMINOLOGY NOTE:
Budgeted financial statements often are referred to as *forecasted financial statements* or *pro forma statements*.

A master budget consists of a set of operating budgets and a set of financial budgets that detail an organization's financial plans for a specific accounting period, generally a year. When a master budget covers an entire year, some of the operating and financial budgets may show planned results by month or by quarter. As the term implies, operating budgets are plans used in daily operations. They are also the basis for preparing the financial budgets, which are projections of financial results for the accounting period. Financial budgets include a budgeted income statement, a capital expenditures budget, a cash budget, and a budgeted balance sheet.

The budgeted financial statements—that is, the budgeted income statement and budgeted balance sheet—are also called pro forma statements, meaning that they show projections rather than actual results. Pro forma statements are often used to communicate business plans to external parties. If, for example, you wanted to obtain a bank loan so you could start a new business, you would have to present the bank with a pro forma, or budgeted, income statement and balance sheet showing that you could repay the loan with cash generated by profitable operations.

Suppose you have started your own business. Whether it is a manufacturing, retail, or service organization, to manage it effectively, you would prepare a master budget each period. A master budget provides the information needed to match long-term goals to short-term activities and to plan the resources needed to ensure an organization's profitability and liquidity.

Figures 2, 3, and 4 display the elements of a master budget for a manufacturing organization, retail organization, and service organization, respectively. As these figures indicate, the process of preparing a master budget is similar in all three types of organizations in that each prepares a set of operating budgets that serve as the basis for preparing the financial budgets. The process differs mainly in the kinds of operating budgets that each type of organization prepares.

The operating budgets of manufacturing organizations like Intel and John Deere include budgets for

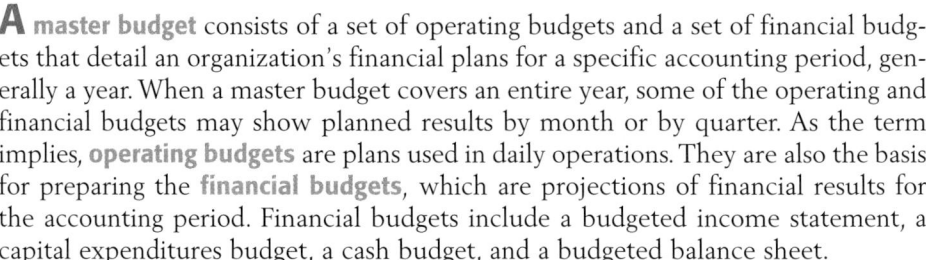

FOCUS ON BUSINESS TECHNOLOGY

Rolling Budgets Never End.
Many companies are shifting their budgeting focus from preparation and revision to an ever-changing budgeting process known as a rolling forecast. With computerized information systems that are able to capture accurate, up-to-the-minute financial and nonfinancial data, a rolling forecast can be refreshed continuously. The rolling forecast differs from a budget revision in that it includes only a few key performance indicators, such as orders, sales, costs, and capital expenditures; can be compiled quickly; has no fixed profit targets; and gives all authorized personnel in an organization immediate access to the same current information.[5]

FIGURE 2
Preparation of a Master Budget for a Manufacturing Organization

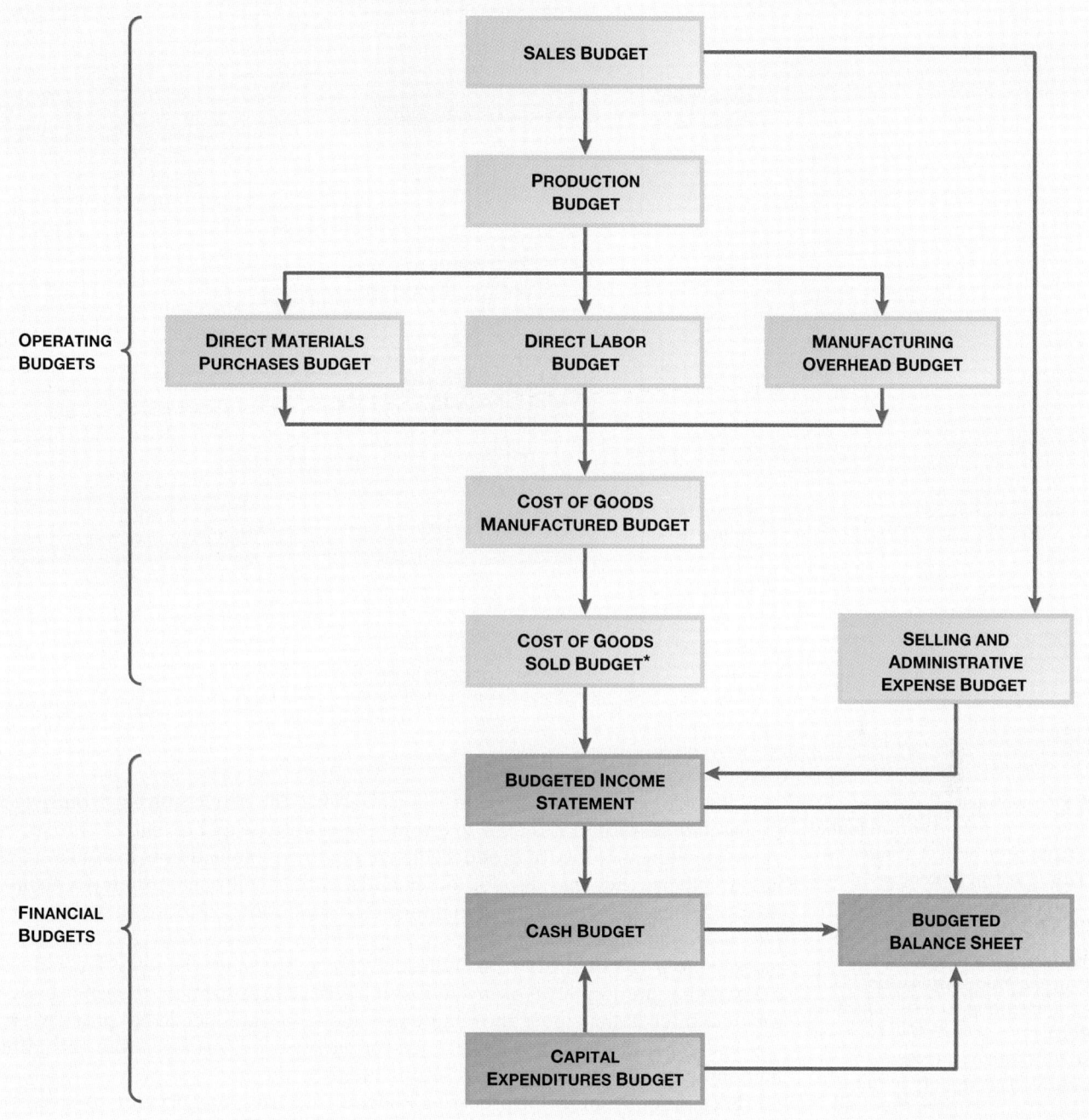

*Some organizations choose to include the cost of goods sold budget in the budgeted income statement.

www.intel.com
www.johndeere.com
www.nordstrom.com
www.talbots.com
www.lowes.com
www.enterprise.com
www.ups.com
www.amtrak.com
sales, production, direct materials purchases, direct labor, manufacturing overhead, selling and administrative expenses, and cost of goods manufactured. Retail organizations, such as Nordstrom, Talbots, and Lowe's, prepare a sales budget, purchases budget, selling and administrative expense budget, and cost of goods sold budget. The operating budgets of service organizations, such as Enterprise Rent-A-Car, UPS, and Amtrak, include budgets for service revenue, labor, services overhead, and selling and administrative expenses.

FIGURE 3
Preparation of a Master Budget for a Retail Organization

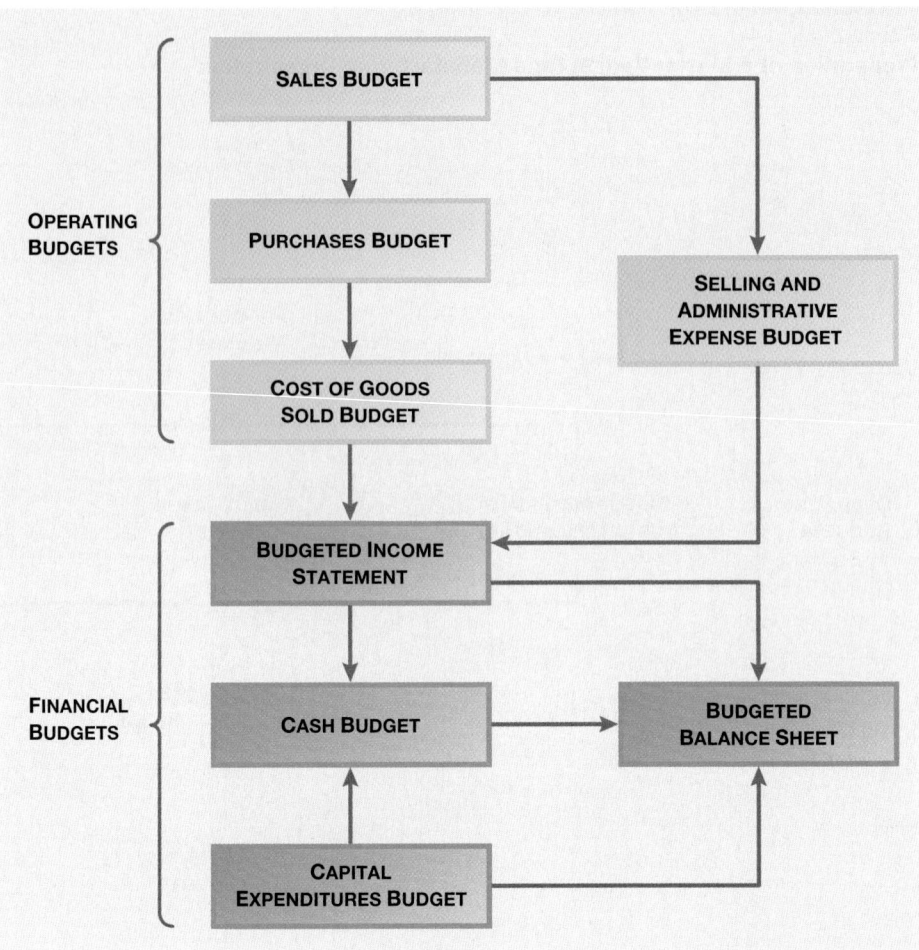

● **STOP AND THINK!**
How is the process of preparing a master budget similar in manufacturing, retail, and service organizations? How does it differ?

All three types of organizations begin the process by developing a set of operating budgets, which provide the data needed to prepare the financial budgets. The process differs mainly in the kinds of operating budgets each type of organization prepares. ■

The sales budget (or in service organizations, the service revenue budget) is prepared first because it is used to estimate sales volume and revenues. Once managers know the quantity of products or services to be sold and how many sales dollars to expect, they can develop other budgets that will enable them to manage their organization's resources so that they generate profits on those sales. For example, in a retail organization, the purchases budget provides managers with information about the quantity of merchandise needed to meet the sales demand and maintain a minimum level of inventory. In a service organization, the labor budget provides information about the labor hours and labor rates needed to provide services and generate the revenues planned for each period; managers use this information in scheduling services and setting prices.

Because procedures for preparing budgets vary from organization to organization, no standard format for budget preparation exists. The only universal requirement is that budgets communicate the appropriate information to the reader in a clear and understandable manner. By keeping that in mind and using the following guidelines, managers can improve the quality of budgets in any type of organization:

1. Know the purpose of the budget.

2. Identify the user group and its information needs.

3. Identify sources of accurate, meaningful budget information. Such information may be gathered from documents or from interviews with employees, suppliers, or managers who work in the related areas.

4. Establish a clear format for the budget. A budget should begin with a clearly stated heading that includes the organization's name, the type of budget, and

Figure 4
Preparation of a Master Budget for a Service Organization

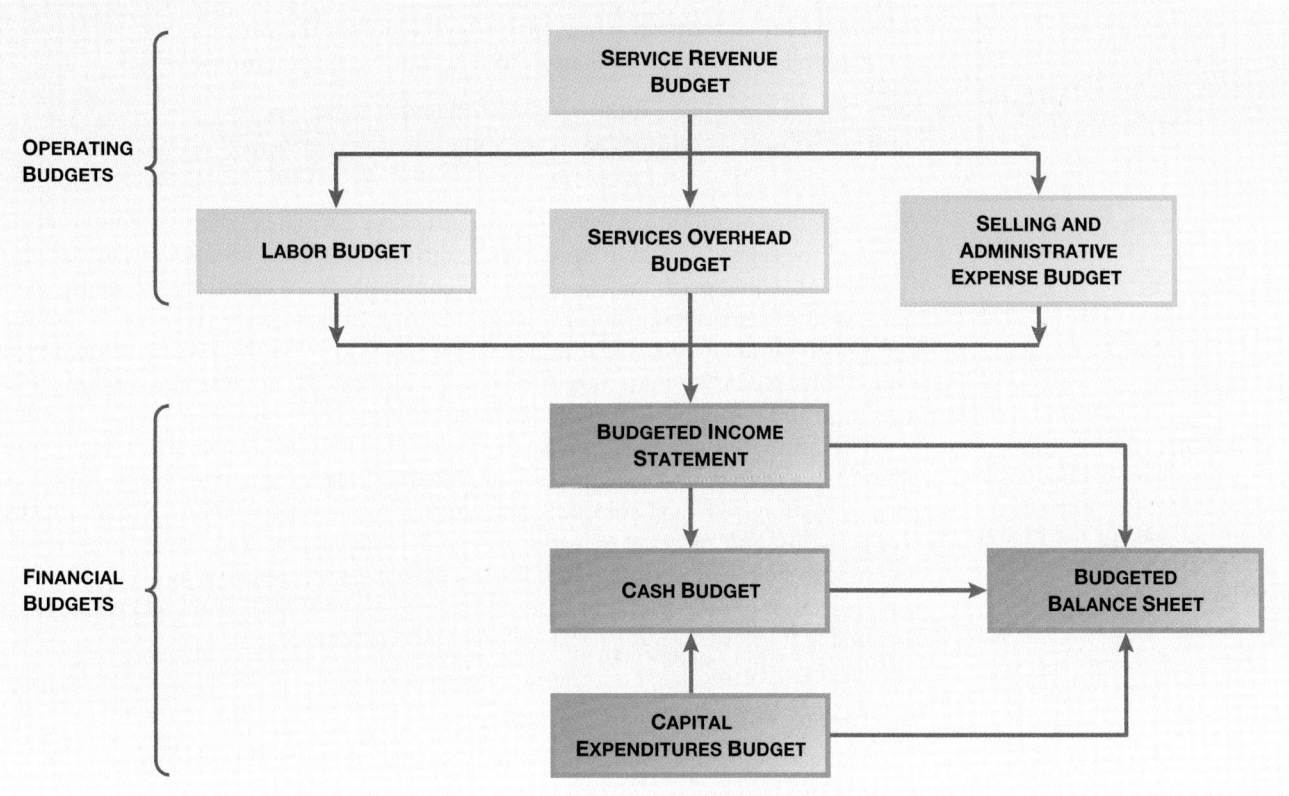

the accounting period under consideration. The budget's components should be clearly labeled, and the unit and financial data should be listed in an orderly manner.

5. Use suitable formulas and calculations to derive the quantitative information.

6. Revise the budget until it includes all planning decisions. Several revisions may be required before the final version is ready for distribution.

   ✓ Check out ACE for a Review Quiz at http://accounting.college.hmco.com/students.

OPERATING BUDGETS

LO3 Prepare the operating budgets that support the financial budgets.

RELATED TEXT ASSIGNMENTS
Q: 13, 14, 15, 16, 17
SE: 5, 6, 7
E: 5, 6, 7, 8, 9, 10, 11, 12
P: 1, 2
SD: 3, 4
MRA: 4

Although procedures for preparing operating budgets vary, the tools used in the process do not. They include cost behavior analysis, cost-volume-profit (C-V-P) analysis, and a product costing method. In this section, we use Framecraft Company to illustrate how a manufacturing organization prepares its operating budgets. Because Framecraft makes only one product—a plastic picture frame—it prepares only one of each type of operating budget. Organizations that manufacture a variety of products or provide many types of services may prepare either separate operating budgets or one comprehensive budget for each product or service.

THE SALES BUDGET

As we indicated earlier, the first step in preparing a master budget is to prepare a sales budget. A **sales budget** is a detailed plan, expressed in both units and dollars, that identifies the product (or service) sales expected in an accounting period. Sales managers use this information to plan sales- and marketing-related activities and to determine human, physical, and technical resource needs. Accountants use the information to determine estimated cash receipts for the cash budget.

The following equation is used to determine the total budgeted sales:

$$\begin{matrix} \text{Total} \\ \text{Budgeted} \\ \text{Sales} \end{matrix} = \begin{matrix} \text{Estimated} \\ \text{Selling Price} \\ \text{per Unit} \end{matrix} \times \begin{matrix} \text{Estimated} \\ \text{Sales in} \\ \text{Units} \end{matrix}$$

Although the calculation is easy, selecting the best estimates for the selling price per unit and the sales demand in units can be difficult. An estimated selling price below the current selling price may be needed if competitors are currently selling the same product at lower prices or if the organization wants to increase its share of the market. On the other hand, if the organization has improved the product's quality by using more expensive materials or production processes, the estimated selling price may have to be higher than the current price.

The estimated sales volume is very important because it will affect the level of operating activities and the amount of resources needed for operations. Resources for production, packing, shipping, accounting, purchasing, selling, and administrative activities will increase in varying degrees with increases in the estimated sales volume. To help estimate sales volume, managers often use a **sales forecast**, which is a projection of sales demand (the estimated sales in units) based on an analysis of external and internal factors. The external factors include

1. The state of the local and national economies
2. The state of the industry's economy
3. The nature of the competition and its sales volume and selling price

Internal factors taken into consideration in a sales forecast include

1. The number of units sold in prior periods
2. The organization's credit policies
3. The organization's collection policies
4. The organization's pricing policies
5. Any new products the organization plans to introduce to the market
6. The capacity of the organization's manufacturing facilities

Exhibit 1 illustrates Framecraft Company's sales budget for 20x7. The budget shows the estimated number of unit sales and dollar revenue amounts for each quarter and for the entire year. Because a sales forecast indicated a highly competitive marketplace, Framecraft's managers have estimated a selling price of $5 per unit. The sales forecast also indicated highly seasonal sales activity; the estimated sales volume therefore varies from 10,000 to 40,000 per quarter.

THE PRODUCTION BUDGET

A **production budget** is a detailed plan showing the number of units a company must produce to meet budgeted sales and inventory needs. Production managers use this information to plan for the materials and human resources that production-related activities will require. To prepare a production budget, managers must know the budgeted number of unit sales (which is specified in the sales budget) and the desired level of ending finished goods inventory for each period in the budget year. That level is often stated as a percentage of the next period's budgeted unit sales. For example, Framecraft Company's desired level of ending finished goods inventory is 10 percent of the next quarter's budgeted unit sales. (Its desired level of beginning finished goods inventory is 10 percent of the current quarter's budgeted unit sales.)

KEY POINT: The sales budget is the only budget subject to customer demand. Other budgets for the period depend on the numbers it provides.

KEY POINT: The production budget must provide for sufficient goods to meet current sales and must ensure that finished goods inventory levels are maintained according to company policy.

EXHIBIT 1
Sales Budget

Framecraft Company
Sales Budget
For the Year Ended December 31, 20x7

	Quarter				
	1	2	3	4	Year
Sales in units	10,000	30,000	10,000	40,000	90,000
× Selling price per unit	× $5	× $5	× $5	× $5	× $5
Total sales	$50,000	$150,000	$50,000	$200,000	$450,000

The following formula identifies the production needs for each accounting period:

$$\begin{array}{c} \text{Total} \\ \text{Production} \\ \text{Units} \end{array} = \begin{array}{c} \text{Budgeted} \\ \text{Sales in} \\ \text{Units} \end{array} + \begin{array}{c} \text{Desired Units of} \\ \text{Ending Finished} \\ \text{Goods Inventory} \end{array} - \begin{array}{c} \text{Desired Units of} \\ \text{Beginning} \\ \text{Finished Goods} \\ \text{Inventory} \end{array}$$

Exhibit 2 shows Framecraft Company's production budget for 20x7. Notice that each quarter's desired total units of ending finished goods inventory become the next quarter's desired total units of beginning finished goods inventory. Because 15,000 unit sales are budgeted for the first quarter of 20x8, the ending finished goods inventory for the fourth quarter of 20x7 is 1,500 units (.10 × 15,000 units), which is the same as the desired number of units of ending finished goods inventory for the entire year. Similarly, the number of desired units for the first quarter's beginning finished goods inventory—1,000—is the same as the desired number of units of beginning finished goods inventory for the entire year.

EXHIBIT 2
Production Budget

Framecraft Company
Production Budget
For the Year Ended December 31, 20x7

	Quarter				
	1	2	3	4	Year
Sales in units	10,000	30,000	10,000	40,000	90,000
Plus desired units of ending finished goods inventory	3,000	1,000	4,000	1,500	1,500
Desired total units	13,000	31,000	14,000	41,500	91,500
Less desired units of beginning finished goods inventory	1,000	3,000	1,000	4,000	1,000
Total production units	12,000	28,000	13,000	37,500	90,500

THE DIRECT MATERIALS PURCHASES BUDGET

KEY POINT: The direct materials purchases budget must reflect both quantities of materials to be acquired and purchase prices. Those quantities and prices will be used again in the preparation of the cash budget.

A **direct materials purchases budget** is a detailed plan that identifies the quantity of purchases required to meet budgeted production and inventory needs and the costs associated with those purchases. A purchasing department uses this information to plan purchases of direct materials. Accountants use the same information to estimate cash payments to suppliers.

To prepare a direct materials purchases budget, managers must know what production needs will be in each accounting period in the budget; this information is provided by the production budget. They must also know the desired level of the direct materials inventory for each period and the per unit cost of direct materials. The desired level of ending direct materials inventory is usually stated as a percentage of the next period's production needs. Framecraft Company's desired level of ending direct materials inventory is 20 percent of the next quarter's budgeted production needs. (Its desired level of beginning direct materials inventory is 20 percent of the current quarter's budgeted production needs.)

The first step in preparing a direct materials purchases budget is to calculate each period's total production needs in units of direct materials. Plastic is the only direct material used in Framecraft Company's picture frames; each frame requires 10 ounces of plastic. Framecraft's managers therefore calculate units of production needs in ounces; they multiply the number of frames budgeted for production in a quarter by the 10 ounces of plastic each frame requires.

In the second step, the following formula is used to determine the quantity of direct materials to be purchased during each accounting period in the budget:

$$
\begin{matrix}
\text{Total Units of} \\ \text{Direct} \\ \text{Materials to} \\ \text{Be Purchased}
\end{matrix}
=
\begin{matrix}
\text{Total Production} \\ \text{Needs in} \\ \text{Units of Direct} \\ \text{Materials}
\end{matrix}
+
\begin{matrix}
\text{Desired Units of} \\ \text{Ending Direct} \\ \text{Materials} \\ \text{Inventory}
\end{matrix}
-
\begin{matrix}
\text{Desired Units of} \\ \text{Beginning Direct} \\ \text{Materials} \\ \text{Inventory}
\end{matrix}
$$

The third step is to calculate the cost of the direct materials purchases by multiplying the total number of unit purchases by the direct materials cost. Framecraft's Purchasing Department has estimated the cost of the plastic used in the picture frames at $.05 per ounce.

Exhibit 3 shows Framecraft's direct materials purchases budget for 20x7. Notice that each quarter's desired units of ending direct materials inventory become the next quarter's desired units of beginning direct materials inventory. The company's budgeted number of units for the first quarter of 20x8 is 150,000 ounces; its ending direct materials inventory for the fourth quarter of 20x7 is therefore 30,000 ounces (.20 × 150,000 ounces), which is the same as the number of desired units of ending direct materials inventory for the entire year. Similarly, the number of desired units for the first quarter's beginning direct materials inventory—24,000 ounces—is the same as the beginning amount for the entire year.

THE DIRECT LABOR BUDGET

A **direct labor budget** is a detailed plan that estimates the direct labor hours needed in an accounting period and the associated costs. Production managers use estimated direct labor hours to plan how many employees will be required during the period and the hours each will work, and accountants use estimated direct labor costs to plan for cash payments to the workers. Managers of human resources use the information in a direct labor budget in deciding whether to hire new employees or reduce the existing work force, as well as a guide in training employees and preparing schedules of employee fringe benefits.

The first step in preparing a direct labor budget is to estimate the total direct labor hours by multiplying the estimated direct labor hours per unit by the anticipated units of production (see Exhibit 2). The second step in preparing such a budget is to calculate the total budgeted direct labor cost by multiplying the esti-

EXHIBIT 3
Direct Materials Purchases Budget

Framecraft Company
Direct Materials Purchases Budget
For the Year Ended December 31, 20x7

	Quarter				Year
	1	2	3	4	
Total production units	12,000	28,000	13,000	37,500	90,500
× 10 ounces per unit	× 10	× 10	× 10	× 10	× 10
Total production needs in ounces	120,000	280,000	130,000	375,000	905,000
Plus desired ounces of ending direct materials inventory	56,000	26,000	75,000	30,000	30,000
	176,000	306,000	205,000	405,000	935,000
Less desired ounces of beginning direct materials inventory	24,000	56,000	26,000	75,000	24,000
Total ounces of direct materials to be purchased	152,000	250,000	179,000	330,000	911,000
× Cost per ounce	× $.05	× $.05	× $.05	× $.05	× $.05
Total cost of direct materials purchases	$ 7,600	$ 12,500	$ 8,950	$ 16,500	$ 45,550

mated total direct labor hours by the estimated direct labor cost per hour. A company's human resources department provides an estimate of the hourly labor wage.

$$\frac{\text{Total Budgeted}}{\text{Direct Labor Cost}} = \frac{\text{Estimated Total Direct}}{\text{Labor Hours}} \times \frac{\text{Estimated Direct}}{\text{Labor Cost per Hour}}$$

Exhibit 4 shows how Framecraft Company uses these formulas to estimate the total direct labor cost. Framecraft's Production Department needs an estimated one-tenth (.10) of a direct labor hour to complete one unit. Its Human Resources Department estimates a direct labor cost of $6 per hour.

THE MANUFACTURING OVERHEAD BUDGET

A **manufacturing overhead budget** is a detailed plan of anticipated manufacturing costs, other than direct materials and direct labor costs, that must be incurred to meet budgeted production needs. A manufacturing overhead budget has two purposes: to integrate the overhead cost budgets developed by the managers of production and production-related departments, and to group information for the calculation of manufacturing overhead rates for the forthcoming accounting period.

The format for presenting information in a manufacturing overhead budget is flexible. Grouping information by activities is useful for organizations that use activity-based costing. This approach makes it easier for accountants to determine the application rates for each cost pool.

As Exhibit 5 shows, Framecraft Company prefers to group information into variable and fixed costs to facilitate C-V-P analysis during the executing stage of the management cycle. The manufacturing overhead rate is the estimated total

● **STOP AND THINK!**

Why are the direct materials purchases, direct labor, and manufacturing overhead budgets prepared after the production budget?

A production budget shows the number of units a company must produce to meet budgeted sales and inventory needs. Managers must have this information to estimate the direct materials, direct labor, and manufacturing overhead that production will require. ■

EXHIBIT 4
Direct Labor Budget

Framecraft Company
Direct Labor Budget
For the Year Ended December 31, 20x7

| | \multicolumn{4}{c}{Quarter} | |
	1	2	3	4	Year
Total production units	12,000	28,000	13,000	37,500	90,500
× Direct labor hours per unit	× .1	× .1	× .1	× .1	× .1
Total direct labor hours	1,200	2,800	1,300	3,750	9,050
× Direct labor cost per hour	× $6	× $6	× $6	× $6	× $6
Total direct labor cost	$ 7,200	$16,800	$ 7,800	$22,500	$54,300

EXHIBIT 5
Manufacturing Overhead Budget

Framecraft Company
Manufacturing Overhead Budget
For the Year Ended December 31, 20x7

| | \multicolumn{4}{c}{Quarter} | |
	1	2	3	4	Year
Variable overhead costs					
Factory supplies	$ 2,160	$ 5,040	$ 2,340	$ 6,750	$ 16,290
Employee benefits	2,880	6,720	3,120	9,000	21,720
Inspection	1,080	2,520	1,170	3,375	8,145
Maintenance and repair	1,920	4,480	2,080	6,000	14,480
Utilities	3,600	8,400	3,900	11,250	27,150
Total variable overhead costs	$11,640	$27,160	$12,610	$36,375	$ 87,785
Fixed overhead costs					
Depreciation, machinery	$ 2,810	$ 2,810	$ 2,810	$ 2,810	$ 11,240
Depreciation, building	3,225	3,225	3,225	3,225	12,900
Supervision	9,000	9,000	9,000	9,000	36,000
Maintenance and repair	2,150	2,150	2,150	2,150	8,600
Other overhead expenses	3,175	3,175	3,175	3,175	12,700
Total fixed overhead costs	$20,360	$20,360	$20,360	$20,360	$ 81,440
Total manufacturing overhead costs	$32,000	$47,520	$32,970	$56,735	$169,225

manufacturing costs divided by the estimated total direct labor hours. Framecraft's predetermined manufacturing overhead rate for 20x7 is $18.70 per direct labor hour ($169,225 ÷ 9,050 direct labor hours), or $1.87 per unit produced ($18.70 per direct labor hour × .10 direct labor hour per unit). The variable portion of the manufacturing overhead rate is $9.70 per direct labor hour ($87,785 ÷ 9,050 direct labor hours), which includes factory supplies, $1.80; employee benefits, $2.40; inspection, $.90; maintenance and repair, $1.60; and utilities, $3.00.

THE SELLING AND ADMINISTRATIVE EXPENSE BUDGET

KEY POINT: Remember that selling and administrative expenses are period costs, not product costs.

A **selling and administrative expense budget** is a detailed plan of operating expenses, other than those related to production, that are needed to support sales and overall operations in an accounting period. Accountants use this budget to estimate cash payments for products or services used in nonproduction-related activities. Framecraft Company's selling and administrative expense budget for 20x7 appears in Exhibit 6. The company groups its selling and administrative expenses into variable and fixed components for purposes of cost behavior analysis, C-V-P analysis, and profit planning. Framecraft Company's estimated variable selling and administrative expense rate for 20x7 is $.29 per unit sold, which includes delivery expenses, $.08; sales commissions, $.10; accounting, $.07; and other administrative expenses, $.04.

EXHIBIT 6
Selling and Administrative Expense Budget

Framecraft Company
Selling and Administrative Expense Budget
For the Year Ended December 31, 20x7

	Quarter				
	1	2	3	4	Year
Variable selling and administrative expenses					
Delivery expenses	$ 800	$ 2,400	$ 800	$ 3,200	$ 7,200
Sales commissions	1,000	3,000	1,000	4,000	9,000
Accounting	700	2,100	700	2,800	6,300
Other administrative expenses	400	1,200	400	1,600	3,600
Total variable selling and administrative expenses	$ 2,900	$ 8,700	$ 2,900	$11,600	$ 26,100
Fixed selling and administrative expenses					
Sales salaries	$ 4,500	$ 4,500	$ 4,500	$ 4,500	$ 18,000
Executive salaries	12,750	12,750	12,750	12,750	51,000
Depreciation, office equipment	925	925	925	925	3,700
Taxes and insurance	1,700	1,700	1,700	1,700	6,800
Total fixed selling and administrative expenses	$19,875	$19,875	$19,875	$19,875	$ 79,500
Total selling and administrative expenses	$22,775	$28,575	$22,775	$31,475	$105,600

EXHIBIT 7
Cost of Goods Manufactured Budget

Framecraft Company
Cost of Goods Manufactured Budget
For the Year Ended December 31, 20x7

			Sources of Data
Direct materials used			
Direct materials inventory, December 31, 20x6	$ 1,200*		Exhibit 3
Purchases for 20x7	45,550		Exhibit 3
Cost of direct materials available for use	$46,750		
Less direct materials inventory, December 31, 20x7	1,500*		Exhibit 3
Cost of direct materials used		$ 45,250	
Direct labor costs		54,300	Exhibit 4
Manufacturing overhead costs		169,225	Exhibit 5
Total manufacturing costs		$268,775	
Work in process inventory, December 31, 20x6		—†	
Less work in process inventory, December 31, 20x7		—†	
Cost of goods manufactured		$268,775	

*The desired direct materials inventory balance at December 31, 20x6, is $1,200 (24,000 ounces × $.05 per ounce); at December 31, 20x7, it is $1,500 (30,000 ounces × $.05 per ounce).

†It is the company's policy to have no units in process at the beginning or end of the year.

THE COST OF GOODS MANUFACTURED BUDGET

A **cost of goods manufactured budget** is a detailed plan that summarizes the estimated costs of production in an accounting period. The sources of information for total manufacturing costs are the direct materials, direct labor, and manufacturing overhead budgets. Most manufacturing organizations anticipate some work in process at the beginning or end of the period covered by a budget. However, Framecraft Company has a policy of no work in process on December 31 of any year. Exhibit 7 summarizes the company's estimated costs of production in 20x7. (The column to the right of the exhibit shows the sources of key data.) The budgeted, or standard, product unit cost for one picture frame is rounded to $2.97 ($268,775 ÷ 90,500 units).

 Check out ACE for a Review Quiz at http://accounting.college.hmco.com/students.

FINANCIAL BUDGETS

LO4 Prepare a budgeted income statement, a cash budget, and a budgeted balance sheet.

RELATED TEXT ASSIGNMENTS
Q: 18, 19
SE: 7, 8, 9, 10
E: 5, 13, 14, 15
P: 2, 3, 4, 5, 6, 7, 8
SD: 2, 4, 5
MRA: 2, 3, 4

With revenues and expenses itemized in the operating budgets, an organization's controller is able to prepare the financial budgets, which, as we noted earlier, are projections of financial results for the accounting period. Financial budgets include a budgeted income statement, a capital expenditures budget, a cash budget, and a budgeted balance sheet.

THE BUDGETED INCOME STATEMENT

A **budgeted income statement** projects an organization's net income in an accounting period based on the revenues and expenses estimated for that period. Exhibit 8

EXHIBIT 8
Budgeted Income Statement

Framecraft Company Budgeted Income Statement For the Year Ended December 31, 20x7			Sources of Data
Sales		$450,000	Exhibit 1
Cost of goods sold			
Finished goods inventory, December 31, 20x6	$ 2,970		
Cost of goods manufactured	268,775		Exhibit 7
Total cost of goods available for sale	$271,745		
Less finished goods inventory, December 31, 20x7	4,455		
Cost of goods sold		267,290	
Gross margin		$182,710	
Selling and administrative expenses		105,600	Exhibit 6
Income from operations		$ 77,110	
Interest expense (8% × $70,000)		5,600	
Income before income taxes		$ 71,510	
Income taxes expense (30%)		21,453	
Net income		$ 50,057	

Note: Finished goods inventory balances assume that product unit costs were the same in 20x6 and 20x7:

December 31, 20x6	December 31, 20x7
1,000 units	1,500 units (Exhibit 2)
× $ 2.97	× $ 2.97
$2,970	$4,455

shows Framecraft Company's budgeted income statement for 20x7. The company's expenses include 8 percent interest paid on a $70,000 note payable and income taxes paid at a rate of 30 percent.

Information about projected sales and costs comes from several operating budgets, as indicated by the column to the right of Exhibit 8, which identifies the sources of key data and makes it possible to trace how Framecraft's budgeted income statement was developed. At this point, you can review the overall preparation of the operating budgets and the budgeted income statement by comparing the preparation flow in Figure 2 with the budgets in Exhibits 1 through 8. You will notice that Framecraft Company has no budget for cost of goods sold; that information is included in its budgeted income statement.

THE CAPITAL EXPENDITURES BUDGET

A **capital expenditures budget** is a detailed plan outlining the anticipated amount and timing of capital outlays for long-term assets in an accounting period. Managers rely on the information in a capital expenditures budget when making decisions about such matters as buying equipment, building a new plant, purchasing and installing a materials handling system, or acquiring another business. Framecraft Company's capital expenditures budget for 20x7 includes $30,000 for the purchase of a new extrusion machine. The company plans to pay $15,000 in the first quarter of 20x7, when the order is placed, and $15,000 in the second quarter of 20x7, when it receives the extrusion machine. This information is necessary in preparing the company's cash budget. We discuss capital expenditures in more detail in another chapter.

THE CASH BUDGET

KEY POINT: The cash budget depends heavily on information from the operating budgets. Therefore, errors in those budgets could be compounded in the cash budget.

A **cash budget** is a projection of the cash an organization will receive and the cash it will pay out in an accounting period. It summarizes the cash flow prospects of all transactions considered in the master budget. The information that the cash budget provides enables managers to plan for short-term loans when the cash balance is low and for short-term investments when the cash balance is high. Table 1 shows how the elements of a cash budget relate to operating, investing, and financing activities.

A cash budget excludes planned noncash transactions, such as depreciation expense, amortization expense, issuance and receipt of stock dividends, uncollectible accounts expense, and gains and losses on sales of assets. Some organizations also exclude deferred taxes and accrued interest from the cash budget.

The following formula is useful in preparing a cash budget:

$$\begin{matrix} \text{Estimated} \\ \text{Ending Cash} \\ \text{Balance} \end{matrix} = \begin{matrix} \text{Total} \\ \text{Estimated} \\ \text{Cash Receipts} \end{matrix} - \begin{matrix} \text{Total} \\ \text{Estimated} \\ \text{Cash Payments} \end{matrix} + \begin{matrix} \text{Estimated} \\ \text{Beginning Cash} \\ \text{Balance} \end{matrix}$$

Estimates of cash receipts are based on information from several sources. Among these sources are the sales budget, the budgeted income statement, cash budgets from previous periods, cash collection records and analyses of collection trends, and records pertaining to notes, stocks, and bonds. Information used in estimating cash payments comes from the operating budgets, the budgeted income statement, the capital expenditures budget, the previous year's financial statements, and loan records.

TABLE 1. Elements of a Cash Budget

Activities	Cash Receipts From	Cash Payments For
Operating	Cash sales Cash collections on credit sales Interest income from investments Cash dividends from investments	Purchases of direct materials Purchases of indirect materials Direct labor Manufacturing overhead expenses Selling expenses Administrative expenses Interest expense Income taxes
Investing	Sale of investments Sale of long-term assets	Purchases of investments Purchases of long-term assets
Financing	Proceeds from loans Proceeds from issue of stock Proceeds from issue of bonds	Loan repayments Cash dividends to stockholders Purchases of treasury stock Retirement of bonds

Note: Classifications of cash receipts and cash payments correspond to those in a statement of cash flows.

EXHIBIT 9
Schedule of Expected Cash Collections from Customers

Framecraft Company
Schedule of Expected Cash Collections from Customers
For the Year Ended December 31, 20x7

	Quarter				
	1	2	3	4	Year
Accounts receivable, Dec. 31, 20x6	$38,000	$ 10,000	—	—	$ 48,000
Cash sales	10,000	30,000	$10,000	$ 40,000	90,000
Collections of credit sales					
First quarter ($40,000)	24,000	12,000	4,000		40,000
Second quarter ($120,000)		72,000	36,000	12,000	120,000
Third quarter ($40,000)			24,000	12,000	36,000
Fourth quarter ($160,000)				96,000	96,000
Total cash to be collected from customers	$72,000	$124,000	$74,000	$160,000	$430,000

In estimating cash receipts and cash payments for the cash budget, many organizations prepare supporting schedules. For example, Framecraft Company's controller converts credit sales to cash inflows and purchases made on credit to cash outflows, and then discloses those conversions on schedules that support the cash budget. The schedule in Exhibit 9 shows the cash that Framecraft Company expects to collect from customers in 20x7. Cash sales represent 20 percent of the company's expected sales; the other 80 percent are credit sales. Experience has shown that Framecraft collects payment of 60 percent of all credit sales in the quarter of sale, 30 percent in the quarter following sale, and 10 percent in the second quarter following sale.

As you can see in Exhibit 9, Framecraft's balance of accounts receivable was $48,000 at December 31, 20x6. The company expects to collect $38,000 of that amount in the first quarter of 20x7 and the remaining $10,000 in the second quarter. At December 31, 20x7, the estimated ending balance of accounts receivable is $68,000—that is, $4,000 from the third quarter's credit sales [($50,000 × .80) × .10] plus $64,000 from the fourth quarter's sales [($200,000 × .80) × .40]. The expected cash collections for each quarter and for the year appear in the total cash receipts section of the cash budget.

Exhibit 10 shows Framecraft's schedule of expected cash payments for direct materials in 20x7. This information is summarized in the first line of the cash payments section of the company's cash budget. Framecraft pays 50 percent of the invoices it receives in the quarter of purchase and the other 50 percent in the following quarter. At December 31, 20x7, the estimated ending balance of accounts payable is $8,250 (50 percent of the $16,500 of direct materials purchases in the fourth quarter).

Framecraft's cash budget for 20x7 appears in Exhibit 11. It shows the estimated cash receipts and cash payments for the period, as well as the cash increase or decrease. The cash increase or decrease plus the period's beginning cash balance equals the ending cash balance anticipated for the period. As you can see in Exhibit 11, the

EXHIBIT 10
Schedule of Expected Cash Payments for Direct Materials

Framecraft Company
Schedule of Expected Cash Payments for Direct Materials
For the Year Ended December 31, 20x7

| | Quarter | | | | |
	1	2	3	4	Year
Accounts payable, Dec. 31, 20x6	$4,200	—	—	—	$ 4,200
First quarter ($7,600)	3,800	$ 3,800			7,600
Second quarter ($12,500)		6,250	$ 6,250		12,500
Third quarter ($8,950)			4,475	$ 4,475	8,950
Fourth quarter ($16,500)				8,250	8,250
Total cash payments for direct materials	$8,000	$10,050	$10,725	$12,725	$41,500

● STOP AND THINK!
Why must a cash budget be prepared before a budgeted balance sheet can be completed?

A budgeted balance sheet must include the ending cash balance that appears in the cash budget. ■

beginning cash balance for the first quarter is $20,000. This amount is also the beginning cash balance for the year. Notice that each quarter's budgeted ending cash balance becomes the next quarter's beginning cash balance. You can trace the development of this budget by referring to the sources listed to the right of the exhibit.

Many organizations maintain a minimum cash balance to provide a margin of safety against uncertainty. If the ending cash balance on the cash budget falls below the minimum level required, short-term borrowing may be necessary to cover planned cash payments during the year. If the ending cash balance is significantly larger than the organization needs, it may invest the excess cash in short-term securities to generate additional income. For example, if Framecraft Company wants a minimum of $10,000 cash available at the end of each quarter, its balance of $7,222 at the end of the first quarter indicates that there is a problem. Framecraft's management has several options for handling this problem. The organization can borrow cash to cover the first quarter's cash needs, delay purchasing the new extrusion machine until the second quarter, or reduce some of the operating expenses. On the other hand, the balance at the end of the fourth quarter may be higher than Framecraft Company wants, in which case management might invest a portion of the idle cash in short-term securities.

THE BUDGETED BALANCE SHEET

A **budgeted balance sheet** projects an organization's financial position at the end of an accounting period. It uses all estimated data compiled in the course of preparing a master budget and is the final step in that process. Exhibit 12 presents Framecraft Company's budgeted balance sheet at December 31, 20x7. Again, to help you follow the development of the statement, the sources of information are listed in the column to the right of the exhibit.

FOCUS ON BUSINESS ETHICS

Does Budgeting Lead to a Breakdown in Corporate Ethics?
When budgets are used to force performance results, as they were at WorldCom <www.mci.com>, breaches in corporate ethics can occur. One former WorldCom employee described the situation at that company as follows: "You would have a budget, and he [WorldCom CEO Bernard Ebbers] would mandate that you had to be 2% under budget. Nothing else was acceptable." This type of restrictive budget policy appears to have been a factor in many of the recent corporate scandals.[6]

Exhibit 11
Cash Budget

<table>
<tr><th colspan="8">Framecraft Company
Cash Budget
For the Year Ended December 31, 20x7</th><th>Sources
of Data</th></tr>
<tr><th></th><th colspan="4">Quarter</th><th></th><th></th></tr>
<tr><th></th><th>1</th><th>2</th><th>3</th><th>4</th><th>Year</th><th></th></tr>
<tr><td>Cash receipts</td><td></td><td></td><td></td><td></td><td></td><td></td></tr>
<tr><td>Expected cash collections from customers</td><td>$ 72,000</td><td>$124,000</td><td>$74,000</td><td>$160,000</td><td>$430,000</td><td>Exhibit 9</td></tr>
<tr><td>Total cash receipts</td><td>$ 72,000</td><td>$124,000</td><td>$74,000</td><td>$160,000</td><td>$430,000</td><td></td></tr>
<tr><td>Cash payments</td><td></td><td></td><td></td><td></td><td></td><td></td></tr>
<tr><td>Direct materials</td><td>$ 8,000</td><td>$ 10,050</td><td>$10,725</td><td>$ 12,725</td><td>$ 41,500</td><td>Exhibit 10</td></tr>
<tr><td>Direct labor</td><td>7,200</td><td>16,800</td><td>7,800</td><td>22,500</td><td>54,300</td><td>Exhibit 4</td></tr>
<tr><td>Factory supplies</td><td>2,160</td><td>5,040</td><td>2,340</td><td>6,750</td><td>16,290</td><td></td></tr>
<tr><td>Employee benefits</td><td>2,880</td><td>6,720</td><td>3,120</td><td>9,000</td><td>21,720</td><td></td></tr>
<tr><td>Inspection</td><td>1,080</td><td>2,520</td><td>1,170</td><td>3,375</td><td>8,145</td><td></td></tr>
<tr><td>Maintenance and repair</td><td>1,920</td><td>4,480</td><td>2,080</td><td>6,000</td><td>14,480</td><td>Exhibit 5</td></tr>
<tr><td>Utilities</td><td>3,600</td><td>8,400</td><td>3,900</td><td>11,250</td><td>27,150</td><td></td></tr>
<tr><td>Supervision</td><td>9,000</td><td>9,000</td><td>9,000</td><td>9,000</td><td>36,000</td><td></td></tr>
<tr><td>Maintenance and repair</td><td>2,150</td><td>2,150</td><td>2,150</td><td>2,150</td><td>8,600</td><td></td></tr>
<tr><td>Other overhead expenses</td><td>3,175</td><td>3,175</td><td>3,175</td><td>3,175</td><td>12,700</td><td></td></tr>
<tr><td>Delivery expenses</td><td>800</td><td>2,400</td><td>800</td><td>3,200</td><td>7,200</td><td></td></tr>
<tr><td>Sales commissions</td><td>1,000</td><td>3,000</td><td>1,000</td><td>4,000</td><td>9,000</td><td></td></tr>
<tr><td>Accounting</td><td>700</td><td>2,100</td><td>700</td><td>2,800</td><td>6,300</td><td></td></tr>
<tr><td>Other administrative expenses</td><td>400</td><td>1,200</td><td>400</td><td>1,600</td><td>3,600</td><td>Exhibit 6</td></tr>
<tr><td>Sales salaries</td><td>4,500</td><td>4,500</td><td>4,500</td><td>4,500</td><td>18,000</td><td></td></tr>
<tr><td>Executive salaries</td><td>12,750</td><td>12,750</td><td>12,750</td><td>12,750</td><td>51,000</td><td></td></tr>
<tr><td>Taxes and insurance</td><td>1,700</td><td>1,700</td><td>1,700</td><td>1,700</td><td>6,800</td><td></td></tr>
<tr><td>Capital expenditures*</td><td>15,000</td><td>15,000</td><td></td><td></td><td>30,000</td><td></td></tr>
<tr><td>Interest expense</td><td>1,400</td><td>1,400</td><td>1,400</td><td>1,400</td><td>5,600</td><td>Exhibit 8</td></tr>
<tr><td>Income taxes</td><td>5,363</td><td>5,363</td><td>5,363</td><td>5,364</td><td>21,453</td><td></td></tr>
<tr><td>Total cash payments</td><td>$ 84,778</td><td>$117,748</td><td>$74,073</td><td>$123,239</td><td>$399,838</td><td></td></tr>
<tr><td>Cash increase (decrease)</td><td>$(12,778)</td><td>$ 6,252</td><td>$ (73)</td><td>$ 36,761</td><td>$ 30,162</td><td></td></tr>
<tr><td>Beginning cash balance</td><td>20,000</td><td>7,222</td><td>13,474</td><td>13,401</td><td>20,000</td><td></td></tr>
<tr><td>Ending cash balance</td><td>$ 7,222</td><td>$ 13,474</td><td>$13,401</td><td>$ 50,162</td><td>$ 50,162</td><td></td></tr>
</table>

*The company plans to purchase an extrusion machine costing $30,000 and to pay for it in two installments of $15,000 each in the first and second quarters of 20x7.

Exhibit 12
Budgeted Balance Sheet

<table>
<tr><td colspan="3" align="center">Framecraft Company
Budgeted Balance Sheet
December 31, 20x7</td><td align="center">Sources
of Data</td></tr>
<tr><td colspan="4" align="center">Assets</td></tr>
<tr><td colspan="4">Current assets</td></tr>
<tr><td>Cash</td><td></td><td>$ 50,162</td><td>Exhibit 11</td></tr>
<tr><td>Accounts receivable</td><td></td><td>68,000[a]</td><td>Exhibit 9</td></tr>
<tr><td>Direct materials inventory</td><td></td><td>1,500</td><td>Exhibit 7</td></tr>
<tr><td>Work in process inventory</td><td></td><td>—</td><td>Exhibit 7, Note</td></tr>
<tr><td>Finished goods inventory</td><td></td><td>4,455</td><td>Exhibit 8, Note</td></tr>
<tr><td>Total current assets</td><td></td><td>$124,117</td><td></td></tr>
<tr><td colspan="4">Property, plant, and equipment</td></tr>
<tr><td>Land</td><td></td><td>$ 50,000</td><td></td></tr>
<tr><td>Plant and equipment[b]</td><td>$200,000</td><td></td><td></td></tr>
<tr><td>Less accumulated depreciation[c]</td><td>45,000</td><td>155,000</td><td></td></tr>
<tr><td>Total property, plant, and equipment</td><td></td><td>205,000</td><td></td></tr>
<tr><td>Total assets</td><td></td><td>$329,117</td><td></td></tr>
<tr><td colspan="4" align="center">Liabilities</td></tr>
<tr><td colspan="4">Current liabilities</td></tr>
<tr><td>Accounts payable</td><td></td><td>$ 8,250[d]</td><td>Exhibit 10</td></tr>
<tr><td>Total current liabilities</td><td></td><td>$ 8,250</td><td></td></tr>
<tr><td colspan="4">Long-term liabilities</td></tr>
<tr><td>Notes payable</td><td></td><td>70,000</td><td></td></tr>
<tr><td>Total liabilities</td><td></td><td>$ 78,250</td><td></td></tr>
<tr><td colspan="4" align="center">Stockholders' Equity</td></tr>
<tr><td>Contributed capital</td><td></td><td></td><td></td></tr>
<tr><td>Common stock</td><td></td><td>$150,000</td><td></td></tr>
<tr><td>Retained earnings[e]</td><td></td><td>100,867</td><td></td></tr>
<tr><td>Total stockholders' equity</td><td></td><td>250,867</td><td></td></tr>
<tr><td>Total liabilities and stockholders' equity</td><td></td><td>$329,117</td><td></td></tr>
</table>

[a]The accounts receivable balance at December 31, 20x7, is $68,000: $4,000 from the third quarter's sales [($50,000 × .80) × .10] plus $64,000 from the fourth quarter's sales [($200,000 × .80) × .40].

[b]The plant and equipment balance includes the $30,000 purchase of an extrusion machine.

[c]The accumulated depreciation balance includes depreciation expense of $27,840 for machinery, building, and office equipment ($11,240, $12,900, and $3,700, respectively).

[d]At December 31, 20x7, the estimated ending balance of accounts payable is $8,250 (50 percent of the $16,500 of direct materials purchases in the fourth quarter).

[e]The retained earnings balance at December 31 equals the beginning retained earnings balance plus the net income projected for 20x7 ($50,810 and $50,057, respectively).

 Check out ACE for a Review Quiz at http://accounting.college.hmco.com/students.

BUDGET IMPLEMENTATION

LO5 Describe management's role in budget implementation.

RELATED TEXT ASSIGNMENTS
Q: 20
P: 6
SD: 3, 5
MRA: 1

● **STOP AND THINK!**

What factors are essential to successful budget implementation?

The success of budget implementation depends on clear communication of performance expectations and budget targets and the support of top management. ■

KEY POINT: Companywide dialogue cannot be overemphasized because good communication can eliminate many of the problems that typically arise in the budget process.

As we noted earlier, an organization's controller plays a central role in designing and coordinating the budgeting process. The controller is part of a **budget committee** that has overall responsibility for budget implementation; the committee oversees each stage in the preparation of the master budget, decides any departmental disputes that may arise in the process, and gives final approval to the budget. Other top managers who make up a budget committee include the company's president and the vice presidents in charge of various functional areas, such as production, purchasing, marketing, and human resources. The make-up of the committee ensures that the budgeting process has a companywide perspective.

A master budget may go through many revisions before it includes all planning decisions and has the approval of the budget committee. After the committee approves the master budget, periodic reports from department managers enable it to monitor the progress the company is making in attaining budget targets.

Successful budget implementation depends on two factors—clear communication and the support of top management. To ensure their cooperation in implementing the budget, all key persons involved must know what roles they are expected to play and have specific directions on how to achieve their performance goals. Thus, the controller and other members of the budget committee must be very clear in communicating performance expectations and budget targets. Equally important, top management must show support for the budget and encourage its implementation. The process will succeed only if middle- and lower-level managers can see that top management is truly interested in the outcome and is willing to reward personnel for meeting the budget targets. Today, many organizations have employee incentive plans that tie the achievement of budget targets to bonuses or other types of compensation.

✔ Check out ACE for a Review Quiz at http://acounting.college.hmco.com/students.

Chapter Review

REVIEW OF LEARNING OBJECTIVES

LO1 Define *budgeting* and explain its role in the management cycle.

Budgeting is the process of identifying, gathering, summarizing, and communicating financial and nonfinancial information about an organization's future activities. During the planning stage of the management cycle, budgeting helps managers relate an organization's long-term goals to short-term activities, plan the distribution of resources, and establish performance measures. During the executing stage, managers use budget information to communicate expectations, measure performance, motivate employees, coordinate activities, and allot resources. In the reviewing stage, they check for variances between planned and actual performance and create solutions to the problems they detect. To provide continuous feedback about an organization's operating, investing, and financing activities, managers prepare and distribute reports based on budget information throughout the year.

LO2 Identify the elements of a master budget in different types of organizations and the guidelines for preparing budgets.

A master budget consists of a set of operating budgets and a set of financial budgets that detail an organization's financial plans for a specific accounting period. The operating budgets serve as the basis for preparing the financial budgets, which include a budgeted income statement, a capital expenditures budget, a cash budget, and a budgeted balance sheet. The operating budgets of a manufacturing organization include budgets for sales, production, direct materials purchases, direct labor, manufacturing overhead, selling and administrative expenses, and cost of goods manufactured; those of a retail organization include budgets for sales, purchases, selling and administrative expenses, and cost of goods sold; those of a service organization include budgets for service revenue, labor, services overhead, and selling and administrative expenses. The guidelines for preparing budgets include identifying the purpose of the budget, the user group and its information needs, and the sources of budget information; establishing a clear format for the budget; and using appropriate formulas and calculations to derive the quantitative information.

LO3 Prepare the operating budgets that support the financial budgets.

The initial step in preparing a master budget in any type of organization is to prepare a sales budget. Once sales have been estimated, the manager of a manufacturing organization's production department is able to prepare a budget that shows how many units of products must be manufactured to meet the projected sales volume. With that information in hand, other managers are able to prepare budgets for direct materials purchases, direct labor, manufacturing overhead, selling and administrative expenses, and cost of goods manufactured. A cost of goods sold budget may be prepared separately, or it may be included in the cost of goods manufactured budget. The operating budgets supply the information needed to prepare the financial budgets.

LO4 Prepare a budgeted income statement, a cash budget, and a budgeted balance sheet.

With estimated revenues and expenses itemized in the operating budgets, a controller is able to prepare the financial budgets. A budgeted income statement projects an organization's net income for a specific accounting period. A capital expenditures budget estimates the amount and timing of its capital outlays during the period. A cash budget projects its cash receipts and cash payments for the period. Estimates of cash receipts and payments are needed to prepare a cash budget. Information about cash receipts comes from several sources, including the sales budget, the budgeted income statement, and various financial records. Sources of information about cash payments include the operating budgets, the budgeted income statement, and the capital expenditures budget. The difference between the total estimated cash receipts and total estimated cash payments is the cash increase or decrease anticipated for the period. That total plus the period's beginning cash balance equals the ending cash balance. The final step in developing a master budget is to prepare a budgeted balance sheet, which projects the organization's financial position at the end of the accounting period. All budgeted data are used in preparing this statement.

LO5 Describe management's role in budget implementation.

A budget committee made up of top management has overall responsibility for budget implementation. The committee oversees each stage in the preparation of the master budget, decides any departmental disputes that may arise in the process, and gives final approval to the budget. After the committee approves the master budget, periodic reports from department managers enable it to monitor the progress the company is making in attaining budget targets. To ensure the cooperation of personnel in implementing the budget, top managers must clearly communicate performance expectations and budget targets. They must also show their support for the budget and encourage its implementation.

REVIEW OF CONCEPTS AND TERMINOLOGY

The following concepts and terms were introduced in this chapter:

LO5 **Budget committee:** A committee made up of top management that has overall responsibility for budget implementation.

LO4 **Budgeted balance sheet:** A statement that projects an organization's financial position at the end of an accounting period.

LO4 **Budgeted income statement:** A projection of an organization's net income in an accounting period based on the revenues and expenses estimated for that accounting period.

LO1 **Budgeting:** The process of identifying, gathering, summarizing, and communicating financial and nonfinancial information about an organization's future activities.

LO1 **Budgets:** Plans of action based on forecasted transactions, activities, and events.

LO4 **Capital expenditures budget:** A detailed plan outlining the anticipated amount and timing of capital outlays for long-term assets in an accounting period.

LO4 **Cash budget:** A projection of the cash an organization will receive and the cash it will pay out in an accounting period.

LO3 **Cost of goods manufactured budget:** A detailed plan that summarizes the estimated costs of production in an accounting period.

LO3 **Direct labor budget:** A detailed plan that estimates the direct labor hours needed in an accounting period and the associated costs.

LO3 **Direct materials purchases budget:** A detailed plan that identifies the quantity of purchases required to meet budgeted production and inventory needs and the costs associated with those purchases.

LO2 **Financial budgets:** Budget projections of the financial results for an accounting period.

LO3 **Manufacturing overhead budget:** A detailed plan of anticipated manufacturing costs, other than direct materials and direct labor costs, that must be incurred to meet budgeted production needs.

LO2 **Master budget:** A set of operating budgets and a set of financial budgets that detail an organization's financial plans for a specific accounting period.

LO2 **Operating budgets:** Budget plans used in daily operations.

LO1 **Participative budgeting:** A process in which personnel at all levels of an organization actively engage in making decisions about a budget.

LO3 **Production budget:** A detailed plan showing the number of units a company must produce to meet budgeted sales and inventory needs.

LO2 **Pro forma statements:** Financial statements that show projections rather than actual results and that are often used to communicate business plans to external parties.

LO3 **Sales budget:** A detailed plan, expressed in both units and dollars, that identifies the product (or service) sales expected in an accounting period.

LO3 **Sales forecast:** A projection of sales demand based on an analysis of external and internal factors.

LO3 **Selling and administrative expense budget:** A detailed plan of operating expenses, other than those related to production, that are needed to support sales and overall operations in an accounting period.

LO1 **Strategic planning:** The process by which management establishes an organization's long-term goals.

REVIEW PROBLEM

Preparing a Cash Budget

LO4 Info Processing Company provides database management services. It uses state-of-the-art equipment and employs five information specialists. Each specialist works an average of 160 hours a month. Info Processing's controller has compiled the following information:

	Actual Data for 20x6		Forecasted Data for 20x7		
	November	December	January	February	March
Client billings (sales)	$25,000	$35,000	$25,000	$20,000	$40,000
Selling and administrative expenses	12,000	13,000	12,000	11,000	12,500
Operating supplies	2,500	3,500	2,500	2,500	4,000
Processing overhead	3,200	3,500	3,000	2,500	3,500

Sixty percent of the client billings are cash sales collected during the month of sale; 30 percent are collected in the first month following the sale; and 10 percent are collected in the second month following the sale. Operating supplies are paid for in the month of purchase. Selling and administrative expenses and processing overhead are paid in the month following the cost's incurrence.

The company has a bank loan of $12,000 at a 12 percent annual interest rate. Interest is paid monthly, and $2,000 of the loan principal is due on February 28, 20x7. Income taxes of $4,550 for calendar year 20x6 are due and payable on March 15, 20x7. The information specialists earn $8.50 an hour, and all payroll-related employee benefit costs are included in processing overhead. The company anticipates no capital expenditures for the first quarter of the coming year. It expects its cash balance on December 31, 20x6, to be $13,840.

REQUIRED ▶ Prepare a monthly cash budget for Info Processing Company for the three-month period ended March 31, 20x7. Comment on whether the ending cash balances are adequate for Info Processing's cash needs.

ANSWER TO REVIEW PROBLEM

Info Processing Company
Monthly Cash Budget
For the Three-Month Period Ended March 31, 20x7

	January	February	March	Totals
Cash receipts				
Client billings	$28,000	$23,000	$32,500	$83,500
Cash payments				
Operating supplies	$ 2,500	$ 2,500	$ 4,000	$ 9,000
Direct labor	6,800	6,800	6,800	20,400
Selling and administrative expenses	13,000	12,000	11,000	36,000
Processing overhead	3,500	3,000	2,500	9,000
Interest expense	120	120	100	340
Loan payment	—	2,000	—	2,000
Income tax payment	—	—	4,550	4,550
Total cash payments	$25,920	$26,420	$28,950	$81,290
Cash increase (decrease)	$ 2,080	($ 3,420)	$ 3,550	$ 2,210
Beginning cash balance	13,840	15,920	12,500	13,840
Ending cash balance	$15,920	$12,500	$16,050	$16,050

The details supporting the individual computations in this cash budget are as follows:

	January	February	March
Client billings			
November	$ 2,500	—	—
December	10,500	$ 3,500	—
January	15,000	7,500	$ 2,500
February	—	12,000	6,000
March	—	—	24,000

	$28,000	$23,000	$32,500
Operating supplies			
Paid for in the month purchased	$ 2,500	$ 2,500	$ 4,000
Direct labor			
5 employees × 160 hours a month			
× $8.50 an hour	6,800	6,800	6,800
Selling and administrative expenses			
Paid in the month following incurrence	13,000	12,000	11,000
Processing overhead			
Paid in the month following incurrence	3,500	3,000	2,500
Interest expense			
January and February = 1% of $12,000	120	120	
March = 1% of $10,000			100
Loan payment	—	2,000	—
Income tax payment		—	4,550

The ending cash balances of $15,920, $12,500, and $16,050 for January, February, and March 20x7, respectively, appear to be comfortable but not too large for Info Processing Company.

Chapter Assignments

BUILDING YOUR KNOWLEDGE FOUNDATION

QUESTIONS

1. Define budgeting.
2. What is a budget? What type of information may a budget include?
3. List three ways in which an organization can use budgets.
4. What is the difference between long-term strategic plans and annual operating plans?
5. What factors should be considered in establishing long-term goals?
6. Explain the purpose of the following budgeting practice: "Restate long-term plans in terms of short-term plans for products or services and in terms of a detailed profit plan."
7. Describe what happens in the budgeting process after management has set short-term goals.
8. Give examples of ways in which budgeting can help managers during the stages of the management cycle.
9. What is a master budget? What is its purpose?
10. In what ways are the master budgets of manufacturing, retail, and service organizations similar?
11. In what ways do the master budgets of a retail organization and a service organization differ?
12. List the guidelines for preparing a budget.
13. What is a sales forecast? What internal and external factors does a sales forecast take into consideration?
14. What are the three steps in preparing a direct materials purchases budget?
15. What are the two steps in preparing a direct labor budget?
16. Why is it useful to distinguish between variable and fixed expenses in a selling and administrative expense budget?
17. Why does a selling and administrative expense budget use units sold rather than units produced?

18. How is the cash budget related to the master budget? What are the purposes of preparing a cash budget?

19. What is the final step in developing a master budget?

20. Who are the people responsible for ensuring that budget implementation is successful? What are their responsibilities?

SHORT EXERCISES

LO1 Budgeting and the Management Cycle

SE 1. All the management activities listed below require the use of budget information. Indicate whether each activity is part of the planning stage (P), executing stage (E), reviewing stage (REV), or reporting stage (REP) of the management cycle.

1. Coordinating purchasing, production, sales, and shipping
2. Selecting performance measures to monitor the timeliness of shipping
3. Calculating variances between the planned direct materials and actual direct materials used in production
4. Developing a budget to distribute the organization's resources among its various departments
5. Preparing a report on the performance of the production department over the last three months

LO1 Budgeting in a Retail Organization

SE 2. Sam Zubac is the manager of the shoe department in a discount department store. During a recent meeting, Zubac and his supervisor agreed that Zubac's goal for the next year would be to increase the number of pairs of shoes sold by 20 percent. The department sold 8,000 pairs of shoes last year. Two salespersons currently work for Zubac. What types of budgets should Zubac use to help him achieve his sales goal? What kinds of information should those budgets provide?

LO1 Budgetary Control

SE 3. Toby Andres owns a tree nursery. She analyzes her business's results by comparing actual operating results with figures budgeted at the beginning of the year. When the business generates large profits, she often overlooks the differences between actual and budgeted data. But when profits are low, she spends many hours analyzing the differences. If you owned Andres's business, would you use her approach to budgetary control? If not, what changes would you make?

LO1 Budgeting and Goals

SE 4. The dashboard assembly team at Rockford Automobile Company is participating in the company's budgeting process for the first time. After the team participated in a discussion of the basic principles of budgeting, one team member asked the controller to explain how the company's long-term goals relate to its short-term plan. How should the controller respond?

LO2 Components of a Master
LO3 Budget

SE 5. A master budget is a compilation of forecasts for the coming year or operating cycle made by various departments or functions within an organization. What is the most basic forecast made in a master budget? List the reasons for your answer. Which budgets must managers prepare before they can prepare a direct materials purchases budget?

LO3 Preparing an Operating Budget

SE 6. Quester Company expects to sell 50,000 units of its product in the coming year. Each unit sells for $45. Sales brochures and supplies for the year are expected to cost $7,000. Three sales representatives cover the southeast region. Each one's base salary is $20,000, and each earns a sales commission of 5 percent of the selling price of the units he or she sells. The sales representatives supply their own transportation; they are reimbursed for travel at a rate of $.40 per mile. The company estimates that the sales representatives will drive a total of 75,000 miles next year.

From the information provided, calculate Quester Company's budgeted selling expenses for the coming year.

LO3 Budgeted Gross Margin
LO4

SE 7. Operating budgets for the DiPaolo Company reveal the following information: net sales, $450,000; beginning materials inventory, $23,000; materials purchased, $185,000; beginning work in process inventory, $64,700; beginning finished goods inventory, $21,600; direct labor costs, $34,000; manufacturing overhead applied, $67,000; ending work in process inventory, $61,200; ending materials inventory, $18,700; and ending finished goods inventory, $16,300.

Compute DiPaola Company's budgeted gross margin.

SE 8.

LO4 Estimating Cash Collections

KD Insurance Company specializes in term life insurance contracts. Cash collection experience shows that 20 percent of billed premiums are collected in the month before they are due, 60 percent are paid in the month they are due, and 16 percent are paid in the month following their due date. Four percent of the billed premiums are paid late (in the second month following their due date) and include a 10 percent penalty payment. Total billing notices in January were $58,000; in February, $62,000; in March, $66,000; in April, $65,000; in May, $60,000; and in June, $62,000. How much cash does the company expect to collect in May?

SE 9.

LO4 Cash Budget

The projections of direct materials purchases that follow are for the Stromboli Corporation.

	Purchases on Account	Cash Purchases
December 20x6	$40,000	$20,000
January 20x7	60,000	30,000
February 20x7	50,000	25,000
March 20x7	70,000	35,000

The company pays for 60 percent of purchases on account in the month of purchase and 40 percent in the month following the purchase. Prepare a monthly schedule of expected cash payments for direct materials for the first quarter of 20x7.

SE 10.

LO4 Budgeted Balance Sheet

Wellman Corporation's budgeted balance sheet for the coming year shows total assets of $4,650,000 and total liabilities of $1,900,000. Common stock and retained earnings make up the entire stockholders' equity section of the balance sheet. Common stock remains at its beginning balance of $1,500,000. The projected net income for the year is $349,600. The company pays no cash dividends. What is the balance of retained earnings at the beginning of the budget period?

EXERCISES

E 1.

LO1 Budgeting and the Management Cycle

All the activities described below require the use of budget information. Indicate whether each activity is part of the planning stage (P), executing stage (E), reviewing stage (REV), or reporting stage (REP) of the management cycle.

1. Vivian Gentry, manager of a golf and tennis resort, develops a budget to distribute limited resources to the resort's pro shop, maintenance department, golf and tennis operations, hotel operations, and restaurant operations.
2. Gentry challenges employees to increase the volume of customers eating in the restaurant by 10 percent, a goal set forth in the restaurant's budget.
3. Gentry selects the number of golf lessons given each month as a measure of performance for the golf operations.
4. The resort's accountant prepares a performance report for the restaurant.
5. Gentry analyzes the restaurant's performance report and finds that sales volume was 25 percent lower than planned.
6. Gentry meets with restaurant managers and employees to discuss the results from a survey of resort guests. Based on her findings, Gentry decides to expand the number of items offered on the menu, increase advertising for the restaurant, and replace the chef.
7. Edgar Thorn, the manager of golf operations, uses the budgeted number of golf lessons to motivate the golf pros to provide more lessons.
8. At the end of the month, Thorn calculates the variance between the actual number of golf lessons given and the budgeted number of golf lessons. He finds that the number of lessons given was fewer than planned.
9. Thorn prepares a variance report and gives it to the golf pros for review.
10. Thorn selects the number of hours of golf instruction as a new performance measure for the remainder of the year.

E 2.

LO1 Characteristics of Budgets

You recently attended a workshop on budgeting and overheard the following comments as you walked to the refreshment table:

1. "Budgets are the same regardless of the size of an organization or management's role in the budgeting process."

2. "Budgets can include financial or nonfinancial data. In our organization, we plan the number of hours to be worked and the number of customer contacts we want our salespeople to make."
3. "All budgets are complicated. You have to be an expert to prepare one."
4. "Budgets don't need to be highly accurate. No one in our company stays within a budget anyway."

Do you agree or disagree with each comment? Explain.

LO1   Budgeting and Goals

E 3. Effective planning of long- and short-term goals has contributed to the success of Multitasker Calendars, Inc. Described below are the actions the company's management team took during a recent planning meeting. Indicate whether the goals related to those actions are short-term or long-term.

1. In forecasting the next ten-year period, the management team considered economic and industry forecasts, employee-management relationships, and the structure and role of management.
2. Based on the ten-year forecast, the team made decisions about next year's sales and profit targets.

LO1   Budgeting and Goals

E 4. Assume that you work in the accounting department of a small wholesale warehousing company. Inspired by a recent seminar on budgeting, the company's president wants to develop a budgeting system and has asked you to direct it. Identify the points about the initial steps in the budgeting process that you should communicate to the president. Concentrate on principles related to long-term goals and short-term goals.

LO2   Components of a Master
LO3   Budget
LO4

E 5. Identify the order in which the following budgets are prepared. Use the letter *a* to indicate the first budget to be prepared, *b* for the second, and so on.

1. Production budget
2. Direct labor budget
3. Direct materials purchases budget
4. Sales budget
5. Budgeted balance sheet
6. Cash budget
7. Budgeted income statement

LO3   Sales Budget

E 6. Quarterly and annual sales for 20x7 for Steen Manufacturing Company are shown below.

Steen Manufacturing Company
Actual Sales Revenue
For the Year Ended December 31, 20x7

Product Class	January–March	April–June	July–September	October–December	Annual Totals	Estimated 20x8 Percent Increases by Product Class
Marine products	$ 44,500	$ 45,500	$ 48,200	$ 47,900	$ 186,100	10%
Mountain products	36,900	32,600	34,100	37,200	140,800	5%
River products	29,800	29,700	29,100	27,500	116,100	30%
Hiking products	38,800	37,600	36,900	39,700	153,000	15%
Running products	47,700	48,200	49,400	49,900	195,200	25%
Biking products	65,400	65,900	66,600	67,300	265,200	20%
Totals	$263,100	$259,500	$264,300	$269,500	$1,056,400	

Prepare a sales budget for 20x8 for the company. Show both quarterly and annual totals for each product class.

E 7.
LO3   Production Budget

Isobel Law, the controller for Aberdeen Lock Company, is preparing a production budget for 20x7. The company's policy is to maintain a finished goods inventory equal to one-half of the following month's sales. Sales of 7,000 locks are budgeted for April. Complete the monthly production budget for the first quarter:

	January	February	March
Sales in units	5,000	4,000	6,000
Add desired units of ending finished goods inventory	2,000	?	?
Desired total units	7,000		
Less desired units of beginning finished goods inventory	2,500	?	?
Total production units	4,500	?	?

E 8.
LO3   Production Budget

Santa Fe Corporation produces and sells a single product. Expected sales for September are 12,000 units; for October, 15,000 units; for November, 9,000 units; for December, 10,000 units; and for January, 14,000 units. The company's desired level of ending finished goods inventory at the end of a month is 10 percent of the following month's sales in units. At the end of August, 1,200 units were on hand. How many units need to be produced in the fourth quarter?

E 9.
LO3   Direct Materials Purchases Budget

The U-Z Door Company manufactures garage door units. The units include hinges, door panels, and other hardware. Prepare a direct materials purchases budget for the first quarter of 20x7 based on budgeted production of 16,000 garage door units. Sandee Morton, the controller, has provided the following information:

Hinges	4 sets per door	$11.00 per set
Door panels	4 panels per door	$27.00 per panel
Other hardware	1 lock per door	$31.00 per lock
	1 handle per door	$22.50 per handle
	2 roller tracks per door	$16.00 per set of 2 roller tracks
	8 rollers per door	$ 4.00 per roller

Assume no beginning or ending quantities of direct materials inventory.

E 10.
LO3   Direct Materials Purchases Budget

Hard Corporation projects sales of $230,000 in May, $250,000 in June, $260,000 in July, and $240,000 in August. The dollar value of the company's cost of goods sold is generally 65 percent of total sales. The dollar value of its desired ending inventory is 25 percent of the following month's cost of goods sold.

Compute the total purchases budgeted for June and the total purchases budgeted for July.

E 11.
LO3   Direct Labor Budget

Paige Metals Company has two departments—Cutting and Grinding—and manufactures three products. Budgeted unit production in 20x7 is 21,000 of Product T, 36,000 of Product M, and 30,000 of Product B. The company is currently analyzing direct labor hour requirements for 20x7.

Data for each department are as follows:

	Cutting	Grinding
Estimated hours per unit		
Product T	1.1	.5
Product M	.6	2.9
Product B	3.2	1.0
Hourly labor rate	$9	$7

Prepare a direct labor budget for 20x7 that shows the budgeted direct labor costs for each department and for the company as a whole.

E 12.
LO3   Manufacturing Overhead Budget

Carole Dahl is chief financial officer of the Phoenix Division of Dahl Corporation, a multinational company with three operating divisions. As part of the budgeting process, Dahl's staff is developing the manufacturing overhead budget for 20x7. The division estimates that it will manufacture 50,000 units during the year. The budgeted cost information is as follows:

	Variable Rate per Unit	Total Fixed Costs
Indirect materials	$1.00	
Indirect labor	4.00	
Supplies	.40	
Repairs and maintenance	3.00	$ 40,000
Electricity	.10	20,000
Factory supervision		180,000
Insurance		25,000
Property taxes		35,000
Depreciation, machinery		82,000
Depreciation, building		72,000

Using the data provided, prepare the division's manufacturing overhead budget for 20x7.

E 13.

LO4   Cash Collections

Dacahr Bros., Inc., is an automobile maintenance and repair company with outlets throughout the western United States. Henley Turlington, the company controller, is starting to assemble the cash budget for the fourth quarter of 20x7. Projected sales for the quarter are as follows:

	On Account	Cash
October	$452,000	$196,800
November	590,000	214,000
December	720,500	218,400

Cash collection records pertaining to sales on account indicate the following collection pattern:

Month of sale	40%
First month following sale	30%
Second month following sale	28%
Uncollectible	2%

Sales on account during August were $346,000. During September, sales on account were $395,000.

Compute the amount of cash to be collected from customers during each month of the fourth quarter.

E 14.

LO4   Cash Collections

XYZ Company collects payment on 50 percent of credit sales in the month of sale, 40 percent in the month following sale, and 5 percent in the second month following the sale. Its sales budget is as follows:

Month	Cash Sales	Credit Sales
May	$20,000	$ 40,000
June	40,000	60,000
July	60,000	80,000
August	80,000	100,000

Compute XYZ Company's total cash collections in July and its total cash collections in August.

E 15.

LO4   Cash Budget

Alberta Limited needs a cash budget for the month of November. The following information is available:

a. The cash balance on November 1 is $6,000.
b. Sales for October and November are $80,000 and $60,000, respectively. Cash collections on sales are 30 percent in the month of sale and 65 percent in the month after the sale; 5 percent of sales are uncollectible.
c. General expenses budgeted for November are $25,000 (depreciation represents $2,000 of this amount).
d. Inventory purchases will total $30,000 in October and $40,000 in November. The company pays for half of its inventory purchases in the month of purchase and for the other half the month after purchase.
e. The company will pay $4,000 in cash for office furniture in November. Sales commissions for November are budgeted at $12,000.

f. The company maintains a minimum ending cash balance of $4,000 and can borrow from the bank in multiples of $100. All loans are repaid after 60 days.

Prepare a cash budget for Alberta Limited for the month of November.

PROBLEMS

P 1.
LO3   Preparing Operating Budgets

The principal product of Yangsoo Enterprises, Inc., is a multipurpose hammer that carries a lifetime guarantee. Listed below are cost and production data for the Yangsoo hammer.

Direct materials
  Anodized steel: 2 kilograms per hammer at $1.60 per kilogram
  Leather strapping for the handle: .5 square meter per hammer at $4.40 per square meter
Direct labor
  Forging operation: $12.50 per labor hour; 6 minutes per hammer
  Leather-wrapping operation: $12.00 per direct labor hour; 12 minutes per hammer
Manufacturing overhead
  Forging operation: rate equals 70 percent of department's direct labor dollars
  Leather-wrapping operation: rate equals 50 percent of department's direct labor dollars

In October, November, and December of 20x7, Yangsoo Enterprises expects to produce 108,000, 104,000, and 100,000 hammers, respectively. The company has no beginning or ending balances of direct materials inventory or work in process inventory for the year.

REQUIRED ▶
1. For the three-month period ending December 31, 20x7, prepare monthly production cost information for the Yangsoo hammer. Classify the costs as direct materials, direct labor, or manufacturing overhead and show your computations.
2. Prepare a cost of goods manufactured budget for the hammer. Show monthly cost data and combined totals for the quarter for each cost category.

P 2.
LO3   Preparing a Comprehensive
LO4   Budget

Bertha's Bathworks began manufacturing hair and bath products in 20x7. Its biggest customer is a national retail chain that specializes in such products. Bertha Jackson, the owner of Bertha's Bathworks, would like to have an estimate of the company's net income in 20x8.

REQUIRED ▶
Calculate Bertha's Bathworks' net income in 20x8 by completing the operating budgets and budgeted income statement that follow.

1. Sales budget:

Bertha's Bathworks
Sales Budget
For the Year Ended December 31, 20x8

| | Quarter | | | | |
	1	2	3	4	Year
Sales in units	4,000	3,000	5,000	5,000	17,000
× Selling price per unit	× $5	× ?	× ?	× ?	× ?
Total sales	$20,000	?	?	?	?

2. Production budget:

Bertha's Bathworks
Production Budget
For the Year Ended December 31, 20x8

	Quarter 1	Quarter 2	Quarter 3	Quarter 4	Year
Sales in units	4,000	?	?	?	?
Plus desired units of ending finished goods inventory*	300	?	?	600	600
Desired total units	4,300				
Less desired units of beginning finished goods inventory†	400	?	?	?	400
Total production units	3,900	?	?	?	?

*Desired units of ending finished goods inventory = 10% of next quarter's budgeted sales.
†Desired units of beginning finished goods inventory = 10% of current quarter's budgeted sales.

3. Direct materials purchases budget:

Bertha's Bathworks
Direct Materials Purchases Budget
For the Year Ended December 31, 20x8

	Quarter 1	Quarter 2	Quarter 3	Quarter 4	Year
Total production units	3,900	3,200	5,000	5,100	17,200
× 3 ounces per unit	× 3	× ?	× ?	× ?	× ?
Total production needs in ounces	11,700	?	?	?	?
Plus desired ounces of ending direct materials inventory*	1,920	?	?	3,600	3,600
	13,620				
Less desired ounces of beginning direct materials inventory†	2,340	?	?	?	2,340
Total ounces of direct materials to be purchased	11,280	?	?	?	?
× Cost per ounce	× $.10	× ?	× ?	× ?	× ?
Total cost of direct materials purchases	$ 1,128	?	?	?	?

Note: Budgeted production needs in ounces for the first quarter of 20x9 = 18,000 ounces.
*Desired ounces of ending direct materials inventory = 20% of next quarter's budgeted production needs in ounces.
†Desired ounces of beginning direct materials inventory = 20% of current quarter's budgeted production needs in ounces.

4. Direct labor budget:

Bertha's Bathworks
Direct Labor Budget
For the Year Ended December 31, 20x8

	Quarter				
	1	2	3	4	Year
Total production units	3,900	?	?	?	?
× Direct labor hours per unit	× .1	× ?	× ?	× ?	× ?
Total direct labor hours	390	?	?	?	?
× Direct labor cost per hour	× $7	× ?	× ?	× ?	× ?
Total direct labor cost	$2,730	?	?	?	?

5. Manufacturing overhead budget:

Bertha's Bathworks
Manufacturing Overhead Budget
For the Year Ended December 31, 20x8

	Quarter				
	1	2	3	4	Year
Variable overhead costs					
Factory supplies ($.05)	$ 195	?	?	?	?
Employee benefits ($.25)	975	?	?	?	?
Inspection ($.10)	390	?	?	?	?
Maintenance and repair ($.15)	585	?	?	?	?
Utilities ($.05)	195	?	?	?	?
Total variable overhead costs	$2,340	?	?	?	?
Fixed overhead costs					
Depreciation, machinery	$ 500	?	?	?	?
Depreciation, building	700	?	?	?	?
Supervision	1,800	?	?	?	?
Maintenance and repair	400	?	?	?	?
Other overhead expenses	600	?	?	?	?
Total fixed overhead costs	$4,000	?	?	?	?
Total manufacturing overhead costs	$6,340	?	?	?	?

Note: The figures in parentheses are variable costs per unit.

6. Selling and administrative expense budget:

Bertha's Bathworks
Selling and Administrative Expense Budget
For the Year Ended December 31, 20x8

	Quarter				Year
	1	2	3	4	
Variable selling and administrative expenses					
Delivery expenses ($.10)	$ 400	?	?	?	?
Sales commissions ($.15)	600	?	?	?	?
Accounting ($.05)	200	?	?	?	?
Other administrative expenses ($.20)	800	?	?	?	?
Total variable selling and administrative expenses	$2,000	?	?	?	?
Fixed selling and administrative expenses					
Sales salaries	$5,000	?	?	?	?
Depreciation, office equipment	900	?	?	?	?
Taxes and insurance	1,700	?	?	?	?
Total fixed selling and administrative expenses	$7,600	?	?	?	?
Total selling and administrative expenses	$9,600	?	?	?	?

Note: The figures in parentheses are variable costs per unit.

7. Cost of goods manufactured budget:

Bertha's Bathworks
Cost of Goods Manufactured Budget
For the Year Ended December 31, 20x8

Direct materials used		
Direct materials inventory, December 31, 20x7	?	
Purchases for 20x8	?	
Cost of direct materials available for use	?	
Less direct materials inventory, December 31, 20x8	?	
Cost of direct materials used		?
Direct labor costs		?
Manufacturing overhead costs		?
Total manufacturing costs		?
Work in process inventory, December 31, 20x7*		?
Less work in process inventory, December 31, 20x8*		?
Cost of goods manufactured		?

*It is the company's policy to have no units in process at the end of the year.

8. Budgeted income statement:

Bertha's Bathworks
Budgeted Income Statement
For the Year Ended December 31, 20x8

Sales		
Cost of goods sold		?
Finished goods inventory, December 31, 20x7	?	
Cost of goods manufactured	?	
Cost of goods available for sale	?	
Less finished goods inventory, December 31, 20x8	?	
Cost of goods sold		?
Gross margin		?
Selling and administrative expenses		?
Income from operations		?
Income taxes expense (30%)*		?
Net income		?

---

*The figure in parentheses is the company's income tax rate.

P 3.

LO4   Basic Cash Budget

Tex Kinkaid's dream was to develop the biggest produce operation with the widest selection of fresh fruits and vegetables in northern Texas. Within three years of opening Minigarden Produce, Inc., Kincaid accomplished his objective. Kinkaid has asked you to prepare monthly cash budgets for Minigarden Produce for the quarter ended September 30, 20x7.

Credit sales to retailers in the area constitute 80 percent of Minigarden Produce's business; cash sales to customers at the company's retail outlet make up the other 20 percent. Collection records indicate that Minigarden Produce collects payment on 50 percent of all credit sales during the month of sale, 30 percent in the month after the sale, and 20 percent in the second month after the sale.

The company's total sales in May were $66,000; in June, they were $67,500. Anticipated sales in July are $69,500; in August, $76,250; and in September, $84,250. The company's purchases are expected to total $43,700 in July, $48,925 in August, and $55,725 in September. The company pays for all purchases in cash.

Projected monthly costs for the quarter include $1,040 for heat, light, and power; $375 for bank fees; $1,925 for rent; $1,120 for supplies; $1,705 for depreciation of equipment; $1,285 for equipment repairs; and $475 for miscellaneous expenses. Other projected costs for the quarter are salaries and wages of $18,370 in July, $19,200 in August, and $20,300 in September.

The company's cash balance at June 30, 20x7, was $2,745. It has a policy of maintaining a minimum monthly cash balance of $1,500.

REQUIRED ▶

1. Prepare a monthly cash budget for Minigarden Produce, Inc., for the quarter ended September 30, 20x7.
2. Should Minigarden Produce anticipate taking out a loan during the quarter? If so, how much should it borrow, and when?

P 4.

LO4   Budgeted Income Statement and Budgeted Balance Sheet

Moontrust Bank has asked the president of Wishware Products, Inc., for a budgeted income statement and budgeted balance sheet for the quarter ended June 30, 20x7. These pro forma statements are needed to support Wishware Product's request for a loan.

Wishware Products routinely prepares a quarterly master budget. The operating budgets prepared for the quarter ending June 30, 20x7, have provided the following information: Projected sales for April are $220,400; for May, $164,220; and for June, $165,980. Direct materials purchases for the period are estimated at $96,840; direct materials usage, at $102,710; direct labor expenses, at $71,460; manufacturing overhead, at $79,940; selling and administrative expenses, at $143,740; capital expenditures, at $125,000 (to be spent on June 29); cost of goods manufactured, at $252,880; and cost of goods sold, at $251,700.

Balance sheet account balances at March 31, 20x7, were as follows: Accounts Receivable, $26,500; Materials Inventory, $23,910; Work in Process Inventory, $31,620; Finished Goods Inventory, $36,220; Prepaid Expenses, $7,200; Plant, Furniture, and Fixtures, $498,600; Accumulated Depreciation, Plant, Furniture, and Fixtures, $141,162; Patents, $90,600; Accounts Payable, $39,600; Notes Payable, $105,500; Common Stock, $250,000; and Retained Earnings, $207,158.

Projected monthly cash balances for the second quarter of 20x7 are as follows: April 30, $20,490; May 31, $35,610; and June 30, $45,400. During the quarter, accounts receivable are expected to increase by 30 percent, patents to go up by $6,500, prepaid expenses to remain constant, and accounts payable to go down by 10 percent (Wishware Products will make a $5,000 payment on a note payable, $4,100 of which is principal reduction).

The federal income tax rate is 34 percent, and the second quarter's tax is paid in July. Depreciation for the quarter will be $6,420, which is included in the manufacturing overhead budget. The company will pay no dividends.

REQUIRED ▶

1. Prepare a budgeted income statement for the quarter ended June 30, 20x7. Round answers to the nearest dollar.
2. Prepare a budgeted balance sheet as of June 30, 20x7.

P 5.
LO4   Comprehensive Cash Budget

Located in Telluride, Colorado, Wellness Centers, Inc., emphasizes the benefits of regular workouts and the importance of physical examinations. The corporation operates three fully equipped fitness centers, as well as a medical center that specializes in preventive medicine. Wellness Center's controller has compiled the following data pertaining to the first quarter of 20x7:

Cash Receipts

Memberships: December 20x6, 870; January 20x7, 880; February, 910; March, 1,030
Membership dues: $90 per month, payable on the 10th of the month (80 percent collected on time; 20 percent collected one month late)
Medical examinations: January, $35,610; February, $41,840; March, $45,610
Special aerobics classes: January, $4,020; February, $5,130; March, $7,130
High-protein food sales: January, $4,890; February, $5,130; March, $6,280

Cash Payments

Salaries and wages:
Corporate officers: 2 at $12,000 per month
Physicians: 2 at $7,000 per month
Nurses: 3 at $2,900 per month
Clerical staff: 2 at $1,500 per month
Aerobics instructors: 3 at $1,100 per month
Clinic staff: 6 at $1,700 per month
Maintenance staff: 3 at $900 per month
Health-food servers: 3 at $750 per month
Purchases:
Muscle-toning machines: January, $14,400; February, $13,800 (no purchases in March)
Pool supplies: $520 per month
Health food: January, $3,290; February, $3,460; March, $3,720
Medical supplies: January, $10,400; February, $11,250; March, $12,640
Medical uniforms and disposable garments: January, $7,410; February, $3,900; March, $3,450
Medical equipment: January, $11,200; February, $3,400; March $5,900
Advertising: January, $2,250; February, $1,190; March, $2,450

Utilities expense: January, $5,450; February, $5,890; March, $6,090
Insurance:
  Fire: January, $3,470
  Liability: March, $3,980
Property taxes: $3,760 due in January
Federal income taxes: 20x6 taxes of $21,000 due in March 20x7
Miscellaneous: January, $2,625; February, $2,800; March, $1,150

Wellness Center's controller anticipates that the beginning cash balance for 20x7 will be $9,840.

REQUIRED ▶ Prepare a cash budget for Wellness Centers, Inc., for the first quarter of 20x7. Use the following column headings:

January   February   March   Quarter

ALTERNATE PROBLEMS

P 6.
LO4 Budgeted Income Statement
LO5

Delft House, Inc., a multinational company based in Amsterdam, organizes and coordinates art shows and auctions throughout the world. Its budgeted and actual costs for last year, 20x4, are as follows:

	Budgeted Cost	Actual Cost
Salaries expense, staging	€ 480,000	€ 512,800
Salaries expense, executive	380,000	447,200
Travel costs	640,000	652,020
Auctioneer services	540,000	449,820
Space rental costs	251,000	246,580
Printing costs	192,000	182,500
Advertising expense	169,000	183,280
Insurance, merchandise	84,800	77,300
Insurance, liability	64,000	67,100
Home office costs	209,200	219,880
Shipping costs	105,000	112,560
Miscellaneous	25,000	25,828
Total expenses	€3,140,000	€3,176,868
Net receipts	€6,200,000	€6,369,200

Delft House has budgeted the following fixed costs for the current year, 20x5: executive salaries, €440,000; advertising expense, €190,000; merchandise insurance, €80,000; and liability insurance, €68,000. Additional information pertaining to the organization's current operations is as follows:

a. Net receipts are estimated at €6,400,000.
b. Salaries expense for staging will increase 20 percent over the actual figures for the previous year.
c. Travel costs are expected to be 11 percent of net receipts.
d. Auctioneer services will be billed at 9.5 percent of net receipts.
e. Space rental costs will be 20 percent higher than the amount budgeted in the previous year.
f. Printing costs are expected to be €190,000.
g. Home office costs are budgeted for €230,000.
h. Shipping costs are expected to be 20 percent higher than the amount budgeted in the previous year.
i. Miscellaneous expenses for the current year will be budgeted at €28,000.

REQUIRED ▶ 1. Prepare the company's budgeted income statement for the current year, 20x5. Since the company sells only services, assume it has expenses only and no cost of sales. (Net receipts equal gross margin.) Use a 34 percent income tax rate.
2. Should the budget committee be worried about the trend in the company's operations? Explain your answer.

LO4   Basic Cash Budget

P 7.   Felasco Nurseries, Inc., has been in business for six years and has four divisions. Ethan Poulis, the corporation's controller, has been asked to prepare a cash budget for the Southern Division for the first quarter of 20x8.

Projected data supporting this budget are as follows:

Sales (60 percent on credit)		Purchases	
November 20x7	$160,000	December 20x7	$ 86,800
December 20x7	200,000	January 20x8	124,700
January 20x8	120,000	February 20x8	99,440
February 20x8	160,000	March 20x8	104,800
March 20x8	140,000		

Collection records of accounts receivable have shown that 30 percent of all credit sales are collected in the month of sale, 60 percent in the month following the sale, and 8 percent in the second month following the sale; 2 percent of the sales are uncollectible. All purchases are paid for in the month after the purchase. Salaries and wages are projected to be $25,200 in January, $33,200 in February, and $21,200 in March. Estimated monthly costs are utilities, $4,220; collection fees, $1,700; rent, $5,300; equipment depreciation, $5,440; supplies, $2,480; small tools, $3,140; and miscellaneous, $1,900.

Each of the corporation's divisions maintains a $6,000 minimum cash balance. As of December 31, 20x7, the Southern Division had a cash balance of $9,600.

REQUIRED ▶

1. Prepare a monthly cash budget for Felasco Nurseries' Southern Division for the first quarter of 20x8.
2. Should Felasco Nurseries anticipate taking out a loan for the Southern Division during the quarter? If so, how much should it borrow, and when?

LO4   Budgeted Income Statement and Budgeted Balance Sheet

P 8.   Whatever Video Company, Inc., produces and markets two popular video games, "High Range" and "Star Boundary." The closing account balances on the company's balance sheet for 20x6 are as follows: Cash, $18,735; Accounts Receivable, $19,900; Materials Inventory, $18,510; Work in Process Inventory, $24,680; Finished Goods Inventory, $21,940; Prepaid Expenses, $3,420; Plant and Equipment, $262,800; Accumulated Depreciation, Plant and Equipment, $55,845; Other Assets, $9,480; Accounts Payable, $52,640; Mortgage Payable, $70,000; Common Stock, $90,000; and Retained Earnings, $110,980.

Operating budgets for the first quarter of 20x7 show the following estimated costs: direct materials purchases, $58,100; direct materials usage, $62,400; direct labor expense, $42,880; manufacturing overhead, $51,910; selling expenses, $35,820; general and administrative expenses, $60,240; cost of goods manufactured, $163,990; and cost of goods sold, $165,440. Estimated ending cash balances are as follows: January, $34,610; February, $60,190; and March, $54,802. The company will have no capital expenditures during the quarter.

Sales are projected to be $125,200 in January, $105,100 in February, and $112,600 in March. Accounts receivable are expected to double during the quarter and accounts payable to decrease by 20 percent. Mortgage payments for the quarter will total $6,000, of which $2,000 will be interest expense. Prepaid expenses are expected to go up by $20,000, and other assets are projected to increase 50 percent over the budget period. Depreciation for plant and equipment (already included in the manufacturing overhead budget) averages 5 percent of total plant and equipment per year. Federal income taxes (34 percent of profits) are payable in April. The company pays no dividends.

REQUIRED ▶

1. Prepare a budgeted income statement for the quarter ended March 31, 20x7.
2. Prepare a budgeted balance sheet as of March 31, 20x7.

SKILLS DEVELOPMENT CASES

Conceptual Analysis

**LO1   The Budgeting Process
LO2**

SD 1.   Many people believe the budgeting process is wasteful and ineffective. They maintain that managers spend too much time focusing on budgeting mechanics and not enough on strategic issues. They believe that emphasis on the budgeting process causes managers to neglect more important matters, such as eliminating nonvalue-adding activities that waste resources. Critics of the budgeting process also maintain that the information and formats that managers use in budgets fail to communicate the short-term business activities needed to achieve long-term goals.

Place yourself in the role of a company's controller and search the Internet for articles on budgeting. Based on your research, prepare a memorandum to your company's owner justifying the need for budgeting. Also suggest ways to make the budgeting process, the budget information, and the budgets themselves efficient, effective, and meaningful.

 Group Activity: Ask students to complete the assignment individually. Then have them work in groups to prepare (1) an argument justifying the use of budgeting and (2) a list of ways to make the budgeting process, the budget information, and the budgets efficient, effective, and meaningful. Select one person from each group to report the group's findings to the class.

SD 2.

LO4   Budgeting for Cash Flows

The nature of a company's business affects its need to budget for cash flows. H&R Block <www.hrblock.com> is a service company whose main business is preparing tax returns. Most tax returns are prepared after January 31 and before April 15. For a fee and interest, the company will advance cash to clients who are due refunds. The clients are then expected to repay the cash advances when they receive their refunds. Although H&R Block has some revenues throughout the year, it devotes most of the nontax season to training potential employees in tax preparation procedures and to laying the groundwork for the next tax season.

Toys "R" Us <www.tru.com> is a toy retailer whose sales are concentrated in October, November, and December of one year and January of the next year. Sales continue at a steady but low level during the rest of the year. The company sells very few products on credit. Its purchases of inventory are concentrated in the period from July to September.

Mitsubishi <www.mitsubishi.com> manufactures large-screen TVs and other electronic products. Its sales tend to be concentrated in the last six months of the year. The company sells its products to retailers, and the retailers sell them to the final customer. Mitsubishi offers retailers credit terms of 60 to 90 days. In addition, when a retailer makes a sale to a buyer who has a good credit rating, Mitsubishi offers the buyer a very generous credit deal that features no payments or interest for one year after the date of the sale.

Discuss the nature of cash receipts and cash disbursements over a calendar year in the three companies we have just described. What are some key estimates that the management of these companies must make when preparing a cash budget?

Ethical Dilemma

SD 3.

LO1   Ethical Considerations in
LO3   Budgeting
LO5

Javier Gonzales is the manager of the Repairs and Maintenance Department of JG Industries. He is responsible for preparing his department's annual budget. Most managers in the company inflate their budget numbers by at least 10 percent because their bonuses depend upon how much below budget their departments operate. Gonzales turned in the following information for his department's 20x8 budget to the company's budget committee:

	Budget 20x7	Actual 20x7	Budget 20x8
Supplies	$ 20,000	$ 16,000	$ 24,000
Labor	80,000	82,000	96,000
Utilities	8,500	8,000	10,200
Tools	12,500	9,000	15,000
Hand-carried equipment	25,000	16,400	30,000
Cleaning materials	4,600	4,200	5,520
Miscellaneous	2,000	2,100	2,400
Totals	$152,600	$137,700	$183,120

Because the figures for 20x8 are 20 percent above those in the 20x7 budget, the budget committee questioned them. Gonzales defended them by saying that he expects a significant increase in activity in his department in 20x8.

What do you think are the real reasons for the increase in the budgeted amounts? What ethical considerations enter into this situation?

Research Activity

LO3   Developing a Budget
LO4

SD 4. Suppose a fundraising club at your school has asked you to manage its bake sales, which are held each weekend in the fall that the football team has a home game. This year, there will be five home games. The club sells only chocolate chip cookies in packages of two dozen; the selling price per package is $5.00. The packaging material costs $.75 per package. Baking utensils and supplies for the entire season will cost $500. Before each game, the cookies are prepared in a school kitchen for a fixed fee of $300 per session; workers are paid a total of $150 to help with the cleanup after each baking session. You estimate that 500 packages of cookies will be baked for each sale and that 96 percent of them will be sold. Alumni volunteers, who receive no compensation, sell half of the packages; students, who receive a commission of $.50 per package, sell the other half. You plan to run an advertisement in the school newspaper before all five games; each advertisement costs $200. The ingredients for four dozen cookies are as follows:

2 1/4 cups all-purpose flour	3/4 cup granulated sugar	2 cups semisweet
1 teaspoon baking soda	3/4 cup brown sugar	chocolate chips
1 teaspoon salt	1 teaspoon vanilla extract	1 cup walnuts
2 sticks butter	2 eggs	

Research the prices of the cookie ingredients at a local supermarket. Then develop a budget for the five bake sales. What is your assessment of the club's fundraising effort?

Decision-Making Practice

LO1   Budgeting Procedures
LO4
LO5

SD 5. Since Rxanne Enterprises inaugurated participative budgeting ten years ago, everyone in the organization—from maintenance personnel to the president's staff—has had a voice in the budgeting process. Until recently, participative budgeting has worked in the best interests of the company as a whole. Now, however, it is becoming evident that some managers are using the practice solely to benefit their own divisions. The budget committee has therefore asked you, the company's controller, to analyze this year's divisional budgets carefully before incorporating them into the company's master budget.

The Motor Division was the first of the company's six divisions to submit its budget request for 20x6. The division's budgeted income statement appears on the opposite page.

1. Recast the Motor Division's budgeted income statement into the following format (round percentages to two places):

	Budget for 12/31/x5			Budget for 12/31/x6	
Account	Amount	Percentage of Sales		Amount	Percentage of Sales

2. Actual results for 20x5 revealed the following information about revenues and cost of goods sold:

	Amount	Percentage of Sales
Net sales		
Radios	$ 780,000	43.94
Appliances	640,000	36.06
Telephones	280,000	15.77
Miscellaneous	75,000	4.23
Net sales	$1,775,000	100.00
Less cost of goods sold	763,425	43.01
Gross margin	$1,011,575	56.99

On the basis of this information and your analysis in **1**, what do you think the budget committee should say to the managers of the Motor Division? Identify any specific areas of the budget that may need to be revised and explain why the revision is needed.

Rxanne Enterprises
Motor Division
Budgeted Income Statement
For the Years Ended December 31, 20x5 and 20x6

	Budget 12/31/x5	Budget 12/31/x6	Increase (Decrease)
Net sales			
Radios	$ 850,000	$ 910,000	$ 60,000
Appliances	680,000	740,000	60,000
Telephones	270,000	305,000	35,000
Miscellaneous	84,400	90,000	5,600
Net sales	$1,884,400	$2,045,000	$160,600
Less cost of goods sold	750,960	717,500*	(33,460)
Gross margin	$1,133,440	$1,327,500	$194,060
Operating expenses			
Wages			
Warehouse	$ 94,500	$ 102,250	$ 7,750
Purchasing	77,800	84,000	6,200
Delivery/shipping	69,400	74,780	5,380
Maintenance	42,650	45,670	3,020
Salaries			
Supervisory	60,000	92,250	32,250
Executive	130,000	164,000	34,000
Purchases, supplies	17,400	20,500	3,100
Merchandise moving equipment			
Maintenance	72,400	82,000	9,600
Depreciation	62,000	74,750†	12,750
Building rent	96,000	102,500	6,500
Sales commissions	188,440	204,500	16,060
Insurance			
Fire	12,670	20,500	7,830
Liability	18,200	20,500	2,300
Utilities	14,100	15,375	1,275
Taxes			
Property	16,600	18,450	1,850
Payroll	26,520	41,000	14,480
Miscellaneous	4,610	10,250	5,640
Total operating expenses	$1,003,290	$1,173,275	$169,985
Income from operations	$ 130,150	$ 154,225	$ 24,075

*Less expensive merchandise will be purchased in 20x6 to boost profits.

†Depreciation is increased because additional equipment must be bought to handle increased sales.

MANAGERIAL REPORTING AND ANALYSIS CASES

Interpreting Management Reports

MRA 1.

LO1   **Policies for Budget**
LO2   **Development**
LO5

Hector Corporation is a manufacturing company with annual sales of $25 million. Its budget committee created a policy that the company uses each year in developing its master budget for the following calendar year. The policy is as follows:

May	The company's controller and corporate officers of the budget committee meet to discuss plans and objectives for next year. The controller conveys all relevant information from this meeting to division managers and department heads.
June	Division managers, department heads, and the controller meet to discuss the corporate plans and objectives for next year. They develop a timetable for developing next year's budget data.
July	Division managers and department heads develop budget data. The vice president of sales provides them with final sales estimates, and they complete monthly sales estimates for each product line.
August	Estimates of next year's monthly production activity and inventory levels are completed. Division managers and department heads communicate these estimates to the controller, who distributes them to other operating areas.
September	All operating areas submit their revised budget data. The controller integrates their labor requirements, direct materials requirements, unit cost estimates, cash requirements, and profit estimates in a preliminary master budget for next year.
October	The budget committee meets to discuss the preliminary master budget and to make any necessary corrections, additions, or deletions. The controller incorporates all authorized changes into a final draft of the master budget.
November	The controller submits the final draft to the corporate officers of the budget committee for approval. If they approve it, it is distributed to all corporate officers, division managers, and department heads.

Comment on this policy. What changes would you recommend?

Formulating Management Reports

MRA 2.

LO1   **Financial Budgets**
LO2
LO4

Suppose you have just signed a partnership agreement with your cousin Eddie to open a bookstore near your college. You believe the store will be able to provide excellent service and undersell the local competition. To fund operations, you and Eddie have applied for a loan from the Small Business Administration. The loan application requires you to submit two financial budgets—a pro forma income statement and a pro forma balance sheet—within six weeks. Because of your expertise in accounting and business, Eddie has asked you to prepare the financial budgets.

1. How do the four *w*'s of preparing an accounting report apply in this situation—that is, *why* are you preparing these financial budgets, *who* needs them, *what* information do you need to prepare for them, and *when* are they due?
2. If you obtain the loan and open the bookstore, how can you and Eddie use the pro forma statements that you prepared?

International Company

MRA 3.

LO4   **Goals and the Cash Budget**

The products of Minnesota Mining and Manufacturing Company (3M) <www.3m.com> range from office supplies, duct tape, and road reflectors to laser imagers for CAT scanners. One of the company's goals is to accelerate sales and product development. Toward that end, it spends over $1 billion a year on research and development and related investment activities. It has also redesigned many of its products to satisfy the needs of its three international operations groups (Asia-Pacific; Europe and Middle East; and Latin American, Africa, and Canada).[7]

Suppose the manager of 3M's Asia-Pacific group is preparing the cash budget for next year's operations. Explain how research and development expenses would affect the cash receipts and cash payments in that cash budget.

Excel Spreadsheet Analysis

MRA 4.

LO3 The Budgeting Process
LO4

Refer to our development of Framecraft Company's master budget for 20x7 in this chapter. Suppose that because of a new customer in Canada, Chase Vittel has decided to increase budgeted sales in the first quarter of 20x7 by 5,000 units. The expenses for this sale will include direct materials, direct labor, variable manufacturing overhead, and variable selling and administrative expenses. The delivery expense for the Canadian customer will be $.18 per unit rather than the regular $.08 per unit. The desired units of beginning finished goods inventory will remain at 1,000 units.

1. Using an Excel spreadsheet, revise Framecraft Company's budgeted income statement and the operating budgets that support it to reflect the changes described above. (Round manufactured cost per unit to three decimals.)
2. What was the change in income from operations? Would you recommend accepting the order from the Canadian customer? If so, why?

Internet Case

MRA 5.

LO1 The Budgeting Process

Some corporate web sites include areas specifically designed for student needs. Search the student area of Johnson & Johnson's web site (www.jnj.com/student_resources/index.htm). What kinds of information does it provide? How does the information apply to the material discussed in this chapter?

This chapter describes how standard costs are computed and how managers use the variances between standard and actual costs to evaluate performance and control costs.

Standard Costing and Variance Analysis

DECISION POINT

A MANAGER'S FOCUS

Coach, Inc. <www.coach.com> The durability of a well-crafted baseball glove was the inspiration for the high-quality leather goods that Coach began making more than fifty years ago. Now sold worldwide, the company's products include not only leather goods, such as handbags and luggage, but also jewelry, shoes, hats, eyewear, scarves, and home furnishings.

Coach's managers value a by-the-numbers approach to business. They keep Coach highly profitable by using design specifications to set standard costs for the company's product lines.[1] How does setting standard costs help control costs?

Managers base standard costs on realistic estimates of operating costs. They use these figures as performance targets and as benchmarks against which to measure actual spending trends. To keep standard costs realistic, they continuously monitor changes in market prices and operating costs and update the estimated figures as conditions warrant. By analyzing variances between standard and actual costs, they gain insight into the causes of those differences. Once they have identified an operating problem that is causing a cost variance, they can devise a solution to the problem.

How do Coach managers control costs by setting performance standards?

STANDARD COSTING

LO1   Define *standard costs* and describe how managers use standard costs in the management cycle.

RELATED TEXT ASSIGNMENTS
Q: 1, 2, 3
SE: 1, 2
E: 1
SD: 2, 3
MRA: 5

Standard costs are realistic estimates of costs based on analyses of both past and projected operating costs and conditions. They are usually stated in terms of cost per unit. They provide a standard, or predetermined, performance level for use in **standard costing,** a method of cost control that also includes a measure of actual performance and a measure of the difference, or **variance,** between standard and actual performance. This method of measuring and controlling costs differs from the actual and normal costing methods in that it uses estimated costs exclusively to compute all three elements of product cost—direct materials, direct labor, and manufacturing overhead.

Using standard costing can be expensive because the estimated costs are based not just on past costs, but also on engineering estimates, forecasted demand, worker input, time and motion studies, and type and quality of direct materials. However, this method can be used in any type of business. Both manufacturers and service businesses use standard costing in conjunction with a job order costing, process costing, or activity-based costing system.

STANDARD COSTS AND THE MANAGEMENT CYCLE

As shown in Figure 1, standard costs are useful tools throughout the management cycle. Managers use them to develop budgets in the planning stage, to control costs as they occur during the executing stage, and to prepare reports. Because of their usefulness in comparing planned and actual costs, standard costs have usually been most closely associated with the performance evaluation that takes place in the reviewing stage.

> **KEY POINT:** Standard costs are necessary for planning and control. Budgets are developed from standard costs, and performance is measured against them.

■ **PLANNING**   During the planning stage, after managers have projected sales and production targets for the next accounting period, standard costs can be used in developing budgets for direct materials, direct labor, and variable manufacturing overhead. These estimated operating costs not only serve as targets for product costing; they are also useful in making decisions about product distribution and pricing.

■ **EXECUTING**   During the executing stage, as actual costs are incurred and recorded, managers apply standard costs to the work in process. By using these standards as yardsticks for measuring expenditures, they can control costs as they occur. For example, when the price a vendor offers is higher than the standard cost, a manager may decide to take the company's business elsewhere.

FOCUS ON BUSINESS PRACTICE

Why Go on a Factory Tour?
If you've had some manufacturing experience, you probably understand the importance of standard costing and variance analysis. If you haven't had any manufacturing experience, gain some insight into the importance of cost planning and control by visiting a factory. Consult your local chamber of commerce for factory tours near you. You can also tour factories online. Check out the production of jellybeans at <www.jellybelly.com> or see how crayons are made at <www.crayola.com>.

■ **REVIEWING**   At the end of an accounting period—whether it is a day, a week, a month, or a quarter—managers compare the actual costs incurred with standard costs and compute the variances. Variances provide measures of performance that can be used to control costs. In reviewing a variance, managers compute its amount, and if the amount is significant, they analyze what is causing it. Their analysis of significant unfavorable variances may reveal operating problems, such as inefficient functions within a department or work cell, which they can then act to correct. Managers also investigate significant favorable variances to determine why and how the positive performance

FIGURE 1
**Standard Costing, Variance
Analysis, and the
Management Cycle**

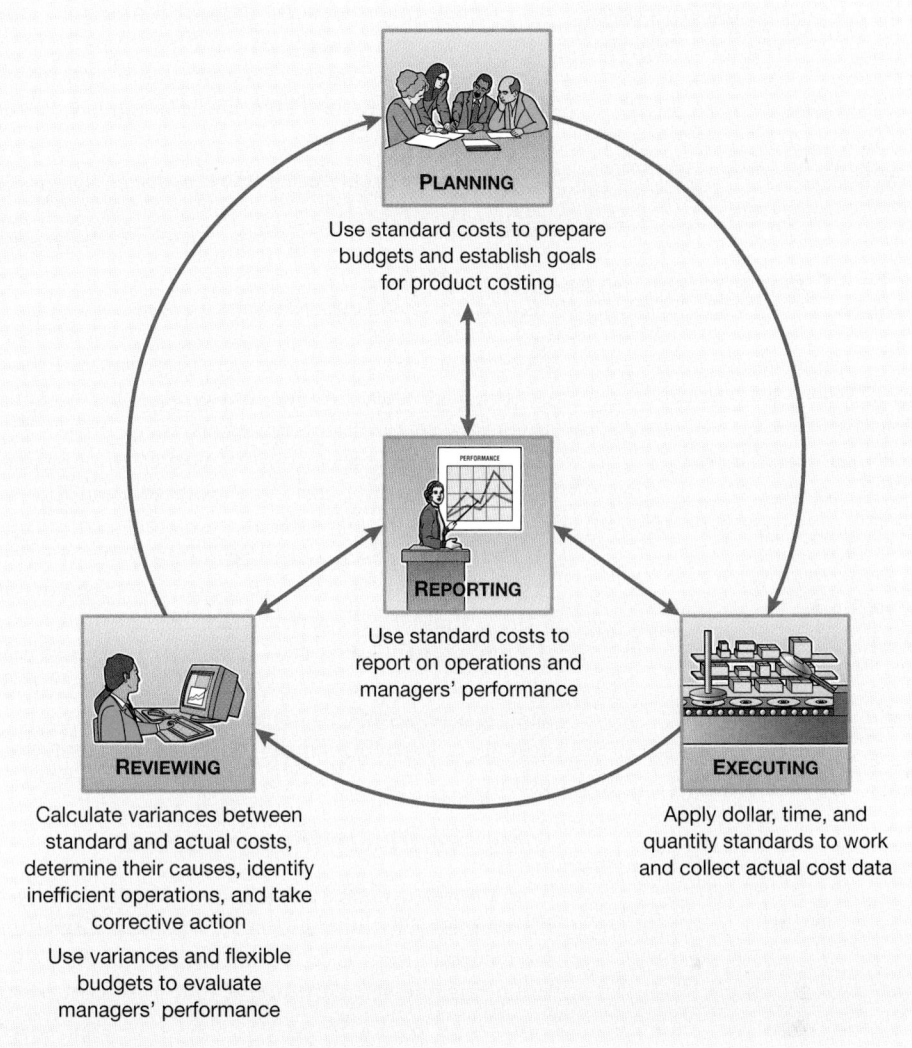

PLANNING

Use standard costs to prepare
budgets and establish goals
for product costing

PERFORMANCE

REPORTING

Use standard costs to
report on operations and
managers' performance

REVIEWING

Calculate variances between
standard and actual costs,
determine their causes, identify
inefficient operations, and take
corrective action

Use variances and flexible
budgets to evaluate
managers' performance

EXECUTING

Apply dollar, time, and
quantity standards to work
and collect actual cost data

⬣ **STOP AND THINK!**
Why should managers be interested in changes in the cost of
materials?
*Information about changes in the
cost of materials enables managers to adjust the prices of goods
to reflect those changes.* ■

occurred. Favorable variances may indicate desirable practices that should be implemented elsewhere or a need to revise the existing standards. Both favorable and
unfavorable variances from standard costs can be used to evaluate an individual
manager's performance.

■ **REPORTING**   During the reporting stage, managers use standard costs to report on
operations and managerial performance. A variance report tailored to a manager's
specific responsibilities provides useful information about how well operations are
proceeding and how well the manager is controlling them.

THE RELEVANCE OF STANDARD COSTING IN TODAY'S BUSINESS ENVIRONMENT

www.coach.com
www.kraft.com
www.boeing.com

In recent years, the increasing automation of manufacturing processes has caused a
significant decrease in direct labor costs and a corresponding decline in the importance of labor-related standard costs and variances. As a result, Coach, Kraft Foods,
Boeing, and many other manufacturers that once used standard costing for all three
elements of product cost now apply this method only to direct materials and manufacturing overhead.

www.bankofamerica.com
www.libertymutual.com

Today, many service organizations, including Bank of America and Liberty Mutual Insurance Company, also use standard costing. Although a service organization has no direct materials costs, labor and overhead costs are very much a part of providing services, and standard costing is an effective way of planning and controlling them.

 Check out ACE for a Review Quiz at http://accounting.college.hmco.com/students.

COMPUTING STANDARD COSTS

LO2 Explain how standard costs are developed and compute a standard unit cost.

RELATED TEXT ASSIGNMENTS
Q: 4, 5, 6, 7, 8
SE: 3
E: 2, 3
P: 1, 6
SD: 2, 3, 4

A fully integrated standard costing system uses standard costs for all the elements of product cost: direct materials, direct labor, and manufacturing overhead. Inventory accounts for materials, work in process, and finished goods, as well as the Cost of Goods Sold account, are maintained and reported in terms of standard costs, and standard unit costs are used to compute account balances. Actual costs are recorded separately so that managers can compare what should have been spent (the standard costs) with the actual costs incurred.

A standard unit cost for a manufactured product has the following six elements: a price standard for direct materials, a quantity standard for direct materials, a standard for direct labor rate, a standard for direct labor time, a standard for variable overhead rate, and a standard for fixed overhead rate. To compute a standard unit cost, it is necessary to identify and analyze each of these elements. (A standard unit cost for a service includes only the elements that relate to direct labor and overhead.)

STANDARD DIRECT MATERIALS COST

The **standard direct materials cost** is found by multiplying the price standard for direct materials by the quantity standard for direct materials. If the price standard for a certain item is $2.75 and a specific job calls for a quantity standard of eight of the items, the standard direct materials cost for that job is computed as follows:

$$\begin{array}{c} \text{Standard Direct} \\ \text{Materials Cost} \end{array} = \begin{array}{c} \text{Direct Materials} \\ \text{Price Standard} \end{array} \times \begin{array}{c} \text{Direct Materials} \\ \text{Quantity Standard} \end{array}$$

$$\$22.00 = \$2.75 \times 8$$

● **STOP AND THINK!**

Why would a purchasing agent or department not always buy the least costly direct materials available?

The quality of the direct materials used in production must remain consistent. Introducing an inexpensive material of an inferior grade can result in excess spoilage and waste and cause unfavorable quantity variances. ■

The **direct materials price standard** is a careful estimate of the cost of a specific direct material in the next accounting period. An organization's purchasing agent or its purchasing department is responsible for developing price standards for all direct materials and for making the actual purchases. When estimating a direct materials price standard, the purchasing agent or department must take into account all possible price increases, changes in available quantities, and new sources of supply.

The **direct materials quantity standard** is an estimate of the amount of direct materials, including scrap and waste, that will be used in an accounting period. It is influenced by product engineering specifications, the quality of direct materials, the age and productivity of machinery, and the quality and experience of the work force. Production managers or management accountants usually establish and monitor standards for direct materials quantity, but engineers, purchasing agents, and machine operators may also contribute to the development of these standards.

STANDARD DIRECT LABOR COST

The **standard direct labor cost** for a product, task, or job order is calculated by multiplying the standard wage for direct labor by the standard hours of direct labor. If the standard direct labor rate is $8.40 per hour and a product takes 1.5 standard direct labor hours to produce, the product's standard direct labor cost is computed as follows:

$$\begin{array}{ccc} \text{Standard Direct} \\ \text{Labor Cost} \end{array} = \begin{array}{c} \text{Direct Labor} \\ \text{Rate Standard} \end{array} \times \begin{array}{c} \text{Direct Labor} \\ \text{Time Standard} \end{array}$$

$$\$12.60 = \$8.40 \times 1.5 \text{ hours}$$

KEY POINT: Both the direct labor rate standard and the direct labor time standard are based on an average of the different levels of skilled workers, and both are related to the production of one unit or batch.

KEY POINT: Updating time and dollar standards for valid reasons produces more meaningful standards. However, if the updates are too frequent, the standards may lose credibility and be perceived as moving targets by managers.

The **direct labor rate standard** is the hourly direct labor rate expected to prevail during the next accounting period for each function or job classification. Although rate ranges are established for each type of worker and rates vary within those ranges according to each worker's experience and length of service, an average standard rate is developed for each task. Even if the person making the product is paid more or less than the standard rate, the standard rate is used to calculate the standard direct labor cost. Standard labor rates are fairly easy to develop because labor rates are either set by a labor union contract or defined by the company.

The **direct labor time standard** is the expected labor time required for each department, machine, or process to complete the production of one unit or one batch of output. In many cases, standard time per unit is a small fraction of an hour. Current time and motion studies of workers and machines, as well as records of their past performance, provide the data for developing this standard. The direct labor time standard should be revised whenever a machine is replaced or the quality of the labor force changes.

STANDARD MANUFACTURING OVERHEAD COST

The **standard manufacturing overhead cost** is the sum of the estimates of variable and fixed overhead costs in the next accounting period. It is based on standard overhead rates that are computed in much the same way as the predetermined overhead rate that we discussed in an earlier chapter. Unlike that rate, however, the standard manufacturing overhead rate has two parts, one for variable costs and one for fixed costs. The reason for computing the standard variable and fixed overhead rates separately is that their cost behavior differs.

The **standard variable overhead rate** is computed by dividing the total budgeted variable overhead costs by an expression of capacity, such as the number of standard machine hours or standard direct labor hours. (Other bases may be used if machine hours or direct labor hours are not good predictors, or drivers, of variable overhead costs.) Using standard machine hours as the base, the formula is as follows:

$$\begin{array}{c} \text{Standard Variable} \\ \text{Overhead Rate} \end{array} = \frac{\text{Total Budgeted Variable Overhead Costs}}{\text{Expected Number of Standard Machine Hours}}$$

The **standard fixed overhead rate** is computed by dividing the total budgeted fixed overhead costs by an expression of capacity, usually normal capacity in terms of standard hours or units. The denominator is expressed in the same terms as the variable overhead rate. Using normal capacity in terms of standard machine hours as the denominator, the formula is as follows:

$$\begin{array}{c} \text{Standard Fixed} \\ \text{Overhead Rate} \end{array} = \frac{\text{Total Budgeted Fixed Overhead Costs}}{\text{Normal Capacity in Terms of Standard Machine Hours}}$$

KEY POINT: Normal capacity is the average annual level of operating capacity needed to meet expected sales demand; it is the level of activity at which a company expects to operate.

Recall that normal capacity is the level of operating capacity needed to meet expected sales demand. Using it as the application base ensures that all fixed overhead costs have been applied to units produced by the time normal capacity is reached.

TOTAL STANDARD UNIT COST

Using standard costs eliminates the need to calculate unit costs from actual cost data every week or month or for each batch of goods produced. Once standard costs for direct materials, direct labor, and variable and fixed overhead have been developed, a total standard unit cost can be computed at any time.

To illustrate how standard costs are used to compute total unit cost, let's suppose that a company called Remember When, Inc., recently updated the standards for its line of watches. Direct materials price standards are now $9.20 per square foot for casing materials and $2.17 for each movement mechanism. Direct materials quantity standards are .025 square foot of casing materials per watch and one movement mechanism per watch. Direct labor time standards are .01 hour per watch for the Case Stamping Department and .05 hour per watch for the Watch Assembly Department. Direct labor rate standards are $8.00 per hour for the Case Stamping Department and $10.20 per hour for the Watch Assembly Department. Standard manufacturing overhead rates are $12.00 per direct labor hour for the standard variable overhead rate and $9.00 per direct labor hour for the standard fixed overhead rate. The standard cost of making one watch would be computed in the following manner:

Direct materials costs:	
Casing ($9.20 per sq. ft. × .025 sq. ft.)	$ .23
One movement mechanism	2.17
Direct labor costs:	
Case Stamping Department ($8.00 per hour × .01 hour per watch)	.08
Watch Assembly Department ($10.20 per hour × .05 hour per watch)	.51
Variable overhead ($12.00 per hour × .06 hour per watch)	.72
Total standard variable cost of one watch	$3.71
Fixed overhead ($9.00 per hour × .06 hour per watch)	.54
Total standard cost of one watch	$4.25

KEY POINT: The total standard cost of $4.25 represents the *desired* cost of producing one watch.

 Check out ACE for a Review Quiz at http://accounting.college.hmco.com/students.

VARIANCE ANALYSIS

LO3 Prepare a flexible budget and describe how variance analysis is used to control costs.

RELATED TEXT ASSIGNMENTS
Q: 9, 10, 11, 12, 13
SE: 4, 5
E: 4
P: 2
SD: 1, 4
MRA: 1, 2, 3, 4

Managers in all types of organizations—manufacturing, retail, and service—constantly compare the costs of what was expected to happen with the costs of what did happen. By examining the differences, or variances, between standard and actual costs, they can gather much valuable information. **Variance analysis** is the process of computing the differences between standard costs and actual costs and identifying the causes of those differences. In this section, we look at how managers use flexible budgets to improve the accuracy of variance analysis and at how they use variance analysis to control costs.

THE ROLE OF FLEXIBLE BUDGETS IN VARIANCE ANALYSIS

The accuracy of variance analysis depends to a large extent on the type of budget managers use when comparing variances. *Static,* or fixed, budgets forecast revenues and expenses for just one level of sales and just one level of output. The budgets that constitute a master budget are usually based on a single level of output, but many things can happen over an accounting period that will cause actual output to differ from the estimated output. If a company produces more products than predicted, total production costs will almost always be greater than predicted. When that is the case, a comparison of actual production costs with fixed budgeted costs will inevitably show variances.

The performance report in Exhibit 1 compares data from Remember When's static master budget with the actual costs of its Watch Division for the year ended December 31, 20x5. As you can see, actual costs exceeded budgeted costs by $5,539, or 7.4 percent. On the face of it, most managers would consider such a cost

EXHIBIT 1
Performance Report Using Data from a Static Budget

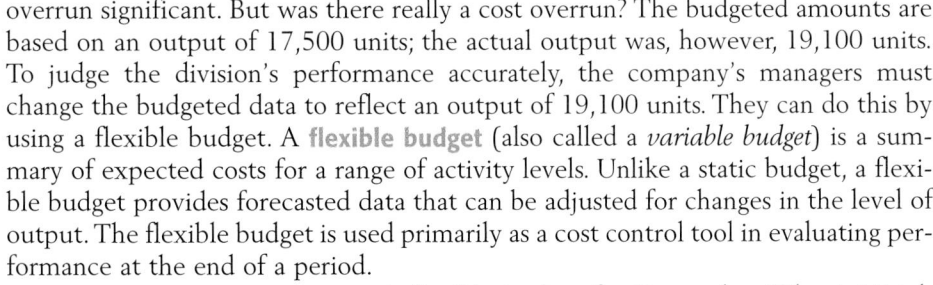

Remember When, Inc.
Performance Report—Watch Division
For the Year Ended December 31, 20x5

Cost Category	Budgeted Costs*	Actual Costs†	Difference Under (Over) Budget
Direct materials	$42,000	$46,000	($4,000)
Direct labor	10,325	11,779	(1,454)
Manufacturing overhead			
Variable			
Indirect materials	3,500	3,600	(100)
Indirect labor	5,250	5,375	(125)
Utilities	1,750	1,810	(60)
Other	2,100	2,200	(100)
Fixed			
Supervisory salaries	4,000	3,500	500
Depreciation	2,000	2,000	—
Utilities	450	450	—
Other	3,000	3,200	(200)
Totals	$74,375	$79,914	($5,539)

*Budgeted costs are based on an output of 17,500 units.
†Actual output was 19,100 units.

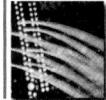

● STOP AND THINK!
When is a flexible budget prepared?

A flexible budget is prepared at the end of an accounting period to evaluate performance; it may then also be used in planning for the next period. ■

FOCUS ON BUSINESS TECHNOLOGY

Why Complicate the Flexible Budget?

Because of the database capabilities of enterprise resource management (ERM) systems and the principles of resource consumption accounting (RCA), what we refer to as the *flexible budget* has become more complicated. This new and more complex version of a flexible budget is called *authorized reporting.* Authorized reporting is like a flexible budget in that it restates an accounting period's costs in terms of different levels of output, but it enhances cost restatement by taking into account all the factors that can influence a cost's behavior. With its more sophisticated cost analyses, authorized reporting is a more relevant yardstick for cost comparison and control than the traditional flexible budget.[3]

overrun significant. But was there really a cost overrun? The budgeted amounts are based on an output of 17,500 units; the actual output was, however, 19,100 units. To judge the division's performance accurately, the company's managers must change the budgeted data to reflect an output of 19,100 units. They can do this by using a flexible budget. A **flexible budget** (also called a *variable budget*) is a summary of expected costs for a range of activity levels. Unlike a static budget, a flexible budget provides forecasted data that can be adjusted for changes in the level of output. The flexible budget is used primarily as a cost control tool in evaluating performance at the end of a period.

A flexible budget for Remember When's Watch Division appears in Exhibit 2. It shows the estimated costs for 15,000, 17,500, and 20,000 units of output. The total cost of a variable cost item is found by multiplying the number of units produced by the item's per unit cost. For example, if the Watch Division produces 15,000 units, direct materials will cost $36,000 (15,000 units × $2.40). An important element in this exhibit is the **flexible budget formula,** an equation that determines the expected, or budgeted, cost for any level of output. Its components include a per unit amount for variable costs and a total amount for fixed costs. (In Exhibit 2, the $3.71 variable cost per unit is computed in the far right column, and the $9,450 is found in the section on fixed manufacturing overhead costs.) Using the flexible budget formula, you can

Exhibit 2
Flexible Budget for Evaluation of Overall Performance

Remember When, Inc.
Flexible Budget–Watch Division
For the Year Ended December 31, 20x5

Cost Category	Units Produced*			Variable Cost per Unit†
	15,000	17,500	20,000	
Direct materials	$36,000	$42,000	$48,000	$2.40
Direct labor	8,850	10,325	11,800	.59
Variable manufacturing overhead				
Indirect materials	3,000	3,500	4,000	.20
Indirect labor	4,500	5,250	6,000	.30
Utilities	1,500	1,750	2,000	.10
Other	1,800	2,100	2,400	.12
Total variable costs	$55,650	$64,925	$74,200	$3.71
Fixed manufacturing overhead				
Supervisory salaries	$ 4,000	$ 4,000	$ 4,000	
Depreciation	2,000	2,000	2,000	
Utilities	450	450	450	
Other	3,000	3,000	3,000	
Total fixed manufacturing overhead costs	$ 9,450	$ 9,450	$ 9,450	
Total costs	$65,100	$74,375	$83,650	

Flexible budget formula:
  Total Budgeted Costs = (Variable Cost per Unit × Number of Units Produced)
              + Budgeted Fixed Costs
            = ($3.71 × Units Produced) + $9,450

*Flexible budgets are commonly used only for overhead costs; when they are, machine hours or direct labor hours are used in place of units produced.

†Computed by dividing the dollar amount in any column by the respective level of output.

KEY POINT: Flexible budgets allow managers to compare budgeted and actual costs at the same level of output.

create a budget for the Watch Division at any level of output in the range of levels given.

The performance report in Exhibit 3 is based on data from the flexible budget shown in Exhibit 2. Variable unit costs have been multiplied by 19,100 units actually produced to arrive at the total budgeted costs, and fixed overhead information has been carried over from Exhibit 2. In this performance report, actual costs are $397 less than the amount budgeted. In other words, when we use a flexible budget, we find that the performance of the Watch Division in this period actually exceeded budget targets by $397.

Using Variance Analysis to Control Costs

As Figure 2 shows, using variance analysis to control costs is a four-step process. First, managers compute the amount of the variance. If the amount is insignificant—meaning actual operating results are close to those anticipated—no corrective action

EXHIBIT 3
Performance Report Using Data from a Flexible Budget

Remember When, Inc.
Performance Report—Watch Division
For the Year Ended December 31, 20x5

Cost Category (Variable Unit Cost)	Budgeted Costs*	Actual Costs	Difference Under (Over) Budget
Direct materials ($2.40)	$45,840	$46,000	($160)
Direct labor ($.59)	11,269	11,779	(510)
Manufacturing overhead			
Variable			
Indirect materials ($.20)	3,820	3,600	220
Indirect labor ($.30)	5,730	5,375	355
Utilities ($.10)	1,910	1,810	100
Other ($.12)	2,292	2,200	92
Fixed			
Supervisory salaries	4,000	3,500	500
Depreciation	2,000	2,000	—
Utilities	450	450	—
Other	3,000	3,200	(200)
Totals	$80,311	$79,914	$397

*Budgeted costs are based on an output of 19,100 units.

FIGURE 2
Variance Analysis: A Four-Step Approach to Controlling Costs

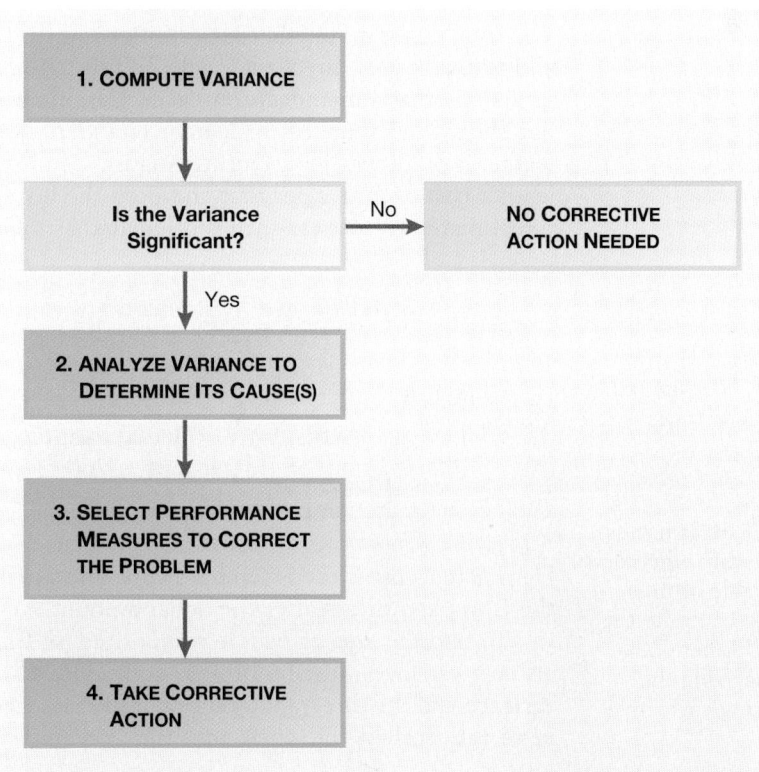

KEY POINT: Many companies use a percentage, such as plus or minus 3 percent of standard, to determine if the dollar amount of a variance is significant.

KEY POINT: Computing variances is only the first step in cost control. Managers must also identify the problem areas causing the variances and take appropriate corrective action.

is needed. If the amount is significant, then managers analyze the variance to identify its cause. In identifying the cause, they are usually able to pinpoint the activities that need to be monitored. They then select performance measures that will enable them to track those activities, analyze the results, and determine the action needed to correct the problem. Their final step is to take the appropriate corrective action.

While computing the amount of a variance is important, it is also important to remember that this computation does nothing to prevent the variance from re-occurring. To control costs, managers must determine the cause of the variance and select performance measures that will help them track the problem and find the best solution for it.

As we focus on the computation and analysis of variances in the next sections, we follow the steps outlined in Figure 2. We limit our analysis to eight variances, two for each of the cost categories of direct materials, direct labor, variable manufacturing overhead, and fixed manufacturing overhead. We give examples of operating problems that might cause each of these variances to occur. We also identify some financial and nonfinancial performance measures that can be used to track the cause of a variance and that can be helpful in correcting it.

 Check out ACE for a Review Quiz at http://accounting.college.hmco.com/students.

COMPUTING AND ANALYZING DIRECT MATERIALS VARIANCES

LO4 Compute and analyze direct materials variances.

RELATED TEXT ASSIGNMENTS
Q: 14, 15, 16
SE: 6
E: 5, 6
P: 3, 4, 7, 8
MRA: 3

To control operations, managers compute and analyze variances for whole cost categories, such as total direct materials costs, as well as variances for elements of those categories, such as the price and quantity of each direct material. The more detailed their analysis of direct materials variances is, the more effective they will be in controlling costs.

COMPUTING DIRECT MATERIALS VARIANCES

The **total direct materials cost variance** is the difference between the standard cost and actual cost of direct materials. To illustrate how this variance is computed, let us assume that a manufacturer called Cambria Company makes leather bags. Each bag should use four feet of leather (standard quantity), and the standard price of leather is $6.00 per foot. During August, Cambria Company purchased 760 feet of leather costing $5.90 per foot and used the leather to produce 180 bags. The total direct materials cost variance is calculated as follows:

Standard cost
Standard price × standard quantity =
$6.00 per foot × (180 bags × 4 feet per bag) =
$6.00 per foot × 720 feet = $4,320

Less actual cost
Actual price × actual quantity =
$5.90 per foot × 760 feet = 4,484

Total direct materials cost variance $ 164 (U)

STUDY NOTE: It is just as important to identify whether a variance is favorable or unfavorable as it is to compute the variance. This information is necessary for analyzing the variance and taking corrective action.

Here, actual cost exceeds standard cost. The situation is unfavorable, as indicated by the U in parentheses after the dollar amount. An F means a favorable situation.

To find the area or people responsible for the variance, the total direct materials cost variance must be broken down into two parts: the direct materials price variance and the direct materials quantity variance. The **direct materials price variance** (also called the *direct material spending or rate variance*) is the difference

● **STOP AND THINK!**

What can cause a direct materials price variance?

Causes of this variance include a change in the quality of materials being used, a change in the price of materials, and a change in vendors. ■

KEY POINT: The direct materials price variance relates to the difference between the standard cost and actual cost of purchased materials. It does not relate to the quantity of materials used in the production process.

between the standard price and the actual price per unit multiplied by the actual quantity purchased. For Cambria Company, the direct materials price variance is computed as follows:

Standard price	$6.00
Less actual price	5.90
Difference per foot	$ .10 (F)

$$\text{Direct Materials Price Variance} = (\text{Standard Price} - \text{Actual Price}) \times \text{Actual Quantity}$$
$$= \$.10 \times 760 \text{ feet}$$
$$= \$76 \text{ (F)}$$

Because the price the company paid for the direct materials was less than the standard price it expected to pay, the variance is favorable.

The **direct materials quantity variance** (also called the *direct material efficiency* or *usage variance*) is the difference between the standard quantity allowed and the actual quantity used multiplied by the standard price. It is computed as follows:

Standard quantity allowed (180 bags × 4 feet per bag)	720 feet
Less actual quantity	760 feet
Difference	40 feet (U)

$$\text{Direct Materials Quantity Variance} = \text{Standard Price} \times (\text{Standard Quantity Allowed} - \text{Actual Quantity})$$
$$= \$6 \times 40 \text{ feet}$$
$$= \$240 \text{ (U)}$$

Because more leather than the standard quantity was used in the production process, the direct materials quantity variance is unfavorable.

If the calculations are correct, the net of the direct materials price variance and the direct materials quantity variance should equal the total direct materials cost variance. The following check shows that the variances were computed correctly:

Direct materials price variance	$ 76 (F)
Direct materials quantity variance	240 (U)
Total direct materials cost variance	$164 (U)

Variance analyses are sometimes easier to interpret in diagram form. Figure 3 illustrates our analysis of Cambria Company's direct materials variances. Notice that although direct materials are purchased at actual cost, they are entered in the Materials Inventory account at standard price; thus, the direct materials price variance of $76 (F) is obvious when the costs are recorded. As Figure 3 shows, the standard price times the standard quantity is the amount entered in the Work in Process Inventory account.

ANALYZING AND CORRECTING DIRECT MATERIALS VARIANCES

Cambria Company's managers were concerned because the company had been experiencing direct materials price variances and quantity variances for some time; moreover, as our analysis shows, the price variances were always favorable, and the quantity variances were always unfavorable. By tracking the purchasing activity for three months, the managers discovered that the company's purchasing agent, without any authorization, had been purchasing a lower grade of leather at a reduced price. After careful analysis, the engineering manager determined that the substitute

FIGURE 3
Diagram of Direct Materials Variance Analysis

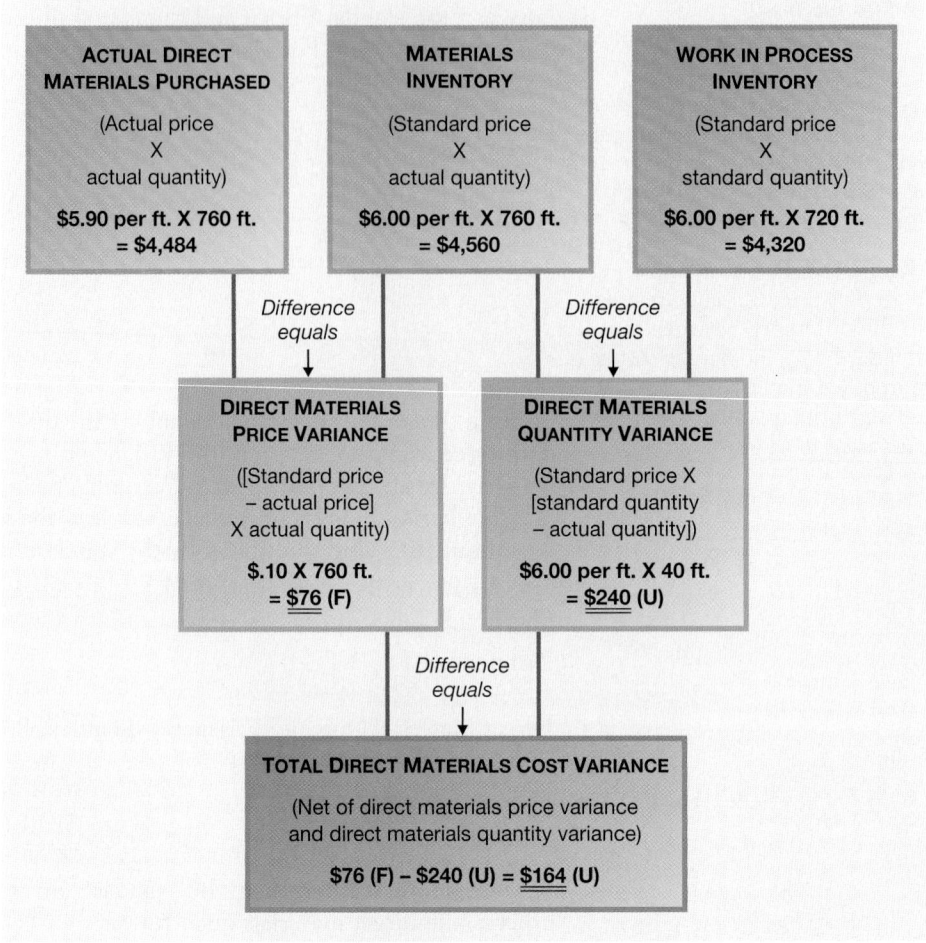

leather was not appropriate and that the company should resume purchasing the grade of leather originally specified. In addition, an analysis of scrap and rework revealed that the inferior quality of the substitute leather was causing the unfavorable quantity variance. By tracking the purchasing activity, Cambria's managers were able to solve the problems the company had been having with direct materials variances.

 Check out ACE for a Review Quiz at http://accounting.college.hmco.com/students.

COMPUTING AND ANALYZING DIRECT LABOR VARIANCES

LO5 Compute and analyze direct labor variances.

RELATED TEXT ASSIGNMENTS
Q: 17
SE: 7
E: 7, 8
P: 3, 4, 7, 8
SD: 5
MRA: 2, 3

The procedure for computing and analyzing direct labor cost variances parallels the procedure for finding direct material variances. Again, the more detailed the analysis is, the more effective managers will be in controlling costs.

COMPUTING DIRECT LABOR VARIANCES

The **total direct labor cost variance** is the difference between the standard direct labor cost for good units produced and actual direct labor costs. (*Good units* are the total units produced less units that are scrapped or need to be reworked.) At Cambria Company, each leather bag requires 2.4 standard direct labor hours, and the standard direct labor rate is $8.50 per hour. During August, 450 direct labor hours were used to make 180 bags at an average pay rate of $9.20 per hour. The total direct labor cost variance is computed as follows:

Standard cost

Standard rate × standard hours allowed =
$8.50 × (180 bags × 2.4 hours per bag) =
$8.50 × 432 hours = $3,672

Less actual cost

Actual rate × actual hours = $9.20 × 450 hours =   4,140

Total direct labor cost variance $ 468 (U)

Both the actual direct labor hours per bag and the actual direct labor rate varied from the standard. For effective performance evaluation, management must know how much of the total cost arose from different direct labor rates and how much from different numbers of direct labor hours. This information is found by computing the direct labor rate variance and the direct labor efficiency variance.

The **direct labor rate variance** (also called the *direct labor spending variance*) is the difference between the standard direct labor rate and the actual direct labor rate multiplied by the actual direct labor hours worked. It is computed as follows:

Standard rate $8.50
Less actual rate   9.20
Difference per hour $0.70 (U)

Direct Labor Rate Variance = (Standard Rate − Actual Rate) × Actual Hours
= $.70 × 450 hours
= $315 (U)

The **direct labor efficiency variance** (also called the *direct labor quantity* or *usage variance*) is the difference between the standard direct labor hours allowed for good units produced and the actual direct labor hours worked multiplied by the standard direct labor rate. It is computed this way:

Standard hours allowed (180 bags × 2.4 hours per bag)   432 hours
Less actual hours   450 hours
Difference   18 hours (U)

Direct Labor Efficiency Variance = Standard Rate × (Standard Hours Allowed − Actual Hours)
= $8.50 × 18 hours
= $153 (U)

If the calculations are correct, the net of the direct labor rate variance and the direct labor efficiency variance should equal the total direct labor cost variance. The following check shows that the variances were computed correctly:

Direct labor rate variance $315 (U)
Direct labor efficiency variance   153 (U)
Total direct labor cost variance $468 (U)

Figure 4 summarizes our analysis of Cambria Company's direct labor variances. Unlike direct materials variances, the direct labor rate and efficiency variances are usually computed and recorded at the same time.

ANALYZING AND CORRECTING DIRECT LABOR VARIANCES

Because Cambria Company's direct labor rate variance and direct labor efficiency variance were unfavorable, its managers investigated the causes of these variances. An analysis of employee time cards revealed that the Bag Assembly Department had replaced an assembly worker who was ill with a machine operator from another department. The machine operator made $9.20 per hour, whereas the assembly

STUDY NOTE: The computation of the direct labor rate variance is very similar to the computation of the direct materials price variance. Computations of the direct labor efficiency variance and the direct materials quantity variance are also similar.

🔴 **STOP AND THINK!**

What can cause a direct labor efficiency variance?

Inadequate labor skills and the condition of equipment are among the factors than can contribute to a direct labor efficiency variance. ∎

FIGURE 4
Diagram of Direct Labor Variance Analysis

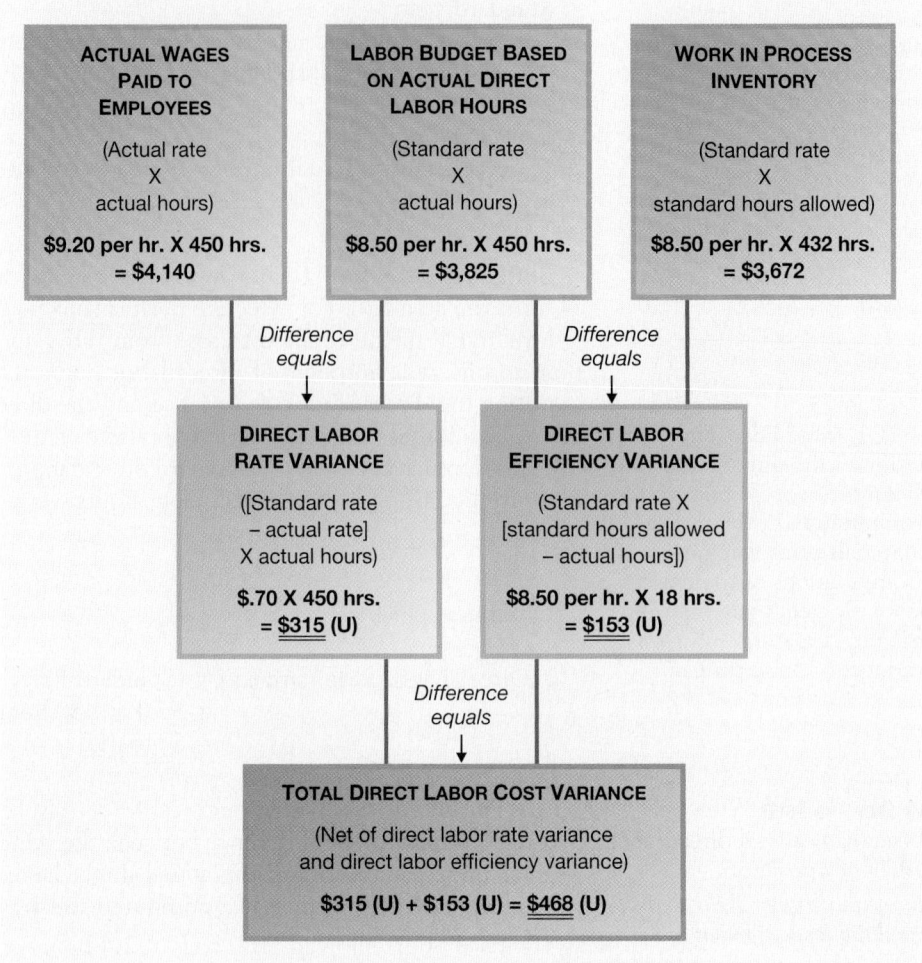

worker earned the standard $8.50 per hour rate. When questioned about the unfavorable efficiency variance, the assembly supervisor identified two causes. First, the machine operator had to learn assembly skills on the job, so his assembly time was longer than the standard time per bag. Second, the materials handling people were partially responsible because they delivered parts late on five different occasions. Because the machine operator was a temporary replacement, Cambria's managers took no corrective action, but they decided to keep a close eye on the materials handling function by tracking delivery times and number of delays for the next three months. Once they have collected and analyzed the new data, they will take whatever action is needed to correct the scheduling problem.

 Check out ACE for a Review Quiz at http://accounting.college.hmco.com/students.

COMPUTING AND ANALYZING MANUFACTURING OVERHEAD VARIANCES

LO6 Compute and analyze manufacturing overhead variances.

RELATED TEXT ASSIGNMENTS
Q: 18, 19
SE: 8, 9
E: 9, 10, 11, 12, 13, 14
P: 4, 5, 8
SD: 5
MRA: 2, 4

Many types of variable and fixed overhead costs may contribute to variances from standard costs. Controlling these costs is more difficult than controlling direct materials and labor costs because the responsibility for overhead costs is hard to assign. Fixed overhead costs are unavoidable past costs, such as depreciation and lease expenses; they are therefore not under the control of any department manager. If variable overhead costs can be related to departments or activities, however, some control is possible.

EXHIBIT 4
Flexible Budget for Evaluation of Manufacturing Overhead Costs

Cambria Company
Flexible Budget—Manufacturing Overhead
Bag Assembly Department
For an Average One-Month Period

Cost Category	Direct Labor Hours (DLH)			Variable Cost per DLH
	400	432	500	
Budgeted variable overhead				
Indirect materials	$ 600	$ 648	$ 750	$1.50
Indirect labor	800	864	1,000	2.00
Supplies	300	324	375	.75
Utilities	400	432	500	1.00
Other	200	216	250	.50
Total budgeted variable overhead costs	$2,300	$2,484	$2,875	$5.75
Budgeted fixed overhead				
Supervisory salaries	$ 600	$ 600	$ 600	
Depreciation	400	400	400	
Other	300	300	300	
Total budgeted fixed overhead costs	$1,300	$1,300	$1,300	
Total budgeted overhead costs	$3,600	$3,784	$4,175	

Flexible budget formula (based on a normal capacity of 400 direct labor hours):
Total Budgeted Overhead Costs = (Variable Costs per Direct Labor Hour × Number of DLH) + Budgeted Fixed Overhead Costs
= ($5.75 × number of DLH) + $1,300

USING A FLEXIBLE BUDGET TO ANALYZE MANUFACTURING OVERHEAD VARIANCES

Earlier in the chapter, we described the flexible budget that the managers of Remember When, Inc., use to evaluate overall performance. That budget, shown in Exhibit 2, is based on units of output. Cambria Company's managers also use a flexible budget but to analyze manufacturing overhead costs only. As you can see in Exhibit 4, Cambria's flexible budget uses direct labor hours as the expression of activity. Thus, variable costs vary with the number of direct labor hours worked. Total fixed overhead costs remain constant. The flexible budget formula in such cases is as follows:

Total Budgeted Overhead Costs = (Variable Costs per Direct Labor Hour × Number of Direct Labor Hours) + Budgeted Fixed Overhead Costs

When applied to Cambria Company's data, the flexible budget formula is as follows:

Total Budgeted Overhead Costs = ($5.75 × Number of Direct Labor Hours) + $1,300

Cambria's flexible budget shows monthly overhead costs for 400, 432, and 500 direct labor hours. To find the total monthly budgeted overhead costs, you simply insert the direct labor hours in the flexible budget formula—for example, ($5.75 × 432 direct labor hours) + $1,300 = $3,784.

COMPUTING MANUFACTURING OVERHEAD VARIANCES

Analyses of overhead variances differ in degree of detail. The basic approach is to compute the total manufacturing overhead variance, which is the difference between actual overhead costs and standard overhead costs. The latter costs are applied to production by using a standard overhead rate.

A standard overhead rate has two parts: a variable rate and a fixed one. For Cambria Company, the standard variable rate is $5.75 per direct labor hour (from the flexible budget). The standard fixed overhead rate is found by dividing total budgeted fixed overhead ($1,300) by normal capacity (Cambria's normal capacity is 400 direct labor hours). The result is a fixed overhead rate of $3.25 per direct labor hour ($1,300 ÷ 400 hours). So, Cambria's total standard overhead rate is $9.00 per direct labor hour ($5.75 + $3.25).

Cambria Company's total manufacturing overhead variance would be computed as follows:

Standard overhead costs applied to good units produced	
$9.00 per direct labor hour × (180 bags × 2.4 hr. per bag)	$3,888
Less actual overhead costs	4,100
Total manufacturing overhead variance	$ 212 (U)

This amount can be divided into variable overhead variances and fixed overhead variances.

■ **VARIABLE OVERHEAD VARIANCES** The total variable overhead variance is the difference between actual variable overhead costs and the standard variable overhead costs that are applied to good units produced using the standard variable rate. The procedure for finding this variance is similar to the procedure for finding direct materials and labor variances.

Figure 5 shows an analysis of Cambria Company's variable overhead variances. At Cambria, each leather bag requires 2.4 standard direct labor hours, and the standard variable overhead rate is $5.75 per direct labor hour. During August, the company incurred $2,500 of variable overhead costs. The total variable overhead cost variance is computed as follows:

Overhead applied to good units produced	
Standard variable rate × standard direct labor hours allowed =	
$5.75 per hour × (180 bags × 2.4 hours per bag) =	
$5.75 × 432 hours =	$2,484
Less actual cost	2,500
Total variable overhead cost variance	$ 16 (U)

Both the actual variable overhead and the direct labor hours per bag may vary from the standard. For effective performance evaluation, managers must know how

FIGURE 5
Diagram of Variable
Overhead Variance Analysis

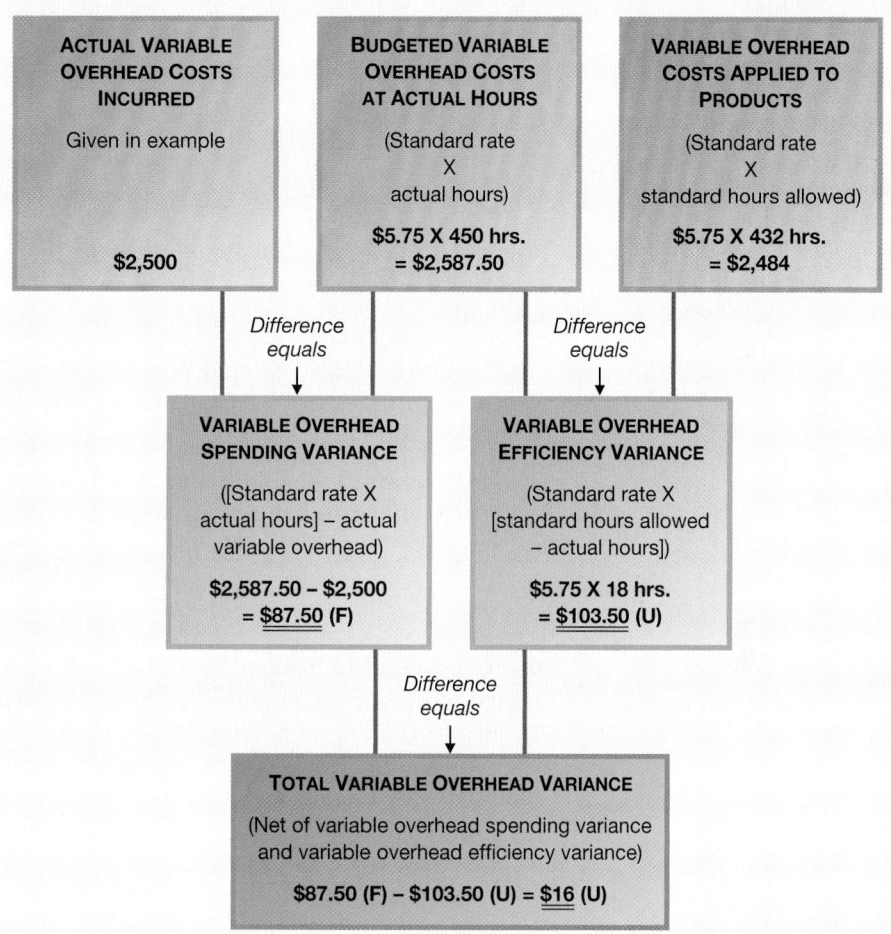

much of the total cost arose from variable overhead spending deviations and how much from variable overhead application deviations (i.e., applied and actual direct labor hours). This information is found by computing the variable overhead spending variance and the variable overhead efficiency variance.

The **variable overhead spending variance** (also called the *variable overhead rate variance*) is computed by multiplying the actual hours worked by the difference between actual variable overhead costs and the standard variable overhead rate, as follows:

$$
\begin{aligned}
\text{Variable Overhead Spending Variance} &= \text{Budgeted Variable Costs at Actual Hours} - \text{Actual Variable Overhead} \\
&= (\text{Standard Variable Rate} \times \text{Actual Hours Worked}) - \text{Actual Variable Overhead} \\
&= (\$5.75 \times 450 \text{ hours}) - \$2,500 \\
&= \$2,587.50 - \$2,500 \\
&= \$87.50 \text{ (F)}
\end{aligned}
$$

The **variable overhead efficiency variance** is the difference between the standard direct labor hours allowed for good units produced and the actual hours worked multiplied by the standard variable overhead rate per hour. It is computed as follows:

Standard direct labor hours allowed (180 bags × 2.4 hours per bag)	432 hours
Less actual hours	450 hours
Difference	18 hours (U)

$$\text{Variable Overhead Efficiency Variance} = \text{Standard Variable Rate} \times (\text{Standard Hours Allowed} - \text{Actual Hours})$$
$$= \$5.75 \times 18 \text{ hours}$$
$$= \$103.50 \text{ (U)}$$

If the calculations are correct, the net of the variable overhead spending variance and the variable overhead efficiency variance should equal the total variable overhead cost variance. The following check shows that these variances have been computed correctly:

Variable overhead spending variance	$ 87.50 (F)
Variable overhead efficiency variance	103.50 (U)
Total variable overhead cost variance	$ 16.00 (U)

■ **FIXED OVERHEAD VARIANCES**   The **total fixed overhead variance** is the difference between actual fixed overhead costs and the standard fixed overhead costs that are applied to good units produced using the standard fixed overhead rate. The procedure for finding this variance differs from the procedure used for finding direct materials, direct labor, and variable overhead variances.

Figure 6 shows an analysis of fixed overhead variances for Cambria Company. At Cambria, each bag requires 2.4 standard direct labor hours, and the standard fixed overhead rate is $3.25 per direct labor hour. As we noted earlier, the standard fixed overhead rate is found by dividing budgeted fixed overhead ($1,300) by normal capacity. In this case, because normal capacity is 400 direct labor hours, the fixed overhead rate is $3.25 per direct labor hour ($1,300 ÷ 400 hours). During August, Cambria incurred $1,600 of actual fixed overhead costs. The total fixed overhead cost variance is computed as follows:

Overhead applied to the good units produced		
Standard fixed rate × standard direct labor hours allowed =		
$3.25 × (180 bags × 2.4 hours per bag) =		
$3.25 × 432 hours =	$1,404	
Less actual cost	1,600	
Total fixed overhead cost variance	$ 196 (U)	

For effective performance evaluation, managers break down the total fixed overhead cost variance into two additional variances: the fixed overhead budget variance and the fixed overhead volume variance.

The **fixed overhead budget variance** (also called the *budgeted fixed overhead variance*) is the difference between budgeted and actual fixed overhead costs, computed as follows:

$$\text{Fixed Overhead Budget Variance} = \text{Budgeted Fixed Overhead} - \text{Actual Fixed Overhead}$$
$$= \$1,300 - \$1,600$$
$$= \$300 \text{ (U)}$$

The **fixed overhead volume variance** is the difference between budgeted fixed overhead costs and the manufacturing overhead costs that are applied to produc-

FIGURE 6
Diagram of Fixed Overhead Variance Analysis

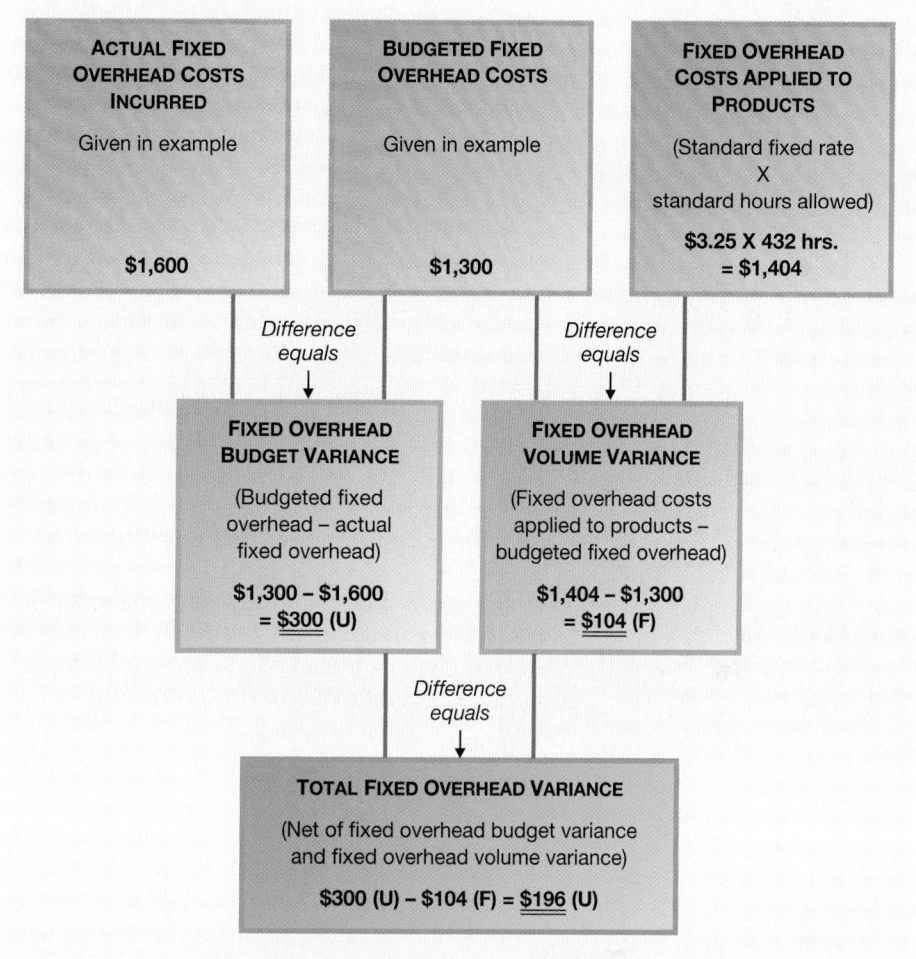

tion using the standard fixed overhead rate. The fixed overhead volume variance is computed as follows:

Standard fixed overhead applied to good units produced
$3.25 per direct labor hour × (180 bags × 2.4 hr. per bag) $1,404
Less total budgeted fixed overhead   1,300
Fixed overhead volume variance $ 104 (F)

Because the fixed overhead volume variance measures the use of existing facilities and capacity, a volume variance will occur if more or less than normal capacity is used. At Cambria Company, 400 direct labor hours are considered normal use of facilities. Because fixed overhead costs are applied on the basis of standard hours allowed, Cambria Company's manufacturing overhead was applied on the basis of 432 hours, even though the fixed overhead rate was computed using 400 hours. Thus, more fixed costs would be applied to products than were budgeted. When capacity exceeds the expected amount, the result is a favorable overhead volume variance.

When a company operates at a level below the normal capacity in units, the result is an unfavorable volume variance. Not all of the fixed overhead costs will be applied to units produced, and it then becomes necessary to add the amount of underapplied fixed overhead to the cost of good units produced, thereby increasing their unit cost.

In some cases, an unfavorable volume variance is in a company's best interest. For example, in a period of slow sales, an unfavorable volume variance would mean the company was not building up excessive inventory that might be subject to obsolescence, weathering, and storage costs. For this reason, a favorable volume variance does not always indicate that a manager has performed well.

■ **SUMMARY OF MANUFACTURING OVERHEAD VARIANCES**   If our calculations of variable and fixed overhead variances are correct, the net of these variances should equal the total manufacturing overhead variance. Checking the computations, we find that the variable and fixed overhead variances do equal the total manufacturing overhead variance:

Variable overhead spending variance	$ 87.50 (F)
Variable overhead efficiency variance	103.50 (U)
Fixed overhead budget variance	300.00 (U)
Fixed overhead volume variance	104.00 (F)
Total manufacturing overhead variance	$212.00 (U)

Figures 5 and 6 summarize our analysis of manufacturing overhead variances. The total manufacturing overhead variance is also the amount of overapplied or underapplied overhead. You may recall from an earlier chapter that actual variable and fixed overhead costs are recorded as they occur, that variable and fixed overhead are applied to products as they are produced, and that the overapplied or underapplied overhead is computed and reconciled at the end of each accounting period. By breaking down the total manufacturing overhead variance into variable and fixed variances, managers can more accurately control costs and reconcile their causes. An analysis of these two overhead variances will help explain why the amount of overhead applied to units produced is different from the actual overhead costs incurred.

ANALYZING AND CORRECTING MANUFACTURING OVERHEAD VARIANCES

In analyzing the unfavorable total manufacturing overhead variance of $212, the manager of Cambria Company's Bag Assembly Department found causes for the variances that contributed to it. Although the variable overhead spending variance was favorable ($87.50 less than expected because of savings on purchases), the inefficiency of the machine operator who substituted for an assembly worker created unfavorable variances for both direct labor efficiency and variable overhead efficiency. As a result, the manager is going to consider the feasibility of implementing a program for cross-training employees.

After reviewing the fixed overhead costs, the manager of the Bag Assembly Department concluded that higher than anticipated factory insurance premiums were the reason for the unfavorable fixed overhead budget variance and were the result of an increase in the number of insurance claims filed by employees. To obtain more specific information, the manager will study the insurance claims filed over a three-month period.

Finally, since the 432 standard hours were well above the normal capacity of 400 direct labor hours, fixed overhead was overapplied, and it resulted in a

FOCUS ON INTERNATIONAL BUSINESS

Have You Bought Gold Medal Sneakers Yet?
Founded by Li-Ning, winner of the 1984 Olympic Gold medal for gymnastics, Beijing Li-Ning Sports Goods Company is aiming to become a dominant force in the global market by 2008, when the Olympic games will be held in Beijing. The company's products include athletic shoes and sportswear. Currently, its sneakers are the best-selling ones in China, a market soon to be the second largest in the world. Controlling costs through the use of standard costing is a key to the company's success. Because its prices are up to two-thirds lower than those of its international competitors and because it controls its costs well, Beijing Li-Ning Sports Goods Company is an up-and-coming global contender.[4]

$104 (F) volume variance. The overutilization of capacity was traced to high seasonal demand that pressed the company to use almost all its capacity. Management decided not to do anything about the fixed overhead volume variance because it fell within an anticipated seasonal range.

 Check out ACE for a Review Quiz at http://accounting.college.hmco.com/students.

USING COST VARIANCES TO EVALUATE MANAGERS' PERFORMANCE

LO7   Explain how variances are used to evaluate managers' performance.

RELATED TEXT ASSIGNMENTS
Q: 20
SE: 10
E: 15

How effectively and fairly a manager's performance is evaluated depends on human factors—the people doing the evaluating—as well as on company policies. The evaluation process becomes more accurate when managerial performance reports include variances from standard costs.

To ensure that the evaluation of a manager's performance is effective and fair, a company's policies should be based on input from managers and employees and should specify the procedures that managers are to use for

- Preparing operational plans
- Assigning responsibility for carrying out the operational plans
- Communicating the operational plans to key personnel
- Evaluating performance in each area of responsibility
- Identifying the causes of significant variances from the operational plan
- Taking corrective action to eliminate problems

Because variance analysis provides detailed data about differences between standard and actual costs and thus helps identify the causes of those differences, it is usually more effective at pinpointing efficient and inefficient operating areas than are basic comparisons of budgeted and actual data. A managerial performance report based on standard costs and related variances should identify the causes of each significant variance, as well as the personnel involved and the corrective actions taken. It should be tailored to the manager's specific areas of responsibility, explaining clearly and accurately in what way the manager's department met or did not meet operating expectations. Managers should be held accountable only for cost areas under their control.

Exhibit 5 shows a performance report for the manager of Cambria Company's Bag Assembly Department. The report summarizes all cost data and variances for direct materials, direct labor, and manufacturing overhead. In addition, it identifies the causes of the variances and the corrective actions taken. Such a report would enable a supervisor to review a manager's actions and evaluate his or her performance.

A point to remember is that the mere occurrence of a variance does not indicate that a manager has performed poorly. However, if a variance consistently occurs and no cause is identified and no corrective action is taken, it may well indicate poor managerial performance.

The report in Exhibit 5 shows that the causes of the variances have been identified and corrective actions have been taken, indicating that the manager of the Cambria Company's Bag Assembly Department has the operation under control.

● **STOP AND THINK!**
Why should evaluations of managers' performance not follow a set pattern?
Because managers have different responsibilities, evaluations of their performance should be tailored to those responsibilities. ■

FOCUS ON BUSINESS ETHICS

Ethics = Profits
According to a recent five-year study, companies that demonstrate a commitment to ethical practices are more profitable than companies that do not demonstrate such a commitment. Conducted by researchers in the United Kingdom and the United States, the study used financial performance measures, including economic value added and return on capital, and nonfinancial performance measures, such as whether a company was on a list of most admired companies. The study found that in the long run, ethical companies outperformed their less ethical peers.[5]

Exhibit 5
Managerial Performance Report Using Variance Analysis

Cambria Company
Managerial Performance Report
Bag Assembly Department
For the Month Ended August 31, 20x6

Productivity Summary:

Normal capacity in units	167 bags
Normal capacity in direct labor hours (DLH)	400 DLH
Good units produced	180 bags
Performance level	
(standard hours allowed for good units produced)	432 DLH

Cost and Variance Analysis:

	Standard Costs	Actual Costs	Total Variance	Variance Breakdown Amount	Variance Breakdown Type
Direct materials	$ 4,320	$ 4,484	$164 (U)	$ 76.00 (F)	Direct materials price variance
				240.00 (U)	Direct materials quantity variance
Direct labor	3,672	4,140	468 (U)	315.00 (U)	Direct labor rate variance
				153.00 (U)	Direct labor efficiency variance
Overhead					
Variable	2,484	2,500	16 (U)	87.50 (F)	Variable overhead spending variance
				103.50 (U)	Variable overhead efficiency variance
Fixed	1,404	1,600	196 (U)	300.00 (U)	Fixed overhead budget variance
				104.00 (F)	Fixed overhead volume variance
Totals	$11,880	$12,724	$844 (U)	$844.00 (U)	

Causes of Variances	Actions Taken
Direct materials price variance:	
New direct material purchased at reduced price	New direct material deemed inappropriate; resumed purchasing material originally specified
Direct materials quantity variance:	
Poor quality of new direct material	New direct material deemed inappropriate; resumed using direct material originally specified
Direct labor rate variance:	
Machine operator who had to learn assembly skills	Temporary replacement; no action taken on the job
Direct labor efficiency variance:	
Machine operator who had to learn assembly skills	Temporary replacement; no action taken on the job
Late delivery of parts to assembly floor	Material delivery times and number of delays being tracked
Variable overhead spending variance:	
Cost savings on purchases	No action necessary
Variable overhead efficiency variance:	
Machine operator who had to learn assembly skills on the job	A cross-training program for employees now under consideration
Fixed overhead budget variance:	
Large number of factory insurance claims	Study of insurance claims being conducted
Fixed overhead volume variance:	
High number of orders caused by seasonal demand	No action necessary

Check out ACE for a Review Quiz at http://accounting.college.hmco.com/students.

Chapter Review

REVIEW OF LEARNING OBJECTIVES

LO1 Define *standard costs* and describe how managers use standard costs in the management cycle.

Standard costs are realistic estimates of costs based on analyses of both past and projected operating costs and conditions. They provide a standard, or predetermined, performance level for use in standard costing, a method of cost control that also includes a measure of actual performance and a measure of the variance between standard and actual performance. In the planning stage of the management cycle, managers use standard costs to develop budgets for direct materials, direct labor, and variable overhead. These estimated costs not only serve as targets for product costing; they are also useful in making decisions about product distribution and pricing. During the executing stage, managers use standard costs to measure expenditures and to control costs as they occur. At the end of an accounting period, they compare actual costs with standard costs and compute the variances. The variances provide measures of performance that can be used to control costs. Managers also use standard costs to report on operations and managerial performance.

LO2 Explain how standard costs are developed and compute a standard unit cost.

A standard unit cost has six elements. The direct materials price standard is based on a careful estimate of all possible price increases, changes in available quantities, and new sources of supply in the next accounting period. The direct materials quantity standard is based on product engineering specifications, the quality of direct materials, the age and productivity of the machines, and the quality and experience of the work force. Labor union contracts or company policies define the direct labor rate standard. Current time and motion studies of workers and machines and records of their past performance provide the data for developing the direct labor time standard. Standard variable and fixed overhead rates are found by dividing total budgeted variable and fixed overhead costs by an appropriate application base.

A total standard unit cost is computed by adding the following costs: direct materials costs (direct materials price standard times direct materials quantity standard), direct labor costs (direct labor rate standard times direct labor time standard), and manufacturing overhead costs (standard variable and standard fixed overhead rate times standard direct labor hours allowed per unit).

LO3 Prepare a flexible budget and describe how variance analysis is used to control costs.

A flexible budget is a summary of anticipated costs for a range of activity levels. It provides forecasted cost data that can be adjusted for changes in level of output. The variable cost per unit and total fixed costs presented in a flexible budget are components of the flexible budget formula, an equation that determines the budgeted cost for any level of output. A flexible budget improves the accuracy of variance analysis, which is a four-step approach to controlling costs. First, managers compute the amount of the variance. If the amount is insignificant, no corrective action is needed. If the amount is significant, managers then analyze the variance to identify its cause. In identifying the cause, they are usually able to pinpoint the activities that need to be monitored. They then select performance measures that will enable them to track those activities, analyze the results, and determine the action needed to correct the problem. Their final step is to take the appropriate corrective action.

LO4 Compute and analyze direct materials variances.

The direct materials price variance is computed by finding the difference between the standard price and the actual price per unit and multiplying it by the actual quantity purchased. The direct materials quantity variance is the difference between the standard quantity that should have been used and the actual quantity used, multiplied by the standard price. An analysis of these variances enables managers to identify what is causing them and to formulate plans for correcting related operating problems.

LO5 Compute and analyze direct labor variances.

The direct labor rate variance is computed by determining the difference between the standard direct labor rate and the actual rate and multiplying it by the actual direct labor hours worked. The direct labor efficiency variance is the difference between the standard hours allowed for the number of good units produced and the actual hours worked multiplied by the standard direct labor rate. Managers analyze these variances to find the causes of differences between standard direct labor costs and actual direct labor costs.

LO6 Compute and analyze manufacturing overhead variances.

The total manufacturing overhead variance is equal to the amount of under- or overapplied overhead costs for an accounting period. An analysis of the variable and fixed overhead variances will help explain why the amount of overhead applied to units produced differs from the actual overhead costs incurred. The total overhead variance can be broken down into a variable overhead spending variance, a variable overhead efficiency variance, a fixed overhead budget variance, and a fixed overhead volume variance.

LO7 Explain how variances are used to evaluate managers' performance.

How effectively and fairly a manager's performance is evaluated depends on human factors—the people doing the evaluating—as well as on company policies. To ensure that performance evaluation is effective and fair, a company's evaluation policies should be based on input from managers and employees and should be specific about the procedures managers are to follow. The evaluation process becomes more accurate when managerial performance reports include variances from standard costs. A managerial performance report based on standard costs and related variances should identify the causes of each significant variance, as well as the personnel involved, and the corrective actions taken. It should be tailored to the manager's specific areas of responsibility.

REVIEW OF CONCEPTS AND TERMINOLOGY

The following concepts and terms were introduced in this chapter:

LO5 **Direct labor efficiency variance:** The difference between the standard direct labor hours allowed for good units produced and the actual direct labor hours worked multiplied by the standard direct labor rate. Also called *direct labor quantity* or *usage variance*.

LO2 **Direct labor rate standard:** The hourly direct labor rate expected to prevail during the next accounting period for each function or job classification.

LO5 **Direct labor rate variance:** The difference between the standard direct labor rate and the actual direct labor rate multiplied by the actual direct labor hours worked. Also called *direct labor spending variance*.

LO2 **Direct labor time standard:** The expected labor time required for each department, machine, or process to complete the production of one unit or one batch of output.

LO2 **Direct materials price standard:** A careful estimate of the cost of a specific direct material in the next accounting period.

LO4 **Direct materials price variance:** The difference between the standard price and the actual price per unit multiplied by the actual quantity purchased. Also called *direct material spending* or *rate variance*.

LO2 **Direct materials quantity standard:** An estimate of the amount of direct materials, including scrap and waste, that will be used in an accounting period.

LO4 **Direct materials quantity variance:** The difference between the standard quantity allowed and the actual quantity used multiplied by the standard price. Also called *direct material efficiency* or *usage variance*.

LO6 **Fixed overhead budget variance:** The difference between budgeted and actual fixed overhead costs. Also called *budgeted fixed overhead variance*.

LO6 **Fixed overhead volume variance:** The difference between budgeted fixed overhead costs and the overhead costs that are applied to production using the standard fixed overhead rate.

LO3 **Flexible budget:** A summary of expected costs for a range of activity levels. Also called *variable budget*.

LO3 **Flexible budget formula:** An equation that determines the expected, or budgeted, cost for any level of productive output.

LO1 **Standard costing:** A method of cost control with three components: a standard, or predetermined, performance level; a measure of actual performance; and a measure of the difference, or variance, between standard and actual performance.

LO1 **Standard costs:** Realistic estimates of costs based on analyses of both past and projected operating costs and conditions.

LO2 **Standard direct labor cost:** The standard wage for direct labor multiplied by the standard hours of direct labor.

LO2 **Standard direct materials cost:** The standard price for direct materials multiplied by the standard quantity for direct materials.

LO2 **Standard fixed overhead rate:** Total budgeted fixed overhead costs divided by an expression of capacity, usually normal capacity in terms of standard hours or units.

LO2 **Standard manufacturing overhead cost:** The sum of the estimates of variable and fixed overhead costs in the next accounting period.

LO2 **Standard variable overhead rate:** Total budgeted variable overhead costs divided by an expression of capacity, such as the expected number of standard machine hours or standard direct labor hours.

LO5 **Total direct labor cost variance:** The difference between the standard direct labor cost for good units produced and actual direct labor costs.

LO4 **Total direct materials cost variance:** The difference between the standard cost and actual cost of direct materials.

LO6 **Total fixed overhead variance:** The difference between actual fixed overhead costs and the standard fixed overhead costs that are applied to good units produced using the standard fixed overhead rate.

LO6 **Total manufacturing overhead variance:** The difference between actual manufacturing overhead costs and standard manufacturing overhead costs.

LO6 **Total variable overhead variance:** The difference between actual variable overhead costs and the standard variable overhead costs that are applied to good units produced using the standard variable overhead rate.

LO6 **Variable overhead efficiency variance:** The difference between the standard direct labor hours allowed for good units produced and the actual hours worked multiplied by the standard variable overhead rate per hour.

LO6 **Variable overhead spending variance:** The difference between actual variable overhead costs and the standard variable overhead rate multiplied by the actual hours used. Also called the *variable overhead rate variance*.

LO1 **Variance:** The difference between a standard cost and an actual cost.

LO3 **Variance analysis:** The process of computing the differences between standard costs and actual costs and identifying the causes of those differences.

REVIEW PROBLEM

Variance Analysis

LO2
LO4
LO5
LO6
Alexa Manufacturing Company has a standard costing system and keeps all its cost standards up to date. The company's main product is copper water pipe, which is made in a single department. The standard variable costs for one unit of finished pipe are as follows:

Direct materials (3 sq. meters @ $12.50 per sq. meter)	$37.50
Direct labor (1.2 hours @ $9.00 per hour)	10.80
Variable overhead (1.2 hours @ $5.00 per direct labor hour)	6.00
Standard variable cost per unit	$54.30

The company's normal capacity is 15,000 direct labor hours. Its budgeted fixed overhead costs for the year were $54,000. During the year, it produced and sold 12,200

5. Variable overhead cost variances:

   a. Variable overhead spending variance:

Budgeted variable overhead for actual hours		
Variable overhead cost		
($5.00 per hour × 15,250 labor hours)	$76,250	
Less actual variable overhead costs incurred	73,200	
Variable overhead spending variance	$ 3,050	(F)

   b. Variable overhead efficiency variance:

Variable overhead applied to good units produced		
(14,640 hours* × $5.00 per hour)	$73,200	
Less budgeted variable overhead for actual hours		
(15,250 hours × $5.00 per hour)	76,250	
Variable overhead efficiency variance	$ 3,050	(U)

   *12,200 units produced × 1.2 hours per unit = 14,640 hours.

   c. Total variable overhead cost variance:

$$\text{Total Variable Overhead Cost Variance} = \text{Net of Variable Overhead Spending Variance and Variable Overhead Efficiency Variance}$$
$$= \$3,050 \text{ (F)} - \$3,050 \text{ (U)}$$
$$= \$0$$

Diagram Form:

	Actual Variable Overhead Costs		Standard Rate × Actual Hours		Standard Rate × Standard Hours
Variable Overhead	$73,200	Spending Variance	$5.00 × 15,250 = $76,250	Efficiency Variance	$5.00 × (12,200 × 1.2) = $73,200
		$3,050 (F)	**Total Variable Overhead Cost Variance**	$3,050 (U)	
			$0		

6. Fixed overhead cost variances:

   a. Fixed overhead budget variance:

Budgeted fixed overhead	$54,000	
Less actual fixed overhead	55,000	
Fixed overhead budget variance	$ 1,000	(U)

   b. Fixed overhead volume variance:

Standard fixed overhead applied		
(14,640 labor hours × $3.60 per hour)	$52,704	
Less total budgeted fixed overhead	54,000	
Fixed overhead volume variance	$ 1,296	(U)

   c. Total fixed overhead cost variance:

$$\text{Total Fixed Overhead Cost Variance} = \text{Net of Fixed Overhead Budget Variance and Fixed Overhead Volume Variance}$$
$$= \$1,000 \text{ (U)} + \$1,296 \text{ (U)}$$
$$= \$2,296 \text{ (U)}$$

Diagram Form:

	Actual Fixed Overhead Costs		Budgeted Fixed Overhead Costs		Standard Rate × Standard Hours
Fixed Overhead	$55,000	Budget Variance	$54,000	Volume Variance	$3.60 × (12,200 × 1.2) = $52,704
		$1,000 (U)	Total Fixed Overhead Variance	$1,296 (U)	
			$2,296 (U)		

Chapter Assignments

BUILDING YOUR KNOWLEDGE FOUNDATION

QUESTIONS

1. What are standard costs?
2. What is a variance?
3. Can a service organization use standard costing? Explain your answer.
4. Explain the following statement: "Standard costing is a total unit cost concept in that standard unit costs are determined for direct materials, direct labor, and manufacturing overhead."
5. What general ledger accounts are affected by a standard costing system?
6. What do a standard overhead manufacturing rate and a predetermined overhead rate have in common? How do they differ?
7. Name the six elements used to compute a standard unit cost.
8. Identify three factors that could affect a direct materials price standard.
9. "Performance is evaluated by comparing what did happen with what should have happened." What does this statement mean? How does it relate to cost control?
10. What is variance analysis?
11. What is a flexible budget? What is its purpose?
12. What are the components of the flexible budget formula? How are they related?
13. How can variances help managers control costs?
14. What is the formula for computing a direct materials price variance?
15. How would you interpret an unfavorable direct materials price variance?
16. Can an unfavorable direct materials quantity variance be caused, at least in part, by a favorable direct materials price variance? Explain your answer.
17. Identify two possible causes of a direct labor rate variance and describe the measures used to track performance in those areas. Then do the same for a direct labor efficiency variance.
18. Distinguish between the fixed overhead budget variance and the fixed overhead volume variance.
19. If standard hours allowed exceed normal hours, will the period's fixed manufacturing overhead volume variance be favorable or unfavorable? Explain your answer.

20. What should a managerial performance report based on standard costs and related variances include? How should it be prepared?

SHORT EXERCISES

SE 1.
LO1 **Uses of Standard Costs**

Lago Corporation is considering adopting the standard costing method. Dan Sarkis, the manager of the Ohio Division, attended a corporate meeting at which Leah Rohr, the controller, discussed the proposal. Sarkis asked, "Leah, how will this new method benefit me? How will I use it?" Prepare Rohr's response to Sarkis.

SE 2.
LO1 **Purposes of Standard Costs**

Suppose you are a management consultant and a client asks you why companies include standard costs in their cost accounting systems. Prepare your response, listing several purposes for using standard costs in a cost accounting system.

SE 3.
LO2 **Computing a Standard Unit Cost**

Using the following information, compute the standard unit cost of Product JLT:

Direct materials quantity standard	5 pounds per unit
Direct materials price standard	$10.20 per pound
Direct labor time standard	.4 hour per unit
Direct labor rate standard	$10.75 per hour
Variable overhead rate standard	$7.00 per machine hour
Fixed overhead rate standard	$11.00 per machine hour
Machine hour standard	2 hours per unit

SE 4.
LO3 **Analyzing Cost Variances**

Garden Metal Works produces lawn sculptures. The company analyzes only variances that differ by more than 5 percent from the standard cost. The controller computed the following direct labor efficiency variances for March:

	Direct Labor Efficiency Variance	Standard Direct Labor Cost
Product 4	$1,240 (U)	$26,200
Product 6	3,290 (F)	41,700
Product 7	2,030 (U)	34,300
Product 9	1,620 (F)	32,560
Product 12	2,810 (U)	59,740

For each product, determine the percentage of the variance to the standard cost (round to one decimal place). Then identify the products whose variances should be analyzed and suggest possible causes for the variances..

SE 5.
LO3 **Preparing a Flexible Budget**

Prepare a flexible budget for 10,000, 12,000, and 14,000 units of output, using the following information:

Variable costs	
Direct materials	$8.00 per unit
Direct labor	$2.50 per unit
Variable overhead	$6.00 per unit
Total budgeted fixed overhead	$81,200

SE 6.
LO4 **Direct Materials Variances**

Using the standard costs in **SE 3** and the following actual cost and usage data, compute the direct materials price and direct materials quantity variances:

Direct materials purchased and used	55,000 pounds
Price paid for direct materials	$10.00 per pound
Number of good units produced	11,000 units

SE 7.
LO5 **Direct Labor Variances**

Using the standard costs in **SE 3** and the following actual cost and usage data, compute the direct labor rate and direct labor efficiency variances:

Direct labor hours used	4,950 hours
Total cost of direct labor	$53,460
Number of good units produced	11,000 units

SE 8.
LO6 **Manufacturing Overhead Variances**

Sutherland Products uses standard costing. The following information about manufacturing overhead was generated during August:

Standard variable overhead rate	$2 per machine hour
Standard fixed overhead rate	$3 per machine hour
Actual variable overhead costs	$443,200
Actual fixed overhead costs	$698,800

Budgeted fixed overhead costs	$700,000
Standard machine hours per unit produced	12
Good units produced	18,940
Actual machine hours	228,400

Compute the variable overhead spending and efficiency variances and the fixed overhead budget and volume variances.

SE 9.
LO6 Fixed Overhead Rate and Variances

To the Point Manufacturing Company uses the standard costing method. The company's main product is a fine quality fountain pen that normally takes 2.5 hours to produce. Normal annual capacity is 30,000 direct labor hours, and budgeted fixed overhead costs for the year were $15,000. During the year, the company produced and sold 14,000 units. Actual fixed overhead costs were $19,000. Compute the fixed overhead rate per direct labor hour and determine the fixed overhead budget and volume variances.

SE 10.
LO7 Evaluating Managerial Performance

Gina Rolando, the controller at WAWA Industries, gave Jason Ponds, the production manager, a report containing the following information:

	Actual Cost	Standard Cost	Variance
Direct materials	$38,200	$36,600	$1,600 (U)
Direct labor	19,450	19,000	450 (U)
Variable overhead	62,890	60,000	2,890 (U)

Rolando asked for a response. If you were Ponds, how would you respond? What additional information might you need to prepare your response?

EXERCISES

E 1.
LO1 Uses of Standard Costs

Summer Diaz has just assumed the duties of controller for Market Research Company. She is concerned that the company's methods of cost planning and control do not accurately track the operations of the business. She plans to suggest to the company's president, Sydney Tyson, that the company start using standard costing for budgeting and cost control. The new method could be incorporated into the existing accounting system. The anticipated cost of adopting it and training managers is around $7,500. Prepare a memo from Summer Diaz to Sydney Tyson that defines standard costing and outlines its uses and benefits.

E 2.
LO2 Computing Standard Costs

Normal Corporation uses standard costing and is in the process of updating its direct materials and direct labor standards for Product 20B. The following data have been accumulated:

Direct materials

In the previous period, 20,500 units were produced, and 32,800 square yards of direct materials at a cost of $122,344 were used to produce them.

Direct labor

During the previous period, 57,400 direct labor hours were worked—34,850 hours on machine H and 22,550 hours on machine K. Machine H operators earned $9.40 per hour, and machine K operators earned $9.20 per hour last period. A new labor union contract calls for a 10 percent increase in labor rates for the coming period.

Using this information as the basis for the new standards, compute the direct materials quantity and price standards and the direct labor time and rate standards for each machine for the coming accounting period.

E 3.
LO2 Computing a Standard Unit Cost

Weather Aerodynamics, Inc., makes electronically equipped weather-detecting balloons for university meteorology departments. Because of recent nationwide inflation, the company's management has ordered that standard costs be recomputed. New direct materials price standards are $600 per set for electronic components and $13.50 per square meter for heavy-duty canvas. Direct materials quantity standards include one set of electronic components and 100 square meters of heavy-duty canvas per balloon. Direct labor time standards are 26 hours per balloon for the Electronics Department and 19 hours per balloon for the Assembly Department. Direct labor rate standards are $11 per hour for the Electronics Department and $10 per hour for the Assembly Department. Standard manufacturing overhead rates are $16 per direct labor hour for the standard variable overhead rate and $12 per direct labor hour for the standard fixed overhead rate. Using these production standards, compute the standard unit cost of one weather balloon.

LO3   Preparing a Flexible Budget

E 4. Keel Company's fixed overhead costs for 20x5 are expected to be as follows: depreciation, $72,000; supervisory salaries, $92,000; property taxes and insurance, $26,000; and other fixed overhead, $14,500. Total fixed overhead is thus expected to be $204,500. Variable costs per unit are expected to be as follows: direct materials, $16.50; direct labor, $8.50; operating supplies, $2.60; indirect labor, $4.10; and other variable overhead costs, $3.20. Prepare a flexible budget for the following levels of production: 18,000 units, 20,000 units, and 22,000 units. What is the flexible budget formula for 20x5?

LO4   Direct Materials Price and Quantity Variances

E 5. SITO Elevator Company manufactures small hydroelectric elevators with a maximum capacity of ten passengers. One of the direct materials used is heavy-duty carpeting for the floor of the elevator. The direct materials quantity standard for April was 8 square yards per elevator. During April, the purchasing agent purchased this carpeting at $11 per square yard; the standard price for the period was $12. Ninety elevators were completed and sold during the month; the Production Department used an average of 8.5 square yards of carpet per elevator. Calculate the company's direct materials price and quantity variances for carpeting for April.

LO4   Direct Materials Variances

E 6. Diekow Productions manufactured and sold 1,000 products at $11,000 each during the past year. At the beginning of the year, production had been set at 1,200 products; direct materials standards had been set at 100 pounds of direct materials at $2 per pound for each product produced. During the year, the company purchased and used 98,000 pounds of direct materials; the cost was $2.04 per pound. Calculate Diekow Production's direct materials price and quantity variances for the year.

LO5   Direct Labor Variances

E 7. At the beginning of last year, Diekow Productions set direct labor standards of 20 hours at $15 per hour for each product produced. During the year, 20,500 direct labor hours were actually worked at an average cost of $16 per hour. Using this information and the applicable information in **E 6,** calculate Diekow Production's direct labor rate and efficiency variances for the year.

LO5   Direct Labor Rate and Efficiency Variances

E 8. NEO Foundry, Inc., manufactures castings that other companies use in the production of machinery. For the past two years, NEO's best-selling product has been a casting for an eight-cylinder engine block. Standard direct labor hours per engine block are 1.8 hours. A labor union contract requires that the company pay all direct labor employees $14 per hour. During June, NEO produced 16,500 engine blocks. Actual direct labor hours and costs for the month were 29,900 hours and $433,550, respectively.

1. Compute the direct labor rate variance for eight-cylinder engine blocks during June.
2. Using the same data, compute the direct labor efficiency variance for eight-cylinder engine blocks during June. Check your answer, assuming that the total direct labor cost variance is $17,750 (U).

LO6   Variable Overhead Variances

E 9. At the beginning of last year, Diekow Productions set standards of 10 machine hours at a variable rate of $10 per hour for each product produced. During the year, 10,800 machine hours were used at a cost of $10.20 per hour. Using this information and the applicable information in **E 6,** calculate Diekow Production's variable overhead spending and efficiency variances for the year.

LO6   Fixed Overhead Variances

E 10. At the beginning of last year, Diekow Productions set budgeted fixed overhead costs at $456,000. During the year, actual fixed overhead costs were $500,000. Using this information and the applicable information in **E 6,** calculate Diekow Production's fixed overhead budget and volume variances for the year.

LO6   Variable Overhead Variances for a Service Business

E 11. Design Architects, LLP, billed clients for 6,000 hours of design work for the month. Actual variable overhead costs for the month were $315,000, and 6,250 hours were worked. At the beginning of the year, a variable overhead standard of $50 per design hour had been developed based on a budget of 5,000 design hours each month. Calculate Design Architect's variable overhead spending and efficiency variances for the month.

LO6   Fixed Overhead Variances for a Service Business

E 12. Engineering Associates billed clients for 11,000 hours of engineering work for the month. Actual fixed overhead costs for the month were $435,000, and 11,850 hours were worked. At the beginning of the year, a fixed overhead standard of $40 per design hour had been developed based on a budget of 10,000 engineering hours each month. Calculate Engineering Associates' fixed overhead budget and volume variances for the month.

E 13.

LO6 Manufacturing Overhead Variances

Cedar Key Company produces handmade clamming buckets and sells them to distributors along the Gulf Coast of Florida. The company incurred $9,400 of actual manufacturing overhead costs ($8,000 variable; $1,400 fixed) in May. Budgeted standard overhead costs for May were $4 of variable overhead costs per direct labor hour and $1,500 of fixed overhead costs. Normal capacity was set at 2,000 direct labor hours per month. In May, the company produced 10,100 clamming buckets by working 1,900 direct labor hours. The time standard is .2 direct labor hour per clamming bucket. Compute (1) the variable overhead spending and efficiency variances and (2) the fixed overhead budget and volume variances for May.

E 14.

LO6 Manufacturing Overhead Variances

Suncoast Industries uses standard costing and a flexible budget for cost planning and control. Its monthly budget for overhead costs is $200,000 of fixed costs plus $5.20 per machine hour. Monthly normal capacity of 100,000 machine hours is used to compute the standard fixed overhead rate. During December, employees worked 105,000 machine hours. Only 98,500 standard machine hours were allowed for good units produced during the month. Actual overhead costs incurred during December totaled $441,000 of variable costs and $204,500 of fixed costs. Compute (1) the under- or over-applied overhead during December and (2) the variable overhead spending and efficiency variances and the fixed overhead budget and volume variances.

E 15.

LO7 Evaluating Managerial Performance

Ron LaTulip oversees projects for ACE Construction Company. Recently, the company's controller sent him a performance report regarding the construction of the Campus Highlands Apartment Complex, a project that LaTulip supervised. Included in the report was an unfavorable direct labor efficiency variance of $1,900 for roof structures. What types of information does LaTulip need to analyze before he can respond to this report?

Problems

P 1.

LO2 Computing and Using Standard Costs

Prefabricated houses are the specialty of Affordable Homes, Inc., of Corsicana, Texas. Although Affordable Homes produces many models, and customers can even place special orders, the company's best-selling model is the Welcome Home, a three-bedroom, 1,400-square-foot house with an impressive front entrance. In 20x5, the standard costs for the six basic direct materials used in manufacturing the entrance were as follows: wood framing materials, $2,140; deluxe front door, $480; door hardware, $260; exterior siding, $710; electrical materials, $580; and interior finishing materials, $1,520. Three types of direct labor are used to build the entrance: carpenter, 30 hours at $12 per hour; door specialist, 4 hours at $14 per hour; and electrician, 8 hours at $16 per hour. In 20x5, the company used a manufacturing overhead rate of 40 percent of total direct materials cost.

During 20x6, the cost of wood framing materials is expected to increase by 20 percent, and a deluxe front door will cost $496. The cost of the door hardware will increase by 10 percent, and the cost of electrical materials will increase by 20 percent. Exterior siding cost should decrease by $16 per unit. The cost of interior finishing materials is expected to remain the same. The carpenter's wages will increase by $1 per hour, and the door specialist's wages should remain the same. The electrician's wages will increase by $.50 per hour. Finally, the manufacturing overhead rate will decrease to 25 percent of total direct materials cost.

REQUIRED ▶

1. Compute the total standard cost of direct materials per entrance for 20x5.
2. Using your answer to item 1, compute the total standard unit cost per entrance for 20x5.
3. Compute the total standard unit cost per entrance for 20x6.

P 2.

LO3 Preparing a Flexible Budget and Evaluating Performance

Home Products Company manufactures a complete line of kitchen glassware. The Beverage Division specializes in 12-ounce drinking glasses. Erin Fisher, the superintendent of the Beverage Division, asked the controller to prepare a report of her division's performance in April 20x4. The following report was handed to her a few days later:

Cost Category (Variable Unit Cost)	Budgeted Costs*	Actual Costs	Difference Under (Over) Budget
Direct materials ($.10)	$ 5,000	$ 4,975	$ 25
Direct labor ($.12)	6,000	5,850	150
Manufacturing overhead			
Variable			
Indirect labor ($.03)	1,500	1,290	210
Supplies ($.02)	1,000	960	40
Heat and power ($.03)	1,500	1,325	175
Other ($.05)	2,500	2,340	160
Fixed			
Heat and power	3,500	3,500	—
Depreciation	4,200	4,200	—
Insurance and taxes	1,200	1,200	—
Other	1,600	1,600	—
Totals	$28,000	$27,240	$760

*Based on normal capacity of 50,000 units.

In discussing the report with the controller, Fisher stated, "Profits have been decreasing in recent months, but this report indicates that our production process is operating efficiently."

REQUIRED ▶

1. Prepare a flexible budget for the Beverage Division using production levels of 45,000 units, 50,000 units, and 55,000 units.
2. What is the flexible budget formula?
3. Assume that the Beverage Division produced 46,560 units in April and that all fixed costs remained constant. Prepare a revised performance report similar to the one above, using actual production in units as a basis for the budget column.
4. Which report is more meaningful for performance evaluation, the original one above or the revised one? Why?

P 3.

LO4 Direct Materials and Direct
LO5 Labor Variances

Winners Trophy Company produces a variety of athletic awards, most of them in the form of trophies. Its deluxe trophy stands three feet tall above the base. The company's direct materials standards for the deluxe trophy include one pound of metal and eight ounces of wood for the base. Standard prices for 20x6 were $3.30 per pound of metal and $.45 per ounce of wood. Direct labor standards for the deluxe trophy specify .2 hour of direct labor in the Molding Department and .4 hour in the Trimming/Finishing Department. Standard direct labor rates are $10.75 per hour in the Molding Department and $12.00 per hour in the Trimming/Finishing Department.

During January 20x6, the company made 16,400 deluxe trophies. Actual production data are as follows:

Direct materials	
Metal	16,640 pounds @ $3.25 per pound
Wood	131,400 ounces @ $.48 per ounce
Direct labor	
Molding	3,400 hours @ $10.60 per hour
Trimming/Finishing	6,540 hours @ $12.10 per hour

REQUIRED ▶

1. Compute the direct materials price and quantity variances for metal and wood.
2. Compute the direct labor rate and efficiency variances for the Molding and the Trimming/Finishing Departments.

P 4.

LO4 Direct Materials, Direct Labor,
LO5 and Manufacturing Overhead
LO6 Variances

The Doormat Division of Clean Sweep Company produces all-vinyl mats. Each doormat calls for .4 meter of vinyl material; the material should cost $3.10 per meter. Standard direct labor hours and labor cost per doormat are .2 hour and $1.84 (.2 hour × $9.20 per hour), respectively. Currently, the division's standard variable overhead rate is $1.50 per direct labor hour, and its standard fixed overhead rate is $.80 per direct labor hour.

In August 20x5, the division manufactured and sold 60,000 doormats. During the month, it used 25,200 meters of vinyl material; the total cost of the material was $73,080. The total actual manufacturing overhead costs for August were $28,200, of which $18,200 was variable. The total number of direct labor hours worked was 10,800, and the factory payroll for direct labor for the month was $95,040. Budgeted fixed overhead for August was $9,280. Normal monthly capacity for the year was set at 58,000 doormats.

REQUIRED ▶

1. Compute for August 20x5 the (a) direct materials price variance, (b) direct materials quantity variance, (c) direct labor rate variance, (d) direct labor efficiency variance, (e) variable overhead spending variance, (f) variable overhead efficiency variance, (g) fixed overhead budget variance, and (h) fixed overhead volume variance.
2. Prepare a performance report based on your variance analysis and suggest possible causes for each variance.

P 5.

LO6   Overhead Variances

Celine Corporation's accountant left for vacation before completing the monthly cost variance report. George Celine, the corporation's president, has asked you to complete the report. The following data are available to you (capacities are expressed in machine hours):

Actual machine hours	17,100
Standard machine hours allowed	17,500
Actual variable overhead	a
Standard variable overhead rate	$2.50
Variable overhead spending variance	$ 250 (F)
Variable overhead efficiency variance	b
Actual fixed overhead	c
Budgeted fixed overhead	$153,000
Fixed overhead cost variance	$1,300 (U)
Fixed overhead volume variance	$4,500 (F)
Normal capacity in machine hours	d
Standard fixed overhead rate	e
Fixed overhead applied	f

REQUIRED ▶

Analyze the data and fill in the missing amounts. (**Hint:** Use the structure of Figures 5 and 6 in this chapter to guide your analysis.)

ALTERNATE PROBLEMS

P 6.

LO2   Computing Standard Costs for Direct Materials

TickTock, Ltd., assembles clock movements for grandfather clocks. Each movement has four components: the clock facing, the clock hands, the time movement, and the spring assembly. For the current year, 20x5, the company used the following standard costs: clock facing, $15.90; clock hands, $12.70; time movement, $66.10; and spring assembly, $52.50.

Prices of materials are expected to change in 20x6. TickTock will purchase 60 percent of the facings from Company A at $18.50 each and the other 40 percent from Company B at $18.80 each. The clock hands, which are produced for TickTock by Hardware, Inc., will cost $15.50 per set in 20x6. TickTock will purchase 30 percent of the time movements from Company Q at $68.50 each, 20 percent from Company R at $69.50 each, and 50 percent from Company S at $71.90 each. The manufacturer that supplies TickTock with spring assemblies has announced that it will increase its prices by 20 percent in 20x6.

REQUIRED ▶

1. Determine the total standard direct materials cost per unit for 20x6.
2. Suppose that because TickTock has guaranteed Hardware, Inc., that it would purchase 2,500 sets of clock hands in 20x6, the cost of a set of clock hands has been reduced by 20 percent. Find the standard direct materials cost per clock.
3. Suppose that to avoid the increase in the cost of spring assemblies, TickTock purchased substandard ones from a different manufacturer at $50 each; 20 percent of them turned out to be unusable and cannot be returned. Assuming that all other data remain the same, compute the standard direct materials unit cost. Spread the cost of the defective materials over good units produced.

P 7.

LO4   Direct Materials and Direct
LO5   Labor Variances

Fruit Packaging Company makes plastic baskets for food wholesalers. Each basket requires .8 gram of liquid plastic and .6 gram of an additive that includes color and hardening agents. The standard prices are $.15 per gram of liquid plastic and $.09 per gram of additive. Two kinds of direct labor—molding and trimming/packing—are required to make the baskets. The direct labor time and rate standards for a batch of 100 baskets are as follows: molding, 1.0 hour per batch at an hourly rate of $12; and trimming/packing, 1.2 hours per batch at $10 per hour.

During 20x9, the company produced 48,000 baskets. It used 38,600 grams of liquid plastic at a total cost of $5,404 and 28,950 grams of additive at $2,895. Actual direct labor included 480 hours for molding at a total cost of $5,664 and 560 hours for trimming/packing at $5,656.

REQUIRED ▶

1. Compute the direct materials price and quantity variances for both the liquid plastic and the additive.
2. Compute the direct labor rate and efficiency variances for the molding and trimming/packing processes.

P 8.

LO4 Computing Variances and
LO5 Evaluating Performance
LO6

During 20x6, Biomed Laboratories, Inc., researched and perfected a cure for the common cold. Called Cold-Gone, the product sells for $28.00 per package, each of which contains five tablets. Standard unit costs for this product were developed in late 20x6 for use in 20x7. Per package, the standard unit costs were as follows: chemical ingredients, 6 ounces at $1.00 per ounce; packaging, $1.20; direct labor, .8 hour at $14.00 per hour; standard variable overhead, $4.00 per direct labor hour; and standard fixed overhead, $6.40 per direct labor hour. Normal capacity is 46,875 units per week.

In the first quarter of 20x7, demand for the new product rose well beyond the expectations of management. During those three months, the peak season for colds, the company produced and sold over 500,000 packages of Cold-Gone. During the first week in April, it produced 50,000 packages but used materials for 50,200 packages costing $60,240. It also used 305,000 ounces of chemical ingredients costing $292,800. The total cost of direct labor for the week was $579,600; direct labor hours totaled 40,250. Total variable overhead was $161,100, and total fixed overhead was $242,000. Budgeted fixed overhead for the week was $240,000.

REQUIRED ▶

1. Compute for the first week of April 20x7 (a) all direct materials price variances, (b) all direct materials quantity variances, (c) the direct labor rate variance, (d) the direct labor efficiency variance, (e) the variable overhead spending variance, (f) the variable overhead efficiency variance, (g) the fixed overhead budget variance, and (h) the fixed overhead volume variance.
2. Prepare a performance report based on your variance analysis and suggest possible causes for each significant variance.

SKILLS DEVELOPMENT CASES

Conceptual Analysis

SD 1.

LO3 Using Variance Analysis to
Control Costs

Holding down operating costs is an ongoing challenge for managers. The lower the costs a company incurs, the higher its profit will be. But two factors can make a target profit difficult to achieve. First, human error and unexpected machine breakdowns may cause dozens of operating inefficiencies, and each inefficiency will cause costs to rise. Second, a company may control its costs so strictly that it will use cheaper materials or labor, which may cause a decline in the quality of its product or service and in its sales. To control costs and still produce high-quality goods or services, managers must continually assess operating activities by analyzing both financial and nonfinancial data.

Write a one-page paper on how variance analysis helps managers control costs. Focus on both the financial and the nonfinancial data used in standard costing.

SD 2.

LO1 Cost Standards for Service
LO2 Companies: A Comparison

Both ChemLawn <www.chemlawn.com> and United Parcel Service (UPS) <www.ups.com> use truck drivers to deliver services to clients. ChemLawn's drivers use a hose connected to the tanks on their trucks to spray liquid fertilizers and weed killers on clients' lawns. Drivers of UPS trucks deliver packages to residences and businesses. If you were setting cost standards for ChemLawn and UPS, what standards would you set that apply to the drivers, and what cost components would you use? What measures would you use to evaluate the drivers' performance? How would cost standards for these two service companies be similar, and how would they differ? How do cost standards for service companies differ from those of manufacturing companies?

Ethical Dilemma

SD 3.

LO1 An Ethical Question Involving
LO2 Standard Costs

Taylor Industries, Inc., develops standard costs for all its direct materials, direct labor, and manufacturing overhead costs. It uses these costs for pricing products, costing inventories, and evaluating the performance of purchasing and production managers. It updates standard costs whenever costs, prices, or rates change by 3 percent or more. It also reviews and updates all standard costs each December; this practice provides current standards appropriate for use in valuing year-end inventories on the company's financial statements.

Jody Elgar is in charge of standard costing at Taylor Industries. On November 30, 20x6, she received a memo from the chief financial officer informing her that Taylor Industries was considering purchasing another company and that she and her staff were to postpone adjusting standard costs until late February; they were instead to concentrate on analyzing the proposed purchase.

In the third week of November, prices on over 20 of Taylor Industries' direct materials had been reduced by 10 percent or more, and a new labor union contract had reduced several categories of labor rates. A revision of standard costs in December would have resulted in lower valuations of inventories, higher cost of goods sold due to inventory write-downs, and lower net income for the year. Elgar believed the company was facing an operating loss and that the assignment to evaluate the proposed purchase was designed primarily to keep her staff from revising and lowering standard costs. She questioned the chief financial officer about the assignment and reiterated the need for updating the standard costs but was again told to ignore the update and concentrate on the proposed purchase. Elgar and her staff were relieved of the assignment in early February. The purchase never materialized.

Assess Jody Elgar's actions in this situation. Did this manager follow all ethical paths to solving the problem? What are the consequences of failing to adjust the standard costs?

Research Activity

SD 4.

LO2 Standard Costs and Variance
LO3 Analysis

Domino's Pizza <www.dominos.com> is a major purveyor of home-delivered pizzas. Although customers can pick up their orders at the shops where Domino's makes its pizzas, employees deliver most orders to customers' homes, and they use their own cars to do it.

Specify what standard costing for a Domino's pizza shop would entail. Where would you obtain the information for determining the cost standards? In what ways would the standards help in managing a pizza shop? If necessary to gain a better understanding of the operation, visit a pizzeria. (It does not have to be a Domino's.)

 Group Activity: Have students work in groups to complete **SD 4.** Select one person from each group to report the group's findings to the class.

Decision-Making Practice

SD 5.

LO5 Standard Costing in a Service
LO6 Company

Annuity Life Insurance Company (ALIC) markets several types of life insurance policies, but P20A—a permanent, 20-year life annuity policy—is its most popular. This policy sells in $10,000 increments and features variable percentages of whole life insurance and single-payment annuities, depending on the policyholder's needs and age. ALIC devotes an entire department to supporting and marketing the P20A policy. Because both the support staff and salespersons contribute to each P20A policy, ALIC categorizes them as direct labor for purposes of variance analysis, cost control, and performance evaluation. For unit costing, each $10,000 increment is considered one unit; thus, a $90,000 policy is counted as nine units. Standard unit cost information for January is as follows:

Direct labor
  Policy support staff
    3 hours at $12.00 per hour $ 36.00
  Policy salesperson
    8.5 hours at $14.20 per hour   120.70
Operating overhead
  Variable operating overhead
    11.5 hours at $26.00 per hour   299.00
  Fixed operating overhead
    11.5 hours at $18.00 per hour   207.00
Standard unit cost $662.70

Actual costs incurred for the 265 units sold during January were as follows:

Direct labor
  Policy support staff
    848 hours at $12.50 per hour $10,600.00
  Policy salespersons
    2,252.5 hours at $14.00 per hour   31,535.00
Operating overhead
  Variable operating overhead   78,440.00
  Fixed operating overhead   53,400.00

Normal monthly capacity is 260 units, and the budgeted fixed operating overhead for January was $53,820.

1. Compute the standard hours allowed in January for policy support staff and policy salespersons.
2. What should the total standard costs for January have been? What were the total actual costs that the company incurred in January? Compute the total cost variance for the month.
3. Compute the direct labor rate and efficiency variances for policy support staff and policy salespersons.
4. Compute the variable and fixed operating overhead variances for January.
5. Identify possible causes for each variance and suggest possible solutions.

MANAGERIAL REPORTING AND ANALYSIS CASES

Interpreting Management Reports

MRA 1.

LO3 Flexible Budgets and Performance Evaluation

Cassen Realtors, Inc., specializes in the sale of residential properties. It earns its revenue by charging a percentage of the sales price. Commissions for salespersons, listing agents, and listing companies are its main costs. Business has improved steadily over the last ten years. Bonnie Cassen, the managing partner of Cassen Realtors, receives a report summarizing the company's performance each year. The report for the most recent year appears at the top of the facing page.

1. Analyze the performance report. What does it say about the company's performance? Is the performance report reliable? Explain your answer.
2. Calculate the budgeted selling fee and budgeted variable costs per sale.
3. Prepare a performance report using a flexible budget based on the actual number of sales.
4. Analyze the report you prepared in **3.** What does it say about the company's performance? Is the performance report reliable? Explain your answer.
5. What recommendations would you make to improve the company's performance next year?

Cassen Realtors, Inc.
Performance Report
For the Year Ended December 31, 20x5

	Budgeted*	Actual†	Difference Under (Over) Budget
Total selling fees	$2,052,000	$2,242,200	($190,200)
Less variable costs			
Sales commissions	$1,102,950	$1,205,183	($102,233)
Automobile	36,000	39,560	(3,560)
Advertising	93,600	103,450	(9,850)
Home repairs	77,400	89,240	(11,840)
General overhead	656,100	716,970	(60,870)
	$1,966,050	$2,154,403	($188,353)
Less fixed costs			
general overhead	60,000	62,300	(2,300)
Total costs	$2,026,050	$2,216,703	($190,653)
Operating income	$ 25,950	$ 25,497	$ 453

*Budgeted data are based on 180 units sold.
†Actual data of 200 units sold.

Formulating Management Reports

MRA 2.

LO3 Preparing Performance
LO5 Reports
LO6

Troy Corrente, the president of Forest Valley Spa, is concerned about the spa's operating performance during March 20x6. He budgeted his costs carefully so that he could reduce the 20x6 membership fees. He now needs to evaluate those costs to make sure the spa's profits are at the level he expected.

He has asked you, the spa's controller, to prepare a performance report on labor and overhead costs for March 20x6. He also wants you to analyze the report and suggest possible causes for any problems you find. He wants to attend to any problems quickly, so he has asked you to submit your report as soon as possible. The following information for the month is available to you:

	Budgeted Costs	Actual Costs
Variable costs		
Operating labor	$10,880	$12,150
Utilities	2,880	3,360
Repairs and maintenance	5,760	7,140
Fixed costs		
Depreciation, equipment	2,600	2,680
Rent	3,280	3,280
Other	1,704	1,860
Totals	$27,104	$30,470

Corrente's budget allows for eight employees to work 160 hours each per month. During March, nine employees worked an average of 150 hours each.

1. Answer the following questions:
   a. Why are you preparing this performance report?
   b. Who will use the report?
   c. What information do you need to develop the report? How will you obtain that information?
   d. When are the performance report and the analysis needed?
2. With the limited information available to you, compute the labor rate variance, the labor efficiency variance, and the variable and fixed overhead variances.
3. Prepare a performance report for the spa for March 20x6. Analyze the report and suggest causes for any problems that you find.

International Company

MRA 3.

LO3   Variance Analysis
LO4
LO5

Ying Zsoa recently became the controller of a joint venture in Hong Kong. He has been using standard costing to plan and control the company's activities. In a meeting with the budget team, which includes managers and employees from purchasing, engineering, and production, Zsoa asked the team members to share any operating problems they had encountered during the last quarter. He explained that his staff would use this information in analyzing the causes of significant cost variances that had occurred in the quarter.

For each of the following situations, identify the direct materials and/or direct labor variance(s) that could be affected and indicate the whether the variances are favorable or unfavorable:

1. The production department used highly skilled, higher-paid workers.
2. Machines were improperly adjusted.
3. Direct labor personnel worked more carefully to manufacture the product.
4. The product design engineer substituted a direct material that was less expensive and of lower quality.
5. The Purchasing Department bought higher-quality materials at a higher price.
6. A major supplier used a less-expensive mode of transportation to deliver the raw materials.
7. Work was halted for two hours because of a power disruption.

Excel Spreadsheet Analysis

MRA 4.

LO3   Developing a Flexible Budget
LO6   and Analyzing Overhead
Variances

Ezelda Marva is the controller at FH Industries. She has asked you, her new assistant, to analyze the following data related to projected and actual overhead costs for October 20x8:

	Standard Variable Costs per Machine Hour (MH)	Actual Variable Costs in October
Indirect materials and supplies	$1.10	$ 2,380
Indirect machine setup labor	2.50	5,090
Materials handling	1.40	3,950
Maintenance and repair	1.50	2,980
Utilities	.80	1,490
Miscellaneous	.10	200
Totals	$7.40	$16,090

	Budgeted Fixed Overhead	Actual Fixed Overhead in October
Supervisory salaries	$ 3,630	$ 3,630
Machine depreciation	8,360	8,580
Other	1,210	1,220
Totals	$13,200	$13,430

For October, the number of good units produced was used to compute the 2,100 standard machine hours allowed.

1. Prepare a monthly flexible budget for operating activity at 2,000 machine hours, 2,200 machine hours, and 2,500 machine hours.
2. Develop a flexible budget formula.
3. The company's normal operating capacity is 2,200 machine hours per month. Compute the fixed overhead rate at this level of activity. Then break the rate down into individual rates for each element of fixed overhead.
4. Prepare a detailed comparative cost analysis for October. Include all variable and fixed overhead costs. Format your analysis by using columns for the following five elements: cost category, cost per machine hour, costs applied, actual costs incurred, and variance.
5. Develop a manufacturing overhead variance analysis for October that identifies the variable overhead spending and efficiency variances and the fixed overhead budget and volume variances.
6. Prepare an analysis of the variances. Could a manager control some of the fixed costs? Defend your answer.

Internet Case

MRA 5.

LO1 Resources for Developing Cost Standards

Suppose you have recently taken a job at a company that manufactures parts for automobiles. You have been assigned the task of developing manufacturing cost standards. You want to gather as much background information as you can about these standards. Using a standard search engine, such as Google, search the Internet for web sites that provide information about cost standards, manufacturing, and automobile manufacturers. Visit the sites that look most interesting. List the five sites you think are most useful. Bring your list to class and compare your findings with those of your classmates.

Chapter 26 discusses performance measurement and describes the role of the balanced scorecard, responsibility accounting, and economic value added as they relate to performance management and evaluation.

Performance Management and Evaluation

LEARNING OBJECTIVES

LO1 Describe how the balanced scorecard aligns performance with organizational goals, and explain the role of the balanced scorecard in the management cycle.

LO2 Discuss performance measurement, and state the issues that affect management's ability to measure performance.

LO3 Define *responsibility accounting,* and describe the role that responsibility centers play in performance management and evaluation.

LO4 Prepare performance reports for cost centers using flexible budgets and for profit centers using variable costing.

LO5 Prepare performance reports for investment centers using traditional measures of return on investment and residual income and the newer measure of economic value added.

LO6 Explain how properly linked performance incentives and measures add value for all stakeholders in performance management and evaluation.

DECISION POINT

A MANAGER'S FOCUS

Vail Resorts <www.vailresorts.com> Vail Resorts PEAKS is an all-in-one card for guests of four Colorado vacation spots: Vail, Breckenridge, Keystone, and Beaver Creek. Guests at all resorts in these areas can use the PEAKS card to pay for lift tickets, skiing and snowboarding lessons, equipment rentals, dining, and more. They like its convenience and its program for earning points toward free or reduced-rate lift tickets, dining, and lodging. They enroll in the PEAKS system by filling out a one-page form that asks for their name, street address, email address, phone number, date of birth, credit card number, and a signed charge privilege authorization. Data for up to eight family members may be linked into one membership account. Each family member receives a bar-coded picture identification card, usually worn on a souvenir cord around the guest's neck, that is scanned each time he or she rides the ski lifts, attends ski school, or charges purchases, dining, or lodging.[1] How can the managers of the Vail Resorts Management Company use the PEAKS card and its integrated database to manage and evaluate the performance of their resorts better?

Managers like PEAKS because it enables them to collect huge amounts of information in a simple way and because the data have so many uses. New data are entered in the system each time a guest's card is scanned. Those data then become part of an integrated management information system that allows managers to measure and control costs, quality, and performance in all four resort areas. The system's abil-

How do managers at Vail Resorts evaluate for peak performance?

ity to store both financial and nonfinancial data about all aspects of the resorts enables managers to learn about and balance the interests of all the company's stakeholders: financial (investors), learning and growth (employees), internal business processes, and customers. The managers can then use the information to answer traditional financial questions about measuring cost of sales and valuing inventory (such as food ingredients in its restaurants and merchandise in its shops) and to obtain performance information about the resorts' activities, products, services, and customers. In addition, managers and employees receive timely feedback about their performance measures so that they can continuously improve.

ORGANIZATIONAL GOALS AND THE BALANCED SCORECARD

LO1   Describe how the balanced scorecard aligns performance with organizational goals, and explain the role of the balanced scorecard in the management cycle.

RELATED TEXT ASSIGNMENTS
Q: 1, 2, 3, 4
SE: 1
E: 1, 2
SD: 1
MRA: 1

The **balanced scorecard**, developed by Robert S. Kaplan and David P. Norton, is a framework that links the perspectives of an organization's four basic stakeholder groups—financial (investors), learning and growth (employees), internal business processes, and customers—with the organization's mission and vision, performance measures, strategic plan, and resources. To succeed, an organization must add value for all groups in both the short and the long terms. Thus, an organization will determine each group's objectives and translate them into performance measures that have specific, quantifiable performance targets. Ideally, managers should be able to see how their actions contribute to the achievement of organizational goals and understand how their compensation is related to their actions. The balanced scorecard assumes that an organization will get only what it measures.

THE BALANCED SCORECARD AND THE MANAGEMENT CYCLE

We will use the Decision Point about the PEAKS card to illustrate the use of the balanced scorecard in the management cycle.

■ **PLANNING**   During the planning stage, the balanced scorecard provides a framework that enables managers to translate their organization's vision and strategy into operational terms. Managers evaluate the company vision from the perspective of each stakeholder group and seek to answer one key question for each group:

● **STOP AND THINK!**
On which perspective do most businesses focus?
Most businesses focus on the financial perspective. ■

- **Financial (investors):** To achieve our organization's vision, how should we appear to our shareholders?
- **Learning and growth (employees):** To achieve our organization's vision, how should we sustain our ability to improve and change?
- **Internal business processes:** To succeed, at what business processes must our organization excel?
- **Customers:** To achieve our organization's vision, how should we appear to our customers?

These key questions align the organization's strategy from all perspectives. The answers to the questions result in performance objectives that are mutually beneficial to all stakeholders. Once the organization's objectives are set, managers can select performance measures and set performance targets to translate objectives into an action plan.

www.vailresorts.com

For example, if Vail Resorts' collective vision and strategy is customer satisfaction, its managers might establish the following overall objectives:

KEY POINT: The alignment of an organization's strategy with all the perspectives of the balanced scorecard results in performance objectives that benefit all stakeholders.

Perspective	Objective
Financial (investors)	Customer satisfaction means revenue growth.
Learning and growth (employees)	Customer satisfaction means cross-trained, customer service–oriented employees.
Internal business processes	Customer satisfaction means reliable products and short delivery cycles.
Customers	Customer satisfaction means keeping customer loyalty through repeat visits and redeemed PEAKS points.

These overall objectives are then translated into specific performance objectives and measures for managers. For example, a ski lift manager's performance objectives might be measured in terms of the following:

Harley-Davidson, Inc.

<**www.harley-davidson.com**>

OBJECTIVES

- To describe the role a performance measurement and evaluation system plays in business today.
- To become familiar with how the balanced scorecard provides a framework for performance management and accountability.
- To show how responsibility accounting is useful in performance evaluation.
- To understand the value of linking organizational goals, objectives, measures, targets, and performance-based pay.

BACKGROUND FOR THE CASE

 Harley-Davidson continues to excel at providing motorcyclists and the general public an expanding line of motorcycles and branded products and services. Strong sales of motorcycles, apparel, parts, insurance, product licensing, and financial services have enabled the company to sustain and improve on its success. Harley's journey to success can be charted through its performance management and evaluation system.

Performance measures like market share, units shipped, revenue, operating profit, and number of employees illustrate its remarkable turnaround. In the 1980s, Harley rose above near bankruptcy to emerge today as the internationally recognized company that "fulfills dreams through the experience of motorcycling." Like many other companies, Harley-Davidson uses a performance management and evaluation system to identify how well it is doing, where it is going, and what improvements will make it more profitable.

For more information about Harley-Davidson, Inc., visit the company's web site directly or access it through the Needles Accounting Resource Center Web Site at **http://accounting.college.hmco.com/students.**

REQUIRED

View the video on Harley-Davidson that accompanies this book. As you are watching the video, take notes related to the following questions:

1. What role does performance measurement and evaluation play in business today?
2. In your own words, describe the balanced scorecard. Who are its stakeholders?
3. Define responsibility accounting. Why is it useful in performance evaluation?
4. Explain how Harley uses Performance Effectiveness Process (PEP) to link performance goals, objectives, measures, and targets. Why does this linking process improve the effectiveness of its performance management and evaluation system?

- **Financial (investors):** hourly lift cost, lift ticket sales in dollars and in units
- **Learning and growth (employees):** number of cross-trained tasks per employee, employee turnover
- **Internal business processes:** number of accident-free days, number and cost of mechanical breakdowns, average lift cycle time (that is, the time between getting in line to ride the ski lift and completing the ski run)
- **Customers:** average number of ski runs per daily lift ticket, number of repeat customers, number of PEAKS points redeemed

 **FOCUS ON BUSINESS PRACTICE**

How Many Stakeholder Groups Has Harley Identified?

Harley-Davidson, Inc., <www.harley-davidson.com> has identified not four but six stakeholder groups. In addition to balancing the needs of investors, employees, business processes, and customers, Harley managers also consider the interests of the community at large and government. Taking a broader perspective enables the company to sustain its competitive advantage and implement effective employee reward programs.[2]

Figure 1 summarizes the planning stage of the management cycle: Vail Resorts' managers link their organization's vision and strategy to objectives, then link the objectives to logical performance measures, and, finally, set performance targets. As a result, a ski lift manager will have a variety of performance measures that balance the perspectives and needs of all stakeholders.

■ **EXECUTING** Managers use the mutually agreed-on strategic objectives for the entire organization as the basis for decision making within their individual areas

FIGURE 1
Sample Balanced Scorecard of Linked Objectives, Performance Measures, and Targets

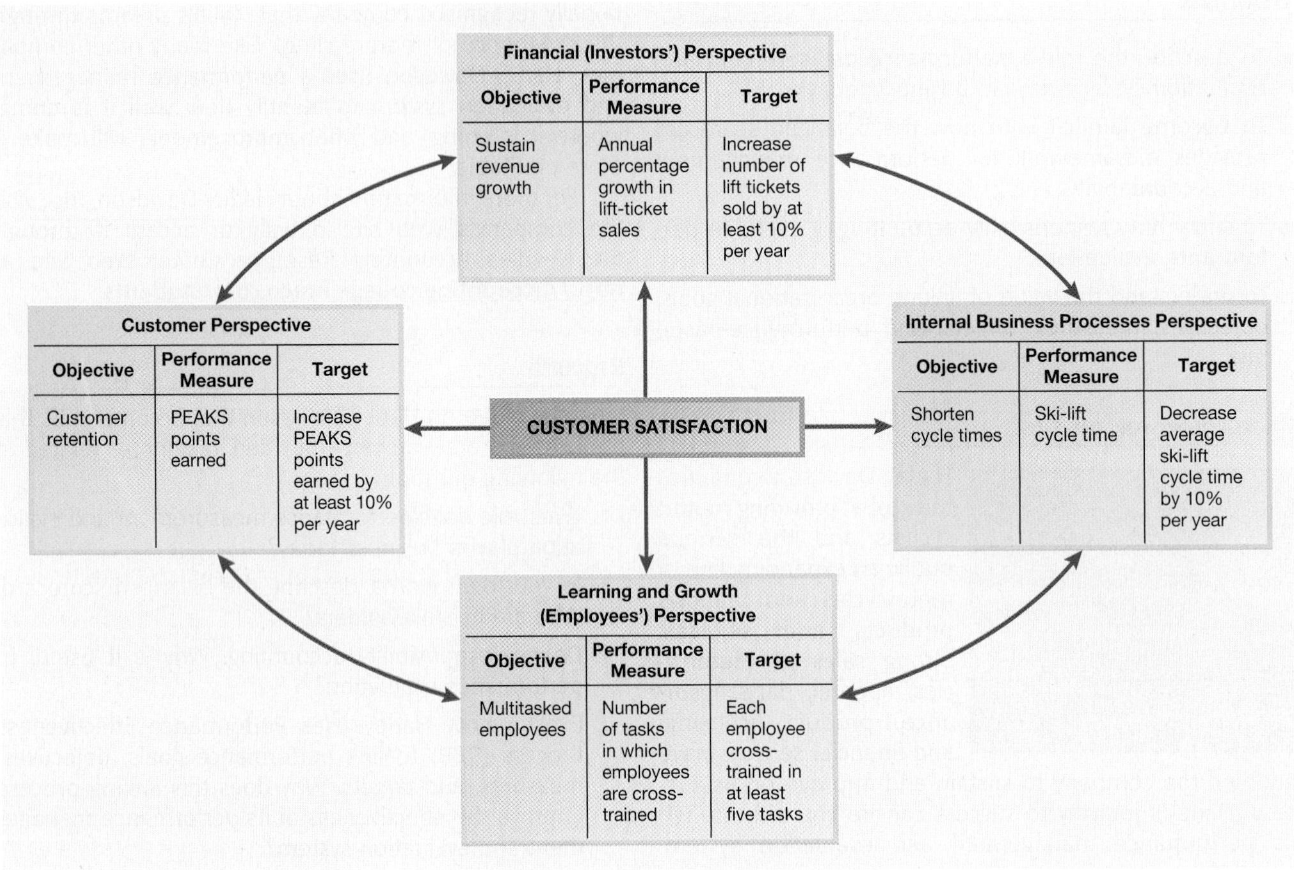

Source: Adapted from Robert S. Kaplan and David P. Norton, "Using the Balanced Scorecard as a Strategic Management System," *Harvard Business Review,* January–February 1996.

ENRICHMENT NOTE: If managers want results, they must understand the causal relationship between their actions and the organization's overall performance. If the relationship can be measured and tracked, it can be improved.

of responsibility. This practice ensures that they consider the needs of all stakeholder groups and how measuring and managing performance for some stakeholder groups can lead to improved performance for another stakeholder group. Specifically, improving performance of internal business processes and learning and growth will lead to improvements for customers, which in turn will result in improved financial performance. For example, when making decisions about available ski lift capacity, the ski lift manager at Vail Resorts will balance such factors as lift ticket sales, snow conditions, equipment reliability, trained staff availability, and length of wait for ski lifts.

When managers understand the causal and linked relationship between their actions and their company's overall performance, they can see new ways to be more effective. For example, a ski lift manager may hypothesize that short waiting lines for the ski lifts would improve customer satisfaction and lead to more visits to the ski lift. The manager could test this possible cause-and-effect relationship by measuring and tracking the length of ski lift waiting lines and the number of visits to the ski lift. If a causal relationship exists, the manager can improve the performance of the ski lift operation by doing everything possible to ensure that waiting lines are short because a quicker ride to the top will result in improved results for the operation and for other perspectives as well.

■ **REVIEWING** Managers will review financial and nonfinancial results frequently during the year, at year end, and over longer periods to evaluate their strategies in

FIGURE 2
The Balanced Scorecard and the Management Cycle

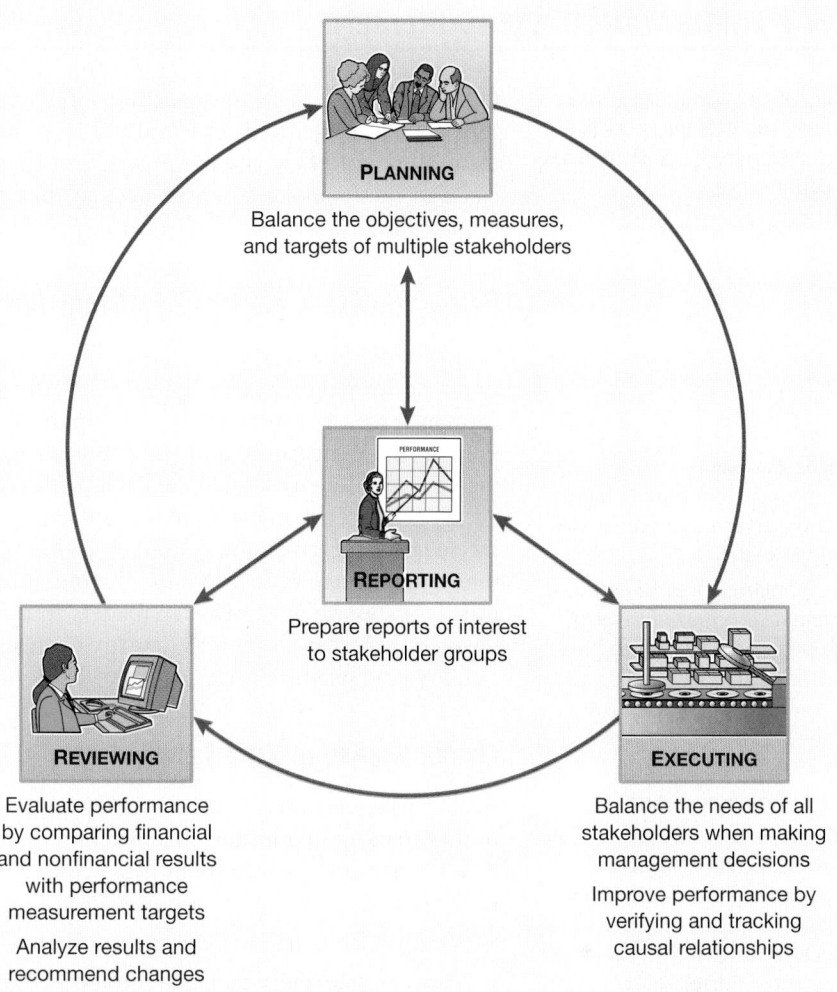

meeting the objectives and performance targets set during the planning stage. They will compare performance objectives and targets with actual results to determine if the targets were met, what measures need to be changed, and what strategies or objectives need revision. For example, the ski lift manager at Vail Resorts would analyze the reasons for performance gaps and make recommendations to improve the performance for the ski lift area.

■ **REPORTING**   Finally, during the reporting stage of the management cycle, a variety of reports are prepared. For example, the database makes it possible to prepare financial performance reports, customer PEAKS statements, internal business process reports for targeted performance measures and results, and performance appraisals of individual employees. Such reports enable managers to monitor and evaluate performance measures that add value for stakeholder groups.

As you can see in Figure 2, the balanced scorecard adds dimension to the management cycle. Managers plan, execute, review, and report on the organization's performance from multiple perspectives. By balancing the needs of all stakeholders, managers are more likely to achieve their objectives in both the short and the long terms.

 Check out ACE for a Review Quiz at http://accounting.college.hmco.com/students.

PERFORMANCE MEASUREMENT

LO2 Discuss performance measurement, and state the issues that affect management's ability to measure performance.

RELATED TEXT ASSIGNMENTS
Q: 5
E: 3, 4
SD: 1, 4, 5
MRA: 2, 3

As a company's management philosophy changes, so must the measures in its performance management and evaluation system. A **performance management and evaluation system** is a set of procedures that account for and report on both financial and nonfinancial performance, so that a company can identify how well it is doing, where it is going, and what improvements will make it more profitable.

WHAT TO MEASURE, HOW TO MEASURE

Performance measurement is the use of quantitative tools to gauge an organization's performance in relation to a specific goal or an expected outcome. For performance measurement to succeed, managers must be able to distinguish between what is being measured and the actual measures used to monitor performance. For instance, product or service quality is *not* a performance measure. It is part of a management strategy: management wants to produce the highest-quality product or service possible, given the resources available. Product or service quality thus is what management *wants* to measure. To measure product or service quality, managers must collaborate with other managers to develop a group of measures, such as the balanced scorecard, that will identify changes in product or service quality and help employees determine what needs to be done to improve quality.

● **STOP AND THINK!**
When managers make changes, should performance measures be reviewed?
Yes. Appropriate financial and nonfinancial performance measures are key to yielding the performance results managers want. ∎

OTHER MEASUREMENT ISSUES

STUDY NOTE: What a manager is measuring—for example, quality—is not the same as the actual measures—for example, the number of defective units per hour—used to monitor performance.

Each organization must develop a unique set of performance measures appropriate to its situation. In addition to answering the basic questions of what to measure and how to measure, management must consider a variety of other issues, including the following:

- What performance measures can be used?
- How can managers monitor the level of product or service quality?
- How can managers monitor production and other business processes to identify areas that need improvement?
- How can managers measure customer satisfaction?
- How can managers monitor financial performance?
- Are there other stakeholders to whom a manager is accountable?
- What performance measures do government entities impose on the company?
- How can a manager measure the company's effect on the environment?

FOCUS ON INTERNATIONAL BUSINESS

"Old" Doesn't Mean "Out-of-Date."

The *tableau de bord*, or "dashboard," was developed by French process engineers around 1900 as a concise performance measurement system that helped managers understand the cause-and-effect relationships between business actions and performance. The indicators, both financial and nonfinancial, allowed managers at any level to monitor their progress in terms of the mission and objectives of their unit and their company overall.

Like a set of nested Russian dolls, each unit's key success factors and key performance indicators were integrated with those of other units with which it was interdependent and needed to collaborate. The dashboard continues to encourage a performance measurement system that focuses on and supports an organization's strategic plan.[3]

  Check out ACE for a Review Quiz at http://accounting.college.hmco.com/students.

RESPONSIBILITY ACCOUNTING

LO3 Define *responsibility account-ing*, and describe the role that responsibility centers play in perform-ance management and evaluation.

RELATED TEXT ASSIGNMENTS
Q: 6, 7, 8, 9, 10, 11, 12
SE: 2, 3
E: 5, 6, 7
P: 1, 3, 7
SD: 2, 5
MRA: 2

● **STOP AND THINK!**

How should managers' per-formance be evaluated?

Evaluation should be based on how managers perform their assigned responsibilities. ■

As part of their performance management systems, many organizations assign resources to specific areas of responsibility and track how the managers of those areas use those resources. For example, DaimlerChrysler Corp. assigns resources to its Jeep, Eagle, and Mercedes automotive divisions and holds the managers of those divisions responsible for generating revenue and managing costs. In addition, the company may give the managers resources to invest in assets that will support the growth of their divisions. Within each division, other managers are assigned respon-sibility for such tasks as manufacturing subassemblies or assembling automobiles. All managers at all levels are then evaluated in terms of their ability to manage their areas of responsibility in keeping with organizational goals.

To assist in performance management and evaluation, many organizations use responsibility accounting. **Responsibility accounting** is an information system that classifies data according to areas of responsibility and reports each area's activities by including only the revenue, cost, and resource categories that the assigned man-ager can control. A **responsibility center** is an organizational unit whose manager has been assigned the responsibility of managing a portion of the organization's resources. The activity of a responsibility center dictates the extent of a manager's responsibility.

TYPES OF RESPONSIBILITY CENTERS

There are five types of responsibility centers: (1) cost centers, (2) discretionary cost centers, (3) revenue centers, (4) profit centers, and (5) investment centers.

■ **COST CENTERS** A responsibility center whose manager is accountable only for controllable costs that have well-defined relationships between the center's resources and products or services is called a **cost center**. Manufacturing companies

www.daimlerchrysler.com
www.apple.com
www.kraft.com

such as DaimlerChrysler, Apple Computer, and Kraft use cost centers to manage assembly plants, where the relationship between the costs of resources (direct mate-rial, direct labor) and the resulting products is well defined.

Nonmanufacturing organizations use cost centers to manage activities in which resources are clearly linked with a service provided at no additional charge. For example, in nursing homes and hospitals, there is a clear relationship between the costs of food and direct labor and the number of inpatient meals served.

The performance of a cost center is usually evaluated by comparing an activity's actual cost with its budgeted cost and analyzing the resulting variances. You may recall this performance evaluation process from the chapter on standard costing.

■ **DISCRETIONARY COST CENTERS** A responsibility center whose manager is account-able for costs only and in which the relationship between resources and products or services produced is not well defined is called a **discretionary cost center**. Units that perform administrative activities, such as accounting, human resources, and legal services, are typical examples of discretionary cost centers. These centers, like cost centers, have approved budgets that set spending limits.

Because the spending and use of resources in discretionary cost centers are not clearly linked to the production of a product or service, cost-based measures cannot usually be used to evaluate performance (although such centers are penalized if they exceed their approved budgets). For example, among the performance meas-ures used to evaluate the research and development activities at manufacturing

www.monsanto.com
www.intel.com

companies such as DaimlerChrysler, Monsanto, and Intel are the number of patents obtained and the number of cost-saving innovations that are developed. At service

national.unitedway.org
organizations, such as the United Way, a common measure of administrative activities is how low their costs are as a percentage of total contributions.

■ **REVENUE CENTERS**   A responsibility center whose manager is accountable primarily for revenue and whose success is based on its ability to generate revenue is called a **revenue center**. Examples of revenue centers are Hertz's national car reservation center and the clothing retailer Nordstrom's ecommerce order department. A revenue center's performance is usually evaluated by comparing its actual revenue with its budgeted revenue and analyzing the resulting variances. Performance measures at both manufacturing and service organizations may include sales dollars, number of customer sales, or sales revenue per minute.

www.hertz.com
www.nordstrom.com

■ **PROFIT CENTERS**   A responsibility center whose manager is accountable for both revenue and costs and for the resulting operating income is called a **profit center**. A good example is the local store of a national chain such as Wal-Mart, Kinko's, or Jiffy Lube. The performance of a profit center is usually evaluated by comparing the figures in its actual income statement with the figures in its master or flexible budget income statement. You may recall this type of comparison from our discussion in previous chapters.

www.walmart.com
www.kinkos.com
www.jiffylube.com

■ **INVESTMENT CENTERS**   A responsibility center whose manager is accountable for profit generation and can also make significant decisions about the resources the center uses is called an **investment center**. For example, the president of DaimlerChrysler's Jeep Division, the president of Harley-Davidson's Buell subsidiary, and the president of Brinker International's Chili's Grill and Bar Concept can control revenues, costs, and the investment of assets to achieve organizational goals. The performance of these centers is evaluated using such measures as return on investment, residual income, and economic value added. These measures are used in all types of organizations, both manufacturing and nonmanufacturing, and are discussed later in this chapter.

www.harley-davidson.com
www.brinker.com

The key characteristics of the five types of responsibility centers are summarized in Table 1.

ORGANIZATIONAL STRUCTURE AND PERFORMANCE MANAGEMENT

Much can be learned about an organization by examining how its managers organize activities and resources. A company's organizational structure formalizes its lines of managerial authority and control. An **organization chart** is a visual representation of an organization's hierarchy of responsibility for the purposes of management control. Within an organization chart, the five types of responsibility centers are arranged by level of management authority and control.

A responsibility accounting system establishes a communications network within an organization that is ideal for gathering and reporting information about the operations of each area of responsibility. The system is used to prepare budgets by responsibility area and to report the actual results of each responsibility center. The report for a responsibility center should contain only the costs, revenues, and resources that the manager of the center can control. Such costs and revenues are called **controllable costs and revenues** because they result from a manager's actions, influence, or decisions. A responsibility accounting system ensures that managers will not be held responsible for items they cannot change.

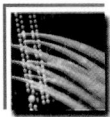

FOCUS ON BUSINESS TECHNOLOGY

Keep It Simple!

There is a new profession: information architect. An information architect develops meaningful ways to report information in print and on the web. In *Understanding USA*, Richard Saul Wurman and a team of twelve information architects have created a graph-rich book (downloadable at www.understandingusa.com and for sale in bookstores) that is the result of a $1 million project backed by many blue-chip organizations. The team's message to managers: Keep it simple. If you define what is important and what you can omit and if you stay honest, reporting information becomes simple.[4]

TABLE 1.   **Types of Responsibility Centers**

Responsibility Center	Manager Accountable For	How Performance Is Measured	Examples
Cost center	Only controllable costs; there are well-defined links between the costs of resources and the resulting products or services	Compare actual costs with flexible and master budget costs Analyze resulting variances	Product: Manufacturing assembly plants Service: Food service for hospital patients
Discretionary cost center	Only controllable costs; the links between the costs of resources and the resulting products or services are *not* well defined	Compare actual noncost-based measures with targets Determine compliance with preapproved budgeted spending limits	Product or service: Administrative activities such as accounting, human resources, and research and development
Revenue center	Revenue generation	Compare actual revenue with budgeted revenue Analyze resulting variances	Product: Phone or ecommerce sales for pizza delivery Service: National car rental reservation center
Profit center	Operating income resulting from controllable revenues and costs	Compare actual variable costing income statement with the budgeted income statement	Product or service: Local store of a national chain such as Wal-Mart <www.walmart.com>, Kinko's <www.kinkos.com>, or Jiffy Lube <www.jiffylube.com>
Investment center	Controllable revenues, costs, and the investment of resources to achieve organizational goals	Return on investment Residual income Economic value added	Product: Jeep Division of DaimlerChrysler <www.daimlerchrysler.com> Service: Chili's Grill and Bar Concept of Brinker International, Inc. <www.brinker.com>

www.brinker.com
www.vicorpinc.com

By examining a typical corporate organization chart, you can see how a responsibility accounting system works. Figure 3 shows part of the management structure for Café Cubano, a multiconcept restaurant chain like Brinker International, Inc., and Vicorp Restaurants. Typically, several vice presidents report to the president of a restaurant division like Chili's or Village Inn. Notice that the figure shows examples of all five types of responsibility centers. The office of Consuelo Jorges, the division president, is an investment center because capital investment decisions are made at the division level. The vice president–restaurants, Ruben Lopez, manages both profit and revenue centers. The vice president–administration, Manuel Segundo, supervises three discretionary cost centers, and the vice president–food products, Orlena Torres, is responsible for the operation of the central kitchen, a cost center.

In a responsibility accounting system, the performance reports for each level of management are tailored to each manager's individual needs for information. Because the system provides a report for every manager and because lower-level

FIGURE 3
Partial Organization Chart of Café Cubano, a Restaurant Chain

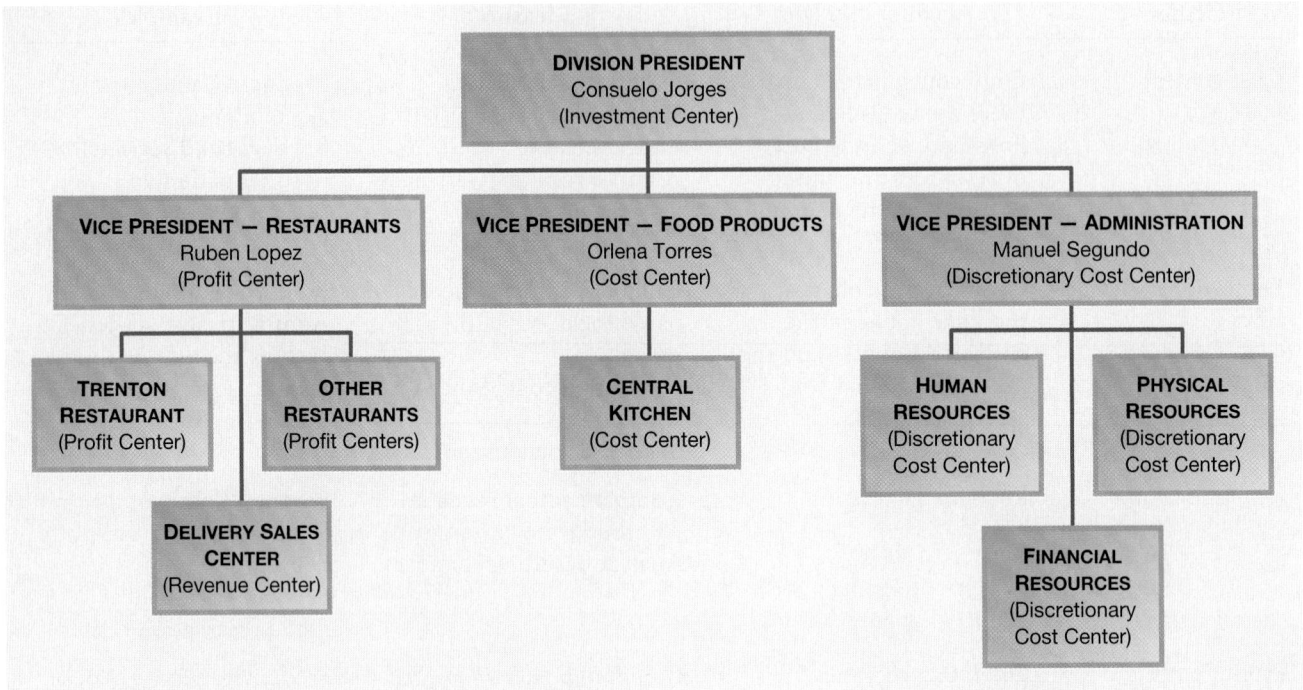

managers report to higher-level managers, the same information may appear in varying formats in several different reports. When information about lower-level operations appears in upper-level managers' reports, it is usually summarized and condensed. Performance reporting by responsibility level enables an organization to trace the source of a cost, revenue, or resource to the manager who controls it and to evaluate that manager's performance accordingly.

 Check out ACE for a Review Quiz at http://accounting.college.hmco.com/students.

PERFORMANCE EVALUATION OF COST CENTERS AND PROFIT CENTERS

LO4 Prepare performance reports for cost centers using flexible budgets and for profit centers using variable costing.

RELATED TEXT ASSIGNMENTS
Q: 13, 14, 15, 16
SE: 4, 5
E: 8, 9, 10, 11
P: 1, 2, 3, 6, 7
SD: 4, 5

KEY POINT: Only controllable items should be included on a manager's performance report.

Because performance reports contain information about costs, revenues, and resources that are controllable by individual managers, they allow comparisons between actual performance and budget expectations. Such comparisons allow management to evaluate an individual's performance with respect to responsibility center objectives and companywide objectives and to recommend changes. It is important to emphasize that performance reports should contain only costs, revenues, and resources that the manager can control. If a performance report includes items that the manager cannot control, the credibility of the entire responsibility accounting system can be called into question. It is up to management to structure and interpret the performance results fairly.

The content and format of a performance report depend on the nature of the responsibility center. Let us take a closer look at the performance reports for cost centers and profit centers.

EVALUATING COST CENTER PERFORMANCE USING FLEXIBLE BUDGETING

Orlena Torres, the vice president–food products at Café Cubano, is responsible for the central kitchen, where basic preparation is done on the food products the restaurants sell. The central kitchen is a cost center because its costs have well-

Exhibit 1
Central Kitchen's Performance Report on Café Cubano's House Dressing

	Actual Results	Variance	Flexible Budget	Variance	Master Budget
Gallons produced	1,200	0	1,200	200 (F)	1,000
Center costs					
Direct materials ($.25 per gallon)	$312	$12 (U)	$300	$50 (U)	$250
Direct labor ($.05 per gallon)	72	12 (U)	60	10 (U)	50
Variable overhead ($.03 per gallon)	33	3 (F)	36	6 (U)	30
Fixed overhead	2	3 (F)	5	0	5
Total cost	$419	$18 (U)	$401	$66 (U)	$335
Performance measures					
Defect-free gallons to total produced	.98	.01 (U)	N/A	N/A	.99
Average throughput time per gallon	11 minutes	1 minute (F)	N/A	N/A	12 minutes

● **STOP AND THINK!**
When is a flexible budget prepared?
A flexible budget is prepared at the end of the period, when performance results are evaluated. ■

defined relationships with the resulting products. To ensure that the central kitchen is meeting its performance goals, Torres has decided to evaluate the performance of each food item produced: she will prepare a separate report for each product that compares its actual costs with the corresponding amounts from the flexible and master budgets. The performance report for Café Cubano's House Dressing, one of the chain's signature menu items, is presented in Exhibit 1.

Recall that favorable (positive, or F) and unfavorable (negative, or U) variances between actual costs and the flexible budget can be further examined by using standard costing to compute specific variances for direct materials, direct labor, and variable and fixed overhead. Also, remember that the flexible budget is a cost control tool used to evaluate performance and is derived by multiplying actual unit output by the standard unit costs. Refer to the chapter on standard costing for further information on performance evaluation using variances or the flexible budget.

EVALUATING PROFIT CENTER PERFORMANCE USING VARIABLE COSTING

Ruben Lopez, the vice president–restaurants, oversees many restaurants. Because the restaurants are profit centers, each is accountable for its own revenues and costs and for the resulting operating income. A profit center's performance is usually evaluated by comparing its actual income statement results to its budgeted income statement.

Variable costing is a method of preparing profit center performance reports that classifies a manager's controllable costs as either variable or fixed. Variable costing produces a variable costing income statement instead of a traditional income statement (also called *full costing* or *absorption costing income statement*), which is used for external reporting purposes. A variable costing income statement is the same as a contribution income statement, the format of which you may recall from its use in cost-volume-profit analysis. Such an income statement is useful in performance management and evaluation because it focuses on cost variability and the profit center's contribution to operating income.

When variable costing is used to evaluate profit center performance, the variable cost of goods sold and the variable selling and administrative expenses are subtracted from sales to arrive at the contribution margin for the center. All controllable fixed costs of a profit center, including those from manufacturing, selling,

EXHIBIT 2
Variable Costing Income Statement Versus Traditional Income Statement for Trenton Restaurant

Variable Costing Income Statement		Traditional Income Statement	
Sales	$2,500	Sales	$2,500
Variable cost of good sold	1,575	Cost of goods sold	1,745
Variable selling expenses	325	(1,575 + $170 = $1,745)	
Contribution margin	$ 600	Gross margin	$ 755
Fixed manufacturing costs	170	Variable selling expenses	325
Fixed selling expenses	230	Fixed selling expenses	230
Profit center income	$ 200	Profit center income	$ 200

and administrative activities, are subtracted from the contribution margin to determine the operating income.

The variable costing income statement differs from the traditional income statement prepared for financial reporting, as shown by the two income statements in Exhibit 2 for Trenton Restaurant, part of the Café Cubano restaurant chain. In the traditional income statement, all manufacturing costs are assigned to cost of goods sold; in the variable costing income statement, only the variable manufacturing costs are included. Under variable costing, direct materials costs, direct labor costs, and variable manufacturing overhead costs are the only cost elements used to compute variable cost of goods sold. Fixed manufacturing costs are considered costs of the current accounting period. Notice that fixed manufacturing costs are listed with fixed selling expenses after the contribution margin has been computed.

The manager of a profit center may also want to measure and evaluate nonfinancial information. For example, Ruben Lopez of Café Cubano may want to track the number of food orders processed and the average amount of a sales order at Trenton Restaurant. The resulting report, based on variable costing and flexible budgeting, is shown in Exhibit 3.

EXHIBIT 3
Performance Report Based on Variable Costing and Flexible Budgeting for Trenton Restaurant

	Actual Results	Variance	Flexible Budget	Variance	Master Budget
Meals served	750	0	750	250 (U)	1,000
Sales (average meal $2.85)	$2,500.00	$362.50 (F)	$2,137.50	$712.50 (U)	$2,850.00
Controllable variable costs					
Variable cost of goods sold ($1.50)	1,575.00	450.00 (U)	1,125.00	375.00 (F)	1,500.00
Variable selling expenses ($.40)	325.00	25.00 (U)	300.00	100.00 (F)	400.00
Contribution margin	$ 600.00	$112.50 (U)	$ 712.50	$237.50 (U)	$ 950.00
Controllable fixed costs					
Fixed manufacturing	170.00	30.00 (F)	200.00	0.00	200.00
Fixed selling	230.00	20.00 (F)	250.00	0.00	250.00
Profit center income	$ 200.00	$ 62.50 (U)	$ 262.50	$237.50 (U)	$ 500.00
Other nonfinancial performance measures					
Number of orders processed	300	50 (F)	N/A		250
Average sales order	$8.34	$3.06 (U)	N/A		$11.40

FOCUS ON BUSINESS ETHICS

Soundproofing with Blue Jeans

In Saarlouis, Germany, old blue jeans have found a new use as sound-deadening material in Ford Motor Company <www.ford.com> cars. Because of Ford's ethical recycling practices, old jeans are shredded, treated, and bonded before they are packed under the hood of every Ford Focus car produced in Ford's German manufacturing facility. What inventive recycling![5]

Although performance reports vary in format depending on the type of responsibility center, they have some common themes. For example, all responsibility center reports compare actual results to budgeted figures and focus on the differences. Often, comparisons are made to a flexible budget as well as to the master budget. Only the items that the manager can control are included in the performance report. Nonfinancial measures are also examined to achieve a more balanced view of the manager's responsibilities.

 Check out ACE for a Review Quiz at http://accounting.college.hmco.com/students.

PERFORMANCE EVALUATION OF INVESTMENT CENTERS

LO5 Prepare performance reports for investment centers using traditional measures of return on investment and residual income and the newer measure of economic value added.

RELATED TEXT ASSIGNMENTS
Q: 17, 18, 19
SE: 6, 7, 8, 9
E: 12, 13
P: 3, 4, 5, 7, 8
SD: 3
MRA: 3, 4

The evaluation of an investment center's performance requires more than a comparison of controllable revenues and costs with budgeted amounts. Because the managers of investment centers also control resources and invest in assets, other performance measures must be used to hold them accountable for revenues, costs, and the capital investments they control. In this section, we focus on the traditional performance evaluation measures of return on investment and residual income and the relatively new performance measure of economic value added.

RETURN ON INVESTMENT

Traditionally, the most common performance measure that takes into account both operating income and the assets invested to earn that income is **return on investment (ROI)**. Return on investment is computed as follows:

$$\text{Return on Investment (ROI)} = \frac{\text{Operating Income}}{\text{Assets Invested}}$$

In this formula, *assets invested* is the average of the beginning and ending asset balances for the period.

Properly measuring the income and the assets specifically controlled by a manager is critical to the quality of this performance measure. Using ROI, it is possible to evaluate the manager of any investment center, whether it is an entire company or a unit within a company, such as a subsidiary, division, or other business segment. For example, assume that the Café Cubano Restaurant Division had actual operating income of $610 and that the average assets invested were $800. The master budget called for $890 in operating income and $1,000 in invested assets. As shown in Exhibit 4, the budgeted ROI for Consuelo Jorges, the president of the division,

EXHIBIT 4
Performance Report Based on Return on Investment for the Café Cubano Restaurant Division

	Actual Results	Variance	Master Budget
Operating income	$610	$280 (U)	$ 890
Assets invested	$800	$200 (F)	$1,000
Performance measure			
ROI	76%	13% (U)	89%

ROI = Operating Income ÷ Assets Invested
    $890 ÷ $1,000 = .89 = 89%
    $610 ÷ $800 = .76 = 76%

would be 89 percent, and the actual ROI would be 76 percent. The actual ROI was lower than the budgeted ROI because the division's actual operating income was lower than expected relative to the actual assets invested.

For investment centers, the ROI computation is really the aggregate measure of many interrelationships. The basic ROI equation, Operating Income ÷ Assets Invested, can be rewritten to show the many elements a manager can influence within the aggregate ROI number. Two important indicators of performance are profit margin and asset turnover. **Profit margin** is the ratio of operating income to sales; it represents the percentage of each sales dollar that results in profit. **Asset turnover** is the ratio of sales to average assets invested; it indicates the productivity of assets, or the number of sales dollars generated by each dollar invested in assets. Return on investment is equal to profit margin multiplied by asset turnover:

KEY POINT: Profit margin focuses on the income statement, and asset turnover focuses on the balance sheet aspects of ROI.

$$ROI = Profit\ Margin \times Asset\ Turnover$$

or

$$ROI = \frac{Operating\ Income}{Sales} \times \frac{Sales}{Assets\ Invested} = \frac{Operating\ Income}{Assets\ Invested}$$

Profit margin and asset turnover help to explain changes in ROI for a single investment center or differences of ROI among investment centers. Therefore, the formula ROI = Profit Margin × Asset Turnover is useful for analyzing and interpreting the elements that make up a business's overall return on investment.

www.dupont.com

DuPont, one of the first organizations to recognize the many interrelationships that affect ROI, designed a formula similar to the one diagrammed in Figure 4. You can see that ROI is affected by a manager's decisions about pricing, product sales mix, capital budgeting for new facilities, product sales volume, and other financial matters. In essence, a single ROI number is a composite index of many cause-and-effect relationships and interdependent financial elements. A manager can improve ROI by increasing sales, decreasing costs, or decreasing assets.

Because of the many factors that affect ROI, management should use this measure cautiously in evaluating performance. If ROI is overemphasized, investment center managers may react with business decisions that favor their personal ROI performance at the expense of companywide profits or the long-term success of other investment centers. To avoid such problems, other performance measures should always be used in conjunction with ROI—for example, comparisons of revenues, costs, and operating income with budget amounts or past trends; sales growth percentages; market share percentages; or other key variables in the organization's activity. ROI should also be compared with budgeted goals and with past ROI trends because changes in this ratio over time can be more revealing than any single number.

RESIDUAL INCOME

Because of the pitfalls of using ROI as a performance measure, other approaches to evaluating investment centers have evolved. For example, companies such as General Motors, General Electric, Coca-Cola, and UPS now use residual income to measure performance. **Residual income** (RI) is the operating income that an investment center earns above a minimum desired return on invested assets. Residual income is not a ratio but a dollar amount: the amount of profit left after subtracting a predetermined desired income target for an investment center. The formula for computing the residual income of an investment center is:

www.gm.com
www.ge.com
www.coca-cola.com
www.ups.com

$$Residual\ Income = Operating\ Income - (Desired\ ROI \times Assets\ Invested)$$

As in the computation of ROI, assets invested is the average of the center's beginning and ending asset balances for the period.

KEY POINT: ROI is expressed as a percentage, and residual income is expressed in dollars.

The desired RI will vary from investment center to investment center depending on the type of business and the level of risk assumed. The performance report

FIGURE 4
Factors That Affect the Return on Investment Calculation

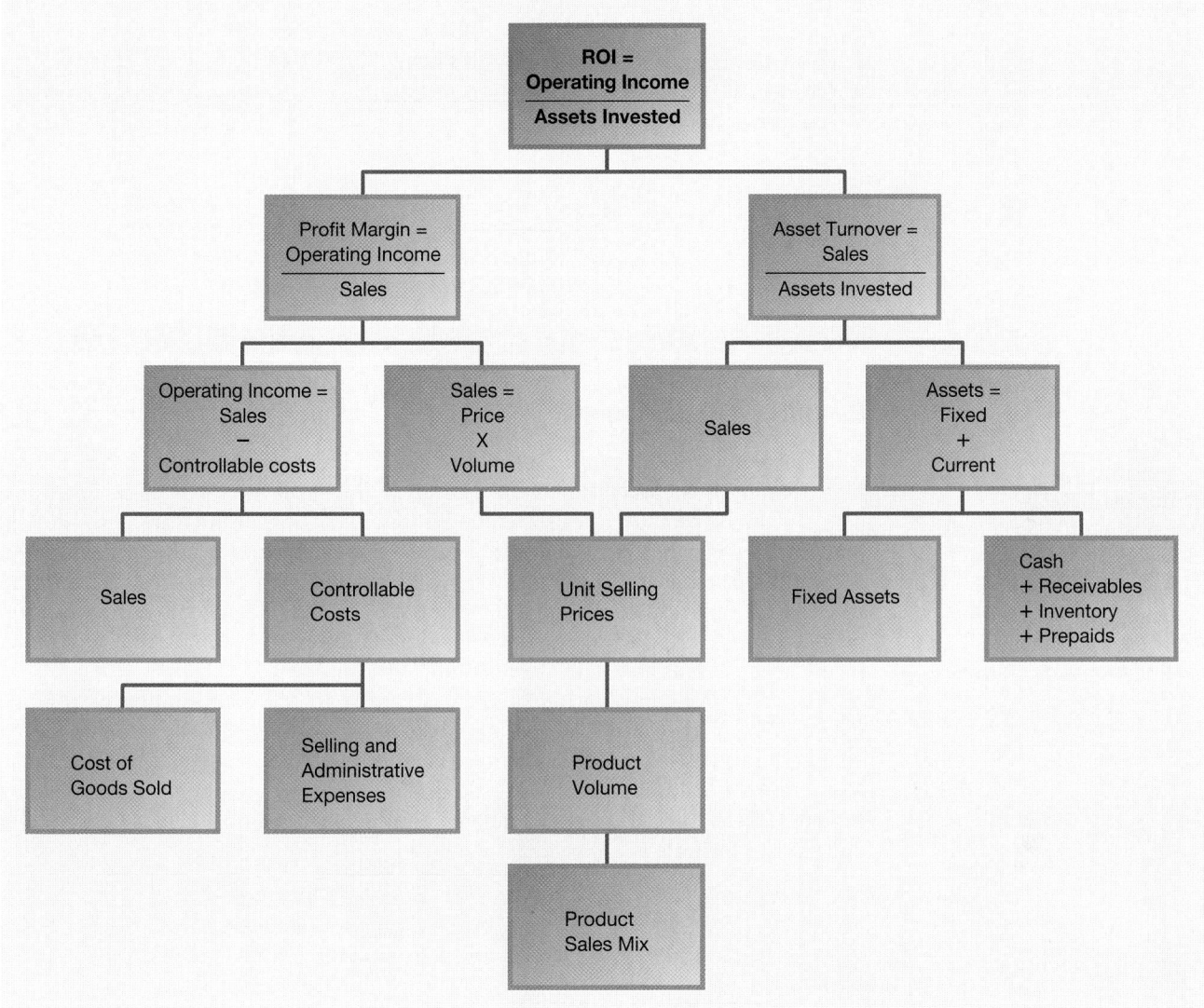

based on residual income for Consuelo Jorges, the president of the Café Cubano Restaurant Division, is shown in Exhibit 5. Assume that the president's residual income performance target is to exceed a 20 percent return on assets invested in the division. Note that the division's residual income is $450, which was lower than the $690 projected in the master budget.

Comparisons with other residual income figures will strengthen the analysis. To add context to the analysis of the division and its manager, questions such as the following need to be answered: How did the division's residual income for this year compare to those of previous years? Did the actual residual income exceed the budgeted residual income? How did this division's residual income compare with amounts generated by other investment centers of the company?

Caution is called for when using residual income to compare investment centers within a company. For their residual income figures to be comparable, all investment centers must have equal access to resources and similar asset investment bases. Some managers may be able to produce larger residual incomes simply because their investment centers are larger rather than because their performance is better. Like ROI, RI has some flaws.

EXHIBIT 5
Performance Report Based on Residual Income for the Café Cubano Restaurant Division

	Actual Results	Variance	Master Budget
Operating income	$610	$280 (U)	$ 890
Assets invested	$800	$200 (F)	$1,000
Desired ROI			20%
Performance measures			
ROI	76%	13% (U)	89%
Residual income	$450	$240 (U)	$ 690

Residual Income = Operating Income − (Desired ROI × Assets Invested)
$$\$890 - 20\%(\$1,000) = \$690$$
$$\$610 - 20\%(\$800) = \$450$$

ECONOMIC VALUE ADDED

STOP AND THINK!
When is the EVA a complex measure?
EVA is complex because it is a composite index drawn from many causal relationships and independent financial elements. ■

More and more businesses are using the shareholder wealth created by an investment center, or the **economic value added (EVA)**, as an indicator of performance. The calculation of EVA, a registered trademark of the consulting firm Stern Stewart & Company, can be quite complex because it makes various cost of capital and accounting principles adjustments. You will learn more about the cost of capital in the chapter that discusses capital investment decisions. However, for the purposes of computing EVA, the **cost of capital** is the minimum desired rate of return on an investment, such as assets invested in an investment center.

Basically, the computation of EVA is similar to the computation of residual income, except that after-tax operating income is used instead of pretax operating income, and a cost of capital percentage is multiplied by the center's invested assets less current liabilities instead of a desired ROI percentage being multiplied by invested assets. Also, like residual income, the economic value added is expressed in dollars. The formula is:

$$\text{EVA} = \text{After-Tax Operating Income} - \text{Cost of Capital in Dollars}$$

or

$$\text{EVA} = \text{After-Tax Operating Income} - [\text{Cost of Capital} \times (\text{Total Assets} - \text{Current Liabilities})]$$

A very basic computation of economic value added for Consuelo Jorges, the president of the Café Cubano Restaurant Division, is shown in Exhibit 6. The report

EXHIBIT 6
Performance Report Based on Economic Value Added for the Café Cubano Restaurant Division

	Actual Results	Variance	Master Budget
Performance measures			
ROI	76%	13% (U)	89%
Residual income	$450	$240 (U)	$690
Economic value added	$334		

Economic Value Added = After-Tax Operating Income − [Cost of Capital × (Total Assets − Current Liabilities)]
$$\$400 - 12\%(\$800 - \$250) = \$334$$

Figure 5

Factors Affecting the Computation of Economic Value Added

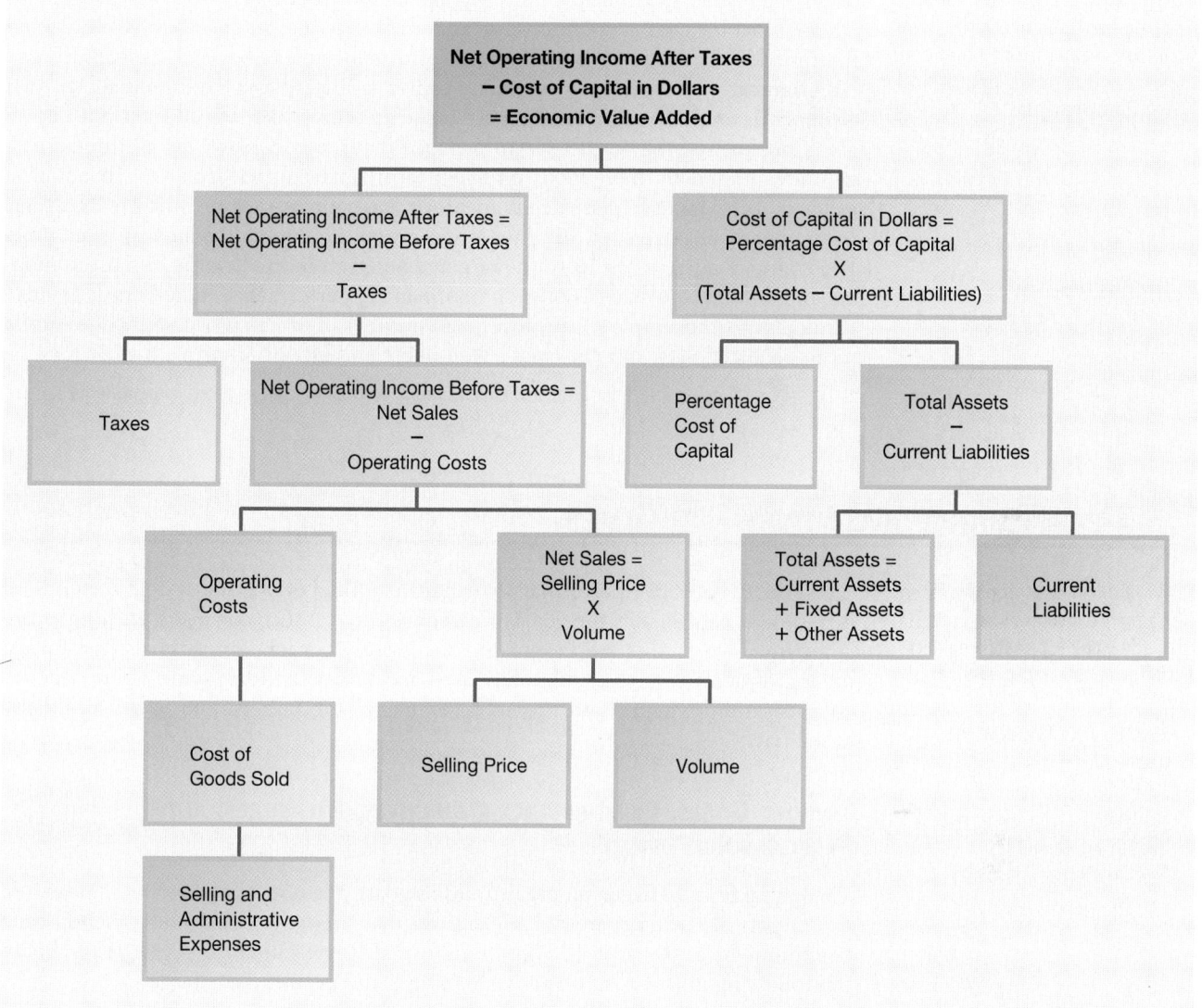

assumes that the division's after-tax operating income is $400, its cost of capital is 12 percent, its total assets are $800, and its current liabilities are $250.

The report shows that the division has added $334 to its economic value after taxes and cost of capital. In other words, the division produced after-tax profits of $334 in excess of the cost of capital required to generate those profits.

Because many factors affect the economic value of an investment center, management should be cautious when drawing conclusions about performance. The evaluation will be more meaningful if the current economic value added is compared to EVAs from previous periods, target EVAs, and EVAs from other investment centers.

The factors that affect the computation of economic value added are illustrated in Figure 5. An investment center's economic value is affected by managers' decisions on pricing, product sales volume, taxes, cost of capital, capital investments, and other financial decisions. In essence, the EVA number is a composite index drawn from many cause-and-effect relationships and interdependent financial elements. A manager can improve the economic value of an investment center by increasing sales, decreasing costs, decreasing assets, or lowering the cost of capital.

THE IMPORTANCE OF MULTIPLE PERFORMANCE MEASURES

KEY POINT: Using multiple measures of both financial and nonfinancial performance over time presents a more balanced view of a business's health and how to improve it.

In summary, to be effective, a performance management system must consider both operating results and multiple performance measures, such as return on investment, residual income, and economic value added. Comparing actual results to budgeted figures adds meaning to the evaluation. Performance measures such as ROI, RI, and EVA indicate whether an investment center is effective in coordinating its own goals with companywide goals because those measures take into account both operating income and the assets used to produce that income. However, all three measures are limited by their focus on short-term financial performance. To obtain a fuller picture, management needs to break these three measures down into their components, analyze such information as responsibility center income over time, and compare current results to the targeted amounts in the flexible or master budgets. In addition, the analysis of such nonfinancial performance indicators as average throughput time, employee turnover, and number of orders processed will ensure a more balanced view of a business's well-being and how to improve it.

 Check out ACE for a Review Quiz at http://accounting.college.hmco.com/students.

PERFORMANCE INCENTIVES AND GOALS

LO6 Explain how properly linked performance incentives and measures add value for all stakeholders in performance management and evaluation.

RELATED TEXT ASSIGNMENTS
Q: 20
SE: 10
E: 14, 15
SD: 4, 5
MRA: 3, 5

The effectiveness of a performance management and evaluation system depends on how well it coordinates the goals of responsibility centers, managers, and the entire company. Two factors are key to the successful coordination of goals: the logical linking of goals to measurable objectives and targets and the tying of appropriate compensation incentives to the achievement of the targets, that is, performance-based pay.

LINKING GOALS, PERFORMANCE OBJECTIVES, MEASURES, AND PERFORMANCE TARGETS

www.bms.com
www.shell.com

KEY POINT: The causal links between an organization's goals, objectives, measures, performance targets, and compensation incentives must be easy to understand.

The causal links between an organization's goals, performance objectives, measures, and targets must be apparent. For example, if a company seeks to be a friend of the environment, as do Bristol-Myers Squibb and Royal Dutch/Shell,[6] it may choose the following linked goal, objective, measure, and performance target:

Goal	Objective	Measure	Performance Target
To be a friend of the environment	To reduce the company's environmental risk	Number of products recycled	To recycle at least 10 percent of products sold

You may recall that the balanced scorecard also links objectives, measures, and targets, as shown in Figure 1 earlier in this chapter.

PERFORMANCE-BASED PAY

www.daimlerchrysler.com

The tying of appropriate compensation incentives to performance targets increases the likelihood that the goals of responsibility centers, managers, and the entire organization will be well coordinated. Unfortunately, this linkage does not always happen. A 1999 survey by AnswerThink reported that only 58 percent of companies link bonuses, merit pay increases, and profit sharing to the measurable performance of strategic and tactical plans.[7] Responsibility center managers are more likely to achieve their performance targets if their compensation depends on it. **Performance-based pay** is the linking of employee compensation to the achievement of measurable business targets. For example, at DaimlerChrysler, all 132,000

German factory employees are eligible for some type of performance-based pay, such as cash bonuses, profit sharing, or stock options.[8]

Cash bonuses, awards, profit-sharing plans, and stock option programs are common types of incentive compensation. Cash bonuses are usually given to reward an individual's short-term performance. A bonus may be stated as a fixed dollar amount or as a percentage of a target figure, such as 5 percent of operating income or 10 percent of the dollar increase in operating income. An award may be a trip or some other form of recognition for desirable individual or group performance. For example, many companies sponsor a trip for all managers who have met their performance targets during a specified period. Other companies award incentive points that employees may redeem for goods or services. (Notice that awards can be used to encourage both short-term and long-term performance.) Profit-sharing plans reward employees with a share of the company's profits. Employees often receive company stock as recognition of their contribution to a profitable period. Using stock as a reward encourages employees to think and act as investors as well as employees and encourages a stable work force. In terms of the balanced scorecard, they assume two stakeholder perspectives and take both a short- and a long-term viewpoint. Stock options give individual employees the right to purchase a certain number of shares at a specific price within a certain period. Companies use stock options to motivate employees to achieve financial targets that increase the company's stock price. Managers like stock options because the options enable them to realize a profit if the actual stock price rises above their granted option price. Stock options usually have specific performance requirements attached to them. Because many of the variables that affect stock price are beyond a manager's control, stock options may not be the best way to promote the coordination of goals.

THE COORDINATION OF GOALS

KEY POINT: Not all businesses have comparable approaches to performance-based pay. Rather, each business will design a compensation program specific to the achievement of its organizational goals.

What performance incentives and measures should a company use to manage and evaluate performance? What actions and behaviors should an organization reward? Which incentive compensation plans work best? The answers to such questions depend on the facts and circumstances of each organization. What promotes the coordination of goals for one organization may not do so for another. To be effective, incentive plans must be developed with input from all employees. All must understand the causal links between goals, objectives, measures, and performance targets. To determine the right performance incentives for their organization, employees and managers must answer several questions:

- When should the reward occur: now or sometime in the future?
- Whose performance should be rewarded: that of responsibility centers, individual managers, or the entire company?
- How should the reward be computed?
- On what should the reward be based?
- What performance criteria should be used?
- Does our performance incentive plan address the interests of all stakeholders?

 STOP AND THINK!
Which performance incentives work best?
Which incentives work best depends on the facts and circumstances of each organization. ■

The effectiveness of a performance management and evaluation system relies on the coordination of responsibility center, managerial, and company goals. Performance can be optimized by linking goals to measurable objectives and targets and by tying appropriate compensation incentives to the achievement of the targets. Common types of incentive compensation are cash bonuses, awards, profit-sharing plans, and stock option programs. Each organization's unique circumstances will determine its correct mix of measures and compensation incentives. If management values the perspectives of all of its stakeholder groups, its performance management and evaluation system will balance and benefit all interests.

Check out ACE for a Review Quiz at http://accounting.college.hmco.com/students.

Chapter Review

REVIEW OF LEARNING OBJECTIVES

LO1 Describe how the balanced scorecard aligns performance with organizational goals, and explain the role of the balanced scorecard in the management cycle.

The balanced scorecard is a framework that links the perspectives of an organization's four basic stakeholder groups—financial, learning and growth, internal business processes, and customers—with its mission and vision, performance measures, strategic plan, and resources. Ideally, managers should see how their actions help to achieve organizational goals and understand how their compensation is linked to their actions. The balanced scorecard assumes that an organization will get what it measures.

LO2 Discuss performance measurement, and state the issues that affect management's ability to measure performance.

An effective performance measurement system accounts for and reports on both financial and nonfinancial performance so an organization can ascertain how well it is doing, where it is going, and what improvements will make it more profitable. Each organization must develop a unique set of performance measures appropriate to its specific situation. Besides answering basic questions about what to measure and how to measure, management must consider a variety of other issues. Managers must collaborate to develop a group of measures, such as the balanced scorecard, that will help them determine how to improve performance.

LO3 Define *responsibility accounting,* and describe the role that responsibility centers play in performance management and evaluation.

Responsibility accounting classifies data according to areas of responsibility and reports each area's activities by including only the revenue, cost, and resource categories that the assigned manager can control. There are five types of responsibility centers: cost, discretionary cost, revenue, profit, and investment. Performance reporting by responsibility center allows the source of a cost, revenue, or resource to be traced to the manager who controls it and thus makes it easier to evaluate a manager's performance.

LO4 Prepare performance reports for cost centers using flexible budgets and for profit centers using variable costing.

Performance reports contain information about costs, revenues, and resources that individual managers can control. The content and format of a performance report depend on the nature of the responsibility center. The performance of a cost center may be evaluated by comparing its actual costs with the corresponding amounts in the flexible and master budgets. A flexible budget is derived by multiplying actual unit output by predetermined standard unit costs for each cost item in the report. The resulting variances between actual costs and the flexible budget can be examined further by using standard costing to compute specific variances for direct materials, direct labor, and overhead. A profit center's performance is usually evaluated by comparing its actual income statement results to its budgeted income statement. When variable costing is used, the profit center manager's controllable costs are classified as variable or fixed. The resulting performance report takes the form of a contribution income statement instead of a traditional income statement. The variable costing income statement is useful because it focuses on cost variability and the profit center's contribution to operating income.

LO5 Prepare performance reports for investment centers using traditional measures of return on investment and residual income and the newer measure of economic value added.

Traditionally, the most common performance measure is return on investment (ROI). Its basic formula is ROI = Operating Income ÷ Assets Invested. Return on investment may also be examined in terms of profit margin and asset turnover. In that case, ROI = Profit Margin × Asset Turnover, where Profit Margin = Operating Income ÷ Sales and Asset Turnover = Sales ÷ Assets Invested. Residual income (RI) is the operating income that an investment center earns above a minimum desired return on invested assets. It is expressed as a dollar amount: Residual Income = Operating Income − (Desired ROI × Assets Invested). It is the amount of profit left after subtracting a predetermined desired income target for an investment. Today, businesses are increasingly using the shareholder wealth created by an investment center, or economic value added (EVA), as a performance measure. The calculation of economic value added can be quite complex because it is a composite of many cause-and-effect relationships and interdependent financial elements. Basically, the concept of economic value added is similar to residual income. EVA = After-Tax Operating Income − Cost of Capital (expressed in dollars). A manager can improve the economic value of an investment center by increasing sales, decreasing costs, decreasing assets, or lowering the cost of capital.

LO6 Explain how properly linked performance incentives and measures add value for all stakeholders in performance management and evaluation.

The effectiveness of a performance management and evaluation system depends on how well it coordinates the goals of responsibility centers, managers, and the entire company. Performance can be optimized by linking goals to measurable objectives and targets and tying appropriate compensation incentives to the achievement of those targets. Common types of incentive compensation are cash bonuses, awards, profit-sharing plans, and stock option programs. Each organization's unique circumstances will determine its correct mix of measures and compensation incentives. If management values the perspectives of all of its stakeholder groups, its performance management and evaluation system will balance and benefit all interests.

REVIEW OF CONCEPTS AND TERMINOLOGY

The following concepts and terms were introduced in this chapter:

LO5 **Asset turnover:** The productivity of assets, or the number of sales dollars generated by each dollar invested in assets; Sales ÷ Assets Invested.

LO1 **Balanced scorecard:** A framework that links the perspectives of an organization's four basic stakeholder groups—financial (investors), learning and growth (employees), internal business processes, and customers—with the organization's mission and vision, performance measures, strategic plan, and resources.

LO3 **Controllable costs and revenues:** Costs and revenues that result from a manager's actions, influence, or decisions.

LO3 **Cost center:** A responsibility center whose manager is accountable only for controllable costs that have well-defined relationships between the center's resources and products or services.

LO5 **Cost of capital:** The minimum desired rate of return on an investment, such as assets invested in an investment center.

LO3 **Discretionary cost center:** A responsibility center whose manager is accountable for costs only and in which the relationship between resources and products or services produced is not well defined.

LO5 **Economic value added (EVA):** The shareholder wealth created by an investment center; Economic Value Added = After-Tax Operating Income − Cost of Capital in Dollars.

LO3 **Investment center:** A responsibility center whose manager is accountable for profit generation and can also make significant decisions about the resources the center uses.

LO3 **Organization chart:** A visual representation of an organization's hierarchy of responsibility for the purposes of management control.

LO6 **Performance-based pay:** The linking of employee compensation to the achievement of measurable business targets.

LO2 **Performance management and evaluation system:** A set of procedures that account for and report on both financial and nonfinancial performance, so that a company can identify how well it is doing, where it is going, and what improvements will make it more profitable.

LO2 **Performance measurement:** The use of quantitative tools to gauge an organization's performance in relation to a specific goal or an expected outcome.

LO3 **Profit center:** A responsibility center whose manager is accountable for both revenue and costs and for the resulting operating income.

LO5 **Profit margin:** The percentage of each sales dollar that results in profit; Operating Income ÷ Sales.

LO5 **Residual income (RI):** The operating income that an investment center earns above a minimum desired return on invested assets; Residual Income = Investment Center's Operating Income − (Desired ROI × Assets Invested).

LO3 **Responsibility accounting:** An information system that classifies data according to areas of responsibility and reports each area's activities by including only the revenue, cost, and resource categories that the assigned manager can control.

LO3   Responsibility center: An organizational unit whose manager has been assigned the responsibility of managing a portion of the organization's resources. The five most common forms of responsibility center are cost centers, discretionary cost centers, revenue centers, profit centers, and investment centers.

LO5   Return on investment (ROI): A traditional performance measure that takes into account both operating income and the assets invested to produce that income; ROI = Operating Income ÷ Assets Invested. ROI can also be expressed as Profit Margin × Asset Turnover.

LO3   Revenue center: A responsibility center whose manager is accountable primarily for revenue and whose success is based on its ability to generate revenue.

LO4   Variable costing: A method of preparing profit center performance reports that classifies a manager's controllable costs as either fixed or variable and produces a contribution income statement.

REVIEW PROBLEM

Evaluating Profit Center and Investment Center Performance

**LO3
LO4
LO5**   Winter Wonderland is a full-service resort and spa. Mary Fortenberry, the resort's general manager, is responsible for guest activities, administration, and food and lodging. In addition, she is solely responsible for the resort's capital investments. The organization chart below shows the resort's various activities and the levels of authority that Fortenberry has established:

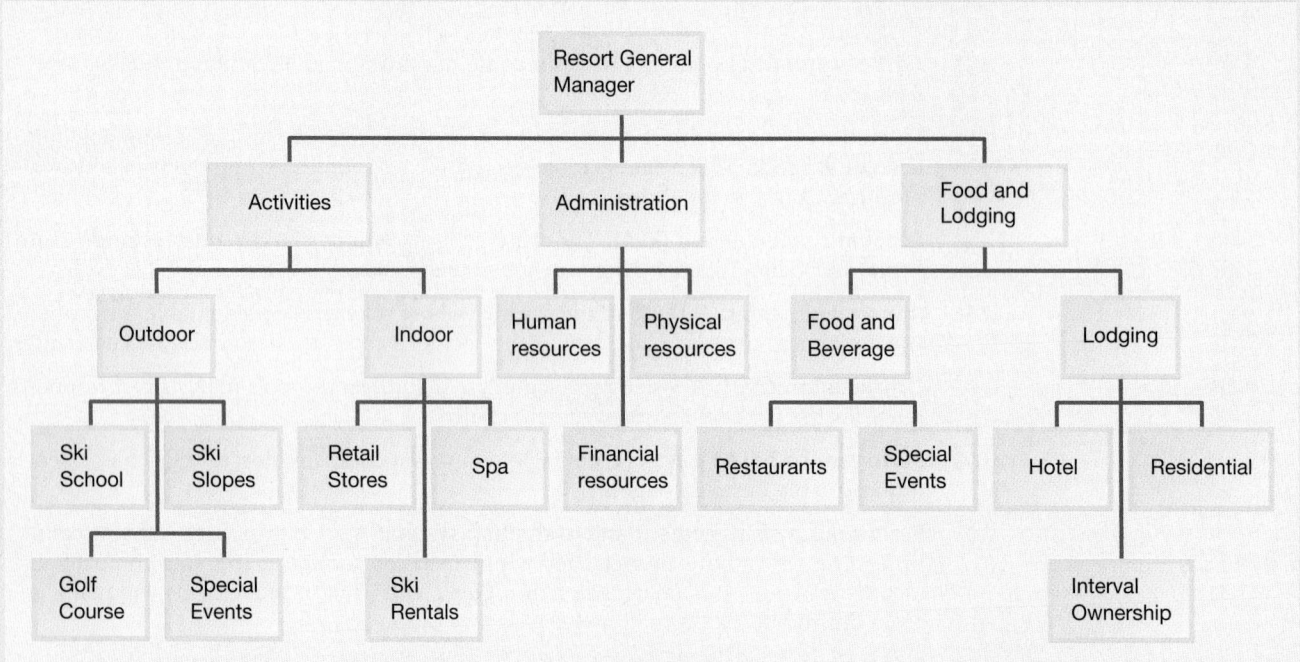

Three divisional managers receive compensation based on their division's performance and have authority to make employee compensation decisions for their division. Alexandra Patel manages the Food and Lodging Division. That division's master budget and actual results for the year ended June 30, 20x8, appear at the top of the opposite page.

REQUIRED ▶

1. What types of responsibility centers are Administration, Food and Lodging, and Resort General Manager?
2. Assume Food and Lodging is a profit center. Prepare a performance report using variable costing and flexible budgeting. Determine the variances between actual results and the corresponding figures in the flexible budget and the master budget.
3. Assume that the divisional managers have been assigned responsibility for capital expenditures and that their divisions are thus investment centers. Food and Lodging

Winter Wonderland
Food and Lodging Division
For the Year Ended June 30, 20x8
(Dollar amounts in thousands)

	Master Budget	Actual Results
Guest days	4,000	4,100
Sales	$38,000	$40,000
Variable cost of sales	24,000	25,000
Variable selling and administrative expenses	4,000	4,250
Fixed cost of sales	2,000	1,800
Fixed selling and administrative expenses	2,500	2,500

is expected to generate a desired ROI of at least 30 percent on average assets invested of $10,000,000.

   a. Compute the division's return on investment and residual income using the average assets invested in both the actual and the budget calculations.
   b. Using the ROI and residual income, evaluate Alexandra Patel's performance as divisional manager.

4. Compute the division's actual economic value added if the division's assets are $12,000,000, current liabilities are $3,000,000, after-tax operating income is $4,500,000, and the cost of capital is 20 percent.

ANSWER TO REVIEW PROBLEM

1. Administration: discretionary cost center; Food and Lodging: profit center; Resort General Manager: investment center.
2. Performance report:

Winter Wonderland
Food and Lodging Division
For the Year Ended June 30, 20x8
(Dollar amounts in thousands)

	Actual Results	Variance	Flexible Budget	Variance	Master Budget
Guest days	4,100	0	4,100	100 (F)	4,000
Sales	$40,000	$1,050 (F)	$38,950	$950 (F)	$38,000
Controllable variable costs					
Variable cost of sales	25,000	400 (U)	24,600	600 (U)	24,000
Variable selling and administrative expenses	4,250	150 (U)	4,100	100 (U)	4,000
Contribution margin	$10,750	$ 500 (F)	$10,250	$250 (F)	$10,000
Controllable fixed costs					
Fixed cost of sales	1,800	200 (F)	2,000	0	2,000
Fixed selling and administrative expenses	2,500	0	2,500	0	2,500
Division operating income	$ 6,450	$ 700 (F)	$ 5,750	$250 (F)	$ 5,500

3. a. **Return on investment**
      Actual results: $6,450,000 ÷ $10,000,000 = 64.50%
      Flexible budget: $5,750,000 ÷ $10,000,000 = 57.50%
      Master budget: $5,500,000 ÷ $10,000,000 = 55.00%

    Residual income
      Actual results: $6,450,000 − 30%($10,000,000) = $3,450,000
      Flexible budget: $5,750,000 − 30%($10,000,000) = $2,750,000
      Master budget: $5,500,000 − 30%($10,000,000) = $2,500,000

   b. Alexandra Patel's performance as the divisional manager of Food and Lodging exceeds company performance expectations. Actual ROI was 64.5 percent, whereas the company expected an ROI of 30 percent and the flexible budget and the master budget showed projections of 57.5 percent and 55.0 percent, respectively. Residual income also exceeded expectations. The Food and Lodging Division generated $3,450,000 in residual income when the flexible budget and master budget had projected RIs of $2,750,000 and $2,500,000, respectively. The performance report for the division shows 100 more guest days than had been anticipated and a favorable controllable fixed cost variance. As a manager, Patel will investigate the unfavorable variances associated with her controllable variable costs.

4. Economic value added:
     $4,500,000 − 20%($12,000,000 − $3,000,000) = $2,700,000

Chapter Assignments

BUILDING YOUR KNOWLEDGE FOUNDATION

QUESTIONS

1. What four basic stakeholder groups are included in the balanced scorecard?
2. Once performance objectives are set in the planning stage of the management cycle, what do managers do?
3. Why is it important for managers to see the causal relationships between their actions and the company's overall performance?
4. How does the balanced scorecard add dimension to the management cycle?
5. What is a performance management and evaluation system?
6. Define responsibility accounting.
7. Describe a responsibility center.
8. Explain the difference between a cost center and a discretionary cost center?
9. What is a revenue center?
10. Compare and contrast a cost center, a profit center, and an investment center.
11. What is the role of a responsibility accounting system in an organization?
12. How does a company's organizational structure affect its responsibility accounting system?
13. What types of information are contained in performance reports?
14. What types of comparisons are contained in a performance report for a cost center?
15. Why is a contribution income statement useful in performance management and evaluation?
16. What are some similarities between the performance reports for the various kinds of responsibility centers?
17. Why is return on investment more than a ratio of two numbers?
18. How does residual income differ from return on investment?
19. What are the similarities and differences between residual income and EVA?
20. Why do incentive plans use performance-based pay?

SHORT EXERCISES

LO1 Balanced Scorecard

SE 1. One of your college's overall goals is customer satisfaction. In the light of that goal, match each of these stakeholders' perspectives with the appropriate objective:

Perspective

1. Financial (investors)
2. Learning and growth (employees)
3. Internal business processes
4. Customers

Objective

a. Customer satisfaction means that the faculty engages in cutting-edge research.
b. Customer satisfaction means that students receive their degrees in four years.
c. Customer satisfaction means that the college has a winning athletics program.
d. Customer satisfaction means that fund-raising campaigns are successful.

LO3 Responsibility Centers

SE 2. Identify each of the following as a cost center, a discretionary cost center, a revenue center, a profit center, or an investment center:

1. The manager of center A is responsible for generating cash inflows and incurring costs with the goal of making money for the company. The manager has no responsibility for assets.
2. Center B produces a product that is not sold to an external party.
3. The manager of center C is responsible for the telephone order operations of a large retailer.
4. Center D designs, produces, and sells products to external parties. The manager makes both long-term and short-term decisions.
5. Center E provides human resource support for the other centers in the company.

LO3 Controllable Costs

SE 3. Adana Kim is the manager of the Paper Cutting Department in the Northwest Division of Williams Paper Products. Identify each of the following costs as either controllable or not controllable by Kim:

1. Salaries of cutting machine workers
2. Cost of cutting machine parts
3. Cost of electricity for the Northwest Division
4. Lumber Department hauling costs
5. Vice president's salary

LO4 Cost Center Performance Report

SE 4. Complete the following performance report for cost center C for the month ended December 31, 20x8:

	Actual Results	Variance	Flexible Budget	Variance	Master Budget
Units produced	80	0	?	20 (U)	100
Center costs					
Direct materials	$ 84	$?	$ 80	$?	$100
Direct labor	150	?	?	40 (F)	200
Variable overhead	?	20 (U)	240	?	300
Fixed overhead	280	?	250	?	250
Total cost	$?	$44 (U)	$?	$120 (F)	$850
Performance measures					
Defect-free units to total produced	75%	?	N/A	N/A	90%
Average throughput time per unit	12 minutes	?	N/A	N/A	10 minutes

LO4 Profit Center Performance Report

SE 5. Complete the following performance report for profit center P for the month ended December 31, 20x8:

	Actual Results	Variance	Master Budget
Sales	$?	$20 (F)	$120
Controllable variable costs			
Variable cost of goods sold	25	10 (U)	?
Variable selling and administrative expenses	15	?	5
Contribution margin	$100	$?	$100
Controllable fixed costs	?	10 (F)	60
Profit center income	$ 50	$10 (F)	$?
Performance measures			
Number of orders processed	50	20 (F)	?
Average daily sales	$?	.66 (F)	$4.00
Number of units sold	100	40 (F)	?

SE 6.

LO5   Return on Investment

Complete the return on investment, profit margin, and asset turnover calculations for investment centers D and V:

	Subsidiary D	Subsidiary V
Total sales	$1,650	$2,840
Operating income	$ 180	$ 210
Average assets invested	$ 940	$1,250
Profit margin	?	7.39%
Asset turnover	1.76 times	?
ROI	?	?

SE 7.

LO5   Return on Investment

Complete the return on investment, profit margin, asset turnover, and average assets invested calculations for investment centers J and K:

	Subsidiary J	Subsidiary K
Total sales	$2,000	$2,000
Operating income	$ 500	$ 800
Beginning assets invested	$4,000	$ 500
Ending assets invested	$6,000	$1,500
Average assets invested	$?	$?
Profit margin	25%	?
Asset turnover	?	2 times
ROI	?	?

SE 8.

LO5   Residual Income

Complete the operating income, ending assets invested, residual income, and average assets invested calculations for investment centers H and F:

	Subsidiary H	Subsidiary F
Total sales	$20,000	$25,000
Operating income	$ 1,500	$?
Beginning assets invested	$ 4,000	$ 500
Ending assets invested	$ 6,000	$?
Average assets invested	$?	$ 1,000
Desired ROI	20%	20%
Residual income	$?	$ 600

SE 9.

LO5   Economic Value Added

Complete the current liabilities, total assets − current liabilities, and economic value added calculations for investment centers M and N:

	Subsidiary M	Subsidiary N
Total sales	$15,000	$18,000
After-tax operating income	$ 1,000	$ 1,100
Total assets	$ 4,000	$ 5,000
Current liabilities	$ 1,000	$?
Total assets − current liabilities	$?	$ 3,500

Cost of capital	15%	15%
Economic value added	$?	$?

LO6 Coordination of Goals

SE 10. One of your college's goals is customer satisfaction. In view of that goal, identify each of the following as a linked objective, a measure, or a performance target.

To have successful fund-raising campaigns
Number of publications per year per tenure-track faculty
To increase the average donation by 10 percent
Average number of dollars raised per donor
To have faculty engage in cutting-edge research
To increase the number of publications per faculty member by at least one per year

EXERCISES

LO1 Balanced Scorecard

E 1. Biggs Industries is considering adopting the balanced scorecard and has compiled the following list of possible performance measures. Select the balanced scorecard perspective that best matches each performance measure.

Performance Measure	Balanced Scorecard Perspective
1. Residual income	a. Financial (investors)
2. Customer satisfaction rating	b. Learning and growth (employees)
3. Employee absentee rate	c. Internal business processes
4. Growth in profits	d. Customers
5. On-time deliveries	
6. Manufacturing process time	

LO1 Balanced Scorecard

E 2. Virtual Online Products is considering adopting the balanced scorecard and has compiled the following list of possible performance measures. Select the balanced scorecard perspective that best matches each performance measure.

Performance Measure	Balanced Scorecard Perspective
1. Economic value added	a. Financial (investors)
2. Employee turnover	b. Learning and growth (employees)
3. Average daily sales	c. Internal business processes
4. Defect-free units	d. Customers
5. Number of repeat customer visits	
6. Employee training hours	

LO2 Performance Measures

E 3. Eva Washington wants to measure her division's product quality. Link an appropriate performance measure with each balanced scorecard perspective:

Product Quality	Possible Performance Measures
1. Financial (investors)	a. Number of defective products returned
2. Learning and growth (employees)	b. Number of products failing inspection
3. Internal business processes	c. Increased market share
4. Customers	d. Savings from employee suggestions

LO2 Performance Measures

E 4. Monty Sams wants to measure customer satisfaction within his region. Link an appropriate performance measure with each balanced scorecard perspective:

Customer Satisfaction	Possible Performance Measures
1. Financial (investors)	a. Number of cross-trained staff
2. Learning and growth (employees)	b. Customer satisfaction rating
3. Internal business processes	c. Time lapse from order to delivery
4. Customers	d. Dollar sales to repeat customers

LO3 Responsibility Centers

E 5. Identify the most appropriate type of responsibility center for each of the following organizational units:

1. A pizza store in a pizza chain
2. The ticket sales center of a major airline
3. The South American segment of a multinational company
4. A subsidiary of a business conglomerate
5. The information technology area of a company
6. A manufacturing department of a large corporation
7. An eye clinic in a community hospital
8. The food service function at a nursing home

9. The food preparation plant of a large restaurant chain
10. The catalog order department of a retailer

LO3   Controllable Costs

E 6.   Angel Sweets produces pies. The company has the following three-tiered manufacturing structure:

Vice President–Production

↑

Plant Manager

↑

Production Supervisors

Identify the manager responsible for each of the following costs.

1. Repair and maintenance costs
2. Materials handling costs
3. Direct labor
4. Supervisors' salaries
5. Maintenance of plant grounds
6. Depreciation, equipment
7. Plant manager's salary
8. Cost of materials used
9. Storage of finished goods
10. Property taxes, plant
11. Depreciation, plant

LO3   Organization Chart

E 7.   Hooper Industries wants to formalize its management structure by designing an organization chart. The company has a president, a board of directors, and two vice presidents. Four discretionary cost centers—Financial Resources, Human Resources, Information Resources, and Physical Resources—report to one of the vice presidents. The other vice president has one manufacturing plant with three subassembly areas reporting to her. Draw the company's organization chart.

LO4   Performance Reports

E 8.   Jackie Jefferson, a new employee at Handown, Inc., is learning about the various types of performance reports. Describe the typical contents of a performance report for each type of responsibility center.

LO4   Variable Costing Income Statement

E 9.   Vegan, LLC, owns a chain of gourmet vegetarian take-out markets. Last month, Store P generated the following information: sales, $890,000; direct materials, $220,000; direct labor, $97,000; variable overhead, $150,000; fixed overhead, $130,000; variable selling and administrative expenses, $44,500; and fixed selling expenses, $82,300. There were no beginning or ending inventories. Average daily sales (25 business days) were $35,600. Customer orders processed totaled 15,000. Vegan had budgeted monthly sales of $900,000; direct materials, $210,000; direct labor, $100,000; variable overhead, $140,000; fixed overhead, $140,000; variable selling and administrative expenses, $45,000; and fixed selling expenses, $85,000. Store P had been projected to do $36,000 in daily sales and process 16,000 customer orders. Using this information, prepare a performance report for Store P.

LO4   Variable Costing Income Statement

E 10.   The income statement in the traditional reporting format for Green Products, Inc., for the year ended December 31, 20x7, is as follows:

Green Products, Inc. Income Statement For the Year Ended December 31, 20x7	
Sales	$296,400
Less Cost of goods sold	112,750
Gross margin	$183,650
Less Operating expenses	
Selling expenses	
Variable	69,820
Fixed	36,980
Administrative expenses	27,410
Operating income	$ 49,440

Total fixed manufacturing costs for 20x7 were $16,750. All administrative expenses are considered to be fixed.

Using this information, prepare an income statement for Green Products, Inc., for the year ended December 31, 20x7, using the variable costing format.

LO4 Performance Report for a Cost Center

E 11. Archer, LLC, owns a blueberry processing plant. Last month, the plant generated the following information: blueberries processed, 50,000 pounds; direct materials, $50,000; direct labor, $10,000; variable overhead, $12,000; and fixed overhead, $13,000. There were no beginning or ending inventories. Average daily pounds processed (25 business days) were 2,000. Average rate of processing was 250 pounds per hour. At the beginning of the month, Archer had budgeted costs of blueberries, $45,000; direct labor, $10,000; variable overhead, $14,000; and fixed overhead, $14,000. The plant had been projected to process 2,000 pounds daily at the rate of 240 pounds per hour.

Using this information, prepare a performance report for the month for the blueberry processing plant. Include a flexible budget and a computation of variances in your report. Indicate whether the variances are favorable (F) or unfavorable (U) to the performance of the plant.

LO5 Investment Center Performance

E 12. Momence Associates is evaluating the performance of three divisions: Maple, Oaks, and Juniper.

Using the following data, compute the return on investment and residual income for each division, compare the divisions' performance, and comment on the factors that influenced performance:

	Maple	Oaks	Juniper
Sales	$100,000	$100,000	$100,000
Operating income	$ 10,000	$ 10,000	$ 20,000
Assets invested	$ 25,000	$ 12,500	$ 25,000
Desired ROI	40%	40%	40%

LO5 Economic Value Added

E 13. Leesburg, LLP, is evaluating the performance of three divisions: Lake, Sumpter, and Poe. Using the following data, compute the economic value added by each division, and comment on each division's performance:

	Lake	Sumpter	Poe
Sales	$100,000	$100,000	$100,000
After-tax operating income	$ 10,000	$ 10,000	$ 20,000
Total assets	$ 25,000	$ 12,500	$ 25,000
Current liabilities	$ 5,000	$ 5,000	$ 5,000
Cost of capital	15%	15%	15%

LO6 Performance Incentives

E 14. Dynamic Consulting is advising Solid Industries on the short-term and long-term effectiveness of cash bonuses, awards, profit sharing, and stock options as performance incentives. Prepare a chart identifying the effectiveness of each incentive as either long-term or short-term or both.

LO6 Goal Congruence

E 15. Necessary Toys, Inc., has adopted the balanced scorecard to motivate its managers to work toward the companywide goal of leading its industry in innovation. Identify the four stakeholder perspectives that would link to the following objectives, measures, and targets:

Perspective	Objective	Measure	Target
	Profitable new products	New product ROI	New product ROI of at least 75%
	Work force with cutting-edge skills	Percentage of employees cross-trained on work-group tasks	100% of work group cross-trained on new tasks within 30 days
	Agile product design and production processes	Time to market (the time between a product idea and its first sales)	Time to market less than one year for 80% of product introductions
	Successful product introductions	New product market share	Capture 80% of new product market within one year

PROBLEMS

P 1.

LO3 **Evaluating Cost Center**
LO4 **Performance**

Beverage Products, LLC, manufactures metal beverage containers. The division that manufactures soft drink beverage cans for the North American market has two plants that operate 24 hours a day, 365 days a year. The plants are evaluated as cost centers. Small tools and plant supplies are considered variable overhead. Depreciation and rent are considered fixed overhead. The master budget for a plant and the operating results of the two North American plants, East Coast and West Coast, are as follows:

	Master Budget	East Coast	West Coast
Center costs			
Rolled aluminum ($.01)	$4,000,000	$3,492,000	$5,040,000
Lids ($.005)	2,000,000	1,980,000	2,016,000
Direct labor ($.0025)	1,000,000	864,000	1,260,000
Small tools and supplies ($.0013)	520,000	432,000	588,000
Depreciation and rent	480,000	480,000	480,000
Total cost	$8,000,000	$7,248,000	$9,384,000
Performance measures			
Cans processed per hour	45,662	41,096	47,945
Average daily pounds of scrap metal	5	6	7
Cans processed (in millions)	400	360	420

REQUIRED ▶

1. Prepare a performance report for the East Coast plant. Include a flexible budget and variance analysis.
2. Prepare a performance report for the West Coast plant. Include a flexible budget and variance analysis.
3. Compare the two plants, and comment on their performance.
4. Explain why a flexible budget should be prepared.

P 2.

LO4 **Traditional and Variable**
   Costing Income Statements

Roofing tile is the major product of the Tops Corporation. The company had a particularly good year in 20x8, as shown by its operating data. It sold 88,400 cases of tile. Variable cost of goods sold was $848,640; variable selling expenses were $132,600; fixed manufacturing overhead was $166,680; fixed selling expenses were $152,048; and fixed administrative expenses were $96,450. Selling price was $18 per case. There were no partially completed jobs in process at the beginning or the end of the year. Finished goods inventory had been used up at the end of the previous year.

REQUIRED ▶

1. Prepare the year-end income statement for the Tops Corporation using the traditional reporting format.
2. Prepare the year-end income statement for the Tops Corporation using the variable costing format.

P 3.

LO3 **Evaluating Profit and**
LO4 **Investment Center**
LO5 **Performance**

Bobbie Howell, the managing partner of the law firm Howell, Bagan, and Clark, LLP, makes asset acquisition and disposal decisions for the firm. As managing partner, she supervises the partners in charge of the firm's three branch offices. Those partners have authority to make employee compensation decisions. The partners' compensation depends on the profitability of their branch office. Victoria Smith manages the City Branch, which has the following master budget and actual results for 20x8:

	Master Budget	Actual Results
Billed hours	5,000	4,900
Revenue	$250,000	$254,800
Controllable variable costs		
Direct labor	120,000	137,200
Variable overhead	40,000	34,300
Contribution margin	$ 90,000	$ 83,300
Controllable fixed costs		
Rent	30,000	30,000
Other administrative expenses	45,000	42,000
Branch operating income	$ 15,000	$ 11,300

REQUIRED ▶

1. Assume that the City Branch is a profit center. Prepare a performance report that includes a flexible budget. Determine the variances between actual results, the flexible budget, and the master budget.

2. Evaluate Victoria Smith's performance as manager of the City Branch.
3. Assume that the branch managers are assigned responsibility for capital expenditures and that the branches are thus investment centers. City Branch is expected to generate a desired ROI of at least 30 percent on average invested assets of $40,000.

   a. Compute the branch's return on investment and residual income.
   b. Using the ROI and residual income, evaluate Victoria Smith's performance as branch manager.

P 4.

LO5 Return on Investment and Residual Income

The financial results for the past two years for Ornamental Iron, a division of the Iron Foundry Company, follow.

Iron Foundry Company
Ornamental Iron Division
Balance Sheet
December 31, 20x7 and 20x8

	20x8	20x7
Assets		
Cash	$ 5,000	$ 3,000
Accounts receivable	10,000	8,000
Inventory	30,000	32,000
Other current assets	600	600
Fixed assets	128,300	120,300
Total assets	$173,900	$163,900
Liabilities and Stockholders' Equity		
Current liabilities	$ 13,900	$ 10,000
Long-term liabilities	90,000	93,900
Stockholders' equity	70,000	60,000
Total liabilities and stockholders' equity	$173,900	$163,900

Iron Foundry Company
Ornamental Iron Division
Income Statement
For the Years Ended December 31, 20x7 and 20x8

	20x8	20x7
Sales	$180,000	$160,000
Cost of goods sold	100,000	90,000
Selling and administrative expenses	27,500	26,500
Operating income	$ 52,500	$ 43,500
Income taxes	17,850	14,790
After-tax operating income	$ 34,650	$ 28,710

REQUIRED ▶   1. Compute the division's profit margin, asset turnover, and return on investment for 20x8 and 20x7. Beginning total assets for 20x7 were $157,900. Round to two decimal places.
2. The desired return on investment for the division has been set at 12 percent. Compute Ornamental Iron's residual income for 20x8 and 20x7.
3. The cost of capital for the division is 8 percent. Compute the division's economic value added for 20x8 and 20x7.
4. Before drawing conclusions on this division's performance, what additional information would you want?

P 5.

LO5   Return on Investment and Economic Value Added

The balance sheet for the New Products Division of NuBone Corporation showed invested assets of $200,000 at the beginning of the year and $300,000 at the end of the year. During the year, the division's operating income was $12,500 on sales of $500,000.

REQUIRED ▶   1. Compute the division's residual income if the desired ROI is 6 percent.
2. Compute the following performance measures for the division: (a) profit margin, (b) asset turnover, and (c) return on investment
3. Recompute the division's ROI under each of the following independent assumptions:

   a. Sales increase from $500,000 to $600,000, causing operating income to rise from $12,500 to $30,000.
   b. Invested assets at the beginning of the year are reduced from $200,000 to $100,000.
   c. Operating expenses are reduced, causing operating income to rise from $12,500 to $20,000.

4. Compute NuBone's EVA if total corporate assets are $500,000, current liabilities are $80,000, after-tax operating income is $50,000, and the cost of capital is 8 percent.

Alternate Problems

P 6.

LO4   Traditional and Variable Costing Income Statements

Interior designers often use the deluxe carpet products of Lux Mills, Inc. The Maricopa blend is the company's top product line. In March 20x9, Lux produced and sold 174,900 square yards of Maricopa blend. Factory operating data for the month included variable cost of goods sold of $2,623,500 and fixed manufacturing overhead of $346,875. Other expenses were variable selling expenses, $166,155; fixed selling expenses, $148,665; and fixed general and administrative expenses, $231,500. Total sales revenue equaled $3,935,250. All production took place in March, and there was no work in process at month end. Goods are usually shipped when completed.

REQUIRED ▶   1. Prepare the March 20x9 income statement for Lux Mills, Inc., using the traditional reporting format.
2. Prepare the March 20x9 income statement for Lux Mills, Inc., using the variable costing format.

P 7.

LO3   Return on Investment and
LO4   Residual Income
LO5

Portia Carter is the president of a company that owns six multiplex movie theaters. Carter has delegated decision-making authority to the theater managers for all decisions except those relating to capital expenditures and film selection. The theater managers' compensation depends on the profitability of their theaters. Max Burgman, the manager of the Park Theater, had the following master budget and actual results for the month:

	Master Budget	Actual Results
Tickets sold	120,000	110,000
Revenue–tickets	$840,000	$880,000
Revenue–concessions	480,000	330,000
Controllable variable costs		
Concessions	120,000	99,000
Direct labor	420,000	330,000
Variable overhead	540,000	550,000
Contribution margin	$240,000	$231,000
Controllable fixed costs		
Rent	55,000	55,000
Other administrative expenses	45,000	50,000
Theater operating income	$140,000	$126,000

REQUIRED ▶ 1. Assuming that the theaters are profit centers, prepare a performance report for the Park Theater. Include a flexible budget. Determine the variances between actual results, the flexible budget, and the master budget.

2. Evaluate Burgman's performance as manager of the Park Theater.

3. Assume that the managers are assigned responsibility for capital expenditures and that the theaters are thus investment centers. Park Theater is expected to generate a desired ROI of at least 6 percent on average invested assets of $2,000,000.

   a. Compute the theater's return on investment and residual income.
   b. Using the ROI and residual income, evaluate Burgman's performance as manager.

P 8.

LO5 Return on Investment and Economic Value Added

Micanopy Company makes replicas of Indian artifacts. The balance sheet for the Arrowhead Division showed that the company had invested assets of $300,000 at the beginning of the year and $500,000 at the end of the year. During the year, the Arrowhead Division's operating income was $80,000 on sales of $1,200,000.

REQUIRED ▶ 1. Compute the Arrowhead Division's residual income if the desired ROI is 20 percent.

2. Compute the following performance measures for the division:

   a. Profit margin
   b. Asset turnover
   c. Return on investment

3. Compute Micanopy Company's economic value added if total corporate assets are $6,000,000, current liabilities are $800,000, after-tax operating income is $750,000, and the cost of capital is 12 percent.

SKILLS DEVELOPMENT CASES

Conceptual Analysis

SD 1.

LO1 Performance Measures and
LO2 the Balanced Scorecard

Identify several performance measures for a business located near you, and link each measure with a specific stakeholder's perspective from the balanced scorecard. Be sure to select at least one performance measure for each perspective. If you were the manager of the business, how would you set performance targets for each measure? Prepare an email-style report stating the business's name, location, and activities and your linked performance measures and perspectives. Be prepared to discuss your business and performance measures in class.

Group Activity: Have students complete this assignment by working in groups of four to six, with each group member assuming a different stakeholder perspective (add government and community if you want more than four perspectives). The group should become familiar with the background of the business, and interview the business's manager or accountant. Ask the group to discuss all perspectives and to prepare a report summarizing their findings.

SD 2.

LO3 Comparison of Business Types Using Responsibility Accounting

The structure of an organization affects its responsibility accounting system. Accenture <www.accenture.com>, a major management consulting firm, organizes its consultants by industry and location. Target <www.target.com>, formerly Dayton-Hudson Corporation, has a division for each major retail department store chain it owns: Target, Mervyn's, Marshall Field's, Dayton's, and Hudson's. Monsanto <www.monsanto.com>, a manufacturer, structures its organization by products: agricultural, pharmaceutical, and nutritional (the last includes NutraSweet).

What is a responsibility accounting system, what is it based on, and what is the criterion for including an item in a manager's operating report? Discuss the general effects that organizational structure has on the creation of a responsibility reporting system and give an example of a cost center, a profit center, and an investment center at Accenture, Target, and Monsanto.

Ethical Dilemma

SD 3.

LO5 Effects of Manager's Decisions on ROI

Cooper Huntington is the manager of the upstate store of a large farm products retailer. His company is a stable, consistently profitable member of the farming industry. The upstate store is doing fine despite severe drought conditions in the area. At the first of the year, corporate headquarters set a targeted return on investment for the store of 20 percent. The upstate store currently averages $140,000 in invested assets (beginning invested assets, $130,000; ending invested assets, $150,000) and is projected to have an operating income of $30,800. Huntington is considering whether to take one or both of the following actions before year end:

- Hold off paying $5,000 in bills owed until the start of the next fiscal year.
- Write down $3,000 in store inventory (nonperishable emergency flood supplies) to zero value because Huntington was unable to sell the items all year.

Currently, Huntington's bonus is based on store profits. Next year, corporate headquarters is changing its performance incentive program so that bonuses will be based on a store's actual return on investment.

1. What effect would each of Huntington's possible actions have on the store's operating income this year? (**Hint:** Use Figure 4 to trace the effects.) In your opinion, is either action unethical?
2. Independent of question 1, if corporate headquarters changes its performance incentive plan for store managers, how will the inventory writedown affect next year's income and return on investment if the items are sold for $4,000 next year? In your opinion, does Huntington have an ethical dilemma?

Research Activity

SD 4.

LO2   Earnings Management
LO4
LO6

Many large multinational companies have recently taken large one-time write-offs or applied other downsizing or reengineering accounting practices that have affected the measurement of the company's performance in only one year. Conduct a search for the financial statements of a company that has recently taken a sizable reduction in income in just one year. Conduct a keyword search using an Internet search engine. Prepare a one-page description of your findings. Include the name of the company, the reason for the large decrease in income, and the probable effect on the company's ROI. Be prepared to present your findings to your classmates.

Decision-Making Practice

SD 5.

LO2   Types of Responsibility Centers
LO3
LO4
LO6

Yuma Foods acquired Aldo's Tortillas several years ago. Aldo's has continued to operate as an independent company, except that Yuma Foods has exclusive authority over capital investments, production quantity, and pricing decisions because Yuma has been Aldo's only customer since the acquisition. Yuma uses return on investment to evaluate the performance of Aldo's manager. The most recent performance report is as follows:

Yuma Foods Performance Report for Aldo's Tortillas For the Year Ended June 30, 20x8	
Sales	$6,000
Variable cost of goods sold	3,000
Variable administrative expenses	1,000
Variable corporate expenses (% of sales)	600
Contribution margin	$1,400
Fixed overhead (includes depreciation of $100)	400
Fixed administrative expenses	500
Operating income	$ 500
Average assets invested	$5,500
Return on investment	9.09%

1. Analyze the items listed in the performance report and identify the items Aldo controls and those Yuma controls. In your opinion, what type of responsibility center is Aldo's Tortillas? Explain your response.
2. Prepare a revised performance report for Aldo's Tortillas and an accompanying memo to the president of Yuma Foods that explains why it is important to change the content of the report. Cite some basic principles of responsibility accounting to support your recommendation.

MANAGERIAL REPORTING AND ANALYSIS CASES

Interpreting Management Reports

MRA 1.
LO1 Balanced Scorecard Results

IT, Inc., has adopted the balanced scorecard approach to motivate the managers of its product divisions to work toward the companywide goal of leading its industry in innovation. The corporation's selected performance measures and scorecard results are as follows:

| | Division | | | Performance |
Measure	A	B	C	Target
New product ROI	80%	75%	70%	75%
Employees cross-trained in new tasks within 30 days	95	96	94	100
New product's time to market less than one year	85	90	86	80
New product's market share one year after introduction	50	100	80	80

Can you effectively compare the performance of three divisions against the targets? What other measures mentioned in this chapter are needed to evaluate performance effectively?

Formulating Management Reports

MRA 2.
LO2 Responsibility Centers
LO3

Wood4Fun makes wooden playground equipment for the institutional and consumer markets. The company strives for low-cost, high-quality production because it operates in a highly competitive market in which product price is set by the marketplace and is not based on production costs. The company is organized into responsibility centers. The vice president of manufacturing is responsible for three manufacturing plants. The vice president of sales is responsible for four sales regions. Recently, these two vice presidents began to disagree about whether the manufacturing plants are cost centers or profit centers. The vice president of manufacturing views the plants as cost centers because the managers of the plants control only product-related costs. The vice president of sales believes the plants are profit centers because product quality and product cost strongly affect company profits.

1. Identify the controllable performance that Wood4Fun values and wants to measure. Give at least three examples of performance measures that Wood4Fun could use to monitor such performance.
2. For the manufacturing plants, what type of responsibility center is most consistent with the controllable performance Wood4Fun wants to measure?
3. For the sales regions, what type of responsibility center is most appropriate?

International Company

MRA 3.
LO2 Economic Value Added and
LO5 Performance
LO6

Sevilla Consulting offers environmental consulting services worldwide. The managers of branch offices are rewarded for superior performance with bonuses based on the economic value the office adds to the company. Last year's operating results for the entire company and for its three offices, expressed in millions of U.S. dollars, follow.

	Worldwide	Europe	Americas	Asia
Cost of capital	9%	10%	8%	12%
Total assets	$210	$70	$70	$70
Current liabilities	80	10	40	30
After-tax operating income	15	5	5	5

1. Compute economic value added for each office and worldwide. What factors affect each office's economic value added? How can an office improve its economic value added?
2. If managers' bonuses are based on economic value added to office performance, what specific actions will managers be motivated to take?
3. Is economic value added the only performance measure needed to evaluate investment centers adequately? Explain your response.

Excel Spreadsheet Analysis

MRA 4.
LO5   Return on Investment and Residual Income

Tina Patel, the manager of the Food and Lodging Division at Winter Wonderland, has hired you as a consultant to help her examine her division's performance under several different circumstances.

1. Type the following format into a spreadsheet to compute the Food and Lodging Division's actual return on investment and residual income. Match your data entry to the rows and columns shown below. Data are from parts **3** and **4** of this chapter's Review Problem. (**Hint:** When entering the formulas, type = in front of the formula in the cell. Then the spreadsheet will know to compute the answer. Remember to format each cell for the type of numbers it holds, such as percentage, currency, or general.)

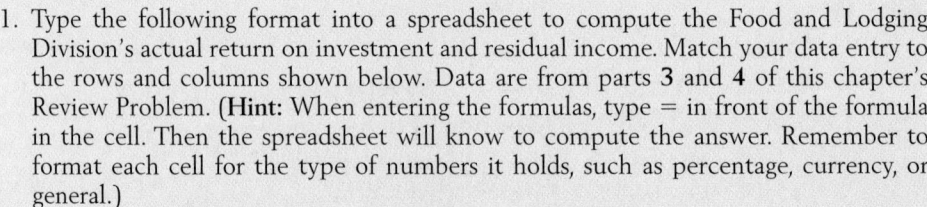

	A	B	C	D	E	F
1						
2	Investment Center		Food and Lodging Division			
3			Actual Results			
4	Sales		$40,000,000			
5	Operating income		$ 6,450,000			
6	Average assets invested		$10,000,000			
7	Desired ROI		30%			
8						
9	Return on Investment		C5/C6			
10						
11	Profit Margin		C5/C4			
12						
13	Asset Turnover		C4/C6			
14						
15	Residual Income		C5-(C7*C6)			
16						

2. Patel would like to know how the figures would change if Food and Lodging had a desired ROI of 40 percent and average assets invested of $10,000,000. Revise your spreadsheet from **1** to compute the division's return on investment and residual income under those conditions.
3. Patel also wants to know how the figures would change if Food and Lodging had a desired ROI of 30 percent and average assets invested of $12,000,000. Revise your spreadsheet from **1** to compute the division's return on investment and residual income under those conditions.
4. Does the use of formatted spreadsheets simplify the computation of ROI and residual income? Do such spreadsheets make it easier to do "what-if" analyses?

Internet Case

MRA 5.

LO6 Top Executive Compensation

Are top executives paid too much? Do the companies run by the most highly paid executives perform better than other companies? Do U.S. executives make more money than their foreign counterparts? These are some of the questions asked routinely in articles and surveys about executive compensation. Use the Internet to locate the top executive salary rankings compiled annually by business publications and other sources. Study the rankings and select several U.S. and foreign companies in the same industry for comparison.

Hint: There are several ways to access this type of information on the Internet. One approach is to do key word searches using search terms like *executive compensation* or *executive salary survey*. Another approach is to access a business publication web site such as <www.forbes.com> and do key word searches of articles. It is also possible to access corporate web sites to view their annual reports. Some corporate web sites are even searchable by key word.

1. In your review of top executive compensation, what types of incentives did you find included in annual compensation?
2. Are the companies with the highest-paid executives the best performers in their industry?
3. Do U.S. executives receive higher pay than their foreign counterparts? If so, do the U.S. companies perform better than their foreign counterparts?

27

Chapter 27 explains how managers make short-run decisions using incremental analysis and long-term capital investment decisions using the net present value method and other methods of capital investment analysis.

Analysis for Decision Making

DECISION POINT

A MANAGER'S FOCUS

Bank of America <www.bankofamerica.com>
Bank of America serves banking clients in over 150 countries worldwide. In its quest to find new ways to meet the needs of its commercial, consumer, global corporate, and investment banking customers, it is conducting more and more of its business over the Internet. As of the end of 2002, Bank of America had more than 4.7 million active online customers. Expectations are that by 2006, nearly half of Bank of America's 15 million active checking account customers will do their banking over the Internet.

Bank management believes this trend is good for business. In a survey of its account holders, Bank of America found that its online users were more likely to stay with the bank and maintain higher account balances and were less likely to make customer service calls. John Rosenfeld, senior vice president for ecommerce, believes that besides making money for the bank, online banking "deepens the relationship" and increases customer satisfaction.[1]

As customers become increasingly familiar with handling their finances online, banks will offer more product and service choices over the Internet. As bank managers make decisions about which business alternatives to pursue, they will ask a number of questions—for example: When should bank products and services be outsourced? When should a special order for service be accepted? When is a bank segment profitable? What is the best sales mix when resource constraints exist? When should bank products be sold as is or processed further into different products? Should

How can incremental analysis help Bank of America take advantage of the business opportunities offered by banking online?

the bank invest in the latest technology, and if so, how should management evaluate the capital investment alternatives? To analyze these types of questions and make informed decisions, bank managers need useful information and analytic methods that will enable them to determine what could happen under the alternative courses of action.

SHORT-RUN DECISION ANALYSIS AND THE MANAGEMENT CYCLE

LO1 Explain how managers make short-run decisions in the management cycle.

RELATED TEXT ASSIGNMENTS
Q: 1, 2, 3
SE: 1
SD: 1

Readers of financial reports are interested in knowing what happened to produce the results that are presented in these reports. The historical information that the reports contain helps answer that question. For planning and control purposes, managers want to know why things happened. They use historical financial and non-financial quantitative information to analyze the results of business actions that will have an effect on their organization's activities in the future. Such information should be relevant, timely, and presented in a format that is easy to use in decision making.

As illustrated in Figure 1, **short-run decision analysis** is the systematic examination of any decision whose effects will be felt over the course of the next year. Although many business problems are unique and cannot be solved by following strict rules, managers frequently take five predictable actions when deciding what to do. The first four actions are taken during the planning stage of the management cycle, and the fifth, and final, action is taken during the reviewing stage.

PLANNING

In the planning stage of the management cycle, managers take the following four actions when performing short-run decision analysis:

1. Discover a problem or need.
2. Identify all reasonable courses of action that can solve the problem or meet the need.
3. Prepare a thorough analysis of each possible solution, identifying its total costs, savings, and other financial effects.
4. Select the best course of action.

www.bankofamerica.com

As a general rule, the managers of companies like Bank of America make decisions that support the company's strategic plan. For example, the managers of a bank may have to make a decision about keeping or eliminating one of the bank's branch locations. Both quantitative and qualitative factors will influence the decision. The quantitative information includes the costs of operating the branch locations and the fee revenues that the branch generates. Management may also want to know the number of customers serviced each year, the types of services offered, and the number and dollar amount of the branch's accounts.

As the managers perform decision analyses, the following qualitative factors will influence their decision to keep or eliminate the branch:

* Competition (Do our competitors have a branch office located here?)
* Economic conditions (Is the community growing?)
* Social issues (Will our offering of this branch location benefit the community we serve?)
* Product or service quality (Can we attract more business because of the service quality of this branch?)
* Timeliness (Does the branch promote customer service?)

Managers must identify and assess the importance of all such qualitative and quantitative factors when they make short-run decisions.

● **STOP AND THINK!**
Are qualitative factors important in short-run decision making?
Yes, because qualitative factors such as competition, economic conditions, social issues, quality, and timeliness influence decision making. ■

EXECUTING

For short-run decisions, we focus on the executing stage of the management cycle—the stage in which managers must adapt to changing environments and take advantage of opportunities that will improve their organization's profitability and liquidity in the short run. During the year, managers may have an opportunity to accept a

FIGURE 1
Short-Run Decisions in the Management Cycle

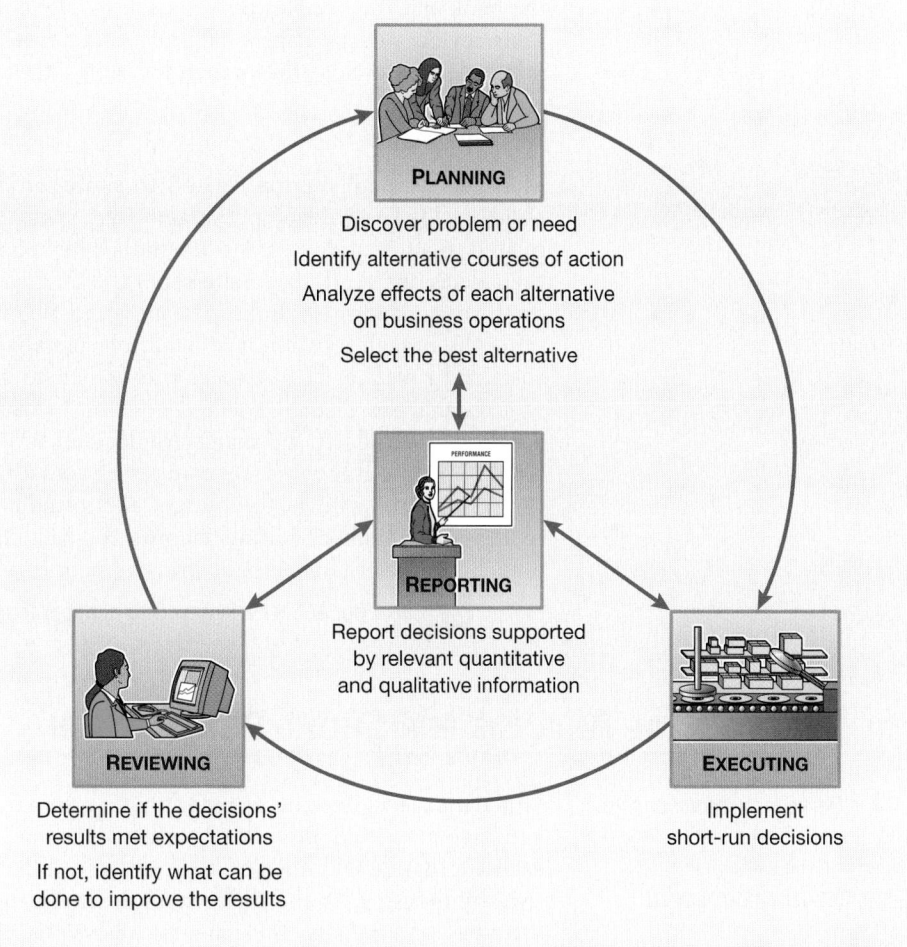

FIGURE 1
Short-Run Decisions in the Management Cycle

special order, examine the profitability of a segment, select the appropriate product mix given a resource constraint, contract with outside suppliers of goods and services, or sell a product as is or process it further. All of those decisions affect operations in the current operating period.

In the executing stage, the bank's management might eliminate a branch if the costs of the branch exceed the revenues generated by it. However, they may choose to keep the branch because the community expects the organization to provide this service.

REVIEWING

It is in the reviewing stage of the management cycle that managers take the fifth predictable action when performing short-run decision analysis: they evaluate each decision to determine whether it produced the forecast results. They examine how each decision was carried out and how it affected the organization. If results fell short, the managers identify and prescribe corrective action. This resulting post-decision audit supplies feedback about the results of the short-run decision. If the solution is not completely satisfactory or if the problem remains, the management cycle begins again. For example, if the bank decided to keep the branch location, the managers would evaluate the results of their decision in many ways. They would probably consider how successful the branch has been, how many people have benefited from the branch, and how well the branch fits in with the other kinds of services the bank offers. They would be interested in knowing how much operating income the branch has produced and in what other ways the branch has benefited the bank and the people the bank serves. Depending on what they discover during their review, the managers might consider ways to improve the branch, or they might decide to close the branch location after all.

REPORTING

Managers prepare reports related to short-run decisions throughout the management cycle. They develop budgets that show the estimated costs and revenues related to alternative courses of action. They compile analyses of data that support their decisions. And they issue reports that measure the effect their decisions had on the organization, including its operating income. When deciding whether to continue the branch location, the bank managers would develop budgets showing the costs and revenues they expect the branch to generate. They would also prepare written analyses of the expected costs and revenues and of the qualitative factors mentioned earlier. If the managers decided to continue the branch location, they would evaluate its success by comparing actual financial and nonfinancial results to the results predicted in the budget and initial analyses. They would create reports telling how much operating income the branch has produced and how else the branch has benefited the bank and the people whom the bank serves.

 Check out ACE for a Review Quiz at http://accounting.college.hmco.com/students.

INCREMENTAL ANALYSIS FOR SHORT-RUN DECISIONS

LO2 Define *incremental analysis* and describe how it applies to short-run decision analysis.

RELATED TEXT ASSIGNMENTS
Q: 4, 5
SE: 2
E: 1
SD: 4
MRA: 3

ENRICHMENT NOTE:
Incremental analysis is a technique used not only by businesses but also by individuals to solve daily problems.

Once managers have determined that a problem or need is worthy of consideration and have identified alternative courses of action, they must evaluate the effect that each alternative will have on their organization. The method of comparing alternatives by focusing on the differences in their projected revenues and costs is called **incremental analysis.** Incremental analysis is also called *differential analysis* if it ignores revenues or costs that stay the same or do not differ among the alternatives.

IRRELEVANT COSTS AND REVENUES

A cost that changes between alternatives is known as a **differential cost** (also referred to as an *incremental cost*). For example, assume that Home State Bank managers are deciding which of two ATM machines—C or W—to buy. The ATMs have the same purchase price, but they have different revenues and cost characteristics. The company currently owns ATM B, which it bought three years ago for $15,000 and which has accumulated depreciation of $9,000 and a book value of $6,000. ATM B is now obsolete as a result of advances in technology and cannot be sold or traded in.

The accountant has collected the following annual revenue and operating cost estimates for the two new machines:

	ATM C	ATM W
Increase in revenue	$16,200	$19,800
Increase in annual operating costs		
Direct materials	4,800	4,800
Direct labor	2,200	4,100
Variable overhead	2,100	3,050
Fixed overhead (depreciation included)	5,000	5,000

The first step in the incremental analysis is to eliminate any irrelevant revenues and costs. Irrelevant revenues are those that will not differ between the alternatives. Irrelevant costs include sunk costs and costs that will not differ between the alternatives. A **sunk cost** is a cost that was incurred because of a previous decision and

EXHIBIT 1
Incremental Analysis

Home State Bank
Incremental Analysis

	ATM C	ATM W	Difference in Favor of ATM W
Increase in revenue	$16,200	$19,800	$3,600
Increase in operating costs that differ between alternatives			
Direct labor	$ 2,200	$ 4,100	($1,900)
Variable overhead	2,100	3,050	(950)
Total relevant operating costs	$ 4,300	$ 7,150	($2,850)
Resulting change in operating income	$11,900	$12,650	$ 750

KEY POINT: Sunk costs cannot be recovered and are irrelevant in short-run decision making.

cannot be recovered through the current decision. An example of a sunk cost is the book value of ATM B. A manager might be tempted to say that the ATM should not be junked because the company still has $6,000 invested in it. However, the manager would be incorrect because the book value of the old ATM represents money that was spent in the past and so does not affect the decision about whether to replace the old ATM with a new one. The old ATM would be of interest only if it could be sold or traded in, and the amount received for it would be different, depending on which new ATM was chosen. In that case, the amount of the sale or trade-in value would be relevant to the decision because it would affect the future cash flows of the alternatives.

Another look at the financial data for ATMs C and W reveals two other irrelevant costs. The costs of direct materials and fixed overhead (depreciation included) can also be eliminated from the analysis because they are the same under both alternatives.

Once the irrelevant revenues and costs have been identified, the incremental analysis may be prepared using only the differential revenues and costs that will change between the alternative ATMs, as shown in Exhibit 1. The analysis shows that ATM W would produce $750 more in operating income than ATM C. Because the costs of buying the two ATMs are the same, this report would favor the purchase of ATM W.

FOCUS ON BUSINESS TECHNOLOGY

How Much Does It Cost to Process a Check?
The banking industry has found that it has options for processing checks. It can outsource the processing of paper checks, use the quasi-paperless system of ATMs, or process transactions over the Internet. Bank managers have concluded that online banking substantially reduces the cost of processing transactions. According to a study by an international consulting firm, the cost of processing a transaction is 1 cent if completed over the Internet, 27 cents using an ATM, and $1.07 if processed by a teller.[2]

OPPORTUNITY COSTS

Because incremental analysis focuses on only the quantitative differences among the alternatives, it simplifies management's evaluation of a decision and reduces the time needed to choose the best course of action. However, incremental analysis is only one input to the final decision. Management needs to consider other issues. For instance, the manufacturer of ATM C might have a reputation for better quality or service than the manufacturer of ATM W. **Opportunity costs** are the benefits that are forfeited or lost when one alternative is chosen over another.

● STOP AND THINK!

When might opportunity costs arise?

Opportunity costs arise when the choice of one course of action eliminates the possibility of another course of action. ■

Consider a plant nursery that has been in business for many years at the intersection of two highways. Suburbs have grown up around the nursery, and a bank has offered the nursery owner a high price for the land. The interest that could be earned from investing the proceeds of the sale is an opportunity cost for the nursery owner. It is revenue that the nursery owner has chosen to forgo to continue operating the nursery in that location.

A bank teller who is deciding whether to go back to school full time to earn a degree in finance also needs to consider opportunity costs. In this case, the opportunity cost is the salary the teller would lose by returning to school. The total cost of the degree includes not only tuition, books, supplies, and living expenses, but also the amount of salary forgone while the teller is a full-time student. This opportunity cost is one reason that many people choose to work full time and attend college part time.

Opportunity costs often come into play when a company is operating at or near capacity and must choose what products or services to offer. For example, assume that The Debit Card Company, which currently services 20,000 cards, has the option of offering 15,000 premium debit cards, a higher-priced product, but it cannot do both. The amount of income from the 20,000 debit cards is an opportunity cost of the premium debit cards.

 Check out ACE for a Review Quiz at http://accounting.college.hmco.com/students.

APPLICATION OF INCREMENTAL ANALYSIS TO SHORT-RUN DECISIONS

LO3   Perform incremental analysis for outsourcing decisions, special order decisions, segment profitability decisions, sales mix decisions involving constrained resources, and sell or process-further decisions.

RELATED TEXT ASSIGNMENTS
Q: 6, 7, 8, 9, 10
SE: 3, 4, 5
E: 2, 3, 4, 5, 6, 7
P: 1, 2, 3, 6, 7
SD: 5

● STOP AND THINK!

Why are depreciation and other fixed costs considered irrelevant when making an outsourcing decision?

Depreciation and other fixed costs do not change, regardless of which alternative is chosen. Only the costs that change—e.g., the cost of direct materials or labor—are included in incremental analysis for outsourcing decisions. ■

www.bankofamerica.com
www.amazon.com

In the course of day-to-day operations, managers are called upon to make many decisions that will have an immediate or short-run effect on current or near-term profitability. In this section, we show how incremental analysis can be applied to the following common situations: (1) outsourcing decisions, (2) special order decisions, (3) segment profitability decisions, (4) sales mix decisions involving constrained resources, and (5) sell or process-further decisions.

INCREMENTAL ANALYSIS FOR OUTSOURCING DECISIONS

Outsourcing is the use of suppliers outside the organization to perform services or produce goods that could be performed or produced internally. **Make-or-buy decisions**, which are decisions about whether to make a part internally or buy it from an external supplier, may lead to outsourcing. Or a company may decide to outsource entire operating activities, such as warehousing and distribution, that it traditionally performed in-house.

To improve operating income and compete effectively in global markets, many companies are focusing their resources on their core competencies—the activities they perform best. One way to obtain the financial, physical, human, and technological resources needed to emphasize those competencies is to outsource expensive, nonvalue-adding activities. Strong candidates for outsourcing include payroll processing, training, managing fleets of vehicles, sales and marketing, custodial services, and information management. Many such areas involve either relatively low skill levels (such as payroll processing or custodial services) or highly specialized knowledge (such as information management) that could be better acquired from experts outside the company.

Outsourcing production or operating activities can reduce a company's investment in physical assets and human resources, which can improve cash flow. It can also help a company reduce operating costs and improve operating income. Many companies like Bank of America and Amazon.com benefit from outsourcing. For example, Amazon.com outsources the distribution of most of its products and has been able to reduce its storage and distribution costs enough to offer product discounts of up to 40 percent off the list price. Outsourcing also enables it to provide additional value-adding services, such as online reviews by customers, personalized recommendations, and discussions and interviews about current products. Banks too are outsourcing to increase their online capabilities, especially in the areas of financial management software and analysis.

In manufacturing companies, a common decision facing managers is whether to make or to buy some or all of the parts used in product assembly. The goal is to select the more profitable choice by identifying the costs of each alternative and their effects on revenues and existing costs. Managers need the following information for this analysis:

Information About Making	Information About Outsourcing
Need for additional machinery	Purchase price of item
Variable costs of making the item	Rent or net cash flow to be generated from vacated space in the factory
Incremental fixed costs	Salvage value of unused machinery

The case of Box Company illustrates an outsourcing decision. For the past five years, the firm has purchased packing cartons from an outside supplier at a cost of $1.25 per carton. The supplier has just informed Box Company that it is raising the price 20 percent, to $1.50 per carton, effective immediately. Box Company has idle machinery that could be adjusted to produce the cartons. Annual production and usage would be 20,000 cartons. The company estimates the cost of direct materials at $.84 per carton. Workers, who will be paid $8.00 per hour, can process 20 cartons per hour ($.40 per carton). The cost of variable manufacturing overhead will be $4 per direct labor hour, and 1,000 direct labor hours will be required. Fixed manufacturing overhead includes $4,000 of depreciation per year and $6,000 of other fixed costs. The company has space and machinery to produce the cartons; the machines are currently idle and will continue to be idle if the part is purchased. Should Box Company continue to outsource the cartons?

Exhibit 2 presents an incremental analysis of the two alternatives. All relevant costs are listed. Because the machinery has already been purchased and neither the machinery nor the required factory space has any other use, the depreciation costs

EXHIBIT 2
Incremental Analysis: Outsourcing Decision

Box Company Outsourcing Decision Incremental Analysis			
	Make	Outsource	Difference in Favor of Make
Direct materials (20,000 × $.84)	$16,800	—	($16,800)
Direct labor (20,000 × $.40)	8,000	—	(8,000)
Variable manufacturing overhead (1,000 hours × $4)	4,000	—	(4,000)
To purchase completed cartons (20,000 × $1.50)	—	$30,000	30,000
Totals	$28,800	$30,000	$ 1,200

and other fixed manufacturing overhead costs are the same for both alternatives; therefore, they are not relevant to the decision. The cost of making the needed cartons is $28,800. The cost of buying 20,000 cartons at the increased purchase price will be $30,000. Since the company would save $1,200 by making the cartons, management will decide to make the cartons.

INCREMENTAL ANALYSIS FOR SPECIAL ORDER DECISIONS

KEY POINT: Special order decisions assume that excess capacity exists to accept the order and that the order, if accepted, will not have an impact on regular sales orders.

Managers are often faced with special order decisions, which are decisions about whether to accept or reject special orders at prices below the normal market prices. Special orders usually involve large numbers of similar products that are sold in bulk. Because these orders are not expected, they are not included in annual cost or sales estimates. And because they are one-time events, they should not be included in revenue or cost estimates for subsequent years. Before a firm accepts a special product order, it must be sure that the products involved are sufficiently different from its regular product line to avoid violating federal price discrimination laws and to avoid reducing unit sales from its full-priced regular product line.

The objective of a special order decision is to determine whether a special order should be accepted. A special order should be accepted only if it maximizes operating income, based on the organization's strategic plan and objectives, the relevant costs of the special order, and qualitative factors. One approach to such a decision is to compare the special order price to the relevant costs to produce, package, and ship the order. The relevant costs include the variable costs, variable selling costs, if any, and other costs directly associated with the special order (for example, freight, insurance, packaging, and labeling the product). Another approach is to prepare a special order bid price by calculating a minimum selling price for the special order. The bid price equals the relevant costs plus an estimated profit.

In many situations, sales commission expenses are excluded from a special order decision analysis because the customer approached the company directly. In addition, the fixed costs of existing facilities usually do not change if a company accepts a special order, and therefore they are usually irrelevant to the decision. If additional fixed costs must be incurred to fill the special order, they would be relevant to the decision. Examples of relevant fixed costs are the purchase of additional machinery, an increase in supervisory help, and an increase in insurance premiums required by a specific order.

For example, Home State Bank has been approved to provide and service four ATMs at a special event. The event sponsors want the fee per ATM transaction reduced to $.50 for these machines. At past special events, ATM use has averaged 2,000 transactions per machine. Home State Bank has located four idle ATMs and determined the following additional information:

ATM Cost Data for 400,000 Transactions (Annual Use for One Machine)

Direct materials	$.10
Direct labor	.05
Overhead	
Variable	.20
Fixed ($100,000 ÷ 400,000)	.25
Advertising ($60,000 ÷ 400,000)	.15
Other fixed selling and administrative	
expenses ($120,000 ÷ 400,000)	.30
Cost per transaction	$1.05
Fee per transaction	$1.50

Should Home State Bank accept the special event offer?

An incremental analysis in the contribution margin reporting format appears in Exhibit 3. The report shows the contribution margin for Home State Bank opera-

EXHIBIT 3
Incremental Analysis: Special Order Decision

Home State Bank
Special Order Decision
Incremental Analysis

	Without Order	With Order	Difference in Favor of Accepting Order
Sales	$2,400,000	$2,404,000	$4,000
Less variable costs			
Direct materials	$ 160,000	$ 160,800	($ 800)
Direct labor	80,000	80,400	(400)
Variable overhead	320,000	321,600	(1,600)
Total variable costs	$ 560,000	$ 562,800	($2,800)
Contribution margin	$1,840,000	$1,841,200	$1,200

tions both with and without the special order. Fixed costs are not included because the only costs affected by the order are direct materials, direct labor, and variable overhead. The net result of accepting the special order is a $1,200 increase in contribution margin (and, correspondingly, in operating income). This amount is verified by the following incremental analysis:

Sales (2,000 transactions × 4) × $.50		$4,000
Less variable costs		
Direct materials (8,000 transactions × $.10)	$ 800	
Direct labor (8,000 transactions × $.05)	400	
Variable overhead (8,000 transactions × $.20)	1,600	
Total variable costs		2,800
Contribution margin		$1,200

The analysis reveals that Home State should accept the special order.

Now let us assume that the event sponsor asks Home State what the minimum special order price is. If the incremental costs for the special order are $2,800, the relevant cost per transaction is $.35 ($2,800 ÷ 8,000). The special order price should cover this cost and generate a profit. If Home State would like to earn $800 from the special order, the special order price should be $.45 ($.35 cost per transaction plus $.10 profit per transaction [$800 ÷ 8,000 transactions]).

Of course, the decision that Home State management makes must be consistent with the bank's strategic plan. Qualitative factors that might influence the decision are (1) the impact of the special order on regular customers, (2) the potential of the special order to lead into new sales areas, and (3) the customer's ability to maintain an ongoing relationship that includes good ordering and paying practices. Notice that the sales of $2,400,000 without the special order absorbed all of the fixed costs of overhead, advertising, and selling and administration.

INCREMENTAL ANALYSIS FOR SEGMENT PROFITABILITY DECISIONS

Another type of operating decision that management must face is whether to keep or to drop unprofitable segments, such as product lines, services, sales territories,

FOCUS ON BUSINESS PRACTICE

To Drop or Not to Drop a Segment?

When Steve Bennett took over as president and CEO of Intuit Corporation <www.intuit.com> in January 2000, he knew the company should have been doing much better than was indicated by its $1 billion in annual revenues from such popular software products as Quicken, QuickBooks, and Turbo Tax. Building on the reliable demand for its tax and accounting software, Bennett has guided Intuit in making acquisitions and building one of the industry's leading online subscription services. At the same time, Bennett began examining parts of Intuit that either weren't producing an adequate return or did not fit well with Intuit's core competencies. Since Bennett's arrival, Intuit has sold its mortgage loan division and eliminated its online insurance business.[3]

BUSINESS WORLD EXAMPLE: Unilever, an English-Dutch Company, is one of the largest consumer goods companies in the world. The company uses segment analysis to evaluate more than 1,400 of its brands.

divisions, departments, stores, or outlets. Management must select the alternative that maximizes operating income, based on the organization's strategic plan and objectives, the relevant revenues and costs, and qualitative factors. The objective of this analysis is to identify the segments that have a negative segment margin.

A **segment margin** is a segment's sales revenue minus its direct costs (direct variable costs and direct fixed costs traceable to the segment). Such costs are assumed to be **avoidable costs**. An avoidable cost could be eliminated if management were to drop the segment. If a segment has a positive segment margin (that is, if the segment's revenue is greater than its direct costs), management should keep the segment. The segment is able to cover its own direct costs and contribute a portion of its revenue to cover common costs and add to operating income. If a segment has a negative segment margin (the segment's revenue is less than its direct costs), management should eliminate the segment. However, certain common costs will be incurred regardless of the decision. Those are unavoidable costs, and the remaining segments must have sufficient contribution margin to cover their own direct costs and the common costs.

An analysis of segment profitability includes the preparation of a segmented income statement using variable costing to identify variable and fixed costs. The fixed costs that are traceable to the segments are called direct fixed costs. The remaining fixed costs are common costs and are not assigned to segments.

Assume that management at Home State Bank wants to determine if the bank should eliminate its Safe Deposit Division. The managers prepare a segmented income statement, separating variable and fixed costs to calculate the contribution margin. They separate the total fixed costs of $84,000 further by directly tracing $55,500 to Bank Operations and $16,500 to Safe Deposit. The remaining $12,000 is considered common fixed costs. The following segmented income statement shows the segment margins for Bank Operations and Safe Deposit and the operating income for the total company:

Home State Bank
Segmented Income Statement
For the Year Ended December 31, 20xx

	Bank Operations	Safe Deposit	Total Company
Sales	$135,000	$15,000	$150,000
Less variable costs	52,500	7,500	60,000
Contribution margin	$ 82,500	$ 7,500	$ 90,000
Less direct fixed costs	55,500	16,500	72,000
Segment margin	$ 27,000	($ 9,000)	$ 18,000
Less common fixed costs			12,000
Operating income			$ 6,000

EXHIBIT 4
Incremental Analysis: Segment Profitability Decision

Home State Bank
Segment Profitability Decision
Incremental Analysis—Situation 1

	Keep Safe Deposit	Drop Safe Deposit	Difference in Favor of Dropping Safe Deposit
Sales	$150,000	$135,000	($15,000)
Less variable costs	60,000	52,500	7,500
Contribution margin	$ 90,000	$ 82,500	($ 7,500)
Less direct fixed costs	72,000	55,500	16,500
Segment margin	$ 18,000	$ 27,000	$ 9,000
Less common fixed costs	12,000	12,000	0
Operating income	$ 6,000	$ 15,000	$ 9,000

Home State Bank
Segment Profitability Decision
Incremental Analysis—Situation 2

	Keep Safe Deposit	Drop Safe Deposit	Difference in Opposition to Dropping Safe Deposit
Sales	$150,000	$108,000	($42,000)
Less variable costs	60,000	42,000	18,000
Contribution margin	$ 90,000	$ 66,000	($24,000)
Less direct fixed costs	72,000	55,500	16,500
Segment margin	$ 18,000	$ 10,500	($ 7,500)
Less common fixed costs	12,000	12,000	0
Operating income	$ 6,000	($ 1,500)	($ 7,500)

FOCUS ON INTERNATIONAL BUSINESS

Why Banks Prefer Ebanking

After performing segment analysis of online banking and face-to-face banking, bank managers worldwide are encouraging customers to do their banking over the Internet. Banks have found that linking worldwide Internet access with customer relationship management (CRM), customer-friendly financial software, and online bill payment in a secure banking environment will reduce costs, increase service and product availability, and boost earnings.[4]

The analysis of Situation 1 in Exhibit 4 shows that dropping the Safe Deposit Division will increase operating income by $9,000. Unless the bank can increase Safe Deposit's segment margin by increasing sales revenue or by reducing direct costs, management should drop the segment. The incremental approach to analyzing this decision isolates the segment and focuses on its segment margin, as shown in the last column of the exhibit.

The decision to drop a segment also requires a careful review of the other segments to see if they will be affected. Let's extend the illustration by assuming that Bank Operation's sales volume and variable costs will decrease 20 percent if management eliminates the Safe Deposit Division. The reduction in sales volume stems from the loss of customers who purchase products from both divisions. The analysis of Situation 2 in Exhibit 4 shows that dropping Safe Deposit would reduce both the segment margin and the bank's operating income by $7,500. In this situation, Home State Bank would want to keep Safe Deposit.

INCREMENTAL ANALYSIS FOR SALES MIX DECISIONS

KEY POINT: When resources such as direct materials, direct labor, or machine time are scarce, the goal is to maximize the contribution margin per unit of scarce resource.

KEY POINT: Selecting an alternative based on contribution margin per unit does not necessarily mean it is the best choice.

A company may not be able to provide the full variety of products or services that customers demand in a given time period. Limits on resources such as machine time or available labor may restrict the types or quantities of products or services. Resource constraints can also be associated with other activities, such as inspection and equipment setup. The question is, Which products or services contribute the most to company profitability in relation to the amount of capital assets or other constrained resources needed to offer those items? To satisfy customers' demands and maximize operating income, management will choose to offer the most profitable product or service first. To identify such products or services, the managers calculate the contribution margin per constrained resource (such as labor hours or machine hours) for each product or service.

The objective of a **sales mix decision** is to select the alternative that maximizes the contribution margin per constrained resource based on the organization's strategic plan and objectives, the relevant revenues and costs, and qualitative factors. The decision analysis, which uses incremental analysis to identify the relevant costs and revenues, consists of two steps. First, calculate the contribution margin per unit for each product or service affected by the constrained resource. The contribution margin per unit equals the selling price per unit less the variable costs per unit. Second, calculate the contribution margin per unit of the constrained resource. The contribution margin per unit of the constrained resource equals the contribution margin per unit divided by the quantity of the constrained resource required per unit.

Assume that Home State Bank offers three types of loans: commercial loans, auto loans and home loans. The product line data are as follows:

	Commercial Loans	Auto Loans	Home Loans
Current loan application demand	20,000	30,000	18,000
Processing hours per loan application	2	1	2.5
Loan origination fee	$24.00	$18.00	$32.00
Variable processing costs	$12.50	$10.00	$18.75
Variable selling costs	$6.50	$5.00	$6.25

The current loan application capacity is 100,000 processing hours.

Question 1: *Which loan type should be advertised and promoted initially because it is the most profitable for the bank? Which should be second? Which last??*

The sales mix analysis is shown in Exhibit 5. It indicates that the auto loans should be sold first because they provide the highest contribution margin per processing hour. Home loans would be sold second, and commercial loans would be sold last.

Question 2: *How many of each type of loan should be sold to maximize the company's contribution margin based on the current loan application activity of 100,000 processing hours? What is the total contribution margin for that combination?*

To begin the analysis, compare the current loan application activity to the required loan activity to meet the current loan demand. The company needs 115,000 processing hours to meet the current loan demand: 40,000 processing hours for commercial loans (20,000 loans × 2 processing hours), 30,000 processing hours for auto loans (30,000 loans × 1 processing hour per loan), and 45,000 processing hours for home loans (18,000 loans × 2.5 processing hours per loan). Because that amount exceeds the current capacity of 100,000 processing hours,

EXHIBIT 5
Incremental Analysis: Sales Mix Decision Involving Constrained Resources

Home State Bank
Sales Mix Decision: Ranking the Order of Loans
Incremental Analysis

	Commercial Loans	Auto Loans	Home Loans
Loan origination fee per loan	$24.00	$18.00	$32.00
Less variable costs			
Processing	$12.50	$10.00	$18.75
Selling	6.50	5.00	6.25
Total variable costs	$19.00	$15.00	$25.00
Contribution margin per loan (A)	$ 5.00	$ 3.00	$ 7.00
Processing hours per loan (B)	2	1	2.5
Contribution margin per processing hour (A ÷ B)	$ 2.50	$ 3.00	$ 2.80

Home State Bank
Sales Mix Decision: Number of Units to Make
Incremental Analysis

	Processing Hours
Total processing hours available	100,000
Less processing hours to produce auto loans (30,000 loans × 1 processing hour)	30,000
Balance of processing hours available	70,000
Less processing hours to produce home loans (18,000 loans × 2.5 processing hours per loan)	45,000
Balance of processing hours available	25,000
Less processing hours to produce commercial loans (12,500 loans × 2 processing hours per loan)	25,000
Balance of processing hours available	0

management must determine the sales mix that maximizes the company's contribution margin, which will also maximize its operating income. The calculations in the second part of Exhibit 5 show that the bank should sell 30,000 auto loans, 18,000 home loans, and 12,500 commercial loans. The total contribution margin is:

	Contribution Margin
Auto loans (30,000 loans × $3.00 per loan)	$ 90,000
Home loans (18,000 loans × $7.00 per loan)	126,000
Commercial loans (12,500 loans × $5.00 per loan)	62,500
Total contribution margin	$278,500

As noted earlier, management makes the final decision based on the company's strategic plan and objectives, all relevant revenues and costs, and qualitative factors.

KEY POINT: Products are made by combining materials or by dividing materials, such as in oil refining or ore extraction.

INCREMENTAL ANALYSIS FOR SELL OR PROCESS-FURTHER DECISIONS

Some companies offer products or services that can either be sold in a basic form or be processed further and sold as a more refined product or service to a different market. For example, a meatpacking company processes cattle into meat and meat-related products, such as bones and hides. The company may choose to sell sides of beef and pounds of bones and hides to other companies for further processing. Alternatively, it could choose to cut and package the meat for immediate sale in grocery stores, process bone into fertilizer for gardeners, or tan hides into refined leather for purses.

A **sell or process-further decision** is a decision about whether to sell a joint product at the split-off point or sell it after further processing. **Joint products** are two or more products, made from a common material or process, that cannot be identified as separate products or services during some or all of the processing. Only at a specific point, called the **split-off point**, do joint products or services become separate and identifiable. At that point, a company may choose to sell the product or service as is or to process it into another form for sale to a different market.

The objective of a sell or process-further decision is to select the alternative that maximizes operating income, based on the organization's strategic plan and objectives, the relevant revenues and costs, and qualitative factors. To complete the analysis, calculate the incremental revenue, which is the difference between the total revenue if the product or service is sold at the split-off point and the total revenue if the product or service is sold after further processing. Compare the incremental revenue to the incremental costs of processing further. Choose to process a product or service further if the incremental revenue is greater than the incremental costs of processing further. If the incremental costs are greater than the incremental revenue, choose to sell the product or service at the split-off point. Be sure to ignore joint costs (or common costs) in your analysis, because they are incurred *before* the split-off point and do not change if further processing occurs. Although accountants assign joint costs to products or services when valuing inventories and calculating cost of goods sold, joint costs are not relevant to a sell or process-further decision and are omitted from the decision analysis

TERMINOLOGY NOTE: The common costs shared by two or more products before they are split off are called *joint costs*. Joint costs are irrelevant in a sell or process-further decision.

For example, as part of the company's strategic plan, Home State Bank's management is looking for new markets for banking services, and management is considering whether it would be profitable to bundle banking services. Home State Bank is considering adding two levels of service, Premier Checking and Personal Banker, beyond its current Basic Checking account services. The three levels have the following features:

- Basic Checking: online checking account, debit card, and online bill payment with a required minimum average balance of $500

- Premier Checking: paper and online checking, a debit card, a credit card, and a small life insurance policy equal to the maximum credit limit on the credit card for customers who maintain a minimum average balance of $1,000

- Personal Banker: all of the features of the Premier Checking plus a safe deposit box, $5,000 personal line of credit at prime, financial investment advice, and a toaster on opening the account for customers who maintain a minimum average balance of $5,000

Assume the bank can earn sales revenue of 5 percent on its checking account balances and that the total cost of Basic Checking is currently $50,000. The bank's accountant provided these data for each level of service:

Product	Sales Revenue	Additional Costs
Basic Checking	$ 25	$ 0
Premier Checking	50	30
Personal Banker	250	200

EXHIBIT 6
Incremental Analysis: Sell or Process-Further Decision

Home State Bank
Sell or Process-Further Decision
Incremental Analysis

	Premier Checking	Personal Banker
Incremental revenue if processed further:		
Process further	$50	$250
Split-off — Basic Checking	25	25
Incremental revenue	$25	$225
Less incremental costs	30	200
Operating income (loss) from processing further	($ 5)	$ 25

The decision analysis in Exhibit 6 indicates that the bank should offer personal banking services in addition to Basic Checking accounts. Notice that the $50,000 joint costs of Basic Checking were ignored because they are sunk costs that will not influence the decision.

As mentioned earlier, management makes the final decision based on the bank's strategic plan and objectives, the relevant revenues and costs, and qualitative factors. A decision to process further must agree with the bank's strategic plan to expand into new markets. In addition, management must consider the bank's ability to obtain favorable returns on its bank deposit investments.

 Check out ACE for a Review Quiz at http://accounting.college.hmco.com/students.

CAPITAL INVESTMENT DECISIONS

LO4 Identify the types of projected costs and revenues used to evaluate alternatives for capital investment.

RELATED TEXT ASSIGNMENTS
Q: 11, 12, 13, 14, 15, 16, 17
SE: 6
E: 8
SD: 2, 3
MRA: 2, 5

www.bankofamerica.com

Among the most significant decisions facing management are **capital investment decisions**, which are decisions about when and how much to spend on capital facilities and other long-term projects. Capital facilities and projects may include machinery, systems, or processes; building additions, renovations, or new structures; entire new divisions or product lines; or distribution and software systems. For example, Bank of America will make decisions about installing new equipment, replacing old equipment, expanding services by buying or building a new facility, and acquiring another company. Capital facilities and projects are expensive. A new building could cost millions of dollars and require several years to complete. Managers must make capital investment decisions carefully to ensure that their choices make the maximum contribution to future profits.

CAPITAL INVESTMENT ANALYSIS

KEY POINT: Capital investment analysis is a decision process for the purchase of capital facilities such as buildings and equipment.

Capital investment analysis, or *capital budgeting*, is the process of making decisions about capital investments. It consists of identifying the need for a capital investment, analyzing courses of action to meet that need, preparing reports for managers, choosing the best alternative, and allocating funds among competing needs.

⬢ **STOP AND THINK!**
How is capital investment analysis part of both the long-term planning and annual budgeting processes?
Capital investment decisions will affect a company for many years, first as broad estimates used for planning purposes and finally, in the year of the expenditure, as specific investment analyses. ■

Every part of the organization participates in this process. Financial analysts supply a target cost of capital or desired rate of return and an estimate of how much money can be spent annually on capital facilities. Marketing specialists predict sales trends and new product demands, which help in determining which operations need expansion or new equipment. Managers at all levels help identify facility needs and often prepare preliminary cost estimates for the desired capital investment. Then they all work together to implement the project selected and to keep the results within revenue and cost estimates.

MEASURES USED IN CAPITAL INVESTMENT ANALYSIS

When evaluating a proposed capital investment, managers must predict how the new asset will perform and how it will benefit the company. Various measures are used to estimate the benefits to be derived from a capital investment.

■ **NET INCOME AND NET CASH INFLOWS**   Each capital investment analysis must include a measure of the expected benefit from the investment project. The measure of expected benefit depends on the method of analyzing capital investment alternatives. One possible measure is net income, calculated in the usual way. Managers determine increases in net income resulting from the capital investment for each alternative.

A more widely used measure of expected benefit is projected cash flows. **Net cash inflows** are the balance of increases in projected cash receipts over increases in projected cash payments resulting from a capital investment. In some cases, equipment replacement decisions involve alternatives when revenues are the same among alternatives. In such cases, **cost savings** measure the benefits, such as reduced costs, from proposed capital investments. Either net cash inflows or cost savings can be used as the basis for an evaluation, but one measure should not be confused with the other. If the analysis involves cash receipts, net cash inflows are used. If the analysis involves only cash outlays, cost savings are used. Managers must measure and evaluate all the investment alternatives consistently.

■ **EQUAL VERSUS UNEQUAL CASH FLOWS**   Projected cash flows may be the same for each year of an asset's life, or they may vary from year to year. Unequal cash flows are common and must be analyzed for each year of an asset's life. Proposed projects with equal annual cash flows require less detailed analysis. Both a project with equal cash flows and one with unequal cash flows are illustrated and explained later in this chapter.

■ **CARRYING VALUE OF ASSETS**   **Carrying value** is the undepreciated portion of the original cost of a fixed asset—that is, the asset's cost less its accumulated depreciation. When a decision to replace an asset is being evaluated, the carrying value of the old asset is irrelevant because it is a past, or historical, cost, and it will therefore not be altered by the decision. Net proceeds from the asset's sale or disposal are relevant, however, because the proceeds affect cash flows and may be different for each alternative.

■ **DEPRECIATION EXPENSE AND INCOME TAXES**   The techniques of capital investment analysis in this chapter compare the relative benefits of proposed capital investments by measuring the cash receipts and payments for a facility or project. Income taxes alter the amount and timing of cash flows of projects under consideration by for-profit companies. To assess the benefits of a capital project, a company must include the effects of income taxes in its capital investment analyses. Depreciation expense is deductible when determining income taxes. (You may recall that the annual depreciation expense computation using the straight-line method is the asset's cost less its residual value, divided by the asset's useful life.) Thus, depreciation expense strongly influences the amount of income taxes a company pays and can lead to significant income tax savings.

Corporate income tax rates vary and can change yearly. To examine how income taxes affect capital investment analysis, assume that a company has a tax rate of 30 percent on taxable income. The company is considering a capital project that will make the following annual contribution to operating income:

Cash revenues	$ 400,000
Cash expenses	(200,000)
Depreciation	(100,000)
Operating income	$ 100,000
Income taxes at 30%	(30,000)
Operating income after income taxes	$ 70,000

The net cash inflows for this project can be determined in two ways:

1. Net cash inflows—receipts and disbursements

Revenues (cash inflows)	$400,000
Cash expenses (outflows)	(200,000)
Income taxes (outflows)	(30,000)
Net cash inflows	$170,000

2. Net cash inflows—income adjustment procedure

Operating income after income taxes	$ 70,000
Add back noncash expenses (depreciation)	100,000
Less noncash revenues	—
Net cash inflows	$170,000

In both computations, the net cash inflows are $170,000, and the total effect of income taxes is to lower the net cash inflows by $30,000.

■ **DISPOSAL OR RESIDUAL VALUES**   Proceeds from the sale of an old asset are current cash inflows and are relevant to evaluating a proposed capital investment. Projected disposal or residual values of replacement equipment are also relevant because they represent future cash inflows and usually differ among alternatives. Remember that the residual value, sometimes called the *disposal* or *salvage value*, of an asset will be received at the end of the asset's estimated life.

FOCUS ON INTERNATIONAL BUSINESS

Why Look Beyond the Cost of a Capital Investment?

Because capital investments are made in long-term facilities and projects that require commitments of large amounts of money to be spent in anticipation of profitable future returns, many things in addition to costs should be evaluated. International trade and logistics can also be part of the capital investment decision. A case in point is Koss Corp. <www.koss.com>, located in Milwaukee, Wisconsin, and maker of high-fidelity headphones used for personal stereos, speakerphones, and other audio equipment. Company managers moved much of the production to China, where costs are low. However, that caused a problem with making timely deliveries to customers.[5] The just-in-time inventory philosophy had to be abandoned, and inventories were tripled from $2 million to $6 million to avoid customer backorders and dissatisfaction. Now, finished products are stacked in the Milwaukee factory to insure against dockworker strikes and missed deliveries. Looking beyond the numbers becomes an important consideration in capital investment decisions.

 Check out ACE for a Review Quiz at http://accounting.college.hmco.com/students.

THE TIME VALUE OF MONEY

An organization has many options for investing capital besides buying fixed assets. Consequently, management expects a fixed asset to yield a reasonable return during its useful life. A key question in capital investment analysis is how to measure the return on a fixed asset. One way is to look at the cash flows the asset will generate during its useful life. When an asset has a long useful life, management will usually analyze those cash flows in terms of the time value of money. The **time value of money** is the concept that cash flows of equal dollar amounts separated by an interval of time have different present values because of the effect of compound interest. The notions of interest, present value, future value, and present value of an ordinary annuity are all related to the time value of money.

INTEREST

KEY POINT: Interest is a cost associated with the passage of time, whether or not there is a stated interest rate.

Interest is the cost associated with the use of money for a specific period of time. Because interest is a cost associated with time and "time is money," interest is an important consideration in any business decision. **Simple interest** is the interest cost for one or more periods when the amount on which the interest is computed stays the same from period to period. **Compound interest** is the interest cost for two or more periods when the amount on which interest is computed changes in each period to include all interest paid in previous periods. In other words, compound interest is interest earned on a principal sum that is increased at the end of each period by the interest for that period.

■ **EXAMPLE: SIMPLE INTEREST** Jo Sanka accepts an 8 percent, $30,000 note due in 90 days. How much will she receive in total when the note comes due? The formula for calculating simple interest is:

$$\text{Interest Expense} = \text{Principal} \times \text{Rate} \times \text{Time}$$
$$= \$30,000 \times 8/100 \times 90/360 = \$600$$

The total that Sanka will receive is computed as follows:

$$\text{Total} = \text{Principal} + \text{Interest}$$
$$= \$30,000 + \$600 = \$30,600$$

If the interest is paid and the note is renewed for an additional 90 days, the interest calculation will remain the same.

■ **EXAMPLE: COMPOUND INTEREST** Andy Clayburn makes a deposit of $5,000 in a savings account that pays 6 percent interest. He expects to leave the principal and accumulated interest in the account for three years. What will be his account total at the end of three years? Assume that the interest is paid at the end of the year, that the interest is added to the principal at that time, and that this total in turn earns interest. The amount at the end of three years is computed as follows:

(1) Year	(2) Principal Amount at Beginning of Year	(3) Annual Amount of Interest (col. 2 × .06)	(4) Accumulated Amount at End of Year (col. 2 + col. 3)
1	$5,000.00	$300.00	$5,300.00
2	5,300.00	318.00	5,618.00
3	5,618.00	337.08	5,955.08

At the end of three years, Clayburn will have $5,955.08 in his savings account. Note that the annual amount of interest increases each year by the interest rate times the interest of the previous year. For example, between year 1 and year 2, the interest increased by $18 ($318 − $300), which exactly equals 6 percent times $300.

PRESENT VALUE

Suppose that you had the choice of receiving $100 either today or one year from today. Intuitively, you would choose to receive the $100 today. Why? You know that if you have the $100 today, you can put it in a savings account to earn interest, so that you will have more than $100 a year from today. Therefore, we can say that an amount to be received in the future (future value) is not worth as much today as the same amount to be received today (present value) because of the cost associated with the passage of time.

Future value and present value are closely related. Future value is the amount an investment will be worth at a future date if invested today at compound interest. Present value is the amount that must be invested today at a given rate of compound interest to produce a given future value.

For example, assume that Daschel Company needs $1,000 one year from now. How much should the company invest today to achieve that goal if the interest rate is 5 percent? The following equation may be used:

STOP AND THINK!
How are present value and future value different?

Present value looks back to determine value in the present, and future value looks forward to determine value at a future time. ∎

$$\text{Present Value} \times (1.0 + \text{Interest Rate}) = \text{Future Value}$$
$$\text{Present Value} \times 1.05 = \$1,000.00$$
$$\text{Present Value} = \$1,000.00 \div 1.05$$
$$\text{Present Value} = \$952.38$$

Thus, to achieve a future value of $1,000.00, a present value of $952.38 must be invested. Interest of 5 percent on $952.38 for one year equals $47.62, and the two amounts added together equal $1,000.00.

PRESENT VALUE OF A SINGLE SUM DUE IN THE FUTURE

When more than one time period is involved, the calculation of present value is more complicated. For example, Reza Company wants to be sure of having $4,000 at the end of three years. How much must the company invest today in a 5 percent savings account to achieve that goal? By adapting the preceding equation, the present value of $4,000 at compound interest of 5 percent for three years in the future may be computed as follows:

Year	Amount at End of Year	Divide by		Present Value at Beginning of Year
3	$4,000.00 ÷	1.05	=	3,809.52
2	3,809.52 ÷	1.05	=	3,628.11
1	3,628.11 ÷	1.05	=	3,455.34

FOCUS ON BUSINESS PRACTICE

How Would You Decide Whether to Buy Rare Dinosaur Bones?

Not-for-profit organizations can also use the techniques of capital investment analysis. For example, the officers of the Field Museum <www.fmnh.org> in Chicago employed these techniques when deciding whether to bid at auction on the most complete skeleton ever found of a *Tyrannosaurus rex*. The museum bought the bones for $8.2 million and spent another $9 million to restore and install the dinosaur, named Sue. The museum projected that Sue would attract 1 million new visitors, who would produce $5 million in admissions and spend several more million dollars on food, gifts, and the like. After deducting operating costs, museum officials used discounted present values to calculate a return on investment of 10.5 percent. Given that the museum's cost of capital was 8.5 percent, Sue's purchase was considered a financial success. Sue has been extremely popular with the public and more than met the museum's attendance goals in the first year after installation.[6]

Reza Company must invest a present value of $3,455.34 to achieve a future value of $4,000 in three years. This calculation is made much easier by using the appropriate table from the appendix on future value and present value tables. In Table 3, we look down the 5 percent column until we reach period 3. There we find the factor .864. This factor when multiplied by $1 gives the present value of $1 to be received three years from now at 5 percent interest. Thus, we solve the problem as follows:

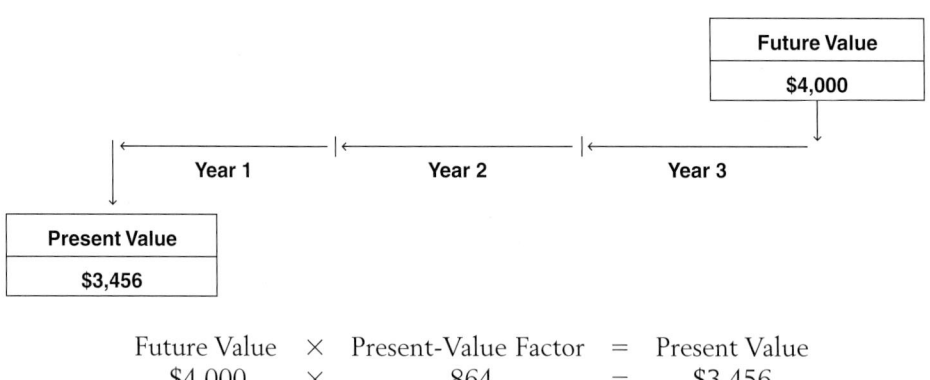

Future Value	×	Present-Value Factor	=	Present Value
$4,000	×	.864	=	$3,456

Except for a rounding difference of $.66, this gives the same result as the previous calculation.

PRESENT VALUE OF AN ORDINARY ANNUITY

STUDY NOTE: The first payment of an ordinary annuity is always made at the end of the first year.

It is often necessary to compute the present value of a series of receipts or payments. When we calculate the present value of equal amounts equally spaced over a period of time, we are computing the present value of an ordinary annuity. An ordinary annuity is a series of equal payments or receipts that will begin one time period from the current date.

For example, assume that Fodor Company has sold a piece of property and is to receive $15,000 in three equal annual cash payments of $5,000, beginning one year from today. What is the present value of this sale, assuming a current interest rate of 5 percent?

We can determine this present value by calculating a separate present value for each of the three payments (using Table 3 in the appendix on future value and present value tables) and summing the results, as follows:

Future Cash Receipts (Annuity)				Present-Value Factor at 5 Percent (from Table 3)		Present Value
Year 1	Year 2	Year 3				
$5,000			×	.952	=	$ 4,760
	$5,000		×	.907	=	4,535
		$5,000	×	.864	=	4,320
Total Present Value						$13,615

The present value of this sale is $13,615. Thus, there is an implied interest cost (given the 5 percent rate) of $1,385 associated with the payment plan that allows the purchaser to pay in three installments.

We can calculate this present value more easily by using Table 4. We look down the 5 percent column until we reach period 3. There we find the factor 2.723. That factor, when multiplied by $1, gives the present value of a series of three $1 payments, spaced one year apart, at compound interest of 5 percent. Thus, we solve the problem as follows:

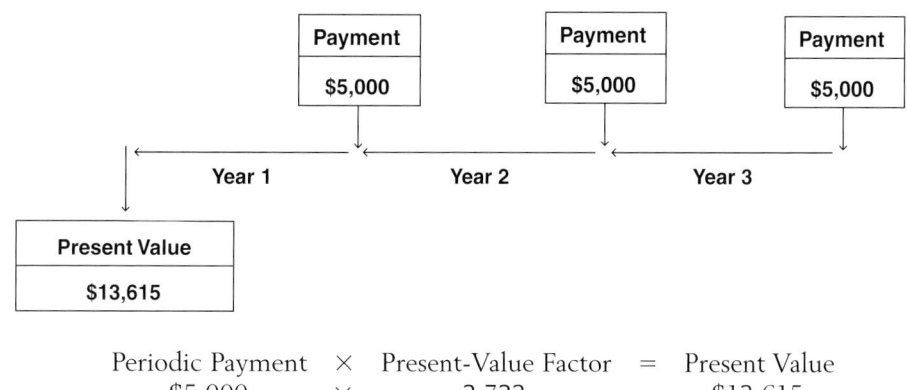

$$\begin{array}{cccccc} \text{Periodic Payment} & \times & \text{Present-Value Factor} & = & \text{Present Value} \\ \$5{,}000 & \times & 2.723 & = & \$13{,}615 \end{array}$$

This result is the same as the one computed earlier. If Fodor Company is willing to accept a 5 percent rate of return, management will be equally satisfied to receive a single cash payment of $13,615 today or three equal annual cash payments of $5,000 spread over the next three years.

✅ Check out ACE for a Review Quiz at http://accounting.college.hmco.com/students.

ANALYZING CAPITAL INVESTMENT PROPOSALS: THE NET PRESENT VALUE METHOD

LO6 Analyze capital investment proposals using the net present value method.

RELATED TEXT ASSIGNMENTS
Q: 20
SE: 8
E: 10, 11, 12
P: 4, 8
SD: 3
MRA: 2

⬤ **STOP AND THINK!**
Why is the net present value method superior to the other methods of capital investment analyses presented in this chapter?
The net present value method takes into account the time value of money, whereas the other methods do not. ∎

BUSINESS WORLD EXAMPLE: State lotteries use the net present value method to compute the lump-sum equivalent of the grand prize.

When evaluating a proposed capital investment, managers must predict how the new asset will perform and how it will benefit the company. Various methods are used to estimate the benefits to be derived from a capital investment. The most important of these is the net present value method. The **net present value method** evaluates a capital investment by discounting its future cash flows to their present values and subtracting the amount of the initial investment from their sum. All proposed capital investments are evaluated in the same way, and the projects with the highest net present value—the amount that exceeds the initial investment—are selected for implementation.

ADVANTAGES OF THE NET PRESENT VALUE METHOD

A significant advantage of the net present value method is that it incorporates the time value of money into the analysis of proposed capital investments. Future cash inflows and outflows are discounted by the company's minimum rate of return to determine their present values. The minimum rate of return should at least equal the company's average cost of capital. **Cost of capital** is the weighted-average rate of return a company must pay to its long-term creditors and shareholders for the use of their funds.

When dealing with the time value of money, use discounting to find the present value of an amount to be received in the future. To determine the present values of future amounts of money, use Tables 3 and 4 in the appendix on future value and present value tables. Remember that Table 3 deals with a single payment or amount, whereas Table 4 is used for a series of equal periodic amounts.

Tables 3 and 4 are used to discount each future cash inflow and cash outflow over the life of the asset to the present. If the net present value is positive (the total of the discounted net cash inflows exceeds the cash investment at the beginning), the rate of return on the investment will exceed the company's minimum rate of return, or hurdle rate, and the project can be accepted. Assuming the project is accepted, investors will be pleased that the company earned a higher rate of return

KEY POINT: If the net present value is zero, the investment will earn the minimum rate of return.

than they expected or required. Conversely, if the net present value is negative (the cash investment at the beginning exceeds the discounted net cash inflows), the return on the investment is less than the minimum rate of return, and the project should be rejected. If the net present value is zero (if discounted cash inflows equal discounted cash outflows), the project meets the minimum rate of return and can be accepted.

THE NET PRESENT VALUE METHOD ILLUSTRATED

Assume that Open Imaging Company is considering the purchase of an ultrasound machine that will improve efficiency in its Radiology Department. The management of Open Imaging Company must decide between two models of the machine, Model M and Model N:

Model M costs $17,500 and will have an estimated residual value of $2,000 after five years. It is projected to produce cash inflows of $6,000, $5,500, $5,000, $4,500, and $4,000 during its five-year life.

Model N costs $21,000 and will have an estimated residual value of $2,000. It is projected to produce cash inflows of $6,000 per year for five years.

ENRICHMENT NOTE:
Because it is based on cash flow, the net present value method is widely used not only in business, but also by individuals.

The company's minimum rate of return is 16 percent.

Because Model M is expected to produce unequal cash inflows, Table 3 in the appendix on future value and present value tables is used to determine the present value of each cash inflow from each year of the machine's life. The net present value of Model M is determined as follows:

Model M

Year	Net Cash Inflows	16% Factor	Present Value
1	$6,000	.862	$ 5,172.00
2	5,500	.743	4,086.50
3	5,000	.641	3,205.00
4	4,500	.552	2,484.00
5	4,000	.476	1,904.00
Residual value	2,000	.476	952.00
Total present value of cash inflows			$17,803.50
Less purchase price of Model M			17,500.00
Net present value			$ 303.50

All the factors for this analysis can be found in the column for 16 percent in Table 3. The factors discount the individual cash flows, including the expected residual value, to the present. The amount of the investment in Model M is deducted from the total present value of the cash inflows to arrive at the net present value of $303.50. Since the entire investment of $17,500 in Model M is a cash outflow at the beginning, that is, time zero, no discounting of the $17,500 purchase price is necessary. Because the net present value is positive, the proposed investment in Model M will achieve at least the minimum rate of return.

Because Model N is expected to produce equal cash receipts in each year of its useful life, Table 4 in the appendix on future value and present value tables is used to determine the combined present value of those future cash inflows. However, Table 3 is used to determine the present value of the machine's residual value because it represents a single payment, not an annuity. The net present value of Model N is calculated as follows:

Model N

Year	Net Cash Inflows	16% Factor	Present Value
1–5	$6,000	3.274	$19,644.00
Residual value	2,000	.476	952.00
Total present value of cash inflows			$20,596.00
Less purchase price of Model N			21,000.00
Net present value			($ 404.00)

Table 4 is used to determine the factor of 3.274, which is found in the column for 16 percent and the row for five periods. Because the residual value is a single inflow in the fifth year, the factor of .476 must be taken from Table 3 (the column for 16 percent and the row for five periods). The result is a net present value of ($404). Because the net present value is negative, the proposed investment in Model N will not achieve the minimum rate of return and should be rejected.

The two analyses show that Model M should be chosen because it has a positive net present value and would exceed the company's minimum rate of return. Model N should be rejected because it does not achieve the minimum rate of return.

 Check out ACE for a Review Quiz at http://accounting.college.hmco.com/students.

OTHER METHODS OF CAPITAL INVESTMENT ANALYSIS

L07 Analyze capital investment proposals using the payback period method and the accounting rate-of-return method.

RELATED TEXT ASSIGNMENTS
Q: 21, 22
SE: 9, 10
E: 13, 14
P: 5, 8
MRA: 2

KEY POINT: The payback period method measures the estimated length of time necessary to recover in cash the cost of an investment.

The net present value method is the best method for capital investment analysis. However, two other commonly used methods provide rough guides to evaluating capital investment proposals. These methods are the payback period method and the accounting rate-of-return method.

THE PAYBACK PERIOD METHOD

Because cash is an essential measure of a business's health, many managers estimate the cash flow that the investment will generate. Their goal is to determine the minimum time it will take to recover the initial investment. If two investment alternatives are being studied, management should choose the investment that pays back its initial cost in the shorter time. That period of time is known as the payback period, and the method of evaluation is called the **payback period method**. Although the payback period method is simple to use, its use has declined since it does not consider the time value of money. The payback period is computed as follows:

$$\text{Payback Period} = \frac{\text{Cost of Investment}}{\text{Annual Net Cash Inflows}}$$

To apply the payback period method, assume the Gordon Company is interested in buying a new bottling machine that costs $51,000 and has a residual value of $3,000. To evaluate the proposed capital investment of the Gordon Company, begin by determining the net cash inflows. First, find and eliminate the effects of all noncash revenue and expense items included in the analysis of net income. Assume that estimates for the proposal include revenue increases of $17,900 a year and operating cost increases of $11,696 a year (including depreciation and taxes). In this case, the only noncash expense or revenue is machine depreciation. To calculate this amount, you must know the asset's life and the depreciation method. Suppose the Gordon Company uses the straight-line method of depreciation, and the new bottling machine will have a ten-year service life. Using this information and the facts given earlier, compute the annual depreciation:

STUDY NOTE: When computing the payback period, omit depreciation from cash expenses since depreciation is a noncash expense.

$$\text{Annual Depreciation} = \frac{\text{Cost} - \text{Residual Value}}{10 \text{ (years)}}$$

$$= \frac{\$51,000 - \$3,000}{10} = \$4,800 \text{ per year}$$

After removing the noncash annual depreciation amount from the operating costs, the payback period is computed as follows:

$$\text{Payback Period} = \frac{\text{Cost of Machine}}{\text{Cash Revenue} - \text{Cash Expenses}}$$

$$= \frac{\$51,000}{\$17,900 - (\$11,696 - \$4,800)}$$

$$= \frac{\$51,000}{\$11,004} = 4.6 \text{ years}$$

If the company's desired payback period is five years or less, this proposal would be approved.

If a proposed capital investment has unequal annual net cash inflows, the payback period is determined by subtracting each annual amount (in chronological order) from the cost of the capital investment. When a zero balance is reached, the payback period has been determined. This will often occur in the middle of a year. The portion of the final year is computed by dividing the amount needed to reach zero (the unrecovered portion of the investment) by the entire year's estimated cash inflow.

The payback period method is widely used because it is easy to compute and understand. It is especially useful in areas in which technology changes rapidly, such as in Internet companies, and when risk is high, such as when investing in emerging countries. However, the disadvantages of this approach far outweigh its advantages. First, the payback period method does not measure profitability. Second, it ignores differences in the present values of cash flows from different periods; thus, it does not adjust cash flows for the time value of money. Finally, the payback period method emphasizes the time it takes to recover the investment rather than the long-term return on the investment. It ignores all future cash flows after the payback period is reached.

THE ACCOUNTING RATE-OF-RETURN METHOD

KEY POINT: The accounting rate-of-return method is appealing because it is easy to understand. It has flaws, however, such as the failure to consider the time value of money.

The **accounting rate-of-return method** is an imprecise but easy way to measure the estimated performance of a capital investment since it uses financial statement information. This method does not use an investment's cash flows but considers the financial reporting effects of the investment instead. The accounting rate-of-return method measures expected performance using two variables: (1) estimated annual net income from the project and (2) average investment cost. The basic equation is

$$\text{Accounting Rate of Return} = \frac{\text{Project's Average Annual Net Income}}{\text{Average Investment Cost}}$$

To compute average annual net income, use the cost and revenue data prepared for evaluating the project. Average investment in a proposed capital investment is calculated as follows:

$$\text{Average Investment Cost} = \left(\frac{\text{Total Investment} - \text{Residual Value}}{2}\right) + \text{Residual Value}$$

To see how this equation is used in evaluating a proposed capital investment, assume the same facts as before for the Gordon Company in its interest in purchasing a new bottling machine. Also assume the company's management will only consider projects that promise to yield more than a 16 percent return. To determine if the company should invest in the machine, compute the accounting rate of return as follows:

$$\text{Accounting Rate of Return} = \frac{\$17,900 - \$11,696}{\left(\frac{\$51,000 - \$3,000}{2}\right) + \$3,000}$$

$$= \frac{\$6,204}{\$27,000}$$

$$= 23\%$$

The projected rate of return is higher than the 16 percent minimum, so management should think seriously about making the investment.

The accounting rate-of-return method has been widely used because it is easy to understand and apply. It does have several disadvantages, however. First, because net income is averaged over the life of the investment, it is not a reliable figure. Actual net income may vary considerably from the estimates. Second, the method is unreliable if estimated annual net incomes differ from year to year. Third, cash flows are ignored. Fourth, the time value of money is not considered in the analysis. Thus, future and present dollars are treated as equal.

● **Stop and Think!**
Why are the payback period method and the accounting rate-of-return method rough estimates?
These methods do not consider the time value of money. ■

✔ Check out ACE for a Review Quiz at http://accounting.college.hmco.com/students.

Chapter Review

REVIEW OF LEARNING OBJECTIVES

LO1 Explain how managers make short-run decisions in the management cycle.

Both quantitative information and qualitative information are important for short-run decision analysis. Such information should be relevant, timely, and presented in a format that is easy to use in decision making. In the planning stage of the management cycle, managers discover a problem or need, identify alternative courses of action to solve the problem or meet the need, perform a complete analysis to determine the effects of each alternative on business operations, and choose the best alternative. Managers during the executing stage accept or reject a special order, examine the profitability of a segment, select the appropriate product mix given a resource constraint, contract with outside suppliers of goods and services, or sell a product as is or process it further. In the reviewing stage, each decision is evaluated to determine if the forecast results were obtained. Reporting occurs throughout the cycle to evaluate the information selected, the decision made, and the impact of that decision on the organization.

LO2 Define *incremental analysis* and describe how it applies to short-run decision analysis.

Incremental analysis helps managers compare alternatives by focusing on the differences in their projected revenues and costs. Any data that relate to future costs, revenues, or uses of resources and that will differ among alternative courses of action are considered relevant decision information. Projected sales or estimated costs, such as direct materials or direct labor, which differ for each decision alternative, are examples of relevant information. The accountant organizes relevant information to determine which alternative contributes the most to profits or incurs the lowest costs. Only data that differ for each alternative appear in the report. Differential or incremental costs are costs that vary among alternatives and thus are relevant to the decision. Sunk costs are past costs that cannot be recovered; they are irrelevant to the decision process. Opportunity costs are revenue or income forgone as a result of choosing an alternative.

LO3 Perform incremental analysis for outsourcing decisions, special order decisions, segment profitability decisions, sales mix decisions involving constrained resources, and sell or process-further decisions.

Outsourcing (including make-or-buy) *decision analysis* helps managers decide whether to use suppliers from outside the organization to perform services or provide goods that could be performed or produced internally. An incremental analysis of the expected costs and revenues for each alternative is used to identify the best alternative. A *special order decision* is a decision about whether to accept or reject a special order at a price below the normal market price. One approach is to compare the special order price to the relevant costs to see if a profit can be generated. Another approach is to prepare a special order bid price by calculating a minimum selling price for the special order. Generally, fixed costs are irrelevant to a special order decision because such costs are covered by regular sales activity and do not differ among alternatives. *Segment profitability decisions* involve the review of segments of an organization, such as product lines, services, sales territories, divisions, or departments. Often managers must decide whether to add or drop a segment. A segment with a negative segment margin may be dropped. A segment margin is a segment's sales revenue minus its direct costs, which include variable costs and avoidable fixed costs. Avoidable costs are costs traceable to a specific segment. If the segment is eliminated, the avoidable costs will also be eliminated. *Sales mix decisions* require the selection of the most profitable combination of sales items when a company makes more than one product or service using a common constrained resource. The product or service generating the highest contribution margin per constrained resource is offered and sold first. *Sell or process-further decisions* require managers to choose between selling a joint product at its split-off point or processing it into a more refined product. The managers compare the incremental revenues and costs of the two alternatives. Joint processing costs are irrelevant to the decision because they are identical for both alternatives. A product should be processed further only if the incremental revenues generated exceed the incremental costs incurred.

LO4 Identify the types of projected costs and revenues used to evaluate alternatives for capital investment.

The accounting rate-of-return method requires measures of net income. Other methods of evaluating capital investments evaluate net cash inflows or cost savings. The analysis process must take into consideration whether each period's cash flows will be equal or unequal. Unless the after-income-tax effects on cash flows are being considered, carrying values and depreciation expense of assets awaiting replacement are irrelevant. Net proceeds from the sale of an old asset and estimated residual value of a new facility represent future cash flows and must be part of the estimated benefit of a project. Depreciation expense on replacement equipment is relevant to evaluations based on after-tax cash flows.

LO5 Apply the concept of the time value of money.

Cash flows of equal dollar amounts at different times have different values because of the effect of compound interest. This phenomenon is known as the time value of money. Of the evaluation methods discussed in this chapter, only the net present value method takes into account the time value of money.

LO6 Analyze capital investment proposals using the net present value method.

The net present value method incorporates the time value of money into the analysis of a proposed capital investment. A minimum required rate of return, usually the average cost of capital, is used to discount an investment's expected future cash flows to their present values. The present values are added together, and the amount of the initial investment is subtracted from their total. If the resulting amount, called the net present value, is positive, the rate of return on the investment will exceed the required rate of return, and the investment should be accepted. If the net present value is negative, the return on the investment will be less than the minimum rate of return, and the investment should be rejected.

LO7 Analyze capital investment proposals using the payback period method and the accounting rate-of-return method.

The payback period method of evaluating a capital investment focuses on the minimum length of time needed to get the amount of the initial investment back in cash. With the accounting rate-of-return method, managers evaluate two or more capital investment proposals and then select the alternative that yields the highest ratio of average annual net income to average cost of investment. Both methods are easy to use, but they are very rough measures that do not consider the time value of money. As a result, the net present value method is preferred.

REVIEW OF CONCEPTS AND TERMINOLOGY

The following concepts and terms were introduced in this chapter:

LO7 **Accounting rate of return method:** A method of evaluating capital investments that does not use an investment's cash flows but considers the financial reporting effects of the investment instead.

LO3 **Avoidable costs:** Costs that can be eliminated by dropping a segment.

LO4 **Capital investment analysis:** The process of making decisions about capital investments. Also called *capital budgeting*.

LO4 **Capital investment decisions:** Management decisions about when and how much to spend on capital facilities and other long-term projects.

LO4 **Carrying value:** The undepreciated portion of the original cost of a fixed asset.

LO5 **Compound interest:** The interest cost for two or more periods when the amount on which interest is computed changes in each period to include all interest paid in previous periods.

LO6 **Cost of capital:** The weighted-average rate of return a company must pay to its long-term creditors and shareholders for the use of their funds.

LO4 **Cost savings:** Benefits, such as reduced costs, from a proposed capital investment.

LO2 **Differential cost:** A cost that changes among alternatives. Also called *incremental cost*.

LO5 **Future value:** The amount an investment will be worth at a future date if invested at compound interest.

LO2 **Incremental analysis:** A technique used in decision analysis that compares alternatives by focusing on the differences in their projected revenues and costs. Also called *differential analysis*.

LO5 **Interest:** The cost associated with the use of money for a specific period of time.

LO3 **Joint products:** Two or more products made from a common material or process that cannot be identified as separate products during some or all of the production process.

LO3 **Make-or-buy decisions:** Decisions about whether to make a part internally or buy it from an external supplier.

LO4 **Net cash inflows:** The balance of increases in projected cash receipts over increases in projected cash payments resulting from a proposed capital investment.

LO6 **Net present value method:** A method of evaluating capital investments in which all future cash flows for each proposed project are discounted to their present values, and the amount of the initial investment is subtracted from their sum. The projects with the highest positive net present value are selected for implementation.

LO2 **Opportunity costs:** The benefits forfeited or lost when one alternative is chosen over another.

LO5 **Ordinary annuity:** A series of equal payments or receipts that will begin one time period from the current date.

LO3 **Outsourcing:** The use of suppliers outside the organization to perform services or produce goods that could be performed or produced internally.

LO7 **Payback period method:** A method of evaluating capital investments that bases the decision to invest in a capital project on the minimum length of time it will take to get the amount of the initial investment back in cash.

LO5 **Present value:** The amount that must be invested today at a given rate of compound interest to produce a given future value.

LO3 **Sales mix decision:** A decision to select the alternative that maximizes the contribution margin per constrained resource.

LO3 **Segment margin:** A segment's sales revenue minus its direct costs (direct variable costs and direct fixed costs traceable to the segment).

LO3 **Sell or process-further decision:** A decision about whether to sell a joint product at the split-off point or sell it after further processing.

LO1 **Short-run decision analysis:** The systematic examination of any decision whose effects will be most felt over the next year or less.

LO5 **Simple interest:** The interest cost for one or more periods when the amount on which the interest is computed stays the same from period to period.

LO3 **Special order decisions:** Decisions about whether to accept or reject a special order at a price below the normal market price.

LO3 **Split-off point:** A specific point in the production process at which two or more joint products become separate and identifiable. At that point, a company may choose to sell the product as is or process it into another form for sale to a different market.

LO2 **Sunk cost:** A cost that was incurred because of a previous decision and cannot be recovered through the current decision.

LO5 **Time value of money:** The concept that cash flows of equal dollar amounts separated by an interval of time have different present values because of the effect of compound interest.

REVIEW PROBLEM

Short-Run Operating Decision Analysis

LO3 Home Services, Inc., specializes in repair and maintenance services. Recently, its profitability has declined, and Dale Bandy, the company's founder, wants to know which service lines are not meeting the company's profit targets. Once the services have been identified, he will either eliminate them or set higher prices. If higher prices are set, the price structure will cover all variable and fixed operating, selling, and general administrative costs. Four service lines are under serious review. Related data are as follows:

	Auto Repair	Boat Repair	Tile Floor Repair	Tree Trimming	Total Impact
Home Services, Inc.					
Segmented Income Statement					
For the Year Ended December 31, 20x8					
Sales	$297,500	$114,300	$126,400	$97,600	$635,800
Less variable costs					
Direct labor	$119,000	$40,005	$44,240	$34,160	$237,405
Operating supplies	14,875	5,715	6,320	4,880	31,790
Small tools	11,900	4,572	5,056	7,808	29,336
Replacement parts	59,500	22,860	25,280	—	107,640
Truck costs	—	11,430	12,640	14,640	38,710
Selling costs	44,625	17,145	18,960	9,760	90,490
Other variable costs	5,950	2,286	2,528	1,952	12,716
Contribution margin	$ 41,650	$ 10,287	$ 11,376	$24,400	$ 87,713
Less direct fixed costs	35,800	16,300	24,100	5,200	81,400
Segment margin	$ 5,850	($ 6,013)	($ 12,724)	$19,200	$ 6,313
Less common fixed costs					32,100
Operating income (loss)					($ 25,787)

REQUIRED ▶ 1. Analyze the performance of the four service lines being reviewed. Should Dale Bandy eliminate any of the service lines? Explain your answer.
2. Why might Bandy want to continue providing unprofitable service lines?
3. Even though some of the unprofitable services can be eliminated, the company still has an operating loss. Identify some possible causes for poor performance by the services. What actions do you recommend?

ANSWER TO REVIEW PROBLEM

1. When deciding whether to eliminate any of the four service lines, Dale Bandy should concentrate on the service lines that have a negative segment margin. If the revenues from a service line are less than the sum of its variable and direct fixed costs, then other service lines must cover some of the losing line's costs while carrying the burden of the common fixed costs.

Home Services, Inc.
Segment Profitability Decision

	Keep Boat Repair and Tile Floor Repair	Drop Boat Repair and Tile Floor Repair	Difference in Favor of Dropping Boat Repair and Tile Floor Repair
Sales	$635,800	$395,100	($240,700)
Less variable costs	548,087	329,050	219,037
Contribution margin	$ 87,713	$ 66,050	($ 21,663)
Less direct fixed costs	81,400	41,000	40,400
Segment margin	$ 6,313	$ 25,050	$ 18,737
Less common fixed costs	32,100	32,100	0
Operating income (loss)	($ 25,787)	($ 7,050)	$ 18,737

By looking at the segmented income statement, Dale Bandy can see that the company will improve its operating income by $18,737 ($6,013 + $12,724) by eliminating the Boat Repair Service and the Tile Floor Repair Service, both of which have a negative segment margin. Bandy's decision can also be supported by the analysis in **2**.

2. Bandy may want to continue offering the unprofitable service lines if their elimination would negatively affect the sale of auto repair or tree trimming services. Bandy may also want to diversify into new markets by offering new services. Bandy should be prepared to suffer some losses initially to enter the new markets.

3. Among the possible causes for poor performance by the company's four services are the following:

   a. Service fees set too low
   b. Inadequate advertising
   c. High direct labor costs
   d. Other variable costs too high
   e. Poor management of fixed costs
   f. Excessive supervision costs

To improve profitability, the organization can eliminate nonvalue-adding costs, increase service fees, or increase the volume of services provided to customers.

Chapter Assignments

BUILDING YOUR KNOWLEDGE FOUNDATION

QUESTIONS

1. Briefly describe how each stage of the management cycle applies to short-run decision analysis.

2. List some common types of short-run decisions that can be made during the executing stage of the management cycle.

3. List qualitative factors that will influence a short-run decision.

4. What is incremental analysis? What types of decision analyses depend on the incremental approach?

5. What is an opportunity cost?

6. List the business activities that are likely to be outsourced. What makes them attractive for outsourcing?

7. Which data are relevant to a make-or-buy decision in a manufacturing operation?

8. What are two approaches to making a special order decision?

9. What are the two steps in the analysis for a sales mix decision?

10. What is the role of joint costs in sell or process-further decision analysis?

11. What are capital investments? Give examples of some capital investments.

12. Define *capital investment analysis*.

13. Distinguish between cost savings and net cash inflows.

14. Why is it important to know whether a capital investment will produce equal cash flows or unequal cash flows?

15. "In capital investment analysis, the carrying value of an asset is irrelevant, whereas current and future residual values are relevant." Is this statement valid? Why or why not?

16. In the evaluation of equipment replacement proposals, why is depreciation of the old equipment ignored?

17. How does the relationship between depreciation and income taxes affect capital investment analysis?

18. Discuss the statement, "To treat all future income flows alike ignores the time value of money."

19. Which table in the appendix on future value and present value tables is used to determine the present value of a single sum to be received in the future? Which table is used to determine the present value of a series of payments (ordinary annuity) to be received in the future? How is each table used in the net present value method?

20. What is the role of the average cost of capital when the net present value method is used to evaluate capital investment proposals?

21. Is the payback period method very accurate? Defend your answer.

22. What formula is used to determine the accounting rate-of-return?

SHORT EXERCISES

SE 1.

LO1 Qualitative and Quantitative Information in Short-Run Decision Analysis

The owner of Mimi's, a French restaurant, is deciding whether to take chicken à l'orange off the menu. Tell whether each of the following pieces of decision information is qualitative or quantitative. If the information is quantitative, specify whether it is financial or nonfinancial.

1. The time needed to prepare the chicken
2. The daily number of customers who order the chicken

3. Whether competing French restaurants have this entrée on the menu
4. The labor cost of the chef who prepares the chicken
5. The fact that the president of a nearby company, who brings ten guests with him each week, always orders chicken à l'orange.

SE 2.

LO2 Using Incremental Analysis

Aries Corporation has assembled the following information related to the purchase of a new automated postage machine.

	Posen Machine	Valuet Machine
Increase in revenue	$43,200	$49,300
Increase in annual operating costs		
Direct materials	12,200	12,200
Direct labor	10,200	10,600
Variable manufacturing overhead	24,500	26,900
Fixed manufacturing overhead (including depreciation)	12,400	12,400

Using incremental analysis and only relevant information, compute the difference in favor of the Valuet machine.

SE 3.

LO3 Outsourcing Decision

Marcus Company assembles products from a group of interconnecting parts. Some of the parts are produced by the company, and some are purchased from outside vendors. The vendor for Part X has just increased its price by 35 percent, to $10 per unit for the first 5,000 units and $9 per additional unit ordered each year. The company uses 7,500 units of Part X each year. Unit costs if the company makes the part are:

Direct materials	$3.50
Direct labor	1.75
Variable manufacturing overhead	4.25
Variable selling costs for the assembled product	3.75

Should the company continue to purchase the part, or should it begin making the part?

SE 4.

LO3 Special Order Decision

Smith Accounting Services is considering a special order that it received from one of its corporate clients. The special order calls for Smith to prepare the individual tax returns of the corporation's four largest shareholders. The company has idle capacity that could be used to complete the special order. The following data have been gathered about the preparation of individual tax returns:

Materials cost per page	$1
Average hourly labor rate	$60
Standard hours per return	4
Standard pages per return	10
Variable overhead cost per page	$.50
Fixed overhead cost per page	$.50

Smith Accounting Services would be satisfied with a $40 gross profit per return. Compute the minimum bid price for the entire order.

SE 5.

LO3 Sales Mix Decision

Snow, Inc., makes three kinds of snowboards, but it has a limited number of machine hours available to make them. Product line data are as follows:

	Wood	Plastic	Graphite
Machine hours per unit	1.25	1.0	1.5
Selling price per unit	$100	$120	$200
Variable manufacturing cost per unit	45	50	100
Variable selling costs per unit	15	26	36

In what order should the snowboard product lines be produced?

SE 6.

LO4 Capital Investment Analysis and Revenue Measures

Maize Corp. is analyzing a proposal to switch its factory over to a lights-out operation. To do so, it must acquire a fully automated machine. The machine will be able to produce an entire product line in a single operation. Projected annual net cash inflows from the machine are $180,000, and projected net income is $120,000. Why is projected net income $60,000 less than projected net cash inflows? Identify possible causes.

SE 7.

LO5 Time Value of Money

Heidi Layne recently inherited a trust fund from a distant relative. On January 2, the bank managing the trust fund notified Layne that she has the option of receiving a lump-sum check for $175,500 or leaving the money in the trust fund and receiving an annual year-end check for $20,000 for each of the next 20 years. Layne likes to earn at least an 8 percent return on her investments. What should she do?

SE 8.
LO6 Capital Investment Decision: Net Present Value Method

Noway Jose Communications, Inc., is considering the purchase of a new piece of computerized data transmission equipment. Estimated annual net cash inflows for the new equipment are $575,000. The equipment costs $2 million, it has a five-year life, and it will have no residual value at the end of the five years. The company has a minimum rate of return of 12 percent. Compute the net present value of the piece of equipment. Should the company purchase it? Use Table 4 in the appendix on future and present value tables.

SE 9.
LO7 Capital Investment Decision: Payback Period Method

East-West Cable, Inc., is considering the purchase of new data transmission equipment. Estimated annual cash revenues for the new equipment are $1 million, and operating costs (including depreciation of $400,000) are $825,000. The equipment costs $2 million, it has a five-year life, and it will have no residual value at the end of the five years. Compute the payback period for the piece of equipment. Does this method yield a positive or a negative response to the proposal to buy the equipment, assuming the company sets a maximum payback period of four years?

SE 10.
LO7 Capital Investment Decision: Accounting Rate-of-Return Method

Best Cleaners is considering whether to purchase a delivery truck that will cost $29,000, last six years, and have an estimated residual value of $5,000. Average annual net income from the delivery service is estimated to be $4,000. Best Cleaners' owners seek to earn an accounting rate of return of 20 percent. Compute the average investment cost and the accounting rate of return. Should the investment be made?

EXERCISES

E 1.
LO2 Incremental Analysis

The managers of Lennox Company must decide which of two mill blade grinders—Y or Z—to buy. The grinders have the same purchase price but different revenues and cost characteristics. The company currently owns Grinder X, which it bought three years ago for $15,000 and which has accumulated depreciation of $9,000 and a book value of $6,000. Grinder X is now obsolete as a result of advances in technology and cannot be sold or traded in.

The accountant has collected the following annual revenue and operating cost estimates for the two new machines:

	Grinder Y	Grinder Z
Increase in revenue	$16,000	$20,000
Increase in annual operating costs		
Direct materials	4,800	4,800
Direct labor	3,000	4,100
Variable manufacturing overhead	2,100	3,000
Fixed manufacturing overhead (depreciation included)	5,000	5,000

1. Identify the relevant data in this problem.
2. Prepare an incremental analysis to aid the managers in their decision.
3. Should the company purchase Grinder Y or Z?

E 2.
LO3 Outsourcing Decision

Sunny Hazel, the manager of Cyber Web Services, must decide whether to hire a new employee or to outsource some of the web design work to Ky To, a freelance graphic designer. If she hires a new employee, she will pay $32 per design hour for the employee to work 600 hours and incur service overhead costs of $2 per design hour. If she outsources the work to Ky To, she will pay $36 per design hour for 600 hours of work. She can also redirect the use of a computer and server to generate $4,000 in additional revenue from web page maintenance work. Should Cyber Web Services hire a new designer or outsource the work to Ky To?

E 3.
LO3 Special Order Decision

Jens Sporting Goods, Inc., manufactures a complete line of sporting equipment. Leiden Enterprises operates a large chain of discount stores. Leiden has approached Jens with a special order for 30,000 deluxe baseballs. Instead of being packaged separately, the balls are to be bulk packed in boxes containing 500 baseballs each. Leiden is willing to pay $2.45 per baseball. Jens knows that annual expected production is 400,000 baseballs. It also knows that the current year's production is 410,000 baseballs and that the maximum production capacity is 450,000 baseballs. The following additional information is available:

Standard unit cost data for 400,000 baseballs

Direct materials	$ .90
Direct labor	.60
Manufacturing overhead	
Variable	.50
Fixed ($100,000 ÷ 400,000)	.25
Packaging per unit	.30
Advertising ($60,000 ÷ 400,000)	.15
Other fixed selling and administrative	
expenses ($120,000 ÷ 400,000)	.30
Product unit cost	$ 3.00
Unit selling price	$ 4.00
Total estimated bulk packaging costs for special order (30,000 baseballs: 500 per box)	$2,500

1. Should Jens Sporting Goods, Inc., accept Leiden's offer?
2. What would be the minimum order price per baseball if Jens would like to earn a profit of $3,000 from the special order?

E 4.   Guld's Glass, Inc., has three divisions: Commercial, Nonprofit, and Residential. The segmented income statement for 20x8 revealed the following:

LO3 Elimination of Unprofitable Segment Decision

Guld's Glass, Inc.
Divisional Profit Summary and Decision Analysis

	Commercial Division	Nonprofit Division	Residential Division	Total Company
Sales	$290,000	$533,000	$837,000	$1,660,000
Less variable costs	147,000	435,000	472,000	1,054,000
Contribution margin	$143,000	$ 98,000	$365,000	$ 606,000
Less direct fixed costs	124,000	106,000	139,000	369,000
Segment margin	$ 19,000	($ 8,000)	$226,000	$ 237,000
Less common fixed costs				168,000
Operating income				$ 69,000

1. How will Guld's Glass, Inc., be affected if the Nonprofit Division is dropped?
2. If the Nonprofit Division is dropped, the sales of the Residential Division will decrease by 10 percent. How will Guld's Glass, Inc., be affected if the Nonprofit Division is dropped?

E 5.   EZ, Inc., manufactures two products that require both machine processing and labor operations. Although there is unlimited demand for both products, EZ could devote all its capacities to a single product. Unit prices, cost data, and processing requirements are:

LO3 Sales Mix Decision

	Product E	Product Z
Unit selling price	$80	$220
Unit variable costs	$40	$90
Machine hours per unit	.4	1.4
Labor hours per unit	2	6

In 20x8 the company will be limited to 160,000 machine hours and 120,000 labor hours. Fixed costs for 20x8 are $1,000,000.

1. Compute the most profitable combination of products to be produced in 20x8.
2. Prepare an income statement using the contribution margin format for the product volume computed in 1.

E 6.

LO3 Sales Mix Decision

Grady Enterprises manufactures three computer games. They are called Rising Star, Ghost Master, and Road Warrior. The product line data are as follows:

	Rising Star	Ghost Master	Road Warrior
Current unit sales demand	20,000	30,000	18,000
Machine hours per unit	2	1	2.5
Selling price per unit	$24.00	$18.00	$32.00
Unit variable manufacturing costs	$12.50	$10.00	$18.75
Unit variable selling costs	$6.50	$5.00	$6.25

The current production capacity is 100,000 machine hours.

1. Which computer game should be manufactured first? Which should be manufactured second? Which last?
2. How many of each type of computer game should be manufactured and sold to maximize the company's contribution margin based on the current production activity of 100,000 machine hours? What is the total contribution margin for that combination?

E 7.

LO3 Sell or Process-Further Decision

Six Star Pizza manufactures frozen pizzas and calzones and sells them for $4 each. Six Star is currently considering a proposal to manufacture and sell fully prepared products. The following relevant information has been gathered by management:

Product	Sales Revenue with No Additional Processing	Sales Revenue if Processed Further	Additional Processing Costs
Pizza	$4	$ 8	$5
Calzone	$4	$10	$5

Use incremental analysis to determine which products Six Star Pizza should offer.

E 8.

LO4 Income Taxes and Net Cash Flow

San Falesco Company has a tax rate of 25 percent on taxable income. It is considering a capital project that will make the following annual contribution to operating income:

Cash revenues	$ 500,000
Cash expenses	(300,000)
Depreciation	(150,000)
Operating income	$ 50,000
Income taxes at 25%	(12,500)
Operating income after income taxes	$ 37,500

1. Determine the net cash inflows for this project in two different ways. Are net cash flows the same under both approaches?
2. What is the impact of income taxes on net cash flows?

E 9.

LO5 Using the Present Value Tables

For each of the following situations, identify the correct factor to use from Table 3 or 4 in the appendix on future value and present value tables. Also, compute the appropriate present value.

1. Annual net cash inflows of $22,500 for twelve years, discounted at 14%
2. The following five years of cash inflows, discounted at 10%:

Year 1	$35,000
Year 2	20,000
Year 3	30,000
Year 4	40,000
Year 5	50,000

3. The amount of $70,000 to be received at the beginning of year 7, discounted at 14%

E 10.

LO6 Capital Investment Decision: Net Present Value Method

Qen and Associates wants to buy an automated coffee roaster/grinder/brewer. This piece of equipment would have a useful life of six years, would cost $219,500, and would increase annual net cash inflows by $57,000. Assume there is no residual value at the end of six years. The company's minimum rate of return is 14 percent.

Using the net present value method, prepare an analysis to determine whether the company should purchase the machine. Use Tables 3 and 4 in the appendix on future value and present value tables.

E 11.

LO6 Capital Investment Decision: Net Present Value Method

H and Y Service Station is planning to invest in automatic car wash equipment valued at $250,000. The owner estimates that the equipment will increase annual net cash inflows by $46,000. The equipment is expected to have a ten-year useful life with an estimated residual value of $50,000. The company requires a 14 percent minimum rate of return. Using the net present value method, prepare an analysis to determine whether the company should purchase the equipment. How important is the estimate of residual value to this decision? Use Tables 3 and 4 in the appendix on future value and present value tables.

E 12.

LO6 Capital Investment Decision: Net Present Value Method

Assume the same facts for H and Y Service Station as in **E11**, except that the company requires a 20 percent minimum rate of return. Using the net present value method, prepare an analysis to determine whether the company should purchase the equipment. How important is the estimate of residual value to this decision? Use Tables 3 and 4 in the appendix on future value and present value tables.

E 13.

LO7 Capital Investment Decision: Payback Period Method

Soaking Wet, Inc., a manufacturer of gears for lawn sprinklers, is thinking about adding a new fully automated machine. This machine can produce gears the company currently produces on its third shift. The machine has an estimated useful life of 10 years and will cost $800,000. Gross cash revenue from the machine will be about $520,000 per year, and related operating expenses, including depreciation, should total $500,000. Depreciation is estimated to be $80,000 annually. The payback period should be five years or less.

Use the payback period method to determine whether the company should invest in the new machine. Show your computations to support your answer.

E 14.

LO7 Capital Investment Decision: Accounting Rate-of-Return Method

Perfection Sound, Inc., a manufacturer of stereo speakers, is thinking about adding a new plastic injection molding machine. This machine can produce speaker parts that the company now buys from outsiders. The machine has an estimated useful life of 14 years and will cost $425,000. Residual value of the new machine is $42,500. Gross cash revenue from the machine will be about $400,000 per year, and related cash expenses should total $310,050. Depreciation is estimated to be $30,350 annually. Management has decided that only capital investments that yield at least a 20 percent return will be accepted.

Using the accounting rate-of-return method, decide whether the company should invest in the machine. Show all computations to support your decision.

PROBLEMS

P 1.

LO3 Sell or Process-Further Decision

Bagels, Inc., produces and sells 20 types of bagels by the dozen. Bagels are priced at $6.00 per dozen and cost $.20 per unit to produce. The company is considering further processing the bagels into two products: bagels with cream cheese and bagel sandwiches. It would cost an additional $.50 per unit to produce bagels with cream cheese, and the new selling price would be $2.50 each. It would cost an additional $1.00 per sandwich to produce bagel sandwiches, and the new selling price would be $3.50 each.

REQUIRED ▶

1. Identify the relevant per unit costs and revenues for the alternatives. Are there any sunk costs?
2. Based on the information in **1**, should Bagels, Inc., expand its product offerings?
3. Suppose that Bagels, Inc., did expand its product line to include bagels with cream cheese and bagel sandwiches. Based on customer feedback, the company determined that it could further process those two products into bagels with fruit and cream cheese and bagel sandwiches with cheese. The company's accountant compiled the following information:

Product (per unit)	Sales Revenue if Sold with No Further Processing	Sales Revenue if Processed Further	Additional Processing Costs
Bagels with cream cheese	$2.50	$3.50	Fruit: $1.00
Bagel sandwiches	$3.50	$4.50	Cheese: $.50

Perform an incremental analysis to determine if Bagels, Inc., should process its products further. Explain your findings.

LO3 Decision to Discontinue Segment

P 2. Seven months ago, Naib Publishing Company published its first book (Book N). Since then, the company has added four more books to its product list (Books S, Q, X, and H). Management is considering proposals for three more new books, but editorial capacity limits the company to producing only seven books annually. Before deciding which of the proposed books to publish, management wants you to evaluate the performance of its existing book list. Recent revenue and cost data appear below.

Naib Publishing Company
Product Profit and Loss Summary
For the Year Ended December 31, 20x8

	Book N	Book S	Book Q	Book X	Book H	Company Totals
Sales	$813,800	$782,000	$634,200	$944,100	$707,000	$3,881,100
Less variable costs						
Materials and binding	$325,520	$312,800	$190,260	$283,230	$212,100	$1,323,910
Editorial services	71,380	88,200	73,420	57,205	80,700	370,905
Author royalties	130,208	125,120	101,472	151,056	113,120	620,976
Sales commissions	162,760	156,400	95,130	141,615	141,400	697,305
Other selling costs	50,682	44,740	21,708	18,334	60,700	196,164
Total variable costs	$740,550	$727,260	$481,990	$651,440	$608,020	$3,209,260
Contribution margin	$ 73,250	$ 54,740	$152,210	$292,660	$ 98,980	$ 671,840
Less total fixed costs	97,250	81,240	89,610	100,460	82,680	451,240
Operating income	($ 24,000)	($ 26,500)	$ 62,600	$192,200	$ 16,300	$ 220,600
Direct fixed costs included in total fixed costs above	$ 51,200	$ 65,100	$ 49,400	$ 69,100	$ 58,800	$ 293,600

Projected data for the proposed new books are Book P, sales, $450,000, contribution margin, $45,000; Book T, sales, $725,000, contribution margin, ($25,200); and Book R, sales, $913,200, contribution margin, $115,500. Projected direct fixed costs are: Book P, $5,000; Book T, $6,000; Book R, $40,000.

REQUIRED ▶
1. Analyze the performance of the five books currently being published.
2. Should the company eliminate any of its present products? If so, which one(s)?
3. Identify the new books you would use to replace those eliminated. Justify your answer.

LO3 Special Order Decision

P 3. Keystone Resorts, Ltd., has approached Crystal Printers, Inc., with a special order to produce 300,000 two-page brochures. Most of Crystal's work consists of recurring short-run orders. Keystone Resorts is offering a one-time order, and Crystal has the capacity to handle the order over a two-month period.

Keystone's management has stated that the company would be unwilling to pay more than $48 per 1,000 brochures. The following cost data were assembled by Crystal's controller for this decision analysis: Direct materials (paper) would be $26.50 per 1,000 brochures. Direct labor costs would be $6.80 per 1,000 brochures. Direct materials (ink) would be $4.40 per 1,000 brochures. Variable production overhead would be $6.20 per 1,000 brochures. Machine maintenance (fixed cost) is $1.00 per direct labor dollar. Other fixed production overhead amounts to $2.40 per direct labor dollar. Variable packing costs would be $4.30 per 1,000 brochures. Also, the share of general and administrative expenses (fixed costs) to be allocated would be $5.25 per direct labor dollar.

REQUIRED ▶

1. Prepare an analysis for Crystal management to use in deciding whether to accept or reject Keystone Resorts' offer. What decision should be made?
2. What is the lowest possible price Crystal can charge per thousand and still make a $6,000 profit on the order?

P 4.

LO5   Net Present Value Method
LO6

Sonja and Sons, Inc., owns and operates a group of apartment buildings. Management wants to sell one of its older four-family buildings and buy a new structure. The old building, which was purchased 25 years ago for $100,000, has a 40-year estimated life. The current market value is $80,000, and if it is sold, the cash inflow will be $67,675. Annual net cash inflows from the old building are expected to average $16,000 for the remainder of its estimated useful life.

The new building being considered will cost $300,000. It has an estimated useful life of 25 years. Net cash inflows are expected to be $50,000 annually.

Assume that (1) all cash flows occur at year end, (2) the company uses straight-line depreciation, (3) the buildings will have a residual value equal to 10 percent of their purchase price, and (4) the minimum rate of return is 14 percent. Use Tables 3 and 4 in the appendix on future value and present value tables.

REQUIRED ▶

1. Compute the net present value of future cash flows from the old building.
2. What will be the net present value of cash flows if the new building is purchased?
3. Should the company keep the old building or purchase the new one?

P 5.

LO7   Accounting Rate-of-Return
and Payback Period Methods

The Raab Company is expanding its production facilities to include a new product line: a sporty automotive tire rim. Using new computerized machinery, tire rims can now be produced with little labor cost. The controller has advised management about two such machines. The details about each machine are as follows:

	XJS Machine	HZT Machine
Cost of machine	$500,000	$550,000
Residual value	50,000	55,000
Average annual net income	34,965	40,670
Annual net cash inflows	91,215	90,170

The minimum rate of return is 12 percent. The maximum payback period is six years. (Where necessary, round calculations to the nearest dollar.)

REQUIRED ▶

1. For each machine, compute the projected accounting rate of return.
2. Compute the payback period for each machine.
3. From the information generated in **1** and **2**, which machine should be purchased? Why?

ALTERNATE PROBLEMS

P 6.

LO3   Outsourcing Decision

The Stainless Refrigerator Company purchases and installs ice makers in its products. The ice makers cost $138 per case, and each case contains 12 ice makers. The supplier recently gave advance notice that the price will rise by 50 percent immediately. Stainless Refrigerator Company has idle equipment that, with only a few minor changes, could be used to produce similar ice makers.

Cost estimates have been prepared under the assumption that the company could make the product itself. Direct materials would cost $100.80 per 12 ice makers. Direct labor required would be 10 minutes per ice maker at a labor rate of $18.00 per hour. Variable manufacturing overhead would be $4.60 per ice maker. Fixed manufacturing overhead, which would be incurred under either decision alternative, would be $32,420 a year for depreciation and $234,000 a year for other costs. Production and usage are estimated at 75,000 ice makers a year. (Assume that any idle equipment cannot be used for any other purpose.)

REQUIRED ▶

1. Prepare an incremental analysis to determine whether the ice makers should be made within the company or purchased from the outside supplier at the higher price.
2. Compute the unit cost to (1) make one ice maker and (2) buy one ice maker.

LO3   Sales Mix Decision

P 7. Dr. Massy, a doctor specializing in internal medicine, wants to analyze his sales mix to find out how the time of his physician assistant, Consuela Ortiz, can be used to generate the highest operating income. Ortiz sees patients in the office, consults with patients over the telephone, and conducts one daily weight-loss support group attended by up to 50 patients. Statistics for the three daily services are:

	Office Visits	Phone Calls	Weight-Loss Support Group
Maximum number of patient billings per day	20	40	50
Minutes per billing	15	6	60
Billing rate	$50	$25	$10
Variable costs	$25	$12	$ 5

Ortiz works seven hours a day.

REQUIRED ▶

1. Determine the best sales mix. Rank the services in order of their profitability.
2. Based on the ranking in **1,** how much time should Ortiz spend on each service in a day? (*Hint:* Remember to consider the maximum number of patient billings per day.) What would be the daily total contribution margin generated by Ortiz?
3. Dr. Massy believes the ranking is incorrect. He knows that the daily 60-minute meeting of the weight-loss support group is attended by 50 patients and should continue to be offered. If the new ranking for the services is (1) weight-loss support group, (2) phone calls, and (3) office visits, how much time should Ortiz spend on each service in a day? What would be the total contribution margin generated by Ortiz, assuming the weight-loss support group has the maximum number of patient billings?
4. Which ranking would you recommend? What additional amount of total contribution margin would be generated if your recommendation is accepted?

LO5   Capital Investment Decision:
LO6   Comprehensive
LO7

P 8. The Arcadia Manufacturing Company, based in Arcadia, Florida, is one of the fastest-growing companies in its industry. According to Ms. Prinze, the company's production vice president, keeping up-to-date with technological changes is what makes the company successful.

Prinze feels that a machine introduced recently would fill an important need. The machine has an estimated useful life of four years, a purchase price of $250,000, and a residual value of $25,000. The company controller has estimated average annual net income of $11,250 and the following cash flows for the new machine:

Year	Cash Inflows	Cash Outflows	Net Cash Inflows
1	$325,000	$250,000	$75,000
2	320,000	250,000	70,000
3	315,000	250,000	65,000
4	310,000	250,000	60,000

Prinze uses a 12 percent minimum rate of return and a three-year payback period for capital investment evaluation purposes.

REQUIRED ▶

1. Analyze the data about the machine and decide if the company should purchase it. Use the following methods in your analysis: (a) the net present value method, (b) the accounting rate-of-return method, and (c) the payback period method. Use Tables 3 and 4 in the appendix on future value and present value tables.
2. Summarize the information generated in **1,** and make a recommendation to Prinze.

SKILLS DEVELOPMENT CASES

Conceptual Analysis

LO1   Management Decision Cycle

SD 1. Two weeks ago your cousin Edna moved from New York City to Houston. She needs a car to drive to work and to run errands but has no experience in selecting a car, and has asked for your help. Using the management cycle presented in this chapter, write her a letter explaining how she can approach making this decision.

How would your response change if the president of your company asked you to help make a decision about acquiring a fleet of cars for use by sales personnel?

SD 2.

LO4   **Factors in Capital Investment**
       Decisions

PPG Industries <www.ppg.com>, founded in 1883, was the first commercially successful plate glass manufacturer in the United States. Today it is a global supplier of coatings, chemicals, and glass. Every year, its management approves capital spending for modernization and productivity improvements, expansion of existing businesses, and environmental control projects.

Because PPG Industries' management receives many proposals for capital investment projects, it must set an appropriate acceptance-rejection standard. What factors should management consider in setting this standard? If more proposed projects meet the minimum standard than can be funded, what other factors should mangement consider, and what should management do?

Ethical Dilemma

SD 3.

LO4   **Ethics, Capital Investment**
LO6   **Decisions, and the New**
       Globally Competitive Business
       Environment

Marika Jonssen is the controller of Bramer Corporation, a globally competitive producer of standard and custom-designed window units for the housing industry. As part of the corporation's move to become automated, Jonssen was asked to prepare a capital investment analysis for a robot-guided aluminum extruding and stamping machine. This machine would automate the entire window-casing manufacturing line.

Jonssen had recently returned from an international seminar on the subject of qualitative inputs into the capital investment decision process, and she was eager to incorporate what she had learned into the analysis. In addition to the normal net present value analysis (which produced a significant negative result) Jonssen factored in figures for customer satisfaction, scrap reduction, reduced inventory needs, and reputation for quality. With the additional information included, the analysis produced a positive response to the decision question.

When the chief financial officer finished reviewing Jonssen's work, he threw the papers on the floor and said, "What kind of garbage is this! You know it's impossible to quantify such things as customer satisfaction and reputation for quality. How do you expect me to go to the board of directors and explain your work? I want you to redo the entire analysis and follow only the traditional approach to net present value. Get it back to me in two hours!"

What is Jonssen's dilemma? What ethical courses of action are available to her?

Research Activity

SD 4.

LO2   **Identifying Relevant Decision**
       Information

Assume you want to take a two-week vacation. Select two destinations for your vacation, and gather information about them from brochures, magazines, travel agents, the Internet, and people you know. Then list the relevant quantitative and qualitative information in its order of importance to your decision. Analyze the information, and select a destination. What factors were the most important to your decision? Why? What factors were the least important to your decision? Why? How would the process of identifying relevant decision information differ if you were asked by the president of your company to prepare a budget for the next training meeting, to be held at a location of your choice?

 Group Activity: Divide the class into groups, and ask them to discuss this skills development case. Then debrief the entire class by asking one person from each group to summarize his or her group's findings.

Decision-Making Practice

SD 5.

LO3   **Decision to Add a New**
       Department

Management at Transco Company is considering a proposal to install a third production department within its factory building. With the company's existing production setup, direct materials are processed through the Mixing Department to produce Materials A

and B in equal proportions. Material A is then processed through the Shaping Department to yield Product C. Material B is sold as is at $20.25 per pound. Product C has a selling price of $100 per pound.

There is a proposal to add a Baking Department to process Material B into Product D. It is expected that any quantity of Product D can be sold for $30 per pound. Costs per pound under this proposal are as follows.

	Mixing Department (Materials A & B)	Shaping Department (Product C)	Baking Department (Product D)
Cost from Mixing Department	—	$33.00	$13.20
Direct materials	$20.00	—	—
Direct labor	6.00	9.00	3.50
Variable manufacturing overhead	4.00	8.00	4.00
Fixed manufacturing overhead			
Traceable (direct, avoidable)	2.25	2.25	1.80
Allocated (common, unavoidable)	.75	.75	.75
	$33.00	$53.00	$23.25

1. If (a) sales and production levels are expected to remain constant in the foreseeable future and (b) there are no foreseeable alternative uses for the factory space, should Transco Company add a Baking Department and produce Product D, if 100,000 pounds of D can be sold? Show calculations of incremental revenues and costs to support your answer.
2. List at least two qualitative reasons that Transco Company may not want to install a Baking Department and produce Product D, even if it appears that this decision is profitable.
3. List at least two qualitative reasons why Transco Company may want to install a Baking Department and produce Product D, even if it appears that this decision is unprofitable.

(CMA adapted)

MANAGERIAL REPORTING AND ANALYSIS CASES

Interpreting Management Reports

MRA 1.
LO5   Capital Investment Analysis

Automated teller machines (ATMs) have become common in the banking industry. San Angelo Federal Bank is planning to replace some old teller machines and has decided to use the York Machine. Nola Chavez, the controller, has prepared the analysis shown at the top of the facing page. She has recommended the purchase of the machine based on the positive net present value shown in the analysis.

The York Machine has an estimated useful life of five years and an expected residual value of $35,000. Its purchase price is $385,000. Two existing ATMs, each having a carrying value of $25,000, can be sold to a neighboring bank for a total of $50,000. Annual operating cash inflows are expected to increase as follows:

Year 1	$79,900
Year 2	76,600
Year 3	79,900
Year 4	83,200
Year 5	86,500

The bank uses straight-line depreciation. The minimum rate of return is 12 percent.

1. Analyze Chavez's work. What changes need to be made in her capital investment analysis?
2. What would be your recommendation to bank management about the purchase of the York Machine?

San Angelo Federal Bank
Capital Investment Analysis
Net Present Value Method
March 2, 20x7

Year	Net Cash Inflows	Present-Value Factors	Present Value
1	$ 85,000	.909	$ 77,265
2	80,000	.826	66,080
3	85,000	.751	63,835
4	90,000	.683	61,470
5	95,000	.621	58,995
5 (residual value)	35,000	.621	21,735
Total present value			$349,380
Initial investment	$385,000		
Less proceeds from the sale of existing ATMs	50,000		
Net capital investment			(335,000)
Net present value			$ 14,380

Formulating Management Reports

MRA 2.

LO4 **Evaluating a Capital**
LO5 **Investment Proposal**
LO6
LO7

Quality work and timely output are the distinguishing characteristics of Smile Photo, Inc. Smile Photo is a nationally franchised company with over 50 outlets located in the southern states. Part of the franchise agreement promises a centralized photo developing process with overnight delivery to the outlets.

Because of the tremendous increase in demand for its photo processing, Emma DuBarry, the corporation's president, is considering the purchase of a new, deluxe photo processing machine by the end of this month. DuBarry wants you to formulate a memo showing your evaluation of this purchase. Your memo will be presented at the board of directors' meeting next week.

According to your research, the new machine will cost $320,000. It will function for an estimated five years and should have a $32,000 residual value. All capital investments are expected to produce a 20 percent minimum rate of return, and the investment should be recovered in three years or less. All fixed assets are depreciated using the straight-line method. The forecast increases in operating results for the new machine are as follows:

Cash Flow Estimates

Year	Cash Inflows	Cash Outflows
1	$310,000	$210,000
2	325,000	220,000
3	340,000	230,000
4	300,000	210,000
5	260,000	180,000

1. In preparation for writing your memo, answer the following questions.

   a. What kinds of information do you need to prepare this memo?
   b. Why is the information relevant?
   c. Where would you find the information?
   d. When would you want to obtain the information?

2. Analyze the purchase of the machine, and decide if the company should purchase it. Use (a) the net present value method, (b) the accounting rate-of-return method, and (c) the payback period method.

International Company

MRA 3.

LO2 Defining and Identifying Relevant Information

Gourmet Burgers is a competitor in the fast-food restaurant business. One component of the company's marketing strategy is to increase sales by expanding in foreign markets. The company uses both financial and nonfinancial quantitative and qualitative information when deciding whether to open restaurants in foreign markets.

Gourmet Burgers decided to open a restaurant in Prague (Czech Republic) five years ago. The following information helped the managers in making that decision.

Financial Quantitative Information

Operating information

Estimated food, labor, and other operating costs (for example, taxes, insurance, utilities, and supplies)
Estimated selling price for each food item

Capital investment information

Cost of land, building, equipment, and furniture
Financing options and amounts

Nonfinancial Quantitative Information

Estimated daily number of customers, hamburgers to be sold, employees to work
High-traffic time periods
Income of people living in the area
Ratio of population to number of restaurants in the market area
Traffic counts in front of similar restaurants in the area

Qualitative Information

Government regulations, taxes, duties, tariffs, political involvement in business operations
Property ownership restrictions
Site visibility
Accessibility of store location
Training process for local managers
Hiring process for employees
Local customs and practices

Gourmet Burgers has hired you as a consultant and has given you an income statement comparing the operating incomes of its five restaurants in Eastern Europe. You have noticed that the Prague location is operating at a loss (including unallocated fixed costs) and must decide whether to recommend closing that restaurant.

Review the information used in making the decision to open the restaurant. Identify the types of information that would also be relevant in deciding whether to close the restaurant. What period or periods of time should be reviewed in making your decision? What additional information would be relevant in making your decision?

Excel Spreadsheet Analysis

MRA 4.

LO3 Sell or Process-Further Decision

Marketeers, Inc., has developed a promotional program for a large shopping center in Sunset Living, Arizona. After investing $360,000 in developing the original promotion campaign, the firm is ready to present its client with an add-on contract offer that includes the original promotion areas of (1) TV advertising campaign, (2) a series of brochures for mass mailing, and (3) a special rotating BIG SALE schedule for 10 of the 28 tenants in the shopping center. Following are the revenue terms from the original contract with the shopping center and the offer for an add-on contract, which extends the original contract terms.

	Contract Terms	
	Original Contract Terms	Extended Contract Including Add-On Terms
TV advertising campaign	$520,000	$ 580,000
Brochure series	210,000	230,000
Rotating BIG SALE schedule	170,000	190,000
Totals	$900,000	$1,000,000

Marketeers estimates that the following additional costs will be incurred by extending the contract:

	TV Campaign	Brochures	BIG SALE Schedule
Direct labor	$30,000	$ 9,000	$7,000
Variable overhead costs	22,000	14,000	6,000
Fixed overhead costs*	12,000	4,000	2,000

*80 percent are direct fixed costs applied to this contract.

1. Using an Excel spreadsheet, compute the costs that will be incurred for each part of the add-on portion of the contract.
2. Should Marketeers, Inc., offer the add-on contract, or should it ask for a final settlement check based on the original contract only? Defend your answer.
3. If management of the shopping center indicated the terms of the add-on contract were negotiable, how should Marketeers respond?

Internet Case

MRA 5.
LO4   **Comparison of Capital Investment Disclosures by Two Large Companies**

Companies vary in the amount of information they disclose about their criteria for selecting capital investments. Access the web sites for two companies—for example, Coca-Cola <www.coca-cola.com> and International Paper <www.internationalpaper. com>. Find management's discussion and analysis (also called the financial review), which precedes the presentation of the financial statements. In that section, find the discussion of capital investments. Which company provides the more in-depth discussion? Does either disclose its criteria for making capital investment decisions? Also look at the investing activities listed in the statement of cash flows for each company. What is the extent of capital expenditures for each company? Compare each company's capital investments with the amount of total assets on the balance sheet. Which company is more of a growth company? Explain.

Appendix A

International Accounting

As businesses grow, they naturally look for new sources of supply and new markets in other countries. Today, it is common for businesses to operate in more than one country, and many of these so-called *multinational* or *transnational corporations* operate throughout the world.

The extent of a company's international operations can be found in its annual report in the segment information note to the financial statements. The annual report will also contain a description of the company's international operations.

www.pepsico.com

For example, the Frito Lay segment of PepsiCo, Inc., obtains more than one-third of its $13 billion in revenues from countries outside the United States. PepsiCo's annual report contains the following description of this division's international operations:

> Frito-Lay International manufactures, markets, sells and distributes salty and sweet snacks. Products include Walkers brand snack foods in the United Kingdom, Smith's brand snack foods in Australia, Sabritas brand snack foods and Alegro and Gamesa brand sweet snacks in Mexico. Many of our U.S. brands have been introduced internationally such as Lay's and Ruffles brand potato chips, Doritos and Tostitos brand tortilla chips, Fritos brand corn chips and Cheetos brand cheese-flavored snacks. Principal international snack markets include Mexico, the United Kingdom, Brazil, Spain, the Netherlands, Australia and South Africa.[1]

Table 1 shows the extent of the foreign revenues of five large U.S. corporations.

www.ibm.com

IBM, for example, has operations in 80 countries and receives almost 60 percent of its sales from outside the United States. Other industrial countries, such as Switzerland, France, Germany, Great Britain, the Netherlands, and Japan, have also

www.nestle.com

given rise to numerous worldwide corporations. Nestlé, the large Swiss food company, makes 98 percent of its sales outside Switzerland. Other companies that make

www.michelin.com
www.unilever.com
www.sony.com

more than half their sales outside their home countries include Michelin, the French tire maker; Unilever, the British/Netherlands consumer products company; and Sony, the Japanese electronics company. More than five hundred companies are listed on at least one stock exchange outside their home countries.

Sophisticated investors no longer restrict their investment activities to domestic securities markets. Many Americans invest in foreign securities markets, and

TABLE 1. Extent of Foreign Revenues for Selected U.S. Companies

Company	Foreign Revenues (millions)	Total Revenues (millions)	Foreign Revenues (percentage)
Exxon Mobil <www.exxonmobil.com>	$158,403	$228,439	69.3
IBM <www.ibm.com>	50,377	87,548	57.5
Ford <www.ford.com>	51,691	170,064	30.4
General Motors <www.gm.com>	48,233	184,632	26.1
PepsiCo <www.pepsico.com>	7,259	20,438	35.5

Source: Form 10-K of each company.

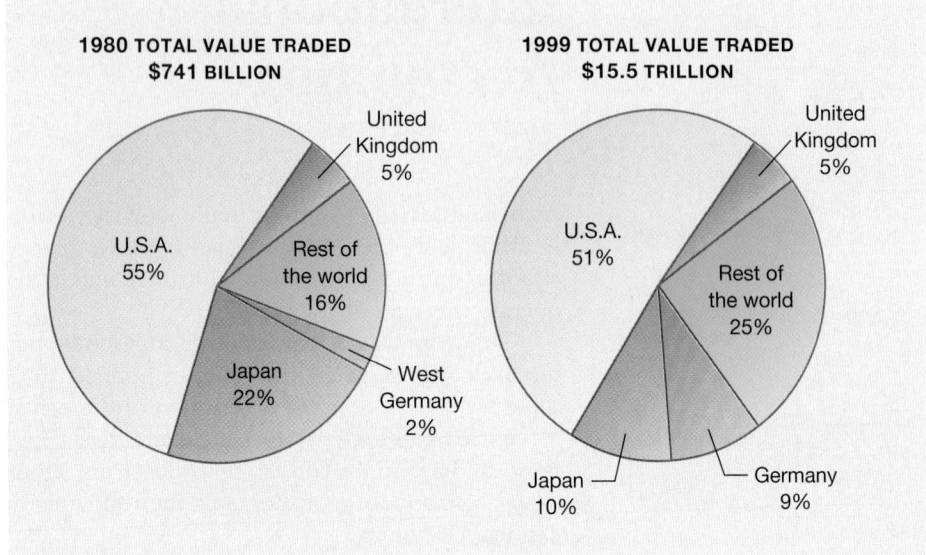

Source: International Finance Corporation, *Emerging Stock Markets Factbook*, © 2000.

non-Americans invest heavily in the stock market in the United States. Figure 1 shows that from 1980 to 1999, the total value of securities traded on the world's stock markets increased over twentyfold, with the U.S. share of the pie declining from 55 to 51 percent.

EFFECTS OF FOREIGN BUSINESS TRANSACTIONS

Foreign business transactions have two major effects on accounting. First, most sales or purchases of goods and services in other countries involve different currencies. Thus, one currency needs to be translated into another, using exchange rates.* An *exchange rate* is the value of one currency stated in terms of another. For example, an English company purchasing goods from a U.S. company and paying in U.S. dollars must exchange British pounds for U.S. dollars before making payment. In effect, currencies are goods that can be bought and sold. Table 2 lists the exchange rates of several currencies in terms of dollars. It shows the exchange rate for the British pound as $1.61. Like the price of any good or service, these prices change daily according to supply and demand. Accounting for these price changes in recording foreign transactions and preparing financial statements for foreign subsidiaries are discussed in the next two sections.

The second major effect of international business on accounting is that financial standards differ from country to country, which makes it difficult to compare companies from different countries. The obstacles to achieving comparability and some of the progress in solving the problem are discussed later in this appendix.

TABLE 2. Partial Listing of Foreign Exchange Rates

Country	Price in $ U.S.	Country	Price in $ U.S.
Britain (pound)	1.61	Hong Kong (dollar)	0.128
Canada (dollar)	0.704	Japan (yen)	0.008
Europe (euro)	1.12	Mexico (peso)	0.10

Source: The Wall Street Journal, May 5, 2003.

*At the time this chapter was written, exchange rates were fluctuating rapidly. The examples, exercises, and probems in this book use exchange rates in the general range for the countries involved.

ACCOUNTING FOR TRANSACTIONS IN FOREIGN CURRENCIES

A U.S. manufacturer may expand by selling its product to foreign customers, or it may lower its product cost by buying a less expensive part from a source in another country. In previous chapters of the text, all purchases and sales were recorded in dollars, and it was assumed that the dollar is a uniform measure in the same way that the inch and the centimeter are. But in the international marketplace, a transaction may take place in Japanese yen, British pounds, or some other currency. The values of these currencies in relation to the dollar rise and fall daily. Thus, if there is a delay between the date of sale or purchase and the date of receipt or payment, the amount of cash involved may differ from that originally agreed upon.

■ **FOREIGN SALES**   When a domestic company sells merchandise abroad, it may bill either in its own country's currency or in the foreign currency. If the billing and payment are both in the domestic currency, no accounting problem arises. For example, assume that a U.S. maker of precision tools sells $160,000 worth of its products to a British company and bills the British company in dollars. The entry to record the sale and receipt of payment is familiar:

Date of Sale

A = L + OE	Accounts Receivable, British company	160,000	
+ +	Sales		160,000

Date of Receipt

A = L + OE	Cash	160,000	
+	Accounts Receivable, British company		160,000
−			

However, if the U.S. company bills the British company in British pounds and accepts payment in pounds, the U.S. company may incur an *exchange gain or loss*. A gain or loss will occur if the exchange rate between dollars and pounds changes between the date of sale and the date of receipt. Since gains and losses tend to offset one another, a single account is used during the year to accumulate the activity. The net exchange gain or loss is reported on the income statement. For example, assume that the sale of $160,000 above was billed at £100,000, reflecting an exchange rate of 1.60 (that is, $1.60 per pound) on the sale date. Now assume that by the date of receipt, the exchange rate has fallen to 1.50. The entries to record the transactions follow:

Date of Sale

A = L + OE	Accounts Receivable, British company	160,000	
+ +	Sales		160,000
	£100,000 × $1.60 = $160,000		

Date of Receipt

A = L + OE	Cash	150,000	
+ −	Exchange Gain or Loss	10,000	
−	Accounts Receivable, British company		160,000
	£100,000 × $1.50 = $150,000		

The U.S. company has incurred an exchange loss of $10,000 because it agreed to accept a fixed number of British pounds in payment for its products, and the value of each pound dropped before the payment was made. Had the value of the pound in relation to the dollar increased, the U.S. company would have made an exchange gain.

■ **FOREIGN PURCHASES**   The same logic applies to purchases as to sales, except that the relationship of exchange gains and losses to changes in exchange rates is reversed. For example, assume that the U.S. toolmaker purchases parts from a Japanese supplier for $15,000. If the purchase and payment are made in U.S. dollars, no accounting problem arises.

Date of Purchase

A = L + OE	Purchases	15,000	
+ −	Accounts Payable, Japanese company		15,000

Date of Payment

A = L + OE	Accounts Payable, Japanese company	15,000	
− −	Cash		15,000

However, the Japanese company may bill the U.S. company in yen and be paid in yen. If so, the U.S. company will incur an exchange gain or loss if the exchange rate changes between the date of purchase and the date of payment. For example, assume that the transaction is for ¥2,500,000 and that the exchange rates on the dates of purchase and payment are $.0090 and $.0085 per yen, respectively. The entries are as follows:

Date of Purchase

A = L + OE	Purchases	22,500	
+ −	Accounts Payable, Japanese company		22,500
	¥2,500,000 × $.0090 = $22,500		

Date of Payment

A = L + OE	Accounts Payable, Japanese company	22,500	
− − +	Exchange Gain or Loss		1,250
	Cash		21,250
	¥2,500,000 × $.0085 = $21,250		

In this case, the U.S. company received an exchange gain of $1,250 because it agreed to pay a fixed ¥2,500,000, and between the dates of purchase and payment, the exchange value of the yen decreased in relation to the dollar.

■ **REALIZED VERSUS UNREALIZED EXCHANGE GAIN OR LOSS**   The preceding illustrations dealt with completed transactions (in the sense that payment was made). In each case, the exchange gain or loss was recognized on the date of receipt or payment. If financial statements are prepared between the sale or purchase and the receipt or payment and exchange rates have changed, there will be unrealized gains or losses. The Financial Accounting Standards Board's *Statement No. 52* requires that exchange gains and losses "be included in determining net income for the period in which the exchange rate changes."[2] The requirement includes interim (quarterly) statements and applies whether or not a transaction is complete.

This ruling has caused much debate. Critics charge that it gives too much weight to fleeting changes in exchange rates, causing random changes in earnings that hide long-run trends. Others believe that the use of current exchange rates to value receivables and payables as of the balance sheet date is a major step toward economic reality (current values). To illustrate, we use the preceding case, in which a U.S. company buys parts from a Japanese supplier. We assume that the transaction has not been completed by the balance sheet date, when the exchange rate is $.0080 per yen:

	Date	Exchange Rate ($ per Yen)
Date of purchase	Dec. 1	.0090
Balance sheet date	Dec. 31	.0080
Date of payment	Feb. 1	.0085

The accounting effects of the unrealized gain are as follows:

	Dec. 1	Dec. 31	Feb. 1
Purchase recorded in U.S. dollars (billed as ¥2,500,000)	$22,500	$22,500	$22,500
Dollars to be paid to equal ¥2,500,000 (¥2,500,000 × exchange rate)	22,500	20,000	21,250
Unrealized gain (or loss)	—	$ 2,500	
Realized gain (or loss)			$ 1,250

A = L + OE + −	Dec. 1	Purchases Accounts Payable, Japanese company	22,500	22,500
A = L + OE − +	Dec. 31	Accounts Payable, Japanese company Exchange Gain or Loss	2,500	2,500
A = L + OE − − −	Feb. 1	Accounts Payable, Japanese company Exchange Gain or Loss Cash	20,000 1,250	21,250

In this case, the original sale was billed in yen by the Japanese company. Following the rules of *Statement No. 52*, an exchange gain of $2,500 is recorded on December 31, and an exchange loss of $1,250 is recorded on February 1. Even though these large fluctuations do not affect the net exchange gain of $1,250 for the whole transaction, the effect on each year's income statements may be important.

RESTATEMENT OF FOREIGN SUBSIDIARY FINANCIAL STATEMENTS

Companies often expand by establishing or buying foreign subsidiaries. If a company owns more than 50 percent of a foreign subsidiary and thus exercises control, then the foreign subsidiary should be included in the consolidated financial statements. The reporting of foreign subsidiaries is covered by FASB *Statement No. 52*. The consolidation procedure is the same as the one we described for domestic subsidiaries, except that the statements of the foreign subsidiary must be restated in the reporting currency before consolidation takes place. The *reporting currency* is the currency in which the consolidated financial statements are presented, which for U.S. companies is usually the U.S. dollar. Clearly, it makes no sense to combine the assets of a Mexican subsidiary stated in pesos with the assets of the U.S. parent company stated in dollars. Thus, *restatement* in the currency of the parent company is necessary.

The method of restatement depends on the foreign subsidiary's *functional currency*, which is the currency of the place where the subsidiary carries on most of its business. Generally, it is the currency in which a company earns and spends its cash. The functional currency used depends on the kind of foreign operation in which the subsidiary takes part.

There are two broad types of foreign operation. Type I includes those that are fairly self-contained and integrated within a certain country or economy. Type II includes those that are mainly a direct and integral part or extension of the parent company's operations. As a rule, Type I subsidiaries use the currency of the country in which they are located, and Type II subsidiaries use the currency of the parent company. If the parent is a U.S. company, the functional currency of a Type I subsidiary will be the currency of the country where the subsidiary carries on its business, and the functional currency of a Type II subsidiary will be the U.S. dollar. *Statement No. 52* makes an exception when a Type I subsidiary operates in a country where there is hyperinflation (as a rule of thumb, more than 100 percent cumulative inflation over three years), such as Brazil or Argentina. In such a case, the subsidiary is treated as a Type II subsidiary, with the functional currency being the U.S. dollar. Restatements in these situations do not affect cash flows because they are done simply for the convenience of preparing consolidated statements.

INTERNATIONAL ACCOUNTING STANDARDS

International investors need to compare the financial position and results of operations of companies from different countries. At present, however, few standards of accounting are recognized worldwide.[3] For example, LIFO is the most popular method of valuing inventory in the United States, but it is not acceptable in most European countries. Historical cost is strictly followed in Germany, replacement cost is used by some companies in the Netherlands, and a mixed system, allowing lower of cost or market in some cases, is used in the United States and Britain. Even the formats of financial statements differ from country to country. In Britain and France, for example, the order of the balance sheets is almost the reverse of that in the United States. In those countries, property, plant, and equipment is the first listing in the assets section.

A number of major problems stand in the way of setting international standards. One is that accountants and users of accounting information have not been able to agree on the goals of financial statements. Differences in the way the accounting profession has developed in various countries, in the laws regulating companies, and in governmental and other requirements present other hurdles. Further difficulties are created by differences among countries in the basic economic factors affecting financial reporting, inconsistencies in practices recommended by the accounting profession in different countries, and the influence of tax laws on financial reporting.

Probably the best hopes for finding areas of agreement among different countries are the International Accounting Standards Board (IASB) and the International Federation of Accountants (IFAC).

The role of the IASB is to contribute to the development and adoption of accounting principles that are relevant, balanced, and comparable throughout the world by formulating and publicizing accounting standards and encouraging their observance in the presentation of financial statements.[4] The standards issued by the IASB are generally followed by large multinational companies that are clients of international accounting firms. The IASB has been especially helpful to companies in developing economies that do not have the financial history or resources to develop accounting standards. The IASB is currently engaged in a major project to improve financial reporting worldwide by introducing a set of international accounting standards that will be acceptable to the world's securities regulators, such as the SEC in the United States. If successful, the effort should make it easier for companies to raise equity capital and list their stocks in other countries.

The IFAC, formed in 1977, also includes most of the world's accountancy organizations. It fully supports the work of the IASB and recognizes the IASB as the sole body with responsibility and authority to issue pronouncements on international accounting standards. The IFAC's principal role is to assure quality audits and financial statements prepared in accordance with international accounting standards. It attempts to accomplish this objective by issuing international auditing standards and monitoring the practice of international firms.

The European Community is also attempting to harmonize accounting standards. One of its directives requires certain minimum, uniform reporting and disclosure standards for financial statements. Other directives deal with uniform rules for preparing consolidated financial statements and qualifications of auditors. More importantly, the European Community has agreed to require international accounting standards beginning in 2005 for all companies that seek financing across borders. This is an important step for recognition of international accounting standards and for the goal of a single European market. It will leave the United States as the only major market that does not accept international accounting standards.

The road to international harmony is not easy. However, there is reason for optimism because an increasing number of countries are recognizing the appropriateness of uniform accounting standards in international trade and commerce.

PROBLEMS

P 1.

Recording International Transactions: Fluctuating Exchange Rate

Part A: Wooster Corporation purchased a special-purpose machine from Konigsberg Corporation on credit for E 50,000. At the date of purchase, the exchange rate was $.90 per euro. On the date of the payment, which was made in euros, the value of the euro was $.95. Prepare entries in journal form to record the purchase and payment in Wooster Corporation's accounting records.

Part B: U.S. Corporation made a sale on account to U.K. Company on November 15 in the amount of £300,000. Payment was to be made in British pounds on February 15. U.S. Corporation's fiscal year is the same as the calendar year. The British pound was worth $1.70 on November 15, $1.58 on December 31, and $1.78 on February 15. Prepare entries in journal form to record the sale, year-end adjustment, and collection on U.S. Corporation's books.

P 2.

International Transactions

Dolfsky Import/Export Company, whose year end is October 31, engaged in the following transactions (exchange rates in parentheses):

Aug. 12 Sold goods to a Mexican firm for $20,000; terms n/30 in U.S. dollars (peso = $.131).

   24 Purchased goods from a Japanese firm for $40,000; terms n/20 in yen (yen = $.0080).

Sept. 2 Sold goods to a British firm for $48,000; terms n/30 in pounds (pound = $1.60).

   11 Received payment in full for August 12 sale (peso = $.128).

   13 Paid for the goods purchased on August 24 (yen = $.0088).

   21 Purchased goods from an Italian firm for $28,000; terms n/10 in U.S. dollars (euro = $.90).

   30 Purchased goods from a Japanese firm for $35,200; terms n/60 in yen (yen = $.0088).

Oct. 2 Paid for the goods purchased on September 21 (euro = $.85).

   3 Received payment in full for the goods sold on September 2 (pound = $1.50).

   8 Sold goods to a French firm for $66,000; terms n/30 in euros (euro = $.88).

   19 Purchased goods from a Mexican firm for $37,000; terms n/30 in U.S. dollars (peso = $.135).

   31 Made year-end adjusting entries for incomplete foreign exchange transactions (euro = $.85; peso = $.130; pound = $1.40; yen = $.0100).

Nov. 9 Received payment for the goods sold on October 8 (euro = $.87).

   18 Paid for the goods purchased on October 19 (peso = $.132).

   28 Paid for the goods purchased on September 30 (yen = $.0090).

REQUIRED ▶ Prepare entries in journal form for these transactions.

Appendix B

Long-Term Investments

www.pepsico.com

Companies make long-term investments for a variety of reasons. For instance, PepsiCo makes investments in operations critical to the distribution of its products, such as its investments in PepsiCo Bottling Company. It also makes investments to expand its markets, as in its purchases of Tropicana, South Beach Beverage, and Quaker Oats. These are stock investments, but a company can also make long-term investments in bonds. Investments in bonds can be a way of ensuring that an affiliate company has sufficient long-term capital, or it can simply be a way of making a relatively secure investment. The following sections discuss the classifications of bonds and stocks and the methods used to account for such investments.

LONG-TERM INVESTMENTS IN BONDS

Like all investments, investments in bonds are recorded at cost, which, in this case, is the price of the bonds plus the broker's commission. When bonds are purchased between interest payment dates, the purchaser must also pay an amount equal to the interest that has accrued on the bonds since the last interest payment date. Then, on the next interest payment date, the purchaser receives an interest payment for the whole period. The payment for accrued interest should be recorded as a debit to Interest Income, which will be offset by a credit to Interest Income when the semiannual interest is received.

Subsequent accounting for a corporation's long-term bond investments depends on the classification of the bonds. If the company plans at some point to sell the bonds, they are classified as *available-for-sale securities*. If the company plans to hold the bonds until they are paid off on their maturity date, they are considered *held-to-maturity securities*. Except in industries like insurance and banking, it is unusual for companies to buy the bonds of other companies with the express purpose of holding them until they mature, which can be in 10 to 30 years. Thus, most long-term bond investments are available-for-sale securities. Such bonds are accounted for at fair value, much as equity or stock investments are; fair value is usually the market value. When bonds are intended to be held to maturity, they are accounted for not at fair value but at cost, adjusted for the amortization of their discount or premium. The procedure is similar to accounting for long-term bond liabilities, except that separate accounts for discounts and premiums are not used.

KEY POINT: The fair value of bonds is closely related to interest rates. An increase in interest rates lowers the fair value of bonds, and vice versa.

LONG-TERM INVESTMENTS IN STOCKS

All long-term investments in stocks are recorded at cost, in accordance with generally accepted accounting principles. The treatment of the investment in the accounting records after the initial purchase depends on the extent to which the investing company can exercise *significant influence* or *control* over the operating and financial policies of the other company. The Accounting Principles Board (APB) defined these important terms in its *Opinion No. 18*.

Significant influence is an investing firm's ability to affect the operating and financial policies of the company whose shares it owns, even though it holds 50 percent or less of the voting stock. Indications of significant influence include representation on the board of directors, participation in policymaking, and material

KEY POINT: Influence and control are related specifically to equity holdings, not debt holdings.

TABLE 1. Accounting Treatments of Long-Term Investments in Stocks		
Level of Ownership	Percentage of Ownership	Accounting Treatment
Noninfluential and noncontrolling	Less than 20%	Cost initially; investment adjusted subsequent to purchase for changes in market value
Influential but noncontrolling	Between 20% and 50%	Equity method; investment valued subsequently at cost plus investor's share of income (or minus investor's share of loss) minus dividends received
Controlling	More than 50%	Financial statements consolidated

transactions, exchange of managerial personnel, and technological dependency between the two companies. For the sake of uniformity, the APB decided that without proof to the contrary, ownership of 20 percent or more of the voting stock should be presumed to confer significant influence.* Ownership of less than 20 percent of the voting stock does not confer significant influence.

Control is an investing firm's ability to decide the operating and financial policies of the other company. Control exists when the investor owns more than 50 percent of the voting stock of the company in which it has invested.

Thus, in the absence of information to the contrary, a noninfluential and noncontrolling investment would be less than 20 percent ownership. An influential but noncontrolling investment would be 20 to 50 percent ownership. And a controlling investment would be more than 50 percent ownership. The accounting treatment differs for each kind of investment. Table 1 summarizes these treatments.

■ **NONINFLUENTIAL AND NONCONTROLLING INVESTMENT** Available-for-sale securities are debt or equity securities that are not classified as trading or held-to-maturity securities. When equity securities are involved, a further criterion is that they be noninfluential and noncontrolling investments of less than 20 percent of the voting stock. The Financial Accounting Standards Board requires a *cost-adjusted-to market method* for accounting for available-for-sale securities. Under this method, available-for-sale securities must be recorded initially at cost and thereafter adjusted periodically through the use of an allowance account to reflect changes in the market value.[1]

Available-for-sale securities are classified as long term if management intends to hold them for more than one year. When accounting for long-term available-for-sale

*The Financial Accounting Standards Board pointed out in its *Interpretation No. 35* (May 1981) that this rule is not a rigid one. All relevant facts and circumstances should be examined to determine whether significant influence exists. The FASB noted five circumstances that may negate significant influence: (1) The company files a lawsuit against the investor or a complaint with a government agency; (2) the investor tries but fails to become a director; (3) the investor agrees not to increase its holdings; (4) the company is operated by a small group that ignores the investor's wishes; (5) the investor tries but fails to obtain company information that is not available to other stockholders.

securities, the unrealized gain or loss resulting from the adjustment is not reported on the income statement. Instead, the gain or loss is reported as a special item in the stockholders' equity section of the balance sheet and in comprehensive income disclosure.

At the end of each accounting period, the total cost and the total market value of these long-term stock investments must be determined. If the total market value is less than the total cost, the difference must be credited to a contra-asset account called Allowance to Adjust Long-Term Investments to Market. Because of the long-term nature of the investment, the debit part of the entry, which represents a decrease in value below cost, is treated as a temporary decrease and does not appear as a loss on the income statement. It is shown in a contra-stockholders' equity account called Unrealized Loss on Long-Term Investments.* Thus, both of these accounts are balance sheet accounts. If the market value exceeds the cost, the allowance account is added to Long-Term Investments, and the unrealized gain appears as an addition to stockholders' equity.

When long-term investments in stock are sold, the difference between the sale price and the cost of the stock is recorded and reported as a realized gain or loss on the income statement. Dividend income from such investments is recorded by a debit to Cash and a credit to Dividend Income. For example, assume the following facts about the long-term stock investments of Coleman Corporation:

June 1, 20x3   Paid cash for the following long-term investments: 10,000 shares of Durbin Corporation common stock (representing 2 percent of outstanding stock) at $25 per share; 5,000 shares of Kotes Corporation common stock (representing 3 percent of outstanding stock) at $15 per share.

Dec. 31, 20x3   Quoted market prices at year end: Durbin common stock, $21; Kotes common stock, $17.

KEY POINT: On April 1, 20x4, a *change in policy* requires the sale. This points out that intent is often the only difference between long-term investments and short-term investments.

Apr. 1, 20x4   Change in policy required sale of 2,000 shares of Durbin common stock at $23.

July 1, 20x4   Received cash dividend from Kotes equal to $.20 per share.

Dec. 31, 20x4   Quoted market prices at year end: Durbin common stock, $24; Kotes common stock, $13.

Entries to record these transactions are as follows:

Investment

	20x3		
A = L + OE	June 1 Long-Term Investments	325,000	
+	Cash		325,000
−	Investments in Durbin common stock (10,000 shares × $25 = $250,000) and Kotes common stock (5,000 shares × $15 = $75,000)		

Year-End Adjustment

	20x3		
A = L + OE	Dec. 31 Unrealized Loss on Long-Term Investments	30,000	
− −	Allowance to Adjust Long-Term Investments to Market		30,000
	To record reduction of long-term investment to market		

---

*If the decrease in market value of the long-term investment is deemed permanent, a different procedure is followed to record the decline. A loss account on the income statement is debited instead of the Unrealized Loss account.

Company	Shares	Market Price	Total Market	Total Cost
Durbin	10,000	$21	$210,000	$250,000
Kotes	5,000	17	85,000	75,000
			$295,000	$325,000

Total Cost − Total Market Value = $325,000 − $295,000 = $30,000

Sale

20x4

A = L + OE   Apr. 1   Cash   46,000

\+   −   Loss on Sale of Investments   4,000

−   Long-Term Investments   50,000

                          Sale of 2,000 shares of Durbin

                          common stock

                          2,000 × $23 = $46,000

                          2,000 × $25 =   50,000

                          Loss $ 4,000

Dividend Received

20x4

A = L + OE   July 1   Cash   1,000

\+   +   Dividend Income   1,000

                          Receipt of cash dividend from Kotes stock

                          5,000 × $.20 = $1,000

Year-End Adjustment

20x4

A = L + OE   Dec. 31   Allowance to Adjust Long-Term

\+   +   Investments to Market   12,000

                          Unrealized Loss on Long-Term

                          Investments   12,000

                          To record the adjustment in long-

                          term investment so it is reported

                          at market

The adjustment equals the previous balance ($30,000 from the December 31, 20x3, entry) minus the new balance ($18,000), or $12,000. The new balance of $18,000 is the difference at the present time between the total market value and the total cost of all investments. It is figured as follows:

Company	Shares	Market Price	Total Market	Total Cost
Durbin	8,000	$24	$192,000	$200,000
Kotes	5,000	13	65,000	75,000
			$257,000	$275,000

Total Cost − Total Market Value = $275,000 − $257,000 = $18,000

The Allowance to Adjust Long-Term Investments to Market and the Unrealized Loss on Long-Term Investments are reciprocal contra accounts, each with the same dollar balance, as shown by the effects of these transactions on the T accounts:

Contra-Asset Account				Contra-Stockholders' Equity Account			
Allowance to Adjust Long-Term Investments to Market				Unrealized Loss on Long-Term Investment			
20x4	12,000	20x3	30,000	20x3	30,000	20x4	12,000
		Bal. 20x4	18,000	Bal. 20x4	18,000		

The Allowance account reduces long-term investments by the amount by which the cost of the investments exceeds market; the Unrealized Loss account reduces stockholders' equity by a similar amount. The opposite effects will exist if market value exceeds cost, resulting in an unrealized gain.

■ **INFLUENTIAL BUT NONCONTROLLING INVESTMENT**   As we have noted, ownership of 20 percent or more of a company's voting stock is considered sufficient to influence the company's operations. When this is the case, the stock investment should be accounted for using the *equity method*. The equity method presumes that an investment of 20 percent or more is not a passive investment and that the investor should therefore share proportionately in the success or failure of the company. The three main features of this method are as follows:

1. The investor records the original purchase of the stock at cost.
2. The investor records its share of the company's periodic net income as an increase in the Investment account, with a corresponding credit to an income account. Similarly, it records its share of a periodic loss as a decrease in the Investment account, with a corresponding debit to a loss account.
3. When the investor receives a cash dividend, the asset account Cash is increased, and the Investment account is decreased.

To illustrate the equity method of accounting, we assume the following facts about an investment by Vassor Corporation: On January 1 of the current year, Vassor acquired 40 percent of the voting common stock of Block Corporation for $180,000. With this share of ownership, Vassor can exert significant influence over Block's operations. During the year, Block reported net income of $80,000 and paid cash dividends of $20,000. Vassor recorded these transactions as follows:

Investment

A = L + OE	Investment in Block Corporation	180,000	
+	Cash		180,000
−	Investment in Block Corporation common stock		

Recognition of Income

A = L + OE	Investment in Block Corporation	32,000	
+ +	Income, Block Corporation Investment		32,000
	Recognition of 40% of income reported by Block Corporation		
	40% × $80,000 = $32,000		

Receipt of Cash Dividend

A = L + OE	Cash	8,000	
+	Investment in Block Corporation		8,000
−	Cash dividend from Block Corporation		
	40% × $20,000 = $8,000		

The balance of the Investment in Block Corporation account after these transactions is $204,000, as shown here:

Investment in Block Corporation

Investment	180,000	Dividend received	8,000
Share of Income	32,000		
Balance	204,000		

STUDY POINT: Under the equity method, dividends received are credited to the Investment account because the dividends represent a return from or a decrease in the investment in Block Corporation.

CONTROLLING INVESTMENT   Some investing firms that own less than 50 percent of the voting stock of a company exercise such powerful influence that for all practical purposes, they control the policies of the other company. Nevertheless, ownership of more than 50 percent of the voting stock is required for accounting recognition of control. When a firm has a controlling interest, a parent-subsidiary relationship is said to exist. The investing company is known as the *parent company*; the other company is a *subsidiary*. Because the two corporations are separate legal entities, each prepares separate financial statements. However, owing to their special relationship, they are viewed for public financial reporting purposes as a single economic entity. For this reason, they must combine their financial statements into a single set of statements called *consolidated financial statements*.

Accounting for consolidated financial statements is complex and is usually the subject of an advanced accounting course. However, most large public corporations have subsidiaries and must prepare consolidated financial statements. It is therefore important to have some understanding of accounting for consolidations.

ENRICHMENT NOTE:
Parents and subsidiaries are separate legal entities even though they combine their financial reports at year end.

PROBLEMS

P 1.

Methods of Accounting for Long-Term Investments

Diversified Corporation has the following long-term investments:

1. 60 percent of the common stock of Down Corporation
2. 13 percent of the common stock of West Lake, Inc.
3. 50 percent of the nonvoting preferred stock of Invole Corporation
4. 100 percent of the common stock of its financing subsidiary, DCF, Inc.
5. 35 percent of the common stock of the French company Maison de Boutaine
6. 70 percent of the common stock of the Canadian company Alberta Mining Company

For each of these investments, tell which of the following methods should be used for external financial reporting, and why.

a. Cost adjusted to market method
b. Equity method
c. Consolidation of parent and subsidiary financial statements

P 2.

Long-Term Investment Transactions

Red Bud Corporation made the following transactions in its Long-Term Investments account over a two-year period:

20x4
Apr. 1   Purchased with cash 20,000 shares of Season Company stock for $152 per share.
June 1   Purchased with cash 15,000 shares of Abbado Corporation stock for $72 per share.
Sept. 1   Received a $1 per share dividend from Season Company.
Nov. 1   Purchased with cash 25,000 shares of Frankel Corporation stock for $110 per share.
Dec. 31   Market values per share of shares held in the Long-Term Investments account were as follows: Season Company, $140; Abbado Corporation, $32; and Frankel Corporation, $122.

20x4
Feb. 1   Because of unfavorable prospects for Abbado Corporation, Abbado stock was sold for cash at $40 per share.
May 1   Purchased with cash 10,000 shares of Schulian Corporation for $224 per share.
Sept. 1   Received $2 per share dividend from Season Company.
Dec. 31   Market values per share of shares held in the Long-Term Investments account were as follows: Season Company, $160; Frankel Corporation, $140; and Schulian Corporation, $200.

Prepare entries to record these transactions in the Red Bud Corporation records. Assume that all investments represent less than 20 percent of the voting stock of the company whose stock was acquired.

P 3.

Long-Term Investments:
Equity Method

The Modi Company owns 40 percent of the voting stock of the Vivanco Company. The Investment account for this company on the Modi Company's balance sheet had a balance of $600,000 on January 1, 20xx. During 20xx, the Vivanco Company reported the following quarterly earnings and dividends paid:

Quarter	Earnings	Dividends Paid
1	$ 80,000	$ 40,000
2	60,000	40,000
3	160,000	40,000
4	(40,000)	40,000
	$260,000	$160,000

The Modi Company exercises a significant influence over the operations of the Vivanco Company and therefore uses the equity method to account for its investment.

REQUIRED ▶

1. Prepare the entries in journal form that the Modi Company must make each quarter in accounting for its investment in the Vivanco Company.

2. Prepare a T account for the investment in common stock of the Vivanco Company. Enter the beginning balance, relevant portions of the entries made in **1**, and the ending balance.

Appendix C

The Time Value of Money

SIMPLE INTEREST AND COMPOUND INTEREST

Interest is the cost associated with the use of money for a specific period of time. Because interest is a cost associated with time, and "time is money," it is also an important consideration in any business decision. *Simple interest* is the interest cost for one or more periods, under the assumption that the amount on which the interest is computed stays the same from period to period. *Compound interest* is the interest cost for two or more periods, under the assumption that after each period the interest of that period is added to the amount on which interest is computed in future periods. In other words, compound interest is interest earned on a principal sum that is increased at the end of each period by the interest for that period.

■ **EXAMPLE—SIMPLE INTEREST**   Joe Sanchez accepts an 8 percent, $30,000 note due in ninety days. How much will he receive in total at that time? Remember that the formula for calculating simple interest is as follows:

$$
\begin{aligned}
\text{Interest} &= \text{Principal} \times \text{Rate} \times \text{Time} \\
&= \$30{,}000 \times 8/100 \times 90/360 \\
&= \$600
\end{aligned}
$$

Therefore, the total that Sanchez will receive is calculated as follows:

$$
\begin{aligned}
\text{Total} &= \text{Principal} + \text{Interest} \\
&= \$30{,}000 + \$600 \\
&= \$30{,}600
\end{aligned}
$$

■ **EXAMPLE—COMPOUND INTEREST**   Ann Clary deposits $5,000 in a savings account that pays 6 percent interest. She expects to leave the principal and accumulated interest in the account for three years. How much will her account total at the end of three years? Assume that the interest is paid at the end of the year and is added to the principal at that time, and that this total in turn earns interest. The amount at the end of three years is computed as follows:

(1) Year	(2) Principal Amount at Beginning of Year	(3) Annual Amount of Interest (Col. 2 × 6%)	(4) Accumulated Amount at End of Year (Col. 2 + Col. 3)
1	$5,000.00	$300.00	$5,300.00
2	5,300.00	318.00	5,618.00
3	5,618.00	337.08	5,955.08

At the end of three years, Clary will have $5,955.08 in her savings account. Note that the annual amount of interest increases each year by the interest rate times the interest of the previous year. For example, between year 1 and year 2, the interest increased by $18 ($318 – $300), which exactly equals 6 percent times $300.

FUTURE VALUE OF A SINGLE INVESTED SUM AT COMPOUND INTEREST

Another way to ask the question in the example of compound interest above is, What is the future value of a single sum ($5,000) at compound interest (6 percent) for three years? *Future value* is the amount that an investment will be worth at a future date if invested at compound interest. A businessperson often wants to know future value, but the method of computing the future value illustrated above is too time-consuming in practice. Imagine how tedious the calculation would be if the example were ten years instead of three. Fortunately, there are tables that simplify solving problems involving compound interest. Table 1, showing the future value of $1 after a given number of time periods, is an example. It is actually part of a larger table, Table 1 in the appendix on future value and present value tables. Suppose that we want to solve the problem of Clary's savings account above. We simply look down the 6 percent column in Table 1 until we reach the line for three periods and find the factor 1.191. This factor, when multiplied by $1, gives the future value of that $1 at compound interest of 6 percent for three periods (years in this case). Thus, we solve the problem as follows:

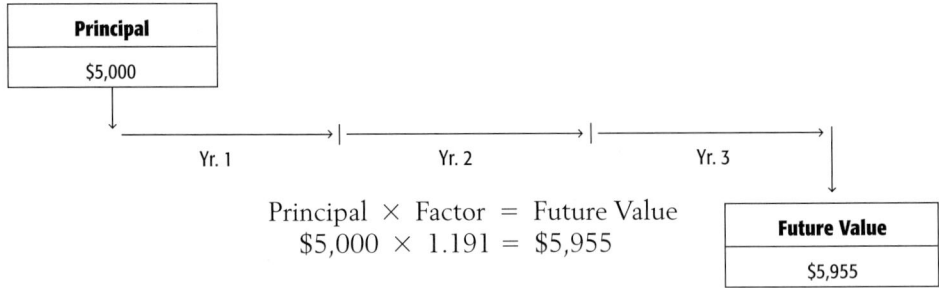

Principal × Factor = Future Value
$5,000 × 1.191 = $5,955

Except for a rounding difference of $.08, the answer is exactly the same as that calculated earlier.

TABLE 1.   Future Value of $1 after a Given Number of Time Periods

Periods	1%	2%	3%	4%	5%	6%	7%	8%	9%	10%	12%	14%	15%
1	1.010	1.020	1.030	1.040	1.050	1.060	1.070	1.080	1.090	1.100	1.120	1.140	1.150
2	1.020	1.040	1.061	1.082	1.103	1.124	1.145	1.166	1.188	1.210	1.254	1.300	1.323
3	1.030	1.061	1.093	1.125	1.158	1.191	1.225	1.260	1.295	1.331	1.405	1.482	1.521
4	1.041	1.082	1.126	1.170	1.216	1.262	1.311	1.360	1.412	1.464	1.574	1.689	1.749
5	1.051	1.104	1.159	1.217	1.276	1.338	1.403	1.469	1.539	1.611	1.762	1.925	2.011
6	1.062	1.126	1.194	1.265	1.340	1.419	1.501	1.587	1.677	1.772	1.974	2.195	2.313
7	1.072	1.149	1.230	1.316	1.407	1.504	1.606	1.714	1.828	1.949	2.211	2.502	2.660
8	1.083	1.172	1.267	1.369	1.477	1.594	1.718	1.851	1.993	2.144	2.476	2.853	3.059
9	1.094	1.195	1.305	1.423	1.551	1.689	1.838	1.999	2.172	2.358	2.773	3.252	3.518
10	1.105	1.219	1.344	1.480	1.629	1.791	1.967	2.159	2.367	2.594	3.106	3.707	4.046

Source: Excerpt from Table 1 in the appendix on future value and present value tables.

FUTURE VALUE OF AN ORDINARY ANNUITY

Another common problem involves an *ordinary annuity*, which is a series of equal payments made at the end of equal intervals of time, with compound interest on these payments.

The following example shows how to find the future value of an ordinary annuity. Assume that Ben Katz makes a $200 payment at the end of each of the next three years into a savings account that pays 5 percent interest. How much money will he have in his account at the end of the three years? One way of computing the amount is shown in the following table.

(1) Year	(2) Beginning Balance	(3) Interest Earned (5% × Col. 2)	(4) Periodic Payment	(5) Accumulated at End of Period (Col. 2 + Col. 3 + Col. 4)
1	—	—	$200	$200.00
2	$200.00	$10.00	200	410.00
3	410.00	20.50	200	630.50

Katz would have $630.50 in his account at the end of three years, consisting of $600.00 in periodic payments and $30.50 in interest.

This calculation can also be simplified by using Table 2. We look down the 5 percent column until we reach three periods and find the factor 3.153. This factor, when multiplied by $1, gives the future value of a series of three $1 payments at compound interest of 5 percent. Thus, we solve the problem as follows:

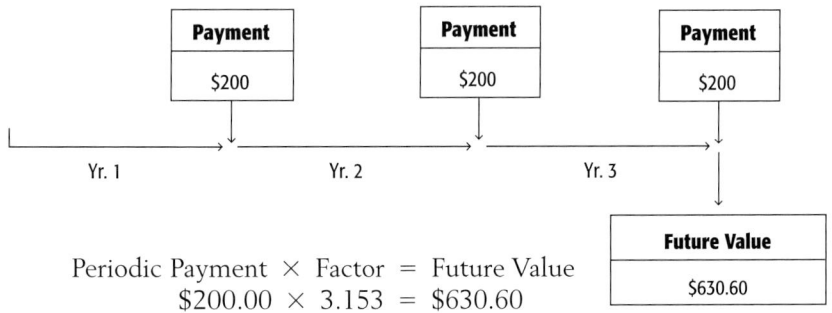

Periodic Payment × Factor = Future Value
$200.00 × 3.153 = $630.60

Except for a rounding difference of $.10, this result is the same as our earlier one.

PRESENT VALUE

Suppose that you had the choice of receiving $100 today or one year from today. Intuitively, you would choose to receive the $100 today. Why? You know that if you have the $100 today, you can put it in a savings account to earn interest, so that you will have more than $100 a year from today. Therefore, we can say that an amount to be received in the future (future value) is not worth as much today as an amount to be received today (present value) because of the cost associated with the passage of time. In fact, present value and future value are closely related. *Present value* is the amount that must be invested now at a given rate of interest to produce a given future value. For example, assume that Sue Dapper needs $1,000 one year from now. How much should she invest today to achieve that goal if the interest rate is 5 percent? From earlier examples, the following equation may be established.

$$\text{Present Value} \times (1.0 + \text{Interest Rate}) = \text{Future Value}$$
$$\text{Present Value} \times 1.05 = \$1,000.00$$
$$\text{Present Value} = \$1,000.00 \div 1.05$$
$$\text{Present Value} = \$952.38$$

Thus, to achieve a future value of $1,000.00, a present value of $952.38 must be invested. Interest of 5 percent on $952.38 for one year equals $47.62, and these two amounts added together equal $1,000.00.

■ **PRESENT VALUE OF A SINGLE SUM DUE IN THE FUTURE**   When more than one time period is involved, the calculation of present value is more complicated. Consider the following example. Don Riley wants to be sure of having $4,000 at the end of three years. How much must he invest today in a 5 percent savings account to achieve this goal? Adapting the above equation, we compute the present value of $4,000 at compound interest of 5 percent for three years in the future.

Year	Amount at End of Year		Divide by		Present Value at Beginning of Year
3	$4,000.00	÷	1.05	=	$3,809.52
2	3,809.52	÷	1.05	=	3,628.11
1	3,628.11	÷	1.05	=	3,455.34

Riley must invest a present value of $3,455.34 to achieve a future value of $4,000.00 in three years.

This calculation is again made much easier by using the appropriate table. In Table 3, we look down the 5 percent column until we reach three periods and find the factor .864. This factor, when multiplied by $1, gives the present value of $1 to be received three years from now at 5 percent interest. Thus, we solve the problem as shown on the next page.

TABLE 2.   Future Value of an Ordinary Annuity of $1 Paid in Each Period for a Given Number of Time Periods

Periods	1%	2%	3%	4%	5%	6%	7%	8%	9%	10%	12%	14%	15%
1	1.000	1.000	1.000	1.000	1.000	1.000	1.000	1.000	1.000	1.000	1.000	1.000	1.000
2	2.010	2.020	2.030	2.040	2.050	2.060	2.070	2.080	2.090	2.100	2.120	2.140	2.150
3	3.030	3.060	3.091	3.122	3.153	3.184	3.215	3.246	3.278	3.310	3.374	3.440	3.473
4	4.060	4.122	4.184	4.246	4.310	4.375	4.440	4.506	4.573	4.641	4.779	4.921	4.993
5	5.101	5.204	5.309	5.416	5.526	5.637	5.751	5.867	5.985	6.105	6.353	6.610	6.742
6	6.152	6.308	6.468	6.633	6.802	6.975	7.153	7.336	7.523	7.716	8.115	8.536	8.754
7	7.214	7.434	7.662	7.898	8.142	8.394	8.654	8.923	9.200	9.487	10.09	10.73	11.07
8	8.286	8.583	8.892	9.214	9.549	9.897	10.26	10.64	11.03	11.44	12.30	13.23	13.73
9	9.369	9.755	10.16	10.58	11.03	11.49	11.98	12.49	13.02	13.58	14.78	16.09	16.79
10	10.46	10.95	11.46	12.01	12.58	13.18	13.82	14.49	15.19	15.94	17.55	19.34	20.30

Source: Excerpt from Table 2 in the appendix on future value and present value tables.

TABLE 3. Present Value of $1 to Be Received at the End of a Given Number of Time Periods

Periods	1%	2%	3%	4%	5%	6%	7%	8%	9%	10%
1	0.990	0.980	0.971	0.962	0.952	0.943	0.935	0.926	0.917	0.909
2	0.980	0.961	0.943	0.925	0.907	0.890	0.873	0.857	0.842	0.826
3	0.971	0.942	0.915	0.889	0.864	0.840	0.816	0.794	0.772	0.751
4	0.961	0.924	0.888	0.855	0.823	0.792	0.763	0.735	0.708	0.683
5	0.951	0.906	0.863	0.822	0.784	0.747	0.713	0.681	0.650	0.621
6	0.942	0.888	0.837	0.790	0.746	0.705	0.666	0.630	0.596	0.564
7	0.933	0.871	0.813	0.760	0.711	0.665	0.623	0.583	0.547	0.513
8	0.923	0.853	0.789	0.731	0.677	0.627	0.582	0.540	0.502	0.467
9	0.914	0.837	0.766	0.703	0.645	0.592	0.544	0.500	0.460	0.424
10	0.905	0.820	0.744	0.676	0.614	0.558	0.508	0.463	0.422	0.386

Source: Excerpt from Table 3 in the appendix on future value and present value tables.

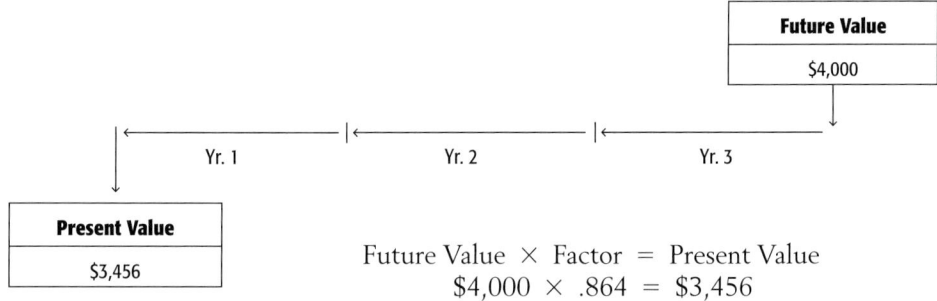

Future Value × Factor = Present Value
$4,000 × .864 = $3,456

Except for a rounding difference of $.66, this result is the same as the one above.

■ **PRESENT VALUE OF AN ORDINARY ANNUITY**   It is often necessary to compute the present value of a series of receipts or payments. When we calculate the present value of equal amounts equally spaced over a period of time, we are computing the present value of an ordinary annuity.

For example, assume that Kathy Foster has sold a piece of property and is to receive $15,000 in three equal annual payments of $5,000, beginning one year from today. What is the present value of this sale, assuming a current interest rate of 5 percent? This present value may be computed by calculating a separate present value for each of the three payments (using Table 3) and summing the results, as shown in the table below.

Future Receipts (Annuity)				Present Value Factor at 5 Percent (from Table 3)		Present Value
Year 1	Year 2	Year 3				
$5,000			×	.952	=	$ 4,760
	$5,000		×	.907	=	4,535
		$5,000	×	.864	=	4,320
Total Present Value						$13,615

The present value of this sale is $13,615. Thus, there is an implied interest cost (given the 5 percent rate) of $1,385 associated with the payment plan that allows the purchaser to pay in three installments.

We can make this calculation more easily by using Table 4. We look down the 5 percent column until we reach three periods and find the factor 2.723. This factor, when multiplied by $1, gives the present value of a series of three $1 payments (spaced one year apart) at compound interest of 5 percent. Thus, we solve the problem as shown below.

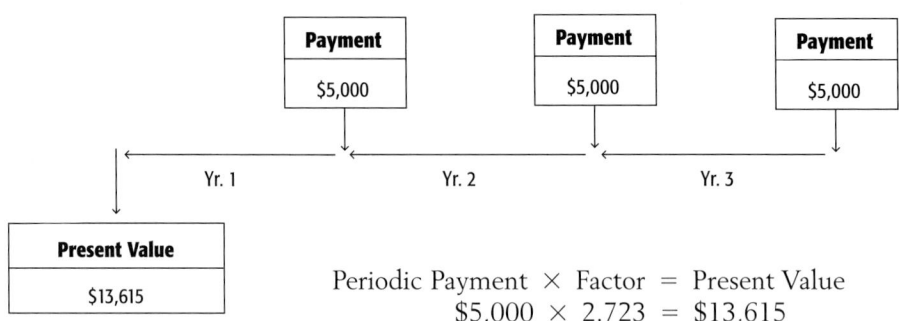

Periodic Payment × Factor = Present Value
$5,000 × 2.723 = $13,615

This result is the same as the one computed earlier.

TIME PERIODS

In all of the previous examples, and in most other cases, the compounding period is one year, and the interest rate is stated on an annual basis. However, in each of the four tables, the left-hand column refers not to years but to periods. This wording is intended to accommodate compounding periods of less than one year. Savings accounts that record interest quarterly and bonds that pay interest semiannually are cases in which the compounding period is less than one year. To use the tables in such cases, it is necessary to (1) divide the annual interest rate by the number of periods in the year, and (2) multiply the number of periods in one year by the number of years.

For example, assume that a $6,000 note is to be paid in two years and carries an annual interest rate of 8 percent. Compute the maturity (future) value of the note, assuming that the compounding period is semiannual. Before using the table, it is

TABLE 4.   Present Value of an Ordinary Annuity of $1 Received Each Period for a Given Number of Time Periods

Periods	1%	2%	3%	4%	5%	6%	7%	8%	9%	10%
1	0.990	0.980	0.971	0.962	0.952	0.943	0.935	0.926	0.917	0.909
2	1.970	1.942	1.913	1.886	1.859	1.833	1.808	1.783	1.759	1.736
3	2.941	2.884	2.829	2.775	2.723	2.673	2.624	2.577	2.531	2.487
4	3.902	3.808	3.717	3.630	3.546	3.465	3.387	3.312	3.240	3.170
5	4.853	4.713	4.580	4.452	4.329	4.212	4.100	3.993	3.890	3.791
6	5.795	5.601	5.417	5.242	5.076	4.917	4.767	4.623	4.486	4.355
7	6.728	6.472	6.230	6.002	5.786	5.582	5.389	5.206	5.033	4.868
8	7.652	7.325	7.020	6.733	6.463	6.210	5.971	5.747	5.535	5.335
9	8.566	8.162	7.786	7.435	7.108	6.802	6.515	6.247	5.995	5.759
10	9.471	8.983	8.530	8.111	7.722	7.360	7.024	6.710	6.418	6.145

Source: Excerpt from Table 4 in the appendix on future value and present value tables.

necessary to compute the interest rate that applies to each compounding period and the total number of compounding periods. First, the interest rate to use is 4 percent (8% annual rate ÷ 2 periods per year). Second, the total number of compounding periods is 4 (2 periods per year × 2 years). From Table 1, therefore, the maturity value of the note is computed as follows:

$$\text{Principal} \times \text{Factor} = \text{Future Value}$$
$$\$6,000 \times 1.170 = \$7,020$$

The note will be worth $7,020 in two years.

This procedure for determining the interest rate and the number of periods when the compounding period is less than one year may be used with all four tables.

APPLICATIONS OF PRESENT VALUE TO ACCOUNTING

The concept of present value is widely applicable in the discipline of accounting. Here, the purpose is to demonstrate its usefulness in some simple applications. In-depth study of present value is deferred to more advanced courses.

■ **IMPUTING INTEREST ON NON-INTEREST-BEARING NOTES**   Clearly there is no such thing as an interest-free debt, regardless of whether the interest rate is explicitly stated. The Accounting Principles Board has declared that when a long-term note does not explicitly state an interest rate (or if the interest rate is unreasonably low), a rate based on the normal interest cost of the company in question should be assigned, or imputed.[1]

The following example applies this principle. On January 1, 20x0, Gato purchased merchandise from Haines by issuing an $8,000 non-interest-bearing note due in two years. Gato can borrow money from the bank at 9 percent interest. Gato paid the note in full after two years.

Note that the $8,000 note represents partly a payment for merchandise and partly a payment of interest for two years. In recording the purchase and sale, it is necessary to use Table 3 to determine the present value of the note. The calculation follows.

$$\text{Future Payment} \times \text{Present Value Factor (9\%, 2 years)} = \text{Present Value}$$
$$\$8,000 \times .842 = \$6,736$$

The imputed interest cost is $1,264 ($8,000 − $6,736) and is recorded as a discount on notes payable in Gato's records and as a discount on notes receivable in Haines's records.

The entries necessary to record the purchase in the Gato records and the sale in the Haines records are as follows:

	Gato Journal			Haines Journal			
A = L + OE	Purchases	6,736		Notes Receivable	8,000		A = L + OE
− −	Discount on			Discount on			+ +
+	Notes Payable	1,264		Notes Receivable		1,264	−
	Notes Payable		8,000	Sales		6,736	

On December 31, 20x0, the adjustments to recognize the interest expense and interest income are as follows:

	Gato Journal			Haines Journal			
A = L + OE	Interest Expense	606.24		Discount on			A = L + OE
+ −	Discount on			Notes Receivable	606.24		+ +
	Notes Payable		606.24	Interest Income		606.24	

The interest is calculated by multiplying the amount of the original purchase by the interest rate for one year ($6,736.00 × .09 = $606.24). When payment is made on December 31, 20x0, the following entries are made in the respective journals.

Gato Journal				Haines Journal		
A = L + OE	Interest Expense	657.76		Discount on		A = L + OE
− + −	Notes Payable	8,000.00		Notes Receivable	657.76	+ +
−	Discount on			Cash	8,000.00	+
	Notes Payable		657.76	Interest Income	657.76	−
	Cash		8,000.00	Notes Receivable	8,000.00	

The interest entries represent the remaining interest to be expensed or realized ($1,264 − $606.24 = $657.76). This amount approximates (because of rounding differences in the table) the interest for one year on the purchase plus last year's interest [($6,736 + $606.24) × .09 = $660.80].

■ **VALUING AN ASSET**   An asset is recorded because it will provide future benefits to the company that owns it. These future benefits are the basis for the definition of an asset. Usually, the purchase price of the asset represents the present value of these future benefits. It is possible to evaluate a proposed purchase price for an asset by comparing that price with the present value of the asset to the company.

For example, Sam Hurst is thinking of buying a new machine that will reduce his annual labor cost by $700 per year. The machine will last eight years. The interest rate that Hurst assumes for making managerial decisions is 10 percent. What is the maximum amount (present value) that Hurst should pay for the machine?

The present value of the machine to Hurst is equal to the present value of an ordinary annuity of $700 per year for eight years at compound interest of 10 percent. Using the factor from Table 4, we compute the value as follows:

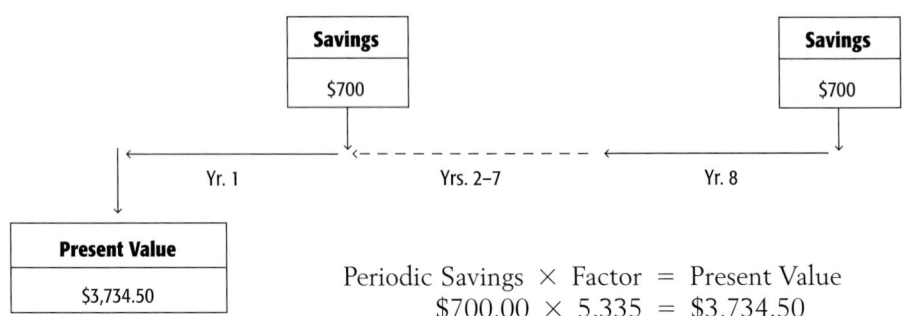

Periodic Savings × Factor = Present Value
$700.00 × 5.335 = $3,734.50

Hurst should not pay more than $3,734.50 for the new machine because this amount equals the present value of the benefits that will be received from owning the machine.

■ **DEFERRED PAYMENT**   A seller will sometimes agree to defer payment for a sale in order to encourage the buyer to make the purchase. This practice is common, for example, in the farm implement industry, where the farmer needs the equipment in the spring but cannot pay for it until the fall crop is in. Assume that Plains Implement Corporation sells a tractor to Dana Washington for $50,000 on February 1, agreeing to take payment ten months later, on December 1. When this type of agreement is made, the future payment includes not only the sales price of the tractor but also an implied (imputed) interest cost. If the prevailing annual interest rate for such transactions is 12 percent compounded monthly, the actual sale (purchase) price of the tractor would be the present value of the future payment, computed using the factor from Table 3 (10 periods, 1 percent), as follows:

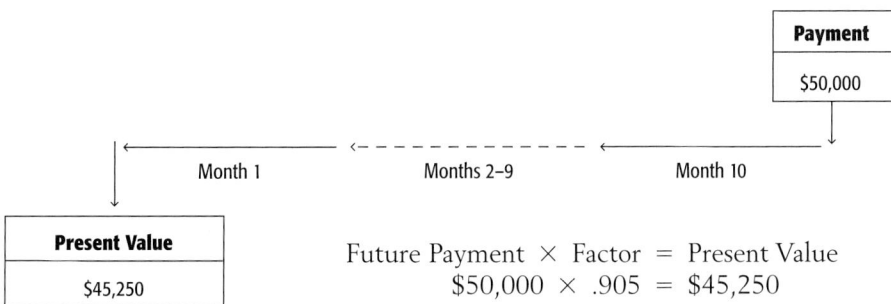

Future Payment × Factor = Present Value
$50,000 × .905 = $45,250

The present value, $45,250, is recorded in Washington's purchase records and in Plains's sale records. The balance consists of interest income. Washington records the purchase and Plains records the sale using the following entries:

Washington Journal			Plains Journal		
A = L + OE Feb. 1 Tractor	45,250		Accounts Receivable	45,250		A = L + OE
+ + Accounts Payable		45,250	Sales		45,250	+ +
Purchased tractor			Sold tractor			

When Washington pays for the tractor, the entries are as follows:

Washington Journal			Plains Journal		
A = L + OE Dec. 1 Accounts Payable	45,250		Cash	50,000		A = L + OE
− − − Interest Expense	4,750		Accounts Receivable		45,250	− +
Cash		50,000	Interest Income		4,750	+
Paid on account,			Received on account			
including imputed			from Washington,			
interest expense			including imputed			
			interest earned			

■ **INVESTMENT OF IDLE CASH**   Childware Corporation, a toy manufacturer, has just completed a successful selling season and has $10,000,000 in cash to invest for six months. The company places the cash in a money market account expected to pay 12 percent annual interest. Interest is compounded and credited to the company's account monthly. How much cash will the company have at the end of six months, and what entries will be made to record the investment and the monthly interest? The future value factor from Table 1 is based on six monthly periods of 1 percent (12 percent divided by 12 months), and the future value is computed as follows:

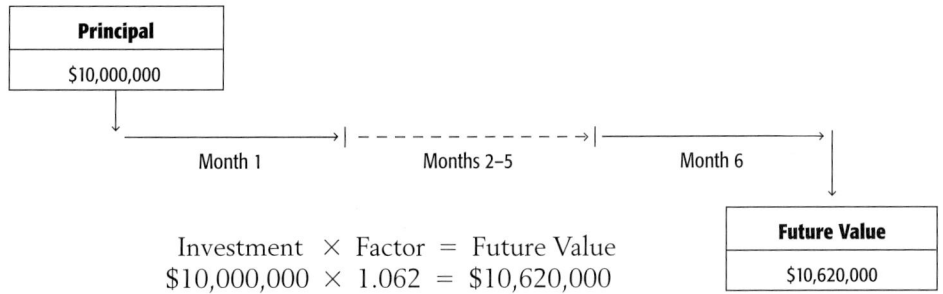

Investment × Factor = Future Value
$10,000,000 × 1.062 = $10,620,000

When the investment is made, the following entry is made:

A = L + OE   Short-Term Investments   10,000,000
+
          Cash   10,000,000
−
             Made investment of cash

After the first month, the interest is recorded by increasing the Short-Term Investments account.

A = L + OE   Short-Term Investments   100,000
+   +
          Interest Income   100,000
             Earned one month's interest income
             $10,000,000 × .01 = $100,000

After the second month, the interest is earned on the new balance of the Short-Term Investments account.

A = L + OE   Short-Term Investments   101,000
+   +
          Interest Income   101,000
             Earned one month's interest income
             $10,100,000 × .01 = $101,000

Entries would continue in a similar manner for four more months, at which time the balance of Short-Term Investments would be about $10,620,000. The actual amount accumulated may vary from this total because the interest rate paid on money market accounts can vary over time as a result of changes in market conditions.

■ **ACCUMULATION OF A FUND**   When a company owes a large fixed amount due in several years, management would be wise to accumulate a fund with which to pay off the debt at maturity. Sometimes creditors, when they agree to provide a loan, require that such a fund be established. In establishing the fund, management must determine how much cash to set aside each period in order to pay the debt. The amount will depend on the estimated rate of interest the investments will earn. Assume that Vason Corporation agrees with a creditor to set aside cash at the end of each year to accumulate enough to pay off a $100,000 note due in five years. Since the first contribution to the fund will be made in one year, five annual contributions will be made by the time the note is due. Assume also that the fund is projected to earn 8 percent, compounded annually. The amount of each annual payment is calculated using Table 2 (5 periods, 8 percent), as follows:

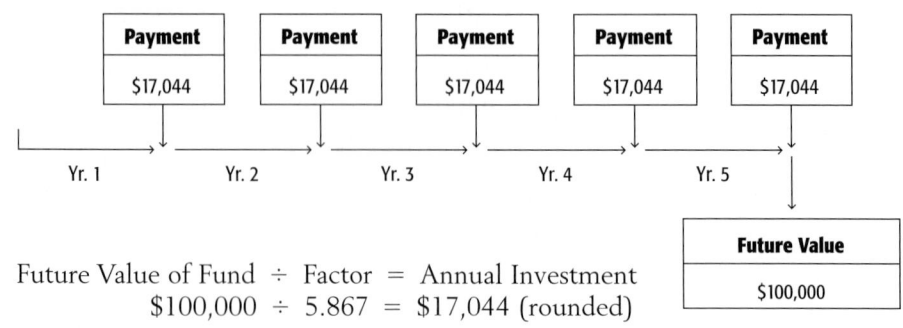

Future Value of Fund ÷ Factor = Annual Investment
$100,000 ÷ 5.867 = $17,044 (rounded)

Each year's contribution to the fund is $17,044, which is recorded as follows:

A = L + OE   Loan Repayment Fund   17,044
+
          Cash   17,044
−
             Recorded annual contribution to loan repayment
             fund

■ **OTHER ACCOUNTING APPLICATIONS** There are many other applications of present value in accounting, including accounting for installment notes, valuing a bond, and recording lease obligations. Present value is also applied in such areas as pension obligations; premium and discount on debt; depreciation of property, plant, and equipment; capital expenditure decisions; and generally any problem in which time is a factor.

EXERCISES

Tables 1 to 4 in the appendix on future value and present value tables may be used where appropriate to solve these exercises.

Future Value Calculations

E 1. Wieland receives a one-year note for $3,000 that carries a 12 percent annual interest rate for the sale of a used car.

Compute the maturity value under each of the following assumptions: (1) The interest is simple interest. (2) The interest is compounded semiannually. (3) The interest is compounded quarterly. (4) The interest is compounded monthly.

Future Value Calculations

E 2. Find the future value of (1) a single payment of $20,000 at 7 percent for ten years, (2) ten annual payments of $2,000 at 7 percent, (3) a single payment of $6,000 at 9 percent for seven years, and (4) seven annual payments of $6,000 at 9 percent.

Future Value Calculations

E 3. Assume that $40,000 is invested today. Compute the amount that would accumulate at the end of seven years when the interest rate is (1) 8 percent compounded annually, (2) 8 percent compounded semiannually, and (3) 8 percent compounded quarterly.

Future Value Calculations

E 4. Calculate the accumulation of periodic payments of $1,000 made at the end of each of four years, assuming (1) 10 percent annual interest compounded annually, (2) 10 percent annual interest compounded semiannually, (3) 4 percent annual interest compounded annually, and (4) 16 percent annual interest compounded quarterly.

Future Value Applications

E 5. a. Two parents have $20,000 to invest for their child's college tuition, which they estimate will cost $40,000 when the child enters college twelve years from now.

Calculate the approximate rate of annual interest that the investment must earn to reach the $40,000 goal in twelve years. (**Hint:** Make a calculation; then use Table 1 in the appendix on future value and present value tables.)

b. Ted Pruitt is saving to purchase a summer home that will cost about $64,000. He has $40,000 now, on which he can earn 7 percent annual interest.

Calculate the approximate length of time he will have to wait to purchase the summer home. (**Hint:** Make a calculation; then use Table 1 in the appendix on future value and present value tables.)

Working Backward from a Future Value

E 6. Gloria Faraquez has a debt of $90,000 due in four years. She wants to save enough money to pay it off by making annual deposits in an investment account that earns 8 percent annual interest.

Calculate the amount she must deposit each year to reach her goal. (**Hint:** Use Table 2 in the appendix on future value and present value tables; then make a calculation.)

Determining an Advance Payment

E 7. Ellen Saber is contemplating paying five years' rent in advance. Her annual rent is $9,600.

Calculate the single sum that would have to be paid now for the advance rent, if we assume compound interest of 8 percent.

Present Value Calculations

E 8.   Find the present value of (1) a single payment of $24,000 at 6 percent for twelve years, (2) twelve annual payments of $2,000 at 6 percent, (3) a single payment of $5,000 at 9 percent for five years, and (4) five annual payments of $5,000 at 9 percent.

Present Value of a Lump-Sum Contract

E 9.   A contract calls for a lump-sum payment of $60,000. Find the present value of the contract, assuming that (1) the payment is due in five years, and the current interest rate is 9 percent; (2) the payment is due in ten years, and the current interest rate is 9 percent; (3) the payment is due in five years, and the current interest rate is 5 percent; and (4) the payment is due in ten years, and the current interest rate is 5 percent.

Present Value of an Annuity Contract

E 10.   A contract calls for annual payments of $1,200. Find the present value of the contract, assuming that (1) the number of payments is seven, and the current interest rate is 6 percent; (2) the number of payments is fourteen, and the current interest rate is 6 percent; (3) the number of payments is seven, and the current interest rate is 8 percent; and (4) the number of payments is fourteen, and the current interest rate is 8 percent.

Non-Interest-Bearing Note

E 11.   On January 1, 20x0, Pendleton purchased a machine from Leyland by signing a two-year, non-interest-bearing $32,000 note. Pendleton currently pays 12 percent interest to borrow money at the bank.
    Prepare entries in Pendleton's and Leyland's journals to (1) record the purchase and the note, (2) adjust the accounts after one year, and (3) record payment of the note after two years (on December 31, 20x2).

Valuing an Asset for the Purpose of Making a Purchasing Decision

E 12.   Oscaro owns a service station and has the opportunity to purchase a car wash machine for $30,000. After carefully studying projected costs and revenues, Oscaro estimates that the car wash machine will produce a net cash flow of $5,200 annually and will last for eight years. Oscaro believes that an interest rate of 14 percent is adequate for his business.
    Calculate the present value of the machine to Oscaro. Does the purchase appear to be a correct business decision?

Deferred Payment

E 13.   Johnson Equipment Corporation sold a precision tool machine with computer controls to Borst Corporation for $800,000 on January 1, agreeing to take payment nine months later, on October 1. Assuming that the prevailing annual interest rate for such a transaction is 16 percent compounded quarterly, what is the actual sale (purchase) price of the machine tool, and what journal entries will be made at the time of the purchase (sale) and at the time of the payment (receipt) on the records of both Borst and Johnson?

Investment of Idle Cash

E 14.   Scientific Publishing Company, a publisher of college books, has just completed a successful fall selling season and has $5,000,000 in cash to invest for nine months, beginning on January 1. The company placed the cash in a money market account that is expected to pay 12 percent annual interest compounded monthly. Interest is credited to the company's account each month. How much cash will the company have at the end of nine months, and what entries are made to record the investment and the first two monthly (February 1 and March 1) interest amounts?

Accumulation of a Fund

E 15.   Laferia Corporation borrowed $3,000,000 from an insurance company on a five-year note. Management agreed to set aside enough cash at the end of each year to accumulate the amount needed to pay off the note at maturity. Since the first contribution to the fund will be made in one year, four annual contributions are needed. Assuming that the fund will earn 10 percent compounded annually, how much will the annual contribution to the fund be (round to nearest dollar), and what will be the journal entry for the first contribution?

E 16.

Negotiating the Sale of a Business

Horace Raftson is attempting to sell his business to Ernando Ruiz. The company has assets of $900,000, liabilities of $800,000, and owner's equity of $100,000. Both parties agree that the proper rate of return to expect is 12 percent; however, they differ on other assumptions. Raftson believes that the business will generate at least $100,000 per year of cash flows for twenty years. Ruiz thinks that $80,000 in cash flows per year is more reasonable and that only ten years in the future should be considered. Using Table 4 in the appendix on future value and present value tables, determine the range for negotiation by computing the present value of Raftson's offer to sell and of Ruiz's offer to buy.

Appendix D

Future Value and Present Value Tables

Table 1 provides the multipliers necessary to compute the future value of a *single* cash deposit made at the *beginning* of year 1. Three factors must be known before the future value can be computed: (1) the time period in years, (2) the stated annual rate of interest to be earned, and (3) the dollar amount invested or deposited.

■ **EXAMPLE—TABLE 1** Determine the future value of $5,000 deposited now that will earn 9 percent interest compounded annually for five years. From Table 1, the necessary multiplier for five years at 9 percent is 1.539, and the answer is

$$\$5,000 \times 1.539 = \$7,695$$

TABLE 1. Future Value of $1 After a Given Number of Time Periods

Periods	1%	2%	3%	4%	5%	6%	7%	8%	9%	10%	12%	14%	15%
1	1.010	1.020	1.030	1.040	1.050	1.060	1.070	1.080	1.090	1.100	1.120	1.140	1.150
2	1.020	1.040	1.061	1.082	1.103	1.124	1.145	1.166	1.188	1.210	1.254	1.300	1.323
3	1.030	1.061	1.093	1.125	1.158	1.191	1.225	1.260	1.295	1.331	1.405	1.482	1.521
4	1.041	1.082	1.126	1.170	1.216	1.262	1.311	1.360	1.412	1.464	1.574	1.689	1.749
5	1.051	1.104	1.159	1.217	1.276	1.338	1.403	1.469	1.539	1.611	1.762	1.925	2.011
6	1.062	1.126	1.194	1.265	1.340	1.419	1.501	1.587	1.677	1.772	1.974	2.195	2.313
7	1.072	1.149	1.230	1.316	1.407	1.504	1.606	1.714	1.828	1.949	2.211	2.502	2.660
8	1.083	1.172	1.267	1.369	1.477	1.594	1.718	1.851	1.993	2.144	2.476	2.853	3.059
9	1.094	1.195	1.305	1.423	1.551	1.689	1.838	1.999	2.172	2.358	2.773	3.252	3.518
10	1.105	1.219	1.344	1.480	1.629	1.791	1.967	2.159	2.367	2.594	3.106	3.707	4.046
11	1.116	1.243	1.384	1.539	1.710	1.898	2.105	2.332	2.580	2.853	3.479	4.226	4.652
12	1.127	1.268	1.426	1.601	1.796	2.012	2.252	2.518	2.813	3.138	3.896	4.818	5.350
13	1.138	1.294	1.469	1.665	1.886	2.133	2.410	2.720	3.066	3.452	4.363	5.492	6.153
14	1.149	1.319	1.513	1.732	1.980	2.261	2.579	2.937	3.342	3.798	4.887	6.261	7.076
15	1.161	1.346	1.558	1.801	2.079	2.397	2.759	3.172	3.642	4.177	5.474	7.138	8.137
16	1.173	1.373	1.605	1.873	2.183	2.540	2.952	3.426	3.970	4.595	6.130	8.137	9.358
17	1.184	1.400	1.653	1.948	2.292	2.693	3.159	3.700	4.328	5.054	6.866	9.276	10.760
18	1.196	1.428	1.702	2.026	2.407	2.854	3.380	3.996	4.717	5.560	7.690	10.580	12.380
19	1.208	1.457	1.754	2.107	2.527	3.026	3.617	4.316	5.142	6.116	8.613	12.060	14.230
20	1.220	1.486	1.806	2.191	2.653	3.207	3.870	4.661	5.604	6.728	9.646	13.740	16.370
21	1.232	1.516	1.860	2.279	2.786	3.400	4.141	5.034	6.109	7.400	10.800	15.670	18.820
22	1.245	1.546	1.916	2.370	2.925	3.604	4.430	5.437	6.659	8.140	12.100	17.860	21.640
23	1.257	1.577	1.974	2.465	3.072	3.820	4.741	5.871	7.258	8.954	13.550	20.360	24.890
24	1.270	1.608	2.033	2.563	3.225	4.049	5.072	6.341	7.911	9.850	15.180	23.210	28.630
25	1.282	1.641	2.094	2.666	3.386	4.292	5.427	6.848	8.623	10.830	17.000	26.460	32.920
26	1.295	1.673	2.157	2.772	3.556	4.549	5.807	7.396	9.399	11.920	19.040	30.170	37.860
27	1.308	1.707	2.221	2.883	3.733	4.822	6.214	7.988	10.250	13.110	21.320	34.390	43.540
28	1.321	1.741	2.288	2.999	3.920	5.112	6.649	8.627	11.170	14.420	23.880	39.200	50.070
29	1.335	1.776	2.357	3.119	4.116	5.418	7.114	9.317	12.170	15.860	26.750	44.690	57.580
30	1.348	1.811	2.427	3.243	4.322	5.743	7.612	10.060	13.270	17.450	29.960	50.950	66.210
40	1.489	2.208	3.262	4.801	7.040	10.290	14.970	21.720	31.410	45.260	93.050	188.900	267.900
50	1.645	2.692	4.384	7.107	11.470	18.420	29.460	46.900	74.360	117.400	289.000	700.200	1,084.000

Where r is the interest rate and n is the number of periods, the factor values for Table 1 are

$$\text{FV Factor} = (1 + r)^n$$

Situations requiring the use of Table 2 are similar to those requiring Table 1 except that Table 2 is used to compute the future value of a *series* of *equal* annual deposits at the end of each period.

■ **EXAMPLE–TABLE 2**   What will be the future value at the end of 30 years if $1,000 is deposited each year on January 1, beginning in one year, assuming 12 percent interest compounded annually? The required multiplier from Table 2 is 241.3, and the answer is

$$\$1,000 \times 241.3 = \$241,300$$

The factor values for Table 2 are

$$\text{FVa Factor} = \frac{(1 + r)^n - 1}{r}$$

TABLE 2.   Future Value of $1 Paid in Each Period for a Given Number of Time Periods

Periods	1%	2%	3%	4%	5%	6%	7%	8%	9%	10%	12%	14%	15%
1	1.000	1.000	1.000	1.000	1.000	1.000	1.000	1.000	1.000	1.000	1.000	1.000	1.000
2	2.010	2.020	2.030	2.040	2.050	2.060	2.070	2.080	2.090	2.100	2.120	2.140	2.150
3	3.030	3.060	3.091	3.122	3.153	3.184	3.215	3.246	3.278	3.310	3.374	3.440	3.473
4	4.060	4.122	4.184	4.246	4.310	4.375	4.440	4.506	4.573	4.641	4.779	4.921	4.993
5	5.101	5.204	5.309	5.416	5.526	5.637	5.751	5.867	5.985	6.105	6.353	6.610	6.742
6	6.152	6.308	6.468	6.633	6.802	6.975	7.153	7.336	7.523	7.716	8.115	8.536	8.754
7	7.214	7.434	7.662	7.898	8.142	8.394	8.654	8.923	9.200	9.487	10.090	10.730	11.070
8	8.286	8.583	8.892	9.214	9.549	9.897	10.260	10.640	11.030	11.440	12.300	13.230	13.730
9	9.369	9.755	10.160	10.580	11.030	11.490	11.980	12.490	13.020	13.580	14.780	16.090	16.790
10	10.460	10.950	11.460	12.010	12.580	13.180	13.820	14.490	15.190	15.940	17.550	19.340	20.300
11	11.570	12.170	12.810	13.490	14.210	14.970	15.780	16.650	17.560	18.530	20.650	23.040	24.350
12	12.680	13.410	14.190	15.030	15.920	16.870	17.890	18.980	20.140	21.380	24.130	27.270	29.000
13	13.810	14.680	15.620	16.630	17.710	18.880	20.140	21.500	22.950	24.520	28.030	32.090	34.350
14	14.950	15.970	17.090	18.290	19.600	21.020	22.550	24.210	26.020	27.980	32.390	37.580	40.500
15	16.100	17.290	18.600	20.020	21.580	23.280	25.130	27.150	29.360	31.770	37.280	43.840	47.580
16	17.260	18.640	20.160	21.820	23.660	25.670	27.890	30.320	33.000	35.950	42.750	50.980	55.720
17	18.430	20.010	21.760	23.700	25.840	28.210	30.840	33.750	36.970	40.540	48.880	59.120	65.080
18	19.610	21.410	23.410	25.650	28.130	30.910	34.000	37.450	41.300	45.600	55.750	68.390	75.840
19	20.810	22.840	25.120	27.670	30.540	33.760	37.380	41.450	46.020	51.160	63.440	78.970	88.210
20	22.020	24.300	26.870	29.780	33.070	36.790	41.000	45.760	51.160	57.280	72.050	91.020	102.400
21	23.240	25.780	28.680	31.970	35.720	39.990	44.870	50.420	56.760	64.000	81.700	104.800	118.800
22	24.470	27.300	30.540	34.250	38.510	43.390	49.010	55.460	62.870	71.400	92.500	120.400	137.600
23	25.720	28.850	32.450	36.620	41.430	47.000	53.440	60.890	69.530	79.540	104.600	138.300	159.300
24	26.970	30.420	34.430	39.080	44.500	50.820	58.180	66.760	76.790	88.500	118.200	158.700	184.200
25	28.240	32.030	36.460	41.650	47.730	54.860	63.250	73.110	84.700	98.350	133.300	181.900	212.800
26	29.530	33.670	38.550	44.310	51.110	59.160	68.680	79.950	93.320	109.200	150.300	208.300	245.700
27	30.820	35.340	40.710	47.080	54.670	63.710	74.480	87.350	102.700	121.100	169.400	238.500	283.600
28	32.130	37.050	42.930	49.970	58.400	68.530	80.700	95.340	113.000	134.200	190.700	272.900	327.100
29	33.450	38.790	45.220	52.970	62.320	73.640	87.350	104.000	124.100	148.600	214.600	312.100	377.200
30	34.780	40.570	47.580	56.080	66.440	79.060	94.460	113.300	136.300	164.500	241.300	356.800	434.700
40	48.890	60.400	75.400	95.030	120.800	154.800	199.600	259.100	337.900	442.600	767.100	1,342.000	1,779.000
50	64.460	84.580	112.800	152.700	209.300	290.300	406.500	573.800	815.100	1,164.000	2,400.000	4,995.000	7,218.000

TABLE 4.   Present Value of $1 Received Each Period for a Given Number of Time Periods

Periods	1%	2%	3%	4%	5%	6%	7%	8%	9%	10%	12%
1	0.990	0.980	0.971	0.962	0.952	0.943	0.935	0.926	0.917	0.909	0.893
2	1.970	1.942	1.913	1.886	1.859	1.833	1.808	1.783	1.759	1.736	1.690
3	2.941	2.884	2.829	2.775	2.723	2.673	2.624	2.577	2.531	2.487	2.402
4	3.902	3.808	3.717	3.630	3.546	3.465	3.387	3.312	3.240	3.170	3.037
5	4.853	4.713	4.580	4.452	4.329	4.212	4.100	3.993	3.890	3.791	3.605
6	5.795	5.601	5.417	5.242	5.076	4.917	4.767	4.623	4.486	4.355	4.111
7	6.728	6.472	6.230	6.002	5.786	5.582	5.389	5.206	5.033	4.868	4.564
8	7.652	7.325	7.020	6.733	6.463	6.210	5.971	5.747	5.535	5.335	4.968
9	8.566	8.162	7.786	7.435	7.108	6.802	6.515	6.247	5.995	5.759	5.328
10	9.471	8.983	8.530	8.111	7.722	7.360	7.024	6.710	6.418	6.145	5.650
11	10.368	9.787	9.253	8.760	8.306	7.887	7.499	7.139	6.805	6.495	5.938
12	11.255	10.575	9.954	9.385	8.863	8.384	7.943	7.536	7.161	6.814	6.194
13	12.134	11.348	10.635	9.986	9.394	8.853	8.358	7.904	7.487	7.103	6.424
14	13.004	12.106	11.296	10.563	9.899	9.295	8.745	8.244	7.786	7.367	6.628
15	13.865	12.849	11.938	11.118	10.380	9.712	9.108	8.559	8.061	7.606	6.811
16	14.718	13.578	12.561	11.652	10.838	10.106	9.447	8.851	8.313	7.824	6.974
17	15.562	14.292	13.166	12.166	11.274	10.477	9.763	9.122	8.544	8.022	7.120
18	16.398	14.992	13.754	12.659	11.690	10.828	10.059	9.372	8.756	8.201	7.250
19	17.226	15.678	14.324	13.134	12.085	11.158	10.336	9.604	8.950	8.365	7.366
20	18.046	16.351	14.878	13.590	12.462	11.470	10.594	9.818	9.129	8.514	7.469
21	18.857	17.011	15.415	14.029	12.821	11.764	10.836	10.017	9.292	8.649	7.562
22	19.660	17.658	15.937	14.451	13.163	12.042	11.061	10.201	9.442	8.772	7.645
23	20.456	18.292	16.444	14.857	13.489	12.303	11.272	10.371	9.580	8.883	7.718
24	21.243	18.914	16.936	15.247	13.799	12.550	11.469	10.529	9.707	8.985	7.784
25	22.023	19.523	17.413	15.622	14.094	12.783	11.654	10.675	9.823	9.077	7.843
26	22.795	20.121	17.877	15.983	14.375	13.003	11.826	10.810	9.929	9.161	7.896
27	23.560	20.707	18.327	16.330	14.643	13.211	11.987	10.935	10.027	9.237	7.943
28	24.316	21.281	18.764	16.663	14.898	13.406	12.137	11.051	10.116	9.307	7.984
29	25.066	21.844	19.189	16.984	15.141	13.591	12.278	11.158	10.198	9.370	8.022
30	25.808	22.396	19.600	17.292	15.373	13.765	12.409	11.258	10.274	9.427	8.055
40	32.835	27.355	23.115	19.793	17.159	15.046	13.332	11.925	10.757	9.779	8.244
50	39.196	31.424	25.730	21.482	18.256	15.762	13.801	12.234	10.962	9.915	8.305

Table 4 is used to compute the present value of a *series* of *equal* annual cash flows.

■ **EXAMPLE–TABLE 4**   Arthur Howard won a contest on January 1, 2002, in which the prize was $30,000, the money was payable in 15 annual installments of $2,000 every December 31, beginning in 2002. Assuming a 9 percent interest rate, what is the present value of Mr. Howard's prize on January 1, 2002? From Table 4, the required multiplier is 8.061, and the answer is:

$$\$2,000 \times 8.061 = \$16,122$$

The factor values for Table 4 are

$$\text{PVa Factor} = \frac{1 - (1 + r)^{-n}}{r}$$

Table 4 is the columnar sum of Table 3. Table 4 applies to *ordinary annuities*, in which the first cash flow occurs one time period beyond the date for which the present value is to be computed.

14%	15%	16%	18%	20%	25%	30%	35%	40%	45%	50%	Periods
0.877	0.870	0.862	0.847	0.833	0.800	0.769	0.741	0.714	0.690	0.667	1
1.647	1.626	1.605	1.566	1.528	1.440	1.361	1.289	1.224	1.165	1.111	2
2.322	2.283	2.246	2.174	2.106	1.952	1.816	1.696	1.589	1.493	1.407	3
2.914	2.855	2.798	2.690	2.589	2.362	2.166	1.997	1.849	1.720	1.605	4
3.433	3.352	3.274	3.127	2.991	2.689	2.436	2.220	2.035	1.876	1.737	5
3.889	3.784	3.685	3.498	3.326	2.951	2.643	2.385	2.168	1.983	1.824	6
4.288	4.160	4.039	3.812	3.605	3.161	2.802	2.508	2.263	2.057	1.883	7
4.639	4.487	4.344	4.078	3.837	3.329	2.925	2.598	2.331	2.109	1.922	8
4.946	4.772	4.607	4.303	4.031	3.463	3.019	2.665	2.379	2.144	1.948	9
5.216	5.019	4.833	4.494	4.192	3.571	3.092	2.715	2.414	2.168	1.965	10
5.453	5.234	5.029	4.656	4.327	3.656	3.147	2.752	2.438	2.185	1.977	11
5.660	5.421	5.197	4.793	4.439	3.725	3.190	2.779	2.456	2.197	1.985	12
5.842	5.583	5.342	4.910	4.533	3.780	3.223	2.799	2.469	2.204	1.990	13
6.002	5.724	5.468	5.008	4.611	3.824	3.249	2.814	2.478	2.210	1.993	14
6.142	5.847	5.575	5.092	4.675	3.859	3.268	2.825	2.484	2.214	1.995	15
6.265	5.954	5.669	5.162	4.730	3.887	3.283	2.834	2.489	2.216	1.997	16
6.373	6.047	5.749	5.222	4.775	3.910	3.295	2.840	2.492	2.218	1.998	17
6.467	6.128	5.818	5.273	4.812	3.928	3.304	2.844	2.494	2.219	1.999	18
6.550	6.198	5.877	5.316	4.844	3.942	3.311	2.848	2.496	2.220	1.999	19
6.623	6.259	5.929	5.353	4.870	3.954	3.316	2.850	2.497	2.221	1.999	20
6.687	6.312	5.973	5.384	4.891	3.963	3.320	2.852	2.498	2.221	2.000	21
6.743	6.359	6.011	5.410	4.909	3.970	3.323	2.853	2.498	2.222	2.000	22
6.792	6.399	6.044	5.432	4.925	3.976	3.325	2.854	2.499	2.222	2.000	23
6.835	6.434	6.073	5.451	4.937	3.981	3.327	2.855	2.499	2.222	2.000	24
6.873	6.464	6.097	5.467	4.948	3.985	3.329	2.856	2.499	2.222	2.000	25
6.906	6.491	6.118	5.480	4.956	3.988	3.330	2.856	2.500	2.222	2.000	26
6.935	6.514	6.136	5.492	4.964	3.990	3.331	2.856	2.500	2.222	2.000	27
6.961	6.534	6.152	5.502	4.970	3.992	3.331	2.857	2.500	2.222	2.000	28
6.983	6.551	6.166	5.510	4.975	3.994	3.332	2.857	2.500	2.222	2.000	29
7.003	6.566	6.177	5.517	4.979	3.995	3.332	2.857	2.500	2.222	2.000	30
7.105	6.642	6.234	5.548	4.997	3.999	3.333	2.857	2.500	2.222	2.000	40
7.133	6.661	6.246	5.554	4.999	4.000	3.333	2.857	2.500	2.222	2.000	50

An *annuity due* is a series of equal cash flows for N time periods, but the first payment occurs immediately. The present value of the first payment equals the face value of the cash flow; Table 4 then is used to measure the present value of $N - 1$ remaining cash flows.

■ **EXAMPLE–TABLE 4**   Determine the present value on January 1, 2002, of 20 lease payments; each payment of $10,000 is due on January 1, beginning in 2002. Assume an interest rate of 8 percent.

$$\text{Present Value} = \text{Immediate Payment} + \left\{ \begin{array}{l} \text{Present Value of 19 Subsequent} \\ \text{Payments at 8\%} \end{array} \right.$$

$$= \$10,000 + (\$10,000 \times 9.604) = \$106,040$$

Endnotes

Chapter 1

1. Walgreen Co., *Annual Report*, 2002.
2. *Statement of Financial Accounting Concepts No. 1*, "Objectives of Financial Reporting by Business Enterprises" (Norwalk, Conn.: Financial Accounting Standards Board, 1978), par. 9.
3. Ibid.
4. Christopher D. Ittner, David F. Larcker, and Madhav V. Rajan, "The Choice of Performance Measures in Annual Bonus Contracts," *The Accounting Review*, April 1997.
5. Walgreen Co., *Annual Report*, 2002.
6. Kathy Williams and James Hart, "Microsoft: Tooling the Information Age," *Management Accounting*, May 1996, p. 42.
7. *Statement of the Accounting Principles Board No. 4*, "Basic Concepts and Accounting Principles Underlying Financial Statements of Business Enterprises" (New York: American Institute of Certified Public Accountants, 1970), par. 138.
8. Touche Ross & Co., "Ethics in American Business" (New York: Touche Ross & Co., 1988), p. 7.
9. "Global Ethics Codes Gain Importance as a Tool to Avoid Litigation and Fines," *The Wall Street Journal*, August 19, 1999.
10. *Statement Number IC*, "Standards of Ethical Conduct for Management Accountants" (Montvale, N.J.: Institute of Management Accountants, 1983, revised 1997).
11. J.C. Penney Company, Inc., *Annual Report*, 1995.
12. Nikhil Deogun, "Coca-Cola Reports 27% Drop in Profits Hurt by Weakness in Foreign Markets," *The Wall Street Journal*, January 27, 1999.
13. Southwest Airlines Co., *Annual Report*, 1996.
14. Queen Sook Kim, "Lechters Inc. Files for Chapter 11, Arranges Financing," *The Wall Street Journal*, May 22, 2001.
15. Charles Schwab Corporation, *Annual Report*, 2001.
16. Robert Frank, "Facing a Loss, Lego Narrates a Sad Toy Story," *The Wall Street Journal*, January 22, 1999.

Chapter 2

1. "Boeing Scores a Deal to Sell 15 Planes for Long-Haul Routes," *The Wall Street Journal*, October 5, 2000.
2. The Boeing Co., *Annual Report*, 1994.
3. Craig S. Smith, "China Halts New Purchases of Jets," *The Wall Street Journal*, February 9, 1999.
4. The Boeing Co., *Annual Report*, 2000.
5. Patricia Kranz, "Rubles? Who Needs Rubles?" *BusinessWeek*, April 13, 1998; Andrew Higgins, "Lacking Money to Pay, Russian Firms Survive on Deft Barter System," *The Wall Street Journal*, August 27, 1998.
6. Intel Corp., *Annual Report*, 2002.
7. Shawn Young, "Lucent Revises Its Revenue Downward," *The Wall Street Journal*, December 22, 2000.
8. Nike, Inc., *Annual Report*, 2002.
9. Mellon Bank, *Annual Report*, 2000.
10. Ajinomoto Company, *Annual Report*, 2000.

Chapter 3

1. Kelly Services, *Annual Report*, 2002.
2. *Statement of Financial Accounting Concepts No. 1*, "Objectives of Financial Reporting by Business Enterprises" (Norwalk, Conn.: Financial Accounting Standards Board, 1978), par. 44.
3. Thomas J. Phillips Jr., Michael S. Luehlfing, and Cynthia M. Daily, "The Right Way to Recognize Revenue," *Journal of Accountancy*, June 2001.
4. "Revenue Recognition in Financial Statements," *Staff Accounting Bulletin No. 10* (Securities and Exchange Commission, 1999).
5. Michael Schroeder and Elizabeth MacDonald, "SEC Expects More Big Cases on Accounting," *The Wall Street Journal*, December 24, 1998.
6. PricewaterhouseCoopers presentation, 1999.
7. Lyric Opera of Chicago, *Annual Report*, 2001.
8. The Walt Disney Company, *Annual Report*, 2001.
9. H. J. Heinz Company, *Annual Report*, 2001.
10. Takashimaya Company, Limited, *Annual Report*, 2000.

Chapter 4

1. Dell Compter Corporation, *Annual Report*, 2002.
2. Adapted from H & R Block, Inc., *Annual Report*, 2002.
3. Nestlé S.A., *Annual Report*, 2000.

Chapter 5

1. Target, *Annual Report*, 2002.
2. Ibid.
3. "Shop Online—Pickup at the Store," *BusinessWeek*, June 12, 2000; Nick Wingfield, "As Web Sales Grow Mail-Order Sellers Are Benefiting the Most," *The Wall Street Journal*, May 2, 2001.
4. Joel Millman, "Here's What Happens to Many Lovely Gifts After Santa Rides Off," *The Wall Street Journal*, December 26, 2001.
5. Matthew Rose, "Magazine Revenue at Newsstands Falls in Worst Year Ever," *The Wall Street Journal*, May 15, 2001.
6. Matthew Schifrin, "The Big Squeeze," *Forbes*, March 11, 1996.
7. Wal-Mart Stores, Inc., *Annual Report*, 2000; Kmart Corp., *Annual Report*, 2000.

Chapter 6

1. General Mills, Inc., *Annual Report*, 2001.
2. "Objectives of Financial Reporting by Business Enterprises," *Statement of Financial Accounting Concepts No. 1* (Norwalk, Conn.: Financial Accounting Standards Board, 1978), pars. 32–54.
3. "Qualitative Characteristics of Accounting Information," *Statement of Financial Accounting Concepts No. 1* (Norwalk, Conn.: Financial Accounting Standards Board, 1980), par. 20.
4. Accounting Principles Board, "Accounting Changes," *Opinion No. 20* (New York: American Institute of Certified Public Accountants, 1971), par. 17.
5. Securities and Exchange Commission, *Staff Accounting Bulletin No. 99*, 1999.
6. Reynolds Metals Company, *Annual Report*, 1998.
7. Ray J. Groves, "Here's the Annual Report. Got a Few Hours?" *The Wall Street Journal Europe*, August 26–27, 1994.
8. Roger Lowenstein, "Investors Will Fish for Footnotes in 'Abbreviated' Annual Reports," *The Wall Street Journal*, September 14, 1995.
9. General Mills, *Annual Report*, 2001.
10. Ibid.
11. National Commission on Fraudulent Financial Reporting, *Report of the National Commission on Fraudulent Financial Reporting* (Washington, D.C., 1987), p. 2.
12. Arthur Levitt, "The Numbers Game," NYU Center for Law and Business, September 28, 1998.
13. "Ex-Chairman of Cendant Is Indicted," *The Wall Street Journal*, March 1, 2001; "SEC Sues Former Sunbeam Executive," *Chicago Tribune*, May 16, 2001; "Enron: A Wake-up Call," *The Wall Street*

Journal, December 4, 2001; "SEC List of Accounting-Fraud Probes Grows," *The Wall Street Journal*, July 6, 2001.

14. *Accounting Research and Terminology Bulletin*, final edition (New York: American Institute of Certified Public Accountants, 1961), p. 20.

15. "Debt vs. Equity: Whose Call Counts," *BusinessWeek*, July 19, 1999.

16. Roger Lowenstein, "The '20% Club' No Longer Is Exclusive," *The Wall Street Journal*, May 4, 1995.

17. "SEC Probes Lucent Accounting Practices," *The Wall Street Journal*, February 9, 2001.

18. Albertson's Inc., *Annual Report*, 2001; Great Atlantic & Pacific Tea Company, *Annual Report*, 2001.

19. GlaxoSmithKline PLC, *Annual Report*, 2000.

20. Toys "R" Us, *Annual Report*, 1987.

Chapter 7

1. Lee Copeland, "Donnelley Goes Dutch in Software Conversion," *Chicago Tribune*, June 3, 2002.

2. News item, *Crain's Chicago Business*, October 2001.

3. AICPA Press Release, Jan. 2, 2003

4. News item, *The Wall Street Journal*, July 29, 1999.

5. Michael Totty, "The Next Phase," *The Wall Street Journal*, May 21, 2001.

6. Frank Potter, "Event-to-Knowledge: A New Metric for Finance Department Efficiency," *Strategic Finance*, July 2001.

7. Walgreens, *Annual Report*, 1993.

8. Anthony Bianco, "Virtual Bookstores to Get Real," *BusinessWeek*, October 27,1997.

Chapter 8

1. Ron Winslow and George Anders, "How New Technology Was Oxford's Nemesis," *The Wall Street Journal*, December 11, 1997.

2. Circuit City Stores, *Annual Report*, 2001.

3. *Professional Standards*, vol. 1 (New York: American Institute of Certified Public Accountants, June 1, 1999), Sec. AU 322.07.

4. "1998 Fraud Survey," KPMG Peat Marwick, 1998.

5. *Professional Standards*, vol. 1, Sec. AU 325.16.

6. Lynette Khalfani, "Information-Destruction Finds Lucrative Business in Going to Waste," *The Wall Street Journal*, December 6, 1996.

7. "B-to-B Communities," *Business 2.0*, December 1999.

8. Amy Merrick, "Starbucks Accuses Employee, Husband of Embezzling $3.7 Million from Firm," *The Wall Street Journal*, November 20, 2000.

Chapter 9

1. Pioneer Corporation, *Annual Report*, 2001.

2. "So Much for Detroit's Cash Cushion," *BusinessWeek*, November 5, 2001.

3. Michael Selz, "Big Customers' Late Bills Choke Small Suppliers," *The Wall Street Journal*, June 22, 1994.

4. Pioneer Corporation, *Annual Report*, 2001.

5. Circuit City Stores, Inc., *Annual Report*, 2001.

6. Pioneer Corporation, *Annual Report*, 2001.

7. *Accounting Trends & Techniques* (New York: American Institute of CPAs, 2000), p. 130.

8. *Statement of Financial Accounting Standards No. 115*, "Accounting for Certain Investments in Debt and Equity Securities" (Norwalk, Conn.: Financial Accounting Standards Board, 1993).

9. Pioneer Corporation, *Annual Report*, 2001.

10. "Bad Loans Rattle Telecom Vendors," *BusinessWeek*, February 19, 2001.

11. Craig S. Smith, "Chinese Companies Writing Off Old Debt," *The Wall Street Journal*, December 28, 1995.

12. Information based on promotional brochures of Mitsubishi Electric Corp.

13. Elizabeth McDonald, "Unhatched Chickens," *Forbes*, February 19, 2001.

14. Philips Electronics N.V., *Annual Report*, 2001; Heineken N.V., *Annual Report*, 2001.

Chapter 10

1. J.C. Penney Company, Inc., *Annual Report*, 2002.

2. Illinois Tool Works, Inc., *Annual Report*, 2002.

3. American Institute of Certified Public Accountants, *Accounting Research Bulletin No. 43* (New York: AICPA, 1953), ch. 4.

4. Gary McWilliams, "Whirlwind on the Web," *BusinessWeek*, April 7, 1997.

5. Karen Lundebaard, "Bumpy Ride," *The Wall Street Journal*, May 21, 2001.

6. American Institute of Certified Public Accountants, *Accounting Research Bulletin No. 43* (New York: AICPA, 1953), ch. 4.

7. Micah Frankel and Robert Trezevant, "The Year-End LIFO Inventory Purchasing Decision: An Empirical Test," *The Accounting Review*, April 1994.

8. American Institute of Certified Public Accountants, *Accounting Trends & Techniques* (New York: AICPA, 2002).

9. "As Rite Aid Grew, CEO Seemed Unable to Manage His Empire," *The Wall Street Journal*, October 20, 1999; "RentWay Details Improper Bookkeeping," *The Wall Street Journal*, June 8, 2001.

10. International Paper Company, *Annual Report*, 2001.

11. American Institute of Certified Public Accountants, *Accounting Trends & Techniques* (New York: AICPA, 2002).

12. "Cisco's Numbers Confound Some," *International Herald Tribune*, April 19, 2001; "Kmart Posts $67 Million Loss Due to Markdowns," *The Wall Street Journal*, November 10, 2000.

13. American Institute of Certified Public Accountants, *Accounting Trends & Techniques* (New York: AICPA, 2002).

14. Exxon Mobil, *Annual Report*, 2000.

15. Adapted from Hershey Foods Corp., *Annual Report*, 2000.

16. "SEC Case Judge Rules Crazy Eddie Principals Must Pay $72.7 Million," *The Wall Street Journal*, May 11, 2000.

17. Crane Company, *Annual Report*, 2000.

18. Pioneer Corporation, *Annual Report*, 2001; Yamaha Motor Co., Ltd., *Annual Report*, 2001.

Chapter 11

1. H. J. Heinz Company, *Annual Report*, 2002.

2. *Statement of Financial Accounting Standards No. 144*, "Accounting for the Impairment or Disposal of Long-Lived Assets" (Norwalk, Conn.: Financial Accounting Standards Board, 2001).

3. David Henry, "The Numbers Game," *BusinessWeek*, May 14, 2001.

4. H. J. Heinz Company, *Annual Report*, 2002.

5. Ford Motor Company, *Annual Report*, 2002.

6. *Statement of Position No. 98-1*, "Accounting for the Costs of Computer Software Developed or Planned for Internal Use" (New York: American Institute of Certified Public Accountants, 1996).

7. *Statement of Financial Accounting Standards No. 34*, "Capitalization of Interest Cost" (Norwalk, Conn.: Financial Accounting Standards Board, 1979), par. 9–11.

8. Jared Sandberg, Deborah Solomon, and Rebecca Blumenstein, "Inside WorldCom's Unearthing of a Vast Accounting Scandal," *The Wall Street Journal*, June 27, 2002.

9. *Financial Accounting Standards: Original Pronouncements as of July 1, 1977* (Norwalk, Conn.: Financial Accounting Standards Board, 1977), ARB No. 43, Ch. 9, Sec. C, par. 5.

10. Accounting Principles Board, *Opinion No. 29*, "Accounting for Nonmonetary Transactions" (New York: American Institute of Certified Public Accountants, 1973); Emerging Issues Task Force, *EITF Issue Summary 86-29*, "Nonmonetary Transactions: Magnitude of Boot and the Exceptions to the Use of Fair Value" (Norwalk, Conn.: Financial Accounting Standards Board, 1986).

11. *Statement of Financial Accounting Standards No. 25*, "Suspension of Certain Accounting Requirements for Oil and Gas Producing

Companies" (Norwalk, Conn.: Financial Accounting Standards Board, 1979).

12. Adapted from Accounting Principles Board, *Opinion No. 17*, "Intangible Assets" (New York: American Institute of Certified Public Accountants, 1970), par. 2.

13. "What's in a Name?" *Time*, May 3, 1993.

14. General Motors, *Annual Report*, 2000.

15. Abbott Laboratories, *Annual Report*, 2000; Roche Group, *Annual Report*, 2000.

16. Allan B. Afterman, *International Accounting, Financial Reporting and Analysis* (New York: Warren, Gorham & Lamont, 1995).

17. *Statement of Financial Accounting Standards No. 2*, "Accounting for Research and Development Costs" (Norwalk, Conn.: Financial Accounting Standards Board, 1974), par. 12.

18. *Statement of Financial Accounting Standards No. 86*, "Accounting for the Costs of Computer Software to be Sold, Leased, or Otherwise Marketed" (Norwalk, Conn.: Financial Accounting Standards Board, 1985).

19. *Accounting Trends & Techniques*, 2002.

20. General Mills, *Annual Report*, 2002; Sara Lee Corporation, *Annual Report*, 2002; Tribune Company, *Annual Report*, 2002.

21. *Statement of Financial Accounting Standards No. 144*, "Accounting for the Impairment or Disposal of Long-Lived Assets" (Norwalk, Conn.: Financial Accounting Standards Board, 2001).

22. Edward P. McTague, "Accounting for Trade-Ins of Operational Assets," *National Public Accountant* (January 1986), p. 39.

23. General Motors Corp., *Annual Report*, 1987.

24. Polaroid Corporation, *Annual Report*, 1997.

25. Hilton Hotels Corporation, *Annual Report*, 2000; Marriott International, *Annual Report*, 2000.

26. "Stock Gives Case the Funds He Needs to Buy New Technology," *BusinessWeek*, April 15, 1996.

27. Roche Group, *Annual Report*, 2000; Baxter International, Inc., *Annual Report*, 2000.

Chapter 12

1. US Airways, Inc., *Annual Report*, 2001.

2. RadioShack Corporation, *Annual Report*, 2002.

3. Pamela L. Moore, "How Xerox Ran Short of Black Ink," *BusinessWeek*, October 30, 2000.

4. Goodyear Tire & Rubber Company, *Annual Report*, 2002.

5. US Airways, Inc., *Annual Report*, 2002.

6. Andersen Enterprise Group, cited in *Crain's Chicago Business*, July 5, 1999.

7. Raju Narisetti, "P&G Ad Chief Plots Demise of the Coupon," *The Wall Street Journal*, April 17, 1996; Renae Merle, "Slowdown Is Business Boon for Coupon Seller Valassis," *The Wall Street Journal*, May 1, 2001.

8. Scott McCartney, "Free Airline Miles Become a Potent Tool for Selling Everything," *The Wall Street Journal*, April 16, 1996; "You've Got Miles," *BusinessWeek*, March 6, 2000.

9. *Statement of Financial Accounting Standards No. 5*, "Accounting for Contingencies" (Norwalk, Conn.: Financial Accounting Standards Board, 1975).

10. American Institute of Certified Public Accountants, *Accounting Trends & Techniques*, 2002.

11. General Motors Corp., *Annual Report*, 2000.

12. American Institute of Certified Public Accountants, *Accounting Trends & Techniques*, 2002.

13. US Airways, Inc., *Annual Report*, 2000.

14. General Motors Corp., *Annual Report*, 2002.

15. Sun Micosystems Inc., *Annual Report*, 2001; Cisco Systems, *Annual Report*, 2001.

16. Texaco, Inc., *Annual Report*, 1986.

17. Man Nutzfahrzeuge Aktiengesellschaft, *Annual Report*, 1997.

Chapter 13

1. KPMG International, Internet site www.kpmg.com, February 10, 2002. KPMG has announced plans to separate its consulting practice as a corporation.

2. Information excerpted from the 1990 and 2002 annual reports of Alliance Capital Management Limited Partnership; *The Wall Street Journal*, February 10, 2003.

3. Anita Raghavan, "Goldman Scrambles to Find $250 Million in Equity Capital from Private Investors," *The Wall Street Journal*, September 15, 1994.

4. "Nokia Unveils Plans for Chinese Centre," *Financial Times London*, May 9, 2000.

Chapter 14

1. Cisco Systems, Inc., *Annual Report*, 2002.

2. Copyright © 2000 by Houghton Mifflin Company. Reproduced by permission from *The American Heritage Dictionary of the English Language, Fourth Edition*.

3. *Statement of Position No. 98-5*, "Report on the Costs of Start up Activities" (New York: American Institute of Certified Public Accountants, 1998).

4. Deborah Solomon, "AT&T Slashes Dividends 83%, Cuts Forecasts," *The Wall Street Journal*, December 21, 2002.

5. Abbott Laboratories, *Annual Report*, 2002.

6. Ibid.

7. American Institute of Certified Public Accountants, *Accounting Trends & Techniques* (New York: AICPA, 2001).

8. *Statement of Accounting Standards No. 123*, "Accounting for Stock-Based Compensation" (Norwalk, Conn.: Financial Accounting Standards Board, 1995).

9. Ruth Simon and Ianthe Jeanne Dugan, "Options Overdose," *The Wall Street Journal*, June 4, 2001.

10. Suzanne McGee, "Europe's New Markets for IPOs of Growth Start-Ups Fly High," *The Wall Street Journal*, February 22, 1999.

11. Microsoft Corporation, Inc., *Annual Report*, 1997.

12. G. Christian Hill, "Microsoft Plans Preferred Issue of $750 Million," *The Wall Street Journal*, December 3, 1996.

13. American Institute of Certified Public Accountants, *Accounting Trends & Techniques* (New York: AICPA, 2001).

14. Robert McGough, Suzanne McGee, and Cassell Bryan-Low, "Buyback Binge Now Creates Big Hangover," *The Wall Street Journal*, December 18, 2000.

15. "Avaya Prices Public Offering of Common Stock" and "Avaya Completes Sale of Approximately $200 Million Common Stock," *The Wall Street Journal Online*, March 22, 2002.

16. Tom Herman, "Preferreds' Rich Yields Blind Some Investors to Risks," *The Wall Street Journal*, March 24, 1992.

17. Stanley Ziemba, "USAir Defers Dividends on Preferred Stock," *Chicago Tribune*, September 30, 1994.

18. Susan Carey, "US Airways to Redeem Preferred Owned by Berkshire Hathaway," *The Wall Street Journal*, February 4, 1998.

19. Roche Group, *Annual Report*, 2001.

Chapter 15

1. AMR Corporation, *Annual Report*, 2002.

2. *Statement of Financial Accounting Standards No. 130*, "Reporting Comprehensive Income" (Norwalk, Conn.: Financial Accounting Standards Board, 1997).

3. American Institute of Certified Public Accountants, *Accounting Trends & Techniques* (New York: American Institute of Certified Public Accountants, 2002).

4. Cited in *The Week in Review* (Deloitte Haskins & Sells), February 28, 1985.

5. "Up to the Minute, Down to the Wire," *Twentieth Century Mutual Funds Newsletter*, 1996.

6. American Institute of Certified Public Accountants, *Accounting Trends & Techniques* (New York: American Institute of Certified Public Accountants, 2001).
7. Robert Manor and Melita Marie Garza, "Company's Accounting May Prove Hard to Criminalize," *Chicago Tribune*, January 11, 2002.
8. Sears, Roebuck and Co., *Annual Report*, 1997.
9. *Statement of Financial Accounting Standards No. 109*, "Accounting for Income Taxes" (Norwalk, Conn.: Financial Accounting Standards Board, 1992).
10. American Institute of Certified Public Accountants, *Accounting Trends & Techniques* (New York: American Institute of Certified Public Accountants, 2002).
11. Accounting Principles Board, *Opinion No. 30*, "Reporting the Results of Operations" (New York: American Institute of Certified Public Accountants, 1973), par. 20.
12. Ibid.
13. American Institute of Certified Public Accountants, *Accounting Trends & Techniques* (New York: American Institute of Certified Public Accountants, 2002).
14. Accounting Principles Board, *Opinion No. 20*, "Accounting Changes" (New York: American Institute of Certified Public Accountants, 1971), par. 20.
15. David Cairns International, *IAS Survey Update*, July 2001.
16. American Institute of Certified Public Accountants, *Accounting Trends & Techniques* (New York: American Institute of Certified Public Accountants, 2002).
17. Accounting Principles Board, *Opinion No. 15*, "Earnings per Share" (New York: American Institute of Certified Public Accountants, 1969), par. 12.
18. Minnesota Mining and Manufacturing Company, *Annual Report*, 2000.
19. *Statement of Financial Accounting Standards No. 128*, "Earnings per Share and the Disclosure of Information About Capital Structure" (Norwalk, Conn.: Financial Accounting Standards Board, 1997).
20. Tribune Company, *Annual Report*, 2002.
21. Skandia Group, *Annual Report*, 2000.
22. *Accounting Research Bulletin No. 43* (New York: American Institute of Certified Public Accountants, 1953), chap. 7, sec. B, par. 10.
23. Ibid., par. 13.
24. Robert O'Brien, "Techs' Chill Fails to Stem Stock Splits," *The Wall Street Journal*, June 8, 2000.
25. Rebecca Buckman, "Microsoft Posts Hefty 18% Revenue Rise," *The Wall Street Journal*, January 18, 2002; William M. Bulkeley, "IBM Reports 13% Decline in Net Income," *The Wall Street Journal*, January 18, 2002.
26. "Technology Firms Post Strong Earnings but Stock Prices Decline Sharply," *The Wall Street Journal*, January 21, 1988; Donald R. Seace, "Industrials Plunge 57.2 Points—Technology Stocks' Woes Cited," *The Wall Street Journal*, January 21, 1988.
27. The Washington Post Company, *Annual Report*, 2000.
28. Yamaha Motor Company, Ltd., *Annual Report*, 2001.

Chapter 16
1. AT&T Corporation, *Annual Report*, 2002.
2. "Canadian Airline's Demise Adds to Industry Woes," *The Washington Post*, November 16, 2001; "A Striking End for Air Afrique," British Broadcasting Company, November 26, 2001; "Small Airlines Adapting Quicker," Associated Press, November 22, 2001; "Swiss Air Rescue Hopes Brighten," British Broadcasting Company, November 21, 2001.
3. AT&T Corporation, *Annual Report*, 2002.
4. Ibid.
5. Quentin Hardy, "Japanese Companies Need to Raise Cash, but First a Bond Market Must Be Built," *The Wall Street Journal*, October 20, 1992.
6. Bill Barnhart, "Bond Bellwether," *Chicago Tribune*, December 4, 1996.
7. Accounting Principles Board, *Opinion No. 21*, "Interest on Receivables and Payables" (New York: American Institute of Certified Public Accountants, 1971), par. 15.
8. *Statement of Financial Accounting Standards No. 13*, "Accounting for Leases" (Norwalk, Conn.: Financial Accounting Standards Board, 1976), par. 10.
9. Philip Morris Companies, Inc., *Annual Report*, 2000.
10. *Statement of Financial Accounting Standards No. 87*, "Employers' Accounting for Pensions" (Norwalk, Conn.: Financial Accounting Standards Board, 1985).
11. *Statement of Financial Accounting Standards No. 106*, "Employers' Accounting for Postretirement Benefits Other than Pensions" (Norwalk, Conn.: Financial Accounting Standards Board, 1990).
12. Stanley Ziemba, "TWA, American Revise O'Hare Gate Agreement," *The Wall Street Journal*, May 13, 1992.
13. FedEx Corporation, *Annual Report*, 2001.
14. "More Hotels Won't Be Able to Pay Debt from Operations, Study Says," *The Wall Street Journal*, October 30, 2001.
15. Amazon.com, Press Release, January 28, 1999.
16. NEC Corporation, *Annual Report*, 2001; Sanyo Electric Co., *Annual Report*, 2001.

Chapter 17
1. Marriott International, Inc., *Annual Report*, 2002, adapted.
2. *Statement of Financial Accounting Standards No. 95*, "Statement of Cash Flows" (Norwalk, Conn.: Financial Accounting Standards Board, 1987); *Statement of Financial Accounting Concepts No. 1*, "Objectives of Financial Reporting for Business Enterprises" (Norwalk, Conn.: Financial Accounting Standards Board, 1978), par. 37–39.
3. Marriott International, Inc., *Annual Report*, 2002.
4. Gary Slutsker, "Look at the Birdie and Say: 'Cash Flow,'" *Forbes*, October 25, 1993.
5. Jonathan Clements, "Yacktman Fund Is Bloodied but Unbowed," *The Wall Street Journal*, November 8, 1993.
6. Jeffrey Laderman, "Earnings, Schmearnings—Look at the Cash," *BusinessWeek*, July 24, 1989.
7. "Deadweight on the Markets," *BusinessWeek*, February 19, 2001.
8. Marriott International, Inc., *Annual Report*, 2002.
9. American Institute of Certified Public Accountants, *Accounting Trends & Techniques* (New York: AICPA, 2001).
10. Pallavi Gogoi, "Cash-Rich, So?" *BusinessWeek*, March 19, 2001.
11. "Cash Flow Shortfall in Quarter May Lead to Default on Loan," *The Wall Street Journal*, September 4, 2001.
12. Enron Corporation, *Press Release*, October 16, 2001.
13. Sony Corporation, *Annual Report*, 2000; Canon, Inc., *Annual Report*, 2000.

Chapter 18
1. Sun Microsystems, *Proxy Statement*, 2001.
2. Phyllis Plitch, "Firms Embrace Pro Forma Way on Earnings," *The Wall Street Journal*, January 22, 2002.
3. David Henry, "The Numbers Game," *BusinessWeek*, May 14, 2001.
4. *Statement of Financial Accounting Standards No. 131*, "Segment Disclosures" (Norwalk, Conn.: Financial Accounting Standards Board, 1997).
5. Sun Microsystems, Inc. *Annual Report*, 2001.
6. William H. Beaver, "Alternative Accounting Measures as Indicators of Failure," *Accounting Review*, January 1968; Edward Altman, "Financial Ratios, Discriminant Analysis and the Prediction of Corporate Bankruptcy," *Journal of Finance*, September 1968.
7. Sun Microsystems, Inc., "Management's Discussion and Analysis," *Annual Report*, 2001.
8. Ibid.
9. *Forbes*, November 13, 1978, p. 154.
10. Elizabeth MacDonald, "Firms Say SEC Earnings Scrutiny Goes Too Far," *The Wall Street Journal*, February 1, 1999.
11. H. J. Heinz Company, *Annual Report*, 2001.
12. Pfizer, Inc., *Annual Report*, 2000; Roche Group, *Annual Report*, 2000.

Chapter 19

1. Frederic M. Biddle, "A Little Gas Fuels Hope for a New Type of Electric Car," *The Wall Street Journal*, July 9, 1999.
2. Northiko Shirouzu, "Honda Bucks Industry Wisdom, Aiming to Be Small and Efficient," *The Wall Street Journal*, July 9, 1999.
3. *Statement No. 1A* (New York: Institute of Management Accountants, 1982).
4. Andra Gumbus and Susan D. Johnson, "The Balanced Scorecard at Futura Industries," *Strategic Finance*, July 2003.
5. Presentation by management of Baxter International, October 2001.
6. American Institute of Certified Public Accountants, "The New Finance," www.aicpa.org.
7. Peter Brewer, "Putting Strategy into the Balanced Scorecard," *Strategic Finance*, January 2002.
8. American Institute of Certified Public Accountants, "Summary of Sarbanes-Oxley Act of 2002," www.aicpa.org/info/sarbanes_oxley_summary.htm; Securities and Exchange Commission, "Final Rule: Certification of Disclosure in Companies' Quarterly and Annual Reports," August 28, 2002, www.sec.gov/rules/final/33-8124.htm.
9. Gregory L. White, "GM Appears to Step Back from Proposal," *The Wall Street Journal*, March 30, 1999.

Chapter 20

1. Southwest Airlines, "Fact Sheet," www.southwest.com.
2. Melanie Trottman, "Vaunted Southwest Slips in On-Time Performance," *The Wall Street Journal*, September 25, 2002.
3. Robert Frank and Sarah Ellison, "Meltdown in Chocolatetown," *The Wall Street Journal*, September 19, 2002.
4. United Parcel Service, "About UPS," www.ups.com.
5. Lisa de Moraes, "Conan the Cost: NBC's Thrifty Numbers Game," *The Washington Post*, February 8, 2002.

Chapter 21

1. Robert L. Simison, "Toyota Finds Way to Make Custom Car in 5 Days," *The Wall Street Journal*, August 6, 1999.
2. John M. Parkinson, "Equivalent Units in Process Costing" (paper presented at the meeting of the American Accounting Association, August 2002).
3. Associated Press, "$75 Screws? The Pentagon Pays It," *The Gainesville Sun*, March 19, 1998.
4. William A. Sahlman, "How to Write a Great Business Plan," *Harvard Business Review*, July–August 1997.

Chapter 22

1. Dan Morse, "Tennessee Producer Tries New Tactic in Sofas: Speed," *The Wall Street Journal*, November 19, 2002.
2. Gary Cokins, "Learning to Love ABC," *Journal of Accountancy*, August 1999.
3. Mylene Mangalindan, "Oracle Puts Priority on Customer Service," *The Wall Street Journal*, January 21, 2003.
4. Lance Thompson, "Examining Methods of VBM," *Strategic Finance*, December 2002.
5. Paulette Thomas, "Electronics Firm Ends Practice Just in Time," *The Wall Street Journal*, October 29, 2002.
6. Gina Imperato, "Time for Zero Time," *Net Company*, Fall 1999.
7. Sally Beatty, "Levi's Strive to Keep a Hip Image," *The Wall Street Journal*, January 23, 2003.

Chapter 23

1. Kraft Foods, "Profile," www.kraft.com.
2. Kraft Foods, "Inside Kraft: A Company Overview," http://164.109.16.145/investors/overview.html.

Chapter 24

1. Johnson & Johnson, "Our Company," www.jnj.com.
2. Omar Aguilar, "How Strategic Performance Management Is Helping Companies Create Business Value," *Strategic Finance*, January 2003.
3. Enterprise Rent-a-Car, "Overview," "Facts," "History," www.enterprise.com.
4. Richard Barrett, "From Fast Close to Fast Forward," *Strategic Finance*, January 2003.

5. Jeremy Hope and Robin Fraser, "Who Needs Budgets?" *Harvard Business Review*, February 2003.
6. Ibid.
7. Minnesota Mining and Manufacturing Company, "About 3M," www.3m.com.

Chapter 25

1. Erin White, "How Stogy Turned Stylish," *The Wall Street Journal*, May 3, 2002.
2. Katy McLaughlin, "Factory Tours," *The Wall Street Journal*, October 29, 2002.
3. David E. Keys and Anton Van Der Merwe, "Gaining Effective Organizational Control with RCA," *Strategic Finance*, May 2002.
4. Gabriel Kahn, "Still Going for Gold," *The Wall Street Journal*, January 28, 2003.
5. Curtis C. Verschoor, "Ethical Corporations Are Still More Profitable," *Strategic Finance*, June 2003.

Chapter 26

1. PEAKS Resorts, www.peakscard.com.
2. Rich Teerlink, "Harley's Leadership U-Turn," *Harvard Business Review*, July–August 2000.
3. Marc J. Epstein and Jean-François Manzoni, "The Balanced Scorecard and Tableau de Bord: Translating Strategy into Action," *Management Accounting*, August 1997.
4. Jill Rosenfeld, "Information as if Understanding Mattered," *Fast Company*, March 2000.
5. "Blue Jeans to Help Keep Cars Quiet: Who Thinks This Stuff Up?" *Fast Company*, May 2000.
6. Ans Kolk, "Green Reporting," *Harvard Business Review*, January–February 2000.
7. Russ Banham, "Better Budgets," *Journal of Accountancy*, February 2000.
8. Julia Flynn, "Use of Performance-Based Pay Spreads Across Continental Europe, Survey Says," *The Wall Street Journal*, November 17, 1999.

Chapter 27

1. Stephanie Miles, "What's a Check?" *Wall Street Journal*, October 21, 2002, p. R5.
2. Miles, p. R5.
3. Michael Liedtke, "Keeping the Books," *The Gainesville Sun*, August 22, 2002.
4. Alan Fuhrman, "Your e-Banking Future," *Strategic Finance*, April, 2002.
5. Paulette Thomas, "Case Study: Electronics Firm Ends Practice Just in Time," *The Wall Street Journal*, October 29, 2002.
6. From a speech by Jim Croft, vice president of finance and administration of the Field Museum, Chicago, November 14, 2000.

Appendix A

1. PepsiCo., Inc., *Annual Report*, 2000.
2. *Statement of Financial Accounting Standards No. 52*, "Foreign Currency Translation" (Norwalk, Conn.: Financial Accounting Standards Board, 1981), par. 15.
3. *Financial Reporting: An International Survey* (New York: Price Waterhouse, May 1995).
4. "International Accounting Standards Committee Objectives and Procedures," *Professional Standards* (New York: American Institute of Certified Public Accountants, 1988), vol. B, sec. 9000, par. 24–27.

Appendix B

1. *Statement of Financial Accounting Standards No. 115*, "Accounting for Certain Investments in Debt and Equity Securities" (Norwalk, Conn.: Financial Accounting Standards Board, 1993).

Appendix C

1. Accounting Principles Board, *Opinion No. 21*, "Interest on Receivables and Payables" (New York: American Institute of Certified Public Accountants, 1971), par. 13.

COMPANY NAME INDEX

Subject Index

Print and Electronic Supplements for Instructors

NEW! Eduspace® Powered by Blackboard™
Houghton Mifflin's homework system, Eduspace, enables students to complete text assignments online. After students complete each text problem, they are asked a series of questions to test their understanding of the problem. They submit their answers online and receive immediate feedback on right and wrong answers. Assignments are automatically graded and entered into a grade book, saving instructors a great deal of time. Eduspace also offers a wealth of other instructor resources, including HMTesting (the computerized test bank), brand new PowerPoint slide presentations, and a complete course manual.

Instructor's Solutions Manual. Contains answers to all text exercises, problems, and cases.

Electronic Solutions. Contains solutions from the printed Instructor's Solutions Manual, allows instructors to manipulate the numbers in the classroom or to distribute solutions electronically.

Solutions Transparencies. More than 1,200 transparencies provide solutions for every exercise, problem, and case in the text, including the appendixes.

Course Manual. Available on the HMClassPrep with HMTesting Instructor CD-ROM. Filled with practical advice and teaching tips, it contains a planning matrix and time/difficulty chart for every chapter and chapter-by-chapter instructional materials and review quizzes.

NEW! PowerPoint Slides. A brand new set of PowerPoint slides is available on the HMClassPrep with HMTesting Instructor CD-ROM. The slides can also be downloaded from the Needles Accounting Resource Center Web Site at http://accounting.college.hmco.com/instructors. The new slides are concise, contain lots of examples of transactions, and explain the accounting process in clear, easy-to-follow steps.

Video Cases. The following video cases are available on the HMClassPrep with HMTesting Instructor CD-ROM: Intel (Chapter 1), **NEW!** Claire's Stores (Chapter 5), **NEW!** J. C. Penney (Chapter 10), Fermi National Accelerator Laboratory (Chapter 11), Goodyear Tire & Rubber Company (Chapter 17), Enterprise Rent-A-Car, and Harley-Davidson, Inc. A corresponding text case relates each video to the themes of the chapter.

Test Bank with Achievement Test Masters and Answers. This printed test bank provides more than 3,000 true-false, multiple choice, short

essay, and critical-thinking questions, as well as exercises and problems.

NEW! HMClassPrep with HMTesting CD-ROM. This CD contains the computerized version of the Test Bank. It allows instructors to select, edit, and add questions, or generate randomly selected questions to produce a test master for easy duplication. The 2005 edition allows tests to be compiled from learning objectives or key words from the text. Online Testing and Gradebook functions allow instructors to administer tests via their local area network or the Web, set up classes, record grades from tests or assignments, analyze grades, and compile class and individual statistics. The instructor CD also contains the Solutions Manual, the complete Course Manual, PowerPoint slides, Video Cases, check figures for end-of-chapter problems, and Web links to the Needles Accounting Resource Center Web Site.

Needles Accounting Resource Center Instructor Web Site (http://accounting.college.hmco.com/instructors). Includes downloadable PowerPoint slides of text presentation materials and text illustrations, electronic solutions, PowerPoint slides, check figures for the end-of-chapter problems, and links to other valuable text resources. In addition, the Instructor Web site includes sample syllabi from other first-year accounting faculty and the *Accounting Instructors' Report* newsletter, which covers a wide range of contemporary teaching issues.

Blackboard Course Cartridges. These cartridges provide flexible, efficient, and creative ways to present learning materials and manage distance learning courses. Specific resources include chapter overviews, check figures for in-text problems, practice quizzes, PowerPoint slides, and Excel Solutions. In addition to course management benefits, instructors may make use of an electronic grade book, receive papers from students enrolled in the course via the Internet, and track student use of the communication and collaboration functions.

WebCT e-Packs. These e-packs provide instructors with a flexible, Internet-based education platform. The WebCT e-packs come with a full array of features to enrich the online learning experience, including online quizzes, bulletin board, chat tool, whiteboard, and other functionality. The e-packs contain text-specific resources, including chapter overviews, check figures, practice quizzes, PowerPoint slides, and Excel Solutions.